The Rolling Stone Index

The Rolling Stone Index

Five More Years of Popular Culture, 1992-1996

Compiled by
Jeffrey N. Gatten

Popular Culture, Ink.

1998

Book design and layout by
Tom Schultheiss.
Computer programs by
Edward S. Przebienda.

ISBN 1-56075-045-6
LC 97-76323

Published by
Popular Culture, Ink.
P.O. Box 1839
Ann Arbor, MI 48106

Home of
"The best rock-and-roll books in the world!"

PCI Collector Editions
are published especially for discerning collectors and libraries.
Each Collector Edition title is released in limited quantities
identified by edition, printing number, and number of copies.
Unlike trade editions, they are not generally available in bookstores.

10 9 8 7 6 5 4 3 2 1
(First edition, first printing: 550 copies)

Printed in the United States of America

Contents

Preface vii
Introduction ix
Letter Group Quick Reference xiii

MAJOR SECTIONS & RELATED INDEXES

ARTICLES & COLUMNS 3
Title Index to Articles & Columns 59
Subject Index to Articles & Columns 81
BOOK REVIEWS 111
Author Index to Book Reviews 115
Reviewer Index to Book Reviews 117
CONCERT REVIEWS 119
Reviewer Index to Concert Reviews 127
Title Index to Concert Reviews 129
COVER APPEARANCES 131
Date & Issue Index to Cover Appearances 135
LETTERS TO THE EDITOR 137
MOVIE REVIEWS 157
Reviewer Index to Movie Reviews 173
PHOTOGRAPHS & ILLUSTRATIONS 175
Photographer & Illustrator Index 513
POETRY 531
RANDOM NOTES 533
RECORD REVIEWS 583
Reviewer Index to Record Reviews 641
Title Index to Record Reviews 647

MASTER INDEXES

MASTER INDEX TO AUTHOR & REVIEWER NAMES 663
MASTER INDEX TO TITLES 681

Preface

to the *Rolling Stone Index* (1967-1991)

Rolling Stone magazine began publication in November 1967. The first twenty-four-page issue featured an article about the Monterey International Pop Festival, and pictured John Lennon on the cover. The price was twenty-five cents.

Over the years, the original target audience of late-1960s hippies has expanded in size and affluence into the phenomenon of the baby-boom generation. A quarter of a century later, *Rolling Stone* is firmly established as America's pop culture magazine of record—twenty-five years of documenting music, politics, fashion, fads, art, cinema, television, sports, health issues, the drug culture, and every other culturally relevant aspect of contemporary society. From Woodstock to Live Aid, from LSD to cocaine, from Watergate to the Iran-Contra affair, from acid rock to disco to punk to new wave to rap, *Rolling Stone* redefined journalism while transforming counterculture into popular culture.

Initially embracing rock music as a cultural catalyst, coverage quickly expanded to a broad range of the arts, including film and literature. Soon after, political issues were featured regularly. In 1971, *Rolling Stone* won a National Magazine Award which acknowledged stories on the Manson family and the Altamont Rock Festival. National media attention focused on the publication in 1975 in response to exclusive articles on the life of Patty Hearst in the underground. *Rolling Stone* continued to experience growth and success due primarily to perceptive, high quality, and often irreverent writing by pioneering journalists. The publication's circulation increased at one of the highest rates among popular magazines, topping the one million mark in 1985. By 1986, *Rolling Stone* was able to proclaim itself number one at reaching 18-to-34 year-olds with incomes exceeding $25,000. Publicity for the *RS* classifieds section today claims an audience of 7.7 million mail-order shoppers. As this book goes to press, *Rolling Stone*'s latest issue announced that *RS* was the recipient of three 1992 ASCAP-Deems Taylor Awards for excellence in music journalism, along with a special twenty-fifth anniversary award "for setting the standards for excellence in rock journalism."

Rolling Stone is a cultural icon. An amazing number of prominent individuals responsible for influencing popular culture have authored, or have been the subject of, articles in the magazine (many have been both!). Dan Rather, Bella Abzug, Timothy Leary, Jane Fonda, Andy Warhol, and William Burroughs are but a small sampling of names. The publication reflects a wide variety of cultural interests, often juxtaposed. My favorite example of this is found in *RS* issue 203, page 21, in which both the Cycle Sluts (a transvestite comedy-song group) and Louisa May Alcott are mentioned in the same sentence.

The *Rolling Stone* Index: Twenty-Five Years of Popular Culture, 1967-1991 is intended to assist researchers, scholars, teachers, librarians, market analysts, agents and publicists, record company staffers, entertainment industry legal counsels—anyone seeking information about popular culture. A much needed reference tool for academic and public libraries, my hope is that any individual or institution with a partial or complete collection of *Rolling Stone* magazine will find this book of great value.

Jeffrey N. Gatten

Introduction

Facilitating research into recent history, and popular culture in particular, through the primary media that document events as they occur was my stated purpose for the compilation of ***The Rolling Stone Index: Twenty-Five Years of Popular Culture, 1967-1991***. Among print media, *Rolling Stone* continues as a premiere source of information on popular culture. With that in mind, the original work is updated here for the years 1992-1996.

Scope & Organization

This volume continues the indexing of *Rolling Stone* magazine from issue No. 615 (October 17, 1991) through issue No. 750/751 (December 26, 1996). With the addition of coverage of photographs and illustrations, ten main sections now categorize more than 33,000 entries, adding to the 73,000 contained in the 1967-1991 volume for a total exceeding 106,000.

This new volume adds over 3,200 citations to articles and columns, more than 1,700 letters to the editor, 5,500-plus "Random Notes" citations, and nearly 3,000 record reviews, as examples. Significantly, and for the first time, over 18,000 citations to the graphic content of *RS* for these five years is included.

Entries within each section are numbered sequentially—picking up the sequence where it left off in the first volume—and are preceded by a two-letter section code. The sections and their respective codes are as follows:

Section Heading	*Code*
Articles & Columns	**AR**
Book Reviews	**BR**
Concert Reviews	**CR**
Cover Appearances	**CV**
Letters to the Editor	**LE**
Movie Reviews	**MR**
Photographs & Illustrations	**PH**
Poetry	**PR**
Random Notes	**RN**
Record Reviews	**RR**

In addition to the main sections, eleven particularized, point-of-use indexes and two master indexes access the information in the main sections through alternative approaches—author, title, or subject (consult the table of contents for a listing of these). Additionally, a quick reference table to letter groups in all sections follows this introduction. It may be necessary to consult several of the sections to insure that a topic has been thoroughly researched.

How to Use this Book

A few comments on using each of the sections and indexes contained in this volume follow:

ARTICLES & COLUMNS (**AR**)

Entries are listed alphabetically by author or by title if author is unknown. Articles published without titles or with vague titles have had descriptive titles created for or information added to them in brackets. If two or more articles have the same title, arrangement is chronological.

This section is supported first by the "Title Index to Articles & Columns." Articles and columns are listed alphabetically by title. (Occasionally, more than one reference to a given title results from the fact that jointly-authored pieces have been listed as by each of several contributors.) All references begin with the two-letter code AR, meaning that the full citation can be found in the preceding ARTICLES & COLUMNS section.

The "Subject Index to Articles & Columns" also accesses this section. Entries are listed alphabetically by subject matter. (Again, several apparently identical citations—except for author name—to a given piece encountered under a subject heading may be an indication of joint participation in an article or column, rather than denoting several different items.)

The subject index does not provide cross references, but most articles have been assigned more than one subject heading. Again, some knowledge and resourcefulness on the part of the reader to search out related subjects which may include their primary subject has been assumed.

For additional subject access to the contents of *RS*, consult the concert review, cover appearances, record review, "Random Notes" and graphics sections of this volume, which are essentially arranged by "subject".

BOOK REVIEWS (**BR**)

Entries are listed alphabetically by book title. For each title, reviews are listed chronologically. Non-review articles about particular books or authors can be located in the "Subject Index to Articles & Columns."

Two point-of-use indexes support this section: the "Author Index to Book Reviews" and the "Reviewer Index to Book Reviews." In each case, names are listed alphabetically. All entry numbers begin with BR, meaning that the full citation can be found in the preceding BOOK REVIEWS section.

CONCERT REVIEWS (**CR**)

Entries are listed alphabetically by performing artist. For each artist, reviews are listed alphabetically by reviewer or by title if reviewer name is unknown. In the case of multiple reviews by the same person, reviews are listed alphabetically by title. Non-review articles about particular concerts or tours can be located in the "Subject Index to Articles & Columns."

This section is cross-indexed in two ways: the "Reviewer Index to Concert Reviews" (entries are alphabetical by reviewer name) and the "Title Index to Concert Reviews" (entries are alphabetical by review title). All entry numbers begin with CR, meaning that the full citation can be found in the preceding CONCERT REVIEWS section.

COVER APPEARANCES (**CV**)

Entries are arranged alphabetically by individual or group name. For each name, entries citing issue and date are arranged chronologically.

This section is supported by the "Date & Issue Index to Cover Appearances." Cover appearances are arranged chronologically by date and issue number.

LETTERS TO THE EDITOR (**LE**)

Entries are listed alphabetically by author. For each author, letters are listed chronologically. If the author indicated a job title or organizational affiliation, this information is included parenthetically following the author's name.

Rolling Stone often publishes rebuttals from prominent personalities as well as its own journalists. See the recommendations made under this heading in the 1967-1991 introductory remarks.

MOVIE REVIEWS (**MR**)

Entries are listed alphabetically by movie title. For each title, reviews are listed chronologically. Non-review articles about particular films and videos can be located in the "Subject Index to Articles & Columns." Articles about film in general (e.g., the movie industry, filmmaking) can be found in the same index under the subject heading "Cinema."

This section is supported by the "Reviewer Index to Movie Reviews." Entries are listed alphabetically by reviewer. All entry numbers begin with MR, meaning that the full citation can be found in the preceding MOVIE REVIEWS section.

PHOTOGRAPHS & ILLUSTRATIONS (**PH**)

Entries are listed under subject headings indicating the primary subject(s) of each photograph or illustration. In many cases, more than one subject heading has been assigned to a given graphic. Within each subject list, graphics are then listed chronologically by date/issue number; if all other information is identical beyond this point, entries are arranged alphabetically by the caption (occasionally, descriptive captions have been added; these appear in brackets); if captions are identical, citations are further arranged by the name of the photographer or illustrator. (In some few instances, this may be misleading for the user, inasmuch as such multiple citations to a given caption are an indication of joint participation in a graphic, rather than denoting several different graphics. Always see the associated credits for clarification.)

Captions associated with graphics have been included as an aid in possibly clarifying graphic content; however, on the assumption that few people would recall captions or prefer them as avenues of access, no alphabetical index to them has been provided.

This section is supported by the "Index to Photographers & Illustrators." Names are listed alphabetically. All references begin with the two-letter code PH, meaning that the full citation can be found in the preceding PHOTOGRAPHS & ILLUSTRATIONS section.

POETRY (**PR**)

A single poem was included in *RS* during the years covered by this volume. For form's, a "Poetry" section appears on page 531.

RANDOM NOTES (**RN**)

Entries are listed alphabetically by individual or group name. For each name, issues are listed chronologically. Each entry is numbered sequentially.

This popular news and gossip column first appeared in issue No. 8 under the title "John J. Rock." RANDOM NOTES often represents the first or only time an individual, musical group, or organization is mentioned in *Rolling Stone*. Therefore, it may be as important as the "Subject Index to Articles & Columns" for locating information on personalities.

RECORD REVIEWS (**RR**)

Entries are listed alphabetically by recording artist or group name. For each artist, records are listed alphabetically by title. For each title, reviews are listed chronologically. Records that are various artists collections, anthologies, soundtracks, etc., appear in a separate sequence (ordered by record title) at the end of the artist list (see page 636). Most reviews are of albums, unless otherwise noted. Nonreview articles about particular recordings can be located in the "Subject Index to Articles & Columns."

The record review section does not include cross-references. Again, use of this section assumes some knowledge and resourcefulness on the part of the reader to search out related subjects.

This section is cross-indexed in two ways: the "Reviewer Index to Record Reviews" (entries are alphabetical by reviewer name) and the "Title Index to Record Reviews" (entries are alphabetical by record title). All entry numbers begin with RR, meaning that the full citation can be found in the preceding RECORD REVIEWS section.

MASTER INDEX TO AUTHOR & REVIEWER NAMES

Entries are listed alphabetically by name. This index provides one-stop access to anything written by an individual within the pages of *Rolling Stone*, including articles, reviews, poetry, and letters to the editor. Also included are the names of authors whose books have been reviewed.

This index does not include references to personal names cited in the capacity of subjects in the "Subject Index to Articles & Columns," or in the cover appearances, concert reviews, "Random Notes," graphics or record reviews sections.

MASTER INDEX TO TITLES

Entries are listed alphabetically by title. This index provides one-stop access to the titles of articles, reviews, and poetry published in *Rolling Stone*. Additionally, the titles of all books and recordings reviewed in *RS* are included.

This index does not include references to titles cited in the capacity of subjects in the "Subject Index to Articles & Columns," nor does it include any references to photo captions, or those sections of the book which do not include title information—the cover appearances, letters, and "Random Notes" sections.

Limitations of this Work

Only a few items have been excluded in compiling this work. These are schedules of upcoming concerts and tours, and lists of top-selling albums. These items do not typically include any commentary.

Acknowledgements

I would like to extend grateful acknowledgement to Megan Gatten and Jennifer Gatten for keeping me current on the latest music; Carolyn Radcliff for advice on this work (and for sharing her life with me); Tom Schultheiss for his continuing efforts at Popular Culture, Ink.; and Kent State University Libraries and Media Services for providing the support to complete this work.

Letter Group Quick Reference

The following two-page table presents the entire alphabetical structure of this book in an easy-to-use format that should prove invaluable to all who consult it. (In this case, citation is to *page* number, rather than to entry number.)

The letters of the alphabet appear down the left-hand side of each page of the table, **A** through **Z**. These correspond to the letters at the beginning of each letter group in each of the sections of this volume.

Across the top of the table pages are codes representing all the sections of the book. A key to these codes and their respective section names appears opposite.

If you wish to determine, for example, whether performer Phil Collins has written any letters to *RS*, find the code **LE** at the top of the table, and scan down the column until you encounter the intersecting row containing the letter **C**. The C's in the "Letters" section begin on page 139 and, after turning one page, you will find the answer—a much simpler process than flipping through the book to find the "Letters" section (assuming you haven't used the Contents page to find the beginning of the section), and then flipping through many more pages until finding the letter C within that section.

Key to Section Codes

AR = Articles & Columns
AR/t = Title Index to Articles & Columns
AR/s = Subject Index to Articles & Columns
BR = Book Reviews
BR/a = Author Index to Book Reviews
BR/r = Reviewer Index to Book Reviews
CR = Concert Reviews
CR/r = Reviewer Index to Concert Reviews
CR/t = Title Index to Concert Reviews
CV = Cover Appearances
CV/d = Date & Issue Index to Cover Appearances (arranged by date)
LE = Letters to the Editor
MR = Movie Reviews
MR/r = Reviewer Index to Movie Reviews
PH = Photographs & Illustrations
PH/p&i = Photographer & Illustrator Index
PR = Poetry
PR/t = Title Index to Poetry (Not included)
RN = Random Notes
RR = Record Reviews
RR/r = Reviewer Index to Record Reviews
RR/t = Title Index to Record Reviews
RR/v = Soundtracks, Anthologies & Various Artists Collections
M/a&r = Master Index to Authors & Reviewers
M/t = Master Index to Titles

	AR	AR/t	AR/s	BR	BR/a	BR/r	CR	CR/r	CR/t	CV	CV/d	LE	MR
A	3	59	81	111	115	117	119	127	129	131	----	137	157
B	5	59	82	111	115	117	119	127	129	131	----	137	157
C	7	61	84	111	115	117	119	127	129	131	----	139	158
D	11	62	86	111	115	117	120	127	129	131	----	140	159
E	14	63	87	111	115	117	120	127	129	131	----	141	160
F	15	64	88	111	115	117	120	127	129	131	----	141	160
G	18	65	89	111	115	117	121	127	129	131	----	142	161
H	23	65	90	111	115	117	121	127	129	131	----	143	162
I	26	67	92	112	----	----	121	----	129	132	----	144	162
J	26	67	93	112	115	----	122	127	129	132	----	144	163
K	27	68	94	----	115	117	122	127	129	132	----	145	163
L	29	68	94	112	115	117	122	127	129	132	----	146	164
M	30	69	95	112	115	117	122	127	130	132	----	146	164
N	34	70	97	112	----	117	123	127	130	132	----	148	165
O	36	71	98	112	----	----	123	127	130	132	----	148	166
P	39	72	99	112	115	117	123	127	130	132	----	149	166
Q	41	73	101	----	----	117	----	127	----	----	----	150	166
R	41	74	101	112	115	117	124	127	130	132	----	150	167
S	44	75	103	112	115	117	124	127	130	133	----	151	167
T	49	77	106	112	115	----	125	127	130	133	----	152	169
U	51	78	107	113	----	----	125	----	130	133	----	153	170
V	51	78	108	113	----	117	125	127	130	133	----	153	170
W	51	78	108	113	115	117	125	127	130	133	----	153	170
X	----	79	109	113	----	----	126	----	----	----	----	----	----
Y	57	79	109	113	115	----	126	----	130	133	----	154	171
Z	58	80	109	----	----	117	126	----	130	133	----	154	171

	MR/r	**PH**	PH/p&i	**PR**	PR/t	**RN**	**RR**	RR/v	RR/r	RR/t	**M/a&r**	**M/t**
A	173	175	513	----	----	533	583	636	641	647	663	681
B	173	186	513	531	----	534	585	636	641	647	663	682
C	----	214	515	----	----	538	590	636	641	648	664	685
D	173	243	516	----	----	542	594	637	641	649	665	687
E	----	260	517	----	----	544	596	637	641	650	666	689
F	----	266	518	----	----	545	597	637	642	650	667	690
G	173	279	518	----	----	547	599	637	643	651	668	691
H	173	297	519	----	----	549	602	637	643	651	669	692
I	----	315	520	----	----	552	604	638	643	652	670	694
J	----	319	520	----	----	553	605	638	643	652	670	695
K	----	331	520	----	----	555	607	638	643	652	671	696
L	----	340	521	----	----	556	608	638	643	653	671	697
M	173	356	521	----	----	558	610	638	643	653	672	698
N	173	383	524	----	----	562	615	638	644	654	674	700
O	----	391	524	----	----	563	616	639	644	654	674	701
P	----	396	525	----	----	564	617	639	644	655	674	703
Q	173	415	526	----	----	567	620	----	644	655	675	705
R	----	415	526	----	----	567	620	639	644	655	675	705
S	----	435	527	----	----	570	623	639	644	656	676	707
T	173	471	529	----	----	575	629	640	644	657	677	710
U	----	483	530	----	----	577	631	640	----	658	679	712
V	----	486	530	----	----	577	631	640	645	658	679	713
W	----	492	530	----	----	578	632	640	645	658	679	713
X	----	507	----	----	----	580	634	----	----	659	----	715
Y	----	507	531	----	----	580	634	640	645	659	680	715
Z	----	510	531	522	----	580	635	----	645	659	680	715

The Rolling Stone Index

Major Sections & Related Indexes

Articles & Columns

A

AARON, CHARLES
"Rappers Get Roughed Up: John 'Ecstacy' Fletcher And Friends File Complaint Against New York Police."
AR12916 651 (March 4, 1993) p24.
ADLER, WILLIAM M.
"Evening The Score: Affirmative Action Cracks Open The Great Divide."
AR12917 714 (August 10, 1995) pp35-38,64,69.
AHEARN, KIM
"Artist Biographies."
AR12918 695 (November 17, 1994) pp154-158,160.
"Artist Biographies [cont.]."
AR12919 695 (November 17, 1994) pp154-158,160.
"Ben Lee."
AR12920 712-713 (July 13, 1995) p42.
"Frente."
AR12921 684 (June 16, 1994) p30.
"Suicide Watch."
AR12922 703 (March 9, 1995) p32.
AIGES, SCOTT
"Let The Good Times Bowl."
AR12923 710 (June 15, 1995) p46.
"Rock & Roll Summer: New Orleans."
AR12924 710 (June 15, 1995) p46.
ALDEN, GRANT
"Country Punk'ins: Nelson Covers Bridge Rebel Cultures."
AR12925 717 (September 21, 1995) p34.
ALEXAKIS, ART
"Raves."
AR12926 732 (April 18, 1996) p38.
ALI, LORRAINE
"Banding Together: Underground Rockers Fight For Abortion Rights."
AR12927 692 (October 6, 1994) p55.
"Boys To Men: The Pharcyde Break Boundaries On 'LabCabin'."
AR12928 722 (November 30, 1995) p38.
"Chemical Brothers Explode Underground With Their New EP, 'Loops Of Fury'."
AR12929 741 (August 22, 1996) p36.
"Critics Comments."
AR12930 726 (January 25, 1996) pp46,50-51.
"Dead Flowers?: Gilbey Clarke Ponders The Troubled State Of Guns N' Roses."
AR12931 691 (September 22, 1994) p28.
"Down-Home Souls: Jayhawks Fly High On Their "Green Grass"."
AR12932 697 (December 15, 1994) p31.
"Exile In Guyville: A Report On How Women Are Faring In The Music Industry."
AR12933 692 (October 6, 1994) pp57-58.
"Funky, Futuristic Beck Channels Cosmic Debris."
AR12934 723 (December 14, 1995) p45.
"K. D. Lang."
AR12935 722 (November 30, 1995) p40.
"The Kids Are Alright: Offspring."
AR12936 691 (September 22, 1994) pp25,27-28.
"Kind Of Blue: Does Songwriter Lou Barlow—The Heart And Soul Of Sebadoh, Sentridoh And The Folk Implosion—Care Too Much?."
AR12937 744 (October 3, 1996) pp54-56,83.
"Message In A Bottle: Shane MacGowan Serves It Straight Up."
AR12938 714 (August 10, 1995) p27.
"Moby: The Great White Wail."
AR12939 707 (May 4, 1995) pp58-61.
"Perry Farrell."
AR12940 686-687 (July 14, 1994) p32.
"The Royal Treatment: The Beastie Boys Fight For Their Right To Prosper."
AR12941 678 (March 24, 1994) pp43-44.
"Social Distortion Find Their New Highs On The Road With 'White Trash'."
AR12942 749 (December 12, 1996) p28.
"Stalkers: Is The Threat To Rock Stars Growing?."
AR12943 747 (November 14, 1996) pp29-30.
"Twisted Twang: Geraldine Fibbers Take It To The Limit."
AR12944 720 (November 2, 1995) p24.
ALICANDRO, BILL
"Our Lives, Our Music: Exile On Main Street."
AR12945 644 (November 26, 1992) pp49-50.
ALLEN, JENNIFER
"Boys: Hanging With The Spur Posse."
AR12946 660-661 (July 8, 1993) pp54-56,58,61 +.
"Young, White And Surrounded."
AR12947 685 (June 30, 1994) pp54-56,59-61 +.
ALTERMAN, ERIC
"Choose Your Poison: Newt & Co. Roll Back A Generation Of Environmental Protections."
AR12948 706 (April 20, 1995) pp41-42,95.
"Clinton Rocked The Vote, Now It's Rocking Him: Young Democrats Are Turning Their Back On The President And Politics."
AR12949 702 (February 23, 1995) pp41-42.
"Culture Wars: The GOP's Version Of American History Is 'Don't Worry, Be Happy'."
AR12950 719 (October 19, 1995) pp45-46,48.
"The GOP's Strike Force: The Right-Wing Propaganda Machine Churns Out Money, Activists And Lies."
AR12951 727 (February 8, 1996) pp30-31,56-57.
"Grace Under Fire: The NRA Takes Potshots At Assault-Weapons Opponents."
AR12952 709 (June 1, 1995) pp32-33,36.
"Losing The Right To Choose: Republicans In Congress Wage War On Abortion."
AR12953 716 (September 7, 1995) pp39-40,42-43.
"Newt Vs. The '60s: The Values Of The Counterculture Top Gingrich's Hit List."
AR12954 698-699 (December 29, 1994) pp164-166.
"Run, Newt, Run: Would A Presidential Bid Finally Expose The Real Newt Gingrich?."
AR12955 717 (September 21, 1995) pp41-42.
"A View To Kill."
AR12956 704 (March 23, 1995) pp48-49,51-52 +.
AMOS, TORI
"Insane In The Brain (song)."
AR12957 681 (May 5, 1994) p16.
"Raves."
AR12958 681 (May 5, 1994) p16.
"AND WE BID YOU GOOD NIGHT: ARTISTS AND COLLEAGUES PAY TRIBUTE TO GARCIA."
AR12959 717 (September 21, 1995) pp31,74-75.
APPLEFORD, STEVE
"Desert Bloom: With Spacey Rock And Country Ballads, Cracker Reinvent Themselves In The California Sun."
AR12960 732 (April 18, 1996) pp47-48.
"The Dread Zone: Bad Brains Are One Of Rock's Most Volatile Bands—In Music And Temper."
AR12961 711 (June 29, 1995) pp15-16.
"Get Happy: Perry Farrell Finds Nirvana On The Way To LollaPalooza

'95 And A New LP."
AR12962 715 (August 24, 1995) pp53-54.
"Heather Nova Weathers The Quiet Storm."
AR12963 723 (December 14, 1995) p41.
"L.A. Confidential."
AR12964 704 (March 23, 1995) p44.
AR12965 708 (May 18, 1995) p32.
AR12966 712-713 (July 13, 1995) p49.
"Mosh Unit: The Muffs' Two-Minute Bursts Of melodic Noise Are Clamorous Punk Postcards From The Edge."
AR12967 718 (October 5, 1995) pp[enc.30-32 +].
"Sponge."
AR12968 706 (April 20, 1995) p36.
"Wayne's World: For The MC5's Kramer, The Future Is Now."
AR12969 708 (May 18, 1995) p30.
ARRINGTON, CARL
"The Astral Jane: Jane Siberry Makes Metaphysical Pop With Heart."
AR12970 680 (April 21, 1994) p18.
"Dawn Of The Dead: The Duo Dead Can Dance Get Back To Nature With Their Album "Into The Labyrinth"."
AR12971 686-687 (July 14, 1994) p35.
"Making Art From Chaos: Jimmy Webb Is Writing His New Songs In The Key Of Life."
AR12972 670 (November 25, 1993) p22.
"Rock's Royal Jesters: King Missile Makes Merry On College Radio With 'Detachable Penis'."
AR12973 654 (April 15, 1993) p17.
"[ART DEPARTMENT]."
AR12974 685 (June 30, 1994) p10.
"ARTISTS' PICKS."
AR12975 726 (January 25, 1996) pp44,48,51.
"ARTISTS' PICKS: 1992 MUSIC AWARDS."
AR12976 625 (March 5, 1992) pp60-61.
"ARTISTS' PICKS: 1993 MUSIC AWARDS."
AR12977 651 (March 4, 1993) pp56-57.
"[ASCAP-DEEMS TAYLOR AWARD]."
AR12978 672-673 (December 23, 1993) p10.
"[ASCAP-DEEMS TAYLOR AWARDS]."
AR12979 621 (January 9, 1992) p7.
AR12980 648 (January 21, 1993) p7.
ATKINS, NORMAN
"The Cost Of Living Clean."
AR12981 681 (May 5, 1994) pp41-42.
"Marian Wright Edelman: On The Front Lines Of The Battle To Save America's Children."
AR12982 645-646 (December 10, 1992) pp126-127,129 +.
"[AWARDS]."
AR12983 634-635 (July 9, 1992) p8.
AR12984 658 (June 10, 1993) p12.
AYKROYD, DAN
"Michael O'Donoghue."
AR12985 698-699 (December 29, 1994) p84.
AZERRAD, MICHAEL
"Angelique Kidjo: Politics With A Beat."
AR12986 630 (May 14, 1992) p32.
"Big Boom In Industrial Metal: Helmet Signs Million-Dollar Deal With Interscope."
AR12987 637 (August 20, 1992) pp15,64.
"Cake Like."
AR12988 703 (March 9, 1995) p29.
"Chris Harford: A Rocker With A Sense Of Direction."
AR12989 640 (October 1, 1992) p25.
"Dada: Strange Characters Take Center Stage In 'Puzzle'."
AR12990 647 (January 7, 1993) p19.
"Does Primus Really Suck?: The San Francisco Trio, Whose Music Mixes Thrash, Funk And Progressive Rock, Has Built A Devoted Following Of Fans On The Alternative Scene."
AR12991 616 (October 31, 1991) pp81-83.
"Follow For Now: A Hard-Rockin' Guitar Band."
AR12992 625 (March 5, 1992) p27.
"Grunge City: For Real Rockers Seattle Is The Ultimate Wet Dream."
AR12993 628 (April 16, 1992) pp43-44,48.
"High Times: Meat Puppets Make Bong Rock Fro Now People."
AR12994 682 (May 19, 1994) pp21-22.
"John Peel."
AR12995 663 (August 19, 1993) p19.
"The Levellers: A Foot-Stompin' News Service."
AR12996 630 (May 14, 1992) p32.
"Live Through This: A Year On The Road With Nirvana."
AR12997 683 (June 2, 1994) pp55-56.
"The Lost Boys: With 'Sweet Oblivion,' Screaming Trees Finally Come Out Of The Woods."
AR12998 650 (February 18, 1993) pp15,25.
"Lotion."
AR12999 685 (June 30, 1994) p28.
"Love Battery: Modifying The Northwest Sound."
AR13000 634-635 (July 9, 1992) p20.
"Luka Bloom Doesn't Want To Be Just Another Boring Folkie: Songs From The Heart."
AR13001 626 (March 19, 1992) pp51-52,104.
"Man With A Plan."
AR13002 712-713 (July 13, 1995) p48.
"New Bands Strike Gold With Majors."
AR13003 637 (August 20, 1992) pp15,64.
"A New 'Girlfriend' For Matthew Sweet: Hard-Edged Album Documents Romantic Turmoil."
AR13004 618 (November 28, 1991) p33.
"1991 CMJ Music Marathon."
AR13005 621 (January 9, 1992) p25.
"Nirvana: Inside The Heart And Mind Of Kurt Cobain."
AR13006 628 (April 16, 1992) pp36-39,41,96 +.
"Nirvana: Noise For '93."
AR13007 647 (January 7, 1993) pp13,25.
"On A High Horse: Shudder To Think Shatter Convention With 'Pony Express'."
AR13008 719 (October 19, 1995) p26.
"PM Dawn: Metaphysical Graffiti."
AR13009 616 (October 31, 1991) p25.
"The Reading Festival."
AR13010 642 (October 29, 1992) p39.
"The Real New Deal: The Breeders Get Wet And Wild As They Dive Back Into Action On 'Last Splash'."
AR13011 668 (October 28, 1993) p18.
"Seven Inches Of Pleasure: For Bands And Fans, The Single Is The New Format Of Choice."
AR13012 649 (February 4, 1993) p18.
"Smashing Pumpkins' Sudden Impact: The Band's 'Siamese Dream' Comes True."
AR13013 667 (October 14, 1993) pp19-20.
"Sonic Youth's 'Dirty' Set For July Release."
AR13014 634-635 (July 9, 1992) p33.
"The Sound Of The Future: With Its First Two Albums, My Bloody Valentine Has Redefined Rock."
AR13015 623 (February 6, 1992) p20.
"This Ain't No Mudd Club: CBGB Celebrates Its 20 Years Of Rock & Roll."
AR13016 675 (February 10, 1994) p14.
"Walt Mink: Power-Trio Rock."
AR13017 637 (August 20, 1992) p20.
"The Watchman: Straightforward Ballsy Folk."
AR13018 615 (October 17, 1991) p28.
"Whigging Out: Afghan Whigs Join Sub Pop Alumni With A Major-Label Debut, 'Gentlemen'."
AR13019 671 (December 9, 1993) p21.

B

BAILEY, ANDREW
"A Day In The Life."
AR13020 641 (October 15, 1992) p161.
BAIRD, ROBERT
"Ex-Blossom Dies: Songwriter Hopkins, 32, Commits Suicide After Battle With Alcohol."
AR13021 675 (February 10, 1994) p15.
BARICH, BILL
"Dead Reckoning: Garcia's Passing Brings To An End A Heroic Journey Of Self-Discovery."
AR13022 717 (September 21, 1995) pp76-78.
BARRON, CHRIS
"Raves."
AR13023 689 (August 25, 1994) p34.
BARTH, JACK
"Hot Drug: Claritin."
AR13024 741 (August 22, 1996) p72.
"Hot Status Symbol: A Tiny Cell Phone."
AR13025 741 (August 22, 1996) p72.
BECK, HENRY CABOT
"'Stock Footage."
AR13026 684 (June 16, 1994) p18.
BEISER, VINCE
"Pop Singer Riles Israeli Right."
AR13027 747 (November 14, 1996) p32.
BELLEN, BRIAN
"Our Lives, Our Music: Workingman's Dead."
AR13028 644 (November 26, 1992) pp54-55.
BERGER, ARION
"The Video File."
AR13029 735 (May 30, 1996) p46.
BERGER, DIANE HARRIS
"Our Lives, Our Music: Songs Of Leonard Cohen."
AR13030 644 (November 26, 1992) p50.
BERK, LORI
"89: Thunderstruck."
AR13031 667 (October 14, 1993) p100.
"30: You Might Think."
AR13032 667 (October 14, 1993) p78.
BERMAN, ERIC
"The Godfathers Of Rap: The Rise And Fall Of The First Heroes Of Hip-Hop."
AR13033 672-673 (December 23, 1993) pp137,139-140+.
BERMANT, CHARLES
"CDs Put A New Spin On Your PC: Multimedia Software Brings Video And Sound Together With Your Computer."
AR13034 638 (September 3, 1992) p77.
BERNHARD, LISA
"Let It Flow: River Phoenix Plays It Cool On And Off The Screen."
AR13035 615 (October 17, 1991) pp83-87.
BILAFER, STEVE
"Guess Who's Coming To Washington."
AR13036 642 (October 29, 1992) pp46,49.
BILYEAU, NANCY
"Walk On The West Side."
AR13037 638 (September 3, 1992) pp[enc.21-26+].
BINELLI, MARK
"Atlanta."
AR13038 736 (June 13, 1996) p47.
"Critics Comments."
AR13039 726 (January 25, 1996) pp46,50-51.
"Just Say Moe: The Heartbeat Of The VU Makes A Solo Noise."
AR13040 696 (December 1, 1994) p36.
"Kelly Hogan."
AR13041 736 (June 13, 1996) p47.
"Rock & Roll Summer: Athens."
AR13042 710 (June 15, 1995) p53.
"BIRMINGHAM, ALABAMA."
AR13043 681 (May 5, 1994) p36.
BLACK, DAVID
"The Plague Years."
AR13044 632 (June 11, 1992) pp150-152.
BLACK, KENT
"Bounty Hunter."
AR13045 741 (August 22, 1996) pp60-62,64,66+.
"'X'treme Prejudice: At The X Games, ESPN's Alterna-Lympics, The Road Lugers Tried To Go Straight, The Network Tried To Get Radical, And Street Cred Was Just A Marketing Concept."
AR13046 742 (September 5, 1996) pp52-54,56-57.
BLACKSTOCK, PETER
"Minor Threat."
AR13047 704 (March 23, 1995) p33.
"Stamping Out Hate."
AR13048 702 (February 23, 1995) p26.
BLAKESBERG, JAY
"Primus Choices."
AR13049 690 (September 8, 1994) p25.
"San Francisco."
AR13050 690 (September 8, 1994) p25.
BLECHMAN, R. O.
"Endpaper."
AR13051 645-646 (December 10, 1992) p208.
"The Year In Movies."
AR13052 645-646 (December 10, 1992) p189.
"The Year In Music."
AR13053 645-646 (December 10, 1992) p23.
"The Year In Records."
AR13054 645-646 (December 10, 1992) p163.
"The Year In Television."
AR13055 645-646 (December 10, 1992) p195.
"BLUESMAN WILLIE DIXON: 1915-1992."
AR13056 625 (March 5, 1992) p22.
BLY, ROBERT
"Heaven Is Under Our Feet: Voices For Walden Woods."
AR13057 615 (October 17, 1991) pp53,55,59,105.
BOEHLERT, ERIC
"Altered Stakes: Don Law Cuts Out The Middleman."
AR13058 730 (March 21, 1996) p22.
"Big Names, Big Bucks."
AR13059 726 (January 25, 1996) p26.
"Buzz Been: Did Radio Kill MTV's Video Star?."
AR13060 733 (May 2, 1996) pp18-20.
"Cheap Trick: Labels Buy Hits By Giving Away Bargain-Price Cassette Singles."
AR13061 728 (February 22, 1996) pp23-24.
"Conventional Wisdom: Why The Bottle Rockets And Other Bands Pay To Play At Industry Schmoozefests."
AR13062 730 (March 21, 1996) pp21-22.
"Crime Pays: Beleaguered Interscope Passes From Hot Potato To Hot Property."
AR13063 731 (April 4, 1996) p30.
"Donald Cammell 1934-1996."
AR13064 737 (June 27, 1996) p24.
"Executive Sweet: Music Execs Name Their Price As Salaries Soar."
AR13065 726 (January 25, 1996) pp26-27.
"Holy Rock & Rollers."
AR13066 744 (October 3, 1996) pp23-24.
"Hot Country Act: BR5-49."
AR13067 741 (August 22, 1996) p71.
"Is Moshing Murder?."
AR13068 738-739 (July 11, 1996) pp19-20.
"Limited Access: Behind-The-Scenes Ticket Maneuvering Leaves Concert Fans With Second-rate Seats."
AR13069 748 (November 28, 1996) p32.
"Live Stiffs: Full-Blown Concert Albums Play To Less Applause."
AR13070 727 (February 8, 1996) pp17-18.

"Lounge's Last Call."
AR13071 728 (February 22, 1996) p26.
"Mall Rats: Beleaguered Chain Record Stores Are Sinking Fast."
AR13072 734 (May 16, 1996) p24.
"Members Only: Record Clubs Feel Retailers' And Artists' Heat."
AR13073 733 (May 2, 1996) pp24,26.
"Mining For Gold: Jewel Takes The Long, Slow Road To Success."
AR13074 736 (June 13, 1996) pp22-24.
"MTV Awards Lure The Stars."
AR13075 743 (September 19, 1996) p32.
"Oh, What A Night."
AR13076 736 (June 13, 1996) p24.
"Pay To Play: Independent Promoters Cash In On The Hits As Alternative Radio Becomes Big Business."
AR13077 741 (August 22, 1996) p34.
"Pearl Jam: Taking On Ticketmaster."
AR13078 724-725 (December 28, 1995) p81.
"Pop Journal."
AR13079 744 (October 3, 1996) p26.
AR13080 745 (October 17, 1996) p41.
AR13081 746 (October 31, 1996) p28.
AR13082 747 (November 14, 1996) p42.
AR13083 748 (November 28, 1996) p36.
AR13084 749 (December 12, 1996) p30.
"Radio Land Rush: The Industry's Biggest Station Owners Get Bigger While The Small Ones Sign Off."
AR13085 745 (October 17, 1996) p40.
"Road Woes: What It Costs."
AR13086 748 (November 28, 1996) p53.
"Rock Radio Make-Over: Two New Formats Echo Listeners' Changing Tastes."
AR13087 701 (February 9, 1995) p24.
"Second Helping."
AR13088 726 (January 25, 1996) p30.
"Sophmore Humps: The Modern-Rock Trail Is Littered With One-Hit Wonders."
AR13089 749 (December 12, 1996) pp22,24.
"Summer Concert Season Comes Up Short."
AR13090 743 (September 19, 1996) p34.
"A Tale Of 2 Indies: Matador...."
AR13091 737 (June 27, 1996) pp19-20.
"Ticket Jam: Pearl Jam's Concert Sales Spur New Controversy."
AR13092 743 (September 19, 1996) p32.
"Ticket Masters: How Smashing Pumpkins, Nine Inch Nails And Others Thwart Concert Scalpers."
AR13093 729 (March 7, 1996) pp12-13.
"Walter Hyatt 1949-1996."
AR13094 737 (June 27, 1996) p24.
"Who Are You? Pearl Jam's Eddie Vedder."
AR13095 748 (November 28, 1996) pp50-54,57+.
AR13096 Number not assigned.
BONO
"Bono On Bob."
AR13097 677 (March 10, 1994) p29.
AR13098 619-620 (December 12, 1991) p32.
AR13099 645-646 (December 10, 1992) pp87-88.
BOOTH, STEPHEN A.
"And A Happy New Gear."
AR13100 700 (January 26, 1995) p70.
"Car Stereos For Spring '96: Roadworthy Companions With Distinct Personalities."
AR13101 731 (April 4, 1996) p70.
"Crossover Acts: Bridging The Gap Between Simplicity And Sophistication, These Cameras Are Shooting For A Wider Audience."
AR13102 623 (February 6, 1992) pp92-93.
"Eco-Tech: Green Components For These PC Times."
AR13103 696 (December 1, 1994) p71.
"Everything Old Is New Again."
AR13104 707 (May 4, 1995) p79.
"Eye Candy."
AR13105 714 (August 10, 1995) p66.
"High Interactivity: CD's Bring Movies, Games And Books To A TV Near You."
AR13106 684 (June 16, 1994) pp85-86.
"High-Quality TV's, Big And Small, For Tight Spaces Or Going Places."
AR13107 726 (January 25, 1996) p79.
"Hot Stuff: Plugging In The New."
AR13108 674 (January 27, 1994) p59.
"How To Be A Road Scholar."
AR13109 666 (September 30, 1993) p119.
"I Want My DVD."
AR13110 748 (November 28, 1996) p112.
"If You Want Your Summer To Be A Movable Feast, You'll Need Tech With Some Get-Up-And-Go."
AR13111 736 (June 13, 1996) p64.
"Improve Your Images."
AR13112 715 (August 24, 1995) p115.
"Isn't That Conveeenient!."
AR13113 705 (April 6, 1995) p73.
"It's All Coming Into Focus."
AR13114 702 (February 23, 1995) p83.
"Let's Interactive."
AR13115 708 (May 18, 1995) pp[enc.18-22+].
"A Little Holiday Gear."
AR13116 670 (November 25, 1993) p129.
"M Speak For Newbies."
AR13117 682 (May 19, 1994) p114.
"Mo' Better Multimedia."
AR13118 678 (March 24, 1994) p107.
"New Film Or No Film? Cameras In The Digital Age Require Your To Choose A Format."
AR13119 729 (March 7, 1996) p59.
"Point And Click Picks."
AR13120 676 (February 24, 1994) p65.
"Power Surge: Multimedia Systems."
AR13121 748 (November 28, 1996) pp103-104,106+.
"The Right Computer For You: It's The Soul Of The System That Counts."
AR13122 696 (December 1, 1994) pp75-76,80-82+.
"Sonic Solutions."
AR13123 719 (October 19, 1995) p163.
"Splash, Point And Shoot: When Your Destination Is All Wet, These Are The Right Cameras to Take Along."
AR13124 649 (February 4, 1993) p79.
"Systems Theory: Carefully Chosen Components + The Right Software = A Computer That Works The Way You Do."
AR13125 722 (November 30, 1995) pp[enc.32-34+].
"Technology: New Home-Theater Products Adapt Themselves To Smaller Spaces."
AR13126 743 (September 19, 1996) p99.
"That's Entertainment."
AR13127 682 (May 19, 1994) pp111-112,114.
"You Can Take it With You."
AR13128 689 (August 25, 1994) p49.
BORRIS, DAN
"Hickory Smoke."
AR13129 684 (June 16, 1994) pp60-61,64,66+.
"Masters Of The Game: Over The Mountain And Through The Woods With Three Young Designers Who Show The Brand Names How To Play."
AR13130 691 (September 22, 1994) pp[enc.25,27+].
BOSS, KIT
"Mr. Microsoftee: Paul Allen, Shy Billionaire, Tries To Rock The I-Way."
AR13131 696 (December 1, 1994) pp53-54,58,138.
BOYLE, T. CORAGHESSAN
"The Road To Wellville."

AR13132 654 (April 15, 1993) pp48-50,52-53+.
BOZZA, ANTHONY
"Bo Diddley."
AR13133 738-739 (July 11, 1996) p31.
"Cub."
AR13134 747 (November 14, 1996) p56.
"Hot Cartoonist: Pat Moriarity."
AR13135 741 (August 22, 1996) p76.
"Hot Hollywood Hangout: Hamilton's."
AR13136 741 (August 22, 1996) p80.
"One Hot Minute."
AR13137 732 (April 18, 1996) pp[enc.28].
"Patti Rothberg Brings Her Subterranean Lovesick Blues To The Surface."
AR13138 744 (October 3, 1996) p30.
BRACKETT, NATHAN
"ENIT Festival."
AR13139 744 (October 3, 1996) pp34-35.
BRADFORD, KRISTA
"The Big Sleaze."
AR13140 650 (February 18, 1993) pp39-43,69.
BRAND, JOEL
"War College."
AR13141 652 (March 18, 1993) pp[enc.43-44+].
BREAM, JON
"His Name Was Prince...."
AR13142 662 (August 5, 1993) p17.
BRESKIN, DAVID
"Clint Eastwood: The Rolling Stone Interview."
AR13143 639 (September 17, 1992) pp66-67,69-71+.
"David Cronenberg: The Rolling Stone Interview."
AR13144 623 (February 6, 1992) pp66-70,96.
"Kids In The Dark."
AR13145 632 (June 11, 1992) pp129-133.
"Robert Altman: The Rolling Stone Interview."
AR13146 628 (April 16, 1992) pp72-77,86,94+.
"Tim Burton: The Rolling Stone Interview."
AR13147 634-635 (July 9, 1992) pp38-42,115+.
"Voodoo Child: The Rolling Stone Interview With Living Colour's Vernon Reid."
AR13148 660-661 (July 8, 1993) pp87-88,90,92+.
"BRIGGS, DAVID 1944-1995."
AR13149 728 (February 22, 1996) p24.
BROTHERS, JOYCE
"On The Couch With Smashing Pumpkins: The Final Analysis."
AR13150 680 (April 21, 1994) p46.
BROUGHTON, FRANK
"Josh Wink Lands Techno At A Major Label."
AR13151 746 (October 31, 1996) p32.
BROWNE, JACKSON
"Raves."
AR13152 676 (February 24, 1994) p17.
BUCHANAN, ROB
"Birth Of The Gearhead Nation: Out For A Clunk With The Pioneers Of Mountain Biking As They Come To Grips With Their Funky Past And Muddy Future."
AR13153 634-635 (July 9, 1992) pp80-82,84,118.
BUCKLEY, JEFF
"Raves."
AR13154 717 (September 21, 1995) p36.
BUFFETT, JIMMY
"Beyond The Low Water Mark: A Treasure Diver Learns That Some Customers Can Drive A Hard Bargain, In This Excerpt From The New Novel 'Where Is Joe Merchant?'."
AR13155 636 (August 6, 1992) pp48-49,51,72+.
"No Vision Whatsoever: Why We Are All Strangers In The Everglades."
AR13156 733 (May 2, 1996) p47.
"BULLETS & BOMBS."
AR13157 727 (February 8, 1996) p18.
BURKETT, ELINOR
"The Secret Of St. Mary's."
AR13158 669 (November 11, 1993) pp48-50,52-54+.
"BURLINGTON, VERMONT."
AR13159 681 (May 5, 1994) p35.
BURNS, JOE
"Provincetown."
AR13160 686-687 (July 14, 1994) p46.
"THE BUZZ AT SUNDANCE."
AR13161 729 (March 7, 1996) p53.

C

CARDWELL, DIANE
"Ephraim Lewis: Sensual Soul."
AR13162 636 (August 6, 1992) p24.
CARROLL, BILL
"Our Lives, Our Music: Murmur."
AR13163 644 (November 26, 1992) p50.
CARSON, TOM
"Don't Try This At Home: At The End Of Its Second Season, 'The Real World' Gets A Reality Check."
AR13164 670 (November 25, 1993) pp99-100,104.
CATALDI, ANNA
"Seizing The Light."
AR13165 702 (February 23, 1995) pp66-67.
CATHY
"Our Lives, Our Music: Appetite For Destruction."
AR13166 644 (November 26, 1992) p50.
"CD NEWS."
AR13167 619-620 (December 12, 1991) p173.
AR13168 622 (January 23, 1992) p45.
"CELEBRITY GUIDANCE COUNSELORS."
AR13169 652 (March 18, 1993) pp[enc.6].
CHAMBERS, GORDON
"Hush."
AR13170 625 (March 5, 1992) p68.
"CHANNEL SURFING."
AR13171 712-713 (July 13, 1995) p119.
AR13172 715 (August 24, 1995) p113.
AR13173 717 (September 21, 1995) p93.
AR13174 718 (January 5, 1995) p81.
AR13175 726 (January 25, 1996) p77.
AR13176 727 (February 8, 1996) p53.
AR13177 729 (March 7, 1996) p57.
AR13178 730 (March 21, 1996) p109.
"[CHARLES BUKOWSKI]."
AR13179 680 (April 21, 1994) p8.
"CHECK IT OUT."
AR13180 690 (September 8, 1994) p16.
AR13181 692 (January 6, 1994) p12.
AR13182 696 (December 1, 1994) p18.
AR13183 697 (December 15, 1994) p14.
CHONIN, NEVA
"Ambersunshower."
AR13184 747 (November 14, 1996) p54.
"CHRONICLE."
AR13185 744 (January 3, 1996) p32.
"[CHRONOLOGY OF FEMALE ROCK MUSICIANS]."
AR13186 692 (January 6, 1994) pp50,52-53.
CLAYPOOL, LES
"Raves."
AR13187 749 (December 12, 1996) p33.
CLEMENTS, MARCELLE
"The Dog Is Us."
AR13188 632 (June 11, 1992) pp139-140.
"CLOSE TO YOU."
AR13189 743 (September 19, 1996) pp[enc.3,5-6+].

COCKER, JARVIS
"Raves."
AR13190 736 (June 13, 1996) p58.
COE, SUE
"The Bush Years: Staying The Course."
AR13191 640 (October 1, 1992) p3.
"The Bush Years: Supreme Cruelty."
AR13192 639 (September 17, 1992) p3.
"The Bush Years: The Environmental President."
AR13193 638 (September 3, 1992) p3.
COFFEY, MICHAEL J.
"In The News."
AR13194 680 (April 21, 1994) p20.
COHEN, ELIZABETH
"A House With No Closets."
AR13195 666 (September 30, 1993) pp87-88,90,95.
COHEN, JASON
"Backbeat: For The Soundtrack Of The Beatles Biopic, An Alternative Supergroup Came Together."
AR13196 680 (April 21, 1994) pp63-64.
"Bill 2982: No Sale."
AR13197 694 (November 3, 1994) p32.
"Clean Sweep: Garbage's Masterminds Craft Murky Pop Into An Album That's Impossible To Refuse."
AR13198 718 (October 5, 1995) pp23-24.
"Cosmic Comeback: Julian Cope's Music Of The Spheres."
AR13199 722 (November 30, 1995) p36.
"Don't Ever Change: Buzzcocks Make Pure Punk-Pop For Now People."
AR13200 675 (February 10, 1994) p16.
"Hole Is A Band: While The Courtney Saga Continues, Hole Prove That A Rock & Roll Band Is The Sum Of Its Parts."
AR13201 715 (August 24, 1995) pp46-51.
"In Through The Back Door: The Butthole Surfers Are The Certified Shock Jocks Of The Next Wave."
AR13202 659 (June 24, 1993) p25.
"Keepers Of The Flame: Defying The Alternative-Rock Trend, Candlebox Break Out Of Seattle With Traditional Pop Metal."
AR13203 702 (February 23, 1995) pp23-25.
"Keeping Up With The Jones: A Colorful Romp From Zeppelin To The Buttholes."
AR13204 659 (June 24, 1993) p25.
"Life Of Brian: Don Was Frames A Beach Boys Saga."
AR13205 707 (May 4, 1995) p33.
"Live: Artist Of The Year."
AR13206 726 (January 25, 1996) pp32-35,81.
"Mark E. Smith's Wrath & Roll: With Their 17th LP, The Fall Are Back In Your Face."
AR13207 665 (September 16, 1993) p20.
"Oasis: The Trouble Boys."
AR13208 708 (May 18, 1995) pp50-52,104.
"The Road Less Traveled: Pavement's Crooked Path To Stardom."
AR13209 686-687 (July 14, 1994) pp19-20.
"Stephen Dorff: Playing The Forgotten Beatle."
AR13210 680 (April 21, 1994) p66.
"Willie Nelson Throws A Reggae Party."
AR13211 743 (September 19, 1996) p40.
COHEN, PATRICIA
"Squeezed Pay."
AR13212 704 (March 23, 1995) p54.
COHEN, RICH
"Acting!!! Genius!!! Brilliant!!!."
AR13213 704 (March 23, 1995) pp102-104,106+.
"Art Students In America."
AR13214 678 (March 24, 1994) pp77-78,80.
"Ballad Of A Teenage Queen."
AR13215 716 (September 7, 1995) pp44-48,50.
"The Big Black Boot: What Do Loggers, Hipsters, Bikers And Hikers Have In Common?."
AR13216 665 (September 16, 1993) pp[enc.39,41+].
"Chuckie's In Love: Triathlete Chuckie V Swims, Cycles And Runs With The Best—And He Doesn't Do it For The Money."
AR13217 665 (September 16, 1993) pp[enc.24-25+].
"Darkness On The Edge of Bedrock: Kyle MacLachlan Brings His All-American Weirdness To "The Flintstones"."
AR13218 685 (June 30, 1994) pp63-64.
"The Girl Friend."
AR13219 729 (March 7, 1996) pp34-38,60-61.
"Hickory Smoke."
AR13220 684 (June 16, 1994) pp60-61,64,66+.
"High School Confidential: Amy Heckerling, The Writer And Director Of 'Clueless," Celebrates Adolescence As A State Of Mind."
AR13221 716 (September 7, 1995) p53.
"The Hood The Bad & The Ugly: For Naughty By Nature, The Question Is Not Can You Take East Orange Out Of The Boyz, But Can You Take The Boyz Out Of East Orange?."
AR13222 663 (August 19, 1993) pp66-68,70.
"Hot Actor."
AR13223 682 (May 19, 1994) p55.
"Hot Actress."
AR13224 682 (May 19, 1994) p57.
"Hot Appliance."
AR13225 682 (May 19, 1994) p58.
"Hot Arms."
AR13226 682 (May 19, 1994) p72.
"Hot Athlete."
AR13227 682 (May 19, 1994) p64.
"Hot Band."
AR13228 682 (May 19, 1994) p56.
"Hot Bulletin Board."
AR13229 682 (May 19, 1994) p56.
"Hot Comic Book."
AR13230 682 (May 19, 1994) p69.
"Hot Country Act."
AR13231 682 (May 19, 1994) p74.
"Hot Designer."
AR13232 682 (May 19, 1994) p64.
"Hot Director."
AR13233 682 (May 19, 1994) p58.
"Hot Exercise."
AR13234 682 (May 19, 1994) p69.
"Hot Jazz Artist."
AR13235 682 (May 19, 1994) pp76-77.
"The Hot List."
AR13236 682 (May 19, 1994) p55.
AR13237 715 (August 24, 1995) pp73-75,77,80+.
"Hot Loser."
AR13238 682 (May 19, 1994) p66.
"Hot Models."
AR13239 682 (May 19, 1994) p63.
"Hot Movie Critic."
AR13240 682 (May 19, 1994) p66.
"Hot Movie Theme."
AR13241 682 (May 19, 1994) p63.
"Hot Performance Artist."
AR13242 682 (May 19, 1994) p74.
"Hot Rapper."
AR13243 682 (May 19, 1994) p64.
"Hot Stand-Up."
AR13244 682 (May 19, 1994) p68.
"Hot Style."
AR13245 656 (May 13, 1993) pp94-98.
"Hot Subculture."
AR13246 682 (May 19, 1994) p68.
"Hot TV Show."
AR13247 682 (May 19, 1994) p56.
"Hot Unprotected Minority."
AR13248 682 (May 19, 1994) p57.

COHEN, RICH (continued)
"Hot Vacation Spot."
AR13249 682 (May 19, 1994) p72.
"Hot Vice."
AR13250 682 (May 19, 1994) p58.
"Insane In The Brain: For Biker Wayne Croasdale Life Is Going Downhill."
AR13251 680 (April 21, 1994) pp[enc.25-29].
"It's Show Time!."
AR13252 689 (August 25, 1994) pp54-61.
"The King & I."
AR13253 747 (November 14, 1996) pp13.
AR13254 747 (November 14, 1996) p74-76, 78-81 +..
"Life In The Indie Cities: From Bad Weather And Obstacles Comes Great Music—If You Know Where To Look."
AR13255 677 (March 10, 1994) pp54-57.
"Liv In The Fast Lane: Actress Liv Tyler Wraps Her Inner Charm In Men's Outerwear."
AR13256 694 (November 3, 1994) pp62-66.
"Master Of War: Novelist Tom Clancy Keeps Making New Enemies."
AR13257 696 (December 1, 1994) pp114-116,118 +.
"Melissa Etheridge: In Through The Out Door."
AR13258 698-699 (December 29, 1994) pp110-114,116.
"Papa Was A Rolling Stone: But Marlon Richards Is Not Just A Chip Off The Old Rock."
AR13259 660-661 (July 8, 1993) pp102-106.
"Pat's Kids."
AR13260 732 (April 18, 1996) pp51-54.
"Red Alert."
AR13261 693 (October 20, 1994) pp97-100,104.
"Shopping At Sal's: Searching For The Look Of The Future At The Salvation Army."
AR13262 680 (April 21, 1994) pp[enc.37-38].
"Skate Dreams: Roller Basketball Is A Game Of Fast Breaks And Fast Breaking."
AR13263 715 (August 24, 1995) pp90-92,94-96.
"Slave To The Grind: Can Eric Nies Escape MTV's Star-Breaker Machinery?."
AR13264 680 (April 21, 1994) pp[enc.17-21].
"Southern Comfort: Hootie And The Blowfish Take Their Deep-Fried Jams And Sweet Love Songs To The Top Of The Charts."
AR13265 714 (August 10, 1995) pp42-45.
"Spin Doctor: Club DJ Junior Vasquez Remixes The Soundtrack Of New York At Night."
AR13266 706 (April 20, 1995) pp[enc.22-24 +].
"Tour De Force: The Rolling Stones Rake It In And Rock The House."
AR13267 694 (November 3, 1994) pp25-26,28 +.
"Wired For Love: Three Tales Of Computer Romance."
AR13268 689 (August 25, 1994) pp77-78,80,83 +.
COHN, JONATHAN
"Anatomy Of A Murder: How Corporate Lobbyists Plotted To Kill Of Direct Student Lending."
AR13269 722 (November 30, 1995) pp45-46,83.
COKE, GORDON P.
"Our Lives, Our Music: Abbey Road."
AR13270 644 (November 26, 1992) p55.
COKER, CHEO H.
"Critics Comments."
AR13271 726 (January 25, 1996) pp46,50-51.
COLAPINTO, JOHN
"Aerosmith In A Hard Place: New Album Is Delayed Amid Rumors Of Drugs, Bickering And Behind-The-Scenes Firings."
AR13272 744 (October 3, 1996) pp22-24,26.
"A Boy And His Gun: An American Tragedy."
AR13273 692 (October 6, 1994) pp64-66,68-70 +.
"Double Fantasy."
AR13274 652 (March 18, 1993) pp[enc.19-20 +].
"[Editorial]."
AR13275 745 (October 17, 1996) p17.
"Getting Lost: Chronicle Of A Death Foretold."
AR13276 745 (October 17, 1996) pp80-82,84,86 +.
"Gold Medals And Platinum Blondes: The Dream Team At Atlanta's Largest Strip Club Gets Pumped For The Summer Olympics."
AR13277 736 (June 13, 1996) pp42-44,46,86 +.
"Heroin."
AR13278 735 (May 30, 1996) pp15-16,18,20 +.
"The Home Front: In The War Against AIDS, Some Of The Bravest Battles Are Fought Far From Laboratories And Demonstrations."
AR13279 619-620 (December 12, 1991) pp122-123,125 +.
"Hot Actress."
AR13280 630 (May 14, 1992) pp60-61,65,67.
"Just Say 'Yes': Morphine Shoot To Low-Fi Stardom."
AR13281 711 (June 29, 1995) p20.
"M. Scott Peck At The End Of The Road."
AR13282 719 (October 19, 1995) pp80-82,86,164.
"Mean & Sober: Ego And Innuendo Run Amok As The Music Industry Feuds Over Drug Treatment."
AR13283 743 (September 19, 1996) p30.
"The Raging Optimism And Multiple Personalities Of Dave Matthews."
AR13284 749 (December 12, 1996) pp52-54,56-57.
"Who Are You? Pearl Jam's Eddie Vedder."
AR13285 748 (November 28, 1996) pp50-54,57 +.
COLE, LEWIS
"HyperViolence: A Generation Of Kids In Richmond, Calif., Is Growing Up In The Shadow Of Guns, Drugs And Death."
AR13286 696 (December 1, 1994) pp106-108,110 +.
COLEMAN, MARK
"Arthur Alexander: 1940-1993."
AR13287 662 (August 5, 1993) p27.
"The Big Show: Hall Of Fame's Labor Day Lineup."
AR13288 712-713 (July 13, 1995) p33.
"Charlie Rich: 1932-1995."
AR13289 716 (September 7, 1995) p35.
"Decking The Hall: As The Hall Of Fame Goes Up, The Collection Comes To Life."
AR13290 706 (April 20, 1995) p29.
"Elvis Costello's Classical Gas: The Pop Poet Teams Up With A String Quartet On 'The Juliet Letters'."
AR13291 651 (March 4, 1993) p23.
"From Graceland To Cleveland."
AR13292 710 (June 15, 1995) p25.
"Gang Starr."
AR13293 695 (November 17, 1994) pp87-89.
"Green Jelly's Bubblegum Punk."
AR13294 660-661 (July 8, 1993) p18.
"Hall Of Fame."
AR13295 698-699 (December 29, 1994) p76.
"Hall Of Fame: See You In September."
AR13296 714 (August 10, 1995) p32.
"Mannequins With A Twist."
AR13297 711 (June 29, 1995) p18.
"Monster Magnetism."
AR13298 656 (May 13, 1993) pp17-18.
"Stone Alone: Pearl Jam's Stone Gossard Goes Solo With Shame."
AR13299 649 (February 4, 1993) p23.
"Stones Uncovered."
AR13300 715 (August 24, 1995) p37.
"We Were Just Happy Freaks, Man: Garcia In His Own Words."
AR13301 717 (September 21, 1995) pp52-56,58-59.
COLEMAN, RICK
"Fats Is Back!."
AR13302 671 (December 9, 1993) p17.
COLLINS, EDWYN
"Raves."
AR13303 721 (November 16, 1995) p43.
"COMEDY."
AR13304 630 (May 14, 1992) p52.

"THE COMPLETE CLAPTON: IN HIS OWN WORDS."
AR13305 655 (April 29, 1993) pp34-35,37-38 +.
"CONGRATS."
AR13306 698-699 (December 29, 1994) p26.
AR13307 708 (May 18, 1995) p14.
"CONGRATULATIONS."
AR13308 705 (April 6, 1995) p14.
AR13309 710 (June 15, 1995) p14.
AR13310 726 (January 25, 1996) p12.
AR13311 735 (May 30, 1996) p10.
CONSIDINE, J. D.
"Bruce: Still The Boss In Europe."
AR13312 636 (August 6, 1992) pp15-16.
"Replays."
AR13313 688 (August 11, 1994) p72.
"Wailing Souls: A Reggae Hall Of Fame."
AR13314 676 (February 24, 1994) pp41-42,44.
"World Music On The Hill: The Grateful Dead Bring The Rain Forest To Washington."
AR13315 655 (April 29, 1993) p24.
CONTRERAS, JOSEPH
"The Long Road Home."
AR13316 698-699 (December 29, 1994) pp120-129.
"THE CONTRIBUTORS."
AR13317 632 (June 11, 1992) p190.
AR13318 641 (January 15, 1992) p204.
COOLIO
"Raves."
AR13319 719 (October 19, 1995) p30.
COOPER, CAROL
"The Big Payback: Coolio Gets A Phat Return On His Dues With "Fantastic Voyage"."
AR13320 691 (September 22, 1994) p37.
"Burn, Baby, Burn: The Women Of TLC Stay Cool Under Fire."
AR13321 715 (August 24, 1995) pp27-28.
"Early Delivery: Brandy Breaks Out at 16 with 'Baby'."
AR13322 705 (April 6, 1995) p32.
COOPER, RICH
"Speed Mettle: The Fastest Americans In Their Sports, These Skaters And Skiers Hope To Bring Home The Olympic Gold."
AR13323 624 (February 20, 1992) pp34-38.
"A Trace Of Gold: The Ace Catches Air On The Way To Lillehammer."
AR13324 676 (February 24, 1994) pp51,53.
"[CORRECTION]."
AR13325 615 (January 17, 1991) p8.
AR13326 617 (November 14, 1991) p8.
AR13327 618 (November 28, 1991) p9.
AR13328 622 (January 23, 1992) p4.
AR13329 644 (November 26, 1992) p11.
AR13330 663 (August 19, 1993) p4.
AR13331 671 (December 9, 1993) p7.
AR13332 675 (February 10, 1994) p6.
AR13333 698-699 (December 29, 1994) p26.
AR13334 700 (January 26, 1995) p14.
AR13335 716 (September 7, 1995) p10.
"[CORRECTIONS]."
AR13336 662 (August 5, 1993) p8.
AR13337 702 (February 23, 1995) p16.
AR13338 703 (March 9, 1995) p16.
COTT, JONATHAN
"Drugstore Cowgirl: It's Sex, Peyote And Poetry As Uma Thurman Thumbs A Ride Aboard A Counterculture Classic."
AR13339 669 (November 11, 1993) pp58-60,62.
"Leonard Bernstein."
AR13340 641 (October 15, 1992) pp197-199.
"Mick Jagger."
AR13341 641 (October 15, 1992) pp84-85.
"Sebastiao Salgado: The Rolling Stone Interview."
AR13342 619-620 (December 12, 1991) pp133,135,138 +.
COTTS, CYNTHIA
"Smart Money."
AR13343 681 (May 5, 1994) pp42-43.
"THE COVERS 1993."
AR13344 672-673 (December 23, 1993) p188.
CRAMER, RICHARD BEN
"The Strange And Mysterious Death Of Mrs. Jerry Lee Lewis."
AR13345 632 (June 11, 1992) pp143-144,147.
CRANSTON, ALAN
"Freddy Krueger Does D.C.: Meet Bob Dole, Nightmare On Capitol Hill."
AR13346 666 (September 30, 1993) pp35-36,120 +.
"The World According To Gorby: Over Lunch In Moscow, The Former Senator From California Talks Politics With The Former Head Of the Soviet Union."
AR13347 689 (August 25, 1994) pp51-53.
"[CREDIT]."
AR13348 626 (March 19, 1992) p6.
CRESSE, MARK E.
"Our Lives, Our Music: Catch Bull At Four."
AR13349 644 (November 26, 1992) p56.
CRISAFULLI, CHUCK
"Critics Comments."
AR13350 726 (January 25, 1996) pp46,50-51.
"Simmering Chili: Peppers Stir Up A Red-Hot New Album."
AR13351 709 (June 1, 1995) p21.
"CRITICS' PICKS: 1992 MUSIC AWARDS."
AR13352 625 (March 5, 1992) p58.
"CRITICS' PICKS: 1993 MUSIC AWARDS."
AR13353 651 (March 4, 1993) p55.
"CRITICS POLL: 1996."
AR13354 726 (January 25, 1996) pp40-43,45,50 +.
CROSS, CHARLES R.
"Can The Presidents Of The United States Of America Live Up To The Majesty & Stupidity Of Their Name?."
AR13355 729 (March 7, 1996) pp30-33.
"Don't Look Back: Two New Films Expand On The Story Of Grunge."
AR13356 748 (November 28, 1996) p36.
"The Joys Of Noise: Soundgarden Throw A High-Frequency Sludgefest."
AR13357 727 (February 8, 1996) p26.
CROWE, CAMERON
"5 Against The World: Pearl Jam Emerge From The Strange Daze Of Superstardom With A New Album Full Of Rage And Warrior Soul."
AR13358 668 (October 28, 1993) pp50-52,55-58 +.
"The 'Jerry Maguire' Journal."
AR13359 750-751 (December 26, 1996) pp137-138,140 +.
"Led Zeppelin."
AR13360 641 (October 15, 1992) pp68-69,71.
"Making The Scene: A Filmmaker's Diary."
AR13361 640 (October 1, 1992) pp57-60.
CULLEY, ERIN
"Breaking Silence: Scott Weiland Of Stone Temple Pilots Opens Up And Gets Busy."
AR13362 710 (June 15, 1995) pp21-22.
"Los Angeles."
AR13363 686-687 (July 14, 1994) p45.
"Orange County Crush."
AR13364 686-687 (July 14, 1994) p45.
"Orange Day: In This Southern California County, The Punk Spirit Never Died."
AR13365 706 (April 20, 1995) pp[enc.14-18].
CUMMINGS, SUE
"Sympathy For The Flip Side: Collector Turns Penchant For The Obscure Into A&R Dream."
AR13366 689 (August 25, 1994) p28.
"Welcome To The Machine: The Music Revolution Comes To Your Town."
AR13367 679 (April 7, 1994) pp15-16,19.

CURTIS, TOM
"Man, Monkeys And Disease."
AR13368 626 (March 19, 1992) p61.
"The Origin Of AIDS: A Startling New Theory Attempts To Answer The Question 'Was It An Act Of God Or An Act Of Man?'."
AR13369 626 (March 19, 1992) pp54-59,61+.

D

DA SILVA, ANA
"Raves."
AR13370 738-739 (July 11, 1996) p31.
DAHL, SHAWN
"My Life With The Thrill Kill Kult: Straight Out Of The Seventies."
AR13371 618 (November 28, 1991) p30.
DALY, JAMES
"Digital Underground: Bootlegging Makes Inroads On The Info Superhighway."
AR13372 690 (September 8, 1994) p40.
"Music By Modem: On-Line Services Provide A High-Tech Option To Music Distribution."
AR13373 686-687 (July 14, 1994) p31.
"Totally Wired."
AR13374 696 (December 1, 1994) p40.
AR13375 702 (February 23, 1995) p39.
DALY, STEVEN
"Britain's Class Act: Blur Stand Up For Their Mod-Rock Roots On "Parklife"."
AR13376 694 (November 3, 1994) p34.
"Bush: Nirvana Wanna Bes."
AR13377 732 (April 18, 1996) pp40-44.
"Depeche Mode: The Rock & Roll Rebirth Of Everybody's Favorite Euroweenies."
AR13378 670 (November 25, 1993) pp90-94,96.
"The Original Riot Grrrl: Joan Jett Lives Up To Her Bad Reputation."
AR13379 678 (March 24, 1994) pp44-45.
"A Rose In Gloom: Madder Rose Balance Prettiness With Dissonance On "Panic On"."
AR13380 688 (August 11, 1994) p29.
"Suede: All That Glitters."
AR13381 657 (May 27, 1993) pp15-16.
"3 Tribes."
AR13382 736 (June 13, 1996) pp37-38,40-41+.
"Totally Stoned: Primal Scream Return To Rock Roots With "Give Out But Don't Give Up"."
AR13383 684 (June 16, 1994) p26.
"Tricky."
AR13384 747 (November 14, 1996) pp46-48.
DAMSKER, MATT
"Critics Comments."
AR13385 726 (January 25, 1996) pp46,50-51.
DANA, WILL
"Hot Mood: Confusion."
AR13386 741 (August 22, 1996) p74.
D'ANTICO, PAUL
"Our Lives, Our Music: Are You Experienced?."
AR13387 644 (November 26, 1992) p52.
D'ARBY, TERENCE TRENT
"People Hold On."
AR13388 675 (February 10, 1994) p18.
"Raves."
AR13389 675 (February 10, 1994) p18.
D'ARCY
AR13390 729 (March 7, 1996) p18.
DARZIN, DAINA
"Ah, The Smell Of It: L7 Bask In The Sweet Stink Of Success."
AR13391 688 (August 11, 1994) pp25-26.
"Astro Freaks: 2000."
AR13392 716 (September 7, 1995) p34.
"Bad Livers."
AR13393 697 (December 15, 1994) p40.
"Dancin' With The Devil: White Zombie Mint Gold From Goth."
AR13394 671 (December 9, 1993) pp13-14.
"[Evan Dando]."
AR13395 695 (November 17, 1994) pp148,150-151.
"Generation Next: The Smokin' Sounds Of Summer '94."
AR13396 686-687 (July 14, 1994) pp72-74.
"Machine Dreams: Rage Take On The Rights Of Native Americans."
AR13397 677 (March 10, 1994) p19.
"Mudhoney: The First Great Seattle Band Of The '80s Has The Last Laugh In The '90s."
AR13398 709 (June 1, 1995) pp46-49.
"The Real Dirt: Alice In Chains Take A Hard Look At The Dark Side Of Seattle On The New EP 'Jar Of Flies'."
AR13399 676 (February 24, 1994) pp18,20.
"Rebel Yellers: Pantera Take Metal To No. 1 With Their New "Far Beyond Driven"."
AR13400 685 (June 30, 1994) p24.
DAVIDSON, JOHN
"Menace To Society."
AR13401 728 (February 22, 1996) pp38-39.
DAVIS, STEPHEN
"This Wheel's On Fire."
AR13402 669 (November 11, 1993) pp66-69,71.
DEAN, CHUCK
"Certified Punk: Claw Hammer Nail It With 'Thank'."
AR13403 715 (August 24, 1995) p36.
"Critics Comments."
AR13404 726 (January 25, 1996) pp46,50-51.
"Evan Dando Of The Lemonheads."
AR13405 747 (November 14, 1996) p40.
"George Jones."
AR13406 748 (November 28, 1996) p45.
"Robyn Hitchcock."
AR13407 710 (June 15, 1995) p26.
"Skids' Mark: Southern Culture Hit It Big With 'Date'."
AR13408 721 (November 16, 1995) p38.
"Trippy Lip Shtick: Flaming Lips Rain Cosmic Debris."
AR13409 703 (March 9, 1995) p26.
"Ween."
AR13410 705 (April 6, 1995) p30.
DEAN, JOHN
"Clarification."
AR13411 693 (October 20, 1994) p22.
"Ghosts In The Machine: The CD-ROM Of "The Haldeman Diaries" And A New Documentary Finally Tell The Full Watergate Story."
AR13412 690 (September 8, 1994) pp47-49,88.
DECURTIS, ANTHONY
"Al Pacino: The Rolling Stone Interview."
AR13413 745 (October 17, 1996) pp62-65,68.
"Bad To The Bone: John Mellencamp Strips Down To Fighting Trim On "Dance Naked"."
AR13414 690 (September 8, 1994) pp62-64,88.
"Bill Monroe: Father Of Bluegrass Is Dead At 84."
AR13415 746 (October 31, 1996) pp20-21,23.
"Bryan Ferry."
AR13416 660-661 (July 8, 1993) p20.
"'Cop Killer': Yielding To Censors Never Works In The Long Run."
AR13417 639 (September 17, 1992) p32.
"Country Music Has Become The Refuge Of Older Rock Fans."
AR13418 644 (November 26, 1992) p23.
"Don Henley & Glenn Frey."
AR13419 641 (October 15, 1992) pp157-158.
"Edie's New "Morning": Solo Brickell Takes It Simple And Soulful."
AR13420 686-687 (July 14, 1994) p38.
"Jackson Browne."
AR13421 641 (October 15, 1992) pp138-139.

DECURTIS, ANTHONY (continued)
"Jonathan Demme: The Rolling STone Interview."
AR13422 678 (March 24, 1994) pp60-61,63,65+.
"Kurt Cobain 1967-1994."
AR13423 683 (June 2, 1994) pp30-33.
"[Michael Stipe]."
AR13424 695 (November 17, 1994) pp34-35,151.
"Monster Madness."
AR13425 693 (October 20, 1994) pp58-62,64+.
"The Music Never Stops: The Rolling Stone Interview With Jerry Garcia."
AR13426 664 (September 2, 1993) pp42-46,76.
"The Naked Transcript."
AR13427 641 (October 15, 1992) p185.
"Naughty By Nature's Surprise Success."
AR13428 615 (October 17, 1991) p27.
"No Mercy: Leonard Cohen's Tales from The Dark Side."
AR13429 648 (January 21, 1993) pp44-46,56.
"Ono's Season Of Grief."
AR13430 682 (May 19, 1994) p29.
"Opera Man: The Rolling Stone Interview With Pete Townshend."
AR13431 672-673 (December 23, 1993) pp105-106,108+.
"Opinion: Chapman Killed Lennon To Achieve This Kind Of Notoriety."
AR13432 648 (January 21, 1993) p19.
"Prince: Free At Last."
AR13433 748 (November 28, 1996) pp61-63,148.
"Prince Records Three Hours Of 'Emancipation'."
AR13434 745 (October 17, 1996) p36.
"Raves."
AR13435 662 (August 5, 1993) p24.
"Refueled & Reborn: While Led Zeppelin Take Their Rightful Place In The Rock & Roll Hall Of Fame, Jimmy Page And Robert Plant Draw Up New Flight Plans."
AR13436 702 (February 23, 1995) pp44-47,86,89.
"Robert Redford: The Rolling Stone Interview."
AR13437 692 (October 6, 1994) pp72-74,76-77+.
"Rock & Roll Must Not Let Broadway Blunt Its Visceral Power."
AR13438 659 (June 24, 1993) p23.
"Ropin' The Whirl Wind: Garth Brooks The Rolling Stone Interview."
AR13439 653 (April 1, 1993) pp30-32,34-35+.
"Television's Refined Tuning: The New York Punk-Guitar Godfathers Pick Up Where They Left Off."
AR13440 647 (January 7, 1993) p22.
"Tipper: Dems Send Wrong Message."
AR13441 638 (September 3, 1992) p17.
"A Tribute To Woody: Artists Gather To Commemorate Singer's Birthday."
AR13442 637 (August 20, 1992) p23.
"'Vibe' Baptized By Fire: Debut Issue Of Hip-Hop Magazine Hits The Street To Attacks And Praise."
AR13443 642 (October 29, 1992) p33.
"WH Down & Dirty: The Rolling Stone Interview."
AR13444 658 (June 10, 1993) pp44-49.
"Woody Allen: The Rolling Stone Interview."
AR13445 665 (September 16, 1993) pp45-46,48-50+.
"The Year In Music."
AR13446 645-646 (December 10, 1992) pp24,26.
"Zoo World Order: With A Lot Of Help From The Edge, U2 Are Reborn With A Case of The Giggles—And A New Sense Of Mission."
AR13447 667 (October 14, 1993) pp48-52,54+.
"DEE MURRAY: 1946-1992."
AR13448 625 (March 5, 1992) p22.
DEPAOLA, JOHN
"Our Lives, Our Music: Armed Forces."
AR13449 644 (November 26, 1992) p58.
D'ERASMO, STACEY
"Melissa Etheridge."
AR13450 683 (June 2, 1994) p20.
DEROGATIS, JIM
"Best New Band: Elastica."
AR13451 726 (January 25, 1996) p44.
"The Boom Goes Bust."
AR13452 724-725 (December 28, 1995) pp83,85.
"Charlie Watts."
AR13453 735 (May 30, 1996) p24.
"Pop Tarts: Orchestrated Rock Maneuvers Its Way Through The Grungy Darkness."
AR13454 729 (March 7, 1996) pp20-21.
"Senator Krist: Krist Novoselic Talks About Politics, Censorship And Life After Nirvana."
AR13455 727 (February 8, 1996) pp19,22,24.
"Shannon Hood: 1967-1995."
AR13456 722 (November 30, 1995) pp23-24.
"Syd Straw Plays With The Skeletons In Her Closet."
AR13457 734 (May 16, 1996) p25.
"Tribute: Pete Grant 1935-1995."
AR13458 726 (January 25, 1996) p28.
"Yum-Yum Make Sugary-Sweet Pop (With Strings)."
AR13459 736 (June 13, 1996) p28.
DERY, MARK
"Master Class."
AR13460 748 (November 28, 1996) pp119-123.
"Terminators: The Robots That Rodney Brooks And Hans Moravec Imagine Will Succeed Humans, Not Serve Them."
AR13461 658 (June 10, 1993) pp[enc.14+].
DIEHL, MATT
"Bassman's Holiday: Mike Watt Casts An All-Star Solo Album."
AR13462 693 (October 20, 1994) p38.
"Chuck D Is Back With More Agendas Than Ever."
AR13463 745 (October 17, 1996) p46.
"David Bowie Rumbles In The Jungle On 'Earthling'."
AR13464 749 (December 12, 1996) p25.
"Fighting Hype And The Weight of His Father's Legend, Jeff Buckley Finds His Own Voice On "Grace"."
AR13465 693 (October 20, 1994) pp68-70,163.
"Fluffy May Be Pretty, But They're Hardly Vacant."
AR13466 746 (October 31, 1996) p28.
"Former Lemonhead Jesse Peretz Gets Behind The Lens."
AR13467 742 (September 5, 1996) p26.
"Head Case."
AR13468 689 (August 25, 1994) pp63-65.
"Hurricane."
AR13469 710 (June 15, 1995) p33.
"Leapin' Lizard: LollaPaloozers Aren't Likely To Forget The Jesus Lizard If Lead Singer David Yow Has Anything To Say About It."
AR13470 714 (August 10, 1995) pp48-51.
"Luscious Jackson Stray From Home On 'Fever In Fever Out'."
AR13471 749 (December 12, 1996) pp23-24.
"Pavement Smooth Out The Edges On 'Corners'."
AR13472 748 (November 28, 1996) p34.
DIZNEY, JOE
"John Campbell: A Modern Bluesman."
AR13473 622 (January 23, 1992) p14.
DOCTOROW, E. L.
"Heaven Is Under Our Feet: Voices For Walden Woods."
AR13474 615 (October 17, 1991) pp53,55,59,105.
DONELLY, TANYA
"Raves."
AR13475 678 (March 24, 1994) p16.
"DON'T CALL ME SLACKER: STUDENT VOLUNTEERS SPEAK FOR THEMSELVES ABOUT CHANGING THE WORLD LITTLE BY LITTLE."
AR13476 678 (March 24, 1994) pp85-86,89.
"THE DOPE ON HEALTH CARE."
AR13477 671 (December 9, 1993) p36.

DOYLE, LARRY
"All They Need To Know They Learned In Hollywood."
AR13478 750-751 (December 26, 1996) pp32-34,36,38+.
DRAKE, PAMELA
"Our Lives, Our Music: Horses."
AR13479 644 (November 26, 1992) p50.
DREYFUSS, ROBERT
"NRA's Last Hurrah?."
AR13480 746 (October 31, 1996) pp52-53,59-60+.
"Portrait Of Defeat: Is The End Near For The NRA?."
AR13481 750-751 (December 26, 1996) pp107,110-111.
DROZDOWSKI, TED
"The Heart Of Darkness: The Boston Band Come Makes Soul Music For The Slacker Generation."
AR13482 654 (April 15, 1993) p22.
"Low-Fi Romantics: Sebadoh Flirt With The Mainstream."
AR13483 704 (March 23, 1995) p43.
DROZDYK, CHARLIE
"Into The Loop: How To Get The Job You Want After Graduation."
AR13484 704 (March 23, 1995) pp95-97,99.
"DRUG NEWS."
AR13485 684 (June 16, 1994) p11.
DUFFY, THOM
"Rock & Roll Summer: London."
AR13486 710 (June 15, 1995) p49.
DUNN, JANCEE
"Aimee Mann."
AR13487 728 (February 22, 1996) p26.
"Are The Kids All Right? As More Moms Enter The Pop-Music Work Force, Rock & Roll Nannies Have Their Hands Full."
AR13488 748 (November 28, 1996) pp30-31.
"Art Garfunkel."
AR13489 670 (November 25, 1993) p28.
"Barry White."
AR13490 701 (February 9, 1995) p30.
"Beck: Resident Alien."
AR13491 738-739 (July 11, 1996) pp51-52,54.
"Billy Joel."
AR13492 672-673 (December 23, 1993) p23.
"Bonnie Raitt."
AR13493 680 (April 21, 1994) p21.
"Boy George."
AR13494 720 (November 2, 1995) p26.
"Cameron Diaz."
AR13495 741 (August 22, 1996) pp50-53,112.
"Carpenters Collection."
AR13496 690 (September 8, 1994) p33.
"Cher."
AR13497 743 (September 19, 1996) p46.
"Chow Manhattan: Parker Posey And Benicio Del Toro Treat Themselves To A Bottle Of Wine, A Little Red Sauce And Some Italian Dressing."
AR13498 718 (October 5, 1995) pp[enc.8-10+].
"Chris Robinson Of The Black Crowes."
AR13499 746 (October 31, 1996) p36.
"Clown 'N' Dirty: Mariah Carey's Twisted 'Fantasy'."
AR13500 721 (November 16, 1995) p33.
"Crowning Moment: Tanya Donelly & Belly Hit The Big Time With King."
AR13501 706 (April 20, 1995) pp46-50,96.
"The Dating Dame."
AR13502 738-739 (July 11, 1996) pp33-34,36,38.
"David Byrne."
AR13503 688 (August 11, 1994) p37.
"Dead Aim: Filter Hit The Bull's Eye With The Controversial Track 'Hey Man, Nice Shot'."
AR13504 715 (August 24, 1995) pp68-70.
"Eddie Spaghetti of Supersuckers."
AR13505 721 (November 16, 1995) p43.
"81: Free Your Mind."
AR13506 667 (October 14, 1993) p98.
"80: Straight Up."
AR13507 667 (October 14, 1993) p98.
"82: Rapture."
AR13508 667 (October 14, 1993) p98.
"Esquivel."
AR13509 719 (October 19, 1995) p30.
"15: Once In A Lifetime."
AR13510 667 (October 14, 1993) p73.
"51: Back To My Roots."
AR13511 667 (October 14, 1993) p90.
"56: Faith."
AR13512 667 (October 14, 1993) p92.
"50: When I Think Of You."
AR13513 667 (October 14, 1993) p87.
"The Fresh Ones: Foo Fighters Weird Candy Fantasies."
AR13514 730 (March 21, 1996) p32.
"Fun Lovin' Criminals Take Their Horseplay Seriously."
AR13515 736 (June 13, 1996) p25.
"Geddy Lee Of Rush."
AR13516 749 (December 12, 1996) p33.
"Generation Next: The Smokin' Sounds Of Summer '94."
AR13517 686-687 (July 14, 1994) pp72-74.
"Getting Better: Work In Progress."
AR13518 745 (October 17, 1996) pp75-79,124+.
"Getting The Led Out: Jimmy Page And Robert Plant Are Back In Business."
AR13519 696 (December 1, 1994) pp29,31.
"Gibby Haynes Of The Butthole Surfers."
AR13520 733 (May 2, 1996) p28.
"Greg Dulli Of Afghan Whigs."
AR13521 690 (September 8, 1994) p34.
"Hail Hail Rock & Roll: Behind The Scenes And Onstage At The Concert For The Hall Of Fame."
AR13522 719 (October 19, 1995) pp35-36,38,40+.
"Hall Of Fame '95: Led Zeppelin And Neil Young Highlight The 10th Anniversary Celebration."
AR13523 702 (February 23, 1995) pp48-50.
"Hall Of Fame '96."
AR13524 728 (February 22, 1996) pp18-19.
"Hot Turn-On: Seventies Porn."
AR13525 741 (August 22, 1996) p82.
"Jennifer Jason Leigh: She's The Queen of The Ravaged, Boozed Up And Strung Out."
AR13526 722 (November 30, 1995) pp57-58,60-61.
"John Lydon."
AR13527 684 (June 16, 1994) p24.
"Johnny Cash."
AR13528 685 (June 30, 1994) p35.
"Joni Mitchell."
AR13529 697 (December 15, 1994) p32.
"Liz Phair."
AR13530 674 (January 27, 1994) p20.
"Losing Their Religion: Rev. Horton Heat Lets The Spirits Move Him."
AR13531 692 (October 6, 1994) p28.
"Magic And Loss: Lida Husik Meshes Indie With Ambient."
AR13532 732 (April 18, 1996) p36.
"Neil Diamond."
AR13533 730 (March 21, 1996) p36.
"Nick Cave."
AR13534 689 (August 25, 1994) p34.
"9: Take On Me."
AR13535 667 (October 14, 1993) p70.
"One Hot Minute."
AR13536 732 (April 18, 1996) pp[enc.10,12].
"One Of Us! One Of Us! One Of...."
AR13537 682 (May 19, 1994) p53.
"Pat Boone."
AR13538 734 (May 16, 1996) p26.

DUNN, JANCEE (continued)
"The Pepper Chase."
AR13539 668 (October 28, 1993) p17.
"Richard Thompson."
AR13540 682 (May 19, 1994) p28.
"Rock & Roll Hall Of Fame."
AR13541 677 (March 10, 1994) pp27-29.
"Rock & Roll Yearbook."
AR13542 672-673 (December 23, 1993) pp15-17,20,27+.
AR13543 750-751 (December 26, 1996) pp45-46,48,50+.
"Rock And Roll Yearbook."
AR13544 698-699 (December 29, 1994) pp36-37,42,50+.
"Ron Wood Of The Rolling Stones."
AR13545 698-699 (December 29, 1994) pp70,72.
"Ruby Doomsday: Ruby Sparkle With Their Bleak Bravado."
AR13546 729 (March 7, 1996) p24.
"Selene Vigil Of 7 Year Bitch."
AR13547 732 (April 18, 1996) p38.
"17: Been Caught Stealing."
AR13548 667 (October 14, 1993) p76.
"79: Voices Carry."
AR13549 667 (October 14, 1993) p98.
"Sir Mix-A-Lot."
AR13550 693 (October 20, 1994) p44.
"62: It's My Life."
AR13551 667 (October 14, 1993) p93.
"Skee-Lo Is As Skee-Lo Does In 'I Wish'."
AR13552 716 (September 7, 1995) p30.
"Soul Asylum."
AR13553 695 (November 17, 1994) pp55-57.
"Soul Asylum: Dave Pirner & Dan Murphy."
AR13554 672-673 (December 23, 1993) p35.
"The Spice Of Life: Salt-N-Pepa Prove That Hip-Hop Is Not Just A Man's Game."
AR13555 685 (June 30, 1994) pp21-22,37.
"Star Trek: Melissa Etheridge Takes The Long Hard Road From The Heartland To Hollywood."
AR13556 709 (June 1, 1995) pp38-41,44-45.
"Stevie Nicks."
AR13557 691 (September 22, 1994) p34.
"10: Express Yourself."
AR13558 667 (October 14, 1993) p70.
"That Girl."
AR13559 692 (October 6, 1994) pp42-46.
"35: Love Shack."
AR13560 667 (October 14, 1993) p80.
"39: In Bloom."
AR13561 667 (October 14, 1993) p82.
"31: Kool Thing."
AR13562 667 (October 14, 1993) p80.
"32: Burning Down The House."
AR13563 667 (October 14, 1993) p80.
"Tom Jones."
AR13564 696 (December 1, 1994) p42.
"Tony Bennett."
AR13565 679 (April 7, 1994) p30.
"28: Vogue."
AR13566 667 (October 14, 1993) p78.
"25: Give It Away."
AR13567 667 (October 14, 1993) p77.
"27: Billie Jean."
AR13568 667 (October 14, 1993) p78.
"26: Hot For Teacher."
AR13569 667 (October 14, 1993) p78.
"22: Girls Just Want To Have Fun."
AR13570 667 (October 14, 1993) p77.
"Wal-Mart: No 'Utero'."
AR13571 669 (November 11, 1993) p13.
"Wide-Lapel Hell: VH1 Drags 'Bandstand' Out Of The Fashion Closet."
AR13572 731 (April 4, 1996) p33.
"Willie Nelson."
AR13573 703 (March 9, 1995) p34.
DURITZ, ADAM
"Raves."
AR13574 677 (March 10, 1994) p19.
DYLAN, JAKOB
AR13575 670 (November 25, 1993) p28.

E

"[E-MAIL]."
AR13576 682 (May 19, 1994) p14.
ECCLES, ANDREW
"Off The Street And Onto Center Stage: Rock Steady Crew And Jossie Harris Turn Break Dancing Into An Art."
AR13577 638 (September 3, 1992) pp[enc.35-36+].
"[EDITORIAL]."
AR13578 750-751 (December 26, 1996) p19.
EFSTATHIOU, JIM
"Oi! Did They Have Troubles."
AR13579 722 (November 30, 1995) p42.
EHRLICH, DIMITRI
"Dionne Farris."
AR13580 692 (October 6, 1994) p32.
"Female Rappers Laud Reno."
AR13581 654 (April 15, 1993) p24.
"Generation Next: The Smokin' Sounds Of Summer '94."
AR13582 686-687 (July 14, 1994) pp72-74.
"Global Village: WOMAD Returns For A Tour Of The U.S.."
AR13583 685 (June 30, 1994) p29.
"Music For Your Mother: Lords Of The Underground Bring Family Values To Hardcore Rap."
AR13584 664 (September 2, 1993) p20.
"The Next Wave: The Fusion Of Jazz And Hip-Hop Is Bringing A New Groove To The Dance Floor."
AR13585 684 (June 16, 1994) p21.
"Not Just Blowing Smoke: Cypress Hill Light Up On 'Black Sunday'."
AR13586 662 (August 5, 1993) p16.
"Phat Cats And Punks: Rappers Meet Metalheads On 'Judgment Night'."
AR13587 663 (August 19, 1993) p20.
"Smokin Suckaz Wit Logic."
AR13588 676 (February 24, 1994) p24.
"Street News."
AR13589 665 (September 16, 1993) p22.
AR13590 676 (February 24, 1994) p25.
AR13591 679 (April 7, 1994) p32.
AR13592 689 (August 25, 1994) p40.
AR13593 694 (November 3, 1994) p40.
AR13594 703 (March 9, 1995) p33.
AR13595 707 (May 4, 1995) p32.
EHRMANN, ERIC
"Toking Down With The MC5."
AR13596 632 (June 11, 1992) pp35-36.
EITZEL, MARK
"Raves."
AR13597 697 (December 15, 1994) p32.
"ELECTION '92."
AR13598 645-646 (December 10, 1992) p98.
ENGELER, AMY
"Tumble Weeds: Competing In A Sport That Demands Youth And Artistry, Gymnasts Shannon Miller And Jarrod Hanks Make The Leap From Athlete To Performer."
AR13599 628 (April 16, 1992) pp[enc.21-23+].
ENO, BRIAN
"Bringing Up Baby: A Behind-The-Scenes Look At The Making Of U2's New Album."

AR13600 618 (November 28, 1991) pp42-48,50,116.
ERICKSON, STEVE
"In The Zone Of Perceived Faith: Report From New Hampshire."
AR13601 726 (January 25, 1996) pp54-56,58-59 +.
"A Nation Of Nomads: As The Presidential Campaign Begins, The Republican Wanna-Be's Encounter An American Electorate Wandering Between Hope And Rage."
AR13602 724-725 (December 28, 1995) pp103-104,107 +.
"Onward Christian Soldiers: Bob Dole, Phil Gramm And The Other Republican Candidates Are Kowtowing To The Religious Right, But Conservative Christians Are Searching For A True Believer."
AR13603 729 (March 7, 1996) pp40-42,44-45 +.
ESZTERHAS, JOE
"King Of The Goons."
AR13604 632 (June 11, 1992) pp61-62,64-65.
ETHERIDGE, ERIC
"The Drug War: Prohibition Fails Again."
AR13605 688 (August 11, 1994) p44.
"A Sacrifice To The Lords Of Yesterday."
AR13606 685 (June 30, 1994) p45.
"A Swing And A Miss: The Senate Crime Bill."
AR13607 680 (April 21, 1994) pp37,40.
ETHERIDGE, MELISSA
"Melissa Etheridge On Janis Joplin."
AR13608 702 (February 23, 1995) p50.
"EUGENE, OREGON."
AR13609 681 (May 5, 1994) p33.
EWALD, RUSS
"Deep Cover."
AR13610 634-635 (July 9, 1992) pp92-94,96-97.

F

"FACES OF VIOLENCE."
AR13611 710 (June 15, 1995) pp57-58,60-65.
FANNON, GARY
"I Am Free And I Want To Thank Rolling Stone And Its Readers For Returning My Life To Me."
AR13612 743 (September 19, 1996) pp48-50.
FARBER, JIM
"Art Versus Commerce."
AR13613 617 (November 14, 1991) p184.
"The GLAAD Hit List."
AR13614 656 (May 13, 1993) p21.
"Music Videos."
AR13615 623 (February 6, 1992) p90.
"New Ragged Glories."
AR13616 621 (January 9, 1992) p56.
"The 100 Top Music Videos."
AR13617 667 (October 14, 1993) p65.
"Rainforest Foundation Benefit."
AR13618 735 (May 30, 1996) p50.
"Superegos On The Loose."
AR13619 615 (October 17, 1991) p102.
"We're Not Gonna Take It: Gay And Lesbian Activists Battle The Rise Of Homophobia In Pop Music."
AR13620 656 (May 13, 1993) p21.
"FAREWELL."
AR13621 619-620 (December 12, 1991) pp109,112.
AR13622 645-646 (December 10, 1992) pp101-102.
AR13623 672-673 (December 23, 1993) pp79-80.
AR13624 698-699 (December 29, 1994) pp80,83,85-86.
FELTON, DAVID
"Brian Wilson."
AR13625 641 (October 15, 1992) pp79,81.
FERNANDO, S. H., JR.
"The B.I.G. Payback: Notorious B.I.G. Is Living Large—The Legal Way."
AR13626 709 (June 1, 1995) p24.
"Mobb Deep Deliver 'Hell On Earth' To The Faithful."
AR13627 749 (December 12, 1996) p32.
"Wu Tang Clan Deliver The Goods With 'Wu Wear'."
AR13628 745 (October 17, 1996) p42.
FINE, JASON
"Beautiful Loser: Video Director Steve Hanft's Scruffy Style Has Taken Him From Beck To Hootie."
AR13629 749 (December 12, 1996) p28.
"The Dust Brothers Take The Past Into The Future."
AR13630 743 (September 19, 1996) p38.
"45 Special: A New Label Flourishes In A Funky Format."
AR13631 709 (June 1, 1995) p27.
"Imperial Teen Chart Their Own Course On 'Seasick'."
AR13632 738-739 (July 11, 1996) p25.
"Jason Bentley."
AR13633 747 (November 14, 1996) p60.
"Screaming Trees."
AR13634 741 (August 22, 1996) pp55-56,108 +.
FISHER, CARRIE
"Madonna."
AR13635 641 (October 15, 1992) pp176-178.
"FIX THE GRAMMYS."
AR13636 680 (April 21, 1994) p33.
FLANAGAN, J. BRIAN
"Our Lives, Our Music: Bringing It All Back Home."
AR13637 644 (November 26, 1992) p49.
FLEISCHMANN, MARK
"All Systems Go: Whether It's Budget Audio For A Dorm Room Or Home Theater For A Mansion, One Of These New Setups Is Right For You."
AR13638 684 (June 16, 1994) pp91-92,94,99 +.
"Audio Power To The People: Now Is The Time To Exercise—And Enjoy—Your Right To Low-Cost Hi-Fi."
AR13639 633 (June 25, 1992) p52.
"Cheap Seats At The Video Revolution: HDTV's On Its Way, But In The Meantime You Still Need Something To Watch."
AR13640 636 (August 6, 1992) p68.
"Disc Contentment: Digital Components Challenge CD-Hating Audiophiles' Claims Of Vinyl Supremacy."
AR13641 627 (April 2, 1992) p48.
"In My Room."
AR13642 621 (January 9, 1992) p41.
"Keep That Wallet Out."
AR13643 658 (June 10, 1993) pp[enc.30].
"Scrambling For Dollars: Will Cable Companies Break The Promise Of New Video Technologies?."
AR13644 616 (October 31, 1991) pp105-106.
"Size Counts: With The Right Audio System, You'll Have A Good Relationship With Music."
AR13645 708 (May 18, 1995) pp[enc.8-12 +].
"Small Audio Dynamite: When It Comes To Stereo Systems, Bigger Is Not Always Better."
AR13646 653 (April 1, 1993) p61.
"So You Finally Put Together The Ideal Audio System."
AR13647 658 (June 10, 1993) pp[enc.26].
"Star Systems 1992."
AR13648 621 (January 9, 1992) pp38-41.
"Star Systems '93: Audio For Every Room And Budget."
AR13649 658 (June 10, 1993) pp[enc.23 +].
"Still Rocking: PCs, The Web, Multimedia...Despite The Hype Computer Technology Can't Compare With The Elegance Reliability And Value Of Today's Audio Systems."
AR13650 735 (May 30, 1996) pp[enc.10-12 +].
FLIPPO, CHET
"Dolly Parton."
AR13651 632 (June 11, 1992) pp114-115,117.
FOEGE, ALEC
"[Billie Joe]."
AR13652 695 (November 17, 1994) pp24-25,77.

"Building On Rock: A Summer '95 Opening Is Expected On The Long-Awaited Rock Hall Of Fame."
AR13653 686-687 (July 14, 1994) p23.
"Candlebox."
AR13654 674 (January 27, 1994) p24.
"Children Of The Damned Never Mind The Sex Pistols: Here's Their Offspring."
AR13655 701 (February 9, 1995) pp42-45.
"Chris Cornell Of Soundgarden: The End Of The Innocence."
AR13656 698-699 (December 29, 1994) pp103-107.
"The Downward Spiral: The Last Days Of Nirvana's Leader."
AR13657 683 (June 2, 1994) pp35-36,38,40 +.
"Fugees: Leaders Of The New Cool."
AR13658 742 (September 5, 1996) pp40-44,72-73.
"Funeral For A Friend: Deadheads Flock To San Francisco To Honor Jerry Garcia."
AR13659 717 (September 21, 1995) pp23-24,26,28.
"Green Day."
AR13660 724-725 (December 28, 1995) pp28-30,32-34.
"Greg Graffin Of Bad Religion."
AR13661 698-699 (December 29, 1994) p52.
"Hollywood Swingin': Film Soundtracks Go Out On The Cutting Edge."
AR13662 688 (August 11, 1994) p34.
"Incense And Insolence: Mazzy Star Carry The Torch For '60s Psychedelia And The Importance Of Being Difficult."
AR13663 693 (October 20, 1994) pp33-34.
"The Kids Are Alright: Green Day."
AR13664 691 (September 22, 1994) pp25,27.
"Once Death-Defying Clowns, The Red Hot Chili Peppers Grow Up To Be Sensitive White Males."
AR13665 719 (October 19, 1995) pp52-58,60.
"Spin Doctors."
AR13666 695 (November 17, 1994) pp135-137.
"Strange Fruit: The Improbable Rise Of Dolores O'Riordan And The Cranberries."
AR13667 704 (March 23, 1995) pp56-60,138 +.
"The Sweet Smell Of Success: The Punks Of Rancid Match Wits With The Corporate Rock Machine."
AR13668 716 (September 7, 1995) pp54-56,58-59.
"Tales From The Downside: Freedy Johnston Writes Perfect pop Songs About Hard Times And Heartbreak."
AR13669 690 (September 8, 1994) pp27,29.
"Three In A Van: Mike Watt Hits The Road Econo Style With Dave Grohl And Eddie Vedder."
AR13670 709 (June 1, 1995) pp19-20.
"The Veldt."
AR13671 683 (June 2, 1994) p24.
"With A Little Help From His Mates: Mick Ronson's Posthumous 'Heaven 'N Hull' To Be Released."
AR13672 681 (May 5, 1994) p13.
FONG-TORRES, BEN
"Land Of The Dead: San Francisco Was Where It All Began."
AR13673 717 (September 21, 1995) pp65-66.
"Ray Charles."
AR13674 641 (October 15, 1992) pp56-58.
"FOR THE RECORD."
AR13675 708 (May 18, 1995) p14.
AR13676 718 (January 5, 1995) p16.
AR13677 719 (January 19, 1995) p10.
AR13678 721 (November 16, 1995) p18.
AR13679 724-725 (December 28, 1995) p24.
AR13680 726 (January 25, 1996) p12.
AR13681 728 (February 22, 1996) p16.
AR13682 731 (April 4, 1996) p14.
AR13683 744 (January 3, 1996) p16.
FOSTER, DOUGLAS
"If The Symptoms Are Rapid Increases In Teen Deaths From Murder, Suicide And Car Crashes, Alcohol And Drugs...The Disease Is Adolescence."
AR13684 671 (December 9, 1993) pp55-57,59-60 +.
FRANCE, KIM
"Becoming Juliana Hatfield."
AR13685 666 (September 30, 1993) p19.
"Eden's Children: 10,000 Maniacs Grapple With The Pleasures & Perils Of Success in The Real World."
AR13686 652 (March 18, 1993) pp34-37,49.
"Grrrls At War."
AR13687 660-661 (July 8, 1993) pp23-24.
"The Spinanes."
AR13688 677 (March 10, 1994) p22.
FRASCELLA, LAWRENCE
"Nora Ephron: On The Front Lines Of The Sexual Battlefield With The Writer And Director Of 'Sleepless In Seattle'."
AR13689 660-661 (July 8, 1993) pp73-75.
FREEDMAN, SAMUEL G.
"Johnny Clegg's War On Apartheid."
AR13690 632 (June 11, 1992) pp181,183-185.
FRICKE, DAVID
"Achtung, Babies! A New U2 Album!."
AR13691 660-661 (July 8, 1993) p17.
"Alejandro Escovedo."
AR13692 733 (May 2, 1996) pp36-37.
"American Stars N' Bars: Living History Steals The Show At SXSW."
AR13693 681 (May 5, 1994) p14.
"Australia's Other Stars: Aboriginal Bands Are Making Their Mark On Music From Down Under."
AR13694 640 (October 1, 1992) p29.
"Big Daze Out: Goin' Off The Deep End At The Big Day Out."
AR13695 705 (April 6, 1995) pp23-24.
"Billy Corgan Talks: The Smashing Pumpkins Leader On Death, Drugs And The Future Of His Band."
AR13696 743 (September 19, 1996) pp26-30,96.
"Boys' Life: Silverchair, Food Fights Are More Fun Than Selling Millions Of Records."
AR13697 728 (February 22, 1996) pp44-47,64.
"Danny Gatton: 1945-1994."
AR13698 696 (December 1, 1994) p49.
"The Dark Side Of 'Amused': Roger Waters Tackles War And Andrew Lloyd Webber On His New Album."
AR13699 639 (September 17, 1992) p28.
"Death Becomes Him: Nick Cave Acquires A Taste For Murder."
AR13700 734 (May 16, 1996) pp34-36.
"Def Leppard: Ready To Roar?."
AR13701 615 (October 17, 1991) p24.
"Don't Tread On Me: Metallica's James Hetfield."
AR13702 654 (April 15, 1993) pp41-46.
"Dutch Treat: The Stones Go Back To Clubland For A New Live LP."
AR13703 712-713 (July 13, 1995) pp34,37.
"Eddie Hinton: 1944-1995."
AR13704 717 (September 21, 1995) p34.
"Exile On Main Street: Small-Town Life Suits Jack Logan Just Fine."
AR13705 730 (March 21, 1996) pp24,26.
"The Fire This Time: Midnight Oil Reignites With A New Album."
AR13706 658 (June 10, 1993) pp19,21.
"Flower Grrrl: After 12 Years With 10,000 Maniacs, Natalie Merchant makes The Most Of Liberation On 'Tigerlily'."
AR13707 721 (November 16, 1995) pp31-32.
"Frank Zappa: 1940-1993."
AR13708 674 (January 27, 1994) pp11-13,15-16.
"The Galactic Boys: Art-Metal Buckaroos."
AR13709 617 (November 14, 1991) p34.
"He Had Faced His Demon: Deborah Koons Garcia Speaks Out."
AR13710 717 (September 21, 1995) p30.
"Heart-Shaped Noise: The Music And The Legacy."
AR13711 683 (June 2, 1994) pp63,66-67.
"Home On The Strange."
AR13712 656 (May 13, 1993) pp28,122.
"Iceland's Sugarcubes."
AR13713 615 (October 17, 1991) p20.

FRICKE, DAVID (continued)
"In Living Color: Vernon Reid Goes Solo With A Stellar Cast."
AR13714 733 (May 2, 1996) p22.
"In With The Outtakes: Def Leppard Issues New Odds & Sods LP."
AR13715 667 (October 14, 1993) p26.
"Jimi: The Man And The Music."
AR13716 623 (February 6, 1992) pp40-42,44-45+.
"Life After Death: The Rolling Stone Interview With Courtney Love."
AR13717 697 (December 15, 1994) pp58-61,64,66+.
"Life After Guns N' Roses: With The Release Of His Album, Izzy Stradlin Finally Breaks His Silence."
AR13718 642 (October 29, 1992) pp23,26.
"Lou Reed: Beyond The Underground."
AR13719 627 (April 2, 1992) p22.
"Married To Metal: The Rolling Stone Interview With Metallica's Lars Ulrich."
AR13720 708 (May 18, 1995) pp72-74,76,93+.
"Metallica: Once The Scourge Of The Mainstream, The Titans Of Thrash Are On Top Of The Charts."
AR13721 617 (November 14, 1991) pp48-50,53-54.
"Michael Stipe."
AR13722 641 (October 15, 1992) pp187-188.
"Michael Stipe: The Rolling Stone Interview."
AR13723 625 (March 5, 1992) pp45-49,72.
"Monster On The Loose: R.E.M. Open Their First Tour In Five Years, In Australia."
AR13724 704 (March 23, 1995) pp27,29-30,32.
"Neil Young: Going To Extremes."
AR13725 618 (November 28, 1991) p20.
"The Next Big Thing."
AR13726 641 (October 15, 1992) p194.
"1994 Music Awards."
AR13727 674 (January 27, 1994) pp40-42,44-45.
"No Pain, No Gain: The Rolling Stone Interview With Henry Rollins."
AR13728 672-673 (December 23, 1993) pp111-112,114.
"On The Edge."
AR13729 730 (March 21, 1996) p98.
AR13730 745 (October 17, 1996) p135.
AR13731 750-751 (December 26, 1996) p192.
"One More Time With Feeling: Defying Time And Trends, The Rolling Stones Return With More Of That Voodoo They Do So Well."
AR13732 686-687 (July 14, 1994) pp68-71,110.
"Opinion: Tribute LPs Filled With Quirky Covers Are Just No Fun Anymore."
AR13733 649 (February 4, 1993) p23.
"Our Man In Nirvana Rages On (And On) About Stardom, Fatherhood, His Feud With Pearl Jam, The Death Of Grunge And Why He's Never Been Happier In His Life: The Rolling Stone Interview."
AR13734 674 (January 27, 1994) pp34-38,56.
"Papa John Creach: 1917-1994."
AR13735 679 (April 7, 1994) p19.
"Patti Smith: The Rolling Stone Interview."
AR13736 738-739 (July 11, 1996) pp42-44,46,48+.
"The Plastic Ono McCartney Band."
AR13737 705 (April 6, 1995) p25.
"Playing In The Band: The Music Of The Grateful Dead."
AR13738 717 (September 21, 1995) pp69,71-73.
"Pretty Hate Machine: On Their New Album, 'Load,' Metallica Explore The Devil Inside."
AR13739 737 (June 27, 1996) pp32-34,36-37+.
"Radio Daze."
AR13740 676 (February 24, 1994) p16.
"Raves."
AR13741 664 (September 2, 1993) p16.
"Red Hot Chili Peppers' Naked Truth."
AR13742 633 (June 25, 1992) pp26-30,50-51.
"Return Of The Crimson King: Robert Fripp And Company Rejoin Forces For The First Time In Ten Years."
AR13743 655 (April 29, 1993) p20.
"Return Of The King: Robert Fripp Keeps His Word."
AR13744 684 (June 16, 1994) p18.
"Rockin' In The Heart Of Texas: Unsigned Bands Reign Supreme At Austin's Annual Music Blowout."
AR13745 629 (April 30, 1992) p28.
"The Rolling Stone Interview With Sonic Youth's Thurston Moore: Better Living Through Feedback."
AR13746 691 (September 22, 1994) pp52-54,56,58+.
"Smashing Pumpkins: The Rolling Stone Interview With Billy Corgan."
AR13747 721 (November 16, 1995) pp50-54,56-59.
"A Smashing Time: At South By Southwest, If You Schmooze, You Lose."
AR13748 707 (May 4, 1995) p29.
"Souled Out: Has The New Technology Finally Sucked The Revolution Out Of Rock & Roll—Or Given It A New Lease On Life?."
AR13749 748 (November 28, 1996) pp91-92,94.
"Sterling Morrison: 1942-1995."
AR13750 719 (October 19, 1995) p22.
"Talk This Way: The Rolling Stone Interview With Aerosmith's Steven Tyler."
AR13751 694 (November 3, 1994) pp56-58,60-61+.
"Television."
AR13752 631 (May 28, 1992) p23.
"This Show Was About Every Critic's Desire: To Rock It Like You Write It."
AR13753 642 (October 29, 1992) p37.
"To Hell & Back: They Say They're Not Jinxed, But The Members Of Def Leppard Have Had To Endure A String Of Tragedies That Would Have Destroyed Most Other Bands."
AR13754 629 (April 30, 1992) pp38-42.
"U2: Finds What It's Looking For."
AR13755 640 (October 1, 1992) pp40-42,47-48+.
"Vision Thing."
AR13756 677 (March 10, 1994) pp51-52.
"Waiting For The Band."
AR13757 659 (June 24, 1993) pp17-18.
"The 'Weird' Side Of R.E.M.: 'Automatic For The People' Features Slow, Dark, Brooding Songs."
AR13758 640 (October 1, 1992) p20.
"You Shoulda Been There."
AR13759 714 (August 10, 1995) p20.
FRISCHMANN, JUSTINE
"Raves."
AR13760 720 (November 2, 1995) p26.
"FROM A (ALLMAN) TO Z (ZAPPA)."
AR13761 696 (December 1, 1994) p38.
FROST, DEBORAH
"Primed And Ticking: PJ Harvey Beat The Sophomore Jinx And Get Their Mojo Workin' With An American Tour And Their Powerful New Album, 'Rid Of Me'."
AR13762 663 (August 19, 1993) pp52-55.
FULLER, GRAHAM
"Ian Anderson."
AR13763 668 (October 28, 1993) p26.
FUTTERMAN, ELLEN
"Axl On Trial."
AR13764 671 (December 9, 1993) p14.
FUTTERMAN, STEVE
"Albert Collins 1932-1993."
AR13765 674 (January 27, 1994) p22.
"Antonio Carlos Jobim: 1927-1994."
AR13766 700 (January 26, 1995) p24.
"BBC Bonanza: Vintage U.K. Radio Concerts Now On CD."
AR13767 648 (January 21, 1993) p23.
"Bluegrass: Then And Now."
AR13768 684 (June 16, 1994) p25.
"Bob Thiele 1922-1996."
AR13769 730 (March 21, 1996) p26.

FUTTERMAN, STEVE (continued)
"The Class Of '92."
AR13770 623 (February 6, 1992) pp50-51,53-54.
"Class Of '93: The Rock And Roll Hall Of Fame."
AR13771 649 (February 4, 1993) pp50-52,54,56.
"The Complete Clapton: Plugged In."
AR13772 655 (April 29, 1993) p42.
"Dizzy Gillespie: 1917-1993."
AR13773 650 (February 18, 1993) p22.
"Fifteen Essential Albums."
AR13774 617 (November 14, 1991) p42.
"Gerry Mulligan 1927-1996."
AR13775 729 (March 7, 1996) p24.
"Hall Of Fame Inductees Announced."
AR13776 670 (November 25, 1993) p17.
"Hot Jazz Artist: Kenny Garrett."
AR13777 741 (August 22, 1996) p82.
"Hot Jazz Artists."
AR13778 656 (May 13, 1993) p72.
"Hot Jazzman."
AR13779 630 (May 14, 1992) p90.
"Jimmy Miller 1942-1994."
AR13780 697 (December 15, 1994) p34.
"Last But Not Lost: Santana's New Label."
AR13781 671 (December 9, 1993) p24.
"[Rock And Roll Hall Of Fame]."
AR13782 702 (February 23, 1995) p49.
"The Rock & Roll Hall Of Fame '94."
AR13783 676 (February 24, 1994) pp45-46,48-49.
"Rock Hall Announces Inductees."
AR13784 642 (October 29, 1992) p32.
"Sun Ra: 1914-1993."
AR13785 660-661 (July 8, 1993) p24.
"Wilbert Harrison 1929-1994."
AR13786 697 (December 15, 1994) p34.

G

GAAR, GILLIAN G.
"The Nerve Of Her."
AR13787 684 (June 16, 1994) p25.
"Radio Free Vedder: Pearl Jam Hijack The Airwaves For A Free-Form Throw-Down."
AR13788 702 (February 23, 1995) p26.
GABOURY, DENNIS
"The Secret Of St. Mary's."
AR13789 669 (November 11, 1993) pp48-50,52-54+.
GAINES, DONNA
"Suicidal Tendencies: Kurt Did Not Die For You."
AR13790 683 (June 2, 1994) pp59-61.
GALLAGHER, HUGH
"An Experiment In Terror: 7 Days And Seven Nights Alone With MTV."
AR13791 655 (April 29, 1993) pp44-48,71,73.
GALLAGHER, NOEL
"Raves."
AR13792 705 (April 6, 1995) p30.
GAMBACCINI, PAUL
"Paul McCartney."
AR13793 641 (October 15, 1992) pp60-62.
GANS, DAVID
"Dead End: The Grateful Dead Call It Quits."
AR13794 726 (January 25, 1996) p23.
GARDNER, ELYSA
"Acquired Taste: G. Love Serves A New Platter With Special Sauce."
AR13795 719 (October 19, 1995) p28.
"After The Storm: Billy Joel Turns To Beethoven For 'Dreams'."
AR13796 658 (June 10, 1993) p32.
"All She Wants."
AR13797 697 (December 15, 1994) pp71-73.
"Black Francis's Name Game: The Pixies Frontman Nutures Another Persona With 'Frank Black'."
AR13798 649 (February 4, 1993) p17.
"Cathy Dennis: One From The Heart."
AR13799 617 (November 14, 1991) p28.
"E: A Tender Pop Sensibility."
AR13800 631 (May 28, 1992) p22.
"87: The Thunder Rolls."
AR13801 667 (October 14, 1993) p100.
"86: Sweet Dreams."
AR13802 667 (October 14, 1993) p100.
"Elton John Leads Fight Against AIDS."
AR13803 644 (November 26, 1992) p22.
"5: Nothing Compares 2 U."
AR13804 667 (October 14, 1993) pp68-69.
"Hit Patrol."
AR13805 652 (March 18, 1993) pp[enc.9-10+].
"Hot Rappers."
AR13806 630 (May 14, 1992) pp79-80.
"In A Bjork State Of Mind: The Former Sugarcube Finds Life Is Sweet As A Soloist."
AR13807 665 (September 16, 1993) pp[enc.17-20].
"INXS Get Real: More Than Hooks And Looks."
AR13808 671 (December 9, 1993) p18.
"The James Gang: With 'Laid,' These British Lads Finally Get Over."
AR13809 680 (April 21, 1994) pp11-12.
"Kenny Wayne Shepherd."
AR13810 742 (September 5, 1996) p76.
"Marxman."
AR13811 690 (September 8, 1994) p44.
"The New Road Warriors: For The Members Of Blues Traveler, Life Is One Big, Happy Tour."
AR13812 622 (January 23, 1992) p10.
"92: Back On The Chain Gang."
AR13813 667 (October 14, 1993) p101.
"Off The Street And Onto Center Stage: Rock Steady Crew And Jossie Harris Turn Break Dancing Into An Art."
AR13814 638 (September 3, 1992) pp[enc.35-36+].
"Peter Gabriel's 'Us': Singer Releases First Album Since 1986's 'So'."
AR13815 639 (September 17, 1992) p27.
"The Pluck Of The Irish: Musicians Unite To Protest Sectarian Violence."
AR13816 656 (May 13, 1993) p18.
"Rock's Dream Team: Legends Meet At Hall Of Fame's Opening-Day Show."
AR13817 716 (September 7, 1995) p22.
"Sarah McLachlan: Happy To Be Unhappy."
AR13818 623 (February 6, 1992) p32.
"70: I Want Your."
AR13819 667 (October 14, 1993) p94.
"71: Rosalita."
AR13820 667 (October 14, 1993) p96.
"76: Mysterious Ways."
AR13821 667 (October 14, 1993) p97.
"73: Wicked Game."
AR13822 667 (October 14, 1993) p96.
"Singer, Actor, Director: With A Movie And A New Album, John Mellencamp Branches Out."
AR13823 623 (February 6, 1992) pp15,33.
"Singin' In The Rain: Artists Unite To Benefit Rain-Forest Charity."
AR13824 693 (October 20, 1994) p37.
"67: Money For Nothing."
AR13825 667 (October 14, 1993) p94.
"Sonic Bloom: Oasis Return With 'Morning Glory' LP."
AR13826 718 (October 5, 1995) p34.
"Those Were The Days: New Home Video Captures The Beatles During Their First Visit To America."

GARDNER, ELYSA (continued)
AR13827 618 (November 28, 1991) p28.
"Tim Finn: Apart From The Crowd."
AR13828 669 (November 11, 1993) p21.
"Tiny Lights: Shining In Hoboken."
AR13829 637 (August 20, 1992) p20.
"Tori Amos: Ethereal Earthquakes."
AR13830 629 (April 30, 1992) p31.
"23: Boys Of Summer."
AR13831 667 (October 14, 1993) p77.
GARELICK, JON
"Critics Comments."
AR13832 726 (January 25, 1996) pp46,50-51.
GARFIELD, SIMON
"Freedom '93: That's What George Michael Gets If He Wins A Groundbreaking Suit Against Sony."
AR13833 671 (December 9, 1993) p16.
GAROFALO, JANEANE
"Janeane Garofalo's Hot List."
AR13834 682 (May 19, 1994) p66.
GEHR, RICHARD
"Critics Comments."
AR13835 726 (January 25, 1996) pp46,50-51.
"Life On The Duplex Planet."
AR13836 679 (April 7, 1994) p20.
"Mickey Hart & Robert Hunter."
AR13837 742 (September 5, 1996) p30.
"Moe."
AR13838 747 (November 14, 1996) p53.
GEITNER, PAUL
"4 Non Blondes."
AR13839 662 (August 5, 1993) p21.
"Muzak Attack."
AR13840 662 (August 5, 1993) p16.
"Playing 'God": The Brains Behind Crash Test Dummies."
AR13841 681 (May 5, 1994) p16.
"GENERATION NEXT."
AR13842 695 (November 17, 1994) p17.
GEORGE-WARREN, HOLLY
"Critics Comments."
AR13843 726 (January 25, 1996) pp46,50-51.
"Divine Inspiration: Sixteen Horsepower Conjure Up That Old-Time Religion."
AR13844 731 (April 4, 1996) p36.
"Honky-Tonk Woman."
AR13845 691 (September 22, 1994) p33.
"Leader Of The Old School: Juggy Gayles Hyped Records The Old-Fashion Way—With Style."
AR13846 678 (March 24, 1994) p14.
"Legends Of Country Music."
AR13847 750-751 (December 26, 1996) pp168-179.
"Marisela Norte."
AR13848 656 (May 13, 1993) p27.
"Mike Scott's Spiritual Renewal: The Leader Of The Waterboys Gets Back To Basics On 'Dream Harder'."
AR13849 658 (June 10, 1993) p26.
"Simon Bonney: The Singer Changes Directions On 'Forever'."
AR13850 648 (January 21, 1993) p22.
GIBBONS, BILLY
"Raves."
AR13851 747 (November 14, 1996) p40.
GIBSON, WILLIAM
"Lo Rez Skyline."
AR13852 735 (May 30, 1996) pp[enc.cover+].
GILES, JEFF
"The Agony And The Ecstasy: Evan Dando On The Highs And Lows Of Being The King Of College Charts."
AR13853 649 (February 4, 1993) p14.
"College Notebook."
AR13854 639 (September 17, 1992) pp79-81.
"'The Crying Game' Star Jaye Davidson Breaks The Silence: Oscar's Big Surprise."
AR13855 653 (April 1, 1993) pp36-37,39,59+.
"Deee-Lusions Of Grandeur: Deee-Lite Searches For A New Groove On 'Infinity Within'."
AR13856 639 (September 17, 1992) pp37,106.
"Fishin' For Tuition: Students Talk About Their Jobs."
AR13857 652 (March 18, 1993) pp[enc.3-4].
"God's Little Monkeys: A Sardonic Political Edge."
AR13858 626 (March 19, 1992) p20.
"Hot Accessory."
AR13859 656 (May 13, 1993) p68.
"Hot Actor."
AR13860 656 (May 13, 1993) p63.
"Hot Actress."
AR13861 656 (May 13, 1993) p62.
"Hot Architect."
AR13862 656 (May 13, 1993) p90.
"Hot Art Form."
AR13863 656 (May 13, 1993) p84.
"Hot Athlete."
AR13864 656 (May 13, 1993) p87.
"Hot Bullshit Compliment."
AR13865 656 (May 13, 1993) p88.
"Hot Car."
AR13866 656 (May 13, 1993) p67.
"Hot Country Singer."
AR13867 656 (May 13, 1993) p65.
"Hot Dates."
AR13868 656 (May 13, 1993) p65.
"Hot Debut."
AR13869 656 (May 13, 1993) p63.
"Hot Designer."
AR13870 656 (May 13, 1993) p73.
"Hot Director."
AR13871 656 (May 13, 1993) p87.
"Hot Drug."
AR13872 656 (May 13, 1993) p90.
"Hot Gadget."
AR13873 656 (May 13, 1993) p65.
"Hot Infomercial."
AR13874 656 (May 13, 1993) p63.
"Hot Judd."
AR13875 656 (May 13, 1993) p84.
"The Hot List."
AR13876 656 (May 13, 1993) pp61-65,67-68+.
"Hot Medical Equipment."
AR13877 656 (May 13, 1993) p64.
"Hot Molecule."
AR13878 656 (May 13, 1993) p90.
"Hot Playwright."
AR13879 656 (May 13, 1993) p73.
"Hot Producer."
AR13880 656 (May 13, 1993) p88.
"Hot Rap Trend."
AR13881 656 (May 13, 1993) p67.
"Hot Record Label."
AR13882 656 (May 13, 1993) p74.
"Hot Resurrection."
AR13883 656 (May 13, 1993) p68.
"Hot Retro Ethos."
AR13884 656 (May 13, 1993) p65.
"Hot Revival."
AR13885 656 (May 13, 1993) p90.
"Hot Scam."
AR13886 656 (May 13, 1993) p88.
"Hot Screenwriter."
AR13887 656 (May 13, 1993) p73.
"Hot Sex Symbol."

GILES, JEFF (continued)
AR13888 656 (May 13, 1993) p68.
"Hot Standup."
AR13889 656 (May 13, 1993) p62.
"Hot Subculture."
AR13890 656 (May 13, 1993) p82.
"Hot Teen Idols."
AR13891 656 (May 13, 1993) p87.
"Hot Threat."
AR13892 656 (May 13, 1993) p64.
"Hot Video Game."
AR13893 656 (May 13, 1993) p67.
"James Carville's Hot List."
AR13894 656 (May 13, 1993) p64.
"Me Phi Me: Up From The Ashes Of Flint."
AR13895 636 (August 6, 1992) p24.
"Michael Richards's Hot List."
AR13896 656 (May 13, 1993) p72.
"Miracle Cure: In The Age Of Grunge, The Spin Doctors Score With A Joyful Noise."
AR13897 647 (January 7, 1993) pp34-39,54.
"No Fear Of Frying: The Hard Rock Cafe Celebrates Twenty Years Of Rock And Rolls."
AR13898 617 (November 14, 1991) pp15,18,21.
"On The Road...Again: A Troupe Of New Bands Is Taking Its Old-Time Rock & Roll Across America."
AR13899 631 (May 28, 1992) pp15-17.
"Panic: Metal Shot Through With Rock."
AR13900 615 (October 17, 1991) p28.
"Richard Linklater's Hot List."
AR13901 656 (May 13, 1993) p82.
"Rock And Roll Yearbook."
AR13902 619-620 (December 12, 1991) pp17-19,22,26+.
"Tough Times For Rock Auctions."
AR13903 626 (March 19, 1992) p18.
"Velocity Girl."
AR13904 655 (April 29, 1993) p24.
"Winona."
AR13905 677 (March 10, 1994) pp44-48.
"Worth Bragging About: Billy Bragg Takes A Leap Forward With A Stunning New Album."
AR13906 622 (January 23, 1992) pp9,17.
GILL, MARK STUART
"Boning Up: Neither Drum-Beating Nor Breast Beating, Men's Studies Comes Into Its Own."
AR13907 626 (March 19, 1992) pp62-65.
GILMORE, MIKAL
"A Death In The Family."
AR13908 632 (June 11, 1992) pp111-112.
"The Devil And Anne Rice."
AR13909 712-713 (July 13, 1995) pp92-94,97-98.
"Easy Target: Why Tupac Should Be Heard Before He's Buried."
AR13910 746 (October 31, 1996) pp49-51,81.
"Ella Fitzgerald: 1917-1996."
AR13911 740 (August 8, 1996) p26.
"Jerry Garcia: 1942-1995."
AR13912 717 (September 21, 1995) pp44-46,48,50+.
"Life After Garcia."
AR13913 724-725 (December 28, 1995) pp85-86.
"The Road From Nowhere: Walking The Streets Of Aberdeen, Wash.."
AR13914 683 (June 2, 1994) pp44-46,53.
"Shot In The Heart."
AR13915 684 (June 16, 1994) pp54-57,118.
"Timothy Leary: 1920-1996."
AR13916 738-739 (July 11, 1996) pp66-68,70,72+.
GILSTRAP, PETER
"Drinkin' And Draggin'."
AR13917 710 (June 15, 1995) p48.
"Rock & Roll Summer: Phoenix."
AR13918 710 (June 15, 1995) p48.
GITTER, MIKE
"Therapy?: From The Land Of Bombings And Bono."
AR13919 654 (April 15, 1993) p21.
"GIVING WORKING PEOPLE A BREAK."
AR13920 694 (November 3, 1994) p54.
GLASER, MILTON
"Jerry Garcia 1942-1995."
AR13921 724-725 (December 28, 1995) p156.
GLICK, DANIEL
"Big Sugar Vs. The Everglades."
AR13922 733 (May 2, 1996) pp44-47,49,64+.
"Twilight Of The Greens."
AR13923 719 (October 19, 1995) pp69-70,72,75+.
GOLD, JONATHAN
"Day Of The Dre: Dr. Dre And His Protege, Snoop Doggy Dogg, Take Hardcore Rap From South Central L.A. To Your House."
AR13924 666 (September 30, 1993) pp38-42,109+.
"Love It To Death: Trent Reznor Of Nine Inch Nails Preaches the Dark Gospel Of Sex, Pain And Rock & Roll."
AR13925 690 (September 8, 1994) pp50-54,88.
"Nothing But A G Thang: Warren G Hits With "Regulate"."
AR13926 690 (September 8, 1994) p37.
"Snoop In The Doghouse: Dr. Dre Protege And Bodyguard Face Murder Charge."
AR13927 667 (October 14, 1993) p21.
GOLDBERG, MICHAEL
"An Abuse Of Trust? Michael Jackson Defends His Honor."
AR13928 667 (October 14, 1993) p21.
"An All-Star Experience: Jimi Hendrix Is Feted On Tribute Album."
AR13929 669 (November 11, 1993) p17.
"The Art Of The Deal: The Real Arithmetic Behind The New Superstar Contracts."
AR13930 647 (January 7, 1993) p18.
"Atco Folds; More Cuts Expected."
AR13931 617 (November 14, 1991) pp15,27.
"Attack Of The Cyber-Rockers: New Computer Rocker Jocks Get Their Modems Working."
AR13932 670 (November 25, 1993) p27.
"Ballroom Blitz."
AR13933 681 (May 5, 1994) p19.
"Big Tours Buoy Promoters' Spirits [and other news]."
AR13934 633 (June 25, 1992) p20.
"Bill Graham's Last Waltz."
AR13935 619-620 (December 12, 1991) p103.
"Billy Joel's New Legal Firestorm."
AR13936 666 (September 30, 1993) p17.
"Bruce Plans Late-Summer Tour [and other news]."
AR13937 631 (May 28, 1992) p23.
"CD-Package Standard Set."
AR13938 627 (April 2, 1992) pp15-16.
"Counting Crows."
AR13939 669 (November 11, 1993) p24.
"Digital-Tape War Heats Up."
AR13940 616 (October 31, 1991) pp15,26.
"Double Dose Of Springsteen."
AR13941 625 (March 5, 1992) pp21,24.
"Elvis's Stamp Of Approval: Postal Service To Pay Tribute To Presley And Other Rock Stars In New Series."
AR13942 626 (March 19, 1992) p18.
"EMI Gives Old Artists New Deal [and other news]."
AR13943 630 (May 14, 1992) p34.
"Fast Start For 'Dangerous'."
AR13944 622 (January 23, 1992) pp9,16.
"Federal Payola Probe Continues [and other news]."
AR13945 617 (November 14, 1991) p26.
"Fortunate Son: John Fogerty Looks Back On The Glory Days Of Creedence Clearwater Revival."
AR13946 649 (February 4, 1993) pp46-48,77.
"Gang Of Seven: All Talk, No Music."
AR13947 640 (October 1, 1992) p26.

GOLDBERG, MICHAEL (continued)
"Garcia: Truckin' Again."
AR13948 648 (January 21, 1993) p20.
"Grand Jury Attacks Arena Security [and other news]."
AR13949 616 (October 31, 1991) p26.
"The Great Price War: Used CDs Become The Center Of A Retail Battle."
AR13950 665 (September 16, 1993) p24.
"Guns N' Roses To Play AIDS Benefit [and other news]."
AR13951 627 (April 2, 1992) p17.
"Hall Of Fame To Break Ground."
AR13952 655 (April 29, 1993) p23.
"In The News."
AR13953 637 (August 20, 1992) p16.
AR13954 638 (September 3, 1992) p16.
AR13955 644 (November 26, 1992) p30.
AR13956 647 (January 7, 1993) p14.
AR13957 648 (January 21, 1993) p20.
AR13958 650 (February 18, 1993) p18.
AR13959 651 (March 4, 1993) p32.
AR13960 652 (March 18, 1993) p27.
AR13961 653 (April 1, 1993) p23.
AR13962 654 (April 15, 1993) p22.
AR13963 655 (April 29, 1993) p18.
AR13964 656 (May 13, 1993) p28.
AR13965 657 (May 27, 1993) p18.
AR13966 658 (June 10, 1993) p26.
AR13967 659 (June 24, 1993) p28.
AR13968 660-661 (July 8, 1993) p30.
AR13969 662 (August 5, 1993) p18.
"Jackson Charity Off To A Slow Start [and other news]."
AR13970 626 (March 19, 1992) p24.
"Jello Biafra Attacked."
AR13971 686-687 (July 14, 1994) p26.
"Jerry Garcia Ill; Dead Cancel Tour."
AR13972 640 (October 1, 1992) pp19,84.
"Lawsuit Over Lymon Song Settled."
AR13973 647 (January 7, 1993) p19.
"Lawyers, Punks And Money: SST Records Battle Of Writs And Wills Against Former Acts."
AR13974 654 (April 15, 1993) p24.
"Madonna To Sign $60 Million Deal [and other news]."
AR13975 628 (April 16, 1992) p22.
"Michael Jackson Plans Summer Tour [and other news]."
AR13976 625 (March 5, 1992) p24.
"Michael Jackson: The Making Of 'The King Of Pop'."
AR13977 621 (January 9, 1992) pp32-37.
"Michael Sues Sony: Fights To Break Contract With Record Company."
AR13978 647 (January 7, 1993) p14.
"Negativland And SST Settle."
AR13979 689 (August 25, 1994) p36.
"New Labels Face Tough Times."
AR13980 618 (November 28, 1991) pp15,22-23.
"No Heat Wave For Summer Tours."
AR13981 637 (August 20, 1992) p19.
"Obscenity Bill Passed In Washington [and other news]."
AR13982 629 (April 30, 1992) p23.
"The Other Summer Tour."
AR13983 658 (June 10, 1993) p29.
"Paisley Is Out."
AR13984 678 (March 24, 1994) p18.
"Perry Farrell Busted For Drugs [and other news]."
AR13985 618 (November 28, 1991) p32.
"Prince Retires—Maybe: He Says He's Quitting Studio Work, But Don't Hold Your Breath."
AR13986 658 (June 10, 1993) p22.
"Promoters Hurt By Summer Flops."
AR13987 622 (January 23, 1992) p16.
"Record High."
AR13988 665 (September 16, 1993) p20.
"Red House Painters."
AR13989 665 (September 16, 1993) p25.
"Red-Hot Lollapalooza: Chili Peppers Will Headline This Summer's Alternative-Music Meld."
AR13990 629 (April 30, 1992) p23.
"Return Of The All-Day Sucker."
AR13991 657 (May 27, 1993) p17.
"Rock's Greatest Showman."
AR13992 619-620 (December 12, 1991) pp97,100,102+.
"Sioux Indians File Suit Against The Cult [and other news]."
AR13993 634-635 (July 9, 1992) p24.
"Springsteen Settles Suits With Roadies [and other news]."
AR13994 615 (October 17, 1991) p27.
"Thorn EMI Buys Virgin."
AR13995 628 (April 16, 1992) p23.
"U2: The Zoo Tour Move Outdoors."
AR13996 636 (August 6, 1992) p21.
"GOLDFINGER."
AR13997 738-739 (July 11, 1996) p116.
GOLDSTEIN, PATRICK
"David Geffen: The Rolling Stone Interview."
AR13998 655 (April 29, 1993) pp50-53,55-56+.
"The Player: Shaquille O'Neal, A Celebrity For The New World."
AR13999 670 (November 25, 1993) pp52-53,55,57+.
"Tom Cruise: Pushing Thirty, The Star Of 'Far And Away' Gets His Life Together With The Help Of Scientology And His Wife Nicole Kidman."
AR14000 631 (May 28, 1992) pp34-37,70.
AR14001 Number not assigned.
GOLLIN, RANDI
"Paleface: Tempering Venom With Glee."
AR14002 626 (March 19, 1992) p20.
"Ugly Kid Joe: Living Out Their Fantasies."
AR14003 629 (April 30, 1992) p31.
GONZALES, LAURENCE
"Lost In Space: Outlaw Engineers Are Struggling To Save NASA With A New Generation Of Secret Technology."
AR14004 705 (April 6, 1995) pp52-54,56-58.
GOODELL, JEFF
"Barry Diller: The Rolling Stone Interview."
AR14005 689 (August 25, 1994) pp66-67,69-70+.
"Chip Trick: Big Brother Is Trying To Get On Line."
AR14006 682 (May 19, 1994) p46.
"Civilizing Cyberspace: The Rolling Stone Interview With Mitch Kapor."
AR14007 658 (June 10, 1993) pp[enc.3-5,8+].
"The Fevered Rise Of America Online."
AR14008 744 (October 3, 1996) pp60-62,64-66.
"Flying Boats: Why 'Netizen' Works And 'Salon' Doesn't."
AR14009 735 (May 30, 1996) pp[enc.22].
"Getting Real: Silicon Flame Out."
AR14010 745 (October 17, 1996) pp119-121,123+.
"Looking For The Next Revolution: The Rolling Stone Interview With Steve Jobs."
AR14011 684 (June 16, 1994) pp73,75,78,80+.
"The Rise And Fall Of Apple Inc."
AR14012 731 (April 4, 1996) pp51-57,72-73.
"The Rise And Fall Of Apple Inc. [Part Two]."
AR14013 732 (April 18, 1996) pp59-63,85,87+.
"The Samurai And The Cyberthief: How The World's Most-Wanted Computer Criminal Was Hunted Down By One Of His Targets—The Master Of Cybersecurity."
AR14014 707 (May 4, 1995) pp40-44,46-47+.
"The Un-Candidate."
AR14015 623 (February 6, 1992) pp57-58,61-64.
"Webheads On Ramona Street: Jonathan 'Dr. Cheeze' Steuer Makes His Million-Dollar Cyborganic Dream Garden Become Reality."
AR14016 722 (November 30, 1995) pp[enc.2-4,6+].

GOODMAN, FRED
"Back To The Garden."
AR14017 683 (June 2, 1994) p16.
"The Big Pay Back: The R&B Foundation Honors Its Stars."
AR14018 681 (May 5, 1994) p15.
"Bittersweet Relief: Rockers Face The Health-Care Blues."
AR14019 664 (September 2, 1993) pp13,77.
"Bone Of Contention: Fishbone Bassist Accused Of Attempted Kidnapping."
AR14020 662 (August 5, 1993) p17.
"Denny Cordell: 1943-1995."
AR14021 706 (April 20, 1995) p32.
"Gettin' Mighty Crowded: Summer Tours '94."
AR14022 683 (June 2, 1994) pp15-17.
"Going For The Gold: Monet Talks As Golden-Circle Seating Divides Concert Audiences."
AR14023 684 (June 16, 1994) p17.
"In The News."
AR14024 664 (September 2, 1993) p22.
AR14025 665 (September 16, 1993) p24.
AR14026 666 (September 30, 1993) p21.
AR14027 667 (October 14, 1993) p28.
AR14028 668 (October 28, 1993) p33.
AR14029 669 (November 11, 1993) p21.
AR14030 670 (November 25, 1993) p27.
AR14031 671 (December 9, 1993) p21.
"More Blues For Music Biz: Layoffs And Cutbacks Continue Into The New Year."
AR14032 621 (January 9, 1992) pp20,22.
"Nirvana To 'Newsweek': Drop Dead."
AR14033 659 (June 24, 1993) p21.
"Paul Rothchild: 1935-1995."
AR14034 708 (May 18, 1995) p33.
"The Price Is Not Right: Is Ticketmaster Taking These People For A Ride?."
AR14035 692 (October 6, 1994) pp21-22.
"Prodigal Son: The Battle Over New Bruce, Dead CDs."
AR14036 678 (March 24, 1994) p12.
"The Times Have Indeed Changed: The Band Follows Dylan In Selling Their Songs As Ads."
AR14037 680 (April 21, 1994) p13.
GOODYEAR, SARAH
"Rebecca Coupe Franks: Young Woman With A Horn."
AR14038 623 (February 6, 1992) p32.
GORDON, ROBERT
"Agony And The Ecstasy: Kevin Salem Turns Bitter Times Into Blissful Blasts."
AR14039 701 (February 9, 1995) p32.
"Sonic Youth: Go Guitar Crazy On Lucky 13th Release."
AR14040 712-713 (July 13, 1995) p32.
GOWEN, ANNE
"Motor Voter: Goin' Mobile."
AR14041 660-661 (July 8, 1993) p18.
"Tipper Gore Quits PMRC: But Has The First Lady of 'Parental Advisory' Really Given Up The Fight?."
AR14042 654 (April 15, 1993) p20.
GRAFF, GARY
"Rock & Roll Summer: Detroit."
AR14043 710 (June 15, 1995) p49.
GRAHAM, LAMAR
"Doomed To Succeed: The Princes Of Twitch Take Cybergore To A New Level."
AR14044 722 (November 30, 1995) pp[enc.47].
"On A Role: What The Jobs Of The 21st Century Will Be—And How To Prepare For Them Now."
AR14045 730 (March 21, 1996) pp71-72,76.
"Whip Smart: The Tricks Of The Trade For Better Grades."
AR14046 704 (March 23, 1995) pp89-90,92,114.
"GRAPEVINE."
AR14047 726 (January 25, 1996) p30.
AR14048 727 (February 8, 1996) p24.
AR14049 728 (February 22, 1996) p25.
AR14050 729 (March 7, 1996) p29.
AR14051 730 (March 21, 1996) p33.
AR14052 731 (April 4, 1996) p30.
"GREAT MOMENTS IN COLLEGE JOURNALISM: 1."
AR14053 652 (March 18, 1993) pp[enc.4].
"GREAT MOMENTS IN COLLEGE JOURNALISM: 2."
AR14054 652 (March 18, 1993) pp[enc.6].
GREEN, ROBIN
"Naked Lunch Box."
AR14055 632 (June 11, 1992) pp51-52.
GREENBERG, COREY
"Honey, I Shrunk The Cineplex: Home Is Where The Theater Is."
AR14056 658 (June 10, 1993) pp[enc.33+].
GREENFIELD, ROBERT
"The Rolling Stones On Tour."
AR14057 632 (June 11, 1992) pp57-59.
"The Secret Life Of Jerry Garcia."
AR14058 740 (August 8, 1996) pp32-36,38-40.
GREIDER, WILLIAM
"After South Central: The White Conscience."
AR14059 633 (June 25, 1992) pp22-23.
"Back To The Back Of The Bus?: Clinton's Mixed Signals On Civil Rights."
AR14060 675 (February 10, 1994) pp25-27.
"Better Workers Or Better Jobs?."
AR14061 654 (April 15, 1993) pp28-29.
"Big Talk In Little Rock."
AR14062 639 (September 17, 1992) pp42-44,109.
"Bill And Hillary Will See You Now."
AR14063 655 (April 29, 1993) pp28-29.
"Bill Clinton: The Rolling Stone Interview."
AR14064 639 (September 17, 1992) pp40-44,47,51+.
"Bill's Mix: Right Ends, Left Means."
AR14065 653 (April 1, 1993) pp28-29.
"Buchanan Rethinks The American Empire."
AR14066 623 (February 6, 1992) pp37-39.
"Bush's Tax-Cut Follies: Rich Entertainment."
AR14067 626 (March 19, 1992) pp31-33.
"Can Clinton Put Life In The Party?."
AR14068 652 (March 18, 1993) pp32-33.
"Citizen GE: How Multinationals Like General Electric Have Seized Power In The United States."
AR14069 628 (April 16, 1992) pp65-66,68-70+.
"Clinton At Midterm? What Went Wrong."
AR14070 694 (November 3, 1994) pp45-46,48,108.
"Clinton Goes Right Toward Consensus."
AR14071 649 (February 4, 1993) pp29-30.
"Clinton's Choice: Jobs Or Mexico."
AR14072 656 (May 13, 1993) pp35-36.
"Colin-Izing America: The Best Thing Colin Powell Could Do For The Nation Is Run For President."
AR14073 721 (November 16, 1995) pp45-46,49,124.
"Congress: Kill NAFTA."
AR14074 668 (October 28, 1993) pp40-41,49,92.
"The Country That Stayed Out In The Cold."
AR14075 622 (January 23, 1992) pp19-20.
"Credit Where Credit's Due."
AR14076 664 (September 2, 1993) pp34-35,74.
"Dead Man Talking: How Newt Gingrich Went From Being The Life Of The Party To The GOP's Pariah In Two Revolutionary Years."
AR14077 744 (October 3, 1996) pp40-43,80.
"Deception & Reality: If You're Wondering Why Bill Clinton And Bob Dole Haven't Addressed The Economic Woes Of The '90s, Don't Ask The Media."
AR14078 733 (May 2, 1996) pp38-40.
"Down But Not Out: Labor Struggles To Find Its Voice."
AR14079 615 (October 17, 1991) pp39-40,106.

GREIDER, WILLIAM (continued)
"Duck And Cover: The Three Most Important Issues Of The Campaign And Why The Candidates Won't Talk About Them."
AR14080 746 (October 31, 1996) pp53-54,56,58.
"Election Post-Mortem: The Price Of Failure."
AR14081 698-699 (December 29, 1994) pp151-154.
"The Emergency Plan To Bail Out The Banks."
AR14082 624 (February 20, 1992) pp20-21.
"The Ex-Im Files: How The Taxpayer-Funded Export-Import Bank Helps Ship Jobs Overseas."
AR14083 740 (August 8, 1996) pp51-55,63,70.
"Eyes Wide Open, Hearts Full Of Hope."
AR14084 632 (June 11, 1992) p196.
"F Troop: The GOP Raids Public Schools."
AR14085 637 (August 20, 1992) pp25-26,62.
"The First Reform: Campaign Finance."
AR14086 650 (February 18, 1993) pp30-31.
"George Herbert Hoover Walker Bush."
AR14087 621 (January 9, 1992) pp27-28.
"The Global Sweatshop: Indonesian Workers Struggle For Rights And Help From Clinton."
AR14088 685 (June 30, 1994) pp43-45.
"Got The Foreclosed, Bankrupt GOP Blues."
AR14089 634-635 (July 9, 1992) pp35-37.
"Grok The Vote."
AR14090 742 (September 5, 1996) pp48-50.
"Guns Or Budget? Clinton's Options."
AR14091 651 (March 4, 1993) pp35-37,77.
"Heard The About The Welfare Queen?."
AR14092 630 (May 14, 1992) pp37-38.
"How Many Times Will Bill Blink?: Courage And The President."
AR14093 657 (May 27, 1993) pp28-29.
"How We Export Jobs And Disease."
AR14094 638 (September 3, 1992) pp32-33.
"Is This Any Way To Renew An Economy?."
AR14095 658 (June 10, 1993) pp37-39.
"Middle-Class Funk."
AR14096 720 (November 2, 1995) pp35-36,82.
"The Money Hunt: A Shrinking Pie Changes D.C. Budget Games."
AR14097 671 (December 9, 1993) pp35-36,84.
"New Deal Redux Or Great Society II?."
AR14098 647 (January 7, 1993) p27.
"Nixon's Record."
AR14099 684 (June 16, 1994) pp40,42,119.
"No More Years: Why George Must Go."
AR14100 640 (October 1, 1992) pp38-39.
"The Pentagon Vs. The Budget: Still Hot For The Cold War."
AR14101 672-673 (December 23, 1993) pp83-85,176.
"A Pistol-Whipped Nation: Pass The Brady Bill—Then Ban Handguns."
AR14102 666 (September 30, 1993) pp31-32,120.
"President Clinton: The Rolling Stone Interview."
AR14103 671 (December 9, 1993) pp40-45,80-81.
"Presidential Candidates Discover America."
AR14104 627 (April 2, 1992) pp25-26,30.
"Race, Money And The Meaningless Search For The Center: Who Really Won The Election Of 1996 And Why."
AR14105 750-751 (December 26, 1996) pp107-108.
"The Remaking Of The President."
AR14106 645-646 (December 10, 1992) pp106-107,109+.
"Ross Perot Talks, Washington Squawks."
AR14107 636 (August 6, 1992) pp31-32,76.
"Rx Now, Pay Later: Will Health Reform Be Clinton's Reaganomics?."
AR14108 670 (November 25, 1993) pp41-42,133.
"Should We Throw The Bums Out?."
AR14109 648 (January 21, 1993) pp27-29.
"Sinful Wages: Clinton Wavers On Raising Workers' Pay."
AR14110 674 (January 27, 1994) pp30-32.
"Smells Like Team Spirit: Clinton Seeks A Few Good Students To Fix Up America."
AR14111 659 (June 24, 1993) pp32-33,90,92.
"Southern Comfort: How Come There Are Billions To Bail Out Mexico But Nada For U.S. Cities?."
AR14112 703 (March 9, 1995) pp40-41,74.
"The Temporary Miracle: How One Good Job Becomes Three Lousy Ones."
AR14113 663 (August 19, 1993) pp32-33,87.
"Up Against The Drywall: Mexican-American Carpenters Remake The U.S. Labor Movement In Orange County, Calif.."
AR14114 669 (November 11, 1993) pp35-37,82.
"What Clinton Can Do For The Economy."
AR14115 642 (October 29, 1992) pp41,44,80.
"What's New, Democrat? Clinton's Politics Look Awfully Familiar."
AR14116 662 (August 5, 1993) pp36-37,80.
"Who Lost Russia?: The Ex-Reds Need Our Greenbacks."
AR14117 678 (March 24, 1994) pp31,33,36-37.
"Who's Pulling Bill Clinton's Strings?."
AR14118 629 (April 30, 1992) pp33,35.
"Why I Don't Believe What He Believes."
AR14119 712-713 (July 13, 1995) pp60,63,66.
"Why The Mighty GE Can't Strike Out."
AR14120 680 (April 21, 1994) p36.
"Why The Rich Get Richer: Because The Fed Is Engineering A Recession For The Rest Of Us."
AR14121 701 (February 9, 1995) pp36-37.
"Will The Fed Stiff Clinton?."
AR14122 665 (September 16, 1993) pp35-36,84.

GROSSMAN, DAN
"Over There: The U.S. Military's Toxic Reach."
AR14123 618 (November 28, 1991) pp39-40.

GUDMUNDSDOTTIR, BJORK
"Raves."
AR14124 683 (June 2, 1994) p20.

"GUNS N' ROSES."
AR14125 619-620 (December 12, 1991) p55.

H

"HALL GETS JOPLIN HAUL."
AR14126 618 (November 28, 1991) p23.
"HALL OF FAME."
AR14127 724-725 (December 28, 1995) pp56-57.
"HALL OF FAME INDUCTEES."
AR14128 746 (January 31, 1996) p27.

HALL, JUSTIN
"Story Of My Life: Personal Publishing On The Web."
AR14129 722 (November 30, 1995) pp[enc.28].

HALL, ROGER
"Our Lives, Our Music: Use Your Illusion I."
AR14130 644 (November 26, 1992) p55.

HAMILTON, TISH
"Personal Best: Whether You're Hitting The Slopes Or An Indoor Pool, You Need Lotions And Shampoos To Counteract The Drying Effects Of The Winter Workout."
AR14131 645-646 (December 10, 1992) pp139-141.
"Rubber Souls."
AR14132 691 (September 22, 1994) pp[enc.36].
"Tri And Mighty: To Brave The Hawaii Ironman, It Takes Big Kahunas."
AR14133 680 (April 21, 1994) pp[enc.33-34].

HAMMER, JOSHUA
"Rwanda: The Death Of A Nation."
AR14134 691 (September 22, 1994) pp67-74,76-80+.

HANDELMAN, DAVID
"Gus Van Sant's Northwest Passage: The Director Of 'Drugstore Cowboy' Continues To Explore Uncharted Territory With 'My Own Private Idaho'."
AR14135 616 (October 31, 1991) pp61-62,64.

"In Their Own Words: Club Series Spawns A Tour By Some Of Music's Most Distinguished Songwriters."
AR14136 630 (May 14, 1992) p35.
"The World's Biggest Rerun: Why Is The Addams Family Making Hollywood Ghoul Crazy?."
AR14137 618 (November 28, 1991) pp43,56,58.
HARDY, ERNEST
"Quad City DJ's Are On The Right Track."
AR14138 743 (September 19, 1996) p38.
HARING, BRUCE
"Channel Surfing: Cable TV Spawns Four New Outlets With Their Eyes On MTV."
AR14139 680 (April 21, 1994) p22.
HARRIS, DAVID
"Ask A Marine."
AR14140 632 (June 11, 1992) pp77-81.
"The Last Stand."
AR14141 727 (February 8, 1996) pp38-43.
"Sao Paulo Megacity."
AR14142 750-751 (December 26, 1996) pp125-133,216.
HARRIS, EMMYLOU
"Raves."
AR14143 744 (October 3, 1996) p36.
HARRIS, JASON C.
"Our Lives, Our Music: The White Album."
AR14144 644 (November 26, 1992) p58.
HATFIELD, JULIANA
"Raves."
AR14145 712-713 (July 13, 1995) p40.
"HEAD COUNT, $ AMOUNT."
AR14146 667 (January 14, 1993) p90.
HEATH, CHRIS
"Dennis Rodman's Floating World."
AR14147 749 (December 12, 1996) pp40-46,50,92.
"R.E.M.."
AR14148 745 (October 17, 1996) pp52-58,148 +.
HELDMAN, KEVIN
"Mean Streaks: Amped, Angry And In Your Face, Graffiti Refuses To Die."
AR14149 701 (February 9, 1995) pp48-49,51-52 +.
"Welcome To The Jungle."
AR14150 716 (September 7, 1995) pp60-62,64,66 +.
HELM, LEVON
"This Wheel's On Fire."
AR14151 669 (November 11, 1993) pp66-69,71.
HENDRICKSON, MATT
"Aerosmith In A Hard Place: New Album Is Delayed Amid Rumors Of Drugs, Bickering And Behind-The-Scenes Firings."
AR14152 744 (October 3, 1996) pp22-24,26.
"Chas Chandler: 1938-1996."
AR14153 742 (September 5, 1996) p26.
"Double Fantasy."
AR14154 703 (March 9, 1995) p25.
"Drugs Claim Sublime's Singer; Depeche Mode's Gahan OD's."
AR14155 738-739 (July 11, 1996) p20.
"Grapevine."
AR14156 732 (April 18, 1996) p32.
AR14157 733 (May 2, 1996) p22.
AR14158 734 (May 16, 1996) p29.
AR14159 735 (May 30, 1996) p27.
AR14160 736 (June 13, 1996) p33.
AR14161 737 (June 27, 1996) p29.
AR14162 738-739 (July 11, 1996) p28.
AR14163 740 (August 8, 1996) p23.
AR14164 741 (August 22, 1996) p36.
AR14165 742 (September 5, 1996) p25.
AR14166 743 (September 19, 1996) p36.
AR14167 744 (October 3, 1996) p30.
AR14168 745 (October 17, 1996) p41.
AR14169 746 (October 31, 1996) p27.
AR14170 747 (November 14, 1996) p36.
AR14171 748 (November 28, 1996) p40.
AR14172 749 (December 12, 1996) p32.
"Hall Of Fame Nominees."
AR14173 741 (August 22, 1996) p40.
"The Jesus & Mazzy Chain."
AR14174 692 (October 6, 1994) p29.
"Joe Henry Bounces From Rural Rock To An Urban Groove."
AR14175 737 (June 27, 1996) p24.
"John Panozzo: 1948-1996."
AR14176 742 (September 5, 1996) p26.
"Magnapop: Georgia's Finest?."
AR14177 696 (December 1, 1994) p33.
"Nice Guys Finish First: Live Make The Leap From Small Town To Big Time."
AR14178 696 (December 1, 1994) pp50-51.
"Nipped In The Bid: High Hopes Dampen Rock Auction."
AR14179 703 (March 9, 1995) p29.
"Oasis."
AR14180 691 (September 22, 1994) p37.
"Polara."
AR14181 711 (June 29, 1995) p23.
"Prai$e The Lord."
AR14182 710 (June 15, 1995) p37.
"Price Busters: Green Day Lower Ticket Prices And One-Up Pearl Jam."
AR14183 697 (December 15, 1994) p28.
"Ralph J. Gleason Awards."
AR14184 744 (October 3, 1996) p30.
"Rancid."
AR14185 701 (February 9, 1995) p29.
"Red Hot + Positive."
AR14186 742 (September 5, 1996) pp23-24.
"Rob Collins: 1963-1996."
AR14187 742 (September 5, 1996) p26.
"Screaming Trees: Woodshed For Success."
AR14188 734 (May 16, 1996) p28.
"Sick Of It All: Searching For Breakthroughs In Musicians' Health Care."
AR14189 704 (March 23, 1995) p44.
"Slash Leaves Guns N' Roses: Cites Differences With Axl Rose."
AR14190 749 (December 12, 1996) p24.
"Smashing Pumpkins' Keyboardist Dies Of Drug Overdose; Drummer Charged With Possession."
AR14191 741 (August 22, 1996) p32.
"Starting Over: Wilco See A New Dawn With 'A.M.'."
AR14192 707 (May 4, 1995) p32.
"A Tale Of 2 Indies: Epitaph Records...."
AR14193 737 (June 27, 1996) pp18-20.
"Weiland In Drug Treatment; Pilots Grounded."
AR14194 736 (June 13, 1996) pp22-23.
"Who Are You? Pearl Jam's Eddie Vedder."
AR14195 748 (November 28, 1996) pp50-54,57 +.
HENKE, JAMES
"Bonnie Raitt."
AR14196 641 (October 15, 1992) pp171-173.
"Bruce's Lucky Touch: Two New Albums Put Springsteen Back In The Rock & Roll Spotlight."
AR14197 628 (April 16, 1992) pp15,23.
"Jerry Garcia."
AR14198 641 (October 15, 1992) pp180-182.
"Neil Young."
AR14199 641 (October 15, 1992) pp145-146.
"The Rolling Stone Interview: Eric Clapton."
AR14200 615 (October 17, 1991) pp42-44,47-49 +.
"The Rolling Stone Interview: Jerry Garcia."
AR14201 616 (October 31, 1991) pp34-35,37-40 +.
"Springsteen: The Rolling Stone Interview."
AR14202 636 (August 6, 1992) pp38-42,44,70.

HENLEY, DON
"Heaven Is Under Our Feet: Voices For Walden Woods."
AR14203 615 (October 17, 1991) pp53,55,59,105.
HERBST, PETER
"James Taylor."
AR14204 641 (October 15, 1992) pp91-92.
HERCZOG, MARY
"AIDS And Rock: Sound Of Silence."
AR14205 629 (April 30, 1992) pp15-16,18,67.
"Rock Against AIDS, 1993."
AR14206 655 (April 29, 1993) pp15-16.
HERNDON, DAVID
"A New World Party: Peter Gabriel brings WOMAD To U.S.."
AR14207 668 (October 28, 1993) p24.
"No Peace In The Valley."
AR14208 667 (October 14, 1993) p36.
HERSH, KRISTIN
"Raves."
AR14209 736 (June 13, 1996) p54.
HERZ, J. C.
"Multimedia."
AR14210 731 (April 4, 1996) p63.
"Welcome To The Information Superdorm: The Digital Future Is Being Shaped On Campus Right Now."
AR14211 719 (October 19, 1995) pp109-110,114+.
"What A Wonderful Web It Could Be: Netscape's Co-Inventor Charts The Digital Future."
AR14212 722 (November 30, 1995) pp[enc.22].
HIGGINBOTHAM, ADAM
"Bis."
AR14213 747 (November 14, 1996) p53.
HIMES, GEOFFREY
"Back In The Saddle: C&W Outlaw Steve Earle Returns From His Lost Years."
AR14214 732 (April 18, 1996) pp34,36.
"Bernard Edwards 1952-1996."
AR14215 736 (June 13, 1996) p25.
"Brownie McGhee 1915-1996."
AR14216 731 (April 4, 1996) p39.
"Don Cherry: 1936-1995."
AR14217 722 (November 30, 1995) p40.
"Tribute: Junior Walker 1931-1995."
AR14218 726 (January 25, 1996) p28.
HINERFELD, DANIEL S.
"Cheating Time: How Some High-School Students From California Improved Their SAT Scores."
AR14219 626 (March 19, 1992) pp73-74,76.
HIRSHEY, GERRI
"The Bat's Meow: Catwoman Michelle Pfeiffer."
AR14220 638 (September 3, 1992) pp36-38,41,82.
"Being There; The History Of Rock & Roll Photography."
AR14221 643 (November 12, 1992) pp53-54,56,60+.
"Mark Morris Says He's Not Just A Hard-Drinking, Chain-Smoking, Long-Haired Beats From Modern-Dance Hell."
AR14222 619-620 (December 12, 1991) pp150-151,153+.
"Michael Jackson."
AR14223 632 (June 11, 1992) pp135-136.
HOCHMAN, STEVE
"AIDS And Rock: Sound Of Silence."
AR14224 629 (April 30, 1992) pp15-16,18,67.
"The Black Crowes."
AR14225 695 (November 17, 1994) pp75-77.
"Burnin' And Lootin': Tony Toni Tone Fire Up The Funk."
AR14226 666 (September 30, 1993) p16.
"Critics Comments."
AR14227 726 (January 25, 1996) pp46,50-51.
"Half Way Home: Soliciting The Hospitality Of Their Extended Family."
AR14228 651 (March 4, 1993) p28.
"Hard To Handle: The Black Crowes Throw A Snit And Toughen Their Sound On The New LP."
AR14229 689 (August 25, 1994) p25.
"Heroin: Back On The Charts."
AR14230 639 (September 17, 1992) pp25,103-104.
"Native American Son: Robbie Robertson Finds A Common Bond Between His Heritage And His Music."
AR14231 692 (October 6, 1994) p27.
"New Jack And Jill."
AR14232 654 (April 15, 1993) pp[enc.4-7+].
"Off The Bandwagon: Teenage Fanclub Battle The Ghost Of Albums Past."
AR14233 701 (February 9, 1995) p33.
"The Pleasure Of Pain: Nine Inch Nails' Trent Reznor Dances On The Edge Of Madness."
AR14234 648 (January 21, 1993) pp13,25.
"Rock Against AIDS, 1993."
AR14235 655 (April 29, 1993) pp15-16.
"'75% Less Fat,' 100% Rock: Former Mat Chris Mars Sheds Some Excess Weight On His Second Solo LP."
AR14236 656 (May 13, 1993) p31.
"Some Kind Of Wonderful: Boz Scaggs Rediscovers The Joys Of Rock & Soul."
AR14237 682 (May 19, 1994) p26.
"Steve Miller: The Space Cowboy And Gangster Of Love Proves There's Life After His Greatest Hits."
AR14238 664 (September 2, 1993) pp21-22.
"A Truly Democratic Party: The MTV And VH-1 Generations Swing Together At Clinton's Inaugural."
AR14239 651 (March 4, 1993) pp21,32.
HODENFIELD, CHRIS
"The Method Of His Madness."
AR14240 632 (June 11, 1992) pp107-108.
HOLLIDAY, ART
"Our Lives, Our Music: What's Going On."
AR14241 644 (November 26, 1992) p55.
"HOLLYWOOD."
AR14242 630 (May 14, 1992) p69.
HONDA, YUKA
"Raves."
AR14243 736 (June 13, 1996) p58.
HOON, SHANNON
AR14244 679 (April 7, 1994) p30.
HOOPER, LAURENCE
"Digital Hollywood: How Computers Are Remaking Movie Making."
AR14245 688 (August 11, 1994) pp54-58,75.
HOPKINS, ELLEN
"Nowhere To Run."
AR14246 632 (June 11, 1992) pp169,171.
HOPKINS, JERRY
"Jim Morrison."
AR14247 641 (October 15, 1992) pp42-43.
"Keith Moon."
AR14248 641 (October 15, 1992) pp53-54.
HOPKINS, TRACY
"Critics Comments."
AR14249 726 (January 25, 1996) pp46,50-51.
"97: Groove Is In The Heart."
AR14250 667 (October 14, 1993) p101.
"33: Mind Playing Tricks On Me."
AR14251 667 (October 14, 1993) p80.
HORTON, TOM
"Paradise Lost."
AR14252 632 (June 11, 1992) pp176-178.
HOSKYNS, BARNEY
"Kula Shaker."
AR14253 748 (November 28, 1996) p152.
"HOT."
AR14254 630 (May 14, 1992) p41.

"HOT PICKS: ROCK & ROLL IS THEIR BUSINESS HERE'S WHO THEY' RE LISTENING TO."
AR14255 660-661 (July 8, 1993) pp100-101.
"HOT PICKS: WHEN MUSIC INSIDERS KICK BACK, THESE ARE THE BANDS THEY LISTEN TO."
AR14256 628 (April 16, 1992) pp62-63.
"HOW TO VOTE IN FIFTY STATES."
AR14257 639 (September 17, 1992) p17.
HOWARD, PETE
"CD News."
AR14258 617 (November 14, 1991) p176.
AR14259 619-620 (December 12, 1991) p173.
AR14260 622 (January 23, 1992) p45.
AR14261 627 (April 2, 1992) p52.
AR14262 630 (May 14, 1992) p106.
AR14263 638 (September 3, 1992) p75.
AR14264 645-646 (December 10, 1992) p184.
AR14265 651 (March 4, 1993) p66.
AR14266 654 (April 15, 1993) p65.
AR14267 657 (May 27, 1993) p50.
AR14268 662 (August 5, 1993) p69.
AR14269 668 (October 28, 1993) p78.
AR14270 674 (January 27, 1994) p56.
AR14271 681 (May 5, 1994) p56.
AR14272 690 (September 8, 1994) p81.
AR14273 698-699 (December 29, 1994) p185.
"Flood Of Box Sets Due."
AR14274 615 (October 17, 1991) pp19,33.
"Monterey Pop, Airplane Sets Due."
AR14275 642 (October 29, 1992) p33.
HUHN, MARY
"Alt.Rock."
AR14276 748 (November 28, 1996) pp97-98,100+.
"Dollars And Dancing Bears."
AR14277 717 (September 21, 1995) p26.
"Web Watch: Because You're Mine, I Walk Online."
AR14278 748 (November 28, 1996) p117.
"(What's The Story) With Brit Pop Sites?."
AR14279 746 (October 31, 1996) p78.
HUNTER, JAMES
"Glam Slam 2: The Auteurs."
AR14280 657 (May 27, 1993) p16.
"Honky-Tonk Men: George Jones And Keith Richards Pair Up For Jones' Upcoming Album."
AR14281 681 (May 5, 1994) p18.
"Shara Nelson."
AR14282 692 (October 6, 1994) p32.
"Sheryl Crow."
AR14283 668 (October 28, 1993) p25.
HUNTER, ROBERT
"An Elegy For Jerry."
AR14284 717 (September 21, 1995) p28.
HUTCHENCE, MICHAEL
"Raves."
AR14285 680 (April 21, 1994) p21.
HYNDE, CHRISSIE
"Raves."
AR14286 674 (January 27, 1994) p20.

I

"I FOUGHT THE LAW."
AR14287 724-725 (December 28, 1995) p60.
"[IN NOVEMBER...]."
AR14288 644 (November 26, 1992) p11.
INFUSINO, DIVINA
"Buy One, Get One Free: Rocket From The Crypt And Drive Like Jehu Put San Diego On The Rock Map."
AR14289 689 (August 25, 1994) p44.
"INTRODUCTION."
AR14290 695 (November 17, 1994) p23.
ISRAEL, DULCY
"Movie Directors Who Toy With Tape."
AR14291 667 (October 14, 1993) p85.
"99: One."
AR14292 667 (October 14, 1993) p101.
"Photographers Who See Some Screen Action."
AR14293 667 (October 14, 1993) p98.
"69: Tennessee."
AR14294 667 (October 14, 1993) p94.
"29: Close."
AR14295 667 (October 14, 1993) p78.
"Videomakers Who Vault To The Big Screen."
AR14296 667 (October 14, 1993) p87.
"IT CAME FROM THE COURSE CATALOG."
AR14297 693 (January 20, 1994) p87.
"IT CAME FROM THE COURSE CATALOG NO. 2."
AR14298 693 (January 20, 1994) p89.
"IT CAME FROM THE COURSE CATALOG NO. 3."
AR14299 693 (January 20, 1994) p90.
"IT CAME FROM THE COURSE CATALOG NO. 4."
AR14300 693 (January 20, 1994) p93.
"IZZY QUITS GUNS N' ROSES."
AR14301 621 (January 9, 1992) p20.

J

JACKSON, DEVON
"China Syndrome: CD Piracy Results In A Trade War."
AR14302 704 (March 23, 1995) p36.
"Well Armed: 'Tank Girl' LP Snags A-List Punks."
AR14303 705 (April 6, 1995) p25.
JACOBS, KARRIE
"Germany Stomps Skinhead Music: Authorities Bust Third Reich & Roll."
AR14304 669 (November 11, 1993) p18.
JACOBS, SALLY
"Wedowee: When An Alabama Principal Said No To Interracial Dating, A Small Community Was Forced To Confront Its Racist Heritage."
AR14305 708 (May 18, 1995) pp55-58,60-61+.
JAMISON, LAURA
"Raw And Chunky: A Tribe Called Quest Go Minimalist."
AR14306 732 (April 18, 1996) p32.
"[JAPAN]."
AR14307 671 (December 9, 1993) p7.
"JEFF PORCARO: 1954-1992."
AR14308 639 (September 17, 1992) p28.
JENKINS, SACHA
"OutKast."
AR14309 747 (November 14, 1996) p136.
"JERRY BROWN'S GRASS-ROOTS CALL TO ARMS: AN INTERVIEW WITH THE EDITORS OF ROLLING STONE."
AR14310 625 (March 5, 1992) pp29-30,40,78.
"JERRY NOLAN: 1946-1992."
AR14311 625 (March 5, 1992) p22.
JOHNSON, ARAN
"Our Lives, Our Music: Appetite For Destruction."
AR14312 644 (November 26, 1992) pp56,58.
JOHNSON, CORY
"Cut To The Chase."
AR14313 633 (June 25, 1992) pp35-37.
"Pedal To The Medal: These Olympic Contenders Shift Into Casual Gear."
AR14314 626 (March 19, 1992) pp79-82.
"School Ties Stars Unbutton Their Shirts."

AR14315 638 (September 3, 1992) pp[enc.45-46 +].
JOHNSON, DEAN
"Rock & Roll Summer: Boston."
AR14316 710 (June 15, 1995) p39.
JOHNSON, HILLARY
"The Forgotten Epidemic."
AR14317 730 (March 21, 1996) pp78-80,82,84 +.
JOHNSON, MARTIN
"Cultural Healing: Choir Marries Gospel And Hip-Hop."
AR14318 686-687 (July 14, 1994) p39.
"Digable Planets: The Trio Pays Homage To Early Jazz Greats."
AR14319 652 (March 18, 1993) p23.
"Onyx: Bringing Old-School Hip-Hop To The Mosh Pit."
AR14320 659 (June 24, 1993) p21.
JOHNSTON, DAVID
"The Enemy Within: An Exclusive Excerpt From The Upcoming Book 'Betrayal' Tells The Inside Story of The Hunt For Aldrich Ames, The Deadliest Traitor In The History Of The CIA."
AR14321 711 (June 29, 1995) pp34-38,53-54 +.
JONES, MICK
"Raves."
AR14322 706 (April 20, 1995) p33.
JONES, RICKIE LEE
"Raves."
AR14323 671 (December 9, 1993) p22.
JOPLIN, JANIS
"Love Janis: Janis Joplin's Rise To Stardom Is Chronicled In These Letters Written To Her Family In Texas."
AR14324 638 (September 3, 1992) pp55-57,59.
JOPLIN, LAURA
"Love Janis: Janis Joplin's Rise To Stardom Is Chronicled In These Letters Written To Her Family In Texas."
AR14325 638 (September 3, 1992) pp55-57,59.

K

KATZ, JON
"AIDS And The Media: Shifting Out Of Neutral."
AR14326 657 (May 27, 1993) pp31-32.
"Animated Arguments: Why The Show's Critics Just Don't Get It."
AR14327 678 (March 24, 1994) p45.
"Bulletin Boards: News From Cyberspace."
AR14328 654 (April 15, 1993) pp35-36,77.
"Can The Media Do The Right Thing?."
AR14329 631 (May 28, 1992) pp30-31.
"The Capital Gang Bang: The Failure Of The Washington Press Corps."
AR14330 663 (August 19, 1993) pp37-39,89.
"Cop Killers? The Media Target The Police."
AR14331 648 (January 21, 1993) pp30-31.
"The Evening Mirror: Can The 'NBC Nightly News' Succeed By Doing Fewer Stories About Washington And More About Peoria?."
AR14332 616 (October 31, 1991) pp101-102.
"The Media's Myth Of The Bloody Campaign."
AR14333 628 (April 16, 1992) pp31-33.
"The Media's War On Kids: From The Beatles To Beavis And Butt-head."
AR14334 670 (November 25, 1993) pp47-49,130.
"Over To You, Dan: How Cronkite's Heir Became Chung's Sidekick."
AR14335 667 (October 14, 1993) pp44-45,130.
"The Plugged-In Voter: The New News Has Reconnected People And Politics."
AR14336 645-646 (December 10, 1992) pp115-117,201.
"The Prince Of Wildwood: Jack Brian Searches The Jersey Shore For Love, Girls And A Future."
AR14337 638 (September 3, 1992) pp45-47,50-51 +.
"Rock, Rap And Movies Bring You The News."
AR14338 625 (March 5, 1992) pp33,36-37,40 +.
"Rom & Roll: Hanging With Wanda The Worm Women And Friends."
AR14339 679 (April 7, 1994) pp43-45.
"Ten Things In 1993 That Didn't Suck."
AR14340 672-673 (December 23, 1993) pp88,90,176.
"Time Warner Runs Up The White Flag: The Media Help Drag Down One Of Their Own."
AR14341 651 (March 4, 1993) pp40-41.
"The War At Home: How The Media Miss The Story On 34,000 Gun Deaths Each Year."
AR14342 660-661 (July 8, 1993) pp37-38,128.
"White Men Can't Rule: A Melting Pot Revolt."
AR14343 636 (August 6, 1992) pp33-34,75.
KEHOE, JOHN
"The Art Of Noise: The New Rock-Poster Genius Of Frank Kozik."
AR14344 672-673 (December 23, 1993) pp131-133.
KELLER, MARTIN
"Space Is The Place: Rockers Look To The Skies In Search Of UFOs."
AR14345 734 (May 16, 1996) pp21-22.
KELLY, CHRIS
"Bush Whacked! An Unknown English Band Takes America By Surprise."
AR14346 712-713 (July 13, 1995) pp29-30.
KELLY, CHRISTINA
"Dad, I'm A Degenerate: New York's D Generation Spark A New Glam-Rock Scene Behind The Green Door."
AR14347 701 (February 9, 1995) pp19-20.
"Dishwalla And Styx Fuse Their Illusions."
AR14348 741 (August 22, 1996) p39.
"Isn't It Alanis? 'Ironic' Parodies Flood The Airwaves."
AR14349 747 (November 14, 1996) p36.
"The Jon Spencer Blues Explosion Throw A Punky, Bluesy Party On 'Now I Got Worry'."
AR14350 745 (October 17, 1996) pp31,36.
KEMP, MARK
"Chill Factor: DJs Cool Down L.A.'s Post-Rave Club Scene."
AR14351 716 (September 7, 1995) p32.
"Critics Comments."
AR14352 726 (January 25, 1996) pp46,50-51.
"Famous By Association: Vic Chestnutt Joins His Rock & Roll Heroes In The Spotlight."
AR14353 743 (September 19, 1996) pp62-65,77,100.
"Geek Love: Stepping Out From John Mellencamp's Shadow, Singer And Violinist Lisa Germano Hits A Nerve On "Geek The Girl"."
AR14354 697 (December 15, 1994) pp23-24.
"Jeffrey Lee Pierce 1958-1996."
AR14355 734 (May 16, 1996) p22.
"Jimmy Buffett."
AR14356 741 (August 22, 1996) p42.
"Paradise Found: Coolio Completes His Fantastic Voyage From The Mean Streets Of Los Angeles To The Top Of The Pop Charts."
AR14357 723 (December 14, 1995) pp33-34.
"Performance."
AR14358 737 (June 27, 1996) p59.
"The Rolling Stones' 'Rock & Roll Circus' Is Back In Town."
AR14359 746 (October 31, 1996) p27.
KENING, DAN
"Marty Brown: More Than A Country Throwback."
AR14360 617 (November 14, 1991) p34.
KENNY, GLENN
"Albert Goldman 1927-1994."
AR14361 682 (May 19, 1994) p22.
"A-Muze Yourself: From Abba To Zappa: A New Computer Gives Fans Fingertip Access To Disc Data."
AR14362 653 (April 1, 1993) p22.
"Beatle On The Block: Rare Tape Of An Early John Lennon Performance To Be Auctioned In London."
AR14363 690 (September 8, 1994) p36.
"Boy George Plays 'The Crying Game'."

KENNY, GLENN (continued)
AR14364 651 (March 4, 1993) p28.
"Brace Yourself! Whale Sink Their Teeth Into Your TV."
AR14365 685 (June 30, 1994) p32.
"Class Conflict: Zappa Vid Gets Teacher Suspended."
AR14366 684 (June 16, 1994) p25.
"8: Leave Me Alone."
AR14367 667 (October 14, 1993) pp69-70.
"18: Kiss."
AR14368 667 (October 14, 1993) p76.
"85: Little Red Corvette."
AR14369 667 (October 14, 1993) p100.
"Feeling The Space: Yoko Ono Enters A New World—The Theater."
AR14370 679 (April 7, 1994) p28.
"55: Wild Thing."
AR14371 667 (October 14, 1993) p90.
"54: And She Was."
AR14372 667 (October 14, 1993) p90.
"59: Justified And Ancient."
AR14373 667 (October 14, 1993) p93.
"57: Fish Heads."
AR14374 667 (October 14, 1993) p92.
"53: Shock The Monkey."
AR14375 667 (October 14, 1993) p90.
"48: China Girl."
AR14376 667 (October 14, 1993) p87.
"45: Whip It."
AR14377 667 (October 14, 1993) p85.
"47: Undercover Of The Night."
AR14378 667 (October 14, 1993) p87.
"Harry Nilsson 1941-1994."
AR14379 677 (March 10, 1994) p25.
"How Swede It Is: Ace Of Base Invade U.S. Airwaves."
AR14380 688 (August 11, 1994) p32.
"In The News."
AR14381 683 (June 2, 1994) p17.
AR14382 684 (June 16, 1994) p26.
"Indie Speedway: Sonicnet Launches An On-Line Service For Music."
AR14383 689 (August 25, 1994) p32.
"Jawbox."
AR14384 678 (March 24, 1994) p20.
"Joey Ramone."
AR14385 678 (March 24, 1994) p16.
"A Little Strange Music."
AR14386 660-661 (July 8, 1993) p23.
"Mercury Rev Rising: They Were Too Weird Even For Lollapalooza."
AR14387 664 (September 2, 1993) p24.
"Metal Metheny Music."
AR14388 685 (June 30, 1994) p32.
"Mike Clarke 1944-1993."
AR14389 675 (February 10, 1994) p15.
"Multimedia."
AR14390 722 (November 30, 1995) p71.
"98: Silent All These Years."
AR14391 667 (October 14, 1993) p101.
"91: Freedom 90."
AR14392 667 (October 14, 1993) p100.
"90: The Perfect Kiss."
AR14393 667 (October 14, 1993) p100.
"93: Orange Crush."
AR14394 667 (October 14, 1993) p101.
"100: Satisfaction."
AR14395 667 (October 14, 1993) p101.
"1: Sledgehammer."
AR14396 667 (October 14, 1993) p67.
"Punk's Holy Rollers: Bad Religion Have Come A Long Way From Their Garage-Rock Roots."
AR14397 670 (November 25, 1993) p30.
"Radiohead: 'Creep' Is The Most Audacious Pop Move Since The Police's 'Every Breath You Take'."
AR14398 665 (September 16, 1993) p22.
"Rock And Rap Comics."
AR14399 667 (October 14, 1993) p26.
"7: Subterranean Homesick Blues."
AR14400 667 (October 14, 1993) p69.
"78: Dirty Boots."
AR14401 667 (October 14, 1993) p97.
"75: One."
AR14402 667 (October 14, 1993) p97.
"74: Psycho Therapy."
AR14403 667 (October 14, 1993) pp96-97.
"72: Shadrach."
AR14404 667 (October 14, 1993) p96.
"60: Epic."
AR14405 667 (October 14, 1993) p93.
"65: Jazzin' For Blue Jean."
AR14406 667 (October 14, 1993) p94.
"63: Rockit."
AR14407 667 (October 14, 1993) p93.
"Sonny Sharrock 1940-1994."
AR14408 686-687 (July 14, 1994) p26.
"Sweet Soul Music: Retro Rockers Collective Soul Take A Shine To The Airwaves."
AR14409 686-687 (July 14, 1994) p30.
"38: Ashes To Ashes."
AR14410 667 (October 14, 1993) p82.
"3: Losing My Religion."
AR14411 667 (October 14, 1993) p68.
"Trash Collection: Sonic Youth Go Artcore On New LP."
AR14412 679 (April 7, 1994) p24.
"Turning Half Japanese."
AR14413 670 (November 25, 1993) p30.
"24: Borderline."
AR14414 667 (October 14, 1993) p77.
"U2 Get Their Wings."
AR14415 675 (February 10, 1994) p13.
KERN, GEOF
"Endpaper."
AR14416 619-620 (December 12, 1991) p220.
KERR, JIM
"Raves."
AR14417 709 (June 1, 1995) p24.
KESEY, KEN
"The Search For The Secret Pyramid."
AR14418 632 (June 11, 1992) pp85-86,88.
KIM, JAE-HA
"Chicago."
AR14419 688 (August 11, 1994) p22.
"Guyville Java Jive."
AR14420 688 (August 11, 1994) p22.
KIM, LINDA
"Camille Paglia: Lit Crit's Snit Fits."
AR14421 693 (October 20, 1994) pp87,92.
KIM, WOOK
"96: Human Behaviour."
AR14422 667 (October 14, 1993) p101.
"Videos By Number."
AR14423 667 (October 14, 1993) p82.
KIRK, DEBORAH
"Space Oddity: Bootsy Collins Orbits Higher With "Zillatron" And "Blasters Of The Universe"."
AR14424 691 (September 22, 1994) p32.
KLEIN, STEVEN
"Snakin Around."
AR14425 638 (September 3, 1992) pp[enc.9-12 +].
KLIEN, JOE
"A Simple Twist Of Fate."
AR14426 641 (October 15, 1992) p74.
KNOPPER, STEVE
"The Battle For Walden Woods: Don Henley Helped Save The Trees,

But Some Preservationists Say He Doesn't Know When To Quit."
AR14427 732 (April 18, 1996) pp22-23,29.
KOHN, HOWARD
"Malignant Giant."
AR14428 632 (June 11, 1992) pp92-93,95,97.
"Tania's World."
AR14429 632 (June 11, 1992) pp100-101,103 +.
KONIGSBERG, ERIC
"The Fall Of Animal House: For Dartmouth's Alpha Delta Fraternity, The Choice Is Change Or Die."
AR14430 639 (September 17, 1992) pp73-76,112.
"Getting In: Everybody Goes To Rusty."
AR14431 745 (October 17, 1996) pp103-104,106 +.
"Justice Denied."
AR14432 706 (April 20, 1995) p45.
KOT, GREG
"The Cradle Will Rock: Silverchair Make Music Beyond Their Years."
AR14433 715 (August 24, 1995) p31.
"Critics Comments."
AR14434 726 (January 25, 1996) pp46,50-51.
"It's The Jesus And Nirvana Chain!."
AR14435 653 (April 1, 1993) p20.
"Les Claypool Of Primus."
AR14436 664 (September 2, 1993) p16.
"Pumpkins Plan Double Disc: Billy Corgan And The Band Have A Smashing Good Time In The Studio."
AR14437 711 (June 29, 1995) p19.
"This Old 'Palooza."
AR14438 741 (August 22, 1996) pp31,33.
"Will Oldham Of Palace: King Of Appalachian Indie Rock."
AR14439 735 (May 30, 1996) p26.
KRAKUER, JON
"Powder To The People: Connoisseurs Of The Cold Rip Through Their Favorite Brand Of Snow."
AR14440 617 (November 14, 1991) pp159-164.
KRANTZ, MICHAEL
"Brave New Home: Couch Potatoes Of The Future, Fear Not."
AR14441 722 (November 30, 1995) pp[enc.45-46].
KRAVITZ, LENNY
"Raves."
AR14442 669 (November 11, 1993) p20.
KRELL, ERIC
"Guitar Note: The DTS-I Changes Tunings In Seconds."
AR14443 708 (May 18, 1995) pp[enc.30-31].
KRUGMAN, MICHAEL
"Critics Comments."
AR14444 726 (January 25, 1996) pp46,50-51.
"The Reading Festival."
AR14445 719 (October 19, 1995) p33.
KUIPERS, DEAN
"The Tracks Of The Coyote."
AR14446 709 (June 1, 1995) pp52-54,56-58 +.
"Update."
AR14447 721 (November 16, 1995) p22.

L

LADYBUG
"Raves."
AR14448 703 (March 9, 1995) p34.
LAXTON, WILLIAM
"Spaghetti Western: The Singing Cowboy Junkie Margo Timmins And The Lone Star State's Own Lyle Lovett Get Duded Up Italian-Like."
AR14449 628 (April 16, 1992) pp[enc.9,11 +].
"LEATHER & LACE."
AR14450 743 (September 19, 1996) pp[enc.28-30].
LEE, RICKY
"Miami."
AR14451 691 (September 22, 1994) p22.
"Pervert Designer."
AR14452 691 (September 22, 1994) p22.
LEIBOVITZ, ANNIE
"Jerry Garcia."
AR14453 717 (September 21, 1995) pp[unnumbered].
"Yoko Ono & John Lennon."
AR14454 643 (November 12, 1992) p256.
LEIBY, RICHARD
"Voodoo Child: Hendrix Jr. Sues Estate."
AR14455 682 (May 19, 1994) p22.
LEONARD, MIKE
"The Big Scare: Heart Attack Trips Up Mellencamp."
AR14456 696 (December 1, 1994) p33.
"Deep-River Blues: John Mellencamp And Blind Melon Rock For Flood Victims."
AR14457 665 (September 16, 1993) p13.
LEVINE, ROBERT
"ABC Television Boots Concert-Tape Traders Off Its America Online Site."
AR14458 742 (September 5, 1996) p25.
"The Noise On The Bus: MTV News & Rock The Vote Put Youth Issues On The '96 Campaign Agenda."
AR14459 745 (October 17, 1996) pp30,33.
LEWIS, NEIL A.
"The Enemy Within: An Exclusive Excerpt From The Upcoming Book 'Betrayal' Tells The Inside Story of The Hunt For Aldrich Ames, The Deadliest Traitor In The History Of The CIA."
AR14460 711 (June 29, 1995) pp34-38,53-54 +.
LEWMAN, MARK
"Tattoo You: Lou Deangelis Gets Crazy On His Mountain Bike."
AR14461 708 (May 18, 1995) pp78-80,82,84 +.
LIEB, KRISTIN
"Simply The Best: Tracy Bonham Enjoys Her Winning Streak."
AR14462 730 (March 21, 1996) p28.
"Studio Of The Moment: At Fort Apache, The Motto Is 'Great Big Guitars And No Rules'."
AR14463 708 (May 18, 1995) p28.
LIGHT, ALAN
"Basehead: Charting A New Course For The Hip-Hop Generation."
AR14464 628 (April 16, 1992) pp51,53.
"Behind The Fly: Bono."
AR14465 651 (March 4, 1993) pp42-43,45-46 +.
"Body Count Shows Canceled, 'Cop Killer' Protest Continues As Police Refuse To Provide Security."
AR14466 649 (February 4, 1993) p16.
"Boys To Men."
AR14467 631 (May 28, 1992) pp40-41.
"Downtown Science: A Broad Spectrum Of Sounds."
AR14468 617 (November 14, 1991) p34.
"Eddie Hazel: 1950-1992."
AR14469 650 (February 18, 1993) p17.
"Eddie Kendricks: 1939-1992."
AR14470 644 (November 26, 1992) p24.
"Forever Young: Neil Young Proves Life In Rock & Roll Can Begin Again At Fortysomething."
AR14471 648 (January 21, 1993) pp34-37,53.
"A 'Heavier, Funkier' Living Colour: Vernon Reid And Company Set To Release 'Stain'."
AR14472 648 (January 21, 1993) p18.
"Ice-T."
AR14473 641 (October 15, 1992) pp162-164.
"Ice-T: The Rolling Stone Interview."
AR14474 637 (August 20, 1992) pp28-32,60.
"Ice-T's Declaration Of Independence: The Truth Behind His Split With Time Warner."
AR14475 652 (March 18, 1993) pp19,31.

LIGHT, ALAN (continued)
"In The News."
AR14476 636 (August 6, 1992) p22.
AR14477 640 (October 1, 1992) p25.
AR14478 642 (October 29, 1992) p28.
AR14479 649 (February 4, 1993) p17.
"Jackson's Dangerous Game: The Self-Crowned King Of Pop Ruled On Prime Time, But Did We Get The Truth?."
AR14480 653 (April 1, 1993) p17.
"L. A. Rappers Speak Out."
AR14481 633 (June 25, 1992) pp15,21.
"A Lasting Impression: The Rolling Stone Interview With Curtis Mayfield."
AR14482 668 (October 28, 1993) pp62-66.
"Mary Wells: 1943-1992."
AR14483 638 (September 3, 1992) p17.
"Motown's Baby Boyz: Philadelphia's Boyz II Men Become The Label's Hottest Act In Years."
AR14484 625 (March 5, 1992) pp21-22.
"Naughty As They Wanna Be: The Hood Comes First When Naughty By Nature Hits The Mike."
AR14485 658 (June 10, 1993) p30.
"Opinion: Blaming Hardcore For Murder Is Taking The Lazy Way Out."
AR14486 650 (February 18, 1993) p28.
"Public Enemy #1: Rap's Top Group Focuses On Gold Brains, Not Gold Chains."
AR14487 622 (January 23, 1992) pp34-37,50-51+.
"Queen Latifah's New Gambit: Her New Album Reaches Out To A Larger Audience."
AR14488 615 (October 17, 1991) pp19,32.
"Rap."
AR14489 645-646 (December 10, 1992) p79.
"Rappers Sound Warning: The Violence In Los Angeles Didn't Surprise Those Who Were Paying Attention."
AR14490 634-635 (July 9, 1992) pp15-17.
"Riots Mar G N' R Tour."
AR14491 639 (September 17, 1992) p32.
"Rock The Vote's New Campaign: Organization Gets Out The Vote In New Hampshire Primary."
AR14492 626 (March 19, 1992) pp17,24.
"Roy Acuff: 1903-1992."
AR14493 647 (January 7, 1993) p16.
"Sinead Speaks."
AR14494 642 (October 29, 1992) pp50-53,80.
"Singing From The Heart: Tracy Chapman Explores Some New Territory On Her Third Album."
AR14495 628 (April 16, 1992) p26.
"Star-Studded Soundtrack: U2, Talking Heads, R.E.M. And Others Provide Music For Wenders Film."
AR14496 623 (February 6, 1992) p34.
"Superbad!: The Elusive Prince Returns Triumphant."
AR14497 655 (April 29, 1993) pp15-16.
"TLC: Street-Level Feminism."
AR14498 631 (May 28, 1992) p22.
"Words From The 'Home' Front."
AR14499 657 (May 27, 1993) pp20-21.
"Wyman Quits The Stones."
AR14500 648 (January 21, 1993) pp13,25.
"Wynonna Leaves Home: One-Half Of Country Music's Judds Declares Her Independence."
AR14501 633 (June 25, 1992) pp15-16.
LIN, EDWARD
"Our Lives, Our Music: Psychocandy."
AR14502 644 (November 26, 1992) p56.
LINDEN, AMY
"Is P.M. Dawn's Prince Be the Brian Wilson Of Hip-Hop? God Only Knows."
AR14503 719 (October 19, 1995) pp19-20.
LIPSKY, DAVID
"Generation Latex: Sex On Campus!!."
AR14504 704 (March 23, 1995) pp80-82,84-85+.
"The Hard-Core Curriculum: Despite A Decade Of 'Just Say No' And Get-Tough Laws, Drugs Are Back On Campus With A Vengeance."
AR14505 719 (October 19, 1995) pp99-105,142.
"Hot List."
AR14506 715 (August 24, 1995) pp73-75,77,80+.
"Junkie Town."
AR14507 735 (May 30, 1996) pp35-40,42-43+.
"The New Skitcoms: Sketches Of Pain."
AR14508 704 (March 23, 1995) p132.
"LITTLE ROCK, ARKANSAS."
AR14509 681 (May 5, 1994) p43.
LOCKHART, JUDY
"Our Lives, Our Music: The White Album."
AR14510 644 (November 26, 1992) p54.
LOCKMAN, DARCY
"Hot Look."
AR14511 741 (August 22, 1996) pp86-88,90,92.
"One Hot Minute."
AR14512 732 (April 18, 1996) pp[enc.14-15].
LODER, KURT
"Bob Dylan."
AR14513 641 (October 15, 1992) pp110-113.
"David Bowie."
AR14514 641 (October 15, 1992) pp141-142.
"Joan Baez."
AR14515 641 (October 15, 1992) pp105,107.
"Keith Richards."
AR14516 641 (October 15, 1992) pp86-87.
"Springsteen."
AR14517 641 (October 15, 1992) pp130-132.
"A Voice In The Night."
AR14518 641 (October 15, 1992) pp121,123.
LOEB, LISA
"Raves."
AR14519 727 (February 8, 1996) p26.
"THE LOOK: IN A NEW BOOK, ROLLING STONE CELEBRATES 40 YEARS OF ROCK PHOTOGRAPHY."
AR14520 720 (November 2, 1995) pp49-51.
LORCH, DONATELLA
"Aftermath: In Rwanda A Year After The Massacre, There Is Still No Justice, No Peace."
AR14521 712-713 (July 13, 1995) pp86-91.
LOVE, COURTNEY
"A Cry In The Dark: Love Reads Cobain's Note To Vigil."
AR14522 683 (June 2, 1994) p40.
LOVE, ROBERT
"Memory Of A Gonzo Christmas Past."
AR14523 748 (November 28, 1996) p13.
"William M. Gaines (1922-1992)."
AR14524 636 (August 6, 1992) p46.
LOVETT, ANTHONY R.
"Wired In California: Meth, The Drug That Snuffed Out The Summer Of Love, Is Back, And California IS Exporting It All Over The Nation."
AR14525 681 (May 5, 1994) pp39-40.
LUOMA, MARC
"Our Lives, Our Music: The Unforgettable Fire."
AR14526 644 (November 26, 1992) p56.

M

MACADAMS, LEWIS
"The Call Of The Wild: To The People On The Edge Of The Environmental Movement, The Program To Bring Back The Wolf Has A

Big Problem—It Isn't Natural."
AR14527 693 (October 20, 1994) pp82-85,160.
"A Gathering Of The Tribes: A Report From The 1993 World Peace And Healing Gathering Of The Rainbow Family Of Living Light."
AR14528 672-673 (December 23, 1993) pp118-120,122+.
"Geronimo Vs. Cochise: As Apaches Fight To Build A Nuclear Waste Dump On Their New Mexico Reservation, The Descendants Of Two Legendary Warriors Are Locked In A Battle For The Soul Of The Tribe."
AR14529 736 (June 13, 1996) pp66-70,73-74.
MACNIE, JIM
"Country Artist Of The Year."
AR14530 726 (January 25, 1996) p48.
"Leann Rimes Sees 'Blue' Skies."
AR14531 744 (October 3, 1996) p32.
MACPHERSON, ANDREW
"Darkness On The Edge of Bedrock: Kyle MacLachlan Brings His All-American Weirdness To "The Flintstones"."
AR14532 685 (June 30, 1994) pp63-64.
"MAKING EDUCATION WORK."
AR14533 694 (November 3, 1994) p52.
MALIGE, DIDIER
"School Ties Stars Unbutton Their Shirts."
AR14534 638 (September 3, 1992) pp[enc.45-46+].
MALLEY, STEPHEN
"Misty Mountain Hop: Amateurs And Pros Jump Around In Aspen Highlands."
AR14535 644 (November 26, 1992) pp60-64.
MANEGOLD, CATHERINE S.
"George Harrison: Live And Low-Key."
AR14536 623 (February 6, 1992) pp15,18.
MANNES, GEORGE
"Metal Machine Music."
AR14537 722 (November 30, 1995) p81.
MANNING, KARA
"Alison Steele: 1937-1995."
AR14538 721 (November 16, 1995) p38.
"Burning Rubber: Elastica Hit The U.S. At Full Throttle."
AR14539 707 (May 4, 1995) pp23-24.
"Close Encounters: Youssou N'Dour And Neneh Cherry Make Record Time In "7 Seconds"."
AR14540 689 (August 25, 1994) p45.
"The Cranberries."
AR14541 664 (September 2, 1993) p28.
"Desert-Island Videos: What's Your No. 1?."
AR14542 667 (October 14, 1993) p93.
"Election Watch."
AR14543 637 (August 20, 1992) p23.
AR14544 639 (September 17, 1992) p28.
AR14545 640 (October 1, 1992) p20.
AR14546 642 (October 29, 1992) p33.
"42: Series Of Dreams."
AR14547 667 (October 14, 1993) p85.
"Generation Next: The Smokin' Sounds Of Summer '94."
AR14548 686-687 (July 14, 1994) pp72-74.
"Hot Picks: An Insider's Guide To the Season's New Faces."
AR14549 686-687 (July 14, 1994) pp78-79.
"In The News."
AR14550 694 (November 3, 1994) p32.
"John Prine."
AR14551 717 (September 21, 1995) p36.
"Leslie Spit Treeo: Canadian Psycho Folk."
AR14552 616 (October 31, 1991) p25.
"Lois."
AR14553 717 (September 21, 1995) p38.
"Party Culture: Strange Customs, Quaint Traditions And Stupid Parlor Tricks."
AR14554 652 (March 18, 1993) pp[enc.4].
"61: Every Breath You Take."
AR14555 667 (October 14, 1993) p93.
"66: Oh Father."
AR14556 667 (October 14, 1993) p94.
"Weezer."
AR14557 694 (November 3, 1994) p40.
"WOMAD On The Road."
AR14558 663 (August 19, 1993) p10.
MANSON, SHIRLEY
"Raves."
AR14559 740 (August 8, 1996) p28.
MARCUS, GREIL
"Blue Hawaii."
AR14560 632 (June 11, 1992) pp119,121.
"Come As You Are."
AR14561 683 (June 2, 1994) p56.
"Is This The Woman Who Invented Rock & Roll?: The Deborah Chessler Story."
AR14562 659 (June 24, 1993) pp41,43,46,48+.
MARGASAK, PETER
"Mo' Wax Captures The Trip-Hop Vibe."
AR14563 738-739 (July 11, 1996) p26.
MARIN, RICK
"40: Baby Got Back."
AR14564 667 (October 14, 1993) p82.
"41: Man On The Moon."
AR14565 667 (October 14, 1993) p85.
"4: This Note's For You."
AR14566 667 (October 14, 1993) p68.
"Man Or Mouth?: The Rolling Stone Interview With Howard Stern."
AR14567 675 (February 10, 1994) pp28-32,53.
"77: White Wedding."
AR14568 667 (October 14, 1993) p97.
"6: Right Now."
AR14569 667 (October 14, 1993) p69.
"68: Smells Like Nirvana."
AR14570 667 (October 14, 1993) p94.
"64: Brilliant Disguise."
AR14571 667 (October 14, 1993) p94.
"36: Jeremy."
AR14572 667 (October 14, 1993) p82.
"37: Atlantic City."
AR14573 667 (October 14, 1993) p82.
"Would You Please Welcome...: Dave, Conan, Jay And Arsenio Pump Up The Volume."
AR14574 677 (March 10, 1994) p17.
MARKUS, KURT
"Kurt Markus."
AR14575 643 (November 12, 1992) pp173-177,179+.
MARSH, DAVE
"Timing Is Everything."
AR14576 641 (October 15, 1992) pp64-65.
MARTEL, JAY
"The Fall Group Grope: The New Season Offers Yuks For Blacks, Fake Feminism For Women, Familiar Faces For The Old, Pecs And Posing For The Young."
AR14577 640 (October 1, 1992) pp77-78,84.
"Getting Ahead: Upgrade Now!."
AR14578 745 (October 17, 1996) pp113-114,116+.
"Hot Actor: Dogging It With Brad Pitt, The Good Ol' Bad Boy From 'Thelma And Louise'."
AR14579 630 (May 14, 1992) pp54-56,59.
"Hot Art Show: The Gramercy Art Fair."
AR14580 741 (August 22, 1996) p78.
"Hot Career Move: Quitting."
AR14581 741 (August 22, 1996) p71.
"Hot Marketing Ploy: Critic Proofing."
AR14582 741 (August 22, 1996) p72.
"Hot Sitcom Twist: Depressing Season Finales."
AR14583 741 (August 22, 1996) p74.

MARTEL, JAY (continued)
"Hot TV Show: Concrete T.V.."
AR14584 741 (August 22, 1996) p77.
"Hot Vacation Spot: Anywhere That's Like Somewhere Else 20 Years Ago."
AR14585 741 (August 22, 1996) p80.
"The Love Boat."
AR14586 618 (November 28, 1991) p106.
"Martin Lawrence."
AR14587 680 (April 21, 1994) pp68-70,74,76+.
"Net Worst" The 'New' Networks Go Where The Boys Already Are."
AR14588 704 (March 23, 1995) pp131-132.
"The Perils Of Pauly."
AR14589 634-635 (July 9, 1992) pp54-57.
"Scenes From The Cast Struggle In Beverly Hills:Mauled In Malls By Rabid Fans, The Stars Of 'Beverly Hills, 90210' Deal With Their Teen Minutes Of Fames."
AR14590 624 (February 20, 1992) pp22-26,45,50.
"True Lies: On "The Larry Sanders Show," Garry Shandling Turns The Talk-Show Brouhaha Into The Funniest Thing On TV."
AR14591 690 (September 8, 1994) pp66-68,70-73.
"Voyage To The Bottom Of The Season."
AR14592 666 (September 30, 1993) pp115-116.
"The Year In Television."
AR14593 619-620 (December 12, 1991) pp199,201-202.
AR14594 645-646 (December 10, 1992) pp196,198.
MARTIN, KEVIN
"Raves."
AR14595 696 (December 1, 1994) p42.
MASSING, MICHAEL
"The Longest War."
AR14596 706 (April 20, 1995) pp44-45.
MASUO, SANDY
"Long Fin Killie."
AR14597 747 (November 14, 1996) p58.
"60 Ft Dolls."
AR14598 747 (November 14, 1996) p52.
"Thermadore Try Not To Get Worried."
AR14599 737 (June 27, 1996) p28.
"311 Kiss Up To Hippies And Skate Punks."
AR14600 743 (September 19, 1996) p37.
MATTHEWS, BRENDA
"Our Lives, Our Music: Get Your Wings."
AR14601 644 (November 26, 1992) p52.
MATTHEWS, DAVE
"Raves."
AR14602 715 (August 24, 1995) p32.
AR14603 737 (June 27, 1996) p26.
"MC5'S ROB TYNER DIES."
AR14604 616 (January 31, 1991) p18.
MCCORMICK, MOIRA
"Jeffrey Gaines: Real-Life Sketches."
AR14605 629 (April 30, 1992) p31.
MCCULLEY, JERRY
"Here, There And Everywhere."
AR14606 722 (November 30, 1995) pp26,28.
MCDONNELL, EVELYN
"Ani DiFranco."
AR14607 721 (November 16, 1995) pp62-63.
"Her Back Pages."
AR14608 682 (May 19, 1994) p29.
"Me'shell NdegeOcello."
AR14609 698-699 (December 29, 1994) p38.
"Native Tongues: New Poets With A Rock & Roll Attitude."
AR14610 662 (August 5, 1993) p20.
"The Olympia Spirit: The Ticket Is Love Rock And Minimalism At Yoyo A Go Go."
AR14611 690 (September 8, 1994) p33.
"Tara Key."
AR14612 679 (April 7, 1994) p32.
"'X's New World Order: L.A.'s Seminal Punkers Reunite On 'Hey Zeus!'."
AR14613 659 (June 24, 1993) p23.
MCGEE, DAVID
"Critics Comments."
AR14614 726 (January 25, 1996) pp46,50-51.
MCGLINN, EVAN
"Double Trouble: Luke And Murphy Jensen Are The new Rude Dudes Of Tennis."
AR14615 665 (September 16, 1993) pp[enc.9-13].
"Emperors Of The Air."
AR14616 668 (October 28, 1993) pp70-73,89,92.
"Masters Of The Game: Over The Mountain And Through The Woods With Three Young Designers Who Show The Brand Names How To Play."
AR14617 691 (September 22, 1994) pp[enc.25,27+].
MCGOVERN, GEORGE
"The Last Nixon."
AR14618 684 (June 16, 1994) pp45,119.
MCKENNA, KRISTINE
"Sting."
AR14619 641 (October 15, 1992) pp115-116.
MCLACHLAN, SARAH
"Raves."
AR14620 690 (September 8, 1994) p34.
MCLANE, DAISANN
"The Girl In The Tweed Jacket."
AR14621 641 (October 15, 1992) pp95-97.
"Jailhouse Ragga: Snow Busts Out Of The Big House And Up The Pop Charts."
AR14622 665 (September 16, 1993) pp11-12.
"A New Wave: Rasin Music Catches Fire At Haitian Fest."
AR14623 718 (October 5, 1995) p25.
MCLEESE, DON
"Acid Damage: The Strange, Tragic Tale Of Psychedelic Icon Roky Erickson's Descent Into Madness."
AR14624 706 (April 20, 1995) pp21,23.
"A Bit Of Guitar Heaven: Austin's Arc Angels Prove They're More Than Just Another Blues-Rock Band."
AR14625 630 (May 14, 1992) p25.
"Blues From On High: The Arc Angels Bring A Li'l Bit Of Heaven To Austin."
AR14626 654 (April 15, 1993) pp[enc.16-20+].
"Blues Power: Stevie Ray Vaughan Honored At Fete."
AR14627 711 (June 29, 1995) p18.
"Conway Twitty: 1933-1993."
AR14628 662 (August 5, 1993) p27.
"Country."
AR14629 645-646 (December 10, 1992) p75.
"The Healing Of Daniel Johnston: A Punk-Rock Cult Hero's Roller-Coaster Ride Toward Wider Recognition."
AR14630 694 (November 3, 1994) pp33-34.
"Rock & Roll Summer: Austin."
AR14631 710 (June 15, 1995) p54.
MCLEESE, MARIA
AR14632 710 (June 15, 1995) p54.
MEEHAN, ARTHUR
"Rubber Souls."
AR14633 691 (September 22, 1994) pp[enc.36].
MERCHANT, ISMAIL
"Bombay: Despite Crushing Poverty And Overpopulation, A Mighty Middle-Class Economy Has Turned Bombay Into A City Of Hope."
AR14634 738-739 (July 11, 1996) pp77-82.
MILLER, ADAM
"Gang Murder In The Heartland."
AR14635 728 (February 22, 1996) pp48-54,72.
"Professors Of Hate: Academia's Dirty Secret."

AR14636 693 (October 20, 1994) pp106-108,110+.
MILLER, BRUCE A.
"Our Lives, Our Music: Out Of Time."
AR14637 644 (November 26, 1992) p54.
MILLER, CHRIS
"If I Only Had A Brain."
AR14638 639 (September 17, 1992) p76.
MILLER, RUSSELL
"Can Doug Wilder's G.O.P. Tricks Save The Democrats?."
AR14639 616 (October 31, 1991) pp31-33.
MILLER, STEVE
"Raves."
AR14640 736 (June 13, 1996) p61.
MILLER, TIM
"One Of Us! One Of Us! One Of...."
AR14641 682 (May 19, 1994) p53.
MILWARD, JOHN
"Blood On The Tracks: Warner Bros. Gets Hit In A Boardroom Shootout."
AR14642 697 (December 15, 1994) pp25,28.
"Filed Of Dreams: The Big Business Behind Woodstock '94."
AR14643 688 (August 11, 1994) pp36-37.
"Joy In Mudville: Against All Odds, Woodstock '94 Gave Another Generation Three Days Of Peace, Muck And Understanding."
AR14644 691 (September 22, 1994) pp61-62,64-65+.
"We Are Golden: Woodstock '94 Is Headed Into The Black."
AR14645 694 (November 3, 1994) p37.
MIRKIN, STEVEN
"Katell Keineg."
AR14646 696 (December 1, 1994) p41.
MITCHELL, DEBORAH
"Working For The Dead."
AR14647 745 (October 17, 1996) p123.
MOLYNEUX, GUY
"The Big Lie: A Republican Majority Doesn't Mean A Reactionary Mandate."
AR14648 698-699 (December 29, 1994) pp154,157.
"But Can He Win?."
AR14649 721 (November 16, 1995) pp46,48.
"When Success fails: What Really Bugs The GOP About Student Loans And Americorps is That They Work."
AR14650 707 (May 4, 1995) pp38-39.
MOON, TOM
"The Roots Roll Away From The Jazz-Hip-Hop Tree."
AR14651 748 (November 28, 1996) p44.
MOORE, THURSTON
"Raves."
AR14652 684 (June 16, 1994) p24.
MORALES, ED
"Clasico Rock."
AR14653 670 (November 25, 1993) p22.
"New Music From Mexico."
AR14654 662 (August 5, 1993) p17.
MORGENSTERN, STEVE
"The Big Three's Best Bets."
AR14655 745 (October 17, 1996) p147.
"Cyberstuff."
AR14656 748 (November 28, 1996) p125.
"The Dish."
AR14657 748 (November 28, 1996) p112.
"The Electric Dorm—Tune In, Turn On, Veg Out With Cool Compact Components."
AR14658 730 (March 21, 1996) p111.
"High-Quality Video Adds Sizzle To CD-ROMs."
AR14659 733 (May 2, 1996) p64.
"Hot Technology."
AR14660 741 (August 22, 1996) pp84-85.
"Multimedia: The Season's Must-Have CD-ROMs."
AR14661 748 (November 28, 1996) p117.
"Players Stumped By Myst Can Now Get Pyst."
AR14662 746 (October 31, 1996) p78.
"Racers, Rockers And Roaches Star In The Best New CD-ROM Games."
AR14663 727 (February 8, 1996) p55.
"Random Access: Dispatches From Cyberspace."
AR14664 735 (May 30, 1996) pp[enc.39-40].
"Rapid Transit."
AR14665 747 (November 14, 1996) p129.
"Technology: A Three-Way Video-Game Battle Begins."
AR14666 745 (October 17, 1996) p147.
"Technology: Getting Up To Speed On The Web With ISDN."
AR14667 747 (November 14, 1996) p129.
MORRIS, BOB
"Range Wars: Should COllege Radio Be Making Waves Or Making Money?."
AR14668 678 (March 24, 1994) pp55-57.
MORRISON, MELISSA
"Tanks For The Memories: Michael Jackson Imposes 'HIStory' On The Czech Republic."
AR14669 746 (October 31, 1996) p26.
MOSER, JEFFREY
"Our Lives, Our Music: Sgt. Pepper's Lonely Hearts Club Band."
AR14670 644 (November 26, 1992) p49.
"MTV TURNS TEN."
AR14671 619-620 (December 12, 1991) pp71,74.
MUNDY, CHRIS
"Achin' To Be Understood: The Rolling Stone Interview With Paul Westerberg."
AR14672 659 (June 24, 1993) pp51-54,92.
"Axl's St. Louis Blues: Singer Arrested In New York For Riot Charges."
AR14673 637 (August 20, 1992) p17.
"Belly: Tanya Donelly Finds Her Lucky 'Star'."
AR14674 649 (February 4, 1993) p16.
"Bob Stinson: 1959-1995."
AR14675 705 (April 6, 1995) p28.
"Buffalo Stance: Boston's Buffalo Tom Steer Clear Of The Musical Wildlife."
AR14676 665 (September 16, 1993) pp[enc.44-45+].
"Cool Jerk: How Sean Penn Reconciles Being The Best Actor Of His Generation With Being A Menace To Society."
AR14677 731 (April 4, 1996) pp44-49.
"Duff's Single-Gun Theory: Duff McKagan Strikes Out On His Own."
AR14678 669 (November 11, 1993) p16.
"88: She Blinded Me With Science."
AR14679 667 (October 14, 1993) p100.
"Ethan Hawke: Renaissance Boy."
AR14680 703 (March 9, 1995) pp44-49,75.
"Eugenius: The Former Captain America Invades The U.S.."
AR14681 642 (October 29, 1992) p32.
"Foo Fighters."
AR14682 718 (October 5, 1995) pp40-43,79,84.
"Generation Next: The Smokin' Sounds Of Summer '94."
AR14683 686-687 (July 14, 1994) pp72-74.
"Green Daze."
AR14684 700 (January 26, 1995) pp40-46,69.
"Henry Rollins: Rocks Angriest Voice Rises From The Ashes Of Black Flag."
AR14685 628 (April 16, 1992) pp58-60.
"The Hidden Power Of Dreams: The Cranberries Speak Softly But Carry A Big Hit."
AR14686 680 (April 21, 1994) pp[enc.6-10+].
"Hot Band: A College-Rock Favorite, Teenage Fanclub Is Now Earning Mainstream Pop Acceptance."
AR14687 630 (May 14, 1992) pp49-51.
"Kat Bjelland Of Babes In Toyland."
AR14688 708 (May 18, 1995) p34.
"Linda Ronstadt."
AR14689 712-713 (July 13, 1995) p40.
"Live, From Vietnam!: Bryan Adams Experiences Life After Wartime

MUNDY, CHRIS (continued)
When He Plays Ho Chi Minh City."
AR14690 677 (March 10, 1994) p18.
"Liz Phair: Last Train To Guyville."
AR14691 667 (October 14, 1993) p24.
"The Lost Boy: The Life Of Kurt Cobain."
AR14692 683 (June 2, 1994) pp51-53.
"Meat Loaf: The Man Who Saw Paradise By The Dashboard Lights Is Back With 'Bat Out Of Hell II'."
AR14693 670 (November 25, 1993) pp15-16.
"Mick Ronson: 1946-1993."
AR14694 658 (June 10, 1993) p30.
"Mr. Natural."
AR14695 657 (May 27, 1993) pp36-40,65.
"Muscle & Melody."
AR14696 674 (January 27, 1994) p17.
"Nicky Hopkins: 1944-1994."
AR14697 693 (October 20, 1994) p37.
"19: Bastards Of Young."
AR14698 667 (October 14, 1993) p76.
"95: Janie's Got A Gun."
AR14699 667 (October 14, 1993) p101.
"Nirvana: After Giving Birth To The Surprise Hit Of The Year, The Guys From Seattle Fight The Demons Of Fame."
AR14700 622 (January 23, 1992) pp38-41.
"Plastic Fantastic Punk Rock: Urge Overkill Bring The '70s Back To Life."
AR14701 664 (September 2, 1993) pp11-12.
"Prescription Refilled: Spin Doctors' "Turn It Upside Down" Is More That Meets The Ear."
AR14702 684 (June 16, 1994) p18.
"Raves."
AR14703 665 (September 16, 1993) p17.
"Rock & Roll Yearbook."
AR14704 672-673 (December 23, 1993) pp15-17,20,27+.
"Rock And Roll Hall Of Fame."
AR14705 625 (March 5, 1992) pp11,13-15,17.
"Rock And Roll Yearbook."
AR14706 619-620 (December 12, 1991) pp17-19,22,26+.
AR14707 698-699 (December 29, 1994) pp36-37,42,50+.
"Ruling Asses: Oasis Have Conquered America, And They Won't Shut Up About It."
AR14708 733 (May 2, 1996) pp32-35,68.
"Seeking Soul Asylum: At Home With The Loud Fast Rulers Of The Minneapolis Music Scene."
AR14709 644 (November 26, 1992) pp31,80.
"Simon LeBon Of Duran Duran."
AR14710 704 (March 23, 1995) p40.
"Slippin' Around On The Road With Brad Pitt."
AR14711 696 (December 1, 1994) pp92-97,136.
"Smashing Pumpkins."
AR14712 680 (April 21, 1994) pp42-446,96.
AR14713 695 (November 17, 1994) pp47,77.
"The Song Remains The Same: L.A.'s Social Distortion Brings Its Punk Roots To The MTV Generation."
AR14714 634-635 (July 9, 1992) pp32-33.
"Soul Asylum: After 11 Long Years Of Virtual Obscurity, The Little Punk Band That Couldn't Finally Does With The Success Of 'Grave Dancers Union'."
AR14715 662 (August 5, 1993) pp38-39,41-43+.
"Speech Therapy: Arrested Development Calls For A Revolution Of The Mind."
AR14716 647 (January 7, 1993) pp13,25.
"Straitjacket Fits: New Zealand's Pop Export."
AR14717 615 (October 17, 1991) p28.
"Sugar: Turning Bitter Into Sweet."
AR14718 694 (November 3, 1994) pp71-73.
"Swervedriver: Chaos, Distortion And Feedback."
AR14719 625 (March 5, 1992) p27.
"Titanic Love Affair: Sunk Once, The Band Returns With 'No Charisma'."
AR14720 658 (June 10, 1993) p32.
"[Tori Amos]."
AR14721 695 (November 17, 1994) pp28-29.
"Toys From The Attic."
AR14722 674 (January 27, 1994) p24.
"Trouble In Paradise: Violence Erupts After MTV Event In New Jersey."
AR14723 636 (August 6, 1992) p16.
"A Truly Democratic Party: The MTV And VH-1 Generations Swing Together At Clinton's Inaugural."
AR14724 651 (March 4, 1993) pp21,32.
"2: Smells Like Teen Spirit."
AR14725 667 (October 14, 1993) pp67-68.
"Velvet Crush: A Slovenly Rock & Roll Spirit."
AR14726 627 (April 2, 1992) p19.
"Voice Of Experience: Iris DeMent Turns Her Life Into Song."
AR14727 693 (October 20, 1994) p47.
"Volley Of The Dolls: The Goo Goo Dolls Turn It Up And Kick Out The Jams, Replacements Style."
AR14728 653 (April 1, 1993) p23.
"Weiland: Of Stone Temple Pilots."
AR14729 675 (February 10, 1994) p18.
"What Does Conan O'Brien Have That You Don't?."
AR14730 743 (September 19, 1996) pp66-69,72,74.
"Where The Wild Things Are: The Beastie Boys Become Kings Of Their Own Urbane Jungle."
AR14731 688 (August 11, 1994) pp46-49,52-53+.
"Whole Lotta Shakin' Up Goin' On."
AR14732 689 (August 25, 1994) p28.
"Wild Thing: Drew Barrymore."
AR14733 710 (June 15, 1995) pp66-73.
"MUSIC AWARDS: 1995."
AR14734 700 (January 26, 1995) pp50-53,55-56.
"MUSIC BIZ BLUES."
AR14735 619-620 (December 12, 1991) p64.

N

NADELMANN, ETHAN
"Europe's Drug Prescription: Innovative Approaches To The Drug Problem From Over There."
AR14736 700 (January 26, 1995) pp38-39.
"Toward A Sane National Drug Policy."
AR14737 681 (May 5, 1994) pp24-26.
NADLER, ERIC
"George Bush's Heroin Connection."
AR14738 692 (October 6, 1994) pp40-41,96.
NEELY, KIM
"Aerosmith Box: A Hard-Rock Primer."
AR14739 618 (November 28, 1991) p28.
"Alternative Music."
AR14740 645-646 (December 10, 1992) p43.
"Axl Rose."
AR14741 641 (October 15, 1992) pp190-192.
"Benedictine Brawl."
AR14742 690 (September 8, 1994) p32.
"The Benefit Blitz: Rockers Put Out For Various Pet Projects."
AR14743 670 (November 25, 1993) p17.
"Caught in The Net: The Cautionary Tale Of A Cornell Student Who Posted A Suicide Note In Cyberspace."
AR14744 696 (December 1, 1994) pp63-66.
"Clinton: I Want The MTV Vote."
AR14745 636 (August 6, 1992) p22.
"Confessions Of Sir Psycho Sexy: The Rolling Stone Interview With Anthony Kiedis Of The Red Hot Chili Peppers."
AR14746 679 (April 7, 1994) pp46-52,85.

NEELY, KIM (continued)
"'Cop Killer' Aftershocks: Labels Asking Rap Artists To Remove Controversial Tracks From Albums."
AR14747 642 (October 29, 1992) p32.
"Courtney Love."
AR14748 672-673 (December 23, 1993) p73.
"84: Alive."
AR14749 667 (October 14, 1993) p100.
"Extreme's Triple Play."
AR14750 636 (August 6, 1992) p21.
"58: Manchild."
AR14751 667 (October 14, 1993) p92.
"The Fight For The Right To Choose: L7 And Friends Rock For Reproductive Freedom."
AR14752 652 (March 18, 1993) pp22-23.
"[Flea]."
AR14753 695 (November 17, 1994) pp66-67,89.
"Frank Zappa Stricken With Cancer: But Family Says He's Fighting It Successfully."
AR14754 621 (January 9, 1992) p22.
"Freedie's Royal Send-Off: Show Also Marks Rock's First Major Rallying Cry In The Fight Against AIDS."
AR14755 633 (June 25, 1992) p17.
"Group Gets Youth Vote On Bandwagon."
AR14756 637 (August 20, 1992) p17.
"Hard To The Core."
AR14757 662 (August 5, 1993) pp50-52,79.
"Help Wanted: Red Hot Guitarist."
AR14758 660-661 (July 8, 1993) p17.
"Homestyle: Neneh Cherry on Love, Music And The Pursuit Of Happiness."
AR14759 649 (February 4, 1993) pp32-35,38.
"Iggy Still Pops: The Original Punk Is In Royal Form On American Caesar."
AR14760 666 (September 30, 1993) pp13-14.
"Into The Unknown: Soundgarden Explore Rock & Roll's Heart Of Darkness."
AR14761 684 (June 16, 1994) pp46-47,49-50 +.
"Izzy Or Isn't He?: Stradlin May Be Splitting With Guns N' Roses."
AR14762 617 (November 14, 1991) p28.
"Joel Sues Lawyers: Singer Claims Fraud In $90 Million Lawsuit."
AR14763 644 (November 26, 1992) p21.
"Keith: Rock's Main Offender."
AR14764 644 (November 26, 1992) p20.
"Knee-Deep In The Hoopla, From Cub Scouts To Bee Girls, With Some Raw Deals & Rough Living In Between, Blind Melon Has Taken The Long, Hard Road To The Top."
AR14765 669 (November 11, 1993) pp38-40,42,46 +.
"Lollapalooza '92."
AR14766 639 (September 17, 1992) pp60-62,64,106.
"Lollapalooza '93."
AR14767 662 (August 5, 1993) pp13-14.
"Misty Mountain Memories: Robert Plant Embraces His Past On 'Fate Of Nations'."
AR14768 660-661 (July 8, 1993) p25.
"Morphine: The Band's Low-Rock Music Is Nearly As Addictive As Its Pharmaceutical Namesake."
AR14769 667 (October 14, 1993) p30.
"Music Versus Muscle."
AR14770 654 (April 15, 1993) pp15-16.
"My Way Or The Highway: Despite Accusations That He's Stuck In The Past, Lenny Kravitz Is Now In Vogue."
AR14771 659 (June 24, 1993) p22.
"94: Beethoven."
AR14772 667 (October 14, 1993) p101.
"Nirvana Tops Album Charts: 'Nevermind' Bumps 'Dangerous' Out Of Number One Position."
AR14773 624 (February 20, 1992) pp15-16.
"Opinion."
AR14774 647 (January 7, 1993) p19.
"Organically Grown: Blind Melon Parlays Its Small-Town Roots Into A Big-City Sound."
AR14775 640 (October 1, 1992) pp27,84.
"Ozzy Osbourne."
AR14776 666 (September 30, 1993) p18.
"Pearl Jam Drummer Beats It."
AR14777 692 (October 6, 1994) p24.
"The Punk-Rock Talking Blues: Henry Rollins Bares All With The Spoken Word."
AR14778 650 (February 18, 1993) p18.
"Raves."
AR14779 663 (August 19, 1993) p19.
AR14780 667 (October 14, 1993) p34.
"Record-Chain Blacklist: Super Club Establishes Policy On Rating Lyrics."
AR14781 637 (August 20, 1992) pp18,62.
"Right Here, Right Now: The Seattle Rock Band Pearl Jam Learns How To Celebrate Life."
AR14782 616 (October 31, 1991) pp15-16.
"The Rolling Stone Interview."
AR14783 627 (April 2, 1992) pp32-37,42,53.
"So Where's The Fire?: Perry Farrell Talks About Sex, Drugs, Karma, Everything But His New Band, Porno For Pyros."
AR14784 656 (May 13, 1993) pp54-57,116.
"Souljah's Bad Rap: Candidate Clinton Thrusts The Rapper-Activist Into The Spotlight."
AR14785 636 (August 6, 1992) pp15,17,72.
"Soundgarden: The Veteran Band From Seattle Proves There's Life After Nirvana."
AR14786 634-635 (July 9, 1992) pp45-46,51 +.
"We Should Have Seen It Coming: Riots Are The Latest Rock Fad."
AR14787 640 (October 1, 1992) p26.
"Where Angels Fear To Tread: Pearl Jam Open Their Spring Tour On A Wing And A Prayer."
AR14788 681 (May 5, 1994) pp11-13.
"[NEW BOOK]."
AR14789 623 (February 6, 1992) p6.
"NEW FACES."
AR14790 619-620 (December 12, 1991) pp44-46,48-49.
AR14791 628 (April 16, 1992) pp55-57.
AR14792 645-646 (December 10, 1992) pp57,59,61-62.
AR14793 672-673 (December 23, 1993) pp45-46,48-49.
AR14794 698-699 (December 29, 1994) pp45-49.
NEWCOMB, DOUG
"Drop In, Turn On, Tune Out: Replacing Factory-Installed Car Speakers Will Change Your Life."
AR14795 657 (May 27, 1993) p61.
NEWMAN, JUDITH
"Out Of The Copy Room: How To Make Your First Job Work For You."
AR14796 719 (October 19, 1995) pp129-133.
"The Real World."
AR14797 666 (September 30, 1993) pp79-80,82.
"NEWPORT, RHODE ISLAND."
AR14798 681 (May 5, 1994) p41.
NEWTON, PHILIP
"Tumble Weeds: Competing In A Sport That Demands Youth And Artistry, Gymnasts Shannon Miller And Jarrod Hanks Make The Leap From Athlete To Performer."
AR14799 628 (April 16, 1992) pp[enc.21-23 +].
"NICHOLAS SCHAFFNER."
AR14800 615 (January 17, 1991) p27.
NICKS, DEWEY
"Looks Like Team Spirit: On Their Way To Barcelona, Four Athletes Take A Break From Their Olympic Training To Try On American Clothes."
AR14801 628 (April 16, 1992) pp[enc.27-29 +].
NICKS, STEVIE
"Raves."
AR14802 686-687 (July 14, 1994) p32.

NIELSON, RICK
AR14803 743 (September 19, 1996) p46.
"THE 1996 PRESIDENTIAL YEARBOOK: WHAT WERE THEY THEN?."
AR14804 730 (March 21, 1996) pp51-52.
"'94 GLEASON AWARDS."
AR14805 683 (June 2, 1994) p17.
NOLAN, A. M.
"Jale."
AR14806 689 (August 25, 1994) p41.
NORMAN, PHILIP
"The Rebirth Of Elton John."
AR14807 626 (March 19, 1992) pp43-44,48-49+.

O

"OBITUARIES."
AR14808 745 (January 17, 1996) p44.
AR14809 747 (November 14, 1996) p32.
AR14810 748 (November 28, 1996) p32.
O'BRIEN, CONAN
"The Year Of The Near Miss."
AR14811 750-751 (December 26, 1996) p222.
O'BRIEN, PATTI
"Acting!!! Genius!!! Brilliant!!!."
AR14812 704 (March 23, 1995) pp102-104,106+.
"Are You Xperienced?: On The Fashion Tip With Kim Gordon Of Sonic Youth."
AR14813 692 (October 6, 1994) pp60-62.
"Bustin' Loose."
AR14814 749 (December 12, 1996) pp75-76,78.
"Chow Manhattan: Parker Posey And Benicio Del Toro Treat Themselves To A Bottle Of Wine, A Little Red Sauce And Some Italian Dressing."
AR14815 718 (October 5, 1995) pp[enc.8-10+].
"Cut To The Chase."
AR14816 633 (June 25, 1992) pp35-37.
"Darkness On The Edge of Bedrock: Kyle MacLachlan Brings His All-American Weirdness To "The Flintstones"."
AR14817 685 (June 30, 1994) pp63-64.
"Deep Cover."
AR14818 634-635 (July 9, 1992) pp92-94,96-97.
"Emperors Of The Air."
AR14819 668 (October 28, 1993) pp70-73,89,92.
"Good Times: Morning Has Broken The Newest Looks Pop And Shine To Keep You Suited Up Long Past The Twilight's Last Gleaming."
AR14820 747 (November 14, 1996) pp100-101,103+.
"Hickory Smoke."
AR14821 684 (June 16, 1994) pp60-61,64,66+.
"The Hidden Power Of Dreams: The Cranberries Speak Softly But Carry A Big Hit."
AR14822 680 (April 21, 1994) pp[enc.6-10+].
"The Hill People: They Only Come Out At Night At Don Hill's, New York's Glam Mecca For The Dusk-Till-Dawn Set."
AR14823 730 (March 21, 1996) pp86-90,92.
"The Hood The Bad & The Ugly: For Naughty By Nature, The Question Is Not Can You Take East Orange Out Of The Boyz, But Can You Take The Boyz Out Of East Orange?."
AR14824 663 (August 19, 1993) pp66-68,70.
"Hot Fashion."
AR14825 630 (May 14, 1992) pp95-99.
"Hot Jazz Artist."
AR14826 682 (May 19, 1994) pp76-77.
"Hot Look."
AR14827 741 (August 22, 1996) pp86-88,90.92.
"Hot Style."
AR14828 656 (May 13, 1993) pp94-98.
"Insane In The Brain: For Biker Wayne Croasdale Life Is Going Downhill."
AR14829 680 (April 21, 1994) pp[enc.25-29].
"It's A Mad, Mad, Mad About You World."
AR14830 706 (April 20, 1995) pp[enc.6-10+].
"Let It Flow: River Phoenix Plays It Cool On And Off The Screen."
AR14831 615 (October 17, 1991) pp83-87.
"Let's Book."
AR14832 693 (October 20, 1994) pp135-137.
"Life In The Indie Cities: From Bad Weather And Obstacles Comes Great Music—If You Know Where To Look."
AR14833 677 (March 10, 1994) pp54-57.
"Liv In The Fast Lane: Actress Liv Tyler Wraps Her Inner Charm In Men's Outerwear."
AR14834 694 (November 3, 1994) pp62-66.
"Misty Mountain Hop: Amateurs And Pros Jump Around In Aspen Highlands."
AR14835 644 (November 26, 1992) pp60-64.
"Mod Squad: With 'I Should Coco' The U.K. Trio Supergrass Bring Their Freshly Manicured Pop To America."
AR14836 718 (October 5, 1995) pp[enc.20-22+].
"Mosh Unit: The Muffs' Two-Minute Bursts Of melodic Noise Are Clamorous Punk Postcards From The Edge."
AR14837 718 (October 5, 1995) pp[enc.30-32+].
"Normal Weirdness In Seattle."
AR14838 652 (March 18, 1993) pp[enc.34-38+].
"One Hot Minute."
AR14839 732 (April 18, 1996) pp[enc.7].
"Orange Day: In This Southern California County, The Punk Spirit Never Died."
AR14840 706 (April 20, 1995) pp[enc.14-18].
"Out Of The Shadows...Into The Night."
AR14841 642 (October 29, 1992) pp64-67.
"Papa Was A Rolling Stone: But Marlon Richards Is Not Just A Chip Off The Old Rock."
AR14842 660-661 (July 8, 1993) pp102-106.
"Pedal To The Medal: These Olympic Contenders Shift Into Casual Gear."
AR14843 626 (March 19, 1992) pp79-82.
"Personal Best: Whether You're Hitting The Slopes Or An Indoor Pool, You Need Lotions And Shampoos To Counteract The Drying Effects Of The Winter Workout."
AR14844 645-646 (December 10, 1992) pp139-141.
"Powder To The People: Connoisseurs Of The Cold Rip Through Their Favorite Brand Of Snow."
AR14845 617 (November 14, 1991) pp159-164.
"Prescentable: This Holiday Season, Make More Than Just A Suitable Impression By Giving—Or Wearing—One Of These Fragrances Or Aftershaves."
AR14846 645-646 (December 10, 1992) pp143,145.
"Pure & Simple: Kelly Willis, County Waif."
AR14847 664 (September 2, 1993) pp56-57.
"Rent Strikes."
AR14848 734 (May 16, 1996) pp54-58.
"Right Hair, Right Now: An Unkempt Mop Top Complements Today's Radical Biker Chic."
AR14849 618 (November 28, 1991) pp79-80,82.
"Scents Of Style: Fragrances For The Holiday Season."
AR14850 618 (November 28, 1991) p84.
"Shop Therapy: Kerri Kenney Of 'The State' Prowls Manhattan's Lower East Side."
AR14851 718 (October 5, 1995) pp[enc.39,41+].
"Shopping At Sal's: Searching For The Look Of The Future At The Salvation Army."
AR14852 680 (April 21, 1994) pp[enc.37-38].
"Skate Dreams: Roller Basketball Is A Game Of Fast Breaks And Fast Breaking."
AR14853 715 (August 24, 1995) pp90-92,94-96.
"Slave To The Grind: Can Eric Nies Escape MTV's Star-Breaker Machinery?."

O'BRIEN, PATTI (continued)
AR14854 680 (April 21, 1994) pp[enc.17-21].
"Soul Asylum."
AR14855 718 (October 5, 1995) pp[enc.45-46].
"Speed Mettle: The Fastest Americans In Their Sports, These Skaters And Skiers Hope To Bring Home The Olympic Gold."
AR14856 624 (February 20, 1992) pp34-38.
"Spin Doctor: Club DJ Junior Vasquez Remixes The Soundtrack Of New York At Night."
AR14857 706 (April 20, 1995) pp[enc.22-24 +].
"Sweet Surrender: Donning Dress-To-Kill Leather Jackets, The Midwestern Singer And The Vampire Slayer Give Themselves Up To A Day At The Beach."
AR14858 637 (August 20, 1992) pp44-47.
"Tattoo You: Lou Deangelis Gets Crazy On His Mountain Bike."
AR14859 708 (May 18, 1995) pp78-80,82,84 +.
"A Trace Of Gold: The Ace Catches Air On The Way To Lillehammer."
AR14860 676 (February 24, 1994) pp51,53.
"Tri And Mighty: To Brave The Hawaii Ironman, It Takes Big Kahunas."
AR14861 680 (April 21, 1994) pp[enc.33-34].
"Two For The Road: On The Move With Those Sexual Screwups From 'Short Cuts,' Matthew Modine & Julianne Moore."
AR14862 667 (October 14, 1993) pp103-106,108 +.
"Unusual Suspects: Loud Lucy & Civ Defy Alterna-Rock Convention And Live To Talk About It."
AR14863 721 (November 16, 1995) pp98-100,103 +.
"Who Is This Guy?."
AR14864 650 (February 18, 1993) pp44-45,47-48.
"Wired For Love: Three Tales Of Computer Romance."
AR14865 689 (August 25, 1994) pp77-78,80,83 +.
O'CONNOR, ROB
"Blur: The New 'Leisure' Class."
AR14866 623 (February 6, 1992) p32.
"Ned's Atomic Dustbin: A Band With A Nonattitude."
AR14867 627 (April 2, 1992) p19.
"School Of Fish: Confounding Critics."
AR14868 618 (November 28, 1991) p30.
O'DAIR, BARBARA
"The King Of Rain."
AR14869 682 (May 19, 1994) p38.
"ON THE ROAD."
AR14870 619-620 (December 12, 1991) p84.
AR14871 645-646 (December 10, 1992) pp35-36.
AR14872 738-739 (July 11, 1996) p25.
"100 CLASSIC ALBUM COVERS."
AR14873 617 (November 14, 1991) pp91-94,97 +.
"100 CLASSIC ALBUM COVERS: A BROKEN FRAME."
AR14874 617 (November 14, 1991) p147.
"100 CLASSIC ALBUM COVERS: ABRAXAS."
AR14875 617 (November 14, 1991) p100.
"100 CLASSIC ALBUM COVERS: ALADDIN SANE."
AR14876 617 (November 14, 1991) p134.
"100 CLASSIC ALBUM COVERS: AMERICA BEAUTY."
AR14877 617 (November 14, 1991) p137.
"100 CLASSIC ALBUM COVERS: AOXOMOXOA."
AR14878 617 (November 14, 1991) p97.
"100 CLASSIC ALBUM COVERS: ARC OF A DIVER."
AR14879 617 (November 14, 1991) p154.
"100 CLASSIC ALBUM COVERS: ATOM HEART MOTHER."
AR14880 617 (November 14, 1991) p149.
"100 CLASSIC ALBUM COVERS: BITCHES BREW."
AR14881 617 (November 14, 1991) p147.
"100 CLASSIC ALBUM COVERS: BLIND FAITH."
AR14882 617 (November 14, 1991) p94.
"100 CLASSIC ALBUM COVERS: BORN TO RUN."
AR14883 617 (November 14, 1991) p110.
"100 CLASSIC ALBUM COVERS: BRAIN SALAD SURGERY."
AR14884 617 (November 14, 1991) p137.
"100 CLASSIC ALBUM COVERS: BREAKFAST IN AMERICA."
AR14885 617 (November 14, 1991) p119.
"100 CLASSIC ALBUM COVERS: BRINGING IT ALL BACK HOME."
AR14886 617 (November 14, 1991) p133.
"100 CLASSIC ALBUM COVERS: CANDY-O."
AR14887 617 (November 14, 1991) p102.
"100 CLASSIC ALBUM COVERS: CATCH A FIRE."
AR14888 617 (November 14, 1991) p132.
"100 CLASSIC ALBUM COVERS: CATS UNDER THE STARS."
AR14889 617 (November 14, 1991) p137.
"100 CLASSIC ALBUM COVERS: CHEAP THRILLS."
AR14890 617 (November 14, 1991) p97.
"100 CLASSIC ALBUM COVERS: COSMIC SLOP."
AR14891 617 (November 14, 1991) p144.
"100 CLASSIC ALBUM COVERS: COUNTRY LIFE."
AR14892 617 (November 14, 1991) pp132-133.
"100 CLASSIC ALBUM COVERS: DARK SIDE OF THE MOON."
AR14893 617 (November 14, 1991) p122.
"100 CLASSIC ALBUM COVERS: DAYDREAM NATION."
AR14894 617 (November 14, 1991) p140.
"100 CLASSIC ALBUM COVERS: DIAMOND DOGS."
AR14895 617 (November 14, 1991) p144.
"100 CLASSIC ALBUM COVERS: DIESEL AND DUST."
AR14896 617 (November 14, 1991) p154.
"100 CLASSIC ALBUM COVERS: DISRAELI GEARS."
AR14897 617 (November 14, 1991) p149.
"100 CLASSIC ALBUM COVERS: DOC AT THE RADAR STATION."
AR14898 617 (November 14, 1991) p134.
"100 CLASSIC ALBUM COVERS: DOCUMENT."
AR14899 617 (November 14, 1991) p149.
"100 CLASSIC ALBUM COVERS: EAT A PEACH."
AR14900 617 (November 14, 1991) p153.
"100 CLASSIC ALBUM COVERS: ELECTRIC LADYLAND."
AR14901 617 (November 14, 1991) p137.
"100 CLASSIC ALBUM COVERS: ELVIS PRESLEY."
AR14902 617 (November 14, 1991) p124.
"100 CLASSIC ALBUM COVERS: EXILE ON MAIN STREET."
AR14903 617 (November 14, 1991) pp93-94.
"100 CLASSIC ALBUM COVERS: FEAR OF MUSIC."
AR14904 617 (November 14, 1991) p128.
"100 CLASSIC ALBUM COVERS: 50,000,000 ELVIS FANS CAN'T BE WRONG."
AR14905 617 (November 14, 1991) p137.
"100 CLASSIC ALBUM COVERS: FRANKS WILD YEARS."
AR14906 617 (November 14, 1991) p144.
"100 CLASSIC ALBUM COVERS: FRESH FRUIT FOR ROTTING VEGETABLES."
AR14907 617 (November 14, 1991) p153.
"100 CLASSIC ALBUM COVERS: GREETINGS FROM ASBURY PARK, N.J.."
AR14908 617 (November 14, 1991) p147.
"100 CLASSIC ALBUM COVERS: HARDCORE JOLLIES."
AR14909 617 (November 14, 1991) p149.
"100 CLASSIC ALBUM COVERS: HEJIRA."
AR14910 617 (November 14, 1991) p100.
"100 CLASSIC ALBUM COVERS: HONEY."
AR14911 617 (November 14, 1991) p149.
"100 CLASSIC ALBUM COVERS: HORSES."
AR14912 617 (November 14, 1991) p113.
"100 CLASSIC ALBUM COVERS: HOT BUTTERED SOUL."
AR14913 617 (November 14, 1991) p144.
"100 CLASSIC ALBUM COVERS: HOTEL CALIFORNIA."
AR14914 617 (November 14, 1991) p94.
"100 CLASSIC ALBUM COVERS: HOUSE OF THE HOLY."
AR14915 617 (November 14, 1991) p134.
"100 CLASSIC ALBUM COVERS: IN THE COURT OF THE CRIMSON KING."
AR14916 617 (November 14, 1991) p140.
"100 CLASSIC ALBUM COVERS: INTO THE PURPLE VALLEY."
AR14917 617 (November 14, 1991) p100.

"100 CLASSIC ALBUM COVERS: IT'S A BEAUTIFUL DAY."
AR14918 617 (November 14, 1991) p110.
"100 CLASSIC ALBUM COVERS: JOURNEY THROUGH THE SECRET LIFE OF PLANTS."
AR14919 617 (November 14, 1991) p137.
"100 CLASSIC ALBUM COVERS: KOO KOO."
AR14920 617 (November 14, 1991) p106.
"100 CLASSIC ALBUM COVERS: LED ZEPPELIN."
AR14921 617 (November 14, 1991) pp122-123.
"100 CLASSIC ALBUM COVERS: LICENSED TO ILL."
AR14922 617 (November 14, 1991) p110.
"100 CLASSIC ALBUM COVERS: LIVE PEACE IN TORONTO."
AR14923 617 (November 14, 1991) p113.
"100 CLASSIC ALBUM COVERS: LONDON CALLING."
AR14924 617 (November 14, 1991) p124.
"100 CLASSIC ALBUM COVERS: LOOK SHARP."
AR14925 617 (November 14, 1991) p108.
"100 CLASSIC ALBUM COVERS: LOS ANGELES."
AR14926 617 (November 14, 1991) p140.
"100 CLASSIC ALBUM COVERS: METAL BOX."
AR14927 617 (November 14, 1991) p132.
"100 CLASSIC ALBUM COVERS: MIDDLE MAN."
AR14928 617 (November 14, 1991) p149.
"100 CLASSIC ALBUM COVERS: NEVER A DULL MOMENT."
AR14929 617 (November 14, 1991) p149.
"100 CLASSIC ALBUM COVERS: NEVER MIND THE BOLLOCKS HERE'S THE SEX PISTOLS."
AR14930 617 (November 14, 1991) pp92-93.
"100 CLASSIC ALBUM COVERS: 1984."
AR14931 617 (November 14, 1991) p144.
"100 CLASSIC ALBUM COVERS: NOTHING'S SHOCKING."
AR14932 617 (November 14, 1991) p106.
"100 CLASSIC ALBUM COVERS: OGDENS' NUT GONE FLAKES."
AR14933 617 (November 14, 1991) p108.
"100 CLASSIC ALBUM COVERS: ONE STEP BEYOND."
AR14934 617 (November 14, 1991) p153.
"100 CLASSIC ALBUM COVERS: OOH LA LA."
AR14935 617 (November 14, 1991) p116.
"100 CLASSIC ALBUM COVERS: PETER GABRIEL."
AR14936 617 (November 14, 1991) p124.
"100 CLASSIC ALBUM COVERS: PHYSICAL GRAFFITI."
AR14937 617 (November 14, 1991) p147.
"100 CLASSIC ALBUM COVERS: PLAYING POSSUM."
AR14938 617 (November 14, 1991) p108.
"100 CLASSIC ALBUM COVERS: POWER, CORRUPTION AND LIES."
AR14939 617 (November 14, 1991) p102.
"100 CLASSIC ALBUM COVERS: RELAYER."
AR14940 617 (November 14, 1991) p102.
"100 CLASSIC ALBUM COVERS: RUMOURS."
AR14941 617 (November 14, 1991) p149.
"100 CLASSIC ALBUM COVERS: SAILIN' SHOES."
AR14942 617 (November 14, 1991) p106.
"100 CLASSIC ALBUM COVERS: SEE JUNGLE! SEE JUNGLE! GO JOIN YOUR GANG YEAH!...."
AR14943 617 (November 14, 1991) p113.
"100 CLASSIC ALBUM COVERS: SELF PORTRAIT."
AR14944 617 (November 14, 1991) p144.
"100 CLASSIC ALBUM COVERS: SGT. PEPPER'S LONELY HEARTS CLUB BAND."
AR14945 617 (November 14, 1991) p92.
"100 CLASSIC ALBUM COVERS: SIGN O' THE TIMES."
AR14946 617 (November 14, 1991) p147.
"100 CLASSIC ALBUM COVERS: SLAVE TO THE RHYTHM."
AR14947 617 (November 14, 1991) p119.
"100 CLASSIC ALBUM COVERS: SOME GIRLS."
AR14948 617 (November 14, 1991) p154.
"100 CLASSIC ALBUM COVERS: STICKY FINGERS."
AR14949 617 (November 14, 1991) p93.
"100 CLASSIC ALBUM COVERS: STRANGE DAYS."
AR14950 617 (November 14, 1991) p116.
"100 CLASSIC ALBUM COVERS: THE BEATLES."
AR14951 617 (November 14, 1991) p93.
"100 CLASSIC ALBUM COVERS: THE IDIOT."
AR14952 617 (November 14, 1991) p144.
"100 CLASSIC ALBUM COVERS: THE JOKER."
AR14953 617 (November 14, 1991) p149.
"100 CLASSIC ALBUM COVERS: THE JOSHUA TREE."
AR14954 617 (November 14, 1991) p154.
"100 CLASSIC ALBUM COVERS: THE LOW SPARK OF HIGH HEELED BOYS."
AR14955 617 (November 14, 1991) p147.
"100 CLASSIC ALBUM COVERS: THE PARKERILLA."
AR14956 617 (November 14, 1991) p140.
"100 CLASSIC ALBUM COVERS: THE RAMONES."
AR14957 617 (November 14, 1991) p137.
"100 CLASSIC ALBUM COVERS: THE SLIDER."
AR14958 617 (November 14, 1991) p123.
"100 CLASSIC ALBUM COVERS: THE SMITHS."
AR14959 617 (November 14, 1991) p140.
"100 CLASSIC ALBUM COVERS: THERE'S A RIOT GOIN' ON."
AR14960 617 (November 14, 1991) p144.
AR14961 Number not assigned.
"100 CLASSIC ALBUM COVERS: TOMMY."
AR14962 617 (November 14, 1991) p119.
"100 CLASSIC ALBUM COVERS: TRUE BLUE."
AR14963 617 (November 14, 1991) p144.
"100 CLASSIC ALBUM COVERS: TRUST."
AR14964 617 (November 14, 1991) p154.
"100 CLASSIC ALBUM COVERS: TURN BACK."
AR14965 617 (November 14, 1991) p137.
"100 CLASSIC ALBUM COVERS: TUTU."
AR14966 617 (November 14, 1991) p153.
"100 CLASSIC ALBUM COVERS: VELVET UNDERGROUND AND NICO."
AR14967 617 (November 14, 1991) p97.
"100 CLASSIC ALBUM COVERS: WAR."
AR14968 617 (November 14, 1991) p128.
"100 CLASSIC ALBUM COVERS: WEASELS RIPPED MY FLESH."
AR14969 617 (November 14, 1991) p116.
"100 CLASSIC ALBUM COVERS: WELCOME TO MY NIGHT-MARE."
AR14970 617 (November 14, 1991) p153.
"100 CLASSIC ALBUM COVERS: WE'RE ONLY IN IT FOR THE MONEY."
AR14971 617 (November 14, 1991) p153.
"100 CLASSIC ALBUM COVERS: WHO'S NEXT."
AR14972 617 (November 14, 1991) p154.
"100 CLASSIC ALBUM COVERS: WISH YOU WERE HERE."
AR14973 617 (November 14, 1991) p128.
"100 CLASSIC ALBUM COVERS: WITH THE BEATLES."
AR14974 617 (November 14, 1991) p137.
"ONLINE."
AR14975 715 (August 24, 1995) p18.
AR14976 716 (September 7, 1995) p10.
AR14977 717 (September 21, 1995) p16.
AR14978 718 (January 5, 1995) p16.
AR14979 719 (January 19, 1995) p10.
AR14980 720 (November 2, 1995) p82.
AR14981 721 (November 16, 1995) p22.
AR14982 722 (November 30, 1995) p16.
AR14983 723 (December 14, 1995) p22.
AR14984 724-725 (December 28, 1995) p24.
AR14985 726 (January 25, 1996) p12.
AR14986 728 (February 22, 1996) p16.
AR14987 729 (March 7, 1996) p6.
AR14988 732 (April 18, 1996) p16.
AR14989 735 (May 30, 1996) p10.
AR14990 736 (June 13, 1996) p16.
"'ORIGIN OF AIDS' UPDATE: CLARIFICATION."

AR14991 671 (December 9, 1993) p39.
"THE ORIOLES DISCOGRAPHY."
AR14992 659 (June 24, 1993) p49.
O'ROURKE, P. J.
"All Guns, No Butter: Inside Somalia, A Starving Nation Armed To The Teeth."
AR14993 653 (April 1, 1993) pp40-41,43,46 +.
"And If You Still Don't Get It...."
AR14994 712-713 (July 13, 1995) p55.
"Bill Clinton: The Rolling Stone Interview."
AR14995 639 (September 17, 1992) pp40-44,47,51 +.
"Cubanomics: In Fidel Castro's Crumbling Socialist Paradise, The Rum Is Older Than The Whores, The Currency Is Worthless, And Everybody's Working For The Yankee Dollar."
AR14996 738-739 (July 11, 1996) pp57-60,62-64 +.
"Deep In The Heart Of Siberia."
AR14997 747 (November 14, 1996) pp86-90,92,94 +.
"Dr. Hunter S. Thompson: On The Occasion Of The 25th Anniversary Of The Publication Of Fear And Loathing In Las Vegas, An Unfettered Discussion On The Values Of The '60s, The Addictive Properties Of Professional Journalism And The Definition of Gonzo."
AR14998 748 (November 28, 1996) pp64-68,70-73 +.
"Earth Summit: Going For The Green In Rio."
AR14999 637 (August 20, 1992) pp36-37,40-41 +.
"The Fifty-First State: P. J. O'Rourke Road-Trips Vietnam."
AR15000 634-635 (July 9, 1992) pp61-62,66,70 +.
"400 Years In A Convent, 50 Years In A Whorehouse."
AR15001 632 (June 11, 1992) pp155-157.
"Gang Bang Bang: Welcome To Ex-Yugoslavia, Land Of A Thousand Grievances, Where The Christians Hate The Muslims, The Serbs Hate The Croats, The Bosnians Hate The Montenegrins, And Everyone Has A Gun."
AR15002 647 (January 7, 1993) pp40-43,55-56.
"Haiti."
AR15003 680 (April 21, 1994) pp48-50,53,56 +.
"Of Lunch And War: There Was Suppose To Be A Revolution In Mexico, But The Mexicans Got In The Way."
AR15004 694 (November 3, 1994) pp83-84,87-88 +.
"P.J. Gets The Last Word: Why I Still Think I'm Right, No Matter What Greider Says."
AR15005 714 (August 10, 1995) pp40-41.
"Pulling The Donkey Lever."
AR15006 639 (September 17, 1992) pp47,51,53,109.
"Russian Roulette."
AR15007 743 (September 19, 1996) pp53-56,58 +].
"Stockholm Syndrome."
AR15008 734 (May 16, 1996) pp47-50,52-53 +.
"Stupid And Contagious."
AR15009 732 (April 18, 1996) pp51,55.
"They Say They Want A Revolution: In The Ukraine And Georgia, Nothing Secedes Like Secession."
AR15010 619-620 (December 12, 1991) pp114-116,118 +.
"Up The Amazon: Chasing Sloths, Drinking Bootleg Rum And Getting Tight With Chiggers."
AR15011 670 (November 25, 1993) pp60-62,64,66 +.
"Waist Deep In Whitewater: P. J. O'Rourke Gets His Mind Right With Pols, Pickles And Catfish."
AR15012 682 (May 19, 1994) pp81-82,85-86.
"Why I Believe What I Believe."
AR15013 712-713 (July 13, 1995) pp53-54,56,67.
ORWELL, BRUCE
"Patrick Lippert: 1958-1993."
AR15014 664 (September 2, 1993) p24.
OSBOURNE, OZZY
"Raves."
AR15015 726 (January 25, 1996) p30.
"OUR LIVES, OUR MUSIC: BY THE READERS OF 'ROLLING STONE'."
AR15016 644 (November 26, 1992) pp49-50,52,54 +.
"OUR LIVES, OUR TIMES: BY THE READERS OF 'ROLLING STONE'."
AR15017 642 (January 29, 1992) pp58-63.
"OUT THERE."
AR15018 747 (November 14, 1996) p53.

P

PALAC, LISA
"Lisa Palac's Hot List."
AR15019 682 (May 19, 1994) p72.
PALMER, ROBERT
"The Complete Clapton: Living On Blues Power."
AR15020 655 (April 29, 1993) pp30-31,33,71.
"Eric Clapton."
AR15021 641 (October 15, 1992) pp126-129.
"1926 Miles 1991: The Man Who Changed Music."
AR15022 617 (November 14, 1991) pp39,41-42,47.
"One Love."
AR15023 676 (February 24, 1994) pp38-41,67.
"Robbie Robertson: The Rolling Stone Interview."
AR15024 617 (November 14, 1991) pp68-69,71-72 +.
"Up The Mountain."
AR15025 632 (June 11, 1992) pp39-40.
"Walk On The Wild Side: The Secret History Of The Alternative-Rock Revolution."
AR15026 718 (October 5, 1995) pp45-46,48,50 +.
"Yoko Ono."
AR15027 729 (March 7, 1996) p18.
PANAHPOUR, NILOU
"Ass Ponys."
AR15028 700 (January 26, 1995) p30.
"The Cardigans Wear Their Loopy '60s Influences On Their Sleeves."
AR15029 743 (September 19, 1996) p41.
"D Generatings."
AR15030 710 (June 15, 1995) p41.
"Hall Of Fame '96."
AR15031 728 (February 22, 1996) pp18-19.
"The Lilys Blossom With Seductive '60s Sounds."
AR15032 749 (December 12, 1996) p30.
"Rock & Roll Summer: New York."
AR15033 710 (June 15, 1995) p41.
"Rock & Roll Yearbook."
AR15034 750-751 (December 26, 1996) pp45-46,48,50 +.
"Shop Therapy: Kerri Kenney Of 'The State' Prowls Manhattan's Lower East Side."
AR15035 718 (October 5, 1995) pp[enc.39,41 +].
"Supermodel City."
AR15036 710 (June 15, 1995) p41.
"Tributes."
AR15037 724-725 (December 28, 1995) pp64,66.
"PEARL JAM ON THE ROAD."
AR15038 660-661 (July 8, 1993) p16.
PENDERGRAST, JAMES T.
"The Campaign."
AR15039 630 (May 14, 1992) p8.
"The Campaign: Clinton Takes A Side Trip."
AR15040 626 (March 19, 1992) p6.
"The Campaign: George B. In Free Fall."
AR15041 625 (March 5, 1992) p4.
"The Campaign: George B. Packs For Japan."
AR15042 624 (February 20, 1992) p7.
"The Campaign: George B's Economic Plan."
AR15043 629 (April 30, 1992) p9.
"The Campaign: George Bush Makes A Decision."
AR15044 621 (January 9, 1992) p7.
"The Campaign: George Bush, The Candidate Of Change."
AR15045 631 (May 28, 1992) p6.

PENDERGRAST, JAMES T. (continued)
"The Campaign: George's Solution For Domestic Problems."
AR15046 623 (February 6, 1992) p6.
"The Campaign: G.H.W. Bush Sees His 1st Bar Code."
AR15047 627 (April 2, 1992) p8.
"The Campaign: G.H.W. Bush Thinks About The Common Man."
AR15048 639 (September 17, 1992) p10.
"The Campaign: GOP Hats In The Ring."
AR15049 622 (January 23, 1992) p4.
"The Campaign: Laid Fresh Every Day!."
AR15050 634-635 (July 9, 1992) p8.
"The Campaign: Movin' On."
AR15051 628 (April 16, 1992) p6.
"The Campaign: Old Math."
AR15052 638 (September 3, 1992) p6.
"The Campaign: President Bush Tours U.S. Cities."
AR15053 633 (June 25, 1992) p5.
"The Campaign: Supreme Court Coatroom, Summer 1992."
AR15054 637 (August 20, 1992) p6.
"The Campaign: Trust-O-Meter."
AR15055 636 (August 6, 1992) p7.
"Empty Gesture Department."
AR15056 659 (June 24, 1993) p10.
"Fame-O-Meter."
AR15057 654 (April 15, 1993) p8.
"How Stardom Works."
AR15058 656 (May 13, 1993) p10.
"The Importance Of Defining Your Terms."
AR15059 651 (March 4, 1993) p10.
AR15060 655 (April 29, 1993) p7.
"Japanese Corporations; U.S. Corporations."
AR15061 640 (October 1, 1992) p6.
"Millie Checks The Pantry."
AR15062 616 (October 31, 1991) p8.
"Millie Comes Upon A Sticky Situation."
AR15063 615 (October 17, 1991) p8.
"Millie Sees Something Scary."
AR15064 617 (November 14, 1991) p8.
"Millie Visits The Senate."
AR15065 618 (November 28, 1991) p9.
"MTV."
AR15066 658 (June 10, 1993) p12.
"1960's - 1990's."
AR15067 648 (January 21, 1993) p7.
"Parkay On Trial."
AR15068 642 (October 29, 1992) p8.
"Playing With Fire."
AR15069 645-646 (December 10, 1992) p20.
"The Sands Of Time."
AR15070 619-620 (December 12, 1991) p14.
"Straight Troops—Gay Troops."
AR15071 652 (March 18, 1993) p10.
"Stress Relief."
AR15072 650 (February 18, 1993) p6.
"Things To Do."
AR15073 653 (April 1, 1993) p8.
"Through The Looking Glass."
AR15074 649 (February 4, 1993) p7.
"Tonight! Sinead Performs!."
AR15075 647 (January 7, 1993) p7.
"U.S. Literacy Sinks To New Low."
AR15076 644 (November 26, 1992) p11.
"Yugoslavian Transportation."
AR15077 657 (May 27, 1993) p6.
PERRY, CHARLES
"The Search For The Secret Pyramid."
AR15078 632 (June 11, 1992) pp85-86,88.
PERSE, TOBIAS
"Enemies Of The Arts: The Republicans' Hit Men."
AR15079 719 (October 19, 1995) pp48-49.
"Mandatory Minimums: Eight More Victims."
AR15080 743 (September 19, 1996) p50.
"Patent Pending."
AR15081 706 (April 20, 1995) pp[enc.32].
"Try A Little Tenderness."
AR15082 693 (October 20, 1994) p132.
"What To Do The Morning After."
AR15083 716 (September 7, 1995) p40.
PHALEN, TOM
"Jampac Benefit."
AR15084 716 (September 7, 1995) p28.
"Murder Mystery."
AR15085 664 (September 2, 1993) p13.
"Rock & Roll Summer: Artist's Picks."
AR15086 710 (June 15, 1995) p40.
"Rock & Roll Summer: Seattle."
AR15087 710 (June 15, 1995) p40.
"Safe & Sound: Home Alive Unites The Seattle Music Community While Teaching Self-Defense."
AR15088 729 (March 7, 1996) p28.
"Straight Shooters: Seattle Rockers Take A Sober Side Trip With Mad Season."
AR15089 704 (March 23, 1995) p33.
PHILIPS, CHUCK
"Domino."
AR15090 680 (April 21, 1994) p29.
"2pac's Gospel Truth: In A Year When His Song Was On Trial For A Murder, The Rapper Seeks Calm In The Storm."
AR15091 668 (October 28, 1993) p22.
PHILLIPS, DAVID
"Our Lives, Our Music: The Wall."
AR15092 644 (November 26, 1992) p50.
PHILLIPS, GLEN
"Raves."
AR15093 693 (October 20, 1994) p44.
PHILLIPS, GRANT LEE
AR15094 736 (June 13, 1996) p51.
PIERSON, KATE
"The Ballad Of Yoko: The B-52's Kate Pierson Talks With Yoko Ono."
AR15095 626 (March 19, 1992) pp17,29.
PIGOZZI, JEAN
"Being There: Wherever The Celebrated And Notorious Set Down In The Eighties, Jean Pigozzi Was There."
AR15096 615 (October 17, 1991) pp63-67.
"POLICE BLOTTER."
AR15097 619-620 (December 12, 1991) p76.
AR15098 645-646 (December 10, 1992) p49.
POND, STEVE
"Daniel Lanois Finds His Own Voice: Known For The LPs He's Made For U2 And Bob Dylan, The Producer Turns One Out For Himself."
AR15099 666 (September 30, 1993) pp24-25.
"From Folk City To Fat City: Shawn Colvin Finds Her Place In The Sun."
AR15100 649 (February 4, 1993) pp58-59.
"Johnny Cash: The Hard Reign Of A Country-Music King."
AR15101 645-646 (December 10, 1992) pp118-119,121+.
"Patti Scialfa."
AR15102 667 (October 14, 1993) p34.
"Roy Orbison."
AR15103 641 (October 15, 1992) pp135-136.
"Victoria's Secret: Victoria Williams Gets Real "Loose" On Her New LP."
AR15104 690 (September 8, 1994) p45.
PORTER, BRUCE
"Blow: How A Small-Town Boy Made $100 Million With The Medellin Cocaine Cartel And Lost It All."
AR15105 660-661 (July 8, 1993) pp76-78,80-82+.
"PORTLAND, MAINE."

AR15106 681 (May 5, 1994) p26.
POWELL, KEVIN
"Arrested Development: Relaying Positive Messages."
AR15107 634-635 (July 9, 1992) p20.
"The Short Life And Death Of Tupac Shakur: Bury Me Like A G."
AR15108 746 (October 31, 1996) pp38-43,46,80.
POWELL, MICHAEL
"Wanted! 10 Things You Can Do To Make A Difference."
AR15109 718 (October 5, 1995) pp37-38.
POWERS, ANN
"Black & Blue: Me'shell NdegeOcello Fights For Your Rights On 'Peace Beyond Passion'."
AR15110 742 (September 5, 1996) pp32-35.
"Grant Lee Buffalo."
AR15111 663 (August 19, 1993) p24.
"Joan Osborne: Holy Roller Finds Salvation In God And Good Sex."
AR15112 730 (March 21, 1996) pp44-49,76.
"The Left Stuff: Consolidated Mix Politics With Humor."
AR15113 697 (December 15, 1994) p33.
"[PRESENT TENSE]."
AR15114 640 (January 1, 1992) p6.
PRINCE, DAVID
"Rhythm Nation."
AR15115 697 (December 15, 1994) p33.
AR15116 705 (April 6, 1995) p33.
AR15117 709 (June 1, 1995) p26.
PRINCE, DAVID J.
"Industrial Era: Jim Nash, Co-Founder Of Wax Trax!, Is Claimed By AIDS."
AR15118 722 (November 30, 1995) p31.
"PROFILES IN COLLEGE: BOOKS, CD-ROMS AND WEB SITES THAT TELL YOU WHERE TO GO."
AR15119 730 (March 21, 1996) p69.
PUTERBAUGH, PARKE
"Big Star: The Strange Life And Resurrection Of An American Power-Pop Legend."
AR15120 668 (October 28, 1993) pp15-16,32.
"The Blues Traveler Rock & Roll Medicine Show."
AR15121 659 (June 24, 1993) pp57-58,60-61.
"Crackers With Attitude: When The Alternative Press Gets Predictable, Cracker Get Weird."
AR15122 679 (April 7, 1994) pp67-69.
"Dan Baird's Dixie-Fried Love: The Former Georgia Satellite Ruffles Some Feathers With His Solo Effort."
AR15123 647 (January 7, 1993) p16.
"Dillon Fence: Pop With A Melody."
AR15124 634-635 (July 9, 1992) p20.
"Fish Out Of Water."
AR15125 710 (June 15, 1995) pp74-76,88.
"Gone But Not Forgotten: Though Virtually Extinct, Vinyl Record Albums Still Have Their Defenders."
AR15126 642 (October 29, 1992) p28.
"Let's Book."
AR15127 693 (October 20, 1994) pp135-137.
"Little Richard."
AR15128 641 (October 15, 1992) pp154-155.
"Robyn Hitchcock's Wild Kingdom: In The Land Of Odds, The Leader Of The Egyptians Rules."
AR15129 654 (April 15, 1993) pp56-58,75.
"The Rock & Roll Hall Of Fame '94."
AR15130 676 (February 24, 1994) pp45-46,48-49.
"Toy Caldwell: 1948-1993."
AR15131 654 (April 15, 1993) p20.
"Tribute: David Briggs 1944-1995."
AR15132 726 (January 25, 1996) p28.
"The Wax Factor: Major Labels Get Back Into The 12-Inch Groove Thang."
AR15133 700 (January 26, 1995) p22.
"Wilmington, N.C.."
AR15134 688 (August 11, 1994) p20.

Q

Q-TIP
"Raves."
AR15135 748 (November 28, 1996) p45.
QUEEN LATIFAH
"Raves."
AR15136 682 (May 19, 1994) p21.

R

"RALPH J. GLEASON AWARDS."
AR15137 629 (April 30, 1992) p28.
RAND, KRISTEN
"Cease Fire."
AR15138 677 (March 10, 1994) pp30-34,36-38+.
"RAP WRAP."
AR15139 619-620 (December 12, 1991) pp86,88.
RATHER, DAN
"Devil Or Angel? Either Way, South Africa's Winnie Mandela Has Grass-Roots Support."
AR15140 693 (October 20, 1994) pp55-57.
RAY, CHRISTOPHER A.
"Our Lives, Our Music: Live At The Apollo."
AR15141 644 (November 26, 1992) pp52,54.
"READERS' PICKS: 1992 MUSIC AWARDS."
AR15142 625 (March 5, 1992) pp53-55.
"READERS' PICKS: 1993 MUSIC AWARDS."
AR15143 651 (March 4, 1993) pp48-50.
"READERS POLL: 1996."
AR15144 726 (January 25, 1996) pp37-38.
"THE READING LIST."
AR15145 652 (March 18, 1993) pp[enc.6].
"REDBAITER LIAR WARMONGER CROOK: RICHARD MILHOUS NIXON 1913-1994."
AR15146 684 (June 16, 1994) p39.
"THE REFRESHMENTS."
AR15147 740 (August 8, 1996) p76.
REICH, ROBERT B.
"Hire Education: The Secretary Of Labor Tells You Where The Jobs Will Be In The New Economy."
AR15148 693 (October 20, 1994) pp119-120,125.
REICHL, PETER
"Our Lives, Our Music: Born To Run."
AR15149 644 (November 26, 1992) p50.
RELIC, PETER J.
"Aunts' Indie Plans."
AR15150 710 (June 15, 1995) p42.
"Rob Zombie."
AR15151 744 (October 3, 1996) p36.
"Rock & Roll Summer: Los Angeles."
AR15152 710 (June 15, 1995) p42.
"REMEMBERING BILL."
AR15153 619-620 (December 12, 1991) pp104,206,208+.
"REMEMBERING MILES."
AR15154 617 (November 14, 1991) pp44,46.
RENO, JAMES
"San Diego."
AR15155 691 (September 22, 1994) p23.
RENSIN, DAVID
"Julia Makes Trouble: The Rolling Stone Interviews."
AR15156 686-687 (July 14, 1994) pp56-60,65.

"Laura Dern."
AR15157 615 (October 17, 1991) pp70-72,108.
"REQUIESCAT IN PACE."
AR15158 717 (September 21, 1995) p104.
RESNICOFF, MATT
"Nathan Daniel: 1912-1994."
AR15159 702 (February 23, 1995) p36.
RESSNER, JEFFREY
"Alice Through The Looking Glass: The Dark Brooding Side Of The Seattle Scene."
AR15160 644 (November 26, 1992) pp45,47,79.
"Bruce Kaplan: 1945-1992."
AR15161 649 (February 4, 1993) p16.
"Casey Scott: 'City' Slacker."
AR15162 656 (May 13, 1993) p27.
"'Cop Killer' Is Iced: Ice-T Pulls Song From His Album In Response To Death Threats."
AR15163 638 (September 3, 1992) p16.
"Freddie Mercury: 1946-1991."
AR15164 621 (January 9, 1992) pp13-14,17.
"Hendrix To Tour U.S.: Traveling Exhibit Hits The States In April."
AR15165 650 (February 18, 1993) p17.
"Jim Lauderdale: An Eclectic 'Debut'."
AR15166 627 (April 2, 1992) p19.
"The Legacy."
AR15167 623 (February 6, 1992) pp45,47-48,94.
"New Kids Top Money List."
AR15168 616 (October 31, 1991) p24.
"Play It By Ear: CD Game A Hit."
AR15169 623 (February 6, 1992) p34.
"Rock & Roll Hall Of Fame."
AR15170 651 (March 4, 1993) pp15-18.
"Stars Sing For Williams."
AR15171 653 (April 1, 1993) p17.
"Stones Sign Deal With Virgin."
AR15172 621 (January 9, 1992) p24.
"Sun-60: A Dynamic Duo."
AR15173 631 (May 28, 1992) p22.
"You Can't Always Get What You Want."
AR15174 638 (September 3, 1992) pp13-14,80.
"RETURN MAIL."
AR15175 688 (August 11, 1994) p10.
REYNOLDS, SIMON
"Jungle Boogie."
AR15176 704 (March 23, 1995) p38.
"The Sea And Cake."
AR15177 721 (November 16, 1995) pp66-67,81.
"Simple Minds: Stereolab Make Suprisingly Seductive Minimalist Pop."
AR15178 731 (April 4, 1996) p40.
RHODES, RICHARD
"Atomic Logic: The Bomb In The Post-Cold War World."
AR15179 676 (February 24, 1994) pp30-33,36-37+.
"Death In The Candy Store: The Prostitution Capital Of The World, Thailand Is Committing Sexual Suicide By HIV Infection."
AR15180 618 (November 28, 1991) pp62-66,69-70+.
"Germ Warfare."
AR15181 616 (October 31, 1991) pp43-44,47-48+.
"The Making Of The Soviet Bomb."
AR15182 657 (May 27, 1993) pp42-46,64.
"Power To The People: Bulgaria Struggles With The Peaceful Atom & Post-Cold War Politics."
AR15183 658 (June 10, 1993) pp50-54,83.
RICE, ANNE
"Memnoch The Devil."
AR15184 712-713 (July 13, 1995) pp98,100-103+.
RICHARDSON, SUSAN
"John Cage: 1912-1992."
AR15185 640 (October 1, 1992) p21.
"John Mellencamp: Gets Serious And Funky."
AR15186 736 (June 13, 1996) p32.
"Marion Williams: 1927-1994."
AR15187 689 (August 25, 1994) p32.
"Push It Good: Salt-N-Pepa Are Going To The Edge."
AR15188 726 (January 25, 1996) p27.
RICKENBACH, JOHN
"Our Lives, Our Music: Goodbye Yellow Brick Road."
AR15189 644 (November 26, 1992) pp55-56.
RIFKIN, GLENN
"Cyber Funk U: Berklee College Of Music Has Seen The Future And Wants You To Write The Score."
AR15190 666 (September 30, 1993) pp71-72,74,96.
RITTS, HERB
"Cindy: A Portfolio."
AR15191 672-673 (December 23, 1993) pp96-103.
"Herb Ritts."
AR15192 643 (November 12, 1992) pp151-158,161+.
RITZ, DAVID
"The Chairman Of The Board: My Life In The Studio With Brother Ray, Lady Soul, Bob Dylan And The Wicked Pickett."
AR15193 650 (February 18, 1993) pp50-52,68.
"Johnny 'Guitar' Watson 1935-1996."
AR15194 738-739 (July 11, 1996) p22.
"Sexual Healing: Janet Jackson Finds Peace, Inspiration And Chart Success Through Carnal Knowledge."
AR15195 665 (September 16, 1993) pp38-41,43,82.
"The Soul Behind The Face: Babyface Steps Out from Behind The Boards To The Top Of The Charts."
AR15196 696 (December 1, 1994) pp103-105.
"Stevie Wonder: Never-Ending Song Of Peace."
AR15197 712-713 (July 13, 1995) pp80-82,84-85+.
"Viva La Divas."
AR15198 660-661 (July 8, 1993) pp64-66,68-69+.
ROBBINS, IRA
"The Alternative Underground: Bands On The Real Cutting Edge Turn Out For Six-day Washington Festival."
AR15199 615 (October 17, 1991) p20.
"Bettie Serveert: A Dutch Band Plays A Sweeter Kind Of Grunge."
AR15200 653 (April 1, 1993) p22.
"Critics Comments."
AR15201 726 (January 25, 1996) pp46,50-51.
"Fountains Of Wayne Bubble With Power Pop."
AR15202 748 (November 28, 1996) p40.
"Gutterball Take A Working Vacation."
AR15203 663 (August 19, 1993) p15.
"New Faces: A Guide To This Summer's Coolest Music—And The Artists Making It."
AR15204 660-661 (July 8, 1993) pp95-97.
"Paul K."
AR15205 666 (September 30, 1993) p16.
"Retread Sneakers: The Duo Releases A Collection Of New Old Songs."
AR15206 655 (April 29, 1993) p19.
"Sleeping With The Enemy?: Indie Meets Major As Matador And Atlantic Records Join Forces."
AR15207 657 (May 27, 1993) p24.
"They're Here, They're The Queers And They're Not What You Think."
AR15208 747 (November 14, 1996) p42.
"Vivian Stanshall: 1943-1995."
AR15209 706 (April 20, 1995) p32.
ROBBINS, MICHAEL
"Our Lives, Our Music: Daydream Nation."
AR15210 644 (November 26, 1992) p56.
ROBERT, FRANCOIS
"The Heart And Sole Of The City: The Right Sneaker Keeps You In The Action."
AR15211 638 (September 3, 1992) pp[enc.53-54].
"Sticks & Stones: Whether You're Heading For The Great Outdoors Or The Urban Jungle, Durable Watches And Rugged Boots Ease

Your Trek Off The Beaten Path."
AR15212 628 (April 16, 1992) pp[enc.37-38 +].
ROBERTS, TODD
"Underworld Find Their Voice Behind Beats And Riffs."
AR15213 744 (October 3, 1996) p32.
ROBICHEAU, PAUL
"Dambuilders."
AR15214 693 (October 20, 1994) p49.
"Webb Of Sound."
AR15215 680 (April 21, 1994) p26.
ROBINSON, CHRIS
"Raves."
AR15216 700 (January 26, 1995) p26.
ROBINSON, SCOTT
"The Plight Of The Crowes: The Band Cancels Show After Trouble With Police."
AR15217 654 (April 15, 1993) p16.
"ROCK & ROLL MUSIC."
AR15218 724-725 (December 28, 1995) pp39-40,42,45 +.
ROGERS, RAY
"A Capital Idea: Rockers Run Labels For Fun 'N' Profit."
AR15219 696 (December 1, 1994) p32.
"Queen's Reich: Queer Punk Comes Out of The Closet—Loudly."
AR15220 708 (May 18, 1995) pp38,42.
"[ROLLING STONE...]."
AR15221 681 (May 5, 1994) p8.
"ROLLING STONE ONLINE."
AR15222 714 (August 10, 1995) p12.
ROLSTON, MATTHEW
"Matthew Rolston."
AR15223 643 (November 12, 1992) pp97-102,105 +.
ROSENBERG, TINA
"On The Row."
AR15224 718 (October 5, 1995) pp56-58,60-62 +.
"The Stealth War Against Abortion: In Rural States Like Mississippi, Abortion May Still Be Legal, But Lawmakers Have Made It Nearly Impossible For Women To Make The Choice For Themselves."
AR15225 737 (June 27, 1996) pp47-50,67-68.
ROTH, MELISSA
"As The World 'Terns: More Weird Tales Of Internships."
AR15226 730 (March 21, 1996) pp51-52.
"College Notebook."
AR15227 719 (October 19, 1995) pp91-92,94-95.
"Hot Founding Father: Ben Franklin."
AR15228 741 (August 22, 1996) p80.
"Hot Revival: The Cold War."
AR15229 741 (August 22, 1996) p74.
"Hot Threat: Cyberterrorism."
AR15230 741 (August 22, 1996) p78.
"Posies: Inside Out."
AR15231 710 (June 15, 1995) p40.
ROWE, JONATHAN
"The Most Dangerous Man In America."
AR15232 721 (November 16, 1995) pp85-86,88-91 +.
ROYTE, ELIZABETH
"Dance Of Death."
AR15233 708 (May 18, 1995) p25.
"Pit Master Wanted: Large, Mellow Men To Keep Peace At Live Shows."
AR15234 708 (May 18, 1995) pp23,25.
RUBINER, MICHAEL
"A.M.C.'s S.F.."
AR15235 690 (September 8, 1994) p25.
"Band On The Run: Life On The Road With The Health And Happiness Show."
AR15236 691 (September 22, 1994) pp[enc.17-20 +].
"Beached Monster."
AR15237 710 (June 15, 1995) p54.
"Bush's Hits."
AR15238 710 (June 15, 1995) p49.
"Cheeky Monkeys."
AR15239 693 (October 20, 1994) pp87,89.
"Cleo's Mass. Appeal."
AR15240 710 (June 15, 1995) p39.
"Dionne Farris."
AR15241 736 (June 13, 1996) p47.
"Eating For A's: Nutrition Experts Chew The No-Fat."
AR15242 693 (October 20, 1994) p90.
"Ezra's Better, Bigger Easy."
AR15243 710 (June 15, 1995) p46.
"The Heat Puppets."
AR15244 710 (June 15, 1995) p48.
"Henry Rollins' L.A.."
AR15245 686-687 (July 14, 1994) p45.
"High-Plains Surfers."
AR15246 710 (June 15, 1995) p54.
"Hot Accessory."
AR15247 656 (May 13, 1993) p68.
"Hot Actor."
AR15248 656 (May 13, 1993) p63.
AR15249 682 (May 19, 1994) p55.
"Hot Actress."
AR15250 656 (May 13, 1993) p62.
AR15251 682 (May 19, 1994) p57.
"Hot Appliance."
AR15252 682 (May 19, 1994) p58.
"Hot Architect."
AR15253 656 (May 13, 1993) p90.
"Hot Arms."
AR15254 682 (May 19, 1994) p72.
"Hot Art Form."
AR15255 656 (May 13, 1993) p84.
"Hot Athlete."
AR15256 656 (May 13, 1993) p87.
AR15257 682 (May 19, 1994) p64.
"Hot Band."
AR15258 682 (May 19, 1994) p56.
"Hot Bulletin Board."
AR15259 682 (May 19, 1994) p56.
"Hot Bullshit Compliment."
AR15260 656 (May 13, 1993) p88.
"Hot Car."
AR15261 656 (May 13, 1993) p67.
"Hot Comic Book."
AR15262 682 (May 19, 1994) p69.
"Hot Country Act."
AR15263 682 (May 19, 1994) p74.
"Hot Country Singer."
AR15264 656 (May 13, 1993) p65.
"Hot Dates."
AR15265 656 (May 13, 1993) p65.
"Hot Debut."
AR15266 656 (May 13, 1993) p63.
"Hot Designer."
AR15267 656 (May 13, 1993) p73.
AR15268 682 (May 19, 1994) p64.
"Hot Director."
AR15269 656 (May 13, 1993) p87.
AR15270 682 (May 19, 1994) p58.
"Hot Drug."
AR15271 656 (May 13, 1993) p90.
"Hot Exercise."
AR15272 682 (May 19, 1994) p69.
"Hot Gadget."
AR15273 656 (May 13, 1993) p65.
"Hot Infomercial."
AR15274 656 (May 13, 1993) p63.

RUBINER, MICHAEL (continued)
"Hot Jazz Artist."
AR15275 682 (May 19, 1994) pp76-77.
"Hot Judd."
AR15276 656 (May 13, 1993) p84.
"The Hot List."
AR15277 656 (May 13, 1993) pp61-65,67-68+.
AR15278 682 (May 19, 1994) p55.
AR15279 715 (August 24, 1995) pp73-75,77,80+.
"Hot Loser."
AR15280 682 (May 19, 1994) p66.
"Hot Medical Equipment."
AR15281 656 (May 13, 1993) p64.
"Hot Models."
AR15282 682 (May 19, 1994) p63.
"Hot Molecule."
AR15283 656 (May 13, 1993) p90.
"Hot Movie Critic."
AR15284 682 (May 19, 1994) p66.
"Hot Movie Theme."
AR15285 682 (May 19, 1994) p63.
"Hot Performance Artist."
AR15286 682 (May 19, 1994) p74.
"Hot Playwright."
AR15287 656 (May 13, 1993) p73.
"Hot Producer."
AR15288 656 (May 13, 1993) p88.
"Hot Rap Trend."
AR15289 656 (May 13, 1993) p67.
"Hot Rapper."
AR15290 682 (May 19, 1994) p64.
"Hot Record Label."
AR15291 656 (May 13, 1993) p74.
"Hot Resurrection."
AR15292 656 (May 13, 1993) p68.
"Hot Retro Ethos."
AR15293 656 (May 13, 1993) p65.
"Hot Revival."
AR15294 656 (May 13, 1993) p90.
"Hot Scam."
AR15295 656 (May 13, 1993) p88.
"Hot Screenwriter."
AR15296 656 (May 13, 1993) p73.
"Hot Sex Symbol."
AR15297 656 (May 13, 1993) p68.
"Hot Stand-Up."
AR15298 682 (May 19, 1994) p68.
"Hot Standup."
AR15299 656 (May 13, 1993) p62.
"Hot Subculture."
AR15300 656 (May 13, 1993) p82.
AR15301 682 (May 19, 1994) p68.
"Hot Teen Idols."
AR15302 656 (May 13, 1993) p87.
"Hot Threat."
AR15303 656 (May 13, 1993) p64.
"Hot TV Show."
AR15304 682 (May 19, 1994) p56.
"Hot Unprotected Minority."
AR15305 682 (May 19, 1994) p57.
"Hot Vacation Spot."
AR15306 682 (May 19, 1994) p72.
"Hot Vice."
AR15307 682 (May 19, 1994) p58.
"Hot Video Game."
AR15308 656 (May 13, 1993) p67.
"I Was A Campus Lab Rat."
AR15309 704 (March 23, 1995) pp67,69-70.
"James Carville's Hot List."
AR15310 656 (May 13, 1993) p64.
"Jon Stewart."
AR15311 700 (January 26, 1995) p26.
"Land O' Babes."
AR15312 710 (June 15, 1995) p52.
"The Mavericks Beach Country."
AR15313 691 (September 22, 1994) p22.
"Michael Richards's Hot List."
AR15314 656 (May 13, 1993) p72.
"Old-School Cool."
AR15315 710 (June 15, 1995) p42.
"Out Of The Shadows...Into The Night."
AR15316 642 (October 29, 1992) pp64-67.
"Planets' World."
AR15317 689 (August 25, 1994) p17.
"Richard Linklater's Hot List."
AR15318 656 (May 13, 1993) p82.
"Rock & Roll Yearbook."
AR15319 750-751 (December 26, 1996) pp45-46,48,50+.
"Saviors' Haven."
AR15320 710 (June 15, 1995) p53.
"Sponge City."
AR15321 710 (June 15, 1995) p49.
"Steal This Diploma: Higher Education At Lower Prices."
AR15322 730 (March 21, 1996) pp65,68.
"Tales From The Crib: Dormitory Resident Advisers Explain How They Deal With Bongs, Beer, Stress And...Uh...Noisy Couples."
AR15323 693 (October 20, 1994) pp89-91.
"Topical Disease."
AR15324 692 (October 6, 1994) p93.
"Urge Overkill Indoors."
AR15325 688 (August 11, 1994) p22.
RUBINSTEIN, JULIAN
"Hot Athlete: Steve Prefontaine."
AR15326 741 (August 22, 1996) p76.
RUCKER, DARIUS
"Raves."
AR15327 704 (March 23, 1995) p40.
RYDER, SHAUN
"Raves."
AR15328 730 (March 21, 1996) p36.

S

SABBAG, ROBERT
"The Cartels Would Like A Second Chance."
AR15329 681 (May 5, 1994) pp35-37,43.
"Lost In America: A Father, A Family And An Entire Community Struggle To Understand How One Of Their Sons Could Go So Wrong."
AR15330 703 (March 9, 1995) pp56-58,60-61+.
"State Of The Reunion."
AR15331 663 (August 19, 1993) pp57-58,60-63.
SAGER, MIKE
"The Devil And John Holmes."
AR15332 632 (June 11, 1992) pp173-174.
"The Dust Of Life."
AR15333 617 (November 14, 1991) pp56-58,61,64+.
"Gut Check In The Heartland."
AR15334 647 (January 7, 1993) pp30-31,54.
"Living In The USA: Revenge Of The Doughnut Boys."
AR15335 640 (October 1, 1992) pp35,80.
"Living In The USA: The Case Of Gary Fannon."
AR15336 638 (September 3, 1992) pp27,30,82.
"The Rise And Fall Of A Super Freak."
AR15337 737 (June 27, 1996) pp38-40,42,44+.
"A Tragic Miscarriage Of Justice Continues: The State Of Michigan Vs. Gary Fannon."
AR15338 664 (September 2, 1993) pp51-53,70.

SALGADO, SEBASTIAO
"Aftermath: In Rwanda A Year After The Massacre, There Is Still No Justice, No Peace."
AR15339 712-713 (July 13, 1995) pp86-91.
"Bombay: Despite Crushing Poverty And Overpopulation, A Mighty Middle-Class Economy Has Turned Bombay Into A City Of Hope."
AR15340 738-739 (July 11, 1996) pp77-82.
"Casualties Of War."
AR15341 702 (February 23, 1995) pp60-65.
"The Long Road Home."
AR15342 698-699 (December 29, 1994) pp120-129.
"Rwanda: The Death Of A Nation."
AR15343 691 (September 22, 1994) pp67-74,76-80 +.
"The Visionary Light."
AR15344 619-620 (December 12, 1991) pp142-147.
"Workers Of The World: A Portfolio."
AR15345 665 (September 16, 1993) pp54-58.
"SALT LAKE CITY, UTAH."
AR15346 681 (May 5, 1994) p38.
SAMUELS, DAVID
"The Big Squeeze: Tuition Is Up, Salaries Are Down, And The Government Couldn't Care Less."
AR15347 719 (October 19, 1995) pp119-120,122.
"The Price Of Politics—Student Loans."
AR15348 719 (October 19, 1995) pp124-125.
"Requiem For A Heavyweight."
AR15349 723 (December 14, 1995) pp77-79.
SANTELLI, ROBERT
"Rock & Roll Summer: Jersey Shore."
AR15350 710 (June 15, 1995) p54.
"Widespread Panic: Not Just Another Southern Band."
AR15351 618 (November 28, 1991) p30.
SANTIAGO, ROBERTO
"Hall Of Fame Groundbreaking: At Long Last, The Site Is Ready For The Country's First Rock Shrine."
AR15352 662 (August 5, 1993) p18.
SAUNDERS, DUDLEY
"Cat Power."
AR15353 747 (November 14, 1996) p58.
"Skeleton Key."
AR15354 747 (November 14, 1996) p56.
SAVAN, LESLIE
"The 'Vad' Fad: Making Music-Video Commercials."
AR15355 667 (October 14, 1993) p80.
SAYLES, JOHN
"Keeping Time."
AR15356 671 (December 9, 1993) pp48-52,82,84.
SCATENA, DINO
"Thunder Down Under: Australia Takes An Alterna-Rock Holiday With Big Day Out."
AR15357 677 (March 10, 1994) pp15-16.
SCAVULLO, FRANCESCO
"It's Pat: Julia Sweeney's Gender-Bending Character Goes To Hollywood."
AR15358 691 (September 22, 1994) pp[enc.9-14].
SCHEMER, KAREN
"Pure & Simple: Kelly Willis, County Waif."
AR15359 664 (September 2, 1993) pp56-57.
SCHIFFMAN, BONNIE
"Kings Of Comedy."
AR15360 616 (October 31, 1991) pp52-56.
SCHIPPER, HENRY
"Clinton And Brown Sound Off: The Candidates Talk About Music, From Miles Davis To The Mothers Of Invention."
AR15361 630 (May 14, 1992) pp17,19,22,120.
SCHMOKE, KURT
"Side Effects: A Concerned Public Official Says We Need To Shift The Way We Think About Drugs Before We Lose Even More Young Lives To AIDS An Violence."
AR15362 681 (May 5, 1994) pp38-39.
SCHNEIDER, FRED
"Raves."
AR15363 734 (May 16, 1996) p26.
SCHOEMER, KAREN
"Big Time: Being Hip Is Something That Dwight Yoakum Does Best."
AR15364 666 (September 30, 1993) pp63-66,96.
"A Breed Apart: Powered by The Musical Vision Of Kim Deal And The Free Spirit Of Her Sister, Kelley, The Breeders Bring Soul And Sass To Punk Rock."
AR15365 682 (May 19, 1994) pp88-90,92-93 +.
"Hot Band."
AR15366 656 (May 13, 1993) pp77-78,80-81.
"Normal Weirdness In Seattle."
AR15367 652 (March 18, 1993) pp[enc.34-38 +].
SCHRUERS, FRED
"Dangerous, Dedicated And Wild At heart, Nicolas Cage Is A Hollywood Samurai."
AR15368 721 (November 16, 1995) pp92-94,96 +.
"Dave Vs. Dave: Forget Leno & Koppel—Letterman May Be His Own Worst Enemy."
AR15369 735 (May 30, 1996) pp28-30,32,62 +.
"Hot Brit: Ewan McGregor."
AR15370 741 (August 22, 1996) p80.
"Jim Carrey: Bare Facts And Shocking Revelations."
AR15371 712-713 (July 13, 1995) pp68-74,124 +.
"The King Of Prime-Time Comedy."
AR15372 691 (September 22, 1994) pp46-50,112 +.
"Man Of The Year: David Letterman."
AR15373 698-699 (December 29, 1994) pp30-34,204 +.
"Matthew McConaughey."
AR15374 741 (August 22, 1996) pp44-46,48,108.
"Neil Jordan."
AR15375 747 (November 14, 1996) pp82-85,132.
"Sheryl Crow: She Only Wants To Be With You."
AR15376 747 (November 14, 1996) pp64-66,68-71.
"Tom Petty: This IS How It Feels On The Road."
AR15377 707 (May 4, 1995) pp48-50,52-54 +.
"Travolta: The Rolling Stone Interview."
AR15378 728 (February 22, 1996) pp40-43,71.
SCRIBNER, SARA
"Presidents Of The United States Of America."
AR15379 718 (October 5, 1995) p35.
"Royal Spoils: Royal Trux Keep Everyone Guessing With 'Thank You'."
AR15380 710 (June 15, 1995) p36.
"Ted Hawkins: 1936-1995."
AR15381 702 (February 23, 1995) p36.
SELIGER, MARK
"Legends Of Country Music."
AR15382 750-751 (December 26, 1996) pp168-179.
"Mark Seliger."
AR15383 643 (November 12, 1992) pp115-125,127 +.
"New Jack And Jill."
AR15384 654 (April 15, 1993) pp[enc.4-7 +].
SEYMOUR, COREY
"Are You Xperienced?: On The Fashion Tip With Kim Gordon Of Sonic Youth."
AR15385 692 (October 6, 1994) pp60-62.
"Lennon's Family Ties: Beatle's Accessories Hot Summer Sellers."
AR15386 660-661 (July 8, 1993) p30.
"Now Ear This: Noses Are Fine, And Navels Are Cool, But This Is Still The Classic Rock & Roll Pierce."
AR15387 662 (August 5, 1993) pp59-60.
"On The Cover Of Rolling Stone."
AR15388 645-646 (December 10, 1992) pp147-149,152 +.
"Picture This: The Best Of Rock-Photography Book."
AR15389 643 (November 12, 1992) pp249-251.

SHARP, MATT
"Raves."
AR15390 710 (June 15, 1995) p26.
SHEFF, DAVID
"Mario's Big Brother: From 'Donkey Kong' To New Super Nintendo, Sigeru Miyamoto Has Shaped A Generation."
AR15391 621 (January 9, 1992) pp45-46.
SHEFF-CAHAN, VICKI
"Robert F. Kennedy Jr.: Getting Down To Earth With A Leading Eco-Activist."
AR15392 645-646 (December 10, 1992) pp133,135-137+.
SHERER, ALAN
"Our Lives, Our Music: Freak Out!."
AR15393 644 (November 26, 1992) p58.
SHERRILL, STEPHEN
"The A List: Celebrity Guidance Counselors Recommend One Book, One Movie, One Recording That Will Change Your Life."
AR15394 666 (September 30, 1993) pp51,55-56.
"Behind The Zines: The Chronic Urges And Ultraobsessions Of Do-It-Yourself Publishing."
AR15395 689 (August 25, 1994) pp73,75,100.
"College 94 Notebook."
AR15396 678 (March 24, 1994) pp49-51.
"The Dropout 'Zine."
AR15397 693 (October 20, 1994) pp92-93.
"Fear Of A Hip Hop Syllabus: Three Professors Reveal What The Required Listening Will Be When Rap Goes To College."
AR15398 666 (September 30, 1993) pp56,59.
"The Frames: Bringing A Different Mix To Their Irish Stew."
AR15399 644 (November 26, 1992) p24.
"The Freewheelers: After-Hours Rock."
AR15400 622 (January 23, 1992) p14.
"Joe Henry: On His Own."
AR15401 637 (August 20, 1992) p20.
"Road Trips."
AR15402 666 (September 30, 1993) pp55-56.
"Slaves To The Grind: The Most Important Job In A College Town Is Supplying The Jolt."
AR15403 666 (September 30, 1993) pp51,55.
SHULMAN, SETH
"Over There: The U.S. Military's Toxic Reach."
AR15404 618 (November 28, 1991) pp39-40.
SIFF, ANDREW E.
"Our Lives, Our Music: The Stranger."
AR15405 644 (November 26, 1992) p52.
SILBERGER, KATHY
"I Am Somebody: After A Wildly Successful Duet With Coolio, L.V. Surfaces With His Own Gangsta's Paradise."
AR15406 733 (May 2, 1996) pp18-20.
SIMMONS, MICHAEL
"Give Pot A Chance: Voters In California And Arizona Strike A Blow Against The War On Drugs."
AR15407 750-751 (December 26, 1996) pp111,113.
SIMONSON, KEVIN P.
"The Millions: A Gimmick-Free Sound."
AR15408 625 (March 5, 1992) p27.
SIMPSON, JOHN
"Our Lives, Our Music: Angel Dust."
AR15409 644 (November 26, 1992) p52.
"SINCE THEN."
AR15410 689 (August 25, 1994) p12.
AR15411 691 (September 22, 1994) p14.
AR15412 694 (November 3, 1994) p14.
AR15413 712-713 (July 13, 1995) p.
SINCLAIR, DAVID
"Beck Is Back: The Reclusive Guitarist Returns With Two Albums."
AR15414 653 (April 1, 1993) pp15-16.
"The British Aren't Coming: Is The Newest Wave From The U.K. A Washout?."
AR15415 703 (March 9, 1995) pp23-24.
"Dear Diary: The Secret World Of Kate Bush."
AR15416 676 (February 24, 1994) pp13-14.
"He's A Loser, Baby: Court Rejects George Michael's Plea To Break His Contract With Sony."
AR15417 688 (August 11, 1994) p28.
"London Calling."
AR15418 660-661 (July 8, 1993) p26.
AR15419 663 (August 19, 1993) p24.
AR15420 668 (October 28, 1993) p25.
AR15421 671 (December 9, 1993) p25.
AR15422 678 (March 24, 1994) p21.
AR15423 682 (May 19, 1994) p32.
AR15424 692 (October 6, 1994) p36.
AR15425 700 (January 26, 1995) p30.
AR15426 706 (April 20, 1995) p36.
AR15427 711 (June 29, 1995) p20.
AR15428 716 (September 7, 1995) p35.
"London Confidential."
AR15429 685 (June 30, 1994) p36.
"Mod Squad: With 'I Should Coco' The U.K. Trio Supergrass Bring Their Freshly Manicured Pop To America."
AR15430 718 (October 5, 1995) pp[enc.20-22+].
"Peter Gabriel's Secret World."
AR15431 663 (August 19, 1993) pp9-10,85.
"Pulp Friction: Frontman Jarvis Cocker Wreaks Revenge For The 'Common People'."
AR15432 732 (April 18, 1996) pp22-25.
"Rory Gallagher: 1948-1995."
AR15433 714 (August 10, 1995) p32.
"Sleeper."
AR15434 709 (June 1, 1995) p27.
"Station To Station: On A Personal Tour Of Ziggy's London, David Bowie Looks Back At His Days As The Glam King Of England."
AR15435 658 (June 10, 1993) pp56-58,60,62+.
"Strange Fruit: Black Grape Uncork A Distinctive Vintage."
AR15436 723 (December 14, 1995) p40.
"Tindersticks."
AR15437 682 (May 19, 1994) p32.
"Tricky."
AR15438 714 (August 10, 1995) p33.
"The Turning Point: Annie Lennox Finds Life After Eurythmics."
AR15439 651 (March 4, 1993) pp58-59,61,77.
"Ziggy's Axeman: Mick Ronson Was A Sideman Extraordinaire."
AR15440 659 (June 24, 1993) p28.
SINCLAIR, TOM
"Chainsaw Kittens: Grungy Glam, Oklahoma Style."
AR15441 630 (May 14, 1992) p32.
"A Tribe Called Quest."
AR15442 660-661 (July 8, 1993) p26.
"SMART ALTERNATIVE."
AR15443 736 (June 13, 1996) p60.
SMEAR, PAT
"Raves."
AR15444 741 (August 22, 1996) p42.
SMITH, DANYEL
"House Of Pain: The Fight Against Gansta Rap Hits Captiol Hill."
AR15445 679 (April 7, 1994) p22.
"Martin Lawrence."
AR15446 669 (November 11, 1993) p20.
"MC Lyte."
AR15447 665 (September 16, 1993) p17.
"Party Out Of Bounds: On The Bus And Out Of Control With The Cypress Hill - House Of Pain Tour."
AR15448 669 (November 11, 1993) pp64-65.
"Positive PE: After A Hiatus, Public Enemy Return With A Fierce But Soulful Album."
AR15449 685 (June 30, 1994) p30.
"Street News."
AR15450 670 (November 25, 1993) p32.

AR15451 681 (May 5, 1994) p18.
AR15452 684 (June 16, 1994) p30.
SMITH, DWIGHT A.
"Our Lives, Our Music: The Joshua Tree."
AR15453 644 (November 26, 1992) p52.
SMITH, KEVIN J.
"Our Lives, Our Music: Mud Slide Slim And The Blue Horizon."
AR15454 644 (November 26, 1992) p55.
SMITH, MAT
"In The News."
AR15455 708 (May 18, 1995) p34.
"Oasis Cancel Last Third Of U.S. Tour After Rocky Start."
AR15456 745 (October 17, 1996) p42.
SOLOTAROFF, PAUL
"Exiles On Main Street."
AR15457 659 (June 24, 1993) pp62-66,68.
"Surviving The Crusades."
AR15458 667 (October 14, 1993) pp57-62.
SOOCHER, STAN
"Supreme Justice: Rap's Day In Court."
AR15459 669 (November 11, 1993) p13.
SPEER, KEITH L.
"Our Lives, Our Music: Scarecrow."
AR15460 644 (November 26, 1992) p52.
SPELLA, ARNOLD R., JR.
"Our Lives, Our Music: Hotcakes."
AR15461 644 (November 26, 1992) p54.
SPENCER, PETER
"Haitian Flight Song: World Music Artists At The Mercy Of Global Politics."
AR15462 691 (September 22, 1994) p36.
SPENCER, SCOTT
"Buddy Guy: His Time Is Now."
AR15463 618 (November 28, 1991) pp72-77,116.
"Hope & Hard Times: For The Workers At Ravenswood Aluminum, The Struggle To Regain Their Union Jobs Took Them From Small-Town Appalachia To The Glass Canyons Of International Finance."
AR15464 629 (April 30, 1992) pp44-46,48,50 +.
"William Kunstler: 1919-1995."
AR15465 719 (October 19, 1995) p89.
SPERA, KEITH
"Luscious Jackson: Record In New Orleans."
AR15466 735 (May 30, 1996) p27.
"Memorial Tribute To Eazy-E."
AR15467 728 (February 22, 1996) p64.
SPRAGUE, DAVID
"Cumbersome Combo: Seven Mary Three Churn It Out."
AR15468 731 (April 4, 1996) pp38-39.
"Devolution Rock: Brainiac Are Taking Retro To The Future."
AR15469 733 (May 2, 1996) p26.
"Girls Against Boys."
AR15470 721 (November 16, 1995) pp74-75,80-81.
"Good Vibrations: The Fugees Score One For Positivity."
AR15471 729 (March 7, 1996) p14.
"Pretty On The Inside: Blur Get Introspective On Their New Album."
AR15472 720 (November 2, 1995) pp19-20.
"Soul Coughing: Hack Out A Hearty Blend Of Beat Poetry, Hip-Hop And Art Rock."
AR15473 735 (May 30, 1996) pp21,23.
"What's In A 'Name'? Goo Goo Dolls Score A Hit Nine Years In The Making."
AR15474 723 (December 14, 1995) p36.
SQUIRES, JIM
"The Crack-Up."
AR15475 640 (October 1, 1992) pp50-52,54-55 +.
ST. LEGER, MARIE ELSIE
"Des'ree Moves On."
AR15476 696 (December 1, 1994) p48.
STAINS, LAURENCE
"Black Like Me."
AR15477 678 (March 24, 1994) pp69-70,72.
"Speech Impediment: How A Penn Freshman Stood Up To The PC Police And Cracked The Campus Speech Code."
AR15478 662 (August 5, 1993) pp45-46,48-49 +.
AR15479 Number not assigned.
"[STAMPS]."
AR15480 644 (November 26, 1992) p24.
"STAR SCRIBES."
AR15481 619-620 (December 12, 1991) p75.
STEELE, BILL
"First Place Watches."
AR15482 638 (September 3, 1992) pp[enc.57].
"Scentsual Pleasures."
AR15483 638 (September 3, 1992) p59.
STERNE, HILARY
"Hot Look."
AR15484 741 (August 22, 1996) pp86-88,90.92.
STEFANI, GWEN
"Rave."
AR15485 735 (May 30, 1996) p24.
STEINBERG, NEIL
"Cutting Edge Colleges: Four Schools That Are Preparing Their Students For The 21st Century."
AR15486 666 (September 30, 1993) pp59-60.
"Gag U.: From Caltech's Card Trick To Amherst's Run-Around Sabrina, These Pranks Are Total Classics."
AR15487 626 (March 19, 1992) pp67-68,70.
"The Law Of Unintended Consequences: Mandatory Minimum Sentencing Puts First-Time Offenders In Jail For Life And Lets Drug Kingpins Bargain For Their Freedom."
AR15488 681 (May 5, 1994) pp33-34.
STEELE, BILL
"Scentsual Pleasures."
AR15489 638 (September 3, 1992) p59.
STERNE, HILARY
"Hot Look."
AR15490 741 (August 22, 1996) pp86-88,90.92.
STEWART, JON
"Jon Stewart's Hot List."
AR15491 682 (May 19, 1994) p63.
STOLDER, STEVEN
"Aren't Stickers Enough? A Revived PMRC Pushes For A Stringent New Record-Ratings System."
AR15492 720 (November 2, 1995) p30.
"Grateful Dead Cut Staff."
AR15493 719 (October 19, 1995) p24.
"Mall Rap: The Million Man March Draws A Crew Of Hip-Hop Artists To Washington, D.C.."
AR15494 722 (November 30, 1995) p37.
"Sole Singers."
AR15495 728 (February 22, 1996) p34.
"We Are Tibet: The Beastie Boys And Smashing Pumpkins Headline The Largest Benefit Concert Of The 1990s."
AR15496 740 (August 8, 1996) pp20-22.
STONE, PETER H.
"Skin Deep: Republican Front-Runner Bob Dole Will Do Anything For A Buck."
AR15497 715 (August 24, 1995) pp39-40,116.
STONE, ROBERT
"End Of The Beginning: Jerry Garcia And The Grateful Dead's Music Was The Last Remnant Of A Magic Vision."
AR15498 717 (September 21, 1995) pp63,67.
STRAUSS, NEIL
"The Acid Test: Deadheads Face Hard Time In LSD Crackdown."
AR15499 686-687 (July 14, 1994) pp24,26.
"A Dose Of Reality: Kurt Cobain Recovers From A Drug-And-Alcohol Induced Coma."
AR15500 680 (April 21, 1994) p20.

"The Downward Spiral: The Last Days Of Nirvana's Leader."
AR15501 683 (June 2, 1994) pp35-36,38,40+.
"Exploding Tickets: Pearl Jam Wage An Anti-Trust War Against Ticketmaster On Capitol Hill."
AR15502 688 (August 11, 1994) p30.
"A Hard Dazed Night: Soul Asylum's Dave Pirner Burns The Midnight Oil, Defending His Band, His Music And His Punk Credibility."
AR15503 711 (June 29, 1995) pp28-33.
"'He Was A Geek And A God:' The Story Behind The Tragic Death Of Kurt Cobain."
AR15504 682 (May 19, 1994) pp17-18,20.
"In The News."
AR15505 674 (January 27, 1994) p22.
AR15506 675 (February 10, 1994) p16.
AR15507 676 (February 24, 1994) p20.
AR15508 677 (March 10, 1994) p18.
AR15509 678 (March 24, 1994) p18.
AR15510 679 (April 7, 1994) p22.
AR15511 680 (April 21, 1994) p20.
AR15512 681 (May 5, 1994) p15.
AR15513 682 (May 19, 1994) p30.
AR15514 685 (June 30, 1994) p30.
AR15515 686-687 (July 14, 1994) p35.
AR15516 690 (September 8, 1994) p40.
AR15517 691 (September 22, 1994) p32.
AR15518 692 (October 6, 1994) p309.
AR15519 693 (October 20, 1994) p43.
AR15520 696 (December 1, 1994) p36.
AR15521 697 (December 15, 1994) p31.
"King For A Day: First Graceland Concert Planned For October."
AR15522 680 (April 21, 1994) p13.
"Kristen Pfaff : 1967-1994."
AR15523 688 (August 11, 1994) p30.
"Lenny Kravitz: Mystic, Mimic, Father, Lover, Which Is The Real Lenny The Kid?."
AR15524 722 (November 30, 1995) pp48-55.
"Lollapalooza Jr.: Tomorrow's Stars Are On The Second Stage Today."
AR15525 689 (August 25, 1994) pp21,24-25.
"Meat Puppets."
AR15526 695 (November 17, 1994) pp145-146.
"[Moby]."
AR15527 695 (November 17, 1994) pp102-103,151.
"Money, It's A Gas: Pink Floyd Eclipse Stones' Ticket-Sales Record."
AR15528 691 (September 22, 1994) p33.
"Moon Struck: Grant Lee Buffalo Roam The Margins Of American Gothic On Might Joe Moon."
AR15529 696 (December 1, 1994) pp98-100.
"Music Biz Rebounds In '93: Sales Increases Give Industry Hope."
AR15530 675 (February 10, 1994) p13.
"My So-Called Double Life: Kristin Hersh Of Throwing Muses Finds The Common Ground Between Motherhood And Rock & Roll."
AR15531 703 (March 9, 1995) pp52-55.
"Nirvana Projects On Hold."
AR15532 684 (June 16, 1994) p17.
"PJ Harvey."
AR15533 724-725 (December 28, 1995) pp68-70,79+.
"Squeeze Box: The Who Get The Deluxe Treatment."
AR15534 678 (March 24, 1994) p18.
"Still First In Space: Pink Floyd Rocket Back To The Top With The Division Bell."
AR15535 684 (June 16, 1994) pp15-16.
"Toasting Townshend: Roger Daltrey Does Carnegie Hall."
AR15536 679 (April 7, 1994) p20.
"Virtual Dylan: Bob Dylan Goes Electric Again—On CD-ROM."
AR15537 706 (April 20, 1995) p25.
"Whole Lotta Lolla."
AR15538 677 (March 10, 1994) p22.
SUDETIC, CHUCK
"Blood And Vengeance: One Family's Story Of The Massacre At Srebrenica And The Unending War In Bosnia."
AR15539 724-725 (December 28, 1995) pp90-91,93-94+.
SUGARMANN, JOSH
"Cease Fire."
AR15540 677 (March 10, 1994) pp30-34,36-38+.
SULLIVAN, RANDALL
"Death Of A Cheerleader."
AR15541 632 (June 11, 1992) pp159,161-163.
"The Seduction Of Peter Jay Rudge: Part One."
AR15542 648 (January 21, 1993) pp38-43,57.
"The Seduction Of Peter Jay Rudge: Part Two."
AR15543 649 (February 4, 1993) pp40-45,76-77.
"The Tonya Harding Fall: The Transformation of A Young Figure-Skating Champion Into The World's Most Visible Villainess."
AR15544 686-687 (July 14, 1994) pp80-82,84,86+.
"Unreasonable Doubt."
AR15545 697 (December 15, 1994) pp77-78,80-82+.
"Unreasonable Doubt: Part 2."
AR15546 698-699 (December 29, 1994) pp130-133,135+.
SULLIVAN, ROBERT
"In Search Of The Cure For AIDS: A Special Report From The Frontiers Of Science."
AR15547 679 (April 7, 1994) pp55,57,59-62+.
"Making Money The Old-Fashion Way: Despite Promises Of A High-Tech Revolution, College-Educated Americans Earn It Working On The Line."
AR15548 702 (February 23, 1995) pp53-56,89.
"The Small One: After Decades Of Preparing For A Big Earthquake Along The San Andreas Fault, California Scientists Now Believe It's The Increasingly Frequent Quakes That May Lay Waste To San Francisco Or Los Angeles."
AR15549 740 (August 8, 1996) pp42-47,72.
SULLIVAN, ROBERT E., JR.
"Great Reduced Expectations."
AR15550 652 (March 18, 1993) pp[enc.29,31+].
"Just Desserts: Can Ben And Jerry Make A Company As Good As Their Ice Cream?."
AR15551 634-635 (July 9, 1992) pp75,77,79.
"SUMMER MOVIE REPORT CARD."
AR15552 639 (September 17, 1992) p102.
"SUN STRATEGIES: THE BEST DEFENSE IS A GOOD DOSE OF SPF."
AR15553 633 (June 25, 1992) p38.
SUPER DJ DMITRY
"Raves."
AR15554 691 (September 22, 1994) p34.
SWEET, MATTHEW
"Raves."
AR15555 701 (February 9, 1995) p30.
SWENSON, JOHN
"Albert King: 1923-1992."
AR15556 649 (February 4, 1993) p12.
"Danny Gatton Tribute."
AR15557 702 (February 23, 1995) p35.
"The Essential Zappa."
AR15558 674 (January 27, 1994) p15.
"H.O.R.D.E. Of Hearing: The New Jamming Generation Hits The Road To Swap Solos And Party Down."
AR15559 663 (August 19, 1993) p12.
"John Campbell: 1952-1993."
AR15560 662 (August 5, 1993) p27.
"Rockin' Dopsie: 1932-1993."
AR15561 667 (October 14, 1993) p36.
SYMAN, STEFANIE
"Next Wave: The Last Word On All Things Computer."
AR15562 696 (December 1, 1994) p91.
"Next Wave: The Last Word On All Things Digital."
AR15563 722 (November 30, 1995) pp[enc.48].
"Peripheral Vision."
AR15564 709 (June 1, 1995) p73.

"Sound Factory: In Computer Labs, Dedicated Wireheads Give Pop Music A Digital Make-Over."
AR15565 708 (May 18, 1995) pp[enc.27-28].

T

TAKACS, ROBERT P.
"Our Lives, Our Music: Shake Your Money Maker."
AR15566 644 (November 26, 1992) p58.
TANNENBAUM, ROB
"Can Seal Handle Fame?: Or Will Success Drive The British Singer 'Crazy'?."
AR15567 618 (November 28, 1991) pp15,18.
"Country Roundup."
AR15568 628 (April 16, 1992) p17.
"Country's New Gold Rush: With Garth Brooks Leading The Way, Nashville Is Booming."
AR15569 628 (April 16, 1992) pp16-17.
"The Disciples Of Pot: Cypress Hill Says Marijuana's Getting A Bad Rap."
AR15570 631 (May 28, 1992) p18.
"The Man Who Would Be King Of Country: Billy Ray Cyrus Scores With 'Some Gave All'."
AR15571 636 (August 6, 1992) p29.
"Neil Tennant Of The Pet Shop Boys."
AR15572 671 (December 9, 1993) p22.
TAYLOR, LILI
"Raves."
AR15573 736 (June 13, 1996) p62.
"TECHNOPOP."
AR15574 658 (June 10, 1993) pp[enc.cover].
"TELL US ABOUT YOUR LIFE."
AR15575 636 (August 6, 1992) p8.
"TELL US ABOUT YOUR MUSIC."
AR15576 637 (August 20, 1992) p4.
TERRY, SARA
"Sins Of The Innocent: Children Are Falling Victim To A New Kind Of Sexual Offender—Other Children."
AR15577 616 (October 31, 1991) pp67,69-70,72.
TESTA, JIM
"Old Punks In Peril: No Green Day For '70s And '80s Pioneers."
AR15578 719 (October 19, 1995) p24.
"The Sounds Of Cyberspace."
AR15579 734 (May 16, 1996) p68.
AR15580 737 (June 27, 1996) p56.
"Unusual Suspects: Loud Lucy & Civ Defy Alterna-Rock Convention And Live To Talk About It."
AR15581 721 (November 16, 1995) pp98-100,103+.
THAYIL, KIM
"Raves."
AR15582 736 (June 13, 1996) p47.
THIGPEN, DAVID
"Eazy-E: Down By Law."
AR15583 657 (May 27, 1993) p24.
"Hammer Hurting; Shops For New Label."
AR15584 668 (October 28, 1993) p17.
"Pearl Jammin'."
AR15585 671 (December 9, 1993) p18.
"Restricted Access: A Major Record Chain Hits Rap And Rock With 18-To-Buy Labels."
AR15586 665 (September 16, 1993) p13.
"Seal, Delivered: "Seal" Chronicles Two Years Of Inner And Outer Turmoil."
AR15587 689 (August 25, 1994) p36.
"'Tommy' Sells Out."
AR15588 658 (June 10, 1993) p22.
"Up Against The Wal: Wal-Mart Keeps Albums—And Customers?—Out."
AR15589 676 (February 24, 1994) p16.
"The Yearn To Earn: Gang Starr Hit Pay Dirt With Streetwise Sounds."
AR15590 682 (May 19, 1994) p30.
"[THIS MONTH...]."
AR15591 616 (January 31, 1991) p8.
THOMAS, MICHAEL
"The Wild Side Of Paradise."
AR15592 632 (June 11, 1992) pp69-70.
THOMPSON, DAVE
"Afghan Whigs Get Soulful On Their New LP 'Black Love'."
AR15593 721 (November 16, 1995) p41.
THOMPSON, HUNTER S.
"Bill Clinton: The Rolling Stone Interview."
AR15594 639 (September 17, 1992) pp40-44,47,51+.
"Fear And Loathing In Elko."
AR15595 622 (January 23, 1992) pp22-29,31,54+.
"Fear And Loathing In Las Vegas."
AR15596 632 (June 11, 1992) pp45-48.
"He Was A Crook."
AR15597 684 (June 16, 1994) pp42,44,119.
"Memo From The National Affairs Desk."
AR15598 715 (August 24, 1995) p40.
"Mr. Bill's Neighborhood."
AR15599 639 (September 17, 1992) pp55-56,108+.
"Polo Is My Life: Fear And Loathing In Horse Country."
AR15600 697 (December 15, 1994) pp44-52,54-56+.
"Trapped in Mr. Bill's Neighborhood."
AR15601 686-687 (July 14, 1994) pp51-52,54-55+.
"25 Years Of Fear And Loathing."
AR15602 748 (November 28, 1996) pp[cover].
THORPE, HELEN
"It's Pat: Julia Sweeney's Gender-Bending Character Goes To Hollywood."
AR15603 691 (September 22, 1994) pp[enc.9-14].
TIEN, ELLEN
"Bustin' Loose."
AR15604 749 (December 12, 1996) pp75-76,78.
"Good Times: Morning Has Broken The Newest Looks Pop And Shine To Keep You Suited Up Long Past The Twilight's Last Gleaming."
AR15605 747 (November 14, 1996) pp100-101,103+.
TIERNEY, MICHAEL
"Our Lives, Our Music: Velvet Underground And Nico."
AR15606 644 (November 26, 1992) p58.
"THE "TIMES" THEY ARE A-CHANGIN'."
AR15607 700 (January 26, 1995) p39.
TIPPENS, ELIZABETH
"Mastering Madonna."
AR15608 639 (September 17, 1992) pp89,111.
TIRELLA, JOSEPH V.
"Police Sweep L.A. In The Wake Of Shakur Murder: Death Row Reportedly Under FBI Investigation."
AR15609 747 (November 14, 1996) p32.
"TO ROLLING STONE READERS."
AR15610 633 (June 25, 1992) p6.
AR15611 634-635 (July 9, 1992) p4.
TOURE
"Born To Be The Boss: All The Hail New Queen Of Hardcore Rap."
AR15612 663 (August 19, 1993) pp14-15.
"Clinton's Health Plan: More Funk 4U."
AR15613 669 (November 11, 1993) pp11-12.
"Dr. Dre Stares Down DWI Rap."
AR15614 693 (October 20, 1994) p47.
"83: It Was A Good Day."
AR15615 667 (October 14, 1993) p98.
"11: Walk This Way."
AR15616 667 (October 14, 1993) p73.
"52: Black Or White."
AR15617 667 (October 14, 1993) p90.

TOURE (continued)
"44: Night Of The Living Baseheads."
AR15618 667 (October 14, 1993) p85.
"49: By The Time I Get To Arizona."
AR15619 667 (October 14, 1993) p87.
"46: Goin' Back To Cali."
AR15620 667 (October 14, 1993) p87.
"43: Justify My Love."
AR15621 667 (October 14, 1993) p85.
"KRS-One."
AR15622 672-673 (December 23, 1993) p61.
"Me'shell NdegeOcello."
AR15623 670 (November 25, 1993) p32.
"'Round Midnight: A Tribe Called Quest Shift Into High Gear With Their New Album."
AR15624 678 (March 24, 1994) pp9-10.
"Run-D.M.C.: Back On The Throne."
AR15625 660-661 (July 8, 1993) pp15-16.
"Sandra Bernhard."
AR15626 692 (October 6, 1994) p30.
"16: Thriller."
AR15627 667 (October 14, 1993) p76.
"Street News."
AR15628 667 (October 14, 1993) p30.
"13: Love Will Never Do."
AR15629 667 (October 14, 1993) p73.
"34: Slave To The Rhythm."
AR15630 667 (October 14, 1993) p80.
"Tori Amos: The Power And The Passion."
AR15631 685 (June 30, 1994) pp66-68.
"12: Beat It."
AR15632 667 (October 14, 1993) p73.
"20: Like A Prayer."
AR15633 667 (October 14, 1993) p76.
"21: Gett Off."
AR15634 667 (October 14, 1993) p77.
"Where There's Smoke: Method Man Ignited Hip-Hop With Blunt Rhyme."
AR15635 702 (February 23, 1995) pp29,32.
"Young, Gifted And Bad."
AR15636 706 (April 20, 1995) p24.
TRAVERS, PETER
"Amateur Home-Theater Setups Created A Look Of High-Tech Chaos That Might Come To Typify Video In The Nineties: The TV Room As Booby Trap."
AR15637 619-620 (December 12, 1991) p197.
"Attack Of The Fall Flicks."
AR15638 743 (September 19, 1996) pp87-88,90.
"The Best In Video Laser."
AR15639 701 (February 9, 1995) p62.
"Big Hits, Bigger Misses."
AR15640 740 (August 8, 1996) p68.
"Bummer Summer: The First Harvest Of A Gutless Film Season Offers Slim Pickings."
AR15641 633 (June 25, 1992) pp47-49.
""Clerks"—Dangerous Talk."
AR15642 694 (November 3, 1994) p104.
"Dinosaur Summer: A T. Rex And A Terminator Aim To Stomp All Rivals, From Clint To The Coneheads."
AR15643 659 (June 24, 1993) pp87-88.
"Dubious Summer Trends."
AR15644 709 (June 1, 1995) p68.
"Dumb About Disc Players: A Guide To Choosing The Best Laser Players Without Straining Brain Or Budget."
AR15645 647 (January 7, 1993) p53.
"Early Starters."
AR15646 709 (June 1, 1995) p70.
"El Mariachi And The Sundance Kid."
AR15647 652 (March 18, 1993) pp45-47,49.
"Great Performances: The Year's Best."
AR15648 674 (January 27, 1994) p48.
AR15649 700 (January 26, 1995) p68.
"Holiday Hits And Misses."
AR15650 750-751 (December 26, 1996) pp206-207.
"Home Video: Broadway Goes Hollywood."
AR15651 683 (June 2, 1994) p76.
"Memo To The Academy On Its 64th Birthday: Retire Or Reform."
AR15652 627 (April 2, 1992) pp39-41.
"More Stunts, More Overpaid Stars, More Demi Moore Naked And More To The Point: Is Anything Any Good?."
AR15653 736 (June 13, 1996) pp56,58,61-62.
"Movie Extras."
AR15654 697 (December 15, 1994) p102.
"1993: The Year In Movies."
AR15655 672-673 (December 23, 1993) pp171-174.
"Oscar '95: The Fix Is In."
AR15656 705 (April 6, 1995) pp68-70.
"Oscar '96: Soo-Ey!."
AR15657 731 (April 4, 1996) pp65-66,68.
"Oscar Blindness."
AR15658 678 (March 24, 1994) pp99-100,104.
"Oscar Rejects: A Racist, Sexist And Gutless Academy Screws Up Big Time."
AR15659 653 (April 1, 1993) pp56-57,59.
"The Players 1992."
AR15660 645-646 (December 10, 1992) pp190,192-193.
"'Posse' Leader Mario Van Peebles Shoots From The Lip."
AR15661 658 (June 10, 1993) p76.
"Report From Sundance."
AR15662 703 (March 9, 1995) p70.
"Robert Rodriguez."
AR15663 652 (March 18, 1993) p47.
"Sally Potter: Introducing 'Orlando' Director."
AR15664 659 (June 24, 1993) p90.
"Saturday Night Jive."
AR15665 706 (April 20, 1995) pp85-86.
"Selling Sex In 'Showgirls'."
AR15666 719 (October 19, 1995) p156.
"Sex At Sundance."
AR15667 679 (April 7, 1994) p82.
"The 'Star Wars' Trilogy On Laser."
AR15668 669 (November 11, 1993) p81.
"Stupid Is As Stupid Does."
AR15669 691 (September 22, 1994) p106.
"Summer Movie Report Card."
AR15670 665 (September 16, 1993) p77.
"Summer With A Vengence: Why Hollywood Will Die Hard Trying To Bust Last Summer's Record."
AR15671 709 (June 1, 1995) pp67-68,70.
"Summer Wrap-Up."
AR15672 743 (September 19, 1996) p90.
"Ten Best Movies Of 1992."
AR15673 648 (January 21, 1993) p56.
"The 10 Best Movies Of 1994."
AR15674 698-699 (December 29, 1994) p196.
"The 10 Worst Movies Of 1994."
AR15675 698-699 (December 29, 1994) p199.
"Tom Hanks Rides Again."
AR15676 716 (September 7, 1995) p78.
""True Lies" And Sexual Violence."
AR15677 689 (August 25, 1994) p96.
"Video Laser Hot Picks."
AR15678 665 (September 16, 1993) p78.
"Video-Laser News."
AR15679 711 (June 29, 1995) p48.
"What TV Movies Are Doing Right."
AR15680 655 (April 29, 1993) p68.
"The Wide-Screen Factor."
AR15681 680 (April 21, 1994) p96.

TRAVERS, PETER (continued)
"Yabba-Dabba-Doo-Doo: A Summer Movie Guide To What's Fun Among The Dumb."
AR15682 684 (June 16, 1994) pp113-116.
"The Year In Movies."
AR15683 619-620 (December 12, 1991) pp191-192,194.
AR15684 698-699 (December 29, 1994) pp193-194,196+.
AR15685 724-725 (December 28, 1995) pp133-134,136+.
AR15686 750-751 (December 26, 1996) pp203-204,206.
"[TRENT HILL'S ESSAY]."
AR15687 672-673 (December 23, 1993) p10.
"TRIBUTE."
AR15688 645-646 (December 10, 1992) p161.
"TRIBUTES."
AR15689 750-751 (December 26, 1996) pp94,95-98.
TROITSKY, ARTEMY
"Moscow's Metal Melee: An Eyewitness Report From The Monsters Of Rock Tour."
AR15690 617 (November 14, 1991) p25.
"Three Days At The Barricades: How Rock & Roll, Fax Machines And The Hip Crowd Helped Crack The Coup."
AR15691 615 (October 17, 1991) pp77,79-81,103.
TUCK, STEPHANIE
"Hot Fashion."
AR15692 630 (May 14, 1992) pp95-99.
"Looks Like Team Spirit: On Their Way To Barcelona, Four Athletes Take A Break From Their Olympic Training To Try On American Clothes."
AR15693 628 (April 16, 1992) pp[enc.27-29+].
"Right Hair, Right Now: An Unkempt Mop Top Complements Today's Radical Biker Chic."
AR15694 618 (November 28, 1991) pp79-80,82.
"Styling A Greater Green Empire: Sebastian Inc. Gives Something Back To The Earth."
AR15695 638 (September 3, 1992) pp[enc.61-62].
"Sweet Surrender: Donning Dress-To-Kill Leather Jackets, The Midwestern Singer And The Vampire Slayer Give Themselves Up To A Day At The Beach."
AR15696 637 (August 20, 1992) pp44-47.

U

UDOVITCH, MIM
"[Bjork]."
AR15697 695 (November 17, 1994) pp68-69,89.
"Demi Moore = Sex."
AR15698 701 (February 9, 1995) pp38-41,67.
"The Girlie Show."
AR15699 667 (October 14, 1993) pp67,69-70.
"K. D. Lang: How Did A Lesbian, Feminist, Vegetarian Canadian Win A Grammy And The Hearts Of America?."
AR15700 662 (August 5, 1993) pp54-57.
"Mothers Of Invention: Women In Rock Talk About Scents, Sensibility And Sexism."
AR15701 692 (October 6, 1994) pp49-50,52-53+.
"Revenge Of The Weezer Nerds: They're Not Punk, They're Not Pop, They're Not Pretty, But They're Huge."
AR15702 704 (March 23, 1995) pp62-64,133.
"RuPaul."
AR15703 662 (August 5, 1993) p24.
"Thoroughly Modern Bjork."
AR15704 712-713 (July 13, 1995) pp76-79.
"UNCHARTED TERRITORY: 12 ARTISTS ON THE EDGE."
AR15705 721 (November 16, 1995) pp61-67,73-76+.
"[UNPRECEDENTED SWEEP]."
AR15706 624 (February 20, 1992) p7.
"[UPDATE]."
AR15707 633 (June 25, 1992) p5.
"UPDATE."
AR15708 722 (November 30, 1995) p16.
AR15709 723 (December 14, 1995) p22.
AR15710 724-725 (December 28, 1995) p24.
AR15711 726 (January 25, 1996) p12.
AR15712 728 (February 22, 1996) p16.
AR15713 729 (March 7, 1996) p6.
AR15714 732 (April 18, 1996) p16.

V

"VALUING THE FAMILY."
AR15715 694 (November 3, 1994) p49.
VAN BAKEL, ROGIER
"Geek Love: Strange But True Tales Of Stereo Obsession."
AR15716 748 (November 28, 1996) pp81-82,84-86.
VAN PARYS, BILL
"Laurie Anderson."
AR15717 706 (April 20, 1995) p33.
"Luscious Life."
AR15718 689 (August 25, 1994) p17.
"New York City."
AR15719 689 (August 25, 1994) p17.
"Two For The Road: On The Move With Those Sexual Screwups From 'Short Cuts,' Matthew Modine & Julianne Moore."
AR15720 667 (October 14, 1993) pp103-106,108+.
"THE VERVE PIPE."
AR15721 741 (August 22, 1996) p116.
VEYSSET, FREDERIQUE
"Walk On The West Side."
AR15722 638 (September 3, 1992) pp[enc.21-26+].
AR15723 Number not assigned.
"VIDEO & LASER HOT SHEET."
AR15724 644 (November 26, 1992) p78.
"VIDEO FILES."
AR15725 619-620 (December 12, 1991) p33.
VIG, BUTCH
"Behind The Sheen: Butch Vig."
AR15726 745 (October 17, 1996) p79.
VINCENTELLI, ELIZABETH
"Critics Comments."
AR15726a 726 (January 25, 1996) pp46,50-51.
"Sleater-Kinney."
AR15727 747 (November 14, 1996) p49.
"Sukia."
AR15728 747 (November 14, 1996) p52.
VIRSHUP, AMY
"Yahoo!: How Two Stanford Students Created The Little Search Engine That Could."
AR15729 722 (November 30, 1995) pp[enc.15-16+].
"THE VISION THING."
AR15730 667 (January 14, 1993) p77.
VIZARD, FRANK
"Let's Interactive: Breakthroughs In Digital Technology Promise To Bring A New Look To Your Television Set."
AR15731 618 (November 28, 1991) pp109,111.
"Lost In America—Not!: Navigation Systems And Cellular Phones Will Help You Get There From Here."
AR15732 631 (May 28, 1992) p67.

W

WALKER, JOHN
"Our Lives, Our Music: Stand!."
AR15733 644 (November 26, 1992) p50.
WALSH, JIM

"Paul Westerberg Looks Back, Moves Forward On New LP."
AR15734 722 (November 30, 1995) p29.
"Rock & Roll Summer: Minneapolis."
AR15735 710 (June 15, 1995) p52.
WALSH, KIRK
"Under Your Thumb: New Hand-Held Electronics Put Technology In The Grasp Of Your Hand."
AR15736 618 (November 28, 1991) p111.
WAREHAM, DEAN
"Raves."
AR15737 733 (May 2, 1996) p29.
WARNOCK, MICKEY
"Our Lives, Our Music: Led Zeppelin IV."
AR15738 644 (November 26, 1992) p58.
WATSON, ALBERT
"Albert Watson."
AR15739 643 (November 12, 1992) pp189-199,201+.
"[WE ARE PROUD...]."
AR15740 750-751 (December 26, 1996) p26.
WEBB, PETE
"Our Lives, Our Music: Nevermind."
AR15741 644 (November 26, 1992) p56.
WEBER, BRUCE
"Bruce Weber."
AR15742 643 (November 12, 1992) pp83-92.
WEIL, ELIZABETH
"Hot Author: Stephen Hunter."
AR15743 741 (August 22, 1996) p82.
"Hot Director: James Mangold."
AR15744 741 (August 22, 1996) p71.
"The Nasty Truth: Field-Tested techniques To Get The Love You Deserve."
AR15745 719 (October 19, 1995) pp137-138,140+.
"One Hot Minute."
AR15746 732 (April 18, 1996) pp[enc.19-20].
WEINER, TIM
"The Enemy Within: An Exclusive Excerpt From The Upcoming Book 'Betrayal' Tells The Inside Story of The Hunt For Aldrich Ames, The Deadliest Traitor In The History Of The CIA."
AR15747 711 (June 29, 1995) pp34-38,53-54+.
WEINGARTEN, MARC
"Not Guided By Voices: The return of Instrumental Rock."
AR15748 723 (December 14, 1995) p44.
"Palmer On Rock."
AR15749 718 (October 5, 1995) p48.
"Rocket Takes Off: San Diego's Favorite Sons Get Fans Fired Up."
AR15750 728 (February 22, 1996) p29.
WEINGER, HARRY
"Robert White 1936-1994."
AR15751 697 (December 15, 1994) p34.
WEIR, DAVID
"Tania's World."
AR15752 632 (June 11, 1992) pp100-101,103+.
WEISEL, AL
"The Braids Update Queen For The Hip-Hop Crowd."
AR15753 748 (November 28, 1996) p34.
"The Chemical Brothers Mix It Up With Noel Gallagher."
AR15754 749 (December 12, 1996) p25.
"Deep Forest's Lush 'Lullaby'."
AR15755 680 (April 21, 1994) p26.
"Freedom Rock: Rock Out Censorship Leads The Fight."
AR15756 693 (October 20, 1994) p50.
"Greed Or Need?: CDs Hit $17.98 In Record Biz's Banner Year."
AR15757 692 (October 6, 1994) p26.
"Hit, With A Bullet: Filter On Target With "Nice Shot"."
AR15758 712-713 (July 13, 1995) p37.
"Hot Alternative Subgenre: One-Hype Wonders."
AR15759 741 (August 22, 1996) p71.
"Hot Label: Ruffhouse."
AR15760 741 (August 22, 1996) p72.
"Hot Producer: Tim Simenon."
AR15761 741 (August 22, 1996) p78.
"Jeff Ament Of Pearl Jam."
AR15762 740 (August 8, 1996) p28.
"John Cale."
AR15763 745 (October 17, 1996) p48.
"LL Cool J."
AR15764 737 (June 27, 1996) p26.
"Maxwell."
AR15765 743 (September 19, 1996) p104.
"Out Of The Closet: Yoko Ono Lends Rare Lennon Gear To The Hall Of Fame."
AR15766 696 (December 1, 1994) p38.
"Portishead."
AR15767 702 (February 23, 1995) p38.
"Primitive Radio Gods Get The Blues."
AR15768 742 (September 5, 1996) p29.
"Ravestock."
AR15769 691 (September 22, 1994) p64.
"Republica."
AR15770 744 (October 3, 1996) p84.
"Saline Solution: Veruca Salt Wrap Their Hardcore Inside A Candy-Pop Coating."
AR15771 700 (January 26, 1995) pp19-20.
"Say Of The Lucas."
AR15772 694 (November 3, 1994) p37.
"Sticky Situation: A New Warning Label On MC Eiht's Hit CD Raises Some Epic Questions."
AR15773 690 (September 8, 1994) p32.
"Unusual Suspects: Loud Lucy & Civ Defy Alterna-Rock Convention And Live To Talk About It."
AR15774 721 (November 16, 1995) pp98-100,103+.
"The Video File."
AR15775 738-739 (July 11, 1996) p87.
WENNER, JANN
"Bill Clinton For President: A Rolling Stone Editorial."
AR15776 639 (September 17, 1992) p15.
"Bill Clinton: The Rolling Stone Interview."
AR15777 639 (September 17, 1992) pp40-44,47,51+.
"Clinton For President."
AR15778 747 (November 14, 1996) p19.
"[Editorial]."
AR15779 733 (May 2, 1996) p9.
AR15780 738-739 (July 11, 1996) p7.
AR15781 740 (August 8, 1996) p7.
AR15782 741 (August 22, 1996) p13.
AR15783 742 (September 5, 1996) p13.
AR15784 743 (September 19, 1996) p9.
AR15785 746 (October 31, 1996) p11.
"Editor's Notebook."
AR15786 734 (May 16, 1996) p11.
AR15787 735 (May 30, 1996) p3.
AR15788 736 (June 13, 1996) p11.
AR15789 737 (June 27, 1996) p7.
"Jagger Remembers: The Rolling Stone Interview."
AR15790 723 (December 14, 1995) pp49-58,60-62+.
"Jerry Brown For President: A Rolling Stone Editorial."
AR15791 629 (April 30, 1992) p7.
"John Lennon."
AR15792 641 (October 15, 1992) pp48-49,51.
"A Letter From The Editor."
AR15793 632 (June 11, 1992) p31.
AR15794 641 (October 15, 1992) p37.
AR15795 643 (November 12, 1992) pp49,51.
"Peter Townshend."
AR15796 641 (October 15, 1992) pp39-40.
"Phil Spector."
AR15797 641 (October 15, 1992) pp45-46.
"Portrait Of The Artist A A Journalist."
AR15798 749 (December 12, 1996) p11.

WENNER, JANN (continued)
"President Clinton: The Rolling Stone Interview."
AR15799 671 (December 9, 1993) pp40-45,80-81.
"To The Readers Of Rolling Stone."
AR15800 698-699 (December 29, 1994) p1.
"Toward A Sane National Drug Policy."
AR15801 681 (May 5, 1994) pp24-26.
WESSEL, CATHRINE
"Band On The Run: Life On The Road With The Health And Happiness Show."
AR15802 691 (September 22, 1994) pp[enc.17-20 +].
"WEST DES MOINES, IOWA."
AR15803 681 (May 5, 1994) p40.
WEXLER, JERRY
"The Chairman Of The Board: My Life In The Studio With Brother Ray, Lady Soul, Bob Dylan And The Wicked Pickett."
AR15804 650 (February 18, 1993) pp50-52,68.
WEYMOUTH, TINA
"Raves."
AR15805 746 (October 31, 1996) p36.
"WHAT YOU CAN DO."
AR15806 664 (September 2, 1993) p53.
"WHERE THE JOBS ARE."
AR15807 652 (March 18, 1993) pp[enc.6].
WHITE, ARMOND
"In Living Color."
AR15808 667 (October 14, 1993) pp73,76-77.
WHITE, TIMOTHY
"Billy Joel."
AR15809 641 (October 15, 1992) pp101-102.
"WHY ARE WE IN HAITI?."
AR15810 694 (November 3, 1994) p46.
"WICHITA, KANSAS."
AR15811 681 (May 5, 1994) p28.
WIEDERHORN, JON
"Blues With A Fuse: Jon Spencer Sparks An Explosive Trio."
AR15812 700 (January 26, 1995) p25.
"Cake."
AR15813 749 (December 12, 1996) p96.
"Cop Killer: The Sequel."
AR15814 711 (June 29, 1995) p19.
"Dwayne Goettel: 1964-1995."
AR15815 718 (October 5, 1995) p25.
"Eazy-E: 1963-1995."
AR15816 707 (May 4, 1995) p25.
"Eels."
AR15817 745 (October 17, 1996) p156.
"Engine Of Aggression: Anthrax Accelerate To The Forefront On 'Stomp 442'."
AR15818 722 (November 30, 1995) p34.
"Everything But The Girl's Ben Watt Makes Pleasant Pop From Personal Misery."
AR15819 738-739 (July 11, 1996) p22.
"Fiona Apple."
AR15820 746 (October 31, 1996) p84.
"In The News."
AR15821 700 (January 26, 1995) p25.
AR15822 702 (February 23, 1995) p25.
AR15823 703 (March 9, 1995) p26.
AR15824 704 (March 23, 1995) p36.
AR15825 706 (April 20, 1995) p32.
AR15826 707 (May 4, 1995) p29.
AR15827 708 (May 18, 1995) p34.
AR15828 709 (June 1, 1995) p21.
AR15829 710 (June 15, 1995) p32.
AR15830 711 (June 29, 1995) p23.
AR15831 712-713 (July 13, 1995) p45.
AR15832 714 (August 10, 1995) p30.
AR15833 715 (August 24, 1995) p30.
AR15834 716 (September 7, 1995) p25.
AR15835 717 (September 21, 1995) p32.
AR15836 718 (October 5, 1995) p26.
AR15837 719 (October 19, 1995) p25.
"The Jesus And Mary Chain Rage Against The Machine On 'I Hate Rock & Roll'."
AR15838 720 (November 2, 1995) p25.
"Kitsch Me, Stupid: Seattle's Super Deluxe Pucker Up."
AR15839 721 (November 16, 1995) p33.
"KMFDM Make Industrial Music The Old-Fashion Way—They Thrash Their Hardware."
AR15840 740 (August 8, 1996) p24.
"Kyuss The Sky: Retrodelic Generator Parties Breed An Electric Genre."
AR15841 692 (October 6, 1994) p24.
"LollaPalooza: Family Affair."
AR15842 715 (August 24, 1995) pp43-45,119.
"London Bridge: Cornershop Curry Western Flavor."
AR15843 728 (February 22, 1996) p32.
"Making History? A Marketing Blitz of Epic Proportions."
AR15844 710 (June 15, 1995) p24.
"Melvin Franklin: 1942-1995."
AR15845 705 (April 6, 1995) p28.
"Not Fade Away: Everclear Triumph Over Demons Of The Past."
AR15846 718 (October 5, 1995) p28.
"Package Goods."
AR15847 709 (June 1, 1995) p23.
"Pretty On The Outside: Echobelly Coat Perversity With Sugar Pop."
AR15848 720 (November 2, 1995) p22.
"R.E.M.: Tour On?."
AR15849 706 (April 20, 1995) p25.
"Rent Strikes."
AR15850 734 (May 16, 1996) pp54-58.
"The Road Less Traveled."
AR15851 714 (August 10, 1995) pp19-20.
"Rock & Roll Yearbook."
AR15852 750-751 (December 26, 1996) pp45-46,48,50 +.
"Rockin' And 'Rolling' Into Cyberspace."
AR15853 712-713 (July 13, 1995) p30.
"The Royalty Scam: R&B Foundation Rewards Underpaid Musical Pioneers."
AR15854 703 (March 9, 1995) p25.
"Scarce Survive Tragedy And Release Belated Debut."
AR15855 745 (October 17, 1996) p42.
"Soaking Up Inspiration From The Local Bowling Alley, Sponge Move From Grim-Faced Grunge To Blue-Collar Glam."
AR15856 742 (September 5, 1996) pp37-38.
"Spacehog: Revive Glam, Gender Bending And Mascara."
AR15857 734 (May 16, 1996) pp32,36.
"Static Electricity: Radiohead Transform Emotional Turmoil Into Kinetic Pop."
AR15858 716 (September 7, 1995) pp19,21.
"Superdrag Take Off For The Big Time At Top Speed."
AR15859 741 (August 22, 1996) p39.
"Tickets To Ride: Pearl Jam Hit The Road Their Way."
AR15860 708 (May 18, 1995) p28.
"To Hell And Back."
AR15861 727 (February 8, 1996) pp32-37.
"Tool Get Spiritual And Scatological With 'Aenima'."
AR15862 748 (November 28, 1996) p41.
"Weiland Arrested For Drugs."
AR15863 711 (June 29, 1995) p16.
"Who's On First?: Lollapalooza Hunts For A Headliner."
AR15864 705 (April 6, 1995) p28.
"Yatsura."
AR15865 747 (November 14, 1996) p60.
WIELENGA, DAVE
"The Dogg Walks."
AR15866 731 (April 4, 1996) pp22-24,26.
"A Free Man On Death Row: White Knight Bails Out Shakur."
AR15867 722 (November 30, 1995) p42.

"Hip-Hop Nation Is Shaken By Tupac Shakur Ambush Off Las Vegas Strip."
AR15868 745 (October 17, 1996) p40.
"In The Dogg House: Tha Dogg Pound Get Caught In The Middle."
AR15869 720 (November 2, 1995) p32.
WILD, DAVID
"The Adventures Of Miss Thing: In 4 Months Alanis Morissette Has Gone From Washed-Up Child Star To Queen Of This Year's Pop Culture Prom."
AR15870 720 (November 2, 1995) pp40-42,44,46+.
"Aerosmith's Hot Grip: Steven Tyler Promises New Album To Be The Band's Biggest, Scariest Yet."
AR15871 647 (January 7, 1993) p14.
"The Andy-Hero: In A Few Minutes, We Learn How Andy Rooney Has Survived 'Dateline,' Molly Ivins And Kurt Cobain."
AR15872 740 (August 8, 1996) p65.
"Anthrax Brings The 'Noise': The Thrash-Metal Kings Find A New Voice."
AR15873 656 (May 13, 1993) p31.
"Artists Join Forces For AIDS Album."
AR15874 636 (August 6, 1992) p21.
"Balancing Act: Eddie Van Halen."
AR15875 705 (April 6, 1995) pp42-46,48-49+.
"Beck: Thanks To 'Loser,' This Hip-Hop Folk Rocker Is The Most Unlikely Success Story Of The Year."
AR15876 680 (April 21, 1994) pp79-80.
"Better Red Than Dead: Learning To Live With Conan O'Brien."
AR15877 715 (August 24, 1995) p113.
"Beyond Cool."
AR15878 712-713 (July 13, 1995) p119.
"Beyond The Reruns."
AR15879 736 (June 13, 1996) p54.
"Birds On A Wire: Counting Crows Fight The Hype And Battle The Backlash As They Revitalize The Sound And Tradition of Classic Rock."
AR15880 685 (June 30, 1994) pp46-48,50,52+.
"Boardroom Shuffle: Baby Boomers Take Over At Major Labels."
AR15881 666 (September 30, 1993) p15.
"Bob Dylan Tribute: All-Star Show Tentatively Set For October."
AR15882 639 (September 17, 1992) p32.
"The Book On Genesis: Collins, Rutherford And Banks Write Another Chapter With Their New Album, 'We Can't Dance'."
AR15883 624 (February 20, 1992) p17.
"Bowie's Wedding Album: The Thin White Duke Returns With His First Solo Album In Six Years."
AR15884 648 (January 21, 1993) p14.
"Brother Ray Is At It Again: Ray Charles Moves Into The Nineties With His New Release, 'My World'."
AR15885 655 (April 29, 1993) p23.
"The Brothers Grim: Ray And Dave Davies Ponder Their Ongoing Sibling Rivalry On 'Phobia'."
AR15886 656 (May 13, 1993) p24.
"The Buddy System: The Networks' New fall Shows Ask, 'Can't We All Be Friends?'."
AR15887 716 (September 7, 1995) pp81,83-84.
"Canter's Rock On Rye: The Kibitz Room Serves Up An Electric Menu Of Matzo And Music."
AR15888 649 (February 4, 1993) pp11,27.
"Channel Surfing."
AR15889 719 (October 19, 1995) p161.
AR15890 720 (November 2, 1995) p79.
AR15891 721 (November 16, 1995) p119.
AR15892 722 (November 30, 1995) p79.
AR15893 738-739 (July 11, 1996) p101.
AR15894 740 (August 8, 1996) p65.
AR15895 741 (August 22, 1996) p107.
AR15896 742 (September 5, 1996) p71.
AR15897 745 (October 17, 1996) p139.
AR15898 746 (October 31, 1996) p73.
AR15899 747 (November 14, 1996) p121.
AR15900 748 (November 28, 1996) p139.
"Chris Isaak's Twin Peaks: The Pop Heartthrob Takes Two Steps Forward With A New Album And Movie."
AR15901 651 (March 4, 1993) p25.
"Chrissie Hynde Of The Pretenders."
AR15902 698-699 (December 29, 1994) p79.
"Clint Eastwood."
AR15903 715 (August 24, 1995) p32.
"Come Gather Round, People."
AR15904 644 (November 26, 1992) pp17,19.
"The Crap Is Out There: The Search For Signs Of Intelligent Life On Fall TV."
AR15905 743 (September 19, 1996) pp93-94,96.
"Crowes Take Flight."
AR15906 628 (April 16, 1992) p26.
"The Cult Of Ray: 'Seinfeld' Meets The Suburbs On CBS' 'Everybody Loves Raymond'."
AR15907 745 (October 17, 1996) p139.
"Cuts Like A Knife."
AR15908 654 (April 15, 1993) pp[enc.29-34].
"Dead Flowers?: Stone Roses Rise For A 'Second Coming'."
AR15909 706 (April 20, 1995) p30.
"The Devil Inside: For Danzig — The Man And The Band — That Old Black Magic Isn't Just A Sales Gimmick."
AR15910 678 (March 24, 1994) pp40-42.
"Donald Fagen: Doing It Again."
AR15911 623 (February 6, 1992) p24.
"Dysfunction Junction: The New Oprahs And Little Rickies Prove Talk Is Cheap."
AR15912 720 (November 2, 1995) p79.
"E!'s So Fine: A Network Boldly Says There's No Business But Show Business."
AR15913 719 (October 19, 1995) p161.
"Eazy-E: 1963-1995."
AR15914 707 (May 4, 1995) p25.
"[Editorial]."
AR15915 744 (October 3, 1996) p11.
"Faith No More."
AR15916 631 (May 28, 1992) p23.
"Forward Into The Past: Paul McCartney Wraps Up A World Tour And Gets Ready For A Beatles Reunion."
AR15917 675 (February 10, 1994) pp11-12.
"The Frat Trap: After A Decade As A Big College Band, Fighting Gravity Are Ready To Move Off Campus."
AR15918 730 (March 21, 1996) pp55-56,60,62+.
"Friends: Six Lives On Videotape."
AR15919 708 (May 18, 1995) pp62-64,67-69.
"Henley To Buy Walden Site."
AR15920 658 (June 10, 1993) p21.
"Hollywood Director David Fincher Returns To Video."
AR15921 745 (October 17, 1996) p44.
"Homeward Bound: Spearhead Redefine The Meaning Of Roots Rock."
AR15922 700 (January 26, 1995) p24.
"House Of Cards: Crowded House Mix Whimsy And Melancholy On 'Together Alone'."
AR15923 676 (February 24, 1994) p17.
"How Bad Can It Be? NBC's Hit Sitcom 'Men Behaving Badly' Is Pretty Good, But It Should Be Worse."
AR15924 748 (November 28, 1996) p139.
"In The News."
AR15925 663 (August 19, 1993) p20.
"It's A Mad, Mad, Mad About You World."
AR15926 706 (April 20, 1995) pp[enc.6-10+].
"Jackson: $20 Million From HBO."
AR15927 640 (October 1, 1992) p21.
"Jackson's Double Play: The Singer Steps Up To The Plate With A New Album And Movie."
AR15928 657 (May 27, 1993) p18.

WILD, DAVID (continued)
"Jay Leno."
AR15929 724-725 (December 28, 1995) pp76-78.
"John Travolta."
AR15930 724-725 (December 28, 1995) pp72-73.
"Johnny B. Gone."
AR15931 738-739 (July 11, 1996) p101.
"Joni Mitchell."
AR15932 641 (October 15, 1992) pp167-169.
"Jurassic Spark: Laura Dern."
AR15933 659 (June 24, 1993) pp34-38.
"Just Desserts."
AR15934 685 (June 30, 1994) p32.
"A Kid Makes 'News': Dave Foley Grows Up To Be A 'Newsradio' Star."
AR15935 729 (March 7, 1996) p57.
"L.A. Confidential."
AR15936 662 (August 5, 1993) p21.
AR15937 664 (September 2, 1993) p28.
AR15938 666 (September 30, 1993) p17.
AR15939 669 (November 11, 1993) p17.
AR15940 677 (March 10, 1994) p24.
AR15941 680 (April 21, 1994) p22.
AR15942 683 (June 2, 1994) p25.
AR15943 688 (August 11, 1994) p33.
AR15944 690 (September 8, 1994) p38.
AR15945 693 (October 20, 1994) p48.
AR15946 704 (March 23, 1995) p44.
"Led Zep: The Boxed Life."
AR15947 670 (November 25, 1993) p19.
"Lemon Fresh Joy."
AR15948 675 (February 10, 1994) pp34-35,38-39+.
"[Lenny Kravitz]."
AR15949 695 (November 17, 1994) pp60-61.
"Life After Def: The Post-Rap, Post-Metal World Of Rick Rubin."
AR15950 719 (October 19, 1995) pp62-64,66-67.
"A Life In The Balance: Jackson Browne Gets Serious About Love."
AR15951 667 (October 14, 1993) p28.
"The Long Road To Little Village: Four Distinguished Musicians Find A New Home."
AR15952 627 (April 2, 1992) pp15-16.
"Loosening The Beltway: Everybody's A Pundit On 'Politically Incorrect'."
AR15953 730 (March 21, 1996) p109.
"Lunatic Behavior: Soul Asylum Fight The Follow-Up-Album Blues."
AR15954 702 (February 23, 1995) p32.
"Majek Faskek: A Messenger Of World Music."
AR15955 626 (March 19, 1992) p20.
"Massive Attack: Infectious Dance Pop."
AR15956 616 (October 31, 1991) p25.
"Maureen Cox Starkey Tigrett: 1946-1994."
AR15957 701 (February 9, 1995) p24.
"'Melrose Place' Is A Really Good Show."
AR15958 682 (May 19, 1994) pp48-50,52-53+.
"Mick: Third Time A Charm?."
AR15959 640 (October 1, 1992) p25.
"Midseason Pre-Mortem."
AR15960 727 (February 8, 1996) p53.
"Mike Love Sues Brian Wilson: Claims He Co-Wrote Several Beach Boys Classics."
AR15961 640 (October 1, 1992) p21.
"The Mitch Is Back: Toweling Off For 'Baywatch Nights'."
AR15962 718 (October 5, 1995) p81.
"Monkees Redux?: Fox's New Show 'The Heights' Zeroes In On A Made-For-Television Blue-Collar Rock Band."
AR15963 642 (October 29, 1992) p36.
"Musical Chairs? Executive-Shuffle Rumors Rage On."
AR15964 715 (August 24, 1995) p37.
"New Facts On Porcaro Death."
AR15965 644 (November 26, 1992) p20.
"Not Out Of The Woods Yet: Don Henley Responds To Developer's Accusations."
AR15966 616 (October 31, 1991) p18.
"One Hot Minute."
AR15967 732 (April 18, 1996) pp[enc.7].
"One Hot Mother Of A Pepper: The Red Hot Chili Peppers Finally Get A New Guitarist And Gear Up To Make Their Next LP."
AR15968 665 (September 16, 1993) p16.
"101 Reasons To Watch TV."
AR15969 750-751 (December 26, 1996) pp209-210.
"One More 'Saturday Night': Will This Season Be A Fresh Start Or The Long Buh-Bye?."
AR15970 721 (November 16, 1995) p119.
"Out Of The Ordinary."
AR15971 653 (April 1, 1993) p20.
"Outtakes: On The Road And Behind The Scenes With Rolling Stone's Chief Photographer."
AR15972 670 (November 25, 1993) pp74-79,81,83+.
"[Paul Westerberg]."
AR15973 695 (November 17, 1994) pp106-107.
"Penn's 'Free-For-All': Singer Releases Stunning Second Effort."
AR15974 636 (August 6, 1992) p22.
"Pete Townshend."
AR15975 736 (June 13, 1996) p30.
"Plans For Dylan Tribute: Clapton, Harrison And Others To Perform."
AR15976 642 (October 29, 1992) pp23,81.
"Post Mac Attack."
AR15977 633 (June 25, 1992) pp32-33,50.
"Pre-Teenage Wasteland: Catching Saturday-Morning Fever."
AR15978 732 (April 18, 1996) p81.
"Quentin Tarantino: The Director Of Pulp Fiction And Reservoir Dogs Guns The Engine On Screen Violence And Twisted Wit."
AR15979 694 (November 3, 1994) pp76-78,80-81+.
"Raves."
AR15980 666 (September 30, 1993) p18.
"Reality Bites Back: In It's Fifth Season, 'The Real World' Spins Off Into Orbit."
AR15981 742 (September 5, 1996) p71.
"The Return Of Dr. Feelgood."
AR15982 666 (September 30, 1993) p21.
"Ringo: Confident And Sober, The Former Beatle Releases His Best Album In Nearly Two Decades."
AR15983 634-635 (July 9, 1992) pp87-89.
"Rock & Roll Hall Of Fame."
AR15984 651 (March 4, 1993) pp15-18.
"Sam Kinison: 1953-1992."
AR15985 631 (May 28, 1992) p26.
"The Second Coming!."
AR15986 717 (September 21, 1995) p93.
"Skit Happens: On HBO's New Sketch-Comedy Series, There's No Business Like 'Mr. Show' Business."
AR15987 747 (November 14, 1996) p121.
"Snakin Around."
AR15988 638 (September 3, 1992) pp[enc.9-12+].
"Sophie's Choice: Sophie B. Hawkins Realizes Her Vision And Creates A Smash Single."
AR15989 638 (September 3, 1992) pp24-25.
"The Soul Of The New Machine: Tin Machine Is More Than David Bowie's Latest Invention."
AR15990 616 (October 31, 1991) pp74-76,78,106.
"Spaghetti Western: The Singing Cowboy Junkie Margo Timmins And The Lone Star State's Own Lyle Lovett Get Duded Up Italian-Like."
AR15991 628 (April 16, 1992) pp[enc.9,11+].
"Spinal Tap."
AR15992 622 (January 23, 1992) p10.
"Starr Time For Ringo."
AR15993 626 (March 19, 1992) p18.
"Stones Take It To The Max: 'At The Max' Shows The Rolling Stones As They've Never Been Seen Before."

WILD, DAVID (continued)
AR15994 621 (January 9, 1992) p24.
"The Strange Loves Of Lyle Lovett."
AR15995 623 (February 6, 1992) p20.
"Surfing's Eco-Warriors: The Members Of The Surfrider Foundation Are Making Waves For Cleaner Coastal Waters."
AR15996 659 (June 24, 1993) pp70-72,74,93.
"The Ted Offensive: How Ted Koppel's 'Nightline' Rules The World."
AR15997 726 (January 25, 1996) p77.
"10,000 Maniacs On The Loose Again."
AR15998 637 (August 20, 1992) p17.
"'Tommy' Scores Again: An Old Tale Gets A New Twist On The Stage."
AR15999 638 (September 3, 1992) p16.
"Topcat: The Making Of "The Lion King"."
AR16000 686-687 (July 14, 1994) pp91-92.
"Tours: From Sex Pistols To Kiss, The Summer Of...'76?."
AR16001 736 (June 13, 1996) p52.
"Tuning Into Prine Time: John Prine Scores High In The Ratings With 'The Missing Years'."
AR16002 624 (February 20, 1992) pp15-16.
"Van Halen: Here, Now."
AR16003 650 (February 18, 1993) p16.
"Van Morrison."
AR16004 641 (October 15, 1992) pp149,152-153.
"War At Warners: Power Struggle Plagues World's Largest Label."
AR16005 714 (August 10, 1995) p24.
"Warner Bros.: A New Regime."
AR16006 700 (January 26, 1995) p22.
"The Weiss Man Cometh: Introducing Rob Weiss—Director, Bigmouth, Suburban Success Story."
AR16007 665 (September 16, 1993) pp[enc.33-34+].
"When Elvis Was King: New Box Set Compiles All Of Presley's Recordings From The Fifties."
AR16008 634-635 (July 9, 1992) p25.
"Who Is This Guy?."
AR16009 650 (February 18, 1993) pp44-45,47-48.
"Whole Lotta Rosie: With 'The Rosie O'Donnell Show' Around, Talk Becomes Slightly Less Cheap."
AR16010 741 (August 22, 1996) p107.
"Who's On Broadway?: Pete Townshend Discusses Bringing The Rock Opera To The Great White Way."
AR16011 652 (March 18, 1993) p21.
"Why Brooke, Why Now."
AR16012 744 (October 3, 1996) pp46-48,50,52+.
"Wilson Phillips."
AR16013 630 (May 14, 1992) p22.
"Win, Lose Or Drawl: Redneck Comic Jeff Foxworthy Tries To Prove That The South Can Do It Again—Again."
AR16014 746 (October 31, 1996) p73.
"Wings Over America: The Eagles Reunite For Their First Tour In 14 Years."
AR16015 685 (June 30, 1994) p23.
"'X' Files: Undercover."
AR16016 734 (May 16, 1996) pp38-42,74.
"'X'-Ploitation: Paranoids Terrorized By Copycat Thriller Series!."
AR16017 722 (November 30, 1995) p79.
"The Year In TV."
AR16018 724-725 (December 28, 1995) p141.
"Zappa Premiere Set: European Ensemble To Debut 'The Yellow Shark'."
AR16019 640 (October 1, 1992) p20.
WILKINSON, FRANCIS
"About Facing Chairman Nunn: Inside The Gay Lobby."
AR16020 656 (May 13, 1993) pp39-42,122.
"All The President's Men."
AR16021 664 (September 2, 1993) pp39-41,74.
"Before You Sign On The Dotted Line...: What The Republicans' Contract With America Means To You."
AR16022 700 (January 26, 1995) pp35-36.
"The Best Little Sinecure In Washington: No One Does Less With More Than The Federal Election Commission."
AR16023 680 (April 21, 1994) pp37-38,40.
"Bruce Babbitt: Is He Tough Enough To Save The Environment?."
AR16024 660-661 (July 8, 1993) pp46-48,51-52+.
"The Campaign-Reform Game."
AR16025 659 (June 24, 1993) p33.
"Can Janet Reno Bust The War On Drugs?: The New Attorney General Tries To Change The Debate On Drugs And Crime."
AR16026 658 (June 10, 1993) pp40-41,43.
"Clinton And Campaign Reform: The Sounds Of Silence."
AR16027 654 (April 15, 1993) pp31-32,72.
"Clinton's Credit: The 72-Hour Student Loan."
AR16028 689 (August 25, 1994) p53.
"The Great Western Cave-In: For Now, Political Forces Beat Market Forces."
AR16029 660-661 (July 8, 1993) p51.
"Guess Who's Coming To Legislate."
AR16030 682 (May 19, 1994) pp43-46,114.
"Gunning For Guns: Clinton Calls For Ideas On Confronting Violence."
AR16031 671 (December 9, 1993) pp36,39.
"The Hate Squad: The Religious Right Is Making A Killing From Bashing Clinton."
AR16032 698-699 (December 29, 1994) pp157,159-160+.
"If You Think You Made A Mistake In 1992, Think Again."
AR16033 694 (November 3, 1994) pp48-49,52,54+.
"Is This Any Way To Run A White House?: Clinton Finally Brings Change To Washington—A New Chief Of Staff."
AR16034 688 (August 11, 1994) pp40-42,44.
"More Washington Show Talk: In Today's Episode, TV Ruins Everything."
AR16035 671 (December 9, 1993) p38.
"None-A-Day: Is The FDA Out To Take Your Vitamins?."
AR16036 674 (January 27, 1994) pp31,33.
"On The Range, Political Forces Still Beat Market Forces."
AR16037 675 (February 10, 1994) p26.
"Phony Campaign Reform: Update."
AR16038 670 (November 25, 1993) p42.
"Pork To The People."
AR16039 691 (September 22, 1994) pp41,44-45.
"Power To The People: Hazel O'Leary Rewires The Department Of Energy."
AR16040 678 (March 24, 1994) pp33-36,108.
"A Separate Peace: The Clinton Administration Has Abandoned The Rhetoric Of The War On Drugs, But It Hasn't Stopped Fighting The War."
AR16041 681 (May 5, 1994) pp26-29.
"Sidewalks For Sale: Libertarians Are Flourishing On Capitol Hill, On Campus And On Line."
AR16042 705 (April 6, 1995) pp40-41,74.
"The Sinkable Carol Browner: New EPA Chief Finds Herself In Over Her Head."
AR16043 668 (October 28, 1993) pp45,47-48.
"When The Senate Comes Around: Cooler Heads Are Prevailing In That Other House On Capitol Hill."
AR16044 708 (May 18, 1995) pp47-49.
"Workers Of The World: A Portfolio."
AR16045 665 (September 16, 1993) pp54-58.
WILKINSON, PETER
"Death Of A Salesman."
AR16046 715 (August 24, 1995) pp58-60,62-65+.
"Dream Girl."
AR16047 693 (October 20, 1994) pp72-77,79-80+.
"Hot Director."
AR16048 630 (May 14, 1992) pp73,75,118.
"The Last Wave."
AR16049 706 (April 20, 1995) pp56-58,60-61+.
"Skate Till You Die: The Fast Times And Tragic Death of Jeff Phillips, The King Of Texas Skateboarding."

AR16050 690 (September 8, 1994) pp56-58,60-61+.
"The Young And The Reckless: The Pot Is Stronger, The Acid Milder, And The Kids Who Are Turning On Are Younger Than Ever."
AR16051 681 (May 5, 1994) pp29,32.
WILLIS, JESSICA
"Our Lives, Our Music: Ritual De Lo Habitual."
AR16052 644 (November 26, 1992) p54.
WILLS, GARRY
"Randy Shilts: The Rolling Stone Interview."
AR16053 666 (September 30, 1993) pp46-49,122+.
WING, ELIZA
"Nanci Griffith Comes Home: The Singer-Songwriter Settles Down After Years Of Late Nights And Hotels."
AR16054 627 (April 2, 1992) p22.
"A Singer Finds Her Voice: Maura O'Connell Redefines The Songstress As A Force To Be Reckoned With."
AR16055 616 (October 31, 1991) p24.
"The Story: A Signature Sound."
AR16056 636 (August 6, 1992) p24.
WITKIN, CHRISTIAN
"One Hot Minute."
AR16057 732 (April 18, 1996) pp[enc.7].
WOLFE, BILL
"These Heads Are Meant To Roll: Manufacturers Put A New—Not To Mention Detachable—Face On Car Audio."
AR16058 656 (May 13, 1993) p121.
WOLFE, TOM
"Ambush At Fort Bragg: Conclusion."
AR16059 750-751 (December 26, 1996) pp147-148,151+.
"Post-Orbal Remorse."
AR16060 632 (June 11, 1992) pp72-73,75.
"When The Mightiest Television Network Meets Up With The Lords Of Testosterone, Someone's Bound To Get Hurt."
AR16061 749 (December 12, 1996) pp61-62,64-66+.
WOLPIN, STEWART
"All I Want For Christmas."
AR16062 697 (December 15, 1994) p107.
"And Don't Forget...."
AR16063 696 (December 1, 1994) p86.
"The Big Noise In The Hood."
AR16064 630 (May 14, 1992) p117.
"Big Sound Tiny Package."
AR16065 691 (September 22, 1994) p109.
"Coming To A Screen Near You."
AR16066 706 (April 20, 1995) p93.
"Disc-O-Mania!!!."
AR16067 718 (October 5, 1995) p83.
"Don't Leave Home Without It."
AR16068 716 (September 7, 1995) p92.
"FAQ: Frequently Asked Questions About The World Wide Web."
AR16069 722 (November 30, 1995) pp[enc.24-28].
"Getting It All On Tape."
AR16070 668 (October 28, 1993) p91.
"Hot Stuff: New Electronics So Cool They Sizzle."
AR16071 664 (September 2, 1993) p73.
"Magnetic Field."
AR16072 625 (March 5, 1992) p81.
"Muscle Machines."
AR16073 721 (November 16, 1995) p122.
"One More For The Road."
AR16074 708 (May 18, 1995) p101.
"Screen Saviors."
AR16075 720 (November 2, 1995) p81.
"The Shape Of Things To Come."
AR16076 708 (May 18, 1995) pp[enc.32].
"Site Seeing On The Web."
AR16077 710 (June 15, 1995) p91.
"Solid-State Family Values: When It Comes Time To Do Something For Posterity, Buy A Camcorder."
AR16078 649 (February 4, 1993) p80.
"Super Highway Sounds."
AR16079 680 (April 21, 1994) p99.
"The Toys Of Summer."
AR16080 686-687 (July 14, 1994) pp46-47.
"Toys Of Summer."
AR16081 712-713 (July 13, 1995) p121.
"Toys Of Summer: Look Here For Something New Under The Sun."
AR16082 660-661 (July 8, 1993) pp123-124.
"Wired For Sound: With The Advent Of Cyberspace, Music May Never Be The Same."
AR16083 696 (December 1, 1994) pp72-73.
"Wysiwys: With These Camcorders, What You See Is What You Shot."
AR16084 693 (October 20, 1994) p139.
"Your Own Private Audio."
AR16085 704 (March 23, 1995) p134.
WOOD, JOE
"Denzel On Malcolm."
AR16086 644 (November 26, 1992) p39.
""X": Can Denzel Washington Make Malcolm Speak To A New Generation Of Americans?."
AR16087 644 (November 26, 1992) pp34-36,39-40+.
WOODARD, JOSEF
"The Pop Wizardry Of Sam Phillips."
AR16088 615 (October 17, 1991) p24.
WOODWARD, FRED
"Blues From On High: The Arc Angels Bring A Li'l Bit Of Heaven To Austin."
AR16089 654 (April 15, 1993) pp[enc.16-20+].
WRIGHT, CHRISTIAN
"Down But Not Out: Chicago's Eleventh Dream Day Picks Up The Pieces With 'El Moodio'."
AR16090 658 (June 10, 1993) p29.
WRIGHT, LAWRENCE
"False Messiah."
AR16091 632 (June 11, 1992) pp164-166.
"The Sensual Christian: Father Matthew Fox Extols The Joys Of Passion And Lust Over The Shame Of Original Sin True Believers."
AR16092 617 (November 14, 1991) pp78-80,84,86+.
WYMAN, BILL
"Fixing The Vote: The Grammys Set Up A Secret Panel To Make Nominations Hipper."
AR16093 729 (March 7, 1996) p13.
"Power Play: Meet The Men Who Rule Modern-Rock Radio."
AR16094 723 (December 14, 1995) pp31-32.
"Selling Out."
AR16095 721 (November 16, 1995) p40.
"Willie's Dream: Blues Heaven Buys Chess Studio."
AR16096 678 (March 24, 1994) p13.

Y

YANKOVIC, AL
"Raves."
AR16097 745 (October 17, 1996) p48.
YAUCH, ADAM
"Holy Rap Session."
AR16098 740 (August 8, 1996) p21.
"THE YEAR IN MUSIC."
AR16099 645-646 (December 10, 1992) pp30-33,39-40+.
"THE YEAR'S BEST IN LASER."
AR16100 727 (February 8, 1996) p46.
YOFFE, EMILY
"It's Party Time—It's Excellent: 'Wayne's World' Will Change The History Of Cinema—And Monkeys Might Fly Out Of Our Butt!."
AR16101 626 (March 19, 1992) pp34-35,37,39+.
YOUNG, BOB

"Toys Of Summer."
AR16102 634-635 (July 9, 1992) pp122-123.
YOUNG, CHARLES M.
"Behind Beavis And Butt-Head: The Stercoraceous Vision Of Mike Judge."
AR16103 663 (August 19, 1993) pp48,50,87.
"The Butthole Surfers."
AR16104 750-751 (December 26, 1996) pp116-118,120+.
"Getting Wise: Howard Zinn's Rage Against The Machine."
AR16105 745 (October 17, 1996) pp93-94,98+.
"Huh-huh, Huh-huh: MTV's Beavis And Butt-Head On What's Cool And What Sucks."
AR16106 663 (August 19, 1993) pp42-43,45,48.
"Meet The Beavis!: The Last Word From America's Phenomenal Pop Combo."
AR16107 678 (March 24, 1994) pp28-40,42.
"Noam Chomsky: Anarchy In The U.S.A.."
AR16108 631 (May 28, 1992) pp42-43,45-47+.
"Son Of Samurai."
AR16109 632 (June 11, 1992) pp124-126.
YOUNGS, BEN
"Our Lives, Our Music: Bat Out Of Hell."
AR16110 644 (November 26, 1992) p54.
YOW, DAVID
"Raves."
AR16111 736 (June 13, 1996) p30.

Z

ZEHME, BILL
"The Cindy Chronicles: The Body, The Marriage, The Mole."
AR16112 672-673 (December 23, 1993) pp93-95.
"Danamania!."
AR16113 656 (May 13, 1993) pp46-50,52,122.
"David Letterman: The Rolling Stone Interview."
AR16114 650 (February 18, 1993) pp32-34,36-37+.
"Hot Cover: Ask Killer Babe Sharon Stone About Sex And You'll Find She Has A Basic Instinct For It."
AR16115 630 (May 14, 1992) pp42-43,45-46+.
"Jerry & George & Kramer & Elaine: Exposing The Secrets Of SEINFELD's Success."
AR16116 660-661 (July 8, 1993) pp40-42,44-45+.
"Kings Of Comedy."
AR16117 616 (October 31, 1991) pp52-56.
"A Sad Day For Comedy."
AR16118 631 (May 28, 1992) p63.
"Tim Robbins: The Running Man."
AR16119 642 (October 29, 1992) pp54-56,78.
"Warren Beatty."
AR16120 632 (June 11, 1992) pp187-189.
ZESKIND, LEONARD
"Armed And Dangerous: The NRA, Militias And White Supremacists Are Fostering A Network Of Right Wing Warriors."
AR16121 720 (November 2, 1995) pp54-58,60-61+.
"The NRA Sees Red."
AR16122 720 (November 2, 1995) p58.
ZEVIN, DAN
"Dancing In The Seats: Roll Over Beethoven, The Professors Of Pop Have Arrived."
AR16123 639 (September 17, 1992) pp83-84,88,112.
"Hot Disease: Ulcers."
AR16124 741 (August 22, 1996) p77.
"Hot Drink: Orbitz."
AR16125 741 (August 22, 1996) p82.
"Hot List."
AR16126 630 (May 14, 1992) pp83-84,89-92.
"Hot Magazine: Loaded."
AR16127 741 (August 22, 1996) p78.
"Hot TV Star: Brandy."
AR16128 741 (August 22, 1996) p74.
"How To Fake A Resume: Entry-Level Lessons For The Real World."
AR16129 678 (March 24, 1994) p51.
"Keep On Pushing!: The Strange And Twisted Tale Of The United States Olympic Bobsled Team."
AR16130 624 (February 20, 1992) pp29,31-32.
"Let's Go Or Let's Not And Say We Did: Why You Can't trust The Best-Selling Harvard Travel Series."
AR16131 704 (March 23, 1995) pp72-77,117.
"Roommatism: How To Live With Others Without Killing Yourself."
AR16132 693 (October 20, 1994) pp131-132.
ZICKLIN, ERIC
"Mod Jobs: Strange And Twisted Paths To Contentment And Prosperity."
AR16133 693 (October 20, 1994) pp125-126,128+.

TITLE INDEX TO ARTICLES & COLUMNS

A

The A List: Celebrity Guidance Counselors Recommend One Book, One Movie, One Recording That Will Change Your Life AR15394
ABC Television Boots Concert-Tape Traders Off Its America Online Site AR14458
About Facing Chairman Nunn: Inside The Gay Lobby AR16020
An Abuse Of Trust? Michael Jackson Defends His Honor AR13928
Achin' To Be Understood: The Rolling Stone Interview With Paul Westerberg AR14672
Achtung, Babies! A New U2 Album! AR13691
Acid Damage: The Strange, Tragic Tale Of Psychedelic Icon Roky Erickson's Descent Into Madness AR14624
The Acid Test: Deadheads Face Hard Time In LSD Crackdown AR15499
Acquired Taste: G. Love Serves A New Platter With Special Sauce AR13795
Acting!!! Genius!!! Brilliant!!! AR13213, AR14812
The Adventures Of Miss Thing: In 4 Months Alanis Morissette Has Gone From Washed-Up Child Star To Queen Of This Year's Pop Culture Prom AR15870
Aerosmith Box: A Hard-Rock Primer AR14739
Aerosmith In A Hard Place: New Album Is Delayed Amid Rumors Of Drugs, Bickering And Behind-The-Scenes Firings AR13272, AR14152
Aerosmith's Hot Grip: Steven Tyler Promises New Album To Be The Band's Biggest, Scariest Yet AR15871
Afghan Whigs Get Soulful On Their New LP 'Black Love' AR15593
After South Central: The White Conscience AR14059
After The Storm: Billy Joel Turns To Beethoven For 'Dreams' AR13796
Aftermath: In Rwanda A Year After The Massacre, There Is Still No Justice, No Peace AR14521, AR15339
The Agony And The Ecstasy: Evan Dando On The Highs And Lows Of Being The King Of College Charts AR13853
Agony And The Ecstasy: Kevin Salem Turns Bitter Times Into Blissful Blasts AR14039
Ah, The Smell Of It: L7 Bask In The Sweet Stink Of Success AR13391
AIDS And Rock: Sound Of Silence AR14205, AR14224
AIDS And The Media: Shifting Out Of Neutral AR14326
Aimee Mann AR13487
Al Pacino: The Rolling Stone Interview AR13413
Albert Collins 1932-1993 AR13765
Albert Goldman 1927-1994 AR14361
Albert King: 1923-1992 AR15556
Albert Watson AR15739
Alejandro Escovedo AR13692
Alice Through The Looking Glass: The Dark Brooding Side Of The Seattle Scene AR15160
Alison Steele: 1937-1995 AR14539
All Guns, No Butter: Inside Somalia, A Starving Nation Armed To The Teeth AR14993
All I Want For Christmas AR16062
All She Wants AR13797
An All-Star Experience: Jimi Hendrix Is Feted On Tribute Album AR13929
All Systems Go: Whether It's Budget Audio For A Dorm Room Or Home Theater For A Mansion, One Of These New Setups Is Right For You AR13638
All The President's Men AR16021
All They Need To Know They Learned In Hollywood AR13478
Altered Stakes: Don Law Cuts Out The Middleman AR13058
Alternative Music AR14740
The Alternative Underground: Bands On The Real Cutting Edge Turn Out For Six-day Washington Festival AR15199
Alt.Rock AR14276
Amateur Home-Theater Setups Created A Look Of High-Tech Chaos That Might Come To Typify Video In The Nineties: The TV Room As Booby Trap AR15637
Ambersunshower AR13184
Ambush At Fort Bragg: Conclusion AR16059
A.M.C.'s S.F. AR15235
American Stars N' Bars: Living History Steals The Show At SXSW AR13693
A-Muze Yourself: From Abba To Zappa: A New Computer Gives Fans Fingertip Access To Disc Data AR14362
Anatomy Of A Murder: How Corporate Lobbyists Plotted To Kill Of Direct Student Lending AR13269
And A Happy New Gear AR13100
And Don't Forget... AR16063
And If You Still Don't Get It... AR14994
And We Bid You Good Night: Artists And Colleagues Pay Tribute To Garcia AR12959
The Andy-Hero: In A Few Minutes, We Learn How Andy Rooney Has Survived 'Dateline,' Molly Ivins And Kurt Cobain AR15872
Angelique Kidjo: Politics With A Beat AR12986
Ani DiFranco AR14607
Animated Arguments: Why The Show's Critics Just Don't Get It AR14327
Anthrax Brings The 'Noise': The Thrash-Metal Kings Find A New Voice AR15873
Antonio Carlos Jobim: 1927-1994 AR13766
Are The Kids All Right? As More Moms Enter The Pop-Music Work Force, Rock & Roll Nannies Have Their Hands Full AR13488
Are You Xperienced?: On The Fashion Tip With Kim Gordon Of Sonic Youth AR14813, AR15385
Aren't Stickers Enough? A Revived PMRC Pushes For A Stringent New Record-Ratings System AR15492
Armed And Dangerous: The NRA, Militias And White Supremacists Are Fostering A Network Of Right Wing Warriors AR16121
Arrested Development: Relaying Positive Messages AR15107
[Art Department] AR12974
Art Garfunkel AR13489
The Art Of Noise: The New Rock-Poster Genius Of Frank Kozik AR14344
The Art Of The Deal: The Real Arithmetic Behind The New Superstar Contracts AR13930
Art Students In America AR13214
Art Versus Commerce AR13613
Arthur Alexander: 1940-1993 AR13287
Artist Biographies AR12918
Artist Biographies [cont.] AR12919
Artists Join Forces For AIDS Album AR15874
Artists' Picks AR12975
Artists' Picks: 1992 Music Awards AR12976
Artists' Picks: 1993 Music Awards AR12977
As The World 'Terns: More Weird Tales Of Internships AR15226
[ASCAP-Deems Taylor Award] AR12978
[ASCAP-Deems Taylor Awards] AR12979, AR12980
Ask A Marine AR14140
Ass Ponys AR15028
The Astral Jane: Jane Siberry Makes Metaphysical Pop With Heart AR12970
Astro Freaks: 2000 AR13392
Atco Folds; More Cuts Expected AR13931
Atlanta AR13038
Atomic Logic: The Bomb In The Post-Cold War World AR15179
Attack Of The Cyber-Rockers: New Computer Rocker Jocks Get Their Modems Working AR13932
Attack Of The Fall Flicks AR15638
Audio Power To The People: Now Is The Time To Exercise—And Enjoy—Your Right To Low-Cost Hi-Fi AR13639
Aunts' Indie Plans AR15150
Australia's Other Stars: Aboriginal Bands Are Making Their Mark On Music From Down Under AR13694
[Awards] AR12983, AR12984
Axl On Trial AR13764
Axl Rose AR14741
Axl's St. Louis Blues: Singer Arrested In New York For Riot Charges AR14673

B

Back In The Saddle: C&W Outlaw Steve Earle Returns From His Lost Years AR14214
Back To The Back Of The Bus?: Clinton's Mixed Signals On Civil Rights AR14060
Back To The Garden AR14017
Backbeat: For The Soundtrack Of The Beatles Biopic, An Alternative Supergroup Came Together AR13196
Bad Livers AR13393
Bad To The Bone: John Mellencamp Strips Down To Fighting Trim On "Dance Naked" AR13414
Balancing Act: Eddie Van Halen AR15875
Ballad Of A Teenage Queen AR13215
The Ballad Of Yoko: The B-52's Kate Pierson Talks With Yoko Ono AR15095
Ballroom Blitz AR13933
Band On The Run: Life On The Road With The Health And Happiness Show AR15236, AR15802
Banding Together: Underground Rockers Fight For Abortion Rights AR12927
Barry Diller: The Rolling Stone Interview AR14005
Barry White AR13490
Basehead: Charting A New Course For The Hip-Hop Generation AR14464
Bassman's Holiday: Mike Watt Casts An All-

Star Solo Album AR13462
The Bat's Meow: Catwoman Michelle Pfeiffer AR14220
The Battle For Walden Woods: Don Henley Helped Save The Trees, But Some Preservationists Say He Doesn't Know When To Quit AR14427
BBC Bonanza: Vintage U.K. Radio Concerts Now On CD AR13767
Beached Monster AR15237
Beatle On The Block: Rare Tape Of An Early John Lennon Performance To Be Auctioned In London AR14363
Beautiful Loser: Video Director Steve Hanft's Scruffy Style Has Taken Him From Beck To Hootie AR13629
Beck Is Back: The Reclusive Guitarist Returns With Two Albums AR15414
Beck: Resident Alien AR13491
Beck: Thanks To 'Loser,' This Hip-Hop Folk Rocker Is The Most Unlikely Success Story Of The Year AR15876
Becoming Juliana Hatfield AR13685
Before You Sign On The Dotted Line...: What The Republicans' Contract With America Means To You AR16022
Behind Beavis And Butt-Head: The Stercoraceous Vision Of Mike Judge AR16103
Behind The Fly: Bono AR14465
Behind The Sheen: Butch Vig AR15726
Behind The Zines: The Chronic Urges And Ultraobsessions Of Do-It-Yourself Publishing AR15395
Being There; The History Of Rock & Roll Photography AR14221
Being There: Wherever The Celebrated And Notorious Set Down In The Eighties, Jean Pigozzi Was There AR15096
Belly: Tanya Donelly Finds Her Lucky 'Star' AR14674
Ben Lee AR12920
Benedictine Brawl AR14742
The Benefit Blitz: Rockers Put Out For Various Pet Projects AR14743
Bernard Edwards 1952-1996 AR14215
The Best In Video Laser AR15639
The Best Little Sinecure In Washington: No One Does Less With More Than The Federal Election Commission AR16023
Best New Band: Elastica AR13451
Better Red Than Dead: Learning To Live With Conan O'Brien AR15877
Better Workers Or Better Jobs? AR14061
Bettie Serveert: A Dutch Band Plays A Sweeter Kind Of Grunge AR15200
Beyond Cool AR15878
Beyond The Low Water Mark: A Treasure Diver Learns That Some Customers Can Drive A Hard Bargain, In This Excerpt From The New Novel 'Where Is Joe Merchant?' AR13155
Beyond The Reruns AR15879
The Big Black Boot: What Do Loggers, Hipsters, Bikers And Hikers Have In Common? AR13216
Big Boom In Industrial Metal: Helmet Signs Million-Dollar Deal With Interscope AR12987
Big Daze Out: Goin' Off The Deep End At The Big Day Out AR13695
Big Hits, Bigger Misses AR15640
The Big Lie: A Republican Majority Doesn't Mean A Reactionary Mandate AR14648
Big Names, Big Bucks AR13059
The Big Noise In The Hood AR16064
The Big Pay Back: The R&B Foundation Honors Its Stars AR14018
The Big Payback: Coolio Gets A Phat Return On His Dues With "Fantastic Voyage" AR13320
The B.I.G. Payback: Notorious B.I.G. Is Living Large—The Legal Way AR13626
The Big Scare: Heart Attack Trips Up Mellencamp AR14456
The Big Show: Hall Of Fame's Labor Day Lineup AR13288
The Big Sleaze AR13140
Big Sound Tiny Package AR16065
The Big Squeeze: Tuition Is Up, Salaries Are Down, And The Government Couldn't Care Less AR15347
Big Star: The Strange Life And Resurrection Of An American Power-Pop Legend AR15120
Big Sugar Vs. The Everglades AR13922
Big Talk In Little Rock AR14062
The Big Three's Best Bets AR14655
Big Time: Being Hip Is Something That Dwight Yoakum Does Best AR15364
Big Tours Buoy Promoters' Spirits [and other news] AR13934
Bill 2982: No Sale AR13197
Bill And Hillary Will See You Now AR14063
Bill Clinton For President: A Rolling Stone Editorial AR15776
Bill Clinton: The Rolling Stone Interview AR14064, AR14995, AR15594, AR15777
Bill Graham's Last Waltz AR13935
Bill Monroe: Father Of Bluegrass Is Dead At 84 AR13415
[Billie Joe] AR13652
Bill's Mix: Right Ends, Left Means AR14065
Billy Corgan Talks: The Smashing Pumpkins Leader On Death, Drugs And The Future Of His Band AR13696
Billy Joel AR13492, AR15809
Billy Joel's New Legal Firestorm AR13936
Birds On A Wire: Counting Crows Fight The Hype And Battle The Backlash As They Revitalize The Sound And Tradition of Classic Rock AR15880
Birmingham, Alabama AR13043
Birth Of The Gearhead Nation: Out For A Clunk With The Pioneers Of Mountain Biking As They Come To Grips With Their Funky Past And Muddy Future AR13153
Bis AR14213
A Bit Of Guitar Heaven: Austin's Arc Angels Prove They're More Than Just Another Blues-Rock Band AR14625
Bittersweet Relief: Rockers Face The Health-Care Blues AR14019
[Bjork] AR15697
Black & Blue: Me'shell NdegeOcello Fights For Your Rights On 'Peace Beyond Passion' AR15110
The Black Crowes AR14225
Black Francis's Name Game: The Pixies Frontman Nutures Another Persona With 'Frank Black' AR13798
Black Like Me AR15477
Blood And Vengeance: One Family's Story Of The Massacre At Srebrenica And The Unending War In Bosnia AR15539
Blood On The Tracks: Warner Bros. Gets Hit In A Boardroom Shootout AR14642
Blow: How A Small-Town Boy Made $100 Million With The Medellin Cocaine Cartel And Lost It All AR15105
Blue Hawaii AR14560
Bluegrass: Then And Now AR13768
Blues From On High: The Arc Angels Bring A Li'l Bit Of Heaven To Austin AR14626, AR16089
Blues Power: Stevie Ray Vaughan Honored At Fete AR14627
The Blues Traveler Rock & Roll Medicine Show AR15121
Blues With A Fuse: Jon Spencer Sparks An Explosive Trio AR15812
Bluesman Willie Dixon: 1915-1992 AR13056
Blur: The New 'Leisure' Class AR14866
Bo Diddley AR13133
Boardroom Shuffle: Baby Boomers Take Over At Major Labels AR15881
Bob Dylan AR14513
Bob Dylan Tribute: All-Star Show Tentatively Set For October AR15882
Bob Stinson: 1959-1995 AR14675
Bob Thiele 1922-1996 AR13769
Body Count Shows Canceled, 'Cop Killer' Protest Continues As Police Refuse To Provide Security AR14466
Bombay: Despite Crushing Poverty And Overpopulation, A Mighty Middle-Class Economy Has Turned Bombay Into A City Of Hope AR14634, AR15340
Bone Of Contention: Fishbone Bassist Accused Of Attempted Kidnapping AR14020
Boning Up: Neither Drum-Beating Nor Breast Beating, Men's Studies Comes Into Its Own AR13907
Bonnie Raitt AR13493, AR14196
Bono On Bob AR13097
The Book On Genesis: Collins, Rutherford And Banks Write Another Chapter With Their New Album, 'We Can't Dance' AR15883
Books AR13098, AR13099
The Boom Goes Bust AR13452
Born To Be The Boss: All The Hail New Queen Of Hardcore Rap AR15612
Bounty Hunter AR13045
Bowie's Wedding Album: The Thin White Duke Returns With His First Solo Album In Six Years AR15884
A Boy And His Gun: An American Tragedy AR13273
Boy George AR13494
Boy George Plays 'The Crying Game' AR14364
Boys: Hanging With The Spur Posse AR12946
Boys' Life: Silverchair, Food Fights Are More Fun Than Selling Millions Of Records AR13697
Boys To Men AR14467
Boys To Men: The Pharcyde Break Boundaries On 'LabCabin' AR12928
Brace Yourself! Whale Sink Their Teeth Into Your TV AR14365
The Braids Update Queen For The Hip-Hop Crowd AR15753
Brave New Home: Couch Potatoes Of The Future, Fear Not AR14441
Breaking Silence: Scott Weiland Of Stone Temple Pilots Opens Up And Gets Busy AR13362
A Breed Apart: Powered by The Musical Vision Of Kim Deal And The Free Spirit Of Her Sister, Kelley, The Breeders Bring Soul And Sass To Punk Rock AR15365
Brian Wilson AR13625
Briggs, David 1944-1995 AR13149
Bringing Up Baby: A Behind-The-Scenes Look At The Making Of U2's New Album AR13600
Britain's Class Act: Blur Stand Up For Their Mod-Rock Roots On "Parklife" AR13376
The British Aren't Coming: Is The Newest Wave From The U.K. A Washout? AR15415

Brother Ray Is At It Again: Ray Charles Moves Into The Nineties With His New Release, 'My World' AR15885
The Brothers Grim: Ray And Dave Davies Ponder Their Ongoing Sibling Rivalry On 'Phobia' AR15886
Brownie McGhee 1915-1996 AR14216
Bruce Babbitt: Is He Tough Enough To Save The Environment? AR16024
Bruce Kaplan: 1945-1992 AR15161
Bruce Plans Late-Summer Tour [and other news] AR13937
Bruce: Still The Boss In Europe AR13312
Bruce Weber AR15742
Bruce's Lucky Touch: Two New Albums Put Springsteen Back In The Rock & Roll Spotlight AR14197
Bryan Ferry AR13416
Buchanan Rethinks The American Empire AR14066
Buddy Guy: His Time Is Now AR15463
The Buddy System: The Networks' New fall Shows Ask, 'Can't We All Be Friends?' AR15887
Buffalo Stance: Boston's Buffalo Tom Steer Clear Of The Musical Wildlife AR14676
Building On Rock: A Summer '95 Opening Is Expected On The Long-Awaited Rock Hall Of Fame AR13653
Bulletin Boards: News From Cyberspace AR14328
Bullets & Bombs AR13157
Bummer Summer: The First Harvest Of A Gutless Film Season Offers Slim Pickings AR15641
Burlington, Vermont AR13159
Burn, Baby, Burn: The Women Of TLC Stay Cool Under Fire AR13321
Burnin' And Lootin': Tony Toni Tone Fire Up The Funk AR14226
Burning Rubber: Elastica Hit The U.S. At Full Throttle AR14540
Bush: Nirvana Wanna Bes AR13377
Bush Whacked! An Unknown English Band Takes America By Surprise AR14346
The Bush Years: Staying The Course AR13191
The Bush Years: Supreme Cruelty AR13192
The Bush Years: The Environmental President AR13193
Bush's Hits AR15238
Bush's Tax-Cut Follies: Rich Entertainment AR14067
Bustin' Loose AR14814, AR15604
But Can He Win? AR14649
The Butthole Surfers AR16104
Buy One, Get One Free: Rocket From The Crypt And Drive Like Jehu Put San Diego On The Rock Map AR14289
The Buzz At Sundance AR13161
Buzz Been: Did Radio Kill MTV's Video Star? AR13060

C

Cake AR15813
Cake Like AR12988
The Call Of The Wild: To The People On The Edge Of The Environmental Movement, The Program To Bring Back The Wolf Has A Big Problem—It Isn't Natural AR14527
Cameron Diaz AR13495
Camille Paglia: Lit Crit's Snit Fits AR14421
The Campaign AR15039
The Campaign: Clinton Takes A Side Trip AR15040
The Campaign: George B. In Free Fall AR15041
The Campaign: George B. Packs For Japan AR15042
The Campaign: George B's Economic Plan AR15043
The Campaign: George Bush Makes A Decision AR15044
The Campaign: George Bush, The Candidate Of Change AR15045
The Campaign: George's Solution For Domestic Problems AR15046
The Campaign: G.H.W. Bush Sees His 1st Bar Code AR15047
The Campaign: G.H.W. Bush Thinks About The Common Man AR15048
The Campaign: GOP Hats In The Ring AR15049
The Campaign: Laid Fresh Every Day! AR15050
The Campaign: Movin' On AR15051
The Campaign: Old Math AR15052
The Campaign: President Bush Tours U.S. Cities AR15053
The Campaign-Reform Game AR16025
The Campaign: Supreme Court Coatroom, Summer 1992 AR15054
The Campaign: Trust-O-Meter AR15055
Can Clinton Put Life In The Party? AR14068
Can Doug Wilder's G.O.P. Tricks Save The Democrats? AR14639
Can Janet Reno Bust The War On Drugs?: The New Attorney General Tries To Change The Debate On Drugs And Crime AR16026
Can Seal Handle Fame?: Or Will Success Drive The British Singer 'Crazy'? AR15567
Can The Media Do The Right Thing? AR14329
Can The Presidents Of The United States Of America Live Up To The Majesty & Stupidity Of Their Name? AR13355
Candlebox AR13654
Canter's Rock On Rye: The Kibitz Room Serves Up An Electric Menu Of Matzo And Music AR15888
The Capital Gang Bang: The Failure Of The Washington Press Corps AR14330
A Capital Idea: Rockers Run Labels For Fun 'N' Profit AR15219
Car Stereos For Spring '96: Roadworthy Companions With Distinct Personalities AR13101
The Cardigans Wear Their Loopy '60s Influences On Their Sleeves AR15029
Carpenters Collection AR13496
The Cartels Would Like A Second Chance AR15329
Casey Scott: 'City' Slacker AR15162
Casualties Of War AR15341
Cat Power AR15353
Cathy Dennis: One From The Heart AR13799
Caught in The Net: The Cautionary Tale Of A Cornell Student Who Posted A Suicide Note In Cyberspace AR14744
CD News AR13167, AR13168, AR14258, AR14259, AR14260, AR14261, AR14262, AR14263, AR14264, AR14265, AR14266, AR14267, AR14268, AR14269, AR14270, AR14271, AR14272, AR14273
CD-Package Standard Set AR13938
CDs Put A New Spin On Your PC: Multimedia Software Brings Video And Sound Together With Your Computer AR13034
Cease Fire AR15138, AR15540
Celebrity Guidance Counselors AR13169
Certified Punk: Claw Hammer Nail It With 'Thank' AR13403
Chainsaw Kittens: Grungy Glam, Oklahoma Style AR15441
The Chairman Of The Board: My Life In The Studio With Brother Ray, Lady Soul, Bob Dylan And The Wicked Pickett AR15193, AR15804
Channel Surfing AR13171, AR13172, AR13173, AR13174, AR13175, AR13176, AR13177, AR13178, AR15889, AR15890, AR15891, AR15892, AR15893, AR15894, AR15895, AR15896, AR15897, AR15898, AR15899, AR15900
Channel Surfing: Cable TV Spawns Four New Outlets With Their Eyes On MTV AR14139
[Charles Bukowski] AR13179
Charlie Rich: 1932-1995 AR13289
Charlie Watts AR13453
Chas Chandler: 1938-1996 AR14153
Cheap Seats At The Video Revolution: HDTV's On Its Way, But In The Meantime You Still Need Something To Watch AR13640
Cheap Trick: Labels Buy Hits By Giving Away Bargain-Price Cassette Singles AR13061
Cheating Time: How Some High-School Students From California Improved Their SAT Scores AR14219
Check It Out AR13180, AR13181, AR13182, AR13183
Cheeky Monkeys AR15239
Chemical Brothers Explode Underground With Their New EP, 'Loops Of Fury' AR12929
The Chemical Brothers Mix It Up With Noel Gallagher AR15754
Cher AR13497
Chicago AR14419
Children Of The Damned Never Mind The Sex Pistols: Here's Their Offspring AR13655
Chill Factor: DJs Cool Down L.A.'s Post-Rave Club Scene AR14351
China Syndrome: CD Piracy Results In A Trade War AR14302
Chip Trick: Big Brother Is Trying To Get On Line AR14006
Choose Your Poison: Newt & Co. Roll Back A Generation Of Environmental Protections AR12948
Chow Manhattan: Parker Posey And Benicio Del Toro Treat Themselves To A Bottle Of Wine, A Little Red Sauce And Some Italian Dressing AR13498, AR14815
Chris Cornell Of Soundgarden: The End Of The Innocence AR13656
Chris Harford: A Rocker With A Sense Of Direction AR12989
Chris Isaak's Twin Peaks: The Pop Heartthrob Takes Two Steps Forward With A New Album And Movie AR15901
Chris Robinson Of The Black Crowes AR13499
Chrissie Hynde Of The Pretenders AR15902
Chronicle AR13185
[Chronology of Female Rock Musicians] AR13186
Chuck D Is Back With More Agendas Than Ever AR13463
Chuckie's In Love: Triathlete Chuckie V Swims, Cycles And Runs With The Best—And He Doesn't Do it For The Money AR13217
Cindy: A Portfolio AR15191
The Cindy Chronicles: The Body, The Marriage, The Mole AR16112
Citizen GE: How Multinationals Like General Electric Have Seized Power In The United States AR14069

Civilizing Cyberspace: The Rolling Stone Interview With Mitch Kapor AR14007
Clarification AR13411
Clasico Rock AR14653
Class Conflict: Zappa Vid Gets Teacher Suspended AR14366
The Class Of '92 AR13770
Class Of '93: The Rock And Roll Hall Of Fame AR13771
Clean Sweep: Garbage's Masterminds Craft Murky Pop Into An Album That's Impossible To Refuse AR13198
Cleo's Mass. Appeal AR15240
"Clerks"—Dangerous Talk AR15642
Clint Eastwood AR15903
Clint Eastwood: The Rolling Stone Interview AR13143
Clinton And Brown Sound Off: The Candidates Talk About Music, From Miles Davis To The Mothers Of Invention AR15361
Clinton And Campaign Reform: The Sounds Of Silence AR16027
Clinton At Midterm? What Went Wrong AR14070
Clinton For President AR15778
Clinton Goes Right Toward Consensus AR14071
Clinton: I Want The MTV Vote AR14745
Clinton Rocked The Vote, Now It's Rocking Him: Young Democrats Are Turning Their Back On The President And Politics AR12949
Clinton's Choice: Jobs Or Mexico AR14072
Clinton's Credit: The 72-Hour Student Loan AR16028
Clinton's Health Plan: More Funk 4U AR15613
Close Encounters: Youssou N'Dour And Neneh Cherry Make Record Time In "7 Seconds" AR14541
Close To You AR13189
Clown 'N' Dirty: Mariah Carey's Twisted 'Fantasy' AR13500
Colin-Izing America: The Best Thing Colin Powell Could Do For The Nation Is Run For President AR14073
College 94 Notebook AR15396
College Notebook AR13854, AR15227
Come As You Are AR14561
Come Gather Round, People AR15904
Comedy AR13304
Coming To A Screen Near You AR16066
The Complete Clapton: In His Own Words AR13305
The Complete Clapton: Living On Blues Power AR15020
The Complete Clapton: Plugged In AR13772
Confessions Of Sir Psycho Sexy: The Rolling Stone Interview With Anthony Kiedis Of The Red Hot Chili Peppers AR14746
Congrats AR13306, AR13307
Congratulations AR13308, AR13309, AR13310, AR13311
Congress: Kill NAFTA AR14074
The Contributors AR13317, AR13318
Conventional Wisdom: Why The Bottle Rockets And Other Bands Pay To Play At Industry Schmoozefests AR13062
Conway Twitty: 1933-1993 AR14628
Cool Jerk: How Sean Penn Reconciles Being The Best Actor Of His Generation With Being A Menace To Society AR14677
'Cop Killer' Aftershocks: Labels Asking Rap Artists To Remove Controversial Tracks From Albums AR14747
'Cop Killer' Is Iced: Ice-T Pulls Song From His Album In Response To Death Threats AR15163
Cop Killer: The Sequel AR15814
'Cop Killer': Yielding To Censors Never Works In The Long Run AR13417
Cop Killers? The Media Target The Police AR14331
[Correction] AR13325, AR13326, AR13327, AR13328, AR13329, AR13330, AR13331, AR13332, AR13333, AR13334, AR13335
[Corrections] AR13336, AR13337, AR13338
Cosmic Comeback: Julian Cope's Music Of The Spheres AR13199
The Cost Of Living Clean AR12981
Counting Crows AR13939
Country AR14629
Country Artist Of The Year AR14530
Country Music Has Become The Refuge Of Older Rock Fans AR13418
Country Punk'ins: Nelson Covers Bridge Rebel Cultures AR12925
Country Roundup AR15568
The Country That Stayed Out In The Cold AR14075
Country's New Gold Rush: With Garth Brooks Leading The Way, Nashville Is Booming AR15569
Courtney Love AR14748
The Covers 1993 AR13344
The Crack-Up AR15475
Crackers With Attitude: When The Alternative Press Gets Predictable, Cracker Get Weird AR15122
The Cradle Will Rock: Silverchair Make Music Beyond Their Years AR14433
The Cranberries AR14542
The Crap Is Out There: The Search For Signs Of Intelligent Life On Fall TV AR15905
[Credit] AR13348
Credit Where Credit's Due AR14076
Crime Pays: Beleaguered Interscope Passes From Hot Potato To Hot Property AR13063
Critics Comments AR12930, AR13039, AR13271, AR13350, AR13385, AR13404, AR13832, AR13835, AR13843, AR14227, AR14249, AR14352, AR14434, AR14444, AR14614, AR15201, AR15726a
Critics' Picks: 1992 Music Awards AR13352
Critics' Picks: 1993 Music Awards AR13353
Critics Poll: 1996 AR13354
Crossover Acts: Bridging The Gap Between Simplicity And Sophistication, These Cameras Are Shooting For A Wider Audience AR13102
Crowes Take Flight AR15906
Crowning Moment: Tanya Donelly & Belly Hit The Big Time With King AR13501
A Cry In The Dark: Love Reads Cobain's Note To Vigil AR14522
'The Crying Game' Star Jaye Davidson Breaks The Silence: Oscar's Big Surprise AR13855
Cub AR13134
Cubanomics: In Fidel Castro's Crumbling Socialist Paradise, The Rum Is Older Than The Whores, The Currency Is Worthless, And Everybody's Working For The Yankee Dollar AR14996
The Cult Of Ray: 'Seinfeld' Meets The Suburbs On CBS' 'Everybody Loves Raymond' AR15907
Cultural Healing: Choir Marries Gospel And Hip-Hop AR14318
Culture Wars: The GOP's Version Of American History Is 'Don't Worry, Be Happy' AR12950
Cumbersome Combo: Seven Mary Three Churn It Out AR15468
Cut To The Chase AR14313, AR14816
Cuts Like A Knife AR15908
Cutting Edge Colleges: Four Schools That Are Preparing Their Students For The 21st Century AR15486
Cyber Funk U: Berklee College Of Music Has Seen The Future And Wants You To Write The Score AR15190
Cyberstuff AR14656

D

D Generatings AR15030
Dad, I'm A Degenerate: New York's D Generation Spark A New Glam-Rock Scene Behind The Green Door AR14347
Dada: Strange Characters Take Center Stage In 'Puzzle' AR12990
Dambuilders AR15214
Dan Baird's Dixie-Fried Love: The Former Georgia Satellite Ruffles Some Feathers With His Solo Effort AR15123
Danamania! AR16113
Dance Of Death AR15233
Dancin' With The Devil: White Zombie Mint Gold From Goth AR13394
Dancing In The Seats: Roll Over Beethoven, The Professors Of Pop Have Arrived AR16123
Dangerous, Dedicated And Wild At heart, Nicolas Cage Is A Hollywood Samurai AR15368
Daniel Lanois Finds His Own Voice: Known For The LPs He's Made For U2 And Bob Dylan, The Producer Turns One Out For Himself AR15099
Danny Gatton: 1945-1994 AR13698
Danny Gatton Tribute AR15557
The Dark Side Of 'Amused': Roger Waters Tackles War And Andrew Lloyd Webber On His New Album AR13699
Darkness On The Edge of Bedrock: Kyle MacLachlan Brings His All-American Weirdness To "The Flintstones" AR13218, AR14532, AR14817
The Dating Dame AR13502
Dave Vs. Dave: Forget Leno & Koppel—Letterman May Be His Own Worst Enemy AR15369
David Bowie AR14514
David Bowie Rumbles In The Jungle On 'Earthling' AR13464
David Byrne AR13503
David Cronenberg: The Rolling Stone Interview AR13144
David Geffen: The Rolling Stone Interview AR13998
David Letterman: The Rolling Stone Interview AR16114
Dawn Of The Dead: The Duo Dead Can Dance Get Back To Nature With Their Album "Into The Labyrinth" AR12971
A Day In The Life AR13020
Day Of The Dre: Dr. Dre And His Protege, Snoop Doggy Dogg, Take Hardcore Rap From South Central L.A. To Your House AR13924
Dead Aim: Filter Hit The Bull's Eye With The Controversial Track 'Hey Man, Nice Shot' AR13504
Dead End: The Grateful Dead Call It Quits AR13794
Dead Flowers?: Gilbey Clarke Ponders The Troubled State Of Guns N' Roses AR12931
Dead Flowers?: Stone Roses Rise For A 'Second Coming' AR15909
Dead Man Talking: How Newt Gingrich Went From Being The Life Of The Party To The

GOP's Pariah In Two Revolutionary Years AR14077
Dead Reckoning: Garcia's Passing Brings To An End A Heroic Journey Of Self-Discovery AR13022
Dear Diary: The Secret World Of Kate Bush AR15416
Death Becomes Him: Nick Cave Acquires A Taste For Murder AR13700
Death In The Candy Store: The Prostitution Capital Of The World, Thailand Is Committing Sexual Suicide By HIV Infection AR15180
A Death In The Family AR13908
Death Of A Cheerleader AR15541
Death Of A Salesman AR16046
Deception & Reality: If You're Wondering Why Bill Clinton And Bob Dole Haven't Addressed The Economic Woes Of The '90s, Don't Ask The Media AR14078
Decking The Hall: As The Hall Of Fame Goes Up, The Collection Comes To Life AR13290
Dee Murray: 1946-1992 AR13448
Deee-Lusions Of Grandeur: Deee-Lite Searches For A New Groove On 'Infinity Within' AR13856
Deep Cover AR13610, AR14818
Deep Forest's Lush 'Lullaby' AR15755
Deep In The Heart Of Siberia AR14997
Deep-River Blues: John Mellencamp And Blind Melon Rock For Flood Victims AR14457
Def Leppard: Ready To Roar? AR13701
Demi Moore = Sex AR15698
Dennis Rodman's Floating World AR14147
Denny Cordell: 1943-1995 AR14021
Denzel On Malcolm AR16086
Depeche Mode: The Rock & Roll Rebirth Of Everybody's Favorite Euroweenies AR13378
Desert Bloom: With Spacey Rock And Country Ballads, Cracker Reinvent Themselves In The California Sun AR12960
Desert-Island Videos: What's Your No. 1? AR14543
Des'ree Moves On AR15476
The Devil And Anne Rice AR13909
The Devil And John Holmes AR15332
The Devil Inside: For Danzig — The Man And The Band — That Old Black Magic Isn't Just A Sales Gimmick AR15910
Devil Or Angel? Either Way, South Africa's Winnie Mandela Has Grass-Roots Support AR15140
Devolution Rock: Brainiac Are Taking Retro To The Future AR15469
Digable Planets: The Trio Pays Homage To Early Jazz Greats AR14319
Digital Hollywood: How Computers Are Remaking Movie Making AR14245
Digital-Tape War Heats Up AR13940
Digital Underground: Bootlegging Makes Inroads On The Info Superhighway AR13372
Dillon Fence: Pop With A Melody AR15124
Dinosaur Summer: A T. Rex And A Terminator Aim To Stomp All Rivals, From Clint To The Coneheads AR15643
Dionne Farris AR13580, AR15241
Disc Contentment: Digital Components Challenge CD-Hating Audiophiles' Claims Of Vinyl Supremacy AR13641
Disc-O-Mania!!! AR16067
The Disciples Of Pot: Cypress Hill Says Marijuana's Getting A Bad Rap AR15570
The Dish AR14657
Dishwalla And Styx Fuse Their Illusions AR14348
Divine Inspiration: Sixteen Horsepower Conjure Up That Old-Time Religion AR13844
Dizzy Gillespie: 1917-1993 AR13773
Dr. Dre Stares Down DWI Rap AR15614
Dr. Hunter S. Thompson: On The Occasion Of The 25th Anniversary Of The Publication Of Fear And Loathing In Las Vegas, An Unfettered Discussion On The Values Of The '60s, The Addictive Properties Of Professional Journalism And The Definition Of Gonzo AR14998
Does Primus Really Suck?: The San Francisco Trio, Whose Music Mixes Thrash, Funk And Progressive Rock, Has Built A Devoted Following Of Fans On The Alternative Scene AR12991
The Dog Is Us AR13188
The Dogg Walks AR15866
Dollars And Dancing Bears AR14277
Dolly Parton AR13651
Domino AR15090
Don Cherry: 1936-1995 AR14217
Don Henley & Glenn Frey AR13419
Donald Cammell 1934-1996 AR13064
Donald Fagen: Doing It Again AR15911
Don't Call Me Slacker: Student Volunteers Speak For Themselves About Changing The World Little By Little AR13476
Don't Ever Change: Buzzcocks Make Pure Punk-Pop For Now People AR13200
Don't Leave Home Without It AR16068
Don't Look Back: Two New Films Expand On The Story Of Grunge AR13356
Don't Tread On Me: Metallica's James Hetfield AR13702
Don't Try This At Home: At The End Of Its Second Season, 'The Real World' Gets A Reality Check AR13164
Doomed To Succeed: The Princes Of Twitch Take Cybergore To A New Level AR14044
The Dope On Health Care AR13477
A Dose Of Reality: Kurt Cobain Recovers From A Drug-And-Alcohol Induced Coma AR15500
Double Dose Of Springsteen AR13941
Double Fantasy AR13274, AR14154
Double Trouble: Luke And Murphy Jensen Are The new Rude Dudes Of Tennis AR14615
Down But Not Out: Chicago's Eleventh Dream Day Picks Up The Pieces With 'El Moodio' AR16090
Down But Not Out: Labor Struggles To Find Its Voice AR14079
Down-Home Souls: Jayhawks Fly High On Their "Green Grass" AR12932
Downtown Science: A Broad Spectrum Of Sounds AR14468
The Downward Spiral: The Last Days Of Nirvana's Leader AR13657, AR15501
The Dread Zone: Bad Brains Are One Of Rock's Most Volatile Bands—In Music And Temper AR12961
Dream Girl AR16047
Drinkin' And Draggin' AR13917
Drop In, Turn On, Tune Out: Replacing Factory-Installed Car Speakers Will Change Your Life AR14795
The Dropout 'Zine AR15397
Drug News AR13485
The Drug War: Prohibition Fails Again AR13605
Drugs Claim Sublime's Singer; Depeche Mode's Gahan OD's AR14155
Drugstore Cowgirl: It's Sex, Peyote And Poetry As Uma Thurman Thumbs A Ride Aboard A Counterculture Classic AR13339
Dubious Summer Trends AR15644
Duck And Cover: The Three Most Important Issues Of The Campaign And Why The Candidates Won't Talk About Them AR14080
Duff's Single-Gun Theory: Duff McKagan Strikes Out On His Own AR14678
Dumb About Disc Players: A Guide To Choosing The Best Laser Players Without Straining Brain Or Budget AR15645
The Dust Brothers Take The Past Into The Future AR13630
The Dust Of Life AR15333
Dutch Treat: The Stones Go Back To Clubland For A New Live LP AR13703
Dwayne Goettel: 1964-1995 AR15815
Dysfunction Junction: The New Oprahs And Little Rickies Prove Talk Is Cheap AR15912

E

E: A Tender Pop Sensibility AR13800
E!'s So Fine: A Network Boldly Says There's No Business But Show Business AR15913
Early Delivery: Brandy Breaks Out at 16 with 'Baby' AR13322
Early Starters AR15646
Earth Summit: Going For The Green In Rio AR14999
Easy Target: Why Tupac Should Be Heard Before He's Buried AR13910
Eating For A's: Nutrition Experts Chew The No-Fat AR15242
Eazy-E: Down By Law AR15583
Eazy-E: 1963-1995 AR15816, AR15914
Eco-Tech: Green Components For These PC Times AR13103
Eddie Hazel: 1950-1992 AR14469
Eddie Hinton: 1944-1995 AR13704
Eddie Kendricks: 1939-1992 AR14470
Eddie Spaghetti of Supersuckers AR13505
Eden's Children: 10,000 Maniacs Grapple With The Pleasures & Perils Of Success in The Real World AR13686
Edie's New "Morning": Solo Brickell Takes It Simple And Soulful AR13420
[Editorial] AR13275, AR13578, AR15779, AR15780, AR15781, AR15782, AR15783, AR15784, AR15785, AR15915
Editor's Notebook AR15786, AR15787, AR15788, AR15789
Eels AR15817
8: Leave Me Alone AR14367
18: Kiss AR14368
88: She Blinded Me With Science AR14679
85: Little Red Corvette AR14369
84: Alive AR14749
89: Thunderstruck AR13031
81: Free Your Mind AR13506
87: The Thunder Rolls AR13801
86: Sweet Dreams AR13802
80: Straight Up AR13507
83: It Was A Good Day AR15615
82: Rapture AR13508
El Mariachi And The Sundance Kid AR15647
Election '92 AR13598
Election Post-Mortem: The Price Of Failure AR14081
Election Watch AR14544, AR14545, AR14546, AR14547
The Electric Dorm—Tune In, Turn On, Veg Out With Cool Compact Components AR14658

An Elegy For Jerry AR14284
11: Walk This Way AR15616
Ella Fitzgerald: 1917-1996 AR13911
Elton John Leads Fight Against AIDS AR13803
Elvis Costello's Classical Gas: The Pop Poet Teams Up With A String Quartet On 'The Juliet Letters' AR13291
Elvis's Stamp Of Approval: Postal Service To Pay Tribute To Presley And Other Rock Stars In New Series AR13942
[E-Mail] AR13576
The Emergency Plan To Bail Out The Banks AR14082
EMI Gives Old Artists New Deal [and other news] AR13943
Emperors Of The Air AR14616, AR14819
Empty Gesture Department AR15056
End Of The Beginning: Jerry Garcia And The Grateful Dead's Music Was The Last Remnant Of A Magic Vision AR15498
Endpaper AR13051, AR14416
Enemies Of The Arts: The Republicans' Hit Men AR15079
The Enemy Within: An Exclusive Excerpt From The Upcoming Book 'Betrayal' Tells The Inside Story of The Hunt For Aldrich Ames, The Deadliest Traitor In The History Of The CIA AR14321, AR14460, AR15747
Engine Of Aggression: Anthrax Accelerate To The Forefront On 'Stomp 442' AR15818
ENIT Festival AR13139
Ephraim Lewis: Sensual Soul AR13162
Eric Clapton AR15021
Esquivel AR13509
The Essential Zappa AR15558
Ethan Hawke: Renaissance Boy AR14680
Eugene, Oregon AR13609
Eugenius: The Former Captain America Invades The U.S. AR14681
Europe's Drug Prescription: Innovative Approaches To The Drug Problem From Over There AR14736
[Evan Dando] AR13395
Evan Dando Of The Lemonheads AR13405
The Evening Mirror: Can The 'NBC Nightly News' Succeed By Doing Fewer Stories About Washington And More About Peoria? AR14332
Evening The Score: Affirmative Action Cracks Open The Great Divide AR12917
Everything But The Girl's Ben Watt Makes Pleasant Pop From Personal Misery AR15819
Everything Old Is New Again AR13104
Ex-Blossom Dies: Songwriter Hopkins, 32, Commits Suicide After Battle With Alcohol AR13021
The Ex-Im Files: How The Taxpayer-Funded Export-Import Bank Helps Ship Jobs Overseas AR14083
Executive Sweet: Music Execs Name Their Price As Salaries Soar AR13065
Exile In Guyville: A Report On How Women Are Faring In The Music Industry AR12933
Exile On Main Street: Small-Town Life Suits Jack Logan Just Fine AR13705
Exiles On Main Street AR15457
An Experiment In Terror: 7 Days And Seven Nights Alone With MTV AR13791
Exploding Tickets: Pearl Jam Wage An Anti-Trust War Against Ticketmaster On Capitol Hill AR15502
Extreme's Triple Play AR14750
Eye Candy AR13105
Eyes Wide Open, Hearts Full Of Hope AR14084
Ezra's Better, Bigger Easy AR15243

F

F Troop: The GOP Raids Public Schools AR14085
Faces Of Violence AR13611
Faith No More AR15916
The Fall Group Grope: The New Season Offers Yuks For Blacks, Fake Feminism For Women, Familiar Faces For The Old, Pecs And Posing For The Young AR14577
The Fall Of Animal House: For Dartmouth's Alpha Delta Fraternity, The Choice Is Change Or Die AR14430
False Messiah AR16091
Fame-O-Meter AR15057
Famous By Association: Vic Chestnutt Joins His Rock & Roll Heroes In The Spotlight AR14353
FAQ: Frequently Asked Questions About The World Wide Web AR16069
Farewell AR13621, AR13622, AR13623, AR13624
Fast Start For 'Dangerous' AR13944
Fats Is Back! AR13302
Fear And Loathing In Elko AR15595
Fear And Loathing In Las Vegas AR15596
Fear Of A Hip Hop Syllabus: Three Professors Reveal What The Required Listening Will Be When Rap Goes To College AR15398
Federal Payola Probe Continues [and other news] AR13945
Feeling The Space: Yoko Ono Enters A New World—The Theater AR14370
Female Rappers Laud Reno AR13581
The Fevered Rise Of America Online AR14008
Fifteen Essential Albums AR13774
15: Once In A Lifetime AR13510
58: Manchild AR14751
The Fifty-First State: P. J. O'Rourke Road-Trips Vietnam AR15000
55: Wild Thing AR14371
54: And She Was AR14372
59: Justified And Ancient AR14373
51: Back To My Roots AR13511
57: Fish Heads AR14374
56: Faith AR13512
53: Shock The Monkey AR14375
52: Black Or White AR15617
50: When I Think Of You AR13513
The Fight For The Right To Choose: L7 And Friends Rock For Reproductive Freedom AR14752
Fighting Hype And The Weight of His Father's Legend, Jeff Buckley Finds His Own Voice On "Grace" AR13465
Filed Of Dreams: The Big Business Behind Woodstock '94 AR14643
Fiona Apple AR15820
The Fire This Time: Midnight Oil Reignites With A New Album AR13706
First Place Watches AR15482
The First Reform: Campaign Finance AR14086
Fish Out Of Water AR15125
Fishin' For Tuition: Students Talk About Their Jobs AR13857
5 Against The World: Pearl Jam Emerge From The Strange Daze Of Superstardom With A New Album Full Of Rage And Warrior Soul AR13358
5: Nothing Compares 2 U AR13804
Fix The Grammys AR13636
Fixing The Vote: The Grammys Set Up A Secret Panel To Make Nominations Hipper AR16093
[Flea] AR14753
Flood Of Box Sets Due AR14274
Flower Grrrl: After 12 Years With 10,000 Maniacs, Natalie Merchant makes The Most Of Liberation On 'Tigerlily' AR13707
Fluffy May Be Pretty, But They're Hardly Vacant AR13466
Flying Boats: Why 'Netizen' Works And 'Salon' Doesn't AR14009
Follow For Now: A Hard-Rockin' Guitar Band AR12992
Foo Fighters AR14682
For The Record AR13675, AR13676, AR13677, AR13678, AR13679, AR13680, AR13681, AR13682, AR13683
Forever Young: Neil Young Proves Life In Rock & Roll Can Begin Again At Fortysomething AR14471
The Forgotten Epidemic AR14317
Former Lemonhead Jesse Peretz Gets Behind The Lens AR13467
Fortunate Son: John Fogerty Looks Back On The Glory Days Of Creedence Clearwater Revival AR13946
40: Baby Got Back AR14564
48: China Girl AR14376
45 Special: A New Label Flourishes In A Funky Format AR13631
45: Whip It AR14377
44: Night Of The Living Baseheads AR15618
49: By The Time I Get To Arizona AR15619
41: Man On The Moon AR14565
47: Undercover Of The Night AR14378
46: Goin' Back To Cali AR15620
43: Justify My Love AR15621
42: Series Of Dreams AR14538
Forward Into The Past: Paul McCartney Wraps Up A World Tour And Gets Ready For A Beatles Reunion AR15917
Fountains Of Wayne Bubble With Power Pop AR15202
400 Years In A Convent, 50 Years In A Whorehouse AR15001
4 Non Blondes AR13839
4: This Note's For You AR14566
The Frames: Bringing A Different Mix To Their Irish Stew AR15399
Frank Zappa: 1940-1993 AR13708
Frank Zappa Stricken With Cancer: But Family Says He's Fighting It Successfully AR14754
The Frat Trap: After A Decade As A Big College Band, Fighting Gravity Are Ready To Move Off Campus AR15918
Freddie Mercury: 1946-1991 AR15164
Freddy Krueger Does D.C.: Meet Bob Dole, Nightmare On Capitol Hill AR13346
A Free Man On Death Row: White Knight Bails Out Shakur AR15867
Freedie's Royal Send-Off: Show Also Marks Rock's First Major Rallying Cry In The Fight Against AIDS AR14755
Freedom '93: That's What George Michael Gets If He Wins A Groundbreaking Suit Against Sony AR13833
Freedom Rock: Rock Out Censorship Leads The Fight AR15756
The Freewheelers: After-Hours Rock AR15400
Frente AR12921
The Fresh Ones: Foo Fighters Weird Candy Fantasies AR13514
Friends: Six Lives On Videotape AR15919
From A (Allman) To Z (Zappa) AR13761
From Folk City To Fat City: Shawn Colvin Finds Her Place In The Sun AR15100

From Graceland To Cleveland AR13292
Fugees: Leaders Of The New Cool AR13658
Fun Lovin' Criminals Take Their Horseplay Seriously AR13515
Funeral For A Friend: Deadheads Flock To San Francisco To Honor Jerry Garcia AR13659
Funky, Futuristic Beck Channels Cosmic Debris AR12934

G

Gag U.: From Caltech's Card Trick To Amherst's Run-Around Sabrina, These Pranks Are Total Classics AR15487
The Galactic Boys: Art-Metal Buckaroos AR13709
Gang Bang Bang: Welcome To Ex-Yugoslavia, Land Of A Thousand Grievances, Where The Christians Hate The Muslims, The Serbs Hate The Croats, The Bosnians Hate The Montenegrins, And Everyone Has A Gun AR15002
Gang Murder In The Heartland AR14635
Gang Of Seven: All Talk, No Music AR13947
Gang Starr AR13293
Garcia: Truckin' Again AR13948
A Gathering Of The Tribes: A Report From The 1993 World Peace And Healing Gathering Of The Rainbow Family Of Living Light AR14528
Geddy Lee Of Rush AR13516
Geek Love: Stepping Out From John Mellencamp's Shadow, Singer And Violinist Lisa Germano Hits A Nerve On "Geek The Girl" AR14354
Geek Love: Strange But True Tales Of Stereo Obsession AR15716
Generation Latex: Sex On Campus!! AR14504
Generation Next AR13842
Generation Next: The Smokin' Sounds Of Summer '94 AR13396, AR13517, AR13582, AR14548, AR14683
George Bush's Heroin Connection AR14738
George Harrison: Live And Low-Key AR14536
George Herbert Hoover Walker Bush AR14087
George Jones AR13406
Germ Warfare AR15181
Germany Stomps Skinhead Music: Authorities Bust Third Reich & Roll AR14304
Geronimo Vs. Cochise: As Apaches Fight To Build A Nuclear Waste Dump On Their New Mexico Reservation, The Descendants Of Two Legendary Warriors Are Locked In A Battle For The Soul Of The Tribe AR14529
Gerry Mulligan 1927-1996 AR13775
Get Happy: Perry Farrell Finds Nirvana On The Way To LollaPalooza '95 And A New LP AR12962
Gettin' Mighty Crowded: Summer Tours '94 AR14022
Getting Ahead: Upgrade Now! AR14578
Getting Better: Work In Progress AR13518
Getting In: Everybody Goes To Rusty AR14431
Getting It All On Tape AR16070
Getting Lost: Chronicle Of A Death Foretold AR13276
Getting Real: Silicon Flame Out AR14010
Getting The Led Out: Jimmy Page And Robert Plant Are Back In Business AR13519
Getting Wise: Howard Zinn's Rage Against The Machine AR16105
Ghosts In The Machine: The CD-ROM Of "The Haldeman Diaries" And A New Documentary Finally Tell The Full Watergate Story AR13412
Gibby Haynes Of The Butthole Surfers AR13520
The Girl Friend AR13219
The Girl In The Tweed Jacket AR14621
The Girlie Show AR15699
Girls Against Boys AR15470
Give Pot A Chance: Voters In California And Arizona Strike A Blow Against The War On Drugs AR15407
Giving Working People A Break AR13920
The GLAAD Hit List AR13614
Glam Slam 2: The Auteurs AR14280
The Global Sweatshop: Indonesian Workers Struggle For Rights And Help From Clinton AR14088
Global Village: WOMAD Returns For A Tour Of The U.S. AR13583
The Godfathers Of Rap: The Rise And Fall Of The First Heroes Of Hip-Hop AR13033
God's Little Monkeys: A Sardonic Political Edge AR13858
Going For The Gold: Monet Talks As Golden-Circle Seating Divides Concert Audiences AR14023
Gold Medals And Platinum Blondes: The Dream Team At Atlanta's Largest Strip Club Gets Pumped For The Summer Olympics AR13277
Goldfinger AR13997
Gone But Not Forgotten: Though Virtually Extinct, Vinyl Record Albums Still Have Their Defenders AR15126
Good Times: Morning Has Broken The Newest Looks Pop And Shine To Keep You Suited Up Long Past The Twilight's Last Gleaming AR14820, AR15605
Good Vibrations: The Fugees Score One For Positivity AR15471
The GOP's Strike Force: The Right-Wing Propaganda Machine Churns Out Money, Activists And Lies AR12951
Got The Foreclosed, Bankrupt GOP Blues AR14089
Grace Under Fire: The NRA Takes Potshots At Assault-Weapons Opponents AR12952
Grand Jury Attacks Arena Security [and other news] AR13949
Grant Lee Buffalo AR15111
Grapevine AR14047, AR14048, AR14049, AR14050, AR14051, AR14052, AR14156, AR14157, AR14158, AR14159, AR14160, AR14161, AR14162, AR14163, AR14164, AR14165, AR14166, AR14167, AR14168, AR14169, AR14170, AR14171, AR14172
Grateful Dead Cut Staff AR15493
Great Moments In College Journalism: 1 AR14053
Great Moments In College Journalism: 2 AR14054
Great Performances: The Year's Best AR15648, AR15649
The Great Price War: Used CDs Become The Center Of A Retail Battle AR13950
Great Reduced Expectations AR15550
The Great Western Cave-In: For Now, Political Forces Beat Market Forces AR16029
Greed Or Need?: CDs Hit $17.98 In Record Biz's Banner Year AR15757
Green Day AR13660
Green Daze AR14684
Green Jelly's Bubblegum Punk AR13294
Greg Dulli Of Afghan Whigs AR13521
Greg Graffin Of Bad Religion AR13661
Grok The Vote AR14090
Group Gets Youth Vote On Bandwagon AR14756
Grrrls At War AR13687
Grunge City: For Real Rockers Seattle Is The Ultimate Wet Dream AR12993
Guess Who's Coming To Legislate AR16030
Guess Who's Coming To Washington AR13036
Guitar Note: The DTS-I Changes Tunings In Seconds AR14443
Gunning For Guns: Clinton Calls For Ideas On Confronting Violence AR16031
Guns N' Roses AR14125
Guns N' Roses To Play AIDS Benefit [and other news] AR13951
Guns Or Budget? Clinton's Options AR14091
Gus Van Sant's Northwest Passage: The Director Of 'Drugstore Cowboy' Continues To Explore Uncharted Territory With 'My Own Private Idaho' AR14135
Gut Check In The Heartland AR15334
Gutterball Take A Working Vacation AR15203
Guyville Java Jive AR14420

H

Hail Hail Rock & Roll: Behind The Scenes And Onstage At The Concert For The Hall Of Fame AR13522
Haiti AR15003
Haitian Flight Song: World Music Artists At The Mercy Of Global Politics AR15462
Half Way Home: Soliciting The Hospitality Of Their Extended Family AR14228
Hall Gets Joplin Haul AR14126
Hall Of Fame AR13295, AR14127
Hall Of Fame '95: Led Zeppelin And Neil Young Highlight The 10th Anniversary Celebration AR13523
Hall Of Fame '96 AR13524, AR15031
Hall Of Fame Groundbreaking: At Long Last, The Site Is Ready For The Country's First Rock Shrine AR15352
Hall Of Fame Inductees AR14128
Hall Of Fame Inductees Announced AR13776
Hall Of Fame Nominees AR14173
Hall Of Fame: See You In September AR13296
Hall Of Fame To Break Ground AR13952
Hammer Hurting; Shops For New Label AR15584
The Hard-Core Curriculum: Despite A Decade Of 'Just Say No' And Get-Tough Laws, Drugs Are Back On Campus With A Vengeance AR14505
A Hard Dazed Night: Soul Asylum's Dave Pirner Burns The Midnight Oil, Defending His Band, His Music And His Punk Credibility AR15503
Hard To Handle: The Black Crowes Throw A Snit And Toughen Their Sound On The New LP AR14229
Hard To The Core AR14757
Harry Nilsson 1941-1994 AR14379
The Hate Squad: The Religious Right Is Making A Killing From Bashing Clinton AR16032
He Had Faced His Demon: Deborah Koons Garcia Speaks Out AR13710
He Was A Crook AR15597
'He Was A Geek And A God:' The Story Behind The Tragic Death Of Kurt Cobain AR15504
Head Case AR13468
Head Count, $ Amount AR14146
The Healing Of Daniel Johnston: A Punk-Rock Cult Hero's Roller-Coaster Ride Toward Wider Recognition AR14630
Heard The About The Welfare Queen?

AR14092
The Heart And Sole Of The City: The Right Sneaker Keeps You In The Action AR15211
The Heart Of Darkness: The Boston Band Come Makes Soul Music For The Slacker Generation AR13482
Heart-Shaped Noise: The Music And The Legacy AR13711
The Heat Puppets AR15244
Heather Nova Weathers The Quiet Storm AR12963
Heaven Is Under Our Feet: Voices For Walden Woods AR13057, AR13474, AR14203
A 'Heavier, Funkier' Living Colour: Vernon Reid And Company Set To Release 'Stain' AR14472
Help Wanted: Red Hot Guitarist AR14758
Hendrix To Tour U.S.: Traveling Exhibit Hits The States In April AR15165
Henley To Buy Walden Site AR15920
Henry Rollins' L.A. AR15245
Henry Rollins: Rocks Angriest Voice Rises From The Ashes Of Black Flag AR14685
Her Back Pages AR14608
Herb Ritts AR15192
Here, There And Everywhere AR14606
Heroin AR13278
Heroin: Back On The Charts AR14230
He's A Loser, Baby: Court Rejects George Michael's Plea To Break His Contract With Sony AR15417
Hickory Smoke AR13129, AR13220, AR14821
The Hidden Power Of Dreams: The Cranberries Speak Softly But Carry A Big Hit AR14686, AR14822
High Interactivity: CD's Bring Movies, Games And Books To A TV Near You AR13106
High-Plains Surfers AR15246
High-Quality TV's, Big And Small, For Tight Spaces Or Going Places AR13107
High-Quality Video Adds Sizzle To CD-ROMs AR14659
High School Confidential: Amy Heckerling, The Writer And Director Of 'Clueless," Celebrates Adolescence As A State Of Mind AR13221
High Times: Meat Puppets Make Bong Rock Fro Now People AR12994
The Hill People: They Only Come Out At Night At Don Hill's, New York's Glam Mecca For The Dusk-Till-Dawn Set AR14823
Hip-Hop Nation Is Shaken By Tupac Shakur Ambush Off Las Vegas Strip AR15868
Hire Education: The Secretary Of Labor Tells You Where The Jobs Will Be In The New Economy AR15148
His Name Was Prince... AR13142
Hit Patrol AR13805
Hit, With A Bullet: Filter On Target With "Nice Shot" AR15758
Hole Is A Band: While The Courtney Saga Continues, Hole Prove That A Rock & Roll Band Is The Sum Of Its Parts AR13201
Holiday Hits And Misses AR15650
Hollywood AR14242
Hollywood Director David Fincher Returns To Video AR15921
Hollywood Swingin': Film Soundtracks Go Out On The Cutting Edge AR13662
Holy Rap Session AR16098
Holy Rock & Rollers AR13066
The Home Front: In The War Against AIDS, Some Of The Bravest Battles Are Fought Far From Laboratories And Demonstrations AR13279
Home On The Strange AR13712
Home Video: Broadway Goes Hollywood AR15651
Homestyle: Neneh Cherry on Love, Music And The Pursuit Of Happiness AR14759
Homeward Bound: Spearhead Redefine The Meaning Of Roots Rock AR15922
Honey, I Shrunk The Cineplex: Home Is Where The Theater Is AR14056
Honky-Tonk Men: George Jones And Keith Richards Pair Up For Jones' Upcoming Album AR14281
Honky-Tonk Woman AR13845
The Hood The Bad & The Ugly: For Naughty By Nature, The Question Is Not Can You Take East Orange Out Of The Boyz, But Can You Take The Boyz Out Of East Orange? AR13222, AR14824
Hope & Hard Times: For The Workers At Ravenswood Aluminum, The Struggle To Regain Their Union Jobs Took Them From Small-Town Appalachia To The Glass Canyons Of International Finance AR15464
H.O.R.D.E. Of Hearing: The New Jamming Generation Hits The Road To Swap Solos And Party Down AR15559
Hot AR14254
Hot Accessory AR13859, AR15247
Hot Actor AR13223, AR13860, AR15248, AR15249
Hot Actor: Dogging It With Brad Pitt, The Good Ol' Bad Boy From 'Thelma And Louise' AR14579
Hot Actress AR13224, AR13280, AR13861, AR15250, AR15251
Hot Alternative Subgenre: One-Hype Wonders AR15759
Hot Appliance AR13225, AR15252
Hot Architect AR13862, AR15253
Hot Arms AR13226, AR15254
Hot Art Form AR13863, AR15255
Hot Art Show: The Gramercy Art Fair AR14580
Hot Athlete AR13227, AR13864, AR15256, AR15257
Hot Athlete: Steve Prefontaine AR15326
Hot Author: Stephen Hunter AR15743
Hot Band AR13228, AR15258, AR15366
Hot Band: A College-Rock Favorite, Teenage Fanclub Is Now Earning Mainstream Pop Acceptance AR14687
Hot Brit: Ewan McGregor AR15370
Hot Bulletin Board AR13229, AR15259
Hot Bullshit Compliment AR13865, AR15260
Hot Car AR13866, AR15261
Hot Career Move: Quitting AR14581
Hot Cartoonist: Pat Moriarity AR13135
Hot Comic Book AR13230, AR15262
Hot Country Act AR13231, AR15263
Hot Country Act: BR5-49 AR13067
Hot Country Singer AR13867, AR15264
Hot Cover: Ask Killer Babe Sharon Stone About Sex And You'll Find She Has A Basic Instinct For It AR16115
Hot Dates AR13868, AR15265
Hot Debut AR13869, AR15266
Hot Designer AR13232, AR13870, AR15267, AR15268
Hot Director AR13233, AR13871, AR15269, AR15270, AR16048
Hot Director: James Mangold AR15744
Hot Disease: Ulcers AR16124
Hot Drink: Orbitz AR16125
Hot Drug AR13872, AR15271
Hot Drug: Claritin AR13024
Hot Exercise AR13234, AR15272
Hot Fashion AR14825, AR15692
Hot Founding Father: Ben Franklin AR15228
Hot Gadget AR13873, AR15273
Hot Hollywood Hangout: Hamilton's AR13136
Hot Infomercial AR13874, AR15274
Hot Jazz Artist AR13235, AR14826, AR15275
Hot Jazz Artist: Kenny Garrett AR13777
Hot Jazz Artists AR13778
Hot Jazzman AR13779
Hot Judd AR13875, AR15276
Hot Label: Ruffhouse AR15760
The Hot List AR13236, AR13237, AR13876, AR14506, AR15277, AR15278, AR15279, AR16126
Hot Look AR14511, AR14827, AR15484, AR15490
Hot Loser AR13238, AR15280
Hot Magazine: Loaded AR16127
Hot Marketing Ploy: Critic Proofing AR14582
Hot Medical Equipment AR13877, AR15281
Hot Models AR13239, AR15282
Hot Molecule AR13878, AR15283
Hot Mood: Confusion AR13386
Hot Movie Critic AR13240, AR15284
Hot Movie Theme AR13241, AR15285
Hot Performance Artist AR13242, AR15286
Hot Picks: An Insider's Guide To the Season's New Faces AR14549
Hot Picks: Rock & Roll Is Their Business Here's Who They're Listening To AR14255
Hot Picks: When Music Insiders Kick Back, These Are The Bands They Listen To AR14256
Hot Playwright AR13879, AR15287
Hot Producer AR13880, AR15288
Hot Producer: Tim Simenon AR15761
Hot Rap Trend AR13881, AR15289
Hot Rapper AR13243, AR15290
Hot Rappers AR13806
Hot Record Label AR13882, AR15291
Hot Resurrection AR13883, AR15292
Hot Retro Ethos AR13884, AR15293
Hot Revival AR13885, AR15294
Hot Revival: The Cold War AR15229
Hot Scam AR13886, AR15295
Hot Screenwriter AR13887, AR15296
Hot Sex Symbol AR13888, AR15297
Hot Sitcom Twist: Depressing Season Finales AR14583
Hot Stand-Up AR13244, AR15298
Hot Standup AR13889, AR15299
Hot Status Symbol: A Tiny Cell Phone AR13025
Hot Stuff: New Electronics So Cool They Sizzle AR16071
Hot Stuff: Plugging In The New AR13108
Hot Style AR13245, AR14828
Hot Subculture AR13246, AR13890, AR15300, AR15301
Hot Technology AR14660
Hot Teen Idols AR13891, AR15302
Hot Threat AR13892, AR15303
Hot Threat: Cyberterrorism AR15230
Hot Turn-On: Seventies Porn AR13525
Hot TV Show AR13247, AR15304
Hot TV Show: Concrete T.V. AR14584
Hot TV Star: Brandy AR16128
Hot Unprotected Minority AR13248, AR15305
Hot Vacation Spot AR13249, AR15306
Hot Vacation Spot: Anywhere That's Like Somewhere Else 20 Years Ago AR14585
Hot Vice AR13250, AR15307

Hot Video Game AR13893, AR15308
House Of Cards: Crowded House Mix Whimsy And Melancholy On 'Together Alone' AR15923
House Of Pain: The Fight Against Gansta Rap Hits Captiol Hill AR15445
A House With No Closets AR13195
How Bad Can It Be? NBC's Hit Sitcom 'Men Behaving Badly' Is Pretty Good, But It Should Be Worse AR15924
How Many Times Will Bill Blink?: Courage And The President AR14093
How Stardom Works AR15058
How Swede It Is: Ace Of Base Invade U.S. Airwaves AR14380
How To Be A Road Scholar AR13109
How To Fake A Resume: Entry-Level Lessons For The Real World AR16129
How To Vote In Fifty States AR14257
How We Export Jobs And Disease AR14094
Huh-huh, Huh-huh: MTV's Beavis And Butt-Head On What's Cool And What Sucks AR16106
Hurricane AR13469
Hush AR13170
HyperViolence: A Generation Of Kids In Richmond, Calif., Is Growing Up In The Shadow Of Guns, Drugs And Death AR13286

I

I Am Free And I Want To Thank Rolling Stone And Its Readers For Returning My Life To Me AR13612
I Am Somebody: After A Wildly Successful Duet With Coolio, L.V. Surfaces With His Own Gangsta's Paradise AR15406
I Fought The Law AR14287
I Want My DVD AR13110
I Was A Campus Lab Rat AR15309
Ian Anderson AR13763
Ice-T AR14473
Ice-T: The Rolling Stone Interview AR14474
Ice-T's Declaration Of Independence: The Truth Behind His Split With Time Warner AR14475
Iceland's Sugarcubes AR13713
If I Only Had A Brain AR14638
If The Symptoms Are Rapid Increases In Teen Deaths From Murder, Suicide And Car Crashes, Alcohol And Drugs...The Disease Is Adolescence AR13684
If You Think You Made A Mistake In 1992, Think Again AR16033
If You Want Your Summer To Be A Movable Feast, You'll Need Tech With Some Get-Up-And-Go AR13111
Iggy Still Pops: The Original Punk Is In Royal Form On American Caesar AR14760
Imperial Teen Chart Their Own Course On 'Seasick' AR13632
The Importance Of Defining Your Terms AR15059, AR15060
Improve Your Images AR13112
In A Bjork State Of Mind: The Former Sugarcube Finds Life Is Sweet As A Soloist AR13807
In Living Color AR15808
In Living Color: Vernon Reid Goes Solo With A Stellar Cast AR13714
In My Room AR13642
[In November...] AR14288
In Search Of The Cure For AIDS: A Special Report From The Frontiers Of Science AR15547
In The Dogg House: Tha Dogg Pound Get Caught In The Middle AR15869
In The News AR13194, AR13953, AR13954, AR13955, AR13956, AR13957, AR13958, AR13959, AR13960, AR13961, AR13962, AR13963, AR13964, AR13965, AR13966, AR13967, AR13968, AR13969, AR14024, AR14025, AR14026, AR14027, AR14028, AR14029, AR14030, AR14031, AR14381, AR14382, AR14476, AR14477, AR14478, AR14479, AR14550, AR15455, AR15505, AR15506, AR15507, AR15508, AR15509, AR15510, AR15511, AR15512, AR15513, AR15514, AR15515, AR15516, AR15517, AR15518, AR15519, AR15520, AR15521, AR15821, AR15822, AR15823, AR15824, AR15825, AR15826, AR15827, AR15828, AR15829, AR15830, AR15831, AR15832, AR15833, AR15834, AR15835, AR15836, AR15837, AR15925
In The Zone Of Perceived Faith: Report From New Hampshire AR13601
In Their Own Words: Club Series Spawns A Tour By Some Of Music's Most Distinguished Songwriters AR14136
In Through The Back Door: The Butthole Surfers Are The Certified Shock Jocks Of The Next Wave AR13202
In With The Outtakes: Def Leppard Issues New Odds & Sods LP AR13715
Incense And Insolence: Mazzy Star Carry The Torch For '60s Psychedelia And The Importance Of Being Difficult AR13663
Indie Speedway: Sonicnet Launches An On-Line Service For Music AR14383
Industrial Era: Jim Nash, Co-Founder Of Wax Trax!, Is Claimed By AIDS AR15118
Insane In The Brain (song) AR12957
Insane In The Brain: For Biker Wayne Croasdale Life Is Going Downhill AR13251, AR14829
Into The Loop: How To Get The Job You Want After Graduation AR13484
Into The Unknown: Soundgarden Explore Rock & Roll's Heart Of Darkness AR14761
Introduction AR14290
INXS Get Real: More Than Hooks And Looks AR13808
Is Moshing Murder? AR13068
Is P.M. Dawn's Prince Be the Brian Wilson Of Hip-Hop? God Only Knows AR14503
Is This Any Way To Renew An Economy? AR14095
Is This Any Way To Run A White House?: Clinton Finally Brings Change To Washington—A New Chief Of Staff AR16034
Is This The Woman Who Invented Rock & Roll?: The Deborah Chessler Story AR14562
Isn't It Alanis? 'Ironic' Parodies Flood The Airwaves AR14349
Isn't That Conveeenient! AR13113
It Came From The Course Catalog AR14297
It Came From The Course Catalog No. 2 AR14298
It Came From The Course Catalog No. 3 AR14299
It Came From The Course Catalog No. 4 AR14300
It's A Mad, Mad, Mad About You World AR14830, AR15926
It's All Coming Into Focus AR13114
It's Party Time—It's Excellent: 'Wayne's World' Will Change The History Of Cinema—And Monkeys Might Fly Out Of Our Butt! AR16101
It's Pat: Julia Sweeney's Gender-Bending Character Goes To Hollywood AR15358, AR15603
It's Show Time! AR13252
It's The Jesus And Nirvana Chain! AR14435
Izzy Or Isn't He?: Stradlin May Be Splitting With Guns N' Roses AR14762
Izzy Quits Guns N' Roses AR14301

J

Jackson Browne AR13421
Jackson Charity Off To A Slow Start [and other news] AR13970
Jackson: $20 Million From HBO AR15927
Jackson's Dangerous Game: The Self-Crowned King Of Pop Ruled On Prime Time, But Did We Get The Truth? AR14480
Jackson's Double Play: The Singer Steps Up To The Plate With A New Album And Movie AR15928
Jagger Remembers: The Rolling Stone Interview AR15790
Jailhouse Ragga: Snow Busts Out Of The Big House And Up The Pop Charts AR14622
Jale AR14806
James Carville's Hot List AR13894, AR15310
The James Gang: With 'Laid,' These British Lads Finally Get Over AR13809
James Taylor AR14204
Jampac Benefit AR15084
Janeane Garofalo's Hot List AR13834
[Japan] AR14307
Japanese Corporations; U.S. Corporations AR15061
Jason Bentley AR13633
Jawbox AR14384
Jay Leno AR15929
Jeff Ament Of Pearl Jam AR15762
Jeff Porcaro: 1954-1992 AR14308
Jeffrey Gaines: Real-Life Sketches AR14605
Jeffrey Lee Pierce 1958-1996 AR14355
Jello Biafra Attacked AR13971
Jennifer Jason Leigh: She's The Queen of The Ravaged, Boozed Up And Strung Out AR13526
Jerry & George & Kramer & Elaine: Exposing The Secrets Of SEINFELD's Success AR16116
Jerry Brown For President: A Rolling Stone Editorial AR15791
Jerry Brown's Grass-Roots Call To Arms: An Interview With The Editors Of Rolling Stone AR14310
Jerry Garcia AR14198, AR14453
Jerry Garcia: 1942-1995 AR13912
Jerry Garcia 1942-1995 AR13921
Jerry Garcia Ill; Dead Cancel Tour AR13972
The 'Jerry Maguire' Journal AR13359
Jerry Nolan: 1946-1992 AR14311
The Jesus & Mazzy Chain AR14174
The Jesus And Mary Chain Rage Against The Machine On 'I Hate Rock & Roll' AR15838
Jim Carrey: Bare Facts And Shocking Revelations AR15371
Jim Lauderdale: An Eclectic 'Debut' AR15166
Jim Morrison AR14247
Jimi: The Man And The Music AR13716
Jimmy Buffett AR14356
Jimmy Miller 1942-1994 AR13780
Joan Baez AR14515
Joan Osborne: Holy Roller Finds Salvation In God And Good Sex AR15112
Joe Henry Bounces From Rural Rock To An Urban Groove AR14175
Joe Henry: On His Own AR15401
Joel Sues Lawyers: Singer Claims Fraud In $90 Million Lawsuit AR14763

Joey Ramone AR14385
John Cage: 1912-1992 AR15185
John Cale AR15763
John Campbell: 1952-1993 AR15560
John Campbell: A Modern Bluesman AR13473
John Lennon AR15792
John Lydon AR13527
John Mellencamp: Gets Serious And Funky AR15186
John Panozzo: 1948-1996 AR14176
John Peel AR12995
John Prine AR14551
John Travolta AR15930
Johnny B. Gone AR15931
Johnny Cash AR13528
Johnny Cash: The Hard Reign Of A Country-Music King AR15101
Johnny Clegg's War On Apartheid AR13690
Johnny 'Guitar' Watson 1935-1996 AR15194
The Jon Spencer Blues Explosion Throw A Punky, Bluesy Party On 'Now I Got Worry' AR14350
Jon Stewart AR15311
Jon Stewart's Hot List AR15491
Jonathan Demme: The Rolling STone Interview AR13422
Joni Mitchell AR13529, AR15932
Josh Wink Lands Techno At A Major Label AR13151
Joy In Mudville: Against All Odds, Woodstock '94 Gave Another Generation Three Days Of Peace, Muck And Understanding AR14644
The Joys Of Noise: Soundgarden Throw A High-Frequency Sludgefest AR13357
Julia Makes Trouble: The Rolling Stone Interviews AR15156
Jungle Boogie AR15176
Junkie Town AR14507
Jurassic Spark: Laura Dern AR15933
Just Desserts AR15934
Just Desserts: Can Ben And Jerry Make A Company As Good As Their Ice Cream? AR15551
Just Say Moe: The Heartbeat Of The VU Makes A Solo Noise AR13040
Just Say 'Yes': Morphine Shoot To Low-Fi Stardom AR13281
Justice Denied AR14432

K

K. D. Lang AR12935
K. D. Lang: How Did A Lesbian, Feminist, Vegetarian Canadian Win A Grammy And The Hearts Of America? AR15700
Kat Bjelland Of Babes In Toyland AR14688
Katell Keineg AR14646
Keep On Pushing!: The Strange And Twisted Tale Of The United States Olympic Bobsled Team AR16130
Keep That Wallet Out AR13643
Keepers Of The Flame: Defying The Alternative-Rock Trend, Candlebox Break Out Of Seattle With Traditional Pop Metal AR13203
Keeping Time AR15356
Keeping Up With The Jones: A Colorful Romp From Zeppelin To The Buttholes AR13204
Keith Moon AR14248
Keith Richards AR14516
Keith: Rock's Main Offender AR14764
Kelly Hogan AR13041
Kenny Wayne Shepherd AR13810
A Kid Makes 'News': Dave Foley Grows Up To Be A 'Newsradio' Star AR15935
The Kids Are Alright: Green Day AR13664
The Kids Are Alright: Offspring AR12936
Kids In The Dark AR13145
Kind Of Blue: Does Songwriter Lou Barlow—The Heart And Soul Of Sebadoh, Sentridoh And The Folk Implosion—Care Too Much? AR12937
The King & I AR13253
The King And I AR13254
King For A Day: First Graceland Concert Planned For October AR15522
The King Of Prime-Time Comedy AR15372
The King Of Rain AR14869
King Of The Goons AR13604
Kings Of Comedy AR15360, AR16117
Kitsch Me, Stupid: Seattle's Super Deluxe Pucker Up AR15839
KMFDM Make Industrial Music The Old-Fashion Way—They Thrash Their Hardware AR15840
Knee-Deep In The Hoopla, From Cub Scouts To Bee Girls, With Some Raw Deals & Rough Living In Between, Blind Melon Has Taken The Long, Hard Road To The Top AR14765
Kristen Pfaff : 1967-1994 AR15523
KRS-One AR15622
Kula Shaker AR14253
Kurt Cobain 1967-1994 AR13423
Kurt Markus AR14575
Kyuss The Sky: Retrodelic Generator Parties Breed An Electric Genre AR15841

L

L.A. Confidential AR12964, AR12965, AR12966, AR15936, AR15937, AR15938, AR15939, AR15940, AR15941, AR15942, AR15943, AR15944, AR15945, AR15946
L. A. Rappers Speak Out AR14481
Land O' Babes AR15312
Land Of The Dead: San Francisco Was Where It All Began AR13673
Last But Not Lost: Santana's New Label AR13781
The Last Nixon AR14618
The Last Stand AR14141
The Last Wave AR16049
A Lasting Impression: The Rolling Stone Interview With Curtis Mayfield AR14482
Laura Dern AR15157
Laurie Anderson AR15717
The Law Of Unintended Consequences: Mandatory Minimum Sentencing Puts First-Time Offenders In Jail For Life And Lets Drug Kingpins Bargain For Their Freedom AR15488
Lawsuit Over Lymon Song Settled AR13973
Lawyers, Punks And Money: SST Records Battle Of Writs And Wills Against Former Acts AR13974
Leader Of The Old School: Juggy Gayles Hyped Records The Old-Fashion Way—With Style AR13846
Leann Rimes Sees 'Blue' Skies AR14531
Leapin' Lizard: LollaPaloozers Aren't Likely To Forget The Jesus Lizard If Lead Singer David Yow Has Anything To Say About It AR13470
Leather & Lace AR14450
Led Zep: The Boxed Life AR15947
Led Zeppelin AR13360
The Left Stuff: Consolidated Mix Politics With Humor AR15113
The Legacy AR15167
Legends Of Country Music AR13847, AR15382
Lemon Fresh Joy AR15948
Lennon's Family Ties: Beatle's Accessories Hot Summer Sellers AR15386
[Lenny Kravitz] AR15949
Lenny Kravitz: Mystic, Mimic, Father, Lover, Which Is The Real Lenny The Kid? AR15524
Leonard Bernstein AR13340
Les Claypool Of Primus AR14436
Leslie Spit Treeo: Canadian Psycho Folk AR14552
Let It Flow: River Phoenix Plays It Cool On And Off The Screen AR13035, AR14831
Let The Good Times Bowl AR12923
Let's Book AR14832, AR15127
Let's Go Or Let's Not And Say We Did: Why You Can't trust The Best-Selling Harvard Travel Series AR16131
Let's Interactive AR13115
Let's Interactive: Breakthroughs In Digital Technology Promise To Bring A New Look To Your Television Set AR15731
A Letter From The Editor AR15793, AR15794, AR15795
The Levellers: A Foot-Stompin' News Service AR12996
Life After Death: The Rolling Stone Interview With Courtney Love AR13717
Life After Def: The Post-Rap, Post-Metal World Of Rick Rubin AR15950
Life After Garcia AR13913
Life After Guns N' Roses: With The Release Of His Album, Izzy Stradlin Finally Breaks His Silence AR13718
A Life In The Balance: Jackson Browne Gets Serious About Love AR15951
Life In The Indie Cities: From Bad Weather And Obstacles Comes Great Music—If You Know Where To Look AR13255, AR14833
Life Of Brian: Don Was Frames A Beach Boys Saga AR13205
Life On The Duplex Planet AR13836
The Lilys Blossom With Seductive '60s Sounds AR15032
Limited Access: Behind-The-Scenes Ticket Maneuvering Leaves Concert Fans With Second-rate Seats AR13069
Linda Ronstadt AR14689
Lisa Palac's Hot List AR15019
A Little Holiday Gear AR13116
Little Richard AR15128
Little Rock, Arkansas AR14509
A Little Strange Music AR14386
Liv In The Fast Lane: Actress Liv Tyler Wraps Her Inner Charm In Men's Outerwear AR13256, AR14834
Live: Artist Of The Year AR13206
Live Stiffs: Full-Blown Concert Albums Play To Less Applause AR13070
Live Through This: A Year On The Road With Nirvana AR12997
Live, From Vietnam!: Bryan Adams Experiences Life After Wartime When He Plays Ho Chi Minh City AR14690
Living In The USA: Revenge Of The Doughnut Boys AR15335
Living In The USA: The Case Of Gary Fannon AR15336
Liz Phair AR13530
Liz Phair: Last Train To Guyville AR14691
LL Cool J AR15764
Lo Rez Skyline AR13852
Lois AR14553
LollaPalooza: Family Affair AR15842
Lollapalooza Jr.: Tomorrow's Stars Are On The Second Stage Today AR15525
Lollapalooza '92 AR14766
Lollapalooza '93 AR14767
London Bridge: Cornershop Curry Western Flavor AR15843

London Calling AR15418, AR15419, AR15420, AR15421, AR15422, AR15423, AR15424, AR15425, AR15426, AR15427, AR15428
London Confidential AR15429
Long Fin Killie AR14597
The Long Road Home AR13316, AR15342
The Long Road To Little Village: Four Distinguished Musicians Find A New Home AR15952
The Longest War AR14596
The Look: In A New Book, Rolling Stone Celebrates 40 Years Of Rock Photography AR14520
Looking For The Next Revolution: The Rolling Stone Interview With Steve Jobs AR14011
Looks Like Team Spirit: On Their Way To Barcelona, Four Athletes Take A Break From Their Olympic Training To Try On American Clothes AR14801, AR15693
Loosening The Beltway: Everybody's A Pundit On 'Politically Incorrect' AR15953
Los Angeles AR13363
Losing The Right To Choose: Republicans In Congress Wage War On Abortion AR12953
Losing Their Religion: Rev. Horton Heat Lets The Spirits Move Him AR13531
The Lost Boy: The Life Of Kurt Cobain AR14692
The Lost Boys: With 'Sweet Oblivion,' Screaming Trees Finally Come Out Of The Woods AR12998
Lost In America: A Father, A Family And An Entire Community Struggle To Understand How One Of Their Sons Could Go So Wrong AR15330
Lost In America—Not!: Navigation Systems And Cellular Phones Will Help You Get There From Here AR15732
Lost In Space: Outlaw Engineers Are Struggling To Save NASA With A New Generation Of Secret Technology AR14004
Lotion AR12999
Lou Reed: Beyond The Underground AR13719
Lounge's Last Call AR13071
Love Battery: Modifying The Northwest Sound AR13000
The Love Boat AR14586
Love It To Death: Trent Reznor Of Nine Inch Nails Preaches the Dark Gospel Of Sex, Pain And Rock & Roll AR13925
Love Janis: Janis Joplin's Rise To Stardom Is Chronicled In These Letters Written To Her Family In Texas AR14324, AR14325
Low-Fi Romantics: Sebadoh Flirt With The Mainstream AR13483
Luka Bloom Doesn't Want To Be Just Another Boring Folkie: Songs From The Heart AR13001
Lunatic Behavior: Soul Asylum Fight The Follow-Up-Album Blues AR15954
Luscious Jackson: Record In New Orleans AR15466
Luscious Jackson Stray From Home On 'Fever In Fever Out' AR13471
Luscious Life AR15718

M

M. Scott Peck At The End Of The Road AR13282
M Speak For Newbies AR13117
Machine Dreams: Rage Take On The Rights Of Native Americans AR13397
Madonna AR13635
Madonna To Sign $60 Million Deal [and other news] AR13975
Magic And Loss: Lida Husik Meshes Indie With Ambient AR13532
Magnapop: Georgia's Finest? AR14177
Magnetic Field AR16072
Majek Faskek: A Messenger Of World Music AR15955
Making Art From Chaos: Jimmy Webb Is Writing His New Songs In The Key Of Life AR12972
Making Education Work AR14533
Making History? A Marketing Blitz of Epic Proportions AR15844
Making Money The Old-Fashion Way: Despite Promises Of A High-Tech Revolution, College-Educated Americans Earn It Working On The Line AR15548
The Making Of The Soviet Bomb AR15182
Making The Scene: A Filmmaker's Diary AR13361
Malignant Giant AR14428
Mall Rap: The Million Man March Draws A Crew Of Hip-Hop Artists To Washington, D.C. AR15494
Mall Rats: Beleaguered Chain Record Stores Are Sinking Fast AR13072
Man, Monkeys And Disease AR13368
Man Of The Year: David Letterman AR15373
Man Or Mouth?: The Rolling Stone Interview With Howard Stern AR14567
The Man Who Would Be King Of Country: Billy Ray Cyrus Scores With 'Some Gave All' AR15571
Man With A Plan AR13002
Mandatory Minimums: Eight More Victims AR15080
Mannequins With A Twist AR13297
Marian Wright Edelman: On The Front Lines Of The Battle To Save America's Children AR12982
Marion Williams: 1927-1994 AR15187
Mario's Big Brother: From 'Donkey Kong' To New Super Nintendo, Sigeru Miyamoto Has Shaped A Generation AR15391
Marisela Norte AR13848
Mark E. Smith's Wrath & Roll: With Their 17th LP, The Fall Are Back In Your Face AR13207
Mark Morris Says He's Not Just A Hard-Drinking, Chain-Smoking, Long-Haired Beats From Modern-Dance Hell AR14222
Mark Seliger AR15383
Married To Metal: The Rolling Stone Interview With Metallica's Lars Ulrich AR13720
Martin Lawrence AR14587, AR15446
Marty Brown: More Than A Country Throwback AR14360
Marxman AR13811
Mary Wells: 1943-1992 AR14483
Massive Attack: Infectious Dance Pop AR15956
Master Class AR13460
Master Of War: Novelist Tom Clancy Keeps Making New Enemies AR13257
Mastering Madonna AR15608
Masters Of The Game: Over The Mountain And Through The Woods With Three Young Designers Who Show The Brand Names How To Play AR13130, AR14617
Matthew McConaughey AR15374
Matthew Rolston AR15223
Maureen Cox Starkey Tigrett: 1946-1994 AR15957
The Mavericks Beach Country AR15313
Maxwell AR15765
MC Lyte AR15447
MC5's Rob Tyner Dies AR14604
Me Phi Me: Up From The Ashes Of Flint AR13895
Mean & Sober: Ego And Innuendo Run Amok As The Music Industry Feuds Over Drug Treatment AR13283
Mean Streaks: Amped, Angry And In Your Face, Graffiti Refuses To Die AR14149
Meat Loaf: The Man Who Saw Paradise By The Dashboard Lights Is Back With 'Bat Out Of Hell II' AR14693
Meat Puppets AR15526
The Media's Myth Of The Bloody Campaign AR14333
The Media's War On Kids: From The Beatles To Beavis And Butt-head AR14334
Meet The Beavis!: The Last Word From America's Phenomenal Pop Combo AR16107
Melissa Etheridge AR13450
Melissa Etheridge: In Through The Out Door AR13258
Melissa Etheridge On Janis Joplin AR13608
'Melrose Place' Is A Really Good Show AR15958
Melvin Franklin: 1942-1995 AR15845
Members Only: Record Clubs Feel Retailers' And Artists' Heat AR13073
Memnoch The Devil AR15184
Memo From The National Affairs Desk AR15598
Memo To The Academy On Its 64th Birthday: Retire Or Reform AR15652
Memorial Tribute To Eazy-E AR15467
Memory Of A Gonzo Christmas Past AR14523
Menace To Society AR13401
Mercury Rev Rising: They Were Too Weird Even For Lollapalooza AR14387
Me'shell NdegeOcello AR14609, AR15623
Message In A Bottle: Shane MacGowan Serves It Straight Up AR12938
Metal Machine Music AR14537
Metal Metheny Music AR14388
Metallica: Once The Scourge Of The Mainstream, The Titans Of Thrash Are On Top Of The Charts AR13721
The Method Of His Madness AR14240
Miami AR14451
Michael Jackson AR14223
Michael Jackson Plans Summer Tour [and other news] AR13976
Michael Jackson: The Making Of 'The King Of Pop' AR13977
Michael O'Donoghue AR12985
Michael Richards's Hot List AR13896, AR15314
[Michael Stipe] AR13424
Michael Stipe AR13722
Michael Stipe: The Rolling Stone Interview AR13723
Michael Sues Sony: Fights To Break Contract With Record Company AR13978
Mick Jagger AR13341
Mick Ronson: 1946-1993 AR14694
Mick: Third Time A Charm? AR15959
Mickey Hart & Robert Hunter AR13837
Middle-Class Funk AR14096
Midseason Pre-Mortem AR15960
Mike Clarke 1944-1993 AR14389
Mike Love Sues Brian Wilson: Claims He Co-Wrote Several Beach Boys Classics AR15961
Mike Scott's Spiritual Renewal: The Leader Of The Waterboys Gets Back To Basics On 'Dream Harder' AR13849
Millie Checks The Pantry AR15062

Millie Comes Upon A Sticky Situation AR15063
Millie Sees Something Scary AR15064
Millie Visits The Senate AR15065
The Millions: A Gimmick-Free Sound AR15408
Mining For Gold: Jewel Takes The Long, Slow Road To Success AR13074
Minor Threat AR13047
Miracle Cure: In The Age Of Grunge, The Spin Doctors Score With A Joyful Noise AR13897
Mr. Bill's Neighborhood AR15599
Mr. Microsoftee: Paul Allen, Shy Billionaire, Tries To Rock The I-Way AR13131
Mr. Natural AR14695
Misty Mountain Hop: Amateurs And Pros Jump Around In Aspen Highlands AR14535, AR14835
Misty Mountain Memories: Robert Plant Embraces His Past On 'Fate Of Nations' AR14768
The Mitch Is Back: Toweling Off For 'Baywatch Nights' AR15962
Mo' Better Multimedia AR13118
Mo' Wax Captures The Trip-Hop Vibe AR14563
Mobb Deep Deliver 'Hell On Earth' To The Faithful AR13627
[Moby] AR15527
Moby: The Great White Wail AR12939
Mod Jobs: Strange And Twisted Paths To Contentment And Prosperity AR16133
Mod Squad: With 'I Should Coco' The U.K. Trio Supergrass Bring Their Freshly Manicured Pop To America AR14836, AR15430
Moe AR13838
The Money Hunt: A Shrinking Pie Changes D.C. Budget Games AR14097
Money, It's A Gas: Pink Floyd Eclipse Stones' Ticket-Sales Record AR15528
Monkees Redux?: Fox's New Show 'The Heights' Zeroes In On A Made-For-Television Blue-Collar Rock Band AR15963
Monster Madness AR13425
Monster Magnetism AR13298
Monster On The Loose: R.E.M. Open Their First Tour In Five Years, In Australia AR13724
Monterey Pop, Airplane Sets Due AR14275
Moon Struck: Grant Lee Buffalo Roam The Margins Of American Gothic On Might Joe Moon AR15529
More Blues For Music Biz: Layoffs And Cutbacks Continue Into The New Year AR14032
More Stunts, More Overpaid Stars, More Demi Moore Naked And More To The Point: Is Anything Any Good? AR15653
More Washington Show Talk: In Today's Episode, TV Ruins Everything AR16035
Morphine: The Band's Low-Rock Music Is Nearly As Addictive As Its Pharmaceutical Namesake AR14769
Moscow's Metal Melee: An Eyewitness Report From The Monsters Of Rock Tour AR15690
Mosh Unit: The Muffs' Two-Minute Bursts Of melodic Noise Are Clamorous Punk Postcards From The Edge AR12967, AR14837
The Most Dangerous Man In America AR15232
Mothers Of Invention: Women In Rock Talk About Scents, Sensibility And Sexism AR15701
Motor Voter: Goin' Mobile AR14041
Motown's Baby Boyz: Philadelphia's Boyz II Men Become The Label's Hottest Act In Years AR14484
Movie Directors Who Toy With Tape AR14291
Movie Extras AR15654
MTV AR15066
MTV Awards Lure The Stars AR13075
MTV Turns Ten AR14671
Mudhoney: The First Great Seattle Band Of The '80s Has The Last Laugh In The '90s AR13398
Multimedia AR14210, AR14390
Multimedia: The Season's Must-Have CD-ROMs AR14661
Murder Mystery AR15085
Muscle & Melody AR14696
Muscle Machines AR16073
Music Awards: 1995 AR14734
Music Biz Blues AR14735
Music Biz Rebounds In '93: Sales Increases Give Industry Hope AR15530
Music By Modem: On-Line Services Provide A High-Tech Option To Music Distribution AR13373
Music For Your Mother: Lords Of The Underground Bring Family Values To Hardcore Rap AR13584
The Music Never Stops: The Rolling Stone Interview With Jerry Garcia AR13426
Music Versus Muscle AR14770
Music Videos AR13615
Musical Chairs? Executive-Shuffle Rumors Rage On AR15964
Muzak Attack AR13840
My Life With The Thrill Kill Kult: Straight Out Of The Seventies AR13371
My So-Called Double Life: Kristin Hersh Of Throwing Muses Finds The Common Ground Between Motherhood And Rock & Roll AR15531
My Way Or The Highway: Despite Accusations That He's Stuck In The Past, Lenny Kravitz Is Now In Vogue AR14771

N

Naked Lunch Box AR14055
The Naked Transcript AR13427
Nanci Griffith Comes Home: The Singer-Songwriter Settles Down After Years Of Late Nights And Hotels AR16054
The Nasty Truth: Field-Tested techniques To Get The Love You Deserve AR15745
Nathan Daniel: 1912-1994 AR15159
A Nation Of Nomads: As The Presidential Campaign Begins, The Republican Wanna-Be's Encounter An American Electorate Wandering Between Hope And Rage AR13602
Native American Son: Robbie Robertson Finds A Common Bond Between His Heritage And His Music AR14231
Native Tongues: New Poets With A Rock & Roll Attitude AR14610
Naughty As They Wanna Be: The Hood Comes First When Naughty By Nature Hits The Mike AR14485
Naughty By Nature's Surprise Success AR13428
Ned's Atomic Dustbin: A Band With A Nonattitude AR14867
Negativland And SST Settle AR13979
Neil Diamond AR13533
Neil Jordan AR15375
Neil Tennant Of The Pet Shop Boys AR15572
Neil Young AR14199
Neil Young: Going To Extremes AR13725
The Nerve Of Her AR13787
Net Worst" The 'New' Networks Go Where The Boys Already Are AR14588
New Bands Strike Gold With Majors AR13003
[New Book] AR14789
New Deal Redux Or Great Society II? AR14098
New Faces AR14790, AR14791, AR14792, AR14793, AR14794
New Faces: A Guide To This Summer's Coolest Music—And The Artists Making It AR15204
New Facts On Porcaro Death AR15965
New Film Or No Film? Cameras In The Digital Age Require Your To Choose A Format AR13119
A New 'Girlfriend' For Matthew Sweet: Hard-Edged Album Documents Romantic Turmoil AR13004
New Jack And Jill AR14232, AR15384
New Kids Top Money List AR15168
New Labels Face Tough Times AR13980
New Music From Mexico AR14654
New Ragged Glories AR13616
The New Road Warriors: For The Members Of Blues Traveler, Life Is One Big, Happy Tour AR13812
The New Skitcoms: Sketches Of Pain AR14508
A New Wave: Rasin Music Catches Fire At Haitian Fest AR14623
A New World Party: Peter Gabriel brings WOMAD To U.S. AR14207
New York City AR15719
Newport, Rhode Island AR14798
Newt Vs. The '60s: The Values Of The Counterculture Top Gingrich's Hit List AR12954
The Next Big Thing AR13726
The Next Wave: The Fusion Of Jazz And Hip-Hop Is Bringing A New Groove To The Dance Floor AR13585
Next Wave: The Last Word On All Things Computer AR15562
Next Wave: The Last Word On All Things Digital AR15563
Nice Guys Finish First: Live Make The Leap From Small Town To Big Time AR14178
Nicholas Schaffner AR14800
Nick Cave AR13534
Nicky Hopkins: 1944-1994 AR14697
9: Take On Me AR13535
19: Bastards Of Young AR14698
1994 Music Awards AR13727
1991 CMJ Music Marathon AR13005
The 1996 Presidential Yearbook: What Were They Then? AR14804
1993: The Year In Movies AR15655
1960's - 1990's AR15067
1926 Miles 1991: The Man Who Changed Music AR15022
98: Silent All These Years AR14391
95: Janie's Got A Gun AR14699
94: Beethoven AR14772
'94 Gleason Awards AR14805
99: One AR14292
91: Freedom 90 AR14392
97: Groove Is In The Heart AR14250
96: Human Behaviour AR14422
90: The Perfect Kiss AR14393
93: Orange Crush AR14394
92: Back On The Chain Gang AR13813
Nipped In The Bid: High Hopes Dampen Rock Auction AR14179
Nirvana: After Giving Birth To The Surprise Hit Of The Year, The Guys From Seattle Fight The Demons Of Fame AR14700

Nirvana: Inside The Heart And Mind Of Kurt Cobain AR13006
Nirvana: Noise For '93 AR13007
Nirvana Projects On Hold AR15532
Nirvana To 'Newsweek': Drop Dead AR14033
Nirvana Tops Album Charts: 'Nevermind' Bumps 'Dangerous' Out Of Number One Position AR14773
Nixon's Record AR14099
No Fear Of Frying: The Hard Rock Cafe Celebrates Twenty Years Of Rock And Rolls AR13898
No Heat Wave For Summer Tours AR13981
No Mercy: Leonard Cohen's Tales from The Dark Side AR13429
No More Years: Why George Must Go AR14100
No Pain, No Gain: The Rolling Stone Interview With Henry Rollins AR13728
No Peace In The Valley AR14208
No Vision Whatsoever: Why We Are All Strangers In The Everglades AR13156
Noam Chomsky: Anarchy In The U.S.A. AR16108
The Noise On The Bus: MTV News & Rock The Vote Put Youth Issues On The '96 Campaign Agenda AR14459
None-A-Day: Is The FDA Out To Take Your Vitamins? AR16036
Nora Ephron: On The Front Lines Of The Sexual Battlefield With The Writer And Director Of 'Sleepless In Seattle' AR13689
Normal Weirdness In Seattle AR14838, AR15367
Not Fade Away: Everclear Triumph Over Demons Of The Past AR15846
Not Guided By Voices: The return of Instrumental Rock AR15748
Not Just Blowing Smoke: Cypress Hill Light Up On 'Black Sunday' AR13586
Not Out Of The Woods Yet: Don Henley Responds To Developer's Accusations AR15966
Nothing But A G Thang: Warren G Hits With "Regulate" AR13926
Now Ear This: Noses Are Fine, And Navels Are Cool, But This Is Still The Classic Rock & Roll Pierce AR15387
Nowhere To Run AR14246
The NRA Sees Red AR16122
NRA's Last Hurrah? AR13480

O

Oasis AR14180
Oasis Cancel Last Third Of U.S. Tour After Rocky Start AR15456
Oasis: The Trouble Boys AR13208
Obituaries AR14808, AR14809, AR14810
Obscenity Bill Passed In Washington [and other news] AR13982
Of Lunch And War: There Was Suppose To Be A Revolution In Mexico, But The Mexicans Got In The Way AR15004
Off The Bandwagon: Teenage Fanclub Battle The Ghost Of Albums Past AR14233
Off The Street And Onto Center Stage: Rock Steady Crew And Jossie Harris Turn Break Dancing Into An Art AR13577, AR13814
Oh, What A Night AR13076
Oi! Did They Have Troubles AR13579
Old Punks In Peril: No Green Day For '70s And '80s Pioneers AR15578
Old-School Cool AR15315
The Olympia Spirit: The Ticket Is Love Rock And Minimalism At Yoyo A Go Go AR14611
On A High Horse: Shudder To Think Shatter Convention With 'Pony Express' AR13008
On A Role: What The Jobs Of The 21st Century Will Be—And How To Prepare For Them Now AR14045
On The Couch With Smashing Pumpkins: The Final Analysis AR13150
On The Cover Of Rolling Stone AR15388
On The Edge AR13729, AR13730, AR13731
On The Range, Political Forces Still Beat Market Forces AR16037
On The Road AR14870, AR14871, AR14872
On The Road...Again: A Troupe Of New Bands Is Taking Its Old-Time Rock & Roll Across America AR13899
On The Row AR15224
Once Death-Defying Clowns, The Red Hot Chili Peppers Grow Up To Be Sensitive White Males AR13665
One Hot Minute AR13137, AR13536, AR14512, AR14839, AR15746, AR15967, AR16057
One Hot Mother Of A Pepper: The Red Hot Chili Peppers Finally Get A New Guitarist And Gear Up To Make Their Next LP AR15968
100 Classic Album Covers AR14873
100 Classic Album Covers: 1984 AR14931
100 Classic Album Covers: 50,000,000 Elvis Fans Can't Be Wrong AR14905
100 Classic Album Covers: A Broken Frame AR14874
100 Classic Album Covers: Abraxas AR14875
100 Classic Album Covers: Aladdin Sane AR14876
100 Classic Album Covers: America Beauty AR14877
100 Classic Album Covers: Aoxomoxoa AR14878
100 Classic Album Covers: Arc Of A Diver AR14879
100 Classic Album Covers: Atom Heart Mother AR14880
100 Classic Album Covers: Bitches Brew AR14881
100 Classic Album Covers: Blind Faith AR14882
100 Classic Album Covers: Born To Run AR14883
100 Classic Album Covers: Brain Salad Surgery AR14884
100 Classic Album Covers: Breakfast In America AR14885
100 Classic Album Covers: Bringing It All Back Home AR14886
100 Classic Album Covers: Candy-O AR14887
100 Classic Album Covers: Catch A Fire AR14888
100 Classic Album Covers: Cats Under The Stars AR14889
100 Classic Album Covers: Cheap Thrills AR14890
100 Classic Album Covers: Cosmic Slop AR14891
100 Classic Album Covers: Country Life AR14892
100 Classic Album Covers: Dark Side Of The Moon AR14893
100 Classic Album Covers: Daydream Nation AR14894
100 Classic Album Covers: Diamond Dogs AR14895
100 Classic Album Covers: Diesel And Dust AR14896
100 Classic Album Covers: Disraeli Gears AR14897
100 Classic Album Covers: Doc At The Radar Station AR14898
100 Classic Album Covers: Document AR14899
100 Classic Album Covers: Eat A Peach AR14900
100 Classic Album Covers: Electric Ladyland AR14901
100 Classic Album Covers: Elvis Presley AR14902
100 Classic Album Covers: Exile On Main Street AR14903
100 Classic Album Covers: Fear Of Music AR14904
100 Classic Album Covers: Franks Wild Years AR14906
100 Classic Album Covers: Fresh Fruit For Rotting Vegetables AR14907
100 Classic Album Covers: Greetings From Asbury Park, N.J. AR14908
100 Classic Album Covers: Hardcore Jollies AR14909
100 Classic Album Covers: Hejira AR14910
100 Classic Album Covers: Honey AR14911
100 Classic Album Covers: Horses AR14912
100 Classic Album Covers: Hot Buttered Soul AR14913
100 Classic Album Covers: Hotel California AR14914
100 Classic Album Covers: House Of The Holy AR14915
100 Classic Album Covers: In The Court Of The Crimson King AR14916
100 Classic Album Covers: Into The Purple Valley AR14917
100 Classic Album Covers: It's A Beautiful Day AR14918
100 Classic Album Covers: Journey Through The Secret Life Of Plants AR14919
100 Classic Album Covers: Koo Koo AR14920
100 Classic Album Covers: Led Zeppelin AR14921
100 Classic Album Covers: Licensed To Ill AR14922
100 Classic Album Covers: Live Peace In Toronto AR14923
100 Classic Album Covers: London Calling AR14924
100 Classic Album Covers: Look Sharp AR14925
100 Classic Album Covers: Los Angeles AR14926
100 Classic Album Covers: Metal Box AR14927
100 Classic Album Covers: Middle Man AR14928
100 Classic Album Covers: Never A Dull Moment AR14929
100 Classic Album Covers: Never Mind The Bollocks Here's The Sex Pistols AR14930
100 Classic Album Covers: Nothing's Shocking AR14932
100 Classic Album Covers: Ogdens' Nut Gone Flakes AR14933
100 Classic Album Covers: One Step Beyond AR14934
100 Classic Album Covers: Ooh La La AR14935
100 Classic Album Covers: Peter Gabriel AR14936
100 Classic Album Covers: Physical Graffiti AR14937
100 Classic Album Covers: Playing Possum AR14938

100 Classic Album Covers: Power, Corruption And Lies AR14939
100 Classic Album Covers: Relayer AR14940
100 Classic Album Covers: Rumours AR14941
100 Classic Album Covers: Sailin' Shoes AR14942
100 Classic Album Covers: See Jungle! See Jungle! Go Join Your Gang Yeah!... AR14943
100 Classic Album Covers: Self Portrait AR14944
100 Classic Album Covers: Sgt. Pepper's Lonely Hearts Club Band AR14945
100 Classic Album Covers: Sign O' The Times AR14946
100 Classic Album Covers: Slave To The Rhythm AR14947
100 Classic Album Covers: Some Girls AR14948
100 Classic Album Covers: Sticky Fingers AR14949
100 Classic Album Covers: Strange Days AR14950
100 Classic Album Covers: The Beatles AR14951
100 Classic Album Covers: The Idiot AR14952
100 Classic Album Covers: The Joker AR14953
100 Classic Album Covers: The Joshua Tree AR14954
100 Classic Album Covers: The Low Spark Of High Heeled Boys AR14955
100 Classic Album Covers: The Parkerilla AR14956
100 Classic Album Covers: The Ramones AR14957
100 Classic Album Covers: The Slider AR14958
100 Classic Album Covers: The Smiths AR14959
100 Classic Album Covers: There's A Riot Goin' On AR14960
100 Classic Album Covers: Tommy AR14962
100 Classic Album Covers: True Blue AR14963
100 Classic Album Covers: Trust AR14964
100 Classic Album Covers: Turn Back AR14965
100 Classic Album Covers: Tutu AR14966
100 Classic Album Covers: Velvet Underground And Nico AR14967
100 Classic Album Covers: War AR14968
100 Classic Album Covers: Weasels Ripped My Flesh AR14969
100 Classic Album Covers: Welcome To My Nightmare AR14970
100 Classic Album Covers: We're Only In It For The Money AR14971
100 Classic Album Covers: Who's Next AR14972
100 Classic Album Covers: Wish You Were Here AR14973
100 Classic Album Covers: With The Beatles AR14974
101 Reasons To Watch TV AR15969
100: Satisfaction AR14395
The 100 Top Music Videos AR13617
One Love AR15023
One More For The Road AR16074
One More 'Saturday Night': Will This Season Be A Fresh Start Or The Long Buh-Bye? AR15970
One More Time With Feeling: Defying Time And Trends, The Rolling Stones Return With More Of That Voodoo They Do So Well AR13732
One Of Us! One Of Us! One Of... AR13537, AR14641
1: Sledgehammer AR14396
Online AR14975, AR14976, AR14977, AR14978, AR14979, AR14980, AR14981, AR14982, AR14983, AR14984, AR14985, AR14986, AR14987, AR14988, AR14989, AR14990
Ono's Season Of Grief AR13430
Onward Christian Soldiers: Bob Dole, Phil Gramm And The Other Republican Candidates Are Kowtowing To The Religious Right, But Conservative Christians Are Searching For A True Believer AR13603
Onyx: Bringing Old-School Hip-Hop To The Mosh Pit AR14320
Opera Man: The Rolling Stone Interview With Pete Townshend AR13431
Opinion AR14774
Opinion: Blaming Hardcore For Murder Is Taking The Lazy Way Out AR14486
Opinion: Chapman Killed Lennon To Achieve This Kind Of Notoriety AR13432
Opinion: Tribute LPs Filled With Quirky Covers Are Just No Fun Anymore AR13733
Orange County Crush AR13364
Orange Day: In This Southern California County, The Punk Spirit Never Died AR13365, AR14840
Organically Grown: Blind Melon Parlays Its Small-Town Roots Into A Big-City Sound AR14775
The Origin Of AIDS: A Startling New Theory Attempts To Answer The Question 'Was It An Act Of God Or An Act Of Man?' AR13369
'Origin Of AIDS' Update: Clarification AR14991
The Original Riot Grrrl: Joan Jett Lives Up To Her Bad Reputation AR13379
The Orioles Discography AR14992
Oscar Blindness AR15658
Oscar '95: The Fix Is In AR15656
Oscar '96: Soo-Ey! AR15657
Oscar Rejects: A Racist, Sexist And Gutless Academy Screws Up Big Time AR15659
The Other Summer Tour AR13983
Our Lives, Our Music: Abbey Road AR13270
Our Lives, Our Music: Angel Dust AR15409
Our Lives, Our Music: Appetite For Destruction AR13166, AR14312
Our Lives, Our Music: Are You Experienced? AR13387
Our Lives, Our Music: Armed Forces AR13449
Our Lives, Our Music: Bat Out Of Hell AR16110
Our Lives, Our Music: Born To Run AR15149
Our Lives, Our Music: Bringing It All Back Home AR13637
Our Lives, Our Music: By The Readers Of 'Rolling Stone' AR15016
Our Lives, Our Music: Catch Bull At Four AR13349
Our Lives, Our Music: Daydream Nation AR15210
Our Lives, Our Music: Exile On Main Street AR12945
Our Lives, Our Music: Freak Out! AR15393
Our Lives, Our Music: Get Your Wings AR14601
Our Lives, Our Music: Goodbye Yellow Brick Road AR15189
Our Lives, Our Music: Horses AR13479
Our Lives, Our Music: Hotcakes AR15461
Our Lives, Our Music: Led Zeppelin IV AR15738
Our Lives, Our Music: Live At The Apollo AR15141
Our Lives, Our Music: Mud Slide Slim And The Blue Horizon AR15454
Our Lives, Our Music: Murmur AR13163
Our Lives, Our Music: Nevermind AR15741
Our Lives, Our Music: Out Of Time AR14637
Our Lives, Our Music: Psychocandy AR14502
Our Lives, Our Music: Ritual De Lo Habitual AR16052
Our Lives, Our Music: Scarecrow AR15460
Our Lives, Our Music: Sgt. Pepper's Lonely Hearts Club Band AR14670
Our Lives, Our Music: Shake Your Money Maker AR15566
Our Lives, Our Music: Songs Of Leonard Cohen AR13030
Our Lives, Our Music: Stand! AR15733
Our Lives, Our Music: The Joshua Tree AR15453
Our Lives, Our Music: The Stranger AR15405
Our Lives, Our Music: The Unforgettable Fire AR14526
Our Lives, Our Music: The Wall AR15092
Our Lives, Our Music: The White Album AR14144, AR14510
Our Lives, Our Music: Use Your Illusion I AR14130
Our Lives, Our Music: Velvet Underground And Nico AR15606
Our Lives, Our Music: What's Going On AR14241
Our Lives, Our Music: Workingman's Dead AR13028
Our Lives, Our Times: By The Readers Of 'Rolling Stone' AR15017
Our Man In Nirvana Rages On (And On) About Stardom, Fatherhood, His Feud With Pearl Jam, The Death Of Grunge And Why He's Never Been Happier In His Life: The Rolling Stone Interview AR13734
Out Of The Closet: Yoko Ono Lends Rare Lennon Gear To The Hall Of Fame AR15766
Out Of The Copy Room: How To Make Your First Job Work For You AR14796
Out Of The Ordinary AR15971
Out Of The Shadows...Into The Night AR14841, AR15316
Out There AR15018
OutKast AR14309
Outtakes: On The Road And Behind The Scenes With Rolling Stone's Chief Photographer AR15972
Over There: The U.S. Military's Toxic Reach AR14123, AR15404
Over To You, Dan: How Cronkite's Heir Became Chung's Sidekick AR14335
Ozzy Osbourne AR14776

P

Package Goods AR15847
Paisley Is Out AR13984
Paleface: Tempering Venom With Glee AR14002
Palmer On Rock AR15749
Panic: Metal Shot Through With Rock AR13900
Papa John Creach: 1917-1994 AR13735
Papa Was A Rolling Stone: But Marlon Richards Is Not Just A Chip Off The Old Rock AR13259, AR14842
Paradise Found: Coolio Completes His Fantastic Voyage From The Mean Streets

Of Los Angeles To The Top Of The Pop Charts AR14357
Paradise Lost AR14252
Parkay On Trial AR15068
Party Culture: Strange Customs, Quaint Traditions And Stupid Parlor Tricks AR14554
Party Out Of Bounds: On The Bus And Out Of Control With The Cypress Hill—House Of Pain Tour AR15448
Pat Boone AR13538
Patent Pending AR15081
Patrick Lippert: 1958-1993 AR15014
Pat's Kids AR13260
Patti Rothberg Brings Her Subterranean Lovesick Blues To The Surface AR13138
Patti Scialfa AR15102
Patti Smith: The Rolling Stone Interview AR13736
Paul K AR15205
Paul McCartney AR13793
Paul Rothchild: 1935-1995 AR14034
[Paul Westerberg] AR15973
Paul Westerberg Looks Back, Moves Forward On New LP AR15734
Pavement Smooth Out The Edges On 'Corners' AR13472
Pay To Play: Independent Promoters Cash In On The Hits As Alternative Radio Becomes Big Business AR13077
Pearl Jam Drummer Beats It AR14777
Pearl Jam On The Road AR15038
Pearl Jam: Taking On Ticketmaster AR13078
Pearl Jammin' AR15585
Pedal To The Medal: These Olympic Contenders Shift Into Casual Gear AR14314, AR14843
Penn's 'Free-For-All': Singer Releases Stunning Second Effort AR15974
The Pentagon Vs. The Budget: Still Hot For The Cold War AR14101
People Hold On AR13388
The Pepper Chase AR13539
Performance AR14358
The Perils Of Pauly AR14589
Peripheral Vision AR15564
Perry Farrell AR12940
Perry Farrell Busted For Drugs [and other news] AR13985
Personal Best: Whether You're Hitting The Slopes Or An Indoor Pool, You Need Lotions And Shampoos To Counteract The Drying Effects Of The Winter Workout AR14131, AR14844
Pervert Designer AR14452
Pete Townshend AR15975
Peter Gabriel's Secret World AR15431
Peter Gabriel's 'Us': Singer Releases First Album Since 1986's 'So' AR13815
Peter Townshend AR15796
Phat Cats And Punks: Rappers Meet Metalheads On 'Judgment Night' AR13587
Phil Spector AR15797
Phony Campaign Reform: Update AR16038
Photographers Who See Some Screen Action AR14293
Picture This: The Best Of Rock-Photography Book AR15389
A Pistol-Whipped Nation: Pass The Brady Bill—Then Ban Handguns AR14102
Pit Master Wanted: Large, Mellow Men To Keep Peace At Live Shows AR15234
P.J. Gets The Last Word: Why I Still Think I'm Right, No Matter What Greider Says AR15005
PJ Harvey AR15533
The Plague Years AR13044
Planets' World AR15317
Plans For Dylan Tribute: Clapton, Harrison And Others To Perform AR15976
Plastic Fantastic Punk Rock: Urge Overkill Bring The '70s Back To Life AR14701
The Plastic Ono McCartney Band AR13737
Play It By Ear: CD Game A Hit AR15169
The Player: Shaquille O'Neal, A Celebrity For The New World AR13999
The Players 1992 AR15660
Players Stumped By Myst Can Now Get Pyst AR14662
Playing 'God": The Brains Behind Crash Test Dummies AR13841
Playing In The Band: The Music Of The Grateful Dead AR13738
Playing With Fire AR15069
The Pleasure Of Pain: Nine Inch Nails' Trent Reznor Dances On The Edge Of Madness AR14234
The Plight Of The Crowes: The Band Cancels Show After Trouble With Police AR15217
The Pluck Of The Irish: Musicians Unite To Protest Sectarian Violence AR13816
The Plugged-In Voter: The New News Has Reconnected People And Politics AR14336
PM Dawn: Metaphysical Graffiti AR13009
Point And Click Picks AR13120
Polara AR14181
Police Blotter AR15097, AR15098
Police Sweep L.A. In The Wake Of Shakur Murder: Death Row Reportedly Under FBI Investigation AR15609
Polo Is My Life: Fear And Loathing In Horse Country AR15600
Pop Journal AR13079, AR13080, AR13081, AR13082, AR13083, AR13084
Pop Singer Riles Israeli Right AR13027
Pop Tarts: Orchestrated Rock Maneuvers Its Way Through The Grungy Darkness AR13454
The Pop Wizardry Of Sam Phillips AR16088
Pork To The People AR16039
Portishead AR15767
Portland, Maine AR15106
Portrait Of Defeat: Is The End Near For The NRA? AR13481
Portrait Of The Artist A A Journalist AR15798
Posies: Inside Out AR15231
Positive PE: After A Hiatus, Public Enemy Return With A Fierce But Soulful Album AR15449
'Posse' Leader Mario Van Peebles Shoots From The Lip AR15661
Post Mac Attack AR15977
Post-Orbal Remorse AR16060
Powder To The People: Connoisseurs Of The Cold Rip Through Their Favorite Brand Of Snow AR14440, AR14845
Power Play: Meet The Men Who Rule Modern-Rock Radio AR16094
Power Surge: Multimedia Systems AR13121
Power To The People: Bulgaria Struggles With The Peaceful Atom & Post-Cold War Politics AR15183
Power To The People: Hazel O'Leary Rewires The Department Of Energy AR16040
Prai$e The Lord AR14182
Pre-Teenage Wasteland: Catching Saturday-Morning Fever AR15978
Prescentable: This Holiday Season, Make More Than Just A Suitable Impression By Giving—Or Wearing—One Of These Fragrances Or Aftershaves AR14846
Prescription Refilled: Spin Doctors' "Turn It Upside Down" Is More That Meets The Ear AR14702
[Present Tense] AR15114
President Clinton: The Rolling Stone Interview AR14103, AR15799
Presidential Candidates Discover America AR14104
Presidents Of The United States Of America AR15379
Pretty Hate Machine: On Their New Album, 'Load,' Metallica Explore The Devil Inside AR13739
Pretty On The Inside: Blur Get Introspective On Their New Album AR15472
Pretty On The Outside: Echobelly Coat Perversity With Sugar Pop AR15848
Price Busters: Green Day Lower Ticket Prices And One-Up Pearl Jam AR14183
The Price Is Not Right: Is Ticketmaster Taking These People For A Ride? AR14035
The Price Of Politics—Student Loans AR15348
Primed And Ticking: PJ Harvey Beat The Sophomore Jinx And Get Their Mojo Workin' With An American Tour And Their Powerful New Album, 'Rid Of Me' AR13762
Primitive Radio Gods Get The Blues AR15768
Primus Choices AR13049
Prince: Free At Last AR13433
The Prince Of Wildwood: Jack Brian Searches The Jersey Shore For Love, Girls And A Future AR14337
Prince Records Three Hours Of 'Emancipation' AR13434
Prince Retires—Maybe: He Says He's Quitting Studio Work, But Don't Hold Your Breath AR13986
Prodigal Son: The Battle Over New Bruce, Dead CDs AR14036
Professors Of Hate: Academia's Dirty Secret AR14636
Profiles In College: Books, CD-ROMs And Web Sites That Tell You Where To Go AR15119
Promoters Hurt By Summer Flops AR13987
Provincetown AR13160
Public Enemy #1: Rap's Top Group Focuses On Gold Brains, Not Gold Chains AR14487
Pulling The Donkey Lever AR15006
Pulp Friction: Frontman Jarvis Cocker Wreaks Revenge For The 'Common People' AR15432
Pumpkins Plan Double Disc: Billy Corgan And The Band Have A Smashing Good Time In The Studio AR14437
The Punk-Rock Talking Blues: Henry Rollins Bares All With The Spoken Word AR14778
Punk's Holy Rollers: Bad Religion Have Come A Long Way From Their Garage-Rock Roots AR14397
Pure & Simple: Kelly Willis, County Waif AR14847, AR15359
Push It Good: Salt-N-Pepa Are Going To The Edge AR15188

Q

Quad City DJ's Are On The Right Track AR14138
Queen Latifah's New Gambit: Her New Album Reaches Out To A Larger Audience AR14488
Queen's Reich: Queer Punk Comes Out of The Closet—Loudly AR15220

R

Race, Money And The Meaningless Search For The Center: Who Really Won The Election Of 1996 And Why AR14105
Racers, Rockers And Roaches Star In The Best New CD-ROM Games AR14663
Radio Daze AR13740
Radio Free Vedder: Pearl Jam Hijack The Airwaves For A Free-Form Throw-Down AR13788
Radio Land Rush: The Industry's Biggest Station Owners Get Bigger While The Small Ones Sign Off AR13085
Radiohead: 'Creep' Is The Most Audacious Pop Move Since The Police's 'Every Breath You Take' AR14398
The Raging Optimism And Multiple Personalities Of Dave Matthews AR13284
Rainforest Foundation Benefit AR13618
Ralph J. Gleason Awards AR14184, AR15137
Rancid AR14185
Random Access: Dispatches From Cyberspace AR14664
Randy Shilts: The Rolling Stone Interview AR16053
Range Wars: Should COllege Radio Be Making Waves Or Making Money? AR14668
Rap AR14489
Rap Wrap AR15139
Rapid Transit AR14665
Rappers Get Roughed Up: John 'Ecstacy' Fletcher And Friends File Complaint Against New York Police AR12916
Rappers Sound Warning: The Violence In Los Angeles Didn't Surprise Those Who Were Paying Attention AR14490
Rave AR15485
Raves AR12926, AR12958, AR13023, AR13152, AR13154, AR13187, AR13190, AR13303, AR13319, AR13370, AR13389, AR13390, AR13435, AR13475, AR13574, AR13575, AR13597, AR13741, AR13760, AR13792, AR13851, AR14124, AR14143, AR14145, AR14209, AR14243, AR14244, AR14285, AR14286, AR14322, AR14323, AR14417, AR14442, AR14448, AR14519, AR14559, AR14595, AR14602, AR14603, AR14620, AR14640, AR14652, AR14703, AR14779, AR14780, AR14802, AR14803, AR15015, AR15093, AR15094, AR15135, AR15136, AR15216, AR15327, AR15328, AR15363, AR15390, AR15444, AR15554, AR15555, AR15573, AR15582, AR15737, AR15805, AR15980, AR16097, AR16111
Ravestock AR15769
Raw And Chunky: A Tribe Called Quest Go Minimalist AR14306
Ray Charles AR13674
Readers' Picks: 1992 Music Awards AR15142
Readers' Picks: 1993 Music Awards AR15143
Readers Poll: 1996 AR15144
The Reading Festival AR13010, AR14445
The Reading List AR15145
The Real Dirt: Alice In Chains Take A Hard Look At The Dark Side Of Seattle On The New EP 'Jar Of Flies' AR13399
The Real New Deal: The Breeders Get Wet And Wild As They Dive Back Into Action On 'Last Splash' AR13011
The Real World AR14797
Reality Bites Back: In It's Fifth Season, 'The Real World' Spins Off Into Orbit AR15981
Rebecca Coupe Franks: Young Woman With A Horn AR14038
Rebel Yellers: Pantera Take Metal To No. 1 With Their New "Far Beyond Driven" AR13400
The Rebirth Of Elton John AR14807
Record-Chain Blacklist: Super Club Establishes Policy On Rating Lyrics AR14781
Record High AR13988
Red Alert AR13261
Red Hot + Positive AR14186
Red Hot Chili Peppers' Naked Truth AR13742
Red-Hot Lollapalooza: Chili Peppers Will Headline This Summer's Alternative-Music Meld AR13990
Red House Painters AR13989
Redbaiter Liar Warmonger Crook: Richard Milhous Nixon 1913-1994 AR15146
The Refreshments AR15147
Refueled & Reborn: While Led Zeppelin Take Their Rightful Place In The Rock & Roll Hall Of Fame, Jimmy Page And Robert Plant Draw Up New Flight Plans AR13436
R.E.M. AR14148
R.E.M.: Tour On? AR15849
The Remaking Of The President AR14106
Remembering Bill AR15153
Remembering Miles AR15154
Rent Strikes AR14848, AR15850
Replays AR13313
Report From Sundance AR15662
Republica AR15770
Requiem For A Heavyweight AR15349
Requiescat In Pace AR15158
Restricted Access: A Major Record Chain Hits Rap And Rock With 18-To-Buy Labels AR15586
Retread Sneakers: The Duo Releases A Collection Of New Old Songs AR15206
Return Mail AR15175
The Return Of Dr. Feelgood AR15982
Return Of The All-Day Sucker AR13991
Return Of The Crimson King: Robert Fripp And Company Rejoin Forces For The First Time In Ten Years AR13743
Return Of The King: Robert Fripp Keeps His Word AR13744
Revenge Of The Weezer Nerds: They're Not Punk, They're Not Pop, They're Not Pretty, But They're Huge AR15702
Rhythm Nation AR15115, AR15116, AR15117
Richard Linklater's Hot List AR13901, AR15318
Richard Thompson AR13540
The Right Computer For You: It's The Soul Of The System That Counts AR13122
Right Hair, Right Now: An Unkempt Mop Top Complements Today's Radical Biker Chic AR14849, AR15694
Right Here, Right Now: The Seattle Rock Band Pearl Jam Learns How To Celebrate Life AR14782
Ringo: Confident And Sober, The Former Beatle Releases His Best Album In Nearly Two Decades AR15983
Riots Mar G N' R Tour AR14491
The Rise And Fall Of A Super Freak AR15337
The Rise And Fall Of Apple Inc AR14012
The Rise And Fall Of Apple Inc. [Part Two] AR14013
The Road From Nowhere: Walking The Streets Of Aberdeen, Wash. AR13914
The Road Less Traveled AR15851
The Road Less Traveled: Pavement's Crooked Path To Stardom AR13209
The Road To Wellville AR13132
Road Trips AR15402
Road Woes: What It Costs AR13086
Rob Collins: 1963-1996 AR14187
Rob Zombie AR15151
Robbie Robertson: The Rolling Stone Interview AR15024
Robert Altman: The Rolling Stone Interview AR13146
Robert F. Kennedy Jr.: Getting Down To Earth With A Leading Eco-Activist AR15392
Robert Redford: The Rolling Stone Interview AR13437
Robert Rodriguez AR15663
Robert White 1936-1994 AR15751
Robyn Hitchcock AR13407
Robyn Hitchcock's Wild Kingdom: In The Land Of Odds, The Leader Of The Egyptians Rules AR15129
Rock & Roll Hall Of Fame AR13541, AR13782, AR15170, AR15984
The Rock & Roll Hall Of Fame '94 AR13783, AR15130
Rock & Roll Music AR15218
Rock & Roll Must Not Let Broadway Blunt Its Visceral Power AR13438
Rock & Roll Summer: Artist's Picks AR15086
Rock & Roll Summer: Athens AR13042
Rock & Roll Summer: Austin AR14631, AR14632
Rock & Roll Summer: Boston AR14316
Rock & Roll Summer: Detroit AR14043
Rock & Roll Summer: Jersey Shore AR15350
Rock & Roll Summer: London AR13486
Rock & Roll Summer: Los Angeles AR15152
Rock & Roll Summer: Minneapolis AR15735
Rock & Roll Summer: New Orleans AR12924
Rock & Roll Summer: New York AR15033
Rock & Roll Summer: Phoenix AR13918
Rock & Roll Summer: Seattle AR15087
Rock & Roll Yearbook AR13542, AR13543, AR14704, AR15034, AR15319, AR15852
Rock Against AIDS, 1993 AR14206, AR14235
Rock And Rap Comics AR14399
Rock And Roll Hall Of Fame AR14705
Rock And Roll Yearbook AR13544, AR13902, AR14706, AR14707
Rock Hall Announces Inductees AR13784
Rock Radio Make-Over: Two New Formats Echo Listeners' Changing Tastes AR13087
Rock, Rap And Movies Bring You The News AR14338
Rock The Vote's New Campaign: Organization Gets Out The Vote In New Hampshire Primary AR14492
Rocket Takes Off: San Diego's Favorite Sons Get Fans Fired Up AR15750
Rockin' And 'Rolling' Into Cyberspace AR15853
Rockin' Dopsie: 1932-1993 AR15561
Rockin' In The Heart Of Texas: Unsigned Bands Reign Supreme At Austin's Annual Music Blowout AR13745
Rock's Dream Team: Legends Meet At Hall Of Fame's Opening-Day Show AR13817
Rock's Greatest Showman AR13992
Rock's Royal Jesters: King Missile Makes Merry On College Radio With 'Detachable Penis' AR12973
[Rolling Stone...] AR15221
The Rolling Stone Interview AR14783
The Rolling Stone Interview: Eric Clapton AR14200
The Rolling Stone Interview: Jerry Garcia AR14201

The Rolling Stone Interview With Sonic Youth's Thurston Moore: Better Living Through Feedback AR13746
Rolling Stone Online AR15222
The Rolling Stones On Tour AR14057
The Rolling Stones' 'Rock & Roll Circus' Is Back In Town AR14359
Rom & Roll: Hanging With Wanda The Worm Women And Friends AR14339
Ron Wood Of The Rolling Stones AR13545
Roommatism: How To Live With Others Without Killing Yourself AR16132
The Roots Roll Away From The Jazz-Hip-Hop Tree AR14651
Ropin' The Whirl Wind: Garth Brooks The Rolling Stone Interview AR13439
Rory Gallagher: 1948-1995 AR15433
A Rose In Gloom: Madder Rose Balance Prettiness With Dissonance On "Panic On" AR13380
Ross Perot Talks, Washington Squawks AR14107
'Round Midnight: A Tribe Called Quest Shift Into High Gear With Their New Album AR15624
Roy Acuff: 1903-1992 AR14493
Roy Orbison AR15103
Royal Spoils: Royal Trux Keep Everyone Guessing With 'Thank You' AR15380
The Royal Treatment: The Beastie Boys Fight For Their Right To Prosper AR12941
The Royalty Scam: R&B Foundation Rewards Underpaid Musical Pioneers AR15854
Rubber Souls AR14132, AR14633
Ruby Doomsday: Ruby Sparkle With Their Bleak Bravado AR13546
Ruling Asses: Oasis Have Conquered America, And They Won't Shut Up About It AR14708
Run-D.M.C.: Back On The Throne AR15625
Run, Newt, Run: Would A Presidential Bid Finally Expose The Real Newt Gingrich? AR12955
RuPaul AR15703
Russian Roulette AR15007
Rwanda: The Death Of A Nation AR14134, AR15343
Rx Now, Pay Later: Will Health Reform Be Clinton's Reaganomics? AR14108

S

A Sacrifice To The Lords Of Yesterday AR13606
A Sad Day For Comedy AR16118
Safe & Sound: Home Alive Unites The Seattle Music Community While Teaching Self-Defense AR15088
Saline Solution: Veruca Salt Wrap Their Hardcore Inside A Candy-Pop Coating AR15771
Sally Potter: Introducing 'Orlando' Director AR15664
Salt Lake City, Utah AR15346
Sam Kinison: 1953-1992 AR15985
The Samurai And The Cyberthief: How The World's Most-Wanted Computer Criminal Was Hunted Down By One Of His Targets—The Master Of Cybersecurity AR14014
San Diego AR15155
San Francisco AR13050
Sandra Bernhard AR15626
The Sands Of Time AR15070
Sao Paulo Megacity AR14142
Sarah McLachlan: Happy To Be Unhappy AR13818
Saturday Night Jive AR15665
Saviors' Haven AR15320
Say Of The Lucas AR15772
Scarce Survive Tragedy And Release Belated Debut AR15855
Scenes From The Cast Struggle In Beverly Hills:Mauled In Malls By Rabid Fans, The Stars Of 'Beverly Hills, 90210' Deal With Their Teen Minutes Of Fames AR14590
Scents Of Style: Fragrances For The Holiday Season AR14850
Scentsual Pleasures AR15483, AR15489
School Of Fish: Confounding Critics AR14868
School Ties Stars Unbutton Their Shirts AR14315, AR14534
Scrambling For Dollars: Will Cable Companies Break The Promise Of New Video Technologies? AR13644
Screaming Trees AR13634
Screaming Trees: Woodshed For Success AR14188
Screen Saviors AR16075
The Sea And Cake AR15177
Seal, Delivered: "Seal" Chronicles Two Years Of Inner And Outer Turmoil AR15587
The Search For The Secret Pyramid AR14418, AR15078
Sebastiao Salgado: The Rolling Stone Interview AR13342
The Second Coming! AR15986
Second Helping AR13088
The Secret Life Of Jerry Garcia AR14058
The Secret Of St. Mary's AR13158, AR13789
The Seduction Of Peter Jay Rudge: Part One AR15542
The Seduction Of Peter Jay Rudge: Part Two AR15543
Seeking Soul Asylum: At Home With The Loud Fast Rulers Of The Minneapolis Music Scene AR14709
Seizing The Light AR13165
Selene Vigil Of 7 Year Bitch AR13547
Selling Out AR16095
Selling Sex In 'Showgirls' AR15666
Senator Krist: Krist Novoselic Talks About Politics, Censorship And Life After Nirvana AR13455
The Sensual Christian: Father Matthew Fox Extols The Joys Of Passion And Lust Over The Shame Of Original Sin True Believers AR16092
A Separate Peace: The Clinton Administration Has Abandoned The Rhetoric Of The War On Drugs, But It Hasn't Stopped Fighting The War AR16041
Seven Inches Of Pleasure: For Bands And Fans, The Single Is The New Format Of Choice AR13012
7: Subterranean Homesick Blues AR14400
17: Been Caught Stealing AR13548
78: Dirty Boots AR14401
75: One AR14402
'75% Less Fat,' 100% Rock: Former Mat Chris Mars Sheds Some Excess Weight On His Second Solo LP AR14236
74: Psycho Therapy AR14403
70: I Want Your AR13819
79: Voices Carry AR13549
71: Rosalita AR13820
77: White Wedding AR14568
76: Mysterious Ways AR13821
73: Wicked Game AR13822
72: Shadrach AR14404
Sex At Sundance AR15667
Sexual Healing: Janet Jackson Finds Peace, Inspiration And Chart Success Through Carnal Knowledge AR15195
Shannon Hood: 1967-1995 AR13456
The Shape Of Things To Come AR16076
Shara Nelson AR14282
Sheryl Crow AR14283
Sheryl Crow: She Only Wants To Be With You AR15376
Shop Therapy: Kerri Kenney Of 'The State' Prowls Manhattan's Lower East Side AR14851, AR15035
Shopping At Sal's: Searching For The Look Of The Future At The Salvation Army AR13262, AR14852
The Short Life And Death Of Tupac Shakur: Bury Me Like A G AR15108
Shot In The Heart AR13915
Should We Throw The Bums Out? AR14109
Sick Of It All: Searching For Breakthroughs In Musicians' Health Care AR14189
Side Effects: A Concerned Public Official Says We Need To Shift The Way We Think About Drugs Before We Lose Even More Young Lives To AIDS An Violence AR15362
Sidewalks For Sale: Libertarians Are Flourishing On Capitol Hill, On Campus And On Line AR16042
Simmering Chili: Peppers Stir Up A Red-Hot New Album AR13351
Simon Bonney: The Singer Changes Directions On 'Forever' AR13850
Simon LeBon Of Duran Duran AR14710
Simple Minds: Stereolab Make Suprisingly Seductive Minimalist Pop AR15178
A Simple Twist Of Fate AR14426
Simply The Best: Tracy Bonham Enjoys Her Winning Streak AR14462
Since Then AR15410, AR15411, AR15412, AR15413
Sinead Speaks AR14494
Sinful Wages: Clinton Wavers On Raising Workers' Pay AR14110
Singer, Actor, Director: With A Movie And A New Album, John Mellencamp Branches Out AR13823
A Singer Finds Her Voice: Maura O'Connell Redefines The Songstress As A Force To Be Reckoned With AR16055
Singin' In The Rain: Artists Unite To Benefit Rain-Forest Charity AR13824
Singing From The Heart: Tracy Chapman Explores Some New Territory On Her Third Album AR14495
The Sinkable Carol Browner: New EPA Chief Finds Herself In Over Her Head AR16043
Sins Of The Innocent: Children Are Falling Victim To A New Kind Of Sexual Offender—Other Children AR15577
Sioux Indians File Suit Against The Cult [and other news] AR13993
Sir Mix-A-Lot AR13550
Site Seeing On The Web AR16077
6: Right Now AR14569
16: Thriller AR15627
68: Smells Like Nirvana AR14570
60: Epic AR14405
65: Jazzin' For Blue Jean AR14406
60 Ft Dolls AR14598
64: Brilliant Disguise AR14571
69: Tennessee AR14294
61: Every Breath You Take AR14555
67: Money For Nothing AR13825
66: Oh Father AR14556
63: Rockit AR14407
62: It's My Life AR13551
Size Counts: With The Right Audio System, You'll Have A Good Relationship With Music AR13645
Skate Dreams: Roller Basketball Is A Game Of Fast Breaks And Fast Breaking AR13263, AR14853

Skate Till You Die: The Fast Times And Tragic Death of Jeff Phillips, The King Of Texas Skateboarding AR16050
Skee-Lo Is As Skee-Lo Does In 'I Wish' AR13552
Skeleton Key AR15354
Skids' Mark: Southern Culture Hit It Big With 'Date' AR13408
Skin Deep: Republican Front-Runner Bob Dole Will Do Anything For A Buck AR15497
Skit Happens: On HBO's New Sketch-Comedy Series, There's No Business Like 'Mr. Show' Business AR15987
Slash Leaves Guns N' Roses: Cites Differences With Axl Rose AR14190
Slave To The Grind: Can Eric Nies Escape MTV's Star-Breaker Machinery? AR13264, AR14854
Slaves To The Grind: The Most Important Job In A College Town Is Supplying The Jolt AR15403
Sleater-Kinney AR15727
Sleeper AR15434
Sleeping With The Enemy?: Indie Meets Major As Matador And Atlantic Records Join Forces AR15207
Slippin' Around On The Road With Brad Pitt AR14711
Small Audio Dynamite: When It Comes To Stereo Systems, Bigger Is Not Always Better AR13646
The Small One: After Decades Of Preparing For A Big Earthquake Along The San Andreas Fault, California Scientists Now Believe It's The Increasingly Frequent Quakes That May Lay Waste To San Francisco Or Los Angeles AR15549
Smart Alternative AR15443
Smart Money AR13343
Smashing Pumpkins AR14712, AR14713
Smashing Pumpkins' Keyboardist Dies Of Drug Overdose; Drummer Charged With Possession AR14191
Smashing Pumpkins' Sudden Impact: The Band's 'Siamese Dream' Comes True AR13013
Smashing Pumpkins: The Rolling Stone Interview With Billy Corgan AR13747
A Smashing Time: At South By Southwest, If You Schmooze, You Lose AR13748
Smells Like Team Spirit: Clinton Seeks A Few Good Students To Fix Up America AR14111
Smokin Suckaz Wit Logic AR13588
Snakin Around AR14425, AR15988
Snoop In The Doghouse: Dr. Dre Protege And Bodyguard Face Murder Charge AR13927
So Where's The Fire?: Perry Farrell Talks About Sex, Drugs, Karma, Everything But His New Band, Porno For Pyros AR14784
So You Finally Put Together The Ideal Audio System AR13647
Soaking Up Inspiration From The Local Bowling Alley, Sponge Move From Grim-Faced Grunge To Blue-Collar Glam AR15856
Social Distortion Find Their New Highs On The Road With 'White Trash' AR12942
Sole Singers AR15495
Solid-State Family Values: When It Comes Time To Do Something For Posterity, Buy A Camcorder AR16078
Some Kind Of Wonderful: Boz Scaggs Rediscovers The Joys Of Rock & Soul AR14237
Son Of Samurai AR16109
The Song Remains The Same: L.A.'s Social Distortion Brings Its Punk Roots To The MTV Generation AR14714
Sonic Bloom: Oasis Return With 'Morning Glory' LP AR13826
Sonic Solutions AR13123
Sonic Youth: Go Guitar Crazy On Lucky 13th Release AR14040
Sonic Youth's 'Dirty' Set For July Release AR13014
Sonny Sharrock 1940-1994 AR14408
Sophie's Choice: Sophie B. Hawkins Realizes Her Vision And Creates A Smash Single AR15989
Sophmore Humps: The Modern-Rock Trail Is Littered With One-Hit Wonders AR13089
Soul Asylum AR13553, AR14855
Soul Asylum: After 11 Long Years Of Virtual Obscurity, The Little Punk Band That Couldn't Finally Does With The Success Of 'Grave Dancers Union' AR14715
Soul Asylum: Dave Pirner & Dan Murphy AR13554
The Soul Behind The Face: Babyface Steps Out from Behind The Boards To The Top Of The Charts AR15196
Soul Coughing: Hack Out A Hearty Blend Of Beat Poetry, Hip-Hop And Art Rock AR15473
The Soul Of The New Machine: Tin Machine Is More Than David Bowie's Latest Invention AR15990
Souled Out: Has The New Technology Finally Sucked The Revolution Out Of Rock & Roll—Or Given It A New Lease On Life? AR13749
Souljah's Bad Rap: Candidate Clinton Thrusts The Rapper-Activist Into The Spotlight AR14785
Sound Factory: In Computer Labs, Dedicated Wireheads Give Pop Music A Digital Make-Over AR15565
The Sound Of The Future: With Its First Two Albums, My Bloody Valentine Has Redefined Rock AR13015
Soundgarden: The Veteran Band From Seattle Proves There's Life After Nirvana AR14786
The Sounds Of Cyberspace AR15579, AR15580
Southern Comfort: Hootie And The Blowfish Take Their Deep-Fried Jams And Sweet Love Songs To The Top Of The Charts AR13265
Southern Comfort: How Come There Are Billions To Bail Out Mexico But Nada For U.S. Cities? AR14112
Space Is The Place: Rockers Look To The Skies In Search Of UFOs AR14345
Space Oddity: Bootsy Collins Orbits Higher With "Zillatron" And "Blasters Of The Universe" AR14424
Spacehog: Revive Glam, Gender Bending And Mascara AR15857
Spaghetti Western: The Singing Cowboy Junkie Margo Timmins And The Lone Star State's Own Lyle Lovett Get Duded Up Italian-Like AR14449, AR15991
Speech Impediment: How A Penn Freshman Stood Up To The PC Police And Cracked The Campus Speech Code AR15478
Speech Therapy: Arrested Development Calls For A Revolution Of The Mind AR14716
Speed Mettle: The Fastest Americans In Their Sports, These Skaters And Skiers Hope To Bring Home The Olympic Gold AR13323, AR14856
The Spice Of Life: Salt-N-Pepa Prove That Hip-Hop Is Not Just A Man's Game AR13555
Spin Doctor: Club DJ Junior Vasquez Remixes The Soundtrack Of New York At Night AR13266, AR14857
Spin Doctors AR13666
Spinal Tap AR15992
The Spinanes AR13688
Splash, Point And Shoot: When Your Destination Is All Wet, These Are The Right Cameras to Take Along AR13124
Sponge AR12968
Sponge City AR15321
Springsteen AR14517
Springsteen Settles Suits With Roadies [and other news] AR13994
Springsteen: The Rolling Stone Interview AR14202
Squeeze Box: The Who Get The Deluxe Treatment AR15534
Squeezed Pay AR13212
Stalkers: Is The Threat To Rock Stars Growing? AR12943
Stamping Out Hate AR13048
[Stamps] AR15480
Star Scribes AR15481
Star-Studded Soundtrack: U2, Talking Heads, R.E.M. And Others Provide Music For Wenders Film AR14496
Star Systems 1992 AR13648
Star Systems '93: Audio For Every Room And Budget AR13649
Star Trek: Melissa Etheridge Takes The Long Hard Road From The Heartland To Hollywood AR13556
The 'Star Wars' Trilogy On Laser AR15668
Starr Time For Ringo AR15993
Stars Sing For Williams AR15171
Starting Over: Wilco See A New Dawn With 'A.M.' AR14192
State Of The Reunion AR15331
Static Electricity: Radiohead Transform Emotional Turmoil Into Kinetic Pop AR15858
Station To Station: On A Personal Tour Of Ziggy's London, David Bowie Looks Back At His Days As The Glam King Of England AR15435
Steal This Diploma: Higher Education At Lower Prices AR15322
The Stealth War Against Abortion: In Rural States Like Mississippi, Abortion May Still Be Legal, But Lawmakers Have Made It Nearly Impossible For Women To Make The Choice For Themselves AR15225
Stephen Dorff: Playing The Forgotten Beatle AR13210
Sterling Morrison: 1942-1995 AR13750
Steve Miller: The Space Cowboy And Gangster Of Love Proves There's Life After His Greatest Hits AR14238
Stevie Nicks AR13557
Stevie Wonder: Never-Ending Song Of Peace AR15197
Sticks & Stones: Whether You're Heading For The Great Outdoors Or The Urban Jungle, Durable Watches And Rugged Boots Ease Your Trek Off The Beaten Path AR15212
Sticky Situation: A New Warning Label On MC Eiht's Hit CD Raises Some Epic Questions AR15773
Still First In Space: Pink Floyd Rocket Back To The Top With The Division Bell AR15535
Still Rocking: PCs, The Web, Multimedia...Despite The Hype Computer Technology Can't Compare With The Elegance Reliability And Value Of

Today's Audio Systems AR13650
Sting AR14619
'Stock Footage AR13026
Stockholm Syndrome AR15008
Stone Alone: Pearl Jam's Stone Gossard Goes Solo With Shame AR13299
Stones Sign Deal With Virgin AR15172
Stones Take It To The Max: 'At The Max' Shows The Rolling Stones As They've Never Been Seen Before AR15994
Stones Uncovered AR13300
The Story: A Signature Sound AR16056
Story Of My Life: Personal Publishing On The Web AR14129
Straight Shooters: Seattle Rockers Take A Sober Side Trip With Mad Season AR15089
Straight Troops—Gay Troops AR15071
Straitjacket Fits: New Zealand's Pop Export AR14717
The Strange And Mysterious Death Of Mrs. Jerry Lee Lewis AR13345
Strange Fruit: Black Grape Uncork A Distinctive Vintage AR15436
Strange Fruit: The Improbable Rise Of Dolores O'Riordan And The Cranberries AR13667
The Strange Loves Of Lyle Lovett AR15995
Street News AR13589, AR13590, AR13591, AR13592, AR13593, AR13594, AR13595, AR15450, AR15451, AR15452, AR15628
Stress Relief AR15072
Studio Of The Moment: At Fort Apache, The Motto Is 'Great Big Guitars And No Rules' AR14463
Stupid And Contagious AR15009
Stupid Is As Stupid Does AR15669
Styling A Greater Green Empire: Sebastian Inc. Gives Something Back To The Earth AR15695
Suede: All That Glitters AR13381
Sugar: Turning Bitter Into Sweet AR14718
Suicidal Tendencies: Kurt Did Not Die For You AR13790
Suicide Watch AR12922
Sukia AR15728
Summer Concert Season Comes Up Short AR13090
Summer Movie Report Card AR15552, AR15670
Summer With A Vengence: Why Hollywood Will Die Hard Trying To Bust Last Summer's Record AR15671
Summer Wrap-Up AR15672
Sun Ra: 1914-1993 AR13785
Sun-60: A Dynamic Duo AR15173
Sun Strategies: The Best Defense Is A Good Dose Of SPF AR15553
Super Highway Sounds AR16079
Superbad!: The Elusive Prince Returns Triumphant AR14497
Superdrag Take Off For The Big Time At Top Speed AR15859
Superegos On The Loose AR13619
Supermodel City AR15036
Supreme Justice: Rap's Day In Court AR15459
Surfing's Eco-Warriors: The Members Of The Surfrider Foundation Are Making Waves For Cleaner Coastal Waters AR15996
Surviving The Crusades AR15458
The Sweet Smell Of Success: The Punks Of Rancid Match Wits With The Corporate Rock Machine AR13668
Sweet Soul Music: Retro Rockers Collective Soul Take A Shine To The Airwaves AR14409
Sweet Surrender: Donning Dress-To-Kill Leather Jackets, The Midwestern Singer And The Vampire Slayer Give Themselves Up To A Day At The Beach AR14858, AR15696
Swervedriver: Chaos, Distortion And Feedback AR14719
A Swing And A Miss: The Senate Crime Bill AR13607
Syd Straw Plays With The Skeletons In Her Closet AR13457
Sympathy For The Flip Side: Collector Turns Penchant For The Obscure Into A&R Dream AR13366
Systems Theory: Carefully Chosen Components + The Right Software = A Computer That Works The Way You Do AR13125

T

A Tale Of 2 Indies: Epitaph Records... AR14193
A Tale Of 2 Indies: Matador... AR13091
Tales From The Crib: Dormitory Resident Advisers Explain How They Deal With Bongs, Beer, Stress And...Uh...Noisy Couples AR15323
Tales From The Downside: Freedy Johnston Writes Perfect pop Songs About Hard Times And Heartbreak AR13669
Talk This Way: The Rolling Stone Interview With Aerosmith's Steven Tyler AR13751
Tania's World AR14429, AR15752
Tanks For The Memories: Michael Jackson Imposes 'HIStory' On The Czech Republic AR14669
Tara Key AR14612
Tattoo You: Lou Deangelis Gets Crazy On His Mountain Bike AR14461, AR14859
Technology: A Three-Way Video-Game Battle Begins AR14666
Technology: Getting Up To Speed On The Web With ISDN AR14667
Technology: New Home-Theater Products Adapt Themselves To Smaller Spaces AR13126
Technopop AR15574
Ted Hawkins: 1936-1995 AR15381
The Ted Offensive: How Ted Koppel's 'Nightline' Rules The World AR15997
Television AR13752
Television's Refined Tuning: The New York Punk-Guitar Godfathers Pick Up Where They Left Off AR13440
Tell Us About Your Life AR15575
Tell Us About Your Music AR15576
The Temporary Miracle: How One Good Job Becomes Three Lousy Ones AR14113
Ten Best Movies Of 1992 AR15673
The 10 Best Movies Of 1994 AR15674
10: Express Yourself AR13558
Ten Things In 1993 That Didn't Suck AR14340
10,000 Maniacs On The Loose Again AR15998
The 10 Worst Movies Of 1994 AR15675
Terminators: The Robots That Rodney Brooks And Hans Moravec Imagine Will Succeed Humans, Not Serve Them AR13461
That Girl AR13559
That's Entertainment AR13127
Therapy?: From The Land Of Bombings And Bono AR13919
Thermadore Try Not To Get Worried AR14599
These Heads Are Meant To Roll: Manufacturers Put A New—Not To Mention Detachable—Face On Car Audio AR16058
They Say They Want A Revolution: In The Ukraine And Georgia, Nothing Secedes Like Secession AR15010
They're Here, They're The Queers And They're Not What You Think AR15208
Things To Do AR15073
13: Love Will Never Do AR15629
38: Ashes To Ashes AR14410
35: Love Shack AR13560
34: Slave To The Rhythm AR15630
39: In Bloom AR13561
31: Kool Thing AR13562
37: Atlantic City AR14573
36: Jeremy AR14572
33: Mind Playing Tricks On Me AR14251
32: Burning Down The House AR13563
30: You Might Think AR13032
This Ain't No Mudd Club: CBGB Celebrates Its 20 Years Of Rock & Roll AR13016
[This Month...] AR15591
This Old 'Palooza AR14438
This Show Was About Every Critic's Desire: To Rock It Like You Write It AR13753
This Wheel's On Fire AR13402, AR14151
Thorn EMI Buys Virgin AR13995
Thoroughly Modern Bjork AR15704
Those Were The Days: New Home Video Captures The Beatles During Their First Visit To America AR13827
Three Days At The Barricades: How Rock & Roll, Fax Machines And The Hip Crowd Helped Crack The Coup AR15691
311 Kiss Up To Hippies And Skate Punks AR14600
Three In A Van: Mike Watt Hits The Road Econo Style With Dave Grohl And Eddie Vedder AR13670
3: Losing My Religion AR14411
3 Tribes AR13382
Through The Looking Glass AR15074
Thunder Down Under: Australia Takes An Alterna-Rock Holiday With Big Day Out AR15357
Ticket Jam: Pearl Jam's Concert Sales Spur New Controversy AR13092
Ticket Masters: How Smashing Pumpkins, Nine Inch Nails And Others Thwart Concert Scalpers AR13093
Tickets To Ride: Pearl Jam Hit The Road Their Way AR15860
Tim Burton: The Rolling Stone Interview AR13147
Tim Finn: Apart From The Crowd AR13828
Tim Robbins: The Running Man AR16119
Time Warner Runs Up The White Flag: The Media Help Drag Down One Of Their Own AR14341
The Times Have Indeed Changed: The Band Follows Dylan In Selling Their Songs As Ads AR14037
The "Times" They Are A-Changin' AR15607
Timing Is Everything AR14576
Timothy Leary: 1920-1996 AR13916
Tindersticks AR15437
Tiny Lights: Shining In Hoboken AR13829
Tipper: Dems Send Wrong Message AR13441
Tipper Gore Quits PMRC: But Has The First Lady of 'Parental Advisory' Really Given Up The Fight? AR14042
Titanic Love Affair: Sunk Once, The Band Returns With 'No Charisma' AR14720
TLC: Street-Level Feminism AR14498
To Hell & Back: They Say They're Not Jinxed, But The Members Of Def Leppard Have Had To Endure A String Of Tragedies That Would Have Destroyed Most Other Bands AR13754
To Hell And Back AR15861
To Rolling Stone Readers AR15610,

AR15611
To The Readers Of Rolling Stone AR15800
Toasting Townshend: Roger Daltrey Does Carnegie Hall AR15536
Toking Down With The MC5 AR13596
Tom Cruise: Pushing Thirty, The Star Of 'Far And Away' Gets His Life Together With The Help Of Scientology And His Wife Nicole Kidman AR14000
Tom Hanks Rides Again AR15676
Tom Jones AR13564
Tom Petty: This IS How It Feels On The Road AR15377
'Tommy' Scores Again: An Old Tale Gets A New Twist On The Stage AR15999
'Tommy' Sells Out AR15588
Tonight! Sinead Performs! AR15075
Tony Bennett AR13565
The Tonya Harding Fall: The Transformation of A Young Figure-Skating Champion Into The World's Most Visible Villainess AR15544
Tool Get Spiritual And Scatological With 'Aenima' AR15862
Topcat: The Making Of "The Lion King" AR16000
Topical Disease AR15324
[Tori Amos] AR14721
Tori Amos: Ethereal Earthquakes AR13830
Tori Amos: The Power And The Passion AR15631
Totally Stoned: Primal Scream Return To Rock Roots With "Give Out But Don't Give Up" AR13383
Totally Wired AR13374, AR13375
Tough Times For Rock Auctions AR13903
Tour De Force: The Rolling Stones Rake It In And Rock The House AR13267
Tours: From Sex Pistols To Kiss, The Summer Of...'76? AR16001
Toward A Sane National Drug Policy AR14737, AR15801
Toy Caldwell: 1948-1993 AR15131
Toys From The Attic AR14722
The Toys Of Summer AR16080
Toys Of Summer AR16081, AR16102
Toys Of Summer: Look Here For Something New Under The Sun AR16082
A Trace Of Gold: The Ace Catches Air On The Way To Lillehammer AR13324, AR14860
The Tracks Of The Coyote AR14446
A Tragic Miscarriage Of Justice Continues: The State Of Michigan Vs. Gary Fannon AR15338
Trapped in Mr. Bill's Neighborhood AR15601
Trash Collection: Sonic Youth Go Artcore On New LP AR14412
Travolta: The Rolling Stone Interview AR15378
[Trent Hill's Essay] AR15687
Tri And Mighty: To Brave The Hawaii Ironman, It Takes Big Kahunas AR14133, AR14861
A Tribe Called Quest AR15442
Tribute AR15688
Tribute: David Briggs 1944-1995 AR15132
Tribute: Junior Walker 1931-1995 AR14218
Tribute: Pete Grant 1935-1995 AR13458
A Tribute To Woody: Artists Gather To Commemorate Singer's Birthday AR13442
Tributes AR15037, AR15689
Tricky AR13384, AR15438
Trippy Lip Shtick: Flaming Lips Rain Cosmic Debris AR13409
Trouble In Paradise: Violence Erupts After MTV Event In New Jersey AR14723
"True Lies" And Sexual Violence AR15677
True Lies: On "The Larry Sanders Show," Garry Shandling Turns The Talk-Show Brouhaha Into The Funniest Thing On TV AR14591
A Truly Democratic Party: The MTV And VH-1 Generations Swing Together At Clinton's Inaugural AR14239, AR14724
Try A Little Tenderness AR15082
Tumble Weeds: Competing In A Sport That Demands Youth And Artistry, Gymnasts Shannon Miller And Jarrod Hanks Make The Leap From Athlete To Performer AR13599, AR14799
Tuning Into Prine Time: John Prine Scores High In The Ratings With 'The Missing Years' AR16002
Turning Half Japanese AR14413
The Turning Point: Annie Lennox Finds Life After Eurythmics AR15439
12: Beat It AR15632
28: Vogue AR13566
25: Give It Away AR13567
25 Years Of Fear And Loathing AR15602
24: Borderline AR14414
20: Like A Prayer AR15633
29: Close AR14295
21: Gett Off AR15634
27: Billie Jean AR13568
26: Hot For Teacher AR13569
23: Boys Of Summer AR13831
22: Girls Just Want To Have Fun AR13570
Twilight Of The Greens AR13923
Twisted Twang: Geraldine Fibbers Take It To The Limit AR12944
Two For The Road: On The Move With Those Sexual Screwups From 'Short Cuts,' Matthew Modine & Julianne Moore AR14862, AR15720
2: Smells Like Teen Spirit AR14725
2pac's Gospel Truth: In A Year When His Song Was On Trial For A Murder, The Rapper Seeks Calm In The Storm AR15091

U

U2: Finds What It's Looking For AR13755
U2 Get Their Wings AR14415
U2: The Zoo Tour Move Outdoors AR13996
Ugly Kid Joe: Living Out Their Fantasies AR14003
The Un-Candidate AR14015
Uncharted Territory: 12 Artists On The Edge AR15705
Under Your Thumb: New Hand-Held Electronics Put Technology In The Grasp Of Your Hand AR15736
Underworld Find Their Voice Behind Beats And Riffs AR15213
[Unprecedented Sweep] AR15706
Unreasonable Doubt AR15545
Unreasonable Doubt: Part 2 AR15546
Unusual Suspects: Loud Lucy & Civ Defy Alterna-Rock Convention And Live To Talk About It AR14863, AR15581, AR15774
Up Against The Drywall: Mexican-American Carpenters Remake The U.S. Labor Movement In Orange County, Calif. AR14114
Up Against The Wal: Wal-Mart Keeps Albums—And Customers?—Out AR15589
Up The Amazon: Chasing Sloths, Drinking Bootleg Rum And Getting Tight With Chiggers AR15011
Up The Mountain AR15025
Update AR14447, AR15707, AR15708, AR15709, AR15710, AR15711, AR15712, AR15713, AR15714
Urge Overkill Indoors AR15325
U.S. Literacy Sinks To New Low AR15076

V

The 'Vad' Fad: Making Music-Video Commercials AR15355
Valuing The Family AR15715
Van Halen: Here, Now AR16003
Van Morrison AR16004
The Veldt AR13671
Velocity Girl AR13904
Velvet Crush: A Slovenly Rock & Roll Spirit AR14726
The Verve Pipe AR15721
'Vibe' Baptized By Fire: Debut Issue Of Hip-Hop Magazine Hits The Street To Attacks And Praise AR13443
Victoria's Secret: Victoria Williams Gets Real "Loose" On Her New LP AR15104
Video & Laser Hot Sheet AR15724
The Video File AR13029, AR15775
Video Files AR15725
Video Laser Hot Picks AR15678
Video-Laser News AR15679
Videomakers Who Vault To The Big Screen AR14296
Videos By Number AR14423
A View To Kill AR12956
Virtual Dylan: Bob Dylan Goes Electric Again—On CD-ROM AR15537
The Vision Thing AR15730
Vision Thing AR13756
The Visionary Light AR15344
Viva La Divas AR15198
Vivian Stanshall: 1943-1995 AR15209
A Voice In The Night AR14518
Voice Of Experience: Iris DeMent Turns Her Life Into Song AR14727
Volley Of The Dolls: The Goo Goo Dolls Turn It Up And Kick Out The Jams, Replacements Style AR14728
Voodoo Child: Hendrix Jr. Sues Estate AR14455
Voodoo Child: The Rolling Stone Interview With Living Colour's Vernon Reid AR13148
Voyage To The Bottom Of The Season AR14592

W

Wailing Souls: A Reggae Hall Of Fame AR13314
Waist Deep In Whitewater: P. J. O'Rourke Gets His Mind Right With Pols, Pickles And Catfish AR15012
Waiting For The Band AR13757
Wal-Mart: No 'Utero' AR13571
Walk On The West Side AR13037, AR15722
Walk On The Wild Side: The Secret History Of The Alternative-Rock Revolution AR15026
Walt Mink: Power-Trio Rock AR13017
Walter Hyatt 1949-1996 AR13094
Wanted! 10 Things You Can Do To Make A Difference AR15109
The War At Home: How The Media Miss The Story On 34,000 Gun Deaths Each Year AR14342
War At Warners: Power Struggle Plagues World's Largest Label AR16005
War College AR13141
Warner Bros.: A New Regime AR16006
Warren Beatty AR16120
The Watchman: Straightforward Ballsy Folk AR13018

The Wax Factor: Major Labels Get Back Into The 12-Inch Groove Thang AR15133
Wayne's World: For The MC5's Kramer, The Future Is Now AR12969
We Are Golden: Woodstock '94 Is Headed Into The Black AR14645
[We Are Proud...] AR15740
We Are Tibet: The Beastie Boys And Smashing Pumpkins Headline The Largest Benefit Concert Of The 1990s AR15496
We Should Have Seen It Coming: Riots Are The Latest Rock Fad AR14787
We Were Just Happy Freaks, Man: Garcia In His Own Words AR13301
Web Watch: Because You're Mine, I Walk Online AR14278
Webb Of Sound AR15215
Webheads On Ramona Street: Jonathan 'Dr. Cheeze' Steuer Makes His Million-Dollar Cyborganic Dream Garden Become Reality AR14016
Wedowee: When An Alabama Principal Said No To Interracial Dating, A Small Community Was Forced To Confront Its Racist Heritage AR14305
Ween AR13410
Weezer AR14557
Weiland Arrested For Drugs AR15863
Weiland In Drug Treatment; Pilots Grounded AR14194
Weiland: Of Stone Temple Pilots AR14729
The 'Weird' Side Of R.E.M.: 'Automatic For The People' Features Slow, Dark, Brooding Songs AR13758
The Weiss Man Cometh: Introducing Rob Weiss—Director, Bigmouth, Suburban Success Story AR16007
Welcome To The Information Superdorm: The Digital Future Is Being Shaped On Campus Right Now AR14211
Welcome To The Jungle AR14150
Welcome To The Machine: The Music Revolution Comes To Your Town AR13367
Well Armed: 'Tank Girl' LP Snags A-List Punks AR14303
We're Not Gonna Take It: Gay And Lesbian Activists Battle The Rise Of Homophobia In Pop Music AR13620
West Des Moines, Iowa AR15803
WH Down & Dirty: The Rolling Stone Interview AR13444
What A Wonderful Web It Could Be: Netscape's Co-Inventor Charts The Digital Future AR14212
What Clinton Can Do For The Economy AR14115
What Does Conan O'Brien Have That You Don't? AR14730
What To Do The Morning After AR15083
What TV Movies Are Doing Right AR15680
What You Can Do AR15806
What's In A 'Name'? Goo Goo Dolls Score A Hit Nine Years In The Making AR15474
What's New, Democrat? Clinton's Politics Look Awfully Familiar AR14116
(What's The Story) With Brit Pop Sites? AR14279
When Elvis Was King: New Box Set Compiles All Of Presley's Recordings From The Fifties AR16008
When Success fails: What Really Bugs The GOP About Student Loans And Americorps is That They Work AR14650
When The Mightiest Television Network Meets Up With The Lords Of Testosterone, Someone's Bound To Get Hurt AR16061
When The Senate Comes Around: Cooler Heads Are Prevailing In That Other House On Capitol Hill AR16044
Where Angels Fear To Tread: Pearl Jam Open Their Spring Tour On A Wing And A Prayer AR14788
Where The Jobs Are AR15807
Where The Wild Things Are: The Beastie Boys Become Kings Of Their Own Urbane Jungle AR14731
Where There's Smoke: Method Man Ignited Hip-Hop With Blunt Rhyme AR15635
Whigging Out: Afghan Whigs Join Sub Pop Alumni With A Major-Label Debut, 'Gentlemen' AR13019
Whip Smart: The Tricks Of The Trade For Better Grades AR14046
White Men Can't Rule: A Melting Pot Revolt AR14343
Who Are You? Pearl Jam's Eddie Vedder AR13095, AR13285, AR14195
Who Is This Guy? AR14864, AR16009
Who Lost Russia?: The Ex-Reds Need Our Greenbacks AR14117
Whole Lotta Lolla AR15538
Whole Lotta Rosie: With 'The Rosie O'Donnell Show' Around, Talk Becomes Slightly Less Cheap AR16010
Whole Lotta Shakin' Up Goin' On AR14732
Who's On Broadway?: Pete Townshend Discusses Bringing The Rock Opera To The Great White Way AR16011
Who's On First?: Lollapalooza Hunts For A Headliner AR15864
Who's Pulling Bill Clinton's Strings? AR14118
Why Are We In Haiti? AR15810
Why Brooke, Why Now AR16012
Why I Believe What I Believe AR15013
Why I Don't Believe What He Believes AR14119
Why The Mighty GE Can't Strike Out AR14120
Why The Rich Get Richer: Because The Fed Is Engineering A Recession For The Rest Of Us AR14121
Wichita, Kansas AR15811
Wide-Lapel Hell: VH1 Drags 'Bandstand' Out Of The Fashion Closet AR13572
The Wide-Screen Factor AR15681
Widespread Panic: Not Just Another Southern Band AR15351
Wilbert Harrison 1929-1994 AR13786
The Wild Side Of Paradise AR15592
Wild Thing: Drew Barrymore AR14733
Will Oldham Of Palace: King Of Appalachian Indie Rock AR14439
Will The Fed Stiff Clinton? AR14122
William Kunstler: 1919-1995 AR15465
William M. Gaines (1922-1992) AR14524
Willie Nelson AR13573
Willie Nelson Throws A Reggae Party AR13211
Willie's Dream: Blues Heaven Buys Chess Studio AR16096
Wilmington, N.C. AR15134
Wilson Phillips AR16013
Win, Lose Or Drawl: Redneck Comic Jeff Foxworthy Tries To Prove That The South Can Do It Again—Again AR16014
Wings Over America: The Eagles Reunite For Their First Tour In 14 Years AR16015
Winona AR13905
Wired For Love: Three Tales Of Computer Romance AR13268, AR14865
Wired For Sound: With The Advent Of Cyberspace, Music May Never Be The Same AR16083
Wired In California: Meth, The Drug That Snuffed Out The Summer Of Love, Is Back, And California IS Exporting It All Over The Nation AR14525
With A Little Help From His Mates: Mick Ronson's Posthumous 'Heaven 'N Hull' To Be Released AR13672
WOMAD On The Road AR14558
Woody Allen: The Rolling Stone Interview AR13445
Words From The 'Home' Front AR14499
Workers Of The World: A Portfolio AR15345, AR16045
Working For The Dead AR14647
The World According To Gorby: Over Lunch In Moscow, The Former Senator From California Talks Politics With The Former Head Of the Soviet Union AR13347
World Music On The Hill: The Grateful Dead Bring The Rain Forest To Washington AR13315
The World's Biggest Rerun: Why Is The Addams Family Making Hollywood Ghoul Crazy? AR14137
Worth Bragging About: Billy Bragg Takes A Leap Forward With A Stunning New Album AR13906
Would You Please Welcome...: Dave, Conan, Jay And Arsenio Pump Up The Volume AR14574
Wu Tang Clan Deliver The Goods With 'Wu Wear' AR13628
Wyman Quits The Stones AR14500
Wynonna Leaves Home: One-Half Of Country Music's Judds Declares Her Independence AR14501
Wysiwys: With These Camcorders, What You See Is What You Shot AR16084

X

X: Can Denzel Washington Make Malcolm Speak To A New Generation Of Americans? AR16087
X Files: Undercover AR16016
X-Ploitation: Paranoids Terrorized By Copycat Thriller Series! AR16017
Xs New World Order: L.A.'s Seminal Punkers Reunite On 'Hey Zeus!' AR14613
X treme Prejudice: At The X Games, ESPN's Alterna-Lympics, The Road Lugers Tried To Go Straight, The Network Tried To Get Radical, And Street Cred Was Just A Marketing Concept AR13046

Y

Yabba-Dabba-Doo-Doo: A Summer Movie Guide To What's Fun Among The Dumb AR15682
Yahoo!: How Two Stanford Students Created The Little Search Engine That Could AR15729
Yatsura AR15865
The Year In Movies AR13052, AR15683, AR15684, AR15685, AR15686
The Year In Music AR13053, AR13446, AR16099
The Year In Records AR13054
The Year In Television AR13055, AR14593, AR14594
The Year In TV AR16018
The Year Of The Near Miss AR14811
The Yearn To Earn: Gang Starr Hit Pay Dirt With Streetwise Sounds AR15590
The Year's Best In Laser AR16100
Yoko Ono AR15027
Yoko Ono & John Lennon AR14454
You Can Take it With You AR13128
You Can't Always Get What You Want

AR15174
You Shoulda Been There AR13759
The Young And The Reckless: The Pot Is Stronger, The Acid Milder, And The Kids Who Are Turning On Are Younger Than Ever AR16051
Young, Gifted And Bad AR15636
Young, White And Surrounded AR12947
Your Own Private Audio AR16085
Yugoslavian Transportation AR15077
Yum-Yum Make Sugary-Sweet Pop (With Strings) AR13459

Z

Zappa Premiere Set: European Ensemble To Debut 'The Yellow Shark' AR16019
Ziggy's Axeman: Mick Ronson Was A Sideman Extraordinaire AR15440
Zoo World Order: With A Lot Of Help From The Edge, U2 Are Reborn With A Case of The Giggles—And A New Sense Of Mission AR13447

Subject Index to Articles & Columns

A

A&M Records AR14031
A-Ha—Videos AR13535
Aaliyah AR14550
Abbey Road (album) AR13270
Abbruzzese, Dave AR14777
ABC Network AR14458
Abdul, Paula AR13993
Abdul, Paula—Recordings AR13975, AR14026
Abdul, Paula—Videos AR13507, AR13615
Aberdeen, Washington AR13914
Aborigines AR13694
Abortions AR12927, AR12953, AR13872, AR14752, AR15083, AR15225, AR15271, AR15458, AR15710, AR15714
Abraxas (album) AR14875
AC-DC—Videos AR13031
Academy Awards AR15652, AR15656, AR15658, AR15659
Ace Of Base AR14380
Achtung Baby (album) AR13755
Ackerman, Paul AR13295, AR13523, AR13782
Ackerman, Will AR13947
Acland, Chris—Obituary AR14810
ACT UP (organization) AR14205, AR14224
Acuff, Roy—Obituary AR14493
Acuff-Rose Music AR15459
Adam, Aslam P. AR14738
Adams, Bryan—Concerts—Ho Chi Minh City, Vietnam AR14690, AR15506
Adams, Bryan—Recordings AR13945
Adamsky, Victor AR15182
The Addams Family (film) AR14137
Addicted To Noise (publication) AR13375
Adler, Steve AR14029
Adolescents AR12946, AR12947, AR13076, AR13273, AR13286, AR13684, AR14150, AR14219, AR14334, AR14635, AR15335, AR15541, AR15542, AR15543, AR15687, AR15712, AR15713
Adolescents—Drug Usage AR13145, AR13684, AR14150, AR15712, AR16051
Adolescents—Suicide AR13684
The Adventures Of Pete And Pete (television show) AR15889
Advertising AR13874, AR14037, AR15274, AR15355
Aerosmith AR13272, AR14050, AR14152, AR15938, AR15972
Aerosmith—Recordings AR14258, AR14601, AR14739, AR15871
Aerosmith—Videos AR14699, AR15616
Affirmative Action AR12917
Afghan Whigs AR12918, AR14255
Afghan Whigs—Recordings AR13019, AR14595, AR15593
Africa AR13369, AR14991
After Midnight (song) AR15355
AIDS AR13044, AR13279, AR13369, AR13684, AR13803, AR14186, AR14205, AR14206, AR14224, AR14235, AR14326, AR14991, AR15362, AR15411, AR15547, AR15874, AR16053
AIDS—Chronology AR13368
AIDS—Concerts AR13951, AR13953, AR14205, AR14224, AR14755
AIDS—Recordings AR14743
Ain't Nuthin' But A She Thing (album) AR15835
Airplanes AR13597
Aladdin Sane (album) AR14876
Albini, Steve AR13880, AR14047, AR14049, AR15288
Album Jackets AR14873
Album Jackets—In Utero AR14271
Alcohol AR13854
Alexakis, Art AR12926
Alexander, Arthur—Obituary AR13287
Alexander, Jason—Profiles AR16116
Alexander, Lamar, Jr. AR14804
Alice In Chains AR12918, AR13399
Alice In Chains—Profiles AR15160, AR15861
Alice In Chains—Recordings AR13399
Alive (video) AR14749
All AR15578
All You Need To Know About The Music Business (book) AR13949
Allen, Janna—Obituary AR14028
Allen, Paul—Profiles AR13131
Allen, Rick AR14287, AR15833
Allen, Woody—Interviews AR13445
Allin, GG—Obituary AR15925
Allman Brothers AR13295, AR13523, AR13761, AR13782
Allman Brothers—Recordings AR14900
Allman, Gregg AR15383, AR16047
Alternative Music AR13005, AR14740, AR15759
Alternative Tentacles Records AR13951
Altman, Robert—Films AR13146
The Amazing Mr. Bickford (video) AR14366
Ambersunshower AR13184
Ambient Music AR14351
Ament, Jeff—Interviews AR15762
Amerasians AR15333
America (book) AR14307
America Beauty (album) AR14877
America Culture AR15595
America Online (company) AR14008
American Bandstand (television show) AR13572
American Culture AR12946, AR12950, AR13188, AR13236, AR13237, AR13246, AR13386, AR13684, AR13865, AR13876, AR13885, AR13907, AR14114, AR14254, AR14329, AR14334, AR14337, AR14338, AR14343, AR14506, AR14581, AR15016, AR15017, AR15109, AR15138, AR15260, AR15277, AR15278, AR15279, AR15294, AR15301, AR15333, AR15334, AR15335, AR15540, AR15542, AR15543, AR15596
American Culture—Asians AR15330, AR15711
American Culture—California AR13286
American Culture—Midwest AR14635
American Culture—Native Americans AR13397
American Culture—South AR14305, AR15413, AR15708
American Indians AR13993, AR14529
American Music Club AR12918, AR13943, AR13949, AR15235
American Music Club—Profiles AR15366
AmeriCorps AR16039
Ames, Aldrich AR14321, AR14460, AR15709, AR15747
Amis, Martin AR13237, AR14506, AR15093, AR15279
Amongst Friends (film) AR16007
Amos, Tori AR12918, AR13830, AR15701
Amos, Tori—Interviews AR14721
Amos, Tori—Profiles AR15631
Amos, Tori—Quotes AR13842
Amos, Tori—Recordings AR14595
Amos, Tori—Tours—North America AR14047
Amos, Tori—Videos AR14391
Amused To Death (album) AR13699
Anastasio, Trey AR12959
And She Was (video) AR14372
And The Band Played On (book) AR14326
Anders, Alison AR15824
Anderson, Brett—Fashion AR15387
Anderson, Gail AR14789
Anderson, Gillian—Interviews AR16016
Anderson, Ian—Interviews AR13763
Anderson, Laurie AR13787
Anderson, Laurie—Interviews AR15717
Andreessen, Marc—Interviews AR14212
Angel Dust (album) AR15409
Animal Farm (store) AR14452
Animal House (film) AR14638
Animal Liberation Front AR14446, AR14447
Animal Rights AR14446, AR14447, AR15705
Animals AR13541, AR13776, AR13783, AR15130
Aniston, Jennifer AR13682, AR15919
Aniston, Jennifer—Profiles AR13219
Anotha Level AR14549
Anquette—Recordings AR13581
Anthony, Christina AR13957
Anthrax AR15818
Anthrax—Recordings AR15873
Anwar, Gabrielle AR13888, AR15297
Aoxomoxoa (album) AR14878
Apartheid AR13690
Appetite For Destruction (album) AR13166, AR14312
Apple Computers AR14012, AR14013, AR15519
Apple, Fiona AR15820
Apple Records AR14259
Appleton, Wisconsin AR14635
Aquino, Corazon—Politics AR15001
Arc (album) AR13725, AR13994
Arc Angels AR14626, AR16089
Arc Angels—Fashion AR14626, AR16089
Arc Angels—Profiles AR14625
Arc Of A Diver (album) AR14879
Architecture AR13862, AR14442, AR15253
Are You Experienced? (album) AR13387
Arizona AR14802, AR15407
Arli$$ (television show) AR15896
Armatrading, Joan—Recordings AR13597
Armed Forces (album) AR13449
Armey, Dick—Politics AR15079
Armstrong, Lance AR14314, AR14843
Arquette, David—Fashion AR13137, AR14839, AR16057
Arrested Development AR15107, AR15451
Arrested Development—Profiles AR14716
Arrested Development—Videos AR14294
Art AR13863, AR14149, AR14580, AR15165, AR15255, AR15795
Art Education AR13214
Art Of Noise—Videos AR14295
Art—Collecting AR13982
Artificial Intelligence AR13461
Artists AR13214, AR15117
Artists—Graham AR15086
Artists—Hoch, Danny AR13242, AR15286
Artists—Judge, Mike AR16103

Artists—Kahlo, Frida AR13475
Artists—Kozik, Frank AR14344
Artists—Kuper, Peter AR13237, AR14506, AR15279
Artists—Lennon, John AR15386
Artists—Mahurin, Matt AR14307
Artists—Matt, Joe AR13230, AR15262
Artists—Mills, Mike AR15018
Artists—Moriarity, Pat AR13135
Artists For A Hate Free America AR13048
ArtRock AR13943
As Nasty As They Wanna Be (album) AR14476
Ashes To Ashes (video) AR14410
Aspin, Les AR14091, AR14101
Ass Ponys AR15028
Astronauts AR16060
Atco Records AR13931
Athens, Georgia AR15320
Athens, Georgia—Rock Scene AR13042
Atlanta, Georgia AR13038, AR13041, AR13277, AR15241
Atlantic City (video) AR14573
Atlantic Records AR13931, AR14261, AR14642, AR14732, AR15207, AR15506, AR16095
Atom Heart Mother (album) AR14880
Atwood, Margaret AR13854
Auctions AR13903, AR13988, AR14179
Auf Der Maur, Melissa AR12975
Augustana College AR15334
Aulerich, Richard AR14446
Austin Music Awards AR13745
Austin, Texas AR13748, AR15246
Austin, Texas—Music Scene AR13745
Austin, Texas—Rock Scene AR14631, AR14632
Austopchuck, Chris AR14873
Australia—Music Scene AR13694, AR13695, AR15357
Auteurs AR14280
Authors—Amis, Martin AR13237, AR14506, AR15279
Authors—Baitz, Jon Robin AR16126
Authors—Boyle, T. Coraghessan AR13132
Authors—Clancy, Tom AR13257
Authors—Hunter, Stephen AR15743
Authors—O'Brian, Patrick AR16126
Authors—Peck, M. Scott AR13282
Authors—Rice, Anne AR13909
Authors—Shilts, Randy AR14326, AR16053
Authors—Thompson, Hunter S. AR14523, AR14998
Authors—Wild, David AR13310
Authors—Wolfe, Tom AR15798
Automatic For The People (album) AR13758
Automobiles AR13866, AR15261, AR15732, AR16126
Ayeroff, Jeff AR14025, AR14873
Azoff, Irving AR13959, AR13980
Azzoli, Val AR14642

B

B-52s—Videos AR13560
B-Real AR14481
Babb-Sprague, Kristen—Fashion AR14825, AR15692
Babbitt, Bruce AR16037
Babbitt, Bruce—Interviews AR16024
Babes In Toyland AR12918, AR14163, AR15312
Babineau, Marko AR13957
Babson College AR15486
Baby Got Back (video) AR14564
Babyface—Profiles AR15196
Baca, Jim—Interviews AR13606
Bacharach, Burt—Recordings AR14052
Back On The Chain Gang (video) AR13813
Back To My Roots (video) AR13511
Back-Packs AR16102
Backbeat (film) AR13196, AR13210
Bad Brains AR12961, AR15834
Bad Livers AR13393
Bad Religion AR12918, AR14397
Bad Religion—Tours—North America AR15829
Badlees AR14052
Baez, Joan AR12959, AR14575
Baez, Joan—Interviews AR14515
Bahamadia AR13592
Bailey, Andrew AR13318
Bailey, David AR14221
Bailey, Jared AR14256
Baird, Dan—Recordings AR15123
Baitz, Jon Robin AR16126
Baker, Steve AR15822
Balin, Marty AR15153
Balkans AR13141, AR13165, AR14985, AR15002, AR15077, AR15539
Balkans—Photography AR15341
Ballard, Glen—Computer Systems AR14276
Baltimore, Maryland AR14113
Bamford, Greg AR15396
Band AR13541, AR13776, AR13783, AR15130
Band—Profiles AR13402, AR14151
Band—Recordings AR14037, AR14267
Banking AR14076
Banking Crisis AR14082, AR14089
Barlow, Lou—Profiles AR12937
Barnes And Barnes—Videos AR14374
Barron, Chris AR14549
Barron, Chris—Fashion AR15387
Barron, Chris—Interviews AR13666
Barron, Chris—Quotes AR13842
Barrymore, Drew AR13169, AR14159
Barrymore, Drew—Profiles AR14733
Baseball AR13129, AR13220, AR13227, AR14821, AR15257
Basehead—Profiles AR14464
Basketball AR13864, AR13999, AR15256
Bastards Of Young (video) AR14698
Bat Out Of Hell (album) AR16110
Bathgate, Lawrence—Profiles AR14089
Batinkoff, Randall AR14315, AR14534
Batlan, Michael AR13994
Batman Returns (film) AR14220
Batteries AR13116
Bauer, Gary AR13603
Bauer, Jill AR16133
Baywatch Nights (television show) AR15962
Be Headed (album) AR12989
Be Still (song) AR13816
Beach Boys AR13625, AR15961
Beach Boys—Recordings AR14157, AR14266, AR15510
Bean-Bayog, Margaret AR13274
Beastie Boys AR12918, AR12941
Beastie Boys—Concerts—San Francisco, California AR14156
Beastie Boys—Profiles AR14731
Beastie Boys—Recordings AR13574, AR14467, AR14922
Beastie Boys—Videos AR14404
Beat Farmers AR15943
Beat Generation AR13884, AR15293
Beat It (video) AR15632
Beatles AR13679, AR13957, AR14171, AR15833, AR15917
Beatles—Films AR13196, AR13965
Beatles—Recordings AR13270, AR14047, AR14144, AR14258, AR14265, AR14273, AR14510, AR14606, AR14670, AR14945, AR14951, AR14974, AR15521, AR15825, AR15830
Beatles—Videos AR13827
The Beatles: The First U.S. Visit (video) AR13827
Beats, Rhymes And Life (album) AR14306
Beatty, Paul AR14610
Beatty, Warren—Interviews AR16120
Beavis & Butt-Head (television show) AR14327, AR16103, AR16106, AR16107
Beavis & Butt-Head (television show)—Films AR13478
Beavis & Butt-Head Do America (film) AR13478
Beck AR12918, AR12975, AR15939
Beck—Profiles AR13491, AR15876
Beck—Recordings AR12934
Beck, Jeff AR13541, AR15383, AR15972
Beck, Jeff—Profiles AR15414
Beck, Jeff—Recordings AR14258, AR15414
Becker, Walter AR15911
Bee Gees AR14128, AR14173, AR15383
Been Caught Stealing (video) AR13548
Beethoven (video) AR14772
Before And After (album) AR13828
Belafonte, Harry AR13524, AR15031
Belafonte, Harry—Quotations AR13524, AR15031
Believe In Me (album) AR14678
Bell, David AR14317
Bella, Manny AR14287
Bellingham, Norman AR14801, AR15693
Bellingham, Norman—Fashion AR14801, AR15693
Belly AR13869, AR14166, AR14674, AR14793, AR15266
Belly—Profiles AR13501
Belushi, John—Profiles AR16109
Ben And Jerry's (company) AR14323 , AR15551
Benedictine Monks Of Santo Domingo De Silos AR14742
Benefit Concerts AR13618, AR14206, AR14235, AR14457, AR14543, AR14752, AR15084, AR15171, AR15496
Bennett, Tony—Interviews AR13565
Bentley, Jason AR13633
Berg, John AR14873
Berklee College Of Music AR15190
Bernard, Walter AR14873
Bernhard, Sandra—Interviews AR15626
Bernstein, Leonard AR13340
Berry, Bill AR15849
Berry, Chuck AR13541, AR15739
Bertelsmann AG (organization) AR13951
Beserkley Records AR13969
Bettencourt, Nuno—Fashion AR15387
Better Than Ezra AR15243
Bettie Serveert AR15200
Betts, Dickey AR15383
Between Thought And Expression (album) AR13719
Beverley, Anne—Obituary AR14809
Beverly Hills, 90210 (television show) AR14590
Biafra, Jello AR13971
Bicycles AR16080, AR16082, AR16102
Bicycling AR13153, AR13251, AR14314, AR14461, AR14829, AR14843, AR14859
Biersach, Bill AR16123
Big Beat Heat (book) AR15137
Big Brother And The Holding Company—Recordings AR14890
Big Daddy Kane AR13592
Big Day Out (rock festival) AR13695, AR14047, AR15357
Big Star—Profiles AR15120
Big Star—Recordings AR14259
Biker Women (television show) AR15895
Bill Graham Presents (book) AR13962
Billboard (publication) AR13945

Billboards (ballet) AR15937
Billie Jean (song) AR15355
Billie Jean (video) AR13568
Billie Joe—Interviews AR13652
Biondi, Matt AR13610, AR14818
Birmingham, Alabama AR13043
Birth Control AR13872, AR14752, AR15225, AR15271, AR15714
Bis AR14213
Bisbee, Arizona AR13237, AR14506, AR15279
Biscuits, Chuck AR14550
Bishop, Sanford—Politics AR13036
Bissett, Josie AR15958
Bitches Brew (album) AR14881
Bjelland, Kat AR14255, AR15701
Bjelland, Kat—Interviews AR14688
Black, Clint AR15568
Black Crowes AR12918, AR14229, AR15972
Black Crowes—Concerts—Houston, Texas AR14770
Black Crowes—Concerts—Louisville, Kentucky AR15217
Black Crowes—Recordings AR14048, AR15566, AR15906
Black Culture AR14329, AR15477, AR15808
Black, David AR13044, AR13317
Black, Frank AR12918
Black Grape AR15436
Black Grape—Concerts—London, England AR15428
Black Grape—Tours—North America AR14052
Black Musicians AR15494, AR15730, AR15808, AR16123
Black Or White (video) AR15617
Black Politicians AR16030
Black Sabbath AR14173
Black Sunday (album) AR13586
Black Uhuru AR13314
Blade Runner (film) AR14620
Blades, Ruben—Politics AR15514
Blaggers ITA AR15419
Blair, Bonnie AR13323, AR14856
Blake, Leigh AR15874
Bland, Bobby AR13770, AR14705
Blige, Mary J. AR14232, AR15384
Blige, Mary J.—Fashion AR14232, AR15384
Blind Faith (album) AR14882
Blind Mellon AR14051
Blind Melon—Profiles AR14765, AR14775
Blind Melon—Recordings AR14170
Blondie AR13962
Blondie—Recordings AR14269
Blondie—Videos AR13508
Bloom, Luka—Profiles AR13001
Bluegrass Music AR13768
Blues Explosion AR14350
Blues Heaven Foundation AR16096
Blues Music AR13994, AR14262
Blues Revue Quarterly (publication) AR13966
Blues Traveler AR13812, AR13899, AR14256
Blues Traveler—Profiles AR15121
Bluetones AR15705
Blur AR14866, AR15425, AR15426, AR15472
Blur—Recordings AR13376
BMG AR13934
Boats AR16102
Bobsledding AR16130
Body Count (album) AR13417, AR13954, AR14341, AR14466, AR14473, AR14474, AR14475, AR14476, AR14499, AR15163
Boiled Crawfish (food) AR13574
Boladian, Armen AR13959
Bolton, Michael AR14382
Bombay, India AR14634, AR15340
Bon Jovi, Jon—Films AR14049
Bone Thugs-N-Harmony AR15837
Bonham, Tracy AR14462
Bonney, Simon AR13850
The Bonnie Hunt Show (television show) AR15891
Bono AR12974, AR13541, AR15153, AR15192, AR15831
Bono—Fashion AR15387
Bono—Interviews AR14465
Boogie Down Productions—Recordings AR13328
Boogie Knights AR12964, AR15946
Boogiemonsters AR13591
Booker T & The M.G.'s AR13770, AR14705
Books AR14184, AR14805, AR15145, AR15389
Boone, Pat—Interviews AR13538
Boots AR15212
Borderline (video) AR14414
Born To Run (album) AR14265, AR14883, AR15149
Bosnia AR13141
Bosnia—Photography AR15341
Bosnia—Politics AR13165, AR14985, AR15002, AR15077, AR15539
Boss AR15612
Boston, Massachusetts—Rock Scene AR14316
Bottle Rockets AR13062
Bottom Line (nightclub) AR14136
Bow Wow Wow—Recordings AR14943
Bowie, David AR13524, AR15026, AR15031, AR15739, AR15830, AR15831, AR15990
Bowie, David—Artworks AR14168
Bowie, David—CD-ROMs AR15516
Bowie, David—Interviews AR14514
Bowie, David—Profiles AR15435
Bowie, David—Recordings AR13464, AR13672, AR14876, AR14895, AR15884
Bowie, David—Tours—North America AR15834
Bowie, David—Videos AR14376, AR14406, AR14410
Boxer, Barbara AR14543
Boy George AR14542, AR15427
Boy George—Interviews AR13494
Boy George—Recordings AR14364
Boys Of Summer (video) AR13831
Boyz II Men AR14256, AR14484
BR5-49 AR13067
Bragg, Billy AR13854, AR13906
Braids—Recordings AR15753
Brain Salad Surgery (album) AR14884
Brainiac AR15469
Brando, Marlon—Profiles AR14240
Brandy AR13322, AR16128
Branton, Leo AR15167
Bravin, Nick AR14801, AR15693
Bravin, Nick—Fashion AR14801, AR15693
Brazil AR14869
Brazil (film) AR15093
Break Like The Wind (album) AR15992
Breakfast In America (album) AR14885
Breeders AR12918, AR13011, AR14255
Breeders—Profiles AR15365
Breeders—Recordings AR15828
Breeze, Joe AR13153
Breskin, David AR13145, AR13317
Brickell, Edie—Recordings AR13420
Briggs, David AR13149
Briggs, David—Obituary AR15132
Brilleaux, Lee—Obituary AR14381
Brilliant Disguise (video) AR14571
Bringing It All Back Home (album) AR13637, AR14886
Brinkley, Christie AR15096, AR15519
Brisebois, Danielle AR15826
BRITS (awards) AR15422
Brodsky Quartet—Recordings AR13291
A Broken Frame (album) AR14874
Brooks, Garth AR13418, AR15569
Brooks, Garth—Interviews AR13439
Brooks, Garth—Videos AR13801
Brooks, Mel—Recordings AR14271
Brooks, Rodney AR13461
Brother Adam—Obituary AR14808
Brown, Bobby AR14287, AR15829
Brown, Bobby—Recordings AR13590
Brown, Dennis AR13314
Brown, James AR14287
Brown, James—Recordings AR14265, AR15141
Brown, Jerry AR14543
Brown, Jerry—Interviews AR14310, AR15361
Brown, Jerry—Politics AR15791
Brown, Junior AR13382
Brown, Lee AR14596
Brown, Marty AR14360
Brown, Ruth AR13771, AR13784, AR15170, AR15984
Browne, Jackson AR14575, AR15098
Browne, Jackson—Computer Systems AR14276
Browne, Jackson—Interviews AR13421
Browne, Jackson—Recordings AR15951
Browner, Carol—Profiles AR16043
Bruce, Neely AR16123
Bryan, Mark AR12975
Bryn Mawr College AR14554
Buchanan, Patrick AR14804
Buchanan, Patrick—Politics AR13260, AR13602, AR14066, AR14104, AR15009
Buckingham, Lindsey—Recordings AR15977
Buckley, Jeff AR12918, AR13154, AR14791, AR14794, AR15944
Buckley, Jeff—Profiles AR13465
Buckley, Tim—Recordings AR14262
Buddies AR13178
Buffalo Springfield AR13761, AR14128, AR14173
Buffalo Tom—Fashion AR14676
Buffett, Jimmy AR14166
Buffett, Jimmy—Interviews AR14356
Build A Fort, Set It On Fire (film) AR13498, AR14815
Bukowski, Charles—Obituary AR13179
Bulgaria AR15183
Bull, Sandy—Recordings AR14052
The Burger And The King (television show) AR15895
Burke, Solomon AR14173
Burkes, Summer AR13805
Burlington, Vermont AR13159
Burning Down The House (video) AR13563
Burning Spear AR13314
Burns, Ed AR13237, AR14506, AR15279
Burroughs, William AR13968
Burton, Tim—Films AR13147
Buscani, Lisa AR14610
Bush AR14346, AR15238
Bush—Profiles AR13377
Bush—Recordings AR14169
Bush, George AR15039, AR15041, AR15042, AR15044, AR15045, AR15047, AR15048, AR15052, AR15053
Bush, George—Politics AR14067, AR14104, AR15043, AR15046
Bush, George—President AR13191, AR13192, AR13193, AR14087, AR14100, AR14738
Bush, Kate—Recordings AR15093, AR15416
Bushnell, George, Jr.—Interviews AR13605

Busta Rhymes AR13382
Busta Rhymes—Videos AR13029
Busweiler, Don AR14452
Butthole Surfers AR13202, AR13204, AR15246
Butthole Surfers—Profiles AR16104
Buzzcocks AR13200
By The Time I Get To Arizona (video) AR15619
Byrd, Robert—Politics AR16044
Byrne, David AR13169, AR13524, AR15031, AR15223
Byrne, David—Interviews AR13503
Byrne, David—Quotations AR13524, AR15031
Byron, Don—Recordings AR15925

C

C-SPAN AR14333
The Cable Guy (film) AR14159
Cage, John—Obituary AR15185
Cage, Nicolas—Profiles AR15368
Caifanes AR14654
Cake AR15813
Cake Like AR12988
Calatrava, Santiago AR13862, AR15253
Calderone, Tom AR14256
Caldwell, Toy—Obituary AR15131
Cale, John—Interviews AR15763
Cale, John—Recordings AR14164, AR14271
California AR14525, AR15407, AR15549
California—Earthquakes AR15940
Calliope Music AR15705
Calvin And Hobbes (comics) AR14595
Cameras AR13102, AR13112, AR13114, AR13116, AR13119, AR13120, AR13124, AR15736, AR16080, AR16081, AR16082, AR16102
Cammell, Donald—Obituary AR13064
Campbell, John AR13473
Campbell, John—Obituary AR15560
Campbell, Luther AR15521
Cancer AR13964
Candlebox AR13203, AR13654
Candy, John AR13624
Candy-O (album) AR14887
Canedo, Ken AR15017
Cantwell, Maria—Politics AR13036
Capitol Records AR14031
Capote, Truman AR15096
Captain America AR14681
Captain Beefheart—Recordings AR14898
Captivated (video) AR13615
Cardigans AR15029
Cardinal—Recordings AR13454
Careers AR14796
Carey, Mariah AR13524, AR15031
Carey, Mariah—Quotations AR13524, AR15031
Carey, Mariah—Videos AR13500
Carlin, John AR15874
Carmichael, Nelson AR13323, AR14856
Carns, Michael P. C. AR12956
Carpenter, Ken AR14314, AR14843
Carpenter, Mary-Chapin AR15568
Carpenters AR13496
Carrey, Jim—Profiles AR15371
Carroll, Dina AR15425
Carroll, Jim—Recordings AR13945
Carrot Top—Profiles AR13261
Cars—Recordings AR14887
Cars—Videos AR13032
Carson, Johnny AR16118
Carter, Chris—Interviews AR16016
Carter, Eden AR14616, AR14819
Carter, James AR13237, AR14506, AR15279
Cartwright, Shawn AR15396
Carvey, Dana—Films AR16101
Carvey, Dana—Profiles AR16113
Carville, James AR13894, AR15310
Carville, James—Interviews AR14090
Cascella, John—Obituary AR13956
Case, Peter AR15942
Case, Steve—Profiles AR14008
Cash, Johnny AR13770, AR13847, AR14705, AR15382, AR15383
Cash, Johnny—Interviews AR13528, AR15101
Cash, Johnny—Recordings AR14050
Cash, Rosanne AR12918, AR13169
Casiraghi, Stefano AR15096
Cassettes AR13061, AR13940, AR16072
Cassidy, David—Profiles AR14055
Cat Power AR15353
Catch A Fire (album) AR14888
Catch Bull At Four (album) AR13349
Catholics AR13158, AR13789, AR16092
Cats Under The Stars (album) AR14889
Cave, Nick AR12918
Cave, Nick—Interviews AR13534
Cave, Nick—Profiles AR13700
Cave, Nick—Recordings AR14049
CB Radios AR13104
CBGB (nightclub) AR13016
CBS Network AR14335
CD-I AR15731
CD-ROMs AR13034, AR13100, AR13104, AR13106, AR13118, AR13374, AR13932, AR13951, AR14339, AR14660, AR14661, AR14662, AR16067
CDnow! (store) AR13375
CDTV AR15731
Censorship AR14486, AR15756
Censorship—Concerts AR15429
Censorship—Films AR14366, AR15642
Censorship—Publishing AR13194, AR15511
Censorship—Records AR13047, AR13081, AR13083, AR13197, AR13417, AR13441, AR13571, AR13954, AR13963, AR13982, AR14042, AR14304, AR14341, AR14381, AR14466, AR14473, AR14474, AR14475, AR14476, AR14499, AR14747, AR14781, AR15163, AR15445, AR15492, AR15514, AR15516, AR15586, AR15589, AR15687, AR15773, AR15814, AR15831, AR15832, AR15836, AR15869
Censorship—Speech AR13330, AR15478
Censorship—Television AR16035
Central Intelligence Agency AR12956, AR14321, AR14460, AR15709, AR15747
Central Park West (television show) AR13677, AR15894
Ceremony (album) AR13993
Cervenka, Exene—Recordings AR14161
Chabot, Steve—Politics AR15079
Chafee, John H. AR14102
Chainsaw Kittens AR15441
Chameleon Records AR13980
Chandler, Chas AR15689
Chandler, Chas—Obituary AR14153
Chandler, Raymond AR13575
Chant (album) AR14742
Chapman, Mark David AR13432
Chapman, Tracy—Recordings AR14495
Chappell, Oliver—Interviews AR13857
Charisma Records AR13980, AR14478
Charlatans U.K. AR15837
Charles Mingus Sextet—Videos AR13741
Charles, Ray AR15742
Charles, Ray—Interviews AR13674
Charles, Ray—Recordings AR15193, AR15804, AR15885
Charley Varrick (film) AR14286
Cheap Thrills (album) AR14890
Chemical Brothers AR12929
Chemical Brothers—Recordings AR14163, AR15754
Cher—Interviews AR13497
Cher—Recordings AR14048
Cherry, Don—Death AR15037
Cherry, Don—Obituary AR14217
Cherry, Neneh—Videos AR14540, AR14751
Cheshire Cat AR15420
Chess AR13023
Chess Records AR16096
Chessler, Deborah AR13523
Chessler, Deborah—Profiles AR14562
Chestnutt, Vic—Profiles AR14353
Chicago, Illinois AR14419, AR14420
Child Abuse AR13158, AR13789, AR15577
Children AR12982, AR13401, AR13488, AR15181, AR15577, AR15978
Children's Defense Fund AR12982
China AR14302
China Girl (video) AR14376
Chippy: Diaries Of A West Texas Hooker (stage musical) AR13845
Cho, Margaret AR13244, AR15298, AR15410
Chomsky, Noam—Interviews AR16108
Christian Rock Music AR13066
Chronic Fatigue Syndrome AR14317
Cibo Matto AR15705
Cinema AR13052, AR13241, AR13871, AR14242, AR14291, AR14296, AR15269, AR15285, AR15639, AR15652, AR15663, AR15665, AR16100
Cinema—Censorship AR14366, AR15642
Cinema—Rock Music AR16123
Cinema—Sex AR15667
Cinema—Sociological Aspects AR14338, AR15677
Cinema—Soundtrack Recordings AR13662
Cinema—Special Effects AR14245
Cinema—Sundance Film Festival AR13161, AR15647, AR15662, AR15667
Cinema (1991) AR15683
Cinema (1992) AR15552, AR15641, AR15660, AR15673
Cinema (1993) AR15643, AR15648, AR15655, AR15658, AR15659, AR15670, AR15678
Cinema (1994) AR15649, AR15654, AR15669, AR15674, AR15675, AR15682, AR15684
Cinema (1995) AR13237, AR14506, AR15279, AR15644, AR15646, AR15656, AR15671, AR15676, AR15679, AR15685
Cinema (1996) AR13161, AR15443, AR15638, AR15640, AR15650, AR15653, AR15657, AR15672, AR15686
Circle Jerks AR15578
Civ—Fashion AR14863, AR15581, AR15774
Civil Rights AR12917, AR14060, AR16020, AR16033
The Civil War (book) AR13574
Clancy, Tom AR13333
Clancy, Tom—Profiles AR13257
Clapton, Eric AR13541, AR13959, AR13970, AR14030, AR14162, AR15170, AR15739, AR15984
Clapton, Eric—Concerts—London, England AR14049
Clapton, Eric—Interviews AR13305, AR14200, AR15021
Clapton, Eric—Profiles AR15020
Clapton, Eric—Recordings AR13772, AR14051, AR15830
Clapton, Eric—Tours AR13943
Clapton, Eric—Tours—North America AR13934
Clapton, Eric—Videos AR15355
Claritin AR13024
Clark, Dave—Recordings AR14267

Clark, Dick AR13771, AR13784, AR15170, AR15984
Clark, Marcia AR15546
Clark, Ozzie—Obituary AR13185
Clarke, Gilbey AR12931
Clarke, Mike—Obituary AR14389
Clash—Recordings AR14258, AR14924
Claw Hammer AR13403
Claypool, Les AR13049, AR13187, AR13327
Claypool, Les—Interviews AR14436
CLE (publication) AR13730
Clements, Marcelle AR13188, AR13317
Cleo—Interviews AR15240
Clerks (film) AR15642
Cleveland, Alfred W.—Obituary AR13185
Cleveland, Ohio—Rock Music AR15352
Cliff, Jimmy AR13314, AR15592
Clinton, Bill AR13240, AR14804, AR15040, AR15284, AR15972
Clinton, Bill—Administration AR13477, AR13581, AR13606, AR14091, AR14330, AR16021, AR16023, AR16024, AR16026, AR16034, AR16037, AR16041, AR16043
Clinton, Bill—Interviews AR14064, AR14103, AR14995, AR15361, AR15594, AR15777, AR15799
Clinton, Bill—Politics AR14062, AR14071, AR14086, AR14098, AR14104, AR14106, AR14115, AR14118, AR14745, AR14785, AR15006, AR15599, AR15601, AR15776, AR15778
Clinton, Bill—President AR12949, AR14060, AR14061, AR14065, AR14068, AR14070, AR14072, AR14074, AR14093, AR14096, AR14101, AR14110, AR14111, AR14116, AR14239, AR14724, AR15778, AR15810, AR16020, AR16025, AR16027, AR16033, AR16034, AR16039
Clinton, Bill—Profiles AR15331
Clinton, Bill—Whitewater AR15012
Clinton, George AR13959, AR15170, AR15554, AR15984
Clinton, George—Profiles AR15613
Clinton, George—Videos AR15937
Clinton, Hillary AR14063
Close (video) AR14295
Club Lingerie (nightclub) AR15937
CMJ Music Marathon AR13005
CNN AR14333
Cobain: A Commemorative Book From The Editors Of Rolling Stone (book) AR13182
Cobain, Kurt AR13278, AR13711, AR13958, AR13969, AR14255, AR14477, AR14595, AR15455, AR15827, AR15833
Cobain, Kurt—Death AR13423, AR13657, AR13790, AR14522, AR14561, AR15501
Cobain, Kurt—Health AR15500
Cobain, Kurt—Interviews AR13734
Cobain, Kurt—Obituary AR15504
Cobain, Kurt—Profiles AR13006, AR13914, AR14692
Cocaine AR13612, AR14432, AR15080, AR15105, AR15336, AR15338, AR15783, AR15806
Cochise, Silas AR14529
Cocker, Jarvis AR13190, AR14052, AR14172
Coffee AR15403
Cohen, Ben—Profiles AR15551
Cohen, Leonard AR13023, AR14273
Cohen, Leonard—Recordings AR13030, AR13429
Cole, David—Obituary AR15823
Cole, Natalie AR13523
Cole, Paul AR14549
Coleman, Ornette AR12959
Coleman, Ray—Obituary AR14809
Coleman, Wanda AR14610
Collective Soul AR14409
Collectors AR13982
Collins, Albert—Obituary AR13765
Collins, Bootsy—Recordings AR14424
Collins, Edwyn AR13303
Collins, Marco AR14256, AR14549
Collins, Michael AR13268, AR14865
Collins, Phil AR14158
Collins, Phil—Videos AR15355
Collins, Rob—Obituary AR14187
Colon, Richard AR13577, AR13814
Coltrane, Ravi AR13778
Columbia AR13485
Colvin, Shawn—Profiles AR15100
Combest, Larry AR12956
Combs, Sean AR15636
Come AR13482, AR14255
Come On Feel The Lemonheads (album) AR15982
Comess, Aaron AR12977
Comics AR13230, AR13969, AR13970, AR14399, AR15262
Compact Discs AR13034, AR13106, AR13375, AR13940, AR13950, AR13954, AR13967, AR14027, AR14258, AR14261, AR14264, AR14270, AR15018, AR15126, AR15169, AR15731, AR16080
Compact Discs—Bootlegs AR14302
Compact Discs—Illustrations AR13167, AR13168
Compact Discs—Manufacturing Quality AR15510
Compact Discs—Packaging AR13938
Compact Discs—Players AR13100, AR13113, AR13641, AR13985, AR15736, AR16065, AR16071
Computers AR13103, AR13106, AR13109, AR13115, AR13116, AR13118, AR13121, AR13122, AR13125, AR13127, AR13128, AR13461, AR14010, AR14011, AR14245, AR14441, AR14658, AR14660, AR14665, AR14667, AR15562, AR15564, AR15736, AR16062, AR16102
Computers—CD-ROMs AR14659, AR14663
Computers—Crime AR14014
Computers—Glossaries AR13117
Computers—Networks AR13131, AR13268, AR13372, AR13374, AR14006, AR14008, AR14009, AR14016, AR14129, AR14211, AR14212, AR14278, AR14328, AR14340, AR14383, AR14458, AR14744, AR14865, AR14985, AR15230, AR15579, AR15729, AR16069, AR16083
Computers—Peripherals AR13105
Computers—Printers AR14658
Computers—Rock Music AR13932
Computers—Software AR13034, AR13114, AR13118, AR13122, AR13125, AR13268, AR13374, AR13951, AR14044, AR14210, AR14339, AR14537, AR14663, AR14664, AR14865, AR15562, AR15563, AR15564, AR16063, AR16066, AR16067
Computers—Viruses AR13477
Computers—World Wide Web AR16077
Conaway, Carrie AR15402
Concert Halls AR15233, AR15234
Concert In The Park (video) AR13615
Concrete T.V. (television show) AR14584
Congress Of The United States AR12948, AR12952, AR12953, AR12956, AR13036, AR13346, AR13480, AR13611, AR13923, AR14077, AR14086, AR14102, AR14109, AR14650, AR15065, AR15138, AR15349, AR15445, AR15497, AR15540, AR16020, AR16030, AR16031, AR16035, AR16044
Conscious Daughters AR15451
Conservatism AR12950, AR14119, AR14994, AR15005, AR15013, AR15598
Consolidated AR15113
Conyers, John AR14059
Cooder, Ry AR13949, AR15938, AR15952
Cooder, Ry—Recordings AR14917
Cook, Stu AR13961
Coolio AR13319, AR13320, AR14794, AR15315
Coolio—Profiles AR14357
Cooper, Alice—Recordings AR14970
Cooper, Michael AR14221
Cop Killer (song) AR13417, AR13954, AR14341, AR14466, AR14473, AR14474, AR14475, AR14476, AR14499, AR14747, AR15163
Cope, Julian AR13199
Copyrights AR13964, AR14302, AR15459
Corbijn, Anton AR14165, AR14873, AR15512
Corbijn, Anton—Videos AR14293
Cordell, Denny—Obituary AR14021
Corea, Chick AR15154
Corgan, Billy—Interviews AR13747, AR14713
Corgan, Billy—Quotations AR13524, AR15031
Cornell, Chris AR12958, AR12993
Cornell, Chris—Interviews AR13656
Cornell University AR14744
Cornershop AR15843
Cornog, F.M. AR15495
Coronado, Rodney AR14447
Coronado, Rodney—Profiles AR14446
Cortese, Dan—Fashion AR14864, AR16009
Cortese, Dan—Profiles AR14864, AR16009
Cortese, Scot—Interviews AR15403
Cosloy, Gerard AR15207
Cosmic Slop (album) AR14891
Costas, Kirsten AR15541
Costello, Elvis AR12959
Costello, Elvis—Recordings AR13291, AR13449, AR14026, AR14052, AR14269, AR14964
Cott, Jonathan AR13318
Counterculture AR14528
Counterculture—Politics AR14429, AR15607, AR15752
Counting Crows AR12918, AR13939, AR14793
Counting Crows—Profiles AR15880
Counting Crows—Recordings AR14047
Country Life (album) AR14892
Country Music AR13418, AR13847, AR14629, AR15382, AR15568, AR15569
Country Music—World Wide Web AR14278
Cowan, Anthony AR15837
Cowboy Junkies AR14449, AR15991
Cows AR14255
Cox, Courteney AR15919
Cracker AR12918
Cracker—Profiles AR12960, AR15122
Cramer, Richard Ben AR13317, AR13345
Cranberries AR12918, AR14541, AR14793
Cranberries—Fashion AR14686, AR14822
Cranberries—Profiles AR13667, AR14686, AR14822
Cranberries—Recordings AR14047
Crane, Phil—Politics AR15079
Crash Test Dummies AR13841
Crawdaddy (publication) AR13959
Crawford, Cindy AR15191
Crawford, Cindy—Profiles AR16112
Crazy Horse—Videos AR13616
Crazy Legs (album) AR15414
Creach, Papa John—Obituary AR13735
Cream AR13771, AR13784, AR15170, AR15984
Cream—Recordings AR14262, AR14897

Cream—Videos AR13619
Creation Rebel AR15554
Creation Records AR16126
Credit To The Nation AR15419, AR15423
Creedence Clearwater Revival AR13784, AR13946, AR13961, AR14164, AR15170, AR15984
Creedence Clearwater Revival—Recordings AR13946
Creep (song) AR14398
Creep (video) AR14323
Crime AR13045, AR13607, AR14014, AR14120, AR14635, AR14737, AR15224, AR15330, AR15335, AR15711, AR15801, AR16026
Criss, Peter AR14287, AR15835
Critics AR13753, AR14582
Croasdale, Wayne—Fashion AR13251, AR14829
Croasdale, Wayne—Profiles AR13251, AR14829
Croatia—Photography AR15341
Croatia—Politics AR13165, AR14985, AR15002, AR15539
Cronenberg, David—Films AR13144
Crooked Officer (song) AR13960
Cropper, Steve AR15383
Crosby, David AR12959
Crosby, Stills & Nash AR14128, AR14173
Crosby, Stills & Nash—Recordings AR14258
Crosby, Stills & Nash—Tours AR15520
Crow, Sheryl AR12918, AR14157, AR14165, AR14283, AR14794
Crow, Sheryl—Profiles AR13797, AR15376
Crow, Sheryl—Recordings AR13081
Crowded House AR15923
Crowe, Cameron AR13318
Crowe, Cameron—Films AR13361
Cruel Inventions (album) AR16088
Cruise, Tom—Films AR13359, AR14000
Cruise, Tom—Profiles AR14000
The Crying Game (film) AR13855
Crystal, Billy AR15170, AR15360, AR15984, AR16117
Cub AR13134
Cuba AR14996, AR16126
Cult AR13993
Cummings, E. E. AR12958
Cunningham, Charlie AR13153
Cure—Tours AR13934
A Current Affair (television show) AR13140
Currie, Justin AR12977
Cusenza, John Sebastian—Interviews AR15695
Cyberspace AR14006, AR14009, AR14016, AR14129, AR14211, AR14212, AR14339, AR14656, AR14985, AR15579, AR15729, AR16069, AR16083
Cypress Hill AR12957, AR15570
Cypress Hill—Recordings AR13586
Cypress Hill—Tours—North America AR15448
Cyrus, Billy Ray AR15571

D

D, Chuck AR12976, AR13463
D., Chuck AR14156, AR15834
D., Chuck—Recordings AR13590
D Generation AR14347, AR15030
D, Mike—Computer Systems AR14276
D., Willie—Recordings AR13954
Da Brat AR13593, AR14794
Da Lench Mob AR15509
Dada AR14255
Dada—Recordings AR12990
Daffan, Ted—Obituary AR14810
Daisy AR14256
Daisy Chainsaw AR14791
Dajae—Recordings AR15115
Dalai Lama—Interview AR16098
Dale, Dick—Recordings AR13937
Daltrey, Roger—Concerts—New York, New York AR15536
Dambuilders AR14549, AR15214
Dance Naked (album) AR13414
Dancing AR13076, AR13079, AR13277, AR14222, AR14774, AR15233, AR15234
Dando, Evan AR12918, AR13853
Dando, Evan—Interviews AR13395, AR13405
Dando, Evan—Profiles AR15948
Dandy Warhols AR15705
Danes, Claire AR13237, AR13247, AR14506, AR15279, AR15304
Dangerous (album) AR13944, AR13977
Daniel, Nathan—Obituary AR15159
Danzig AR12918, AR14550, AR15821, AR15910
Danzig, Glenn AR14550
D'Arcy AR13390
Dare International Records AR14036
Dark Side Of The Moon (album) AR14893
Dark Star (book) AR14058
The Darker Side Of Black (film) AR13592
Dartmouth College AR14430, AR14638, AR15486
Dashboard Saviors AR15320
DAT AR13940
Davidson, Jaye—Interviews AR13855
Davies, Ray AR15383
Davies, Richard—Recordings AR13454
Davis, Clive AR12959
Davis, Larry—Obituary AR15514
Davis, Miles AR15154
Davis, Miles—Discography AR13774
Davis, Miles—Obituary AR15022
Davis, Miles—Recordings AR14259, AR14273, AR14881, AR14966
Davis, Tamra—Videos AR14296
Daydream Nation (album) AR14894, AR15210
DCC Compact Classics AR14261
De La Hoya, Oscar—Fashion AR14825, AR15692
De La Soul AR12918
De Silva, Ana AR13370
Dead Can Dance AR12971
Dead Elvis (book) AR15137
Dead Kennedys AR13951
Dead Kennedys—Recordings AR14907
Deadheads AR15499
Deal, Kelley AR15821, AR15831
Deal, Kim AR15830, AR15831
Dean, Roger AR14873
Deangelis, Lou—Profiles AR14461, AR14859
Death Penalty AR13908, AR15224
Death Row Records AR13082, AR15609
DeBell, Sara—Recordings AR13840
Decathlon AR14314, AR14843
DeCurtis, Anthony AR13318, AR14873
Deee-Lite—Profiles AR13856
Deee-Lite—Videos AR14250
Deep Forest—Videos AR15755
Def American Records AR13589, AR15938
Def Leppard—Concerts—Norfolk, Virginia AR13329
Def Leppard—Profiles AR13754
Def Leppard—Recordings AR13701, AR13715
Del Amitri AR14841, AR15316
Del Toro, Benicio—Films AR13498, AR14815
DeMann, Freddy AR13937
DeMent, Iris AR13867, AR14256, AR14727, AR15264
Demme, Jonathan AR13854
Demme, Jonathan—Films AR13422
Demme, Jonathan—Videos AR14291
Democratic Party AR12949, AR13441, AR14015, AR14068, AR14079, AR14081, AR14104, AR14106, AR14116, AR14310, AR14639, AR15349
Democratic Party—Conventions (1992) AR14543
Dennis, Cathy—Recordings AR13799
Denzil AR15424
DePalma—Videos AR14291
Depeche Mode AR14160
Depeche Mode—Profiles AR13378
Depeche Mode—Recordings AR13943, AR14874
Derek And The Dominos—Recordings AR14268
Dern, Laura—Profiles AR15157, AR15933
Desmond, L. R. AR15017
Des'ree AR15476
Detachable Penis (song) AR12973
Detroit, Michigan AR15321
Detroit, Michigan—Rock Scene AR14043
Devo AR13883, AR15292
Devo—Videos AR14377, AR14395
DGC Records AR13980
Diamond Dogs (album) AR14895
Diamond, Neil—Interviews AR13533
Diaz, Cameron—Profiles AR13495
DiCaprio, Leonardo AR13223, AR15249
Dickins, Rob AR14642
Diddley, Bo AR14049, AR15739
Diddley, Bo—Interviews AR13133
Diesel And Dust (album) AR14896
DiFranco, Ani AR14607
Digable Planets AR13591, AR13595, AR14319, AR14793, AR15317
Digital Cultural Stream (publication) AR13374
Digital Hardcore Records AR15018
Diller, Barry—Interviews AR14005
Dillon Fence AR15124
Dinosaur Jr AR12918, AR13298
Dion AR15170, AR15984
Dire Straits—Videos AR13825
Dirty (album) AR13014
Dirty Boots (video) AR14401
Dirty, Ike AR13591
Disarm (song) AR15726
Diseases AR15181
Dishwalla—Recordings AR14348
DiSipio, Fred AR13963
Disney, Walt—Films AR15521
Disney, Walt—Videos AR13613
Disposable Heroes Of Hiphoprisy AR13590, AR14256
Disposable Heroes Of Hiphoprisy—Recordings AR13968
Disraeli Gears (album) AR14897
Diving AR14801, AR15693
Dixon, Jimmy AR13129, AR13220, AR14821
Dixon, Marie AR16096
Dixon, Willie AR13541, AR13783, AR15130, AR16096
Dixon, Willie—Obituary AR13056
Dixon, Willie—Recordings AR14273
DJ Premier AR13591, AR13592
DJ Red Alert AR12918
DJ Spooky AR13237, AR14506, AR15279
Do Wop AR15452
Doc At The Radar Station (album) AR14898
Document (album) AR14899
Doherty, Shannen—Profiles AR14590
Dolby, Thomas—Videos AR14679
Dole, Robert AR14804, AR15831
Dole, Robert—Politics AR13079, AR13601, AR15497

Dole, Robert—Profiles AR13346, AR15497
Domino AR15090
Domino, Fats AR15383
Domino, Fats—Recordings AR13302
Dominoes AR14173
Don Byron Plays The Music Of Mickey Katz (album) AR15925
Don Caballero AR15748
Donahue, Tom AR13524, AR15031
Donelly, Tanya AR14674
Don't Blame Me (video) AR13613
Doors AR13771, AR13784, AR15170, AR15984
Doors—Recordings AR14950, AR15455, AR15827
Dorff, Stephen—Films AR13210
Dornan, Robert—Politics AR15079
Dorschester, Massachusetts AR16039
Dorsey, Tommy—Recordings AR14271
Double Trouble—Videos AR13616
Doughty, M.—Computer Systems AR14276
Douglas, Alan AR15167
Douglas, Steve—Obituary AR13967
Dowd, Maureen AR14333
Down Home Guide To The Blues (book) AR13994
Downtown Science AR14468
Dr. Dre AR12918, AR13954, AR15098, AR15614, AR15628, AR15824, AR15972
Dr. Dre—Profiles AR13924
Dr. Dre—Tours—North America AR15925
Dr. Katz, Professional Therapist (television show) AR13171
Dr. Offfff AR14442
Drake, Nick—Recordings AR13597
Drama AR13213, AR13879, AR13887, AR14812, AR15287, AR15296, AR15651
Dream Harder (album) AR13849
Dreamworldnews (publication) AR15395
Drew University AR14554
Drive Like Jehu AR14289
Droge, Pete—Recordings AR12922
Drop The Dead Donkey (television show) AR13171
Drug Culture AR12981, AR13145, AR13188, AR13278, AR13283, AR13286, AR13612, AR14155, AR14230, AR14432, AR14507, AR14525, AR14736, AR15080, AR15332, AR15336, AR15338, AR15499, AR15596, AR15783, AR15806, AR16051, AR16126
Drug Culture—Higher Education AR14505
Drug Policy Foundation (organization) AR13343
Drug Smuggling—United States AR14596, AR14738, AR15105, AR16041
Drugs AR12981, AR13024, AR13043, AR13159, AR13283, AR13609, AR14230, AR14509, AR14525, AR14596, AR14798, AR15106, AR15329, AR15346, AR15803, AR15811, AR16026, AR16041, AR16126
Drugs—Legislation AR13343, AR13485, AR13605, AR13612, AR14432, AR14596, AR14737, AR15080, AR15336, AR15338, AR15362, AR15407, AR15488, AR15783, AR15801, AR15806, AR16026
Drugs—Legislation—Europe AR14736
Duchovny, David—Interview AR16016
Duckworth, William AR16123
Dulli, Greg—Interviews AR13521
Duo (book) AR15591
The Duplex Planet (book) AR13836
Duran Duran AR15971
Dust Brothers AR13630
Dye, David AR14255
Dylan, Bob AR12959, AR13023, AR14037, AR15519, AR15521
Dylan, Bob—CD-ROMs AR13374, AR15516
Dylan, Bob—Concerts—New York, New York AR15882, AR15904, AR15976
Dylan, Bob—Concerts—San Diego, California AR14024
Dylan, Bob—Interviews AR14513
Dylan, Bob—Recordings AR13637, AR14167, AR14270, AR14273, AR14886, AR14944, AR15193, AR15804
Dylan, Bob—Software AR15537
Dylan, Bob—Videos AR14400, AR14547

E

E AR13800, AR15937
E! (television network) AR15913
E-Mail AR13229, AR15259
Eagles—Recordings AR14914
Eagles—Tours AR15520, AR16015
Earl, Robert AR13898
Earle, Steve AR14214, AR15821
Early Works (book) AR14608
Earrings AR15387
Earth And Sun And Moon (album) AR13706
Earth Summit (1992) AR14999
Earthquakes AR15549
Earthquakes—California AR15940
Earthrise (album) AR13824
Eastern Mind (software) AR14210
Eastwood, Clint—Films AR13143
Eastwood, Clint—Interviews AR15903
Eat A Peach (album) AR14900
Eazy-E AR12965, AR15467, AR15583
Eazy-E—Death AR15037
Eazy-E—Obituary AR15816, AR15914
Echobelly AR15423, AR15848
Echobelly—Recordings AR15424
Eckardt, Shawn AR15544
Economics AR14070, AR14072, AR14074, AR14080, AR14115, AR16033
Economy AR13191, AR13920, AR14063, AR14067, AR14071, AR14082, AR14083, AR14088, AR14091, AR14092, AR14094, AR14095, AR14096, AR14100, AR14108, AR14110, AR14112, AR14113, AR14114, AR14115, AR14116, AR14121, AR14122, AR15041, AR15045, AR15148, AR15548, AR15550, AR16133
Economy—Minimum Wage AR13212
Economy—National Service AR14061, AR14111
Eddy, Duane AR13541, AR13776, AR13783, AR15130
Edelman, Marian Wright—Interviews AR12982
Edge AR12976, AR14705
Edge—Fashion AR15387
Editorials AR13254, AR13275, AR14737, AR15776, AR15778, AR15781, AR15782, AR15783, AR15784, AR15785, AR15786, AR15787, AR15788, AR15789, AR15791, AR15798, AR15800, AR15801, AR15915
Education AR12950, AR14085, AR14533, AR16033
Education—Testing AR14219
Edwards, Anthony AR14052
Edwards, Bernard—Obituary AR14215
Edwards, Frank AR12916
Eels AR15817
Ehrmann, Eric AR13317, AR13596
Eickhoff, Janie AR14314, AR14843
8-Track Mind (publication) AR13741
Eitzel, Mark AR15366
Elastica AR13451, AR14165, AR14539, AR15422, AR15836
Elections AR14086, AR14109, AR16023, AR16025, AR16027, AR16038
Elections (1972) AR15597
Elections (1992) AR13441, AR13598, AR14015, AR14062, AR14064, AR14066, AR14100, AR14104, AR14106, AR14107, AR14118, AR14310, AR14333, AR14336, AR14492, AR14543, AR14544, AR14545, AR14546, AR14594, AR14745, AR14756, AR14785, AR14995, AR15006, AR15039, AR15040, AR15041, AR15045, AR15046, AR15049, AR15051, AR15055, AR15475, AR15594, AR15599, AR15601, AR15776, AR15777, AR15791
Elections (1994) AR14081, AR14648
Elections (1996) AR12951, AR12955, AR13079, AR13082, AR13260, AR13480, AR13481, AR13601, AR13602, AR13603, AR14073, AR14078, AR14080, AR14105, AR14459, AR14649, AR15009, AR15778
Electric Factory (organization) AR13954
Electric Ladyland (album) AR14901
Electronic Bulletin Boards AR13229, AR15259
Elektra Entertainment AR13934
Elektra Records AR14550, AR14642
Eleventh Dream Day AR16090
Elliott, Joe—Recordings AR13672
Elliott, Lee Ann AR16023
Ellis, Terry AR13980
Ellison, Jim—Obituary AR14163
Ellison, Ronald AR13945, AR13949
Ellsberg, Daniel AR13411
Elvis Presley (album) AR14902
Emelien, Jean AR13945
Emerson, Lake & Palmer—Recordings AR14884
EMI Music AR13943
EMI Records AR13963, AR14742
Emmons, Andrea AR15323
The Empire Strikes Back (film) AR15668
Employment AR13484, AR13892, AR14796, AR15148, AR15303
En Vogue—Profiles AR15198
En Vogue—Videos AR13506
Engine AR13574
England—Rock Scene AR15419
England's Dreaming (book) AR13962
English, Karan—Politics AR13036
ENIT Festival AR13139, AR14163
Eno, Brian AR13951
Eno, Brian—CD-ROMs AR15516
Entertainment Tonight (television show) AR15931
Entertainment Weekly (publication) AR14338
Environment AR12948, AR13193, AR13315, AR13606, AR13824, AR13923, AR14094, AR14123, AR14252, AR14527, AR14999, AR15392, AR15404, AR15695, AR15996, AR16024, AR16029, AR16033, AR16037, AR16043
Environment—Brazil AR14869
Environment—Everglades AR13156, AR13922, AR15779
Environment—Redwood Forests AR14141
Environment—Walden Woods AR13057, AR13474, AR14203, AR14427, AR15920, AR15966
Environmental Protection Agency AR16043
Ephron, Nora—Interviews AR13689
Epic (video) AR14405
Epic Records AR15773
Epitaph Records AR14193
Eric B AR13593
Erickson, Roky—Profiles AR14624
Ertegun, Ahmet AR13523
Escape From L.A. (film) AR14162
Escovedo, Alejandro AR13692
ESPN Network AR13046
Esquivel—Interviews AR13509
Eszterhas, Joe AR13317, AR13604
Etheridge, Melissa AR12975, AR13523, AR13608
Etheridge, Melissa—Interviews AR13258,

AR13450
Etheridge, Melissa—Profiles AR13556
Etheridge, Melissa—Tours AR14049
Eugene, Oregon AR13609
Eugenius AR14681
Europe AR14736
Eurythmics—Videos AR13802, AR14772
Even Cowgirls Get The Blues (film) AR13339
Everclear AR14167, AR15846
Everclear—Tours—North America AR14047
Everglades AR13156, AR13922
Everlast AR13591
Everly Brothers—Recordings AR14272
Everly, Erin AR13194, AR15511
Every Breath You Take (video) AR14555
Everything But The Girl AR15819
Exercise AR16126
Exercise—Spinning AR13234, AR15272
Exile In Guyville (album) AR14691
Exile On Main Street (album) AR12945, AR14903
Exit 57 (television show) AR14508
Experimental Jet Set, Trash And No Star (album) AR14412
Express Yourself (video) AR13558
Extreme AR12976
Extreme III Sides To Every Story (album) AR14750
Extremely Live (album) AR13328
Exxon (company) AR14252

F

Faces—Recordings AR14935
Fagen, Donald AR15911
Fagen, Donald—Recordings AR13945
Faith (video) AR13512
Faith No More AR15507
Faith No More—Recordings AR13985, AR15409, AR15916
Faith No More—Videos AR14405
Faithfull, Marianne AR14050, AR15742
Fall—Recordings AR13207
Falling From Grace (film) AR13823
Family And Medical Leave Act AR15715
Famines—Africa AR14993
Fan Clubs AR15505
Fancher, Lisa AR14255
Fannon, Gary AR14432, AR15783, AR15806
Fannon, Gary—Profiles AR13612, AR15336, AR15338
Fans AR13949, AR14770
Fantasia (film) AR15521
Fantasy Records AR13982
Far And Away (film) AR14000
Farming AR13922
Farrell, Perry AR12918, AR13985, AR13990, AR14287, AR15515, AR15823
Farrell, Perry—Fashion AR15387
Farrell, Perry—Interviews AR12940, AR12962
Farrell, Perry—Profiles AR14784
Farris, Dionne AR13580, AR15241
Fashek, Majek AR15955
Fashion AR12967, AR13037, AR13129, AR13152, AR13189, AR13213, AR13216, AR13218, AR13220, AR13222, AR13235, AR13237, AR13239, AR13255, AR13262, AR13263, AR13266, AR13268, AR13323, AR13324, AR13365, AR13498, AR13577, AR13599, AR13610, AR13675, AR13814, AR13859, AR14131, AR14133, AR14313, AR14314, AR14315, AR14425, AR14440, AR14449, AR14450, AR14461, AR14506, AR14511, AR14532, AR14534, AR14535, AR14616, AR14799, AR14801, AR14812, AR14813, AR14814, AR14815, AR14816, AR14817, AR14818, AR14819, AR14820, AR14821, AR14823, AR14824, AR14825, AR14826, AR14827, AR14830, AR14832, AR14833, AR14835, AR14836, AR14837, AR14838, AR14839, AR14840, AR14841, AR14843, AR14844, AR14845, AR14846, AR14848, AR14849, AR14851, AR14852, AR14853, AR14855, AR14856, AR14857, AR14858, AR14859, AR14860, AR14861, AR14862, AR14864, AR14865, AR15035, AR15081, AR15127, AR15211, AR15212, AR15236, AR15247, AR15275, AR15279, AR15282, AR15316, AR15358, AR15367, AR15385, AR15386, AR15396, AR15425, AR15430, AR15482, AR15483, AR15484, AR15553, AR15603, AR15604, AR15605, AR15692, AR15693, AR15694, AR15696, AR15720, AR15722, AR15802, AR15850, AR15926, AR15988, AR15991, AR15996, AR16009, AR16057
Fashion—Blass, Bill AR15396
Fashion—Cusenza, John Sebastian AR15695
Fashion—Earrings AR15387
Fashion—Hilfiger, Tommy AR15396
Fashion—Kallen, Peter AR13130, AR14617
Fashion—Karan, Donna AR15396
Fashion—Leach, Conrad AR13130, AR14617
Fashion—Lola AR14442
Fashion—Mirzrahi, Isaac AR15396
Fashion—Oldham, Todd AR16126
Fashion—Sui, Anna AR13870, AR15267, AR15396
Fashion—Tappan, Heidi AR13130, AR14617
Fashion—Tyler, Richard AR13232, AR15268
Fat Joe AR15452
Fate Of Nations (album) AR14768
Fatima Mansions AR13325
Fear And Loathing In Las Vegas (book) AR15602
Fear Of Music (album) AR14904
Fearing, Stephen AR14620
Fechner, Andrew AR14832, AR15127
Federal Bureau Of Alcohol, Tobacco And Firearms AR15138, AR15540
Federal Bureau Of Investigation AR14476
Federal Communications Commission AR13085
Federal Reserve System AR14121, AR14122
Feingold, Russ—Politics AR13036
Feldman, Corey AR15945
Felton, David AR13318
Fencing AR14801, AR15693
Fender Guitars AR13976
Fender, Leo AR13770, AR14705
Ferguson, Kent AR14801, AR15693
Ferguson, Kent—Fashion AR14801, AR15693
Ferrick, Melissa AR15939
Ferry, Bryan—Interviews AR13416
Festivals—1993 World Peace And Healing Gathering Of The Rainbow Family Of Living Light AR14528
Fiction AR13132, AR13155, AR13852, AR15184, AR15356, AR16059, AR16061
50,000,000 Elvis Fans Can't Be Wrong (album) AR14905
Fighting Gravity—Profiles AR15918
Fillmore Auditorium—San Francisco, California AR13933
Filo, David AR15729
Filter AR13504
Filter—Recordings AR15758
Fincher, David AR15921
Fincher, David—Videos AR14296
Finck, Robin AR14156
Finn, Neil AR14160
Finn, Tim—Recordings AR13828
Fish Heads (video) AR14374
Fishbone AR14020
Fisher, Carrie AR13318
Fisher, Christopher AR12947
Fisher, Gary AR13153
Fisher, John Norwood AR14020
Fitzgerald, Ella AR14381, AR15689
Fitzgerald, Ella—Obituary AR13911
Flack, Roberta AR15154
Flaim, Eric AR13323, AR14856
Flaming Lips AR13409, AR15525
Flavor Flav AR13590, AR14287, AR15098, AR15831, AR15834
Flea AR12977
Flea—Interviews AR14753
Fleetwood Mac AR15972
Fleetwood Mac—Recordings AR14271, AR14941
Fleetwood, Mick AR15383
Fletcher, John AR12916
Fletcher, Matthew—Obituary AR14163
Flipper—Recordings AR13976
Flippo, Chet AR13317, AR13651
Florida—Everglades AR13156, AR13922, AR15779
Flowbee Infomercial (television show) AR13575
Fluffy AR13466
Fly Girls—Fashion AR13245, AR14828
Fogerty, John AR13194, AR13961, AR13969, AR13982, AR14164, AR14705, AR15170, AR15383, AR15511, AR15940, AR15984
Fogerty, John—Interviews AR13946
Folds, Ben AR15705
Foley, Dave—Interviews AR15935
Follow For Now AR12992
Fong-Torres, Ben AR13318
Foo Fighters AR14172
Foo Fighters—Concerts AR15084
Foo Fighters—Profiles AR14682
Foo Fighters—Recordings AR14050
Foo Fighters—Tours—North America AR14047, AR15825
Foo Fighters—Videos AR13514
Foo, Mark—Profiles AR16049
Food AR13574, AR13597, AR14442, AR15093, AR15242, AR15551, AR16125
Football AR15334
For Squirrels AR14050, AR15837
Forbes (publication) AR15168
Forbes, Steve AR14804
Ford (company) AR15515
Fordham, Johanna—Fashion AR13365, AR14840
Forrest, Bob AR13957
Fort Apache (recording studio) AR14463
Fountains Of Wayne AR15202
4 Non Blondes AR13839, AR14793
Fourth Reich (organization) AR12947
Fowler, Bernard—Recordings AR14167
Fox, Matthew—Profiles AR16092
Foxworthy, Jeff—Television AR16014
Frames AR15399
Francis, Black—Recordings AR13798
Frank, Anthony M. AR13942
Frankie's House (album) AR15414
Franklin, Aretha AR15192
Franklin, Aretha—Recordings AR14263, AR15193, AR15804
Franklin, Benjamin AR15228
Franklin, Melvin—Obituary AR15845
Franks Wild Years (album) AR14906
Franks, Rebecca Coupe AR14038
Franti, Michael AR15452
Fraser, Brendan AR14315, AR14534
Freak Out! (album) AR15393
Freakwater AR13396, AR13517, AR13582, AR14548, AR14683
Free Your Mind (video) AR13506

Free-For-All (album) AR15974
Freedman, Samuel G. AR13317, AR13690
Freedom (video) AR13397
Freedom 90 (video) AR14392
Freewheelers AR15400
Freiberg, David AR12959
Frente AR12921
Fresh Fruit For Rotting Vegetables (album) AR14907
Frey, Glenn AR12966
Frey, Glenn—Interviews AR13419
Fricke, David AR13318, AR14873
Friedman, Steve AR14332
Friends (television show) AR15919
Friends: The Official Companion (book) AR13310
Fripp, Robert AR13743
Frischmann, Justine AR13760
Frischmann, Justine—Interviews AR13451
From Cakewalks to Concert Halls (book) AR13962
Frykowski, Voytek AR15512
F.S.K. AR14549
Fuchs, Michael AR15835, AR15836
Fugees AR15471
Fugees—Profiles AR13658
Fuhrman, Mark AR15545
Full Moon, Dirty Hearts (album) AR13808
Fuller, Charles AR15824
Fun Lovin' Criminals AR13515
Fun Lovin' Criminals—Videos AR13081
Fun-Da-Mental AR13593
Funkadelic AR13761, AR14128, AR14173
Funkadelic—Recordings AR14891, AR14909
Funkdoobiest—Tours—North America AR15448
Funkmaster Flex—Recordings AR13594
Furse, Elizabeth—Politics AR13036
Further Festival AR14159
The Future (album) AR13429
Future Sound Of London AR15705

G

G., Warren AR15628
Gabler, Milt AR13771, AR13784, AR15170, AR15984
Gabriel, Peter AR14549
Gabriel, Peter—CD-ROMs AR13932
Gabriel, Peter—Recordings AR13815, AR14620, AR14936
Gabriel, Peter—Tours—Europe AR15431
Gabriel, Peter—Tours—North America AR13583, AR14207
Gabriel, Peter—Videos AR14375, AR14396
Gahan, Dave AR14155, AR14542, AR15836
Gahr, David AR14221
Gaines, Jeffrey AR14605
Gaines, William—Obituary AR14524
Galactic Cowboys AR13709
Galaxie 500—Recordings AR14169
Gale, Eric—Obituary AR15515
Gallagher, Noel AR13792, AR15754
Gallagher, Rory—Obituary AR15433
Gallen, Joel AR15170, AR15984
Gallo, Robert AR13369
Galvin, Peter AR16095
Gambaccini, Paul AR13318
Games AR15169
Gang Of Seven Records AR13947
Gang Starr AR12918
Gang Starr—Recordings AR15590
Gans, David AR12959
Gap Band—Recordings AR13313
Garbage AR13198
Garbage—Profiles AR13518
Garcia, Jerry AR13948, AR13972, AR14198, AR14453, AR15383, AR15781
Garcia, Jerry—Death AR12959, AR13022, AR13659, AR13673, AR13710, AR13738, AR14284, AR15158, AR15498
Garcia, Jerry—Interviews AR13426, AR14198, AR14201
Garcia, Jerry—Obituary AR13912
Garcia, Jerry—Profiles AR14058
Garcia, Jerry—Quotes AR13301, AR13921
Garcia, Jerry—Recordings AR14051, AR14889
Garfunkel, Art—Interviews AR13489
Garofalo, Janeane AR13834, AR15410
Garrett, Kenny AR13777
Gates, Daryl AR14343
Gates, Robert AR12956
Gatorade Ironman Triathlon World Championship AR14133, AR14861
Gatton, Danny AR15557
Gatton, Danny—Obituary AR13698
Gaudi AR14442
Gay And Lesbian Alliance Against Defamation (organization) AR13614, AR13620
Gaye, Marvin AR14273
Gaye, Marvin—Recordings AR13313, AR14241, AR14268, AR14270, AR14272
Gayles, Juggy—Profiles AR13846
Geffen, Aviv AR13027
Geffen, David AR13934, AR14027
Geffen, David—Interviews AR13998
Geffen, David—Quotes AR13954
Geffen Records AR13957, AR13960, AR13980, AR14027, AR15532, AR15828
Geggy Tah—Recordings AR15093
Geiger, Marc AR14256, AR16126
Gene AR15425
General Electric(company) AR14069, AR14120
Genesis AR14158, AR15883
Genesis—Tours AR13934
Genocide AR14134, AR14521, AR15339, AR15343
Gentlemen (album) AR13019
Georgetown University AR15331
Georgia (Europe) AR15010
Geraldine Fibbers AR12944
Gergen, David—Profiles AR16021
Germano, Lisa AR14354
Germany AR13485
Germany—Rock Scene AR14304
Geronimo, Joe AR14529
Gerry Spence (television show) AR13172
Gersh, Gary AR13968, AR14031
Gessner, Sandra AR15510
Get Your Wings (album) AR14601
Geto Boys—Recordings AR13960
Geto Boys—Videos AR14251
Gett Off (video) AR15634
Getty, Jean Paul, III AR13020
Giant Records AR13980
Gibbons, Billy AR13851
Gibson, Bob—Obituary AR14810
Giesen, Bobby AR14616, AR14819
Gill, Vince AR15568
Gillespie, Dizzy—Obituary AR13773
Gilmore, Gary AR13908, AR13915
Gilmore, Jimmie Dale—Profiles AR13756
Gilmore, Mikal AR13308, AR13317, AR13908
Gimme Shelter (film) AR13993
Gin Blossoms AR13089, AR14047, AR14793
Gingrich, Newt AR14081
Gingrich, Newt—Politics AR12954, AR12955, AR15079, AR16044
Gingrich, Newt—Profiles AR14077
Ginn, Greg AR13974, AR13979
Giovanni, Nikki AR15136
Girlfriend (album) AR13004
Girls Against Boys AR15470
Girls Against Boys—Tours—North America AR14047
Girls Just Want To Have Fun (video) AR13570
Gits AR15455, AR15827
Give It Away (video) AR13567
Give Out But Don't Give Up (album) AR13383
Glover, Corey AR12977
Glover, Crispin AR15554
Go Fish (film) AR13233, AR15270
Go-Go's AR15945
God's Favorite Band AR14794
God's Little Monkeys AR13858
Godunov, Alexander AR15096
Goettel, Dwayne—Obituary AR15815
Goin' Back To Cali (video) AR15620
Goldberg, Danny AR14642, AR14732, AR15207, AR15506, AR15835, AR15964, AR16006
Golden Smog AR14048
Goldfinger AR13997
Goldie AR14172, AR15705
Goldman, Albert—Obituary AR14361
Goldman, Ron AR13337, AR15545
Goldner, George AR13973
Golf AR14167
Goo Goo Dolls AR14728, AR15474
Good Guys (store) AR13575
Good To The Last Drop (album) AR15944
Good Vibrations (album) AR14266
Goodbye Yellow Brick Road (album) AR15189
Goode Behavior (television show) AR15897
Gopalan, Geetha AR14832, AR15127
Gorbachev, Mikhail AR13347
Gordon, Kim AR12977, AR15701
Gordon, Kim—Fashion AR14813, AR15385
Gordon, Mike—Computer Systems AR14276
Gordon, Nina AR12975
Gore, Karenna AR13868, AR15265
Gore, Kristin AR13868, AR15265
Gore, Sarah AR13868, AR15265
Gore, Tipper AR13441, AR14042
Gorecki, Henryk AR13389
Gossard, Stone AR12977
Gossard, Stone—Recordings AR13299
Goude, Jean-Paul—Videos AR14293
Government (United States) AR14069, AR14119, AR14994, AR15005, AR15013, AR15138, AR15540, AR15598, AR16033, AR16121
Government (United States)—Attorney General AR13581, AR16026
Government (United States)—Budget AR14067, AR14080, AR14097, AR14101, AR16027
Government (United States)—Department Of Defense AR14080, AR14101
Government (United States)—Department Of Energy AR16040
Government (United States)—Department Of Interior AR16024, AR16040
Government (United States)—Environmental Protection Agency AR16043
Government (United States)—Export-Import Bank AR14083
Government (United States)—Federal Elections Commission AR16023
Government (United States)—Food And Drug Administration AR16036
Government (United States)—Postal Service AR13942, AR15480
Government (United States)—Social Security AR14080
Graceland (estate) AR15522
Graffin, Greg—Interviews AR13661
Graffiti AR14149
Graham AR15086
Graham, Bill AR13770, AR13935, AR13955,

AR13993, AR14477, AR14705, AR15153
Graham, Bill—Obituary AR13992
Graham, David AR15153
Gramercy International Contemporary Art Fair AR14580
Gramm, Phil AR14804
Gramm, Phil—Politics AR15079
Grammy Awards AR13636, AR16093
Grand Juries AR13945, AR13949
Grand Puba Maxwell AR14791
Grand Royal Records AR14031
Graning, Chick AR15832
Granite, Tom AR14256
Grant, Amy AR12976
Grant Lee Buffalo AR12918, AR14156, AR15111
Grant Lee Buffalo—Profiles AR15529
Grant, Peter—Obituary AR13458
Graphic Witt: The Art Of Humor In Design (book) AR14789
Grateful Dead AR13374, AR13541, AR13673, AR13776, AR13783, AR13794, AR13912, AR13913, AR13966, AR14277, AR14647, AR15130, AR15493, AR15498, AR15499, AR15835
Grateful Dead—Concerts AR15833
Grateful Dead—Concerts—Meadowlands, New Jersey AR13949, AR14770, AR15509
Grateful Dead—Concerts—Orlando, Florida AR14381
Grateful Dead—Concerts—Washington, D.C. AR15832
Grateful Dead—Profiles AR13738
Grateful Dead—Recordings AR13028, AR13951, AR14036, AR14877, AR14878
Grateful Dead—Tours AR13934
Grateful Dead Productions AR14277
Grease (stage musical) AR15651
Great Britain—Fashion AR15425
Great Britain—Music Scene AR15176, AR15415, AR15429
Green, Al AR13295, AR13523, AR13761, AR13782, AR15739
Green Day AR12918, AR13228, AR13664, AR14157, AR14183, AR14794, AR15258
Green Day—Profiles AR13660, AR14684
Green Day—Recordings AR13678
Green Day—Videos AR15775
Green Jelly—Videos AR13294
Green, Jim AR14256
Green, Robin AR13317, AR14055
Green, Susannah AR15017
Greenberger, David AR13836
Greene, Graham AR15096
Greene, Herb AR14221
Greenfield, Jerry—Profiles AR15551
Greenfield, Robert AR13317, AR14057
Greenspan, Alan AR14122
Greetings From Asbury Park, N.J. (album) AR14908
Greider, William AR13317, AR14084
Grenier, Amanda AR13273, AR15713
Greta AR15936
Griffith, Nanci AR12918, AR16054
Griffith, Nanci—Tours AR14165
Grisham, John AR13854
Grisman, David AR12959
Groening, Matt AR15394
Grohl, Dave—Recordings AR15823
Groove Is In The Heart (video) AR14250
Gruber, Gerri Lynne AR15017
Grubman, Allen AR14031, AR14763
Grunge Lite (album) AR13840
Guatemala AR15181
Gudmundsdottir, Bjork AR12918, AR12958, AR14158, AR14169, AR14285, AR14323, AR15832, AR15833
Gudmundsdottir, Bjork—Fashion AR13807
Gudmundsdottir, Bjork—Interviews AR15697
Gudmundsdottir, Bjork—Profiles AR13807, AR15704
Gudmundsdottir, Bjork—Videos AR14422
Guess Who—Recordings AR14259
Guided By Voices AR13396, AR13517, AR13582, AR14548, AR14683
Guinier, Lani AR14060
Guitar For The Practicing Musician (publication) AR15837
Guitars AR14443, AR14537
Gulliver's Travels (television show) AR13176
Gun Control AR12952, AR13273, AR13480, AR13481, AR13611, AR14102, AR14342, AR15138, AR15412, AR15506, AR15540, AR15713, AR15785, AR16031, AR16121, AR16122
Guns N' Roses AR12931, AR13976, AR14029, AR14125, AR14190, AR14301, AR14491, AR14741, AR14762
Guns N' Roses—Concerts—St. Louis, Missouri AR13764, AR14673
Guns N' Roses—Recordings AR13166, AR14130, AR14312, AR15505, AR15512
Guns N' Roses—Tours AR13982
Guns N' Roses—Tours—North America AR13934
Guns N' Roses—Videos AR15938
Guralnick, Peter AR13307
Guru—Interviews AR13293
Gustafsson, Per AR14442
Guthrie, Arlo AR14426
Guthrie, Woody AR13442, AR14426
Guts And Grace Records AR13781
Gutterball AR14255
Gutterball—Recordings AR15203
Guy, Buddy AR15829
Guy, Buddy—Profiles AR15463
Gymnastics AR13599, AR14799, AR14801, AR15693

H

Haggard, Merle AR13847, AR15382
Haiti AR15003, AR15462, AR15810
Haiti—Music Scene AR14623
Hakmoun, Hassan AR14549
Haldeman, H. R. AR13412
Hale House AR13593
Half Japanese AR14413
Half Way Home AR14228
Half-Cocked (album) AR15705
Hall, Jerry AR15096
Hamilton, Mark AR13260
Hamilton, Suzy AR14313, AR14816
Hamilton's (nightclub) AR13136
Hammer AR13955, AR14051, AR15584, AR15823
Hammonds, Jeffrey AR13227, AR15257
Hampden-Sydney College AR14554
Hancock, Herbie AR15154
Hancock, Herbie—Videos AR14407
Handsome—Recordings AR14162
Hanft, Steve—Videos AR13629
Hanks, Jarrod AR13599, AR14799
Hanks, Jarrod—Fashion AR13599, AR14799
Hannah, Daryl AR15098
Hanson, Richard AR14366
Happy Mondays AR13962
A Hard Day's Night (CD-ROM) AR13965
Hard Rock Cafe (nightclub) AR13898
Hardcore Jollies (album) AR14909
Harding, John Wesley AR13037, AR14048, AR15722
Harding, Tonya AR15837
Harding, Tonya—Profiles AR15544
Hardkiss—Recordings AR15116
Harford, Chris—Recordings AR12989
Harper, Ben AR12975, AR15705, AR15941
Harris, David AR13317, AR14140
Harris, Emmylou AR14143
Harris, Jared—Fashion AR14839, AR15746, AR16057
Harris, Jordan AR14025
Harris, Jossie AR13577, AR13814
Harrison, George AR14030, AR15383
Harrison, George—Tours—Japan AR14536
Harrison, Wilbert—Obituary AR13786
Harry Pussy AR14652
Harry, Debbie AR13962, AR15742
Harry, Debbie—Recordings AR14920
Hart, Mickey AR15153
Hart, Mickey—Interviews AR13837
Hart, Mickey—Recordings AR13315
Harte, Brian AR13537, AR14641
Hartman, Dan—Obituary AR15513
Hartnoll, Paul—Computer Systems AR14276
Harvard University AR16131
Harvest Of Seven Years (video) AR13619
Harvey, Polly Jean AR12958, AR15939
Harvey, Polly Jean—Interviews AR15533
Harvey, Polly Jean—Profiles AR13762
Harvey, Polly Jean—Recordings AR14162
Hassan, Umar Bin AR13590
Hatfield, Juliana AR12918, AR12975, AR13685, AR13854, AR14145
Hawke, Ethan—Profiles AR14680
Hawkins, Sophie B.—Profiles AR15989
Hawkins, Ted AR15937
Hawkins, Ted—Obituary AR15381
Haydn, Lili AR12965
Hayes, Isaac—Recordings AR13594, AR14913
Haynes, Gibby—Interviews AR13520
Haynes, Rusty—Profiles AR14431
Hazel, Eddie—Obituary AR14469
Hazelwood, Joseph AR14252
HBO AR15927
Headman Shabalala AR13956
Headphones AR16065
Heads AR14161
Heal The World (organization) AR13970
Healey, Jack AR15153
Health AR12927, AR12981, AR13044, AR13234, AR13279, AR13369, AR13872, AR13877, AR14186, AR14205, AR14224, AR14317, AR14326, AR14987, AR14991, AR15083, AR15181, AR15225, AR15242, AR15271, AR15272, AR15281, AR15362, AR15411, AR15547, AR15714, AR16036, AR16124, AR16126
Health—Insurance AR14019, AR14063, AR14108, AR14189
Health—Politics AR13477, AR14063, AR14108
Health And Happiness Show AR15236, AR15802
Health And Happiness Show—Fashion AR15236, AR15802
Hearst, Patty AR14429, AR15096, AR15752
Heart-Shaped Box (video) AR12958, AR15512
Heaven Is Under Our Feet: A Book For Walden Woods (book) AR13057, AR13474, AR14203
Heaven 'N Hull (album) AR13672
Heavy D.—Recordings AR13591
Heavy Metal Music AR14160, AR15690
Heckerling, Amy—Interviews AR13221
The Heights (television show) AR15963
Hejira (album) AR14910
Hell On Earth (album) AR13627
Helm, Levon—Profiles AR13402, AR14151
Helmet AR12918, AR14165

Helmet—Profiles AR12987, AR13468
Helms, Jesse—Politics AR15079
Hendrix, Al AR13965, AR14455, AR15167, AR15834, AR15835
Hendrix, Jimi AR13929, AR13965, AR14165, AR14455, AR14705, AR15165, AR15831, AR15834, AR15835
Hendrix, Jimi—Death AR15507
Hendrix, Jimi—Profiles AR13716, AR15167
Hendrix, Jimi—Recordings AR13387, AR14271, AR14901
Hendrix, Jimi, Jr. AR14455
Henke, James AR13318, AR14722
Henley, Don AR12966, AR13960, AR14026, AR14027, AR14427, AR15223, AR15920
Henley, Don—Interviews AR13419, AR15966
Henley, Don—Videos AR13831
Henry, Joe AR15401
Henry, Joe—Recordings AR14175
Herbst, Peter AR13318
Hercules: The Legendary Journeys (television show) AR13237, AR14506, AR15279
Herod, Galen AR14256
Heroin AR13278, AR13283, AR14230, AR14507, AR15329
Hersh, Kristin AR14209
Hersh, Kristin—Profiles AR15531
Herzigova, Eva AR16126
Hetfield, James AR14491, AR15972
Hetfield, James—Interviews AR13702
Heymann, Philip B.—Interviews AR13607
Hiatt, John AR13949, AR15952
Hicks, Bill AR13889, AR15299
High Incident AR13178
High Lonesome: The Story Of Bluegrass Music (film) AR13768
High School High (soundtrack) AR13081
High Society (television show) AR15892
Higher Education AR12917, AR13195, AR13214, AR13476, AR13854, AR13857, AR13907, AR14045, AR14053, AR14054, AR14219, AR14431, AR14554, AR14578, AR14636, AR14797, AR15060, AR15082, AR15119, AR15145, AR15148, AR15226, AR15227, AR15309, AR15323, AR15396, AR15398, AR15402, AR15477, AR15487, AR15548, AR15550, AR15608, AR15745, AR15807, AR16123, AR16132, AR16133
Higher Education—Augustana College AR15334
Higher Education—Babson College AR15486
Higher Education—Bryn Mawr College AR14554
Higher Education—Censorship AR13330, AR15478
Higher Education—College Radio Stations AR14668
Higher Education—Cornell University AR14744
Higher Education—Curricula AR14297, AR14298, AR14299, AR14300
Higher Education—Dartmouth College AR14430, AR14638, AR15486
Higher Education—Drew University AR14554
Higher Education—Drug Culture AR14505
Higher Education—Finances AR13269, AR13680, AR15322, AR15347, AR15348, AR16028
Higher Education—Georgetown University AR15331
Higher Education—Hampden-Sydney College AR14554
Higher Education—Harvard University AR16131
Higher Education—Internet AR14211
Higher Education—National Technological University AR15486
Higher Education—Recreation AR14832, AR15127, AR15239
Higher Education—Reed College AR14554
Higher Education—Ringling School Of Art And Design AR15486
Higher Education—Sex AR14504
Higher Education—Sports AR13574, AR15334
Higher Education—Studying AR14046
Higher Education—Tulane University AR14554
Higher Education—University Of Minnesota AR14554
Higher Education—University Of Pennsylvania AR13330, AR15478
Higher Education—University Of Texas AR12917
Higher Education—Yale University AR13213, AR14812, AR16126
Hijazi, Tanya AR13945
Hilburn, Robert AR14873
Hinton, Eddie—Obituary AR13704
Hip-Hop AR13585
Hippies AR14528
Hiroshima, Mon Amour (film) AR13597
Hirshey, Gerri AR13317, AR14223
History AR12950, AR16105
History—1960s AR15017
History—Nuclear Weapons AR15179
History—Photography AR14221
History—Rap Music AR13033
History—Rock Music AR13186, AR13726, AR14221, AR14345, AR14562, AR15016, AR15026, AR15749, AR16123
History—Soviet Union AR15182
HIStory (album) AR15844
Hitchcock, Robyn—Interviews AR13407
Hitchcock, Robyn—Profiles AR15129
Hitting Birth AR14256
Hobbs, Elsbeary—Obituary AR14163
Hobo Humpin' Slobo Babe (video) AR14365
Hoch, Danny AR13242, AR15286
Hodenfield, Chris AR13317, AR14240
Hoffman, Dezo AR14221
Hogan, Kelly AR13041
Hogan, Marty AR15017
Hogshire, Jim—Interviews AR15395
Hole AR15828
Hole—Profiles AR13201
Hole—Recordings AR14595, AR15825
Holland, Annie AR15836
Holland, Nicky AR14841, AR15316
Hollies—Recordings AR14267
Hollywood Records AR13980
Holmes, John—Profiles AR15332
Holt, Jefferson AR14161
Home Alive (album) AR15088
Home Taping AR14029
Homosexuality AR13044, AR13195, AR13614, AR13620, AR13890, AR15071, AR15300, AR16020, AR16053, AR16095, AR16126
Homosexuality—Rock Music AR15220
Honda, Yuka AR14243
Honey (album) AR14911
Honor (album) AR14164
Hooker, John Lee AR14172, AR14575, AR15154
Hooker, John Lee—Recordings AR13958
Hoon, Shannon AR13278
Hoon, Shannon—Obituary AR13456
Hooper, Tobe—Videos AR14291
Hootie And The Blowfish—Concerts AR14164
Hootie And The Blowfish—Profiles AR13265, AR15125
Hootie And The Blowfish—Recordings AR14050
Hopkins, Anthony AR14323
Hopkins, Doug—Obituary AR13021
Hopkins, Ellen AR13317, AR14246
Hopkins, Jerry AR13318
Hopkins, Nicky—Obituary AR14697
Hopper, Dennis AR15096
H.O.R.D.E. AR15559
Horn, Shirley—Recordings AR13597
Horn, Stacy AR13268, AR14865
Hornsby, Bruce AR12959, AR13541
Horses AR15600
Horses (album) AR13479, AR14912
Horton, Tom AR13317, AR14252
Hot Buttered Soul (album) AR14913
Hot For Teacher (video) AR13569
Hotcakes (album) AR15461
Hotel California (album) AR14914
House Music AR13367
House Of Blues (nightclub) AR15942, AR15943, AR15944
House Of Buggin' (television show) AR14508
House Of Pain—Tours—North America AR15448
House Of The Holy (album) AR14915
Houston, Texas—Adolescents AR14150, AR15712
Houston, Whitney AR15832
Houston, Whitney—Interviews AR13444
Hovercraft—Tours—North America AR13670
Hudgins, Joseph AR15224
Hudlin, Reginald—Videos AR14291
Hudson, Mark AR15826
Huffington, Michael—Politics AR13036
Hughes, Albert--Videos AR14296
Human Behaviour (video) AR14422
Human Body AR14131, AR14844
Human Touch (album) AR13941, AR14197
Humanitarian Efforts AR13088
Humble Pie—Recordings AR13313
Humor AR13304, AR13854, AR14054, AR14416, AR14811, AR15039, AR15040, AR15041, AR15042, AR15043, AR15044, AR15045, AR15046, AR15047, AR15048, AR15049, AR15050, AR15051, AR15052, AR15053, AR15054, AR15055, AR15057, AR15058, AR15059, AR15060, AR15061, AR15062, AR15063, AR15064, AR15065, AR15066, AR15067, AR15068, AR15070, AR15071, AR15072, AR15073, AR15074, AR15075, AR15076, AR15077, AR15309, AR15360, AR15992, AR16106, AR16107, AR16117, AR16129
Humphries, Hulond AR14305
Huncke, Herbert—Obituary AR13185
Hunt, Chris—Interviews AR13195
Hunter, Robert AR14244
Hunter, Robert—Interviews AR13837
Hunter, Stephen AR15743
Huntington Beach High Surf Team—Fashion AR13365, AR14840
Hurricane AR13469
Hurricane—Recordings AR13594
Husik, Lida AR13532
Husker Du—Recordings AR15510
Hussein, Saddam AR14100
Huston, Anjelica AR15096
Huxley, Trev AR14362
Hyatt, Walter—Obituary AR13094
Hynde, Chrissie AR14542, AR15701, AR15739
Hynde, Chrissie—Interviews AR15902
Hynde, Chrissie—Recordings AR13672, AR13982
Hype! (film) AR13356, AR15829

I

I Hate Rock & Roll (song) AR15838
I Photograph To Remember (CD-ROM) AR14339
I Want Your (video) AR13819
Ian, Scott AR12976
Ibuprofen AR16126
Ice Cream AR15551
Ice Cube AR12918, AR13592, AR14549, AR15628
Ice Cube—Concerts—Seattle, Washington AR14479
Ice Cube—Recordings AR13590
Ice Cube—Videos AR15615
Ice Skating AR13323, AR14856, AR15544
Ice-T AR14323, AR14473, AR14477, AR14481, AR15383
Ice-T—Fashion AR15387
Ice-T—Films AR13589
Ice-T—Interviews AR14473, AR14474, AR14499
Ice-T—Recordings AR13417, AR13590, AR13954, AR14341, AR14466, AR14473, AR14474, AR14475, AR14476, AR14499, AR14747, AR15163
Ice-T—Tours AR14466
Iceland AR14124
The Idiot (album) AR14952
Idol, Billy AR13943, AR15098
Idol, Billy—Videos AR14568
If At All Possible, Involve A Cow (book) AR15487
If I Were A Carpenter (album) AR13496
If Not For You (television show) AR15890
If You Don't Love Me (song) AR12922
Iha, James AR14549
I'm Alive (album) AR15951
Immigrants AR15330, AR15711
Imperial Teen AR13632
In Bloom (video) AR13561
In Cold Blood (television show) AR15900
In The Court Of The Crimson King (album) AR14916
In Utero (album) AR13571, AR14271
Incest AR13241, AR15285
Incognito AR15452
Incredibly Strange Music, Volume I (book) AR14386
Indians AR13248, AR15305
Indigo Girls AR12918
Indigo Girls—Tours AR15831
Indonesia AR14088
Indursky, Arthur AR14763
Industry AR14069, AR14094, AR15464, AR15548, AR15707
Industry—Sweatshops AR14088
Infinity Within (album) AR13856
Information Superhighway AR13131, AR13372, AR14006, AR14007, AR14008, AR14009, AR14016, AR14129, AR14211, AR14212, AR14328, AR14985, AR15579, AR15729, AR16069, AR16083
Infotainment Scam (album) AR13207
Inner Views: Filmmakers In Conversation (book) AR14288
Insomniac (album) AR13678
An Inspector Calls (drama) AR15651
Instruments—Guitars AR14443, AR14537
Instruments—Interactive AR13108
Instruments—Keyboards AR14537, AR15018, AR16082
International Pop Underground Convention AR15199
Internet AR13131, AR13237, AR13372, AR13373, AR13374, AR13375, AR14006, AR14008, AR14009, AR14016, AR14129, AR14212, AR14278, AR14328, AR14383, AR14458, AR14506, AR14744, AR14985, AR15230, AR15279, AR15579, AR15580, AR15729, AR16069, AR16083
Internet—Higher Education AR14211
Internet Underground Music Archive (IUMA) AR13373
Interscope Records AR13063, AR13980, AR15835
Interviews—Allen, Woody AR13445
Interviews—Altman, Robert AR13146
Interviews—Ament, Jeff AR15762
Interviews—Amos, Tori AR14721
Interviews—Anderson, Gillian AR16016
Interviews—Anderson, Ian AR13763
Interviews—Anderson, Laurie AR15717
Interviews—Andreessen, Marc AR14212
Interviews—Babbitt, Bruce AR16024
Interviews—Baca, Jim AR13606
Interviews—Baez, Joan AR14515
Interviews—Barron, Chris AR13666
Interviews—Beatty, Warren AR16120
Interviews—Bennett, Tony AR13565
Interviews—Bernhard, Sandra AR15626
Interviews—Bernstein, Leonard AR13340
Interviews—Billie Joe AR13652
Interviews—Bjelland, Kat AR14688
Interviews—Bono AR14465
Interviews—Boone, Pat AR13538
Interviews—Bowie, David AR14514
Interviews—Boy George AR13494
Interviews—Brooks, Garth AR13439
Interviews—Brown, Jerry AR14310, AR15361
Interviews—Browne, Jackson AR13421
Interviews—Buffett, Jimmy AR14356
Interviews—Burton, Tim AR13147
Interviews—Bushnell, George, Jr. AR13605
Interviews—Byrne, David AR13503
Interviews—Cale, John AR15763
Interviews—Carter, Chris AR16016
Interviews—Carville, James AR14090
Interviews—Cash, Johnny AR13528, AR15101
Interviews—Cave, Nick AR13534
Interviews—Chappell, Oliver AR13857
Interviews—Charles, Ray AR13674
Interviews—Cher AR13497
Interviews—Chomsky, Noam AR16108
Interviews—Clapton, Eric AR13305, AR14200, AR15021
Interviews—Claypool, Les AR14436
Interviews—Cleo AR15240
Interviews—Clinton, Bill AR14064, AR14103, AR14995, AR15361, AR15594, AR15777, AR15799
Interviews—Cobain, Kurt AR13734
Interviews—Corgan, Billy AR13747, AR14713
Interviews—Cornell, Chris AR13656
Interviews—Cortese, Scot AR15403
Interviews—Cronenberg, David AR13144
Interviews—Cusenza, John Sebastian AR15695
Interviews—Dalai Lama AR16098
Interviews—Dando, Evan AR13395, AR13405
Interviews—Davidson, Jaye AR13855
Interviews—Demme, Jonathan AR13422
Interviews—Diamond, Neil AR13533
Interviews—Diddley, Bo AR13133
Interviews—Diller, Barry AR14005
Interviews—Duchovny, David AR16016
Interviews—Dulli, Greg AR13521
Interviews—Dylan, Bob AR14513
Interviews—Eastwood, Clint AR13143, AR15903
Interviews—Edelman, Marian Wright AR12982
Interviews—Ephron, Nora AR13689
Interviews—Esquivel AR13509
Interviews—Etheridge, Melissa AR13258, AR13450
Interviews—Farrell, Perry AR12940, AR12962
Interviews—Ferry, Bryan AR13416
Interviews—Flea AR14753
Interviews—Fogerty, John AR13946
Interviews—Foley, Dave AR15935
Interviews—Frey, Glenn AR13419
Interviews—Frischmann, Justine AR13451
Interviews—Garcia, Jerry AR13426, AR14198, AR14201
Interviews—Garfunkel, Art AR13489
Interviews—Geffen, David AR13998
Interviews—Graffin, Greg AR13661
Interviews—Gudmundsdottir, Bjork AR15697
Interviews—Guru AR13293
Interviews—Hart, Mickey AR13837
Interviews—Harvey, Polly Jean AR15533
Interviews—Haynes, Gibby AR13520
Interviews—Heckerling, Amy AR13221
Interviews—Henley, Don AR13419, AR15966
Interviews—Hetfield, James AR13702
Interviews—Heymann, Philip B. AR13607
Interviews—Hitchcock, Robyn AR13407
Interviews—Hogshire, Jim AR15395
Interviews—Houston, Whitney AR13444
Interviews—Hunt, Chris AR13195
Interviews—Hunter, Robert AR13837
Interviews—Hynde, Chrissie AR15902
Interviews—Ice-T AR14473, AR14474, AR14499
Interviews—Jagger, Mick AR13341, AR15790
Interviews—Jobs, Steve AR14011
Interviews—Joel, Billy AR13492, AR15809
Interviews—Jones, George AR13406
Interviews—Jones, Tom AR13564
Interviews—Jordan, Neil AR15375
Interviews—Kapor, Mitch AR14007
Interviews—Kennedy, Robert F., Jr. AR15392
Interviews—Kiedis, Anthony AR14746
Interviews—Kirkwood, Curt AR15526
Interviews—Krauss, Alison AR14530
Interviews—Kravitz, Lenny AR15949
Interviews—KRS-One AR15622
Interviews—L. L. Cool J AR15764
Interviews—Lang, K. D. AR12935
Interviews—Lawrence, Martin AR15446
Interviews—LeBon, Simon AR14710
Interviews—Led Zeppelin AR13360
Interviews—Lee, Geddy AR13516
Interviews—Leigh, Jennifer Jason AR13526
Interviews—Lennon, John AR15792
Interviews—Leno, Jay AR15929
Interviews—Letterman, David AR16114
Interviews—Lewis, Juliette AR13280
Interviews—Link, Norman AR13857
Interviews—Little Richard AR15128
Interviews—Love, Courtney AR13717, AR14748
Interviews—Lydon, John AR13527
Interviews—Lyte, MC AR15447
Interviews—Madonna AR13635
Interviews—Mann, Aimee AR13487
Interviews—Marchand, Shoshana AR15395
Interviews—Mayfield, Curtis AR14482
Interviews—McCartney, Paul AR13793
Interviews—Mitchell, Joni AR13529, AR15932
Interviews—Moby AR15527
Interviews—Moon, Keith AR14248
Interviews—Moore, Demi AR15698
Interviews—Moore, Thurston AR13746

Interviews—Morrison, Jim AR14247
Interviews—Morrison, Van AR16004
Interviews—Murphy, Dan AR13554
Interviews—Nader, Ralph AR15232
Interviews—NdegeOcello, Me'shell AR14609
Interviews—Nelson, Willie AR13573
Interviews—Nick, Stevie AR13557
Interviews—Novoselic, Krist AR13455
Interviews—O'Connor, Sinead AR14494
Interviews—Ono, Yoko AR15027, AR15095
Interviews—Orbison, Roy AR15103
Interviews—Osbourne, Ozzy AR14776
Interviews—Pacino, Al AR13413
Interviews—Palmer, Robert AR15749
Interviews—Peel, John AR12995
Interviews—Phair, Liz AR13530
Interviews—Pirner, Dave AR13553, AR13554
Interviews—Potter, Sally AR15664
Interviews—Prine, John AR14551
Interviews—Raitt, Bonnie AR13493, AR14196
Interviews—Ramone, Joey AR14385
Interviews—Redford, Robert AR13437
Interviews—Reid, Vernon AR13148
Interviews—Rice, Anne AR13909
Interviews—Richards, Keith AR14516
Interviews—Ritcher, Scott AR15397
Interviews—Roberts, Julia AR15156
Interviews—Robertson, Robbie AR15024
Interviews—Robinson, Chris AR13499, AR14225
Interviews—Rodriguez, Robert AR15663
Interviews—Rollins, Henry AR13728
Interviews—Romano, Ray AR15907
Interviews—Ronstadt, Linda AR14689
Interviews—Rose, Axl AR14741, AR14783
Interviews—Rubin, Rick AR15950
Interviews—RuPaul AR15703
Interviews—Salgado, Sebastiao AR13342
Interviews—Scialfa, Patti AR15102
Interviews—Shilts, Randy AR16053
Interviews—Sir Mix-A-Lot AR13550
Interviews—Smith, Erin AR15395
Interviews—Smith, Patti AR13736
Interviews—Spaghetti, Eddie AR13505
Interviews—Spector, Phil AR15797
Interviews—Springsteen, Bruce AR14202, AR14517
Interviews—St. Lawrence, Jes AR15403
Interviews—Starr, Ringo AR15983
Interviews—Steele, Robert D. AR14006
Interviews—Stern, Howard AR14567
Interviews—Stewart, Jon AR15311
Interviews—Sting AR14619, AR14869
Interviews—Stipe, Michael AR13424, AR13722, AR13723
Interviews—Taylor, James AR14204
Interviews—Tennant, Neil AR15572
Interviews—Thompson, Hunter S. AR14998
Interviews—Thompson, Richard AR13540
Interviews—Thorn, Emily AR15403
Interviews—Toohey, Sherri AR13857
Interviews—Townshend, Peter AR13431, AR15796, AR15975, AR16011
Interviews—Travolta, John AR15378, AR15930
Interviews—Tyler, Steven AR13751
Interviews—U2 AR13447
Interviews—Ulrich, Lars AR13720
Interviews—Van Halen, Eddie AR15875
Interviews—Van Peebles, Mario AR15661
Interviews—Vigil, Selene AR13547
Interviews—Vinge, Vernor AR13460
Interviews—Washington, Denzel AR16086
Interviews—Watts, Charlie AR13453
Interviews—Ween AR13410
Interviews—Weiland AR14729
Interviews—Westerberg, Paul AR14672, AR15973
Interviews—White, Barry AR13490
Interviews—Wilbur, Jay AR14044
Interviews—Wilson, Brian AR13625
Interviews—Wilson, Mike AR14044
Interviews—Wood, Ron AR13545
Interviews—Wyndorf, Dave AR15237
Interviews—Young, Neil AR14199
Interviews—Zinn, Howard AR16105
Interviews—Zombie, Rob AR15151
Into The Purple Valley (album) AR14917
INXS—Recordings AR13808
Ionesco, Eugene AR13624
Iovine, Jimmy AR13980
Iraq—Politics AR14100
Isaak, Chris AR13949
Isaak, Chris—Films AR15901
Isaak, Chris—Videos AR13822
Isgro, Joe AR13945, AR14478
Island Records AR13985
Isle Of Wight Festival Of Music AR14171
Isley Brothers AR13770, AR14705
Israel—Politics AR13027
It Was A Good Day (video) AR15615
It's A Beautiful Day (album) AR14918
It's My Life (video) AR13551
It's Too Soon To Know (song) AR14562
Ivey, Michael—Profiles AR14464

J

J Mascis AR13298, AR14255
Jabberjaw (nightclub) AR14167
Jack, Wolfman—Obituary AR15832
Jackson, Alan AR15568
Jackson Family Honors (television show) AR15513
Jackson Five AR13761, AR14128, AR14173
Jackson, Janet AR12974, AR14481, AR15192, AR15451
Jackson, Janet—Profiles AR15195
Jackson, Janet—Recordings AR15928
Jackson, Janet—Videos AR13513, AR15629
Jackson, Joe—Recordings AR14925
Jackson, John A. AR15137
Jackson, Mahalia AR14128
Jackson, Michael AR13084, AR13928, AR13951, AR13970, AR14028, AR14029, AR14052, AR14480, AR15192
Jackson, Michael—Concerts—Bucharest, Romania AR15927
Jackson, Michael—Concerts—Malaysia AR14171
Jackson, Michael—Concerts—Prague, Czechoslovakia AR14669
Jackson, Michael—Concerts—Rome, Italy AR13953
Jackson, Michael—Profiles AR13977, AR14223
Jackson, Michael—Recordings AR13944, AR13977, AR14273, AR15832, AR15844
Jackson, Michael—Tours—World AR13976
Jackson, Michael—Videos AR13568, AR14367, AR15355, AR15617, AR15627, AR15632, AR15775
Jackson, Oliver, Jr.—Obituary AR15515
Jacksons AR13965
Jacobowitz, Eden AR13330, AR15478
Jacobs, Mark AR14652
Jager, Tom AR13610, AR14818
Jagged Little Pill (album) AR13083, AR15870
Jagger, Jade AR15096
Jagger, Mick AR14985, AR15096, AR15739
Jagger, Mick—Films AR14163
Jagger, Mick—Interviews AR13341, AR15790
Jagger, Mick—Recordings AR15959
Jajouka, Morocco AR15025
Jale AR14806
Jamaica AR15592
James AR13809
James, Elmore AR13770, AR14705
James, Elmore—Recordings AR13313
James, Etta AR13023, AR13541, AR13771, AR13784, AR15170, AR15984
James, Richey AR15426
James, Rick AR13945, AR14028, AR15938
James, Rick—Profiles AR15337
Jane's Addiction—Recordings AR14932, AR16052
Jane's Addiction—Videos AR13548
Janet (album) AR15928
Janet Reno (song) AR13581
Janie's Got A Gun (video) AR14699
Jansen, Dan AR13323, AR14856
Jansson, Tove AR14124
Japan AR13238, AR14307, AR15280
Jarmusch, Jim AR13854
Jasmine AR15096
Jawbox AR14384
Jawbreakers AR14164, AR14255
Jayhawks AR14050, AR14791
Jayhawks—Recordings AR12932
Jazz AR13585, AR13881, AR15289
Jazz Festivals—New Orleans Jazz & Heritage Festival AR13574
Jazz Musicians AR13778, AR13779
Jazzin' For Blue Jean (video) AR14406
J.D. AR15824
The Jeff Foxworthy Show (television show) AR15890, AR16014
Jefferson Airplane AR13524, AR13761, AR15031
Jefferson Airplane—Recordings AR14275
Jeffrey, Michael AR15167
Jennifer 8 (film) AR14053
Jensen, Luke—Fashion AR14615
Jeremy (video) AR14572
Jerry Maguire (film) AR13359
Jeru The Damaja—Recordings AR15451
Jesus And Mary Chain—Recordings AR14174, AR14502, AR15518, AR15838
Jesus Lizard—Profiles AR13470
Jesus Lizard—Recordings AR14435
Jethro Tull—Recordings AR14266
Jett, Joan AR13379, AR15455, AR15701, AR15827
Jewel AR13074
JFK (film) AR14338
The Jim Rose Circus Sideshow (video) AR14780
Jimi Hendrix Exhibition (art show) AR15165
Joanou, Phil—Videos AR14291
Job Hunting AR13484
Jobim, Antonio Carlos—Obituary AR13766
Jobs, Steve AR14012, AR14013
Jobs, Steve—Interviews AR14011
Joel, Billy AR13936, AR13963, AR14031, AR14705, AR14763, AR15096, AR15383, AR15519, AR15809
Joel, Billy—Interviews AR13492, AR15809
Joel, Billy—Recordings AR13796, AR14026, AR15405
John Woo's Once A Thief (film) AR15897
John, Elton AR13541, AR13776, AR13783, AR13803, AR13949, AR14164, AR15130, AR15192
John, Elton—Concerts—Great Britain AR15418
John, Elton—Profiles AR14807
John, Elton—Recordings AR15189
John, Elton—Tours AR13943
John, Elton—Tours—North America AR13934

Johnson, Christopher Lynn AR15413, AR15708
Johnson, Derwin AR13537, AR14641
Johnson, Gregory AR13970
Johnson, Marv—Obituary AR13967
Johnson, Michael AR14313, AR14816
Johnston, Daniel AR14630
Johnston, Freddy—Recordings AR15726
Johnston, Freedy AR13669
Joint Artists And Music Promotions Political Action Committee (organization) AR15084
The Joker (album) AR14953
Jones, Booker T. AR15383
Jones, Brian—Death AR15515
Jones, George AR13847, AR15382
Jones, George—Interviews AR13406
Jones, George—Recordings AR14281
Jones, Grace—Recordings AR14947
Jones, Grace—Videos AR15630
Jones, John Paul AR13202, AR13204, AR14170
Jones, Kendall AR12976, AR14020
Jones, Mick AR13541, AR14322
Jones, Quincy AR15154
Jones, Rickie Lee AR15742
Jones, Stacy AR15831
Jones, Tom—Interviews AR13564
Jonze, Spike AR14160
Joplin, Janis AR13295, AR13523, AR13608, AR13761, AR13782, AR14126, AR14324, AR14325
Joplin, Janis—Recordings AR14269, AR14890
Jordan, Loretta AR13920
Jordan, Neil AR13169
Jordan, Neil—Films AR15375
The Joshua Tree (album) AR14954, AR15453
Joshua Tree National Monument AR15554
Jourgensen, Al AR14287, AR15837
Journalism AR14053, AR14054, AR14334, AR14336, AR14338
Journey Through The Secret Life Of Plants (album) AR14919
Joy Division—Recordings AR15455, AR15827
Ju, Zhang—Obituary AR15831
Judd, Ashley AR13875, AR15276
Judd, Naomi AR14501
Judge, Mike AR14327
Judge, Mike—Profiles AR16103
Judgment Night (album) AR13587
The Juliet Letters (album) AR13291
Jung, George—Profiles AR15105
Jungle Music AR15116, AR15176
Justified And Ancient (video) AR14373
Justify My Love (video) AR15621
Juvenile Delinquency AR14150, AR14635, AR15335, AR15712

K

K Composite (publication) AR15397
K Foundation AR15420
K, Paul AR15205
K-Dee AR14549
Kaelin, Kato AR15545
Kahlo, Frida AR13475
Kahn, John—Obituary AR14163
Kallen, Peter AR13130, AR14617
Kalobius, Ernie AR13273, AR15713
Kantner, Paul AR12959, AR15153
Kaplan, Bruce—Obituary AR15161
Kapor, Mitch—Interviews AR14007
Kasso, Ricky—Profiles AR13145
Katz, Adam AR13949, AR14770, AR15509
Kaufman, Matthew King AR13969
Kaukonen, Jorma AR12959
Kayaking AR14801, AR15693
KCMU (radio station) AR14668
Keineg, Katell AR14646
Keiser, Christopher AR16133
Kelly, Charles AR13153
Kelly, R. AR14550, AR15519
Keltner, Jim AR13949, AR15952
Kendricks, Eddie AR13388
Kendricks, Eddie—Obituary AR14470
Kennedy AR14780
Kennedy, Robert F., Jr.—Interviews AR15392
Kenny, Kerri—Profiles AR14851, AR15035
Kerr, Jim AR14417
Kerrey, Bob AR12956
Kerrey, Bob—Profiles AR14015
Kerrigan, Nancy AR15544
Kershenbaum, David AR13980
Kerslake, Kevin AR15512
Kesey, Ken AR12959, AR13317, AR14418, AR15078
Kevorkian, Jack AR13475
Key, Tara AR14612
Keyboards AR14537, AR15018
Khan, Chaka AR15554
Kibitz Room, Cantor's (nightclub) AR15888
Kick Boxing AR14285
Kid Frost AR14481
Kidjo, Angelique AR12986
Kidnappings AR15542, AR15543
Kids In The Hall (television show) AR13475
Kiedis, Anthony AR15507
Kiedis, Anthony—Interviews AR14746
King, Albert—Obituary AR15556
King, B. B. AR14575, AR14705
King, Carole AR14575
King Coffey—Computer Systems AR14276
King Crimson AR13743, AR13744
King Crimson—Recordings AR14916
King Just AR13592
King, Larry AR13254
King, Larry—Profiles AR13253
King Missile AR12973
King, Richard AR12916
King, Rodney AR14059, AR14481, AR14490, AR15583
Kinison, Sam—Obituary AR15985
Kinks—Recordings AR15886
Kirkwood, Curt—Interviews AR15526
Kiss AR13951
Kiss—Tours—World AR14052
Kiss (video) AR14368
Kissinger, Henry AR13411
Kitt, A. J. AR13323, AR14856
Klegg, Johnny—Profiles AR13690
Klein, Howard AR15822
Klein, Joe AR13318
Klenfner, Michael AR15153
KLF—Videos AR14373
KLIT (radio station) AR15944
KMD—Recordings AR13589
KMFDM AR15840
Knab, Chris AR14668
Knapp, Cheryl Davis—Politics AR13036
Knievel, Evel AR13604
Knight, Gladys AR13524, AR15031
Knight, Marion AR15867
Knopfler, Mark AR15739
Knuckles, Frankie AR14256
Kohn, Howard AR13317, AR14428, AR14429, AR15752
Koo Koo (album) AR14920
Kool DJ Red Alert AR13591, AR13594
Kool Thing (video) AR13562
Koons Garcia, Deborah AR13710
Koprowski, Hilary AR13369, AR14991
Korine, Harmony AR13237, AR14506, AR15279
Kosh, John AR14873
Kovic, Ron—Profiles AR14140
Kozik, Frank AR13631, AR14344
Kraft, Cathy AR15402
Kramer, Wayne AR12969
Kramer, Wayne—Recordings AR14049
Krasnow, Bob AR13524, AR14642, AR14732, AR15031
Kratochvil, Laurie AR14873
Krauss, Alison—Interviews AR14530
Kravitz, Lenny AR12918, AR12976, AR14051, AR14771
Kravitz, Lenny—Fashion AR15387
Kravitz, Lenny—Interviews AR15949
Kravitz, Lenny—Profiles AR15524
Kravitz, Lenny—Videos AR13615
Kriegsmann, James AR14221
Krim, Rick AR14256
KRS-One—Interviews AR15622
KRS-One—Recordings AR14048
KTWV (radio station) AR14802
Ku Klux Klan AR15056
Kudrow, Lisa AR15919
Kula Shaker AR14253
Kunstler, William—Death AR15037
Kunstler, William—Obituary AR15465
Kuper, Peter AR13237, AR14506, AR15279
Kurious AR15452
Kurious Jorge—Recordings AR13589
Kushner, Tony AR13879, AR15287, AR15394
Kyuss AR15841

L

L. A. Firefighters (television show) AR15893
L. L. Cool J—Interviews AR15764
L. L. Cool J—Videos AR15620
L7 AR13391, AR12918, AR14165, AR14170, AR14752, AR14791
La Femme Nikita (film) AR14595
La Super-Rica (restaurant) AR13152
Lactose Intolerance AR16126
Lady Day (book) AR15137
Lady of Rage AR13592
Ladybug AR14448
Ladysmith Black Mambazo AR13956
LaFollette, Tavia AR15464, AR15707
Lake, Ricki AR15394
Lambert, Mary—Videos AR14296
Lance, Major AR13624
Landis, John—Videos AR14291
Landy, Eugene AR13625
Lane, Tony AR14873
Lang, K. D.—Interviews AR12935
Lang, K. D.—Profiles AR15700
Lang, K. D.—Videos AR13619
Langston, Adreana Patricia AR15017
Lanois, Daniel AR15099
Largent, Steve—Politics AR15079
The Larry Sanders Show (television show) AR14591
Larsen, Kristina AR15017
Last Poets—Recordings AR13595
Late Show (television show) AR15369, AR15373
Lauderdale, Jim AR15166
Laughlin, Lynne Hughes—Obituary AR13964
Lauper, Cyndi AR13169
Lauper, Cyndi—Videos AR13570
Lauwers, Gary AR13145
Lavine, Michael AR14170
Law, Don AR13058
Lawrence, Martin—Interviews AR15446
Lawrence, Martin—Profiles AR14587
Leach, Conrad AR13130, AR14617
Leary, Paul AR14052
Leary, Timothy AR15689, AR15780
Leary, Timothy—Obituary AR13916

Leave Me Alone (video) AR14367
LeBlanc, Matt AR15919
LeBon, Simon AR14542
LeBon, Simon—Interviews AR14710
Led Zeppelin AR13295, AR13360, AR13436, AR13523, AR13761, AR13782
Led Zeppelin—Interviews AR13360
Led Zeppelin—Recordings AR14265, AR14266, AR14269, AR14272, AR14915, AR14921, AR14937, AR15738, AR15947
Led Zeppelin (album) AR14921
Led Zeppelin IV (album) AR15738
Led Zeppelin: Live Dreams (book) AR14051
Lee, Ben AR12920, AR14052
Lee, Geddy—Interviews AR13516
Lee, Spike AR13970
Lee, Spike—Videos AR14291
Leeds, Harvey AR13805
Leeds, Peter AR13962
Legacy Records AR14272
Leibovitz, Annie AR14221
Leigh, Jennifer Jason AR13854
Leigh, Jennifer Jason—Interviews AR13526
Leighton, Laura AR15958
Lemay, Rodney AR15832
Lemonheads AR15936, AR15948
Lemonheads—Profiles AR13853
Lemonheads—Recordings AR14163, AR15982
Lennon, John AR13295, AR13541, AR13776, AR13783, AR14476, AR14560, AR15130, AR15386, AR15766, AR15831, AR15834, AR15837
Lennon, John—CD-ROMs AR15516
Lennon, John—Death AR13432
Lennon, John—Interviews AR15792
Lennon, John—Recordings AR14154, AR14363, AR14550, AR14923
Lennon, Sean—Recordings AR13737
Lennox, Annie—Profiles AR15439
Leno, Jay—Interviews AR15929
Leonowicz, Chuck AR16130
Lerner-Shaev, Hilary AR13805
Lesh, Phil—Quotations AR13524, AR15031
Leslie Spit Treeo AR14552
Let's Go (books) AR16131
Letterman, David AR15972
Letterman, David—Interviews AR16114
Letterman, David—Profiles AR15369, AR15373
Letters To Cleo AR15831
Leturgez, Bryan AR16130
Levellers AR12996, AR14256, AR15421
Leventhal, Rachel AR13268, AR14865
Levin, Jack AR15153
Lewis, Arthur AR13276
Lewis, Emmanuel AR13237, AR14506, AR15279
Lewis, Ephraim AR13162
Lewis, Ephraim—Obituary AR15943
Lewis, Jerry Lee AR13345, AR13967, AR16091
Lewis, Juliette—Interviews AR13280
Lewis, Richard AR15360, AR16117
Lewis, Shawn AR13345
Liberalism AR14119, AR14994, AR15005, AR15013, AR15598
Libertarianism AR16042
Licensed To Ill (album) AR14922
Liddy, G. Gordon AR13412
Liebler, Bob AR13854
LIFEbeat (organization) AR14206, AR14235
Light, Alan AR13306, AR13318
Like A Prayer (song) AR15355
Like A Prayer (video) AR15633
Lil' Kim—Recordings AR13083
Lilys AR15032
Lind, Michael AR13237, AR14506, AR15279
Link, Norman—Interviews AR13857
Linklater, Richard AR13901, AR15318
Linton, Renee AR14246
The Lion King (film) AR16000
Lippert, Patrick—Obituary AR15014
Lipuma, Tommy AR15154
Liquid Courage AR15215
Liquid Sky D-Sign (company) AR15554
Listening At The Luncheonette (film) AR15898
Litt, Scott AR14256
Little Feat—Recordings AR14942
Little Red Corvette (video) AR14369
Little Richard AR14705, AR15192
Little Richard—Interviews AR15128
Little Rock, Arkansas AR14509, AR15012
Little Village AR13949
Little Village—Profiles AR15952
Little Willie John AR13524, AR13761, AR15031
Live AR14160, AR14168, AR14256
Live—Fashion AR14178
Live—Profiles AR13206
Live At The Apollo (album) AR15141
Live At The BBC (album) AR15521
Live At The El Mocambo (video) AR13616
Live Hardcore Worldwide (album) AR13328
Live Peace In Toronto (album) AR14923
Living Colour AR12918, AR13726, AR15823
Living Colour—Recordings AR14472
Lo, Wayne AR14486
Loaded (publication) AR16127
Local H—Recordings AR13080
Locklear, Heather AR15958
Loder, Kurt AR13318, AR14542, AR14873
Loeb, Lisa AR14519
Lofgren, Nils AR14030
Logan, Jack AR13396, AR13517, AR13582, AR13705, AR14548, AR14683, AR14794
Lola AR14442
LollaPalooza '92 AR13934, AR13937, AR13976, AR13990, AR14766
LollaPalooza '93 AR13961, AR13964, AR13991, AR14767
LollaPalooza 94 AR15525, AR15538, AR15831
LollaPalooza '95 AR15842, AR15864
LollaPalooza '96 AR14438
London Calling (album) AR14924
London, England AR15238
London, England—Rock Scene AR13486
The Long And Winding Road (documentary) AR13957
Long Fin Killie AR14597
Long Gone John AR13366
Longanecker, David—Interviews—Interviews—Longanecker, David AR16028
Look Sharp (album) AR14925
Loose (album) AR15104
Lord, Mary Lou AR14182, AR14549
Lords Of The Underground AR13584
Los Angeles (album) AR14926
Los Angeles, California AR13363, AR14059, AR14242, AR14481, AR14490, AR15245, AR15583, AR15609
Los Angeles, California—Music Scene AR14351
Los Angeles, California—Rock Scene AR15152, AR15888
Los Illegals AR12966
Losing My Religion (video) AR14411, AR14620
Lost Soul Band From Edinburgh AR15418
Lotion AR12999
Loud Family AR15204
Loud Lucy—Fashion AR14863, AR15581, AR15774
The Louie Show (television show) AR13177
Louis-Dreyfus, Julia—Profiles AR16116
Louisiana—Censorship AR15832
Louvin, Charlie AR13847, AR15382
Love And Rockets AR15828
Love Battery AR13000
Love, Courtney AR12918, AR13854, AR13969, AR14287, AR14382, AR14477, AR14522, AR15455, AR15517, AR15701, AR15827, AR15831, AR15833
Love, Courtney—Films AR14049
Love, Courtney—Interviews AR13717, AR14748
Love, G. AR13795
Love Janis (book) AR14324, AR14325
Love, Mike AR15510, AR15961
Love, Monie AR13592
Love Shack (video) AR13560
Love Songs For The Hearing Impaired (album) AR15123
Love Stories (television show) AR14586
Love Will Never Do (video) AR15629
Loveless (album) AR13015
Lovett, Lyle AR12976, AR14705
Lovett, Lyle—Concerts—Santa Barbara, California AR15980
Lovett, Lyle—Fashion AR14449, AR15991
Lovett, Lyle—Recordings AR15995
Lovitz, Jon AR15360, AR16117
The Low Spark Of High Heeled Boys (album) AR14955
Lowe, Nick AR13949, AR15952
Lowery, David AR14549
Lozano, Paul AR13274
LSD AR15499, AR16051
Lucas, Gary AR14791
Lucas—Videos AR15772
Lucky Town (album) AR13941, AR14197
Lugar, Richard AR14804
Lundqvist, Alex AR14511, AR14827, AR15490
Luquire, Rusty AR13854
Luscious Jackson AR13471, AR14052, AR15204, AR15525, AR15718
Luscious Jackson—Recordings AR15466
Lush—Recordings AR14050
Lush—Tours AR13937
L.V. AR15406
Lydon, Johnny AR15739
Lydon, Johnny—Interviews AR13527
Lymon, Frankie AR13771, AR13784, AR13973, AR15170, AR15984
Lyndonville, New York AR14317
Lynn, Loretta AR13847, AR15382
Lynn, O. V., Jr.—Obituary AR14808
Lynyrd Skynyrd AR14173
Lyte, MC AR15451
Lyte, MC—Interviews AR15447
Lyte, MC—Recordings AR13590

M

Ma, Yo-Yo AR13170
Macarena (dance) AR13079
MacDonald, Norm AR13237, AR14506, AR15279
Macedonia—Politics AR14985, AR15002, AR15539
MacGowan, Shane AR12938
Mack, Connie—Politics AR15079
MacLachlan—Fashion AR13218, AR14532, AR14817
Mad (publication) AR14524
Mad Season AR15089
Madden, Danny AR14256
Madder Rose AR13380
Maddern, Steve AR15323
Madness—Recordings AR14934
Madonna AR13524, AR13937, AR13943, AR13953, AR13975, AR13982, AR13993,

AR15031, AR15517, AR15608, AR15701
Madonna—Interviews AR13635
Madonna—Recordings AR14963
Madonna—Videos AR13558, AR13566, AR14414, AR14556, AR15355, AR15621, AR15633
Madsen, Michael AR13860, AR15248
Maffeo, Lois AR14553
Maggie's Dream AR14256
Maglia, Lou AR13980
Magnapop AR13080, AR14177
Mahurin, Matt AR14307
Mahurin, Matt—Videos AR14293
Main Offender (album) AR14764
Main One AR15452
Malcolm X (film) AR16087
Malik AR13927
Mamas And The Papas AR14173
A Man Called E AR15944
Man On The Moon (video) AR14565
Manchild (video) AR14751
Mandela, Winnie—Politics AR15140
Mangold, James AR15744
Manic Street Preachers AR14162, AR15419
Mann, Aimee AR14255
Mann, Aimee—Interviews AR13487
Mann, Aimee—Recordings AR12964, AR15946
Manning, Barbara AR14791
Man's Ruin Records AR13631
Manson, Charles AR15505, AR15512
Manson, Charles—Recordings AR15834
Manson, Shirley AR14559
Marchand, Shoshana—Interviews AR15395
Marcos, Ferdinand—Politics AR15001
Marcus, Greil AR13317, AR14560, AR15137
Margulies, Julianna AR14052
Marijuana AR13188, AR15570, AR16051
Marijuana—Legislation AR15407
Marilyn Manson AR14165
Marilyn Manson—Videos AR13029
Marin County—California AR13153
Marine, Yvette AR13975, AR13993, AR14026
Mark, Marky AR14425, AR15988
Mark, Marky—Concerts—Portland, Maine AR15510
Markus, Kurt AR14575
Marley, Bob AR13097, AR13541, AR13776, AR14051, AR15592
Marley, Bob—Profiles AR15023
Marley, Bob—Recordings AR14263, AR14888
Mars, Chris AR14256
Mars, Chris—Recordings AR14236
Marsalis, Branford AR12959, AR13591, AR14549
Marsalis, Wynton AR15154
Marsh, Dave AR13318
Marshall, Jim AR14221
Marshall Tucker Band AR15131
Martha And The Vandellas AR13295, AR13523, AR13761, AR13782
Martin, George AR14163
Martin, Jim AR15507
Martinez, Jack—Fashion AR13365, AR14840
Martinez, Melissa—Fashion AR13365, AR14840
Marvel Comics AR13969
Marxman AR13811
Massive Attack AR15956
Massive Attack—Videos AR14124
Matador Records AR13091, AR14157, AR15207
Matt, Joe AR13230, AR15262
Matters Of The Heart (album) AR14495
Matthews, Dave AR14602, AR14603, AR14794
Matthews, Dave—Computer Systems AR14276
Matthews, Dave—Profiles AR13284
Matthews, Eric AR15705
Matthews, Eric—Recordings AR13454
Maultsby, Portia AR16123
Maverick (company) AR13937
Mavericks AR13231, AR15263, AR15313
Maxwell AR15765
Mayfield, Curtis AR15518
Mayfield, Curtis—Interviews AR14482
Mazza, Jim AR13980
Mazzocchi, Tony AR14079
Mazzy Star AR12918, AR13663, AR15937
MC Eiht—Recordings AR15773
MC5 AR12969, AR14604, AR15026
MC5—Profiles AR13596
MCA AR13965
MCA Records AR13063, AR13959, AR14272, AR15964
McAlmont And Butler AR15427
McBride, Christian AR13779
Mccarron, Doug AR14114
McCarthy, Jenny—Profiles AR13502
McCartney, Paul AR13541, AR13793, AR15739, AR15835
McCartney, Paul—Interviews AR13793
McCartney, Paul—Recordings AR13737, AR13957, AR14266
McCartney, Paul—Tours—World AR15917
McCaughan, Mac AR12975
McClain, Steve AR14162
McConaughey, Matthew—Profiles AR15374
McCulloch, Jamie AR14255
McDaniel, Melodie—Videos AR14293
McDonald, Danny Lee AR16023
McDonnell, Sean—Obituary AR15822
McEntire, John AR15705
McFerrin, Bobby AR13170
McGhee, Brownie—Obituary AR14216
McGregor, Ewan AR15370
McGuinn, Roger AR14575
McKagan, Duff—Recordings AR14678
McKenna, Kristine AR13318
McKenna, Terence AR13152, AR15554
McKinney, Cynthia—Politics AR13036
McLachlan, Sarah AR13818, AR14802
McLachlan, Sarah—Computer Systems AR14276
McLane, Daisann AR13318
McMillan, Terry AR13854
McNally, Dennis AR14647
McNaughton, John—Films AR16048
McVie, John AR15383
Me Phi Me AR13895
Meat Loaf AR15837
Meat Loaf—Profiles AR14693
Meat Loaf—Recordings AR16110
Meat Puppets AR12918, AR12994, AR13966, AR13974, AR14244, AR15244
Mecca Normal AR15204
Medellin Cocaine Cartel AR15105
Meisel, Steven AR14221, AR15096
Mellencamp, John AR14051, AR14158, AR14456, AR15519
Mellencamp, John—Concerts AR14457
Mellencamp, John—Fashion AR15387
Mellencamp, John—Films AR13823
Mellencamp, John—Profiles AR13414
Mellencamp, John—Recordings AR13672, AR13823, AR15186, AR15460
Mellencamp, John—Videos AR15508
Melrose Baking Company (Los Angeles, California) AR14323
Melrose Place (television show) AR13537, AR14641, AR15958
Melvoin, Jonathan—Obituary AR14191
Memnoch The Devil (book) AR15184
Men AR13907
Men Behaving Badly (television show) AR15924
Mera Laung Gawacha (song) AR15420
Merchant, Jimmy AR13973
Merchant, Natalie AR12918, AR13707, AR14051
Mercury, Freddie AR13953, AR14205, AR14224, AR14755
Mercury, Freddie—Obituary AR15164
Mercury Rev AR14387
Mercy Rule AR14794
Merritt, Stephin AR15495
Merritt, Stephin—Recordings AR13002
Messiaen, Olivier AR14124
Metal Box (album) AR14927
Metallica AR14550, AR15821
Metallica—Profiles AR13721, AR13739
Metallica—Recordings AR14049, AR14159
Metallica—Tours AR13982
Metallica—Tours—North America AR13934
Metallica—Videos AR14402
Meters AR14173
Methamphetamine AR14525
Metheny, Pat—Recordings AR14388
Method Man AR15635
Mexican-Americans AR14114
Mexico AR14072, AR14074, AR14094, AR14112, AR15004
Mexico—Rock Music AR14654
Miami, Florida AR14451
Miami Rhapsody (film) AR13338
Michael, George AR13833, AR13978, AR14030, AR15417, AR15422, AR15427, AR15517, AR15832
Michael, George—Fashion AR15387
Michael, George—Videos AR13512, AR14392
Michigan AR15336, AR15338, AR15806
Middle Man (album) AR14928
Midnight Oil—Recordings AR13706, AR14896
Military (China) AR15179
Military (United States) AR14123, AR14140, AR14993, AR15071, AR15179, AR15404, AR15457, 16033
Military (United States)—Budget AR14075, AR14091, AR14101
Military (United States)—Homosexuality AR16020
Militias AR16121
Milk—Recordings AR13593
Miller, Jimmy—Death AR15520
Miller, Jimmy—Obituary AR13780
Miller, Kenny AR13268, AR14865
Miller, Marcus AR15154
Miller, Shannon AR13599, AR14799
Miller, Shannon—Fashion AR13599, AR14799
Miller, Steve AR14640
Miller, Steve—Profiles AR14238
Miller, Steve—Recordings AR14953
Million Man March AR15494
Millionaire Of Combustible Edison AR12975
Millions AR15408
Mills, Mike AR15018
Mind Playing Tricks On Me (video) AR14251
Ministry AR15837
Minneapolis, Minnesota AR15312
Minneapolis, Minnesota—Rock Scene AR15735
Minor, Charlie—Obituary AR15826
Minor, Charlie—Profiles AR16046
Mitchell, Joni AR13761, AR14128, AR14173, AR15192
Mitchell, Joni—Interviews AR13529, AR15932
Mitchell, Joni—Recordings AR14910

Mitchell, Mitch AR14705
Mitchum, Robert AR14242
Mitnick, Kevin AR14014
Mixmaster Morris—Recordings AR15117
Miyamoto, Sigeru—Profiles AR15391
Mo' Wax Records AR14050, AR14563, AR15117
Mobb Deep—Recordings AR13627
Moby AR12918, AR12975, AR14159
Moby—CD-ROMs AR14390
Moby—Interviews AR15527
Moby—Profiles AR12939
Moby Grape—Recordings AR14267, AR14286
Modine, Matthew—Fashion AR14862, AR15720
Modine, Matthew—Films AR14862, AR15720
Moe. AR13838
Moe, Tommy AR13323, AR14856
Moline, Jack, Rabbi AR13537, AR14641
Mondino, Jean Baptiste—Videos AR14293
Money Don't Matter 2 Night (video) AR13970
Money For Nothing (video) AR13825
Money Mark—Recordings AR14563
Monroe, Bill AR13768, AR14128, AR15689
Monroe, Bill—Obituary AR14808
Monroe, Bill—Profiles AR13415
Monster (album) AR13375
Monster Magnet AR13392, AR15237
Monsters Of Rock AR15418
Montenegro—Politics AR14985, AR15002, AR15539
Monterey International Pop Festival AR14275
Montes, Nene AR13959
Moon, Keith—Interviews AR14248
Moon, Slim AR14549
Moonglows AR14173
Moore, Demi—Interviews AR15698
Moore, Julianne—Fashion AR14862, AR15720
Moore, Sam AR13079, AR15518
Moore, Thurston—Interviews AR13746
Morales, Pablo AR13610, AR14818
Moravec, Hans AR13461
Morello, Mary AR14157
Morey, Douglas G. AR15017
Morgado, Robert AR14642
Morgan Creek Records AR13980
Moriarity, Pat AR13135
Morissette, Alanis—Concerts—New Orleans, Louisiana AR14172
Morissette, Alanis—Profiles AR15870
Morissette, Alanis—Recordings AR13083, AR15870
Morissette, Alanis—Tours—North America AR14048
Morissette, Alanis—Videos AR14349, AR15775
Morning Glory (album) AR13826
Morphine AR13281, AR14769, AR14793, AR15940
Morris, Doug AR14642, AR14732, AR15964
Morris, Keith AR15578
Morris, Mark—Profiles AR14222
Morrison, Jim AR14052, AR15507
Morrison, Jim—Interviews AR14247
Morrison, Sterling—Death AR15037
Morrison, Sterling—Obituary AR13750
Morrison, Toni AR13854
Morrison, Van AR13771, AR13784, AR14163, AR14172, AR15093, AR15170, AR15984, AR16004
Morrison, Van—Recordings AR13958
Morrissey—Recordings AR14267
Morton, Peter AR13898
Moshing AR13068, AR13082, AR15233, AR15234
Motherhead Bug AR14255
Mothers Of Invention AR15822
Mothers Of Invention—Recordings AR15393
Motley Crue AR13994
Motown Records AR13949, AR14025, AR14268
Mott The Hoople—Recordings AR14258
Mould, Bob AR12977, AR14051
Mouse, Stanley AR13966
Move—Recordings AR14267
Moynihan, Patrick AR12956
Mozambique AR13316, AR15342
Mozart AR13389, AR15939
Mr. Show With Bob And David (television show) AR15892, AR15987
Mr. T—Fashion AR15387
MSNBC Network AR15896
MTV AR13060, AR13075, AR13079, AR13081, AR13164, AR13264, AR13791, AR14146, AR14327, AR14459, AR14589, AR14653, AR14671, AR14723, AR14745, AR14854, AR14864, AR15066, AR15505, AR15508, AR15519, AR16009, AR16103, AR16106, AR16107
MTV's Supermodel Summit (television show) AR14703
Muck, Penny AR13957
Mud Slide Slim And The Blue Horizon (album) AR15454
Mudhoney AR12918, AR12993, AR13398
Muffs—Profiles AR12967, AR14837
Mulcahy, Russell—Videos AR14296
Muldaur, Maria AR12959
Mulligan, Gerry—Obituary AR13775
Muratore, John AR14004
Murder Ballads (album) AR13700
Murder One (television show) AR15899
Murders AR12943, AR13145, AR13273, AR13337, AR13432, AR13908, AR13949, AR14102, AR14246, AR14342, AR14635, AR14770, AR15085, AR15224, AR15332, AR15541, AR15545, AR15713, AR15835, AR16046
Murmur (album) AR13163
Murphy, Dan—Interviews AR13554
Murphy, Elliott—Recordings AR14262
Murray, Dee—Obituary AR13448
Music AR15018, AR15705
Music—Television AR15878
Music Festivals—South By Southwest Music And Media Conference AR13712
Music Festivals—Southwest Music And Media Conference AR13693
Music Industry AR12933, AR13062, AR13070, AR13089, AR13157, AR13283, AR13488, AR13712, AR13951, AR14032, AR14383, AR14735, AR15018, AR15074
Music Industry—Business Aspects AR13003, AR13058, AR13059, AR13061, AR13065, AR13069, AR13072, AR13073, AR13078, AR13091, AR13092, AR13093, AR13452, AR13805, AR13833, AR13899, AR13930, AR13931, AR13945, AR13950, AR14022, AR14023, AR14035, AR14189, AR14193, AR14642, AR15168, AR15508, AR15517, AR15530, AR15757, AR15833, AR15860, AR16005, AR16095, AR16123
Music Industry—Charities AR14186
Music Industry—Concerts And Tours AR13058, AR13069, AR13078, AR13082, AR13088, AR13090, AR13092, AR13093, AR13382, AR13899, AR13981, AR13987, AR13990, AR13991, AR14023, AR14035, AR14047, AR14048, AR14183, AR14479, AR14770, AR14871, AR14872, AR15502, AR15528, AR15690, AR15833, AR15847, AR15860, AR16001
Music Industry—Fraud AR14302
Music Industry—Geffen, David AR13998
Music Industry—Geiger, Marc AR16126
Music Industry—Health Care AR14019
Music Industry—Higher Education AR14832, AR15127
Music Industry—Minor, Charlie AR16046
Music Industry—Promoters AR13077, AR13953, AR13982
Music Industry—Tours And Concerts AR13934
Music Videos AR13029, AR13617, AR13619, AR13629, AR14146, AR14291, AR14293, AR14296, AR14349, AR14423, AR15355, AR15518, AR15699, AR15730, AR15808
Musicals (stage)—Chippy: Diaries Of A West Texas Hooker AR13845
Musicals (stage)—New York Rock AR13430, AR14370
Musicals (stage)—Passion AR15651
Musicians AR13488, AR14019, AR14792, AR15495, AR15701, AR15705
Musicians—Education AR15190
Muze (computer system) AR14362
My Bloody Valentine AR13015
My Life With Evan Dando Pop Star (publication) AR14652
My Life With The Thrill Kill Kult AR13371
My Own Private Idaho (film) AR14135
My So-Called Life (television show) AR13247, AR15304
My World (album) AR15885
Myers, Mike—Films AR16101
Myst (CD-ROM) AR14339
Mysterious Ways (video) AR13821
Mystery Science Theater 3000 (television show) AR14703

N

Nader, Ralph—Interviews AR15232
Naftaly, Keith AR14256
Nall, Anita AR14818
Nannies AR13488
Nas AR13243, AR15290
NASA AR14004, AR16060
Nascimento, Milton AR14124
Nash, Eddie AR15332
Nash, Graham AR14027
Nash, Jim—Obituary AR15118
Nathan, Syd AR14128
National Endowment For The Arts AR15079
National Institute Of Bail Enforcement (organization) AR13045
National Multiple Sclerosis Society AR14208
National Organization For Reform Of Marijuana Laws AR13343, AR15570
National Rifle Association AR12952, AR13480, AR13481, AR13611, AR14102, AR15138, AR15540, AR15785, AR16121, AR16122
National Service Initiative AR14061, AR14111, AR16039
National Technological University AR15486
National Wildlife Federation AR13923
Native Americans AR13397
Naughty By Nature AR12918, AR14485
Naughty By Nature—Fashion AR13222, AR14824
Naughty By Nature—Profiles AR13222, AR14824
Naughty By Nature—Recordings AR13428
Navarro, Dave AR13382, AR13539
Navarro, Nick AR14476
NBC Nightly News (television show) AR14332
NdegeOcello, Me'shell AR12918, AR15623,

AR15701
NdegeOcello, Me'shell—Interviews AR14609
NdegeOcello, Me'shell—Profiles AR15110
N'Dour, Youssou—Videos AR14540
Ned's Atomic Dustbin AR14867
Neely, Kim AR13318
Nefertiti AR15452
Negativland AR13974, AR13979
Neil Young: The Rolling Stone Files (book) AR13182
Neil, Vince AR13934, AR15936
Nelson, Harriet AR13624
Nelson, Shara AR14282
Nelson, Willie AR13523, AR13847, AR15382
Nelson, Willie—Interviews AR13573
Nelson, Willie—Recordings AR12925, AR13211
Neneh, Cherry—Profiles AR14759
Nepkie, Janet AR16123
Neruda, Pablo AR14285
Netherlands AR14736
Never A Dull Moment (album) AR14929
Never Mind The Bollocks Here's The Sex Pistols (album) AR14930
Nevermind (album) AR14773, AR15741
Neville, Aaron AR14705
Nevolo, Greg AR14616, AR14819
New Age AR16092, AR16126
New England Shelter For Homeless Veterans AR15457
New Hampshire—Elections AR14492
New Hampshire—Politics AR14104
New Jersey AR15237
New Jersey—Rock Scene AR15350
New Order—Recordings AR14939
New Order—Videos AR14393
New Orleans Jazz & Heritage Festival AR13574
New Orleans, Louisiana AR12923, AR13475
New Orleans, Louisiana—Rock Scene AR12924
The New Rolling Stone Encyclopedia Of Rock & Roll (book) AR15740
New York News (television show) AR15891
New York Rock (stage musical) AR13430, AR14370
New York Times (publication) AR14078, AR14333, AR15607
New York Undercover (television show) AR13175
New York, New York AR14149, AR15030, AR15036, AR15719
New York, New York—Rock Scene AR15033
Newark, New Jersey AR15335
Newman, Randy—Recordings AR14026
Newport, Rhode Island AR14798
News Media AR13140, AR14078, AR14326, AR14328, AR14329, AR14330, AR14331, AR14332, AR14334, AR14335, AR14336, AR14338, AR14340, AR14341, AR14342
News Media—Elections AR14333
Newsted, Jason AR13169
The Newz (television show) AR14508
Next Ticketing (company) AR13058
Nice And Smooth—Recordings AR13590
Nicholson, Jack AR15096
Nickles, Don—Politics AR15079
Nicks, Stevie AR15153, AR15223
Nicks, Stevie—Films AR14052
Nicks, Stevie—Interviews AR13557
Nielson, Rick AR14803
Nies, Eric—Fashion AR13264, AR14854
Nies, Eric—Profiles AR13264, AR14854
Night Games (television show) AR14586
Night Of The Living Baseheads (video) AR15618
Nightclubs AR13854, AR16126
Nightline (television show) AR15997
Nilsson, Harry AR13624, AR13962
Nilsson, Harry—Death AR15507
Nilsson, Harry—Obituary AR14379
Nine Inch Nails AR12918, AR14234
Nine Inch Nails—Profiles AR13925
Nine Inch Nails—Tours—North America AR15834
1980s AR15017
1984 (album) AR14931
1990s AR15017
1992—Music AR13446
1995—Cinema AR15644, AR15646, AR15671, AR15676, AR15685, AR16100
1995—Highlights AR14287, AR15037, AR15218
1995—Music AR12930, AR13350, AR13354, AR13385, AR13404, AR13832, AR13835, AR13843, AR14227, AR14249, AR14352, AR14434, AR14444, AR14614, AR15144, AR15201, AR15218, AR15726a
1995—Television AR15887, AR15986, AR16018
1995—Music AR13039, AR13271
1994—Cinema AR15649
1994—Highlights AR13544, AR14707
1994—Music AR14734
1991 AR15070
1991—Cinema AR15683
1991—Highlights AR13902, AR14706, AR15097
1991—Music AR14790, AR14870, AR15139
1991—Publications AR13098, AR15481
1991—Television AR14593
1991—Videos AR15725
1996 AR13386, AR13578, AR15782
1996—Cinema AR15443, AR15638, AR15640, AR15650, AR15653, AR15657, AR15672, AR15686
1996—Highlights AR13543, AR15034, AR15319, AR15852
1996—Humor AR14811
1996—Music AR13090, AR13382, AR13543, AR15034, AR15319, AR15852
1996—Obituaries AR15689
1996—Television AR15879, AR15905, AR15960, AR15969
1993—Highlights AR14340
1993—Music AR13542, AR14704
1993—Personalities AR13344
1992 AR13051
1992—Books AR13099
1992—Cinema AR15641, AR15660
1992—Highlights AR15069, AR15098, AR16099
1992—Music AR13054, AR14489, AR14629, AR14740, AR14792, AR14871, AR16099
1992—Television AR14594
1970s AR15017
1960s AR13673, AR15017, AR15331, AR15498
1960s—Sociological Aspects AR12954
Nintendo (company) AR15391
Nirvana AR12918, AR12976, AR15516, AR15532, AR15972
Nirvana—Profiles AR13006, AR13914, AR14700
Nirvana—Recordings AR13007, AR13571, AR13711, AR13951, AR14033, AR14165, AR14260, AR14271, AR14435, AR14773, AR15726, AR15741
Nirvana—Tours—North America AR12997, AR13976
Nirvana—Videos AR12958, AR13561, AR14725, AR15512
Nissan AR13943
Nitric Oxide AR13878, AR15283
Nixon, Richard AR13237, AR13334, AR14099, AR14506, AR14618, AR15279, AR15597
Nixon, Richard—Obituary AR15146
Nixon, Richard—President AR14618
Nixon, Richard—Watergate AR13411, AR13412, AR15597
No Alternative (album) AR14743
No Quarter (album) AR13436
No World Order (album) AR13932
Noise Addict AR14052
Nolan, Jerry—Obituary AR14311
Norte, Marisela AR13848
North American Concert Promoters Association AR13982
North American Free Trade Agreement AR14072, AR14074, AR14080
Northern Ireland—Politics AR13816
Not Bad For A Girl (film) AR13356
Nothing Compares 2 U (video) AR13804
Nothing's Shocking (album) AR14932
Notorious B.I.G. AR13626, AR15830
Nova, Heather AR12963
Novoselic, Krist AR15826
Novoselic, Krist—Interviews AR13455
Nowell, Brad—Death AR14155
Nuclear Power AR14428, AR14529, AR15183
Nuclear Testing AR16040
Nuclear Weapons AR14075, AR15179, AR15182
Nudity AR15239
Nunn, Sam AR16020
N.W.A. AR13955
Nyro, Laura AR15154

O

Oasis AR14158, AR14166, AR14169, AR14180, AR14794, AR15829
Oasis—Profiles AR13208, AR14708
Oasis—Recordings AR13826, AR14172
Oasis—Tours—North America AR15456
Obituaries (1991) AR13621
Obituaries (1992) AR13622
Obituaries (1993) AR13623
Obituaries (1994) AR13624
Obituaries (1996) AR15689
Obituaries—Acland, Chris AR14810
Obituaries—Acuff, Roy AR14493
Obituaries—Alexander, Arthur AR13287
Obituaries—Allen, Janna AR14028
Obituaries—Allin, GG AR15925
Obituaries—Beverley, Anne AR14809
Obituaries—Briggs, David AR15132
Obituaries—Brilleaux, Lee AR14381
Obituaries—Brother Adam AR14808
Obituaries—Bukowski, Charles AR13179
Obituaries—Cage, John AR15185
Obituaries—Caldwell, Toy AR15131
Obituaries—Cammell, Donald AR13064
Obituaries—Campbell, John AR15560
Obituaries—Cascella, John AR13956
Obituaries—Chandler, Chas AR14153
Obituaries—Cherry, Don AR14217
Obituaries—Clark, Ozzie AR13185
Obituaries—Clarke, Mike AR14389
Obituaries—Cleveland, Alfred W. AR13185
Obituaries—Cobain, Kurt AR15504
Obituaries—Cole, David AR15823
Obituaries—Coleman, Ray AR14809
Obituaries—Collins, Albert AR13765
Obituaries—Collins, Rob AR14187
Obituaries—Cordell, Denny AR14021
Obituaries—Creach, Papa John AR13735
Obituaries—Daffan, Ted AR14810
Obituaries—Daniel, Nathan AR15159
Obituaries—Davis, Larry AR15514

Obituaries—Davis, Miles AR15022
Obituaries—Dixon, Willie AR13056
Obituaries—Douglas, Steve AR13967
Obituaries—Eazy-E AR15816, AR15914
Obituaries—Edwards, Bernard AR14215
Obituaries—Ellison, Jim AR14163
Obituaries—Fitzgerald, Ella AR13911
Obituaries—Fletcher, Matthew AR14163
Obituaries—Franklin, Melvin AR15845
Obituaries—Gaines, William AR14524
Obituaries—Gale, Eric AR15515
Obituaries—Gallagher, Rory AR15433
Obituaries—Garcia, Jerry AR13912
Obituaries—Gatton, Danny AR13698
Obituaries—Gibson, Bob AR14810
Obituaries—Gillespie, Dizzy AR13773
Obituaries—Goettel, Dwayne AR15815
Obituaries—Goldman, Albert AR14361
Obituaries—Graham, Bill AR13992
Obituaries—Grant, Peter AR13458
Obituaries—Harrison, Wilbert AR13786
Obituaries—Hartman, Dan AR15513
Obituaries—Hawkins, Ted AR15381
Obituaries—Hazel, Eddie AR14469
Obituaries—Hinton, Eddie AR13704
Obituaries—Hobbs, Elsbeary AR14163
Obituaries—Hood, Shannon AR13456
Obituaries—Hopkins, Doug AR13021
Obituaries—Hopkins, Nicky AR14697
Obituaries—Huncke, Herbert AR13185
Obituaries—Hyatt, Walter AR13094
Obituaries—Jackson, Oliver, Jr. AR15515
Obituaries—Jobim, Antonio Carlos AR13766
Obituaries—Johnson, Marv AR13967
Obituaries—Ju, Zhang AR15831
Obituaries—Kahn, John AR14163
Obituaries—Kaplan, Bruce AR15161
Obituaries—Kendricks, Eddie AR14470
Obituaries—King, Albert AR15556
Obituaries—Kinison, Sam AR15985
Obituaries—Kunstler, William AR15465
Obituaries—Laughlin, Lynne Hughes AR13964
Obituaries—Leary, Timothy AR13916
Obituaries—Lewis, Ephraim AR15943
Obituaries—Lippert, Patrick AR15014
Obituaries—Lynn, O. V., Jr. AR14808
Obituaries—McDonnell, Sean AR15822
Obituaries—McGhee, Brownie AR14216
Obituaries—Melvoin, Jonathan AR14191
Obituaries—Mercury, Freddie AR15164
Obituaries—Miller, Jimmy AR13780
Obituaries—Minor, Charlie AR15826
Obituaries—Monroe, Bill AR14808
Obituaries—Morrison, Sterling AR13750
Obituaries—Mulligan, Gerry AR13775
Obituaries—Murray, Dee AR13448
Obituaries—Nash, Jim AR15118
Obituaries—Nilsson, Harry AR14379
Obituaries—Nixon, Richard AR15146
Obituaries—Nolan, Jerry AR14311
Obituaries—O'Donoghue, Michael AR12985
Obituaries—Panozzo, John AR14176
Obituaries—Paskow, Bruce Jay AR15508
Obituaries—Pass, Joe AR15515
Obituaries—Pfaff, Kristen AR15523
Obituaries—Pierce, Jeffrey Lee AR14355
Obituaries—Porcaro, Jeff AR14308
Obituaries—Ra, Sun AR13785
Obituaries—Rich, Charlie AR13289
Obituaries—Rockin' Dopsie AR15561
Obituaries—Rodney, Red AR15515
Obituaries—Ronson, Mick AR14694
Obituaries—Rothchild, Paul AR14034
Obituaries—Savio, Mario AR15689
Obituaries—Schaffner, Nicholas AR14800
Obituaries—Scott, Raymond AR15509
Obituaries—Seymour, Phil AR15938
Obituaries—Shakur, Tupac AR15108
Obituaries—Sharrock, Sonny AR14408
Obituaries—Silk, Garnet AR15821
Obituaries—Smith, Fred AR15521
Obituaries—Snyder, Patrick AR14025
Obituaries—Stanshall, Vivian AR15209
Obituaries—Steele, Alison AR14538
Obituaries—Stinson, Bob AR14675
Obituaries—Subroc AR13589
Obituaries—Sunnyland Slim AR15826
Obituaries—Taylor, Mel AR13185
Obituaries—Tee, Richard AR14024
Obituaries—Thiele, Bob AR13769
Obituaries—Tigrett, Maureen Cox Starkey AR15957
Obituaries—Twitty, Conway AR14628
Obituaries—Tyner, Rob AR14604
Obituaries—Walker, Junior AR14218
Obituaries—Warren, Earle AR15515
Obituaries—Watson, Johnny AR15194
Obituaries—Wells, Mary AR14483
Obituaries—White, Robert AR15751
Obituaries—Williams, Marion AR15187
Obituaries—Williams-Chappel, Fiona AR14808
Obituaries—Wolfman Jack AR15832
Obituaries—Zapata, Mia AR15085
Obituaries—Zappa, Frank AR13708
O'Brian, Patrick AR16126
O'Brien, Conan AR15877
O'Brien, Conan—Profiles AR14730
O'Brien, Dan AR14314, AR14843
O'Brien, Glen AR13953
Obscenity AR13982
O'Connell, Maura—Profiles AR16055
O'Connor, Sinead AR15075, AR15742, AR15832
O'Connor, Sinead—Interviews AR14494
O'Connor, Sinead—Videos AR13804, AR13819
O'Donnell, Rosie AR16010
O'Donoghue, Michael—Obituary AR12985
Oedipus AR14255
Offspring AR12918, AR12936, AR13338, AR13364, AR14156, AR14160, AR14171, AR14794, AR15943
Offspring—Profiles AR13655
Ogdens' Nut Gone Flakes (album) AR14933
Oh Father (video) AR14556
Oh, Pretty Woman (song) AR15459
Ohio Players—Recordings AR14911
Ojai, California AR14323
Oldham, Todd AR16126
Oldham, Will AR14439
O'Leary, Hazel—Profiles AR16040
Olympia, Washington—Music Scene AR14611
Olympics AR14801, AR15693
Olympics (1992) AR13323, AR13610, AR14313, AR14314, AR14816, AR14818, AR14825, AR14843, AR14856, AR15692, AR16130
Olympics (1994) AR15544
Olympics (1996) AR13277
O'Meally, Robert AR15137
Once In A Lifetime (video) AR13510
One (video) AR14292, AR14402
One Dove AR15421
One Records AR13960
One Step Beyond (album) AR14934
O'Neal, Shaquille AR13332, AR13864, AR15256
O'Neal, Shaquille—Profiles AR13999
Ono, Yoko AR13430, AR14370, AR14454, AR15223, AR15831
Ono, Yoko—Interviews AR15027, AR15095
Ono, Yoko—Recordings AR13737, AR14260
Onyx AR14320, AR14793
Ooh La La (album) AR14935
Opal Fox Quartet AR14256
O.P.P. (song) AR13428
Orange County, California AR13365, AR14840
Orange Crush (video) AR14394
Orb AR15554
Orb—Recordings AR15115
Orbison, Roy AR15103
Oregon AR14544
Organic (rave) AR14161
Orioles AR13295, AR13523, AR13782
Orioles—Discography AR14992
Orioles—Profiles AR14562
O'Riordan, Dolores AR13667
Orlando (film) AR15664
O'Rourke, P. J. AR13317, AR15001
Osborne, Joan AR14791
Osborne, Joan—Profiles AR15112
Osborne, Joan—Tours AR14049
Osbourne, Ozzy AR14050, AR15015, AR15383
Osbourne, Ozzy—Fashion AR15387
Osbourne, Ozzy—Interviews AR14776
Osbourne, Ozzy—Videos AR13613
Oseary, Guy—Fashion AR14839, AR15967, AR16057
Osler's Web (book) AR14317
Ostin, Mo AR14642, AR14732, AR15517, AR15835
Otis! (album) AR14268
Otis, Johnny AR13541, AR13783, AR15130
Our House (song) AR14027
Out (publication) AR16126
Out Of The Cradle (album) AR15977
Out Of Time (album) AR14637
OutKast AR14309, AR14549
Over The Rhine AR15945
Overnight Sensation (book) AR15934
Ovis AR15945
Owen, Judith AR12964, AR15946
Owens, Buck AR13847, AR15382

P

Pacino, Al—Films AR13413
Page, Jimmy AR13519, AR14157, AR14170, AR15383, AR15424, AR15516, AR15833, AR15947
Page, Jimmy—Profiles AR13436
Paglia, Camille—Quotes AR14421
Paisley Park Records AR13984
Pakistan AR14738
Pakistanis AR13248, AR15305
Palac, Lisa AR15019
Palace Brothers AR13597
Paleface AR14002
Palmer, Robert AR13317, AR13318, AR15025
Palmer, Robert—Interviews AR15749
Palmer, Robert—Videos AR15355
Paltrow, Gwyneth AR13224, AR15251
Pamplin, Rick—Politics AR13036
Pan American Health Organization AR15181
Pandora's Box (album) AR14739
Panic AR13900
Panozzo, John—Obituary AR14176
Pantera AR13400
Papa's Culture AR15204
Paradinas, Michael—Recordings AR15115
Paraskevin-Young, Connie AR14314, AR14843
Parents For Rock And Rap (organization) AR14157
Parents Music Resource Center AR13441, AR14042, AR15492
Parker, Graham—Recordings AR14956
Parker, Sarah Jessica AR13854
The Parkerilla (album) AR14956

Parliament AR13761, AR14128, AR14173
Partners (television show) AR13677
Parton, Dolly—Profiles AR13651
The Partridge Family (television show) AR14703
Paskow, Bruce Jay—Obituary AR15508
Pass, Joe—Obituary AR15515
Passman, Don AR13949
Paterno, Peter AR13980
Patra AR12918
Paul Smith Boutique (company) AR13152
Paul, Les AR14595, AR15833
Pavement AR12918, AR13209, AR15512
Pavement—Recordings AR13472
Pavitt, Bruce AR12993
Payola AR13077, AR13945, AR13970
Payton, John AR14060
Pearl Jam AR12918, AR13078, AR13092, AR13788, AR14035, AR14164, AR14777, AR15502, AR15515, AR15516, AR15833, AR15860
Pearl Jam—Concerts—Atlanta, Georgia AR15513
Pearl Jam—Profiles AR13095, AR13285, AR13358, AR14195, AR14782
Pearl Jam—Recordings AR14048, AR15514, AR15520, AR15585, AR15824
Pearl Jam—Tours AR14788, AR15834, AR15851
Pearl Jam—Tours—Europe AR15038
Pearl Jam—Tours—North America AR13086, AR13759, AR15517, AR15829, AR15851
Pearl Jam—Videos AR14572, AR14749
Peck, M. Scott—Profiles AR13282
Peckinpah, Sam—Videos AR14291
Peel, John—Interviews AR12995
Pell Mell AR15748
Penn, Michael AR15943
Penn, Michael—Recordings AR15974
Penn, Sean—Profiles AR14677
Pennsylvania—Censorship AR13197, AR15516
Peoples, David Webb AR13887, AR15296
Pepper, Allan AR14136
Pepsi Cola AR14029
Perella, Marco AR15017
Peretz, Jesse—Videos AR13467
The Perfect Kiss (video) AR14393
Perfumes AR14846, AR14850, AR15489
Perkins, Carl—Tours—United Kingdom AR13954
Perlich, Max AR14242
Perlich, Max—Fashion AR13536, AR14839, AR16057
Perot, Ross—Politics AR14107, AR14336, AR15475
Perry, Charles AR13317, AR14418, AR15078
Perry, Joe AR13523, AR15739
Perry, Luke—Profiles AR14590
Perry, Matthew AR15919
Persian Gulf War AR14100
Personalities AR12943, AR13239, AR13278, AR13344, AR13488, AR14221, AR15058, AR15096, AR15168, AR15282
Personals (television show) AR14586
Perspective Records AR14031
Peru AR15011
Peter Gabriel (album) AR14936
Peterson, Donna—Politics AR13036
Petit Basset Griffon Vendeen (PBGV) AR16126
Pets AR13886, AR15295
Petty, Tom AR15383, AR15972
Petty, Tom—Profiles AR15377
Petty, Tom—Recordings AR13943
Petty, Tom—Tours AR13970
Petty, Tom—Tours—North America AR15377
Pfaff, Kristen—Obituary AR15523
Pfeiffer, Michelle—Films AR14220
Phair, Liz AR12918, AR15204
Phair, Liz—Interviews AR13530
Phair, Liz—Profiles AR13559
Phair, Liz—Recordings AR14047, AR14691
Pharcyde AR12928, AR14793, AR15204
Phelan, Jacquie AR13153
Phifer, Mekhi—Fashion AR14839, AR15746, AR16057
Philadelphia (film) AR13422
Philippines—Politics AR15001
Philips AR13985
Phillips, Grant Lee AR15094
Phillips, Jeff—Profiles AR16050
Phillips, Randy AR13976
Phillips, Sam (singer)—Recordings AR15093, AR15938, AR16088
Philosophy AR13250, AR13282, AR14418, AR15078, AR15307, AR16092, AR16108
Phish AR13899, AR15175
Phobia (album) AR15886
Phoenix, Arizona AR13917
Phoenix, Arizona—Rock Scene AR13918
Phoenix, River AR13035, AR14831
Phoenix, River—Fashion AR13035, AR14831
Photographers AR14221, AR14293, AR15795
Photographers—Bailey, David AR14221
Photographers—Corbijn, Anton AR14165
Photographers—Gahr, David AR14221
Photographers—Gustafsson, Per AR14442
Photographers—Hoffman, Dezo AR14221
Photographers—Lavine, Michael AR14170
Photographers—Leibovitz, Annie AR14221
Photographers—Markus, Kurt AR14575
Photographers—Marshall, Jim AR14221
Photographers—Pigozzi, Jean AR15096
Photographers—Randolph, Popsie AR14221
Photographers—Ritts, Herb AR15192
Photographers—Rolston, Matthew AR14221, AR15223
Photographers—Russell, Ethan AR14221
Photographers—Salgado, Sebastiao AR13165, AR13311, AR13342, AR15345, AR16045
Photographers—Scavullo, Francesco AR14221
Photographers—Seliger, Mark AR15383, AR15972
Photographers—Watson, Albert AR15739
Photographers—Weber, Bruce AR14221, AR15742
Photographers—Wertheimer, Alfred AR14221
Photography AR12984, AR13344, AR14520, AR15191, AR15341, AR15344, AR15345, AR15388, AR15389, AR15591, AR15688, AR15795, AR16045
Photography—Equipment AR13102, AR13114, AR13119, AR13120, AR13124, AR16078, AR16102
Photography—History AR14221
Physical Graffiti (album) AR14937
The Piano (film) AR14620
Pickett, Wilson—Recordings AR15193, AR15804
Picnic (drama) AR15651
Pierce, Jeffrey Lee—Obituary AR14355
Pierson, Kate AR13523, AR14256
Pigozzi, Jean AR15096
Pilate, Felton C., II AR15823
Pills-A-Go-Go (publication) AR15395
Pink Floyd AR13524, AR15031, AR15423
Pink Floyd—Recordings AR14880, AR14893, AR14973, AR15092, AR15535
Pink Floyd—Tours—North America AR15528
Pioneer Fund AR14636
Pirner, Dave AR13541, AR15503
Pirner, Dave—Interviews AR13553, AR13554
Pirro, Mark AR15835
Pisello, Sal AR13959
Pitney, Gene AR14173
Pitt, Brad—Films AR14711
Pitt, Brad—Profiles AR14579, AR14711
PJ Harvey AR12918
PJ Harvey—Profiles AR13762
Plant, Robert AR13519, AR14157, AR14170, AR15424, AR15516
Plant, Robert—Profiles AR13436
Plant, Robert—Recordings AR14768
Plastikman AR15829
Play It By Ear (game) AR15169
The Player (film) AR15660
Playing Possum (album) AR14938
PM Dawn AR13009
PM Dawn—Profiles AR13806
PM Dawn—Recordings AR14048, AR14503
Poe—Computer Systems AR14276
Poetry AR14284, AR14608, AR14610
Pogues AR14166
Pohlmann, Ken AR16123
Polara AR14181
Police AR13023
Police—Recordings AR14272
Police—Videos AR14555
Police Officers AR14331, AR14466
Police Officers—Los Angeles, California AR14059, AR14481, AR14490, AR15583
Police Officers—Louisville, Kentucky AR15217
Police Officers—New York, New York AR12916
Poliomyelitis AR13369, AR14991, AR15181
Poliomyelitis—Chronology AR13368
Politically Incorrect (television show) AR15953
Politics AR12948, AR13602, AR13894, AR14069, AR14084, AR14106, AR14116, AR14119, AR14343, AR14544, AR14994, AR15005, AR15013, AR15109, AR15179, AR15229, AR15310, AR15349, AR15396, AR15598, AR16020, AR16025, AR16031, AR16038, AR16042, AR16108, AR16121
Politics—Aquino, Corazon AR15001
Politics—Armey, Dick AR15079
Politics—Bauer, Gary AR13603
Politics—Bishop, Sanford AR13036
Politics—Blacks AR16030
Politics—Brown, Jerry AR14310, AR15791
Politics—Buchanan, Patrick AR13260, AR13602, AR14066, AR14104, AR15009
Politics—Bush, George AR14067, AR14104, AR15043, AR15046
Politics—Byrd, Robert AR16044
Politics—Cantwell, Maria AR13036
Politics—Chabot, Steve AR15079
Politics—Clinton, Bill AR14062, AR14071, AR14086, AR14098, AR14104, AR14106, AR14115, AR14118, AR14745, AR14785, AR15006, AR15599, AR15776, AR15778
Politics—Counterculture AR14429, AR15607, AR15752
Politics—Crane, Phil AR15079
Politics—Dole, Robert AR13601, AR15497
Politics—Dornan, Robert AR15079
Politics—English, Karan AR13036
Politics—Foreign Affairs AR14075, AR14100, AR14117, AR15462
Politics—Furse, Elizabeth AR13036
Politics—Gingrich, Newt AR12955, AR14077, AR15079, AR16044
Politics—Gramm, Phil AR15079

Politics—Health AR13477, AR14063, AR14108
Politics—Helms, Jesse AR15079
Politics—Huffington, Michael AR13036
Politics—Kerrey, Bob AR14015
Politics—Knapp, Cheryl Davis AR13036
Politics—Largent, Steve AR15079
Politics—Marcos, Ferdinand AR15001
Politics—McKinney, Cynthia AR13036
Politics—Nickles, Don AR15079
Politics—Nunn, Sam AR16020
Politics—Pamplin, Rick AR13036
Politics—Perot, Ross AR14107, AR14336, AR15475
Politics—Peterson, Donna AR13036
Politics—Powell, Colin AR14073, AR14649
Politics—Religion AR13603, AR16032
Politics—Rock Music AR13027, AR13048, AR13082, AR13397, AR13598, AR13816, AR14041, AR14162, AR14239, AR14338, AR14459, AR14492, AR14543, AR14544, AR14545, AR14546, AR14724, AR14743, AR14752, AR14756
Politics—Rohrabacher, Dana AR15079
Politics—Rush, Bobby AR13036
Politics—Stearns, Cliff AR15079
Politics—Tsongas, Paul AR14104
Politics—Watt, Mel AR13036
Politics—Wilder, Doug AR14639
Politics—Women AR16030
Politics—Woolsey, Lynn AR13036
Pollack, Jeff AR14256
Pollution AR14094, AR14123, AR15404
Polo AR15600
Polonsky, Jonny AR15495
PolyGram Records AR13937
Pomus, Doc AR13770, AR14273, AR14705
Pond, Steve AR13318
Poneman, Jonathan AR12993
Poor Righteous Teachers AR13592
Pop Art AR13943
Pop, Iggy AR13382
Pop, Iggy—Profiles AR14760
Pop, Iggy—Recordings AR13597, AR14952
Popeil, Ron AR13874, AR15274
Population AR14142
Porcaro, Jeff AR15965
Porcaro, Jeff—Obituary AR14308
Porno For Pyros AR13982
Porno For Pyros—Recordings AR12962, AR14047
Pornography AR13525, AR15332, AR16047
Porter, Chris AR14549
Porter, James, Father AR13158, AR13789
Portishead AR15767
Portland, Maine AR15106
Portland, Oregon—Music Scene AR16126
Posey, Parker—Films AR13498, AR14815
Posies AR14255, AR15231
Posse (film) AR15661
Poster Art AR13943, AR14344
Poster Children AR14256
Potter, Sally AR13336
Potter, Sally—Interviews AR15664
Poverty AR12982, AR13920, AR14092, AR15003
Powell, Colin—Politics AR14073, AR14649
Powell, Colin—Profiles AR14073
Power, Corruption And Lies (album) AR14939
POZ (publication) AR13237, AR14506, AR15279
Prefontaine, Steve AR15326
Pregnancy AR13684
Present Tense: Rock & Roll And Culture (book) AR15114
Presidents Of The United States Of America AR14166, AR15379
Presidents Of The United States Of America—Profiles AR13355
Presley, Elvis AR13181, AR13292, AR13942, AR14560, AR15522
Presley, Elvis—Death AR15518
Presley, Elvis—Recordings AR14262, AR14271, AR14272, AR14273, AR14902, AR14905, AR16008
Pretenders—Videos AR13813
Price, Lloyd AR14173
Pride And Glory AR13396, AR13517, AR13582, AR14548, AR14683
Priestley, Jason—Profiles AR14590
Primal Scream—Recordings AR13383
Primitive Radio Gods—Recordings AR15768
Primus AR13327, AR14165
Primus—Profiles AR12991
Prince AR13142, AR13961, AR13970, AR13984, AR13986, AR14158, AR14478, AR14497
Prince—Profiles AR13433
Prince—Recordings AR13434, AR14946
Prince—Tours—North America AR14497
Prince—Videos AR13970, AR14368, AR14369, AR15634
Prince Be—Fashion AR15387
Prince William Sound, Alaska AR14252
Princess Caroline AR15096
Prine, John AR14256
Prine, John—Interviews AR14551
Prine, John—Profiles AR16002
Priority Records AR13080, AR13882, AR15291
Professor Longhair AR13770, AR14705
Prostitution AR15180
Provincetown, Massachusetts AR13160
Psycho Therapy (video) AR14403
Psychocandy (album) AR14502
Psychology AR13274
Ptacek, Rainer AR14156
Public Enemy AR15449
Public Enemy—Profiles AR14487
Public Enemy—Recordings AR15450
Public Enemy—Tours—Africa AR13976
Public Enemy—Videos AR13619, AR15618, AR15619
Public Image, Ltd.—Recordings AR14927
Publications AR15137, AR15389, AR15395
Publishing AR13099, AR15395
Puente, Tito AR15153
Pulp AR15432
Punk Rock AR15220, AR15578
Puterbaugh, Parke AR13318
Puzzle (album) AR12990
Pyramids AR14418, AR15078
Pyst (CD-ROM) AR14662

Q

Q-Tip AR15135
Quad City DJ's—Recordings AR14138
Quarry Men—Recordings AR14363
Quartararo, Phil AR13980
Quayle, Dan AR15050
Queen AR13953, AR14755
Queen—Recordings AR13937
Queen Bitch (song) AR13083
Queen Latifah AR15450, AR15833
Queen Latifah—Profiles AR14488
Queen Of Soul (album) AR14263
Queers AR15208
The Question Of Equality (television show) AR13174
QVC (television network) AR14005

R

Ra, Sun—Obituary AR13785
Racism AR12947, AR13330, AR14059, AR14305, AR14329, AR14636, AR15056, AR15064, AR15413, AR15478, AR15708, AR16121
Racket (album) AR15206
Radio Stations AR13085, AR13152, AR13740, AR14124
Radio Stations—Censorship AR13083
Radio Stations—College Stations AR14668
Radio Stations—KLIT AR15944
Radio Stations—Programming AR13077, AR13081, AR13087, AR16094
Radio Stations—WEDG AR13681
Radio XFM (radio station) AR15426
Radiohead AR14793, AR15204, AR15420, AR15858
Radiohead—Recordings AR14398
Radiohead—Videos AR14323
Radios AR16062, AR16065, AR16080
Rage Against The Machine AR14159, AR14285
Rage Against The Machine—Videos AR13397
Rain Forests AR13315, AR13824, AR14141, AR14869, AR15011
Rain Forests—Benefit Concerts AR13618
Rainbow Family Of Living Light AR14528
Raitt, Bonnie AR13023, AR15170, AR15742, AR15984
Raitt, Bonnie—Interviews AR13493, AR14196
Rakim AR13593
Rakim—Recordings AR13595
Ralph J. Gleason Music Book Awards AR13962, AR14805, AR15137
Rammellzee AR13595
Ramone, Joey AR12975, AR14160, AR14172
Ramone, Joey—Interviews AR14385
Ramones AR15830
Ramones—Videos AR14403
The Ramones (album) AR14957
Ranaldo, Lee AR12959
Rancid AR14185
Rancid—Profiles AR13668
Randolph County, Alabama AR14305, AR15413, AR15708
Randolph, Popsie AR14221
Ranks, Shabba AR13314
Rap Music AR13237, AR13328, AR13881, AR13910, AR14338, AR14473, AR14477, AR14481, AR14489, AR14490, AR14506, AR14747, AR15139, AR15279, AR15289, AR15445, AR15514, AR15628
Rap Music—History AR13033
Rape AR12946, AR15577
Rapture (video) AR13508
Rascals AR14173
Rascoff, Joseph AR15516
Rasin Music AR14623
Raspberries AR15934
Rastafarians AR15592
Rather, Dan—Profiles AR14335
Ratner, Laurence AR14051
Ravel AR14595
Ravenswood Aluminum Corporation AR15464, AR15707
Ravenswood, West Virginia AR15464, AR15707
Raves AR13367
Raw Fusion—Recordings AR15451
Rea, Chris AR15421
Reading Festival AR13010, AR14445
Real TV (television show) AR15900
The Real World (television show) AR13164, AR15981
Recoil AR13943
Record Companies AR13003, AR13059, AR13061, AR13091, AR13366, AR13805, AR13930, AR13931, AR13950, AR13980,

AR14027, AR14029, AR14032, AR14162, AR14193, AR14642, AR14732, AR14740, AR15207, AR15219, AR15518, AR15824, AR15881, AR15964, AR16005
Record Producers AR13255, AR14833
Record Producers—Albini, Steve AR13880, AR15288
Record Producers—Dust Brothers AR13630
Record Producers—Jones, John Paul AR13204
Record Producers—Lanois, Daniel AR15099
Record Producers—McEntire, John AR15705
Record Producers—Simenon, Tim AR15761
Record Producers—Vig, Butch AR15726, AR16126
Record Producers—Wexler, Jerry AR15193, AR15804
Record Stores AR13072, AR13575, AR14027, AR14362, AR14781, AR15174, AR15508
Record Stores—Musicland AR15586
Recording Studios—Cambridge, Massachusetts AR14463
Recording Studios—Chess AR16096
Records AR13767, AR13994, AR14264, AR14743, AR15133
Records—Bootlegs AR13372, AR14458
Records—Box Sets AR14274
Records—Care And Handling AR13104
Records—Collecting AR13988, AR14386
Records—Popularity AR15016, AR15126
Records—Prices AR14478, AR15757
Records—Sales AR13061, AR13070, AR13073, AR13084, AR13089, AR13157, AR13446, AR13452, AR13930, AR13931, AR13944, AR13945, AR13950, AR13958, AR13963, AR14027, AR14259, AR14274, AR14773, AR15530, AR15569, AR15585
Records—Tributes AR13733
Recreation—Bicycling AR13153
Recreation—Chess AR13023
Recreation—Skateboarding AR16050
Recreation—Skiing AR14440, AR14535, AR14616, AR14819, AR14835, AR14845
Recreation—Snow Boarding AR14049
Recreation—Surfing AR15996
Red Aunts AR15150
Red Hot & Dance (album) AR15874
Red Hot Chili Peppers AR12918, AR13539, AR14157, AR14758, AR15837, AR15968, AR15972
Red Hot Chili Peppers—Profiles AR13665, AR13742
Red Hot Chili Peppers—Recordings AR13351
Red Hot Chili Peppers—Tours—North America AR13990
Red Hot Chili Peppers—Videos AR13567
Red Hot Organization (organization) AR14186
Red House Painters AR13934, AR13989
Red House Painters—Recordings AR15093
The Red Shoes (album) AR15416
Red Wing Shoes (company) AR13575
Redding, Noel AR14705
Redding, Otis—Recordings AR14260, AR14268
Redford, Robert—Interviews AR13437
Redman, Josh AR13778
Reed College AR14554
Reed, Eric AR14549
Reed, Johnny AR13523
Reed, Lou AR15505, AR15739
Reed, Lou—Recordings AR13719
Reed, Lou—Videos AR15355
Reed, Ralph AR16032
Reel Wild Cinema (television show) AR15893
Refreshments AR15147
Reggae Music AR13314, AR15592
Reid, Vernon AR12977, AR15154
Reid, Vernon—Computer Systems AR14276
Reid, Vernon—Interviews AR13148
Reid, Vernon—Recordings AR13714
Reiner, Carl—Recordings AR14271
Reiser, Paul AR13169
Reiser, Paul—Fashion AR14830, AR15926
Reiser, Paul—Profiles AR14830, AR15926
Relayer (album) AR14940
Religion AR13066, AR13603, AR16032, AR16091, AR16092
R.E.M. AR12918, AR13374, AR13723, AR14158, AR14161, AR14575, AR15833, AR15835, AR15837
R.E.M.—Concerts—Slane Castle, Ireland AR15834
R.E.M.—Films AR14166
R.E.M.—Profiles AR13425, AR14148
R.E.M.—Recordings AR13163, AR13375, AR13758, AR14263, AR14637, AR14899
R.E.M.—Tours AR13724
R.E.M.—Tours—United States AR15849
R.E.M.—Videos AR13613, AR14394, AR14411, AR14565, AR14620
R.E.M. Rough Cut (television show) AR13174
The Ren & Stimpy Show (television show) AR13304
Reno, Janet AR13581, AR16026
Rent (rock opera) AR14358, AR14848, AR15850
Replacements—Videos AR14698
The Reporters (television show) AR13140
Reprise Records AR15822
Republica AR15770
Republican Party AR12950, AR12951, AR12953, AR13260, AR13346, AR13603, AR14066, AR14077, AR14081, AR14104, AR14106, AR14648, AR14649, AR14650, AR15009, AR15049, AR15079, AR15497, AR15607, AR16022
Rescue Unit AR13899
Residents—CD-ROMs AR14339
Retro Active (album) AR13715
Retrospective (video) AR13615
Return Of The Jedi (film) AR15668
Rev Run Records AR15836
Reverend Horton Heat AR13382, AR13531, AR15204
Reznor, Trent AR14165
Reznor, Trent—Computer Systems AR14276
Reznor, Trent—Profiles AR13925, AR14234
Reznor, Trent—Recordings AR14049
Rhino Records AR14261, AR14479
Rhythm & Blues Foundation (organization) AR14018, AR15854
Rhythm And The Blues: A Life In American Music (book) AR15193, AR15804
Rice, Anne AR13854
Rice, Anne—Interviews AR13909
Rich, Charlie—Death AR15037
Rich, Charlie—Obituary AR13289
Rich, Marc AR15464, AR15707
Rich, Tony—Fashion AR14839, AR15967, AR16057
Richards, Keith AR14705, AR15153, AR15739
Richards, Keith—Fashion AR15387
Richards, Keith—Interviews AR14516
Richards, Keith—Recordings AR13993, AR14281, AR14764
Richards, Keith—Videos AR13616
Richards, Marlon AR13259, AR14842
Richards, Marlon—Fashion AR13259, AR14842
Richards, Michael AR13896, AR15314
Richards, Michael—Profiles AR16116
Richmond, California AR13286
Right Now (video) AR14569
The Right Stuff (book) AR16060
Rilke, Rainer Maria AR14620
Rimes, Leann AR14531
Ringling School Of Art And Design AR15486
Rio de Janeiro, Brazil AR14999
Riot Grrrls AR13687
Riots AR14787
Riots—Los Angeles, California AR14059, AR14343, AR14481, AR14490, AR15583
Riots—St. Louis, Missouri AR13764, AR14673
Ritcher, Scott—Interviews AR15397
Ritchey, Tom AR13153
Ritts, Herb AR14221, AR15096, AR15192, AR15591
Ritts, Herb—Videos AR14293
Ritual De Lo Habitual (album) AR16052
River Of Dreams (album) AR13796
Roach Archie AR13694
Roach, Max AR15154
Road Rules (television show) AR13172
The Road To Wellville (book) AR13132
Robbins, Tim—Profiles AR16119
Robbins, Tom AR12959, AR13339
Roberts, Julia—Interviews AR15156
Robertson, Robbie AR14231, AR14705, AR15153, AR15154, AR15170, AR15742, AR15984
Robertson, Robbie—Interviews AR15024
Robertson, Robbie—Tours AR13994
Robin, Alyson AR15402
Robinson, Chris AR12976, AR15216
Robinson, Chris—Interviews AR13499, AR14225
Robinson, Chris—Quotes AR13842
Robinson, Smokey AR15223
Robotics AR13461
Rock & Roll (television show) AR13174
Rock & Roll: An Unruly History (book) AR15026
Rock & Roll In Literature (performance) AR12966
Rock And Roll Circus (album) AR14359
Rock And Roll Hall Of Fame AR13097, AR13290, AR13292, AR13295, AR13296, AR13297, AR13300, AR13523, AR13524, AR13541, AR13653, AR13716, AR13761, AR13770, AR13771, AR13776, AR13782, AR13783, AR13784, AR13817, AR13952, AR13953, AR13961, AR14126, AR14127, AR14128, AR14159, AR14173, AR14705, AR14722, AR15031, AR15130, AR15170, AR15352, AR15766, AR15940, AR15972, AR15984
Rock And Roll Hall Of Fame—Concert AR13288, AR13292, AR13296, AR13522, AR13817, AR14127
Rock And Roll Hall Of Fame—Recordings AR14173
Rock Festivals AR13382
Rock Festivals—Big Day Out AR13695, AR14047, AR15357
Rock Festivals—CMJ Music Marathon AR13005
Rock Festivals—England AR15418
Rock Festivals—ENIT Festival AR13139
Rock Festivals—Further Festival AR14159
Rock Festivals—H.O.R.D.E. AR15559
Rock Festivals—International Pop Underground Convention AR15199
Rock Festivals—Isle Of Wight Festival Of Music AR14171
Rock Festivals—LollaPalooza '92 AR13976, AR13990, AR14766
Rock Festivals—LollaPalooza '93 AR13961,

AR13991, AR14767
Rock Festivals—LollaPalooza '94 AR15525, AR15538
Rock Festivals—LollaPalooza '95 AR15842, AR15864
Rock Festivals—Monsters Of Rock AR15418
Rock Festivals—Monterey International Pop Festival AR14275
Rock Festivals—Reading Festival AR13010, AR14445
Rock Festivals—Tibetan Freedom Concert AR15496
Rock Festivals—Violence AR14723, AR14770
Rock Festivals—Woodstock AR14208
Rock Festivals—Woodstock '94 AR14017, AR14643, AR14645
Rock Festivals—Yoyo A Go Go AR14611
Rock Music AR13053, AR13066, AR13438, AR13749, AR14198, AR14290, AR15748, AR16123
Rock Music—AIDS AR14205, AR14224
Rock Music—Cinema AR16123
Rock Music—Computers AR13932
Rock Music—History AR13726, AR14221, AR14345, AR14562, AR15016, AR15026, AR15749, AR16123
Rock Music—Homosexuality AR15220
Rock Music—Politics AR13027, AR13048, AR13082, AR13397, AR13598, AR13816, AR14041, AR14162, AR14239, AR14338, AR14459, AR14492, AR14543, AR14544, AR14545, AR14546, AR14724, AR14743, AR14752, AR14756
Rock Music—Sociological Aspects AR13614, AR13620, AR14205, AR14224, AR15016, AR15017, AR16123
Rock Music—Television AR13060, AR13079, AR13572, AR13791, AR14028, AR14139, AR14574, AR14653
Rock Music—Violence AR12943, AR13068, AR13614, AR13949, AR14479, AR14486, AR14770, AR14774, AR14787, AR15233, AR15234
Rock Music—Women AR13687
Rock Operas—Rent AR14358, AR14848, AR15850
Rock Operas—Tommy AR15999
Rock Steady Crew AR13577, AR13814
Rock The Vote AR14257, AR14492, AR14756
Rock-It Comix AR14399
Rocket From The Crypt AR14289, AR15750
Rockin' Dopsie—Obituary AR15561
Rockit (video) AR14407
Rodan AR13396, AR13517, AR13582, AR14548, AR14683
Rodman, Dennis—Profiles AR14147
Rodney, Red—Obituary AR15515
Rodriguez, Robert—Interviews AR15663
Rohrabacher, Dana—Politics AR15079
ROIR AR13767
Roller Basketball AR13263, AR14853
Roller Skates AR16080
Rollerblades AR16082
Rolling Stone (publication) AR12974, AR12979, AR12980, AR12983, AR12984, AR13194, AR13309, AR13344, AR13576, AR14267, AR15221, AR15511, AR15794, AR15800, AR15972
Rolling Stone (publication)—Advertising AR13335
Rolling Stone (publication)—History AR13020, AR13044, AR13145, AR13188, AR13340, AR13345, AR13360, AR13427, AR13596, AR13604, AR13651, AR13674, AR13690, AR13908, AR14055, AR14057, AR14084, AR14140, AR14198, AR14223, AR14240, AR14246, AR14248, AR14252, AR14418, AR14426, AR14428, AR14429, AR14473, AR14518, AR14560, AR14576, AR14621, AR15001, AR15017, AR15025, AR15078, AR15103, AR15332, AR15388, AR15541, AR15592, AR15596, AR15688, AR15752, AR15793, AR15795, AR16060, AR16091, AR16109, AR16120
Rolling Stone (publication)—Manuscripts AR15575, AR15576, AR15610, AR15611
Rolling Stone (publication)—Music Awards AR12976, AR12977, AR13352, AR13353, AR13727, AR13740, AR15142, AR15143
Rolling Stone (publication)—Staff AR12978, AR13183, AR13317, AR13318, AR14789, AR15114, AR15591, AR15706
The Rolling Stone Album Guide (book) AR14288
The Rolling Stone Book Of Comedy (book) AR13326, AR15360, AR16117
The Rolling Stone Illustrated History Of Rock & Roll (book) AR14288
Rolling Stone Images Of Rock & Roll (book) AR14520, AR15740
Rolling Stone Online (electronic publication) AR14975, AR14976, AR14977, AR14978, AR14979, AR14980, AR14981, AR14982, AR14983, AR14984, AR14986, AR14987, AR14988, AR14989, AR14990, AR15222, AR15853
Rolling Stones AR13300, AR13676, AR14500, AR15172, AR15831, AR15941
Rolling Stones—Films AR13993, AR14359, AR15994
Rolling Stones—Profiles AR13252, AR13732
Rolling Stones—Recordings AR12945, AR13313, AR13703, AR14271, AR14359, AR14903, AR14948, AR14949, AR15829
Rolling Stones—Tours—Great Britain AR14057
Rolling Stones—Tours—World AR13071, AR13252, AR13267, AR15528
Rolling Stones—Videos AR14378
Rollins, Henry AR12918, AR12977, AR13960, AR15245, AR15829
Rollins, Henry—Interviews AR13728
Rollins, Henry—Profiles AR14685
Rollins, Henry—Recordings AR14778
Rollins, Riz AR14668
Rolston, Matthew AR14221, AR15223
Rolston, Matthew—Videos AR14293
Romance AR15745
Romano, Ray—Interviews AR15907
Ronson, Mick—Obituary AR14694
Ronson, Mick—Profiles AR15440
Ronson, Mick—Recordings AR13672
Ronstadt, Linda—Interviews AR14689
Rooney, Andy AR15872
Roots AR13237, AR14506, AR14651, AR15279
Roots 'N' Blues: An American Music Retrospective 1925-1950 (album) AR14262
Rosalita (video) AR13820
Rose, Axl AR13194, AR13541, AR13764, AR13976, AR14673, AR15098, AR15192, AR15511
Rose, Axl—Fashion AR15387
Rose, Axl—Interviews AR14741, AR14783
Rose, Jim—Videos AR14780
Rosen, Fred AR14035
Rosen, Hilary AR15514
Rosenberg, Tina AR13311
Rosenthal, Jack AR13942
The Rosie O'Donnell Show (television show) AR16010
Ross, Diana AR15739
Rossellini, Isabella AR15096
Rossington, Gary AR15153
Roth, David Lee AR14163
Rothberg, Patti AR13138
Rothchild, Paul—Obituary AR14034
Roxy Music—Recordings AR14892
Roy Ayers Ubiquity AR15554
Royal Trux AR15380
Royalties AR15854
RU-486 AR13872, AR15271
Rubin, Rick AR13960
Rubin, Rick—Interviews AR15950
Ruby AR13546
Rucker, Darius AR15327
Rudge, Peter Jay AR15542, AR15543
Ruffhouse Records AR15760
Rumours (album) AR14941
Run-D.M.C. AR15625
Run-D.M.C.—Videos AR15616
Rundgren, Todd AR15940
Rundgren, Todd—Recordings AR13932
RuPaul AR15036
RuPaul—Interviews AR15703
RuPaul—Videos AR13511
Rush, Bobby—Politics AR13036
Russell, Ethan AR14221
Russia AR13347, AR14117, AR15784
Russia—Profiles AR14997, AR15007
Rwanda AR14134, AR14521, AR15339, AR15343
Ryder, Shaun AR13962, AR15328
Ryder, Winona—Profiles AR13905

S

S*M*A*S*H* AR15423
Sabato, Antonio, Jr. AR14511, AR14827, AR15490
Sabbe, John AR13854
Sabelle AR13591
Sabin, Albert AR13369
Sager, Mike AR13317, AR15332
Sagoo, Bally AR15420
Sailin' Shoes (album) AR14942
Salem, Kevin AR14039
Salgado, Sebastiao AR13165, AR13311
Salgado, Sebastiao—Interviews AR13342
Salk, Jonas AR13369
Salt Lake City, Utah AR15346
Salt-N-Pepa AR12918
Salt-N-Pepa—Profiles AR13555
Salt-N-Pepa—Recordings AR14049, AR15188
Salvation Army (organization) AR13262, AR14852
Sam And Dave AR13770, AR14705
San Diego, California AR15155
San Diego, California—Music Scene AR14289
San Francisco, California AR13049, AR13050, AR13673, AR15498
San Francisco Days (album) AR15901
Santana—Concerts—San Diego, California AR14024
Santana—Recordings AR14875
Santana, Carlos AR12959, AR13781, AR15153, AR15383
Santiago, Herman AR13973
Sao Paulo, Brazil—Profiles AR14142
Sarajevo, Bosnia AR13141
Satisfaction (video) AR14395
Saturday Morning (album) AR15836
Saturday Night Live (television show) AR14157, AR14159, AR15665, AR15970
Savage Records AR13968
Savalas, Telly AR13624
Savio, Mario—Obituary AR15689
Sayles, John AR13169
Sayles, John—Videos AR14291
Scaccia, Mike AR14287, AR15837

Scaggs, Boz AR13970
Scaggs, Boz—Recordings AR14237, AR14928
Scanner AR15832, AR15833
Scarce AR15855
Scarecrow (album) AR15460
Scavullo, Francesco AR14221, AR15096
Scelsa, Vin AR13574
Schader, Seth Cash AR15017
Schaffner, Nicholas—Obituary AR14800
Schellenbach, Kate AR15701
Schemel, Patty AR12975
Schenkenberg, Marcus AR16126
Schiffman, Bonnie AR14221
Schillaci, John AR15944
Schmoke, Kurt AR14113
Schneider, Fred AR13523, AR14542, AR15363
Scholastic Aptitude Test AR14219
School Of Fish AR14868
School Ties (film) AR14315, AR14534
Schools AR13076, AR13859, AR14085, AR15247
Schrader, Paul—Videos AR14291
Schreifels, Walter AR14165
Schumacher, Joel—Videos AR14291
Schwarzenegger, Arnold AR15096
Schwimmer, David AR13237, AR14506, AR15279, AR15919
Scialfa, Patti—Interviews AR15102
Science AR13461, AR13872, AR13878, AR15271, AR15283
Science—AIDS AR15411, AR15547
Scientology AR15830
Scofield, John AR15154
Scooby Snacks (video) AR13081
Scorsese, Martin AR14620
Scorsese, Martin—Videos AR14291
Scott, Campbell—Films AR13361
Scott, Casey AR15162
Scott, Jimmy AR13597
Scott, Raymond—Obituary AR15509
Screaming Trees AR12918
Screaming Trees—Profiles AR12998, AR13634
Screaming Trees—Recordings AR14188
Screaming Trees—Tours—North America AR13983
Scruggs, Earl AR13847, AR15382
Sculley, John AR14012, AR14013
Sea And Cake AR15177
Seal AR12918, AR15587
Seal—Profiles AR15567
Seattle, Washington AR14507, AR14838, AR15086, AR15367
Seattle, Washington—Rock Music AR12993, AR15087
Sebadoh AR13483
Sebastian AR15972
Sebastian International Inc. (company) AR15695
Second Noah (television show) AR13177
Sednaoui, Stephane—Videos AR14293
See Jungle! See Jungle! Go Join Your Gang Yeah!... (album) AR14943
Seeff, Norman AR14221
Seeger, Pete AR13524, AR15031
Seidemann, Bob AR14221
Seinfeld (television show) AR13336, AR16116
Seinfeld, Jerry AR13304
Seinfeld, Jerry—Profiles AR15372, AR16116
Selena—Death AR15037
Self Portrait (album) AR14944
Self-Defense AR15088
Seliger, Mark AR14221, AR15383, AR15972
Seliger, Mark—Videos AR14293
Sen Dog AR14052
Sena, Dominic—Videos AR14296
Serbia—Photography AR15341
Serbia—Politics AR13165, AR14985, AR15002, AR15077, AR15539
Series Of Dreams (video) AR14547
Sermon, Erick—Recordings AR13589
Seven Mary Three AR15468
7 Seconds (video) AR14540
7 Year Bitch AR14166
75% Less Fat (album) AR14236
Sex AR12946, AR13044, AR13241, AR13274, AR13684, AR14504, AR15019, AR15285, AR15745, AR16092
Sex (book) AR13953
Sex Pistols—Recordings AR14930
Sex Pistols—Tours AR14156, AR14158
Sexism AR15677, AR15699
Sexual Harassment AR15595
Sexually Transmitted Diseases AR13044, AR13279, AR13369, AR13684, AR14186, AR14205, AR14224, AR14326, AR14991, AR15180, AR15411, AR15547, AR16053
Seymour, Indiana AR13194, AR15511
Seymour, Phil—Obituary AR15938
Sgt. Pepper's Lonely Hearts Club Band (album) AR14670, AR14945
Shadrach (video) AR14404
Shaggy AR14793
Shake Your Money Maker (album) AR15566
Shakur, TuPac AR14287, AR14481, AR15091, AR15452, AR15509, AR15824, AR15830, AR15832 , AR15867, AR15868
Shakur, Tupac—Death AR15609
Shakur, Tupac—Obituary AR15108
Shakur, Tupac—Recordings AR13910
Shamanism AR16126
Shame—Recordings AR13299
Shampoos AR14131, AR14844
Shana—Fashion AR14425, AR15988
Shandling, Garry—Profiles AR14591
Shapiro, Robert AR15546
Sharp, Jonah AR15115
Sharp, Matt AR15390
Sharrock, Sonny—Obituary AR14408
She Blinded Me With Science (video) AR14679
Shepherd, Kenny Wayne AR13810
Shields, Brooke—Profiles AR16012
Shilts, Randy AR13624, AR14326
Shilts, Randy—Interviews AR16053
Shimomura, Tsutomu AR14014
Shinas, Sofia AR13037, AR15722
Shirelles AR13524, AR13761, AR15031
Shock The Monkey (video) AR14375
Shocklee, Hank AR15450
Shoes AR14132, AR14633, AR14855, AR15211
Shonen Knife—Fashion AR15908
Shore, Pauly—Profiles AR14589
Short Cuts (film) AR14862, AR15720
A Short Visit To Planet Earth (book) AR15096
Shorter, Wayne AR15154
Shot In The Heart (book) AR13915
The Show (film) AR15831
Showgirls (film) AR15666
Shudder To Think AR13008, AR13396, AR13517, AR13582, AR14548, AR14549, AR14683
Siberia, Russia AR14997
Siberry, Jane AR12970, AR14620
Sidi Bou Said—Recordings AR15421
Sightings (television show) AR15899
Sign O' The Times (album) AR14946
Silent All These Years (video) AR14391
Silk, Garnet—Obituary AR15821
Silkwood, Karen AR14428
Silva, John AR14255
Silverchair AR14172, AR14433
Silverchair—Profiles AR13697
Silverstone, Alicia—Profiles AR13215
Simenon, Tim AR15761
Simmons, Bonnie AR13574, AR14549
Simmons, Gene AR15394
Simmons, Jan AR15153
Simon And The Bar Sinister AR14549
Simon, Carly AR15481
Simon, Carly—Recordings AR14938, AR15461
Simon, Paul AR13956, AR14575, AR15481
Simon, Paul—Videos AR13615
Simone, Nina AR15836
Simply Irresistible (song) AR15355
Simply Mad About The Mouse (video) AR13613
Simpson, Nicole Brown AR13337, AR15545
Simpson, O. J.—Profiles AR13337, AR15545, AR15546
Sinatra, Frank—Recordings AR14271
Sinclair, John AR13596
Singles (film) AR13361
Singles (records) AR13012, AR13631
Singleton, John—Videos AR14291
Sir Mix-A-Lot AR13589
Sir Mix-A-Lot—Interviews AR13550
Sir Mix-A-Lot—Videos AR14564
Sister Souljah AR14785
Sixteen Horsepower AR13844
60 Ft Dolls AR14598
Skatalites AR13314
Skateboarding AR16050
Skee-Lo—Videos AR13552
Skeleton Key AR15354
Skiing AR13323, AR13324, AR13348, AR14440, AR14535, AR14616, AR14819, AR14835, AR14845, AR14856, AR14860
Skin AR14131, AR14844, AR15553
Skinheads AR12947, AR14304
Slash AR14190, AR15223, AR15972, AR16047
Slave To The Rhythm (album) AR14947
Slave To The Rhythm (video) AR15630
Slayer—Recordings AR15836
Sleater-Kinney AR15727
Sledgehammer (video) AR14396
Sleeper AR15434
Sleepless In Seattle (film) AR13689
Slick, Grace AR12959
The Slider (album) AR14958
Sloan, Ross AR12916
Slovenia—Photography AR15341
Slovenia—Politics AR13165, AR14985, AR15002, AR15539
Slow Train Coming (album) AR15193, AR15804
Sly And The Family Stone AR13771, AR13784, AR15170, AR15554, AR15984
Sly And The Family Stone—Recordings AR14960, AR15733
Small Faces—Recordings AR14933
Smallpox AR15181
Smashing Pumpkins AR12918, AR13013, AR13150, AR13747, AR14191, AR14255, AR15512
Smashing Pumpkins—Concerts—Dublin, Ireland AR13068
Smashing Pumpkins—Profiles AR13696, AR14712
Smashing Pumpkins—Recordings AR14169, AR14437, AR15726
Smear, Pat AR15444
Smells Like Nirvana (video) AR14570
Smells Like Teen Spirit (video) AR14725
Smif N Wessun AR13396, AR13517, AR13582, AR14548, AR14683
Smith, Clifford AR15635

Smith, Erin—Interviews AR15395
Smith, Fred AR13624
Smith, Fred—Obituary AR15521
Smith, Ken AR15457
Smith, Patti AR13524, AR13957, AR14159, AR14576, AR14608, AR15031
Smith, Patti—Interviews AR13736
Smith, Patti—Quotations AR13524, AR15031
Smith, Patti—Recordings AR13479, AR14912
Smiths AR14171
The Smiths (album) AR14959
Smokin Suckaz Wit Logic AR13588
Smooth—Videos AR15450
Smulders, Sherry AR14616, AR14819
Snake River Canyon AR13604
Snavely, Todd AR16130
Sneakers—Recordings AR15206
Snoop Doggy Dogg AR12918, AR13924, AR13927, AR14793, AR15822, AR15972
Snoop Doggy Dogg—Lyrics AR15628
Snoop Doggy Dogg—Profiles AR15866
Snoop Doggy Dogg—Tours AR14550
Snow—Profiles AR14622
Snow Boarding AR14049
Snyder, Patrick—Obituary AR14025
Sobule, Jill—Recordings AR15830
Social Distortion AR12942, AR14163
Social Distortion—Profiles AR14714
Softley, Iain—Films AR13196
Somalia—Politics AR14993
Some Girls (album) AR14948
Something In The Way (song) AR15726
Sometime In New York City (book) AR15831
Son Of Beserkley Entertainment AR13969
Songs Of Freedom (album) AR14263
Songs Of Leonard Cohen (album) AR13030
Songwriters AR14136
Sonic Youth AR12918, AR14040, AR14158
Sonic Youth—Recordings AR13014, AR14168, AR14412, AR14894, AR15210, AR15726
Sonic Youth—Videos AR13562, AR14401
SonicNet (company) AR14383
Sonnenfeld, Barry—Films AR14137
Sony AR13833, AR13978, AR13985, AR13994, AR14030, AR15417, AR15422, AR15517
Soul Asylum AR12918, AR14542, AR15954, AR15972
Soul Asylum—Profiles AR14709, AR14715, AR15503
Soul Asylum—Tours—North America AR13983
Soul Coughing AR15473
Sound Patrol—Recordings AR15117
Soundgarden AR12918
Soundgarden—CD-ROMs AR14390
Soundgarden—Profiles AR14761, AR14786
Soundgarden—Recordings AR13357, AR14696
Sounds Of Blackness—Recordings AR14318
Source (publication) AR15520
South Africa—Politics AR13690, AR15140
South America AR15011
South By Southwest Music And Media Conference AR13712, AR13745
Southern Culture On The Skids—Recordings AR13408
Southern Utah Wilderness Alliance (organization) AR13923
Southern, Terry—Death AR15037
Southwest Music And Media Conference AR13693, AR13748
Soviet Union AR15010
Soviet Union—Politics AR15182, AR15691
Soviet Union—Rock Scene AR15690
Space Jam (film) AR14169
Space Shuttle Flights AR14004
Spacehog AR15857
Spacetime Continuum AR15115
Spacey, Kevin AR13237, AR14506, AR15279
Spaghetti, Eddie—Interviews AR13505
Speakers AR14660, AR16080
Spearhead AR13590, AR15452, AR15922
Special Ed—Recordings AR15450
Special Sauce AR13795
Specter, Arlen AR12956
Spector, Phil AR14705
Spector, Phil—Interviews AR15797
Spector, Phil—Recordings AR14258
Speech AR14542
Speeris, Penelope—Films AR16101
Spencer, James AR15323
Spencer, Jon AR14350, AR15812
Spice 1—Recordings AR15450
Spin Doctors AR12918, AR13899
Spin Doctors—Profiles AR13897
Spin Doctors—Recordings AR14702
Spin Doctors—Tours—North America AR13983
Spinal Tap—Recordings AR15992
Spinanes AR13688
The Spirit Cries (album) AR13315
Spivak, Allen AR13966
Sponge AR12968, AR14156, AR15321
Sponge—Profiles AR15856
Sports—Baseball AR13129, AR13220, AR13227, AR14821, AR15257, AR16082
Sports—Basketball AR13864, AR13999, AR15256
Sports—Bicycling AR13251, AR14314, AR14461, AR14829, AR14843, AR14859
Sports—Bobsledding AR16130
Sports—Decathlon AR14314, AR14843
Sports—Diving AR14801, AR15693
Sports—Fencing AR14801, AR15693
Sports—Football AR15334
Sports—Golf AR14167
Sports—Gymnastics AR13599, AR14799, AR14801, AR15693
Sports—Higher Education AR13574, AR15334
Sports—Ice Skating AR13323, AR14856, AR15544
Sports—Kayaking AR14801, AR15693
Sports—Kick Boxing AR14285
Sports—Polo AR15600
Sports—Roller Basketball AR13263, AR14853
Sports—Skiing AR13323, AR13324, AR13348, AR14535, AR14835, AR14856, AR14860
Sports—Surfing AR16049
Sports—Swimming AR13610, AR14818
Sports—Triathlons AR14133, AR14861
Sports—X Games AR13046
Sports Equipment—Helmets AR16081
Sports Weekend (album) AR14476
Spouse Abuse AR14246
Springsteen, Bruce AR13994, AR15170, AR15192, AR15984
Springsteen, Bruce—Concerts—Stockholm, Sweden AR13312
Springsteen, Bruce—Concerts—Tacoma, Washington AR13955
Springsteen, Bruce—Interviews AR14202, AR14517
Springsteen, Bruce—Recordings AR13941, AR13970, AR14036, AR14197, AR14265, AR14267, AR14883, AR14908, AR15149
Springsteen, Bruce—Tours—Europe AR14048
Springsteen, Bruce—Tours—North America AR13934, AR13937
Springsteen, Bruce—Videos AR13820, AR14571, AR14573
Spying AR14006
Squire, John AR14158
SST Records AR13966, AR13974, AR13979
SST Superstore (record store) AR13575
St. Lawrence, Jes—Interviews AR15403
St. Louis, Missouri AR13764, AR14673
Staggers, Barbara AR13684
Stain (album) AR14472
Stalin, Joseph AR15182
Stalking AR12943
Stallone, Sylvester AR15096
Stamps AR13942, AR15480
Stand! (album) AR15733
Stanshall, Vivian—Obituary AR15209
Staple Singers AR13152
Star Wars (film) AR15668
Stark, Koo AR15096
Starr, Ringo AR15383, AR15957
Starr, Ringo—Interviews AR15983
Starr, Ringo—Recordings AR15993
Starr, Ringo—Tours—North America AR15837
The State (television show) AR14508
Stearns, Cliff—Politics AR15079
Steckler, Jeremy AR14832, AR15127
Steel Pole Bath Tub AR15705
Steele, Alison—Obituary AR14538
Steele, Robert D.—Interviews AR14006
Steely Dan—Tours—North America AR13968
Stefani, Gwen AR15485
Stein, Seymour AR15822
Stephens, Jody AR14255
Stephens, Victor AR12916
Stepping Razor-Red X (film) AR13435
Stereo Equipment AR13108, AR13111, AR13575, AR13639, AR13643, AR13645, AR13646, AR13647, AR13648, AR13649, AR13650, AR15716, AR16062, AR16065, AR16071, AR16081, AR16082, AR16102
Stereo Equipment—Amplifiers AR13648, AR13649
Stereo Equipment—Automobiles AR13101, AR14795, AR16058, AR16064, AR16074, AR16079
Stereo Equipment—Cassette Decks AR13639, AR13648, AR13649, AR13940, AR13993
Stereo Equipment—Compact Discs Players AR13641, AR13648, AR13649, AR13985, AR14658, AR15736, AR16079
Stereo Equipment—Converters AR13641
Stereo Equipment—Headphones AR13108, AR14658, AR16085
Stereo Equipment—Mini Disc Players AR13108, AR16079
Stereo Equipment—Receivers AR13648, AR13649
Stereo Equipment—Speakers AR13123, AR13639, AR13648, AR13649, AR14660, AR14795, AR15736, AR16071, AR16079
Stereo Equipment—Tuners AR13648
Stereo Equipment—Turntables AR13104, AR13648, AR13649
Stereolab AR15178
Stern, Howard—Interviews AR14567
Steuer, Jonathan AR14016
The Steve Harvey Show (television show) AR15898
Stevens, Cat—Recordings AR13349
Stevenson, Bill AR15578
Stewart, Jim AR14705
Stewart, Jon AR15410, AR15491
Stewart, Jon—Interviews AR15311
Stewart, Melvin AR14818
Stewart, Rod AR13776, AR13783, AR13976, AR15130, AR15383, AR15833, AR15940
Stewart, Rod—Recordings AR14929

Sticky Fingers (album) AR14949
Stiffed: The True Story Of MCA, The Music Business, And The Mafia (book) AR13959
Stills, Stephen—Quotes AR14543
Sting AR15739
Sting—Interviews AR14619, AR14869
Sting—Profiles AR14695
Stinson, Bob—Death AR15037
Stinson, Bob—Obituary AR14675
Stipe, Michael AR14159, AR15835
Stipe, Michael—Interviews AR13424, AR13722, AR13723
Stone Free (album) AR13929
Stone Roses AR14158, AR14172, AR15425, AR15455, AR15827, AR15909
Stone Roses—Tours—Great Britain AR15428
Stone Roses—Tours—North America AR15831
Stone Temple Pilots AR12918, AR13362, AR14171, AR14194, AR14793
Stone Temple Pilots—Profiles AR14757
Stone Temple Pilots—Tours AR14170
Stone, Oliver—Films AR14338
Stone, Sharon—Profiles AR16115
Stooges AR14173, AR15026
Story AR16056
Storytellers (television show) AR15894
Stradlin, Izzy AR14301, AR14762
Stradlin, Izzy—Profiles AR13718
Straight Up (video) AR13507
Straitjacket Fits AR14717
Strange Brew (video) AR13619
Strange Days (album) AR14950
The Stranger (album) AR15405
Straw, Syd AR13457
Straw, Syd—Recordings AR14048
Street Musicians AR13575
Streisand, Barbara AR13597
Stripped (album) AR13703
Strippers AR13277
Studs (television show) AR14586, AR16126
Styx—Concerts And Tours AR14348
Sub Pop AR12993, AR15821
Sublime AR12965, AR14052
Subroc—Obituary AR13589
Subterranean Homesick Blues (video) AR14400
Suede AR13381, AR15418, AR15420
Sugar AR12918, AR14051, AR15945
Sugar—Profiles AR14718
Sugarcubes—Recordings AR13713
Sugarplastic—Fashion AR14512, AR14839, AR16057
Suggs, Donald AR13620
Sui, Anna AR13870, AR15267
Suicide AR13275, AR13276, AR13790, AR14744
Sukia AR15728
Sullivan, Randall AR13317, AR15541
Summerall, Sharon AR12966
Sun-60 AR15173
Sundance Film Festival AR15662
Sunglasses AR16080
Sunnyland Slim—Obituary AR15826
Super Deluxe AR15839
Supercop (soundtrack) AR14164
Superdrag AR15859
Supergrass—Profiles AR14836, AR15430
Supertramp—Recordings AR14885
Support Program For Abuse-Reactive Kids AR15577
Supreme Court Of The United States AR13192, AR15054
Surfing AR15996, AR16049
Surfrider Foundation (organization) AR15996
Sutcliffe, Stuart AR13210
Sutphin, Michael AR13994
Swaggart, Jimmy—Profiles AR16091
Swanson, Kristy AR14858
Sweden—Profiles AR15008
Sweeney, Julia—Fashion AR15358, AR15603
Sweet Dreams (video) AR13802
Sweet, Katrina AR14616, AR14819
Sweet Lullaby (video) AR15755
Sweet, Matthew AR12918, AR14255, AR14858, AR15555
Sweet, Matthew—Recordings AR13004
Sweet Relief II (album) AR14157
Swervedriver AR14719
Swift, Ken AR13577, AR13814
Swimming AR13610, AR14818
Switzerland AR14736
Symbionese Liberation Army AR14429, AR15752
Sympathy For The Record Industry (company) AR13366

T

T-Bone AR14285, AR15824, AR15826
T Rex—Recordings AR14958
Taj Mahal (nightclub) AR13277
Take On Me (video) AR13535
Take That AR13891, AR14052, AR15302, AR15428
Talk Soup (television show) AR15980
Talk Talk—Recordings AR14620
Talk Talk—Videos AR13551
Talking Heads AR14161, AR14167
Talking Heads—Recordings AR14904
Talking Heads—Videos AR13510, AR13563, AR14372
Tank Girl (album) AR14303
Tappan, Heidi AR13130, AR14617
Tarantino, Quentin—Films AR15979
Tarsem AR15755
Tartt, Donna AR13169
Taupin, Bernie AR13949, AR14161
Taxes AR14067
Taylor, Christopher AR15224
Taylor, James AR14026, AR15192
Taylor, James—Interviews AR14204
Taylor, James—Recordings AR15454
Taylor, Lili AR14652, AR15573
Taylor, Mel—Obituary AR13185
Teach Your Children (song) AR14027
Team Dresch AR14549
Techno Music AR13367, AR15116
Technology AR13105, AR13106, AR13113, AR13749, AR14006, AR14339, AR14664, AR15183, AR15574, AR15732, AR16076, AR16080, AR16102
Technology—Artificial Life AR13461
Technology—Cassettes AR16072
Technology—CD-I AR15731
Technology—Communications AR16068
Technology—Computers AR13118
Technology—Digital AR13034, AR13110, AR13641, AR13932, AR13940, AR13967, AR14441, AR14660, AR15565, AR15731, AR16064
Technology—Fax Machines AR16082
Technology—Sound Systems AR13638
Technology—Stereo AR16085
Technology—Television AR13107, AR13116, AR13126, AR13640, AR13642, AR13644, AR14056, AR14657, AR14658, AR15637, AR15681, AR15731, AR16062, AR16070, AR16075
Technology—Video AR15637
Technology—Video Discs AR15645
Tee, Richard—Obituary AR14024
Teenage Fanclub AR14233, AR14256
Teenage Fanclub—Profiles AR14687
Teenage Fanclub—Recordings AR13331
Teenage Gang Debs (publication) AR15395
Telephones AR13025, AR13113, AR13225, AR15252, AR15732, AR16071
TelePrompTer AR13951
Telescopes AR16102
Television AR13055, AR13140, AR14056, AR14334, AR14340, AR14583, AR14671, AR15518, AR15915, AR15960, AR15978, AR16035, AR16071, AR16080
Television—A Current Affair AR13140
Television—America Bandstand AR13572
Television—Arli$$ AR15896
Television—Beavis & Butt-Head AR14327, AR16103, AR16106, AR16107
Television—Buddies AR13178
Television—Central Park West AR15894
Television—Concrete T.V. AR14584
Television—Entertainment Tonight AR15931
Television—Exit 57 AR14508
Television—Flowbee Infomercial AR13575
Television—Goode Behavior AR15897
Television—Gulliver's Travels AR13176
Television—High Incident AR13178
Television—House Of Buggin' AR14508
Television—In Cold Blood AR15900
Television—Kids In The Hall AR13475
Television—L. A. Firefighters AR15893
Television—Late Show AR15369
Television—Love Stories AR14586
Television—Melrose Place AR13537, AR14641, AR15958
Television—Men Behaving Badly AR15924
Television—Mr. Show With Bob And David AR15987
Television—MTV's Supermodel Summit AR14703
Television—Murder One AR15899
Television—Music AR15878
Television—My So-Called Life AR13247, AR15304
Television—Mystery Science Theater 3000 AR14703
Television—NBC Nightly News AR14332
Television—New York Undercover AR13175
Television—Night Games AR14586
Television—Nightline AR15997
Television—Personals AR14586
Television—Politically Incorrect AR15953
Television—Real TV AR15900
Television—Reel Wild Cinema AR15893
Television—Rock Music AR13060, AR13079, AR13572, AR13791, AR14028, AR14139, AR14574, AR14653
Television—Saturday Night Live AR14157, AR14159
Television—Second Noah AR13177
Television—Seinfeld AR16116
Television—Sightings AR15899
Television—Sociological Aspects AR14338
Television—Storytellers AR15894
Television—Studs AR14586, AR16126
Television—Talk Soup AR15980
Television—Talk Shows AR15912
Television—Technology AR13107, AR13126, AR13640, AR13642, AR13644, AR14657, AR14658, AR15637, AR15681, AR15731, AR16062, AR16070, AR16075
Television—The Adventures Of Pete And Pete AR15889
Television—The Heights AR15963
Television—The Jeff Foxworthy Show AR16014
Television—The Larry Sanders Show AR14591
Television—The Louie Show AR13177
Television—The Newz AR14508
Television—The Partridge Family AR14703
Television—The Real World AR13164,

AR15981
Television—The Reporters AR13140
Television—The Rosie O'Donnell Show AR16010
Television—The State AR14508
Television—The Steve Harvey Show AR15898
Television—Tonight Show AR16118
Television—29 Minutes AR14779
Television—Violence AR13401, AR16035
Television—X-Files AR16016
Television—Xena AR15889
Television (1991) AR14593
Television (1992) AR14577, AR14594
Television (1993) AR14592, AR15680
Television (1994) AR15324
Television (1995) AR14588, AR15887, AR15986, AR16018
Television (1996) AR15879, AR15905, AR15969
Television (music group)—Profiles AR13440
Television (music group)—Recordings AR13752
Temple, Johnny—Computer Systems AR14276
Temple, Julien—Videos AR14296
Temptations—Recordings AR14272
10,000 Maniacs—Profiles AR13686
10,000 Maniacs—Recordings AR15998
Tennant, Neil—Interviews AR15572
Tennessee (video) AR14294
Tenuta, Judy AR15360, AR16117
Terminator X—Recordings AR13590
Terrorism AR15230
Tesh, John AR15931
Tha Dogg Pound—Recordings AR15869
Thailand AR15180
That Dog AR15937
Thayil, Kim AR15582
Thelonious Monster AR13957
Therapy? AR13919, AR14158
There's A Riot Goin' On (album) AR14960
Theresa's Sound-World (song) AR15726
Thermadore AR14599
Thermadore—Recordings AR14049
They Don't Care About Us (song) AR15832
Thiele, Bob—Obituary AR13769
Thirteen (album) AR13331
Thirty Years Of Maximum R&B (album) AR15534
This Film Is On (video) AR13613
This Is Spinal Tap (CD-ROM) AR13375
This Note's For You (video) AR14566
This Perfect World (song) AR15726
This Wheel's On Fire (book) AR13402, AR14151
Thomas, Clarence AR15595
Thomas, Michael AR13317, AR15592
Thompson, Bill AR15153
Thompson, Hunter S. AR13317, AR14523, AR15596
Thompson, Hunter S.—Interviews AR14998
Thompson, Richard AR14259
Thompson, Richard—Interviews AR13540
Thoreau, Henry David AR13057, AR13474, AR14203, AR14427
Thorn EMI AR13995
Thorn, Emily—Interviews AR15403
Thorne-Smith, Courtney AR15958
Thoroughgood, Frank AR15515
311 AR14600
311—Recordings AR15946, AR12964
Three Little Pigs (video) AR13294
Thriller (video) AR15627
Throwing Muses AR15531
The Thunder Rolls (video) AR13801
Thunder, Shelly AR13314
Thunderstruck (video) AR13031
Thurman, Uma—Films AR13339
Tibetan Freedom Concert AR15496
Ticket Scalping AR13069, AR13976
Ticketmaster (company) AR13058, AR13078, AR13092, AR14035, AR14183, AR15502, AR15515, AR15516, AR15833, AR15860
Tigrett, Isaac AR13898, AR15957
Til Tuesday—Videos AR13549
Tillis, Pam AR15568
Tim-Kerr Records AR15705
Time-Warner AR13417, AR13937, AR13993, AR14341, AR14475, AR15814, AR15831, AR15836, AR15964, AR16005
Timmons, Margo—Fashion AR14449, AR15991
Timony, Simon Fair AR13237, AR14506, AR15279
Tin Machine—Profiles AR15990
Tindersticks AR15437
Tiny Lights AR13829
Tiny Tim AR14170
Titanic Love Affair AR14720
TLC AR14498, AR15832
TLC—Profiles AR13321
Tofino AR14620
Tomei, Marisa AR13861, AR15250
Tommy (album) AR13438, AR14962
Tommy (opera) AR13438, AR15588, AR15999, AR16011
Tone Loc AR12965, AR12966
Tone-Loc—Videos AR14371
Tonight Show AR16118
Tonight, Tonight, Tonight (song) AR15355
Tony! Toni! Tone! AR12918, AR14226
Too Many Walls (song) AR13799
Toohey, Sherri—Interviews AR13857
Tool AR15862
Toots And The Maytals AR13314
Torres, Dara AR13610, AR14818
Torres, Edwin AR14610
Tortoise AR15748
Toto—Recordings AR14965
Touhouliotis, George AR14256
Tour Of A Black Planet (video) AR13619
Townshend, Peter AR13080, AR15153, AR15536, AR15588
Townshend, Peter—Concerts—London, England AR15419
Townshend, Peter—Interviews AR13431, AR15796, AR15975, AR16011
Toys AR13873, AR15169, AR15273
Traffic—Recordings AR14955
Trains AR14095
Trainspotting (soundtrack album) AR14161
Transmissions From The Planet Dog (album) AR15117
Travel AR14585, AR15011, AR15396, AR16131
Travolta, John—Interviews AR15378, AR15930
Treach AR15835
Triathlons AR14133, AR14861
Tribe 8 AR15705
A Tribe Called Quest AR12918, AR13683, AR15442, AR15452, AR15624
A Tribe Called Quest—Recordings AR14306
Tricky AR13384, AR15426, AR15438
Tritt, Travis AR15568
Troche, Rose AR13233, AR15270
Troubadour (nightclub) AR15942
Trucks, Derek AR16126
True Blue (album) AR14963
True Lies (film) AR15677
Trust (album) AR14964
Trynin, Jennifer—Recordings AR13237, AR14506, AR15279
Tsongas, Paul—Politics AR14104
Tuba Frenzy (publication) AR13729
Tucker, C. DeLores AR15445
Tucker, Maureen AR13040, AR15701
Tuff City Records AR13594
Tulane University AR14554
Turn Back (album) AR14965
Turn It Upside Down (album) AR14702
Turner, Ike AR13985
Turner, Janine AR15394
Turner, Tina AR15739
Turner, Tina—Profiles AR14518
Turnout Brothers AR14256
Turow, Scott AR15394
Tutu (album) AR14966
TV Nation (television show) AR13172
25th Anniversary Box (album) AR14266
29 Minutes (television show) AR14779
22 Jacks AR14172
Twilley, Dwight AR15944
Twist—Fashion AR13245, AR14828
Twitty, Conway—Obituary AR14628
2 Guitars Bass And Drums AR13985
2 Live Crew AR13964
2 Live Crew—Recordings AR13194, AR14476, AR15459, AR15511
Two Rooms (album) AR13949
Two Rooms (video) AR13616
Tyler, Liv—Fashion AR13256, AR14834
Tyler, Richard AR13232, AR15268
Tyler, Steven AR13523, AR15739
Tyler, Steven—Interviews AR13751
Tyner, Rob—Obituary AR14604
Tyson, Mike AR15098

U

U Roy AR13314
U2 AR14172, AR14465, AR15192, AR15505
U2—Concerts—Sydney, Australia AR14030
U2—Interviews AR13447
U2—Profiles AR13755
U2—Recordings AR13600, AR13691, AR14047, AR14168, AR14526, AR14954, AR14968, AR15453, AR15832
U2—Tours AR13934
U2—Tours—North America AR13996
U2—Tours—World AR14024
U2—Videos AR13821, AR14292, AR14415
U2: The Rolling Stone Files (book) AR13180
UB40—Recordings AR15834
Udris, David—Fashion AR14512, AR14839, AR16057
Udris, Michael—Fashion AR14512, AR14839, AR16057
UFOs AR14345
Ugly Kid Joe AR14003
Ugly Things (publication) AR13729
U.K.-L.A. Festival 1994 AR15945
Ukraine AR15010
Ulrich, Lars AR12977
Ulrich, Lars—Interviews AR13720
Undercover Of The Night (video) AR14378
Undertones—Recordings AR13313
Underworld AR15213
Unfinished Sympathy (video) AR14124
The Unforgettable Fire (album) AR14526
Unions AR14079, AR15464, AR15707
United Nations AR14999
United Steelworkers Of America AR15464, AR15707
Universal Studios—Orlando, Florida AR14051
University Of California Bears AR13574
University Of Minnesota AR14554
University Of Pennsylvania AR13330, AR15478
University Of Texas AR12917
Until The End Of The World (film) AR14496
Urb (publication) AR15115

Urbus Orbis (coffeehouse) AR14420
Urge Overkill AR12918, AR14286, AR15325
Urge Overkill—Profiles AR14701
Us (album) AR13815
Us And Them (album) AR15705
Use Your Illusion I (album) AR14130
Usenet Newsgroups AR15580
Utensil AR13753
Utter Confusion AR13579

V

V, Chuckie—Fashion AR13217
Van Damme, Jean-Claude AR13169
Van Halen AR14163, AR14170, AR15383
Van Halen—Recordings AR14168, AR14931, AR16003
Van Halen—Videos AR13569, AR14569
Van Halen, Alex AR14542
Van Halen, Eddie—Interviews AR15875
Van Meter, Jonathan AR13443, AR14382
Van Peebles, Mario—Interviews AR15661
Van Peebles, Melvin AR14287, AR15829
Van Sant, Gus AR13854
Van Sant, Gus—Films AR14135
Van Seenus AR14511, AR14827, AR15490
Vanilla Ice—Recordings AR13328
Vasquez, Junior AR13266, AR14051, AR14857
Vasquez, Junior—Fashion AR13266, AR14857
Vaughan, Stevie Ray AR13976
Vaughan, Stevie Ray—Tributes AR14627
Vaughan, Stevie Ray—Videos AR13616
Vedder, Eddie AR13523, AR15170, AR15513, AR15984
Vedder, Eddie—Profiles AR13095, AR13285, AR14195
Veg AR15939
Vega, Suzanne AR12959
Vega, Suzanne—Recordings AR14156
Veldt AR13671
Velocity Girl AR13904
Velvet Crush AR14726
Velvet Underground AR13524, AR13761, AR14244, AR15026, AR15031
Velvet Underground—Concerts AR13731
Velvet Underground—Profiles AR13757
Velvet Underground—Recordings AR14967, AR15606
Velvet Underground And Nico (album) AR14967, AR15606
Verlaine, Tom—Recordings AR13985
Veruca Salt AR13396, AR13517, AR13582, AR14548, AR14683, AR14794, AR15771
Verve AR14793, AR15204, AR15836
Verve Pipe AR15721
VH1 (television network) AR15878
Vibe (publication) AR13443, AR14382
Victor, Jessica AR13854
Video AR15637
Video Cameras AR13100, AR13112, AR16070, AR16073, AR16078, AR16082, AR16084, AR16102
Video Discs AR15639, AR15645, AR15724
Video Discs—Players AR16075
Video Games AR13100, AR13893, AR14655, AR14658, AR14666, AR15308, AR15391
Video Mixers AR13108
Video Projectors AR16102
Video Recorders AR13112, AR13113, AR13642, AR15736, AR16070, AR16075
Videotapes AR15724, AR16070
Vietnam AR13249, AR15000, AR15306
Vietnam—Refugees AR15333
Vietnam War AR14140, AR15000
Vietnam War—Veterans AR14140, AR15457
Vig, Butch AR14256, AR15726, AR16126
Vigil, Selene—Interviews AR13547
Vinge, Vernor—Interviews AR13460
Vinie—Computer Systems AR14276
Violence AR13226, AR13273, AR13286, AR13432, AR13611, AR13684, AR13859, AR14059, AR14150, AR14246, AR14331, AR14342, AR14481, AR14490, AR14635, AR15059, AR15073, AR15138, AR15247, AR15254, AR15540, AR15583, AR15712, AR15713, AR16031
Violence—Rock Festivals AR14723, AR14770
Violence—Rock Music AR12943, AR13068, AR13614, AR13949, AR14479, AR14486, AR14770, AR14774, AR14787, AR15233, AR15234
Violence—Television AR13401, AR16035
Viper Room (nightclub) AR15939, AR15942
Virgin Music Group AR13993
Virgin Records AR13934, AR13995, AR14025, AR14478, AR15172, AR15428
Vitamins AR16036
Vogt, Ali AR15402
Vogue (video) AR13566
Voices Carry (video) AR13549
Vollmann, William T. AR14382
Volunteers AR13476
Voodoo Glow Skulls AR12964, AR15946
Voodoo Glow Skulls—Fashion AR13365, AR14840
Voting AR14041, AR14159, AR14257
Vreeland, Diana AR15096

W

Wailer, Bunny AR13314
Wailers—Recordings AR14888
Waits, Tom AR15519
Waits, Tom—Recordings AR13985, AR14906
Waking Up The Neighbors (album) AR13945
Wal-Mart (company) AR13081, AR13571, AR15589
Walden Woods AR13057, AR13474, AR14203, AR14427, AR15920, AR15966
Walden, Diane Lyn AR15542, AR15543
Walk On The Wild Side (song) AR15355
Walk This Way (video) AR15616
Walker, Junior—Obituary AR14218
Walker, Scott AR15427
Walker, Wyatt Tee AR14059
The Wall (album) AR15092
Wallflowers AR14156
Walt Mink AR13017
Walters, Happy AR15836
War—Recordings AR14595
War (album) AR14968
Wareham, Dean AR15737
Warhol, Andy AR14595, AR15096
Warner Brothers AR14732
Warner Brothers Records AR13986, AR14341, AR14642, AR15520, AR15822, AR15835, AR15836, AR16006
Warner Music Group AR15829, AR15835, AR15836, AR15964, AR16005
Waronker, Lenny AR14642, AR15835
Warp Records AR14124
Warren G AR13926, AR14794
Warren, Earle—Obituary AR15515
Warwick, Dionne AR15505
Was (Not Was)—Recordings AR13985
Was, Don AR13196, AR15170, AR15984
Was, Don—Films AR13205, AR13970
Washington—Censorship AR13047, AR13963, AR13982, AR14381, AR14476
Washington, Denzel—Films AR16087
Washington, Denzel—Interviews AR16086
Washington, Dinah AR13771, AR13784, AR15170, AR15984
Wasps' Nest (album) AR13002
Wasserman, Rob AR12959
Watches AR15212, AR15482, AR16081, AR16082
Watchman AR13018
Waterboys—Recordings AR13849, AR15093
Watergate AR13411, AR13412, AR15597
Waterman, Chris AR16123
Waters, John AR15096
Waters, Roger—Recordings AR13699
Watley, Jody AR14481
Watson, Albert AR15739
Watson, Albert—Videos AR14293
Watson, Johnny—Obituary AR15194
Watt, Ben AR14168, AR15819
Watt, Mel—Politics AR13036
Watt, Mike—Computer Systems AR14276
Watt, Mike—Recordings AR13462
Watt, Mike—Tours—North America AR13670
Watts, Charlie—Interviews AR13453
Waugh, Bob AR14256
Wax Trax! Records AR15118
Wayne's World (film) AR16101
We Come Strapped (album) AR15773
Weasels Ripped My Flesh (album) AR14969
Webb, Jimmy—Recordings AR12972
Weber, Bruce AR14221, AR15742
Weber, Bruce—Videos AR14293
Weber, Frank AR13963, AR14031, AR14763
WEDG (radio station) AR13681
Wedowee, Alabama AR14305, AR15413, AR15708
Ween—Interviews AR13410
Weezer AR14165, AR14557, AR15832
Weezer—Profiles AR15702
Weiland AR14194, AR15831, AR15863
Weiland—Interviews AR14729
Weinberg, Jay AR14095
Weinberg, Max AR14030
Weinbrecht, Donna AR13323, AR14856
Weinstein, Deena AR16123
Weir, Bob AR13382, AR15481
Weir, David AR13317, AR14429, AR15752
Weird TV (television show) AR15892
Weiss, Rob—Fashion AR16007
Welcome To My Nightmare (album) AR14970
Weld (album) AR13725, AR13994
Weld (video) AR13616
Welfare AR14092
Wells, Kitty AR13847, AR15382
Wells, Mary—Obituary AR14483
Wenders, Wim—Films AR14496
Wenders, Wim—Videos AR14415
Wenner, Jann AR13523, AR15153
We're Only In It For The Money (album) AR14971
Wertheimer, Alfred AR14221
West Des Moines, Iowa AR15803
Westerberg, Paul AR12919
Westerberg, Paul—Concerts—Los Angeles, California AR15937
Westerberg, Paul—Interviews AR14672, AR15973
Westerberg, Paul—Recordings AR15734
Wexler, Jerry—Profiles AR15193, AR15804
Weymouth, Tina AR15805
Whale—Videos AR14365
What's Going On (album) AR14241
When I Think Of You (video) AR13513
Whenever We Wanted (album) AR13823
Where Is Joe Merchant? (book) AR13155
Whip It (video) AR14377
Whitaker, Lisa AR15402
White Album (album) AR14144, AR14510, AR14951
White Wedding (video) AR14568

White Zombie AR12919, AR13394
White, Barry—Interviews AR13490
White, Mark AR12977
White, Robert—Obituary AR15751
White, Timothy AR13318
Whiteside, Everett AR15477
Whitley, Chris AR12976
Whitman, Walt AR13389
Who AR14165, AR14273
Who—CD-ROMs AR15516
Who—Concerts—London, England AR14160
Who—Recordings AR14270, AR14272, AR14962, AR14972, AR15534
Who Will Tell The People (book) AR14069
Whodini—Recordings AR13590
Whooliganz—Tours—North America AR15448
Who's Next (album) AR14972
Why Do Fools Fall In Love (song) AR13973
Wichita, Kansas AR15811
Wicked Game (video) AR13822
Widespread Panic AR13899, AR15351
Wiener, Jon AR14476
Wilbur, Jay—Interviews AR14044
Wilco AR13083, AR14192
Wild Colonials AR15937
Wild, David AR13310, AR13318
Wild Thing (video) AR14371
Wilder, Alan AR15831
Wilder, Doug—Politics AR14639
Wildwood, New Jersey AR14337
Wilhelm, David—Profiles AR14068
Williams, Marion AR13435, AR13624
Williams, Marion—Obituary AR15187
Williams, Paul AR13959
Williams, Robbie AR15428
Williams, Robin AR15360, AR15972, AR16117
Williams, Tony AR15154
Williams, Vanessa AR14481
Williams, Victoria AR12919, AR15171
Williams, Victoria—Recordings AR15104
Williams, Wendy AR14801, AR15693
Williams, Wendy—Fashion AR14801, AR15693
Williams-Chappel, Fiona—Obituary AR14808
Willie Nelson Twisted (album) AR12925
Willis, Kelly—Fashion AR14847, AR15359
Wilmington, North Carolina AR15134
Wilsey, James Calvin AR13943
Wilsey, Shannon—Profiles AR16047
Wilson, Brian AR15223, AR15510, AR15961
Wilson, Brian—Films AR13173, AR13205, AR13970
Wilson, Brian—Interviews AR13625
Wilson, Brian—Recordings AR13965
Wilson, Cassandra AR13235, AR14826, AR15275
Wilson, Cassandra—Fashion AR13235, AR14826, AR15275
Wilson, Mary AR15508
Wilson, Mike—Interviews AR14044
Wilson Phillips—Recordings AR16013
Windle, Patricia—Profiles AR15458
Wink, Josh AR13151
Winston, Clifford AR13537, AR14641
Winters, Jonathan AR15360, AR16117
Winwood, Steve AR15739
Winwood, Steve—Recordings AR14879
Wiseman, Bob AR15093
Wish You Were Here (album) AR14973
With The Beatles (album) AR14974
Woldemariam, Phillip AR13927, AR15866
Wolf, Peter AR15943
Wolfe, Tom AR13317, AR15798, AR16060
Wolman, Baron AR14221
Wolves AR14527
WOMAD (organization) AR13583, AR14207, AR14558, AR15431
Women AR12933, AR13687, AR13907, AR14246, AR15699, AR15701
Women Politicians AR16030
Wonder, Stevie AR13524, AR15031
Wonder, Stevie—Profiles AR15197
Wonder, Stevie—Recordings AR14919, AR15136
Woo, John AR13871, AR15269
Wood, Andy AR12993
Wood, Ron AR14160
Wood, Ron—Interviews AR13545
Wood, Ron—Recordings AR13953, AR14167
Woodard, Jeff AR16130
Woodstock AR14208
Woodstock (film) AR13026
Woodstock '94 AR14017, AR14643, AR14644, AR14645, AR15769
Woodstock Ventures AR14208
Woodward, Fred AR14873
Woodward, Fred—Videos AR14293
Wool Gathering (book) AR13957
Woolsey, Lynn—Politics AR13036
Woolsey, R. James AR14091
WORK Records AR15824
Workers: An Archaeology Of The Industrial Age (book) AR15345, AR16045
Workingman's Dead (album) AR13028
Workplace AR14796
Worl-A-Girl AR13396, AR13517, AR13582, AR14548, AR14683
World Health Organization AR15181
World Music AR13315, AR15462, AR16123
World Population AR14142
World Wide Web AR14008, AR14009, AR14010, AR14016, AR14129, AR14212, AR14278, AR14279, AR14458, AR14665, AR14667, AR14985, AR14986, AR15018, AR15579, AR15729, AR16069, AR16077
Worthington, Trace—Fashion AR13324, AR14860
Wozniak, Steve AR14012, AR14013
Wreckx-n-Effect AR14232, AR15384
Wreckx-n-Effect—Fashion AR14232, AR15384
Wright, Johnny AR13847, AR15382
Wright, Lawrence AR13317, AR16091
Wright, Tony AR14873
Wu Tang Clan AR13590, AR15512
Wu Tang Clan—Recordings AR13628
Wu, Jennifer S. AR15017
WUFX (radio station) AR13681
Wyatt, Barbara AR15492
Wyman, Bill AR14500
Wyndorf, Dave—Interviews AR15237
Wynette, Tammy AR13847, AR15382

X

X AR14613, AR15936
X—Recordings AR14926
X, Malcolm AR15067
X-Files (television show) AR16016, AR16017
X-Pensive Winos—Videos AR13616
Xenz (television show) AR15889
Xplora 1 (CD-ROM) AR13932
XTC AR15834
Xu, Li AR15017

Y

Yahoo (software) AR15729
Yakuza (publication) AR13730
Yale University AR13213, AR14812, AR16126
Yang, Jerry AR15729
Yang, Ne Yeng AR15330, AR15711
Yang, Xou AR15330, AR15711
Yankovic, Al AR16097
Yankovic, Al—Videos AR13029, AR14570
Yardbirds AR13770, AR14705
Yatsura AR15865
Yearwood, Trisha AR12977
Yes—Recordings AR14940
Yo-Yo AR14481
Yoakum, Dwight—Profiles AR15364
Yothu Yindi AR13694
You Might Think (video) AR13032
Young, Charles M. AR13317, AR16109
Young Disciples AR14791
Young MC AR15394
Young, Neil AR13295, AR13523, AR13761, AR13782, AR14027, AR14161, AR14244, AR14705, AR15739, AR15825
Young, Neil—Interviews AR14199
Young, Neil—Profiles AR14471
Young, Neil—Recordings AR13725, AR13994, AR14270, AR14471, AR15824
Young, Neil—Tours—North America AR15517
Young, Neil—Videos AR13616, AR14566
Young Rascals AR14128
Yow, David AR14287, AR15836, AR16111
Yoyo A Go Go AR14611
Yugoslavia AR13141
Yugoslavia—Photography AR15341
Yugoslavia—Politics AR13165, AR14985, AR15002, AR15077, AR15539
Yum-Yum—Recordings AR13459

Z

Z Z Top AR14476
Z Z Top—Recordings AR13982
Zaire AR14134, AR14521, AR15339, AR15343
Zapata, Mia AR15088, AR15455, AR15827
Zapata, Mia—Obituary AR15085
Zappa, Frank AR13295, AR13523, AR13761, AR13782, AR14754, AR16019
Zappa, Frank—Discographies AR15558
Zappa, Frank—Obituary AR13708
Zappa, Frank—Recordings AR14969, AR14971, AR15393
Zappa, Gail AR15822
Zappa, Moon Unit AR13523
Zard, David AR13953
Zehme, Bill AR13317, AR16120
Zehr, Mindy—Fashion AR13365, AR14840
Zellar, Martin AR14168
Zero Tolerance For Silence (album) AR14388
Zevon, Warren—Recordings AR14262
Zimmerman, Gary AR13936
Zinn, Howard—Interviews AR16105
Zombie, Rob—Interviews AR15151
Zoo Records AR13980
Zooropa (album) AR13691
Zuckerman, Mort AR14427, AR15966
Zug, Switzerland AR15464, AR15707
Zuniga, Daphne AR15958

Book Reviews

A

ALL YOU NEED IS EARS (Martin, George)
BR01040 698-699 (December 29, 1994) pp63-65. (Coleman, Mark)
AMERICAN LABOR STRUGGLES (Yellen, Samuel)
BR01041 745 (October 17, 1996) p94. (Zinn, Howard)
THE ART OF WAR (Tzu, Sun)
BR01042 679 (April 7, 1994) p30. (Hoon, Shannon)
AS NASTY AS THEY WANNA BE (Campbell, Luther/Miller, John R.)
BR01043 668 (October 28, 1993) p26. (DeCurtis, Anthony)
AWOPBOPALOOBOP: THE GOLDEN AGE OF ROCK (Cohn, Nik)
BR01044 750-751 (December 26, 1996) p196. (Coleman, Mark)

B

BABES IN TOYLAND: THE MAKING AND SELLING OF A ROCK AND ROLL BAND (Karlen, Neal)
BR01045 692 (October 6, 1994) p37. (Damsker, Matt)
BR01046 698-699 (December 29, 1994) pp63-65. (Coleman, Mark)
THE BIBLE
BR01047 669 (November 11, 1993) p20. (Kravitz, Lenny)
BIG PICTURES (Rolston, Matthew)
BR01048 616 (October 31, 1991) p99. (Frascella, Lawrence)
BILL GRAHAM PRESENTS (Graham, Bill/Greenfield, Robert)
BR01049 662 (August 5, 1993) p24. (DeCurtis, Anthony)
BLACK MONK TIME (Klemke, Anita/Shaw, Thomas Edward)
BR01050 712-713 (July 13, 1995) p42. (George-Warren, Holly)
BLACK NOISE (Rose, Tricia)
BR01051 698-699 (December 29, 1994) pp63-65. (Coleman, Mark)
BLUES ALL AROUND ME (King, B. B./Ritz, David)
BR01052 750-751 (December 26, 1996) p196. (Coleman, Mark)
BOB DYLAN: THE RECORDING SESSIONS (1960-1994) (Heylin, Clinton)
BR01053 750-751 (December 26, 1996) p196. (Coleman, Mark)
THE BOWIE COMPANION (Gutman, David/Thomson, Elizabeth)
BR01054 750-751 (December 26, 1996) p196. (Coleman, Mark)
BURY MY HEART AT WOUNDED KNEE (Brown, Dee)
BR01055 745 (October 17, 1996) p94. (Zinn, Howard)

C

COME AS YOU ARE: THE STORY OF NIRVANA (Azerrad, Michael)
BR01056 666 (September 30, 1993) p15. (Mundy, Chris)
CONFUSION IS NEXT (Foege, Alec)
BR01057 698-699 (December 29, 1994) pp63-65. (Coleman, Mark)
THE CORAL SEA (Smith, Patti)
BR01058 750-751 (December 26, 1996) p196. (Coleman, Mark)
COUNTRY: THE TWISTED ROOTS OF ROCK & ROLL (Tosches, Nick)
BR01059 750-751 (December 26, 1996) p196. (Coleman, Mark)

D

DARK STAR (Greenfield, Robert)
BR01060 750-751 (December 26, 1996) p196. (Coleman, Mark)
THE DARK STUFF (Kent, Nick)
BR01061 727 (February 8, 1996) p51. (Hunter, James)
DIARY OF A DRUG FIEND (Crowley, Aleister)
BR01062 686-687 (July 14, 1994) p32. (Nicks, Stevie)
A DIFFERENT MIRROR (Takaki, Ron)
BR01063 745 (October 17, 1996) p94. (Zinn, Howard)

E

EARLY WORK (Smith, Patti)
BR01064 698-699 (December 29, 1994) pp63-65. (Coleman, Mark)
ENGLAND'S DREAMING: ANARCHY, SEX PISTOLS, PUNK ROCK AND BEYOND (Savage, Jon)
BR01065 630 (May 14, 1992) p114. (Fricke, David)

F

FACING WEST (Drinnon, Richard)
BR01066 745 (October 17, 1996) p94. (Zinn, Howard)
FAITHFULL (Faithfull, Marianne)
BR01067 698-699 (December 29, 1994) pp63-65. (Coleman, Mark)
THE FEMALE EXPERIENCE (Lerner, Gerda)
BR01068 745 (October 17, 1996) p94. (Zinn, Howard)
FIVE HUNDRED YEARS OF CHICANO HISTORY IN PICTURES (Martinez, Elizabeth)
BR01069 745 (October 17, 1996) p94. (Zinn, Howard)
FROM METAL TO MOZART (Heller, Chris)
BR01070 693 (October 20, 1994) p51. (Richardson, Susan)

G

GLIMPSES (Shiner, Lewis)
BR01071 679 (April 7, 1994) p29. (Damsker, Matt)
GO, CAT GO! (McGee, David/Perkins, Carl)
BR01072 750-751 (December 26, 1996) p196. (Coleman, Mark)
GOING DOWN WITH JANIS (Caserta, Peggy)
BR01073 668 (October 28, 1993) p26. (DeCurtis, Anthony)
THE GRAVEST SHOW ON EARTH (Burkett, Elinor)
BR01074 722 (November 30, 1995) p77. (Love, Robert)
THE GUINNESS ENCYCLOPEDIA OF POPULAR MUSIC (Larkin, Carol)
BR01075 656 (May 13, 1993) p26. (Robbins, Ira)
GUNS N' ROSES: THE PHOTOGRAPHIC HISTORY (John, Robert)
BR01076 663 (August 19, 1993) p19. (Neely, Kim)

H

HANK WILLIAMS: THE BIOGRAPHY (Escott, Colin)
BR01077 698-699 (December 29, 1994) pp63-65. (Coleman, Mark)
HOLE IN OUR SOLE (Bayles, Martha)
BR01078 698-699 (December 29, 1994) pp63-65. (Coleman, Mark)
HOLLYWOOD ROCK (Crenshaw, Marshall)
BR01079 690 (September 8, 1994) p38. (Weisel, Al)

I

THE ILIAD (Homer)
BR01080 689 (August 25, 1994) p34. (Barron, Chris)

J

JESUS' SON (Johnson, Denis)
BR01081 662 (August 5, 1993) p24. (DeCurtis, Anthony)
JIMI HENDRIX: ELECTRIC GYPSY (Glebbeek, Caesar/Shapiro, Harry)
BR01082 615 (October 17, 1991) p105. (Fricke, David)

L

THE L. A. MUSICAL HISTORY TOUR (Fein, Art)
BR01083 615 (October 17, 1991) p105. (Fricke, David)
LAST TRAIN TO MEMPHIS (Guralnick, Peter)
BR01084 698-699 (December 29, 1994) pp63-65. (Coleman, Mark)
LIES MY TEACHER TOLD ME (Loewen, James W.)
BR01085 745 (October 17, 1996) p94. (Zinn, Howard)
LOUIE LOUIE (Marsh, Dave)
BR01086 664 (September 2, 1993) p20. (Kenny, Glenn)
LUSH LIFE (Hajdu, David)
BR01087 750-751 (December 26, 1996) p196. (Coleman, Mark)

M

MAN ENOUGH TO BE A WOMAN (County, Jayne)
BR01088 734 (May 16, 1996) p64. (Van Parys, Bill)
MONSTER (Shakur, Sanyika)
BR01089 682 (May 19, 1994) p21. (Queen Latifah)

N

THE NEAREST FARAWAY PLACE (White, Timothy)
BR01090 707 (May 4, 1995) p33. (Damsker, Matt)
NONVIOLENCE IN AMERICA (Lynd, Alice/Lynd, Staughton)
BR01091 745 (October 17, 1996) p94. (Zinn, Howard)
NUEVA OLA PORTORICENSIS (Santiago, Javier)
BR01092 709 (June 1, 1995) p62. (McLane, Daisann)

O

OFF THE CHARTS (Haring, Bruce)
BR01093 740 (August 8, 1996) p60. (Cross, Charles R.)
OPEN VIEWS OF LATIN AMERICA (Galeano, Eduardo)
BR01094 745 (October 17, 1996) p94. (Zinn, Howard)
ORANGES ARE NOT THE ONLY FRUIT (Winterson, Jeanette)
BR01095 678 (March 24, 1994) p16. (Donelly, Tanya)

P

PLAYING IT STRAIGHT (Dodd, David)
BR01096 750-751 (December 26, 1996) p196. (Coleman, Mark)
PLEASE KILL ME (McCain, Gillian/McNeil, Legs)
BR01097 737 (June 27, 1996) p55. (Schruers, Fred)
BR01098 750-751 (December 26, 1996) p196. (Coleman, Mark)
POLAROIDS FROM THE DEAD (Coupland, Douglas)
BR01099 738-739 (July 11, 1996) p90. (DeRogatis, Jim)
POSSESSING THE SECRET OF JOY (Walker, Alice)
BR01100 681 (May 5, 1994) p16. (Amos, Tori)
PUNK DIARY 1970-1979 (Gimarc, George)
BR01101 690 (September 8, 1994) p38. (Van Parys, Bill)

R

RAGE TO SURVIVE (James, Etta/Ritz, David)
BR01102 720 (November 2, 1995) p33. (Richardson, Susan)
RANTERS AND CROWD PLEASERS: PUNK IN POP MUSIC 1977-92 (Marcus, Greil)
BR01103 658 (June 10, 1993) p33. (Damsker, Matt)
RIDING THE YELLOW TROLLEY CAR (Kennedy, William)
BR01104 666 (September 30, 1993) p18. (Wild, David)
RINGOLEVIO (Grogan, Emmett)
BR01105 684 (June 16, 1994) p24. (Moore, Thurston)
ROCK & ROLL COOKBOOK (Des Barres, Pamela/St. John, Dick/St. John, Sandy)
BR01106 670 (November 25, 1993) p19. (Dunn, Jancee)
ROCK & ROLL TRAVELER USA (Glinert, Ed/Perry, Jim)
BR01107 748 (November 28, 1996) p44. (Brackett, Nathan)
ROCK SHE WROTE (McDowell, Evelyn/Powers, Ann)
BR01108 723 (December 14, 1995) p96. (Coleman, Mark)
ROCK: THE ROUGH GUIDE
BR01109 748 (November 28, 1996) p44. (Brackett, Nathan)
ROTTEN: NO IRISH—NO BLACKS—NO DOGS (Lyden, John/Zimmerman, Keith/Zimmerman, Kent)
BR01110 680 (April 21, 1994) p28. (Damsker, Matt)
ROUTE 666: ON THE ROAD TO NIRVANA (Arnold, Gina)
BR01111 665 (September 16, 1993) p25. (Damsker, Matt)
RUNNING WITH THE DEVIL (Walser, Robert)
BR01112 669 (November 11, 1993) p24. (Powers, Ann)
THE RUSHDIE LETTERS
BR01113 676 (February 24, 1994) p17. (Browne, Jackson)

S

SCREAMING LIFE (Peterson, Charles)
BR01114 724-725 (December 28, 1995) p128. (Coleman, Mark)
SESSIONS! (Seeff, Norman)
BR01115 698-699 (December 29, 1994) pp63-65. (Coleman, Mark)
SHE'S A REBEL (Gaar, Gillian G.)
BR01116 652 (March 18, 1993) p30. (Gardner, Elysa)
SKELETON KEY (Shenk, David/Silberman, Steve)
BR01117 693 (October 20, 1994) p43. (Futterman, Steve)
STAN GETZ: A LIFE IN JAZZ (Maggin, Donald L.)
BR01118 750-751 (December 26, 1996) p196. (Coleman, Mark)
STIFFED: A TRUE STORY OF MCA, THE MUSIC BUSINESS, AND THE MAFIA (Knoedelseder, William)
BR01119 656 (May 13, 1993) p26. (Soocher, Stan)
STORY OF THE EYE (Bataille, Georges)
BR01120 683 (June 2, 1994) p20. (Gudmundsdottir, Bjork)
SUMMER OF LOVE (Selvin, Joel)
BR01121 697 (December 15, 1994) p41. (Damsker, Matt)

T

TAKE ANOTHER LITTLE PIECE OF MY HEART (Des Barres, Pamela)
BR01122 652 (March 18, 1993) p30. (Gardner, Elysa)
TARANTULA (Dylan, Bob)
BR01123 679 (April 7, 1994) p29. (Damsker, Matt)
THIS WHEEL'S ON FIRE (Helm, Levon)
BR01124 698-699 (December 29, 1994) pp63-65. (Coleman, Mark)

TO BE LOVED (Gordy, Berry)
BR01125 698-699 (December 29, 1994) pp63-65. (Coleman, Mark)

U

UNDER A HOODOO MOON (Dr. John)
BR01126 698-699 (December 29, 1994) pp63-65. (Coleman, Mark)

V

THE VIETNAM WARS (Young, Marilyn)
BR01127 745 (October 17, 1996) p94. (Zinn, Howard)
VINDICATION (Sherwood, Frances)
BR01128 686-687 (July 14, 1994) p32. (Nicks, Stevie)
VOICES OF FREEDOM (Fayer, Steve/Hampton, Henry)
BR01129 745 (October 17, 1996) p94. (Zinn, Howard)

W

WAITING FOR THE SUN (Hoskyns, Barney)
BR01130 750-751 (December 26, 1996) p196. (Coleman, Mark)
WAYLON: AN AUTOBIOGRAPHY (Jennings, Waylon/Kaye, Lenny)
BR01131 750-751 (December 26, 1996) p196. (Coleman, Mark)
THE WHITE HOTEL (Thomas, D. M.)
BR01132 680 (April 21, 1994) p21. (Hutchence, Michael)
THE WORLD OF ZINES (Gunderloy, Mike/Janice, Cari Goldberg)
BR01133 660-661 (July 8, 1993) p20. (Fricke, David)

X

X-RAY (Davies, Ray)
BR01134 721 (November 16, 1995) p34. (Wild, David)

Y

YOU SEND ME (Wolff, Daniel)
BR01135 701 (February 9, 1995) p28. (Richardson, Susan)

Author Index to Book Reviews

A

Arnold, Gina BR01111
Azerrad, Michael BR01056

B

Bataille, Georges BR01120
Bayles, Martha BR01078
Brown, Dee BR01055
Burkett, Elinor BR01074

C

Campbell, Luther BR01043
Caserta, Peggy BR01073
Cohn, Nik BR01044
County, Jayne BR01088
Coupland, Douglas BR01099
Crenshaw, Marshall BR01079
Crowley, Aleister BR01062

D

Davies, Ray BR01134
Des Barres, Pamela BR01106, BR01122
Dodd, David BR01096
Dr. John BR01126
Drinnon, Richard BR01066
Dylan, Bob BR01123

E

Escott, Colin BR01077

F

Faithfull, Marianne BR01067
Fayer, Steve BR01129
Fein, Art BR01083
Foege, Alec BR01057

G

Gaar, Gillian G. BR01116
Galeano, Eduardo BR01094
Gimarc, George BR01101
Glebbeek, Caesar BR01082
Glinert, Ed BR01107
Gordy, Berry BR01125
Graham, Bill BR01049
Greenfield, Robert BR01060
Grogan, Emmett BR01105
Gunderloy, Mike BR01133
Guralnick, Peter BR01084
Gutman, David BR01054

H

Hajdu, David BR01087
Hampton, Henry BR01129
Haring, Bruce BR01093
Heller, Chris BR01070
Helm, Levon BR01124
Heylin, Clinton BR01053
Homer BR01080
Hoskyns, Barney BR01130

J

James, Etta BR01102
Janice, Cari Goldberg BR01133
Jennings, Waylon BR01131
John, Robert BR01076
Johnson, Denis BR01081

K

Karlen, Neal BR01045, BR01046
Kaye, Lenny BR01131
Kennedy, William BR01104
Kent, Nick BR01061
King, B. B. BR01052
Klemke, Anita BR01050
Knoedelseder, William BR01119

L

Larkin, Carol BR01075
Lerner, Gerda BR01068
Loewen, James W. BR01085
Lyden, John BR01110
Lynd, Alice BR01091

M

Maggin, Donald L. BR01118
Marcus, Greil BR01103
Marsh, Dave BR01086
Martin, George BR01040
Martinez, Elizabeth BR01069
McCain, Gillian BR01097, BR01098
McDowell, Evelyn BR01108
McGee, David BR01072
McNeil, Legs BR01097, BR01098
Miller, John R. BR01043

P

Perkins, Carl BR01072
Perry, Jim BR01107
Peterson, Charles BR01114
Powers, Ann BR01108

R

Ritz, David BR01052, BR01102
Rolston, Matthew BR01048
Rose, Tricia BR01051

S

Santiago, Javier BR01092
Savage, Jon BR01065
Seeff, Norman BR01115
Selvin, Joel BR01121
Shakur, Sanyika BR01089
Shapiro, Harry BR01082
Shaw, Thomas Edward BR01050
Shenk, David BR01117
Sherwood, Frances BR01128
Shiner, Lewis BR01071
Silberman, Steve BR01117
Smith, Patti BR01058, BR01064
St. John, Dick BR01106

T

Takaki, Ron BR01063
Thomas, D. M. BR01132
Thomson, Elizabeth BR01054
Tosches, Nick BR01059
Tzu, Sun BR01042

W

Walker, Alice BR01100
Walser, Robert BR01112
White, Timothy BR01090
Winterson, Jeanette BR01095
Wolff, Daniel BR01135

Y

Yellen, Samuel BR01041
Young, Marilyn BR01127
Zimmerman, Keith BR01110

Reviewer Index to Book Reviews

A

Amos, Tori BR01100

B

Barron, Chris BR01080
Brackett, Nathan BR01107, BR01109
Browne, Jackson BR01113

C

Coleman, Mark BR01040, BR01044, BR01046, BR01051, BR01052, BR01053, BR01054, BR01057, BR01058, BR01059, BR01060, BR01064, BR01067, BR01072, BR01077, BR01078, BR01084, BR01087, BR01096, BR01098, BR01108, BR01114, BR01115, BR01118, BR01124, BR01125, BR01126, BR01130, BR01131
Cross, Charles R. BR01093

D

Damsker, Matt BR01045, BR01071, BR01090, BR01103, BR01110, BR01111, BR01121, BR01123
DeCurtis, Anthony BR01043, BR01049, BR01073, BR01081
DeRogatis, Jim BR01099
Donelly, Tanya BR01095
Dunn, Jancee BR01106

F

Frascella, Lawrence BR01048
Fricke, David BR01065, BR01082, BR01083, BR01133
Futterman, Steve BR01117

G

Gardner, Elysa BR01116, BR01122
George-Warren, Holly BR01050
Gudmundsdottir, Bjork BR01120

H

Hoon, Shannon BR01042
Hunter, James BR01061
Hutchence, Michael BR01132

K

Kenny, Glenn BR01086
Kravitz, Lenny BR01047

L

Love, Robert BR01074

M

McLane, Daisann BR01092
Moore, Thurston BR01105
Mundy, Chris BR01056

N

Neely, Kim BR01076
Nicks, Stevie BR01062, BR01128

P

Powers, Ann BR01112

Q

Queen Latifah BR01089

R

Richardson, Susan BR01070, BR01102, BR01135
Robbins, Ira BR01075

S

Schruers, Fred BR01097
Soocher, Stan BR01119

V

Van Parys, Bill BR01088, BR01101

W

Weisel, Al BR01079
Wild, David BR01104, BR01134

Z

Zinn, Howard BR01041, BR01055, BR01063, BR01066, BR01068, BR01069, BR01085, BR01091, BR01094, BR01127, BR01129

Concert Reviews

A

ADAMS, BRYAN

CR00634 Robbins, Ira. "Bryan Adams. " 625 (March 5, 1992) p25.

AEROSMITH

CR00635 Milward, John. "Aerosmith: Albany, N.Y." 669 (November 11, 1993) p25.

AFGHAN WHIGS

CR00636 Panahpour, Nilou. "Afghan Whigs: Washington." 684 (June 16, 1994) p32.

ALICE IN CHAINS

CR00637 Puterbaugh, Parke. "Van Halen." 615 (October 17, 1991) p34.

B

B-52S

CR00638 Gardner, Elysa. "The B-52s, Juliana Hatfield: Radio City Music Hall." 652 (March 18, 1993) p27.

BASH AND POP

CR00639 McLeese, Don. "Paul Westerberg—Bash And Pop: Austin, Texas." 666 (September 30, 1993) p20.

BATS

CR00640 Goldberg, Michael. "Straitjacket Fits—The Bats—The Jean-Paul Sarte Experience: San Francisco." 665 (September 16, 1993) p26.

BEASTIE BOYS

CR00641 Azerrad, Michael. "Beastie Boys, Rollins Band: Roseland Ballroom." 648 (January 21, 1993) p24.

CR00642 Darzin, Daina. "Beastie Boys: New York." 712-713 (July 13, 1995) p46.

BEAUSOLEIL

CR00643 Swenson, John. "Beausoleil." 623 (February 6, 1992) p29.

BECK

CR00644 Kot, Greg. "Beck: The Metro." 744 (October 3, 1996) p34.

CR00645 Walsh, Jim. "Beck: Minneapolis." 688 (August 11, 1994) p38.

BECK, JEFF

CR00646 Fricke, David. "Santana-Jeff Beck." 722 (November 30, 1995) p70.

BIG AUDIO DYNAMITE II

CR00647 McLeese, Don. "Big Audio Dynamite II; Public Image Ltd.; Live; Blind Melon." 630 (May 14, 1992) p28.

BLACK CROWES

CR00648 Creswell, Toby. "The Black Crowes." 637 (August 20, 1992) p22.

CR00649 Damsker, Matt. "The Black Crowes: Upper Darby, PA." 708 (May 18, 1995) p42.

BLIGE, MARY J.

CR00650 McLeese, Don. "Bobby Brown, Shabba Ranks, TLC, Mary J. Blige: Reunion Arena." 651 (March 4, 1993) p31.

BLIND MELON

CR00651 McCormick, Moira. "Blind Melon: Chicago." 681 (May 5, 1994) p19.

CR00652 McLeese, Don. "Big Audio Dynamite II; Public Image Ltd.; Live; Blind Melon." 630 (May 14, 1992) p28.

BLOOM, LUKA

CR00653 Jones, Rickie Lee. "Luka Bloom: The Troubadour." 671 (December 9, 1993) p22.

CR00654 Powers, Ann. "Luka Bloom, David Byrne, Rosanne Cash, Lou Reed: The Bottom Line." 653 (April 1, 1993) p24.

BODY COUNT

CR00655 Sinclair, Tom. "Body Count: The Academy." 649 (February 4, 1993) p22.

BON JOVI

CR00656 Santelli, Robert. "Bon Jovi." 644 (November 26, 1992) p27.

BOOKER T & THE M.G.'S

CR00657 Futterman, Steve. "Booker T. And The MG's." 625 (March 5, 1992) p25.

BOWIE, DAVID

CR00658 Weisel, Al. "Nine Inch Nails—David Bowie: Camden, N.J. " 720 (November 2, 1995) p28.

CR00659 Wiederhorn, Jon. "David Bowie: Roseland Ballroom." 746 (October 31, 1996) pp34-35.

BOYZ II MEN

CR00660 Light, Alan. "Hammer; Boyz II Men; Jodeci." 634-635 (July 9, 1992) p27.

BRAND NEW HEAVIES

CR00661 St. Leger, Marie Elsie. "The Brand New Heavies: New York City." 692 (October 6, 1994) p35.

BROOKS, GARTH

CR00662 Puterbaugh, Parke. "Garth Brooks: Charlotte, N.C. " 670 (November 25, 1993) p33.

BROWN, BOBBY

CR00663 McLeese, Don. "Bobby Brown, Shabba Ranks, TLC, Mary J. Blige: Reunion Arena." 651 (March 4, 1993) p31.

BROWN, JUNIOR

CR00664 Dylan, Jakob. "Junior Brown: Warfield Theater." 670 (November 25, 1993) p28.

CR00665 Swenson, John. "Junior Brown: New York." 696 (December 1, 1994) p44.

BROWNE, JACKSON

CR00666 McAlley, John. "Jackson Browne: New York City." 679 (April 7, 1994) p34.

BUCKINGHAM, LINDSEY

CR00667 Wild, David. "Lindsey Buckingham: The Wiltern Theater." 654 (April 15, 1993) p19.

BUCKLEY, JEFF

CR00668 Darzin, Daina. "Jeff Buckley: New York City." 676 (February 24, 1994) p26.

BUSTA RHYMES

CR00669 Fine, Jason. "Smokin' Groovies." 742 (September 5, 1996) p28.

BUTTHOLE SURFERS

CR00670 Darzin, Daina. "Butthole Surfers—Stone Temple Pilots—Flaming Lips: New York Coty." 665 (September 16, 1993) p26.

BYRNE, DAVID

CR00671 Powers, Ann. "Luka Bloom, David Byrne, Rosanne Cash, Lou Reed: The Bottom Line." 653 (April 1, 1993) p24.

C

CALHOUN, WILL

CR00672 Futterman, Steve. "Vernon Reid, Will Calhoun And Melvin Gibbs." 622 (January 23, 1992) p11.

CASH, JOHNNY

CR00673 Coleman, Mark. "Johnny Cash: New York." 694 (November 3, 1994) p42.

CASH, ROSANNE

CR00674 Powers, Ann. "Luka Bloom, David Byrne, Rosanne Cash,

Lou Reed: The Bottom Line." 653 (April 1, 1993) p24.

CHAPMAN, TRACY

CR00675 DeCurtis, Anthony. "Tracy Chapman." 743 (September 19, 1996) pp44-45.

CLAPTON, ERIC

CR00676 Fricke, David. "Eric Clapton: New York City." 684 (June 16, 1994) p32.

CR00677 Sinclair, David. "Eric Clapton: Royal Albert Hall." 654 (April 15, 1993) p19.

CLARK, GUY

CR00678 Pond, Steve. "Guy Clark, Joe Ely, Paul Kelly, Michelle Shocked, Allen Toussaint: The Troubadour." 653 (April 1, 1993) p24.

CLINTON, GEORGE

CR00679 Fricke, David. "George Clinton And The P-Funk All-Stars." 741 (August 22, 1996) p41.

CR00680 Puterbaugh, Parke. "George Clinton And The P-Funk All-Stars." 655 (April 29, 1993) p25.

COCTEAU TWINS

CR00681 Hunter, James. "Cocteau Twins—Moose: Atlanta." 680 (April 21, 1994) p30.

COHEN, LEONARD

CR00682 Gardner, Elysa. "Leonard Cohen: New York City." 662 (August 5, 1993) p28.

COLE, LLOYD

CR00683 Azerrad, Michael. "Lloyd Cole." 623 (February 6, 1992) p29.

COLVIN, SHAWN

CR00684 Browne, Jackson. "The Strand, Los Angeles." 676 (February 24, 1994) p17.

CONCRETE BLONDE

CR00685 McCormick, Moira. "Concrete Blonde: Chicago." 678 (March 24, 1994) p22.

COSTELLO, ELVIS

CR00686 Harris, Michael C. "Elvis Costello And The Attractions: Tinley Park, Ill. " 686-687 (July 14, 1994) p36.

COUNTING CROWS

CR00687 Jurek, Thom. "Counting Crows: Detroit." 674 (January 27, 1994) p25.

COWBOY JUNKIES

CR00688 Puterbaugh, Parke. "Cowboy Junkies; John Prine." 631 (May 28, 1992) p24.

CRANBERRIES

CR00689 Cross, Charles R. "The Cranberries." 743 (September 19, 1996) p44.

CR00690 Duffy, Thom. "The Cranberries: London." 696 (December 1, 1994) p44.

CRANES

CR00691 McLeese, Don. "The Cure." 636 (August 6, 1992) p27.

CYPRESS HILL

CR00692 Fine, Jason. "Smokin' Groovies." 742 (September 5, 1996) p28.

CROW, SHERYL

CR00693 Hunter, James. "Crowded House, Sheryl Crow: Atlanta." 684 (June 16, 1994) p32.

CROWDED HOUSE

CR00693 Hunter, James. "Crowded House, Sheryl Crow: Atlanta." 684 (June 16, 1994) p32.

CRUEL SEA

CR00694 Donald, Tom. "Cruel Sea: New York." 712-713 (July 13, 1995) p46.

CURE

CR00695 McLeese, Don. "The Cure." 636 (August 6, 1992) p27.

D

DANZIG

CR00696 Gitter, Mike. "Danzig: Roseland." 650 (February 18, 1993) p29.

DAVIES, RAY

CR00697 DeRogatis, Jim. "Ray Davies." 732 (April 18, 1996) p71.

DEF LEPPARD

CR00698 Puterbaugh, Parke. "Def Leppard." 640 (October 1, 1992) p34.

DESCENDENTS

CR00699 Abowitz, Richard. "Descendents: The Warehouse." 746 (October 31, 1996) p35.

DIGABLE PLANETS

CR00700 Hopkins, Tracy. "Digable Planets: New York." 707 (May 4, 1995) p36.

DINOSAUR JR.

CR00701 Anderson, Mark Kendall. "Dinosaur Jr.: Northhampton, Mass. " 693 (October 20, 1994) p52.

CR00702 McLeese, Don. "My Bloody Valentine; Dinosaur Jr. " 627 (April 2, 1992) p23.

DIRE STRAITS

CR00703 Tannenbaum, Rob. "Dire Straits." 629 (April 30, 1992) p29.

DOOBIE BROTHERS

CR00704 Robicheau, Paul. "Foreigner—The Doobie Brothers: Mansfield, Mass. " 692 (October 6, 1994) p35.

DURAN DURAN

CR00705 Foege, Alec. "Duran Duran: New York City." 676 (February 24, 1994) p26.

DYLAN, BOB

CR00706 Darzin, Daina. "Bob Dylan—Santana: Wantagh, N.Y. " 668 (October 28, 1993) p30.

CR00707 DeCurtis, Anthony. "Bob Dylan: Jones Beach, N.Y. " 668 (October 28, 1993) p26.

CR00708 DeRogatis, Jim. "Bob Dylan: The Beacon Theater." 726 (January 25, 1996) p74.

CR00709 Richardson, Susan. "Bob Dylan: New York." 697 (December 15, 1994) p38.

E

EAGLES

CR00710 Wild, David. "The Eagles: Irvine, Calif. " 686-687 (July 14, 1994) p36.

ECHOBELLY

CR00711 Sinclair, David. "Echobelly: London." 694 (November 3, 1994) p42.

ELY, JOE

CR00712 Pond, Steve. "Guy Clark, Joe Ely, Paul Kelly, Michelle Shocked, Allen Toussaint: The Troubadour." 653 (April 1, 1993) p24.

ESTEP, MAGGIE

CR00713 McDonnell, Evelyn. "The Free Your Mind Spoken-Word Tour." 680 (April 21, 1994) p30.

ETHERIDGE, MELISSA

CR00714 Abowitz, Richard. "Melissa Etheridge: Target Center." 747 (November 14, 1996) p44.

F

FATEH ALI KHAN, NUSRAT

CR00715 Richardson, Susan. "Nusrat Fateh Ali Khan: Radio City Music Hall." 744 (October 3, 1996) p35.

FAUST

CR00716 Fricke, David. "Faust: Hartford, Conn. " 685 (June 30, 1994) p38.

FERGUSON, TIM

CR00717 Dylan, Jakob. "Tim Ferguson: The Mint." 670 (November 25, 1993) p28.

FERRY, BRYAN
CR00718 Manning, Kara. "Bryan Ferry: New York." 700 (January 26, 1995) p32.
FIREHOSE
CR00719 Gitter, Mike. "Firehose: The Grand." 658 (June 10, 1993) p34.
FLAMING LIPS
CR00720 Darzin, Daina. "Butthole Surfers—Stone Temple Pilots—Flaming Lips: New York Coty." 665 (September 16, 1993) p26.
FOREIGNER
CR00721 Robicheau, Paul. "Foreigner—The Doobie Brothers: Mansfield, Mass. " 692 (October 6, 1994) p35.
FUGAZI
CR00722 Azerrad, Michael. "Fugazi." 633 (June 25, 1992) p18.
CR00723 Darzin, Daina. "Fugazi: New York City." 670 (November 25, 1993) p33.
FUGEES
CR00724 Fine, Jason. "Performance." 734 (May 16, 1996) p66.

G

GABRIEL, PETER
CR00725 Ehrlich, Dimitri. "Peter Gabriel: The Academy." 657 (May 27, 1993) p25.
GAINES, REG E.
CR00726 McDonnell, Evelyn. "The Free Your Mind Spoken-Word Tour." 680 (April 21, 1994) p30.
GERMANO, LISA
CR00727 Considine, J. D. "Voters For A Choice Benefit: Washington." 703 (March 9, 1995) p36.
GIANT SAND
CR00728 Tannenbaum, Rob. "Giant Sand: Hoboken, N.J. " 662 (August 5, 1993) p28.
GIBBS, MELVIN
CR00729 Futterman, Steve. "Vernon Reid, Will Calhoun And Melvin Gibbs." 622 (January 23, 1992) p11.
GOLDEN SMOG
CR00730 Kemp, Mark. "Golden Smog." 735 (May 30, 1996) p50.
GOO GOO DOLLS
CR00731 Walsh, Jim. "Goo Goo Dolls: Minneapolis." 710 (June 15, 1995) p31.
GRATEFUL DEAD
CR00732 Hochman, Steve. "The Grateful Dead, Sting: Las Vegas, Nevada." 660-661 (July 8, 1993) p29.
GUMBALL
CR00733 Darzin, Daina. "Gumball: New York." 691 (September 22, 1994) p38.
GUNS N' ROSES
CR00734 Fricke, David. "Guns N' Roses." 622 (January 23, 1992) p11.
CR00735 Gitter, Mike. "Guns N' Roses: New Haven Coliseum." 655 (April 29, 1993) p25.
CR00736 Sinclair, Tom. "Guns N' Roses; Metallica." 638 (September 3, 1992) p18.
GUY, BUDDY
CR00737 Milward, John. "Buddy Guy: The Chance." 656 (May 13, 1993) p32.

H

HALL, JOHN S.
CR00738 McDonnell, Evelyn. "The Free Your Mind Spoken-Word Tour." 680 (April 21, 1994) p30.
HAMMER
CR00739 Light, Alan. "Hammer; Boyz II Men; Jodeci." 634-635 (July 9, 1992) p27.
HARVEY, POLLY JEAN
CR00740 Harrison, Andrew. "John Parish & Polly Jean Harvey: Fleece And Firkin." 748 (November 28, 1996) p47.
HATFIELD, JULIANA
CR00741 Drozdowski, Ted. "Lemonheads." 637 (August 20, 1992) p22.
CR00742 Gardner, Elysa. "The B-52s, Juliana Hatfield: Radio City Music Hall." 652 (March 18, 1993) p27.
HIATT, JOHN
CR00743 Kenny, Glenn. "John Hiatt: New York City." 669 (November 11, 1993) p25.
HIGH PLAINS DRIFTERS
CR00744 Swenson, John. "G. E. Smith & The High Plains Drifters: Amagansett, N. Y. " 668 (October 28, 1993) p30.
HITCHCOCK, ROBYN
CR00745 Fricke, David. "Raves." 660-661 (July 8, 1993) p20.
CR00746 Fricke, David. "Robyn Hitchcock And The Egyptians." 617 (November 14, 1991) p32.
HOLE
CR00747 O'Dair, Barbara. "Hole: New York." 694 (November 3, 1994) p42.
HOOTIE AND THE BLOWFISH
CR00748 Aiges, Scott. "Hootie And The Blowfish: New Orleans." 705 (April 6, 1995) p36.

I

ICE-T
CR00749 Sinclair, Tom. "Body Count: The Academy." 649 (February 4, 1993) p22.
INXS
CR00750 Ehrlich, Dimitri. "INXS: New York City." 660-661 (July 8, 1993) p29.
ISAAK, CHRIS
CR00751 Gardner, Elysa. "Chris Isaak: Beacon Theater." 748 (November 28, 1996) p47.

J

J MASCIS
CR00752 Diehl, Matt. "J Mascis: New York City." 678 (March 24, 1994) p22.
JACKSON, JANET
CR00753 Kot, Greg. "Janet Jackson: Rosemont, Ill. " 674 (January 27, 1994) p25.
JACKSON, MICHAEL
CR00754 Light, Alan. "Michael Jackson." 639 (September 17, 1992) p38.
JAMES
CR00755 Kim, Jae-Ha. "James." 629 (April 30, 1992) p29.
JAYHAWKS
CR00756 Gardner, Elysa. "The Jayhawks." 644 (November 26, 1992) p27.
JEAN-PAUL SARTE EXPERIENCE
CR00757 Goldberg, Michael. "Straitjacket Fits—The Bats—The Jean-Paul Sarte Experience: San Francisco." 665 (September 16, 1993) p26.
JESUS AND MARY CHAIN
CR00758 Gladstone, Eric. "The Jesus And Mary Chain: Washington, D.C. " 697 (December 15, 1994) p38.
JESUS JONES
CR00759 Gardner, Elysa. "Jesus Jones, Stereo MC's: Roseland." 659 (June 24, 1993) p30.
JETT, JOAN
CR00760 Ahearn, Kim. "Joan Jett And The Blackhearts: New York City." 689 (August 25, 1994) p46.

JIAN, CUI
CR00761 Fricke, David. "Cui Jian: New York." 720 (November 2, 1995) p28.
JODECI
CR00762 Light, Alan. "Hammer; Boyz II Men; Jodeci." 634-635 (July 9, 1992) p27.
JOEL, BILLY
CR00763 Gardner, Elysa. "Billy Joel & Elton John: East Rutherford, N.J." 690 (September 8, 1994) p42.
JOHN, ELTON
CR00763 Gardner, Elysa. "Billy Joel & Elton John: East Rutherford, N.J." 690 (September 8, 1994) p42.
JOHNSON, JOHNNIE
CR00764 Harris, Michael C. "Johnnie Johnson & The Kentucky Headhunters: Chicago." 668 (October 28, 1993) p30.
JONES, GEORGE
CR00765 Tannenbaum, Rob. "George Jones: Tramps." 647 (January 7, 1993) p24.
JONES, RICKIE LEE
CR00766 Ehrlich, Dimitri. "Rickie Lee Jones: New York." 682 (May 19, 1994) p34.

K

KAISER, HENRY
CR00767 Fine, Jason. "Henry Kaiser: San Francisco." 708 (May 18, 1995) p42.
KELLY, PAUL
CR00768 Pond, Steve. "Guy Clark, Joe Ely, Paul Kelly, Michelle Shocked, Allen Toussaint: The Troubadour." 653 (April 1, 1993) p24.
KELLY, R.
CR00769 Jamison, Laura. "R. Kelly." 736 (June 13, 1996) p80.
KENTUCKY HEADHUNTERS
CR00770 Harris, Michael C. "Johnnie Johnson & The Kentucky Headhunters: Chicago." 668 (October 28, 1993) p30.
KING CRIMSON
CR00771 Futterman, Steve. "King Crimson: New York." 712-713 (July 13, 1995) p46.
KISS
CR00772 Wild, David. "Kiss: Tiger Stadium." 740 (August 8, 1996) p31.
KNOX, CHRIS
CR00773 McDonnell, Evelyn. "Chris Knox: New York." 709 (June 1, 1995) p30.

L

L7
CR00774 Considine, J. D. "Voters For A Choice Benefit: Washington." 703 (March 9, 1995) p36.
LAMB, ANDREW
CR00775 Moore, Thurston. "Raves." 684 (June 16, 1994) p24.
LEE, ARTHUR
CR00776 Fricke, David. "Love Featuring Arthur Lee: New York." 681 (May 5, 1994) p19.
LEMONHEADS
CR00777 Cohen, Jason. "Lemonheads: New York City." 674 (January 27, 1994) p25.
CR00778 Drozdowski, Ted. "Lemonheads." 637 (August 20, 1992) p22.
CR00779 Robbins, Ira. "Lemonheads: The Academy." 658 (June 10, 1993) p34.
LENNOX, ANNIE
CR00780 Panahpour, Nilou. "Annie Lennox: New York." 720 (November 2, 1995) p28.
LETTERS TO CLEO
CR00781 Darzin, Daina. "Letters To Cleo: New York City." 690 (September 8, 1994) p42.
LIVE
CR00782 Binelli, Mark. "Live: Athens, Ga." 710 (June 15, 1995) p31.
CR00783 McLeese, Don. "Big Audio Dynamite II; Public Image Ltd.; Live; Blind Melon." 630 (May 14, 1992) p28.
LOGAN, JACK
CR00784 Moon, Tom. "Jack Logan: New York." 702 (February 23, 1995) p35.
LOS LOBOS
CR00785 Hochman, Steve. "Los Lobos." 640 (October 1, 1992) p34.
LOVE
CR00786 Fricke, David. "Love Featuring Arthur Lee: New York." 681 (May 5, 1994) p19.
LOW POP SUICIDE
CR00787 Robbins, Ira. "Lemonheads: The Academy." 658 (June 10, 1993) p34.
LUNA
CR00788 Manning, Kara. "The Sundays: The Academy." 655 (April 29, 1993) p25.
CR00789 Sprague, David. "Luna." 728 (February 22, 1996) p64.

M

MADONNA
CR00790 Duffy, Thom. "Madonna: London." 669 (November 11, 1993) p25.
MARILYN MANSON
CR00791 Kelly, Christina. "Marilyn Manson: Convention Hall." 749 (December 12, 1996) p36.
MARLEY, ZIGGY
CR00792 Fine, Jason. "Smokin' Groovies." 742 (September 5, 1996) p28.
MASSIVE ATTACK
CR00793 Fernando, S. H., Jr. "Massive Attack: New York." 718 (October 5, 1995) p32.
MATTHEWS, DAVE
CR00794 Puterbaugh, Parke. "Dave Matthews Band: Raleigh, N.C." 718 (October 5, 1995) p32.
MAVERICKS
CR00795 Darzin, Daina. "The Mavericks: New York City." 693 (October 20, 1994) p52.
MAY, BRIAN
CR00796 Gitter, Mike. "Guns N' Roses: New Haven Coliseum." 655 (April 29, 1993) p25.
MCCARTNEY, PAUL
CR00797 Wild, David. "Paul McCartney: Sam Boyd Silver Bowl." 658 (June 10, 1993) p34.
MEAT LOAF
CR00798 Arrington, Carl. "Meat Loaf: New York City." 678 (March 24, 1994) p22.
MEGADETH
CR00799 Darzin, Daina. "Megadeth: New York." 704 (March 23, 1995) p46.
MEKONS
CR00800 Cohen, Jason. "Mekons: New York City." 667 (October 14, 1993) p37.
MELLENCAMP, JOHN
CR00801 DeCurtis, Anthony. "John Mellencamp: Grand Rapids, Mich." 703 (March 9, 1995) p36.
CR00802 Jurek, Thom. "John Mellencamp." 627 (April 2, 1992) p23.
MERCURY REV
CR00803 Coleman, Mark. "Mercury Rev: Irving Plaza." 652 (March 18, 1993) p27.

METALLICA
CR00804 Jurek, Thom. "Metallica: Clarkston, Mich. " 688 (August 11, 1994) p38.
CR00805 McLeese, Don. "Metallica." 626 (March 19, 1992) p25.
CR00806 Sinclair, Tom. "Guns N' Roses; Metallica." 638 (September 3, 1992) p18.
MICHAEL, GEORGE
CR00807 Wild, David. "George Michael." 618 (November 28, 1991) p35.
MINISTRY
CR00808 Sinclair, Tom. "Ministry: The Paramount." 648 (January 21, 1993) p24.
MITCHELL, JONI
CR00809 Wild, David. "Joni Mitchell: Los Angeles." 704 (March 23, 1995) p46.
MOOSE
CR00810 Hunter, James. "Cocteau Twins—Moose: Atlanta." 680 (April 21, 1994) p30.
MORPHINE
CR00811 Drozdowski, Ted. "Morphine: Boston." 686-687 (July 14, 1994) p36.
MORRISON, VAN
CR00812 Futterman, Steve. "Van Morrison." 736 (June 13, 1996) p80.
CR00813 Wild, David. "Van Morrison: The Nob Hill Masonic Center." 651 (March 4, 1993) p31.
MORRISSEY
CR00814 Evans, Paul. "Morrissey: Atlantic Civic Center." 648 (January 21, 1993) p24.
MOULD, BOB
CR00815 Diehl, Matt. "Bob Mould: Irving Plaza." 747 (November 14, 1996) p44.
CR00816 McCormick, Moira. "Bob Mould: Chicago." 670 (November 25, 1993) p33.
CR00817 Puterbaugh, Parke. "Sugar: Cat's Cradle." 647 (January 7, 1993) p24.
MUDHONEY
CR00818 Fine, Jason. "Mudhoney: San Francisco." 700 (January 26, 1995) p32.
MY BLOODY VALENTINE
CR00819 McLeese, Don. "My Bloody Valentine; Dinosaur Jr. " 627 (April 2, 1992) p23.

N

NAS
CR00820 Fine, Jason. "Smokin' Groovies." 742 (September 5, 1996) p28.
NAUGHTY BY NATURE
CR00821 Echlin, Hobey. "Naughty By Nature: Detroit." 715 (August 24, 1995) p34.
CR00822 Tannenbaum, Rob. "Run-D.M.C., Naughty By Nature: Radio City Music Hall." 656 (May 13, 1993) p32.
NDEGEOCELLO, ME'SHELL
CR00823 Panahpour, Nilou. "Me'shell NdegeOcello: New York City." 693 (October 20, 1994) p52.
CR00824 Queen Latifah. "The Grand, New York." 682 (May 19, 1994) p21.
NESMITH, MIKE
CR00825 Pond, Steve. "Michael Nesmith." 626 (March 19, 1992) p25.
NINE INCH NAILS
CR00826 Weisel, Al. "Nine Inch Nails—David Bowie: Camden, N.J. " 720 (November 2, 1995) p28.
CR00827 Wiederhorn, Jon. "Nine Inch Nails: Irving Plaza." 745 (October 17, 1996) p47.
NIRVANA
CR00828 Arnold, Gina. "Red Hot Chili Peppers Nirvana Pearl Jam." 624 (February 20, 1992) p19.
CR00829 Powers, Ann. "Nirvana: Cow Palace." 657 (May 27, 1993) p25.
NO DOUBT
CR00830 Holthouse, David. "No Doubt." 742 (September 5, 1996) p28.
NRBQ
CR00831 Azerrad, Michael. "NRBQ: New York City." 676 (February 24, 1994) p26.

O

OASIS
CR00832 Cohen, Jason. "Oasis: Hoboken, N.J. " 697 (December 15, 1994) p38.
OFFSPRING
CR00833 Darzin, Daina. "The Offspring: New York." 706 (April 20, 1995) p38.
ORB
CR00834 Kot, Greg. "The Orb: Chicago." 671 (December 9, 1993) p26.
OSBOURNE, OZZY
CR00835 Puterbaugh, Parke. "Ozzy Osbourne." 738-739 (July 11, 1996) p92.

P

PAGE, JIMMY
CR00836 Puterbaugh, Parke. "Jimmy Page And Robert Plant: Miami." 706 (April 20, 1995) p38.
PARISH, JOHN
CR00837 Harrison, Andrew. "John Parish & Polly Jean Harvey: Fleece And Firkin." 748 (November 28, 1996) p47.
PAVEMENT
CR00838 Mundy, Chris. "Pavement: London." 682 (May 19, 1994) p34.
PEARL JAM
CR00839 Arnold, Gina. "Red Hot Chili Peppers Nirvana Pearl Jam." 624 (February 20, 1992) p19.
CR00840 Considine, J. D. "Neil Young—Pearl Jam: Stockholm, Sweden." 664 (September 2, 1993) p29.
CR00841 Considine, J. D. "Voters For A Choice Benefit: Washington." 703 (March 9, 1995) p36.
CR00842 Cross, Charles R. "Pearl Jam: Key Arena." 746 (October 31, 1996) p34.
CR00843 Goldberg, Michael. "Pearl Jam: San Francisco." 671 (December 9, 1993) p26.
PETTY, TOM
CR00844 Okamoto, Chris. "Tom Petty And The Heartbreakers—Chris Whitley." 616 (October 31, 1991) p21.
PHAIR, LIZ
CR00845 Schruers, Fred. "Liz Phair: Los Angeles." 709 (June 1, 1995) p30.
PHISH
CR00846 . "[Correction]." 704 (March 23, 1995) p18.
CR00847 Robicheau, Paul. "Phish: Boston." 702 (February 23, 1995) p35.
PJ HARVEY
CR00848 Azerrad, Michael. "PJ Harvey." 640 (October 1, 1992) p34.
CR00849 Perse, Tobias. "PJ Harvey: London." 707 (May 4, 1995) p36.
PLANT, ROBERT
CR00850 Puterbaugh, Parke. "Jimmy Page And Robert Plant: Miami." 706 (April 20, 1995) p38.
POE
CR00851 Saunders, Dudley. "Poe: Toad's Place." 747 (November

14, 1996) p44.
PORNO FOR PYROS
CR00852 Hochman, Steve. "Porno For Pyros." 638 (September 3, 1992) p18.
PRETENDERS
CR00853 Sinclair, David. "The Pretenders: London." 685 (June 30, 1994) p38.
PRINE, JOHN
CR00854 Puterbaugh, Parke. "Cowboy Junkies; John Prine." 631 (May 28, 1992) p24.
PRODIGY
CR00855 Gaar, Gillian G. "Prodigy." 743 (September 19, 1996) p45.
CR00856 Owen, Frank. "The Prodigy: New York." 715 (August 24, 1995) p34.
PUBLIC IMAGE, LTD.
CR00857 McLeese, Don. "Big Audio Dynamite II; Public Image Ltd.; Live; Blind Melon." 630 (May 14, 1992) p28.
PULP
CR00858 Goodwin, Andrew. "Pulp." 738-739 (July 11, 1996) p92.

R

RAGE AGAINST THE MACHINE
CR00859 McDonnell, Evelyn. "Rage Against The Machine: Roseland Ballroom." 744 (October 3, 1996) p34.
RAITT, BONNIE
CR00860 DeLuca, Dan. "Bonnie Raitt: Philadelphia." 691 (September 22, 1994) p38.
RANKS, SHABBA
CR00861 McLeese, Don. "Bobby Brown, Shabba Ranks, TLC, Mary J. Blige: Reunion Arena." 651 (March 4, 1993) p31.
RED HOT CHILI PEPPERS
CR00862 Arnold, Gina. "Red Hot Chili Peppers Nirvana Pearl Jam." 624 (February 20, 1992) p19.
REED, LOU
CR00863 Powers, Ann. "Luka Bloom, David Byrne, Rosanne Cash, Lou Reed: The Bottom Line." 653 (April 1, 1993) p24.
REID, VERNON
CR00864 Futterman, Steve. "Vernon Reid, Will Calhoun And Melvin Gibbs." 622 (January 23, 1992) p11.
R.E.M.
CR00865 Foege, Alec. "R.E.M.: Mountain View, Calif." 711 (June 29, 1995) p26.
REVEREND HORTON HEAT
CR00866 Foege, Alec. "Reverend Horton Heat: New York City." 667 (October 14, 1993) p37.
RICHARDS, KEITH
CR00867 Sinclair, David. "Keith Richards And The X-Pensive Winos: Town And Country." 649 (February 4, 1993) p22.
ROLLINS BAND
CR00868 Azerrad, Michael. "Beastie Boys, Rollins Band: Roseland Ballroom." 648 (January 21, 1993) p24.
RUN-D.M.C.
CR00869 Tannenbaum, Rob. "Run-D.M.C., Naughty By Nature: Radio City Music Hall." 656 (May 13, 1993) p32.

S

SANTANA
CR00870 Darzin, Daina. "Bob Dylan—Santana: Wantagh, N.Y." 668 (October 28, 1993) p30.
CR00871 Fricke, David. "Santana-Jeff Beck." 722 (November 30, 1995) p70.
CR00872 Futterman, Steve. "Santana." 618 (November 28, 1991) p35.
SCOTT-HERON, GIL
CR00873 Ehrlich, Dimitri. "Gil Scott-Heron: New York City." 689 (August 25, 1994) p46.
SEX PISTOLS
CR00874 Sinclair, David. "The Sex Pistols: Finsbury Park." 740 (August 8, 1996) pp30-31.
SHANKAR, RAVI
CR00875 DeCurtis, Anthony. "Ravi Shankar At Carnegie Hall." 662 (August 5, 1993) p24.
SHOCKED, MICHELLE
CR00876 Pond, Steve. "Guy Clark, Joe Ely, Paul Kelly, Michelle Shocked, Allen Toussaint: The Troubadour." 653 (April 1, 1993) p24.
SHORT, BOBBY
CR00877 Kravitz, Lenny. "Bobby Short: Live At New York City's Cafe Carlyle." 669 (November 11, 1993) p20.
SIMPLE MINDS
CR00878 Gaar, Gillian G. "Simple Minds: Seattle." 704 (March 23, 1995) p46.
SIMPLY RED
CR00879 Gardner, Elysa. "Simply Red." 636 (August 6, 1992) p27.
SIOUXSIE AND THE BANSHEES
CR00880 Van Parys, Bill. "Siouxsie And The Banshees: New York." 710 (June 15, 1995) p31.
SLAYER
CR00881 Darzin, Daina. "Slayer: New York." 705 (April 6, 1995) p36.
SLOAN
CR00882 Robbins, Ira. "Lemonheads: The Academy." 658 (June 10, 1993) p34.
SMASHING PUMPKINS
CR00883 Chonin, Neva. "The Smashing Pumpkins: Thomas And Mack Center." 745 (October 17, 1996) p47.
CR00884 Harris, Michael C. "Smashing Pumpkins: Chicago." 666 (September 30, 1993) p20.
SMITH, G. E.
CR00885 Swenson, John. "G. E. Smith & The High Plains Drifters: Amagansett, N. Y." 668 (October 28, 1993) p30.
SMITH, PATTI
CR00886 DeRogatis, Jim. "Patti Smith." 726 (January 25, 1996) p74.
CR00887 Frost, Deborah. "Patti Smith: New York City." 663 (August 19, 1993) p25.
CR00888-92 Numbers not assigned.
SOUNDGARDEN
CR00893 McLeese, Don. "Soundgarden: Houston." 690 (September 8, 1994) p42.
SPLIT RAIL
CR00894 Moerer, Keith. "Performance." 733 (May 2, 1996) p57.
SPRINGSTEEN, BRUCE
CR00895 Sinclair, David. "Bruce Springsteen: Sheffield Arena." 659 (June 24, 1993) p30.
STEELY DAN
CR00896 D'Arby, Terence Trent. "The Greek Theater, Los Angeles." 675 (February 10, 1994) p18.
CR00897 Shirley, David. "Steely Dan: New York City." 667 (October 14, 1993) p37.
STEREO MC'S
CR00898 Gardner, Elysa. "Jesus Jones, Stereo MC's: Roseland." 659 (June 24, 1993) p30.
STEREOLAB
CR00899 Flaum, Eric. "Stereolab: Hoboken, N.J." 691 (September 22, 1994) p38.
STEWART, ROD
CR00900 Hochman, Steve. "Rod Stewart: Anaheim, Calif." 682 (May 19, 1994) p34.
STING
CR00901 Hochman, Steve. "The Grateful Dead, Sting: Las Vegas, Nevada." 660-661 (July 8, 1993) p29.

STONE TEMPLE PILOTS
CR00902 Darzin, Daina. "Butthole Surfers—Stone Temple Pilots—Flaming Lips: New York Coty." 665 (September 16, 1993) p26.
CR00903 DiMartino, Dave. "Stone Temple Pilots: Universal Amphitheater." 749 (December 12, 1996) p36.
CR00904 Moon, Tom. "Stone Temple Pilots: Philadelphia." 692 (October 6, 1994) p35.

STRAITJACKET FITS
CR00905 Goldberg, Michael. "Straitjacket Fits—The Bats—The Jean-Paul Sarte Experience: San Francisco." 665 (September 16, 1993) p26.

STREISAND, BARBRA
CR00906 Travers, Peter. "Barbra Streisand: New York City." 688 (August 11, 1994) p38.

SUEDE
CR00907 Cohen, Jason. "The London Suede: New York." 705 (April 6, 1995) p36.
CR00908 Foege, Alec. "Suede: New York City." 671 (December 9, 1993) p26.

SUGAR
CR00909 Puterbaugh, Parke. "Sugar: Cat's Cradle." 647 (January 7, 1993) p24.

SUN RA ARKESTRA
CR00910 Neely, Kim. "Sun Ra Arkestra At The Bottom Line." 663 (August 19, 1993) p19.

SUNDAYS
CR00911 Manning, Kara. "The Sundays: The Academy." 655 (April 29, 1993) p25.

SWEET, MATTHEW
CR00912 Jurek, Thom. "Matthew Sweet: Detroit." 663 (August 19, 1993) p25.

T

TEENAGE FANCLUB
CR00913 Kot, Greg. "Yo La Tengo—Teenage Fanclub." 679 (April 7, 1994) p34.

THEY MIGHT BE GIANTS
CR00914 Panahpour, Nilou. "They Might Be Giants: New York." 709 (June 1, 1995) p30.
CR00915 Ressner, Jeffrey. "They Might Be Giants." 637 (August 20, 1992) p22.

THROWING MUSES: SAN FRANCISCO
CR00916 Stolder, Steve. "Throwing Muses." 707 (May 4, 1995) p36.

TLC
CR00917 McLeese, Don. "Bobby Brown, Shabba Ranks, TLC, Mary J. Blige: Reunion Arena." 651 (March 4, 1993) p31.

TOOL
CR00918 Drozdowski, Ted. "Tool: Boston." 679 (April 7, 1994) p34.

TOUSSAINT, ALLEN
CR00919 Pond, Steve. "Guy Clark, Joe Ely, Paul Kelly, Michelle Shocked, Allen Toussaint: The Troubadour." 653 (April 1, 1993) p24.

TOWNSHEND, PETER
CR00920 Gardner, Elysa. "Pete Townshend: New York City." 664 (September 2, 1993) p29.

TRAFFIC
CR00921 Dean, Chuck. "Traffic: Charlotte, N.C. " 689 (August 25, 1994) p46.

A TRIBE CALLED QUEST
CR00922 Fine, Jason. "Smokin' Groovies." 742 (September 5, 1996) p28.

U

U2
CR00923 Puterbaugh, Parke. "U2." 628 (April 16, 1992) p29.

V

VAN HALEN
CR00924 Jurek, Thom. "Van Halen: Clarkston, Michigan." 663 (August 19, 1993) p25.
CR00925 Puterbaugh, Parke. "Van Halen." 615 (October 17, 1991) p34.

VEGA, SUZANNE
CR00926 Santelli, Robert. "Suzanne Vega: The Academy." 656 (May 13, 1993) p32.

VELVET UNDERGROUND
CR00927 Fricke, David. "The Velvet Underground: London." 662 (August 5, 1993) p28.

VERVE
CR00928 Fricke, David. "Verve At The Anshe Slonim Synagogue." 664 (September 2, 1993) p16.
CR00929 Panahpour, Nilou. "The Verve: New York." 718 (October 5, 1995) p32.

W

WACO BROTHERS
CR00930 Moerer, Keith. "Performance." 733 (May 2, 1996) p57.

WAITS, TOM
CR00931 Stolder, Steven. "Tom Waits: Paramount Theater." 730 (March 21, 1996) p100.

WALLFLOWERS
CR00932 DeCurtis, Anthony. "The Wallflowers At The Chance, Poughkeepsie, N.Y. " 662 (August 5, 1993) p24.

WALSER, DON
CR00933 Moerer, Keith. "Performance." 733 (May 2, 1996) p57.

WATTS, CHARLIE
CR00934 Futterman, Steve. "Charlie Watts." 638 (September 3, 1992) p18.

WELCH, GILLIAN
CR00935 Lozaw, Tristram. "Gillian Welch: Cajun And Bluegrass Festival." 745 (October 17, 1996) p47.

WESTERBERG, PAUL
CR00936 McLeese, Don. "Paul Westerberg—Bash And Pop: Austin, Texas." 666 (September 30, 1993) p20.

WHITE ZOMBIE
CR00937 Drozdowski, Ted. "White Zombie: Mansfield, Mass. " 715 (August 24, 1995) p34.

WHITLEY, CHRIS
CR00938 Okamoto, Chris. "Tom Petty And The Heartbreakers—Chris Whitley." 616 (October 31, 1991) p21.

WILLIAMS, LUCINDA
CR00939 McLeese, Don. "Lucinda Williams: La Zona Rosa." 650 (February 18, 1993) p29.

WILLIAMS, VICTORIA
CR00940 Moon, Tom. "Victoria Williams: New York." 700 (January 26, 1995) p32.

WOLF, PETER
CR00941 Foege, Alec. "Peter Wolf: New York." 696 (December 1, 1994) p44.

WOOD, RON
CR00942 Evans, Paul. "Ronnie Wood: The Roxy Theater." 647 (January 7, 1993) p24.

X

X-PENSIVE WINOS
CR00943 Sinclair, David. "Keith Richards And The X-Pensive Winos: Town And Country." 649 (February 4, 1993) p22.

Y

YO LA TENGO
CR00944 Kot, Greg. "Yo La Tengo—Teenage Fanclub." 679 (April 7, 1994) p34.
YOUNG, NEIL
CR00945 Considine, J. D. "Neil Young—Pearl Jam: Stockholm, Sweden." 664 (September 2, 1993) p29.
CR00946 Considine, J. D. "Voters For A Choice Benefit: Washington." 703 (March 9, 1995) p36.
CR00947 Light, Alan. "Neil Young." 628 (April 16, 1992) p29.
CR00948 Puterbaugh, Parke. "Neil Young: Virginia Beach Amphitheater." 744 (October 3, 1996) p35.

Z

Z
CR00949 Swenson, John. "Z: New York City." 680 (April 21, 1994) p30.
Z Z TOP
CR00950 Puterbaugh, Parke. "Z Z Top." 685 (June 30, 1994) p38.

Reviewer Index to Concert Reviews

A

Abowitz, Richard CR00699, CR00714
Ahearn, Kim CR00760
Aiges, Scott CR00748
Anderson, Mark Kendall CR00701
Arnold, Gina CR00828, CR00839, CR00862
Arrington, Carl CR00798
Azerrad, Michael CR00641, CR00683, CR00722, CR00831, CR00848, CR00868

B

Binelli, Mark CR00782
Browne, Jackson CR00684

C

Chonin, Neva CR00883
Cohen, Jason CR00777, CR00800, CR00832, CR00907
Coleman, Mark CR00673, CR00803
Considine, J. D. CR00727, CR00774, CR00840, CR00841, CR00945, CR00946, CR00846
Creswell, Toby CR00648
Cross, Charles R. CR00689, CR00842

D

Damsker, Matt CR00649
D'Arby, Terence Trent CR00896
Darzin, Daina CR00642, CR00668, CR00670, CR00706, CR00720, CR00723, CR00733, CR00781, CR00795, CR00799, CR00833, CR00870, CR00881, CR00902
Dean, Chuck CR00921
DeCurtis, Anthony CR00675, CR00707, CR00801, CR00875, CR00932
DeLuca, Dan CR00860
DeRogatis, Jim CR00697, CR00708, CR00886
Diehl, Matt CR00752, CR00815
DiMartino, Dave CR00903
Donald, Tom CR00694
Drozdowski, Ted CR00741, CR00778, CR00811, CR00918, CR00937
Duffy, Thom CR00690, CR00790
Dylan, Jakob CR00664, CR00717

E

Echlin, Hobey CR00821
Ehrlich, Dimitri CR00725, CR00750, CR00766, CR00873
Evans, Paul CR00814, CR00942

F

Fernando, S. H., Jr. CR00793
Fine, Jason CR00669, CR00692, CR00724, CR00767, CR00792, CR00818, CR00820, CR00922
Flaum, Eric CR00899
Foege, Alec CR00705, CR00865, CR00866, CR00908, CR00941
Fricke, David CR00646,CR00676, CR00679, CR00716, CR00734, CR00745, CR00746, CR00761, CR00776, CR00786, CR00871, CR00927, CR00928
Frost, Deborah CR00887
Futterman, Steve CR00657, CR00672, CR00729, CR00771, CR00812, CR00864, CR00872, CR00934

G

Gaar, Gillian G. CR00855, CR00878
Gardner, Elysa CR00638, CR00682, CR00742, CR00751, CR00756, CR00759, CR00763, CR00879, CR00898, CR00920
Gitter, Mike CR00696, CR00719, CR00735, CR00796
Gladstone, Eric CR00758
Goldberg, Michael CR00640, CR00757, CR00843, CR00905
Goodwin, Andrew CR00858

H

Harris, Michael C. CR00686, CR00764, CR00770, CR00884
Harrison, Andrew CR00740, CR00837
Hochman, Steve CR00732, CR00785, CR00852, CR00900, CR00901
Holthouse, David CR00830
Hopkins, Tracy CR00700
Hunter, James CR00681, CR00693, CR00810

J

Jamison, Laura CR00769
Jones, Rickie Lee CR00653
Jurek, Thom CR00687, CR00802, CR00804, CR00912, CR00924

K

Kelly, Christina CR00791
Kemp, Mark CR00730
Kenny, Glenn CR00743
Kim, Jae-Ha CR00755
Kot, Greg CR00644, CR00753, CR00834, CR00913, CR00944
Kravitz, Lenny CR00877

L

Light, Alan CR00660, CR00739, CR00754, CR00762, CR00947
Lozaw, Tristram CR00935

M

Manning, Kara CR00718, CR00788, CR00911
McAlley, John CR00666
McCormick, Moira CR00651, CR00685, CR00816
McDonnell, Evelyn CR00713, CR00726, CR00738, CR00773, CR00859
McLeese, Don CR00639, CR00647, CR00650, CR00652, CR00663, CR00691, CR00695, CR00702, CR00783, CR00805, CR00819, CR00857, CR00861, CR00893, CR00917, CR00936, CR00939
Milward, John CR00635, CR00737
Moerer, Keith CR00894, CR00930, CR00933
Moon, Tom CR00784, CR00904, CR00940
Moore, Thurston CR00775
Mundy, Chris CR00838

N

Neely, Kim CR00910

O

O'Dair, Barbara CR00747
Okamoto, Chris CR00844, CR00938
Owen, Frank CR00856

P

Panahpour, Nilou CR00636, CR00780, CR00823, CR00914, CR00929
Perse, Tobias CR00849
Pond, Steve CR00678, CR00712, CR00768, CR00825, CR00876, CR00919
Powers, Ann CR00654, CR00671, CR00674, CR00829, CR00863
Puterbaugh, Parke CR00637, CR00662, CR00680, CR00688, CR00698, CR00794, CR00817, CR00835, CR00836, CR00850, CR00854, CR00909, CR00923, CR00925, CR00948, CR00950

Q

Queen Latifah CR00824

R

Ressner, Jeffrey CR00915
Richardson, Susan CR00709, CR00715
Robbins, Ira CR00634, CR00779, CR00787, CR00882
Robicheau, Paul CR00704, CR00721, CR00847

S

Santelli, Robert CR00656, CR00926
Saunders, Dudley CR00851
Schruers, Fred CR00845
Shirley, David CR00897
Sinclair, David CR00677, CR00711, CR00853, CR00867, CR00874, CR00895, CR00943
Sinclair, Tom CR00655, CR00736, CR00749, CR00806, CR00808
Sprague, David CR00789
St. Leger, Marie Elsie CR00661
Stolder, Steve CR00916, CR00931
Swenson, John CR00643, CR00665, CR00744, CR00885, CR00949

T

Tannenbaum, Rob CR00703, CR00728, CR00765, CR00822, CR00869
Travers, Peter CR00906

V

Van Parys, Bill CR00880

W

Walsh, Jim CR00645, CR00731
Weisel, Al CR00658, CR00826
Wiederhorn, Jon CR00659, CR00827
Wild, David CR00667, CR00710, CR00772, CR00797, CR00807, CR00809, CR00813

Title Index to Concert Reviews

A

Aerosmith: Albany, N.Y. CR00635
Afghan Whigs: Washington CR00636
Annie Lennox: New York CR00780

B

The B-52s, Juliana Hatfield: Radio City Music Hall CR00638, CR00742
Barbra Streisand: New York City CR00906
Beastie Boys: New York CR00642
Beastie Boys, Rollins Band: Roseland Ballroom CR00641, CR00868
Beausoleil CR00643
Beck: Minneapolis CR00645
Beck: The Metro CR00644
Big Audio Dynamite II; Public Image Ltd.; Live; Blind Melon CR00647, CR00652, CR00783, CR00857
Billy Joel & Elton John: East Rutherford, N.J. CR00763
The Black Crowes CR00648
The Black Crowes: Upper Darby, PA CR00649
Blind Melon: Chicago CR00651
Bob Dylan—Santana: Wantagh, N.Y. CR00706, CR00870
Bob Dylan: Jones Beach, N.Y. CR00707
Bob Dylan: New York CR00709
Bob Dylan: The Beacon Theater CR00708
Bob Mould: Chicago CR00816
Bob Mould: Irving Plaza CR00815
Bobby Brown, Shabba Ranks, TLC, Mary J. Blige: Reunion Arena CR00650, CR00663, CR00861, CR00917
Bobby Short: Live At New York City's Cafe Carlyle CR00877
Body Count: The Academy CR00655, CR00749
Bon Jovi CR00656
Bonnie Raitt: Philadelphia CR00860
Booker T. And The MG's CR00657
The Brand New Heavies: New York City CR00661
Bruce Springsteen: Sheffield Arena CR00895
Bryan Adams CR00634
Bryan Ferry: New York CR00718
Buddy Guy: The Chance CR00737
Butthole Surfers—Stone Temple Pilots—Flaming Lips: New York Coty CR00670, CR00720, CR00902

C

Charlie Watts CR00934
Chris Isaak: Beacon Theater CR00751
Chris Knox: New York CR00773
Cocteau Twins—Moose: Atlanta CR00681, CR00810
Concrete Blonde: Chicago CR00685
[Correction] CR00846
Counting Crows: Detroit CR00687
Cowboy Junkies; John Prine CR00688, CR00854
The Cranberries CR00689
The Cranberries: London CR00690
Crowded House, Sheryl Crow: Atlanta CR00693
Cruel Sea: New York CR00694
Cui Jian: New York CR00761
The Cure CR00691, CR00695

D

Danzig: Roseland CR00696
Dave Matthews Band: Raleigh, N.C. CR00794
David Bowie: Roseland Ballroom CR00659
Def Leppard CR00698
Descendents: The Warehouse CR00699
Digable Planets: New York CR00700
Dinosaur Jr.: Northhampton, Mass. CR00701
Dire Straits CR00703
Duran Duran: New York City CR00705

E

The Eagles: Irvine, Calif. CR00710
Echobelly: London CR00711
Elvis Costello And The Attractions: Tinley Park, Ill. CR00686
Eric Clapton: New York City CR00676
Eric Clapton: Royal Albert Hall CR00677

F

Faust: Hartford, Conn. CR00716
Firehose: The Grand CR00719
Foreigner—The Doobie Brothers: Mansfield, Mass. CR00704, CR00721
The Free Your Mind Spoken-Word Tour CR00713, CR00726, CR00738
Fugazi CR00722
Fugazi: New York City CR00723

G

G. E. Smith & The High Plains Drifters: Amagansett, N. Y. CR00744, CR00885
Garth Brooks: Charlotte, N.C. CR00662
George Clinton And The P-Funk All-Stars CR00679, CR00680
George Jones: Tramps CR00765
George Michael CR00807
Giant Sand: Hoboken, N.J. CR00728
Gil Scott-Heron: New York City CR00873
Gillian Welch: Cajun And Bluegrass Festival CR00935
Golden Smog CR00730
Goo Goo Dolls: Minneapolis CR00731
The Grand, New York CR00824
The Grateful Dead, Sting: Las Vegas, Nevada CR00732, CR00901
The Greek Theater, Los Angeles CR00896
Gumball: New York CR00733
Guns N' Roses CR00734
Guns N' Roses: New Haven Coliseum CR00735, CR00796
Guns N' Roses; Metallica CR00736, CR00806
Guy Clark, Joe Ely, Paul Kelly, Michelle Shocked, Allen Toussaint: The Troubadour CR00678, CR00712, CR00768, CR00876, CR00919

H

Hammer; Boyz II Men; Jodeci CR00660, CR00739, CR00762
Henry Kaiser: San Francisco CR00767
Hole: New York CR00747
Hootie And The Blowfish: New Orleans CR00748

I

INXS: New York City CR00750

J

J Mascis: New York City CR00752
Jack Logan: New York CR00784
Jackson Browne: New York City CR00666
James CR00755
Janet Jackson: Rosemont, Ill. CR00753
The Jayhawks CR00756
Jeff Buckley: New York City CR00668
The Jesus And Mary Chain: Washington, D.C. CR00758
Jesus Jones, Stereo MC's: Roseland CR00759, CR00898
Jimmy Page And Robert Plant: Miami CR00836, CR00850
Joan Jett And The Blackhearts: New York City CR00760
John Hiatt: New York City CR00743
John Mellencamp CR00802
John Mellencamp: Grand Rapids, Mich. CR00801
John Parish & Polly Jean Harvey: Fleece And Firkin CR00740, CR00837
Johnnie Johnson & The Kentucky Headhunters: Chicago CR00764, CR00770
Johnny Cash: New York CR00673
Joni Mitchell: Los Angeles CR00809
Junior Brown: New York CR00665
Junior Brown: Warfield Theater CR00664

K

Keith Richards And The X-Pensive Winos: Town And Country CR00867, CR00943
King Crimson: New York CR00771
Kiss: Tiger Stadium CR00772

L

Lemonheads CR00741, CR00778
Lemonheads: New York City CR00777
Lemonheads: The Academy CR00779, CR00787, CR00882
Leonard Cohen: New York City CR00682
Letters To Cleo: New York City CR00781
Lindsey Buckingham: The Wiltern Theater CR00667
Live: Athens, Ga. CR00782
Liz Phair: Los Angeles CR00845
Lloyd Cole CR00683
The London Suede: New York CR00907
Los Lobos CR00785

Love Featuring Arthur Lee: New York CR00776, CR00786
Lucinda Williams: La Zona Rosa CR00939
Luka Bloom, David Byrne, Rosanne Cash, Lou Reed: The Bottom Line CR00654, CR00671, CR00674, CR00863
Luka Bloom: The Troubadour CR00653
Luna CR00789

M

Madonna: London CR00790
Marilyn Manson: Convention Hall CR00791
Massive Attack: New York CR00793
Matthew Sweet: Detroit CR00912
The Mavericks: New York City CR00795
Meat Loaf: New York City CR00798
Megadeth: New York CR00799
Mekons: New York City CR00800
Melissa Etheridge: Target Center CR00714
Mercury Rev: Irving Plaza CR00803
Me'shell NdegeOcello: New York City CR00823
Metallica CR00805
Metallica: Clarkston, Mich. CR00804
Michael Jackson CR00754
Michael Nesmith CR00825
Ministry: The Paramount CR00808
Morphine: Boston CR00811
Morrissey: Atlantic Civic Center CR00814
Mudhoney: San Francisco CR00818
My Bloody Valentine; Dinosaur Jr. CR00702, CR00819

N

Naughty By Nature: Detroit CR00821
Neil Young CR00947
Neil Young—Pearl Jam: Stockholm, Sweden CR00840, CR00945
Neil Young: Virginia Beach Amphitheater CR00948
Nine Inch Nails—David Bowie: Camden, N.J. CR00658, CR00826
Nine Inch Nails: Irving Plaza CR00827
Nirvana: Cow Palace CR00829
No Doubt CR00830
NRBQ: New York City CR00831
Nusrat Fateh Ali Khan: Radio City Music Hall CR00715

O

Oasis: Hoboken, N.J. CR00832
The Offspring: New York CR00833
The Orb: Chicago CR00834
Ozzy Osbourne CR00835

P

Patti Smith CR00886
Patti Smith: New York City CR00887
Paul McCartney: Sam Boyd Silver Bowl CR00797
Paul Westerberg—Bash And Pop: Austin, Texas CR00639, CR00936
Pavement: London CR00838
Pearl Jam: Key Arena CR00842
Pearl Jam: San Francisco CR00843
Performance CR00724, CR00894, CR00930, CR00933
Pete Townshend: New York City CR00920
Peter Gabriel: The Academy CR00725
Peter Wolf: New York CR00941
Phish: Boston CR00847
PJ Harvey CR00848
PJ Harvey: London CR00849
Poe: Toad's Place CR00851
Porno For Pyros CR00852
The Pretenders: London CR00853
Prodigy CR00855
The Prodigy: New York CR00856
Pulp CR00858

R

R. Kelly CR00769
Rage Against The Machine: Roseland Ballroom CR00859
Raves CR00745, CR00775
Ravi Shankar At Carnegie Hall CR00875
Ray Davies CR00697
Red Hot Chili Peppers Nirvana Pearl Jam CR00828, CR00839, CR00862
R.E.M.: Mountain View, Calif. CR00865
Reverend Horton Heat: New York City CR00866
Rickie Lee Jones: New York CR00766
Robyn Hitchcock And The Egyptians CR00746
Rod Stewart: Anaheim, Calif. CR00900
Ronnie Wood: The Roxy Theater CR00942
Run-D.M.C., Naughty By Nature: Radio City Music Hall CR00822, CR00869

S

Santana CR00872
Santana-Jeff Beck CR00646, CR00871
The Sex Pistols: Finsbury Park CR00874
Simple Minds: Seattle CR00878
Simply Red CR00879
Siouxsie And The Banshees: New York CR00880
Slayer: New York CR00881
Smashing Pumpkins: Chicago CR00884
The Smashing Pumpkins: Thomas And Mack Center CR00883
Smokin' Groovies CR00669, CR00692, CR00792, CR00820, CR00892
Soundgarden: Houston CR00922
Steely Dan: New York City CR00897
Stereolab: Hoboken, N.J. CR00899
Stone Temple Pilots: Philadelphia CR00904
Stone Temple Pilots: Universal Amphitheater CR00903
Straitjacket Fits—The Bats—The Jean-Paul Sarte Experience: San Francisco CR00640, CR00757, CR00905
The Strand, Los Angeles CR00684
Suede: New York City CR00908
Sugar: Cat's Cradle CR00817, CR00909
Sun Ra Arkestra At The Bottom Line CR00910
The Sundays: The Academy CR00788, CR00911
Suzanne Vega: The Academy CR00926

T

They Might Be Giants CR00915
They Might Be Giants: New York CR00914
Throwing Muses CR00916
Tim Ferguson: The Mint CR00717
Tom Petty And The Heartbreakers—Chris Whitley CR00844, CR00938
Tom Waits: Paramount Theater CR00931
Tool: Boston CR00918
Tracy Chapman CR00675
Traffic: Charlotte, N.C. CR00921

U

U2 CR00923

V

Van Halen CR00637, CR00925
Van Halen: Clarkston, Michigan CR00924
Van Morrison CR00812
Van Morrison: The Nob Hill Masonic Center CR00813
The Velvet Underground: London CR00927
Vernon Reid, Will Calhoun And Melvin Gibbs CR00672, CR00729, CR00864
Verve At The Anshe Slonim Synagogue CR00928
The Verve: New York CR00929
Victoria Williams: New York CR00940
Voters For A Choice Benefit: Washington CR00727, CR00774, CR00841, CR00946

W

The Wallflowers At The Chance, Poughkeepsie, N.Y. CR00932
White Zombie: Mansfield, Mass. CR00937

Y

Yo La Tengo—Teenage Fanclub CR00913, CR00944

Z

Z: New York City CR00949
ZZTop CR00950

Cover Appearances

A

ALEXANDER, JASON
CV01042 660-661 (July 8, 1993)
ANDERSON, GILLIAN
CV01043 734 (May 16, 1996)
ANISTON, JENNIFER
CV01044 708 (May 18, 1995)
CV01045 729 (March 7, 1996)

B

BACH, SEBASTIAN
CV01046 619-620 (December 12, 1991)
BARRYMORE, DREW
CV01047 710 (June 15, 1995)
BATMAN
CV01048 634-635 (July 9, 1992)
CV01049 645-646 (December 10, 1992)
BEASTIE BOYS
CV01050 688 (August 11, 1994)
BEAVIS & BUTT-HEAD
CV01051 663 (August 19, 1993)
CV01052 678 (March 24, 1994)
CV01053 750-751 (December 26, 1996)
BECK
CV01054 736 (June 13, 1996)
BELLY
CV01055 706 (April 20, 1995)
BISSETT, JOSIE
CV01056 682 (May 19, 1994)
BLACK CROWES
CV01057 619-620 (December 12, 1991)
BLIND MELON
CV01058 669 (November 11, 1993)
BONO
CV01059 640 (October 1, 1992)
CV01060 645-646 (December 10, 1992)
CV01061 651 (March 4, 1993)
BROOKS, GARTH
CV01062 653 (April 1, 1993)
BUFFETT, JIMMY
CV01063 736 (June 13, 1996)
BULLOCK, SANDRA
CV01063 736 (June 13, 1996)

C

CARREY, JIM
CV01064 712-713 (July 13, 1995)
CARVEY, DANA
CV01065 626 (March 19, 1992)
CV01066 645-646 (December 10, 1992)
CV01067 656 (May 13, 1993)
CHERRY, NENEH
CV01068 649 (February 4, 1993)
CLAPTON, ERIC
CV01069 615 (October 17, 1991)
CV01070 619-620 (December 12, 1991)
CV01071 655 (April 29, 1993)
CLINTON, BILL
CV01072 639 (September 17, 1992)
CV01073 645-646 (December 10, 1992)
CV01074 671 (December 9, 1993)
COBAIN, KURT
CV01075 683 (June 2, 1994)
COOLIO
CV01076 724-725 (December 28, 1995)
CORGAN, BILLY
CV01076 724-725 (December 28, 1995)
CV01077 736 (June 13, 1996)
CORNELL, CHRIS
CV01077 736 (June 13, 1996)
COUNTING CROWS
CV01078 685 (June 30, 1994)
COX, COURTENEY
CV01079 708 (May 18, 1995)
CRAWFORD, CINDY
CV01080 672-673 (December 23, 1993)
CROW, SHERYL
CV01081 724-725 (December 28, 1995)
CV01082 747 (November 14, 1996)
CRUISE, TOM
CV01083 631 (May 28, 1992)
CV01084 645-646 (December 10, 1992)

D

DEF LEPPARD
CV01085 629 (April 30, 1992)
CV01086 645-646 (December 10, 1992)
DEPP, JOHNNY
CV01087 619-620 (December 12, 1991)
DERN, LAURA
CV01088 659 (June 24, 1993)
DIAZ, CAMERON
CV01089 741 (August 22, 1996)
DOHERTY, SHANNEN
CV01090 624 (February 20, 1992)
CV01091 645-646 (December 10, 1992)
DR. DRE
CV01092 666 (September 30, 1993)
DRUGS
CV01093 681 (May 5, 1994)
DUCHOVNY, DAVID
CV01094 734 (May 16, 1996)

E

EDGE
CV01095 667 (October 14, 1993)
ETHERIDGE, MELISSA
CV01096 709 (June 1, 1995)

F

FARRELL, PERRY
CV01097 736 (June 13, 1996)
FOO FIGHTERS
CV01098 718 (October 5, 1995)
FOSTER, JODIE
CV01099 619-620 (December 12, 1991)
FUGEES
CV01100 742 (September 5, 1996)
FUTURE OF ROCK
CV01101 695 (November 17, 1994)

G

GARCIA, JERRY
CV01102 616 (October 31, 1991)
CV01103 619-620 (December 12, 1991)
CV01104 664 (September 2, 1993)
CV01105 717 (September 21, 1995)
CV01106 724-725 (December 28, 1995)
CV01107 740 (August 8, 1996)
GOLD LAME SUIT (ELVIS PRESLEY'S)
CV01108 643 (November 12, 1992)
CV01109 645-646 (December 10, 1992)
GREEN DAY
CV01110 700 (January 26, 1995)
CV01111 724-725 (December 28, 1995)
GUNS N' ROSES
CV01112 619-620 (December 12, 1991)

H

HAWKE, ETHAN
CV01113 703 (March 9, 1995)
HENDRIX, JIMI
CV01114 623 (February 6, 1992)
CV01115 645-646 (December 10, 1992)
HERMAN, PEE-WEE
CV01116 619-620 (December 12, 1991)
HETFIELD, JAMES
CV01117 654 (April 15, 1993)
HOLE
CV01118 715 (August 24, 1995)

HOOTIE AND THE BLOWFISH
CV01119 714 (August 10, 1995)
HOUSTON, WHITNEY
CV01120 658 (June 10, 1993)
HUNTER, RACHEL
CV01121 619-620 (December 12, 1991)

I

ICE-T
CV01122 637 (August 20, 1992)
CV01123 645-646 (December 10, 1992)

J

JACKSON, JANET
CV01124 665 (September 16, 1993)
JACKSON, MICHAEL
CV01125 621 (January 9, 1992)
CV01126 645-646 (December 10, 1992)
JAGGER, MICK
CV01127 723 (December 14, 1995)

K

KIEDIS, ANTHONY
CV01128 679 (April 7, 1994)
KISS
CV01129 736 (June 13, 1996)
KRAVITZ, LENNY
CV01130 722 (November 30, 1995)
KUDROW, LISA
CV01131 708 (May 18, 1995)

L

LEBLANC, MATT
CV01131 708 (May 18, 1995)
LEE, PAMELA ANDERSON
CV01132 750-751 (December 26, 1996)
LEIGHTON, LAURA
CV01133 682 (May 19, 1994)
LETTERMAN, DAVID
CV01134 650 (February 18, 1993)
CV01135 698-699 (December 29, 1994)
CV01136 735 (May 30, 1996)
LIVE
CV01137 726 (January 25, 1996)
LOCKLEAR, HEATHER
CV01138 682 (May 19, 1994)
LOUIS-DREYFUS, JULIA
CV01139 660-661 (July 8, 1993)
LOVE, COURTNEY
CV01140 697 (December 15, 1994)
CV01141 724-725 (December 28, 1995)

M

MADONNA
CV01142 619-620 (December 12, 1991)
MARLEY, BOB
CV01143 676 (February 24, 1994)
MCCARTHY, JENNY
CV01144 738-739 (July 11, 1996)
MERCHANT, NATALIE
CV01145 652 (March 18, 1993)
METALLICA
CV01146 617 (November 14, 1991)
CV01147 619-620 (December 12, 1991)
CV01148 737 (June 27, 1996)
MOORE, DEMI
CV01149 701 (February 9, 1995)
MORISSETTE, ALANIS
CV01150 720 (November 2, 1995)
CV01151 724-725 (December 28, 1995)
CV01152 736 (June 13, 1996)
MORRISON, JIM
CV01153 619-620 (December 12, 1991)
MYERS, MIKE
CV01154 626 (March 19, 1992)
CV01155 645-646 (December 10, 1992)

N

NIRVANA
CV01156 628 (April 16, 1992)
CV01157 645-646 (December 10, 1992)
CV01158 674 (January 27, 1994)

O

OASIS
CV01159 733 (May 2, 1996)
O'BRIEN, CONAN
CV01160 743 (September 19, 1996)
O'CONNOR, SINEAD
CV01161 619-620 (December 12, 1991)
CV01162 642 (October 29, 1992)
CV01163 645-646 (December 10, 1992)
O'NEAL, SHAQUILLE
CV01164 670 (November 25, 1993)
O'RIORDAN, DOLORES
CV01165 704 (March 23, 1995)
OSBORNE, JOAN
CV01166 730 (March 21, 1996)

P

PAGE, JIMMY
CV01167 702 (February 23, 1995)
PEARL JAM
CV01168 668 (October 28, 1993)
PENN, SEAN
CV01169 731 (April 4, 1996)
PERRY, LUKE
CV01170 624 (February 20, 1992)
CV01171 645-646 (December 10, 1992)
PERRY, MATTHEW
CV01172 708 (May 18, 1995)
PETTY, TOM
CV01173 619-620 (December 12, 1991)
CV01174 707 (May 4, 1995)
PFEIFFER, MICHELLE
CV01175 638 (September 3, 1992)
CV01176 645-646 (December 10, 1992)
PHAIR, LIZ
CV01177 692 (October 6, 1994)
PITT, BRAD
CV01178 696 (December 1, 1994)
PLANT, ROBERT
CV01179 702 (February 23, 1995)
POPPER, JOHN
CV01180 736 (June 13, 1996)
PRIESTLEY, JASON
CV01181 624 (February 20, 1992)
CV01182 645-646 (December 10, 1992)

R

RED HOT CHILI PEPPERS
CV01183 633 (June 25, 1992)
CV01184 645-646 (December 10, 1992)
CV01185 719 (October 19, 1995)
R.E.M.
CV01186 619-620 (December 12, 1991)
CV01187 625 (March 5, 1992)
CV01188 645-646 (December 10, 1992)
CV01189 693 (October 20, 1994)
CV01190 745 (October 17, 1996)
REZNOR, TRENT
CV01191 690 (September 8, 1994)
RICHARDS, MICHAEL
CV01192 660-661 (July 8, 1993)
ROBERTS, JULIA
CV01193 686-687 (July 14, 1994)
RODMAN, DENNIS
CV01194 749 (December 12, 1996)
ROLLING STONES
CV01195 689 (August 25, 1994)
ROSE, AXL
CV01196 627 (April 2, 1992)
CV01197 645-646 (December 10, 1992)
ROSSDALE, GAVIN
CV01198 732 (April 18, 1996)
RYDER, WINONA
CV01199 619-620 (December 12, 1991)
CV01200 677 (March 10, 1994)

S

SCHWARZENEGGER, ARNOLD
CV01201 619-620 (December 12, 1991)
SCHWIMMER, DAVID
CV01202 708 (May 18, 1995)
SEINFELD, JERRY
CV01203 660-661 (July 8, 1993)
CV01204 691 (September 22, 1994)
SHAKUR, TUPAC
CV01205 746 (October 31, 1996)
SHIELDS, BROOKE
CV01206 744 (October 3, 1996)
SILVERSTONE, ALICIA
CV01207 716 (September 7, 1995)
SLASH
CV01208 619-620 (December 12, 1991)
SMASHING PUMPKINS
CV01209 680 (April 21, 1994)
CV01210 721 (November 16, 1995)
SNOOP DOGGY DOGG
CV01211 666 (September 30, 1993)
SOUL ASYLUM
CV01212 662 (August 5, 1993)
CV01213 711 (June 29, 1995)
SOUNDGARDEN
CV01214 684 (June 16, 1994)
SPIN DOCTORS
CV01215 647 (January 7, 1993)
SPRINGSTEEN, BRUCE
CV01216 636 (August 6, 1992)
CV01217 645-646 (December 10, 1992)
STALEY, LAYNE
CV01218 727 (February 8, 1996)
STERN, HOWARD
CV01219 675 (February 10, 1994)
STEWART, ROD
CV01220 619-620 (December 12, 1991)
STING
CV01220 619-620 (December 12, 1991)
CV01221 657 (May 27, 1993)
STONE, SHARON
CV01222 630 (May 14, 1992)
CV01223 645-646 (December 10, 1992)

T

TAYLOR, JAMES
CV01224 736 (June 13, 1996)
THOMPSON, HUNTER S.
CV01225 622 (January 23, 1992)
CV01226 645-646 (December 10, 1992)
THORNE-SMITH, COURTNEY
CV01227 682 (May 19, 1994)
TRAVOLTA, JOHN
CV01228 724-725 (December 28, 1995)
CV01229 728 (February 22, 1996)
TWENTY-FIFTH ANNIVERSARY
CV01230 632 (June 11, 1992)
CV01231 641 (October 15, 1992)
TYLER, LIV
CV01232 694 (November 3, 1994)
TYLER, STEVEN
CV01232 694 (November 3, 1994)

U

U2
CV01233 618 (November 28, 1991)
CV01234 619-620 (December 12, 1991)

V

VAN HALEN, EDDIE
CV01235 705 (April 6, 1995)
VEDDER, EDDIE
CV01236 748 (November 28, 1996)

W

WASHINGTON, DENZEL
CV01237 644 (November 26, 1992)
CV01238 645-646 (December 10, 1992)
WILLIAMS, ROBIN
CV01239 619-620 (December 12, 1991)
WILSON PHILLIPS
CV01239 619-620 (December 12, 1991)

Y

YOUNG, NEIL
CV01240 648 (January 21, 1993)

Z

ZUNIGA, DAPHNE
CV01241 682 (May 19, 1994)

Date & Issue Index to Cover Appearances

1991

OCTOBER 17, 1991 (615)
- Clapton, Eric

OCTOBER 31, 1991 (616)
- Garcia, Jerry

NOVEMBER 14, 1991 (617)
- Metallica

NOVEMBER 28, 1991 (618)
- U2

DECEMBER 12, 1991 (619-620)
- Bach, Sebastian
- Black Crowes
- Clapton, Eric
- Depp, Johnny
- Foster, Jodie
- Garcia, Jerry
- Guns N' Roses
- Herman, Pee-Wee
- Hunter, Rachel
- Madonna
- Metallica
- Morrison, Jim
- O'Connor, Sinead
- Petty, Tom
- R.E.M.
- Ryder, Winona
- Schwarzenegger, Arnold
- Slash
- Stewart, Rod
- Sting
- U2
- Williams, Robin
- Wilson Phillips

1992

JANUARY 9, 1992 (621)
- Jackson, Michael

JANUARY 23, 1992 (622)
- Thompson, Hunter S.

FEBRUARY 6, 1992 (623)
- Hendrix, Jimi

FEBRUARY 20, 1992 (624)
- Doherty, Shannen
- Perry, Luke
- Priestley, Jason

MARCH 5, 1992 (625)
- R.E.M.

MARCH 19, 1992 (626)
- Carvey, Dana
- Myers, Mike

APRIL 2, 1992 (627)
- Rose, Axl

APRIL 16, 1992 (628)
- Nirvana

APRIL 30, 1992 (629)
- Def Leppard

MAY 14, 1992 (630)
- Stone, Sharon

MAY 28, 1992 (631)
- Cruise, Tom

JUNE 11, 1992 (632)
- Twenty-Fifth Anniversary

JUNE 25, 1992 (633)
- Red Hot Chili Peppers

JULY 9, 1992 (634-635)
- Batman

AUGUST 6, 1992 (636)
- Springsteen, Bruce

AUGUST 20, 1992 (637)
- Ice-T

SEPTEMBER 3, 1992 (638)
- Pfeiffer, Michelle

SEPTEMBER 17, 1992 (639)
- Clinton, Bill

OCTOBER 1, 1992 (640)
- Bono

OCTOBER 15, 1992 (641)
- Twenty-Fifth Anniversary

OCTOBER 29, 1992 (642)
- O'Connor, Sinead

NOVEMBER 12, 1992 (643)
- Gold Lame Suit (Elvis Presley's)

NOVEMBER 26, 1992 (644)
- Washington, Denzel

DECEMBER 10, 1992 (645-646)
- Batman
- Bono
- Carvey, Dana
- Clinton, Bill
- Cruise, Tom
- Def Leppard
- Doherty, Shannen
- Gold Lame Suit (Elvis Presley's)
- Hendrix, Jimi
- Ice-T
- Jackson, Michael
- Myers, Mike
- Nirvana
- O'Connor, Sinead
- Perry, Luke
- Pfeiffer, Michelle
- Priestley, Jason
- Red Hot Chili Peppers
- R.E.M.
- Rose, Axl
- Springsteen, Bruce
- Stone, Sharon
- Thompson, Hunter S.
- Washington, Denzel

1993

JANUARY 7, 1993 (647)
- Spin Doctors

JANUARY 21, 1993 (648)
- Young, Neil

FEBRUARY 4, 1993 (649)
- Cherry, Neneh

FEBRUARY 18, 1993 (650)
- Letterman, David

MARCH 4, 1993 (651)
- Bono

MARCH 18, 1993 (652)
- Merchant, Natalie

APRIL 1, 1993 (653)
- Brooks, Garth

APRIL 15, 1993 (654)
- Hetfield, James

APRIL 29, 1993 (655)
- Clapton, Eric

MAY 13, 1993 (656)
- Carvey, Dana

MAY 27, 1993 (657)
- Sting

JUNE 10, 1993 (658)
- Houston, Whitney

JUNE 24, 1993 (659)
- Dern, Laura

JULY 8, 1993 (660-661)
- Alexander, Jason
- Louis-Dreyfus, Julia
- Richards, Michael
- Seinfeld, Jerry

AUGUST 5, 1993 (662)
- Soul Asylum

AUGUST 19, 1993 (663)
- Beavis & Butt-Head

SEPTEMBER 2, 1993 (664)
- Garcia, Jerry

SEPTEMBER 16, 1993 (665)
- Jackson, Janet

SEPTEMBER 30, 1993 (666)
- Dr. Dre
- Snoop Doggy Dogg

OCTOBER 14, 1993 (667)
- Edge

OCTOBER 28, 1993 (668)
- Pearl Jam

NOVEMBER 11, 1993 (669)
- Blind Melon

NOVEMBER 25, 1993 (670)
- O'Neal, Shaquille

DECEMBER 9, 1993 (671)
- Clinton, Bill

DECEMBER 23, 1993 (672-673)
- Crawford, Cindy

1994

JANUARY 27, 1994 (674)
- Nirvana

FEBRUARY 10, 1994 (675)
- Stern, Howard

FEBRUARY 24, 1994 (676)
- Marley, Bob

MARCH 10, 1994 (677)
- Ryder, Winona

MARCH 24, 1994 (678)
- Beavis & Butt-Head

APRIL 7, 1994 (679)
- Kiedis, Anthony

APRIL 21, 1994 (680)
- Smashing Pumpkins

MAY 5, 1994 (681)
- Drugs

MAY 19, 1994 (682)
- Bissett, Josie
- Leighton, Laura
- Locklear, Heather
- Thorne-Smith, Courtney
- Zuniga, Daphne

JUNE 2, 1994 (683)
- Cobain, Kurt

JUNE 16, 1994 (684)
- Soundgarden

JUNE 30, 1994 (685)
- Counting Crows

JULY 14, 1994 (686-687)
- Roberts, Julia

AUGUST 11, 1994 (688)
- Beastie Boys

AUGUST 25, 1994 (689)
- Rolling Stones

SEPTEMBER 8, 1994 (690)
- Reznor, Trent

SEPTEMBER 22, 1994 (691)
- Seinfeld, Jerry

OCTOBER 6, 1994 (692)
- Phair, Liz

OCTOBER 20, 1994 (693)
- R.E.M.

NOVEMBER 3, 1994 (694)
- Tyler, Liv
- Tyler, Steven

NOVEMBER 17, 1994 (695)
- Future Of Rock

DECEMBER 1, 1994 (696)
- Pitt, Brad

DECEMBER 15, 1994 (697)
- Love, Courtney

DECEMBER 29, 1994 (698-699)
- Letterman, David

1995

JANUARY 26, 1995 (700)
- Green Day

FEBRUARY 9, 1995 (701)
- Moore, Demi

FEBRUARY 23, 1995 (702)
- Page, Jimmy
- Plant, Robert

MARCH 9, 1995 (703)
- Hawke, Ethan

MARCH 23, 1995 (704)
- O'Riordan, Dolores

APRIL 6, 1995 (705)
- Van Halen, Eddie

APRIL 20, 1995 (706)
- Belly

MAY 4, 1995 (707)
- Petty, Tom

MAY 18, 1995 (708)
- Aniston, Jennifer

Cox, Courteney
Kudrow, Lisa
LeBlanc, Matt
Perry, Matthew
Schwimmer, David
JUNE 1, 1995 (709)
Etheridge, Melissa
JUNE 15, 1995 (710)
Barrymore, Drew
JUNE 29, 1995 (711)
Soul Asylum
JULY 13, 1995 (712-713)
Carrey, Jim
AUGUST 10, 1995 (714)
Hootie And The Blowfish
AUGUST 24, 1995 (715)
Hole
SEPTEMBER 7, 1995 (716)
Silverstone, Alicia
SEPTEMBER 21, 1995 (717)
Garcia, Jerry
OCTOBER 5, 1995 (718)
Foo Fighters
OCTOBER 19, 1995 (719)
Red Hot Chili Peppers
NOVEMBER 2, 1995 (720)
Morissette, Alanis
NOVEMBER 16, 1995 (721)
Smashing Pumpkins
NOVEMBER 30, 1995 (722)
Kravitz, Lenny
DECEMBER 14, 1995 (723)
Jagger, Mick
DECEMBER 28, 1995 (724-725)
Coolio
Corgan, Billy
Crow, Sheryl
Garcia, Jerry
Green Day
Love, Courtney
Morissette, Alanis
Travolta, John

1996

JANUARY 25, 1996 (726)
Live
FEBRUARY 8, 1996 (727)
Staley, Layne
FEBRUARY 22, 1996 (728)
Travolta, John
MARCH 7, 1996 (729)
Aniston, Jennifer
MARCH 21, 1996 (730)
Osborne, Joan
APRIL 4, 1996 (731)
Penn, Sean
APRIL 18, 1996 (732)
Rossdale, Gavin
MAY 2, 1996 (733)
Oasis
MAY 16, 1996 (734)
Anderson, Gillian
Duchovny, David
MAY 30, 1996 (735)
Letterman, David
JUNE 13, 1996 (736)
Beck
Buffett, Jimmy
Bullock, Sandra
Corgan, Billy
Cornell, Chris
Farrell, Perry
Kiss
Morissette, Alanis
Popper, John
Taylor, James
JUNE 27, 1996 (737)
Metallica
JULY 11, 1996 (738-739)
McCarthy, Jenny
AUGUST 8, 1996 (740)
Garcia, Jerry
AUGUST 22, 1996 (741)
Diaz, Cameron
SEPTEMBER 5, 1996 (742)
Fugees
SEPTEMBER 19, 1996 (743)
O'Brien, Conan
OCTOBER 3, 1996 (744)
Shields, Brooke
OCTOBER 17, 1996 (745)
R.E.M.
OCTOBER 31, 1996 (746)
Shakur, Tupac
NOVEMBER 14, 1996 (747)
Crow, Sheryl
NOVEMBER 28, 1996 (748)
Vedder, Eddie
DECEMBER 12, 1996 (749)
Rodman, Dennis
DECEMBER 26, 1996 (750-751)
Beavis & Butt-Head
Lee, Pamela Anderson

Letters to the Editor

A

AASEN, ARIN
LE08034 749 (December 12, 1996) p16.
ABBEY, MARC
LE08035 677 (March 10, 1994) p12.
ABBRING, LANCE
LE08036 666 (September 30, 1993) p10.
ABEL, BRAD
LE08037 681 (May 5, 1994) p8.
ABERNATHY, BRIAN
LE08038 636 (August 6, 1992) p7.
ABRAHAM, JACOB (RESIDENT PSYCHIATRIST, COLUMBIA-PRESBYTERIAN MEDICAL CENTER)
LE08039 622 (January 23, 1992) p4.
ABRAMOWITZ, ANDY
LE08040 727 (February 8, 1996) p10.
ABRAMSON, GREG
LE08041 664 (September 2, 1993) p8.
ACOSTA, JOSHUA
LE08042 659 (June 24, 1993) p10.
ADAMIDIS, HARRY
LE08043 683 (June 2, 1994) p11.
ADAMS, JEFF
LE08044 639 (September 17, 1992) p10.
ADAMS, SCOTT
LE08045 683 (June 2, 1994) p11.
ADAMS, TODD
LE08046 708 (May 18, 1995) p14.
ADKINS, G. P., CAPTAIN (FORT LEONARD WOOD)
LE08047 617 (November 14, 1991) p8.
ADKINS, SUZI L.
LE08048 627 (April 2, 1992) p8.
AGGERS, WILLIAM
LE08049 678 (March 24, 1994) p6.
ALATORRE, LAURA
LE08050 694 (November 3, 1994) p14.
ALBANO, DAWN
LE08051 615 (October 17, 1991) p8.
ALEJANDRO, HANNAH
LE08052 654 (April 15, 1993) p8.
ALLEN, LAURA
LE08053 694 (November 3, 1994) p14.
ALLGOOD, DESIREE
LE08054 689 (August 25, 1994) p12.
ALTMAN, ANN
LE08055 707 (May 4, 1995) p16.
AMBS, DARYL
LE08056 734 (May 16, 1996) p14.
AMENT, JEFF
LE08057 645-646 (December 10, 1992) p20.
AMERMAN, DALE
LE08058 638 (September 3, 1992) p6.
AMSDEN, STEPHEN E.
LE08059 667 (October 14, 1993) p14.
ANDERSON, DAVID J.
LE08060 684 (June 16, 1994) p11.
ANDERSON, PHYLLIS (U.S. DEPARTMENT OF ENERGY)
LE08061 660-661 (July 8, 1993) p10.
ANDLER, MATTHEW
LE08062 664 (September 2, 1993) p8.
ANDREWS, PAUL D.
LE08063 698-699 (December 29, 1994) p26.
ANGELINE, MARY
LE08064 617 (November 14, 1991) p8.
ANSTADT, DOUGLAS
LE08065 625 (March 5, 1992) p4.
APODACA, TIM
LE08066 615 (October 17, 1991) p8.
APTER, LAUREN E.
LE08067 638 (September 3, 1992) p6.
ARCHER, BRIAN
LE08068 627 (April 2, 1992) p8.
ARCHER-WEINSTEIN, LINDA (T.J. MARTELL FOUNDATION)
LE08069 682 (May 19, 1994) p14.
ARENDT, A. J.
LE08070 644 (November 26, 1992) p11.
ARMOR, PERRY
LE08071 694 (November 3, 1994) p14.
ARMSTRONG, ADAM
LE08072 660-661 (July 8, 1993) p10.
ARMSTRONG, LYNN
LE08073 718 (October 5, 1995) p16.
ARMSTRONG, SHERRI
LE08074 683 (June 2, 1994) p11.
ARNOLD, KERRY
LE08075 712-713 (July 13, 1995) p20.
ARTLEY, MELANIE
LE08076 723 (December 14, 1995) p20.
ASEL, ERIC
LE08077 722 (November 30, 1995) p14.
ASH, DEBBIE
LE08078 648 (January 21, 1993) p7.
ASHBY, KELSO, III
LE08079 657 (May 27, 1993) p6.
ASHDOWN, DAVID
LE08080 650 (February 18, 1993) p6.
ASKEW, ROGER
LE08081 702 (February 23, 1995) p16.
ATKINS, VANCE
LE08082 676 (February 24, 1994) p10.
ATKINSON, BISHOP
LE08083 650 (February 18, 1993) p6.
AUBREY, JOY
LE08084 706 (April 20, 1995) p12.
AUBUCHON, MARK
LE08085 698-699 (December 29, 1994) p26.
AUDEVART, PETE
LE08086 681 (May 5, 1994) p8.
AUER, NICOLE J.
LE08087 697 (December 15, 1994) p14.
AUFDENKAMPE, NICK
LE08088 727 (February 8, 1996) p10.
AUSTIN, MICHAEL D.
LE08089 670 (November 25, 1993) p8.
AZEVEDO, ROB.
LE08090 734 (May 16, 1996) p14.

B

B., ANNA
LE08091 720 (November 2, 1995) p12.
BABER, MICHAEL
LE08092 748 (November 28, 1996) p22.
BACH, SEBASTIAN
LE08093 645-646 (December 10, 1992) p20.
LE08094 689 (August 25, 1994) p12.
BACKOUS, MIKE
LE08095 657 (May 27, 1993) p6.
BAE, NELSON
LE08096 665 (September 16, 1993) p6.
BAERWALD, DAVID
LE08097 750-751 (December 26, 1996) p26.
BAICH, KARIELLE
LE08098 658 (June 10, 1993) p12.
BAIKAL, ALISON
LE08099 664 (September 2, 1993) p8.
BAILEY, B. J.
LE08100 666 (September 30, 1993) p10.
BAKER, ALEX
LE08101 670 (November 25, 1993) p8.
BAKER, CARL F.
LE08102 722 (November 30, 1995) p14.
BAKER, ERIC
LE08103 676 (February 24, 1994) p10.
BAKER, JOSH
LE08104 642 (October 29, 1992) p8.
BAKER, ROGER
LE08105 717 (September 21, 1995) p16.
BALLARD, CHRIS
LE08106 658 (June 10, 1993) p12.
BALLOU, MELISSA
LE08107 647 (January 7, 1993) p7.
BARBER, SCOTT
LE08108 669 (November 11, 1993) p8.
BARENDSE, NATHAN
LE08109 625 (March 5, 1992) p4.
BARLOW, J. A.
LE08110 694 (November 3, 1994) p14.
BARRETT, JOHANNA
LE08111 680 (April 21, 1994) p8.
BARRIS, LYN
LE08112 626 (March 19, 1992) p6.
BARRITT, T. R.
LE08113 652 (March 18, 1993) p10.
BARRYMORE, DREW
LE08114 645-646 (December 10, 1992) p20.
BARTHOLOMEW, DANIELLE
LE08115 642 (October 29, 1992) p8.
BASSON, DUNCAN
LE08116 693 (October 20, 1994) p22.
BATTIS, AMY
LE08117 670 (November 25, 1993) p8.
BAUER, NANCI
LE08118 682 (May 19, 1994) p14.
BAUGH, DANNY SCOTT
LE08119 625 (March 5, 1992) p4.
BEAM, M. J.

LE08120 634-635 (July 9, 1992) p8.
BEARD, MICHAEL A.
LE08121 730 (March 21, 1996) p14.
BEARDEN, DONNA
LE08122 627 (April 2, 1992) p8.
BEARE, STEPHEN
LE08123 617 (November 14, 1991) p8.
BEATTY, DAN
LE08124 705 (April 6, 1995) p14.
LE08125 743 (September 19, 1996) p12.
BECKER, MATT
LE08126 681 (May 5, 1994) p8.
BEDWELL, AUDREY
LE08127 730 (March 21, 1996) p14.
BEJARANO, RICHARD XAVIER, SR.
LE08128 671 (December 9, 1993) p7.
BELCH, JOHN
LE08129 665 (September 16, 1993) p6.
BELDEN, HEATH
LE08130 724-725 (December 28, 1995) p20.
BELINSKI, JULES
LE08131 721 (November 16, 1995) p18.
BELLACE, MATT
LE08132 685 (June 30, 1994) p10.
BELLINO, TERESA
LE08133 726 (January 25, 1996) p12.
BENN, EVAN
LE08134 729 (March 7, 1996) p6.
BENNETT, BILL
LE08135 629 (April 30, 1992) p9.
BENNETT, COURTNEY
LE08136 649 (February 4, 1993) p7.
BENOIT, RAYMOND S.
LE08137 667 (October 14, 1993) p14.
BENSRETI, E.
LE08138 703 (March 9, 1995) p16.
BENTLEY, CORY ANN
LE08139 648 (January 21, 1993) p7.
BENZAKEIN, ARIEL
LE08140 668 (October 28, 1993) p8.
BENZIE, ROBERT
LE08141 656 (May 13, 1993) p10.
BERAN, GEOFF
LE08142 679 (April 7, 1994) p10.
BERCE, STEVEN
LE08143 724-725 (December 28, 1995) p20.
BERGMAN, BARRY
LE08144 640 (October 1, 1992) p6.
BERKA, ANTHONY S.
LE08145 679 (April 7, 1994) p10.
BERKOWITZ, ROGER
LE08146 726 (January 25, 1996) p12.
BERMAN, JOSEPH
LE08147 616 (October 31, 1991) p8.
BERTRAM, MICHELLE
LE08148 662 (August 5, 1993) p8.
BERUBE, MICHAEL
LE08149 696 (December 1, 1994) p18.
BEST, DAISY
LE08150 647 (January 7, 1993) p7.
BETTS, MICHAEL C.
LE08151 677 (March 10, 1994) p12.
BEZZAG, LOESA
LE08152 665 (September 16, 1993) p6.
BIBLER, JON
LE08153 707 (May 4, 1995) p16.
BILENKIN, SHARONE
LE08154 689 (August 25, 1994) p12.
BILLERA, JOE
LE08155 692 (October 6, 1994) p12.
BIRT, RAYMOND
LE08156 715 (August 24, 1995) p18.
BISHOP, ELAINE
LE08157 652 (March 18, 1993) p10.
BISHOP, JAKE
LE08158 743 (September 19, 1996) p12.
BITOPOULOS, BILL
LE08159 662 (August 5, 1993) p8.
BITTNER, MARLENA
LE08160 680 (April 21, 1994) p8.
BLACK, CLINT
LE08161 672-673 (December 23, 1993) p10.
BLACK, JASON
LE08162 655 (April 29, 1993) p7.
BLACKBURN, JAY
LE08163 674 (January 27, 1994) p8.
BLACKSTONE, EVE
LE08164 692 (October 6, 1994) p12.
BLAIR, TIFFANY
LE08165 633 (June 25, 1992) p5.
BLAKE, D. M.
LE08166 704 (March 23, 1995) p18.
BLANCHARD, JAKE
LE08167 711 (June 29, 1995) p10.
BLANKHOLM, BECKY
LE08168 629 (April 30, 1992) p9.
BLECKSMITH, EMILY
LE08169 677 (March 10, 1994) p12.
BLUM, MATTHEW GREGG
LE08170 634-635 (July 9, 1992) p8.
BOGGERI, LISA
LE08171 675 (February 10, 1994) p6.
BOHANNON, ALLEN
LE08172 674 (January 27, 1994) p8.
BON JOVI, JON
LE08173 672-673 (December 23, 1993) p10.
BONSOL, ALLAN
LE08174 737 (June 27, 1996) p12.
BOOK, KEVIN
LE08175 638 (September 3, 1992) p6.
BOOPKINS, BILLY
LE08176 710 (June 15, 1995) p14.
BOSCH, NIKA
LE08177 746 (October 31, 1996) p14.
BOSLEY, RACHAEL K.
LE08178 654 (April 15, 1993) p8.
BOSWINKLE, BILL
LE08179 711 (June 29, 1995) p10.
BOVE, RICHIE X.
LE08180 681 (May 5, 1994) p8.
BOWERS, CAROL
LE08181 662 (August 5, 1993) p8.
BOWIE, DAVID
LE08182 619-620 (December 12, 1991) p14.
BOYDSTON, BARBARA
LE08183 653 (April 1, 1993) p8.
BOYKIN, BEN
LE08184 629 (April 30, 1992) p8.
BOZOWSKI, NICOLE
LE08185 616 (October 31, 1991) p8.
BRAAM, THOMAS
LE08186 692 (October 6, 1994) p12.
BRADFORD, MEREDITH
LE08187 703 (March 9, 1995) p16.
BRADSHAW, MIKE
LE08188 693 (October 20, 1994) p22.
BRADY, SARAH (CHAIR, HANDGUN CONTROL, INC.)
LE08189 669 (November 11, 1993) p8.
BRANNON, PATRICK T.
LE08190 694 (November 3, 1994) p14.
LE08191 709 (June 1, 1995) p14.
BRANT, JAMES
LE08192 678 (March 24, 1994) p6.
BRATTO, DAVID
LE08193 679 (April 7, 1994) p10.
BRECKENRIDGE, DARCY
LE08194 660-661 (July 8, 1993) p10.
BRET, KATHRYN A.
LE08195 694 (November 3, 1994) p14.
BREWER, LYNN A.
LE08196 642 (October 29, 1992) p8.
BREWSTER, JOSH
LE08197 708 (May 18, 1995) p14.
BRILLMAN, DAN
LE08198 721 (November 16, 1995) p18.
BRODSKY, ANDREW
LE08199 698-699 (December 29, 1994) p26.
BROOKS, DAVID
LE08200 720 (November 2, 1995) p12.
BROOKS, ROBERT A.
LE08201 616 (October 31, 1991) p8.
BROSCHEID, DEBORAH
LE08202 621 (January 9, 1992) p6.
BROWN, ELISSA
LE08203 656 (May 13, 1993) p10.
BROWN, JEFFREY C.
LE08204 692 (October 6, 1994) p12.
BROWN, JENNIE
LE08205 637 (August 20, 1992) p6.
BROWN, JOSEPH
LE08206 727 (February 8, 1996) p10.
BROWN, KEVIN
LE08207 616 (October 31, 1991) p8.
BROWN, LEE P. (DIRECTOR, OFFICE OF NATIONAL DRUG CONTROL POLICY)
LE08208 714 (August 10, 1995) p12.
BROWN, MARTHA
LE08209 630 (May 14, 1992) p8.
BROWN, PATSY
LE08210 615 (October 17, 1991) p8.
BRUNETTI, MAUREEN
LE08211 738-739 (July 11, 1996) p12.
BRYAN, MATTHEW W.
LE08212 716 (September 7, 1995) p10.
BRYANT, KEVIN
LE08213 683 (June 2, 1994) p11.
BRYANT, MERRIKEN
LE08214 653 (April 1, 1993) p8.
BUCKINGHAM, BRIAN
LE08215 640 (October 1, 1992) p6.
BUCKLEY, CHRISTOPHER
LE08216 700 (January 26, 1995) p14.
BUDOFF, IRENE
LE08217 633 (June 25, 1992) p5.
BUELL, BEBE
LE08218 697 (December 15, 1994) p14.
BUFFKIN, MEG
LE08219 658 (June 10, 1993) p12.
BUKOVICA, EMIR
LE08220 728 (February 22, 1996) p16.
BUNCH, AIMEE J.
LE08221 686-687 (July 14, 1994) p14.

BUNN, TORIE
LE08222 663 (August 19, 1993) p4.
BURES, JULIANA
LE08223 731 (April 4, 1996) p14.
BURFORD, KATIE
LE08224 748 (November 28, 1996) p22.
BURGER, BOB
LE08225 625 (March 5, 1992) p4.
BURK, RONNIE
LE08226 647 (January 7, 1993) p7.
BURKE, J. MICHAEL
LE08227 649 (February 4, 1993) p7.
BURKERT, TIM
LE08228 719 (October 19, 1995) p10.
BURKHARDT, LOUIS
LE08229 708 (May 18, 1995) p14.
BURNS, RICK, JR.
LE08230 720 (November 2, 1995) p12.
BUSBY, ROBERT
LE08231 663 (August 19, 1993) p4.
BUSSELL, ADAM
LE08232 745 (October 17, 1996) p24.
BUTH, MARIANNE
LE08233 689 (August 25, 1994) p12.
BUTLER, DAVE
LE08234 627 (April 2, 1992) p8.
BUTLER, KEITH D. (MILITARY JOURNALIST - STAFF SERGEANT, U.S. ARMY)
LE08235 670 (November 25, 1993) p8.
BYRD, ESTHER BROCK
LE08236 745 (October 17, 1996) p24.

C

CAIN, DAVID
LE08237 679 (April 7, 1994) p10.
CALCAGNO, JO ANN (ASSISTANT PROGRAM DIRECTOR, WQBK-FM)
LE08238 690 (September 8, 1994) p16.
CALDWELL, MIKIE
LE08239 633 (June 25, 1992) p5.
CALE, JOHN
LE08240 672-673 (December 23, 1993) p10.
CALHOUN, AARON
LE08241 654 (April 15, 1993) p8.
CALHOUN, MIKE
LE08242 663 (August 19, 1993) p4.
CALLAHAN, JIM
LE08243 652 (March 18, 1993) p10.
CAMERON, SEAN
LE08244 644 (November 26, 1992) p11.
CAMINO, ANNA
LE08245 732 (April 18, 1996) p16.
CAMPBELL, ARCHIBALD W.
LE08246 724-725 (December 28, 1995) p20.
CAMPBELL, JACK
LE08247 678 (March 24, 1994) p6.
CAMPBELL, LEANN
LE08248 650 (February 18, 1993) p6.
CANADY, CHARLES T.
LE08249 722 (November 30, 1995) pp14,16.
CANDLER, JONAS
LE08250 634-635 (July 9, 1992) p8.
CANEDO, KEN, FATHER
LE08251 621 (January 9, 1992) p7.
CAO, ANDY
LE08252 633 (June 25, 1992) p5.
CAPPELLO, ROBIN
LE08253 686-687 (July 14, 1994) p14.
CAPPELLO, VICTORIA
LE08254 651 (March 4, 1993) p10.
CARLIN, T. M.
LE08255 676 (February 24, 1994) p10.
CARMAN, COLIN
LE08256 715 (August 24, 1995) p18.
CARMICHAEL, MARNI
LE08257 664 (September 2, 1993) p8.
CARMONA, OLIVER
LE08258 656 (May 13, 1993) p10.
CAROTHERS, FRANK
LE08259 711 (June 29, 1995) p10.
CARR, TIMOTHY M.
LE08260 747 (November 14, 1996) p20.
CARRICO, MONICA A.
LE08261 627 (April 2, 1992) p8.
CARROLL, GREGG
LE08262 621 (January 9, 1992) p6.
CARROLL, LISA
LE08263 657 (May 27, 1993) p6.
CARTER, STACIE
LE08264 706 (April 20, 1995) p12.
CARTER, THOMAS
LE08265 668 (October 28, 1993) p8.
CARULLI, FRANK
LE08266 627 (April 2, 1992) p8.
CARVAINES, MICHAEL
LE08267 702 (February 23, 1995) p16.
CASANTA, SHARON
LE08268 700 (January 26, 1995) p14.
CASE, J. MARSHALL
LE08269 746 (October 31, 1996) p14.
CASE, RACHEL
LE08270 677 (March 10, 1994) p12.
CASELNOVA, ANDREW
LE08271 716 (September 7, 1995) p10.
CASERTANO, MATT
LE08272 717 (September 21, 1995) p16.
CASEY, MIKE
LE08273 677 (March 10, 1994) p12.
CASH, ROSANNE
LE08274 736 (June 13, 1996) p16.
CASIDA, CHRIS
LE08275 690 (September 8, 1994) p16.
CASTLEBERRY, JANET
LE08276 718 (October 5, 1995) p16.
CATE, THOM
LE08277 686-687 (July 14, 1994) p14.
CATFISH
LE08278 736 (June 13, 1996) p16.
CAUDELL, KIM FEATHERS
LE08279 664 (September 2, 1993) p8.
CAULDER, LISA
LE08280 697 (December 15, 1994) p14.
CAUTHEN, KARIN
LE08281 651 (March 4, 1993) p10.
CAVE, NICK
LE08282 619-620 (December 12, 1991) p14.
CAVENDISH, DAVE
LE08283 707 (May 4, 1995) p16.
C.D.
LE08284 720 (November 2, 1995) p12.
CEJAS, F.
LE08285 690 (September 8, 1994) p16.
CEKINOVICH, NICHOLAS
LE08286 668 (October 28, 1993) p8.
CENOTE, MONARCHA
LE08287 675 (February 10, 1994) p6.
CHAFEE, JOHN H. (U.S. SENATE)
LE08288 737 (June 27, 1996) p12.
CHATFIELD, LUCAS
LE08289 680 (April 21, 1994) p8.
CHEEK, WILLIAM
LE08290 702 (February 23, 1995) p16.
CHENEY, ALAN
LE08291 668 (October 28, 1993) p8.
LE08292 707 (May 4, 1995) p16.
CHENEY, DEIDRE
LE08293 707 (May 4, 1995) p16.
CHERICO, MARK A.
LE08294 626 (March 19, 1992) p6.
CHERNIAVSKY, NEVA
LE08295 680 (April 21, 1994) p8.
CHETWIN, SUSAN (GENERAL MANAGER, MUZAK)
LE08296 665 (September 16, 1993) p6.
CHILD, DESMOND
LE08297 619-620 (December 12, 1991) p14.
CHILDS, CLANCY
LE08298 650 (February 18, 1993) p6.
CHOATE, ROB
LE08299 637 (August 20, 1992) p6.
CHOY, CINDY CUP
LE08300 659 (June 24, 1993) p10.
CHRISTIANSON, DAN
LE08301 732 (April 18, 1996) p16.
CHRISTMAS, ANDREW
LE08302 710 (June 15, 1995) p14.
CHUNG, BERNARD
LE08303 724-725 (December 28, 1995) p20.
CHUNG, JAE
LE08304 684 (June 16, 1994) p11.
CIGNOLI, CHRISTINE
LE08305 728 (February 22, 1996) p16.
CILUFFO, JASON
LE08306 667 (October 14, 1993) p14.
CIOFFI, TARA M.
LE08307 689 (August 25, 1994) p12.
CIOLEK, DANNA G.
LE08308 669 (November 11, 1993) p8.
CIPOLLO, LISA
LE08309 740 (August 8, 1996) p14.
CLARK, AARON
LE08310 750-751 (December 26, 1996) p26.
CLARK, BEKI
LE08311 622 (January 23, 1992) p4.
CLARK, CHARITY
LE08312 648 (January 21, 1993) p7.
CLARK, TIM
LE08313 704 (March 23, 1995) p18.
CLARK, WILLIAM SCOTT
LE08314 709 (June 1, 1995) p14.
CLARKE, ZANE
LE08315 722 (November 30, 1995) p14.
CLAYPOOL, LES
LE08316 619-620 (December 12, 1991) p14.
LE08317 669 (November 11, 1993) p8.
CLEAR, RANDY
LE08318 628 (April 16, 1992) p6.

CLEMENS, JIM
LE08319 683 (June 2, 1994) p11.
CLOHESSY, DAVID (SURVIVORS NETWORK OF THOSE ABUSED BY PRIESTS)
LE08320 675 (February 10, 1994) p6.
COCCOLI, CHRISTINE
LE08321 677 (March 10, 1994) p12.
COHEN, RANDEE DAWN
LE08322 707 (May 4, 1995) p16.
COLALILLO, CHRISTINA
LE08323 633 (June 25, 1992) p5.
COLATRELLA, ELIZABETH
LE08324 683 (June 2, 1994) p11.
COLBY, SHANNON
LE08325 705 (April 6, 1995) p14.
COLE, NATALIE
LE08326 619-620 (December 12, 1991) p14.
COLLINS, BARBARA (LIBRARIAN, CENTRAL HIGH SCHOOL, KNOXVILLE, TENNESSEE)
LE08327 636 (August 6, 1992) p7.
COLLINS, PHIL
LE08328 672-673 (December 23, 1993) p10.
COLMAN, CHRIS
LE08329 678 (March 24, 1994) p6.
COMES, JOHN F.
LE08330 709 (June 1, 1995) p14.
COMPTON, JEFFREY R.
LE08331 712-713 (July 13, 1995) p20.
COMSTOCK, CHRISTINA
LE08332 615 (October 17, 1991) p8.
CONCERNED READER
LE08333 729 (March 7, 1996) p6.
CONLON, CINDER
LE08334 636 (August 6, 1992) p7.
CONNELL, DAVID
LE08335 743 (September 19, 1996) p12.
CONNER, KATHY
LE08336 637 (August 20, 1992) p6.
CONNERS, JANET
LE08337 665 (September 16, 1993) p6.
CONROD, JONAN
LE08338 749 (December 12, 1996) p16.
CONSTANTINO, MARIO T.
LE08339 681 (May 5, 1994) p8.
CONTRERAS, FRANKIE
LE08340 735 (May 30, 1996) p10.
CONTY, TONY
LE08341 709 (June 1, 1995) p14.
CONYERS, JOHN (UNITED STATES HOUSE OF REPRESENTATIVES-DEMOCRAT, MICHIGAN)
LE08342 746 (October 31, 1996) p14.
COOK, CHRISTINE A.
LE08343 640 (October 1, 1992) p6.
COOK, JIM
LE08344 633 (June 25, 1992) p5.
COOK, STU
LE08345 652 (March 18, 1993) p10.
COON, KIERSTEN
LE08346 640 (October 1, 1992) p6.
LE08347 Number not assigned.
COOVER, KRIS W.
LE08348 665 (September 16, 1993) p6.
COPPOLA, ANGELA
LE08349 696 (December 1, 1994) p18.
CORBIN, ROSEMARY M. (MAYOR, RICHMOND, CALIFORNIA)
LE08350 706 (April 20, 1995) p12.
CORCORAN, JOEL
LE08351 658 (June 10, 1993) p12.
CORRIGAN, JEFF
LE08352 706 (April 20, 1995) p12.
CORSETTI, LORRIE
LE08353 657 (May 27, 1993) p6.
COSTELLO, ELVIS
LE08354 722 (November 30, 1995) p14.
COSTIC, JEFF
LE08355 721 (November 16, 1995) p18.
COTTON, MARK
LE08356 667 (October 14, 1993) p14.
COUNTS, KYLE
LE08357 737 (June 27, 1996) p12.
COYLE, JOHN
LE08358 696 (December 1, 1994) p18.
CRAIN, WILLIAM
LE08359 734 (May 16, 1996) p14.
CRAMER, ERIN
LE08360 719 (October 19, 1995) p10.
CRAN, KATHY
LE08361 728 (February 22, 1996) p16.
CRANE, JESSICA
LE08362 676 (February 24, 1994) p10.
LE08363 682 (May 19, 1994) p14.
CRANSTON, MICHAEL S.
LE08364 617 (November 14, 1991) p8.
CRAWFORD, MILES
LE08365 651 (March 4, 1993) p10.
LE08366 658 (June 10, 1993) p12.
CRAWFORD, PAUL, J.
LE08367 622 (January 23, 1992) p4.
CREASY
LE08368 703 (March 9, 1995) p16.
CRIBLEZ, DAVID J.
LE08369 615 (October 17, 1991) p8.
LE08370 644 (November 26, 1992) p11.
CRIM, RICK
LE08371 662 (August 5, 1993) p8.
CROGHAN, PEGGY
LE08372 690 (September 8, 1994) p16.
CROWE, JOSHUA
LE08373 655 (April 29, 1993) p7.
CRUTCHER, MICHAEL J.
LE08374 621 (January 9, 1992) p7.
CRUTCHER, WILL
LE08375 650 (February 18, 1993) p6.
CRUZ, BRIAN
LE08376 615 (October 17, 1991) p8.
CUNNINGHAM, CARL
LE08377 712-713 (July 13, 1995) p20.
CURRAN, BETSY
LE08378 741 (August 22, 1996) p20.
CURTIS, JEFF
LE08379 663 (August 19, 1993) p4.
CUTHBERTSON, TIMOTHY
LE08380 737 (June 27, 1996) p12.

D

D.A.
LE08381 662 (August 5, 1993) p8.
DAGELEN, MARK
LE08382 625 (March 5, 1992) p4.
DALBESIO, JAMIE
LE08383 692 (October 6, 1994) p12.
DAMRON, VICKI L.
LE08384 679 (April 7, 1994) p10.
D'ARBY, TERENCE TRENT
LE08385 672-673 (December 23, 1993) p10.
DARLING, NICOLETT
LE08386 734 (May 16, 1996) p14.
DAVIES, JIM
LE08387 684 (June 16, 1994) p11.
DAVIES, PETE
LE08388 717 (September 21, 1995) p16.
DAVIS, CHRISTINE
LE08389 733 (May 2, 1996) p10.
DAVIS, ELITE (ELITE PROFESSIONAL SERVICES)
LE08390 657 (May 27, 1993) p6.
DAVIS, FRANCIS
LE08391 680 (April 21, 1994) p8.
DAVIS, GREG
LE08392 745 (October 17, 1996) p24.
DAVIS, RACHEL
LE08393 714 (August 10, 1995) p12.
DAVIS, STEVEN
LE08394 658 (June 10, 1993) p12.
DAVIS, VIRGINIA B.
LE08395 711 (June 29, 1995) p10.
DAWSON, AMY E.
LE08396 664 (September 2, 1993) p8.
DAY, PAMELA
LE08397 642 (October 29, 1992) p8.
DAYTON, ELIZABETH
LE08398 689 (August 25, 1994) p12.
DAYTON, MARK
LE08399 658 (June 10, 1993) p12.
DE JONG, JONATHAN
LE08400 750-751 (December 26, 1996) p26.
DE ROSIER, SARAH
LE08401 742 (September 5, 1996) p16.
DE VAUL, PHILIP HART, ESQ.
LE08402 716 (September 7, 1995) p10.
DEAN, ROGER
LE08403 616 (October 31, 1991) p8.
DEAN, WAYNE
LE08404 628 (April 16, 1992) p6.
DEFALCO, RITCH
LE08405 634-635 (July 9, 1992) p8.
DEFOER, DAMON
LE08406 647 (January 7, 1993) p7.
DEGRAZIA-SANDERS, JOHN
LE08407 709 (June 1, 1995) p14.
DEITZ, ALEX
LE08408 723 (December 14, 1995) p20.
DELUCA, SHANNON
LE08409 736 (June 13, 1996) p16.
DENNY, JYRONE, JR.
LE08410 701 (February 9, 1995) p14.
DENTICO, TODD
LE08411 650 (February 18, 1993) p6.
DEPARRIE, PAUL (EDITOR, LIFE ADVOCATE)
LE08412 714 (August 10, 1995) p12.
DEPOTO, MARC D.
LE08413 708 (May 18, 1995) p14.
DERY, JOHANNA
LE08414 726 (January 25, 1996) p12.
DEWITT, CAREY A.
LE08415 639 (September 17, 1992) p10.

DIANE
LE08416 728 (February 22, 1996) p16.
DICKSON, HARVEY
LE08417 653 (April 1, 1993) p8.
DIEHL, MINDY
LE08418 629 (April 30, 1992) p8.
DIGBY, ALAN
LE08419 723 (December 14, 1995) p20.
DILLARD, L. R.
LE08420 618 (November 28, 1991) p9.
DILLON, ALEX
LE08421 730 (March 21, 1996) p14.
DINSMORE, JEFF
LE08422 719 (October 19, 1995) p10.
DIONNE, PAUL A.
LE08423 723 (December 14, 1995) p20.
D.J.
LE08424 732 (April 18, 1996) p16.
DMYTRYK, VICKY
LE08425 671 (December 9, 1993) p7.
DOCKERY, SUE ELLEN
LE08426 665 (September 16, 1993) p6.
DODGE, BRIAN
LE08427 707 (May 4, 1995) p16.
DOMINICIS, JORGE (FLO-SUN INC.)
LE08428 736 (June 13, 1996) p16.
DONAHOE, TOM
LE08429 721 (November 16, 1995) p18.
DONALD, KYRA
LE08430 690 (September 8, 1994) p16.
DONNELLY, JASON
LE08431 716 (September 7, 1995) p10.
DONNERSTAG, ROSLYN
LE08432 711 (June 29, 1995) p10.
DONOHUE, JOHN
LE08433 654 (April 15, 1993) p8.
DONOVAN, SCOTT
LE08434 694 (November 3, 1994) p14.
DOUGLASS, AMY
LE08435 735 (May 30, 1996) p10.
DOWDY, JULIE
LE08436 730 (March 21, 1996) p14.
DOWELL, SUSANNAH
LE08437 736 (June 13, 1996) p16.
DOYLE, MACREENA
LE08438 656 (May 13, 1993) p10.
DRAGO, KAREN
LE08439 719 (October 19, 1995) p10.
DRAKE, G. L.
LE08440 743 (September 19, 1996) p12.
DRAKE, JOANNE
LE08441 710 (June 15, 1995) p14.
DRAKEFORD, DALE B.
LE08442 707 (May 4, 1995) p16.
DREW, DAN
LE08443 747 (November 14, 1996) p20.
DREW, MARILYN
LE08444 747 (November 14, 1996) p20.
DRISCOLL, KEVIN
LE08445 621 (January 9, 1992) p6.
DU PLESSIS, ADRIAN
LE08446 750-751 (December 26, 1996) p26.
DUBIN, K. L.
LE08447 749 (December 12, 1996) p16.
DUDMAN, JOE
LE08448 722 (November 30, 1995) p14.
DUEX, STEVEN
LE08449 684 (June 16, 1994) p11.
DUGAN, RENEE
LE08450 621 (January 9, 1992) pp6-7.
DUGAN, SARAH
LE08451 705 (April 6, 1995) p14.
DUNLAP, BARBARA J.
LE08452 677 (March 10, 1994) p12.
DUNNING, THOMAS N.
LE08453 683 (June 2, 1994) p11.
DURANT, WENDY
LE08454 665 (September 16, 1993) p6.
DURHAM, CURTIS W., JR.
LE08455 651 (March 4, 1993) p10.
DYREK, MARK
LE08456 625 (March 5, 1992) p4.

E

E., REBECCA
LE08457 724-725 (December 28, 1995) p20.
EARLE, SIMON
LE08458 742 (September 5, 1996) p16.
EASTERLING, SHAN
LE08459 650 (February 18, 1993) p6.
LE08460 665 (September 16, 1993) p6.
E.B.
LE08461 706 (April 20, 1995) p12.
EBERT, CRISSY
LE08462 736 (June 13, 1996) p16.
EBERTH, GARRETT
LE08463 697 (December 15, 1994) p14.
ECCLES, BERT
LE08464 622 (January 23, 1992) p4.
ECKE, RAY
LE08465 691 (September 22, 1994) p14.
EDMONSON, G. HUEY, JR.
LE08466 730 (March 21, 1996) p14.
EDWARDS, LEW
LE08467 697 (December 15, 1994) p14.
EGGERS, PAUL W.
LE08468 716 (September 7, 1995) p10.
EHRMANN, ERIC
LE08469 668 (October 28, 1993) p8.
EICHHORN, DENNIS
LE08470 658 (June 10, 1993) p12.
EIDSON, MATT
LE08471 724-725 (December 28, 1995) p20.
EILBERG, JONATHAN S.
LE08472 740 (August 8, 1996) p14.
EISENHOUR, ANDREW
LE08473 651 (March 4, 1993) p10.
ELDRIDGE, CORINNE
LE08474 616 (October 31, 1991) p8.
ELDRIDGE, MATT
LE08475 726 (January 25, 1996) p12.
ELIAS
LE08476 733 (May 2, 1996) p10.
ELLINGSWORTH, LINDA
LE08477 675 (February 10, 1994) p6.
ELLIOT, JOE
LE08478 619-620 (December 12, 1991) p14.
ELLSWORTH, MATT
LE08479 700 (January 26, 1995) p14.
EMANUEL, MATT
LE08480 625 (March 5, 1992) p4.
ENGLENDER, JONATHAN
LE08481 666 (September 30, 1993) p10.
ENGLERT, FRANCIS
LE08482 707 (May 4, 1995) p16.
ENO, BRIAN
LE08483 621 (January 9, 1992) p6.
ENRIQUEZ, ERIC
LE08484 738-739 (July 11, 1996) p12.
ERDMAN, ED
LE08485 712-713 (July 13, 1995) p20.
ERSTAD, SPED
LE08486 705 (April 6, 1995) p14.
ESHLEMAN, KRISTEN
LE08487 684 (June 16, 1994) p11.
ESQUERRA, TERESA C.
LE08488 721 (November 16, 1995) p18.
ETHAN S.
LE08489 691 (September 22, 1994) p14.
ETHERIDGE, MELISSA
LE08490 750-751 (December 26, 1996) p26.
EVANGELISTO, CHRISTIE
LE08491 678 (March 24, 1994) p6.
EVANS, BOB
LE08492 640 (October 1, 1992) p6.
EVANS, DANIEL R.
LE08493 678 (March 24, 1994) p6.
EVANS, JOHN G.
LE08494 652 (March 18, 1993) p10.
EVANS, KRISTA
LE08495 729 (March 7, 1996) p6.
EVISTON, TODD
LE08496 717 (September 21, 1995) p16.
EWERT, MARC E.
LE08497 634-635 (July 9, 1992) p8.
LE08498 655 (April 29, 1993) p7.
EWING, ROSE
LE08499 628 (April 16, 1992) p6.

F

FABB, CHARLIE
LE08500 708 (May 18, 1995) p14.
FAILOR, THOMAS
LE08501 723 (December 14, 1995) pp20,22.
FALK, BRADLEY
LE08502 748 (November 28, 1996) p22.
FALK, STEPHEN
LE08503 731 (April 4, 1996) p14.
FALLON, MELANIE
LE08504 715 (August 24, 1995) p18.
FALLOW, JOHN
LE08505 745 (October 17, 1996) p24.
FANNON, GARY
LE08506 667 (October 14, 1993) p14.
FANNON, LINDA
LE08507 644 (November 26, 1992) p11.
FARGO, HANK
LE08508 749 (December 12, 1996) p16.
FARKAS, RACHEL
LE08509 729 (March 7, 1996) p6.
FARLAND, ADAM
LE08510 669 (November 11, 1993) p8.
FARMER, GREG
LE08511 675 (February 10, 1994) p6.
FARRELL, KEVIN
LE08512 700 (January 26, 1995) p14.
FARSI, LINDA

LE08513 724-725 (December 28, 1995) p20.
FAYNER, SCOTT
LE08514 701 (February 9, 1995) p14.
FEATHERSTONE, PETER J.
LE08515 678 (March 24, 1994) p6.
FELDMAN, MARK
LE08516 690 (September 8, 1994) p16.
FELDMAN, RICHARD J. (EXECUTIVE DIRECTOR, AMERICAN SHOOTING SPORTS COUNCIL)
LE08517 714 (August 10, 1995) p12.
FELDT, GLORIA (PRESIDENT, PLANNED PARENTHOOD OF AMERICA)
LE08518 741 (August 22, 1996) p20.
FENTOFF, HERB
LE08519 750-751 (December 26, 1996) p26.
FERDON, RICKY
LE08520 654 (April 15, 1993) p8.
FERGUSON, JEANNE
LE08521 640 (October 1, 1992) p6.
FERRARO, TONY
LE08522 703 (March 9, 1995) p16.
FERREN, SCOTT
LE08523 724-725 (December 28, 1995) p20.
FIDLER, DANIELLE
LE08524 674 (January 27, 1994) p8.
FIERST, DAVID
LE08525 642 (October 29, 1992) p8.
FINCH, JANNETTE
LE08526 662 (August 5, 1993) p8.
FINNEY, STEPHEN C., JR.
LE08527 726 (January 25, 1996) p12.
FISCHER, RON
LE08528 709 (June 1, 1995) p14.
FISCHIA
LE08529 731 (April 4, 1996) p14.
FISHER, CHASE
LE08530 733 (May 2, 1996) p10.
FISHER, LIZ
LE08531 712-713 (July 13, 1995) p20.
FITZGERALD, MIKE
LE08532 658 (June 10, 1993) p12.
FITZHUGH, CHRISSIE
LE08533 659 (June 24, 1993) p10.
FITZPATRICK, SEAN
LE08534 707 (May 4, 1995) p16.
FLECK, JOE
LE08535 735 (May 30, 1996) p10.
FLEMING, ROSS
LE08536 710 (June 15, 1995) p14.
FLETCHER, ANDREW
LE08537 672-673 (December 23, 1993) p10.
FLETCHER, DOUG (PUBLISHER, JOURNAL OF NURSING JOCULARITY)
LE08538 677 (March 10, 1994) p12.
FLETCHER, MATTHEW J.
LE08539 678 (March 24, 1994) p6.
FLOWERS, STEPHEN W.
LE08540 680 (April 21, 1994) p8.
FOGARTY, KELLY P.
LE08541 664 (September 2, 1993) p8.
FOGG, ERIC
LE08542 729 (March 7, 1996) p6.
FOGLE, THOMAS
LE08543 715 (August 24, 1995) p18.
FONTAINE, HEATHER
LE08544 629 (April 30, 1992) p8.
FONTENOTE, TROY
LE08545 650 (February 18, 1993) p6.
FORTINI, ELLEN J.
LE08546 711 (June 29, 1995) p10.
FORTNER, LYNN
LE08547 657 (May 27, 1993) p6.
FOSS, NICHOLAS
LE08548 651 (March 4, 1993) p10.
FOSTER, NICK
LE08549 706 (April 20, 1995) p12.
FRANCINE, LISA
LE08550 638 (September 3, 1992) p6.
FRANK, PHILLY
LE08551 729 (March 7, 1996) p6.
FRANKEL, ALEX
LE08552 722 (November 30, 1995) p14.
FRASER, DONOVAN
LE08553 640 (October 1, 1992) p6.
FREAM, ROB
LE08554 677 (March 10, 1994) p12.
FREDRICKSON, DAN
LE08555 735 (May 30, 1996) p10.
FREEMAN, PRISCILLA (HUMANS AGAINST NUCLEAR-WASTE DUMPS)
LE08556 740 (August 8, 1996) p14.
FRENCH, DAVID T.
LE08557 686-687 (July 14, 1994) p14.
FRENCH, VALERIE
LE08558 650 (February 18, 1993) p6.
FRIEDLINE, RICK
LE08559 654 (April 15, 1993) p8.
FRIEDMAN, CAROLINE
LE08560 682 (May 19, 1994) p14.
FRIEDMAN, DAVID BENIOFF
LE08561 664 (September 2, 1993) p8.
FRIEL, GILLIAN
LE08562 735 (May 30, 1996) p10.
FRIESEN, DALE
LE08563 682 (May 19, 1994) p14.
FRIESEN, JEFFREY
LE08564 671 (December 9, 1993) p7.
FRISBIE, FRITZ
LE08565 720 (November 2, 1995) p12.
FRITZ, MATTHEW
LE08566 697 (December 15, 1994) p14.
FRITZ, MATTHEW R.
LE08567 708 (May 18, 1995) p14.
FROST, NICHOLAS
LE08568 710 (June 15, 1995) p14.
FRYMAN, AVI
LE08569 616 (October 31, 1991) p8.
FULLER, JOHN
LE08570 702 (February 23, 1995) p16.
FULLER, KIMBERLY A.
LE08571 657 (May 27, 1993) p6.
FUTEY, JASON
LE08572 716 (September 7, 1995) p10.

G

G., JENNY
LE08573 718 (October 5, 1995) p16.
GAAL, GARY
LE08574 669 (November 11, 1993) p8.
GAENIR, PALYNE
LE08575 658 (June 10, 1993) p12.
GAINES, GREGORY
LE08576 727 (February 8, 1996) p10.
GARDNER, M. VICTORIA
LE08577 652 (March 18, 1993) p10.
GARLAND, ERIC
LE08578 621 (January 9, 1992) p6.
GARLICK, ERIN
LE08579 690 (September 8, 1994) p16.
GARNEAU, BILL
LE08580 726 (January 25, 1996) p12.
GARRARD, DALE
LE08581 660-661 (July 8, 1993) p10.
GARRETT, LARRY ALTON
LE08582 710 (June 15, 1995) p14.
GAUTHIER, MARTINA
LE08583 691 (September 22, 1994) p14.
GELBER, ERIC
LE08584 724-725 (December 28, 1995) p20.
GELLER, KEITH
LE08585 736 (June 13, 1996) p16.
GEORGE, JENNY
LE08586 683 (June 2, 1994) p11.
GERARDO
LE08587 619-620 (December 12, 1991) p14.
GERSTEIN, LAWRENCE (DIRECTOR, INTERNATIONAL TIBET MOVEMENT)
LE08588 743 (September 19, 1996) p12.
GETMAN, JOSH
LE08589 749 (December 12, 1996) p16.
GHOSSTMYST@AOL.COM
LE08590 747 (November 14, 1996) p20.
GIDEON, TIM
LE08591 667 (October 14, 1993) p14.
GILBERT, DEBBIE
LE08592 748 (November 28, 1996) p22.
GILLEN, JAMES
LE08593 682 (May 19, 1994) p14.
GILMARTIN, ERIC
LE08594 692 (October 6, 1994) p12.
GIONFRIDDO, GINA
LE08595 733 (May 2, 1996) p10.
GIORDANO, A. J.
LE08596 706 (April 20, 1995) p12.
GIRAUDO, ANGIE
LE08597 747 (November 14, 1996) p20.
GLASS, DANIEL
LE08598 624 (February 20, 1992) p7.
GLENN, AMANDA
LE08599 653 (April 1, 1993) p8.
GNOSHITA, MIKK
LE08600 675 (February 10, 1994) p6.
GOLDAMMER, ROSMARIE
LE08601 666 (September 30, 1993) p10.
GOLDSCHMID, EYAL
LE08602 686-687 (July 14, 1994) p14.
GOLDSTEIN, PAUL
LE08603 724-725 (December 28, 1995) p20.
GOLDSTEIN, STEVE
LE08604 616 (October 31, 1991) p8.
GOLPINAR, DERYA
LE08605 686-687 (July 14, 1994) p14.
GONOS, MICHAEL
LE08606 630 (May 14, 1992) p8.
GONZALES, MINDY
LE08607 714 (August 10, 1995) p12.
GONZALEZ, J.
LE08608 691 (September 22, 1994) p14.

GONZALEZ, JIM
LE08609 644 (November 26, 1992) p11.
GOODMAN, RYAN J.
LE08610 654 (April 15, 1993) p8.
GOOSENS, MILES
LE08611 660-661 (July 8, 1993) p10.
GORAIEB, ROB
LE08612 731 (April 4, 1996) p14.
GORENFELD, JOHN
LE08613 692 (October 6, 1994) p12.
GOSLOW, PAUL
LE08614 674 (January 27, 1994) p8.
GOULD, SEAN
LE08615 658 (June 10, 1993) p12.
GOWDY, STEPHANIE
LE08616 630 (May 14, 1992) p8.
GRACZYK, T. J.
LE08617 693 (October 20, 1994) p22.
GRAHAM, GARY
LE08618 750-751 (December 26, 1996) p26.
GRAHAM, HOLLY A.
LE08619 631 (May 28, 1992) p6.
GRAHAM, KEN
LE08620 660-661 (July 8, 1993) p10.
GRANT, DUNCAN
LE08621 691 (September 22, 1994) p14.
GRAVES, D'ANN
LE08622 616 (October 31, 1991) p8.
GRAVES, TROY C.
LE08623 740 (August 8, 1996) p14.
GRAYSON, GEORGE T.
LE08624 693 (October 20, 1994) p22.
GREBER, JONATHAN
LE08625 705 (April 6, 1995) p14.
GREEDER, CHRIS
LE08626 679 (April 7, 1994) p10.
GREEN, JOHN
LE08627 639 (September 17, 1992) p10.
GREENFIELD, STEVE
LE08628 655 (April 29, 1993) p7.
GREENLAW, ROB
LE08629 708 (May 18, 1995) p14.
GREENLEES, TERESA
LE08630 704 (March 23, 1995) p18.
GREENWOOD, JANE A.
LE08631 654 (April 15, 1993) p8.
GREGERSEN, ANDREA M.
LE08632 636 (August 6, 1992) p7.
GREGG, ALLISON
LE08633 702 (February 23, 1995) p16.
GREGORY, V.
LE08634 650 (February 18, 1993) p6.
GREIDER, WILLIAM
LE08635 660-661 (July 8, 1993) p10.
GREY, ELLEN
LE08636 623 (February 6, 1992) p6.
GRIFFIN, ROB
LE08637 748 (November 28, 1996) p22.
GRIGSBY, CAMILLA
LE08638 709 (June 1, 1995) p14.
GROSHNER, GARY
LE08639 670 (November 25, 1993) p8.
GROSS, ALLISON
LE08640 703 (March 9, 1995) p16.
GROSS, ALLISON LEVIE
LE08641 657 (May 27, 1993) p6.
GROSS, WENDY
LE08642 723 (December 14, 1995) p20.
GRUBB, KAREN
LE08643 617 (November 14, 1991) p8.
GRUNKE, CHRIS
LE08644 648 (January 21, 1993) p7.
GUENDER, SUKI
LE08645 684 (June 16, 1994) p11.
GUIDA-COLONNO, LAURIE
LE08646 705 (April 6, 1995) p14.
GUILL, MARK
LE08647 625 (March 5, 1992) p4.
GUNNING, JONATHAN
LE08648 721 (November 16, 1995) p18.
GUSTAFSON, CAREY
LE08649 627 (April 2, 1992) p8.
GUY, ED
LE08650 678 (March 24, 1994) p6.
GYDE, AMELIA
LE08651 730 (March 21, 1996) p14.

H

HABER, MATT
LE08652 664 (September 2, 1993) p8.
HABERMAN, MARY
LE08653 747 (November 14, 1996) p20.
HADLEY, JESS
LE08654 659 (June 24, 1993) p10.
HAEFEKER, AMY
LE08655 726 (January 25, 1996) p12.
HAGADORN, N.
LE08656 714 (August 10, 1995) p12.
HAGAN, BRIAN
LE08657 703 (March 9, 1995) p16.
HAIK, MAC
LE08658 616 (October 31, 1991) p8.
LE08659 637 (August 20, 1992) p6.
HAIK, MACK
LE08660 621 (January 9, 1992) p7.
HAISLIP, THERESA
LE08661 659 (June 24, 1993) p10.
HALL, JANE
LE08662 703 (March 9, 1995) p16.
HALL, KAYLAN
LE08663 623 (February 6, 1992) p6.
HAMERLINCK, JOHN
LE08664 628 (April 16, 1992) p6.
HAMILTON, DIANE
LE08665 617 (November 14, 1991) p8.
HAMILTON, JOHN
LE08666 644 (November 26, 1992) p11.
HAMILTON, WOODY
LE08667 625 (March 5, 1992) p4.
HANAUER, AMY
LE08668 717 (September 21, 1995) p16.
HANFMAN, EDWARD
LE08669 731 (April 4, 1996) p14.
HANNIGAN, JIM
LE08670 642 (October 29, 1992) p8.
HANSEN, PETER
LE08671 748 (November 28, 1996) p22.
HANSEN, ROBYN
LE08672 656 (May 13, 1993) p10.
HANSON, MARY KAY
LE08673 623 (February 6, 1992) p6.
HARDY, JON A.
LE08674 628 (April 16, 1992) p6.
HARGETT, GAYLE
LE08675 653 (April 1, 1993) p8.
HARLAND, DAVE
LE08676 732 (April 18, 1996) p16.
HARP, NICHOLAS ALLEN
LE08677 706 (April 20, 1995) p12.
HARRELSON, WOODY
LE08678 645-646 (December 10, 1992) p20.
HARRIS, ANTHONY
LE08679 733 (May 2, 1996) p10.
HARRIS, PATRICIA
LE08680 666 (September 30, 1993) p10.
HARRISON, JODY-KATE FISHER
LE08681 618 (November 28, 1991) p9.
HARRISON, LISA A.
LE08682 691 (September 22, 1994) p14.
HARROLD, JAMIE
LE08683 684 (June 16, 1994) p11.
HARSTAD, DAVE
LE08684 628 (April 16, 1992) p6.
HART, DANIEL WAR
LE08685 663 (August 19, 1993) p4.
LE08686 671 (December 9, 1993) p7.
LE08687 681 (May 5, 1994) p8.
HARTLEY, BRUCE (MERCURY RECORDS)
LE08688 675 (February 10, 1994) p6.
HARTLEY, K.
LE08689 665 (September 16, 1993) p6.
HARTNER, GEORGE
LE08690 736 (June 13, 1996) p16.
HARTSIG, BETH
LE08691 670 (November 25, 1993) p8.
HARTWIGER, ALEXANDER G.
LE08692 676 (February 24, 1994) p10.
HARVEY, KEVIN
LE08693 678 (March 24, 1994) p6.
HASELMANN, RALPH, JR.
LE08694 658 (June 10, 1993) p12.
HATCH, MICHAEL
LE08695 652 (March 18, 1993) p10.
HATTO, MELISSA
LE08696 741 (August 22, 1996) p20.
HAUN, TOM
LE08697 652 (March 18, 1993) p10.
HAUSER, ROBERT
LE08698 734 (May 16, 1996) p14.
HAVEMAN, KATHY
LE08699 659 (June 24, 1993) p10.
HAWK, R. D.
LE08700 636 (August 6, 1992) p7.
HAWTHORNE, KATE
LE08701 727 (February 8, 1996) p10.
HAYDOCK, PATRICIA
LE08702 618 (November 28, 1991) p9.
HAYES, JEN
LE08703 723 (December 14, 1995) p20.
HAYES, MISTY
LE08704 678 (March 24, 1994) p6.
HEATOM, CAMBRIAH
LE08705 693 (October 20, 1994) p22.
HECHINGER, BRIAN
LE08706 718 (October 5, 1995) p16.
HEFFNER, JOSH
LE08707 707 (May 4, 1995) p16.
HEIDGERKEN, TANYA
LE08708 628 (April 16, 1992) p6.
HELIN, JEANINE
LE08709 629 (April 30, 1992) p9.
HELMECZI, MONICA L.
LE08710 724-725 (December 28, 1995) p20.

HELMUTH, TINA
LE08711 716 (September 7, 1995) p10.
HELTON, SHANNON
LE08712 659 (June 24, 1993) p10.
HENDRICKSON, F.
LE08713 685 (June 30, 1994) p10.
HENDRIKSON, ANDREW
LE08714 704 (March 23, 1995) p18.
HENERA, RICHARD
LE08715 686-687 (July 14, 1994) p14.
HENNIGER, MICHAEL
LE08716 710 (June 15, 1995) p14.
HENRY, GEORGE
LE08717 717 (September 21, 1995) p16.
HENRY, MEGAN ANNE
LE08718 624 (February 20, 1992) p7.
HERLANDS, JASON
LE08719 625 (March 5, 1992) p4.
HERRERA, TIMOTHY
LE08720 744 (October 3, 1996) p16.
HERZ, DAYNA
LE08721 728 (February 22, 1996) p16.
HESSE, ANGUS
LE08722 644 (November 26, 1992) p11.
HETZEL, KAREN
LE08723 622 (January 23, 1992) p4.
HIATT, JOHN
LE08724 645-646 (December 10, 1992) p20.
HILDEBRAND, LARRY
LE08725 674 (January 27, 1994) p8.
HILL, MEG
LE08726 640 (October 1, 1992) p6.
HILLER, EDDIE
LE08727 637 (August 20, 1992) p6.
HINKLE, KATIE J.
LE08728 718 (October 5, 1995) p16.
HOFFER, JULIE
LE08729 655 (April 29, 1993) p7.
HOFFMAN, A. M.
LE08730 642 (October 29, 1992) p8.
HOFFMAN, ALAN
LE08731 701 (February 9, 1995) p14.
HOFFMAN, JOHN
LE08732 670 (November 25, 1993) p8.
HOFFMAN, LEN
LE08733 736 (June 13, 1996) p16.
HOFFNER, AIDAN
LE08734 737 (June 27, 1996) p12.
HOLDEN, CHRIS
LE08735 747 (November 14, 1996) p20.
HOLDEN, JOY
LE08736 664 (September 2, 1993) p8.
HOLDEN, RYAN
LE08737 720 (November 2, 1995) p12.
LE08738 750-751 (December 26, 1996) p26.
HOLLAND, PAM
LE08739 642 (October 29, 1992) p8.
HOLLINGER, ANDREW
LE08740 669 (November 11, 1993) p8.
HOLORAN, MICHAEL (PROGRAM DIRECTOR, KUPR)
LE08741 744 (October 3, 1996) p16.
HONECK, JOHN
LE08742 642 (October 29, 1992) p8.
HOOD, S.
LE08743 717 (September 21, 1995) p16.
HOOTEN, JOE
LE08744 627 (April 2, 1992) p8.
HOOTON, RACHEL
LE08745 723 (December 14, 1995) p20.
HOPPER, JUSTIN
LE08746 651 (March 4, 1993) p10.
HORN, LINDA J.
LE08747 700 (January 26, 1995) p14.
HORNE, PAULA MAJOR
LE08748 719 (October 19, 1995) p10.
HORNSBY, MARK
LE08749 667 (October 14, 1993) p14.
HOROVITZ, PAMELA (NATIONAL ASSOCIATION OF RECORDING MERCHANDISERS)
LE08750 647 (January 7, 1993) p7.
HORRIGAN, TIMOTHY
LE08751 685 (June 30, 1994) p10.
HORTON, LORI
LE08752 648 (January 21, 1993) p7.
HORTON, RICH
LE08753 648 (January 21, 1993) p7.
HOSSELTON, GAROLD
LE08754 633 (June 25, 1992) p5.
HOUCHINS, ELIZABETH
LE08755 715 (August 24, 1995) p18.
LE08756 734 (May 16, 1996) p14.
HOUGHTON, LEAH
LE08757 716 (September 7, 1995) p10.
HOUSER, MELISSA
LE08758 683 (June 2, 1994) p11.
HOVAV, ADI
LE08759 733 (May 2, 1996) p10.
HOWELL, JACKIE
LE08760 730 (March 21, 1996) p14.
HOWELL, SCOTT
LE08761 640 (October 1, 1992) p6.
HUBBARD, MARK A.
LE08762 680 (April 21, 1994) p8.
HUBER, KEVIN R., REV.
LE08763 647 (January 7, 1993) p7.
HUDGINS, CONNY
LE08764 727 (February 8, 1996) p10.
HUDSON, ANGELA
LE08765 629 (April 30, 1992) p8.
HUEGELMANN, MARK
LE08766 708 (May 18, 1995) p14.
HUGHES, CHRIS
LE08767 688 (August 11, 1994) p10.
HUGHES, KATHIE
LE08768 678 (March 24, 1994) p6.
HULKA, EVAN
LE08769 702 (February 23, 1995) p16.
HUML, A.
LE08770 630 (May 14, 1992) p8.
HUNT, J.
LE08771 650 (February 18, 1993) p6.

LE08772 750-751 (December 26, 1996) p26.
HUTCHINSON, JAMES
LE08773 701 (February 9, 1995) p14.

I

IAN, JANIS
LE08774 649 (February 4, 1993) p7.
IAN, SCOTT
LE08775 619-620 (December 12, 1991) p14.
ICE CUBE
LE08776 645-646 (December 10, 1992) p20.
IDZKOWSKI, MAI
LE08777 617 (November 14, 1991) p8.
INGRAM, SUSAN
LE08778 628 (April 16, 1992) p6.
IRVING, DAVID
LE08779 693 (October 20, 1994) p22.
ISAACS, STEVE (MTV)
LE08780 631 (May 28, 1992) p6.
IVESON, SUZANNE
LE08781 637 (August 20, 1992) p6.

J

JACKSON, BIFF
LE08782 624 (February 20, 1992) p7.
JACKSON, LARA
LE08783 626 (March 19, 1992) p6.
JACOBOWITZ, EDEN
LE08784 666 (September 30, 1993) p10.
JAFFE, ERIQ
LE08785 616 (October 31, 1991) p8.
JAFFE, JONATHAN
LE08786 704 (March 23, 1995) p18.
JAFLOAT, CRAIG
LE08787 656 (May 13, 1993) p10.
J.A.M.
LE08788 702 (February 23, 1995) p16.
JANCZYN, MELINDA
LE08789 664 (September 2, 1993) p8.
JANECEK, REBECCA
LE08790 621 (January 9, 1992) p6.
JASNIEWICZ, LISABETH
LE08791 691 (September 22, 1994) p14.
JAYNES, SIMON
LE08792 744 (October 3, 1996) p16.
J.D.
LE08793 709 (June 1, 1995) p14.
J.E.B.
LE08794 707 (May 4, 1995) p16.
JEFF
LE08795 710 (June 15, 1995) p14.
LE08796 718 (October 5, 1995) p16.
JEFFRIES, SARA
LE08797 626 (March 19, 1992) p6.
JENNINGS, MATT
LE08798 746 (October 31, 1996) p14.
JENSEN, SHEILA
LE08799 636 (August 6, 1992) p7.
J.J.
LE08800 691 (September 22, 1994) p14.
JOEL, BILLY
LE08801 651 (March 4, 1993) p10.
JOHANSSEN, PASCAL
LE08802 745 (October 17, 1996) p24.
JOHNSON, AMBER
LE08803 697 (December 15, 1994) p14.
JOHNSON, CHARLES
LE08804 744 (October 3, 1996) p16.
JOHNSON, DEBRA A.
LE08805 727 (February 8, 1996) p10.
JOHNSON, JERRY C.
LE08806 703 (March 9, 1995) p16.
JOHNSON, RAY
LE08807 662 (August 5, 1993) p8.
JOHNSON, SARAH

LE08808 719 (October 19, 1995) p10.
JOHNSON, SHAUN
LE08809 636 (August 6, 1992) p7.
JOHNSON, TANYA
LE08810 746 (October 31, 1996) p14.
JOHNSON, TIFFANY D.
LE08811 691 (September 22, 1994) p14.
JONES, ADAM
LE08812 628 (April 16, 1992) p6.
JONES, J. MARCUS
LE08813 717 (September 21, 1995) p16.
JONES, KELLY
LE08814 681 (May 5, 1994) p8.
JONES, KRISTINE
LE08815 674 (January 27, 1994) p8.
JONES, NATALIE
LE08816 740 (August 8, 1996) p14.
JONES, PATRIC
LE08817 677 (March 10, 1994) p12.
JONES, TIM A.
LE08818 747 (November 14, 1996) p20.
JORGENSEN, LORI
LE08819 660-661 (July 8, 1993) p10.
JORGENSEN, VIDAR J. (THOREAU COUNTRY CONSERVATION ALLIANCE)
LE08820 735 (May 30, 1996) p10.
JOYCE, MATT
LE08821 630 (May 14, 1992) p8.
JOYNER, DAN
LE08822 629 (April 30, 1992) p8.
J.T.
LE08823 717 (September 21, 1995) p16.
JUDD, BRIAN
LE08824 623 (February 6, 1992) p6.
JULIG, LOUISE
LE08825 732 (April 18, 1996) p16.
JUON, STEVE ▒FLASH▒
LE08826 693 (October 20, 1994) p22.

K

KAHLMORGAN, ANDREE
LE08827 733 (May 2, 1996) p10.
KAHN, CAROLE E.
LE08828 655 (April 29, 1993) p7.
KALINOSKI, PAMELA
LE08829 706 (April 20, 1995) p12.
KALITOWSKI, SUSANNA
LE08830 701 (February 9, 1995) p14.
KAPRELIAN, PETER
LE08831 653 (April 1, 1993) p8.
KARNES, RANDALL T.
LE08832 649 (February 4, 1993) p7.
KARR, KATHY JO
LE08833 683 (June 2, 1994) p11.
KARR, SUNNY
LE08834 669 (November 11, 1993) p8.
KASENDORF, JESSE
LE08835 705 (April 6, 1995) p14.
KASPRZAK, MICHELLE
LE08836 650 (February 18, 1993) p6.
KATHOL, JON
LE08837 621 (January 9, 1992) p6.
KATSON, TRISHA
LE08838 671 (December 9, 1993) p7.
KATZ, ADAM
LE08839 702 (February 23, 1995) p16.
KAY, JILL
LE08840 696 (December 1, 1994) p18.
KAZDOY, AMANDA
LE08841 704 (March 23, 1995) p18.
K.B.
LE08842 709 (June 1, 1995) p14.
KEADLE, DIANNE L.
LE08843 664 (September 2, 1993) p8.
KEARSE, ASHLEY
LE08844 689 (August 25, 1994) p12.
KEEBLER, ED
LE08845 708 (May 18, 1995) p14.
KEEFE, TOM
LE08846 720 (November 2, 1995) p12.
KEIGWIN, MARK
LE08847 637 (August 20, 1992) p6.
KELLER, EUGENE
LE08848 743 (September 19, 1996) p12.
KELLEY, COLLIN
LE08849 679 (April 7, 1994) p10.
KELLY, CHAZ
LE08850 644 (November 26, 1992) p11.
KELLY, KATE
LE08851 649 (February 4, 1993) p7.
KELLY, ROB
LE08852 638 (September 3, 1992) p6.
KENDALL, STEVEN L.
LE08853 656 (May 13, 1993) p10.
KENNEDY, DANIEL
LE08854 629 (April 30, 1992) p8.
KENNEDY, MIKE
LE08855 744 (October 3, 1996) p16.
KESTER, T. S.
LE08856 628 (April 16, 1992) p6.
KEVORKIAN, MAUREEN
LE08857 658 (June 10, 1993) p12.
KIBLER, MARTHA
LE08858 654 (April 15, 1993) p8.
KIGHT, MATT
LE08859 682 (May 19, 1994) p14.
KILPATRICK, EVA
LE08860 668 (October 28, 1993) p8.
KIM, BEN
LE08861 636 (August 6, 1992) p7.
KIMBALL, JACLYN
LE08862 666 (September 30, 1993) p10.
KIMBROUGH, WALTER
LE08863 750-751 (December 26, 1996) p26.
KINEL, TRACI
LE08864 615 (October 17, 1991) p8.
KING, BILL
LE08865 658 (June 10, 1993) p12.
KING, KELLI
LE08866 719 (October 19, 1995) p10.
KINGSLEY, KIM
LE08867 618 (November 28, 1991) p9.
LE08868 Numer not assigned.
KINKADA, CHRIS
LE08869 748 (November 28, 1996) p22.
KIPP, BRIAN K.
LE08870 681 (May 5, 1994) p8.
KIRIE, V.
LE08871 652 (March 18, 1993) p10.
KIRK, KEN
LE08872 631 (May 28, 1992) p6.
KIRKA, MIKE
LE08873 664 (September 2, 1993) p8.
KISS
LE08874 624 (February 20, 1992) p7.
KJELDERGAARD, DENNIS
LE08875 708 (May 18, 1995) p14.
KLAVANS, ANNE
LE08876 729 (March 7, 1996) p6.
KLEIN, MORGAN
LE08877 729 (March 7, 1996) p6.
KLOCKNER, CATHY LUTE
LE08878 618 (November 28, 1991) p9.
KLOFKORN, WARREN
LE08879 680 (April 21, 1994) p8.
KLOP, J. MICHAEL
LE08880 671 (December 9, 1993) p7.
K.M.
LE08881 686-687 (July 14, 1994) p14.
KNAPP, JOHN R., JR.
LE08882 616 (October 31, 1991) p8.
KNIGHT, KRISTY
LE08883 663 (August 19, 1993) p4.
KNUDSON, HEATHER
LE08884 734 (May 16, 1996) p14.
KOBACK, TODD J.
LE08885 657 (May 27, 1993) p6.
KOENIGSMANN, HEIDI
LE08886 748 (November 28, 1996) p22.
KOLLOCK, PAUL
LE08887 657 (May 27, 1993) p6.
KONLACK, SHANNA
LE08888 669 (November 11, 1993) p8.
KOPPEL, JEFFREY
LE08889 662 (August 5, 1993) p8.
KOPPEL, JEFFREY D.
LE08890 649 (February 4, 1993) p7.
KORTHALS, JIM
LE08891 698-699 (December 29, 1994) p26.
KOSSLOW, KENNY
LE08892 730 (March 21, 1996) p14.
KOURI, JAMES J. (VICE-PRESIDENT AND ASSOCIATE EDITOR, 'CHIEF OF POLICE')
LE08893 651 (March 4, 1993) p10.
KOWALESKI, MICHAEL
LE08894 628 (April 16, 1992) p6.
KRAEMER, GEORGE P.
LE08895 642 (October 29, 1992) p8.
KRAKORA, CHRISTOPHER
LE08896 731 (April 4, 1996) p14.
KRAMER, B.
LE08897 711 (June 29, 1995) p10.
KRAMER, DAN
LE08898 651 (March 4, 1993) p10.
KRAMER, KATHLEEN J.
LE08899 700 (January 26, 1995) p14.
KRIEGER, CHRIS
LE08900 618 (November 28, 1991) p9.
KRS-ONE METAPHYSICIAN
LE08901 619-620 (December 12, 1991) p14.
KRUBECK, JIM
LE08902 656 (May 13, 1993) p10.
KUHN, KELLY
LE08903 647 (January 7, 1993) p7.
KULICK, BRUCE
LE08904 624 (February 20, 1992) p7.
KUTCH, STEPHANI
LE08905 685 (June 30, 1994) p10.
KYRIAZI, LINDA
LE08906 694 (November 3, 1994) p14.

L

L., JOHN
LE08907 639 (September 17, 1992) p10.
LADD, CAROL
LE08908 652 (March 18, 1993) p10.
LAGUERRE, HARVEY
LE08909 696 (December 1, 1994) p18.
LAING, D. BRENT
LE08910 689 (August 25, 1994) p12.
LAMBERT, KELSEY
LE08911 722 (November 30, 1995) p14.
LAMSSIES, DOMINIQUE
LE08912 676 (February 24, 1994) p10.
LANDSEA, CHRIS
LE08913 700 (January 26, 1995) p14.
LANE, KAREN
LE08914 740 (August 8, 1996) p14.
LANGBEHN, JOSH
LE08915 735 (May 30, 1996) p10.
LANGENBURG, LEA
LE08916 624 (February 20, 1992) p7.
LANGIE, MATTHEW
LE08917 697 (December 15, 1994) p14.
LANGRO, ROBERT
LE08918 663 (August 19, 1993) p4.
LANIER, EMMETT MIKE
LE08919 708 (May 18, 1995) p14.
LAPIERRE, WAYNE R., JR. (NATIONAL RIFLE ASSOCIATION OF AMERICA)
LE08920 669 (November 11, 1993) p8.
LARGE, KIM
LE08921 656 (May 13, 1993) p10.
LARI, ERIKA
LE08922 665 (September 16, 1993) p6.
LE08923 683 (June 2, 1994) p11.
LASHER, GRANT B.
LE08924 653 (April 1, 1993) p8.
LAUDATI, NIEL
LE08925 626 (March 19, 1992) p6.
LAUZON, TIMOTHY
LE08926 709 (June 1, 1995) p14.
LAWRENCE, DANA J.
LE08927 618 (November 28, 1991) p9.
LAWRENCE, SHARRON LESLEY
LE08928 720 (November 2, 1995) p12.
LAWRENCE, TINA
LE08929 667 (October 14, 1993) p14.
LAY, CARRIE
LE08930 683 (June 2, 1994) p11.
LAZAR, SHELLEY
LE08931 721 (November 16, 1995) p18.
LEACH, STEVE
LE08932 621 (January 9, 1992) p6.
LEAHY, DEBORAH
LE08933 670 (November 25, 1993) p8.
LEAHY, JOSIE
LE08934 656 (May 13, 1993) p10.
LEBER, REBECCA (RHODE ISLAND SCHOOL OF DESIGN)
LE08935 681 (May 5, 1994) p8.
LEBLANC, ANGIE
LE08936 648 (January 21, 1993) p7.
LECONTE, ROBERT (PRESIDENT, NATIONAL ASSOCIATION OF VETERAN POLICE OFFICERS)
LE08937 640 (October 1, 1992) p6.
LE08938 Number not assigned.
LEE, JANET
LE08939 622 (January 23, 1992) p4.
LEE, MEE SUN
LE08940 721 (November 16, 1995) p18.
LEE, ROBERTA
LE08941 724-725 (December 28, 1995) p20.
LE08942 742 (September 5, 1996) p16.
LEE, ROY
LE08943 655 (April 29, 1993) p7.
LEECH, JOHN
LE08944 749 (December 12, 1996) p16.
LEFSETZ, ROBERT SCOTT
LE08945 693 (October 20, 1994) p22.
LEHRER, ELI
LE08946 750-751 (December 26, 1996) p26.
LEIGH, VIVIAN
LE08947 675 (February 10, 1994) p6.
LENQUETTE, YOURI
LE08948 705 (April 6, 1995) p14.
LEONETTI, CHUCK
LE08949 711 (June 29, 1995) p10.
LEPSCHE, MICHELE
LE08950 682 (May 19, 1994) p14.
LESCO, BARBARA
LE08951 730 (March 21, 1996) p14.
LEURQUIN, CHRIS
LE08952 657 (May 27, 1993) p6.
LEVESQUE, RICHARD L.
LE08953 648 (January 21, 1993) p7.
LEVIN, MICHAEL
LE08954 696 (December 1, 1994) p18.
LEVY, DOUGLAS
LE08955 689 (August 25, 1994) p12.
LEWIS, JENNIFER
LE08956 703 (March 9, 1995) p16.
LEWIS, JEREMY
LE08957 723 (December 14, 1995) p20.
LEWIS, MONNICA
LE08958 688 (August 11, 1994) p10.
LEWIS, RICHARD
LE08959 672-673 (December 23, 1993) p10.
L'HEUREUX, SUSAN A.
LE08960 656 (May 13, 1993) p10.
LIDMAN, ERIC
LE08961 723 (December 14, 1995) p22.
LILLY, JEAN
LE08962 706 (April 20, 1995) p12.
LILLY, NED
LE08963 660-661 (July 8, 1993) p10.
LIMES, PATRICK
LE08964 658 (June 10, 1993) p12.
LINDERMAN, ALLISON
LE08965 719 (October 19, 1995) p10.
LINDSAY, K.
LE08966 737 (June 27, 1996) p12.
LITTLE, CRAIG (LIBRARIAN, RICH CENTRAL HIGH SCHOOL)
LE08967 659 (June 24, 1993) p10.
L.M.W.
LE08968 636 (August 6, 1992) p7.
LOCHRIDGE, ERIC
LE08969 625 (March 5, 1992) p4.
LOGAN, PENELOPE
LE08970 644 (November 26, 1992) p11.
LOMAX, LOUISA
LE08971 718 (October 5, 1995) p16.
LOMBARDO, DAVE
LE08972 619-620 (December 12, 1991) p14.
LONG, DANIEL M.
LE08973 649 (February 4, 1993) p7.
LOSE, E. HEATHER
LE08974 680 (April 21, 1994) p8.
LOUDERBACK, DAYLIN C.
LE08975 693 (October 20, 1994) p22.
LOUIE, LISA
LE08976 682 (May 19, 1994) p14.
LOUIS, PAUL C.
LE08977 711 (June 29, 1995) p10.
LOUIS, SCOTT M.
LE08978 678 (March 24, 1994) p6.
LOVE, MARY JANE
LE08979 696 (December 1, 1994) p18.
LOWENSTEIN, TIM
LE08980 629 (April 30, 1992) p8.
LOWRY, PAM
LE08981 706 (April 20, 1995) p12.
LUCIANO, MANFREDI
LE08982 674 (January 27, 1994) p8.
LUDWIG, ERIN Z.
LE08983 665 (September 16, 1993) p6.
LUDWIG, LOUIE
LE08984 735 (May 30, 1996) p10.
LUEDERS, JANE
LE08985 742 (September 5, 1996) p16.
LUGAR, RICHARD (CHAIRMAN, U.S. SENATE AGRICULTURE COMMITTEE)
LE08986 736 (June 13, 1996) p16.
LUKIN, CHLOE
LE08987 631 (May 28, 1992) p6.
LUNDGREN, ERIC
LE08988 634-635 (July 9, 1992) p8.
LUNDGREN, JULIE
LE08989 670 (November 25, 1993) p8.
LURIE, ELIZABETH B. (PRESIDENT AND COO, NET, INC.)
LE08990 731 (April 4, 1996) p14.
LYNCH, AMANDA
LE08991 747 (November 14, 1996) p20.
LYNN, ADAM
LE08992 681 (May 5, 1994) p8.
LE08993 712-713 (July 13, 1995) p20.
LYON, DENNIS
LE08994 662 (August 5, 1993) p8.
LE08995 677 (March 10, 1994) p12.
LE08996 685 (June 30, 1994) p10.
LE08997 724-725 (December 28, 1995) p24.

M

MAASZ
LE08998 731 (April 4, 1996) p14.
MACALLISTER, JULES
LE08999 683 (June 2, 1994) p11.
MACANKE, MIKE
LE09000 719 (October 19, 1995) p10.
MACAYEAL, JAMES
LE09001 732 (April 18, 1996) p16.
MACAYEAL, JIM
LE09002 689 (August 25, 1994) p12.
MACE, LUTHER, III
LE09003 662 (August 5, 1993) p8.
MACHCINSKI, DAWN
LE09004 639 (September 17, 1992) p10.
MACHT, DAVE

LE09005 667 (October 14, 1993) p14.
MACKEY, KRISTOPHER
LE09006 693 (October 20, 1994) p22.
MACNEIL, TIMOTHY L.
LE09007 732 (April 18, 1996) p16.
MADORSKY, JORDAN
LE09008 664 (September 2, 1993) p8.
MADRID, BEN, III
LE09009 702 (February 23, 1995) p16.
MAHAFFY, SCOTT WILLIAM
LE09010 627 (April 2, 1992) p8.
LE09011 650 (February 18, 1993) p6.
MAJERUS, ELIZABETH
LE09012 616 (October 31, 1991) p8.
MALONE, RYAN
LE09013 671 (December 9, 1993) p7.
MALONEE, JAMES
LE09014 721 (November 16, 1995) p18.
MALOOF, AARON
LE09015 683 (June 2, 1994) p11.
MANCINI, DANTE
LE09016 678 (March 24, 1994) p6.
MANDEL, GERRY
LE09017 743 (September 19, 1996) p12.
MANDELBAUM, SYD
LE09018 729 (March 7, 1996) p6.
MANKAD, NIMITT
LE09019 685 (June 30, 1994) p10.
MANNING, TODD M.
LE09020 651 (March 4, 1993) p10.
MANOS, JESSICA
LE09021 730 (March 21, 1996) p14.
MANSON, MIKE
LE09022 638 (September 3, 1992) p6.
MANTICOS, STEPHANIE
LE09023 664 (September 2, 1993) p8.
MARGEAS, SAM
LE09024 708 (May 18, 1995) p14.
MARKOTAY, JOHN
LE09025 622 (January 23, 1992) p4.
MARKUNAS, CHRISTINA
LE09026 668 (October 28, 1993) p8.
MARSH, DAVE
LE09027 730 (March 21, 1996) p14.
MARTENS, PATRICK
LE09028 668 (October 28, 1993) p8.
MARTIN, CHERIE A.
LE09029 708 (May 18, 1995) p14.
MARTIN, MARY
LE09030 664 (September 2, 1993) p8.
MARTIN, SARAH
LE09031 639 (September 17, 1992) p10.
MARTIN, V. N.
LE09032 666 (September 30, 1993) p10.
MARTINEZ, JANIE
LE09033 636 (August 6, 1992) p7.
MASLINE, GARY W.
LE09034 625 (March 5, 1992) p4.
MASON, STEWART ALLENSWORTH
LE09035 625 (March 5, 1992) p4.
MASSERAT, SASSAN
LE09036 743 (September 19, 1996) p12.
MASTERSON, HOLLY
LE09037 701 (February 9, 1995) p14.
MATHEWS, RANDY
LE09038 675 (February 10, 1994) p6.
MATTHEI, JULIE
LE09039 702 (February 23, 1995) p16.
MATTHEWS, MERILL
LE09040 723 (December 14, 1995) p20.
MATTHEWS, NICK
LE09041 703 (March 9, 1995) p16.
MATTHEWS, TOM
LE09042 714 (August 10, 1995) p12.
MATTSON, ROSEMARY
LE09043 714 (August 10, 1995) p12.
MATUSAK, RON
LE09044 651 (March 4, 1993) p10.
MAY, ALEX
LE09045 618 (November 28, 1991) p9.
MAYNOR, L. BRYCE
LE09046 749 (December 12, 1996) p16.
MAYNTHER, ANDREA
LE09047 741 (August 22, 1996) p20.
MCALLEN, JIM
LE09048 729 (March 7, 1996) p6.
MCCARTY, KELLY S.
LE09049 655 (April 29, 1993) p7.
MCCLAFFERTY, JENNIFER
LE09050 630 (May 14, 1992) p8.
MCCLELLAN, MIKE
LE09051 703 (March 9, 1995) p16.
MCDONALD, MIKE
LE09052 685 (June 30, 1994) p10.
MCDOUGAL, ROGER
LE09053 651 (March 4, 1993) p10.
MCEWEN, MATT
LE09054 704 (March 23, 1995) p18.
MCGANN, RACHEL
LE09055 728 (February 22, 1996) p16.
MCGARR, MICHAEL
LE09056 680 (April 21, 1994) p8.
MCGARRAH, C.
LE09057 636 (August 6, 1992) p7.
MCGASKO, J.
LE09058 696 (December 1, 1994) p18.
MCGEE, MATT J.
LE09059 670 (November 25, 1993) p8.
MCGRATH, JUDITH (PRESIDENT, MTV)
LE09060 737 (June 27, 1996) p12.
MCGUIGAN, CHRISTINE
LE09061 712-713 (July 13, 1995) p20.
MCGUIRE, ROXANNE
LE09062 642 (October 29, 1992) p8.
MCINTYRE, ROGER
LE09063 626 (March 19, 1992) p6.
MCKAGAN, DUFF
LE09064 672-673 (December 23, 1993) p10.
MCLAUGHLIN, KELLY
LE09065 719 (October 19, 1995) p10.
MCLEMORE, TOD
LE09066 709 (June 1, 1995) p14.
MCLEOD, ERNEST
LE09067 681 (May 5, 1994) p8.
MCMANUS, SAM
LE09068 728 (February 22, 1996) p16.
MCNAUGHTON, CRAIG
LE09069 710 (June 15, 1995) p14.
MCNEILL, REBECCA
LE09070 710 (June 15, 1995) p14.
MCNULTY, BILL (GENERAL MANAGER, KCXX)
LE09071 744 (October 3, 1996) p16.
MCNUTLY, LORI
LE09072 674 (January 27, 1994) p8.
MCPHERSON, RICH
LE09073 712-713 (July 13, 1995) p20.
MCQUEEN, GREGG
LE09074 644 (November 26, 1992) p11.
MCRAE, VICTORIA
LE09075 653 (April 1, 1993) p8.
MCTIG, ALEX
LE09076 680 (April 21, 1994) p8.
MCTIGUE, LEO
LE09077 639 (September 17, 1992) p10.
MEATHRELL, CARRIE
LE09078 698-699 (December 29, 1994) p26.
MEDA, TONY
LE09079 722 (November 30, 1995) p14.
MEGAN, SHEILA
LE09080 630 (May 14, 1992) p8.
MEIS, MARCIA
LE09081 707 (May 4, 1995) p16.
MELARA, JOHN
LE09082 681 (May 5, 1994) p8.
MER
LE09083 693 (October 20, 1994) p22.
MERCER, MICHAEL
LE09084 708 (May 18, 1995) p14.
MERCER, MIKE
LE09085 679 (April 7, 1994) p10.
MEROVICH, HEATHER
LE09086 719 (October 19, 1995) p10.
MESSICK, JAYMELIN
LE09087 737 (June 27, 1996) p12.
METALLICA
LE09088 619-620 (December 12, 1991) p14.
METZLER, JEFF
LE09089 709 (June 1, 1995) p14.
MEYER, SHARON
LE09090 659 (June 24, 1993) p10.
MIKE L.
LE09091 691 (September 22, 1994) p14.
MIKESELL, BRIAN G.
LE09092 656 (May 13, 1993) p10.
MIKLAS, JOLENE
LE09093 717 (September 21, 1995) p16.
MILAM, DOUG
LE09094 748 (November 28, 1996) p22.
MILCHEN, JEFF
LE09095 712-713 (July 13, 1995) p20.
MILES, FRANK
LE09096 681 (May 5, 1994) p8.
MILITANO, M.
LE09097 624 (February 20, 1992) p7.
MILLER, DAN (U.S. HOUSE OF REPRESENTATIVES)
LE09098 736 (June 13, 1996) p16.
MILLER, ELLEN
LE09099 707 (May 4, 1995) p16.
MILLER, GREG
LE09100 731 (April 4, 1996) p14.
MILLER, HILLARY
LE09101 709 (June 1, 1995) p14.
MILLER, JENNIFER
LE09102 697 (December 15, 1994) p14.
MILLER, JOANNA
LE09103 653 (April 1, 1993) p8.
MILLER, JUSTIN
LE09104 721 (November 16, 1995) p18.
MILLER, RHONDA
LE09105 748 (November 28, 1996) p22.
MILLER, SUSAN S.
LE09106 665 (September 16, 1993) p6.
MILLIKEN, SKYE
LE09107 640 (October 1, 1992) p6.
MILLS, SOPHIE

LE09108 734 (May 16, 1996) p14.
MILNER, ANDREW
LE09109 681 (May 5, 1994) p8.
MINARD, RON
LE09110 679 (April 7, 1994) p10.
MINOR, MARGO
LE09111 616 (October 31, 1991) p8.
MINTON, JONATHAN
LE09112 640 (October 1, 1992) p6.
MISLOW, BRADLEY S.
LE09113 655 (April 29, 1993) p7.
MITANI, KAREN
LE09114 690 (September 8, 1994) p16.
MITCHELL, LEE
LE09115 625 (March 5, 1992) p4.
MITRO, TINA
LE09116 711 (June 29, 1995) p10.
MOBLEY, DIANE
LE09117 663 (August 19, 1993) p4.
MOE, JACKIE
LE09118 743 (September 19, 1996) p12.
MOELLER, KARIN
LE09119 634-635 (July 9, 1992) p8.
MOFFITT, GARY S.
LE09120 702 (February 23, 1995) p16.
MOLANPHY, CHRIS
LE09121 681 (May 5, 1994) p8.
MOLIDOR, ROD, JR.
LE09122 716 (September 7, 1995) p10.
MONICA AND GABRIELLA
LE09123 628 (April 16, 1992) p6.
MONK
LE09124 702 (February 23, 1995) p16.
MONTALBANO, LIZ
LE09125 652 (March 18, 1993) p10.
MONTGOMERY, LIZ
LE09126 659 (June 24, 1993) p10.
MONTGOMERY, MATT
LE09127 628 (April 16, 1992) p6.
MONTGOMERY, SARAH
LE09128 625 (March 5, 1992) p4.
MONTGOMERY, STEPHANIE
LE09129 712-713 (July 13, 1995) p20.
MOODY, EUGENIE
LE09130 674 (January 27, 1994) p8.
MOOMAW, BRUCE
LE09131 737 (June 27, 1996) p12.
MOON, ROBYN
LE09132 681 (May 5, 1994) p8.
LE09133 707 (May 4, 1995) p16.
MOORE, DAVID
LE09134 655 (April 29, 1993) p7.
MOORE, DOUGLAS
LE09135 671 (December 9, 1993) p7.
MOORE, KIMBERLY
LE09136 626 (March 19, 1992) p6.
MOORE, THOMAS
LE09137 731 (April 4, 1996) p14.
MOORE, THURSTON
LE09138 645-646 (December 10, 1992) p20.
MORGENSTERN, HANS
LE09139 676 (February 24, 1994) p10.
MORRIS, JASON
LE09140 648 (January 21, 1993) p7.
MORRIS, KARLENE
LE09141 642 (October 29, 1992) p8.
MORRISSEY, SANDY
LE09142 709 (June 1, 1995) p14.
MOSS, SHAYNA
LE09143 630 (May 14, 1992) p8.
MOSZYNSKI, MEEGAN
LE09144 670 (November 25, 1993) p8.
MOTT, DAVID
LE09145 715 (August 24, 1995) p18.
MOUNT, JIMMY
LE09146 636 (August 6, 1992) p7.
MR. RIOT
LE09147 731 (April 4, 1996) p14.
MUELLER, FREDERICK
LE09148 642 (October 29, 1992) p8.
MUETZ, ROMAN
LE09149 631 (May 28, 1992) p6.
MULROONEY, C.
LE09150 733 (May 2, 1996) p10.
MURPHY, DARREN
LE09151 744 (October 3, 1996) p16.
MURPHY, ELLIOTT
LE09152 675 (February 10, 1994) p6.
MURPHY, JOSEPH
LE09153 674 (January 27, 1994) p8.
MUSIL, ROBERT K. (PHYSICIANS FOR SOCIAL RESPONSIBILITY)
LE09154 696 (December 1, 1994) p18.
MUSTAFAA, I'DRIS ABDUL
LE09155 666 (September 30, 1993) p10.
MYERS, MIKE
LE09156 645-646 (December 10, 1992) p20.
MYNATT, JULIE
LE09157 616 (October 31, 1991) p8.

N

NAKAMURA, LAUREN
LE09158 717 (September 21, 1995) p16.
NAME WITHHELD
LE09159 630 (May 14, 1992) p8.
LE09160 634-635 (July 9, 1992) p8.
LE09161 640 (October 1, 1992) p6.
LE09162 652 (March 18, 1993) p10.
LE09163 702 (February 23, 1995) p16.
LE09164 707 (May 4, 1995) p16.
LE09165 710 (June 15, 1995) p14.
LE09166 712-713 (July 13, 1995) p20.
LE09167 719 (October 19, 1995) p10.
LE09168 722 (November 30, 1995) p14.
LE09169 723 (December 14, 1995) p20.
LE09170 727 (February 8, 1996) p10.
LE09171 738-739 (July 11, 1996) p12.
LE09172 746 (October 31, 1996) p14.
LE09173 747 (November 14, 1996) p20.
NEAL, MIM (ROTARY INTERNATIONAL)
LE09174 618 (November 28, 1991) p9.
NEFSKY, BRIAN
LE09175 732 (April 18, 1996) p16.
NEILL, DANIELLE
LE09176 701 (February 9, 1995) p14.
NEISWENDER, KATE M.
LE09177 674 (January 27, 1994) p8.
NEMEC, MICHAEL PAUL
LE09178 680 (April 21, 1994) p8.
NEUMANN, RITA E.
LE09179 732 (April 18, 1996) p16.
NEWBAUER, JAMES L.
LE09180 629 (April 30, 1992) pp8-9.
NEWBOLD, RENEE
LE09181 627 (April 2, 1992) p8.
NEWMAN, ELIZABETH
LE09182 637 (August 20, 1992) p6.
NEWMAN, HERBERT E.
LE09183 711 (June 29, 1995) p10.
NICHOLSON, ANTHONY
LE09184 691 (September 22, 1994) p14.
NICKELS, MARK
LE09185 723 (December 14, 1995) p22.
NIGARA, MARK
LE09186 683 (June 2, 1994) p11.
NILAN
LE09187 663 (August 19, 1993) p4.
NILSON, KAI
LE09188 654 (April 15, 1993) p8.
NOBIS, J. G.
LE09189 710 (June 15, 1995) p14.
NOBLE, DANIELLE
LE09190 623 (February 6, 1992) p6.
NOON, REBECCA
LE09191 690 (September 8, 1994) p16.
NORLAND, JOHN
LE09192 717 (September 21, 1995) p16.
NORLANDER, LINDA
LE09193 677 (March 10, 1994) p12.
NOTORIOUS B.A.E.
LE09194 730 (March 21, 1996) p14.
NOVOSELIC, KRIST
LE09195 688 (August 11, 1994) p10.
LE09196 738-739 (July 11, 1996) p12.
NUDO, SAL
LE09197 681 (May 5, 1994) p8.

O

O'BRIEN, JILL
LE09198 633 (June 25, 1992) p5.
LE09199 Number not assigned.
OCEL, NATALIE
LE09200 693 (October 20, 1994) p22.
O'CONNELL, TOM
LE09201 718 (October 5, 1995) p16.
ODOM, GARY
LE09202 671 (December 9, 1993) p7.
OEHLING, RICK
LE09203 669 (November 11, 1993) p8.
OESER, KRISTEN
LE09204 686-687 (July 14, 1994) p14.
OLSZEWSKI, SHELLIE
LE09205 704 (March 23, 1995) p18.
OLTARZEWSKI, JOHN
LE09206 624 (February 20, 1992) p7.
LE09207 692 (October 6, 1994) p12.
132 UNIVERSITY OF WISCONSIN STUDENTS
LE09208 618 (November 28, 1991) p9.
O'NEILL, DAN
LE09209 708 (May 18, 1995) p14.
ONO, YOKO
LE09210 645-646 (December 10, 1992) p20.
ORANSKY, MICHAEL
LE09211 627 (April 2, 1992) p8.
ORLOFF, PETER
LE09212 680 (April 21, 1994) p8.
ORLOFFSKY, GEORGE
LE09213 744 (October 3, 1996) p16.
OROSCO, JANICE L.

LE09214 642 (October 29, 1992) p8.
ORSBORN, MIKEL
LE09215 674 (January 27, 1994) p8.
OSBOURNE, SHARON
LE09216 741 (August 22, 1996) p20.
OSOJNAK, JAKE S.
LE09217 705 (April 6, 1995) p14.
OSSIAN, RICHARD E.
LE09218 623 (February 6, 1992) p6.
OSWALD, ERIC
LE09219 629 (April 30, 1992) p9.
OZEGOVIX, GEORGIANA
LE09220 742 (September 5, 1996) p16.

P

PABST, BOBBI
LE09221 639 (September 17, 1992) p10.
PAGAZA, JOY
LE09222 627 (April 2, 1992) p8.
PAGE, CAROLYN D.
LE09223 679 (April 7, 1994) p10.
PAGNAC, DAWN
LE09224 638 (September 3, 1992) p6.
PAGUAGA, A.
LE09225 617 (November 14, 1991) p8.
PALMER, BRYANT (NEWS EDITOR, VANDERBILT HUSTLER, VANDERBILT UNIVERSITY)
LE09226 666 (September 30, 1993) p10.
PAN, WILBER
LE09227 628 (April 16, 1992) p6.
PARK, BRAD
LE09228 746 (October 31, 1996) p14.
PARK, EMMET
LE09229 745 (October 17, 1996) p24.
PARKER, CHRIS
LE09230 732 (April 18, 1996) p16.
PARKER, CHRISS
LE09231 704 (March 23, 1995) p18.
PARKER, JOHN
LE09232 746 (October 31, 1996) p14.
PARKER, RENEE
LE09233 637 (August 20, 1992) p6.
PARKINSON, MANDY
LE09234 657 (May 27, 1993) p6.
PARKS, CHERI
LE09235 667 (October 14, 1993) p14.
PARROTT, DAVID
LE09236 658 (June 10, 1993) p12.
PARTRIDGE, MARGARET
LE09237 630 (May 14, 1992) p8.
PASHA, J.
LE09238 738-739 (July 11, 1996) p12.
PASSALAQUA, WILLIAM
LE09239 662 (August 5, 1993) p8.
PATELLIS, TONY
LE09240 617 (November 14, 1991) p8.
PATRIAS, R. J.
LE09241 667 (October 14, 1993) p14.
PATRICK, BRIAN
LE09242 686-687 (July 14, 1994) p14.
PATRICK, DEVAL L. (ASSISTANT ATTORNEY GENERAL)
LE09243 711 (June 29, 1995) p10.
PEACHES
LE09244 675 (February 10, 1994) p6.
PEARCE, GREG
LE09245 716 (September 7, 1995) p10.
PEARCE, MATT
LE09246 724-725 (December 28, 1995) p20.
PEAVY, ALLISON
LE09247 626 (March 19, 1992) p6.
PECKHAM, DAVID
LE09248 625 (March 5, 1992) p4.
PEERS, JAMES H., III
LE09249 692 (October 6, 1994) p12.
PELEKAKIS, STEVE
LE09250 665 (September 16, 1993) p6.
PELL, SAINT JAMES
LE09251 626 (March 19, 1992) p6.
PELLEGRINI, CHRISTINA
LE09252 654 (April 15, 1993) p8.
PELLONE, MICHELLE
LE09253 729 (March 7, 1996) p6.
PENDON, MIKE
LE09254 634-635 (July 9, 1992) p8.
PENSIERO, NICOLE
LE09255 679 (April 7, 1994) p10.
PEREIRA, CHRIS
LE09256 741 (August 22, 1996) p20.
PEREZ, JENNIFER
LE09257 718 (October 5, 1995) p16.
PEREZ, SOMER
LE09258 707 (May 4, 1995) p16.
PEROLLI, AGIM
LE09259 700 (January 26, 1995) p14.
PERRIN, DEBBIE
LE09260 655 (April 29, 1993) p7.
PERRY, JOE
LE09261 672-673 (December 23, 1993) p10.
PERRY, LUKE
LE09262 645-646 (December 10, 1992) p20.
PERRY, TOM
LE09263 653 (April 1, 1993) p8.
PERSINGER, MICHAEL
LE09264 679 (April 7, 1994) p10.
PETERS, ANTHONY
LE09265 703 (March 9, 1995) p16.
PETERS, MATT
LE09266 746 (October 31, 1996) p14.
PETERSON, DELE
LE09267 682 (May 19, 1994) p14.
PETERSON, GARY
LE09268 681 (May 5, 1994) p8.
PETRI, TOM (HOUSE OF REPRESENTATIVES)
LE09269 710 (June 15, 1995) p14.
PETRONE, JOE
LE09270 719 (October 19, 1995) p10.
PETTE, FINN J.
LE09271 686-687 (July 14, 1994) p14.
PETTY, ALAN
LE09272 629 (April 30, 1992) p8.
PFEIFFER, KAPPY
LE09273 670 (November 25, 1993) p8.
PFLIEGER, AIMEE
LE09274 702 (February 23, 1995) p16.
PHYTHIAN, MICHAEL
LE09275 640 (October 1, 1992) p6.
PICARD, BILLY
LE09276 724-725 (December 28, 1995) p24.
PICHA, BILL
LE09277 742 (September 5, 1996) p16.
PICKERING, JAKE
LE09278 736 (June 13, 1996) p16.
PIERSON, ERICA
LE09279 647 (January 7, 1993) p7.
PIETRADURA, EDIE
LE09280 631 (May 28, 1992) p6.
PIGZA, JEFF
LE09281 679 (April 7, 1994) p10.
PIKE, MELISSA
LE09282 701 (February 9, 1995) p14.
PILAR SOARING HAWK
LE09283 615 (October 17, 1991) p8.
PINHEAD THE CENOBITE
LE09284 724-725 (December 28, 1995) pp20,24.
PIROZZI, ANTHONY A.
LE09285 666 (September 30, 1993) p10.
PITTS, CINDY
LE09286 648 (January 21, 1993) p7.
PLACE, MICHELLE
LE09287 697 (December 15, 1994) p14.
PLAKE, JONATHAN
LE09288 749 (December 12, 1996) p16.
PLATT, AREN
LE09289 650 (February 18, 1993) p6.
PLOSZAY, AIMEE
LE09290 660-661 (July 8, 1993) p10.
POLASEK, ARON
LE09291 683 (June 2, 1994) p11.
POLLARD, ROCK & ROLL PEG
LE09292 727 (February 8, 1996) p10.
POPE, CHRISTY LYNN
LE09293 694 (November 3, 1994) p14.
POSIES
LE09294 672-673 (December 23, 1993) p10.
POTTER, CHRISTOPHER BEACH
LE09295 630 (May 14, 1992) p8.
POTTER, ELAINE
LE09296 685 (June 30, 1994) p10.
POULIN, DAVID J.
LE09297 654 (April 15, 1993) p8.
POWELL, BRYAN C.
LE09298 722 (November 30, 1995) p14.
PRATER, FRANCINE
LE09299 668 (October 28, 1993) p8.
PRATT, JENNIFER
LE09300 721 (November 16, 1995) p18.
PRATT, MONICA (PROJECT DIRECTOR, FAMILIES AGAINST MANDATORY MINIMUMS)
LE09301 746 (October 31, 1996) p14.
PREPSKY, TODD ALAN
LE09302 626 (March 19, 1992) p6.
PRESCOTT, NORMA
LE09303 627 (April 2, 1992) p8.
PRICE, ANNA
LE09304 728 (February 22, 1996) p16.
PRICE, MARK
LE09305 659 (June 24, 1993) p10.
PRICE, MICHAEL L.
LE09306 743 (September 19, 1996) p12.
PRICONE, STEVEN
LE09307 668 (October 28, 1993) p8.
PRINCE, MALCOLM D.
LE09308 747 (November 14, 1996) p20.
PROCTOR, MAGGIE
LE09309 735 (May 30, 1996) p10.
PUGH, MONICA
LE09310 678 (March 24, 1994) p6.

PUNKY II
LE09311 717 (September 21, 1995) p16.

Q

QUATTLEBAUM, JON
LE09312 636 (August 6, 1992) p7.
QUIRK, MICHAEL ▓UCKING▓
LE09313 714 (August 10, 1995) p12.

R

RABBAT, PAUL
LE09314 644 (November 26, 1992) p11.
RACHEL
LE09315 721 (November 16, 1995) p18.
RAFTER, JIM
LE09316 720 (November 2, 1995) p12.
RAFTERY, BRIAN M.
LE09317 698-699 (December 29, 1994) p26.
RAINES, GREG
LE09318 709 (June 1, 1995) p14.
RAINNIE, MICHAEL
LE09319 629 (April 30, 1992) p8.
RAIS, MICHAEL
LE09320 704 (March 23, 1995) p18.
RAK, JOHN L.
LE09321 634-635 (July 9, 1992) p8.
RALPH, ANNE ELIZABETH
LE09322 703 (March 9, 1995) p16.
RAMIREZ, ALFONSO
LE09323 625 (March 5, 1992) p4.
RAMIREZ, JOAN
LE09324 675 (February 10, 1994) p6.
RAMIREZ, ROBERT
LE09325 654 (April 15, 1993) p8.
RAML, JOHN
LE09326 711 (June 29, 1995) p10.
RAMON, VIDA
LE09327 652 (March 18, 1993) p10.
RAMONE, JOEY
LE09328 672-673 (December 23, 1993) p10.
RAMSEY, LEAH
LE09329 653 (April 1, 1993) p8.
RANDALL, LEO
LE09330 639 (September 17, 1992) p10.
RANDALL, ROBERT
LE09331 644 (November 26, 1992) p11.
LE09332 654 (April 15, 1993) p8.
RAPATTONI, R.
LE09333 706 (April 20, 1995) p12.
RASCHER, J.
LE09334 721 (November 16, 1995) p18.
RAWLEY, KIM
LE09335 709 (June 1, 1995) p14.
RAY, ERIC
LE09336 734 (May 16, 1996) p14.
RAY, MICHAEL
LE09337 630 (May 14, 1992) p8.
RAY, MICHAEL K.
LE09338 688 (August 11, 1994) p10.
REDMOND, TODD
LE09339 628 (April 16, 1992) p6.
REED, ANDREW D.
LE09340 716 (September 7, 1995) p10.
REED, THOMAS GRADY, III
LE09341 685 (June 30, 1994) p10.
REEHER, JASON CHAFFEY
LE09342 700 (January 26, 1995) p14.
REES, ROBERT
LE09343 677 (March 10, 1994) p12.
REEVES, JOHN
LE09344 680 (April 21, 1994) p8.
REGER, NATHAN
LE09345 701 (February 9, 1995) p14.
REICH, ROBERT (SECRETARY OF LABOR)
LE09346 723 (December 14, 1995) p20.
REICHART, JOEL
LE09347 738-739 (July 11, 1996) p12.
REIMELT, CHRISTINE
LE09348 639 (September 17, 1992) p10.
REINARDT, TONY
LE09349 704 (March 23, 1995) p18.
REINDOLLAR, BRETT
LE09350 689 (August 25, 1994) p12.
REINHARDT, MEL
LE09351 686-687 (July 14, 1994) p14.
REINICHE, JOSH
LE09352 650 (February 18, 1993) p6.
RENFRO, RODNEY
LE09353 640 (October 1, 1992) p6.
LE09354 750-751 (December 26, 1996) p26.
RESSLER, ROBIN E.
LE09355 674 (January 27, 1994) p8.
RESSLER-BUNK, AMANDA
LE09356 737 (June 27, 1996) p12.
REZNIKOFF, CHARLIE
LE09357 627 (April 2, 1992) p8.
RHODES, DAVID C.
LE09358 723 (December 14, 1995) p20.
RICE, NOAH
LE09359 736 (June 13, 1996) p16.
RICHARDS, B. J.
LE09360 722 (November 30, 1995) p14.
RICHARDS, BRIGID (PROJECT ASSISTANT, RICHMOND HIGH SCHOOL)
LE09361 700 (January 26, 1995) p14.
RICHARDSON, J.
LE09362 684 (June 16, 1994) p11.
RICHART, M.
LE09363 634-635 (July 9, 1992) p8.
RICHMOND, REBECCA
LE09364 682 (May 19, 1994) p14.
RIDENOUR, HEATHER AMANDA
LE09365 669 (November 11, 1993) p8.
RIEDMULLER, KEVIN G.
LE09366 616 (October 31, 1991) p8.
RIEGLER, JENNIFER
LE09367 668 (October 28, 1993) p8.
RIFFLE, DALE (DIRECTOR, P.I.G.S.)
LE09368 659 (June 24, 1993) p10.
RIFKIND, NINA F.
LE09369 664 (September 2, 1993) p8.
RING, JAMES
LE09370 749 (December 12, 1996) p16.
RIPLEY, J. F.
LE09371 737 (June 27, 1996) p12.
RIZER, JASMINE
LE09372 710 (June 15, 1995) p14.
RIZZI, DANNY
LE09373 698-699 (December 29, 1994) p26.
ROBB, PHILLIP MICHAEL
LE09374 650 (February 18, 1993) p6.
ROBERTS, CHRISTA A.
LE09375 636 (August 6, 1992) p7.
ROBERTS, ELIZA
LE09376 689 (August 25, 1994) p12.
ROBERTS, SARA
LE09377 691 (September 22, 1994) p14.
ROBINSON, BRENT
LE09378 660-661 (July 8, 1993) p10.
ROBINSON, CHRIS
LE09379 619-620 (December 12, 1991) p14.
ROBINSON, KATHERINE
LE09380 701 (February 9, 1995) p14.
ROBINSON, TODD
LE09381 744 (October 3, 1996) p16.
ROCHE, LAURA ANNE
LE09382 690 (September 8, 1994) p16.
ROCHESTER, AARON
LE09383 644 (November 26, 1992) p11.
A ROCK & ROLL FAN
LE09384 692 (October 6, 1994) p12.
RODIN, JENNY
LE09385 704 (March 23, 1995) p18.
RODRICK, TAMARA
LE09386 683 (June 2, 1994) p11.
RODRIGUES, MARCUS
LE09387 722 (November 30, 1995) p14.
ROGERS, SARA
LE09388 654 (April 15, 1993) p8.
ROLLINS, HENRY
LE09389 645-646 (December 10, 1992) p20.
ROOF, DENNIS
LE09390 693 (October 20, 1994) p22.
ROSADO, JEN
LE09391 638 (September 3, 1992) p6.
ROSE, CATHERINE
LE09392 638 (September 3, 1992) p6.
ROSE, STARLETTE
LE09393 681 (May 5, 1994) p8.
ROSEEN, ERYK
LE09394 653 (April 1, 1993) p8.
ROSENBAUM, DAVID
LE09395 656 (May 13, 1993) p10.
ROSEWALL, LAURA
LE09396 657 (May 27, 1993) p6.
ROSS, KRISTIN
LE09397 718 (October 5, 1995) p16.
ROSS, LINDA
LE09398 692 (October 6, 1994) p12.
ROSS, MICHAEL (PRESIDENT, DELICIOUS VINYL)
LE09399 670 (November 25, 1993) p8.
ROTHWELL, ADAM
LE09400 648 (January 21, 1993) p7.
ROWELL, BOB
LE09401 649 (February 4, 1993) p7.
ROZELL, TERESA
LE09402 629 (April 30, 1992) p8.
RUBRIGHT, JEANNIE
LE09403 629 (April 30, 1992) p8.
RUBSAM, DAVID
LE09404 686-687 (July 14, 1994) p14.
RUDD, LARRY
LE09405 720 (November 2, 1995) p12.
RUDE GRRL
LE09406 718 (October 5, 1995) p16.
RUEF, BILL A.
LE09407 718 (October 5, 1995) p16.

RUGGIERO, BOB
LE09408 628 (April 16, 1992) p6.
RULE, KRISTIN
LE09409 615 (October 17, 1991) p8.
RUSCITTO, CHRIS
LE09410 653 (April 1, 1993) p8.
RUSH, TODD
LE09411 649 (February 4, 1993) p7.
RUSHTON, J. PHILIPPE
LE09412 696 (December 1, 1994) p18.
RUSHTON, JERRY L.
LE09413 676 (February 24, 1994) p10.
RUZICKA, ALEXANDER
LE09414 649 (February 4, 1993) p7.
RYALL, RICH
LE09415 702 (February 23, 1995) p16.
RYAN, JENN
LE09416 731 (April 4, 1996) p14.
RYE, RAMSEY
LE09417 633 (June 25, 1992) p5.

S

S., KYLE
LE09418 666 (September 30, 1993) p10.
S., LILY
LE09419 734 (May 16, 1996) p14.
SAALBERG, AMY
LE09420 678 (March 24, 1994) p6.
SAHM, DOUG
LE09421 696 (December 1, 1994) p18.
SAIA, GEOFFREY
LE09422 705 (April 6, 1995) p14.
SALCEDO, HELEN
LE09423 615 (October 17, 1991) p8.
SALTZMAN, TANYA
LE09424 679 (April 7, 1994) p10.
SAMSON, KATE
LE09425 692 (October 6, 1994) p12.
SAMUELS, WENDELL, JR.
LE09426 675 (February 10, 1994) p6.
SANAULLA, JABEEN
LE09427 697 (December 15, 1994) p14.
SANDERS, JACK P.
LE09428 668 (October 28, 1993) p8.
SANE, HOON
LE09429 662 (August 5, 1993) p8.
SANGER, BRIAN
LE09430 660-661 (July 8, 1993) p10.
SANTOS, TONY
LE09431 703 (March 9, 1995) p16.
SATTLER, TINA
LE09432 638 (September 3, 1992) p6.
SAUDER, R. L.
LE09433 670 (November 25, 1993) p8.
SAUER, LUCAS K.
LE09434 650 (February 18, 1993) p6.
SAUL, THOMAS
LE09435 662 (August 5, 1993) p8.
SAUNDERS, MARGUERITE T.
LE09436 663 (August 19, 1993) p4.
SAUTNER, GRANT
LE09437 680 (April 21, 1994) p8.
SAVAGE, CHAD L.
LE09438 674 (January 27, 1994) p8.
SAVAGE, JOHN C.
LE09439 665 (September 16, 1993) p6.
SAVAGLIA, KENNY
LE09440 644 (November 26, 1992) p11.
SCALZO, GREG J.
LE09441 653 (April 1, 1993) p8.
SCHANSBERG, D. ERIC (INDIANA UNIVERSITY-SOUTHEAST)
LE09442 666 (September 30, 1993) p10.
SCHEEL, MICHELLE
LE09443 640 (October 1, 1992) p6.
SCHILDBACH, J. C.
LE09444 676 (February 24, 1994) p10.
SCHIRMER, DAVID W.
LE09445 625 (March 5, 1992) p4.
SCHLEICH, KATHRYN
LE09446 675 (February 10, 1994) p6.
SCHLOSBERG, JEREMY
LE09447 649 (February 4, 1993) p7.
SCHLOSSER, KURT
LE09448 657 (May 27, 1993) p6.
SCHMIDT, BILL
LE09449 721 (November 16, 1995) p18.
SCHMIDT, GEORGE
LE09450 653 (April 1, 1993) p8.
SCHMIDT, PATTY
LE09451 733 (May 2, 1996) p10.
SCHMOLL, DAVID
LE09452 706 (April 20, 1995) p12.
SCHNABEL, JASON
LE09453 685 (June 30, 1994) p10.
SCHNECK, DIANE
LE09454 633 (June 25, 1992) p5.
SCHOONBECK, LUCINDA
LE09455 667 (October 14, 1993) p14.
SCHOTT, JOHN
LE09456 749 (December 12, 1996) p16.
SCHWARTZ, STEPHEN (STAFF WRITER, SAN FRANCISCO CHRONICLE)
LE09457 728 (February 22, 1996) p16.
SCHWINGHAMMER, MICHELLE
LE09458 629 (April 30, 1992) p8.
SCOTT, TAYLOR
LE09459 720 (November 2, 1995) p12.
S.E.A.
LE09460 717 (September 21, 1995) p16.
SEDGWICK, KYRA
LE09461 645-646 (December 10, 1992) p20.
SEEBOTH, MARTIN
LE09462 667 (October 14, 1993) p14.
SEGAL, ELI J.
LE09463 694 (November 3, 1994) p14.
SEGAL, ROBERT
LE09464 634-635 (July 9, 1992) p8.
SEGAL, STEPHANIE
LE09465 701 (February 9, 1995) p14.
SEGALE, LISA
LE09466 702 (February 23, 1995) p16.
SEIBEL, BOB
LE09467 651 (March 4, 1993) p10.
SEKULIC, MIKE
LE09468 680 (April 21, 1994) p8.
SENDECKE, ANNE C.
LE09469 630 (May 14, 1992) p8.
SEXTON, SCOTT
LE09470 708 (May 18, 1995) p14.
SHABINO, BRUCE
LE09471 677 (March 10, 1994) p12.
SHANNON, DAVID
LE09472 654 (April 15, 1993) p8.
SHARP, RAE
LE09473 640 (October 1, 1992) p6.
SHATURD, PAULIE
LE09474 665 (September 16, 1993) p6.
SHAW, DANA
LE09475 659 (June 24, 1993) p10.
SHAW, JOCELYN
LE09476 718 (October 5, 1995) p16.
SHAW, STEVE
LE09477 732 (April 18, 1996) p16.
SHAWNA J
LE09478 715 (August 24, 1995) p18.
SHEA, BRIAN
LE09479 733 (May 2, 1996) p10.
SHEA, MACK D.
LE09480 638 (September 3, 1992) p6.
SHELLEY, N.
LE09481 685 (June 30, 1994) p10.
SHEPHERD JOHN
LE09482 675 (February 10, 1994) p6.
SHEPPARD, SCOTT ROBERT
LE09483 684 (June 16, 1994) p11.
SHETLER, DARREN
LE09484 694 (November 3, 1994) p14.
SHIELDS, BEN
LE09485 718 (October 5, 1995) p16.
SHIPLEY, JAMES
LE09486 704 (March 23, 1995) p18.
SHOEMAKER, BILL
LE09487 637 (August 20, 1992) p6.
SHORE, TONY
LE09488 628 (April 16, 1992) p6.
SHRIVER, SARGENT
LE09489 688 (August 11, 1994) p10.
SIDDOWAY, MARK
LE09490 629 (April 30, 1992) p9.
SIELER, MARK J.
LE09491 625 (March 5, 1992) p4.
SILMAN, S. JACK
LE09492 647 (January 7, 1993) p7.
SILVERSHER, MICHAEL
LE09493 734 (May 16, 1996) p14.
SILVIDI, ALAN
LE09494 709 (June 1, 1995) p14.
SIMMONS, D. MICHAEL
LE09495 698-699 (December 29, 1994) p26.
SIMMONS, GENE
LE09496 624 (February 20, 1992) p7.
SIMON, PAUL (SENATOR)
LE09497 726 (January 25, 1996) p12.
SIMON, SUSAN
LE09498 659 (June 24, 1993) p10.
SIMPSON, PETER G.
LE09499 639 (September 17, 1992) p10.
SINGH, MATT
LE09500 680 (April 21, 1994) p8.
SINGLETARY, M. J.
LE09501 683 (June 2, 1994) p11.
SINGLETON, JOHN
LE09502 645-646 (December 10, 1992) p20.
SINTES, MAC
LE09503 728 (February 22, 1996) p16.
SIRLOIN
LE09504 724-725 (December 28, 1995) p20.
SKAALRUD, LEE
LE09505 701 (February 9, 1995) p14.
SKALA, GENE
LE09506 748 (November 28, 1996) p22.
SKALSKI, PAUL

LE09507 721 (November 16, 1995) p18.
SKORIC, IVO
LE09508 650 (February 18, 1993) p6.
SKROK, RACHEL
LE09509 665 (September 16, 1993) p6.
SLATER, CHRISTIAN
LE09510 672-673 (December 23, 1993) p10.
SLICK, LAURIE L.
LE09511 633 (June 25, 1992) p5.
SMALL, JOHN
LE09512 616 (October 31, 1991) p8.
SMICKLAS, LISA
LE09513 720 (November 2, 1995) p12.
SMITH, ADAM
LE09514 676 (February 24, 1994) p10.
SMITH, CHRISTINE
LE09515 712-713 (July 13, 1995) p20.
SMITH, ERIN
LE09516 742 (September 5, 1996) p16.
SMITH, G. E. (MUSIC DIRECTOR, SATURDAY NIGHT LIVE)
LE09517 622 (January 23, 1992) p4.
SMITH, JEN
LE09518 733 (May 2, 1996) p10.
SMITH, JENNIFER
LE09519 682 (May 19, 1994) p14.
SMITH, JONATHAN
LE09520 618 (November 28, 1991) p9.
SMITH, KEN (EXECUTIVE DIRECTOR, NEW ENGLAND SHELTER FOR HOMELESS VETERANS)
LE09521 665 (September 16, 1993) p6.
SMITH, MARTY
LE09522 639 (September 17, 1992) p10.
SMITH, MATT
LE09523 697 (December 15, 1994) p14.
SMITH, PATTI
LE09524 730 (March 21, 1996) p14.
SMITH, R.
LE09525 639 (September 17, 1992) p10.
SMITH, STEPHANIE LYNN
LE09526 729 (March 7, 1996) p6.
SMITH, VIRGINIA A.
LE09527 690 (September 8, 1994) p16.
SMITH-PEARSON, STEPHANY
LE09528 628 (April 16, 1992) p6.
SNYDER, ED B.
LE09529 623 (February 6, 1992) p6.
SNYDER, JULENE
LE09530 730 (March 21, 1996) p14.
SNYDER, KENNETH
LE09531 668 (October 28, 1993) p8.
SO, CONWAY
LE09532 709 (June 1, 1995) p14.
SODANO, TODD M.
LE09533 717 (September 21, 1995) p16.
SOMACH, DENNY (PRESIDENT, CINEMA RECORDS)
LE09534 628 (April 16, 1992) p6.
LE09535 Number not assigned.
SORENSEN, CHARLIE
LE09536 711 (June 29, 1995) p10.
SOTO, ALFRED
LE09537 716 (September 7, 1995) p10.
SOUTHER, MATT
LE09538 689 (August 25, 1994) p12.
SOUZA, KENNETH J.
LE09539 625 (March 5, 1992) p4.
SPARACIO, BOB
LE09540 676 (February 24, 1994) p10.
SPARLING, STEVEN W.
LE09541 670 (November 25, 1993) p8.
SPECTOR, PHIL
LE09542 685 (June 30, 1994) p10.
SPEECE, ANDY
LE09543 742 (September 5, 1996) p16.
SPINELLI, NICOLE K.
LE09544 671 (December 9, 1993) p7.
SPINNEY, CONSTANCE
LE09545 662 (August 5, 1993) p8.
SPRIGGS, JAMES D.
LE09546 729 (March 7, 1996) p6.
S.R.M.
LE09547 698-699 (December 29, 1994) p26.
STACEY C.
LE09548 636 (August 6, 1992) p7.
STACHLER, JOSEPH
LE09549 711 (June 29, 1995) p10.
STAGGS, JEFFREY
LE09550 690 (September 8, 1994) p16.
STAMBAUGH, SCOTT
LE09551 618 (November 28, 1991) p9.
STAMBERG, ERIC
LE09552 622 (January 23, 1992) p4.
STANKOVICH, HAJIRA D.
LE09553 728 (February 22, 1996) p16.
STANKOWITZ, ANNE M.
LE09554 624 (February 20, 1992) p7.
STANLEY, GINGER
LE09555 630 (May 14, 1992) p8.
STANLEY, PAUL
LE09556 624 (February 20, 1992) p7.
STARNES, G. BRIAN
LE09557 681 (May 5, 1994) p8.
STASKO, MICHAEL A.
LE09558 653 (April 1, 1993) p8.
STEINHAUER, JOSIE
LE09559 675 (February 10, 1994) p6.
STENMO, ART
LE09560 663 (August 19, 1993) p4.
STEPHENS, MARC
LE09561 657 (May 27, 1993) p6.
STEPHENS, RON
LE09562 682 (May 19, 1994) p14.
STEPHENSON, LISA
LE09563 719 (October 19, 1995) p10.
STEVENS, PHIL
LE09564 654 (April 15, 1993) p8.
STEWART, JENN
LE09565 615 (October 17, 1991) p8.
STIPE, MICHAEL
LE09566 627 (April 2, 1992) p8.
STONE, KASSY
LE09567 678 (March 24, 1994) p6.
STONE, KELLY
LE09568 658 (June 10, 1993) p12.
LE09569 714 (August 10, 1995) p12.
STONE, OLIVER
LE09570 626 (March 19, 1992) p6.
STOTT, DAEMON
LE09571 705 (April 6, 1995) p14.
STRITTMATTER, GRETA
LE09572 668 (October 28, 1993) p8.
STROMME, RENEE D.
LE09573 656 (May 13, 1993) p10.
STUDLEY, KEVIN A.
LE09574 623 (February 6, 1992) p6.
STURDIVANT, WADE
LE09575 660-661 (July 8, 1993) p10.
SUEMATSU, DAISUKE
LE09576 701 (February 9, 1995) p14.
SULIKOWSKI, STEFAN
LE09577 630 (May 14, 1992) p8.
SULLIVAN, ANDY
LE09578 720 (November 2, 1995) p12.
SUMMERS, AUDREY
LE09579 647 (January 7, 1993) p7.
SUMMERS, COREY
LE09580 745 (October 17, 1996) p24.
SUNDBERG, GREG
LE09581 622 (January 23, 1992) p4.
SUSKIND, CHAD
LE09582 738-739 (July 11, 1996) p12.
SUTTER, J. PAUL
LE09583 686-687 (July 14, 1994) p14.
SVABODAN, CHELSEA
LE09584 666 (September 30, 1993) p10.
SWALLOW, ERIK
LE09585 733 (May 2, 1996) p10.
SWANSON, PETE
LE09586 639 (September 17, 1992) p10.
SWEENEY, JAN
LE09587 712-713 (July 13, 1995) p20.
SWIERCZYNSKI, DUANE (RESEARCH EDITOR, PHILADELPHIA MAGAZINE)
LE09588 670 (November 25, 1993) p8.
SWISHER, SHAWN
LE09589 723 (December 14, 1995) p20.
SZADA, SHELLY
LE09590 726 (January 25, 1996) p12.

T

T.
LE09591 694 (November 3, 1994) p14.
TADDEO, ANNIE
LE09592 710 (June 15, 1995) p14.
TAGUE, SUSAN MATHIS
LE09593 717 (September 21, 1995) p16.
TALLEY, JOHN
LE09594 712-713 (July 13, 1995) p20.
TANKERSLEY, JOEL
LE09595 680 (April 21, 1994) p8.
TANT, ED
LE09596 714 (August 10, 1995) p12.
TARANTO, MICHAEL
LE09597 640 (October 1, 1992) p6.
TAREE, AERLE
LE09598 645-646 (December 10, 1992) p20.
TAROLI, GARRY S.
LE09599 676 (February 24, 1994) p10.
TAYLOR, COREY
LE09600 711 (June 29, 1995) p10.
TAYLOR, DANE
LE09601 712-713 (July 13, 1995) p20.
TAYLOR, JEREMY
LE09602 675 (February 10, 1994) p6.
TAYLOR, JODI
LE09603 703 (March 9, 1995) p16.
TAYLOR, KRISTEN
LE09604 624 (February 20, 1992) p7.
LE09605 Number not assigned.
TAYLOR, LINDA
LE09606 649 (February 4, 1993) p7.

TEITSWORTH, CHARLES
LE09607 720 (November 2, 1995) p12.
TEMONEY, KATE E.
LE09608 691 (September 22, 1994) p14.
TERENCE, DANIELLE
LE09609 684 (June 16, 1994) p11.
TEWS, EDDIE
LE09610 679 (April 7, 1994) p10.
THAYIL, KIM
LE09611 619-620 (December 12, 1991) p14.
THELANDER, MARI
LE09612 735 (May 30, 1996) p10.
THOMAS, STEWART
LE09613 674 (January 27, 1994) p8.
THOMPSON, BRUCE
LE09614 647 (January 7, 1993) p7.
THOMPSON, CHRISTOPHER L.
LE09615 651 (March 4, 1993) p10.
THOMPSON, GAVIN
LE09616 638 (September 3, 1992) p6.
THOMPSON, HUNTER S.
LE09617 674 (January 27, 1994) p8.
LE09618 740 (August 8, 1996) p14.
THOMPSON, PAGE
LE09619 692 (October 6, 1994) p12.
THOMPSON, STEPHEN
LE09620 666 (September 30, 1993) p10.
THOMSON, STEPHANIE
LE09621 723 (December 14, 1995) p20.
THORNE-SMITH, COURTNEY
LE09622 672-673 (December 23, 1993) p10.
THORNTON, JERRY
LE09623 659 (June 24, 1993) p10.
THORNTON, KYAN
LE09624 666 (September 30, 1993) p10.
THURMAN, POPPY
LE09625 662 (August 5, 1993) p8.
TIM
LE09626 707 (May 4, 1995) p16.
TIMMINS, MARGO
LE09627 619-620 (December 12, 1991) p14.
TIMS, STAN
LE09628 656 (May 13, 1993) p10.
TISCH, JERRY
LE09629 623 (February 6, 1992) p6.
TODD, E.
LE09630 656 (May 13, 1993) p10.
TOLLEY, BRIDGET
LE09631 629 (April 30, 1992) p8.
TOMASELLI, MINDY RUBEN
LE09632 644 (November 26, 1992) p11.
TOUT, DEBORAH
LE09633 722 (November 30, 1995) p14.
TOWEY, SHAUN
LE09634 676 (February 24, 1994) p10.
TRAVERS, PETER
LE09635 626 (March 19, 1992) p6.
TRE
LE09636 672-673 (December 23, 1993) p10.
TREADAWAY, TREY
LE09637 668 (October 28, 1993) p8.
TREGUBOFF, JEFF
LE09638 705 (April 6, 1995) p14.
TREMAIN, KERRY
LE09639 642 (October 29, 1992) p8.
TREMBLAY, MIKE
LE09640 636 (August 6, 1992) p7.
TREUBIG, DENNIS
LE09641 634-635 (July 9, 1992) p8.
TRINCHERA, TOM
LE09642 722 (November 30, 1995) p14.
TRISHA
LE09643 689 (August 25, 1994) p12.
TRITT, TRAVIS
LE09644 672-673 (December 23, 1993) p10.
TROIANO, LARRY
LE09645 627 (April 2, 1992) p8.
TRUMBO, KEITH
LE09646 617 (November 14, 1991) p8.
TUDIR, SUSAN
LE09647 696 (December 1, 1994) p18.
TULLOS, JULIE
LE09648 700 (January 26, 1995) p14.
TURKMAN, S. U.
LE09649 651 (March 4, 1993) p10.
TURNER, KIRK
LE09650 734 (May 16, 1996) p14.
TURNER, MARK
LE09651 648 (January 21, 1993) p7.
TYLER, SARAH
LE09652 741 (August 22, 1996) p20.
TYLER, STEVEN
LE09653 619-620 (December 12, 1991) p14.
LE09654 633 (June 25, 1992) p5.
LE09655 645-646 (December 10, 1992) p20.
LE09656 672-673 (December 23, 1993) p10.

U

ULLENBERG, SUSAN
LE09657 729 (March 7, 1996) p6.
UNGER, RUSS
LE09658 714 (August 10, 1995) p12.
UNHOLZ, JOHN
LE09659 685 (June 30, 1994) p10.
UNTERMYER, ALEXANDER
LE09660 678 (March 24, 1994) p6.

V

VAGELATOS, ALEX
LE09661 750-751 (December 26, 1996) p26.
VALENCE, RICK
LE09662 719 (October 19, 1995) p10.
VALIUM, JUDEA
LE09663 718 (October 5, 1995) p16.
VAN BUSKIRK, ELIZABETH M.
LE09664 715 (August 24, 1995) p18.
VAN DO, DAVE
LE09665 679 (April 7, 1994) p10.
VAN DUSEN, CHRISTIE
LE09666 691 (September 22, 1994) p14.
VAN WAGNER, CHAD
LE09667 731 (April 4, 1996) p14.
VAN ZEIPEL, JAYSON
LE09668 654 (April 15, 1993) p8.
VANALSTYNE, KIRSTIE
LE09669 702 (February 23, 1995) p16.
VANTO-FHYM, ASER
LE09670 669 (November 11, 1993) p8.
VARELA, ROGER
LE09671 663 (August 19, 1993) p4.
VAUGHN, WENDI
LE09672 723 (December 14, 1995) p20.
VEDDER, EDDIE
LE09673 619-620 (December 12, 1991) p14.
VELAZQUEZ, BRIAN
LE09674 715 (August 24, 1995) p18.
VILLASANA, TINA
LE09675 630 (May 14, 1992) p8.
VISHNESKY, PHILLIP C.
LE09676 688 (August 11, 1994) p10.
VITAS, JASON A.
LE09677 617 (November 14, 1991) p8.
VITEK, ROBIN L.
LE09678 701 (February 9, 1995) p14.
VLLER, JOSH
LE09679 664 (September 2, 1993) p8.
VOIDA, STEVEN M.
LE09680 711 (June 29, 1995) p10.
VYKRUTA, RON
LE09681 631 (May 28, 1992) p6.

W

WACHELDORF, SHELLEY
LE09682 701 (February 9, 1995) p14.
WADE, JESSE
LE09683 723 (December 14, 1995) p20.
WALK, HUNTER
LE09684 722 (November 30, 1995) p14.
WALKER, MURRAY
LE09685 692 (October 6, 1994) p12.
WALKER, SCOTT
LE09686 728 (February 22, 1996) p16.
WALLACE, KRISTIN
LE09687 621 (January 9, 1992) p6.
WALLIOR, SUSAN M.
LE09688 677 (March 10, 1994) p12.
WALSH, JOHN
LE09689 741 (August 22, 1996) p20.
WALTERS, JAMES
LE09690 744 (October 3, 1996) p16.
WARD, MATTHEW B.
LE09691 642 (October 29, 1992) p8.
WARD, SANDY
LE09692 633 (June 25, 1992) p5.
WARNER, JUSTIN
LE09693 727 (February 8, 1996) p10.
WARREN, BRAD
LE09694 663 (August 19, 1993) p4.
WASYLKIW, BLAINE
LE09695 735 (May 30, 1996) p10.
WATERS, MARTHA
LE09696 642 (October 29, 1992) p8.
WATKINS, GLENN A.
LE09697 682 (May 19, 1994) p14.
WATKINS, NEIL
LE09698 658 (June 10, 1993) p12.
WATLEY, JODY
LE09699 639 (September 17, 1992) p10.
WATSON, DAVE
LE09700 660-661 (July 8, 1993) p10.

WATSON, JASON R.
LE09701 679 (April 7, 1994) p10.
WATSON, KEVIN
LE09702 723 (December 14, 1995) p22.
WATSON, MELISSA AUDRA
LE09703 674 (January 27, 1994) p8.
WATSON, TERRI M.
LE09704 669 (November 11, 1993) p8.
WEBER, KURT T. (PROGRAM DIRECTOR, CASCADE POLICY INSTITUTE)
LE09705 668 (October 28, 1993) p8.
WEBSTER, CHRISTOPHER A.
LE09706 667 (October 14, 1993) p14.
WEEDMAN, JEFF
LE09707 630 (May 14, 1992) p8.
WEICKER, LOWELL P., JR.
LE09708 714 (August 10, 1995) p12.
WEIDLER, BOB
LE09709 638 (September 3, 1992) p6.
WEIL, HOLLY J.
LE09710 652 (March 18, 1993) p10.
WEILL, SUE
LE09711 715 (August 24, 1995) p18.
WEINER, KIRSTEN
LE09712 664 (September 2, 1993) p8.
WEIS, SHYAMA
LE09713 712-713 (July 13, 1995) p20.
WEISNER, ARON
LE09714 697 (December 15, 1994) p14.
WEISS, MICHAEL F.
LE09715 630 (May 14, 1992) p8.
WELLS, JO ANN
LE09716 698-699 (December 29, 1994) p26.
WENTWORTH, LIZ
LE09717 706 (April 20, 1995) p12.
WEST, FAITH
LE09718 715 (August 24, 1995) p18.
WEST, JILL
LE09719 677 (March 10, 1994) p12.
WESTFIELD, ALISHA
LE09720 648 (January 21, 1993) p7.
WHEATLEY, JACK
LE09721 675 (February 10, 1994) p6.
WHINERY, MEGAN
LE09722 698-699 (December 29, 1994) p26.
WHISLER, CASEY
LE09723 709 (June 1, 1995) p14.
WHITE, AARON
LE09724 684 (June 16, 1994) p11.
WHITE, CHRIS
LE09725 636 (August 6, 1992) p7.
WHITE, RICHARD
LE09726 738-739 (July 11, 1996) p12.
WHITE, RICHARD J.
LE09727 676 (February 24, 1994) p10.
WHITE, S. TRACY
LE09728 617 (November 14, 1991) p8.
WHITEHEAD, JOHN C. (ASST. PROF., DEPT. OF ECONOMICS, EAST CAROLINA UNIV.)
LE09729 671 (December 9, 1993) p7.
WHITELEY, STEPHEN
LE09730 660-661 (July 8, 1993) p10.
WHITMER, MIKE
LE09731 617 (November 14, 1991) p8.
WHITNEY, STU
LE09732 634-635 (July 9, 1992) p8.
WIATT, JODY
LE09733 698-699 (December 29, 1994) p26.
WIESER, ADAM J.
LE09734 731 (April 4, 1996) p14.
WIEST, RANDY
LE09735 701 (February 9, 1995) p14.
WILBER, CATIE
LE09736 627 (April 2, 1992) p8.
WILEY, AUDREY
LE09737 708 (May 18, 1995) p14.
WILKINSON, GEORGE MARK
LE09738 678 (March 24, 1994) p6.
WILKISON, CHAD
LE09739 657 (May 27, 1993) p6.
WILKOFSKY, MARC
LE09740 719 (October 19, 1995) p10.
WILLEY, LISA
LE09741 658 (June 10, 1993) p12.
WILLIAMS, A.
LE09742 703 (March 9, 1995) p16.
WILLIAMS, ALLEN
LE09743 691 (September 22, 1994) p14.
WILLIAMS, FERN BAUM
LE09744 705 (April 6, 1995) p14.
WILLIAMS, ISAAC
LE09745 719 (October 19, 1995) p10.
WILLIAMS, JENNY
LE09746 693 (October 20, 1994) p22.
WILLIAMS, LINDA
LE09747 703 (March 9, 1995) p16.
WILLIAMS, S.
LE09748 703 (March 9, 1995) p16.
WILLIAMSON, ROGER
LE09749 634-635 (July 9, 1992) p8.
WILLIS, AARON
LE09750 656 (May 13, 1993) p10.
WILSON, BOB
LE09751 684 (June 16, 1994) p11.
WILSON, IAN
LE09752 640 (October 1, 1992) p6.
WILSON, LARRY
LE09753 621 (January 9, 1992) p6.
WILSON, LEANNE
LE09754 681 (May 5, 1994) p8.
WILSON, LINDA M.
LE09755 704 (March 23, 1995) p18.
WILSON, PETER
LE09756 742 (September 5, 1996) p16.
WILSON, RONA H.
LE09757 637 (August 20, 1992) p6.
WILSON, SUSAN
LE09758 633 (June 25, 1992) p5.
WINTHROP, D. L.
LE09759 617 (November 14, 1991) p8.
WISCHER, DAVID
LE09760 655 (April 29, 1993) p7.
WITHYCOMBE, MARY
LE09761 724-725 (December 28, 1995) p24.
WOFFORD, EMMETT
LE09762 690 (September 8, 1994) p16.
WOLF, JOHN A.
LE09763 678 (March 24, 1994) p6.
WOLMAN, KRIS
LE09764 701 (February 9, 1995) p14.
WOOD, T. (ANDY WOOD'S MOTHER)
LE09765 647 (January 7, 1993) p7.
WOODIE, JOHN D. F.
LE09766 682 (May 19, 1994) p14.
WOODWARD, MIKE
LE09767 634-635 (July 9, 1992) p8.
WOOL, RACHEL
LE09768 666 (September 30, 1993) p10.
WOOSTER, CHRIS
LE09769 674 (January 27, 1994) p8.
WORTHINGTON, BETH
LE09770 678 (March 24, 1994) p6.
WRIGHT, KELLY
LE09771 712-713 (July 13, 1995) p20.
WYAR, SUE
LE09772 644 (November 26, 1992) p11.
WYMAN, BEN
LE09773 630 (May 14, 1992) p8.
WYNDHAM, CHARLES
LE09774 686-687 (July 14, 1994) p14.

Y

YACKLEY, AYLA JEAN
LE09775 636 (August 6, 1992) p7.
YAEGEL, MARK S.
LE09776 630 (May 14, 1992) p8.
LE09777 677 (March 10, 1994) p12.
YARLAS, AARON
LE09778 660-661 (July 8, 1993) p10.
YEARWOOD, TRISHA
LE09779 672-673 (December 23, 1993) p10.
YEDNOCK, KIMBERLY
LE09780 649 (February 4, 1993) p7.
YO-YO
LE09781 645-646 (December 10, 1992) p20.
YOCKEY, W. H.
LE09782 616 (October 31, 1991) p8.
YOCOM, TRAVIS C.
LE09783 633 (June 25, 1992) p5.
YORK, KRISTI
LE09784 717 (September 21, 1995) p16.
YOUCHISON, STEVEN
LE09785 703 (March 9, 1995) p16.
YOUELLS, M.
LE09786 663 (August 19, 1993) p4.
YOUNG, AMY
LE09787 630 (May 14, 1992) p8.
YOUNG, HILARIE
LE09788 705 (April 6, 1995) p14.
YOUNG, J. A.
LE09789 664 (September 2, 1993) p8.
YOUNG, JOHN
LE09790 628 (April 16, 1992) p6.
YOUSUF, SARA
LE09791 719 (October 19, 1995) p10.

Z

ZACCHERIO, MICHAEL
LE09792 633 (June 25, 1992) p5.
LE09793 644 (November 26, 1992) p11.
LE09794 667 (October 14, 1993) p14.
ZANI, CHERI
LE09795 624 (February 20, 1992) p7.
LE09796 677 (March 10, 1994) p12.
ZANTI, HOPE
LE09797 747 (November 14, 1996) p20.

ZARTMAN, DAVID C.
LE09798 642 (October 29, 1992) p8.
ZARZECKI, TOM
LE09799 625 (March 5, 1992) p4.
ZAWADZKI, TRINETTE
LE09800 662 (August 5, 1993) p8.
ZAY, LAURA
LE09801 684 (June 16, 1994) p11.
ZERBE, ALLISON
LE09802 642 (October 29, 1992) p8.
ZIMA, DAN
LE09803 676 (February 24, 1994) p10.
ZULAICA, DON
LE09804 618 (November 28, 1991) p9.
ZWEIBACK, RICHARD
LE09805 720 (November 2, 1995) p12.

MOVIE REVIEWS

A

ABOVE THE RIM
MR01189 680 (April 21, 1994) pp93,95. (Travers, Peter)
ACE VENTURA: PET DETECTIVE
MR01190 679 (April 7, 1994) p83. (Travers, Peter)
ACE VENTURA: WHEN NATURE CALLS
MR01191 722 (November 30, 1995) pp73-75. (Travers, Peter)
THE ADDAMS FAMILY
MR01192 621 (January 9, 1992) p55. (Travers, Peter)
MR01193 634-635 (July 9, 1992) p111.
ADDAMS FAMILY VALUES
MR01194 671 (December 9, 1993) p78. (Travers, Peter)
THE ADDICTION
MR01195 719 (October 19, 1995) p159. (Travers, Peter)
THE ADVENTURES OF PRISCILLA, QUEEN OF THE DESERT
MR01196 689 (August 25, 1994) p97. (Travers, Peter)
THE AGE OF INNOCENCE
MR01197 666 (September 30, 1993) pp111-112. (Travers, Peter)
MR01198 672-673 (December 23, 1993) p174. (Travers, Peter)
AILEEN WUORNOS: THE SELLING OF A SERIAL KILLER
MR01199 677 (March 10, 1994) p60. (Travers, Peter)
AIRHEADS
MR01200 689 (August 25, 1994) p97. (Travers, Peter)
ALADDIN
MR01201 644 (November 26, 1992) pp77-78. (Travers, Peter)
ALAN & NAOMI
MR01202 624 (February 20, 1992) p50. (Travers, Peter)
ALBINO ALLIGATOR
MR01203 748 (November 28, 1996) p142. (Travers, Peter)
ALIEN
MR01204 651 (March 4, 1993) p72. (Travers, Peter)
ALIEN 3
MR01205 633 (June 25, 1992) pp48-49. (Travers, Peter)
ALIVE
MR01206 649 (February 4, 1993) p75. (Travers, Peter)
ALL THE VERMEERS IN NEW YORK
MR01207 630 (May 14, 1992) p114. (Travers, Peter)
AMATEUR
MR01208 706 (April 20, 1995) pp88-89. (Travers, Peter)
AMERICAN BUFFALO
MR01209 744 (October 3, 1996) p78. (Travers, Peter)
AMERICAN DREAM
MR01210 628 (April 16, 1992) p91. (Travers, Peter)
AMERICAN FRIENDS
MR01211 655 (April 29, 1993) p69. (Travers, Peter)
AMERICAN HEART
MR01212 658 (June 10, 1993) pp74,78. (Travers, Peter)
AMERICAN ME
MR01213 627 (April 2, 1992) p42. (Travers, Peter)
THE AMERICAN PRESIDENT
MR01214 722 (November 30, 1995) p76. (Travers, Peter)
AMONGST FRIENDS
MR01215 662 (August 5, 1993) p73. (Travers, Peter)
AMOS AND ANDREW
MR01216 653 (April 1, 1993) p59. (Travers, Peter)
AND THE BAND PLAYED ON
MR01217 666 (September 30, 1993) p113. (Travers, Peter)
ANGELS AND INSECTS
MR01218 731 (April 4, 1996) p68. (Travers, Peter)
ANGIE
MR01219 678 (March 24, 1994) p104. (Travers, Peter)
ANOTHER STAKEOUT
MR01220 664 (September 2, 1993) p70. (Travers, Peter)
APOLLO 13
MR01221 712-713 (July 13, 1995) pp113-116. (Travers, Peter)
ARTICLE 99
MR01222 628 (April 16, 1992) p93. (Travers, Peter)
THE ASSOCIATE
MR01223 748 (November 28, 1996) p143. (Travers, Peter)
AT PLAY IN THE FIELDS OF THE LORD
MR01224 621 (January 9, 1992) p55. (Travers, Peter)
MR01225 629 (April 30, 1992) p65.
AN AWFULLY BIG ADVENTURE
MR01226 714 (August 10, 1995) p62. (Travers, Peter)

B

THE BABE
MR01227 630 (May 14, 1992) pp112-113. (Travers, Peter)
BABY, IT'S YOU
MR01228 677 (March 10, 1994) p18. (Duritz, Adam)
BABYFEVER
MR01229 682 (May 19, 1994) pp106-107. (Travers, Peter)
BACKBEAT
MR01230 680 (April 21, 1994) pp92-93. (Travers, Peter)
BAD BEHAVIOR
MR01231 667 (October 14, 1993) p128. (Travers, Peter)
BAD BOYS
MR01232 707 (May 4, 1995) pp73-74,76. (Travers, Peter)
BAD GIRLS
MR01233 683 (June 2, 1994) p76. (Travers, Peter)
BAD LIEUTENANT
MR01234 644 (November 26, 1992) pp77-78. (Travers, Peter)
MR01235 648 (January 21, 1993) p56. (Travers, Peter)
MR01236 679 (April 7, 1994) p30. (Hoon, Shannon)
BAD MOON
MR01237 748 (November 28, 1996) p143. (Travers, Peter)
THE BALLAD OF LITTLE JO
MR01238 663 (August 19, 1993) p83. (Travers, Peter)
BARB WIRE
MR01239 734 (May 16, 1996) p72. (Travers, Peter)
BARCELONA
MR01240 688 (August 11, 1994) p63. (Travers, Peter)
BARTON FINK
MR01241 622 (January 23, 1992) p49. (Travers, Peter)
MR01242 634-635 (July 9, 1992) p111.
BASIC INSTINCT
MR01243 628 (April 16, 1992) pp89-90. (Travers, Peter)
THE BASKETBALL DIARIES
MR01244 704 (March 23, 1995) pp127-128. (Travers, Peter)
BASQUIAT
MR01245 741 (August 22, 1996) p105. (Travers, Peter)
BATMAN FOREVER
MR01246 712-713 (July 13, 1995) pp113-116. (Travers, Peter)
BATMAN RETURNS
MR01247 634-635 (July 9, 1992) pp109,111. (Travers, Peter)
BEAUTIFUL GIRLS
MR01248 729 (March 7, 1996) p53. (Travers, Peter)
BEAUTY AND THE BEAST
MR01249 622 (January 23, 1992) p49. (Travers, Peter)
MR01250 651 (March 4, 1993) p72. (Travers, Peter)
BEFORE AND AFTER
MR01251 730 (March 21, 1996) p106. (Travers, Peter)
BEFORE SUNRISE
MR01252 702 (February 23, 1995) pp79-80. (Travers, Peter)

BEFORE THE RAIN
MR01253 704 (March 23, 1995) p128. (Travers, Peter)
BEING HUMAN
MR01254 683 (June 2, 1994) pp76,78. (Travers, Peter)
BELLE EPOQUE
MR01255 681 (May 5, 1994) p49. (Travers, Peter)
BENNY AND JOON
MR01256 656 (May 13, 1993) pp114,116. (Travers, Peter)
THE BEST INTENTIONS
MR01257 636 (August 6, 1992) p66. (Travers, Peter)
THE BEVERLY HILLBILLIES
MR01258 669 (November 11, 1993) pp80-81. (Travers, Peter)
BEVERLY HILLS COP III
MR01259 685 (June 30, 1994) p81. (Travers, Peter)
BEYOND RANGOON
MR01260 716 (September 7, 1995) p77. (Travers, Peter)
BIG NIGHT
MR01261 744 (October 3, 1996) p78. (Travers, Peter)
BILLY BATHGATE
MR01262 618 (November 28, 1991) p103. (Travers, Peter)
MR01263 629 (April 30, 1992) p65.
BILLY MADISON
MR01264 703 (March 9, 1995) p72. (Travers, Peter)
THE BIRDCAGE
MR01265 731 (April 4, 1996) p68. (Travers, Peter)
BITTER MOON
MR01266 676 (February 24, 1994) p62. (Travers, Peter)
BLACK BEAUTY
MR01267 688 (August 11, 1994) p63. (Travers, Peter)
BLACK CHRISTMAS
MR01268 669 (November 11, 1993) p80. (Travers, Peter)
BLACK ROBE
MR01269 618 (November 28, 1991) p104. (Travers, Peter)
BLACK SHEEP
MR01270 729 (March 7, 1996) p54. (Travers, Peter)
BLANKMAN
MR01271 690 (September 8, 1994) p87. (Travers, Peter)
BLINK
MR01272 675 (February 10, 1994) p52. (Travers, Peter)
BLOWN AWAY
MR01273 686-687 (July 14, 1994) p99. (Travers, Peter)
BLUE
MR01274 671 (December 9, 1993) p78. (Travers, Peter)
MR01275 702 (February 23, 1995) p80. (Travers, Peter)
BLUE IN THE FACE
MR01276 718 (October 5, 1995) pp77,79. (Travers, Peter)
BLUE SKY
MR01277 692 (October 6, 1994) p81. (Travers, Peter)
BOB ROBERTS
MR01278 639 (September 17, 1992) pp101-102. (Travers, Peter)
MR01279 656 (May 13, 1993) p114. (Travers, Peter)
BODIES, REST AND MOTION
MR01280 655 (April 29, 1993) pp68-69. (Travers, Peter)
BODY OF EVIDENCE
MR01281 649 (February 4, 1993) pp71-72. (Travers, Peter)
MR01282 650 (February 18, 1993) p67. (Travers, Peter)
BODY SNATCHERS
MR01283 669 (November 11, 1993) pp79-80. (Travers, Peter)
THE BODYGUARD
MR01284 647 (January 7, 1993) p51. (Travers, Peter)
BOGUS
MR01285 744 (October 3, 1996) p78. (Travers, Peter)
BOOMERANG
MR01286 636 (August 6, 1992) pp63-64. (Travers, Peter)
MR01287 649 (February 4, 1993) p72. (Travers, Peter)
BORN YESTERDAY
MR01288 655 (April 29, 1993) p69. (Travers, Peter)
BOTTLE ROCKET
MR01289 728 (February 22, 1996) p70. (Travers, Peter)
BOUND
MR01290 745 (October 17, 1996) p142. (Travers, Peter)
BOXING HELENA
MR01291 665 (September 16, 1993) p77. (Travers, Peter)
BOYS DANCE
MR01292 735 (May 30, 1996) pp56-57. (Travers, Peter)
THE BOYS OF ST. VINCENT
MR01293 686-687 (July 14, 1994) p99. (Travers, Peter)
BOYS ON THE SIDE
MR01294 702 (February 23, 1995) pp80-81. (Travers, Peter)
BOYZ N THE HOOD
MR01295 622 (January 23, 1992) p49. (Travers, Peter)
MR01296 629 (April 30, 1992) p65.
THE BRADY BUNCH
MR01297 703 (March 9, 1995) p72. (Travers, Peter)
BRAVEHEART
MR01298 710 (June 15, 1995) pp85-86,88. (Travers, Peter)
BREAKFAST AT TIFFANY'S
MR01299 675 (February 10, 1994) p18. (D'Arby, Terence Trent)
BREAKING THE WAVES
MR01300 748 (November 28, 1996) p143. (Travers, Peter)
BRENDA STARR
MR01301 622 (January 23, 1992) p49. (Travers, Peter)
BRIDGES OF MADISON COUNTY
MR01302 711 (June 29, 1995) pp47-48. (Travers, Peter)
A BRIEF HISTORY OF TIME
MR01303 638 (September 3, 1992) p75. (Travers, Peter)
BROKEN ARROW
MR01304 729 (March 7, 1996) p54. (Travers, Peter)
A BRONX TALE
MR01305 668 (October 28, 1993) p88. (Travers, Peter)
THE BROOD
MR01306 669 (November 11, 1993) p80. (Travers, Peter)
BROTHER'S KEEPER
MR01307 649 (February 4, 1993) p75. (Travers, Peter)
THE BROTHERS MCMULLEN
MR01308 715 (August 24, 1995) p110. (Travers, Peter)
THE BROWNING VERSION
MR01309 696 (December 1, 1994) p132. (Travers, Peter)
BUCCANEER
MR01310 638 (September 3, 1992) p72. (Travers, Peter)
BUFFY THE VAMPIRE SLAYER
MR01311 638 (September 3, 1992) p75. (Travers, Peter)
BUGSY
MR01312 621 (January 9, 1992) p56. (Travers, Peter)
MR01313 622 (January 23, 1992) p49. (Travers, Peter)
MR01314 634-635 (July 9, 1992) p111.
BULLETPROOF
MR01315 744 (October 3, 1996) p78. (Travers, Peter)
BULLETS OVER BROADWAY
MR01316 694 (November 3, 1994) pp103-104. (Travers, Peter)
BURNT BY THE SUN
MR01317 708 (May 18, 1995) pp97-98. (Travers, Peter)
THE BUTCHER'S WIFE
MR01318 617 (November 14, 1991) p182. (Travers, Peter)
MR01319 631 (May 28, 1992) p60. (Travers, Peter)
BYE, BYE, LOVE
MR01320 705 (April 6, 1995) p70. (Travers, Peter)

C

THE CABLE GUY
MR01321 738-739 (July 11, 1996) pp95-96, 98. (Travers, Peter)
CALENDAR GIRL
MR01322 665 (September 16, 1993) pp77-78. (Travers, Peter)
CANADIAN BACON
MR01323 718 (October 5, 1995) p79. (Travers, Peter)
CANDYMAN

MR01324 642 (October 29, 1992) p77. (Travers, Peter)
CAPE FEAR
MR01325 618 (November 28, 1991) pp101,103. (Travers, Peter)
MR01326 622 (January 23, 1992) p49. (Travers, Peter)
MR01327 634-635 (July 9, 1992) p111.
CARLITO'S WAY
MR01328 671 (December 9, 1993) pp75-76. (Travers, Peter)
CARNIVAL OF SOULS
MR01329 669 (November 11, 1993) p80. (Travers, Peter)
CARRINGTON
MR01330 722 (November 30, 1995) pp73-75. (Travers, Peter)
CASINO
MR01331 723 (December 14, 1995) pp89-90,92. (Travers, Peter)
CB4
MR01332 653 (April 1, 1993) p59. (Travers, Peter)
THE CELLULOID CLOSET
MR01333 730 (March 21, 1996) p106. (Travers, Peter)
THE CEMENT GARDEN
MR01334 675 (February 10, 1994) p52. (Travers, Peter)
CHAIN REACTION
MR01335 742 (September 5, 1996) p68. (Travers, Peter)
THE CHAMBER
MR01336 747 (November 14, 1996) p124. (Travers, Peter)
CHAPLIN
MR01337 647 (January 7, 1993) pp50-51. (Travers, Peter)
CHILDREN OF PARADISE
MR01338 617 (November 14, 1991) p184. (Travers, Peter)
CHINA MOON
MR01339 678 (March 24, 1994) p104. (Travers, Peter)
CHUNKING EXPRESS
MR01340 729 (March 7, 1996) pp53-54. (Travers, Peter)
CIRCLE OF FRIENDS
MR01341 704 (March 23, 1995) p129. (Travers, Peter)
CITY HALL
MR01342 729 (March 7, 1996) pp52-53. (Travers, Peter)
CITY OF HOPE
MR01343 616 (October 31, 1991) p97. (Travers, Peter)
CITY OF JOY
MR01344 629 (April 30, 1992) pp64-65. (Travers, Peter)
CITY SLICKERS II
MR01345 685 (June 30, 1994) pp80-81. (Travers, Peter)
CLASS ACT
MR01346 633 (June 25, 1992) p48. (Travers, Peter)
CLEAN SLATE
MR01347 682 (May 19, 1994) p107. (Travers, Peter)
CLEAN, SHAVEN
MR01348 704 (March 23, 1995) p129. (Travers, Peter)
CLEAR AND PRESENT DANGER
MR01349 690 (September 8, 1994) p84. (Travers, Peter)
THE CLIENT
MR01350 688 (August 11, 1994) pp61-62. (Travers, Peter)
CLIFFHANGER
MR01351 660-661 (July 8, 1993) p121. (Travers, Peter)
CLOCKERS
MR01352 717 (September 21, 1995) pp89-90. (Travers, Peter)
CLOSE MY EYES
MR01353 624 (February 20, 1992) p50. (Travers, Peter)
CLUELESS
MR01354 714 (August 10, 1995) pp61-62,64. (Travers, Peter)
COBB
MR01355 697 (December 15, 1994) p104. (Travers, Peter)
COCKSUCKER BLUES
MR01356 668 (October 28, 1993) p26. (DeCurtis, Anthony)
COLD COMFORT FARM
MR01357 735 (May 30, 1996) p57. (Travers, Peter)
COLOR OF NIGHT
MR01358 691 (September 22, 1994) p106. (Travers, Peter)
THE COMMITMENTS
MR01359 629 (April 30, 1992) p65.
THE COMPANY OF WOLVES
MR01360 669 (November 11, 1993) p80. (Travers, Peter)
CONEHEADS
MR01361 664 (September 2, 1993) p70. (Travers, Peter)
CONGO
MR01362 711 (June 29, 1995) pp48-49. (Travers, Peter)
MR01363 715 (August 24, 1995) p108. (Travers, Peter)
CONSENTING ADULTS
MR01364 644 (November 26, 1992) p80. (Travers, Peter)
COPYCAT
MR01365 721 (November 16, 1995) p117. (Travers, Peter)
CORRINA, CORRINA
MR01366 689 (August 25, 1994) pp96-97. (Travers, Peter)
COURAGE UNDER FIRE
MR01367 740 (August 8, 1996) pp67-68,70. (Travers, Peter)
THE COWBOY WAY
MR01368 685 (June 30, 1994) pp81-82. (Travers, Peter)
CRONOS
MR01369 680 (April 21, 1994) p95. (Travers, Peter)
CROOKLYN
MR01370 683 (June 2, 1994) pp75-76. (Travers, Peter)
THE CROSSING GUARD
MR01371 722 (November 30, 1995) pp75-76. (Travers, Peter)
THE CROW
MR01372 682 (May 19, 1994) pp105-106. (Travers, Peter)
MR01373 743 (September 19, 1996) p90. (Travers, Peter)
THE CRUCIBLE
MR01374 749 (December 12, 1996) pp89-90. (Travers, Peter)
CRUMB
MR01375 707 (May 4, 1995) pp73-74,76. (Travers, Peter)
THE CRYING GAME
MR01376 644 (November 26, 1992) p80. (Travers, Peter)
MR01377 648 (January 21, 1993) p56. (Travers, Peter)
CUTTHROAT ISLAND
MR01378 726 (January 25, 1996) p67. (Travers, Peter)
THE CUTTING EDGE
MR01379 629 (April 30, 1992) p65. (Travers, Peter)

D

DAMAGE
MR01380 647 (January 7, 1993) p51. (Travers, Peter)
DANGEROUS GAME
MR01381 671 (December 9, 1993) p78. (Travers, Peter)
DANGEROUS MINDS
MR01382 715 (August 24, 1995) pp107-108,110. (Travers, Peter)
A DANGEROUS WOMAN
MR01383 671 (December 9, 1993) p78. (Travers, Peter)
THE DARK HALF
MR01384 656 (May 13, 1993) pp113-114. (Travers, Peter)
DAVE
MR01385 657 (May 27, 1993) pp55-56. (Travers, Peter)
DAVID MAMET'S OLEANNA
MR01386 696 (December 1, 1994) pp132,134. (Travers, Peter)
DAZED AND CONFUSED
MR01387 665 (September 16, 1993) p17. (Mundy, Chris)
MR01388 667 (October 14, 1993) p128. (Travers, Peter)
MR01389 672-673 (December 23, 1993) p174. (Travers, Peter)
DEAD AGAIN
MR01390 629 (April 30, 1992) p65.
DEAD MAN
MR01391 735 (May 30, 1996) p56. (Travers, Peter)
DEAD MAN WALKING
MR01392 724-725 (December 28, 1995) p139. (Travers, Peter)
DEAD PRESIDENTS
MR01393 719 (October 19, 1995) p159. (Travers, Peter)

DEAR GOD?
MR01394 748 (November 28, 1996) p143. (Travers, Peter)
DEATH AND THE MAIDEN
MR01395 700 (January 26, 1995) p68. (Travers, Peter)
DEATH BECOMES HER
MR01396 637 (August 20, 1992) p57. (Travers, Peter)
DECEIVED
MR01397 617 (November 14, 1991) p182. (Travers, Peter)
DEEP BLUES
MR01398 639 (September 17, 1992) p26. (DeCurtis, Anthony)
DEEP COVER
MR01399 630 (May 14, 1992) p114. (Travers, Peter)
DELICATESSEN
MR01400 628 (April 16, 1992) p93. (Travers, Peter)
DEMOLITION MAN
MR01401 669 (November 11, 1993) pp79-80. (Travers, Peter)
DESOLATION ANGELS
MR01402 737 (June 27, 1996) p62. (Travers, Peter)
DESPERADO
MR01403 716 (September 7, 1995) pp76-77. (Travers, Peter)
DESTINY TURNS ON THE RADIO
MR01404 708 (May 18, 1995) p98. (Travers, Peter)
DEVIL IN A BLUE DRESS
MR01405 718 (October 5, 1995) pp75-77. (Travers, Peter)
DIABOLIQUE
MR01406 732 (April 18, 1996) p78. (Travers, Peter)
DIE HARD WITH A VENGEANCE
MR01407 710 (June 15, 1995) pp85-86,88. (Travers, Peter)
DIGGSTOWN
MR01408 638 (September 3, 1992) p75. (Travers, Peter)
THE DISTINGUISHED GENTLEMAN
MR01409 647 (January 7, 1993) p51. (Travers, Peter)
DIVORCE ITALIAN STYLE
MR01410 634-635 (July 9, 1992) p111.
THE DOCTOR
MR01411 629 (April 30, 1992) p65.
DOLORES CLAIBORNE
MR01412 706 (April 20, 1995) p88. (Travers, Peter)
DON JUAN DEMARCO
MR01413 707 (May 4, 1995) pp73-74,76. (Travers, Peter)
DON'T LOOK NOW
MR01414 669 (November 11, 1993) p80. (Travers, Peter)
THE DOOM GENERATION
MR01415 721 (November 16, 1995) p117. (Travers, Peter)
THE DOORS
MR01416 615 (October 17, 1991) p102. (Travers, Peter)
THE DOUBLE LIFE OF VERONIQUE
MR01417 618 (November 28, 1991) p103. (Travers, Peter)
DR. JEKYLL AND MS. HYDE
MR01418 715 (August 24, 1995) p108. (Travers, Peter)
DR. STRANGELOVE
MR01419 634-635 (July 9, 1992) p111.
DRACULA
MR01420 649 (February 4, 1993) p72. (Travers, Peter)
DRACULA: DEAD AND LOVING IT
MR01421 726 (January 25, 1996) p67. (Travers, Peter)
DRAGON
MR01422 657 (May 27, 1993) pp56,58. (Travers, Peter)
DRAGONHEART
MR01423 737 (June 27, 1996) p62. (Travers, Peter)
MR01424 738-739 (July 11, 1996) p98. (Travers, Peter)
DREAM LOVER
MR01425 683 (June 2, 1994) p78. (Travers, Peter)

E

ED WOOD
MR01426 693 (October 20, 1994) pp153,155. (Travers, Peter)
EDWARD II
MR01427 627 (April 2, 1992) pp41-42. (Travers, Peter)
EL MARIACHI
MR01428 652 (March 18, 1993) pp45-47,49. (Travers, Peter)
EMMA
MR01429 741 (August 22, 1996) pp103-104. (Travers, Peter)
ENCHANTED APRIL
MR01430 637 (August 20, 1992) p60. (Travers, Peter)
ENCINO MAN
MR01431 633 (June 25, 1992) p48. (Travers, Peter)
THE ENDLESS SUMMER II
MR01432 685 (June 30, 1994) p82. (Travers, Peter)
THE ENGLISH PATIENT
MR01433 748 (November 28, 1996) p142. (Travers, Peter)
EQUINOX
MR01434 660-661 (July 8, 1993) pp120-121. (Travers, Peter)
ERASER
MR01435 738-739 (July 11, 1996) p98. (Travers, Peter)
ESCAPE FROM L.A.
MR01436 742 (September 5, 1996) pp68-69. (Travers, Peter)
ETHAN FROME
MR01437 653 (April 1, 1993) p59. (Travers, Peter)
EUROPA, EUROPA
MR01438 634-635 (July 9, 1992) p111.
EVEN COWGIRLS GET THE BLUES
MR01439 682 (May 19, 1994) p107. (Travers, Peter)
THE EXECUTION PROTOCOL
MR01440 656 (May 13, 1993) p116. (Travers, Peter)
EXIT TO EDEN
MR01441 694 (November 3, 1994) p106. (Travers, Peter)
EXOTICA
MR01442 704 (March 23, 1995) p129. (Travers, Peter)
EXTREME MEASURES
MR01443 745 (October 17, 1996) p144. (Travers, Peter)
EYE FOR AN EYE
MR01444 727 (February 8, 1996) p47. (Travers, Peter)

F

FAIR GAME
MR01445 715 (August 24, 1995) pp107-108,110. (Travers, Peter)
MR01446 722 (November 30, 1995) p76. (Travers, Peter)
FAITHFUL
MR01447 733 (May 2, 1996) p62. (Travers, Peter)
FALLING DOWN
MR01448 651 (March 4, 1993) pp71-72. (Travers, Peter)
FALLING FROM GRACE
MR01449 625 (March 5, 1992) p78. (Travers, Peter)
A FAMILY THING
MR01450 732 (April 18, 1996) p78. (Travers, Peter)
THE FAN
MR01451 742 (September 5, 1996) pp67-68. (Travers, Peter)
FAR AND AWAY
MR01452 633 (June 25, 1992) p48. (Travers, Peter)
FARAWAY, SO CLOSE
MR01453 682 (May 19, 1994) p21. (Queen Latifah)
FAREWELL MY CONCUBINE
MR01454 668 (October 28, 1993) p86. (Travers, Peter)
FARGO
MR01455 730 (March 21, 1996) p104. (Travers, Peter)
FARINELLI
MR01456 704 (March 23, 1995) p129. (Travers, Peter)
FATAL ATTRACTION
MR01457 629 (April 30, 1992) p65.
FATAL INSTINCT
MR01458 669 (November 11, 1993) p81. (Travers, Peter)
FATHER OF THE BRIDE

MR01459 622 (January 23, 1992) p50. (Travers, Peter)
MR01460 631 (May 28, 1992) p60. (Travers, Peter)
FEAR OF A BLACK HAT
MR01461 686-687 (July 14, 1994) p99. (Travers, Peter)
FEARLESS
MR01462 668 (October 28, 1993) pp85-86. (Travers, Peter)
MR01463 672-673 (December 23, 1993) p174. (Travers, Peter)
FEDERAL HILL
MR01464 696 (December 1, 1994) p134. (Travers, Peter)
FEED
MR01465 642 (October 29, 1992) p78. (Travers, Peter)
FEELING MINNESOTA
MR01466 744 (October 3, 1996) pp78-79. (Travers, Peter)
A FEW GOOD MEN
MR01467 647 (January 7, 1993) pp49-50. (Travers, Peter)
MR01468 648 (January 21, 1993) p56. (Travers, Peter)
FINAL ANALYSIS
MR01469 625 (March 5, 1992) pp77-78. (Travers, Peter)
THE FIRM
MR01470 662 (August 5, 1993) pp72-73. (Travers, Peter)
FIRST KNIGHT
MR01471 714 (August 10, 1995) p64. (Travers, Peter)
THE FIRST WIVES CLUB
MR01472 744 (October 3, 1996) pp77-78. (Travers, Peter)
THE FISHER KING
MR01473 615 (October 17, 1991) pp99-100. (Travers, Peter)
MR01474 622 (January 23, 1992) p49. (Travers, Peter)
MR01475 629 (April 30, 1992) p65.
MR01476 651 (March 4, 1993) p72. (Travers, Peter)
FLED
MR01477 741 (August 22, 1996) p105. (Travers, Peter)
FLESH AND BONES
MR01478 670 (November 25, 1993) pp125-126. (Travers, Peter)
THE FLINTSTONES
MR01479 684 (June 16, 1994) p115. (Travers, Peter)
FLIRTING WITH DISASTER
MR01480 732 (April 18, 1996) p78. (Travers, Peter)
FLOUNDERING
MR01481 696 (December 1, 1994) p132. (Travers, Peter)
THE FLOWER OF MY SECRET
MR01482 731 (April 4, 1996) p68. (Travers, Peter)
FLY AWAY HOME
MR01483 745 (October 17, 1996) p142. (Travers, Peter)
FLY BY NIGHT
MR01484 681 (May 5, 1994) p49. (Travers, Peter)
FOR LOVE OR MONEY
MR01485 667 (October 14, 1993) p128. (Travers, Peter)
FOR THE BOYS
MR01486 621 (January 9, 1992) p55. (Travers, Peter)
MR01487 622 (January 23, 1992) p49. (Travers, Peter)
MR01488 631 (May 28, 1992) p60. (Travers, Peter)
FOREIGN STUDENT
MR01489 690 (September 8, 1994) p87. (Travers, Peter)
FOREVER YOUNG
MR01490 647 (January 7, 1993) p51. (Travers, Peter)
FORREST GUMP
MR01491 686-687 (July 14, 1994) pp97-99. (Travers, Peter)
FOUR ROOMS
MR01492 726 (January 25, 1996) p67. (Travers, Peter)
FOUR WEDDINGS AND A FUNERAL
MR01493 678 (March 24, 1994) p104. (Travers, Peter)
1492
MR01494 642 (October 29, 1992) pp76-78. (Travers, Peter)
MR01495 649 (February 4, 1993) p72. (Travers, Peter)
FRANKIE AND JOHNNY
MR01496 616 (October 31, 1991) pp95,97. (Travers, Peter)
MR01497 631 (May 28, 1992) p60. (Travers, Peter)
FREE WILLY
MR01498 662 (August 5, 1993) p72. (Travers, Peter)
FREEJACK
MR01499 631 (May 28, 1992) p60. (Travers, Peter)
FRENCH KISS
MR01500 708 (May 18, 1995) pp96-97. (Travers, Peter)
FRESH
MR01501 690 (September 8, 1994) p87. (Travers, Peter)
FRIED GREEN TOMATOES
MR01502 622 (January 23, 1992) p50. (Travers, Peter)
MR01503 638 (September 3, 1992) p72. (Travers, Peter)
THE FRIGHTENERS
MR01504 741 (August 22, 1996) p105. (Travers, Peter)
FROM DUSK TILL DAWN
MR01505 728 (February 22, 1996) p70. (Travers, Peter)
FROM RUSSIA WITH LOVE
MR01506 651 (March 4, 1993) p72. (Travers, Peter)
FROM THE JOURNALS OF JEAN SEBERG
MR01507 730 (March 21, 1996) pp104,106. (Travers, Peter)
THE FUGITIVE
MR01508 663 (August 19, 1993) p84. (Travers, Peter)
FUN
MR01509 707 (May 4, 1995) p74. (Travers, Peter)
THE FUNERAL
MR01510 747 (November 14, 1996) p126. (Travers, Peter)
FUNNY BONES
MR01511 706 (April 20, 1995) pp86,88. (Travers, Peter)

G

GAS FOOD LODGING
MR01512 637 (August 20, 1992) p60. (Travers, Peter)
THE GATEWAY
MR01513 676 (February 24, 1994) p62. (Travers, Peter)
GEORGIA
MR01514 722 (November 30, 1995) pp73-75. (Travers, Peter)
GERMANY YEAR 90 NINE ZERO
MR01515 702 (February 23, 1995) p81. (Travers, Peter)
GET ON THE BUS
MR01516 746 (October 31, 1996) p76. (Travers, Peter)
GET SHORTY
MR01517 720 (November 2, 1995) pp73-74. (Travers, Peter)
GETTING EVEN WITH DAD
MR01518 686-687 (July 14, 1994) p99. (Travers, Peter)
GETTYSBURG
MR01519 670 (November 25, 1993) p127. (Travers, Peter)
THE GHOST AND THE DARKNESS
MR01520 746 (October 31, 1996) p78. (Travers, Peter)
GIANT
MR01521 744 (October 3, 1996) p78. (Travers, Peter)
GIRL 6
MR01522 732 (April 18, 1996) pp77-78. (Travers, Peter)
GIRLS TOWN
MR01523 742 (September 5, 1996) p69. (Travers, Peter)
GLADIATOR
MR01524 626 (March 19, 1992) p102. (Travers, Peter)
THE GLASS SHIELD
MR01525 711 (June 29, 1995) p49. (Travers, Peter)
GLENGARRY GLEN ROSS
MR01526 640 (October 1, 1992) p74. (Travers, Peter)
MR01527 648 (January 21, 1993) p56. (Travers, Peter)
GO FISH
MR01528 685 (June 30, 1994) p82. (Travers, Peter)
THE GODFATHER PART III
MR01529 615 (October 17, 1991) p102. (Travers, Peter)
THE GODFATHER TRILOGY
MR01530 651 (March 4, 1993) p72. (Travers, Peter)
GOD'S MOVIE, VOLUME 1
MR01531 667 (October 14, 1993) p34. (Neely, Kim)
GOLDEN GATE

MR01532 675 (February 10, 1994) pp52-53. (Travers, Peter)
GOLDENEYE
MR01533 722 (November 30, 1995) pp73-75. (Travers, Peter)
A GOOD MAN IN AFRICA
MR01534 691 (September 22, 1994) p106. (Travers, Peter)
THE GOOD SON
MR01535 668 (October 28, 1993) p88. (Travers, Peter)
GRACE OF MY HEART
MR01536 744 (October 3, 1996) p79. (Travers, Peter)
GRAND CANYON
MR01537 622 (January 23, 1992) pp49-50. (Travers, Peter)
THE GREAT WHITE HYPE
MR01538 735 (May 30, 1996) p57. (Travers, Peter)
GREATEST SHOW ON EARTH
MR01539 638 (September 3, 1992) p72. (Travers, Peter)
GRUMPIER OLD MEN
MR01540 726 (January 25, 1996) p67. (Travers, Peter)
GRUMPY OLD MEN
MR01541 674 (January 27, 1994) pp47-48. (Travers, Peter)
GUARDING TESS
MR01542 679 (April 7, 1994) pp82-83. (Travers, Peter)
GUILTY AS SIN
MR01543 660-661 (July 8, 1993) p121. (Travers, Peter)
GUILTY BY SUSPICION
MR01544 622 (January 23, 1992) p49. (Travers, Peter)
GUNCRAZY
MR01545 650 (February 18, 1993) p67. (Travers, Peter)
GUNMEN
MR01546 675 (February 10, 1994) p52. (Travers, Peter)

H

THE HAIRDRESSER'S HUSBAND
MR01547 633 (June 25, 1992) p49. (Travers, Peter)
THE HAND THAT ROCKS THE CRADLE
MR01548 623 (February 6, 1992) p88. (Travers, Peter)
MR01549 634-635 (July 9, 1992) p111.
HANGIN' WITH THE HOMEBOYS
MR01550 629 (April 30, 1992) p65.
HARD PROMISES
MR01551 624 (February 20, 1992) pp49-50. (Travers, Peter)
HARD TARGET
MR01552 665 (September 16, 1993) pp76-77. (Travers, Peter)
HATE
MR01553 728 (February 22, 1996) p70. (Travers, Peter)
HEAR MY SONG
MR01554 624 (February 20, 1992) p50. (Travers, Peter)
MR01555 638 (September 3, 1992) p72. (Travers, Peter)
HEARTS AND SOULS
MR01556 664 (September 2, 1993) pp69-70. (Travers, Peter)
HEARTS OF DARKNESS
MR01557 622 (January 23, 1992) p50. (Travers, Peter)
MR01558 634-635 (July 9, 1992) p111.
HEAT
MR01559 724-725 (December 28, 1995) p138. (Travers, Peter)
HEAVENLY CREATURES
MR01560 694 (November 3, 1994) pp104,106. (Travers, Peter)
HEAVY
MR01561 737 (June 27, 1996) p62. (Travers, Peter)
HELAS POUR MOI
MR01562 680 (April 21, 1994) p95. (Travers, Peter)
HERO
MR01563 642 (October 29, 1992) pp76-78. (Travers, Peter)
MR01564 649 (February 4, 1993) p72. (Travers, Peter)
HIDEAWAY
MR01565 705 (April 6, 1995) p70. (Travers, Peter)
HIGH HEELS
MR01566 621 (January 9, 1992) p56. (Travers, Peter)
HIGH SCHOOL HIGH
MR01567 748 (November 28, 1996) p143. (Travers, Peter)
HIGHER LEARNING
MR01568 700 (January 26, 1995) pp66,68. (Travers, Peter)
HOCUS POCUS
MR01569 664 (September 2, 1993) p70. (Travers, Peter)
HOFFA
MR01570 647 (January 7, 1993) pp49-50. (Travers, Peter)
HOME FOR THE HOLIDAYS
MR01571 721 (November 16, 1995) pp116-117. (Travers, Peter)
HOMICIDE
MR01572 616 (October 31, 1991) p99. (Travers, Peter)
MR01573 629 (April 30, 1992) p65.
HONEYMOON IN VEGAS
MR01574 639 (September 17, 1992) pp102-103. (Travers, Peter)
HOOK
MR01575 621 (January 9, 1992) pp54-55. (Travers, Peter)
MR01576 638 (September 3, 1992) p72. (Travers, Peter)
HOOP DREAMS
MR01577 694 (November 3, 1994) p106. (Travers, Peter)
HOT SHOTS! PART DEUX
MR01578 659 (June 24, 1993) pp88-89. (Travers, Peter)
THE HOURS AND TIMES
MR01579 631 (May 28, 1992) pp60-61. (Travers, Peter)
THE HOUSE OF THE SPIRITS
MR01580 677 (March 10, 1994) p60. (Travers, Peter)
HOUSEHOLD SAINTS
MR01581 667 (October 14, 1993) p128. (Travers, Peter)
HOUSESITTER
MR01582 634-635 (July 9, 1992) p114. (Travers, Peter)
HOW GREEN WAS MY VALLEY
MR01583 634-635 (July 9, 1992) p111.
HOW TO MAKE AN AMERICAN QUILT
MR01584 720 (November 2, 1995) p77. (Travers, Peter)
HOWARDS END
MR01585 627 (April 2, 1992) p41. (Travers, Peter)
MR01586 648 (January 21, 1993) p56. (Travers, Peter)
HUDSON HAWK
MR01587 622 (January 23, 1992) p49. (Travers, Peter)
THE HUDSUCKER PROXY
MR01588 678 (March 24, 1994) p105. (Travers, Peter)
THE HUNCHBACK OF NOTRE DAME
MR01589 738-739 (July 11, 1996) pp96,98. (Travers, Peter)
MR01589 738-739 (July 11, 1996) p98. (Travers, Peter)
HUSBANDS AND WIVES
MR01590 640 (October 1, 1992) pp71-72. (Travers, Peter)
MR01591 648 (January 21, 1993) p56. (Travers, Peter)
MR01592 656 (May 13, 1993) p114. (Travers, Peter)

I

I JUST WASN'T MADE FOR THESE TIMES
MR01593 717 (September 21, 1995) p89. (Travers, Peter)
I LIKE IT LIKE THAT
MR01594 694 (November 3, 1994) p106. (Travers, Peter)
I LOVE TROUBLE
MR01595 688 (August 11, 1994) p62. (Travers, Peter)
I SHOT ANDY WARHOL
MR01596 734 (May 16, 1996) pp71-72,74. (Travers, Peter)
IF LUCY FELL
MR01597 730 (March 21, 1996) p106. (Travers, Peter)
I'LL DO ANYTHING
MR01598 676 (February 24, 1994) p62. (Travers, Peter)
I'M NOT RAPPAPORT
MR01599 748 (November 28, 1996) p143. (Travers, Peter)
IMMORTAL BELOVED
MR01600 700 (January 26, 1995) p66. (Travers, Peter)
IN THE ARMY NOW

MR01601 690 (September 8, 1994) p87. (Travers, Peter)
IN THE LINE OF FIRE
MR01602 662 (August 5, 1993) pp71-72. (Travers, Peter)
IN THE MOUTH OF MADNESS
MR01603 703 (March 9, 1995) p72. (Travers, Peter)
IN THE NAME OF THE FATHER
MR01604 674 (January 27, 1994) pp47-48. (Travers, Peter)
IN THE SOUP
MR01605 642 (October 29, 1992) p77. (Travers, Peter)
INCIDENT AT OGLALA
MR01606 631 (May 28, 1992) p61. (Travers, Peter)
THE INCREDIBLY TRUE ADVENTURE OF TWO GIRLS IN LOVE
MR01607 711 (June 29, 1995) p49. (Travers, Peter)
INDECENT PROPOSAL
MR01608 655 (April 29, 1993) pp67-68. (Travers, Peter)
INDEPENDENCE DAY
MR01609 738-739 (July 11, 1996) p98. (Travers, Peter)
INDIANA JONES AND THE TEMPLE OF DOOM
MR01610 638 (September 3, 1992) p72. (Travers, Peter)
INDOCHINE
MR01611 648 (January 21, 1993) pp55-56. (Travers, Peter)
THE INNER CIRCLE
MR01612 623 (February 6, 1992) pp88,90. (Travers, Peter)
INNOCENT BLOOD
MR01613 642 (October 29, 1992) p77. (Travers, Peter)
INTERSECTION
MR01614 676 (February 24, 1994) p62. (Travers, Peter)
INTERVIEW WITH THE VAMPIRE
MR01615 697 (December 15, 1994) pp101-102,104. (Travers, Peter)
INTO THE SUN
MR01616 623 (February 6, 1992) p88. (Travers, Peter)
INTO THE WEST
MR01617 657 (May 27, 1993) p59. (Travers, Peter)
I.Q.
MR01618 700 (January 26, 1995) p66. (Travers, Peter)
THE ISLAND OF DR. MOREAU
MR01619 743 (September 19, 1996) p90. (Travers, Peter)
IT COULD HAPPEN TO YOU
MR01620 688 (August 11, 1994) pp62-63. (Travers, Peter)
IT'S MY PARTY
MR01621 731 (April 4, 1996) p68. (Travers, Peter)

J

JACK
MR01622 742 (September 5, 1996) p68. (Travers, Peter)
JACK THE BEAR
MR01623 655 (April 29, 1993) p69. (Travers, Peter)
JACQUOT
MR01624 662 (August 5, 1993) p72. (Travers, Peter)
JADE
MR01625 721 (November 16, 1995) p116. (Travers, Peter)
JAMES AND THE GIANT PEACH
MR01626 734 (May 16, 1996) p72. (Travers, Peter)
JANE EYRE
MR01627 733 (May 2, 1996) p62. (Travers, Peter)
JASON'S LYRIC
MR01628 693 (October 20, 1994) p157. (Travers, Peter)
JAWS
MR01629 638 (September 3, 1992) p72. (Travers, Peter)
MR01630 651 (March 4, 1993) p72. (Travers, Peter)
JEFFERSON IN PARIS
MR01631 706 (April 20, 1995) p89. (Travers, Peter)
JEFFREY
MR01632 715 (August 24, 1995) p110. (Travers, Peter)
THE JERKY BOYS
MR01633 703 (March 9, 1995) p72. (Travers, Peter)
JFK
MR01634 622 (January 23, 1992) pp48-49. (Travers, Peter)
MR01635 631 (May 28, 1992) p60. (Travers, Peter)
JIMMY HOLLYWOOD
MR01636 680 (April 21, 1994) p95. (Travers, Peter)
JINGLE ALL THE WAY
MR01637 749 (December 12, 1996) p90. (Travers, Peter)
JOE'S APARTMENT
MR01638 741 (August 22, 1996) p105. (Travers, Peter)
JOHNNY MNEMONIC
MR01639 711 (June 29, 1995) p49. (Travers, Peter)
JOHNNY STECCHINO
MR01640 640 (October 1, 1992) p72. (Travers, Peter)
JOHNNY SUEDE
MR01641 638 (September 3, 1992) pp72,75. (Travers, Peter)
JOURNEY OF HOPE
MR01642 622 (January 23, 1992) p49. (Travers, Peter)
THE JOY LUCK CLUB
MR01643 666 (September 30, 1993) p113. (Travers, Peter)
JUDGE DREDD
MR01644 714 (August 10, 1995) p64. (Travers, Peter)
JUICE
MR01645 623 (February 6, 1992) p90. (Travers, Peter)
JUNGLE FEVER
MR01646 623 (February 6, 1992) p90. (Travers, Peter)
JUNIOR
MR01647 697 (December 15, 1994) p104. (Travers, Peter)
JURASSIC PARK
MR01648 660-661 (July 8, 1993) p120. (Travers, Peter)
THE JUROR
MR01649 729 (March 7, 1996) p54. (Travers, Peter)
JUST ANOTHER GIRL ON THE I.R.T.
MR01650 650 (February 18, 1993) pp66-67. (Travers, Peter)

K

K2
MR01651 618 (November 28, 1991) p103. (Travers, Peter)
KAFKA
MR01652 623 (February 6, 1992) pp87-88. (Travers, Peter)
KALIFORNIA
MR01653 665 (September 16, 1993) p78. (Travers, Peter)
KANSAS CITY
MR01654 741 (August 22, 1996) pp104-105. (Travers, Peter)
KAZAAM
MR01655 741 (August 22, 1996) p105. (Travers, Peter)
KICKING AND SCREAMING
MR01656 717 (September 21, 1995) p90. (Travers, Peter)
KIDS
MR01657 714 (August 10, 1995) pp61-62,64. (Travers, Peter)
KIDS IN THE HALL: BRAIN CANDY
MR01658 733 (May 2, 1996) pp61-62. (Travers, Peter)
KIKA
MR01659 682 (May 19, 1994) p106. (Travers, Peter)
KILLER
MR01660 741 (August 22, 1996) p105. (Travers, Peter)
KILLING ZOE
MR01661 690 (September 8, 1994) p87. (Travers, Peter)
KING OF THE HILL
MR01662 664 (September 2, 1993) p70. (Travers, Peter)
KISS OF DEATH
MR01663 707 (May 4, 1995) pp73-74,76. (Travers, Peter)
KUFFS
MR01664 623 (February 6, 1992) p88. (Travers, Peter)

L

LA BELLE NOISEUSE
MR01665 616 (October 31, 1991) p99. (Travers, Peter)
LADYBIRD, LADYBIRD
MR01666 697 (December 15, 1994) p104. (Travers, Peter)
LARGER THAN LIFE
MR01667 748 (November 28, 1996) p143. (Travers, Peter)
THE LAST BOY SCOUT
MR01668 622 (January 23, 1992) p49. (Travers, Peter)
MR01669 629 (April 30, 1992) p65.
LAST DANCE
MR01670 735 (May 30, 1996) pp55-56. (Travers, Peter)
THE LAST DAYS OF CHEZ NOUS
MR01671 651 (March 4, 1993) p74. (Travers, Peter)
LAST MAN STANDING
MR01672 745 (October 17, 1996) p144. (Travers, Peter)
THE LAST OF THE MOHICANS
MR01673 642 (October 29, 1992) pp76-78. (Travers, Peter)
THE LAST SEDUCTION
MR01674 693 (October 20, 1994) p157. (Travers, Peter)
LAST SUMMER IN THE HAMPTONS
MR01675 722 (November 30, 1995) p76. (Travers, Peter)
THE LAST SUPPER
MR01676 732 (April 18, 1996) p80. (Travers, Peter)
A LEAGUE OF THEIR OWN
MR01677 634-635 (July 9, 1992) pp109,111. (Travers, Peter)
LEAP OF FAITH
MR01678 648 (January 21, 1993) p55. (Travers, Peter)
LEAVING LAS VEGAS
MR01679 720 (November 2, 1995) pp74,76. (Travers, Peter)
LEAVING NORMAL
MR01680 630 (May 14, 1992) p114. (Travers, Peter)
LEGENDS OF THE FALL
MR01681 700 (January 26, 1995) pp65-66. (Travers, Peter)
LEOLO
MR01682 654 (April 15, 1993) p72. (Travers, Peter)
LEON THE PIG FARMER
MR01683 667 (October 14, 1993) p128. (Travers, Peter)
LET HIM HAVE IT
MR01684 618 (November 28, 1991) pp103-104. (Travers, Peter)
LETHAL WEAPON 3
MR01685 633 (June 25, 1992) p49. (Travers, Peter)
LIEBESTRAUM
MR01686 616 (October 31, 1991) p97. (Travers, Peter)
MR01687 631 (May 28, 1992) p60. (Travers, Peter)
THE LIFE AND TIMES OF ALLEN GINSBERG
MR01688 677 (March 10, 1994) p60. (Travers, Peter)
LIFE IS SWEET
MR01689 617 (November 14, 1991) pp182,184. (Travers, Peter)
MR01690 638 (September 3, 1992) p72. (Travers, Peter)
LIFE WITH MIKEY
MR01691 660-661 (July 8, 1993) p121. (Travers, Peter)
LIGHT SLEEPER
MR01692 626 (March 19, 1992) pp102,104. (Travers, Peter)
LIKE WATER FOR CHOCOLATE
MR01693 678 (March 24, 1994) p16. (Donelly, Tanya)
THE LION KING
MR01694 686-687 (July 14, 1994) pp97-99. (Travers, Peter)
LITTLE BUDDHA
MR01695 685 (June 30, 1994) p82. (Travers, Peter)
LITTLE MAN TATE
MR01696 616 (October 31, 1991) pp97,99. (Travers, Peter)
LITTLE ODESSA
MR01697 710 (June 15, 1995) p86. (Travers, Peter)
LITTLE WOMEN
MR01698 700 (January 26, 1995) p66. (Travers, Peter)
LIVIN' LARGE!
MR01699 615 (October 17, 1991) p100. (Travers, Peter)
THE LIVING END
MR01700 638 (September 3, 1992) p75. (Travers, Peter)
LIVING IN OBLIVION
MR01701 712-713 (July 13, 1995) p116. (Travers, Peter)
LONDON KILLS ME
MR01702 636 (August 6, 1992) p66. (Travers, Peter)
LONE STAR
MR01703 738-739 (July 11, 1996) p98. (Travers, Peter)
THE LONG DAY CLOSES
MR01704 658 (June 10, 1993) p78. (Travers, Peter)
THE LONG KISS GOODNIGHT
MR01705 746 (October 31, 1996) p76. (Travers, Peter)
LOOKING FOR RICHARD
MR01706 746 (October 31, 1996) p78. (Travers, Peter)
LORD OF ILLUSIONS
MR01707 717 (September 21, 1995) p90. (Travers, Peter)
LORENZO'S OIL
MR01708 648 (January 21, 1993) pp54-55. (Travers, Peter)
LOSING ISAIAH
MR01709 705 (April 6, 1995) p70. (Travers, Peter)
LOST IN YONKERS
MR01710 657 (May 27, 1993) p58. (Travers, Peter)
LOVE AFFAIR
MR01711 696 (December 1, 1994) p134. (Travers, Peter)
LOVE AND A .45
MR01712 696 (December 1, 1994) p132. (Travers, Peter)
LOVE AND HUMAN REMAINS
MR01713 710 (June 15, 1995) p88. (Travers, Peter)
LOVE FIELD
MR01714 648 (January 21, 1993) pp54-55. (Travers, Peter)
THE LOVER
MR01715 640 (October 1, 1992) p74. (Travers, Peter)

M

M. BUTTERFLY
MR01716 668 (October 28, 1993) p86. (Travers, Peter)
MAD DOG TIME
MR01717 749 (December 12, 1996) p90. (Travers, Peter)
MAD LOVE
MR01718 710 (June 15, 1995) p88. (Travers, Peter)
MADAME BOVARY
MR01719 621 (January 9, 1992) p56. (Travers, Peter)
MR01720 634-635 (July 9, 1992) p111.
MADE IN AMERICA
MR01721 659 (June 24, 1993) p88. (Travers, Peter)
THE MADNESS OF KING GEORGE
MR01722 700 (January 26, 1995) p68. (Travers, Peter)
MADONNA: TRUTH OR DARE
MR01723 615 (October 17, 1991) p102. (Travers, Peter)
MALCOLM X
MR01724 645-646 (December 10, 1992) p192. (Travers, Peter)
MR01725 648 (January 21, 1993) p56. (Travers, Peter)
MALICE
MR01726 667 (October 14, 1993) p128. (Travers, Peter)
MALLRATS
MR01727 720 (November 2, 1995) p74. (Travers, Peter)
THE MAMBO KINGS
MR01728 626 (March 19, 1992) pp101-102. (Travers, Peter)
MR01729 638 (September 3, 1992) p72. (Travers, Peter)
MR01730 651 (March 4, 1993) p72. (Travers, Peter)
THE MAN IN THE MOON
MR01731 616 (October 31, 1991) p97. (Travers, Peter)
A MAN OF NO IMPORTANCE
MR01732 697 (December 15, 1994) p104. (Travers, Peter)
MAN OF THE HOUSE
MR01733 705 (April 6, 1995) p70. (Travers, Peter)
MAN TROUBLE

MR01734 649 (February 4, 1993) p72. (Travers, Peter)
THE MAN WITHOUT A FACE
MR01735 665 (September 16, 1993) pp75-76. (Travers, Peter)
MANHATTAN MURDER MYSTERY
MR01736 664 (September 2, 1993) pp68-69. (Travers, Peter)
THE MARRYING MAN
MR01737 622 (January 23, 1992) p49. (Travers, Peter)
MARTHA AND ETHEL
MR01738 702 (February 23, 1995) p81. (Travers, Peter)
MARY SHELLEY'S FRANKENSTEIN
MR01739 696 (December 1, 1994) pp131-132. (Travers, Peter)
THE MASK
MR01740 689 (August 25, 1994) pp95-96. (Travers, Peter)
MATINEE
MR01741 651 (March 4, 1993) p74. (Travers, Peter)
MAVERICK
MR01742 684 (June 16, 1994) p115. (Travers, Peter)
MEDICINE MAN
MR01743 626 (March 19, 1992) p102. (Travers, Peter)
MR01744 638 (September 3, 1992) p72. (Travers, Peter)
MEDITERRANEO
MR01745 628 (April 16, 1992) p93. (Travers, Peter)
MEETING VENUS
MR01746 618 (November 28, 1991) p104. (Travers, Peter)
MR01747 631 (May 28, 1992) p60. (Travers, Peter)
MEMOIRS OF AN INVISIBLE MAN
MR01748 626 (March 19, 1992) p104. (Travers, Peter)
MENACE II SOCIETY
MR01749 660-661 (July 8, 1993) p121. (Travers, Peter)
MR01750 672-673 (December 23, 1993) p174. (Travers, Peter)
MI VIDA LOCA
MR01751 686-687 (July 14, 1994) p99. (Travers, Peter)
MIAMI RHAPSODY
MR01752 701 (February 9, 1995) pp61-62. (Travers, Peter)
MICHAEL COLLINS
MR01753 746 (October 31, 1996) p76. (Travers, Peter)
A MIDNIGHT CLEAR
MR01754 626 (March 19, 1992) p102. (Travers, Peter)
A MIDWINTER'S TALE
MR01755 728 (February 22, 1996) p70. (Travers, Peter)
MIGHTY APHRODITE
MR01756 721 (November 16, 1995) pp115-116. (Travers, Peter)
THE MIRACLE
MR01757 623 (February 6, 1992) p90. (Travers, Peter)
THE MIRROR HAS TWO FACES
MR01758 749 (December 12, 1996) pp90,92. (Travers, Peter)
THE MISFITS
MR01759 678 (March 24, 1994) p16. (Donelly, Tanya)
THE MISSION
MR01760 629 (April 30, 1992) p65.
MISSION IMPOSSIBLE
MR01761 738-739 (July 11, 1996) p98. (Travers, Peter)
MISSISSIPPI MASALA
MR01762 624 (February 20, 1992) p50. (Travers, Peter)
MISTRESS
MR01763 637 (August 20, 1992) pp57,60. (Travers, Peter)
MIXED NUTS
MR01764 700 (January 26, 1995) p66. (Travers, Peter)
MODERN TIMES
MR01765 651 (March 4, 1993) p72. (Travers, Peter)
MOLL FLANDERS
MR01766 738-739 (July 11, 1996) p98. (Travers, Peter)
MONEY TRAIN
MR01767 723 (December 14, 1995) p92. (Travers, Peter)
MONSTER IN A BOX
MR01768 631 (May 28, 1992) p61. (Travers, Peter)
MOONLIGHT AND VALENTINO
MR01769 720 (November 2, 1995) p77. (Travers, Peter)
MOTHER NIGHT
MR01770 748 (November 28, 1996) p143. (Travers, Peter)
MR. HOLLAND'S OPUS
MR01771 727 (February 8, 1996) pp46-47. (Travers, Peter)
MR. SATURDAY NIGHT
MR01772 642 (October 29, 1992) p78. (Travers, Peter)
MR. WONDERFUL
MR01773 669 (November 11, 1993) p81. (Travers, Peter)
MRS. DOUBTFIRE
MR01774 671 (December 9, 1993) p78. (Travers, Peter)
MRS. PARKER AND THE VICIOUS CIRCLE
MR01775 697 (December 15, 1994) p104. (Travers, Peter)
MUCH ADO ABOUT NOTHING
MR01776 657 (May 27, 1993) p56. (Travers, Peter)
MULHOLLAND FALLS
MR01777 735 (May 30, 1996) p56. (Travers, Peter)
MULTIPLICITY
MR01778 740 (August 8, 1996) p70. (Travers, Peter)
MURDER IN THE FIRST
MR01779 701 (February 9, 1995) pp62-63. (Travers, Peter)
MURIEL'S WEDDING
MR01780 704 (March 23, 1995) p128. (Travers, Peter)
MUTE WITNESS
MR01781 712-713 (July 13, 1995) p116. (Travers, Peter)
MY COUSIN VINNY
MR01782 627 (April 2, 1992) p42. (Travers, Peter)
MY FAMILY
MR01783 708 (May 18, 1995) p98. (Travers, Peter)
MY GIRL
MR01784 631 (May 28, 1992) p60. (Travers, Peter)
MY LIFE
MR01785 670 (November 25, 1993) p127. (Travers, Peter)
MY NEW GUN
MR01786 644 (November 26, 1992) p80. (Travers, Peter)
MY OWN PRIVATE IDAHO
MR01787 615 (October 17, 1991) p100. (Travers, Peter)
MR01788 629 (April 30, 1992) p65.
MYSTERY SCIENCE THEATER 3000: THE MOVIE
MR01789 733 (May 2, 1996) pp61-62. (Travers, Peter)

N

NADJA
MR01790 715 (August 24, 1995) p108. (Travers, Peter)
NAKED
MR01791 672-673 (December 23, 1993) p174. (Travers, Peter)
MR01792 674 (January 27, 1994) pp47-48. (Travers, Peter)
NAKED GUN 33 1/3
MR01793 680 (April 21, 1994) p93. (Travers, Peter)
NAKED IN NEW YORK
MR01794 681 (May 5, 1994) pp48-49. (Travers, Peter)
NAKED LUNCH
MR01795 623 (February 6, 1992) pp87-88. (Travers, Peter)
MR01796 634-635 (July 9, 1992) p111.
NATURAL BORN KILLERS
MR01797 690 (September 8, 1994) pp83-84,87. (Travers, Peter)
NEAR DARK
MR01798 669 (November 11, 1993) p80. (Travers, Peter)
NELLY AND MONSIEUR ARNAUD
MR01799 733 (May 2, 1996) p62. (Travers, Peter)
THE NET
MR01800 715 (August 24, 1995) pp107-108,110. (Travers, Peter)
THE NEW AGE
MR01801 692 (October 6, 1994) p81. (Travers, Peter)
NEW JERSEY DRIVE
MR01802 708 (May 18, 1995) p98. (Travers, Peter)
NEWSIES
MR01803 630 (May 14, 1992) p114. (Travers, Peter)
THE NEXT KARATE KID

MR01804 691 (September 22, 1994) p106. (Travers, Peter)
NICK OF TIME
MR01805 723 (December 14, 1995) p92. (Travers, Peter)
NIGHT AND THE CITY
MR01806 642 (October 29, 1992) p77. (Travers, Peter)
NIGHT ON EARTH
MR01807 630 (May 14, 1992) pp111-112. (Travers, Peter)
NIGHTMARE BEFORE CHRISTMAS
MR01808 669 (November 11, 1993) pp79-80. (Travers, Peter)
NIGHTS OF CABIRIA
MR01809 676 (February 24, 1994) p17. (Browne, Jackson)
NINE MONTHS
MR01810 714 (August 10, 1995) p62. (Travers, Peter)
NIXON
MR01811 726 (January 25, 1996) pp63-64. (Travers, Peter)
NO ESCAPE
MR01812 682 (May 19, 1994) p107. (Travers, Peter)
NORMA JEAN AND MARILYN
MR01813 735 (May 30, 1996) p56. (Travers, Peter)
NORMAL LIFE
MR01814 747 (November 14, 1996) p126. (Travers, Peter)
NOW AND THEN
MR01815 720 (November 2, 1995) p77. (Travers, Peter)
THE NUTTY PROFESSOR
MR01816 738-739 (July 11, 1996) p96. (Travers, Peter)

O

OF MICE AND MEN
MR01817 642 (October 29, 1992) p77. (Travers, Peter)
OLIVER OLIVER
MR01818 650 (February 18, 1993) p66. (Travers, Peter)
ON DEADLY GROUND
MR01819 679 (April 7, 1994) p83. (Travers, Peter)
ONE FALSE MOVE
MR01820 637 (August 20, 1992) p60. (Travers, Peter)
101 DALMATIANS
MR01821 749 (December 12, 1996) p90. (Travers, Peter)
ONLY YOU
MR01822 693 (October 20, 1994) pp156-157. (Travers, Peter)
ORLANDO
MR01823 659 (June 24, 1993) p88. (Travers, Peter)
OTHELLO
MR01824 626 (March 19, 1992) p104. (Travers, Peter)
MR01825 726 (January 25, 1996) p64. (Travers, Peter)
OTHER PEOPLE'S MONEY
MR01826 617 (November 14, 1991) pp179,182. (Travers, Peter)
OUTBREAK
MR01827 706 (April 20, 1995) p89. (Travers, Peter)

P

THE PALLBEARER
MR01828 733 (May 2, 1996) pp61-62. (Travers, Peter)
PANTHER
MR01829 708 (May 18, 1995) pp95-96. (Travers, Peter)
THE PAPER
MR01830 679 (April 7, 1994) pp81-82. (Travers, Peter)
PARADISE
MR01831 615 (October 17, 1991) pp101-102. (Travers, Peter)
PARIS IS BURNING
MR01832 622 (January 23, 1992) p49. (Travers, Peter)
PARTY GIRL
MR01833 704 (March 23, 1995) p128. (Travers, Peter)
PASSION FISH
MR01834 648 (January 21, 1993) pp54-55. (Travers, Peter)
PATRIOT GAMES
MR01835 634-635 (July 9, 1992) pp111,114. (Travers, Peter)
PEEPING TOM
MR01836 669 (November 11, 1993) p80. (Travers, Peter)
THE PELICAN BRIEF
MR01837 674 (January 27, 1994) pp47-48. (Travers, Peter)
A PERFECT CANDIDATE
MR01838 741 (August 22, 1996) p104. (Travers, Peter)
A PERFECT WORLD
MR01839 671 (December 9, 1993) pp76,78. (Travers, Peter)
PERSUASION
MR01840 719 (October 19, 1995) p159. (Travers, Peter)
PETER'S FRIENDS
MR01841 647 (January 7, 1993) p51. (Travers, Peter)
THE PHANTOM
MR01842 737 (June 27, 1996) pp62-63. (Travers, Peter)
MR01843 738-739 (July 11, 1996) p98. (Travers, Peter)
PHENOMENON
MR01844 738-739 (July 11, 1996) p98. (Travers, Peter)
THE PIANO
MR01845 671 (December 9, 1993) p76. (Travers, Peter)
MR01846 672-673 (December 23, 1993) p174. (Travers, Peter)
THE PLAYBOYS
MR01847 630 (May 14, 1992) p114. (Travers, Peter)
THE PLAYER
MR01848 629 (April 30, 1992) pp63-64. (Travers, Peter)
MR01849 648 (January 21, 1993) p56. (Travers, Peter)
MR01850 656 (May 13, 1993) p114. (Travers, Peter)
POCAHONTAS
MR01851 712-713 (July 13, 1995) pp113-116. (Travers, Peter)
POETIC JUSTICE
MR01852 663 (August 19, 1993) pp81-82. (Travers, Peter)
POINT OF NO RETURN
MR01853 654 (April 15, 1993) pp69,72. (Travers, Peter)
POISON IVY
MR01854 631 (May 28, 1992) pp59-60. (Travers, Peter)
POSSE
MR01855 658 (June 10, 1993) pp73-74. (Travers, Peter)
THE POWER OF ONE
MR01856 628 (April 16, 1992) p93. (Travers, Peter)
PRELUDE TO A KISS
MR01857 637 (August 20, 1992) p57. (Travers, Peter)
PRIEST
MR01858 705 (April 6, 1995) p70. (Travers, Peter)
PRIMAL FEAR
MR01859 732 (April 18, 1996) pp78,80. (Travers, Peter)
THE PRINCE OF TIDES
MR01860 621 (January 9, 1992) p55. (Travers, Peter)
MR01861 622 (January 23, 1992) p49. (Travers, Peter)
MR01862 638 (September 3, 1992) p72. (Travers, Peter)
PRINCESS CARABOO
MR01863 692 (October 6, 1994) p81. (Travers, Peter)
THE PROFESSIONAL
MR01864 694 (November 3, 1994) p106. (Travers, Peter)
PROOF
MR01865 628 (April 16, 1992) p93. (Travers, Peter)
PROSPERO'S BOOKS
MR01866 617 (November 14, 1991) p184. (Travers, Peter)
THE PUBLIC EYE
MR01867 642 (October 29, 1992) p77. (Travers, Peter)
PULP FICTION
MR01868 692 (October 6, 1994) pp79-81. (Travers, Peter)

Q

QUEEN MARGOT
MR01869 700 (January 26, 1995) p66. (Travers, Peter)
THE QUEST

MR01870 734 (May 16, 1996) p72. (Travers, Peter)
THE QUICK AND THE DEAD
MR01871 703 (March 9, 1995) pp69-70. (Travers, Peter)
THE QUIET MAN
MR01872 634-635 (July 9, 1992) p111.
QUIZ SHOW
MR01873 691 (September 22, 1994) pp103-104. (Travers, Peter)

R

RADIO FLYER
MR01874 626 (March 19, 1992) p104. (Travers, Peter)
RADIOLAND MURDERS
MR01875 696 (December 1, 1994) p134. (Travers, Peter)
RAIDERS OF THE LOST ARK
MR01876 638 (September 3, 1992) p72. (Travers, Peter)
RAISE RED LANTERN
MR01877 626 (March 19, 1992) p102. (Travers, Peter)
RAISING CAIN
MR01878 636 (August 6, 1992) pp64-65. (Travers, Peter)
MR01879 649 (February 4, 1993) p72. (Travers, Peter)
RAMBLING ROSE
MR01880 622 (January 23, 1992) p49. (Travers, Peter)
RAMPAGE
MR01881 644 (November 26, 1992) p80. (Travers, Peter)
RANSOM
MR01882 748 (November 28, 1996) pp141-142. (Travers, Peter)
THE RAPTURE
MR01883 615 (October 17, 1991) pp100-101. (Travers, Peter)
MR01884 622 (January 23, 1992) p49. (Travers, Peter)
RARA NUI
MR01885 691 (September 22, 1994) p106. (Travers, Peter)
THE REAL MCCOY
MR01886 666 (September 30, 1993) p113. (Travers, Peter)
REALITY BITES
MR01887 677 (March 10, 1994) pp59-60. (Travers, Peter)
A REASON TO BELIEVE
MR01888 717 (September 21, 1995) p90. (Travers, Peter)
RECKLESS
MR01889 722 (November 30, 1995) p76. (Travers, Peter)
RED
MR01890 702 (February 23, 1995) p80. (Travers, Peter)
RED ROCK WEST
MR01891 681 (May 5, 1994) p48. (Travers, Peter)
RED SORGHUM
MR01892 681 (May 5, 1994) p16. (Amos, Tori)
THE REF
MR01893 679 (April 7, 1994) p83. (Travers, Peter)
REGARDING HENRY
MR01894 622 (January 23, 1992) p49. (Travers, Peter)
THE REMAINS OF THE DAY
MR01895 670 (November 25, 1993) p125. (Travers, Peter)
MR01896 672-673 (December 23, 1993) p174. (Travers, Peter)
RENAISSANCE MAN
MR01897 685 (June 30, 1994) p82. (Travers, Peter)
RESERVOIR DOGS
MR01898 642 (October 29, 1992) p77. (Travers, Peter)
MR01899 648 (January 21, 1993) p56. (Travers, Peter)
MR01900 656 (May 13, 1993) p114. (Travers, Peter)
RESTORATION
MR01901 726 (January 25, 1996) p67. (Travers, Peter)
RHAPSODY IN AUGUST
MR01902 622 (January 23, 1992) p50. (Travers, Peter)
RHYTHM THIEF
MR01903 722 (November 30, 1995) p74. (Travers, Peter)
RICHARD III
MR01904 726 (January 25, 1996) p64. (Travers, Peter)
RICOCHET
MR01905 617 (November 14, 1991) p182. (Travers, Peter)
RIFF-RAFF
MR01906 650 (February 18, 1993) p67. (Travers, Peter)
RISING SUN
MR01907 664 (September 2, 1993) p69. (Travers, Peter)
A RIVER RUNS THROUGH IT
MR01908 642 (October 29, 1992) p78. (Travers, Peter)
THE RIVER WILD
MR01909 693 (October 20, 1994) pp155-156. (Travers, Peter)
THE ROAD TO WELLVILLE
MR01910 696 (December 1, 1994) p134. (Travers, Peter)
ROB ROY
MR01911 707 (May 4, 1995) pp73-74,76. (Travers, Peter)
ROBIN HOOD: MEN IN TIGHTS
MR01912 664 (September 2, 1993) p70. (Travers, Peter)
ROBIN HOOD: PRINCE OF THIEVES
MR01913 617 (November 14, 1991) p184. (Travers, Peter)
THE ROCK
MR01914 737 (June 27, 1996) pp61-62. (Travers, Peter)
MR01915 738-739 (July 11, 1996) p98. (Travers, Peter)
ROCK HUDSON'S HOME MOVIES
MR01916 656 (May 13, 1993) p116. (Travers, Peter)
ROMEO IS BLEEDING
MR01917 675 (February 10, 1994) pp51-52. (Travers, Peter)
ROMPER STOMPER
MR01918 658 (June 10, 1993) p78. (Travers, Peter)
ROOMMATES
MR01919 705 (April 6, 1995) p70. (Travers, Peter)
RUBY
MR01920 628 (April 16, 1992) pp91,93. (Travers, Peter)
RUBY IN PARADISE
MR01921 668 (October 28, 1993) pp86,88. (Travers, Peter)
RUDY
MR01922 669 (November 11, 1993) p81. (Travers, Peter)
THE RUN OF THE COUNTRY
MR01923 718 (October 5, 1995) p79. (Travers, Peter)
RUSH
MR01924 621 (January 9, 1992) pp55-56. (Travers, Peter)

S

SABRINA
MR01925 726 (January 25, 1996) pp66-67. (Travers, Peter)
SAFE
MR01926 714 (August 10, 1995) p64. (Travers, Peter)
SAFE PASSAGE
MR01927 700 (January 26, 1995) p66. (Travers, Peter)
SAMSON AND DELILAH
MR01928 638 (September 3, 1992) p72. (Travers, Peter)
SARAFINA!
MR01929 642 (October 29, 1992) p77. (Travers, Peter)
SAVAGE NIGHTS
MR01930 675 (February 10, 1994) p53. (Travers, Peter)
THE SCARLET LETTER
MR01931 721 (November 16, 1995) p117. (Travers, Peter)
SCENT OF A WOMAN
MR01932 647 (January 7, 1993) p50. (Travers, Peter)
SCHINDLER'S LIST
MR01933 672-673 (December 23, 1993) p174. (Travers, Peter)
SCHOOL TIES
MR01934 640 (October 1, 1992) p72. (Travers, Peter)
SEANCE ON A WET AFTERNOON
MR01935 669 (November 11, 1993) p80. (Travers, Peter)
SEARCH AND DESTROY
MR01936 708 (May 18, 1995) p97. (Travers, Peter)
THE SEARCH FOR SIGNS OF INTELLIGENT LIFE IN THE UNIVERSE
MR01937 615 (October 17, 1991) p100. (Travers, Peter)

THE SEARCHERS
MR01938 658 (June 10, 1993) p74. (Travers, Peter)
SEARCHING FOR BOBBY FISCHER
MR01939 664 (September 2, 1993) p70. (Travers, Peter)
SECRET FRIENDS
MR01940 624 (February 20, 1992) p50. (Travers, Peter)
THE SECRET OF ROAN INISH
MR01941 702 (February 23, 1995) p81. (Travers, Peter)
THE SECRET RAPTURE
MR01942 681 (May 5, 1994) p48. (Travers, Peter)
SECRETS AND LIES
MR01943 745 (October 17, 1996) pp142,144. (Travers, Peter)
SENSE AND SENSIBILITY
MR01944 724-725 (December 28, 1995) p139. (Travers, Peter)
SERIAL MOM
MR01945 681 (May 5, 1994) pp47-48. (Travers, Peter)
SERVING IN SILENCE
MR01946 702 (February 23, 1995) p81. (Travers, Peter)
SET IT OFF
MR01947 748 (November 28, 1996) p143. (Travers, Peter)
SEVEN
MR01948 718 (October 5, 1995) pp75-77. (Travers, Peter)
1776
MR01949 651 (March 4, 1993) p72. (Travers, Peter)
SEX IS...
MR01950 667 (October 14, 1993) p128. (Travers, Peter)
S.F.W.
MR01951 694 (November 3, 1994) p106. (Travers, Peter)
MR01952 701 (February 9, 1995) p63. (Travers, Peter)
THE SHADOW
MR01953 688 (August 11, 1994) p62. (Travers, Peter)
SHADOWLANDS
MR01954 674 (January 27, 1994) pp47-48. (Travers, Peter)
SHADOWS AND FOG
MR01955 628 (April 16, 1992) p91. (Travers, Peter)
MR01956 649 (February 4, 1993) p72. (Travers, Peter)
SHAKES THE CLOWN
MR01957 626 (March 19, 1992) p102. (Travers, Peter)
SHALLOW GRAVE
MR01958 702 (February 23, 1995) p81. (Travers, Peter)
SHANGHAI TRIAD
MR01959 726 (January 25, 1996) p67. (Travers, Peter)
SHATTERED
MR01960 616 (October 31, 1991) p97. (Travers, Peter)
THE SHAWSHANK REDEMPTION
MR01961 692 (October 6, 1994) p81. (Travers, Peter)
SHE'S THE ONE
MR01962 741 (August 22, 1996) p105. (Travers, Peter)
SHINE
MR01963 749 (December 12, 1996) p92. (Travers, Peter)
SHINING THROUGH
MR01964 624 (February 20, 1992) pp47,49. (Travers, Peter)
MR01965 634-635 (July 9, 1992) p111.
SHORT CUTS
MR01966 667 (October 14, 1993) pp125-126,128. (Travers, Peter)
MR01967 672-673 (December 23, 1993) p174. (Travers, Peter)
SHOUT
MR01968 617 (November 14, 1991) p182. (Travers, Peter)
THE SILENCE OF THE LAMBS
MR01969 617 (November 14, 1991) p184. (Travers, Peter)
SILENT FALL
MR01970 694 (November 3, 1994) p106. (Travers, Peter)
SILENT TONGUE
MR01971 676 (February 24, 1994) pp61-62. (Travers, Peter)
SIMPLE MEN
MR01972 640 (October 1, 1992) p74. (Travers, Peter)
MR01973 689 (August 25, 1994) p34. (Barron, Chris)
SINGIN' IN THE RAIN
MR01974 629 (April 30, 1992) p65.
A SINGLE GIRL
MR01975 749 (December 12, 1996) p90. (Travers, Peter)
SINGLE WHITE FEMALE
MR01976 638 (September 3, 1992) pp71-72. (Travers, Peter)
MR01977 649 (February 4, 1993) p72. (Travers, Peter)
SINGLES
MR01978 640 (October 1, 1992) p72. (Travers, Peter)
SIR DRONE
MR01979 684 (June 16, 1994) p24. (Moore, Thurston)
SISTER ACT
MR01980 633 (June 25, 1992) p48. (Travers, Peter)
SLEEP WITH ME
MR01981 692 (October 6, 1994) p81. (Travers, Peter)
SLEEPERS
MR01982 746 (October 31, 1996) pp75-76. (Travers, Peter)
SLEEPLESS IN SEATTLE
MR01983 660-661 (July 8, 1993) pp119-120. (Travers, Peter)
SLING BLADE
MR01984 749 (December 12, 1996) p90. (Travers, Peter)
SMOKE
MR01985 711 (June 29, 1995) p49. (Travers, Peter)
THE SNAPPER
MR01986 671 (December 9, 1993) p78. (Travers, Peter)
SNEAKERS
MR01987 640 (October 1, 1992) p72. (Travers, Peter)
SO I MARRIED AN AXE MURDERER
MR01988 663 (August 19, 1993) pp82-83. (Travers, Peter)
SOMETHING TO TALK ABOUT
MR01989 715 (August 24, 1995) pp107-108,110. (Travers, Peter)
SOMMERSBY
MR01990 650 (February 18, 1993) pp65-66. (Travers, Peter)
SPANKING THE MONKEY
MR01991 686-687 (July 14, 1994) p98. (Travers, Peter)
SPARTACUS
MR01992 651 (March 4, 1993) p72. (Travers, Peter)
THE SPECIALIST
MR01993 694 (November 3, 1994) p106. (Travers, Peter)
SPECIES
MR01994 714 (August 10, 1995) p64. (Travers, Peter)
MR01995 715 (August 24, 1995) pp107-108,110. (Travers, Peter)
MR01995 715 (August 24, 1995) p108. (Travers, Peter)
SPEECHLESS
MR01996 700 (January 26, 1995) p66. (Travers, Peter)
SPEED
MR01997 685 (June 30, 1994) pp79-80. (Travers, Peter)
THE SPITFIRE GRILL
MR01998 742 (September 5, 1996) p69. (Travers, Peter)
SPY HARD
MR01999 738-739 (July 11, 1996) p98. (Travers, Peter)
STAR TREK: FIRST CONTACT
MR02000 749 (December 12, 1996) p90. (Travers, Peter)
STAR TREK VI
MR02001 621 (January 9, 1992) p55. (Travers, Peter)
MR02002 634-635 (July 9, 1992) p111.
STARGATE
MR02003 696 (December 1, 1994) p134. (Travers, Peter)
STEAL BIG, STEAL LITTLE
MR02004 720 (November 2, 1995) p74. (Travers, Peter)
STEALING BEAUTY
MR02005 737 (June 27, 1996) p63. (Travers, Peter)
THE STEPFATHER
MR02006 669 (November 11, 1993) p80. (Travers, Peter)
STEPPING OUT
MR02007 617 (November 14, 1991) p182. (Travers, Peter)
STONEWALL
MR02008 741 (August 22, 1996) p105. (Travers, Peter)
THE STORY OF QIU JU
MR02009 654 (April 15, 1993) p72. (Travers, Peter)

STORYVILLE
MR02010 639 (September 17, 1992) p103. (Travers, Peter)
STRANGE DAYS
MR02011 719 (October 19, 1995) pp156,158. (Travers, Peter)
A STRANGER AMONG US
MR02012 636 (August 6, 1992) pp65-66. (Travers, Peter)
STRANGERS IN GOOD COMPANY
MR02013 623 (February 6, 1992) p88. (Travers, Peter)
MR02014 638 (September 3, 1992) p72. (Travers, Peter)
STRAWBERRY AND CHOCOLATE
MR02015 701 (February 9, 1995) p63. (Travers, Peter)
A STREET CAR NAMED DESIRE
MR02016 680 (April 21, 1994) p21. (Hutchence, Michael)
STREET FIGHTERS
MR02017 701 (February 9, 1995) p63. (Travers, Peter)
STRICTLY BALLROOM
MR02018 651 (March 4, 1993) p74. (Travers, Peter)
STRIPTEASE
MR02019 738-739 (July 11, 1996) p98. (Travers, Peter)
SUDDEN DEATH
MR02020 726 (January 25, 1996) p67. (Travers, Peter)
THE SUGARLAND EXPRESS
MR02021 638 (September 3, 1992) p72. (Travers, Peter)
SUNCHASER
MR02022 748 (November 28, 1996) p143. (Travers, Peter)
SUNDAY'S CHILDREN
MR02023 681 (May 5, 1994) p48. (Travers, Peter)
SUPER MARIO BROS.
MR02024 660-661 (July 8, 1993) p121. (Travers, Peter)
SURVIVING PICASSO
MR02025 744 (October 3, 1996) pp77-78. (Travers, Peter)
SWEET NOTHING
MR02026 744 (October 3, 1996) p78. (Travers, Peter)
SWIMMING WITH SHARKS
MR02027 708 (May 18, 1995) p98. (Travers, Peter)
SWING KIDS
MR02028 653 (April 1, 1993) p59. (Travers, Peter)
SWINGERS
MR02029 746 (October 31, 1996) p78. (Travers, Peter)
SWITCHBLADE SISTERS
MR02030 737 (June 27, 1996) p62. (Travers, Peter)
SWOON
MR02031 640 (October 1, 1992) pp72,74. (Travers, Peter)
MR02032 656 (May 13, 1993) p114. (Travers, Peter)

T

TALES FROM THE HOOD
MR02033 710 (June 15, 1995) p86. (Travers, Peter)
TANK GIRL
MR02034 707 (May 4, 1995) p74. (Travers, Peter)
THE TEN COMMANDMENTS
MR02035 638 (September 3, 1992) p72. (Travers, Peter)
TERMINATOR 2: JUDGMENT DAY
MR02036 623 (February 6, 1992) p90. (Travers, Peter)
THANK YOU AND GOODNIGHT!
MR02037 624 (February 20, 1992) p50. (Travers, Peter)
THAT NIGHT
MR02038 663 (August 19, 1993) p83. (Travers, Peter)
THAT THING YOU DO!
MR02039 745 (October 17, 1996) pp141-142. (Travers, Peter)
THAT'S ENTERTAINMENT! III
MR02040 682 (May 19, 1994) p108. (Travers, Peter)
THELMA & LOUISE
MR02041 622 (January 23, 1992) p49. (Travers, Peter)
MR02042 623 (February 6, 1992) p90. (Travers, Peter)
THEREMIN: AN ELECTRONIC ODYSSEY
MR02043 717 (September 21, 1995) p89. (Travers, Peter)
THINGS TO DO IN DENVER WHEN YOU'RE DEAD
MR02044 719 (October 19, 1995) pp158-159. (Travers, Peter)
THINNER
MR02045 748 (November 28, 1996) p143. (Travers, Peter)
THIS BOY'S LIFE
MR02046 654 (April 15, 1993) pp67,69. (Travers, Peter)
THIS IS MY LIFE
MR02047 625 (March 5, 1992) pp75-77. (Travers, Peter)
THE THREE MUSKETEERS
MR02048 670 (November 25, 1993) pp124-125. (Travers, Peter)
THREE OF HEARTS
MR02049 657 (May 27, 1993) pp58-59. (Travers, Peter)
THREE WISHES
MR02050 722 (November 30, 1995) p76. (Travers, Peter)
THREESOME
MR02051 680 (April 21, 1994) p93. (Travers, Peter)
THUNDERHEART
MR02052 628 (April 16, 1992) p93. (Travers, Peter)
TIE-DYED
MR02053 718 (October 5, 1995) p79. (Travers, Peter)
TIME COP
MR02054 692 (October 6, 1994) p81. (Travers, Peter)
A TIME TO KILL
MR02055 740 (August 8, 1996) pp67-68,70. (Travers, Peter)
TIN CUP
MR02056 743 (September 19, 1996) p90. (Travers, Peter)
THE TIN DRUM
MR02057 683 (June 2, 1994) p20. (Gudmundsdottir, Bjork)
TO DIE FOR
MR02058 719 (October 19, 1995) pp155-156. (Travers, Peter)
TO GILLIAN ON HER 37TH BIRTHDAY
MR02059 746 (October 31, 1996) p78. (Travers, Peter)
TO LIVE
MR02060 696 (December 1, 1994) p132. (Travers, Peter)
TO WONG FOO, THANKS FOR EVERYTHING! JULIE NEWMAR
MR02061 717 (September 21, 1995) pp87,89. (Travers, Peter)
TOM AND VIV
MR02062 700 (January 26, 1995) p66. (Travers, Peter)
TOM JONES
MR02063 629 (April 30, 1992) p65.
TOTAL ECLIPSE
MR02064 722 (November 30, 1995) p76. (Travers, Peter)
TOTO THE HERO
MR02065 625 (March 5, 1992) p78. (Travers, Peter)
TOUS LES MATINS DU MONDE
MR02066 644 (November 26, 1992) p80. (Travers, Peter)
TOY STORY
MR02067 723 (December 14, 1995) p90. (Travers, Peter)
TOYS
MR02068 648 (January 21, 1993) p55. (Travers, Peter)
MR02069 649 (February 4, 1993) p72. (Travers, Peter)
TRACES OF RED
MR02070 644 (November 26, 1992) pp78,80. (Travers, Peter)
TRAINSPOTTING
MR02071 740 (August 8, 1996) pp67-68,70. (Travers, Peter)
TREES LOUNGE
MR02072 747 (November 14, 1996) p126. (Travers, Peter)
TRESPASS
MR02073 649 (February 4, 1993) p75. (Travers, Peter)
TRIAL BY JURY
MR02074 691 (September 22, 1994) pp104,106. (Travers, Peter)
THE TRIGGER EFFECT
MR02075 743 (September 19, 1996) p90. (Travers, Peter)
TRUE ROMANCE
MR02076 666 (September 30, 1993) pp112-113. (Travers, Peter)
TRULY, MADLY, DEEPLY
MR02077 631 (May 28, 1992) p60. (Travers, Peter)
THE TRUTH ABOUT CATS AND DOGS
MR02078 734 (May 16, 1996) p74. (Travers, Peter)

TWELFTH NIGHT
MR02079 747 (November 14, 1996) p124. (Travers, Peter)
12 MONKEYS
MR02080 726 (January 25, 1996) pp64,66. (Travers, Peter)
29TH STREET
MR02081 616 (October 31, 1991) p97. (Travers, Peter)
TWENTY-ONE
MR02082 615 (October 17, 1991) p102. (Travers, Peter)
MR02083 629 (April 30, 1992) p65.
TWIN PEAKS: FIRE WALK WITH ME
MR02084 639 (September 17, 1992) p103. (Travers, Peter)
TWISTER
MR02085 738-739 (July 11, 1996) p98. (Travers, Peter)
TWO BITS
MR02086 723 (December 14, 1995) p92. (Travers, Peter)
2 DAYS IN THE VALLEY
MR02087 745 (October 17, 1996) p142. (Travers, Peter)
TWO IF BY SEA
MR02088 727 (February 8, 1996) pp45-46. (Travers, Peter)

U

THE UMBRELLAS OF CHERBOURG
MR02089 734 (May 16, 1996) p72. (Travers, Peter)
UN COEUR EN HIVER
MR02090 662 (August 5, 1993) p72. (Travers, Peter)
UNDER SIEGE
MR02091 644 (November 26, 1992) p80. (Travers, Peter)
UNDER SUSPICION
MR02092 626 (March 19, 1992) p102. (Travers, Peter)
THE UNDERNEATH
MR02093 708 (May 18, 1995) p98. (Travers, Peter)
UNDERTOW
MR02094 615 (October 17, 1991) p100. (Travers, Peter)
UNFORGIVEN
MR02095 637 (August 20, 1992) pp55,57. (Travers, Peter)
UNHOOK THE STARS
MR02096 748 (November 28, 1996) p143. (Travers, Peter)
UNIVERSAL SOLDIER
MR02097 636 (August 6, 1992) p66. (Travers, Peter)
UNLAWFUL ENTRY
MR02098 636 (August 6, 1992) p66. (Travers, Peter)
UNSTRUNG HEROES
MR02099 717 (September 21, 1995) p90. (Travers, Peter)
UNTAMED HEART
MR02100 651 (March 4, 1993) pp72,74. (Travers, Peter)
UNTIL THE END OF THE WORLD
MR02101 622 (January 23, 1992) p50. (Travers, Peter)
UNZIPPED
MR02102 715 (August 24, 1995) p110. (Travers, Peter)
UP CLOSE AND PERSONAL
MR02103 730 (March 21, 1996) pp103-104. (Travers, Peter)
USED PEOPLE
MR02104 648 (January 21, 1993) p56. (Travers, Peter)
MR02105 649 (February 4, 1993) p72. (Travers, Peter)
THE USUAL SUSPECTS
MR02106 716 (September 7, 1995) pp75-76. (Travers, Peter)

V

VALLEY OF THE DOLLS
MR02107 629 (April 30, 1992) p65.
VAMPIRE IN BROOKLYN
MR02108 722 (November 30, 1995) p76. (Travers, Peter)
THE VANISHING
MR02109 623 (February 6, 1992) p90. (Travers, Peter)
VANYA ON 42ND STREET
MR02110 694 (November 3, 1994) p106. (Travers, Peter)
VENICE-VENICE
MR02111 642 (October 29, 1992) p77. (Travers, Peter)
VERTIGO
MR02112 745 (October 17, 1996) p144. (Travers, Peter)
A VERY BRADY SEQUEL
MR02113 743 (September 19, 1996) p90. (Travers, Peter)
VIRTUOSITY
MR02114 716 (September 7, 1995) p77. (Travers, Peter)
VISIONS OF LIGHT
MR02115 656 (May 13, 1993) p116. (Travers, Peter)
MR02116 672-673 (December 23, 1993) p174. (Travers, Peter)
THE VISITORS
MR02117 741 (August 22, 1996) p105. (Travers, Peter)
VOYAGER
MR02118 617 (November 14, 1991) p184. (Travers, Peter)

W

WAGONS EAST!
MR02119 691 (September 22, 1994) p106. (Travers, Peter)
WAITING TO EXHALE
MR02120 724-725 (December 28, 1995) pp138-139. (Travers, Peter)
A WALK IN THE CLOUDS
MR02121 715 (August 24, 1995) p110. (Travers, Peter)
WALKING AND TALKING
MR02122 741 (August 22, 1996) p105. (Travers, Peter)
THE WAR
MR02123 696 (December 1, 1994) p134. (Travers, Peter)
THE WAR ROOM
MR02124 670 (November 25, 1993) pp126-127. (Travers, Peter)
THE WATERDANCE
MR02125 631 (May 28, 1992) p60. (Travers, Peter)
MR02126 651 (March 4, 1993) p72. (Travers, Peter)
WATERLAND
MR02127 642 (October 29, 1992) p77. (Travers, Peter)
WAYNE'S WORLD
MR02128 626 (March 19, 1992) p102. (Travers, Peter)
WES CRAVEN'S NEW NIGHTMARE
MR02129 694 (November 3, 1994) p106. (Travers, Peter)
WHAT HAPPENED WAS...
MR02130 691 (September 22, 1994) p106. (Travers, Peter)
WHAT'S EATING GILBERT GRAPE
MR02131 674 (January 27, 1994) pp47-48. (Travers, Peter)
WHAT'S LOVE GOT TO DO WITH IT
MR02132 659 (June 24, 1993) p88. (Travers, Peter)
WHEN A MAN LOVES A WOMAN
MR02133 682 (May 19, 1994) p107. (Travers, Peter)
WHEN WE WERE KINGS
MR02134 747 (November 14, 1996) p126. (Travers, Peter)
WHERE ANGELS FEAR TO TREAD
MR02135 625 (March 5, 1992) p78. (Travers, Peter)
WHERE THE DAY TAKES YOU
MR02136 640 (October 1, 1992) p72. (Travers, Peter)
WHILE YOU WERE SLEEPING
MR02137 708 (May 18, 1995) p97. (Travers, Peter)
WHISPERS IN THE DARK
MR02138 638 (September 3, 1992) p72. (Travers, Peter)
WHITE
MR02139 702 (February 23, 1995) p80. (Travers, Peter)
WHITE MAN'S BURDEN
MR02140 723 (December 14, 1995) p92. (Travers, Peter)
WHITE MEN CAN'T JUMP
MR02141 629 (April 30, 1992) p65. (Travers, Peter)
MR02142 638 (September 3, 1992) p72. (Travers, Peter)
WHITE OF THE EYE

MR02143 669 (November 11, 1993) p80. (Travers, Peter)
WHITE SANDS
MR02144 630 (May 14, 1992) pp113-114. (Travers, Peter)
WHITE SQUALL
MR02145 728 (February 22, 1996) pp69-70. (Travers, Peter)
WHORE
MR02146 615 (October 17, 1991) p100. (Travers, Peter)
WIDE SARGASSO SEA
MR02147 656 (May 13, 1993) p116. (Travers, Peter)
WIDOWS' PEAK
MR02148 683 (June 2, 1994) p76. (Travers, Peter)
WILD BILL
MR02149 723 (December 14, 1995) p92. (Travers, Peter)
THE WILD BUNCH
MR02150 703 (March 9, 1995) pp70,72. (Travers, Peter)
WILD REEDS
MR02151 711 (June 29, 1995) p49. (Travers, Peter)
WILLIAM SHAKESPEARE'S ROMEO AND JULIET
MR02152 747 (November 14, 1996) pp123-124. (Travers, Peter)
WITH HONORS
MR02153 682 (May 19, 1994) p106. (Travers, Peter)
WOLF
MR02154 686-687 (July 14, 1994) pp97-99. (Travers, Peter)
A WOMAN'S TALE
MR02155 624 (February 20, 1992) p50. (Travers, Peter)
THE WONDERFUL, HORRIBLE LIFE OF LENI RIEFENSTAHL
MR02156 680 (April 21, 1994) p95. (Travers, Peter)
WOODSTOCK
MR02157 688 (August 11, 1994) p63. (Travers, Peter)
WRESTLING ERNEST HEMINGWAY
MR02158 674 (January 27, 1994) pp47-48. (Travers, Peter)
WYATT EARP
MR02159 688 (August 11, 1994) p62. (Travers, Peter)

Y

YEAR OF THE GUN
MR02160 618 (November 28, 1991) p103. (Travers, Peter)
YOU SO CRAZY
MR02161 677 (March 10, 1994) p60. (Travers, Peter)

Z

ZEBRAHEAD
MR02162 642 (October 29, 1992) p77. (Travers, Peter)

Reviewer Index to Movie Reviews

A

Amos, Tori MR01892

B

Barron, Chris MR01973

Browne, Jackson MR01809

D

D'Arby, Terence Trent MR01299

DeCurtis, Anthony MR01356, MR01398

Donelly, Tanya MR01693, MR01759

Duritz, Adam MR01228

G

Gudmundsdottir, Bjork MR02057, MR01549

H

Hoon, Shannon MR01236

Hutchence, Michael MR02016

M

Moore, Thurston MR01979

Mundy, Chris MR01387

N

Neely, Kim MR01531

Q

Queen Latifah MR01453

T

Travers, Peter MR01189, MR01190, MR01191, MR01192, MR01194, MR01195, MR01196, MR01197, MR01198, MR01199, MR01200, MR01201, MR01202, MR01203, MR01204, MR01205, MR01206, MR01207, MR01208, MR01209, MR01210, MR01211, MR01212, MR01213, MR01214, MR01215, MR01216, MR01217, MR01218, MR01219, MR01220, MR01221, MR01222, MR01223, MR01224, MR01226, MR01227, MR01229, MR01230, MR01231, MR01232, MR01233, MR01234, MR01235, MR01237, MR01238, MR01239, MR01240, MR01241, MR01243, MR01244, MR01245, MR01246, MR01247, MR01248, MR01249, MR01250, MR01251, MR01252, MR01253, MR01254, MR01255, MR01256, MR01257, MR01258, MR01259, MR01260, MR01261, MR01262, MR01264, MR01265, MR01266, MR01267, MR01268, MR01269, MR01270, MR01271, MR01272, MR01273, MR01274, MR01275, MR01276, MR01277, MR01278, MR01279, MR01280, MR01281, MR01282, MR01283, MR01284, MR01285, MR01286, MR01287, MR01288, MR01289, MR01290, MR01291, MR01292, MR01293, MR01294, MR01295, MR01297, MR01298, MR01300, MR01301, MR01302, MR01303, MR01304, MR01305, MR01306, MR01307, MR01308, MR01309, MR01310, MR01311, MR01312, MR01313, MR01315, MR01316, MR01317, MR01318, MR01319, MR01320, MR01321, MR01322, MR01323, MR01324, MR01325, MR01326, MR01328, MR01329, MR01330, MR01331, MR01332, MR01333, MR01334, MR01335, MR01336, MR01337, MR01338, MR01339, MR01340, MR01341, MR01342, MR01343, MR01344, MR01345, MR01346, MR01347, MR01348, MR01349, MR01350, MR01351, MR01352, MR01353, MR01354, MR01355, MR01357, MR01358, MR01360, MR01361, MR01362, MR01363, MR01364, MR01365, MR01366, MR01367, MR01368, MR01369, MR01370, MR01371, MR01372, MR01373, MR01374, MR01375, MR01376, MR01377, MR01378, MR01379, MR01380, MR01381, MR01382, MR01383, MR01384, MR01385, MR01386, MR01388, MR01389, MR01391, MR01392, MR01393, MR01394, MR01395, MR01396, MR01397, MR01399, MR01400, MR01401, MR01402, MR01403, MR01404, MR01405, MR01406, MR01407, MR01408, MR01409, MR01412, MR01413, MR01414, MR01415, MR01416, MR01417, MR01418, MR01420, MR01421, MR01422, MR01423, MR01424, MR01425, MR01426, MR01427, MR01428, MR01429, MR01430, MR01431, MR01432, MR01433, MR01434, MR01435, MR01436, MR01437, MR01439, MR01440, MR01441, MR01442, MR01443, MR01444, MR01445, MR01446, MR01447, MR01448, MR01449, MR01450, MR01451, MR01452, MR01454, MR01455, MR01456, MR01458, MR01459, MR01460, MR01461, MR01462, MR01463, MR01464, MR01465, MR01466, MR01467, MR01468, MR01469, MR01470, MR01471, MR01472, MR01473, MR01474, MR01476, MR01477, MR01478, MR01479, MR01480, MR01481, MR01482, MR01483, MR01484, MR01485, MR01486, MR01487, MR01488, MR01489, MR01490, MR01491, MR01492, MR01493, MR01494, MR01495, MR01496, MR01497, MR01498, MR01499, MR01500, MR01501, MR01502, MR01503, MR01504, MR01505, MR01506, MR01507, MR01508, MR01509, MR01510, MR01511, MR01512, MR01513, MR01514, MR01515, MR01516, MR01517, MR01518, MR01519, MR01520, MR01521, MR01522, MR01523, MR01524, MR01525, MR01526, MR01527, MR01528, MR01529, MR01530, MR01532, MR01533, MR01534, MR01535, MR01536, MR01537, MR01538, MR01539, MR01540, MR01541, MR01542, MR01543, MR01544, MR01545, MR01546, MR01547, MR01548, MR01551, MR01552, MR01553, MR01554, MR01555, MR01556, MR01557, MR01559, MR01560, MR01561, MR01562, MR01563, MR01564, MR01565, MR01566, MR01567, MR01568, MR01569, MR01570, MR01571, MR01572, MR01574, MR01575, MR01576, MR01577, MR01578, MR01579, MR01580, MR01581, MR01582, MR01584, MR01585, MR01586, MR01587, MR01588, MR01589, MR01590, MR01591, MR01592, MR01593, MR01594, MR01595, MR01596, MR01597, MR01598, MR01599, MR01600, MR01601, MR01602, MR01603, MR01604, MR01605, MR01606, MR01607, MR01608, MR01609, MR01610, MR01611, MR01612, MR01613, MR01614, MR01615, MR01616, MR01617, MR01618, MR01619, MR01620, MR01621, MR01622, MR01623, MR01624, MR01625, MR01626, MR01627, MR01628, MR01629, MR01630, MR01631, MR01632, MR01633, MR01634, MR01635, MR01636, MR01637, MR01638, MR01639, MR01640, MR01641, MR01642, MR01643, MR01644, MR01645, MR01646, MR01647, MR01648, MR01649, MR01650, MR01651, MR01652, MR01653, MR01654, MR01655, MR01656, MR01657, MR01658, MR01659, MR01660, MR01661, MR01662, MR01663, MR01664, MR01665, MR01666, MR01667, MR01668, MR01670, MR01671, MR01672, MR01673, MR01674, MR01675, MR01676, MR01677, MR01678, MR01679, MR01680, MR01681, MR01682, MR01683, MR01684, MR01685, MR01686, MR01687, MR01688, MR01689, MR01690, MR01691, MR01692, MR01694, MR01695, MR01696, MR01697, MR01698, MR01699, MR01700, MR01701, MR01702, MR01703, MR01704, MR01705, MR01706, MR01707, MR01708, MR01709, MR01710, MR01711, MR01712, MR01713, MR01714, MR01715, MR01716, MR01717, MR01718, MR01719, MR01721, MR01722, MR01723, MR01724, MR01725, MR01726, MR01727, MR01728, MR01729, MR01730, MR01731, MR01732, MR01733, MR01734, MR01735, MR01736, MR01737, MR01738, MR01739, MR01740, MR01741, MR01742, MR01743, MR01744, MR01745, MR01746, MR01747, MR01748, MR01749, MR01750, MR01751, MR01752, MR01753, MR01754, MR01755, MR01756, MR01757, MR01758, MR01761, MR01762, MR01763, MR01764, MR01765, MR01766, MR01767, MR01768, MR01769, MR01770, MR01771, MR01772, MR01773, MR01774, MR01775, MR01776, MR01777, MR01778, MR01779, MR01780, MR01781, MR01782, MR01783, MR01784, MR01785, MR01786, MR01787, MR01789, MR01790, MR01791, MR01792, MR01793, MR01794, MR01795, MR01797, MR01798, MR01799, MR01800, MR01801, MR01802, MR01803, MR01804, MR01805, MR01806, MR01807, MR01808, MR01810, MR01811, MR01812, MR01813, MR01814, MR01815, MR01816, MR01817, MR01818, MR01819, MR01820, MR01821, MR01822, MR01823, MR01824, MR01825, MR01826, MR01827, MR01828, MR01829, MR01830, MR01831, MR01832, MR01833, MR01834, MR01835, MR01836, MR01837, MR01838, MR01839, MR01840, MR01841, MR01842, MR01843, MR01844 MR01845, MR01846, MR01847, MR01848, MR01849, MR01850, MR01851, MR01852, MR01853, MR01854, MR01855, MR01856, MR01857, MR01858, MR01859, MR01860, MR01861, MR01862, MR01863, MR01864, MR01865, MR01866, MR01867, MR01868, MR01869, MR01870, MR01871, MR01873, MR01874, MR01875, MR01876, MR01877, MR01878, MR01879, MR01880, MR01881, MR01882, MR01883,

Travers, Peter (continued)
MR01884, MR01885, MR01886, MR01887, MR01888, MR01889, MR01890, MR01891, MR01893, MR01894, MR01895, MR01896, MR01897, MR01898, MR01899, MR01900, MR01901, MR01902, MR01903, MR01904, MR01905, MR01906, MR01907, MR01908, MR01909, MR01910, MR01911, MR01912, MR01913, MR01914, MR01915, MR01916, MR01917, MR01918, MR01919, MR01920, MR01921, MR01922, MR01923, MR01924, MR01925, MR01926, MR01927, MR01928, MR01929, MR01930, MR01931, MR01932, MR01933, MR01934, MR01935, MR01936, MR01937, MR01938, MR01939, MR01940, MR01941, MR01942, MR01943, MR01944, MR01945, MR01946, MR01947, MR01948, MR01949, MR01950, MR01951, MR01952, MR01953, MR01954, MR01955, MR01956, MR01957, MR01958, MR01959, MR01960, MR01961, MR01962, MR01963, MR01964, MR01966, MR01967, MR01968, MR01969, MR01970, MR01971, MR01972, MR01975, MR01976, MR01977, MR01978, MR01980, MR01981, MR01982, MR01983, MR01984, MR01985, MR01986, MR01987, MR01988, MR01989, MR01990, MR01991, MR01992, MR01993, MR01994, MR01995, MR01996, MR01997, MR01998, MR01999, MR02000, MR02001, MR02003, MR02004, MR02005, MR02006, MR02007, MR02008, MR02009, MR02010, MR02011, MR02012, MR02013, MR02014, MR02015, MR02017, MR02018, MR02019, MR02020, MR02021, MR02022, MR02023, MR02024, MR02025, MR02026, MR02027, MR02028, MR02029, MR02030, MR02031, MR02032, MR02033, MR02034, MR02035, MR02036, MR02037, MR02038, MR02039, MR02040, MR02041, MR02042, MR02043, MR02044, MR02045, MR02046, MR02047, MR02048, MR02049, MR02050, MR02051, MR02052, MR02053, MR02054, MR02055, MR02056, MR02058, MR02059, MR02060, MR02061, MR02062, MR02064, MR02065, MR02066, MR02067, MR02068, MR02069, MR02070, MR02071, MR02072, MR02073, MR02074, MR02075, MR02076, MR02077, MR02078, MR02079, MR02080, MR02081, MR02082, MR02084, MR02085, MR02086, MR02087, MR02088, MR02089, MR02090, MR02091, MR02092, MR02093, MR02094, MR02095, MR02096, MR02097, MR02098, MR02099, MR02100, MR02101, MR02102, MR02103, MR02104, MR02105, MR02106, MR02108, MR02109, MR02110, MR02111, MR02112, MR02113, MR02114, MR02115, MR02116, MR02117, MR02118, MR02119, MR02120, MR02121, MR02122, MR02123, MR02124, MR02125, MR02126, MR02127, MR02128, MR02129, MR02130, MR02131, MR02132, MR02133, MR02134, MR02135, MR02136, MR02137, MR02138, MR02139, MR02140, MR02141, MR02142, MR02143, MR02144, MR02145, MR02146, MR02147, MR02148, MR02149, MR02150, MR02151, MR02152, MR02153, MR02154, MR02155, MR02156, MR02157, MR02158, MR02159, MR02160, MR02161, MR02162

Photographs & Illustrations

A

A-HA—PHOTOGRAPHS
PH00001 667 (October 14, 1993) p70. "A-Ha: Through The Looking Glass, To The Top"
ABBRUZZESE, DAVE—PHOTOGRAPHS
PH00002 616 (October 31, 1991) p15. "Pearl Jam (from left): Mike McCready, Dave Abbruzzese, Eddie Vedder, Jeff Ament And Stone Gossard" (Cuffaro, Chris)
PH00003 634-635 (July 9, 1992) p13. "Pearl Jam's Mike McCready, Dave Abbruzzese, Eddie Vedder, Gossard And Jeff Ament (from left)" (Mercer, Lance)
PH00004 668 (October 28, 1993) p58. "Pre-Show Shenanigans: Ament Drops His Drawers..." (Seliger, Mark)
PH00005 668 (October 28, 1993) p51. "The Sun Shines On The Five Musketeers: Jeff Ament, Eddie Vedder (We're Not Kidding), Dave Abbruzzese, Stone Gossard And Mike McCready (from left)" (Seliger, Mark)
PH00006 668 (October 28, 1993) p58. "...While Dave Abbruzzese Takes Five And Vedder Mops Up" (Seliger, Mark)
PH00007 672-673 (December 23, 1993) p69. "Us 'Vs.' The World: Gossard, Mike McCready, Dave Abbruzzese, Vedder, Jeff Ament (from left)" (Seliger, Mark)
PH00008 681 (May 5, 1994) p13. "Abbruzzese: The Secret Weapon Of 'Vs.'" (Mercer, Lance)
PH00009 692 (October 6, 1994) p24. "Pearl Jam, With Abbruzzese (left)" (Rikken, Clemens)
PH00010 703 (March 9, 1995) p21. "'It's Still Evolving,' Says Abbruzzese (right), With Pals"
ABDUL, PAULA—ALBUMS
PH00011 715 (August 24, 1995) p102. "Head Over Heals"
ABDUL, PAULA—PHOTOGRAPHS
PH00012 619-620 (December 12, 1991) p37. "Paula Abdul Steps Up To The Mike" (Zuffante, Vincent)
PH00013 619-620 (December 12, 1991) p33. "Paula Abdul's 'Rush Rush'"
PH00014 622 (January 23, 1992) p7. "Paula Abdul"
PH00015 625 (March 5, 1992) p53. "Abdul Isn't Forever The Readers' Girl" (Silfen, Alan)
ABDUL, PAULA—PHOTOGRAPHS—PORTRAITS
PH00016 667 (October 14, 1993) p98. "Forever Your Girl: Paula Abdul's 'Straight Up' Video Tap-Dances Onto The List"
PH00017 730 (March 21, 1996) p18. "Oh, Kermie! Abdul And Kermit"
ABERDEEN, WASHINGTON—PHOTOGRAPHS
PH00018 683 (June 2, 1994) p45. "Cobain Once Called North Aberdeen Bridge Home" (Berry, Jim)
PH00019 683 (June 2, 1994) p44. "Cobain's Hometown: A Recent Aberdeen Scene" (Winters, Dan)
PH00020 683 (June 2, 1994) p53. "O'Connor's Aberdeen Home" (Berry, Jim)
ABORTIONS—ILLUSTRATIONS
PH00021 670 (November 25, 1993) p8. "Life" (Pendergrast, James T.)
PH00022 716 (September 7, 1995) p39. "Take A Right..." (Witte, Michael)
PH00023 719 (October 19, 1995) p10. "My Body, Your Business" (Pendergrast, James T.)
PH00024 741 (August 22, 1996) p20. "Choice" (Pendergrast, James T.)
ABRAMOVITZ, RAFAEL—PHOTOGRAPHS
PH00025 650 (February 18, 1993) p43. "'The Reporters': Jim Paymar, Dunlop, Bradford, Abramovitz, And Dunleavy (from left)"
ABRIL, VICTORIA—PHOTOGRAPHS
PH00026 621 (January 9, 1992) p56. "Abril (center) And Jailbirds In Fashion"
ABZUG, BELLA—ILLUSTRATIONS
PH00027 645-646 (December 10, 1992) p148. "Bella Abzug, 1977"
ABZUG, BELLA—PHOTOGRAPHS
PH00028 745 (October 17, 1996) p28. "Bonnie Raitt (left) Joins Bella Abzug In Mocking Bob Dole In Chicago" (Natkin, Paul)
AC-DC—ALBUMS
PH00029 721 (November 16, 1995) p112. "Ballbreaker"
AC-DC—ILLUSTRATIONS
PH00030 721 (November 16, 1995) p128. "AC-DC: Big Balls O'Fire" (Gabor, Tim)
ACADEMY AWARDS—ILLUSTRATIONS
PH00031 653 (April 1, 1993) p56. "[Oscars]" (Brodner, Steve)
ACCIDENTALLY ON PURPOSE (TELEVISION SHOW)—PHOTOGRAPHS
PH00032 617 (November 14, 1991) p11. "Cinque And Joie Lee With Pop" (Busacca, Larry)
ACE OF BASE—ALBUMS
PH00033 681 (May 5, 1994) p60. "The Sign"
PH00034 686-687 (July 14, 1994) p124. "The Sign"
ACE OF BASE—ILLUSTRATIONS
PH00035 682 (May 19, 1994) p120. "Swede Success: Ace of Base" (Allen, Terry)
ACE OF BASE—PHOTOGRAPHS—PORTRAITS
PH00036 688 (August 11, 1994) p32. "Aces Jonas, Linn, Ekberg And Jenny (from left)" (Danelian, Stephen)
ACE VENTURA: PET DETECTIVE (FILM)—PHOTOGRAPHS
PH00037 698-699 (December 29, 1994) p196. "The Stupidity Of "Ace Ventura" (top) And "The Flintstones" (above) Mined Gold"
ACE VENTURA: WHEN NATURE CALLS (FILM)—PHOTOGRAPHS
PH00038 722 (November 30, 1995) p74. "Is Jonathan Pryce's Lytton Strachey Wittier Than Jim Carrey's Ace? You Betcha"
ACKER, KATHY—ALBUMS
PH00039 729 (March 7, 1996) p50. "Pussy, King Of The Pirates"
ACKERMAN, WILL—PHOTOGRAPHS—PORTRAITS
PH00040 640 (October 1, 1992) p26. "[Will Ackerman]" (Reitzel, Bill)
ACKERSON, ED—PHOTOGRAPHS
PH00041 711 (June 29, 1995) p23. "Blending '60s Who With Atmospheric Noise: Jurgens, Orris, Ackerson And Wilson (from left)" (Elledge, Paul)
ACLAND, CHRIS—PHOTOGRAPHS—PORTRAITS
PH00042 729 (March 7, 1996) p29. "Lush Members Emma Anderson, Phil King, Miki Berenyi And Chris Acland (from left)" (Anker, Matt)
PH00043 748 (November 28, 1996) p32. "[Chris Acland]"
ACUFF, ROY—PHOTOGRAPHS
PH00044 672-673 (December 23, 1993) p80. "Roy Acuff" (Fowler, Simon)
AD-ROCK—PHOTOGRAPHS
PH00045 726 (January 25, 1996) p17. "Keepin',It Real: Beasties Ad-Rock (left) And MCA" (Papas, B. J.)
ADALITA—PHOTOGRAPHS
PH00046 705 (April 6, 1995) p23. "The Joys Of Noise: Adalita Of Magic Dirt (left) And You Am I's Tim Rogers" (Mott, Tony)
ADAMS, BRYAN—ALBUMS
PH00047 615 (October 17, 1991) p92. "Waking Up The Neighbours"
ADAMS, BRYAN—ILLUSTRATIONS
PH00048 625 (March 5, 1992) p3. "Bryan Adams" (Burke,

Philip)
ADAMS, BRYAN—PHOTOGRAPHS
PH00049 625 (March 5, 1992) p25. "[Bryan Adams]" (Mazur, Kevin)
PH00050 640 (October 1, 1992) p10. "Adams (left) And Def Leppard's Joe Elliott" (Mazur, Kevin)
PH00051 654 (April 15, 1993) p13. "Tina Turner And Bryan Adams" (Mazur, Kevin)
PH00052 672-673 (December 23, 1993) p74. "Below: Sting, Adams And Stewart Pay Homage To Men In Tights" (Wessel, Cathrine)
PH00053 677 (March 10, 1994) p18. "He Does It For Them: Adams With His Fans, Who Sang Along With Him" (Regan, Ken)
PH00054 677 (March 10, 1994) p18. "Hey, Ho, Let's Go: Adams Atop The American Embassy (above)" (Regan, Ken)
PH00055 677 (March 10, 1994) p18. "On The Streets (below)" (Regan, Ken)
PH00056 694 (November 3, 1994) p22. "Pavarotti (left) And Adams"
PH00057 698-699 (December 29, 1994) p36. "Hello, Ho Chi Minh! Adams Rocks Vietnam" (Regan, Ken)
PH00058 736 (June 13, 1996) p19. "The Iggy-esque Guy With Joan Osborne At The VH1 Honors' Benefit? Bryan Adams" (Mazur, Kevin)
PH00059 750-751 (December 26, 1996) p67. "[Bryan Adams]" (Rolston, Matthew)
PH00060 750-751 (December 26, 1996) p67. "Make-Over" (Rama, Raj)
ADAMS, BRYAN—PHOTOGRAPHS—PORTRAITS
PH00061 619-620 (December 12, 1991) p60. "...While Bryan Adams (below) Rolled"
ADAMS, CAROLYN—PHOTOGRAPHS
PH00062 717 (September 21, 1995) p46. "A Moment Of Repose: Jerry Garcia With Carolyn 'Mountain Girl' Adams And Her Daughter, Sunshine, In 1966" (Anthony, Gene)
ADAMS, OLETA—ALBUMS
PH00063 671 (December 9, 1993) p72. "Evolution"
ADAMS, RICHARD—PHOTOGRAPHS
PH00064 628 (April 16, 1992) p56. "Gray, Garside, Johnson And Adams (from left)" (Double, Steve)
ADAMSON, BARRY—ALBUMS
PH00065 665 (September 16, 1993) p72. "The Negro Inside Me"
PH00066 746 (October 31, 1996) p70. "Oedipus Schmoedipus"
THE ADDAMS FAMILY (FILM)—PHOTOGRAPHS
PH00067 618 (November 28, 1991) p53. "They're Altogether Ooky" (Seliger, Mark)
PH00068 618 (November 28, 1991) p56. "They're Creepy, And They're Kooky" (Seliger, Mark)
THE ADDICTION (FILM)—PHOTOGRAPHS
PH00069 719 (October 19, 1995) p159. "Vampire Lili Taylor Stalks The Streets"
ADJANI, ISABELLE—PHOTOGRAPHS
PH00070 700 (January 26, 1995) p66. "Smart Women, Foolish Choices"
PH00071 732 (April 18, 1996) p78. "Stone And Adjani"
ADKINS, MARK—PHOTOGRAPHS
PH00072 715 (August 24, 1995) p23. "Miranda, My Ass: Adkins And His Newfound Friends" (Bain, Rick)
ADOLESCENTS—ILLUSTRATIONS
PH00073 704 (March 23, 1995) p25. "House Arrest" (Fisher, Carolyn)
PH00074 717 (September 21, 1995) p16. "Welcome" (Pendergrast, James T.)
PH00075 719 (October 19, 1995) p10. "Jump Here" (Pendergrast, James T.)
ADOLESCENTS—PHOTOGRAPHS
PH00076 648 (January 21, 1993) p39. "[Seduction]" (Winters, Dan)
PH00077 649 (February 4, 1993) p41. "[Seduction]" (Winters, Dan)
PH00078 716 (September 7, 1995) pp60-62,64,67. "[Montrose]" (Exum)
ADOLPHSON, MATT—PHOTOGRAPHS
PH00079 719 (October 19, 1995) p70. "Adolphson (left) And Scholten Collecting Petition Signatures At Utah's Arches National Park" (McDonough, Patricia)
THE ADVENTURES OF BRISCO COUNTY JR. (TELEVISION SHOW)—PHOTOGRAPHS
PH00080 666 (September 30, 1993) p116. "'Brisco County Jr.'"
THE ADVENTURES OF PRISCILLA, QUEEN OF THE DESERT (FILM)—PHOTOGRAPHS
PH00081 689 (August 25, 1994) p97. "Drag Queens On A Bus: Pearce, Stamp And Weaving"
PH00082 705 (April 6, 1995) p69. "Oscar Rejects"
AEROSMITH—ALBUMS
PH00083 619-620 (December 12, 1991) p177. "Pandora's Box"
PH00084 656 (May 13, 1993) p103. "Get A Grip"
PH00085 658 (June 10, 1993) p86. "Get A Grip"
AEROSMITH—ILLUSTRATIONS
PH00086 672-673 (December 23, 1993) p10. "Mosh Pit" (Pendergrast, James T.)
AEROSMITH—PHOTOGRAPHS
PH00087 626 (March 19, 1992) p13. "Aerosmith" (Granitz, Steve)
PH00088 634-635 (July 9, 1992) p11. "Tom Hamilton, Joe Perry And Tyler (from left) With Museum Curator Helaine Posner" (Putnam, Sarah)
PH00089 647 (January 7, 1993) p14. "Aerosmith In The Studio" (Rubinstein, Bill)
PH00090 657 (May 27, 1993) p11. "Alan Dershowitz (center) With Aerosmith At The Boston Music Awards" (Robicheau, Paul)
PH00091 668 (October 28, 1993) p36. "Steven Tyler (left) And Joe Perry At The Walden Woods Benefit" (Robicheau, Paul)
PH00092 683 (June 2, 1994) p25. "Aerosmith Kickin' In The House Of Blues" (Kirkland, Gene)
PH00093 688 (August 11, 1994) p36. "More Days Of Peace And Music: Aerosmith (above) And Rollins (right)" (Davis, Katharine)
PH00094 688 (August 11, 1994) p36. "More Days Of Peace And Music: Aerosmith (above) And Rollins (right)" (Hutson, Mick)
PH00095 694 (November 3, 1994) p58. "Aerodynamics: Tyler (left) And Joe Perry Live" (Mazur, Kevin)
PH00096 694 (November 3, 1994) p61. "Before The Fall: Aerosmith In 1977 While recording "Draw The Line"" (Pownall, Ron)
PH00097 694 (November 3, 1994) p60. "Early Daze: Whitford, Tyler, Hamilton, Perry And Kramer At Boston College, 1973" (Pownall, Ron)
PH00098 696 (December 1, 1994) p73. "Crazy: Aerosmith Tours Compuserve's Headquarters In September" (Dodge, Tom)
PH00099 700 (January 26, 1995) p55. "Aerosmith's Steven Tyler Recommends The Jon Spencer Blues Explosion" (Seeff, Norman)
PH00100 701 (February 9, 1995) p16. "Aerosmith Score One For The Home Crowd: Onstage At Boston's Mama Kin Music Hall" (Robicheau, Paul)
PH00101 702 (February 23, 1995) p48. "Aerosmith's Joe Perry And Steven Tyler Get Chummy With Led Zep's Robert Plant And Jimmy Page" (Mazur, Kevin)
PH00102 724-725 (December 28, 1995) p40. "Aerosmith's Tom Hamilton, Joey Kramer, Brad Whitford And Steven Tyler (from left)" (Robicheau, Paul)
PH00103 744 (October 3, 1996) p26. "Aerosmith's Joey Kramer, Brad Whitford, Tyler, Perry And Tom Hamilton (from left) At The 1994 MTV Video Music Awards" (Del Grecco, Maria)
AEROSMITH—PHOTOGRAPHS—PORTRAITS
PH00104 670 (November 25, 1993) p85. "[Aerosmith]" (Seliger, Mark)
AFFLECK, CASEY—PHOTOGRAPHS
PH00105 719 (October 19, 1995) p156. "She Glides Her TV-Form Divine Past Gawkers Phoenix, Affleck And Folland"

AFGHAN WHIGS—ALBUMS
PH00106 674 (January 27, 1994) p52. "Gentlemen"
PH00107 730 (March 21, 1996) p95. "Black Love"
AFGHAN WHIGS—ILLUSTRATIONS
PH00108 730 (March 21, 1996) p95. "Heart Of Darkness" (Dodson, Jeff)
AFGHAN WHIGS—PHOTOGRAPHS
PH00109 691 (September 22, 1994) p21. "[Afghan Whigs]" (Moore, Michael)
PH00110 695 (November 17, 1994) p78. "Afghan Whigs" (Lixenberg, Dana)
PH00111 721 (November 16, 1995) p41. "Greg Dulli (left) and John Curley In Robert Lang's Studio, In Seattle" (Peterson, Charles)
AFGHAN WHIGS—PHOTOGRAPHS—PORTRAITS
PH00112 671 (December 9, 1993) p21. "The Whig Club: Rick McCollum, Greg Dulli, Steve Earle And John Curley" (Broad, Julian)
AFRICA—ILLUSTRATIONS
PH00113 626 (March 19, 1992) p54. "Site Of Mass Polio Vaccination, 1957-1960: 325,000 Known Inoculations" (Prato, Rodica)
AFRICA—PHOTOGRAPHS
PH00114 626 (March 19, 1992) p55. "An Africa Child Receives The Polio Vaccine In The Belgian Congo In 1957" (Phillips, Robert)
AFRIKA BAMBAATAA—PHOTOGRAPHS
PH00115 670 (November 25, 1993) p37. "Grandmaster Flash, Herc, Afrika Bambaataa And Chuck D" (Mazur, Kevin)
PH00116 672-673 (December 23, 1993) p142. "Planet Rock's Rap Visionary Afrika Bambaataa" (Low, Dorothy)
AGASSI, ANDRE—PHOTOGRAPHS
PH00117 721 (November 16, 1995) p26. "[Elton John & Andre Agassi]" (Jacobs, Michael)
PH00118 744 (October 3, 1996) p48. "Brooke Shields And Her Fiances, Andre Agassi: 'She Gave Great Fax'"
THE AGE OF INNOCENCE (FILM)—ILLUSTRATIONS
PH00119 666 (September 30, 1993) p111. "Mean Street Circa 1870" (De Seve, Peter)
THE AGE OF INNOCENCE (FILM)—PHOTOGRAPHS
PH00120 666 (September 30, 1993) p112. "Daniel Day-Lewis Nuzzles Michelle Pfeiffer"
PH00121 666 (September 30, 1993) p112. "Director Martin Scorsese Sets Up A Lavish Dinner Party"
PH00122 672-673 (December 23, 1993) p172. "Hot Romance"
PH00123 677 (March 10, 1994) p47. "With Daniel Day-Lewis In 'The Age Of Innocence'"
PH00124 680 (April 21, 1994) p96. "The Age Of Innocence"
PH00125 Number not assigned.
AGNEW, VALERIE—PHOTOGRAPHS
PH00126 722 (November 30, 1995) p19. "Who Are You Callin' A Bitch?: To Wit, Elizabeth Davis, Selene Vigil, Agnew And Roisin Dunne Of 7 Year Bitch (from left)" (Blakesberg, Jay)
AGUILAR, SLICK—PHOTOGRAPHS
PH00127 644 (November 26, 1992) p15. "Kantner, Darby Gould, Jack Casady, Tim Gorman, Prairie Prince, Papa John Creach, McGuinn And Slick Aguilar (from left)" (Mazur, Kevin)
AIDS—ILLUSTRATIONS
PH00128 632 (June 11, 1992) pp150-151. "[AIDS]" (Mahurin, Matt)
PH00129 679 (April 7, 1994) p60. "A Viral Family Tree: The Millions Of Different Variants Of HIV Around The World Are Grouped Into Seven Categories Called Clades"
AIDS—PHOTOGRAPHS
PH00130 618 (November 28, 1991) p65. "At 5:00 a.m., Near The End Of Another Long Night In Patpong, Some Locals Wait For Their Girlfriends, Who Work As Bar Girls" (Zachmann, Patrick)
PH00131 618 (November 28, 1991) p70. "Bangkok Prostitutes Await The Results Of HIV Tests For Their Health Identity Cards, Which Are Demanded By Some Bars" (Zachmann, Patrick)
PH00132 618 (November 28, 1991) p66. "A Bankok Streetwalker Reads A Pamphlet On AIDS Distributed By A Support Organization For Prostitutes, Empower" (Zachmann, Patrick)
PH00133 618 (November 28, 1991) p66. "A Health Worker Gives A Lesson In AIDS Prevention In A Red-Light District" (Zachmann, Patrick)
PH00134 618 (November 28, 1991) pp62-66,69-70. "In A Bangkok Hospital, An Eight-Month-Old Child Suffers From AIDS" (Zachmann, Patrick)
PH00135 618 (November 28, 1991) p65. "In A Bar In Pattaya, A Beach Resort, A Customer Tries To Examine A Possible Purchase" (Zachmann, Patrick)
PH00136 618 (November 28, 1991) p69. "Male Dancers Perform At A Bar In Patpong" (Zachmann, Patrick)
PH00137 618 (November 28, 1991) p69. "A Male Sex Worker Displays His Government Health Identity Card, Which Certifies He's Been Tested This Month For HIV" (Zachmann, Patrick)
PH00138 618 (November 28, 1991) p62. "The Red-Light District Of Patpong" (Zachmann, Patrick)
PH00139 618 (November 28, 1991) p64. "Some Children Are Sold Into Prostitution By Their Parents" (Zachmann, Patrick)
PH00140 618 (November 28, 1991) p63. "Streetwalkers In Another Of The City's Night-Life Sections" (Zachmann, Patrick)
PH00141 618 (November 28, 1991) pp62-66,69-70. "Two Addicts With AIDS Who Have Found Refuge In A Shelter In Bangkok" (Zachmann, Patrick)
PH00142 618 (November 28, 1991) p64. "Where East Meets West: A Bar Girl Encourages A Client" (Zachmann, Patrick)
PH00143 619-620 (December 12, 1991) pp122-123. "[AIDS Victims]" (Nofziger, Christopher)
PH00144 619-620 (December 12, 1991) p125. "Bruce, 27, Moved Home To Maine In March 1991 After He Was Hospitalized" (Nofziger, Christopher)
PH00145 619-620 (December 12, 1991) p130. "Rick, 27, Had To Battle The Virus Without Drugs Like AZT And DDI" (Nofziger, Christopher)
PH00146 633 (June 25, 1992) p6. "[AIDS]" (Fox, Robert)
PH00147 636 (August 6, 1992) p8. "[AIDS}" (Fox, Robert)
PH00148 679 (April 7, 1994) p59. "A Cluster From The Lung Of An AIDS Patient" (Cushion, Melanie)
PH00149 679 (April 7, 1994) p59. "A Cluster Of Pneumocystis From A Rat Lung Shows Many Of Its Forms, Including Spherical Cysts With Daughter Forms Inside" (Ruffolo, John)
PH00150 679 (April 7, 1994) p59. "DuPont Merck's Patrick Lam Between Two Computer Models That Show The Virus's Protease Enzyme Successfully Jammed" (Eckstein, Ed)
PH00151 679 (April 7, 1994) p55. "Some Of The Earliest HIV Variants Ever Identified In The United States Are Among The Virus Samples Kept In Freezers At Northwestern University" (Winters, Dan)
PH00152 742 (September 5, 1996) p24. "Moby Inside Manhattan's Lower East Side Needle Exchange" (Tavee, Tom)
PH00153 742 (September 5, 1996) p24. "Volunteers Distribute Free Condoms And Clean Needles To Clients" (Tavee, Tom)
AIELLO, DANNY—PHOTOGRAPHS
PH00154 628 (April 16, 1992) p93. "Danny Aiello As Jack Ruby Chats Up Sherilyn Fenn"
AILEEN WUORNOS: THE SELLING OF A SERIAL KILLER (FILM)—PHOTOGRAPHS
PH00155 677 (March 10, 1994) p60. "[Aileen Wuornos]"
AIRHEADS (FILM)—PHOTOGRAPHS
PH00156 689 (August 25, 1994) p97. "Rock Wanna-Be's: Sandler, Fraser, Buscemi"
AIRPLANES—PHOTOGRAPHS
PH00157 676 (February 24, 1994) p37. "In 1983, A Field Of B-52s Retired Under The SALT Disarmament Treaty Bask In The Arizona Sun" (Taylor, Randy)

AKER, ALP—PHOTOGRAPHS
PH00158 704 (March 23, 1995) p74. "Nathan's Boss Alp Aker (right) With other Guide Editors" (Asnin, Marc)
ALADDIN (FILM)—ILLUSTRATIONS
PH00159 644 (November 26, 1992) p78. "...And A Cartoon Williams"
PH00160 653 (April 1, 1993) p57. "Aladdin"
ALAN, CARTER—BOOKS
PH00161 645-646 (December 10, 1992) p87. "[Outside Is America]"
ALARD, NELLY—PHOTOGRAPHS
PH00162 642 (October 29, 1992) p77. "Venice-Venice"
ALBARN, DAMON—ILLUSTRATIONS
PH00163 720 (November 2, 1995) p9. "Damon Albarn Of Blur" (Burke, Philip)
ALBARN, DAMON—PHOTOGRAPHS
PH00164 694 (November 3, 1994) p34. "Social Distortion: Blur's Coxon, Albarn, Rowntree And James (from left)" (Westenberg, Kevin)
PH00165 706 (April 20, 1995) p36. "Big Mouth Albarn (center) And Blur" (Lenquette)
PH00166 720 (November 2, 1995) p20. "Coxon (left) And Albarn At A BBC Radio One Gig In London On Sept. 7" (Westenberg, Kevin)
PH00167 737 (June 27, 1996) p16. "Albarn's Bum"
PH00168 737 (June 27, 1996) p16. "Liam Gallagher (left) Of Oasis And Albarn"
ALBARN, DAMON—PHOTOGRAPHS—PORTRAITS
PH00169 623 (February 6, 1992) p32. "Alex James, Damon Albarn, Graham Coxon, Dave Rowntree (clockwise from top)" (Lavine, Michael)
PH00170 720 (November 2, 1995) p19. "'Great Escape' Artists Coxon, Albarn, James And Rountree (from left)" (Westenberg, Kevin)
ALBERT, EDDIE—PHOTOGRAPHS—PORTRAITS
PH00171 666 (September 30, 1993) p116. "Out Of This World 'Green Acres' (left)"
ALBINI, STEVE—PHOTOGRAPHS
PH00172 656 (May 13, 1993) p88. "[Big Black]"
ALDA, ALAN—PHOTOGRAPHS
PH00173 639 (September 17, 1992) p102. "Worst Supporting Actor"
ALDRIN, BUZZ—PHOTOGRAPHS
PH00174 705 (April 6, 1995) p58. "Glory Days: Buzz Aldrin Does The Moonwalk"
ALEXAKIS, ART—PHOTOGRAPHS
PH00175 709 (June 1, 1995) p17. "Alexakis, Craig Montoya And Greg Eklund With Banner From Kids" (Grossman, Amanda)
PH00176 718 (October 5, 1995) p28. "Distortion-Fuzzed Alterna-Rockers Montoya, Alexakis And Eklund (from left)" (Westenberg, Kevin)
PH00177 726 (January 25, 1996) p18. "Everclear's Alexakis (left) And Bassist Craig Montoya Treat The Crowd To A Free Gig In Cali."
PH00178 735 (May 30, 1996) p20. "Everclear's Art Alexakis On Getting Clean: 'You Have To Reinvent Yourself Totally'" (Peterson, Charles)
PH00179 742 (September 5, 1996) p20. "Selene Vigil Of 7 Year Bitch, Langdon, Alexakis And Bonham" (Morganstein, Barry)
ALEXANDER, ARTHUR—ALBUMS
PH00180 662 (August 5, 1993) p64. "Lonely Just Like Me"
ALEXANDER, ARTHUR—PHOTOGRAPHS
PH00181 656 (May 13, 1993) p28. "Soul Legend Arthur Alexander" (Virobik-Adams, Kevin)
ALEXANDER, ARTHUR—PHOTOGRAPHS—PORTRAITS
PH00182 662 (August 5, 1993) p27. "[Arthur Alexander]" (Ockenfels, Frank W.)
ALEXANDER, JASON—PHOTOGRAPHS
PH00183 660-661 (July 8, 1993) p44. "[George Gets Great Women]" (Seliger, Mark)
PH00184 660-661 (July 8, 1993) p41. "Nothing On: Jason Alexander, Julia Louis-Dreyfus, Jerry Seinfeld And Michael Richards" (Seliger, Mark)
PH00185 660-661 (July 8, 1993) pp[cover]. "Seinfeld Rules!" (Seliger, Mark)
PH00186 672-673 (December 23, 1993) p188. "[Covers]" (Seliger, Mark)
ALEXANDER, LAMAR—PHOTOGRAPHS—PORTRAITS
PH00187 730 (March 21, 1996) p51. "Alexander"
ALEXANDER, TIM—PHOTOGRAPHS
PH00188 662 (August 5, 1993) p14. "Les Claypool, Tim Alexander And Larry LaLonde (from left) Of Primus" (Blakesberg, Jay)
ALEXANDER, TIM—PHOTOGRAPHS—PORTRAITS
PH00189 616 (October 31, 1991) p81. "Smooth Sailing: Guitarist Larry Lalonde, Drummer Tim Alexander And Bassist Les Claypool (clockwise from left)" (Seliger, Mark)
ALEXANDER, WILLIE—PHOTOGRAPHS—PORTRAITS
PH00190 736 (June 13, 1996) p20. "Willie, We're Pulling For Ya! Willie Alexander (left) And Peter Wolf, Together Again" (Robicheau, Paul)
ALI, MUHAMMAD—PHOTOGRAPHS
PH00191 645-646 (December 10, 1992) p157. "Muhammad Ali, 1971"
PH00192 712-713 (July 13, 1995) p26. "The Mouths That Roar: Muhammad Ali, Madonna" (Mazur, Kevin)
ALI, MUHAMMAD—PHOTOGRAPHS—PORTRAITS
PH00193 747 (November 14, 1996) p124. "Now Playing"
ALICE IN CHAINS—ALBUMS
PH00194 625 (March 5, 1992) p60. "Facelift"
PH00195 645-646 (December 10, 1992) p179. "Dirt"
PH00196 651 (March 4, 1993) p56. "Dirt"
PH00197 722 (November 30, 1995) p63. "Alice In Chains"
PH00198 744 (October 3, 1996) p71. "Unplugged"
ALICE IN CHAINS—ILLUSTRATIONS
PH00199 695 (November 17, 1994) p129. "Alice In Chains" (Holley, Jason)
PH00200 722 (November 30, 1995) p63. "Alice Comes Clean" (Niemann, Christoph)
ALICE IN CHAINS—PHOTOGRAPHS
PH00201 644 (November 26, 1992) p45. "[Alice In Chains]" (Winters, Dan)
PH00202 662 (August 5, 1993) p13. "Mike Inez, Layne Staley, Jerry Cantrell And Sean Kinney (clockwise from top left) Of Alice In Chains" (Blakesberg, Jay)
PH00203 676 (February 24, 1994) p18. "Chain Reaction: Sean Kinney, Jerry Cantrell, Layne Staley And Mike Inez (from left)" (Moskowitz, Karen)
PH00204 714 (August 10, 1995) p32. "Alice In Chains Join The Hall Of Fame Concert Lineup" (Vadukul, Nitin)
PH00205 723 (December 14, 1995) p28. "Mike Inez, A Fan, Layne Staley, Cantrell (from left) And Ghoulish Pals" (Doughty, Curt)
PH00206 727 (February 8, 1996) p33. "Kinney, Cantrell, Staley And Inez (from left)" (Seliger, Mark)
PH00207 727 (February 8, 1996) p35. "Kinney, Cantrell, Staley And Mike Starr In 1990 (from left)"
PH00208 727 (February 8, 1996) p36. "Staley (left) And Cantrell Performing During LollaPalooza '93" (Eichner, Steve)
ALIEN 3 (FILM)—PHOTOGRAPHS
PH00209 633 (June 25, 1992) p48. "Weaver Is More Sinead Than Sigourney"
ALISON—PHOTOGRAPHS
PH00210 747 (November 14, 1996) p36. "'Ironic Traffic Jam'"
ALIVE (FILM)—PHOTOGRAPHS
PH00211 649 (February 4, 1993) p75. "Ethan Hawke (center) Survives A Plane Crash In The Andes"
ALIVE (VIDEO)—PHOTOGRAPHS
PH00212 667 (October 14, 1993) p100. "It's 'Alive'! 'Give The People A Chance To Visualize Their Own Ideas,' Says Ament"

ALL—PHOTOGRAPHS
PH00213 719 (October 19, 1995) p24. "No Mall Punks For All: Chad Price, Stephen Egerton, Karl Alvarez, Bill Stevenson (from left)" (Corrigan, Daniel)
ALLEN, DAVE—PHOTOGRAPHS
PH00214 626 (March 19, 1992) p20. "God's Little Monkeys (from left): Dave Allen, Jo Swiss, Dave Wall, Jon Townend" (Byrne, Peter)
ALLEN, JOAN—PHOTOGRAPHS
PH00215 726 (January 25, 1996) p64. "Oliver Stone Directs Joan Allen And Anthony Hopkins"
PH00216 749 (December 12, 1996) p90. "Day-Lewis And Allen Fight Back"
ALLEN, PAUL—PHOTOGRAPHS
PH00217 696 (December 1, 1994) p58. "Billionaire Boys' Club: Allen (seated) And Bill Gates Hack At High School"
PH00218 696 (December 1, 1994) p54. "[Paul Allen]" (Seliger, Mark)
ALLEN, RICK—PHOTOGRAPHS
PH00219 667 (October 14, 1993) p26. "Rick Savage, Phil Collen, Vivian Campbell, Rick Allen And Joe Elliott" (Halfin, Ross)
PH00220 715 (August 24, 1995) p30. "Def Leppard's Allen Faces The Music" (Blakesberg, Jay)
PH00221 724-725 (December 28, 1995) p60. "Allen" (Seliger, Mark)
ALLEN, RICK—PHOTOGRAPHS—PORTRAITS
PH00222 629 (April 30, 1992) pp38-39,41. "After The Crash, Allen Had To Battle Drugs And Alcohol" (Seliger, Mark)
ALLEN, WOODY—ILLUSTRATIONS
PH00223 640 (October 1, 1992) p71. "Trouble In Paradise" (Sorel, Edward)
PH00224 664 (September 2, 1993) p68. "Annie Small" (Blitt, Barry)
PH00225 668 (October 28, 1993) p8. "Life—Art" (Pendergrast, James T.)
PH00226 694 (November 3, 1994) p103. "Woody's Comic Gunfire" (Allen, Terry)
PH00227 721 (November 16, 1995) p115. "Woody's Hooker Adventure" (Brodner, Steve)
ALLEN, WOODY—PHOTOGRAPHS
PH00228 628 (April 16, 1992) p91. "Woody Allen Directs Malkovich, Farrow And Madonna"
PH00229 640 (October 1, 1992) p72. "Allen And Farrow Reach An Impasse"
PH00230 640 (October 1, 1992) p72. "Allen Meets Danner, The Mother Of Infatuated Student Lewis"
PH00231 645-646 (December 10, 1992) p190. "Woody Allen And Mia Farrow"
PH00232 648 (January 21, 1993) p56. "Husbands And Wives"
PH00233 649 (February 4, 1993) p72. "[Shadows And Fog]"
PH00234 659 (June 24, 1993) p87. "Dinosaur Summer" (Witte, Michael)
PH00235 664 (September 2, 1993) p69. "'Annie Hall' Lovers Keaton And Allen (left) Reteam In A Romantic 'Mystery'"
PH00236 665 (September 16, 1993) p49. "Filming 'Sleeper' (1973) With Diane Keaton"
PH00237 665 (September 16, 1993) p50. "Pondering The Future In His Penthouse, 1993" (Hamill, Brian)
PH00238 665 (September 16, 1993) p45. "[Woody Allen]" (Hamill, Brian)
PH00239 678 (March 24, 1994) p100. "Missing In Oscar Action"
PH00240 721 (November 16, 1995) p116. "Mira Sorvino's Hooker And Woody Allen"
ALLEN, WOODY—PHOTOGRAPHS—PORTRAITS
PH00241 665 (September 16, 1993) p48. "As A Stand-Up In The Early '60s"
PH00242 665 (September 16, 1993) p46. "As A Young Boy In Brooklyn, N.Y."
ALLISON, LORI—PHOTOGRAPHS
PH00243 625 (March 5, 1992) p27. "Lori Allison, Marty Amsler, Harry Dingman II, Greg Hill (from left)" (Natkin, Paul)
ALLMAN BROTHERS—ALBUMS
PH00244 617 (November 14, 1991) p153. "Eat A Peach" (Holmes, J. F.)
PH00245 617 (November 14, 1991) p153. "Eat A Peach" (Powell, D.)
PH00246 711 (June 29, 1995) p45. "2nd Street"
ALLMAN BROTHERS—PHOTOGRAPHS
PH00247 624 (February 20, 1992) p12. "Gregg Allman (left) And Dickey Betts" (West, Kirk)
PH00248 702 (February 23, 1995) pp48-49. "The Allman Brothers Band" (Mazur, Kevin)
ALLMAN, GREGG—ILLUSTRATIONS
PH00249 686-687 (July 14, 1994) p104. "Gregg Allman" (Cowles, David)
ALLMAN, GREGG—PHOTOGRAPHS
PH00250 617 (November 14, 1991) p13. "Allman (right) In 'Rush'" (Birmelin, Bruce)
PH00251 623 (February 6, 1992) p11. "Toys For Tots: Bob Weir With Gregg Allman" (Blakesberg, Jay)
PH00252 624 (February 20, 1992) p12. "Gregg Allman (left) And Dickey Betts" (West, Kirk)
PH00253 672-673 (December 23, 1993) p28. "Above: Gregg Allman, John Fogerty And Neil Young" (Blakesberg, Jay)
PH00254 693 (October 20, 1994) p80. "Allman And Shannon, Circa 1986"
PH00255 702 (February 23, 1995) p50. "Party On! A Merry-Makin' Allman With Dickey Betts" (Mazur, Kevin)
PH00256 719 (October 19, 1995) p40. "Sheryl Crow And Gregg Allman Chat During Rehearsals" (Corbijn, Anton)
PH00257 746 (October 31, 1996) p18. "Gregg Allman At The Fillmore, Trying To Make A Livin' And Doin' The Best He Can" (Blakesberg, Jay)
ALLMAN, GREGG—PHOTOGRAPHS—PORTRAITS
PH00258 643 (November 12, 1992) p136. "Dickey Betts & Gregg Allman" (Seliger, Mark)
ALMANAC OF THE DEAD (BOOK)—PHOTOGRAPHS
PH00259 652 (March 18, 1993) pp[enc.6]. "Almanac Of The Dead"
ALPERT, RICHARD—PHOTOGRAPHS
PH00260 738-739 (July 11, 1996) p68. "With Alpert At Harvard, 1961"
ALPHIN, KENT—PHOTOGRAPHS—PORTRAITS
PH00261 634-635 (July 9, 1992) p20. "Dillon Fence (from left): Chris Goode, Kent Alphin, Greg Humphreys And Scott Carle" (Thompson, D. Kent)
ALSTON, SHIRLEY—PHOTOGRAPHS
PH00262 728 (February 22, 1996) p18. "Shirelles Shirley Alston, Lee, Doris Kenner (from left): Dedicating It To The Ones They Love" (Mazur, Kevin)
A.L.T.—ALBUMS
PH00263 676 (February 24, 1994) p59. "Stone Cold World"
ALTERNATIVE MUSIC—ILLUSTRATIONS
PH00264 741 (August 22, 1996) p71. "[One-Hype Wonders]" (Hungry Dog Studio)
ALTERNATIVE MUSIC—PHOTOGRAPHS—ILLUSTRATIONS
PH00265 645-646 (December 10, 1992) p43. "[Alternative Music]" (Aitken, Doug)
ALTMAN, ROBERT—PHOTOGRAPHS
PH00266 628 (April 16, 1992) p75. "In 1971, Altman Directed Hollywood Player Warren Beatty In 'McCabe And Mrs. Miller'"
PH00267 645-646 (December 10, 1992) p190. "Artists Or Hitmakers? You Decide: Director Robert Altman And Tim Robbins"
PH00268 667 (October 14, 1993) p126. "Below: Director Robert Altman (right) Catches The Spirit Of Writer Raymond Carver"
PH00269 667 (October 14, 1993) p109. "Director Robert Altman On The Set of 'Short Cuts'" (Rudolph, Joyce)
PH00270 741 (August 22, 1996) p104. "Altman In For The Jazz"

ALTMAN, ROBERT—PHOTOGRAPHS—PORTRAITS
PH00271 628 (April 16, 1992) p73. "[Robert Altman]" (Watson, Albert)
ALTSHULER, LEV—PHOTOGRAPHS—PORTRAITS
PH00272 657 (May 27, 1993) p46. "Physicists Lev Altshuler (above)..." (Altshuler, Lev)
ALVAREZ, KARL—PHOTOGRAPHS
PH00273 719 (October 19, 1995) p24. "No Mall Punks For All: Chad Price, Stephen Egerton, Karl Alvarez, Bill Stevenson (from left)" (Corrigan, Daniel)
ALVIN, DAVE—ALBUMS
PH00274 619-620 (December 12, 1991) p168. "Blue Blvd"
ALVIN, DAVE—ILLUSTRATIONS
PH00275 686-687 (July 14, 1994) p104. "Dave Alvin" (Cowles, David)
ALVIN, DAVE—PHOTOGRAPHS
PH00276 629 (April 30, 1992) p28. "Dave Alvin (right) With Skeletons Lou Whitney (left) And Bobby Lloyd Hicks" (Carrico, John)
AMATEUR (FILM)—PHOTOGRAPHS
PH00277 706 (April 20, 1995) p88. "Young, Huppert, Donovan And Lowensohn Run"
THE AMAZING MR. BICKFORD (VIDEO)—PHOTOGRAPHS
PH00278 684 (June 16, 1994) p25. "The Animation Of Bruce Bickford Outraged Some Pennsylvania Educators" (Gougenheim, Kim)
AMAZING MR. LIFTO—PHOTOGRAPHS
PH00279 639 (September 17, 1992) p62. "Jim Rose And The Amazing Mr. Lifto" (Blakesberg, Jay)
AMBERSUNSHOWER—PHOTOGRAPHS
PH00280 747 (November 14, 1996) p54. "[Ambersunshower]" (Guip, Amy)
AMELIO, GIL—PHOTOGRAPHS
PH00281 732 (April 18, 1996) p62. "New CEO Gil Amelio" (Gropp, Gerry)
AMENT, JEFF—PHOTOGRAPHS
PH00282 616 (October 31, 1991) p15. "Pearl Jam (from left): Mike McCready, David Abbruzzese, Eddie Vedder, Jeff Ament And Stone Gossard" (Cuffaro, Chris)
PH00283 634-635 (July 9, 1992) p13. "Pearl Jam's Mike McCready, Dave Abbruzzese, Eddie Vedder, Gossard And Jeff Ament (from left)" (Mercer, Lance)
PH00284 639 (September 17, 1992) p60. "Eddie Vedder, Mike McCready, Jeff Ament And Stone Gossard (from left) Of Pearl Jam" (Blakesberg, Jay)
PH00285 659 (June 24, 1993) p15. "McCready, Eitzel, Ament, AMC's Vudi And Dan Pearson (from left)" (Blakesberg, Jay)
PH00286 662 (August 5, 1993) p34. "Vedder (left) With Jeff Ament" (Rachlin, Amy)
PH00287 665 (September 16, 1993) p31. "[Elvis Costello, Jeff Ament, Mike McCready]" (Mercer, Lance)
PH00288 668 (October 28, 1993) p60. "Ament, Vedder And McCready Write A Set List" (Seliger, Mark)
PH00289 668 (October 28, 1993) p58. "Pre-Show Shenanigans: Ament Drops His Drawers..." (Seliger, Mark)
PH00290 668 (October 28, 1993) p51. "The Sun Shines On The Five Musketeers: Jeff Ament, Eddie Vedder (We're Not Kidding), Dave Abbruzzese, Stone Gossard And Mike McCready (from left)" (Seliger, Mark)
PH00291 668 (October 28, 1993) p56. "Vedder (on his back) And Bassist Jeff Ament Get Crazy Onstage" (Preston, Neal)
PH00292 668 (October 28, 1993) p57. "Vedder And Ament (flying): Thriving On The Weirdness" (Preston, Neal)
PH00293 672-673 (December 23, 1993) p69. "Us 'Vs.' The World: Gossard, Mike McCready, Dave Abbruzzese, Vedder, Jeff Ament (from left)" (Seliger, Mark)
PH00294 681 (May 5, 1994) p12. "Jeff Ament: Pearl Jam's Ace Of Bass" (Mercer, Lance)
PH00295 688 (August 11, 1994) p30. "Ament (left) And Gossard To Testify Before A House Subcommittee" (Brennan, Shayna)
PH00296 696 (December 1, 1994) p23. "The Annual Bridge School Benefit: Pearl Jam's Jeff Ament And Eddie Vedder (above)" (Blakesberg, Jay)
PH00297 698-699 (December 29, 1994) p60. "Pearl Jam's Jeff Ament And Stone Gossard"
PH00298 702 (February 23, 1995) p26. "Pirate Music: McCready, Vedder, Ament, Irons And Stone Gossard (from left)" (Mercer, Lance)
PH00299 714 (August 10, 1995) p20. "Bassist Jeff Ament: Rocky Mountain High" (Mazur, Kevin)
PH00300 726 (January 25, 1996) p17. "Mike McCready, Jeff Ament, Harper, Eddie Vedder, Jack Irons And Stone Gossard (from left)"
PH00301 727 (February 8, 1996) p17. "Mike McReady, Jeff Ament And Eddie Vedder (from left) Dropped Plans For A Live Pearl Jam Album But Allowed Radio Stations To Distribute Their '95 Concert Recordings For Free" (Ge
PH00302 733 (May 2, 1996) p24. "Pearl Jam's Jeff Ament And Eddie Vedder" (Popplewell, John)
AMENT, JEFF—PHOTOGRAPHS—PORTRAITS
PH00303 740 (August 8, 1996) p28. "[Jeff Ament]" (Mercer, Lance)
AMERASIANS—PHOTOGRAPHS
PH00304 617 (November 14, 1991) p58. "Five Years Ago, Minh Van Truong, 21, Worked As A Farmer Plowing Rice Paddies With Water Buffalos" (Winters, Dan)
PH00305 617 (November 14, 1991) p57. "Nathan Duong, 20, Mary Nguyen's Tenth Adopted Child, Came To The U.S. In November 1990" (Winters, Dan)
PH00306 617 (November 14, 1991) p61. "Nga Thanh Tu, 20, A Black Amerasian, Has No Memory Of Her Father Or Mother" (Winters, Dan)
PH00307 617 (November 14, 1991) p58. "Phung Minh Ton, 19, Was Abandoned In Vietnam And Raised By Buddhist Nuns" (Winters, Dan)
PH00308 617 (November 14, 1991) p61. "Thai The Pham, 21, Arrived In California Just Two Months Ago" (Winters, Dan)
PH00309 617 (November 14, 1991) p56. "Tu-Nga Thi Van, 20, Was Born In Nha Trang, Vietnam, And Arrived In The United States In March, 1991" (Winters, Dan)
AMERICA IS DYING SLOWLY (ALBUM)—PHOTOGRAPHS
PH00310 742 (September 5, 1996) p23. "Red Hot's Rainbow Coalition"
AMERICA ONLINE (COMPANY)—ILLUSTRATIONS
PH00311 747 (November 14, 1996) p20. "Modem-Condom" (Pendergrast, James T.)
AMERICAN BANDSTAND (TELEVISION SHOW)—PHOTOGRAPHS
PH00312 731 (April 4, 1996) p33. "'70s Style Gods Get Down"
PH00313 731 (April 4, 1996) p33. "Bicentennial Sock Patrol, 1976"
PH00314 750-751 (December 26, 1996) p46. "We Are The Goon Squad, And We're Coming To Town: American Bandstand"
AMERICAN BUFFALO (FILM)—PHOTOGRAPHS
PH00315 744 (October 3, 1996) p78. "Now Playing"
AMERICAN CULTURE—ILLUSTRATIONS
PH00316 636 (August 6, 1992) p33. "[America]" (Cronin, Brian)
PH00317 656 (May 13, 1993) p88. "[Old Soul]" (Clayton, Christian)
PH00318 741 (August 22, 1996) p74. "[Confusion]" (Clarke, Greg)
AMERICAN CULTURE—ILLUSTRATIONS—LETTERING
PH00319 630 (May 14, 1992) pp41-43,45-46+. "Hot" (Ortiz-Lopez, Dennis)
AMERICAN CULTURE—PHOTOGRAPHS
PH00320 656 (May 13, 1993) pp61,63,65,67+. "Hot" (Rosa, Doug)
PH00321 660-661 (July 8, 1993) p58. "Is She A Spur Girl?" (Smale, Brian)
PH00322 660-661 (July 8, 1993) p58. "Posse Within A Posse: A rat Packer Flying Colors" (Smale, Brian)

AMERICAN GOTHIC (TELEVISION SHOW)—PHOTOGRAPHS
PH00323 716 (September 7, 1995) p84. "Gary Cole's Psycho Psychic Cop From American Gothic"
AMERICAN HEART (FILM)—PHOTOGRAPHS
PH00324 658 (June 10, 1993) p74. "Jailbird Bridges Finds A Son To Protect In Furlong"
AMERICAN INDIAN RESERVATIONS—PHOTOGRAPHS
PH00325 736 (June 13, 1996) p67. "Petroglyphs Overlook The Proposed Site Where 4,000 Bunkers Would Be Built" (Barker, Kent)
AMERICAN INDIANS—ILLUSTRATIONS
PH00326 740 (August 8, 1996) p14. "[Rabbit]" (Pendergrast, James T.)
AMERICAN MUSIC CLUB—ALBUMS
PH00327 619-620 (December 12, 1991) p187. "Everclear"
PH00328 654 (April 15, 1993) p61. "Mercury"
PH00329 696 (December 1, 1994) p122. "San Francisco"
AMERICAN MUSIC CLUB—PHOTOGRAPHS
PH00330 659 (June 24, 1993) p15. "McCready, Eitzel, Ament, AMC's Vudi And Dan Pearson (from left)" (Blakesberg, Jay)
PH00331 690 (September 8, 1994) p25. "[American Music Club]" (Blakesberg, Jay)
PH00332 695 (November 17, 1994) p131. "American Music Club" (Duke, William)
PH00333 698-699 (December 29, 1994) p68. "AMC: Down And Out In San Francisco" (Keeley, Dennis)
PH00334 742 (September 5, 1996) p23. "[American Music Club]" (Blakesberg, Jay)
AMERICAN MUSIC CLUB—PHOTOGRAPHS—PORTRAITS
PH00335 656 (May 13, 1993) p77. "American Music Club (from left): Danny Pearson, Tim Mooney, Vudi, Bruce Kaphan And Mark Eitzel" (Ockenfels, Frank, 3)
THE AMERICAN PRESIDENT (FILM)—PHOTOGRAPHS
PH00336 722 (November 30, 1995) p76. "Annette Bening As His Hot Date"
PH00337 722 (November 30, 1995) p76. "Michael J. Fox As His Trouble-Shooter"
AMES, ALDRICH—PHOTOGRAPHS
PH00338 704 (March 23, 1995) p52. "Spy-Turned-Traitor Aldrich Ames Tried To Undermine The CIA"
PH00339 711 (June 29, 1995) p38. "After A Hearing, The Couple Says Goodbye"
PH00340 711 (June 29, 1995) pp34-35. "FBI Tapes Show Ames Trying To Meet With The KGB In Bogota In 1993"
PH00341 711 (June 29, 1995) p37. "Feb. 21, 1994: FBI Agents Blocked Ames' Car And Arrested Him" (Hallisey, John)
PH00342 711 (June 29, 1995) p38. "'Money Was The Motivation,' Ames Says Now"
AMES, ALDRICH—PHOTOGRAPHS—PORTRAITS
PH00343 711 (June 29, 1995) p36. "Aldrich Ames (right) Began Working With His Father, Carleton, At The CIA In High School"
PH00344 711 (June 29, 1995) p37. "Ames And his Wife, Rosario, Whom he Met While Stationed In Mexico City, Were Both Charged With Espionage"
AMES, CARLETON—PHOTOGRAPHS—PORTRAITS
PH00345 711 (June 29, 1995) p36. "Aldrich Ames (right) Began Working With His Father, Carleton, At The CIA In High School"
AMES, ROSARIO—PHOTOGRAPHS
PH00346 711 (June 29, 1995) p38. "After A Hearing, The Couple Says Goodbye"
PH00347 711 (June 29, 1995) p38. "Rosario Ames Received A Five-Year Sentence"
AMES, ROSARIO—PHOTOGRAPHS—PORTRAITS
PH00348 711 (June 29, 1995) p37. "Ames And his Wife, Rosario, Whom he Met While Stationed In Mexico City, Were Both Charged With Espionage"
AMHERST COLLEGE—PHOTOGRAPHS
PH00349 626 (March 19, 1992) p70. "Hard To Handle: Long Coveted By Amherst's Student Body, Sabrina Gets Around"
AMICK, MADCHEN—PHOTOGRAPHS
PH00350 683 (June 2, 1994) p78. "Amick Gets Spader In Her Sex Vise"
AMIS, MARTIN—PHOTOGRAPHS—PORTRAITS
PH00351 715 (August 24, 1995) p82. "Hot Writers" (Cook, Nick)
AMIS, SUZY—PHOTOGRAPHS
PH00352 663 (August 19, 1993) p83. "Suzy Amis As The Beautiful Josephine (left) And As Little Jo, A Tough Hombre In The Wild, Sexist West"
AMONGST FRIENDS (FILM)—PHOTOGRAPHS
PH00353 662 (August 5, 1993) p73. "Guy Talk From Parlavecchio, McGaw And Lambson"
AMOS, TORI—ALBUMS
PH00354 627 (April 2, 1992) p46. "Little Earthquakes"
PH00355 676 (February 24, 1994) p59. "Under The Pink"
PH00356 698-699 (December 29, 1994) p185. "Under The Pink"
PH00357 727 (February 8, 1996) p48. "Boys For Pele"
AMOS, TORI—ILLUSTRATIONS
PH00358 685 (June 30, 1994) p7. "Tori Amos" (Burke, Philip)
PH00359 690 (September 8, 1994) p16. "Famous Tori Amos Cookies" (Pendergrast, James T.)
PH00360 727 (February 8, 1996) p48. "She Walks The Line" (Mahurin, Matt)
AMOS, TORI—PHOTOGRAPHS
PH00361 685 (June 30, 1994) p68. "Amos Playing Piano For A Church Program At 15"
PH00362 685 (June 30, 1994) p68. "Behind The Keys In North Carolina At Age 2"
PH00363 691 (September 22, 1994) p20. "[Michael Stipe & Tori Amos]" (Diamond, Rick)
PH00364 701 (February 9, 1995) p17. "Spicy (left) And Yogurt, But Shaved, Take A Break" (Kravitz, Jeff)
PH00365 737 (June 27, 1996) p15. "Valletta (left) Hugs Amos, Who Introduced Her Onstage Piano As "My New Little Friend"" (Busacca, Larry)
AMOS, TORI—PHOTOGRAPHS—PORTRAITS
PH00366 629 (April 30, 1992) p31. "[Tori Amos]" (Counts, Wyatt)
PH00367 645-646 (December 10, 1992) p59. "Tori Amos" (Counts, Wyatt)
PH00368 651 (March 4, 1993) p48. "New Kid On The Block: Tori Amos" (Blakesberg, Jay)
PH00369 685 (June 30, 1994) p67. "[Tori Amos]" (Meier, Raymond)
PH00370 692 (October 6, 1994) p49. "Tori Amos" (Counts, Wyatt)
PH00371 695 (November 17, 1994) p28. "Tori Amos" (Mahurin, Matt)
PH00372 698-699 (December 29, 1994) p37. "Tori-osity: (In)famous Amos" (Ridgers, Derek)
AMPS—ALBUMS
PH00373 723 (December 14, 1995) p82. "Pacer"
AMSLER, MARTY—PHOTOGRAPHS
PH00374 625 (March 5, 1992) p27. "Lori Allison, Marty Amsler, Harry Dingman II, Greg Hill (from left)" (Natkin, Paul)
AMSTERDAM, NETHERLANDS—PHOTOGRAPHS
PH00375 700 (January 26, 1995) p38. "The Dutch Solution: A "Coffee Shop" In Amsterdam" (Merillon, Georges)
ANASTASI, AMRIN—PHOTOGRAPHS
PH00376 706 (April 20, 1995) pp[enc.14]. "Huntington Beach High Surf Team" (Seliger, Mark)
ANASTASIO, TREY—PHOTOGRAPHS
PH00377 631 (May 28, 1992) p16. "Phish (from left): Trey Anastasio, Mike Gordon, Page McConnell, Jon Fishman" (Halsband, Michael)
PH00378 702 (February 23, 1995) p35. "Phishman Trey Anastasio Comes Up For Air" (Robicheau, Paul)
ANCHORAGE, KENTUCKY—ILLUSTRATIONS
PH00379 733 (May 2, 1996) p10. "Entering Anchorage"

(Pendergrast, James T.)
AND THE BAND PLAYED ON (FILM)—PHOTOGRAPHS
PH00380 666 (September 30, 1993) p113. "A TV Movie That Matters"
ANDERSEN, ERIC—ALBUMS
PH00381 674 (January 27, 1994) p54. "Danko-Fjeld-Andersen"
ANDERSON, BRETT—ILLUSTRATIONS
PH00382 657 (May 27, 1993) p3. "Brett Anderson Of Suede" (Burke, Philip)
ANDERSON, BRETT—PHOTOGRAPHS
PH00383 657 (May 27, 1993) p15. "Ultra Suede: Gilbert, Anderson, Osman, Butler (from left)" (Broad, Julian)
PH00384 657 (May 27, 1993) p16. "Wilde Thing: Anderson"
PH00385 671 (December 9, 1993) p26. "Ultra-Suede: Frontman Brett Anderson" (Mazur, Kevin)
PH00386 705 (April 6, 1995) p36. "Brett Anderson: Pirouettes And Pounding Power" (Capak, R. J.)
ANDERSON, BRETT—PHOTOGRAPHS—PORTRAITS
PH00387 662 (August 5, 1993) p60. "Brett Anderson" (Lenquette)
ANDERSON, BRIAN—PHOTOGRAPHS
PH00388 705 (April 6, 1995) p57. "Mutiny On The Bounty: NASA's Pirates Perrine, Anderson And Muratore (from left)" (Turner, Danny)
ANDERSON, CARLEEN—PHOTOGRAPHS
PH00389 628 (April 16, 1992) p57. "Carleen Anderson, Marc Nelson And Femi Williams (from left)"
ANDERSON, EMMA—PHOTOGRAPHS
PH00390 729 (March 7, 1996) p29. "Lush Members Emma Anderson, Phil King, Miki Berenyi And Chris Acland (from left)" (Anker, Matt)
ANDERSON, GILLIAN—PHOTOGRAPHS
PH00391 734 (May 16, 1996) pp38-39. "David Duchovny, Gillian Anderson & Chris Carter" (Montalbetti-Campbell)
PH00392 734 (May 16, 1996) p42. "Gillian Anderson During Her Punk Phase, In London In 1985"
PH00393 734 (May 16, 1996) pp[cover]. "'X' Files Under Cover" (Montalbetti-Campbell)
ANDERSON, IAN—PHOTOGRAPHS
PH00394 668 (October 28, 1993) p26. "[Ian Anderson]" (Jana)
ANDERSON, JEFF—PHOTOGRAPHS
PH00395 694 (November 3, 1994) p104. "Clerks Anderson And O'Halloran Discuss The Forbidden"
ANDERSON, LAURIE—ALBUMS
PH00396 697 (December 15, 1994) p95. "Bright Red"
ANDERSON, LAURIE—PHOTOGRAPHS
PH00397 684 (June 16, 1994) p25. "Anderson: Traveling Bible Show" (Victor, Pascal)
PH00398 706 (April 20, 1995) p33. "Laurie Anderson" (Leibovitz, Annie)
PH00399 719 (October 19, 1995) p42. "This Magic Moment: Lou Reed Gives His Best To Laurie Anderson Backstage" (Corbijn, Anton)
PH00400 735 (May 30, 1996) p13. "Laurie Anderson, Reed And Wareham (from left) Post-Gig At Josie's, In New York" (Roberts, Ebet)
ANDERSON, MICHAEL—PHOTOGRAPHS
PH00401 639 (September 17, 1992) p103. "Anderson (left) And MacLachlan Lost In Lynchland"
ANDERSON, PAMELA—PHOTOGRAPHS
PH00402 705 (April 6, 1995) p17. "[Pamela Anderson]"
PH00403 706 (April 20, 1995) p15. "Tommy Lee And Pamela Anderson Still Married At Press Time" (Kravitz, Jeff)
PH00404 708 (May 18, 1995) p18. "[Tommy Lee & Pamela Anderson]" (Gerber, M.)
PH00405 724-725 (December 28, 1995) p46. "[Pamela Anderson & Tommy Lee]" (Gerber, Mitch)
PH00405a 734 (May 16, 1996) p72. "Pamela Anderson Lee"
PH00405b 750 (December 26, 1996) pp[cover]. "Beavis & Butthead Go To Hollywood: Guesr Starring Pamela Anderson Lee" (Seliger, Mark)
ANDERSON, THOMAS—ALBUMS
PH00406 653 (April 1, 1993) p54. "Blues For The Flying Dutchman"
ANDRE, ALFONSO—PHOTOGRAPHS
PH00407 662 (August 5, 1993) p17. "Andre, Saul Hernandez, Alejando Marcovech" (Mazur, Kevin)
ANDREESSEN, MARC—PHOTOGRAPHS
PH00408 722 (November 30, 1995) pp[enc.22]. "[Marc Andreessen]" (McLeod, William Mercer)
ANDREWS, JASON—PHOTOGRAPHS
PH00409 722 (November 30, 1995) p74. "Quick Sex: Flynn, Andrews"
ANGIE (FILM)—PHOTOGRAPHS
PH00410 678 (March 24, 1994) p104. "Two Babes And A Hunk: Davis (Angie); Stowe (China Moon); Grant (Four Weddings)"
ANGUS, DAVID—PHOTOGRAPHS
PH00411 631 (May 28, 1992) p61. "Angus (left) And Hart Probe A Beatles Love Story"
ANIMAL RIGHTS—ILLUSTRATIONS
PH00412 712-713 (July 13, 1995) p20. "Glue" (Pendergrast, James T.)
ANIMALS—ILLUSTRATIONS
PH00413 694 (November 3, 1994) p33. "[Artwork]" (Johnston, Daniel)
ANIMALS—PHOTOGRAPHS
PH00414 676 (February 24, 1994) p48. "The Angry Young Animals (from left): Drummer John Steel, Organist Alan Price, bass Player Chas Chandler, Lead Singer Eric Burdon And Guitarist Hilton Valentine"
PH00415 677 (March 10, 1994) p28. "Pirner With Animals Valentine, Chas Chandler And John Steel" (Mazur, Kevin)
ANISTON, JENNIFER—ILLUSTRATIONS
PH00416 732 (April 18, 1996) p16. "Rolling Stone" (Pendergrast, James T.)
ANISTON, JENNIFER—PHOTOGRAPHS
PH00417 708 (May 18, 1995) pp[cover]. "Fast Friends: No Sex Bad Jobs Hit Show Go Figure" (Seliger, Mark)
PH00418 708 (May 18, 1995) p. "Matt LeBlanc, Jennifer Aniston, David Schwimmer, Courteney Cox, Lisa Kudrow, Matthew Perry" (Seliger, Mark)
PH00419 729 (March 7, 1996) p38. "Aniston (bottom right) In The Zitcom Ferris Bueller"
PH00420 729 (March 7, 1996) pp[cover[. "The Girl Friend: Jennifer Aniston" (Seliger, Mark)
PH00421 729 (March 7, 1996) pp34-35,37. "[Jennifer Aniston]" (Seliger, Mark)
PH00422 741 (August 22, 1996) p105. "Burns, Bahns, Diaz, Aniston, McGlone"
ANISTON, JENNIFER—PHOTOGRAPHS—PORTRAITS
PH00423 729 (March 7, 1996) p36. "In 1987, In The Fame-School Yearbook"
ANNIE HALL (FILM)—PHOTOGRAPHS
PH00424 664 (September 2, 1993) p69. "'Annie Hall' Lovers Keaton And Allen (left) Reteam In A Romantic 'Mystery'"
ANSANI, TED—PHOTOGRAPHS
PH00425 712-713 (July 13, 1995) p25. "[Liz Phair & Material Issue]" (Natkin, Paul)
ANSELMO, PHIL—PHOTOGRAPHS
PH00426 685 (June 30, 1994) p24. "Rex, Dimebag Darrell, Vinnie Paul And Phil Anselmo (clockwise from left)" (Winters, Dan)
ANT, ADAM—ILLUSTRATIONS
PH00427 706 (April 20, 1995) p80. "Adam Ant" (Carroll, Tim)
ANT, ADAM—PHOTOGRAPHS
PH00428 702 (February 23, 1995) p19. "[Trent Reznor & Adam Ant]" (Cultice, Joseph)
PH00429 724-725 (December 28, 1995) p39. "Goody-Two-Shoes

Trent Reznor Helped Resurrect Adam Ant (left)" (Cultice, Joseph)
ANTENNA—ALBUMS
PH00430 618 (November 28, 1991) p96. "Sway"
PH00431 655 (April 29, 1993) p65. "Hideout"
ANTENNAS—PHOTOGRAPHS
PH00432 670 (November 25, 1993) p129. "AudioPrism High-Q 6500 FM Indoor Antenna, $70" (Miller, Greg)
ANTHONY, MICHAEL—PHOTOGRAPHS
PH00433 650 (February 18, 1993) p16. "Alex, Eddie, Anthony, Hagar (from left)"
ANTHONY, TREVOR—PHOTOGRAPHS
PH00434 704 (March 23, 1995) pp102-103. "Class of '95" (Tavee, Tom)
ANTHRAX—ALBUMS
PH00435 659 (June 24, 1993) p83. "Sound Of White Noise"
ANTHRAX—PHOTOGRAPHS
PH00436 619-620 (December 12, 1991) p88. "PE And Anthrax" (Natkin, Paul)
PH00437 656 (May 13, 1993) p31. "Noisemakers Ian, Dan Spitz, Bush, Frankie Bello And Benante (from left)" (Mazur, Kevin)
PH00438 722 (November 30, 1995) p34. "Totally Ruled By Instinct: Band Members Charlie Benante, Scott Ian, John Bush And Frank Bello (from left)" (Cultice, Joseph)
ANWAR, GABRIELLE—PHOTOGRAPHS
PH00439 647 (January 7, 1993) p50. "Blind Al Pacino Savors A Last Tango With Gabrielle Anwar"
PH00440 669 (November 11, 1993) p80. "Fright Sights (from left): 'Body Snatchers' 1956, 1978, 1993"
PH00441 719 (October 19, 1995) p158. "Andy Garcia Sweet-Talks Gabrielle Anwar Into Danger"
ANWAR, GABRIELLE—PHOTOGRAPHS—PORTRAITS
PH00442 656 (May 13, 1993) p68. "[Gabrielle Anwar]" (Guzman)
APACHE INDIAN—PHOTOGRAPHS
PH00443 668 (October 28, 1993) p25. "Apache Indian: Summer Sound"
APARTHEID—ILLUSTRATIONS
PH00444 632 (June 11, 1992) p181. "[Apartheid]" (Cronin, Brian)
APARTMENTS—ALBUMS
PH00445 711 (June 29, 1995) p43. "A Life Full Of Farewells"
APHEX TWIN—ALBUMS
PH00446 685 (June 30, 1994) p72. "Selected Ambient Works Vol. II"
PH00447 707 (May 4, 1995) p65. "I Care Because You Do"
APOLLO 9—PHOTOGRAPHS
PH00447a 689 (August 25, 1994) p44. "All Together Now: Trombino, Atom, Kennedy, Reis, N.D., Petey X, Apollo 9, Froberg (from left)" (Cuffaro, Chris)
APOLLO THEATER—PHOTOGRAPHS
PH00447b 643 (November 12, 1992) p56. "...Popsie Covered The Action At Places Like Harlem's Apollo Theater" (Randolph, Popsie)
APOLLO 13 (FILM)—ILLUSTRATIONS
PH00448 712-713 (July 13, 1995) p113. "Fire Rockets 1, 2, 3" (Allen, Terry)
APOLLO 13 (FILM)—PHOTOGRAPHS
PH00449 709 (June 1, 1995) p68. "Oscar Seekers"
PH00450 712-713 (July 13, 1995) p116. "'Apollo 13' Astronauts Hanks And Bacon Blast Off; And Harris Waits In Houston"
PH00451 724-725 (December 28, 1995) p136. "The 10 Best movies Of 1995 (degrees of size)"
PH00452 731 (April 4, 1996) p66. "'Apollo 13,' With Tom Hanks"
PH00453 Number not assigned.
PH00454 Number not assigned.
APPLE COMPUTERS—ILLUSTRATIONS
PH00455 735 (May 30, 1996) p10. "Before Media—After Media" (Pendergrast, James T.)
APPLE COMPUTERS—PHOTOGRAPHS
PH00456 Number not assigned.
PH00457 731 (April 4, 1996) p55. "Flags Flying High At Apple's Cupertino, Calif., Headquarters"
PH00458 731 (April 4, 1996) p54. "Jobs' Mythical Garage"
PH00458a 731 (April 4, 1996) p56. "The '1984' Super Bowl Spot, Which Ridley Scott Directed"
PH00459 731 (April 4, 1996) p54. "The Original Apple"
PH00460 731 (April 4, 1996) p52. "Several Members Of Team Mac Showing Off The Fruits Of Their Labor" (Seeff, Norman)
APPLE, FIONA—PHOTOGRAPHS
PH00461 746 (October 31, 1996) p84. "[Fiona Apple]" (Rolston, Matthew)
APPLETON, WISCONSIN—PHOTOGRAPHS
PH00462 728 (February 22, 1996) p54. "Baker Of The Langlade Sheriff's Department..." (Smale, Brian)
PH00463 728 (February 22, 1996) p53. "The Last Ride: Cops Inspect The Mysterious Bullet Hole In The Windshield" (Courtney, Mark)
PH00464 728 (February 22, 1996) p48. "Near The North Lot: 'The Cops Won't Acknowledge The Truth,' Says An 18-Year-Old Gang Member" (Smale, Brian)
PH00465 728 (February 22, 1996) p49. "Suicide Or Murder? Either Way The Weapon Was The Raven .25-Caliber Semiautomatic Handgun" (Smale, Brian)
APT. Q258—PHOTOGRAPHS
PH00466 631 (May 28, 1992) p16. "The Rescue Unit (from left): Matt Mundy, Oteil Burbridge, Col. Bruce Hampton, Jimmy Herring And Apt. Q258" (Frazier, Jeff)
AQUANETTAS—PHOTOGRAPHS
PH00467 668 (October 28, 1993) p36. "The Aquanettas: Say It, Don't Spray It" (Govoni, Tricia)
ARAYA, TOM—PHOTOGRAPHS
PH00468 705 (April 6, 1995) p36. "Live Evil: Araya (left) And King" (Mazur, Kevin)
ARC ANGELS—ALBUMS
PH00469 634-635 (July 9, 1992) p107. "Arc Angels"
ARC ANGELS—PHOTOGRAPHS
PH00470 630 (May 14, 1992) p25. "Chris Layton, Tommy Shannon, Doyle Bramhall II, Charlie Sexton (from left)" (Pumphrey, Steve)
ARCHER, ANNE—PHOTOGRAPHS
PH00471 667 (October 14, 1993) p126. "Above: A Cop (Tim Robbins) And A Clown (Anne Archer) Enjoy A Chance Encounter"
ARCHER, TASMIN—ALBUMS
PH00472 659 (June 24, 1993) p83. "Great Expectations"
ARCHER, WINSTON—PHOTOGRAPHS
PH00473 715 (August 24, 1995) pp90-91. "On The Court In Thompkins Park" (Danelian, Stephen)
ARCHERS OF LOAF—ALBUMS
PH00474 710 (June 15, 1995) p96. "Vee Vee"
ARCHITECTURE—PHOTOGRAPHS
PH00475 656 (May 13, 1993) p90. "[Kuwait Pavilion]" (Linden, John Edward)
ARISTIDE, JEAN-BERTRAND—PHOTOGRAPHS
PH00476 704 (March 23, 1995) p52. "The CIA Tried To Undermine Haiti's Jean-Bertrand Aristide" (Stone, Les)
PH00477 Number not assigned.
ARM, MARK—ILLUSTRATIONS
PH00478 709 (June 1, 1995) p9. "Mudhoney's Mark Arm" (Burke, Philip)
ARM, MARK—PHOTOGRAPHS
PH00479 628 (April 16, 1992) p48. "Mudhoney's Lukin, Turner, Peters And Arm (from left)" (Seliger, Mark)
PH00480 642 (October 29, 1992) p39. "Beery But Brutal: Mark Arm Of Mudhoney" (Taylor, Chris)
PH00480a 655 (April 29, 1993) p11. "Charo Relives The 'Love Boat' Days With Mark Arm"
PH00481 668 (October 28, 1993) p35. "Mudhoney's Mark Arm"

(Dugdale, Bruce)
PH00482 670 (November 25, 1993) p38. "Mudhoney Guitarist Steve Turner, Gilmore And Guitarist Mark Arm" (Peterson, Charles)
PH00483 679 (April 7, 1994) p38. "Arm In Arms: Arm, Vedder And Gilmore"
PH00484 695 (November 17, 1994) p90. "Mudhoney" (Ragel, Jon)
PH00485 700 (January 26, 1995) p32. "Lukin, Arm, Turner (from left)" (Blakesberg, Jay)
PH00486 709 (June 1, 1995) p47. "Mark Arm" (Winters, Dan)
PH00487 709 (June 1, 1995) p48. "Seattle Mudslingers: Turner, Arm, Lukin And Peters (from left)" (Winters, Dan)
ARMANI, GIORGIO—PHOTOGRAPHS
PH00488 750-751 (December 26, 1996) p81. "Winona Ryder, Giorgio Armani, And Jakob Dylan (from left)" (Mazur, Kevin)
ARMEY, DICK—PHOTOGRAPHS—PORTRAITS
PH00489 719 (October 19, 1995) p49. "Armey"
PH00490 720 (November 2, 1995) p60. "Armey, One Of Congress' Most Powerful Republicans, Has Ties To Pratt" (Markowitz, Jeffrey)
ARMSTRONG, BILLIE JOE—PHOTOGRAPHS
PH00491 724-725 (December 28, 1995) p32. "[Billie Joe Armstrong]" (Seliger, Mark)
PH00492 724-725 (December 28, 1995) p34. "Billie Joe Armstrong Lets His Slip Show In Berkeley, June 1993" (Popplewell, John)
PH00493 724-725 (December 28, 1995) p30. "Punk Rock In Action: Armstrong Onstage In San Francisco Last June" (Jennings, Steve)
PH00494 724-725 (December 28, 1995) p29. "Tre Cool, Billy Joe Armstrong, Mike Dirnt" (Seliger, Mark)
PH00495 726 (January 25, 1996) p38. "Billie Joe Armstrong (left) And Mike Dirnt Of Green Day" (Olson, Sheryl)
ARMSTRONG, BILLIE JOE—PHOTOGRAPHS—PORTRAITS
PH00496 738-739 (July 11, 1996) p87. "Green Day's Billie Joe Armstrong Acts Oblivious"
ARMSTRONG, LANCE—PHOTOGRAPHS
PH00497 626 (March 19, 1992) p82. "[Lance Armstrong]" (Hanauer, Mark)
ARMSTRONG, TIM—ILLUSTRATIONS
PH00498 716 (September 7, 1995) p7. "Rancid's Tim Armstrong" (Burke, Philip)
ARMSTRONG, TIM—PHOTOGRAPHS
PH00499 712-713 (July 13, 1995) p25. "Hey Who's Working The Door?" (Aguiar, Mariah)
PH00500 716 (September 7, 1995) p56. "Frederiksen And Armstrong Perfect The Art Of Speed Skanking At A Milwaukee Gig" (Garrity, Brian)
PH00501 716 (September 7, 1995) p59. "Gilman Street, Back In The Day: Armstrong Bodysurfs At An Operation Ivy Show In 1987" (Bowles, Murray)
PH00502 716 (September 7, 1995) pp54-55. "Rancid: Lars Frederiksen, Tim Armstrong, Brett Reed, Matt Freeman (clockwise from top left)" (Vadukul, Nitin)
PH00503 718 (October 5, 1995) p20. "[Tim Armstrong]" (Cadiente, Tim)
PH00504 726 (January 25, 1996) p38. "Rancid's Tim Armstrong (left) And Lara Frederiksen" (Garrity, Brian)
PH00505 727 (February 8, 1996) p12. "Woodpussy's Michel Cicero, Rancid's Tim Armstrong, Iggy, The Offspring's Dexter Holland (from left)" (Buzzerio, Johnny)
PH00506 735 (May 30, 1996) p13. "Do You Feel Lucky Today?"
ARMSTRONG, TIM—PHOTOGRAPHS—PORTRAITS
PH00507 701 (February 9, 1995) p29. "Mohawk Nation: Reed, Freeman, Armstrong And Frederiksen (from left)" (Muller, Michael)
ARNAUD, DELMAR—PHOTOGRAPHS
PH00508 720 (November 2, 1995) p32. "Demons Of The Week: Kurupt And Daz (from left)"
ARNOLD, GINA—BOOKS
PH00509 665 (September 16, 1993) p25. "Route 666: On The Road To Nirvana"
ARNOLD, TOM—ILLUSTRATIONS
PH00510 682 (May 19, 1994) p68. "[White Trash]" (Friedman, Drew)
ARNOLD, TOM—PHOTOGRAPHS
PH00511 678 (March 24, 1994) p28. "[MTV's Rock n' Jock Softball Challenge]"
ARQUETTE, DAVID—PHOTOGRAPHS
PH00512 732 (April 18, 1996) pp[enc.cover+]. "[David Arquette]" (Witkin, Christian)
ARQUETTE, PATRICIA—PHOTOGRAPHS
PH00513 666 (September 30, 1993) p112. "Slater (right) Comforts A Bloody Arquette"
PH00514 709 (June 1, 1995) p68. "Oscar Seekers"
PH00515 716 (September 7, 1995) p77. "Patricia Arquette Finds It's A Jungle Out There"
PH00516 721 (November 16, 1995) p96. "Cage, With Patricia Arquette, Calls Their Surprise Marriage 'Off-The-Wall'" (P.A.G.)
ARQUETTE, ROSANNA—PHOTOGRAPHS
PH00517 692 (October 6, 1994) p45. "Winona Ryder, Phair And Rosanna Arquette In Santa Monica, 1994" (Kravitz, Jeff)
ARQUETTE, ROSANNA—PHOTOGRAPHS—PORTRAITS
PH00518 692 (October 6, 1994) p80. "Arquette Gets Pierced"
ARRESTED DEVELOPMENT—ALBUMS
PH00519 645-646 (December 10, 1992) p164. "3 Years, 5 Months And 2 Days In The Life Of..."
PH00520 651 (March 4, 1993) p56. "3 Years, 5 Months And 2 Days In The Life Of..."
PH00521 685 (June 30, 1994) p71. "Zingalamaduni"
ARRESTED DEVELOPMENT—ILLUSTRATIONS
PH00522 685 (June 30, 1994) p71. "Afro Eccentric" (Shurley, Hugh)
ARRESTED DEVELOPMENT—PHOTOGRAPHS
PH00523 645-646 (December 10, 1992) p96. "[Arrested Development]"
PH00524 647 (January 7, 1993) p13. "Arrested Development's Headliner, Taree, Eshe And Speech (from left): Talkin' About A Different Kind Of Nirvana" (States, Ann)
PH00525 648 (January 21, 1993) p9. "Arrested Development (from left): Speech, Aerle Taree, Headliner, Rasa Don, Baba Oje And Montsho Eshe" (Mazur, Kevin)
PH00526 651 (March 4, 1993) p55. "Artist Of The Year" (Yurkovic, Gerhard)
PH00527 651 (March 4, 1993) p49. "Everyday People: Arrested Development" (Mazur, Kevin)
PH00528 654 (April 15, 1993) p11. "Best New Artist Arrested Development With Peter Gabriel (second from right)" (Mazur, Kevin)
PH00529 657 (May 27, 1993) p17. "Arrested Development's Aerle taree, Headliner And Speech (from left)" (Arnold, Alice)
PH00530 660-661 (July 8, 1993) p33. "Lollapaloosin' It: Arrested Development"
PH00531 662 (August 5, 1993) p14. "Arrested Development" (Blakesberg, Jay)
ARRESTED DEVELOPMENT—PHOTOGRAPHS—PORTRAITS
PH00532 634-635 (July 9, 1992) p20. "Arrested Development (from left): Headliner, Montsho Eshe, Aerle Taree, Rasa Don And Speech" (Lavine, Michael)
PH00533 634-635 (July 9, 1992) p20. "Love Battery (from left): Kevin Whitworth, Rod Rudzitis And Jason Finn" (Lavine, Michael)
PH00534 645-646 (December 10, 1992) p57. "Arrested Development" (Natkin, Paul)
ARSENIO (TELEVISION SHOW)—PHOTOGRAPHS
PH00535 645-646 (December 10, 1992) p196. "Bill Clinton (above) Had Nearly Blown It Before He Blew It On 'Arsenio'"
ART—ILLUSTRATIONS
PH00536 703 (March 9, 1995) p21. "Net Works" (O'Connell,

Mitch)
ART—PHOTOGRAPHS
PH00537 656 (May 13, 1993) p84. "Scene Of The Crime (Whose Crime?)" (Clements, Geoffrey)
PH00538 741 (August 22, 1996) p78. "[The Gramercy Art Fair]"
ART OF NOISE—PHOTOGRAPHS
PH00539 667 (October 14, 1993) p78. "Art(ful) Destruction: 'Close (To The Edit)'"
ARTHUR—PHOTOGRAPHS
PH00540 721 (November 16, 1995) p98. "Sammy, Arthur, Charlie And Civ (from left)" (GS, Jamil)
ARTHURS, PAUL—PHOTOGRAPHS
PH00541 691 (September 22, 1994) p37. "Arthurs, McCarroll, Liam Gallagher, McGuigan, Noel Gallagher (from left)"
PH00542 718 (October 5, 1995) p34. "White, Arthurs, Liam Gallagher, Noel Gallagher, McGuigan (from left)" (Jones, Michael Spenser)
PH00543 733 (May 2, 1996) p34. "Liam And Arthurs (right) Onstage In ;95" (Rasic, Brian)
ARTHURS, PAUL—PHOTOGRAPHS—PORTRAITS
PH00544 708 (May 18, 1995) p52. "From Left: McGuigan, McCarroll And 'Bonehead'" (Bailey, David)
ARTIS THE SPOON—PHOTOGRAPHS
PH00545 681 (May 5, 1994) p21. "Cornell (left) With Seattle Spoon Artist Artis" (Peterson, Charles)
PH00546 700 (January 26, 1995) p16. "[Soundgarden]" (Doughty, Curt)
ARTURRO, MICHAEL—PHOTOGRAPHS
PH00547 665 (September 16, 1993) pp[enc.36]. "[Rob Weiss & Michael Arturro]" (Nystrom, Dick)
PH00548 665 (September 16, 1993) pp[enc.34]. "[Rob Weiss, Steve Parlavecchio, Michael Arturro]" (Nystrom, Dick)
ASH—PHOTOGRAPHS
PH00549 719 (October 19, 1995) p33. "Tim Wheeler (left), Mark Hamilton Of Ash" (Page, Scarlet)
ASHCROFT, RICHARD—PHOTOGRAPHS
PH00550 660-661 (July 8, 1993) p96. "Verve (clockwise from top left): Ashcroft, Peter Salisbury, Simon Jones And McCabe" (Sharp, Ken)
PH00551 689 (August 25, 1994) p25. "Rock On: The Verve's Richard Ashcroft" (Blakesberg, Jay)
PH00552 718 (October 5, 1995) p32. "Richard Ashcroft: The British Chris Robinson?" (Capak, R. J.)
ASHER, TONY—PHOTOGRAPHS
PH00553 733 (May 2, 1996) p22. "Wilson (right) With Collaborator Tony Asher" (Schwartz, Michael)
ASHES TO ASHES (VIDEO)—PHOTOGRAPHS
PH00554 667 (October 14, 1993) p82. "'Ashes To Ashes': In This David Bowie Video, Major Tom Falls To Earth"
ASLAKSEN, DUANE—PHOTOGRAPHS
PH00555 706 (April 20, 1995) p21. "Erickson (right) In '76 With Guitarist Duane Aslaksen" (Gindreau, J. C.)
ASPINAL, JEZ—PHOTOGRAPHS
PH00556 660-661 (July 8, 1993) p101. "Motherhead Bug (from left): Anthony Lee, Steven Ovenden, April Chung, Cyril Mazzard, Jez Aspinal, Tomoyo, And Dave Ouimet" (Leopardi, N.)
ASS PONYS—PHOTOGRAPHS
PH00557 700 (January 26, 1995) p30. "From Left: Morrison, Cheek, Erhardt, Cleaver" (Ockenfels, Frank, 3)
ASSANTE, ARMAND—ILLUSTRATIONS
PH00558 626 (March 19, 1992) p101. "Playing Songs Of Love" (Kelley, Gary)
ASSANTE, ARMAND—PHOTOGRAPHS
PH00559 626 (March 19, 1992) p102. "Banderas (left) And Assante Say It With Music"
PH00560 669 (November 11, 1993) p81. "Assante And Young Get Smoke In Their Eyes"
ASSASSINS (FILM)—PHOTOGRAPHS
PH00561 718 (October 5, 1995) p76. "Pulp To Come"
THE ASSOCIATE (FILM)—PHOTOGRAPHS
PH00562 748 (November 28, 1996) p143. "Dead On Arrival"
ASTIN, SEAN—PHOTOGRAPHS
PH00563 633 (June 25, 1992) p48. "Shore (left) And Astin Flank Cave Man Fraser"
ASTLE, KEVIN—PHOTOGRAPHS
PH00564 652 (March 18, 1993) pp[enc.36]. "Kevin Astle And Heather Freeman" (Seliger, Mark)
AT THE ZOO (BOOK)—ILLUSTRATIONS
PH00565 619-620 (December 12, 1991) p75. "[At The Zoo]" (Michaut, Valerie)
ATKINS, CHOLLY—PHOTOGRAPHS
PH00566 720 (November 2, 1995) p49. "Aretha Franklin & Cholly Atkins"
ATKINS, CHRISTOPHER—PHOTOGRAPHS
PH00567 744 (October 3, 1996) p50. "Island Girl: With Christopher Atkins In 'The Blue Lagoon'"
ATKINS, JAMES—PHOTOGRAPHS
PH00568 636 (August 6, 1992) p13. "EMF's James Atkins" (Cohen, Lester)
ATOM—PHOTOGRAPHS
PH00569 689 (August 25, 1994) p44. "All Together Now: Trombino, Atom, Kennedy, Reis, N.D., Petey X, Apollo 9, Froberg (from left)" (Cuffaro, Chris)
ATTAR, BACHIR—ALBUMS
PH00570 637 (August 20, 1992) p52. "Apocalypse Across The Sky"
ATTAR, BACHIR—PHOTOGRAPHS
PH00571 632 (June 11, 1992) p40. "In 1988, Robert Palmer Gets Back Into The Mystic With Master Musician Bachir Attar" (Katzenstein, David)
ATTAWAY, MURRAY—ALBUMS
PH00572 662 (August 5, 1993) p64. "In Thrall"
AUER, JON—PHOTOGRAPHS
PH00573 658 (June 10, 1993) p17. "Auer, Chilton, Stephens And Stringfellow" (Perez, Marty)
PH00574 660-661 (July 8, 1993) p101. "The Posies (from left): Jon Auer, Dave Fox, Ken Stringfellow And Mike Musburger" (Natkin, Paul)
PH00575 710 (June 15, 1995) p40. "Posies Brian Young, Auer, Stringfellow, Joe Bass (from left)" (Moskowitz, Karen)
AUF DER MAUR, MELISSA—PHOTOGRAPHS
PH00576 697 (December 15, 1994) p67. "Hole As One: Bassist Melissa Auf Der Maur (who replaced Kristen Pfaff), Guitarist Eric Erlandson, Drummer Patty Schemel And Love (from left)" (Seliger, Mark)
PH00577 698-699 (December 29, 1994) p50. "Doll Parts: Hole's Eric Erlandson, Melissa Auf der Maur, Patty Schemel And Love" (Seliger, Mark)
PH00578 715 (August 24, 1995) p51. "Auf Der Maur Onstage In Washington" (Blakesberg, Jay)
PH00579 715 (August 24, 1995) p46. "Courtney Love, Eric Erlandson, Patty Schemel, Melissa Auf Der Maur" (Seliger, Mark)
AUGUSTE, ANNE—PHOTOGRAPHS
PH00580 701 (February 9, 1995) p16. "Gabriel Honors Rose-Anne Auguste Of Haiti" (Robicheau, Paul)
AUGUSTYNIAK, JEROME—PHOTOGRAPHS—PORTRAITS
PH00581 652 (March 18, 1993) pp34-35. "Rob Buck, Dennis Drew, Natalie Merchant, Jerome Augustyniak, Steven Gustafson (from left)" (Ockenfels, Frank W.)
AULERICH, RICHARD—PHOTOGRAPHS
PH00582 709 (June 1, 1995) p57. "Richard Aulerich In His Office At Michigan State University After The ALF Attack" (Aguilera-Hellweg, Max)
AUSTIN, MARY—PHOTOGRAPHS
PH00583 621 (January 9, 1992) p17. "Mercury With Longtime Friend Mary Austin" (Davidson, Alan)
AUSTIN, SIMON—PHOTOGRAPHS—PORTRAITS
PH00584 684 (June 16, 1994) p30. "Simon Austin, Angie Hart,

Alistair Barden And Tim O'Connor (from left)" (Westenberg, Kevin)
AUTEURS—PHOTOGRAPHS
PH00585 657 (May 27, 1993) p16. "Auteur, Auteur: Banbury, Haines, Collins And Readman (clockwise from left)" (Lass, Imke)
AUTOMOBILES—PHOTOGRAPHS
PH00586 630 (May 14, 1992) p92. "[1986 Camaro]"
PH00587 656 (May 13, 1993) p67. "[Cadillac STS]"
AVERILL, STEVE—PHOTOGRAPHS
PH00588 618 (November 28, 1991) pp42-48,50. "Dublin: Making Cutouts For The Album Cover Under The Guidance Of Steve Averill (second from left)" (Corbijn, Anton)
AVERRE, BURTON—PHOTOGRAPHS
PH00589 617 (November 14, 1991) p13. "Burton Averre, Dallas Taylor, Wilson And Was (from left)" (Preston, Neal)
AVERY, ERIC—PHOTOGRAPHS
PH00590 653 (April 1, 1993) p11. "Navarro, Michael Murphy And Avery" (Cohen, Lester)
PH00591 715 (August 24, 1995) p54. "Jane's Addiction, 1990: Farrell, Perkins, Dave Navarro And Eric Avery (from left)" (Miller, Peter Darley)
AN AWFULLY BIG ADVENTURE (FILM)—PHOTOGRAPHS
PH00592 709 (June 1, 1995) p68. "Too Much Hugh Grant"
PH00593 714 (August 10, 1995) p62. "An Awfully Big Adventure"
AXIOM FUNK—ALBUMS
PH00594 712-713 (July 13, 1995) p108. "Funkcronomicon"
AYKROYD, DAN—PHOTOGRAPHS
PH00595 664 (September 2, 1993) p70. "Conehead Movies"
PH00596 684 (June 16, 1994) p116. "Kinky: O'Donnell And Aykroyd In "Eden""
PH00597 696 (December 1, 1994) p25. "Ms. Aykroyd (Donna Dixon), Eric Clapton, Uma Thurman And Dan Aykroyd (from left)" (Allen, David)
AYKROYD, DAN—PHOTOGRAPHS—PORTRAITS
PH00598 706 (April 20, 1995) p86. "The 'SNL' Legacy Of Screen Shame"
AYRES, BEN—PHOTOGRAPHS
PH00599 728 (February 22, 1996) p32. "Cornershop's Simms, Saffery, Tjinder Singh, Ayres And Hall (from left)" (Wonderland, Alison)
AZERRAD, MICHAEL—BOOKS
PH00600 666 (September 30, 1993) p15. "Come As You Are: The Story Of Nirvana"
AZTEC CAMERA—ALBUMS
PH00601 666 (September 30, 1993) p104. "Dreamland"

B

B, ROB—PHOTOGRAPHS
PH00602 659 (June 24, 1993) p30. "Stereo's Rob B" (Capak, R. J.)
B-52S—ALBUMS
PH00603 634-635 (July 9, 1992) p101. "Good Stuff"
B-52S—PHOTOGRAPHS
PH00604 630 (May 14, 1992) p13. "Kate Pierson, Fred Schneider And Kim Bassinger (from left) At The Brown Fund-Raiser" (Mazur, Kevin)
PH00605 637 (August 20, 1992) p11. "The B-52's (from left): Fred Schneider, Kate Pierson, Julee Cruise, Keith Strickland, Sue Hadjopoulos And Pat Irwin" (Michelson, Eric T.)
PH00606 652 (March 18, 1993) p27. "Kate Pierson And Fred Schneider"
PH00607 667 (October 14, 1993) p80. "'Love Shack': The B-52's Rock The House"
PH00608 683 (June 2, 1994) p27. "Below: Schneider, Kate Pierson, Keith Strickland" (Batzdorff, Rob)
B-REAL—ILLUSTRATIONS
PH00609 669 (November 11, 1993) p5. "Cypress Hill's B-Real" (Burke, Philip)
B-REAL—PHOTOGRAPHS
PH00610 631 (May 28, 1992) p18. "Muggs, Sen Dog And B-Real (from left)" (Moss, Gary)
PH00611 662 (August 5, 1993) p16. "Just Another Band From L.A.? Sen Dog, B-Real And DJ Muggs (from left)"
PH00612 672-673 (December 23, 1993) p53. "Muggs, B-Real And Sen-Dog (from left) Pay Homage To The Wicked Weed On 'Black Sunday'" (Borris, Dan)
PH00613 715 (August 24, 1995) p44. "Sen Dog, B-Real, Bobo (from left)" (Blakesberg, Jay)
PH00614 718 (October 5, 1995) p20. "B-Real Flanked By Carl Hinds (left) And Morpurgo" (Shapiro, Stephen)
PH00615 729 (March 7, 1996) p10. "Baseball Been Bery, Bery Good To Me: Morris, Monica And B-Real (from left)" (Kravitz, Jeff)
PH00616 731 (April 4, 1996) p30. "Sen Dog, Muggs, B-Real (from left)" (McClelland, P.)
B-REAL—PHOTOGRAPHS—PORTRAITS
PH00617 669 (November 11, 1993) p64. "The Dope On The Hill: B-real, Sen Dog And Muggs (bottom row, from left)" (Borris, Dan)
PH00618 671 (December 9, 1993) p31. "House's Danny Boy, DJ Lethal And Everlast With Cypress' B-Real And Muggs (from left)" (Blakesberg, Jay)
BABA, MEHER—PHOTOGRAPHS—PORTRAITS
PH00619 645-646 (December 10, 1992) p156. "Meher Baba, 1970"
BABB-SPRAGUE, KRISTEN—PHOTOGRAPHS
PH00620 630 (May 14, 1992) pp95,99. "[Kristen Babb-Sprague]" (Nystrom, Dick)
BABBITT, BRUCE—PHOTOGRAPHS
PH00621 660-661 (July 8, 1993) p51. "Babbitt At His Confirmation Hearing Talking With Arizona Senator Dennis DeConcini" (Binder, Donna)
PH00622 660-661 (July 8, 1993) p52. "Babbitt On The Campaign Trail: Presidential Candidates Michael Dukakis, Babbitt, Paul Simon, Richard Gephardt, Jesse Jackson And Al Gore (from left) At A New York Forum In December....
PH00623 660-661 (July 8, 1993) p48. "With The Vice-President: Al Gore And Babbitt After One Of Their Weekly Breakfast Meetings On The Environment" (Ockenfels, Frank W.)
BABBITT, BRUCE—PHOTOGRAPHS—PORTRAITS
PH00624 660-661 (July 8, 1993) p47. "[Bruce Babbitt]" (Ockenfels, Frank W.)
BABE (FILM)—PHOTOGRAPHS
PH00625 724-725 (December 28, 1995) p136. "Unusual Pleasure"
PH00626 731 (April 4, 1996) p66. "'Babe,' With James Cromwell And Pig"
PH00627 750-751 (December 26, 1996) p57. "'Babe'—Good Movie! Family Values! Animals!"
THE BABE (FILM)—PHOTOGRAPHS
PH00628 630 (May 14, 1992) p113. "John Goodman Tries Hard But Can't Win One For The Babe"
BABES IN TOYLAND—ILLUSTRATIONS
PH00629 709 (June 1, 1995) p64. "Babes In Toyland" (Mericle, Charise)
BABES IN TOYLAND—PHOTOGRAPHS
PH00630 657 (May 27, 1993) p17. "The Female Minority: Babes In Toyland" (Anker, Matt)
PH00631 662 (August 5, 1993) p13. "Maureen Herman, Kat Bjelland And Lori Barbero Of Babes in Toyland" (Blakesberg, Jay)
PH00632 692 (October 6, 1994) p37. "Babes In Toyland"
PH00633 710 (June 15, 1995) p51. "Bjelland, Maureen Herman, Barbero (from left)" (Sferra, Rik)

BABES IN TOYLAND—PHOTOGRAPHS—PORTRAITS
PH00634 695 (November 17, 1994) p71. "Babes In Toyland" (Borris, Dan)
BABSON COLLEGE—ILLUSTRATIONS
PH00635 666 (September 30, 1993) p60. "[Higher Education]"
BABY GOT BACK (VIDEO)—PHOTOGRAPHS
PH00636 667 (October 14, 1993) p82. "Butt Seriously, Folks: MTV Kicked Sir Mix-A-Lot's Ass Off The Air"
BABYFACE—ALBUMS
PH00637 668 (October 28, 1993) p76. "For The Cool In You"
BABYFACE—PHOTOGRAPHS
PH00638 696 (December 1, 1994) p103. "[Babyface]" (Camp, E. J.)
PH00639 696 (December 1, 1994) p105. "The Dream Team: Daryl Simmons, Babyface And L.A. Reid At The 1993 Grammys" (Deguire, Greg)
PH00640 696 (December 1, 1994) p104. "Rhythm Nation: With Toni Braxton" (Deguire, Greg)
PH00641 738-739 (July 11, 1996) p15. "Clapton And Babyface In Hoboken, N.J. (really), For The 'Change The World'"
BABYFACE—PHOTOGRAPHS—PORTRAITS
PH00642 704 (March 23, 1995) p24. "Babyface And Madonna Take In The AMAs" (Nannarello, Spike)
PH00643 724-725 (December 28, 1995) p45. "Babyface (top) And L.A. Reid"
BACA, JIM—PHOTOGRAPHS—PORTRAITS
PH00644 685 (June 30, 1994) p45. "Jim Baca: Bounced For Doing His Job"
BACCHUS, RICHARD—PHOTOGRAPHS
PH00645 701 (February 9, 1995) p19. "D Gen (from left): Danny Sage, Richard Bacchus, Howie Pyro, Jesse Malin, Michael Wildwood" (Seliger, Mark)
PH00646 710 (June 15, 1995) p41. "D Gen (from left): Pyro, Michael Wildwood, Malin, Sage, Richard Bacchus And Gomez" (Ragel, Jon)
BACH, SEBASTIAN—PHOTOGRAPHS
PH00647 619-620 (December 12, 1991) pp[cover]. "1991 Yearbook" (Seliger, Mark)
PH00648 619-620 (December 12, 1991) p53. "Skid Row, Prison Row, Memory Lane: Sebastian Bach (below left)..." (Kirkland, Gene)
BACK TO MY ROOTS (VIDEO)—PHOTOGRAPHS
PH00649 667 (October 14, 1993) p90. "Work It, Girl: RuPaul Shows His Roots"
PH00650 Number not assigned.
BACKBEAT (FILM)—ILLUSTRATIONS
PH00651 680 (April 21, 1994) p92. "Underground Beatles" (Drawson, Blair)
BACKBEAT (FILM)—PHOTOGRAPHS
PH00652 680 (April 21, 1994) p93. "Dorff And Hart Flank Lee In A Beatles Love Triangle"
PH00653 680 (April 21, 1994) p64. "There's A Place: Backbeatles With Sutcliffe (Dorff, Right)"
PH00654 697 (December 15, 1994) p102. ""Backbeat" On Laserdisc Recalls The Days of Five Beatles"
BACKDRAFT (FILM)—PHOTOGRAPHS
PH00655 654 (April 15, 1993) p69. "Backdraft"
BACK-PACKS—PHOTOGRAPHS
PH00655a 634-635 (July 9, 1992) pp122-123. "[Toys]" (Goldin, David)
BACON, KEVIN—PHOTOGRAPHS
PH00656 693 (October 20, 1994) p156. "Woman Warrior Streep (above, with Reilly and Bacon) Braves The Rapids To Save Son Mazzello And Husband Strathairn (left)"
PH00657 701 (February 9, 1995) p63. "Slater And Bacon Fight Injustice"
PH00658 712-713 (July 13, 1995) p116. "'Apollo 13' Astronauts Hanks And Bacon Blast Off; And Harris Waits In Houston"
BACON, KEVIN—PHOTOGRAPHS—PORTRAITS
PH00659 731 (April 4, 1996) p66. "Bacon, 'Murder'"
BAD BOYS (FILM)—PHOTOGRAPHS
PH00660 707 (May 4, 1995) p74. "Lawrence And Smith In 'Bad Boys'"
BAD BRAINS—ALBUMS
PH00661 710 (June 15, 1995) p81. "God Of Love"
BAD BRAINS—ILLUSTRATIONS
PH00662 715 (August 24, 1995) p18. "Bad Equation" (Pendergrast, James T.)
BAD BRAINS—PHOTOGRAPHS
PH00663 706 (April 20, 1995) p16. "'God' Producer Ocasek (left) And Bad Brains" (Johnson, Lisa)
PH00664 711 (June 29, 1995) p15. "Cosmic Agit Pop And Measured Fury: Dr. Know, H.R., Darryl Jenifer And Earl Hudson of Bad Brains (from left)" (Cuffaro, Chris)
PH00665 724-725 (December 28, 1995) p49. "[Bad Brains]" (Settle, Ken)
BAD GIRLS (FILM)—PHOTOGRAPHS
PH00666 683 (June 2, 1994) p76. "Drew Barrymore ("Bad Girls")"
BAD LIEUTENANT (FILM)—ILLUSTRATIONS
PH00667 644 (November 26, 1992) p77. "Killer Ratings" (Burns, Charles)
BAD LIEUTENANT (FILM)—PHOTOGRAPHS
PH00668 644 (November 26, 1992) p78. "Running The Ratings Gamut: Keitel..."
PH00669 648 (January 21, 1993) p56. "Bad Lieutenant"
BAD LIVERS—PHOTOGRAPHS—PORTRAITS
PH00670 697 (December 15, 1994) p40. "Bad Boys: Barnes, Rubin And White (from left)" (Cardillicchio, Nick)
BAD RADIO—PHOTOGRAPHS
PH00671 748 (November 28, 1996) p53. "A 1989 Publicity Shot Of Bad Radio" (Gaynor, Adrian)
BAD RELIGION—ALBUMS
PH00672 694 (November 3, 1994) p98. "Stranger Than Fiction"
PH00673 729 (March 7, 1996) p48. "The Gray Race"
BAD RELIGION—PHOTOGRAPHS
PH00674 670 (November 25, 1993) p30. "Hetson, Bobby Schayer, Bentley, Gurewitz And Graffin (clockwise from top left)" (Zlozower, Neil)
PH00675 700 (January 26, 1995) p17. "Bad Religion's Brian Baker, Greg Graffin, Bobby Schayer, Jay Bentley and Greg Hetson" (Kravitz, Jeff)
PH00676 722 (November 30, 1995) p19. "Graffin, Ocasek, Jay Bentley, Brian Baker, Greg Hetson And Bobby Schayer (from left)" (Mazur, Kevin)
BAD SEEDS—ALBUMS
PH00677 636 (August 6, 1992) p57. "Henry's Dream"
PH00678 684 (June 16, 1994) p110. "Let Love In"
PH00679 730 (March 21, 1996) p96. "Murder Ballads"
PH00680 733 (May 2, 1996) p72. "Murder Ballads"
BAD SEEDS—PHOTOGRAPHS
PH00681 692 (October 6, 1994) p16. "At Philly's Lollapalooza: L7's Donita Sparks (left), Dee Plakas, Suzi Gardner And Jennifer Finch With Bad Seeds Mick Harvey, James Johnston And Nick Cave" (Weiner, Scott)
BADALAMENTI, ANGELO—ALBUMS
PH00682 745 (October 17, 1996) p134. "Booth And The Bad Angel"
BADER, DIEDRICH—PHOTOGRAPHS
PH00683 669 (November 11, 1993) p81. "Tomlin's Miss Hathaway Welcomes The Clampetts To 90210"
BAERWALD, DAVID—ALBUMS
PH00684 653 (April 1, 1993) p54. "Triage"
BAEZ, JOAN—ALBUMS
PH00685 648 (January 21, 1993) p49. "Play Me Backwards"
BAEZ, JOAN—ILLUSTRATIONS
PH00686 641 (October 15, 1992) p105. "[Joan Baez]" (Flesher, Vivienne)
BAEZ, JOAN—ILLUSTRATIONS—PORTRAITS
PH00686a 675 (February 10, 1994) p43. "Voices Of The People"

(Deacon, Jim)
BAEZ, JOAN—PHOTOGRAPHS
PH00687 645-646 (December 10, 1992) p152. "Bob Dylan And Joan Baez, 1976"
PH00688 648 (January 21, 1993) p11. "Baez, Gabriel, Richie Havens And Stipe (from left) At The Reebok Awards" (Robicheau, Paul)
PH00689 649 (February 4, 1993) p9. "Joan Baez (left) With Harding" (Blakesberg, Jay)
BAEZ, JOAN—PHOTOGRAPHS—PORTRAITS
PH00690 643 (November 12, 1992) p185. "Joan Baez" (Markus, Kurt)
BAGAROZZI, CHRIS—PHOTOGRAPHS
PH00691 715 (August 24, 1995) p36. "Bagarozzi, Walther, Lee And Wahl" (Peterson, Charles)
BAHCALL, STEVE—PHOTOGRAPHS
PH00692 722 (November 30, 1995) pp[enc.3]. " ing Went The Strings: Steve Bahcall In His Studio Using A Program Called Sound Designer With His Strat" (McLeod, William Mercer)
BAHIA BLACK—ALBUMS
PH00693 629 (April 30, 1992) p59. "Ritual Beating System"
BAHNS, MAXINE—PHOTOGRAPHS
PH00694 715 (August 24, 1995) p110. "Mulcahy, Burns, Bahns And McGlone (from left)"
PH00695 741 (August 22, 1996) p105. "Burns, Bahns, Diaz, Aniston, McGlone"
BAILEY, ANDREW—PHOTOGRAPHS
PH00696 632 (June 11, 1992) p62. "Staff Members And Contributing Writers At The 1971 Editorial Conference, At Esalen, In Big Sur" (Leibovitz, Annie)
BAILEY, EARNIE—PHOTOGRAPHS
PH00697 692 (October 6, 1994) p15. "Novoselic, Vedder And Earnie Bailey (from left) Get Loose" (Van Wey, Charles)
BAILEY, F. LEE—PHOTOGRAPHS
PH00698 724-725 (December 28, 1995) p58. "The American Way: F. Lee Bailey, Simpson, Johnnie Cochran" (Chun, Myung J.)
BAIO, SCOTT—PHOTOGRAPHS
PH00699 697 (December 15, 1994) p18. "Etheridge, Waters, "Politically Incorrect" Host Bill Maher, Molinari And Baio (from left)"
BAIOCCHI, JUDITH—PHOTOGRAPHS
PH00700 663 (August 19, 1993) p61. "College Cabinet: William Clinton, Judith Baiocchi, David Kammer, Paul Maloy (from left)"
BAIRD, DAN—ALBUMS
PH00701 648 (January 21, 1993) p49. "Love Songs For The Hearing Impaired"
BAIRD, DAN—PHOTOGRAPHS
PH00702 647 (January 7, 1993) p16. "[Dan Baird]" (Camp, E. J.)
PH00703 650 (February 18, 1993) p13. "Baird, Kevin Kinney And Richards (from left)" (Diamond, Rick)
BAITZ, JON ROBIN—PHOTOGRAPHS—PORTRAITS
PH00704 630 (May 14, 1992) p91. "[Jon Robin Baitz]" (Shacter, Susan)
BAKER, BRIAN—PHOTOGRAPHS
PH00705 700 (January 26, 1995) p17. "Bad Religion's Brian Baker, Greg Graffin, Bobby Schayer, Jay Bentley and Greg Hetson" (Kravitz, Jeff)
PH00706 722 (November 30, 1995) p19. "Graffin, Ocasek, Jay Bentley, Brian Baker, Greg Hetson And Bobby Schayer (from left)" (Mazur, Kevin)
BAKER, BRIAN—PHOTOGRAPHS—PORTRAITS
PH00707 695 (November 17, 1994) p40. "Bad Religion" (Guip, Amy)
BAKER, CHET—PHOTOGRAPHS—PORTRAITS
PH00708 643 (November 12, 1992) p230. "Weber Purveyed The Masculine Appeal Of Artists Like Chet Baker" (Weber, Bruce)
BAKER, DAVE—PHOTOGRAPHS
PH00709 664 (September 2, 1993) p24. "They're All Revved Up: Donahue, Thorpe, Baker, Chambers, Fridmann And Grasshopper (from left)" (Gullick, Steve)
BAKER, EARL, JR.—PHOTOGRAPHS
PH00710 704 (March 23, 1995) pp102-103. "Class of '95" (Tavee, Tom)
PH00711 704 (March 23, 1995) p102. "Onstage" (Tavee, Tom)
BAKER, GINGER—ALBUMS
PH00712 693 (October 20, 1994) p148. "Going Back Home"
BAKER, GINGER—PHOTOGRAPHS
PH00713 649 (February 4, 1993) p51. "Clapton, Baker And Bruce Of Cream"
PH00714 655 (April 29, 1993) p35. "The Aptly Named Blind Faith: Steve Winwood, Rick Grech, Ginger Baker And Clapton (from left)"
PH00715 655 (April 29, 1993) p38. "Rock's First Power Trio (Clapton, Baker and Bruce, from left) Basking In The Sunshine of History Backstage At The Hall Of Fame" (Mazur, Kevin)
BAKER, GINGER—PHOTOGRAPHS—PORTRAITS
PH00716 655 (April 29, 1993) p34. "Cream In November 1996, Shortly Before The U.K. Release Of The Group's debut Album, Fresh Cream: Jack Bruce, Ginger Baker And Clapton (clockwise from left)" (Gale, Tony)
BAKER, NADIENE—PHOTOGRAPHS
PH00717 719 (October 19, 1995) p25. "Cowan Signs To Motown: Motown's Nadiene Baker, Manager Bill Dern, Jackson, Cowan (clockwise from top left)"
BAKER, SUSAN—PHOTOGRAPHS
PH00718 654 (April 15, 1993) p20. "PMRC Cofounders Gore And Susan Baker" (Brack, Dennis)
BAKULA, SCOTT—PHOTOGRAPHS
PH00719 717 (September 21, 1995) p90. "Private Eye Bakula Tracks The Undead"
BALAMUTH, FRAN—PHOTOGRAPHS
PH00720 678 (March 24, 1994) p85. "Let's Talk About Sex: Balamuth Teaches Teens At State-Run Gorup Homes In Rhode Island" (Marsel, Steve)
BALDWIN, ALEC—PHOTOGRAPHS
PH00721 637 (August 20, 1992) p57. "Soul-Searching: Ryan (left) And Baldwin"
PH00722 667 (October 14, 1993) p128. "Evil Doings For Alec Baldwin And Nicole Kidman"
PH00723 676 (February 24, 1994) p62. "Glam Gun Toters: Kim Basinger And Alec Baldwin"
PH00724 688 (August 11, 1994) p62. "The Shadow"
PH00725 690 (September 8, 1994) p72. "Many Celebrities Who Appear On "The Larry Sanders Show" Are Fans, Like Alec Baldwin" (Tepper, Randy)
BALDWIN, STEPHEN—ILLUSTRATIONS
PH00726 716 (September 7, 1995) p75. "A Summer Sleeper" (Ulriksen, Mark)
BALDWIN, STEPHEN—PHOTOGRAPHS
PH00727 658 (June 10, 1993) p74. "The Magnificent Six (from left): Stephen Baldwin, Big Daddy Kane, Mario Van Peebles, Tiny Lister Jr., Charles Lane, Tone Loc"
PH00728 680 (April 21, 1994) p93. "Student Union For Charles, Boyle And Baldwin"
BALDWIN, WILLIAM—PHOTOGRAPHS
PH00729 659 (June 24, 1993) p88. "Lust: 'Sliver,' With William Baldwin And Sharon Stone"
PH00730 660-661 (July 8, 1993) p120. "Snow White And Stone (with Baldwin)"
BALKANS—ILLUSTRATIONS
PH00731 657 (May 27, 1993) p6. "Yugoslavian Transportation" (Pendergrast, James T.)
BALKANS—PHOTOGRAPHS
PH00732 702 (February 23, 1995) pp60-65. "[Bosnian Refugees]" (Salgado, Sebastiao)
BALL, LUCILLE—PHOTOGRAPHS
PH00733 682 (May 19, 1994) p108. "MTV-Ready Lucille Ball Cracks The Whip"

BALL, MARCIA—ALBUMS
PH00734 701 (February 9, 1995) p57. "Blue House"
THE BALLAD OF LITTLE JO (FILM)—PHOTOGRAPHS
PH00735 663 (August 19, 1993) p83. "Suzy Amis As The Beautiful Josephine (left) And As Little Jo, A Tough Hombre In The Wild, Sexist West"
BALLEW, CHRIS—ILLUSTRATIONS
PH00736 729 (March 7, 1996) p3. "PUSA's Chris Ballew" (Niemann, Christoph)
BALLEW, CHRIS—PHOTOGRAPHS
PH00737 718 (October 5, 1995) p35. "The Right Stuff: Jason Finn, Chris Ballew And Dave Dederer (from left)" (Mason, Karen)
PH00738 727 (February 8, 1996) p24. "Chris Ballew Gives A Presidential Turn" (Cassidy, Chris)
PH00739 729 (March 7, 1996) p32. "The Presidents Pay Tribute To The Seattle Sonics" (Westenberg, Kevin)
BALLEW, CHRIS—PHOTOGRAPHS—PORTRAITS
PH00740 729 (March 7, 1996) p30. "One Band Indivisible With Power, Pop And Jokes For All" (Westenberg, Kevin)
BALLY'S CASINO—PHOTOGRAPHS
PH00741 634-635 (July 9, 1992) p13. "[Bally's]" (Scheid, Jeff)
BALMER, JEAN-FRANCOIS—PHOTOGRAPHS
PH00742 621 (January 9, 1992) p56. "Isabelle Huppert And Jean-Francois Balmer In Turmoil"
BALTIMORE, MARYLAND—PHOTOGRAPHS
PH00743 691 (September 22, 1994) p41. "Young Baltimore Participants Perform Calisthenics Weekday Mornings At City Hall" (Wolfe, Tom)
BAM-BAM—PHOTOGRAPHS
PH00744 672-673 (December 23, 1993) p118. "A Rainbow Named Bam-Bam (above) Howls At The Sky" (Borris, Dan)
BAM-BAM—PHOTOGRAPHS—PORTRAITS
PH00745 672-673 (December 23, 1993) p120. "Bam-Bam In The Drummers' Circle, 'Blasting Out Babylon'" (Borris, Dan)
BAMFORD, GREG—PHOTOGRAPHS
PH00746 678 (March 24, 1994) p50. "In The Belly Of The Beast: Bamford On Campus In D.C." (Wolff, Tom)
BAMONTE, PERRY—PHOTOGRAPHS
PH00747 631 (May 28, 1992) p11. "Simon Gallup, Porl Thompson, Perry Bamonte, Robert Smith, Boris Williams (from left)" (Cox, Paul)
PH00748 633 (June 25, 1992) p12. "The Cure's Simon Gallup, Perry Bamonte And Smith (from left)" (Elgar, Nick)
PH00749 733 (May 2, 1996) p22. "Partial To Shades: The Cure's New Lineup Is Simon Gallup, Roger O'Donnell, Robert Smith, Perry Bamonte And Jason Cooper (from left)" (Cox, Paul)
BANANARAMA—PHOTOGRAPHS
PH00750 731 (April 4, 1996) p33. "Bananarama's High-Fashion Holocaust, 1982" (Schwartz, Murray)
BANBURY, JAMES—PHOTOGRAPHS
PH00751 657 (May 27, 1993) p16. "Auteur, Auteur: Banbury, Haines, Collins And Readman (clockwise from left)" (Lass, Imke)
BANCROFT, ANNE—PHOTOGRAPHS
PH00752 721 (November 16, 1995) p116. "Hunter (left) At Home With Mom Bancroft"
BAND—ALBUMS
PH00753 676 (February 24, 1994) p57. "Jericho"
PH00754 698-699 (December 29, 1994) p188. "Across The Great Divide"
BAND—PHOTOGRAPHS
PH00755 617 (November 14, 1991) p75. "The Last Waltz, 1976: Robertson, Danko And Manuel, With Neil Young (left), Bob Dylan (back to camera) And Van Morrison" (Leibovitz, Annie)
PH00756 669 (November 11, 1993) p66. "The Hawks At Ontario's Brass Rail Circa '63: Danko, Manuel, Hawkins, Helm, Robertson And Hudson (from left)"
PH00757 669 (November 11, 1993) p67. "Shooting The Band For Music From Big Pink (left)" (Landy, Elliott)
PH00758 676 (February 24, 1994) p46. "The Band (clockwise from top left): Guitarist Robbie Robertson, Drummer Levon Helm, Organist Garth Hudson, Bassist Rock Danko And Pianist Richard Manuel" (Gahr, David)
PH00759 680 (April 21, 1994) p13. "Rock Marries Commerce Again: The Band (above) shill For Diet Coke With 'The Weight,' Which Is Owned By Dylan (left)" (Landy, Elliott)
BAND OF SUSANS—ALBUMS
PH00760 664 (September 2, 1993) p62. "Veil"
BANDERAS, ANTONIO—PHOTOGRAPHS
PH00761 626 (March 19, 1992) p102. "Banderas (left) And Assante Say It With Music"
PH00762 677 (March 10, 1994) p60. "Streep And Close Play Ball (left), While Ryder And Her Lover, Banderas, Play Around"
PH00763 678 (March 24, 1994) p63. "Demme, Flanked By Hanks And Banderas, Denies That The Positive Gay Images In 'Philadelphia' Are A Reaction Against The Gay Killer in 'Lambs' (left)"
PH00764 701 (February 9, 1995) p62. "Farrow Catches Parker And Banderas"
PH00765 716 (September 7, 1995) p76. "Antonio Banderas Takes Aim At Being An Action Hero"
BANKING—ILLUSTRATIONS
PH00766 667 (October 14, 1993) p14. "Welcome To The Bank" (Pendergrast, James T.)
BANKING CRISIS—ILLUSTRATIONS
PH00767 624 (February 20, 1992) p20. "[Banks]" (Cronin, Brian)
PH00768 634-635 (July 9, 1992) p35. "[Banking Crisis]" (Tanhauser, Gary)
BANKS, NICK—PHOTOGRAPHS
PH00769 732 (April 18, 1996) p24. "A Wildly Unorthodox Mixture Of Influence Gathered Around The Table: Pulp's Candida Doyle, Mark Webber, Cocker, Steve Mackey, Russell Senior And Nick Banks (from left)" (Rankin)
BANKS, TONY—PHOTOGRAPHS
PH00770 624 (February 20, 1992) p17. "Genesis, From Left: Tony Banks, Mike Rutherford And Phil Collins" (Ockenfels, Frank W.)
BANNING, CALIFORNIA—PHOTOGRAPHS
PH00771 030 (March 9, 1995) p60. "In Hmong Families It Is Typically The Children Who Become Fluent In English" (Llewellyn, Michael)
PH00772 703 (March 9, 1995) p58. "Guys Just Want To Be Cool: Westernized Hmong-American Teen-Agers Pose On The Streets Of Banning" (Llewellyn, Michael)
PH00773 703 (March 9, 1995) p57. "Tradition: Performing At The Funeral Of An Elder In Banning, January 1995" (Llewellyn, Michael)
BARANCIK, ELLIE—PHOTOGRAPHS
PH00774 743 (September 19, 1996) p72. "Comedy Is A Great Passive-Aggressive Tool" (Seliger, Mark)
BARB WIRE (FILM)—PHOTOGRAPHS
PH00775 734 (May 16, 1996) p72. "Pamela Anderson Lee"
BARBARIANS AT THE GATE (TELEVISION FILM)—PHOTOGRAPHS
PH00776 655 (April 29, 1993) p68. "Barbarians At The Gate"
BARBE, DAVID—PHOTOGRAPHS
PH00777 637 (August 20, 1992) p9. "Sugar (clockwise from left): Bob Mould, Malcolm Travis And David Barbe"
PH00778 694 (November 3, 1994) p73. "Barbe (left) And Mould, Athens, Ga. July 1992" (Double, Steve)
PH00779 694 (November 3, 1994) p71. "David Barbe, Malcolm Travis Ad Bob Mould (from left)" (Broad, Julian)
PH00780 701 (February 9, 1995) p17. "[Sugar]" (Hermer, Ken)
BARBER, TONY—PHOTOGRAPHS
PH00781 675 (February 10, 1994) p16. "Chemistry Club: Buzzcocks' Diggle, Barber, Shelley And Barker (from left)"
BARBERO, LORI—PHOTOGRAPHS
PH00782 662 (August 5, 1993) p13. "Maureen Herman, Kat

Bjelland And Lori Barbero Of Babes in Toyland" (Blakesberg, Jay)
PH00783 710 (June 15, 1995) p51. "Bjelland, Maureen Herman, Barbero (from left)" (Sferra, Rik)
BARBERO, LORI—PHOTOGRAPHS—PORTRAITS
PH00784 695 (November 17, 1994) p71. "Babes In Toyland" (Borris, Dan)
BARBIE DOLL (TOY)—ILLUSTRATIONS
PH00785 722 (November 30, 1995) p20. "Doll Partners" (Bartholomew, Beth)
BARBOT, BILL—PHOTOGRAPHS
PH00786 678 (March 24, 1994) p20. "Barocas, Robbins, Coletta, Barbot (from left)" (Falls, John)
BARCELONA (FILM)—PHOTOGRAPHS
PH00787 688 (August 11, 1994) p63. "It's Ole To Nichols, Bergen, Eigeman And Sorvino"
BARDEN, ALISTAIR—PHOTOGRAPHS
PH00788 684 (June 16, 1994) p30. "Simon Austin, Angie Hart, Alistair Barden And Tim O'Connor (from left)" (Westenberg, Kevin)
BARENAKED LADIES—PHOTOGRAPHS
PH00789 662 (August 5, 1993) p34. "Barenaked Ladies: They're Really Big In Canada"
BARILE, RICHARD—PHOTOGRAPHS—PORTRAITS
PH00790 660-661 (July 8, 1993) p82. "Richard Barile And George Jung, Arrested For Possession On Cape Cod in 1980"
BARKER, PHIL—PHOTOGRAPHS
PH00791 675 (February 10, 1994) p16. "Chemistry Club: Buzzcocks' Diggle, Barber, Shelley And Barker (from left)"
BARKIN, ELLEN—PHOTOGRAPHS
PH00792 654 (April 15, 1993) p69. "Pick The Psycho: De Niro, Dushku, Barkin Or DiCaprio?"
PH00793 657 (May 27, 1993) p59. "Questing: Gabriel Byrne, Ellen Barkin"
BARLEY, MARY—PHOTOGRAPHS
PH00794 733 (May 2, 1996) p46. "Barley And Reed, The Greens' Secret Weapons" (Tavee, Tom)
BARLOW, JOHN PERRY—PHOTOGRAPHS
PH00795 717 (September 21, 1995) p28. "Not Fade Away: Barlow, Hart, Kantner And Weir (from left) Celebrate Garcia In Golden Gate Park" (Blakesberg, Jay)
PH00796 717 (September 21, 1995) p28. "Olatunji With Kantner, Two Drummers, John Perry Barlow, Weir And Koons Garcia (from left) At The Aug. 13 Memorial At The Polo Field" (Blakesberg, Jay)
BARLOW, LOU—ILLUSTRATIONS
PH00797 747 (November 14, 1996) p20. "In Case Of Emergency Break Glass" (Pendergrast, James T.)
BARLOW, LOU—PHOTOGRAPHS
PH00798 704 (March 23, 1995) p43. "The Sensitive Souls Of Sebadoh: Fay, Barlow And Loewenstein (from left)" (Ockenfels, Frank, 3)
PH00799 706 (April 20, 1995) p17. "Barlow (right) Grudgingly Strikes Back" (Hole, Danny)
PH00800 736 (June 13, 1996) p53. "Sebadoh's Natural Ones: Bob Fay, Jason Lowenstein And Lou Barlow" (Van Iperen, Neils)
PH00801 750-751 (December 26, 1996) p57. "Multiband Lou Barlow With His Gee-Tar" (Soares, John)
BARLOW, LOU—PHOTOGRAPHS—PORTRAITS
PH00802 744 (October 3, 1996) p56. "Barlow, At 17, During A Photo Shoot For The Cover Of A Deep Wound EP"
PH00803 744 (October 3, 1996) p54. "[Lou Barlow]" (Ragel, Jon)
BARNES, DANNY—PHOTOGRAPHS—PORTRAITS
PH00804 697 (December 15, 1994) p40. "Bad Boys: Barnes, Rubin And White (from left)" (Cardillicchio, Nick)
BARNETT, RONNIE—PHOTOGRAPHS
PH00805 735 (May 30, 1996) p13. "Muffs Roy McDonald And Kim Shattuck, Sean Ono Lennon, Muff Ronnie Barnett, Sideman Bill Bartell, And Eric Erlandson" (Phalen, Tom)
BARNEY—ALBUMS
PH00806 669 (November 11, 1993) p74. "Barney's Favorites Vol. 1"
BARNSTABLE, DEREK—PHOTOGRAPHS—PORTRAITS
PH00807 728 (February 22, 1996) p52. "Nov. 23, 1995: Derek, Charged With Conspiracy To Commit Murder, At A Bond Hearing At The Outagamie County Courthouse" (Powers, Dan)
BAROCAS, ZACH—PHOTOGRAPHS
PH00808 678 (March 24, 1994) p20. "Barocas, Robbins, Coletta, Barbot (from left)" (Falls, John)
BARONE, RICHARD—ALBUMS
PH00809 675 (February 10, 1994) p45. "Clouds Over Eden"
BARR, BOB—PHOTOGRAPHS—PORTRAITS
PH00810 710 (June 15, 1995) p62. "Barr" (Marquette, Joe)
BARRON, CHRIS—ILLUSTRATIONS
PH00811 684 (June 16, 1994) p7. "Spin Doctors' Chris Barron" (Burke, Philip)
BARRON, CHRIS—PHOTOGRAPHS
PH00812 631 (May 28, 1992) p15. "The Spin Doctors' Chris Barron, Eric Schenkman And Aaron Comess (from left)" (Mazur, Kevin)
PH00813 647 (January 7, 1993) p36. "...And Practices Some Pretzel-Shape-Yogi Exercises In The Privacy Of His Hotel Room" (Seliger, Mark)
PH00814 647 (January 7, 1993) p36. "Barron As Mr. Bubble" (Seliger, Mark)
PH00815 647 (January 7, 1993) p39. "Barron Takes A Breather In New Hampshire Before Show Time" (Seliger, Mark)
PH00816 647 (January 7, 1993) p36. "Barron, A Health-Juice Freak, gets Ready For The Evening's Festivities By Whipping Up One Of His Special Vegetable Energy Cocktails" (Seliger, Mark)
PH00817 647 (January 7, 1993) p38. "Chris Barron Puts His Best Foot Forward" (Seliger, Mark)
PH00818 647 (January 7, 1993) p36. "Chris Barron Shows off His Double-Platinum Tonsils In Extreme Close-Up" (Seliger, Mark)
PH00819 647 (January 7, 1993) p39. "In Rochester, New York, Chris Barron Connects With The Kids" (Seliger, Mark)
PH00820 647 (January 7, 1993) p36. "...While Chris Barron Goes Into Rubber-Legs Overdrive Onstage..." (Seliger, Mark)
PH00820a 647 (August 5, 1993) p60. "Christopher Barron" (Atashian, John)
PH00821 672 (December 23, 1993) p40. "Left: Head Doctor Chris Barron" (Mazur, Kevin)
PH00822 684 (June 16, 1994) p18. "A Force Of Hobbit: Schenkman, White, Barron And Comess Back In The Studio"
PH00823 695 (November 17, 1994) p135. "Spin Doctors" (Seeff, Norman)
BARRON, CHRIS—PHOTOGRAPHS—PORTRAITS
PH00824 647 (January 7, 1993) p34. "[Spin Doctors]" (Seliger, Mark)
BARROW, GEOFF—PHOTOGRAPHS
PH00825 702 (February 23, 1995) p38. "Noir-Agers Beth Gibbons (left) And Geoff Barrow" (Cultice, Joseph)
BARRY, DAVE—PHOTOGRAPHS
PH00826 634-635 (July 9, 1992) p13. "Authorial Intrusion: Stephen King, Dave Barry And Ridley Pearson (from left)" (Foothorap, Robert)
BARRY, JACK—PHOTOGRAPHS
PH00827 691 (September 22, 1994) p104. "Van Doren, Left, And Stemple Flank Host Jack Barry On "Twenty-One," Circa 1956"
BARRY, JENNIFER—PHOTOGRAPHS
PH00828 651 (March 4, 1993) p28. "Dean Zuckerman, Kevin Costigan, Jennifer Barry, Eddie Fagin (from left)" (Lavine, Michael)
BARRY, MARION—PHOTOGRAPHS
PH00829 698-699 (December 29, 1994) p55. "Hizzoner Marion "Bitch Set Me Up" Barry, Mayor Of Our Nation's Capital" (Palmer, Brian)

BARRYMORE, DREW
PH00830 710 (June 15, 1995) pp[cover]. "Wild Thing: Drew Barrymore" (Seliger, Mark)
BARRYMORE, DREW—ILLUSTRATIONS
PH00831 631 (May 28, 1992) p59. "A Nineties Lolita From Hell" (Drawson, Blair)
PH00832 714 (August 10, 1995) p12. "Doesn't Matter" (Pendergrast, James T.)
BARRYMORE, DREW—PHOTOGRAPHS
PH00833 631 (May 28, 1992) p60. "Barrymore Flashes Tattoo And Toes To Lure Skerritt"
PH00834 631 (May 28, 1992) p60. "Barrymore Plays Moody Babe With Costar Gilbert"
PH00835 644 (November 26, 1992) p78. "[Poison Ivy]"
PH00836 650 (February 18, 1993) p67. "A Pensive Drew Barrymore Packs A Rod And A Conscience"
PH00837 681 (May 5, 1994) p22. "Drewlywed" (Galella, Ron)
PH00838 683 (June 2, 1994) p76. "Drew Barrymore ("Bad Girls")"
PH00839 690 (September 8, 1994) p21. "Mad Lovers Drew Barrymore (top right) And 7 Year Bitch" (Marshak, Bob)
PH00840 694 (November 3, 1994) p17. "[Drew Barrymore & Eric Erlandson]" (Allen, David)
PH00841 702 (February 23, 1995) p81. "Actresses Goldberg, Parker And Barrymore Blow It"
PH00842 710 (June 15, 1995) p88. "Barrymore And O'Donnell Before The Fall"
PH00843 710 (June 15, 1995) p70. "Barrymore At 7—Even Then A Flower Child"
PH00844 710 (June 15, 1995) pp66,69,71. "[Drew Barrymore]" (Seliger, Mark)
PH00845 710 (June 15, 1995) p68. "In New York, Barrymore Snuggles With Boyfriend Eric Erlandson Of Hole"
PH00846 712-713 (July 13, 1995) p115. "Villians: Carrey's Riddler, Jones' Two-face With Sirens Barrymore And Mazar"
PH00847 734 (May 16, 1996) p18. "[Drew Barrymore & Courtney Love]" (Granitz, Steve)
PH00848 741 (August 22, 1996) p48. "McConaughey Onscreen"
PH00849 750-751 (December 26, 1996) p206. "Drew Barrymore"
BARRYMORE, DREW—PHOTOGRAPHS—PORTRAITS
PH00850 652 (March 18, 1993) pp[enc.6]. "[Drew Barrymore]" (Staedler, Lance)
BARTELL, BILL—PHOTOGRAPHS
PH00851 735 (May 30, 1996) p13. "Muffs Roy McDonald And Kim Shattuck, Sean Ono Lennon, Muff Ronnie Barnett, Sideman Bill Bartell, And Eric Erlandson" (Phalen, Tom)
BARTON FINK (FILM)—PHOTOGRAPHS
PH00852 627 (April 2, 1992) p41. "'Barton Fink,' With John Turturro And John Goodman"
BARYSHNIKOV, MIKHAIL—PHOTOGRAPHS
PH00853 619-620 (December 12, 1991) p154. "'He's An Old-Fashioned Choreographer,' Says Baryshnikov (left), Rehearsing With Morris At White Oak Plantation" (Leibovitz, Annie)
BASEBALL—PHOTOGRAPHS
PH00854 660-661 (July 8, 1993) p124. "Franklin Sports Diamond Master Collector's Gloves, &8 Each" (Miller, Greg)
PH00855 660-661 (July 8, 1993) p124. "Franklin Sports Tropical Brite Two-Tone Baseballs, $5 Each" (Miller, Greg)
PH00856 660-661 (July 8, 1993) p124. "Franklin Sports Tee-Ball Set With Colorado Rockies Logo, $16" (Miller, Greg)
PH00857 684 (June 16, 1994) p64. "The Crawdads Remove Their Hats For The National Anthem" (Borris, Dan)
PH00858 684 (June 16, 1994) p61. "Game Time At The Crawdads' Dugout, In L.P. Frans Stadium, Hickory, N.C." (Borris, Dan)
BASEHART, RICHARD—PHOTOGRAPHS
PH00859 666 (September 30, 1993) p115. "All Wet: Basehart (far left) In 'Bottom Of The Sea'"
BASEHEAD—ALBUMS
PH00860 634-635 (July 9, 1992) p102. "Play With Toys"
PH00861 656 (May 13, 1993) p108. "Not In Kansas Anymore"
BASEHEAD—ILLUSTRATIONS—LETTERING
PH00862 628 (April 16, 1992) p51. "[Basehead]" (Allen, Terry)
BASEHEAD—PHOTOGRAPHS
PH00863 628 (April 16, 1992) p51. "Basehead, The Band (from left): Brian Hendrix, Keith Lofton, Bill Conway And Michael Ivey" (Ockenfels, Frank W.)
BASH AND POP—RECORDS
PH00864 649 (February 4, 1993) p64. "Friday Night Is Killing Me"
BASIC INSTINCT (FILM)—ILLUSTRATIONS
PH00865 628 (April 16, 1992) p89. "'Jagged Edge' Meets 'Fatal Attraction'" (Maffia, Daniel)
BASIC INSTINCT (FILM)—PHOTOGRAPHS
PH00866 628 (April 16, 1992) p90. "Clothes Off, Heat On, Douglas Romances The Stone"
PH00867 644 (November 26, 1992) p78. "[Basic Instinct]"
PH00868 645-646 (December 10, 1992) p190. "Sharon Stone"
PH00869 649 (February 4, 1993) p72. "Homage Of Ripoff? In 'Body of Evidence,' Madonna And Dafoe (left) Share Stone And Douglas's Basic Instincts"
BASINGER, KIM—ILLUSTRATIONS
PH00870 639 (September 17, 1992) p102. "Worst Supporting Actress"
BASINGER, KIM—PHOTOGRAPHS
PH00871 625 (March 5, 1992) p77. "Kim Basinger And Richard Gere Make Strange Bedfellows"
PH00872 630 (May 14, 1992) p13. "Kate Pierson, Fred Schneider And Kim Basinger (from left) At The Brown Fund-Raiser" (Mazur, Kevin)
PH00873 676 (February 24, 1994) p62. "Glam Gun Toters: Kim Basinger And Alec Baldwin"
THE BASKETBALL DIARIES (FILM)—PHOTOGRAPHS
PH00874 704 (March 23, 1995) p128. "Dicaprio, With McGaw (left), Takes A Dive"
BASQUIAT (FILM)—PHOTOGRAPHS
PH00875 741 (August 22, 1996) p105. "Wright, Bowie, Oldman, Hopper"
BASS, JOE—PHOTOGRAPHS
PH00876 710 (June 15, 1995) p40. "Posies Brian Young, Auer, Stringfellow, Joe Bass (from left)" (Moskowitz, Karen)
BASSETT, ANGELA—PHOTOGRAPHS
PH00877 659 (June 24, 1993) p89. "Biography: "What's Love Got To Do With It,' With Lawrence Fishburne And Angela Bassett As Ike And Tina Turner (left)"
PH00878 660-661 (July 8, 1993) p33. "What's Love Got To Do With It?" (Stevens, D.)
PH00879 665 (September 16, 1993) p77. "Best Actress"
PH00880 719 (October 19, 1995) p158. "Kathryn Bigelow (left) Directs Bassett And Fiennes In A Brutal Parable"
PH00881 724-725 (December 28, 1995) p138. "Houston, Devine, Rochon And Bassett In 'Exhale' (from left)"
BATES, ALAN—PHOTOGRAPHS
PH00882 624 (February 20, 1992) p50. "Alan Bates (left) And Friends At Dinner"
BATES, KATHY—PHOTOGRAPHS
PH00883 656 (May 13, 1993) p114. "Above, More King Characters Show Their Dark Side: Kathy Bates ('Misery'), Jack Nicholson ('The Shining'), Sissy Spacek ('Carrie')"
PH00884 706 (April 20, 1995) p88. "Kathy Bates And Jennifer Jason Leigh Hide Secrets"
BATES, SEAN—PHOTOGRAPHS—PORTRAITS
PH00885 652 (March 18, 1993) pp[enc.37]. "Podge And Sean Bates" (Seliger, Mark)
BATES, TODD—PHOTOGRAPHS
PH00886 652 (March 18, 1993) pp[enc.37]. "Todd Bates" (Seliger, Mark)

BATINKOFF, RANDALL—PHOTOGRAPHS—PORTRAITS
PH00887 638 (September 3, 1992) pp[enc.45-46]. "[Randall Batinkoff]" (Malige, Didier)
BATMAN (FILM)—PHOTOGRAPHS
PH00887a 634-635 (July 9, 1992) pp[cover]. "Inside Batman: The Rolling Stone Interview With Director Tim Burton" (Ritts, Herb)
PH00887b 645-646 (December 10, 1992) pp[cover]. "1992 Yearbook" (Ritts, Herb)
BATMAN FOREVER (FILM)—ILLUSTRATIONS
PH00888 712-713 (July 13, 1995) p113. "Fire Rockets 1, 2, 3" (Allen, Terry)
BATMAN FOREVER (FILM)—PHOTOGRAPHS
PH00889 709 (June 1, 1995) p68. "Potential Goldmines"
PH00890 712-713 (July 13, 1995) p114. "Good Guys: Kilmer's Batman, Kidman's Dr. Chase Meridian, O'Donnell's Robin"
PH00891 712-713 (July 13, 1995) p115. "Villians: Carrey's Riddler, Jones' Two-face With Sirens Barrymore And Mazar"
PH00892 716 (September 7, 1995) p78. "Summer Wrap-Up]"
PH00893 Number not assigned.
PH00894 Number not assigned.
BATMAN RETURNS (FILM)—ILLUSTRATIONS
PH00895 634-635 (July 9, 1992) p109. "Bat Girls On The Line" (Risko, Robert)
BATMAN RETURNS (FILM)—PHOTOGRAPHS
PH00896 634-635 (July 9, 1992) p42. "Danny DeVito's Penguin Is Another Of Burton's Mutated Children Of The Night" (Pedota, Jack)
PH00897 634-635 (July 9, 1992) p41. "Michelle Pfeiffer's Sexy, Leather-Bound Catwoman Reveals A Soul In Torment" (Rosenthal, Zade)
PH00898 634-635 (July 9, 1992) p111. "Pfeiffer Puts Keaton In His Place"
PH00899 639 (September 17, 1992) p102. "Best Actress"
PH00900 644 (November 26, 1992) p78. "[Batman Returns]"
PH00901 645-646 (December 10, 1992) p190. "Michelle Pfeiffer"
BATT, BRYAN—PHOTOGRAPHS
PH00902 715 (August 24, 1995) p110. "Friends United: Batt, Stewart, Weber And Weiss"
BATTAGLIA, FRAN—PHOTOGRAPHS
PH00903 669 (November 11, 1993) p49. "Battaglia Today" (Hom, Marc)
PH00904 669 (November 11, 1993) p49. "Suffer The Little Children"
BATTERIES—PHOTOGRAPHS
PH00905 670 (November 25, 1993) p129. "Rayovac Renewal Battery System, $15" (Miller, Greg)
BAUCUS, MAX—PHOTOGRAPHS
PH00906 660-661 (July 8, 1993) p51. "Montana Senator Max Baucus" (Walker, Diana)
BAUCUS, MAX—PHOTOGRAPHS—PORTRAITS
PH00907 709 (June 1, 1995) p36. "The Unforgiven: The NRA Targets Baucus" (Brack, Dennis)
BAUER, GARY—PHOTOGRAPHS
PH00908 729 (March 7, 1996) p45. "Gary Bauer Spearheads The Anti-Powellmania Crusade" (Simon, Martin)
BAUER, JILL—PHOTOGRAPHS—PORTRAITS
PH00909 693 (October 20, 1994) p129. "Bauer Of QVC: Exploiting Her Gift Of Gab"
BAUER, JUDAH—PHOTOGRAPHS
PH00910 700 (January 26, 1995) p25. "Blues Demolition Squad: Judah Bauer, Spencer, Russell Simins (from left)" (Ockenfels, Frank, 3)
PH00911 745 (October 17, 1996) p31. "Primitive Cool: Russell Simins, Jon Spencer And Judah Bauer (from left)" (Ockenfels, Frank W.)
BAULIEU, ETIENNE-EMILE—PHOTOGRAPHS
PH00912 656 (May 13, 1993) p90. "[RU-486]" (Mack, Andrew)
BAXTER, JEFF—PHOTOGRAPHS
PH00913 652 (March 18, 1993) p15. "Cheap Dates (from left): Phantom, Baxter, Sales, Stanton And James" (Matheu, Robert)
BAYE, NATHALIE—PHOTOGRAPHS
PH00914 650 (February 18, 1993) p66. "A Decade After 'The Return Of Martin Guerre' With Depardieu And Baye (top)..."
BAYLES, MARTHA—BOOKS
PH00915 698-699 (December 29, 1994) p64. "Hole In Our Soul"
BAYNTON-POWER, DAVID—PHOTOGRAPHS—PORTRAITS
PH00916 680 (April 21, 1994) p11. "[James]" (Borris, Dan)
BAYWATCH NIGHTS (TELEVISION SHOW)—ILLUSTRATIONS
PH00917 718 (October 5, 1995) p81. "[Baywatch Nights]" (Fishman, Miriam)
BEACH BOYS—ALBUMS
PH00918 663 (August 19, 1993) p73. "Good Vibrations"
BEACH BOYS—PHOTOGRAPHS
PH00919 707 (May 4, 1995) p33. "Wilson (standing) In The Studio"
BEALS, JENNIFER—ILLUSTRATIONS
PH00920 718 (October 5, 1995) p75. "Crime Fiction" (Kelley, Gary)
BEALS, JENNIFER—PHOTOGRAPHS—PORTRAITS
PH00921 718 (October 5, 1995) p76. "Detective Denzil Washington Falls Under The Spell Of Devil Jennifer Beals"
BEAM, LEWIS—PHOTOGRAPHS—PORTRAITS
PH00922 710 (June 15, 1995) p64. "Beam"
BEAN, JANET BEVERIDGE—PHOTOGRAPHS
PH00923 658 (June 10, 1993) p29. "Wink O'Bannon, Janet Beveridge Bean, Rick Rizzo And Doug McCombs (from left)" (Guip, Andy)
PH00924 686-687 (July 14, 1994) p74. "Erwin, Bean, Touring Member Bob Egan And Gay (from left); Mascot Matthew Bean-Rizzo (front)" (Elledge, Paul)
BEAN-BAYOG, MARGARET—PHOTOGRAPHS
PH00925 652 (March 18, 1993) pp[enc.22]. "Margaret Bean-Bayog At A State Medical Board Hearing In 1992"
BEAN-RIZZO, MATTHEW—PHOTOGRAPHS
PH00926 686-687 (July 14, 1994) p74. "Erwin, Bean, Touring Member Bob Egan And Gay (from left); Mascot Matthew Bean-Rizzo (front)" (Elledge, Paul)
BEARD, FRANK—PHOTOGRAPHS
PH00927 631 (May 28, 1992) p11. "ZZ Top's Dusty Hill, Frank Beard And Billy Gibbons (from left)" (Reitzel, Bill)
BEART, EMMANUELLE—PHOTOGRAPHS
PH00928 616 (October 31, 1991) p99. "Artist And Model: Michel Piccoli And Emmanuelle Beart"
BEASTIE BOYS—ALBUMS
PH00929 617 (November 14, 1991) p110. "Licensed To Ill" (Byram, Stephen)
PH00930 617 (November 14, 1991) p110. "Licensed To Ill" (Omes, World B.)
PH00931 633 (June 25, 1992) p41. "Check Your Head"
PH00932 651 (March 4, 1993) p56. "Check Your Head"
PH00933 683 (June 2, 1994) p68. "Ill Communication"
PH00934 689 (August 25, 1994) p104. "Ill Communication"
PH00935 700 (January 26, 1995) p55. "Ill Communication"
BEASTIE BOYS—ILLUSTRATIONS
PH00936 683 (June 2, 1994) p68. "'94 And Illin'" (Brown, Calef)
BEASTIE BOYS—PHOTOGRAPHS
PH00937 631 (May 28, 1992) p40. "The Beastie Boys (from left): Adam Yauch, Mike Diamond And Adam Horovitz" (Camp, E. J.)
PH00938 648 (January 21, 1993) p24. "MCA (left) And King Ad Rock Of The Beasties" (Mazur, Kevin)
PH00939 660-661 (July 8, 1993) p32. "Boys In The Hood: The Beasties In The Studio" (Powell, Ricky)
PH00940 677 (March 10, 1994) p22. "The Beastie Boys Are Among The Bands Up For Lollapalooza 1994" (Kino)
PH00941 678 (March 24, 1994) p43. "Beasties In The Jungle: Mike Diamond, Adam Horovitz And Adam Yauch (clockwise

from top left)" (Simons, Chip)
PH00942 683 (June 2, 1994) p16. "The Beastie Boys Rock" (Mazur, Kevin)
PH00943 684 (June 16, 1994) p36. "United Beastie Service: Adam Horowitz, Mike Diamond, Adam Yauch" (Kravitz, Jeff)
PH00944 688 (August 11, 1994) pp[cover]. "Beastie-ality: The Beastie Boys Funk Up Lollapalooza" (Rolston, Matthew)
PH00945 688 (August 11, 1994) p53. "The Beasties Onstage On Long Island, N.Y., During "Licensed To Ill" Tour" (Powell, Ricky)
PH00946 688 (August 11, 1994) p49. "Yaugh, Diamond, Horovitz (clockwise from top) In 1986"
PH00947 693 (October 20, 1994) p28. "Beasties Adam Yauch, Mike D, Adam Horowitz Warming Up At Radio City Music Hall During Rehearsal (from left)" (Mazur, Kevin)
PH00948 698-699 (December 29, 1994) p55. "[Beastie Boys]" (Rolston, Matthew)
PH00949 719 (October 19, 1995) p64. "Rubin, In White T-Shirt And Beard, With Members Of The Beasties, Slayer And Run-D.M.C. In 1985"
PH00950 726 (January 25, 1996) p17. "Keepin',It Real: Beasties Ad-Rock (left) And MCA" (Papas, B. J.)
PH00951 732 (April 18, 1996) p32. "Ad-Rock, Adam Yauch, Mike D. (from left)"
PH00952 736 (June 13, 1996) p19. "Beastie Boys Mike D, Adam Yauch And Adam Horovitz (from left)" (Baehler, Chapman)
PH00953 740 (August 8, 1996) pp20-21. "The Beasties' Mike D." (Blakesberg, Jay)

BEASTIE BOYS—PHOTOGRAPHS—PORTRAITS
PH00954 645-646 (December 10, 1992) p45. "[Beastie Boys]" (Springsteen, Pam)
PH00955 695 (November 17, 1994) p139. "Beastie Boys" (Rolston, Matthew)

BEAT GENERATION—PHOTOGRAPHS
PH00956 656 (May 13, 1993) p65. "[Beatnik]"

BEAT HAPPENING—PHOTOGRAPHS
PH00957 615 (October 17, 1991) p20. "Fest Organizer Calvin Johnson's Beat Happening" (Harrison, Mark)

BEAT HAPPENING—RECORDS
PH00958 649 (February 4, 1993) p68. "You Turn Me On"

BEATLES—ALBUMS
PH00959 617 (November 14, 1991) p92. "Sgt. Pepper's Lonely Hearts Club Band" (Blake, Peter)
PH00960 617 (November 14, 1991) p92. "Sgt. Pepper's Lonely Hearts Club Band" (Haworth, Jann)
PH00961 617 (November 14, 1991) p92. "Sgt. Pepper's Lonely Hearts Club Band" (Cooper, Michael)
PH00962 617 (November 14, 1991) p93. "White Album" (Hamilton, Richard)
PH00963 617 (November 14, 1991) p137. "With The Beatles" (Freeman, Robert)
PH00964 700 (January 26, 1995) p59. "Live At The BBC"
PH00965 726 (January 25, 1996) p43. "Anthology 1"
PH00966 731 (April 4, 1996) p59. "Anthology 2"
PH00967 749 (December 12, 1996) p84. "Anthology 3"

BEATLES—ILLUSTRATIONS
PH00968 700 (January 26, 1995) p59. "Beatles '95" (Risko, Robert)
PH00969 701 (February 9, 1995) p72. "The Beatles: Absolutely Fab-ulous" (Bartholomew, Caty)
PH00970 731 (April 4, 1996) p59. "Act Naturally" (Ventura, Andrea)

BEATLES—PHOTOGRAPHS
PH00971 618 (November 28, 1991) p28. "[Beatles]"
PH00972 643 (November 12, 1992) p63. "The Fab Four Pose For Dezo Hoffmann In 1963" (Hoffman, Dezo)
PH00973 645-646 (December 10, 1992) p88. "[The Complete Beatles Chronicle]"
PH00974 665 (September 16, 1993) p20. "Fab Score: Rights To Rare Beatles Pic"
PH00975 670 (November 25, 1993) p47. "The Old Find The Young Ever Threatening: In '66, Lennon Said The Beatles Topped Jesus On The Charts"
PH00976 680 (April 21, 1994) p63. "Hamburg Days: George Harrison, Stuart Sutcliffe And John Lennon" (Kirchherr, Astrid)
PH00977 680 (April 21, 1994) p64. "Ticket To Ride: Starr And Lennon With Photographer Astrid Kirchherr" (Scheler, Max)
PH00978 698-699 (December 29, 1994) p64. "All You Need Is Ears"
PH00979 711 (June 29, 1995) p23. "The Beatles At A Party For 'Sgt. Pepper,' 1967"
PH00980 718 (October 5, 1995) pp[enc.22]. "In The Living Room At Their House, In Oxford" (GS, Jamil)
PH00981 720 (November 2, 1995) p49. "Stu Sutcliffe & Paul McCartney" (Kirchherr, Astrid)
PH00982 722 (November 30, 1995) p28. "It Won't Be Long: The Fab Four In 1963"
PH00983 722 (November 30, 1995) p26. "Ringo Starr, John Lennon, Paul McCartney And George Harrison During The Filming Of 'Help!' In 1965: 'So Much Younger Than Today'" (Kindahl, Chris)
PH00984 724-725 (December 28, 1995) p63. "From Left: Joey, Johnny, Marky...Whoops!"
PH00985 726 (January 25, 1996) p46. "Starr, McCartney, Harrison, Lennon"
PH00986 748 (November 28, 1996) p40. "'Closure' Achieved: The Beatles Call It A Day, One More Time"

BEATTY, PAUL—PHOTOGRAPHS—PORTRAITS
PH00987 662 (August 5, 1993) p20. "[Paul Beatty]" (Borris, Dan)

BEATTY, WARREN—ILLUSTRATIONS
PH00988 632 (June 11, 1992) p187. "[Warren Beatty]" (Cronin, Brian)

BEATTY, WARREN—PHOTOGRAPHS
PH00989 621 (January 9, 1992) p56. "Warren Beatty And Annette Bening In Love"
PH00990 628 (April 16, 1992) p75. "In 1971, Altman Directed Hollywood Player Warren Beatty In 'McCabe And Mrs. Miller'"
PH00991 632 (June 11, 1992) p188. "'I Don't Hate It,' Warren Said When He Read The Published Story, 'And I Don't Like It'" (Ritts, Herb)

BEAUSOLEIL—PHOTOGRAPHS
PH00992 623 (February 6, 1992) p29. "Michael Doucet (left) And Beausoleil" (Mazur, Kevin)

BEAUTIFUL GIRLS (FILM)—PHOTOGRAPHS
PH00993 729 (March 7, 1996) p53. "Crazy Love Timothy Hutton And Natalie Portman"

BEAUTY AND THE BEAST (FILM)—ILLUSTRATIONS
PH00994 619-620 (December 12, 1991) p192. "In 'Beauty And The Beast,' Belle Sees Beneath The Surface To The Man Inside"

BEAVIS & BUTT-HEAD—ALBUMS
PH00995 671 (December 9, 1993) p66. "The Beavis And Butt-Head Experience"
PH00996 676 (February 24, 1994) p16. "The Beavis & Butt-Head Experience"
PH00997 Number not assigned.
PH00998 Number not assigned.

BEAVIS & BUTT-HEAD—ILLUSTRATIONS
PH00999 663 (August 19, 1993) p45. "[Beavis & Butt-Head]" (Judge, Mike)
PH01000 663 (August 19, 1993) pp[cover]. "Beavis & Butt-Head: The Voice Of A New Generation" (Judge, Mike)
PH01001 663 (August 19, 1993) p50. "Judge: 'It's This Funny, Awkward Moment In Life When You Want To Be Supermacho And Show You're Not A Kid.'" (Judge, Mike)
PH01002 672-673 (December 23, 1993) p188. "[Covers]" (Judge, Mike)
PH01003 674 (January 27, 1994) p41. "'Beavis & Butt-Head' Takes The Best With The Worst"

PH01004 678 (March 24, 1994) pp[cover]. "50,000,000 Beavis & Butt-head Fans Can't Be Wrong" (Judge, Mike)
PH01005 678 (March 24, 1994) pp38-39,41-42. "[Beavis & Butt-Head]" (Judge, Mike)
PH01006 681 (May 5, 1994) p8. "Instant Amnesia" (Pendergrast, James T.)

BEAVIS & BUTT-HEAD DO AMERICA (FILM)—ILLUSTRATIONS
PH01006a 750-751 (December 26, 1996) p34. "A Billion Dollars Worth Of Boys: Beavis And Butthead Nail A Take With A Heavily Disguised Demi Moore"
PH01006b 750-751 (December 26, 1996) p38. "Fame Is Cool: Beavis And Butt-Head Tangle With An Actor Who Is Said To Be Bruce Willis"

BEAVIS & BUTTHEAD DO AMERICA (FILM)—PHOTOGRAPHS
PH01007 743 (September 19, 1996) p88. "Dickheads"

BECK—ALBUMS
PH01008 679 (April 7, 1994) p72. "Mellow Gold"
PH01009 698-699 (December 29, 1994) p190. "Mellow Gold"
PH01010 736 (June 13, 1996) p77. "Odelay"

BECK—ILLUSTRATIONS
PH01011 680 (April 21, 1994) p3. "Beck" (Burke, Philip)
PH01012 683 (June 2, 1994) p82. "Loser Gets Lucky: Beck" (Allen, Terry)
PH01013 695 (November 17, 1994) p73. "Beck" (Brown, Calef)
PH01014 736 (June 13, 1996) p77. "Surrealistic Pillar" (Clarke, Greg)

BECK—PHOTOGRAPHS
PH01015 669 (November 11, 1993) p17. "Beck: L.A.'s Latest Label Interest" (Dipaola, Debra)
PH01016 674 (January 27, 1994) p29. "Backstage At McCabe's" (Kravitz, Jeff)
PH01017 680 (April 21, 1994) p80. "Do Not Call Him A Slacker" (Hales-Tooke, Hugh)
PH01018 688 (August 11, 1994) p38. "In Search of The Perfect Groove: Beck" (Garrity, Brian)
PH01019 698-699 (December 29, 1994) p37. "[Beck]" (Keeley, Dennis)
PH01020 714 (August 10, 1995) p15. "Shandling, Left, And Beck On The Set Of 'Larry Sanders'" (Hole, Danny)
PH01021 715 (August 24, 1995) p43. "The Visionary Iconoclast Beck Brings The Tribes Together With Head Swimming, Low-Fi Boogie" (Blakesberg, Jay)
PH01022 723 (December 14, 1995) p45. "Beck In The Saddle Again In Los Angeles" (Annalisa)
PH01023 723 (December 14, 1995) p27. "The Show-Stealin' Beck" (Blakesberg, Jay)
PH01024 730 (March 21, 1996) p17. "Beck, Devo's Mark Mothersbaugh, Bob Casale, Josh Freese, Bob Mothersbaugh, Jerry Casale" (Anderson, Vera)
PH01025 738-739 (July 11, 1996) p51. "[Beck]" (Winters, Dan)
PH01026 738-739 (July 11, 1996) p52. "Seeing Beck In Concert Is A Crapshoot That Can Either Exhilerate Or Aggravate" (Mazur, Kevin)
PH01027 743 (September 19, 1996) p19. "Beck, Presumably In Mid-Beck Thing (pretending to eat a burger, perhaps)" (Phalen, Tom)
PH01028 744 (October 3, 1996) p34. "Beck Rejoices At The Alter Of Elvis" (Zielenbach, Tim)
PH01029 745 (October 17, 1996) p27. "Beck (left) And Foo Fighter Dave Grohl" (Mazur, Kevin)

BECK—PHOTOGRAPHS—PORTRAITS
PH01030 680 (April 21, 1994) p79. "[Beck]" (Hales-Tooke, Hugh)
PH01031 736 (June 13, 1996) pp[cover]. "Rock & Roll Summer!" (Ockenfels, Frank W.)
PH01032 750-751 (December 26, 1996) p78. "Beck Outside The Legendary Cain's Ballroom, In Tulsa, Okla." (Basil)

BECK, JEFF—ALBUMS
PH01033 665 (September 16, 1993) p70. "Crazy Legs"

BECK, JEFF—ILLUSTRATIONS
PH01034 653 (April 1, 1993) p5. "Jeff Beck" (Burke, Philip)

BECK, JEFF—PHOTOGRAPHS
PH01035 625 (March 5, 1992) p11. "Jeff Beck (left) And Jimmy Page" (Mazur, Kevin)
PH01036 636 (August 6, 1992) p13. "Beck (left) With Waters" (Adebari, Eugene)
PH01037 653 (April 1, 1993) p15. "[Jeff Beck]" (Seliger, Mark)
PH01038 653 (April 1, 1993) p16. "The Jeff Beck group Circa 1968: Mickey Waller, Beck, Stewart And Wood (from left)"
PH01039 655 (April 29, 1993) p37. "Clapton, Bill Wyman And Jeff Beck Onstage At London's Royal Albert Hall In September 1983, Performing At The ARMS Benefit Concerts" (Zuffante, Vinnie)
PH01040 670 (November 25, 1993) pp74-75. "[Jeff Beck]" (Seliger, Mark)
PH01041 677 (March 10, 1994) p27. "Jeff Beck Gets Ready To Induct Stewart" (Mazur, Kevin)
PH01042 722 (November 30, 1995) p70. "Beck: Conjuring Lusty Voices From His Strat" (Pulin, Chuck)

BECK, JEFF—PHOTOGRAPHS—PORTRAITS
PH01043 625 (March 5, 1992) pp14-15. "On The Evening Of The Seventh Annual Hall Of Fame Induction Ceremony, 'Rolling Stone' Gathered These Nine Legendary Guitarists At The Waldorf-Astoria For A Once-In-A-Lifetime Pho
PH01044 643 (November 12, 1992) p119. "Jeff Beck" (Seliger, Mark)

BECKER, JOZEF—PHOTOGRAPHS
PH01045 660-661 (July 8, 1993) p97. "The Loud Family: Paul Wieneke, Zachary Smith, Miller, Jozef Becker And Rob Poor" (Blakesberg, Jay)

BECKER, WALTER—PHOTOGRAPHS
PH01046 637 (August 20, 1992) p11. "Rock And Soul (from left): Boz Scaggs, Walter Becker, Donald Fagen, Michael McDonald, Phoebe Snow And Chuck Jackson" (Hamilton, James)
PH01047 664 (September 2, 1993) p32. "Walter Becker And Donald Fagen" (Mazur, Kevin)
PH01048 667 (October 14, 1993) p37. "Walter Becker (left), Donald Fagen Get Back, Jack" (Mazur, Kevin)
PH01049 672-673 (December 23, 1993) p58. "Below: Walter Becker And Donald Fagen" (Mazur, Kevin)

BECKER, WES—PHOTOGRAPHS
PH01050 706 (April 20, 1995) pp[enc.14]. "Huntington Beach High Surf Team" (Seliger, Mark)

BECKINSALE, KATE—PHOTOGRAPHS
PH01051 735 (May 30, 1996) p57. "Life On The Farm"

BEDARD, IRENE—PHOTOGRAPHS
PH01052 736 (June 13, 1996) p54. "Irene Bedard And A Martinez In HBO's Tribal Drama 'Grand Avenue'"

BEDLAM ROVERS—PHOTOGRAPHS—PORTRAITS
PH01053 619-620 (December 12, 1991) p49. "...And San Francisco's Bedlam Rovers (below)" (Blakesberg, Jay)

BEE GEES—PHOTOGRAPHS—PORTRAITS
PH01054 643 (November 12, 1992) p143. "The Bee Gees" (Seliger, Mark)

BEERS, GARRY—PHOTOGRAPHS
PH01055 663 (August 19, 1993) p27. "INXS's Garry Gary Beers, Iggy Pop, Andrew Fariss And Jon Fariss (from left)" (Mazur, Kevin)
PH01056 671 (December 9, 1993) p18. "INXS Marks Their Spot: Pengilly; Beers, Tim, Andrew And Jon Farriss; Hutchence (from left)" (Borris, Dan)

BEFORE AND AFTER (FILM)—PHOTOGRAPHS
PH01057 730 (March 21, 1996) p106. ""Before" (from left): Neeson, Furlong And Streep"

BEFORE SUNRISE (FILM)—ILLUSTRATIONS
PH01058 702 (February 23, 1995) p79. "Sex And The Single Slacker" (Schumaker, Ward)

BEFORE SUNRISE (FILM)—PHOTOGRAPHS
PH01059 702 (February 23, 1995) p80. "And Enjoy A Night In Vienna"
PH01060 702 (February 23, 1995) p80. "Julie Delpy And Ethan Hawke Share A Kiss"
PH01061 702 (February 23, 1995) p80. "Take Direction From Richard Linklater"
PH01062 703 (March 9, 1995) p48. "Let's Go! Austria: Hawke Meets Delpy On A Eurailpass In 'Before Sunrise'" (Brandenstein, Gabriela)
BEFORE THE RAIN (FILM)—PHOTOGRAPHS
PH01063 704 (March 23, 1995) p128. "Manchevski Directs Lovers Cartlidge And Serbedzija"
BEING HUMAN (FILM)—PHOTOGRAPHS
PH01064 683 (June 2, 1994) p76. "Robin Williams Plays The Ages Of Man"
BEINHORN, MICHAEL—PHOTOGRAPHS
PH01065 634-635 (July 9, 1992) p11. "Booker T. In The Studio With Producer Michael Beinhorn And Dave Pirner (from left)" (Soica, Alex)
BELAFONTE, HARRY—PHOTOGRAPHS
PH01066 723 (December 14, 1995) p92. "Race As An Issue: Belafonte And Travolta"
PH01067 728 (February 22, 1996) pp18-19. "Belafonte, Seeger And Guthrie (from left)" (Mazur, Kevin)
BELANOFF, CANDICE—PHOTOGRAPHS—PORTRAITS
PH01068 637 (August 20, 1992) p20. "Candice Belanoff, John Kimbrough And Joey Waronker (from left)" (Cuffaro, Chris)
BELEW, ADRIAN—PHOTOGRAPHS
PH01069 712-713 (July 13, 1995) p46. "Adrian Belew: Animated Art Rock" (Capak, R. J.)
BELEW, ADRIAN—PHOTOGRAPHS—PORTRAITS
PH01070 684 (June 16, 1994) p18. "Belew, Fripp, Bruford And Levin"
BELL BIV DEVOE—ALBUMS
PH01071 663 (August 19, 1993) p74. "Hootie Mack"
BELL JET RANGER (HELICOPTER)—PHOTOGRAPHS
PH01072 619-620 (December 12, 1991) p100. "The Bell Jet Ranger Copter After The Crash" (Trott, Greg)
BELL, ANDY—PHOTOGRAPHS
PH01073 722 (November 30, 1995) p20. "Hello, Darkness! Andy Bell, Johnston And Clarke (from left)" (Mazur, Kevin)
BELL, BRIAN—PHOTOGRAPHS
PH01074 694 (November 3, 1994) p40. "Matt Sharp, Patrick Wilson, Brian Bell And Rivers Cuomo (from left)" (Elledge, Paul)
PH01075 704 (March 23, 1995) pp62-63. "Matt Sharp, Rivers Cuomo, Brian Bell, Pat Wilson (from left)" (Corbijn, Anton)
BELL, CHRIS—PHOTOGRAPHS
PH01076 668 (October 28, 1993) p15. "Big Star On The Steps Of Alex Chilton's Memphis, Tenn., Home In 1972: Andy Hummel, Jody Stephens, Chris Bell And Chilton (above, from left)" (Manning, Carole)
BELL, DAVID—PHOTOGRAPHS
PH01077 730 (March 21, 1996) p79. "Lyndonville Pediatrician David Bell (above, examining a patient who doesn't have CFS), Was Initially Baffled By The Children's Symptoms" (Tavee, Tom)
BELL, JOHN—PHOTOGRAPHS
PH01078 631 (May 28, 1992) p17. "Widespread Panic (from left): John Bell, Michael Houser, Todd Nance, David Schools And Domingo Ortiz" (Messer, Alan)
BELL, RICO—PHOTOGRAPHS
PH01079 736 (June 13, 1996) p19. "Where's Sammy And Frank?" (Herdon, David)
BELL, TRENT—PHOTOGRAPHS—PORTRAITS
PH01080 630 (May 14, 1992) p32. "Chainsaw Kittens (clockwise from top left): McBay, Meade, Preston, Bell And Metzger" (Mazur, Kevin)
BELLE EPOQUE (FILM)—PHOTOGRAPHS
PH01081 681 (May 5, 1994) p49. "Sanz Nuzzles Verdu For A Beautiful Time"
BELLINGHAM, NORMAN—PHOTOGRAPHS
PH01082 628 (April 16, 1992) pp[enc.27]. "[Norman Bellingham, Wendy Williams, Kent Ferguson]" (Nicks, Dewey)
PH01083 628 (April 16, 1992) pp[enc.31]. "[Norman Bellingham]" (Nicks, Dewey)
PH01084 628 (April 16, 1992) pp[enc.34]. "[Wendy Williams, Norman Bellingham]" (Nicks, Dewey)
BELLO, FRANK—PHOTOGRAPHS
PH01085 656 (May 13, 1993) p31. "Noisemakers Ian, Dan Spitz, Bush, Frank Bello And Benante (from left)" (Mazur, Kevin)
PH01086 722 (November 30, 1995) p34. "Totally Ruled By Instinct: Band Members Charlie Benante, Scott Ian, John Bush And Frank Bello (from left)" (Cultice, Joseph)
BELLUM, SLADE—PHOTOGRAPHS
PH01087 721 (November 16, 1995) p81. "The Tribe That Sticks Together: Slade Bellum, Lynn Breedlove, Leslie Mah, Lynn Payne, Lynn Flipper (from left)" (Yemchuk, Yelena)
BELLY—ALBUMS
PH01088 653 (April 1, 1993) p68. "Star"
PH01089 654 (April 15, 1993) p64. "Star"
PH01090 655 (April 29, 1993) p80. "Star"
PH01091 656 (May 13, 1993) p128. "Star"
PH01092 674 (January 27, 1994) p44. "Star"
BELLY—ILLUSTRATIONS
PH01093 709 (June 1, 1995) p14. "Sold Out" (Pendergrast, James T.)
BELLY—PHOTOGRAPHS
PH01094 659 (June 24, 1993) p15. "Belly At The Santa Monica Pier" (Allen, Greg)
PH01095 663 (August 19, 1993) p27. "Belly's Tanya Donelly (left) And Gail Greenwood With Robyn Hitchcock" (Mazur, Kevin)
PH01096 691 (September 22, 1994) p20. "Members Of Bettie Serveert And Belly With Singer Jim Lauderdale (far right) And Juliana Hatfield (seated, right) At Central Park" (Roberts, Ebet)
PH01097 706 (April 20, 1995) pp[cover]. "Belly gets Big" (Seliger, Mark)
PH01098 749 (December 12, 1996) p22. "[Belly]" (Seliger, Mark)
BELLY—PHOTOGRAPHS—PORTRAITS
PH01099 649 (February 4, 1993) p16. "Chris Gorman, Tanya Donelly And Tom Gorman (from left)" (Feingold, Deborah)
PH01100 656 (May 13, 1993) p63. "[Belly]" (Anchor, Mat)
PH01101 672-673 (December 23, 1993) p45. "[Belly]" (Double, Stephen)
BELMAN, DANA—PHOTOGRAPHS
PH01102 660-661 (July 8, 1993) p61. "Twenty Years Old And What Next?" (Smale, Brian)
BELMAN, KRIS—PHOTOGRAPHS
PH01103 660-661 (July 8, 1993) p56. "A 'Virile Specimen' Is What Kris Belman's Father Called His Son After He Was Arrested" (Smale, Brian)
BELMAR, NEW JERSEY—PHOTOGRAPHS
PH01104 636 (August 6, 1992) p16. "A Confrontation After Two Cars Collide" (Costello, Thomas P.)
BELOVED (BOOK)—PHOTOGRAPHS
PH01105 639 (September 17, 1992) p80. "Beloved"
BELTON, DON—PHOTOGRAPHS
PH01106 651 (March 4, 1993) p23. "Michael Thomas, Jaqueline Thomas, Paul Cassidy, Elvis Costello, Don Belton" (Westenberg, Kevin)
BELUSHI, JIM—PHOTOGRAPHS
PH01107 655 (April 29, 1993) p68. "Wild Palms"
PH01108 720 (November 2, 1995) p17. "Good Lovin', They Got A Truckload: Belushi, Clinton And Gore In L.A."
BELUSHI, JOHN—ILLUSTRATIONS
PH01109 632 (June 11, 1992) p124. "[John Belushi]" (Cronin,

Brian)
BELUSHI, JOHN—PHOTOGRAPHS
PH01110 632 (June 11, 1992) p126. "Young And Belushi Meet The Dead Boys, December 1977" (Kearney, Mitch)
BELUSHI, JOHN—PHOTOGRAPHS—PORTRAITS
PH01111 632 (June 11, 1992) p125. "[John Belushi]" (Hiro)
PH01112 645-646 (December 10, 1992) p161. "John Belushi, 1982"
PH01113 706 (April 20, 1995) p86. "The 'SNL' Legacy Of Screen Shame"
BEN—PHOTOGRAPHS
PH01114 730 (March 21, 1996) p52. "Ben Scalps Strangers"
BENANTE, CHARLIE—PHOTOGRAPHS
PH01115 656 (May 13, 1993) p31. "Noisemakers Ian, Dan Spitz, Bush, Frankie Bello And Benante (from left)" (Mazur, Kevin)
PH01116 722 (November 30, 1995) p34. "Totally Ruled By Instinct: Band Members Charlie Benante, Scott Ian, John Bush And Frank Bello (from left)" (Cultice, Joseph)
BENATAR, PAT—ALBUMS
PH01117 666 (September 30, 1993) p108. "Gravity's Rainbow"
BENEDICTINE MONKS OF SANTO DOMINGO DE SILOS—ILLUSTRATIONS
PH01118 685 (June 30, 1994) p88. "Enchanted: Benedictine Monks" (Levine, Laura)
BENEDICTINE MONKS OF SANTO DOMINGO DE SILOS—PHOTOGRAPHS
PH01119 690 (September 8, 1994) p32. "[Benedictine Monks Of Santo Domingo De Silos]"
BENING, ANNETTE—PHOTOGRAPHS
PH01120 621 (January 9, 1992) p56. "Warren Beatty And Annette Bening In Love"
PH01121 722 (November 30, 1995) p76. "Annette Bening As His Hot Date"
BENNETT, JAY—PHOTOGRAPHS
PH01122 658 (June 10, 1993) p32. "Clockwise From Left: Lars Gustafsson, Jay Bennett, Ken Hartz And Mike Hazelrigg" (Elledge, Paul)
PH01123 707 (May 4, 1995) p32. "The Buddy System: Johnston, Coomer, Stirratt, Tweedy And Bennett (from left)" (Miller, Brad)
BENNETT, TONY—PHOTOGRAPHS
PH01124 654 (April 15, 1993) p11. "Chili Peppers Kiedis And Flea Flank Fan Tony Bennett" (Downie, Scott)
PH01125 667 (October 14, 1993) p39. "Flea, Bennett And Anthony Kiedis" (Mazur, Kevin)
PH01126 672-673 (December 23, 1993) p63. "Left: Flea, Bennett And Kiedis" (Kravitz, Jeff)
PH01127 675 (February 10, 1994) p23. "Tony Bennett Meets His Teenage Fanclub"
PH01128 714 (August 10, 1995) p17. "Absolut-ly Fabulous: Bennett And Stewart In New York" (Mazur, Kevin)
BENNETT, TONY—PHOTOGRAPHS—PORTRAITS
PH01129 679 (April 7, 1994) p30. "[Tony Bennett]" (Irish, Len)
PH01130 683 (June 2, 1994) p27. "Above: Lang, Bennett, Costello" (Mazur, Kevin)
PH01131 706 (April 20, 1995) p15. "Bennett (left) And Springsteen Bagged A Few" (Mazur, Kevin)
BENNY AND JOON (FILM)—PHOTOGRAPHS
PH01132 656 (May 13, 1993) p116. "Sex Is Sweet For Depp (left) And Masterson"
BENTLEY, JASON—PHOTOGRAPHS
PH01133 716 (September 7, 1995) p32. "Jason Bentley Rides On The Wheels Of Steel" (Villand, Kiino)
BENTLEY, JASON—PHOTOGRAPHS—PORTRAITS
PH01134 747 (November 14, 1996) p60. "[Jason Bentley]" (Ockenfels, Frank W.)
BENTLEY, JAY—PHOTOGRAPHS
PH01135 700 (January 26, 1995) p17. "Bad Religion's Brian Baker, Greg Graffin, Bobby Schayer, Jay Bentley and Greg Hetson" (Kravitz, Jeff)
PH01136 722 (November 30, 1995) p19. "Graffin, Ocasek, Jay Bentley, Brian Baker, Greg Hetson And Bobby Schayer (from left)" (Mazur, Kevin)
BENTLEY, JAY—PHOTOGRAPHS—PORTRAITS
PH01137 695 (November 17, 1994) p40. "Bad Religion" (Guip, Amy)
BENTLEY, PATRICK—PHOTOGRAPHS
PH01138 660-661 (July 8, 1993) p96. "The Reverend Horton Heat: Jimbo Wallace, Jim Heath And Patrick 'Taz' Bentley" (Watermann, Greg)
BENTLEY, SCHAYER—PHOTOGRAPHS
PH01139 670 (November 25, 1993) p30. "Hetson, Bobby Schayer, Bentley, Gurewitz And Graffin (clockwise from top left)" (Zlozower, Neil)
BENTSEN, LLOYD—PHOTOGRAPHS
PH01140 664 (September 2, 1993) p35. "President Clinton And Treasury Secretary Lloyd Bentsen In The Rose Garden In July For The Announcement Of The Administration's New Community-Banking Initiative"
BERDAHL, BLAZE—PHOTOGRAPHS
PH01141 671 (December 9, 1993) p31. "Spinderella, Blaze Berdahl Of 'Ghostwriter,' Pepa And Salt (from left)" (Leibowitz, Eric)
BERENYI, MIKI—PHOTOGRAPHS
PH01142 639 (September 17, 1992) p64. "Miki Berenyi Of Lush" (Blakesberg, Jay)
BERENYI, MIKI—PHOTOGRAPHS—PORTRAITS
PH01143 729 (March 7, 1996) p29. "Lush Members Emma Anderson, Phil King, Miki Berenyi And Chris Acland (from left)" (Anker, Matt)
BERG, MATRACA—ALBUMS
PH01144 682 (May 19, 1994) p100. "The Speed Of Grace"
BERG, PETER—PHOTOGRAPHS
PH01145 735 (May 30, 1996) p57. "Preening"
BERG, TONY—PHOTOGRAPHS
PH01146 636 (August 6, 1992) p22. "Penn (left) In The Studio With Berg" (Cohen, Lester)
BERGEN, CANDICE—PHOTOGRAPHS
PH01147 619-620 (December 12, 1991) p202. "Anything For A Ratings Point: Candice Bergen's Murphy Brown Got Pregnant In A Season-Ending Cliffhanger"
BERGEN, POLLY—PHOTOGRAPHS
PH01148 618 (November 28, 1991) p103. "Robert Mitchum Harassed Polly Bergen In 1962"
BERGEN, TUSHKA—PHOTOGRAPHS
PH01149 688 (August 11, 1994) p63. "It's Ole To Nichols, Bergen, Eigeman And Sorvino"
BERGGREN, JENNY—PHOTOGRAPHS—PORTRAITS
PH01150 688 (August 11, 1994) p32. "Aces Jonas, Linn, Ekberg And Jenny (from left)" (Danelian, Stephen)
BERGGREN, JONAS—PHOTOGRAPHS—PORTRAITS
PH01150 688 (August 11, 1994) p32. "Aces Jonas, Linn, Ekberg And Jenny (from left)" (Danelian, Stephen)
BERGGREN, LINN—PHOTOGRAPHS—PORTRAITS
PH01150 688 (August 11, 1994) p32. "Aces Jonas, Linn, Ekberg And Jenny (from left)" (Danelian, Stephen)
BERGGREN, WES—PHOTOGRAPHS
PH01151 716 (September 7, 1995) p13. "Dye Hard: Daisy's DeLaughter (left) And Wes Berggren" (George, Tryan)
BERIA, LAVRENTI PAVLOVICH—PHOTOGRAPHS—PORTRAITS
PH01152 657 (May 27, 1993) p46. "Beria, Stalin's Man, Kept Watch Over The Scientists"
BERKLEE COLLEGE OF MUSIC—PHOTOGRAPHS
PH01153 666 (September 30, 1993) p72. "Students At Guitar Hall: There Is A Concern That The General Level Of Musicianship Has Gone Down" (Hill, Britain)
BERKLEY, ELIZABETH—PHOTOGRAPHS
PH01154 719 (October 19, 1995) p156. "Elizabeth Berkley Showing Off"

PH01155 724-725 (December 28, 1995) p134. "The 10 Worst Movies Of 1995 (degrees of sleaze)"
BERLE, PETER—PHOTOGRAPHS
PH01156 719 (October 19, 1995) p78. "Under The Egret: Berle, Former CEO Of The National Audubon Society" (McDonough, Patricia)
BERLIN WALL—PHOTOGRAPHS
PH01157 704 (March 23, 1995) p51. "And The Walls Came Tumbling Down: A Chunk Of The Berlin Wall, A Nostalgic Memento From The Good Ol' Days Of The Cold War, Now Sits In The CIA's Compound" (Alfred)
BERLIN, STEVE—PHOTOGRAPHS
PH01158 616 (October 31, 1991) p13. "Cesar Rosas, Louis Perez, Conrad Lozano, David Hidalgo And Steve Berlin (from left)" (Granitz, Steve)
BERMET, ZOE—PHOTOGRAPHS
PH01159 729 (March 7, 1996) p28. "Lawless, Harley And Zoe Bermet (from left) Hone Their Skills At The Home Alive Classroom, In Seattle" (Wescott, Stacey)
BERNHARD, SANDRA—PHOTOGRAPHS
PH01160 700 (January 26, 1995) p16. "Farrell, Bernhard And Doe Ham It Up" (Winter, Kevin)
PH01161 705 (April 6, 1995) p16. "[Sandra Bernhard & Courtney Love]" (McMullan, Patrick)
BERNHARD, SANDRA—PHOTOGRAPHS—PORTRAITS
PH01162 692 (October 6, 1994) p30. "[Sandra Bernhard]" (Von Unwerth, Ellen)
BERNSTEIN, LEONARD—ILLUSTRATIONS—PORTRAITS
PH01163 641 (October 15, 1992) p197. "[Leonard Bernstein]" (Summers, Mark)
BERRY, BILL—PHOTOGRAPHS
PH01164 628 (April 16, 1992) p11. "R.E.M.'s Mike Mills, Michael Stipe, Peter Buck And Bill Berry (from left)" (Mazur, Kevin)
PH01165 640 (October 1, 1992) p20. "Michael Stipe, Peter Buck, Mike Mills And Bill Berry (clockwise from left)" (Corbijn, Anton)
PH01166 647 (January 7, 1993) p9. "From Left: Mike Mills, Buck, Bill Berry and Stipe" (Colletti, Steve)
PH01167 693 (October 20, 1994) p27. "R.E.M.'s Bill Berry, Michael Stipe, Peter Buck, Mike Mills" (Mazur, Kevin)
PH01168 704 (March 23, 1995) p32. "Band On The Run: Berry, Mills, Stipe And Buck (above, from left)" (Sheehan, Tom)
PH01169 704 (March 23, 1995) p30. "Bill Berry Told R.E.M. He'd Quit If They Didn't Get Back To Rock & Roll Basics" (Liguz, Andrzej)
PH01170 724-725 (December 28, 1995) p46. "R.E.M.'s Berry Revealed A Lot" (Jensen, David)
PH01171 726 (January 25, 1996) p42. "Peter Buck, Michael Stipe, Bill Berry, Mike Mills" (Jensen, David)
PH01172 737 (June 27, 1996) p29. "R.E.M.'s Mike Mills, Bill Berry, Stipe And Buck (from left) Have Split With Their Longtime Manager" (Rider, Paul)
BERRY, BILL—PHOTOGRAPHS—PORTRAITS
PH01173 693 (October 20, 1994) p61. "Bill Berry" (Seliger, Mark)
PH01174 706 (April 20, 1995) p25. "Berry: Healing" (Crum, Lee)
BERRY, CHUCK—PHOTOGRAPHS
PH01175 662 (August 5, 1993) p18. "Architect I. M. Pei Greets Chuck Berry" (Mazur, Kevin)
PH01176 662 (August 5, 1993) p18. "Diggin' In The Dirt: The Celebrity Crew Does The Honors" (Mazur, Kevin)
PH01177 662 (August 5, 1993) p18. "One Big Happy Family: Pirner, Berry, Townshend, Joel (from left)" (Mazur, Kevin)
PH01178 663 (August 19, 1993) p62. "Chuck Berry, Who Performed At The Reunion, And Kalell"
PH01179 672-673 (December 23, 1993) p39. "Diggin' In The Dirt: Soul Asylum's Dave Pirner, Chuck Berry, Townshend, Billy Joel" (Mazur, Kevin)
PH01180 677 (March 10, 1994) p28. "Berry, Weir And Shirli Dixon (from left)" (Mazur, Kevin)
PH01181 677 (March 10, 1994) p27. "Willie Dixon's Daughter Shirli (left) And Widow, Marie, With Presenter Chuck Berry" (Mazur, Kevin)
PH01182 719 (October 19, 1995) p35. "Chuck Berry Backstage At Cleveland Stadium" (Corbijn, Anton)
PH01183 719 (October 19, 1995) p42. "Chuck Berry, Bob Dylan And James Brown Head Toward The Artists' Tents At The Close Of The Show" (Corbijn, Anton)
PH01184 724-725 (December 28, 1995) p56. "Hail Hail: Berry And Brown" (Mazur, Kevin)
BERRY, CHUCK—PHOTOGRAPHS—PORTRAITS
PH01185 643 (November 12, 1992) p211. "Chuck Berry" (Watson, Albert)
BERRY, HALLE—ILLUSTRATIONS
PH01186 636 (August 6, 1992) p63. "Depreciating Eddie Murphy" (Brodner, Steven)
BERRY, HALLE—PHOTOGRAPHS
PH01187 627 (April 2, 1992) p41. "Jackson, With Halle Berry, In 'Jungle Fever'"
BERRY, MARK—PHOTOGRAPHS—PORTRAITS
PH01188 723 (December 14, 1995) p40. "Kermit, Bez And Ryder (from left) Mix An Intoxicating Musical Cocktail" (Westenberg, Kevin)
BERTINELLI, VALERIE—PHOTOGRAPHS
PH01189 619-620 (December 12, 1991) p31. "Van Halen And Bertinelli Wait For Wolfgang" (Granitz, Steve)
PH01190 645-646 (December 10, 1992) p98. "Valerie Bertinelli, Van Halen And James Wood At A Clinton Rally" (Jacobs, Michael)
BETTENCOURT, NUNO—PHOTOGRAPHS
PH01191 636 (August 6, 1992) p21. "Extreme's Nuno Bettencourt (seated, right) At The Boards With Bob St. John"
BETTENCOURT, NUNO—PHOTOGRAPHS—PORTRAITS
PH01192 662 (August 5, 1993) p59. "Nuno Bettencourt" (Seliger, Mark)
BETTER THAN EZRA—ALBUMS
PH01193 743 (September 19, 1996) p82. "Friction, Baby"
BETTER THAN EZRA—PHOTOGRAPHS
PH01194 710 (June 15, 1995) p46. "Griffin, Bonnecaze And Drummond (from left) Veg In The Garden District" (Chiasson, John)
BETTIE SERVEERT—ALBUMS
PH01195 655 (April 29, 1993) p61. "Palomine"
PH01196 702 (February 23, 1995) p77. "Lamprey"
BETTIE SERVEERT—PHOTOGRAPHS
PH01197 653 (April 1, 1993) p22. "Peter Visser, Herman Bunskoeke, Carol Van Dijk And Berend Dubbe (from left)" (Doove, Hester)
PH01198 691 (September 22, 1994) p20. "Members Of Bettie Serveert And Belly With Singer Jim Lauderdale (far right) And Juliana Hatfield (seated, right) At Central Park" (Roberts, Ebet)
BETTS, DICKEY—PHOTOGRAPHS
PH01199 624 (February 20, 1992) p12. "Gregg Allman (left) And Dickey Betts" (West, Kirk)
PH01200 702 (February 23, 1995) p50. "Party On! A Merry-Makin' Allman With Dickey Betts" (Mazur, Kevin)
BETTS, DICKEY—PHOTOGRAPHS—PORTRAITS
PH01201 643 (November 12, 1992) p136. "Dickey Betts & Gregg Allman" (Seliger, Mark)
BEVERLEY, ANNE—PHOTOGRAPHS—PORTRAITS
PH01202 747 (November 14, 1996) p32. "[Anne Beverley]"
THE BEVERLY HILLBILLIES (FILM)—PHOTOGRAPHS
PH01203 669 (November 11, 1993) p81. "Tomlin's Miss Hathaway Welcomes The Clampetts To 90210"
THE BEVERLY HILLBILLIES (TELEVISION SHOW)—PHOTOGRAPHS
PH01204 656 (May 13, 1993) p90. "[The Beverly Hillbillies]"

BEVERLY HILLS COP III (FILM)—PHOTOGRAPHS
PH01205 685 (June 30, 1994) p81. "Eddie Murphy Fires Off A New Volley Of "Cop" Action"
PH01206 684 (June 16, 1994) p114. "Potential Headaches"
PH01207 691 (September 22, 1994) p106. "Falling Ego"
BEYOND RANGOON (FILM)—PHOTOGRAPHS
PH01208 709 (June 1, 1995) p68. "Oscar Seekers"
PH01209 716 (September 7, 1995) p77. "Patricia Arquette Finds It's A Jungle Out There"
BEZ—PHOTOGRAPHS
PH01210 727 (February 8, 1996) p13. "Run For The Border: Ryder (left) And Bez In Cuba" (Ayanian, Ryan)
BHATT, V. M.—ALBUMS
PH01211 656 (May 13, 1993) p108. "A Meeting By The River"
BICYCLES—PHOTOGRAPHS
PH01212 634-635 (July 9, 1992) pp122-123. "[Toys]" (Goldin, David)
PH01213 660-661 (July 8, 1993) p123. "Cannondale b106 Expanding Bicycle-Seat Bag, $24" (Miller, Greg)
PH01214 660-661 (July 8, 1993) p123. "Cannondale Super V 3000 Suspension Bicycle, $3500" (Miller, Greg)
PH01215 686-687 (July 14, 1994) pp46-47. "[Toys]" (Grant, Bob)
BICYCLING—PHOTOGRAPHS
PH01216 630 (May 14, 1992) p90. "[Ibuprofen]" (Beck, Robert)
BIERSACH, BILL—PHOTOGRAPHS
PH01217 639 (September 17, 1992) p84. "Bill Biersach Was There, Man" (Grecco, Michael)
BIG AUDIO DYNAMITE II—PHOTOGRAPHS
PH01218 630 (May 14, 1992) p28. "B.A.D.'s Nick Hawkins (left) And Mick Jones" (Kraft, Chris)
BIG BLACK—PHOTOGRAPHS
PH01219 656 (May 13, 1993) p88. "[Big Black]"
BIG BLACK—RECORDS
PH01220 649 (February 4, 1993) p66. "The Rich Man's Eight Track Tape"
BIG BROTHER AND THE HOLDING COMPANY—ALBUMS
PH01221 617 (November 14, 1991) p97. "Cheap Thrills" (Crumb, R.)
BIG DADDY KANE—PHOTOGRAPHS
PH01222 659 (June 24, 1993) p15. "Ride 'Em, Cowboy: Big Daddy Kane (left) And Tone Loc Take New York" (Shaw, Gene)
BIG DAY OUT (ROCK FESTIVAL)—PHOTOGRAPHS
PH01223 677 (March 10, 1994) p16. "The Kids" (Mott, Tony)
PH01224 705 (April 6, 1995) p24. "Manic Nirvana: The View From The Skate Stagepit In Sydney As The Fans Turn On The Heat For Silverchair" (Mott, Tony)
BIG D.S.—PHOTOGRAPHS—PORTRAITS
PH01225 659 (June 24, 1993) p21. "Fredro Starr, Suave Sonny Caesar, Sticky Fingaz And Big D.S. (from left)" (Spector, Gary)
BIG HEAD TODD AND THE MONSTERS—PHOTOGRAPHS
PH01226 663 (August 19, 1993) p12. "Home-State Boys Big Head Todd And The Monsters (below)" (Caudle, Todd)
BIG NIGHT (FILM)—PHOTOGRAPHS
PH01227 744 (October 3, 1996) p78. "Cooking With Shalhoub (left) And Tucci"
BIG STAR—ALBUMS
PH01228 626 (March 19, 1992) p87. "Third-Sister Lovers"
PH01229 645-646 (December 10, 1992) p180. "No. 1 Record"
PH01230 645-646 (December 10, 1992) p180. "Radio City"
PH01231 670 (November 25, 1993) p117. "Columbia"
BIG STAR—ILLUSTRATIONS
PH01232 626 (March 19, 1992) p87. "The Great American Pop Band" (Guarnaccia, Steven)
BIG STAR—PHOTOGRAPHS
PH01233 668 (October 28, 1993) p15. "Big Star On The Steps Of Alex Chilton's Memphis, Tenn., Home In 1972: Andy Hummel, Jody Stephens, Chris Bell And Chilton (above, from left)" (Manning, Carole)
PH01234 668 (October 28, 1993) p16. "The Original Big Star Quartet In 1971" (Manning, Carole)
BIG TOWN PLAYBOYS—ALBUMS
PH01235 665 (September 16, 1993) p70. "Crazy Legs"
BIGELOW, KATHRYN—PHOTOGRAPHS
PH01236 719 (October 19, 1995) p158. "Kathryn Bigelow (left) Directs Bassett And Fiennes In A Brutal Parable"
BIHAR, INDIA—PHOTOGRAPHS
PH01237 619-620 (December 12, 1991) pp144-145. "A Coal Worker In The Indian State Of Bihar, 1989" (Salgado, Sebastiao)
BIKINI KILL—ALBUMS
PH01238 666 (September 30, 1993) p104. "Yeah Yeah Yeah Yeah"
BIKINI KILL—PHOTOGRAPHS
PH01239 660-661 (July 8, 1993) p23. "Riot Squads: Bikini Kill In New York (above)..." (Rich, Nina)
BIKINI KILL—RECORDS
PH01240 649 (February 4, 1993) p68. "Bikini Kill"
BILLIE JOE—ILLUSTRATIONS
PH01241 691 (September 22, 1994) p11. "Green Day's Billie Joe" (Burke, Philip)
BILLIE JOE—PHOTOGRAPHS
PH01242 689 (August 25, 1994) p15. ""Saturday Night Fever" Star Billie Joe" (Blakesberg, Jay)
PH01243 691 (September 22, 1994) p27. "Green Day's Billie Joe At Lollapalooza '94" (Gershoff, Gary)
PH01244 691 (September 22, 1994) p25. "Punk's New Breed: Mike Dirnt, Billie Joe And Tre Cool (from left)" (Seliger, Mark)
PH01245 693 (October 20, 1994) p27. "Green Day's Billie Joe" (Mazur, Kevin)
PH01246 694 (November 3, 1994) p17. "C'mere You Little Punk: Green Day's Billie Joe Is Escorted From The Stage" (Pollock, Arthur)
PH01247 695 (November 17, 1994) p25. "Billie Joe of Green day" (Watson, Albert)
PH01248 697 (December 15, 1994) p28. "Road Warrior: Green Day Lead Singer Billie Joe" (Davis, Katharine)
PH01249 700 (January 26, 1995) pp40-41. "Billie Joe (Opposite), Mike Dirnt And Tre Cool" (Winters, Dan)
BILLY BATHGATE (FILM)—PHOTOGRAPHS
PH01250 618 (November 28, 1991) p103. "Gangsters Hoffman, Hill And Dean (from left)"
BILLY PILGRIM—ALBUMS
PH01251 683 (June 2, 1994) p72. "Billy Pilgrim"
BINDER, JUDITH—PHOTOGRAPHS
PH01252 672-673 (December 23, 1993) p88. "Binder (left) And Cain" (Sibert, Jody)
BINOCHE, JULIETTE—PHOTOGRAPHS
PH01253 647 (January 7, 1993) p51. "Juliette Binoche And Jeremy Irons Play Sex Dangerously"
PH01254 702 (February 23, 1995) p80. "Blue"
BINOCHE, JULIETTE—PHOTOGRAPHS—PORTRAITS
PH01255 748 (November 28, 1996) p142. "Scott Thomas, Left, Binoche"
BIONDI, MATT—PHOTOGRAPHS
PH01256 634-635 (July 9, 1992) p94. "Matt Biondi, Dara Torres And Tom Jager (from left)" (Zander, Peter)
THE BIRDCAGE (FILM)—PHOTOGRAPHS
PH01257 731 (April 4, 1996) p67. "Now Playing"
BIS—PHOTOGRAPHS
PH01258 747 (November 14, 1996) p53. "[Bis]" (Broad, Julian)
BISBEE, ARIZONA—PHOTOGRAPHS
PH01259 715 (August 24, 1995) p84. "Hot Vacation Spot" (Gipe, Jon)
BISCUITS, CHUCK—PHOTOGRAPHS
PH01260 678 (March 24, 1994) p42. "Those Evil Mothers In Danzig: Chuck Biscuits, Glenn Danzig, John Christ, Eerie Von (from left)" (Seliger, Mark)
BISSETT, JOSIE—PHOTOGRAPHS
PH01261 682 (May 19, 1994) pp48-49. "[Melrose Place]"

(Seliger, Mark)
PH01262 682 (May 19, 1994) p50. "Good Girl Josie Bissett (left) And Bad Girl Heather Locklear, Who Thinks Her Character Is Just Misunderstood" (Seliger, Mark)
PH01263 682 (May 19, 1994) pp48-49. "[Melrose Place]" (Seliger, Mark)
PH01264 682 (May 19, 1994) pp[cover]. "Melrose Place's Bod Squad" (Seliger, Mark)
BITTAN, ROY—PHOTOGRAPHS
PH01265 629 (April 30, 1992) p11. "Chapman Onstage With Accordionist Roy Bittan And Vernon Reid" (Mazur, Kevin)
BITTER MOON (FILM)—PHOTOGRAPHS
PH01266 676 (February 24, 1994) p62. "Shipboard Romance Seigner (left) And Scott-Thomas"
BJELLAND, KAT—PHOTOGRAPHS
PH01267 662 (August 5, 1993) p13. "Maureen Herman, Kat Bjelland And Lori Barbero Of Babes in Toyland" (Blakesberg, Jay)
PH01268 672-673 (December 23, 1993) p39. "Babes' Kat Bjelland Got Misty-Eyed" (Blakesberg, Jay)
PH01269 710 (June 15, 1995) p51. "Bjelland, Maureen Herman, Barbero (from left)" (Sferra, Rik)
BJELLAND, KAT—PHOTOGRAPHS—PORTRAITS
PH01270 695 (November 17, 1994) p71. "Babes In Toyland" (Borris, Dan)
PH01271 708 (May 18, 1995) p34. "[Kat Bjelland]" (Borris, Dan)
PH01272 748 (November 28, 1996) p36. "Babes In Toyland's Kat Bjelland In 'Not Bad'"
BLACK BEAUTY (FILM)—PHOTOGRAPHS
PH01273 688 (August 11, 1994) p63. "[Black Beauty]"
BLACK, CLINT—PHOTOGRAPHS
PH01274 628 (April 16, 1992) p17. "Clint Black: Country's Cary Grant?" (Camp, E. J.)
PH01275 660-661 (July 8, 1993) p33. "Clint Black And Wynonna At Radio City" (Mazur, Kevin)
BLACK CROWES—ALBUMS
PH01276 633 (June 25, 1992) p40. "The Southern Harmony And Musical Companion"
PH01277 651 (March 4, 1993) p56. "The Southern Harmony And Musical Companion"
PH01278 694 (November 3, 1994) p95. "Amorica"
BLACK CROWES—ILLUSTRATIONS
PH01279 633 (June 25, 1992) p40. "Solid At The Crowes Rock" (Delessert, Etienne)
BLACK CROWES—PHOTOGRAPHS
PH01280 619-620 (December 12, 1991) pp[cover]. "1991 Yearbook" (Seliger, Mark)
PH01281 619-620 (December 12, 1991) p31. "The Black Crowes (above) Broke Out" (Mottram, Tony)
PH01282 619-620 (December 12, 1991) p26. "Metallica (left) And The Black Crowes (right)" (Seliger, Mark)
PH01283 631 (May 28, 1992) p9. "Chris (left) And Rich Robinson" (Diamond, Rick)
PH01284 642 (October 29, 1992) p19. "Black Crowes Marc Ford, Johnny Colt And Chris Robinson (from left) With Guest Rehearser And Show Host Dana Carvey" (Mazur, Kevin)
PH01285 645-646 (December 10, 1992) p47. "The Smokin' Black Crowes" (Diamond, Rick)
PH01286 670 (November 25, 1993) p74. "[Black Crowes]" (Seliger, Mark)
PH01287 689 (August 25, 1994) p25. "Silent Partners: Chris (left) And Rich Robinson Share A Happy Moment" (Dyer, Alison)
PH01288 695 (November 17, 1994) p75. "The Black Crowes" (Luchford, Glen)
PH01289 709 (June 1, 1995) p16. "Jayhawk Gary Louris, Crowes Marc Ford And Robinson, Perlman (from left)" (Diamond, Rick)
PH01290 736 (June 13, 1996) p41. "The Black Crowes In '94: Chris Robinson, Chris Trujilo, Rich Robinson (from left)" (Blakesberg, Jay)
BLACK CROWES—PHOTOGRAPHS—PORTRAITS
PH01291 645-646 (December 10, 1992) p54. "Reefer Madness: The Black Crowes" (Seliger, Mark)
BLACK FLAG—PHOTOGRAPHS—PORTRAITS
PH01292 672-673 (December 23, 1993) p112. "Hardcore Heroes Black Flag In March 1984: Bill Stevenson, Kira Roessler, Greg Ginn And Rollins (from left)" (Rosenberg, Howard)
BLACK, FRANK—ALBUMS
PH01293 653 (April 1, 1993) p54. "Frank Black"
PH01294 657 (May 27, 1993) p63. "Frank Black"
PH01295 658 (June 10, 1993) p86. "Frank Black"
PH01296 659 (June 24, 1993) p96. "Frank Black"
PH01297 689 (August 25, 1994) p89. "Teenager Of The Year"
BLACK, FRANK—ILLUSTRATIONS
PH01298 734 (May 16, 1996) p21. "The Truth, And The Tunes, Are Out There..." (Friedman, Drew)
BLACK, FRANK—PHOTOGRAPHS
PH01299 693 (October 20, 1994) p30. "[Frank Black]" (Rasic, Brian)
PH01300 695 (November 17, 1994) p70. "Frank Black" (Hanauer, Mark)
BLACK GRAPE—ALBUMS
PH01301 721 (November 16, 1995) p111. "It's Great When You're Straight...Yeah"
BLACK GRAPE—PHOTOGRAPHS—PORTRAITS
PH01302 723 (December 14, 1995) p40. "Kermit, Bez And Ryder (from left) Mix An Intoxicating Musical Cocktail" (Westenberg, Kevin)
BLACK MUSICIANS—ILLUSTRATIONS
PH01303 667 (October 14, 1993) pp73,76-77. "[Afro-American Musicians]" (Isip, Jordin)
PH01304 667 (October 14, 1993) p118. "Essential Funk"
PH01305 723 (December 14, 1995) p81. "Young Gifted And Black" (Todd, Mark)
BLACK OR WHITE (VIDEO)—PHOTOGRAPHS
PH01306 667 (October 14, 1993) p90. "'Black Or White': Jackson's Original Ending Got Cut"
BLACK ROBE (FILM)—PHOTOGRAPHS
PH01307 618 (November 28, 1991) p104. "Missionary Lothaire Bluteau Preaches To The Indians"
BLACK ROCK COALITION—ALBUMS
PH01308 617 (November 14, 1991) p173. "The History Of Our Future"
BLACK, ROGER—PHOTOGRAPHS
PH01309 643 (November 12, 1992) p49. "'Rolling Stone' Art Directors (from left): Bob Kingsbury (1968-73), Tony Lane (1974-76), Annie Leibovitz, Mike Salisbury (1973-74), Roger Black (1976-78), Jann S. Wenner...
BLACK SABBATH—PHOTOGRAPHS
PH01310 647 (January 7, 1993) p9. "Ozzy (center) With Members Of Black Sabbath" (Granitz, Steve)
BLACK SHEEP (FILM)—PHOTOGRAPHS
PH01311 729 (March 7, 1996) p54. "Now Playing"
BLACK UHURU—PHOTOGRAPHS—PORTRAITS
PH01312 676 (February 24, 1994) p44. "Tuff Vocal Trio Black Uhuru" (Goldsmith, Lynn)
BLACK VELVET FLAG—PHOTOGRAPHS
PH01313 690 (September 8, 1994) p24. "Members Of The Combustible Edison And Black Velvet Flag Pay Homage To Their Mentor" (Mazur, Kevin)
PH01314 Number not assigned.
BLACKIE—PHOTOGRAPHS
PH01315 677 (March 10, 1994) p16. "From Above Left: Guitarist Blackie Of The Hard-Ons" (Mott, Tony)
PH01316 695 (November 17, 1994) p84. "Urge Overkill" (Clinch, Danny)
BLACKMAN, MARC—PHOTOGRAPHS
PH01317 649 (February 4, 1993) p43. "Diane And Lawyer Marc Blackman, Before She Was Charged With Sexual Abuse" (Jewett,

Tim)
PH01318 649 (February 4, 1993) p44. "Diane Walden And Lawyer Blackman Await The Jury's Verdict On April 28th, 1992" (Ellis, Bob)
BLACK-OUTS—PHOTOGRAPHS
PH01318a 674 (January 27, 1994) p12. "Greasy Kids Stuff: Zappa Behind The Drums With The Black-Outs (above)"
BLACKWELL, ED—ALBUMS
PH01319 679 (April 7, 1994) p74. "What It Is?"
BLACKWOOD, NINA—PHOTOGRAPHS
PH01320 619-620 (December 12, 1991) p71. "The Original VJs (Clockwise from bottom left): Nina Blackwood, Mark Goodman, Martha Quinn, J. J. Jackson, Alan Hunter"
BLADES, RUBEN—PHOTOGRAPHS
PH01321 692 (October 6, 1994) p76. "Redford Shares A Laugh With Freddy Fender And Ruben Blades On "The Milagro Beanfield War" Set"
BLAIR, BONNIE—PHOTOGRAPHS
PH01322 624 (February 20, 1992) p35. "[Bonnie Blair]" (Eccles, Andrew)
BLAIR, LINDA—PHOTOGRAPHS
PH01323 737 (June 27, 1996) p42. "Linda Blair And Rick James, 1982"
BLAKE, BRADEN—PHOTOGRAPHS
PH01324 721 (November 16, 1995) p33. "John Kirsch, Braden Blake, Jake Nesheim And Chris Lockwood (from left)" (Moskowitz, Karen)
BLAKE, CHRIS—PHOTOGRAPHS
PH01325 660-661 (July 8, 1993) p100. "Jawbreaker (from left): Adam Pfahler, Chris Blake And Blake Schwarzenbach" (Lewis, Don)
BLAKE, NORMAN—PHOTOGRAPHS
PH01326 630 (May 14, 1992) p49. "Fanclub Guru Norman Blake" (Broad, Julian)
PH01327 630 (May 14, 1992) p50. "Guitarist Norman Blake, Bassist Gerry Love, Drummer Brendan O'Hare And Guitarist Raymond McGinley (from left)" (Broad, Julian)
PH01328 701 (February 9, 1995) p33. "Join The Club: Norman Blake, Raymond McGinley, Paul Quinn And Gerard Love (clockwise from top left)" (Dyer, Alison)
BLAND, BOBBY—PHOTOGRAPHS
PH01329 625 (March 5, 1992) p13. "Bobby 'Blue' Bland (left) With B. B. King" (Elgar, Nick)
PH01330 628 (April 16, 1992) p13. "Mavis Staples, MC Lyte, Sam Moore And Bobby 'Blue' Bland (from left)" (Mazur, Kevin)
PH01331 746 (October 31, 1996) p17. "Bland (left) Duets With A Disturbingly Fit Slash" (De Leon, John)
BLAND, BOBBY—PHOTOGRAPHS—PORTRAITS
PH01332 623 (February 6, 1992) p50. "[Bobby 'Blue' Bland]"
BLAND, JOHN—PHOTOGRAPHS
PH01333 704 (March 23, 1995) p111. "Bland" (Tavee, Tom)
PH01334 704 (March 23, 1995) pp102-103. "Class of '95" (Tavee, Tom)
BLANDING, TOM—PHOTOGRAPHS
PH01335 732 (April 18, 1996) p29. "[Tom Blanding]" (Wyman, Ira)
BLANKMAN (FILM)—PHOTOGRAPHS
PH01336 690 (September 8, 1994) p87. "Damon Wayans Is A Tacky Caped Crusader"
BLASHFIELD, JIM—PHOTOGRAPHS—PORTRAITS
PH01337 667 (October 14, 1993) p70. "'Leave Me Alone' Director Jim Blashfield" (Trappe, David)
BLASS, BILL—PHOTOGRAPHS—PORTRAITS
PH01338 678 (March 24, 1994) p50. "Bill Blass" (Eccles, Andrew)
BLEGVAD, PETER—ALBUMS
PH01339 728 (February 22, 1996) p62. "Just Woke Up"
BLESS THIS HOUSE (TELEVISION SHOW)—PHOTOGRAPHS
PH01340 716 (September 7, 1995) p84. "Bless This House (left) With Cathy Moriarty And Andrew Clay: No Dice"
BLETHYN, BRENDA—PHOTOGRAPHS
PH01341 743 (September 19, 1996) p90. "Quality Control"
PH01342 745 (October 17, 1996) p142. "Jean-Bapiste (left) And Blethyn Flank Mike Leigh"
BLIGE, MARY J.—ALBUMS
PH01343 645-646 (December 10, 1992) p166. "What's The 411?"
BLIGE, MARY J.—ILLUSTRATIONS
PH01344 654 (April 15, 1993) p3. "Mary J. Blige: In Spring Fashion 1993" (Burke, Philip)
BLIGE, MARY J.—PHOTOGRAPHS
PH01345 704 (March 23, 1995) p25. "[Flavor Flav & Mary J. Blige]" (Mazur, Kevin)
PH01346 707 (May 4, 1995) p20. "Mary J. Blige Supports 'Panther'" (Turner, Arnold)
BLIGE, MARY J.—PHOTOGRAPHS—PORTRAITS
PH01347 654 (April 15, 1993) pp[enc.5]. "Mary J. Blige" (Seliger, Mark)
PH01348 654 (April 15, 1993) pp[enc.12]. "[Mary J. Blige]" (Seliger, Mark)
PH01349 717 (September 21, 1995) p19. "Yo, Girl, What's The 411?: The Queen Of Soul, Aretha Franklin (left), With Mary J. Blige"
BLIND FAITH—ALBUMS
PH01350 617 (November 14, 1991) p94. "Blind Faith" (Seidemann, Bob)
PH01351 655 (April 29, 1993) p42. "Blind Faith"
BLIND FAITH—PHOTOGRAPHS
PH01352 655 (April 29, 1993) p35. "The Aptly Named Blind Faith: Steve Winwood, Rick Grech, Ginger Baker And Clapton (from left)"
BLIND MELON—ALBUMS
PH01353 651 (March 4, 1993) p57. "Blind Melon"
PH01354 716 (September 7, 1995) p72. "Soup"
BLIND MELON—PHOTOGRAPHS
PH01355 630 (May 14, 1992) p28. "Blind Melon's Hoon (left) And Rogers Stevens" (Kraft, Chris)
PH01356 639 (September 17, 1992) p20. "Shannon Hoon, Christopher Thorn, Glen Graham, Brad Smith And Rogers Stevens (clockwise from top left)" (Clinch, Danny)
PH01357 640 (October 1, 1992) p27. "Blind Melon (from left): Smith, Stevens, Thorn, Hoon And Graham" (Clinch, Danny)
PH01358 645-646 (December 10, 1992) p62. "Blind Melon" (Mason, Karen)
PH01359 666 (September 30, 1993) p27. "Media Darlings Blind Melon" (Tisman, Jeff)
PH01360 669 (November 11, 1993) pp[cover]. "Blind Melon: Ripe & Ready" (Seliger, Mark)
PH01361 669 (November 11, 1993) pp38-39. "Brad Smith, Glen Graham, Shannon Hood, Rogers Stevens & Christopher Thorn (from left)" (Seliger, Mark)
PH01362 669 (November 11, 1993) p40. "Hoon Abandoned Jockdom For The Slacker Lifestyle" (Gerber, Mitchell)
PH01363 669 (November 11, 1993) p42. "Hoon's Mother Was Bailing Him Out So Often That At One Point She Had Four Separate Bonds In Her Wallet" (Wessel, Cathrine)
PH01364 669 (November 11, 1993) p46. "Performing On MTV's 120 Minutes Tour, January 1992, Austin, Texas" (Clinch, Danny)
PH01365 672-673 (December 23, 1993) p188. "[Covers]" (Seliger, Mark)
PH01366 722 (November 30, 1995) p24. "The Gig That Never happened: A Flier For Blind Melon's Show At Tipitina's" (Smith, Sean)
PH01367 722 (November 30, 1995) p23. "Hoon (foreground) With Members Of Blind Melon In 1993" (Seliger, Mark)
BLINK (FILM)—PHOTOGRAPHS
PH01368 675 (February 10, 1994) p52. "Cop Aidan Quinn Beds Angel Madeleine Stowe"
BLINK FAITH—PHOTOGRAPHS
PH01369 655 (April 29, 1993) p35. "The Aptly Named Blind

Faith: Steve Winwood, Rick Grech, Ginger Baker And Clapton (from left)"
BLK—ALBUMS
PH01370 626 (March 19, 1992) p93. "Black 47"
BLOCH, KURT—PHOTOGRAPHS
PH01371 730 (March 21, 1996) p17. "Fastbacks' Kurt Bloch, Mike Musburger, Vedder, Fastbacks' Kim Warnick, Lu Lu Gargiulo" (Michelson, Randall)
BLOCK PARTY (COMPANY)—ILLUSTRATIONS
PH01372 702 (February 23, 1995) p19. "Chuck E. Cheesier" (Mats)
BLOOD OF ABRAHAM—ALBUMS
PH01373 675 (February 10, 1994) p43. "Future Profits"
BLOOD ORANGES—ALBUMS
PH01374 685 (June 30, 1994) p74. "The Crying Tree"
BLOOM, LUKA—PHOTOGRAPHS
PH01375 645-646 (December 10, 1992) p31. "Irish Biker Luka Bloom" (Goldsmith, Lynn)
PH01376 653 (April 1, 1993) p24. "Cash, Reed And Bloom Onstage In New York" (Capak, R. J.)
BLOOM, LUKA—PHOTOGRAPHS—PORTRAITS
PH01377 626 (March 19, 1992) p51. "[Luka Bloom]" (Ockenfels, Frank W.)
BLOWN AWAY (FILM)—PHOTOGRAPHS
PH01378 686-687 (July 14, 1994) p99. "Jeff Bridges And Forest Whitaker Go Boom"
BLUE (FILM)—PHOTOGRAPHS
PH01379 702 (February 23, 1995) p80. "Blue"
BLUE AEROPLANES—ALBUMS
PH01380 619-620 (December 12, 1991) p187. "Beatsongs"
BLUE IN THE FACE (FILM)—PHOTOGRAPHS
PH01381 718 (October 5, 1995) p77. "Rupal, Keitel And Gorham Boogie"
THE BLUE LAGOON (FILM)—PHOTOGRAPHS
PH01382 744 (October 3, 1996) p50. "Island Girl: With Christopher Atkins In 'The Blue Lagoon'"
BLUE NILE—ALBUMS
PH01383 737 (June 27, 1996) p56. "Peace At Last"
BLUE RODEO—ALBUMS
PH01384 648 (January 21, 1993) p52. "Lost Together"
BLUE SKY (FILM)—PHOTOGRAPHS
PH01385 692 (October 6, 1994) p81. "Now Playing"
BLUES ALL AROUND ME (BOOK)—PHOTOGRAPHS
PH01386 750-751 (December 26, 1996) p196. "Books"
BLUES BROTHERS—PHOTOGRAPHS—PORTRAITS
PH01387 645-646 (December 10, 1992) p156. "The Blues Brothers, 1979"
BLUES EXPLOSION—ALBUMS
PH01388 744 (October 3, 1996) p72. "Now I Got Worry"
BLUES EXPLOSION—PHOTOGRAPHS
PH01389 745 (October 17, 1996) p31. "Primitive Cool: Russell Simins, Jon Spencer And Judah Bauer (from left)" (Ockenfels, Frank W.)
BLUES TRAVELER—ALBUMS
PH01390 714 (August 10, 1995) p72. "Four"
PH01391 741 (August 22, 1996) p96. "Live From The Fall"
BLUES TRAVELER—ILLUSTRATIONS
PH01392 715 (August 24, 1995) p124. "Blues Traveler: Four Times Lucky" (Rosen, Jonathon)
BLUES TRAVELER—PHOTOGRAPHS
PH01393 622 (January 23, 1992) p10. "Clockwise From Top Left: Bobby Sheehan, Brendan Hill, John Popper, Chan Kinchla" (Carroll, Chris)
PH01394 631 (May 28, 1992) p17. "Blues Traveler (from left): Chan Kinchla, John Popper, Brendan Hill And Bobby Sheehan" (Aresu, Paul)
PH01395 659 (June 24, 1993) p57. "Band Of Gypsies: Brendan Hill, Chan Kinchla, John Popper And Bobby Sheehan (from left)" (Fink, Larry)
PH01396 659 (June 24, 1993) p61. "Popper Rises Unsteadily To His Feet In A Climatic Moment, As If On Cue From A Faith Healer" (Fink, Larry)
PH01397 659 (June 24, 1993) p61. "'The Shape Of The Wave Is By Them,' Says Sheenan, 'But The Force Of The Wave Is From Us.'" (Fink, Larry)
PH01398 659 (June 24, 1993) p60. "With Blues Traveler's Unadulterated Live Music, No Two Shows Are Ever The Same" (Fink, Larry)
PH01399 714 (August 10, 1995) p16. "Blues Traveler's Chan Kinchla, Bobby Sheehan, Brendan Hill And Popper (from left) With Ice-T (second from left)" (Kravitz, Jeff)
PH01400 727 (February 8, 1996) p17. "Popper And Blues Traveler Will Release A Live Album This Spring" (Atashian, John)
BLUETONES—ALBUMS
PH01401 742 (September 5, 1996) p62. "Expecting To Fly"
BLUR—ALBUMS
PH01402 719 (October 19, 1995) p172. "Country House"
BLUR—PHOTOGRAPHS
PH01403 694 (November 3, 1994) p34. "Social Distortion: Blur's Coxon, Albarn, Rowntree And James (from left)" (Westenberg, Kevin)
PH01404 706 (April 20, 1995) p36. "Big Mouth Albarn (center) And Blur" (Lenquette)
PH01405 720 (November 2, 1995) p20. "Coxon (left) And Albarn At A BBC Radio One Gig In London On Sept. 7" (Westenberg, Kevin)
BLUR—PHOTOGRAPHS—PORTRAITS
PH01406 623 (February 6, 1992) p32. "Alex James, Damon Albarn, Graham Coxon, Dave Rowntree (clockwise from top)" (Lavine, Michael)
PH01407 720 (November 2, 1995) p19. "'Great Escape' Artists Coxon, Albarn, James And Rountree (from left)" (Westenberg, Kevin)
BLUTEAU, LOTHAIRE—PHOTOGRAPHS
PH01408 618 (November 28, 1991) p104. "Missionary Lothaire Bluteau Preaches To The Indians"
BOATS—PHOTOGRAPHS
PH01409 634-635 (July 9, 1992) pp122-123. "[Toys]" (Goldin, David)
BOB DYLAN: HIGHWAY 61 INTERACTIVE (CD-ROM)—PHOTOGRAPHS
PH01410 706 (April 20, 1995) p25. "Here It Is: Interactive Bob"
BOB ROBERTS (FILM)—ILLUSTRATIONS
PH01411 639 (September 17, 1992) p101. "The Player As Candidate" (Kunz, Anita)
BOB ROBERTS (FILM)—PHOTOGRAPHS
PH01412 639 (September 17, 1992) p102. "Robbins (right) And Rickman Hit The Campaign Trail"
BOB, TIM—PHOTOGRAPHS
PH01413 735 (May 30, 1996) p27. "Rage Against The Machine"
BOBBITT, JOHN—ILLUSTRATIONS
PH01414 682 (May 19, 1994) p68. "[White Trash]" (Friedman, Drew)
BOBBY (ALBUM)—PHOTOGRAPHS
PH01415 645-646 (December 10, 1992) p168. ""
BOBLE, JASON—PHOTOGRAPHS
PH01416 686-687 (July 14, 1994) p74. "Getting The Point Across: Rodan's Tara Jane O'Neil, Noble, Mueller And Kevin Coultas (from left)" (Clinch, Danny)
BOBO—PHOTOGRAPHS
PH01417 715 (August 24, 1995) p44. "Sen Dog, B-Real, Bobo (from left)" (Blakesberg, Jay)
BOBSLEDDING—PHOTOGRAPHS
PH01418 624 (February 20, 1992) p32. "May The G-Force Be With You: Don't Ask About The Mush Run" (Smale, Brian)
BOCKRIS, VICTOR—BOOKS
PH01419 645-646 (December 10, 1992) p87. "[Keith Richards]"

BODEANS—ALBUMS
PH01420 677 (March 10, 1994) p64. "Go Slow Down"
BODIES, REST AND MOTION (FILM)—PHOTOGRAPHS
PH01421 655 (April 29, 1993) p68. "Bridget Fonda (left) And Phoebe Cates Stalling"
BODY OF EVIDENCE (FILM)—ILLUSTRATIONS
PH01422 649 (February 4, 1993) p71. "Madonna's Come On" (Piven, Hanoch Ernesto)
BODY OF EVIDENCE (FILM)—PHOTOGRAPHS
PH01423 649 (February 4, 1993) p72. "Homage Of Ripoff? In 'Body of Evidence,' Madonna And Dafoe (left) Share Stone And Douglas's Basic Instincts"
PH01424 672-673 (December 23, 1993) p172. "Dud Sex"
PH01425 672-673 (December 23, 1993) p16. "Left: Willem Dafoe Sucks Face With Madonna"
BODY SNATCHERS (FILM)—PHOTOGRAPHS
PH01426 669 (November 11, 1993) p80. "Fright Sights (from left): 'Body Snatchers' 1956, 1978, 1993"
BOGDAN, HENRY—PHOTOGRAPHS
PH01427 637 (August 20, 1992) p15. "Helmet (from left): Stanier, Bogdan, Mengede And Hamilton" (Ockenfels, Frank W.)
PH01428 689 (August 25, 1994) p63. "John Stanier, Henry Bogdan, Page Hamilton And Rob Echeverria (clockwise from top left)" (Wessel, Cathrine)
PH01429 689 (August 25, 1994) p64. "Original Guitarist Mengede, Bogdan, Hamilton, Stanier (from left)" (Brice, Lindsay)
PH01430 695 (November 17, 1994) p92. "Helmet" (Huba, John)
BOGOSIAN, ERIC—PHOTOGRAPHS
PH01431 621 (January 9, 1992) p10. "Eric Bogosian (above)..." (Mazur, Kevin)
BOHRINGER, ROMANE—PHOTOGRAPHS
PH01432 675 (February 10, 1994) p53. "Unsafe Sex: Collard (left) And Bohringer"
BOISSONNEAU, HEIDI—PHOTOGRAPHS—PORTRAITS
PH01433 676 (February 24, 1994) p53. "At The Wasatch Brew Pub With Heidi Boissonneau..." (Hanauer, Mark)
BOLLIN, ZUZU—ALBUMS
PH01434 624 (February 20, 1992) p42. "Texas Bluesman"
BOLTON, DAN—PHOTOGRAPHS
PH01435 719 (October 19, 1995) p15. "Eddie Spaghetti And Dan Bolton Of The Supersuckers (top) And Cult Folkie Ani DiFranco Get Down At Seattle's Bumbershoot" (Doughty, Curt)
PH01436 721 (November 16, 1995) p25. "Nelson, Supersuckers Eddie Spaghetti And Dan Bolton (from left) Lend A Hand" (Roberts, Ebet)
PH01437 731 (April 4, 1996) p18. "Jennings (center) With Suckers, Dan Siegel, Dan Bolton, Ron Heathman And Singer Eddie Spaghetti (from left)" (Diamond, Rick)
BOLTON, MICHAEL—PHOTOGRAPHS
PH01438 628 (April 16, 1992) p11. "Michael Bolton Wants YOU To Kiss His Ass" (Mazur, Kevin)
BOLTON, MICHAEL—PHOTOGRAPHS—PORTRAITS
PH01439 619-620 (December 12, 1991) p42. "Sitting Pretty: Michael Bolton"
BOMB THE BASS—ALBUMS
PH01440 732 (April 18, 1996) p69. "Clear"
BOMBAY, INDIA—PHOTOGRAPHS
PH01441 738-739 (July 11, 1996) pp77-82. "[Bombay]" (Salgado, Sebastiao)
BON JOVI—ALBUMS
PH01442 645-646 (December 10, 1992) p168. "Keep The Faith"
PH01443 711 (June 29, 1995) p42. "These Days"
BON JOVI, JON—PHOTOGRAPHS
PH01444 615 (October 17, 1991) p14. "Sambora (left), Bon Jovi" (Mazur, Kevin)
PH01445 623 (February 6, 1992) p13. "Jon Bon Jovi" (Mazur, Kevin)
PH01446 644 (November 26, 1992) p27. "Jon Bon Jovi" (Busacca, Larry)
PH01447 650 (February 18, 1993) p11. "The Boss And Bon Jovi Share A Stage" (Picknally, Pete)
PH01448 709 (June 1, 1995) p16. "Joel, John And Jon Bon Jovi At Carnegie Hall (from left)" (Mazur, Kevin)
PH01449 715 (August 24, 1995) p25. "Bon Jovi (left) Geldof"
PH01450 719 (October 19, 1995) p40. "Eric Burdon And Jon Bon Jovi Hang Before The Show" (Corbijn, Anton)
BON JOVI, JON—PHOTOGRAPHS—PORTRAITS
PH01451 692 (October 6, 1994) p17. "Bon Jovi, Foster, Sambora (from left)" (Mazur, Kevin)
BONADUCE, DANNY—PHOTOGRAPHS
PH01452 678 (March 24, 1994) p28. "Bonaduce And Osmond"
BONE THUGS-N-HARMONY—ALBUMS
PH01453 720 (November 2, 1995) p69. "E. 1999 Eternal"
BONE THUGS-N-HARMONY—ILLUSTRATIONS
PH01454 718 (October 5, 1995) p88. "Bone Thugs-N-Harmony: Eternally Yours" (Menchin, Scott)
BONEBRAKE, D. J.—PHOTOGRAPHS
PH01455 659 (June 24, 1993) p23. "'Xdream: Gilkyson, Doe, Cervenka, Bonebrake (from left)"
BONET, LISA—PHOTOGRAPHS
PH01456 722 (November 30, 1995) p53. "Lenny The Family Man: With Lisa Bonet And Baby Zoe In 1989" (Zuffante, Vinnie)
BONET, LISA—PHOTOGRAPHS—PORTRAITS
PH01457 645-646 (December 10, 1992) p153. "Lisa Bonet, 1988"
BONHAM, JOHN—PHOTOGRAPHS
PH01458 702 (February 23, 1995) p46. "The Golden Boys: Page, Jones, Bonham And Plant (from left)"
BONHAM, TRACY—PHOTOGRAPHS
PH01459 723 (December 14, 1995) p28. "Robert Plant And Tracy Bonham" (Robicheau, Paul)
PH01460 730 (March 21, 1996) p28. "[Tracy Bonham]" (Clinch, Danny)
PH01461 742 (September 5, 1996) p20. "Selene Vigil Of 7 Year Bitch, Langdon, Alexakis And Bonham" (Morganstein, Barry)
PH01462 743 (September 19, 1996) p36. "Safe And Sound: Bonham Contributes To A Benefit Album" (Ockenfels, Frank W.)
PH01463 750-751 (December 26, 1996) p54. "[Tracy Bonham]" (Otte, Sylvia)
BONNAR, GRAHAM—PHOTOGRAPHS
PH01464 625 (March 5, 1992) p27. "Jimmy Hartridge, Graham Bonnar, Adam Franklin, Adi Vynes (from left)" (Anker, Matt)
BONNECAZE, CARY—PHOTOGRAPHS
PH01465 710 (June 15, 1995) p46. "Griffin, Bonnecaze And Drummond (from left) Veg In The Garden District" (Chiasson, John)
BONNEY, SIMON—PHOTOGRAPHS
PH01466 648 (January 21, 1993) p22. "[Simon Bonney]" (Schacher, Stephen)
BONO—ILLUSTRATIONS
PH01467 662 (August 5, 1993) p63. "Mac Phisto: U2" (Ryden, Mark)
BONO—ILLUSTRATIONS—PORTRAITS
PH01468 651 (March 4, 1993) p42. "U2: Artist Of The Year" (Burns, Charles)
BONO—ILLUSTRATIONS—LETTERING
PH01469 651 (March 4, 1993) p43. "Behind The Fly" (Karl, Anita)
BONO—PHOTOGRAPHS
PH01470 618 (November 28, 1991) p50. "Berlin" 'Bono's Halo Explodes'" (Corbijn, Anton)
PH01471 618 (November 28, 1991) p46. "Dan Lanois Takes Careful Notes As The Singer Practices His Bongolese During Vocal Sessions At Dogtown Studio" (Corbijn, Anton)
PH01472 618 (November 28, 1991) p46. "Flood With Bono And Edge In Berlin" (Corbijn, Anton)
PH01473 618 (November 28, 1991) p46. "Lanois, Eno, Edge And Bono In The Control Room At Hansa Studios, In Berlin" (Corbijn, Anton)

PH01474 618 (November 28, 1991) pp44-45. "Larry And Bono In Berlin, Where Much Of The Album Was Recorded" (Corbijn, Anton)
PH01475 618 (November 28, 1991) pp42-43. "[U2]" (Corbijn, Anton)
PH01476 619-620 (December 12, 1991) p94. "Bono (left) And Edge" (Stone, Dennis)
PH01477 627 (April 2, 1992) p11. "U2 Performs At A London Clothing Store: Bono (left) And Adam Clayton"
PH01478 628 (April 16, 1992) p29. "Where Was Bono's Vox?" (Mazur, Kevin)
PH01479 636 (August 6, 1992) p11. "Adam Clayton, The Edge, Bono And Larry Mullen Jr. (from left)" (Thomas, Justin)
PH01480 636 (August 6, 1992) p21. "Zoo TV: Bono Onstage"
PH01481 639 (September 17, 1992) p19. "His Bononess" (Double, Steve)
PH01482 640 (October 1, 1992) p40. "[Bono]" (Ritts, Herb)
PH01483 640 (October 1, 1992) pp40-41. "Bono As The Fly: 'Some Of This Bullshit Is Pretty Cool'" (Ritts, Herb)
PH01484 640 (October 1, 1992) pp[cover]. "U2: Serious Fun" (Preston, Neal)
PH01485 645-646 (December 10, 1992) p77. "Bono: Man Or Fly?" (Mazur, Kevin)
PH01486 645-646 (December 10, 1992) p35. "Rock Star Bono" (Mazur, Kevin)
PH01487 651 (March 4, 1993) p48. "Bono And..." (Mazur, Kevin)
PH01488 660-661 (July 8, 1993) p17. "Bono As His Latest Stage Manifestation, MacPhisto" (Cummins, Kevin)
PH01489 662 (August 5, 1993) p59. "Bono" (Cummins, Kevin)
PH01490 663 (August 19, 1993) p27. "Bono MacPhisto: The Chess King?" (Cummins, Kevin)
PH01491 666 (September 30, 1993) p27. "Salman Rushdie (left) Give Bono Macphisto An Earful Of Fashion Advice" (Rasic, Brian)
PH01492 667 (October 14, 1993) p52. "Bono Kisses The Hands That Feed Him: 'Macphisto Is The Fly When He's Fat And Playing Las Vegas'" (MacPherson, Andrew)
PH01493 667 (October 14, 1993) p54. "Their Satanic Majesties: Bono As The Fly And Salman Rushdie" (Corbijn, Anton)
PH01494 667 (October 14, 1993) p54. "The Zoo Gang On Tour: The Edge, Bono, Larry Mullen Jr. And Adam Clayton (from left)" (Corbijn, Anton)
PH01495 672-673 (December 23, 1993) p37. "Above: His Bononess, In All His Splendor" (Preston, Neal)
PH01496 672-673 (December 23, 1993) p57. "Satan, In Disguise (left) Meets The 'Outed' Author Of 'The Santanic Verse' In London" (Corbijn, Anton)
PH01497 675 (February 10, 1994) p13. "[Bono]"
PH01498 675 (February 10, 1994) p22. "[Bono & Sinead O'Connor]"
PH01499 676 (February 24, 1994) p28. "[Bono & Frank Sinatra]" (Corbijn, Anton)
PH01500 677 (March 10, 1994) p29. "Ziggy And Rita Marley With Bono" (Mazur, Kevin)
PH01501 680 (April 21, 1994) p33. "Bono, Still Getting Under Sinatra's Skin" (Mazur, Kevin)
PH01502 686-687 (July 14, 1994) p41. "[U2]" (Fisher, David)
PH01503 698-699 (December 29, 1994) p36. "The Marleys, Bono (above)" (Mazur, Kevin)
PH01504 698-699 (December 29, 1994) p42. "Post-Grammy Bono And Frank Sinatra" (Mazur, Kevin)
PH01505 698-699 (December 29, 1994) p63. "U2 Far Away So Close"
PH01506 704 (March 23, 1995) p24. "Million-Dollar Movie Mogul: U2's Bono"
PH01507 714 (August 10, 1995) p30. "U2 Can Do Film Scores: Adam Clayton, Bono, The Edge, Larry Mullen (from left)" (Mazur, Kevin)
PH01508 721 (November 16, 1995) p25. "[Bono]" (Masi, Agenzia)
PH01509 726 (January 25, 1996) p30. "U2's Bono, Adam Clayton, The Edge And Larry Mullen Jr. (from left)" (Pasley, Richard)
PH01510 728 (February 22, 1996) p20. "[Bono]" (Haley, Thomas)
PH01511 735 (May 30, 1996) p13. "[Bono & Liam Gallagher]"
PH01512 750-751 (December 26, 1996) p46. "Yet Another Inspirational Comment From Bono On His Bosnia Visit: 'There Was A Light In The Eyes Of The People'" (Stoddart)

BONO—PHOTOGRAPHS—PORTRAITS
PH01513 643 (November 12, 1992) p152. "Bono" (Ritts, Herb)
PH01514 645-646 (December 10, 1992) pp[cover]. "1992 Yearbook" (Preston, Neal)
PH01515 651 (March 4, 1993) pp[cover]. "Bono: The Rolling Stone Interview" (MacPherson, Andrew)
PH01516 672-673 (December 23, 1993) p188. "[Covers]" (MacPherson, Andrew)
PH01517 726 (January 25, 1996) p17. "La Liaison Dangereuse: Bono And Tina Turner, Livin' On The Edge"

BOO RADLEYS—PHOTOGRAPHS
PH01518 748 (November 28, 1996) p40. "The Boo Radleys (above) Join Therapy? And Supergrass To Toast The Smiths" (Sheehan, Tom)

BOO-YAA TRIBE—PHOTOGRAPHS
PH01519 639 (September 17, 1992) p64. "Ice-T And The Boo-Yaa Tribe Join The Chili Peppers" (Blakesberg, Jay)

BOOKER T & THE M.G.'S—ALBUMS
PH01520 693 (October 20, 1994) p148. "That's The Way It Should Be"

BOOKER T & THE M.G.'S—PHOTOGRAPHS
PH01521 625 (March 5, 1992) p25. "Booker T. And The MG's, With Neil Young" (Mazur, Kevin)
PH01522 625 (March 5, 1992) p13. "Lewis Steinberg, Steve Cropper, Booker T. Jones, Marion Jackson, Randall Jackson, Duck Dunn, Jim Stewart (from left)" (Elgar, Nick)
PH01523 674 (January 27, 1994) p42. "Forever Young: With Booker T.,MG's" (Blakesberg, Jay)

BOOKER T & THE M.G.'S—PHOTOGRAPHS—PORTRAITS
PH01524 623 (February 6, 1992) p50. "Booker T. And The MGs (from left): Donald 'Duck' Dunn, Booker T., Steve Cropper And Al Jackson Jr."
PH01525 685 (June 30, 1994) p41. "Booker T. Jones, Steve Cropper, Dave Edmunds And Donald "Duck" Dunn (from left)" (Cohen, Lester)
PH01526 703 (March 9, 1995) p25. "Memphis-Soul Stew: The MG's"

BOOKER, KEVIN—PHOTOGRAPHS
PH01527 684 (June 16, 1994) p60. "Kevin Booker" (Borris, Dan)

BOOMERANG (FILM)—ILLUSTRATIONS
PH01528 636 (August 6, 1992) p63. "Depreciating Eddie Murphy" (Brodner, Steven)

BOOMERANG (FILM)—PHOTOGRAPHS
PH01529 636 (August 6, 1992) p64. "Robin Givens Has The Nails, But Eddie Murphy's Got The Claws"
PH01530 639 (September 17, 1992) p102. "Worst Picture, Worst Actor"
PH01531 649 (February 4, 1993) p72. "[Boomerang]"
PH01532 680 (April 21, 1994) p74. "With His Co-Stars In 'Boomerang' David Alan Grier (left) And Eddie Murphy"

BOON, D.—PHOTOGRAPHS
PH01533 693 (October 20, 1994) p38. "Minutemen D. Boon, Watt And George Hurley In 1985 (from left)" (Pasley, Richard)

BOONE, PAT—PHOTOGRAPHS
PH01534 734 (May 16, 1996) p26. "[Pat Boone]" (Cuffaro, Chris)
PH01535 Number not assigned.

BOOTH, TIM—ALBUMS
PH01536 745 (October 17, 1996) p134. "Booth And The Bad Angel"
BOOTH, TIM—PHOTOGRAPHS
PH01537 680 (April 21, 1994) p12. "Booth: 'There Were These Screaming Girls In Front'" (Mosenfelder, Tim)
PH01537a 686-687 (July 14, 1994) p41. "James' Lead Singer, Tim Booth, In Atlanta" (Stratton, Jim)
BOOTH, TIM—PHOTOGRAPHS—PORTRAITS
PH01538 680 (April 21, 1994) p11. "[James]" (Borris, Dan)
BOOTLEG RECORDINGS—PHOTOGRAPHS
PH01539 717 (September 21, 1995) p39. "Dylan Outtakes On 'Basement Tapes'"
PH01540 717 (September 21, 1995) p39. "Hot Hendrix Tracks"
PH01541 717 (September 21, 1995) p39. "Live—From A Houston Soundboard"
BOOTS—PHOTOGRAPHS
PH01542 628 (April 16, 1992) pp[enc.38,40]. "[Boots]" (Robert, Francois)
PH01543 665 (September 16, 1993) pp[enc.39,41+]. "[Boots]" (Hranek, Matthew)
BOQUIST, DAVE—PHOTOGRAPHS
PH01544 716 (September 7, 1995) p14. "Son Burning: David Boquist, Farrar, Heidorn And Jim Boquist (from left) Crank Up The Voltage" (Lucas, J.)
BOQUIST, JIM—PHOTOGRAPHS
PH01544 716 (September 7, 1995) p14. "Son Burning: David Boquist, Farrar, Heidorn And Jim Boquist (from left) Crank Up The Voltage" (Lucas, J.)
BORCHARDT, JEFFREY—PHOTOGRAPHS
PH01545 627 (April 2, 1992) p19. "Jeffrey Borchardt, Paul Chastain And Ric Menck (from left)" (Lavine, Michael)
PH01546 685 (June 30, 1994) p40. "Velvet's Paul Chastain, Jeffrey Borchardt And Menck With McGuinn (from left)"
BORDELLO OF BLOOD (FILM)—PHOTOGRAPHS
PH01547 736 (June 13, 1996) p62. "Fierce Women"
BORDEN, JACK—PHOTOGRAPHS
PH01548 732 (April 18, 1996) p29. "[Jack Borden]" (Sinclair, Jodie)
BOREDOMS—ALBUMS
PH01549 712-713 (July 13, 1995) p111. "Chocolate Synthesizer"
BOREN, DAVID—PHOTOGRAPHS
PH01550 670 (November 25, 1993) p42. "Boren: Not A PAC-Man" (Ashe, Terry)
BORN YESTERDAY (FILM)—PHOTOGRAPHS
PH01551 655 (April 29, 1993) p69. "Crawford And Holliday (left) Reborn As Goodman And Griffith"
BOSNIA—ILLUSTRATIONS
PH01552 705 (April 6, 1995) p14. "Old Product, New Label" (Pendergrast, James T.)
PH01553 724-725 (December 28, 1995) p97. "[Maps]"
PH01554 728 (February 22, 1996) p16. "The Heart..." (Pendergrast, James T.)
BOSNIA—PHOTOGRAPHS
PH01555 702 (February 23, 1995) pp60-65. "[Bosnian Refugees]" (Salgado, Sebastiao)
PH01556 724-725 (December 28, 1995) p93. "July 11, 1995: Muslim Prisoners Board A Truck After The Serbs Overrun Srebrenica; 8,000 Men Are Missing Or Dead"
PH01557 724-725 (December 28, 1995) p97. "July 12, 1995: Muslim Refugees Flee The Unprotected 'Safe Area' Of Srebrenica" (McNamara-Zamur)
PH01558 724-725 (December 28, 1995) p94. "Lies: Mladic (left) Toasts Karremans"
PH01559 724-725 (December 28, 1995) p93. "A Woman From Srebrenica Hanged Herself Near The U.N. Base At Tuzla"
BOSS—PHOTOGRAPHS—PORTRAITS
PH01560 663 (August 19, 1993) p14. "Boss: 'A Bitch Is Just A Hard, Straight-Up Real Woman'"
BOSS HOG—ALBUMS
PH01561 721 (November 16, 1995) p113. "Boss Hog"
PH01562 726 (January 25, 1996) p84. "Boss Hog"
BOSTON, MASSACHUSETTS—PHOTOGRAPHS
PH01563 694 (November 3, 1994) p52. "In The Protech Program, These Boston High-School Students Learn Marketable Skills Before Graduation" (Harders, Marian)
BOSTROM, DERRICK—PHOTOGRAPHS
PH01564 682 (May 19, 1994) p21. "Puppet Masters: Curt And Cris Kirkwood And Derrick Bostrom (from left)" (Halsband, Michael)
PH01565 695 (November 17, 1994) p145. "Meat Puppets" (Seliger, Mark)
PH01566 710 (June 15, 1995) p48. "Hey, Mow! Cris And Curt Kirkwood And Derrick Bostrom (from left)" (Gipe, Jon)
BOTTLE ROCKETS—ALBUMS
PH01567 719 (October 19, 1995) p150. "The Brooklyn Side"
BOTTLE ROCKETS—PHOTOGRAPHS
PH01568 730 (March 21, 1996) p22. "At Atlanta's Hard Rock Cafe, "The Best-Smelling Place We've Ever Played"" (Diamond, Rick)
PH01569 730 (March 21, 1996) p21. "Bottle Rockets Tom Parr, Tom Ray, Brian Henneman, Mark Ortmann (from left)"
BOUKMAN EKSPERYANS—ALBUMS
PH01570 707 (May 4, 1995) p68. "Libete"
BOUKMAN EKSPERYANS—PHOTOGRAPHS
PH01571 718 (October 5, 1995) p25. "Boukman Eksperyans" (Corio, David)
BOULANGER, RICHARD—PHOTOGRAPHS
PH01572 666 (September 30, 1993) p74. "Boulanger Demonstrating The Interactive Radio Baton" (Hill, Britain)
BOULWARE, BEN—PHOTOGRAPHS
PH01573 684 (June 16, 1994) p61. "Ben Boulware" (Borris, Dan)
BOUND (FILM)—PHOTOGRAPHS
PH01574 745 (October 17, 1996) p142. "Now Playing"
BOW WOW WOW—ALBUMS
PH01575 617 (November 14, 1991) p113. "See Jungle! See Jungle! Go Join Your Gang Yeah!..." (Egan, Nick)
PH01576 617 (November 14, 1991) p113. "See Jungle! See Jungle! Go Join Your Gang Yeah!..." (Earl, Andy)
BOWEN, REVONDA—PHOTOGRAPHS
PH01577 708 (May 18, 1995) p56. "A Preprom Revonda Bowen, With Boyfriend Chris Brown: The Daughter Of An Interracial Marriage, Revonda Dates Without Regard To Color" (Glackmeyer, Kevin)
PH01578 708 (May 18, 1995) p57. "Revonda Bowen And Son Saeje: Vice president Of The Student Body, Bowen Is Considering Going To Bartending School In Atlanta After Graduation" (Mark, Mary Ellen)
BOWIE, DAVID—ALBUMS
PH01579 617 (November 14, 1991) p134. "Aladdin Sane" (Philo, Duffy)
PH01580 617 (November 14, 1991) p134. "Aladdin Sane" (Philo, Celia)
PH01581 617 (November 14, 1991) p144. "Diamond Dogs" (Peellart, Guy)
PH01582 655 (April 29, 1993) p59. "Black Tie White Noise"
PH01583 719 (October 19, 1995) p148. "Outside"
BOWIE, DAVID—ILLUSTRATIONS
PH01584 616 (October 31, 1991) p3. "David Bowie" (Burke, Philip)
PH01585 619-620 (December 12, 1991) p5. "[David Bowie]" (Burke, Philip)
PH01586 655 (April 29, 1993) p59. "Bowie '93: Soul To Soul" (Calver, Dave)
BOWIE, DAVID—ILLUSTRATIONS—PORTRAITS
PH01587 641 (October 15, 1992) p141. "[David Bowie]" (Eidrigevicius, Stasys)

PH01588 719 (October 19, 1995) p148. "Art Crime" (Gabor, Tim)
BOWIE, DAVID—PHOTOGRAPHS
PH01589 619-620 (December 12, 1991) p68. "Bowie At The Hangar" (Mazur, Kevin)
PH01590 621 (January 9, 1992) p17. "Mercury Joins Paul McCartney And Other Stars In The Live Aid Finale, 1985" (Preston, Neal)
PH01591 622 (January 23, 1992) p7. "Brad Whitford, David Bowie, Steven Tyler, Hunt Sales, Tony Sales, Reeves Gabrels, Joey Kramer" (McAlpine, Paul)
PH01592 643 (November 12, 1992) p225. "Taking The Photo Op To Another Galaxy And Back: Bowie In 1987" (Ritts, Herb)
PH01593 645-646 (December 10, 1992) p53. "Nearly Newlywed Iman And Bowie" (Mazur, Kevin)
PH01594 645-646 (December 10, 1992) p45. "Saluting Freddie: Lennox And Bowie (above)" (Mazur, Kevin)
PH01595 647 (January 7, 1993) p9. "Bowie (left) And Glass" (Mazur, Kevin)
PH01596 647 (January 7, 1993) p11. "David Bowie" (Lowitt, Roxanne)
PH01597 658 (June 10, 1993) p60. "As Ziggy, With Iggy Pop And Lou Reed Circa 1972: 'We Knew We Were On The Wave Of Something'"
PH01598 658 (June 10, 1993) p58. "[David Bowie]" (Ritts, Herb)
PH01599 658 (June 10, 1993) p64. "In The Studio Recording 'Let's Dance' With Nile Rodgers, 1983" (Rosenthal, Cindy)
PH01600 658 (June 10, 1993) p62. "On American TV With Marianne Faithfull, 1973" (Rock, Mick)
PH01601 658 (June 10, 1993) p64. "Onstage With His Longtime Collaborator Mick Ronson During The Spiders' 1973 Japanese Tour"
PH01602 658 (June 10, 1993) p62. "Starring In 'The Man Who Fell To Earth,' 1975"
PH01603 659 (June 24, 1993) p28. "Bowie (with sax) And Ronson (with axe) Were Reunited On Record This Year"
PH01604 667 (October 14, 1993) p87. "'China Girl': Bowie Takes On Imperialism, Takes Off Trousers (above)"
PH01605 704 (March 23, 1995) p25. "Bowie (left) Greets Art Lover Meat Loaf" (Bentham, John)
PH01606 712-713 (July 13, 1995) p25. "With Honors" (Dilyard, Matt)
PH01607 714 (August 10, 1995) p15. "Bowie And A 'Basquiat' Assistant On Set" (Conde, Dominick)
PH01608 718 (October 5, 1995) p45. "Bowie" (Putland, Michael)
PH01609 718 (October 5, 1995) p48. "David Bowie In His 'Aladdin Sane' Period"
PH01610 720 (November 2, 1995) p50. "David Bowie" (Putland, Michael)
PH01611 720 (November 2, 1995) p28. "David Bowie (left) Tangos With Trent Reznor" (Capak, R. J.)
PH01612 720 (November 2, 1995) p16. "Funtime: Iggy Caught Bowie's Set During A Public Theater Benefit, In New York" (Mazur, Kevin)
PH01613 723 (December 14, 1995) p27. "[David Bowie & Johnny Lydon]" (Mazur, Kevin)
PH01614 723 (December 14, 1995) p53. "Jagger (middle) Celebrating Androgyny In The Glam-Rock '70s With Lou Reed (left) And David Bowie, Two Of The Many Who Followed In Jagger's Gender-Bending Footsteps"
PH01615 737 (June 27, 1996) p42. "With David Bowie In 1983" (Butler, Geoff)
PH01616 738-739 (July 11, 1996) p28. "David Bowie Does Andy Warhol" (Bayer, Sam)
PH01617 741 (August 22, 1996) p105. "Wright, Bowie, Oldman, Hopper"
PH01618 746 (October 31, 1996) p35. "This Year's Bowie: The Thin White Duke Governs Roseland" (Mazur, Kevin)
PH01619 749 (December 12, 1996) p25. "[David Bowie]" (Cardillicchio, Nick)
BOWIE, DAVID—PHOTOGRAPHS—PORTRAITS
PH01620 616 (October 31, 1991) p76. "David Bowie, Hunt Sales, Tony Sales And Reeves Gabrels (from left)" (Uchitel, Diego)
PH01621 616 (October 31, 1991) pp74-75. "[Tim Machine]" (Uchitel, Diego)
PH01622 643 (November 12, 1992) p78. "Bailey Captured Bowie's High-Fashion Look" (Bailey, David)
PH01623 643 (November 12, 1992) pp194-195. "David Bowie" (Watson, Albert)
PH01624 648 (January 21, 1993) p14. "[David Bowie]" (Ockenfels, Frank W.)
PH01625 658 (June 10, 1993) p56. "[David Bowie]" (Ritts, Herb)
PH01626 658 (June 10, 1993) p60. "Time May Change Me: Bowie In The Late Sixties"
PH01627 667 (October 14, 1993) p82. "'Ashes To Ashes': In This David Bowie Video, Major Tom Falls To Earth"
BOWMAN, STEVE—PHOTOGRAPHS
PH01628 669 (November 11, 1993) p24. "A '90s Sensibility: Vickrey, Gillingham, Duritz, Bowman, Malley, Bryson (from left)" (Blakesberg, Jay)
PH01629 685 (June 30, 1994) pp[cover]. "Counting Crows: The Biggest New Band In America" (Seliger, Mark)
PH01630 685 (June 30, 1994) p46. "Free Men In Paris: Dave Bryson, Steve Bowman, Dan Vickrey, Matt Malley And Charlie Gillingham (from left)" (Seliger, Mark)
BOY GEORGE—PHOTOGRAPHS—PORTRAITS
PH01631 651 (March 4, 1993) p28. "Boys Keep Swinging: George (left)..."
PH01632 672-673 (December 23, 1993) p28. "Above: Boy George, Remodeled For The '90s"
PH01633 720 (November 2, 1995) p26. "[Boy George]" (Weber, Uli)
BOYD, MALAIKA—PHOTOGRAPHS
PH01634 745 (October 17, 1996) p82. "[Malaika Boyd]" (Watson, Albert)
BOYD, MIKE—PHOTOGRAPHS
PH01635 730 (March 21, 1996) p55. "The Boys In The Bus: Schiavone McGee, David Triano, Eric Lawson, Chris Leitch, Karl Vonklein, David Peterson And Mike Boyd (clockwise from left)" (Clinch, Danny)
BOYD, PATTIE—PHOTOGRAPHS
PH01636 655 (April 29, 1993) p35. "Clapton In The Mid-Seventies With The Real-Life Layla, Pattie Boyd" (Wiltshire, Graham)
BOYLE, LARA FLYNN—PHOTOGRAPHS
PH01637 680 (April 21, 1994) p93. "Student Union For Charles, Boyle And Baldwin"
PH01638 705 (April 6, 1995) p17. "Lara Flynn Boyle And Jon Stewart Groping At The ESPY Awards" (Mazur, Kevin)
BOYLE, RAYMOND—PHOTOGRAPHS—PORTRAITS
PH01639 642 (October 29, 1992) p32. "Eugenius (clockwise from upper left): Boyle, Kelly, Keen, Lawrence" (Lavine, Michael)
BOYS (FILM)—PHOTOGRAPHS
PH01640 735 (May 30, 1996) p56. "Preppy Haas His Way With Ryder"
BOYS OF ST. VINCENT (FILM)-PHOTOGRAPHS
PH01641 705 (April 6, 1995) p69. "Oscar Rejects"
BOYS OF SUMMER (VIDEO)—PHOTOGRAPHS
PH01642 667 (October 14, 1993) p77. "Henley: Bittersweet 'Boys Of Summer' Hit One Out"
BOYS ON THE SIDE (FILM)—PHOTOGRAPHS
PH01643 702 (February 23, 1995) p81. "Actresses Goldberg, Parker And Barrymore Blow It"
PH01644 741 (August 22, 1996) p48. "McConaughey Onscreen"

BOYZ II MEN—ALBUMS
PH01645 693 (October 20, 1994) p168. "II"
PH01646 698-699 (December 29, 1994) p176. "II"
BOYZ II MEN—ILLUSTRATIONS
PH01647 694 (November 3, 1994) p120. "Boyz II Men: Making Love II You" (Gorgun, Ahmet)
BOYZ II MEN—PHOTOGRAPHS
PH01648 625 (March 5, 1992) p21. "Michael McCary, Wanya Morris, Shawn Stockman And Nate Morris (clockwise from top left)" (Graham, Jim)
PH01649 645-646 (December 10, 1992) p92. "[Boyz II Men]"
PH01650 651 (March 4, 1993) p18. "Boyz II Men In Top Doo-Wop Form" (Mazur, Kevin)
PH01651 653 (April 1, 1993) p57. "Boomerang"
PH01652 700 (January 26, 1995) p51. "Motown To Philly, '70s To '90s: Boyz II Men Rule R&B" (Trachtenberg, Robert)
PH01653 709 (June 1, 1995) p23. "Boyz II Men: Shawn Stockman, Michael McCary, Wanya Morris, Nate Morris" (Granitz, Steve)
BOYZ II MEN—PHOTOGRAPHS—PORTRAITS
PH01654 628 (April 16, 1992) p62. "Boyz II Men" (Graham, Jim)
BOYZ IN THE HOOD (FILM)—PHOTOGRAPHS
PH01655 619-620 (December 12, 1991) p60. "Ice Cube In 'Boyz In The Hood'"
BOZEMAN, MONTANA—PHOTOGRAPHS
PH01656 693 (October 20, 1994) p85. "Locals Demonstrate Outside The Montana Fish And Game Headquarters, In Bozeman" (Wuerthner, George)
BOZULICH, CARLA—PHOTOGRAPHS
PH01657 720 (November 2, 1995) p24. "Bozulich, Keenan, Tutton, Fitzgerald, Greene (from left)" (Toy, Joann)
BR5-49—ALBUMS
PH01658 748 (November 28, 1996) p132. "BR5-49"
BR5-49—PHOTOGRAPHS
PH01659 741 (August 22, 1996) p71. "[BR5-49]" (Herrington, Jim)
BRADFORD, JESSE—PHOTOGRAPHS
PH01660 664 (September 2, 1993) p70. "Krabbe Leaves Bradford Home Alone"
BRADFORD, KRISTA—PHOTOGRAPHS
PH01661 650 (February 18, 1993) p41. "After Five Years In Tabloid TV, Bradford (pictured here) Reached 'A Point At Which I Concluded I Was Not Going To Take This Anymore'" (Ockenfels, Frank W.)
PH01662 650 (February 18, 1993) p43. "'The Reporters': Jim Paymar, Dunlop, Bradford, Abramovitz, And Dunleavy (from left)"
BRADFORD, RODERICK—PHOTOGRAPHS
PH01663 678 (March 24, 1994) p69. "Brothers Under The Skin: Martin Phillips, Greg Parker, Mike Williams, Dexter Wilson, Rick Brown, Greg Jackson, Everett Whiteside, Roderick Bradford, Lacell Sherman, Daniel..." (Smi
BRADY, JIM—PHOTOGRAPHS
PH01664 666 (September 30, 1993) p31. "Pushing Gun Control: Sarah And Jim Brady With New York Mayor David Dinkins In 1991" (Markel, B.)
BRADY, SARAH—PHOTOGRAPHS
PH01664 666 (September 30, 1993) p31. "Pushing Gun Control: Sarah And Jim Brady With New York Mayor David Dinkins In 1991" (Markel, B.)
BRAGG, BILLY—ALBUMS
PH01665 616 (October 31, 1991) p92. "Don't Try This At Home"
PH01666 743 (September 19, 1996) p84. "William Bloke"
BRAGG, BILLY—PHOTOGRAPHS
PH01667 616 (October 31, 1991) p13. "Black Francis, Billy Bragg And Robyn Hitchcock (from left)" (Mazur, Kevin)
PH01668 619-620 (December 12, 1991) p81. "Billy Bragg" (Mazur, Kevin)
PH01669 619-620 (December 12, 1991) p37. "Billy Bragg (second from right) Joins R.E.M. On 'Mountain Stage'" (Cohrssen, James)
PH01670 622 (January 23, 1992) p17. "[Billy Bragg]" (Gershoff, Gary)
PH01671 623 (February 6, 1992) p13. "Billy Bragg Leads An All-Star Jam For ACT UP" (Cleland, Jane)
PH01672 667 (October 14, 1993) p40. "Below: Merchant, Bragg, Founder Harry Horgan, Tanya Donelly, Janovitz" (Robicheau, Paul)
PH01673 702 (February 23, 1995) p19. "Front: Hatfield, Donelly, Bragg. Rear: Dean Fraser, Gary Smith, Sean Slade" (Robicheau, Paul)
PH01674 747 (November 14, 1996) p25. "This Hall Was Made For You And Me: Arlo Guthrie, Bruce Springsteen, Tim Robbins, Dave Pirner And Billy Bragg (from left) At The Rock & Roll Hall Of Fame's Woody Guthrie Celebrati
BRAGG, BILLY—PHOTOGRAPHS—PORTRAITS
PH01675 622 (January 23, 1992) p9. "[Billy Bragg]" (Nofziger, Christopher)
PH01676 639 (September 17, 1992) p80. "" (Rider, Paul)
BRAIDS—PHOTOGRAPHS
PH01677 748 (November 28, 1996) p34. "'Rhapsody' In Rhythm & Blues: Braids Cornwell (left) And Ellis" (Ockenfels, Frank W.)
BRAIMES, JEFF—PHOTOGRAPHS
PH01678 615 (October 17, 1991) p28. "Jack Coy, George Hernandez, Jeff Braimes, Martin Chandler (from left)" (Mason, Karen)
BRAIN SURGEONS—ALBUMS
PH01679 701 (February 9, 1995) p59. "Eponymous"
BRAINIAC—PHOTOGRAPHS—PORTRAITS
PH01680 733 (May 2, 1996) p26. "Killing Retro: Tim Taylor, Juan Monasterio, John Schmersal And Tyler Trent (from top)" (McGuire, Leeann)
BRAMHALL, DOYLE, II—PHOTOGRAPHS
PH01681 630 (May 14, 1992) p25. "Chris Layton, Tommy Shannon, Doyle Bramhall II, Charlie Sexton (from left)" (Pumphrey, Steve)
BRAMHALL, DOYLE, II—PHOTOGRAPHS—PORTRAITS
PH01682 654 (April 15, 1993) pp[enc.17]. "[Doyle Bramhall II]" (Woodward, Fred)
BRANAGH, KENNETH—PHOTOGRAPHS
PH01683 657 (May 27, 1993) p56. "Awry: Washington, Branagh, Thompson"
PH01684 696 (December 1, 1994) p132. "Branagh's Dr. Frankenstein Lip Locks Bonham Carter"
PH01685 728 (February 22, 1996) p70. "The Actor's Life: Branagh (right) Directs Maloney"
BRANCA, GLENN—PHOTOGRAPHS
PH01686 691 (September 22, 1994) p58. "Moore (right) And Ranaldo (center) With Glenn Branca"
BRANCATO, LILLO—PHOTOGRAPHS
PH01687 668 (October 28, 1993) p88. "Are You Talking To Me? De Niro Directs Brancato (left)"
BRAND NEW HEAVIES—ALBUMS
PH01688 639 (September 17, 1992) p94. "Heavy Rhyme Experience: Vol. 1"
PH01689 679 (April 7, 1994) pp74,76. "Brother Sister"
BRAND, JOEL—PHOTOGRAPHS
PH01690 652 (March 18, 1993) pp[enc.44]. "The Author With His Trusty, Taped Renault At The Start Of The Airport Road, The Lifeline For The City Of Sarajevo" (Haley, Tom)
BRANDO, MARLON—ILLUSTRATIONS
PH01691 632 (June 11, 1992) p107. "[Marlon Brando]" (Cronin, Brian)
PH01692 707 (May 4, 1995) p73. "Bad Boys On The Prowl" (Kelley, Gary)
BRANDO, MARLON—PHOTOGRAPHS
PH01693 632 (June 11, 1992) p108. "Always A Presence: Brando In Costume For 'The Missouri Breaks'" (Mark, Mary Ellen)

PH01694 707 (May 4, 1995) p74. "Depp And Brando In 'Don Juan'"
PH01695 745 (October 17, 1996) p65. "'The Godfather' (1972): Brando And Pacino Flank Director Coppola"

BRANDY—PHOTOGRAPHS
PH01696 705 (April 6, 1995) p32. "Really Hot In The Church: Brandy" (Smith, Matthew Jordan)
PH01697 711 (June 29, 1995) p13. "Brandy (left) With A Newly Shorn Janet Jackson" (Mazur, Kevin)
PH01698 741 (August 22, 1996) p74. "[Brandy]" (Dah-Len)

BRANDY—PHOTOGRAPHS—PORTRAITS
PH01699 748 (November 28, 1996) p26. "Brandy, Left, With Lyte, Who Calls Her Friend 'An Old Soul'" (Maloney, Wren)

BRAUN, BILL—PHOTOGRAPHS
PH01700 665 (September 16, 1993) pp[enc.29]. "[Chuckie V & Bill Braun]" (Hanauer, Mark)
PH01701 665 (September 16, 1993) pp[enc.25]. "From Left: Greg Welsh, Ray Browning, Mike Pigg, Wes Hobson, Chuckie V, Scott Tinley, Nate Llerandi And Bill Braun" (Hanauer, Mark)

BRAVEHEART (FILM)—PHOTOGRAPHS
PH01702 709 (June 1, 1995) p68. "Men In Wigs"
PH01703 710 (June 15, 1995) p86. "Gibson Directs A 'Braveheart' Battle"
PH01704 731 (April 4, 1996) p66. "'Braveheart,' With Gibson"
PH01705 750-751 (December 26, 1996) p57. "'Braveheart'—Bad Movie! Blood! Gore! Boobs!"

BRAVIN, NICK—PHOTOGRAPHS
PH01706 628 (April 16, 1992) pp[enc.32]. "[Nick Bravin]" (Nicks, Dewey)

BRAXTON, TONI—ALBUMS
PH01707 670 (November 25, 1993) p114. "Toni Braxton"
PH01708 680 (April 21, 1994) p104. "Toni Braxton"

BRAXTON, TONI—PHOTOGRAPHS
PH01709 680 (April 21, 1994) p33. "Curtis Mayfield, Toni Braxton" (Jackson, Gregory)
PH01710 696 (December 1, 1994) p104. "Rhythm Nation: With Toni Braxton" (Deguire, Greg)

BRAZ, CLAUDIO—PHOTOGRAPHS
PH01711 706 (April 20, 1995) pp[enc.22]. "At Big Coffee Shop, In New York" (Tavee, Tom)

BREAKING THE WAVES (FILM)—PHOTOGRAPHS
PH01712 748 (November 28, 1996) p143. "Wave Maker Emily Watson"

BREEDERS—ALBUMS
PH01713 667 (October 14, 1993) p116. "Last Splash"
PH01714 668 (October 28, 1993) p96. "Last Splash"
PH01715 669 (November 11, 1993) p88. "Last Splash"
PH01716 670 (November 25, 1993) p140. "Last Splash"
PH01717 672-673 (December 23, 1993) p162. "Last Splash"
PH01718 674 (January 27, 1994) p44. "Last Splash"

BREEDERS—ILLUSTRATIONS
PH01719 685 (June 30, 1994) p10. "Thigh-O-Meter" (Pendergrast, James T.)

BREEDERS—PHOTOGRAPHS
PH01720 668 (October 28, 1993) p18. "Not Just Another Girl Group: Wiggs, Kim Deal, Macpherson And Kelley Deal (from left)" (Lass, Imke)
PH01721 682 (May 19, 1994) p89. "[The Breeders]" (Seliger, Mark)
PH01722 695 (November 17, 1994) p131. "The Breeders" (Seliger, Mark)
PH01723 698-699 (December 29, 1994) p36. "[Breeders]" (Mott, Tony)

BREEDERS—PHOTOGRAPHS—PORTRAITS
PH01724 660-661 (July 8, 1993) p101. "Breeders: Jim MacPherson, Kelley Deal, Kim Deal And Josephine Wiggs" (Mart, K.)
PH01725 672-673 (December 23, 1993) p57. "The Breeders: Last Splash? Let's Hope Not" (Blakesberg, Jay)

BREEDLOVE, LYNN—PHOTOGRAPHS
PH01726 721 (November 16, 1995) p81. "The Tribe That Sticks Together: Slade Bellum, Lynn Breedlove, Leslie Mah, Lynn Payne, Lynn Flipper (from left)" (Yemchuk, Yelena)

BREEZE, JOE—PHOTOGRAPHS
PH01727 634-635 (July 9, 1992) pp80-81. "By Their Jerseys Ye Shall Know Them: The Original Ballooners Charles Kelly, Joe Breeze And Gary Fisher (from left)" (Stone, Pete)

BREHENEY, CHRISTIAN—PHOTOGRAPHS
PH01728 704 (March 23, 1995) p97. "Former 'Late Night' Intern Breheney: It Wasn't Too Late To Work For Free—And It Paid Off" (Pluchino, Joseph)

BREMSER, WAYNE—PHOTOGRAPHS
PH01729 745 (October 17, 1996) p120. "Wayne Bremser, 24, Who Migrated To San Francisco To Work On The Web, Says 'You're Basically Just A Hamster—An Infinitely Replaceable Resources" (Duke, William)

BRENNAN, PAUL—PHOTOGRAPHS
PH01730 644 (November 26, 1992) p24. "Hansard, Noreen O'Donnell, Colm Mac Con Iomaire, Brennan, David Odlum And John Carney (from left)" (Marsden, Barry)

BRESKIN, DAVID—PHOTOGRAPHS
PH01731 632 (June 11, 1992) p133. "Breskin, Often Mistaken For 'One Of Them'"

BRICKELL, EDIE—ALBUMS
PH01732 697 (December 15, 1994) p97. "Picture Perfect Morning"

BRICKELL, EDIE—PHOTOGRAPHS
PH01733 659 (June 24, 1993) p13. "Edie Brickell And Paul Simon Join Nelson (left) For His Televised Birthday Celebration" (Kennedy, Bill)
PH01734 686-687 (July 14, 1994) p38. "Brickell, Assistant Engineer Andy Smith And Halee (from left)" (Mazur, Kevin)
PH01735 Number not assigned.

BRIDGES OF MADISON COUNTY (FILM)—ILLUSTRATIONS
PH01736 711 (June 29, 1995) p47. "Bridge Of Tides" (MacDonald, Ross)

BRIDGES OF MADISON COUNTY (FILM)—PHOTOGRAPHS
PH01736a 709 (June 1, 1995) p68. "Oscar Seekers"
PH01737 711 (June 29, 1995) p48. "New Romantic Triangle: Woman (Meryl Streep), man (Clint Eastwood) And Bridge"

BRIDGES, BEAU—PHOTOGRAPHS
PH01738 666 (September 30, 1993) p116. "'Harts Of The West'"

BRIDGES, JEFF—ILLUSTRATIONS
PH01739 728 (February 22, 1996) p69. "The Unsinkable Jeff Bridges" (Allen, Julian)

BRIDGES, JEFF—PHOTOGRAPHS
PH01740 658 (June 10, 1993) p74. "Jailbird Bridges Finds A Son To Protect In Furlong"
PH01741 668 (October 28, 1993) p86. "Jeff Bridges Survives A Plane Crash As A Man His Wife And Family Cannot Recognize"
PH01742 678 (March 24, 1994) p100. "Missing In Oscar Action"
PH01743 686-687 (July 14, 1994) p99. "Jeff Bridges And Forest Whitaker Go Boom"
PH01744 723 (December 14, 1995) p92. "Jeff Bridges"
PH01745 728 (February 22, 1996) p70. "Bridges At The Helm: Strong Actor, Shaky Career"
PH01746 728 (February 22, 1996) p70. "Bridges Finds Home Sweet Hell On Water"

BRIDGES, JEFF—PHOTOGRAPHS—PORTRAITS
PH01747 728 (February 22, 1996) p70. "Bridges At The Helm: Strong Actor, Shaky Career"
PH01748 728 (February 22, 1996) p70. "Bridges Finds Home Sweet Hell On Water"

BRIDGES, LLOYD—PHOTOGRAPHS
PH01749 666 (September 30, 1993) p116. "'Harts Of The West'"

BRIDGES, TODD—PHOTOGRAPHS
PH01750 665 (September 16, 1993) p41. "Todd Bridges And Janet On 'Different Strokes'"

BRIGGS, DAVID—PHOTOGRAPHS
PH01751 728 (February 22, 1996) p24. "Young And Briggs At 1995's Rock & Roll Hall Of Fame Inductions" (Briggs, Bettina)
BRIGGS, DAVID—PHOTOGRAPHS—PORTRAITS
PH01752 726 (January 25, 1996) p28. "Briggs, Co-Producer Of 17 Young LPs"
BRIGGS, PAT—PHOTOGRAPHS
PH01753 741 (August 22, 1996) p31. "Soundgarden's Cornell,. Psychotica's Briggs And Joey Ramone" (Blakesberg, Jay)
BRILL, DMITRY—PHOTOGRAPHS—PORTRAITS
PH01754 639 (September 17, 1992) p37. "Super DJ Dmitry Brill, Lady Kier Kirby And Towa 'Towa' Tei (clockwise from top left)" (Anderson, Patrick)
BRILLIANT DISGUISE (VIDEO)—PHOTOGRAPHS
PH01755 667 (October 14, 1993) p94. "'Brilliant Disguise': Bruce Springsteen Wears It Well"
BRINKLEY, CHRISTIE—PHOTOGRAPHS
PH01756 615 (October 17, 1991) p66. "Christie Brinkley And Billy Joel, Long Island, 1989" (Pigozzi, Jean)
BRISENO, THEODORE—PHOTOGRAPHS
PH01757 657 (May 27, 1993) p24. "Police Escort: Eazy-E With Briseno"
PH01758 672-673 (December 23, 1993) p30. "Strange Bedfellows: Eazy-E With Briseno" (Nelson, Mike)
BRODERICK, MATTHEW—PHOTOGRAPHS
PH01759 686-687 (July 14, 1994) p92. "Broderick Speaks For The King"
BRODIE, V. S.—PHOTOGRAPHS
PH01760 685 (June 30, 1994) p82. "Director Troche (left) With Stars Brodie And Turner"
BRODSKY QUARTET—ALBUMS
PH01761 652 (March 18, 1993) p39. "The Juliet Letters" (Gardner, Elysa)
BRODSKY QUARTET—PHOTOGRAPHS
PH01762 651 (March 4, 1993) p23. "Michael Thomas, Jaqueline Thomas, Paul Cassidy, Elvis Costello, Don Belton" (Westenberg, Kevin)
BRODUS, BEVERLY—PHOTOGRAPHS
PH01763 750-751 (December 26, 1996) p50. "Snoop Leaving A Los Angeles Courthouse With His Mother, Beverly Brodus, And His On, Corde" (Ruymen, Jim)
BROKAW, CHRIS—PHOTOGRAPHS
PH01764 621 (January 9, 1992) p25. "Codeine (from left): John Engle, Chris Brokaw And Stephen Immerwahr" (Capak, R. J.)
PH01765 654 (April 15, 1993) p22. "They've Arrived: Arthur Johnson, Sean O'Brien, Thalia Zedek And Chris Brokaw" (Westenberg, Kevin)
PH01766 660-661 (July 8, 1993) p100. "Come (from left): Arthur Johnson, Sean O'Brien, Chris Brokaw And Thalia Zedek" (Apicella-Hitchcock, Stephen)
BROKEN ARROW (FILM)—PHOTOGRAPHS
PH01767 728 (February 22, 1996) p43. "Travolta Puts On The Moves In 'Pulp Fiction,' 'Saturday Night Fever' And 'Broken Arrow'"
BRONX STYLE BOB—ALBUMS
PH01768 645-646 (December 10, 1992) p182. "Grandma's Ghost"
A BRONX TALE (FILM)—PHOTOGRAPHS
PH01769 668 (October 28, 1993) p88. "Are You Talking To Me? De Niro Directs Brancato (left)"
BROOKE, JONATHA—PHOTOGRAPHS—PORTRAITS
PH01770 636 (August 6, 1992) p24. "Jennifer Kimball (left) And Jonatha Brooke" (Horner, Carl J.)
BROOKS AND DUNN—ALBUMS
PH01771 656 (May 13, 1993) p107. "Hard Workin' Man"
BROOKS, GARTH—ALBUMS
PH01772 616 (October 31, 1991) p114. "Ropin' The Wind"
PH01773 618 (November 28, 1991) p120. "Ropin' The Wind"
PH01774 619-620 (December 12, 1991) p162. "Ropin' The Wind"
PH01775 624 (February 20, 1992) p53. "Ropin' The Wind"
PH01776 626 (March 19, 1992) p112. "Ropin' The Wind"
PH01777 627 (April 2, 1992) p50. "Ropin' The Wind"
PH01778 628 (April 16, 1992) p100. "Ropin' The Wind"
PH01779 629 (April 30, 1992) p72. "Ropin' The Wind"
PH01780 644 (November 26, 1992) p84. "The Chase"
PH01781 645-646 (December 10, 1992) p184. "The Chase"
PH01782 667 (October 14, 1993) p114. "In Pieces"
PH01783 668 (October 28, 1993) p96. "In Pieces"
PH01784 670 (November 25, 1993) p140. "In Pieces"
BROOKS, GARTH—PHOTOGRAPHS
PH01785 619-620 (December 12, 1991) p79. "Garth Brooks (right)..." (St. Nicholas, Randee)
PH01786 627 (April 2, 1992) p13. "Garth Brooks: Are We Clear For A Landing?" (Wolfson, Ron)
PH01787 628 (April 16, 1992) p13. "One Giddy Garth Brooks" (Gwinn, Beth)
PH01788 630 (May 14, 1992) p15. "Garth Brooks: His Star Has Fallen" (Diltz, Henry)
PH01789 649 (February 4, 1993) p8. "Garth Brooks" (Schwab, Bill)
PH01790 651 (March 4, 1993) p49. "Garth Brooks, Man Of A Thousand Hats" (Blakesberg, Jay)
PH01791 653 (April 1, 1993) p30. "[Garth Brooks]" (Markus, Kurt)
PH01792 670 (November 25, 1993) p33. "Garth-Mania, Alive And Well" (Natkin, Paul)
PH01793 688 (August 11, 1994) p18. "Garth And The Closest Thing To God, James Taylor" (Kravitz, Jeff)
PH01794 700 (January 26, 1995) p51. "Garth Brooks Wins Best Country Artist" (Butler, Henrietta)
BROOKS, GARTH—PHOTOGRAPHS—PORTRAITS
PH01795 628 (April 16, 1992) p16. "King Of The Hill: Garth Brooks" (Tucker, Mark)
PH01796 653 (April 1, 1993) p32. "[Garth Brooks]" (Markus, Kurt)
PH01797 653 (April 1, 1993) pp[cover]. "Garth Brooks: The Cat In The Hat Meets Rolling Stone" (Markus, Kurt)
PH01798 672-673 (December 23, 1993) p188. "[Covers]" (Markus, Kurt)
BROOKS, HADDA—ALBUMS
PH01799 729 (March 7, 1996) p50. "Time Was When"
BROOKS, RICKY—PHOTOGRAPHS
PH01800 733 (May 2, 1996) p14. "Nixons' Bassist Ricky Brooks (left) And Maloy" (Burton, Eric)
BROOKS, RODNEY—PHOTOGRAPHS
PH01801 658 (June 10, 1993) pp[enc.21]. "Rodney Brooks Poses With Genghis II, One Of His Insectoid Creations" (Llewellyn, Michael)
BROOME, CURTIS—PHOTOGRAPHS
PH01802 684 (June 16, 1994) p68. "Curtis Broome" (Borris, Dan)
PH01803 684 (June 16, 1994) p66. "Curtis Broome Takes Batting Practice" (Borris, Dan)
BROSNAN, PIERCE—ILLUSTRATIONS
PH01804 722 (November 30, 1995) p73. "Big Fish Little Fish" (Allen, Terry)
BROSNAN, PIERCE—PHOTOGRAPHS—PORTRAITS
PH01805 722 (November 30, 1995) p74. "Is Jennifer Jason Leigh's Rocker Hotter Than Pierce Brosnan's Bond? No Contest"
BROTHERLY LOVE (TELEVISION SHOW)—PHOTOGRAPHS
PH01806 716 (September 7, 1995) p84. "Brotherly Love With The Lawrence Clones"
BROTHER'S KEEPER (FILM)—PHOTOGRAPHS
PH01807 653 (April 1, 1993) p57. "Brother's Keeper"
THE BROTHERS MCMULLEN (FILM)—PHOTOGRAPHS
PH01808 709 (June 1, 1995) p70. "Rebel Voices"
PH01809 715 (August 24, 1995) p110. "Mulcahy, Burns, Bahns And McGlone (from left)"

PH01810 731 (April 4, 1996) p66. "McMullen"
BROUGH, ANDREW—PHOTOGRAPHS
PH01811 615 (October 17, 1991) p28. "John Collie, Shayne Carter, Andrew Brough, David Wood (from left)" (Blakesberg, Jay)
BROWN, BOBBY—ALBUMS
PH01812 639 (September 17, 1992) p90. "Bobby"
PH01813 645-646 (December 10, 1992) p168. ""
BROWN, BOBBY—ILLUSTRATIONS
PH01814 639 (September 17, 1992) p90. "It's Not His Prerogative" (Burke, Philip)
BROWN, BOBBY—PHOTOGRAPHS
PH01815 622 (January 23, 1992) p6. "Brown And Houston, Giddy With Love" (Shaw, Eugene)
PH01816 645-646 (December 10, 1992) p71. "Bobby Brown And Whitney Houston"
PH01817 645-646 (December 10, 1992) p77. "Mr. Whitney Houston" (Benabib, Michael)
PH01818 651 (March 4, 1993) p31. "Bobby Brown" (Kraft, Chris)
PH01819 710 (June 15, 1995) p32. "Mama Said Knock You Out: Brown" (Talesnick, Barry)
PH01820 726 (January 25, 1996) p26. "Whitney Houston, Clive Davis Of Arista And Bobby Brown (from left)" (Hurschmann, Paul)
BROWN, BOBBY—PHOTOGRAPHS—PORTRAITS
PH01821 658 (June 10, 1993) p47. "[Bobby Brown]" (Watson, Albert)
PH01822 680 (April 21, 1994) p33. "The Bobby Browns Greet Aretha" (Mazur, Kevin)
PH01823 724-725 (December 28, 1995) p60. "Bobby Brown" (Oliver, Benjamin)
BROWN, CHARLES—ALBUMS
PH01824 702 (February 23, 1995) p76. "These Blues"
BROWN, CHRIS—PHOTOGRAPHS
PH01825 708 (May 18, 1995) p56. "A Preprom Revonda Bowen, With Boyfriend Chris Brown: The Daughter Of An Interracial Marriage, Revonda Dates Without Regard To Color" (Glackmeyer, Kevin)
BROWN, DAN—PHOTOGRAPHS
PH01826 710 (June 15, 1995) p36. "Brown, Herrema, Hagerty And Pyle (from left): 'We're A Marketing Nightmare'" (Westenberg, Kevin)
BROWN, DENNIS—PHOTOGRAPHS
PH01827 676 (February 24, 1994) p44. "Lover's Rock Man Dennis Brown" (Corio, David)
BROWN, DIVINE MARIE—PHOTOGRAPHS—PORTRAITS
PH01828 716 (September 7, 1995) p78. "Summer Wrap-Up]"
BROWN, GREG—ALBUMS
PH01829 669 (November 11, 1993) p74. "Friend Of Mine"
PH01830 748 (November 28, 1996) p137. "Further In"
BROWN, IAN—PHOTOGRAPHS
PH01831 712-713 (July 13, 1995) p26. "Stone Roses Frontman Ian Brown Wilts At The Atlanta Fest" (Diamond, Rick)
PH01832 724-725 (December 28, 1995) p39. "Stoned, Dethroned: Mani, Squire, Brown, Reni (from left)" (Otte, Sylvia)
BROWN, IAN—PHOTOGRAPHS—PORTRAITS
PH01833 706 (April 20, 1995) p30. "The Stone Roses (clockwise from top left): Mountfield, Wren, Squire And Brown" (Ragel, Jon)
BROWN, JAMES—ALBUMS
PH01834 619-620 (December 12, 1991) p162. "Star Time"
BROWN, JAMES—PHOTOGRAPHS
PH01835 615 (October 17, 1991) p14. "Arsenio Hall, James Brown And M. C. Hammer (from left)" (Mazur, Kevin)
PH01836 619-620 (December 12, 1991) p22. "James Brown (above) Tastes Freedom, While Mariah Carey (below) Tastes Victory" (Mazur, Kevin)
PH01837 619-620 (December 12, 1991) p53. "...James Brown (above)..." (De Guire, Gregg)
PH01838 626 (March 19, 1992) p11. "Mariah Carey, James Brown" (Mazur, Kevin)
PH01839 645-646 (December 10, 1992) p31. "AMA Winner James Brown"
PH01840 654 (April 15, 1993) p13. "Hammer, Pickett And Brown (from left)" (Mazur, Kevin)
PH01841 684 (June 16, 1994) p35. "Magic Johnson, Springsteen, James Brown" (Kravitz, Jeff)
PH01842 684 (June 16, 1994) p36. "[Wheel Of Fortune]" (Slenzak, Ron)
PH01843 716 (September 7, 1995) p22. "James Brown: On The Good Foot" (Natkin, Paul)
PH01844 719 (October 19, 1995) p42. "Chuck Berry, Bob Dylan And James Brown Head Toward The Artists' Tents At The Close Of The Show" (Corbijn, Anton)
PH01845 719 (October 19, 1995) p36. "James Brown, The Godfather Of Soul, Warms Up" (Corbijn, Anton)
PH01846 724-725 (December 28, 1995) p56. "Hail Hail: Berry And Brown" (Mazur, Kevin)
PH01847 737 (June 27, 1996) p16. "[James Brown]" (Cleere, Carol)
BROWN, JERRY—ILLUSTRATIONS—PORTRAITS
PH01848 625 (March 5, 1992) p29. "[Jerry Brown]" (Payne, C. F.)
BROWN, JERRY—PHOTOGRAPHS
PH01849 630 (May 14, 1992) p17. "[Jerry Brown]" (Eichner, Steve)
PH01850 630 (May 14, 1992) p22. "Jerry Brown In The Late Seventies With Linda Ronstadt, Jackson Browne (right), The Eagles And Other West Coast Musicians" (Pulin, Chuck)
BROWN, JULIE—PHOTOGRAPHS
PH01851 619-620 (December 12, 1991) p74. "Downtown Julie Brown With L. L. Cool J"
BROWN, JUNIOR—ILLUSTRATIONS
PH01852 736 (June 13, 1996) p40. "Junior Brown" (Cowles, David)
BROWN, JUNIOR—PHOTOGRAPHS
PH01853 696 (December 1, 1994) p44. "Layne, Mr. Brown, Smith, Mrs. Brown" (Capak, R. J.)
PH01854 742 (September 5, 1996) p29. "Junior Brown"
BROWN, JUNIOR—PHOTOGRAPHS—PORTRAITS
PH01855 691 (September 22, 1994) p21. "Junior Brown (left) With Nick Lowe"
BROWN, LEE—PHOTOGRAPHS
PH01856 706 (April 20, 1995) p44. "Brown Can Inspect The Haul From A Raid In Bolivia, But The Drug Czar Still Can't Control His Kingdom"
BROWN, MARTY—ALBUMS
PH01857 660-661 (July 8, 1993) p116. "Wild Kentucky Skies"
BROWN, MARTY—PHOTOGRAPHS—PORTRAITS
PH01858 617 (November 14, 1991) p34. "[Marty Brown]" (Dixon, Dean)
BROWN, OSCAR, JR.—PHOTOGRAPHS
PH01859 668 (October 28, 1993) p66. "Mayfield (seated) Meeting With Singer Oscar Brown Jr."
BROWN, RICARDO—PHOTOGRAPHS
PH01860 720 (November 2, 1995) p32. "Demons Of The Week: Kurupt And Daz (from left)"
BROWN, RICK—PHOTOGRAPHS
PH01861 678 (March 24, 1994) p69. "Brothers Under The Skin: Martin Phillips, Greg Parker, Mike Williams, Dexter Wilson, Rick Brown, Greg Jackson, Everett Whiteside, Roderick Bradford, Lacell Sherman, Daniel..." (Smi
BROWN, RUTH—PHOTOGRAPHS
PH01862 651 (March 4, 1993) p15. "Ruth Brown With Bonnie Raitt (left)" (Mazur, Kevin)
PH01863 681 (May 5, 1994) p15. "Martha Reeves, Brown, Fred Schneider, Richard And Raitt At The Recent Awards (from left)" (Micelotta, Frank)

PH01864 697 (December 15, 1994) p34. "White (center) With Ruth Brown (left) In The Mid-'60s"
BROWN, RUTH—PHOTOGRAPHS—PORTRAITS
PH01865 649 (February 4, 1993) p50. "[Ruth Brown]"
BROWN, TANYA RAE—PHOTOGRAPHS
PH01866 696 (December 1, 1994) p44. "Layne, Mr. Brown, Smith, Mrs. Brown" (Capak, R. J.)
BROWN, THURLOW—PHOTOGRAPHS
PH01867 669 (November 11, 1993) p66. "A Performance At Marvell High School Circa '55, With Thurlow Brown, Linda And Levon Helm (above, from left)"
BROWN, VINCENT—PHOTOGRAPHS
PH01868 615 (October 17, 1991) p27. "Naughty By Nature: DJ Kay Gee, Treach And Vinnie (from left)" (Larsen, Kristine)
BROWN, VINNIE—PHOTOGRAPHS
PH01869 663 (August 19, 1993) pp66-68,70. "[Naughty By Nature]" (Gregoire, Jean Louis)
BROWN, WILBUR—PHOTOGRAPHS
PH01870 691 (September 22, 1994) p44. "Boston Director Ron Homer Jr. (center left) And Supervisor Wilbur Brown (center, right) Let The Kids Find Their Own Remedies To Urban Blight" (Ng, Karjean)
BROWNBACK, SAM—PHOTOGRAPHS—PORTRAITS
PH01871 746 (October 31, 1996) p59. "Sam Brownback"
BROWNE, JACKSON—ALBUMS
PH01872 672-673 (December 23, 1993) p162. "I'm Alive"
PH01873 729 (March 7, 1996) p48. "Looking East"
BROWNE, JACKSON—ILLUSTRATIONS
PH01874 641 (October 15, 1992) p138. "[Jackson Browne]" (McMullan, James)
BROWNE, JACKSON—ILLUSTRATIONS—PORTRAITS
PH01875 645-646 (December 10, 1992) p152. "Jackson Browne, 1976"
BROWNE, JACKSON—PHOTOGRAPHS
PH01876 618 (November 28, 1991) p11. "Byrne (left) And Browne" (Mazur, Kevin)
PH01877 619-620 (December 12, 1991) p18. "The Rock And Roll Hall Of Fame Jam" (Bellissimo, J.)
PH01878 630 (May 14, 1992) p22. "Jerry Brown In The Late Seventies With Linda Ronstadt, Jackson Browne (right), The Eagles And Other West Coast Musicians" (Pulin, Chuck)
PH01879 645-646 (December 10, 1992) p49. "Browne And Hannah In Happier Times" (Guastella, Mike)
PH01880 651 (March 4, 1993) p17. "The New P-Folk? George Clinton, Jackson Browne And Don Was (from left)" (Mazur, Kevin)
PH01881 667 (October 14, 1993) p28. "I Suppose This Album's More Personal..." (Danelian, Stephen)
PH01882 671 (December 9, 1993) p32. "Raitt, Wallace And Browne (from left)" (Gardner, Christopher M.)
PH01883 672-673 (December 23, 1993) p69. "Jackson Browne: Lucky In Love?" (Danelian, Stephen)
PH01884 679 (April 7, 1994) p34. "He's Live" Jackson Browne In New York" (Mazur, Kevin)
PH01885 684 (June 16, 1994) p36. "Indigo Girl Emily Saliers, Nanci Griffith, Browne, Carpenter, Indigo Girl Amy Ray" (Diamond, Rick)
PH01886 686-687 (July 14, 1994) p42. "My Old School Chum: Markiewicz, Browne"
PH01887 718 (October 5, 1995) p21. "[Bonnie Raitt & Jackson Browne]" (Paul, Jonathan)
PH01888 719 (October 19, 1995) p41. "Jackson Browne Rehearsing" (Corbijn, Anton)
PH01889 724-725 (December 28, 1995) p56. "The Time Was Right: Crow, Hynde, Browne And Reeves (from left)" (Mazur, Kevin)
PH01890 748 (November 28, 1996) p98. "Browne Began Using E-Mail As AN Easy Way To Communicate With His Son In Australia" (Seliger, Mark)
BROWNE, JACKSON—PHOTOGRAPHS—PORTRAITS
PH01891 643 (November 12, 1992) p186. "Jackson Browne" (Markus, Kurt)
PH01892 705 (April 6, 1995) p17. "Sauce Du Jour, Brown Gravy: Said Sauce Jackson Browne (left), Gravy" (Blakesberg, Jay)
PH01893 741 (August 22, 1996) p40. "[Jackson Browne]" (Israelson, Nels)
BROWNER, CAROL—PHOTOGRAPHS
PH01894 668 (October 28, 1993) p45. "Carol Browner Is Not In Florida Anymore: The EPA Head In Her D.C. Office" (Eccles, Andrew)
PH01895 668 (October 28, 1993) p47. "Welcome To The Shark Tank: Browner With Her Mentor, Al Gore"
BROWNING, RAY—PHOTOGRAPHS
PH01896 665 (September 16, 1993) pp[enc.25]. "From Left: Greg Welsh, Ray Browning, Mike Pigg, Wes Hobson, Chuckie V, Scott Tinley, Nate Llerandi And Bill Braun" (Hanauer, Mark)
BRUCE, JACK—PHOTOGRAPHS
PH01897 649 (February 4, 1993) p51. "Clapton, Baker And Bruce Of Cream"
PH01898 651 (March 4, 1993) p18. "Bob Dylan (in disguise) Greets Jack Bruce" (Mazur, Kevin)
PH01899 655 (April 29, 1993) p38. "Rock's First Power Trio (Clapton, Baker and Bruce, from left) Basking In The Sunshine of History Backstage At The Hall Of Fame" (Mazur, Kevin)
BRUCE, JACK—PHOTOGRAPHS—PORTRAITS
PH01900 655 (April 29, 1993) p34. "Cream In November 1996, Shortly Before The U.K. Release Of The Group's debut Album, Fresh Cream: Jack Bruce, Ginger Baker And Clapton (clockwise from left)" (Gale, Tony)
BRUCE, LENNY—ALBUMS
PH01901 627 (April 2, 1992) p46. "Lenny Bruce Originals: Volume 1"
BRUCE, NEELY—PHOTOGRAPHS—PORTRAITS
PH01902 639 (September 17, 1992) p84. "Neely Bruce Works Undercover" (Borris, Dan)
BRUFORD, BILL—PHOTOGRAPHS
PH01903 655 (April 29, 1993) p20. "The Great Deceivers: John Wetton, David Cross, Fripp And Bill Bruford (from left)"
BRUFORD, BILL—PHOTOGRAPHS—PORTRAITS
PH01904 684 (June 16, 1994) p18. "Belew, Fripp, Bruford And Levin"
BRYAN, MARK—PHOTOGRAPHS
PH01905 691 (September 22, 1994) p19. "Hootie Goes to Washington: Soni, Dean Felber, The Prez, Darius Rucker, Bryan (from left)"
PH01906 714 (August 10, 1995) pp42-43. "Darius Rucker, Dean Felber, Mark Bryan And Jim Sonefeld" (Seliger, Mark)
PH01907 726 (January 25, 1996) p37. "Hootie And The Blowfish: Jim Sonefeld, Darius Rucker, Dean Felber And Mark Bryan (from left)" (Seliger, Mark)
BRYSON, DAVE—PHOTOGRAPHS
PH01908 669 (November 11, 1993) p24. "A '90s Sensibility: Vickrey, Gillingham, Duritz, Bowman, Malley, Bryson (from left)" (Blakesberg, Jay)
PH01909 685 (June 30, 1994) pp[cover]. "Counting Crows: The Biggest New Band In America" (Seliger, Mark)
PH01910 685 (June 30, 1994) p46. "Free Men In Paris: Dave Bryson, Steve Bowman, Dan Vickrey, Matt Malley And Charlie Gillingham (from left)" (Seliger, Mark)
BUCHANAN, PATRICK—ILLUSTRATIONS
PH01911 623 (February 6, 1992) p37. "[Globe]" (Cronin, Brian)
PH01912 732 (April 18, 1996) p53. "[Pat Buchanan]" (Burke, Philip)
PH01913 735 (May 30, 1996) p10. "Ol' Ignorance" (Pendergrast, James T.)
BUCHANAN, PATRICK—PHOTOGRAPHS
PH01914 724-725 (December 28, 1995) p110. "Buchanan Has The Right Eating Out Of His Hands" (Fink, Larry)

PH01915 724-725 (December 28, 1995) p104. "Republican Hopeful Pat Buchanan At New Hampshire's Thomas More College, Pressing The Flesh" (Fink, Larry)
PH01916 724-725 (December 28, 1995) p103. "Trailblazers: Buchanan Supporters Meet Their Man In New Hampshire" (Fink, Larry)
PH01917 750-751 (December 26, 1996) p50. "The Man From Fear: Buchanan Tried To Scare Us And Ended Up Scaring Us Off" (Sanders, David)

BUCHANAN, PATRICK—PHOTOGRAPHS—PORTRAITS
PH01918 730 (March 21, 1996) p51. "Buchanan"

BUCK, PETER—ILLUSTRATIONS
PH01919 704 (March 23, 1995) p13. "R.E.M.'s Peter Buck" (Burke, Philip)

BUCK, PETER—PHOTOGRAPHS
PH01920 618 (November 28, 1991) p11. "Clockwise From Left: Buck, Enrique, Ryan-Harris, Chris Tinsley, Kinney, Billy Fields And Jamie Turner (wearing glasses)" (Diamond, Rick)
PH01921 628 (April 16, 1992) p11. "R.E.M.'s Mike Mills, Michael Stipe, Peter Buck And Bill Berry (from left)" (Mazur, Kevin)
PH01922 640 (October 1, 1992) p20. "Michael Stipe, Peter Buck, Mike Mills And Bill Berry (clockwise from left)" (Corbijn, Anton)
PH01923 647 (January 7, 1993) p9. "From Left: Mike Mills, Buck, Bill Berry and Stipe" (Colletti, Steve)
PH01924 667 (October 14, 1993) p39. "Below: Dave Pirner (left) With Peter Buck" (Mazur, Kevin)
PH01925 693 (October 20, 1994) p59. "Peter Buck" (Seliger, Mark)
PH01926 693 (October 20, 1994) p27. "R.E.M.'s Bill Berry, Michael Stipe, Peter Buck, Mike Mills" (Mazur, Kevin)
PH01927 704 (March 23, 1995) p32. "Band On The Run: Berry, Mills, Stipe And Buck (above, from left)" (Sheehan, Tom)
PH01928 704 (March 23, 1995) p30. "Married With Children: Peter Buck" (Liguz, Andrzej)
PH01929 711 (June 29, 1995) p12. "Barrett Martin, Peter Buck And Mike McCready (from left)" (Mercer, Lance)
PH01930 711 (June 29, 1995) p26. "Buck On Opening Night" (Blakesberg, Jay)
PH01931 714 (August 10, 1995) p16. "The New Math: McCaughey, Buck, Tweedy And Greenberg (from left)" (Perez, Marty)
PH01932 717 (September 21, 1995) p20. "Three Beatle Maniacs: Lord, Buck And McCaughey (from left)" (Clinch, Danny)
PH01933 726 (January 25, 1996) p42. "Peter Buck, Michael Stipe, Bill Berry, Mike Mills" (Jensen, David)
PH01934 737 (June 27, 1996) p29. "R.E.M.'s Mike Mills, Bill Berry, Stipe And Buck (from left) Have Split With Their Longtime Manager" (Rider, Paul)
PH01935 748 (November 28, 1996) p26. "Tuatara's Martin, Harwood And Buck (from left)" (Doughty, Curt)

BUCK, ROB—PHOTOGRAPHS—PORTRAITS
PH01936 652 (March 18, 1993) pp34-35. "Rob Buck, Dennis Drew, Natalie Merchant, Jerome Augustyniak, Steven Gustafson (from left)" (Ockenfels, Frank W.)

BUCKINGHAM, LINDSEY—ALBUMS
PH01937 634-635 (July 9, 1992) p99. "Out Of The Cradle"
PH01938 645-646 (December 10, 1992) p169. "Out Of The Cradle"

BUCKINGHAM, LINDSEY—ILLUSTRATIONS
PH01939 633 (June 25, 1992) p3. "Lindsey Buckingham" (Burke, Philip)
PH01940 634-635 (July 9, 1992) p99. "'Out Of The Cradle': Going His Own Way" (Fish, James)

BUCKINGHAM, LINDSEY—PHOTOGRAPHS
PH01941 633 (June 25, 1992) pp32-33. "[Lindsey Buckingham]" (Camp, E. J.)
PH01942 654 (April 15, 1993) p19. "[Lindsey Buckingham]" (Granitz, Steve)

BUCKINGHAM, LINDSEY—PHOTOGRAPHS—PORTRAITS
PH01943 630 (May 14, 1992) p15. "Lindsey Buckingham" (Guzman)

BUCKLEY, JEFF—ALBUMS
PH01944 694 (November 3, 1994) p101. "Grace"

BUCKLEY, JEFF—ILLUSTRATIONS—PORTRAITS
PH01945 677 (March 10, 1994) p65. "Jeff Buckley" (Preuitt, Clayton)

BUCKLEY, JEFF—PHOTOGRAPHS
PH01946 628 (April 16, 1992) p55. "Buckley (left) And Lucas" (Buck, Chris)
PH01947 676 (February 24, 1994) p26. "Buckley: Dylan Meets Diamanda" (Capak, R. J.)
PH01948 690 (September 8, 1994) p38. "Jeff Buckley Goes West" (Gahr, David)
PH01949 693 (October 20, 1994) pp68-69. "[Jeff Buckley]" (Thurnher, Jeffrey)
PH01950 693 (October 20, 1994) p70. "Jeff Buckley Live: His Voice Is The Main Event" (Capak, R. J.)
PH01951 695 (November 17, 1994) p49. "Jeff Buckley" (Thurnher, Jeffrey)
PH01952 703 (March 9, 1995) p20. "Whitley (left) With Fan Jeff Buckley" (Busacca, Larry)
PH01953 710 (June 15, 1995) p18. "Salt Of The Earth: Buckley Does His Part In Atlanta" (Diamond, Rick)
PH01954 727 (February 8, 1996) p13. "Fateh Ali Khan And Buckley, Sharing And Caring" (Vartoogian, Jack)

BUCKLEY, JEFF—PHOTOGRAPHS—PORTRAITS
PH01955 698-699 (December 29, 1994) p49. "Jeff Buckley" (Dill, Nicola)
PH01956 700 (January 26, 1995) p52. "Jeff Buckley Emerged As best New Male Singer" (Lavine, Michael)
PH01957 702 (February 23, 1995) p50. "Tears Of A Clown: Buckley, Etheridge" (Mazur, Kevin)

BUCKLEY, TIM—PHOTOGRAPHS
PH01958 693 (October 20, 1994) p70. "Hip Troubadour Tim Buckley"

BUELL, BEBE—PHOTOGRAPHS
PH01959 694 (November 3, 1994) p67. "Rad Dad: Bebe Buell, Tyler And Liv (age 11) In 1988" (Hall, Charles)

BUERSTATTE, PHIL—PHOTOGRAPHS
PH01960 671 (December 9, 1993) p13. "Beavis And Butt-head Faves J., Philo, Rob And Sean (from left)" (Ragel, Jon)

BUFFALO TOM—PHOTOGRAPHS
PH01961 665 (September 16, 1993) pp[enc.45]. "Above From Left: Chris Colbourn, Friend Debra Monaco, Tom Maginnis And Bill Janovitz" (Newton, Philip)
PH01962 665 (September 16, 1993) pp[enc.5]. "[Buffalo Tom]" (Newton, Philip)
PH01963 665 (September 16, 1993) pp[enc.54]. "Buffalo Tom Performing On Tour At Sheehan's Cafe, In Northampton" (Newton, Philip)
PH01964 665 (September 16, 1993) pp[enc.48]. "Onstage At Sheehan's Cafe, Northampton, Mass." (Newton, Philip)
PH01965 672-673 (December 23, 1993) p65. "Tom Maginnis, Janovitz And Chris Colbourn" (Robicheau, Paul)

BUFFETT, JIMMY—ILLUSTRATIONS
PH01966 744 (October 3, 1996) p16. "J. Buffett Fan's Apt." (Pendergrast, James T.)

BUFFETT, JIMMY—PHOTOGRAPHS
PH01967 741 (August 22, 1996) p42. "[Jimmy Buffett]" (Haynsworth, John)
PH01968 743 (September 19, 1996) p36. "It's About Showtunes! Buffett Goes Broadway" (Cardenas, Jeffrey)
PH01969 750-751 (December 26, 1996) p90. "Buffett" (Braley, Colin)

BUFFETT, JIMMY—PHOTOGRAPHS—PORTRAITS
PH01970 642 (October 29, 1992) p21. "Jimmy Buffett"
PH01971 736 (June 13, 1996) pp[cover]. "Rock & Roll Summer!" (Davey, Randy)

BUFFY THE VAMPIRE SLAYER (FILM)—PHOTOGRAPHS
PH01972 638 (September 3, 1992) p75. "Luke Perry And Kristy Swanson Fight The Bloodsuckers"
BUGSY (FILM)—PHOTOGRAPHS
PH01973 621 (January 9, 1992) p56. "Warren Beatty And Annette Bening In Love"
BUICK MACKANE—PHOTOGRAPHS
PH01974 707 (May 4, 1995) p29. "Escovedo With Buick MacKane" (Wolfson, Todd V.)
BUKEM, L. T. J.—ALBUMS
PH01975 744 (October 3, 1996) p74. "Logical Progression"
BULLETPROOF (FILM)—PHOTOGRAPHS
PH01976 743 (September 19, 1996) p88. "Dickheads"
PH01977 744 (October 3, 1996) p78. "Now Playing"
BULLETS OVER BROADWAY (FILM)—PHOTOGRAPHS
PH01978 694 (November 3, 1994) p104. "Palminteri Runs With No-Talent Boss Tilly"
PH01979 694 (November 3, 1994) p104. "Wiest Puts The Make On Cusack In Central Park"
PH01980 700 (January 26, 1995) p68. "Best Supporting Actress"
BULLOCK, SANDRA—PHOTOGRAPHS
PH01981 685 (June 30, 1994) p80. "Swat Dude Keanu Reeves Puts Sandra Bullock In The Driver's Seat"
PH01982 694 (November 3, 1994) p18. "[Eric Stoltz, Sandra Bullock, Samantha Mathis]"
PH01983 698-699 (December 29, 1994) p194. "Reeves And Bullock Ride In "Speed""
PH01984 705 (April 6, 1995) p69. "Oscar Rejects"
PH01985 708 (May 18, 1995) p97. "Sandra Bullock Wears Down Bill Pullman's Resistance"
PH01986 715 (August 24, 1995) p108. "Dangerous Women: Michelle Pfeiffer, Sandra Bullock, Julia Roberts, Cindy Crawford And Natasha Henstridge"
PH01987 727 (February 8, 1996) p46. "Denis Leary And Sandra Bullock Mug And Kiss As Lovers On The Run In The First And Maybe Worst Comedy Of 1996"
BULLOCK, SANDRA—PHOTOGRAPHS—PORTRAITS
PH01988 736 (June 13, 1996) pp[cover]. "Rock & Roll Summer!" (Garner, Kate)
BUNSKOEKE, HERMAN—PHOTOGRAPHS
PH01989 653 (April 1, 1993) p22. "Peter Visser, Herman Bunskoeke, Carol Van Dijk And Berend Dubbe (from left)" (Doove, Hester)
BURBRIDGE, OTEIL—PHOTOGRAPHS
PH01990 631 (May 28, 1992) p16. "The Rescue Unit (from left): Matt Mundy, Oteil Burbridge, Col. Bruce Hampton, Jimmy Herring And Apt. Q258" (Frazier, Jeff)
BURDON, ERIC—PHOTOGRAPHS
PH01991 676 (February 24, 1994) p48. "The Angry Young Animals (from left): Drummer John Steel, Organist Alan Price, bass Player Chas Chandler, Lead Singer Eric Burdon And Guitarist Hilton Valentine"
PH01992 719 (October 19, 1995) p40. "Eric Burdon And Jon Bon Jovi Hang Before The Show" (Corbijn, Anton)
BURKE, SUMMER—PHOTOGRAPHS
PH01993 652 (March 18, 1993) pp[enc.14]. "Rep Summer Burke Says, 'I'd Love To Be Able To Let Artists Know That Record Companies Aren't All Terribly Evil.'" (Barry, David)
BURNETT, ROB—PHOTOGRAPHS
PH01994 735 (May 30, 1996) p30. "Letterman With New Executive Producer Rob Burnett, Who Survived 'Uma, Oprah'"
BURNETT, T-BONE—ALBUMS
PH01995 638 (September 3, 1992) p67. "The Criminal Under My Own Hat"
BURNETT, T-BONE—PHOTOGRAPHS
PH01996 639 (September 17, 1992) p20. "T Bone Burnett"
BURNING SPEAR—ALBUMS
PH01997 676 (February 24, 1994) p42. "Marcus Garvey"
BURNING SPEAR—PHOTOGRAPHS
PH01998 676 (February 24, 1994) p42. "Burning Spear, The Voice Of Righteousness (below)"
BURNS, BOB—PHOTOGRAPHS
PH01999 727 (February 8, 1996) p12. "Skynyrd's Bob Burns, Leon Wilkeson, Artimus Pyle (from left)" (Diamond, Rick)
BURNS, ED—PHOTOGRAPHS
PH02000 715 (August 24, 1995) p80. "Hot Movie Director" (Cuffaro, Chris)
PH02001 715 (August 24, 1995) p110. "Mulcahy, Burns, Bahns And McGlone (from left)"
PH02002 741 (August 22, 1996) p105. "Burns, Bahns, Diaz, Aniston, McGlone"
BURNS, JOEY—PHOTOGRAPHS
PH02003 662 (August 5, 1993) p28. "Sandman Joey Burns (left) And Howe Gelb" (Gershoff, Gary)
BURNS, STEF—PHOTOGRAPHS
PH02004 616 (October 31, 1991) p11. "Greg Smith, Pete Freezin', Alice Cooper And Stef Burns (from left)" (Mazur, Kevin)
BURNSIDE, R. L.—ALBUMS
PH02005 690 (September 8, 1994) p80. "Too Bad Jim"
PH02006 741 (August 22, 1996) p100. "A Ass Pocket Of Whiskey"
BURR, J. M.—PHOTOGRAPHS
PH02007 722 (November 30, 1995) p42. "Utter Confusion Caused Exactly That: Albert Min, Len Longo And J. M. Burr" (Dipeso, Debra)
BURRIS, DAVID—PHOTOGRAPHS
PH02008 683 (June 2, 1994) p24. "Twin Tones: Daniel Chavis, Burris, Danny Chavis And Levi (from left)" (Cardillicchio, Nick)
BURRIS, JAMIE—PHOTOGRAPHS
PH02009 748 (November 28, 1996) p52. "Mueller, Voted Most Talented At San Dieguito High In 1982, And Jamie Burris"
BURROUGHS, WILLIAM—ALBUMS
PH02010 670 (November 25, 1993) p116. "Spare Ass Annie And Other Tales"
BURROUGHS, WILLIAM—PHOTOGRAPHS
PH02011 675 (February 10, 1994) p23. "'Black Rider' Creators Wilson, Burroughs And Waits (from left)" (Brinkhoff, Ralf)
BURROUGHS, WILLIAM—PHOTOGRAPHS—PORTRAITS
PH02012 735 (May 30, 1996) p18. "Junkie Icon William Burroughs" (Natkin, Paul)
BURSTYN, ELLEN—PHOTOGRAPHS
PH02013 742 (September 5, 1996) p68. "Elliott, Burstyn And Harden"
BURTON, BOB—PHOTOGRAPHS
PH02014 741 (August 22, 1996) p64. "Professor Bounty Hunter Bob Burton" (Maxwell, Robert)
BURTON, DON—PHOTOGRAPHS
PH02015 690 (September 8, 1994) p24. "The Newlyweds Greet Fans Outside The Abbey" (Boland, Laurence)
PH02016 704 (March 23, 1995) p60. "O'Riordan And Don Burton On Their Wedding Day, July 1994"
BURTON, TIM—PHOTOGRAPHS
PH02017 634-635 (July 9, 1992) p40. "Burton Identifies With The Dark Knight Of 'Batman Returns' (Michael Keaton)" (Rosenthal, Zade)
PH02018 634-635 (July 9, 1992) pp38-39. "[Tim Burton]" (Watson, Albert)
BUSCANI, LISA—PHOTOGRAPHS—PORTRAITS
PH02019 662 (August 5, 1993) p20. "[Lisa Buscani]" (Alicino, Christine)
BUSCEMI, STEVE—PHOTOGRAPHS
PH02020 680 (April 21, 1994) p34. "Airheads Buscemi, Sandler And Fraser" (Wallace, Merie W.)
PH02021 689 (August 25, 1994) p97. "Rock Wanna-Be's: Sandler, Fraser, Buscemi"
PH02022 730 (March 21, 1996) p104. "Steve Buscemi Takes A Hit"
PH02023 747 (November 14, 1996) p26. "Buscemi (left) With Canadian Punk-Rock Folk Singer Hayden" (Clinch, Danny)

BUSEY, GARY—PHOTOGRAPHS
PH02024 662 (August 5, 1993) p73. "Busey, Hunter And Cruise In Jeopardy"
BUSH—ALBUMS
PH02025 732 (April 18, 1996) p84. "Sixteen Stone"
PH02026 749 (December 12, 1996) p84. "Razorblade Suitcase"
BUSH—ILLUSTRATIONS
PH02027 717 (September 21, 1995) p16. "Bush" (Pendergrast, James T.)
PH02028 735 (May 30, 1996) p10. "Seattle" (Pendergrast, James T.)
BUSH—PHOTOGRAPHS
PH02029 710 (June 15, 1995) p49. "Dave Parsons, Rossdale, Robin Goodridge, Pulsford (from left)" (Westenberg, Kevin)
PH02030 712-713 (July 13, 1995) p30. "Pulsford (left) And Rossdale In New York In March" (Olson, Sheryl)
PH02031 712-713 (July 13, 1995) p29. "Zen Careerists: Pulsford, Parsons, Rossdale, And Goodridge (from left)" (Mahurin, Matt)
BUSH—PHOTOGRAPHS—PORTRAITS
PH02032 732 (April 18, 1996) p41. "Robin Goodridge, Gavin Rossdale, Dave Parsons And Nigel Pulsford" (Seliger, Mark)
BUSH, GEORGE—ILLUSTRATIONS
PH02033 621 (January 9, 1992) p7. "George Bush Makes A Decision" (Pendergrast, James T.)
PH02034 623 (February 6, 1992) p6. "George's Solution For Domestic Problems" (Pendergrast, James T.)
PH02035 624 (February 20, 1992) p7. "George B. Packs For Japan" (Pendergrast, James T.)
PH02036 625 (March 5, 1992) p4. "George B. In Free Fall" (Pendergrast, James T.)
PH02037 627 (April 2, 1992) p8. "G.H.W. Bush Sees His 1st Bar Code" (Pendergrast, James T.)
PH02038 629 (April 30, 1992) p9. "George B's Economic Plan" (Pendergrast, James T.)
PH02039 630 (May 14, 1992) p8. "Air Force One" (Pendergrast, James T.)
PH02040 633 (June 25, 1992) p5. "President Bush Tours U.S. Cities" (Pendergrast, James T.)
PH02041 638 (September 3, 1992) p3. "The Bush Years: The Environmental President" (Coe, Sue)
PH02042 638 (September 3, 1992) p6. "Old Math" (Pendergrast, James T.)
PH02043 639 (September 17, 1992) p10. "G.H.W. Bush Thinks About The Common Man" (Pendergrast, James T.)
PH02044 640 (October 1, 1992) p3. "The Bush Years: Staying The Course" (Coe, Sue)
PH02045 640 (October 1, 1992) p38. "[George Bush]" (Cronin, Brian)
PH02046 692 (October 6, 1994) p40. "[George Bush]" (Friedman, Drew)
BUSH, GEORGE—PHOTOGRAPHS
PH02047 642 (October 29, 1992) p78. "Bush And Clinton Fuss Before Air Time"
BUSH, GEORGE, JR.—PHOTOGRAPHS
PH02048 698-699 (December 29, 1994) p66. "Bush Does His Bit For Population Control"
BUSH, JOHN—PHOTOGRAPHS
PH02049 656 (May 13, 1993) p31. "Noisemakers Ian, Dan Spitz, Bush, Frankie Bello And Benante (from left)" (Mazur, Kevin)
PH02050 722 (November 30, 1995) p34. "Totally Ruled By Instinct: Band Members Charlie Benante, Scott Ian, John Bush And Frank Bello (from left)" (Cultice, Joseph)
BUSH, KATE—ALBUMS
PH02051 670 (November 25, 1993) p120. "The Red Shoes"
BUSH, KATE—ILLUSTRATIONS
PH02052 676 (February 24, 1994) p7. "Kate Bush" (Burke, Philip)
PH02053 679 (April 7, 1994) p10. "[Slice Of heaven]" (Pendergrast, James T.)
BUSH, KATE—PHOTOGRAPHS
PH02054 676 (February 24, 1994) p14. "The Sensual Woman: Bush In Europe In '79" (Rex)
BUSH, KATE—PHOTOGRAPHS—PORTRAITS
PH02055 676 (February 24, 1994) p13. "[Kate Bush]" (Snowden, Lord)
PH02056 692 (October 6, 1994) p53. "Kate Bush"
BUSHNELL, GEORGE, JR.—PHOTOGRAPHS—PORTRAITS
PH02057 688 (August 11, 1994) p44. "Bushnell: The Lessons of History"
BUSHWICK BILL—PHOTOGRAPHS
PH02058 619-620 (December 12, 1991) p76. "Bushwick Bill Outta Sight" (Vallbona, Nuri)
BUSTA RHYMES—ALBUMS
PH02059 733 (May 2, 1996) p54. "The Coming"
BUSTA RHYMES—ILLUSTRATIONS
PH02060 734 (May 16, 1996) p80. "Busta Rhymes: Kingdom's Coming" (Hungry Dog Studio)
PH02061 736 (June 13, 1996) p40. "Busta Rhymes" (Cowles, David)
BUSTA RHYMES—PHOTOGRAPHS
PH02062 742 (September 5, 1996) p21. "Busta Rhymes: Smokin'—And Not Just Onstage" (Blakesberg, Jay)
BUSTA RHYMES—PHOTOGRAPHS—PORTRAITS
PH02063 750-751 (December 26, 1996) p68. "Busta Rhymes" (Paniccioli, Ernie)
BUSWEILER, DON—PHOTOGRAPHS—PORTRAITS
PH02064 691 (September 22, 1994) p22. "[Don Busweiler]" (Tytler, Scott)
BUTCHER, BILINDA—PHOTOGRAPHS
PH02065 627 (April 2, 1992) p23. "Bilinda Butcher Of My Bloody Valentine" (Pool, Smiley)
BUTCHER, BILINDA—PHOTOGRAPHS—PORTRAITS
PH02066 623 (February 6, 1992) p20. "Clockwise From Top Left: Butcher, Shields, Googe, O'Ciosoig" (Double, Steve)
THE BUTCHER'S WIFE (FILM)—PHOTOGRAPHS
PH02067 617 (November 14, 1991) p182. "Jeff Daniels Seeks The Truth From Clairvoyant Demi Moore"
BUTLER, BERNARD—PHOTOGRAPHS
PH02068 657 (May 27, 1993) p15. "Ultra Suede: Gilbert, Anderson, Osman, Butler (from left)" (Broad, Julian)
BUTLER, ISHMAEL—PHOTOGRAPHS
PH02069 652 (March 18, 1993) p23. "Doodlebug, Ladybug, Butterfly (from left)" (Guzman)
BUTLER, JERRY—PHOTOGRAPHS—PORTRAITS
PH02070 668 (October 28, 1993) p65. "The Impressions: Butler (top left) And Mayfield (bottom right)"
BUTTER—ALBUMS
PH02071 747 (November 14, 1996) p116. "Butter"
BUTTERFIELD, PAUL—ALBUMS
PH02072 710 (June 15, 1995) p81. "Strawberry Jam"
PH02073 748 (November 28, 1996) p136. "East-West Live"
BUTTHOLE SURFERS—ALBUMS
PH02074 658 (June 10, 1993) p70. "Independent Worm Saloon"
BUTTHOLE SURFERS—PHOTOGRAPHS
PH02075 659 (June 24, 1993) p25. "Gibby Haynes, Jeff Pinkus, Paul Leary And King Coffey (clockwise from top)" (Watermann, Greg)
PH02076 665 (September 16, 1993) p26. "Surfers Paul Leary (left) And Gibby Haynes" (Mazur, Kevin)
PH02077 710 (June 15, 1995) p54. "Surf Thing: Coffey, Haynes, Leary (from left)" (Van Overbeek, Will)
PH02078 738-739 (July 11, 1996) p28. "Surfers' King Coffey, Gibby Haynes, Paul Leary (from left)" (Van Overbeek, Will)
PH02079 750-751 (December 26, 1996) p116. "Buttholes For Breakfast" (Vadukul, Nitin)
PH02080 750-751 (December 26, 1996) p117. "Gibby Haynes, Paul Leary, Kyle Ellison, Owen McMahon And King Coffey (clockwise from left)" (Vadukul, Nitin)

PH02081 750-751 (December 26, 1996) p116. "Leary, Coffey, And A Driver (from left) On The Road" (Vadukul, Nitin)
BUZZCOCKS—PHOTOGRAPHS
PH02082 675 (February 10, 1994) p16. "Chemistry Club: Buzzcocks' Diggle, Barber, Shelley And Barker (from left)"
BYE, BYE, LOVE (FILM)—PHOTOGRAPHS
PH02083 705 (April 6, 1995) p70. "Bye, Bye, Love"
BYRD, ALEXANDER—PHOTOGRAPHS
PH02084 625 (March 5, 1992) p11. "Neville, Longhair's Son Alexander Byrd" (Mazur, Kevin)
BYRD, BOBBY—ALBUMS
PH02085 718 (October 5, 1995) p70. "Bobby Byrd Got Soul"
BYRD, DONALD—PHOTOGRAPHS
PH02086 715 (August 24, 1995) p23. "Guru, Patra And Byrd At The 'Jazzmatazz II' Release Party" (Capak, R. J.)
BYRDS—PHOTOGRAPHS
PH02087 619-620 (December 12, 1991) p18. "The Byrds" (Mazur, Kevin)
PH02088 619-620 (December 12, 1991) p18. "The Rock And Roll Hall Of Fame Jam" (Bellissimo, J.)
BYRNE, DAVID—ALBUMS
PH02089 626 (March 19, 1992) p89. "Uh-Oh"
PH02090 686-687 (July 14, 1994) p110. "David Byrne"
BYRNE, DAVID—PHOTOGRAPHS
PH02091 618 (November 28, 1991) p11. "Byrne (left) And Browne" (Mazur, Kevin)
PH02092 630 (May 14, 1992) p13. "David Byrne, Richard Thompson And John Cale (from left) After The Saint Ann Show" (Vartoogian, Jack)
PH02093 653 (April 1, 1993) p24. "Talking Head: David Byrne At The Bottom Line" (Capak, R. J.)
PH02094 688 (August 11, 1994) p37. "[David Byrne]" (Seliger, Mark)
PH02095 706 (April 20, 1995) p17. "Tibet House Supporters Byrne (left) And Gilmore" (Capak, R. J.)
PH02096 719 (October 19, 1995) p15. "Talk About It: Doughty (left) And David Byrne Get Funky" (Capak, R. J.)
PH02097 728 (February 22, 1996) p19. "Bowie's Eloquent Disciples Byrne And Madonna" (Mazur, Kevin)
PH02098 733 (May 2, 1996) p13. "David Byrne Visits Rankine's After-Show Party"
BYRNE, DAVID—PHOTOGRAPHS—PORTRAITS
PH02099 629 (April 30, 1992) p18. "David Byrne: 'It Does Seem Odd That More People [in rock] Haven't Gotten Sick'" (Wexler, Lane)
PH02100 643 (November 12, 1992) pp98-99. "David Byrne" (Rolston, Matthew)
PH02101 643 (November 12, 1992) p234. "Hommage To Hollywood: Hurrell's David Byrne..." (Hurrell, George)

C

C+C MUSIC FACTORY—PHOTOGRAPHS
PH02102 619-620 (December 12, 1991) p44. "You Can Dance If You Wanna: The Hit-making C+C Music Factory (above)..." (Lavine, Michael)
PH02103 626 (March 19, 1992) p11. "Freedom Williams, David Cole, Robert Clivilles, Zelma Davis (from left)" (Mazur, Kevin)
C., TIMMY—PHOTOGRAPHS
PH02104 664 (September 2, 1993) p31. "Rage's Timmy C., Zack De La Rocha, Brad Wilk And Tom Morello (from left)" (Johnson, William)
CAAN, JAMES—PHOTOGRAPHS
PH02105 639 (September 17, 1992) p103. "Cage (left) And Caan Vie For Parker"
THE CABLE GUY (FILM)—PHOTOGRAPHS
PH02106 736 (June 13, 1996) p61. "Funny Guys"
PH02107 738-739 (July 11, 1996) p96. "Carrey's Cable Guy Goes From The Life Of The Party (left) To Deranged Creep"
CAESAR, SUAVE SONNY—PHOTOGRAPHS—PORTRAITS
PH02108 659 (June 24, 1993) p21. "Fredro Starr, Suave Sonny Caesar, Sticky Fingaz And Big D.S. (from left)" (Spector, Gary)
CAFFEY, CHARLOTTE—PHOTOGRAPHS
PH02109 616 (October 31, 1991) p11. "Cervenka, Gina Schock, Jane Wiedlin, Kathy Valentine, Charlotte Caffey (clockwise from top left)" (Granitz, Steve)
CAGE, JOHN—PHOTOGRAPHS—PORTRAITS
PH02110 640 (October 1, 1992) p21. "[John Cage]" (Sanders, Timothy Greenfield)
PH02111 645-646 (December 10, 1992) p101. "Musical Innovator John Cage" (Gunther, Steve A.)
CAGE, NICOLAS—ILLUSTRATIONS
PH02112 737 (June 27, 1996) p61. "Bad Boy Son Alcatraz" (Brodner, Steve)
PH02113 750-751 (December 26, 1996) p54. "[Nicolas Cage]" (Burke, Philip)
CAGE, NICOLAS—PHOTOGRAPHS
PH02114 639 (September 17, 1992) p103. "Cage (left) And Caan Vie For Parker"
PH02115 688 (August 11, 1994) p62. "It's A Jackpot-Lottery Win For Fonda, Cage And Perez"
PH02116 707 (May 4, 1995) p74. "Caruso And Cage In 'Kiss Of Death'"
PH02117 720 (November 2, 1995) p76. "He (Nicolas Cage) Is An Alcoholic"
PH02118 720 (November 2, 1995) p76. "Together: cage And Shue Are Lovers Battling The Odds"
PH02119 721 (November 16, 1995) p94. "And The Drunk (with Elizabeth Shue) In 'Leaving Las Vegas'" (Hanover, Suzanne)
PH02120 721 (November 16, 1995) p94. "The Baker In 'Moonstruck'"
PH02121 721 (November 16, 1995) p96. "Cage, With Patricia Arquette, Calls Their Surprise Marriage 'Off-The-Wall'" (P.A.G.)
PH02122 721 (November 16, 1995) p94. "The Elvis Wanna-Be (with William Dafoe) In 'Wild At Heart'"
PH02122a 737 (June 27, 1996) p62. "Sean Connery Watches Nicolas Cage Defuse A Poison-Gas Bomb On Alcatraz"
CAGE, NICOLAS—PHOTOGRAPHS—PORTRAITS
PH02123 721 (November 16, 1995) p93. "[Nicolas Cage]" (Winters, Dan)
CAGED HEAT (FILM)—PHOTOGRAPHS
PH02124 678 (March 24, 1994) p65. "Working In Roger Corman's B-Movie Factory, Demme Made his Directing Debut In 1974 With 'Caged Heat' And Found Humor And Humanity Even In Schlock"
CAHILL, TIM—PHOTOGRAPHS
PH02125 632 (June 11, 1992) p62. "Staff Members And Contributing Writers At The 1971 Editorial Conference, At Esalen, In Big Sur" (Leibovitz, Annie)
CAIFANES—ALBUMS
PH02126 696 (December 1, 1994) p122. "El Nervio Del Volcan"
CAIFANES—PHOTOGRAPHS
PH02127 662 (August 5, 1993) p17. "Andre, Saul Hernandez, Alejando Marcovech" (Mazur, Kevin)
CAIN, NANCY—PHOTOGRAPHS
PH02128 672-673 (December 23, 1993) p88. "Binder (left) And Cain" (Sibert, Jody)
CAIN, SIM—PHOTOGRAPHS
PH02129 686-687 (July 14, 1994) p45. "[Rollins Band]" (Halfin, Ross)
CAIRNS, ANDY—PHOTOGRAPHS—PORTRAITS
PH02130 654 (April 15, 1993) p21. "In Need Of Therapy?: Fyfe Ewing, Michael McKeegan And Andy Cairns (from left)" (Gullick, Steve)
CAKE LIKE—ALBUMS
PH02131 702 (February 23, 1995) p76. "Delicious"
CAKE LIKE—PHOTOGRAPHS
PH02132 703 (March 9, 1995) p29. "Easy As Pie: Jody Seifert,

Nina Hellman And Kerri Kenney (from left)" (Falls, John)
CAKE—PHOTOGRAPHS
PH02133 749 (December 12, 1996) p96. "Rising" (Chavez, Marina)
CALANDRA, JOE—PHOTOGRAPHS
PH02134 710 (June 15, 1995) p54. "Boys In The Attic (clockwise from upper left): Ed Mundell, Jon Kleiman, Wyndorf And Joe Calandra" (Toliver, Chris)
CALANDRA, JOE—PHOTOGRAPHS—PORTRAITS
PH02135 716 (September 7, 1995) p34. "Dopes To Infinity: Wyndorf, Mundell, Kleiman And Calandra (from left)" (Lavine, Michael)
CALDERONE, PAUL—PHOTOGRAPHS
PH02136 669 (November 11, 1993) p49. "Little Leaguer Peter Calderone (second from left, bottom row) In 1959..."
CALDERONE, PETER—PHOTOGRAPHS
PH02136 669 (November 11, 1993) p49. "Little Leaguer Peter Calderone (second from left, bottom row) In 1959..."
PH02137 669 (November 11, 1993) p50. "Seven-Year-Old Calderone At His Parents' Home In 1957, On His Way To First Holy Communion At St. Mary's..."
PH02138 669 (November 11, 1993) p50. "A Survivor: Calderone, Who Was A Familiar Face At The North Attleboro, Mass., Post Office, Said, 'Take It Or Leave It,' As He Delivered The Group's Final Nonnegotiable Demand..."
CALDWELL, TOY—PHOTOGRAPHS—PORTRAITS
PH02139 654 (April 15, 1993) p20. "[Toy Caldwell]" (Abbott, Waring)
CALE, JOHN—ALBUMS
PH02140 700 (January 26, 1995) p61. "Last Day On Earth"
CALE, JOHN—PHOTOGRAPHS
PH02141 630 (May 14, 1992) p13. "David Byrne, Richard Thompson And John Cale (from left) After The Saint Ann Show" (Vartoogian, Jack)
PH02142 648 (January 21, 1993) p11. "Lou Reed, John Cale And Sterling Morrison (from left) At NYU" (Andersen, Nancy)
PH02143 662 (August 5, 1993) p28. "John Cale (left) And Lou Reed Doing The Velvet Underground" (Paton, Tim)
PH02144 678 (March 24, 1994) p27. "Bob Neuwirth (left) And John Cale" (Mark, Mary Ellen)
PH02145 692 (October 6, 1994) p16. "{Siouxsie Sioux And John Cale]" (Berg, Bob)
PH02146 718 (October 5, 1995) p46. "The Velvet Underground (clockwise from bottom left): Nico, Reed, Morrison, Cale And Tucker"
PH02147 728 (February 22, 1996) p18. "Martha Morrison, Tucker, Cale And Reed (from left) Celebrate The Velvets' Induction" (Mazur, Kevin)
CALE, JOHN—PHOTOGRAPHS—PORTRAITS
PH02148 659 (June 24, 1993) p17. "Tucker, Morrison, Cale And Reed Today (from left)" (Wood, Graham)
PH02149 745 (October 17, 1996) p48. "[John Cale]" (Irish, Len)
CALHOUN, ATEN JULIUS BUSHAW—PHOTOGRAPHS—PORTRAITS
PH02150 666 (September 30, 1993) p28. "[Elizabeth Ann Wiles & Aten Julius Bushaw Calhoun]"
CALHOUN, WILL—PHOTOGRAPHS
PH02151 623 (February 6, 1992) p13. "Vernon Reid, Will Calhoun And Melvin Gibbs (from left)" (Mazur, Kevin)
PH02152 648 (January 21, 1993) p18. "Corey Glover, Will Calhoun, Vernon Reid And Doug Wimbish (from left)" (Leialoha, Mark)
CALHOUN, WILL—PHOTOGRAPHS—PORTRAITS
PH02153 660-661 (July 8, 1993) p88. "The Band (from left): Will Calhoun, Vernon Reid, Doug Wimbish And Corey Glover" (Malfer)
CALIFORNIA—ILLUSTRATIONS
PH02154 664 (September 2, 1993) p59. "...And Menace For All" (Bustamante, Gerald)
CALIFORNIA INSTITUTE OF TECHNOLOGY—PHOTOGRAPHS
PH02155 626 (March 19, 1992) p70. "A Crooked Deck: The University Of Washington Flips The Cards For Caltech At The 1961 Rose Bowl"
CALIO, JOIE—PHOTOGRAPHS
PH02156 647 (January 7, 1993) p19. "Michael Gurley, Joie Calio And Phil Leavitt (from left)" (Mauro, Aldo)
PH02157 660-661 (July 8, 1993) p101. "Dada (from left): Michael Gurley, Phil Leavitt And Joie Calio" (Lass, Imke)
CALLAHAN, KEN—PHOTOGRAPHS
PH02158 644 (November 26, 1992) p27. "Louris, Callahan, Olson And Perlman (from left)" (Capak, R. J.)
CALLAHAN, KEN—PHOTOGRAPHS—PORTRAITS
PH02159 628 (April 16, 1992) p57. "Perlman, Olson, Louris And Callahan (from left)" (Crouser, Michael)
CAMBERLIN, JIMMY—PHOTOGRAPHS
PH02160 680 (April 21, 1994) pp42-43. "All Pumped Up: Jimmy Chamberlin, James Iha, Billy Corgan And D'Arcy (from left)" (Luchford, Glen)
CAMBODIA—PHOTOGRAPHS
PH02161 619-620 (December 12, 1991) p146. "In 1990 A Cambodian Child Recovers In A Hospital After Losing A Leg To A Land Mine Placed By The Khmer Rouge" (Salgado, Sebastiao)
CAMERAS—PHOTOGRAPHS
PH02162 623 (February 6, 1992) p92. "[Cameras]" (Grant, Bob)
PH02163 634-635 (July 9, 1992) pp122-123. "[Toys]" (Goldin, David)
PH02164 649 (February 4, 1993) p79. "Beach Equipment: Minolta Weathermatic Dual 35 And Pentax IQZoom 90-WR" (Llewellyn, Michael)
PH02165 660-661 (July 8, 1993) p123. "Olympus Infinity Stylus Zoom Autoflash 35-mm Camera, $325" (Miller, Greg)
PH02166 670 (November 25, 1993) p129. "Pentax IQZoom 28W Camera" (Miller, Greg)
PH02167 676 (February 24, 1994) p65. "Cannon Sure Shot Z115 ($500)" (Miller, Greg)
PH02168 676 (February 24, 1994) p65. "Contax TVS Compact With Carl Zeiss Zoom ($1,695)" (Miller, Greg)
PH02169 676 (February 24, 1994) p65. "Minolta Maxxum 700SI ($1,026, Body Only)" (Miller, Greg)
PH02170 676 (February 24, 1994) p65. "Nikon 35TI Compact Camera ($1,120)" (Miller, Greg)
PH02171 686-687 (July 14, 1994) pp46-47. "[Toys]" (Grant, Bob)
PH02172 697 (December 15, 1994) p107. "[Technology]" (Grant, Bob)
PH02173 702 (February 23, 1995) p83. "[Cameras]" (Grant, Bob)
PH02174 712-713 (July 13, 1995) p121. "[Technology]" (Grant, Bob)
PH02175 715 (August 24, 1995) p115. "[Video]" (Grant, Bob)
PH02176 729 (March 7, 1996) p59. "[Digital Cameras]" (Grant, Bob)
CAMERON, JAMES—PHOTOGRAPHS
PH02177 688 (August 11, 1994) p58. "On The Miami Set, James Cameron Does Some "Image Capturing" For "True Lies"" (Rosenthal, Zade)
CAMERON, MATT—PHOTOGRAPHS
PH02178 621 (January 9, 1992) p11. "Ben Shepherd, Kim Thayil, Chris Cornell And Matt Cameron (from left)"
PH02179 667 (October 14, 1993) p40. "John Waterman, Brian Wood, John McBain, Ben Shepherd And Matt Cameron" (Hapke, Fran)
PH02180 674 (January 27, 1994) p17. "Cameron, Shepherd, Cornell, Thayil (from left)" (Westenberg, Kevin)
PH02181 684 (June 16, 1994) p52. "Cameron, Thayil, Yamamoto, Cornell, Silver, Tour Manager Eric Johnson (from left) In 1988" (Peterson, Charles)
PH02182 684 (June 16, 1994) p49. "Sit 'N' Spin: Cameron,

Shepherd, Thayil And Cornell (from left) In Seattle" (Seliger, Mark)

PH02183 695 (November 17, 1994) p131. "Soundgarden" (Seliger, Mark)

PH02184 698-699 (December 29, 1994) p106. "From Sub Pop To Superstardom: Kim Thayil, Cornell, Ben Shepherd And Matt Cameron (from left)" (Seliger, Mark)

PH02185 727 (February 8, 1996) p26. "Soundgarden's Chris Cornell, Kim Thayil, Ben Shepherd And Matt Cameron (from left) In Seattle's Studio Litho" (Westenberg, Kevin)

PH02186 737 (June 27, 1996) p56. "Soundgarden's Cornell, Ben Shepherd, Thayil And Matt Cameron (from left)"

CAMERON, MATT—PHOTOGRAPHS—PORTRAITS

PH02187 634-635 (July 9, 1992) p45. "[Soundgarden]" (Seliger, Mark)

CAMPANELLA, HEATHER—PHOTOGRAPHS

PH02188 728 (February 22, 1996) p51. "Heather Campanella, A Close Friend Of Jermaine's, At His Grave In Milwaukee" (Smale, Brian)

CAMPBELL, BRUCE—PHOTOGRAPHS

PH02189 666 (September 30, 1993) p116. "'Brisco County Jr.'"

CAMPBELL, JOHN—ALBUMS

PH02190 653 (April 1, 1993) p53. "Howlin Mercy"

CAMPBELL, JOHN—PHOTOGRAPHS

PH02191 662 (August 5, 1993) p27. "[John Campbell]" (Ockenfels, Frank W.)

CAMPBELL, JOHN—PHOTOGRAPHS—PORTRAITS

PH02192 622 (January 23, 1992) p14. "[John Campbell]" (White, Brian Ashley)

PH02193 672-673 (December 23, 1993) p80. "Above: Blues Guitarist John Campbell" (Ockenfels, Frank W.)

CAMPBELL, LUTHER—PHOTOGRAPHS

PH02194 669 (November 11, 1993) p13. "The 2 Live Crew's Luther Campbell: Rappers Just Wanna Have Fun" (Keiser, Beth)

CAMPBELL, MIKE—PHOTOGRAPHS

PH02195 707 (May 4, 1995) p52. "Backstage With The Boss And The Band (below, from left): Steve Ferrone, Mike Campbell, Petty, Benmont Tench, Howie Epstein And Scott Thurston" (Seliger, Mark)

CAMPBELL, NAOMI—PHOTOGRAPHS

PH02196 630 (May 14, 1992) p15. "Michael Jackson Surrounded By MTV Winners And Other Charming Dinner Companions"

PH02197 715 (August 24, 1995) p87. "Hot Career Move" (Sands, Steve)

CAMPBELL, NELL—PHOTOGRAPHS

PH02198 617 (November 14, 1991) p11. "Nell Campbell And Sting" (Granitz, Steve)

CAMPBELL, STERLING—PHOTOGRAPHS

PH02199 711 (June 29, 1995) p31. "'I Want To Put Myself On A Pedestal And Hate Myself For Being There': Pirner, Murphy, Mueller, Campbell (from left)" (Mahurin, Matt)

CAMPBELL, TISHA—PHOTOGRAPHS

PH02200 680 (April 21, 1994) p77. "As Sheneneh, With His 'Martin' Girlfriend, Tisha Campbell"

CAMPBELL, VIVIAN—PHOTOGRAPHS

PH02201 667 (October 14, 1993) p26. "Rick Savage, Phil Collen, Vivian Campbell, Rick Allen And Joe Elliott" (Halfin, Ross)

CAMPION, JANE—PHOTOGRAPHS

PH02202 672-673 (December 23, 1993) p173. "Power Women Of The Year"

CANDLEBOX—ALBUMS

PH02203 720 (November 2, 1995) p70. "Lucy"

CANDLEBOX—PHOTOGRAPHS

PH02204 674 (January 27, 1994) p24. "Bardi Martin, Klett, Kevin Martin, Mercado (from left)" (Knight, Kevin)

PH02205 686-687 (July 14, 1994) p42. "Bardie Martin (left), Kevin Martin" (Mason, Karen)

PH02206 702 (February 23, 1995) p23. "Candlebox (from left): Peter Klett, Scott Mercado, Kevin Martin, Bardi Martin" (Ford, Charles)

CANDLEBOX—PHOTOGRAPHS—PORTRAITS

PH02207 749 (December 12, 1996) p22. "[Candlebox]" (Schafer, F. Scott)

CANDY, JOHN—PHOTOGRAPHS

PH02208 698-699 (December 29, 1994) p85. "John Candy" (Moss, Gary)

CANEDO, KEN—PHOTOGRAPHS—PORTRAITS

PH02209 642 (October 29, 1992) p61. "This Is Your Brain"

PH02210 642 (October 29, 1992) p61. "This Is Your Brain On God"

PH02211 642 (October 29, 1992) p61. "This Is Your Brain On Rock & Roll"

CANNES FILM FESTIVAL (1987)—PHOTOGRAPHS

PH02212 615 (October 17, 1991) p63. "Paparazzi At Cannes Film Festival, 1987" (Pigozzi, Jean)

CANNING, KURK—PHOTOGRAPHS

PH02213 698-699 (December 29, 1994) p42. "L7's Donita Sparks, Vedder, L7's Dee Plakas And Her Husband, Kurk Canning (from left)" (Mercer, Lance)

CANTRELL, JERRY—ILLUSTRATIONS

PH02214 695 (November 17, 1994) p129. "Alice In Chains" (Holley, Jason)

CANTRELL, JERRY—PHOTOGRAPHS

PH02215 624 (February 20, 1992) p12. "From Left: Layne Staley, Ann Wilson, Stone Gossard, Jerry Cantrell" (Mason, Karen)

PH02216 644 (November 26, 1992) p45. "[Alice In Chains]" (Winters, Dan)

PH02217 662 (August 5, 1993) p13. "Mike Inez, Layne Staley, Jerry Cantrell And Sean Kinney (clockwise from top left) Of Alice In Chains" (Blakesberg, Jay)

PH02218 676 (February 24, 1994) p18. "Chain Reaction: Sean Kinney, Jerry Cantrell, Layne Staley And Mike Inez (from left)" (Moskowitz, Karen)

PH02219 723 (December 14, 1995) p28. "Mike Inez, A Fan, Layne Staley, Cantrell (from left) And Ghoulish Pals" (Doughty, Curt)

PH02220 727 (February 8, 1996) p33. "Kinney, Cantrell, Staley And Inez (from left)" (Seliger, Mark)

PH02221 727 (February 8, 1996) p35. "Kinney, Cantrell, Staley And Mike Starr In 1990 (from left)"

PH02222 727 (February 8, 1996) p36. "Staley (left) And Cantrell Performing During LollaPalooza '93" (Eichner, Steve)

PH02223 735 (May 30, 1996) p27. "Stupid Pet Tricks"

CANTRELL, JERRY—PHOTOGRAPHS—PORTRAITS

PH02224 727 (February 8, 1996) p37. "Guitarist, Whirlyball Fan And Gross-Out King Cantrell" (Seliger, Mark)

CANTWELL, MARIA—PHOTOGRAPHS—PORTRAITS

PH02225 642 (October 29, 1992) p46. "[Maria Cantwell]"

CAPALDI, JIM—PHOTOGRAPHS

PH02226 680 (April 21, 1994) p34. "Capaldi Backs Winwood" (Corbijn, Anton)

CAPE FEAR (FILM)—ILLUSTRATIONS

PH02227 618 (November 28, 1991) p101. "Through A Lens Darkly" (Rosen, Jonathon)

CAPE FEAR (FILM)—PHOTOGRAPHS

PH02228 618 (November 28, 1991) p103. "Now Robert De Niro Terrorizes Jessica Lange"

PH02229 618 (November 28, 1991) p103. "Robert Mitchum Harassed Polly Bergen In 1962"

PH02230 742 (September 5, 1996) p68. "With Nolte In 'Cape Fear'"

CAPITALISM—ILLUSTRATIONS

PH02231 678 (March 24, 1994) p31. "How Capitalism Creates Democracy" (Rall, Ted)

CAPOTE, TRUMAN—PHOTOGRAPHS

PH02232 615 (October 17, 1991) p66. "Truman Capote And Francesco Scavullo, Studio 54, 1979" (Pigozzi, Jean)

CAPPS, STEVE—PHOTOGRAPHS

PH02233 731 (April 4, 1996) p55. "Steve Capps (third from

right) And The Mac Software Team Taking A Rare Break In '84" (Seeff, Norman)

CAPTAIN AND TENNILLE—PHOTOGRAPHS

PH02234 653 (April 1, 1993) p13. "Toni Tennille And Captain (background)" (Erbland, Peter)

CAPTAIN BEEFHEART—ALBUMS

PH02235 617 (November 14, 1991) p134. "Doc At The Radar Station" (Van Vliet, Don)

CAPTAIN BEEFHEART—PHOTOGRAPHS

PH02236 674 (January 27, 1994) p13. "Zappa With Captain Beefheart (left)" (Pulin, Chuck)

CARDIGANS—ALBUMS

PH02237 747 (November 14, 1996) p112. "First Band On The Moon"

CARDIGANS—PHOTOGRAPHS

PH02238 743 (September 19, 1996) p41. "Dressed For Success" (Bogren, Martin)

CAREY, MARIAH—ALBUMS

PH02239 617 (November 14, 1991) p170. "Emotions"

PH02240 668 (October 28, 1993) p76. "Music Box"

PH02241 674 (January 27, 1994) p64. "Music Box"

PH02242 675 (February 10, 1994) p60. "Music Box"

PH02243 676 (February 24, 1994) p72. "Music Box"

PH02244 677 (March 10, 1994) p72. "Music Box"

PH02245 679 (April 7, 1994) p88. "Music Box"

CAREY, MARIAH—PHOTOGRAPHS

PH02246 615 (October 17, 1991) p14. "Mariah Carey, David Cole" (Mazur, Kevin)

PH02247 619-620 (December 12, 1991) p22. "James Brown (above) Tastes Freedom, While Mariah Carey (below) Tastes Victory" (Mazur, Kevin)

PH02248 619-620 (December 12, 1991) p33. "Mariah Carey's 'Someday'"

PH02249 625 (March 5, 1992) p55. "Readers Wanna Sex Mariah Up" (Vaccaro, Nick)

PH02250 626 (March 19, 1992) p11. "Mariah Carey, James Brown" (Mazur, Kevin)

PH02251 645-646 (December 10, 1992) p30. "The Sex-Stifling Carey" (Mazur, Kevin)

PH02252 672-673 (December 23, 1993) p41. "Right: Carey And Mottola" (Somoza, Gerardo)

PH02253 721 (November 16, 1995) p33. "The Many Moods Of Mariah"

PH02254 721 (November 16, 1995) p33. "O.D.B. And Carey On The Set At Rye beach, N.Y." (Toy, Joann)

PH02255 726 (January 25, 1996) p26. "Mariah Carey And Sony Music Chief Tommy Mottola With Cyndi Lauper (from left)" (Capak, R. J.)

PH02256 728 (February 22, 1996) p19. "Knight (left) And Carey" (Mazur, Kevin)

CARLE, SCOTT—PHOTOGRAPHS—PORTRAITS

PH02257 634-635 (July 9, 1992) p20. "Dillon Fence (from left): Chris Goode, Kent Alphin, Greg Humphreys And Scott Carle" (Thompson, D. Kent)

CARLISLE, BELINDA—ALBUMS

PH02258 622 (January 23, 1992) p44. "Live Your Life Be Free"

CARLITO'S WAY (FILM)—ILLUSTRATIONS

PH02259 671 (December 9, 1993) p75. "Son Of Scarface" (Cober, Alan E.)

CARLITO'S WAY (FILM)—PHOTOGRAPHS

PH02260 671 (December 9, 1993) p76. "Deja Vu: Pacino's Carlito With Miller (left)"

PH02261 678 (March 24, 1994) p100. "Missing In Oscar Action"

CARLOS, BUN E.—PHOTOGRAPHS

PH02262 723 (December 14, 1995) p27. "The Chicago Eight: D'Arcy, Petersson, Carlos, Corgan, Nielsen, Iha, Chamberlin And Zander (from left)" (Elledge, Paul)

CARMICHAEL, NELSON—PHOTOGRAPHS

PH02263 624 (February 20, 1992) p36. "[Nelson Carmichael]" (Eccles, Andrew)

CARNEY, JOHN—PHOTOGRAPHS

PH02264 644 (November 26, 1992) p24. "Hansard, Noreen O'Donnell, Colm Mac Con Iomaire, Brennan, David Odlum And John Carney (from left)" (Marsden, Barry)

CARNS, MICHAEL P. C.—PHOTOGRAPHS

PH02265 704 (March 23, 1995) p49. "Hail To The Chief: Clinton Introduces His Pick To Lead The CIA, Retired Air Force Gen. Carns" (Mills, Doug)

CARONE, RICK—PHOTOGRAPHS

PH02266 684 (June 16, 1994) p66. "Rick Carone" (Borris, Dan)

CARPENTER, KAREN—ALBUMS

PH02267 746 (October 31, 1996) p68. "Karen Carpenter"

CARPENTER, KAREN—ILLUSTRATIONS

PH02268 693 (October 20, 1994) p142. "More Than Ever" (Ascencios, N.)

CARPENTER, KAREN—PHOTOGRAPHS—PORTRAITS

PH02269 690 (September 8, 1994) p33. "Swinging Siblings: Richard And Karen"

CARPENTER, KEN—PHOTOGRAPHS

PH02270 626 (March 19, 1992) p80. "[Ken Carpenter]" (Hanauer, Mark)

CARPENTER, MARY-CHAPIN—ALBUMS

PH02271 638 (September 3, 1992) p68. "Come On Come On"

CARPENTER, MARY-CHAPIN—PHOTOGRAPHS

PH02272 625 (March 5, 1992) p18. "Sara Lee, Crimmins, Graham Nash, Amy Ray, Emily Saliers, David Crosby, Etheridge, Carpenter (from left)" (Berg, Lisa)

PH02273 638 (September 3, 1992) p9. "Mary-Chapin Carpenter" (Campbell, William)

PH02274 662 (August 5, 1993) p33. "Chris Guest, Harry Shearer, Michael McKean, With Carpenter" (Cohen, Lester)

PH02275 684 (June 16, 1994) p36. "Indigo Girl Emily Saliers, Nanci Griffith, Browne, Carpenter, Indigo Girl Amy Ray" (Diamond, Rick)

PH02276 697 (December 15, 1994) p17. "All For A Good Cause: Carpenter Strums One For The Native Americans" (Young, Dale)

CARPENTER, RICHARD—PHOTOGRAPHS—PORTRAITS

PH02277 690 (September 8, 1994) p33. "Swinging Siblings: Richard And Karen"

CARPENTERS—PHOTOGRAPHS—PORTRAITS

PH02277 690 (September 8, 1994) p33. "Swinging Siblings: Richard And Karen"

CARRERE, TIA—PHOTOGRAPHS

PH02278 626 (March 19, 1992) p39. "Myers Parties On With Babe Tia Carrere And Carvey" (Schiffman, Bonnie)

PH02279 748 (November 28, 1996) p143. "Dead On Arrival"

CARREY, JIM—ILLUSTRATIONS

PH02280 689 (August 25, 1994) p95. "Ace Of Face" (Ryden, Mark)

PH02281 716 (September 7, 1995) p10. "Artistic Release" (Pendergrast, James T.)

PH02282 722 (November 30, 1995) p73. "Big Fish Little Fish" (Allen, Terry)

PH02283 738-739 (July 11, 1996) p95. "Freaks Of Comedy" (Brodner, Steve)

CARREY, JIM—PHOTOGRAPHS

PH02284 684 (June 16, 1994) p115. "Jim Carrey's Grin Equals A Box-Office Ace"

PH02285 689 (August 25, 1994) p96. "Jim Carrey Shows His Delicate Approach To Comedy As The Man Behind The Mask"

PH02286 691 (September 22, 1994) p106. "Rising Star"

PH02287 698-699 (December 29, 1994) p199. "Carrey And Daniels In "Dumb""

PH02288 698-699 (December 29, 1994) p61. "Unmasked: Carrey Licks The Box Office"

PH02289 705 (April 6, 1995) p69. "Oscar Rejects"

PH02290 712-713 (July 13, 1995) p74. "Carrey In Disguise Again As The Riddler"

PH02291 712-713 (July 13, 1995) pp68-72. "[Jim Carrey]" (Ritts, Herb)

PH02292 712-713 (July 13, 1995) pp[cover]. "Jim Carrey: Bare Facts And Shocking Revelations" (Ritts, Herb)
PH02293 712-713 (July 13, 1995) p73. "The Puckish Jim Carrey (right) Was Already A Bad-Boy Clown At Age 3, With brother John In Ontario In 1965"
PH02294 712-713 (July 13, 1995) p115. "Villians: Carrey's Riddler, Jones' Two-face With Sirens Barrymore And Mazar"
PH02295 712-713 (July 13, 1995) p74. "Who Is That Masked Man?"
PH02296 716 (September 7, 1995) p78. "Summer Wrap-Up]"
PH02297 735 (May 30, 1996) p27. "Stupid Pet Tricks"
PH02298 738-739 (July 11, 1996) p96. "Carrey's Cable Guy Goes From The Life Of The Party (left) To Deranged Creep"

CARREY, JIM—PHOTOGRAPHS—PORTRAITS
PH02299 722 (November 30, 1995) p74. "Is Jonathan Pryce's Lytton Strachey Wittier Than Jim Carrey's Ace? You Betcha"

CARREY, JOHN—PHOTOGRAPHS
PH02300 712-713 (July 13, 1995) p73. "The Puckish Jim Carrey (right) Was Already A Bad-Boy Clown At Age 3, With brother John In Ontario In 1965"

CARRIE (FILM)—PHOTOGRAPHS
PH02301 656 (May 13, 1993) p114. "Above, More King Characters Show Their Dark Side: Kathy Bates ('Misery'), Jack Nicholson ('The Shining'), Sissy Spacek ('Carrie')"

CARRINGTON (FILM)—PHOTOGRAPHS
PH02302 722 (November 30, 1995) p74. "Is Jonathan Pryce's Lytton Strachey Wittier Than Jim Carrey's Ace? You Betcha"
PH02303 731 (April 4, 1996) p66. "Pryce, 'Carrington'"

CARROLL, DIAHANN—PHOTOGRAPHS—PORTRAITS
PH02304 666 (September 30, 1993) p116. "Mommy Track: Diahann Carroll In 'Julia'"

CARROLL, DINA—PHOTOGRAPHS
PH02305 700 (January 26, 1995) p30. "Dina Carroll, Poised" (Croft, Richard)

CARROLL, ROSEMARY—PHOTOGRAPHS
PH02306 714 (August 10, 1995) p24. "Courtney Love; Goldberg's Wife, Rosemary Carroll; Goldberg; Kurt Cobain In '93" (Kravitz, Jeff)

CARROT TOP—PHOTOGRAPHS
PH02307 693 (October 20, 1994) p100. "The College Comedian Of The Year With His "Party Hat" (above) And Lip-Syncing To "Mellow Yellow" (above right)" (Diamond, Rick)

CARROT TOP—PHOTOGRAPHS—PORTRAITS
PH02308 693 (October 20, 1994) p97. "For Scott Thompson, AKA Carrot Top, Everything Can Be A Prop, Even His Hair" (Seliger, Mark)
PH02309 693 (October 20, 1994) pp98-99. "[Scott Thompson, AKA Carrot Top]" (Seliger, Mark)

CARS—ALBUMS
PH02310 617 (November 14, 1991) p102. "Candy-O" (Coro, Ron)
PH02311 617 (November 14, 1991) p102. "Candy-O" (Lee, Johnny)
PH02312 617 (November 14, 1991) p102. "Candy-O" (Vargas, Alberto)

CARS—PHOTOGRAPHS
PH02313 667 (October 14, 1993) p78. "The Cars' 'You Might Think': When Ric Ocasek Sang It, He Sang A Mouthful"

CARSON, JOHNNY—ILLUSTRATIONS
PH02314 631 (May 28, 1992) p63. "[Johnny Carson]" (Cowles, David)
PH02315 698-699 (December 29, 1994) p33. "[Johnny Carson & David Letterman]" (Blitt, Barry)

CARSON, LORI—ALBUMS
PH02316 708 (May 18, 1995) p90. "Where It Goes"

CARSON, LORI—PHOTOGRAPHS—PORTRAITS
PH02317 712-713 (July 13, 1995) p26. "[Lori Carson & Adam Duritz]" (Erikson, Wendy)

CARSTENS, ARLIE—PHOTOGRAPHS
PH02318 652 (March 18, 1993) pp[enc.40]. "Arlie Carstens" (Seliger, Mark)

CARTER, BILL—PHOTOGRAPHS
PH02319 709 (June 1, 1995) p16. "[P]" (Smith, Kelly)

CARTER, CARLENE—ALBUMS
PH02320 664 (September 2, 1993) p66. "Little Love Letters"

CARTER, CHRIS—ILLUSTRATIONS
PH02321 734 (May 16, 1996) p21. "The Truth, And The Tunes, Are Out There..." (Friedman, Drew)

CARTER, CHRIS—PHOTOGRAPHS
PH02322 734 (May 16, 1996) pp38-39. "David Duchovny, Gillian Anderson & Chris Carter" (Montalbetti-Campbell)

CARTER, EDEN—PHOTOGRAPHS
PH02323 668 (October 28, 1993) p73. "At The Bridge Tender" (Newton, Philip)
PH02324 668 (October 28, 1993) p73. "Eden At Squaw Valley" (Newton, Philip)
PH02325 668 (October 28, 1993) p71. "Eden Bungee Jumping At High Camp" (Newton, Philip)
PH02326 668 (October 28, 1993) p72. "[Eden Carter & Sherry Smulders]" (Newton, Philip)

CARTER, HELENA BONHAM—PHOTOGRAPHS
PH02327 696 (December 1, 1994) p132. "Branagh's Dr. Frankenstein Lip Locks Bonham Carter"

CARTER, JAMES—ALBUMS
PH02328 696 (December 1, 1994) p129. "JC On The Set"

CARTER, JAMES—PHOTOGRAPHS
PH02329 715 (August 24, 1995) p73. "Hot Jazzman" (Schafer, F. Scott)

CARTER, JIMMY—ILLUSTRATIONS
PH02330 645-646 (December 10, 1992) p148. "Jimmy Carter, 1976"

CARTER, JIMMY—PHOTOGRAPHS
PH02331 698-699 (December 29, 1994) p58. "Jimmy Carter Bonds With The Late Kim Il Sung"

CARTER, JUNE—PHOTOGRAPHS
PH02332 719 (October 19, 1995) p38. "Johnny And June Carter Cash" (Corbijn, Anton)

CARTER, SHAYNE—PHOTOGRAPHS
PH02333 615 (October 17, 1991) p28. "John Collie, Shayne Carter, Andrew Brough, David Wood (from left)" (Blakesberg, Jay)
PH02334 665 (September 16, 1993) p26. "If The Jacket Fits: Shayne Carter" (Blakesberg, Jay)

CARTLIDGE, KATRIN—PHOTOGRAPHS
PH02335 704 (March 23, 1995) p128. "Manchevski Directs Lovers Cartlidge And Serbedzija"

CARTWRIGHT, SHAWN—PHOTOGRAPHS
PH02336 678 (March 24, 1994) p49. "Shawn Cartwright Of UCLA: He's 7-0 And Dating The President" (Azimi, Mojgan B.)

CARUSO, DAVID—PHOTOGRAPHS
PH02337 707 (May 4, 1995) p74. "Caruso And Cage In 'Kiss Of Death'"

CARVER, RAYMOND—PHOTOGRAPHS—PORTRAITS
PH02338 667 (October 14, 1993) p126. "Below: Director Robert Altman (right) Catches The Spirit Of Writer Raymond Carver"

CARVEY, DANA—PHOTOGRAPHS
PH02339 626 (March 19, 1992) p40. "Director Spheeris Advised Her Stars To 'Keep It Subtle'" (Schiffman, Bonnie)
PH02340 626 (March 19, 1992) p39. "Myers Parties On With Babe Tia Carrere And Carvey" (Schiffman, Bonnie)
PH02341 626 (March 19, 1992) pp34-35. "[Wayne's World]" (Schiffman, Bonnie)
PH02342 626 (March 19, 1992) pp[cover]. "Wayne's World: It's Party Time! It's Excellent!" (Schiffman, Bonnie)
PH02343 642 (October 29, 1992) p19. "Black Crowes Marc Ford, Johnny Colt And Chris Robinson (from left) With Guest Rehearser And Show Host Dana Carvey" (Mazur, Kevin)
PH02344 645-646 (December 10, 1992) p198. "Possible Talk-Show Host Dana Carvey With Fake Talk-Show Host Garry Shandling"

PH02345 656 (May 13, 1993) p50. "Carvey: A Better Bush Than Bush Himself"
PH02346 656 (May 13, 1993) p48. "[Church Lady]"
PH02347 656 (May 13, 1993) pp46-47,49. "[Dana Carvey]" (Seliger, Mark)
PH02348 656 (May 13, 1993) p52. "Myers And Carvey: Partners Who Aren't Really Partners"
PH02349 706 (April 20, 1995) p86. "The 'SNL' Legacy Of Screen Shame"

CARVEY, DANA—PHOTOGRAPHS—PORTRAITS
PH02350 645-646 (December 10, 1992) pp[cover]. "1992 Yearbook" (Schiffman, Bonnie)
PH02351 645-646 (December 10, 1992) p190. "Mike Myers And Dana Carvey"
PH02352 656 (May 13, 1993) pp[cover]. "Dana Carvey Quits" (Seliger, Mark)
PH02353 672-673 (December 23, 1993) p188. "[Covers]" (Seliger, Mark)

CARVILLE, JAMES—ILLUSTRATIONS
PH02354 742 (September 5, 1996) p48. "[James Carville]" (Payne, C. F.)

CARVILLE, JAMES—PHOTOGRAPHS
PH02355 670 (November 25, 1993) p126. "Stephanopoulos (left) And Carville Cheer For Clinton"

CARVILLE, JAMES—PHOTOGRAPHS—PORTRAITS
PH02356 656 (May 13, 1993) p64. "[James Carville]" (Borris, Dan)

CASADY, JACK—PHOTOGRAPHS
PH02357 644 (November 26, 1992) p15. "Kantner, Darby Gould, Jack Casady, Tim Gorman, Prairie Prince, Papa John Creach, McGuinn And Slick Aguilar (from left)" (Mazur, Kevin)

CASALE, BOB—PHOTOGRAPHS
PH02358 730 (March 21, 1996) p17. "Beck, Devo's Mark Mothersbaugh, Bob Casale, Josh Freese, Bob Mothersbaugh, Jerry Casale" (Anderson, Vera)

CASALE, JERRY—PHOTOGRAPHS
PH02358 730 (March 21, 1996) p17. "Beck, Devo's Mark Mothersbaugh, Bob Casale, Josh Freese, Bob Mothersbaugh, Jerry Casale" (Anderson, Vera)

CASE, PETER—PHOTOGRAPHS
PH02359 623 (February 6, 1992) p13. "Peter Case" (Keeley, Dennis)
PH02360 683 (June 2, 1994) p25. "Case Studies The Standards" (Allen, Greg)

CASE, PETER—PHOTOGRAPHS—PORTRAITS
PH02361 645-646 (December 10, 1992) p40. "[Peter Case]"

CASE, STEVE—PHOTOGRAPHS—PORTRAITS
PH02362 744 (October 3, 1996) p62. "[Steve Case]" (Kelly, James M.)

THE CASH BOX (PUBLICATION)—PHOTOGRAPHS
PH02363 659 (June 24, 1993) p48. "The Orioles And Chessler Honored At The Apollo (1950)"

CASH, FRED—PHOTOGRAPHS
PH02364 668 (October 28, 1993) p66. "The Impressions Circa '67: Mayfield, Fred Cash And Gooden"

CASH, JOHNNY—ALBUMS
PH02365 698-699 (December 29, 1994) p176. "American Recordings"

CASH, JOHNNY—ILLUSTRATIONS
PH02366 682 (May 19, 1994) p97. "Their Way" (Day, Robert)

CASH, JOHNNY—ILLUSTRATIONS—LETTERING
PH02367 645-646 (December 10, 1992) pp118-119. "[Johnny Cash]" (Ortiz-Lopez, Dennis)

CASH, JOHNNY—PHOTOGRAPHS
PH02368 625 (March 5, 1992) p11. "Johnny Cash" (Mazur, Kevin)
PH02369 625 (March 5, 1992) p17. "Neil Young Takes Center Stage During The All-Star-Jam Finale" (Gershoff, Gary)
PH02370 644 (November 26, 1992) p17. "The Great Garden Party: Dylan Center Stage For The Grand Finale" (Mazur, Kevin)
PH02371 645-646 (December 10, 1992) p121. "Cash Started Out Selling Home Appliances; By 1969 He Had His Own Prime-Time TV Series"
PH02372 645-646 (December 10, 1992) p30. "Inductee Johnny Cash (below)" (Mazur, Kevin)
PH02373 674 (January 27, 1994) p28. "Jeff Lynne, Tom Petty, Johnny Cash And Rick Rubin (from left) At The Viper Room" (Kirkland, Gene)
PH02374 681 (May 5, 1994) p14. "Johnny Cash" (Dye, Bruce)
PH02375 694 (November 3, 1994) p42. "Country Legend Johnny Cash: Back In Black" (Mazur, Kevin)
PH02376 700 (January 26, 1995) p53. "Country legend Cash" (Seliger, Mark)
PH02377 702 (February 23, 1995) p19. "Henry Rollins And Joe Strummer With Cash In L.A. (from left)" (Granitz, Steve)
PH02378 719 (October 19, 1995) p38. "Johnny And June Carter Cash" (Corbijn, Anton)
PH02379 719 (October 19, 1995) p64. "Johnny Cash Was The First Music Veteran Whose Career Rubin Revitalized" (McDaniel, Melodie)
PH02380 720 (November 2, 1995) p49. "Johnny Cash" (Marshall, Jim)
PH02381 724-725 (December 28, 1995) p56. "Cash And Green Went Well Together" (Mazur, Kevin)
PH02382 724-725 (December 28, 1995) p40. "[Johnny Cash]" (Krementz, Jill)
PH02383 729 (March 7, 1996) p29. "Back In The Saddle Again: Cash Is Recording With Tom Petty's Band And The Former Jayhawks" (Gwinn, Beth)
PH02384 750-751 (December 26, 1996) p169. "Johnny Cash" (Seliger, Mark)
PH02385 750-751 (December 26, 1996) p88. "Producer Rick Rubin, Benmont Tench, Petty And Cash (from left) Work Their Magic"

CASH, JOHNNY—PHOTOGRAPHS—PORTRAITS
PH02386 623 (February 6, 1992) p51. "[Johnny Cash]"
PH02387 643 (November 12, 1992) p125. "Johnny Cash" (Seliger, Mark)
PH02388 645-646 (December 10, 1992) pp118-119. "[Johnny Cash]" (Seliger, Mark)
PH02389 685 (June 30, 1994) p35. "Johnny Cash" (Seliger, Mark)
PH02390 694 (November 3, 1994) p22. "[Johnny Cash & Anthony Kiedis]" (Roberts, Ebet)
PH02391 716 (September 7, 1995) p22. "Johnny Cash Connects Rock To Its Country Roots" (Afanador, Ruven)
PH02392 717 (September 21, 1995) p34. "Johnny Cash Chimes In With Seattle Superstars On 'Willie Nelson Twisted'" (Peterson, Charles)
PH02393 742 (September 5, 1996) p23. "[Johnny Cash]" (Afanador, Ruven)

CASH, JUNE CARTER—PHOTOGRAPHS
PH02394 644 (November 26, 1992) p17. "The Great Garden Party: Dylan Center Stage For The Grand Finale" (Mazur, Kevin)

CASH, ROSANNE—ALBUMS
PH02395 652 (March 18, 1993) p40. "The Wheel"
PH02396 733 (May 2, 1996) p52. "10 Song Demo"

CASH, ROSANNE—PHOTOGRAPHS
PH02397 637 (August 20, 1992) p11. "Williams (left) And Cash" (Gershoff, Gary)
PH02398 649 (February 4, 1993) p8. "Cash, Cockburn And Reed (from left)" (Ienner, Jimmy, Jr.)
PH02399 653 (April 1, 1993) p24. "Cash, Reed And Bloom Onstage In New York" (Capak, R. J.)
PH02400 703 (March 9, 1995) p29. "Rosanne Cash And Marshall With His Classic Shot Of Her Dad" (Mazur, Kevin)

CASH, ROSANNE—PHOTOGRAPHS—PORTRAITS
PH02401 652 (March 18, 1993) pp[enc.6]. "[Rosanne Cash]" (Springsteen, Pam)

PH02402 695 (November 17, 1994) p65. "Rosanne Cash" (Lacombe, Brigitte)
CASHMERE—PHOTOGRAPHS
PH02403 747 (November 14, 1996) p71. "Mizzou, 1980: Crow Played In A Band Called Cashmere While At The University Of Missouri"
CASINO (FILM)—ILLUSTRATIONS
PH02404 723 (December 14, 1995) p89. "Goodfellas Go Vegas" (Brodner, Steve)
CASINO (FILM)—PHOTOGRAPHS
PH02405 718 (October 5, 1995) p76. "Pulp To Come"
PH02406 723 (December 14, 1995) p90. "The Lady Gambles: Stone With The Dice; With Jealous Husband Robert De Niro; Gangster Lover Joe Pesci; And Director Martin Scorsese (from top)"
CASIRAGHI, STEFANO—PHOTOGRAPHS
PH02407 615 (October 17, 1991) p65. "Stefano Casiraghi And Princess Caroline, 1990" (Pigozzi, Jean)
CASSEL, VINCENT—PHOTOGRAPHS
PH02408 728 (February 22, 1996) p70. "Hot With Hate: Cassel Takes Aim At A Violent World"
CASSETTES—PHOTOGRAPHS
PH02409 625 (March 5, 1992) p81. "[Cassettes]" (Coleman, Gene)
PH02410 728 (February 22, 1996) p23. "Budget Singles: A Boon For Consumers, A Tool To Pump Up Rock Stars' Egos" (Lego)
CASSIDY, DAVID—PHOTOGRAPHS
PH02411 645-646 (December 10, 1992) p153. "David Cassidy, 1972"
PH02412 664 (September 2, 1993) p32. "Paul Stanley (left) With David Cassidy" (Plummer, Sue)
PH02413 678 (March 24, 1994) p28. "[MTV's Rock n' Jock Softball Challenge]"
PH02414 689 (August 25, 1994) p16. "David "Donk" Cassidy"
CASSIDY, DAVID—PHOTOGRAPHS—PORTRAITS
PH02415 632 (June 11, 1992) p52. "Some Of David Cassidy's Fans Wrote In To Say He Couldn't Possibly Possess Pubic Hair" (Leibovitz, Annie)
CASSIDY, PAUL—PHOTOGRAPHS
PH02416 651 (March 4, 1993) p23. "Michael Thomas, Jaqueline Thomas, Paul Cassidy, Elvis Costello, Don Belton" (Westenberg, Kevin)
CASTLE, DESHONN—PHOTOGRAPHS
PH02417 642 (October 29, 1992) p77. "Zebrahead"
CAT POWER—PHOTOGRAPHS
PH02418 747 (November 14, 1996) p58. "[Cat Power]" (Irish, Len)
CATALOGS—ILLUSTRATIONS
PH02419 696 (December 1, 1994) p25. "Fan Mail Order" (Goldin, David)
CATES, PHOEBE—PHOTOGRAPHS
PH02420 655 (April 29, 1993) p68. "Bridget Fonda (left) And Phoebe Cates Stalling"
PH02421 722 (November 30, 1995) p60. "Leigh (with Phoebe Cates) Had Her First Hit With 'Fast Times At Ridgemont High'"
CATHERINE WHEEL—ALBUMS
PH02422 710 (June 15, 1995) p80. "Happy Days"
CATHOLICS—ILLUSTRATIONS
PH02423 669 (November 11, 1993) p8. "Tolerance" (Pendergrast, James T.)
CATTLE—PHOTOGRAPHS
PH02424 675 (February 10, 1994) p26. "[Grazing Fees]" (Cancalosi, John)
CAUTY, JIMMY—PHOTOGRAPHS
PH02425 668 (October 28, 1993) p25. "Drummond And Cauty Of K" (Cummins, Kevin)
CAVANAGH, FRANK—PHOTOGRAPHS
PH02426 715 (August 24, 1995) pp68-69. "Brian Liesegang, Richard Patrick, Geno Lenardo, Matt Walker, Frank Cavanagh (from left)" (Ockenfels, Frank W.)
CAVE, NICK—ALBUMS
PH02427 636 (August 6, 1992) p57. "Henry's Dream"
PH02428 684 (June 16, 1994) p110. "Let Love In"
PH02429 730 (March 21, 1996) p96. "Murder Ballads"
PH02430 733 (May 2, 1996) p72. "Murder Ballads"
CAVE, NICK—PHOTOGRAPHS
PH02431 642 (October 29, 1992) p39. "Blues And Brecht: Nick Cave" (Taylor, Chris)
PH02432 664 (September 2, 1993) p32. "Nick Cave With Syd Straw" (Mazur, Kevin)
PH02433 692 (October 6, 1994) p16. "At Philly's Lollapalooza: L7's Donita Sparks (left), Dee Plakas, Suzi Gardner And Jennifer Finch With Bad Seeds Mick Harvey, James Johnston And Nick Cave" (Weiner, Scott)
PH02434 695 (November 17, 1994) p108. "Nick Cave" (Kern, Geof)
PH02435 733 (May 2, 1996) p13. "I Vant To Bite Your Neck: Harvey, Left, And Cave" (Young, Richard)
CAVE, NICK—PHOTOGRAPHS—PORTRAITS
PH02436 645-646 (December 10, 1992) p54. "[Nick Cave]" (Anker, Matt)
PH02437 689 (August 25, 1994) p34. "[Nick Cave]" (Lavine, Michael)
PH02438 728 (February 22, 1996) p25. "Nick Cave, Murder Buff And 'X-Files' Fan"
PH02439 734 (May 16, 1996) p35. "[Nick Cave]" (Burbridge, Richard)
CB RADIOS—PHOTOGRAPHS
PH02440 707 (May 4, 1995) p79. "[Technology]" (Grant, Bob)
CD-ROMS—ILLUSTRATIONS
PH02441 700 (January 26, 1995) p17. "Virtual Raving" (Fisher, Carolyn)
PH02442 733 (May 2, 1996) p64. "[Technology]"
PH02443 748 (November 28, 1996) p117. "[CD-ROMs]"
CD-ROMS—PHOTOGRAPHS
PH02444 638 (September 3, 1992) p77. "[CD-ROM]" (Tavee, Tom)
PH02445 706 (April 20, 1995) p93. "[CD-ROMs]"
PH02446 707 (May 4, 1995) p79. "[Technology]" (Grant, Bob)
PH02447 718 (October 5, 1995) p83. "[Unplugged]" (Grant, Bob)
PH02448 741 (August 22, 1996) pp84-85. "[Hot Technology]" (Grant, Bob)
CDTV—PHOTOGRAPHS
PH02449 618 (November 28, 1991) p109. "Facing The Audio-Video Future: The Philips 910 CD-I Player" (Westheimer, Bill)
CELL—RECORDS
PH02450 650 (February 18, 1993) p59. "Slo-Blo"
CENSORSHIP—ILLUSTRATIONS
PH02451 662 (August 5, 1993) p8. "Free Speech Store" (Pendergrast, James T.)
PH02452 679 (April 7, 1994) p10. "Controversy-Profits" (Pendergrast, James T.)
PH02453 693 (October 20, 1994) p50. "[Censorship]" (Steinberg, James)
PH02454 694 (November 3, 1994) p32. "Pennsylvania Debates A Tough CD Warning-Label Law" (Bishofs, Maris)
PH02455 697 (December 15, 1994) p14. "Music Store" (Pendergrast, James T.)
PH02456 720 (November 2, 1995) p30. "Unfit" (Rosenthal, Marc)
PH02457 723 (December 14, 1995) p28. "Ban 'Zine" (Meshon, Aaron)
PH02458 723 (December 14, 1995) p20. "Free Speech" (Pendergrast, James T.)
PH02459 731 (April 4, 1996) p14. "Vol-Ch" (Pendergrast, James T.)
CENTRAL INTELLIGENCE AGENCY—ILLUSTRATIONS
PH02460 704 (March 23, 1995) p48. "[CIA]" (Witte, Michael)
PH02461 Number not assigned.

PH02462 715 (August 24, 1995) p18. "CIA Cash Machine" (Pendergrast, James T.)
CENTRAL INTELLIGENCE AGENCY—PHOTOGRAPHS
PH02462a 711 (June 29, 1995) p36. "The Smoking Gun (above)" (Trippett, Robert)
CENTRAL PARK WEST (TELEVISION SHOW)—PHOTOGRAPHS
PH02463 716 (September 7, 1995) p83. "Central Park West: A Bon-Ton John-John Bonbon"
CERVENKA, EXENE—PHOTOGRAPHS
PH02464 616 (October 31, 1991) p11. "Cervenka, Gina Schock, Jane Wiedlin, Kathy Valentine, Charlotte Caffey (clockwise from top left)" (Granitz, Steve)
PH02465 659 (June 24, 1993) p23. "'Xdream: Gilkyson, Doe, Cervenka, Bonebrake (from left)"
PH02466 666 (September 30, 1993) p28. "Exene Cervenka" (Mercer, Lance)
CERVENKA, EXENE—PHOTOGRAPHS—PORTRAITS
PH02467 737 (June 27, 1996) p29. "Poet And Bomb Buff Cervenkova" (Brice, Lindsay)
CERVERIS, MICHAEL—PHOTOGRAPHS
PH02468 672-673 (December 23, 1993) p106. "A Chorus Line: 'Tommy' Director Des McAnuff, Townshend And Michael Cerveris, Who Plays Tommy (from left)" (Cunningham, Peter)
CHADWICK, MARK—PHOTOGRAPHS
PH02469 630 (May 14, 1992) p32. "The Levellers (from left): Friend, Sevink, Chadwick, Heather And Cunningham" (Doove, Hester)
CHAIN REACTION (FILM)—PHOTOGRAPHS
PH02470 742 (September 5, 1996) p68. "Now Playing"
CHAINSAW KITTENS—PHOTOGRAPHS
PH02471 680 (April 21, 1994) p34. "[Iggy Pop, Evan Dando, Chainsaw Kittens]" (Peterson, Charles)
CHAINSAW KITTENS—PHOTOGRAPHS—PORTRAITS
PH02472 630 (May 14, 1992) p32. "Chainsaw Kittens (clockwise from top left): McBay, Meade, Preston, Bell And Metzger" (Mazur, Kevin)
THE CHAMBER (FILM)—PHOTOGRAPHS
PH02473 747 (November 14, 1996) p124. "The Chamber: John Grisham's First Screen Strikeout"
CHAMBERLIN, JIMMY—PHOTOGRAPHS
PH02474 660-661 (July 8, 1993) p100. "Smashing Pumpkins (from left): Billy Corgan, D'Arcy, Jimmy Chamberlin And James Iha" (Johnson, Lisa)
PH02475 695 (November 17, 1994) p47. "Smashing Pumpkins" (Ockenfels, Frank, 3)
PH02476 705 (April 6, 1995) p16. "Billy Corgan, Drummer Jimmy Chamberlin And James Iha (from left)" (Natkin, Paul)
PH02477 711 (June 29, 1995) p19. "Billy Corgan, D'Arcy, Jimmy Chamberlin, James Iha (from left)" (Elledge, Paul)
PH02478 721 (November 16, 1995) p52. "Cutting Up: James Iha (left) And Jimmy Chamberlin" (Seliger, Mark)
PH02479 721 (November 16, 1995) p56. "Ready To Rock You: D'Arcy, Iha, Corgan, Chamberlin (from left) In 1992" (Lenquette)
PH02480 723 (December 14, 1995) p27. "The Chicago Eight: D'Arcy, Petersson, Carlos, Corgan, Nielsen, Iha, Chamberlin And Zander (from left)" (Elledge, Paul)
PH02481 724-725 (December 28, 1995) p40. "Corgan, Jimmy Chamberlin, James Iha (from left)" (Natkin, Paul)
PH02482 726 (January 25, 1996) p43. "Smashing Pumpkins' Billy Corgan, D'Arcy, James Iha, Jimmy Chamberlin (from left)" (Seliger, Mark)
PH02483 743 (September 19, 1996) p28. "Before The Fall: Chamberlin Onstage (top)" (Page, Scarlet)
CHAMBERLIN, JIMMY—PHOTOGRAPHS—PORTRAITS
PH02484 667 (October 14, 1993) p19. "D'Arcy, Jimmy Chamberlin, Billy Corgan, James Iha (clockwise from top left)" (Hom, Marc)
PH02485 741 (August 22, 1996) p32. "Melvoin (left) And Chamberlin" (Colver, Ed)
CHAMBERS, JIMY—PHOTOGRAPHS
PH02486 664 (September 2, 1993) p24. "They're All Revved Up: Donahue, Thorpe, Baker, Chambers, Fridmann And Grasshopper (from left)" (Gullick, Steve)
CHANDLER, CHAS—PHOTOGRAPHS
PH02487 676 (February 24, 1994) p48. "The Angry Young Animals (from left): Drummer John Steel, Organist Alan Price, bass Player Chas Chandler, Lead Singer Eric Burdon And Guitarist Hilton Valentine"
PH02488 677 (March 10, 1994) p28. "Pirner With Animals Valentine, Chas Chandler And John Steel" (Mazur, Kevin)
PH02489 742 (September 5, 1996) p26. "[Chas Chandler]"
PH02490 750-751 (December 26, 1996) p97. "[Chas Chandler]"
CHANDLER, MARTIN—PHOTOGRAPHS
PH02491 615 (October 17, 1991) p28. "Jack Coy, George Hernandez, Jeff Braimes, Martin Chandler (from left)" (Mason, Karen)
CHANNING, CHAD—PHOTOGRAPHS
PH02492 674 (January 27, 1994) p38. "Young Nirvana: Ex-Drummer Chad Channing, Novoselic, Cobain In '88 (from left)" (Peterson, Charles)
PH02493 683 (June 2, 1994) p52. "Channing, Short-term Guitarist Jason Everman, Novoselic, Cobain 1989" (Wheeler, Alice)
CHANNING, STOCKARD—PHOTOGRAPHS
PH02494 672-673 (December 23, 1993) p174. "[Six Degrees Of Separation]"
PH02495 711 (June 29, 1995) p49. "Stockard Channing Blows Smoke At A Wary Harvey Keitel"
CHAPLIN (FILM)—PHOTOGRAPHS
PH02496 647 (January 7, 1993) p51. "Robert Downey Jr. Is The Little Tramp"
CHAPLIN, BEN—PHOTOGRAPHS
PH02497 734 (May 16, 1996) p74. "Chaplin, Thurman And Garofalo In Love"
CHAPMAN, MARK DAVID—PHOTOGRAPHS—PORTRAITS
PH02498 747 (November 14, 1996) p30. "Lennon And His Murderer, Mark David Chapman"
CHAPMAN, TOM—PHOTOGRAPHS
PH02499 693 (October 20, 1994) p74. "Actors Tom Chapman And Marc Wallice"
CHAPMAN, TRACY—ALBUMS
PH02500 630 (May 14, 1992) p103. "Matters Of The Heart"
PH02501 721 (November 16, 1995) p111. "New Beginning"
CHAPMAN, TRACY—ILLUSTRATIONS
PH02502 737 (June 27, 1996) p72. "Chapman's 'New Beginning'" (Ciardiello, Joe)
CHAPMAN, TRACY—PHOTOGRAPHS
PH02503 619-620 (December 12, 1991) p94. "The All-Star Jam Finale At The Bridge Concert" (Blakesberg, Jay)
PH02504 629 (April 30, 1992) p11. "Chapman Onstage With Accordionist Roy Bittan And Vernon Reid" (Mazur, Kevin)
PH02505 645-646 (December 10, 1992) p47. "Chapman Takes Matters To Heart" (Mazur, Kevin)
PH02506 743 (September 19, 1996) p45. "Chapman Scores When She's Loose" (Mazur, Kevin)
PH02507 750-751 (December 26, 1996) p62. "Tracy Chapman Lodged Herself In The Top 10 In May" (Estrada, Kevin)
CHAPMAN, TRACY—PHOTOGRAPHS—PORTRAITS
PH02508 628 (April 16, 1992) p26. "[Tracy Chapman]" (Ockenfels, Frank W.)
CHAPPELL, OLIVER—PHOTOGRAPHS
PH02509 652 (March 18, 1993) pp[enc.3]. "[Oliver Chappell]" (Calahan, Walter)
CHARLATANS UK—ALBUMS
PH02510 634-635 (July 9, 1992) p105. "Between 10th And 11th"
CHARLATANS UK—PHOTOGRAPHS
PH02511 619-620 (December 12, 1991) p46. "The Charlatans UK" (Seliger, Mark)

CHARLES, JOSH—PHOTOGRAPHS
PH02512 680 (April 21, 1994) p93. "Student Union For Charles, Boyle And Baldwin"
CHARLES, RAY—ALBUMS
PH02513 619-620 (December 12, 1991) p177. "The Birth Of Soul"
CHARLES, RAY—ILLUSTRATIONS—PORTRAITS
PH02514 641 (October 15, 1992) p56. "[Ray Charles]" (Holland, Brad)
CHARLES, RAY—PHOTOGRAPHS
PH02515 650 (February 18, 1993) p50. "Wexler And Ray Charles Share A Laugh Backstage"
PH02516 655 (April 29, 1993) p23. "[Ray Charles]" (Weber, Bruce)
PH02517 662 (August 5, 1993) p33. "Billy Joel And Ray Charles In New York City" (Mazur, Kevin)
PH02518 668 (October 28, 1993) p35. "Charles" (Dugdale, Bruce)
PH02519 669 (November 11, 1993) p27. "Brother Ray With Hutchence" (Granitz, Steve)
PH02520 698-699 (December 29, 1994) p63. "Sessions" (Seeff, Norman)
PH02521 720 (November 2, 1995) p49. "Ray Charles" (Marshall, Jim)
CHARLES, RAY—PHOTOGRAPHS—PORTRAITS
PH02522 643 (November 12, 1992) p84. "Ray Charles" (Weber, Bruce)
CHARLIE—PHOTOGRAPHS
PH02523 721 (November 16, 1995) p106. "Civ: Charlie" (GS, Jamil)
PH02524 721 (November 16, 1995) p98. "Sammy, Arthur, Charlie And Civ (from left)" (GS, Jamil)
CHARMAINE—PHOTOGRAPHS
PH02525 686-687 (July 14, 1994) p72. "Girl World: Sensi, Linda, Charmaine, Sabrina (from left)" (Borris, Dan)
CHARO—PHOTOGRAPHS
PH02526 655 (April 29, 1993) p11. "Charo Relives The 'Love Boat' Days With Mark Arm"
CHASE, CHEVY—PHOTOGRAPHS
PH02527 626 (March 19, 1992) p104. "Invisibility Hampers Chevy Chase's Game"
PH02528 706 (April 20, 1995) p86. "The 'SNL' Legacy Of Screen Shame"
CHASE, COURTNEY—PHOTOGRAPHS
PH02529 723 (December 14, 1995) p92. "Race Against Time: Chase And Depp"
CHASTAIN, PAUL—PHOTOGRAPHS
PH02530 627 (April 2, 1992) p19. "Jeffrey Borchardt, Paul Chastain And Ric Menck (from left)" (Lavine, Michael)
PH02531 685 (June 30, 1994) p40. "Velvet's Paul Chastain, Jeffrey Borchardt And Menck With McGuinn (from left)"
CHAVEZ, FELIPE—PHOTOGRAPHS
PH02532 672-673 (December 23, 1993) p. "Felipe And Lynn Chavez And Children (opposite) Were The Seed People For Kid Village" (Borris, Dan)
CHAVEZ, LYNN—PHOTOGRAPHS
PH02532 672-673 (December 23, 1993) p. "Felipe And Lynn Chavez And Children (opposite) Were The Seed People For Kid Village" (Borris, Dan)
CHAVIS, DANIEL—PHOTOGRAPHS
PH02533 683 (June 2, 1994) p24. "Twin Tones: Daniel Chavis, Burris, Danny Chavis And Levi (from left)" (Cardillicchio, Nick)
CHAVIS, DANNY—PHOTOGRAPHS
PH02533 683 (June 2, 1994) p24. "Twin Tones: Daniel Chavis, Burris, Danny Chavis And Levi (from left)" (Cardillicchio, Nick)
CHAYKIN, MAURY—PHOTOGRAPHS
PH02534 717 (September 21, 1995) p90. "Watt Is Flanked By Uncles Chaykin And Richards"
CHEADLE, DON—PHOTOGRAPHS
PH02535 731 (April 4, 1996) p66. "Cheadle And Washington, 'Devil'"
CHEAP DATES—PHOTOGRAPHS
PH02536 652 (March 18, 1993) p15. "Cheap Dates (from left): Phantom, Baxter, Sales, Stanton And James" (Matheu, Robert)
CHEAP TRICK—ALBUMS
PH02537 683 (June 2, 1994) p69. "Woke Up With A Monster"
PH02538 727 (February 8, 1996) p18. "At Budokan"
PH02539 746 (October 31, 1996) p68. "Sex, America, Cheap Trick"
CHEAP TRICK—PHOTOGRAPHS
PH02540 706 (April 20, 1995) p17. "[Seattle]" (Doughty, Curt)
PH02541 723 (December 14, 1995) p27. "The Chicago Eight: D'Arcy, Petersson, Carlos, Corgan, Nielsen, Iha, Chamberlin And Zander (from left)" (Elledge, Paul)
CHEBA, EDDIE—PHOTOGRAPHS
PH02542 672-673 (December 23, 1993) p139. "Lovebug (left) With Early Rapper Eddie Cheba In 1978"
CHECKER, CHUBBY—PHOTOGRAPHS
PH02543 720 (November 2, 1995) p50. "Chubby Checker" (Ray, Bill)
CHEEK, RANDY—PHOTOGRAPHS
PH02544 700 (January 26, 1995) p30. "From Left: Morrison, Cheek, Erhardt, Cleaver" (Ockenfels, Frank, 3)
CHEEK, TERRY—PHOTOGRAPHS
PH02545 718 (October 5, 1995) p64. "Public Defender Robert Gamble At The Arraignment Of Cheek And Hudgins (from left)" (Beckner, Greg)
CHEERLEADING—ILLUSTRATIONS
PH02546 717 (September 21, 1995) p20. "Sidelined" (Angel, Vinnie)
CHELIK, EDIN—PHOTOGRAPHS
PH02547 724-725 (December 28, 1995) p91. "The Chelik Family (clockwise from top): Paya, Hiba, Sanela With Nehrudin, Mirza, Edin, Zlatiya" (Cobb, Rachel)
CHELIK, HIBA—PHOTOGRAPHS
PH02547 724-725 (December 28, 1995) p91. "The Chelik Family (clockwise from top): Paya, Hiba, Sanela With Nehrudin, Mirza, Edin, Zlatiya" (Cobb, Rachel)
CHELIK, HUSO—PHOTOGRAPHS
PH02548 724-725 (December 28, 1995) p94. "Huso Chelik In Mostar For Salena's High School Equivalency Exam" (Cobb, Rachel)
CHELIK, MIRZA—PHOTOGRAPHS
PH02549 724-725 (December 28, 1995) p91. "The Chelik Family (clockwise from top): Paya, Hiba, Sanela With Nehrudin, Mirza, Edin, Zlatiya" (Cobb, Rachel)
CHELIK, PAYA—PHOTOGRAPHS
PH02549 724-725 (December 28, 1995) p91. "The Chelik Family (clockwise from top): Paya, Hiba, Sanela With Nehrudin, Mirza, Edin, Zlatiya" (Cobb, Rachel)
CHELIK, ZLATIYA—PHOTOGRAPHS
PH02549 724-725 (December 28, 1995) p91. "The Chelik Family (clockwise from top): Paya, Hiba, Sanela With Nehrudin, Mirza, Edin, Zlatiya" (Cobb, Rachel)
CHEMICAL BROTHERS—PHOTOGRAPHS
PH02550 741 (August 22, 1996) p36. "The Future Is Now: Rowlands And Simons" (Sundland, Steen)
PH02551 749 (December 12, 1996) p25. "Just Say Noel" (Double, Steve)
CHENEY, PAUL—PHOTOGRAPHS
PH02552 730 (March 21, 1996) p85. "In 1984, Dr. Paul Cheney Observed An Outbreak Of CFS At Lake Tahoe, Nev." (McIntyre, Will)
CHER—PHOTOGRAPHS
PH02553 733 (May 2, 1996) p62. "'Faithfull': Cher, Palminteri, O'Neal"
PH02554 740 (August 8, 1996) p18. "[Cher]" (Usa, Rex)
CHER—PHOTOGRAPHS—PORTRAITS
PH02555 692 (October 6, 1994) p52. "Cher"
PH02556 743 (September 19, 1996) p46. "[Cher]" (Scheinmann, David)

CHERONE, GARY—PHOTOGRAPHS
PH02557 683 (June 2, 1994) p28. "Extreme's Gary Cherone, Rock Star, In The Title Role Of "Jesus Christ Superstar"" (Robicheau, Paul)
CHERRY, DON—PHOTOGRAPHS
PH02558 722 (November 30, 1995) p40. "[Don Cherry]" (Putland, Michael)
PH02559 724-725 (December 28, 1995) p66. "[Don Cherry]" (Teller, Juergen)
CHERRY, NENEH—ALBUMS
PH02560 644 (November 26, 1992) p69. "Homebrew"
CHERRY, NENEH—ILLUSTRATIONS
PH02561 644 (November 26, 1992) p69. "Neneh's Hot 'Homebrew'" (Guy, Edmund)
CHERRY, NENEH—PHOTOGRAPHS
PH02562 642 (October 29, 1992) p21. "Cherry And Stipe" (Keeley, Dennis)
PH02563 645-646 (December 10, 1992) p92. "Neneh Cherry"
PH02564 649 (February 4, 1993) pp32-34,38. "[Neneh Cherry]" (Von Unwerth, Ellen)
PH02565 649 (February 4, 1993) pp[cover]. "Neneh Cherry: Beauty And The Beat" (Von Unwerth, Ellen)
PH02566 655 (April 29, 1993) p12. "Cherry (left) And N'Dour" (Gershoff, Gary)
PH02567 662 (August 5, 1993) p34. "D'Arby, Cherry And White (from left)" (Robicheau, Paul)
PH02568 667 (October 14, 1993) p92. "Cherry: 'Manchild' Takes First Steps Into New World"
PH02569 686-687 (July 14, 1994) p42. "Seven Seconds With Cherry And N'Dour"
PH02570 692 (October 6, 1994) p53. "Neneh Cherry"
CHERRY, NENEH—PHOTOGRAPHS—PORTRAITS
PH02571 649 (February 4, 1993) p35. "[Neneh Cherry]" (Von Unwerth, Ellen)
PH02572 672-673 (December 23, 1993) p188. "[Covers]" (Von Unwerth, Ellen)
PH02573 689 (August 25, 1994) p45. "Timekeeper Cherry" (Gougenheim, Kim)
CHESSLER, DEBORAH—PHOTOGRAPHS
PH02574 659 (June 24, 1993) p46. "Chessler Managing Her Accounts"
PH02575 659 (June 24, 1993) p43. "Chessler, Til (on her right) And The Orioles After A Show In 1952, No Longer Penniless"
PH02576 659 (June 24, 1993) p41. "[Deborah Chessler]" (Seliger, Mark)
PH02577 659 (June 24, 1993) p48. "The Orioles And Chessler Honored At The Apollo (1950)"
CHESTNUTT, VIC—ALBUMS
PH02578 749 (December 12, 1996) p86. "About To Choke"
CHESTNUTT, VIC—ILLUSTRATIONS
PH02579 741 (August 22, 1996) p95. "Covered With Love" (Kunz, Anita)
CHESTNUTT, VIC—PHOTOGRAPHS
PH02580 689 (August 25, 1994) p16. "Jack Logan (second from left) With Vic Chestnutt (front) And Other Enablers" (Torno, Pattiy)
PH02581 743 (September 19, 1996) p65. "Fast Times At Pike County High: Chestnutt As Class Clown"
PH02582 743 (September 19, 1996) p64. "Gone Fishin': Chestnutt With A Swell Head At Age 11"
PH02583 743 (September 19, 1996) p62. "[Vic Chestnutt]" (Mark, Mary Ellen)
PH02584 750-751 (December 26, 1996) p67. "Vic Chestnutt Gets By With A Little Help From His Friends" (Bozi, Tibor)
CHIC—ALBUMS
PH02585 626 (March 19, 1992) p89. "Chic-ism"
CHIEFTAINS—ALBUMS
PH02586 619-620 (December 12, 1991) p189. "The Bells Of Dublin"
PH02587 625 (March 5, 1992) p72. "An Irish Evening"
PH02588 701 (February 9, 1995) p56. "The Long Black Veil"
CHILD ABUSE—ILLUSTRATIONS
PH02589 616 (October 31, 1991) pp67,70. "[Child Abuse]" (Kunz, Anita)
CHILDREN—ILLUSTRATIONS
PH02590 715 (August 24, 1995) p25. "Schoolhouse Rock" (Mericle, Cherise)
PH02591 720 (November 2, 1995) p17. "Radio Ga-Ga" (Freda, Anthony)
CHILDRESS, ROSS—PHOTOGRAPHS
PH02592 686-687 (July 14, 1994) p30. "Soul Men: Childress, Evans, Dean Roland, Turpin And Ed Roland (clockwise from top left)" (Callahan, Kristin)
CHILDS, BERT—PHOTOGRAPHS
PH02593 666 (September 30, 1993) p88. "Wade Price, Steivan Oligmueller And Bert Childs (from left)" (Himmel, Lizzie)
CHILLS—ALBUMS
PH02594 638 (September 3, 1992) p68. "Soft Bomb"
CHILTON, ALEX—PHOTOGRAPHS
PH02595 658 (June 10, 1993) p17. "Auer, Chilton, Stephens And Stringfellow" (Perez, Marty)
PH02596 668 (October 28, 1993) p15. "Big Star On The Steps Of Alex Chilton's Memphis, Tenn., Home In 1972: Andy Hummel, Jody Stephens, Chris Bell And Chilton (above, from left)" (Manning, Carole)
PH02597 668 (October 28, 1993) p32. "Chilton And His Box Tops Gold Records In 1970" (Manning, Carole)
PH02598 668 (October 28, 1993) p15. "Chilton And Stephens On Reunion Day 1993 (left)" (Rosenberg, Merlyn)
PH02599 668 (October 28, 1993) p16. "A Rare Stage Shot Of Chilton With Big Star" (Margolis, Lisa B.)
PH02600 688 (August 11, 1994) p17. "Star Quality: Alex Chilton At The Fillmore" (Jennings, Steve)
CHINA GIRL (VIDEO)—PHOTOGRAPHS
PH02601 667 (October 14, 1993) p87. "'China Girl': Bowie Takes On Imperialism, Takes Off Trousers (above)"
CHINA MOON (FILM)—PHOTOGRAPHS
PH02602 678 (March 24, 1994) p104. "Two Babes And A Hunk: Davis (Angie); Stowe (China Moon); Grant (Four Weddings)"
CHINO, WENDELL—PHOTOGRAPHS—PORTRAITS
PH02603 736 (June 13, 1996) p70. "Wendell Chino, The Mescalero's President, Is Considered By Many To Be The Apache Nelson Mandela" (Barker, Kent)
CHISUM, GLORIA—PHOTOGRAPHS
PH02604 662 (August 5, 1993) p46. "Four Of The Five Delta Sigma Theta Sisters With Peggy Reeves Sanday, Who Replaced Zolla Airall [Photo is Gloria Chisum, not Peggy Reeves Sanday]"
CHO, MARGARET—PHOTOGRAPHS
PH02605 682 (May 19, 1994) p68. "[Margaret Cho]" (Ragel, Jon)
CHOICE—ALBUMS
PH02606 631 (May 28, 1992) p55. "Stick-N-Moove"
CHOMSKY, NOAM—PHOTOGRAPHS—PORTRAITS
PH02607 631 (May 28, 1992) pp43,45. "[Noam Chomsky]" (Winters, Dan)
CHONG, MARCUS—PHOTOGRAPHS
PH02608 708 (May 18, 1995) p96. "Vance And Chong Front The Panthers"
CHORUSH, BOB—PHOTOGRAPHS
PH02609 632 (June 11, 1992) p62. "Staff Members And Contributing Writers At The 1971 Editorial Conference, At Esalen, In Big Sur" (Leibovitz, Annie)
CHOUDHURY, SARITA—PHOTOGRAPHS
PH02610 624 (February 20, 1992) p50. "Washington And Choudhury At Odds"
CHRIST, JOHN—PHOTOGRAPHS
PH02611 678 (March 24, 1994) p42. "Those Evil Mothers In Danzig: Chuck Biscuits, Glenn Danzig, John Christ, Eerie Von (from left)" (Seliger, Mark)

CHRISTIAN ROCK MUSIC—ILLUSTRATIONS
PH02612 747 (November 14, 1996) p20. "[Christian Rockers]" (Pendergrast, James T.)
CHRISTIANS—PHOTOGRAPHS
PH02613 729 (March 7, 1996) p44. "At A Christian Coalition Convention, The Faithful Give Vent To Their Political Fervor" (Fink, Larry)
CHRISTIANSEN, HELENA—PHOTOGRAPHS
PH02614 667 (October 14, 1993) p96. "From Her To Eternity: In 'Wicked Game,' Isaak Nuzzles Christiansen Beachside"
CHRISTMAS—ILLUSTRATIONS
PH02615 689 (August 25, 1994) p16. "Is Nothing Sacred?" (Martin, Matthew)
CHUNG, APRIL—PHOTOGRAPHS
PH02616 660-661 (July 8, 1993) p101. "Motherhead Bug (from left): Anthony Lee, Steven Ovenden, April Chung, Cyril Mazzard, Jez Aspinal, Tomoyo, And Dave Ouimet" (Leopardi, N.)
CHUNG, CONNIE—PHOTOGRAPHS
PH02617 667 (October 14, 1993) p45. "Bussing Connie Chung At A Press Conference Earlier This Year"
CHURCH—ALBUMS
PH02618 628 (April 16, 1992) p84. "Priest = Aura"
PH02619 693 (October 20, 1994) p151. "Sometime Anywhere"
CHUVAKHIN, SERGEI—PHOTOGRAPHS
PH02620 711 (June 29, 1995) p36. "Ames KGB Link, Sergei Chuvakhin (left)"
CIBO MATTO—ALBUMS
PH02621 727 (February 8, 1996) p50. "Viva! La Woman"
CIBO MATTO—PHOTOGRAPHS
PH02622 721 (November 16, 1995) p76. "Yuka Honda (left) And Miho Hatori: Galloping Gourmets With A Taste For Big Beats And Pop Exotica" (Exum)
PH02623 729 (March 7, 1996) p9. "Cibo Matto's Honda And Miho Hatori Gettin' Down With Sean Lennon" (Kleiman, Dennis)
PH02624 750-751 (December 26, 1996) p46. "Cibo Matto Performing With Special Guest Sean Ono Lennon (right) In New York" (Kleiman, Dennis)
CICCONE, CHRIS—PHOTOGRAPHS
PH02625 748 (November 28, 1996) p30. "Papa, Don't Preach: A Very Pregnant Madonna In Los Angeles, With Her Brother, Chris Ciccone, In Early September" (Lewis, Gary)
CICERO, MICHEL—PHOTOGRAPHS
PH02626 727 (February 8, 1996) p12. "Woodpussy's Michel Cicero, Rancid's Tim Armstrong, Iggy, The Offspring's Dexter Holland (from left)" (Buzzerio, Johnny)
CINEMA (1993)—ILLUSTRATIONS
PH02627 659 (June 24, 1993) p87. "Dinosaur Summer" (Witte, Michael)
CINEMA (1994)—ILLUSTRATIONS
PH02628 684 (June 16, 1994) p113. "[Movies]" (Blitt, Barry)
CINEMA (1995)—ILLUSTRATIONS
PH02629 724-725 (December 28, 1995) p134. "Usual Suspects" (Brodner, Steve)
CINEMA (1996)—ILLUSTRATIONS
PH02630 743 (September 19, 1996) p87. "[Mars Attacks..]" (Brodner, Steve)
CINEMA—ILLUSTRATIONS
PH02631 615 (October 17, 1991) p100. "Now Playing"
PH02632 616 (October 31, 1991) p97. "Now Playing"
PH02633 617 (November 14, 1991) p182. "Star Snores"
PH02634 618 (November 28, 1991) p103. "Now Playing"
PH02635 621 (January 9, 1992) p55. "Now Playing"
PH02636 622 (January 23, 1992) p49. "1991 Ten Best & Worst" (Kroninger, Stephen)
PH02637 622 (January 23, 1992) p50. "Now Playing"
PH02638 623 (February 6, 1992) p88. "Now Playing"
PH02639 624 (February 20, 1992) p50. "Now Playing"
PH02640 626 (March 19, 1992) p102. "Now Playing"
PH02641 627 (April 2, 1992) p39. "Memo To The Academy On Its 64th Birthday: Retire Or Reform" (Cowles, David)
PH02642 628 (April 16, 1992) p93. "Now Playing"
PH02643 630 (May 14, 1992) p114. "Now Playing"
PH02644 633 (June 25, 1992) p47. "The First Harvest Of A Gutless Film Season Offers Slim Pickings" (Smith, Elwood)
PH02645 633 (June 25, 1992) p49. "Now Playing"
PH02646 636 (August 6, 1992) p66. "Now Playing"
PH02647 637 (August 20, 1992) p60. "Now Playing"
PH02648 638 (September 3, 1992) p75. "Now Playing"
PH02649 640 (October 1, 1992) p72. "Now Playing"
PH02650 644 (November 26, 1992) p80. "An Identity Crisis For Jaye Davidson (left) And Stephen Rea"
PH02651 644 (November 26, 1992) p80. "Now Playing"
PH02652 645-646 (December 10, 1992) p189. "The Year In Movies" (Blechman, R. O.)
PH02653 647 (January 7, 1993) p51. "Stinkers"
PH02654 650 (February 18, 1993) p67. "Now Playing"
PH02655 653 (April 1, 1993) p59. "Now Playing"
PH02656 656 (May 13, 1993) p116. "Now Playing"
PH02657 660-661 (July 8, 1993) p121. "Summer Bummers"
PH02658 662 (August 5, 1993) p72. "Now Playing"
PH02659 667 (October 14, 1993) p128. "Now Playing"
PH02660 669 (November 11, 1993) p79. "Scare Tactics" (Guy, Edmund)
PH02661 671 (December 9, 1993) p78. "Now Playing"
PH02662 678 (March 24, 1994) p99. "[Academy Awards]" (Vellekoop, Maurice)
PH02663 691 (September 22, 1994) p14. "Rolling Stone" (Pendergrast, James T.)
PH02664 691 (September 22, 1994) p106. "Summer Wrap-Up" (Corio, Paul)
PH02665 701 (February 9, 1995) p62. "[Video Disc Films]"
PH02666 705 (April 6, 1995) p68. "The Clueless Academy Has An Unofficial Motto For Picking Winners This Year: In Gump We trust" (Yaccarino, Dan)
PH02667 709 (June 1, 1995) p67. "[Cinema 1995]" (Smith, Elwood)
PH02668 719 (October 19, 1995) p95. "The Look Of The Perverse"
PH02669 731 (April 4, 1996) p65. "Feeding At The Trough Of Censorship And Political Scare Tactics, The Academy Slops Of Slops And Sciences Ushers In The Season Of The Pig" (Brodner, Steve)
PH02670 733 (May 2, 1996) p61. "Invasion Of The TV Brain Snatchers" (Brodner, Steve)
CINEMA—PHOTOGRAPHS
PH02671 630 (May 14, 1992) p69. "[Psychiatrists, Indians And Vampires]" (Seliger, Mark)
CIRCLE JERKS—PHOTOGRAPHS
PH02672 719 (October 19, 1995) p24. "Reuniting Hasn't Been Easy For The Circle Jerks: Keith Morris, Zander Schloss And Keith Clark (from left)" (Garcia, Willie)
CIRCLE OF FRIENDS (FILM)—PHOTOGRAPHS
PH02673 704 (March 23, 1995) p129. "Driver's Irish Eyes Smile At O'Donnell"
CITY COLLEGE OF NEW YORK—PHOTOGRAPHS
PH02674 645-646 (December 10, 1992) p30. "After The Storm At CCNY"
CITY HALL (FILM)—ILLUSTRATIONS
PH02675 729 (March 7, 1996) p52. "Hizzoner And Dishonor" (Brodner, Steve)
CITY HALL (FILM)—PHOTOGRAPHS
PH02676 729 (March 7, 1996) p53. "Pacino Says His Piece As A Mayor Under Suspicion"
CITY OF JOY (FILM)—PHOTOGRAPHS
PH02677 629 (April 30, 1992) p65. "Patrick Swayze Does His Bit For The Poor"
CITY SLICKERS II (FILM)—PHOTOGRAPHS
PH02678 685 (June 30, 1994) p80. "Crystal, Lovitz And Stern Go West For Box-Office Gold"
PH02679 684 (June 16, 1994) p114. "Potential Blockbusters"

CIV—PHOTOGRAPHS
PH02680 721 (November 16, 1995) p103. "Civ" (GS, Jamil)
PH02681 721 (November 16, 1995) p98. "Sammy, Arthur, Charlie And Civ (from left)" (GS, Jamil)
CLANCY, CHARLES—PHOTOGRAPHS
PH02682 678 (March 24, 1994) p69. "Brothers Under The Skin: Martin Phillips, Greg Parker, Mike Williams, Dexter Wilson, Rick Brown, Greg Jackson, Everett Whiteside, Roderick Bradford, Lacell Sherman, Daniel..." (Smi
CLANCY, TOM—ILLUSTRATIONS
PH02683 696 (December 1, 1994) p115. "[Tom Clancy]" (Rosen, Jonathon)
CLAPTON, BONNIE—PHOTOGRAPHS
PH02684 637 (August 20, 1992) p11. "Raitt And Clapton At Wembley" (Ollerenshow, Philip)
CLAPTON, CONOR—PHOTOGRAPHS
PH02685 615 (October 17, 1991) p44. "Clapton's Next LP Will Be A Tribute To His Son" (Usa, Rex)
CLAPTON, ERIC—ALBUMS
PH02686 616 (October 31, 1991) p91. "24 Nights"
PH02687 619-620 (December 12, 1991) p174. "24 Nights"
PH02688 645-646 (December 10, 1992) p180. "Unplugged"
PH02689 654 (April 15, 1993) p80. "Unplugged"
PH02690 655 (April 29, 1993) p80. "Unplugged"
PH02691 693 (October 20, 1994) p141. "From The Cradle"
PH02692 694 (November 3, 1994) p120. "From The Cradle"
CLAPTON, ERIC—ILLUSTRATIONS
PH02693 641 (October 15, 1992) p126. "[Clapton Is God]" (Kelley, Gary)
PH02694 693 (October 20, 1994) p141. "Gospel Blues" (Collier, John)
PH02695 696 (December 1, 1994) p144. "Eric Clapton: True Blues" (Clayton, Christian)
CLAPTON, ERIC—ILLUSTRATIONS—LETTERING
PH02695a 615 (October 17, 1991) p42. "RS+EC" (Hoeffler, Jonathan)
CLAPTON, ERIC—ILLUSTRATIONS—PORTRAITS
PH02696 655 (April 29, 1993) p30. "1952" (Liepke, Skip)
PH02697 655 (April 29, 1993) p31. "1993" (Liepke, Skip)
PH02698 Number not assigned.
CLAPTON, ERIC—PHOTOGRAPHS
PH02699 615 (October 17, 1991) p14. "Buddy Guy, Eric Clapton" (Mazur, Kevin)
PH02700 615 (October 17, 1991) p44. "Clapton's Next LP Will Be A Tribute To His Son" (Usa, Rex)
PH02701 615 (October 17, 1991) p47. "Cray, Clapton And Vaughan (from left) On The Night Of The Crash" (Knight, Robert)
PH02702 615 (October 17, 1991) p49. "Road Warriors: Clapton And His Pal Harrison" (Rider, Paul)
PH02703 619-620 (December 12, 1991) p22. "Clapton Leads The Royal Albert Hall Band"
PH02704 623 (February 6, 1992) p18. "Clapton (right) Got A Warmer Welcome" (Studna, Carl)
PH02705 623 (February 6, 1992) p51. "The Yardbirds, Circa 1964 (from left): Chris Dreja, Keith Reif, Paul Samwell-Smith, Eric Clapton And Jim McCarty"
PH02706 643 (November 12, 1992) p65. "Clapton, Lennon, Mitchell And Richards (from left) In 1968" (Russell, Ethan)
PH02707 645-646 (December 10, 1992) p66. "Raitt Joins Slowhand Onstage At Wembley" (Ollerenshaw, Philip)
PH02708 647 (January 7, 1993) p11. "Eric Clapton" (Lowitt, Roxanne)
PH02709 649 (February 4, 1993) p51. "Clapton, Baker And Bruce Of Cream"
PH02710 651 (March 4, 1993) p50. "[Eric Clapton]" (Mazur, Kevin)
PH02711 651 (March 4, 1993) p16. "Eric Clapton And Robbie Robertson" (Granitz, Steve)
PH02712 654 (April 15, 1993) p11. "Eric Clapton" (Mayer, Jeffrey)
PH02713 654 (April 15, 1993) p19. "[Eric Clapton]" (Rasic, Brian)
PH02714 655 (April 29, 1993) p35. "The Aptly Named Blind Faith: Steve Winwood, Rick Grech, Ginger Baker And Clapton (from left)"
PH02715 655 (April 29, 1993) p35. "Clapton (right) On Tour With Delaney And Bonnie" (Cummins, Jim)
PH02716 655 (April 29, 1993) p34. "Clapton In 1969 Outside Olympic Studios, In Barnes, England, Where Blind Faith Recorded Its One And Only Album" (Gahr, David)
PH02717 655 (April 29, 1993) p34. "Clapton In 1969, As Blind Faith Skidded To Its Ignoble Halt..." (Wentzell, Barrie)
PH02718 655 (April 29, 1993) p35. "Clapton In The Mid-Seventies With The Real-Life Layla, Pattie Boyd" (Wiltshire, Graham)
PH02719 655 (April 29, 1993) p35. "Clapton In The Studio In 1971 With Howlin' Wolf, Recording The Wolf's Album London Sessions" (McDermand, Jo)
PH02720 655 (April 29, 1993) p38. "Clapton Onstage In January, Kicking Out The Jams Again With The Reunited Cream At The Rock & Roll Hall Of Fame Induction Ceremony" (Mazur, Kevin)
PH02721 655 (April 29, 1993) p38. "Clapton Performing This Year In London" (Rasic, Brian)
PH02722 655 (April 29, 1993) p37. "Clapton Taping The Original Video For 'Tears In Heaven,' His Tribute To His Late Son" (Blanshard, Richard)
PH02723 655 (April 29, 1993) p37. "Clapton With His Son Conor" (Young, Richard)
PH02724 655 (April 29, 1993) p34. "Clapton With John Mayall's Bluesbreakers At The Height Of God-mania in '66: Mayall, Hughie Flint, God And John McVie (from left)"
PH02725 655 (April 29, 1993) p37. "Clapton, Bill Wyman And Jeff Beck Onstage At London's Royal Albert Hall In September 1983, Performing At The ARMS Benefit Concerts" (Zuffante, Vinnie)
PH02726 655 (April 29, 1993) p35. "Derek And The Dominos: Jim Gordon, Carl Radle, Bobby Whitlock And Clapton (from left)..."
PH02727 655 (April 29, 1993) p34. "Eric Clapton As A Teenage Mod Lounging In London's Hyde Park In 1964, Halfway Through His Tenure With The Yardbirds"
PH02728 655 (April 29, 1993) p38. "The Guitarist At The Grammys In February" (Zuffante, Vinnie)
PH02729 655 (April 29, 1993) p35. "Muddy Waters, One Of Clapton's Earliest Blues Idols, Joins The Guitarist Onstage In Chicago In 1979..." (Natkin, Paul)
PH02730 655 (April 29, 1993) p37. "A Portrait Of The Guitarist As Journeyman In The Eighties" (Furmanovsky, Jill)
PH02731 655 (April 29, 1993) p38. "Rock's First Power Trio (Clapton, Baker and Bruce, from left) Basking In The Sunshine of History Backstage At The Hall Of Fame" (Mazur, Kevin)
PH02732 669 (November 11, 1993) p17. "Hendrix With Eric Clapton In London, Circa 1966"
PH02733 670 (November 25, 1993) p37. "[Eric Clapton, Z Z Top]" (Mason, Colin)
PH02734 672-673 (December 23, 1993) p20. "Grammy Gobblers Eric Clapton (left)..." (Meyer, Jeffrey)
PH02735 675 (February 10, 1994) p13. "'Unplugged' Put Clapton On Top" (Mazur, Kevin)
PH02736 677 (March 10, 1994) p29. "With The Band: Clapton And Robertson" (Mazur, Kevin)
PH02737 684 (June 16, 1994) p32. "The Bluesman Cometh: Clapton Plays To The Biz" (Beccaris, Rob)
PH02738 696 (December 1, 1994) p25. "Ms. Aykroyd (Donna Dixon), Eric Clapton, Uma Thurman And Dan Aykroyd (from left)" (Allen, David)
PH02739 698-699 (December 29, 1994) p36. "Famers Eric Clapton And Robbie Robertson (below)" (Mazur, Kevin)

PH02740 711 (June 29, 1995) p18. "B. B. King, Robert Cray, Buddy Guy, Art Neville, Jimmie Vaughan, Clapton, Raitt And Tommy Shannon" (Long, Andrew)
PH02741 730 (March 21, 1996) p33. "A Cool Clapton In Philadelphia, '77" (Putland, Michael)
PH02742 731 (April 4, 1996) p61. "Clapton Plays New Haven, Conn., In 1975" (Sia, Joe)
PH02743 738-739 (July 11, 1996) p15. "Clapton And Babyface In Hoboken, N.J. (really), For The 'Change The World'"
PH02744 746 (October 31, 1996) p17. "Clapton And Jakob Dylan, Who Did A Short Set With His Band, The Wallflowers" (Mazur, Kevin)
PH02745 Eri (December 12, 1991) p95. "" (Mazur, Kevin)
CLAPTON, ERIC—PHOTOGRAPHS—PORTRAITS
PH02746 615 (October 17, 1991) p43. "[Eric Clapton]" (Watson, Albert)
PH02747 615 (October 17, 1991) pp[cover]. "Eric Clapton's Blues" (Watson, Albert)
PH02748 619-620 (December 12, 1991) pp[cover]. "1991 Yearbook" (Watson, Albert)
PH02749 643 (November 12, 1992) p218. "Eric Clapton" (Watson, Albert)
PH02750 645-646 (December 10, 1992) p147. "Eric Clapton, 1968"
PH02751 655 (April 29, 1993) p35. "Clapton Announcing His Return To Active Duty At A Press Party In London On April 10th, 1974" (Stevens, Joseph)
PH02752 655 (April 29, 1993) p35. "Clapton taking A Rare Breather During An Otherwise Hectic Decade" (Preston, Neal)
PH02753 655 (April 29, 1993) pp[cover]. "Clapton: The Man & His Music" (Watson, Albert)
PH02754 655 (April 29, 1993) p34. "Cream In November 1996, Shortly Before The U.K. Release Of The Group's debut Album, Fresh Cream: Jack Bruce, Ginger Baker And Clapton (clockwise from left)" (Gale, Tony)
PH02755 655 (April 29, 1993) p35. "A Drug-Free Clapton During The Sessions For 461 Ocean Boulevard" (Gahr, David)
PH02756 655 (April 29, 1993) p34. "Slowhand (at bottom left) With The Yardbirds: Chris Dreja, Jim McCarty, Paul Samwell-Smith And Keith Relf (clockwise from top left)"
PH02757 672-673 (December 23, 1993) p188. "[Covers]" (Watson, Albert)
PH02758 735 (May 30, 1996) p3. "[The Faces Of Heroin]"
CLARIDGE, ERIC—PHOTOGRAPHS
PH02759 721 (November 16, 1995) p67. "The Sea And Cake: Art-Pop Aficionados Sam Prekop, John McEntire, Archer Prewitt And Eric Claridge (middle row, from left)" (Guip, Amy)
CLARK, DICK—PHOTOGRAPHS
PH02760 649 (February 4, 1993) p56. "[Dick Clark]"
PH02761 651 (March 4, 1993) p16. "Dick Clark With Teenagers Herman Santiago (left) And Jimmy Merchant" (Mazur, Kevin)
PH02762 731 (April 4, 1996) p33. "Clark With Madonna In 1984"
CLARK, GENE—PHOTOGRAPHS
PH02763 619-620 (December 12, 1991) p109. "Gene Clark"
CLARK, GUY—PHOTOGRAPHS
PH02764 653 (April 1, 1993) p24. "Backstage At The Troubadour In L.A." (Granitz, Steve)
CLARK, KEITH—PHOTOGRAPHS
PH02765 719 (October 19, 1995) p24. "Reuniting Hasn't Been Easy For The Circle Jerks: Keith Morris, Zander Schloss And Keith Clark (from left)" (Garcia, Willie)
CLARK, STEVE—PHOTOGRAPHS—PORTRAITS
PH02766 619-620 (December 12, 1991) p109. "Steve Clark" (Halfin, Ross)
CLARK-FRIESON, CHARLOTTE—PHOTOGRAPHS
PH02767 708 (May 18, 1995) p61. "The Head Of The Local NAACP Chapter, Charlotte Clark-Frieson, Was Also The Sole Black School-Board Member" (Mark, Mary Ellen)
CLARKE, GILBEY—ILLUSTRATIONS
PH02768 689 (August 25, 1994) p90. "Gilbey Clarke" (Fish, Jim)
CLARKE, GILBEY—PHOTOGRAPHS
PH02769 676 (February 24, 1994) p28. "Producer Waddy Wachtel And Gunmen Gilbey And Axl" (John, Robert)
CLARKE, GILBEY—PHOTOGRAPHS—PORTRAITS
PH02770 691 (September 22, 1994) p28. "Gilbey Clarke Seeks Solace In A Solo Album" (Johnson, Lisa)
CLARKE, MIKE—PHOTOGRAPHS—PORTRAITS
PH02771 675 (February 10, 1994) p15. "[Mike Clarke]"
CLARKE, VINCE—PHOTOGRAPHS
PH02772 722 (November 30, 1995) p20. "Hello, Darkness! Andy Bell, Johnston And Clarke (from left)" (Mazur, Kevin)
CLASH—ALBUMS
PH02773 617 (November 14, 1991) p124. "London Calling" (Lowry, Ray)
PH02774 617 (November 14, 1991) p124. "London Calling" (Smith, Pennie)
PH02775 634-635 (July 9, 1992) p4. "London Calling"
PH02776 637 (August 20, 1992) p4. "London Calling"
CLASS ACT (FILM)—PHOTOGRAPHS
PH02777 633 (June 25, 1992) p48. "Kid (left) 'N Play Rap With Rogers (left) And Parsons"
CLASS OF '61 (TELEVISION FILM)—PHOTOGRAPHS
PH02778 655 (April 29, 1993) p68. "Class Of '61"
CLAW HAMMER—PHOTOGRAPHS
PH02779 715 (August 24, 1995) p36. "Bagarozzi, Walther, Lee And Wahl" (Peterson, Charles)
CLAY, ANDREW DICE—PHOTOGRAPHS
PH02780 716 (September 7, 1995) p84. "Bless This House (left) With Cathy Moriarty And Andrew Clay: No Dice"
CLAYPOOL, LES—ILLUSTRATIONS
PH02781 664 (September 2, 1993) p5. "Les Claypool Of Primus" (Burke, Philip)
CLAYPOOL, LES—PHOTOGRAPHS
PH02782 654 (April 15, 1993) p16. "Les Claypool Of Primus Flanked By Two Guards Manning The Mosh Pit" (Blakesberg, Jay)
PH02783 662 (August 5, 1993) p14. "Les Claypool, Tim Alexander And Larry LaLonde (from left) Of Primus" (Blakesberg, Jay)
PH02784 664 (September 2, 1993) p16. "[Les Claypool]" (Blakesberg, Jay)
PH02785 681 (May 5, 1994) p21. "Primus's Les Claypool And Metallica's Jason Newsted" (Blakesberg, Jay)
PH02786 686-687 (July 14, 1994) p41. "Sausage Daze: Les Claypool" (Blakesberg, Jay)
PH02787 690 (September 8, 1994) p25. "[Les Claypool]" (Blakesberg, Jay)
CLAYPOOL, LES—PHOTOGRAPHS—PORTRAITS
PH02788 616 (October 31, 1991) p81. "Smooth Sailing: Guitarist Larry Lalonde, Drummer Tim Alexander And Bassist Les Claypool (clockwise from left)" (Seliger, Mark)
CLAYTON, ADAM—PHOTOGRAPHS
PH02789 627 (April 2, 1992) p11. "U2 Performs At A London Clothing Store: Bono (left) And Adam Clayton"
PH02790 636 (August 6, 1992) p11. "Adam Clayton, The Edge, Bono And Larry Mullen Jr. (from left)" (Thomas, Justin)
PH02791 640 (October 1, 1992) p48. "Bassist Adam Clayton (above)..." (Solomon, Mark)
PH02792 651 (March 4, 1993) p32. "Ad-hoc Automatic Baby: Mike Mills, Adam Clayton, Michael Stipe, Larry Mullen Jr." (Mazur, Kevin)
PH02793 667 (October 14, 1993) p54. "The Zoo Gang On Tour: The Edge, Bono, Larry Mullen Jr. And Adam Clayton (from left)" (Corbijn, Anton)
PH02794 672-673 (December 23, 1993) p16. "Mills, Clayton, Stipe And Mullen (from left)" (Mazur, Kevin)

PH02795 710 (June 15, 1995) p17. "[u2]" (Mazur, Kevin)
PH02796 714 (August 10, 1995) p30. "U2 Can Do Film Scores: Adam Clayton, Bono, The Edge, Larry Mullen (from left)" (Mazur, Kevin)
PH02797 726 (January 25, 1996) p30. "U2's Bono, Adam Clayton, The Edge And Larry Mullen Jr. (from left)" (Pasley, Richard)

CLAYTON, EVA—PHOTOGRAPHS
PH02798 682 (May 19, 1994) p43. "Reps. Cynthia McKinney, D-Ga., Carrie Meek, D-Fla., And Eva Clayton, D-N.C. (from left), Are Among The New Black Congresswomen..." (Borris, Dan)

CLEAN, SHAVEN (FILM)—PHOTOGRAPHS
PH02799 704 (March 23, 1995) p129. "Peter Greene Listens To Strange Voices"

CLEAR AND PRESENT DANGER (FILM)—PHOTOGRAPHS
PH02800 690 (September 8, 1994) p84. "[Clear And Present Danger]"

CLEAVER, CHUCK—PHOTOGRAPHS
PH02801 700 (January 26, 1995) p30. "From Left: Morrison, Cheek, Erhardt, Cleaver" (Ockenfels, Frank, 3)

CLEAVER, ELDRIDGE—PHOTOGRAPHS
PH02802 738-739 (July 11, 1996) p70. "With Eldridge Cleaver, 1970"

CLEGG, JOHNNY—PHOTOGRAPHS
PH02803 632 (June 11, 1992) p184. "The Nexus Between Music And Social Change: Clegg And Dudu Zulu (left) In Johannesburg" (Katzenstein, David)
PH02804 632 (June 11, 1992) p183. "'There's Always Been A Hidden, Invisible Middle Ground In South Africa Of Connections Between People And Cultures,' Said Clegg, Shown Here With Savuka Percussionist Dudu Zulu" (Kat

CLEMENTS, MARCELLE—PHOTOGRAPHS
PH02805 632 (June 11, 1992) p140. "The Author (center) With Some Friends In The Sixties" (Aaron, Peter)

CLEMONS, CLARENCE—PHOTOGRAPHS
PH02806 644 (November 26, 1992) p15. "Max Weinberg, Clarence Clemons, Darlene Love, Little Steven, Garry Tallent And Danny Federici (from left)" (Mazur, Kevin)

CLEO—PHOTOGRAPHS
PH02807 710 (June 15, 1995) p39. "Eisenstein, Scott Riebling, Hanley, Stacy Jones, Greg McKenna (from left)" (McDonough, Patricia)

CLERKS (FILM)—PHOTOGRAPHS
PH02808 694 (November 3, 1994) p104. "Clerks Anderson And O'Halloran Discuss The Forbidden"

CLEVELAND, ALFRED W.—PHOTOGRAPHS—PORTRAITS
PH02809 744 (October 3, 1996) p32. "[Alfred W. Cleveland]"

CLEVELAND, JAMES—PHOTOGRAPHS
PH02810 619-620 (December 12, 1991) p112. "The Reverend James Cleveland"

CLEWISTON, FLORIDA—PHOTOGRAPHS
PH02811 733 (May 2, 1996) p49. "Clewiston, Fla.: Workers Mill Cane Into Raw Sugar" (Tavee, Tom)

THE CLIENT (FILM)—ILLUSTRATIONS
PH02812 688 (August 11, 1994) p61. "Grisham's Law" (Woodruff, Thomas)

THE CLIENT (FILM)—PHOTOGRAPHS
PH02813 684 (June 16, 1994) p114. "Potential Blockbusters"
PH02814 688 (August 11, 1994) p62. "It's A Day In Court For Lawyer Sarandon And Renfro"
PH02815 691 (September 22, 1994) p106. "Woman Redeemed"

CLIFF, JIMMY—PHOTOGRAPHS
PH02816 676 (February 24, 1994) p41. "Veteran Reggae Vocalist Jimmy Cliff" (Barrett, Fitzroy)

CLIFFHANGER (FILM)—PHOTOGRAPHS
PH02817 659 (June 24, 1993) p88. "Thrills: 'Cliffhanger,' With Stallone"

CLIFFORD BALL (ROCK FESTIVAL)—PHOTOGRAPHS
PH02818 744 (October 3, 1996) p19. "Phish Fans At Clifford Ball, In Upstate New York" (Costello, Paul)
PH02819 750-751 (December 26, 1996) p74. "Phish Fans Overtake Plattsburgh, N.Y., Shrouding The City In A Los Angeles-Like Haze Of Pot Smoke"

CLIFFORD, DOUG—PHOTOGRAPHS—PORTRAITS
PH02820 649 (February 4, 1993) p48. "Drummer Clifford, Bassist Cook, Rhythm Guitarist Fogerty, Frontman Fogerty (clockwise from left)" (Wolman, Baron)

CLINE, PATSY—ALBUMS
PH02821 619-620 (December 12, 1991) p177. "The Patsy Cline Collection"

CLINTON, BILL—ILLUSTRATIONS
PH02822 626 (March 19, 1992) p6. "Clinton Takes A Trip" (Pendergrast, James T.)
PH02823 629 (April 30, 1992) p33. "[Bill Clinton]" (Cronin, Brian)
PH02824 630 (May 14, 1992) p3. "Bill Clinton" (Burke, Philip)
PH02825 630 (May 14, 1992) p89. "[Yale]" (Cowles, David)
PH02826 647 (January 7, 1993) p27. "[Politics]" (Cronin, Brian)
PH02827 649 (February 4, 1993) p29. "[Bill Clinton]" (Bishofs, Maris)
PH02828 653 (April 1, 1993) p28. "[Bill Clinton's Presidency]" (Cronin, Brian)
PH02829 657 (May 27, 1993) p28. "[Bill Clinton]" (Cronin, Brian)
PH02830 670 (November 25, 1993) p41. "[Health Care Reform]" (Oliphant)
PH02831 674 (January 27, 1994) p8. "Change Ahead: Watch Out For First Step" (Pendergrast, James T.)
PH02832 674 (January 27, 1994) p8. "Change: Apply Liberally" (Pendergrast, James T.)
PH02833 674 (January 27, 1994) p8. "Forward-Right-Backward-Left" (Pendergrast, James T.)
PH02834 675 (February 10, 1994) p25. "Clintonian Logic At Work" (Rall, Ted)
PH02835 678 (March 24, 1994) p6. "Plans-Reality" (Pendergrast, James T.)
PH02836 680 (April 21, 1994) p36. "Three Strikes And...We're Out...Of Money!!" (Morin, Jim)
PH02837 682 (May 19, 1994) p66. "[Bill Clinton]" (Friedman, Drew)
PH02838 688 (August 11, 1994) pp40-41. "[Bill Clinton]" (Kunz, Anita)
PH02839 694 (November 3, 1994) p45. "[Bill Clinton]" (Collier, John)
PH02840 702 (February 23, 1995) p41. "Stop The Bus, Bill, I Want To Get Off" (Witte, Michael)
PH02841 703 (March 9, 1995) p40. "Business As Usual: Wall Street Floats On A Multibillion-Dollar Life Preserver" (Witte, Michael)
PH02842 707 (May 4, 1995) p38. "A Tough Row To Hoe: Gingrich Trims The Federal Budget" (Witte, Michael)
PH02843 720 (November 2, 1995) p35. "I've Been Waiting Years For Someone To Dump Greenspan" (Witte, Michael)
PH02844 733 (May 2, 1996) p39. "[Bill Clinton & Bob Dole]" (Payne, C. F.)

CLINTON, BILL—PHOTOGRAPHS
PH02845 630 (May 14, 1992) p17. "[Bill Clinton]" (Trippett, Robert)
PH02846 630 (May 14, 1992) p19. "Clinton And A Member Of Jackie Lee And The Stickem Up Posse Band At A Fund-Raiser"
PH02847 636 (August 6, 1992) p22. "Clinton (left) 'Facing The Future' With The MTV Audience"
PH02848 639 (September 17, 1992) p42. "At The Table (from left): Greider, O'Rourke, Wenner, Thompson And Clinton" (Seliger, Mark)
PH02849 639 (September 17, 1992) p51. "Clinton: 'We're Still Fighting Yesterday's Battles'" (Seliger, Mark)
PH02850 639 (September 17, 1992) p55. "Dr. Thompson Ponders Clinton's Call For More Cops In The Street" (Seliger, Mark)

PH02851 642 (October 29, 1992) p78. "Bush And Clinton Fuss Before Air Time"
PH02852 645-646 (December 10, 1992) p196. "Bill Clinton (above) Had Nearly Blown It Before He Blew It On 'Arsenio'"
PH02853 645-646 (December 10, 1992) p98. "Clinton With Bonnie Raitt And Her Husband, Michael O'Keefe" (Jacobs, Michael)
PH02854 645-646 (December 10, 1992) p66. "Clinton With MTV's Soren" (Cohen, Lester)
PH02855 645-646 (December 10, 1992) p98. "Stills Greets Clinton At The Convention" (Jacobs, Michael)
PH02856 651 (March 4, 1993) p21. "Gala Groove: Hillary, Chelsea, Bill, Michael Jackson And Stevie Nicks" (Mazur, Kevin)
PH02857 660-661 (July 8, 1993) p18. "President Clinton Joins Living Colour During The Celebration"
PH02858 662 (August 5, 1993) p37. "Al Gore And Bill Clinton Introducing Newest Democrat, David Gergen, In May"
PH02859 663 (August 19, 1993) p61. "College Cabinet: William Clinton, Judith Baiocchi, David Kammer, Paul Maloy (from left)"
PH02860 663 (August 19, 1993) p63. "The Running Man: Bill Clinton Campaigned For Student Council President In 1967..."
PH02861 664 (September 2, 1993) p35. "President Clinton And Treasury Secretary Lloyd Bentsen In The Rose Garden In July For The Announcement Of The Administration's New Community-Banking Initiative"
PH02862 664 (September 2, 1993) p39. "With Bill Clinton And George Stephanopoulos, may 1993"
PH02863 670 (November 25, 1993) p85. "[Bill Clinton]" (Seliger, Mark)
PH02864 671 (December 9, 1993) pp[cover]. "President Clinton: Life In The Fast Lane" (Seliger, Mark)
PH02865 671 (December 9, 1993) p42. "[The Rolling Stone Interview of Bill Clinton]" (Seliger, Mark)
PH02866 672-673 (December 23, 1993) p188. "[Covers]" (Seliger, Mark)
PH02867 672-673 (December 23, 1993) p16. "Mr. And Mrs. President At The MTV Gala" (Mazur, Kevin)
PH02868 691 (September 22, 1994) p19. "Hootie Goes to Washington: Soni, Dean Felber, The Prez, Darius Rucker, Bryan (from left)"
PH02869 704 (March 23, 1995) p49. "Hail To The Chief: Clinton Introduces His Pick To Lead The CIA, Retired Air Force Gen. Carns" (Mills, Doug)
PH02870 711 (June 29, 1995) p33. "Ryder, Pirner, Band Manager Heaps, Murphy (background) And Ex-Drummer Young Greet Clinton (foreground) At The White House (from left)" (Markowitz, Jeffrey)
PH02871 720 (November 2, 1995) p17. "Good Lovin', They Got A Truckload: Belushi, Clinton And Gore In L.A."
CLINTON, BILL—PHOTOGRAPHS—PORTRAITS
PH02872 639 (September 17, 1992) p41. "[Bill Clinton]" (Seliger, Mark)
PH02873 639 (September 17, 1992) p41. "[Bill Clinton]" (Gagnon, Mark)
PH02874 639 (September 17, 1992) pp[cover]. "Bill Clinton: The Rolling Stone Interview" (Seliger, Mark)
PH02875 645-646 (December 10, 1992) pp[cover]. "1992 Yearbook" (Seliger, Mark)
PH02876 645-646 (December 10, 1992) p148. "Bill Clinton, 1992"
PH02877 663 (August 19, 1993) p57. "Bill Clinton At Georgetown: Not Rich Or Catholic But Still The BMOC"
PH02878 671 (December 9, 1993) pp41,44-45. "[Bill Clinton]" (Seliger, Mark)
PH02879 698-699 (December 29, 1994) p152. "[Bill Clinton]"
PH02880 730 (March 21, 1996) p51. "Clinton"
CLINTON, BILL—ADMINISTRATION—PHOTOGRAPHS
PH02881 663 (August 19, 1993) p37. "Please, Please, Please: The White House 'Oral Briefer Band' Serenading The Media At A Picnic In June" (Markel, Brad)
CLINTON, CHELSEA—PHOTOGRAPHS
PH02882 651 (March 4, 1993) p21. "Gala Groove: Hillary, Chelsea, Bill, Michael Jackson And Stevie Nicks" (Mazur, Kevin)
PH02883 743 (September 19, 1996) p19. "[Chelsea Clinton & George Clinton]" (Charbonneau, Eric)
PH02884 750-751 (December 26, 1996) p70. "Chelsea Clinton (center) And Long-Lost Uncle George Clinton (right) At Atlanta's House Of Blues" (Charbonneau, Eric)
CLINTON, GEORGE—ALBUMS
PH02885 674 (January 27, 1994) p54. "Hey Man...Smell My Finger"
PH02886 738-739 (July 11, 1996) p87. "T.A.P.O.A.F.O.M."
CLINTON, GEORGE—PHOTOGRAPHS
PH02887 651 (March 4, 1993) p17. "The New P-Folk? George Clinton, Jackson Browne And Don Was (from left)" (Mazur, Kevin)
PH02888 655 (April 29, 1993) p25. "Funk Meister Extraordinaire: Clinton" (Bauknight, Catherine)
PH02889 667 (October 14, 1993) p39. "Snoop, Shaquille O'Neal, George Clinton" (Mazur, Kevin)
PH02890 669 (November 11, 1993) p12. "Clinton Onstage With P-Funk In The Mid-1970s" (England, Thomas S.)
PH02891 669 (November 11, 1993) p11. "[George Clinton]" (Ragel, Jon)
PH02892 680 (April 21, 1994) p34. "Originator Little Richard With George Clinton" (Mazur, Kevin)
PH02893 712-713 (July 13, 1995) p25. "Don't Fear The Reefer" (Blakesberg, Jay)
PH02894 736 (June 13, 1996) p53. "Clinton (above right) Reunites With P-Funk"
PH02895 741 (August 22, 1996) p41. "The Mothership Connection: Clinton (left) And Bootsy Collins" (Watts, Mychal)
PH02896 743 (September 19, 1996) p19. "[Chelsea Clinton & George Clinton]" (Charbonneau, Eric)
PH02897 750-751 (December 26, 1996) p70. "Chelsea Clinton (center) And Long-Lost Uncle George Clinton (right) At Atlanta's House Of Blues" (Charbonneau, Eric)
CLINTON, GEORGE—PHOTOGRAPHS—PORTRAITS
PH02898 669 (November 11, 1993) p11. "[George Clinton]" (Ragel, Jon)
PH02899 696 (December 1, 1994) p38. "Clinton" (Ockenfels, Frank, 3)
CLINTON, HILLARY RODHAM—ILLUSTRATIONS
PH02900 670 (November 25, 1993) p41. "[Health Care Reform]" (Oliphant)
CLINTON, HILLARY RODHAM—PHOTOGRAPHS
PH02901 651 (March 4, 1993) p21. "Gala Groove: Hillary, Chelsea, Bill, Michael Jackson And Stevie Nicks" (Mazur, Kevin)
PH02902 665 (September 16, 1993) p35. "Federal Reserve Chairman Alan Greenspan With The First Lady And Tipper Gore At The State Of The Union"
PH02903 672-673 (December 23, 1993) p16. "Mr. And Mrs. President At The MTV Gala" (Mazur, Kevin)
PH02904 698-699 (December 29, 1994) p37. "David Letterman's Mom (left) Bonds With Hillary Clinton"
PH02905 732 (April 18, 1996) p61. "John Sculley (left) With Hillary Clinton"
CLINTON, ROGER—PHOTOGRAPHS
PH02906 645-646 (December 10, 1992) p196. "His Half-Brother, Roger, Serenaded John Ritter And Markie Post On 'Hearts Afire'"
CLIVILLES, ROBERT—PHOTOGRAPHS
PH02907 626 (March 19, 1992) p11. "Freedom Williams, David Cole, Robert Clivilles, Zelma Davis (from left)" (Mazur, Kevin)
CLOCKERS (FILM)—PHOTOGRAPHS
PH02908 717 (September 21, 1995) p89. "Keitel And Lee On The Case"

PH02909 717 (September 21, 1995) p89. "Phifer On The Spot"
CLOONEY, GEORGE—PHOTOGRAPHS
PH02910 728 (February 22, 1996) p70. "Now Playing"
CLOSE (VIDEO)—PHOTOGRAPHS
PH02911 667 (October 14, 1993) p78. "Art(ful) Destruction: 'Close (To The Edit)'"
CLOSE, GLENN—PHOTOGRAPHS
PH02912 618 (November 28, 1991) p104. "Diva Glenn Close Enjoys A Nonfatal Attraction"
PH02913 677 (March 10, 1994) p60. "Streep And Close Play Ball (left), While Ryder And Her Lover, Banderas, Play Around"
PH02914 697 (December 15, 1994) p102. "Glenn Close Onstage Recalls Swanson In "Sunset Blvd.""
PH02915 702 (February 23, 1995) p81. "Atten-tion! Close"
CLOUTIER, SUZANNE—PHOTOGRAPHS
PH02916 626 (March 19, 1992) p104. "Jealousy Destroys Welles And Cloutier"
CLUB 662 (NIGHTCLUB)—PHOTOGRAPHS
PH02917 746 (October 31, 1996) p40. "[Club 662]"
CLUELESS (FILM)—ILLUSTRATIONS
PH02918 714 (August 10, 1995) p61. "Kids Today" (Tillery, Bob)
PH02919 714 (August 10, 1995) p61. "Kids Today" (Tillery, Val)
CLUELESS (FILM)—PHOTOGRAPHS
PH02920 709 (June 1, 1995) p68. "back-To-School Bashes"
PH02921 714 (August 10, 1995) p62. "Dash And Silverstone Phone It In At High School"
PH02922 716 (September 7, 1995) p78. "Summer Wrap-Up]"
PH02923 731 (April 4, 1996) p66. "Clueless"
PH02924 741 (August 22, 1996) p104. "Silverstone As Her Clueless Update"
COATS, DAN—PHOTOGRAPHS—PORTRAITS
PH02925 722 (November 30, 1995) p47. "[Dan Coats]" (Downing, Larry)
COBAIN, FRANCES BEAN—ILLUSTRATIONS
PH02926 672-673 (December 23, 1993) p73. "[Courtney Love]" (Ryden, Mark)
COBAIN, FRANCES BEAN—PHOTOGRAPHS
PH02927 672-673 (December 23, 1993) p39. "Family Feud: Frances Bean, Kurt, Courtney" (Mazur, Kevin)
PH02928 682 (May 19, 1994) p18. "Frances, Love And Cobain" (Kravitz, Jeff)
PH02929 683 (June 2, 1994) p55. "Cobain And Daughter Backstage Last Fall" (Mazur, Kevin)
PH02930 683 (June 2, 1994) p33. "Father And Daughter" (Guzman)
PH02931 683 (June 2, 1994) p36. "The Mourning After: Love Wanders With Frances Bean In A Park Near Their Home On April 9" (Rexroad, James)
PH02932 683 (June 2, 1994) p32. "With Wife Love And Daughter Frances Bean" (Guzman)
PH02933 697 (December 15, 1994) p66. "In Happier Times: Love And Cobain Celebrate Frances Bean's First Christmas, In 1992"
PH02934 720 (November 2, 1995) p16. "[Courtney Love]"
PH02935 748 (November 28, 1996) p30. "Holding Pattern: Frances Bean Cobain With One Of The Many Nannies She's Known, Stacey Hubbard" (Seliger, Mark)
COBAIN, FRANCES—PHOTOGRAPHS
PH02936 667 (October 14, 1993) p39. "Above: Nirvana's Dave Grohl And Kurt Cobain Flanking RuPaul And Frances Cobain" (Kravitz, Jeff)
COBAIN, GARY—PHOTOGRAPHS
PH02937 721 (November 16, 1995) p73. "Brian Dougans (left) And Gary Cobain: Future Shock And Techno Reflections" (Broad, Julian)
COBAIN, KURT—ILLUSTRATIONS
PH02938 622 (January 23, 1992) p3. "Kurt Cobain Of Nirvana" (Burke, Philip)
PH02939 677 (March 10, 1994) p12. "Neurosis-Psychosis" (Pendergrast, James T.)
PH02940 683 (June 2, 1994) p11. "[Kurt Cobain]" (Watson, Esther)
PH02941 683 (June 2, 1994) p7. "Kurt Cobain" (Burke, Philip)
PH02942 686-687 (July 14, 1994) p14. "Kurt" (Pendergrast, James T.)
PH02943 692 (October 6, 1994) p12. "Entering Nirvana" (Pendergrast, James T.)
PH02944 692 (October 6, 1994) p12. "Human Enough" (Pendergrast, James T.)
PH02945 695 (November 17, 1994) p58. "Nirvana" (Ryden, Mark)
COBAIN, KURT—PHOTOGRAPHS
PH02946 622 (January 23, 1992) pp38-39. "Kurt Cobain" (Broad, Julian)
PH02947 624 (February 20, 1992) p19. "Kurt Cobain" (Constanini, Mark)
PH02948 628 (April 16, 1992) pp36-37. "Guitarist Kurt Cobain" (Seliger, Mark)
PH02949 642 (October 29, 1992) p19. "Cobain, Love And Baby Frances" (Mazur, Kevin)
PH02950 642 (October 29, 1992) p39. "Loving Husband And Father: Kurt Cobain" (Taylor, Chris)
PH02951 647 (January 7, 1993) p13. "Kurt Cobain" (Hutson, Mick)
PH02952 653 (April 1, 1993) p20. "Nirvana's Chris Novoselic, Kurt Cobain And Dave Grohl (clockwise from top)" (Watermann, Greg)
PH02953 655 (April 29, 1993) p11. "Hurt Cobain" (Day, Jeff)
PH02954 657 (May 27, 1993) p25. "Never Mind: Kurt Cobain" (Blakesberg, Jay)
PH02955 659 (June 24, 1993) p21. "Nirvs: Grohl, Novoselic, Cobain (from left)" (Sirrs, Ed)
PH02956 664 (September 2, 1993) p31. "Feedback Freak: Nirvana's Kurt Cobain" (Mazur, Kevin)
PH02957 666 (September 30, 1993) p28. "Kurt Cobain (left) And Chris Novoselic" (Andeel, Michael)
PH02958 667 (October 14, 1993) p39. "Above: Nirvana's Dave Grohl And Kurt Cobain Flanking RuPaul And Frances Cobain" (Kravitz, Jeff)
PH02959 672-673 (December 23, 1993) p64. "Cobain: This Is What He Looks Like Out Of Utero" (Mazur, Kevin)
PH02960 672-673 (December 23, 1993) p39. "Family Feud: Frances Bean, Kurt, Courtney" (Mazur, Kevin)
PH02961 672-673 (December 23, 1993) p54. "Kurt Cobain: Seminar Surprise" (Mazur, Kevin)
PH02962 674 (January 27, 1994) p36. "Team Spirit: Novoselic, Smear, Grohl, Cobain And Touring Cellist Lori Goldston (from left)" (Seliger, Mark)
PH02963 674 (January 27, 1994) p38. "Young Nirvana: Ex-Drummer Chad Channing, Novoselic, Cobain In '88 (from left)" (Peterson, Charles)
PH02964 676 (February 24, 1994) p29. "Nirvana's Kurt Cobain: A Lollapaloozer" (Blakesberg, Jay)
PH02965 682 (May 19, 1994) p20. "Angel Of America: Cobain On 'In Utero' Tour In '93" (Kravitz, Jeff)
PH02966 682 (May 19, 1994) p18. "The Band And The Family: Grohl, Novoselic And Cobain (above)" (Huntington, Jane)
PH02967 682 (May 19, 1994) p18. "Frances, Love And Cobain" (Kravitz, Jeff)
PH02968 683 (June 2, 1994) p63. "Booming Catharsis: Kurt Cobain Onstage At Vancouver's Commodore Ballroom In April 1991" (Peterson, Charles)
PH02969 683 (June 2, 1994) p52. "Channing, Short-term Guitarist Jason Everman, Novoselic, Cobain 1989" (Wheeler, Alice)
PH02970 683 (June 2, 1994) p55. "Cobain And Daughter Backstage Last Fall" (Mazur, Kevin)

PH02971 683 (June 2, 1994) p67. "Cobain At England's 1992 Reading Festival"
PH02972 683 (June 2, 1994) p31. "Cobain At Home In L.A., Fall 1992" (Guzman)
PH02973 683 (June 2, 1994) p56. "Cobain Enters Reading In Wheelchair" (Peterson, Charles)
PH02974 683 (June 2, 1994) p35. "Cobain Lay Dead In A Room Above His Garage For Days" (Reese, Tom)
PH02975 683 (June 2, 1994) p61. "Cobain On New Year's Day, Seattle 1993" (Peterson, Charles)
PH02976 683 (June 2, 1994) p45. "Cobain Photographed By Girlfriend Tracy Marander In Their Olympia Home, 1989" (Marander, Tracy)
PH02977 683 (June 2, 1994) p33. "Father And Daughter" (Guzman)
PH02978 683 (June 2, 1994) p35. "Headed To The Hospital After Rome Suicide Attempt" (Sestini, Massimo)
PH02979 683 (June 2, 1994) p32. "With Wife Love And Daughter Frances Bean" (Guzman)
PH02980 691 (September 22, 1994) p54. "Kurt Cobain With Kim Gordon On Nirvana's 1991 Tour With Sonic Youth" (Moore, T.)
PH02981 697 (December 15, 1994) p66. "In Happier Times: Love And Cobain Celebrate Frances Bean's First Christmas, In 1992"
PH02982 697 (December 15, 1994) p64. "Love And Cobain In A Quiet Embrace" (Guzman)
PH02983 698-699 (December 29, 1994) p50. "[Kurt Cobain]" (Micelotta, Frank)
PH02984 698-699 (December 29, 1994) p86. "Kurt Cobain" (Seliger, Mark)
PH02985 700 (January 26, 1995) p50. "Rock & Roll Never Forgets: Kurt Cobain, 1967-1994" (Ockenfels, Frank W.)
PH02986 714 (August 10, 1995) p24. "Courtney Love; Goldberg's Wife, Rosemary Carroll; Goldberg; Kurt Cobain In '93" (Kravitz, Jeff)
PH02987 724-725 (December 28, 1995) p128. "Kurt Cobain Performs A Drum Solo—His Way" (Peterson, Charles)
PH02988 727 (February 8, 1996) p22. "Nirvana Was Always Political: Novoselic, Cobain And Grohl (from left) In London, 1993"
PH02989 735 (May 30, 1996) p16. "[Kurt Cobain]" (Peterson, Charles)

COBAIN, KURT—PHOTOGRAPHS—PORTRAITS
PH02990 669 (November 11, 1993) p13. "Kurt Cobain: Off The Wal-Mart" (Kravitz, Jeff)
PH02991 674 (January 27, 1994) p35. "[Kurt Cobain]" (Seliger, Mark)
PH02992 680 (April 21, 1994) p20. "[Kurt Cobain]" (Hoselton, Charles B.)
PH02993 682 (May 19, 1994) p17. "[Kurt Cobain]" (Micelotta, Frank)
PH02994 683 (June 2, 1994) p51. "Kurt At 5: He Was An Artistic, Inquisitive And Energetic Child"
PH02995 683 (June 2, 1994) pp[cover]. "Kurt Cobain 1967-1994" (Seliger, Mark)
PH02996 683 (June 2, 1994) p40. "Tributes To Cobain Burned Bright At The Seattle Vigil" (Winters, Dan)
PH02997 697 (December 15, 1994) p60. "Till Death Do Us Part"
PH02998 698-699 (December 29, 1994) p1. "Kurt Cobain 1967-1994" (Seliger, Mark)
PH02999 718 (October 5, 1995) p43. "Nirvana In 1993 During The 'In Utero' Tour: Pat Smear, Kurt Cobain, Dave Grohl, Krist Novoselic (clockwise from right)" (Lenquette, Youri)
PH03000 735 (May 30, 1996) p3. "[The Faces Of Heroin]"

COBB (FILM)—PHOTOGRAPHS
PH03001 697 (December 15, 1994) p104. "Tommy Lee Jones Plays Ty Cobb In Glory And In Disgrace"
PH03002 698-699 (December 29, 1994) p194. "Jones Swings In "Cobb""
PH03003 705 (April 6, 1995) p69. "Oscar Rejects"

COCA-COLA—ILLUSTRATIONS
PH03004 688 (August 11, 1994) p17. "I Hate Myself And Want A Soda" (Rosenthal, Marc)

COCAINE—PHOTOGRAPHS
PH03005 660-661 (July 8, 1993) p82. "'Tom' (left), 'Greg' (third from left) And Coke After Lauderdale Bust"

COCHISE, SILAS—PHOTOGRAPHS—PORTRAITS
PH03006 736 (June 13, 1996) p68. "Silas Cochise, Great-Grandson Of The Warrior" (Barker, Kent)

COCHRAN, JOHNNIE—PHOTOGRAPHS
PH03007 724-725 (December 28, 1995) p58. "The American Way: F. Lee Bailey, Simpson, Johnnie Cochran" (Chun, Myung J.)

COCHRANE, RORY—PHOTOGRAPHS
PH03008 667 (October 14, 1993) p128. "School Daze For Cochrane, London And Jenson"

COCKBURN, BRUCE—PHOTOGRAPHS
PH03009 623 (February 6, 1992) p11. "Sam Phillips Joins Bruce Cockburn Onstage" (Ienner, Jimmy, Jr.)
PH03010 638 (September 3, 1992) p11. "Rob Wasserman, Bob Weir, Michelle Shocked And Bruce Cockburn (from left)" (Kravitz, Jeff)
PH03011 649 (February 4, 1993) p8. "Cash, Cockburn And Reed (from left)" (Ienner, Jimmy, Jr.)

COCKER, JARVIS—ILLUSTRATIONS
PH03012 736 (June 13, 1996) p58. "Jarvis Cocker" (Cowles, David)

COCKER, JARVIS—PHOTOGRAPHS
PH03013 731 (April 4, 1996) p30. "Feeling Cheeky: Pulp's Jarvis Cocker" (Double, Steve)
PH03014 732 (April 18, 1996) p24. "A Wildly Unorthodox Mixture Of Influence Gathered Around The Table: Pulp's Candida Doyle, Mark Webber, Cocker, Steve Mackey, Russell Senior And Nick Banks (from left)" (Rankin)
PH03015 738-739 (July 11, 1996) p92. "Cocker Launches Pulp's U.S. Tour In San Francisco" (Blakesberg, Jay)
PH03016 742 (September 5, 1996) p20. "[Jarvis Cocker & Karen Mulder]" (Barritt, Craig)
PH03017 750-751 (December 26, 1996) p50. "Who's Bad? Cheeky Brit Jarvis Cocker Of Pulp" (Young, Richard)

COCTEAU TWINS—ALBUMS
PH03018 677 (March 10, 1994) p64. "Four-Calendar Cafe"

CODEINE—ALBUMS
PH03019 682 (May 19, 1994) p120. "The White Birch"

CODEINE—PHOTOGRAPHS
PH03020 621 (January 9, 1992) p25. "Codeine (from left): John Engle, Chris Brokaw And Stephen Immerwahr" (Capak, R. J.)

COEN, ETHAN—PHOTOGRAPHS
PH03021 730 (March 21, 1996) p104. "The Coens Flank Deakins"

COEN, JOEL—PHOTOGRAPHS
PH03021 730 (March 21, 1996) p104. "The Coens Flank Deakins"

COFFEE SHOPS—ILLUSTRATIONS
PH03022 727 (February 8, 1996) p13. "The Anti-Spago" (Sutton, Ward)

COFFEY, KING—PHOTOGRAPHS
PH03023 659 (June 24, 1993) p25. "Gibby Haynes, Jeff Pinkus, Paul Leary And King Coffey (clockwise from top)" (Watermann, Greg)
PH03024 710 (June 15, 1995) p54. "Surf Thing: Coffey, Haynes, Leary (from left)" (Van Overbeek, Will)
PH03025 738-739 (July 11, 1996) p28. "Surfers' King Coffey, Gibby Haynes, Paul Leary (from left)" (Van Overbeek, Will)
PH03026 750-751 (December 26, 1996) p116. "King Coffey Lounges (below)" (Vadukul, Nitin)

COHEN, GREG—PHOTOGRAPHS
PH03027 743 (September 19, 1996) p72. "Comedy Is A Great Passive-Aggressive Tool" (Seliger, Mark)

COHEN, HERB—PHOTOGRAPHS
PH03028 747 (November 14, 1996) p76. "Joe Garagiola, Larry And Herb Cohen (from left) In 1988"

PH03029 747 (November 14, 1996) p78. "Larry And Herbie (top row, from left), Warriors On The Stoop In Bensonhurst"
PH03030 747 (November 14, 1996) p81. "Live From New York's Governors Island, 1984: Larry, Gov. Mario Cuomo, Herb Cohen (from left)"
PH03031 747 (November 14, 1996) p78. "Warriors, 1946: Larry (with bottle) Standing Next To Herbie (center)"
PH03032 747 (November 14, 1996) p81. "Washington, D.C., 1988: Writer George Will With Larry And Herb Cohen (from left)" (Naltchayan, Neshan)
COHEN, JASON—PHOTOGRAPHS
PH03033 694 (November 3, 1994) p17. "Pumpkin Billy Corgan, Love, Cohen, Krugman (from left)"
COHEN, LEONARD—ALBUMS
PH03034 647 (January 7, 1993) p45. "The Future"
COHEN, LEONARD—ILLUSTRATIONS
PH03035 647 (January 7, 1993) p44. "Bob Dylan Looks Back, But For Leonard Cohen, The Future Is Murder" (Cowles, David)
COHEN, LEONARD—PHOTOGRAPHS
PH03036 618 (November 28, 1991) p12. "Leonard Cohen"
PH03037 648 (January 21, 1993) p44. "[Leonard Cohen]" (Weber, Bruce)
PH03038 662 (August 5, 1993) p28. "Leonard Cohen In New York" (Busacca, Larry)
COHEN, RICH—PHOTOGRAPHS
PH03039 747 (November 14, 1996) p76. "Larry (center) With The Author (second from right) In 1995 At A Fund-Raiser"
COHN, MARK—PHOTOGRAPHS—PORTRAITS
PH03040 619-620 (December 12, 1991) p49. "Mark Cohn (left)..." (Carroll, Chris)
COLBOURN, CHRIS—PHOTOGRAPHS
PH03041 665 (September 16, 1993) pp[enc.45]. "Above From Left: Chris Colbourn, Friend Debra Monaco, Tom Maginnis And Bill Janovitz" (Newton, Philip)
PH03042 665 (September 16, 1993) pp[enc.5]. "[Buffalo Tom]" (Newton, Philip)
PH03043 665 (September 16, 1993) pp[enc.54]. "[Chris Colbourn]" (Newton, Philip)
PH03044 672-673 (December 23, 1993) p65. "Tom Maginnis, Janovitz And Chris Colbourn" (Robicheau, Paul)
PH03045 683 (June 2, 1994) p27. "Race Music: B.T.'s Chris Colbourn" (Robicheau, Paul)
COLD COMFORT FARM (FILM)—PHOTOGRAPHS
PH03046 735 (May 30, 1996) p57. "Life On The Farm"
COLD WAR—ILLUSTRATIONS
PH03047 676 (February 24, 1994) p10. "[Market Solution]" (Pendergrast, James T.)
COLE, DAVID—PHOTOGRAPHS
PH03048 615 (October 17, 1991) p14. "Mariah Carey, David Cole" (Mazur, Kevin)
PH03049 626 (March 19, 1992) p11. "Freedom Williams, David Cole, Robert Clivilles, Zelma Davis (from left)" (Mazur, Kevin)
COLE, GARY—PHOTOGRAPHS
PH03050 716 (September 7, 1995) p84. "Gary Cole's Psycho Psychic Cop From American Gothic"
COLE, LLOYD—ALBUMS
PH03051 623 (February 6, 1992) p83. "Don't Get Weird On Me, Babe"
PH03052 693 (October 20, 1994) p150. "Bad Vibes"
COLE, LLOYD—PHOTOGRAPHS
PH03053 623 (February 6, 1992) p29. "Lloyd Cole" (Mazur, Kevin)
COLE, LLOYD—PHOTOGRAPHS—PORTRAITS
PH03054 619-620 (December 12, 1991) p79. "[Lloyd Cole]" (Donaldson, Matthew)
COLE, NAT KING—PHOTOGRAPHS
PH03055 678 (March 24, 1994) p14. "Juggy Gayles, The Moses Of Promo..."
COLE, NATALIE—ALBUMS
PH03056 664 (September 2, 1993) p61. "Take A Look"
COLE, NATALIE—PHOTOGRAPHS
PH03057 628 (April 16, 1992) p11. "Metallica (from left): Ulrich, James Hetfield, Kirk Hammett And Jason Newsted" (Mazur, Kevin)
PH03058 628 (April 16, 1992) p11. "Natalie Cole Shows Off Her Hardware" (Mazur, Kevin)
PH03059 629 (April 30, 1992) p11. "Dress Rehearsal For The Rain-Forest Benefit: Sting, John, Goldberg, Cole, Henley And Taylor (from left)" (Regan, Ken)
PH03060 629 (April 30, 1992) p11. "Natalie Cole Waltzes Sting" (Regan, Ken)
PH03061 645-646 (December 10, 1992) p32. "Natalie Cole"
PH03062 651 (March 4, 1993) p17. "Natalie Cole Inducting Dinah Washington" (Mazur, Kevin)
COLE, NATALIE—PHOTOGRAPHS—PORTRAITS
PH03063 619-620 (December 12, 1991) p53. "...And Natalie Cole (below)" (Grecco, Michael)
COLE, PAULA—PHOTOGRAPHS
PH03064 686-687 (July 14, 1994) p78. "[Paula Cole]"
PH03065 707 (May 4, 1995) p20. "[Sarah McLaughlan & Paula Cole]" (Olson, Sheryl)
COLE, RICHARD—BOOKS
PH03066 645-646 (December 10, 1992) p88. "[Stairway To Heaven]"
COLEMAN, CLAUDE—PHOTOGRAPHS
PH03067 705 (April 6, 1995) p30. "Claude Coleman, Drums" (Clinch, Danny)
COLEMAN, DABNEY—PHOTOGRAPHS
PH03068 692 (October 6, 1994) p94. "Working Girl: Mad dad Dabney Coleman With Cynthia Gibb"
COLEMAN, JAMIE—ILLUSTRATIONS
PH03069 748 (November 28, 1996) p139. "[Men Behaving Badly]" (Ciardiello, Joe)
COLEMAN, JAZ—PHOTOGRAPHS
PH03070 692 (October 6, 1994) p17. "Strange Bedfellows: Iggy Pop (left) And Killing Joke's Jaz Coleman" (Knaeps, Gie)
COLEMAN, ORNETTE—ALBUMS
PH03071 723 (December 14, 1995) p84. "Tone Dialing"
COLEMAN, RAY—PHOTOGRAPHS—PORTRAITS
PH03072 747 (November 14, 1996) p32. "[Ray Coleman]" (Plummer, Barry)
COLEMAN, WANDA—PHOTOGRAPHS
PH03073 662 (August 5, 1993) p20. "[Wanda Coleman]" (Estrine, Darryl)
COLETTA, KIM—PHOTOGRAPHS
PH03074 678 (March 24, 1994) p20. "Barocas, Robbins, Coletta, Barbot (from left)" (Falls, John)
COLIN, GREGOIRE—PHOTOGRAPHS
PH03075 650 (February 18, 1993) p66. "Gregoire Colin Is More Than A Brother To Marina Golovine"
COLLARD, CYRIL—PHOTOGRAPHS
PH03076 675 (February 10, 1994) p53. "Unsafe Sex: Collard (left) And Bohringer"
COLLECTIVE SOUL—ALBUMS
PH03077 710 (June 15, 1995) p83. "Collective Soul"
COLLECTIVE SOUL—PHOTOGRAPHS
PH03078 686-687 (July 14, 1994) p30. "Soul Men: Childress, Evans, Dean Roland, Turpin And Ed Roland (clockwise from top left)" (Callahan, Kristin)
COLLEN, PHIL—PHOTOGRAPHS
PH03079 629 (April 30, 1992) p39. "Def Leppard Guitarist Phil Collen And Bass Player Rick Savage" (Seliger, Mark)
PH03080 667 (October 14, 1993) p26. "Rick Savage, Phil Collen, Vivian Campbell, Rick Allen And Joe Elliott" (Halfin, Ross)
PH03081 724-725 (December 28, 1995) p58. "Def Leppard's Phil Collen And Joe Elliot Flank Fans In Tangier"
COLLETTE, TONI—PHOTOGRAPHS
PH03082 704 (March 23, 1995) p128. "The Big Day Is Here At Last For Toni Collette"

COLLEY, DANA—PHOTOGRAPHS
PH03083 686-687 (July 14, 1994) p36. "Morphine's Sandman, Conway And Colley (from left)" (Lyden, Paul)
PH03084 711 (June 29, 1995) p20. "Masters Of 'Implied Grunge': Colley, Sandman, Conway (from left)" (Ockenfels, Frank W.)
COLLEY, DANA—PHOTOGRAPHS—PORTRAITS
PH03085 667 (October 14, 1993) p30. "Mark Sandman, Dana Colley And Bill Conway" (Eichner, Steve)
COLLIE, JOHN—PHOTOGRAPHS
PH03086 615 (October 17, 1991) p28. "John Collie, Shayne Carter, Andrew Brough, David Wood (from left)" (Blakesberg, Jay)
COLLINS, ALBERT—PHOTOGRAPHS
PH03087 674 (January 27, 1994) p22. "[Albert Collins]" (Sievert, Jon)
COLLINS, BOOTSY—PHOTOGRAPHS
PH03088 723 (December 14, 1995) p28. "Kravitz (left) And Collins Funk It Up In Los Angeles"
PH03089 741 (August 22, 1996) p41. "The Mothership Connection: Clinton (left) And Bootsy Collins" (Watts, Mychal)
COLLINS, BOOTSY—PHOTOGRAPHS—PORTRAITS
PH03090 691 (September 22, 1994) p32. "[Bootsy Collins]" (Rice, Ted)
COLLINS, EDWYN—ALBUMS
PH03091 719 (October 19, 1995) p153. "Gorgeous George"
COLLINS, GLENN—PHOTOGRAPHS
PH03092 657 (May 27, 1993) p16. "Auteur, Auteur: Banbury, Haines, Collins And Readman (clockwise from left)" (Lass, Imke)
COLLINS, MARCO—PHOTOGRAPHS
PH03093 723 (December 14, 1995) p32. "Seattle Programmer Collins (center) With Members Of Elastica" (Mason, Karen)
COLLINS, MICHAEL—PHOTOGRAPHS
PH03094 689 (August 25, 1994) p84. "Michael Collins At The Reach Networks Office, in Manhattan" (Newton, Philip)
COLLINS, PHIL—ALBUMS
PH03095 675 (February 10, 1994) p43. "Both Sides"
COLLINS, PHIL—ILLUSTRATIONS
PH03096 672-673 (December 23, 1993) p10. "It's All About Me!" (Pendergrast, James T.)
COLLINS, PHIL—PHOTOGRAPHS
PH03097 624 (February 20, 1992) p17. "Genesis, From Left: Tony Banks, Mike Rutherford And Phil Collins" (Ockenfels, Frank W.)
PH03098 734 (May 16, 1996) p29. "Collins: Too Talented For One Band" (Douglas Brothers)
COLLINS, ROB—PHOTOGRAPHS—PORTRAITS
PH03099 742 (September 5, 1996) p26. "[Rob Collins]" (Sheehan, Tom)
COLLISTER, CRAIG—PHOTOGRAPHS
PH03100 704 (March 23, 1995) p69. "Collister Of Michigan Bit Bands To Be Butch" (Mastroianni, Roger)
COLOHAN, PETER—PHOTOGRAPHS
PH03101 666 (September 30, 1993) p90. "Hunt (third from left, bottom row) With Delta Lambda Phi Brothers (clockwise from top right): Peter Colohan, Sean McClafferty, Rob Corwin, Price, Stephen Smith And Oligmueller"
COLON, RICHARD—PHOTOGRAPHS
PH03102 638 (September 3, 1992) pp[enc.42]. "[Jossie Harris, Ken Swift, Richard Colon]" (Eccles, Andrew)
PH03103 638 (September 3, 1992) pp[enc.40-41]. "[Richard Colon]" (Eccles, Andrew)
COLOR OF NIGHT (FILM)—PHOTOGRAPHS
PH03104 691 (September 22, 1994) p106. "Bombs Away"
COLT, JOHNNY—PHOTOGRAPHS
PH03105 642 (October 29, 1992) p19. "Black Crowes Marc Ford, Johnny Colt And Chris Robinson (from left) With Guest Rehearser And Show Host Dana Carvey" (Mazur, Kevin)
COLTRANE, JOHN—ALBUMS
PH03106 708 (May 18, 1995) p87. "Live In Seattle"
COLTRANE, JOHN—PHOTOGRAPHS
PH03107 617 (November 14, 1991) p42. "Miles With John Coltrane (right), 1955"
COLTRANE, RAVI—PHOTOGRAPHS—PORTRAITS
PH03108 656 (May 13, 1993) p72. "[Ravi Coltrane]" (Douthart, Bill)
COLVIN, MONTY—PHOTOGRAPHS
PH03109 617 (November 14, 1991) p34. "Ben Huggins, Alan Doss, Monty Colvin And Dane Sonnier (from left)" (Carter, Keith)
COLVIN, SHAWN—ALBUMS
PH03110 647 (January 7, 1993) p47. "Fat City"
PH03111 697 (December 15, 1994) p98. "Cover Girl"
COLVIN, SHAWN—PHOTOGRAPHS
PH03112 649 (February 4, 1993) p58. "[Shawn Colvin]" (Camp, E. J.)
PH03113 667 (October 14, 1993) p40. "Steady On: Shawn Colvin For Choice" (Diltz, Henry)
COMBS, SEAN—PHOTOGRAPHS
PH03114 706 (April 20, 1995) p24. "Combs: 'When I'm Hearing Sounds, I'm Always Looking For Something Different'" (Lavine, Michael)
COMBUSTIBLE EDISON—PHOTOGRAPHS
PH03115 690 (September 8, 1994) p24. "Members Of The Combustible Edison And Black Velvet Flag Pay Homage To Their Mentor" (Mazur, Kevin)
COME—ALBUMS
PH03116 655 (April 29, 1993) p63. "Eleven: Eleven"
PH03117 740 (August 8, 1996) p58. "Near Life Experience"
COME—PHOTOGRAPHS
PH03118 654 (April 15, 1993) p22. "They've Arrived: Arthur Johnson, Sean O'Brien, Thalia Zedek And Chris Brokaw" (Westenberg, Kevin)
PH03119 660-661 (July 8, 1993) p100. "Come (from left): Arthur Johnson, Sean O'Brien, Chris Brokaw And Thalia Zedek" (Apicella-Hitchcock, Stephen)
COMESS, AARON—PHOTOGRAPHS
PH03120 631 (May 28, 1992) p15. "The Spin Doctors' Chris Barron, Eric Schenkman And Aaron Comess (from left)" (Mazur, Kevin)
PH03121 647 (January 7, 1993) p39. "Later, Aaron Comess Double-Checks The Set List" (Seliger, Mark)
PH03122 647 (January 7, 1993) p36. "Schenkman, In The Top Bunk, And Comess, Down Below, Enjoy A Rare Moment Of Midtour Shut-Eye" (Seliger, Mark)
PH03123 684 (June 16, 1994) p18. "A Force Of Hobbit: Schenkman, White, Barron And Comess Back In The Studio"
PH03124 695 (November 17, 1994) p135. "Spin Doctors" (Seeff, Norman)
COMESS, AARON—PHOTOGRAPHS—PORTRAITS
PH03125 647 (January 7, 1993) p34. "[Spin Doctors]" (Seliger, Mark)
COMICS—ILLUSTRATIONS
PH03126 741 (August 22, 1996) p76. "[Pat Moriarity]" (Moriarity, Pat)
COMMERCIALISM—ILLUSTRATIONS
PH03127 702 (February 23, 1995) p20. "Fan Plastic" (Blackwell, Patrick)
THE COMMITMENTS (FILM)—PHOTOGRAPHS
PH03128 619-620 (December 12, 1991) p79. "...And The Commitments (below) Try A Little Tenderness" (Appleby, David)
COMMON SENSE—ALBUMS
PH03129 701 (February 9, 1995) p55. "Resurrection"
COMPACT DISC PLAYERS—PHOTOGRAPHS
PH03130 676 (February 24, 1994) p65. "Kodak Portable Photo CD Player, PCD 970 ($449)" (Miller, Greg)
PH03131 684 (June 16, 1994) p86. "3DO Challenger: The 64-Bit

Atari Jaguar" (Rosa & Rosa)
PH03132 684 (June 16, 1994) p86. "3DO Player: Panasonic's FZ-I Real" (Rosa & Rosa)
PH03133 684 (June 16, 1994) p85. "Arcade-Style Interactive: JVC's Sega-Compatible X' Eye (above)" (Rosa & Rosa)
PH03134 684 (June 16, 1994) p85. "Compact-Disc Interactive: Magnavox's CDI200" (Rosa & Rosa)
PH03135 684 (June 16, 1994) p86. "Laseractive Champion: Pioneer's CLD-A100" (Rosa & Rosa)

COMPACT DISCS—ILLUSTRATIONS
PH03136 617 (November 14, 1991) p176. "CD News"
PH03137 619-620 (December 12, 1991) p168. "On The Edge"
PH03138 625 (March 5, 1992) p70. "On The Edge"
PH03139 628 (April 16, 1992) p85. "On The Edge"
PH03140 630 (May 14, 1992) p106. "CD News"
PH03141 638 (September 3, 1992) p75. "CD News"
PH03142 642 (October 29, 1992) p28. "[CD]" (Corio, Paul)
PH03143 645-646 (December 10, 1992) p184. "CD News"
PH03144 651 (March 4, 1993) p66. "CD News"
PH03145 652 (March 18, 1993) p42. "On The Edge"
PH03146 654 (April 15, 1993) p65. "[CD News]"
PH03147 655 (April 29, 1993) p62. "[Replays]"
PH03148 657 (May 27, 1993) p50. "CD News"
PH03149 662 (August 5, 1993) p69. "CD News"
PH03150 665 (September 16, 1993) p24. "[Used CDs]" (Yaccarino, Dan)
PH03151 668 (October 28, 1993) p78. "CD News"
PH03152 668 (October 28, 1993) p8. "Inflated CD Prices—Used Cd's" (Pendergrast, James T.)
PH03153 672-673 (December 23, 1993) p169. "CD News"
PH03154 674 (January 27, 1994) p56. "[Compact Discs]"
PH03155 676 (February 24, 1994) p57. "On The Edge"
PH03156 677 (March 10, 1994) p67. "Replays"
PH03157 681 (May 5, 1994) p56. "CD News"
PH03158 688 (August 11, 1994) p72. "[Replays]"
PH03159 690 (September 8, 1994) p81. "[Compact Discs]"
PH03160 694 (November 3, 1994) p100. "Replays"
PH03161 698-699 (December 29, 1994) p185. "CD News"
PH03162 704 (March 23, 1995) p36. "[CD Piracy]" (Stubbs, Charles)
PH03163 706 (April 20, 1995) p72. "On The Edge"
PH03164 716 (September 7, 1995) p73. "On The Edge"
PH03165 730 (March 21, 1996) p98. "On The Edge"
PH03166 745 (October 17, 1996) p135. "On The Edge"

COMPACT DISCS—PHOTOGRAPHS
PH03167 686-687 (July 14, 1994) pp46-47. "[Toys]" (Grant, Bob)

THE COMPLETE BEATLES CHRONICLE (BOOK)—PHOTOGRAPHS
PH03168 645-646 (December 10, 1992) p88. "[The Complete Beatles Chronicle]"

COMPUTER SOFTWARE—PHOTOGRAPHS
PH03169 678 (March 24, 1994) p107. "Media Vision Quantum Gate Interactive Adventure ($80)" (Miller, Greg)

COMPUTERS—ILLUSTRATIONS
PH03170 654 (April 15, 1993) p35. "[Internet]" (Guy, Edmund)
PH03171 670 (November 25, 1993) p27. "[Cyber-Rockers]" (Cowles, David)
PH03172 707 (May 4, 1995) pp40-41. "[Cyberthief]" (Allen, Terry)
PH03173 710 (June 15, 1995) p14. "[Eye]" (Pendergrast, James T.)
PH03174 734 (May 16, 1996) p14. "Only Window(s)" (Pendergrast, James T.)
PH03175 741 (August 22, 1996) p78. "[Cyberterrorism]" (Hungry Dog Studio)

COMPUTERS—PHOTOGRAPHS
PH03176 618 (November 28, 1991) p111. "Pocketful Of Miracles: The Sharp OZ-8000 Wizard" (Butler, Robert)
PH03177 634-635 (July 9, 1992) pp122-123. "[Toys]" (Goldin, David)
PH03178 666 (September 30, 1993) p119. "Apple Newton Messagepad" (Miller, Greg)
PH03179 666 (September 30, 1993) p119. "Canon Notejet 486" (Miller, Greg)
PH03180 666 (September 30, 1993) p119. "Hewlett-Packard Omnibook 300" (Miller, Greg)
PH03181 666 (September 30, 1993) p119. "IBM Thinkpad 500" (Miller, Greg)
PH03182 666 (September 30, 1993) p119. "Panasonic CF-1000A" (Miller, Greg)
PH03183 670 (November 25, 1993) p129. "Compaq Presario 425 Computer, $1,399" (Miller, Greg)
PH03184 678 (March 24, 1994) p107. "Media Vision Memphis Multimedia Upgrade Kit ($999)" (Miller, Greg)
PH03185 678 (March 24, 1994) p107. "Multiwave Innovation Audiowave Platinum 16 Soundcard ($299)" (Miller, Greg)
PH03186 678 (March 24, 1994) p107. "Sigma Designs Reel Magic Video Card ($449)" (Miller, Greg)
PH03187 682 (May 19, 1994) p112. "I" (Miller, Greg)
PH03188 682 (May 19, 1994) p111. "System 2..." (Miller, Greg)
PH03189 682 (May 19, 1994) p112. "System 3: The Apple Power Mac Line Can Run Software Written For IBM Compatibles" (Miller, Greg)
PH03190 682 (May 19, 1994) p112. "System 4: Packard Bell's Pentium With Samsung's Synmaster Monitor IS Geared For Graphics" (Miller, Greg)
PH03191 682 (May 19, 1994) p112. "System 5: Reelmagics Puts Full-Motion Video On IBM's Basic Valuepoint 433DX" (Miller, Greg)
PH03192 682 (May 19, 1994) p111. "System I: Tandy's Sensation! With VGM-390 Monitor And Okidata OL-400E Printer" (Miller, Greg)
PH03193 689 (August 25, 1994) p49. "[Portable Computers]" (Grant, Bob)
PH03194 696 (December 1, 1994) p71. "[Computer Equipment]" (Grant, Bob)
PH03195 696 (December 1, 1994) pp75-76,80-82 +. "[Computer Equipment]" (Rosa And Rosa)
PH03196 696 (December 1, 1994) p91. "[Computer Software]" (Grant, Bob)
PH03197 708 (May 18, 1995) pp[enc.18-22 +]. "[Computers]" (Rosa And Rosa)
PH03198 709 (June 1, 1995) p73. "[Computers]" (Grant, Bob)
PH03199 714 (August 10, 1995) p66. "[Computer Peripherals]" (Grant, Bob)
PH03200 722 (November 30, 1995) pp[enc.45,47]. "[Computer Technology]" (McLeod, William Mercer)
PH03201 722 (November 30, 1995) pp[enc.32-33 +]. "[Computers]" (Richardson, Alan)
PH03202 722 (November 30, 1995) pp[enc.9]. "Even The Loo Is An Experience In Virtual Reality" (McLeod, William Mercer)
PH03203 722 (November 30, 1995) pp[enc.2]. "Windows On World Domination: The Cyborganics' Shrine To Microsoft's Windows 95" (McLeod, William Mercer)
PH03204 730 (March 21, 1996) p111. "[Technology]" (Grant, Bob)
PH03205 735 (May 30, 1996) pp[enc.39-40]. "[Computers]" (Grant, Bob)
PH03206 741 (August 22, 1996) pp84-85. "[Hot Technology]" (Grant, Bob)
PH03207 747 (November 14, 1996) p129. "[Computers & Modems]" (Grant, Bob)
PH03208 748 (November 28, 1996) pp103,104,106 +. "[Computers]" (Grant, Bob)

CONCRETE BLONDE—ALBUMS
PH03209 627 (April 2, 1992) p45. "Walking In London"
PH03210 630 (May 14, 1992) p124. "Walking In London"

CONCRETE BLONDE—PHOTOGRAPHS
PH03211 670 (November 25, 1993) p37. "Johnette Napolitano Toasts Johnny Depp" (Kravitz, Jeff)

CONEHEADS (FILM)—PHOTOGRAPHS
PH03212 664 (September 2, 1993) p70. "Conehead Movies"
CONGO (FILM)—PHOTOGRAPHS
PH03213 711 (June 29, 1995) p48. "Laura Linney (center) Holds Off Jungle Fever"
PH03214 715 (August 24, 1995) p108. "The Man Eaters"
CONGRESS OF THE UNITED STATES—ILLUSTRATIONS
PH03215 618 (November 28, 1991) p9. "Millie Visits The Senate" (Pendergrast, James T.)
PH03216 648 (January 21, 1993) p27. "[Elections]" (Bishofs, Maris)
CONNEFF, KEVIN—PHOTOGRAPHS
PH03217 621 (January 9, 1992) p10. "Kevin Conneff, Paddy Moloney, Charlie Watts And Matt Molloy (from left)"
CONNELL, MIKE—PHOTOGRAPHS
PH03218 633 (June 25, 1992) p11. "Greg Humphreys, Mike Watt, Doug Macmillan, Bill Janovitz, Tom Maginnis And Mike Connell (from left) In Raleigh"
CONNELLY, JENNIFER—PHOTOGRAPHS
PH03219 700 (January 26, 1995) p68. "Swanson, Connelly, Epps And Cube Tackle "Learning""
CONNER, GARY LEE—PHOTOGRAPHS
PH03220 650 (February 18, 1993) p15. "Gary Lee Conner, Barrett Martin, Mark Lanegan And Van Conner (from left)" (Winters, Dan)
PH03221 695 (November 17, 1994) p110. "Screaming Trees" (Ragel, Jon)
PH03222 734 (May 16, 1996) p28. "The Album That Wouldn't Die: Gary Lee Conner Lays Down Another Guitar Part" (Strauss, Jay)
CONNER, LEE—PHOTOGRAPHS
PH03223 658 (June 10, 1993) p29. "Screaming Trees' Lee Conner" (Eichner, Steve)
CONNER, VAN—PHOTOGRAPHS
PH03224 650 (February 18, 1993) p15. "Gary Lee Conner, Barrett Martin, Mark Lanegan And Van Conner (from left)" (Winters, Dan)
CONNER, VAN—PHOTOGRAPHS—PORTRAITS
PH03225 695 (November 17, 1994) p110. "Screaming Trees" (Ragel, Jon)
CONNERY, SEAN—ILLUSTRATIONS
PH03226 737 (June 27, 1996) p61. "Bad Boy Son Alcatraz" (Brodner, Steve)
CONNERY, SEAN—PHOTOGRAPHS
PH03227 664 (September 2, 1993) p69. "Thriller Tempura: Connery And Snipes Dine Japanese"
PH03228 714 (August 10, 1995) p64. "Gere And Connery Deconstruct Camelot"
PH03229 737 (June 27, 1996) p62. "Sean Connery Watches Nicholas Cage Defuse A Poison-Gas Bomb On Alcatraz"
CONNICK, HARRY, JR.—PHOTOGRAPHS
PH03230 650 (February 18, 1993) p11. "Gun-Toting Connick Is Hustled Into Custody"
CONRAD, ROBERT—PHOTOGRAPHS—PORTRAITS
PH03231 666 (September 30, 1993) p116. "Gee-Whiz Men: 'Wild, Wild West' (left)"
CONSOLIDATED—PHOTOGRAPHS
PH03232 671 (December 9, 1993) p32. "Members Of Consolidated And 4 Non Blondes Unite For Critters Big And Small" (Blakesberg, Jay)
PH03233 697 (December 15, 1994) p33. "[Consolidated]" (Arnold, Alice)
CONSTANTEN, TOM—PHOTOGRAPHS
PH03234 717 (September 21, 1995) p73. "marrying Acid-Damaged Art Music And The Funky Snort Of Live Rock & Roll: The Dead As A Lysergic-Dance Band In 1969 With Tom Constanten, Weir, Kreutzmann, Pigpen, Lesh, Hart..."
CONSTITUTION OF THE UNITED STATES—ILLUSTRATIONS
PH03235 689 (August 25, 1994) p12. "Mind Altering Substance" (Pendergrast, James T.)
CONVERSATIONS WITH THE DEAD (BOOK)—PHOTOGRAPHS
PH03236 619-620 (December 12, 1991) p32. "[Conversations With The Dead]"
CONWAY, BILL—PHOTOGRAPHS
PH03237 628 (April 16, 1992) p51. "Basehead, The Band (from left): Brian Hendrix, Keith Lofton, Bill Conway And Michael Ivey" (Ockenfels, Frank W.)
CONWAY, BILLY—PHOTOGRAPHS
PH03238 686-687 (July 14, 1994) p36. "Morphine's Sandman, Conway And Colley (from left)" (Lyden, Paul)
PH03239 711 (June 29, 1995) p20. "Masters Of 'Implied Grunge': Colley, Sandman, Conway (from left)" (Ockenfels, Frank W.)
CONWAY, BILLY—PHOTOGRAPHS—PORTRAITS
PH03240 667 (October 14, 1993) p30. "Mark Sandman, Dana Colley And Bill Conway" (Eichner, Steve)
COODER, RY—ALBUMS
PH03241 617 (November 14, 1991) p100. "Into The Purple Valley" (Salisbury, Mike)
PH03242 617 (November 14, 1991) p100. "Into The Purple Valley" (Evans, Marty)
PH03243 652 (March 18, 1993) p42. "Rising Sons"
PH03244 656 (May 13, 1993) p108. "A Meeting By The River"
COODER, RY—PHOTOGRAPHS
PH03245 624 (February 20, 1992) p11. "Ry Cooder (left) Joins Bluesman John Lee Hooker Onstage" (Blakesberg, Jay)
PH03246 627 (April 2, 1992) p15. "Jim Keltner, Ry Cooder, Nick Lowe And John Hiatt (from left)" (Hanauer, Mark)
PH03247 697 (December 15, 1994) p28. "[Ry Cooder]" (Navizet, Albane)
COOK, PAUL—PHOTOGRAPHS
PH03248 734 (May 16, 1996) p17. "Matlock, Rotten, Jones And Cook Now" (Gruen, Bob)
PH03249 734 (May 16, 1996) p17. "The Pistols' Rotten, Glen Matlock, Steve Jones And Paul Cook In '76" (Gruen, Bob)
PH03250 736 (June 13, 1996) p52. "Pistols '96: Glen Matlock, Steve Jones, Paul Cook And Johnny Rotten (from left)" (Thomas, Justin)
COOK, STU—PHOTOGRAPHS—PORTRAITS
PH03251 649 (February 4, 1993) p48. "Drummer Clifford, Bassist Cook, Rhythm Guitarist Fogerty, Frontman Fogerty (clockwise from left)" (Wolman, Baron)
COOKE, SAM—ILLUSTRATIONS
PH03252 696 (December 1, 1994) p121. "[Sam Cooke]" (Adolphe, Joseph)
COOKE, SAM—PHOTOGRAPHS
PH03253 701 (February 9, 1995) p28. "You Send Me"
COOL WORLD (FILM)—ILLUSTRATIONS
PH03254 639 (September 17, 1992) p102. "Worst Supporting Actress"
COOL, JENNY—PHOTOGRAPHS
PH03255 722 (November 30, 1995) pp[enc.6]. "Jenny Cool (left) And Trisha" (McLeod, William Mercer)
COOLIDGE, MARTHA—PHOTOGRAPHS
PH03256 657 (May 27, 1993) p58. "Lost: Coolidge And Ruehl Flank Simon"
COOLIO—ILLUSTRATIONS
PH03257 692 (October 6, 1994) p104. "Coolio: Baby, You Can Drive My Car" (Gorgun, Ahmet)
PH03258 723 (December 14, 1995) p15. "Coolio" (Burke, Philip)
COOLIO—PHOTOGRAPHS
PH03259 700 (January 26, 1995) p55. "Coolio: Best Rapper Runner-Up In The Readers' Poll" (Miller, Michael)
PH03260 703 (March 9, 1995) p20. "Coolio (FYI: Dreads Underneath Cap)" (Kravitz, Jeff)
PH03261 710 (June 15, 1995) p42. "[Coolio]" (Danelian, Stephen)
PH03262 720 (November 2, 1995) p17. "Hoop Dreams: Latifah And Teammate Coolio" (Kravitz, Jeff)

PH03263 723 (December 14, 1995) p34. "Coolio: A Far Cry From Your Average Gat-Toting Rapper" (Mosenfeld, Tim)
PH03264 723 (December 14, 1995) p33. "'I'm Trying To Get Rid Of The Jacket That's Been Put On My Back—That I'm A Gangsta Rapper,' Coolio Says" (Watson, Albert)
PH03265 724-725 (December 28, 1995) p42. "Gangsta's Paradise: Coolio, Des'ree" (Mazur, Kevin)
PH03266 726 (January 25, 1996) p41. "He Spent Most Of The Year Livin' In A Critics' Paradise: The Always Stylish Coolio" (Watson, Albert)
PH03267 731 (April 4, 1996) p17. "I'm Too Sexy For My Shirt—Coolio Twirls" (Somoza, Gerardo)
PH03268 732 (April 18, 1996) p19. "Joni Mitchell And Coolio Reminisce About All The Good Times They've Shared Together" (Mazur, Kevin)

COOLIO—PHOTOGRAPHS—PORTRAITS
PH03269 691 (September 22, 1994) p37. "Coolio: Journey To The Land Of Funk"
PH03270 698-699 (December 29, 1994) p48. "Coolio"
PH03271 710 (June 15, 1995) p17. "Sage Beyond His Age: Coolio In L.A."
PH03272 733 (May 2, 1996) p20. "Throwing Signs: Coolio And L.V. (right) Goofing On 'Saturday Night Live,' Feb. 10, 1996" (Ng, Norman)
PH03273 742 (September 5, 1996) p23. "[Coolio]" (Elledge, Paul)

COOMBES, GAZ—PHOTOGRAPHS
PH03274 718 (October 5, 1995) pp[enc.28]. "Coombes At Sheidonian Theater, Oxford" (GS, Jamil)
PH03275 726 (January 25, 1996) p18. "Me Public: Bratty Brit Coombes Of Supergrass"

COOMER, KEN—PHOTOGRAPHS
PH03276 707 (May 4, 1995) p32. "The Buddy System: Johnston, Coomer, Stirratt, Tweedy And Bennett (from left)" (Miller, Brad)

COOPER UNION FOR THE ADVANCEMENT OF SCIENCE AND ART—ILLUSTRATIONS
PH03277 730 (March 21, 1996) p65. "New York's Cooper Union"

COOPER, ALICE—ALBUMS
PH03278 617 (November 14, 1991) p153. "Welcome To My Nightmare" (Struzan, Drew)
PH03279 617 (November 14, 1991) p153. "Welcome To My Nightmare" (Lopex, Bret)
PH03280 686-687 (July 14, 1994) p110. "The Last Temptation"

COOPER, ALICE—PHOTOGRAPHS
PH03281 616 (October 31, 1991) p11. "Greg Smith, Pete Freezin', Alice Cooper And Stef Burns (from left)" (Mazur, Kevin)
PH03282 631 (May 28, 1992) p11. "Alice Cooper, Smokey Robinson And Bob Seger (from left)" (Plummer, Sue)

COOPER, JASON—PHOTOGRAPHS
PH03283 733 (May 2, 1996) p22. "Partial To Shades: The Cure's New Lineup Is Simon Gallup, Roger O'Donnell, Robert Smith, Perry Bamonte And Jason Cooper (from left)" (Cox, Paul)

COOPER, MICHAEL—PHOTOGRAPHS
PH03284 643 (November 12, 1992) p70. "Michael Cooper (left) Photographed The Cover Of 'Sgt. Pepper'" (Cooper, Michael)

COP KILLER (SONG)—PHOTOGRAPHS
PH03285 652 (March 18, 1993) p31. "A 'Cop Killer' Protest Last Summer" (Reuters)

COPE, JULIAN—ALBUMS
PH03286 619-620 (December 12, 1991) p178. "Peggy Suicide"
PH03287 647 (January 7, 1993) p47. "Jehovahkill"

COPE, JULIAN—ILLUSTRATIONS
PH03288 693 (October 20, 1994) p148. "Julian Cope" (Gallagher, James)

COPE, JULIAN—PHOTOGRAPHS
PH03289 722 (November 30, 1995) p36. "[Julian Cope]" (Westenberg, Kevin)

COPPOLA, FRANCIS FORD—PHOTOGRAPHS
PH03290 745 (October 17, 1996) p65. "'The Godfather' (1972): Brando And Pacino Flank Director Coppola"
PH03291 745 (October 17, 1996) p65. "'The Godfather III' (1990): Coppola Directs Pacino As The Aging Don"

COPPOLA, FRANCIS FORD—PHOTOGRAPHS—PORTRAITS
PH03292 742 (September 5, 1996) p68. "Francis Ford Coppola Directs Robin Williams To Act Like A 10-Year-Old In 'Jack'"

COPS (TELEVISION SHOW)—PHOTOGRAPHS
PH03293 672-673 (December 23, 1993) p90. "Into The Streets With 'Cops'" (Slobin, Barry)

COPYCAT (FILM)—PHOTOGRAPHS
PH03294 721 (November 16, 1995) p117. "Sigourney Weaver (left) Plays Victim While Cop Holly Hunter Packs Heat"

CORDELL, DENNY—PHOTOGRAPHS
PH03295 706 (April 20, 1995) p32. "Producer Denny Cordell Takes Five" (Thomas, Huw)

COREA, CHICK—ALBUMS
PH03296 625 (March 5, 1992) p68. "Play"

CORGAN, BILLY—ILLUSTRATIONS
PH03297 667 (October 14, 1993) p11. "Smashing Pumpkins' Billy Corgan" (Burke, Philip)
PH03298 750-751 (December 26, 1996) p68. "[Smashing Pumpkins]" (Drawson, Blair)

CORGAN, BILLY—PHOTOGRAPHS
PH03299 655 (April 29, 1993) p12. "Pumpkins D'Arcy (left) And Corgan" (Diamond, Rick)
PH03300 660-661 (July 8, 1993) p100. "Smashing Pumpkins (from left): Billy Corgan, D'Arcy, Jimmy Chamberlin And James Iha" (Johnson, Lisa)
PH03301 666 (September 30, 1993) p20. "Smashing Pumpkins' Frontman, Billy Corgan" (Natkin, Paul)
PH03302 667 (October 14, 1993) p20. "Corgan: His Love-Hate Affair With The Indie Community Goes Way Back" (Bodtke, Peter)
PH03303 677 (March 10, 1994) p15. "Billy Corgan Of Smashing Pumpkins" (Mott, Tony)
PH03304 680 (April 21, 1994) pp42-43. "All Pumped Up: Jimmy Chamberlin, James Iha, Billy Corgan And D'Arcy (from left)" (Luchford, Glen)
PH03305 680 (April 21, 1994) p45. "Corgan: 'My Rep AS A Tyrant, There's Truth In It'" (Jana)
PH03306 683 (June 2, 1994) p16. "Lollapalooza Dreams For Smashing Pumpkins' Billy Corgan" (Dexters, Bernaded)
PH03307 689 (August 25, 1994) p24. "Pumpkins' Corgan Joins The Frogs' Damien Strigens And Jimmy Fleming" (Blakesberg, Jay)
PH03308 694 (November 3, 1994) p17. "Pumpkin Billy Corgan, Love, Cohen, Krugman (from left)"
PH03309 695 (November 17, 1994) p47. "Smashing Pumpkins" (Ockenfels, Frank W.)
PH03310 705 (April 6, 1995) p16. "Billy Corgan, Drummer Jimmy Chamberlin And James Iha (from left)" (Natkin, Paul)
PH03311 711 (June 29, 1995) p19. "Billy Corgan, D'Arcy, Jimmy Chamberlin, James Iha (from left)" (Elledge, Paul)
PH03312 721 (November 16, 1995) p54. "'A Corny Boy From Chicago': Corgan At The Piano In His Home" (Seliger, Mark)
PH03313 721 (November 16, 1995) pp50-51. "Billy Corgan Levitates D'Arcy" (Seliger, Mark)
PH03314 721 (November 16, 1995) p53. "Corgan" (Seliger, Mark)
PH03315 721 (November 16, 1995) p56. "Ready To Rock You: D'Arcy, Iha, Corgan, Chamberlin (from left) In 1992" (Lenquette)
PH03316 721 (November 16, 1995) p57. "'Throwing Down The Gauntlet': Corgan At LollaPalooza '94" (Mosenfelder, Tim)
PH03317 726 (January 25, 1996) p43. "Smashing Pumpkins' Billy Corgan, D'Arcy, James Iha, Jimmy Chamberlin (from left)" (Seliger, Mark)

PH03318 728 (February 22, 1996) p19. "Pink Floyd's Richard Wright (left) And Gilmour Flank Special Guest Corgan" (Mazur, Kevin)
PH03319 729 (March 7, 1996) p12. "A Tale Of Two Tours: The Small-Theater Tour By Springsteen (left) Was A Field Day For Scalpers, But Corgan And The Pumpkins Shut Them Out" (Capak, R. J.)
PH03320 729 (March 7, 1996) p12. "A Tale Of Two Tours: The Small-Theater Tour By Springsteen (left) Was A Field Day For Scalpers, But Corgan And The Pumpkins Shut Them Out" (Liu, Brian)
PH03321 736 (June 13, 1996) pp[cover]. "Rock & Roll Summer!" (Mazur, Kevin)
PH03322 740 (August 8, 1996) p20. "Smashing Pumpkin's Billy Corgan..." (Mazur, Kevin)
PH03323 745 (October 17, 1996) p47. "Back On Track: Pumpkinhead Corgan" (Miller, Ethan)
PH03324 745 (October 17, 1996) p27. "David Lee Roth With Pumpkin Billy Corgan And Eddie Van Halen" (Kravitz, Jeff)
PH03325 750-751 (December 26, 1996) p45. "Corgan (left) With David Gilmour" (Mazur, Kevin)

CORGAN, BILLY—PHOTOGRAPHS—PORTRAITS
PH03326 667 (October 14, 1993) p19. "D'Arcy, Jimmy Chamberlim, Billy Corgan, James Iha (clockwise from top left)" (Hom, Marc)
PH03327 680 (April 21, 1994) p44. "Young Pumpkin: Corgan At 13"
PH03328 724-725 (December 28, 1995) pp[cover]. "Rock & Roll Yearbook" (Seliger, Mark)
PH03329 728 (February 22, 1996) p20. "Who Loves Ya, Baby? Billy Corgan Does" (Liu, Brian)
PH03330 743 (September 19, 1996) pp26-27. "[Billy Corgan]" (Ockenfels, Frank W.)

CORINA—PHOTOGRAPHS
PH03331 619-620 (December 12, 1991) p59. "Women In Rock Band Together For Prochoice" (Berkwitz, David Neil)

CORINA, SARAH—PHOTOGRAPHS
PH03332 667 (October 14, 1993) p37. "Mekons Sarah Corina (left) And Jon Langford" (Mazur, Kevin)
PH03333 Number not assigned.

CORNELL, CHRIS—ILLUSTRATIONS
PH03334 634-635 (July 9, 1992) p3. "Chris Cornell Of Soundgarden" (Burke, Philip)

CORNELL, CHRIS—PHOTOGRAPHS
PH03335 621 (January 9, 1992) p11. "Ben Shepherd, Kim Thayil, Chris Cornell And Matt Cameron (from left)"
PH03336 634-635 (July 9, 1992) p46. "Jesus Christ Pose? Above: Chris Cornell Onstage" (Blakesberg, Jay)
PH03337 638 (September 3, 1992) p9. "...And Soundgarden's Chris Cornell" (Blakesberg, Jay)
PH03338 674 (January 27, 1994) p17. "Cameron, Shepherd, Cornell, Thayil (from left)" (Westenberg, Kevin)
PH03339 677 (March 10, 1994) p15. "Chris Cornell Of Soundgarden" (Mott, Tony)
PH03340 684 (June 16, 1994) p52. "Cameron, Thayil, Yamamoto, Cornell, Silver, Tour Manager Eric Johnson (from left) In 1988" (Peterson, Charles)
PH03341 684 (June 16, 1994) p50. "Cornell, Thayil, Sundquist, Yamamoto In Mid-'80s" (Peterson, Charles)
PH03342 684 (June 16, 1994) p50. "Ditto Tavern, '86: Thayil And Cornell" (Peterson, Charles)
PH03343 684 (June 16, 1994) p49. "Sit 'N' Spin: Cameron, Shepherd, Thayil And Cornell (from left) In Seattle" (Seliger, Mark)
PH03344 690 (September 8, 1994) p42. "Cornell Combating The Sonic Sludge" (Virobik-Adams, Kevin)
PH03345 695 (November 17, 1994) p131. "Soundgarden" (Seliger, Mark)
PH03346 698-699 (December 29, 1994) p103. "[Chris Cornell]" (Ockenfels, Frank W.)
PH03347 698-699 (December 29, 1994) p106. "From Sub Pop To Superstardom: Kim Thayil, Cornell, Ben Shepherd And Matt Cameron (from left)" (Seliger, Mark)
PH03348 698-699 (December 29, 1994) p104. "In Bloom: Cornell With Soundgarden At The Vogue Tavern In Seattle In '86" (Peterson, Charles)
PH03349 698-699 (December 29, 1994) p107. "Sorry, Wrong Bus: Reluctant Heroes Eddie Vedder (center) And Cornell (right) During The 1992 Lollapalooza Tour" (Mercer, Lance)
PH03350 719 (October 19, 1995) p15. "[Chris Cornell]" (Callahan, Kristin)
PH03351 727 (February 8, 1996) p26. "Soundgarden's Chris Cornell, Kim Thayil, Ben Shepherd And Matt Cameron (from left) In Seattle's Studio Litho" (Westenberg, Kevin)
PH03352 737 (June 27, 1996) p56. "Soundgarden's Cornell, Ben Shepherd, Thayil And Matt Cameron (from left)"
PH03353 741 (August 22, 1996) p31. "Soundgarden's Cornell,. Psychotica's Briggs And Joey Ramone" (Blakesberg, Jay)
PH03354 743 (September 19, 1996) p19. "Soundgarden's Chris Cornell (left) With Joey Ramone And His Little Pals, The New York Dolls" (Di Santo, Anna)

CORNELL, CHRIS—PHOTOGRAPHS—PORTRAITS
PH03355 634-635 (July 9, 1992) p45. "[Soundgarden]" (Seliger, Mark)
PH03356 681 (May 5, 1994) p21. "Cornell (left) With Seattle Spoon Artist Artis" (Peterson, Charles)
PH03357 684 (June 16, 1994) pp46-47. "[Chris Cornell]" (Seliger, Mark)
PH03358 693 (October 20, 1994) p28. "Krist Novoselic And Chris Cornell" (Mazur, Kevin)
PH03359 698-699 (December 29, 1994) p103. "[Chris Cornell]" (Ockenfels, Frank W.)
PH03360 706 (April 20, 1995) p15. "You, Too, Can BE A Winner: Crow, Soundgarden's Chris Cornell And Etheridge" (Mazur, Kevin)
PH03361 720 (November 2, 1995) p51. "Chris Cornell" (Ockenfels, Frank W.)
PH03362 736 (June 13, 1996) pp[cover]. "Rock & Roll Summer!" (Seliger, Mark)

CORNERSHOP—PHOTOGRAPHS
PH03363 728 (February 22, 1996) p32. "Cornershop's Simms, Saffery, Tjinder Singh, Ayres And Hall (from left)" (Wonderland, Alison)

CORNOG, F. M.—PHOTOGRAPHS
PH03364 728 (February 22, 1996) p34. "Solo Act F. M. Cornog, Better Known As East River Pipe" (Lantry, Christian)

CORONADO, RAY, JR.—PHOTOGRAPHS
PH03365 709 (June 1, 1995) p54. "Ray Coronado Jr. And His Wife, Sunday, Support Rodney's Ecological Awakening And Have Faith In Their Son's Innocence" (Aguilera-Hellweg, Max)

CORONADO, RODNEY—PHOTOGRAPHS
PH03366 709 (June 1, 1995) p58. "Coronado Going Into Federal Court In Tucson For A Bail Hearing In October '94" (Aguilera-Hellweg, Max)
PH03367 709 (June 1, 1995) p53. "[Rodney Coronado]" (Aguilera-Hellweg, Max)

CORONADO, SUNDAY—PHOTOGRAPHS
PH03368 709 (June 1, 1995) p54. "Ray Coronado Jr. And His Wife, Sunday, Support Rodney's Ecological Awakening And Have Faith In Their Son's Innocence" (Aguilera-Hellweg, Max)

CORPSE—ILLUSTRATIONS
PH03369 712-713 (July 13, 1995) p26. "Slice Of Life" (Faiola, Susan)

CORRINA, CORRINA (FILM)—PHOTOGRAPHS
PH03370 689 (August 25, 1994) p96. "Whoopi Goldberg And Ray Liotta Get It On In The '50s"

CORTESE, DAN—PHOTOGRAPHS—PORTRAITS
PH03371 650 (February 18, 1993) p47. "[Dan Cortese]" (Nystrom, Dick)

CORTESE, SCOT—PHOTOGRAPHS
PH03372 666 (September 30, 1993) p51. "Cortese Of Espresso Roma: 'It's A Labor Of Love'" (Van Ess, Mark)
CORWIN, ROB—PHOTOGRAPHS
PH03373 666 (September 30, 1993) p90. "Hunt (third from left, bottom row) With Delta Lambda Phi Brothers (clockwise from top right): Peter Colohan, Sean McClafferty, Rob Corwin, Price, Stephen Smith And Oligmueller"
COSBY (TELEVISION SHOW)—PHOTOGRAPHS
PH03374 743 (September 19, 1996) pp94,96. "[Television]"
COSLOY, GERARD—PHOTOGRAPHS
PH03375 737 (June 27, 1996) p19. "Matador Honchos Lombardi (left) And Cosloy" (Clinch, Danny)
COSTAS, KIRSTEN—PHOTOGRAPHS
PH03376 632 (June 11, 1992) p161. "Costas: Straight, Popular, Attractive And A Social Butterfly"
COSTELLO, ELVIS—ALBUMS
PH03377 617 (November 14, 1991) p154. "Trust" (Davies And Starr)
PH03378 652 (March 18, 1993) p39. "The Juliet Letters" (Gardner, Elysa)
PH03379 678 (March 24, 1994) p96. "Brutal Youth"
PH03380 711 (June 29, 1995) p43. "Kojak Variety"
COSTELLO, ELVIS—PHOTOGRAPHS
PH03381 651 (March 4, 1993) p23. "Michael Thomas, Jaqueline Thomas, Paul Cassidy, Elvis Costello, Don Belton" (Westenberg, Kevin)
PH03382 665 (September 16, 1993) p31. "[Elvis Costello, Jeff Ament, Mike McCready]" (Mercer, Lance)
PH03383 686-687 (July 14, 1994) p36. "Nothing Here Has Changed: Elvis Costello Live" (Natkin, Paul)
COSTELLO, ELVIS—PHOTOGRAPHS—PORTRAITS
PH03384 683 (June 2, 1994) p27. "Above: Lang, Bennett, Costello" (Mazur, Kevin)
PH03385 734 (May 16, 1996) p18. "Kinky Attraction: Davies (left) And Costello Compare Scarves" (White, E. Lee)
COSTIGAN, KEVIN—PHOTOGRAPHS
PH03386 651 (March 4, 1993) p28. "Dean Zuckerman, Kevin Costigan, Jennifer Barry, Eddie Fagin (from left)" (Lavine, Michael)
COSTNER, KEVIN—PHOTOGRAPHS
PH03387 617 (November 14, 1991) p184. "Is Mastrantonio Wondering If Costner's Aim Is True?"
PH03388 622 (January 23, 1992) p49. "Kevin Costner Conspires With Director Oliver Stone"
PH03389 671 (December 9, 1993) p76. "Star Team: Ranger Eastwood (left) And Convict Costner"
PH03390 684 (June 16, 1994) p114. "TV Echoes"
PH03391 688 (August 11, 1994) p62. "Wyatt Earp"
PH03392 696 (December 1, 1994) p134. "Father, Son: Kevin Costner, Elijah Wood"
COTE, BILLY—PHOTOGRAPHS
PH03393 688 (August 11, 1994) p29. "Drummer Johnny Kick, Cote, Lorson And Bassist Chris Giammalvo (from left)" (Berg, Bob)
COULTAS, KEVIN—PHOTOGRAPHS
PH03394 686-687 (July 14, 1994) p74. "Getting The Point Across: Rodan's Tara Jane O'Neil, Noble, Mueller And Kevin Coultas (from left)" (Clinch, Danny)
COUNTING CROWS—ALBUMS
PH03395 668 (October 28, 1993) p76. "August And Everything After"
PH03396 672-673 (December 23, 1993) p153. "August And Everything After"
PH03397 700 (January 26, 1995) p55. "August And Everything After"
COUNTING CROWS—ILLUSTRATIONS
PH03398 690 (September 8, 1994) p16. "Reincarnation" (Pendergrast, James T.)
COUNTING CROWS—PHOTOGRAPHS
PH03399 669 (November 11, 1993) p24. "A '90s Sensibility: Vickrey, Gillingham, Duritz, Bowman, Malley, Bryson (from left)" (Blakesberg, Jay)
PH03400 672-673 (December 23, 1993) p48. "[Counting Crows]" (Blakesberg, Jay)
PH03401 674 (January 27, 1994) p25. "Crows (from left): Vickrey, Malley, Duritz" (Blakesberg, Jay)
PH03402 685 (June 30, 1994) pp[cover]. "Counting Crows: The Biggest New Band In America" (Seliger, Mark)
PH03403 685 (June 30, 1994) p50. "The Crows Onstage At The Rock & Roll Hall Of Fame Ceremony, January 1993" (Mazur, Kevin)
PH03404 685 (June 30, 1994) p46. "Free Men In Paris: Dave Bryson, Steve Bowman, Dan Vickrey, Matt Malley And Charlie Gillingham (from left)" (Seliger, Mark)
PH03405 748 (November 28, 1996) p134. "Recovering The Satellites"
COUNTRY MUSIC—ILLUSTRATIONS
PH03406 637 (August 20, 1992) p53. "Country & Western"
PH03407 645-646 (December 10, 1992) p174. "Country & Western"
PH03408 645-646 (December 10, 1992) p75. "[Country Music]" (Aitken, Doug)
PH03409 647 (January 7, 1993) p54. "Country & Western"
PH03410 656 (May 13, 1993) p110. "[Country & Western]"
PH03411 663 (August 19, 1993) p77. "Country & Western"
PH03412 666 (September 30, 1993) p105. "[Country & Western]"
PH03413 672-673 (December 23, 1993) pp15158. "Country & Western"
PH03414 675 (February 10, 1994) p46. "Country & Western"
PH03415 679 (April 7, 1994) p77. "Country & Western"
PH03416 683 (June 2, 1994) p70. "[Country & Western]"
PH03417 686-687 (July 14, 1994) p107. "Country & Western"
PH03418 693 (October 20, 1994) p150. "Country & Western"
PH03419 698-699 (December 29, 1994) p178. "Country & Western"
PH03420 707 (May 4, 1995) p70. "Country & Western"
PH03421 748 (November 28, 1996) p117. "[World Wide Web]"
COUNTY, JAYNE—PHOTOGRAPHS
PH03422 734 (May 16, 1996) p64. "Crossing The County Line"
COUPLAND, DOUGLAS—BOOKS
PH03423 738-739 (July 11, 1996) p90. "Polaroids From The Dead"
COURAGE UNDER FIRE (FILM)—PHOTOGRAPHS
PH03424 736 (June 13, 1996) p62. "Fierce Women"
PH03425 740 (August 8, 1996) p68. "Moriarty (left), Washington"
PH03426 740 (August 8, 1996) p68. "Ryan Under Fire"
PH03427 743 (September 19, 1996) p90. "[Summer...]"
COVERDALE, DAVID—ALBUMS
PH03428 654 (April 15, 1993) p62. "Coverdale-Page"
COVINGTON CROSS (TELEVISION SHOW)—PHOTOGRAPHS
PH03429 640 (October 1, 1992) p78. "'Beverly Hills, 902 A.D.': The Grays Of 'Covington Cross'" (Seliger, Mark)
COWAN, ANTHONY—PHOTOGRAPHS
PH03430 719 (October 19, 1995) p25. "Cowan Signs To Motown: Motown's Nadiene Baker, Manager Bill Dern, Jackson, Cowan (clockwise from top left)"
COWBOY JUNKIES—ALBUMS
PH03431 623 (February 6, 1992) p73. "Black Eyed Man"
PH03432 677 (March 10, 1994) p66. "Pale Sun Crescent Moon"
THE COWBOY WAY (FILM)—PHOTOGRAPHS
PH03433 685 (June 30, 1994) p81. "Urban Riders: Sutherland And Harrelson"
COX, COURTENEY—PHOTOGRAPHS
PH03434 708 (May 18, 1995) pp[cover]. "Fast Friends: No Sex Bad Jobs Hit Show Go Figure" (Seliger, Mark)

PH03435 708 (May 18, 1995) p. "Matt LeBlanc, Jennifer Aniston, David Schwimmer, Courteney Cox, Lisa Kudrow, Matthew Perry" (Seliger, Mark)
PH03436 Number not assigned.
COXON, GRAHAM—PHOTOGRAPHS
PH03437 694 (November 3, 1994) p34. "Social Distortion: Blur's Coxon, Albarn, Rowntree And James (from left)" (Westenberg, Kevin)
PH03437a 709 (June 1, 1995) p17. "[Graham Coxon]" (Peters, Doug)
PH03438 720 (November 2, 1995) p20. "Coxon (left) And Albarn At A BBC Radio One Gig In London On Sept. 7" (Westenberg, Kevin)
COXON, GRAHAM—PHOTOGRAPHS—PORTRAITS
PH03439 623 (February 6, 1992) p32. "Alex James, Damon Albarn, Graham Coxon, Dave Rowntree (clockwise from top)" (Lavine, Michael)
PH03440 720 (November 2, 1995) p19. "'Great Escape' Artists Coxon, Albarn, James And Rountree (from left)" (Westenberg, Kevin)
COY, JACK—PHOTOGRAPHS
PH03441 615 (October 17, 1991) p28. "Jack Coy, George Hernandez, Jeff Braimes, Martin Chandler (from left)" (Mason, Karen)
COYNE, WAYNE—PHOTOGRAPHS
PH03442 689 (August 25, 1994) p21. "The Flaming Lips' Michael Ivins, Steven Drozd, Wayne Coyne (from left)" (Blakesberg, Jay)
PH03443 703 (March 9, 1995) p26. "Imagine The Beatles Drunk On Robitussin: Coyne, Drozd, Ivins And Jones (from left)" (Lavine, Michael)
PH03444 736 (June 13, 1996) p33. "The Flaming Lips' Steven Drozd, Michael Ivins, Wayne Coyne And Ronald Jones (from left)" (Martin, J. Michelle)
CRACKER—PHOTOGRAPHS
PH03445 626 (March 19, 1992) p13. "Cracker's Johnny Hickman, David Lowery And Davey Faragher (from left)" (Young, Russell)
PH03446 679 (April 7, 1994) p68. "Cracked: David Lovering, David Lowery, Bruce Hughes, Johnny Hickman (from left)" (Wolff, Tom)
PH03447 695 (November 17, 1994) p143. "Cracker" (Guzman)
PH03448 732 (April 18, 1996) p47. "Playing Cowboys In The Desert: Bob Rupe, Charlie Quintana, David Lowery And Johnny Hickman (from left)" (Maxwell, Robert)
PH03449 737 (June 27, 1996) p15. "Tjinder Singh With Cracker's Johnny Hickman And Bob Rupe (from left)" (Roberts, Ebet)
CRACKER—PHOTOGRAPHS—PORTRAITS
PH03450 645-646 (December 10, 1992) p57. "Cracker" (Young, Russell)
CRAGG, JONNY—PHOTOGRAPHS
PH03451 734 (May 16, 1996) p32. "Fighting For Time In Front Of The Mirror: Brothers Antony And Royston Langdon, Richard Steel, And Jonny Cragg (from left)" (Clinch, Danny)
CRANBERRIES—ALBUMS
PH03452 697 (December 15, 1994) p94. "No Need To Argue"
PH03453 735 (May 30, 1996) p46. "To The Faithful Departed"
CRANBERRIES—ILLUSTRATIONS
PH03454 702 (February 23, 1995) p84. "The Cranberries: Strange Fruit" (Bartholomew, Caty)
PH03455 707 (May 4, 1995) p16. "Guilt Berries" (Pendergrast, James T.)
CRANBERRIES—PHOTOGRAPHS
PH03456 664 (September 2, 1993) p28. "Lawler, Mike Hogan, O'Riordan, Noel Hogan"
PH03457 672-673 (December 23, 1993) p48. "[The Cranberries]"
PH03458 680 (April 21, 1994) pp[enc.6-10+]. "[The Cranberries]" (Broad, Julian)
PH03459 695 (November 17, 1994) p37. "The Cranberries" (Meeks, Raymond)
PH03460 704 (March 23, 1995) pp56-57. "[Strange Fruit]" (Day, Corinne)
PH03461 724-725 (December 28, 1995) p46. "O'Riordan In D.C." (Liu, Brian)
CRANE, PHIL—PHOTOGRAPHS—PORTRAITS
PH03462 719 (October 19, 1995) p49. "Crane"
CRANE, WHITFIELD—PHOTOGRAPHS
PH03463 629 (April 30, 1992) p31. "Ugly Kid Joe (from left): Roger Lahr, Klaus Eichstadt, Whitfield Crane, Cordell Crockett And Mark Davis" (O'Beirne, Andy)
CRANES—ALBUMS
PH03464 627 (April 2, 1992) p46. "Wings Of Joy"
CRASH TEST DUMMIES—PHOTOGRAPHS
PH03465 681 (May 5, 1994) p16. "Big Dummies: Dan And Brad Roberts, Darvill, Dorge And Reid (from left)" (Blakesberg, Jay)
CRAVEN, JOE—PHOTOGRAPHS
PH03466 717 (September 21, 1995) p75. "Grisman, Jim Kerwin, Garcia, Joe Craven (from left) In San Francisco, 1991" (Millman, Susana)
CRAWFORD, BRODERICK—PHOTOGRAPHS
PH03467 655 (April 29, 1993) p69. "Crawford And Holliday (left) Reborn As Goodman And Griffith"
CRAWFORD, CINDY—ILLUSTRATIONS
PH03468 715 (August 24, 1995) p107. "Woman As Male Fear & Fantasy" (Ryden, Mark)
CRAWFORD, CINDY—PHOTOGRAPHS
PH03469 672-673 (December 23, 1993) pp96-103. "[Cindy]" (Ritts, Herb)
PH03470 672-673 (December 23, 1993) pp[cover]. "[Cindy Crawford]" (Ritts, Herb)
PH03471 672-673 (December 23, 1993) p94. "Cindy The Brownie With Her Siblings In 1972"
PH03472 672-673 (December 23, 1993) p188. "[Covers]" (Ritts, Herb)
PH03473 715 (August 24, 1995) p108. "Dangerous Women: Michelle Pfeiffer, Sandra Bullock, Julia Roberts, Cindy Crawford And Natasha Henstridge"
CRAWFORD, CINDY—PHOTOGRAPHS—PORTRAITS
PH03474 672-673 (December 23, 1993) p94. "Before The Calendars And Videos Was Cindy The Student, Age 5"
PH03475 672-673 (December 23, 1993) p93. "[Cindy Crawford]" (Ritts, Herb)
PH03476 672-673 (December 23, 1993) p95. "Cindy The Model On An Early Job In San Francisco, Circa 1988" (Watson, Albert)
CRAY, ROBERT—ALBUMS
PH03477 642 (October 29, 1992) p70. "I Was Warned"
PH03478 669 (November 11, 1993) p73. "Shame + A Sin"
CRAY, ROBERT—PHOTOGRAPHS
PH03479 615 (October 17, 1991) p47. "Cray, Clapton And Vaughan (from left) On The Night Of The Crash" (Knight, Robert)
PH03480 616 (October 31, 1991) p13. "B. B. King (left) And Robert Cray" (Blakesberg, Jay)
PH03481 658 (June 10, 1993) p17. "Robert Cray At Earth Day" (Mazur, Kevin)
PH03482 711 (June 29, 1995) p18. "B. B. King, Robert Cray, Buddy Guy, Art Neville, Jimmie Vaughan, Clapton, Raitt And Tommy Shannon" (Long, Andrew)
CRAZY HORSE—ALBUMS
PH03483 617 (November 14, 1991) p171. "Weld"
PH03484 619-620 (December 12, 1991) p165. "Weld"
PH03485 689 (August 25, 1994) p87. "Sleeps With Angels"
PH03486 740 (August 8, 1996) p58. "Broken Arrow"
CRAZY HORSE—VIDEOS
PH03487 621 (January 9, 1992) p56. "New Ragged Glories"
CREACH, PAPA JOHN—PHOTOGRAPHS
PH03488 644 (November 26, 1992) p15. "Kantner, Darby Gould, Jack Casady, Tim Gorman, Prairie Prince, Papa John Creach,

McGuinn And Slick Aguilar (from left)" (Mazur, Kevin)
CREAM—ALBUMS
PH03489 617 (November 14, 1991) p149. "Disraeli Gears" (Sharp, Martin)
PH03490 617 (November 14, 1991) p149. "Disraeli Gears" (Whitaker, Bob)
PH03491 655 (April 29, 1993) p42. "Disraeli Gears"
CREAM—PHOTOGRAPHS
PH03492 649 (February 4, 1993) p51. "Clapton, Baker And Bruce Of Cream"
PH03493 651 (March 4, 1993) p15. "Cream Brings Some 'Sunshine' To The Show" (Mazur, Kevin)
PH03494 655 (April 29, 1993) p38. "Rock's First Power Trio (Clapton, Baker and Bruce, from left) Basking In The Sunshine of History Backstage At The Hall Of Fame" (Mazur, Kevin)
PH03495 655 (April 29, 1993) p34. "The Various Sartorial Incarnatios Of Cream, From Acid Dandies To Proto-Grunge" (Sharratt, Marc)
PH03496 672-673 (December 23, 1993) p17. "Below: The Reunited Cream" (Mazur, Kevin)
CREAM—PHOTOGRAPHS—PORTRAITS
PH03497 655 (April 29, 1993) p34. "Cream In November 1996, Shortly Before The U.K. Release Of The Group's debut Album, Fresh Cream: Jack Bruce, Ginger Baker And Clapton (clockwise from left)" (Gale, Tony)
CREDIT TO THE NATION—PHOTOGRAPHS
PH03498 682 (May 19, 1994) p32. "Nation's M. C. Fusion (center)" (Double, Steve)
CREEDENCE CLEARWATER REVIVAL—PHOTOGRAPHS—PORTRAITS
PH03499 649 (February 4, 1993) p48. "Drummer Clifford, Bassist Cook, Rhythm Guitarist Fogerty, Frontman Fogerty (clockwise from left)" (Wolman, Baron)
CREMIN, SUSAN—PHOTOGRAPHS
PH03500 704 (March 23, 1995) pp102-103. "Class of '95" (Tavee, Tom)
CRENSHAW, MARSHALL—ALBUMS
PH03501 743 (September 19, 1996) p84. "Miracle Of Science"
CRENSHAW, MARSHALL—BOOKS
PH03502 690 (September 8, 1994) p38. "Hollywood Rock"
CRENSHAW, MARSHALL—PHOTOGRAPHS
PH03503 619-620 (December 12, 1991) p42. "Recognize This Man? Marshall Crenshaw" (White, Timothy)
CRIME—ILLUSTRATIONS
PH03504 733 (May 2, 1996) p10. "$125 Fine For Public Urination" (Pendergrast, James T.)
PH03505 744 (October 3, 1996) p16. "$50 Bounty Hunter Kit" (Pendergrast, James T.)
CRIME—PHOTOGRAPHS
PH03506 741 (August 22, 1996) p60. "The Tools Of The Bounty Hunter's Trade" (Maxwell, Robert)
CRIMMINS, BARRY—PHOTOGRAPHS
PH03507 625 (March 5, 1992) p18. "Sara Lee, Crimmins, Graham Nash, Amy Ray, Emily Saliers, David Crosby, Etheridge, Carpenter (from left)" (Berg, Lisa)
CRIMSON TIDE (FILM)—PHOTOGRAPHS
PH03508 709 (June 1, 1995) p70. "Early Starters"
CRISS, ANTHONY—PHOTOGRAPHS
PH03509 615 (October 17, 1991) p27. "Naughty By Nature: DJ Kay Gee, Treach And Vinnie (from left)" (Larsen, Kristine)
CRISS, PETER—PHOTOGRAPHS
PH03510 724-725 (December 28, 1995) p60. "Criss" (Criss, Lydia)
PH03511 727 (February 8, 1996) p18. "Gene Simmons, Peter Criss And Ace Frehley (from left) Rode 'Kiss Alive!' To Stardom In 1975 And Scored A Second Hit Concert Album With 'Kiss Alive II' In 1977" (Putland, Michael)
PH03512 732 (April 18, 1996) p19. "Ace Frehley, Paul Stanley, 2Pac, Peter Criss And Gene Simmons (from left)" (Mazur, Kevin)
PH03513 736 (June 13, 1996) p52. "Kiss Come Back With Their Makeup Intact: Ace Frehley, Gene Simmons, Peter Criss And Paul Stanley" (Malluk, Eddie)
CRISS, PETER—PHOTOGRAPHS—PORTRAITS
PH03514 717 (September 21, 1995) p32. "Packing Heat: Criss" (Goldsmith, Lynn)
CRIST, JOHN—PHOTOGRAPHS
PH03515 710 (June 15, 1995) p52. "At The Uptown: McBride, Veal, John Crist, Michael Gibson (from left)" (Clinch, Danny)
CRITCHLEY, JOHN—PHOTOGRAPHS
PH03516 676 (February 24, 1994) p28. "John Critchley (left) And 13 Engines" (Sigusmondi, Floris)
CROASDALE, CRYSTAL—PHOTOGRAPHS
PH03517 680 (April 21, 1994) pp[enc.26]. "Above With Little Wayne And Crystal" (Halles-Tooke, Hugh)
CROASDALE, WAYNE—PHOTOGRAPHS
PH03517 680 (April 21, 1994) pp[enc.26]. "Above With Little Wayne And Crystal" (Halles-Tooke, Hugh)
PH03518 680 (April 21, 1994) pp[enc.26]. "Above, In His Bike Shop" (Halles-Tooke, Hugh)
PH03519 680 (April 21, 1994) pp[enc.26]. "Below Right, At The Carwash" (Halles-Tooke, Hugh)
PH03520 680 (April 21, 1994) pp[enc.28]. "Below, At Home With Little Wayne" (Halles-Tooke, Hugh)
PH03521 680 (April 21, 1994) pp[enc.29]. "Opposite Page, Riding Off-Road" (Halles-Tooke, Hugh)
PH03522 680 (April 21, 1994) pp[enc.5]. "[Wayne Croasdale]" (Hales-Tooke, Hugh)
PH03523 680 (April 21, 1994) pp[enc.25,27+]. "[Wayne Croasdale]" (Halles-Tooke, Hugh)
CROASDALE, WAYNE, JR.—PHOTOGRAPHS
PH03524 680 (April 21, 1994) pp[enc.26]. "Above With Little Wayne And Crystal" (Halles-Tooke, Hugh)
PH03525 680 (April 21, 1994) pp[enc.28]. "Below, At Home With Little Wayne" (Halles-Tooke, Hugh)
CROATIA—ILLUSTRATIONS
PH03526 728 (February 22, 1996) p16. "The Heart..." (Pendergrast, James T.)
CROCKETT, CORDELL—PHOTOGRAPHS
PH03527 629 (April 30, 1992) p31. "Ugly Kid Joe (from left): Roger Lahr, Klaus Eichstadt, Whitfield Crane, Cordell Crockett And Mark Davis" (O'Beirne, Andy)
CROMWELL, JAMES—PHOTOGRAPHS
PH03528 731 (April 4, 1996) p66. "'Babe,' With James Cromwell And Pig"
CRONENBERG, DAVID—ILLUSTRATIONS—LETTERING
PH03529 623 (February 6, 1992) pp66-70. "[David Cronenberg]" (Ortiz-Lopez, Dennis)
CRONENBERG, DAVID—PHOTOGRAPHS
PH03530 623 (February 6, 1992) p66. "[David Cronenberg]" (Watson, Albert)
CROPPER, STEVE—PHOTOGRAPHS
PH03531 625 (March 5, 1992) p13. "Lewis Steinberg, Steve Cropper, Booker T. Jones, Marion Jackson, Randall Jackson, Duck Dunn, Jim Stewart (from left)" (Elgar, Nick)
PH03532 664 (September 2, 1993) p29. "Grunge Guru Young (left) And Steve Cropper" (Mikrut, Jack)
PH03533 697 (December 15, 1994) p20. "Steve Cropper, King And Lowell Fulson Pay Tribute To Dixon (from left)" (Mosenfelder, Tim)
CROPPER, STEVE—PHOTOGRAPHS—PORTRAITS
PH03534 623 (February 6, 1992) p50. "Booker T. And The MGs (from left): Donald 'Duck' Dunn, Booker T., Steve Cropper And Al Jackson Jr."
PH03535 625 (March 5, 1992) pp14-15. "On The Evening Of The Seventh Annual Hall Of Fame Induction Ceremony, 'Rolling Stone' Gathered These Nine Legendary Guitarists At The Waldorf-Astoria For A Once-In-A-Lifetime..."
PH03536 643 (November 12, 1992) p141. "Booker T. & Steve Cropper" (Seliger, Mark)

PH03537 685 (June 30, 1994) p41. "Booker T. Jones, Steve Cropper, Dave Edmunds And Donald "Duck" Dunn (from left)" (Cohen, Lester)
CROSBY, DAVID—ALBUMS
PH03538 665 (September 16, 1993) p72. "Thousand Roads"
CROSBY, DAVID—PHOTOGRAPHS
PH03539 625 (March 5, 1992) p18. "Sara Lee, Crimmins, Graham Nash, Amy Ray, Emily Saliers, David Crosby, Etheridge, Carpenter (from left)" (Berg, Lisa)
PH03540 679 (April 7, 1994) p37. "Ain't Gonna Work On Yasgur's Farm No More: Phil Lesh, Crosby, Nash, Jorma Kaukonen" (Blakesberg, Jay)
CROSBY, STILLS & NASH—ILLUSTRATIONS
PH03541 645-646 (December 10, 1992) p152. "Crosby, Stills And Nash, 1977"
CROSS, DAVID—ILLUSTRATIONS
PH03542 747 (November 14, 1996) p121. "[Mr. Show With Bob And David]" (Ciardiello, Joe)
CROSS, DAVID—PHOTOGRAPHS
PH03543 655 (April 29, 1993) p20. "The Great Deceivers: John Wetton, David Cross, Fripp And Bill Bruford (from left)"
CROSS, MIKE—PHOTOGRAPHS
PH03544 706 (April 20, 1995) p36. "Motor City Five: Mazzola, Grover, Dombrowski, Tim And Mike Cross (from left)" (Halsband, Michael)
PH03545 708 (May 18, 1995) p17. "Mike Cross (left), Dombrowski Rock Detroit" (Schwab, Bill)
PH03546 710 (June 15, 1995) p49. "Mike Cross, Dombrowski, Charlie Grover, Joey Mazzola, Tim Cross (from left)" (Tavee, Tom)
CROSS, TIM—PHOTOGRAPHS
PH03547 706 (April 20, 1995) p36. "Motor City Five: Mazzola, Grover, Dombrowski, Tim And Mike Cross (from left)" (Halsband, Michael)
PH03548 710 (June 15, 1995) p49. "Mike Cross, Dombrowski, Charlie Grover, Joey Mazzola, Tim Cross (from left)" (Tavee, Tom)
THE CROSSING GUARD (FILM)—PHOTOGRAPHS
PH03549 722 (November 30, 1995) p75. "Regrets For Nicholson And Huston"
CROUGHN, DONNA—PHOTOGRAPHS—PORTRAITS
PH03550 637 (August 20, 1992) p20. "John Hamilton, Donna Croughn, Andy Demos, Dave Dreiwitz And Stuart Hake (from left)" (Borris, Dan)
CROUSE, TIMOTHY—PHOTOGRAPHS
PH03551 632 (June 11, 1992) p62. "Staff Members And Contributing Writers At The 1971 Editorial Conference, At Esalen, In Big Sur" (Leibovitz, Annie)
CROVER, DALE—PHOTOGRAPHS
PH03552 675 (February 10, 1994) p22. "Crover, Simmons, King Buzzo And Mark Deutrom" (Cohen, Lester)
THE CROW (FILM)—ILLUSTRATIONS
PH03553 682 (May 19, 1994) p105. "Enter The Phantom" (Rosen, Jonathon)
THE CROW (FILM)—PHOTOGRAPHS
PH03554 682 (May 19, 1994) p106. "Lee's Inspiration: Black Crowe Robinson"
PH03555 743 (September 19, 1996) p90. "Now Playing"
CROW, BERNICE—PHOTOGRAPHS
PH03556 747 (November 14, 1996) p66. "Down Home In Kennett, 1969: Wendell And Bernice Crow With 6-Year-Old Sheryl And Siblings Kathy (left), Karen (right) And Steve"
CROW, KAREN—PHOTOGRAPHS
PH03556 747 (November 14, 1996) p66. "Down Home In Kennett, 1969: Wendell And Bernice Crow With 6-Year-Old Sheryl And Siblings Kathy (left), Karen (right) And Steve"
CROW, KATHY—PHOTOGRAPHS
PH03556 747 (November 14, 1996) p66. "Down Home In Kennett, 1969: Wendell And Bernice Crow With 6-Year-Old Sheryl And Siblings Kathy (left), Karen (right) And Steve"
CROW, SHERYL—ALBUMS
PH03557 744 (October 3, 1996) p69. "Sheryl Crow"
CROW, SHERYL—ILLUSTRATIONS
PH03558 697 (December 15, 1994) p11. "Sheryl Crow" (Burke, Philip)
PH03559 744 (October 3, 1996) p69. "Jagged Little Frills: Sheryl Crow Makes Bittersweet Pop With Sexy Assurance" (Baseman, Gary)
PH03560 750-751 (December 26, 1996) p26. "Rolling Stone" (Pendergrast, James T.)
CROW, SHERYL—PHOTOGRAPHS
PH03561 681 (May 5, 1994) p22. "Eagle Backs Up Crow" (Cohen, Lester)
PH03562 684 (June 16, 1994) p32. "Together Alone: Crowded House's Neil Finn; Sheryl Crow" (Diamond, Rick)
PH03563 695 (November 17, 1994) p30. "Sheryl Crow" (Kaltman, Naomi)
PH03564 697 (December 15, 1994) p72. "1987's "Bad" Tour: Sheryl Crow (in wig) With Michael Jackson" (Mazur, Kevin)
PH03565 697 (December 15, 1994) p71. "[Sheryl Crow]" (Kaltman, Naomi)
PH03566 697 (December 15, 1994) p73. "Solo Crow: Behind The Scenes No More" (Hutson, Mick)
PH03567 698-699 (December 29, 1994) p45. "Sheryl Crow"
PH03568 706 (April 20, 1995) p15. "Bonnie Raitt, Mistress Of Sensitivity Lennox, Carly Simon And Crow (from left)" (Busacca, Larry)
PH03569 707 (May 4, 1995) p19. "Farrell Tackled The Slopes With An Apres-Ski Aperitif And Sartorial Flair, While The Equally Fly Crow beat Bono At His Own Game In Vegas" (Kravitz, Jeff)
PH03570 719 (October 19, 1995) p40. "Sheryl Crow And Gregg Allman Chat During Rehearsals" (Corbijn, Anton)
PH03571 724-725 (December 28, 1995) p42. "Sheryl Crow Pretended She Was Having Fun" (Mazur, Kevin)
PH03572 724-725 (December 28, 1995) p56. "The Time Was Right: Crow, Hynde, Browne And Reeves (from left)" (Mazur, Kevin)
PH03573 732 (April 18, 1996) p20. "Great Bar Mitzvah, Huh? Crow Perches On John Popper Of Blues Travelers" (Mazur, Kevin)
PH03574 742 (September 5, 1996) p25. "Sheryl Crow Is Serving Seconds" (Sundland, Steen)
PH03575 746 (October 31, 1996) p28. "Join The Club: Wal-Mart Bans Sheryl Crow's New Album" (Sundland, Steen)
PH03576 747 (November 14, 1996) p66. "Down Home In Kennett, 1969: Wendell And Bernice Crow With 6-Year-Old Sheryl And Siblings Kathy (left), Karen (right) And Steve"
PH03577 747 (November 14, 1996) p71. "Mizzou, 1980: Crow Played In A Band Called Cashmere While At The University Of Missouri"
PH03578 747 (November 14, 1996) p70. "The Performer At 15: Center Stage Held Few Terrors"
PH03579 747 (November 14, 1996) pp65,68-69. "[Sheryl Crow]" (Seliger, Mark)
PH03580 747 (November 14, 1996) pp[cover]. "Sheryl Crow: Why The Hell Is She So Sad?" (Seliger, Mark)
PH03581 748 (November 28, 1996) p25. "Crow Flirting With Matthew McConaughey" (Kravitz, Jeff)
PH03582 750-751 (December 26, 1996) p81. "[Sheryl Crow]" (Sundland, Steen)
CROW, SHERYL—PHOTOGRAPHS—PORTRAITS
PH03583 668 (October 28, 1993) p25. "As Crow Flies: The Singer Looks To 'Let It Bleed' For Inspiration On Her New LP" (Ng, Karjean)
PH03584 700 (January 26, 1995) p50. "All I Wanna Do Is Win Best New Female Singer: Sheryl Crow" (Preston, Neal)
PH03585 706 (April 20, 1995) p15. "You, Too, Can BE A Winner: Crow, Soundgarden's Chris Cornell And Etheridge" (Mazur, Kevin)

PH03586 724-725 (December 28, 1995) pp[cover]. "Rock & Roll Yearbook" (Seliger, Mark)
PH03587 750-751 (December 26, 1996) p81. "Make-Over" (Jennings, Steve)

CROW, STEVE—PHOTOGRAPHS
PH03588 747 (November 14, 1996) p66. "Down Home In Kennett, 1969: Wendell And Bernice Crow With 6-Year-Old Sheryl And Siblings Kathy (left), Karen (right) And Steve"

CROW, WENDELL—PHOTOGRAPHS
PH03588 747 (November 14, 1996) p66. "Down Home In Kennett, 1969: Wendell And Bernice Crow With 6-Year-Old Sheryl And Siblings Kathy (left), Karen (right) And Steve"

CROWDED HOUSE—ALBUMS
PH03589 679 (April 7, 1994) p76. "Together Alone"

CROWDED HOUSE—PHOTOGRAPHS
PH03590 676 (February 24, 1994) p17. "Four's A Crowd: Neil Finn, Mark Hart, Paul Hester And Nick Seymour (from left)" (Broad, Julian)

CROWDED HOUSE—PHOTOGRAPHS—PORTRAITS
PH03591 619-620 (December 12, 1991) p60. "Crowded House (above) Rocked..." (Cuffaro, Chris)

CROWE, CAMERON—PHOTOGRAPHS
PH03592 638 (September 3, 1992) p11. "Josh Taft, Paul Westerberg And Cameron Crowe (from left)" (Mercer, Lance)
PH03593 640 (October 1, 1992) p59. "Crowe Wore A Woeful Countenance During Filming" (O'Neal, Jane)
PH03594 647 (January 7, 1993) p11. "RS Alumni Photog Annie Leibovitz, Thompson, David Felton, Cameron Crowe, Chris Hodenfield, Ben Fong-Torres, Paul Scanlon (from left)" (Elgar, Nick)
PH03595 750-751 (December 26, 1996) p138. "Crowe—Script In Hand—Directs Cruise And Zellweger"

CROWELL, RODNEY—ALBUMS
PH03596 636 (August 6, 1992) p60. "Life Is Messy"
PH03597 691 (September 22, 1994) p99. "Let The Picture Paint Itself"

THE CRUCIBLE (FILM)—ILLUSTRATIONS
PH03598 749 (December 12, 1996) p89. "The Devil Made Them Do It" (Brodner, Steve)

THE CRUCIBLE (FILM)—PHOTOGRAPHS
PH03599 743 (September 19, 1996) p88. "The Young And The Restless"
PH03600 749 (December 12, 1996) p90. "Day-Lewis And Allen Fight Back"
PH03601 749 (December 12, 1996) p90. "Ryder And Woodard Cast A Spell"
PH03602 749 (December 12, 1996) p90. "Scofield Drives A Girl To Hysteria"

CRUEL SEA—ALBUMS
PH03603 704 (March 23, 1995) p124. "The Honeymoon Is Over"

CRUEL SEA—PHOTOGRAPHS
PH03604 712-713 (July 13, 1995) p46. "High Sea: Gormly, Elliot, And Perkins (from left)" (Capak, R. J.)

CRUISE, JULEE—PHOTOGRAPHS
PH03605 637 (August 20, 1992) p11. "The B-52's (from left): Fred Schneider, Kate Pierson, Julee Cruise, Keith Strickland, Sue Hadjopoulos And Pat Irwin" (Michelson, Eric T.)

CRUISE, TOM—ILLUSTRATIONS
PH03606 659 (June 24, 1993) p87. "Dinosaur Summer" (Witte, Michael)
PH03607 697 (December 15, 1994) p101. "The Dying Game" (Kelley, Gary)

CRUISE, TOM—ILLUSTRATIONS—LETTERING
PH03608 631 (May 28, 1992) p34. "Tom Cruise" (Karl, Anita)

CRUISE, TOM—PHOTOGRAPHS
PH03609 633 (June 25, 1992) p48. "Cruise And Kidman Get Their Irish Up"
PH03610 647 (January 7, 1993) p50. "Jack Nicholson: On The Spot With To Cruise (left)..."
PH03611 648 (January 21, 1993) p56. "A Few Good Men"
PH03612 653 (April 1, 1993) p57. "A Few Good Men"
PH03613 659 (June 24, 1993) p88. "Suspense: 'The Firm' With Jeanne Tripplehorn And Cruise"
PH03614 662 (August 5, 1993) p73. "Busey, Hunter And Cruise In Jeopardy"
PH03615 696 (December 1, 1994) p94. "In "Vampire," Pitt And Tom Cruise Are Star Bloodsuckers"
PH03616 697 (December 15, 1994) p17. "[Keith Richards, Tom Cruise, & Bruce Springsteen]" (Ferreira, Albert)
PH03617 697 (December 15, 1994) p102. "Prowling Vampires Kirsten Dunst, Brad Pitt And Tom Cruise"
PH03618 698-699 (December 29, 1994) p74. "Cruise And Nicole Kidman Put The Media Bite On Film Fans" (Trapper, Frank)
PH03619 698-699 (December 29, 1994) p194. "Cruise Bites Pitt In "Vampire""
PH03620 705 (April 6, 1995) p69. "Oscar Rejects"
PH03621 750-751 (December 26, 1996) p138. "Crowe—Script In Hand—Directs Cruise And Zellweger"
PH03622 750-751 (December 26, 1996) p207. "Tom Cruise And Renee Zellweger"

CRUISE, TOM—PHOTOGRAPHS—PORTRAITS
PH03623 631 (May 28, 1992) pp35,37. "[Tom Cruise]" (Watson, Albert)
PH03624 631 (May 28, 1992) pp[cover]. "Tom Cruise: The Human Touch" (Watson, Albert)
PH03625 645-646 (December 10, 1992) pp[cover]. "1992 Yearbook" (Watson, Albert)
PH03626 750-751 (December 26, 1996) p138. "Cruise Makes A Point"
PH03627 750-751 (December 26, 1996) p137. "[Tom Cruise]"

CRUMB (FILM)—ILLUSTRATIONS
PH03628 724-725 (December 28, 1995) p136. "Unusual Pleasure"

CRUMB (FILM)—PHOTOGRAPHS
PH03629 707 (May 4, 1995) p74. "R. Crumb In 'Crumb'"
PH03630 724-725 (December 28, 1995) p136. "The 10 Best movies Of 1995 (degrees of size)"

CRUMB, R.—ILLUSTRATIONS—PORTRAITS
PH03631 707 (May 4, 1995) p76. "Self-Portrait: I'm Just A Bitter, Mean Spirited Dude" (Crumb, R.)

CRUMB, R.—PHOTOGRAPHS
PH03632 707 (May 4, 1995) p74. "R. Crumb In 'Crumb'"

THE CRUSH (FILM)—PHOTOGRAPHS
PH03633 716 (September 7, 1995) p50. "Lethal Lolita: Silverstone Does Her Thing In 'The Crush'" (McEwan, Rob)

CRUZ, BRANDON—PHOTOGRAPHS
PH03634 702 (February 23, 1995) p20. "Thrashin' To The Oldies: Cruz (left) and Dolenz" (Mayer, Jeffrey)

CRUZ, VLADIMIR—PHOTOGRAPHS
PH03635 701 (February 9, 1995) p63. "Perrugoria And Cruz Do The Forbidden"

CRYER, SUZANNE—PHOTOGRAPHS
PH03636 704 (March 23, 1995) pp102-103. "Class of '95" (Tavee, Tom)

THE CRYING GAME (FILM)—PHOTOGRAPHS
PH03637 644 (November 26, 1992) p80. "An Identity Crisis For Jaye Davidson (left) And Stephen Rea"
PH03638 648 (January 21, 1993) p56. "The Crying Game"
PH03639 653 (April 1, 1993) p57. "The Crying Game"

CRYNER, BOBBIE—ALBUMS
PH03640 726 (January 25, 1996) p73. "Girl Of Your Dreams"

CRYSTAL, BILLY—PHOTOGRAPHS
PH03641 616 (October 31, 1991) p52. "With A Face Made For Pathos, He Is Our Preeminent Sad, Smiling Medium For Disembodied Pain And Reckoning" (Schiffman, Bonnie)
PH03642 642 (October 29, 1992) p78. "In Or Out Of Old-Age Makeup, Billy Crystal Gets Laughs"
PH03643 651 (March 4, 1993) p18. "Billy Crystal Presenting The Award To His Uncle Milt Gabler" (Mazur, Kevin)

PH03644 678 (March 24, 1994) p100. "Missing In Oscar Action"
PH03645 685 (June 30, 1994) p80. "Crystal, Lovitz And Stern Go West For Box-Office Gold"
CUB—ALBUMS
PH03646 729 (March 7, 1996) p64. "Volcano"
CUB—PHOTOGRAPHS
PH03647 747 (November 14, 1996) p56. "[Cub]" (Chavez, Marina)
CUBA—ILLUSTRATIONS
PH03648 630 (May 14, 1992) p91. "[Cuba]" (Cowles, David)
PH03649 738-739 (July 11, 1996) p60. "P. J. O'Rourke's Cuba" (Blitt, Barry)
PH03650 742 (September 5, 1996) p16. "Cuban Economy" (Pendergrast, James T.)
CUBA—PHOTOGRAPHS
PH03651 619-620 (December 12, 1991) p146. "Sugar-Cane Cutters In Their Quarters Near Havana, 1988" (Salgado, Sebastiao)
CUCCURULLO, WARREN—PHOTOGRAPHS
PH03652 653 (April 1, 1993) p20. "Nick Rhodes, Simon LeBon, John Taylor And Warren Cuccurullo (from left)" (Heungman)
PH03653 708 (May 18, 1995) p17. "Simon LeBon, Grandmaster Flash And Warren Cuccurullo In New York (from left)" (Olson, Sheryl)
CULKIN, MACAULAY—PHOTOGRAPHS
PH03654 645-646 (December 10, 1992) p190. "Macaulay Culkin"
PH03655 668 (October 28, 1993) p88. "Mac The Knife"
PH03656 686-687 (July 14, 1994) p99. "[Macaulay Culkin]"
CULT—ALBUMS
PH03657 698-699 (December 29, 1994) p173. "The Cult"
CUNNIFF, JILL—PHOTOGRAPHS
PH03658 660-661 (July 8, 1993) p97. "Luscious Jackson (clockwise from top left): Glaser, Schellenbach, Cunniff, Trimble" (Minchin, James R., III)
PH03659 689 (August 25, 1994) p24. "Luscious' Gabby Glaser, Jill Cunniff" (Blakesberg, Jay)
PH03660 710 (June 15, 1995) p17. "LJ's Schellenbach, Gabby Glaser, Vivian trimble And Jill Cunniff At The Rally For Women's Lives, in D.C. (from left)" (Harrington, John)
CUNNINGHAM, CHARLIE—PHOTOGRAPHS
PH03661 634-635 (July 9, 1992) p84. "Bike Builder Charlie Cunningham With His Legendary Racer Wife, Jacquie Phelan" (Stone, Pete)
CUNNINGHAM, JEREMY—PHOTOGRAPHS
PH03662 630 (May 14, 1992) p32. "The Levellers (from left): Friend, Sevink, Chadwick, Heather And Cunningham" (Doove, Hester)
CUNNINGHAM, REBECCA—PHOTOGRAPHS
PH03663 736 (June 13, 1996) p46. "As An Integral Part Of Their Training Regimen, Rebecca (left) And Karey Visit A Tanning Salon Daily" (Seliger, Mark)
PH03664 736 (June 13, 1996) p44. "Rebecca Cunningham (left) And Karey 'Harley' Tynes In The Atlanta Apartment The Two Dancers Share" (Seliger, Mark)
CUOMO, MARIO—PHOTOGRAPHS
PH03665 747 (November 14, 1996) p81. "Live From New York's Governors Island, 1984: Larry, Gov. Mario Cuomo, Herb Cohen (from left)"
CUOMO, RIVERS—PHOTOGRAPHS
PH03666 694 (November 3, 1994) p40. "Matt Sharp, Patrick Wilson, Brian Bell And Rivers Cuomo (from left)" (Elledge, Paul)
PH03667 704 (March 23, 1995) pp62-63. "Matt Sharp, Rivers Cuomo, Brian Bell, Pat Wilson (from left)" (Corbijn, Anton)
PH03668 704 (March 23, 1995) p64. "The Ultrasensitive Rivers Cuomo" (Corbijn, Anton)
CURE—ALBUMS
PH03669 630 (May 14, 1992) p101. "Wish"
PH03670 645-646 (December 10, 1992) p179. "Wish"
PH03671 672-673 (December 23, 1993) p168. "Show"
PH03672 736 (June 13, 1996) p83. "Wild Mood Swings"
CURE—ILLUSTRATIONS
PH03673 630 (May 14, 1992) p101. "Healing For A Cult Of Millions" (Rosen, Jonathon)
CURE—PHOTOGRAPHS
PH03674 631 (May 28, 1992) p11. "Simon Gallup, Porl Thompson, Perry Bamonte, Robert Smith, Boris Williams (from left)" (Cox, Paul)
PH03675 633 (June 25, 1992) p12. "The Cure's Simon Gallup, Perry Bamonte And Smith (from left)" (Elgar, Nick)
PH03676 733 (May 2, 1996) p22. "Partial To Shades: The Cure's New Lineup Is Simon Gallup, Roger O'Donnell, Robert Smith, Perry Bamonte And Jason Cooper (from left)" (Cox, Paul)
CURLEY, JOHN—PHOTOGRAPHS
PH03677 695 (November 17, 1994) p78. "Afghan Whigs" (Lixenberg, Dana)
PH03678 721 (November 16, 1995) p41. "Greg Dulli (left) and John Curley In Robert Lang's Studio, In Seattle" (Peterson, Charles)
CURLEY, JOHN—PHOTOGRAPHS—PORTRAITS
PH03679 671 (December 9, 1993) p21. "The Whig Club: Rick McCollum, Greg Dulli, Steve Earle And John Curley" (Broad, Julian)
CURRIE, JUSTIN—PHOTOGRAPHS—PORTRAITS
PH03680 642 (October 29, 1992) pp64-65. "[Justin Currie]" (Salvatori, Lou)
CURTIN, JANE—PHOTOGRAPHS
PH03681 664 (September 2, 1993) p70. "Conehead Movies"
CURTIN, JANE—PHOTOGRAPHS—PORTRAITS
PH03682 706 (April 20, 1995) p86. "The 'SNL' Legacy Of Screen Shame"
CURTIS, JAMIE LEE—PHOTOGRAPHS
PH03683 689 (August 25, 1994) p96. "Schwarzenegger And Curtis Work Out The Kinks"
PH03684 691 (September 22, 1994) p106. "Woman Demeaned"
CURVE—ALBUMS
PH03685 630 (May 14, 1992) p107. "Doppelganger"
PH03686 631 (May 28, 1992) p69. "Doppleganger"
CUSACK, JOHN—PHOTOGRAPHS
PH03687 694 (November 3, 1994) p104. "Wiest Puts The Make On Cusack In Central Park"
CUSENZA, JOHN SEBASTIAN—PHOTOGRAPHS—PORTRAITS
PH03688 638 (September 3, 1992) pp[enc.61]. "[John Sebastian Cusenza]" (Eccles, Andrew)
CUSHION, MELANIE—PHOTOGRAPHS
PH03689 679 (April 7, 1994) p64. "[University Of Cincinnati, Melanie Cushion]" (Winters, Dan)
CYBERSPACE—PHOTOGRAPHS
PH03690 696 (December 1, 1994) p72. " Interactive "Monster" Press kit On America Online"
PH03691 696 (December 1, 1994) p72. "Hard-Core Music Newsgroups On Cyberden"
PH03692 696 (December 1, 1994) p73. "Level Playing Field: Any Band Gets On-Line Exposure"
PH03693 696 (December 1, 1994) p72. "A Music Bulletin Board On Prodigy"
PH03694 696 (December 1, 1994) p72. "R.E.M."
PH03695 748 (November 28, 1996) p125. "[Cyberspace]" (Grant, Bob)
CYBORGANICS—PHOTOGRAPHS
PH03696 722 (November 30, 1995) pp[enc.2-3]. "The Ramona Street Gang At Home: Welcome To Ground Zero Of The Information Explosion" (McLeod, William Mercer)
PH03697 722 (November 30, 1995) pp[enc.4]. "Some Guests From Mills College Mixing At T.N.D." (McLeod, William Mercer)
PH03698 722 (November 30, 1995) pp[enc.10]. "Some Of The Regulars At White Trash Night" (McLeod, William Mercer)

CYPHER, JULIE—PHOTOGRAPHS
PH03699 698-699 (December 29, 1994) p114. "With Live-In Lover Julie Cypher"
PH03700 709 (June 1, 1995) p45. "Etheridge With Cypher" (Sirota, Peggy)

CYPRESS HILL—ALBUMS
PH03701 665 (September 16, 1993) p64. "Black Sunday"
PH03702 721 (November 16, 1995) p109. "Temples Of Boom"

CYPRESS HILL—ILLUSTRATIONS
PH03703 721 (November 16, 1995) p109. "High Priests" (Coe, Sue)
PH03704 731 (April 4, 1996) p18. "[The Simpsons]" (Groening, Matt)

CYPRESS HILL—PHOTOGRAPHS
PH03705 631 (May 28, 1992) p18. "Muggs, Sen Dog And B-Real (from left)" (Moss, Gary)
PH03706 662 (August 5, 1993) p16. "Just Another Band From L.A.? Sen Dog, B-Real And DJ Muggs (from left)"
PH03707 663 (August 19, 1993) p20. "Future New Wave? Sonic Youth In The Studio With Cypress Hill" (Callahan, Kristin)
PH03708 672-673 (December 23, 1993) p53. "Muggs, B-Real And Sen-Dog (from left) Pay Homage To The Wicked Weed On 'Black Sunday'" (Borris, Dan)
PH03709 715 (August 24, 1995) p44. "Sen Dog, B-Real, Bobo (from left)" (Blakesberg, Jay)
PH03710 731 (April 4, 1996) p30. "Sen Dog, Muggs, B-Real (from left)" (McClelland, P.)

CYPRESS HILL—PHOTOGRAPHS—PORTRAITS
PH03711 669 (November 11, 1993) p64. "The Dope On The Hill: B-real, Sen Dog And Muggs (bottom row, from left)" (Borris, Dan)
PH03712 674 (January 27, 1994) p41. "Cypress Hill: Smokin'" (Blakesberg, Jay)
PH03713 705 (April 6, 1995) p28. "Rappers Cypress Hill" (Brusso, Andrew)

CYRUS, BILLY RAY—ALBUMS
PH03714 636 (August 6, 1992) p60. "Some Gave All"
PH03715 637 (August 20, 1992) p68. "Some Gave All"
PH03716 638 (September 3, 1992) p88. "Some Gave All"
PH03717 639 (September 17, 1992) p116. "Some Gave All"
PH03718 640 (October 1, 1992) p88. "Some Gave All"
PH03719 642 (October 29, 1992) p84. "Some Gave All"
PH03720 645-646 (December 10, 1992) p166. "Some Gave All"
PH03721 665 (September 16, 1993) p66. "It Won't Be The Last"

CYRUS, BILLY RAY—PHOTOGRAPHS
PH03722 636 (August 6, 1992) p29. "[Billy Ray Cyrus]" (Nash, Peter)
PH03723 645-646 (December 10, 1992) p65. "Achy Breaky Billy" (Baker, Lenny)

D

D GENERATION—ALBUMS
PH03724 743 (September 19, 1996) p84. "No Lunch" (Fricke, David)

D GENERATION—PHOTOGRAPHS
PH03725 701 (February 9, 1995) p19. "D Gen (from left): Danny Sage, Richard Bacchus, Howie Pyro, Jesse Malin, Michael Wildwood" (Seliger, Mark)
PH03726 701 (February 9, 1995) p20. "Glam Rabble-Rousers Wildwood, Malin And Sage (from left) In New York City" (Mazur, Kevin)
PH03727 705 (April 6, 1995) p16. "Label Flava Of The Month: D Gen's Jesse malin (left) And Danny Sage" (Brown, Christy)
PH03728 710 (June 15, 1995) p41. "D Gen (from left): Pyro, Michael Wildwood, Malin, Sage, Richard Bacchus And Gomez" (Ragel, Jon)

D, CHUCK—ALBUMS
PH03729 744 (October 3, 1996) p72. "Autobiography Of Mistachuck"

D, CHUCK—PHOTOGRAPHS
PH03730 624 (February 20, 1992) p12. "PE's Chuck D"
PH03731 664 (September 2, 1993) p32. "Speaker Of The House: PE's Chuck D" (Wise, Alexandra)
PH03732 670 (November 25, 1993) p37. "Grandmaster Flash, Herc, Afrika Bambaataa And Chuck D" (Mazur, Kevin)
PH03733 685 (June 30, 1994) p30. "New "Mess Age": Flavor Flav, Chuck D And Terminator X (from front)" (Seliger, Mark)
PH03734 733 (May 2, 1996) p14. "Vote-Getters Ice-T, Hayes And Chuck D (from left) Do The Right Thing" (Mazur, Kevin)

D, CHUCK—PHOTOGRAPHS—PORTRAITS
PH03735 716 (September 7, 1995) p25. "On Hiatus: P.E.'s Flavor Flav (left), Chuck D" (Tonge, David)
PH03736 745 (October 17, 1996) p46. "[Chuck D]" (Leitman, Ruth)

D, MIKE—ILLUSTRATIONS
PH03737 631 (May 28, 1992) p3. "The Beasties' Mike D" (Burke, Philip)

D, MIKE—PHOTOGRAPHS
PH03738 631 (May 28, 1992) p40. "The Beastie Boys (from left): Adam Yauch, Mike Diamond And Adam Horovitz" (Camp, E. J.)
PH03739 681 (May 5, 1994) p21. "Beasties Adam Yauch (left) And Mike D With Joey DiPaolo"
PH03740 693 (October 20, 1994) p28. "Beasties Adam Yauch, Mike D, Adam Horowitz Warming Up At Radio City Music Hall During Rehearsal (from left)" (Mazur, Kevin)

D, MIKE—PHOTOGRAPHS—PORTRAITS
PH03741 695 (November 17, 1994) p139. "Beastie Boys" (Rolston, Matthew)
PH03742 750-751 (December 26, 1996) p56. "Mike D Of The Beastie Boys" (Kessler, Joshua)

D-SMOOTH—PHOTOGRAPHS
PH03743 676 (February 24, 1994) p24. "Spank Dog, Money Mike, Mr. Watts, Peter Jorge, D-Smooth, G (from left)" (Hastings, Daniel)

DA BRAT—PHOTOGRAPHS
PH03744 694 (November 3, 1994) p40. "Da Brat: One Nasty Girl" (Otte, Sylvia)
PH03745 698-699 (December 29, 1994) p46. "Da Brat"
PH03746 707 (May 4, 1995) p19. "[Da Brat]" (De Guire, Gregg)

DADA—PHOTOGRAPHS
PH03747 647 (January 7, 1993) p19. "Michael Gurley, Joie Calio And Phil Leavitt (from left)" (Mauro, Aldo)
PH03748 660-661 (July 8, 1993) p101. "Dada (from left): Michael Gurley, Phil Leavitt And Joie Calio" (Lass, Imke)

DADDY G—PHOTOGRAPHS
PH03749 616 (October 31, 1991) p25. "Massive Attack (from left): 3-D, Mushroom And Daddy G"
PH03750 718 (October 5, 1995) p32. "Nicolette, Stephen Lewinson, Daddy G (from left)" (Mazur, Kevin)

DADDY RICH—ALBUMS
PH03751 669 (November 11, 1993) p76. "Dust To Dust"

DAFOE, WILLEM—PHOTOGRAPHS
PH03752 626 (March 19, 1992) p104. "Sarandon And Dafoe Try To Find A New Life After Drug Dealing"
PH03753 630 (May 14, 1992) p114. "Dafoe (left) Suspects Rourke And Mastrantonio"
PH03754 649 (February 4, 1993) p72. "Homage Of Ripoff? In 'Body of Evidence,' Madonna And Dafoe (left) Share Stone And Douglas's Basic Instincts"
PH03755 672-673 (December 23, 1993) p172. "Dud Sex"
PH03756 672-673 (December 23, 1993) p16. "Left: Willem Dafoe Sucks Face With Madonna"
PH03757 700 (January 26, 1995) p66. "Dafoe, Richardson"
PH03758 721 (November 16, 1995) p94. "The Elvis Wanna-Be (with Willem Dafoe) In 'Wild At Heart'"

DAHLHEIMER, PATRICK—PHOTOGRAPHS
PH03759 696 (December 1, 1994) p51. "Patrick Dahlheimer" (Fleischauer, Robert)
PH03760 716 (September 7, 1995) p13. "Chad Taylor, Kowalezyk, Patrick Dahlheimer (from left)" (Callahan, Kristin)
PH03761 726 (January 25, 1996) p35. "Dahlheimer, Taylor, Kowalczyk And Gracey (from left) At Their York, Pa., High School In 1989" (Broad, Julian)
DAHLHEIMER, PATRICK—PHOTOGRAPHS—PORTRAITS
PH03762 726 (January 25, 1996) p34. "Taylor, Kowalczyk, Gracey And Dahlheimer (from left) In New York In Late 1995" (Broad, Julian)
DAISY—PHOTOGRAPHS
PH03763 628 (April 16, 1992) p63. "Daisy" (DeJoseph, Dominic)
DAISY CHAINSAW—PHOTOGRAPHS
PH03764 628 (April 16, 1992) p56. "Gray, Garside, Johnson And Adams (from left)" (Double, Steve)
DALAI LAMA—PHOTOGRAPHS
PH03765 740 (August 8, 1996) p21. "The Dalai Lama And Yauch Meet In Rome" (Suekwon)
DALE, DICK—ALBUMS
PH03766 668 (October 28, 1993) p81. "Tribal Thunder"
DALTON, NIC—PHOTOGRAPHS
PH03767 675 (February 10, 1994) p39. "The Squeaky Clean, Endlessly Cute Power-Pop Trio: Drummer Ryan, Dando And Bassist Dalton" (Rheims, Bettina)
DALTREY, ROGER—PHOTOGRAPHS
PH03768 619-620 (December 12, 1991) p100. "Graham With The Who's Roger Daltrey, Keith Moon And Pete Townshend, In 1976" (Zagaris, Michael)
PH03769 678 (March 24, 1994) p18. "Who Wants A Box Set? Daltrey (left) With Band"
PH03770 679 (April 7, 1994) p20. "Join Together: Daltrey Onstage With Townshend" (Mazur, Kevin)
DALY, BOB—PHOTOGRAPHS
PH03771 726 (January 25, 1996) p26. "Warner's Bob Daly (left), Terry Semel" (Smeal, Jim)
DAMAGE (FILM)—PHOTOGRAPHS
PH03772 647 (January 7, 1993) p51. "Juliette Binoche And Jeremy Irons Play Sex Dangerously"
DAMBUILDERS—PHOTOGRAPHS
PH03773 686-687 (July 14, 1994) p79. "[The Dambuilders]" (Berg, Bob)
PH03774 693 (October 20, 1994) p30. "Cleo's Hanley, Stacy Jones, Manning; Builders Joan Wasser, Eric Masunaga" (Robicheau, Paul)
PH03775 693 (October 20, 1994) p49. "Kevin March, Dave Derby, Joan Wasser, Eric Masunaga (from left)" (Lass, Imke)
DANCE HALL CRASHERS—PHOTOGRAPHS
PH03776 721 (November 16, 1995) p25. "DHC's Rogers (left) And Karina Denike" (Chambers, Brian)
DANCERS—PHOTOGRAPHS
PH03777 736 (June 13, 1996) p43. "Backstage At The Taj Mahal, Dancers Prepare For A Evening's Work" (Seliger, Mark)
PH03778 736 (June 13, 1996) p42. "[Strip Club Dancers]" (Seliger, Mark)
DANCING—PHOTOGRAPHS
PH03779 736 (June 13, 1996) p24. "[Proms]"
DANDO, EVAN—ILLUSTRATIONS
PH03780 675 (February 10, 1994) p3. "Evan Dando" (Burke, Philip)
DANDO, EVAN—PHOTOGRAPHS
PH03781 627 (April 2, 1992) p13. "Juliana Hatfield And The Lemonheads' Evan Dando In The Studio" (Shulman, Scott C.)
PH03782 637 (August 20, 1992) p22. "Hatfield (left) With Dando" (Pasley, Richard)
PH03783 658 (June 10, 1993) p34. "Head Lemonhead Evan Dando" (Capak, R. J.)
PH03784 662 (August 5, 1993) p33. "Michael Hutchence (left) With Dando" (Florence, John)
PH03785 666 (September 30, 1993) p21. "Evan Dando: 'My Only Goal For This Album Was To Have Enough Songs'" (Cuffaro, Chris)
PH03786 674 (January 27, 1994) p25. "Dando: Hysteria In New York" (Mazur, Kevin)
PH03787 675 (February 10, 1994) p38. "6-Year-Old Evan And Family In St. Croix In 1973"
PH03788 675 (February 10, 1994) p38. "At Home In Boston"
PH03789 675 (February 10, 1994) pp34-35. "[Evan Dando]" (Rheims, Bettina)
PH03790 675 (February 10, 1994) p38. "Jeffrey, Holly, Evan And Susan Dando In 1975"
PH03791 675 (February 10, 1994) p39. "The Squeaky Clean, Endlessly Cute Power-Pop Trio: Drummer Ryan, Dando And Bassist Dalton" (Rheims, Bettina)
PH03792 680 (April 21, 1994) p34. "[Iggy Pop, Evan Dando, Chainsaw Kittens]" (Peterson, Charles)
PH03793 695 (November 17, 1994) p148. "Evan Dando" (Klein, Steven)
PH03794 700 (January 26, 1995) p17. "[John Giorno's AIDS Treatment Project]" (Gruen, Bob)
PH03795 708 (May 18, 1995) p17. "Love, On The Rocks: Dando And Date" (Mazur, Kevin)
PH03796 721 (November 16, 1995) p40. "Evan Dando: Can 'Big Gay Heart' Play To The Truly Alternative?" (Levine, Laura)
PH03797 742 (September 5, 1996) p21. "Fruit O' the Loon: Lemonhead Dando Rocks Hard (can't ya tell?) With Patrick Murphy, Dina Waxman And Bill Gibson (from left)"
PH03798 747 (November 14, 1996) p40. "[Evan Dando]" (Churilla, Lynda)
DANDO, EVAN—PHOTOGRAPHS—PORTRAITS
PH03799 649 (February 4, 1993) p14. "Alterna-hunk Dando" (Peretz, Jesse)
PH03800 672-673 (December 23, 1993) p69. "Left: Evan Dando, This Year's Model" (Factor, Davis)
PH03801 675 (February 10, 1994) p38. "Dando's Skidmore ID"
PH03802 740 (August 8, 1996) p23. "Evan Dando Gets Out Of The Clubs And Into The Studio" (Cuffaro, Chris)
DANDO, HOLLY—PHOTOGRAPHS
PH03803 675 (February 10, 1994) p38. "6-Year-Old Evan And Family In St. Croix In 1973"
PH03804 675 (February 10, 1994) p38. "At Home In Boston"
PH03805 675 (February 10, 1994) p38. "Jeffrey, Holly, Evan And Susan Dando In 1975"
DANDO, JEFFREY—PHOTOGRAPHS
PH03806 675 (February 10, 1994) p38. "6-Year-Old Evan And Family In St. Croix In 1973"
PH03807 675 (February 10, 1994) p38. "At Home In Boston"
PH03808 675 (February 10, 1994) p38. "Jeffrey, Holly, Evan And Susan Dando In 1975"
DANDO, SUSAN—PHOTOGRAPHS
PH03809 675 (February 10, 1994) p38. "6-Year-Old Evan And Family In St. Croix In 1973"
PH03810 675 (February 10, 1994) p38. "At Home In Boston"
PH03811 675 (February 10, 1994) p38. "Jeffrey, Holly, Evan And Susan Dando In 1975"
DANDY WARHOLS—PHOTOGRAPHS
PH03812 721 (November 16, 1995) p78. "Peter Holmstrom, Courtney Taylor, Zia McCabe, Eric Hedford (from left): They're Exploding, Plastic And Inevitable, Andy Would Approve!" (Winters, Dan)
DANELL, DENNIS—PHOTOGRAPHS
PH03813 634-635 (July 9, 1992) p32. "Chris Reece, Mike Ness, John Maurer And Dennis Danell (from left)" (Cuffaro, Chris)
DANES, CLAIRE—ILLUSTRATIONS
PH03814 747 (November 14, 1996) p123. "Just Two Kids In Love" (Brodner, Steve)

DANES, CLAIRE—PHOTOGRAPHS
PH03815 682 (May 19, 1994) p56. "[Claire Danes]"
PH03816 700 (January 26, 1995) p17. "Hatfield, "Lifer" Claire Danes" (Wolfe, Jerry)
PH03817 715 (August 24, 1995) p73. "Hot Actress" (Duttmann, Uwe)
PH03818 740 (August 8, 1996) p18. "Samantha Mathis (left) And Claire Danes At The MTV Movie Awards" (Kravitz, Jeff)
PH03819 747 (November 14, 1996) p124. "The Bright Angel Meets Her Knight At A Costume Ball"
PH03820 747 (November 14, 1996) p124. "Danes Juliet Pines For Her Love"
PH03821 747 (November 14, 1996) p124. "Dicaprio's Desperate Romeo Takes A Hostage"
PH03822 749 (December 12, 1996) p19. "[Leonardo Dicaprio & Claire Danes]" (Kravitz, Jeff)
D'ANGELO—ALBUMS
PH03823 716 (September 7, 1995) p71. "Brown Sugar"
D'ANGELO—PHOTOGRAPHS
PH03824 732 (April 18, 1996) p19. "Open Up And Say Ah: D'Angelo (left) And Three-Time Winner Seal Get A Little Crazy" (Mazur, Kevin)
DANGEROUS GAME (FILM)—PHOTOGRAPHS
PH03825 671 (December 9, 1993) p78. "Impossible Dream: Keitel Teaches Madonna To Act"
DANGEROUS MINDS (FILM)—PHOTOGRAPHS
PH03826 715 (August 24, 1995) p108. "Dangerous Women: Michelle Pfeiffer, Sandra Bullock, Julia Roberts, Cindy Crawford And Natasha Henstridge"
DANIEL, CASEY—PHOTOGRAPHS
PH03827 731 (April 4, 1996) p36. "The Two Jasons (Pollock and Ross), Khalsa And Daniel" (Clinch, Danny)
DANIEL, NATHAN—PHOTOGRAPHS
PH03828 702 (February 23, 1995) p36. "Daniel Wields Two Of His Axes" (Soest, Steve)
DANIELS, JEFF—PHOTOGRAPHS
PH03829 617 (November 14, 1991) p182. "Jeff Daniels Seeks The Truth From Clairvoyant Demi Moore"
PH03830 698-699 (December 29, 1994) p199. "Carrey And Daniels In "Dumb""
DANIELS, JEFF—PHOTOGRAPHS—PORTRAITS
PH03831 670 (November 25, 1993) p127. "Jeff Daniels: Bad Hair, Bold Performance"
DANKO, RICK—ALBUMS
PH03832 674 (January 27, 1994) p54. "Danko-Fjeld-Andersen"
DANKO, RICK—PHOTOGRAPHS
PH03833 617 (November 14, 1991) p75. "The Last Waltz, 1976: Robertson, Danko And Manuel, With Neil Young (left), Bob Dylan (back to camera) And Van Morrison" (Leibovitz, Annie)
PH03834 617 (November 14, 1991) p72. "Levon And The Hawks, Circa 1963: Sax Player Jerry Field, Rick Danko, Levon Helm, Richard Manuel, Garth Hudson And Robertson (from left)"
PH03835 669 (November 11, 1993) p66. "The Hawks At Ontario's Brass Rail Circa '63: Danko, Manuel, Hawkins, Helm, Robertson And Hudson (from left)"
PH03836 669 (November 11, 1993) p67. "Sredni Vollmer, Helm, Dylan And Danko In NYC in '83 (above)" (Landy, Elliott)
PH03837 676 (February 24, 1994) p46. "The Band (clockwise from top left): Guitarist Robbie Robertson, Drummer Levon Helm, Organist Garth Hudson, Bassist Rock Danko And Pianist Richard Manuel" (Gahr, David)
PH03838 677 (March 10, 1994) p28. "Rick Danko, Hudson And Arlie Manuel" (Mazur, Kevin)
DANNER, BLYTHE—PHOTOGRAPHS
PH03839 640 (October 1, 1992) p72. "Allen And Farrow Reach An Impasse"
PH03840 640 (October 1, 1992) p72. "Allen Meets Danner, The Mother Of Infatuated Student Lewis"
DANNY BOY—PHOTOGRAPHS—PORTRAITS
PH03841 671 (December 9, 1993) p31. "House's Danny Boy, DJ Lethal And Everlast With Cypress' B-Real And Muggs (from left)" (Blakesberg, Jay)
DANSIE, LEE—PHOTOGRAPHS
PH03842 742 (September 5, 1996) pp52-53. "World-Class Road-Luge Pilots Lee Dansie, Bob Stiles And Shawn Goulet (from left) Take A Break Near The Top Of The X Games' 'Crash Alley'" (Seliger, Mark)
DANSON, TED—PHOTOGRAPHS
PH03843 659 (June 24, 1993) p88. "Love: 'America,' With Goldberg And Danson"
PH03844 665 (September 16, 1993) p77. "Worst Actor"
PH03845 672-673 (December 23, 1993) p172. "Unfunny"
DANZIG—ALBUMS
PH03846 634-635 (July 9, 1992) p105. "Danzig III: How The Gods Kill"
DANZIG—PHOTOGRAPHS
PH03847 678 (March 24, 1994) p42. "Those Evil Mothers In Danzig: Chuck Biscuits, Glenn Danzig, John Christ, Eerie Von (from left)" (Seliger, Mark)
DANZIG, GLENN—ILLUSTRATIONS
PH03848 678 (March 24, 1994) p3. "Glenn Danzig" (Burke, Philip)
PH03849 681 (May 5, 1994) p8. "Try 'Em All!" (Pendergrast, James T.)
DANZIG, GLENN—PHOTOGRAPHS
PH03850 650 (February 18, 1993) p29. "Glenn Danzig" (Mazur, Kevin)
PH03851 678 (March 24, 1994) pp40-41. "[Glenn Danzig]" (Seliger, Mark)
PH03852 678 (March 24, 1994) p42. "Those Evil Mothers In Danzig: Chuck Biscuits, Glenn Danzig, John Christ, Eerie Von (from left)" (Seliger, Mark)
PH03853 695 (November 17, 1994) p62. "Glenn Danzig" (Seliger, Mark)
D'ARBY, TERENCE TRENT—ALBUMS
PH03854 660-661 (July 8, 1993) p110. "Symphony Or Damn"
PH03855 709 (June 1, 1995) p61. "Vibrator"
D'ARBY, TERENCE TRENT—PHOTOGRAPHS
PH03856 662 (August 5, 1993) p34. "D'Arby, Cherry And White (from left)" (Robicheau, Paul)
D'ARCY—PHOTOGRAPHS
PH03857 660-661 (July 8, 1993) p100. "Smashing Pumpkins (from left): Billy Corgan, D'Arcy, Jimmy Chamberlin And James Iha" (Johnson, Lisa)
PH03858 680 (April 21, 1994) pp42-43. "All Pumped Up: Jimmy Chamberlin, James Iha, Billy Corgan And D'Arcy (from left)" (Luchford, Glen)
PH03859 680 (April 21, 1994) p45. "D'Arcy: 'If You Don't Have Anything Nice To Say...'" (Mott, Tony)
PH03859a 695 (November 17, 1994) p47. "Smashing Pumpkins" (Ockenfels, Frank W.)
PH03860 711 (June 29, 1995) p19. "Billy Corgan, D'Arcy, Jimmy Chamberlin, James Iha (from left)" (Elledge, Paul)
PH03861 721 (November 16, 1995) pp50-51. "Billy Corgan Levitates D'Arcy" (Seliger, Mark)
PH03862 721 (November 16, 1995) p56. "Ready To Rock You: D'Arcy, Iha, Corgan, Chamberlin (from left) In 1992" (Lenquette)
PH03863 723 (December 14, 1995) p27. "The Chicago Eight: D'Arcy, Petersson, Carlos, Corgan, Nielsen, Iha, Chamberlin And Zander (from left)" (Elledge, Paul)
PH03864 726 (January 25, 1996) p43. "Smashing Pumpkins' Billy Corgan, D'Arcy, James Iha, Jimmy Chamberlin (from left)" (Seliger, Mark)
D'ARCY—PHOTOGRAPHS—PORTRAITS
PH03865 667 (October 14, 1993) p19. "D'Arcy, Jimmy Chamberlim, Billy Corgan, James Iha (clockwise from top left)" (Hom, Marc)
THE DARK HALF (FILM)—PHOTOGRAPHS
PH03866 656 (May 13, 1993) p114. "Top, Timothy Hutton And

His Evil Twin"
DARK SKIES (TELEVISION SHOW)—PHOTOGRAPHS
PH03867 743 (September 19, 1996) pp94,96. "[Television]"
DARK, GREGORY—PHOTOGRAPHS—PORTRAITS
PH03868 693 (October 20, 1994) p74. "Director Gregory Dark"
DARLING, CANDY—PHOTOGRAPHS
PH03869 734 (May 16, 1996) p72. "Warhol With Candy Darling"
DARLING, HELEN—RECORDS
PH03870 716 (September 7, 1995) p70. "Jenny Come Back (song)"
DARTMOUTH COLLEGE—ILLUSTRATIONS
PH03871 666 (September 30, 1993) p59. "[Higher Education]"
DARTMOUTH COLLEGE—PHOTOGRAPHS
PH03872 639 (September 17, 1992) p75. "Drink Till You Boot: Green Key Party, 1989" (Fox, John Gilbert)
PH03873 639 (September 17, 1992) p75. "Fraternity Initiation At Dartmouth College, Circa 1950"
PH03874 639 (September 17, 1992) pp74-75. "Green Key Party At AD, 1989" (Fox, John Gilbert)
PH03875 639 (September 17, 1992) p74. "In The Doghouse: Jacobs, Goldfarb And Schane Of Alpha Delta (from left)" (Smale, Brian)
DARVILL, BENJAMIN—PHOTOGRAPHS
PH03876 681 (May 5, 1994) p16. "Big Dummies: Dan And Brad Roberts, Darvill, Dorge And Reid (from left)" (Blakesberg, Jay)
DAS EFX—ALBUMS
PH03877 631 (May 28, 1992) p55. "Dead Serious"
DASH, STACEY—PHOTOGRAPHS
PH03878 714 (August 10, 1995) p62. "Dash And Silverstone Phone It In At High School"
DASHBOARD SAVIORS—ILLUSTRATIONS
PH03879 736 (June 13, 1996) p16. "Not So Fast!" (Pendergrast, James T.)
DASHBOARD SAVIORS—PHOTOGRAPHS
PH03880 689 (August 25, 1994) p16. "Jack Logan (second from left) With Vic Chesnutt (front) And Other Enablers" (Torno, Pattiy)
PH03881 710 (June 15, 1995) p52. "At The Uptown: McBride, Veal, John Crist, Michael Gibson (from left)" (Clinch, Danny)
DASHBOARD SAVIORS—PHOTOGRAPHS—PORTRAITS
PH03882 645-646 (December 10, 1992) p62. "Dashboard Saviors" (Diamond, Rick)
DAUGHERTY, JAY DEE—PHOTOGRAPHS
PH03883 738-739 (July 11, 1996) p44. "Smith's Great '70s Band"
DAVE (FILM)—ILLUSTRATIONS
PH03884 657 (May 27, 1993) p55. "Mr. Myth Goes To Washington" (Risko, Robert)
DAVE (FILM)—PHOTOGRAPHS
PH03885 657 (May 27, 1993) p56. "Dave Practices His Moves"
PH03886 657 (May 27, 1993) p56. "Dave The Fake Prez (Kevin Kline) Waves With The Real First Lady (Sigourney Weaver)"
DAVENPORT, N'DEA—PHOTOGRAPHS
PH03887 692 (October 6, 1994) p35. "Boogie Nights: The Brand New Heavies' Davenport" (Diamond, Rick)
DAVID MAMET'S OLEANNA (FILM)—PHOTOGRAPHS
PH03888 696 (December 1, 1994) p132. "Sex Combat: Debra Eisenstadt And William H. Macy"
PH03889 Number not assigned.
DAVIDSON, AQIL—PHOTOGRAPHS—PORTRAITS
PH03890 654 (April 15, 1993) pp[enc.6]. "[Aqil Davidson]" (Seliger, Mark)
PH03891 654 (April 15, 1993) pp[enc.4]. "Wreckx-n-Effect's Markell Riley And Aqil Davidson" (Seliger, Mark)
DAVIDSON, JAYE—PHOTOGRAPHS
PH03892 644 (November 26, 1992) p80. "An Identity Crisis For Jaye Davidson (left) And Stephen Rea"
PH03892a 653 (April 1, 1993) p57. "The Crying Game"
DAVIDSON, JAYE—PHOTOGRAPHS—PORTRAITS
PH03893 653 (April 1, 1993) p37. "[Jaye Davidson]" (Watson, Albert)
DAVIDTZ, EMBETH—PHOTOGRAPHS—PORTRAITS
PH03894 678 (March 24, 1994) p100. "Missing In Oscar Action"
DAVIES, DAVE—PHOTOGRAPHS
PH03895 656 (May 13, 1993) p24. "The Klash Of The Kinks: Dave (left) And Brother Ray" (Rapoport, Aaron)
DAVIES, DAVE—PHOTOGRAPHS—PORTRAITS
PH03896 672-673 (December 23, 1993) p37. "The Brothers Grim: Dave And Ray Davies" (Rapoport, Aaron)
DAVIES, JEREMY—PHOTOGRAPHS
PH03897 682 (May 19, 1994) p63. "[Incest]"
PH03898 686-687 (July 14, 1994) p98. "Mom Watson And Son Davies"
DAVIES, RAY—PHOTOGRAPHS
PH03899 656 (May 13, 1993) p24. "The Klash Of The Kinks: Dave (left) And Brother Ray" (Rapoport, Aaron)
PH03900 721 (November 16, 1995) p34. " -Ray"
PH03901 732 (April 18, 1996) p71. "Ray Davies: Doing The Best Things So Conservatively" (Capak, R. J.)
PH03902 746 (October 31, 1996) p32. "[Ray Davies]"
DAVIES, RAY—PHOTOGRAPHS—PORTRAITS
PH03903 643 (November 12, 1992) p124. "Ray Davies" (Seliger, Mark)
PH03904 672-673 (December 23, 1993) p37. "The Brothers Grim: Dave And Ray Davies" (Rapoport, Aaron)
PH03905 734 (May 16, 1996) p18. "Kinky Attraction: Davies (left) And Costello Compare Scarves" (White, E. Lee)
DAVIES, RICHARD—PHOTOGRAPHS
PH03906 742 (September 5, 1996) p21. "Are We Having Fun Yet?" (Kessler, Joshua)
DAVIES, RICHARD—PHOTOGRAPHS—PORTRAITS
PH03907 729 (March 7, 1996) p21. "Alone Again, Naturally: A Post-Moles Davies" (Peterson, Charles)
DAVIES, SAUL—PHOTOGRAPHS—PORTRAITS
PH03908 680 (April 21, 1994) p11. "[James]" (Borris, Dan)
DAVIS, BLAKE—PHOTOGRAPHS—PORTRAITS
PH03909 660-661 (July 8, 1993) p96. "Papa's Culture: White (left) And Davis" (Alicino, Christine)
DAVIS, CLIVE—PHOTOGRAPHS
PH03910 644 (November 26, 1992) p17. "The Great Garden Party: Dylan Center Stage For The Grand Finale" (Mazur, Kevin)
PH03911 726 (January 25, 1996) p26. "Whitney Houston, Clive Davis Of Arista And Bobby Brown (from left)" (Hurschmann, Paul)
DAVIS, ELIZABETH—PHOTOGRAPHS
PH03912 722 (November 30, 1995) p19. "Who Are You Callin' A Bitch?: To Wit, Elizabeth Davis, Selene Vigil, Agnew And Roisin Dunne Of 7 Year Bitch (from left)" (Blakesberg, Jay)
PH03913 731 (April 4, 1996) p17. "7 Year Bitch's Davis, Selene Vigil (from left)" (Eichner, Steve)
DAVIS, GEENA—ILLUSTRATIONS
PH03914 634-635 (July 9, 1992) p109. "Bat Girls On The Line" (Risko, Robert)
DAVIS, GEENA—PHOTOGRAPHS
PH03915 619-620 (December 12, 1991) p194. "Male Wimps And Female Warriors"
PH03916 623 (February 6, 1992) p90. "Susan Sarandon (left) And Geena Davis Get Even"
PH03917 634-635 (July 9, 1992) p111. "Davis, O'Donnell, Madonna And Petty In A Man's Game"
PH03918 653 (April 1, 1993) p57. "League"
PH03919 696 (December 1, 1994) p96. "Pitt Has Dated "Thelma And Louise" Co-Star Davis (top) And "Kalifornia" Girl Lewis (below)"
PH03920 746 (October 31, 1996) p76. "La Femme Geena Davis Packs A License To Kill"
DAVIS, GEENA—PHOTOGRAPHS—PORTRAITS
PH03921 678 (March 24, 1994) p104. "Two Babes And A Hunk: Davis (Angie); Stowe (China Moon); Grant (Four Weddings)"
PH03922 700 (January 26, 1995) p66. "Smart Women, Foolish Choices"

DAVIS, JONATHAN—PHOTOGRAPHS
PH03923 660-661 (July 8, 1993) p26. "Tribe's Malik 'Phife' Taylor, Ali Shaheed Muhammed And Jonathan 'Q-Tip' Davis (from left)" (Mazur, Kevin)
DAVIS, JUDY—PHOTOGRAPHS
PH03924 679 (April 7, 1994) p83. "Denis Leary Refs Judy Davis And Kevin Spacey"
DAVIS, MARK—PHOTOGRAPHS
PH03925 629 (April 30, 1992) p31. "Ugly Kid Joe (from left): Roger Lahr, Klaus Eichstadt, Whitfield Crane, Cordell Crockett And Mark Davis" (O'Beirne, Andy)
DAVIS, MARTIN—PHOTOGRAPHS
PH03926 660-661 (July 8, 1993) p121. "Turner Menaces Martin Davis"
DAVIS, MICHAEL—PHOTOGRAPHS
PH03927 632 (June 11, 1992) p36. "MC5 (clockwise from top left): Thompson, Tyner, Kramer, Smith"
PH03928 708 (May 18, 1995) p30. "MC5: Michael Davis, Dennis Thompson, Kramer, Smith, Tyner (from left)"
DAVIS, MILES—ALBUMS
PH03929 617 (November 14, 1991) p147. "Bitches Brew" (Berg, John)
PH03930 617 (November 14, 1991) p147. "Bitches Brew" (Klarwein, Mati)
PH03931 617 (November 14, 1991) p153. "Tutu" (Ishioka, Eiko)
PH03932 617 (November 14, 1991) p153. "Tutu" (Welt, Susan)
PH03933 617 (November 14, 1991) p153. "Tutu" (Penn, Irving)
PH03934 636 (August 6, 1992) p60. "Doo-Bop"
DAVIS, MILES—ILLUSTRATIONS
PH03935 617 (November 14, 1991) p3. "Miles Davis" (Burke, Philip)
PH03936 619-620 (December 12, 1991) p5. "[Miles Davis]" (Burke, Philip)
DAVIS, MILES—PHOTOGRAPHS
PH03937 617 (November 14, 1991) p42. "A 'Birth Of The Cool' Session, 1949"
PH03938 617 (November 14, 1991) p42. "Miles (second from right) With Charlie Parker's Band, 1947"
PH03939 617 (November 14, 1991) p44. "Miles At Home, 1969"
PH03940 617 (November 14, 1991) p47. "Miles At The Montreux Jazz Festival, 1991" (Leonard, Herman)
PH03941 617 (November 14, 1991) p41. "Miles At The Royal Roost, 1948" (Leonard, Herman)
PH03942 617 (November 14, 1991) p46. "Miles In Concert, 1970" (Gahr, David)
PH03943 617 (November 14, 1991) p42. "Miles With John Coltrane (right), 1955"
DAVIS, MILES—PHOTOGRAPHS—PORTRAITS
PH03944 617 (November 14, 1991) p39. "1926 Miles 1991" (Hiro)
PH03945 619-620 (December 12, 1991) p109. "Miles Davis"
DAVIS, PHIL—PHOTOGRAPHS
PH03946 718 (October 5, 1995) p24. "Erikson, Vig And Phil Davis (from left) As Firetown, 1989" (Pantsios, A. J.)
DAVIS, TRACY—PHOTOGRAPHS
PH03947 714 (August 10, 1995) p35. "Law Student Tracy Davis: An Unabashed Beneficiary Of Affirmative Action" (Turner, Danny)
DAVIS, ZELMA—PHOTOGRAPHS
PH03948 626 (March 19, 1992) p11. "Freedom Williams, David Cole, Robert Clivilles, Zelma Davis (from left)" (Mazur, Kevin)
DAY-LEWIS, DANIEL—ILLUSTRATIONS
PH03949 642 (October 29, 1992) p76. "Hard Times For Heroes" (Blitt, Barry)
PH03950 666 (September 30, 1993) p111. "Mean Street Circa 1870" (De Seve, Peter)
DAY-LEWIS, DANIEL—PHOTOGRAPHS
PH03951 645-646 (December 10, 1992) p190. "Daniel Day-Lewis"
PH03952 666 (September 30, 1993) p112. "Daniel Day-Lewis Nuzzles Michelle Pfeiffer"
PH03953 672-673 (December 23, 1993) p172. "Hot Romance"
PH03954 674 (January 27, 1994) p48. "Acting Vehicles Include 'The Pelican Brief,' 'In The Name Of The Father,' 'What's Eating Gilbert Grape,' 'Shadowlands,' 'Naked,' And 'Grumpy Old Men'"
PH03955 677 (March 10, 1994) p47. "With Daniel Day-Lewis In 'The Age Of Innocence'"
PH03956 678 (March 24, 1994) p100. "Oscar's Choices: 'Schindler's List,' 'The Piano,' 'The Remains Of the Day,' 'In The Name Of The Father,' 'The Fugitive' (from left)"
PH03957 749 (December 12, 1996) p90. "Day-Lewis And Allen Fight Back"
DAY-LEWIS, DANIEL—PHOTOGRAPHS—PORTRAITS
PH03958 674 (January 27, 1994) p48. "Best Actor"
DAZED AND CONFUSED (FILM)—PHOTOGRAPHS
PH03959 667 (October 14, 1993) p128. "School Daze For Cochrane, London And Jenson"
PH03960 672-673 (December 23, 1993) p172. "Funny"
PH03961 741 (August 22, 1996) p48. "McConaughey Onscreen"
DE GLI ANTONI, MARK—PHOTOGRAPHS—PORTRAITS
PH03962 735 (May 30, 1996) p21. "Frontman M. Doughty, Sebastian Steinberg, Mark De Gli Antoni And Yuval Gabay" (Vadukul, Nitin)
DE LA FALAISE, LUCIE—PHOTOGRAPHS
PH03963 660-661 (July 8, 1993) pp104-106. "[Marlon Richards & Lucie De La Falaise]" (Pfriender, Stephanie)
PH03964 748 (November 28, 1996) p25. "Richards And Hansen With De La Falaise Holding Little Ella Rose At The New York Film Festival" (Brady, Jay)
DE LA HOYA, OSCAR—PHOTOGRAPHS—PORTRAITS
PH03965 630 (May 14, 1992) p96. "[Oscar De La Hoya]" (Nystrom, Dick)
DE LA ROCHA, ZACK—PHOTOGRAPHS
PH03966 664 (September 2, 1993) p31. "Rage's Timmy C., Zack De La Rocha, Brad Wilk And Tom Morello (from left)" (Johnson, William)
PH03967 677 (March 10, 1994) p19. "Freedom Fighter: Rage's De La Rocha Hopes President Clinton Will Pay Attention" (Gougenheim, Kim)
PH03968 718 (October 5, 1995) p20. "Rant 'N' Rage: Zack De La Rocha In D.C." (Liu, Brian)
PH03969 735 (May 30, 1996) p27. "Rage Against The Machine"
PH03970 740 (August 8, 1996) p21. "Rage Against The Machine's Zack De La Rocha" (Blakesberg, Jay)
DE LA SOUL—ALBUMS
PH03971 672-673 (December 23, 1993) p156. "Buhloone Mind State"
DE LA SOUL—PHOTOGRAPHS
PH03972 695 (November 17, 1994) p99. "De La Soul" (Astor, Josef)
DE LA SOUL—PHOTOGRAPHS—PORTRAITS
PH03973 672-673 (December 23, 1993) p70. "De La Soul Are Most Definitely Not Dead" (Wessel, Cathrine)
DE MEDEIROS, MARIA—PHOTOGRAPHS
PH03974 692 (October 6, 1994) p80. "Willis And De Medeiros Screw"
DE MORNAY, REBECCA—PHOTOGRAPHS
PH03975 623 (February 6, 1992) p88. "Nanny Rebecca DeMornay Terrorizes Ernie Hudson"
PH03976 670 (November 25, 1993) p125. "De Mornay Seduces Guppy O'Donnell (below)"
DE NIRO, ROBERT—ILLUSTRATIONS
PH03977 618 (November 28, 1991) p101. "Through A Lens Darkly" (Rosen, Jonathon)
PH03978 723 (December 14, 1995) p89. "Goodfellas Go Vegas" (Brodner, Steve)
PH03979 742 (September 5, 1996) p67. "The Psycho Guy" (Brodner, Steve)

DE NIRO, ROBERT—ILLUSTRATIONS—PORTRAITS
PH03980 654 (April 15, 1993) p67. "Is De Niro Slipping?" (Collier, John)
DE NIRO, ROBERT—PHOTOGRAPHS
PH03981 618 (November 28, 1991) p103. "Now Robert De Niro Terrorizes Jessica Lange"
PH03982 637 (August 20, 1992) p60. "Deal Makings: De Niro (left) And Wuhl"
PH03983 642 (October 29, 1992) p77. "Night And The City"
PH03984 654 (April 15, 1993) p69. "Backdraft"
PH03985 654 (April 15, 1993) p69. "Deer Hunter"
PH03986 654 (April 15, 1993) p69. "The Godfather Part II"
PH03987 654 (April 15, 1993) p69. "Guilty By Suspicion"
PH03988 654 (April 15, 1993) p69. "Mad Dog"
PH03989 654 (April 15, 1993) p69. "Pick The Psycho: De Niro, Dushku, Barkin Or DiCaprio?"
PH03990 654 (April 15, 1993) p69. "Raging Bull"
PH03991 654 (April 15, 1993) p69. "Taxi Driver"
PH03992 654 (April 15, 1993) p69. "We're No Angels"
PH03993 668 (October 28, 1993) p88. "Are You Talking To Me? De Niro Directs Brancato (left)"
PH03994 696 (December 1, 1994) p132. "De Niro's Monster And Karloff's 1931 Model"
PH03995 723 (December 14, 1995) p90. "The Lady Gambles: Stone With The Dice; With Jealous Husband Robert De Niro; Gangster Lover Joe Pesci; And Director Martin Scorsese (from top)"
PH03996 724-725 (December 28, 1995) p138. "De Niro, Pacino And Kilmer In 'Heat'"
PH03997 742 (September 5, 1996) p68. "Fan De Niro Stalks Snipes At A Ballgame"
PH03998 742 (September 5, 1996) p68. "In 'Taxi Driver'"
PH03999 742 (September 5, 1996) p68. "With Dicaprio In 'This Boy's Life'"
PH04000 742 (September 5, 1996) p68. "With Lewis In 'The King Of Comedy'"
PH04001 742 (September 5, 1996) p68. "With Nolte In 'Cape Fear'"
PH04002 746 (October 31, 1996) p76. "De Niro's Priest Lies On The Stand"
DE PAULA, SIMONE—PHOTOGRAPHS
PH04003 680 (April 21, 1994) pp[enc.38]. "It's Not Just Shopping, It's An Adventure" (Ragel, Jon)
DE QUADROS, CIRO—PHOTOGRAPHS
PH04004 616 (October 31, 1991) p47. "The Inventor Of Polio Vaccine, Jonas Salk (left), And Dr. Ciro de Quadros" (Gaggero, Carlos)
DEACON, JOHN—PHOTOGRAPHS
PH04005 621 (January 9, 1992) p14. "Queen In The Mid-Seventies (from left): Deacon, Mercury, May And Taylor" (Rock, Mick)
DEAD BOYS—PHOTOGRAPHS
PH04006 632 (June 11, 1992) p126. "Young And Belushi Meet The Dead Boys, December 1977" (Kearney, Mitch)
DEAD CAN DANCE—PHOTOGRAPHS
PH04007 686-687 (July 14, 1994) p35. ""We Aim To Wake up That Other Self We Have": Lisa Gerrard And Brendan Perry" (Grecco, Michael)
DEAD HOT WORKSHOP—PHOTOGRAPHS
PH04008 722 (November 30, 1995) p20. "Gin Blossom's Scott Johnson, Dead Hot's Brian Griffith, Blossom Valenzuela And Dead Hot Curtis Grippe (from left)"
DEAD KENNEDYS—ALBUMS
PH04009 617 (November 14, 1991) p153. "Fresh Fruit For Rotting Vegetables" (Biafra, Jello)
PH04010 617 (November 14, 1991) p153. "Fresh Fruit For Rotting Vegetables" (Horwood, Annie)
PH04011 617 (November 14, 1991) p153. "Fresh Fruit For Rotting Vegetables" (Calson, Judith)
DEAD MAN WALKING (FILM)—ILLUSTRATIONS
PH04012 726 (January 25, 1996) p69. "The Last Waltz" (Collier, John)
DEAD MAN WALKING (FILM)—PHOTOGRAPHS
PH04013 724-725 (December 28, 1995) p139. "An Image To Remember: Penn And Sarandon"
DEAD PRESIDENTS (FILM)—PHOTOGRAPHS
PH04014 718 (October 5, 1995) p76. "Pulp To Come"
PH04015 719 (October 19, 1995) p159. "Black Thief On The Run In Whiteface"
DEADHEADS—PHOTOGRAPHS
PH04016 686-687 (July 14, 1994) p24. "Are Deadheads Now In Danger?" (Blakesberg, Jay)
PH04017 686-687 (July 14, 1994) p24. "Following The Grateful Dead Has New Complications" (Blakesberg, Jay)
PH04018 686-687 (July 14, 1994) p26. "Need A Miracle: Ticketless At A Dead Show" (Blakesberg, Jay)
PH04019 717 (September 21, 1995) p59. "Deadheads In Ecstasy At A 1987 Show" (Blakesberg, Jay)
PH04020 717 (September 21, 1995) p63. "Fans A A Dead Show On New Year's Eve, 1968, At Winterland, In San Francisco" (Marshall, Jim)
DEAKIN, PAUL—PHOTOGRAPHS
PH04021 691 (September 22, 1994) p22. "[The Mavericks]" (Harris, Brad)
DEAKIN, PAUL—PHOTOGRAPHS—PORTRAITS
PH04022 682 (May 19, 1994) p74. "[Mavericks]" (Tucker, Mark)
DEAKINS, ROGER—PHOTOGRAPHS
PH04023 730 (March 21, 1996) p104. "The Coens Flank Deakins"
DEAL, KELLEY—ALBUMS
PH04024 744 (October 3, 1996) p74. "Go To The Sugar Alter"
DEAL, KELLEY—ILLUSTRATIONS
PH04025 676 (February 24, 1994) p72. "Kim And Kelley Deal Of The Breeders" (Cowles, David)
DEAL, KELLEY—PHOTOGRAPHS
PH04026 668 (October 28, 1993) p18. "Not Just Another Girl Group: Wiggs, Kim Deal, Macpherson And Kelley Deal (from left)" (Lass, Imke)
PH04027 682 (May 19, 1994) p89. "[The Breeders]" (Seliger, Mark)
PH04028 695 (November 17, 1994) p131. "The Breeders" (Seliger, Mark)
DEAL, KELLEY—PHOTOGRAPHS—PORTRAITS
PH04029 660-661 (July 8, 1993) p101. "Breeders: Jim MacPherson, Kelley Deal, Kim Deal And Josephine Wiggs" (Mart, K.)
PH04030 677 (March 10, 1994) p16. "Kim Thayil And Breeder Kelley Deal" (Mott, Tony)
DEAL, KIM—ILLUSTRATIONS
PH04031 676 (February 24, 1994) p72. "Kim And Kelley Deal Of The Breeders" (Cowles, David)
PH04032 682 (May 19, 1994) p11. "The Breeders' Kim Deal" (Burke, Philip)
DEAL, KIM—PHOTOGRAPHS
PH04033 668 (October 28, 1993) p18. "Not Just Another Girl Group: Wiggs, Kim Deal, Macpherson And Kelley Deal (from left)" (Lass, Imke)
PH04034 677 (March 10, 1994) p15. "The Breeders' Kim Deal" (Mott, Tony)
PH04035 682 (May 19, 1994) p92. "New Deal: Kim Onstage Recently In Australia" (Walsh, Nick)
PH04036 682 (May 19, 1994) p90. "Old Deal: Kim With Pixies David Lovering, Black Francis, Joey Santiago (from left)" (Blakesberg, Jay)
PH04037 682 (May 19, 1994) p89. "[The Breeders]" (Seliger, Mark)
PH04038 695 (November 17, 1994) p131. "The Breeders" (Seliger, Mark)

PH04039 724-725 (December 28, 1995) p46. "The New Deal: Kim Cranked Up Her Amps" (Schultz, Nina)

DEAL, KIM—PHOTOGRAPHS—PORTRAITS

PH04040 652 (March 18, 1993) p15. "Ex-Pixies David Lovering, Deal, Joey Santiago, Black Francis (clockwise from left)" (Catlin, A.)

PH04041 660-661 (July 8, 1993) p101. "Breeders: Jim MacPherson, Kelley Deal, Kim Deal And Josephine Wiggs" (Mart, K.)

DEAN, JOHN—PHOTOGRAPHS

PH04042 690 (September 8, 1994) p48. "Dean At The Senate Watergate Hearings"

DEAN, LOREN—PHOTOGRAPHS

PH04043 618 (November 28, 1991) p103. "Gangsters Hoffman, Hill And Dean (from left)"

DEAN, SHIRLEY—PHOTOGRAPHS

PH04044 724-725 (December 28, 1995) p63. "MacDonald (with Berkeley Mayor Shirley Dean) Lest Go"

DEANGELIS, LOU—PHOTOGRAPHS

PH04045 708 (May 18, 1995) p78. "At Tail O' The Pup, In West Hollywood" (Seliger, Mark)

PH04046 708 (May 18, 1995) p80. "At Vasquez Rocks, In California" (Seliger, Mark)

PH04047 708 (May 18, 1995) pp78-79. "[Lou Deangelis]" (Seliger, Mark)

PH04048 708 (May 18, 1995) p85. "[Lou Deangelis & Camille Donatacci]" (Seliger, Mark)

PH04049 708 (May 18, 1995) p82. "On Muscle Beach, In Venice, Calif." (Seliger, Mark)

PH04050 708 (May 18, 1995) p84. "On Venice Beach" (Seliger, Mark)

DEAR, TRACY—PHOTOGRAPHS

PH04051 733 (May 2, 1996) p57. "Durante, Schlabowske, Langford, Dear (from left)" (Swider, Frank)

DEATH AND THE MAIDEN (FILM)—PHOTOGRAPHS

PH04052 700 (January 26, 1995) p68. "Weaver And Kingsley Talk "Death""

DEATH BECOMES HER (FILM)—PHOTOGRAPHS

PH04053 637 (August 20, 1992) p57. "Youth Seeking: Hawn (left) And Streep"

DEATH PENALTY—ILLUSTRATIONS

PH04054 721 (November 16, 1995) p18. "Booster Seat" (Pendergrast, James T.)

DEBARGE, EL—ALBUMS

PH04055 631 (May 28, 1992) p55. "In The Storm"

DEBARGE, JAMES—PHOTOGRAPHS

PH04056 665 (September 16, 1993) p43. "With Ex-Husband James DeBarge (left) And With Her Current Boyfriend, Rene Elizondo" (Zuffante, Vinnie)

DEBELL, SARA—ALBUMS

PH04057 662 (August 5, 1993) p16. "Grunge Lite"

DECARLO, MARK—PHOTOGRAPHS

PH04058 618 (November 28, 1991) p106. "'Studs' Host Mark DeCarlo And Contestants: Men Who Date Women And The Women Who Trash Them"

PH04059 630 (May 14, 1992) p89. "[Studs]"

DECONCINI, DENNIS—PHOTOGRAPHS

PH04060 660-661 (July 8, 1993) p51. "Babbitt At His Confirmation Hearing Talking With Arizona Senator Dennis DeConcini" (Binder, Donna)

DECONSTRUCTION—ALBUMS

PH04061 693 (October 20, 1994) p151. "Deconstruction"

DECONSTRUCTION—PHOTOGRAPHS

PH04062 653 (April 1, 1993) p11. "Navarro, Michael Murphy And Avery" (Cohen, Lester)

DEDERER, DAVE—PHOTOGRAPHS

PH04063 718 (October 5, 1995) p35. "The Right Stuff: Jason Finn, Chris Ballew And Dave Dederer (from left)" (Mason, Karen)

PH04064 729 (March 7, 1996) p32. "The Presidents Pay Tribute To The Seattle Sonics" (Westenberg, Kevin)

DEDERER, DAVE—PHOTOGRAPHS—PORTRAITS

PH04065 729 (March 7, 1996) p30. "One Band Indivisible With Power, Pop And Jokes For All" (Westenberg, Kevin)

DEEE-LITE—ALBUMS

PH04066 634-635 (July 9, 1992) p101. "Infinity Within"

DEEE-LITE—PHOTOGRAPHS—PORTRAITS

PH04067 639 (September 17, 1992) p37. "Super DJ Dmitry Brill, Lady Kier Kirby And Towa 'Towa' Tei (clockwise from top left)" (Anderson, Patrick)

DEEP FOREST—PHOTOGRAPHS—PORTRAITS

PH04068 680 (April 21, 1994) p26. "Deep Forest's Sanchez And Mouquet And Director Tarsem (from left)" (Kuczala, John)

DEEP THROAT (FILM)—PHOTOGRAPHS

PH04069 741 (August 22, 1996) p82. "[Seventies Porn]"

DEER HUNTER (FILM)—PHOTOGRAPHS

PH04070 654 (April 15, 1993) p69. "Deer Hunter"

DEF LEPPARD—ALBUMS

PH04071 628 (April 16, 1992) p79. "Adrenalize"

PH04072 631 (May 28, 1992) p69. "Adrenalize"

PH04073 670 (November 25, 1993) p114. "Retro Active"

DEF LEPPARD—ILLUSTRATIONS

PH04074 628 (April 16, 1992) p79. "Back Again And Deffer Than Ever" (Marek, Mark)

DEF LEPPARD—PHOTOGRAPHS

PH04075 629 (April 30, 1992) p39. "Def Leppard Guitarist Phil Collen And Bass Player Rick Savage" (Seliger, Mark)

PH04076 645-646 (December 10, 1992) p47. "[Def Leppard]" (Mazur, Kevin)

PH04077 667 (October 14, 1993) p26. "Rick Savage, Phil Collen, Vivian Campbell, Rick Allen And Joe Elliott" (Halfin, Ross)

PH04078 724-725 (December 28, 1995) p58. "Def Leppard's Phil Collen And Joe Elliot Flank Fans In Tangier"

DEF LEPPARD—PHOTOGRAPHS—PORTRAITS

PH04079 629 (April 30, 1992) pp[cover]. "Def Leppard: To Hell And Back" (Seliger, Mark)

PH04080 645-646 (December 10, 1992) pp[cover]. "1992 Yearbook" (Seliger, Mark)

DEFINITION OF SOUND—ALBUMS

PH04081 736 (June 13, 1996) p85. "Experience"

DEFORREST, CALVERT—PHOTOGRAPHS

PH04082 692 (October 6, 1994) p17. "[Nine Inch Nails & Larry "Bud" Melman]" (Cultice, Joseph)

DEFREITAS, ELAINE—PHOTOGRAPHS

PH04083 730 (March 21, 1996) p84. "Elaine Defreitas Identified A Virus That Some Think Causes CFS" (Weller, Bonnie)

DEGENERES, ELLEN—PHOTOGRAPHS

PH04084 750-751 (December 26, 1996) p85. "Left-Handed Woman? Ellen DeGeneres' Sitcom Self Crawled Halfway Out Of The Closet" (Pfriender, Stephanie)

DEL TORO, BENICIO—ILLUSTRATIONS

PH04085 716 (September 7, 1995) p75. "A Summer Sleeper" (Ulriksen, Mark)

DEL TORO, BENICIO—PHOTOGRAPHS

PH04086 718 (October 5, 1995) pp[enc.10]. "[Benicio Del Toro]" (Seliger, Mark)

PH04087 718 (October 5, 1995) pp[enc.14]. "Del Toro At The Elizabeth Street Garden" (Seliger, Mark)

PH04088 718 (October 5, 1995) pp[enc.8-9]. "Parker Posey And Benicio Del Toro At La Meia Ristorante, In Little Italy, In New York" (Seliger, Mark)

DELANEY AND BONNIE—PHOTOGRAPHS

PH04089 655 (April 29, 1993) p35. "Clapton (right) On Tour With Delaney And Bonnie" (Cummins, Jim)

DELAUGHTER, TIM—PHOTOGRAPHS

PH04090 716 (September 7, 1995) p13. "Dye Hard: Daisy's DeLaughter (left) And Wes Berggren" (George, Tryan)

DELEO, DEAN—PHOTOGRAPHS

PH04091 662 (August 5, 1993) p50. "Stone Temple Pilots Eric

Kretz, Dean DeLeo, Robert DeLeo And Weiland (from left)" (Ragel, Jon)
PH04092 710 (June 15, 1995) p22. "STP, From Left: Robert And Dean DeLeo, Weiland, Kretz" (Haynes, Loren)

DELEO, ROBERT—PHOTOGRAPHS
PH04093 662 (August 5, 1993) p50. "Stone Temple Pilots Eric Kretz, Dean DeLeo, Robert DeLeo And Weiland (from left)" (Ragel, Jon)
PH04094 710 (June 15, 1995) p22. "STP, From Left: Robert And Dean DeLeo, Weiland, Kretz" (Haynes, Loren)

DELEVANTES—ALBUMS
PH04095 709 (June 1, 1995) p64. "Long About That Time"

DELIRIUM (PUBLICATION)—ILLUSTRATIONS
PH04096 701 (February 9, 1995) p17. "Hot Serial" (Preuitt, Clayton)

DELLA PENNA, ERIK—PHOTOGRAPHS
PH04097 691 (September 22, 1994) pp[enc.18]. "Della Penna At Gibson Guitars Showroom" (Wessel, Cathrine)
PH04098 691 (September 22, 1994) pp[enc.cover]. "Erik Della Penna From The Health And Happiness Show" (Wessel, Cathrine)
PH04099 691 (September 22, 1994) pp[enc.17]. "Erik Della Penna in Nashville" (Wessel, Cathrine)
PH04100 691 (September 22, 1994) pp[enc.18]. "Murphy And Della Penna At 12th And Porter In Nashville" (Wessel, Cathrine)
PH04101 691 (September 22, 1994) pp[enc.5]. "Style 94" (Wessel, Cathrine)
PH04102 691 (September 22, 1994) pp[enc.20]. "Della Penna At The Stanhope House, In New Jersey" (Wessel, Cathrine)

DELPY, JULIE—ILLUSTRATIONS
PH04103 702 (February 23, 1995) p79. "Sex And The Single Slacker" (Schumaker, Ward)

DELPY, JULIE—PHOTOGRAPHS
PH04104 617 (November 14, 1991) p184. "Delpy Hides The Truth From Shepard"
PH04105 702 (February 23, 1995) p80. "And Enjoy A Night In Vienna"
PH04106 702 (February 23, 1995) p80. "Julie Delpy And Ethan Hawke Share A Kiss"
PH04107 702 (February 23, 1995) p80. "Take Direction From Richard Linklater"
PH04108 702 (February 23, 1995) p80. "White"
PH04109 703 (March 9, 1995) p48. "Let's Go! Austria: Hawke Meets Delpy On A Eurailpass In 'Before Sunrise'" (Brandenstein, Gabriela)

DELTA LAMBDA PHI—PHOTOGRAPHS
PH04110 666 (September 30, 1993) p88. "[Delta Lambda Phi]" (Himmel, Lizzie)
PH04111 666 (September 30, 1993) p90. "Hunt (third from left, bottom row) With Delta Lambda Phi Brothers (clockwise from top right): Peter Colohan, Sean McClafferty, Rob Corwin, Price, Stephen Smith And Oligmueller"
PH04112 666 (September 30, 1993) p90. "Picnic At Rock Creek Park In Washington" (Himmel, Lizzie)

DEMENT, IRIS—ALBUMS
PH04113 672-673 (December 23, 1993) p168. "Infamous Angel"
PH04114 688 (August 11, 1994) pp6669. "My Life"

DEMENT, IRIS—PHOTOGRAPHS
PH04115 656 (May 13, 1993) p65. "[Iris DeMent]" (Tucker, Mark)

DEMENT, IRIS—PHOTOGRAPHS—PORTRAITS
PH04116 693 (October 20, 1994) p47. "'It's Satisfying," Says DeMent, "To Have Something To Give To People"" (Broad, Julian)

DEMESKI, STANLEY—PHOTOGRAPHS
PH04117 728 (February 22, 1996) p64. "Luna's Wareham, Demeski And Eden (from left)" (Capak, R. J.)

DEMME, JONATHAN—ILLUSTRATIONS
PH04118 681 (May 5, 1994) p8. "Burp" (Pendergrast, James T.)

DEMME, JONATHAN—PHOTOGRAPHS
PH04119 678 (March 24, 1994) p63. "Demme, Flanked By Hanks And Banderas, Denies That The Positive Gay Images In 'Philadelphia' Are A Reaction Against The Gay Killer in 'Lambs' (left)"

DEMME, JONATHAN—PHOTOGRAPHS—PORTRAITS
PH04120 678 (March 24, 1994) p61. "[Jonathan Demme]" (Watson, Albert)

DEMOCRACY—ILLUSTRATIONS
PH04121 678 (March 24, 1994) p31. "How Capitalism Creates Democracy" (Rall, Ted)

DEMOCRATIC PARTY—ILLUSTRATIONS
PH04122 616 (October 31, 1991) p31. "[Democratic Party]" (Cronin, Brian)
PH04123 627 (April 2, 1992) p25. "[Democratic Party, Republican Party]" (Cronin, Brian)
PH04124 652 (March 18, 1993) p32. "[Democratic Party]" (Cronin, Brian)
PH04125 662 (August 5, 1993) p36. "The New Democratic Jello Mold" (Brodner, Steven)
PH04126 702 (February 23, 1995) p41. "Stop The Bus, Bill, I Want To Get Off" (Witte, Michael)
PH04127 723 (December 14, 1995) p77. "It Looks Like The Democrats Have Lost Another Seat" (Witte, Michael)
PH04128 746 (October 31, 1996) p56. "[Democratics-Republicans]"

DEMOLITION MAN (FILM)—PHOTOGRAPHS
PH04129 669 (November 11, 1993) p80. "'Demolition' Men Wesley Snipes And Sylvester Stallone"

DEMOS, ANDY—PHOTOGRAPHS—PORTRAITS
PH04130 637 (August 20, 1992) p20. "John Hamilton, Donna Croughn, Andy Demos, Dave Dreiwitz And Stuart Hake (from left)" (Borris, Dan)

DEMOS, GREG—PHOTOGRAPHS—PORTRAITS
PH04131 686-687 (July 14, 1994) p74. "Kevin Fennell, Toby Sprout, Pollard, Jim Pollard, Greg Demos (from left)" (Rice, Ted)

DENIKE, KARINA—PHOTOGRAPHS
PH04132 721 (November 16, 1995) p25. "DHC's Rogers (left) And Karina Denike" (Chambers, Brian)

DENISON, DUANE—PHOTOGRAPHS
PH04133 653 (April 1, 1993) p20. "The Jesus Lizard (clockwise from top left): McNeilly, Yow, Denison And Sims" (Ewolf)
PH04134 714 (August 10, 1995) p48. "David Sims, Mac McNeilly, David Yow, Duane Denison, From Left" (Seliger, Mark)
PH04135 714 (August 10, 1995) p51. "The Ones To Watch At LollaPalooza: Denison, Yow And Sims (from left)" (Perez, Marty)
PH04136 736 (June 13, 1996) p20. "Jockey Lavern Hostetler Has A Lot To Discuss With Jesus Lizard Members David Sims, David Yow, Mac McNeilly And Duane Denison (from left)" (Gilson, Matthew)

DENNIS, CATHY—PHOTOGRAPHS—PORTRAITS
PH04137 617 (November 14, 1991) p28. "[Cathy Dennis]"

DENSMORE, JOHN—PHOTOGRAPHS
PH04138 649 (February 4, 1993) p52. "The Doors (from left): keyboardist Ray Manzarek, Drummer John Densmore, Guitarist Robbie Krieger, Shaman Jim Morrison" (Diltz, Henry)
PH04139 724-725 (December 28, 1995) p46. "Doors John Densmore, Manzarek And Robby Krieger (from left)" (Kaplin, Todd)

DENUNZIO, VINNY—PHOTOGRAPHS
PH04140 691 (September 22, 1994) pp[enc.17]. "Mastro And Vinny DeNunzio At The Sutler, Nashville" (Wessel, Cathrine)

DENZIL—PHOTOGRAPHS
PH04141 692 (October 6, 1994) p36. "Denzil Squeezes Out A Spark"

DEPARDIEU, GERARD—ILLUSTRATIONS
PH04142 642 (October 29, 1992) p76. "Hard Times For Heroes" (Blitt, Barry)

DEPARDIEU, GERARD—PHOTOGRAPHS
PH04143 649 (February 4, 1993) p72. "[1492]"
PH04144 650 (February 18, 1993) p66. "A Decade After 'The Return Of Martin Guerre' With Depardieu And Baye (top)..."
PH04145 680 (April 21, 1994) p95. "Now Playing"
DEPECHE MODE—ALBUMS
PH04146 617 (November 14, 1991) p147. "A Broken Frame" (Atkins, Martin)
PH04147 617 (November 14, 1991) p147. "A Broken Frame" (Griffin, Brian)
PH04148 654 (April 15, 1993) p65. "Songs Of Faith And Devotion"
PH04149 656 (May 13, 1993) p128. "Songs Of Faith And Devotion"
PH04150 672-673 (December 23, 1993) p151. "Songs Of Faith And Devotion"
DEPECHE MODE—PHOTOGRAPHS
PH04151 650 (February 18, 1993) p13. "Depeche Mode"
PH04152 669 (November 11, 1993) p27. "Lou Reed (left) Dropped In On Depeche Mode During Their Plugged Press Conference" (Mazur, Kevin)
PH04153 670 (November 25, 1993) p94. "1982: Fletcher, Gahan, Gore And Wilder (from left)"
PH04154 670 (November 25, 1993) p94. "1985: Gore, Wilder, Gahan And Fletcher (clockwise from left)" (Nosotti, Fabio)
PH04155 670 (November 25, 1993) p92. "In Madrid, Making Their Last Record: Gahan, Gore, Wilder, Fletcher (from left)" (Corbijn, Anton)
DEPP, JOHNNY—ILLUSTRATIONS
PH04156 693 (October 20, 1994) p153. "Autuer In Angora" (Risko, Robert)
PH04157 707 (May 4, 1995) p73. "Bad Boys On The Prowl" (Kelley, Gary)
DEPP, JOHNNY—PHOTOGRAPHS
PH04158 656 (May 13, 1993) p116. "Sex Is Sweet For Depp (left) And Masterson"
PH04159 674 (January 27, 1994) p48. "Acting Vehicles Include 'The Pelican Brief,' 'In The Name Of The Father,' 'What's Eating Gilbert Grape,' 'Shadowlands,' 'Naked,' And 'Grumpy Old Men'"
PH04160 683 (June 2, 1994) p28. "Depp (left) And Pop At The "Serial Mom" Premiere" (Banks, Kathy)
PH04161 693 (October 20, 1994) p155. "Depp As Ed Wood And Landau As Bela "Dracula" Lugosi"
PH04162 696 (December 1, 1994) p24. "[Johnny Depp & Shane MacGowan]" (Woode, Theodore)
PH04163 698-699 (December 29, 1994) p194. "Depp And Landau Team In "Ed Wood""
PH04164 698-699 (December 29, 1994) p66. "Depp Goes For A Stroll With A Friend"
PH04165 707 (May 4, 1995) p74. "Depp And Brando In 'Don Juan'"
PH04166 709 (June 1, 1995) p16. "[P]" (Smith, Kelly)
PH04167 723 (December 14, 1995) p92. "Race Against Time: Chase And Depp"
PH04168 734 (May 16, 1996) p17. "[Johnny Depp & Al Pacino]" (Davila, Bill)
PH04169 738-739 (July 11, 1996) p15. "Johnny Depp, About Whom Ramone Has More To Say..." (Ferreira, Albert)
PH04170 747 (November 14, 1996) p25. "Hunter Thompson (right) Flogs A Blow-Up Doll As Johnny Depp Takes In The Good Doctor's, Er, Lecture" (Kravitz, Jeff)
DEPP, JOHNNY—PHOTOGRAPHS—PORTRAITS
PH04171 619-620 (December 12, 1991) pp[cover]. "1991 Yearbook" (Ritts, Herb)
PH04172 735 (May 30, 1996) p56. "Johnny Depp (left) Draws, While Director Jim Jarmusch Dawdles"
DEPRUME, IVAN—PHOTOGRAPHS
PH04173 695 (November 17, 1994) p50. "White Zombie" (Winter, Dan)
DERBY, DAVE—PHOTOGRAPHS
PH04174 693 (October 20, 1994) p49. "Kevin March, Dave Derby, Joan Wasser, Eric Masunaga (from left)" (Lass, Imke)
DEREK AND THE DOMINOS—ALBUMS
PH04175 655 (April 29, 1993) p42. "Layla"
DEREK AND THE DOMINOS—PHOTOGRAPHS
PH04176 655 (April 29, 1993) p35. "Derek And The Dominos: Jim Gordon, Carl Radle, Bobby Whitlock And Clapton (from left)..."
DEREK, BO—PHOTOGRAPHS
PH04177 750-751 (December 26, 1996) p88. "He Don't Want To Cause No Fuss: Bo Derek And Bob Dole, Scamming A Ticket To Ride"
DERN, BILL—PHOTOGRAPHS
PH04178 719 (October 19, 1995) p25. "Cowan Signs To Motown: Motown's Nadiene Baker, Manager Bill Dern, Jackson, Cowan (clockwise from top left)"
DERN, LAURA—PHOTOGRAPHS
PH04179 659 (June 24, 1993) p36. "Dern (with Joseph Mazzello And Sam Neill) Perks Up A Sick Dino" (Close, Murray)
PH04180 659 (June 24, 1993) p36. "Dern And Jeff Goldblum, Flanking Steven Spielberg, Fell In Love On The Set" (Close, Murray)
PH04181 659 (June 24, 1993) p35. "[Laura Dern]" (Markus, Kurt)
PH04182 659 (June 24, 1993) pp[cover]. "Laura Dern: The Spark In Jurassic Park" (Markus, Kurt)
PH04183 659 (June 24, 1993) p37. "Star Child: Laura And Mother Diane Ladd Hit The Town In 1975"
PH04184 672-673 (December 23, 1993) p188. "[Covers]" (Markus, Kurt)
DERN, LAURA—PHOTOGRAPHS—PORTRAITS
PH04185 615 (October 17, 1991) pp70-71. "[Laura Dern]" (Rolston, Matthew)
DEROSA, STEPHEN—PHOTOGRAPHS
PH04186 704 (March 23, 1995) pp102-103. "Class of '95" (Tavee, Tom)
PH04187 704 (March 23, 1995) p104. "Derosa" (Tavee, Tom)
DERSHOWITZ, ALAN—PHOTOGRAPHS
PH04188 657 (May 27, 1993) p11. "Alan Dershowitz (center) With Aerosmith At The Boston Music Awards" (Robicheau, Paul)
DES BARRES, PAMELA—BOOKS
PH04189 670 (November 25, 1993) p19. "Rock & Roll Cook-book"
DESPERADO (FILM)—PHOTOGRAPHS
PH04190 716 (September 7, 1995) p76. "Antonio Banderas Takes Aim At Being An Action Hero"
DES'REE—PHOTOGRAPHS
PH04191 724-725 (December 28, 1995) p42. "Gangsta's Paradise: Coolio, Des'ree" (Mazur, Kevin)
DES'REE—PHOTOGRAPHS—PORTRAITS
PH04192 696 (December 1, 1994) p48. "No Disco Diva, Des'ree Follows Her Own Drummer" (Cultice, Joseph)
DESTINY TURNS ON THE RADIO (FILM)—PHOTOGRAPHS
PH04193 708 (May 18, 1995) p98. "Tarantino As Destiny"
DEUTROM, MARK—PHOTOGRAPHS
PH04194 675 (February 10, 1994) p22. "Crover, Simmons, King Buzzo And Mark Deutrom" (Cohen, Lester)
DEVIL IN A BLUE DRESS (FILM)—ILLUSTRATIONS
PH04195 718 (October 5, 1995) p75. "Crime Fiction" (Kelley, Gary)
DEVIL IN A BLUE DRESS (FILM)—PHOTOGRAPHS
PH04196 718 (October 5, 1995) p76. "Detective Denzil Washington Falls Under The Spell Of Devil Jennifer Beals"
PH04197 731 (April 4, 1996) p66. "Cheadle And Washington, 'Devil'"
DEVINE, LORETTA—PHOTOGRAPHS
PH04198 724-725 (December 28, 1995) p138. "Houston, Devine, Rochon And Bassett In 'Exhale' (from left)"

PH04199 731 (April 4, 1996) p66. "Bassett And Devine, 'Exhale'"
DEVITO, DANNY—ILLUSTRATIONS
PH04200 617 (November 14, 1991) p179. "Selling Short" (Cowles, David)
DEVITO, DANNY—PHOTOGRAPHS
PH04201 617 (November 14, 1991) p182. "DeVito Turns On The Charm For Legal Cupcake Miller"
PH04202 634-635 (July 9, 1992) p42. "Danny DeVito's Penguin Is Another Of Burton's Mutated Children Of The Night" (Pedota, Jack)
PH04203 644 (November 26, 1992) p78. "[Batman Returns]"
PH04204 647 (January 7, 1993) p50. "...And Danny DeVito"
PH04205 655 (April 29, 1993) p69. "DeVito Is Dad To Steinmiller And Hughes"
PH04206 684 (June 16, 1994) p116. "Funny: DeVito Instructs Mark In "Renaissance man""
PH04207 697 (December 15, 1994) p104. "Dr. DeVito Examines A Very Pregnant Ah-nuld"
PH04208 720 (November 2, 1995) p74. "DeVito Takes Aim"
PH04209 720 (November 2, 1995) p74. "Hackman (in brace) And DeVito Watch Travolta Operate, Hollywood Style"
DEVITO, KARLA—PHOTOGRAPHS
PH04210 670 (November 25, 1993) p16. "With Singer Karla De Vito On Tour During 'Bat I'" (Putland, Michael)
DEVLINS—ALBUMS
PH04211 658 (June 10, 1993) p70. "Drift"
DEVO—PHOTOGRAPHS
PH04212 656 (May 13, 1993) p68. "[Devo]" (De Roos, Govert)
PH04213 730 (March 21, 1996) p17. "Beck, Devo's Mark Mothersbaugh, Bob Casale, Josh Freese, Bob Mothersbaugh, Jerry Casale" (Anderson, Vera)
DEYOUNG, DENNIS—ALBUMS
PH04214 696 (December 1, 1994) p129. "10 On Broadway"
DEYOUNG, DENNIS—PHOTOGRAPHS
PH04215 743 (September 19, 1996) p34. "Summer's Young And Old" (Spencer, Robert)
DHANBAD, BIHAR STATE, INDIA—PHOTOGRAPHS
PH04216 665 (September 16, 1993) pp54-58. "Workers of The World" (Salgado, Sebastiao)
DIABOLIQUE (FILM)—PHOTOGRAPHS
PH04217 732 (April 18, 1996) p78. "Stone And Adjani"
DIAMOND, DEBI—PHOTOGRAPHS
PH04218 693 (October 20, 1994) p74. "Actress Debi Diamond Takes A Break Between Takes"
DIAMOND, MICHAEL—PHOTOGRAPHS
PH04219 678 (March 24, 1994) p43. "Beasties In The Jungle: Michael Diamond, Adam Horovitz And Adam Yauch (clockwise from top left)" (Simons, Chip)
PH04219a 684 (June 16, 1994) p36. "United Beastie Service: Adam Horowitz, Michael Diamond, Adam Yauch" (Kravitz, Jeff)
PH04220 688 (August 11, 1994) p49. "Yaugh, Diamond, Horovitz (clockwise from top) In 1986"
DIAMOND, MICHAEL—PHOTOGRAPHS—PORTRAITS
PH04221 688 (August 11, 1994) p46. "Michael Diamond" (Rolston, Matthew)
PH04222 Number not assigned.
DIAMOND, NEIL—ALBUMS
PH04223 636 (August 6, 1992) p56. "The Greatest Hits 1966-1992"
DIAMOND, NEIL—PHOTOGRAPHS
PH04224 659 (June 24, 1993) p13. "Fight The Power: L.L. With Neil Diamond" (Mazur, Kevin)
PH04225 665 (September 16, 1993) p32. "Neil Diamond (center) With Mary's Danish" (Preston, Neal)
PH04226 711 (June 29, 1995) p13. "Fine Artist Diamond In Graduation Garb" (Mazur, Kevin)
PH04227 730 (March 21, 1996) p36. "[Neil Diamond]" (Preston, Neal)
DIAZ, CAMERON—ILLUSTRATIONS
PH04228 744 (October 3, 1996) p16. "Finger Lickin' Good!" (Pendergrast, James T.)
DIAZ, CAMERON—PHOTOGRAPHS
PH04229 732 (April 18, 1996) p80. "Ron Eldard And Cameron Diaz Eat Till They Drop"
PH04230 741 (August 22, 1996) pp[cover]. "The 1996 Hot Issue Starring Cameron Diaz" (Seliger, Mark)
PH04231 741 (August 22, 1996) p52. "Brace Yourself: That's Diaz (right) With A Pal In 1986"
PH04232 741 (August 22, 1996) p105. "Burns, Bahns, Diaz, Aniston, McGlone"
PH04233 741 (August 22, 1996) pp50-51. "[Cameron Diaz]" (Seliger, Mark)
PH04234 744 (October 3, 1996) p78. "Cameron Diaz, Keanu Reeves" With 'Feeling'"
DICAPRIO, LEONARDO—ILLUSTRATIONS
PH04235 704 (March 23, 1995) p127. "He Shoots, he Scores" (Ulriksen, Mark)
PH04236 747 (November 14, 1996) p123. "Just Two Kids In Love" (Brodner, Steve)
DICAPRIO, LEONARDO—PHOTOGRAPHS
PH04237 654 (April 15, 1993) p69. "Pick The Psycho: De Niro, Dushku, Barkin Or Dicaprio?"
PH04238 674 (January 27, 1994) p48. "Acting Vehicles Include 'The Pelican Brief,' 'In The Name Of The Father,' 'What's Eating Gilbert Grape,' 'Shadowlands,' 'Naked,' And 'Grumpy Old Men'"
PH04239 703 (March 9, 1995) p70. "Leonardo Dicaprio And Gene Hackman Face Off In Familial Fury"
PH04240 704 (March 23, 1995) p128. "Dicaprio, With McGaw (left), Takes A Dive"
PH04241 710 (June 15, 1995) p18. "[Leonardo Dicaprio & Marky Mark]" (Mazur, Kevin)
PH04242 742 (September 5, 1996) p68. "With Dicaprio In 'This Boy's Life'"
PH04243 747 (November 14, 1996) p124. "The Bright Angel Meets Her Knight At A Costume Ball"
PH04244 747 (November 14, 1996) p124. "Danes Juliet Pines For Her Love"
PH04245 747 (November 14, 1996) p124. "Dicaprio's Desperate Romeo Takes A Hostage"
PH04246 749 (December 12, 1996) p19. "[Leonardo Dicaprio & Claire Danes]" (Kravitz, Jeff)
DICAPRIO, LEONARDO—PHOTOGRAPHS—PORTRAITS
PH04247 682 (May 19, 1994) p55. "[Leonardo Dicaprio]" (Seliger, Mark)
PH04248 750-751 (December 26, 1996) p207. "Diane Keaton, Leonardo Dicaprio"
DICKIES—PHOTOGRAPHS
PH04249 743 (September 19, 1996) p29. "Melvoin (left) With L.A. Punk Band The Dickies In The Early '90s" (Colver, Ed)
DIDDLEY, BO—PHOTOGRAPHS—PORTRAITS
PH04250 643 (November 12, 1992) p217. "Bo Diddley" (Watson, Albert)
PH04251 738-739 (July 11, 1996) p31. "[Bo Diddley]" (Schafer, F. Scott)
DIE HARD WITH A VENGEANCE (FILM)—PHOTOGRAPHS
PH04252 709 (June 1, 1995) p68. "Potential Goldmines"
PH04253 710 (June 15, 1995) p86. "Jackson And Willis Try To Undo A Bad Situation In 'Die Hard With A Vengeance'"
DIED PRETTY—ALBUMS
PH04254 625 (March 5, 1992) p70. "Doughboy Hollow"
DIET COKE (COMMERCIAL)—PHOTOGRAPHS
PH04255 680 (April 21, 1994) p13. "Rock Marries Commerce Again: The Band (above) shill For Diet Coke With 'The Weight,' Which Is Owned By Dylan (left)"
DIEYI, CHENG—PHOTOGRAPHS
PH04256 668 (October 28, 1993) p86. "Cheng Dieyi As Concubine"

DIFFERENT STROKES (TELEVISION SHOW)—PHOTOGRAPHS
PH04257 665 (September 16, 1993) p41. "Todd Bridges And Janet On 'Different Strokes'"
DIFRANCO, ANI—ALBUMS
PH04258 715 (August 24, 1995) p102. "Not A Pretty Girl"
DIFRANCO, ANI—ILLUSTRATIONS
PH04259 721 (November 16, 1995) p11. "Ani DiFranco On The Edge" (Burke, Philip)
DIFRANCO, ANI—PHOTOGRAPHS
PH04260 719 (October 19, 1995) p15. "Eddie Spaghetti And Dan Bolton Of The Supersuckers (top) And Cult Folkie Ani DiFranco Get Down At Seattle's Bumbershoot" (Doughty, Curt)
PH04261 721 (November 16, 1995) p63. "[Ani DiFranco]" (Exum)
PH04262 738-739 (July 11, 1996) p16. "Franti (left) And Ani DiFranco, Who Is An Avid Spearhead Fan" (Blakesberg, Jay)
DIFRANCO, ANI—PHOTOGRAPHS—PORTRAITS
PH04263 750-751 (December 26, 1996) p82. "Ani DiFranco" (Franckling, Ken)
DIGABLE PLANETS—ALBUMS
PH04264 672-673 (December 23, 1993) p157. "Reachin'"
PH04265 696 (December 1, 1994) p127. "Blowout Comb"
DIGABLE PLANETS—PHOTOGRAPHS
PH04266 652 (March 18, 1993) p23. "Doodlebug, Ladybug, Butterfly (from left)" (Guzman)
PH04267 656 (May 13, 1993) p67. "[Hip Bop]" (Guzman)
PH04268 689 (August 25, 1994) p17. "[Digable Planets]"
PH04269 707 (May 4, 1995) p36. "Doodlebug (left) And Ladybug Shock The House" (Capak, R. J.)
DIGABLE PLANETS—PHOTOGRAPHS—PORTRAITS
PH04270 672-673 (December 23, 1993) p46. "[Digable Planets]" (Wessel, Cathrine)
DIGABLE PLANETS—RECORDS
PH04271 650 (February 18, 1993) p60. "Reachin'"
DIGGLE, STEVE—PHOTOGRAPHS
PH04272 675 (February 10, 1994) p16. "Chemistry Club: Buzzcocks' Diggle, Barber, Shelley And Barker (from left)"
DIGITAL UNDERGROUND—PHOTOGRAPHS
PH04273 746 (October 31, 1996) p42. "Shakur With Digital Underground's Money B. (from left) And The D.U. Posse On A Video Shoot In 1991" (Posey, Carl)
DILLER, BARRY—PHOTOGRAPHS
PH04274 689 (August 25, 1994) p69. "Diller With John Malone, The Cable Magnate With A Stake In QVC, Before Senate Testimony On The Info Highway Last Winter"
DILLER, BARRY—PHOTOGRAPHS—PORTRAITS
PH04275 689 (August 25, 1994) p70. "Diller, With Close Friend Diane Von Furstenberg, At CBS' 25th-Anniversary Party For "60 Minutes" In 1993" (Lennihn, Mark)
PH04276 689 (August 25, 1994) p69. "Those Were The Days: CBS President Howard Stringer, QVC Chairman Barry Diller And CBS Chairman Larry Tisch, from left"
DILLON FENCE—PHOTOGRAPHS—PORTRAITS
PH04277 634-635 (July 9, 1992) p20. "Dillon Fence (from left): Chris Goode, Kent Alphin, Greg Humphreys And Scott Carle" (Thompson, D. Kent)
DILLON, MATT—PHOTOGRAPHS
PH04278 719 (October 19, 1995) p156. "Kidman Gets Dillon In A Sexual Vise"
PH04279 748 (November 28, 1996) p142. "Kevin Spacey, Left, Directs Matt Dillon"
DIM STARS—PHOTOGRAPHS
PH04280 633 (June 25, 1992) p12. "Dim Stars (from left): Richard Hell, Steve Shelley, Thurston Moore And Don Fleming" (Busacca, Larry)
DIMEBAG DARRELL—PHOTOGRAPHS
PH04281 685 (June 30, 1994) p24. "Rex, Dimebag Darrell, Vinnie Paul And Phil Anselmo (clockwise from left)" (Winters, Dan)
PH04282 689 (August 25, 1994) p16. "Dimebag (left) With hair Mate Kisser" (Settle, Ken)
DIMEBAG DARRELL—PHOTOGRAHS
PH04283 707 (May 4, 1995) p20. "Icky Wail's Mike Teis, Pantera's Dimebag Darrell And Vinnie Paul (from left)" (Stone, John)
DINGMAN, HARRY, III—PHOTOGRAPHS
PH04284 625 (March 5, 1992) p27. "Lori Allison, Marty Amsler, Harry Dingman II, Greg Hill (from left)" (Natkin, Paul)
DINIZIO, PAT—PHOTOGRAPHS
PH04285 648 (January 21, 1993) p11. "The Smithereens' Pat Dinizio" (Capak, R. J.)
DINKENS, RON—PHOTOGRAPHS
PH04286 736 (June 13, 1996) p20. "Miranda Molen, Ron 'Rondonna' Dinkens, Watt And Daniela Eden (from left)" (Temme, Marty)
DINKINS, DAVID—PHOTOGRAPHS
PH04287 666 (September 30, 1993) p31. "Pushing Gun Control: Sarah And Jim Brady With New York Mayor David Dinkins In 1991" (Markel, B.)
DINOSAUR JR.—ALBUMS
PH04288 619-620 (December 12, 1991) p182. "Green Mind"
PH04289 692 (October 6, 1994) p90. "Without A Sound"
DINOSAUR JR.—PHOTOGRAPHS
PH04290 656 (May 13, 1993) p17. "Don't Call Us Slackers: Mike Johnson, Murph And J Mascis" (Ockenfels, Frank W.)
DINOSAUR JR.—RECORDS
PH04291 650 (February 18, 1993) p58. "Where You Been"
DION—PHOTOGRAPHS
PH04292 651 (March 4, 1993) p17. "Dion, Phil Spector And Springsteen" (Mazur, Kevin)
DIONISI, STEFANO—PHOTOGRAPHS—PORTRAITS
PH04293 704 (March 23, 1995) p129. "Dionisi As Farinelli"
DIPAOLO, JOEY—PHOTOGRAPHS
PH04294 681 (May 5, 1994) p21. "Beasties Adam Yauch (left) And Mike D With Joey DiPaolo"
DIRE STRAITS—ALBUMS
PH04295 615 (October 17, 1991) p91. "On Every Street"
DIRNT, MIKE—PHOTOGRAPHS
PH04296 691 (September 22, 1994) p25. "Punk's New Breed: Mike Dirnt, Billie Joe And Tre Cool (from left)" (Seliger, Mark)
PH04297 700 (January 26, 1995) pp40-41. "Billie Joe (Opposite), Mike Dirnt And Tre Cool" (Winters, Dan)
PH04298 707 (May 4, 1995) p20. "Dirnt (left) And Perennial Bammie Fave Carlos Santana" (Blakesberg, Jay)
PH04299 724-725 (December 28, 1995) p29. "Tre Cool, Billy Joe Armstrong, Mike Dirnt" (Seliger, Mark)
PH04300 726 (January 25, 1996) p38. "Billie Joe Armstrong (left) And Mike Dirnt Of Green Day" (Olson, Sheryl)
DIRTY BOOTS (VIDEO)—PHOTOGRAPHS
PH04301 667 (October 14, 1993) p97. "Sonic Youth: This 'Boots' Is Made For Watching"
DIRTY THREE—ALBUMS
PH04302 746 (October 31, 1996) p70. "Horse Stories"
DISCLOSURE (FILM)—PHOTOGRAPHS
PH04303 698-699 (December 29, 1994) p199. "Moore And Douglas In "Disclosure""
PH04304 711 (June 29, 1995) p48. "Rentals: 'Vampires,' 'Disclosure'"
DISHWALLA—PHOTOGRAPHS
PH04305 741 (August 22, 1996) p39. "Dishwalla" (Clinch, Danny)
DISNEY STUDIOS—PHOTOGRAPHS
PH04306 686-687 (July 14, 1994) p92. "Artists At Team Disney Study A Real Lion For Inspiration"
DISPOSABLE HEROES OF HIPHOPRISY—ALBUMS
PH04307 630 (May 14, 1992) p108. "Hypocrisy Is The Greatest Luxury"
PH04307a 651 (March 4, 1993) p57. "Hypocrisy Is The Greatest Luxury"

DISPOSABLE HEROES OF HIPHOPRISY—PHOTOGRAPHS—PORTRAITS
PH04308 628 (April 16, 1992) .63. ▒Disposable Heroes Of Hiphoprisy▒Blakesberg, Jay)
PH04309 Number not assigned.
DISTEFANO, PETE—PHOTOGRAPHS—PORTRAITS
PH04310 656 (May 13, 1993) p54. "Pete Distefano" (Seliger, Mark)
DIVINE—PHOTOGRAPHS
PH04311 681 (May 5, 1994) p48. "Momhood, John Waters Style: Divine (left) And Turner"
DIVINYLS—PHOTOGRAPHS
PH04312 619-620 (December 12, 1991) p18. "The Divinyls: A Touching Success Story" (Feingold, Deborah)
DIXON, DONNA—PHOTOGRAPHS
PH04313 696 (December 1, 1994) p25. "Ms. Aykroyd (Donna Dixon), Eric Clapton, Uma Thurman And Dan Aykroyd (from left)" (Allen, David)
DIXON, JIMMY—PHOTOGRAPHS
PH04314 684 (June 16, 1994) p61. "James Dixon (center) With Teammates Shane Spry And Mickey McKinion" (Borris, Dan)
PH04315 684 (June 16, 1994) p64. "Jimmy Dixon" (Borris, Dan)
DIXON, MARIE—PHOTOGRAPHS
PH04316 677 (March 10, 1994) p27. "Willie Dixon's Daughter Shirli (left) And Widow, Marie, With Presenter Chuck Berry" (Mazur, Kevin)
DIXON, SHIRLI—PHOTOGRAPHS
PH04317 677 (March 10, 1994) p28. "Berry, Weir And Shirli Dixon (from left)" (Mazur, Kevin)
PH04318 677 (March 10, 1994) p27. "Willie Dixon's Daughter Shirli (left) And Widow, Marie, With Presenter Chuck Berry" (Mazur, Kevin)
DIXON, WILLIE—PHOTOGRAPHS—PORTRAITS
PH04319 645-646 (December 10, 1992) p101. "Bluesman Willie Dixon"
PH04320 676 (February 24, 1994) p49. "Dixon Made The Blues Rock And Rock Bluesier" (Gahr, David)
DJ ALAMO—PHOTOGRAPHS
PH04321 628 (April 16, 1992) p55. "DJ Alamo, Grand Puba Maxwell And Ron Stud (from left)" (Seliger, Mark)
DJ KAYGEE—PHOTOGRAPHS
PH04322 658 (June 10, 1993) p30. "From Illtown To Chilltown: Naughty's Treach, Vinnie And DJ KayGee" (Larsen, Kristine)
DJ LETHAL—PHOTOGRAPHS—PORTRAITS
PH04323 671 (December 9, 1993) p31. "House's Danny Boy, DJ Lethal And Everlast With Cypress' B-Real And Muggs (from left)" (Blakesberg, Jay)
DJ LORD JAZZ—PHOTOGRAPHS
PH04324 664 (September 2, 1993) p20. "The Lords Of Newark (from left): DJ Lord Jazz, Mr. Funke And DoItAll" (Apicella-Hitchcock, Stephen)
DJ MINUTEMIX—PHOTOGRAPHS
PH04325 672-673 (December 23, 1993) p27. "Hippie, Dippy DJ Minutemix (left) And Prince Be" (Natkin, Paul)
DJ MINUTEMIX—PHOTOGRAPHS—PORTRAITS
PH04326 616 (October 31, 1991) p25. "DJ Minutemix (left) And Prince Be" (Brusso, Andrew)
PH04327 630 (May 14, 1992) p79. "Prince Be (left) And His Brother DJ Minutemix" (Watson, Albert)
DJ MUGGS—PHOTOGRAPHS
PH04328 662 (August 5, 1993) p16. "Just Another Band From L.A.? Sen Dog, B-Real And DJ Muggs (from left)"
DJ PREMIER—PHOTOGRAPHS
PH04329 682 (May 19, 1994) p30. "Back To The Razzmatazz: DJ Premier (left) And Guru Return To Their Roots" (Seliger, Mark)
PH04330 695 (November 17, 1994) p87. "Gang Starr" (Irish, Len)
DJ PREMIER—PHOTOGRAPHS—PORTRAITS
PH04331 685 (June 30, 1994) p40. "Partners LeFonque: Premier, Marsalis"
DJ RED ALERT—PHOTOGRAPHS
PH04332 695 (November 17, 1994) p31. "DJ Red Alert" (Exum)
DJ SHADOW—PHOTOGRAPHS
PH04333 738-739 (July 11, 1996) p26. "Mo' Wax Founder And Trip-Hop Enthusiast James Lavelle (left) With DJ Shadow" (Cardillicchio, Nick)
DJ SPOOKY—PHOTOGRAPHS
PH04334 715 (August 24, 1995) p82. "Hot DJ" (Johnson, Eric)
D.J. YELLA—PHOTOGRAPHS
PH04335 639 (September 17, 1992) p19. "N.W.A. (from left): D.J. Yella, Dr. Dre, Eazy-E And M.C. Ren"
DOCKING, JILL—PHOTOGRAPHS
PH04336 746 (October 31, 1996) p62. "Anti-Gun Senate Candidate Jill Docking Of Kansas: Dodging NRA Bullets"
THE DOCTOR (FILM)—PHOTOGRAPHS
PH04337 619-620 (December 12, 1991) p194. "Male Wimps And Female Warriors"
DODD, BUBBA—PHOTOGRAPHS
PH04338 685 (June 30, 1994) p40. "[Willie Nelson & Bubba Dodd]" (Sanchez, Bobby)
DOE, JOHN—ALBUMS
PH04339 717 (September 21, 1995) p84. "Kissingsohard"
DOE, JOHN—PHOTOGRAPHS
PH04340 650 (February 18, 1993) p11. "Doe's Other 'Love'" (Granitz, Steve)
PH04341 659 (June 24, 1993) p23. "'Xdream: Gilkyson, Doe, Cervenka, Bonebrake (from left)"
DOGG POUND—ILLUSTRATIONS
PH04342 724-725 (December 28, 1995) p124. "Filter Out All The Fool Talk About Women And 'Dogg Food' Is Lithe, Slow-Rollin' 70s Funk, Stripped Back Like P-Funk Dub Plates" (Hungry Dog Studio)
DOGS—PHOTOGRAPHS
PH04343 654 (April 15, 1993) pp[enc.17]. "[Dog]" (Woodward, Fred)
PH04344 656 (May 13, 1993) p74. "[Bulldog]"
DOGTOWN STUDIO—PHOTOGRAPHS
PH04345 618 (November 28, 1991) p46. "Producer Lanois's Progress Chart At Dogtown Studio, Outside Of Dublin" (Corbijn, Anton)
DOHERTY, SHANNEN—PHOTOGRAPHS—PORTRAITS
PH04346 624 (February 20, 1992) pp[cover]. "Beverly Hills, 90210: Smells Like Teen Spirit" (Eccles, Andrew)
PH04347 624 (February 20, 1992) p25. "Teen From A Mall: Doherty's Brenda Is Still Recovering From The Bang Heard Around The World" (Eccles, Andrew)
PH04348 645-646 (December 10, 1992) pp[cover]. "1992 Yearbook" (Eccles, Andrew)
DOHRN, WALT—PHOTOGRAPHS
PH04349 678 (March 24, 1994) p77. "Like Studying Sex? Cal Artists Walt Dohrn (left) And Eric Koenig In A Student-Designed Dorm Room" (Little, Blake)
DOITALL—PHOTOGRAPHS
PH04350 664 (September 2, 1993) p20. "The Lords Of Newark (from left): DJ Lord Jazz, Mr. Funke And DoItAll" (Apicella-Hitchcock, Stephen)
DOLAN, MIKE—PHOTOGRAPHS
PH04351 626 (March 19, 1992) p24. "Jackson And Dolan (right) In Durham" (Mazur, Kevin)
DOLBY, THOMAS—PHOTOGRAPHS
PH04352 667 (October 14, 1993) p100. "Dolby's Human 'Science' Project"
DOLE, ELIZABETH—PHOTOGRAPHS
PH04353 666 (September 30, 1993) p36. "Politicking With Wife Elizabeth In New Hampshire, '87" (Wyman, Ira)
DOLE, ROBERT—ILLUSTRATIONS
PH04354 708 (May 18, 1995) p47. "Chock-Full Of Nuts: Dole's Senate Chills Gingrich's Overheated House" (Witte, Michael)
PH04355 715 (August 24, 1995) p39. "Just Put It In The Dole Hole" (Witte, Michael)

PH04356 733 (May 2, 1996) p39. "[Bill Clinton & Bob Dole]" (Payne, C. F.)
DOLE, ROBERT—PHOTOGRAPHS
PH04357 666 (September 30, 1993) p36. "Politicking With Wife Elizabeth In New Hampshire, '87" (Wyman, Ira)
PH04358 726 (January 25, 1996) p54. "Organization, Endorsements And Cash Have Propelled Dole To The Top"
PH04359 744 (October 3, 1996) p26. "Dole Brother No. 1: Presidential Candidate Robert Dole (left) Clinches With Sam Moore Of Sam And Dave At A GOP Rally"
PH04360 745 (October 17, 1996) p33. "Fear And Loathing: Bob Dole With Tabitha Soren (top); A Choose Or Lose Representative Talks With Potential Young Voters"
PH04361 750-751 (December 26, 1996) p88. "He Don't Want To Cause No Fuss: Bo Derek And Bob Dole, Scamming A Ticket To Ride"
DOLE, ROBERT—PHOTOGRAPHS—PORTRAITS
PH04362 666 (September 30, 1993) p35. "Dole In His Senate Office, In Front Of A Portrait Of Fellow Kansan Dwight Eisenhower" (Downing, Larry)
PH04363 666 (September 30, 1993) p36. "During His First Senate Term, '72" (Halstead, Dirk)
PH04364 710 (June 15, 1995) p57. "Dole" (Simon, Martin)
PH04365 724-725 (December 28, 1995) p46. "Bob Dole Preferred Family Fun" (Gifford)
PH04366 730 (March 21, 1996) p52. "Dole"
DOLENZ, MICKEY—PHOTOGRAPHS
PH04367 702 (February 23, 1995) p20. "Thrashin' To The Oldies: Cruz (left) and Dolenz" (Mayer, Jeffrey)
DOLORES CLAIBORNE (FILM)—PHOTOGRAPHS
PH04368 706 (April 20, 1995) p88. "Kathy Bates And Jennifer Jason Leigh Hide Secrets"
DOLPHINS—ILLUSTRATIONS
PH04369 670 (November 25, 1993) p64. "Amazon Dolphins Actually Do Like Songs By Judy Collins" (Peck, Everett)
DOMBROWSKI, VINNIE—PHOTOGRAPHS
PH04370 706 (April 20, 1995) p36. "Motor City Five: Mazzola, Grover, Dombrowski, Tim And Mike Cross (from left)" (Halsband, Michael)
PH04371 708 (May 18, 1995) p17. "Mike Cross (left), Dombrowski Rock Detroit" (Schwab, Bill)
PH04372 710 (June 15, 1995) p49. "Mike Cross, Dombrowski, Charlie Grover, Joey Mazzola, Tim Cross (from left)" (Tavee, Tom)
DOMINO—PHOTOGRAPHS
PH04373 690 (September 8, 1994) p24. "[Guru & Domino]"
DOMINO—PHOTOGRAPHS—PORTRAITS
PH04374 680 (April 21, 1994) p29. "Oh, Oh, Domino: Straight Outta Long Beach, Calif., This Hardcore Rapper With A Sweet Side Has Been Called Snoop Puppy Pupp As He Follows His Fellow Rapper Up The Charts" (Miller, M
DOMINO, FATS—PHOTOGRAPHS
PH04375 703 (March 9, 1995) p25. "Fats Domino: The Spirit Of new Orleans"
DOMINO, FATS—PHOTOGRAPHS—PORTRAITS
PH04376 643 (November 12, 1992) p146. "Fats Domino" (Seliger, Mark)
PH04377 671 (December 9, 1993) p17. "Domino's New Studio LP Is His First Since 1968" (Seliger, Mark)
DOMMARTIN, SOLVEIG—PHOTOGRAPHS
PH04378 622 (January 23, 1992) p50. "William Hurt And Solveig Dommartin Face The End"
DON CABALLERO—PHOTOGRAPHS
PH04379 723 (December 14, 1995) p44. "Don Caballero: Polyrhythmic Punk" (Vogt, Andy)
DON JUAN DEMARCO (FILM)—PHOTOGRAPHS
PH04380 707 (May 4, 1995) p74. "Depp And Brando In 'Don Juan'"
DON, RASA—PHOTOGRAPHS
PH04381 648 (January 21, 1993) p9. "Arrested Development (from left): Speech, Aerle Taree, Headliner, Rasa Don, Baba Oje And Montsho Eshe" (Mazur, Kevin)
DON, RASA—PHOTOGRAPHS—PORTRAITS
PH04382 634-635 (July 9, 1992) p20. "Arrested Development (from left): Headliner, Montsho Eshe, Aerle Taree, Rasa Don And Speech" (Lavine, Michael)
PH04383 634-635 (July 9, 1992) p20. "Love Battery (from left): Kevin Whitworth, Rod Rudzitis And Jason Finn" (Lavine, Michael)
DONAHUE, JONATHAN—PHOTOGRAPHS
PH04384 652 (March 18, 1993) p27. "Jonathan Donahue (left) And Grasshopper"
PH04385 664 (September 2, 1993) p24. "They're All Revved Up: Donahue, Thorpe, Baker, Chambers, Fridmann And Grasshopper (from left)" (Gullick, Steve)
DONALDSON, CALEB—PHOTOGRAPHS
PH04386 722 (November 30, 1995) pp[enc.6]. "Caleb Donaldson Cruising The Net" (McLeod, William Mercer)
DONATACCI, CAMILLE—PHOTOGRAPHS
PH04387 708 (May 18, 1995) p85. "[Lou Deangelis & Camille Donatacci]" (Seliger, Mark)
DONELLY, TANYA—PHOTOGRAPHS
PH04388 663 (August 19, 1993) p27. "Belly's Tanya Donelly (left) And Gail Greenwood With Robyn Hitchcock" (Mazur, Kevin)
PH04389 667 (October 14, 1993) p40. "Below: Merchant, Bragg, Founder Harry Horgan, Tanya Donelly, Janovitz" (Robicheau, Paul)
PH04390 671 (December 9, 1993) p31. "Yorke And Donelly Share A Moment"
PH04391 702 (February 23, 1995) p19. "Front: Hatfield, Donelly, Bragg. Rear: Dean Fraser, Gary Smith, Sean Slade" (Robicheau, Paul)
PH04392 703 (March 9, 1995) p55. "The Throwing Muses Lineup In 1989 (from left): Hersh, Leslie Langston, Tanya Donelly And Narcizo" (Musto, Ilpo)
PH04393 706 (April 20, 1995) p50. "Onstage In London, January '95"
DONELLY, TANYA—PHOTOGRAPHS—PORTRAITS
PH04394 649 (February 4, 1993) p16. "Chris Gorman, Tanya Donelly And Tom Gorman (from left)" (Feingold, Deborah)
PH04395 706 (April 20, 1995) p46. "[Tanya Donelly]" (Seliger, Mark)
PH04396 743 (September 19, 1996) p36. "Sologirl Donelly" (Catlin, Andrew)
DONOVAN—ALBUMS
PH04397 645-646 (December 10, 1992) p166. "Troubadour: The Definitive Collection 1964-1976"
PH04398 748 (November 28, 1996) p134. "Sutras"
DONOVAN—PHOTOGRAPHS
PH04399 719 (October 19, 1995) p67. "Rubin In A Los Angeles Studio Working With Donovan On The Singer's Comeback" (McDaniel, Melodie)
DONOVAN, MARTIN—PHOTOGRAPHS
PH04400 706 (April 20, 1995) p88. "Young, Huppert, Donovan And Lowensohn Run"
DON'T LOOK BACK (FILM)—PHOTOGRAPHS
PH04401 667 (October 14, 1993) p69. "Pennebaker's Answer To What About Bob"
DOO WOP MUSIC—ILLUSTRATIONS
PH04402 686-687 (July 14, 1994) p108. "[Doo Wop Music]" (Plunkert, David)
DOODLEBUG—PHOTOGRAPHS
PH04403 707 (May 4, 1995) p36. "Doodlebug (left) And Ladybug Shock The House" (Capak, R. J.)
THE DOOM GENERATION (FILM)—PHOTOGRAPHS
PH04404 721 (November 16, 1995) p117. "Duval, McGowan, Schaech (from left)"

DOONESBURY—ILLUSTRATIONS
PH04405 645-646 (December 10, 1992) p156. "Garry Trudeau's Uncle Duke, 1975"
DOORS—ALBUMS
PH04406 617 (November 14, 1991) p116. "Strange Days" (Harvey, William S.)
PH04407 617 (November 14, 1991) p116. "Strange Days" (Brodsky, Joel)
DOORS—PHOTOGRAPHS
PH04408 649 (February 4, 1993) p52. "The Doors (from left): keyboardist Ray Manzarek, Drummer John Densmore, Guitarist Robbie Krieger, Shaman Jim Morrison" (Diltz, Henry)
PH04409 651 (March 4, 1993) p16. "Eddie Vedder And The Surviving Doors Light A Fire Together" (Granitz, Steve)
PH04410 672-673 (December 23, 1993) p17. "Above: The Dorrs With Vedder" (Mazur, Kevin)
PH04411 686-687 (July 14, 1994) p23. "Jim Morrison (above left) And Janis Joplin (left) Are Both Represented With Collections" (Teske, Edmund)
PH04412 718 (October 5, 1995) p51. "Jim Morrison With The Doors: 'The Shadow Side Of Rock & Roll's Dionysian Impulse'"
PH04413 724-725 (December 28, 1995) p46. "Doors John Densmore, Manzarek And Robby Krieger (from left)" (Kaplin, Todd)
DOORS (FILM)—PHOTOGRAPHS
PH04414 619-620 (December 12, 1991) p31. "Val Kilmer Gets Oliver Stoned"
DORFF, STEPHEN—PHOTOGRAPHS
PH04415 680 (April 21, 1994) p93. "Dorff And Hart Flank Lee In A Beatles Love Triangle"
PH04416 680 (April 21, 1994) p64. "There's A Place: Backbeatles With Sutcliffe (Dorff, Right)"
PH04417 734 (May 16, 1996) p72. "Stephen Dorff"
PH04418 750-751 (December 26, 1996) p74. "Stipe, Rick Rubin, Nusrat Ali Khan, Stephen Dorff And Flea (from left)" (Cohen, Lester)
DORFF, STEPHEN—PHOTOGRAPHS—PORTRAITS
PH04419 680 (April 21, 1994) p66. "[Stephen Dorff]" (Cuffaro, Chris)
DORGAN, BILLY—PHOTOGRAPHS
PH04420 723 (December 14, 1995) p27. "The Chicago Eight: D'Arcy, Petersson, Carlos, Corgan, Nielsen, Iha, Chamberlin And Zander (from left)" (Elledge, Paul)
DORGE, MICHEL—PHOTOGRAPHS
PH04421 681 (May 5, 1994) p16. "Big Dummies: Dan And Brad Roberts, Darvill, Dorge And Reid (from left)" (Blakesberg, Jay)
DORNAN, ROBERT—PHOTOGRAPHS—PORTRAITS
PH04422 719 (October 19, 1995) p49. "Dornan" (Kraft, Brooks)
DOSS, ALAN—PHOTOGRAPHS
PH04423 617 (November 14, 1991) p34. "Ben Huggins, Alan Doss, Monty Colvin And Dane Sonnier (from left)" (Carter, Keith)
DOUCET, MICHAEL—PHOTOGRAPHS
PH04424 623 (February 6, 1992) p29. "Michael Doucet (left) And Beausoleil" (Mazur, Kevin)
DOUCETT, LINDA—PHOTOGRAPHS
PH04425 690 (September 8, 1994) p70. "Shandling With Real-Life Fiancee And Fictional Co-Worker Linda Doucett" (Kravitz, Jeff)
DOUGANS, BRIAN—PHOTOGRAPHS
PH04426 721 (November 16, 1995) p73. "Brian Dougans (left) And Gary Cobain: Future Shock And Techno Reflections" (Broad, Julian)
DOUGHTY—PHOTOGRAPHS
PH04427 719 (October 19, 1995) p15. "Talk About It: Doughty (left) And David Byrne Get Funky" (Capak, R. J.)
DOUGHTY, M.—PHOTOGRAPHS
PH04428 734 (May 16, 1996) p18. "Soul Brothas M. Doughty (left) And Sebastian Steinberg" (Callahan, Kristin)
PH04429 735 (May 30, 1996) p23. "The Rock & Roll Zelig: Doughty Mouthing Off Onstage, 1994" (Banjee)
DOUGHTY, M.—PHOTOGRAPHS—PORTRAITS
PH04430 735 (May 30, 1996) p21. "Frontman M. Doughty, Sebastian Steinberg, Mark De Gli Antoni And Yuval Gabay" (Vadukul, Nitin)
DOUGLAS, ALAN—PHOTOGRAPHS
PH04431 623 (February 6, 1992) p48. "Producer Alan Douglas Now Controls Jimi's Musical Legacy" (Estrine, Darryl)
DOUGLAS, ILLEANA—PHOTOGRAPHS
PH04432 708 (May 18, 1995) p97. "A Deadly Drive For Dunne, Douglas And Walken"
PH04433 744 (October 3, 1996) p79. "Illeana Douglas Meets A '50s Girl Group"
DOUGLAS, MICHAEL—ILLUSTRATIONS
PH04434 651 (March 4, 1993) p71. "He's Mad As Hell" (Peck, Everett)
DOUGLAS, MICHAEL—PHOTOGRAPHS
PH04435 624 (February 20, 1992) p49. "Michael Douglas And Secretary Melanie Griffith At War"
PH04436 628 (April 16, 1992) p90. "Clothes Off, Heat On, Douglas Romances The Stone"
PH04437 644 (November 26, 1992) p78. "[Basic Instinct]"
PH04438 649 (February 4, 1993) p72. "Homage Of Ripoff? In 'Body of Evidence,' Madonna And Dafoe (left) Share Stone And Douglas's Basic Instincts"
PH04439 651 (March 4, 1993) p72. "Michael Douglas Turns L.A. Vigilante After Losing Both His Job And His Family"
PH04440 698-699 (December 29, 1994) p199. "Moore And Douglas In "Disclosure""
PH04441 722 (November 30, 1995) p76. "Rob Reiner Directs Michael Douglas As The Prez"
PH04442 746 (October 31, 1996) p78. "Great White Hunter Michael Douglas"
DOW, JOHN—PHOTOGRAPHS
PH04443 700 (January 26, 1995) p16. "Farrell, Bernhard And Doe Ham It Up" (Winter, Kevin)
DOWN BY LAW—ALBUMS
PH04444 709 (June 1, 1995) p80. "Punkrockacademyfightsong"
DOWN THUNDER ROAD (BOOK)—PHOTOGRAPHS
PH04445 645-646 (December 10, 1992) p87. "[Down Thunder Road]"
DOWNEY, ROBERT, JR.—PHOTOGRAPHS
PH04446 647 (January 7, 1993) p51. "Robert Downey Jr. Is The Little Tramp"
PH04447 664 (September 2, 1993) p69. "Charles Grodin, Robert Downey Jr., Kyra Sedgwick, Alfre Woodard And Tom Sizemore"
PH04448 693 (October 20, 1994) p157. "Tomei, Downey And Scene-Stealing Italy"
PH04449 726 (January 25, 1996) p67. "Dressed To Kill: Robert Downey Jr."
DOWNTOWN SCIENCE—PHOTOGRAPHS
PH04450 617 (November 14, 1991) p34. "Bosco Money (left) And Sam Sever" (Lavine, Michael)
DOYLE, CANDIDA—PHOTOGRAPHS
PH04451 732 (April 18, 1996) p24. "A Wildly Unorthodox Mixture Of Influence Gathered Around The Table: Pulp's Candida Doyle, Mark Webber, Cocker, Steve Mackey, Russell Senior And Nick Banks (from left)" (Rankin)
DOYLE, MARK—PHOTOGRAPHS
PH04452 721 (November 16, 1995) p100. "Loud Lucy: Furar, Lane And Doyle (from left)" (GS, Jamil)
DOYLE, TAD—PHOTOGRAPHS
PH04453 708 (May 18, 1995) p18. "Light And Sweet: Tad, Matthew" (Olson, Sheryl)
DR. DRE—ALBUMS
PH04454 652 (March 18, 1993) p40. "The Chronic"
PH04455 672-673 (December 23, 1993) p146. "The Chronic"
DR. DRE—PHOTOGRAPHS
PH04456 619-620 (December 12, 1991) p74. "The Stars Of 'Yo!

MTV Raps': Ed Lover (left) And Dr. Dre"
PH04457 634-635 (July 9, 1992) p17. "N.W.A. (clockwise from top left): MC Ren, Yella, Eazy-E And Dr. Dre" (Preston, Neal)
PH04458 639 (September 17, 1992) p19. "N.W.A. (from left): D.J. Yella, Dr. Dre, Eazy-E And M.C. Ren"
PH04459 659 (June 24, 1993) p15. "Russian Summit: Ed Lover, Henry Kissinger And Dr. Dre (from left)" (Mazur, Kevin)
PH04460 666 (September 30, 1993) pp38-39. "[Dr. Dre & Snoop Doggy Dogg]" (Seliger, Mark)
PH04461 666 (September 30, 1993) p40. "Dr. Dre With Extras At The Video Shoot For 'Let Me Ride'" (Seliger, Mark)
PH04462 666 (September 30, 1993) p41. "Dre Directs At Audubon Junior High" (Seliger, Mark)
PH04463 666 (September 30, 1993) p41. "Dre With An Assistant Camerawoman And His Cinematographer" (Seliger, Mark)
PH04464 666 (September 30, 1993) p42. "Serious Attitude: Ex-N.W.A. Members Ice Cube, Yella, Eazy-E, Dre And MC Ren" (Rosenberg, Howard)
PH04465 670 (November 25, 1993) p83. "[Snoop Doggy Dogg & Dr. Dre]" (Seliger, Mark)
PH04466 674 (January 27, 1994) p41. "Rapper Du Jour Dre" (Mazur, Kevin)
PH04467 695 (November 17, 1994) p154. "Dr. Dre" (Seliger, Mark)
PH04468 700 (January 26, 1995) p16. "Big Brother Is Watching: Dr. Dre (left) With The Birthday Boy" (Cross, Brian)
PH04469 712-713 (July 13, 1995) p33. "Dr. Dre (left), Snoop Doggy Dogg" (Seliger, Mark)
PH04470 750-751 (December 26, 1996) p90. "[Dr. Dre]" (Nahoum, Ken)
PH04471 750-751 (December 26, 1996) p90. "Make-Over" (Goldsmith, Lynn)

DR. DRE—PHOTOGRAPHS—PORTRAITS
PH04472 645-646 (December 10, 1992) p49. "Dr. Dre Mugs It Up" (Ruthless)
PH04473 666 (September 30, 1993) pp[cover]. "Dr Dre And Snoop Doggy Dogg: One Nation Under A G Thang" (Seliger, Mark)
PH04474 666 (September 30, 1993) p42. "Early Dre: Young In 11th Grade At Compton's Centennial High"
PH04475 672-673 (December 23, 1993) p188. "[Covers]" (Seliger, Mark)
PH04476 672-673 (December 23, 1993) p20. "Left: Dr. Dre's 'The Chronic' Hits No. 1" (Benabib, Michael)
PH04477 693 (October 20, 1994) p47. "[Dr. Dre]" (Benabib, Michael)

DR. HOOK AND THE MEDICINE SHOW—ILLUSTRATIONS
PH04478 645-646 (December 10, 1992) p148. "Dr. Hook And The Medicine Show, 1973"

DR. JEKYLL AND MRS. HYDE (FILM)—PHOTOGRAPHS
PH04479 715 (August 24, 1995) p108. "The Man Eaters"

DR. JOHN—ALBUMS
PH04480 639 (September 17, 1992) p96. "Goin' Back To New Orleans"

DR. JOHN—PHOTOGRAPHS
PH04481 626 (March 19, 1992) p13. "Dave Stewart, Robin Zander And Dr. John (from left)" (Tallman, Susie)

DR. KNOW—PHOTOGRAPHS
PH04482 711 (June 29, 1995) p15. "Cosmic Agit Pop And Measured Fury: Dr. Know, H.R., Darryl Jenifer And Earl Hudson of Bad Brains (from left)" (Cuffaro, Chris)

DR. SEUSS—BOOKS
PH04483 639 (September 17, 1992) p81. "Green Eggs And Ham"

DRACULA (FILM)—PHOTOGRAPHS
PH04484 649 (February 4, 1993) p72. "[Dracula]"

DRAGON (FILM)—PHOTOGRAPHS
PH04485 657 (May 27, 1993) p56. "Tormented: Bruce Lee (Jason Scott Lee) Battles A Nightmare"

DRAGONHEART (FILM)—PHOTOGRAPHS
PH04486 736 (June 13, 1996) p58. "Headaches"
PH04487 737 (June 27, 1996) p62. "Dennis Quaid's Knight Feels Sean Connery's Dragon Breath"

DREAM LOVER (FILM)—PHOTOGRAPHS
PH04488 683 (June 2, 1994) p78. "Amick Gets Spader In Her Sex Vise"

DREAM WARRIORS—PHOTOGRAPHS
PH04489 619-620 (December 12, 1991) p46. "The Dream Warriors" (Burniston, Ray)

DREIWITZ, DAVE—PHOTOGRAPHS—PORTRAITS
PH04490 637 (August 20, 1992) p20. "John Hamilton, Donna Croughn, Andy Demos, Dave Dreiwitz And Stuart Hake (from left)" (Borris, Dan)

DREJA, CHRIS—PHOTOGRAPHS
PH04491 623 (February 6, 1992) p51. "The Yardbirds, Circa 1964 (from left): Chris Dreja, Keith Reif, Paul Samwell-Smith, Eric Clapton And Jim McCarty"
PH04492 655 (April 29, 1993) p34. "Slowhand (at bottom left) With The Yardbirds: Chris Dreja, Jim McCarty, Paul Samwell-Smith And Keith Relf (clockwise from top left)"

DREW, DENNIS—PHOTOGRAPHS—PORTRAITS
PH04493 652 (March 18, 1993) pp34-35. "Rob Buck, Dennis Drew, Natalie Merchant, Jerome Augustyniak, Steven Gustafson (from left)" (Ockenfels, Frank W.)

DREYER, CRAIG—PHOTOGRAPHS
PH04494 730 (March 21, 1996) p46. "Osborne With Bobby Sheehan Of Blues Traveler (left) And Craig Dreyer, 1991"

DREYFUSS, RICHARD—PHOTOGRAPHS
PH04495 727 (February 8, 1996) p46. "Richard Dreyfuss Teaches Music To Alicia Witt"

DRIVE LIKE JEHU—ALBUMS
PH04496 683 (June 2, 1994) p72. "Yank Crime"

DRIVE LIKE JEHU—PHOTOGRAPHS
PH04497 689 (August 25, 1994) p44. "All Together Now: Trombino, Atom, Kennedy, Reis, N.D., Petey X, Apollo 9, Froberg (from left)" (Cuffaro, Chris)

DRIVER, MINNIE—PHOTOGRAPHS
PH04498 704 (March 23, 1995) p129. "Driver's Irish Eyes Smile At O'Donnell"

DRIVIN' N' CRYIN'—ALBUMS
PH04499 657 (May 27, 1993) p52. "Smoke"

DROGE, PETE—ALBUMS
PH04500 737 (June 27, 1996) p55. "Find A Door"

DROGE, PETE—PHOTOGRAPHS
PH04501 697 (December 15, 1994) p20. "Petty, Droge And Dylan At The Viper Room (from left)"
PH04502 701 (February 9, 1995) p16. "Louise Post, Johnston, Nina Gordon And Pete Droge do D.C." (Harrington, John)

DROGE, PETE—PHOTOGRAPHS—PORTRAITS
PH04503 703 (March 9, 1995) p32. "Droge: Smart Move Playing 'Dumb'" (Moskowitz, Karen)

DROGE, PETE—SINGLES
PH04504 703 (March 9, 1995) p32. "If You Don't Love Me"

DROZD, STEVEN—PHOTOGRAPHS
PH04505 689 (August 25, 1994) p21. "The Flaming Lips' Michael Ivins, Steven Drozd, Wayne Coyne (from left)" (Blakesberg, Jay)
PH04506 703 (March 9, 1995) p26. "Imagine The Beatles Drunk On Robitussin: Coyne, Drozd, Ivins And Jones (from left)" (Lavine, Michael)
PH04507 736 (June 13, 1996) p33. "The Flaming Lips' Steven Drozd, Michael Ivins, Wayne Coyne And Ronald Jones (from left)" (Martin, J. Michelle)

DRUG CULTURE—ILLUSTRATIONS
PH04508 663 (August 19, 1993) p4. "Instant Addiction" (Pendergrast, James T.)
PH04509 681 (May 5, 1994) p26. "[Drugs]" (Guy, Edmund)
PH04510 681 (May 5, 1994) p34. "[Drugs]" (Mahurin, Matt)
PH04511 681 (May 5, 1994) p36. "[Heroin]" (Duke, William)
PH04512 681 (May 5, 1994) p32. "[Marijuana]" (Frampton, Jerald)

DRUG CULTURE—PHOTOGRAPHS
PH04513 681 (May 5, 1994) p39. "[Methamphetamine]" (Frailey, Stephen)
PH04514 719 (October 19, 1995) p99. "[Drugs]" (Ravid, Joyce)
DRUGS—ILLUSTRATIONS
PH04515 684 (June 16, 1994) p11. "Dead End" (Pendergrast, James T.)
PH04516 703 (March 9, 1995) p20. "Huff Baked" (O'Connell, Mitch)
PH04517 703 (March 9, 1995) p16. "Moral High Road" (Pendergrast, James T.)
PH04518 714 (August 10, 1995) p12. "Drugs" (Pendergrast, James T.)
PH04519 722 (November 30, 1995) p14. "Entering Zero Tolerance, Next Stop Hard Drugs" (Pendergrast, James T.)
DRUGS—ILLUSTRATIONS—LETTERING
PH04520 681 (May 5, 1994) pp[cover]. "Drugs In America"
DRUGS—PHOTOGRAPHS
PH04521 639 (September 17, 1992) p81. "Famous Brains On Drugs"
DRUMMERS OF BURUNDI—PHOTOGRAPHS
PH04522 668 (October 28, 1993) p24. "The Drummers Of Burundi Put The Beat In World Beat For WOMAD's Rousing Finale" (Capak, R. J.)
DRUMMOND, BILL—PHOTOGRAPHS
PH04523 668 (October 28, 1993) p25. "Drummond And Cauty Of K" (Cummins, Kevin)
DRUMMOND, TOM—PHOTOGRAPHS
PH04524 710 (June 15, 1995) p46. "Griffin, Bonnecaze And Drummond (from left) Veg In The Garden District" (Chiasson, John)
DUBBE, BEREND—PHOTOGRAPHS
PH04525 653 (April 1, 1993) p22. "Peter Visser, Herman Bunskoeke, Carol Van Dijk And Berend Dubbe (from left)" (Doove, Hester)
DUCHOVNY, DAVID—ILLUSTRATIONS
PH04526 737 (June 27, 1996) p12. "Internat'l Ass-kicking Line" (Pendergrast, James T.)
DUCHOVNY, DAVID—PHOTOGRAPHS
PH04527 734 (May 16, 1996) pp38-39. "David Duchovny, Gillian Anderson & Chris Carter" (Montalbetti-Campbell)
PH04528 734 (May 16, 1996) p41. "The Novice Actor Goes Soft-Core In 'Red Shoe Diaries'"
PH04529 734 (May 16, 1996) pp[cover]. "'X' Files Under Cover" (Montalbetti-Campbell)
DUCHOVNY, DAVID—PHOTOGRAPHS—PORTRAITS
PH04530 734 (May 16, 1996) p41. "David Duchovny (right), Age 7, With His Father And Brother Danny"
PH04531 734 (May 16, 1996) p41. "With His Fictional Vampire Lover And Real-Life Ex-Girlfriend, Perrey Reeves"
DUFF—PHOTOGRAPHS
PH04532 622 (January 23, 1992) p6. "From Left: Hoon, Slash And Duff" (White, Frank)
DUFFY, MARTIN—PHOTOGRAPHS—PORTRAITS
PH04533 684 (June 16, 1994) p26. "A Slice Of Scream: Keyboardist Martin Duffy, Gillespie And Innes (from left)" (Sheehan, Tom)
DUKAKIS, MICHAEL—PHOTOGRAPHS
PH04534 660-661 (July 8, 1993) p52. "Babbitt On The Campaign Trail: Presidential Candidates Michael Dukakis, Babbitt, Paul Simon, Richard Gephardt, Jesse Jackson And Al Gore (from left) At A New York Forum ..." (Peterso
DULLI, GREG—PHOTOGRAPHS
PH04535 674 (January 27, 1994) p29. "Heat Wave: Dulli Onstage With Reeves" (Schwab, Bill)
PH04536 676 (February 24, 1994) p29. "'Backbeat' Boys: Dulli, Fleming, Mike Mills, Dave Grohl And Thurston Moore"
PH04537 680 (April 21, 1994) p64. "Twist And Shout: Fleming, Dulli, Grohl And Mills (from left) At A 'Backbeat' Session" (Cuffaro, Chris)
PH04538 684 (June 16, 1994) p32. "Gentleman And Head Whig Dulli" (Mazur, Kevin)
PH04539 688 (August 11, 1994) p17. "At The Movie Awards: Backbeaters Mike Mills, Don Fleming, Dave Pirner, Greg Dulli, Dave Grohl And Thurston Moore (above, from left)" (Kravitz, Jeff)
PH04540 691 (September 22, 1994) p21. "[Afghan Whigs]" (Moore, Michael)
PH04541 695 (November 17, 1994) p78. "Afghan Whigs" (Lixenberg, Dana)
PH04542 698-699 (December 29, 1994) p50. "Dulli, Fleming, Mills, Grohl, Moore, Pirner Went Out For A Smoke" (Cuffaro, Chris)
PH04543 721 (November 16, 1995) p41. "Greg Dulli (left) and John Curley In Robert Lang's Studio, In Seattle" (Peterson, Charles)
PH04544 730 (March 21, 1996) p17. "You Are So Beautiful To Me: Dulli, Sorvino" (Mazur, Kevin)
PH04545 740 (August 8, 1996) p17. "Dulli Superstar" (Liu, Brian)
DULLI, GREG—PHOTOGRAPHS—PORTRAITS
PH04546 671 (December 9, 1993) p21. "The Whig Club: Rick McCollum, Greg Dulli, Steve Earle And John Curley" (Broad, Julian)
PH04547 690 (September 8, 1994) p34. "[Greg Dulli]"
PH04548 750-751 (December 26, 1996) p48. "Greg Dulli Of Afghan Wigs" (Kessler, Joshua)
DUMB AND DUMBER (FILM)—PHOTOGRAPHS
PH04549 698-699 (December 29, 1994) p199. "Carrey And Daniels In "Dumb""
DUNLAP, SLIM—PHOTOGRAPHS
PH04550 659 (June 24, 1993) p52. "The Later Mats Incarnation: Tommy Stinson, Westerberg, Slim Dunlap And Chris Mars (from left)" (Matheu, Robert)
DUNLAVY, BRIAN—PHOTOGRAPHS
PH04551 647 (January 7, 1993) p30. "Dunlavy, Dominic Pasquini, Matt Hensler" (Mark, Mary Ellen)
DUNLEAVY, STEVE—PHOTOGRAPHS
PH04552 650 (February 18, 1993) p43. "'The Reporters': Jim Paymar, Dunlop, Bradford, Abramovitz, And Dunleavy (from left)"
DUNLOP, STEVE—PHOTOGRAPHS
PH04552 650 (February 18, 1993) p43. "'The Reporters': Jim Paymar, Dunlop, Bradford, Abramovitz, And Dunleavy (from left)"
DUNN, DUCK—PHOTOGRAPHS
PH04553 625 (March 5, 1992) p13. "Lewis Steinberg, Steve Cropper, Booker T. Jones, Marion Jackson, Randall Jackson, Duck Dunn, Jim Stewart (from left)" (Elgar, Nick)
PH04554 625 (March 5, 1992) p17. "Neil Young Takes Center Stage During The All-Star-Jam Finale" (Gershoff, Gary)
DUNN, DUCK—PHOTOGRAPHS—PORTRAITS
PH04555 623 (February 6, 1992) p50. "Booker T. And The MGs (from left): Donald 'Duck' Dunn, Booker T., Steve Cropper And Al Jackson Jr."
PH04556 685 (June 30, 1994) p41. "Booker T. Jones, Steve Cropper, Dave Edmunds And Donald "Duck" Dunn (from left)" (Cohen, Lester)
DUNNE, GRIFFIN—PHOTOGRAPHS
PH04557 708 (May 18, 1995) p97. "A Deadly Drive For Dunne, Douglas And Walken"
DUNNE, ROISIN—PHOTOGRAPHS
PH04558 722 (November 30, 1995) p19. "Who Are You Callin' A Bitch?: To Wit, Elizabeth Davis, Selene Vigil, Agnew And Roisin Dunne Of 7 Year Bitch (from left)" (Blakesberg, Jay)
DUNST, KIRSTEN—PHOTOGRAPHS
PH04559 697 (December 15, 1994) p102. "Prowling Vampires Kirsten Dunst, Brad Pitt And Tom Cruise"
PH04560 705 (April 6, 1995) p69. "Oscar Rejects"

DUPLEX PLANET ILLUSTRATED (PUBLICATION)—PHOTOGRAPHS
PH04561 679 (April 7, 1994) p20. "Duplex Planet Illustrated"
DURAN DURAN—ALBUMS
PH04562 651 (March 4, 1993) p65. "Duran Duran"
PH04563 672-673 (December 23, 1993) p156. "Duran Duran"
PH04564 709 (June 1, 1995) p62. "Thank You"
DURAN DURAN—PHOTOGRAPHS
PH04565 653 (April 1, 1993) p20. "Nick Rhodes, Simon LeBon, John Taylor And Warren Cuccurullo (from left)" (Heungman)
PH04566 674 (January 27, 1994) p41. "They're Back: Duran Duran" (Otte, Sylvia)
DURANGO, SANTIAGO—PHOTOGRAPHS
PH04567 656 (May 13, 1993) p88. "[Big Black]"
DURANTE, MARK—PHOTOGRAPHS
PH04568 733 (May 2, 1996) p57. "Durante, Schlabowske, Langford, Dear (from left)" (Swider, Frank)
DURITZ, ADAM—ILLUSTRATIONS
PH04569 679 (April 7, 1994) p88. "Adam Duritz Of Counting Crows" (Brown, Calef)
DURITZ, ADAM—PHOTOGRAPHS
PH04570 669 (November 11, 1993) p24. "A '90s Sensibility: Vickrey, Gillingham, Duritz, Bowman, Malley, Bryson (from left)" (Blakesberg, Jay)
PH04571 674 (January 27, 1994) p25. "Crows (from left): Vickrey, Malley, Duritz" (Blakesberg, Jay)
PH04572 685 (June 30, 1994) p46. "Adam Duritz in Paris" (Seliger, Mark)
PH04573 685 (June 30, 1994) p53. "Chasing A Dream: Duritz (second from left) With Fellow Himalayans, Circa 1988"
PH04574 685 (June 30, 1994) pp[cover]. "Counting Crows: The Biggest New Band In America" (Seliger, Mark)
PH04575 695 (November 17, 1994) p84. "Adam Duritz Of Counting Crows" (Seliger, Mark)
DURITZ, ADAM—PHOTOGRAPHS—PORTRAITS
PH04576 712-713 (July 13, 1995) p26. "[Lori Carson & Adam Duritz]" (Erikson, Wendy)
DUSHKU, ELIZA—PHOTOGRAPHS
PH04577 654 (April 15, 1993) p69. "Pick The Psycho: De Niro, Dushku, Barkin Or DiCaprio?"
DUST BROTHERS—PHOTOGRAPHS
PH04578 743 (September 19, 1996) p38. "Producers For The New Millennium" (Garner, Kate)
DUVAL, JAMES—PHOTOGRAPHS
PH04579 721 (November 16, 1995) p117. "Duval, McGowan, Schaech (from left)"
DYLAN, BOB—ALBUMS
PH04580 617 (November 14, 1991) p133. "Bringing It All Back Home" (Berg, John)
PH04581 617 (November 14, 1991) p133. "Bringing It All Back Home" (Kramer, Daniel)
PH04582 617 (November 14, 1991) p144. "Self Portrait" (Coro, Ron)
PH04583 617 (November 14, 1991) p144. "Self Portrait" (Dylan, Bob)
PH04584 647 (January 7, 1993) p45. "Good As I Been To You"
PH04585 707 (May 4, 1995) p63. "Greatest Hits, Vol. III"
DYLAN, BOB—ILLUSTRATIONS
PH04586 642 (October 29, 1992) p5. "Bob Dylan" (Burke, Philip)
PH04587 647 (January 7, 1993) p44. "Bob Dylan Looks Back, But For Leonard Cohen, The Future Is Murder" (Cowles, David)
PH04588 707 (May 4, 1995) p63. "His Back Pages" (Piven, Hanoch)
DYLAN, BOB—ILLUSTRATIONS—PORTRAITS
PH04589 641 (October 15, 1992) p111. "[Bob Dylan]" (Liepke, Skip)
PH04590 645-646 (December 10, 1992) p152. "Bob Dylan, 1974"
DYLAN, BOB—PHOTOGRAPHS
PH04591 617 (November 14, 1991) p75. "The Last Waltz, 1976: Robertson, Danko And Manuel, With Neil Young (left), Bob Dylan (back to camera) And Van Morrison" (Leibovitz, Annie)
PH04592 619-620 (December 12, 1991) p39. "Dylan Hits The Big Five-Oh" (Feingold, Deborah)
PH04593 619-620 (December 12, 1991) p104. "Graham And Bob Dylan At A 1975 Benefit" (Regan, Ken)
PH04594 619-620 (December 12, 1991) p22. "Lifer Bob Dylan With Jack Nicholson" (Mazur, Kevin)
PH04595 619-620 (December 12, 1991) p90. "Like A Rolling Stone: Richards With Dylan (above)..." (Putland, Michael)
PH04596 643 (November 12, 1992) p23. "Before The Flood: Jim Marshall Photographed The Pre-Electrified Bob Dylan In 1963" (Marshall, Jim)
PH04597 643 (November 12, 1992) p63. "David Gahr Catches A Freewheelin' Bob Dylan At The 1963 Newport Folk Festival" (Gahr, David)
PH04598 644 (November 26, 1992) p17. "The Great Garden Party: Dylan Center Stage For The Grand Finale" (Mazur, Kevin)
PH04599 645-646 (December 10, 1992) p91. "[Bob Dylan]" (Mazur, Kevin)
PH04600 645-646 (December 10, 1992) p152. "Bob Dylan And Joan Baez, 1976"
PH04601 645-646 (December 10, 1992) p152. "Bob Dylan, 1968"
PH04602 645-646 (December 10, 1992) p153. "Bob Dylan, 1978"
PH04603 650 (February 18, 1993) p51. "Bob Dylan and Wexler In 1972 During A Doug Sahm Session" (Gahr, David)
PH04604 651 (March 4, 1993) p18. "Bob Dylan (in disguise) Greets Jack Bruce" (Mazur, Kevin)
PH04605 658 (June 10, 1993) p16. "Bob Dylan" (Sigmon, Jim)
PH04606 665 (September 16, 1993) p31. "Carlos Santana And Bob Dylan" (Granitz, Steven)
PH04607 667 (October 14, 1993) p69. "Bob Dylan (With Allen Ginsberg At Left): You Don't Need A Weatherman"
PH04608 667 (October 14, 1993) p69. "Pennebaker's Answer To What About Bob"
PH04609 668 (October 28, 1993) p30. "Dylan: Subfreezing" (Capak, R. J.)
PH04610 669 (November 11, 1993) p67. "Sredni Vollmer, Helm, Dylan And Danko In NYC in '83 (above)" (Landy, Elliott)
PH04611 672-673 (December 23, 1993) p30. "Above: Nelson (left) With Well_wisher Dylan" (Kennedy, Bill)
PH04612 686-687 (July 14, 1994) p41. "A Buddha-less Bob Dylan"
PH04613 691 (September 22, 1994) p65. "Dylan In His First Woodstock Appearance" (Mazur, Kevin)
PH04614 697 (December 15, 1994) p38. "Dylan High-Steps Through His History And Ours" (Busacca, Larry)
PH04615 706 (April 20, 1995) p25. "Out On Info Highway 61: A Digitized Dylan On The '60s Folk-Coffeehouse Circuit"
PH04616 717 (September 21, 1995) p19. "[Bob Dylan & Mick Jagger]" (Gassian, Claude)
PH04617 717 (September 21, 1995) p24. "Bob Dylan At The Funeral In Belvedere, Calif." (Stewart, Chris)
PH04618 717 (September 21, 1995) p31. "Dylan And Garcia, Oakland Coliseum, 1987" (Blakesberg, Jay)
PH04619 719 (October 19, 1995) p38. "Bob Dylan Takes A Break From Signing Autographs Out By His Trailer" (Corbijn, Anton)
PH04620 719 (October 19, 1995) p42. "Chuck Berry, Bob Dylan And James Brown Head Toward The Artists' Tents At The Close Of The Show" (Corbijn, Anton)
PH04621 720 (November 2, 1995) p51. "Jesse & Bob Dylan" (Landy, Elliott)
PH04622 724-725 (December 28, 1995) p49. "Dylan And Jagger Jammed In Montpellier, France" (Gassian, Claude)

PH04623 724-725 (December 28, 1995) p56. "Forever Young: Bob Dylan And Bruce Springsteen" (Mazur, Kevin)
PH04624 726 (January 25, 1996) p74. "Divine Intervention: Dylan And Smith Duet On 'Dark Eyes' At The Beacon" (Beccaris, Rob)
PH04625 726 (January 25, 1996) p17. "You Hockey Puck! Dylan, Rickles And Bruce Springsteen" (Mazur, Kevin)
PH04626 736 (June 13, 1996) p33. "Bob Dylan: Shares A Bill With The Who" (Mazur, Kevin)
PH04627 738-739 (July 11, 1996) p48. "And Patti Singing With Her Hero Bob Dylan In New York During Their 1995 Tour" (Mazur, Kevin)
PH04628 741 (August 22, 1996) p25. "Pete Townshend And Bob Dylan Bond Backstage At The Prince's Trust Concert" (Mazur, Kevin)
PH04629 743 (September 19, 1996) p20. "Dylan With Young Pal Matthews At The Zelt Festival (Zelt: 'tent')" (Erickson, Sam)

DYLAN, BOB—PHOTOGRAPHS—PORTRAITS
PH04630 619-620 (December 12, 1991) p31. "While Dylan (below) Boxed Himself In" (Feingold, Deborah)
PH04631 645-646 (December 10, 1992) p153. "Bob Dylan, 1978"
PH04632 645-646 (December 10, 1992) p153. "Tom Petty And Bob Dylan, 1986"
PH04633 680 (April 21, 1994) p13. "Rock Marries Commerce Again: The Band (above) shill For Diet Coke With 'The Weight,' Which Is Owned By Dylan (left)" (Feingold, Deborah)

DYLAN, JAKOB—PHOTOGRAPHS
PH04634 636 (August 6, 1992) p13. "The Wallflowers (from left): Barrie Maguire, Jakob Dylan, Rami Jaffee, Peter Yanowitz And Tobi Miller" (Mark, Mary Ellen)
PH04635 649 (February 4, 1993) p27. "Jakob Dylan (second from left) And Friends Outside The Kibitz Room"
PH04636 657 (May 27, 1993) p11. "Natalie Merchant Croons With The Wallflowers' Jakob Dylan" (Taft, Mike)
PH04637 697 (December 15, 1994) p20. "Petty, Droge And Dylan At The Viper Room (from left)"
PH04638 746 (October 31, 1996) p17. "Clapton And Jakob Dylan, Who Did A Short Set With His Band, The Wallflowers" (Mazur, Kevin)
PH04639 750-751 (December 26, 1996) p81. "Winona Ryder, Giorgio Armani, And Jakob Dylan (from left)" (Mazur, Kevin)

DYLAN, JAKOB—PHOTOGRAPHS—PORTRAITS
PH04640 670 (November 25, 1993) p28. "[Jakob Dylan]"

DYLAN, JESSE—PHOTOGRAPHS
PH04641 720 (November 2, 1995) p51. "Jesse & Bob Dylan" (Landy, Elliott)

E

E—PHOTOGRAPHS—PORTRAITS
PH04642 631 (May 28, 1992) p22. "[E]" (Cuffaro, Chris)

E! (TELEVISION NETWORK)—ILLUSTRATIONS
PH04643 719 (October 19, 1995) p161. "[E!]" (Fishman, Miriam)

EAGLES—ALBUMS
PH04644 617 (November 14, 1991) p94. "Hotel California" (Kosh)
PH04645 617 (November 14, 1991) p94. "Hotel California" (Henley, Don)
PH04646 617 (November 14, 1991) p94. "Hotel California" (Alexander, David)

EAGLES—PHOTOGRAPHS
PH04647 630 (May 14, 1992) p22. "Jerry Brown In The Late Seventies With Linda Ronstadt, Jackson Browne (right), The Eagles And Other West Coast Musicians" (Pulin, Chuck)
PH04648 685 (June 30, 1994) p23. "Birds Of A Feather: Joe Walsh, Timothy B. Schmit, Don Henley, Don Felder And Glenn Frey (from left)"
PH04649 686-687 (July 14, 1994) p36. "Frey (left) And Henley in Eagles' Hell" (Granitz, Steve)
PH04650 698-699 (December 29, 1994) p55. "Glenn Frey (left) And Don Henley" (Mazur, Kevin)

EAGLES—PHOTOGRAPHS—PORTRAITS
PH04651 645-646 (December 10, 1992) p152. "The Eagles, 1979"

EARL, ROBERT—PHOTOGRAPHS
PH04652 617 (November 14, 1991) p21. "Earl Outside The Orlando Hard Rock" (Smith, Brian)

EARL, THERESA—PHOTOGRAPHS
PH04653 702 (February 23, 1995) p53. "Theresa Earl Paints By The Numbers" (Kuehn, Karen)

EARLE, STEVE—ALBUMS
PH04654 729 (March 7, 1996) p47. "I Feel Alright"

EARLE, STEVE—ILLUSTRATIONS
PH04655 729 (March 7, 1996) p47. "The Pleasure Principle" (Cronin, Brian)

EARLE, STEVE—PHOTOGRAPHS
PH04656 695 (November 17, 1994) p78. "Afghan Whigs" (Lixenberg, Dana)
PH04657 732 (April 18, 1996) p34. "[Steve Earle]" (Reynolds, Tamara)
PH04658 741 (August 22, 1996) p26. "Earle Treated Inmates To 'Feel Alright' And 'Ellis Unit One.'" (Kahn, Lee)
PH04659 750-751 (December 26, 1996) p67. "Steve Earle Entertaining Well-Behaved Inmates" (Cahn, Lee)

EARLE, STEVE—PHOTOGRAPHS—PORTRAITS
PH04660 671 (December 9, 1993) p21. "The Whig Club: Rick McCollum, Greg Dulli, Steve Earle And John Curley" (Broad, Julian)

EARTH—ALBUMS
PH04661 746 (October 31, 1996) p66. "Pentastar"

EARTHQUAKES—ILLUSTRATIONS
PH04662 740 (August 8, 1996) p46. "Each Big Bay Area Quake Has Followed A Clump Of Smaller Ones" (Chambers, Bruce)
PH04663 743 (September 19, 1996) p12. "[West Coast]" (Pendergrast, James T.)

EAST RIVER PIPE—ALBUMS
PH04663a 745 (January 17, 1996) p136. "[East River Pipe]"

EASTER, MITCH—PHOTOGRAPHS—PORTRAITS
PH04664 655 (April 29, 1993) p19. "Mitch Easter (left) And Chris Stamey" (Register, Charles)

EASTERN MIND (SOFTWARE)—ILLUSTRATIONS
PH04665 731 (April 4, 1996) p63. "Blow Your Eastern Mind: A Scene From Sato's CD-ROM"

EASTON, SHEENA—PHOTOGRAPHS
PH04666 624 (February 20, 1992) p11. "Sheena Easton In 'Man Of La Mancha'" (Marcus, Joan)

EASTWOOD, CLINT—ILLUSTRATIONS
PH04667 637 (August 20, 1992) p55. "An Outlaw At Twilight" (Unruh, Jack)
PH04668 662 (August 5, 1993) p71. "The Real Action Hero" (Guy, Edmund)
PH04669 711 (June 29, 1995) p47. "Bridge Of Tides" (MacDonald, Ross)

EASTWOOD, CLINT—ILLUSTRATIONS—LETTERING
PH04669a 639 (September 17, 1992) p66. "Clint Eastwood: The Rolling Stone Interview" (Karl, Anita)

EASTWOOD, CLINT—ILLUSTRATIONS—PORTRAITS
PH04670 645-646 (December 10, 1992) p152. "Clint Eastwood, 1985"
PH04671 Number not assigned.

EASTWOOD, CLINT—PHOTOGRAPHS
PH04672 637 (August 20, 1992) p57. "Eastwood's Grizzled Face Reflects The Long Road He's Traveled Since 'Rawhide' (right)"
PH04673 639 (September 17, 1992) p102. "Best Picture, Best Actor"

PH04674 645-646 (December 10, 1992) p190. "Clint Eastwood"
PH04675 648 (January 21, 1993) p56. "Unforgiven"
PH04676 653 (April 1, 1993) p57. "Unforgiven"
PH04677 659 (June 24, 1993) p87. "Dinosaur Summer" (Witte, Michael)
PH04678 662 (August 5, 1993) p72. "In 'Fire' (above), Eastwood Guards A President"
PH04679 665 (September 16, 1993) p77. "Best Actor"
PH04680 671 (December 9, 1993) p76. "Star Team: Ranger Eastwood (left) And Convict Costner"
PH04681 678 (March 24, 1994) p100. "Missing In Oscar Action"
PH04682 709 (June 1, 1995) p68. "Oscar Seekers"
PH04683 711 (June 29, 1995) p48. "New Romantic Triangle: Woman (Meryl Streep), man (Clint Eastwood) And Bridge"
PH04684 742 (September 5, 1996) p25. "Corbijn Shot Clint Eastwood" (Corbijn, Anton)

EASTWOOD, CLINT—PHOTOGRAPHS—PORTRAITS
PH04685 639 (September 17, 1992) p67. "[Clint Eastwood]"
PH04686 715 (August 24, 1995) p32. "[Clint Eastwood]" (Maser, Wayne)

EAZY-E—PHOTOGRAPHS
PH04687 619-620 (December 12, 1991) p29. "Mr. E Goes To Washington" (Granitz, Steve)
PH04688 634-635 (July 9, 1992) p17. "N.W.A. (clockwise from top left): MC Ren, Yella, Eazy-E And Dr. Dre" (Preston, Neal)
PH04689 639 (September 17, 1992) p19. "N.W.A. (from left): D.J. Yella, Dr. Dre, Eazy-E And M.C. Ren"
PH04690 657 (May 27, 1993) p24. "Police Escort: Eazy-E With Briseno"
PH04691 666 (September 30, 1993) p42. "Serious Attitude: Ex-N.W.A. Members Ice Cube, Yella, Eazy-E, Dre And MC Ren" (Rosenberg, Howard)
PH04692 670 (November 25, 1993) p38. "Eazy-E: Takin' On Dr. Dre And Snoop"
PH04693 672-673 (December 23, 1993) p30. "Strange Bedfellows: Eazy-E With Briseno" (Nelson, Mike)
PH04694 707 (May 4, 1995) p25. "Eazy-E (taking aim) With N.W.A. In 1991"
PH04695 707 (May 4, 1995) p25. "Onstage With N.W.A. In 1990" (Hogan, Dave)

EAZY-E—PHOTOGRAPHS—PORTRAITS
PH04696 707 (May 4, 1995) p25. "The Player: Eazy-E Was A Successful Businessman As Well As A Platinum Rapper"
PH04697 724-725 (December 28, 1995) p64. "[Eazy-E]" (Dokus, Peter)

ECCLESTON, CHRISTOPHER—PHOTOGRAPHS
PH04698 702 (February 23, 1995) p81. "Fox, McGregor And Eccleston Find The Body"

ECHEVERRIA, ROB—PHOTOGRAPHS
PH04699 689 (August 25, 1994) p63. "John Stanier, Henry Bogdan, Page Hamilton And Rob Echeverria (clockwise from top left)" (Wessel, Cathrine)
PH04700 695 (November 17, 1994) p92. "Helmet" (Huba, John)

ECHOBELLY—PHOTOGRAPHS
PH04701 692 (October 6, 1994) p36. "Echobelly: Heaven-Sent Pop"
PH04702 703 (March 9, 1995) p23. "Echobelly (above) Are One Of Many Bands Trying To Break Through To The U.S. Market" (Eichner, Steve)
PH04703 720 (November 2, 1995) p22. "On: Echobelly's Harris, Smith, Johansson, Madan And Henderson (from left)" (Claiborne, Barron)

ECKARDT, SHAWN—PHOTOGRAPHS
PH04704 686-687 (July 14, 1994) p86. "Eckardt Arrested In Portland (left)" (Wojahn, Brent)

ECONOMY—ILLUSTRATIONS
PH04705 621 (January 9, 1992) p27. "[Economy]" (Cronin, Brian)
PH04706 631 (May 28, 1992) p6. "George Bush, The Candidate Of Change" (Pendergrast, James T.)
PH04707 640 (October 1, 1992) p6. "Japanese Corporations—U.S. Corporations" (Pendergrast, James T.)
PH04708 642 (October 29, 1992) p41. "[Economy]" (Cronin, Brian)
PH04709 654 (April 15, 1993) p28. "[National Service]" (Cronin, Brian)
PH04710 662 (August 5, 1993) p8. "Instant Prosperity" (Pendergrast, James T.)
PH04711 665 (September 16, 1993) p36. "What's The Fed To Do?" (Klein, Renee)
PH04712 674 (January 27, 1994) p30. "[What Do Americans Really Want]" (Rall, Ted)
PH04713 685 (June 30, 1994) pp43-44. "[Sweatshops]" (Kuper, Peter)
PH04714 693 (October 20, 1994) pp119-120. "[Higher Education]" (Kuper, Peter)
PH04715 698-699 (December 29, 1994) p154. "[Economic Charts]" (Klein, Renee)
PH04716 704 (March 23, 1995) p18. "Blame-O-Meter" (Pendergrast, James T.)
PH04717 720 (November 2, 1995) p35. "I've Been Waiting Years For Someone To Dump Greenspan" (Witte, Michael)
PH04718 723 (December 14, 1995) p20. "The Economy" (Pendergrast, James T.)

ECONOMY—PHOTOGRAPHS
PH04719 704 (March 23, 1995) p54. "Minimum Wagers: The Young And The Paid Less" (Berman, Nina)

ECUADOR—PHOTOGRAPHS
PH04720 619-620 (December 12, 1991) p146. "A Community Above Chimborazo, Ecuador, 1982" (Salgado, Sebastiao)
PH04721 619-620 (December 12, 1991) p146. "A Drunken Man In The High Plains Of Ecuador, 1982" (Salgado, Sebastiao)
PH04722 619-620 (December 12, 1991) p146. "A Meeting Of A Religious Community On The Road To Chimborazo, Ecuador, In 1982" (Salgado, Sebastiao)

ED WOOD (FILM)—ILLUSTRATIONS
PH04723 693 (October 20, 1994) p153. "Autuer In Angora" (Risko, Robert)

ED WOOD (FILM)—PHOTOGRAPHS
PH04724 693 (October 20, 1994) p155. "Depp As Ed Wood And Landau As Bela "Dracula" Lugosi"
PH04725 698-699 (December 29, 1994) p194. "Depp And Landau Team In "Ed Wood""
PH04726 700 (January 26, 1995) p68. "Best Supporting Actor"
PH04726a 705 (April 6, 1995) p69. "Oscar Rejects"

EDDIE (FILM)—PHOTOGRAPHS
PH04727 736 (June 13, 1996) p62. "Fierce Women"

EDDY, DUANE—PHOTOGRAPHS
PH04728 676 (February 24, 1994) p49. "Duane Eddy, The Man Who Made The Guitar Twang"

EDDY, DUANE—PHOTOGRAPHS—PORTRAITS
PH04729 677 (March 10, 1994) p29. "Duane Eddy (left) With Mick Jones" (Mazur, Kevin)

EDELMAN, MARIAN WRIGHT—ILLUSTRATIONS—LETTERING
PH04730 645-646 (December 10, 1992) p127. "[Marian Wright Edelman]" (Karl, Anita)

EDELMAN, MARIAN WRIGHT—PHOTOGRAPHS—PORTRAITS
PH04731 645-646 (December 10, 1992) p126. "[Marian Wright Edelman]" (Irish, Len)

EDEN, DANIELA—PHOTOGRAPHS
PH04732 736 (June 13, 1996) p20. "Miranda Molen, Ron 'Rondonna' Dinkens, Watt And Daniela Eden (from left)" (Temme, Marty)

EDEN, SEAN—PHOTOGRAPHS
PH04733 728 (February 22, 1996) p64. "Luna's Wareham, Demeski And Eden (from left)" (Capak, R. J.)

EDGE—PHOTOGRAPHS
PH04734 618 (November 28, 1991) p46. "Flood With Bono And Edge In Berlin" (Corbijn, Anton)

PH04735 618 (November 28, 1991) p46. "Lanois, Eno, Edge And Bono In The Control Room At Hansa Studios, In Berlin" (Corbijn, Anton)
PH04736 619-620 (December 12, 1991) p94. "Bono (left) And Edge" (Stone, Dennis)
PH04737 625 (March 5, 1992) p11. "Edge, Robertson" (Mazur, Kevin)
PH04738 636 (August 6, 1992) p11. "Adam Clayton, The Edge, Bono And Larry Mullen Jr. (from left)" (Thomas, Justin)
PH04739 640 (October 1, 1992) pp40-41. "[The Edge]" (Ritts, Herb)
PH04740 645-646 (December 10, 1992) p30. "The Famous Party-Ending Jam (above)" (Mazur, Kevin)
PH04741 667 (October 14, 1993) pp48,51. "[The Edge]" (MacPherson, Andrew)
PH04742 667 (October 14, 1993) p54. "The Zoo Gang On Tour: The Edge, Bono, Larry Mullen Jr. And Adam Clayton (from left)" (Corbijn, Anton)
PH04743 674 (January 27, 1994) p41. "U2's The Edge" (Mazur, Kevin)
PH04744 686-687 (July 14, 1994) p41. "[U2]" (Fisher, David)
PH04745 714 (August 10, 1995) p30. "U2 Can Do Film Scores: Adam Clayton, Bono, The Edge, Larry Mullen (from left)" (Mazur, Kevin)
PH04746 726 (January 25, 1996) p30. "U2's Bono, Adam Clayton, The Edge And Larry Mullen Jr. (from left)" (Pasley, Richard)

EDGE—PHOTOGRAPHS—PORTRAITS
PH04747 625 (March 5, 1992) pp14-15. "On The Evening Of The Seventh Annual Hall Of Fame Induction Ceremony, 'Rolling Stone' Gathered These Nine Legendary Guitarists At The Waldorf-Astoria For A Once-In-A-Lifetime..."
PH04748 662 (August 5, 1993) p60. "The Edge" (Busacca, Larry)
PH04749 667 (October 14, 1993) pp[cover]. "U2's Zoo World Order: The Edge Takes Charge" (MacPherson, Andrew)
PH04750 672-673 (December 23, 1993) p188. "[Covers]" (MacPherson, Andrew)

EDMUNDS, DAVE—ILLUSTRATIONS
PH04751 691 (September 22, 1994) p98. "Dave Edmunds" (Ascencios, N.)

EDMUNDS, DAVE—PHOTOGRAPHS—PORTRAITS
PH04752 685 (June 30, 1994) p41. "Booker T. Jones, Steve Cropper, Dave Edmunds And Donald "Duck" Dunn (from left)" (Cohen, Lester)

EDMUNDSON, DAVE—PHOTOGRAPHS—PORTRAITS
PH04753 720 (November 2, 1995) p58. "Former NRA Board-Member-Turned-Critic Dave Edmundson" (Warburg, Jennifer)

EDUCATION—ILLUSTRATIONS
PH04754 626 (March 19, 1992) p73. "[Education]" (Stasys)
PH04755 637 (August 20, 1992) p25. "School" (Cronin, Brian)
PH04756 644 (November 26, 1992) p11. "U.S. Literacy Sinks To New Low" (Pendergrast, James T.)

EDWARD—PHOTOGRAPHS
PH04757 707 (May 4, 1995) p29. "Hamell: Attack-Dog Folk" (Green, Martha)

EDWARD II (FILM)—PHOTOGRAPHS
PH04758 627 (April 2, 1992) p42. "Gay King Waddongton Nuzzles A Frustrated Swinton"

EDWARDS, BERNARD—PHOTOGRAPHS—PORTRAITS
PH04759 736 (June 13, 1996) p25. "[Bernard Edwards]"

EDWARDS, DAVE EUGENE—PHOTOGRAPHS
PH04760 731 (April 4, 1996) p36. "Roots-Gloom Trio: Sixteen Horsepower's Soll, Tola And Edwards (from left)" (Keeley, Dennis)

EDWARDS, FRANK—PHOTOGRAPHS
PH04761 651 (March 4, 1993) p24. "Sloan, Edwards, Fletcher, Stephens" (Roca, John)

EDWARDS, MIKE—PHOTOGRAPHS
PH04762 659 (June 24, 1993) p30. "Right Here: Jesus Jones's Mike Edwards" (Capak, R. J.)

EDWARDS, TEDDY—ALBUMS
PH04763 623 (February 6, 1992) p79. "Mississippi Lad"

EELS—PHOTOGRAPHS
PH04764 745 (October 17, 1996) p156. "[Eels]" (Fink, Larry)

EGAN, BOB—PHOTOGRAPHS
PH04765 686-687 (July 14, 1994) p74. "Erwin, Bean, Touring Member Bob Egan And Gay (from left); Mascot Matthew Bean-Rizzo (front)" (Elledge, Paul)

EGERTON, STEPHEN—PHOTOGRAPHS
PH04766 719 (October 19, 1995) p24. "No Mall Punks For All: Chad Price, Stephen Egerton, Karl Alvarez, Bill Stevenson (from left)" (Corrigan, Daniel)
PH04767 746 (October 31, 1996) p35. "Stephen Egerton Of Descendents" (Garrity, Brian)

EHRLICHMAN, JOHN—PHOTOGRAPHS
PH04768 690 (September 8, 1994) p48. "Above, In A Photo From The CD-ROM: Nixon, Ehrlichman, Kissinger, Haldeman"

EICHSTADT, KLAUS—PHOTOGRAPHS
PH04769 629 (April 30, 1992) p31. "Ugly Kid Joe (from left): Roger Lahr, Klaus Eichstadt, Whitfield Crane, Cordell Crockett And Mark Davis" (O'Beirne, Andy)

EICKHOFF, JANIE—PHOTOGRAPHS
PH04770 626 (March 19, 1992) p80. "[Janie Eickhoff]" (Hanauer, Mark)

EIGEMAN, CHRIS—PHOTOGRAPHS
PH04771 688 (August 11, 1994) p63. "It's Ole To Nichols, Bergen, Eigeman And Sorvino"

EISENSTADT, DEBRA—PHOTOGRAPHS
PH04772 696 (December 1, 1994) p132. "Sex Combat: Debra Eisenstadt And William H. Macy"

EISENSTEIN, MIKE—PHOTOGRAPHS
PH04773 710 (June 15, 1995) p39. "Eisenstein, Scott Riebling, Hanley, Stacy Jones, Greg McKenna (from left)" (McDonough, Patricia)

EISNER, MICHAEL—PHOTOGRAPHS
PH04774 724-725 (December 28, 1995) p51. "Disney's Michael Eisner (left), ABC's Thomas Murphy" (Tannenbaum)

EITZEL, MARK—ALBUMS
PH04775 730 (March 21, 1996) p100. "60 Watt Silver Lining"

EITZEL, MARK—PHOTOGRAPHS
PH04776 659 (June 24, 1993) p15. "McCready, Eitzel, Ament, AMC's Vudi And Dan Pearson (from left)" (Blakesberg, Jay)
PH04777 670 (November 25, 1993) p37. "It's Not For Me to Say: Mathis And Eitzel" (Pereira, Al)
PH04778 690 (September 8, 1994) p25. "[American Music Club]" (Blakesberg, Jay)
PH04779 695 (November 17, 1994) p131. "American Music Club" (Duke, William)

EITZEL, MARK—PHOTOGRAPHS—PORTRAITS
PH04780 656 (May 13, 1993) p77. "American Music Club (from left): Danny Pearson, Tim Mooney, Vudi, Bruce Kaphan And Mark Eitzel" (Ockenfels, Frank W.)
PH04781 656 (May 13, 1993) p78. "Mark Eitzel" (Ockenfels, Frank W.)

EKBERG, ULF—PHOTOGRAPHS—PORTRAITS
PH04782 688 (August 11, 1994) p32. "Aces Jonas, Linn, Ekberg And Jenny (from left)" (Danelian, Stephen)

EKLUND, GREG—PHOTOGRAPHS
PH04783 709 (June 1, 1995) p17. "Alexakis, Craig Montoya And Greg Eklund With Banner From Kids" (Grossman, Amanda)
PH04784 718 (October 5, 1995) p28. "Distortion-Fuzzed Alterna-Rockers Montoya, Alexakis And Eklund (from left)" (Westenberg, Kevin)

EL DIN, HAMZA—PHOTOGRAPHS
PH04785 740 (August 8, 1996) p35. "Egypt, September 1978" (Boot, Adrian)

EL MARIACHI (FILM)—ILLUSTRATIONS
PH04786 652 (March 18, 1993) p45. "El Mariachi And The Sundance Kid" (Allen, Terry)

ELASTICA—ALBUMS
PH04787 708 (May 18, 1995) p88. "Elastica"
ELASTICA—PHOTOGRAPHS
PH04788 678 (March 24, 1994) p21. "Elastica With Frischman (front)" (Paton, Tim)
PH04789 707 (May 4, 1995) p23. "Donna Matthews, Justine Frischmann, Annie Holland And Justin Welch (from left)" (Camp, E. J.)
PH04790 707 (May 4, 1995) p23. "Matthews (left), Frischmann In Manchester, England, '93" (Hening, Lu)
PH04791 723 (December 14, 1995) p32. "Seattle Programmer Collins (center) With Members Of Elastica" (Mason, Karen)
PH04792 724-725 (December 28, 1995) p42. "[Elastica]" (Bell, Colin)
PH04793 746 (October 31, 1996) p17. "Bush, Matthews, Frischmann, Chipperfield And Justin Welch (from left)" (Milne, Donald)
ELDARD, RON—PHOTOGRAPHS
PH04794 732 (April 18, 1996) p80. "Ron Eldard And Cameron Diaz Eat Till They Drop"
ELDERS, JOYCE—PHOTOGRAPHS
PH04795 693 (October 20, 1994) p90. "[Nutrition]" (Klein, Renee)
ELECTIONS (1992)—ILLUSTRATIONS
PH04796 622 (January 23, 1992) p4. "GOP Hats In The Ring" (Pendergrast, James T.)
PH04797 628 (April 16, 1992) p6. "Movin' On" (Pendergrast, James T.)
PH04798 636 (August 6, 1992) p7. "Trust-O-Meter" (Pendergrast, James T.)
PH04799 645-646 (December 10, 1992) pp107,109. "[Elections]" (Cronin, Brian)
PH04800 686-687 (July 14, 1994) pp51-52. "[Elections 1992]" (Kuper, Peter)
ELECTIONS (1996)—ILLUSTRATIONS
PH04801 749 (December 12, 1996) p16. "Public Clamors For More VS!" (Pendergrast, James T.)
ELECTIONS (1996)—PHOTOGRAPHS
PH04802 726 (January 25, 1996) p55. "Dole Supporters In Orlando, Fla. Celebrate His Straw-Poll Victory In November 1995 And Hope For An Even Bigger Win In The New Hampshire Primary" (Fink, Larry)
PH04803 745 (October 17, 1996) p30. "[Choose Or Lose]" (Elledge, Paul)
PH04804 745 (October 17, 1996) p33. "Fear And Loathing: Bob Dole With Tabitha Soren (top); A Choose Or Lose Representative Talks With Potential Young Voters"
ELECTIONS (1993)—ILLUSTRATIONS
PH04805 650 (February 18, 1993) p30. "Present-Proposed" (Bishofs, Maris)
PH04806 654 (April 15, 1993) p31. "[Campaign Reform]" (Lins, Rico)
ELECTRA, CARMEN—PHOTOGRAPHS
PH04807 750-751 (December 26, 1996) p90. "Russ Meyer Flick? No, McCarthy (left) And Electra" (Rose, Lisa)
ELECTRIC GYPSY (BOOK)—PHOTOGRAPHS
PH04808 619-620 (December 12, 1991) p32. "[Electric Gypsy]"
ELECTRONIC MAIL—ILLUSTRATIONS
PH04809 732 (April 18, 1996) p20. "Geek Letters"
ELENIAK, ERIKA—PHOTOGRAPHS
PH04810 669 (November 11, 1993) p81. "Tomlin's Miss Hathaway Welcomes The Clampetts To 90210"
ELEPHANT'S MEMORY—PHOTOGRAPHS
PH04811 626 (March 19, 1992) p29. "Performing With Elephant's Memory On The 'Dick Cavett Show' 1972" (Gruen, Bob)
ELEVENTH DAY DREAM—ALBUMS
PH04812 660-661 (July 8, 1993) p116. "El Moodio"
ELEVENTH DAY DREAM—PHOTOGRAPHS
PH04813 658 (June 10, 1993) p29. "Wink O'Bannon, Janet Beveridge Bean, Rick Rizzo And Doug McCombs (from left)" (Guip, Andy)
ELIOT, MARC—BOOKS
PH04814 645-646 (December 10, 1992) p87. "[Down Thunder Road]"
ELISE—PHOTOGRAPHS
PH04815 736 (June 13, 1996) p54. "L.A. Firefighters: Alexandra Hedison, Jarrod Emick, Elise (from left)"
ELIZONDO, RENE—PHOTOGRAPHS
PH04816 665 (September 16, 1993) p43. "With Ex-Husband James DeBarge (left) And With Her Current Boyfriend, Rene Elizondo" (Zuffante, Vinnie)
ELLINGTON, DUKE—ILLUSTRATIONS
PH04817 680 (April 21, 1994) p87. "Wrap Up" (Cowles, David)
ELLIOT, CASS—PHOTOGRAPHS
PH04818 692 (October 6, 1994) p50. "Mama Cass Elliot" (Diltz, Henry)
PH04819 Number not assigned.
ELLIOTT, ALISON—PHOTOGRAPHS
PH04820 708 (May 18, 1995) p98. "Alison Elliott And Peter Gallagher Conspire"
PH04821 742 (September 5, 1996) p68. "Elliott, Burstyn And Harden"
ELLIOTT, CHRIS—PHOTOGRAPHS
PH04822 706 (April 20, 1995) p86. "The 'SNL' Legacy Of Screen Shame"
ELLIOTT, JIM—PHOTOGRAPHS
PH04823 712-713 (July 13, 1995) p46. "High Sea: Gormly, Elliot, And Perkins (from left)" (Capak, R. J.)
ELLIOTT, JOE—PHOTOGRAPHS
PH04824 640 (October 1, 1992) p10. "Adams (left) And Def Leppard's Joe Elliott" (Mazur, Kevin)
PH04825 640 (October 1, 1992) p34. "Def Leppard's Joe Elliott" (Fitzgerald, Ralph)
PH04826 667 (October 14, 1993) p26. "Rick Savage, Phil Collen, Vivian Campbell, Rick Allen And Joe Elliott" (Halfin, Ross)
PH04826a 724-725 (December 28, 1995) p58. "Def Leppard's Phil Collen And Joe Elliot Flank Fans In Tangier"
ELLIOTT, JOE—PHOTOGRAPHS—PORTRAITS
PH04827 629 (April 30, 1992) pp38-39. "Lead Singer Joe Elliott" (Seliger, Mark)
ELLIOTT, LEE ANN—PHOTOGRAPHS
PH04828 680 (April 21, 1994) p40. "Lee Ann Elliott Helped The FEC Move To A Building Owned By Her Former Employer" (Martin, Christopher T.)
ELLIS, TERRY—PHOTOGRAPHS
PH04829 709 (June 1, 1995) p17. "Maxine Jones, Robinson, O'Donnell, Cindy Herron, Terry Ellis" (Nelson, Ralph)
ELLIS, TERRY—PHOTOGRAPHS—PORTRAITS
PH04830 660-661 (July 8, 1993) pp64-65. "En Vogue's Sheer Beauties: Terry Ellis, Maxine Jones, Dawn Robinson And Cindy Herron (from left)" (Rolston, Matthew)
PH04831 660-661 (July 8, 1993) p69. "Terry Ellis" (Rolston, Matthew)
ELLISON, JIM—PHOTOGRAPHS
PH04832 712-713 (July 13, 1995) p25. "[Liz Phair & Material Issue]" (Natkin, Paul)
ELLISON, KYLE—PHOTOGRAPHS
PH04833 750-751 (December 26, 1996) p116. "A Fog-Shrouded Ellison (above)" (Vadukul, Nitin)
ELY, JOE—PHOTOGRAPHS
PH04834 653 (April 1, 1993) p24. "Backstage At The Troubadour In L.A." (Granitz, Steve)
EMERSON, LAKE & PALMER—ALBUMS
PH04835 617 (November 14, 1991) p137. "Brain Salad Surgery" (Nicoli, Fabio)
PH04836 617 (November 14, 1991) p137. "Brain Salad Surgery" (Giger, H. R.)
EMERY, JILL—PHOTOGRAPHS—PORTRAITS
PH04837 637 (August 20, 1992) p15. "Hole's Jill Emery, Eric

Erlandson, Love And Caroline Rue (from left)" (Lavine, Michael)

EMF—PHOTOGRAPHS

PH04838 619-620 (December 12, 1991) p44. "...And EMF (below)" (Double, Steve)

EMICK, JARROD—PHOTOGRAPHS

PH04839 736 (June 13, 1996) p54. "L.A. Firefighters: Alexandra Hedison, Jarrod Emick, Elise (from left)"

EMMA (FILM)—ILLUSTRATIONS

PH04840 741 (August 22, 1996) p103. "Hot And Bothered" (Brodner, Steve)

EMMA (FILM)—PHOTOGRAPHS

PH04841 741 (August 22, 1996) p104. "Paltrow As Matchmaking Emma"

PH04842 743 (September 19, 1996) p90. "[Summer...]"

EMMONS, ANDREA—PHOTOGRAPHS

PH04843 693 (October 20, 1994) p89. "Oberlin R.A. Andrea Emmons (top left) Leads A Stress-Reliever Session"

EMPLOYMENT—ILLUSTRATIONS

PH04844 707 (May 4, 1995) p16. "Ideal Job—Your Job" (Pendergrast, James T.)

EMPLOYMENT—PHOTOGRAPHS

PH04845 741 (August 22, 1996) p71. "[Quitting]"

EN VOGUE—ALBUMS

PH04846 629 (April 30, 1992) p56. "Funky Divas"

PH04847 645-646 (December 10, 1992) p166. "Funky Divas"

EN VOGUE—PHOTOGRAPHS

PH04848 709 (June 1, 1995) p17. "Maxine Jones, Robinson, O'Donnell, Cindy Herron, Terry Ellis" (Nelson, Ralph)

EN VOGUE—PHOTOGRAPHS—PORTRAITS

PH04849 645-646 (December 10, 1992) p40. "En Vogue" (Roth, David)

PH04850 660-661 (July 8, 1993) pp64-65. "En Vogue's Sheer Beauties: Terry Ellis, Maxine Jones, Dawn Robinson And Cindy Herron (from left)" (Rolston, Matthew)

ENCINO MAN (FILM)—PHOTOGRAPHS

PH04851 633 (June 25, 1992) p48. "Shore (left) And Astin Flank Cave Man Fraser"

ENDLESS LOVE (FILM)—PHOTOGRAPHS

PH04852 744 (October 3, 1996) p50. "Teen Idyll: Steaming It Up With Martin Hewitt In 1981's 'Endless Love'"

THE ENDLESS SUMMER II (FILM)—PHOTOGRAPHS

PH04853 685 (June 30, 1994) p82. "Now Playing"

ENGLAND'S DREAMING: ANARCHY, SEX PISTOLS, PUNK ROCK AND BEYOND (BOOK)—PHOTOGRAPHS

PH04854 630 (May 14, 1992) p114. "No Future: Looking Back At The Punk Revolution"

ENGLE, JOHN—PHOTOGRAPHS

PH04855 621 (January 9, 1992) p25. "Codeine (from left): John Engle, Chris Brokaw And Stephen Immerwahr" (Capak, R. J.)

THE ENGLISH PATIENT (FILM)—PHOTOGRAPHS

PH04856 743 (September 19, 1996) p90. "Quality Control"

PH04857 748 (November 28, 1996) p142. "Fiennes"

PH04858 748 (November 28, 1996) p142. "Scott Thomas, Left, Binoche"

THE ENGLISHMAN WHO WENT UP A HILL, BUT CAME DOWN A MOUNTAIN (FILM)—PHOTOGRAPHS

PH04859 709 (June 1, 1995) p70. "Early Starters"

ENO, BRIAN—ALBUMS

PH04860 645-646 (December 10, 1992) p182. "Nerve Net"

ENO, BRIAN—PHOTOGRAPHS

PH04861 618 (November 28, 1991) pp42-48,50. "Dublin: Making Cutouts For The Album Cover Under The Guidance Of Steve Averill (second from left)" (Corbijn, Anton)

PH04862 618 (November 28, 1991) p44. "Flood, The Album's Engineer, And Eno, Who Coproduced Several Tracks, Work On The Final Mixes" (Corbijn, Anton)

PH04863 618 (November 28, 1991) p46. "Lanois, Eno, Edge And Bono In The Control Room At Hansa Studios, In Berlin" (Corbijn, Anton)

ENRIQUE—PHOTOGRAPHS

PH04864 618 (November 28, 1991) p11. "Clockwise From Left: Buck, Enrique, Ryan-Harris, Chris Tinsley, Kinney, Billy Fields And Jamie Turner (wearing glasses)" (Diamond, Rick)

PH04865 625 (March 5, 1992) p27. "Jamie Turner, David Ryan-Harris, Billy Fields, Chris Tinsley, Enrique (from left)" (Leitman, Ruth)

ENVIRONMENT—ILLUSTRATIONS

PH04866 638 (September 3, 1992) p3. "The Bush Years: The Environmental President" (Coe, Sue)

PH04867 660-661 (July 8, 1993) p10. "Saved" (Pendergrast, James T.)

PH04868 706 (April 20, 1995) p41. "The GOP's Trojan Horse Is Trampling Environmental Safeguards" (Witte, Michael)

PH04869 722 (November 30, 1995) p14. "Walden Pond Water" (Pendergrast, James T.)

PH04870 730 (March 21, 1996) p14. "[The Last Stand]" (Pendergrast, James T.)

ENYA—ALBUMS

PH04871 726 (January 25, 1996) p73. "The Memory Of Trees"

EPHRON, NORA—PHOTOGRAPHS

PH04872 660-661 (July 8, 1993) p75. "Ephron On The 'Sleepless In Seattle' Set With Tom Hanks: 'You Hope To Get The Guys To Cry, Too.'" (McBroom, Bruce)

PH04873 660-661 (July 8, 1993) p74. "[Nora Ephron]" (Camp, E. J.)

EPHRON, NORA—PHOTOGRAPHS—PORTRAITS

PH04874 660-661 (July 8, 1993) p73. "At Home In Manhattan: Doing Scripts Saved Me From Having To Live In The Country" (Camp, E. J.)

EPMD—ALBUMS

PH04875 639 (September 17, 1992) p95. "Business Never Personal"

EPPS, OMAR—PHOTOGRAPHS

PH04876 623 (February 6, 1992) p90. "Cindy Herron And Omar Epps Take Time Out From Fighting"

PH04877 700 (January 26, 1995) p68. "Swanson, Connelly, Epps And Cube Tackle "Learning""

EPSTEIN, HOWIE—PHOTOGRAPHS

PH04878 707 (May 4, 1995) p52. "Backstage With The Boss And The Band (below, from left): Steve Ferrone, Mike Campbell, Petty, Benmont Tench, Howie Epstein And Scott Thurston" (Seliger, Mark)

E.R. (TELEVISION SHOW)—PHOTOGRAPHS

PH04879 692 (October 6, 1994) p94. "Health-Care Woes: The Docs Of "E.R.""

ERASER (FILM)—PHOTOGRAPHS

PH04880 736 (June 13, 1996) p58. "Headaches"

PH04881 738-739 (July 11, 1996) p98. "Bang For The Buck Movie Chart"

PH04882 740 (August 8, 1996) p68. "'Independence Day,' Travolta In 'Phenomenon,' Schwarzenegger In 'Eraser,' Moore In 'Striptease'"

PH04883 743 (September 19, 1996) p90. "[Summer...]"

ERASURE—ALBUMS

PH04884 645-646 (December 10, 1992) p182. "Abba-Esque"

PH04885 697 (December 15, 1994) p96. "I Say, I Say, I Say"

ERASURE—PHOTOGRAPHS

PH04886 722 (November 30, 1995) p20. "Hello, Darkness! Andy Bell, Johnston And Clarke (from left)" (Mazur, Kevin)

ERDRICH, LOUISE—BOOKS

PH04887 639 (September 17, 1992) p80. "Love Medicine"

PH04888 Number not assigned.

ERHARDT, JOHN—PHOTOGRAPHS

PH04889 700 (January 26, 1995) p30. "From Left: Morrison, Cheek, Erhardt, Cleaver" (Ockenfels, Frank W.)

ERIC B. AND RAKIM—ALBUMS

PH04890 634-635 (July 9, 1992) p106. "Don't Sweat The Technique"

ERICKSON, ROKY—ALBUMS
PH04891 708 (May 18, 1995) p90. "All That may Do My Rhyme"
ERICKSON, ROKY—PHOTOGRAPHS
PH04892 656 (May 13, 1993) p28. "Psychedelic Ranger Roky Erickson (center) Howling About His Two-Headed Dog" (Grenon, Martha)
PH04893 706 (April 20, 1995) p21. "Erickson (right) In '76 With Guitarist Duane Aslaksen" (Gindreau, J. C.)
PH04894 706 (April 20, 1995) p23. "Spaced Rangers: Erickson (center) With The Elevators Onstage In 1966" (Simmons, Bob)
ERICKSON, ROKY—PHOTOGRAPHS—PORTRAITS
PH04895 706 (April 20, 1995) p23. "Erickson In The Mid-'70s (left) And In 1994" (Chernikowski, Stephanie)
PH04896 708 (May 18, 1995) p17. "Erickson (left) And Rollins In Austin" (Chernikowski, Stephanie)
ERIKSON, DUKE—PHOTOGRAPHS
PH04897 718 (October 5, 1995) p24. "Erikson, Vig And Phil Davis (from left) As Firetown, 1989" (Pantsios, A. J.)
PH04898 718 (October 5, 1995) p23. "Trash Is Where It's At: Erikson, Marker, Vig, Manson (clockwise from left)" (Ockenfels, Frank W.)
ERLANDSON, ERIC—PHOTOGRAPHS
PH04899 683 (June 2, 1994) p42. "Hole: Patty Schemel, Love, Kristen Pfaff, Eric Erlandson" (Seliger, Mark)
PH04900 694 (November 3, 1994) p17. "[Drew Barrymore & Eric Erlandson]" (Allen, David)
PH04901 697 (December 15, 1994) p67. "Hole As One: Bassist Melissa Auf Der Maur (who replaced Kristen Pfaff), Guitarist Eric Erlandson, Drummer Patty Schemel And Love (from left)" (Seliger, Mark)
PH04902 698-699 (December 29, 1994) p50. "Doll Parts: Hole's Eric Erlandson, Melissa Auf der Maur, Patty Schemel And Love" (Seliger, Mark)
PH04903 710 (June 15, 1995) p68. "In New York, Barrymore Snuggles With Boyfriend Eric Erlandson Of Hole"
PH04904 715 (August 24, 1995) p46. "Courtney Love, Eric Erlandson, Patty Schemel, Melissa Auf Der Maur" (Seliger, Mark)
PH04905 735 (May 30, 1996) p13. "Muffs Roy McDonald And Kim Shattuck, Sean Ono Lennon, Muff Ronnie Barnett, Sideman Bill Bartell, And Eric Erlandson" (Phalen, Tom)
ERLANDSON, ERIC—PHOTOGRAPHS—PORTRAITS
PH04906 637 (August 20, 1992) p15. "Hole's Jill Emery, Eric Erlandson, Love And Caroline Rue (from left)" (Lavine, Michael)
ERRICO, GREG—PHOTOGRAPHS
PH04907 649 (February 4, 1993) p51. "Rose Stone, Sly, Freddie Stone, Graham, Robinson, Errico And Martini Of Sly And The Family Stone"
ERTEGUN, AHMET—PHOTOGRAPHS
PH04908 650 (February 18, 1993) p52. "White, Franklin, Wexler And Nesuhi And Ahmet Ertegun (from left)" (Gahr, David)
PH04909 655 (April 29, 1993) p55. "With Mentor Ahmet Ertegun, Cofounder Of Atlantic Records, 1973" (Leibovitz, Annie)
PH04910 702 (February 23, 1995) p49. "Wenner (left) And Ertegun" (Mazur, Kevin)
ERTEGUN, NESUHI—PHOTOGRAPHS
PH04911 650 (February 18, 1993) p52. "White, Franklin, Wexler And Nesuhi And Ahmet Ertegun (from left)" (Gahr, David)
ERWIN, CATHERINE—PHOTOGRAPHS
PH04912 686-687 (July 14, 1994) p74. "Erwin, Bean, Touring Member Bob Egan And Gay (from left); Mascot Matthew Bean-Rizzo (front)" (Elledge, Paul)
ESCAPE FROM L.A. (FILM)—PHOTOGRAPHS
PH04913 742 (September 5, 1996) p68. "Kurt Russell Returns AS Snake Plissken"
ESCOVEDO, ALEJANDRO—ALBUMS
PH04914 640 (October 1, 1992) p67. "Gravity"
PH04915 682 (May 19, 1994) p102. "Thirteen Years"
PH04916 732 (April 18, 1996) p71. "With These Hands"
ESCOVEDO, ALEJANDRO—PHOTOGRAPHS
PH04917 629 (April 30, 1992) p28. "Alejandro Escovedo (right) With His Stunning Chamber-Rock Ensemble" (Davis, Lisa)
PH04918 707 (May 4, 1995) p29. "Escovedo With Buick MacKane" (Wolfson, Todd V.)
ESCOVEDO, ALEJANDRO—PHOTOGRAPHS—PORTRAITS
PH04919 733 (May 2, 1996) pp36-37. "[Alejandro Escovedo]" (Ford, Charles)
ESHE, MONTSHO—PHOTOGRAPHS
PH04920 647 (January 7, 1993) p13. "Arrested Development's Headliner, Taree, Eshe And Speech (from left): Talkin' About A Different Kind Of Nirvana" (States, Ann)
PH04921 648 (January 21, 1993) p9. "Arrested Development (from left): Speech, Aerle Taree, Headliner, Rasa Don, Baba Oje And Montsho Eshe" (Mazur, Kevin)
ESHE, MONTSHO—PHOTOGRAPHS—PORTRAITS
PH04922 634-635 (July 9, 1992) p20. "Arrested Development (from left): Headliner, Montsho Eshe, Aerle Taree, Rasa Don And Speech" (Lavine, Michael)
PH04923 634-635 (July 9, 1992) p20. "Love Battery (from left): Kevin Whitworth, Rod Rudzitis And Jason Finn" (Lavine, Michael)
ESQUIVEL—PHOTOGRAPHS
PH04924 719 (October 19, 1995) p30. "[Esquivel]" (Debourbon, Yvonne)
ESTEFAN, GLORIA—PHOTOGRAPHS
PH04925 658 (June 10, 1993) p16. "Gloria Estefan, Smokey Robinson, Franklin, John (from left)" (Mazur, Kevin)
ESTEP, MAGGIE—ALBUMS
PH04926 684 (June 16, 1994) p106. "No More Mister Nice Girl"
ESTEP, MAGGIE—PHOTOGRAPHS
PH04927 680 (April 21, 1994) p30. "Word Goddess: Maggie Estep" (Cheuse, Josh)
ESZTERHAS, JOE—PHOTOGRAPHS
PH04928 632 (June 11, 1992) p62. "Staff Members And Contributing Writers At The 1971 Editorial Conference, At Esalen, In Big Sur" (Leibovitz, Annie)
ET TU, BABE (BOOK)—PHOTOGRAPHS
PH04929 652 (March 18, 1993) pp[enc.6]. "Et Tu, Babe"
ETERNAL—ALBUMS
PH04930 692 (October 6, 1994) p87. "Always And Forever"
ETHERIDGE, ERIC—PHOTOGRAPHS
PH04931 639 (September 17, 1992) p42. "At The Table (from left): Greider, O' Rourke, Wenner, Thompson And Clinton" (Seliger, Mark)
ETHERIDGE, MELISSA—ALBUMS
PH04932 630 (May 14, 1992) p103. "Never Enough"
PH04933 722 (November 30, 1995) p68. "Your Little Secret"
ETHERIDGE, MELISSA—ILLUSTRATIONS
PH04934 712-713 (July 13, 1995) p20. "Welcome" (Pendergrast, James T.)
ETHERIDGE, MELISSA—PHOTOGRAPHS
PH04935 625 (March 5, 1992) p18. "Sara Lee, Crimmins, Graham Nash, Amy Ray, Emily Saliers, David Crosby, Etheridge, Carpenter (from left)" (Berg, Lisa)
PH04936 685 (June 30, 1994) p40. "Etheridge With Kato, Tony Stull, Blackie Onassis And "Eddie" King Roeser (from left)" (Mazur, Kevin)
PH04937 697 (December 15, 1994) p18. "Etheridge, Waters, "Politically Incorrect" Host Bill Maher, Molinari And Baio (from left)"
PH04938 698-699 (December 29, 1994) p111. "[Melissa Etheridge]" (Danelian, Stephen)
PH04939 698-699 (December 29, 1994) p114. "Onstage In San Francisco, September '92"
PH04940 698-699 (December 29, 1994) p113. "Performing At A Leavenworth, Kan., Talent Show, Age 11"

PH04941 698-699 (December 29, 1994) p116. "With K. D. Lang At A LifeBeat benefit In New York City, June '94" (Eichner, Steve)
PH04942 698-699 (December 29, 1994) p114. "With Live-In Lover Julie Cypher"
PH04943 703 (March 9, 1995) p21. "Bonnie Raitt, Tom Hanks, Melissa Etheridge (from left)" (Berliner, A.)
PH04944 705 (April 6, 1995) p17. "Springsteen And Etheridge team Up For 'MTV Unplugged'" (Micelotta, Frank)
PH04945 709 (June 1, 1995) p45. "Etheridge With Cypher" (Sirota, Peggy)
PH04946 709 (June 1, 1995) p40. "Etheridge, Age 10, And Guitar"
PH04947 709 (June 1, 1995) p41. "Everyone Who Knew Me Knew I Was Going To Be A Rock Star, Because I Told Them" (Sirota, Peggy)
PH04948 709 (June 1, 1995) p39. "[Melissa Etheridge]" (Sirota, Peggy)
PH04949 709 (June 1, 1995) pp[cover]. "Melissa Etheridge: She's The Boss" (Sirota, Peggy)
PH04950 709 (June 1, 1995) p40. "With Her Grammy For 'Come To My Window,' March" (Granitz, Steve)
PH04951 719 (October 19, 1995) p40. "Melissa Etheridge Watches From Backstage" (Corbijn, Anton)
PH04952 728 (February 22, 1996) p20. "Etheridge: Check Out Any Time You Like"
PH04953 747 (November 14, 1996) p44. "[Melissa Etheridge]" (Garrity, Brian)

ETHERIDGE, MELISSA—PHOTOGRAPHS—PORTRAITS
PH04954 683 (June 2, 1994) p20. "Melissa Etheridge" (Cuffaro, Chris)
PH04955 702 (February 23, 1995) p50. "Tears Of A Clown: Buckley, Etheridge" (Mazur, Kevin)
PH04956 706 (April 20, 1995) p15. "You, Too, Can Be A Winner: Crow, Soundgarden's Chris Cornell And Etheridge" (Mazur, Kevin)
PH04957 738-739 (July 11, 1996) p16. "Etheridge And Mullen At A Party In A UCLA Parking Lot" (Berliner, Alan)

ETHYL MEATPLOW—ALBUMS
PH04958 664 (September 2, 1993) p61. "Happy Days, Sweetheart"

ETZIONI, MARVIN—ALBUMS
PH04959 626 (March 19, 1992) p97. "The Mandolin Man"

ETZIONI, MARVIN—PHOTOGRAPHS
PH04960 660-661 (July 8, 1993) p33. "Almost Lone Justice: Marvin Etzioni, McKee And Don Heffington" (Cohen, Lester)

EUGENIUS—ILLUSTRATIONS
PH04961 678 (March 24, 1994) p95. "Eugenius" (Friske, Maria)

EUGENIUS—PHOTOGRAPHS—PORTRAITS
PH04962 642 (October 29, 1992) p32. "Eugenius (clockwise from upper left): Boyle, Kelly, Keen, Lawrence" (Lavine, Michael)
PH04963 645-646 (December 10, 1992) p61. "Eugenius" (Lavine, Michael)

EVANGELISTA, LINDA—PHOTOGRAPHS
PH04964 685 (June 30, 1994) pp63-64. "With Linda Evangelista" (MacPherson, Andrew)

EVANS, SHANE—PHOTOGRAPHS
PH04965 686-687 (July 14, 1994) p30. "Soul Men: Childress, Evans, Dean Roland, Turpin And Ed Roland (clockwise from top left)" (Callahan, Kristin)

EVEN COWGIRLS GET THE BLUES (FILM)—PHOTOGRAPHS
PH04966 669 (November 11, 1993) p62. "'Cowgirls' Lineup: Rain Phoenix, Victoria Williams And Heather Graham" (Markus, Kurt)
PH04967 682 (May 19, 1994) p107. "Now Playing"

EVERCLEAR—PHOTOGRAPHS
PH04968 718 (October 5, 1995) p28. "Distortion-Fuzzed Alterna-Rockers Montoya, Alexakis And Eklund (from left)" (Westenberg, Kevin)
PH04969 726 (January 25, 1996) p18. "Everclear's Alexakis (left) And Bassist Craig Montoya Treat The Crowd To A Free Gig In Cali."
PH04970 744 (October 3, 1996) p30. "Smiths Fans: Everclear (above) Cover 'How Soon Is Now?'" (Dyer, Alison)

EVERGLADES—ILLUSTRATIONS
PH04971 733 (May 2, 1996) p46. "[Florida]"
PH04972 736 (June 13, 1996) p16. "Sugar" (Pendergrast, James T.)

EVERGLADES—PHOTOGRAPHS
PH04973 733 (May 2, 1996) pp45-44. "Florida's Everglades, A River Of Grass That Once Flowed Across 50 Uninterupted Miles" (Tavee, Tom)
PH04974 733 (May 2, 1996) p44. "The Machinery Of Big Sugar Brings In The Harvest" (Tavee, Tom)

EVERLAST—PHOTOGRAPHS—PORTRAITS
PH04975 671 (December 9, 1993) p31. "House's Danny Boy, DJ Lethal And Everlast With Cypress' B-Real And Muggs (from left)" (Blakesberg, Jay)
PH04976 679 (April 7, 1994) p32. "Everlast In-House" (Pizzarello, Charlie)

EVERLY BROTHERS—ALBUMS
PH04977 698-699 (December 29, 1994) p188. "Heartaches And Harmonies"

EVERMAN, JASON—PHOTOGRAPHS
PH04978 683 (June 2, 1994) p52. "Channing, Short-term Guitarist Jason Everman, Novoselic, Cobain 1989" (Wheeler, Alice)

EVERYBODY LOVES RAYMOND (TELEVISION SHOW)—PHOTOGRAPHS
PH04979 743 (September 19, 1996) pp94,96. "[Television]"

EVERYTHING BUT THE GIRL—ILLUSTRATIONS
PH04980 738-739 (July 11, 1996) p7. "Everything But The Girl's Ben Watt And Tracey Thorn" (Risko, Robert)

EVERYTHING BUT THE GIRL—PHOTOGRAPHS
PH04981 738-739 (July 11, 1996) p22. "Watt And Thorn: Their Relationship Survived His Illness, And Their Music Thrived" (Alston, Kwaku)

EVITA (FILM)—PHOTOGRAPHS
PH04982 743 (September 19, 1996) p88. "Divas"

EWELL, DWIGHT—PHOTOGRAPHS
PH04983 718 (October 5, 1995) pp[enc.13]. "[Parker Posey]" (Seliger, Mark)

EWING, FYFE—PHOTOGRAPHS—PORTRAITS
PH04984 654 (April 15, 1993) p21. "In Need Of Therapy?: Fyfe Ewing, Michael McKeegan And Andy Cairns (from left)" (Gullick, Steve)

EXECUTIVE GRANT OF CLEMENCY (ASLAM P. ADAM)—PHOTOGRAPHS
PH04985 692 (October 6, 1994) p41. "Adam's Commutation: A Kinder, Gentler Drug War?"

F

FACES—ALBUMS
PH04986 617 (November 14, 1991) p116. "Ooh La La" (Ladwig, Jim)
PH04987 617 (November 14, 1991) p116. "Ooh La La" (Wright, Tom)
PH04988 617 (November 14, 1991) p116. "Ooh La La" (Kilby, Jak)

FACES—PHOTOGRAPHS
PH04989 653 (April 1, 1993) p11. "Kenny Jones, Stewart, Wyman, Wood And Ian McLagan" (Hutchson, Mick)

FAGEN, DONALD—ALBUMS
PH04990 662 (August 5, 1993) p65. "Kamakiriad"

FAGEN, DONALD—PHOTOGRAPHS
PH04991 637 (August 20, 1992) p11. "Rock And Soul (from

left): Boz Scaggs, Walter Becker, Donald Fagen, Michael McDonald, Phoebe Snow And Chuck Jackson" (Hamilton, James)

PH04992 664 (September 2, 1993) p32. "Walter Becker And Donald Fagen" (Mazur, Kevin)

PH04993 667 (October 14, 1993) p37. "Walter Becker (left), Donald Fagen Get Back, Jack" (Mazur, Kevin)

PH04994 672-673 (December 23, 1993) p58. "Below: Walter Becker And Donald Fagen" (Mazur, Kevin)

FAGEN, DONALD—PHOTOGRAPHS—PORTRAITS

PH04995 623 (February 6, 1992) p24. "[Donald Fagen]" (Ockenfels, Frank W.)

FAGIN, EDDIE—PHOTOGRAPHS

PH04996 651 (March 4, 1993) p28. "Dean Zuckerman, Kevin Costigan, Jennifer Barry, Eddie Fagin (from left)" (Lavine, Michael)

FAIR GAME (FILM)—PHOTOGRAPHS

PH04997 715 (August 24, 1995) p108. "Dangerous Women: Michelle Pfeiffer, Sandra Bullock, Julia Roberts, Cindy Crawford And Natasha Henstridge"

FAIR, DAVID—PHOTOGRAPHS

PH04998 670 (November 25, 1993) p30. "'King' Director Jeff Feuerzeig (left) With Jad And David Fair"

FAIR, JAD—PHOTOGRAPHS

PH04998 670 (November 25, 1993) p30. "'King' Director Jeff Feuerzeig (left) With Jad And David Fair"

FAIR, SIMON—PHOTOGRAPHS

PH04999 691 (September 22, 1994) p19. "Nirvana's Grohl (drums), Simon Fair (at mike), Novoselic (bass)" (Doughty, Curt)

FAIRPORT CONVENTION—PHOTOGRAPHS

PH05000 691 (September 22, 1994) p21. "Ric Sanders, Simon Nicol And Richard Thompson (from left)" (Robicheau, Paul)

FAITH NO MORE—ALBUMS

PH05001 638 (September 3, 1992) p65. "Angel Dust"

PH05002 709 (June 1, 1995) p61. "King For A Day, Fool For A Lifetime"

FAITH NO MORE—PHOTOGRAPHS

PH05003 652 (March 18, 1993) p13. "Faith No More" (Roberts, Ebet)

FAITHFULL (FILM)—PHOTOGRAPHS

PH05004 733 (May 2, 1996) p62. "'Faithfull': Cher, Palminteri, O'Neal"

FAITHFULL, MARIANNE—ALBUMS

PH05005 693 (October 20, 1994) p150. "A Collection Of Her Best Recordings"

FAITHFULL, MARIANNE—PHOTOGRAPHS

PH05006 658 (June 10, 1993) p62. "On American TV With Marianne Faithfull, 1973" (Rock, Mick)

PH05007 723 (December 14, 1995) p53. "Jagger Stepping Out In London With Girlfriend Marianne Faithful (sans bearskin rug), 1967" (Kelly, John)

PH05008 730 (March 21, 1996) p17. "You Can't Always Get What You Want: Richards And Mick Jagger's Ex Faithfull" (Goldsmith, Lynn)

FAITHFULL, MARIANNE—PHOTOGRAPHS—PORTRAITS

PH05009 643 (November 12, 1992) p89. "Marianne Faithfull" (Weber, Bruce)

PH05010 735 (May 30, 1996) p18. "[Marianne Faithfull]" (Putland, Michael)

PH05011 735 (May 30, 1996) p3. "[The Faces Of Heroin]"

FALL—ALBUMS

PH05012 657 (May 27, 1993) p24. "The Infotainment Scan"

FALLING DOWN (FILM)—ILLUSTRATIONS

PH05013 651 (March 4, 1993) p71. "He's Mad As Hell" (Peck, Everett)

FALLING DOWN (FILM)—PHOTOGRAPHS

PH05014 651 (March 4, 1993) p72. "Michael Douglas Turns L.A. Vigilante After Losing Both His Job And His Family"

FALLING FROM GRACE (FILM)—ILLUSTRATIONS

PH05015 627 (April 2, 1992) p44. "Mellencamp's Uneasy State Of Grace" (MacDonald, Ross)

FALLING FROM GRACE (FILM)—PHOTOGRAPHS

PH05016 625 (March 5, 1992) p78. "Hemingway And Mellencamp Make Peace"

FALLON, B. P.—BOOKS

PH05017 698-699 (December 29, 1994) p63. "U2 Far Away So Close"

THE FAN (FILM)—ILLUSTRATIONS

PH05018 742 (September 5, 1996) p67. "The Psycho Guy" (Brodner, Steve)

THE FAN (FILM)—PHOTOGRAPHS

PH05019 742 (September 5, 1996) p68. "Fan De Niro Stalks Snipes At A Ballgame"

FANNON, GARY—ILLUSTRATIONS

PH05020 667 (October 14, 1993) p14. "Justice—Reality" (Pendergrast, James T.)

PH05021 709 (June 1, 1995) p14. "Life Sentence" (Pendergrast, James T.)

PH05022 746 (October 31, 1996) p14. "Wrong Tool" (Pendergrast, James T.)

FANNON, GARY—PHOTOGRAPHS

PH05023 638 (September 3, 1992) p27. "Fannon: Life Without Parole" (Mark, Ellen)

PH05024 658 (June 10, 1993) p40. "[Gary Fannon]" (Mark, Ellen)

PH05025 664 (September 2, 1993) p51. "Fannon At Ryan Regional Correctional Facility, 1993" (Borris, Dan)

PH05026 664 (September 2, 1993) p52. "Gary (right) With His Younger Brother, Robert"

PH05027 664 (September 2, 1993) p52. "Gary And His Mother At His High-School Graduation, 1986"

PH05028 743 (September 19, 1996) p49. "Gary And His Mother, Linda, 10 Days After Gary's Release From Prison" (Mark, Mary Ellen)

PH05029 743 (September 19, 1996) p48. "Gary Fannon In 1992 At Michigan's Medium-Security Ryan Correctional Facility" (Mark, Mary Ellen)

PH05030 743 (September 19, 1996) p50. "Gary, Right, With His Mother And Younger Brother, Robert, Weeks Before Beginning His Life-Without-Parole Prison Sentence"

FANNON, LINDA—PHOTOGRAPHS

PH05031 664 (September 2, 1993) p52. "Gary And His Mother At His High-School Graduation, 1986"

PH05032 664 (September 2, 1993) p53. "Heidi Miller And Linda Fannon At Gary's Benefit In Pittsburgh, 1993" (Borris, Dan)

PH05033 743 (September 19, 1996) p49. "Gary And His Mother, Linda, 10 Days After Gary's Release From Prison" (Mark, Mary Ellen)

PH05034 743 (September 19, 1996) p50. "Gary, Right, With His Mother And Younger Brother, Robert, Weeks Before Beginning His Life-Without-Parole Prison Sentence"

FANNON, ROBERT—PHOTOGRAPHS

PH05035 664 (September 2, 1993) p52. "Gary (right) With His Younger Brother, Robert"

PH05036 743 (September 19, 1996) p50. "Gary, Right, With His Mother And Younger Brother, Robert, Weeks Before Beginning His Life-Without-Parole Prison Sentence"

FANS—PHOTOGRAPHS

PH05037 715 (August 24, 1995) p30. "Parts Of Deadhead Culture May Be On The Way Out" (Otte, Sylvia)

PH05038 748 (November 28, 1996) p32. "Some Fans Will Give Anything For Tickets" (Kraft, Brooks)

FAR AND AWAY (FILM)—PHOTOGRAPHS

PH05039 633 (June 25, 1992) p48. "Cruise And Kidman Get Their Irish Up"

FARAGHER, DAVEY—PHOTOGRAPHS

PH05040 626 (March 19, 1992) p13. "Cracker's Johnny Hickman, David Lowery And Davey Faragher (from left)" (Young, Russell)

FAREWELL MY CONCUBINE (FILM)—PHOTOGRAPHS
PH05041 668 (October 28, 1993) p86. "Cheng Dieyi As Concubine"
FARGO (FILM)—PHOTOGRAPHS
PH05042 730 (March 21, 1996) p104. "Steve Buscemi Takes A Hit"
FARINA, DENNIS—PHOTOGRAPHS
PH05043 720 (November 2, 1995) p74. "Dennis Farina Takes The Throne"
FARINELLI (FILM)—PHOTOGRAPHS
PH05044 704 (March 23, 1995) p129. "Dionisi As Farinelli"
FARISS, ANDREW—PHOTOGRAPHS
PH05045 663 (August 19, 1993) p27. "INXS's Garry Gary Beers, Iggy Pop, Andrew Fariss And Jon Fariss (from left)" (Mazur, Kevin)
FARISS, JON—PHOTOGRAPHS
PH05045 663 (August 19, 1993) p27. "INXS's Garry Gary Beers, Iggy Pop, Andrew Fariss And Jon Fariss (from left)" (Mazur, Kevin)
FARLEY, CHRIS—PHOTOGRAPHS
PH05046 706 (April 20, 1995) p86. "'SNL' Movie Hell: Chris Farley With David Spade In 'Tommy Boy,' Al Franken With Bear In 'Stuart' And Adam Sandler With Dunces In 'Billy Madison' (from left)"
PH05047 729 (March 7, 1996) p54. "Now Playing"
FARRAKHAM, LOUIS—PHOTOGRAPHS
PH05048 750-751 (December 26, 1996) p50. "Marching To Pretoria: Louis Farrakham Meeting With President Nelson Mandela In South Africa" (Silva, Joao)
FARRAR, JAY—PHOTOGRAPHS
PH05049 684 (June 16, 1994) p35. "Tupelo's Last Stand: Farrar (left), Tweedy" (Defilippo, Michael)
PH05050 716 (September 7, 1995) p14. "Son Burning: David Boquist, Farrar, Heidorn And Jim Boquist (from left) Crank Up The Voltage" (Lucas, J.)
FARRELL, PERRY—ILLUSTRATIONS
PH05051 660-661 (July 8, 1993) p10. "Genius-Misdirected Immaturity" (Pendergrast, James T.)
PH05052 734 (May 16, 1996) p21. "The Truth, And The Tunes, Are Out There..." (Friedman, Drew)
PH05053 736 (June 13, 1996) p11. "Enit's Perry Farrell And H.O.R.D.E.'s John Popper" (Grossman, Robert)
FARRELL, PERRY—PHOTOGRAPHS
PH05054 617 (November 14, 1991) p11. "Perry Farrell's Grand Finale" (Cuffaro, Chris)
PH05055 619-620 (December 12, 1991) p59. "Perry Farrell" (Busacca, Larry)
PH05056 631 (May 28, 1992) p9. "Perry Farrell" (Cadiente, Tim)
PH05057 638 (September 3, 1992) p9. "Farrell (left)..." (Blakesberg, Jay)
PH05058 639 (September 17, 1992) p61. "Perry Farrell" (Blakesberg, Jay)
PH05059 645-646 (December 10, 1992) p45. "Farrell Debuts Pyros"
PH05060 648 (January 21, 1993) p11. "[Perry Farrell, Stacey Lowe]"
PH05061 656 (May 13, 1993) p54. "[Perry Farrell]" (Seliger, Mark)
PH05062 676 (February 24, 1994) p29. "Pyro Perry Farrell" (Mayer, Jeffrey)
PH05063 686-687 (July 14, 1994) p32. "Perry Farrell" (Garner, Kate)
PH05064 700 (January 26, 1995) p16. "Farrell, Bernhard And Doe Ham It Up" (Winter, Kevin)
PH05065 707 (May 4, 1995) p19. "Farrell Tackled The Slopes With An Apres-Ski Aperitif And Sartorial Flair, While The Equally Fly Crow beat Bono At His Own Game In Vegas" (Kravitz, Jeff)
PH05066 715 (August 24, 1995) p54. "Jane's Addiction, 1990: Farrell, Perkins, Dave Navarro And Eric Avery (from left)" (Miller, Peter Darley)
PH05067 715 (August 24, 1995) p53. "[Perry Farrell]" (Seliger, Mark)
PH05068 715 (August 24, 1995) p43. "S.Y.'s Kim Gordon Backstage With proud Lolla Papa Perry Farrell" (Blakesberg, Jay)
PH05069 727 (February 8, 1996) p12. "Perry Farrell Lets The Spirits Move Him" (Doughty, Curt)
PH05070 733 (May 2, 1996) p13. "Nothing's Shocking: Perry Farrell Gazes Fondly At His Unlikely New Pal Yoko Ono"
PH05071 736 (June 13, 1996) p38. "Farrell Performing With Jane's Addiction, 1991" (Busacca, Larry)
PH05072 736 (June 13, 1996) pp[cover]. "Rock & Roll Summer!" (Mazur, Kevin)
PH05073 744 (October 3, 1996) p34. "Cowboy Perry Gets Happy" (Mazur, Kevin)
PH05074 750-751 (December 26, 1996) p73. "Farrell Launches ENIT, Calling It The Happiest Night Of His Life" (Mazur, Kevin)
FARRELL, PERRY—PHOTOGRAPHS—PORTRAITS
PH05075 625 (March 5, 1992) p58. "Artist Of The Year" (Blakesberg, Jay)
PH05076 656 (May 13, 1993) p55. "[Perry Farrell]" (Seliger, Mark)
PH05077 662 (August 5, 1993) p59. "Perry Farrell" (Seliger, Mark)
PH05078 695 (November 17, 1994) p27. "Perry Farrell" (Seliger, Mark)
PH05079 705 (April 6, 1995) p28. "Lollapalooza Co-Founder Perry Farrell (left)" (Blakesberg, Jay)
PH05080 724-725 (December 28, 1995) p60. "Farrell" (Blakesberg, Jay)
FARRIS, DIONNE—PHOTOGRAPHS
PH05081 736 (June 13, 1996) p47. "Dionne Farris" (Leitman, Ruth)
FARRIS, DIONNE—PHOTOGRAPHS—PORTRAITS
PH05082 692 (October 6, 1994) p32. "She's No Diva: Atlanta-Based Singer Dionne Farris Tends To Her Solo Career" (Roth, David)
FARRISS, ANDREW—PHOTOGRAPHS
PH05083 671 (December 9, 1993) p18. "INXS Marks Their Spot: Pengilly; Beers, Tim, Andrew And Jon Farriss; Hutchence (from left)" (Borris, Dan)
FARRISS, JON—PHOTOGRAPHS
PH05083 671 (December 9, 1993) p18. "INXS Marks Their Spot: Pengilly; Beers, Tim, Andrew And Jon Farriss; Hutchence (from left)" (Borris, Dan)
FARRISS, TIM—PHOTOGRAPHS
PH05083 671 (December 9, 1993) p18. "INXS Marks Their Spot: Pengilly; Beers, Tim, Andrew And Jon Farriss; Hutchence (from left)" (Borris, Dan)
FARROW, MIA—ILLUSTRATIONS
PH05084 640 (October 1, 1992) p71. "Trouble In Paradise" (Sorel, Edward)
FARROW, MIA—PHOTOGRAPHS
PH05085 628 (April 16, 1992) p91. "Woody Allen Directs Malkovich, Farrow And Madonna"
PH05086 640 (October 1, 1992) p72. "Allen And Farrow Reach An Impasse"
PH05087 640 (October 1, 1992) p72. "Allen Meets Danner, The Mother Of Infatuated Student Lewis"
PH05088 645-646 (December 10, 1992) p190. "Woody Allen And Mia Farrow"
PH05089 648 (January 21, 1993) p56. "Husbands And Wives"
PH05090 649 (February 4, 1993) p72. "[Shadows And Fog]"
PH05091 683 (June 2, 1994) p76. "Mia Farrow ("Widows' Peak")"
PH05092 701 (February 9, 1995) p62. "Farrow Catches Parker And Banderas"

FASHEK, MAJEK—PHOTOGRAPHS
PH05093 626 (March 19, 1992) p20. "[Majek Fashek]" (Pessin, Annalisa)
FASHION—ILLUSTRATIONS
PH05094 680 (April 21, 1994) pp[enc.5-6 +]. "Style" (Hambly, Bob)
PH05095 692 (October 6, 1994) p16. "Body Talk" (Blackwell, Patrick)
PH05096 715 (August 24, 1995) p87. "Hot Female Look" (Faiola, Susan)
PH05097 733 (May 2, 1996) p10. "Scales Of Beauty" (Pendergrast, James T.)
PH05098 746 (October 31, 1996) p14. "Rolling Stone" (Pendergrast, James T.)
FASHION—PHOTOGRAPHS
PH05099 618 (November 28, 1991) pp79-80,82. "[Models]" (Abrahams, Mark)
PH05100 656 (May 13, 1993) p68. "[Mesh Backpack]" (Porto, Jim)
PH05101 732 (April 18, 1996) pp[enc.31]. "[Shoes]" (Witkin, Christian)
PH05102 743 (September 19, 1996) pp[enc.3,5-6 +]. "[Fashion]" (Maxwell, Robert Paul)
PH05103 747 (November 14, 1996) pp100-101,103 +. "[Fashion]" (Maxwell, Robert Paul)
PH05104 749 (December 12, 1996) pp75-76,78. "[Fashion]" (Maxwell, Robert Paul)
FAST TIMES AT RIDGEMONT HIGH (FILM)—PHOTOGRAPHS
PH05105 639 (September 17, 1992) p81. "You Must Remember This Line"
PH05106 722 (November 30, 1995) p60. "Leigh (with Phoebe Cates) Had Her First Hit With 'Fast Times At Ridgemont High'"
FASTBACKS—ALBUMS
PH05107 655 (April 29, 1993) p63. "Zucker"
FASTBACKS—PHOTOGRAPHS
PH05108 730 (March 21, 1996) p17. "Fastbacks' Kurt Bloch, Mike Musburger, Vedder, Fastbacks' Kim Warnick, Lu Lu Gargiulo" (Michelson, Randall)
FAT JOE DA GANGSTA—ALBUMS
PH05109 668 (October 28, 1993) p83. "Represent"
FATAL INSTINCT (FILM)—PHOTOGRAPHS
PH05110 669 (November 11, 1993) p81. "Assante And Young Get Smoke In Their Eyes"
FATEH ALI KHAN, NUSRAT—ALBUMS
PH05111 728 (February 22, 1996) p60. "Night Song"
FATEH ALI KHAN, NUSRAT—ILLUSTRATIONS
PH05112 744 (October 3, 1996) p11. "Nusrat Fateh Ali Khan In Performance" (Kelley, Gary)
FATEH ALI KHAN, NUSRAT—PHOTOGRAPHS
PH05113 727 (February 8, 1996) p13. "Fateh Ali Khan And Buckley, Sharing And Caring" (Vartoogian, Jack)
PH05114 744 (October 3, 1996) p35. "Fateh Ali Khan Gets A Witness In New York" (Capak, R. J.)
PH05115 750-751 (December 26, 1996) p74. "Stipe, Rick Rubin, Nusrat Ali Khan, Stephen Dorff And Flea (from left)" (Cohen, Lester)
FATIMA MANSIONS—ALBUMS
PH05116 619-620 (December 12, 1991) p187. "Viva Dead Ponies"
FATIMA MANSIONS—PHOTOGRAPHS
PH05117 619-620 (December 12, 1991) p48. "...And Fatima Mansions" (Veronsky, Frank)
FAVREAU, JON—PHOTOGRAPHS
PH05118 746 (October 31, 1996) p78. "Now Playing"
FAY, BOB—PHOTOGRAPHS
PH05119 704 (March 23, 1995) p43. "The Sensitive Souls Of Sebadoh: Fay, Barlow And Loewenstein (from left)" (Ockenfels, Frank W.)
PH05120 736 (June 13, 1996) p53. "Sebadoh's Natural Ones: Bob Fay, Jason Lowenstein And Lou Barlow" (Van Iperen, Neils)
FEAR AND LOATHING IN LAS VEGAS (BOOK)—ILLUSTRATIONS
PH05121 748 (November 28, 1996) pp[cover]. "[Fear And Loathing In Las Vegas]" (Steadman, Ralph)
FEARLESS (FILM)—ILLUSTRATIONS
PH05122 668 (October 28, 1993) p85. "Flying Blind" (Woodruff, Thomas)
FEARLESS (FILM)—PHOTOGRAPHS
PH05123 668 (October 28, 1993) p86. "Jeff Bridges Survives A Plane Crash As A Man His Wife And Family Cannot Recognize"
PH05124 674 (January 27, 1994) p48. "Best Supporting Actress"
PH05125 678 (March 24, 1994) p100. "Missing In Oscar Action"
FECHNER, ANDREW—PHOTOGRAPHS
PH05126 693 (October 20, 1994) p135. "Fechner In Page Auditorium At Duke University" (White, Steven)
FEDERAL HILL (FILM)—PHOTOGRAPHS
PH05127 696 (December 1, 1994) p134. "Libby Langdon Gets A Leg Up On The Hill's Men"
FEDERICI, DANNY—PHOTOGRAPHS
PH05128 644 (November 26, 1992) p15. "Max Weinberg, Clarence Clemons, Darlene Love, Little Steven, Garry Tallent And Danny Federici (from left)" (Mazur, Kevin)
FEED (FILM)—PHOTOGRAPHS
PH05129 642 (October 29, 1992) p78. "Bush And Clinton Fuss Before Air Time"
FEELING MINNESOTA (FILM)—PHOTOGRAPHS
PH05130 744 (October 3, 1996) p78. "Cameron Diaz, Keanu Reeves" With 'Feeling'"
FELBER, DEAN—PHOTOGRAPHS
PH05131 691 (September 22, 1994) p19. "Hootie Goes to Washington: Soni, Dean Felber, The Prez, Darius Rucker, Bryan (from left)"
PH05132 714 (August 10, 1995) pp42-43. "Darius Rucker, Dean Felber, Mark Bryan And Jim Sonefeld" (Seliger, Mark)
PH05133 726 (January 25, 1996) p37. "Hootie And The Blowfish: Jim Sonefeld, Darius Rucker, Dean Felber And Mark Bryan (from left)" (Seliger, Mark)
FELDER, DON—PHOTOGRAPHS
PH05134 685 (June 30, 1994) p23. "Birds Of A Feather: Joe Walsh, Timothy B. Schmit, Don Henley, Don Felder And Glenn Frey (from left)"
FELDMANN, JOHN—PHOTOGRAPHS
PH05135 738-739 (July 11, 1996) p116. "Pfeiffer, Feldmann, Williams And Paulson (from left)"
FELL, NORMAN—PHOTOGRAPHS
PH05136 678 (March 24, 1994) p28. "[MTV's Rock n' Jock Softball Challenge]"
FELTON, DAVID—PHOTOGRAPHS
PH05137 632 (June 11, 1992) p62. "Staff Members And Contributing Writers At The 1971 Editorial Conference, At Esalen, In Big Sur" (Leibovitz, Annie)
PH05138 647 (January 7, 1993) p11. "RS Alumni Photog Annie Leibovitz, Thompson, David Felton, Cameron Crowe, Chris Hodenfield, Ben Fong-Torres, Paul Scanlon (from left)" (Elgar, Nick)
FENDER, FREDDY—PHOTOGRAPHS
PH05139 692 (October 6, 1994) p76. "Redford Shares A Laugh With Freddy Fender And Ruben Blades On "The Milagro Beanfield War" Set"
FENDER, LEO—PHOTOGRAPHS
PH05140 623 (February 6, 1992) p54. "[Leo Fender]" (Strick, David)
FENDER, LEO—PHOTOGRAPHS—PORTRAITS
PH05141 619-620 (December 12, 1991) p112. "Leo Fender"
FENDER, PHYLLIS—PHOTOGRAPHS
PH05142 625 (March 5, 1992) p13. "Phyllis Fender" (Mazur, Kevin)
FENN, SHERILYN—PHOTOGRAPHS
PH05143 628 (April 16, 1992) p93. "Danny Aiello As Jack Ruby Chats Up Sherilyn Fenn"

PH05144 657 (May 27, 1993) p58. "Gay: Lovers Kelly Lynch And Sherilyn Fenn Before The Fall"
FENNELL, KEVIN—PHOTOGRAPHS—PORTRAITS
PH05145 686-687 (July 14, 1994) p74. "Kevin Fennell, Toby Sprout, Pollard, Jim Pollard, Greg Demos (from left)" (Rice, Ted)
FENSKE, MARK—PHOTOGRAPHS
PH05146 667 (October 14, 1993) p69. "Van Halen And Fenske At '92 MTV Awards" (Micelotta, Frank)
FERGIE—PHOTOGRAPHS
PH05147 621 (January 9, 1992) p11. "Fergie And John Mellencamp" (Bernstein, Bill)
FERGUSON, BILL—PHOTOGRAPHS—PORTRAITS
PH05148 685 (June 30, 1994) p28. "Tragi-Pop Wuss Rockers: Lotion's Youngberg, Zajkowski, Bill And Jim Ferguson (from left)" (Cardillicchio, Nick)
FERGUSON, JIM—PHOTOGRAPHS—PORTRAITS
PH05148 685 (June 30, 1994) p28. "Tragi-Pop Wuss Rockers: Lotion's Youngberg, Zajkowski, Bill And Jim Ferguson (from left)" (Cardillicchio, Nick)
FERGUSON, KENT—PHOTOGRAPHS
PH05149 628 (April 16, 1992) pp[enc.27]. "[Norman Bellingham, Wendy Williams, Kent Ferguson]" (Nicks, Dewey)
PH05150 628 (April 16, 1992) pp[enc.29]. "[Wendy Williams, Kent Ferguson]" (Nicks, Dewey)
FERGUSON, KENT—PHOTOGRAPHS—PORTRAITS
PH05151 628 (April 16, 1992) pp[enc.cover]. "Fashion Collection" (Nicks, Dewey)
FERRICK, MELISSA—PHOTOGRAPHS—PORTRAITS
PH05152 669 (November 11, 1993) p17. "Ferrick: Song For Juliana"
FERRIS, TIMOTHY—PHOTOGRAPHS
PH05153 632 (June 11, 1992) p62. "Staff Members And Contributing Writers At The 1971 Editorial Conference, At Esalen, In Big Sur" (Leibovitz, Annie)
FERRONE, STEVE—PHOTOGRAPHS
PH05154 707 (May 4, 1995) p52. "Backstage With The Boss And The Band (below, from left): Steve Ferrone, Mike Campbell, Petty, Benmont Tench, Howie Epstein And Scott Thurston" (Seliger, Mark)
FERRY, BRYAN—ALBUMS
PH05155 659 (June 24, 1993) p78. "Taxi"
PH05156 696 (December 1, 1994) p124. "Mamouna"
FERRY, BRYAN—PHOTOGRAPHS
PH05157 700 (January 26, 1995) p32. "Bryan Ferry: A Studio Perfectionist Lets Loose" (Bellissimo, John)
FERRY, BRYAN—PHOTOGRAPHS—PORTRAITS
PH05158 657 (May 27, 1993) p11. "Ferry" (Miller, Karen)
PH05159 660-661 (July 8, 1993) p20. "Bryan Ferry" (White, James)
FEUERZEIG, JEFF—PHOTOGRAPHS
PH05160 670 (November 25, 1993) p30. "'King' Director Jeff Feuerzeig (left) With Jad And David Fair"
A FEW GOOD MEN (FILM)—PHOTOGRAPHS
PH05161 645-646 (December 10, 1992) p190. "Jack Nicholson"
PH05162 647 (January 7, 1993) p50. "Jack Nicholson: On The Spot With To Cruise (left)..."
PH05163 648 (January 21, 1993) p56. "A Few Good Men"
PH05164 653 (April 1, 1993) p57. "A Few Good Men"
FICCA, BILLY—PHOTOGRAPHS
PH05165 647 (January 7, 1993) p22. "Tom Verlaine, Richard Lloyd, Billy Ficca And Fred Smith (from left)" (Buck, Chris)
FICTION—ILLUSTRATIONS
PH05166 671 (December 9, 1993) p49. "[Keeping Time]" (Mahurin, Matt)
FIDRYCH, MARK—PHOTOGRAPHS—PORTRAITS
PH05167 645-646 (December 10, 1992) p157. "Mark Fidrych, 1977"
FIELD, JERRY—PHOTOGRAPHS
PH05168 617 (November 14, 1991) p72. "Levon And The Hawks, Circa 1963: Sax Player Jerry Field, Rick Danko, Levon Helm, Richard Manuel, Garth Hudson And Robertson (from left)"
FJELD, JONAS—ALBUMS
PH05168a 674 (January 27, 1994) p54. "Danko-Fjeld-Andersen"
FIELD, SALLY—PHOTOGRAPHS
PH05169 727 (February 8, 1996) p47. "Worst Nightmare: Field With A Gun"
FIELDS, BILLY—PHOTOGRAPHS
PH05170 618 (November 28, 1991) p11. "Clockwise From Left: Buck, Enrique, Ryan-Harris, Chris Tinsley, Kinney, Billy Fields And Jamie Turner (wearing glasses)" (Diamond, Rick)
PH05171 625 (March 5, 1992) p27. "Jamie Turner, David Ryan-Harris, Billy Fields, Chris Tinsley, Enrique (from left)" (Leitman, Ruth)
FIELDS, TED—PHOTOGRAPHS—PORTRAITS
PH05172 731 (April 4, 1996) p30. "Interscope's Ted Fields (left) And Jimmy Iovine"
FIENNES, RALPH—PHOTOGRAPHS
PH05173 691 (September 22, 1994) p104. "Onscreen It's Ralph Fiennes, Left, As Van Doren, And John Turturro As Stemple"
PH05174 692 (October 6, 1994) p74. "In "Quiz Show," Director Redford (with actor Ralph Fiennes) Exposes An Infamous 1950s Television Scandal"
PH05175 719 (October 19, 1995) p158. "Kathryn Bigelow (left) Directs Bassett And Fiennes In A Brutal Parable"
PH05176 743 (September 19, 1996) p90. "Quality Control"
PH05177 748 (November 28, 1996) p142. "Fiennes"
FIENNES, RALPH—PHOTOGRAPHS—PORTRAITS
PH05178 674 (January 27, 1994) p48. "Best Supporting Actor"
FIERLINGER, PETER—PHOTOGRAPHS
PH05179 745 (October 17, 1996) p123. "CD-ROM Creators Philip (left) And Peter Fierlinger In Their San Francisco Office" (Duke, William)
FIERLINGER, PHILIP—PHOTOGRAPHS
PH05179 745 (October 17, 1996) p123. "CD-ROM Creators Philip (left) And Peter Fierlinger In Their San Francisco Office" (Duke, William)
FIGHTING GRAVITY—PHOTOGRAPHS
PH05180 730 (March 21, 1996) p55. "The Boys In The Bus: Schiavone McGee, David Triano, Eric Lawson, Chris Leitch, Karl Vonklein, David Peterson And Mike Boyd (clockwise from left)" (Clinch, Danny)
PH05181 730 (March 21, 1996) p56. "McGee, Peterson, Triano And Lawson (from left) Rehearse In The Bus" (Clinch, Danny)
PH05182 730 (March 21, 1996) p62. "Peterson (left) And Leitch Rest For The Next Show" (Clinch, Danny)
FILLMORE AUDITORIUM—PHOTOGRAPHS
PH05183 717 (September 21, 1995) p48. "The Openning Weekend At Concert Promoter Bill Graham's Fabled San Francisco Venue The Fillmore West, June 1968" (Marshall, Jim)
FILO, DAVID—PHOTOGRAPHS
PH05184 722 (November 30, 1995) pp[enc.15]. "Yang (left) And Filo, Creators Of The Yahoo! Directory: They Found A Way To 'Deliver Eyeballs'" (Winters, Dan)
PH05185 722 (November 30, 1995) pp[enc.19]. "Young, In Charge And Tired: Yang (left) And Filo" (Blakesberg, Jay)
FILTER—ILLUSTRATIONS
PH05186 715 (August 24, 1995) p13. "Filter" (Burke, Philip)
FILTER—PHOTOGRAPHS
PH05187 712-713 (July 13, 1995) p37. "The Touring Filter, With Patrick (left) And Liesegang (foreground)" (Norcross, Deborah)
PH05188 715 (August 24, 1995) pp68-69. "Brian Liesegang, Richard Patrick, Geno Lenardo, Matt Walker, Frank Cavanagh (from left)" (Ockenfels, Frank W.)
PH05189 715 (August 24, 1995) p70. "Liesegang (left) And Patrick Crank It Out In Houston" (Haveman, Kathy)
FINAL ANALYSIS (FILM)—PHOTOGRAPHS
PH05190 625 (March 5, 1992) p77. "Kim Basinger And Richard Gere Make Strange Bedfellows"
FINCH, JENNIFER—PHOTOGRAPHS

PH05191 628 (April 16, 1992) p56. "Finch, Sparks, Gardner And Plakas (from left)" (Cuffaro, Chris)
PH05192 644 (November 26, 1992) p15. "Dee Plakas, Jennifer Finch, Jett, Donita Sparks And Suzi Gardner (clockwise from left)" (Lewis, Don)
PH05193 652 (March 18, 1993) p22. "Feminist Majority Rules: L7's Finch, Gardner, Sparks, Dee Plakas (from left)" (Johnson, Lisa)
PH05194 688 (August 11, 1994) p25. "Dee Plakas, Donita Sparks, Jennifer Finch, Suzi Gardner (from left)" (Broad, Julian)
PH05195 688 (August 11, 1994) p26. "Smell The Magic: Finch Wails For A Frenzied Pit In Nashville, 1993" (Salvadori, Honey)
PH05196 692 (October 6, 1994) p16. "At Philly's Lollapalooza: L7's Donita Sparks (left), Dee Plakas, Suzi Gardner And Jennifer Finch With Bad Seeds Mick Harvey, James Johnston And Nick Cave" (Weiner, Scott)
PH05197 695 (November 17, 1994) p52. "L7" (Broad, Julian)
PH05198 696 (December 1, 1994) p23. "Elvismania: L7's Suzi Gardner, Dee Plakas, Sparks And Jennifer Finch (from left)" (Mazur, Kevin)
PH05199 718 (October 5, 1995) p20. "Read My Lips: Jennifer Finch Of L7 In Austin, Texas" (Crawford, Michael)

FINCHER, DAVID—PHOTOGRAPHS—PORTRAITS
PH05200 745 (October 17, 1996) p44. "Slumming: Fincher Shoots Wallflowers"

FINCK, ROBIN—PHOTOGRAPHS
PH05201 690 (September 8, 1994) p54. "Vrenna, Woolley, Reznor, Finck, Lohner (from left)" (Cultice, Joseph)

FINN, JASON—PHOTOGRAPHS
PH05202 718 (October 5, 1995) p35. "The Right Stuff: Jason Finn, Chris Ballew And Dave Dederer (from left)" (Mason, Karen)
PH05203 729 (March 7, 1996) p32. "The Presidents Pay Tribute To The Seattle Sonics" (Westenberg, Kevin)

FINN, JASON—PHOTOGRAPHS—PORTRAITS
PH05204 634-635 (July 9, 1992) p20. "Love Battery (from left): Kevin Whitworth, Rod Rudzitis And Jason Finn" (Lavine, Michael)
PH05205 729 (March 7, 1996) p30. "One Band Indivisible With Power, Pop And Jokes For All" (Westenberg, Kevin)

FINN, NEIL—PHOTOGRAPHS
PH05206 676 (February 24, 1994) p17. "Four's A Crowd: Neil Finn, Mark Hart, Paul Hester And Nick Seymour (from left)" (Broad, Julian)
PH05207 684 (June 16, 1994) p32. "Together Alone: Crowded House's Neil Finn; Sheryl Crow" (Diamond, Rick)

FINN, TIM—PHOTOGRAPHS
PH05208 662 (August 5, 1993) p34. "Finn (left) With Thompson" (Roth, Greg)

FINN, TIM—PHOTOGRAPHS—PORTRAITS
PH05209 669 (November 11, 1993) p21. "'I Think That I've Escaped The Clutches Of The Romantic Myth,' Says Finn" (Clinch, Danny)

FINNEY, ALBERT—PHOTOGRAPHS
PH05210 653 (April 1, 1993) p57. "Playboys"
PH05211 697 (December 15, 1994) p104. "Albert Finney"

FIORENTINO, LINDA—PHOTOGRAPHS
PH05212 693 (October 20, 1994) p157. "Now Playing"
PH05213 700 (January 26, 1995) p68. "Best Actress"
PH05214 705 (April 6, 1995) p70. "Shafted: Linda Fiorentino In 'Last Seduction'"
PH05215 721 (November 16, 1995) p116. "Linda Fiorentino Does The 'Jade' Thing"

FIREHOSE—ALBUMS
PH05216 623 (February 6, 1992) p82. "The Live Totem Pole EP"
PH05217 657 (May 27, 1993) p52. "Mr. Machinery Operator"

FIREHOSE—PHOTOGRAPHS
PH05218 658 (June 10, 1993) p34. "Firehose's Watt And Hurley" (Mazur, Kevin)

FIREMAN—ALBUMS
PH05219 685 (June 30, 1994) p76. "Strawberries Oceans Ships Forest"

FIRETOWN—PHOTOGRAPHS
PH05220 718 (October 5, 1995) p24. "Erikson, Vig And Phil Davis (from left) As Firetown, 1989" (Pantsios, A. J.)

THE FIRM (BOOK)—PHOTOGRAPHS
PH05221 639 (September 17, 1992) p81. "The Firm"

THE FIRM (FILM)—PHOTOGRAPHS
PH05222 659 (June 24, 1993) p88. "Suspense: 'The Firm' With Jeanne Tripplehorn And Cruise"
PH05223 662 (August 5, 1993) p73. "Busey, Hunter And Cruise In Jeopardy"
PH05224 665 (September 16, 1993) p77. "Best Supporting Actress"

FIRST KNIGHT (FILM)—PHOTOGRAPHS
PH05225 714 (August 10, 1995) p64. "Gere And Connery Deconstruct Camelot"

THE FIRST WIVES CLUB (FILM)—PHOTOGRAPHS
PH05226 736 (June 13, 1996) p62. "Fierce Women"
PH05227 744 (October 3, 1996) p78. "First Wives Keaton, Midler And Hawn Out For Revenge"

FISCH, TONY—PHOTOGRAPHS—PORTRAITS
PH05228 685 (June 30, 1994) p61. ""Black People Be Like 'At Least You're Down For Your Shit,'" Says Tony Fisch" (Winters, Dan)

FISHBONE—ALBUMS
PH05229 619-620 (December 12, 1991) p178. "The Reality Of My Surroundings"

FISHBONE—PHOTOGRAPHS
PH05230 662 (August 5, 1993) p17. "Fishbone: Jones (third from left) And Fisher (far right)" (Katz, Jeff)

FISHBURNE, LAURENCE—PHOTOGRAPHS
PH05231 660-661 (July 8, 1993) p33. "What's Love Got To Do With It?" (Stevens, D.)
PH05232 664 (September 2, 1993) p70. "Fishburne Challenges Chess Prodigy Pomeranc"
PH05233 726 (January 25, 1996) p64. "Othello"

FISHBURNE, LAWRENCE—PHOTOGRAPHS
PH05234 659 (June 24, 1993) p89. "Biography: "What's Love Got To Do With It,' With Lawrence Fishburne And Angela Bassett As Ike And Tina Turner (left)"

THE FISHER KING (FILM)—ILLUSTRATIONS
PH05235 615 (October 17, 1991) p99. "That Old Black Magic" (Payne, C. F.)

THE FISHER KING (FILM)—PHOTOGRAPHS
PH05236 615 (October 17, 1991) p100. "Street Sorcery From Robin Williams And His Homeless Knights"

FISHER, CHRISTOPHER—PHOTOGRAPHS
PH05237 685 (June 30, 1994) p56. "Debi Holds A Photo Of Her Boyfriend, Skins Founder Christopher Fisher" (Yoder, Dave)

FISHER, CHRISTOPHER—PHOTOGRAPHS—PORTRAITS
PH05238 685 (June 30, 1994) p56. "Fisher's Senior Yearbook Photo"

FISHER, GARY—PHOTOGRAPHS
PH05239 634-635 (July 9, 1992) pp80-81. "By Their Jerseys Ye Shall Know Them: The Original Ballooners Charles Kelly, Joe Breeze And Gary Fisher (from left)" (Stone, Pete)

FISHER, JOHN NORWOOD—PHOTOGRAPHS
PH05240 662 (August 5, 1993) p17. "Fishbone: Jones (third from left) And Fisher (far right)" (Katz, Jeff)

THE FISHERMAN'S SONG (BOOK)—ILLUSTRATIONS
PH05241 619-620 (December 12, 1991) p75. "[The Fisherman's Song]" (Datz, Margot)

FISHMAN, JON—PHOTOGRAPHS
PH05242 631 (May 28, 1992) p16. "Phish (from left): Trey Anastasio, Mike Gordon, Page McConnell, Jon Fishman" (Halsband, Michael)

FITZGERALD, ELLA—ILLUSTRATIONS
PH05243 743 (September 19, 1996) p12. "[Butterfly]" (Pendergrast, James T.)

FITZGERALD, ELLA—PHOTOGRAPHS
PH05244 740 (August 8, 1996) p26. "[Ella Fitzgerald]"
FITZGERALD, ELLA—PHOTOGRAPHS—PORTRAITS
PH05245 750-751 (December 26, 1996) p94. "[Ella Fitzgerald]"
FITZGERALD, KEVIN—PHOTOGRAPHS
PH05246 720 (November 2, 1995) p24. "Bozulich, Keenan, Tutton, Fitzgerald, Greene (from left)" (Toy, Joann)
FITZGERALD, TARA—PHOTOGRAPHS
PH05247 679 (April 7, 1994) p82. "Flanked By Sirens, Fitzgerald Is Erotically Awakened"
FITZPATRICK, LEO—PHOTOGRAPHS
PH05248 714 (August 10, 1995) p62. "Fitzpatrick Kisses A New Virgin"
FIVE BLIND BOYS OF ALABAMA—RECORDS
PH05249 649 (February 4, 1993) p68. "Deep River"
5 ROYALS—ALBUMS
PH05250 688 (August 11, 1994) p71. "Monkey Hips And Rice"
PH05251 674 Number not assigned.
FLAIM, ERIC—PHOTOGRAPHS
PH05252 624 (February 20, 1992) p38. "[Eric Flaim]" (Eccles, Andrew)
FLAMING LIPS—ALBUMS
PH05253 668 (October 28, 1993) p81. "Transmissions From The Satellite Heart"
PH05254 720 (November 2, 1995) p68. "Clouds Taste Metallic"
FLAMING LIPS—ILLUSTRATIONS
PH05255 706 (April 20, 1995) p12. "Gasoline-Matches-Seltzer" (Pendergrast, James T.)
FLAMING LIPS—PHOTOGRAPHS
PH05256 689 (August 25, 1994) p21. "The Flaming Lips' Michael Ivins, Steven Drozd, Wayne Coyne (from left)" (Blakesberg, Jay)
PH05257 703 (March 9, 1995) p26. "Imagine The Beatles Drunk On Robitussin: Coyne, Drozd, Ivins And Jones (from left)" (Lavine, Michael)
PH05258 736 (June 13, 1996) p33. "The Flaming Lips' Steven Drozd, Michael Ivins, Wayne Coyne And Ronald Jones (from left)" (Martin, J. Michelle)
FLANAGAN, MIKE—PHOTOGRAPHS
PH05259 746 (October 31, 1996) p59. "Mike Flanagan"
FLANERY, SEAN PATRICK—PHOTOGRAPHS—PORTRAITS
PH05260 724-725 (December 28, 1995) p134. "The 10 Worst Movies Of 1995 (degrees of sleaze)"
FLANSBURGH, JOHN—PHOTOGRAPHS
PH05261 709 (June 1, 1995) p30. "Giant Flansburgh Serenades Geek-Rock Lovers" (Capak, R. J.)
FLATT, LESTER—PHOTOGRAPHS
PH05262 746 (October 31, 1996) p23. "Pride Of The Opry: The Legendary Bluegrass Boys Lineup Of Monroe, Chubby Wise, Flatt, Scruggs And Monroe's Brother Birch, Circa 1947 (from left)"
FLATTUM, DALE—PHOTOGRAPHS
PH05263 721 (November 16, 1995) p78. "Mike Morasky, Darren Mor-X And Dale Flattum (from left) Briefly Considered The Name Rusty Nail Shower Stall But Soon Thought Better of It" (Winters, Dan)
FLAVOR FLAV—PHOTOGRAPHS
PH05264 622 (January 23, 1992) p36. "Comic Relief: Chuck's Sidekick, Flavor, Works The Crowd" (Callahan, Kristin)
PH05265 624 (February 20, 1992) p12. "Flavor And A Fellow Arrestee" (Smith, Jack)
PH05266 645-646 (December 10, 1992) p49. "Flavor Flav Shows Off His New Do" (Stabile, K. Wiles)
PH05267 656 (May 13, 1993) p32. "Naughty By Nature With Flavor Flav (center)" (Capak, R. J.)
PH05268 667 (October 14, 1993) p85. "'Baseheads': PE's Flav Brings The News"
PH05269 672-673 (December 23, 1993) p74. "Flavor Flav: Once A Felon..." (Goldsmith, Lynn)
PH05270 685 (June 30, 1994) p30. "New "Mess Age": Flavor Flav, Chuck D And Terminator X (from front)" (Seliger, Mark)
PH05271 689 (August 25, 1994) p16. "[Flavor Flav]" (Berman, Steve)
PH05272 704 (March 23, 1995) p25. "[Flavor Flav & Mary J. Blige]" (Mazur, Kevin)
PH05273 724-725 (December 28, 1995) p51. "P.E.'s Flavor Flav: A Better Rapper Than Driver" (Weiner, Scott)
FLAVOR FLAV—PHOTOGRAPHS—PORTRAITS
PH05274 716 (September 7, 1995) p25. "On Hiatus: P.E.'s Flavor Flav (left), Chuck D" (Tonge, David)
FLEA—PHOTOGRAPHS
PH05275 625 (March 5, 1992) p54. "Readers Find This Pepper Red Hot" (Haddi, Michael)
PH05276 629 (April 30, 1992) p23. "John Frusciante, Anthony Kiedis, Chad Smith And Flea (from left)" (Cuffaro, Chris)
PH05277 639 (September 17, 1992) p60. "Chili Peppers Flea (left) And Kiedis" (Blakesberg, Jay)
PH05278 642 (October 29, 1992) p19. "Chili Pepper Flea And Friends Onstage" (Kravitz, Jeff)
PH05279 654 (April 15, 1993) p11. "Chili Peppers Kiedis And Flea Flank Fan Tony Bennett" (Downie, Scott)
PH05280 660-661 (July 8, 1993) p17. "Man Overboard: Smith, Kiedis, Marshall And Flea" (Leialoha, Mark)
PH05281 665 (September 16, 1993) p16. "Anthony Kiedis And Flea (below)" (Seliger, Mark)
PH05282 667 (October 14, 1993) p39. "Flea, Bennett And Anthony Kiedis" (Mazur, Kevin)
PH05283 672-673 (December 23, 1993) p63. "Left: Flea, Bennett And Kiedis" (Kravitz, Jeff)
PH05284 674 (January 27, 1994) p28. "Nirvana's Dave Grohl And Krist Novoselic With Madcap MTV Hosts Anthony Kiedis And Flea" (Mazur, Kevin)
PH05285 679 (April 7, 1994) p49. "We Three: Hillel Slovak, Kiedis And Flea In '82 (from left)" (Shear, Jack)
PH05286 692 (October 6, 1994) p17. "Peppers Roast: Flea, Anthony Kiedis, Dave Navarro, Chad Smith (from left)" (Mazur, Kevin)
PH05287 695 (November 17, 1994) pp66-67. "Flea Of The Red Hot Chili Peppers" (Mark, Mary Ellen)
PH05288 709 (June 1, 1995) p21. "RHCPs (from left): Flea, Chad Smith, Dave Navarro And Anthony Kiedis" (Streiber, Art)
PH05289 719 (October 19, 1995) p56. "'86: Irons, Slovak, Flea, Kiedis (from left) Backstage At The Ritz, In New York" (Gershoff, Gary)
PH05290 719 (October 19, 1995) pp52-53. "Anthony Kiedis And Flea" (Corbijn, Anton)
PH05291 719 (October 19, 1995) pp54-55. "Flea, Kiedis" (Corbijn, Anton)
PH05292 719 (October 19, 1995) p58. "Red Hot Chili Peppers, '95: Dave Navarro, Anthony Kiedis, Flea An Chad Smith (from left)" (Corbijn, Anton)
PH05293 719 (October 19, 1995) p60. "Woodstock 1994: Flea And Kiedis" (Weiner, Scott)
PH05294 731 (April 4, 1996) p17. "Bush Covers? Chili Peppers Frontman Anthony Kiedis, Bassist Flea, The Not-Unattractive Navarro And Drummer Chad Smith (from left)" (Baehler, Chapman)
PH05295 744 (October 3, 1996) p19. "[Flea]" (Knaeps, Gie)
PH05296 750-751 (December 26, 1996) p74. "Stipe, Rick Rubin, Nusrat Ali Khan, Stephen Dorff And Flea (from left)" (Cohen, Lester)
PH05297 Number not assigned.
FLEETWOOD MAC—ALBUMS
PH05298 617 (November 14, 1991) p149. "Rumours" (Strobel, Desmond)
PH05299 617 (November 14, 1991) p149. "Rumours" (Worthington, Herbert)
FLEETWOOD MAC—PHOTOGRAPHS
PH05300 670 (November 25, 1993) pp78-79. "[Fleetwood Mac]"

(Seliger, Mark)
PH05301 720 (November 2, 1995) p49. "Mick Fleetwood & John McVie" (Seliger, Mark)
FLEETWOOD, MICK—PHOTOGRAPHS
PH05302 655 (April 29, 1993) p11. "From Left: A Bongo, Fleetwood, Keyboardist Nicky Hopkins And Sweet" (Di Santo, Annamaria)
PH05303 670 (November 25, 1993) pp78-79. "[Fleetwood Mac]" (Seliger, Mark)
PH05304 720 (November 2, 1995) p49. "Mick Fleetwood & John McVie" (Seliger, Mark)
FLEETWOOD, MICK—PHOTOGRAPHS—PORTRAITS
PH05305 643 (November 12, 1992) p117. "Mick Fleetwood & John McVie" (Seliger, Mark)
FLEISIG, ALEXIS—PHOTOGRAPHS
PH05306 721 (November 16, 1995) p75. "Johnny Temple, Scott McCloud, Alexis Fleisig And Eli Janney (from left) Enjoy An All-American Snack" (Exum)
FLEMING, DON—PHOTOGRAPHS
PH05307 633 (June 25, 1992) p12. "Dim Stars (from left): Richard Hell, Steve Shelley, Thurston Moore And Don Fleming" (Busacca, Larry)
PH05308 656 (May 13, 1993) p15. "Moore, Fleming, Firehose's Mike Watt And J Mascis (from left)" (Callahan, Kristin)
PH05309 676 (February 24, 1994) p29. "'Backbeat' Boys: Dulli, Fleming, Mike Mills, Dave Grohl And Thurston Moore"
PH05310 680 (April 21, 1994) p64. "Twist And Shout: Fleming, Dulli, Grohl And Mills (from left) At A 'Backbeat' Session" (Cuffaro, Chris)
PH05311 688 (August 11, 1994) p17. "At The Movie Awards: Backbeaters Mike Mills, Don Fleming, Dave Pirner, Greg Dulli, Dave Grohl And Thurston Moore (above, from left)" (Kravitz, Jeff)
PH05312 691 (September 22, 1994) p38. "Revoke-Your-License Velocity: Gumball Drummer Jay Spiegel, Fleming And Bassist Eric Vermillion (from left)" (Capak, R. J.)
PH05313 698-699 (December 29, 1994) p50. "Dulli, Fleming, Mills, Grohl, Moore, Pirner Went Out For A Smoke" (Cuffaro, Chris)
FLEMING, JIMMY—PHOTOGRAPHS
PH05314 689 (August 25, 1994) p24. "Pumpkins' Corgan Joins The Frogs' Damien Strigens And Jimmy Fleming" (Blakesberg, Jay)
FLESH AND BONE (FILM)—PHOTOGRAPHS
PH05315 670 (November 25, 1993) p126. "Dennis Quaid And Meg Ryan Steal A Kiss"
PH05316 670 (November 25, 1993) p126. "Gwyneth Paltrow (right) Steals The Film"
PH05316a 678 (March 24, 1994) p100. "Missing In Oscar Action"
FLESHER, DANNIE—PHOTOGRAPHS
PH05317 722 (November 30, 1995) p31. "Industrial-Music Pioneers Dannie Flesher And Jim Nash At The Wax Trax! Offices In Chicago's Wicker Park, October 1994" (Chung, Andre F.)
FLETCHER, ANDREW—PHOTOGRAPHS
PH05318 670 (November 25, 1993) p94. "1982: Fletcher, Gahan, Gore And Wilder (from left)"
PH05319 670 (November 25, 1993) p94. "1985: Gore, Wilder, Gahan And Fletcher (clockwise from left)" (Nosotti, Fabio)
PH05320 670 (November 25, 1993) p92. "In Madrid, Making Their Last Record: Gahan, Gore, Wilder, Fletcher (from left)" (Corbijn, Anton)
FLETCHER, JOHN—PHOTOGRAPHS
PH05321 651 (March 4, 1993) p24. "Sloan, Edwards, Fletcher, Stephens" (Roca, John)
FLINT, HUGHIE—PHOTOGRAPHS
PH05322 655 (April 29, 1993) p34. "Clapton With John Mayall's Bluesbreakers At The Height Of God-mania in '66: Mayall, Hughie Flint, God And John McVie (from left)"
FLINT, KEITH—PHOTOGRAPHS
PH05323 715 (August 24, 1995) p34. "Reality Raps While Flint Gets Down (from left)" (Capak, R. J.)
PH05324 749 (December 12, 1996) p19. "Prodigy's Keith Flint, Midmosh At MTV's Fete In New York" (Mazur, Kevin)
THE FLINTSTONES (FILM)—PHOTOGRAPHS
PH05325 683 (June 2, 1994) p27. "Below: Schneider, Kate Pierson, Keith Strickland" (Batzdorff, Rob)
PH05326 684 (June 16, 1994) p115. "Now Playing"
PH05327 684 (June 16, 1994) p114. "Potential Headaches"
PH05328 698-699 (December 29, 1994) p196. "The Stupidity Of "Ace Ventura" (top) And "The Flintstones" (above) Mined Gold"
FLIPPEN, BENTON—ALBUMS
PH05329 698-699 (December 29, 1994) p174. "Old Times, New Times"
FLIPPER, LYNN—PHOTOGRAPHS
PH05330 721 (November 16, 1995) p81. "The Tribe That Sticks Together: Slade Bellum, Lynn Breedlove, Leslie Mah, Lynn Payne, Lynn Flipper (from left)" (Yemchuk, Yelena)
FLIPPO, CHET—PHOTOGRAPHS
PH05331 632 (June 11, 1992) p117. "Parton And Flippo In 1977 At The Waldorf-Astoria Hotel In New York City" (Gahr, David)
FLIRTING WITH DISASTER (FILM)—PHOTOGRAPHS
PH05332 732 (April 18, 1996) p78. "Kelly And Stiller"
FLOOD—PHOTOGRAPHS
PH05333 618 (November 28, 1991) p46. "Flood With Bono And Edge In Berlin" (Corbijn, Anton)
PH05334 618 (November 28, 1991) p44. "Flood, The Album's Engineer, And Eno, Who Coproduced Several Tracks, Work On The Final Mixes" (Corbijn, Anton)
FLORIDA—PHOTOGRAPHS
PH05335 632 (June 11, 1992) p75. "Moonshot Fever: Like The World Series, A Championship Fight, The Bicentennial" (Leibovitz, Annie)
FLORIO, JIM—PHOTOGRAPHS—PORTRAITS
PH05336 671 (December 9, 1993) p36. "Profiles In Courage"
FLOWERED UP—ALBUMS
PH05337 625 (March 5, 1992) p68. "A Life With Brian"
FLUFFY—PHOTOGRAPHS
PH05338 746 (October 31, 1996) p28. "Right Honorable: Adams, Rootes, Jones And Storer (from left)" (Constantine, Elaine)
PH05339 750-751 (December 26, 1996) p80. "Breakthrough" (Blakesberg, Jay)
FLY GIRLS—PHOTOGRAPHS—PORTRAITS
PH05340 656 (May 13, 1993) p94. "Deidre Lang, Jennifer Lopez, Twist, Jossie Harris, Lisa Thompson (from left)"
FLYING SAUCER ATTACK—ALBUMS
PH05341 731 (April 4, 1996) p61. "Chorus"
FLYNN, KIMBERLY—PHOTOGRAPHS
PH05342 722 (November 30, 1995) p74. "Quick Sex: Flynn, Andrews"
FLYNT, LARRY—PHOTOGRAPHS
PH05343 750-751 (December 26, 1996) p204. "'ID4' (above) Is Biggest, But 'Larry Flynt' (left), With Harrelson And Love Flanking Flynt, Is The Best"
FOETUS—ALBUMS
PH05344 709 (June 1, 1995) p62. "Gash"
FOGELNES, JAKE—PHOTOGRAPHS
PH05345 709 (June 1, 1995) p16. "Flava In Ya Ear: Wax's Loomis, Joe Sib, Dave Georgeff And Soda Drop In On Fogelnes In His 'Squirt TV' Bedroom Studio (from left)" (Brown, Christy)
FOGELSONG, CORI—PHOTOGRAPHS
PH05346 683 (June 2, 1994) p61. "Aberdeen High Freshman Cori Fogelsong (center) Holds Homemade Tribute" (Berry, Jim)
FOGERTY, JOHN—ILLUSTRATIONS
PH05347 649 (February 4, 1993) p3. "John Fogerty" (Burke, Philip)
FOGERTY, JOHN—PHOTOGRAPHS
PH05348 630 (May 14, 1992) p13. "John Fogerty" (Granitz, Steve)

PH05349 651 (March 4, 1993) p17. "Creedence Clearwater Revisited: Springsteen, Was, Fogerty And Robertson" (Mazur, Kevin)
PH05350 672-673 (December 23, 1993) p28. "Above: Gregg Allman, John Fogerty And Neil Young" (Blakesberg, Jay)
FOGERTY, JOHN—PHOTOGRAPHS—PORTRAITS
PH05351 625 (March 5, 1992) pp14-15. "On The Evening Of The Seventh Annual Hall Of Fame Induction Ceremony, 'Rolling Stone' Gathered These Nine Legendary Guitarists At The Waldorf-Astoria For A Once-In-A-Lifetime..."
PH05352 643 (November 12, 1992) p145. "John Fogerty" (Seliger, Mark)
PH05353 649 (February 4, 1993) p48. "Drummer Clifford, Bassist Cook, Rhythm Guitarist Fogerty, Frontman Fogerty (clockwise from left)" (Wolman, Baron)
PH05354 649 (February 4, 1993) p46. "[John Fogerty]" (Seliger, Mark)
FOGERTY, TOM—PHOTOGRAPHS—PORTRAITS
PH05355 649 (February 4, 1993) p48. "Drummer Clifford, Bassist Cook, Rhythm Guitarist Fogerty, Frontman Fogerty (clockwise from left)" (Wolman, Baron)
FOLDS, BEN—ALBUMS
PH05356 718 (October 5, 1995) p70. "Ben Folds Five"
FOLDS, BEN—PHOTOGRAPHS
PH05357 721 (November 16, 1995) p73. "Power Trio With A Twist: Darren Jessee, Ben Folds And Robert Sledge (from left) Make Absurdity Swing Like Mad" (Guip, Amy)
PH05358 749 (December 12, 1996) p20. "BFF's Robert Sledge, Darren Jessee; Klezmatics Frank London, Alicia Svigals; And Folds" (Mazur, Kevin)
FOLEY, DAVE—ILLUSTRATIONS
PH05359 729 (March 7, 1996) p57. "[Dave Foley]" (Fishman, Miriam)
FOLEY, DAVID—PHOTOGRAPHS—PORTRAITS
PH05360 733 (May 2, 1996) p62. "Kids Foley, McKinney, McCulloch, McDonald And Thompson"
FOLEY, TOM—PHOTOGRAPHS—PORTRAITS
PH05361 698-699 (December 29, 1994) p152. "[Tom Foley]" (Downing, Larry)
FOLKSMEN—PHOTOGRAPHS
PH05362 662 (August 5, 1993) p33. "Chris Guest, Harry Shearer, Michael McKean, With Carpenter" (Cohen, Lester)
FOLLAND, ALISON—PHOTOGRAPHS
PH05363 719 (October 19, 1995) p156. "She Glides Her TV-Form Divine Past Gawkers Phoenix, Affleck And Folland"
FOLLOW FOR NOW—ALBUMS
PH05364 618 (November 28, 1991) p98. "Follow For Now"
FOLLOW FOR NOW—PHOTOGRAPHS
PH05365 619-620 (December 12, 1991) p48. "Follow For Now (above)..." (Leitman, Ruth)
PH05366 625 (March 5, 1992) p27. "Jamie Turner, David Ryan-Harris, Billy Fields, Chris Tinsley, Enrique (from left)" (Leitman, Ruth)
FONDA, BRIDGET—ILLUSTRATIONS
PH05367 638 (September 3, 1992) p71. "Achy Breaky And Deadly" (Sadowski, Wiktor)
FONDA, BRIDGET—PHOTOGRAPHS
PH05368 638 (September 3, 1992) p72. "Bonding With Leigh (left) Is A Living Hell For Fonda"
PH05369 649 (February 4, 1993) p72. "[Single White Female]"
PH05370 654 (April 15, 1993) p72. "Bridget Fonda (left) Can't Match The Sizzle of Anne Parillaud in 'Le Femme Nikita'"
PH05371 655 (April 29, 1993) p68. "Bridget Fonda (left) And Phoebe Cates Stalling"
PH05372 688 (August 11, 1994) p62. "It's A Jackpot-Lottery Win For Fonda, Cage And Perez"
FONDA, PETER—PHOTOGRAPHS
PH05373 657 (May 27, 1993) p11. "Yoakum (left, no tongue) And Fonda" (Kravitz, Jeff)
FONG-TORRES, BEN—PHOTOGRAPHS
PH05374 632 (June 11, 1992) p62. "Staff Members And Contributing Writers At The 1971 Editorial Conference, At Esalen, In Big Sur" (Leibovitz, Annie)
PH05375 647 (January 7, 1993) p11. "RS Alumni Photog Annie Leibovitz, Thompson, David Felton, Cameron Crowe, Chris Hodenfield, Ben Fong-Torres, Paul Scanlon (from left)" (Elgar, Nick)
FONGHEISER, DENNY—PHOTOGRAPHS
PH05376 696 (December 1, 1994) p25. "Howard Leese, John Paul Jones, Ann Wilson, Denny Fongheiser And Nancy Wilson"
FOO FIGHTERS—ALBUMS
PH05377 714 (August 10, 1995) p56. "Foo Fighters"
PH05378 715 (August 24, 1995) p124. "Foo Fighters"
PH05379 718 (October 5, 1995) p88. "Foo Fighters"
FOO FIGHTERS—ILLUSTRATIONS
PH05380 724-725 (December 28, 1995) p120. "The Might And melody That Ex-Nirvana Drummer Dave Grohl Puts Into His Foo Fighters Songs Are The Stuff Of New Beginnings" (Angel, Vinnie)
FOO FIGHTERS—PHOTOGRAPHS
PH05381 718 (October 5, 1995) p40. "[Foo Fighters]" (Winters, Dan)
PH05382 718 (October 5, 1995) pp[cover]. "Invasion Of Foo Fighters: Dave Grohl Takes Command" (Winters, Dan)
PH05383 726 (January 25, 1996) p37. "Foo Fighters Are, From Left, Nate Mendel, Pat Smear, Dave Grohl And William Goldsmith" (Seliger, Mark)
PH05384 730 (March 21, 1996) p32. "Horsing Around: David Grohl (top and bottom) And Fellow Foo Fighters William Goldsmith, Pat Smear And Nate Mendel (middle, from left)" (Gougenheim, Kim)
PH05385 736 (June 13, 1996) p20. "[Foo Fighters]" (Mazur, Kevin)
PH05386 749 (December 12, 1996) p32. "The Foo Fighters' Next LP Won't Be The Dave Grohl Project Part 2" (Mott, Tony)
FOO, MARK—ILLUSTRATIONS
PH05387 706 (April 20, 1995) p59. "[Mark Foo]" (Baseman, Gary)
FOO, MARK—PHOTOGRAPHS
PH05388 706 (April 20, 1995) p64. "Anatomy Of A Fatal Wipeout" (Beck, Lawrence)
PH05389 706 (April 20, 1995) p58. "And At Rest" (Baker, Bernie)
PH05390 706 (April 20, 1995) p58. "Foo: A Legend At Work..." (Barbour, Bob)
PH05391 706 (April 20, 1995) p61. "Foo At Oahu's North Shore: Lack Of Big Waves Drove Him To California" (King, Don)
PH05392 706 (April 20, 1995) p60. "Foo In 1978: Already A Small-Wave Professional" (Foo, Sharlyn)
PH05393 706 (April 20, 1995) p66. "January 1995, Waimea Bay, Hawaii: 200 Friends And Fellow Riders Gather To Honor The Memory Of Mark Foo, Surfer, Salesman And Now A Genuine Legend" (Baker, Bernie)
PH05394 706 (April 20, 1995) p66. "January 1995, Waimea Bay, Hawaii: 200 Friends And Fellow Riders Gather To Honor The Memory Of Mark Foo, Surfer, Salesman And Now A Genuine Legend" (Bilderback)
FOOD—ILLUSTRATIONS
PH05395 706 (April 20, 1995) p15. "Big Mac Attack" (Corio, Paul)
FOOD—PHOTOGRAPHS
PH05396 750-751 (December 26, 1996) p90. "[Jellybeans]"
FOR SQUIRRELS—ALBUMS
PH05397 726 (January 25, 1996) p72. "Example"
PH05398 727 (February 8, 1996) p60. "Example"
FORBES, STEVE—PHOTOGRAPHS
PH05399 726 (January 25, 1996) p58. "Forbes Preaches The Flat-Tax Gospel To Republicans At Hofstra University, In New York" (Fink, Larry)

FORBES, STEVE—PHOTOGRAPHS—PORTRAITS
PH05400 730 (March 21, 1996) p52. "Forbes"
FORD, HARRISON—PHOTOGRAPHS
PH05401 619-620 (December 12, 1991) p194. "Male Wimps And Female Warriors"
PH05402 634-635 (July 9, 1992) p114. "A Flag-Waving Thriller Pits Ford Against Terrorists"
PH05403 663 (August 19, 1993) p84. "Harrison Ford (right) Puts A '90s Twist On A '60s TV Series, Starring David Janssen (left)"
PH05404 678 (March 24, 1994) p100. "Oscar's Choices: 'Schindler's List,' 'The Piano,' 'The Remains Of the Day,' 'In The Name Of The Father,' 'The Fugitive' (from left)"
PH05405 680 (April 21, 1994) p96. "The Fugitive"
PH05406 690 (September 8, 1994) p84. "[Clear And Present Danger]"
PH05407 696 (December 1, 1994) p116. "Tom Clancy And Harrison Ford On The Set Of "Clear And Present Danger""
PH05408 726 (January 25, 1996) p66. "Unlucky In Love: Ormond Flanked By Kinnear And Ford"
FORD, MARC—PHOTOGRAPHS
PH05409 621 (January 9, 1992) p11. "Marc Ford (left) And Chris Robinson" (Matheu, Robert)
PH05410 642 (October 29, 1992) p19. "Black Crowes Marc Ford, Johnny Colt And Chris Robinson (from left) With Guest Rehearser And Show Host Dana Carvey" (Mazur, Kevin)
PH05411 709 (June 1, 1995) p16. "Jayhawk Gary Louris, Crowes Marc Ford And Robinson, Perlman (from left)" (Diamond, Rick)
FORDHAM, JOHANNA—PHOTOGRAPHS
PH05412 706 (April 20, 1995) pp[enc.17]. "At Garf's" (Seliger, Mark)
FORDHAM, JULIA—ALBUMS
PH05413 691 (September 22, 1994) p97. "Falling Forward"
FOREIGNER—ALBUMS
PH05414 707 (May 4, 1995) p68. "Mr. Moonlight"
FOREIGNER—PHOTOGRAPHS
PH05415 692 (October 6, 1994) p35. "Foreigner's Lou Gramm (left) And Mick Jones" (Robicheau, Paul)
PH05416 718 (October 5, 1995) p21. "Fans Got Behind Foreigner In A Big Way At Nudestock '95" (Whitall, Robert)
FOREMAN, DAVE—PHOTOGRAPHS—PORTRAITS
PH05417 693 (October 20, 1994) p84. "Dave Foreman, An Earth First! Founder" (Dykinga, Jack W.)
FORESKIN—ILLUSTRATIONS
PH05418 716 (September 7, 1995) p14. "Tips Appreciated" (Angel, Vinnie)
FOREVER BAD BLUES BAND—ALBUMS
PH05419 669 (November 11, 1993) p77. "Just Stompin'"
FORGET PARIS (FILM)—PHOTOGRAPHS
PH05420 709 (June 1, 1995) p70. "Early Starters"
FORMAN, MILOS—PHOTOGRAPHS
PH05421 741 (August 22, 1996) p25. "Love (center) And Forman With Friend Miss Martina On Location In A Rented House In Memphis, Tenn." (Von Jansky, Ladi)
FORREST GUMP (FILM)—ILLUSTRATIONS
PH05422 686-687 (July 14, 1994) p97. "The Wolf, The Lion And The Lamb" (Fisher, Jeffrey)
PH05423 708 (May 18, 1995) p14. "Chocolates" (Pendergrast, James T.)
FORREST GUMP (FILM)—PHOTOGRAPHS
PH05424 684 (June 16, 1994) p116. "Weepy: Hanks Alone In "Forrest Gump""
PH05425 686-687 (July 14, 1994) p98. "Robin Wright And Hanks ("Forrest Gump")"
PH05426 688 (August 11, 1994) p56. "[Forrest Gump]"
PH05427 691 (September 22, 1994) p106. "Acting Peaks"
PH05428 698-699 (December 29, 1994) p194. "Hanks Sits In "Gump""
PH05429 698-699 (December 29, 1994) p60. "Simple Minds: Forrest Gump"
PH05430 705 (April 6, 1995) p69. "The Envelope, Please: Nominated For best Picture: Forrest Gump, Pulp Fiction, Quiz Show, Four Weddings And A Funeral, And The Shawshank Redemption"
FORSYTHE, WILLIAM—PHOTOGRAPHS
PH05431 631 (May 28, 1992) p60. "Forsythe, Stoltz And Snipes (from left) Battle Paralysis"
FOSTER, HENRY—PHOTOGRAPHS
PH05432 724-725 (December 28, 1995) p40. "Henry Foster"
FOSTER, JODIE—ILLUSTRATIONS
PH05433 650 (February 18, 1993) p65. "Con With The Wind" (Cowles, David)
FOSTER, JODIE—PHOTOGRAPHS
PH05434 616 (October 31, 1991) p97. "Gifted Son And Mother: Adam Hann-Byrd And Jodie Foster"
PH05435 617 (November 14, 1991) p184. "Art Versus Commerce"
PH05436 619-620 (December 12, 1991) pp[cover]. "1991 Yearbook" (Rolston, Matthew)
PH05437 619-620 (December 12, 1991) p192. "In 'The Silence Of The Lambs,' Jodie Foster Finds An Affinity With The Male Monster (Anthony Hopkins)"
PH05438 650 (February 18, 1993) p66. "...Richard Gere Plays Tricks On Jodie Foster"
PH05439 698-699 (December 29, 1994) p199. "Foster And Neeson In "Nell""
FOSTER, JODIE—PHOTOGRAPHS—PORTRAITS
PH05440 692 (October 6, 1994) p17. "Bon Jovi, Foster, Sambora (from left)" (Mazur, Kevin)
FOSTER, SABINE—PHOTOGRAPHS
PH05441 680 (April 21, 1994) pp[enc.38]. "It's Not Just Shopping, It's An Adventure" (Ragel, Jon)
FOUNTAIN, CLARENCE—RECORDS
PH05442 649 (February 4, 1993) p68. "Deep River"
FOUNTAINS OF WAYNE—PHOTOGRAPHS
PH05443 748 (November 28, 1996) p40. "Running Over" (Annalisa)
FOUR HORSEMEN—PHOTOGRAPHS
PH05444 619-620 (December 12, 1991) p26. "The Four Horsemen" (Dokus, Peter)
PH05445 619-620 (December 12, 1991) p45. "The Four Horsemen's Debut Came Through Loud And Clear" (Giron, Joe)
4 NON BLONDES—PHOTOGRAPHS
PH05446 662 (August 5, 1993) p21. "Brunets Have Fun, Too: Hillhouse, Rocha, Perry And Richardson (from left)" (MacNaughtan, Andrew)
PH05447 671 (December 9, 1993) p32. "Members Of Consolidated And 4 Non Blondes Unite For Critters Big And Small" (Blakesberg, Jay)
4 NON BLONDES—PHOTOGRAPHS—PORTRAITS
PH05448 672-673 (December 23, 1993) p46. "[4 Non Blondes]"
FOUR ROOMS (FILM)—PHOTOGRAPHS
PH05449 718 (October 5, 1995) p76. "Pulp To Come"
FOUR WEDDINGS AND A FUNERAL (FILM)—PHOTOGRAPHS
PH05450 678 (March 24, 1994) p104. "Two Babes And A Hunk: Davis (Angie); Stowe (China Moon); Grant (Four Weddings)"
PH05451 698-699 (December 29, 1994) p194. "Grant Gets MacDowell In "Weddings""
PH05452 705 (April 6, 1995) p69. "The Envelope, Please: Nominated For best Picture: Forrest Gump, Pulp Fiction, Quiz Show, Four Weddings And A Funeral, And The Shawshank Redemption"
PH05453 705 (April 6, 1995) p69. "Oscar Rejects"
1492 (FILM)—ILLUSTRATIONS
PH05454 642 (October 29, 1992) p76. "Hard Times For Heroes" (Blitt, Barry)
1492 (FILM)—PHOTOGRAPHS
PH05455 649 (February 4, 1993) p72. "[1492]"
FOWLER, BERNARD—PHOTOGRAPHS
PH05456 647 (January 7, 1993) p24. "Bernard Fowler (left) And

Wood" (Diamond, Richard)
PH05457 734 (May 16, 1996) p18. "Wood, Richards And Fowler (from left) Kicking It"
FOWLER, CHRIS—PHOTOGRAPHS
PH05458 715 (August 24, 1995) p94. "[Chris Fowler]" (Danelian, Stephen)
PH05459 715 (August 24, 1995) pp90-91. "On The Court In Thompkins Park" (Danelian, Stephen)
FOX, DAVE—PHOTOGRAPHS
PH05460 660-661 (July 8, 1993) p101. "The Posies (from left): Jon Auer, Dave Fox, Ken Stringfellow And Mike Musburger" (Natkin, Paul)
FOX, JOHN—PHOTOGRAPHS
PH05461 746 (October 31, 1996) p59. "John Fox"
FOX, KERRY—PHOTOGRAPHS
PH05462 702 (February 23, 1995) p81. "Fox, McGregor And Eccleston Find The Body"
FOX, MATTHEW—ILLUSTRATIONS—LETTERING
PH05463 617 (November 14, 1991) p79. "The Sensual Christian By Lawrence Wright: Father Matthew Fox Extols The Joys Of Passion And Lust Over The Shame Of Original Sin True Believers" (Karl, Anita)
FOX, MATTHEW—PHOTOGRAPHS
PH05464 617 (November 14, 1991) p79. "[Matthew Fox]" (Winters, Dan)
PH05465 617 (November 14, 1991) p80. "Matthew With His "Spiritual Director," Tristan, A Fifteen-Year-Old Spitz" (Winters, Dan)
FOX, MICHAEL J.—PHOTOGRAPHS
PH05466 722 (November 30, 1995) p76. "Michael J. Fox As His Trouble-Shooter"
FOX, PAUL—PHOTOGRAPHS
PH05467 637 (August 20, 1992) p17. "Natalie Merchant With Producer Paul Fox" (Granitz, Steve)
FOXWORTHY, JEFF—ILLUSTRATIONS
PH05468 746 (October 31, 1996) p73. "[Jeff Foxworthy]" (Witte, Michael)
FOXX, REDD—PHOTOGRAPHS
PH05469 619-620 (December 12, 1991) p202. "Redd Foxx (with his 'Royal Family' costar, Della Reese) Died In 'Real Life'"
FRAGO (FILM)—PHOTOGRAPHS
PH05470 730 (March 21, 1996) p104. "Frances McDormand On Duty"
FRAMES—PHOTOGRAPHS
PH05471 644 (November 26, 1992) p24. "Hansard, Noreen O'Donnell, Colm Mac Con Iomaire, Brennan, David Odlum And John Carney (from left)" (Marsden, Barry)
FRANCIS, BLACK—PHOTOGRAPHS
PH05472 616 (October 31, 1991) p13. "Black Francis, Billy Bragg And Robyn Hitchcock (from left)" (Mazur, Kevin)
PH05473 649 (February 4, 1993) p17. "One Of The Many Faces Of Frank Black" (Halsband, Michael)
PH05474 682 (May 19, 1994) p90. "Old Deal: Kim With Pixies David Lovering, Black Francis, Joey Santiago (from left)" (Blakesberg, Jay)
FRANCIS, BLACK—PHOTOGRAPHS—PORTRAITS
PH05475 652 (March 18, 1993) p15. "Ex-Pixies David Lovering, Deal, Joey Santiago, Black Francis (clockwise from left)" (Catlin, A.)
FRANKEN, AL—PHOTOGRAPHS
PH05476 750-751 (December 26, 1996) p74. "Al Franken And Arianna Huffington In Bed" (Blankenhorn, Craig)
FRANKEN, AL—PHOTOGRAPHS—PORTRAITS
PH05477 706 (April 20, 1995) p86. "'SNL' Movie Hell: Chris Farley With David Spade In 'Tommy Boy,' Al Franken With Bear In 'Stuart' And Adam Sandler With Dunces In 'Billy Madison' (from left)"
FRANKIE AND JOHNNY (FILM)—ILLUSTRATIONS
PH05478 616 (October 31, 1991) p95. "Love In A Greasy Spoon" (Risko, Robert)
FRANKIE AND JOHNNY (FILM)—PHOTOGRAPHS
PH05479 616 (October 31, 1991) p97. "Pacino And Pfeiffer Hit A Brick Wall In Love"
FRANKLIN, ADAM—PHOTOGRAPHS
PH05480 625 (March 5, 1992) p27. "Jimmy Hartridge, Graham Bonnar, Adam Franklin, Adi Vynes (from left)" (Anker, Matt)
FRANKLIN, ARETHA—ALBUMS
PH05481 645-646 (December 10, 1992) p170. "Queen Of Soul: The Atlantic Recordings"
FRANKLIN, ARETHA—PHOTOGRAPHS
PH05482 650 (February 18, 1993) p51. "Aretha Franklin 'Making Miracles' In The Studio With Wexler In 1969"
PH05483 650 (February 18, 1993) p52. "White, Franklin, Wexler And Nesuhi And Ahmet Ertegun (from left)" (Gahr, David)
PH05484 658 (June 10, 1993) p16. "Gloria Estefan, Smokey Robinson, Franklin, John (from left)" (Mazur, Kevin)
PH05485 719 (October 19, 1995) p36. "Aretha Franklin, The Fan, Backstage" (Corbijn, Anton)
PH05486 720 (November 2, 1995) p49. "Aretha Franklin & Cholly Atkins"
PH05487 724-725 (December 28, 1995) p56. "Queen of Soul Aretha Franklin" (Mazur, Kevin)
FRANKLIN, ARETHA—PHOTOGRAPHS—PORTRAITS
PH05488 643 (November 12, 1992) p155. "Aretha Franklin" (Ritts, Herb)
PH05489 680 (April 21, 1994) p33. "The Bobby Browns Greet Aretha" (Mazur, Kevin)
PH05490 692 (October 6, 1994) p50. "Aretha Franklin"
PH05491 717 (September 21, 1995) p19. "Yo, Girl, What's The 411?: The Queen Of Soul, Aretha Franklin (left), With Mary J. Blige"
FRANKLIN, BEN—ILLUSTRATIONS
PH05492 741 (August 22, 1996) p80. "[Ben Franklin]"
FRANKLIN, MELVIN—PHOTOGRAPHS—PORTRAITS
PH05493 705 (April 6, 1995) p28. "Stylish And Electrifying: Franklin"
FRANKS, REBECCA COUPE—PHOTOGRAPHS—PORTRAITS
PH05494 623 (February 6, 1992) p32. "[Rebecca Coupe Franks]" (Mundahl, Kurt)
FRANTI, MICHAEL—PHOTOGRAPHS
PH05495 684 (June 16, 1994) p30. "Franti (foreground) With Spearhead" (Miller, Michael)
PH05496 708 (May 18, 1995) p18. "Members Of Zap mama With Spearhead's Michael Franti (rear)" (Roberts, Ebet)
PH05497 733 (May 2, 1996) p20. "Buzz Clips: Spearhead's Michael Franti (below); Radioheads' Thom Yorke (above, left)"
PH05498 738-739 (July 11, 1996) p16. "Franti (left) And Ani DiFranco, Who Is An Avid Spearhead Fan" (Blakesberg, Jay)
FRANTI, MICHAEL—PHOTOGRAPHS—PORTRAITS
PH05499 700 (January 26, 1995) p24. "[Spearhead]"
FRANTION, MICHAEL—PHOTOGRAPHS
PH05500 747 (November 14, 1996) p42. "Was Spearhead's Michael Frantion On The Last Big Rap Tour?" (Baehler, Chapman)
FRANTZ, CHRIS—PHOTOGRAPHS
PH05501 637 (August 20, 1992) p9. "Fred Schneider, Kwame, Weymouth And Frantz (from left) At The 'Paper' Bash"
PH05502 638 (September 3, 1992) p11. "Weymouth, Shaun Ryder, Frantz And Paul Ryder (clockwise from lower left)" (Gershoff, Gary)
PH05503 744 (October 3, 1996) p30. "Will The Heads (above) Roll? The Band Was Sued By Byrne" (Ockenfels, Frank W.)
FRANZ, DENNIS—PHOTOGRAPHS
PH05504 744 (October 3, 1996) p78. "Now Playing"
FRASER, BRENDAN—PHOTOGRAPHS
PH05505 633 (June 25, 1992) p48. "Shore (left) And Astin Flank Cave Man Fraser"
PH05506 680 (April 21, 1994) p34. "Airheads Buscemi, Sandler And Fraser" (Wallace, Merie W.)

PH05507 682 (May 19, 1994) p106. "Higher Education For Pesci (right) And Fraser"
PH05508 689 (August 25, 1994) p97. "Rock Wanna-Be's: Sandler, Fraser, Buscemi"
FRASER, BRENDAN—PHOTOGRAPHS—PORTRAITS
PH05509 638 (September 3, 1992) pp[enc.49-50]. "[Brendan Fraser]" (Malige, Didier)
FRASER, DEAN—PHOTOGRAPHS
PH05510 702 (February 23, 1995) p19. "Front: Hatfield, Donelly, Bragg. Rear: Dean Fraser, Gary Smith, Sean Slade" (Robicheau, Paul)
FRAZER, ELIZABETH—PHOTOGRAPHS
PH05511 680 (April 21, 1994) p30. "Trilling Singer: Cocteau Twin Elizabeth Fraser" (Diamond, Rick)
FREAKWATER—PHOTOGRAPHS
PH05512 686-687 (July 14, 1994) p74. "Erwin, Bean, Touring Member Bob Egan And Gay (from left); Mascot Matthew Bean-Rizzo (front)" (Elledge, Paul)
FREDERIKSEN, LARS—PHOTOGRAPHS
PH05513 716 (September 7, 1995) p56. "Frederiksen And Armstrong Perfect The Art Of Speed Skanking At A Milwaukee Gig" (Garrity, Brian)
PH05514 716 (September 7, 1995) pp54-55. "Rancid: Lars Frederiksen, Tim Armstrong, Brett Reed, Matt Freeman (clock-wise from top left)" (Vadukul, Nitin)
PH05515 726 (January 25, 1996) p38. "Rancid's Tim Armstrong (left) And Lars Frederiksen" (Garrity, Brian)
FREDERIKSEN, LARS—PHOTOGRAPHS—PORTRAITS
PH05516 701 (February 9, 1995) p29. "Mohawk Nation: Reed, Freeman, Armstrong And Frederiksen (from left)" (Muller, Michael)
FREE WILLY (FILM)—PHOTOGRAPHS
PH05517 659 (June 24, 1993) p88. "Tears: 'Free Willy,' With A Boy And A Whale"
FREEDMAN, SAMUEL G.—PHOTOGRAPHS
PH05518 632 (June 11, 1992) p183. "Freedman With The Elders Of A Church In Sebokeng" (Katzenstein, David)
FREEDOM (VIDEO)—PHOTOGRAPHS
PH05519 677 (March 10, 1994) p19. "Freedom Fighter: Rage's De La Rocha Hopes President Clinton Will Pay Attention" (Gougenheim, Kim)
FREEMAN, HEATHER—PHOTOGRAPHS
PH05520 652 (March 18, 1993) pp[enc.35]. "Hilary Wall, Julie French And Heather Freeman" (Seliger, Mark)
PH05521 652 (March 18, 1993) pp[enc.36]. "Kevin Astle And Heather Freeman" (Seliger, Mark)
FREEMAN, MATT—PHOTOGRAPHS
PH05522 716 (September 7, 1995) pp54-55. "Rancid: Lars Frederiksen, Tim Armstrong, Brett Reed, Matt Freeman (clock-wise from top left)" (Vadukul, Nitin)
FREEMAN, MATT—PHOTOGRAPHS—PORTRAITS
PH05523 701 (February 9, 1995) p29. "Mohawk Nation: Reed, Freeman, Armstrong And Frederiksen (from left)" (Muller, Michael)
FREEMAN, MORGAN—PHOTOGRAPHS
PH05524 692 (October 6, 1994) p81. "Morgan Freeman And Tim Robbins Plot An Escape"
PH05525 731 (April 4, 1996) p66. "Freeman, 'Seven'"
PH05526 738-739 (July 11, 1996) p98. "Robin Wright Relies On Morgan Freeman"
FREESE, JOSH—PHOTOGRAPHS
PH05527 730 (March 21, 1996) p17. "Beck, Devo's Mark Mothersbaugh, Bob Casale, Josh Freese, Bob Mothersbaugh, Jerry Casale" (Anderson, Vera)
FREEWHEELERS—PHOTOGRAPHS
PH05528 622 (January 23, 1992) p14. "Clockwise From Top Left: Davel Sobel, Luther Russell, Chris Joyner, John Hofer, Jason Hiller" (Annalisa)
FREEZIN', PETE—PHOTOGRAPHS
PH05529 616 (October 31, 1991) p11. "Greg Smith, Pete Freezin', Alice Cooper And Stef Burns (from left)" (Mazur, Kevin)
FREHLEY, ACE—PHOTOGRAPHS
PH05530 727 (February 8, 1996) p18. "Gene Simmons, Peter Criss And Ace Frehley (from left) Rode 'Kiss Alive!' To Stardom In 1975 And Scored A Second Hit Concert Album With 'Kiss Alive II' In 1977" (Putland, Michael)
PH05531 732 (April 18, 1996) p19. "Ace Frehley, Paul Stanley, 2Pac, Peter Criss And Gene Simmons (from left)" (Mazur, Kevin)
PH05532 736 (June 13, 1996) p52. "Kiss Come Back With Their Makeup Intact: Ace Frehley, Gene Simmons, Peter Criss And Paul Stanley" (Malluk, Eddie)
FRENCH KISS (FILM)—PHOTOGRAPHS
PH05533 708 (May 18, 1995) p96. "Meg Ryan Mixes It Up With French Kisser Kevin Kline"
FRENCH, JULIE—PHOTOGRAPHS
PH05534 652 (March 18, 1993) pp[enc.35]. "Hilary Wall, Julie French And Heather Freeman" (Seliger, Mark)
FRENTE—ALBUMS
PH05535 681 (May 5, 1994) p60. "Labour Of Love"
FRENTE—PHOTOGRAPHS—PORTRAITS
PH05536 684 (June 16, 1994) p30. "Simon Austin, Angie Hart, Alistair Barden And Tim O' Connor (from left)" (Westenberg, Kevin)
FRESH (FILM)—PHOTOGRAPHS
PH05537 690 (September 8, 1994) p87. "Drug Runner Nelson Plays Chess With Dad Jackson"
FRESH FLY FLAVOR (BOOK)—PHOTOGRAPHS
PH05538 645-646 (December 10, 1992) p88. "[Fresh Fly Flavor]"
FRESH PRINCE—PHOTOGRAPHS
PH05539 672-673 (December 23, 1993) p174. "[Six Degrees Of Separation]"
FREY, GLENN—ILLUSTRATIONS
PH05540 641 (October 15, 1992) p157. "[Don Henley, Glenn Frey]" (Russo, Anthony)
PH05541 697 (December 15, 1994) p92. "Glen Frey And Don Henley" (Cowles, David)
FREY, GLENN—PHOTOGRAPHS
PH05542 685 (June 30, 1994) p23. "Birds Of A Feather: Joe Walsh, Timothy B. Schmit, Don Henley, Don Felder And Glenn Frey (from left)"
PH05543 686-687 (July 14, 1994) p36. "Frey (left) And Henley in Eagles' Hell" (Granitz, Steve)
PH05544 698-699 (December 29, 1994) p55. "Glenn Frey (left) And Don Henley" (Mazur, Kevin)
FRIDMANN, DAVE—PHOTOGRAPHS
PH05545 664 (September 2, 1993) p24. "They're All Revved Up: Donahue, Thorpe, Baker, Chambers, Fridmann And Grasshopper (from left)" (Gullick, Steve)
FRIEDMAN, KINKY—ALBUMS
PH05546 656 (May 13, 1993) p107. "Old Testaments And New Revelations"
FRIEND, SIMON—PHOTOGRAPHS
PH05547 630 (May 14, 1992) p32. "The Levellers (from left): Friend, Sevink, Chadwick, Heather And Cunningham" (Doove, Hester)
FRIENDS (TELEVISION SHOW)—ILLUSTRATIONS
PH05548 711 (June 29, 1995) p10. "It's Friends!" (Pendergrast, James T.)
PH05549 750-751 (December 26, 1996) p82. "[Friends]" (Friedman, Drew)
FRIENDS (TELEVISION SHOW)—PHOTOGRAPHS
PH05550 692 (October 6, 1994) p93. "Gen X "Friends": Postcollege, Pre-"Seinfeld""
PH05551 708 (May 18, 1995) p64. "Hey, Hey, Where's The Monkey? (Marcel Is Leaving)"
PH05552 720 (November 2, 1995) p17. "[Friends]"
FRIPP, ROBERT—ALBUMS
PH05553 670 (November 25, 1993) p114. "The First Day"

FRIPP, ROBERT—PHOTOGRAPHS
PH05554 655 (April 29, 1993) p20. "The Great Deceivers: John Wetton, David Cross, Fripp And Bill Bruford (from left)"
PH05555 655 (April 29, 1993) p20. "Guitar Craftsman Fripp" (Westenberg, Kevin)
FRIPP, ROBERT—PHOTOGRAPHS—PORTRAITS
PH05556 684 (June 16, 1994) p18. "Belew, Fripp, Bruford And Levin"
FRISA, DAN—PHOTOGRAPHS—PORTRAITS
PH05557 746 (October 31, 1996) p59. "Dan Frisa"
FRISCHMANN, JUSTINE—PHOTOGRAPHS
PH05558 678 (March 24, 1994) p21. "Elastica With Frischmann (front)" (Paton, Tim)
PH05559 707 (May 4, 1995) p23. "Donna Matthews, Justine Frischmann, Annie Holland And Justin Welch (from left)" (Camp, E. J.)
PH05560 707 (May 4, 1995) p23. "Matthews (left), Frischmann In Manchester, England, '93" (Hening, Lu)
PH05561 712-713 (July 13, 1995) p25. "Hey Who's Working The Door?" (Aguiar, Mariah)
PH05562 723 (December 14, 1995) p28. "Justin Welch, Justine Frischmann And MTV's Daisy Fuentes (from left)" (Mazur, Kevin)
PH05563 726 (January 25, 1996) p44. "Justine Frischmann" (Bell, Colin)
FRISELL, BILL—ALBUMS
PH05564 656 (May 13, 1993) p107. "Have A Little Faith"
FROBERG, RICK—PHOTOGRAPHS
PH05565 689 (August 25, 1994) p44. "All Together Now: Trombino, Atom, Kennedy, Reis, N.D., Petey X, Apollo 9, Froberg (from left)" (Cuffaro, Chris)
FROGS—PHOTOGRAPHS
PH05566 689 (August 25, 1994) p24. "Pumpkins' Corgan Joins The Frogs' Damien Strigens And Jimmy Fleming" (Blakesberg, Jay)
FROM DUSK TILL DAWN (FILM)—PHOTOGRAPHS
PH05567 718 (October 5, 1995) p76. "Pulp To Come"
PH05568 728 (February 22, 1996) p70. "Now Playing"
FROM THE JOURNALS OF JEAN SEBERG (FILM)—PHOTOGRAPHS
PH05569 730 (March 21, 1996) p104. "Hurt (left) Reflects On Seberg As Saint Joan"
FRUSCIANTE, JOHN—PHOTOGRAPHS
PH05570 629 (April 30, 1992) p23. "John Frusciante, Anthony Kiedis, Chad Smith And Flea (from left)" (Cuffaro, Chris)
F.S.K.—PHOTOGRAPHS
PH05571 686-687 (July 14, 1994) p79. "[F.S.K.]"
FUCHS, MICHAEL—PHOTOGRAPHS—PORTRAITS
PH05572 714 (August 10, 1995) p24. "The Players: Michael Fuchs (left)" (Bauer, Randy)
FUENTES, DAISY—PHOTOGRAPHS
PH05573 723 (December 14, 1995) p28. "Justin Welch, Justine Frischmann And MTV's Daisy Fuentes (from left)" (Mazur, Kevin)
FUGAZI—ALBUMS
PH05574 666 (September 30, 1993) p106. "In On The Kill Taker"
PH05575 712-713 (July 13, 1995) p109. "Red Medicine"
FUGAZI—PHOTOGRAPHS
PH05576 633 (June 25, 1992) p18. "Guy Picciotto" (Callahan, Kristin)
PH05577 670 (November 25, 1993) p33. "Ian MacKaye Flanked By Guy Piciotto (left) And Joe Lally" (Mazur, Kevin)
PH05578 744 (October 3, 1996) p19. "Mackaye (left) Points In The General Direction Of Guitarist Guy Picciotto" (Fine, Sean)
FUGEES—ALBUMS
PH05579 730 (March 21, 1996) p96. "The Score"
FUGEES—ILLUSTRATIONS
PH05580 733 (May 2, 1996) p72. "They Shoot! They Score! Fugees!" (Hungry Dog Studio)
PH05581 745 (October 17, 1996) p24. "[Fugees]" (Pendergrast, James T.)
FUGEES—PHOTOGRAPHS
PH05582 729 (March 7, 1996) p14. "The Fugees Channel The Ghetto Vibe: Clef Jean, Pras Michel And Lauryn Hill (from left)" (Keeling, Jason)
PH05583 734 (May 16, 1996) p66. "Rappin' At The House Of Blues: Fugees' Hill, Jean And Michel (from left)" (Kravitz, Jeff)
PH05584 742 (September 5, 1996) pp[cover]. "Are The Fugees The Future Of Rock & Roll?" (Rolston, Matthew)
PH05585 742 (September 5, 1996) p44. "Fugees At The Tibetan Freedom Concert, In San Francisco" (Mazur, Kevin)
PH05586 742 (September 5, 1996) pp40-41. "Prakazrel Michel, Lauryn Hill, Wyclef Jean" (Rolston, Matthew)
PH05587 750-751 (December 26, 1996) p70. "The Smokin' Grooves Tour: The Fugees Killed Us Softly With Their Beats" (Blakesberg, Jay)
THE FUGITIVE (FILM)—PHOTOGRAPHS
PH05588 663 (August 19, 1993) p84. "Harrison Ford (right) Puts A '90s Twist On A '60s TV Series, Starring David Janssen (left)"
PH05589 665 (September 16, 1993) p77. "Best Supporting Actor"
PH05590 678 (March 24, 1994) p100. "Oscar's Choices: 'Schindler's List,' 'The Piano,' 'The Remains Of the Day,' 'In The Name Of The Father,' 'The Fugitive' (from left)"
PH05591 680 (April 21, 1994) p96. "The Fugitive"
THE FUGITIVE (TELEVISION SHOW)—PHOTOGRAPHS
PH05592 663 (August 19, 1993) p84. "Harrison Ford (right) Puts A '90s Twist On A '60s TV Series, Starring David Janssen (left)"
FUGS—ALBUMS
PH05593 670 (November 25, 1993) p112. "The Fugs First Album"
FULSON, LOWELL—PHOTOGRAPHS
PH05594 697 (December 15, 1994) p20. "Steve Cropper, King And Lowell Fulson Pay Tribute To Dixon (from left)" (Mosenfelder, Tim)
FUN (FILM)—PHOTOGRAPHS
PH05595 707 (May 4, 1995) p74. "Humphrey, Witt ('Fun')"
FUN LOVIN' CRIMINALS—ALBUMS
PH05596 731 (April 4, 1996) p60. "Come Find Yourself"
FUN LOVIN' CRIMINALS—PHOTOGRAPHS
PH05597 736 (June 13, 1996) p25. "Three Fun-Lovin' Guys: Fast, Huey And Steve (from left)" (Johnson, Eric)
PH05598 746 (October 31, 1996) p28. "Whacked For 'Scooby Snacks': Fun Lovin' Criminals Fast, Huey And Steve (from left)" (Tobiishi, Tsukasa)
FUN-DA-MENTAL—PHOTOGRAPHS
PH05599 694 (November 3, 1994) p40. "A Fun-Da-Mental Counter to Racism" (Bright, Matt)
THE FUNERAL (FILM)—PHOTOGRAPHS
PH05600 747 (November 14, 1996) p126. "Gretchen Mol Mourns Vincent Gallo"
FUNKADELIC—ALBUMS
PH05601 617 (November 14, 1991) p144. "Cosmic Slop" (Bell, Pedro)
PH05602 617 (November 14, 1991) p144. "Cosmic Slop" (Bell, Bruse)
PH05603 617 (November 14, 1991) p149. "Hardcore Jollies" (Clinton, George)
PH05604 617 (November 14, 1991) p149. "Hardcore Jollies" (Bell, Pedro)
FUNKI PORCINI—ALBUMS
PH05605 748 (November 28, 1996) p136. "Love, Pussycats And Carwrecks"
FUNNY BONES (FILM)—PHOTOGRAPHS
PH05606 706 (April 20, 1995) p88. "Jerry Lewis And Oliver Platt Do Battle"
FUR—PHOTOGRAPHS
PH05607 705 (April 6, 1995) p23. "Mosh City: Fur (above) And The Mark Of Cain (below)" (Mott, Tony)

FURAR, TOMMY—PHOTOGRAPHS
PH05608 721 (November 16, 1995) p100. "Loud Lucy: Furar, Lane And Doyle (from left)" (GS, Jamil)
PH05609 721 (November 16, 1995) p104. "Loud Lucy: Tommy Furar" (GS, Jamil)
FURLONG, EDWARD—PHOTOGRAPHS
PH05610 658 (June 10, 1993) p74. "Jailbird Bridges Finds A Son To Protect In Furlong"
PH05611 730 (March 21, 1996) p106. ""Before" (from left): Neeson, Furlong And Streep"
FURSE, ELIZABETH—PHOTOGRAPHS—PORTRAITS
PH05612 642 (October 29, 1992) p46. "[Elizabeth Furse]"
FUTURE SOUND OF LONDON—PHOTOGRAPHS
PH05613 721 (November 16, 1995) p73. "Brian Dougans (left) And Gary Cobain: Future Shock And Techno Reflections" (Broad, Julian)

G

G—PHOTOGRAPHS
PH05614 676 (February 24, 1994) p24. "Spank Dog, Money Mike, Mr. Watts, Peter Jorge, D-Smooth, G (from left)" (Hastings, Daniel)
G. LOVE—ALBUMS
PH05615 684 (June 16, 1994) p108. "G. Love And Special Sauce"
GABAY, YUVAL—PHOTOGRAPHS—PORTRAITS
PH05616 735 (May 30, 1996) p21. "Frontman M. Doughty, Sebastian Steinberg, Mark De Gli Antoni And Yuval Gabay" (Vadukul, Nitin)
GABLER, MILT—PHOTOGRAPHS
PH05617 649 (February 4, 1993) p56. "[Milt Gabler]"
PH05618 651 (March 4, 1993) p18. "Billy Crystal Presenting The Award To His Uncle Milt Gabler" (Mazur, Kevin)
GABOR, EVA—PHOTOGRAPHS—PORTRAITS
PH05619 666 (September 30, 1993) p116. "Out Of This World 'Green Acres' (left)"
GABOURY, DENNIS—PHOTOGRAPHS
PH05620 669 (November 11, 1993) p54. "Gaboury Today (above): I Tried 'To Reach Out To The Church, But It Was Futile.'" (Hom, Marc)
GABOURY, DENNIS—PHOTOGRAPHS—PORTRAITS
PH05621 669 (November 11, 1993) p54. "Innocence Crushed: Dennis Gaboury (right) In The Early 1960s, When He Believed That Being An Alter Boy Was A Privilege"
GABRELS, REEVES—PHOTOGRAPHS
PH05622 622 (January 23, 1992) p7. "Brad Whitford, David Bowie, Steven Tyler, Hunt Sales, Tony Sales, Reeves Gabrels, Joey Kramer" (McAlpine, Paul)
GABRELS, REEVES—PHOTOGRAPHS—PORTRAITS
PH05623 616 (October 31, 1991) p76. "David Bowie, Hunt Sales, Tony Sales And Reeves Gabrels (from left)" (Uchitel, Diego)
PH05624 616 (October 31, 1991) pp74-75. "[Tim Machine]" (Uchitel, Diego)
GABRIEL, PETER—ALBUMS
PH05625 617 (November 14, 1991) p124. "Peter Gabriel" (Thorgerson, Strom)
PH05626 617 (November 14, 1991) p124. "Peter Gabriel" (Powell, Aubrey)
PH05627 640 (October 1, 1992) p63. "Us"
PH05628 693 (October 20, 1994) p142. "Secret World Live"
GABRIEL, PETER—ILLUSTRATIONS
PH05629 663 (August 19, 1993) p3. "Peter Gabriel" (Burke, Philip)
GABRIEL, PETER—PHOTOGRAPHS
PH05630 617 (November 14, 1991) p13. "Lanois (left) And Gabriel" (Hildenhagen, Michael)
PH05631 619-620 (December 12, 1991) p39. "Sting, Sinead O'Connor, Peter Gabriel (from left)" (Linsen, M.)
PH05632 648 (January 21, 1993) p11. "Baez, Gabriel, Richie Havens And Stipe (from left) At The Reebok Awards" (Robicheau, Paul)
PH05633 653 (April 1, 1993) p11. "Gabriel" (Hutchson, Mick)
PH05634 654 (April 15, 1993) p11. "Best New Artist Arrested Development With Peter Gabriel (second from right)" (Mazur, Kevin)
PH05635 657 (May 27, 1993) p25. "[Peter Gabriel]" (Mazur, Kevin)
PH05636 663 (August 19, 1993) p9. "[Peter Gabriel]" (Mahurin, Matt)
PH05637 663 (August 19, 1993) p10. "The Wizard Of Odds At A Recent New York Show" (Mazur, Kevin)
PH05638 667 (October 14, 1993) p66. "Gabriel: 'Sledgehammer' Pounded The Competition With Its Outrageous And Zany Animation"
PH05639 667 (October 14, 1993) p67. "Personal Trainer: Johnson Outfits Gabriel"
PH05640 668 (October 28, 1993) p24. "Gabriel: Showing Real World Roots" (Capak, R. J.)
PH05641 672-673 (December 23, 1993) p65. "[Peter Gabriel]" (Natkin, Paul)
PH05642 674 (January 27, 1994) p29. "Gabriel, Merchant And Odetta In Boston" (Robicheau, Paul)
PH05643 685 (June 30, 1994) p29. "WOMAD Ringleader Peter Gabriel" (Blakesberg, Jay)
PH05644 691 (September 22, 1994) p19. "Gabriel, Kidjo And Marsalis (from left)" (Smith, Robert)
PH05645 701 (February 9, 1995) p16. "Gabriel Honors Rose-Anne Auguste Of Haiti" (Robicheau, Paul)
GABRIEL, PETER—PHOTOGRAPHS—PORTRAITS
PH05646 639 (September 17, 1992) p27. "[Peter Gabriel]" (Schienmann, David)
PH05647 645-646 (December 10, 1992) p79. "The Introspective Gabriel" (Beukers, Alan)
GACY BUNCH—PHOTOGRAPHS
PH05648 697 (December 15, 1994) p17. "Clowin' Around: Gacy Fans McCready (left) And Staley" (Mercer, Lance)
GAHAN, DAVE—ILLUSTRATIONS
PH05649 670 (November 25, 1993) p5. "Depeche Mode's Dave Gahan" (Burke, Philip)
GAHAN, DAVE—PHOTOGRAPHS
PH05650 670 (November 25, 1993) p94. "1982: Fletcher, Gahan, Gore And Wilder (from left)"
PH05651 670 (November 25, 1993) p94. "1985: Gore, Wilder, Gahan And Fletcher (clockwise from left)" (Nosotti, Fabio)
PH05652 670 (November 25, 1993) p92. "In Madrid, Making Their Last Record: Gahan, Gore, Wilder, Fletcher (from left)" (Corbijn, Anton)
PH05653 670 (November 25, 1993) pp90-91. "Mode Indigo: Depeche's Lead Singer, Dave Gahan (right)..." (Watson, Albert)
PH05654 670 (November 25, 1993) p96. "Paint It Black: Gahan Sings 'Walking In My Shoes' On The Current Tour, In Zurich" (Corbijn, Anton)
PH05655 718 (October 5, 1995) p26. "On The Mend: Dave Gahan Of Depeche Mode" (Gehring, Karl A.)
PH05656 724-725 (December 28, 1995) p51. "Singer Gahan In Less Miserable Times" (Gehring, Karl A.)
PH05657 738-739 (July 11, 1996) p20. "Gahan: Hospitalized Once Again" (Slattery, Paul)
GAHAN, DAVE—PHOTOGRAPHS—PORTRAITS
PH05658 696 (December 1, 1994) p25. "[Joan Jett & Dave Gahan]" (Williamson, Tucker)
GAINES, JEFFREY—PHOTOGRAPHS—PORTRAITS
PH05659 629 (April 30, 1992) p31. "[Jeffrey Gaines]" (Feingold, Deborah)
GAINES, REG E.—ILLUSTRATIONS
PH05660 684 (June 16, 1994) p108. "[Reg E. Gaines]"

(Steinberg, James)
GAINES, WILLIAM—PHOTOGRAPHS
PH05661 636 (August 6, 1992) p46. "[William M. Gaines]" (Cantor, David)
PH05662 645-646 (December 10, 1992) p102. "[William Gaines]" (Sterkel, Mark P.)
GAITHER, TOMMY—PHOTOGRAPHS—PORTRAITS
PH05663 659 (June 24, 1993) p48. "The Orioles: Sonny Til, Johnny Reed, Tommy Gaither, George Nelson And Alexander Sharp"
GALACTIC COWBOYS—PHOTOGRAPHS
PH05664 617 (November 14, 1991) p34. "Ben Huggins, Alan Doss, Monty Colvin And Dane Sonnier (from left)" (Carter, Keith)
GALAS, DIAMANDA—ALBUMS
PH05665 633 (June 25, 1992) p44. "The Singer"
GALAXIE 500—ALBUMS
PH05666 747 (November 14, 1996) p116. "Galaxie 500"
GALAXIE 500—PHOTOGRAPHS
PH05667 746 (October 31, 1996) p27. "This Is Their Music: Rykodisc Releases A Galaxie 500 Box Set"
GALLAGHER, HUGH—PHOTOGRAPHS
PH05668 655 (April 29, 1993) pp44-45. "[MTV]" (Seliger, Mark)
GALLAGHER, LIAM—ILLUSTRATIONS
PH05669 708 (May 18, 1995) p11. "Oasis' Liam Gallagher" (Burke, Philip)
GALLAGHER, LIAM—PHOTOGRAPHS
PH05670 691 (September 22, 1994) p37. "Arthurs, McCarroll, Liam Gallagher, McGuigan, Noel Gallagher (from left)"
PH05671 697 (December 15, 1994) p38. "Oasis Lead Singer Liam Gallagher" (Capak, R. J.)
PH05672 718 (October 5, 1995) p34. "White, Arthurs, Liam Gallagher, Noel Gallagher, McGuigan (from left)" (Jones, Michael Spenser)
PH05673 727 (February 8, 1996) p13. "The Brothers Grim: Liam (left) And Noel Gallagher Of Oasis" (Hole, Danny)
PH05674 731 (April 4, 1996) p18. "[Liam Gallagher & Patsy Kensit]" (Murray, Andrew)
PH05675 733 (May 2, 1996) p34. "Liam And Arthurs (right) Onstage In ;95" (Rasic, Brian)
PH05676 733 (May 2, 1996) p35. "Liam Catches Up On His Reading, Early '95" (Sheehan, Tom)
PH05677 733 (May 2, 1996) p35. "Liam Pays His Respects At The Brit Awards In February" (Hogan, Dave)
PH05678 733 (May 2, 1996) p35. "Noel, Liam And Hutchence (from left) At Awards" (Fisher, David)
PH05679 735 (May 30, 1996) p13. "[Bono & Liam Gallagher]"
PH05680 737 (June 27, 1996) p16. "Liam Gallagher (left) Of Oasis And Albarn"
PH05681 749 (December 12, 1996) p20. "[Liam Gallagher]" (Fenton, Steve)
GALLAGHER, LIAM—PHOTOGRAPHS—PORTRAITS
PH05682 708 (May 18, 1995) pp50-51. "Noel Gallagher—Liam Gallagher" (Bailey, David)
PH05683 733 (May 2, 1996) p33. "[Liam Gallagher]" (Robathon, Peter)
PH05684 745 (October 17, 1996) p42. "[Liam Gallagher]" (Pope, Pat)
GALLAGHER, NOEL—PHOTOGRAPHS
PH05685 691 (September 22, 1994) p37. "Arthurs, McCarroll, Liam Gallagher, McGuigan, Noel Gallagher (from left)"
PH05686 718 (October 5, 1995) p34. "White, Arthurs, Liam Gallagher, Noel Gallagher, McGuigan (from left)" (Jones, Michael Spenser)
PH05687 724-725 (December 28, 1995) p63. "Noel Gallagher Shook Things Up In November"
PH05688 727 (February 8, 1996) p13. "The Brothers Grim: Liam (left) And Noel Gallagher Of Oasis" (Hole, Danny)
PH05689 733 (May 2, 1996) p34. "McGuigan, White And Noel (from left)" (Goldberg, Nathaniel)
PH05690 733 (May 2, 1996) p35. "Noel, Liam And Hutchence (from left) At Awards" (Fisher, David)
GALLAGHER, NOEL—PHOTOGRAPHS—PORTRAITS
PH05691 708 (May 18, 1995) pp50-51. "Noel Gallagher—Liam Gallagher" (Bailey, David)
PH05692 733 (May 2, 1996) p32. "[Noel Gallagher]" (Robathon, Peter)
PH05693 749 (December 12, 1996) p25. "Just Say Noel" (Double, Steve)
GALLAGHER, PETER—PHOTOGRAPHS
PH05694 629 (April 30, 1992) p64. "Mill Watches Rival Larry Levy (Peter Gallagher)"
PH05695 708 (May 18, 1995) p98. "Alison Elliott And Peter Gallagher Conspire"
GALLAGHER, RORY—PHOTOGRAPHS
PH05696 714 (August 10, 1995) p32. "[Rory Gallagher]" (Rider, Paul)
GALLO, VINCENT—PHOTOGRAPHS
PH05697 747 (November 14, 1996) p126. "Gretchen Mol Mourns Vincent Gallo"
GALLUP, SIMON—PHOTOGRAPHS
PH05698 631 (May 28, 1992) p11. "Simon Gallup, Porl Thompson, Perry Bamonte, Robert Smith, Boris Williams (from left)" (Cox, Paul)
PH05699 633 (June 25, 1992) p12. "The Cure's Simon Gallup, Perry Bamonte And Smith (from left)" (Elgar, Nick)
PH05700 733 (May 2, 1996) p22. "Partial To Shades: The Cure's New Lineup Is Simon Gallup, Roger O'Donnell, Robert Smith, Perry Bamonte And Jason Cooper (from left)" (Cox, Paul)
GAMBLE, ROBERT—PHOTOGRAPHS
PH05701 718 (October 5, 1995) p64. "Public Defender Robert Gamble At The Arraignment Of Cheek And Hudgins (from left)" (Beckner, Greg)
GANE, TIM—PHOTOGRAPHS
PH05702 731 (April 4, 1996) p40. "Always The Same, Always Different: Stereolab's Mary Hansen, Tim Gane, Laetitia Sadier And Morgane Lhote (from left)" (Perou, Ralph)
GANG STARR—ALBUMS
PH05703 634-635 (July 9, 1992) p105. "Daily Operation"
PH05704 683 (June 2, 1994) p70. "Hard To Earn"
PH05705 698-699 (December 29, 1994) p173. "Hard To Earn"
GANG STARR—PHOTOGRAPHS
PH05706 695 (November 17, 1994) p87. "Gang Starr" (Irish, Len)
GANG STARR—PHOTOGRAPHS—PORTRAITS
PH05707 682 (May 19, 1994) p30. "Back To The Razzmatazz: DJ Premier (left) And Guru Return To Their Roots" (Seliger, Mark)
GANO, GORDON—PHOTOGRAPHS
PH05708 665 (September 16, 1993) p32. "Gano, Lou Reed And Penn Jillette" (Capak, R. J.)
GARAGIOLA, JOE—PHOTOGRAPHS
PH05709 747 (November 14, 1996) p76. "Joe Garagiola, Larry And Herb Cohen (from left) In 1988"
GARBAGE—ALBUMS
PH05710 717 (September 21, 1995) p82. "Garbage"
GARBAGE—ILLUSTRATIONS
PH05711 717 (September 21, 1995) p82. "Garbage Strike" (Ascencios, N.)
PH05712 748 (November 28, 1996) p22. "Experimental Realms" (Pendergrast, James T.)
GARBAGE—PHOTOGRAPHS
PH05713 718 (October 5, 1995) p23. "Trash Is Where It's At: Erikson, Marker, Vig, Manson (clockwise from left)" (Ockenfels, Frank W.)
PH05714 745 (October 17, 1996) p78. "I Have Bent Over Backward For You People" (Seliger, Mark)

PH05715 Number not assigned.
GARCIA, ANDY—PHOTOGRAPHS
PH05716 652 (March 18, 1993) pp[enc.4]. "[Jennifer 8]"
PH05717 682 (May 19, 1994) p107. "Stormy Triangle Garcia, Ryan And Booze"
PH05718 719 (October 19, 1995) p158. "Andy Garcia Sweet-Talks Gabrielle Anwar Into Danger"
GARCIA, CAROLYN—PHOTOGRAPHS
PH05719 740 (August 8, 1996) p35. "Egypt, September 1978" (Boot, Adrian)
GARCIA, JERRY—ALBUMS
PH05720 617 (November 14, 1991) p137. "Cats Under The Stars" (Kelly-Mouse Studios)
PH05721 672-673 (December 23, 1993) p151. "Not For Kids Only"
GARCIA, JERRY—ILLUSTRATIONS
PH05722 641 (October 15, 1992) p181. "[Jerry Garcia]" (Woolley, Janet)
PH05723 717 (September 21, 1995) p11. "[Jerry Garcia]" (Burke, Philip)
PH05724 717 (September 21, 1995) p104. "Requiescat In Pace"
PH05725 717 (September 21, 1995) p32. "A Timely Tribute From Central Africa"
PH05726 720 (November 2, 1995) p12. "Still Grateful" (Pendergrast, James T.)
PH05727 743 (September 19, 1996) p12. "Not Perfect, Still Grateful" (Pendergrast, James T.)
GARCIA, JERRY—ILLUSTRATIONS—LETTERING
PH05728 616 (October 31, 1991) p34. "Jerry Garcia: The Rolling Stone Interview By James Henke" (Ortiz-Lopez, Dennis)
GARCIA, JERRY—ILLUSTRATIONS—PORTRAITS
PH05729 740 (August 8, 1996) pp[cover]. "Exclusive: The Secret Life Of Jerry Garcia" (Davis, Paul)
GARCIA, JERRY—PHOTOGRAPHS
PH05730 616 (October 31, 1991) p40. "Bill Kreutzmann, Ron "Pigpen" McKernan, Bob Weir, Garcia And Phil Lesh (clockwise from top left) In 1966" (Greene, Herb)
PH05731 616 (October 31, 1991) p40. "Jerry Garcia And Mountain Girl At Golden Gate Park In 1968" (Greene, Herb)
PH05732 619-620 (December 12, 1991) p102. "Graham And Jerry Garcia At One Of The Dead's 'Farewell' Concerts In 1974" (Leibovitz, Annie)
PH05733 619-620 (December 12, 1991) p29. "Jerry Garcia, Artist Extraordinaire" (Adaskaveg, Michael)
PH05734 619-620 (December 12, 1991) p103. "Phil Lesh, Bob Weir, Neil Young And Jerry Garcia (from left) Pay Tribute To Bill Graham" (Blakesberg, Jay)
PH05735 645-646 (December 10, 1992) p77. "A Preexhaustion Jerry Garcia" (Blakesberg, Jay)
PH05736 648 (January 21, 1993) p20. "The New And Improved Garcia" (Caudle, Todd)
PH05737 655 (April 29, 1993) p24. "Garcia And Hart At The Library Of Congress" (Mazur, Kevin)
PH05738 656 (May 13, 1993) p13. "Garcia: Art And The Artist" (Capak, R. J.)
PH05739 657 (May 27, 1993) p9. "Oh Say Can You See?: The Dead's Vince Welnick, Bob Weir And Jerry Garcia" (Blakesberg, Jay)
PH05740 660-661 (July 8, 1993) p29. "The Dead's Phil Lesh, Bob Weir And Jerry Garcia (from left)" (Blakesberg, Jay)
PH05741 664 (September 2, 1993) p46. "The Dead At Rest in 1966: Phil Lesh, Bill Kreutzman, Ron 'Pigpen' McKernan, Bob Weir And Jerry Garcia (clockwise from left)" (Greene, Herb)
PH05742 664 (September 2, 1993) p43. "[Jerry Garcia]" (Seliger, Mark)
PH05743 664 (September 2, 1993) pp[cover]. "Jerry Garcia: The Road Goes On Forever" (Seliger, Mark)
PH05744 676 (February 24, 1994) p46. "The Early Grateful Dead (clockwise from left): Jerry Garcia, Bill Kreutzmann, Ron 'Pigpen' McKernan, Bob Weir, Percussionist Mickey Hart And Phil Lesh" (Marshall, Jim)
PH05745 679 (April 7, 1994) p38. "The Garcias" (Frost, Frankie)
PH05746 691 (September 22, 1994) p20. "[Jerry Garcia & Deborah Koons]" (Ferreira, Albert)
PH05747 696 (December 1, 1994) p24. "Bob Weir, Lesh And Garcia (from left)" (Blakesberg, Jay)
PH05748 717 (September 21, 1995) p52. "Before The Dead, They Were The Warlocks" (Greene, Herbi)
PH05749 717 (September 21, 1995) p78. "Bringing In The Sheaves: Jerry Garcia Plays In A Field Of Wheat Outside Indianapolis In June 1993" (Seliger, Mark)
PH05750 717 (September 21, 1995) p71. "A Couple Of Good-Time Pirates: Garcia (left) With Pigpen In 1967" (Marshall, Jim)
PH05751 717 (September 21, 1995) p54. "The Dead In '66 At The Crossroads, the Corner Of Haight And Ashbury: Garcia, Pigpen, Lesh, Weir, Kreutzmann (from left)" (Greene, Herbi)
PH05752 717 (September 21, 1995) p65. "The Dead In Front Of Their Ashbury St. House, 1967: Jerry Garcia, Ron 'Pigpen' McKernan, Bob Weir, Phil Lesh, Co-Managers Danny Rifkin And Rock Scully, And Bill Kreutzmann..."
PH05753 717 (September 21, 1995) p31. "Dylan And Garcia, Oakland Coliseum, 1987" (Blakesberg, Jay)
PH05754 717 (September 21, 1995) p24. "Garcia At Three Rivers Stadium, In Pittsburgh, June 30, 1995" (Rieker, Edward)
PH05755 717 (September 21, 1995) p50. "Garcia Plays A Show At The Las Vegas Silver Bowl, May 1993" (Blakesberg, Jay)
PH05756 717 (September 21, 1995) p75. "Grisman, Jim Kerwin, Garcia, Joe Craven (from left) In San Francisco, 1991" (Millman, Susana)
PH05757 717 (September 21, 1995) p45. "[Jerry Garcia]" (Greene, Herbi)
PH05758 717 (September 21, 1995) pp[unnumbered]. "[Jerry Garcia]" (Leibovitz, Annie)
PH05759 717 (September 21, 1995) p67. "Jerry Garcia, Phil Lesh, Bill Kreutzmann, Bob Weir And Ron 'Pigpen' McKernan (clockwise from bottom right) Huddled In San Francisco's Golden Gate Park, 1967" (Marshall, Jim)
PH05760 717 (September 21, 1995) p66. "Lesh, Early Dead Co-Managers Scully And Rifkin, Weir And Garcia At A Press Conference Following The Oct. 2, 1967, drug Bust At The Dead's House" (Wolman, Baron)
PH05761 717 (September 21, 1995) p73. "marrying Acid-Damaged Art Music And The Funky Snort Of Live Rock & Roll: The Dead As A Lysergic-Dance Band In 1969 With Tom Constanten, Weir, Kreutzmann, Pigpen, Lesh, Hart..."
PH05762 717 (September 21, 1995) p46. "A Moment Of Repose: Jerry Garcia With Carolyn 'Mountain Girl' Adams And Her Daughter, Sunshine, In 1966" (Anthony, Gene)
PH05763 717 (September 21, 1995) p72. "The Music Never Stopped: Garcia, Weir, Lesh, Brent Mydland, Kreutzmann And Hart (from left) In 1979" (Greene, Herbi)
PH05764 717 (September 21, 1995) p69. "The Original Quintet At Home At 710 Ashbury St., In 1966: Phil Lesh, Bob Weir, Bill Kreutzmann, Ron 'Pigpen' McKernan And Jerry Garcia (from left)" (Anthony, Gene)
PH05765 717 (September 21, 1995) p56. "'The Dressing Room Is This Way, Jerry': Garcia Takes A Desert Stroll During The Dead's Historic Run Of Shows At The Great Pyramid, in Egypt, In September 1978" (Boot, Adrian)
PH05766 717 (September 21, 1995) p46. "A Young Jerry Garcia"
PH05767 720 (November 2, 1995) p49. "Jerry Garcia" (Greene, Herb)
PH05768 726 (January 25, 1996) p23. "The Last Incarnation Of The Dead Perform In February 1995: Phil Lesh, Mickey Hart, Bob Weir, Jerry Garcia And Vince Welnick (from left)" (Blakesberg, Jay)
PH05768a 735 (May 30, 1996) p3. "[The Faces Of Heroin]"
PH05769 740 (August 8, 1996) p36. "1990: Diving Off The Coast Of Kona, Hawaii, With Steve Parish" (Jensen, Victoria)

PH05770 740 (August 8, 1996) p35. "Egypt, September 1978" (Boot, Adrian)
PH05771 740 (August 8, 1996) p40. "Highgate, Vt., June 1995: Garcia At One Of The Final Shows" (Galbraith, Robert)
PH05772 740 (August 8, 1996) p39. "Maui, Hawaii, January 1993: Meier And Garcia"
PH05773 740 (August 8, 1996) p36. "Paris 1990: A Break From Touring, With Keelin (left) And Manasha Garcia" (Di Biase, Vince)

GARCIA, JERRY—PHOTOGRAPHS—PORTRAITS
PH05774 616 (October 31, 1991) p37. "Garcia: "We're Going To Have To Figure Out To Make The Dead Fun Again."" (Seliger, Mark)
PH05775 616 (October 31, 1991) p35. "[Jerry Garcia]" (Seliger, Mark)
PH05776 616 (October 31, 1991) pp[cover]. "Jerry Garcia: The Rolling Stone Interview" (Seliger, Mark)
PH05777 619-620 (December 12, 1991) pp[cover]. "1991 Yearbook" (Seliger, Mark)
PH05778 640 (October 1, 1992) p19. "[Jerry Garcia]" (Seliger, Mark)
PH05779 643 (November 12, 1992) p127. "Jerry Garcia" (Seliger, Mark)
PH05780 664 (September 2, 1993) p44. "Garcia Then (1966) And Now" (Greene, Herb)
PH05781 664 (September 2, 1993) p45. "[Jerry Garcia]" (Seliger, Mark)
PH05782 672-673 (December 23, 1993) p188. "[Covers]" (Seliger, Mark)
PH05783 704 (March 23, 1995) p25. "Jerry Garcia Goes Gaga For Abbott And Costello On AMC"
PH05784 717 (September 21, 1995) p58. "Garcia In '66 At Rancho Olompali, In Marin County" (Greene, Herbi)
PH05785 717 (September 21, 1995) p74. "Garcia With Carlos Santana In Oakland, 1988" (Blakesberg, Jay)
PH05786 717 (September 21, 1995) p53. "[Jerry Garcia]" (Greene, Herbi)
PH05787 717 (September 21, 1995) pp54-55. "[Jerry Garcia]" (Wolman, Baron)
PH05788 717 (September 21, 1995) p76. "[Jerry Garcia]" (Seliger, Mark)
PH05789 717 (September 21, 1995) pp[cover]. "Jerry Garcia: 1942-1995" (Greene, Herbi)
PH05790 717 (September 21, 1995) p72. "Nonstop Truckin' And Retooled Roots: The Dead's 1970s Lineup, With Keith Godchaux, Garcia, Lesh, kreutzmann, Donna Godchaux And Weir (clockwise from top left)"
PH05791 717 (September 21, 1995) p73. "Poet And Picker: Hunter And Garcia" (Blakesberg, Jay)
PH05792 724-725 (December 28, 1995) pp[cover]. "Rock & Roll Yearbook" (Seliger, Mark)
PH05793 740 (August 8, 1996) p33. "[Jerry Garcia]" (Seliger, Mark)

GARCIA, JOE—PHOTOGRAPHS—PORTRAITS
PH05794 717 (September 21, 1995) p46. "Joe Garcia, Jerry's Father, Never Heard His Son's Music"

GARCIA, JOHN—PHOTOGRAPHS
PH05795 692 (October 6, 1994) p24. "Desert Storm: Kyuss' Homme, Reeder, Garcia And Hernandez (from left)" (Miller, Michael)

GARCIA, MANASHA—PHOTOGRAPHS
PH05796 740 (August 8, 1996) p36. "Paris 1990: A Break From Touring, With Keelin (left) And Manasha Garcia" (Di Biase, Vince)

GARCIA, MAYTE—PHOTOGRAPHS
PH05797 733 (May 2, 1996) p13. "[Prince & Mayte Garcia]" (Amati, Ray)
PH05798 750-751 (December 26, 1996) p48. "Happy Couple Garcia And Prince" (Rasic, Brian)

GARDNER, ERIC—PHOTOGRAPHS
PH05799 616 (October 31, 1991) p13. "Rundgren, Eric Gardner, Janis Gardner, Little Richard, Spector (from left)" (Granitz, Steve)

GARDNER, JAMES—PHOTOGRAPHS
PH05800 655 (April 29, 1993) p68. "Barbarians At The Gate"

GARDNER, JAMES—PHOTOGRAPHS—PORTRAITS
PH05801 684 (June 16, 1994) p114. "TV Echoes"

GARDNER, JANIS—PHOTOGRAPHS
PH05802 616 (October 31, 1991) p13. "Rundgren, Eric Gardner, Janis Gardner, Little Richard, Spector (from left)" (Granitz, Steve)

GARDNER, SUZI—ILLUSTRATIONS
PH05803 688 (August 11, 1994) p7. "L7's Suzi Gardner" (Burke, Philip)

GARDNER, SUZI—PHOTOGRAPHS
PH05804 628 (April 16, 1992) p56. "Finch, Sparks, Gardner And Plakas (from left)" (Cuffaro, Chris)
PH05805 644 (November 26, 1992) p15. "Dee Plakas, Jennifer Finch, Jett, Donita Sparks And Suzi Gardner (clockwise from left)" (Lewis, Don)
PH05806 652 (March 18, 1993) p22. "Feminist Majority Rules: L7's Finch, Gardner, Sparks, Dee Plakas (from left)" (Johnson, Lisa)
PH05807 688 (August 11, 1994) p25. "Dee Plakas, Donita Sparks, Jennifer Finch, Suzi Gardner (from left)" (Broad, Julian)
PH05808 692 (October 6, 1994) p16. "At Philly's Lollapalooza: L7's Donita Sparks (left), Dee Plakas, Suzi Gardner And Jennifer Finch With Bad Seeds Mick Harvey, James Johnston And Nick Cave" (Weiner, Scott)
PH05809 695 (November 17, 1994) p52. "L7" (Broad, Julian)
PH05810 696 (December 1, 1994) p23. "Elvismania: L7's Suzi Gardner, Dee Plakas, Sparks And Jennifer Finch (from left)" (Mazur, Kevin)

GARDNER, TED—PHOTOGRAPHS
PH05811 736 (June 13, 1996) p38. "Part Of The Current Lollapalooza Brain Trust: Grosslight, Gardner And Geiger (from left)" (Dyer, Alison)

GARFUNKEL, ART—PHOTOGRAPHS
PH05812 672-673 (December 23, 1993) p70. "Garfunkel And His Soul Mate Simon" (Mazur, Kevin)

GARFUNKEL, ART—PHOTOGRAPHS—PORTRAITS
PH05813 670 (November 25, 1993) p28. "[Art Garfunkel]" (Feingold, Deborah)

GARGIULO, LU LU—PHOTOGRAPHS
PH05814 730 (March 21, 1996) p17. "Fastbacks' Kurt Bloch, Mike Musburger, Vedder, Fastbacks' Kim Warnick, Lu Lu Gargiulo" (Michelson, Randall)

GARLAND, BILLY—PHOTOGRAPHS
PH05815 746 (October 31, 1996) p43. "Billy Garland (right), Shakur's Father, At A Memorial Service On Sept. 22" (Muhammad, Ozier)

GAROFALO, JANEANE—ILLUSTRATIONS
PH05816 677 (March 10, 1994) p59. "Twenty Something" (Ryden, Mark)
PH05817 736 (June 13, 1996) p56. "Janeane Garofalo" (Cowles, David)

GAROFALO, JANEANE—PHOTOGRAPHS
PH05818 677 (March 10, 1994) p60. "Zahn, Ryder, Garofalo And Hawke Face A Shaky Future (from left)"
PH05819 682 (May 19, 1994) p66. "[Janeane Garofalo]" (Ragel, Jon)
PH05820 734 (May 16, 1996) p74. "Chaplin, Thurman And Garofalo In Love"
PH05821 734 (May 16, 1996) p17. "Garofalo (left) And Vega Waxin' And Relaxin'" (Murray, Rebecca)

GARRETT, KENNY—PHOTOGRAPHS—PORTRAITS
PH05822 741 (August 22, 1996) p82. "[Kenny Garrett]"

GARRETT, PETER—ILLUSTRATIONS
PH05823 658 (June 10, 1993) p7. "Peter Garrett Of Midnight

Oil" (Burke, Philip)
GARRETT, PETER—PHOTOGRAPHS
PH05824 633 (June 25, 1992) p11. "Peter Garrett (below)..." (Robicheau, Paul)
PH05825 645-646 (December 10, 1992) p47. "Peter Garrett" (Robicheau, Paul)
PH05826 658 (June 10, 1993) p21. "Bald And Brassy: Peter Garrett" (Seliger, Mark)
PH05827 658 (June 10, 1993) p19. "Burnin' Again: Hillman, Garrett, Moginie, Hirst, Rotsey (from left)" (Seliger, Mark)
PH05828 669 (November 11, 1993) p28. "The Oils' Peter Garrett With Guitarist Martin Rotsey" (Blakesberg, Jay)
PH05829 690 (September 8, 1994) p21. "Say "Ah"; Garrett At The WOMAD Finale" (Robicheau, Paul)
GARSIDE, KATIE-JANE—PHOTOGRAPHS
PH05830 628 (April 16, 1992) p56. "Gray, Garside, Johnson And Adams (from left)" (Double, Steve)
GASSEE, JEAN-LOUIS—PHOTOGRAPHS
PH05831 732 (April 18, 1996) p62. "Apple's Flamboyant Frenchman Jean-Louis Gassee" (Kashi, Ed)
GATES, BILL—PHOTOGRAPHS
PH05832 696 (December 1, 1994) p58. "Billionaire Boys' Club: Allen (seated) And Bill Gates Hack At High School"
PH05833 731 (April 4, 1996) pp54-55. "The King Of Software, Bill Gates (right), In '92" (Payne, Gary)
PH05834 732 (April 18, 1996) p61. "Citizen Gates"
GATES, REBECCA—PHOTOGRAPHS
PH05835 690 (September 8, 1994) p33. "Woman On The Front: Spinanes' Rebecca Gates" (Wheeler, Alice)
GATORADE IRONMAN TRIATHLON WORLD CHAMPIONSHIP—PHOTOGRAPHS
PH05836 680 (April 21, 1994) pp[enc.5]. "[Hawaii Ironman]" (Kron, Daniel)
GATTON, DANNY—ALBUMS
PH05837 750-751 (December 26, 1996) p192. "The Humbler"
GATTON, DANNY—PHOTOGRAPHS
PH05838 696 (December 1, 1994) p49. "Gatton And His Daughter, Holly Anne, In 1989" (Southam, Andrew)
GATTON, HOLLY ANNE—PHOTOGRAPHS
PH05838 696 (December 1, 1994) p49. "Gatton And His Daughter, Holly Anne, In 1989" (Southam, Andrew)
GAULTIER, JEAN PAUL—PHOTOGRAPHS
PH05839 694 (November 3, 1994) p18. "Gaultier Snuggles Glam Pal Madonna" (Allen, David)
GAVIRIA, PABLO ESCOBAR—PHOTOGRAPHS—PORTRAITS
PH05840 660-661 (July 8, 1993) p81. "El Padrino: Pablo Escobar Gaviria"
GAY, DAVE—PHOTOGRAPHS
PH05841 686-687 (July 14, 1994) p74. "Erwin, Bean, Touring Member Bob Egan And Gay (from left); Mascot Matthew Bean-Rizzo (front)" (Elledge, Paul)
GAYE, MARVIN—PHOTOGRAPHS—PORTRAITS
PH05842 645-646 (December 10, 1992) p161. "Marvin Gaye, 1984"
GAYLE, CHARLES—ALBUMS
PH05843 702 (February 23, 1995) p84. "Kingdom Come"
GAYLES, JUGGY—PHOTOGRAPHS—PORTRAITS
PH05844 678 (March 24, 1994) p14. "Juggy Gayles, The Moses Of Promo..."
PH05845 678 (March 24, 1994) p14. "Juggy Gayles, The Moses Of Promo..." (Carroll, Chris)
GEE, KAY—PHOTOGRAPHS
PH05846 695 (November 17, 1994) p110. "Naughty By Nature" (Callis, Chris)
GEFFEN, AVIV—PHOTOGRAPHS
PH05847 747 (November 14, 1996) p32. "'Draft Dodger Rag': Geffen In Performance"
GEFFEN, DAVID—PHOTOGRAPHS
PH05848 655 (April 29, 1993) p56. "Geffen With John Lennon And Yoko Ono, New York, 1980" (Senecal, Michel)
PH05849 655 (April 29, 1993) p52. "'I Couldn't Wait To Move To California,' He Says"
PH05850 655 (April 29, 1993) p53. "In 1971 The Boy Genius Of Asylum Bared All For Annie Leibovitz: "She Dared Me'" (Leibovitz, Annie)
PH05851 655 (April 29, 1993) p55. "Manager Geffen With An Early Client, Singer-Songwriter Laura Nyro, 1968" (Paley, Stephen)
PH05852 655 (April 29, 1993) p56. "Michael Jackson And Madonna Celebrate Geffen's Birthday In 1991"
PH05853 655 (April 29, 1993) p55. "With Mentor Ahmet Ertegun, Cofounder Of Atlantic Records, 1973" (Leibovitz, Annie)
GEFFEN, DAVID—PHOTOGRAPHS—PORTRAITS
PH05854 655 (April 29, 1993) p50. "[David Geffen]" (Ritts, Herb)
PH05855 655 (April 29, 1993) p52. "Geffen's High-School Yearbook Photo, 1960"
PH05856 698-699 (December 29, 1994) p68. "Geffen, Katzenberg, Spielberg (from left)" (Berliner)
GEIGER, MARC—PHOTOGRAPHS
PH05857 630 (May 14, 1992) p84. "[Marc Geiger]" (Little, Blake)
PH05858 736 (June 13, 1996) p38. "Part Of The Current Lollapalooza Brain Trust: Grosslight, Gardner And Geiger (from left)" (Dyer, Alison)
GELB, HOWE—PHOTOGRAPHS
PH05859 662 (August 5, 1993) p28. "Sandman Joey Burns (left) And Howe Gelb" (Gershoff, Gary)
GELDOF, BOB—ALBUMS
PH05860 663 (August 19, 1993) p78. "The Happy Club"
GELDOF, BOB—PHOTOGRAPHS
PH05861 621 (January 9, 1992) p17. "Mercury Joins Paul McCartney And Other Stars In The Live Aid Finale, 1985" (Preston, Neal)
PH05862 715 (August 24, 1995) p25. "Bon Jovi (left) Geldof"
GENE—ALBUMS
PH05863 711 (June 29, 1995) p45. "Olympian"
GENE—PHOTOGRAPHS
PH05864 700 (January 26, 1995) p30. "Gene: This Week's Next Big Thing" (Double, Steve)
GENERAL ELECTRIC—ILLUSTRATIONS
PH05865 628 (April 16, 1992) pp65,66. "[General Electric]" (Drescher, Henrik)
GENERAL PUBIC—ALBUMS
PH05866 708 (May 18, 1995) p92. "Rub It Better"
GENERATION ECCH! (BOOK)—ILLUSTRATIONS
PH05867 690 (September 8, 1994) p21. "Days Of Wine And Poses" (Mayo, Martin)
GENERATION GAP—ILLUSTRATIONS
PH05868 666 (September 30, 1993) p10. "Choose A Generation" (Pendergrast, James T.)
GENESIS—ALBUMS
PH05869 621 (January 9, 1992) p51. "We Can't Dance"
GENESIS—PHOTOGRAPHS
PH05870 624 (February 20, 1992) p17. "Genesis, From Left: Tony Banks, Mike Rutherford And Phil Collins" (Ockenfels, Frank W.)
GENIUS—ALBUMS
PH05871 722 (November 30, 1995) p66. "Liquid Swords"
GEORGEFF, DAVE—PHOTOGRAPHS
PH05872 709 (June 1, 1995) p16. "Flava In Ya Ear: Wax's Loomis, Joe Sib, Dave Georgeff And Soda Drop In On Fogelnes In His 'Squirt TV' Bedroom Studio (from left)" (Brown, Christy)
GEORGES, BERNARD—PHOTOGRAPHS
PH05873 703 (March 9, 1995) p54. "Giving In To The Muses: Drummer David Narcizo, Hersh And Bassist Bernard Georges (from left)" (Seliger, Mark)
PH05874 707 (May 4, 1995) p36. "Georges (left) And Hersh Throw Down" (Blakesberg, Jay)

GEORGIA (EUROPE)—PHOTOGRAPHS
PH05875 619-620 (December 12, 1991) p116. "Both Supporters And Opponents Of President Zviad Gamsakhurdia's Government Cobbled Together Barricades In The Streets Of Tbilisi, Georgia" (Nubile, James)
PH05876 619-620 (December 12, 1991) p115. "[Georgia]" (Nubile, James)
PH05877 619-620 (December 12, 1991) p120. "Outside Opposition Headquarters: The Urban Elite Were Pitted Against The President's Supporters—Peasants And Villagers Who Were Bused In From The Countryside For The Occasion"
PH05878 619-620 (December 12, 1991) p119. "Renegade National Guardsmen And Civilians Defending The Offices Of The State TV Station" (Nubile, James)
GEORGIA (FILM)—PHOTOGRAPHS
PH05879 722 (November 30, 1995) p74. "Is Jennifer Jason Leigh's Rocker Hotter Than Pierce Brosnan's Bond? No Contest"
PH05880 731 (April 4, 1996) p66. "Leigh, 'Georgia'"
GEORGIA—PHOTOGRAPHS
PH05881 698-699 (December 29, 1994) p157. "Clinton-Hating Venom Erupts At An Anti-Gay Rally In Georgia" (Clark, Bill)
PH05882 698-699 (December 29, 1994) p58. "The Day After: Rison's Georgia Manse" (Ivansco, Joey)
GEPHARDT, RICHARD—PHOTOGRAPHS
PH05883 660-661 (July 8, 1993) p52. "Babbitt On The Campaign Trail: Presidential Candidates Michael Dukakis, Babbitt, Paul Simon, Richard Gephardt, Jesse Jackson And Al Gore (from left) At A New York Forum ..." (Peterso
GERALDINE FIBBERS—PHOTOGRAPHS
PH05884 720 (November 2, 1995) p24. "Bozulich, Keenan, Tutton, Fitzgerald, Greene (from left)" (Toy, Joann)
GERARDO—PHOTOGRAPHS
PH05885 619-620 (December 12, 1991) p88. "Latin Rapper Gerardo" (St. Nicholas, Randee)
GERE, RICHARD—ILLUSTRATIONS
PH05886 650 (February 18, 1993) p65. "Con With The Wind" (Cowles, David)
GERE, RICHARD—PHOTOGRAPHS
PH05887 625 (March 5, 1992) p77. "Kim Basinger And Richard Gere Make Strange Bedfellows"
PH05888 650 (February 18, 1993) p66. "...Richard Gere Plays Tricks On Jodie Foster"
PH05889 714 (August 10, 1995) p64. "Gere And Connery Deconstruct Camelot"
PH05890 732 (April 18, 1996) p80. "From Left: Linney And Gere Huddle; Norton Broods"
GERE, RICHARD—PHOTOGRAPHS—PORTRAITS
PH05891 676 (February 24, 1994) p62. "[Intersection]"
GERGEN, DAVID—PHOTOGRAPHS
PH05892 662 (August 5, 1993) p37. "Al Gore And Bill Clinton Introducing Newest Democrat, David Gergen, In May"
PH05893 664 (September 2, 1993) p41. "Fielding Questions In The White House After Reagan Was Shot In March 1981"
PH05894 664 (September 2, 1993) p41. "In Gerald Ford's White House, 1976"
PH05895 664 (September 2, 1993) p40. "An Officer And A Gentleman: In Naval Officer Candidate School In The Mid-'60s"
PH05896 664 (September 2, 1993) p39. "What Difference Does A Decade Make? Gergen With Ronald Reagan And Larry Speakes, May 1982" (Kennerly, David Hume)
PH05897 664 (September 2, 1993) p39. "With Bill Clinton And George Stephanopoulos, may 1993"
PH05898 671 (December 9, 1993) p42. "[The Rolling Stone Interview of Bill Clinton]" (Seliger, Mark)
GERMANO, LISA—ALBUMS
PH05899 617 (November 14, 1991) p177. "On The Way Down From The Moon Palace"
PH05900 666 (September 30, 1993) p106. "Happiness"
PH05901 742 (September 5, 1996) p64. "Excerpts From A Love Circus"
GERMANO, LISA—ILLUSTRATIONS
PH05902 694 (November 3, 1994) p98. "Lisa Germano" (Von Buhler, Cynthia)
GERMANO, LISA—PHOTOGRAPHS
PH05903 697 (December 15, 1994) p23. "[Lisa Germano]" (McDaniel, Melodie)
PH05904 697 (December 15, 1994) p24. "Proud To Be Uncool: Germano In The Solo Spotlight" (Herzhaft, Beth)
GERMS—ALBUMS
PH05905 676 (February 24, 1994) p57. "MIA"
GERONIMO (FILM)—PHOTOGRAPHS
PH05906 672-673 (December 23, 1993) p174. "[Geronimo]"
GERONIMO, JOE—PHOTOGRAPHS
PH05907 736 (June 13, 1996) p66. "Joe Geronimo Has Vowed To Keep The Reservation Nuclear-Free" (Barker, Kent)
GERRARD, LISA—PHOTOGRAPHS
PH05908 686-687 (July 14, 1994) p35. ""We Aim To Wake up That Other Self We Have": Lisa Gerrard And Brendan Perry" (Grecco, Michael)
GERSHON, GINA—PHOTOGRAPHS
PH05909 745 (October 17, 1996) p142. "Now Playing"
GET ON THE BUS (FILM)—PHOTOGRAPHS
PH05910 746 (October 31, 1996) p76. "Get On The Bus"
GET SHORTY (FILM)—ILLUSTRATIONS
PH05911 720 (November 2, 1995) p73. "The Mob Goes Hollywood" (Linn, Warren)
GET SHORTY (FILM)—PHOTOGRAPHS
PH05912 718 (October 5, 1995) p76. "Pulp To Come"
PH05913 720 (November 2, 1995) p74. "Dennis Farina Takes The Throne"
PH05914 720 (November 2, 1995) p74. "DeVito Takes Aim"
PH05915 720 (November 2, 1995) p74. "Hackman (in brace) And DeVito Watch Travolta Operate, Hollywood Style"
PH05916 720 (November 2, 1995) p74. "Travolta And Russo Take A Meeting"
PH05917 724-725 (December 28, 1995) p136. "Unusual Pleasure"
PH05918 731 (April 4, 1996) p66. "Travolta, 'Shorty'"
THE GETAWAY (FILM)—PHOTOGRAPHS
PH05919 676 (February 24, 1994) p62. "Glam Gun Toters: Kim Basinger And Alec Baldwin"
GETO BOYS—ALBUMS
PH05920 619-620 (December 12, 1991) p184. "We Can't Be Stopped"
PH05921 658 (June 10, 1993) p69. "Till Death Do Us Part"
GETO BOYS—PHOTOGRAPHS
PH05922 667 (October 14, 1993) p80. "Geto Boys: 'Playing' With Our Minds"
GETTING EVEN WITH DAD (FILM)—PHOTOGRAPHS
PH05923 686-687 (July 14, 1994) p99. "[Macaulay Culkin]"
GETTY, JEAN PAUL, III—ILLUSTRATIONS
PH05924 641 (October 15, 1992) p161. "[Jean Paul Getty III]" (Dunnick, Regan)
GETTYSBURG (FILM)—PHOTOGRAPHS
PH05925 670 (November 25, 1993) p127. "Jeff Daniels: Bad Hair, Bold Performance"
GETZ, STAN—PHOTOGRAPHS
PH05926 619-620 (December 12, 1991) p112. "Stan Getz"
THE GHOST AND THE DARKNESS (FILM)—PHOTOGRAPHS
PH05927 746 (October 31, 1996) p78. "Great White Hunter Michael Douglas"
GHOSTFACE KILLAH—ALBUMS
PH05928 749 (December 12, 1996) p82. "Ironman"
GHOSTS OF MISSISSIPPI (FILM)—PHOTOGRAPHS
PH05929 743 (September 19, 1996) p90. "Quality Control"
GIAMMALVO, CHRIS—PHOTOGRAPHS
PH05930 688 (August 11, 1994) p29. "Drummer Johnny Kick, Cote, Lorson And Bassist Chris Giammalvo (from left)" (Berg, Bob)

GIANT SAND—ALBUMS
PH05931 689 (August 25, 1994) p92. "Purge And Slouch"
PH05932 690 (September 8, 1994) p78. "Glum"
GIANT SAND—PHOTOGRAPHS
PH05933 662 (August 5, 1993) p28. "Sandman Joey Burns (left) And Howe Gelb" (Gershoff, Gary)
GIBB, CYNTHIA—PHOTOGRAPHS
PH05934 692 (October 6, 1994) p94. "Working Girl: Mad dad Dabney Coleman With Cynthia Gibb"
GIBBONS, BETH—PHOTOGRAPHS
PH05935 702 (February 23, 1995) p38. "Noir-Agers Beth Gibbons (left) And Geoff Barrow" (Cultice, Joseph)
GIBBONS, BILLY—PHOTOGRAPHS
PH05936 631 (May 28, 1992) p11. "ZZ Top's Dusty Hill, Frank Beard And Billy Gibbons (from left)" (Reitzel, Bill)
PH05937 685 (June 30, 1994) p38. "Blues Beard: ZZ's Billy Gibbons" (Dorst, Chris)
GIBBS, MELVIN—PHOTOGRAPHS
PH05938 622 (January 23, 1992) p11. "Vernon Reid (left) And Melvin Gibbs" (Mazur, Kevin)
PH05939 623 (February 6, 1992) p13. "Vernon Reid, Will Calhoun And Melvin Gibbs (from left)" (Mazur, Kevin)
PH05940 686-687 (July 14, 1994) p45. "[Rollins Band]" (Halfin, Ross)
GIBSON, BILL—PHOTOGRAPHS
PH05941 742 (September 5, 1996) p21. "Fruit O' the Loon: Lemonhead Dando Rocks Hard (can't ya tell?) With Patrick Murphy, Dina Waxman And Bill Gibson (from left)"
GIBSON, BOB—PHOTOGRAPHS—PORTRAITS
PH05942 748 (November 28, 1996) p32. "[Bob Gibson]"
GIBSON, DEBBIE—ALBUMS
PH05943 651 (March 4, 1993) p65. "Body Mind Soul"
GIBSON, DEBBIE—PHOTOGRAPHS
PH05944 624 (February 20, 1992) p11. "Debbie Gibson In 'Les Miserables'" (Mazur, Kevin)
PH05945 712-713 (July 13, 1995) p25. "Zander Schloss (left), Gibson And Morris At CBGB" (Toliver, Chris)
PH05946 724-725 (December 28, 1995) p42. "Guest Punkette Debbie Gibson Joined Circle Jerks' Keith Morris" (Toliver, Chris)
GIBSON, MEL—ILLUSTRATIONS
PH05947 665 (September 16, 1993) p75. "The Melephant Man" (Guy, Edmund)
PH05948 710 (June 15, 1995) p85. "Die Hard In A Kilt" (Payne, C. F.)
PH05949 748 (November 28, 1996) p141. "Daddy Braveheart: Mel Gibson Shows The Rebel Chops Of A Scottish Warrior As A New York Tycoon Out To Save His Kidnapped Son By Whatever Means Necessary" (Brodner, Steve)
GIBSON, MEL—PHOTOGRAPHS
PH05950 633 (June 25, 1992) p49. "A Trio For Glover (left), Gibson And Gun"
PH05951 644 (November 26, 1992) p78. "[Lethal Weapon 3]"
PH05952 665 (September 16, 1993) p76. "Mel Gibson Shows A Different Side"
PH05953 674 (January 27, 1994) p31. "Mel Gibson In A Pro-Supplements Video" (Gougenheim, Kim)
PH05954 710 (June 15, 1995) p86. "Gibson Directs A 'Braveheart' Battle"
PH05955 731 (April 4, 1996) p66. "'Braveheart,' With Gibson"
PH05956 748 (November 28, 1996) p142. "Gibson With Son Nolte"
PH05957 748 (November 28, 1996) p142. "With 'Ransom' Director Ron Howard"
GIBSON, MEL—PHOTOGRAPHS—PORTRAITS
PH05958 684 (June 16, 1994) p114. "TV Echoes"
PH05959 709 (June 1, 1995) p68. "Men In Wigs"
GIBSON, MICHAEL—PHOTOGRAPHS
PH05960 710 (June 15, 1995) p52. "At The Uptown: McBride, Veal, John Crist, Michael Gibson (from left)" (Clinch, Danny)
GIELGUD, JOHN—PHOTOGRAPHS
PH05961 617 (November 14, 1991) p184. "Gielgud (with two lovers) Can't Tell Truth From Illusion"
GIESEN, BOBBY—PHOTOGRAPHS
PH05962 668 (October 28, 1993) p73. "At Cafe O'Lake" (Newton, Philip)
PH05963 668 (October 28, 1993) p73. "Bobby At Passage Restaurant" (Newton, Philip)
GIFFORD, KATHIE LEE—PHOTOGRAPHS—PORTRAITS
PH05964 750-751 (December 26, 1996) p58. "Kathie Lee Gifford Arranges Her Eyebrows Into A Sincere Position"
GIL, GILBERTO—ILLUSTRATIONS
PH05965 688 (August 11, 1994) p69. "[Caetano Veloso & Gil Gilberto]" (Menchin, Scott)
GILBERT, JAMES—PHOTOGRAPHS
PH05966 708 (May 18, 1995) p58. "Bryant Heard, Left, And Buddy James Gilbert: Students Often Went To School, Gun Racks Loaded, Camouflage Bloodied From An Early-Morning Hunt" (Mark, Mary Ellen)
GILBERT, SARA—PHOTOGRAPHS
PH05967 631 (May 28, 1992) p60. "Barrymore Plays Moody Babe With Costar Gilbert"
PH05968 644 (November 26, 1992) p78. "[Poison Ivy]"
GILBERT, SIMON—PHOTOGRAPHS
PH05969 657 (May 27, 1993) p15. "Ultra Suede: Gilbert, Anderson, Osman, Butler (from left)" (Broad, Julian)
GILKYSON, TONY—PHOTOGRAPHS
PH05970 659 (June 24, 1993) p23. "'Xdream: Gilkyson, Doe, Cervenka, Bonebrake (from left)"
GILLESPIE, BOBBY—PHOTOGRAPHS—PORTRAITS
PH05971 684 (June 16, 1994) p26. "A Slice Of Scream: Keyboardist Martin Duffy, Gillespie And Innes (from left)" (Sheehan, Tom)
GILLESPIE, DIZZY—ILLUSTRATIONS
PH05972 650 (February 18, 1993) p3. "Dizzy Gillespie: 1917-1993" (Burke, Philip)
GILLESPIE, DIZZY—PHOTOGRAPHS—PORTRAITS
PH05973 650 (February 18, 1993) p22. "[Dizzy Gillespie]" (Ritts, Herb)
PH05974 672-673 (December 23, 1993) p79. "Above: Dizzy Gillespie" (Ritts, Herb)
GILLIES, BEN—PHOTOGRAPHS
PH05975 715 (August 24, 1995) p31. "Chris Joannou, Ben Gillies And Daniel Johns (from left): Could You Just Say We're 18?" (Clinch, Danny)
PH05976 726 (January 25, 1996) p38. "Silverchair: Young, Hard-Rocking Aussies Chris Joannou, Daniel Johns And Ben Gillies (from left)" (Anderson, David)
PH05977 728 (February 22, 1996) p46. "Gut Feeling: Johns, Joannou And Gillies, From Left, In A Sophisticated Pose (left)" (Seliger, Mark)
PH05978 728 (February 22, 1996) p47. "Johns, Joannou And Gillies (from left) Goof Around—As Usual" (Seliger, Mark)
GILLIES, BEN—PHOTOGRAPHS—PORTRAITS
PH05979 728 (February 22, 1996) p45. "Silverchair's Daniel Johns, Ben Gillies And Chris Joannou (from left) Turn On The Charm" (Seliger, Mark)
GILLINGHAM, CHARLIE—PHOTOGRAPHS
PH05980 669 (November 11, 1993) p24. "A '90s Sensibility: Vickrey, Gillingham, Duritz, Bowman, Malley, Bryson (from left)" (Blakesberg, Jay)
PH05981 685 (June 30, 1994) pp[cover]. "Counting Crows: The Biggest New Band In America" (Seliger, Mark)
PH05982 685 (June 30, 1994) p46. "Free Men In Paris: Dave Bryson, Steve Bowman, Dan Vickrey, Matt Malley And Charlie Gillingham (from left)" (Seliger, Mark)
GILLOOLY, JEFF—PHOTOGRAPHS
PH05983 686-687 (July 14, 1994) p86. "Gillooly Arraigned In Portland" (Bechtel, Doug)

GILMORE, BESSIE—PHOTOGRAPHS
PH05984 684 (June 16, 1994) p55. "Bessie And Her Youngest, Mikal, Ca. 1957"
PH05985 684 (June 16, 1994) p55. "The Gilmores Circa 1950: Father Frank, Mother Bessie, Gaylen, Gary, Frank Jr. In Portland, Ore. (clockwise from left)"
GILMORE, FRANK—PHOTOGRAPHS
PH05986 684 (June 16, 1994) p57. "Frank Gilmore Jr. And Sr."
PH05987 684 (June 16, 1994) p55. "The Gilmores Circa 1950: Father Frank, Mother Bessie, Gaylen, Gary, Frank Jr. In Portland, Ore. (clockwise from left)"
GILMORE, FRANK, JR.—PHOTOGRAPHS
PH05988 684 (June 16, 1994) p56. "Blood Brothers: Gary, Mikal, Gaylen And Frank Jr. (from left) At Portland Home In 1957"
PH05989 684 (June 16, 1994) p57. "Frank Gilmore Jr. And Sr."
PH05990 684 (June 16, 1994) p55. "The Gilmores Circa 1950: Father Frank, Mother Bessie, Gaylen, Gary, Frank Jr. In Portland, Ore. (clockwise from left)"
GILMORE, GARY—ILLUSTRATIONS
PH05991 632 (June 11, 1992) p111. "[Gary Gilmore]" (Cronin, Brian)
GILMORE, GARY—PHOTOGRAPHS
PH05992 632 (June 11, 1992) p112. "Gary Mark Gilmore At Oregon State Prison"
PH05993 684 (June 16, 1994) p56. "Blood Brothers: Gary, Mikal, Gaylen And Frank Jr. (from left) At Portland Home In 1957"
PH05994 684 (June 16, 1994) p54. "Gary Gilmore At The Marion, Ill., Penitentiary, 1975"
PH05995 684 (June 16, 1994) p55. "The Gilmores Circa 1950: Father Frank, Mother Bessie, Gaylen, Gary, Frank Jr. In Portland, Ore. (clockwise from left)"
GILMORE, GAYLEN—PHOTOGRAPHS
PH05996 684 (June 16, 1994) p56. "Blood Brothers: Gary, Mikal, Gaylen And Frank Jr. (from left) At Portland Home In 1957"
PH05997 684 (June 16, 1994) p55. "The Gilmores Circa 1950: Father Frank, Mother Bessie, Gaylen, Gary, Frank Jr. In Portland, Ore. (clockwise from left)"
GILMORE, JIMMIE DALE—ALBUMS
PH05998 619-620 (December 12, 1991) p184. "After Awhile"
PH05999 667 (October 14, 1993) p114. "Spinning Around The Sun"
PH06000 738-739 (July 11, 1996) p87. "Braver Newer World"
GILMORE, JIMMIE DALE—PHOTOGRAPHS
PH06001 665 (September 16, 1993) p32. "Jimmie Dale Gilmore At The Tribute" (Mazur, Kevin)
PH06002 674 (January 27, 1994) p42. "Winner Jimmie Dale Gilmore" (Mazur, Kevin)
PH06003 677 (March 10, 1994) p52. "'I'm An Expressive Actor,' Says Gilmore. 'The Songs Are My Lines.'" (Mazur, Kevin)
PH06004 679 (April 7, 1994) p38. "Arm In Arms: Arm, Vedder And Gilmore"
PH06005 706 (April 20, 1995) p17. "Tibet House Supporters Byrne (left) And Gilmore" (Capak, R. J.)
GILMORE, JIMMIE DALE—PHOTOGRAPHS—PORTRAITS
PH06006 670 (November 25, 1993) p38. "Mudhoney Guitarist Steve Turner, Gilmore And Guitarist Mark Arm" (Peterson, Charles)
PH06007 672-673 (December 23, 1993) p58. "Jimmie Dale Gilmore: High Cool Factor" (Springsteen, Pamela)
PH06008 677 (March 10, 1994) p51. "[Jimmie Dale Gilmore]" (Carter, Keith)
GILMORE, MIKAL—PHOTOGRAPHS
PH06009 684 (June 16, 1994) p55. "Bessie And Her Youngest, Mikal, Ca. 1957"
PH06010 684 (June 16, 1994) p56. "Blood Brothers: Gary, Mikal, Gaylen And Frank Jr. (from left) At Portland Home In 1957"
GILMOUR, DAVID—PHOTOGRAPHS
PH06011 684 (June 16, 1994) p16. "This One's Pink: David Gilmour" (Mazur, Kevin)
PH06012 691 (September 22, 1994) p33. "Hands Off My Stash: David Gilmour" (Mazur, Kevin)
PH06013 728 (February 22, 1996) p19. "Pink Floyd's Richard Wright (left) And Gilmour Flank Special Guest Corgan" (Mazur, Kevin)
PH06014 750-751 (December 26, 1996) p45. "Corgan (left) With David Gilmour" (Mazur, Kevin)
GIMARC, GEORGE—BOOKS
PH06015 690 (September 8, 1994) p38. "Punk Diary 1970-1979"
GIN BLOSSOMS—ALBUMS
PH06016 672-673 (December 23, 1993) p146. "New Miserable Experience"
PH06017 730 (March 21, 1996) p98. "Congratulations I'm Sorry"
GIN BLOSSOMS—PHOTOGRAPHS
PH06018 665 (September 16, 1993) p31. "Phoenix's Chart-Friendly Gin Blossoms" (Mazur, Kevin)
PH06019 672-673 (December 23, 1993) p49. "[Gin Blossoms]" (Ragel, Jon)
PH06020 722 (November 30, 1995) p20. "Gin Blossom's Scott Johnson, Dead Hot's Brian Griffith, Blossom Valenzuela And Dead Hot Curtis Grippe (from left)"
PH06021 726 (January 25, 1996) p30. "Gin Blossoms: Robin Wilson, Phillip Rhodes, Bill Lien, Jesse Valenzuela, Scott Johnson (from left)" (Jennings, Steve)
PH06022 749 (December 12, 1996) p22. "[Gin Blossoms]" (Clinch, Danny)
GINEN, BOUKAN—PHOTOGRAPHS
PH06023 718 (October 5, 1995) p25. "Boukan Ginen" (Corio, David)
GINGERBREAD MAN (CD-ROM)—ILLUSTRATIONS
PH06024 702 (February 23, 1995) p39. "Screen Shots From 'Gingerbread Man'"
GINGRICH, NEWT—ILLUSTRATIONS
PH06025 698-699 (December 29, 1994) p13. "Newt Gingrich Election Post-Mortem" (Burke, Philip)
PH06026 700 (January 26, 1995) pp35-36. "[Contract With America]" (Kuper, Peter)
PH06027 703 (March 9, 1995) p40. "Business As Usual: Wall Street Floats On A Multibillion-Dollar Life Preserver" (Witte, Michael)
PH06028 707 (May 4, 1995) p38. "A Tough Row To Hoe: Gingrich Trims The Federal Budget" (Witte, Michael)
PH06029 708 (May 18, 1995) p47. "Chock-Full Of Nuts: Dole's Senate Chills Gingrich's Overheated House" (Witte, Michael)
PH06030 717 (September 21, 1995) p41. "Now That's My Kind Of Contract" (Witte, Michael)
PH06031 744 (October 3, 1996) p41. "[Newt Gingrich]" (Payne, C. F.)
PH06032 747 (November 14, 1996) p20. "Voting Booth" (Pendergrast, James T.)
GINGRICH, NEWT—PHOTOGRAPHS
PH06033 698-699 (December 29, 1994) p151. "Gingrich Gives Himself A Thumbs-Up On Election"
PH06034 698-699 (December 29, 1994) p164. "Once A Backbencher, Gingrich Now Basks In The Spotlight"
PH06035 698-699 (December 29, 1994) p165. "Wave Of The Future: Conservatives Gingrich And Barry Goldwater In 1976"
PH06036 724-725 (December 28, 1995) p39. "[Newt Gingrich]" (Westenberger)
GINGRICH, NEWT—PHOTOGRAPHS—PORTRAITS
PH06037 710 (June 15, 1995) p62. "Gingrich" (Clark, Bill)
GINN, GREG—PHOTOGRAPHS
PH06038 654 (April 15, 1993) p24. "SST's Greg Ginn Gets Even" (Little, Blake)
GINN, GREG—PHOTOGRAPHS—PORTRAITS
PH06039 672-673 (December 23, 1993) p112. "Hardcore Heroes Black Flag In March 1984: Bill Stevenson, Kira Roessler, Greg

Ginn And Rollins (from left)" (Rosenberg, Howard)
GINSBERG, ALLEN—PHOTOGRAPHS
PH06040 667 (October 14, 1993) p69. "Bob Dylan (With Allen Ginsberg At Left): You Don't Need A Weatherman"
PH06041 690 (September 8, 1994) p21. "Tin Man, Ginsberg, Kesey, Dorothy (from left)" (Miles, Steve)
PH06042 738-739 (July 11, 1996) p70. "With Allen Ginsberg At A Be-In, 1967" (Marshall, Jim)
PH06043 744 (October 3, 1996) p20. "Young At Heart, McCartney, Right, Accompanies Ginsberg In London" (McCartney, Linda)
GIORDANO, LOU—PHOTOGRAPHS
PH06044 722 (November 30, 1995) p29. "Giordano, Westerberg And Assistant Engineer Eddie Miller (from left)" (Keeley, Dennis)
GIRL 6 (FILM)—ILLUSTRATIONS
PH06045 732 (April 18, 1996) p77. "Phone Sex, Spike Style" (Brodner, Steve)
GIRL 6 (FILM)—PHOTOGRAPHS
PH06046 732 (April 18, 1996) p78. "Girl 6 Theresa Randle Heats Up The Line"
PH06047 732 (April 18, 1996) p78. "Leonard Thomas And Randle Fulfill A Blaxploitation Fantasy"
GIRLS AGAINST BOYS—ALBUMS
PH06048 733 (May 2, 1996) p54. "House Of GVSB"
PH06049 734 (May 16, 1996) p80. "House Of GVSB"
GIRLS AGAINST BOYS—PHOTOGRAPHS
PH06050 721 (November 16, 1995) p75. "Johnny Temple, Scott McCloud, Alexis Fleisig And Eli Janney (from left) Enjoy An All-American Snack" (Exum)
GIRLS TOWN (FILM)—PHOTOGRAPHS
PH06051 742 (September 5, 1996) p68. "Girls Taylor, Grace And Harris"
PH06052 743 (September 19, 1996) p90. "[Summer...]"
GISH, LILLIAN—PHOTOGRAPHS
PH06053 721 (November 16, 1995) p117. "Lillian Gish (1926)"
GIST, KIER—PHOTOGRAPHS
PH06054 615 (October 17, 1991) p27. "Naughty By Nature: DJ Kay Gee, Treach And Vinnie (from left)" (Larsen, Kristine)
GIULIANI, RUDY—PHOTOGRAPHS
PH06055 716 (September 7, 1995) p13. "Wanna Be Schools Chancellor?: Giuliani And Jacko" (Mazur, Kevin)
GIVE IT AWAY (VIDEO)—PHOTOGRAPHS
PH06056 667 (October 14, 1993) p77. "Peppers: The Video That Keeps On Giving"
GIVENS, ROBIN—ILLUSTRATIONS
PH06057 636 (August 6, 1992) p63. "Depreciating Eddie Murphy" (Brodner, Steven)
GIVENS, ROBIN—PHOTOGRAPHS
PH06058 636 (August 6, 1992) p64. "Robin Givens Has The Nails, But Eddie Murphy's Got The Claws"
GLADIATOR (FILM)—PHOTOGRAPHS
PH06059 626 (March 19, 1992) p102. "Race Divides Gooding And Marshall"
GLASER, GABBY—PHOTOGRAPHS
PH06060 689 (August 25, 1994) p24. "Luscious' Gabby Glaser, Jill Cunniff" (Blakesberg, Jay)
PH06061 710 (June 15, 1995) p17. "LJ's Schellenbach, Gabby Glaser, Vivian trimble And Jill Cunniff At The Rally For Women's Lives, in D.C. (from left)" (Harrington, John)
PH06062 735 (May 30, 1996) p27. "Glaser, Schellenbach, Producer Lanois And Trimble (from left)" (Olivier, Rick)
GLASER, GABBY—PHOTOGRAPHS—PORTRAITS
PH06063 660-661 (July 8, 1993) p97. "Luscious Jackson (clockwise from top left): Glaser, Schellenbach, Cunniff, Trimble" (Minchin, James R., III)
GLASS, PHILIP—PHOTOGRAPHS
PH06064 647 (January 7, 1993) p9. "Bowie (left) And Glass" (Mazur, Kevin)
GLENGARRY GLEN ROSS (FILM)—PHOTOGRAPHS
PH06065 648 (January 21, 1993) p56. "Glengarry Glen Ross"
PH06066 Lem (October 1, 1992) p74. ""
GLENNIE, JIM—PHOTOGRAPHS
PH06067 680 (April 21, 1994) p12. "Glennie: Mixing Hard And Heavy With Atmospheric" (Mosenfelder, Tim)
GLENNIE, JIM—PHOTOGRAPHS—PORTRAITS
PH06068 680 (April 21, 1994) p11. "[James]" (Borris, Dan)
GLIMPSES (BOOK)—PHOTOGRAPHS
PH06069 679 (April 7, 1994) p29. "The Way We Were"
GLOVER, COREY—PHOTOGRAPHS
PH06070 637 (August 20, 1992) p9. "Living Colour's Vernon Reid, Corey Glover And Doug Wimbish (from left)" (Mazur, Kevin)
PH06071 648 (January 21, 1993) p18. "Corey Glover, Will Calhoun, Vernon Reid And Doug Wimbish (from left)" (Leialoha, Mark)
GLOVER, COREY—PHOTOGRAPHS—PORTRAITS
PH06072 660-661 (July 8, 1993) p88. "The Band (from left): Will Calhoun, Vernon Reid, Doug Wimbish And Corey Glover" (Malfer)
GLOVER, DANNY—PHOTOGRAPHS
PH06073 633 (June 25, 1992) p49. "A Trio For Glover (left), Gibson And Gun"
PH06074 644 (November 26, 1992) p78. "[Lethal Weapon 3]"
GO-GO'S—PHOTOGRAPHS
PH06075 616 (October 31, 1991) p11. "Cervenka, Gina Schock, Jane Wiedlin, Kathy Valentine, Charlotte Caffey (clockwise from top left)" (Granitz, Steve)
PH06076 693 (October 20, 1994) p48. "Oh, God, Here They Go-Go Again" (Preston, Neal)
GOATS—ALBUMS
PH06077 696 (December 1, 1994) p127. "No Goats, No Glory"
GOATS—RECORDS
PH06078 650 (February 18, 1993) p60. "Tricks Of The Shade"
GOD IS MY CO-PILOT—PHOTOGRAPHS
PH06079 708 (May 18, 1995) p38. "N.Y.'s Jazzy Punks God Is My Co-Pilot" (Clinch, Danny)
GODCHAUX, DONNA—PHOTOGRAPHS—PORTRAITS
PH06080 717 (September 21, 1995) p72. "Nonstop Truckin' And Retooled Roots: The Dead's 1970s Lineup, With Keith Godchaux, Garcia, Lesh, Kreutzmann, Donna Godchaux And Weir (clockwise from top left)"
GODCHAUX, KEITH—PHOTOGRAPHS—PORTRAITS
PH06080 717 (September 21, 1995) p72. "Nonstop Truckin' And Retooled Roots: The Dead's 1970s Lineup, With Keith Godchaux, Garcia, Lesh, Kreutzmann, Donna Godchaux And Weir (clockwise from top left)"
THE GODFATHER PART II (FILM)—PHOTOGRAPHS
PH06081 654 (April 15, 1993) p69. "The Godfather Part II"
THE GODFATHER PART III (FILM)—PHOTOGRAPHS
PH06082 615 (October 17, 1991) p102. "Superegos On The Loose"
GOD'S FAVORITE BAND—PHOTOGRAPHS
PH06083 698-699 (December 29, 1994) p49. "God's Favorite Band" (McLeah, Jill)
GOD'S LITTLE MONKEYS—PHOTOGRAPHS
PH06084 626 (March 19, 1992) p20. "God's Little Monkeys (from left): Dave Allen, Jo Swiss, Dave Wall, Jon Townend" (Byrne, Peter)
GODUNOV, ALEXANDER—PHOTOGRAPHS
PH06085 615 (October 17, 1991) p67. "Diana Vreeland And Alexander Godunov, New York City, 1981" (Pigozzi, Jean)
GODZILLA—PHOTOGRAPHS
PH06086 682 (May 19, 1994) p66. "[Japan]"
GOENAGA, ANTHONY—PHOTOGRAPHS
PH06087 730 (March 21, 1996) p51. "Knickerophilliac Goenaga" (Cardillicchio, Nick)
GOETTEL, DWAYNE—PHOTOGRAPHS—PORTRAITS
PH06088 718 (October 5, 1995) p25. "[Dwayne Goettel]"

(Bilham, Maryanne)
GOFFEY, DANNY—PHOTOGRAPHS
PH06089 718 (October 5, 1995) pp[enc.24]. "Goffey In His Living Room" (GS, Jamil)
GOLD LAME SUIT (ELVIS PRESLEY'S)—PHOTOGRAPHS
PH06090 643 (November 12, 1992) pp[cover]. "Portraits" (Watson, Albert)
PH06091 645-646 (December 10, 1992) pp[cover]. "1992 Yearbook" (Watson, Albert)
GOLDBERG, ALEX—PHOTOGRAPHS
PH06092 615 (October 17, 1991) p14. "Hagar, Goldberg, Van Halen And Goldberg's Daughter, Alex" (Mazur, Kevin)
GOLDBERG, DANNY—PHOTOGRAPHS
PH06093 714 (August 10, 1995) p24. "Courtney Love; Goldberg's Wife, Rosemary Carroll; Goldberg; Kurt Cobain In '93" (Kravitz, Jeff)
GOLDBERG, WHOOPI—PHOTOGRAPHS
PH06094 615 (October 17, 1991) p14. "Hagar, Goldberg, Van Halen And Goldberg's Daughter, Alex" (Mazur, Kevin)
PH06095 629 (April 30, 1992) p11. "Dress Rehearsal For The Rain-Forest Benefit: Sting, John, Goldberg, Cole, Henley And Taylor (from left)" (Regan, Ken)
PH06096 633 (June 25, 1992) p48. "Goldberg (left) And Najimy Are Singing Nuns On The Run"
PH06097 642 (October 29, 1992) p77. "Sarafina!"
PH06098 644 (November 26, 1992) p22. "Goldberg, Richie, Taylor, John, Michael And Hornsby (from left) At The Garden" (Mazur, Kevin)
PH06099 644 (November 26, 1992) p78. "[Sister Act]"
PH06100 645-646 (December 10, 1992) p39. "[Rain Forest Redux]" (Regan, Ken)
PH06101 659 (June 24, 1993) p88. "Love: 'America,' With Goldberg And Danson"
PH06102 672-673 (December 23, 1993) p172. "Unfunny"
PH06103 689 (August 25, 1994) p96. "Whoopi Goldberg And Ray Liotta Get It On In The '50s"
PH06104 702 (February 23, 1995) p81. "Actresses Goldberg, Parker And Barrymore Blow It"
PH06105 741 (August 22, 1996) p48. "McConaughey Onscreen"
PH06106 748 (November 28, 1996) p143. "Dead On Arrival"
GOLDBLUM, JEFF—PHOTOGRAPHS
PH06107 659 (June 24, 1993) p36. "Dern And Jeff Goldblum, Flanking Steven Spielberg, Fell In Love On The Set" (Close, Murray)
GOLDEN PALOMINOS—ALBUMS
PH06108 618 (November 28, 1991) p98. "Drunk With Passion"
GOLDEN SMOG—ALBUMS
PH06109 729 (March 7, 1996) p50. "Down By The Old Mainstream"
GOLDEN SMOG—PHOTOGRAPHS
PH06110 633 (June 25, 1992) p11. "Golden Smog (from left): Gary Louris, Chris Mars, Dan Murphy, Craig Johnson And Marc Perlman" (Butler, Bonnie Lynn)
PH06111 735 (May 30, 1996) p50. "Golden Smog's Murphy And Kraig Johnson (from left)" (Capak, R. J.)
GOLDENEYE (FILM)—PHOTOGRAPHS
PH06112 718 (October 5, 1995) p76. "Pulp To Come"
PH06113 722 (November 30, 1995) p74. "Is Jennifer Jason Leigh's Rocker Hotter Than Pierce Brosnan's Bond? No Contest"
GOLDFINGER—PHOTOGRAPHS
PH06114 738-739 (July 11, 1996) p116. "Pfeiffer, Feldmann, Williams And Paulson (from left)"
PH06115 745 (October 17, 1996) p28. "[Goldfinger]" (Johnson, Lisa)
GOLDIE—PHOTOGRAPHS
PH06116 721 (November 16, 1995) p80. "Goldie" (Westenberg, Kevin)
PH06117 745 (October 17, 1996) p28. "Goldie And His Luv, Bjork" (Capak, R. J.)
GOLDIE—PHOTOGRAPHS—PORTRAITS
PH06118 704 (March 23, 1995) p38. "Artist Goldie" (Double, Steve)
PH06119 749 (December 12, 1996) p32. "Goldie Breathes Nice And Easy" (MacLennan, Philippe)
GOLDMAN, ALBERT—ILLUSTRATIONS
PH06120 685 (June 30, 1994) p10. "Ouch!" (Pendergrast, James T.)
GOLDSMITH, WILLIAM—PHOTOGRAPHS
PH06121 726 (January 25, 1996) p37. "Foo Fighters Are, From Left, Nate Mendel, Pat Smear, Dave Grohl And William Goldsmith" (Seliger, Mark)
PH06122 730 (March 21, 1996) p32. "Horsing Around: David Grohl (top and bottom) And Fellow Foo Fighters William Goldsmith, Pat Smear And Nate Mendel (middle, from left)" (Gougenheim, Kim)
PH06123 736 (June 13, 1996) p20. "[Foo Fighters]" (Mazur, Kevin)
GOLDSTON, LORI—PHOTOGRAPHS
PH06124 674 (January 27, 1994) p36. "Team Spirit: Novoselic, Smear, Grohl, Cobain And Touring Cellist Lori Goldston (from left)" (Seliger, Mark)
GOLDWATER, BARRY—PHOTOGRAPHS
PH06125 698-699 (December 29, 1994) p165. "Wave Of The Future: Conservatives Gingrich And Barry Goldwater In 1976"
GOLINO, VALERIA—PHOTOGRAPHS
PH06126 659 (June 24, 1993) p88. "Farce: 'Hot Shots! Part Deux,' With Sheen And Golino"
GOLOVINE, MARINA—PHOTOGRAPHS
PH06127 650 (February 18, 1993) p66. "Gregoire Colin Is More Than A Brother To Marina Golovine"
GOMEZ—PHOTOGRAPHS
PH06128 710 (June 15, 1995) p41. "D Gen (from left): Pyro, Michael Wildwood, Malin, Sage, Richard Bacchus And Gomez" (Ragel, Jon)
GOMEZ, CHICO—PHOTOGRAPHS
PH06129 706 (April 20, 1995) pp[enc.18]. "Skating At Chicken's Pool" (Seliger, Mark)
GOMEZ, JESUS—PHOTOGRAPHS
PH06130 669 (November 11, 1993) p35. "Rebuilding The Carpenters Union: Ubaldo Vasquez, Mike Olds And Jesus Gomez (foreground, from left)" (Reed, Dudley)
GOMI—PHOTOGRAPHS
PH06131 706 (April 20, 1995) pp[enc.22]. "At Big Coffee Shop, In New York" (Tavee, Tom)
GONE WITH THE WIND (FILM)—PHOTOGRAPHS
PH06132 724-725 (December 28, 1995) p42. "Pancakes, My Ass! Mississippi Entered The 20th Century"
GONZO—PHOTOGRAPHS
PH06133 618 (November 28, 1991) p11. "Kirk Kammett, Slash, Lars Ulrich, Geoff Tate And Armored Saint Drummer Gonzo (from left)" (Blakesberg, Jay)
GOO GOO DOLLS—PHOTOGRAPHS
PH06134 653 (April 1, 1993) p23. "Serious Fun: The Goos Rock With An Adolescent Passion And Grown-Up Themes" (Lass, Imke)
PH06135 723 (December 14, 1995) p36. "Hungry For Success And Searching For Dinner: Johnny Rzeznik, Robby Takac And Mike Malinin" (Ockenfels, Frank W.)
GOOD ROCKIN' TONIGHT (BOOK)—PHOTOGRAPHS
PH06136 619-620 (December 12, 1991) p32. "[Good Rockin' Tonight]"
THE GOOD SON (FILM)—PHOTOGRAPHS
PH06137 668 (October 28, 1993) p88. "Mac The Knife"
GOODE, CHRIS—PHOTOGRAPHS—PORTRAITS
PH06138 634-635 (July 9, 1992) p20. "Dillon Fence (from left): Chris Goode, Kent Alphin, Greg Humphreys And Scott Carle" (Thompson, D. Kent)
GOODEN, SAM—PHOTOGRAPHS
PH06139 668 (October 28, 1993) p66. "The Impressions Circa

'67: Mayfield, Fred Cash And Gooden"
GOODING, CUBA—PHOTOGRAPHS
PH06140 626 (March 19, 1992) p102. "Race Divides Gooding And Marshall"
PH06141 750-751 (December 26, 1996) p140. "Gooding Plays Dress-Up At The King Of Sports Endorsements"
GOODLING, WILLIAM—PHOTOGRAPHS—PORTRAITS
PH06142 719 (October 19, 1995) p125. "Goodling: Greed Guarantor" (Trippett, Robert)
GOODMAN, GREER—PHOTOGRAPHS
PH06143 704 (March 23, 1995) pp102-103. "Class of '95" (Tavee, Tom)
GOODMAN, JOHN—PHOTOGRAPHS
PH06144 627 (April 2, 1992) p41. "'Barton Fink,' With John Turturro And John Goodman"
PH06145 630 (May 14, 1992) p113. "John Goodman Tries Hard But Can't Win One For The Babe"
PH06146 651 (March 4, 1993) p74. "John Goodman Directs Cathy Moriarty And Tacky Monster"
PH06147 655 (April 29, 1993) p69. "Crawford And Holliday (left) Reborn As Goodman And Griffith"
PH06148 685 (June 30, 1994) p64. "Maclachlan As Cliff Vandercave With John Goodman On The Set Of "Flintstones""
GOODMAN, MARK—PHOTOGRAPHS
PH06149 619-620 (December 12, 1991) p71. "The Original VJs (Clockwise from bottom left): Nina Blackwood, Mark Goodman, Martha Quinn, J. J. Jackson, Alan Hunter"
GOODRIDGE, ROBIN—PHOTOGRAPHS
PH06150 710 (June 15, 1995) p49. "Dave Parsons, Rossdale, Robin Goodridge, Pulsford (from left)" (Westenberg, Kevin)
PH06151 712-713 (July 13, 1995) p29. "Zen Careerists: Pulsford, Parsons, Rossdale, And Goodridge (from left)" (Mahurin, Matt)
GOODRIDGE, ROBIN—PHOTOGRAPHS—PORTRAITS
PH06152 732 (April 18, 1996) p41. "Robin Goodridge, Gavin Rossdale, Dave Parsons And Nigel Pulsford" (Seliger, Mark)
GOOGE, DEB—PHOTOGRAPHS—PORTRAITS
PH06153 623 (February 6, 1992) p20. "Clockwise From Top Left: Butcher, Shields, Googe, O'Ciosoig" (Double, Steve)
GOPALAN, GEETHA—PHOTOGRAPHS
PH06154 693 (October 20, 1994) p136. "Gopalan" (White, Steven)
GORBACHEV, MIKHAIL—ILLUSTRATIONS
PH06155 615 (October 17, 1991) p8. "Millie Comes Upon A Sticky Situation" (Pendergrast, James T.)
GORBACHEV, MIKHAIL—PHOTOGRAPHS
PH06156 623 (February 6, 1992) p11. "Mikhail Gorbachev Greets Members Of Scorpions In Moscow" (Regan, Ken)
PH06157 689 (August 25, 1994) p52. "The Man Who Helped Topple The Iron Curtain Visits The Iron Lady: Gorbachev With Lady Thatcher Late Last Year"
GORBACHEV, MIKHAIL—PHOTOGRAPHS—PORTRAITS
PH06158 689 (August 25, 1994) p51. "[Mikhail Gorbachev]" (Kidd, Tom)
GORDON, JIM—PHOTOGRAPHS
PH06159 655 (April 29, 1993) p35. "Derek And The Dominos: Jim Gordon, Carl Radle, Bobby Whitlock And Clapton (from left)..."
GORDON, KIM—PHOTOGRAPHS
PH06160 619-620 (December 12, 1991) p59. "Women In Rock Band Together For Prochoice" (Berkwitz, David Neil)
PH06161 634-635 (July 9, 1992) p33. "Steve Shelley, Kim Gordon, Lee Ranaldo And Thurston Moore (from left)"
PH06162 637 (August 20, 1992) p9. "Steve Shelley, Kim Gordon, Lee Ranaldo, Shake-A-Leg's Harry Horgan, Moore, Hersh And David Narcizo (from left)" (Robicheau, Paul)
PH06163 691 (September 22, 1994) p54. "Kurt Cobain With Kim Gordon On Nirvana's 1991 Tour With Sonic Youth" (Moore, T.)
PH06164 691 (September 22, 1994) p56. "Moore And Gordon In '87" (Moore-Erdman, Susan)
PH06165 691 (September 22, 1994) p56. "Ranaldo, Gordon, Moore, Shelley (from left)" (Petersen, Naomi)
PH06166 692 (October 6, 1994) p62. "Gordon In Manhattan" (Hom, Marc)
PH06167 692 (October 6, 1994) p53. "Kim Gordon" (Levine, Linda)
PH06168 692 (October 6, 1994) p61. "Kim Gordon In Bed At Von Furth's" (Hom, Marc)
PH06169 695 (November 17, 1994) p84. "Sonic Youth" (Mark, Mary Ellen)
PH06170 700 (January 26, 1995) p17. "[John Giorno's AIDS Treatment Project]" (Gruen, Bob)
PH06171 712-713 (July 13, 1995) p32. "All The Way To Memphis: Moore, Shelley, Gordon And Ranaldo (from left)" (Day, Corinne)
PH06172 715 (August 24, 1995) p43. "S.Y.'s Kim Gordon Backstage With proud Lolla Papa Perry Farrell" (Blakesberg, Jay)
PH06173 721 (November 16, 1995) p25. "Sonic Youth's Lee Ranaldo, Thurston Moore, Kim Gordon And Steve Shelley (from left) After Their 'State' Taping In New York" (Capak, R. J.)
GORDON, KIM—PHOTOGRAPHS—PORTRAITS
PH06174 679 (April 7, 1994) p24. "The SOnic Set: Gordon, Moore, Ranaldo, Shelley (clockwise from top left)" (Watson, Norman)
PH06175 691 (September 22, 1994) p54. "Sonic Parents: Moore And Kim Gordon" (Vadukal, Nitin)
PH06176 692 (October 6, 1994) p49. "Kim Gordon" (Levine, Laura)
GORDON, MIKE—PHOTOGRAPHS
PH06177 631 (May 28, 1992) p16. "Phish (from left): Trey Anastasio, Mike Gordon, Page McConnell, Jon Fishman" (Halsband, Michael)
GORDON, NINA—PHOTOGRAPHS
PH06178 686-687 (July 14, 1994) p73. "Salt Of The Earth: Lack, Gordon, Post And Shapiro (from left)" (Elledge, Paul)
PH06179 700 (January 26, 1995) p20. "Angry Post-Feminists Don't Wear Fur: Post And Gordon" (Seliger, Mark)
PH06180 700 (January 26, 1995) p19. "Gordon, Lack, Post And Shapiro (from left)" (Seliger, Mark)
PH06181 701 (February 9, 1995) p16. "Louise Post, Johnston, Nina Gordon And Pete Droge do D.C." (Harrington, John)
PH06182 709 (June 1, 1995) p17. "Veruca Salt's Louise Post, Jim Shapiro And Gordon (from left)" (Peters, Karen A.)
GORDON, ROBERT—ALBUMS
PH06183 750-751 (December 26, 1996) p192. "The Humbler"
GORDY, BERRY—BOOKS
PH06184 698-699 (December 29, 1994) p64. "To Be Loved"
GORDY, BERRY—PHOTOGRAPHS
PH06184 698-699 (December 29, 1994) p64. "To Be Loved"
GORE, ALBERT—ILLUSTRATIONS
PH06185 671 (December 9, 1993) p7. "On This Site" (Pendergrast, James T.)
GORE, ALBERT—PHOTOGRAPHS
PH06186 660-661 (July 8, 1993) p52. "Babbitt On The Campaign Trail: Presidential Candidates Michael Dukakis, Babbitt, Paul Simon, Richard Gephardt, Jesse Jackson And Al Gore (from left) At A New York Forum ..." (Peterso
PH06187 660-661 (July 8, 1993) p48. "With The Vice-President: Al Gore And Babbitt After One Of Their Weekly Breakfast Meetings On The Environment" (Ockenfels, Frank W.)
PH06188 662 (August 5, 1993) p37. "Al Gore And Bill Clinton Introducing Newest Democrat, David Gergen, In May"
PH06189 668 (October 28, 1993) p47. "Welcome To The Shark Tank: Browner With Her Mentor, Al Gore"
PH06190 698-699 (December 29, 1994) p61. "Tipper And Al "Achilles" Gore" (Neema, Frederic)
PH06191 720 (November 2, 1995) p17. "Good Lovin', They Got A Truckload: Belushi, Clinton And Gore In L.A."

GORE, KARENNA—PHOTOGRAPHS
PH06192 656 (May 13, 1993) p65. "[The Gore Girls]" (Adams, Eddie)
GORE, KRISTIN—PHOTOGRAPHS
PH06192 656 (May 13, 1993) p65. "[The Gore Girls]" (Adams, Eddie)
GORE, MARTIN—PHOTOGRAPHS
PH06193 670 (November 25, 1993) p94. "1982: Fletcher, Gahan, Gore And Wilder (from left)"
PH06194 670 (November 25, 1993) p94. "1985: Gore, Wilder, Gahan And Fletcher (clockwise from left)" (Nosotti, Fabio)
PH06195 670 (November 25, 1993) p91. "...And Martin Gore (far right)" (Watson, Albert)
PH06196 670 (November 25, 1993) p92. "In Madrid, Making Their Last Record: Gahan, Gore, Wilder, Fletcher (from left)" (Corbijn, Anton)
GORE, SARAH—PHOTOGRAPHS
PH06197 656 (May 13, 1993) p65. "[The Gore Girls]" (Adams, Eddie)
GORE, TIPPER—PHOTOGRAPHS
PH06198 654 (April 15, 1993) p20. "PMRC Cofounders Gore And Susan Baker" (Brack, Dennis)
PH06199 665 (September 16, 1993) p35. "Federal Reserve Chairman Alan Greenspan With The First Lady And Tipper Gore At The State Of The Union"
PH06200 698-699 (December 29, 1994) p61. "Tipper And Al "Achilles" Gore" (Neema, Frederic)
GORECKI, HENRYK—ALBUMS
PH06201 655 (April 29, 1993) p65. "Symphony No. 3"
GORHAM, MEL—PHOTOGRAPHS
PH06202 718 (October 5, 1995) p77. "Rupal, Keitel And Gorham Boogie"
GORKY'S ZYGOTIC MYNCI—ALBUMS
PH06203 745 (October 17, 1996) p132. "Introducing Gorky's Zygotic Mynci"
GORMAN, CHRIS—PHOTOGRAPHS
PH06204 706 (April 20, 1995) p48. "Chris Gorman & Gail Greenwood" (Seliger, Mark)
GORMAN, CHRIS—PHOTOGRAPHS—PORTRAITS
PH06205 649 (February 4, 1993) p16. "Chris Gorman, Tanya Donelly And Tom Gorman (from left)" (Feingold, Deborah)
GORMAN, TIM—PHOTOGRAPHS
PH06206 644 (November 26, 1992) p15. "Kantner, Darby Gould, Jack Casady, Tim Gorman, Prairie Prince, Papa John Creach, McGuinn And Slick Aguilar (from left)" (Mazur, Kevin)
GORMAN, TOM—PHOTOGRAPHS
PH06207 706 (April 20, 1995) p49. "Tom Gorman" (Seliger, Mark)
GORMAN, TOM—PHOTOGRAPHS—PORTRAITS
PH06208 649 (February 4, 1993) p16. "Chris Gorman, Tanya Donelly And Tom Gorman (from left)" (Feingold, Deborah)
GORMLY, KEN—PHOTOGRAPHS
PH06209 712-713 (July 13, 1995) p46. "High Sea: Gormly, Elliot, And Perkins (from left)" (Capak, R. J.)
GOSPEL MUSIC—ILLUSTRATIONS
PH06210 668 (October 28, 1993) p75. "Every Day Is Sunday" (Barbour, Karen)
GOSSARD, STONE—PHOTOGRAPHS
PH06211 616 (October 31, 1991) p15. "Pearl Jam (from left): Mike McCready, David Abbruzzese, Eddie Vedder, Jeff Ament And Stone Gossard" (Cuffaro, Chris)
PH06212 624 (February 20, 1992) p12. "From Left: Layne Staley, Ann Wilson, Stone Gossard, Jerry Cantrell" (Mason, Karen)
PH06213 634-635 (July 9, 1992) p13. "Pearl Jam's Mike McCready, Dave Abbruzzese, Eddie Vedder, Gossard And Jeff Ament (from left)" (Mercer, Lance)
PH06214 639 (September 17, 1992) p60. "Eddie Vedder, Mike McCready, Jeff Ament And Stone Gossard (from left) Of Pearl Jam" (Blakesberg, Jay)
PH06215 649 (February 4, 1993) p23. "Jeremy Toback, Shawn Smith, Regan Hagar And Stone Gossard (from left)"
PH06216 668 (October 28, 1993) p51. "The Sun Shines On The Five Musketeers: Jeff Ament, Eddie Vedder (We're Not Kidding), Dave Abbruzzese, Stone Gossard And Mike McCready (from left)" (Seliger, Mark)
PH06217 672-673 (December 23, 1993) p69. "Us 'Vs.' The World: Gossard, Mike McCready, Dave Abbruzzese, Vedder, Jeff Ament (from left)" (Seliger, Mark)
PH06218 688 (August 11, 1994) p30. "Ament (left) And Gossard To Testify Before A House Subcommittee" (Brennan, Shayna)
PH06219 698-699 (December 29, 1994) p60. "Pearl Jam's Jeff Ament And Stone Gossard"
PH06220 698-699 (December 29, 1994) p68. "Young, Vedder And Stone Gossard (from left) Do The Right Thing For The Kids" (Hashimoto, Mike)
PH06221 702 (February 23, 1995) p26. "Pirate Music: McCready, Vedder, Ament, Irons And Stone Gossard (from left)" (Mercer, Lance)
PH06222 726 (January 25, 1996) p17. "Mike McCready, Jeff Ament, Harper, Eddie Vedder, Jack Irons And Stone Gossard (from left)"
PH06223 728 (February 22, 1996) p25. "Pearl Jam's Gossard Monkeys Around" (Jonze, Spike)
GOTT, LARRY—PHOTOGRAPHS—PORTRAITS
PH06224 680 (April 21, 1994) p11. "[James]" (Borris, Dan)
GOULD, DARBY—PHOTOGRAPHS
PH06225 644 (November 26, 1992) p15. "Kantner, Darby Gould, Jack Casady, Tim Gorman, Prairie Prince, Papa John Creach, McGuinn And Slick Aguilar (from left)" (Mazur, Kevin)
GOULET, SHAWN—PHOTOGRAPHS
PH06226 742 (September 5, 1996) pp52-53. "World-Class Road-Luge Pilots Lee Dansie, Bob Stiles And Shawn Goulet (from left) Take A Break Near The Top Of The X Games' 'Crash Alley'" (Seliger, Mark)
GOVERNMENT (UNITED STATES)—ILLUSTRATIONS
PH06227 671 (December 9, 1993) p35. "Start-Finish" (Klein, Renee)
PH06228 672-673 (December 23, 1993) p83. "What A 25% Defense Cut Could Buy" (Rall, Ted)
GRACE OF MY HEART (FILM)—PHOTOGRAPHS
PH06229 744 (October 3, 1996) p79. "Illeana Douglas Meets A '50s Girl Group"
GRACE, ANNA—PHOTOGRAPHS
PH06230 742 (September 5, 1996) p68. "Girls Taylor, Grace And Harris"
GRACELAND (ESTATE)—PHOTOGRAPHS
PH06231 680 (April 21, 1994) p13. "Elvis Site: A Convergence Of Stars" (Nation, Bill)
GRACEY, CHAD—PHOTOGRAPHS
PH06232 696 (December 1, 1994) p50. "Chad Gracey" (Fleischauer, Robert)
PH06233 726 (January 25, 1996) p35. "Dahlheimer, Taylor, Kowalczyk And Gracey (from left) At Their York, Pa., High School In 1989" (Broad, Julian)
GRACEY, CHAD—PHOTOGRAPHS—PORTRAITS
PH06234 726 (January 25, 1996) p34. "Taylor, Kowalczyk, Gracey And Dahlheimer (from left) In New York In Late 1995" (Broad, Julian)
GRAFFIN, GREG—ILLUSTRATIONS
PH06235 698-699 (December 29, 1994) p52. "[Greg Graffin]" (Todd, Mark)
GRAFFIN, GREG—PHOTOGRAPHS
PH06236 670 (November 25, 1993) p30. "Hetson, Bobby Schayer, Bentley, Gurewitz And Graffin (clockwise from top left)" (Zlozower, Neil)
PH06237 700 (January 26, 1995) p17. "Bad Religion's Brian Baker, Greg Graffin, Bobby Schayer, Jay Bentley and Greg Hetson" (Kravitz, Jeff)

PH06238 722 (November 30, 1995) p19. "Graffin, Ocasek, Jay Bentley, Brian Baker, Greg Hetson And Bobby Schayer (from left)" (Mazur, Kevin)
GRAFFIN, GREG—PHOTOGRAPHS—PORTRAITS
PH06239 695 (November 17, 1994) p40. "Bad Religion" (Guip, Amy)
GRAFFITI—ILLUSTRATIONS
PH06240 704 (March 23, 1995) p18. "Road To Hell" (Pendergrast, James T.)
GRAHAM—PHOTOGRAPHS
PH06241 710 (June 15, 1995) p40. "[Graham]" (Mafford, Spike)
GRAHAM, BILL—PHOTOGRAPHS
PH06242 619-620 (December 12, 1991) p100. "Graham (lower right) With His Mother (top right) And Sisters, In Berlin In 1938"
PH06243 619-620 (December 12, 1991) p104. "Graham And Bob Dylan At A 1975 Benefit" (Regan, Ken)
PH06244 619-620 (December 12, 1991) p104. "Graham And Close Friend Carlos Santana" (Roberts, Ebet)
PH06245 619-620 (December 12, 1991) p102. "Graham And Janis Joplin At Winterland, One Of His Regular Venues, In 1968" (Marshall, Jim)
PH06246 619-620 (December 12, 1991) p102. "Graham And Jerry Garcia At One Of The Dead's 'Farewell' Concerts In 1974" (Leibovitz, Annie)
PH06247 619-620 (December 12, 1991) p104. "Graham And Keith Richards In 1972" (Regan, Ken)
PH06248 619-620 (December 12, 1991) p100. "Graham In 'Guys And Dolls,' Circa 1958"
PH06249 619-620 (December 12, 1991) p97. "Graham Onstage During The U.S. Portion Of Live Aid, In July 1985" (Regan, Ken)
PH06250 619-620 (December 12, 1991) p100. "Graham With Former Girlfriend Marcia Sult, Son David And Stepson Thomas Sult" (Regan, Ken)
PH06251 619-620 (December 12, 1991) p100. "Graham With The Who's Roger Daltrey, Keith Moon And Pete Townshend, In 1976" (Zagaris, Michael)
GRAHAM, BILL—PHOTOGRAPHS—PORTRAITS
PH06252 619-620 (December 12, 1991) p97. "[Bill Graham]" (Feingold, Deborah)
PH06253 623 (February 6, 1992) p54. "[Bill Graham]" (Greene, Herb)
GRAHAM, DAVID—PHOTOGRAPHS
PH06254 619-620 (December 12, 1991) p100. "Graham With Former Girlfriend Marcia Sult, Son David And Stepson Thomas Sult" (Regan, Ken)
GRAHAM, GLEN—PHOTOGRAPHS
PH06255 639 (September 17, 1992) p20. "Shannon Hoon, Christopher Thorn, Glen Graham, Brad Smith And Rogers Stevens (clockwise from top left)" (Clinch, Danny)
PH06256 640 (October 1, 1992) p27. "Blind Melon (from left): Smith, Stevens, Thorn, Hoon And Graham" (Clinch, Danny)
PH06257 669 (November 11, 1993) pp38-39. "Brad Smith, Glen Graham, Shannon Hood, Rogers Stevens & Christopher Thorn (from left)" (Seliger, Mark)
GRAHAM, HEATHER—PHOTOGRAPHS
PH06258 669 (November 11, 1993) p62. "'Cowgirls' Lineup: Rain Phoenix, Victoria Williams And Heather Graham" (Markus, Kurt)
GRAHAM, LARRY—PHOTOGRAPHS
PH06259 649 (February 4, 1993) p51. "Rose Stone, Sly, Freddie Stone, Graham, Robinson, Errico And Martini Of Sly And The Family Stone"
GRAMLICH, EDWARD—ILLUSTRATIONS
PH06260 746 (October 31, 1996) p54. "[Edward Gramlich]"
GRAMM, LOU—PHOTOGRAPHS
PH06261 692 (October 6, 1994) p35. "Foreigner's Lou Gramm (left) And Mick Jones" (Robicheau, Paul)
GRAMM, LOU—PHOTOGRAPHS—PORTRAITS
PH06262 642 (October 29, 1992) p21. "Mick Jones (left) And Lou Gramm" (Sullivan, Lorinda)
GRAMM, PHIL—PHOTOGRAPHS—PORTRAITS
PH06263 710 (June 15, 1995) p57. "Gramm" (Sharp, Tim)
GRANATIR, SARAH—PHOTOGRAPHS—PORTRAITS
PH06264 652 (March 18, 1993) pp[enc.37]. "Sarah Granatir" (Seliger, Mark)
GRAND PUBA—ALBUMS
PH06265 647 (January 7, 1993) p46. "Reel To Reel"
GRAND PUBA MAXWELL—PHOTOGRAPHS
PH06266 628 (April 16, 1992) p55. "DJ Alamo, Grand Puba Maxwell And Ron Stud (from left)" (Seliger, Mark)
GRANDMASTER FLASH—PHOTOGRAPHS
PH06267 670 (November 25, 1993) p37. "Grandmaster Flash, Herc, Afrika Bambaataa And Chuck D" (Mazur, Kevin)
PH06268 672-673 (December 23, 1993) p140. "Before The Split: Flash (center) And His Furious Crew Spreading 'The Message' In 1983" (Saunders, Red)
PH06269 708 (May 18, 1995) p17. "Simon LeBon, Grandmaster Flash And Warren Cuccurullo In New York (from left)" (Olson, Sheryl)
GRANDMASTER FLASH—PHOTOGRAPHS—PORTRAITS
PH06270 672-673 (December 23, 1993) p140. "Grandmaster Flash Today" (Wessel, Cathrine)
GRANDSTAFF, TRACY—PHOTOGRAPHS
PH06271 663 (August 19, 1993) p48. "Writer Tracy Grandstaff, Judge And MTV Exec Abby Terkuhle" (Ockenfels, Frank W.)
PH06272 704 (March 23, 1995) p95. "Tracy Grandstaff Of MTV Said To Her Interviewer, 'What Do I Have Say To Get This Job? What Do I Have To Do?'" (Pluchino, Joseph)
GRANT, HUGH—PHOTOGRAPHS
PH06273 698-699 (December 29, 1994) p194. "Grant Gets MacDowell In "Weddings""
PH06274 714 (August 10, 1995) p62. "An Awfully Big Adventure"
PH06275 714 (August 10, 1995) p62. "Nine Months"
PH06276 745 (October 17, 1996) p144. "Grant And Parker Do The ER Thing"
GRANT, HUGH—PHOTOGRAPHS—PORTRAITS
PH06277 678 (March 24, 1994) p104. "Two Babes And A Hunk: Davis (Angie); Stowe (China Moon); Grant (Four Weddings)"
PH06278 705 (April 6, 1995) p69. "Oscar Rejects"
PH06279 709 (June 1, 1995) p68. "Too Much Hugh Grant"
PH06280 716 (September 7, 1995) p78. "Summer Wrap-Up]"
GRANT LEE BUFFALO—ALBUMS
PH06281 692 (October 6, 1994) p84. "Mighty Joe Moon"
PH06282 698-699 (December 29, 1994) p190. "Mighty Joe Moon"
PH06283 736 (June 13, 1996) p78. "Copperopolis"
GRANT LEE BUFFALO—PHOTOGRAPHS
PH06284 663 (August 19, 1993) p24. "[Grant Lee Buffalo]" (Azimi, Mojgan B.)
PH06285 695 (November 17, 1994) p94. "Grant Lee Buffalo" (Samuel, Deborah)
PH06286 696 (December 1, 1994) pp98-99. "American Icons: Joey Peters, Grant Lee Phillips And Paul Kimble (from left)" (Ockenfels, Frank, 3)
GRANT, PETER—PHOTOGRAPHS
PH06287 726 (January 25, 1996) p28. "Page, Grant And Plant (from left) In 1975" (Preston, Neal)
GRASSHOPPER—PHOTOGRAPHS
PH06288 652 (March 18, 1993) p27. "Jonathan Donahue (left) And Grasshopper"
PH06289 664 (September 2, 1993) p24. "They're All Revved Up: Donahue, Thorpe, Baker, Chambers, Fridmann And Grasshopper (from left)" (Gullick, Steve)
GRATEFUL DEAD—ALBUMS
PH06290 617 (November 14, 1991) p137. "American Beauty" (Kelly-Mouse Studios)
PH06291 617 (November 14, 1991) p97. "Aoxomoxoa" (Griffin, Rick)

GRATEFUL DEAD—ILLUSTRATIONS
PH06292 619-620 (December 12, 1991) p32. "[Conversations With The Dead]"
PH06293 666 (September 30, 1993) p27. "[Grateful Dead]" (Griffin, Rick)
PH06294 667 (October 14, 1993) p14. "Dead Ahead" (Pendergrast, James T.)
PH06295 693 (October 20, 1994) p43. "Dead Center"
GRATEFUL DEAD—PHOTOGRAPHS
PH06296 616 (October 31, 1991) p40. "Bill Kreutzmann, Ron "Pigpen" McKernan, Bob Weir, Garcia And Phil Lesh (clockwise from top left) In 1966" (Greene, Herb)
PH06297 619-620 (December 12, 1991) p84. "The Grateful Dead" (Blakesberg, Jay)
PH06298 619-620 (December 12, 1991) p103. "Phil Lesh, Bob Weir, Neil Young And Jerry Garcia (from left) Pay Tribute To Bill Graham" (Blakesberg, Jay)
PH06299 643 (November 12, 1992) p63. "The Grateful Dead Mug For Baron Wolman After Their 1967 Bust" (Wolman, Baron)
PH06300 645-646 (December 10, 1992) p36. "The Grateful Dead Before The Fall" (Blakesberg, Jay)
PH06301 657 (May 27, 1993) p9. "Oh Say Can You See?: The Dead's Vince Welnick, Bob Weir And Jerry Garcia" (Blakesberg, Jay)
PH06302 660-661 (July 8, 1993) p29. "The Dead's Phil Lesh, Bob Weir And Jerry Garcia (from left)" (Blakesberg, Jay)
PH06303 664 (September 2, 1993) p46. "The Dead At Rest in 1966: Phil Lesh, Bill Kreutzman, Ron 'Pigpen' McKernan, Bob Weir And Jerry Garcia (clockwise from left)" (Greene, Herb)
PH06304 672-673 (December 23, 1993) p37. "Left; The Dead In San Francisco" (Blakesberg, Jay)
PH06305 676 (February 24, 1994) p46. "The Early Grateful Dead (clockwise from left): Jerry Garcia, Bill Kreutzmann, Ron 'Pigpen' McKernan, Bob Weir, Percussionist Mickey Hart And Phil Lesh" (Marshall, Jim)
PH06306 677 (March 10, 1994) p27. "The Dead's Lesh, Weir, Vince Welnick, Hornsby, Bill Kreutzmann, Mickey Hart" (Mazur, Kevin)
PH06307 693 (October 20, 1994) p43. ""Dark Star" Gazing: The Grateful Dead In A 1971 New York City Concert" (Pulin, Chuck)
PH06308 696 (December 1, 1994) p24. "Bob Weir, Lesh And Garcia (from left)" (Blakesberg, Jay)
PH06309 717 (September 21, 1995) p52. "Before The Dead, They Were The Warlocks" (Greene, Herbi)
PH06310 717 (September 21, 1995) p71. "The Dawn Of A New Euphoria: The Grateful Dead Let The Good Times Roll With A Free Show At The Panhandle, By San Francisco's Golden Gate Park, In 1966" (Marshall, Jim)
PH06311 717 (September 21, 1995) p54. "The Dead In '66 At The Crossroads, the Corner Of Haight And Ashbury: Garcia, Pigpen, Lesh, Weir, Kreutzmann (from left)" (Greene, Herbi)
PH06312 717 (September 21, 1995) p65. "The Dead In Front Of Their Ashbury St. House, 1967: Jerry Garcia, Ron 'Pigpen' McKernan, Bob Weir, Phil Lesh, Co-Managers Danny Rifkin And Rock Scully, And Bill Kreutzmann..."
PH06313 717 (September 21, 1995) p48. "The Dead Play To A Packed Crowd On Haight Street In 1968, At One Of The Band's Many Free Concerts" (Marshall, Jim)
PH06314 717 (September 21, 1995) p67. "Jerry Garcia, Phil Lesh, Bill Kreutzmann, Bob Weir And Ron 'Pigpen' McKernan (clockwise from bottom right) Huddled In San Francisco's Golden Gate Park, 1967" (Marshall, Jim)
PH06315 717 (September 21, 1995) p66. "Lesh, Early Dead Co-Managers Scully And Rifkin, Weir And Garcia At A Press Conference Following The Oct. 2, 1967, drug Bust At The Dead's House" (Wolman, Baron)
PH06316 717 (September 21, 1995) p73. "marrying Acid-Damaged Art Music And The Funky Snort Of Live Rock & Roll: The Dead As A Lysergic-Dance Band In 1969 With Tom Constanten, Weir, Kreutzmann, Pigpen, Lesh, Hart..."
PH06317 717 (September 21, 1995) p72. "The Music Never Stopped: Garcia, Weir, Lesh, Brent Mydland, Kreutzmann And Hart (from left) In 1979" (Greene, Herbi)
PH06318 717 (September 21, 1995) p69. "The Original Quintet At Home At 710 Ashbury St., In 1966: Phil Lesh, Bob Weir, Bill Kreutzmann, Ron 'Pigpen' McKernan And Jerry Garcia (from left)" (Anthony, Gene)
PH06319 717 (September 21, 1995) p51. "Past And Present Members of The Grateful Dead Fronted By A Cardboard Garcia At The Band's Induction Into The Rock & Roll Hall Of Fame, January 1994" (Elgar, Nick)
PH06320 726 (January 25, 1996) p23. "The Last Incarnation Of The Dead Perform In February 1995: Phil Lesh, Mickey Hart, Bob Weir, Jerry Garcia And Vince Welnick (from left)" (Blakesberg, Jay)
PH06321 740 (August 8, 1996) p34. "The Dead's House At 710 Ashbury St., In San Francisco, 1966" (Greene, Herb)
GRATEFUL DEAD—PHOTOGRAPHS—PORTRAITS
PH06322 717 (September 21, 1995) p72. "Nonstop Truckin' And Retooled Roots: The Dead's 1970s Lineup, With Keith Godchaux, Garcia, Lesh, kreutzmann, Donna Godchaux And Weir (clockwise from top left)"
GRAVEDIGGAZ—ALBUMS
PH06323 692 (October 6, 1994) p90. "Six Feet Deep"
GRAY, CRISPIN—PHOTOGRAPHS
PH06324 628 (April 16, 1992) p56. "Gray, Garside, Johnson And Adams (from left)" (Double, Steve)
GRAY, JAMES—PHOTOGRAPHS
PH06325 700 (January 26, 1995) p24. "[Spearhead]"
GRAY, JERMAINE—PHOTOGRAPHS
PH06326 728 (February 22, 1996) p48. "March 1995: D-Mac Crew Parties With Jazz At Mitch Weller's" (Smale, Brian)
GRAY, SHANE—PHOTOGRAPHS
PH06326 728 (February 22, 1996) p48. "March 1995: D-Mac Crew Parties With Jazz At Mitch Weller's" (Smale, Brian)
PH06327 728 (February 22, 1996) p49. "Shane Gray: He Went Out Like A Real Gangster" (Smale, Brian)
GREASE (STAGE MUSICAL)—PHOTOGRAPHS
PH06328 683 (June 2, 1994) p76. "Grease"
GREAT SOCIETY—ALBUMS
PH06329 741 (August 22, 1996) p100. "Born To Be Burned"
THE GREAT WHITE HYPE (FILM)—PHOTOGRAPHS
PH06330 735 (May 30, 1996) p57. "Preening"
GRECH, RICK—PHOTOGRAPHS
PH06331 655 (April 29, 1993) p35. "The Aptly Named Blind Faith: Steve Winwood, Rick Grech, Ginger Baker And Clapton (from left)"
GREEN ACRES (TELEVISION SHOW)—PHOTOGRAPHS
PH06332 666 (September 30, 1993) p116. "Out Of This World 'Green Acres' (left)"
GREEN DAY—ALBUMS
PH06333 698-699 (December 29, 1994) p191. "Dookie"
PH06334 706 (April 20, 1995) p104. "Dookie"
PH06335 720 (November 2, 1995) p65. "Insomniac"
GREEN DAY—ILLUSTRATIONS
PH06336 694 (November 3, 1994) p14. "Green Day" (Pendergrast, James T.)
PH06337 720 (November 2, 1995) p65. "Ode To Billie Joe" (Panter, Gary)
PH06338 728 (February 22, 1996) p16. "Punk-Platinum" (Pendergrast, James T.)
GREEN DAY—PHOTOGRAPHS
PH06339 682 (May 19, 1994) p56. "[Green Day]" (Seliger, Mark)
PH06340 691 (September 22, 1994) p64. "Mud As The Punk Accessory Of Choice: Green Day Being Bombarded On The South Stage by Enthusiastic Fans" (Olson, Jonathan)

PH06341 691 (September 22, 1994) p25. "Punk's New Breed: Mike Dirnt, Billie Joe And Tre Cool (from left)" (Seliger, Mark)
PH06342 698-699 (December 29, 1994) p46. "Green Day" (Watson, Albert)
PH06343 700 (January 26, 1995) p46. "All Dressed Up: Onstage In New York City, December 1994" (Cassidy, Chris)
PH06344 700 (January 26, 1995) pp40-41. "Billie Joe (Opposite), Mike Dirnt And Tre Cool" (Winters, Dan)
PH06345 700 (January 26, 1995) p42. "[Green Day]" (Winters, Dan)
PH06346 700 (January 26, 1995) p45. "The Now-Famous Mud Fight At Woodstock" (Olson, Jonathan)
PH06347 701 (February 9, 1995) p16. "[Green Day]" (Reilly, John)
PH06348 724-725 (December 28, 1995) p33. "[Green Day]" (Seliger, Mark)
PH06349 724-725 (December 28, 1995) pp[cover]. "Rock & Roll Yearbook" (Seliger, Mark)
PH06350 724-725 (December 28, 1995) p29. "Tre Cool, Billy Joe Armstrong, Mike Dirnt" (Seliger, Mark)
PH06351 726 (January 25, 1996) p38. "Billie Joe Armstrong (left) And Mike Dirnt Of Green Day" (Olson, Sheryl)

GREEN DAY—PHOTOGRAPHS—PORTRAITS
PH06352 698-699 (December 29, 1994) p37. "[Green Day]" (Muller, Michael)
PH06353 700 (January 26, 1995) pp[cover]. "Green Day: Best New Band" (Winters, Dan)

GREEN EGGS AND HAM (BOOK)—PHOTOGRAPHS
PH06354 639 (September 17, 1992) p81. "Green Eggs And Ham"

GREEN JELLY—PHOTOGRAPHS
PH06355 660-661 (July 8, 1993) p18. "Jelly On A Roll: A Current Lineup Of Visionaries" (Smith, Brian)
PH06356 672-673 (December 23, 1993) p54. "Green Jelly: A Mistake, Nothing More" (Smith, Brian)

GREEN, AL—PHOTOGRAPHS
PH06357 702 (February 23, 1995) p48. "Willie Nelson (left) With Rev. Al Green" (Mazur, Kevin)
PH06358 724-725 (December 28, 1995) p56. "Cash And Green Went Well Together" (Mazur, Kevin)
PH06359 726 (January 25, 1996) p46. "Hall Of Fame Legend Al Green In Action" (Elgar, Nick)

GREEN, AL—PHOTOGRAPHS—PORTRAITS
PH06360 643 (November 12, 1992) p197. "Al Green" (Watson, Albert)

GREEN, BRIAN—PHOTOGRAPHS
PH06361 750-751 (December 26, 1996) p62. "Brian Green Would Just As Soon Kill You As Look At You" (Cuta, Anthony)

GREEN, MARK—PHOTOGRAPHS
PH06362 721 (November 16, 1995) p88. "Nader's Devotion To Real Democracy Led Him To Endorse Mark Green For New York's Public Advocate In 1993" (Albans, Michael)

GREENBERG, MARK—PHOTOGRAPHS
PH06363 714 (August 10, 1995) p16. "The New Math: McCaughey, Buck, Tweedy And Greenberg (from left)" (Perez, Marty)

GREENE, GRAHAM—PHOTOGRAPHS
PH06364 615 (October 17, 1991) p66. "Graham Greene And Koo Stark, 1986" (Pigozzi, Jean)

GREENE, JESSY—PHOTOGRAPHS
PH06365 720 (November 2, 1995) p24. "Bozulich, Keenan, Tutton, Fitzgerald, Greene (from left)" (Toy, Joann)

GREENE, MICHAEL—PHOTOGRAPHS
PH06366 729 (March 7, 1996) p13. "Grammy Guy: NARAS' Michael Greene" (Spellman, John)

GREENE, PETER—PHOTOGRAPHS—PORTRAITS
PH06367 704 (March 23, 1995) p129. "Peter Greene Listens To Strange Voices"

GREENFIELD, JERRY—PHOTOGRAPHS
PH06368 634-635 (July 9, 1992) p75. "[Jerry Greenfield]" (Heisler, Gregory)

GREENFIELD, ROBERT—PHOTOGRAPHS
PH06369 632 (June 11, 1992) p62. "Staff Members And Contributing Writers At The 1971 Editorial Conference, At Esalen, In Big Sur" (Leibovitz, Annie)

GREENHALGH, TOM—PHOTOGRAPHS
PH06370 736 (June 13, 1996) p19. "Where's Sammy And Frank?" (Herdon, David)

GREENSPAN, ALAN—ILLUSTRATIONS
PH06371 701 (February 9, 1995) p36. "Cruel To Be Kind: Greenspan Brakes The Economy" (Witte, Michael)
PH06372 703 (March 9, 1995) p40. "Business As Usual: Wall Street Floats On A Multibillion-Dollar Life Preserver" (Witte, Michael)
PH06373 720 (November 2, 1995) p35. "I've Been Waiting Years For Someone To Dump Greenspan" (Witte, Michael)

GREENSPAN, ALAN—PHOTOGRAPHS
PH06374 665 (September 16, 1993) p35. "Federal Reserve Chairman Alan Greenspan With The First Lady And Tipper Gore At The State Of The Union"

GREENWAY, BARNEY—PHOTOGRAPHS
PH06375 694 (November 3, 1994) p18. "Dynamic Duo: Greenway (left), Perry" (Mayer, Jeffrey)

GREENWOOD, COLIN—PHOTOGRAPHS
PH06376 660-661 (July 8, 1993) p95. "Radiohead: Ed O'Brien, Colin Greenwood, Phil Selway, Yorke, Jonny Greenwood" (Sharp, Ken)
PH06377 716 (September 7, 1995) p19. "Colin Greenwood, Ed O'Brien, Thom Yorke, Jonny Greenwood And Phil Selway (from left)" (Blakesberg, Jay)
PH06378 738-739 (July 11, 1996) p15. "Thom Yorke, Colin Greenwood, Roseanne, Ed O'Brien, Phil Selway And Jonny Greenwood" (Diltz, Henry)

GREENWOOD, GAIL—PHOTOGRAPHS
PH06379 663 (August 19, 1993) p27. "Belly's Tanya Donelly (left) And Gail Greenwood With Robyn Hitchcock" (Mazur, Kevin)
PH06380 706 (April 20, 1995) p48. "Chris Gorman & Gail Greenwood" (Seliger, Mark)

GREENWOOD, JONNY—PHOTOGRAPHS
PH06381 660-661 (July 8, 1993) p95. "Radiohead: Ed O'Brien, Colin Greenwood, Phil Selway, Yorke, Jonny Greenwood" (Sharp, Ken)
PH06382 716 (September 7, 1995) p19. "Colin Greenwood, Ed O'Brien, Thom Yorke, Jonny Greenwood And Phil Selway (from left)" (Blakesberg, Jay)
PH06383 738-739 (July 11, 1996) p15. "Thom Yorke, Colin Greenwood, Roseanne, Ed O'Brien, Phil Selway And Jonny Greenwood" (Diltz, Henry)

GREGG, JONATHAN—ALBUMS
PH06384 625 (March 5, 1992) p72. "Blue On Blonde"

GREGURICH, DANNY—PHOTOGRAPHS
PH06385 728 (February 22, 1996) p48. "March 1995: D-Mac Crew Parties With Jazz At Mitch Weller's" (Smale, Brian)

GREIDER, WILLIAM—ILLUSTRATIONS
PH06386 712-713 (July 13, 1995) p60. "[William Greider]" (Witte, Michael)
PH06386a 712-713 (July 13, 1995) p67. "[William Greider & P.J. O'Rourke]]" (Witte, Michael)

GREIDER, WILLIAM—PHOTOGRAPHS
PH06387 639 (September 17, 1992) p42. "At The Table (from left): Greider, O'Rourke, Wenner, Thompson And Clinton" (Seliger, Mark)
PH06388 671 (December 9, 1993) p42. "[The Rolling Stone Interview of Bill Clinton]" (Seliger, Mark)

GRENIER, AMANDA—PHOTOGRAPHS
PH06389 692 (October 6, 1994) p66. "Amanda As A Cheerleader, Fall '91"
PH06390 692 (October 6, 1994) p66. "Until '93, The Grenier Sisters' Garage Knew Only Happy Times"

GRENIER, AMANDA—PHOTOGRAPHS—PORTRAITS
PH06391 692 (October 6, 1994) p65. "Amanda's Mother, Linda, And Stepfather, Steve, Outside Their Sicklerville, N.J., Home" (Lixenberg, Dana)
GRENIER, HEATHER—PHOTOGRAPHS
PH06392 692 (October 6, 1994) p69. "Heather By Her Pool: She Didn't Think Ernie Was A Bad Guy, Just A Pest" (Lixenberg, Dana)
GRETA—PHOTOGRAPHS
PH06393 662 (August 5, 1993) p21. "Greta: Label-War Heroes"
PH06394 Number not assigned.
GRIER, DAVID ALAN—PHOTOGRAPHS
PH06395 680 (April 21, 1994) p74. "With His Co-Stars In 'Boomerang' David Alan Grier (left) And Eddie Murphy"
GRIFFIN, KEVIN—PHOTOGRAPHS
PH06396 710 (June 15, 1995) p46. "Griffin, Bonnecaze And Drummond (from left) Veg In The Garden District" (Chiasson, John)
GRIFFIN, RICK—PHOTOGRAPHS—PORTRAITS
PH06397 619-620 (December 12, 1991) p112. "Rick Griffin" (Greene, Herb)
GRIFFIN'S MICKEY MOUSE—ILLUSTRATIONS
PH06398 645-646 (December 10, 1992) p156. "Zap Comix, 1968"
GRIFFITH, BRIAN—PHOTOGRAPHS
PH06399 722 (November 30, 1995) p20. "Gin Blossom's Scott Johnson, Dead Hot's Brian Griffith, Blossom Valenzuela And Dead Hot Curtis Grippe (from left)"
GRIFFITH, MELANIE—ILLUSTRATIONS
PH06400 624 (February 20, 1992) p47. "Achtung Baby" (Kunz, Anita)
GRIFFITH, MELANIE—PHOTOGRAPHS
PH06401 624 (February 20, 1992) p49. "Michael Douglas And Secretary Melanie Griffith At War"
PH06402 636 (August 6, 1992) p65. "New York Cop Melanie Griffith Goes Undercover As A Hasidic Jew"
PH06403 639 (September 17, 1992) p102. "Worst Actress"
PH06404 655 (April 29, 1993) p69. "Crawford And Holliday (left) Reborn As Goodman And Griffith"
GRIFFITH, NANCI—ALBUMS
PH06405 654 (April 15, 1993) p62. "Other Voices, Other Rooms"
PH06406 696 (December 1, 1994) p122. "Flyer"
GRIFFITH, NANCI—PHOTOGRAPHS
PH06407 684 (June 16, 1994) p36. "Indigo Girl Emily Saliers, Nanci Griffith, Browne, Carpenter, Indigo Girl Amy Ray" (Diamond, Rick)
GRIFFITH, NANCI—PHOTOGRAPHS—PORTRAITS
PH06408 627 (April 2, 1992) p22. "[Nanci Griffith]" (Broad, Julian)
PH06409 695 (November 17, 1994) p140. "Nanci Griffith" (Woodward, Fred)
GRIFTERS—ALBUMS
PH06410 701 (February 9, 1995) p57. "Crappin' You Negative"
PH06411 728 (February 22, 1996) p62. "Ain't My Lookout"
GRILLO, DAVID—PHOTOGRAPHS
PH06412 704 (March 23, 1995) pp102-103. "Class of '95" (Tavee, Tom)
GRILLO, STEVE—PHOTOGRAPHS
PH06413 730 (March 21, 1996) p52. "Stern-Task Master"
GRINNEL COLLEGE—PHOTOGRAPHS
PH06414 730 (March 21, 1996) p65. "Grinnel College: Granola U"
GRIPPE, CURTIS—PHOTOGRAPHS
PH06415 722 (November 30, 1995) p20. "Gin Blossom's Scott Johnson, Dead Hot's Brian Griffith, Blossom Valenzuela And Dead Hot Curtis Grippe (from left)"
GRISHAM, JOHN—BOOKS
PH06416 639 (September 17, 1992) p81. "The Firm"
GRISMAN, DAVID—ALBUMS
PH06417 672-673 (December 23, 1993) p151. "Not For Kids Only"
GRISMAN, DAVID—PHOTOGRAPHS
PH06418 717 (September 21, 1995) p75. "Grisman, Jim Kerwin, Garcia, Joe Craven (from left) In San Francisco, 1991" (Millman, Susana)
GRITZ, JAMES—PHOTOGRAPHS—PORTRAITS
PH06419 710 (June 15, 1995) p64. "Gritz"
GRODIN, CHARLES—PHOTOGRAPHS
PH06420 664 (September 2, 1993) p69. "Charles Grodin, Robert Downey Jr., Kyra Sedgwick, Alfre Woodard And Tom Sizemore"
GROENE, SCOTT—PHOTOGRAPHS
PH06421 719 (October 19, 1995) p70. "Far From The Madding Crowd: Groene During A Recent Visit To Albuquerque, N. M." (McDonough, Patricia)
GROENING, MATT—PHOTOGRAPHS—PORTRAITS
PH06422 666 (September 30, 1993) p56. "[Matt Groening]"
GROHL, DAVE—ILLUSTRATIONS
PH06423 695 (November 17, 1994) p58. "Nirvana" (Ryden, Mark)
PH06424 721 (November 16, 1995) p18. "Nirvana" (Pendergrast, James T.)
GROHL, DAVE—PHOTOGRAPHS
PH06425 622 (January 23, 1992) p41. "Dave Grohl" (Broad, Julian)
PH06426 628 (April 16, 1992) p41. "Drummer Dave Grohl" (Seliger, Mark)
PH06427 653 (April 1, 1993) p20. "Nirvana's Chris Novoselic, Kurt Cobain And Dave Grohl (clockwise from top)" (Watermann, Greg)
PH06428 659 (June 24, 1993) p21. "Nirvs: Grohl, Novoselic, Cobain (from left)" (Sirrs, Ed)
PH06429 667 (October 14, 1993) p39. "Above: Nirvana's Dave Grohl And Kurt Cobain Flanking RuPaul And Frances Cobain" (Kravitz, Jeff)
PH06430 674 (January 27, 1994) p28. "Nirvana's Dave Grohl And Krist Novoselic With Madcap MTV Hosts Anthony Kiedis And Flea" (Mazur, Kevin)
PH06431 674 (January 27, 1994) p36. "Team Spirit: Novoselic, Smear, Grohl, Cobain And Touring Cellist Lori Goldston (from left)" (Seliger, Mark)
PH06432 676 (February 24, 1994) p29. "'Backbeat' Boys: Dulli, Fleming, Mike Mills, Dave Grohl And Thurston Moore"
PH06433 680 (April 21, 1994) p64. "Twist And Shout: Fleming, Dulli, Grohl And Mills (from left) At A 'Backbeat' Session" (Cuffaro, Chris)
PH06434 682 (May 19, 1994) p18. "The Band And The Family: Grohl, Novoselic And Cobain (above)" (Huntington, Jane)
PH06435 683 (June 2, 1994) p38. "Dave Grohl And Fiancee Jennifer Youngblood, Krist Novoselic And Wife Shelli Enter The Memorial Service On April 10" (Banner, Ellen M.)
PH06436 688 (August 11, 1994) p17. "At The Movie Awards: Backbeaters Mike Mills, Don Fleming, Dave Pirner, Greg Dulli, Dave Grohl And Thurston Moore (above, from left)" (Kravitz, Jeff)
PH06437 691 (September 22, 1994) p19. "Nirvana's Grohl (drums), Simon Fair (at mike), Novoselic (bass)" (Doughty, Curt)
PH06438 698-699 (December 29, 1994) p50. "Dulli, Fleming, Mills, Grohl, Moore, Pirner Went Out For A Smoke" (Cuffaro, Chris)
PH06439 698-699 (December 29, 1994) p60. "Yoyo A Gaga: Stinky Puffs With Special Guests Dave Grohl And Krist Novoselic" (Doughty, Curt)
PH06440 706 (April 20, 1995) p16. "Fists Were Fast As Lightning: Foo Fighter Grohl Knocks Out Portland" (Doughty, Curt)
PH06441 709 (June 1, 1995) p20. "From Left: Eddie Vedder, Dave Grohl; And Their Guiding Light, Mike Watt" (Mazur, Kevin)

PH06442 718 (October 5, 1995) p42. "Dave Grohl: 'Out Of The Four Of Us, I'm The Least Charismatic'" (Mazur, Kevin)
PH06443 724-725 (December 28, 1995) p45. "Dave Grohl And Foo Fighters Shone In Watt's Current" (Mazur, Kevin)
PH06444 726 (January 25, 1996) p37. "Foo Fighters Are, From Left, Nate Mendel, Pat Smear, Dave Grohl And William Goldsmith" (Seliger, Mark)
PH06445 727 (February 8, 1996) p22. "Nirvana Was Always Political: Novoselic, Cobain And Grohl (from left) In London, 1993"
PH06446 730 (March 21, 1996) p32. "Horsing Around: Dave Grohl (top and bottom) And Fellow Foo Fighters William Goldsmith, Pat Smear And Nate Mendel (middle, from left)" (Gougenheim, Kim)
PH06447 732 (April 18, 1996) p20. "Pat Smear ('This is my first suit') And Dave Grohl" (Mazur, Kevin)
PH06448 736 (June 13, 1996) p20. "[Foo Fighters]" (Mazur, Kevin)
PH06449 745 (October 17, 1996) p27. "Beck (left) And Foo Fighter Dave Grohl" (Mazur, Kevin)

GROHL, DAVE—PHOTOGRAPHS—PORTRAITS
PH06450 718 (October 5, 1995) p43. "Nirvana In 1993 During The 'In Utero' Tour: Pat Smear, Kurt Cobain, Dave Grohl, Krist Novoselic (clockwise from right)" (Lenquette, Youri)

GROOVE COLLECTIVE—PHOTOGRAPHS
PH06451 684 (June 16, 1994) p21. "New York City's Groove Collective" (Micelotta, Frank)

GROOVE IS IN THE HEART (VIDEO)—PHOTOGRAPHS
PH06452 667 (October 14, 1993) p101. "Deee-Lite: Lady Kier In The 'Groove'"

GROSSLIGHT, PETER—PHOTOGRAPHS
PH06453 736 (June 13, 1996) p38. "Part Of The Current Lollapalooza Brain Trust: Grosslight, Gardner And Geiger (from left)" (Dyer, Alison)

GROSSMAN, PATTY—PHOTOGRAPHS
PH06454 664 (September 2, 1993) p34. "Where Bankers Fear To Tread" (Rystedt, Rex)

GROUP HOME—ALBUMS
PH06455 729 (March 7, 1996) p50. "Livin' Proof"

GROUPIES—PHOTOGRAPHS
PH06456 645-646 (December 10, 1992) p149. "Groupies, 1969"

GROVER, CHARLIE—PHOTOGRAPHS
PH06457 706 (April 20, 1995) p36. "Motor City Five: Mazzola, Grover, Dombrowski, Tim And Mike Cross (from left)" (Halsband, Michael)
PH06458 710 (June 15, 1995) p49. "Mike Cross, Dombrowski, Charlie Grover, Joey Mazzola, Tim Cross (from left)" (Tavee, Tom)

GRUBER, GERRI LUNNE—PHOTOGRAPHS
PH06459 642 (October 29, 1992) p60. "College: Dressed For Protest"
PH06460 642 (October 29, 1992) p60. "Eighties: Dressed For Success"
PH06461 642 (October 29, 1992) p60. "Today: Dressed To De-Stress"

GRUMPY OLD MEN (FILM)—PHOTOGRAPHS
PH06462 674 (January 27, 1994) p48. "Acting Vehicles Include 'The Pelican Brief,' 'In The Name Of The Father,' 'What's Eating Gilbert Grape,' 'Shadowlands,' 'Naked,' And 'Grumpy Old Men'"

GRUNGE MUSIC—ILLUSTRATIONS
PH06463 648 (January 21, 1993) p48. "The Remains Of Grunge" (Krueger, Brian)
PH06464 706 (April 20, 1995) p12. "[Plaid]" (Pendergrast, James T.)

GUARAT, INDIA—PHOTOGRAPHS
PH06465 665 (September 16, 1993) pp54-58. "Workers of The World" (Salgado, Sebastiao)

GUATEMALA—PHOTOGRAPHS
PH06466 616 (October 31, 1991) p44. "One Step At A Time: Part Of A National Immunization Campaign In Guatemala" (Gaggero, Carlos)
PH06467 741 (August 22, 1996) p80. "[Guatemala]" (Nachtwey, James)

GUDMUNDSDOTTIR, BJORK—ALBUMS
PH06468 664 (September 2, 1993) p66. "Debut"
PH06469 711 (June 29, 1995) p41. "Post"

GUDMUNDSDOTTIR, BJORK—ILLUSTRATIONS
PH06470 711 (June 29, 1995) p41. "Wild Kingdom" (Dervaux, Isabelle)
PH06471 712-713 (July 13, 1995) p13. "Bjork" (Burke, Philip)

GUDMUNDSDOTTIR, BJORK—PHOTOGRAPHS
PH06472 658 (June 10, 1993) p16. "Gudmundsdottir, Captain Of Her Own Ship" (Mondino, Jean Baptiste)
PH06473 665 (September 16, 1993) pp[enc.18-20]. "[Bjork]" (Woodard, Fred)
PH06474 665 (September 16, 1993) pp[enc.18]. "Onstage In New York" (Woodard, Fred)
PH06475 665 (September 16, 1993) pp[enc.18]. "With Lucy Hatschek, The Queen Mother" (Woodard, Fred)
PH06476 667 (October 14, 1993) p101. "Bjork: A Study In 'Human Behaviour'"
PH06477 677 (March 10, 1994) p15. "Wizards In Oz: Bjork As An Icelandic Angel In Pigtails" (Mott, Tony)
PH06478 678 (March 24, 1994) p21. "International Female: Bjork" (Jennings, Steve)
PH06479 679 (April 7, 1994) p37. "Bjork And Harvey, Puttin' On The Brits" (Young, Richard)
PH06480 716 (September 7, 1995) p28. "Bjork Casts A Spell On Seattle's Grunge Mafia" (Peterson, Charles)
PH06481 720 (November 2, 1995) p50. "Bjork" (Levine, Laura)
PH06482 724-725 (December 28, 1995) p49. "Bjork Sang For Free Speech" (Peterson, Charles)
PH06483 726 (January 25, 1996) p42. "Shh! Bjork Gets Oh So Quiet" (Olson, Sheryl)
PH06484 734 (May 16, 1996) p29. "Bjork: Fixin' To Get Hitched To Goldie" (Rankin)
PH06485 745 (October 17, 1996) p28. "Goldie And His Luv, Bjork" (Capak, R. J.)
PH06486 750-751 (December 26, 1996) p48. "Bjork Looks Like Pebbles, Acts Like Bam-Bam" (Wells, Tony)

GUDMUNDSDOTTIR, BJORK—PHOTOGRAPHS—PORTRAITS
PH06487 665 (September 16, 1993) pp[enc.17]. "[Bjork]" (Woodard, Fred)
PH06488 672-673 (December 23, 1993) p54. "Bjork: Expert On Human Behavior" (Lenquette, Youri)
PH06489 695 (November 17, 1994) p68. "Bjork" (Sednaoui, Stephane)
PH06490 697 (December 15, 1994) p18. "Man Of The Hour With Bjork In L.A." (Cohen, Lester)
PH06491 712-713 (July 13, 1995) p76. "[Bjork]" (McDean, Craig)
PH06492 747 (November 14, 1996) p29. "Bjork And Her Stalker Ricardo Lopez" (Cultice, Joseph)

GUERRA, JUAN LUIS—ALBUMS
PH06493 654 (April 15, 1993) p65. "Areito"

GUEST, CHRISTOPHER—PHOTOGRAPHS
PH06494 662 (August 5, 1993) p33. "Chris Guest, Harry Shearer, Michael McKean, With Carpenter" (Cohen, Lester)

GUIDED BY VOICES—ALBUMS
PH06495 688 (August 11, 1994) p66. "Bee Thousand"
PH06496 700 (January 26, 1995) p56. "Bee Thousand"
PH06497 704 (March 23, 1995) p119. "Box"
PH06498 731 (April 4, 1996) p60. "Under The Bushes Under The Stars"

GUIDED BY VOICES—PHOTOGRAPHS—PORTRAITS
PH06499 686-687 (July 14, 1994) p74. "Kevin Fennell, Toby Sprout, Pollard, Jim Pollard, Greg Demos (from left)" (Rice, Ted)

GUILTY BY SUSPICION (FILM)—PHOTOGRAPHS
PH06500 654 (April 15, 1993) p69. "Guilty By Suspicion"

GUIRY, TOM—PHOTOGRAPHS
PH06501 684 (June 16, 1994) p114. "TV Echoes"
GUITARS—ILLUSTRATIONS
PH06502 708 (May 18, 1995) p31. "[Guitar]"
GUITARS—PHOTOGRAPHS
PH06503 670 (November 25, 1993) p86. "[Guitar With Autographs]" (Seliger, Mark)
PH06504 722 (November 30, 1995) p81. "[Instruments]" (Grant, Bob)
PH06505 724-725 (December 28, 1995) p39. "Cobain's Bloodied Guitar Fetched 17 Grand At Auction" (Eichner, Steve)
GUMBALL—PHOTOGRAPHS
PH06506 668 (October 28, 1993) p36. "Shonen Knife (front) Hang With Gumball" (Boland, Laurence)
PH06507 691 (September 22, 1994) p38. "Revoke-Your-License Velocity: Gumball Drummer Jay Spiegel, Fleming And Bassist Eric Vermillion (from left)" (Capak, R. J.)
GUMBO—ALBUMS
PH06508 667 (October 14, 1993) p123. "Basement Music"
GUMBS, TRENTEN—PHOTOGRAPHS
PH06509 626 (March 19, 1992) p11. "Michael Jackson With Eddie Murphy And Producer Trenten Gumbs (from left)"
PH06510 633 (June 25, 1992) p12. "Murphy With McCartney And Producer Trenten Gumbs (from left)"
GUN CONTROL—ILLUSTRATIONS
PH06511 664 (September 2, 1993) p8. "Welcome To NRA Land!" (Pendergrast, James T.)
PH06512 667 (October 14, 1993) p14. "Bullets Lite!" (Pendergrast, James T.)
PH06513 669 (November 11, 1993) p8. "Rolling Stone" (Pendergrast, James T.)
PH06514 680 (April 21, 1994) p8. "[Gun Control]" (Pendergrast, James T.)
PH06515 680 (April 21, 1994) p8. "Gun Control Laws" (Pendergrast, James T.)
PH06516 712-713 (July 13, 1995) p20. "[Duck]" (Pendergrast, James T.)
PH06517 714 (August 10, 1995) p12. "Baby's First Revolver" (Pendergrast, James T.)
GUN CONTROL—PHOTOGRAPHS
PH06518 660-661 (July 8, 1993) p37. "In April, Demonstrators Gathered In Dallas, Texas To Show Their Support For The Right To Keep And Bear Arms" (Woo, David)
PH06519 720 (November 2, 1995) p54. "[Gun Control]" (Winters, Dan)
GUNCRAZY (FILM)—PHOTOGRAPHS
PH06520 650 (February 18, 1993) p67. "A Pensive Drew Barrymore Packs A Rod And A Conscience"
GUNMEN (FILM)—PHOTOGRAPHS
PH06521 675 (February 10, 1994) p52. "Now Playing"
GUNN, DAVID, JR.—PHOTOGRAPHS
PH06522 671 (December 9, 1993) p32. "L7 Beauties Pose Backstage With Gunn" (Johnson, Lisa)
PH06523 692 (October 6, 1994) p55. "David Gunn Jr. (center) Son Of Slain Clinic Doctor, Backstage With L7 At A Rock For Choice Show In L.A. This Year" (Johnson, Lisa)
GUNS N' ROSES—ALBUMS
PH06524 615 (October 17, 1991) p89. "Use Your Illusion I"
PH06525 615 (October 17, 1991) p89. "Use Your Illusion II"
PH06526 617 (November 14, 1991) p196. "Use Your Illusion II"
PH06527 619-620 (December 12, 1991) p162. "Use Your Illusion I"
PH06528 671 (December 9, 1993) p65. "The Spaghetti Incident?"
GUNS N' ROSES—ILLUSTRATIONS
PH06529 615 (October 17, 1991) p89. "Guns N' Roses Blazing: Choose Your Illusion" (Drescher, Henrik)
PH06530 615 (October 17, 1991) p89. "Guns N' Roses Blazing: Choose Your Illusion" (Rosen, Jonathon)
PH06531 671 (December 9, 1993) p65. "Guns N' Poses" (Corio, Paul)
GUNS N' ROSES—PHOTOGRAPHS
PH06532 619-620 (December 12, 1991) pp[cover]. "1991 Yearbook" (Ritts, Herb)
PH06533 619-620 (December 12, 1991) p55. "The Dynamic Duo? Axl And Slash (above)" (Mazur, Kevin)
PH06534 625 (March 5, 1992) p19. "Axl Rose (left) And Slash" (Mazur, Kevin)
PH06535 625 (March 5, 1992) p55. "'Comeback' From The 'Worst' Band" (Kirkland, Gene)
PH06536 633 (June 25, 1992) p6. "[Guns N' Roses]" (Kirkland, Gene)
PH06537 636 (August 6, 1992) p8. "[Guns N' Roses]" (Kirkland, Gene)
PH06538 642 (October 29, 1992) p26. "Happier Days: Izzy With Axl" (Funk, Harrison)
PH06539 663 (August 19, 1993) p27. "Izzy (left) Cuddles Up To Buddy Slash" (Kirkland, Greg)
PH06540 666 (September 30, 1993) p17. "Guns N' Roses Get 'Estranged'" (Mazur, Kevin)
PH06541 672-673 (December 23, 1993) p74. "Slash And Axl: Punks For A Day" (Mazur, Kevin)
GURALNICK, PETER—BOOKS
PH06542 698-699 (December 29, 1994) p63. "Last Train To Memphis"
GUREWITZ, BRETT—PHOTOGRAPHS
PH06543 670 (November 25, 1993) p30. "Hetson, Bobby Schayer, Bentley, Gurewitz And Graffin (clockwise from top left)" (Zlozower, Neil)
PH06544 737 (June 27, 1996) p18. "Punk-Rock Record Mogul: Epitaph Owner Brett Gurewitz In His Los Angeles Office" (Azimi, Mojgan B.)
GURLEY, MICHAEL—PHOTOGRAPHS
PH06545 647 (January 7, 1993) p19. "Michael Gurley, Joie Calio And Phil Leavitt (from left)" (Mauro, Aldo)
PH06546 660-661 (July 8, 1993) p101. "Dada (from left): Michael Gurley, Phil Leavitt And Joie Calio" (Lass, Imke)
GURU—ALBUMS
PH06547 659 (June 24, 1993) p83. "Jazzmatazz Volume 1: An Experimental Fusion Of Hip-Hop And Jazz"
PH06548 715 (August 24, 1995) p102. "Jazzmatazz: Volume II"
GURU—PHOTOGRAPHS
PH06549 690 (September 8, 1994) p24. "[Guru & Domino]"
PH06550 695 (November 17, 1994) p87. "Gang Starr" (Irish, Len)
PH06551 715 (August 24, 1995) p23. "Guru, Patra And Byrd At The 'Jazzmatazz II' Release Party" (Capak, R. J.)
GURU—PHOTOGRAPHS—PORTRAITS
PH06552 682 (May 19, 1994) p30. "Back To The Razzmatazz: DJ Premier (left) And Guru Return To Their Roots" (Seliger, Mark)
GUSTAFSON, STEVEN—PHOTOGRAPHS—PORTRAITS
PH06553 652 (March 18, 1993) pp34-35. "Rob Buck, Dennis Drew, Natalie Merchant, Jerome Augustyniak, Steven Gustafson (from left)" (Ockenfels, Frank W.)
GUSTAFSSON, LARS—PHOTOGRAPHS
PH06554 658 (June 10, 1993) p32. "Clockwise From Left: Lars Gustafsson, Jay Bennett, Ken Hartz And Mike Hazelrigg" (Elledge, Paul)
GUTHRIE, ARLO—ILLUSTRATIONS
PH06555 641 (October 15, 1992) p74. "[Arlo & Woody Guthrie]" (Ulriksen, Mark)
GUTHRIE, ARLO—PHOTOGRAPHS
PH06556 637 (August 20, 1992) p23. "The All-Star Lineup Onstage In Central Park" (Mazur, Kevin)
PH06557 728 (February 22, 1996) pp18-19. "Belafonte, Seeger And Guthrie (from left)" (Mazur, Kevin)
PH06558 747 (November 14, 1996) p25. "This Hall Was Made For You And Me: Arlo Guthrie, Bruce Springsteen, Tim Robbins, Dave Pirner And Billy Bragg (from left) At The Rock & Roll Hall Of Fame's Woody Guthrie ..."

GUTHRIE, WOODY—ILLUSTRATIONS
PH06559 641 (October 15, 1992) p74. "[Arlo & Woody Guthrie]" (Ulriksen, Mark)
GUTTERBALL—ALBUMS
PH06560 666 (September 30, 1993) p108. "Gutterball"
GUTTERBALL—PHOTOGRAPHS
PH06561 660-661 (July 8, 1993) p101. "Gutterball: Johnny Hott, Bryan Harvey, Steve Wynn, Bob Rupe, Stephen McCarthy"
PH06562 663 (August 19, 1993) p15. "Rupe, Hott, Harvey, Wynn And McCarthy (from left)" (Callahan, Walter)
GUY, BUDDY—ALBUMS
PH06563 623 (February 6, 1992) p79. "Damn Right, I've Got The Blues"
PH06564 653 (April 1, 1993) p53. "Feels Like Rain"
GUY, BUDDY—PHOTOGRAPHS
PH06565 615 (October 17, 1991) p14. "Buddy Guy, Eric Clapton" (Mazur, Kevin)
PH06566 618 (November 28, 1991) p74. "Guy, B. B. King And Junior Wells At The 1968 Newport Folk Festival" (Gahr, David)
PH06567 640 (October 1, 1992) p10. "Santana (left) And Guy" (Granitz, Steve)
PH06568 656 (May 13, 1993) p32. "Buddy Guy" (Mazur, Kevin)
PH06569 676 (February 24, 1994) p29. "Slash And Buddy Guy" (Lines, Edward G., Jr.)
PH06570 711 (June 29, 1995) p18. "B. B. King, Robert Cray, Buddy Guy, Art Neville, Jimmie Vaughan, Clapton, Raitt And Tommy Shannon" (Long, Andrew)
GUY, BUDDY—PHOTOGRAPHS—PORTRAITS
PH06571 618 (November 28, 1991) p73. "[Buddy Guy]" (Watson, Albert)
GWYNNE, FRED—PHOTOGRAPHS
PH06572 627 (April 2, 1992) p42. "Fred Gwynne Referees For Joe Pesci And Marisa Tomei"
GZA—ALBUMS
PH06573 722 (November 30, 1995) p66. "Liquid Swords"

H

H-TOWN—ALBUMS
PH06574 662 (August 5, 1993) p65. "Fever For Da Flavor"
HAAS, LUKAS—PHOTOGRAPHS
PH06575 735 (May 30, 1996) p56. "Preppy Haas His Way With Ryder"
HACKMAN, GENE—PHOTOGRAPHS
PH06576 703 (March 9, 1995) p70. "Leonardo Dicaprio And Gene Hackman Face Off In Familial Fury"
PH06577 720 (November 2, 1995) p74. "Hackman (in brace) And DeVito Watch Travolta Operate, Hollywood Style"
HACKMAN, GENE—PHOTOGRAPHS—PORTRAITS
PH06578 747 (November 14, 1996) p124. "The Chamber: John Grisham's First Screen Strikeout"
HACKNEY, SHELDON—PHOTOGRAPHS
PH06579 662 (August 5, 1993) p49. "Penn's President Sheldon Hackney: A 'Hopeless Weenie'?" (Johnson, C.)
HADJOPOULOS, SUE—PHOTOGRAPHS
PH06580 637 (August 20, 1992) p11. "The B-52's (from left): Fred Schneider, Kate Pierson, Julee Cruise, Keith Strickland, Sue Hadjopoulos And Pat Irwin" (Michelson, Eric T.)
HAGAR, REGAN—PHOTOGRAPHS
PH06581 649 (February 4, 1993) p23. "Jeremy Toback, Shawn Smith, Regan Hagar And Stone Gossard (from left)"
HAGAR, SAMMY—PHOTOGRAPHS
PH06582 615 (October 17, 1991) p34. "Eddie Van Halen (left) And Sammy Hagar" (Mazur, Kevin)
PH06583 615 (October 17, 1991) p14. "Hagar, Goldberg, Van Halen And Goldberg's Daughter, Alex" (Mazur, Kevin)
PH06584 622 (January 23, 1992) p7. "Eddie Van HAlen And Hagar" (Clark, Shaun)
PH06585 645-646 (December 10, 1992) p96. "Vedder (left) With Sammy Hagar" (Blakesberg, Jay)
PH06586 650 (February 18, 1993) p16. "Alex, Eddie, Anthony, Hagar (from left)"
PH06587 663 (August 19, 1993) p25. "Sammy Hagar And Eddie Van Halen" (Settle, Ken)
PH06588 729 (March 7, 1996) p10. "[Sammy Hagar]" (Stahnke, Paul)
HAGERTY, NEIL—PHOTOGRAPHS
PH06589 710 (June 15, 1995) p36. "Brown, Herrema, Hagerty And Pyle (from left): 'We're A Marketing Nightmare'" (Westenberg, Kevin)
HAGGARD, MERLE—ALBUMS
PH06590 733 (May 2, 1996) p54. "Down Every Road"
HAGGARD, MERLE—PHOTOGRAPHS
PH06591 750-751 (December 26, 1996) p174. "Merle Haggard" (Seliger, Mark)
HAINES, LUKE—ILLUSTRATIONS
PH06592 684 (June 16, 1994) p106. "Luke Haines" (Skwish, Andrew)
HAINES, LUKE—PHOTOGRAPHS
PH06593 657 (May 27, 1993) p16. "Auteur, Auteur: Banbury, Haines, Collins And Readman (clockwise from left)" (Lass, Imke)
HAITI—ILLUSTRATIONS
PH06594 680 (April 21, 1994) p49. "[Haiti]" (Payne, C. F.)
PH06595 680 (April 21, 1994) p50. "[Haiti]" (Kuper, Peter)
PH06596 680 (April 21, 1994) p53. "[Haiti]" (Isip, Jordin)
PH06597 680 (April 21, 1994) p60. "[Haiti]" (Linn, Warren)
PH06598 691 (September 22, 1994) p36. "[Haiti]" (Martin, Matthew)
HAKE, STUART—PHOTOGRAPHS—PORTRAITS
PH06599 637 (August 20, 1992) p20. "John Hamilton, Donna Croughn, Andy Demos, Dave Dreiwitz And Stuart Hake (from left)" (Borris, Dan)
HAKMOUN, HASSAN—PHOTOGRAPHS
PH06600 686-687 (July 14, 1994) p79. "[Hassan Hakmoun]"
HALDEMAN, H. R.—PHOTOGRAPHS
PH06601 690 (September 8, 1994) p48. "Above, In A Photo From The CD-ROM: Nixon, Ehrlichman, Kissinger, Haldeman"
PH06602 690 (September 8, 1994) p47. "The Author's Bosses: Future Chief Of Staff H. R. Haldeman (left) And Richard Nixon During The 1968 Campaign"
HALEE, ROY—PHOTOGRAPHS
PH06603 686-687 (July 14, 1994) p38. "Brickell, Assistant Engineer Andy Smith And Halee (from left)" (Mazur, Kevin)
HALF WAY HOME—PHOTOGRAPHS
PH06604 651 (March 4, 1993) p28. "Dean Zuckerman, Kevin Costigan, Jennifer Barry, Eddie Fagin (from left)" (Lavine, Michael)
HALILOVIC, MUHAMED—PHOTOGRAPHS—PORTRAITS
PH06605 724-725 (December 28, 1995) p98. "Sanela Halilovic With Nehrudin And Photo Of Husband Muhamed" (Cobb, Rachel)
HALILOVIC, NEHRUDIN—PHOTOGRAPHS
PH06606 724-725 (December 28, 1995) p91. "The Chelik Family (clockwise from top): Paya, Hiba, Sanela With Nehrudin, Mirza, Edin, Zlatiya" (Cobb, Rachel)
PH06607 724-725 (December 28, 1995) p98. "Sanela Halilovic With Nehrudin And Photo Of Husband Muhamed" (Cobb, Rachel)
HALILOVIC, SANELA—PHOTOGRAPHS
PH06608 724-725 (December 28, 1995) p91. "The Chelik Family (clockwise from top): Paya, Hiba, Sanela With Nehrudin, Mirza, Edin, Zlatiya" (Cobb, Rachel)
PH06609 724-725 (December 28, 1995) p98. "Sanela Halilovic With Nehrudin And Photo Of Husband Muhamed" (Cobb, Rachel)
HALL, ARSENIO—PHOTOGRAPHS
PH06610 615 (October 17, 1991) p14. "Arsenio Hall, James

Brown And M. C. Hammer (from left)" (Mazur, Kevin)

PH06611 615 (October 17, 1991) p13. "Michael Stipe, Arsenio Hall" (Mazur, Kevin)

PH06612 645-646 (December 10, 1992) p196. "Bill Clinton (above) Had Nearly Blown It Before He Blew It On 'Arsenio'"

HALL, JERRY—PHOTOGRAPHS

PH06613 615 (October 17, 1991) p63. "Jasmine, Jean Pigozzi And Jerry Hall, 1987" (Pigozzi, Jean)

PH06614 615 (October 17, 1991) p64. "Massai, Jade Jagger And Jerry Hall, Nassau, 1983" (Pigozzi, Jean)

PH06615 723 (December 14, 1995) p57. "Jagger With Wife Jerry Hall At The Palladium In New York, 1979"

PH06616 748 (November 28, 1996) p25. "Jagger And Hall In The Proverbial Happier Times" (Allen, David)

PH06617 750-751 (December 26, 1996) p85. "Jagger And Hall" (Young, Richard)

HALL, JOHN S.—PHOTOGRAPHS

PH06618 659 (June 24, 1993) p15. "Weiland (left) With King Missile's John S. Hall" (Kravitz, Jeff)

HALL, JOHN S.—PHOTOGRAPHS—PORTRAITS

PH06619 654 (April 15, 1993) p17. "Murdock, Hall, Xefos, Rick (from left)" (Seliger, Mark)

HALL, PETE—PHOTOGRAPHS

PH06620 728 (February 22, 1996) p32. "Cornershop's Simms, Saffery, Tjinder Singh, Ayres And Hall (from left)" (Wonderland, Alison)

HALL, RICHARD—PHOTOGRAPHS

PH06621 679 (April 7, 1994) p16. "The Face Of techno: Moby Is Its Most Marketable Star" (Greenberg, Jill)

HALLETT, JAMES—PHOTOGRAPHS

PH06622 704 (March 23, 1995) pp102-103. "Class of '95" (Tavee, Tom)

PH06623 704 (March 23, 1995) p109. "Hallett In Jong's Produce Market" (Tavee, Tom)

HALO BENDERS

PH06624 690 (September 8, 1994) p96. "God Don't Make No Junk"

HAMILL, MARK—PHOTOGRAPHS

PH06625 669 (November 11, 1993) p81. "[Star Wars Trilogy]"

HAMILTON, GEORGE—PHOTOGRAPHS

PH06626 741 (August 22, 1996) p80. "[Hamilton's]" (Schiffman, Bonnie)

HAMILTON, JOHN—PHOTOGRAPHS—PORTRAITS

PH06627 637 (August 20, 1992) p20. "John Hamilton, Donna Croughn, Andy Demos, Dave Dreiwitz And Stuart Hake (from left)" (Borris, Dan)

HAMILTON, LINDA—PHOTOGRAPHS

PH06628 619-620 (December 12, 1991) p194. "Male Wimps And Female Warriors"

HAMILTON, MARK—PHOTOGRAPHS

PH06629 719 (October 19, 1995) p33. "Tim Wheeler (left), Mark Hamilton Of Ash" (Page, Scarlet)

HAMILTON, PAGE—ILLUSTRATIONS

PH06630 689 (August 25, 1994) p11. "Helmet's Page Hamilton" (Burke, Philip)

HAMILTON, PAGE—PHOTOGRAPHS

PH06631 621 (January 9, 1992) p25. "Helmet's Page Hamilton" (Capak, R. J.)

PH06632 637 (August 20, 1992) p15. "Helmet (from left): Stanier, Bogdan, Mengede And Hamilton" (Ockenfels, Frank W.)

PH06633 672-673 (December 23, 1993) p70. "Live From New York: Hamilton, Pirner, Williams, Henry And Murphy (clockwise from top left)" (Mazur, Kevin)

PH06634 689 (August 25, 1994) p65. ""I Was A Nice Little Small-Town Geek": Hamilton, 1992" (Callahan, Kristin)

PH06635 689 (August 25, 1994) p64. "Original Guitarist Mengede, Bogdan, Hamilton, Stanier (from left)" (Brice, Lindsay)

PH06636 695 (November 17, 1994) p92. "Helmet" (Huba, John)

HAMILTON, PAGE—PHOTOGRAPHS—PORTRAITS

PH06637 689 (August 25, 1994) p63. "John Stanier, Henry Bogdan, Page Hamilton And Rob Echeverria (clockwise from top left)" (Wessel, Cathrine)

HAMILTON, SUZY—PHOTOGRAPHS—PORTRAITS

PH06638 633 (June 25, 1992) p36. "Suzy Hamilton" (Ford, Charles)

HAMILTON, TOM—PHOTOGRAPHS

PH06639 634-635 (July 9, 1992) p11. "Tom Hamilton, Joe Perry And Tyler (from left) With Museum Curator Helaine Posner" (Putnam, Sarah)

PH06640 659 (June 24, 1993) p13. "Kuriansky, Tyler And Hamilton" (Paul, Tina)

PH06641 694 (November 3, 1994) p60. "Early Daze: Whitford, Tyler, Hamilton, Perry And Kramer At Boston College, 1973" (Pownall, Ron)

PH06642 724-725 (December 28, 1995) p40. "Aerosmith's Tom Hamilton, Joey Kramer, Brad Whitford And Steven Tyler (from left)" (Robicheau, Paul)

HAMMER—ILLUSTRATIONS

PH06643 618 (November 28, 1991) p90. "Hammer Gets Serious; Loc Gets Down" (Schwartz, Sara)

PH06644 619-620 (December 12, 1991) p88. "'Hammerman' Fights The Forces Of Evil"

HAMMER—PHOTOGRAPHS

PH06645 615 (October 17, 1991) p14. "Arsenio Hall, James Brown And M. C. Hammer (from left)" (Mazur, Kevin)

PH06646 619-620 (December 12, 1991) p39. "M. C. Hammer" (Putland, Michael)

PH06647 634-635 (July 9, 1992) p27. "Hammer: Onstage Chaos" (Micelotta, Frank)

PH06648 654 (April 15, 1993) p13. "Hammer, Pickett And Brown (from left)" (Mazur, Kevin)

PH06649 668 (October 28, 1993) p17. "Hammer: The Singer Wants $25 Million For A New Deal—With No Takers" (Mazur, Kevin)

HAMMETT, KIRK—PHOTOGRAPHS

PH06650 618 (November 28, 1991) p11. "Kirk Kammett, Slash, Lars Ulrich, Geoff Tate And Armored Saint Drummer Gonzo (from left)" (Blakesberg, Jay)

PH06651 708 (May 18, 1995) p74. "Metallica In 1991, From Left: Hammett, Ulrich, Newsted, Hetfield" (Seliger, Mark)

PH06652 727 (February 8, 1996) p12. "Fifty And Fabulous! Kilmister (center) Flanked By Metallica's Jason Newsted, James Hetfield, Kirk Hammett And Lars Ulrich (from left)" (Disanto, Annamaria)

PH06653 728 (February 22, 1996) p25. "Metallica's James Hetfield, Kirk Hammett, Lars Ulrich And Jason Newsted (from left)"

PH06654 737 (June 27, 1996) p36. "Not Just Riding Shotgun: Newsted (left), Hammett" (Corbijn, Anton)

PH06655 742 (September 5, 1996) p20. "Kirk Hammett With Model Julie Skinner" (Jordan, Kelly)

HAMMONDS, JEFFREY—PHOTOGRAPHS

PH06656 682 (May 19, 1994) p64. "[Jeffrey Hammonds]" (Telemans, Al)

HAMPTON BEACH, NEW HAMPSHIRE—PHOTOGRAPHS

PH06657 717 (September 21, 1995) p26. "On The Night Of Garcia's Death, Fans Flocked To Bob Weir's Sold-Out Performance At The Hampton Beach Casino Ballroom, In New Hampshire" (Seliger, Mark)

HAMPTON, BRUCE—ALBUMS

PH06658 626 (March 19, 1992) p95. "Col. Bruce Hampton And The Aquarium Rescue Unit"

HAMPTON, BRUCE—PHOTOGRAPHS

PH06659 631 (May 28, 1992) p16. "The Rescue Unit (from left): Matt Mundy, Oteil Burbridge Bruce Hampton, Jimmy Herring And Apt. Q258" (Frazier, Jeff)

PH06660 663 (August 19, 1993) p12. "Colonel Bruce Hampton And His Chazoid (left)" (Caudle, Todd)

HAMPTON GREASE BAND—ALBUMS
PH06661 750-751 (December 26, 1996) p189. "Music To Eat"
HANCOCK, BUTCH—ALBUMS
PH06662 706 (April 20, 1995) p78. "Eats Away The Night"
HANCOCK, HERBIE—ALBUMS
PH06663 710 (June 15, 1995) p83. "Dis Is Da Drum"
HANCOCK, POLLY—PHOTOGRAPHS
PH06664 650 (February 18, 1993) p13. "Peter Tork (left) With The 'Jays' Hancock, Robinson And Ben Kesteven" (Mayer, Jeffrey)
THE HAND THAT ROCKS THE CRADLE (FILM)—PHOTOGRAPHS
PH06665 623 (February 6, 1992) p88. "Nanny Rebecca DeMornay Terrorizes Ernie Hudson"
HAND, JOHN—PHOTOGRAPHS
PH06666 702 (February 23, 1995) p53. "John Hand Serves As Door Checker And Bouncer" (Kuehn, Karen)
HANFT, STEVE—PHOTOGRAPHS
PH06667 749 (December 12, 1996) p28. "[Steve Hanft]" (Lujan, Marcos)
HANKS, JARROD—PHOTOGRAPHS
PH06668 628 (April 16, 1992) pp[enc.21,23]. "[Jarrod Hanks]" (Newton, Philip)
HANKS, TOM—ILLUSTRATIONS
PH06669 660-661 (July 8, 1993) p119. "Date-Night Film Frenzy" (Blitt, Barry)
PH06670 698-699 (December 29, 1994) p193. "The Year In Movies" (Kunz, Anita)
PH06671 712-713 (July 13, 1995) p113. "Fire Rockets 1, 2, 3" (Allen, Terry)
PH06672 716 (September 7, 1995) p78. "[Tom Hanks]" (Mats)
PH06673 745 (October 17, 1996) p141. "Tom Hank Turns Auteur" (Brodner, Steve)
HANKS, TOM—PHOTOGRAPHS
PH06674 660-661 (July 8, 1993) p75. "Ephron On The 'Sleepless In Seattle' Set With Tom Hanks: 'You Hope To Get The Guys To Cry, Too.'" (McBroom, Bruce)
PH06675 660-661 (July 8, 1993) p120. "'Someday My Prince Will Come' Is A Theme For Ryan (with Hanks, above)"
PH06676 672-673 (December 23, 1993) p174. "[Philadelphia]"
PH06677 678 (March 24, 1994) p63. "Demme, Flanked By Hanks And Banderas, Denies That The Positive Gay Images In 'Philadelphia' Are A Reaction Against The Gay Killer in 'Lambs' (left)"
PH06678 684 (June 16, 1994) p116. "Weepy: Hanks Alone In "Forrest Gump""
PH06679 686-687 (July 14, 1994) p98. "Robin Wright And Hanks ("Forrest Gump")"
PH06680 691 (September 22, 1994) p106. "Acting Peaks"
PH06681 698-699 (December 29, 1994) p194. "Hanks Sits In "Gump""
PH06682 698-699 (December 29, 1994) p60. "Simple Minds: Forrest Gump"
PH06683 703 (March 9, 1995) p21. "Bonnie Raitt, Tom Hanks, Melissa Etheridge (from left)" (Berliner, A.)
PH06684 712-713 (July 13, 1995) p116. "'Apollo 13' Astronauts Hanks And Bacon Blast Off; And Harris Waits In Houston"
PH06685 745 (October 17, 1996) p142. "Tom Hanks Directs The Band"
HANKS, TOM—PHOTOGRAPHS—PORTRAITS
PH06686 731 (April 4, 1996) p66. "'Apollo 13,' With Tom Hanks"
HANLEY, KAY—PHOTOGRAPHS
PH06687 690 (September 8, 1994) p42. "Cleo's Hanley, McKenna And Scott Riebling (from left)" (Capak, R. J.)
PH06688 693 (October 20, 1994) p30. "Cleo's Hanley, Stacy Jones, Manning; Builders Joan Wasser, Eric Masunaga" (Robicheau, Paul)
PH06689 710 (June 15, 1995) p39. "Eisenstein, Scott Riebling, Hanley, Stacy Jones, Greg McKenna (from left)" (McDonough, Patricia)
HANN-BYRD, ADAM—PHOTOGRAPHS
PH06690 616 (October 31, 1991) p97. "Gifted Son And Mother: Adam Hann-Byrd And Jodie Foster"
HANNA, KATHLEEN—PHOTOGRAPHS
PH06691 690 (September 8, 1994) p21. "Jett (left) With Bikini Kill's Hanna" (Capak, R. J.)
PH06692 738-739 (July 11, 1996) p16. "[Kathleen Hanna]" (Wheat, Jody)
HANNAH, DARYL—PHOTOGRAPHS
PH06693 645-646 (December 10, 1992) p49. "Browne And Hannah In Happier Times" (Guastella, Mike)
HANOI, VIETNAM—PHOTOGRAPHS
PH06694 634-635 (July 9, 1992) p62. "Every Boy Needs One: Toy U.S. Air Force F-111 Fighters For Sale In Hanoi" (Giannini, John)
PH06695 682 (May 19, 1994) p72. "[Vietnam]"
HANSARD, GLEN—PHOTOGRAPHS
PH06696 644 (November 26, 1992) p24. "Hansard, Noreen O'Donnell, Colm Mac Con Iomaire, Brennan, David Odlum And John Carney (from left)" (Marsden, Barry)
HANSEN, MARY—PHOTOGRAPHS
PH06697 691 (September 22, 1994) p38. "Stereolab's Hansen (left) And Sadier Wax Etheral" (Clinch, Danny)
PH06698 731 (April 4, 1996) p40. "Always The Same, Always Different: Stereolab's Mary Hansen, Tim Gane, Laetitia Sadier And Morgane Lhote (from left)" (Perou, Ralph)
HANSEN, PATTI—PHOTOGRAPHS
PH06699 647 (January 7, 1993) p11. "Keith Richards And Patti Hansen" (Elgar, Nick)
PH06700 748 (November 28, 1996) p25. "Richards And Hansen With De La Falaise Holding Little Ella Rose At The New York Film Festival" (Brady, Jay)
HARD ROCK CAFE (LAS VEGAS, NEVADA)—ILLUSTRATIONS
PH06701 617 (November 14, 1991) p21. "Artist's Rendering Of The Proposed Hard Rock Hotel And Casino In Las Vegas" (Smith, Brian)
HARD ROCK CAFE (LAS VEGAS, NEVADA)—PHOTOGRAPHS
PH06702 617 (November 14, 1991) p21. "The Las Vegas Hard Rock" (Smith, Brian)
HARD ROCK CAFE (ORLANDO, FLORIDA)—PHOTOGRAPHS
PH06703 617 (November 14, 1991) p15. "Robert Earl's Hard Rock Cafe In Orlando, Florida"
HARD TARGET (FILM)—PHOTOGRAPHS
PH06704 665 (September 16, 1993) p76. "Woo (left) Directs Van Damme For Action"
HARDEN, MARCIA GAY—PHOTOGRAPHS
PH06705 742 (September 5, 1996) p68. "Elliott, Burstyn And Harden"
HARDIE, GEORGE—PHOTOGRAPHS
PH06706 669 (November 11, 1993) p53. "Hardie With His Sister, Anne Carol, At A Press Conference In New Bedford, Mass..." (Stockwell, Mark)
HARDIE, GEORGE—PHOTOGRAPHS—PORTRAITS
PH06707 669 (November 11, 1993) p52. "George Hardie Was Wound Tight During The Negotiations: 'I Don't Think You Understand What We're Saying; We're Going To Destroy The Church'" (Hom, Marc)
HARDIN, GARRETT—PHOTOGRAPHS—PORTRAITS
PH06708 693 (October 20, 1994) p110. "Garrett Hardin: University Of California At Santa Barbara"
HARDIN, TIM—ALBUMS
PH06709 692 (October 6, 1994) p90. "Hang On To A Dream"
HARDING, JOHN WESLEY—PHOTOGRAPHS
PH06710 638 (September 3, 1992) pp[enc.22-25]. "[John Wesley Harding]" (Veyssey, Frederique)
PH06710 638 (September 3, 1992) pp[enc.30]. "[John Wesley Harding]" (Veyssey, Frederique)
PH06711 638 (September 3, 1992) pp[enc.26]. "[Sofia Shinas, John Wesley Harding]" (Veyssey, Frederique)

PH06712 649 (February 4, 1993) p9. "Joan Baez (left) With Harding" (Blakesberg, Jay)
PH06713 688 (August 11, 1994) p20. "Pull Up A Stool: John Wesley Harding (left) Is Joined By Buddy Bruce Springsteen" (Glade, Gary)
HARDING, TONYA—ILLUSTRATIONS
PH06714 682 (May 19, 1994) p68. "[White Trash]" (Friedman, Drew)
PH06715 686-687 (July 14, 1994) p81. "[Tonya Harding]" (Collins, John)
PH06716 689 (August 25, 1994) p12. "Rolling Stone" (Pendergrast, James T.)
HARDING, TONYA—PHOTOGRAPHS
PH06717 686-687 (July 14, 1994) p84. "At 21, She Flaunts Her Style" (Quintero, John)
PH06718 686-687 (July 14, 1994) p82. "The Broken Boot Lace That Sabotaged Tonya's Long Program" (Treick, Tom)
PH06719 686-687 (July 14, 1994) p84. "Tonya At Age 4—Her Teachers Were Amazed"
PH06720 686-687 (July 14, 1994) p88. "Tonya Takes A Break From Her Community-Service Job At A Senior Citizens Center" (Starr, Steve)
PH06721 719 (October 19, 1995) p25. "Tonya Harding: As Popular Onstage As On Ice" (Tapogna, Mary)
PH06722 724-725 (December 28, 1995) p54. "Harding Took Another Swipe At Stardom And Failed" (Wojahn, Brent)
PH06723 750-751 (December 26, 1996) p46. "Harding And Michael Smith, Her Future Ex-Hubby" (McKiernan, Scott)
HARDING, TORBIN—PHOTOGRAPHS
PH06724 666 (September 30, 1993) p71. "Harding In The Synth Lab: 'I'm Pushing The Boundaries'" (Hill, Britain)
HARDSON, TRE—PHOTOGRAPHS
PH06725 660-661 (July 8, 1993) p97. "The Pharcyde: Romye Robinson, Imani Wilcox, Derrick Stewart And Tre Hardson" (Azimi, Mojgan B.)
PH06726 722 (November 30, 1995) p38. "Hip-Hop's Cosmic Voyagers: Wilcox, Robinson, Hardson And Stewart (from left)" (McClelland, Philippe)
HARDWARE—ILLUSTRATIONS
PH06727 715 (August 24, 1995) p73. "Hot Gadget" (Faiola, Susan)
HARDWICK, CHRIS—PHOTOGRAPHS
PH06728 748 (November 28, 1996) p25. "[Chris Hardwick]" (Garner, Kate)
HARFORD, CHRIS—PHOTOGRAPHS
PH06729 621 (January 9, 1992) p25. "Chris Harford" (Capak, R. J.)
HARFORD, CHRIS—PHOTOGRAPHS—PORTRAITS
PH06730 640 (October 1, 1992) p25. "[Chris Harford]" (Feingold, Deborah)
PH06731 645-646 (December 10, 1992) p59. "Chris Harford" (Feingold, Deborah)
HARING, BRUCE—BOOKS
PH06732 740 (August 8, 1996) p60. "Off The Charts"
HARLEY, GRETTA—PHOTOGRAPHS
PH06733 729 (March 7, 1996) p28. "Lawless, Harley And Zoe Bermet (from left) Hone Their Skills At The Home Alive Classroom, In Seattle" (Wescott, Stacey)
HARLOW, LISA—PHOTOGRAPHS
PH06734 700 (January 26, 1995) p16. "[Soundgarden]" (Doughty, Curt)
HARPER, BEN—PHOTOGRAPHS
PH06735 680 (April 21, 1994) p22. "Harper: Singing The Folk Blues"
PH06736 717 (September 21, 1995) p20. "Get Up, Stand Up: Harper Does His Soul Funk Hip-Hop Thing" (Diamond, Rick)
PH06737 721 (November 16, 1995) p65. "[Ben Harper]" (Winters, Dan)
PH06738 726 (January 25, 1996) p17. "Mike McCready, Jeff Ament, Harper, Eddie Vedder, Jack Irons And Stone Gossard (from left)"
HARPER, JESSICA—PHOTOGRAPHS
PH06739 690 (September 8, 1994) p70. "With Real-Life Co-Worker And Fictional Girlfriend Jessica harper, From "It's Garry Shandling's Show""
HARRELSON, WOODY—ILLUSTRATIONS
PH06740 655 (April 29, 1993) p67. "Fiscal Attraction" (Friedman, Drew)
PH06741 690 (September 8, 1994) p83. "Blood From A Stone" (Gosfield, Josh)
HARRELSON, WOODY—PHOTOGRAPHS
PH06742 655 (April 29, 1993) p68. "Demi's Choice: Robert Redford (left) Or Woody Harrelson?"
PH06743 685 (June 30, 1994) p81. "Urban Riders: Sutherland And Harrelson"
PH06744 684 (June 16, 1994) p116. "Bloody: Lewis And Harrelson In "Natural Born Killers""
PH06745 690 (September 8, 1994) p84. "Lewis And Harrelson"
PH06746 691 (September 22, 1994) p21. "Natural-Born Killer Woody Harrelson" (Papas, B. J.)
PH06747 723 (December 14, 1995) p92. "Race For The Money: Harrelson And Snipes"
PH06748 748 (November 28, 1996) p26. "[Courtney Love & Woody Harrelson]" (Oliveira, Alex)
PH06749 750-751 (December 26, 1996) p204. "'ID4' (above) Is Biggest, But 'Larry Flynt' (left), With Harrelson And Love Flanking Flynt, Is The Best"
HARRELSON, WOODY—PHOTOGRAPHS—PORTRAITS
PH06750 690 (September 8, 1994) p84. "Killer Lover Boy Woody Harrelson"
HARRIS, BRUKLIN—PHOTOGRAPHS
PH06751 742 (September 5, 1996) p68. "Girls Taylor, Grace And Harris"
HARRIS, DAVID—PHOTOGRAPHS
PH06752 632 (June 11, 1992) p80. "David Harris In California, 1969" (Marshall, Jim)
HARRIS, ED—PHOTOGRAPHS
PH06753 712-713 (July 13, 1995) p116. "'Apollo 13' Astronauts Hanks And Bacon Blast Off; And Harris Waits In Houston"
HARRIS, EMMYLOU—ALBUMS
PH06754 625 (March 5, 1992) p70. "At The Ryman"
PH06755 669 (November 11, 1993) p73. "Cowgirl's Prayer"
PH06756 721 (November 16, 1995) p110. "Wrecking Ball"
HARRIS, EMMYLOU—PHOTOGRAPHS
PH06757 746 (October 31, 1996) p18. "Sisters Are Doin' It For Themselves: McLachlan (left) And Harris At Lilith Fair" (Nemchin, Tracy)
PH06758 749 (December 12, 1996) p24. "Harris (left) Onstage With Luscious Jackson" (Lance, James L.)
HARRIS, JAMES—PHOTOGRAPHS
PH06759 720 (November 2, 1995) p22. "On: Echobelly's Harris, Smith, Johansson, Madan And Henderson (from left)" (Claiborne, Barron)
HARRIS, JARED—ILLUSTRATIONS
PH06760 734 (May 16, 1996) p71. "Scum Manifesto" (Brodner, Steve)
HARRIS, JARED—PHOTOGRAPHS
PH06761 732 (April 18, 1996) pp[enc.24,28]. "[Jared Harris]" (Witkin, Christian)
HARRIS, JARED—PHOTOGRAPHS—PORTRAITS
PH06762 734 (May 16, 1996) p72. "Jared Harris"
HARRIS, JOSSIE—PHOTOGRAPHS
PH06763 638 (September 3, 1992) pp[enc.42]. "[Jossie Harris, Ken Swift, Richard Colon]" (Eccles, Andrew)
HARRIS, JOSSIE—PHOTOGRAPHS—PORTRAITS
PH06764 638 (September 3, 1992) pp[enc.35-36]. "[Jossie Harris]" (Eccles, Andrew)
PH06765 656 (May 13, 1993) p94. "Deidre Lang, Jennifer Lopez, Twist, Jossie Harris, Lisa Thompson (from left)"

PH06766 656 (May 13, 1993) p96. "Harris"
HARRIS, LESLIE—PHOTOGRAPHS
PH06767 652 (March 18, 1993) p47. "'I.R.T.' Director Harris" (Michaelson, Randall)
HARRIS, LISA—PHOTOGRAPHS
PH06768 749 (December 12, 1996) p20. "It's A Family Affair: Jam's Wife, Lisa Harris, Holding Tyler; Jam; Jackson; And Lewis (from left)"
HARRIS, MARY—PHOTOGRAPHS—PORTRAITS
PH06769 700 (January 26, 1995) p24. "[Spearhead]"
HARRIS, RALPH—PHOTOGRAPHS—PORTRAITS
PH06770 692 (October 6, 1994) p93. "Family In Crisis: Ralph Harris Of "On Our Own" Wears His Mom's Clothes"
HARRISON, GEORGE—PHOTOGRAPHS
PH06771 615 (October 17, 1991) p49. "Road Warriors: Clapton And His Pal Harrison" (Rider, Paul)
PH06772 623 (February 6, 1992) p18. "Clapton (right) Got A Warmer Welcome" (Studna, Carl)
PH06773 623 (February 6, 1992) p18. "Harrison: Visibly Nervous And Ultracareful" (Studna, Carl)
PH06774 630 (May 14, 1992) p13. "Tom Petty, George Harrison, Gary Moore And B. B. King (from left)"
PH06775 631 (May 28, 1992) p9. "Ringo Starr, Julian Lennon And George Harrison (from left)" (Young, Richard)
PH06776 644 (November 26, 1992) p17. "The Great Garden Party: Dylan Center Stage For The Grand Finale" (Mazur, Kevin)
PH06777 648 (January 21, 1993) p9. "Tom Petty And Harrison" (Mazur, Kevin)
PH06778 649 (February 4, 1993) p8. "Van Halen (left) And George Harrison At The Jeff Porcaro Tribute" (Granitz, Steve)
PH06779 680 (April 21, 1994) p63. "Hamburg Days: George Harrison, Stuart Sutcliffe And John Lennon" (Kirchherr, Astrid)
PH06780 722 (November 30, 1995) p26. "Ringo Starr, John Lennon, Paul McCartney And George Harrison During The Filming Of 'Help!' In 1965: 'So Much Younger Than Today'" (Kindahl, Chris)
PH06781 726 (January 25, 1996) p46. "Starr, McCartney, Harrison, Lennon"
HARRISON, GEORGE—PHOTOGRAPHS—PORTRAITS
PH06782 643 (November 12, 1992) p134. "George Harrison" (Seliger, Mark)
HARRISON, JERRY—PHOTOGRAPHS
PH06783 744 (October 3, 1996) p30. "Will The Heads (above) Roll? The Band Was Sued By Byrne" (Ockenfels, Frank W.)
HARRISON, PHILLIP—PHOTOGRAPHS
PH06784 670 (November 25, 1993) p58. "Home Boy: With Father Philip, Mother Lucille, Brother Jamal And Sister Lateefah (from left) In His Parents' Orlando Home Last Year" (Chiasson, John)
HARRISON, WILBERT—PHOTOGRAPHS—PORTRAITS
PH06785 697 (December 15, 1994) p34. "Wilbert Harrison In The Late '50s"
HARRY, DEBBIE—ALBUMS
PH06786 617 (November 14, 1991) p106. "Koo Koo" (Giger, H. R.)
PH06787 617 (November 14, 1991) p106. "Koo Koo" (Wagg, Peter)
PH06788 617 (November 14, 1991) p106. "Koo Koo" (Aris, Brian)
PH06789 667 (October 14, 1993) p118. "Debravation"
HARRY, DEBBIE—PHOTOGRAPHS
PH06790 621 (January 9, 1992) p10. "...And Debbie Harry (right) Lend A Hand To Benefit AIDS" (Wyman, Jay)
PH06791 667 (October 14, 1993) p98. "'Rapture': Debbie Harry's Rap Video"
PH06792 688 (August 11, 1994) p18. "Debbie Harry Greets Joey, The Big Birthday Boy" (Banks, Paul)
PH06793 700 (January 26, 1995) p17. "[John Giorno's AIDS Treatment Project]" (Gruen, Bob)
HARRY, DEBBIE—PHOTOGRAPHS—PORTRAITS
PH06794 643 (November 12, 1992) pp90-91. "Debbie Harry" (Weber, Bruce)
PH06795 692 (October 6, 1994) p52. "Debbie Harry"
HART, ANGIE—ILLUSTRATIONS
PH06796 685 (June 30, 1994) p73. "Angie Hart" (Deacon, Jim)
HART, ANGIE—PHOTOGRAPHS—PORTRAITS
PH06797 684 (June 16, 1994) p30. "Simon Austin, Angie Hart, Alistair Barden And Tim O'Connor (from left)" (Westenberg, Kevin)
HART, GARY—ILLUSTRATIONS
PH06798 630 (May 14, 1992) p89. "[Yale]" (Cowles, David)
HART, GRANT—PHOTOGRAPHS
PH06799 694 (November 3, 1994) p72. "Poison Years: Husker Du's Grant Hart, Greg Norton And Mould" (Corrigan, Daniel)
PH06800 729 (March 7, 1996) p9. "Dave Pirner (left) And Danny Murphy Of Soul Asylum Flank Grant Hart" (Garrity, Brian)
HART, IAN—PHOTOGRAPHS
PH06801 631 (May 28, 1992) p61. "Angus (left) And Hart Probe A Beatles Love Story"
PH06802 680 (April 21, 1994) p93. "Dorff And Hart Flank Lee In A Beatles Love Triangle"
HART, MARK—PHOTOGRAPHS
PH06803 676 (February 24, 1994) p17. "Four's A Crowd: Neil Finn, Mark Hart, Paul Hester And Nick Seymour (from left)" (Broad, Julian)
HART, MICKEY—PHOTOGRAPHS
PH06804 655 (April 29, 1993) p24. "Garcia And Hart At The Library Of Congress" (Mazur, Kevin)
PH06805 676 (February 24, 1994) p46. "The Early Grateful Dead (clockwise from left): Jerry Garcia, Bill Kreutzmann, Ron 'Pigpen' McKernan, Bob Weir, Percussionist Mickey Hart And Phil Lesh" (Marshall, Jim)
PH06806 677 (March 10, 1994) p27. "The Dead's Lesh, Weir, Vince Welnick, Hornsby, Bill Kreutzmann, Mickey Hart" (Mazur, Kevin)
PH06807 717 (September 21, 1995) p73. "marrying Acid-Damaged Art Music And The Funky Snort Of Live Rock & Roll: The Dead As A Lysergic-Dance Band In 1969 With Tom Constanten, Weir, Kreutzmann, Pigpen, Lesh, H..." (G
PH06808 717 (September 21, 1995) p72. "The Music Never Stopped: Garcia, Weir, Lesh, Brent Mydland, Kreutzmann And Hart (from left) In 1979" (Greene, Herbi)
PH06809 717 (September 21, 1995) p28. "Not Fade Away: Barlow, Hart, Kantner And Weir (from left) Celebrate Garcia In Golden Gate Park" (Blakesberg, Jay)
PH06810 726 (January 25, 1996) p24. "Drums In Space: Hart At Work In The Studio" (Dyer, Alison)
PH06811 726 (January 25, 1996) p23. "The Last Incarnation Of The Dead Perform In February 1995: Phil Lesh, Mickey Hart, Bob Weir, Jerry Garcia And Vince Welnick (from left)" (Blakesberg, Jay)
PH06812 742 (September 5, 1996) p30. "[Mickey Hart]" (Werner, John)
HARTLING, EVE—PHOTOGRAPHS
PH06813 689 (August 25, 1994) p41. "Pierce, MacLeod, Hartling, Stein (from top)" (Crump, James)
HARTMAN, DAVE—PHOTOGRAPHS
PH06814 721 (November 16, 1995) p38. "The Party Has Rolled Back Into Town: Huff, Miller And Hartman (from left)" (Elledge, Paul)
HARTRIDGE, JIMMY—PHOTOGRAPHS
PH06815 625 (March 5, 1992) p27. "Jimmy Hartridge, Graham Bonnar, Adam Franklin, Adi Vynes (from left)" (Anker, Matt)
HARTS OF THE WEST (TELEVISION SHOW)—PHOTOGRAPHS
PH06816 666 (September 30, 1993) p116. "'Harts Of The West'"
HARTZ, KEN—PHOTOGRAPHS
PH06817 658 (June 10, 1993) p32. "Clockwise From Left: Lars Gustafsson, Jay Bennett, Ken Hartz And Mike Hazelrigg" (Elledge, Paul)

HARVARD UNIVERSITY—PHOTOGRAPHS
PH06818 626 (March 19, 1992) p68. "Bye-Bye, Birdie: 'Crimson' Editors Turn The Ibis Over To Another Shade Of Red"
PH06819 704 (March 23, 1995) p74. "Editorial Director Pete Keith (standing) Rallies The '95 Staff" (Asnin, Marc)
PH06820 704 (March 23, 1995) p75. "The Editors Of the British Guide: All Copy Is Screened For Libel" (Asnin, Marc)
PH06821 704 (March 23, 1995) p75. "The Itineraries For The Students Researching The U.S. Guide" (Asnin, Marc)
PH06822 704 (March 23, 1995) p74. "Nathan's Boss Alp Aker (right) With other Guide Editors" (Asnin, Marc)
HARVEY, ALEX—ALBUMS
PH06823 648 (January 21, 1993) p23. "The Sensational Alex Harvey Band: BBC Radio Live In Concert"
HARVEY, BRYAN—PHOTOGRAPHS
PH06824 660-661 (July 8, 1993) p101. "Gutterball: Johnny Hott, Bryan Harvey, Steve Wynn, Bob Rupe, Stephen McCarthy"
PH06825 663 (August 19, 1993) p15. "Rupe, Hott, Harvey, Wynn And McCarthy (from left)" (Callahan, Walter)
HARVEY, MICK—PHOTOGRAPHS
PH06826 692 (October 6, 1994) p16. "At Philly's Lollapalooza: L7's Donita Sparks (left), Dee Plakas, Suzi Gardner And Jennifer Finch With Bad Seeds Mick Harvey, James Johnston And Nick Cave" (Weiner, Scott)
HARVEY, POLLY JEAN—ALBUMS
PH06827 745 (October 17, 1996) p130. "Dance Hall At Louse Point"
HARVEY, POLLY JEAN—ILLUSTRATIONS
PH06828 703 (March 9, 1995) p63. "Voodoo Child" (Jetter, Frances)
PH06829 724-725 (December 28, 1995) p13. "Polly Jean Harvey" (Burke, Philip)
HARVEY, POLLY JEAN—PHOTOGRAPHS
PH06830 640 (October 1, 1992) p34. "Polly Harvey At CBGB" (Mazur, Kevin)
PH06831 663 (August 19, 1993) p54. "'These Costumes Aren't Sexy,' She Says, 'They're Ridiculous...'" (Natkin, Paul)
PH06832 669 (November 11, 1993) p27. "Harvey" (Kravitz, Jeff)
PH06833 674 (January 27, 1994) p42. "Best Singer: Polly Harvey Of PJ Harvey" (Watermann, Greg)
PH06834 677 (March 10, 1994) p17. "Polly Jean Harvey Makes Small Talk With Jay Leno" (Norton, Margaret)
PH06835 679 (April 7, 1994) p37. "Bjork And Harvey, Puttin' On The Brits" (Young, Richard)
PH06836 695 (November 17, 1994) p109. "PJ Harvey" (Corbijn, Anton)
PH06837 707 (May 4, 1995) p36. "Polly Jean Harvey: Rock's Psychodrama Queen" (Westenberg, Kevin)
PH06838 714 (August 10, 1995) p15. "Polly Jean Harvey At The HFS-tival, In Washington, D. C." (Liu, Brian)
PH06839 721 (November 16, 1995) p26. "Harvey And Kowalczyk, Sharing And Caring In Pennsylvania" (Oleski, Dan)
PH06840 724-725 (December 28, 1995) p70. "Glam Slam: Polly Jean Harvey During A July Performance In Belgium" (Knaeps, Gie)
PH06841 724-725 (December 28, 1995) pp68-69. "[Polly Jean Harvey]" (Garner, Kate)
PH06842 726 (January 25, 1996) p40. "Artist Of The Year: PJ Harvey" (McDean, Craig)
PH06843 733 (May 2, 1996) p13. "I Vant To Bite Your Neck: Harvey, Left, And Cave" (Young, Richard)
PH06844 738-739 (July 11, 1996) p28. "John Parish And Polly Jean Harvey Team Up"
PH06845 748 (November 28, 1996) p47. "[Polly Jean Harvey]" (Madden, Hayley)
HARVEY, POLLY JEAN—PHOTOGRAPHS—PORTRAITS
PH06846 645-646 (December 10, 1992) p59. "PJ Harvey's Polly Harvey" (Double, Steve)
PH06847 651 (March 4, 1993) p55. "Best Songwriter" (Blakesberg, Jay)
PH06848 663 (August 19, 1993) p53. "[Polly Jean Harvey]" (Ockenfels, Frank W.)
HARVIE, IAIN—PHOTOGRAPHS—PORTRAITS
PH06849 642 (October 29, 1992) pp66-67. "[Iain Harvie]" (Salvatori, Lou)
HARWOOD, JUSTIN—PHOTOGRAPHS
PH06850 748 (November 28, 1996) p26. "Tuatara's Martin, Harwood And Buck (from left)" (Doughty, Curt)
HASKETT, CHRIS—PHOTOGRAPHS
PH06851 686-687 (July 14, 1994) p42. "Media Ho Henry Rollins, Vernon Reid And Rollins Guitarist Chris Haskett" (Malluk, Eddie)
PH06852 686-687 (July 14, 1994) p45. "[Rollins Band]" (Halfin, Ross)
HASLOCK, CHRIS—PHOTOGRAPHS
PH06853 676 (February 24, 1994) p51. "[Coach Chris "Hatchet' Haslock]" (Hanauer, Mark)
HASSAN, UMAR BIN—PHOTOGRAPHS—PORTRAITS
PH06854 676 (February 24, 1994) p25. "Last poet: Umar Bin Hassan" (Le, Thi-Linh)
HATCH, ORRIN—PHOTOGRAPHS—PORTRAITS
PH06855 710 (June 15, 1995) p62. "Hatch" (Simon, Martin)
HATE (FILM)—PHOTOGRAPHS
PH06856 728 (February 22, 1996) p70. "Hot With Hate: Cassel Takes Aim At A Violent World"
HATFIELD, JULIANA—ALBUMS
PH06857 634-635 (July 9, 1992) p106. "Hey Babe"
PH06858 645-646 (December 10, 1992) p182. "Hey Babe"
PH06859 668 (October 28, 1993) p81. "Become What You Are"
PH06860 704 (March 23, 1995) p124. "Only Everything"
HATFIELD, JULIANA—PHOTOGRAPHS
PH06861 627 (April 2, 1992) p13. "Juliana Hatfield And The Lemonheads' Evan Dando In The Studio" (Shulman, Scott C.)
PH06862 637 (August 20, 1992) p22. "Hatfield (left) With Dando" (Pasley, Richard)
PH06863 662 (August 5, 1993) p33. "Juliana Hatfield"
PH06864 666 (September 30, 1993) p19. "[Juliana Hatfield]" (Danelian, Stephen)
PH06865 671 (December 9, 1993) p32. "Happy Birthday: Hatfield With Henry" (Treml, Alex)
PH06866 691 (September 22, 1994) p20. "Members Of Bettie Serveert And Belly With Singer Jim Lauderdale (far right) And Juliana Hatfield (seated, right) At Central Park" (Roberts, Ebet)
PH06867 695 (November 17, 1994) p101. "Juliana Hatfield" (White, Steven)
PH06868 700 (January 26, 1995) p17. "Hatfield, "Lifer" Claire Danes" (Wolfe, Jerry)
PH06869 702 (February 23, 1995) p19. "Front: Hatfield, Donelly, Bragg. Rear: Dean Fraser, Gary Smith, Sean Slade" (Robicheau, Paul)
HATFIELD, JULIANA—PHOTOGRAPHS—PORTRAITS
PH06870 672-673 (December 23, 1993) p65. "Above: Juliana Hatfield" (Danelian, Stephen)
HATORI, HONDA—PHOTOGRAPHS
PH06871 729 (March 7, 1996) p9. "Cibo Matto's Honda And Miho Hatori Gettin' Down With Sean Lennon" (Kleiman, Dennis)
HATORI, MIHO—PHOTOGRAPHS
PH06872 721 (November 16, 1995) p76. "Yuka Honda (left) And Miho Hatori: Galloping Gourmets With A Taste For Big Beats And Pop Exotica" (Exum)
PH06873 729 (March 7, 1996) p9. "Cibo Matto's Honda And Miho Hatori Gettin' Down With Sean Lennon" (Kleiman, Dennis)
HATSCHEK, LUCY—PHOTOGRAPHS
PH06874 665 (September 16, 1993) pp[enc.18]. "With Lucy Hatschek, The Queen Mother" (Woodard, Fred)
HAVEL, VACLAV—PHOTOGRAPHS
PH06875 746 (October 31, 1996) p26. "Czech President Vaclav Havel With Jackson In Prague"

HAVENS, RICHIE—PHOTOGRAPHS
PH06876 648 (January 21, 1993) p11. "Baez, Gabriel, Richie Havens And Stipe (from left) At The Reebok Awards" (Robicheau, Paul)
HAWKE, ETHAN—ILLUSTRATIONS
PH06877 677 (March 10, 1994) p59. "Twenty Something" (Ryden, Mark)
PH06878 702 (February 23, 1995) p79. "Sex And The Single Slacker" (Schumaker, Ward)
PH06879 706 (April 20, 1995) p12. "Hawke 'N' Eggs" (Pendergrast, James T.)
HAWKE, ETHAN—PHOTOGRAPHS
PH06880 649 (February 4, 1993) p75. "Ethan Hawke (center) Survives A Plane Crash In The Andes"
PH06881 677 (March 10, 1994) p47. "Future Hazy, Try Again: Ryder And Her 'Reality Bites' Boyfriend, Ethan Hawke"
PH06882 677 (March 10, 1994) p60. "Zahn, Ryder, Garofalo And Hawke Face A Shaky Future (from left)"
PH06883 688 (August 11, 1994) p18. "[Madonna & Ethan Hawke]" (Amati, Ray)
PH06884 702 (February 23, 1995) p80. "And Enjoy A Night In Vienna"
PH06885 702 (February 23, 1995) p80. "Julie Delpy And Ethan Hawke Share A Kiss"
PH06886 702 (February 23, 1995) p80. "Take Direction From Richard Linklater"
PH06887 703 (March 9, 1995) pp44-45,47. "[Ethan Hawke]" (Seliger, Mark)
PH06888 703 (March 9, 1995) p46. "Ethan, 8, In Brooklyn Heights, N.Y."
PH06889 703 (March 9, 1995) p48. "Let's Go! Austria: Hawke Meets Delpy On A Eurailpass In 'Before Sunrise'" (Brandenstein, Gabriela)
PH06890 703 (March 9, 1995) p49. "Reality Bites Back: Hawke On The Set With Ryder" (Redin, Van)
PH06891 744 (October 3, 1996) p20. "Ethan 'Pip' Hawke And Gwyneth 'Stella' Paltrow" (Schwartzwald, Lawrence)
PH06892 749 (December 12, 1996) p20. "Great Expectations: Hawke At Signing" (Olson, Sheryl)
HAWKE, ETHAN—PHOTOGRAPHS—PORTRAITS
PH06893 703 (March 9, 1995) pp[cover]. "Fool For Love: Ethan HAwke" (Seliger, Mark)
HAWKINS, NICK—PHOTOGRAPHS
PH06894 630 (May 14, 1992) p28. "B.A.D.'s Nick Hawkins (left) And Mick Jones" (Kraft, Chris)
HAWKINS, SOPHIE B.—ALBUMS
PH06895 631 (May 28, 1992) p53. "Tongues And Tails"
HAWKINS, SOPHIE B.—PHOTOGRAPHS
PH06896 631 (May 28, 1992) p11. "Sophie B. Hawkins" (Ienner, Jimmy, Jr.)
PH06897 638 (September 3, 1992) pp24-25. "" ([Sophie B. Hawkins])
HAWKINS, TED—ALBUMS
PH06898 689 (August 25, 1994) p90. "The Next Hundred Years"
HAWKINS, TED—PHOTOGRAPHS
PH06899 702 (February 23, 1995) p36. "Jaws Dropped, And There Was Complete Silence: Hawkins" (Dipaolo, Debra)
HAWKS—PHOTOGRAPHS
PH06900 669 (November 11, 1993) p66. "The Hawks At Ontario's Brass Rail Circa '63: Danko, Manuel, Hawkins, Helm, Robertson And Hudson (from left)"
HAWN, GOLDIE—ILLUSTRATIONS
PH06901 744 (October 3, 1996) p77. "Men Behaving Badly" (Brodner, Steve)
HAWN, GOLDIE—PHOTOGRAPHS
PH06902 634-635 (July 9, 1992) p114. "A Coy Comedy Defeats The Efforts Of Hawn And Martin"
PH06903 637 (August 20, 1992) p57. "Youth Seeking: Hawn (left) And Streep"
PH06904 744 (October 3, 1996) p78. "First Wives Keaton, Midler And Hawn Out For Revenge"
HAWTHORNE, EBONY—PHOTOGRAPHS
PH06905 671 (December 9, 1993) p60. "Ebony Hawthorne (left) With Her Mother" (Light, Ken)
HAWTHORNE, NIGEL—PHOTOGRAPHS
PH06906 700 (January 26, 1995) p68. "Hawthorne Chases "madness""
HAYDEN—PHOTOGRAPHS
PH06907 747 (November 14, 1996) p26. "Buscemi (left) With Canadian Punk-Rock Folk Singer Hayden" (Clinch, Danny)
PH06908 750-751 (December 26, 1996) p63. "[Hayden]" (Giordano, Ann)
HAYES, BOB—PHOTOGRAPHS
PH06909 659 (June 24, 1993) p63. "Bob Hayes, Who Runs The Shelter's Housing Office, On His Harley" (Agulera-Helwig, Max)
HAYES, ISAAC—ALBUMS
PH06910 617 (November 14, 1991) p144. "Hot Buttered Soul" (Whorf, Christopher)
PH06911 617 (November 14, 1991) p144. "Hot Buttered Soul" (Smith, Bob)
HAYES, ISAAC—PHOTOGRAPHS
PH06912 733 (May 2, 1996) p14. "Vote-Getters Ice-T, Hayes And Chuck D (from left) Do The Right Thing" (Mazur, Kevin)
HAYES, ISAAC—PHOTOGRAPHS—PORTRAITS
PH06913 703 (March 9, 1995) p33. "Hayes: Back In Action" (Double, Steve)
HAYNES, GIBBY—ILLUSTRATIONS
PH06914 750-751 (December 26, 1996) p19. "Gibby Haynes Of Butthole Surfers" (Pilon, Alain)
HAYNES, GIBBY—PHOTOGRAPHS
PH06915 659 (June 24, 1993) p25. "Gibby Haynes, Jeff Pinkus, Paul Leary And King Coffey (clockwise from top)" (Watermann, Greg)
PH06916 665 (September 16, 1993) p26. "Surfers Paul Leary (left) And Gibby Haynes" (Mazur, Kevin)
PH06917 674 (January 27, 1994) p28. "Vedder And haynes Do The Bus Jam" (Spinelli, Edward)
PH06918 694 (November 3, 1994) p22. "Mekons Singer Sally Timms, Gibby Haynes And Jon Langford Belt It Out Onstage" (Crawford, Michael)
PH06919 709 (June 1, 1995) p16. "[P]" (Smith, Kelly)
PH06920 710 (June 15, 1995) p54. "Surf Thing: Coffey, Haynes, Leary (from left)" (Van Overbeek, Will)
PH06921 733 (May 2, 1996) p28. "[Gibby Haynes]" (Cardillicchio, Nick)
PH06922 738-739 (July 11, 1996) p28. "Surfers' King Coffey, Gibby Haynes, Paul Leary (from left)" (Van Overbeek, Will)
PH06923 747 (November 14, 1996) p26. "'Incorrect' Host Bill Maher (left) With Haynes"
PH06924 750-751 (December 26, 1996) p116. "Gibby Haynes Caught With His Pants Down" (Vadukul, Nitin)
PH06925 750-751 (December 26, 1996) p116. "A Sleeping Haynes (right)" (Vadukul, Nitin)
HAYNES, RUSTY—PHOTOGRAPHS
PH06926 745 (October 17, 1996) p103. "Headed For Brown? Mica Rosenberg, A High-School Senior In Albuquerque, With Consultant Rusty Haynes" (Ford, Charles)
HAYS, CINDY—PHOTOGRAPHS
PH06927 698-699 (December 29, 1994) p160. "Cindy Hays (above)"
HAZELRIGG, MIKE—PHOTOGRAPHS
PH06928 658 (June 10, 1993) p32. "Clockwise From Left: Lars Gustafsson, Jay Bennett, Ken Hartz And Mike Hazelrigg" (Elledge, Paul)
HEADLINER—PHOTOGRAPHS
PH06929 647 (January 7, 1993) p25. "AD's Headliner (left) And Speech" (States, Ann)
PH06930 647 (January 7, 1993) p13. "Arrested Development's Headliner, Taree, Eshe And Speech (from left): Talkin' About A

Different Kind Of Nirvana" (States, Ann)
PH06931 648 (January 21, 1993) p9. "Arrested Development (from left): Speech, Aerle Taree, Headliner, Rasa Don, Baba Oje And Montsho Eshe" (Mazur, Kevin)
PH06932 657 (May 27, 1993) p17. "Arrested Development's Aerle taree, Headliner And Speech (from left)" (Arnold, Alice)
HEADLINER—PHOTOGRAPHS—PORTRAITS
PH06933 634-635 (July 9, 1992) p20. "Arrested Development (from left): Headliner, Montsho Eshe, Aerle Taree, Rasa Don And Speech" (Lavine, Michael)
PH06934 634-635 (July 9, 1992) p20. "Love Battery (from left): Kevin Whitworth, Rod Rudzitis And Jason Finn" (Lavine, Michael)
HEADPHONES—PHOTOGRAPHS
PH06935 674 (January 27, 1994) p59. "Koss Quiet Zone Noise-Reduction Headphones, $149" (Miller, Greg)
PH06936 704 (March 23, 1995) p134. "[Headphones]" (Grant, Bob)
HEADS—ALBUMS
PH06937 745 (October 17, 1996) p130. "No Talking Just Head"
HEALTH—ILLUSTRATIONS
PH06938 655 (April 29, 1993) p28. "[Health Care Reform]" (Cronin, Brian)
HEALTH—PHOTOGRAPHS
PH06939 616 (October 31, 1991) p44. "One Step At A Time: Part Of A National Immunization Campaign In Guatemala" (Gaggero, Carlos)
PH06940 616 (October 31, 1991) p48. "A Peruvian Mother Has Her Baby Immunized For Polio" (Gaggero, Carlos)
PH06941 626 (March 19, 1992) p55. "An Africa Child Receives The Polio Vaccine In The Belgian Congo In 1957" (Phillips, Robert)
PH06942 630 (May 14, 1992) p84. "[I Just Don't Have Any Energy]"
PH06943 630 (May 14, 1992) p92. "[Lactose Intolerance]"
PH06944 656 (May 13, 1993) p74. "[Slipped Disk]"
PH06945 741 (August 22, 1996) p77. "[Ulcers]"
HEALTH AND HAPPINESS SHOW—PHOTOGRAPHS
PH06946 691 (September 22, 1994) pp[enc.22]. "At The Elliston Place Soda Shop, In Nashville" (Wessel, Cathrine)
PH06947 691 (September 22, 1994) pp[enc.20]. "At The Mercury Lounge, In New York" (Wessel, Cathrine)
PH06948 691 (September 22, 1994) pp[enc.19]. "The Health And Happiness Show On The Road" (Wessel, Cathrine)
PH06949 691 (September 22, 1994) pp[enc.22]. "The Health And Happiness Show In Nashville" (Wessel, Cathrine)
HEAPS, DANNY—PHOTOGRAPHS
PH06950 711 (June 29, 1995) p33. "Ryder, Pirner, Band Manager Heaps, Murphy (background) And Ex-Drummer Young Greet Clinton (foreground) At The White House (from left)" (Markowitz, Jeffrey)
HEARD, BRYANT—PHOTOGRAPHS
PH06951 708 (May 18, 1995) p58. "Bryant Heard, Left, And Buddy James Gilbert: Students Often Went To School, Gun Racks Loaded, Camouflage Bloodied From An Early-Morning Hunt" (Mark, Mary Ellen)
HEARST, PATTY—ILLUSTRATIONS
PH06952 632 (June 11, 1992) p100. "[Patty Hearst]" (Putnam, Jamie)
PH06953 645-646 (December 10, 1992) p149. "Patty Hearst, 1975"
HEARST, PATTY—PHOTOGRAPHS
PH06954 615 (October 17, 1991) p64. "Patty Hearst And John Waters, 1988" (Pigozzi, Jean)
HEART—PHOTOGRAPHS
PH06955 696 (December 1, 1994) p25. "Howard Leese, John Paul Jones, Ann Wilson, Denny Fongheiser And Nancy Wilson"
HEARTS AFIRE (TELEVISION SHOW)—PHOTOGRAPHS
PH06956 645-646 (December 10, 1992) p196. "His Half-Brother, Roger, Serenaded John Ritter And Markie Post On 'Hearts Afire'"
HEARTS AND SOULS (FILM)—PHOTOGRAPHS
PH06957 664 (September 2, 1993) p69. "Charles Grodin, Robert Downey Jr., Kyra Sedgwick, Alfre Woodard And Tom Sizemore"
HEAT (FILM)—PHOTOGRAPHS
PH06958 724-725 (December 28, 1995) p138. "De Niro, Pacino And Kilmer In 'Heat'"
PH06959 731 (April 4, 1996) p66. "Heat"
HEAT, REVEREND HORTON—PHOTOGRAPHS
PH06960 685 (June 30, 1994) p41. "Heat's band Mates Taz And Jimbo; Jourgensen And Heat" (Bland, James)
HEATH, JIM—PHOTOGRAPHS
PH06961 660-661 (July 8, 1993) p96. "The Reverend Horton Heat: Jimbo Wallace, Jim Heath And Patrick 'Taz' Bentley" (Watermann, Greg)
PH06962 667 (October 14, 1993) p37. "Horton Heat: Rockabilly Madness" (Capak, R. J.)
HEATH, JIM—PHOTOGRAPHS—PORTRAITS
PH06963 692 (October 6, 1994) p28. "Country-Fried Rock: Taz, Jimbo And The Sultan Of Psychobilly, The Rev. Horton Heat" (Seliger, Mark)
HEATHER, CHARLIE—PHOTOGRAPHS
PH06964 630 (May 14, 1992) p32. "The Levellers (from left): Friend, Sevink, Chadwick, Heather And Cunningham" (Doove, Hester)
HEATHMAN, RON—PHOTOGRAPHS
PH06965 731 (April 4, 1996) p18. "Jennings (center) With Suckers, Dan Siegel, Dan Bolton, Ron Heathman And Singer Eddie Spaghetti (from left)" (Diamond, Rick)
HEAVEN AND EARTH (FILM)—PHOTOGRAPHS
PH06966 672-673 (December 23, 1993) p174. "[Heaven And Earth]"
HEAVENLY CREATURES (FILM)—PHOTOGRAPHS
PH06967 705 (April 6, 1995) p69. "Oscar Rejects"
HEAVY (FILM)—PHOTOGRAPHS
PH06968 737 (June 27, 1996) p62. "Now Playing"
HEAVY D AND THE BOYS—ALBUMS
PH06969 654 (April 15, 1993) p62. "Blue Funk"
HEAVY METAL MUSIC—ILLUSTRATIONS
PH06970 681 (May 5, 1994) p52. "Metal Thunder" (Corio, Paul)
PH06971 715 (August 24, 1995) p104. "Jurassic Rock" (Freda, Anthony)
HECKERLING, AMY—PHOTOGRAPHS
PH06972 716 (September 7, 1995) p53. "[Amy Heckerling]" (Marks, Elliot)
HEDFORD, ERIC—PHOTOGRAPHS
PH06973 721 (November 16, 1995) p78. "Peter Holmstrom, Courtney Taylor, Zia McCabe, Eric Hedford (from left): They're Exploding, Plastic And Inevitable, Andy Would Approve!" (Winters, Dan)
HEDISON, ALEXANDRA—PHOTOGRAPHS
PH06974 736 (June 13, 1996) p54. "L.A. Firefighters: Alexandra Hedison, Jarrod Emick, Elise (from left)"
HEFFINGTON, DON—PHOTOGRAPHS
PH06975 660-661 (July 8, 1993) p33. "Almost Lone Justice: Marvin Etzioni, McKee And Don Heffington" (Cohen, Lester)
HEIDORN, MIKE—PHOTOGRAPHS
PH06976 716 (September 7, 1995) p14. "Son Burning: David Boquist, Farrar, Heidorn And Jim Boquist (from left) Crank Up The Voltage" (Lucas, J.)
THE HEIGHTS (TELEVISION SHOW)—PHOTOGRAPHS
PH06977 640 (October 1, 1992) p77. "'The Heights': We're The Young Generation, And We've Got Nothing To Say" (Thurnher, Jeffrey)
PH06978 642 (October 29, 1992) p36. "The Cast Of 'The Heights': A Cross-Marketing Bonanza Or A Big Flop?"
HELAS POUR MOI (FILM)—PHOTOGRAPHS
PH06979 680 (April 21, 1994) p95. "Now Playing"
HELL, RICHARD—PHOTOGRAPHS
PH06980 633 (June 25, 1992) p12. "Dim Stars (from left): Richard Hell, Steve Shelley, Thurston Moore And Don Fleming"

(Busacca, Larry)
HELLER, CRAIG—BOOKS
PH06981 693 (October 20, 1994) p51. "From Metal To Mozart"
HELLMAN, NINA—PHOTOGRAPHS
PH06982 703 (March 9, 1995) p29. "Easy As Pie: Jody Seifert, Nina Hellman And Kerri Kenney (from left)" (Falls, John)
HELM, LEVON—PHOTOGRAPHS
PH06983 617 (November 14, 1991) p72. "Levon And The Hawks, Circa 1963: Sax Player Jerry Field, Rick Danko, Levon Helm, Richard Manuel, Garth Hudson And Robertson (from left)"
PH06984 669 (November 11, 1993) p67. "At Filmore East, '70 (top)" (Landy, Elliott)
PH06985 669 (November 11, 1993) p66. "The Hawks At Ontario's Brass Rail Circa '63: Danko, Manuel, Hawkins, Helm, Robertson And Hudson (from left)"
PH06986 669 (November 11, 1993) p66. "Levon Helm With Madolin In '70 (top)" (Landy, Elliott)
PH06987 669 (November 11, 1993) p66. "A Performance At Marvell High School Circa '55, With Thurlow Brown, Linda And Levon Helm (above, from left)"
PH06988 669 (November 11, 1993) p67. "Sredni Vollmer, Helm, Dylan And Danko In NYC in '83 (above)" (Landy, Elliott)
PH06989 669 (November 11, 1993) p66. "A Talent Show Circa '53 (left)"
PH06990 676 (February 24, 1994) p46. "The Band (clockwise from top left): Guitarist Robbie Robertson, Drummer Levon Helm, Organist Garth Hudson, Bassist Rock Danko And Pianist Richard Manuel" (Gahr, David)
HELM, LINDA—PHOTOGRAPHS
PH06991 669 (November 11, 1993) p66. "A Performance At Marvell High School Circa '55, With Thurlow Brown, Linda And Levon Helm (above, from left)"
HELMET—ALBUMS
PH06992 639 (September 17, 1992) p91. "Meantime"
PH06993 651 (March 4, 1993) p57. "Strap It On"
PH06994 692 (October 6, 1994) p91. "Betty"
HELMET—PHOTOGRAPHS
PH06995 637 (August 20, 1992) p15. "Helmet (from left): Stanier, Bogdan, Mengede And Hamilton" (Ockenfels, Frank W.)
PH06996 689 (August 25, 1994) p64. "Original Guitarist Mengede, Bogdan, Hamilton, Stanier (from left)" (Brice, Lindsay)
PH06997 695 (November 17, 1994) p92. "Helmet" (Huba, John)
HELMETS—PHOTOGRAPHS
PH06998 712-713 (July 13, 1995) p121. "[Technology]" (Grant, Bob)
HELMS, JESSE—PHOTOGRAPHS—PORTRAITS
PH06999 719 (October 19, 1995) p49. "Helms" (Trippett, Robert)
HELTAH SKELTAH—ALBUMS
PH07000 741 (August 22, 1996) p98. "Nocturnal"
HEMINGWAY, MARIEL—PHOTOGRAPHS
PH07001 625 (March 5, 1992) p78. "Hemingway And Mellencamp Make Peace"
HEMP—ILLUSTRATIONS
PH07002 705 (April 6, 1995) p17. "Hemp, Hemp, Hooray!" (Todd, Mark)
HENDERSON, ANDY—PHOTOGRAPHS
PH07003 720 (November 2, 1995) p22. "On: Echobelly's Harris, Smith, Johansson, Madan And Henderson (from left)" (Claiborne, Barron)
HENDERSON, BRUCE—PHOTOGRAPHS
PH07004 668 (October 28, 1993) p30. "G. E. Smith (left) And Bruce Henderson" (Mazur, Kevin)
HENDERSON, D. A.—PHOTOGRAPHS
PH07005 616 (October 31, 1991) p43. "D. A. Henderson Is A Leader In The Fight To Eradicate Polio" (Heisler, George)
HENDRIX, AL—PHOTOGRAPHS
PH07006 623 (February 6, 1992) p47. "One Room Of Al Hendrix's Home Is A Shrine To His Late Son" (Estrine, Darryl)
PH07007 625 (March 5, 1992) p17. "Al Hendrix" (Elgar, Nick)
PH07008 625 (March 5, 1992) p17. "Mitch Mitchell, Noel Redding, Young And Al Hendrix (from left)" (Elgar, Nick)
PH07009 716 (September 7, 1995) p25. "Al Hendrix Has Gained Control Of His Son's Legacy"
PH07010 724-725 (December 28, 1995) p51. "Why Is This Man Smiling?: Hendrix" (Estrine, Darryl)
HENDRIX, AL—PHOTOGRAPHS—PORTRAITS
PH07011 623 (February 6, 1992) p42. "'Johnny Allen' Hendrix With His Father, Al, In Seattle In 1945"
HENDRIX, BRIAN—PHOTOGRAPHS
PH07012 628 (April 16, 1992) p51. "Basehead, The Band (from left): Brian Hendrix, Keith Lofton, Bill Conway And Michael Ivey" (Ockenfels, Frank W.)
HENDRIX, JIMI—ALBUMS
PH07013 617 (November 14, 1991) p137. "Electric Ladyland" (King, David)
PH07014 617 (November 14, 1991) p137. "Electric Ladyland" (Montgomery, David)
PH07015 726 (January 25, 1996) p38. "Jimi Hendrix: The Ultimate Experience"
HENDRIX, JIMI—ILLUSTRATIONS—LETTERING
PH07016 623 (February 6, 1992) pp40-45,47-48+. "[Jimi Hendrix]" (Ortiz-Lopez, Dennis)
HENDRIX, JIMI—PHOTOGRAPHS
PH07017 615 (October 17, 1991) p105. "From Electric Ladyland To The Tour Of La-La Land"
PH07018 623 (February 6, 1992) p44. "Hendrix (second from left) With His First Band, The Rocking Kings"
PH07019 638 (September 3, 1992) p59. "Janis Backstage Being Filmed By Jimi Hendrix, 1968" (Marshall, Jim)
PH07020 669 (November 11, 1993) p17. "Hendrix With Eric Clapton In London, Circa 1966"
PH07021 682 (May 19, 1994) p22. "Father And Son? Jimi Hendrix Jr. (below) And Jimi Hendrix (above)"
PH07022 712-713 (July 13, 1995) p45. "The Experience, Circa '67: Drummer Mitch Mitchell (left), Hendrix, bassist Redding"
PH07023 720 (November 2, 1995) p51. "Jimi Hendrix" (Kelly, Roz)
HENDRIX, JIMI—PHOTOGRAPHS—PORTRAITS
PH07024 619-620 (December 12, 1991) p32. "[Electric Gypsy]"
PH07025 623 (February 6, 1992) p45. "Hendrix Found His Perfect Musical Accomplices In Noel Redding (left) And Mitch Mitchell (right)" (Mankowitz, Gered)
PH07026 623 (February 6, 1992) pp40-41. "[Jimi Hendrix]" (Mankowitz, Gered)
PH07027 623 (February 6, 1992) pp[cover]. "Jimi Hendrix: The Greatest Guitarist Of All Time" (Mankowitz, Gered)
PH07028 623 (February 6, 1992) p42. "'Johnny Allen' Hendrix With His Father, Al, In Seattle In 1945"
PH07029 645-646 (December 10, 1992) pp[cover]. "1992 Yearbook" (Mankowitz, Gered)
PH07030 645-646 (December 10, 1992) p161. "Jimi Hendrix, 1970"
PH07031 650 (February 18, 1993) p17. "[Jimi Hendrix]"
PH07032 697 (December 15, 1994) p28. "[Jimi Hendrix]"
HENDRIX, JIMI, JR.—PHOTOGRAPHS
PH07033 682 (May 19, 1994) p22. "Father And Son? Jimi Hendrix Jr. (below) And Jimi Hendrix (above)" (Boot, Adrian)
HENKE, JAMES—BOOKS
PH07034 645-646 (December 10, 1992) p87. "[History Of Rock & Roll]"
HENLEY, DON—ILLUSTRATIONS
PH07035 641 (October 15, 1992) p157. "[Don Henley, Glenn Frey]" (Russo, Anthony)
PH07036 697 (December 15, 1994) p92. "Glen Frey And Don Henley" (Cowles, David)
PH07037 732 (April 18, 1996) p11. "Don Henley" (Payne, C. F.)

HENLEY, DON—PHOTOGRAPHS
PH07038 615 (October 17, 1991) p13. "Steven Tyler, Don Henley" (Mazur, Kevin)
PH07039 619-620 (December 12, 1991) p90. "Henley, Sting, Joel, Raitt" (Kaplan, Todd)
PH07040 619-620 (December 12, 1991) p68. "Joel, Don Henley, Mick Jones" (Mazur, Kevin)
PH07041 626 (March 19, 1992) p13. "Don Henley Performs At The Pollack Radio Conference" (Granitz, Steve)
PH07042 629 (April 30, 1992) p11. "Dress Rehearsal For The Rain-Forest Benefit: Sting, John, Goldberg, Cole, Henley And Taylor (from left)" (Regan, Ken)
PH07043 647 (January 7, 1993) p11. "Don Henley (left) With Billy Joel" (Elgar, Nick)
PH07044 657 (May 27, 1993) p9. "Alert The Media: Don Henley Smiles" (Preston, Neal)
PH07045 681 (May 5, 1994) p22. "Eagle Backs Up Crow" (Cohen, Lester)
PH07046 685 (June 30, 1994) p23. "Birds Of A Feather: Joe Walsh, Timothy B. Schmit, Don Henley, Don Felder And Glenn Frey (from left)"
PH07047 683 (June 2, 1994) p16. "Don Henley Breaks The Bank With The Eagles" (Mazur, Kevin)
PH07048 686-687 (July 14, 1994) p36. "Frey (left) And Henley in Eagles' Hell" (Granitz, Steve)
PH07049 698-699 (December 29, 1994) p55. "Glenn Frey (left) And Don Henley" (Mazur, Kevin)
PH07050 712-713 (July 13, 1995) p49. "Henley And Bride Summerall" (Dominguez, Miguel)
PH07051 732 (April 18, 1996) pp23-24. "[Don Henley]" (Sinclair, Jodie)
PH07052 735 (May 30, 1996) p12. "If You're Gonna Love, Wear The Glove" (Mazur, Kevin)
PH07053 750-751 (December 26, 1996) p57. "The Rainforest All-Star Supremes Tribute" (Mazur, Kevin)
HENLEY, DON—PHOTOGRAPHS—PORTRAITS
PH07054 616 (October 31, 1991) p18. "[Don Henley]"
PH07055 643 (November 12, 1992) p102. "Don Henley" (Rolston, Matthew)
PH07056 667 (October 14, 1993) p77. "Henley: Bittersweet 'Boys Of Summer' Hit One Out"
HENNEMAN, BRIAN—PHOTOGRAPHS
PH07057 721 (November 16, 1995) p26. "Bottle Rocket Henneman (left) And Jeff Tweedy Of Wilco" (Ellenby, Peter)
PH07058 730 (March 21, 1996) p21. "Bottle Rockets Tom Parr, Tom Ray, Brian Henneman, Mark Ortmann (from left)"
HENRY, JOE—ALBUMS
PH07059 732 (April 18, 1996) p69. "Trampoline"
HENRY, JOE—PHOTOGRAPHS
PH07060 671 (December 9, 1993) p32. "Happy Birthday: Hatfield With Henry" (Treml, Alex)
PH07061 672-673 (December 23, 1993) p70. "Live From New York: Hamilton, Pirner, Williams, Henry And Murphy (clockwise from top left)" (Mazur, Kevin)
PH07062 737 (June 27, 1996) p24. "[Joe Henry]" (Welch, Matthew)
HENRY, JOE—PHOTOGRAPHS—PORTRAITS
PH07063 637 (August 20, 1992) p20. "[Joe Henry]" (Perry, David)
HENSLER, MATT—PHOTOGRAPHS
PH07064 647 (January 7, 1993) p30. "Dunlavy, Dominic Pasquini, Matt Hensler" (Mark, Mary Ellen)
HENSTRIDGE, NATASHA—PHOTOGRAPHS—PORTRAITS
PH07065 715 (August 24, 1995) p108. "Dangerous Women: Michelle Pfeiffer, Sandra Bullock, Julia Roberts, Cindy Crawford And Natasha Henstridge"
HERCULES: THE LEGENDARY JOURNEYS (TELEVISION SHOW)—PHOTOGRAPHS
PH07066 715 (August 24, 1995) p74. "Hot TV Show"
HEREDIA, WILSON JERMAINE—PHOTOGRAPHS
PH07067 734 (May 16, 1996) p56. "[Wilson Jermaine Heredia]" (Hom, Marc)
HERMAN, MAUREEN—PHOTOGRAPHS
PH07068 662 (August 5, 1993) p13. "Maureen Herman, Kat Bjelland And Lori Barbero Of Babes in Toyland" (Blakesberg, Jay)
PH07069 710 (June 15, 1995) p51. "Bjelland, Maureen Herman, Barbero (from left)" (Sferra, Rik)
HERMAN, MAUREEN—PHOTOGRAPHS—PORTRAITS
PH07070 695 (November 17, 1994) p71. "Babes In Toyland" (Borris, Dan)
HERMAN, PEE-WEE—PHOTOGRAPHS
PH07071 615 (October 17, 1991) p13. "Pee-Wee Herman" (Mazur, Kevin)
HERMAN, PEE-WEE—PHOTOGRAPHS—PORTRAITS
PH07072 619-620 (December 12, 1991) pp[cover]. "1991 Yearbook" (Beckman, Janette)
HERMAN, WOODY—PHOTOGRAPHS
PH07073 678 (March 24, 1994) p14. "Juggy Gayles, The Moses Of Promo..."
HERNANDEZ, ALFREDO—PHOTOGRAPHS
PH07074 692 (October 6, 1994) p24. "Desert Storm: Kyuss' Homme, Reeder, Garcia And Hernandez (from left)" (Miller, Michael)
HERNANDEZ, GEORGE—PHOTOGRAPHS
PH07075 615 (October 17, 1991) p28. "Jack Coy, George Hernandez, Jeff Braimes, Martin Chandler (from left)" (Mason, Karen)
HERNANDEZ, SAUL—PHOTOGRAPHS
PH07076 662 (August 5, 1993) p17. "Andre, Saul Hernandez, Alejando Marcovech" (Mazur, Kevin)
HERO (FILM)—ILLUSTRATIONS
PH07077 642 (October 29, 1992) p76. "Hard Times For Heroes" (Blitt, Barry)
HERO (FILM)—PHOTOGRAPHS
PH07078 649 (February 4, 1993) p72. "[Hero]"
HEROIN—ILLUSTRATIONS
PH07079 681 (May 5, 1994) p36. "[Heroin]" (Duke, William)
PH07080 738-739 (July 11, 1996) p12. "Addiction" (Pendergrast, James T.)
PH07081 738-739 (July 11, 1996) p12. "In Case Of Addiction Break Glass" (Pendergrast, James T.)
HEROIN—PHOTOGRAPHS
PH07082 639 (September 17, 1992) p25. "[Heroin]" (Winters, Dan)
PH07083 735 (May 30, 1996) pp35-40. "[Seattle & Heroin]" (Exum)
HERREMA, JENNIFER—PHOTOGRAPHS
PH07084 710 (June 15, 1995) p36. "Brown, Herrema, Hagerty And Pyle (from left): 'We're A Marketing Nightmare'" (Westenberg, Kevin)
HERRERO, MERCEDES—PHOTOGRAPHS
PH07085 704 (March 23, 1995) pp102-103. "Class of '95" (Tavee, Tom)
HERRING, JIMMY—PHOTOGRAPHS
PH07086 631 (May 28, 1992) p16. "The Rescue Unit (from left): Matt Mundy, Oteil Burbridge, Col. Bruce Hampton, Jimmy Herring And Apt. Q258" (Frazier, Jeff)
HERRON, CINDY—PHOTOGRAPHS
PH07087 623 (February 6, 1992) p90. "Cindy Herron And Omar Epps Take Time Out From Fighting"
PH07088 709 (June 1, 1995) p17. "Maxine Jones, Robinson, O'Donnell, Cindy Herron, Terry Ellis" (Nelson, Ralph)
HERRON, CINDY—PHOTOGRAPHS—PORTRAITS
PH07089 660-661 (July 8, 1993) p68. "Cindy Herron" (Rolston, Matthew)
PH07090 660-661 (July 8, 1993) pp64-65. "En Vogue's Sheer Beauties: Terry Ellis, Maxine Jones, Dawn Robinson And Cindy Herron (from left)" (Rolston, Matthew)

HERSH, KRISTEN—ALBUMS
PH07091 678 (March 24, 1994) p112. "Hips And Makers"
PH07092 679 (April 7, 1994) p72. "Hips And Makers"
HERSH, KRISTIN—ILLUSTRATIONS
PH07093 703 (March 9, 1995) p11. "Throwing Muses' Kristin Hersh" (Burke, Philip)
HERSH, KRISTIN—PHOTOGRAPHS
PH07094 637 (August 20, 1992) p9. "Steve Shelley, Kim Gordon, Lee Ranaldo, Shake-A-Leg's Harry Horgan, Moore, Hersh And David Narcizo (from left)" (Robicheau, Paul)
PH07095 674 (January 27, 1994) p28. "Guided By Voices: Hersh And Stipe"
PH07096 703 (March 9, 1995) p54. "Giving In To The Muses: Drummer David Narcizo, Hersh And Bassist Bernard Georges (from left)" (Seliger, Mark)
PH07097 703 (March 9, 1995) p55. "The Throwing Muses Lineup In 1989 (from left): Hersh, Leslie Langston, Tanya Donelly And Narcizo" (Musto, Ilpo)
PH07098 704 (March 23, 1995) p25. "Buffalo Tom's Bill Janovitz, Kristin Hersh, Morphine's Mark Sandman, Gigolo Aunts' Steve Hurley (from left)" (Robicheau, Paul)
PH07099 707 (May 4, 1995) p36. "Georges (left) And Hersh Throw Down" (Blakesberg, Jay)
PH07100 718 (October 5, 1995) p21. "Kristin Hersh Of Throwing Muses In Seattle" (Moore, Michael)
PH07101 748 (November 28, 1996) p30. "Hersh, On Tour With Her Husband, Billy O'Connell, And Son Ryder" (Chiarella, Frank)
HERSH, KRISTIN—PHOTOGRAPHS—PORTRAITS
PH07102 688 (August 11, 1994) p20. "Sisters in Charity: Milla And Kristin Hersh (right)"
PH07103 703 (March 9, 1995) p53. "[Kristin Hersh]" (Seliger, Mark)
HERZIGOVA, EVA—PHOTOGRAPHS
PH07104 747 (November 14, 1996) p25. "[Bon Jovi & Friends]" (Souliers, Philippe)
HERZIGOVA, EVA—PHOTOGRAPHS—PORTRAITS
PH07105 630 (May 14, 1992) p84. "[Eva]" (Von Unwerth, Ellen)
HESS, ANN—PHOTOGRAPHS
PH07106 722 (November 30, 1995) pp[enc.6]. "'Web Godfather': Ann 'Sonic' Hess" (McLeod, William Mercer)
HESTER, PAUL—PHOTOGRAPHS
PH07107 676 (February 24, 1994) p17. "Four's A Crowd: Neil Finn, Mark Hart, Paul Hester And Nick Seymour (from left)" (Broad, Julian)
HETFIELD, JAMES—PHOTOGRAPHS
PH07108 615 (October 17, 1991) p13. "Metallica's Ulrich (left), James Hetfield" (Mazur, Kevin)
PH07109 626 (March 19, 1992) p25. "James Hetfield (above)" (Pool, Smiley)
PH07110 637 (August 20, 1992) p19. "Metallica's James Hetfield" (Hutson, Mick)
PH07111 638 (September 3, 1992) p18. "Metallica's James Hetfield" (Capak, R. J.)
PH07112 645-646 (December 10, 1992) p35. "Hetfield And Co. Went At It With G N' R" (Mazur, Kevin)
PH07113 645-646 (December 10, 1992) p71. "Metallica's James Hetfield" (Mazur, Kevin)
PH07114 654 (April 15, 1993) pp[cover]. "James Hetfield Of Metallica: The Leader Of The Real Free World Speaks" (Seliger, Mark)
PH07115 655 (April 29, 1993) p11. "Ulrich, Young And Hetfield (from left)" (Blakesberg, Jay)
PH07116 670 (November 25, 1993) p83. "[James Hetfield]" (Seliger, Mark)
PH07117 672-673 (December 23, 1993) p188. "[Covers]" (Seliger, Mark)
PH07118 688 (August 11, 1994) p38. "Enough Energy For A Reactor" Metallica's Hetfield" (Settle, Ken)
PH07119 708 (May 18, 1995) p74. "Metallica In 1991, From Left: Hammett, Ulrich, Newsted, Hetfield" (Seliger, Mark)
PH07120 727 (February 8, 1996) p12. "Fifty And Fabulous! Kilmister (center) Flanked By Metallica's Jason Newsted, James Hetfield, Kirk Hammett And Lars Ulrich (from left)" (Disanto, Annamaria)
PH07121 728 (February 22, 1996) p25. "Metallica's James Hetfield, Kirk Hammett, Lars Ulrich And Jason Newsted (from left)"
PH07122 737 (June 27, 1996) p34. "Hetfield: Now He Apologizes" (Corbijn, Anton)
PH07123 741 (August 22, 1996) p31. "Metallica's Hetfield" (Jennings, Steve)
HETFIELD, JAMES—PHOTOGRAPHS—PORTRAITS
PH07124 654 (April 15, 1993) pp41,43. "[James Hetfield]" (Seliger, Mark)
PH07125 750-751 (December 26, 1996) p67. "James Hetfield Of Metallica Rockin' Out At Lollapalooza" (Blakesberg, Jay)
HETSON, GREG—PHOTOGRAPHS
PH07126 670 (November 25, 1993) p30. "Hetson, Bobby Schayer, Bentley, Gurewitz And Graffin (clockwise from top left)" (Zlozower, Neil)
PH07127 700 (January 26, 1995) p17. "Bad Religion's Brian Baker, Greg Graffin, Bobby Schayer, Jay Bentley and Greg Hetson" (Kravitz, Jeff)
PH07128 722 (November 30, 1995) p19. "Graffin, Ocasek, Jay Bentley, Brian Baker, Greg Hetson And Bobby Schayer (from left)" (Mazur, Kevin)
HETSON, GREG—PHOTOGRAPHS—PORTRAITS
PH07129 695 (November 17, 1994) p40. "Bad Religion" (Guip, Amy)
HEWITT, MARTIN—PHOTOGRAPHS—PORTRAITS
PH07130 744 (October 3, 1996) p50. "Teen Idyll: Steaming It Up With Martin Hewitt In 1981's 'Endless Love'"
HEYMAN, ALISSA—PHOTOGRAPHS—PORTRAITS
PH07131 745 (October 17, 1996) p86. "'Gifted And Talented' Friends (from left): Nicole Mauro, Arthur Lewis And Alissa Heyman As They Appeared In The 1991 Middletown High School South Yearbook, Aquiline"
HEYMANN, PHILIP B.—PHOTOGRAPHS
PH07132 680 (April 21, 1994) p37. "[Philip B. Heymann]" (Ashe, Terry)
HOON, SHANNON—PHOTOGRAPHS
PH07133 669 (November 11, 1993) pp38-39. "Brad Smith, Glen Graham, Shannon Hoon, Rogers Stevens & Christopher Thorn (from left)" (Seliger, Mark)
HIATT, JOHN—ALBUMS
PH07134 668 (October 28, 1993) p78. "Perfectly Good Guitar"
HIATT, JOHN—PHOTOGRAPHS
PH07135 627 (April 2, 1992) p15. "Jim Keltner, Ry Cooder, Nick Lowe And John Hiatt (from left)" (Hanauer, Mark)
PH07136 665 (September 16, 1993) p32. "Perfectly Good John Hiatt" (Seliger, Mark)
HICKMAN, JOHNNY—PHOTOGRAPHS
PH07137 626 (March 19, 1992) p13. "Cracker's Johnny Hickman, David Lowery And Davey Faragher (from left)" (Young, Russell)
PH07138 679 (April 7, 1994) p68. "Cracked: David Lovering, David Lowery, Bruce Hughes, Johnny Hickman (from left)" (Wolff, Tom)
PH07139 695 (November 17, 1994) p143. "Cracker" (Guzman)
PH07140 732 (April 18, 1996) p47. "Playing Cowboys In The Desert: Bob Rupe, Charlie Quintana, David Lowery And Johnny Hickman (from left)" (Maxwell, Robert)
PH07141 737 (June 27, 1996) p15. "Tjinder Singh With Cracker's Johnny Hickman And Bob Rupe (from left)" (Roberts, Ebet)
HICKOR WIND (BOOK)—PHOTOGRAPHS
PH07142 619-620 (December 12, 1991) p32. "[Hickory Wind]"

HICKS, BILL—PHOTOGRAPHS
PH07143 656 (May 13, 1993) p62. "[Bill Hicks]"
HICKS, DARREN—PHOTOGRAPHS
PH07144 715 (August 24, 1995) p94. "Keane With Empire State Building Guards Darren Hicks, Lance Pelt And Peter Vargas" (Danelian, Stephen)
HICKS, LLOYD—PHOTOGRAPHS
PH07145 629 (April 30, 1992) p28. "Dave Alvin (right) With Skeletons Lou Whitney (left) And Bobby Lloyd Hicks" (Carrico, John)
HIDALGO, DAVID—PHOTOGRAPHS
PH07146 616 (October 31, 1991) p13. "Cesar Rosas, Louis Perez, Conrad Lozano, David Hidalgo And Steve Berlin (from left)" (Granitz, Steve)
PH07147 679 (April 7, 1994) p39. "Isaak With Lobo David Hidalgo" (Kravitz, Jeff)
HIGH HEELS (FILM)—PHOTOGRAPHS
PH07148 621 (January 9, 1992) p56. "Abril (center) And Jailbirds In Fashion"
HIGH SCHOOL HIGH (FILM)—PHOTOGRAPHS
PH07149 748 (November 28, 1996) p143. "Dead On Arrival"
HIGHER EDUCATION—ILLUSTRATIONS
PH07150 639 (September 17, 1992) pp79-81. "[College Notebook]" (Mayforth, Hal)
PH07151 639 (September 17, 1992) p89. "[Madonna]" (Mayforth, Hal)
PH07152 652 (March 18, 1993) pp[enc.29,31]. "[Higher Education]" (Bustamante, Gerald)
PH07153 652 (March 18, 1993) pp[enc.4]. "[Party Culture]" (Turk, Steve)
PH07154 655 (April 29, 1993) p7. "The Importance Of Defining Your Terms" (Pendergrast, James T.)
PH07155 670 (November 25, 1993) p8. "Interns" (Pendergrast, James T.)
PH07156 678 (March 24, 1994) pp50-51. "Spring Break News" (Klein, Renee)
PH07157 693 (October 20, 1994) pp131-132. "[College Roomates]" (Corio, Paul)
PH07158 693 (October 20, 1994) pp87,89-90,93. "[Curricula]" (Goldin, David)
PH07159 694 (November 3, 1994) p17. "Grubby Grub Grubbers" (Menchin, Scott)
PH07160 701 (February 9, 1995) p16. "Work Study" (Preuitt, Clayton)
PH07161 704 (March 23, 1995) p24. "970-Coed" (Fisher, Carolyn)
PH07162 704 (March 23, 1995) pp67,69. "[College 1995]" (Mats)
PH07163 704 (March 23, 1995) p70. "It Came With The Application Form!" (Klein, Renee)
PH07164 704 (March 23, 1995) p89. "Time Management, Yes; Highlighters, No" (Goldin, David)
PH07165 705 (April 6, 1995) p14. "Real World Mfg. Co." (Pendergrast, James T.)
PH07166 710 (June 15, 1995) p17. "Whip Smart" (Angel, Vinnie)
PH07167 719 (October 19, 1995) p119. "[Higher Education Costs]" (Allen, Terry)
PH07168 719 (October 19, 1995) pp92,94-95. "Money For Nothing" (Angel, Vinnie)
PH07169 719 (October 19, 1995) p124. "[Student Loans]" (Allen, Terry)
PH07170 722 (November 30, 1995) p45. "This Way For High-Cost, High-Hassle Student Loans" (Witte, Michael)
PH07171 726 (January 25, 1996) p12. "The Future!" (Pendergrast, James T.)
PH07172 745 (October 17, 1996) pp113-114,117. "[Higher Education]" (Corio, Paul)
HIGHER EDUCATION—ILLUSTRATIONS—LETTERING
PH07173 678 (March 24, 1994) pp49-51,55-57+. "[College 94]" (Hoefler, Jonathan)
PH07174 678 (March 24, 1994) pp49-51,55-57+. "[College 94]" (Siry, Eric)
HIGHER EDUCATION—PHOTOGRAPHS
PH07175 639 (September 17, 1992) pp79-81. "[College Notebook]"
PH07176 704 (March 23, 1995) p70. "Beer And Gefilte Fish: Two Great Tastes That Go Great Together" (Wayland, Pat)
PH07177 704 (March 23, 1995) p82. "The Object of My Infection: Many Students Will Graduate With An STD—Along With A B.A. Or B.S." (Kuehn, Karen)
PH07178 704 (March 23, 1995) p82. "'This Is Our Chance, We're Young Now. This Is Our Time'" (Kuehn, Karen)
PH07179 730 (March 21, 1996) p72. "All Those Old Folks Will Need Medical Professionals, Like Pharmacists; Later, They'll Need Funeral Directors" (Frailey, Stephen)
PH07180 730 (March 21, 1996) p71. "What Can We Do?" (Frailey, Stephen)
HIGHER LEARNING (FILM)—PHOTOGRAPHS
PH07181 700 (January 26, 1995) p68. "Swanson, Connelly, Epps And Cube Tackle "Learning""
HIGHWAYMEN—ALBUMS
PH07182 712-713 (July 13, 1995) p110. "The Road Goes On Forever"
HIJAZI, TANYA—PHOTOGRAPHS
PH07183 619-620 (December 12, 1991) p76. "Superfreak Rick James And Tanya Anne Hijazi Face The Music" (Barr, John)
PH07184 737 (June 27, 1996) p40. "Rick James Fiancee, Tanya Hijazi, And Their Son, Tazman, Age 3, In Hollywood, Calif., 1995" (Winters, Dan)
HILFIGER, TOMMY—PHOTOGRAPHS—PORTRAITS
PH07185 678 (March 24, 1994) p50. "Tommy Hilfiger" (McGee, Henry)
HILL, ANITA—ILLUSTRATIONS
PH07186 630 (May 14, 1992) p89. "[Yale]" (Cowles, David)
HILL, BRENDAN—PHOTOGRAPHS
PH07187 622 (January 23, 1992) p10. "Clockwise From Top Left: Bobby Sheehan, Brendan Hill, John Popper, Chan Kinchla" (Carroll, Chris)
PH07188 631 (May 28, 1992) p17. "Blues Traveler (from left): Chan Kinchla, John Popper, Brendan Hill And Bobby Sheehan" (Aresu, Paul)
PH07189 659 (June 24, 1993) p57. "Band Of Gypsies: Brendan Hill, Chan Kinchla, John Popper And Bobby Sheehan (from left)" (Fink, Larry)
PH07190 714 (August 10, 1995) p16. "Blues Traveler's Chan Kinchla, Bobby Sheehan, Brendan Hill And Popper (from left) With Ice-T (second from left)" (Kravitz, Jeff)
HILL, DON—PHOTOGRAPHS
PH07191 730 (March 21, 1996) p90. "Don Hill Is The Owner Of Don Hill's At 511 Greenwich St., In New York" (Witkin, Christian)
HILL, DUSTY—PHOTOGRAPHS
PH07192 631 (May 28, 1992) p11. "ZZ Top's Dusty Hill, Frank Beard And Billy Gibbons (from left)" (Reitzel, Bill)
HILL, GREG—PHOTOGRAPHS
PH07193 625 (March 5, 1992) p27. "Lori Allison, Marty Amsler, Harry Dingman II, Greg Hill (from left)" (Natkin, Paul)
HILL, LAURYN—PHOTOGRAPHS
PH07194 734 (May 16, 1996) p66. "Rappin' At The House Of Blues: Fugees' Hill, Jean And Michel (from left)" (Kravitz, Jeff)
PH07195 736 (June 13, 1996) p52. "Summer Of '96 Road Warriors" (Kleiman, Dennis)
PH07196 741 (August 22, 1996) p25. "[Fugees]" (Capak, R. J.)
PH07197 742 (September 5, 1996) p43. "Lauryn Hill" (Rolston, Matthew)
PH07198 742 (September 5, 1996) p44. "Lauryn Hill In 'Sister Act 2: Back In The Habit'"
HILL, STEPHEN—PHOTOGRAPHS
PH07199 618 (November 28, 1991) p103. "Gangsters Hoffman,

Hill And Dean (from left)"
HILL, STUART—PHOTOGRAPHS
PH07200 686-687 (July 14, 1994) p73. "Cute-Band Alert: Shudder To Think's Werdren, Wade, Larson And Hill (from left)" (Clinch, Danny)
HILL, STUART—PHOTOGRAPHS—PORTRAITS
PH07201 719 (October 19, 1995) p26. "Truly Baroque—Like A Strange Union Of R.E.M. And Queen: Larson, Hill, Wedren And Wade (from left)" (Clinch, Danny)
HILLER, JASON—PHOTOGRAPHS
PH07202 622 (January 23, 1992) p14. "Clockwise From Top Left: Davel Sobel, Luther Russell, Chris Joyner, John Hofer, Jason Hiller" (Annalisa)
HILLHOUSE, CHRISTA—PHOTOGRAPHS
PH07203 662 (August 5, 1993) p21. "Brunets Have Fun, Too: Hillhouse, Rocha, Perry And Richardson (from left)" (MacNaughtan, Andrew)
HILLMAN, BONES—PHOTOGRAPHS
PH07204 658 (June 10, 1993) p19. "Burnin' Again: Hillman, Garrett, Moginie, Hirst, Rotsey (from left)" (Seliger, Mark)
HIMALAYANS—PHOTOGRAPHS
PH07205 685 (June 30, 1994) p53. "Chasing A Dream: Duritz (second from left) With Fellow Himalayans, Circa 1988"
HIMMELMAN, PETER—PHOTOGRAPHS
PH07206 675 (February 10, 1994) p22. "Penn, Williams And Himmelman At The Gimme Shelter Benefit For The Homeless" (Mayer, Jeffrey)
HINDS, CARL—PHOTOGRAPHS
PH07207 718 (October 5, 1995) p20. "B-Real Flanked By Carl Hinds (left) And Morpurgo" (Shapiro, Stephen)
HINTON, EDDIE—PHOTOGRAPHS—PORTRAITS
PH07208 717 (September 21, 1995) p34. "[Eddie Hinton]"
HINTON, NATHAN—PHOTOGRAPHS
PH07209 704 (March 23, 1995) pp102-103. "Class of '95" (Tavee, Tom)
PH07210 704 (March 23, 1995) p102. "Onstage" (Tavee, Tom)
HIP-HOP MUSIC—ILLUSTRATIONS
PH07211 670 (November 25, 1993) p121. "In The House?" (Brown, Calef)
PH07212 701 (February 9, 1995) p55. "Hip-Hop Slide" (Barbour, Karen)
PH07213 721 (November 16, 1995) p113. "New York Groove" (Corio, Paul)
HIPPIES—PHOTOGRAPHS
PH07214 633 (June 25, 1992) p6. "[Hippies]"
PH07215 636 (August 6, 1992) p8. "[Hippies]"
HIRST, ROB—PHOTOGRAPHS
PH07216 658 (June 10, 1993) p19. "Burnin' Again: Hillman, Garrett, Moginie, Hirst, Rotsey (from left)" (Seliger, Mark)
HISTORY—PHOTOGRAPHS
PH07217 668 (October 28, 1993) p41. "Ford Goons Attack A UAW Organizer In 1937..."
HITCHCOCK, ROBYN—ALBUMS
PH07218 615 (October 17, 1991) p112. "Perspex Island"
PH07219 616 (October 31, 1991) p114. "Perspex Island"
PH07220 619-620 (December 12, 1991) p182. "Perspex Island"
PH07221 654 (April 15, 1993) p62. "Respect"
PH07222 745 (October 17, 1996) p137. "Moss Elixir"
HITCHCOCK, ROBYN—ILLUSTRATIONS—LETTERING
PH07223 654 (April 15, 1993) p57. "Wild Kingdom" (Stevens, John)
HITCHCOCK, ROBYN—PHOTOGRAPHS
PH07224 616 (October 31, 1991) p13. "Black Francis, Billy Bragg And Robyn Hitchcock (from left)" (Mazur, Kevin)
PH07225 617 (November 14, 1991) p32. "[Robyn Hitchcock]" (Mazur, Kevin)
PH07226 626 (March 19, 1992) p11. "Robyn Hitchcock (left), Matthew Sweet" (Capak, R. J.)
PH07227 663 (August 19, 1993) p27. "Belly's Tanya Donelly (left) And Gail Greenwood With Robyn Hitchcock" (Mazur, Kevin)
PH07228 710 (June 15, 1995) p26. "[Robyn Hitchcock]" (Borris, Dan)
HITCHCOCK, ROBYN—PHOTOGRAPHS—PORTRAITS
PH07229 619-620 (December 12, 1991) p68. "Robyn Hitchcock" (Carroll, Chris)
PH07230 654 (April 15, 1993) p56. "[Robyn Hitchcock]" (Borris, Dan)
HITTING BIRTH—PHOTOGRAPHS
PH07231 628 (April 16, 1992) p62. "Hitting Birth" (Gonson, J. J.)
HOBO HUMPIN' SLOBO BABE (VIDEO)—PHOTOGRAPHS
PH07232 685 (June 30, 1994) p32. "[Whale]" (Gougenheim, Kim)
HOBSON, WES—PHOTOGRAPHS
PH07233 665 (September 16, 1993) pp[enc.25]. "From Left: Greg Welsh, Ray Browning, Mike Pigg, Wes Hobson, Chuckie V, Scott Tinley, Nate Llerandi And Bill Braun" (Hanauer, Mark)
HOCH, DANNY—PHOTOGRAPHS
PH07234 682 (May 19, 1994) p74. "[Danny Hoch]" (Wakefield, Michael)
HODENFIELD, CHRIS—PHOTOGRAPHS
PH07235 632 (June 11, 1992) p108. "Hodenfield, Back From Mondo Brando" (Bernstein, Andrea)
PH07236 647 (January 7, 1993) p11. "RS Alumni Photog Annie Leibovitz, Thompson, David Felton, Cameron Crowe, Chris Hodenfield, Ben Fong-Torres, Paul Scanlon (from left)" (Elgar, Nick)
HOFER, JOHN—PHOTOGRAPHS
PH07237 622 (January 23, 1992) p14. "Clockwise From Top Left: Davel Sobel, Luther Russell, Chris Joyner, John Hofer, Jason Hiller" (Annalisa)
HOFFA (FILM)—PHOTOGRAPHS
PH07238 647 (January 7, 1993) p50. "...And Danny DeVito"
HOFFMAN, ABBIE—PHOTOGRAPHS
PH07239 738-739 (July 11, 1996) p70. "Leary Plotting With Abbie Hoffman (left) And Jerry Rubin, 1968"
HOFFMAN, DUSTIN—ILLUSTRATIONS
PH07240 621 (January 9, 1992) p54. "Nothing To Crow About" (Payne, C. F.)
PH07241 642 (October 29, 1992) p76. "Hard Times For Heroes" (Blitt, Barry)
HOFFMAN, DUSTIN—PHOTOGRAPHS
PH07242 618 (November 28, 1991) p103. "Gangsters Hoffman, Hill And Dean (from left)"
PH07243 621 (January 9, 1992) p55. "Robin Williams (left) And Dustin Hoffman In Conflict"
PH07244 649 (February 4, 1993) p72. "[Hero]"
PH07245 744 (October 3, 1996) p78. "Now Playing"
HOFFMAN, DUSTIN—PHOTOGRAPHS—PORTRAITS
PH07246 706 (April 20, 1995) p89. "Now Playing"
HOFFMAN, GABY—PHOTOGRAPHS
PH07247 625 (March 5, 1992) p76. "Hoffman, Kavner And Mathis Turn Trauma Into Laughter"
HOGAN, KELLY—ALBUMS
PH07248 742 (September 5, 1996) p65. "The Whistle Only Dogs Can Hear"
HOGAN, KELLY—PHOTOGRAPHS—PORTRAITS
PH07249 736 (June 13, 1996) p47. "Kelly Hogan" (Verene, Chris)
HOGAN, MARTY—PHOTOGRAPHS
PH07250 642 (October 29, 1992) p61. "Out Of The Blues"
HOGAN, MIKE—PHOTOGRAPHS
PH07251 664 (September 2, 1993) p28. "Lawler, Mike Hogan, O'Riordan, Noel Hogan"
PH07252 695 (November 17, 1994) p37. "The Cranberries" (Meeks, Raymond)
PH07253 704 (March 23, 1995) pp56-57. "[Strange Fruit]" (Day, Corinne)

HOGAN, NOEL—PHOTOGRAPHS
PH07254 664 (September 2, 1993) p28. "Lawler, Mike Hogan, O'Riordan, Noel Hogan"
PH07255 695 (November 17, 1994) p37. "The Cranberries" (Meeks, Raymond)
PH07256 704 (March 23, 1995) pp56-57. "[Strange Fruit]" (Day, Corinne)
HOGSHIRE, JIM—PHOTOGRAPHS
PH07257 689 (August 25, 1994) p75. "Don't Try This At Home: Hogshire Of "Pills-A-Go-Go"" (Mercer, Lance)
HOLCOMB, ROBIN—ALBUMS
PH07258 642 (October 29, 1992) p69. "Rockabye"
HOLDEN, WILLIAM—PHOTOGRAPHS
PH07259 703 (March 9, 1995) p72. "Aging Cowboy William Holden Goes For The Big Gun In The Final Shootout"
HOLE—ALBUMS
PH07260 680 (April 21, 1994) p83. "Live Through This"
PH07261 683 (June 2, 1994) p82. "Live Through This"
PH07262 698-699 (December 29, 1994) p191. "Live Through This"
HOLE—ILLUSTRATIONS
PH07263 718 (October 5, 1995) p16. "Publicity-Press Kit" (Pendergrast, James T.)
HOLE—PHOTOGRAPHS
PH07264 683 (June 2, 1994) p42. "Hole: Patty Schemel, Love, Kristen Pfaff, Eric Erlandson" (Seliger, Mark)
PH07265 692 (October 6, 1994) p53. "Courtney Love And Hole" (Moskowitz, Karen)
PH07266 697 (December 15, 1994) p67. "Hole As One: Bassist Melissa Auf Der Maur (who replaced Kristen Pfaff), Guitarist Eric Erlandson, Drummer Patty Schemel And Love (from left)" (Seliger, Mark)
PH07267 698-699 (December 29, 1994) p50. "Doll Parts: Hole's Eric Erlandson, Melissa Auf der Maur, Patty Schemel And Love" (Seliger, Mark)
PH07268 715 (August 24, 1995) p46. "Courtney Love, Eric Erlandson, Patty Schemel, Melissa Auf Der Maur" (Seliger, Mark)
PH07269 715 (August 24, 1995) p49. "Endless Summer: Hole On The Beach At Coney Island, N.Y., June 1995" (Seliger, Mark)
PH07270 715 (August 24, 1995) pp[cover]. "Hole Is A Band: Courtney Love Is A Soap Opera" (Seliger, Mark)
HOLE—PHOTOGRAPHS—PORTRAITS
PH07271 637 (August 20, 1992) p15. "Hole's Jill Emery, Eric Erlandson, Love And Caroline Rue (from left)" (Lavine, Michael)
HOLIDAY, BILLIE—ILLUSTRATIONS—PORTRAITS
PH07272 616 (October 31, 1991) p89. "The Light And Dark Of Lady Day" (Dionisi, Sandra)
HOLIDAY, BILLIE—PHOTOGRAPHS—PORTRAITS
PH07273 692 (October 6, 1994) p50. "Billie Holiday"
PH07274 735 (May 30, 1996) p3. "[The Faces Of Heroin]"
HOLLAND, ANNIE—PHOTOGRAPHS
PH07275 707 (May 4, 1995) p23. "Donna Matthews, Justine Frischmann, Annie Holland And Justin Welch (from left)" (Camp, E. J.)
HOLLAND, ANNIE—PHOTOGRAPHS—PORTRAITS
PH07276 718 (October 5, 1995) p26. "Sprung: Elastica's Holland" (Bell, Colin)
HOLLAND, BRYAN—ILLUSTRATIONS
PH07277 701 (February 9, 1995) p9. "The Offspring's Dexter Holland" (Burke, Philip)
HOLLAND, BRYAN—PHOTOGRAPHS
PH07278 686-687 (July 14, 1994) p45. "[Offspring]" (Johnson, Lisa)
PH07279 691 (September 22, 1994) p25. "Shakin' Thing Up: Ron Welty, Greg K, Noodles, Bryan Holland (from left)" (Seliger, Mark)
PH07280 695 (November 17, 1994) p78. "Offspring" (Danelian, Stephen)
PH07281 700 (January 26, 1995) p16. "Bryan "Dexter" Holland Of Offspring At The "Billboard" Awards" (Kravitz, Jeff)
PH07282 701 (February 9, 1995) p44. "Bryan "Dexter" Holland In L.A., December '94" (Kravitz, Jeff)
PH07283 701 (February 9, 1995) pp42-43. "Greg Kriesel, Bryan Holland, Kevin Wasserman And Ron Welty (from left)" (Seliger, Mark)
PH07284 706 (April 20, 1995) p38. "Bryan Holland: Keeping 'Em Separated, For Now" (Capak, R. J.)
PH07285 711 (June 29, 1995) p12. "The Offspring's Bryan Holland Takes On The Spitting Crowd At The Skatefest" (Johnson, Lisa)
PH07286 727 (February 8, 1996) p12. "Woodpussy's Michel Cicero, Rancid's Tim Armstrong, Iggy, The Offspring's Bryan Holland (from left)" (Buzzerio, Johnny)
HOLLAND, NICKY—PHOTOGRAPHS—PORTRAITS
PH07287 642 (October 29, 1992) pp64,67. "[Nicky Holland]" (Salvatori, Lou)
HOLLAND, SUSAN BANE—PHOTOGRAPHS
PH07288 678 (March 24, 1994) p78. "Susan Bane Holland At RISD's Glass-Blowing Furnace" (Hill, Britain)
HOLLIDAY, JUDY—PHOTOGRAPHS
PH07289 655 (April 29, 1993) p69. "Crawford And Holliday (left) Reborn As Goodman And Griffith"
HOLLIS—PHOTOGRAPHS
PH07290 690 (September 8, 1994) p44. "K1, Oisin, Phrase And Hollis (from left)" (Cross, Brian)
HOLLY, BUDDY—ALBUMS
PH07291 672-673 (December 23, 1993) p148. "The Buddy Holly Collection"
HOLMES BROTHERS—ALBUMS
PH07292 624 (February 20, 1992) p45. "Where It's At"
PH07293 636 (August 6, 1992) p59. "Jubilation"
HOLMES, CHRIS—PHOTOGRAPHS—PORTRAITS
PH07294 736 (June 13, 1996) p28. "Chicagoan Chris Holmes Is A Man Of Many Bands And Esoteric Interests" (Miller, Brad)
HOLMES, JOHN—ILLUSTRATIONS
PH07295 632 (June 11, 1992) p13. "[John Holmes]" (Cronin, Brian)
HOLMES, JOHN—PHOTOGRAPHS—PORTRAITS
PH07296 632 (June 11, 1992) p174. "Holmes: Everyman's Gigolo, A Polyester Smoothie"
HOLMSTROM, PETER—PHOTOGRAPHS
PH07297 721 (November 16, 1995) p78. "Peter Holmstrom, Courtney Taylor, Zia McCabe, Eric Hedford (from left): They're Exploding, Plastic And Inevitable, Andy Would Approve!" (Winters, Dan)
HOLSAPPLE, PETER—ALBUMS
PH07298 619-620 (December 12, 1991) p184. "Mavericks"
HOME ALONE 2 (FILM)—PHOTOGRAPHS
PH07299 645-646 (December 10, 1992) p190. "Macaulay Culkin"
HOME FOR THE HOLIDAYS (FILM)—PHOTOGRAPHS
PH07300 721 (November 16, 1995) p116. "Hunter (left) At Home With Mom Bancroft"
HOMER, RON, JR.—PHOTOGRAPHS
PH07301 691 (September 22, 1994) p44. "Boston Director Ron Homer Jr. (center left) And Supervisor Wilbur Brown (center, right) Let The Kids Find Their Own Remedies To Urban Blight" (Ng, Karjean)
HOMME, JOSH—PHOTOGRAPHS
PH07302 692 (October 6, 1994) p24. "Desert Storm: Kyuss' Homme, Reeder, Garcia And Hernandez (from left)" (Miller, Michael)
HOMOSEXUALITY—ILLUSTRATIONS
PH07303 632 (June 11, 1992) pp150-151. "[AIDS]" (Mahurin, Matt)
HONDA, YUKA—ILLUSTRATIONS
PH07304 736 (June 13, 1996) p58. "Yuka Honda" (Cowles, David)

HONDA, YUKA—PHOTOGRAPHS
PH07305 721 (November 16, 1995) p76. "Yuka Honda (left) And Miho Hatori: Galloping Gourmets With A Taste For Big Beats And Pop Exotica" (Exum)
HONEYMOON IN VEGAS (FILM)—PHOTOGRAPHS
PH07306 639 (September 17, 1992) p103. "Cage (left) And Caan Vie For Parker"
HONG, YU FEI—PHOTOGRAPHS
PH07307 666 (September 30, 1993) p113. "Yu Fei Hong Finds No Joy Dancing With Russell Wong"
HOOK (FILM)—ILLUSTRATIONS
PH07308 621 (January 9, 1992) p54. "Nothing To Crow About" (Payne, C. F.)
HOOK (FILM)—PHOTOGRAPHS
PH07309 621 (January 9, 1992) p55. "Robin Williams (left) And Dustin Hoffman In Conflict"
HOOKER, JOHN LEE—ALBUMS
PH07310 619-620 (December 12, 1991) p174. "Mr. Lucky"
PH07311 655 (April 29, 1993) p65. "Boom Boom"
HOOKER, JOHN LEE—PHOTOGRAPHS
PH07312 624 (February 20, 1992) p11. "Ry Cooder (left) Joins Bluesman John Lee Hooker Onstage" (Blakesberg, Jay)
PH07313 629 (April 30, 1992) p12. "Chris Isaak (left) With John Lee Hooker" (Blakesberg, Jay)
HOOKER, JOHN LEE—PHOTOGRAPHS—PORTRAITS
PH07314 643 (November 12, 1992) p174. "John Lee Hooker" (Markus, Kurt)
HOON, SHANNON—ILLUSTRATIONS
PH07315 726 (January 25, 1996) p12. "No-Fault Plan" (Pendergrast, James T.)
HOON, SHANNON—PHOTOGRAPHS
PH07316 622 (January 23, 1992) p6. "From Left: Hoon, Slash And Duff" (White, Frank)
PH07317 630 (May 14, 1992) p28. "Blind Melon's Hoon (left) And Rogers Stevens" (Kraft, Chris)
PH07318 639 (September 17, 1992) p20. "Shannon Hoon, Christopher Thorn, Glen Graham, Brad Smith And Rogers Stevens (clockwise from top left)" (Clinch, Danny)
PH07319 640 (October 1, 1992) p27. "Blind Melon (from left): Smith, Stevens, Thorn, Hoon And Graham" (Clinch, Danny)
PH07320 669 (November 11, 1993) p40. "Hoon Abandoned Jockdom For The Slacker Lifestyle" (Gerber, Mitchell)
PH07321 674 (January 27, 1994) p29. "A Clothed Shannon Hoon" (Kirkland, Gene)
PH07322 681 (May 5, 1994) p19. "'Rain' Supreme: Blind Melon's Shannon Hoon" (Natkin, Paul)
PH07323 691 (September 22, 1994) p62. "A Festival Highlight: Blind Melon's Shannon Hoon, Complete With Pink Barrettes (left)" (Mazur, Kevin)
PH07324 722 (November 30, 1995) p23. "Hoon (foreground) With Members Of Blind Melon In 1993" (Seliger, Mark)
PH07325 747 (November 14, 1996) p36. "One More Time For Hoon" (Clinch, Danny)
HOON, SHANNON—PHOTOGRAPHS—PORTRAITS
PH07326 735 (May 30, 1996) p16. "The Same Night Shannon Hoon (right) Heard The News Of Kurt Cobain's Suicide, He Appeared On TV Posing The Question On Everyone's Mind" (Gougenheim, Kim)
PH07327 735 (May 30, 1996) p3. "[The Faces Of Heroin]"
HOOP DREAMS (FILM)—PHOTOGRAPHS
PH07328 698-699 (December 29, 1994) p194. "Agee Reaches In "Hoop Dreams""
PH07329 705 (April 6, 1995) p69. "Oscar Rejects"
HOOTIE AND THE BLOWFISH—ALBUMS
PH07330 710 (June 15, 1995) p96. "Cracked Rear View"
PH07331 711 (June 29, 1995) p60. "Cracked Rear View"
PH07332 712-713 (July 13, 1995) p132. "Cracked Rear View"
PH07333 716 (September 7, 1995) p100. "Cracked Rear View"
PH07334 717 (September 21, 1995) p98. "Cracked Rear View"
PH07335 719 (October 19, 1995) p172. "Cracked Rear View"
PH07336 734 (May 16, 1996) p63. "Fairweather Johnson"
HOOTIE AND THE BLOWFISH—ILLUSTRATIONS
PH07337 706 (April 20, 1995) p104. "Hootie And The Blowfish: Super Grouper" (Marten, Ruth)
PH07338 714 (August 10, 1995) p12. "Sign Here" (Pendergrast, James T.)
PH07339 717 (September 21, 1995) p16. "Hiss" (Pendergrast, James T.)
PH07340 729 (March 7, 1996) p6. "Welcome To Success!" (Pendergrast, James T.)
PH07341 734 (May 16, 1996) p63. "Everyday People" (Adel, Daniel)
HOOTIE AND THE BLOWFISH—PHOTOGRAPHS
PH07342 691 (September 22, 1994) p19. "Hootie Goes to Washington: Soni, Dean Felber, The Prez, Darius Rucker, Bryan (from left)"
PH07343 710 (June 15, 1995) pp74-75. "[Hootie And The Blowfish]" (Tavee, Tom)
PH07344 710 (June 15, 1995) p76. "Warming Up And Taking Five At Wittenberg University, In Springfield, Ohio" (Tavee, Tom)
PH07345 714 (August 10, 1995) pp42-43. "Darius Rucker, Dean Felber, Mark Bryan And Jim Sonefeld" (Seliger, Mark)
PH07346 714 (August 10, 1995) p45. "Decadent Rock Stars At Play: The Guys Love A Round Of Golf" (Seliger, Mark)
PH07347 714 (August 10, 1995) pp[cover]. "Hootie And The Blowfish: Sex, Golf And Rock & Roll" (Seliger, Mark)
PH07348 714 (August 10, 1995) p45. "Multiplatinum Bar Band: We're Breaking Ground By Being Normal" (Seliger, Mark)
PH07349 726 (January 25, 1996) p37. "Hootie And The Blowfish: Jim Sonefeld, Darius Rucker, Dean Felber And Mark Bryan (from left)" (Seliger, Mark)
PH07350 741 (August 22, 1996) p36. "Scalpers, Beware! Hootie And The Blowfish Don't Take No Mess" (Clark, John)
PH07351 742 (September 5, 1996) p25. "Hootie And The Blowfish Just Say No To Bootlegging On The Internet" (Seliger, Mark)
HOPKINS, ANTHONY—ILLUSTRATIONS
PH07352 726 (January 25, 1996) p63. "Natural Born Tricksters" (Coe, Sue)
PH07353 744 (October 3, 1996) p77. "Men Behaving Badly" (Brodner, Steve)
HOPKINS, ANTHONY—PHOTOGRAPHS
PH07354 619-620 (December 12, 1991) p192. "In 'The Silence Of The Lambs,' Jodie Foster Finds An Affinity With The Male Monster (Anthony Hopkins)"
PH07355 627 (April 2, 1992) p41. "Hopkins And Thompson Battle For Home And England"
PH07356 670 (November 25, 1993) p125. "Love Unspoken: Anthony Hopkins And Emma Thompson"
PH07357 674 (January 27, 1994) p48. "Acting Vehicles Include 'The Pelican Brief,' 'In The Name Of The Father,' 'What's Eating Gilbert Grape,' 'Shadowlands,' 'Naked,' And 'Grumpy Old Men'"
PH07358 726 (January 25, 1996) p64. "Nixon Confers With Haldeman (James Woods)"
PH07359 726 (January 25, 1996) p64. "Nixon Say's He's 'Not A Crook'"
PH07360 726 (January 25, 1996) p64. "Oliver Stone Directs Joan Allen And Anthony Hopkins"
PH07361 744 (October 3, 1996) p78. "Hopkins As Picasso With Mistress McElhone"
HOPKINS, ANTHONY—PHOTOGRAPHS—PORTRAITS
PH07362 672-673 (December 23, 1993) p173. "Repressed Man Of The Year"
PH07363 678 (March 24, 1994) p100. "Oscar's Choices: 'Schindler's List,' 'The Piano,' 'The Remains Of the Day,' 'In The Name Of The Father,' 'The Fugitive' (from left)"

HOPKINS, DOUG—PHOTOGRAPHS—PORTRAITS
PH07364 675 (February 10, 1994) p15. "Hopkins: The Former Gin Blossom Wrote The Band's Hit Song 'Hey Jealousy'" (Archibald, Timothy)
HOPKINS, JERRY—PHOTOGRAPHS
PH07365 632 (June 11, 1992) p62. "Staff Members And Contributing Writers At The 1971 Editorial Conference, At Esalen, In Big Sur" (Leibovitz, Annie)
HOPKINS, LIGHTNIN'—ALBUMS
PH07366 640 (October 1, 1992) p67. "The Complete Candid Otis Spann-Lightnin' Hopkins Sessions"
HOPKINS, NICKY—PHOTOGRAPHS
PH07367 655 (April 29, 1993) p11. "From Left: A Bongo, Fleetwood, Keyboardist Nicky Hopkins And Sweet" (Di Santo, Annamaria)
PH07368 693 (October 20, 1994) p37. "[Nicky Hopkins]"
HOPPER, DENNIS—ILLUSTRATIONS
PH07369 685 (June 30, 1994) p79. "Die Hard On A Bus" (Pastrana, Robert M.)
HOPPER, DENNIS—PHOTOGRAPHS
PH07370 615 (October 17, 1991) p67. "Dennis Hopper, Christmas Day, Nassau, 1985" (Pigozzi, Jean)
PH07371 741 (August 22, 1996) p105. "Wright, Bowie, Oldman, Hopper"
HOPWOOD, CHERYL—PHOTOGRAPHS
PH07372 714 (August 10, 1995) p36. "Witness For The Prosecution: Cheryl Hopwood With Her Daughter, Tara" (Turner, Danny)
HOPWOOD, TARA—PHOTOGRAPHS
PH07372 714 (August 10, 1995) p36. "Witness For The Prosecution: Cheryl Hopwood With Her Daughter, Tara" (Turner, Danny)
H.O.R.D.E.—PHOTOGRAPHS
PH07373 663 (August 19, 1993) p12. "The Bird's-Eye View (top)" (Caudle, Todd)
HORGAN, HARRY—PHOTOGRAPHS
PH07374 637 (August 20, 1992) p9. "Steve Shelley, Kim Gordon, Lee Ranaldo, Shake-A-Leg's Harry Horgan, Moore, Hersh And David Narcizo (from left)" (Robicheau, Paul)
PH07375 667 (October 14, 1993) p40. "Below: Merchant, Bragg, Founder Harry Horgan, Tanya Donelly, Janovitz" (Robicheau, Paul)
HORN, STACY—PHOTOGRAPHS
PH07376 689 (August 25, 1994) p83. "Horn At The Office In Her Apartment In New York City" (Newton, Philip)
PH07377 689 (August 25, 1994) p80. "Stacy Horn At Black Medicine Coffee Shop, In Manhattan" (Newton, Philip)
HORNSBY, BRUCE—ALBUMS
PH07378 658 (June 10, 1993) p69. "Harbor Lights"
HORNSBY, BRUCE—PHOTOGRAPHS
PH07379 644 (November 26, 1992) p22. "Goldberg, Richie, Taylor, John, Michael And Hornsby (from left) At The Garden" (Mazur, Kevin)
PH07380 677 (March 10, 1994) p27. "The Dead's Lesh, Weir, Vince Welnick, Hornsby, Bill Kreutzmann, Mickey Hart" (Mazur, Kevin)
PH07381 683 (June 2, 1994) p28. "Weir, Bruce Hornsby, Reed And Wasserman (from left) At The Trios Show" (Mazur, Kevin)
HOROVITZ, ADAM—PHOTOGRAPHS
PH07382 631 (May 28, 1992) p40. "The Beastie Boys (from left): Adam Yauch, Mike Diamond And Adam Horovitz" (Camp, E. J.)
PH07383 631 (May 28, 1992) p9. "Skate-Master Tate, MCA, Ad-Rock, Anthony Kiedis, Henry Rollins (from left)" (Cohen, Lester)
PH07384 678 (March 24, 1994) p43. "Beasties In The Jungle: Mike Diamond, Adam Horovitz And Adam Yauch (clockwise from top left)" (Simons, Chip)
PH07385 684 (June 16, 1994) p36. "United Beastie Service: Adam Horovitz, Mike Diamond, Adam Yauch" (Kravitz, Jeff)
PH07386 688 (August 11, 1994) p49. "Yaugh, Diamond, Horovitz (clockwise from top) In 1986"
PH07387 693 (October 20, 1994) p28. "Beasties Adam Yauch, Mike D, Adam Horovitz Warming Up At Radio City Music Hall During Rehearsal (from left)" (Mazur, Kevin)
PH07388 700 (January 26, 1995) p51. "Beastie Boy Adam Horovitz Performs "Sabotage"" (Micelotta, Frank)
PH07389 712-713 (July 13, 1995) p46. "Adam Horovitz: Hyped-Up Guy" (Callahan, Kristin)
HOROVITZ, ADAM—PHOTOGRAPHS—PORTRAITS
PH07390 688 (August 11, 1994) pp46-47. "Adam Horovitz" (Rolston, Matthew)
HORROCKS, JANE—PHOTOGRAPHS
PH07391 627 (April 2, 1992) p41. "'Life Is Sweet' And Stars Horrocks And Alison Steadman"
HORTON, TOM—PHOTOGRAPHS
PH07392 632 (June 11, 1992) p178. "Author Horton Interviewed Oscar The Otter, The Mascot Of Valdez Harbor" (Kirschbaum, Jed)
HOSKINS, ROBERT DEWEY—PHOTOGRAPHS—PORTRAITS
PH07393 747 (November 14, 1996) p30. "Madonna And Her Now-Imprisoned Stalker, Robert Dewey Hoskins"
PH07394 750-751 (December 26, 1996) p45. "Looking For Madonna: Robert Dewey Hoskins"
HOSTETLER, LAVERN—PHOTOGRAPHS
PH07395 736 (June 13, 1996) p20. "Jockey Lavern Hostetler Has A Lot To Discuss With Jesus Lizard Members David Sims, David Yow, Mac McNeilly And Duane Denison (from left)" (Gilson, Matthew)
HOT FOR TEACHER (VIDEO)—PHOTOGRAPHS
PH07396 667 (October 14, 1993) p78. "Van Halen's 'Teacher'"
HOT SHOTS! PART DEUX (FILM)—PHOTOGRAPHS
PH07397 659 (June 24, 1993) p88. "Farce: 'Hot Shots! Part Deux,' With Sheen And Golino"
HOTHOUSE FLOWERS—ALBUMS
PH07398 657 (May 27, 1993) p52. "Songs From The Rain"
HOTT, JOHNNY—PHOTOGRAPHS
PH07399 660-661 (July 8, 1993) p101. "Gutterball: Johnny Hott, Bryan Harvey, Steve Wynn, Bob Rupe, Stephen McCarthy"
PH07400 663 (August 19, 1993) p15. "Rupe, Hott, Harvey, Wynn And McCarthy (from left)" (Callahan, Walter)
THE HOURS AND THE TIMES (FILM)—PHOTOGRAPHS
PH07401 631 (May 28, 1992) p61. "Angus (left) And Hart Probe A Beatles Love Story"
HOUSE OF PAIN—ALBUMS
PH07402 642 (October 29, 1992) p70. "Fine Malt Lyrics"
HOUSE OF PAIN—ILLUSTRATIONS
PH07403 689 (August 25, 1994) p104. "House Of Pain: Celtic Chaos" (Todd, Mark)
HOUSE OF PAIN—PHOTOGRAPHS
PH07404 645-646 (December 10, 1992) p62. "House Of Pain" (Pizzarello, Charlie)
THE HOUSE OF SPIRITS (FILM)—PHOTOGRAPHS
PH07405 677 (March 10, 1994) p60. "Streep And Close Play Ball (left), While Ryder And Her Lover, Banderas, Play Around"
HOUSE PARTY 2 (FILM)—PHOTOGRAPHS
PH07406 680 (April 21, 1994) p74. "In 'House Party 2,' Lawrence Reprises His Role As A Tone-Deaf DJ"
HOUSER, MICHAEL—PHOTOGRAPHS
PH07407 631 (May 28, 1992) p17. "Widespread Panic (from left): John Bell, Michael Houser, Todd Nance, David Schools And Domingo Ortiz" (Messer, Alan)
HOUSESITTER (FILM)—PHOTOGRAPHS
PH07408 634-635 (July 9, 1992) p114. "A Coy Comedy Defeats The Efforts Of Hawn And Martin"
HOUSTON, PENELOPE—ALBUMS
PH07409 731 (April 4, 1996) p62. "Cut You"
HOUSTON, TEXAS—PHOTOGRAPHS
PH07410 654 (April 15, 1993) p15. "The Enforcers: Security Personnel Line The Stage In Houston" (Kneten, Rocky)

PH07411 716 (September 7, 1995) pp60-62,64,67. "[Montrose]" (Exum)
HOUSTON, WHITNEY—PHOTOGRAPHS
PH07412 622 (January 23, 1992) p6. "Brown And Houston, Giddy With Love" (Shaw, Eugene)
PH07413 645-646 (December 10, 1992) p71. "Bobby Brown And Whitney Houston"
PH07414 682 (May 19, 1994) p37. "John And Houston At The Rain-Forest Benefit" (Mazur, Kevin)
PH07415 682 (May 19, 1994) p37. "No Rap, No Hard Stuff: Taylor, Houston, Wynette, John, Sting (from left) At Rehearsal" (Mazur, Kevin)
PH07416 724-725 (December 28, 1995) p138. "Houston, Devine, Rochon And Bassett In 'Exhale' (from left)"
PH07417 726 (January 25, 1996) p26. "Whitney Houston, Clive Davis Of Arista And Bobby Brown (from left)" (Hurschmann, Paul)
HOUSTON, WHITNEY—PHOTOGRAPHS—PORTRAITS
PH07418 658 (June 10, 1993) pp44,46-47. "[Whitney Houston]" (Watson, Albert)
PH07419 658 (June 10, 1993) pp[cover]. "Whitney Houston Gets Nasty" (Watson, Albert)
PH07420 672-673 (December 23, 1993) p188. "[Covers]" (Watson, Albert)
PH07421 680 (April 21, 1994) p33. "The Bobby Browns Greet Aretha" (Mazur, Kevin)
PH07422 682 (May 19, 1994) p38. "Houston Sings That Song Again" (Mazur, Kevin)
PH07423 743 (September 19, 1996) p88. "Divas"
HOW TO MAKE AN AMERICAN QUILT (FILM)—PHOTOGRAPHS
PH07424 720 (November 2, 1995) p77. "Female-Bonding Movies"
HOWARD, ADINA—ILLUSTRATIONS
PH07425 708 (May 18, 1995) p90. "Adina Howard" (Tanabe, Hiroshi)
HOWARD, RON—PHOTOGRAPHS
PH07426 748 (November 28, 1996) p142. "With 'Ransom' Director Ron Howard"
HOWARDS END (FILM)—PHOTOGRAPHS
PH07427 627 (April 2, 1992) p41. "Hopkins And Thompson Battle For Home And England"
PH07428 648 (January 21, 1993) p56. "Howards End"
PH07429 653 (April 1, 1993) p57. "Howards End"
HOWLE, DANIELLE—PHOTOGRAPHS
PH07430 742 (September 5, 1996) p21. "Are We Having Fun Yet?" (Kessler, Joshua)
HOWLIN' WOLF—PHOTOGRAPHS
PH07431 655 (April 29, 1993) p35. "Clapton In The Studio In 1971 With Howlin' Wolf, Recording The Wolf's Album London Sessions" (McDermand, Jo)
PH07432 720 (November 2, 1995) p51. "Howlin' Wolf" (Gahr, David)
H.R.—PHOTOGRAPHS
PH07433 711 (June 29, 1995) p15. "Cosmic Agit Pop And Measured Fury: Dr. Know, H.R., Darryl Jenifer And Earl Hudson of Bad Brains (from left)" (Cuffaro, Chris)
PH07434 711 (June 29, 1995) p16. "H.R. At A 1990 New York Show" (Eichner, Steve)
HSIUNG, PEARL—PHOTOGRAPHS
PH07435 680 (April 21, 1994) pp[enc.38]. "It's Not Just Shopping, It's An Adventure" (Ragel, Jon)
HUALTLA DE JIMENEZ, MEXICO—PHOTOGRAPHS
PH07436 619-620 (December 12, 1991) p146. "The Cemetery In The Town Of Hualtla De Jimenez, Mexico, 1980" (Salgado, Sebastiao)
HUBBARD, STACEY—PHOTOGRAPHS
PH07437 748 (November 28, 1996) p30. "Holding Pattern: Frances Bean Cobain With One Of The Many Nannies She's Known, Stacey Hubbard" (Seliger, Mark)
HUBERT, LAURA—PHOTOGRAPHS
PH07438 616 (October 31, 1991) p25. "The Leslie Spit Treeo (from left): Jack Nicholsen, Laura Hubert, Pat Langner And Tag" (Counts, Wyatt)
HUCKNALL, MICK—PHOTOGRAPHS
PH07439 636 (August 6, 1992) p27. "Blue-Eyed Soul: Mick Hucknall" (Mazur, Kevin)
HUDGINS, CONNY—PHOTOGRAPHS
PH07440 718 (October 5, 1995) p58. "Family Portrait: Conny Surrounded By Children, Grandchildren And His Ceramic Creations" (Mark, Mary Ellen)
PH07441 718 (October 5, 1995) pp56-57. "Joseph's Father, Conny, With His Grandchildren Jared, 3, And Kristin, 2" (Mark, Mary Ellen)
HUDGINS, JOSEPH—PHOTOGRAPHS
PH07442 718 (October 5, 1995) p64. "Public Defender Robert Gamble At The Arraignment Of Cheek And Hudgins (from left)" (Beckner, Greg)
HUDGINS, JOSEPH—PHOTOGRAPHS—PORTRAITS
PH07443 718 (October 5, 1995) p57. "[Joseph Hudgins]" (Mark, Mary Ellen)
HUDSON, EARL—PHOTOGRAPHS
PH07444 711 (June 29, 1995) p15. "Cosmic Agit Pop And Measured Fury: Dr. Know, H.R., Darryl Jenifer And Earl Hudson of Bad Brains (from left)" (Cuffaro, Chris)
HUDSON, ERNIE—PHOTOGRAPHS
PH07445 623 (February 6, 1992) p88. "Nanny Rebecca DeMornay Terrorizes Ernie Hudson"
HUDSON, GARTH—PHOTOGRAPHS
PH07446 617 (November 14, 1991) p72. "Levon And The Hawks, Circa 1963: Sax Player Jerry Field, Rick Danko, Levon Helm, Richard Manuel, Garth Hudson And Robertson (from left)"
PH07447 669 (November 11, 1993) p66. "The Hawks At Ontario's Brass Rail Circa '63: Danko, Manuel, Hawkins, Helm, Robertson And Hudson (from left)"
PH07448 676 (February 24, 1994) p46. "The Band (clockwise from top left): Guitarist Robbie Robertson, Drummer Levon Helm, Organist Garth Hudson, Bassist Rock Danko And Pianist Richard Manuel" (Gahr, David)
PH07449 677 (March 10, 1994) p28. "Rick Danko, Hudson And Arlie Manuel" (Mazur, Kevin)
HUDSON, PAUL—PHOTOGRAPHS
PH07450 716 (September 7, 1995) p25. "Busted: H.R. Of Bad Brains" (Mosenfeld, Tim)
THE HUDSUCKER PROXY (FILM)—PHOTOGRAPHS
PH07451 678 (March 24, 1994) p105. "Robbins (left) And Newman Play Office Politics, While Leigh (far right) Gets The Story"
HUFF, MARY—PHOTOGRAPHS
PH07452 721 (November 16, 1995) p38. "The Party Has Rolled Back Into Town: Huff, Miller And Hartman (from left)" (Elledge, Paul)
PH07453 746 (October 31, 1996) p18. "[Mary Huff]" (Basil)
HUFFINGTON, ARIANNA—PHOTOGRAPHS
PH07454 750-751 (December 26, 1996) p74. "Al Franken And Arianna Huffington In Bed" (Blankenhorn, Craig)
HUGGHINS, JOEL—PHOTOGRAPHS
PH07455 704 (March 23, 1995) p67. "Hugghins Of MIT: The Pink-Glop Amino-Acid Test" (Huber, William)
HUGGINS, BEN—PHOTOGRAPHS
PH07456 617 (November 14, 1991) p34. "Ben Huggins, Alan Doss, Monty Colvin And Dane Sonnier (from left)" (Carter, Keith)
HUGGY BEAR—PHOTOGRAPHS
PH07457 660-661 (July 8, 1993) p23. "...And Huggy Bear's Chris, Jon, Karen, Nikki And Jo (clockwise from left)" (O'Keefe, Cora)
HUGHES, ALBERT—PHOTOGRAPHS
PH07458 660-661 (July 8, 1993) p121. "'Menace' Directors Albert (left) And Allen Hughes"

HUGHES, BRUCE—PHOTOGRAPHS
PH07459 679 (April 7, 1994) p68. "Cracked: David Lovering, David Lowery, Bruce Hughes, Johnny Hickman (from left)" (Wolff, Tom)
HUGHES, LANGSTON—ILLUSTRATIONS
PH07460 706 (April 20, 1995) p78. "Langston Hughes (left) And Ol' Dirty Bastard" (Pauley, Lynn)
HUGHES, MIKO—PHOTOGRAPHS
PH07461 655 (April 29, 1993) p69. "DeVito Is Dad To Steinmiller And Hughes"
HULCE, TOM—PHOTOGRAPHS
PH07462 623 (February 6, 1992) p90. "Tom Hulce Is Burdened By Stalin Idolatry"
HUMAN BEHAVIOUR (VIDEO)—PHOTOGRAPHS
PH07463 667 (October 14, 1993) p101. "Bjork: A Study In 'Human Behaviour'"
HUMAN BODY—ILLUSTRATIONS
PH07464 719 (October 19, 1995) p92. "The Body Shop" (Rosen, Jonathon)
HUMAN CELLS—PHOTOGRAPHS
PH07465 679 (April 7, 1994) p55. "[Viral RNA]"
HUMMEL, ANDY—PHOTOGRAPHS
PH07466 668 (October 28, 1993) p15. "Big Star On The Steps Of Alex Chilton's Memphis, Tenn., Home In 1972: Andy Hummel, Jody Stephens, Chris Bell And Chilton (above, from left)" (Manning, Carole)
HUMOR—ILLUSTRATIONS
PH07467 630 (May 14, 1992) p52. "[Comedy]" (Cowles, David)
PH07468 632 (June 11, 1992) pp46-47. "[Fear And Loathing]" (Steadman, Ralph)
PH07469 678 (March 24, 1994) p31. "How Capitalism Creates Democracy" (Rall, Ted)
HUMOR—PHOTOGRAPHS
PH07470 619-620 (December 12, 1991) p220. "Endpaper" (Kern, Geof)
PH07471 619-620 (December 12, 1991) p17. "Rock & Roll Yearbook" (Kern, Geof)
PH07472 619-620 (December 12, 1991) p191. "The Year In Movies" (Kern, Geof)
PH07473 619-620 (December 12, 1991) p161. "The Year In Records" (Kern, Geof)
PH07474 619-620 (December 12, 1991) p199. "The Year In Television" (Kern, Geof)
PH07475 630 (May 14, 1992) p84. "[I Just Don't Have Any Energy]"
PH07476 630 (May 14, 1992) p92. "[Lactose Intolerance]"
PH07477 630 (May 14, 1992) p69. "[Lounges]" (Little, Blake)
PH07478 630 (May 14, 1992) p69. "[Max Perlich]" (Little, Blake)
PH07479 630 (May 14, 1992) p69. "[Psychiatrists, Indians And Vampires]" (Seliger, Mark)
HUMPERDINCK, ENGELBERT—PHOTOGRAPHS
PH07480 744 (October 3, 1996) p19. "Humperdinck, Who Looks Like A Senator From Nevada, And His Pal Rotton"
HUMPHREY, RENEE—PHOTOGRAPHS
PH07481 707 (May 4, 1995) p74. "Humphrey, Witt ('Fun')"
HUMPHREYS, GREG—PHOTOGRAPHS
PH07482 633 (June 25, 1992) p11. "Greg Humphreys, Mike Watt, Doug Macmillan, Bill Janovitz, Tom Maginnis And Mike Connell (from left) In Raleigh"
HUMPHREYS, GREG—PHOTOGRAPHS—PORTRAITS
PH07483 634-635 (July 9, 1992) p20. "Dillon Fence (from left): Chris Goode, Kent Alphin, Greg Humphreys And Scott Carle" (Thompson, D. Kent)
HUMPHRIES, HULOND—PHOTOGRAPHS
PH07484 708 (May 18, 1995) p55. "Humphries Addresses A Crowd In 1994" (Gates, Stephen)
THE HUNCHBACK OF NOTRE DAME (FILM)—ILLUSTRATIONS
PH07485 736 (June 13, 1996) p58. "Blockbusters"
PH07486 738-739 (July 11, 1996) p96. "A Cartoon Moore (left) In 'Hunchback'; In 'Striptease'"
PH07487 738-739 (July 11, 1996) p95. "Freaks Of Comedy" (Brodner, Steve)
HUNT, CHRIS—PHOTOGRAPHS
PH07488 666 (September 30, 1993) p87. "Chris Hunt, President Of Delta Lambda Phi's D.C. Chapter, At His Apartment" (Himmel, Lizzie)
PH07489 666 (September 30, 1993) p90. "Hunt (third from left, bottom row) With Delta Lambda Phi Brothers (clockwise from top right): Peter Colohan, Sean McClafferty, Rob Corwin, Price, Stephen Smith And Oligmueller"
HUNT, HELEN—PHOTOGRAPHS
PH07490 672-673 (December 23, 1993) p88. "Larry (right) With Helen Hunt" (Fallon, Brenda)
HUNT, MILES—PHOTOGRAPHS
PH07491 719 (October 19, 1995) p33. "Vent's reluctant Anti-Star Hunt" (Sirrs, Ed)
HUNTER, ALAN—PHOTOGRAPHS
PH07492 619-620 (December 12, 1991) p71. "The Original VJs (Clockwise from bottom left): Nina Blackwood, Mark Goodman, Martha Quinn, J. J. Jackson, Alan Hunter"
HUNTER, BOB—PHOTOGRAPHS
PH07493 683 (June 2, 1994) p46. "Bob Hunter Holds An Art Project On Metamorphosis From Cobain's Junior Year" (Berry, Jim)
HUNTER, HOLLY—PHOTOGRAPHS
PH07494 655 (April 29, 1993) p68. "Cheerleader-Murdering Mom"
PH07495 662 (August 5, 1993) p73. "Busey, Hunter And Cruise In Jeopardy"
PH07496 665 (September 16, 1993) p77. "Best Supporting Actress"
PH07497 671 (December 9, 1993) p76. "Grace Notes: Holly Hunter (left) And Anna Paquin"
PH07498 672-673 (December 23, 1993) p173. "Power Women Of The Year"
PH07499 674 (January 27, 1994) p48. "Best Actress"
PH07500 678 (March 24, 1994) p100. "Oscar's Choices: 'Schindler's List,' 'The Piano,' 'The Remains Of the Day,' 'In The Name Of The Father,' 'The Fugitive' (from left)"
PH07501 721 (November 16, 1995) p116. "Hunter (left) At Home With Mom Bancroft"
PH07502 721 (November 16, 1995) p117. "Sigourney Weaver (left) Plays Victim While Cop Holly Hunter Packs Heat"
HUNTER, IAN—PHOTOGRAPHS
PH07503 681 (May 5, 1994) p13. "Ronson On Stage With His Old Pal Ian Hunter (left) Back In 1975" (Putland, Michael)
HUNTER, MARK—PHOTOGRAPHS—PORTRAITS
PH07504 680 (April 21, 1994) p11. "[James]" (Borris, Dan)
HUNTER, RACHEL—PHOTOGRAPHS
PH07505 619-620 (December 12, 1991) pp[cover]. "1991 Yearbook" (Eccles, Andrew)
PH07506 619-620 (December 12, 1991) p19. "[Rod Stewart, Rachel Hunter]" (Smeal, James)
HUNTER, ROBERT—PHOTOGRAPHS—PORTRAITS
PH07507 717 (September 21, 1995) p73. "Poet And Picker: Hunter And Garcia" (Blakesberg, Jay)
PH07508 742 (September 5, 1996) p30. "[Robert Hunter]"
HUNTER, STEPHEN—PHOTOGRAPHS
PH07509 741 (August 22, 1996) p82. "[Stephen Hunter]"
HUPPERT, ISABELLE—PHOTOGRAPHS
PH07510 621 (January 9, 1992) p56. "Isabelle Huppert And Jean-Francois Balmer In Turmoil"
PH07511 706 (April 20, 1995) p88. "Young, Huppert, Donovan And Lowensohn Run"
HURLEY, GEORGE—PHOTOGRAPHS
PH07512 658 (June 10, 1993) p34. "Firehose's Watt And Hurley" (Mazur, Kevin)
PH07513 693 (October 20, 1994) p38. "Minutemen D. Boon, Watt And George Hurley In 1985 (from left)" (Pasley, Richard)

HURLEY, STEVE—PHOTOGRAPHS
PH07514 704 (March 23, 1995) p25. "Buffalo Tom's Bill Janovitz, Kristin Hersh, Morphine's Mark Sandman, Gigolo Aunts' Steve Hurley (from left)" (Robicheau, Paul)
HURRICANE—ALBUMS
PH07515 709 (June 1, 1995) p65. "The Hurra"
HURRICANE—PHOTOGRAPHS
PH07516 703 (March 9, 1995) p33. "Hurricane Unleashed"
PH07517 710 (June 15, 1995) p33. "Grand Royalty: DJ-Cum-Rapper Hurricane" (Arnold, Alice)
HURT, MARY BETH—PHOTOGRAPHS
PH07518 730 (March 21, 1996) p104. "Hurt (left) Reflects On Seberg As Saint Joan"
HURT, WILLIAM—PHOTOGRAPHS
PH07519 619-620 (December 12, 1991) p194. "Male Wimps And Female Warriors"
PH07520 622 (January 23, 1992) p50. "William Hurt And Solveig Dommartin Face The End"
PH07521 691 (September 22, 1994) p106. "Cop Hurt Moves In On Juror Whalley-Kilmer"
HURWITZ, CHARLES—PHOTOGRAPHS
PH07522 727 (February 8, 1996) p41. "Those Who Have The Gold, Rule: Maxxam's Maxim According To Hurwitz (above, in 1993)" (Mella, Michael)
HUSBANDS AND WIVES (FILM)—ILLUSTRATIONS
PH07523 640 (October 1, 1992) p71. "Trouble In Paradise" (Sorel, Edward)
HUSBANDS AND WIVES (FILM)—PHOTOGRAPHS
PH07524 640 (October 1, 1992) p72. "Allen And Farrow Reach An Impasse"
PH07525 640 (October 1, 1992) p72. "Allen Meets Danner, The Mother Of Infatuated Student Lewis"
PH07526 648 (January 21, 1993) p56. "Husbands And Wives"
HUSIK, LIDA—PHOTOGRAPHS
PH07527 732 (April 18, 1996) p36. "[Lida Husik]" (Alston, Kwaku)
HUSKER DU—ALBUMS
PH07528 681 (May 5, 1994) p53. "The Living End"
HUSKER DU—PHOTOGRAPHS
PH07529 694 (November 3, 1994) p72. "Poison Years: Husker Du's Grant Hart, Greg Norton And Mould" (Corrigan, Daniel)
HUSTON, ANJELICA—ILLUSTRATIONS
PH07530 618 (November 28, 1991) p3. "Anjelica Huston In 'The World's Biggest Rerun'" (Burke, Philip)
PH07531 619-620 (December 12, 1991) p5. "[Anjelica Huston]" (Burke, Philip)
HUSTON, ANJELICA—PHOTOGRAPHS
PH07532 615 (October 17, 1991) p64. "Anjelica Huston And Isabella Rossellini, 1990" (Pigozzi, Jean)
PH07533 618 (November 28, 1991) p53. "They're Altogether Ooky" (Seliger, Mark)
PH07534 722 (November 30, 1995) p75. "Regrets For Nicholson And Huston"
HUTCHENCE, MICHAEL—PHOTOGRAPHS
PH07535 659 (June 24, 1993) p13. "INXS's Michael Hutchence In Santa Monica" (Cohen, Lester)
PH07536 660-661 (July 8, 1993) p29. "INXS's Michael Hutchence" (Mazur, Kevin)
PH07537 662 (August 5, 1993) p33. "Michael Hutchence (left) With Dando" (Florence, John)
PH07538 669 (November 11, 1993) p27. "Brother Ray With Hutchence" (Granitz, Steve)
PH07539 671 (December 9, 1993) p18. "INXS Marks Their Spot: Pengilly; Beers, Tim, Andrew And Jon Farriss; Hutchence (from left)" (Borris, Dan)
PH07540 733 (May 2, 1996) p35. "Noel, Liam And Hutchence (from left) At Awards" (Fisher, David)
HUTCHENCE, MICHAEL—PHOTOGRAPHS—PORTRAITS
PH07541 686-687 (July 14, 1994) p41. "INXS's Michael Hutchence And Joni Mitchell"
HUTTON, TIMOTHY—ILLUSTRATIONS
PH07542 656 (May 13, 1993) p113. "Stephen King Divided" (Cober, Alan E.)
HUTTON, TIMOTHY—PHOTOGRAPHS
PH07543 656 (May 13, 1993) p114. "Top, Timothy Hutton And His Evil Twin"
PH07544 692 (October 6, 1994) p76. "Redford And Actor Timothy Hutton Both Earned Oscars For "Ordinary People""
PH07545 729 (March 7, 1996) p53. "Crazy Love Timothy Hutton And Natalie Portman"
HYENAS IN THE DESERT—ALBUMS
PH07546 742 (September 5, 1996) p62. "Die Laughing"
HYNDE, CHRISSIE—ILLUSTRATIONS
PH07547 698-699 (December 29, 1994) p79. "[Chrissie Hynde]" (Hungry Dog Studio)
HYNDE, CHRISSIE—PHOTOGRAPHS
PH07548 650 (February 18, 1993) p13. "Hynde: Vegged Out In Amsterdam" (Hess, Fred)
PH07549 655 (April 29, 1993) p12. "Even Chrissie Hynde Gets The Blues" (Hirst, Edward)
PH07550 685 (June 30, 1994) p685. "Hardly Pretending: Chrissie Hynde Revs It Up" (Coles, Rogan)
PH07551 712-713 (July 13, 1995) p33. "The Pretenders With Chrissie Hynde" (Fowler, Simon)
PH07552 719 (October 19, 1995) p41. "Chrissie Hynde Of The Pretenders Leaving The Stage" (Corbijn, Anton)
PH07553 720 (November 2, 1995) p17. "[Friends]"

I

I LIKE IT LIKE THAT (FILM)—PHOTOGRAPHS
PH07554 694 (November 3, 1994) p106. "Now Playing"
I LOVE TROUBLE (FILM)—PHOTOGRAPHS
PH07555 684 (June 16, 1994) p116. "Flirty: Roberts And Nolte In "Trouble""
PH07556 688 (August 11, 1994) p62. "I Love Trouble"
PH07557 691 (September 22, 1994) p106. "Acting Valleys"
I PHOTOGRAPH TO REMEMBER (CD-ROM)—PHOTOGRAPHS
PH07558 679 (April 7, 1994) p44. "Pedro Meyer Depicts His Parents' Dying On 'I Photograph To Remember'"
I SHOT ANDY WARHOL (FILM)—ILLUSTRATIONS
PH07559 734 (May 16, 1996) p71. "Scum Manifesto" (Brodner, Steve)
I SHOT ANDY WARHOL (FILM)—PHOTOGRAPHS
PH07560 734 (May 16, 1996) p72. "Jared Harris"
PH07561 734 (May 16, 1996) p72. "Lili Taylor"
PH07562 734 (May 16, 1996) p72. "Stephen Dorff"
IAN, JANIS—ALBUMS
PH07563 665 (September 16, 1993) p65. "Breaking Silence"
IAN, SCOTT—PHOTOGRAPHS
PH07564 656 (May 13, 1993) p31. "Noisemakers Ian, Dan Spitz, Bush, Frankie Bello And Benante (from left)" (Mazur, Kevin)
PH07565 665 (September 16, 1993) p31. "Scott Ian (left) With Unannounced Guest Al Jourgensen" (Murrey, Ron)
PH07566 722 (November 30, 1995) p34. "Totally Ruled By Instinct: Band Members Charlie Benante, Scott Ian, John Bush And Frank Bello (from left)" (Cultice, Joseph)
IBOLD, MARK—PHOTOGRAPHS
PH07567 686-687 (July 14, 1994) p20. "Ibold, Nastanovich And Kannberg (from left)" (Blakesberg, Jay)
PH07568 686-687 (July 14, 1994) p19. "Pavement (clockwise from left): Mark Ibold, Steve West, Bob Nastanovich And Stephen Malkmus" (Blakesberg, Jay)
PH07569 695 (November 17, 1994) p78. "Pavement" (Hanauer, Mark)
PH07570 709 (June 1, 1995) p23. "Lollapalooza Puts Pavement's Mark Ibold (left) And Stephen Malkmus On The Road" (Corio, David)

ICE CUBE—ALBUMS

PH07571 619-620 (December 12, 1991) p165. "Death Certificate"

PH07572 647 (January 7, 1993) p60. "The Predator"

ICE CUBE—ILLUSTRATIONS

PH07573 647 (January 7, 1993) p46. "[Ice Cube]" (Cowles, David)

PH07574 674 (January 27, 1994) p51. "Snoop & Cube" (Linn, Warren)

PH07575 695 (November 17, 1994) p127. "Ice Cube" (Hungry Dog Studio)

ICE CUBE—PHOTOGRAPHS

PH07576 618 (November 28, 1991) p12. "MC Lyte And Ice Cube" (Michelson, Eric T.)

PH07577 619-620 (December 12, 1991) p60. "Ice Cube In 'Boyz In The Hood'"

PH07578 621 (January 9, 1992) p11. "Ice-T (left) With Ice Cube" (Emerson, Sam)

PH07579 639 (September 17, 1992) p60. "Ice Cube (left) And Ice-T" (Blakesberg, Jay)

PH07580 645-646 (December 10, 1992) p33. "Ice Cube Hit The Lolla Trail" (Blakesberg, Jay)

PH07581 645-646 (December 10, 1992) p97. "Ice-T (left) And Ice Cube" (Gray, Todd)

PH07582 649 (February 4, 1993) p75. "Ice Cube (left) And Ice-T Get Fired Up"

PH07583 665 (September 16, 1993) p13. "[Ice Cube]" (Springsteen, Pam)

PH07584 666 (September 30, 1993) p42. "Serious Attitude: Ex-N.W.A. Members Ice Cube, Yella, Eazy-E, Dre And MC Ren" (Rosenberg, Howard)

PH07585 675 (February 10, 1994) p22. "Ice Cube"

PH07586 700 (January 26, 1995) p68. "Swanson, Connelly, Epps And Cube Tackle "Learning""

PH07587 702 (February 23, 1995) p19. "Wesley Snipes (left) Hands It To Ice Cube" (Mazur, Kevin)

ICE CUBE—PHOTOGRAPHS—PORTRAITS

PH07588 634-635 (July 9, 1992) p15. "[Ice-T]" (Ford, Larry)

PH07589 638 (September 3, 1992) p9. "Ice Cube" (Blakesberg, Jay)

PH07590 656 (May 13, 1993) p74. "[Ice Cube & Ice-T]" (Frohman, Jesse)

ICE-T—ALBUMS

PH07591 630 (May 14, 1992) p105. "Body Count"

PH07592 653 (April 1, 1993) p51. "Home Invasion"

PH07593 672-673 (December 23, 1993) p165. "Home Invasion"

PH07594 737 (June 27, 1996) p56. "VI: Return Of The Real"

ICE-T—ILLUSTRATIONS

PH07595 641 (October 15, 1992) p162. "[Ice-T]" (Cober, Alan E.)

PH07596 651 (March 4, 1993) p40. "[Ice-T]" (Guy, Edmund)

PH07597 652 (March 18, 1993) p7. "Ice-T" (Burke, Philip)

PH07598 653 (April 1, 1993) p51. "Ice-T Fires: Black Rage, Dope Beats" (Panter, Gary)

ICE-T—PHOTOGRAPHS

PH07599 619-620 (December 12, 1991) p31. "Ice-T In 'New Jack City'"

PH07600 619-620 (December 12, 1991) p84. "Ice-T Wows The Lollapalooza Crowd" (Preston, Neal)

PH07601 621 (January 9, 1992) p11. "Ice-T (left) With Ice Cube" (Emerson, Sam)

PH07602 636 (August 6, 1992) p11. "Ice-T At The New Music Seminar" (Pulin, Chuck)

PH07603 639 (September 17, 1992) p60. "Ice Cube (left) And Ice-T" (Blakesberg, Jay)

PH07604 639 (September 17, 1992) p64. "Ice-T And The Boo-Yaa Tribe Join The Chili Peppers" (Blakesberg, Jay)

PH07605 645-646 (December 10, 1992) p97. "Ice-T (left) And Ice Cube" (Gray, Todd)

PH07606 649 (February 4, 1993) p75. "Ice Cube (left) And Ice-T Get Fired Up"

PH07607 649 (February 4, 1993) p22. "Ice-T" (Mazur, Kevin)

PH07608 672-673 (December 23, 1993) p17. "Hot Potato: Ice-T" (Mazur, Kevin)

PH07609 683 (June 2, 1994) p27. "[Ice-T and Janet Jackson]"

PH07610 714 (August 10, 1995) p16. "Blues Traveler's Chan Kinchla, Bobby Sheehan, Brendan Hill And Popper (from left) With Ice-T (second from left)" (Kravitz, Jeff)

PH07611 722 (November 30, 1995) p37. "Brother To Brother: Ice-T Was Among The Throng At The National Mall" (Tolbert, Mpozi)

PH07612 724-725 (December 28, 1995) p58. "Marcher And Rapper Ice-T (center)" (Konte, Keba)

PH07613 733 (May 2, 1996) p14. "Vote-Getters Ice-T, Hayes And Chuck D (from left) Do The Right Thing" (Mazur, Kevin)

ICE-T—PHOTOGRAPHS—PORTRAITS

PH07614 619-620 (December 12, 1991) p86. "Ice-T, Rap-Thrash-Movie Star" (Blakesberg, Jay)

PH07615 634-635 (July 9, 1992) p16. "Ice-T: The Riots Were 'Vindicating'" (Smith, Brian)

PH07616 637 (August 20, 1992) pp28,31. "[Ice-T]" (Seliger, Mark)

PH07617 637 (August 20, 1992) pp[cover]. "Ice-T Talks Back (You Got A Problem With That?)" (Seliger, Mark)

PH07618 642 (October 29, 1992) p32. "[Ice-T]" (Ockenfels, Frank W.)

PH07619 643 (November 12, 1992) p132. "Van Halen" (Seliger, Mark)

PH07620 645-646 (December 10, 1992) pp[cover]. "1992 Yearbook" (Seliger, Mark)

PH07621 645-646 (December 10, 1992) p65. "Ice-T Dukes It Out" (Seliger, Mark)

PH07622 645-646 (December 10, 1992) p149. "Ice-T, 1992"

PH07623 649 (February 4, 1993) p16. "[Ice-T]" (Rapport, Steve)

PH07624 651 (March 4, 1993) p49. "Ice-T: Cool And Refreshing" (Frohman, Jesse)

PH07625 652 (March 18, 1993) p19. "[Ice-T]" (Seliger, Mark)

PH07626 656 (May 13, 1993) p74. "[Ice Cube & Ice-T]" (Frohman, Jesse)

PH07627 657 (May 27, 1993) p21. "[Ice-T]" (Seliger, Mark)

PH07628 662 (August 5, 1993) p60. "Ice-T" (Seliger, Mark)

PH07629 678 (March 24, 1994) p27. "Actor Ice-T: The Most Dreadly Game" (Stevens, D.)

PH07630 720 (November 2, 1995) p51. "Ice-T" (Seliger, Mark)

IDOL, BILLY—ALBUMS

PH07631 662 (August 5, 1993) p64. "Cyberpunk"

IDOL, BILLY—PHOTOGRAPHS

PH07632 615 (October 17, 1991) p14. "Queensryche's Geoff Tate, Billy Idol" (Mazur, Kevin)

PH07633 622 (January 23, 1992) p7. "Billy Idol" (Farrington, Tom)

PH07634 645-646 (December 10, 1992) p49. "Billy Idol Contemplates His Future"

PH07635 749 (December 12, 1996) p19. "Yes, That's Billy Idol (right), Who Also Performed" (Blakesberg, Jay)

IDOL, BILLY—PHOTOGRAPHS—PORTRAITS

PH07636 667 (October 14, 1993) p97. "Idol Pleasures: 'White Wedding'"

IF LUCY FELL (FILM)—PHOTOGRAPHS

PH07637 730 (March 21, 1996) p106. "Now Playing"

IGUANAS—PHOTOGRAPHS

PH07638 627 (April 2, 1992) p11. "Springsteen Onstage With The Iguanas" (Gerber, Cheryl)

IHA, JAMES—ILLUSTRATIONS

PH07639 711 (June 29, 1995) p7. "Pumpkins' James Iha" (Burke, Philip)

IHA, JAMES—PHOTOGRAPHS

PH07640 660-661 (July 8, 1993) p100. "Smashing Pumpkins (from left): Billy Corgan, D'Arcy, Jimmy Chamberlin And James

Iha" (Johnson, Lisa)
PH07641 680 (April 21, 1994) pp42-43. "All Pumped Up: Jimmy Chamberlin, James Iha, Billy Corgan And D'Arcy (from left)" (Luchford, Glen)
PH07642 695 (November 17, 1994) p47. "Smashing Pumpkins" (Ockenfels, Frank, 3)
PH07643 705 (April 6, 1995) p16. "Billy Corgan, Drummer Jimmy Chamberlin And James Iha (from left)" (Natkin, Paul)
PH07644 711 (June 29, 1995) p19. "Billy Corgan, D'Arcy, Jimmy Chamberlin, James Iha (from left)" (Elledge, Paul)
PH07645 721 (November 16, 1995) p52. "Cutting Up: James Iha (left) And Jimmy Chamberlin" (Seliger, Mark)
PH07646 721 (November 16, 1995) p56. "Ready To Rock You: D'Arcy, Iha, Corgan, Chamberlin (from left) In 1992" (Lenquette)
PH07647 723 (December 14, 1995) p27. "The Chicago Eight: D'Arcy, Petersson, Carlos, Corgan, Nielsen, Iha, Chamberlin And Zander (from left)" (Elledge, Paul)
PH07648 724-725 (December 28, 1995) p40. "Corgan, Jimmy Chamberlin, James Iha (from left)" (Natkin, Paul)
PH07649 726 (January 25, 1996) p43. "Smashing Pumpkins' Billy Corgan, D'Arcy, James Iha, Jimmy Chamberlin (from left)" (Seliger, Mark)
PH07650 735 (May 30, 1996) p12. "James Iha Finds That Pimpin' Ain't Easy" (Gerber, M.)
PH07651 745 (October 17, 1996) p27. "Pumpkin James Iha (left) With Foo Fighter Smear" (Mazur, Kevin)

IHA, JAMES—PHOTOGRAPHS—PORTRAITS
PH07652 667 (October 14, 1993) p19. "D'Arcy, Jimmy Chamberlim, Billy Corgan, James Iha (clockwise from top left)" (Hom, Marc)

ILE DE LA REUNION—PHOTOGRAPHS
PH07653 619-620 (December 12, 1991) p143. "A Wedding Party In A Farming Village On The Ile De La Reunion, In The Indian Ocean, In 1989" (Salgado, Sebastiao)

I'M NOT RAPPAPORT (FILM)—PHOTOGRAPHS
PH07654 748 (November 28, 1996) p143. "Matthau"

IMAN—PHOTOGRAPHS
PH07655 645-646 (December 10, 1992) p53. "Nearly Newlywed Iman And Bowie" (Mazur, Kevin)

IMMERWAHR, STEPHEN—PHOTOGRAPHS
PH07656 621 (January 9, 1992) p25. "Codeine (from left): John Engle, Chris Brokaw And Stephen Immerwahr" (Capak, R. J.)

IMMORTAL BELOVED (FILM)—PHOTOGRAPHS
PH07657 700 (January 26, 1995) p66. "Oldman, Rossellini"

IMPERIAL TEEN—ALBUMS
PH07658 734 (May 16, 1996) p68. "Seasick"

IMPERIAL TEEN—PHOTOGRAPHS
PH07659 738-739 (July 11, 1996) p25. "Teen Angels In Love" (Chavez, Marina)

IMPRESSIONS—PHOTOGRAPHS
PH07660 668 (October 28, 1993) p66. "The Impressions Circa '67: Mayfield, Fred Cash And Gooden"

IMPRESSIONS—PHOTOGRAPHS—PORTRAITS
PH07661 668 (October 28, 1993) p65. "The Impressions: Butler (top left) And Mayfield (bottom right)"

IMPRESSIONS—RECORDS
PH07662 649 (February 4, 1993) p69. "The Anthology 1961-1977"

IN MY LIFE (SONG)—PHOTOGRAPHS
PH07663 696 (December 1, 1994) p38. "Lennon Song Lyrics"

IN THE LINE OF FIRE (FILM)—ILLUSTRATIONS
PH07664 662 (August 5, 1993) p71. "The Real Action Hero" (Guy, Edmund)

IN THE LINE OF FIRE (FILM)—PHOTOGRAPHS
PH07665 662 (August 5, 1993) p72. "In 'Fire' (above), Eastwood Guards A President"
PH07666 665 (September 16, 1993) p77. "Best Actor"
PH07667 678 (March 24, 1994) p100. "Missing In Oscar Action"

IN THE MOUTH OF MADNESS (FILM)—PHOTOGRAPHS
PH07668 703 (March 9, 1995) p72. "Sam Neill Flares Up"

IN THE NAME OF THE FATHER (FILM)—PHOTOGRAPHS
PH07669 674 (January 27, 1994) p48. "Acting Vehicles Include 'The Pelican Brief,' 'In The Name Of The Father,' 'What's Eating Gilbert Grape,' 'Shadowlands,' 'Naked,' And 'Grumpy Old Men'"
PH07670 674 (January 27, 1994) p48. "Best Actor"
PH07671 678 (March 24, 1994) p100. "Oscar's Choices: 'Schindler's List,' 'The Piano,' 'The Remains Of the Day,' 'In The Name Of The Father,' 'The Fugitive' (from left)"

IN THE SOUP (FILM)—PHOTOGRAPHS
PH07672 642 (October 29, 1992) p77. "In The Soup"

INCOGNITO—ALBUMS
PH07673 719 (October 19, 1995) p150. "100 Degrees And Rising"

INDECENT PROPOSAL (FILM)—ILLUSTRATIONS
PH07674 655 (April 29, 1993) p67. "Fiscal Attraction" (Friedman, Drew)

INDECENT PROPOSAL (FILM)—PHOTOGRAPHS
PH07675 655 (April 29, 1993) p68. "Demi's Choice: Robert Redford (left) Or Woody Harrelson?"

INDEPENDENCE DAY (FILM)—PHOTOGRAPHS
PH07676 736 (June 13, 1996) p58. "Blockbusters"
PH07677 738-739 (July 11, 1996) p98. "Bang For The Buck Movie Chart"
PH07678 740 (August 8, 1996) p68. "'Independence Day,' Travolta In 'Phenomenon,' Schwarzenegger In 'Eraser,' Moore In 'Striptease'"
PH07679 743 (September 19, 1996) p90. "[Summer...]"
PH07680 750-751 (December 26, 1996) p204. "'ID4' (above) Is Biggest, But 'Larry Flynt' (left), With Harrelson And Love Flanking Flynt, Is The Best"

INDIA—PHOTOGRAPHS
PH07681 665 (September 16, 1993) pp54-58. "Workers of The World" (Salgado, Sebastiao)

INDIGO GIRLS—ALBUMS
PH07682 689 (August 25, 1994) p89. "Swamp Ophelia"

INDIGO GIRLS—ILLUSTRATIONS
PH07683 686-687 (July 14, 1994) p124. "Indigo Girls: Touch Of Blue" (Levine, Laura)

INDIGO GIRLS—PHOTOGRAPHS
PH07684 645-646 (December 10, 1992) p54. "Indigo Girls" (Levine, Laura)
PH07685 684 (June 16, 1994) p36. "Indigo Girl Emily Saliers, Nanci Griffith, Browne, Carpenter, Indigo Girl Amy Ray" (Diamond, Rick)
PH07686 695 (November 17, 1994) p95. "Indigo Girls" (Ford, Charles)
PH07687 712-713 (July 13, 1995) p45. "Indigo Girls Emily Saliers (left), Amy Ray (center) On The White Earth Reservation, In Minnesota" (Pickett, Keri)
PH07688 733 (May 2, 1996) p22. "Indigo Girls Emily Saliers (left) And Amy Ray"

INDONESIA—PHOTOGRAPHS
PH07689 665 (September 16, 1993) pp54-58. "Workers of The World" (Salgado, Sebastiao)

INDUSTRY—ILLUSTRATIONS
PH07690 638 (September 3, 1992) p32. "[Industry]" (Cronin, Brian)

INEZ, MIKE—ILLUSTRATIONS
PH07691 695 (November 17, 1994) p129. "Alice In Chains" (Holley, Jason)

INEZ, MIKE—PHOTOGRAPHS
PH07692 662 (August 5, 1993) p13. "Mike Inez, Layne Staley, Jerry Cantrell And Sean Kinney (clockwise from top left) Of Alice In Chains" (Blakesberg, Jay)
PH07693 676 (February 24, 1994) p18. "Chain Reaction: Sean Kinney, Jerry Cantrell, Layne Staley And Mike Inez (from left)" (Moskowitz, Karen)

PH07694 723 (December 14, 1995) p28. "Mike Inez, A Fan, Layne Staley, Cantrell (from left) And Ghoulish Pals" (Doughty, Curt)
PH07695 727 (February 8, 1996) p33. "Kinney, Cantrell, Staley And Inez (from left)" (Seliger, Mark)
INFARINATO, RUTH—PHOTOGRAPHS
PH07696 670 (November 25, 1993) p22. "Lewin, Infarinato, Morales (from left)"
INFIDELS—ALBUMS
PH07697 621 (January 9, 1992) p53. "Infidels"
INHOFE, JAMES—PHOTOGRAPHS—PORTRAITS
PH07698 710 (June 15, 1995) p62. "Inhofe" (Trippett, Robert)
THE INNER CIRCLE (FILM)—PHOTOGRAPHS
PH07699 623 (February 6, 1992) p90. "Tom Hulce Is Burdened By Stalin Idolatry"
INNES, ANDREW—PHOTOGRAPHS
PH07700 684 (June 16, 1994) p26. "A Slice Of Scream: Keyboardist Martin Duffy, Gillespie And Innes (from left)" (Sheehan, Tom)
INNOCENT BLOOD (FILM)—PHOTOGRAPHS
PH07701 642 (October 29, 1992) p77. "Innocent Blood"
THE INNOCENTS (FILM)—PHOTOGRAPHS
PH07702 727 (February 8, 1996) p46. "Home Video"
INSECTS—ILLUSTRATIONS
PH07703 728 (February 22, 1996) p20. "Grub" (Sutton, Ward)
INSTRUMENTS—PHOTOGRAPHS
PH07704 674 (January 27, 1994) p59. "Lonestar Technologies Key Interactive Instrument, $400" (Miller, Greg)
INTERNET—ILLUSTRATIONS
PH07705 689 (August 25, 1994) p32. "[Internet]" (Clayton, Chris)
PH07706 690 (September 8, 1994) p40. "[Internet]" (Deen, Georganne)
PH07707 696 (December 1, 1994) p63. "[Internet]" (Cronin, Brian)
PH07708 700 (January 26, 1995) p14. "Just Kidding" (Pendergrast, James T.)
PH07709 700 (January 26, 1995) p14. "Welcome To The Infobahn!" (Pendergrast, James T.)
PH07710 714 (August 10, 1995) p16. "Blank Pages" (Mericle, Charise)
PH07711 719 (October 19, 1995) p109. "[Internet]" (Stauffer, Brian)
INTERNET—PHOTOGRAPHS
PH07712 715 (August 24, 1995) p81. "Hot Web Whatzit"
PH07713 719 (October 19, 1995) p117. "Click On This To Hear The Princeton Tigertones"
PH07714 719 (October 19, 1995) p110. "Crackbaby Calls His Home Page 'A Snapshot Into My Soul'"
PH07715 719 (October 19, 1995) p114. "Frisbee Anyone? Intramural Sports On The Web"
PH07716 719 (October 19, 1995) p116. "The Home Pages Of Student Web Publishing Wizards Scott Banister (top) And Justin Hall"
PH07717 719 (October 19, 1995) p110. "One-Stop Shopping On University Home Pages"
PH07718 719 (October 19, 1995) p114. "Personal Home Pages: Scrapbooks For A New Generation"
PH07719 719 (October 19, 1995) p114. "The Web Welcomes All, Greek Or Geek"
INTERNET UNDERGROUND MUSIC ARCHIVE—PHOTOGRAPHS
PH07720 686-687 (July 14, 1994) p31. "The Look Of Sounds To Come: IUMA Screen Shot" (Davis, Chris)
INTERSECTION (FILM)—PHOTOGRAPHS
PH07721 676 (February 24, 1994) p62. "[Intersection]"
INTERVIEW WITH THE VAMPIRE (FILM)—PHOTOGRAPHS
PH07722 696 (December 1, 1994) p94. "In "Vampire," Pitt And Tom Cruise Are Star Bloodsuckers"
PH07723 697 (December 15, 1994) p102. "Prowling Vampires Kirsten Dunst, Brad Pitt And Tom Cruise"
PH07724 698-699 (December 29, 1994) p194. "Cruise Bites Pitt In "Vampire""
PH07725 705 (April 6, 1995) p69. "Oscar Rejects"
PH07726 711 (June 29, 1995) p48. "Rentals: 'Vampires,' 'Disclosure'"
INTO THE WEST (FILM)—PHOTOGRAPHS
PH07727 657 (May 27, 1993) p59. "Questing: Gabriel Byrne, Ellen Barkin"
INVASION OF THE BODY SNATCHERS (FILM)—PHOTOGRAPHS
PH07728 669 (November 11, 1993) p80. "Fright Sights (from left): 'Body Snatchers' 1956, 1978, 1993"
INXS—ALBUMS
PH07729 638 (September 3, 1992) p65. "Welcome To Wherever You Are"
PH07730 676 (February 24, 1994) p56. "Full Moon, Dirty Hearts"
INXS—PHOTOGRAPHS
PH07731 631 (May 28, 1992) p9. "INXS Onstage In Sydney"
PH07732 663 (August 19, 1993) p27. "INXS's Garry Gary Beers, Iggy Pop, Andrew Fariss And Jon Fariss (from left)" (Mazur, Kevin)
PH07733 671 (December 9, 1993) p18. "INXS Marks Their Spot: Pengilly; Beers, Tim, Andrew And Jon Farriss; Hutchence (from left)" (Borris, Dan)
INXS—PHOTOGRAPHS—PORTRAITS
PH07734 645-646 (December 10, 1992) p69. "INXS: Welcome To Wherever We Are" (Sirota, Peggy)
IOMAIRE, COLM MAC CON—PHOTOGRAPHS
PH07735 644 (November 26, 1992) p24. "Hansard, Noreen O'Donnell, Colm Mac Con Iomaire, Brennan, David Odlum And John Carney (from left)" (Marsden, Barry)
IONESCO, EUGENE—PHOTOGRAPHS
PH07736 698-699 (December 29, 1994) p85. "Eugene Ionesco"
IOVINE, JIMMY—PHOTOGRAPHS—PORTRAITS
PH07737 731 (April 4, 1996) p30. "Interscope's Ted Fields (left) And Jimmy Iovine"
I.Q. (FILM)—PHOTOGRAPHS
PH07738 700 (January 26, 1995) p66. "Smart Women, Foolish Choices"
IRONS, JACK—PHOTOGRAPHS
PH07739 702 (February 23, 1995) p26. "Pirate Music: McCready, Vedder, Ament, Irons And Stone Gossard (from left)" (Mercer, Lance)
PH07740 719 (October 19, 1995) p56. "'86: Irons, Slovak, Flea, Kiedis (from left) Backstage At The Ritz, In New York" (Gershoff, Gary)
PH07741 726 (January 25, 1996) p17. "Mike McCready, Jeff Ament, Harper, Eddie Vedder, Jack Irons And Stone Gossard (from left)"
IRONS, JEREMY—PHOTOGRAPHS
PH07742 623 (February 6, 1992) p88. "Jeremy Irons Hides In Terror From The Forces Of Darkness"
PH07743 647 (January 7, 1993) p51. "Juliette Binoche And Jeremy Irons Play Sex Dangerously"
PH07744 703 (March 9, 1995) p20. "Terrorist Sam Phillips Shares A Love Scene With Jeremy Irons"
PH07745 737 (June 27, 1996) p63. "Irons (left) And Tyler Talk Sex And Art"
IRVING, CRAIG—PHOTOGRAPHS
PH07746 652 (March 18, 1993) p23. "Doodlebug, Ladybug, Butterfly (from left)" (Guzman)
IRWIN, ELAINE—PHOTOGRAPHS
PH07747 640 (October 1, 1992) p9. "[John Mellencamp, Elaine Irwin]" (Ortega, Albert)
PH07748 690 (September 8, 1994) p64. "On The Beach: Mellencamp With His Wife, Elaine Irwin" (Seliger, Mark)
IRWIN, PAT—PHOTOGRAPHS
PH07749 637 (August 20, 1992) p11. "The B-52's (from left): Fred Schneider, Kate Pierson, Julee Cruise, Keith Strickland, Sue Hadjopoulos And Pat Irwin" (Michelson, Eric T.)

ISAAK, CHRIS—ALBUMS
PH07750 656 (May 13, 1993) p104. "San Francisco Days"
ISAAK, CHRIS—PHOTOGRAPHS
PH07751 623 (February 6, 1992) p11. "Isaak With Todd Rundgren" (Blakesberg, Jay)
PH07752 629 (April 30, 1992) p12. "Chris Isaak (left) With John Lee Hooker" (Blakesberg, Jay)
PH07753 644 (November 26, 1992) p13. "Chris Isaak In The Studio" (Diltz, Henry)
PH07754 651 (March 4, 1993) p25. "[Chris Isaak]" (Tighe, Michael)
PH07755 667 (October 14, 1993) p96. "From Her To Eternity: In 'Wicked Game,' Isaak Nuzzles Christiansen Beachside"
PH07756 668 (October 28, 1993) p35. "Drummer Kenney Dale Johnson With Isaak" (Plummer, Sue)
PH07757 679 (April 7, 1994) p39. "Isaak With Lobo David Hidalgo" (Kravitz, Jeff)
PH07758 716 (September 7, 1995) p14. "Chaka Khan And Chris Isaak At LIFEbeat" (Mazur, Kevin)
PH07759 748 (November 28, 1996) p47. "Aw, Shucks: Chris Isaak Slings The Sad Stuff" (Callahan, Kristin)
ISLEY BROTHERS—PHOTOGRAPHS
PH07760 623 (February 6, 1992) p52. "Brothers Kelly, Ronald And Rudolph Isley (from left)"
PH07761 625 (March 5, 1992) p13. "Rockin' And Rollin' (above, from left): Little Richard, Ronald Isley, Ernie Isley, Chris Jasper, Marvin Isley" (Mazur, Kevin)
ISLEY, ERNIE—PHOTOGRAPHS
PH07761 625 (March 5, 1992) p13. "Rockin' And Rollin' (above, from left): Little Richard, Ronald Isley, Ernie Isley, Chris Jasper, Marvin Isley" (Mazur, Kevin)
ISLEY, KELLY—PHOTOGRAPHS
PH07762 623 (February 6, 1992) p52. "Brothers Kelly, Ronald And Rudolph Isley (from left)"
ISLEY, MARVIN—PHOTOGRAPHS
PH07763 625 (March 5, 1992) p13. "Rockin' And Rollin' (above, from left): Little Richard, Ronald Isley, Ernie Isley, Chris Jasper, Marvin Isley" (Mazur, Kevin)
ISLEY, RONALD—PHOTOGRAPHS
PH07764 623 (February 6, 1992) p52. "Brothers Kelly, Ronald And Rudolph Isley (from left)"
PH07765 625 (March 5, 1992) p13. "Rockin' And Rollin' (above, from left): Little Richard, Ronald Isley, Ernie Isley, Chris Jasper, Marvin Isley" (Mazur, Kevin)
ISLEY, RUDOLPH—PHOTOGRAPHS
PH07766 623 (February 6, 1992) p52. "Brothers Kelly, Ronald And Rudolph Isley (from left)"
ISRAEL, DREW—PHOTOGRAPHS—PORTRAITS
PH07767 680 (April 21, 1994) p26. "Israel Webb, Lords (from left)" (Marsel, Steve)
IT COULD HAPPEN TO YOU (FILM)—PHOTOGRAPHS
PH07768 688 (August 11, 1994) p62. "It's A Jackpot-Lottery Win For Fonda, Cage And Perez"
ITALY—PHOTOGRAPHS
PH07769 665 (September 16, 1993) pp54-58. "Workers of The World" (Salgado, Sebastiao)
IT'S A BEAUTIFUL DAY—ALBUMS
PH07770 617 (November 14, 1991) p110. "It's A Beautiful Day" (Hunter, George)
IVEY, MICHAEL—PHOTOGRAPHS
PH07771 628 (April 16, 1992) p51. "Basehead, The Band (from left): Brian Hendrix, Keith Lofton, Bill Conway And Michael Ivey" (Ockenfels, Frank W.)
IVINS, MICHAEL—PHOTOGRAPHS
PH07772 689 (August 25, 1994) p21. "The Flaming Lips' Michael Ivins, Steven Drozd, Wayne Coyne (from left)" (Blakesberg, Jay)
PH07773 703 (March 9, 1995) p26. "Imagine The Beatles Drunk On Robitussin: Coyne, Drozd, Ivins And Jones (from left)" (Lavine, Michael)
PH07774 736 (June 13, 1996) p33. "The Flaming Lips' Steven Drozd, Michael Ivins, Wayne Coyne And Ronald Jones (from left)" (Martin, J. Michelle)

J

J.—PHOTOGRAPHS
PH07775 648 (January 21, 1993) p9. "German Rapper J."
PH07776 671 (December 9, 1993) p13. "Beavis And Butt-head Faves J., Philo, Rob And Sean (from left)" (Ragel, Jon)
PH07777 695 (November 17, 1994) p50. "White Zombie" (Winter, Dan)
PH07778 726 (January 25, 1996) p50. "White Zombie: J., Rob Zombie, John Tempesta And Sean Yseult (from left)" (Cuffaro, Chris)
J MASCIS—ALBUMS
PH07779 733 (May 2, 1996) p56. "Martin And Me"
J MASCIS—PHOTOGRAPHS
PH07780 656 (May 13, 1993) p17. "Don't Call Us Slackers: Mike Johnson, Murph And J Mascis" (Ockenfels, Frank, 3)
PH07781 656 (May 13, 1993) p15. "Moore, Fleming, Firehose's Mike Watt And J Mascis (from left)" (Callahan, Kristin)
PH07782 656 (May 13, 1993) p18. "Unlikely Messiah: Mascis" (Roberts, Ebet)
PH07783 693 (October 20, 1994) p52. "Dinosaur Jr's Mascis: Still Life With Feedback" (Pasley, Richard)
J MASCIS—PHOTOGRAPHS—PORTRAITS
PH07784 695 (November 17, 1994) p38. "J Mascis Of Dinosaur Jr" (Fink, Larry)
JACK (FILM)—PHOTOGRAPHS
PH07785 742 (September 5, 1996) p68. "Francis Ford Coppola Directs Robin Williams To Act Like A 10-Year-Old In 'Jack'"
JACK THE BEAR (FILM)—PHOTOGRAPHS
PH07786 655 (April 29, 1993) p69. "DeVito Is Dad To Steinmiller And Hughes"
JACKSON, AL, JR.—PHOTOGRAPHS—PORTRAITS
PH07787 623 (February 6, 1992) p50. "Booker T. And The MGs (from left): Donald 'Duck' Dunn, Booker T., Steve Cropper And Al Jackson Jr."
JACKSON, ALAN—PHOTOGRAPHS
PH07788 628 (April 16, 1992) p17. "Video Star Alan Jackson" (St. Nicholas, Randee)
JACKSON, CHUCK—PHOTOGRAPHS
PH07789 637 (August 20, 1992) p11. "Rock And Soul (from left): Boz Scaggs, Walter Becker, Donald Fagen, Michael McDonald, Phoebe Snow And Chuck Jackson" (Hamilton, James)
JACKSON FAMILY HONORS (TELEVISION SHOW)—PHOTOGRAPHS
PH07790 679 (April 7, 1994) p37. "[Jacksons]"
JACKSON FIVE—ALBUMS
PH07791 724-725 (December 28, 1995) p122. "Soulsation!"
JACKSON, GREG—PHOTOGRAPHS
PH07792 678 (March 24, 1994) p69. "Brothers Under The Skin: Martin Phillips, Greg Parker, Mike Wiliams, Dexter Wilson, Rick Brown, Greg Jackson, Everettt Whiteside, Roderick Bradford, Lacell Sherman..." (Smith, Bria
PH07793 678 (March 24, 1994) p72. "Williams, Whiteside, Jackson, Sherman (from left) On The Library Steps" (Smith, Brian)
JACKSON, J. J.—PHOTOGRAPHS
PH07794 619-620 (December 12, 1991) p71. "The Original VJs (Clockwise from bottom left): Nina Blackwood, Mark Goodman, Martha Quinn, J. J. Jackson, Alan Hunter"
JACKSON, JAMES—PHOTOGRAPHS
PH07795 719 (October 19, 1995) p25. "Cowan Signs To Motown: Motown's Nadiene Baker, Manager Bill Dern, Jackson, Cowan (clockwise from top left)"

JACKSON, JANET—ALBUMS
PH07796 660-661 (July 8, 1993) p136. "Janet"
PH07797 662 (August 5, 1993) p77. "Janet"
PH07798 672-673 (December 23, 1993) p152. "Janet"
JACKSON, JANET—ILLUSTRATIONS
PH07799 659 (June 24, 1993) p78. "She Wants To Sex You Up" (Cowles, David)
PH07800 663 (August 19, 1993) p81. "Girlz N The Hood" (Kelley, Gary)
JACKSON, JANET—PHOTOGRAPHS
PH07801 654 (April 15, 1993) p11. "Janet And Michael Jackson" (Mazur, Kevin)
PH07802 657 (May 27, 1993) p18. "[Janet Jackson]" (Ritts, Herb)
PH07803 663 (August 19, 1993) p82. "Janet Jackson With Her Boyz: Director John Singleton (left) And Co-Star Tupac Shakur"
PH07804 665 (September 16, 1993) p41. "Backstage With Brother Michael In His Afro Days"
PH07805 665 (September 16, 1993) p39. "[Janet Jackson]" (Von Unwerth, Ellen)
PH07806 665 (September 16, 1993) pp[cover]. "Janet Jackson: The Joy Of Sex" (Demarchelier, Patrick)
PH07807 665 (September 16, 1993) p41. "Lounging With LaToya (right)" (Salicki)
PH07808 665 (September 16, 1993) p40. "Sweet Thing: A Young Janet" (Gruen, Bob)
PH07809 665 (September 16, 1993) p41. "Todd Bridges And Janet On 'Different Strokes'"
PH07810 665 (September 16, 1993) p43. "With Ex-Husband James DeBarge (left) And With Her Current Boyfriend, Rene Elizondo" (Zuffante, Vinnie)
PH07811 667 (October 14, 1993) p39. "Left: Axl? No, Janet Jackson" (Mazur, Kevin)
PH07812 667 (October 14, 1993) p73. "'Love Will Never Do Without You': Janet Comes Out"
PH07813 672-673 (December 23, 1993) p188. "[Covers]" (Demarchelier, Patrick)
PH07814 674 (January 27, 1994) p41. "Janet Jackson"
PH07815 674 (January 27, 1994) p25. "Janet Jackson: The Focus Is Below The Belt" (Wolfe, Eddie)
PH07816 683 (June 2, 1994) p27. "[Ice-T and Janet Jackson]"
PH07817 698-699 (December 29, 1994) p58. "Jackson With "Seinfeld" Ham Michael Richards" (Kravitz, Jeff)
PH07818 711 (June 29, 1995) p13. "Brandy (left) With A Newly Shorn Janet Jackson" (Mazur, Kevin)
PH07819 715 (August 24, 1995) p62. "With Janet Jackson And Her Producer Jimmy Jam, '90"
PH07820 746 (October 31, 1996) p42. "Shakur With Janet Jackson On The Set Of The Film 'Poetic Justice' In 1993"
PH07821 749 (December 12, 1996) p20. "It's A Family Affair: Jam's Wife, Lisa Harris, Holding Tyler; Jam; Jackson; And Lewis (from left)"
JACKSON, JANET—PHOTOGRAPHS—PORTRAITS
PH07822 619-620 (December 12, 1991) p29. "Janet (below and rich)" (Granitz, Steve)
PH07823 643 (November 12, 1992) p166. "Janet Jackson" (Ritts, Herb)
PH07824 665 (September 16, 1993) p38. "[Janet Jackson]" (Von Unwerth, Ellen)
PH07825 665 (September 16, 1993) p43. "Michael And Janet At Last Year's Grammys" (Emerson, Sam)
PH07826 672-673 (December 23, 1993) p37. "Jackson: Like A Virgin, But Not Really" (Demarchelier, Patrick)
JACKSON, JESSE—PHOTOGRAPHS
PH07827 626 (March 19, 1992) p24. "Jackson And Dolan (right) In Durham" (Mazur, Kevin)
PH07828 660-661 (July 8, 1993) p52. "Babbitt On The Campaign Trail: Presidential Candidates Michael Dukakis, Babbitt, Paul Simon, Richard Gephardt, Jesse Jackson And Al Gore (from left) At A New York Forum ..." (Peterson, Charles)
PH07829 750-751 (December 26, 1996) p90. "Jesse Jackson And Bruce Springsteen Led The Rally"
JACKSON, JOE—ALBUMS
PH07830 617 (November 14, 1991) p108. "Look Sharp" (Ross, Michael)
PH07831 617 (November 14, 1991) p108. "Look Sharp" (Griffin, Brian)
JACKSON, LATOYA—PHOTOGRAPHS
PH07832 665 (September 16, 1993) p41. "Lounging With LaToya (right)" (Salicki)
JACKSON, MARION—PHOTOGRAPHS
PH07833 625 (March 5, 1992) p13. "Lewis Steinberg, Steve Cropper, Booker T. Jones, Marion Jackson, Randall Jackson, Duck Dunn, Jim Stewart (from left)" (Elgar, Nick)
JACKSON, MICHAEL—ALBUMS
PH07834 621 (January 9, 1992) p49. "Dangerous"
PH07835 623 (February 6, 1992) p100. "Dangerous"
PH07836 710 (June 15, 1995) p24. "History"
PH07837 714 (August 10, 1995) p55. "History"
JACKSON, MICHAEL—ILLUSTRATIONS
PH07838 621 (January 9, 1992) p49. "Michael Jackson: Art And Life As Performance" (Gosfield, Josh)
PH07839 621 (January 9, 1992) p49. "Michael Jackson: Art And Life As Performance" (Smith, Lane)
PH07840 632 (June 11, 1992) p135. "[Michael Jackson]" (Cronin, Brian)
PH07841 645-646 (December 10, 1992) p152. "Michael Jackson, 1987"
PH07842 653 (April 1, 1993) p17. "[Michael Jackson]" (Sweeny, Glynis)
PH07843 714 (August 10, 1995) p55. "King Of Pain" (Drawson, Blair)
PH07844 750-751 (December 26, 1996) p45. "[Michael Jackson & Lisa Marie Presley]" (Ryden, Mark)
JACKSON, MICHAEL—PHOTOGRAPHS
PH07845 619-620 (December 12, 1991) p31. "Madonna And Michael Jackson Took In The Oscars" (Elgar, Nick)
PH07846 619-620 (December 12, 1991) p29. "Michael (right and richer) Jackson" (Mazur, Kevin)
PH07847 621 (January 9, 1992) pp[cover]. "Michael Jackson: The Making Of 'The King Of Pop'" (Ritts, Herb)
PH07848 626 (March 19, 1992) p11. "Michael Jackson With Eddie Murphy And Producer Trenten Gumbs (from left)"
PH07849 630 (May 14, 1992) p15. "Michael Jackson Surrounded By MTV Winners And Other Charming Dinner Companions"
PH07850 639 (September 17, 1992) p38. "[Michael Jackson]" (Mazur, Kevin)
PH07851 640 (October 1, 1992) p21. "[Michael Jackson]" (Sands, Steve)
PH07852 645-646 (December 10, 1992) p36. "The King Of Pepsi" (Mazur, Kevin)
PH07853 645-646 (December 10, 1992) p66. "Michael Does Europe" (Mazur, Kevin)
PH07854 651 (March 4, 1993) p21. "Gala Groove: Hillary, Chelsea, Bill, Michael Jackson And Stevie Nicks" (Mazur, Kevin)
PH07855 654 (April 15, 1993) p11. "Janet And Michael Jackson" (Mazur, Kevin)
PH07856 655 (April 29, 1993) p56. "Michael Jackson And Madonna Celebrate Geffen's Birthday In 1991"
PH07857 665 (September 16, 1993) p41. "Backstage With Brother Michael In His Afro Days"
PH07858 667 (October 14, 1993) p90. "'Black Or White': Jackson's Original Ending Got Cut"
PH07859 667 (October 14, 1993) p69. "Jackson: A video Taylored To His Dreams"
PH07860 667 (October 14, 1993) p21. "Jackson At The Super Bowl: The Scandal Has Already Taken Its Toll" (Morse, Paul)
PH07861 672-673 (December 23, 1993) p58. "Jackson: He's Bad, He's Bad, He's Bad, Bad, Bad" (Mazur, Kevin)

PH07862 672-673 (December 23, 1993) p74. "Right: Michael Jackson" (Garcia, Frederic)
PH07863 672-673 (December 23, 1993) p20. "Winfrey And Jackson Yukking It Up On The Air" (Emerson, Sam)
PH07864 679 (April 7, 1994) p37. "[Jacksons]"
PH07865 691 (September 22, 1994) p19. "[Michael Jackson & Lisa Marie Presley]" (Zimmerman, Dick)
PH07866 693 (October 20, 1994) p28. "Mr. (left) And Mrs. Michael Jackson" (Kravitz, Jeff)
PH07867 697 (December 15, 1994) p72. "1987's "Bad" Tour: Sheryl Crow (in wig) With Michael Jackson" (Mazur, Kevin)
PH07868 716 (September 7, 1995) p13. "Wanna Be Schools Chancellor?: Giuliani And Jacko" (Mazur, Kevin)
PH07869 719 (October 19, 1995) p16. "Michael Jackson And The Missis" (Kravitz, Jeff)
PH07870 720 (November 2, 1995) p50. "Michael Jackson" (Plummer, Barry)
PH07871 724-725 (December 28, 1995) p48. "No Glove, And Definitely No Love: Sawyer, Jacksons"
PH07872 724-725 (December 28, 1995) p49. "Some Of My Best Friends Are Jewish, Jackson Said" (Micelotta, Frank)
PH07873 726 (January 25, 1996) p17. "[Michael Jackson]" (Schwartzwald, Lawrence)
PH07874 726 (January 25, 1996) p42. "Michael Jackson, King Of Hype" (Preston, Neal)
PH07875 737 (June 27, 1996) p15. "Let The Little Children Come Unto Me" (Niviere, D.)
PH07876 746 (October 31, 1996) p26. "Czech President Vaclav Havel With Jackson In Prague"
PH07877 749 (December 12, 1996) p30. "A New Book Threatens To Reignite Jackson's Child-Abuse Controversy" (Rabbo, Ammar Abd)
PH07878 750-751 (December 26, 1996) p54. "[Michael Jackson & Prince Alwaleed Bin Talal Bin Abdulaziz Al-Saud]" (Rabbo, Ammar Abd)

JACKSON, MICHAEL—PHOTOGRAPHS—PORTRAITS
PH07879 619-620 (December 12, 1991) p94. "Michael Jackson Begins His 'Dangerous' Business" (Berliner, Alex)
PH07880 621 (January 9, 1992) p37. "Jackson In His First Photo Session For 'Rolling Stone,' 1971" (Diltz, Henry)
PH07881 621 (January 9, 1992) pp33,35. "[Michael Jackson]" (Ritts, Herb)
PH07882 632 (June 11, 1992) p136. "Michael Jackson In Early 1983: Healthy, Handsome And Robustly African American" (Schiffman, Bonnie)
PH07883 636 (August 6, 1992) p11. "Michael Jackson In London" (Loftus, Phil)
PH07884 643 (November 12, 1992) p154. "Michael Jackson" (Ritts, Herb)
PH07885 645-646 (December 10, 1992) pp[cover]. "1992 Yearbook" (Ritts, Herb)
PH07886 650 (February 18, 1993) p13. "Michael Jackson, White Like Me" (Diltz, Henry)
PH07887 656 (May 13, 1993) p13. "[Michael Jackson]"
PH07888 660-661 (July 8, 1993) p32. "[Michael Jackson]" (Kravitz, Jeff)
PH07889 665 (September 16, 1993) p43. "Michael And Janet At Last Year's Grammys" (Emerson, Sam)
PH07890 667 (October 14, 1993) p78. "Michael Jackson: Ode To 'Bille Jean'" (Adebari, Eugene)
PH07891 698-699 (December 29, 1994) p55. "[Michael Jackson & Lisa Marie Presley]" (Zimmerman, Dick)
PH07892 710 (June 15, 1995) p24. "Jackson: Still The King Of Pop?"

JACKSON, RANDALL—PHOTOGRAPHS
PH07893 625 (March 5, 1992) p13. "Lewis Steinberg, Steve Cropper, Booker T. Jones, Marion Jackson, Randall Jackson, Duck Dunn, Jim Stewart (from left)" (Elgar, Nick)

JACKSON, RANDY—PHOTOGRAPHS
PH07894 679 (April 7, 1994) p37. "[Jacksons]"

JACKSON, RANDY, JR.—PHOTOGRAPHS
PH07894 679 (April 7, 1994) p37. "[Jacksons]"

JACKSON, SAMUEL L.—PHOTOGRAPHS
PH07895 627 (April 2, 1992) p41. "Jackson, With Halle Berry, In 'Jungle Fever'"
PH07896 690 (September 8, 1994) p87. "Drug Runner Nelson Plays Chess With Dad Jackson"
PH07897 692 (October 6, 1994) p80. "Travolta And Jackson Shoot"
PH07898 700 (January 26, 1995) p68. "Best Actor (tie)"
PH07899 710 (June 15, 1995) p86. "Jackson And Willis Try To Undo A Bad Situation In 'Die Hard With A Vengeance'"
PH07900 735 (May 30, 1996) p57. "Preening"

JACKSON, SAMUEL L.—PHOTOGRAPHS—PORTRAITS
PH07901 743 (September 19, 1996) p90. "[Summer...]"

JACKSON, WANDA—PHOTOGRAPHS—PORTRAITS
PH07902 692 (October 6, 1994) p50. "Wanda Jackson"

JACOB, IRENE—PHOTOGRAPHS
PH07903 702 (February 23, 1995) p80. "Red"

JACOBOWITZ, EDEN—PHOTOGRAPHS
PH07904 662 (August 5, 1993) p45. "Jacobowitz On The Dock In Woodmere, Long Island: 'Why Am I Being Blamed For History?'" (Irish, Len)
PH07905 662 (August 5, 1993) p48. "Jacobowitz With Kors: 'There Ought To Be Truth In Advertising,' Says The History Professor" (Massar, Eli)

JACOBSON, SCOTT—PHOTOGRAPHS
PH07906 617 (November 14, 1991) pp159-163. "[Scott Jacobson]" (Noble, Chris)

JADE (FILM)—PHOTOGRAPHS
PH07907 721 (November 16, 1995) p116. "Linda Fiorentino Does The 'Jade' Thing"

JAFFEE, RAMI—PHOTOGRAPHS
PH07908 636 (August 6, 1992) p13. "The Wallflowers (from left): Barrie Maguire, Jakob Dylan, Rami Jaffee, Peter Yanowitz And Tobi Miller" (Mark, Mary Ellen)

JAGER, TOM—PHOTOGRAPHS
PH07909 634-635 (July 9, 1992) p94. "Matt Biondi, Dara Torres And Tom Jager (from left)" (Zander, Peter)

JAGGER, BIANCA—PHOTOGRAPHS
PH07910 632 (June 11, 1992) p58. "This Time Let's Do It Plane, Not Train, Eh? Mick And Bianca Jagger Somewhere Over North America During The Stones' 1972 Tour" (Leibovitz, Annie)
PH07911 723 (December 14, 1995) p53. "A Newly Wed Jagger Popping The Cork In A Limo With Bianca On Their Wedding Day, 1971" (Lichfield, P.)

JAGGER, CHRIS—PHOTOGRAPHS
PH07912 731 (April 4, 1996) p17. "Mick (for our cave-dwelling readers) And Brother Chris" (Allocca, Dave)

JAGGER, ELIZABETH—PHOTOGRAPHS
PH07913 723 (December 14, 1995) p74. "Jagger Enjoys The Sun With Daughter Elizabeth (on his lap) And Her Friend: A New Version Of 'Mother's Little Helper'" (Raban, Duncan)

JAGGER, JADE—PHOTOGRAPHS
PH07914 615 (October 17, 1991) p64. "Massai, Jade Jagger And Jerry Hall, Nassau, 1983" (Pigozzi, Jean)

JAGGER, MICK—ALBUMS
PH07915 650 (February 18, 1993) p56. "Wandering Spirit"
PH07916 672-673 (December 23, 1993) p146. "Wandering Spirit"

JAGGER, MICK—ILLUSTRATIONS
PH07917 641 (October 15, 1992) p85. "[Mick Jagger]" (Glaser, Milton)
PH07918 650 (February 18, 1993) p56. "Is This The Summer Of Love?" (Guy, Edmund)
PH07919 686-687 (July 14, 1994) p11. "Mick Jagger" (Burke, Philip)
PH07920 727 (February 8, 1996) p10. "[Mick Jagger]" (Pendergrast, James T.)

JAGGER, MICK—PHOTOGRAPHS

PH07921 615 (October 17, 1991) p64. "Mick Jagger And Arnold Schwarzenegger, 1990" (Pigozzi, Jean)

PH07922 615 (October 17, 1991) p67. "Mick Jagger, Madrid, 1981" (Pigozzi, Jean)

PH07923 619-620 (December 12, 1991) p90. "...And Jagger (left)" (Mazur, Kevin)

PH07924 625 (March 5, 1992) p19. "Jagger At The 'Freejack' Premiere" (Ortega, Albert)

PH07925 632 (June 11, 1992) p59. "Mick Disembarking From The Stones' DC-7, At An Unidentified Stop On The 1972 Tour" (Leibovitz, Annie)

PH07926 632 (June 11, 1992) p58. "This Time Let's Do It Plane, Not Train, Eh? Mick And Bianca Jagger Somewhere Over North America During The Stones' 1972 Tour" (Leibovitz, Annie)

PH07927 637 (August 20, 1992) p9. "Jagger (left) With Bluesman Jimmy Rogers" (Dent, Phil)

PH07928 643 (November 12, 1992) p74. "On The Rolling Stones' 1975 Tour, Annie Leibovitz's Lens Captured Keith, Mick And Real-Life Rock & Roll" (Leibovitz, Annie)

PH07929 644 (November 26, 1992) p15. "Rubin (left) And Jagger" (Mazur, Kevin)

PH07930 645-646 (December 10, 1992) p69. "Jagger And Jimmy Rogers Share The Stage"

PH07931 645-646 (December 10, 1992) p156. "Mick Jagger, 1968"

PH07932 645-646 (December 10, 1992) p156. "Mick Jagger, 1970"

PH07933 645-646 (December 10, 1992) p157. "Mick Jagger, 1973"

PH07934 652 (March 18, 1993) p15. "Mick Jagger" (Wolman, Baron)

PH07935 653 (April 1, 1993) p11. "Start Me Up: Mick Jagger At Webster Hall" (Mazur, Kevin)

PH07936 662 (August 5, 1993) p33. "Watts, Jagger And Richards In Barbados"

PH07937 667 (October 14, 1993) p87. "'Undercover': Latin Jagger"

PH07938 668 (October 28, 1993) p35. "[Rolling Stones]"

PH07939 672-673 (December 23, 1993) p20. "Above: Mick Jagger In The Wandering Spirit" (Mazur, Kevin)

PH07940 683 (June 2, 1994) p16. "Jagger And Richards Roll It Out One More Time" (Mazur, Kevin)

PH07941 686-687 (July 14, 1994) pp68-69. "And Then There Were Four: Charlie Watts, Ron Wood, Mick Jagger And Keith Richards" (Seliger, Mark)

PH07942 686-687 (July 14, 1994) p71. "Lounge Lizards: Don Was Confers With Keith Richards And Mick Jagger In The Studio" (Adebari, Eugene)

PH07943 689 (August 25, 1994) pp56-57. "Four Play In Toronto..." (Corbijn, Anton)

PH07944 689 (August 25, 1994) p61. "The Glimmer Twins, Still In The Swing Of Things: "It's Just You And Your mates," Says Richards" (Corbijn, Anton)

PH07945 689 (August 25, 1994) p55. "[Mick Jagger]" (Corbijn, Anton)

PH07946 689 (August 25, 1994) pp58-59. "[Mick Jagger & Keith Richards]" (Corbijn, Anton)

PH07947 690 (September 8, 1994) p21. "Mick Jagger, Charlie Watts And Keith Richards (from left) Get Warmed Up In Toronto" (Halsband, Michael)

PH07948 692 (October 6, 1994) p15. "[Mick Jagger]" (Mazur, Kevin)

PH07949 694 (November 3, 1994) p26. "Jagger In His Private Trailer, Columbia, Mo." (Seliger, Mark)

PH07950 694 (November 3, 1994) p26. "Putting The Squeeze Play On Watts" (Seliger, Mark)

PH07951 712-713 (July 13, 1995) p34. "Stoned In Amsterdam: Wood, Jagger, Richards And Watts (from left) Get Their Ya-Yas Out At The Paradiso" (Corbijn, Anton)

PH07952 715 (August 24, 1995) p37. "Jones, Richards, Watts, Jagger, Wyman (from left) [Watts, Richards, Jones, Jagger, Wyman (from left)]" (Mankowitz, Gered)

PH07953 717 (September 21, 1995) p19. "[Bob Dylan & Mick Jagger]" (Gassian, Claude)

PH07954 720 (November 2, 1995) p50. "Mick Jagger" (O'Neill, Terry)

PH07955 723 (December 14, 1995) p57. "Backstage At The Los Angeles Forum, 1972" (Marshall, Jim)

PH07956 723 (December 14, 1995) p52. "During Downtime On Tour, Jagger Lounging On A Hotel Bed With Watts On The Isle Of Man, 1964"

PH07957 723 (December 14, 1995) p53. "Jagger (middle) Celebrating Androgyny In The Glam-Rock '70s With Lou Reed (left) And David Bowie, Two Of The Many Who Followed In Jagger's Gender-Bending Footsteps"

PH07958 723 (December 14, 1995) p56. "Jagger (with Charlie Watts, right) Performing 'Brown Sugar' From A Flatbed Truck In New York to Publicize The Stones' 1975 Tour Of The Americas" (Laffont, Jean Pierre)

PH07959 723 (December 14, 1995) p50. "Jagger And Richards Performing With The Stones At The Tower Ballroom, Near Liverpool, 1964"

PH07960 723 (December 14, 1995) p74. "Jagger Enjoys The Sun With Daughter Elizabeth (on his lap) And Her Friend: A New Version Of 'Mother's Little Helper'" (Raban, Duncan)

PH07961 723 (December 14, 1995) p58. "Jagger Gets His Ya-Yas Out During A Spring And Summer 1976 Tour Of Europe"

PH07962 723 (December 14, 1995) p52. "Jagger Meeting Faithful Fans In The Dressing Room While Touring The United States, 1965" (Mankowitz, Gered)

PH07963 723 (December 14, 1995) p53. "Jagger Stepping Out In London With Girlfriend Marianne Faithful (sans bearskin rug), 1967" (Kelly, John)

PH07964 723 (December 14, 1995) p57. "Jagger With Wife Jerry Hall At The Palladium In New York, 1979"

PH07965 723 (December 14, 1995) p54. "[Mick Jagger]" (Marshall, Jim)

PH07966 723 (December 14, 1995) p53. "A Newly Wed Jagger Popping The Cork In A Limo With Bianca On Their Wedding Day, 1971" (Lichfield, P.)

PH07967 723 (December 14, 1995) p53. "A Pensive Moment In The Studio During The Recording Of 'Aftermath,' 1966" (Mankowitz, Gered)

PH07968 723 (December 14, 1995) p62. "Wasted Elegance: Jagger And Richards Together In The 1970s"

PH07969 724-725 (December 28, 1995) p49. "Dylan And Jagger Jammed In Montpellier, France" (Gassian, Claude)

PH07970 731 (April 4, 1996) p17. "Mick (for our cave-dwelling readers) And Brother Chris" (Allocca, Dave)

PH07971 738-739 (July 11, 1996) p15. "[Mick Jagger]" (Aslan)

PH07972 746 (October 31, 1996) p27. "Ono, Richards, Watts, Jagger And Jones (from left) With Circus Friends"

PH07973 748 (November 28, 1996) p25. "Jagger And Hall In The Proverbial Happier Times" (Allen, David)

PH07974 750-751 (December 26, 1996) p85. "Jagger And Hall" (Young, Richard)

JAGGER, MICK—PHOTOGRAPHS—PORTRAITS

PH07975 643 (November 12, 1992) p67. "England's David Bailey First Introduced Rock Stars Like Mick Jagger To The World Of High Fashion" (Bailey, David)

PH07976 643 (November 12, 1992) p190. "Mick Jagger" (Watson, Albert)

PH07977 645-646 (December 10, 1992) p157. "Mick Jagger And Keith Richards, 1989"

PH07978 645-646 (December 10, 1992) p157. "Mick Jagger And Keith Richards, 1975"

PH07979 645-646 (December 10, 1992) p157. "Mick Jagger, 1978"

PH07980 645-646 (December 10, 1992) p157. "Mick Jagger, 1983"
PH07981 680 (April 21, 1994) p22. "Jagger: Of Viper And Virgin" (Mazur, Kevin)
PH07982 723 (December 14, 1995) p52. "Jagger Hamming It Up Backstage Before Performing On 'Top Of The Pops,' In England, 1964" (Goodwin, Harry)
PH07983 723 (December 14, 1995) p52. "Jagger Looking Like A Mod On Yet Another TV Show, 'Ready Steady, Go!,' In 1965" (Redfern, David)
PH07984 723 (December 14, 1995) pp[cover]. "Jagger Remembers: The Rolling Stone Interview By Jann S. Wenner" (Lindberg, Peter)
PH07985 723 (December 14, 1995) p49. "[Mick Jagger]" (Lindberg, Peter)
PH07986 723 (December 14, 1995) p51. "Portrait Of The R&B Singer As A Young Man, 1966" (Mankowitz, Gered)
JAGLOM, HENRY—PHOTOGRAPHS
PH07987 642 (October 29, 1992) p77. "Venice-Venice"
JAH-T—PHOTOGRAPHS
PH07988 634-635 (July 9, 1992) p11. "Yes, He Is: Izzy Stradlin In A Chicago Studio With Jah-T" (Natkin, Paul)
JAJOUKA, MOROCCO—ILLUSTRATIONS
PH07989 632 (June 11, 1992) p39. "[Jajouka, Morocco]" (Cronin, Brian)
JALE—PHOTOGRAPHS
PH07990 689 (August 25, 1994) p41. "Pierce, MacLeod, Hartling, Stein (from top)" (Crump, James)
JAM—ALBUMS
PH07991 693 (October 20, 1994) p146. "Live Jam"
JAM, JIMMY—PHOTOGRAPHS
PH07992 749 (December 12, 1996) p20. "It's A Family Affair: Jam's Wife, Lisa Harris, Holding Tyler; Jam; Jackson; And Lewis (from left)"
JAMAICA—ILLUSTRATIONS
PH07993 632 (June 11, 1992) p69. "[Jamaica]" (Cronin, Brian)
JAMES—ALBUMS
PH07994 677 (March 10, 1994) p72. "Laid"
PH07995 698-699 (December 29, 1994) p190. "Wah Wah"
JAMES—PHOTOGRAPHS—PORTRAITS
PH07996 680 (April 21, 1994) p11. "[James]" (Borris, Dan)
JAMES, ALEX—PHOTOGRAPHS
PH07997 694 (November 3, 1994) p34. "Social Distortion: Blur's Coxon, Albarn, Rowntree And James (from left)" (Westenberg, Kevin)
JAMES, ALEX—PHOTOGRAPHS—PORTRAITS
PH07998 623 (February 6, 1992) p32. "Alex James, Damon Albarn, Graham Coxon, Dave Rowntree (clockwise from top)" (Lavine, Michael)
PH07999 720 (November 2, 1995) p19. "'Great Escape' Artists Coxon, Albarn, James And Rountree (from left)" (Westenberg, Kevin)
JAMES, DAVID—PHOTOGRAPHS
PH08000 700 (January 26, 1995) p24. "[Spearhead]"
JAMES, ELMORE—PHOTOGRAPHS—PORTRAITS
PH08001 623 (February 6, 1992) p52. "[Elmore James]"
JAMES, ETTA—ALBUMS
PH08002 644 (November 26, 1992) p75. "The Right Time"
JAMES, ETTA—PHOTOGRAPHS
PH08003 630 (May 14, 1992) p15. "Steve Winwood And Etta James" (Cooper, Dick)
PH08004 651 (March 4, 1993) p15. "Etta James (left) With K. D. Lang" (Mazur, Kevin)
JAMES, ETTA—PHOTOGRAPHS—PORTRAITS
PH08005 649 (February 4, 1993) p51. "[Etta James]"
PH08006 720 (November 2, 1995) p33. "Rage To Survive"
JAMES, JAMIE—PHOTOGRAPHS
PH08007 652 (March 18, 1993) p15. "Cheap Dates (from left): Phantom, Baxter, Sales, Stanton And James" (Matheu, Robert)
JAMES, RICK—ILLUSTRATIONS
PH08008 737 (June 27, 1996) p7. "Rick James" (Payne, C. F.)
PH08009 741 (August 22, 1996) p20. "Court Room" (Pendergrast, James T.)
JAMES, RICK—PHOTOGRAPHS
PH08010 619-620 (December 12, 1991) p76. "Superfreak Rick James And Tanya Anne Hijazi Face The Music" (Barr, John)
PH08011 737 (June 27, 1996) p42. "The King Of Funk Plays A TV Gig On 'Solid Gold,' 1983" (Wolfson, Ron)
PH08012 737 (June 27, 1996) p42. "Linda Blair And Rick James, 1982"
PH08013 737 (June 27, 1996) p42. "Performing In 1982" (Simon, Peter)
PH08014 737 (June 27, 1996) p39. "[Rick James]" (Winters, Dan)
PH08015 737 (June 27, 1996) p44. "Rick James At Limelight In New York, 1985" (Winters, Dan)
PH08016 737 (June 27, 1996) p42. "With David Bowie In 1983" (Butler, Geoff)
PH08017 744 (October 3, 1996) p21. "[Rick James]"
PH08018 750-751 (December 26, 1996) p73. "Rick James. We're Pulling For You, Rick!"
JAMES, RICK—PHOTOGRAPHS—PORTRAITS
PH08019 737 (June 27, 1996) p42. "Bustin' Out With Pal Eddie Murphy At New York's Paladium Nightclub For A 'Saturday Night Live' Party, 1985"
JAMES, WENDY—ALBUMS
PH08020 665 (September 16, 1993) p70. "Now Ain't The Time For Your Tears"
JAMIROQUAI—ILLUSTRATIONS
PH08020a 704 (March 23, 1995) p125. "The Return Of The Space Cowboy" (Evans, Paul)
JAMISON, LIANE—PHOTOGRAPHS—PORTRAITS
PH08021 700 (January 26, 1995) p24. "[Spearhead]"
JANE'S ADDICTION—ALBUMS
PH08022 617 (November 14, 1991) p106. "Nothing's Shocking" (Champagne, Kim)
PH08023 617 (November 14, 1991) p106. "Nothing's Shocking" (Farrell, Perry)
PH08024 625 (March 5, 1992) p61. "Nothing's Shocking"
PH08025 634-635 (July 9, 1992) p4. "Nothing's Shocking"
PH08026 637 (August 20, 1992) p4. "Nothing's Shocking"
JANE'S ADDICTION—PHOTOGRAPHS
PH08027 715 (August 24, 1995) p54. "Jane's Addiction, 1990: Farrell, Perkins, Dave Navarro And Eric Avery (from left)" (Miller, Peter Darley)
JANIE'S GOT A GUN (VIDEO)—PHOTOGRAPHS
PH08028 667 (October 14, 1993) p101. "Aerosmith: Steve Tyler Acts Out For 'Janie's'"
JANNEY, ELI—PHOTOGRAPHS
PH08029 721 (November 16, 1995) p75. "Johnny Temple, Scott McCloud, Alexis Fleisig And Eli Janney (from left) Enjoy An All-American Snack" (Exum)
JANOVITZ, BILL—PHOTOGRAPHS
PH08030 633 (June 25, 1992) p11. "Greg Humphreys, Mike Watt, Doug Macmillan, Bill Janovitz, Tom Maginnis And Mike Connell (from left) In Raleigh"
PH08031 665 (September 16, 1993) pp[enc.45]. "Above From Left: Chris Colbourn, Friend Debra Monaco, Tom Maginnis And Bill Janovitz" (Newton, Philip)
PH08032 665 (September 16, 1993) pp[enc.48,54]. "[Bill Janovitz]" (Newton, Philip)
PH08033 665 (September 16, 1993) pp[enc.44]. "[Bill Janovitz & Debra Monaco]" (Newton, Philip)
PH08034 665 (September 16, 1993) pp[enc.48]. "Bill On Tour" (Newton, Philip)
PH08035 665 (September 16, 1993) pp[enc.5]. "[Buffalo Tom]" (Newton, Philip)
PH08036 667 (October 14, 1993) p40. "Below: Merchant, Bragg,

Founder Harry Horgan, Tanya Donelly, Janovitz" (Robicheau, Paul)
PH08037 667 (October 14, 1993) p40. "Right: The Tom's Bill Janovitz" (Robicheau, Paul)
PH08038 672-673 (December 23, 1993) p65. "Tom Maginnis, Janovitz And Chris Colbourn" (Robicheau, Paul)
PH08039 704 (March 23, 1995) p25. "Buffalo Tom's Bill Janovitz, Kristin Hersh, Morphine's Mark Sandman, Gigolo Aunts' Steve Hurley (from left)" (Robicheau, Paul)
JANSEN, DAN—PHOTOGRAPHS
PH08040 624 (February 20, 1992) p35. "[Dan Jansen]" (Eccles, Andrew)
JANSSEN, DAVID—PHOTOGRAPHS
PH08041 663 (August 19, 1993) p84. "Harrison Ford (right) Puts A '90s Twist On A '60s TV Series, Starring David Janssen (left)"
JARMUSCH, JIM—PHOTOGRAPHS
PH08042 630 (May 14, 1992) p112. "Jim Jarmusch Dispatches Driver Winona Ryder"
PH08043 731 (April 4, 1996) p17. "[Neil Young & Jim Jarmusch]" (Hashimoto, Mike)
PH08044 735 (May 30, 1996) p56. "Johnny Depp (left) Draws, While Director Jim Jarmusch Dawdles"
JARMUSCH, JIM—PHOTOGRAPHS—PORTRAITS
PH08045 639 (September 17, 1992) p81. "Filmmaker"
JARS OF CLAY—PHOTOGRAPHS
PH08046 744 (October 3, 1996) p24. "Dan Haseltine (left) And Steve Mason Of Jars Of Clay" (Blakesberg, Jay)
JARVIS, KATHY—PHOTOGRAPHS
PH08047 617 (November 14, 1991) pp161,164. "[Kathy Jarvis]" (Noble, Chris)
JASMINE—PHOTOGRAPHS
PH08048 615 (October 17, 1991) p63. "Jasmine, Jean Pigozzi And Jerry Hall, 1987" (Pigozzi, Jean)
JASON—ALBUMS
PH08049 637 (August 20, 1992) p52. "One Foot In The Honky Tonk"
JASON AND THE SCORCHERS—ALBUMS
PH08050 703 (March 9, 1995) p66. "A Blazing Grace"
JASPER, CHRIS—PHOTOGRAPHS
PH08051 625 (March 5, 1992) p13. "Rockin' And Rollin' (above, from left): Little Richard, Ronald Isley, Ernie Isley, Chris Jasper, Marvin Isley" (Mazur, Kevin)
JAWBOX—PHOTOGRAPHS
PH08052 678 (March 24, 1994) p20. "Barocas, Robbins, Coletta, Barbot (from left)" (Falls, John)
JAWBREAKER—PHOTOGRAPHS
PH08053 660-661 (July 8, 1993) p100. "Jawbreaker (from left): Adam Pfahler, Chris Blake And Blake Schwarzenbach" (Lewis, Don)
JAYHAWKS—ALBUMS
PH08054 642 (October 29, 1992) p70. "Hollywood Town Hall"
PH08055 651 (March 4, 1993) p57. "Hollywood Town Hall"
PH08056 703 (March 9, 1995) p66. "Tomorrow The Green Grass"
JAYHAWKS—PHOTOGRAPHS
PH08057 644 (November 26, 1992) p27. "Louris, Callahan, Olson And Perlman (from left)" (Capak, R. J.)
PH08058 658 (June 10, 1993) p17. "The Jayhawks And Waylon Jennings At Farm Aid" (Natkin, Paul)
PH08059 697 (December 15, 1994) p31. ""We Had A Retro Tag, But This Isn't Like Our Last Album," Says Olson (center), With Perlman And Louris" (Dyer, Alison)
PH08060 709 (June 1, 1995) p16. "Jayhawk Gary Louris, Crowes Marc Ford And Robinson, Perlman (from left)" (Diamond, Rick)
JAYHAWKS—PHOTOGRAPHS—PORTRAITS
PH08061 628 (April 16, 1992) p57. "Perlman, Olson, Louris And Callahan (from left)" (Crouser, Michael)
JAZZ—ILLUSTRATIONS
PH08062 618 (November 28, 1991) p96. "Jazz Notes"
PH08063 623 (February 6, 1992) p80. "Jazz Notes"
PH08064 631 (May 28, 1992) p61. "Jazz Notes"
PH08065 642 (October 29, 1992) p75. "Jazz Notes"
PH08066 645-646 (December 10, 1992) p180. "Jazz Notes"
PH08067 653 (April 1, 1993) p53. "Jazz Notes"
PH08068 659 (June 24, 1993) p84. "Jazz Notes"
PH08069 665 (September 16, 1993) p67. "Jazz Notes"
PH08070 671 (December 9, 1993) p70. "Jazz Notes"
PH08071 672-673 (December 23, 1993) p164. "Jazz Notes"
PH08072 678 (March 24, 1994) p97. "Jazz Notes"
PH08073 692 (October 6, 1994) p89. "Jazz Notes"
PH08074 698-699 (December 29, 1994) p180. "Jazz Notes"
PH08075 708 (May 18, 1995) p87. "Jazz Fission" (King, J. D.)
PH08076 711 (June 29, 1995) p44. "Jazz Notes"
J.C. THE ETERNAL—PHOTOGRAPHS
PH08077 719 (October 19, 1995) p19. "P.M. Dawn's Prince Be (left) And J.C. The Eternal Are Redefining What It Means To Be A Black Artists" (Thomas, Katrin)
JEAN, WYCLEF—PHOTOGRAPHS
PH08078 734 (May 16, 1996) p66. "Rappin' At The House Of Blues: Fugees' Hill, Jean And Michel (from left)" (Kravitz, Jeff)
JEAN, WYCLEF—PHOTOGRAPHS—PORTRAITS
PH08079 742 (September 5, 1996) p42. "Wyclef Jean" (Rolston, Matthew)
JEAN-BAPTISTE, MARIANNE—PHOTOGRAPHS
PH08080 745 (October 17, 1996) p142. "Jean-Bapiste (left) And Blethyn Flank Mike Leigh"
JEE, RUPERT—PHOTOGRAPHS
PH08081 735 (May 30, 1996) p32. "For The 'Video Special,' Dave Relayed Obnoxious Instructions To Rupert Jee (top), Co-Owner Of The Hello Deli"
JEFFERIES, PETER—ALBUMS
PH08082 693 (October 20, 1994) p168. "Electricity"
JEFFERSON AIRPLANE—PHOTOGRAPHS
PH08083 728 (February 22, 1996) p19. "The Airplane's Paul Kantner (left) And Jorma Kaukonen" (Mazur, Kevin)
JEFFERSON AIRPLANE—PHOTOGRAPHS—PORTRAITS
PH08084 643 (November 12, 1992) p70. "Herb Greene Shot Jefferson Airplane's 'Surrealistic Pillow' Cover In His Apartment" (Greene, Herb)
JEFFERSON IN PARIS (FILM)—PHOTOGRAPHS
PH08085 706 (April 20, 1995) p89. "Nolte's Jefferson Toys With Slave Thandie Newton"
JEFFREY (FILM)—PHOTOGRAPHS
PH08086 709 (June 1, 1995) p70. "Rebel Voices"
PH08087 715 (August 24, 1995) p110. "Friends United: Batt, Stewart, Weber And Weiss"
JEFFREYS, GARLAND—ALBUMS
PH08088 628 (April 16, 1992) p80. "Don't Call Me Buckwheat"
PH08089 645-646 (December 10, 1992) p178. "Don't Call Me Buckwheat"
JENCO, SAL—PHOTOGRAPHS
PH08090 709 (June 1, 1995) p16. "[P]" (Smith, Kelly)
JENIFER, DARRYL—PHOTOGRAPHS
PH08091 711 (June 29, 1995) p15. "Cosmic Agit Pop And Measured Fury: Dr. Know, H.R., Darryl Jenifer And Earl Hudson of Bad Brains (from left)" (Cuffaro, Chris)
JENNIFER 8 (FILM)—PHOTOGRAPHS
PH08092 652 (March 18, 1993) pp[enc.4]. "[Jennifer 8]"
JENNINGS, PETER—PHOTOGRAPHS
PH08093 715 (August 24, 1995) p25. "Jennings, Son Christopher And Pal Kevin (from right)" (Eichner, Steve)
JENNINGS, WAYLON—PHOTOGRAPHS
PH08094 658 (June 10, 1993) p17. "The Jayhawks And Waylon Jennings At Farm Aid" (Natkin, Paul)
PH08095 731 (April 4, 1996) p18. "Jennings (center) With Suckers, Dan Siegel, Dan Bolton, Ron Heathman And Singer Eddie Spaghetti (from left)" (Diamond, Rick)
JENNINGS, WAYLON—PHOTOGRAPHS—PORTRAITS
PH08096 750-751 (December 26, 1996) p196. "Books"

JENSEN, HOWARD—PHOTOGRAPHS
PH08097 665 (September 16, 1993) pp[enc.12]. "The Jensen Brothers At Home In Ludington, Mich., With Their Father, Howard Jensen" (Borris, Dan)
JENSEN, LUKE—PHOTOGRAPHS
PH08097 665 (September 16, 1993) pp[enc.12]. "The Jensen Brothers At Home In Ludington, Mich., With Their Father, Howard Jensen" (Borris, Dan)
PH08098 665 (September 16, 1993) pp[enc.9]. "Luke And Murphy Jensen Shooting Pool At Le Swimming In Montreal" (Borris, Dan)
PH08099 665 (September 16, 1993) pp[enc.10]. "Luke And Murphy At The French Open" (Borris, Dan)
PH08100 665 (September 16, 1993) pp[enc.11-12]. "[Luke And Murphy Jensen]" (Borris, Dan)
PH08101 665 (September 16, 1993) pp[enc.10]. "[Luke Jensen]" (Borris, Dan)
PH08102 665 (September 16, 1993) pp[enc.13]. "[Luke Jensen, Murphy Jensen, Rachel Jensen, Rebecca Jensen]" (Borris, Dan)
PH08103 665 (September 16, 1993) pp[enc.12]. "Luke With Sister Rebecca" (Borris, Dan)
JENSEN, MURPHY—PHOTOGRAPHS
PH08104 665 (September 16, 1993) pp[enc.12]. "The Jensen Brothers At Home In Ludington, Mich., With Their Father, Howard Jensen" (Borris, Dan)
PH08105 665 (September 16, 1993) pp[enc.9]. "Luke And Murphy Jensen Shooting Pool At Le Swimming In Montreal" (Borris, Dan)
PH08106 665 (September 16, 1993) pp[enc.10]. "Luke And Murphy At The French Open" (Borris, Dan)
PH08107 665 (September 16, 1993) pp[enc.11-12]. "[Luke And Murphy Jensen]" (Borris, Dan)
PH08108 665 (September 16, 1993) pp[enc.13]. "[Luke Jensen, Murphy Jensen, Rachel Jensen, Rebecca Jensen]" (Borris, Dan)
PH08109 665 (September 16, 1993) pp[enc.12]. "[Murphy Jensen]" (Borris, Dan)
JENSEN, RACHEL—PHOTOGRAPHS
PH08110 665 (September 16, 1993) pp[enc.13]. "[Luke Jensen, Murphy Jensen, Rachel Jensen, Rebecca Jensen]" (Borris, Dan)
JENSEN, REBECCA—PHOTOGRAPHS
PH08110 665 (September 16, 1993) pp[enc.13]. "[Luke Jensen, Murphy Jensen, Rachel Jensen, Rebecca Jensen]" (Borris, Dan)
PH08111 665 (September 16, 1993) pp[enc.12]. "Luke With Sister Rebecca" (Borris, Dan)
JENSON, SASHA—PHOTOGRAPHS
PH08112 667 (October 14, 1993) p128. "School Daze For Cochrane, London And Jenson"
PH08113 741 (August 22, 1996) p48. "McConaughey Onscreen"
JEREMY (VIDEO)—PHOTOGRAPHS
PH08114 667 (October 14, 1993) p82. "'Jeremy': Pearl Jam's Video Of One Boy's Despair"
JEREMY, RON—PHOTOGRAPHS
PH08115 693 (October 20, 1994) p79. "A Friend In Deed: Jeremy (left) And Axl Rose At Ciro's" (Jeremy, Ron)
PH08116 693 (October 20, 1994) p74. "Ron Jeremy At Home"
JERRY MAGUIRE (FILM)—PHOTOGRAPHS
PH08117 750-751 (December 26, 1996) p138. "Cruise Makes A Point"
PH08118 750-751 (December 26, 1996) p141. "Zellweger Won The Hardest Part To Cast"
JERU THE DAMAJA—PHOTOGRAPHS
PH08119 681 (May 5, 1994) p18. "He's The Man: Jeru The Damaja"
JESPERSON, PETER—PHOTOGRAPHS
PH08120 677 (March 10, 1994) p57. "Left: Twin Tone's McLean And Jesperson" (Smale, Brian)
JESSEE, DARREN—PHOTOGRAPHS
PH08121 721 (November 16, 1995) p73. "Power Trio With A Twist: Darren Jessee, Ben Folds And Robert Sledge (from left) Make Absurdity Swing Like Mad" (Guip, Amy)
PH08122 749 (December 12, 1996) p20. "BFF's Robert Sledge, Darren Jessee; Klezmatics Frank London, Alicia Svigals; And Folds" (Mazur, Kevin)
JESUS AND MARY CHAIN—ALBUMS
PH08123 630 (May 14, 1992) p107. "Honey's Dead"
PH08124 633 (June 25, 1992) p56. "Honey's Dead"
PH08125 697 (December 15, 1994) p94. "Stoned And De-throned"
JESUS AND MARY CHAIN—PHOTOGRAPHS
PH08126 697 (December 15, 1994) p38. "Happy When It Rains: The Jesus And Mary Chain" (O'Leary, Bill)
PH08127 720 (November 2, 1995) p25. "JAMC's Jim (left) And William Reid Vent"
JESUS CHRIST SUPERSTAR (STAGE MUSICAL)—PHOTOGRAPHS
PH08128 683 (June 2, 1994) p28. "Extreme's Gary Cherone, Rock Star, In The Title Role Of "Jesus Christ Superstar"" (Robicheau, Paul)
JESUS JONES—ALBUMS
PH08129 619-620 (December 12, 1991) p182. "Doubt"
PH08129a 650 (February 18, 1993) p60. "Perverse"
JESUS JONES—PHOTOGRAPHS
PH08130 619-620 (December 12, 1991) p22. "[Jesus Jones]" (St. Nicholas, Randee)
PH08131 Number not assigned.
JESUS LIZARD—ALBUMS
PH08132 697 (December 15, 1994) p97. "Down"
PH08133 733 (May 2, 1996) p52. "Shot"
JESUS LIZARD—ILLUSTRATIONS
PH08134 717 (September 21, 1995) p16. "Hiss" (Pendergrast, James T.)
JESUS LIZARD—PHOTOGRAPHS
PH08135 653 (April 1, 1993) p20. "The Jesus Lizard (clockwise from top left): McNeilly, Yow, Denison And Sims" (Ewolf)
PH08136 714 (August 10, 1995) p48. "David Sims, Mac McNeilly, David Yow, Duane Denison, From Left" (Seliger, Mark)
PH08137 714 (August 10, 1995) p51. "The Ones To Watch At LollaPalooza: Denison, Yow And Sims (from left)" (Perez, Marty)
PH08138 716 (September 7, 1995) p13. "[David Yow]" (Oh, Viviane)
PH08139 736 (June 13, 1996) p20. "Jockey Lavern Hostetler Has A Lot To Discuss With Jesus Lizard Members David Sims, David Yow, Mac McNeilly And Duane Denison (from left)" (Gilson, Matthew)
JESUS LIZARD—SINGLES
PH08140 653 (April 1, 1993) p20. "Puss (song)"
JETT, JOAN—ALBUMS
PH08141 615 (October 17, 1991) p93. "Notorious"
JETT, JOAN—PHOTOGRAPHS
PH08142 616 (October 31, 1991) p11. "Westerberg And Jett" (Busacca, Larry)
PH08143 644 (November 26, 1992) p15. "Dee Plakas, Jennifer Finch, Jett, Donita Sparks And Suzi Gardner (clockwise from left)" (Lewis, Don)
PH08144 652 (March 18, 1993) p23. "Jett Joins Two Ramones At New York Gig" (Mazur, Kevin)
PH08145 675 (February 10, 1994) p14. "Joan Jett At Birthday Gig" (Roberts, Ebet)
PH08146 678 (March 24, 1994) p44. "[Joan Jett]" (Lavine, Michael)
PH08147 689 (August 25, 1994) p46. "Rocking Harder Than A Wee Runaway: Jett" (Mazur, Kevin)
PH08148 690 (September 8, 1994) p21. "Jett (left) With Bikini Kill's Hanna" (Capak, R. J.)
PH08149 740 (August 8, 1996) p17. "Smear With, Yes, Joan Jett" (Liu, Brian)
JETT, JOAN—PHOTOGRAPHS—PORTRAITS
PH08150 692 (October 6, 1994) p49. "Joan Jett" (Lavine, Michael)

PH08151 692 (October 6, 1994) p53. "Joan Jett"
PH08152 696 (December 1, 1994) p25. "[Joan Jett & Dave Gahan]" (Williamson, Tucker)
PH08153 705 (April 6, 1995) p25. "Jett Does Porter With Westerberg"
PH08154 736 (June 13, 1996) p78. "Who Can Turn The World On With Her Smile? Joan Jett"
JEWEL—PHOTOGRAPHS
PH08155 736 (June 13, 1996) pp22-23. "[Jewel]" (Southam, Andrew)
JFK (FILM)—ILLUSTRATIONS
PH08156 622 (January 23, 1992) p48. "Oh, What A Tangled Web" (Tarlofsky, Malcolm)
JIAN, CUI—PHOTOGRAPHS
PH08157 720 (November 2, 1995) p28. "Up Against The Great Wall: Liu (left) And Cui" (Pulin, Chuck)
JILLETTE, PENN—PHOTOGRAPHS
PH08158 665 (September 16, 1993) p32. "Gano, Lou Reed And Penn Jillette" (Capak, R. J.)
JIMBO—PHOTOGRAPHS
PH08159 685 (June 30, 1994) p41. "Heat's band Mates Taz And Jimbo; Jourgensen And Heat" (Bland, James)
JIMBO—PHOTOGRAPHS—PORTRAITS
PH08160 692 (October 6, 1994) p28. "Country-Fried Rock: Taz, Jimbo And The Sultan Of Psychobilly, The Rev. Horton Heat" (Seliger, Mark)
JIMI HENDRIX: ELECTRIC GYPSY (BOOK)—PHOTOGRAPHS
PH08161 615 (October 17, 1991) p105. "From Electric Ladyland To The Tour Of La-La Land"
JIMI HENDRIX EXPERIENCE—PHOTOGRAPHS—PORTRAITS
PH08162 623 (February 6, 1992) p45. "Hendrix Found His Perfect Musical Accomplices In Noel Redding (left) And Mitch Mitchell (right)" (Mankowitz, Gered)
JIMMY HOLLYWOOD (FILM)—PHOTOGRAPHS
PH08163 680 (April 21, 1994) p95. "Christian Slater And Joe Pesci Go Hollywood"
JIMMY JAM—PHOTOGRAPHS
PH08164 715 (August 24, 1995) p62. "With Janet Jackson And Her Producer Jimmy Jam, '90"
JOANNOU, CHRIS—PHOTOGRAPHS
PH08165 715 (August 24, 1995) p31. "Chris Joannou, Ben Gillies And Daniel Johns (from left): Could You Just Say We're 18?" (Clinch, Danny)
PH08166 726 (January 25, 1996) p38. "Silverchair: Young, Hard-Rocking Aussies Chris Joannou, Daniel Johns And Ben Gillies (from left)" (Anderson, David)
PH08167 728 (February 22, 1996) p46. "Gut Feeling: Johns, Joannou And Gillies, From Left, In A Sophisticated Pose (left)" (Seliger, Mark)
PH08168 728 (February 22, 1996) p47. "Johns, Joannou And Gillies (from left) Goof Around—As Usual" (Seliger, Mark)
JOANNOU, CHRIS—PHOTOGRAPHS—PORTRAITS
PH08169 728 (February 22, 1996) p45. "Silverchair's Daniel Johns, Ben Gillies And Chris Joannou (from left) Turn On The Charm" (Seliger, Mark)
JOBIM, ANTONIO CARLOS—PHOTOGRAPHS—PORTRAITS
PH08170 700 (January 26, 1995) p24. "[Antonio Carlos Jobim]"
JOBS, STEVE—PHOTOGRAPHS
PH08171 684 (June 16, 1994) p78. "Jobs At A MacIntosh meeting In Late 1982, Just Over A Year before The Mac's Release" (Walker, Diana)
PH08172 684 (June 16, 1994) p75. "A MacIntosh In 1984" (Walker, Diana)
PH08173 684 (June 16, 1994) p75. "A Next In 1988" (Walker, Diana)
PH08174 684 (June 16, 1994) p75. "Steve Jobs Posing With An Apple II In 1979" (Morse, Ralph)
PH08175 731 (April 4, 1996) pp54-55. "Jobs And Sculley In '84" (Kashi, Ed)
PH08176 731 (April 4, 1996) p54. "Jobs Kicking Back In '81" (Korody, T.)
PH08177 731 (April 4, 1996) p54. "Jobs Leads A Meeting In '88" (Kirkland, Douglas)
PH08178 731 (April 4, 1996) p54. "Jobs, Sculley And Wozniak (from left) Unveil The Apple IIC In '84"
PH08179 731 (April 4, 1996) p55. "Woz (left), Jobs And Some Serious Circuitry In '76"
PH08180 731 (April 4, 1996) p53. "Young, Smart And Rich: By The Time He Was 25, Steve Jobs Would Be Worth $165 Million" (Seeff, Norman)
JOBS, STEVE—PHOTOGRAPHS—PORTRAITS
PH08181 684 (June 16, 1994) p73. "[Steve Jobs]" (Duke, William)
JODECI—ALBUMS
PH08182 719 (October 19, 1995) p152. "The Show, The After-Party, The Hotel"
JOEL, BILLY—ALBUMS
PH08183 663 (August 19, 1993) p74. "River Of Dreams"
PH08184 666 (September 30, 1993) p128. "River Of Dreams"
PH08185 667 (October 14, 1993) p136. "River Of Dreams"
PH08186 672-673 (December 23, 1993) p156. "River Of Dreams"
JOEL, BILLY—ILLUSTRATIONS
PH08187 672-673 (December 23, 1993) p23. "[Billy Joel]" (Cowles, David)
JOEL, BILLY—ILLUSTRATIONS—PORTRAITS
PH08188 641 (October 15, 1992) p101. "[Billy Joel]" (Kunz, Anita)
JOEL, BILLY—PHOTOGRAPHS
PH08189 615 (October 17, 1991) p66. "Christie Brinkley And Billy Joel, Long Island, 1989" (Pigozzi, Jean)
PH08190 619-620 (December 12, 1991) p42. "Billy Joel, Gentleman Scholar" (Corkery, R.)
PH08191 619-620 (December 12, 1991) p90. "Henley, Sting, Joel, Raitt" (Kaplan, Todd)
PH08192 619-620 (December 12, 1991) p68. "Joel, Don Henley, Mick Jones" (Mazur, Kevin)
PH08193 625 (March 5, 1992) p13. "Billy Joel (left) With Sam Moore" (Elgar, Nick)
PH08194 634-635 (July 9, 1992) p11. "Paul Simon (left) And Billy Joel" (Busacca, Larry)
PH08195 642 (October 29, 1992) p21. "Joel Adds The Bass To A Fishing Protest" (Brinkley, Christie)
PH08196 645-646 (December 10, 1992) p85. "Billy Joel" (Mazur, Kevin)
PH08197 645-646 (December 10, 1992) p54. "Billy Joel (left) And Paul Simon" (Busacca, Larry)
PH08198 647 (January 7, 1993) p11. "Don Henley (left) With Billy Joel" (Elgar, Nick)
PH08199 657 (May 27, 1993) p11. "Artist Peter Max (left) And Billy Joel" (Mazur, Kevin)
PH08200 658 (June 10, 1993) p32. "[Billy Joel]" (White, Timothy)
PH08201 662 (August 5, 1993) p33. "Billy Joel And Ray Charles In New York City" (Mazur, Kevin)
PH08202 662 (August 5, 1993) p18. "Diggin' In The Dirt: The Celebrity Crew Does The Honors" (Mazur, Kevin)
PH08203 662 (August 5, 1993) p18. "One Big Happy Family: Pirner, Berry, Townshend, Joel (from left)" (Mazur, Kevin)
PH08204 666 (September 30, 1993) p17. "The Singer Is Accused Of Song Plagiarism" (Busacca, Larry)
PH08205 672-673 (December 23, 1993) p57. "Billy Joel: Exploring Middle Age" (Busacca, Larry)
PH08206 672-673 (December 23, 1993) p39. "Diggin' In The Dirt: Soul Asylum's Dave Pirner, Chuck Berry, Townshend, Billy Joel" (Mazur, Kevin)
PH08207 683 (June 2, 1994) p17. "Double Indemnity: Cash Cows Elton John (top) And Billy Joel Split The Bill To Up The Ante" (Mazur, Kevin)

PH08208 689 (August 25, 1994) p15. "Piano Men Joel And John" (Capak, R. J.)
PH08209 690 (September 8, 1994) p42. "Don't Shoot: Pianomen John (left) And Joel" (Mazur, Kevin)
PH08210 698-699 (December 29, 1994) p61. "Get This Man A Stool: Joel (left) And John" (Mazur, Kevin)
PH08211 709 (June 1, 1995) p16. "Joel, John And Jon Bon Jovi At Carnegie Hall (from left)" (Mazur, Kevin)

JOEL, BILLY—PHOTOGRAPHS—PORTRAITS
PH08212 643 (November 12, 1992) p123. "Billy Joel" (Seliger, Mark)

JOE'S APARTMENT (FILM)—PHOTOGRAPHS
PH08213 741 (August 22, 1996) p105. "Now Playing"

JOHANSSON, GLENN—PHOTOGRAPHS
PH08214 720 (November 2, 1995) p22. "On: Echobelly's Harris, Smith, Johansson, Madan And Henderson (from left)" (Claiborne, Barron)

JOHN AND MARY—ALBUMS
PH08215 656 (May 13, 1993) p104. "The Weedkiller's Daughter"

JOHN, DARLYNN—PHOTOGRAPHS
PH08216 728 (February 22, 1996) p19. "Stevie Wonder With Darlynn And Keith John, The Son Of The Late Soul Singer Little Willie John" (Mazur, Kevin)

JOHN, ELTON—ALBUMS
PH08217 638 (September 3, 1992) p67. "The One"
PH08218 671 (December 9, 1993) p66. "Duets"
PH08219 707 (May 4, 1995) p65. "Made In England"

JOHN, ELTON—ILLUSTRATIONS
PH08220 626 (March 19, 1992) p3. "Elton John" (Burke, Philip)
PH08221 709 (June 1, 1995) p80. "Elton John: Hitsville, U.K." (Bartholomew, Beth)

JOHN, ELTON—PHOTOGRAPHS
PH08222 617 (November 14, 1991) p13. "John (left) And Michael" (Mazur, Kevin)
PH08223 618 (November 28, 1991) p12. "Bernie Taupin (left) And Elton John" (Mazur, Kevin)
PH08224 619-620 (December 12, 1991) p37. "Rod Stewart (right) And His John" (Adebari, Eugene)
PH08225 626 (March 19, 1992) pp43-44. "[Elton John]" (Ritts, Herb)
PH08226 629 (April 30, 1992) p18. "AIDS Victim Ryan White With Elton John" (Slocomb, Jeff)
PH08227 629 (April 30, 1992) p11. "Dress Rehearsal For The Rain-Forest Benefit: Sting, John, Goldberg, Cole, Henley And Taylor (from left)" (Regan, Ken)
PH08228 629 (April 30, 1992) p12. "Elton At The Opry" (Mazur, Kevin)
PH08229 633 (June 25, 1992) p17. "An Emotional High Point: Elton And Axl At The End Of 'Bohemian Rhapsody'" (Mazur, Kevin)
PH08230 642 (October 29, 1992) p19. "Elton John (left) And Axl Rose" (Mazur, Kevin)
PH08231 644 (November 26, 1992) p22. "Goldberg, Richie, Taylor, John, Michael And Hornsby (from left) At The Garden" (Mazur, Kevin)
PH08232 645-646 (December 10, 1992) p45. "John And Rose (below)" (Mazur, Kevin)
PH08233 645-646 (December 10, 1992) p96. "Taylor, Young And Elton John" (Blakesberg, Jay)
PH08234 655 (April 29, 1993) p11. "Elton John" (Mazur, Kevin)
PH08235 656 (May 13, 1993) p15. "Mike Myers (left) And Elton John" (Mazur, Kevin)
PH08236 658 (June 10, 1993) p16. "Gloria Estefan, Smokey Robinson, Franklin, John (from left)" (Mazur, Kevin)
PH08237 664 (September 2, 1993) p24. "Elton John With Lippert" (Mazur, Kevin)
PH08238 669 (November 11, 1993) p28. "[Elton John]" (Granitz, Steve)
PH08239 677 (March 10, 1994) pp28-29. "John Salutes Longtime Colaborator Bernie Taupin" (Mazur, Kevin)
PH08240 682 (May 19, 1994) p37. "John And Houston At The Rain-Forest Benefit" (Mazur, Kevin)
PH08241 682 (May 19, 1994) p37. "No Rap, No Hard Stuff: Taylor, Houston, Wynette, John, Sting (from left) At Rehearsal" (Mazur, Kevin)
PH08242 683 (June 2, 1994) p17. "Double Indemnity: Cash Cows Elton John (top) And Billy Joel Split The Bill To Up The Ante" (Mazur, Kevin)
PH08243 686-687 (July 14, 1994) p91. "Elton John Makes Music For Simba (top), The Animated Lion King Of The Disney Jungle"
PH08244 689 (August 25, 1994) p15. "Piano Men Joel And John" (Capak, R. J.)
PH08245 690 (September 8, 1994) p42. "Don't Shoot: Pianomen John (left) And Joel" (Mazur, Kevin)
PH08246 698-699 (December 29, 1994) p61. "Get This Man A Stool: Joel (left) And John" (Mazur, Kevin)
PH08247 703 (March 9, 1995) p20. "Sting And Man Of The Hour Elton John" (Mazur, Kevin)
PH08248 709 (June 1, 1995) p16. "Joel, John And Jon Bon Jovi At Carnegie Hall (from left)" (Mazur, Kevin)
PH08249 720 (November 2, 1995) p50. "Elton John" (Wentzell, Barry)
PH08250 721 (November 16, 1995) p26. "[Elton John & Andre Agassi]" (Jacobs, Michael)
PH08251 724-725 (December 28, 1995) p39. "Behind Closed Doors: Sting And John" (Mazur, Kevin)
PH08252 730 (March 21, 1996) p17. "[Elton John & Pete Sampras]" (Diamond, Rick)
PH08253 735 (May 30, 1996) p12. "Williams Gives A Big 'Nanu, Nanu' To Pal Elton John" (Mazur, Kevin)
PH08254 740 (August 8, 1996) p18. "John Happily Displays Some Tasteful, Understated Merchandise" (Diamond, Rick)
PH08255 750-751 (December 26, 1996) p57. "The Rainforest All-Star Supremes Tribute" (Mazur, Kevin)

JOHN, ELTON—PHOTOGRAPHS—PORTRAITS
PH08256 643 (November 12, 1992) p164. "Elton John" (Ritts, Herb)
PH08257 676 (February 24, 1994) p48. "Elton John, Still Standing At The Top Of The Charts" (Leibovitz, Annie)
PH08258 681 (May 5, 1994) p22. "Neil Young (left) And Elton John Go Hollywood At Elton's Oscar Party" (Mazur, Kevin)
PH08259 697 (December 15, 1994) p18. "[Elton John & Sting]" (Fisher, David)

JOHN, KEITH—PHOTOGRAPHS
PH08260 728 (February 22, 1996) p19. "Stevie Wonder With Darlynn And Keith John, The Son Of The Late Soul Singer Little Willie John" (Mazur, Kevin)

JOHNNY MNEMONIC (FILM)—PHOTOGRAPHS
PH08261 709 (June 1, 1995) p68. "Potential Trouble Spots"
PH08262 711 (June 29, 1995) p49. "Reeves in Something Fishy"

JOHNNY SUEDE (FILM)—PHOTOGRAPHS
PH08263 638 (September 3, 1992) p72. "Brad Pitt Worships At The Altar Of Idol Ricky Nelson"

JOHNS, DANIEL—ILLUSTRATIONS
PH08264 728 (February 22, 1996) p9. "Silverchair's Daniel Johns" (Hungry Dog Studio)

JOHNS, DANIEL—PHOTOGRAPHS
PH08265 705 (April 6, 1995) p23. "The Hardcore Roar Of Silverchair (Daniel Johns, left) And Spiderbait" (Mott, Tony)
PH08266 715 (August 24, 1995) p31. "Chris Joannou, Ben Gillies And Daniel Johns (from left): Could You Just Say We're 18?" (Clinch, Danny)
PH08267 720 (November 2, 1995) p16. "It's My Blood! It's My Blood! Silverchair's Daniel Johns In A Rock & Roll Rite Of Passage" (Dunne, John)
PH08268 726 (January 25, 1996) p38. "Silverchair: Young, Hard-Rocking Aussies Chris Joannou, Daniel Johns And Ben Gillies (from left)" (Anderson, David)

PH08269 728 (February 22, 1996) p46. "Gut Feeling: Johns, Joannou And Gillies, From Left, In A Sophisticated Pose (left)" (Seliger, Mark)
PH08270 728 (February 22, 1996) p46. "Johns Rocks Out In New York City (below)" (Seliger, Mark)
PH08271 728 (February 22, 1996) p47. "Johns, Joannou And Gillies (from left) Goof Around—As Usual" (Seliger, Mark)
JOHNS, DANIEL—PHOTOGRAPHS—PORTRAITS
PH08272 728 (February 22, 1996) p45. "Silverchair's Daniel Johns, Ben Gillies And Chris Joannou (from left) Turn On The Charm" (Seliger, Mark)
PH08273 684 Number not assigned.
JOHNSON, ARIYAN—PHOTOGRAPHS
PH08274 650 (February 18, 1993) p66. "Ariyan Johnson Makes A Dazzling Debut"
JOHNSON, ARTHUR—PHOTOGRAPHS
PH08275 654 (April 15, 1993) p22. "They've Arrived: Arthur Johnson, Sean O'Brien, Thalia Zedek And Chris Brokaw" (Westenberg, Kevin)
PH08276 660-661 (July 8, 1993) p100. "Come (from left): Arthur Johnson, Sean O'Brien, Chris Brokaw And Thalia Zedek" (Apicella-Hitchcock, Stephen)
JOHNSON, BETSEY—PHOTOGRAPHS—PORTRAITS
PH08277 678 (March 24, 1994) p50. "Betsey Johnson" (Ford, Larry)
JOHNSON, BIG JACK—ILLUSTRATIONS—PORTRAITS
PH08278 679 (April 7, 1994) p74. "Big Jack Johnson" (Fish, Jim)
JOHNSON, BRIAN—PHOTOGRAPHS
PH08279 743 (September 19, 1996) p20. "Johnson, With Stern And Angus Young (from left), Calls Stern 'A Good Kid. And His Fans Are A Rowdy Bunch Of Buggers'"
JOHNSON, CRAIG—PHOTOGRAPHS
PH08280 633 (June 25, 1992) p11. "Golden Smog (from left): Gary Louris, Chris Mars, Dan Murphy, Craig Johnson And Marc Perlman" (Butler, Bonnie Lynn)
JOHNSON, DON—PHOTOGRAPHS
PH08281 702 (February 23, 1995) p50. "Johnson, Tyler, Springsteen And Patti Scialfa Schmooze" (Mazur, Kevin)
JOHNSON, ERIC—PHOTOGRAPHS
PH08281a 684 (June 16, 1994) p52. "Cameron, Thayil, Yamamoto, Cornell, Silver, Tour Manager Eric Johnson (from left) In 1988" (Peterson, Charles)
JOHNSON, JOHNNIE—PHOTOGRAPHS
PH08282 668 (October 28, 1993) p30. "Greg Martin, Johnnie Johnson And Richard Young (from left)" (Natkin, Paul)
JOHNSON, KENNEY DALE—PHOTOGRAPHS
PH08283 668 (October 28, 1993) p35. "Drummer Kenney Dale Johnson With Isaak" (Plummer, Sue)
JOHNSON, KRAIG—PHOTOGRAPHS
PH08284 735 (May 30, 1996) p50. "Golden Smog's Murphy And Kraig Johnson (from left)" (Capak, R. J.)
JOHNSON, MAGIC—PHOTOGRAPHS
PH08285 684 (June 16, 1994) p35. "Magic Johnson, Springsteen, James Brown" (Kravitz, Jeff)
JOHNSON, MICHAEL—PHOTOGRAPHS
PH08286 633 (June 25, 1992) pp35,37. "[Michael Johnson]" (Ford, Charles)
JOHNSON, MIKE—PHOTOGRAPHS
PH08287 656 (May 13, 1993) p17. "Don't Call Us Slackers: Mike Johnson, Murph And J Mascis" (Ockenfels, Frank, 3)
JOHNSON, NICHOLAS—PHOTOGRAPHS—PORTRAITS
PH08288 645-646 (December 10, 1992) p156. "Nicholas Johnson, 1971"
JOHNSON, SCOTT—PHOTOGRAPHS
PH08289 722 (November 30, 1995) p20. "Gin Blossom's Scott Johnson, Dead Hot's Brian Griffith, Blossom Valenzuela And Dead Hot Curtis Grippe (from left)"
PH08290 726 (January 25, 1996) p30. "Gin Blossoms: Robin Wilson, Phillip Rhodes, Bill Lien, Jesse Valenzuela, Scott Johnson (from left)" (Jennings, Steve)
JOHNSON, STEPHEN—PHOTOGRAPHS
PH08291 667 (October 14, 1993) p67. "Personal Trainer: Johnson Outfits Gabriel"
JOHNSON, VINCE—PHOTOGRAPHS
PH08292 628 (April 16, 1992) p56. "Gray, Garside, Johnson And Adams (from left)" (Double, Steve)
JOHNSTON, DANIEL—ALBUMS
PH08293 624 (February 20, 1992) p41. "Artistic Vice"
JOHNSTON, DANIEL—PHOTOGRAPHS
PH08294 694 (November 3, 1994) p33. "Genius Or Geek? Daniel Johnston (above) And His Artwork (right)" (Beauvais, Yves)
JOHNSTON, FREEDY—ALBUMS
PH08295 686-687 (July 14, 1994) p102. "This Perfect World"
JOHNSTON, FREEDY—ILLUSTRATIONS
PH08296 690 (September 8, 1994) p9. "Freedy Johnston" (Burke, Philip)
JOHNSTON, FREEDY—PHOTOGRAPHS
PH08297 690 (September 8, 1994) p29. ""I Don't Expect To Be A Star," Says Johnston. "But Making A Good Record Never Hurts You."" (Apicella-Hitchcock, Stephen)
PH08298 701 (February 9, 1995) p16. "Louise Post, Johnston, Nina Gordon And Pete Droge do D.C." (Harrington, John)
PH08299 716 (September 7, 1995) p14. "[Jill Sobule & Freedy Johnston]" (Spellan, Jim)
JOHNSTON, FREEDY—PHOTOGRAPHS—PORTRAITS
PH08300 690 (September 8, 1994) p27. "[Freedy Johnston]" (Borris, Dan)
JOHNSTON, JAMES—PHOTOGRAPHS
PH08301 692 (October 6, 1994) p16. "At Philly's Lollapalooza: L7's Donita Sparks (left), Dee Plakas, Suzi Gardner And Jennifer Finch With Bad Seeds Mick Harvey, James Johnston And Nick Cave" (Weiner, Scott)
JOHNSTON, LLOYD—PHOTOGRAPHS
PH08302 719 (October 19, 1995) p102. "Dr. Lloyd Johnston Blames Increased Drug Use On The Lack Of Bad Examples" (Ravid, Joyce)
JOHNSTON, MAX—PHOTOGRAPHS
PH08303 707 (May 4, 1995) p32. "The Buddy System: Johnston, Coomer, Stirratt, Tweedy And Bennett (from left)" (Miller, Brad)
JOHNSTON, NICK—PHOTOGRAPHS
PH08304 722 (November 30, 1995) p20. "Hello, Darkness! Andy Bell, Johnston And Clarke (from left)" (Mazur, Kevin)
JOI—ALBUMS
PH08305 700 (January 26, 1995) p62. "The Pendulum Vibe"
JONAS—PHOTOGRAPHS
PH08306 730 (March 21, 1996) p52. "Jonas Fills Clubs With The Girl Next Dorm" (Lego)
JONES, BOOKER T.—PHOTOGRAPHS
PH08307 625 (March 5, 1992) p13. "Lewis Steinberg, Steve Cropper, Booker T. Jones, Marion Jackson, Randall Jackson, Duck Dunn, Jim Stewart (from left)" (Elgar, Nick)
PH08308 634-635 (July 9, 1992) p11. "Booker T. In The Studio With Producer Michael Beinhorn And Dave Pirner (from left)" (Soica, Alex)
JONES, BOOKER T.—PHOTOGRAPHS—PORTRAITS
PH08309 623 (February 6, 1992) p50. "Booker T. And The MGs (from left): Donald 'Duck' Dunn, Booker T., Steve Cropper And Al Jackson Jr."
PH08310 643 (November 12, 1992) p141. "Booker T. & Steve Cropper" (Seliger, Mark)
PH08311 685 (June 30, 1994) p41. "Booker T. Jones, Steve Cropper, Dave Edmunds And Donald "Duck" Dunn (from left)" (Cohen, Lester)
JONES, BRIAN—PHOTOGRAPHS
PH08312 715 (August 24, 1995) p37. "Jones, Richards, Watts, Jagger, Wyman (from left) [Watts, Richards, Jones, Jagger, Wyman (from left)]" (Mankowitz, Gered)
PH08313 746 (October 31, 1996) p27. "Ono, Richards, Watts, Jagger And Jones (from left) With Circus Friends"

JONES, DUNCAN—PHOTOGRAPHS
PH08314 712-713 (July 13, 1995) p25. "With Honors" (Dilyard, Matt)
JONES, GEORGE—PHOTOGRAPHS
PH08315 647 (January 7, 1993) p24. "George Jones" (Mazur, Kevin)
PH08316 681 (May 5, 1994) p18. "Nashville Cats: Jones And Richards"
PH08317 748 (November 28, 1996) p45. "[George Jones]" (Seliger, Mark)
JONES, GEORGE—PHOTOGRAPHS—PORTRAITS
PH08318 750-751 (December 26, 1996) p177. "George Jones" (Seliger, Mark)
JONES, GRACE—ALBUMS
PH08319 617 (November 14, 1991) p119. "Slave To The Rhythm" (Goude, Jean-Paul)
JONES, GRACE—ILLUSTRATIONS
PH08320 636 (August 6, 1992) p63. "Depreciating Eddie Murphy" (Brodner, Steven)
JONES, HOWARD—ALBUMS
PH08321 630 (May 14, 1992) p103. "In The Running"
JONES, JOAN—PHOTOGRAPHS—PORTRAITS
PH08322 631 (May 28, 1992) p22. "David Russo And Joan Jones" (Lewis, Robert)
JONES, JOHN PAUL—PHOTOGRAPHS
PH08323 696 (December 1, 1994) p25. "Howard Leese, John Paul Jones, Ann Wilson, Denny Fongheiser And Nancy Wilson"
PH08324 702 (February 23, 1995) p46. "The Golden Boys: Page, Jones, Bonham And Plant (from left)"
PH08325 702 (February 23, 1995) p47. "Jones, Plant And Page Trample England Underfoot On Tour In 1970"
JONES, KENDALL REY—PHOTOGRAPHS
PH08326 662 (August 5, 1993) p17. "Fishbone: Jones (third from left) And Fisher (far right)" (Katz, Jeff)
JONES, KENNY—PHOTOGRAPHS
PH08327 653 (April 1, 1993) p11. "Kenny Jones, Stewart, Wyman, Wood And Ian McLagan" (Hutchson, Mick)
JONES, MAXINE—PHOTOGRAPHS
PH08328 709 (June 1, 1995) p17. "Maxine Jones, Robinson, O'Donnell, Cindy Herron, Terry Ellis" (Nelson, Ralph)
JONES, MAXINE—PHOTOGRAPHS—PORTRAITS
PH08329 660-661 (July 8, 1993) pp64-65. "En Vogue's Sheer Beauties: Terry Ellis, Maxine Jones, Dawn Robinson And Cindy Herron (from left)" (Rolston, Matthew)
PH08330 660-661 (July 8, 1993) p69. "Maxine Jones" (Rolston, Matthew)
JONES, MICK—PHOTOGRAPHS
PH08331 618 (November 28, 1991) p12. "Mick Jones (left) And Joe Strummer" (Gruen, Bob)
PH08332 619-620 (December 12, 1991) p68. "Joel, Don Henley, Mick Jones" (Mazur, Kevin)
PH08333 630 (May 14, 1992) p28. "B.A.D.'s Nick Hawkins (left) And Mick Jones" (Kraft, Chris)
PH08334 692 (October 6, 1994) p35. "Foreigner's Lou Gramm (left) And Mick Jones" (Robicheau, Paul)
JONES, MICK—PHOTOGRAPHS—PORTRAITS
PH08335 642 (October 29, 1992) p21. "Mick Jones (left) And Lou Gramm" (Sullivan, Lorinda)
PH08336 677 (March 10, 1994) p29. "Duane Eddy (left) With Mick Jones" (Mazur, Kevin)
JONES, PAULA—PHOTOGRAPHS
PH08337 698-699 (December 29, 1994) p160. "Paula Jones (below) And her Alleged Description Of Clinton's Penis"
JONES, PETE 'DJ'—PHOTOGRAPHS
PH08338 672-673 (December 23, 1993) p139. "Pete 'DJ' Jones, Lovebug's Mentor, In The Early 1970s"
JONES, QUINCY—PHOTOGRAPHS
PH08339 619-620 (December 12, 1991) p22. "Six-Timer Quincy Jones" (Mazur, Kevin)
JONES, RICKIE LEE—ALBUMS
PH08340 616 (October 31, 1991) p93. "Pop Pop"
PH08341 668 (October 28, 1993) p80. "Traffic From Paradise"
JONES, RICKIE LEE—PHOTOGRAPHS
PH08342 669 (November 11, 1993) p28. "Peculiar Pairing: Jones And Kottke"
JONES, RICKIE LEE—PHOTOGRAPHS—PORTRAITS
PH08343 643 (November 12, 1992) p85. "Rickie Lee Jones" (Weber, Bruce)
JONES, RON—PHOTOGRAPHS
PH08344 733 (May 2, 1996) p46. "Jones At Work" (Tavee, Tom)
JONES, RONALD—PHOTOGRAPHS
PH08345 703 (March 9, 1995) p26. "Imagine The Beatles Drunk On Robitussin: Coyne, Drozd, Ivins And Jones (from left)" (Lavine, Michael)
PH08346 736 (June 13, 1996) p33. "The Flaming Lips' Steven Drozd, Michael Ivins, Wayne Coyne And Ronald Jones (from left)" (Martin, J. Michelle)
JONES, SIMON—PHOTOGRAPHS
PH08347 660-661 (July 8, 1993) p96. "Verve (clockwise from top left): Ashcroft, Peter Salisbury, Simon Jones And McCabe" (Sharp, Ken)
JONES, SPIKE—ILLUSTRATIONS
PH08348 691 (September 22, 1994) p93. "Musical Mayhem" (Hungry Dog Studio)
JONES, STACY—PHOTOGRAPHS
PH08349 693 (October 20, 1994) p30. "Cleo's Hanley, Stacy Jones, Manning; Builders Joan Wasser, Eric Masunaga" (Robicheau, Paul)
PH08350 710 (June 15, 1995) p39. "Eisenstein, Scott Riebling, Hanley, Stacy Jones, Greg McKenna (from left)" (McDonough, Patricia)
JONES, STEVE—PHOTOGRAPHS
PH08351 721 (November 16, 1995) p26. "Momentary Hipster McKagan With Jones And Pop (from left)" (Kravitz, Jeff)
PH08352 731 (April 4, 1996) p18. "Jones (left) And McKagan In Seattle" (Doughty, Curt)
PH08353 734 (May 16, 1996) p17. "Matlock, Rotten, Jones And Cook Now" (Gruen, Bob)
PH08354 734 (May 16, 1996) p17. "The Pistols' Rotten, Glen Matlock, Steve Jones And Paul Cook In '76" (Gruen, Bob)
PH08355 736 (June 13, 1996) p52. "Pistols '96: Glen Matlock, Steve Jones, Paul Cook And Johnny Rotten (from left)" (Thomas, Justin)
JONES, TOM—PHOTOGRAPHS
PH08356 653 (April 1, 1993) p13. "Tom Jones And Shakespear's Sister"
PH08357 696 (December 1, 1994) p42. "[Tom Jones]" (Seliger, Mark)
PH08358 741 (August 22, 1996) p36. "Jones And Rankine Try 'Kung Fu'" (Temme, Marty)
JONES, TOM—PHOTOGRAPHS—PORTRAITS
PH08359 697 (December 15, 1994) p18. "Man Of The Hour With Bjork In L.A." (Cohen, Lester)
JONES, TOMMY LEE—PHOTOGRAPHS
PH08360 665 (September 16, 1993) p77. "Best Supporting Actor"
PH08361 692 (October 6, 1994) p81. "Now Playing"
PH08362 697 (December 15, 1994) p104. "Tommy lee Jones Plays Ty Cobb In Glory And In Disgrace"
PH08363 698-699 (December 29, 1994) p194. "Jones Swings In "Cobb""
PH08364 705 (April 6, 1995) p69. "Oscar Rejects"
PH08365 712-713 (July 13, 1995) p115. "Villians: Carrey's Riddler, Jones' Two-face With Sirens Barrymore And Mazar"
JONES, VALENTINA—PHOTOGRAPHS
PH08366 680 (April 21, 1994) pp[enc.38]. "It's Not Just Shopping, It's An Adventure" (Ragel, Jon)

JOPLIN, JANIS—ALBUMS
PH08367 617 (November 14, 1991) p97. "Cheap Thrills" (Crumb, R.)
PH08368 672-673 (December 23, 1993) p148. "Janis"
JOPLIN, JANIS—ILLUSTRATIONS—LETTERING
PH08369 638 (September 3, 1992) p55. "Love, Janis" (Lee, Lilly)
JOPLIN, JANIS—PHOTOGRAPHS
PH08370 619-620 (December 12, 1991) p102. "Graham And Janis Joplin At Winterland, One Of His Regular Venues, In 1968" (Marshall, Jim)
PH08371 638 (September 3, 1992) pp55-56. "Janis (left) With Her Mother And Sister"
PH08372 638 (September 3, 1992) p57. "Janis And Her Dog George In Her San Francisco Apartment, 1968" (Marshall, Jim)
PH08373 638 (September 3, 1992) p59. "Janis Backstage Being Filmed By Jimi Hendrix, 1968" (Marshall, Jim)
PH08374 638 (September 3, 1992) p59. "Onstage With Tina Turner, 1969"
PH08375 643 (November 12, 1992) p64. "Legendary San Francisco Shooter Jim Marshall With Joplin" (Marshall, Jim)
PH08376 692 (October 6, 1994) p50. "Janis Joplin"
PH08377 717 (September 21, 1995) p48. "Janis Joplin And Ron 'Pigpen' McKernan At The Northern California Folk Rock, In San Jose, Calif., 1968" (Marshall, Jim)
JOPLIN, JANIS—PHOTOGRAPHS—PORTRAITS
PH08378 638 (September 3, 1992) p56. "Janis In San Francisco, 1963"
PH08379 643 (November 12, 1992) p70. "Bob Seidemann Captured Janis Joplin's Dark Side" (Seidmann, Bob)
PH08380 643 (November 12, 1992) p73. "The San Francisco Queen Bees Of Rock, Slick And Joplin, Sat For Marshall" (Marshall, Jim)
PH08381 645-646 (December 10, 1992) p161. "Janis Joplin, 1970"
PH08382 686-687 (July 14, 1994) p23. "Jim Morrison (above left) And Janis Joplin (left) Are Both Represented With Collections" (Wolman, Baron)
PH08383 735 (May 30, 1996) p3. "[The Faces Of Heroin]"
JOPLIN, LAURA—PHOTOGRAPHS
PH08384 638 (September 3, 1992) pp55-56. "Janis (left) With Her Mother And Sister"
JORDAN, AKAI—PHOTOGRAPHS
PH08385 694 (November 3, 1994) p54. "A Tax Credit Gave Loretta Jordan A Little Breathing Room" (Barocas, Melanie)
JORDAN, KYLE—PHOTOGRAPHS
PH08385 694 (November 3, 1994) p54. "A Tax Credit Gave Loretta Jordan A Little Breathing Room" (Barocas, Melanie)
JORDAN, LORETTA—PHOTOGRAPHS
PH08385 694 (November 3, 1994) p54. "A Tax Credit Gave Loretta Jordan A Little Breathing Room" (Barocas, Melanie)
JORDAN, MICHAEL—PHOTOGRAPHS
PH08386 743 (September 19, 1996) p88. "Dickheads"
PH08387 745 (October 17, 1996) p40. "Westinghouse's Michael Jordan (left), Infinity's Mel Karmazin"
JORDAN, MICHAEL—PHOTOGRAPHS—PORTRAITS
PH08388 750-751 (December 26, 1996) p57. "None-Too-Fragrant 11-Year-Old Sneakers! Any Takers?"
JORDAN, NEIL—PHOTOGRAPHS
PH08389 747 (November 14, 1996) p84. "Jordan Directs The Troops On The 'Collins' Set"
PH08390 747 (November 14, 1996) pp82-83. "[Neil Jordan]" (Corbijn, Anton)
JORGE, PETER—PHOTOGRAPHS
PH08391 676 (February 24, 1994) p24. "Spank Dog, Money Mike, Mr. Watts, Peter Jorge, D-Smooth, G (from left)" (Hastings, Daniel)
JOURGENSEN, AL—ILLUSTRATIONS
PH08392 700 (January 26, 1995) p63. "Al Jourgensen" (Greve, Margie)
JOURGENSEN, AL—PHOTOGRAPHS
PH08393 639 (September 17, 1992) p60. "Ministry's Al Jourgensen" (Blakesberg, Jay)
PH08394 648 (January 21, 1993) p24. "Ministry's Al Jourgensen Raises Hell" (Mazur, Kevin)
PH08395 665 (September 16, 1993) p31. "Scott Ian (left) With Unannounced Guest Al Jourgensen" (Murrey, Ron)
PH08396 685 (June 30, 1994) p41. "Heat's band Mates Taz And Jimbo; Jourgensen And Heat" (Bland, James)
PH08397 719 (October 19, 1995) p25. "Jourgensen Finds Himself In A Fix In Texas" (Schwab, Bill)
JOURGENSEN, AL—PHOTOGRAPHS—PORTRAITS
PH08398 724-725 (December 28, 1995) p60. "Jourgensen"
JOURNALISM—ILLUSTRATIONS
PH08399 641 (October 15, 1992) p185. "[Rolling Stone]" (Smith, Lane)
PH08400 652 (March 18, 1993) pp[enc.6]. "[College Journalism]"
PH08401 660-661 (July 8, 1993) p10. "Goldilocks, The Journalist" (Pendergrast, James T.)
JOVOVICH, MILLA—PHOTOGRAPHS—PORTRAITS
PH08402 688 (August 11, 1994) p20. "Sisters in Charity: Milla And Kristin Hersh (right)"
THE JOY LUCK CLUB (FILM)—PHOTOGRAPHS
PH08403 666 (September 30, 1993) p113. "Yu Fei Hong Finds No Joy Dancing With Russell Wong"
JOYNER, CHRIS—PHOTOGRAPHS
PH08404 622 (January 23, 1992) p14. "Clockwise From Top Left: Davel Sobel, Luther Russell, Chris Joyner, John Hofer, Jason Hiller" (Annalisa)
JU JU HOUNDS—ALBUMS
PH08405 645-646 (December 10, 1992) p179. "Izzy Stradlin And The Ju Ju Hounds"
JU JU HOUNDS—PHOTOGRAPHS—PORTRAITS
PH08406 645-646 (December 10, 1992) p93. "Stradlin And The Ju Ju Hounds Come Out From Under The Gunners' Shadow"
JUAZEIRO DO NORTE, BRAZIL—PHOTOGRAPHS
PH08407 619-620 (December 12, 1991) p142. "Girls At Their First Communion, In Juazeiro Do Norte, Brazil, 1981" (Salgado, Sebastiao)
JUDD, ASHLEY—PHOTOGRAPHS
PH08408 652 (March 18, 1993) p47. "'Ruby In Paradise' Starr Judd" (Michaelson, Randall)
PH08409 670 (November 25, 1993) p37. "Naomi Judd, Phillips, Ashley And Wynonna (from left)" (Kravitz, Jeff)
PH08410 678 (March 24, 1994) p100. "Missing In Oscar Action"
PH08411 735 (May 30, 1996) p56. "Now Playing"
PH08412 741 (August 22, 1996) p48. "McConaughey Onscreen"
PH08413 747 (November 14, 1996) p124. "Mad Housewife Judd"
JUDD, ASHLEY—PHOTOGRAPHS—PORTRAITS
PH08414 656 (May 13, 1993) p84. "[Ashley Judd]" (Seliger, Mark)
PH08415 672-673 (December 23, 1993) p172. "Debut"
JUDD, NAOMI—PHOTOGRAPHS
PH08416 633 (June 25, 1992) p16. "Wynonna (left) And Naomi On Their Front Porch In Franklin, Tennessee, In 1979"
PH08417 670 (November 25, 1993) p37. "Naomi Judd, Phillips, Ashley And Wynonna (from left)" (Kravitz, Jeff)
JUDD, WYNONNA—ALBUMS
PH08418 631 (May 28, 1992) p51. "Wynonna"
PH08419 645-646 (December 10, 1992) p164. "Wynonna"
PH08420 660-661 (July 8, 1993) p114. "Tell Me Why"
JUDD, WYNONNA—ILLUSTRATIONS
PH08421 631 (May 28, 1992) p51. "'Wynonna': A Faith Supreme" (Nakamura, Joel)
JUDD, WYNONNA—PHOTOGRAPHS
PH08422 633 (June 25, 1992) p16. "Wynonna (left) And Naomi On Their Front Porch In Franklin, Tennessee, In 1979"

PH08423 645-646 (December 10, 1992) p98. "Wynonna Judd Croons For The GOP" (Katz, Shelly)
PH08424 660-661 (July 8, 1993) p33. "Clint Black And Wynonna At Radio City" (Mazur, Kevin)
PH08425 670 (November 25, 1993) p37. "Naomi Judd, Phillips, Ashley And Wynonna (from left)" (Kravitz, Jeff)
JUDD, WYNONNA—PHOTOGRAPHS—PORTRAITS
PH08426 633 (June 25, 1992) p15. "[Wynonna Judd]" (Smith, Brian)
PH08427 645-646 (December 10, 1992) p40. "Wynonna Judd" (Smith, Brian)
JUDDS—PHOTOGRAPHS
PH08428 633 (June 25, 1992) p16. "Wynonna (left) And Naomi On Their Front Porch In Franklin, Tennessee, In 1979"
JUDGE DREDD (FILM)—PHOTOGRAPHS
PH08429 709 (June 1, 1995) p68. "Potential Trouble Spots"
PH08430 716 (September 7, 1995) p78. "Summer Wrap-Up]"
JUDGE, MIKE—PHOTOGRAPHS
PH08431 663 (August 19, 1993) p42. "Creator Mike Judge Hatches More Sordid Tales" (Ockenfels, Frank W.)
PH08432 663 (August 19, 1993) p48. "Writer Tracy Grandstaff, Judge And MTV Exec Abby Terkuhle" (Ockenfels, Frank W.)
PH08433 678 (March 24, 1994) p45. "Kiss My Butt-Head: Judge Defends His Creations" (Ockenfels, Frank W.)
JUDGMENT NIGHT (FILM)—ILLUSTRATIONS
PH08434 666 (September 30, 1993) p100. "Rock & Rap Will Stand" (Bartholomew, Beth)
JUICE (FILM)—PHOTOGRAPHS
PH08435 623 (February 6, 1992) p90. "Cindy Herron And Omar Epps Take Time Out From Fighting"
JULIA, RAUL—PHOTOGRAPHS
PH08436 618 (November 28, 1991) p53. "They're Altogether Ooky" (Seliger, Mark)
JULIA, RAUL—PHOTOGRAPHS—PORTRAITS
PH08437 701 (February 9, 1995) p63. "The Late Raul Julia"
JUNG, GEORGE—PHOTOGRAPHS
PH08438 660-661 (July 8, 1993) p84. "Broke But Free: Jung Today At His Cottage In Scrub-Oak Forest On Cape Cod" (Seliger, Mark)
PH08439 660-661 (July 8, 1993) p77. "[George Jung]" (Seliger, Mark)
JUNG, GEORGE—PHOTOGRAPHS—PORTRAITS
PH08440 660-661 (July 8, 1993) p76. "[George Jung]"
PH08441 660-661 (July 8, 1993) p78. "Jung, 1968: Two Decades In The Drug Trade Awaited"
PH08442 660-661 (July 8, 1993) p82. "Richard Barile And George Jung, Arrested For Possession On Cape Cod in 1980"
JUNGLE BROTHERS—ALBUMS
PH08443 668 (October 28, 1993) p83. "J. Beez Wit The Remedy"
JUNGLE FEVER (FILM)—PHOTOGRAPHS
PH08444 623 (February 6, 1992) p90. "[Jungle Fever]"
PH08445 627 (April 2, 1992) p41. "Jackson, With Halle Berry, In 'Jungle Fever'"
JUNIOR (FILM)—PHOTOGRAPHS
PH08446 697 (December 15, 1994) p104. "Dr. De Vito Examines A Very Pregnant Ah-nuld"
JURASSIC PARK (FILM)—ILLUSTRATIONS
PH08447 659 (June 24, 1993) p87. "Dinosaur Summer" (Witte, Michael)
JURASSIC PARK (FILM)—PHOTOGRAPHS
PH08448 659 (June 24, 1993) p36. "Dern (with Joseph Mazzello And Sam Neill) Perks Up A Sick Dino" (Close, Murray)
PH08449 659 (June 24, 1993) p36. "Dern And Jeff Goldblum, Flanking Steven Spielberg, Fell In Love On The Set" (Close, Murray)
PH08450 660-661 (July 8, 1993) p120. "Meet Steven Spielberg's New Jaws: A T. Rex At Mealtime"
PH08451 672-673 (December 23, 1993) p172. "Monster Hit"
PH08452 678 (March 24, 1994) p100. "Missing In Oscar Action"
JURGENS, JENNIFER—PHOTOGRAPHS
PH08453 711 (June 29, 1995) p23. "Blending '60s Who With Atmospheric Noise: Jurgens, Orris, Ackerson And Wilson (from left)" (Elledge, Paul)
JUROR (FILM)—PHOTOGRAPHS
PH08454 718 (October 5, 1995) p76. "Pulp To Come"
JUST ANOTHER GIRL ON THE I.R.T. (FILM)—PHOTOGRAPHS
PH08455 650 (February 18, 1993) p66. "Ariyan Johnson Makes A Dazzling Debut"
JUSTIFY MY LOVE (VIDEO)—PHOTOGRAPHS
PH08456 667 (October 14, 1993) p85. "'Justify' A Trip To Paris: Madonna Heated The Hotel"

K

K COMPOSITE (PUBLICATION)—PHOTOGRAPHS
PH08457 693 (October 20, 1994) p93. "[K Composite]"
K FOUNDATION—PHOTOGRAPHS
PH08458 668 (October 28, 1993) p25. "Drummond And Cauty Of K" (Cummins, Kevin)
K, GREG—PHOTOGRAPHS
PH08459 695 (November 17, 1994) p78. "Offspring" (Danelian, Stephen)
K, PAUL—PHOTOGRAPHS—PORTRAITS
PH08460 666 (September 30, 1993) p16. "[Paul K]" (Irish, Len)
K1—PHOTOGRAPHS
PH08461 690 (September 8, 1994) p44. "K1, Oisin, Phrase And Hollis (from left)" (Cross, Brian)
KACZYNSKI, TED—PHOTOGRAPHS
PH08462 750-751 (December 26, 1996) p56. "Kaczynski At A Courthouse In Helena, Mont."
KAFKA (FILM)—ILLUSTRATIONS
PH08463 623 (February 6, 1992) p87. "Literary Freak Shows" (Rosen, Jonathon)
KAFKA (FILM)—PHOTOGRAPHS
PH08464 623 (February 6, 1992) p88. "Jeremy Irons Hides In Terror From The Forces Of Darkness"
KALELL, JOHN—PHOTOGRAPHS
PH08465 663 (August 19, 1993) p62. "Chuck Berry, Who Performed At The Reunion, And Kalell"
KALIFORNIA (FILM)—PHOTOGRAPHS
PH08466 665 (September 16, 1993) p78. "Lewis (left) And Pitt Share A Kiss"
PH08467 696 (December 1, 1994) p96. "Pitt Has Dated "Thelma And Louise" Co-Star Davis (top) And "Kalifornia" Girl Lewis (below)"
KALLEN, PETER—PHOTOGRAPHS
PH08468 691 (September 22, 1994) pp[enc.30]. "Climbing On The Outer Wall At Nike Headquarters" (Borris, Dan)
PH08469 691 (September 22, 1994) pp[enc.32]. "Kallen In Downtown Portland, Ore., With His Skateboard" (Borris, Dan)
PH08470 691 (September 22, 1994) pp[enc.cover]. "Nike's Peter Kallen" (Borris, Dan)
PH08471 691 (September 22, 1994) pp[enc.30]. "Peter Kallen In His Office At Nike World Campus In Beaverton, Ore." (Borris, Dan)
KAMMER, DAVID—PHOTOGRAPHS
PH08472 663 (August 19, 1993) p61. "College Cabinet: William Clinton, Judith Baiocchi, David Kammer, Paul Maloy (from left)"
KANE, BIG DADDY—PHOTOGRAPHS
PH08473 658 (June 10, 1993) p74. "The Magnificent Six (from left): Stephen Baldwin, Big Daddy Kane, Mario Van Peebles, Tiny Lister Jr., Charles Lane, Tone Loc"
KANE, BIG DADDY—PHOTOGRAPHS
PH08474 689 (August 25, 1994) p40. "Big Daddy Kane: New LP, Movie" (Benabib, Michael)
KANE, NICK—PHOTOGRAPHS
PH08475 691 (September 22, 1994) p22. "[The Mavericks]"

(Harris, Brad)
KANE, NICK—PHOTOGRAPHS—PORTRAITS
PH08476 682 (May 19, 1994) p74. "[Mavericks]" (Tucker, Mark)
KANNBERG, SCOTT—PHOTOGRAPHS
PH08477 686-687 (July 14, 1994) p20. "Ibold, Nastanovich And Kannberg (from left)" (Blakesberg, Jay)
KANPECH—PHOTOGRAPHS
PH08478 718 (October 5, 1995) p25. "Kanpech Reaches Out" (Corio, David)
KANSAS CITY (FILM)—PHOTOGRAPHS
PH08479 736 (June 13, 1996) p58. "Oscar Seekers"
PH08480 741 (August 22, 1996) p104. "Richardson (left) And Leigh In Peril In Kansas City"
KANTNER, PAUL—ALBUMS
PH08481 747 (November 14, 1996) p114. "A Guide Through The Chaos"
KANTNER, PAUL—PHOTOGRAPHS
PH08482 644 (November 26, 1992) p15. "Kantner, Darby Gould, Jack Casady, Tim Gorman, Prairie Prince, Papa John Creach, McGuinn And Slick Aguilar (from left)" (Mazur, Kevin)
PH08483 717 (September 21, 1995) p28. "Not Fade Away: Barlow, Hart, Kantner And Weir (from left) Celebrate Garcia In Golden Gate Park" (Blakesberg, Jay)
PH08484 717 (September 21, 1995) p28. "Olatunji With Kantner, Two Drummers, John Perry Barlow, Weir And Koons Garcia (from left) At The Aug. 13 Memorial At The Polo Field" (Blakesberg, Jay)
PH08485 728 (February 22, 1996) p19. "The Airplane's Paul Kantner (left) And Jorma Kaukonen" (Mazur, Kevin)
KAPHAN, BRUCE—PHOTOGRAPHS—PORTRAITS
PH08486 656 (May 13, 1993) p77. "American Music Club (from left): Danny Pearson, Tim Mooney, Vudi, Bruce Kaphan And Mark Eitzel" (Ockenfels, Frank, 3)
KAPLAN, IRA—PHOTOGRAPHS
PH08487 679 (April 7, 1994) p34. "American Band: Yo La's Kaplan" (Natkin, Paul)
KAPOR, MITCH—PHOTOGRAPHS
PH08488 658 (June 10, 1993) pp[enc.3,5]. "[Mitch Kapor]" (Borris, Dan)
KARAN, DONNA—PHOTOGRAPHS—PORTRAITS
PH08489 678 (March 24, 1994) p49. "Donna Karan" (Sanders, Timothy Greenfield)
KARE, SUSAN—PHOTOGRAPHS
PH08490 731 (April 4, 1996) p57. "The Iconographic Graphic Designer Susan Kare In 1984" (Seeff, Norman)
KARLEN, NEAL—BOOKS
PH08491 692 (October 6, 1994) p37. "Babes In Toyland"
KARLOFF, BORIS—PHOTOGRAPHS
PH08492 696 (December 1, 1994) p132. "De Niro's Monster And Karloff's 1931 Model"
KARMAZIN, MEL—PHOTOGRAPHS
PH08493 745 (October 17, 1996) p40. "Westinghouse's Michael Jordan (left), Infinity's Mel Karmazin"
KASSEBAUM, NANCY—PHOTOGRAPHS—PORTRAITS
PH08494 722 (November 30, 1995) p47. "[Nancy Kassebaum]" (Markowitz, Jeffrey)
KASSO, RICKY—PHOTOGRAPHS
PH08495 632 (June 11, 1992) p130. "After His Arrest, Ricky Kasso Hanged Himself In Prison" (Jerome, Tony)
KATO, NASH—PHOTOGRAPHS
PH08496 664 (September 2, 1993) p12. "Urge A Go-Go (clockwise from left): Onassis, Kato, Roeser" (Robert, Francis)
PH08497 668 (October 28, 1993) p35. "Urge Guitarist Nash Kato With Hynde"
PH08498 685 (June 30, 1994) p40. "Etheridge With Kato, Tony Stull, Blackie Onassis And "Eddie" King Roeser (from left)" (Mazur, Kevin)
PH08499 695 (November 17, 1994) p84. "Urge Overkill" (Clinch, Danny)
KATO, NASH—PHOTOGRAPHS—PORTRAITS
PH08500 664 (September 2, 1993) p11. "[Urge Overkill]" (Robert, Francis)
KATZENBERG, JEFFREY—PHOTOGRAPHS—PORTRAITS
PH08501 698-699 (December 29, 1994) p68. "Geffen, Katzenberg, Spielberg (from left)" (Berliner)
KAUFMAN, ANDY—ILLUSTRATIONS
PH08502 705 (April 6, 1995) p16. "Andy Lives" (Todd, Mark)
KAUKONEN, JORMA—PHOTOGRAPHS
PH08503 679 (April 7, 1994) p37. "Ain't Gonna Work On Yasgur's Farm No More: Phil Lesh, Crosby, Nash, Jorma Kaukonen" (Blakesberg, Jay)
PH08504 728 (February 22, 1996) p19. "The Airplane's Paul Kantner (left) And Jorma Kaukonen" (Mazur, Kevin)
KAVNER, JULIE—ILLUSTRATIONS
PH08505 625 (March 5, 1992) p75. "A Sundance Spotlight On Women" (Risko, Robert)
KAVNER, JULIE—PHOTOGRAPHS
PH08506 625 (March 5, 1992) p76. "Hoffman, Kavner And Mathis Turn Trauma Into Laughter"
KAWAH IDJEN, INDONESIA—PHOTOGRAPHS
PH08507 665 (September 16, 1993) pp54-58. "Workers of The World" (Salgado, Sebastiao)
KAY GEE—PHOTOGRAPHS
PH08508 663 (August 19, 1993) pp66-68,70. "[Naughty By Nature]" (Gregoire, Jean Louis)
KAY, MICHAEL—PHOTOGRAPHS
PH08509 748 (November 28, 1996) p82. "At Michael Kay's High-End Store, Insatiable Customers Fall Prey To The 'Upgrade Virus'" (Pluchino, Joseph)
KAYE, LENNY—PHOTOGRAPHS
PH08510 728 (February 22, 1996) p18. "Smith And Her Guitarist Lenny Kaye" (Mazur, Kevin)
PH08511 738-739 (July 11, 1996) p55. "Calling Radio Ethiopia: Smith With Lenny Kaye In 1976" (Goldsmith, Lynn)
PH08512 738-739 (July 11, 1996) p44. "Smith's Great '70s Band"
KEANE, AARON—PHOTOGRAPHS
PH08513 715 (August 24, 1995) p92. "Keane On The Observation Deck At The Empire State Building" (Danelian, Stephen)
PH08514 715 (August 24, 1995) p94. "Keane With Empire State Building Guards Darren Hicks, Lance Pelt And Peter Vargas" (Danelian, Stephen)
PH08515 715 (August 24, 1995) pp90-91. "On The Court In Thompkins Park" (Danelian, Stephen)
KEARNS, TOM—PHOTOGRAPHS
PH08515 715 (August 24, 1995) pp90-91. "On The Court In Thompkins Park" (Danelian, Stephen)
KEATON, DIANE—ILLUSTRATIONS
PH08516 664 (September 2, 1993) p68. "Annie Small" (Blitt, Barry)
PH08517 744 (October 3, 1996) p77. "Men Behaving Badly" (Brodner, Steve)
KEATON, DIANE—PHOTOGRAPHS
PH08518 664 (September 2, 1993) p69. "'Annie Hall' Lovers Keaton And Allen (left) Reteam In A Romantic 'Mystery'"
PH08519 665 (September 16, 1993) p49. "Filming 'Sleeper' (1973) With Diane Keaton"
PH08520 678 (March 24, 1994) p100. "Missing In Oscar Action"
PH08521 744 (October 3, 1996) p78. "First Wives Keaton, Midler And Hawn Out For Revenge"
KEATON, DIANE—PHOTOGRAPHS—PORTRAITS
PH08522 750-751 (December 26, 1996) p207. "Diane Keaton, Leonardo Dicaprio"
KEATON, MICHAEL—PHOTOGRAPHS
PH08523 634-635 (July 9, 1992) p40. "Burton Identifies With The Dark Knight Of 'Batman Returns' (Michael Keaton)" (Rosenthal, Zade)
PH08524 634-635 (July 9, 1992) p111. "Pfeiffer Puts Keaton In His Place"

PH08525 644 (November 26, 1992) p78. "[Batman Returns]"
PH08526 670 (November 25, 1993) p127. "Pregnant Nicole Kidman Toasts Dying Michael Keaton"
PH08527 679 (April 7, 1994) p82. "Metro Editor Michael Keaton (standing) Rouses The Staff For A Hot Story"
PH08528 740 (August 8, 1996) p70. "Close Shave For Keaton And Keaton"
KEB' MO'—ALBUMS
PH08529 697 (December 15, 1994) p98. "Keb' Mo'"
KEEN, GORDON—PHOTOGRAPHS—PORTRAITS
PH08530 642 (October 29, 1992) p32. "Eugenius (clockwise from upper left): Boyle, Kelly, Keen, Lawrence" (Lavine, Michael)
KEEN, ROBERT EARL—ALBUMS
PH08531 698-699 (December 29, 1994) p181. "Gringo Honey-moon"
KEENAN, DANIEL—PHOTOGRAPHS
PH08532 720 (November 2, 1995) p24. "Bozulich, Keenan, Tutton, Fitzgerald, Greene (from left)" (Toy, Joann)
KEENAN, MAYNARD JAMES—PHOTOGRAPHS
PH08533 679 (April 7, 1994) p34. "Power Tool: Maynard James Keenan" (Capak, R. J.)
KEESLER, MATT—PHOTOGRAPHS
PH08534 718 (October 5, 1995) p79. "Matt Keesler And Victoria Smurfit Skinny-Dip"
KEINEG, KATELL—PHOTOGRAPHS—PORTRAITS
PH08535 696 (December 1, 1994) p41. "[Katell Keineg]" (France, Neil A.)
KEISER, CHRISTOPHER—PHOTOGRAPHS
PH08536 693 (October 20, 1994) p126. "[Christopher Keiser]" (Gipe, Jon)
PH08537 693 (October 20, 1994) p125. ""I Just Realized That I Could Really Have A Future Here," Says Blading Instructor Christopher Keiser (right)" (Gipe, Jon)
KEITA, SALIF—ALBUMS
PH08538 727 (February 8, 1996) p51. "Folon...The Past"
KEITEL, HARVEY—ILLUSTRATIONS
PH08539 644 (November 26, 1992) p77. "Killer Ratings" (Burns, Charles)
KEITEL, HARVEY—PHOTOGRAPHS
PH08540 644 (November 26, 1992) p78. "Running The Ratings Gamut: Keitel..."
PH08541 671 (December 9, 1993) p78. "Impossible Dream: Keitel Teaches Madonna To Act"
PH08542 692 (October 6, 1994) p80. "Keitel Deals"
PH08543 711 (June 29, 1995) p49. "Stockard Channing Blows Smoke At A Wary Harvey Keitel"
PH08544 717 (September 21, 1995) p89. "Keitel And Lee On The Case"
PH08545 717 (September 21, 1995) p89. "Phifer On The Spot"
PH08546 718 (October 5, 1995) p77. "Rupal, Keitel And Gorham Boogie"
KEITH RICHARDS: THE BIOGRAPHY (BOOK)—PHOTOGRAPHS
PH08547 645-646 (December 10, 1992) p87. "[Keith Richards]"
KEITH, PETE—PHOTOGRAPHS
PH08548 704 (March 23, 1995) p74. "Editorial Director Pete Keith (standing) Rallies The '95 Staff" (Asnin, Marc)
KELLEGHER, TINA—PHOTOGRAPHS
PH08549 671 (December 9, 1993) p78. "Daddy's Girl: Kellegher With Meaney"
KELLY, CHARLES—PHOTOGRAPHS
PH08550 634-635 (July 9, 1992) pp80-81. "By Their Jerseys Ye Shall Know Them: The Original Ballooners Charles Kelly, Joe Breeze And Gary Fisher (from left)" (Stone, Pete)
KELLY, DAVID PATRICK—PHOTOGRAPHS
PH08551 732 (April 18, 1996) p78. "Kelly And Stiller"
KELLY, EUGENE—PHOTOGRAPHS—PORTRAITS
PH08552 642 (October 29, 1992) p32. "Eugenius (clockwise from upper left): Boyle, Kelly, Keen, Lawrence" (Lavine, Michael)
KELLY, GENE—PHOTOGRAPHS
PH08553 741 (August 22, 1996) p72. "[Claritin]"
KELLY, JOHN—ILLUSTRATIONS
PH08554 693 (October 20, 1994) p27. "Go Farther East, Young Loaf" (Watson, Esther)
KELLY, PAUL—ALBUMS
PH08555 698-699 (December 29, 1994) p176. "Wanted Man"
PH08556 747 (November 14, 1996) p116. "The Best Of Paul Kelly"
KELLY, PAUL—PHOTOGRAPHS
PH08557 653 (April 1, 1993) p24. "Backstage At The Trouba-dour In L.A." (Granitz, Steve)
KELLY, R.—ALBUMS
PH08558 726 (January 25, 1996) p72. "R. Kelly"
KELLY, R.—ILLUSTRATIONS
PH08559 726 (January 25, 1996) p84. "R. Kelly: Tough Love" (Angel, Vinnie)
KELLY, R.—PHOTOGRAPHS
PH08560 736 (June 13, 1996) p80. "Kelly Gets Sexual (and nasty and freaky) In New Jersey" (Capak, R. J.)
PH08561 736 (June 13, 1996) p19. "[R. Kelly]"
PH08562 746 (October 31, 1996) p27. "You Remind Me Of E.T.: R. Kelly Is Joining The 'Space Jam' Media Blitz"
KELTNER, JIM—PHOTOGRAPHS
PH08563 627 (April 2, 1992) p15. "Jim Keltner, Ry Cooder, Nick Lowe And John Hiatt (from left)" (Hanauer, Mark)
KEMP, GARY—PHOTOGRAPHS
PH08564 627 (April 2, 1992) p11. "Gary Kemp"
KENDRICKS, EDDIE—PHOTOGRAPHS—PORTRAITS
PH08565 644 (November 26, 1992) p24. "[Eddie Kendricks]" (Abbott, Waring)
PH08566 645-646 (December 10, 1992) p101. "Singer Eddie Kendricks"
KENEIPP, KELLY—PHOTOGRAPHS
PH08567 730 (March 21, 1996) p26. "Logan (left) And Keneipp Talk Drag-Racing" (Torno, Pattiy)
KENNEDY, EDWARD—PHOTOGRAPHS—PORTRAITS
PH08568 722 (November 30, 1995) p47. "[Ted Kennedy]" (Wyman, Ira)
KENNEDY, MIKE—PHOTOGRAPHS
PH08569 689 (August 25, 1994) p44. "All Together Now: Trombino, Atom, Kennedy, Reis, N.D., Petey X, Apollo 9, Froberg (from left)" (Cuffaro, Chris)
KENNEDY, ROBERT—PHOTOGRAPHS
PH08570 698-699 (December 29, 1994) p166. "Bobby Kennedy, A Hero To The Counterculture, Reaches Out To The Voters In 1966" (Capa, Cornell)
KENNEDY, ROBERT F., JR.—PHOTOGRAPHS—PORTRAITS
PH08571 645-646 (December 10, 1992) p133. "[Robert F. Kennedy, Jr.]" (Eccles, Andrew)
KENNER, DORIS—PHOTOGRAPHS
PH08572 728 (February 22, 1996) p18. "Shirelles Shirley Alston, Lee, Doris Kenner (from left): Dedicating It To The Ones They Love" (Mazur, Kevin)
KENNEY, KERRI—PHOTOGRAPHS
PH08573 703 (March 9, 1995) p29. "Easy As Pie: Jody Seifert, Nina Hellman And Kerri Kenney (from left)" (Falls, John)
PH08574 718 (October 5, 1995) pp[enc.39,41+]. "[Kerri Kenney]" (Tavee, Tom)
KENSIT, PATSY—PHOTOGRAPHS
PH08575 615 (October 17, 1991) p102. "Patsy Kensit Ponders Sex In The Nineties"
PH08576 731 (April 4, 1996) p18. "[Liam Gallagher & Patsy Kensit]" (Murray, Andrew)
KENT, NICK—BOOKS
PH08577 727 (February 8, 1996) p51. "The Dark Stuff"
KENTUCKY HEADHUNTERS—PHOTOGRAPHS
PH08578 668 (October 28, 1993) p30. "Greg Martin, Johnnie Johnson And Richard Young (from left)" (Natkin, Paul)

KERMIT THE FROG—PHOTOGRAPHS
PH08579 730 (March 21, 1996) p18. "Oh, Kermie! Abdul And Kermit"
KERR, JIM—PHOTOGRAPHS
PH08580 704 (March 23, 1995) p46. "Jim Kerr: Promising A Miracle And Delivering" (Mercer, Lance)
KERR-MCGEE (COMPANY)—PHOTOGRAPHS
PH08581 632 (June 11, 1992) p95. "The Kerr-McGee Plutonium Plant In Crescent, Oklahoma, Where Silkwood Worked"
KERREY, BOB—PHOTOGRAPHS
PH08582 623 (February 6, 1992) pp57-58,62,64. "[Bob Kerrey]" (Berndt, Jerry)
PH08583 709 (June 1, 1995) p33. "Kerrey Wasn't Intimidated By A Moses Impression" (Roemer, Mike)
KERRIGAN, NANCY—PHOTOGRAPHS
PH08584 686-687 (July 14, 1994) p87. ""This Is So Corny," Kerrigan Told The Mouse. "This Is So Dumb.""
KERWIN, JIM—PHOTOGRAPHS
PH08585 717 (September 21, 1995) p75. "Grisman, Jim Kerwin, Garcia, Joe Craven (from left) In San Francisco, 1991" (Millman, Susana)
KESEY, KEN—PHOTOGRAPHS
PH08586 690 (September 8, 1994) p21. "Tin Man, Ginsberg, Kesey, Dorothy (from left)" (Miles, Steve)
KESTEVEN, BEN—PHOTOGRAPHS
PH08587 650 (February 18, 1993) p13. "Peter Tork (left) With The 'Jays' Hancock, Robinson And Ben Kesteven" (Mayer, Jeffrey)
KETCHUM, HAL—ALBUMS
PH08588 653 (April 1, 1993) p52. "Sure Love"
KEVORKIAN, JACK—PHOTOGRAPHS
PH08589 681 (May 5, 1994) p21. "Ryder And Dr. Death: Devil With A Blue Sweater On?"
KEY, TARA—PHOTOGRAPHS—PORTRAITS
PH08590 679 (April 7, 1994) p32. "[Tara Key]" (Knight, Kevin)
KEYBOARDS—PHOTOGRAPHS
PH08591 722 (November 30, 1995) p81. "[Instruments]" (Grant, Bob)
KEYES, ALAN—PHOTOGRAPHS
PH08592 729 (March 7, 1996) p45. "The Truest Believer: Alan Keyes, Who Calls Himself An Abolitionist, Campaigns In Des Moines, Iowa" (Feanny, Najlah)
KHALSA, GITI—PHOTOGRAPHS
PH08593 731 (April 4, 1996) p36. "The Two Jasons (Pollock and Ross), Khalsa And Daniel" (Clinch, Danny)
KHAN, CHAKA—ALBUMS
PH08594 628 (April 16, 1992) p84. "The Woman I Am"
KHAN, CHAKA—PHOTOGRAPHS
PH08595 716 (September 7, 1995) p14. "Chaka Khan And Chris Isaak At LIFEbeat" (Mazur, Kevin)
KHAN, CHAKA—PHOTOGRAPHS—PORTRAITS
PH08596 692 (October 6, 1994) p52. "Chaka Khan" (Abbott, Waring)
KIBITZ ROOM, CANTER'S—PHOTOGRAPHS
PH08597 649 (February 4, 1993) p11. "[Canter's Kibitz Room]"
KICK, JOHNNY—PHOTOGRAPHS
PH08598 688 (August 11, 1994) p29. "Drummer Johnny Kick, Cote, Lorson And Bassist Chris Giammalvo (from left)" (Berg, Bob)
KICKING AND SCREAMING (FILM)—PHOTOGRAPHS
PH08599 717 (September 21, 1995) p90. "Parker Posey As A Coed From Hell"
KID FROST—ALBUMS
PH08600 631 (May 28, 1992) p54. "East Side Story"
KID 'N PLAY—PHOTOGRAPHS
PH08601 633 (June 25, 1992) p48. "Kid (left) 'N Play Rap With Rogers (left) And Parsons"
KIDJO, ANGELIQUE—PHOTOGRAPHS
PH08602 691 (September 22, 1994) p19. "Gabriel, Kidjo And Marsalis (from left)" (Smith, Robert)
KIDJO, ANGELIQUE—PHOTOGRAPHS—PORTRAITS
PH08603 630 (May 14, 1992) p32. "[Angelique Kidjo]" (Cultice, Joseph)
KIDMAN, NICOLE—ILLUSTRATIONS
PH08604 719 (October 19, 1995) p155. "Lethal Seduction" (Hungry Dog Studio)
KIDMAN, NICOLE—PHOTOGRAPHS
PH08605 633 (June 25, 1992) p48. "Cruise And Kidman Get Their Irish Up"
PH08606 667 (October 14, 1993) p128. "Evil Doings For Alec Baldwin And Nicole Kidman"
PH08607 670 (November 25, 1993) p127. "Pregnant Nicole Kidman Toasts Dying Michael Keaton"
PH08608 698-699 (December 29, 1994) p74. "Cruise And Nicole Kidman Put The Media Bite On Film Fans" (Trapper, Frank)
PH08609 712-713 (July 13, 1995) p114. "Good Guys: Kilmer's Batman, Kidman's Dr. Chase Meridian, O'Donnell's Robin"
PH08610 719 (October 19, 1995) p156. "Kidman Gets Dillon In A Sexual Vise"
PH08611 719 (October 19, 1995) p156. "She Glides Her TV-Form Divine Past Gawkers Phoenix, Affleck And Folland"
PH08612 731 (April 4, 1996) p66. "Kidman, 'To Die For'"
KIDMAN, NICOLE—PHOTOGRAPHS—PORTRAITS
PH08613 743 (September 19, 1996) p90. "Quality Control"
KIDS (FILM)—ILLUSTRATIONS
PH08614 714 (August 10, 1995) p61. "Kids Today" (Tillery, Bob)
PH08615 714 (August 10, 1995) p61. "Kids Today" (Tillery, Val)
KIDS (FILM)—PHOTOGRAPHS
PH08616 709 (June 1, 1995) p70. "Rebel Voices"
PH08617 714 (August 10, 1995) p62. "Fitzpatrick Kisses A New Virgin"
PH08618 714 (August 10, 1995) p62. "The Kids Of 'Kids' Prowl"
PH08619 716 (September 7, 1995) p78. "Summer Wrap-Up]"
PH08620 724-725 (December 28, 1995) p136. "Unusual Pleasure"
KIDS IN THE HALL—PHOTOGRAPHS—PORTRAITS
PH08621 733 (May 2, 1996) p62. "Kids Foley, McKinney, McCulloch, McDonald And Thompson"
KIEDIS, ANTHONY—ILLUSTRATIONS
PH08622 624 (February 20, 1992) p5. "The Pepper's Anthony Kiedis" (Burke, Philip)
PH08623 682 (May 19, 1994) p14. "Freedom" (Pendergrast, James T.)
PH08624 682 (May 19, 1994) p14. "Rolling Stone" (Pendergrast, James T.)
KIEDIS, ANTHONY—PHOTOGRAPHS
PH08625 624 (February 20, 1992) p19. "Anthony Kiedis" (Constanini, Mark)
PH08626 629 (April 30, 1992) p23. "John Frusciante, Anthony Kiedis, Chad Smith And Flea (from left)" (Cuffaro, Chris)
PH08627 631 (May 28, 1992) p9. "Skate-Master Tate, MCA, Ad-Rock, Anthony Kiedis, Henry Rollins (from left)" (Cohen, Lester)
PH08628 638 (September 3, 1992) p9. "Anthony Kiedis Proves Red Hot" (Blakesberg, Jay)
PH08629 639 (September 17, 1992) p61. "Anthony Kiedis" (Blakesberg, Jay)
PH08630 639 (September 17, 1992) p60. "Chili Peppers Flea (left) And Kiedis" (Blakesberg, Jay)
PH08631 642 (October 29, 1992) p19. "Kiedis (left) And Vedder Get Tender" (Mazur, Kevin)
PH08632 654 (April 15, 1993) p11. "Chili Peppers Kiedis And Flea Flank Fan Tony Bennett" (Downie, Scott)
PH08633 655 (April 29, 1993) p16. "Michael (left) And The Chili Peppers' Kiedis Are Raising Money For AIDS Patients" (Mazur, Kevin)

PH08634 660-661 (July 8, 1993) p17. "Man Overboard: Smith, Kiedis, Marshall And Flea" (Leialoha, Mark)
PH08635 665 (September 16, 1993) p16. "Anthony Kiedis And Flea (below)" (Seliger, Mark)
PH08636 667 (October 14, 1993) p39. "Flea, Bennett And Anthony Kiedis" (Mazur, Kevin)
PH08637 672-673 (December 23, 1993) p63. "Left: Flea, Bennett And Kiedis" (Kravitz, Jeff)
PH08638 674 (January 27, 1994) p28. "Nirvana's Dave Grohl And Krist Novoselic With Madcap MTV Hosts Anthony Kiedis And Flea" (Mazur, Kevin)
PH08639 679 (April 7, 1994) pp48,51-52. "[Anthony Kiedis]" (Rolston, Matthew)
PH08640 679 (April 7, 1994) p49. "We Three: Hillel Slovak, Kiedis And Flea In '82 (from left)" (Shear, Jack)
PH08641 692 (October 6, 1994) p17. "Peppers Roast: Flea, Anthony Kiedis, Dave Navarro, Chad Smith (from left)" (Mazur, Kevin)
PH08642 709 (June 1, 1995) p21. "RHCPs (from left): Flea, Chad Smith, Dave Navarro And Anthony Kiedis" (Streiber, Art)
PH08643 719 (October 19, 1995) p56. "'86: Irons, Slovak, Flea, Kiedis (from left) Backstage At The Ritz, In New York" (Gershoff, Gary)
PH08644 719 (October 19, 1995) p16. "Anthony Kiedis And The Divine Miss M" (Mazur, Kevin)
PH08645 719 (October 19, 1995) pp52-53. "Anthony Kiedis And Flea" (Corbijn, Anton)
PH08646 719 (October 19, 1995) pp54-55. "Flea, Kiedis" (Corbijn, Anton)
PH08647 719 (October 19, 1995) p58. "Red Hot Chili Peppers, '95: Dave Navarro, Anthony Kiedis, Flea An Chad Smith (from left)" (Corbijn, Anton)
PH08648 719 (October 19, 1995) p60. "Woodstock 1994: Flea And Kiedis" (Weiner, Scott)
PH08649 722 (November 30, 1995) p19. "[Red Hot Chili Peppers]" (Musto, Ilpo)
PH08650 731 (April 4, 1996) p17. "Bush Covers? Chili Peppers Frontman Anthony Kiedis, Bassist Flea, The Not-Unattractive Navarro And Drummer Chad Smith (from left)" (Baehler, Chapman)

KIEDIS, ANTHONY—PHOTOGRAPHS—PORTRAITS
PH08651 679 (April 7, 1994) pp46-47,50. "[Anthony Kiedis]" (Rolston, Matthew)
PH08652 679 (April 7, 1994) pp[cover]. "Red Hot Chili Peppers' Anthony Kiedis: Confessions Of Sir Psycho Sexy" (Rolston, Matthew)
PH08653 694 (November 3, 1994) p22. "[Johnny Cash & Anthony Kiedis]" (Roberts, Ebet)
PH08654 703 (March 9, 1995) p21. "Red Hot Chili Peppers Anthony Kiedis (left) And Dave Navarro At The Slayer Blowout In Los Angeles" (Cohen, Lester)

KIER, LADY MISS—PHOTOGRAPHS
PH08655 667 (October 14, 1993) p101. "Deee-Lite: Lady Kier In The 'Groove'"

KIG MISSILE—ALBUMS
PH08656 652 (March 18, 1993) p39. "Happy Hour" (.)

KILCHER, JEWEL—PHOTOGRAPHS
PH08657 716 (September 7, 1995) p14. "Jewel Of The Aisle: Kilcher And Penn Get Acquainted Backstage" (Young, P.)

KILLER JOE—ALBUMS
PH08658 622 (January 23, 1992) p46. "Scene Of The Crime"

KILLING ZOE (FILM)—PHOTOGRAPHS
PH08659 690 (September 8, 1994) p87. "[Killing Zoe]"

KILMER, VAL—ILLUSTRATIONS
PH08660 712-713 (July 13, 1995) p113. "Fire Rockets 1, 2, 3" (Allen, Terry)

KILMER, VAL—PHOTOGRAPHS
PH08661 619-620 (December 12, 1991) p31. "Val Kilmer Gets Oliver Stoned"
PH08662 724-725 (December 28, 1995) p138. "De Niro, Pacino And Kilmer In 'Heat'"

KILMER, VAL—PHOTOGRAPHS—PORTRAITS
PH08663 712-713 (July 13, 1995) p114. "Good Guys: Kilmer's Batman, Kidman's Dr. Chase Meridian, O'Donnell's Robin"

KILMISTER, LEMMY—PHOTOGRAPHS
PH08664 727 (February 8, 1996) p12. "Fifty And Fabulous! Kilmister (center) Flanked By Metallica's Jason Newsted, James Hetfield, Kirk Hammett And Lars Ulrich (from left)" (Disanto, Annamaria)

KIMBALL, JENNIFER—PHOTOGRAPHS—PORTRAITS
PH08665 636 (August 6, 1992) p24. "Jennifer Kimball (left) And Jonatha Brooke" (Horner, Carl J.)

KIMBLE, PAUL—PHOTOGRAPHS
PH08666 663 (August 19, 1993) p24. "[Grant Lee Buffalo]" (Azimi, Mojgan B.)
PH08667 695 (November 17, 1994) p94. "Grant Lee Buffalo" (Samuel, Deborah)
PH08668 696 (December 1, 1994) pp98-99. "American Icons: Joey Peters, Grant Lee Phillips And Paul Kimble (from left)" (Ockenfels, Frank, 3)

KIMBROUGH, JOHN—PHOTOGRAPHS—PORTRAITS
PH08669 637 (August 20, 1992) p20. "Candice Belanoff, John Kimbrough And Joey Waronker (from left)" (Cuffaro, Chris)

KIMBROUGH, JUNIOR—ALBUMS
PH08670 649 (February 4, 1993) p69. "All Night Long"
PH08671 698-699 (December 29, 1994) p181. "Sad Days, Lonely Nights"

KINCHLA, CHAN—PHOTOGRAPHS
PH08672 622 (January 23, 1992) p10. "Clockwise From Top Left: Bobby Sheehan, Brendan Hill, John Popper, Chan Kinchla" (Carroll, Chris)
PH08673 631 (May 28, 1992) p17. "Blues Traveler (from left): Chan Kinchla, John Popper, Brendan Hill And Bobby Sheehan" (Aresu, Paul)
PH08674 659 (June 24, 1993) p58. "After Eight Months Off, Kinchla Finally Said: 'Enough! Touring Is What I Want To Do!'" (Fink, Larry)
PH08675 659 (June 24, 1993) p57. "Band Of Gypsies: Brendan Hill, Chan Kinchla, John Popper And Bobby Sheehan (from left)" (Fink, Larry)
PH08676 714 (August 10, 1995) p16. "Blues Traveler's Chan Kinchla, Bobby Sheehan, Brendan Hill And Popper (from left) With Ice-T (second from left)" (Kravitz, Jeff)

KING AD-ROCK—PHOTOGRAPHS
PH08677 648 (January 21, 1993) p24. "MCA (left) And King Ad Rock Of The Beasties" (Mazur, Kevin)

KING AD-ROCK—PHOTOGRAPHS—PORTRAITS
PH08678 695 (November 17, 1994) p139. "Beastie Boys" (Rolston, Matthew)

KING, AL—PHOTOGRAPHS
PH08679 741 (August 22, 1996) p66. "In Tombstone, Everything's Fake But The Guns: Bounty Hunter Al King" (Maxwell, Robert)

KING, ALBERT—PHOTOGRAPHS—PORTRAITS
PH08680 649 (February 4, 1993) p12. "[Albert King]"
PH08681 672-673 (December 23, 1993) p79. "Right: Albert King" (Watson, Albert)

KING, B. B.—ALBUMS
PH08682 645-646 (December 10, 1992) p170. "King Of The Blues"

KING, B. B.—PHOTOGRAPHS
PH08683 616 (October 31, 1991) p13. "B. B. King (left) And Robert Cray" (Blakesberg, Jay)
PH08684 618 (November 28, 1991) p74. "Guy, B. B. King And Junior Wells At The 1968 Newport Folk Festival" (Gahr, David)
PH08685 625 (March 5, 1992) p13. "Bobby 'Blue' Bland (left) With B. B. King" (Elgar, Nick)
PH08686 630 (May 14, 1992) p13. "Tom Petty, George Harrison, Gary Moore And B. B. King (from left)"

PH08687 697 (December 15, 1994) p20. "Steve Cropper, King And Lowell Fulson Pay Tribute To Dixon (from left)" (Mosenfelder, Tim)
PH08688 711 (June 29, 1995) p18. "B. B. King, Robert Cray, Buddy Guy, Art Neville, Jimmie Vaughan, Clapton, Raitt And Tommy Shannon" (Long, Andrew)
PH08689 720 (November 2, 1995) p50. "B. B. King" (Hooks Brothers)
PH08690 748 (November 28, 1996) p26. "King And Shepherd At A Tour Stop In Minneapolis"
PH08691 750-751 (December 26, 1996) p196. "Books"
KING, B. B.—PHOTOGRAPHS—PORTRAITS
PH08692 625 (March 5, 1992) pp14-15. "On The Evening Of The Seventh Annual Hall Of Fame Induction Ceremony, 'Rolling Stone' Gathered These Nine Legendary Guitarists At The Waldorf-Astoria For A Once-In-A-Lifetime..."
PH08693 643 (November 12, 1992) p180. "B. B. King" (Markus, Kurt)
KING, BEN E.—PHOTOGRAPHS
PH08694 681 (May 5, 1994) p15. "Ben E. King And Irma Thomas Are Besides Themselves" (Micelotta, Frank)
KING, BEN E.—PHOTOGRAPHS—PORTRAITS
PH08695 681 (May 5, 1994) p15. "Ben E. King And Irma Thomas Are Besides Themselves"
KING BUZZO—PHOTOGRAPHS
PH08696 675 (February 10, 1994) p22. "Crover, Simmons, King Buzzo And Mark Deutrom" (Cohen, Lester)
KING, CAROLE—ALBUMS
PH08697 659 (June 24, 1993) p80. "Colour Of Your Dreams"
KING, CAROLE—PHOTOGRAPHS
PH08698 633 (June 25, 1992) p12. "Slash: Carole King And I" (Whitall, Bob)
PH08699 692 (October 6, 1994) p52. "Carole King"
KING, CAROLE—PHOTOGRAPHS—PORTRAITS
PH08700 636 (August 6, 1992) p13. "Carole King" (Greyshock, Caroline)
PH08701 643 (November 12, 1992) pp176-177. "Carole King" (Markus, Kurt)
KING COFFEY—PHOTOGRAPHS
PH08702 696 (December 1, 1994) p32. "The Butthole Surfer's King Coffey" (Eder, John)
KING CRIMSON—ALBUMS
PH08703 617 (November 14, 1991) p140. "In The Court Of The Crimson King" (Godber, Barry)
PH08704 698-699 (December 29, 1994) p174. "Vroom"
PH08705 711 (June 29, 1995) p43. "Thrak"
KING CRIMSON—PHOTOGRAPHS
PH08706 655 (April 29, 1993) p20. "The Great Deceivers: John Wetton, David Cross, Fripp And Bill Bruford (from left)"
KING CRIMSON—PHOTOGRAPHS—PORTRAITS
PH08707 684 (June 16, 1994) p18. "Belew, Fripp, Bruford And Levin"
KING, KERRY—PHOTOGRAPHS
PH08708 705 (April 6, 1995) p36. "Live Evil: Araya (left) And King" (Mazur, Kevin)
KING, LARRY—ILLUSTRATIONS
PH08709 747 (November 14, 1996) p74. "[Larry King]" (Hirschfeld, Al)
PH08710 750-751 (December 26, 1996) p26. "Answer Machine" (Pendergrast, James T.)
KING, LARRY—PHOTOGRAPHS
PH08711 747 (November 14, 1996) p76. "Joe Garagiola, Larry And Herb Cohen (from left) In 1988"
PH08712 747 (November 14, 1996) p76. "Larry (center) With The Author (second from right) In 1995 At A Fund-Raiser"
PH08713 747 (November 14, 1996) p78. "Larry And Herbie (top row, from left), Warriors On The Stoop In Bensonhurst"
PH08714 747 (November 14, 1996) p81. "Live From New York's Governors Island, 1984: Larry, Gov. Mario Cuomo, Herb Cohen (from left)"
PH08715 747 (November 14, 1996) p78. "Warriors, 1946: Larry (with bottle) Standing Next To Herbie (center)"
PH08716 747 (November 14, 1996) p81. "Washington, D.C., 1988: Writer George Will With Larry And Herb Cohen (from left)" (Naltchayan, Neshan)
PH08717 747 (November 14, 1996) p76. "With Presidential Candidate Ross Perot In October 1992"
KING, LARRY—PHOTOGRAPHS—PORTRAITS
PH08718 747 (November 14, 1996) p79. "Larry During The Miami Days, Circa 1959"
KING, LITTLE JIMMY—PHOTOGRAPHS
PH08719 697 (December 15, 1994) p17. "[Rolling Stones]" (Jones, Steve)
KING MISSILE—PHOTOGRAPHS—PORTRAITS
PH08720 654 (April 15, 1993) p17. "Murdock, Hall, Xefos, Rick (from left)" (Seliger, Mark)
THE KING OF COMEDY (FILM)—PHOTOGRAPHS
PH08721 742 (September 5, 1996) p68. "With Lewis In 'The King Of Comedy'"
KING OF THE HILL (FILM)—PHOTOGRAPHS
PH08722 664 (September 2, 1993) p70. "Krabbe Leaves Bradford Home Alone"
KING, PHIL—PHOTOGRAPHS—PORTRAITS
PH08723 729 (March 7, 1996) p29. "Lush Members Emma Anderson, Phil King, Miki Berenyi And Chris Acland (from left)" (Anker, Matt)
KING, STEPHEN—PHOTOGRAPHS
PH08724 634-635 (July 9, 1992) p13. "Authorial Intrusion: Stephen King, Dave Barry And Ridley Pearson (from left)" (Foothorap, Robert)
KINGPIN (FILM)—PHOTOGRAPHS
PH08725 736 (June 13, 1996) p61. "Funny Guys"
KING'S X—ALBUMS
PH08726 629 (April 30, 1992) p56. "King's X"
KINGSBURY, BOB—PHOTOGRAPHS
PH08727 632 (June 11, 1992) p62. "Staff Members And Contributing Writers At The 1971 Editorial Conference, At Esalen, In Big Sur" (Leibovitz, Annie)
PH08728 643 (November 12, 1992) p49. "'Rolling Stone' Art Directors (from left): Bob Kingsbury (1968-73), Tony Lane (1974-76), Annie Leibovitz, Mike Salisbury (1973-74), Roger Black (1976-78), Jann S. Wenner..."
KINGSLEY, BEN—PHOTOGRAPHS
PH08729 640 (October 1, 1992) p72. "Kingsley (left) Puts Redford On The Spot"
PH08730 700 (January 26, 1995) p68. "Weaver And Kingsley Talk "Death""
KINISON, SAM—PHOTOGRAPHS—PORTRAITS
PH08731 631 (May 28, 1992) p26. "[Sam Kinison]" (Seliger, Mark)
PH08732 645-646 (December 10, 1992) p101. "Comedian Sam Kinison" (Seliger, Mark)
KINKS—ALBUMS
PH08733 654 (April 15, 1993) p64. "Phobia"
KINNEAR, GREG—PHOTOGRAPHS
PH08734 726 (January 25, 1996) p66. "Unlucky In Love: Ormond Flanked By Kinnear And Ford"
KINNEY, JONATHAN—PHOTOGRAPHS—PORTRAITS
PH08735 728 (February 22, 1996) p50. "Oct. 12, 1995: Jonathan Kinney Waits To Be Arraigned At The Outagamie County Courthouse" (Powers, Dan)
KINNEY, KEVIN—PHOTOGRAPHS
PH08736 650 (February 18, 1993) p13. "Baird, Kevin Kinney And Richards (from left)" (Diamond, Rick)
KINNEY, SEAN—ILLUSTRATIONS
PH08737 695 (November 17, 1994) p129. "Alice In Chains" (Holley, Jason)
KINNEY, SEAN—PHOTOGRAPHS
PH08738 644 (November 26, 1992) p45. "[Alice In Chains]" (Winters, Dan)

PH08739 662 (August 5, 1993) p13. "Mike Inez, Layne Staley, Jerry Cantrell And Sean Kinney (clockwise from top left) Of Alice In Chains" (Blakesberg, Jay)
PH08740 676 (February 24, 1994) p18. "Chain Reaction: Sean Kinney, Jerry Cantrell, Layne Staley And Mike Inez (from left)" (Moskowitz, Karen)
PH08741 727 (February 8, 1996) p33. "Kinney, Cantrell, Staley And Inez (from left)" (Seliger, Mark)
PH08742 727 (February 8, 1996) p35. "Kinney, Cantrell, Staley And Mike Starr In 1990 (from left)"
KINSKI, NASTASSIA—PHOTOGRAPHS
PH08743 645-646 (December 10, 1992) p153. "Nastassia Kinski, 1982"
KIRCHHERR, ASTRID—PHOTOGRAPHS
PH08744 680 (April 21, 1994) p64. "Ticket To Ride: Starr And Lennon With Photographer Astrid Kirchherr" (Scheler, Max)
KIRKWOOD, CRIS—PHOTOGRAPHS
PH08745 682 (May 19, 1994) p21. "Puppet Masters: Curt And Cris Kirkwood And Derrick Bostrom (from left)" (Halsband, Michael)
PH08746 695 (November 17, 1994) p145. "Meat Puppets" (Seliger, Mark)
PH08747 710 (June 15, 1995) p48. "Hey, Mow! Cris And Curt Kirkwood And Derrick Bostrom (from left)" (Gipe, Jon)
KIRKWOOD, CURT—PHOTOGRAPHS
PH08748 682 (May 19, 1994) p21. "Puppet Masters: Curt And Cris Kirkwood And Derrick Bostrom (from left)" (Halsband, Michael)
PH08749 694 (November 3, 1994) p22. "Stern And Puppet Curt Kirkwood" (Mazur, Kevin)
PH08750 695 (November 17, 1994) p145. "Meat Puppets" (Seliger, Mark)
PH08751 710 (June 15, 1995) p48. "Hey, Mow! Cris And Curt Kirkwood And Derrick Bostrom (from left)" (Gipe, Jon)
KIRSCH, JOHN—PHOTOGRAPHS
PH08752 721 (November 16, 1995) p33. "John Kirsch, Braden Blake, Jake Nesheim And Chris Lockwood (from left)" (Moskowitz, Karen)
KIRSHNER, MIA—PHOTOGRAPHS
PH08753 708 (May 18, 1995) p17. "Love, On The Rocks: Dando And Date" (Mazur, Kevin)
PH08754 743 (September 19, 1996) p90. "Now Playing"
KISS—ILLUSTRATIONS
PH08755 750-751 (December 26, 1996) p64. "[Kiss]" (Piven, Hanoch)
KISS—PHOTOGRAPHS
PH08756 715 (August 24, 1995) p25. "Paul Stanley, Gene Simmons, Eric Singer, Bruce Kulick (from left)" (Blakesberg, Jay)
PH08757 724-725 (December 28, 1995) p51. "Kiss' Simmons, Eric Singer, Stanley And Bruce Kulick (from left)" (Blakesberg, Jay)
PH08758 727 (February 8, 1996) p18. "Gene Simmons, Peter Criss And Ace Frehley (from left) Rode 'Kiss Alive!' To Stardom In 1975 And Scored A Second Hit Concert Album With 'Kiss Alive II' In 1977" (Putland, Michael)
PH08759 732 (April 18, 1996) p19. "Ace Frehley, Paul Stanley, 2Pac, Peter Criss And Gene Simmons (from left)" (Mazur, Kevin)
PH08760 736 (June 13, 1996) p52. "Kiss Come Back With Their Makeup Intact: Ace Frehley, Gene Simmons, Peter Criss And Paul Stanley" (Malluk, Eddie)
KISS—PHOTOGRAPHS—PORTRAITS
PH08761 736 (June 13, 1996) pp[cover]. "Rock & Roll Summer!" (Costello)
KISS OF DEATH (FILM)—PHOTOGRAPHS
PH08762 707 (May 4, 1995) p74. "Caruso And Cage In 'Kiss Of Death'"
KISSER, ANDREAS—PHOTOGRAPHS
PH08763 689 (August 25, 1994) p16. "Dimebag (left) With hair Mate Kisser" (Settle, Ken)
KISSINGER, HENRY—PHOTOGRAPHS
PH08764 659 (June 24, 1993) p15. "Russian Summit: Ed Lover, Henry Kissinger And Dr. Dre (from left)" (Mazur, Kevin)
PH08765 690 (September 8, 1994) p48. "Above, In A Photo From The CD-ROM: Nixon, Ehrlichman, Kissinger, Haldeman"
KITT, A. J.—PHOTOGRAPHS
PH08766 624 (February 20, 1992) p37. "[A. J. Kitt]" (Eccles, Andrew)
KITT, ERTHA—ILLUSTRATIONS
PH08767 636 (August 6, 1992) p63. "Depreciating Eddie Murphy" (Brodner, Steven)
KLAAS, JOE—PHOTOGRAPHS
PH08768 677 (March 10, 1994) p48. "Ryder, With Klaas' Grandfather Joe Klaas And A Neighbor, Learns Of Polly's Death" (Manchester, Scott)
KLEIMAN, JON—PHOTOGRAPHS
PH08769 710 (June 15, 1995) p54. "Boys In The Attic (clockwise from upper left): Ed Mundell, Jon Kleiman, Wyndorf And Joe Calandra" (Toliver, Chris)
KLEIMAN, JON—PHOTOGRAPHS—PORTRAITS
PH08770 716 (September 7, 1995) p34. "Dopes To Infinity: Wyndorf, Mundell, Kleiman And Calandra (from left)" (Lavine, Michael)
KLEMKE, ANITA—PHOTOGRAPHS—PORTRAITS
PH08771 712-713 (July 13, 1995) p42. "Klemke And Shaw In '66"
KLETT, PETER—PHOTOGRAPHS
PH08772 674 (January 27, 1994) p24. "Bardi Martin, Klett, Kevin Martin, Mercado (from left)" (Knight, Kevin)
PH08773 702 (February 23, 1995) p23. "Candlebox (from left): Peter Klett, Scott Mercado, Kevin Martin, Bardi Martin" (Ford, Charles)
PH08774 702 (February 23, 1995) p25. "Guitarist Klett Before The "Smashing" Finale" (Mazur, Kevin)
KLEYN, DUARD—PHOTOGRAPHS
PH08775 730 (March 21, 1996) pp86-87. "Duard Kleyn (opposite) Is The Drummer For Friday Nights' Squeezebox, And Larry Mitchell Is A Solo Performer" (Witkin, Christian)
KLINE, KEVIN—ILLUSTRATIONS
PH08776 657 (May 27, 1993) p55. "Mr. Myth Goes To Washington" (Risko, Robert)
KLINE, KEVIN—PHOTOGRAPHS
PH08777 657 (May 27, 1993) p56. "Dave Practices His Moves"
PH08778 657 (May 27, 1993) p56. "Dave The Fake Prez (Kevin Kline) Waves With The Real First Lady (Sigourney Weaver)"
PH08779 708 (May 18, 1995) p96. "Meg Ryan Mixes It Up With French Kisser Kevin Kline"
KMFDM—PHOTOGRAPHS—PORTRAITS
PH08780 740 (August 8, 1996) p24. "Scary Monsters: KMFDM's Schulz, Connelly, Konietzko, En Esch (from left)" (Elledge, Paul)
KNAB, CHRIS—PHOTOGRAPHS
PH08781 678 (March 24, 1994) p57. "Cursed? KCMU-FM Management: Knab, Now Resigned, Yates And Mara (from left)" (Lavine, Michael)
KNAPP, CHERYL DAVIS—PHOTOGRAPHS—PORTRAITS
PH08782 642 (October 29, 1992) p49. "[Cheryl Davis Knapp]"
KNIEVEL, EVEL—ILLUSTRATIONS
PH08783 632 (June 11, 1992) p61. "[Evel Knievel]" (Cronin, Brian)
KNIEVEL, EVEL—PHOTOGRAPHS
PH08784 632 (June 11, 1992) p64. "Evel Knievel: Ready For The Greatest Day Of His Life" (Krueger, Gary)
PH08785 632 (June 11, 1992) p65. "The Skycycle On Its Way To The Floor Of The Snake" (Krueger, Gary)
KNIGHT, GLADYS—PHOTOGRAPHS
PH08786 728 (February 22, 1996) p19. "Knight (left) And Carey" (Mazur, Kevin)
KNIGHT, LOVELL—PHOTOGRAPHS
PH08787 708 (May 18, 1995) p58. "Karren Parker, Right, With Boyfriend Lovell Knight, Claims Humphries Asked Her 'Why

Can't You Black Girls Not Have So Many Babies?'" (Mark, Mary Ellen)
KNIGHT, MARION—PHOTOGRAPHS
PH08788 745 (October 17, 1996) p40. "Tupac Shakur (left) With Death Row's 'Suge' Knight This Summer"
KNIGHT, SUGE—PHOTOGRAPHS
PH08789 746 (October 31, 1996) p41. "Shakur (left) And Knight Sitting In Knight's Black BMW Sedan In Las Vegas On Sept. 7, Only Moments Before The Shooting" (Corjuni)
PH08790 746 (October 31, 1996) p46. "Shakur (left) And Suge Knight In 1995 At Club 662 On Flamingo Road In Downtown Las Vegas"
KNOEDELSEDER, WILLIAM—BOOKS
PH08791 656 (May 13, 1993) p26. "Stiffed: A True Story Of MCA, The Music Business, And The Mafia"
KNOPFLER, MARK—PHOTOGRAPHS
PH08792 629 (April 30, 1992) p29. "Mark Knopfler" (Mazur, Kevin)
KNOPFLER, MARK—PHOTOGRAPHS—PORTRAITS
PH08793 643 (November 12, 1992) p215. "Mark Knopfler" (Watson, Albert)
KNOX, CHRIS—PHOTOGRAPHS
PH08794 709 (June 1, 1995) p30. "Chris Knox Bares All" (Kravitz, Jeff)
KNOX, NEAL—PHOTOGRAPHS
PH08795 710 (June 15, 1995) p58. "Knox" (Brack, Dennis)
PH08796 746 (October 31, 1996) p52. "Flirting With Disaster? The NRA's Neal Knox, The Gun Lobby's Wizard Of Oz" (Berman, Nina)
KNUTSEN, LEIF—PHOTOGRAPHS
PH08797 664 (September 2, 1993) p34. "Where Bankers Fear To Tread" (Rystedt, Rex)
KOA, CHRISTIANO—PHOTOGRAPHS
PH08798 730 (March 21, 1996) p88. "Christiano Koa (opposite) Is The Manager Of Don Hill's" (Witkin, Christian)
KOBE, JAPAN—PHOTOGRAPHS
PH08799 740 (August 8, 1996) p45. "Kobe, Japan, January 1995" (Iwasa)
KOENIG, ERIC—PHOTOGRAPHS
PH08800 678 (March 24, 1994) p77. "Like Studying Sex? Cal Artists Walt Dohrn (left) And Eric Koenig In A Student-Designed Dorm Room" (Little, Blake)
KOHN, HOWARD—PHOTOGRAPHS
PH08801 632 (June 11, 1992) p97. "Kohn At A Rally In California In 1978"
PH08802 632 (June 11, 1992) p103. "Kohn, Alison And David Weir And Wenner (from left) In 1975" (Kohn, Diana)
KONICKE, TOM—PHOTOGRAPHS—PORTRAITS
PH08803 747 (November 14, 1996) p26. "Deadhead Tom Konicke (left) With Wavy Gravy" (Mazur, Kevin)
KOOL DJ HERC—PHOTOGRAPHS
PH08804 670 (November 25, 1993) p37. "Grandmaster Flash, Herc, Afrika Bambaataa And Chuck D" (Mazur, Kevin)
KOOL DJ RED ALERT—PHOTOGRAPHS—PORTRAITS
PH08805 679 (April 7, 1994) p32. "Dance-Hall Disc: Red Alert"
KOONS, DEBORAH—PHOTOGRAPHS
PH08806 679 (April 7, 1994) p38. "The Garcias" (Frost, Frankie)
PH08807 691 (September 22, 1994) p20. "[Jerry Garcia & Deborah Koons]" (Ferreira, Albert)
PH08807a 717 (September 21, 1995) p28. "Olatunji With Kantner, Two Drummers, John Perry Barlow, Weir And Koons Garcia (from left) At The Aug. 13 Memorial At The Polo Field" (Blakesberg, Jay)
KOPPEL, TED—ILLUSTRATIONS
PH08808 726 (January 25, 1996) p77. "[Ted Koppel]" (Fishman, Miriam)
KOPROWSKI, HILARY—PHOTOGRAPHS
PH08809 626 (March 19, 1992) p59. "Dr. Hilary Koprowski And An Assistant Making Polio Vaccine In 1956" (Joel, Yale)
KORINE, HARMONY—PHOTOGRAPHS—PORTRAITS
PH08810 715 (August 24, 1995) p84. "Harmony Korine's Hot List" (Irish, Len)
KORS, ALAN CHARLES—PHOTOGRAPHS
PH08811 662 (August 5, 1993) p48. "Jacobowitz With Kors: 'There Ought To Be Truth In Advertising,' Says The History Professor" (Massar, Eli)
KOTTKE, LEO—PHOTOGRAPHS
PH08812 669 (November 11, 1993) p28. "Peculiar Pairing: Jones And Kottke"
KOUTSOS, ANTHONY—PHOTOGRAPHS
PH08813 665 (September 16, 1993) p25. "In The Red: Mack, Vessel, Kozelek, Koutsos (from left)" (Blakesberg, Jay)
KOVIC, RON—ILLUSTRATIONS
PH08814 632 (June 11, 1992) p77. "[Ron Kovic]" (Cronin, Brian)
KOVIC, RON—PHOTOGRAPHS—PORTRAITS
PH08815 632 (June 11, 1992) pp78-79. "[Ron Kovic]" (Leibovitz, Annie)
KOWALCZYK, ED—PHOTOGRAPHS
PH08816 630 (May 14, 1992) p28. "Live's Edward Kowalczyk" (Kraft, Chris)
PH08817 696 (December 1, 1994) p51. "Ed Kowalczyk" (Fleischauer, Robert)
PH08818 714 (August 10, 1995) p15. "[Ed Kowalczyk]" (Rikken, Clemens)
PH08819 721 (November 16, 1995) p26. "Harvey And Kowalczyk, Sharing And Caring In Pennsylvania" (Oleski, Dan)
PH08820 724-725 (December 28, 1995) p54. "MTV Video Music Award Performers: Live's Ed Kowalczyk, Michael Stipe And White Zombie's Sean Yseult (from left)" (Mazur, Kevin)
PH08821 726 (January 25, 1996) p35. "Dahlheimer, Taylor, Kowalczyk And Gracey (from left) At Their York, Pa., High School In 1989" (Broad, Julian)
PH08822 726 (January 25, 1996) p37. "Singer, Natty Dresser And The Readers' Fave: Live's Ed Kowalczyk Gives His All Onstage" (Micelotta, Frank)
KOWALCZYK, ED—PHOTOGRAPHS—PORTRAITS
PH08823 726 (January 25, 1996) pp32-33. "Ed Kowalczyk" (Broad, Julian)
PH08824 726 (January 25, 1996) p34. "Taylor, Kowalczyk, Gracey And Dahlheimer (from left) In New York In Late 1995" (Broad, Julian)
KOWALEZYK, ED—PHOTOGRAPHS
PH08825 710 (June 15, 1995) p31. "Live And Let Live: Ed Kowalezyk" (Diamond, Rick)
PH08826 716 (September 7, 1995) p13. "Chad Taylor, Kowalezyk, Pat Dahlheimer (from left)" (Callahan, Kristin)
KOZELEK, MARK—PHOTOGRAPHS
PH08827 665 (September 16, 1993) p25. "In The Red: Mack, Vessel, Kozelek, Koutsos (from left)" (Blakesberg, Jay)
KOZIK, FRANK—PHOTOGRAPHS
PH08828 672-673 (December 23, 1993) p133. "Frank Kozik Outside CBGB In N.Y.C." (Danelian, Steve)
KRAL, IVAN—PHOTOGRAPHS
PH08829 738-739 (July 11, 1996) p44. "Smith's Great '70s Band"
KRAMER, JOEY—PHOTOGRAPHS
PH08830 622 (January 23, 1992) p7. "Brad Whitford, David Bowie, Steven Tyler, Hunt Sales, Tony Sales, Reeves Gabrels, Joey Kramer" (McAlpine, Paul)
PH08831 694 (November 3, 1994) p60. "Early Daze: Whitford, Tyler, Hamilton, Perry And Kramer At Boston College, 1973" (Pownall, Ron)
PH08832 724-725 (December 28, 1995) p40. "Aerosmith's Tom Hamilton, Joey Kramer, Brad Whitford And Steven Tyler (from left)" (Robicheau, Paul)
KRAMER, WAYNE—ALBUMS
PH08833 704 (March 23, 1995) p122. "The Hard Stuff"

KRAMER, WAYNE—PHOTOGRAPHS

PH08834 632 (June 11, 1992) p36. "MC5 (clockwise from top left): Thompson, Tyner, Kramer, Smith"

PH08835 708 (May 18, 1995) p30. "MC5: Michael Davis, Dennis Thompson, Kramer, Smith, Tyner (from left)"

PH08836 708 (May 18, 1995) p30. "[Wayne Kramer]" (Dyer, Alison)

KRATOCHVIL, LAURIE—PHOTOGRAPHS

PH08837 643 (November 12, 1992) p49. "'Rolling Stone' Art Directors (from left): Bob Kingsbury (1968-73), Tony Lane (1974-76), Annie Leibovitz, Mike Salisbury (1973-74), Roger Black (1976-78), Jann S. Wenner..." (Le

KRAUSS, ALISON—ILLUSTRATIONS

PH08838 712-713 (July 13, 1995) p132. "Alison Krauss: Fiddler On The Loose" (Martin, Matthew)

KRAUSS, ALISON—PHOTOGRAPHS—PORTRAITS

PH08839 726 (January 25, 1996) p48. "Alison Krauss" (Harrington, Russ)

KRAVITZ, LENNY—ALBUMS

PH08840 655 (April 29, 1993) p61. "Are You Gonna Go My Way"

PH08841 672-673 (December 23, 1993) p153. "Are You Gonna Go My Way"

PH08842 717 (September 21, 1995) p81. "Circus"

KRAVITZ, LENNY—ILLUSTRATIONS

PH08843 717 (September 21, 1995) p81. "Led Love Rules" (Brown, Calef)

PH08844 726 (January 25, 1996) p12. "The Hip Club" (Pendergrast, James T.)

KRAVITZ, LENNY—PHOTOGRAPHS

PH08845 669 (November 11, 1993) p20. "[Lenny Kravitz]" (Gustafsson, Per)

PH08846 671 (December 9, 1993) p32. "[Slash & Lenny Kravitz]" (Mayer, Jeffrey)

PH08847 672-673 (December 23, 1993) p27. "Right: Ultracool Lenny Kravitz" (Blakesberg, Jay)

PH08848 695 (November 17, 1994) p61. "Lenny Kravitz" (Afanador, Ruven)

PH08849 722 (November 30, 1995) p52. "Fun In The Sun: Kravitz And Mom Roxie Roker On The Beach In California, 1967"

PH08850 722 (November 30, 1995) p55. "Kravitz Rocks Out In 1992: 'Every Riff Sounds Like Something Else'" (Somoza, Gerardo)

PH08851 722 (November 30, 1995) pp48-49,50. "[Lenny Kravitz]" (Rolston, Matthew)

PH08852 722 (November 30, 1995) p53. "Lenny The Family man: With Lisa Bonet And Baby Zoe In 1989" (Zuffante, Vinnie)

PH08853 722 (November 30, 1995) pp[cover]. "What's So Funny About Peace, Love And Lenny Kravitz" (Rolston, Matthew)

PH08854 723 (December 14, 1995) p28. "Kravitz (left) And Collins Funk It Up In Los Angeles"

PH08855 735 (May 30, 1996) p12. "[Lenny Kravitz & Vanessa Paradis]"

PH08856 750-751 (December 26, 1996) p56. "Paradis (left) And Kravitz In Midscuffle"

KRAVITZ, LENNY—PHOTOGRAPHS—PORTRAITS

PH08857 659 (June 24, 1993) p22. "[Lenny Kravitz]" (Gustafsson, Per)

PH08858 662 (August 5, 1993) p59. "Lenny Kravitz" (Rider, Paul)

PH08859 711 (June 29, 1995) p13. "[Trouble With Tribbles]" (Mazur, Kevin)

KRETZ, ERIC—PHOTOGRAPHS

PH08860 662 (August 5, 1993) p50. "Stone Temple Pilots Eric Kretz, Dean DeLeo, Robert DeLeo And Weiland (from left)" (Ragel, Jon)

PH08861 710 (June 15, 1995) p22. "STP, From Left: Robert And Dean DeLeo, Weiland, Kretz" (Haynes, Loren)

KREUTZMANN, BILL—PHOTOGRAPHS

PH08862 616 (October 31, 1991) p40. "Bill Kreutzmann, Ron "Pigpen" McKernan, Bob Weir, Garcia And Phil Lesh (clockwise from top left) In 1966" (Greene, Herb)

PH08863 664 (September 2, 1993) p46. "The Dead At Rest in 1966: Phil Lesh, Bill Kreutzmann, Ron 'Pigpen' McKernan, Bob Weir And Jerry Garcia (clockwise from left)" (Greene, Herb)

PH08864 676 (February 24, 1994) p46. "The Early Grateful Dead (clockwise from left): Jerry Garcia, Bill Kreutzmann, Ron 'Pigpen' McKernan, Bob Weir, Percussionist Mickey Hart And Phil Lesh" (Marshall, Jim)

PH08865 677 (March 10, 1994) p27. "The Dead's Lesh, Weir, Vince Welnick, Hornsby, Bill Kreutzmann, Mickey Hart" (Mazur, Kevin)

PH08866 717 (September 21, 1995) p52. "Before The Dead, They Were The Warlocks" (Greene, Herbi)

PH08867 717 (September 21, 1995) p54. "The Dead In '66 At The Crossroads, the Corner Of Haight And Ashbury: Garcia, Pigpen, Lesh, Weir, Kreutzmann (from left)" (Greene, Herbi)

PH08868 717 (September 21, 1995) p65. "The Dead In Front Of Their Ashbury St. House, 1967: Jerry Garcia, Ron 'Pigpen' McKernan, Bob Weir, Phil Lesh, Co-Managers Danny Rifkin And Rock Scully, And Bill Kreutzmann..."

PH08869 717 (September 21, 1995) p67. "Jerry Garcia, Phil Lesh, Bill Kreutzmann, Bob Weir And Ron 'Pigpen' McKernan (clockwise from bottom right) Huddled In San Francisco's Golden Gate Park, 1967" (Marshall, Jim)

PH08870 717 (September 21, 1995) p73. "marrying Acid-Damaged Art Music And The Funky Snort Of Live Rock & Roll: The Dead As A Lysergic-Dance Band In 1969 With Tom Constanten, Weir, Kreutzmann, Pigpen, Lesh, H..." (G

PH08871 717 (September 21, 1995) p72. "The Music Never Stopped: Garcia, Weir, Lesh, Brent Mydland, Kreutzmann And Hart (from left) In 1979" (Greene, Herbi)

PH08872 717 (September 21, 1995) p69. "The Original Quintet At Home At 710 Ashbury St., In 1966: Phil Lesh, Bob Weir, Bill Kreutzmann, Ron 'Pigpen' McKernan And Jerry Garcia (from left)" (Anthony, Gene)

KREUTZMANN, BILL—PHOTOGRAPHS—PORTRAITS

PH08873 717 (September 21, 1995) p72. "Nonstop Truckin' And Retooled Roots: The Dead's 1970s Lineup, With Keith Godchaux, Garcia, Lesh, kreutzmann, Donna Godchaux And Weir (clockwise from top left)"

KRIEGER, ROBBIE—PHOTOGRAPHS

PH08874 649 (February 4, 1993) p52. "The Doors (from left): keyboardist Ray Manzarek, Drummer John Densmore, Guitarist Robbie Krieger, Shaman Jim Morrison" (Diltz, Henry)

PH08875 724-725 (December 28, 1995) p46. "Doors John Densmore, Manzarek And Robbie Krieger (from left)" (Kaplin, Todd)

KRIESEL, GREG—PHOTOGRAPHS

PH08876 686-687 (July 14, 1994) p45. "[Offspring]" (Johnson, Lisa)

PH08877 691 (September 22, 1994) p25. "Shakin' Thing Up: Ron Welty, Greg K, Noodles, Dexter Holland (from left)" (Seliger, Mark)

PH08878 701 (February 9, 1995) pp42-43. "Greg Kriesel, Bryan Holland, Kevin Wasserman And Ron Welty (from left)" (Seliger, Mark)

KRIM, MATHILDE—PHOTOGRAPHS

PH08879 710 (June 15, 1995) p18. "AmFar Head Mathilde Krim With Ono" (Mazur, Kevin)

KRIS KROSS—ALBUMS

PH08880 633 (June 25, 1992) p56. "Totally Krossed Out"

PH08881 634-635 (July 9, 1992) p128. "Totally Krossed Out"

PH08882 667 (October 14, 1993) p117. "Da Bomb"

KRIS KROSS—PHOTOGRAPHS—PORTRAITS

PH08883 645-646 (December 10, 1992) p57. "Kris Kross" (Lavine, Michael)

KRISOLOGO, AMANDA—PHOTOGRAPHS—PORTRAITS
PH08884 652 (March 18, 1993) pp[enc.37]. "Amanda Krisologo" (Seliger, Mark)
KRISTAL, HILLY—PHOTOGRAPHS—PORTRAITS
PH08885 675 (February 10, 1994) p14. "The Inveterate Hilly Kristal" (Knight, Kevin)
KRISTOFFERSON, KRIS—PHOTOGRAPHS
PH08886 678 (March 24, 1994) p28. "Kristofferson, Williams, Vega, DJ Vin Scelsa And Lou Reed (from left)" (Roberts, Ebet)
PH08887 741 (August 22, 1996) p48. "McConaughey Onscreen"
KRONOS QUARTET—ALBUMS
PH08888 628 (April 16, 1992) p86. "Pieces Of Africa"
PH08889 658 (June 10, 1993) p71. "Short Stories"
KRS-ONE—ALBUMS
PH08890 670 (November 25, 1993) p120. "Return Of The Boom Bap"
KRS-ONE—ILLUSTRATIONS
PH08891 672-673 (December 23, 1993) p61. "[KRS-One]" (Allen, Terry)
PH08892 676 (February 24, 1994) p10. "[KRS-One]" (Pendergrast, James T.)
KRS-ONE—PHOTOGRAPHS
PH08893 667 (October 14, 1993) p30. "The Return Of Boom Bap: KRS-One"
KRS-ONE—PHOTOGRAPHS—PORTRAITS
PH08894 727 (February 8, 1996) p24. "KRS-One To Release A Rage-Filled Remix" (Turnball, Ann)
KRUGMAN, MICHAEL—PHOTOGRAPHS
PH08895 694 (November 3, 1994) p17. "Pumpkin Billy Corgan, Love, Cohen, Krugman (from left)"
KU KLUX KLAN—ILLUSTRATIONS
PH08896 659 (June 24, 1993) p10. "Empty Gesture Department" (Pendergrast, James T.)
KU KLUX KLAN—PHOTOGRAPHS
PH08897 708 (May 18, 1995) p61. "Klansmen From Franklin, Ga., Hold A Membership Drive Just Outside Wedowee" (Edmondson, Vanessa)
KUDROW, LISA—PHOTOGRAPHS
PH08898 708 (May 18, 1995) pp[cover]. "Fast Friends: No Sex Bad Jobs Hit Show Go Figure" (Seliger, Mark)
PH08899 708 (May 18, 1995) p. "Matt LeBlanc, Jennifer Aniston, David Schwimmer, Courteney Cox, Lisa Kudrow, Matthew Perry" (Seliger, Mark)
KULA SHAKER—PHOTOGRAPHS
PH08900 748 (November 28, 1996) p152. "Sanskirt Mantras And The Stone Roses" (Broad, Julian)
PH08901 750-751 (December 26, 1996) p85. "[Kula Shaker]" (Double, Steve)
KULICK, BRUCE—PHOTOGRAPHS
PH08902 715 (August 24, 1995) p25. "Paul Stanley, Gene Simmons, Eric Singer, Bruce Kulick (from left)" (Blakesberg, Jay)
PH08903 724-725 (December 28, 1995) p51. "Kiss' Simmons, Eric Singer, Stanley And Bruce Kulick (from left)" (Blakesberg, Jay)
KUNSTLER, WILLIAM—PHOTOGRAPHS
PH08904 719 (October 19, 1995) p89. "My Role Is To Fight Government,' Said Kunstler In '93" (Pugliano, Bill)
KUNSTLER, WILLIAM—PHOTOGRAPHS—PORTRAITS
PH08905 724-725 (December 28, 1995) p64. "[William Kunstler]"
KUPER, PETER—ILLUSTRATIONS
PH08906 715 (August 24, 1995) p74. "Hot Comic Book Artist" (Kuper, Peter)
KURCHATOV, IGOR—PHOTOGRAPHS
PH08907 657 (May 27, 1993) p46. "...And Igor Kurchatov Were Crucial To The Soviet Bomb Effort"
KURIANSKY, JUDY—PHOTOGRAPHS
PH08908 659 (June 24, 1993) p13. "Kuriansky, Tyler And Hamilton" (Paul, Tina)
KUSHNER, TONY—PHOTOGRAPHS—PORTRAITS
PH08909 656 (May 13, 1993) p73. "[Tony Kushner]" (Braun, Cory Wells)
KUSTOMIZED—ALBUMS
PH08910 706 (April 20, 1995) p81. "The Battle For Space"
KUWAIT—PHOTOGRAPHS
PH08911 619-620 (December 12, 1991) p147. "A Member Of The Team Working To Cap The Burning Wells In The Oil Fields Of Kuwait" (Salgado, Sebastiao)
KWAME—PHOTOGRAPHS
PH08912 637 (August 20, 1992) p9. "Fred Schneider, Kwame, Weymouth And Frantz (from left) At The 'Paper' Bash"
KYUSS—PHOTOGRAPHS
PH08913 692 (October 6, 1994) p24. "Desert Storm: Kyuss' Homme, Reeder, Garcia And Hernandez (from left)" (Miller, Michael)

L

THE L. A. MUSICAL HISTORY TOUR (BOOK)—PHOTOGRAPHS
PH08914 615 (October 17, 1991) p105. "From Electric Ladyland To The Tour Of La-La Land"
L. L. COOL J—ALBUMS
PH08915 619-620 (December 12, 1991) p184. "Mama Said Knock You Out"
PH08916 656 (May 13, 1993) p107. "14 Shots To The Dome"
PH08917 727 (February 8, 1996) p49. "Mr. Smith"
L. L. COOL J—ILLUSTRATIONS
PH08918 727 (February 8, 1996) p60. "The Rebirth Of Cool J" (Angel, Vinnie)
L. L. COOL J—PHOTOGRAPHS
PH08919 615 (October 17, 1991) p13. "L. L. Cool J" (Mazur, Kevin)
PH08920 619-620 (December 12, 1991) p74. "Downtown Julie Brown With L. L. Cool J"
PH08921 619-620 (December 12, 1991) p37. "L. L. Cool J Undressed And 'Unplugged'" (Micelotta, Frank)
PH08922 619-620 (December 12, 1991) p33. "L. L. Cool J:"Mama Said Knock You Out'"
PH08923 645-646 (December 10, 1992) p97. "[Toys]" (Baldwin, Sidney)
PH08924 648 (January 21, 1993) p55. "Robin Williams (left) And A Huggy L. L. Cool J Play Cousins"
PH08925 659 (June 24, 1993) p13. "Fight The Power: L.L. With Neil Diamond" (Mazur, Kevin)
PH08926 664 (September 2, 1993) p31. "L.L. Gets To Strut His Stuff In New York" (Capak, R. J.)
L. L. COOL J—PHOTOGRAPHS—PORTRAITS
PH08927 619-620 (December 12, 1991) p86. "Hip-Hop Hero L. L. Cool J" (Watermann, Greg)
PH08928 737 (June 27, 1996) p26. "[LL Cool J]" (Kuhmsted, B.)
L7—ALBUMS
PH08929 639 (September 17, 1992) p80. "Bricks Are Heavy"
PH08930 698-699 (December 29, 1994) p182. "Hungry For Stink"
L7—PHOTOGRAPHS
PH08931 628 (April 16, 1992) p56. "Finch, Sparks, Gardner And Plakas (from left)" (Cuffaro, Chris)
PH08932 644 (November 26, 1992) p15. "Dee Plakas, Jennifer Finch, Jett, Donita Sparks And Suzi Gardner (clockwise from left)" (Lewis, Don)
PH08933 652 (March 18, 1993) p22. "Feminist Majority Rules: L7's Finch, Gardner, Sparks, Dee Plakas (from left)" (Johnson, Lisa)
PH08934 659 (June 24, 1993) p13. "Waters And Turner (second from right) With Members Of L7" (Caruso, Phillip)
PH08935 671 (December 9, 1993) p32. "L7 Beauties Pose

Backstage With Gunn" (Johnson, Lisa)
PH08936 688 (August 11, 1994) p25. "Dee Plakas, Donita Sparks, Jennifer Finch, Suzi Gardner (from left)" (Broad, Julian)
PH08937 692 (October 6, 1994) p16. "At Philly's Lollapalooza: L7's Donita Sparks (left), Dee Plakas, Suzi Gardner And Jennifer Finch With Bad Seeds Mick Harvey, James Johnston And Nick Cave" (Weiner, Scott)
PH08938 692 (October 6, 1994) p55. "David Gunn Jr. (center) Son Of Slain Clinic Doctor, Backstage With L7 At A Rock For Choice Show In L.A. This Year" (Johnson, Lisa)
PH08939 695 (November 17, 1994) p52. "L7" (Broad, Julian)
PH08940 696 (December 1, 1994) p23. "Elvismania: L7's Suzi Gardner, Dee Plakas, Sparks And Jennifer Finch (from left)" (Mazur, Kevin)
PH08941 698-699 (December 29, 1994) p60. "[L7]" (Hanauer, Mark)
PH08942 698-699 (December 29, 1994) p42. "L7's Donita Sparks, Vedder, L7's Dee Plakas And Her Husband, Kurk Canning (from left)" (Mercer, Lance)

L7—PHOTOGRAPHS—PORTRAITS
PH08943 645-646 (December 10, 1992) p45. "L7: Heavier Than Bricks" (Hames, William)

LA BELLE NOISEUSE (FILM)—PHOTOGRAPHS
PH08944 616 (October 31, 1991) p99. "Artist And Model: Michel Piccoli And Emmanuelle Beart"

LA FEMME NIKITA (FILM)—PHOTOGRAPHS
PH08945 619-620 (December 12, 1991) p194. "Male Wimps And Female Warriors"
PH08946 654 (April 15, 1993) p72. "Bridget Fonda (left) Can't Match The Sizzle of Anne Parillaud in 'Le Femme Nikita'"

LA LANNE, JACK—PHOTOGRAPHS
PH08947 693 (October 20, 1994) p90. "[Nutrition]" (Klein, Renee)

LA PALAIS DU FESTIVAL—PHOTOGRAPHS
PH08948 615 (October 17, 1991) p67. "Leaving La Palais du Festival, 1987" (Pigozzi, Jean)

LACK, STEVE—PHOTOGRAPHS
PH08949 686-687 (July 14, 1994) p73. "Salt Of The Earth: Lack, Gordon, Post And Shapiro (from left)" (Elledge, Paul)
PH08950 700 (January 26, 1995) p19. "Gordon, Lack, Post And Shapiro (from left)" (Seliger, Mark)

LADD, DIANE—PHOTOGRAPHS
PH08951 659 (June 24, 1993) p37. "Star Child: Laura And Mother Diane Ladd Hit The Town In 1975"

LADY KIER—PHOTOGRAPHS
PH08952 619-620 (December 12, 1991) p59. "Women In Rock Band Together For Prochoice" (Berkwitz, David Neil)
PH08953 622 (January 23, 1992) p6. "Phoebe Snow (left) And Lady Kier At The Reebok Awards" (Robicheau, Paul)

LADY KIER—PHOTOGRAPHS—PORTRAITS
PH08954 639 (September 17, 1992) p37. "Super DJ Dmitry Brill, Lady Kier Kirby And Towa 'Towa' Tei (clockwise from top left)" (Anderson, Patrick)

LADYBIRD, LADYBIRD (FILM)—PHOTOGRAPHS
PH08955 697 (December 15, 1994) p104. "Crissy Rock"

LADYBUG—PHOTOGRAPHS
PH08956 707 (May 4, 1995) p36. "Doodlebug (left) And Ladybug Shock The House" (Capak, R. J.)

LAGARDE, TOM—PHOTOGRAPHS
PH08957 715 (August 24, 1995) p91. "Tom LaGarde (in khaki T-shirt) On The Court During Practice" (Danelian, Stephen)

LAHR, ROGER—PHOTOGRAPHS
PH08958 629 (April 30, 1992) p31. "Ugly Kid Joe (from left): Roger Lahr, Klaus Eichstadt, Whitfield Crane, Cordell Crockett And Mark Davis" (O'Beirne, Andy)

LAKE, RICKI—PHOTOGRAPHS—PORTRAITS
PH08959 666 (September 30, 1993) p55. "[Ricki Lake]"

LAKEWOOD, CALIFORNIA—ILLUSTRATIONS
PH08960 664 (September 2, 1993) p8. "Welcome To Lakewood High" (Pendergrast, James T.)

LAKEWOOD, CALIFORNIA—PHOTOGRAPHS
PH08961 660-661 (July 8, 1993) p62. "Lakewood High Uses Cameras To Monitor Its Campus" (Smale, Brian)
PH08962 660-661 (July 8, 1993) p63. "Spurs Lunch Often At The Lakewood Taco Bell" (Smale, Brian)

LALONDE, LARRY—PHOTOGRAPHS
PH08963 662 (August 5, 1993) p14. "Les Claypool, Tim Alexander And Larry LaLonde (from left) Of Primus" (Blakesberg, Jay)

LALONDE, LARRY—PHOTOGRAPHS—PORTRAITS
PH08964 616 (October 31, 1991) p81. "Smooth Sailing: Guitarist Larry Lalonde, Drummer Tim Alexander And Bassist Les Claypool (clockwise from left)" (Seliger, Mark)

LAM, PATRICK—PHOTOGRAPHS
PH08965 679 (April 7, 1994) p59. "DuPont Merck's Patrick Lam Between Two Computer Models That Show The Virus's Protease Enzyme Successfully Jammed" (Eckstein, Ed)

LAMBERT, RICK—PHOTOGRAPHS
PH08966 723 (December 14, 1995) p32. "Lambert (in back) And My Life With The Thrill Kill Kult"

LAMBSON, BRETT—PHOTOGRAPHS
PH08967 662 (August 5, 1993) p73. "Guy Talk From Parlavecchio, McGaw And Lambson"

LANCE, MAJOR—PHOTOGRAPHS—PORTRAITS
PH08968 698-699 (December 29, 1994) p80. "Chicago Soul Singer Major Lance (above)"

LANDAU, JON—PHOTOGRAPHS
PH08969 632 (June 11, 1992) p62. "Staff Members And Contributing Writers At The 1971 Editorial Conference, At Esalen, In Big Sur" (Leibovitz, Annie)

LANDAU, MARTIN—PHOTOGRAPHS
PH08970 693 (October 20, 1994) p155. "Depp As Ed Wood And Landau As Bela "Dracula" Lugosi"
PH08971 698-699 (December 29, 1994) p194. "Depp And Landau Team In "Ed Wood""
PH08972 700 (January 26, 1995) p68. "Best Supporting Actor"

LANDAU, MICHAEL—PHOTOGRAPHS
PH08973 704 (March 23, 1995) p96. "Landau With His Boss Nicole Miller: He Was Told The Company Wasn't Hiring, But He Didn't Buy It" (Pluchino, Joseph)

LANE, CHARLES—PHOTOGRAPHS
PH08974 658 (June 10, 1993) p74. "The Magnificent Six (from left): Stephen Baldwin, Big Daddy Kane, Mario Van Peebles, Tiny Lister Jr., Charles Lane, Tone Loc"

LANE, CHRISTIAN—PHOTOGRAPHS
PH08975 721 (November 16, 1995) p99. "Loud Lucy: Christian Lane" (GS, Jamil)
PH08976 721 (November 16, 1995) p100. "Loud Lucy: Furar, Lane And Doyle (from left)" (GS, Jamil)

LANE, TONY—PHOTOGRAPHS
PH08977 643 (November 12, 1992) p49. "'Rolling Stone' Art Directors (from left): Bob Kingsbury (1968-73), Tony Lane (1974-76), Annie Leibovitz, Mike Salisbury (1973-74), Roger Black (1976-78), Jann S. Wenner..." (Le

LANEGAN, MARK—ALBUMS
PH08978 680 (April 21, 1994) p89. "Whiskey For The Holy Ghost"

LANEGAN, MARK—ILLUSTRATIONS
PH08979 741 (August 22, 1996) p13. "Mark Lanegan Of Screaming Trees" (Grahn, Geoffrey)

LANEGAN, MARK—PHOTOGRAPHS
PH08980 650 (February 18, 1993) p15. "Gary Lee Conner, Barrett Martin, Mark Lanegan And Van Conner (from left)" (Winters, Dan)
PH08981 650 (February 18, 1993) p25. "Screaming Tree Mark Lanegan" (Winters, Dan)
PH08982 695 (November 17, 1994) p110. "Screaming Trees" (Ragel, Jon)

LANG, DEIDRE—PHOTOGRAPHS—PORTRAITS
PH08983 656 (May 13, 1993) p94. "Deidre Lang, Jennifer Lopez,

Twist, Jossie Harris, Lisa Thompson (from left)"
PH08984 656 (May 13, 1993) p98. "Left Thompson, Right Lang"
LANG, K. D.—ALBUMS
PH08985 629 (April 30, 1992) p57. "Ingenue"
PH08986 651 (March 4, 1993) p56. "Ingenue"
PH08987 721 (November 16, 1995) p112. "All You Can Eat"
LANG, K. D.—ILLUSTRATIONS
PH08988 662 (August 5, 1993) p5. "K. D. Lang" (Burke, Philip)
PH08989 665 (September 16, 1993) p6. "Hearts Of America" (Pendergrast, James T.)
LANG, K. D.—PHOTOGRAPHS
PH08990 640 (October 1, 1992) p9. "...And Lang (right)" (Kraft, Chris)
PH08991 651 (March 4, 1993) p17. "Bonnie Raitt, K. D. Lang And Barbara Orbison (from left)" (Mazur, Kevin)
PH08992 651 (March 4, 1993) p15. "Etta James (left) With K. D. Lang" (Mazur, Kevin)
PH08993 652 (March 18, 1993) p13. "Lang Adds Life To The AMAs" (Mazur, Kevin)
PH08994 657 (May 27, 1993) p9. "Lang And McCartney Onstage" (Preston, Neal)
PH08995 662 (August 5, 1993) p46. "'I Won't Sleep With A Fan, Because K. D. Lang the Performer Is So Much Cooler Than Me'" (Staedler, Lance)
PH08996 672-673 (December 23, 1993) p37. "Above: Linda, Paul And Lang At Earth Day" (Preston, Neal)
PH08997 672-673 (December 23, 1993) p20. "...And K. D. Lang (below) Show Us Their Pearly Whites" (Mazur, Kevin)
PH08998 672-673 (December 23, 1993) p16. "Billy Ray's Heartbreak: K.D. Lang" (Mazur, Kevin)
PH08999 674 (January 27, 1994) p28. "[K. D. Lang]" (Mazur, Kevin)
PH09000 698-699 (December 29, 1994) p116. "With K. D. Lang At A LifeBeat benefit In New York City, June '94" (Eichner, Steve)
PH09001 720 (November 2, 1995) p49. "K. D. Lang" (Danelian, Stephen)
LANG, K. D.—PHOTOGRAPHS—PORTRAITS
PH09002 645-646 (December 10, 1992) p39. "The World's Newest Chanteuse, K. D. Lang" (Danelian, Stephen)
PH09003 662 (August 5, 1993) p55. "[K. D. Lang]" (Staedler, Lance)
PH09004 683 (June 2, 1994) p27. "Above: Lang, Bennett, Costello" (Mazur, Kevin)
PH09005 722 (November 30, 1995) p40. "[K. D. Lang]" (Seliger, Mark)
LANGDON, ANTONY—PHOTOGRAPHS
PH09006 734 (May 16, 1996) p36. "All The Young Dudes: Antony Onstage" (Callahan, Kristin)
PH09007 734 (May 16, 1996) p32. "Fighting For Time In Front Of The Mirror: Brothers Antony And Royston Langdon, Richard Steel, And Jonny Cragg (from left)" (Clinch, Danny)
LANGDON, ANTONY—PHOTOGRAPHS—PORTRAITS
PH09008 750-751 (December 26, 1996) p64. "Antony Langdon Of Spacehog" (Hershiko, Eli)
LANGDON, LIBBY—PHOTOGRAPHS
PH09009 696 (December 1, 1994) p134. "Libby Langdon Gets A Leg Up On The Hill's Men"
LANGDON, ROYSTON—ILLUSTRATIONS
PH09010 734 (May 16, 1996) p11. "Spacehog's Royston Langdon" (Green And Read)
LANGDON, ROYSTON—PHOTOGRAPHS
PH09011 734 (May 16, 1996) p32. "Fighting For Time In Front Of The Mirror: Brothers Antony And Royston Langdon, Richard Steel, And Jonny Cragg (from left)" (Clinch, Danny)
PH09012 742 (September 5, 1996) p20. "Selene Vigil Of 7 Year Bitch, Langdon, Alexakis And Bonham" (Morganstein, Barry)
LANGE, JESSICA—PHOTOGRAPHS
PH09013 618 (November 28, 1991) p103. "Now Robert De Niro Terrorizes Jessica Lange"
PH09014 692 (October 6, 1994) p81. "Now Playing"
LANGFORD, JON—PHOTOGRAPHS
PH09015 667 (October 14, 1993) p37. "Mekons Sarah Corina (left) And Jon Langford" (Mazur, Kevin)
PH09016 694 (November 3, 1994) p22. "Mekons Singer Sally Timms, Gibby Haynes And Jon Langford Belt It Out Onstage" (Crawford, Michael)
PH09017 733 (May 2, 1996) p57. "Durante, Schlabowske, Langford, Dear (from left)" (Swider, Frank)
PH09018 736 (June 13, 1996) p19. "Where's Sammy And Frank?" (Herdon, David)
LANGNER, PAT—PHOTOGRAPHS
PH09019 616 (October 31, 1991) p25. "The Leslie Spit Treeo (from left): Jack Nicholsen, Laura Hubert, Pat Langner And Tag" (Counts, Wyatt)
LANGSTON, ANDREANA PATRICIA—PHOTOGRAPHS
PH09020 642 (October 29, 1992) p62. "Protesting The Rodney King Verdict"
LANGSTON, LESLIE—PHOTOGRAPHS
PH09021 703 (March 9, 1995) p55. "The Throwing Muses Lineup In 1989 (from left): Hersh, Leslie Langston, Tanya Donelly And Narcizo" (Musto, Ilpo)
LANOIS, DANIEL—ALBUMS
PH09022 657 (May 27, 1993) p49. "For The Beauty Of Wynona"
LANOIS, DANIEL—PHOTOGRAPHS
PH09023 617 (November 14, 1991) p13. "Lanois (left) And Gabriel" (Hildenhagen, Michael)
PH09024 618 (November 28, 1991) p46. "Dan Lanois Takes Careful Notes As The Singer Practices His Bongolese During Vocal Sessions At Dogtown Studio" (Corbijn, Anton)
PH09025 618 (November 28, 1991) p46. "Lanois, Eno, Edge And Bono In The Control Room At Hansa Studios, In Berlin" (Corbijn, Anton)
PH09026 666 (September 30, 1993) pp24-25. "[Daniel Lanois]" (Levine, Laura)
PH09027 735 (May 30, 1996) p27. "Glaser, Schellenbach, Producer Lanois And Trimble (from left)" (Olivier, Rick)
LAPIERRE, WAYNE—PHOTOGRAPHS—PORTRAITS
PH09028 710 (June 15, 1995) p58. "Lapierre"
LARA, VICTOR—PHOTOGRAPHS
PH09029 678 (March 24, 1994) p78. "Victor Lara, A Professor At RISD" (Hill, Britain)
LARGENT, STEVE—PHOTOGRAPHS—PORTRAITS
PH09030 719 (October 19, 1995) p49. "Largent"
LARGER THAN LIFE (FILM)—PHOTOGRAPHS
PH09031 743 (September 19, 1996) p88. "Dickheads"
PH09032 748 (November 28, 1996) p143. "Dead On Arrival"
LARKIN, COLIN—BOOKS
PH09033 656 (May 13, 1993) p26. "The Guinness Encyclopedia Of Popular Music"
LARROQUETTE, JOHN—PHOTOGRAPHS
PH09034 666 (September 30, 1993) p116. "Night Hawk: Larroquette"
THE LARRY SANDERS SHOW (TELEVISION SHOW)—PHOTOGRAPHS
PH09035 645-646 (December 10, 1992) p198. "Possible Talk-Show Host Dana Carvey With Fake Talk-Show Host Garry Shandling"
PH09036 672-673 (December 23, 1993) p88. "Larry (right) With Helen Hunt" (Fallon, Brenda)
PH09037 690 (September 8, 1994) p72. "Many Celebrities Who Appear On "The Larry Sanders Show" Are Fans, Like Alec Baldwin" (Tepper, Randy)
PH09038 690 (September 8, 1994) p68. "Sidekick Hank Kingsley (Jeffrey Tambor), Producer Arthur (Rip Torn) And Host Larry Sanders (Shandling)"
LARSEN, KRISTINA—PHOTOGRAPHS
PH09039 642 (October 29, 1992) p63. "Teen To Sixties People: Drop Dead!"

LARSON, NATHAN—PHOTOGRAPHS
PH09040 686-687 (July 14, 1994) p73. "Cute-Band Alert: Shudder To Think's Werdren, Wade, Larson And Hill (from left)" (Clinch, Danny)
LARSON, NATHAN—PHOTOGRAPHS—PORTRAITS
PH09041 719 (October 19, 1995) p26. "Truly Baroque—Like A Strange Union Of R.E.M. And Queen: Larson, Hill, Wedren And Wade (from left)" (Clinch, Danny)
LA'S—PHOTOGRAPHS
PH09042 619-620 (December 12, 1991) p46. "Ride (above) And The La's (below) Brought The Guitar Back To Pop"
LAS VEGAS, NEVADA—ILLUSTRATIONS
PH09043 746 (October 31, 1996) p40. "Night Of The Shooting" (General Cartography)
LAS VEGAS, NEVADA—PHOTOGRAPHS
PH09044 746 (October 31, 1996) p46. "Shakur's Fans Gathered With Candles And Prayers In Las Vegas On Sept. 14, The Day After The Rapper Died, To Eulogize Him"
PH09045 746 (October 31, 1996) p41. "[Tupac Shakur's Death Scene]" (Payne, Malcolm)
LAST ACTION HERO (FILM)—PHOTOGRAPHS
PH09046 662 (August 5, 1993) p72. "In 'Hero,' Schwarzenegger Carries A Stiff, And We Do Mean The Film"
PH09047 665 (September 16, 1993) p77. "Worst Picture"
PH09048 672-673 (December 23, 1993) p172. "Fattest Flop"
LAST DANCE (FILM)—ILLUSTRATIONS
PH09049 735 (May 30, 1996) p55. "Dead Babe Walking" (Brodner, Steve)
LAST DANCE (FILM)—PHOTOGRAPHS
PH09050 735 (May 30, 1996) p56. "Jailbird"
LAST EXIT TO BROOKLYN (FILM)—PHOTOGRAPHS
PH09051 722 (November 30, 1995) p58. "The Gang-Raped Hooker In 'Last Exit' Appealed To Leigh: 'I Have A Problem With Generic Female Roles'"
LAST MAN STANDING (FILM)—PHOTOGRAPHS
PH09052 736 (June 13, 1996) p58. "Headaches"
PH09053 745 (October 17, 1996) p144. "Bruce Willis Plays Samurai In A Suit"
THE LAST OF THE MOHICANS (FILM)—ILLUSTRATIONS
PH09054 642 (October 29, 1992) p76. "Hard Times For Heroes" (Blitt, Barry)
THE LAST OF THE MOHICANS (FILM)—PHOTOGRAPHS
PH09055 645-646 (December 10, 1992) p190. "Daniel Day-Lewis"
PH09056 653 (April 1, 1993) p57. "Mohicans"
LAST POETS—PHOTOGRAPHS
PH09057 707 (May 4, 1995) p32. "Torch Song Trilogy: The Last Poets"
THE LAST SEDUCTION (FILM)—PHOTOGRAPHS
PH09058 693 (October 20, 1994) p157. "Now Playing"
PH09059 700 (January 26, 1995) p68. "Best Actress"
PH09060 705 (April 6, 1995) p70. "Shafted: Linda Fiorentino In 'Last Seduction'"
THE LAST SUPPER (FILM)—PHOTOGRAPHS
PH09061 732 (April 18, 1996) p80. "Ron Eldard And Cameron Diaz Eat Till They Drop"
THE LAST WALTZ (CONCERT)—PHOTOGRAPHS
PH09062 617 (November 14, 1991) p75. "The Last Waltz, 1976: Robertson, Danko And Manuel, With Neil Young (left), Bob Dylan (back to camera) And Van Morrison" (Leibovitz, Annie)
L'ATALANTE (FILM)—PHOTOGRAPHS
PH09063 644 (November 26, 1992) p78. "[L'Atalante]"
LATE NIGHT (TELEVISION SHOW)—PHOTOGRAPHS
PH09064 677 (March 10, 1994) p17. "Morphine Make 'Late Night' Noise For Conan O'Brien" (Mazur, Kevin)
LATE SHOW (TELEVISION SHOW)—PHOTOGRAPHS
PH09065 698-699 (December 29, 1994) p42. "[Madonna & David Letterman]"
LATHAN, SANAA—PHOTOGRAPHS
PH09066 704 (March 23, 1995) pp102-103. "Class of '95" (Tavee, Tom)
PH09067 704 (March 23, 1995) p106. "Lathan At The Yale Repertory Theater" (Tavee, Tom)
LATIN PLAYBOYS—ALBUMS
PH09068 684 (June 16, 1994) p109. "Latin Playboys"
LAUDERDALE, JIM—ALBUMS
PH09069 623 (February 6, 1992) p83. "Planet Of Love"
LAUDERDALE, JIM—PHOTOGRAPHS
PH09070 691 (September 22, 1994) p20. "Members Of Bettie Serveert And Belly With Singer Jim Lauderdale (far right) And Juliana Hatfield (seated, right) At Central Park" (Roberts, Ebet)
LAUDERDALE, JIM—PHOTOGRAPHS—PORTRAITS
PH09071 627 (April 2, 1992) p19. "[Jim Lauderdale]" (Buchsbaum, Jay David)
LAUPER, CYNDI—ALBUMS
PH09072 664 (September 2, 1993) p60. "Hat Full Of Stars"
LAUPER, CYNDI—PHOTOGRAPHS
PH09073 619-620 (December 12, 1991) p71. "Cyndi Lauper"
PH09074 717 (September 21, 1995) p20. "[Cyndi Lauper]" (Keyser, James)
PH09075 726 (January 25, 1996) p26. "Mariah Carey And Sony Music Chief Tommy Mottola With Cyndi Lauper (from left)" (Capak, R. J.)
LAUPER, CYNDI—PHOTOGRAPHS—PORTRAITS
PH09076 616 (October 31, 1991) p99. "The Varied Images Of A Camera Chameleon" (Rolston, Matthew)
PH09077 643 (November 12, 1992) p234. "...And Rolston's Cyndi Lauper" (Rolston, Matthew)
PH09078 692 (October 6, 1994) p53. "Cyndi Lauper" (Bellissimo, John)
LAVELLE, JAMES—PHOTOGRAPHS
PH09079 738-739 (July 11, 1996) p26. "Mo' Wax Founder And Trip-Hop Enthusiast James Lavelle (left) With DJ Shadow" (Cardillichio, Nick)
LAWLER, FERGAL—PHOTOGRAPHS
PH09080 664 (September 2, 1993) p28. "Lawler, Mike Hogan, O'Riordan, Noel Hogan"
PH09081 695 (November 17, 1994) p37. "The Cranberries" (Meeks, Raymond)
PH09082 704 (March 23, 1995) pp56-57. "[Strange Fruit]" (Day, Corinne)
LAWLESS, JESSICA—PHOTOGRAPHS
PH09083 729 (March 7, 1996) p28. "Lawless, Harley And Zoe Bermet (from left) Hone Their Skills At The Home Alive Classroom, In Seattle" (Wescott, Stacey)
LAWRENCE, JOEY—PHOTOGRAPHS
PH09084 678 (March 24, 1994) p28. "[MTV's Rock n' Jock Softball Challenge]"
LAWRENCE, MARTIN—ILLUSTRATIONS
PH09085 707 (May 4, 1995) p73. "Bad Boys On The Prowl" (Kelley, Gary)
LAWRENCE, MARTIN—PHOTOGRAPHS
PH09086 677 (March 10, 1994) p60. "Martin Lawrence From Sitcom To Stand-Up"
PH09087 680 (April 21, 1994) p77. "As Sheneneh, With His 'Martin' Girlfriend, Tisha Campbell"
PH09088 680 (April 21, 1994) p74. "In 'House Party 2,' Lawrence Reprises His Role As A Tone-Deaf DJ"
PH09089 680 (April 21, 1994) pp68-70. "[Martin Lawrence]" (Seliger, Mark)
PH09090 680 (April 21, 1994) p74. "With His Co-Stars In 'Boomerang' David Alan Grier (left) And Eddie Murphy"
PH09091 707 (May 4, 1995) p74. "Lawrence And Smith In 'Bad Boys'"
LAWRENCE, MARTIN—PHOTOGRAPHS—PORTRAITS
PH09092 669 (November 11, 1993) p20. "[Martin Lawrence]" (Cuffaro, Chris)
LAWRENCE, ROY—PHOTOGRAPHS—PORTRAITS
PH09093 642 (October 29, 1992) p32. "Eugenius (clockwise from upper left): Boyle, Kelly, Keen, Lawrence" (Lavine,

Michael)
LAWS, RUFINA—PHOTOGRAPHS—PORTRAITS
PH09094 736 (June 13, 1996) p73. "Woman With A Mission: Rufina Laws Opposes The Waste Project" (Barker, Kent)
LAWSON, ERIC—PHOTOGRAPHS
PH09095 730 (March 21, 1996) p55. "The Boys In The Bus: Schiavone McGee, David Triano, Eric Lawson, Chris Leitch, Karl Vonklein, David Peterson And Mike Boyd (clockwise from left)" (Clinch, Danny)
PH09096 730 (March 21, 1996) p56. "McGee, Peterson, Triano And Lawson (from left) Rehearse In The Bus" (Clinch, Danny)
LAYNE, STEVE—PHOTOGRAPHS
PH09097 696 (December 1, 1994) p44. "Layne, Mr. Brown, Smith, Mrs. Brown" (Capak, R. J.)
LAYTON, CHRIS—PHOTOGRAPHS
PH09098 630 (May 14, 1992) p25. "Chris Layton, Tommy Shannon, Doyle Bramhall II, Charlie Sexton (from left)" (Pumphrey, Steve)
PH09099 654 (April 15, 1993) pp[enc.23]. "[Chris Layton]" (Woodward, Fred)
PH09100 654 (April 15, 1993) pp[enc.18]. "[Chris Layton & Joe]" (Woodward, Fred)
LAYTON, CHRIS—PHOTOGRAPHS—PORTRAITS
PH09101 654 (April 15, 1993) pp[enc.17]. "[Chris Layton]" (Woodward, Fred)
LAYTON, JOE—PHOTOGRAPHS
PH09102 654 (April 15, 1993) pp[enc.18]. "[Chris Layton & Joe]" (Woodward, Fred)
LE, HIEP THI—PHOTOGRAPHS
PH09103 672-673 (December 23, 1993) p174. "[Heaven And Earth]"
LE NOBLE, MARTYN—PHOTOGRAPHS—PORTRAITS
PH09104 656 (May 13, 1993) p54. "Martyn Le Noble" (Seliger, Mark)
LEACH, CONRAD—PHOTOGRAPHS
PH09105 691 (September 22, 1994) pp[enc.25]. "Conrad Leach At Canal Jeans, New York City" (Borris, Dan)
PH09106 691 (September 22, 1994) pp[enc.cover]. "Dr. Martens Designer Conrad Leach" (Borris, Dan)
PH09107 691 (September 22, 1994) pp[enc.5]. "Style 94" (Borris, Dan)
LEACHMAN, CLORIS—PHOTOGRAPHS
PH09108 669 (November 11, 1993) p81. "Tomlin's Miss Hathaway Welcomes The Clampetts To 90210"
A LEAGUE OF THEIR OWN (FILM)—ILLUSTRATIONS
PH09109 634-635 (July 9, 1992) p109. "Bat Girls On The Line" (Risko, Robert)
A LEAGUE OF THEIR OWN (FILM)—PHOTOGRAPHS
PH09110 634-635 (July 9, 1992) p111. "Davis, O'Donnell, Madonna And Petty In A Man's Game"
PH09111 639 (September 17, 1992) p102. "Best Supporting Actor"
PH09112 653 (April 1, 1993) p57. "League"
LEAP OF FAITH (FILM)—PHOTOGRAPHS
PH09113 648 (January 21, 1993) p55. "Preacher Steve Martin Can't Save His Movie"
LEARY, DENIS—ALBUMS
PH09114 651 (March 4, 1993) p65. "No Cure For Cancer"
LEARY, DENIS—PHOTOGRAPHS
PH09115 679 (April 7, 1994) p83. "Denis Leary Refs Judy Davis And Kevin Spacey"
PH09116 727 (February 8, 1996) p46. "Denis Leary And Sandra Bullock Mug And Kiss As Lovers On The Run In The First And Maybe Worst Comedy Of 1996"
LEARY, MARIANNE—PHOTOGRAPHS—PORTRAITS
PH09117 738-739 (July 11, 1996) p72. "First Wife Marianne"
LEARY, PAUL—PHOTOGRAPHS
PH09118 659 (June 24, 1993) p25. "Gibby Haynes, Jeff Pinkus, Paul Leary And King Coffey (clockwise from top)" (Watermann, Greg)
PH09119 665 (September 16, 1993) p26. "Surfers Paul Leary (left) And Gibby Haynes" (Mazur, Kevin)
PH09120 710 (June 15, 1995) p54. "Surf Thing: Coffey, Haynes, Leary (from left)" (Van Overbeek, Will)
PH09121 738-739 (July 11, 1996) p28. "Surfers' King Coffey, Gibby Haynes, Paul Leary (from left)" (Van Overbeek, Will)
LEARY, ROSEMARY—PHOTOGRAPHS
PH09122 738-739 (July 11, 1996) p72. "Leary With Rosemary In Berkeley, 1969" (Altman, Robert)
PH09123 738-739 (July 11, 1996) p68. "Tommy Smothers, John Lennon, Yoko Ono, Rosemary And Timothy Leary (from left) During The Bed-In For Peace In Montreal, 1969"
LEARY, SUSAN—PHOTOGRAPHS
PH09124 738-739 (July 11, 1996) p72. "With Daughter Susan In 1966"
LEARY, TIMOTHY—ILLUSTRATIONS
PH09125 740 (August 8, 1996) p14. "Still Trippin'" (Pendergrast, James T.)
LEARY, TIMOTHY—PHOTOGRAPHS
PH09126 738-739 (July 11, 1996) p68. "At West Point, 1940"
PH09127 738-739 (July 11, 1996) p66. "Leary At Millbrook, N. Y., 1967"
PH09128 738-739 (July 11, 1996) p70. "Leary Plotting With Abbie Hoffman (left) And Jerry Rubin, 1968"
PH09129 738-739 (July 11, 1996) p72. "Leary With Rosemary In Berkeley, 1969" (Altman, Robert)
PH09130 738-739 (July 11, 1996) p74. "Timothy Leary At His Home In Beverly Hills, April 1996" (Seliger, Mark)
PH09131 738-739 (July 11, 1996) p68. "Tommy Smothers, John Lennon, Yoko Ono, Rosemary And Timothy Leary (from left) During The Bed-In For Peace In Montreal, 1969"
PH09132 738-739 (July 11, 1996) p70. "With Allen Ginsberg At A Be-In, 1967" (Marshall, Jim)
PH09133 738-739 (July 11, 1996) p68. "With Alpert At Harvard, 1961"
PH09134 738-739 (July 11, 1996) p72. "With Daughter Susan In 1966"
PH09135 738-739 (July 11, 1996) p70. "With Eldridge Cleaver, 1970"
PH09136 738-739 (July 11, 1996) p72. "With Stepson Zachary And Granddaughter Sarah, 1996" (Kuhn, Shane)
LEARY, TIMOTHY—PHOTOGRAPHS—PORTRAITS
PH09137 738-739 (July 11, 1996) p70. "Hard Time, 1970"
PH09138 738-739 (July 11, 1996) p67. "In The 'Rolling Stone' Offices, 1969" (Wolman, Baron)
PH09139 750-751 (December 26, 1996) p96. "[Timothy Leary]" (Wolman, Baron)
LEAVE ME ALONE (VIDEO)—PHOTOGRAPHS
PH09140 667 (October 14, 1993) p69. "Jackson: A video Taylor-ed To His Dreams"
LEAVING LAS VEGAS (FILM)—ILLUSTRATIONS
PH09141 734 (May 16, 1996) p14. "Leaving Las Vegas" (Pendergrast, James T.)
LEAVING LAS VEGAS (FILM)—PHOTOGRAPHS
PH09142 720 (November 2, 1995) p76. "He (Nicolas Cage) Is An Alcoholic"
PH09143 720 (November 2, 1995) p76. "She (Elizabeth Shue) Is A Hooker"
PH09144 720 (November 2, 1995) p76. "Together: cage And Shue Are Lovers Battling The Odds"
PH09145 721 (November 16, 1995) p94. "And The Drunk (with Elizabeth Shue) In 'Leaving Las Vegas'" (Hanover, Suzanne)
PH09146 724-725 (December 28, 1995) p136. "Unusual Pleasure"
LEAVITT, PHIL—PHOTOGRAPHS
PH09147 647 (January 7, 1993) p19. "Michael Gurley, Joie Calio And Phil Leavitt (from left)" (Mauro, Aldo)
PH09148 660-661 (July 8, 1993) p101. "Dada (from left): Michael Gurley, Phil Leavitt And Joie Calio" (Lass, Imke)

LEBLANC, MATT—PHOTOGRAPHS
PH09149 708 (May 18, 1995) pp[cover]. "Fast Friends: No Sex Bad Jobs Hit Show Go Figure" (Seliger, Mark)
PH09150 708 (May 18, 1995) p. "Matt LeBlanc, Jennifer Aniston, David Schwimmer, Courteney Cox, Lisa Kudrow, Matthew Perry" (Seliger, Mark)
LEBON, SIMON—PHOTOGRAPHS
PH09151 653 (April 1, 1993) p20. "Nick Rhodes, Simon LeBon, John Taylor And Warren Cuccurullo (from left)" (Heungman)
PH09152 676 (February 24, 1994) p26. "Simon LeBon: Ignoring The Vegas Within" (Mazur, Kevin)
PH09153 704 (March 23, 1995) p40. "[Simon LeBon]" (Von Unwerth, Ellen)
PH09154 708 (May 18, 1995) p17. "Simon LeBon, Grandmaster Flash And Warren Cuccurullo In New York (from left)" (Olson, Sheryl)
LED ZEPPELIN—ALBUMS
PH09155 617 (November 14, 1991) p134. "House Of The Holy" (Thorgerson, Strom)
PH09156 617 (November 14, 1991) p134. "House Of The Holy" (Powell, Aubrey)
PH09157 617 (November 14, 1991) p123. "Led Zeppelin" (Hardie, George)
PH09158 617 (November 14, 1991) p147. "Physical Graffiti" (Doud, Mike)
PH09159 617 (November 14, 1991) p147. "Physical Graffiti" (Corriston, Peter)
PH09160 617 (November 14, 1991) p147. "Physical Graffiti" (Erwitt, Elliot)
PH09161 634-635 (July 9, 1992) p4. "Houses Of The Holy"
PH09162 637 (August 20, 1992) p4. "Houses Of The Holy"
LED ZEPPELIN—ILLUSTRATIONS
PH09163 705 (April 6, 1995) p14. "The Future" (Pendergrast, James T.)
LED ZEPPELIN—PHOTOGRAPHS
PH09164 696 (December 1, 1994) p31. "Plant (left) And Page On Led Zep's 1975 U.S. Tour" (Preston, Neal)
PH09165 702 (February 23, 1995) p48. "Aerosmith's Joe Perry And Steven Tyler Get Chummy With Led Zep's Robert Plant And Jimmy Page" (Mazur, Kevin)
PH09166 702 (February 23, 1995) p46. "...Getting Chummy With Plant In Rehearsal In 1975" (Preston, Neal)
PH09167 702 (February 23, 1995) p47. "Getting Ledded At Live Aid In '85: 'It Made Us Look Like Loonies,' Says Plant"
PH09168 702 (February 23, 1995) p46. "The Golden Boys: Page, Jones, Bonham And Plant (from left)"
PH09169 702 (February 23, 1995) p47. "Jones, Plant And Page Trample England Underfoot On Tour In 1970"
PH09170 702 (February 23, 1995) p47. "Whole Lotta Led: Hanging Loose In England In '69" (Thompson, Jay)
PH09171 720 (November 2, 1995) p49. "Robert Plant & Jimmy Page" (Greene, Herb)
PH09172 726 (January 25, 1996) p28. "Page, Grant And Plant (from left) In 1975" (Preston, Neal)
LEDOYEN, VIRGINIE—PHOTOGRAPHS
PH09173 749 (December 12, 1996) p90. "Now Playing"
LEE, ALBERT—PHOTOGRAPHS
PH09174 655 (April 29, 1993) p35. "Muddy Waters, One Of Clapton's Earliest Blues Idols, Joins The Guitarist Onstage In Chicago In 1979..." (Natkin, Paul)
PH09175 702 (February 23, 1995) p35. "Albert Lee, Arlen Roth And Les Paul (from left)" (Capak, R. J.)
LEE, ANG—PHOTOGRAPHS
PH09176 724-725 (December 28, 1995) p138. "Lee Directs Winslet, Thompson And Imogen Stubbs In 'Sense' (from left)"
LEE, ANTHONY—PHOTOGRAPHS
PH09177 660-661 (July 8, 1993) p101. "Motherhead Bug (from left): Anthony Lee, Steven Ovenden, April Chung, Cyril Mazzard, Jez Aspinal, Tomoyo, And Dave Ouimet" (Leopardi, N.)
LEE, ARTHUR—PHOTOGRAPHS
PH09178 681 (May 5, 1994) p19. "No Love Lost Here: Arthur Lee" (Mazur, Kevin)
LEE, BEN—ALBUMS
PH09179 708 (May 18, 1995) p92. "Grandpaw Would"
LEE, BEN—PHOTOGRAPHS
PH09180 710 (June 15, 1995) p18. "Make Love, Not Bore: Ben Lee At His L.A. Strum-Along" (Hole, Danny)
LEE, BEN—PHOTOGRAPHS—PORTRAITS
PH09181 712-713 (July 13, 1995) p42. "[Ben Lee]" (Rosa, Alison)
LEE, BEVERLY—PHOTOGRAPHS
PH09182 728 (February 22, 1996) p18. "Shirelles Shirley Alston, Lee, Doris Kenner (from left): Dedicating It To The Ones They Love" (Mazur, Kevin)
LEE, BOB—PHOTOGRAPHS
PH09183 715 (August 24, 1995) p36. "Bagarozzi, Walther, Lee And Wahl" (Peterson, Charles)
LEE, BRANDON—ILLUSTRATIONS
PH09184 682 (May 19, 1994) p105. "Enter The Phantom" (Rosen, Jonathon)
LEE, BRANDON—PHOTOGRAPHS
PH09185 682 (May 19, 1994) p106. "Lee's Inspiration: Black Crowe Robinson"
LEE, BRENDA—PHOTOGRAPHS
PH09186 720 (November 2, 1995) p50. "Brenda Lee"
LEE, CINQUE—PHOTOGRAPHS
PH09187 617 (November 14, 1991) p11. "Cinque And Joie Lee With Pop" (Busacca, Larry)
LEE, GEDDY—PHOTOGRAPHS
PH09188 749 (December 12, 1996) p33. "[Geddy Lee]" (Whiteside, George)
LEE, JASON SCOTT—PHOTOGRAPHS
PH09189 657 (May 27, 1993) p56. "Tormented: Bruce Lee (Jason Scott Lee) Battles A Nightmare"
LEE, JOIE—PHOTOGRAPHS
PH09190 617 (November 14, 1991) p11. "Cinque And Joie Lee With Pop" (Busacca, Larry)
LEE, LAURA—PHOTOGRAPHS—PORTRAITS
PH09191 692 (October 6, 1994) p52. "Laura Lee"
LEE, MCKINLEY—PHOTOGRAPHS
PH09192 731 (April 4, 1996) p26. "Lee And Snoop Give Each Other Support"
PH09193 731 (April 4, 1996) p24. "Snoop (right) And Former Bodyguard McKinley Lee Listen To Trial Testimony"
LEE, PAMELA ANDERSON—PHOTOGRAPHS
PH09194 734 (May 16, 1996) p72. "Pamela Anderson Lee"
PH09195 750-751 (December 26, 1996) pp[cover]. "Beavis & Butthead Go To Hollywood: Guest Starring Pamela Anderson Lee" (Seliger, Mark)
PH09196 750-751 (December 26, 1996) pp32-33. "[Pamela Anderson Lee & Beavis & Butt-Head]" (Seliger, Mark)
LEE, SARA—PHOTOGRAPHS
PH09197 625 (March 5, 1992) p18. "Sara Lee, Crimmins, Graham Nash, Amy Ray, Emily Saliers, David Crosby, Etheridge, Carpenter (from left)" (Berg, Lisa)
LEE, SHERYL—PHOTOGRAPHS
PH09198 680 (April 21, 1994) p93. "Dorff And Hart Flank Lee In A Beatles Love Triangle"
PH09199 748 (November 28, 1996) p143. "Nick Nolte And Sheryl Lee Get Cozy"
LEE, SPIKE—ILLUSTRATIONS
PH09200 732 (April 18, 1996) p77. "Phone Sex, Spike Style" (Brodner, Steve)
LEE, SPIKE—ILLUSTRATIONS—PORTRAITS
PH09201 683 (June 2, 1994) p75. "Spike Lee Grows Up" (Liepke, Skip)
LEE, SPIKE—PHOTOGRAPHS
PH09202 644 (November 26, 1992) p39. "Denzel And Spike On Location In Egypt" (Lee, David)

PH09203 644 (November 26, 1992) p40. "Denzel And Spike (seated) Prepare For The Film's Barbershop Sequence" (Lee, David)
PH09204 645-646 (December 10, 1992) p190. "Spike Lee"
PH09205 653 (April 1, 1993) p57. "Lee"
PH09206 717 (September 21, 1995) p89. "Keitel And Lee On The Case"
PH09207 717 (September 21, 1995) p89. "Phifer On The Spot"
PH09208 732 (April 18, 1996) p78. "Madonna And Randle Flank Director Spike Lee"
LEE, TOMMY—PHOTOGRAPHS
PH09209 706 (April 20, 1995) p15. "Tommy Lee And Pamela Anderson Still Married At Press Time" (Kravitz, Jeff)
PH09210 708 (May 18, 1995) p18. "[Tommy Lee & Pamela Anderson]" (Gerber, M.)
PH09211 724-725 (December 28, 1995) p46. "[Pamela Anderson & Tommy Lee]" (Gerber, Mitch)
LEE, TOMMY—PHOTOGRAPHS—PORTRAITS
PH09212 627 (April 2, 1992) p13. "Motley Crue's Tommy Lee, Nikki Sixx, Mick Mars And The Defrocked Vince Neil (clockwise from top left)" (Double, Steve)
LEECHES—ILLUSTRATIONS
PH09213 656 (May 13, 1993) p64. "[Leeches]" (Corio, Paul)
LEEDS, HARVEY—PHOTOGRAPHS
PH09214 652 (March 18, 1993) pp[enc.10]. "Epic Exec Harvey Leeds Repped At Syracuse: 'When I Was In College,' He Says, 'I Lived The record And radio Business.'" (Barry, David)
LEESE, HOWARD—PHOTOGRAPHS
PH09215 696 (December 1, 1994) p25. "Howard Leese, John Paul Jones, Ann Wilson, Denny Fongheiser And Nancy Wilson"
LEFLEUR, JELANNA—PHOTOGRAPHS
PH09216 743 (September 19, 1996) p38. "Vocalist 'Lana' LeFleur And Producer 'Jay Ski' McGowan"
LEGAT, JASON—PHOTOGRAPHS
PH09217 652 (March 18, 1993) pp[enc.37]. "Jason Legat" (Seliger, Mark)
LEGENDS OF THE FALL (FILM)—ILLUSTRATIONS
PH09218 700 (January 26, 1995) p65. "Legends For The Mall" (Osborn, Kathy)
LEGENDS OF THE FALL (FILM)—PHOTOGRAPHS
PH09219 700 (January 26, 1995) p66. "Film Legends In The Making: Julia Ormond And Brad Pitt"
PH09220 705 (April 6, 1995) p69. "Oscar Rejects"
LEGUIZAMO, JOHN—PHOTOGRAPHS
PH09221 717 (September 21, 1995) p89. "Patrick Swayze, Wesley Snipes And John Leguizamo (from left) Hit The Road"
PH09222 731 (April 4, 1996) p66. "Leguizamo, 'Wong Foo'"
LEHDER, CARLOS—PHOTOGRAPHS
PH09223 660-661 (July 8, 1993) p80. "Lehder, Now Serving Life Plus 135 Years" (Medina, Lope)
LEIBOVITZ, ANNIE—PHOTOGRAPHS
PH09224 643 (November 12, 1992) p49. "'Rolling Stone' Art Directors (from left): Bob Kingsbury (1968-73), Tony Lane (1974-76), Annie Leibovitz, Mike Salisbury (1973-74), Roger Black (1976-78), Jann S. Wenner...
PH09225 647 (January 7, 1993) p11. "RS Alumni Photog Annie Leibovitz, Thompson, David Felton, Cameron Crowe, Chris Hodenfield, Ben Fong-Torres, Paul Scanlon (from left)" (Elgar, Nick)
LEIGH, JENNIFER JASON—PHOTOGRAPHS
PH09226 621 (January 9, 1992) p55. "Jason Patric And Jennifer Jason Leigh In Danger"
PH09227 638 (September 3, 1992) p72. "Bonding With Leigh (left) Is A Living Hell For Fonda"
PH09228 649 (February 4, 1993) p72. "[Single White Female]"
PH09229 678 (March 24, 1994) p105. "Robbins (left) And Newman Play Office Politics, While Leigh (far right) Gets The Story"
PH09230 697 (December 15, 1994) p104. "Leigh, Third From Left, At The Famed Round Table"
PH09231 705 (April 6, 1995) p69. "Oscar Rejects"
PH09232 706 (April 20, 1995) p88. "Kathy Bates And Jennifer Jason Leigh Hide Secrets"
PH09233 722 (November 30, 1995) p58. "The Gang-Raped Hooker In 'Last Exit' Appealed To Leigh: 'I Have A Problem With Generic Female Roles'"
PH09234 722 (November 30, 1995) p74. "Is Jennifer Jason Leigh's Rocker Hotter Than Pierce Brosnan's Bond? No Contest"
PH09235 722 (November 30, 1995) p57. "[Jennifer Jason Leigh]" (Demarchelier, Patrick)
PH09236 722 (November 30, 1995) p60. "Leigh (with Phoebe Cates) Had Her First Hit With 'Fast Times At Ridgemont High'"
PH09237 722 (November 30, 1995) p61. "Leigh Didn't Have To Walk Out Of 'Miami Blues'—Her Work Opposite Balwin Ranks With Her Best"
PH09238 722 (November 30, 1995) p60. "Leigh Hit A Career Low Point In 1986: getting Stretched Between Two Vehicles In 'The Hitcher'"
PH09239 731 (April 4, 1996) p66. "Leigh, 'Georgia'"
PH09240 741 (August 22, 1996) p104. "Richardson (left) And Leigh In Peril In Kansas City"
LEIGH, JENNIFER JASON—PHOTOGRAPHS—PORTRAITS
PH09241 722 (November 30, 1995) p58. "Leigh (with 'Georgia' sister Winningham) Would Like An Oscar But Says, 'It Doesn't Change Your Life'" (Demarchelier, Patrick)
LEIGH, MIKE—PHOTOGRAPHS
PH09242 745 (October 17, 1996) p142. "Jean-Bapiste (left) And Blethyn Flank Mike Leigh"
LEIGHTON, BRENNEN—PHOTOGRAPHS
PH09243 652 (March 18, 1993) pp[enc.36]. "Brennen Leighton" (Seliger, Mark)
LEIGHTON, LAURA—PHOTOGRAPHS
PH09244 682 (May 19, 1994) p52. "Bad Girl Leighton (right) Makes Trouble..." (Seliger, Mark)
PH09245 682 (May 19, 1994) pp48-49. "[Melrose Place]" (Seliger, Mark)
PH09246 682 (May 19, 1994) pp[cover]. "Melrose Place's Bod Squad" (Seliger, Mark)
LEITCH, CHRIS—PHOTOGRAPHS
PH09247 730 (March 21, 1996) p55. "The Boys In The Bus: Schiavone McGee, David Triano, Eric Lawson, Chris Leitch, Karl Vonklein, David Peterson And Mike Boyd (clockwise from left)" (Clinch, Danny)
PH09248 730 (March 21, 1996) p62. "Peterson (left) And Leitch Rest For The Next Show" (Clinch, Danny)
LEITCH, DONOVAN—PHOTOGRAPHS
PH09249 682 (May 19, 1994) p63. "[Models]" (Hollywood, Barry)
LEMMON, JACK—PHOTOGRAPHS
PH09250 674 (January 27, 1994) p48. "Acting Vehicles Include 'The Pelican Brief,' 'In The Name Of The Father,' 'What's Eating Gilbert Grape,' 'Shadowlands,' 'Naked,' And 'Grumpy Old Men'"
PH09251 Lem (October 1, 1992) p74. ""
LEMONHEADS—ALBUMS
PH09252 637 (August 20, 1992) p68. "It's A Shame About Ray"
PH09253 670 (November 25, 1993) p108. "Come On Feel The Lemonheads"
PH09254 748 (November 28, 1996) p132. "Car Button Cloth"
LEMONHEADS—ILLUSTRATIONS
PH09255 678 (March 24, 1994) p6. "A Lemonhead Meets A Picklehead" (Pendergrast, James T.)
LEMONHEADS—PHOTOGRAPHS
PH09256 637 (August 20, 1992) p22. "Hatfield (left) With Dando" (Pasley, Richard)
PH09257 645-646 (December 10, 1992) p53. "[Lemonheads]"
PH09258 675 (February 10, 1994) p39. "The Squeaky Clean, Endlessly Cute Power-Pop Trio: Drummer Ryan, Dando And Bassist Dalton" (Rheims, Bettina)

LENARDO, GENO—PHOTOGRAPHS
PH09259 715 (August 24, 1995) pp68-69. "Brian Liesegang, Richard Patrick, Geno Lenardo, Matt Walker, Frank Cavanagh (from left)" (Ockenfels, Frank W.)
LENNON, JOHN—ALBUMS
PH09260 617 (November 14, 1991) p113. "Live Peace In Toronto" (Lennon, John)
PH09261 617 (November 14, 1991) p113. "Live Peace In Toronto" (Ono, Yoko)
LENNON, JOHN—ILLUSTRATIONS
PH09262 645-646 (December 10, 1992) p149. "John Lennon, 1990"
PH09263 722 (November 30, 1995) p9. "John Lennon" (Burke, Philip)
LENNON, JOHN—ILLUSTRATIONS—PORTRAITS
PH09264 641 (October 15, 1992) p49. "[John Lennon]" (Bralds, Braldt)
PH09265 710 (June 15, 1995) p18. "From Abkhazia With Love: The Stamp Of Marx And Lennon"
LENNON, JOHN—PHOTOGRAPHS
PH09266 626 (March 19, 1992) p29. "Performing With Elephant's Memory On The 'Dick Cavett Show' 1972" (Gruen, Bob)
PH09267 633 (June 25, 1992) p6. "[John Lennon]" (Franken, O.)
PH09268 636 (August 6, 1992) p8. "[John Lennon]" (Franken, O.)
PH09269 643 (November 12, 1992) p65. "Clapton, Lennon, Mitchell And Richards (from left) In 1968" (Russell, Ethan)
PH09270 645-646 (December 10, 1992) p148. "John Lennon And Yoko Ono, 1968"
PH09271 645-646 (December 10, 1992) p148. "John Lennon, 1967"
PH09272 655 (April 29, 1993) p56. "Geffen With John Lennon And Yoko Ono, New York, 1980" (Senecal, Michel)
PH09273 660-661 (July 8, 1993) p38. "In 1990, People Gathered In New York's Central Park To Mark The Tenth Anniversary Of John Lennon's Murder" (Everke, Tobias)
PH09274 674 (January 27, 1994) p13. "Jamming With John And Yoko In 1971 (below)" (Sia, Joseph)
PH09275 680 (April 21, 1994) p63. "Hamburg Days: George Harrison, Stuart Sutcliffe And John Lennon" (Kirchherr, Astrid)
PH09276 680 (April 21, 1994) p64. "Ticket To Ride: Starr And Lennon With Photographer Astrid Kirchherr" (Scheler, Max)
PH09277 690 (September 8, 1994) p36. "Lennon (center) With The Quarry Men, In Liverpool, England, July 1957" (Rhind, Geoff)
PH09278 722 (November 30, 1995) p26. "Ringo Starr, John Lennon, Paul McCartney And George Harrison During The Filming Of 'Help!' In 1965: 'So Much Younger Than Today'" (Kindahl, Chris)
PH09279 726 (January 25, 1996) p46. "Starr, McCartney, Harrison, Lennon"
PH09280 738-739 (July 11, 1996) p68. "Tommy Smothers, John Lennon, Yoko Ono, Rosemary And Timothy Leary (from left) During The Bed-In For Peace In Montreal, 1969"
LENNON, JOHN—PHOTOGRAPHS—PORTRAITS
PH09281 643 (November 12, 1992) p256. "Yoko Ono & John Lennon" (Leibovitz, Annie)
PH09282 645-646 (December 10, 1992) p149. "The Gun Lobby, 1981"
PH09283 645-646 (December 10, 1992) p149. "John Lennon And Yoko Ono, 1982"
PH09284 645-646 (December 10, 1992) p161. "John Lennon And Yoko Ono, 1981"
PH09285 645-646 (December 10, 1992) p149. "John Lennon, 1971"
PH09286 676 (February 24, 1994) p45. "John Lennon's Impact Remains Universal, His Influence Undiminished" (Leibovitz, Annie)
PH09287 703 (March 9, 1995) p25. "The Late John Lennon" (Gruen, Bob)
PH09288 720 (November 2, 1995) p49. "John Lennon" (Kirchherr, Astrid)
PH09289 747 (November 14, 1996) p30. "[John Lennon]" (Wolff, Richard)
LENNON, JULIAN—ALBUMS
PH09290 616 (October 31, 1991) p93. "Help Yourself"
LENNON, JULIAN—PHOTOGRAPHS
PH09291 631 (May 28, 1992) p9. "Ringo Starr, Julian Lennon And George Harrison (from left)" (Young, Richard)
LENNON, SEAN—PHOTOGRAPHS
PH09292 729 (March 7, 1996) p9. "Cibo Matto's Honda And Miho Hatori Gettin' Down With Sean Lennon" (Kleiman, Dennis)
PH09293 735 (May 30, 1996) p13. "Muffs Roy McDonald And Kim Shattuck, Sean Ono Lennon, Muff Ronnie Barnett, Sideman Bill Bartell, And Eric Erlandson" (Phalen, Tom)
PH09294 742 (September 5, 1996) p21. "[Yoko Ono, Sean Lennon, Adam Yauch]" (Atlas, David)
PH09295 750-751 (December 26, 1996) p46. "Cibo Matto Performing With Special Guest Sean Ono Lennon (right) In New York" (Kleiman, Dennis)
LENNOX, ANNIE—ALBUMS
PH09296 633 (June 25, 1992) p41. "Diva"
PH09297 706 (April 20, 1995) p70. "Medusa"
LENNOX, ANNIE—ILLUSTRATIONS
PH09298 651 (March 4, 1993) p5. "Annie Lennox" (Burke, Philip)
LENNOX, ANNIE—PHOTOGRAPHS
PH09299 645-646 (December 10, 1992) p45. "Saluting Freddie: Lennox And Bowie (above)" (Mazur, Kevin)
PH09300 651 (March 4, 1993) p59. "[Annie Lennox]" (Broad, Julian)
PH09301 651 (March 4, 1993) p48. "The Readers' Choice Is...Annie Lennox" (Mazur, Kevin)
PH09302 706 (April 20, 1995) p15. "Bonnie Raitt, Mistress Of Sensitivity Lennox, Carly Simon And Crow (from left)" (Busacca, Larry)
PH09303 720 (November 2, 1995) p28. "Lennox: Flamboyant Diva" (Mazur, Kevin)
LENNOX, ANNIE—PHOTOGRAPHS—PORTRAITS
PH09304 651 (March 4, 1993) p58. "[Annie Lennox]" (Broad, Julian)
PH09305 667 (October 14, 1993) p100. "Taking Care Of Business In 'Sweet Dreams'"
PH09306 716 (September 7, 1995) p22. "Annie Lennox: Ruling U.K. Diva" (Seidman, Amy)
PH09307 742 (September 5, 1996) p23. "[Annie Lennox]" (Lavine, Michael)
LENO, JAY—PHOTOGRAPHS
PH09308 677 (March 10, 1994) p17. "Polly Jean Harvey Makes Small Talk With Jay Leno" (Norton, Margaret)
PH09309 686-687 (July 14, 1994) p20. "Crooked Reign: Pavement Take Over "The Tonight Show""
LENO, JAY—PHOTOGRAPHS—PORTRAITS
PH09310 724-725 (December 28, 1995) pp76-77. "[Jay Leno]" (Seliger, Mark)
LEONOWICZ, CHUCK—PHOTOGRAPHS
PH09311 624 (February 20, 1992) p32. "May The G-Force Be With You: Don't Ask About The Mush Run" (Smale, Brian)
PH09312 624 (February 20, 1992) p29. "Today Calgary, Tomorrow Albertville? From Left: Woodard, Leturgez, Snavely And Leonowicz" (Smale, Brian)
LEONSIS, TED—PHOTOGRAPHS—PORTRAITS
PH09313 744 (October 3, 1996) p66. "[Ted Leonsis]"
LERNER-SHAEV, HILARY—PHOTOGRAPHS
PH09314 652 (March 18, 1993) pp[enc.9]. "Hilary Lerner-Shaev Has Gone From Working For CBS At Duke To Running EMI's Video And Alternative Promotion" (Barry, David)

LES MISERABLES (STAGE MUSICAL)—PHOTOGRAPHS
PH09315 624 (February 20, 1992) p11. "Debbie Gibson In 'Les Miserables'" (Mazur, Kevin)
LESH, PHIL—PHOTOGRAPHS
PH09316 616 (October 31, 1991) p40. "Bill Kreutzmann, Ron "Pigpen" McKernan, Bob Weir, Garcia And Phil Lesh (clockwise from top left) In 1966" (Greene, Herb)
PH09317 619-620 (December 12, 1991) p103. "Phil Lesh, Bob Weir, Neil Young And Jerry Garcia (from left) Pay Tribute To Bill Graham" (Blakesberg, Jay)
PH09318 660-661 (July 8, 1993) p29. "The Dead's Phil Lesh, Bob Weir And Jerry Garcia (from left)" (Blakesberg, Jay)
PH09319 664 (September 2, 1993) p46. "The Dead At Rest in 1966: Phil Lesh, Bill Kreutzman, Ron 'Pigpen' McKernan, Bob Weir And Jerry Garcia (clockwise from left)" (Greene, Herb)
PH09320 676 (February 24, 1994) p46. "The Early Grateful Dead (clockwise from left): Jerry Garcia, Bill Kreutzmann, Ron 'Pigpen' McKernan, Bob Weir, Percussionist Mickey Hart And Phil Lesh" (Marshall, Jim)
PH09321 677 (March 10, 1994) p27. "The Dead's Lesh, Weir, Vince Welnick, Hornsby, Bill Kreutzmann, Mickey Hart" (Mazur, Kevin)
PH09322 679 (April 7, 1994) p37. "Ain't Gonna Work On Yasgur's Farm No More: Phil Lesh, Crosby, Nash, Jorma Kaukonen" (Blakesberg, Jay)
PH09323 696 (December 1, 1994) p24. "Bob Weir, Lesh And Garcia (from left)" (Blakesberg, Jay)
PH09324 717 (September 21, 1995) p52. "Before The Dead, They Were The Warlocks" (Greene, Herbi)
PH09325 717 (September 21, 1995) p54. "The Dead In '66 At The Crossroads, the Corner Of Haight And Ashbury: Garcia, Pigpen, Lesh, Weir, Kreutzmann (from left)" (Greene, Herbi)
PH09326 717 (September 21, 1995) p65. "The Dead In Front Of Their Ashbury St. House, 1967: Jerry Garcia, Ron 'Pigpen' McKernan, Bob Weir, Phil Lesh, Co-Managers Danny Rifkin And Rock Scully, And Bill Kreutzmann..."
PH09327 717 (September 21, 1995) p67. "Jerry Garcia, Phil Lesh, Bill Kreutzmann, Bob Weir And Ron 'Pigpen' McKernan (clockwise from bottom right) Huddled In San Francisco's Golden Gate Park, 1967" (Marshall, Jim)
PH09328 717 (September 21, 1995) p66. "Lesh, Early Dead Co-Managers Scully And Rifkin, Weir And Garcia At A Press Conference Following The Oct. 2, 1967, drug Bust At The Dead's House" (Wolman, Baron)
PH09329 717 (September 21, 1995) p73. "marrying Acid-Damaged Art Music And The Funky Snort Of Live Rock & Roll: The Dead As A Lysergic-Dance Band In 1969 With Tom Constanten, Weir, Kreutzmann, Pigpen, Lesh, H..." (G
PH09330 717 (September 21, 1995) p72. "The Music Never Stopped: Garcia, Weir, Lesh, Brent Mydland, Kreutzmann And Hart (from left) In 1979" (Greene, Herbi)
PH09331 717 (September 21, 1995) p69. "The Original Quintet At Home At 710 Ashbury St., In 1966: Phil Lesh, Bob Weir, Bill Kreutzmann, Ron 'Pigpen' McKernan And Jerry Garcia (from left)" (Anthony, Gene)
PH09332 717 (September 21, 1995) p28. "Phil Lesh Joined 20,000 Fans In A Massive Tribute To Garcia At The Sunday Memorial" (Blakesberg, Jay)
PH09333 726 (January 25, 1996) p23. "The Last Incarnation Of The Dead Perform In February 1995: Phil Lesh, Mickey Hart, Bob Weir, Jerry Garcia And Vince Welnick (from left)" (Blakesberg, Jay)
LESH, PHIL—PHOTOGRAPHS—PORTRAITS
PH09334 717 (September 21, 1995) p72. "Nonstop Truckin' And Retooled Roots: The Dead's 1970s Lineup, With Keith Godchaux, Garcia, Lesh, kreutzmann, Donna Godchaux And Weir (clockwise from top left)"
LESLIE SPIT TREEO—PHOTOGRAPHS
PH09335 616 (October 31, 1991) p25. "The Leslie Spit Treeo (from left): Jack Nicholsen, Laura Hubert, Pat Langner And Tag" (Counts, Wyatt)
LESTER, DAVID—PHOTOGRAPHS—PORTRAITS
PH09336 660-661 (July 8, 1993) p95. "Mecca Normal: David Lester, Jean Smith" (Karpa, Robert)
LETHAL WEAPON 3 (FILM)—PHOTOGRAPHS
PH09337 633 (June 25, 1992) p49. "A Trio For Glover (left), Gibson And Gun"
PH09338 644 (November 26, 1992) p78. "[Lethal Weapon 3]"
LET'S GO (PUBLICATION)—ILLUSTRATIONS
PH09339 707 (May 4, 1995) p16. "Let's Go" (Pendergrast, James T.)
LETTERMAN, DAVID—ILLUSTRATIONS
PH09340 650 (February 18, 1993) p32. "[David Letterman]" (Hirschfeld, Al)
PH09341 698-699 (December 29, 1994) p30. "[David Letterman]" (Cowles, David)
PH09342 698-699 (December 29, 1994) p33. "[Johnny Carson & David Letterman]" (Blitt, Barry)
PH09343 698-699 (December 29, 1994) p32. "[Madonna & David Letterman]" (Ryden, Mark)
PH09344 702 (February 23, 1995) p16. "Big Ass" (Pendergrast, James T.)
PH09345 738-739 (July 11, 1996) p12. "Dave's Tricks" (Pendergrast, James T.)
LETTERMAN, DAVID—PHOTOGRAPHS
PH09346 693 (October 20, 1994) p28. "Letterman, Madonna" (Mazur, Kevin)
PH09347 698-699 (December 29, 1994) p42. "[Madonna & David Letterman]"
PH09348 735 (May 30, 1996) p28. "[David Letterman]" (Watson, Albert)
PH09349 735 (May 30, 1996) p32. "For The 'Video Special,' Dave Relayed Obnoxious Instructions To Rupert Jee (top), Co-Owner Of The Hello Deli"
PH09350 735 (May 30, 1996) p30. "In The Pre-Suit, Pre-CBS Days, Producer Robert Morton Backs Up Dave" (Smeal, James)
PH09351 735 (May 30, 1996) p30. "Letterman With New Executive Producer Rob Burnett, Who Survived 'Uma, Oprah'"
LETTERMAN, DAVID—PHOTOGRAPHS—PORTRAITS
PH09352 650 (February 18, 1993) pp[cover]. "Heeeeeeeeerrre's Dave!" (Seliger, Mark)
PH09353 670 (November 25, 1993) pp76-77. "[David Letterman]" (Seliger, Mark)
PH09354 672-673 (December 23, 1993) p188. "[Covers]" (Seliger, Mark)
PH09355 698-699 (December 29, 1994) pp[cover]. "Man Of The Year: It's Dave's World, We Only Live In It" (Ockenfels, Frank, 3)
PH09356 735 (May 30, 1996) pp[cover]. "Dave Vs. Dave: Is Letterman His Own Worst Enemy?" (Watson, Albert)
LETTERMAN, DOROTHY—ILLUSTRATIONS
PH09357 698-699 (December 29, 1994) p34. "[Dorothy Letterman]" (Friedman, Drew)
LETTERMAN, DOROTHY—PHOTOGRAPHS
PH09358 698-699 (December 29, 1994) p37. "David Letterman's Mom (left) Bonds With Hillary Clinton"
LETTERS TO CLEO—PHOTOGRAPHS
PH09359 690 (September 8, 1994) p42. "Cleo's Hanley, McKenna And Scott Riebling (from left)" (Capak, R. J.)
PH09360 693 (October 20, 1994) p30. "Cleo's Hanley, Stacy Jones, Manning; Builders Joan Wasser, Eric Masunaga" (Robicheau, Paul)
LETURGEZ, BRYAN—PHOTOGRAPHS
PH09361 624 (February 20, 1992) p32. "May The G-Force Be With You: Don't Ask About The Mush Run" (Smale, Brian)
PH09362 624 (February 20, 1992) p29. "Today Calgary, Tomorrow Albertville? From Left: Woodard, Leturgez, Snavely And Leonowicz" (Smale, Brian)
LEVELLERS—ALBUMS
PH09363 633 (June 25, 1992) p45. "Levelling The Land"

LEVELLERS—PHOTOGRAPHS
PH09364 628 (April 16, 1992) p63. "The Levellers"
PH09365 630 (May 14, 1992) p32. "The Levellers (from left): Friend, Sevink, Chadwick, Heather And Cunningham" (Doove, Hester)
PH09366 685 (June 30, 1994) p36. "Levellers: Tomorrow's Criminals?" (Double, Steve)
LEVELLERS—PHOTOGRAPHS—PORTRAITS
PH09367 645-646 (December 10, 1992) p61. "The Levellers" (Sheehan, Tom)
LEVENTHAL, RACHEL—PHOTOGRAPHS
PH09368 689 (August 25, 1994) p77. "Kenny Miller And Rachel Leventhal At The Viacom Office In Times Square, New York City" (Newton, Philip)
PH09369 689 (August 25, 1994) p78. "Miller And Leventhal At Their Loft in Tribeca, New York City" (Newton, Philip)
LEVERIDGE, PAUL—PHOTOGRAPHS—PORTRAITS
PH09370 723 (December 14, 1995) p40. "Kermit, Bez And Ryder (from left) Mix An Intoxicating Musical Cocktail" (Westenberg, Kevin)
LEVI, MARVIN—PHOTOGRAPHS
PH09371 683 (June 2, 1994) p24. "Twin Tones: Daniel Chavis, Burris, Danny Chavis And Levi (from left)" (Cardillicchio, Nick)
LEVIN, MICHAEL—PHOTOGRAPHS
PH09372 693 (October 20, 1994) p108. "Michael Levin: City College of New York" (Barry, David)
LEVIN, TONY—PHOTOGRAPHS—PORTRAITS
PH09373 684 (June 16, 1994) p18. "Belew, Fripp, Bruford And Levin"
LEVON AND THE HAWKS—PHOTOGRAPHS
PH09374 617 (November 14, 1991) p72. "Levon And The Hawks, Circa 1963: Sax Player Jerry Field, Rick Danko, Levon Helm, Richard Manuel, Garth Hudson And Robertson (from left)"
LEVY, ERIK—PHOTOGRAPHS
PH09375 693 (October 20, 1994) p128. "[Erik Levy]" (Rapp, Frank)
LEVY, NOAH—PHOTOGRAPHS
PH09376 691 (September 22, 1994) p20. "Hawks Gary Louris, Mark Perlman, Dan Murphy, Noah Levy, Tweedy" (Smiley, Jay)
LEW, JAMES—PHOTOGRAPHS
PH09377 692 (October 6, 1994) p81. "Van Damme Aims A Lethal Kick At Assassin James Lew"
LEWD, TREY—ALBUMS
PH09378 645-646 (December 10, 1992) p180. "Drop Of The Line"
LEWIN, ALFREDO—PHOTOGRAPHS
PH09379 670 (November 25, 1993) p22. "Lewin, Infarinato, Morales (from left)"
LEWINSON, STEPHEN—PHOTOGRAPHS
PH09380 718 (October 5, 1995) p32. "Nicolette, Stephen Lewinson, Daddy G (from left)" (Mazur, Kevin)
LEWIS, ARTHUR—PHOTOGRAPHS
PH09381 745 (October 17, 1996) p84. "[Arthur Lewis]" (Watson, Albert)
PH09382 745 (October 17, 1996) p88. "Arthur Lewis, During The Winter Of 1992, Outside His Parent's Home, In Locust, N.J."
LEWIS, ARTHUR—PHOTOGRAPHS—PORTRAITS
PH09383 745 (October 17, 1996) p86. "'Gifted And Talented' Friends (from left): Nicole Mauro, Arthur Lewis And Alissa Heyman As They Appeared In The 1991 Middletown High School South Yearbook, Aquiline"
LEWIS, BARBARA—PHOTOGRAPHS
PH09384 745 (October 17, 1996) p81. "[Barbara Lewis]" (Watson, Albert)
LEWIS, EMMANUEL—PHOTOGRAPHS
PH09385 715 (August 24, 1995) p89. "Hot International Star" (Jones, Sam)
LEWIS, EPHRAIM—ALBUMS
PH09386 637 (August 20, 1992) p53. "Skin"
LEWIS, EPHRAIM—PHOTOGRAPHS—PORTRAITS
PH09387 636 (August 6, 1992) p24. "[Ephraim Lewis]" (Low, Dorothy)
PH09388 645-646 (December 10, 1992) p59. "Ephraim Lewis" (Schultz, Nina)
PH09389 688 (August 11, 1994) p33. "The Late Ephraim Lewis"
LEWIS, GROVER—PHOTOGRAPHS
PH09390 632 (June 11, 1992) p62. "Staff Members And Contributing Writers At The 1971 Editorial Conference, At Esalen, In Big Sur" (Leibovitz, Annie)
LEWIS, JAMES—PHOTOGRAPHS
PH09391 730 (March 21, 1996) p91. "James Lewis Is Vaporhead's Singer" (Witkin, Christian)
LEWIS, JERRY—PHOTOGRAPHS
PH09392 706 (April 20, 1995) p88. "Jerry Lewis And Oliver Platt Do Battle"
PH09393 738-739 (July 11, 1996) p96. "Jerry Lewis: The Original Mr. Two-Face"
PH09394 742 (September 5, 1996) p68. "With Lewis In 'The King Of Comedy'"
LEWIS, JERRY LEE—ALBUMS
PH09395 712-713 (July 13, 1995) p111. "Young Blood"
LEWIS, JERRY LEE—ILLUSTRATIONS
PH09396 694 (November 3, 1994) p18. "Disgraceland" (Menchin, Scott)
LEWIS, JERRY LEE—PHOTOGRAPHS
PH09397 619-620 (December 12, 1991) p32. "[Good Rockin' Tonight]"
PH09398 632 (June 11, 1992) p147. "Shawn And Jerry Lee Lewis At Their Wedding, Seventy-Seven Days Before Her Death" (Diamond, Rick)
PH09399 690 (September 8, 1994) p24. "Jerry Lee Entertains The Cleveland Crowd"
PH09400 719 (October 19, 1995) p36. "Jerry Lee Lewis At Cleveland Stadium" (Corbijn, Anton)
LEWIS, JERRY LEE—PHOTOGRAPHS—PORTRAITS
PH09401 632 (June 11, 1992) p144. "Jerry Lee Lewis Was The Spendingest Man In The County" (Dickson, Nigel)
LEWIS, JULIETTE—ILLUSTRATIONS
PH09402 690 (September 8, 1994) p83. "Blood From A Stone" (Gosfield, Josh)
LEWIS, JULIETTE—PHOTOGRAPHS
PH09403 640 (October 1, 1992) p72. "Allen And Farrow Reach An Impasse"
PH09404 640 (October 1, 1992) p72. "Allen Meets Danner, The Mother Of Infatuated Student Lewis"
PH09405 663 (August 19, 1993) p83. "Juliette Lewis Prepares For The Big Night"
PH09406 665 (September 16, 1993) p78. "Lewis (left) And Pitt Share A Kiss"
PH09407 684 (June 16, 1994) p116. "Bloody: Lewis And Harrelson In "Natural Born Killers""
PH09408 690 (September 8, 1994) p84. "Crimescape: Juliette Lewis With Cop Tom Sizemore"
PH09409 690 (September 8, 1994) p84. "Lewis And Harrelson"
PH09410 696 (December 1, 1994) p96. "Pitt Has Dated "Thelma And Louise" Co-Star Davis (top) And "Kalifornia" Girl Lewis (below)"
LEWIS, JULIETTE—PHOTOGRAPHS—PORTRAITS
PH09411 630 (May 14, 1992) pp60-61,65. "[Juliette Lewis]" (Maser, Wayne)
LEWIS, PETER—PHOTOGRAPHS
PH09412 670 (November 25, 1993) p38. "Jerry Miller, Don Stevenson, Plant, Peter Lewis And Skip Spence" (Blakesberg, Jay)
LEWIS, RICHARD—PHOTOGRAPHS
PH09413 616 (October 31, 1991) p56. "Quite Frankly, Do Not Mock His Posture, For Life's Gravity Pulls On Him More Unforgivingly Than It Does Us" (Schiffman, Bonnie)

LEWIS, SHAWN—ILLUSTRATIONS
PH09414 632 (June 11, 1992) p13. "[Shawn Lewis]" (Cronin, Brian)
LEWIS, SHAWN—PHOTOGRAPHS
PH09415 632 (June 11, 1992) p147. "Shawn And Jerry Lee Lewis At Their Wedding, Seventy-Seven Days Before Her Death" (Diamond, Rick)
LEWIS, TERRY—PHOTOGRAPHS
PH09416 749 (December 12, 1996) p20. "It's A Family Affair: Jam's Wife, Lisa Harris, Holding Tyler; Jam; Jackson; And Lewis (from left)"
LEWISOHN, MARK—BOOKS
PH09417 645-646 (December 10, 1992) p88. "[The Complete Beatles Chronicle]"
LHOTE, MORGANE—PHOTOGRAPHS
PH09418 731 (April 4, 1996) p40. "Always The Same, Always Different: Stereolab's Mary Hansen, Tim Gane, Laetitia Sadier And Morgane Lhote (from left)" (Perou, Ralph)
LI, GONG—PHOTOGRAPHS
PH09419 653 (April 1, 1993) p57. "Red Lantern"
PH09420 654 (April 15, 1993) p72. "Gong Li May Be The Biggest Star You've Never Heard Of"
PH09421 726 (January 25, 1996) p67. "Shanghai Triad"
LIBERTARIANS—ILLUSTRATIONS
PH09422 708 (May 18, 1995) p14. "Libertarian" (Pendergrast, James T.)
LIBRARIANS—ILLUSTRATIONS
PH09423 697 (December 15, 1994) p14. "Librarians: See "Babes"" (Pendergrast, James T.)
LIBRARIES—ILLUSTRATIONS
PH09424 706 (April 20, 1995) p17. "Shelf Destruction" (Corio, Paul)
LIDDY, G. GORDON—PHOTOGRAPHS
PH09425 690 (September 8, 1994) p49. "Liddy At The Courthouse In 1972 After Pleading Not Guilty"
LIDDY, G. GORDON—PHOTOGRAPHS—PORTRAITS
PH09426 710 (June 15, 1995) p57. "Liddy" (Trippett, Robert)
LIEBERMAN, JUDY—PHOTOGRAPHS
PH09427 679 (April 7, 1994) p62. "Since 1989, Judy Lieberman Has Been Pioneering An AIDS Therapy Based On Boosting The Immune-System Response Of Patients" (Winters, Dan)
LIEBLING, BETH—PHOTOGRAPHS
PH09428 688 (August 11, 1994) p17. "[Eddie Vedder & Beth Liebling]"
PH09429 732 (April 18, 1996) p19. "Smokin'! Vedder And Wife Beth Liebling" (Mazur, Kevin)
PH09430 748 (November 28, 1996) p54. "Beth Liebling And Vedder At The VH1 Honors At The Universal Amphitheater, In L.A., April 1996" (Mazur, Kevin)
LIEN, BILL—PHOTOGRAPHS
PH09431 726 (January 25, 1996) p30. "Gin Blossoms: Robin Wilson, Phillip Rhodes, Bill Lien, Jesse Valenzuela, Scott Johnson (from left)" (Jennings, Steve)
LIESEGANG, BRIAN—PHOTOGRAPHS
PH09432 712-713 (July 13, 1995) p37. "The Touring Filter, With Patrick (left) And Liesegang (foreground)" (Norcross, Deborah)
PH09433 715 (August 24, 1995) pp68-69. "Brian Liesegang, Richard Patrick, Geno Lenardo, Matt Walker, Frank Cavanagh (from left)" (Ockenfels, Frank W.)
PH09434 715 (August 24, 1995) p70. "Liesegang (left) And Patrick Crank It Out In Houston" (Haveman, Kathy)
PH09435 720 (November 2, 1995) p16. "Robert And Richard Patrick With Brian Liesegang In L.A. (from left)" (Phillips, Ken)
LIESEGANG, BRIAN—PHOTOGRAPHS—PORTRAITS
PH09436 715 (August 24, 1995) p70. "For All Filter's Noisy, Bile-Soaked Music, Liesegang (left) And Patrick Are Shy, Thoughtful Guys—Eggheads, Really" (Ockenfels, Frank W.)
LIFE (FILM)—PHOTOGRAPHS
PH09436a 747 (November 14, 1996) p124. "'Mad Housewife Judd"
LIFE IS SWEET (FILM)—PHOTOGRAPHS
PH09437 627 (April 2, 1992) p41. "'Life Is Sweet' And Stars Horrocks And Alison Steadman"
LIGHT SLEEPER (FILM)—PHOTOGRAPHS
PH09438 626 (March 19, 1992) p104. "Sarandon And Dafoe Try To Find A New Life After Drug Dealing"
LIGHTFOOT, GORDON—ALBUMS
PH09439 664 (September 2, 1993) p62. "Waiting For You"
LIKE A PRAYER (VIDEO)—PHOTOGRAPHS
PH09440 667 (October 14, 1993) p76. "Jail-House Rock: Madonna's 'Prayer' Pissed Off Both The Pope And Pepsi"
LIL' KIM—PHOTOGRAPHS
PH09441 748 (November 28, 1996) p36. "Queen 'Itch: Lil' Kim Gets Bleeped" (Lavine, Michael)
LILYS—PHOTOGRAPHS
PH09442 749 (December 12, 1996) p30. "This Year's Model" (Millson, P. J.)
LIMBAUGH, RUSH—PHOTOGRAPHS—PORTRAITS
PH09443 672-673 (December 23, 1993) p90. "Don't Shush Rush" (Butler, Kimberly)
LIND, MICHAEL—PHOTOGRAPHS—PORTRAITS
PH09444 715 (August 24, 1995) p88. "Michael Lind's Hot List" (Irish, Len)
LINDA, MISS—PHOTOGRAPHS—PORTRAITS
PH09445 686-687 (July 14, 1994) p72. "Girl World: Sensi, Linda, Charmaine, Sabrina (from left)" (Borris, Dan)
LINDGREN, YVONNE—PHOTOGRAPHS
PH09446 702 (February 23, 1995) p54. "Woman In The Machine: Working On The Line Means Lindgren Can Afford An Apartment Of Her Own" (Kuehn, Karen)
LINDSEY, JOSEPH—PHOTOGRAPHS
PH09447 652 (March 18, 1993) p47. "Patrick McGaw, Joseph Lindsey And Steve Parlavecchio (from left) Of 'Amongst Friends'" (Michaelson, Randall)
LINKLATER, RICHARD—PHOTOGRAPHS
PH09448 656 (May 13, 1993) p82. "[Richard Linklater]" (Seliger, Mark)
PH09449 702 (February 23, 1995) p80. "And Enjoy A Night In Vienna"
PH09450 702 (February 23, 1995) p80. "Julie Delpy And Ethan Hawke Share A Kiss"
PH09451 702 (February 23, 1995) p80. "Take Direction From Richard Linklater"
LINKLATER, RICHARD—PHOTOGRAPHS—PORTRAITS
PH09452 730 (March 21, 1996) p18. "Keep It In Your Pants: Tarantino (left) And Linklater" (Crawford, Michael)
LINNEY, LAURA—PHOTOGRAPHS
PH09453 711 (June 29, 1995) p48. "Laura Linney (center) Holds Off Jungle Fever"
PH09454 732 (April 18, 1996) p80. "From Left: Linney And Gere Huddle; Norton Broods"
THE LION KING (FILM)—ILLUSTRATIONS
PH09455 684 (June 16, 1994) p114. "Potential Blockbusters"
PH09456 686-687 (July 14, 1994) p98. "Scar And Hyenas ("The Lion King")"
PH09457 686-687 (July 14, 1994) p91. "[The Lion King]"
PH09458 686-687 (July 14, 1994) p97. "The Wolf, The Lion And The Lamb" (Fisher, Jeffrey)
PH09459 698-699 (December 29, 1994) p194. "Uncle Scar Reigns In "The Lion King""
PH09460 705 (April 6, 1995) p69. "Oscar Rejects"
LIOTTA, RAY—PHOTOGRAPHS
PH09461 689 (August 25, 1994) p96. "Whoopi Goldberg And Ray Liotta Get It On In The '50s"
LIPMICKI, JONATHAN—PHOTOGRAPHS
PH09462 750-751 (December 26, 1996) p142. "Jonathan Lipmicki, 6, A Cruise Fan From Way Back To 'Top Gun,' Plays Jerry's Stepson"
LIPPERT, PATRICK—PHOTOGRAPHS
PH09463 664 (September 2, 1993) p24. "Elton John With

Lippert" (Mazur, Kevin)
LIQUID COURAGE—PHOTOGRAPHS—PORTRAITS
PH09464 680 (April 21, 1994) p26. "Israel Webb, Lords (from left)" (Marsel, Steve)
LIQUOR CABINET—ALBUMS
PH09465 726 (January 25, 1996) p71. "Mood Elevator"
LISA LISA—ILLUSTRATIONS
PH09466 681 (May 5, 1994) p54. "Lisa Lisa" (Skwish, Andrew)
LISTER, TINY, JR.—PHOTOGRAPHS
PH09467 658 (June 10, 1993) p74. "The Magnificent Six (from left): Stephen Baldwin, Big Daddy Kane, Mario Van Peebles, Tiny Lister Jr., Charles Lane, Tone Loc"
LITHGOW, JOHN—PHOTOGRAPHS
PH09468 636 (August 6, 1992) p65. "Psychotic John Lithgow Lends A Hand"
LITHUANIAN BASKETBALL TEAM—PHOTOGRAPHS
PH09469 640 (October 1, 1992) p10. "The Lithuanian Basketball Team" (Capozzola, Lou)
LITTLE FEAT—ALBUMS
PH09470 617 (November 14, 1991) p106. "Sailin' Shoes" (Park, Neon)
LITTLE MAN TATE (FILM)—PHOTOGRAPHS
PH09471 616 (October 31, 1991) p97. "Gifted Son And Mother: Adam Hann-Byrd And Jodie Foster"
LITTLE RICHARD—ILLUSTRATIONS
PH09472 641 (October 15, 1992) p154. "[Little Richard]" (Burns, Charles)
LITTLE RICHARD—PHOTOGRAPHS
PH09473 616 (October 31, 1991) p13. "Rundgren, Eric Gardner, Janis Gardner, Little Richard, Spector (from left)" (Granitz, Steve)
PH09474 625 (March 5, 1992) p13. "Rockin' And Rollin' (above, from left): Little Richard, Ronald Isley, Ernie Isley, Chris Jasper, Marvin Isley" (Mazur. Kevin)
PH09475 680 (April 21, 1994) p34. "Originator Little Richard With George Clinton" (Mazur, Kevin)
PH09476 681 (May 5, 1994) p15. "Martha Reeves, Brown, Fred Schneider, Richard And Raitt At The Recent Awards (from left)" (Micelotta, Frank)
PH09477 684 (June 16, 1994) p36. "[Wheel Of Fortune]" (Slenzak, Ron)
PH09478 724-725 (December 28, 1995) p56. "Jann Wenner, Yoko Ono, Little Richard, Paul Shaffer Cut Loose" (Mazur, Kevin)
LITTLE RICHARD—PHOTOGRAPHS—PORTRAITS
PH09479 643 (November 12, 1992) pp156-157. "Little Richard" (Ritts, Herb)
PH09480 720 (November 2, 1995) p50. "Little Richard"
LITTLE ROCK, ARKANSAS—ILLUSTRATIONS
PH09481 682 (May 19, 1994) pp81,85. "[Little Rock]" (Burns, Charles)
LITTLE VILLAGE—ALBUMS
PH09482 624 (February 20, 1992) p42. "Little Village"
LITTLE VILLAGE—PHOTOGRAPHS
PH09483 627 (April 2, 1992) p15. "Jim Keltner, Ry Cooder, Nick Lowe And John Hiatt (from left)" (Hanauer, Mark)
LITTLE WOMEN (FILM)—PHOTOGRAPHS
PH09484 700 (January 26, 1995) p66. "Smart Women, Foolish Choices"
LIVE—ALBUMS
PH09485 709 (June 1, 1995) p80. "Throwing Copper"
PH09486 715 (August 24, 1995) p124. "Throwing Copper"
LIVE—ILLUSTRATIONS
PH09487 714 (August 10, 1995) p72. "Live: Throwing Platinum" (Rosen, Jonathon)
LIVE—PHOTOGRAPHS
PH09488 628 (April 16, 1992) p62. "Live"
PH09489 716 (September 7, 1995) p13. "Chad Taylor, Kowalezyk, Pat Dahlheimer (from left)" (Callahan, Kristin)
PH09490 726 (January 25, 1996) p35. "Dahlheimer, Taylor, Kowalczyk And Gracey (from left) At Their York, Pa., High School In 1989" (Broad, Julian)
PH09491 745 (October 17, 1996) p41. "In L.A., Live Put The Finishing Touches On Their Third Album"
LIVE—PHOTOGRAPHS—PORTRAITS
PH09492 726 (January 25, 1996) pp[cover]. "Live (Artist Of The Year)" (Broad, Julian)
PH09493 726 (January 25, 1996) p34. "Taylor, Kowalczyk, Gracey And Dahlheimer (from left) In New York In Late 1995" (Broad, Julian)
LIVE AID—PHOTOGRAPHS
PH09494 621 (January 9, 1992) p17. "Mercury Joins Paul McCartney And Other Stars In The Live Aid Finale, 1985" (Preston, Neal)
PH09495 633 (June 25, 1992) p6. "[Live Aid]" (Regan, Ken)
PH09496 636 (August 6, 1992) p8. "[Live Aid]" (Regan, Ken)
LIVE FROM THE HOUSE OF BLUES (TELEVISION SHOW)—PHOTOGRAPHS
PH09497 702 (February 23, 1995) p20. "[Public Enemy]"
LIVING COLOUR—ALBUMS
PH09498 652 (March 18, 1993) p39. "Stain"
PH09499 672-673 (December 23, 1993) p157. "Stain"
LIVING COLOUR—ILLUSTRATIONS
PH09500 641 (October 15, 1992) p194. "[Living Colour]" (Paraskevas, Michael)
LIVING COLOUR—PHOTOGRAPHS
PH09501 637 (August 20, 1992) p9. "Living Colour's Vernon Reid, Corey Glover And Doug Wimbish (from left)" (Mazur, Kevin)
PH09502 645-646 (December 10, 1992) p71. "Living Colour At New York's CBGB" (Mazur, Kevin)
PH09503 648 (January 21, 1993) p18. "Corey Glover, Will Calhoun, Vernon Reid And Doug Wimbish (from left)" (Leialoha, Mark)
PH09504 660-661 (July 8, 1993) p18. "President Clinton Joins Living Colour During The Celebration"
LIVING COLOUR—PHOTOGRAPHS—PORTRAITS
PH09505 660-661 (July 8, 1993) p88. "The Band (from left): Will Calhoun, Vernon Reid, Doug Wimbish And Corey Glover" (Malfer)
PH09506 660-661 (July 8, 1993) p90. "The 'Vivid' Incarnations Of Living Colour, With Muzz Skillings (far right)" (Lavine, Michael)
THE LIVING END (FILM)—PHOTOGRAPHS
PH09507 653 (April 1, 1993) p57. "The Living End"
LIVING IN OBLIVION (FILM)—PHOTOGRAPHS
PH09508 712-713 (July 13, 1995) p116. "Big Winners On Small Budgets"
LLERANDI, NATE—PHOTOGRAPHS
PH09509 665 (September 16, 1993) pp[enc.25]. "From Left: Greg Welsh, Ray Browning, Mike Pigg, Wes Hobson, Chuckie V, Scott Tinley, Nate Llerandi And Bill Braun" (Hanauer, Mark)
LLOYD, CHRISTOPHER—PHOTOGRAPHS
PH09510 618 (November 28, 1991) p53. "They're Altogether Ooky" (Seliger, Mark)
LLOYD, RICHARD—PHOTOGRAPHS
PH09511 647 (January 7, 1993) p22. "Tom Verlaine, Richard Lloyd, Billy Ficca And Fred Smith (from left)" (Buck, Chris)
LOADED (PUBLICATION)—PHOTOGRAPHS
PH09512 741 (August 22, 1996) p78. "[Loaded]"
LOCAL H—PHOTOGRAPHS
PH09513 745 (October 17, 1996) p41. "Jealous And Petty: Joe Daniels (left) And Lucas Of Local H Spoof Eddie Vedder" (Chavez, Marina)
LOCKLEAR, HEATHER—PHOTOGRAPHS
PH09514 682 (May 19, 1994) p50. "Good Girl Josie Bissett (left) And Bad Girl Heather Locklear, Who Thinks Her Character Is Just Misunderstood" (Seliger, Mark)

PH09515 682 (May 19, 1994) pp48-49. "[Melrose Place]" (Seliger, Mark)
PH09516 682 (May 19, 1994) pp[cover]. "Melrose Place's Bod Squad" (Seliger, Mark)
PH09517 747 (November 14, 1996) p25. "[Bon Jovi & Friends]" (Souliers, Philippe)
LOCKWOOD, CHRIS—PHOTOGRAPHS
PH09518 721 (November 16, 1995) p33. "John Kirsch, Braden Blake, Jake Nesheim And Chris Lockwood (from left)" (Moskowitz, Karen)
LOEWENSTEIN, JASON—PHOTOGRAPHS
PH09519 704 (March 23, 1995) p43. "The Sensitive Souls Of Sebadoh: Fay, Barlow And Loewenstein (from left)" (Ockenfels, Frank, 3)
LOFTON, KEITH—PHOTOGRAPHS
PH09520 628 (April 16, 1992) p51. "Basehead, The Band (from left): Brian Hendrix, Keith Lofton, Bill Conway And Michael Ivey" (Ockenfels, Frank W.)
LOGAN, JACK—ALBUMS
PH09521 691 (September 22, 1994) p100. "Bulk"
PH09522 726 (January 25, 1996) p71. "Mood Elevator"
LOGAN, JACK—ILLUSTRATIONS—PORTRAITS
PH09523 730 (March 21, 1996) p11. "Jack Logan" (Allen, Julian)
LOGAN, JACK—PHOTOGRAPHS
PH09524 686-687 (July 14, 1994) p74. "Jack Logan" (Leitman, Ruth)
PH09525 689 (August 25, 1994) p16. "Jack Logan (second from left) With Vic Chesnutt (front) And Other Enablers" (Torno, Pattiy)
PH09526 702 (February 23, 1995) p35. "Home-Studio Maven Jack Logan" (Mazur, Kevin)
PH09527 730 (March 21, 1996) p24. "[Jack Logan]" (Alston, Kwaku)
PH09528 730 (March 21, 1996) p26. "Logan (left) And Keneipp Talk Drag-Racing" (Torno, Pattiy)
LOGAN, JACK—PHOTOGRAPHS—PORTRAITS
PH09529 698-699 (December 29, 1994) p47. "Jack Logan" (Leitman, Ruth)
LOGSDON, JEFF—PHOTOGRAPHS
PH09530 722 (November 30, 1995) pp[enc.8]. "Jeff Logsdon Gives Two Housemates Tips In Web-Page Building" (McLeod, William Mercer)
LOHNER, DANNY—PHOTOGRAPHS
PH09531 690 (September 8, 1994) p54. "Vrenna, Woolley, Reznor, Finck, Lohner (from left)" (Cultice, Joseph)
LOLLAPALOOZA—PHOTOGRAPHS
PH09532 619-620 (December 12, 1991) p84. "One Of The Sideshow Attractions" (Buscarro, Larry)
LOLLAPALOOZA '93—PHOTOGRAPHS
PH09533 662 (August 5, 1993) p14. "Cattle Call: 'It's Not The First Time My Art Has been Censored,' Said Scarification Buff John Patrick Sullivan (bottom), Whose Body-Branding Booth Was Quickly Shut Down..." (Blakes
PH09534 662 (August 5, 1993) p14. "Lollapaloozers Line Up For A Pseudo-LSD Trip" (Blakesberg, Jay)
PH09535 736 (June 13, 1996) p40. "Alternative-Rock Fans Mosh At Lollapalooza '93 During It's Stop At The Gorge, In George, Washington" (Blakesberg, Jay)
LOLLAPALOOZA '94—PHOTOGRAPHS
PH09536 689 (August 25, 1994) p24. "[Lollapalooza]" (Blakesberg, Jay)
LOLLAPALOOZA '95—ILLUSTRATIONS
PH09537 718 (October 5, 1995) p16. "Better Luck Next Time" (Pendergrast, James T.)
LOLLAPALOOZA '95—PHOTOGRAPHS
PH09538 715 (August 24, 1995) p45. "Opening-Day Fireworks: The Action In The Pit At The Gorge On July Fourth" (Blakesberg, Jay)
LOLLAPALOOZA II—ILLUSTRATIONS—LETTERING
PH09539 639 (September 17, 1992) pp60-62,64. "LollaPalooza '92" (Lee, John)
LOLLAPALOOZA II—PHOTOGRAPHS
PH09540 639 (September 17, 1992) p62. "The Safe Sex Wheel Of Fortune (above)" (Blakesberg, Jay)
LOMBARD, KARINA—PHOTOGRAPHS
PH09541 656 (May 13, 1993) p116. "Sex Is Hot For Lombard (top) And Parker"
LOMBARDI, CHRIS—PHOTOGRAPHS
PH09542 737 (June 27, 1996) p19. "Matador Honchos Lombardi (left) And Cosloy" (Clinch, Danny)
LOMENZO, JAMES—PHOTOGRAPHS
PH09543 686-687 (July 14, 1994) p72. "LoMenzo, Wylde And Tischy (from left)" (Ragel, Jon)
LONDON SINFONIETTA—ALBUMS
PH09544 655 (April 29, 1993) p65. "Symphony No. 3"
LONDON SUEDE—ALBUMS
PH09545 698-699 (December 29, 1994) p185. "Dog Man Star"
LONDON, FRANK—PHOTOGRAPHS
PH09546 749 (December 12, 1996) p20. "BFF's Robert Sledge, Darren Jessee; Klezmatics Frank London, Alicia Svigals; And Folds" (Mazur, Kevin)
LONDON, JASON—PHOTOGRAPHS
PH09547 667 (October 14, 1993) p128. "School Daze For Cochrane, London And Jenson"
LONE STAR (FILM)—PHOTOGRAPHS
PH09548 736 (June 13, 1996) p60. "Smart Alternatives"
PH09549 741 (August 22, 1996) p48. "McConaughey Onscreen"
PH09550 743 (September 19, 1996) p90. "[Summer...]"
LONE, JOHN—PHOTOGRAPHS
PH09551 668 (October 28, 1993) p86. "John Lone (left) As Butterfly"
LONESOME DEBONAIRES—ALBUMS
PH09552 625 (March 5, 1992) p72. "Blue On Blonde"
THE LONG DAY CLOSES (FILM)—PHOTOGRAPHS
PH09553 658 (June 10, 1993) p78. "Fifties Kid McCormack Finds Magic At The Movies"
LONG FIN KILLIE—PHOTOGRAPHS
PH09554 747 (November 14, 1996) p58. "[Long Fin Killie]" (Clinch, Danny)
LONG GONE JOHN—PHOTOGRAPHS
PH09555 689 (August 25, 1994) p28. "Sympathy For The Record Industry's Long Gone John" (Dipaolo, Debra)
THE LONG KISS GOODNIGHT (FILM)—PHOTOGRAPHS
PH09556 746 (October 31, 1996) p76. "La Femme Geena Davis Packs A License To Kill"
LONGANECKER, DAVID—PHOTOGRAPHS—PORTRAITS
PH09557 689 (August 25, 1994) p53. "Longanecker: Cheaper College Funds" (Kittner, Sam)
LONGO, LEN—PHOTOGRAPHS
PH09558 722 (November 30, 1995) p42. "Utter Confusion Caused Exactly That: Albert Min, Len Longo And J. M. Burr" (Dipeso, Debra)
LONSTEIN, SHOSHANNA—PHOTOGRAPHS
PH09559 691 (September 22, 1994) p50. "A 21-Year Age Gap Doesn't Faze Seinfeld Or Shoshanna Lonstein" (Gerber, M.)
LOOKING FOR RICHARD (FILM)—PHOTOGRAPHS
PH09560 746 (October 31, 1996) p78. "Big, Bad Hunchbacked King Al Pacino"
LOOMIS—PHOTOGRAPHS
PH09561 709 (June 1, 1995) p16. "Flava In Ya Ear: Wax's Loomis, Joe Sib, Dave Georgeff And Soda Drop In On Fogelnes In His 'Squirt TV' Bedroom Studio (from left)" (Brown, Christy)
LOPES, LISA—PHOTOGRAPHS
PH09562 631 (May 28, 1992) p22. "TLC (clockwise from top): T-Boz, Chilli, Left Eye" (Cuffaro, Chris)
PH09563 688 (August 11, 1994) p20. "[Lisa "left Eye" Lopes]"
LOPES, LISA—PHOTOGRAPHS—PORTRAITS
PH09564 715 (August 24, 1995) p27. "'Left Eye' Lopes, 'T-Boz'

Watkins And 'Chilli' Thomas (from left)" (White, Steve)
PH09565 715 (August 24, 1995) p28. "The Younger, Wilder TLC: Watkins, Lopes And Thomas In 1992 (from left)" (Green, Adrian)
LOPEZ, JENNIFER—PHOTOGRAPHS—PORTRAITS
PH09566 656 (May 13, 1993) p94. "Deidre Lang, Jennifer Lopez, Twist, Jossie Harris, Lisa Thompson (from left)"
PH09567 656 (May 13, 1993) p95. "Lopez"
LOPEZ, RICARDO—PHOTOGRAPHS—PORTRAITS
PH09568 747 (November 14, 1996) p29. "[Ricardo Lopez]"
LOPEZ-LEZCANO, FERNANDO—PHOTOGRAPHS
PH09569 708 (May 18, 1995) p28. "Lopez-Lezcano Programs 'Scenes' On The Radio Drum" (Gipe, Jon)
LORD OF ILLUSIONS (FILM)—PHOTOGRAPHS
PH09570 717 (September 21, 1995) p90. "Private Eye Bakula Tracks The Undead"
LORD, MARY LOU—PHOTOGRAPHS
PH09571 686-687 (July 14, 1994) p79. "[Mary Lou Lord]" (Wheeler, Alice)
PH09572 690 (September 8, 1994) p33. "Super Trouper: Mary Lou Lord" (Wheeler, Alice)
PH09573 710 (June 15, 1995) p37. "Lord: The Girl With The Most Cake" (Peterson, Charles)
PH09574 717 (September 21, 1995) p20. "Three Beatle Maniacs: Lord, Buck And McCaughey (from left)" (Clinch, Danny)
PH09575 742 (September 5, 1996) p21. "Are We Having Fun Yet?" (Kessler, Joshua)
LORDS OF THE UNDERGROUND—PHOTOGRAPHS
PH09576 664 (September 2, 1993) p20. "The Lords Of Newark (from left): DJ Lord Jazz, Mr. Funke And DoItAll" (Apicella-Hitchcock, Stephen)
LORDS, NEAL—PHOTOGRAPHS—PORTRAITS
PH09577 680 (April 21, 1994) p26. "Israel Webb, Lords (from left)" (Marsel, Steve)
LOREN, RICHARD—PHOTOGRAPHS
PH09578 740 (August 8, 1996) p35. "Egypt, September 1978" (Boot, Adrian)
LORENZO'S OIL (FILM)—ILLUSTRATIONS
PH09579 648 (January 21, 1993) p54. "A Few Good Women" (Witte, Michael)
LORENZO'S OIL (FILM)—PHOTOGRAPHS
PH09580 648 (January 21, 1993) p55. "Sarandon Tackles Medicine"
LORSON, MARY—PHOTOGRAPHS
PH09581 688 (August 11, 1994) p29. "Drummer Johnny Kick, Cote, Lorson And Bassist Chris Giammalvo (from left)" (Berg, Bob)
LOS ANGELES, CALIFORNIA—ILLUSTRATIONS
PH09582 740 (August 8, 1996) pp42-43. "[California Earthquake]" (Allen, Julian)
PH09583 740 (August 8, 1996) p45. "Faults Crisscross L.A.'s Downtown"
LOS ANGELES, CALIFORNIA—PHOTOGRAPHS
PH09584 615 (October 17, 1991) p105. "From Electric Ladyland To The Tour Of La-La Land"
PH09585 740 (August 8, 1996) p47. "Los Angeles, January 1994" (Heller, Steven A.)
LOS LOBOS—ALBUMS
PH09586 633 (June 25, 1992) p41. "Kiko"
PH09587 732 (April 18, 1996) p70. "Colossal Head"
LOS LOBOS—PHOTOGRAPHS
PH09588 616 (October 31, 1991) p13. "Cesar Rosas, Louis Perez, Conrad Lozano, David Hidalgo And Steve Berlin (from left)" (Granitz, Steve)
PH09589 619-620 (December 12, 1991) p37. "Bob Weir (left) Digs Los Lobos And, In Turn, Is Dug, At The "Deadicated' Party"
LOSING ISAIAH (FILM)—PHOTOGRAPHS
PH09590 705 (April 6, 1995) p70. "Losing Isaiah"
LOSING MY RELIGION (VIDEO)—PHOTOGRAPHS
PH09591 619-620 (December 12, 1991) p33. "R.E.M.'s 'Losing My Religion'"
PH09592 667 (October 14, 1993) p68. "'Losing' Is Winning: Stipe And Company Make R.E.M.'s Video A Religious Experience"
LOST IN YONKERS (FILM)—PHOTOGRAPHS
PH09593 657 (May 27, 1993) p58. "Lost: Coolidge And Ruehl Flank Simon"
LOTION—PHOTOGRAPHS—PORTRAITS
PH09594 685 (June 30, 1994) p28. "Tragi-Pop Wuss Rockers: Lotion's Youngberg, Zajkowski, Bill And Jim Ferguson (from left)" (Cardillicchio, Nick)
LOUD FAMILY—ALBUMS
PH09595 656 (May 13, 1993) p104. "Plants And Birds And Rocks And Things" (.)
PH09596 698-699 (December 29, 1994) p182. "The Tape Of Only Linda"
LOUD FAMILY—PHOTOGRAPHS
PH09597 660-661 (July 8, 1993) p97. "The Loud Family: Paul Wieneke, Zachary Smith, Miller, Jozef Becker And Rob Poor" (Blakesberg, Jay)
LOUD LUCY—PHOTOGRAPHS
PH09598 721 (November 16, 1995) p100. "Loud Lucy: Furar, Lane And Doyle (from left)" (GS, Jamil)
LOUIS-DREYFUS, JULIA—PHOTOGRAPHS
PH09599 660-661 (July 8, 1993) p41. "Nothing On: Jason Alexander, Julia Louis-Dreyfus, Jerry Seinfeld And Michael Richards" (Seliger, Mark)
PH09600 660-661 (July 8, 1993) pp[cover]. "Seinfeld Rules!" (Seliger, Mark)
PH09601 660-661 (July 8, 1993) p44. "'These Four Characters Are A Pathetic Group,' Says Julia Louis-Dreyfus" (Seliger, Mark)
PH09602 672-673 (December 23, 1993) p188. "[Covers]" (Seliger, Mark)
PH09603 691 (September 22, 1994) p49. "Jerry And Elaine (Julia Louis-Dreyfus) Won't Get Back In The Sack" (Sonnemair, Jan)
LOURIS, GARY—PHOTOGRAPHS
PH09604 633 (June 25, 1992) p11. "Golden Smog (from left): Gary Louris, Chris Mars, Dan Murphy, Craig Johnson And Marc Perlman" (Butler, Bonnie Lynn)
PH09605 644 (November 26, 1992) p27. "Louris, Callahan, Olson And Perlman (from left)" (Capak, R. J.)
PH09606 691 (September 22, 1994) p20. "Hawks Gary Louris, Mark Perlman, Dan Murphy, Noah Levy, Tweedy" (Smiley, Jay)
PH09607 697 (December 15, 1994) p31. ""We Had A Retro Tag, But This Isn't Like Our Last Album," Says Olson (center), With Perlman And Louris" (Dyer, Alison)
PH09608 709 (June 1, 1995) p16. "Jayhawk Gary Louris, Crowes Marc Ford And Robinson, Perlman (from left)" (Diamond, Rick)
PH09609 718 (October 5, 1995) p21. "Gary Louris Of The Jayhawks In Newport, R.I." (Hendrickson, Matt)
LOURIS, GARY—PHOTOGRAPHS—PORTRAITS
PH09610 628 (April 16, 1992) p57. "Perlman, Olson, Louris And Callahan (from left)" (Crouser, Michael)
LOUVIN BROTHERS—ALBUMS
PH09611 750-751 (December 26, 1996) p189. "Satan Is Real"
LOUVIN, CHARLIE—PHOTOGRAPHS
PH09612 750-751 (December 26, 1996) p178. "Charlie Louvin" (Seliger, Mark)
LOVE AFFAIRS (FILM)—PHOTOGRAPHS
PH09613 696 (December 1, 1994) p134. "Misfires"
LOVE AND A .45 (FILM)—PHOTOGRAPHS
PH09614 696 (December 1, 1994) p132. "Now Playing"
LOVE AND HUMAN REMAINS (FILM)—PHOTOGRAPHS
PH09615 710 (June 15, 1995) p88. "'Friends' Canadian Style: Reality Bites"
LOVE BATTERY—PHOTOGRAPHS—PORTRAITS
PH09616 634-635 (July 9, 1992) p20. "Love Battery (from left): Kevin Whitworth, Rod Rudzitis And Jason Finn" (Lavine, Michael)

LOVE FIELD (FILM)—ILLUSTRATIONS
PH09617 648 (January 21, 1993) p54. "A Few Good Women" (Witte, Michael)
LOVE FIELD (FILM)—PHOTOGRAPHS
PH09618 648 (January 21, 1993) p55. "Pfeiffer (left) Battles Racism"
LOVE MEDICINE (BOOK)—PHOTOGRAPHS
PH09619 639 (September 17, 1992) p80. "Love Medicine"
LOVE SHACK (VIDEO)—PHOTOGRAPHS
PH09620 667 (October 14, 1993) p80. "'Love Shack': The B-52's Rock The House"
LOVE SPIT LOVE—ALBUMS
PH09621 697 (December 15, 1994) p95. "Love Spit Love"
LOVE WILL NEVER DO (VIDEO)—PHOTOGRAPHS
PH09622 667 (October 14, 1993) p73. "'Love Will Never Do Without You': Janet Comes Out"
LOVE, COURTNEY—ILLUSTRATIONS
PH09623 672-673 (December 23, 1993) p73. "[Courtney Love]" (Ryden, Mark)
PH09624 680 (April 21, 1994) p83. "Pretty Hate Machines" (Habermacher, Rene)
PH09625 701 (February 9, 1995) p14. "Hole" (Pendergrast, James T.)
PH09626 703 (March 9, 1995) p16. "Puke Gland" (Pendergrast, James T.)
PH09627 750-751 (December 26, 1996) p88. "[Courtney Love & Madonna]" (Banyai, Istvan)
LOVE, COURTNEY—PHOTOGRAPHS
PH09628 642 (October 29, 1992) p19. "Cobain, Love And Baby Frances" (Mazur, Kevin)
PH09629 660-661 (July 8, 1993) p32. "Courtney Does CounterAid" (Granitz, Steve)
PH09630 672-673 (December 23, 1993) p39. "Family Feud: Frances Bean, Kurt, Courtney" (Mazur, Kevin)
PH09631 682 (May 19, 1994) p18. "Frances, Love And Cobain" (Kravitz, Jeff)
PH09632 683 (June 2, 1994) p35. "Headed To The Hospital After Rome Suicide Attempt" (Sestini, Massimo)
PH09633 683 (June 2, 1994) p42. "Hole: Patty Schemel, Love, Kristen Pfaff, Eric Erlandson" (Seliger, Mark)
PH09634 683 (June 2, 1994) p36. "The Mourning After: Love Wanders With Frances Bean In A Park Near Their Home On April 9" (Rexroad, James)
PH09635 683 (June 2, 1994) p32. "With Wife Love And Daughter Frances Bean" (Guzman)
PH09636 688 (August 11, 1994) p17. "Courtney Love And Michael Stipe (right)" (Kravitz, Jeff)
PH09637 689 (August 25, 1994) p15. "[Lemonheads-Buffalo Tom-Gigolo Aunts]" (Busacca, Larry)
PH09638 692 (October 6, 1994) p52. "Courtney Love" (Thurnher, Jeffrey)
PH09639 692 (October 6, 1994) p53. "Courtney Love And Hole" (Moskowitz, Karen)
PH09640 694 (November 3, 1994) p42. "New York Doll: Courtney Conquers Manhattan" (Mazur, Kevin)
PH09641 694 (November 3, 1994) p17. "Pumpkin Billy Corgan, Love, Cohen, Krugman (from left)"
PH09642 695 (November 17, 1994) p63. "Courtney Love" (Seliger, Mark)
PH09643 697 (December 15, 1994) pp58-59. "[Courtney Love]" (Seliger, Mark)
PH09644 697 (December 15, 1994) p67. "Hole As One: Bassist Melissa Auf Der Maur (who replaced Kristen Pfaff), Guitarist Eric Erlandson, Drummer Patty Schemel And Love (from left)" (Seliger, Mark)
PH09645 697 (December 15, 1994) p66. "In Happier Times: Love And Cobain Celebrate Frances Bean's First Christmas, In 1992"
PH09646 697 (December 15, 1994) p64. "Love And Cobain In A Quiet Embrace" (Guzman)
PH09647 697 (December 15, 1994) p60. "Love In The Front Of The Family Christmas Tree In Portland, ore., 1977"
PH09648 697 (December 15, 1994) p61. "[Sugar Babylon]"
PH09649 698-699 (December 29, 1994) p50. "Doll Parts: Hole's Eric Erlandson, Melissa Auf der Maur, Patty Schemel And Love" (Seliger, Mark)
PH09650 700 (January 26, 1995) p52. "Courtney Love With Hole" (Mazur, Kevin)
PH09651 705 (April 6, 1995) p28. "Love: On Or Off?" (Jennings, Steve)
PH09652 705 (April 6, 1995) p16. "[Sandra Bernhard & Courtney Love]" (McMullan, Patrick)
PH09653 714 (August 10, 1995) p24. "Courtney Love; Goldberg's Wife, Rosemary Carroll; Goldberg; Kurt Cobain In '93" (Kravitz, Jeff)
PH09654 715 (August 24, 1995) p43. "Courtney Love Falls Down On The Job" (Blakesberg, Jay)
PH09655 715 (August 24, 1995) p46. "Courtney Love, Eric Erlandson, Patty Schemel, Melissa Auf Der Maur" (Seliger, Mark)
PH09656 715 (August 24, 1995) p48. "Lolla Darling: Love In Uniform" (Blakesberg, Jay)
PH09657 720 (November 2, 1995) p16. "[Courtney Love]"
PH09658 720 (November 2, 1995) p49. "Courtney Love" (Guzman)
PH09659 724-725 (December 28, 1995) p45. "Courtney Love Got Unplugged All Around"
PH09660 726 (January 25, 1996) p51. "Courtney Love: What Else Needs To Be Said?" (Davila, Bill)
PH09661 734 (May 16, 1996) p18. "[Drew Barrymore & Courtney Love]" (Granitz, Steve)
PH09662 741 (August 22, 1996) p25. "Love (center) And Forman With Friend Miss Martina On Location In A Rented House In Memphis, Tenn." (Von Jansky, Ladi)
PH09663 743 (September 19, 1996) p88. "Divas"
PH09664 745 (October 17, 1996) p27. "Steven Tyler With Courtney Love" (Mazur, Kevin)
PH09665 748 (November 28, 1996) p26. "[Courtney Love & Woody Harrelson]" (Oliveira, Alex)
PH09666 750-751 (December 26, 1996) p204. "'ID4' (above) Is Biggest, But 'Larry Flynt' (left), With Harrelson And Love Flanking Flynt, Is The Best"
LOVE, COURTNEY—PHOTOGRAPHS—PORTRAITS
PH09667 637 (August 20, 1992) p15. "Hole's Jill Emery, Eric Erlandson, Love And Caroline Rue (from left)" (Lavine, Michael)
PH09668 639 (September 17, 1992) p81. "" (Levenson, Alan)
PH09669 640 (October 1, 1992) p25. "Courtney Love" (Levenson, Alan)
PH09670 660-661 (July 8, 1993) p24. "Former Grrrlfriend: Courtney Love Gets Annoyed" (Ockenfels, Frank W.)
PH09671 697 (December 15, 1994) pp[cover]. "Courtney Love: Talks About Music, Madness And The Last Days Of Kurt Cobain" (Seliger, Mark)
PH09672 697 (December 15, 1994) p60. "Till Death Do Us Part"
PH09673 724-725 (December 28, 1995) p60. "Love" (Scheltema, Sandy)
PH09674 724-725 (December 28, 1995) pp[cover]. "Rock & Roll Yearbook" (Seliger, Mark)
PH09675 735 (May 30, 1996) p3. "[The Faces Of Heroin]"
PH09676 750-751 (December 26, 1996) p90. "[Courtney Love]" (Allen, David)
PH09677 750-751 (December 26, 1996) p90. "[Courtney Love]" (Gallo, Armando)
LOVE, DARLENE—PHOTOGRAPHS
PH09678 639 (September 17, 1992) p20. "Love (left) With Spector" (Granitz, Steve)
PH09679 644 (November 26, 1992) p15. "Max Weinberg, Clarence Clemons, Darlene Love, Little Steven, Garry Tallent And Danny Federici (from left)" (Mazur, Kevin)

LOVE, G.—PHOTOGRAPHS
PH09680 719 (October 19, 1995) p28. "G. Love: 'Blues Is Just A Feel Of What's Going On, Whether You're An Old Black Guy Or A White Kid From Philly'" (Cardillicchio, Nick)
LOVE, GERARD—PHOTOGRAPHS
PH09681 701 (February 9, 1995) p33. "Join The Club: Norman Blake, Raymond McGinley, Paul Quinn And Gerard Love (clockwise from top left)" (Dyer, Alison)
LOVE, GERRY—PHOTOGRAPHS
PH09682 630 (May 14, 1992) p50. "Guitarist Norman Blake, Bassist Gerry Love, Drummer Brendan O'Hare And Guitarist Raymond McGinley (from left)" (Broad, Julian)
LOVE, MIKE—PHOTOGRAPHS
PH09683 640 (October 1, 1992) p10. "Endless Bummer: Mike Love" (Corkery, Richard)
LOVE, MONIE—ALBUMS
PH09684 658 (June 10, 1993) p69. "In A Word Or 2"
LOVE, MONIE—PHOTOGRAPHS
PH09685 625 (March 5, 1992) p18. "Pepa, Salt, Monie Love And Spinderella (from left)" (Shaw, Gene)
PH09686 689 (August 25, 1994) p40. "Paying Lip Service To MTV: Rapper Monie Love" (Llewellyn, Michael)
LOVER, ED—PHOTOGRAPHS
PH09687 619-620 (December 12, 1991) p74. "The Stars Of 'Yo! MTV Raps': Ed Lover (left) And Dr. Dre"
PH09688 653 (April 1, 1993) p13. "Ed Lover And Yo-Yo"
PH09689 659 (June 24, 1993) p15. "Russian Summit: Ed Lover, Henry Kissinger And Dr. Dre (from left)" (Mazur, Kevin)
LOVERING, DAVID—PHOTOGRAPHS
PH09690 679 (April 7, 1994) p68. "Cracked: David Lovering, David Lowery, Bruce Hughes, Johnny Hickman (from left)" (Wolff, Tom)
PH09691 682 (May 19, 1994) p90. "Old Deal: Kim With Pixies David Lovering, Black Francis, Joey Santiago (from left)" (Blakesberg, Jay)
LOVERING, DAVID—PHOTOGRAPHS—PORTRAITS
PH09692 652 (March 18, 1993) p15. "Ex-Pixies David Lovering, Deal, Joey Santiago, Black Francis (clockwise from left)" (Catlin, A.)
LOVETT, LYLE—ALBUMS
PH09693 629 (April 30, 1992) p56. "Joshua Judges Ruth"
PH09694 692 (October 6, 1994) p88. "I Love Everybody"
LOVETT, LYLE—PHOTOGRAPHS
PH09695 628 (April 16, 1992) pp[enc.5,14]. "[Lyle Lovett]" (Laxton, William)
PH09696 628 (April 16, 1992) pp[enc.9]. "[Lyle Lovett, Margo Timmins]" (Laxton, William)
PH09697 645-646 (December 10, 1992) p40. "Lyle Lovett" (Hutson, Mick)
PH09698 648 (January 21, 1993) p9. "Lyle Lovett And Cake"
PH09699 663 (August 19, 1993) p28. "Lyle Lovett And Julia Roberts"
PH09700 672-673 (December 23, 1993) p41. "Above: Roberts Poses With Her Best man, Lovett"
PH09701 686-687 (July 14, 1994) p65. "The Sneak Wedding Day: June 27, 1993"
PH09702 686-687 (July 14, 1994) p65. "While Divorce Rumors Swirl, Mr. And Mrs. Lovett Stroll In Paris" (Ginies, Michael)
PH09703 693 (October 20, 1994) p30. "Lyle Lovett" (Burrington, Robert)
LOVETT, LYLE—PHOTOGRAPHS—PORTRAITS
PH09704 628 (April 16, 1992) pp[enc.11,16]. "[Lyle Lovett]" (Laxton, William)
PH09705 672-673 (December 23, 1993) p174. "[Short Cuts]"
LOVITZ, JON—PHOTOGRAPHS
PH09706 639 (September 17, 1992) p102. "Best Supporting Actor"
PH09707 685 (June 30, 1994) p80. "Crystal, Lovitz And Stern Go West For Box-Office Gold"
PH09708 748 (November 28, 1996) p143. "Dead On Arrival"
LOVITZ, JON—PHOTOGRAPHS—PORTRAITS
PH09709 616 (October 31, 1991) pp52-53. "The Matinee Idol Drives Beautiful Women To Despair, For His Greatest Mistress, Alas, Must Always Be Act-ing!" (Schiffman, Bonnie)
LOWE, CHRIS—PHOTOGRAPHS—PORTRAITS
PH09710 651 (March 4, 1993) p28. "...Tennant And Lowe"
LOWE, NICK—ALBUMS
PH09711 698-699 (December 29, 1994) p190. "The Impossible Bird"
LOWE, NICK—PHOTOGRAPHS
PH09712 627 (April 2, 1992) p15. "Jim Keltner, Ry Cooder, Nick Lowe And John Hiatt (from left)" (Hanauer, Mark)
LOWE, NICK—PHOTOGRAPHS—PORTRAITS
PH09713 691 (September 22, 1994) p21. "Junior Brown (left) With Nick Lowe"
LOWE, STACEY—PHOTOGRAPHS
PH09714 648 (January 21, 1993) p11. "[Perry Farrell, Stacey Lowe]"
LOWENSOHN, ELINA—PHOTOGRAPHS
PH09715 706 (April 20, 1995) p88. "Young, Huppert, Donovan And Lowensohn Run"
LOWENSTEIN, JASON—PHOTOGRAPHS
PH09716 736 (June 13, 1996) p53. "Sebadoh's Natural Ones: Bob Fay, Jason Lowenstein And Lou Barlow" (Van Iperen, Neils)
LOWERY, DAVID—ILLUSTRATIONS
PH09717 679 (April 7, 1994) p7. "Cracker's David Lowery" (Burke, Philip)
LOWERY, DAVID—PHOTOGRAPHS
PH09718 626 (March 19, 1992) p13. "Cracker's Johnny Hickman, David Lowery And Davey Faragher (from left)" (Young, Russell)
PH09719 679 (April 7, 1994) p68. "Cracked: David Lovering, David Lowery, Bruce Hughes, Johnny Hickman (from left)" (Wolff, Tom)
PH09720 679 (April 7, 1994) p67. "From Camper To Cracker: David Lowery" (Wolff, Tom)
PH09721 695 (November 17, 1994) p143. "Cracker" (Guzman)
PH09722 732 (April 18, 1996) p48. "Lowery Likes Playing To A Larger Audience" (Eichner, Steve)
PH09723 732 (April 18, 1996) p47. "Playing Cowboys In The Desert: Bob Rupe, Charlie Quintana, David Lowery And Johnny Hickman (from left)" (Maxwell, Robert)
PH09724 745 (October 17, 1996) p40. "Cracker's Lowery" (Jennings, Steve)
LOYOLA COLLEGE—PHOTOGRAPHS
PH09725 704 (March 23, 1995) p70. "Power Hour At Loyola: Kids, Don't Try This At Home" (Olson, Sheryl)
LOZANO, CONRAD—PHOTOGRAPHS
PH09726 616 (October 31, 1991) p13. "Cesar Rosas, Louis Perez, Conrad Lozano, David Hidalgo And Steve Berlin (from left)" (Granitz, Steve)
LOZANO, EPIFANIA—PHOTOGRAPHS
PH09727 652 (March 18, 1993) pp[enc.25]. "Lozano's Family Gathered At The Evergreen East Cemetery In El Paso On The First Anniversary Of His Death" (Smith, F. Carter)
LOZANO, EPIFANIA—PHOTOGRAPHS—PORTRAITS
PH09728 652 (March 18, 1993) pp[enc.24]. "Lozano's Parent's, Epifania And Marcos, Blamed Bean-Bayog" (Garcia, Fernie)
LOZANO, MARCOS—PHOTOGRAPHS
PH09729 652 (March 18, 1993) pp[enc.25]. "Lozano's Family Gathered At The Evergreen East Cemetery In El Paso On The First Anniversary Of His Death" (Smith, F. Carter)
LOZANO, MARCOS—PHOTOGRAPHS—PORTRAITS
PH09730 652 (March 18, 1993) pp[enc.24]. "Lozano's Parent's, Epifania And Marcos, Blamed Bean-Bayog" (Garcia, Fernie)
LOZANO, PAUL—PHOTOGRAPHS—PORTRAITS
PH09731 652 (March 18, 1993) pp[enc.20]. "Lozano, Later Diagnosed With Borderline-Personality Disorder"
LUCAS—PHOTOGRAPHS
PH09732 694 (November 3, 1994) p37. "Lucas (right) Creates

Seamless Cinema In "Lucas With The Lid Off"" (Gougenheim, Kim)

LUCAS, GARY—PHOTOGRAPHS

PH09733 628 (April 16, 1992) p55. "Buckley (left) And Lucas" (Buck, Chris)

LUCAS, GARY—RECORDS

PH09734 649 (February 4, 1993) p68. "Gods And Monsters"

LUGAR, RICHARD—PHOTOGRAPHS—PORTRAITS

PH09735 730 (March 21, 1996) p52. "Lugar"

LUKIN, MATT—PHOTOGRAPHS

PH09736 695 (November 17, 1994) p90. "Mudhoney" (Ragel, Jon)

PH09737 700 (January 26, 1995) p32. "Lukin, Arm, Turner (from left)" (Blakesberg, Jay)

PH09738 709 (June 1, 1995) p48. "Seattle Mudslingers: Turner, Arm, Lukin And Peters (from left)" (Winters, Dan)

LULU—ALBUMS

PH09739 663 (August 19, 1993) p78. "Independence"

LULU—PHOTOGRAPHS

PH09740 658 (June 10, 1993) p16. "Lulu And Pirner" (Mazur, Kevin)

LUNA—PHOTOGRAPHS

PH09741 728 (February 22, 1996) p64. "Luna's Wareham, Demeski And Eden (from left)" (Capak, R. J.)

LUNA2—PHOTOGRAPHS—PORTRAITS

PH09742 645-646 (December 10, 1992) p61. "Luna2" (Lavine, Michael)

LUNACHICKS—ALBUMS

PH09743 653 (April 1, 1993) p54. "Binge And Purge"

LUNDGREN, DOLPH—PHOTOGRAPHS

PH09744 636 (August 6, 1992) p66. "Van Damme (right) And Lundgren (center) Play Robots"

LUNDQVIST, ALEX—PHOTOGRAPHS

PH09745 741 (August 22, 1996) pp87-88. "[Alex Lundqvist]" (Churilla, Lynda)

LUSCIOUS JACKSON—ALBUMS

PH09746 691 (September 22, 1994) p92. "Natural Ingredients"

LUSCIOUS JACKSON—PHOTOGRAPHS

PH09747 685 (June 30, 1994) p41. "Gotta Dance: Luscious Jackson's "Easy" Performance" (Mazur, Kevin)

PH09748 689 (August 25, 1994) p24. "Luscious' Gabby Glaser, Jill Cunniff" (Blakesberg, Jay)

PH09749 689 (August 25, 1994) p17. "[Luscious Jackson]" (Lavine, Michael)

PH09750 710 (June 15, 1995) p17. "LJ's Schellenbach, Gabby Glaser, Vivian trimble And Jill Cunniff At The Rally For Women's Lives, in D.C. (from left)" (Harrington, John)

PH09751 716 (September 7, 1995) p13. "Clued In: America's 'As If' Girl Alicia Silverstone (center) With Luscious Jackson" (Cohen, Lester)

PH09752 735 (May 30, 1996) p27. "Glaser, Schellenbach, Producer Lanois And Trimble (from left)" (Olivier, Rick)

PH09753 749 (December 12, 1996) p24. "Harris (left) Onstage With Luscious Jackson" (Lance, James L.)

PH09754 749 (December 12, 1996) p23. "Life Of Leisure" (Clinch, Danny)

LUSCIOUS JACKSON—PHOTOGRAPHS—PORTRAITS

PH09755 660-661 (July 8, 1993) p97. "Luscious Jackson (clockwise from top left): Glaser, Schellenbach, Cunniff, Trimble" (Minchin, James R., III)

LUSH—ALBUMS

PH09756 628 (April 16, 1992) p100. "Spooky"

PH09757 629 (April 30, 1992) p72. "Spooky"

PH09758 691 (September 22, 1994) p120. "Split"

LUSH—PHOTOGRAPHS

PH09759 729 (March 7, 1996) p29. "Lush Members Emma Anderson, Phil King, Miki Berenyi And Chris Acland (from left)" (Anker, Matt)

L.V.—PHOTOGRAPHS

PH09760 733 (May 2, 1996) p19. "[L.V.]" (Cuffaro, Chris)

L.V.—PHOTOGRAPHS—PORTRAITS

PH09761 733 (May 2, 1996) p20. "Throwing Signs: Coolio And L.V. (right) Goofing On 'Saturday Night Live,' Feb. 10, 1996" (Ng, Norman)

LYCETT, KEVIN—PHOTOGRAPHS

PH09762 736 (June 13, 1996) p19. "Where's Sammy And Frank?" (Herdon, David)

LYDON, JOHNNY—BOOKS

PH09763 680 (April 21, 1994) p28. "Rotten: No Irish, No Blacks, No Dogs"

LYDON, JOHNNY—PHOTOGRAPHS

PH09764 630 (May 14, 1992) p28. "Public Image's Lydon" (Kraft, Chris)

PH09765 645-646 (December 10, 1992) p36. "Public Image Ltd.'s Lydon" (Corio, David)

PH09766 655 (April 29, 1993) p12. "Authors Lydon (right) And Jon Savage Fly The British Bird"

PH09767 723 (December 14, 1995) p27. "[David Bowie & Johnny Lydon]" (Mazur, Kevin)

PH09768 732 (April 18, 1996) p32. "John Lydon Is Rotten Once Again" (Hogan, Dave)

LYDON, JOHNNY—PHOTOGRAPHS—PORTRAITS

PH09769 643 (November 12, 1992) p198. "John Lydon" (Watson, Albert)

PH09770 684 (June 16, 1994) p24. "[John Lydon]" (MacPherson, Andrew)

LYMAN, MEL—PHOTOGRAPHS—PORTRAITS

PH09771 645-646 (December 10, 1992) p156. "Mel Lyman, 1971"

LYMON, FRANKIE—PHOTOGRAPHS—PORTRAITS

PH09772 649 (February 4, 1993) p54. "From The Streets Of The Bronx To The Top Of The Charts: Frankie Lymon (center) And The Teenagers In The Mid-Fifties"

LYNCH, JENNIFER—PHOTOGRAPHS

PH09773 652 (March 18, 1993) p47. "Sands And Lynch Of 'Boxing Helena'" (Michaelson, Randall)

LYNCH, KELLY—PHOTOGRAPHS

PH09774 657 (May 27, 1993) p58. "Gay: Lovers Kelly Lynch And Sherilyn Fenn Before The Fall"

LYNN, LORETTA—PHOTOGRAPHS

PH09775 750-751 (December 26, 1996) p176. "Loretta Lynn" (Seliger, Mark)

LYNN, LORETTA—PHOTOGRAPHS—PORTRAITS

PH09776 692 (October 6, 1994) p52. "Loretta Lynn"

LYNN, O. V., JR.—PHOTOGRAPHS—PORTRAITS

PH09777 745 (October 17, 1996) p44. "[O. V. Lynn, Jr.]"

LYNNE, JEFF—PHOTOGRAPHS

PH09778 674 (January 27, 1994) p28. "Jeff Lynne, Tom Petty, Johnny Cash And Rick Rubin (from left) At The Viper Room" (Kirkland, Gene)

LYNYRD SKYNYRD—PHOTOGRAPHS

PH09779 727 (February 8, 1996) p12. "Skynyrd's Bob Burns, Leon Wilkeson, Artimus Pyle (from left)" (Diamond, Rick)

LYONS, JIM—PHOTOGRAPHS

PH09780 664 (September 2, 1993) p34. "Where Bankers Fear To Tread" (Rystedt, Rex)

LYONS, KIRK—PHOTOGRAPHS—PORTRAITS

PH09781 720 (November 2, 1995) p57. "Kirk Lyons, Who Called Himself A White Separatist On 'Sally Jesse Rafael,' At The NRA Convention" (Warburg, Jennifer)

LYTE, MC—ALBUMS

PH09782 668 (October 28, 1993) p78. "Ain't No Other"

M

M. BUTTERFLY (FILM)—PHOTOGRAPHS

PH09783 668 (October 28, 1993) p86. "John Lone (left) As Butterfly"

M PEOPLE—ALBUMS
PH09784 714 (August 10, 1995) p58. "Bizarre Fruit"
MACCOLL, KIRSTY—ALBUMS
PH09785 675 (February 10, 1994) p44. "Titanic Days"
MACDONALD, COUNTRY JOE—PHOTOGRAPHS
PH09786 724-725 (December 28, 1995) p63. "MacDonald (with Berkeley Mayor Shirley Dean) Lest Go"
MACDONALD, JASON—PHOTOGRAPHS
PH09787 706 (April 20, 1995) pp[enc.14]. "Huntington Beach High Surf Team" (Seliger, Mark)
MACDONALD, NORM—PHOTOGRAPHS
PH09788 715 (August 24, 1995) p77. "Norm MacDonald's Hot List" (Pluchino, Joseph)
MACDONALD, NORM—PHOTOGRAPHS—PORTRAITS
PH09789 750-751 (December 26, 1996) p88. "Norm MacDonald Of 'Saturday Night Live'" (Baskin, Edie)
MACERO, TEO—PHOTOGRAPHS
PH09790 733 (May 2, 1996) p22. "From Left: Prince Paul, Reid And Teo Macero At The Manhattan Center" (Gershoff, Gary)
MACGOWAN, SHANE—ALBUMS
PH09791 715 (August 24, 1995) p100. "The Snake"
MACGOWAN, SHANE—PHOTOGRAPHS
PH09792 668 (October 28, 1993) p36. "[Van Morrison, Shane MacGowan, Fiachna O'Braonain]"
PH09793 696 (December 1, 1994) p24. "[Johnny Depp & Shane MacGowan]" (Woode, Theodore)
PH09794 714 (August 10, 1995) p27. "[Shane MacGowan]" (Nissen, Melanie)
MACK, CONNIE—PHOTOGRAPHS—PORTRAITS
PH09795 719 (October 19, 1995) p49. "Mack" (Stavato, Michael)
MACK, GORDEN—PHOTOGRAPHS
PH09796 665 (September 16, 1993) p25. "In The Red: Mack, Vessel, Kozelek, Koutsos (from left)" (Blakesberg, Jay)
MACK, RICHARD—PHOTOGRAPHS
PH09797 720 (November 2, 1995) p61. "Mack Attack: The Arizona Sheriff Was Named NRA's Officer Of The Year" (Warburg, Jennifer)
MACKAYE, IAN—PHOTOGRAPHS
PH09798 633 (June 25, 1992) p18. "Ian MacKaye" (Callahan, Kristin)
PH09799 670 (November 25, 1993) p33. "Ian MacKaye Flanked By Guy Piciotto (left) And Joe Lally" (Mazur, Kevin)
MACKLEY, STEVE—PHOTOGRAPHS
PH09800 732 (April 18, 1996) p24. "A Wildly Unorthodox Mixture Of Influence Gathered Around The Table: Pulp's Candida Doyle, Mark Webber, Cocker, Steve Mackey, Russell Senior And Nick Banks (from left)" (Rankin)
MACLACHLAN, KYLE—PHOTOGRAPHS
PH09801 639 (September 17, 1992) p103. "Anderson (left) And MacLachlan Lost In Lynchland"
PH09802 685 (June 30, 1994) pp63-64. "[Kyle MacLachlan]" (MacPherson, Andrew)
PH09803 685 (June 30, 1994) p64. "Maclachlan As Cliff Vandercave With John Goodman On The Set Of "Flintstones""
PH09804 685 (June 30, 1994) pp63-64. "With Linda Evangelista" (MacPherson, Andrew)
MACLAINE, SHIRLEY—PHOTOGRAPHS
PH09805 649 (February 4, 1993) p72. "[Used People]"
MACLEOD, ALYSON—PHOTOGRAPHS
PH09806 689 (August 25, 1994) p41. "Pierce, MacLeod, Hartling, Stein (from top)" (Crump, James)
MACMILLAN, DOUG—PHOTOGRAPHS
PH09807 633 (June 25, 1992) p11. "Greg Humphreys, Mike Watt, Doug Macmillan, Bill Janovitz, Tom Maginnis And Mike Connell (from left) In Raleigh"
MACPHERSON, ELLE—PHOTOGRAPHS
PH09808 715 (August 24, 1995) p87. "Hot Career Move" (Sands, Steve)
PH09809 727 (February 8, 1996) p13. "[Jack Nicholson & Elle MacPherson]"
PH09810 731 (April 4, 1996) p48. "Out On The Town With Supermodel Elle MacPherson In 1996"
MACPHERSON, JIM—PHOTOGRAPHS
PH09811 668 (October 28, 1993) p18. "Not Just Another Girl Group: Wiggs, Kim Deal, MacPherson And Kelley Deal (from left)" (Lass, Imke)
PH09812 682 (May 19, 1994) p89. "[The Breeders]" (Seliger, Mark)
PH09813 695 (November 17, 1994) p131. "The Breeders" (Seliger, Mark)
MACPHERSON, JIM—PHOTOGRAPHS—PORTRAITS
PH09814 660-661 (July 8, 1993) p101. "Breeders: Jim MacPherson, Kelley Deal, Kim Deal And Josephine Wiggs" (Mart, K.)
MACY, WILLIAM H.—PHOTOGRAPHS
PH09815 696 (December 1, 1994) p132. "Sex Combat: Debra Eisenstadt And William H. Macy"
MAD (PUBLICATION)—PHOTOGRAPHS
PH09816 636 (August 6, 1992) p46. "[Mad Magazine]"
MAD ABOUT YOU (TELEVISION SHOW)—PHOTOGRAPHS
PH09817 741 (August 22, 1996) p74. "[Depressing Season Finales]"
MAD DOG (FILM)—PHOTOGRAPHS
PH09818 654 (April 15, 1993) p69. "Mad Dog"
MAD LOVE (FILM)—PHOTOGRAPHS
PH09819 709 (June 1, 1995) p68. "Sappy Love Stories"
PH09820 710 (June 15, 1995) p88. "Barrymore And O'Donnell Before The Fall"
MAD PROFESSOR—ALBUMS
PH09821 705 (April 6, 1995) p65. "It's A Mad, Mad, Mad, Mad Professor"
PH09822 734 (May 16, 1996) p64. "No Protection"
MAD SEASON—ALBUMS
PH09823 706 (April 20, 1995) p74. "Above"
MAD SEASON—PHOTOGRAPHS—PORTRAITS
PH09824 704 (March 23, 1995) p33. "Barrett Martin, Layne Staley, Baker Saunder And Mike McCready (from left)" (Mercer, Lance)
MADAME BOVARY (FILM)—PHOTOGRAPHS
PH09825 621 (January 9, 1992) p56. "Isabelle Huppert And Jean-Francois Balmer In Turmoil"
MADAN, SONYA AURORA—PHOTOGRAPHS
PH09826 694 (November 3, 1994) p42. "Echobelly Lead Singer Madan" (Sirrs, Ed)
PH09827 720 (November 2, 1995) p22. "On: Echobelly's Harris, Smith, Johansson, Madan And Henderson (from left)" (Claiborne, Barron)
MADDER ROSE—ALBUMS
PH09828 685 (June 30, 1994) p76. "Panic On"
MADDER ROSE—PHOTOGRAPHS
PH09829 688 (August 11, 1994) p29. "Drummer Johnny Kick, Cote, Lorson And Bassist Chris Giammalvo (from left)" (Berg, Bob)
MADDERN, STEVE—PHOTOGRAPHS
PH09830 693 (October 20, 1994) p91. "Maddern, Helping To Educate People"
PH09831 693 (October 20, 1994) p90. "Stall Tactics Of Emory's Maddern"
MADE IN AMERICA (FILM)—PHOTOGRAPHS
PH09832 659 (June 24, 1993) p88. "Love: 'America,' With Goldberg And Danson"
PH09833 665 (September 16, 1993) p77. "Worst Actor"
PH09834 672-673 (December 23, 1993) p172. "Unfunny"
MADMAN OF THE PEOPLE (TELEVISION SHOW)—PHOTOGRAPHS
PH09835 692 (October 6, 1994) p94. "Working Girl: Mad dad Dabney Coleman With Cynthia Gibb"

MADNESS—ALBUMS

PH09836 617 (November 14, 1991) p153. "One Step Beyond" (McVey, Cameron)

THE MADNESS OF KING GEORGE (FILM)—PHOTOGRAPHS

PH09837 700 (January 26, 1995) p68. "Hawthorne Chases "madness""

MADONNA—ALBUMS

PH09838 617 (November 14, 1991) p144. "True Blue" (McManus, Jeri)

PH09839 617 (November 14, 1991) p144. "True Blue" (Ayeroff, Jeffrey Kent)

PH09840 617 (November 14, 1991) p144. "True Blue" (Ritts, Herb)

PH09841 644 (November 26, 1992) p70. "Erotica"

PH09842 697 (December 15, 1994) p93. "Bedtime Stories"

MADONNA—ILLUSTRATIONS

PH09843 634-635 (July 9, 1992) p109. "Bat Girls On The Line" (Risko, Robert)

PH09844 639 (September 17, 1992) p89. "[Madonna]" (Mayforth, Hal)

PH09845 641 (October 15, 1992) p176. "[Madonna]" (Davis, Paul)

PH09846 649 (February 4, 1993) p71. "Madonna's Come On" (Piven, Hanoch Ernesto)

PH09847 692 (October 6, 1994) p5. "Madonna" (Burke, Philip)

PH09848 698-699 (December 29, 1994) p32. "[Madonna & David Letterman]" (Ryden, Mark)

PH09849 748 (November 28, 1996) p13. "Will Madonna's Child Join The Ranks Of Kids Reared By Rock & Roll Nannies?" (Hungry Dog Studio)

PH09850 750-751 (December 26, 1996) p88. "[Courtney Love & Madonna]" (Banyai, Istvan)

MADONNA—PHOTOGRAPHS

PH09851 619-620 (December 12, 1991) pp[cover]. "1991 Yearbook" (Meisel, Steven)

PH09852 619-620 (December 12, 1991) p31. "Madonna And Michael Jackson Took In The Oscars" (Elgar, Nick)

PH09853 619-620 (December 12, 1991) p71. "Madonna At The First MTV Awards Show"

PH09854 619-620 (December 12, 1991) p39. "Madonna With Her Material Girl-ettes" (Mazur, Kevin)

PH09855 625 (March 5, 1992) p55. "Madonna's Still In Vogue"

PH09856 628 (April 16, 1992) p91. "Woody Allen Directs Malkovich, Farrow And Madonna"

PH09857 629 (April 30, 1992) p16. "Madonna Accepting The AmFAR Award" (Berliner, Alex)

PH09858 634-635 (July 9, 1992) p111. "Davis, O'Donnell, Madonna And Petty In A Man's Game"

PH09859 643 (November 12, 1992) p230. "Ritts Got Ahead By Teaming Up With Madonna" (Day, Lorraine)

PH09860 643 (November 12, 1992) p240. "Shooting Stars: Madonna And Steven Meisel At Work On Her New Book, 'Sex'" (Lew, Darren)

PH09861 644 (November 26, 1992) p13. "Madonna Risks Overexposure With Photographer Steven Meisel" (Mazur, Kevin)

PH09862 645-646 (December 10, 1992) p47. "Madonna" (Mazur, Kevin)

PH09863 645-646 (December 10, 1992) p91. "Madonna And Photog Steven Meisel Do 'Sex'" (Mazur, Kevin)

PH09864 645-646 (December 10, 1992) p153. "Madonna, 1991"

PH09865 649 (February 4, 1993) p72. "Homage Of Ripoff? In 'Body of Evidence,' Madonna And Dafoe (left) Share Stone And Douglas's Basic Instincts"

PH09866 649 (February 4, 1993) p8. "Madonna" (Colliton, Paul O.)

PH09867 655 (April 29, 1993) p56. "Michael Jackson And Madonna Celebrate Geffen's Birthday In 1991"

PH09868 667 (October 14, 1993) p70. "Expressing Herself: Of Madonna's Sizable Body Of Work, This Video Stands Out"

PH09869 667 (October 14, 1993) p85. "'Justify' A Trip To Paris: Madonna Heated The Hotel"

PH09870 669 (November 11, 1993) p25. "Exotica: Madonna At The Girlie Show Opener" (Preston, Neal)

PH09871 671 (December 9, 1993) p78. "Impossible Dream: Keitel Teaches Madonna To Act"

PH09872 672-673 (December 23, 1993) p172. "Dud Sex"

PH09873 672-673 (December 23, 1993) p16. "Left: Willem Dafoe Sucks Face With Madonna"

PH09874 672-673 (December 23, 1993) p63. "[Madonna]" (Preston, Neal)

PH09875 688 (August 11, 1994) p18. "[Madonna & Ethan Hawke]" (Amati, Ray)

PH09876 693 (October 20, 1994) p28. "Letterman, Madonna" (Mazur, Kevin)

PH09877 694 (November 3, 1994) p18. "Gaultier Snuggles Glam Pal Madonna" (Allen, David)

PH09878 698-699 (December 29, 1994) p42. "[Madonna & David Letterman]"

PH09879 703 (March 9, 1995) p21. "Madonna Sucks—Not! According To 'Encyclopedia Madonnica,' The 'Sex' Queen Don't Play The Skin Flute" (Gerber, M.)

PH09880 712-713 (July 13, 1995) p26. "The Mouths That Roar: Muhammad Ali, Madonna" (Mazur, Kevin)

PH09881 715 (August 24, 1995) p25. "[Madonna]" (Davis, Ron)

PH09882 719 (October 19, 1995) p16. "Anthony Kiedis And The Divine Miss M" (Mazur, Kevin)

PH09883 720 (November 2, 1995) p50. "Madonna" (Lindbergh, Peter)

PH09884 728 (February 22, 1996) p19. "Bowie's Eloquent Disciples Byrne And Madonna" (Mazur, Kevin)

PH09885 729 (March 7, 1996) p9. "[Madonna]" (Liotta Patrick)

PH09886 731 (April 4, 1996) p33. "Clark With Madonna In 1984"

PH09887 731 (April 4, 1996) p48. "Penn Protecting Then Wife Madonna From The Paparazzi In 1986" (Savignano, Anthony)

PH09888 732 (April 18, 1996) p78. "Madonna And Randle Flank Director Spike Lee"

PH09889 748 (November 28, 1996) p30. "Papa, Don't Preach: A Very Pregnant Madonna In Los Angeles, With Her Brother, Chris Ciccone, In Early September" (Lewis, Gary)

PH09890 750-751 (December 26, 1996) p82. "Oh, Baby! After All Her Various Incarnations, Now, Finally, Madonna Is Just Mom" (Lewis, Gary)

MADONNA—PHOTOGRAPHS—PORTRAITS

PH09891 643 (November 12, 1992) pp244-245. "Fifties Glamour Meets Nineties High Concept: Madonna In Miami, 1992" (Meisel, Steven)

PH09892 651 (March 4, 1993) p50. "Madonna: Evidence Of A Body" (Meisel, Steven)

PH09893 667 (October 14, 1993) p76. "Jail-House Rock: Madonna's 'Prayer' Pissed Off Both The Pope And Pepsi"

PH09894 667 (October 14, 1993) p78. "'Vogue': Madonna's Video Is Burning"

PH09895 692 (October 6, 1994) p49. "Madonna"

PH09896 704 (March 23, 1995) p24. "Babyface And Madonna Take In The AMAs" (Nannarello, Spike)

PH09897 743 (September 19, 1996) p88. "Divas"

PH09898 747 (November 14, 1996) p30. "[Madonna]" (Sands, Steve)

MAFFEO, LOIS—PHOTOGRAPHS

PH09899 717 (September 21, 1995) p38. "Reaching For The Sky: Songstress Lois Maffeo" (Lavine, Michael)

MAGGIE'S DREAM—PHOTOGRAPHS

PH09900 628 (April 16, 1992) p63. "Maggie's Dream" (Tisman, Jeff)

MAGIC DIRT—ALBUMS

PH09901 732 (April 18, 1996) p68. "Magic Dirt"

MAGINNIS, TOM—PHOTOGRAPHS

PH09902 633 (June 25, 1992) p11. "Greg Humphreys, Mike

Watt, Doug Macmillan, Bill Janovitz, Tom Maginnis And Mike Connell (from left) In Raleigh"
PH09903 665 (September 16, 1993) pp[enc.45]. "Above From Left: Chris Colbourn, Friend Debra Monaco, Tom Maginnis And Bill Janovitz" (Newton, Philip)
PH09904 665 (September 16, 1993) pp[enc.5]. "[Buffalo Tom]" (Newton, Philip)
PH09905 665 (September 16, 1993) pp[enc.50,54]. "[Tom Maginnis]" (Newton, Philip)
PH09906 665 (September 16, 1993) pp[enc.50]. "[Tom Maginnis & Debra Monaco]" (Newton, Philip)
PH09907 672-673 (December 23, 1993) p65. "Tom Maginnis, Janovitz And Chris Colbourn" (Robicheau, Paul)
MAGNAPOP—ALBUMS
PH09908 698-699 (December 29, 1994) p190. "Hot Boxing"
MAGNAPOP—PHOTOGRAPHS
PH09909 696 (December 1, 1994) p33. "Magnapop: Next Wave From Atlanta" (Cardillicchio, Nick)
MAGUIRE, BARRY—PHOTOGRAPHS
PH09910 636 (August 6, 1992) p13. "The Wallflowers (from left): Barrie Maguire, Jakob Dylan, Rami Jaffee, Peter Yanowitz And Tobi Miller" (Mark, Mary Ellen)
MAH, LESLIE—PHOTOGRAPHS
PH09911 721 (November 16, 1995) p81. "The Tribe That Sticks Together: Slade Bellum, Lynn Breedlove, Leslie Mah, Lynn Payne, Lynn Flipper (from left)" (Yemchuk, Yelena)
MAHAL, TAJ—ALBUMS
PH09912 652 (March 18, 1993) p42. "Rising Sons"
MAHER, BILL—PHOTOGRAPHS
PH09913 697 (December 15, 1994) p18. "Etheridge, Waters, "Politically Incorrect" Host Bill Maher, Molinari And Baio (from left)"
PH09914 747 (November 14, 1996) p26. "'Incorrect' Host Bill Maher (left) With Haynes"
MAIER, JEFFREY—PHOTOGRAPHS
PH09915 750-751 (December 26, 1996) p85. "Rookie Of The Year: Maier (top, second from right) Propelled The Yankees"
MAILBOX—PHOTOGRAPHS
PH09916 711 (June 29, 1995) p36. "One Of Ames' Signaling Points" (Trippett, Robert)
MALCOLM X (FILM)—PHOTOGRAPHS
PH09917 645-646 (December 10, 1992) p192. "Denzel Washington: Trying To Do The Right Thing By Malcolm"
PH09918 648 (January 21, 1993) p56. "Malcolm X"
MALI—PHOTOGRAPHS
PH09919 619-620 (December 12, 1991) p145. "In A Nutritional Center In Mali In 1985, A Child Is Weighed In Order To Determine His Rations" (Salgado, Sebastiao)
MALICE (FILM)—PHOTOGRAPHS
PH09920 667 (October 14, 1993) p128. "Evil Doings For Alec Baldwin And Nicole Kidman"
MALIK—PHOTOGRAPHS—PORTRAITS
PH09921 667 (October 14, 1993) p21. "Snoop Dogg (left) And Malik" (Seliger, Mark)
MALIN, JESSE—PHOTOGRAPHS
PH09922 701 (February 9, 1995) p19. "D Gen (from left): Danny Sage, Richard Bacchus, Howie Pyro, Jesse Malin, Michael Wildwood" (Seliger, Mark)
PH09923 701 (February 9, 1995) p20. "Glam Rabble-Rousers Wildwood, Malin And Sage (from left) In New York City" (Mazur, Kevin)
PH09924 705 (April 6, 1995) p16. "Label Flava Of The Month: D Gen's Jesse malin (left) And Danny Sage" (Brown, Christy)
PH09925 710 (June 15, 1995) p41. "D Gen (from left): Pyro, Michael Wildwood, Malin, Sage, Richard Bacchus And Gomez" (Ragel, Jon)
MALINA, JUDITH—PHOTOGRAPHS
PH09926 618 (November 28, 1991) p53. "They're Altogether Ooky" (Seliger, Mark)
MALININ, MIKE—PHOTOGRAPHS
PH09927 723 (December 14, 1995) p36. "Hungry For Success And Searching For Dinner: Johnny Rzeznik, Robby Takac And Mike Malinin" (Ockenfels, Frank W.)
MALKMUS, STEPHEN—PHOTOGRAPHS
PH09928 682 (May 19, 1994) p34. "Pavement's Stephen Malkmus" (Sirrs, Ed)
PH09929 685 (June 30, 1994) p40. "Pavement's Stephen Malkmus In D.C." (Liu, Brian)
PH09930 686-687 (July 14, 1994) p19. "Pavement (clockwise from left): Mark Ibold, Steve West, Bob Nastanovich And Stephen Malkmus" (Blakesberg, Jay)
PH09931 695 (November 17, 1994) p78. "Pavement" (Hanauer, Mark)
PH09932 709 (June 1, 1995) p23. "Lollapalooza Puts Pavement's Mark Ibold (left) And Stephen Malkmus On The Road" (Corio, David)
MALKOVICH, JOHN—PHOTOGRAPHS
PH09933 628 (April 16, 1992) p91. "Woody Allen Directs Malkovich, Farrow And Madonna"
MALLEY, MATT—PHOTOGRAPHS
PH09934 669 (November 11, 1993) p24. "A '90s Sensibility: Vickrey, Gillingham, Duritz, Bowman, Malley, Bryson (from left)" (Blakesberg, Jay)
PH09935 674 (January 27, 1994) p25. "Crows (from left): Vickrey, Malley, Duritz" (Blakesberg, Jay)
PH09936 685 (June 30, 1994) pp[cover]. "Counting Crows: The Biggest New Band In America" (Seliger, Mark)
PH09937 685 (June 30, 1994) p46. "Free Men In Paris: Dave Bryson, Steve Bowman, Dan Vickrey, Matt Malley And Charlie Gillingham (from left)" (Seliger, Mark)
MALLRATS (FILM)—PHOTOGRAPHS
PH09938 720 (November 2, 1995) p74. "Mallrats Smith And Mewes"
MALO, RAUL—PHOTOGRAPHS
PH09939 691 (September 22, 1994) p22. "[The Mavericks]" (Harris, Brad)
PH09940 693 (October 20, 1994) p52. "Raul Malo Of The Mavericks Sees The Light" (Capak, R. J.)
PH09941 707 (May 4, 1995) p19. "Maverick's Raul Malo (left) And Reynolds In L.A." (Soqui, Ted)
MALO, RAUL—PHOTOGRAPHS—PORTRAITS
PH09942 682 (May 19, 1994) p74. "[Mavericks]" (Tucker, Mark)
MALONE, JOHN—PHOTOGRAPHS
PH09943 689 (August 25, 1994) p69. "Diller With John Malone, The Cable Magnate With A Stake In QVC, Before Senate Testimony On The Info Highway Last Winter"
MALONEY, MICHAEL—PHOTOGRAPHS
PH09944 728 (February 22, 1996) p70. "The Actor's Life: Branagh (right) Directs Maloney"
MALOY, PAUL—PHOTOGRAPHS
PH09945 663 (August 19, 1993) p61. "College Cabinet: William Clinton, Judith Baiocchi, David Kammer, Paul Maloy (from left)"
MALOY, ZAC—PHOTOGRAPHS
PH09946 733 (May 2, 1996) p14. "Nixons' Bassist Ricky Brooks (left) And Maloy" (Burton, Eric)
MAMA SAID KNOCK YOU OUT (VIDEO)—PHOTOGRAPHS
PH09947 619-620 (December 12, 1991) p33. "L. L. Cool J:"Mama Said Knock You Out'"
THE MAMBO KINGS (FILM)—ILLUSTRATIONS
PH09948 626 (March 19, 1992) p101. "Playing Songs Of Love" (Kelley, Gary)
THE MAMBO KINGS (FILM)—PHOTOGRAPHS
PH09949 626 (March 19, 1992) p102. "Banderas (left) And Assante Say It With Music"
MAMET, DAVID—PHOTOGRAPHS
PH09950 616 (October 31, 1991) p99. "Actor And Director: Mantegna And Mamet"

A MAN CALLED E—PHOTOGRAPHS
PH09951 690 (September 8, 1994) p38. "E, Starring At A Club Near You"
MAN OF LA MANCHA (STAGE MUSICAL)—PHOTOGRAPHS
PH09952 624 (February 20, 1992) p11. "Sheena Easton In 'Man Of La Mancha'" (Marcus, Joan)
A MAN OF NO IMPORTANCE (FILM)—PHOTOGRAPHS
PH09953 697 (December 15, 1994) p104. "Albert Finney"
MAN ON THE MOON (VIDEO)—PHOTOGRAPHS
PH09954 667 (October 14, 1993) p85. "Stipe: R.E.M.'s Man On The Street"
MAN TROUBLE (FILM)—PHOTOGRAPHS
PH09955 649 (February 4, 1993) p72. "[Man Trouble]"
THE MAN WHO FELL TO EARTH (FILM)—PHOTOGRAPHS
PH09956 658 (June 10, 1993) p62. "Starring In 'The Man Who Fell To Earth,' 1975"
THE MAN WITHOUT A FACE (FILM)—PHOTOGRAPHS
PH09957 665 (September 16, 1993) p76. "Mel Gibson Shows A Different Side"
MANCHEVSKI, MILCHO—PHOTOGRAPHS
PH09958 704 (March 23, 1995) p128. "Manchevski Directs Lovers Cartlidge And Serbedzija"
MANCHILD (VIDEO)—PHOTOGRAPHS
PH09959 667 (October 14, 1993) p92. "Cherry: 'Manchild' Takes First Steps Into New World"
MANDELA, NELSON—PHOTOGRAPHS
PH09960 688 (August 11, 1994) p17. "Nelson Mandela (left) And AD's Speech"
PH09961 750-751 (December 26, 1996) p50. "Marching To Pretoria: Louis Farrakham Meeting With President Nelson Mandela In South Africa" (Silva, Joao)
MANDELA, WINNIE—ILLUSTRATIONS
PH09962 693 (October 20, 1994) pp55-56. "[Winnie Mandela]" (Dionisi, Sandra)
MANGOLD, JAMES—PHOTOGRAPHS
PH09963 741 (August 22, 1996) p71. "[James Mangold]" (Mantel, John M.)
MANHATTAN MURDER MYSTERY (FILM)—ILLUSTRATIONS
PH09964 664 (September 2, 1993) p68. "Annie Small" (Blitt, Barry)
MANHATTAN MURDER MYSTERY (FILM)—PHOTOGRAPHS
PH09965 664 (September 2, 1993) p69. "'Annie Hall' Lovers Keaton And Allen (left) Reteam In A Romantic 'Mystery'"
PH09966 678 (March 24, 1994) p100. "Missing In Oscar Action"
MANI—PHOTOGRAPHS
PH09967 724-725 (December 28, 1995) p39. "Stoned, Dethroned: Mani, Squire, Brown, Reni (from left)" (Otte, Sylvia)
MANIC STREET PREACHERS—PHOTOGRAPHS
PH09968 663 (August 19, 1993) p24. "The Manics: Riot Guys On The Road"
MANN, AIMEE—ALBUMS
PH09969 662 (August 5, 1993) p68. "Whatever"
MANN, AIMEE—PHOTOGRAPHS
PH09970 660-661 (July 8, 1993) p100. "'Til Tuesday No More: Aimee Mann" (Levine, Laura)
PH09971 674 (January 27, 1994) p29. "Mann Is Joined by Troubadour Partridge" (Busacca, Larry)
PH09972 728 (February 22, 1996) p26. "[Aimee Mann]" (Garner, Kate)
MANN, AIMEE—PHOTOGRAPHS—PORTRAITS
PH09973 704 (March 23, 1995) p44. "Mann: Edgier But Still Infectious" (Feingold, Deborah)
MANNING, BARBARA—PHOTOGRAPHS
PH09974 693 (October 20, 1994) p30. "Cleo's Hanley, Stacy Jones, Manning; Builders Joan Wasser, Eric Masunaga" (Robicheau, Paul)
MANNING, BARBARA—PHOTOGRAPHS—PORTRAITS
PH09975 628 (April 16, 1992) p56. "[Barbara Mannning]" (Alicino, Christine)
MANSON, CHARLES—PHOTOGRAPHS—PORTRAITS
PH09976 724-725 (December 28, 1995) p54. "[Charles Manson]" (Darrios, H.)
MANSON, SHIRLEY—ILLUSTRATIONS
PH09977 718 (October 5, 1995) p9. "Shirley Manson Of Garbage" (Burke, Philip)
MANSON, SHIRLEY—PHOTOGRAPHS
PH09978 718 (October 5, 1995) p24. "Manson Performing With Angelfish In 1993" (Eichner, Steve)
PH09979 718 (October 5, 1995) p23. "Trash Is Where It's At: Erikson, Marker, Vig, Manson (clockwise from left)" (Ockenfels, Frank W.)
PH09980 740 (August 8, 1996) p17. "Stefani, Left, And Manson, Who Obviously Eats Her Spinach" (Cohen, Lester)
PH09981 745 (October 17, 1996) p75. "Garbage's Shirley Manson" (Seliger, Mark)
PH09982 745 (October 17, 1996) pp76-77. "[Shirley Manson]" (Rolston, Matthew)
MANSON, SHIRLEY—PHOTOGRAPHS—PORTRAITS
PH09983 745 (October 17, 1996) p79. "Manson, Age 12, At Broughton High"
MANTEGNA, JOE—PHOTOGRAPHS
PH09984 616 (October 31, 1991) p99. "Actor And Director: Mantegna And Mamet"
PH09985 748 (November 28, 1996) p143. "Dead On Arrival"
M.A.N.T.I.S. (TELEVISION SHOW)—PHOTOGRAPHS
PH09986 692 (October 6, 1994) p94. ""M.A.N.T.I.S." Metro-Area nerd Turns Into Stud"
MANUEL, ARLIE—PHOTOGRAPHS
PH09987 677 (March 10, 1994) p28. "Rick Danko, Hudson And Arlie Manuel" (Mazur, Kevin)
MANUEL, RICHARD—PHOTOGRAPHS
PH09988 617 (November 14, 1991) p75. "The Last Waltz, 1976: Robertson, Danko And Manuel, With Neil Young (left), Bob Dylan (back to camera) And Van Morrison" (Leibovitz, Annie)
PH09989 617 (November 14, 1991) p72. "Levon And The Hawks, Circa 1963: Sax Player Jerry Field, Rick Danko, Levon Helm, Richard Manuel, Garth Hudson And Robertson (from left)"
PH09990 669 (November 11, 1993) p66. "The Hawks At Ontario's Brass Rail Circa '63: Danko, Manuel, Hawkins, Helm, Robertson And Hudson (from left)"
PH09991 676 (February 24, 1994) p46. "The Band (clockwise from top left): Guitarist Robbie Robertson, Drummer Levon Helm, Organist Garth Hudson, Bassist Rock Danko And Pianist Richard Manuel" (Gahr, David)
MANZAREK, RAY—ALBUMS
PH09992 747 (November 14, 1996) p114. "Myth And Reality"
MANZAREK, RAY—PHOTOGRAPHS
PH09993 649 (February 4, 1993) p52. "The Doors (from left): keyboardist Ray Manzarek, Drummer John Densmore, Guitarist Robbie Krieger, Shaman Jim Morrison" (Diltz, Henry)
PH09994 724-725 (December 28, 1995) p46. "Doors John Densmore, Manzarek And Robby Krieger (from left)" (Kaplin, Todd)
MANZELLA, RAY—PHOTOGRAPHS
PH09995 738-739 (July 11, 1996) p38. "In L.A. With Agent-Boyfriend Manzella" (Kravitz, Jeff)
MAO—PHOTOGRAPHS
PH09996 741 (August 22, 1996) p74. "[The Cold War]"
MARA, TOM—PHOTOGRAPHS
PH09997 678 (March 24, 1994) p57. "Cursed? KCMU-FM Management: Knab, Now Resigned, Yates And Mara (from left)" (Lavine, Michael)
MARCH, JANE—PHOTOGRAPHS
PH09998 691 (September 22, 1994) p106. "Bombs Away"
MARCH, KEVIN—PHOTOGRAPHS
PH09999 693 (October 20, 1994) p49. "Kevin March, Dave Derby, Joan Wasser, Eric Masunaga (from left)" (Lass, Imke)
MARCHAND, LUKE—PHOTOGRAPHS
PH10000 689 (August 25, 1994) p75. "Marchand Of "DWN"

With Husband Luke And Rafael Harpo" (Hill, Britain)
MARCHAND, RAFAEL HARPO—PHOTOGRAPHS
PH10000 689 (August 25, 1994) p75. "Marchand Of "DWN" With Husband Luke And Rafael Harpo" (Hill, Britain)
MARCHAND, SHOSHANA—PHOTOGRAPHS
PH10000 689 (August 25, 1994) p75. "Marchand Of "DWN" With Husband Luke And Rafael Harpo" (Hill, Britain)
MARCOVECH, ALEJANDO—PHOTOGRAPHS
PH10001 662 (August 5, 1993) p17. "Andre, Saul Hernandez, Alejando Marcovech" (Mazur, Kevin)
MARCUS, GREIL—BOOKS
PH10002 658 (June 10, 1993) p33. "Ranters And Crowd Pleasers: Punk In Pop Music 1977-92"
MARCUS, GREIL—PHOTOGRAPHS
PH10003 632 (June 11, 1992) p121. "Greil Marcus And His Daughter On Vacation In Maui, In August 1977"
MARIJUANA—ILLUSTRATIONS
PH10004 632 (June 11, 1992) p139. "[Marijuana]" (Cronin, Brian)
PH10005 681 (May 5, 1994) p32. "[Marijuana]" (Frampton, Jerald)
MARILYN MANSON—ALBUMS
PH10006 748 (November 28, 1996) p129. "Antichrist Superstar"
MARILYN MANSON—ILLUSTRATIONS
PH10007 748 (November 28, 1996) p129. "Shtick Or Treat?" (Burns, Charles)
MARILYN MANSON—PHOTOGRAPHS
PH10008 735 (May 30, 1996) p46. "The Insectoid Marilyn Manson" (Gougenheim, Kim)
PH10009 749 (December 12, 1996) p36. "Manson Gets Blasphemous" (Callahan, Kristin)
PH10010 750-751 (December 26, 1996) p85. "[Marilyn Manson]" (Cultice, Joseph)
MARIO—ILLUSTRATIONS
PH10011 621 (January 9, 1992) p46. "[Mario]"
MARK OF CAIN—PHOTOGRAPHS
PH10012 705 (April 6, 1995) p23. "Mosh City: Fur (above) And The Mark Of Cain (below)" (Mott, Tony)
MARK, MARKY—PHOTOGRAPHS
PH10013 638 (September 3, 1992) pp[enc.10-11]. "[Marky Mark]" (Klein, Steven)
PH10014 638 (September 3, 1992) pp[enc.2,12]. "[Marky Mark, Shana]" (Klein, Steven)
PH10015 656 (May 13, 1993) p21. "Main Offenders: Mark (left)..." (Quigley, Brian)
PH10016 684 (June 16, 1994) p116. "Funny: DeVito Instructs Mark In "Renaissance man""
MARK, MARKY—PHOTOGRAPHS—PORTRAITS
PH10017 638 (September 3, 1992) pp[enc.. "Fall Fashion 1992" (Klein, Steven)
PH10018 672-673 (December 23, 1993) p20. "Mark: How About A Calvin Undershirt?" (Contratto, Mark)
MARKER, STEVE—PHOTOGRAPHS
PH10019 718 (October 5, 1995) p23. "Trash Is Where It's At: Erikson, Marker, Vig, Manson (clockwise from left)" (Ockenfels, Frank W.)
MARKIE, BIZ—ALBUMS
PH10020 666 (September 30, 1993) p101. "All Samples Cleared!"
MARKIEWICZ, CLARISSA—PHOTOGRAPHS
PH10021 686-687 (July 14, 1994) p42. "My Old School Chum: Markiewicz, Browne"
MARKKULA, MIKE—PHOTOGRAPHS
PH10022 732 (April 18, 1996) p63. "Spindler (left) And Markkula Were Barraged By Questions At Apple's 1996 Shareholders' Meeting"
MARKS, DAVE—PHOTOGRAPHS
PH10023 652 (March 18, 1993) pp[enc.37]. "Dave Marks" (Seliger, Mark)
MARKUS, KURT—ILLUSTRATIONS
PH10024 643 (November 12, 1992) p173. "[Kurt Markus]" (Russo, Anthony)
MARKUS, KURT—ILLUSTRATIONS—LETTERING
PH10025 643 (November 12, 1992) p173. "[Kurt Markus]" (Karl, Anita)
MARLEY, BOB—ALBUMS
PH10026 617 (November 14, 1991) p132. "Catch A Fire" (Dyer, Rod)
PH10027 617 (November 14, 1991) p132. "Catch A Fire" (Weiner, Bob)
PH10028 645-646 (December 10, 1992) p170. "Songs Of Freedom"
MARLEY, BOB—PHOTOGRAPHS
PH10029 632 (June 11, 1992) p70. "The Rudies Still Rules Kingston, And Bob Marley's Dreadlocks Were Just Starting To Sprout" (Gorson, Arthur H.)
PH10030 Number not assigned.
PH10031 676 (February 24, 1994) p40. "Bob Marley—In Concert And In Ecstasy—At The Paramount Theater, In Oakland, Calif., In July 1976" (Leibovitz, Annie)
PH10032 676 (February 24, 1994) pp[cover]. "Bob Marley's Reggae Legacy" (Leibovitz, Annie)
PH10033 676 (February 24, 1994) p40. "Marley And His Entourage Leaving His Last London Concert In June 1980" (Corio, David)
PH10033a 676 (February 24, 1994) p40. "Marley As A Rude Boy In The Early '60s"
PH10034 676 (February 24, 1994) p40. "Marley At Home In Jamaica With Members Of His Family In The Mid-'70s" (Boot, Adrian)
PH10035 749 (December 12, 1996) p30. "Moldy Oldies? Sales Drop For Evergreens Such As Marley's "Legend'"
MARLEY, BOB—PHOTOGRAPHS—PORTRAITS
PH10036 676 (February 24, 1994) p39. "[Bob Marley]" (Morris, Dennis)
PH10037 720 (November 2, 1995) p50. "Bob Marley" (Morris, Dennis)
MARLEY, CEDELLA—PHOTOGRAPHS
PH10038 626 (March 19, 1992) p13. "Sharon Marley Prendergrast, Cedella Marley, Ziggy, Stephen Marley (from left)"
MARLEY, RITA—PHOTOGRAPHS
PH10039 677 (March 10, 1994) p29. "Ziggy And Rita Marley With Bono" (Mazur, Kevin)
MARLEY, STEPHEN—PHOTOGRAPHS
PH10040 626 (March 19, 1992) p13. "Sharon Marley Prendergrast, Cedella Marley, Ziggy, Stephen Marley (from left)"
MARLEY, ZIGGY—ALBUMS
PH10041 664 (September 2, 1993) p62. "Joy And Blues"
MARLEY, ZIGGY—PHOTOGRAPHS
PH10042 626 (March 19, 1992) p13. "Sharon Marley Prendergrast, Cedella Marley, Ziggy, Stephen Marley (from left)"
PH10043 634-635 (July 9, 1992) p11. "Ziggy Marley At The United Nations" (Bryan-Brown, Marc)
PH10044 653 (April 1, 1993) p13. "Ziggy Marley Takes Seattle" (Mercer, Lance)
PH10045 677 (March 10, 1994) p29. "Ziggy And Rita Marley With Bono" (Mazur, Kevin)
PH10046 694 (November 3, 1994) p18. "Son Splash: Ziggy MArley" (Missbrenner, Kevin)
PH10047 734 (May 16, 1996) p17. "Ziggy Marley, Who Looks So Much Like His Father It's Scary" (Olsen, K. Thor)
MARRIOTT, STEVE—PHOTOGRAPHS
PH10048 619-620 (December 12, 1991) p109. "Steve Marriott" (Walter, Chris)
MARS ATTACKS (FILM)—PHOTOGRAPHS
PH10049 743 (September 19, 1996) p88. "Going For The Gold"
MARS, CHRIS—ALBUMS
PH10050 657 (May 27, 1993) p50. "75% Less Fat"

MARS, CHRIS—PHOTOGRAPHS

PH10051 633 (June 25, 1992) p11. "Golden Smog (from left): Gary Louris, Chris Mars, Dan Murphy, Craig Johnson And Marc Perlman" (Butler, Bonnie Lynn)

PH10052 656 (May 13, 1993) p31. "[Chris Mars]" (Crouser, Michael)

PH10053 659 (June 24, 1993) p54. "Early Mats: Westerberg, Bob Stinson, Mars And Tommy Stinson (from left)" (Pasley, Richard)

PH10054 659 (June 24, 1993) p52. "The Later Mats Incarnation: Tommy Stinson, Westerberg, Slim Dunlap And Chris Mars (from left)" (Matheu, Robert)

PH10055 712-713 (July 13, 1995) p26. "The Show Must Go On—But Without Chris Mars" (Nelson, Tony)

MARS, CHRIS—PHOTOGRAPHS—PORTRAITS

PH10056 627 (April 2, 1992) p13. "Chris Mars (no relation to Mick)" (Umland, Steve)

PH10057 628 (April 16, 1992) p63. "Chris Mars" (Umland, Steve)

MARS, MICK—PHOTOGRAPHS—PORTRAITS

PH10058 627 (April 2, 1992) p13. "Motley Crue's Tommy Lee, Nikki Sixx, Mick Mars And The Defrocked Vince Neil (clockwise from top left)" (Double, Steve)

MARSALIS, BRANFORD—PHOTOGRAPHS

PH10059 682 (May 19, 1994) p38. "Marsalis (left) And Neville, Pre-Show" (Mazur, Kevin)

PH10060 691 (September 22, 1994) p19. "Gabriel, Kidjo And Marsalis (from left)" (Smith, Robert)

MARSALIS, BRANFORD—PHOTOGRAPHS—PORTRAITS

PH10061 624 (February 20, 1992) p12. "'Tonight Show' Bandleader Marsalis" (Hamilton, James)

PH10062 685 (June 30, 1994) p40. "Partners LeFonque: Premier, Marsalis"

MARSALIS, WYNTON—ALBUMS

PH10063 637 (August 20, 1992) p52. "Blue Interlude"

PH10064 653 (April 1, 1993) p52. "Citi Movement"

MARSH, DAVE—BOOKS

PH10065 664 (September 2, 1993) p20. "Louie Louie"

MARSHALL, ARIK—PHOTOGRAPHS

PH10066 660-661 (July 8, 1993) p17. "Man Overboard: Smith, Kiedis, Marshall And Flea" (Leialoha, Mark)

MARSHALL, JAMES—PHOTOGRAPHS

PH10067 626 (March 19, 1992) p102. "Race Divides Gooding And Marshall"

MARSHALL, JIM—PHOTOGRAPHS

PH10068 643 (November 12, 1992) p64. "Legendary San Francisco Shooter Jim Marshall With Joplin" (Marshall, Jim)

PH10069 703 (March 9, 1995) p29. "Rosanne Cash And Marshall With His Classic Shot Of Her Dad" (Mazur, Kevin)

MARTHA AND THE VANDELLAS—PHOTOGRAPHS

PH10070 702 (February 23, 1995) p49. "Schneider And Pierson Sandwich The Vandellas" (Mazur, Kevin)

MARTIN (TELEVISION SHOW)—PHOTOGRAPHS

PH10071 680 (April 21, 1994) p77. "As Sheneneh, With His 'Martin' Girlfriend, Tisha Campbell"

MARTIN, BARDI—PHOTOGRAPHS

PH10072 674 (January 27, 1994) p24. "Bardi Martin, Klett, Kevin Martin, Mercado (from left)" (Knight, Kevin)

PH10073 686-687 (July 14, 1994) p42. "Bardie Martin (left), Kevin Martin" (Mason, Karen)

PH10074 702 (February 23, 1995) p23. "Candlebox (from left): Peter Klett, Scott Mercado, Kevin Martin, Bardi Martin" (Ford, Charles)

MARTIN, BARRETT—PHOTOGRAPHS

PH10075 650 (February 18, 1993) p15. "Gary Lee Conner, Barrett Martin, Mark Lanegan And Van Conner (from left)" (Winters, Dan)

PH10076 695 (November 17, 1994) p110. "Screaming Trees" (Ragel, Jon)

PH10077 711 (June 29, 1995) p12. "Barrett Martin, Peter Buck And Mike McCready (from left)" (Mercer, Lance)

PH10078 748 (November 28, 1996) p26. "Tuatara's Martin, Harwood And Buck (from left)" (Doughty, Curt)

MARTIN, BARRETT—PHOTOGRAPHS—PORTRAITS

PH10079 704 (March 23, 1995) p33. "Barrett Martin, Layne Staley, Baker Saunder And Mike McCready (from left)" (Mercer, Lance)

MARTIN, GEORGE—BOOKS

PH10080 698-699 (December 29, 1994) p64. "All You Need Is Ears"

MARTIN, GEORGE—PHOTOGRAPHS

PH10080 698-699 (December 29, 1994) p64. "All You Need Is Ears"

MARTIN, GREG—PHOTOGRAPHS

PH10081 668 (October 28, 1993) p30. "Greg Martin, Johnnie Johnson And Richard Young (from left)" (Natkin, Paul)

MARTIN, JESSE L.—PHOTOGRAPHS

PH10082 734 (May 16, 1996) p57. "[Jesse L. Martin]" (Hom, Marc)

MARTIN, KEVIN—ILLUSTRATIONS

PH10083 702 (February 23, 1995) p9. "Candlebox's Kevin Martin" (Burke, Philip)

MARTIN, KEVIN—PHOTOGRAPHS

PH10084 674 (January 27, 1994) p24. "Bardi Martin, Klett, Kevin Martin, Mercado (from left)" (Knight, Kevin)

PH10085 686-687 (July 14, 1994) p42. "Bardie Martin (left), Kevin Martin" (Mason, Karen)

PH10086 702 (February 23, 1995) p23. "Candlebox (from left): Peter Klett, Scott Mercado, Kevin Martin, Bardi Martin" (Ford, Charles)

PH10087 702 (February 23, 1995) p24. "Kevin Martin In Between Bouts Of Stage Diving" (Mazur, Kevin)

MARTIN, STEVE (PUBLICIST)—PHOTOGRAPHS

PH10088 677 (March 10, 1994) p57. "Nasty Men: Martin And Perry Serpa" (Smale, Brian)

MARTIN, STEVE—PHOTOGRAPHS

PH10089 634-635 (July 9, 1992) p114. "A Coy Comedy Defeats The Efforts Of Hawn And Martin"

PH10090 648 (January 21, 1993) p55. "Preacher Steve Martin Can't Save His Movie"

MARTINA—PHOTOGRAPHS

PH10091 706 (April 20, 1995) p36. "Trip-Hop Hooray: Martina And Tricky" (Rider, Paul)

PH10092 726 (January 25, 1996) p50. "Trip-Hopper Tricky (right) With Singer Martine" (Double, Steve)

MARTINEZ, A—PHOTOGRAPHS

PH10093 736 (June 13, 1996) p54. "Irene Bedard And A Martinez In HBO's Tribal Drama 'Grand Avenue'"

MARTINEZ, JACK—PHOTOGRAPHS

PH10094 706 (April 20, 1995) pp[enc.15]. "Jack And Melissa Martinez At Garf's, In Costa Mesa" (Seliger, Mark)

MARTINEZ, MELISSA—PHOTOGRAPHS

PH10094 706 (April 20, 1995) pp[enc.15]. "Jack And Melissa Martinez At Garf's, In Costa Mesa" (Seliger, Mark)

MARTINI, JERRY—PHOTOGRAPHS

PH10095 649 (February 4, 1993) p51. "Rose Stone, Sly, Freddie Stone, Graham, Robinson, Errico And Martini Of Sly And The Family Stone"

MARTINOV, VALERY—PHOTOGRAPHS—PORTRAITS

PH10096 711 (June 29, 1995) p38. "Martinov, KGB: Killed"

MARVELETTES—PHOTOGRAPHS—PORTRAITS

PH10097 703 (March 9, 1995) p25. "The Marvelettes: Motown Legends"

MARX, GROUCHO—ILLUSTRATIONS—PORTRAITS

PH10098 710 (June 15, 1995) p18. "From Abkhazia With Love: The Stamp Of Marx And Lennon"

MARXMAN—PHOTOGRAPHS

PH10099 690 (September 8, 1994) p44. "K1, Oisin, Phrase And Hollis (from left)" (Cross, Brian)

MARY SHELLEY'S FRANKENSTEIN (FILM)—ILLUSTRATIONS

PH10100 696 (December 1, 1994) p131. "You Talking To Me?"

(Guy, Edmund)
MARY SHELLEY'S FRANKENSTEIN (FILM)—PHOTOGRAPHS
PH10101 696 (December 1, 1994) p132. "De Niro's Monster And Karloff's 1931 Model"
PH10102 696 (December 1, 1994) p132. "Branagh's Dr. Frankenstein Lip Locks Bonham Carter"
MARY'S DANISH—ALBUMS
PH10103 647 (January 7, 1993) p47. "American Standard"
MARY'S DANISH—PHOTOGRAPHS
PH10104 619-620 (December 12, 1991) p59. "Mary's Danish Releases A Spectacular Sophomore Effort" (Allen, Ethan)
PH10105 665 (September 16, 1993) p32. "Neil Diamond (center) With Mary's Danish" (Preston, Neal)
MASH, DAVID—PHOTOGRAPHS
PH10106 666 (September 30, 1993) p74. "David Mash, Center, Architect Of Berklee's Brave New World, Teaching" (Hill, Britain)
THE MASK (FILM)—ILLUSTRATIONS
PH10107 689 (August 25, 1994) p95. "Ace Of Face" (Ryden, Mark)
THE MASK (FILM)—PHOTOGRAPHS
PH10108 684 (June 16, 1994) p115. "Jim Carrey's Grin Equals A Box-Office Ace"
PH10109 689 (August 25, 1994) p96. "Jim Carrey Shows His Delicate Approach To Comedy As The Man Behind The Mask"
PH10110 691 (September 22, 1994) p106. "Rising Star"
PH10111 698-699 (December 29, 1994) p61. "Unmasked: Carrey Licks The Box Office"
PH10112 705 (April 6, 1995) p69. "Oscar Rejects"
MASLIAH, LAURENCE—PHOTOGRAPHS
PH10113 680 (April 21, 1994) p95. "Now Playing"
MASSAI—PHOTOGRAPHS
PH10114 615 (October 17, 1991) p64. "Massai, Jade Jagger And Jerry Hall, Nassau, 1983" (Pigozzi, Jean)
MASSIVE ATTACK—ALBUMS
PH10115 734 (May 16, 1996) p64. "No Protection"
MASSIVE ATTACK—ILLUSTRATIONS
PH10116 705 (April 6, 1995) p64. "Massive Attack" (Meshon, Aaron)
MASSIVE ATTACK—PHOTOGRAPHS
PH10117 616 (October 31, 1991) p25. "Massive Attack (from left): 3-D, Mushroom And Daddy G"
PH10118 718 (October 5, 1995) p32. "Nicolette, Stephen Lewinson, Daddy G (from left)" (Mazur, Kevin)
MASTER MUSICIANS OF JAJOUKA—ALBUMS
PH10119 637 (August 20, 1992) p52. "Apocalypse Across The Sky"
MASTER MUSICIANS OF JAJOUKA—PHOTOGRAPHS
PH10120 722 (November 30, 1995) p20. "[Master Musicians Of Jajouka]" (Robicheau, Paul)
MASTERS OF REALITY—ALBUMS
PH10121 652 (March 18, 1993) p40. "Sunrise On The Sufferbus"
MASTERSON, MARY STUART—PHOTOGRAPHS
PH10122 656 (May 13, 1993) p116. "Sex Is Sweet For Depp (left) And Masterson"
MASTRANTONIO, MARY ELIZABETH—PHOTOGRAPHS
PH10123 617 (November 14, 1991) p184. "Is Mastrantonio Wondering If Costner's Aim Is True?"
PH10124 630 (May 14, 1992) p114. "Dafoe (left) Suspects Rourke And Mastrantonio"
MASTRO, JAMES—PHOTOGRAPHS
PH10125 691 (September 22, 1994) pp[enc.19]. "[James Mastro]" (Wessel, Cathrine)
PH10126 691 (September 22, 1994) pp[enc.cover]. "James Mastro Of The Health And Happiness Show" (Wessel, Cathrine)
PH10127 691 (September 22, 1994) pp[enc.17]. "James Mastro Onstage" (Wessel, Cathrine)
PH10128 691 (September 22, 1994) pp[enc.cover]. "Mastro" (Wessel, Cathrine)
PH10129 691 (September 22, 1994) pp[enc.17]. "Mastro And Vinny DeNunzio At The Sutler, Nashville" (Wessel, Cathrine)
PH10130 691 (September 22, 1994) pp[enc.18]. "Mastro At Tower Records In Nashville" (Wessel, Cathrine)
MASUNAGA, ERIC—PHOTOGRAPHS
PH10131 693 (October 20, 1994) p30. "Cleo's Hanley, Stacy Jones, Manning; Builders Joan Wasser, Eric Masunaga" (Robicheau, Paul)
PH10132 693 (October 20, 1994) p49. "Kevin March, Dave Derby, Joan Wasser, Eric Masunaga (from left)" (Lass, Imke)
MATARAZZO, HEATHER—PHOTOGRAPHS
PH10133 743 (September 19, 1996) p90. "[Summer...]"
MATERIAL ISSUE—PHOTOGRAPHS
PH10134 712-713 (July 13, 1995) p25. "[Liz Phair & Material Issue]" (Natkin, Paul)
MATHIS, JOHNNY—PHOTOGRAPHS
PH10135 670 (November 25, 1993) p37. "It's Not For Me to Say: Mathis And Eitzel" (Pereira, Al)
MATHIS, SAMANTHA—PHOTOGRAPHS
PH10136 625 (March 5, 1992) p76. "Hoffman, Kavner And Mathis Turn Trauma Into Laughter"
PH10137 694 (November 3, 1994) p18. "[Eric Stoltz, Sandra Bullock, Samantha Mathis]"
PH10138 740 (August 8, 1996) p18. "Samantha Mathis (left) And Claire Danes At The MTV Movie Awards" (Kravitz, Jeff)
MATINEE (FILM)—PHOTOGRAPHS
PH10139 651 (March 4, 1993) p74. "John Goodman Directs Cathy Moriarty And Tacky Monster"
MATLOCK, GLEN—PHOTOGRAPHS
PH10140 734 (May 16, 1996) p17. "Matlock, Rotten, Jones And Cook Now" (Gruen, Bob)
PH10141 734 (May 16, 1996) p17. "The Pistols' Rotten, Glen Matlock, Steve Jones And Paul Cook In '76" (Gruen, Bob)
PH10142 736 (June 13, 1996) p52. "Pistols '96: Glen Matlock, Steve Jones, Paul Cook And Johnny Rotten (from left)" (Thomas, Justin)
MATTESON, MOLLIE—PHOTOGRAPHS
PH10143 693 (October 20, 1994) p84. "Matteson And Wuerthner In Absaroka-Bear Tooth Wilderness" (Wuerthner, George)
MATTHAU, WALTER—PHOTOGRAPHS
PH10144 674 (January 27, 1994) p48. "Acting Vehicles Include 'The Pelican Brief,' 'In The Name Of The Father,' 'What's Eating Gilbert Grape,' 'Shadowlands,' 'Naked,' And 'Grumpy Old Men'"
MATTHAU, WALTER—PHOTOGRAPHS—PORTRAITS
PH10145 748 (November 28, 1996) p143. "Matthau"
MATTHEWS, DAVE—ALBUMS
PH10146 696 (December 1, 1994) p144. "Under The Table And Dreaming"
PH10147 698-699 (December 29, 1994) p181. "Under The Table And Dreaming"
MATTHEWS, DAVE—ILLUSTRATIONS
PH10148 711 (June 29, 1995) p60. "Dave Matthews Band: Whaddya Say!" (Martin, Matthew)
MATTHEWS, DAVE—PHOTOGRAPHS
PH10149 698-699 (December 29, 1994) p47. "Dave Matthews Band" (Falls, John)
PH10150 718 (October 5, 1995) p32. "Dave Matthews Serenades The World's Gentlest Mosh Pit" (Brainard, George)
PH10151 743 (September 19, 1996) p20. "Dylan With Young Pal Matthews At The Zelt Festival (Zelt: 'tent')" (Erickson, Sam)
PH10152 743 (September 19, 1996) p34. "Summer's Young And Old" (Van Iperen, Neils)
PH10153 749 (December 12, 1996) p52. "[Dave Matthews Band]" (Maxwell, Robert Paul)
MATTHEWS, DAVE—PHOTOGRAPHS—PORTRAITS
PH10154 749 (December 12, 1996) p54. "[Dave Matthews]" (Maxwell, Robert Paul)
MATTHEWS, DONNA—PHOTOGRAPHS
PH10155 707 (May 4, 1995) p23. "Donna Matthews, Justine

Frischmann, Annie Holland And Justin Welch (from left)" (Camp, E. J.)
PH10156 707 (May 4, 1995) p23. "Matthews (left), Frischmann In Manchester, England, '93" (Hening, Lu)
MATTHEWS, ERIC—ALBUMS
PH10157 719 (October 19, 1995) p150. "It's Heavy In Here"
MATTHEWS, ERIC—PHOTOGRAPHS
PH10158 721 (November 16, 1995) p64. "[Eric Matthews]" (Winters, Dan)
MATTHEWS, ERIC—PHOTOGRAPHS—PORTRAITS
PH10159 729 (March 7, 1996) p20. "Matthews: A Classically Trained Trumpeter Turned Solo Indie Rocker" (Peterson, Charles)
MATURANA, MATILDE—PHOTOGRAPHS
PH10160 666 (September 30, 1993) p79. "Maturana: A Lesson In Pulling Together" (Irish, Len)
MAULTSBY, PORTIA—PHOTOGRAPHS—PORTRAITS
PH10161 639 (September 17, 1992) p84. "Portia Maultsby Says It Loud" (Counts, Wyatt)
MAURER, JOHN—PHOTOGRAPHS
PH10162 634-635 (July 9, 1992) p32. "Chris Reece, Mike Ness, John Maurer And Dennis Danell (from left)" (Cuffaro, Chris)
MAURO, NICOLE—PHOTOGRAPHS—PORTRAITS
PH10163 745 (October 17, 1996) p86. "'Gifted And Talented' Friends (from left): Nicole Mauro, Arthur Lewis And Alissa Heyman As They Appeared In The 1991 Middletown High School South Yearbook, Aquiline"
MAVERICK (FILM)—PHOTOGRAPHS
PH10164 684 (June 16, 1994) p115. "Now Playing"
MAVERICKS—PHOTOGRAPHS
PH10165 691 (September 22, 1994) p22. "[The Mavericks]" (Harris, Brad)
PH10166 707 (May 4, 1995) p19. "Maverick's Raul Malo (left) And Reynolds In L.A." (Soqui, Ted)
MAVERICKS—PHOTOGRAPHS—PORTRAITS
PH10167 682 (May 19, 1994) p74. "[Mavericks]" (Tucker, Mark)
MAX, PETER—PHOTOGRAPHS
PH10168 657 (May 27, 1993) p11. "Artist Peter Max (left) And Billy Joel" (Mazur, Kevin)
MAXIMUM REALITY—PHOTOGRAPHS
PH10169 743 (September 19, 1996) p45. "Maximum Reality Floors End Fest" (Mercer, Lance)
MAXWELL—PHOTOGRAPHS
PH10170 743 (September 19, 1996) p104. "[Maxwell]" (Johnson, Eric)
PH10171 750-751 (December 26, 1996) p46. "Maxwell"
MAXX—PHOTOGRAPHS
PH10172 730 (March 21, 1996) p89. "[Amnesia's Guitarist Maxx]" (Witkin, Christian)
MAY, BRIAN—ALBUMS
PH10173 657 (May 27, 1993) p50. "Back To The Light"
MAY, BRIAN—PHOTOGRAPHS
PH10174 650 (February 18, 1993) p11. "Slash (left) And May Play Dueling Guitars" (Mazur, Kevin)
MAY, BRIAN—PHOTOGRAPHS—PORTRAITS
PH10175 621 (January 9, 1992) p14. "Queen In The Mid-Seventies (from left): Deacon, Mercury, May And Taylor" (Rock, Mick)
MAYALL, JOHN—PHOTOGRAPHS
PH10176 655 (April 29, 1993) p34. "Clapton With John Mayall's Bluesbreakers At The Height Of God-mania in '66: Mayall, Hughie Flint, God And John McVie (from left)"
MAYFIELD, CURTIS—ALBUMS
PH10176a 649 (February 4, 1993) p69. "The Anthology 1961-1977"
PH10177 747 (November 14, 1996) p112. "New World Order"
PH10178 750-751 (December 26, 1996) p189. "People Get Ready!"
MAYFIELD, CURTIS—ILLUSTRATIONS
PH10179 668 (October 28, 1993) p5. "Curtis Mayfield" (Burke, Philip)
MAYFIELD, CURTIS—PHOTOGRAPHS
PH10180 668 (October 28, 1993) p62. "[Curtis Mayfield]" (Seliger, Mark)
PH10181 668 (October 28, 1993) p66. "The Impressions Circa '67: Mayfield, Fred Cash And Gooden"
PH10182 668 (October 28, 1993) p66. "Mayfield (seated) Meeting With Singer Oscar Brown Jr."
PH10183 680 (April 21, 1994) p33. "Curtis Mayfield, Toni Braxton" (Jackson, Gregory)
MAYFIELD, CURTIS—PHOTOGRAPHS—PORTRAITS
PH10184 668 (October 28, 1993) p63. "[Curtis Mayfield]" (Seliger, Mark)
PH10185 668 (October 28, 1993) p65. "The Impressions: Butler (top left) And Mayfield (bottom right)"
PH10186 Number not assigned.
MAYFIELD, PERCY—RECORDS
PH10187 649 (February 4, 1993) p66. "Percy Mayfield Live"
MAZAR, DEBI—PHOTOGRAPHS
PH10188 712-713 (July 13, 1995) p115. "Villians: Carrey's Riddler, Jones' Two-face With Sirens Barrymore And Mazar"
MAZUR, MANET—PHOTOGRAPHS
PH10189 749 (December 12, 1996) p19. "Rhapsody In Blues: Navarro And His Lady Friend, Monet Mazur" (Mazur, Kevin)
MAZZARD, CYRIL—PHOTOGRAPHS
PH10190 660-661 (July 8, 1993) p101. "Motherhead Bug (from left): Anthony Lee, Steven Ovenden, April Chung, Cyril Mazzard, Jez Aspinal, Tomoyo, And Dave Ouimet" (Leopardi, N.)
MAZZELLO, JOSEPH—PHOTOGRAPHS
PH10191 659 (June 24, 1993) p36. "Dern (with Joseph Mazzello And Sam Neill) Perks Up A Sick Dino" (Close, Murray)
PH10192 693 (October 20, 1994) p156. "Woman Warrior Streep (above, with Reilly and Bacon) Braves The Rapids To Save Son Mazzello And Husband Strathairn (left)"
MAZZOLA, JOEY—PHOTOGRAPHS
PH10193 706 (April 20, 1995) p36. "Motor City Five: Mazzola, Grover, Dombrowski, Tim And Mike Cross (from left)" (Halsband, Michael)
PH10194 710 (June 15, 1995) p49. "Mike Cross, Dombrowski, Charlie Grover, Joey Mazzola, Tim Cross (from left)" (Tavee, Tom)
MAZZY STAR—ALBUMS
PH10195 671 (December 9, 1993) p73. "So Tonight That I Might See"
MAZZY STAR—PHOTOGRAPHS—PORTRAITS
PH10196 693 (October 20, 1994) p33. "[Mazzy Star]" (Sebring, Steven)
PH10197 695 (November 17, 1994) p49. "Mazzy Star" (Sebring, Steven)
MC EIHT—ALBUMS
PH10198 690 (September 8, 1994) p32. "We Come Strapped"
MC FUSION—PHOTOGRAPHS
PH10199 682 (May 19, 1994) p32. "Nation's M. C. Fusion (center)" (Double, Steve)
MC REN—PHOTOGRAPHS
PH10200 634-635 (July 9, 1992) p17. "N.W.A. (clockwise from top left): MC Ren, Yella, Eazy-E And Dr. Dre" (Preston, Neal)
PH10201 639 (September 17, 1992) p19. "N.W.A. (from left): D.J. Yella, Dr. Dre, Eazy-E And M.C. Ren"
PH10202 666 (September 30, 1993) p42. "Serious Attitude: Ex-N.W.A. Members Ice Cube, Yella, Eazy-E, Dre And MC Ren" (Rosenberg, Howard)
MC SOLAAR—ALBUMS
PH10203 697 (December 15, 1994) p97. "Prose Combat"
MC5—ALBUMS
PH10204 645-646 (December 10, 1992) p174. "Back In The USA"

MC5—ILLUSTRATIONS
PH10205 632 (June 11, 1992) p11. "[MC5]" (Cronin, Brian)
MC5—PHOTOGRAPHS
PH10206 632 (June 11, 1992) p36. "MC5 (clockwise from top left): Thompson, Tyner, Kramer, Smith"
PH10207 708 (May 18, 1995) p30. "MC5: Michael Davis, Dennis Thompson, Kramer, Smith, Tyner (from left)"
MC5—PHOTOGRAPHS—PORTRAITS
PH10208 718 (October 5, 1995) p48. "Detroit's Legendary MC5, Victims Of 'The American Ruse'"
MCA—PHOTOGRAPHS
PH10209 631 (May 28, 1992) p40. "The Beastie Boys (from left): Adam Yauch, Mike Diamond And Adam Horovitz" (Camp, E. J.)
PH10210 631 (May 28, 1992) p9. "Skate-Master Tate, MCA, Ad-Rock, Anthony Kiedis, Henry Rollins (from left)" (Cohen, Lester)
PH10211 648 (January 21, 1993) p24. "MCA (left) And King Ad Rock Of The Beasties" (Mazur, Kevin)
PH10212 695 (November 17, 1994) p139. "Beastie Boys" (Rolston, Matthew)
PH10213 726 (January 25, 1996) p17. "Keepin',It Real: Beasties Ad-Rock (left) And MCA" (Papas, B. J.)
MCALLISTER, BEN—PHOTOGRAPHS
PH10214 652 (March 18, 1993) pp[enc.37]. "Ben McAllister" (Seliger, Mark)
MCANUFF, DES—PHOTOGRAPHS
PH10215 672-673 (December 23, 1993) p106. "A Chorus Line: 'Tommy' Director Des McAnuff, Townshend And Michael Cerveris, Who Plays Tommy (from left)" (Cunningham, Peter)
MCBAIN, JOHN—PHOTOGRAPHS
PH10216 667 (October 14, 1993) p40. "John Waterman, Brian Wood, John McBain, Ben Shepherd And Matt Cameron" (Hapke, Fran)
MCBAY, CLINT—PHOTOGRAPHS—PORTRAITS
PH10217 630 (May 14, 1992) p32. "Chainsaw Kittens (clockwise from top left): McBay, Meade, Preston, Bell And Metzger" (Mazur, Kevin)
MCBRIDE, CHRISTIAN—PHOTOGRAPHS—PORTRAITS
PH10218 630 (May 14, 1992) p90. "[Christian McBride]" (Carroll, Chris)
MCBRIDE, JIMMY—PHOTOGRAPHS—PORTRAITS
PH10219 747 (November 14, 1996) p36. "'Ironic Traffic Jam'"
MCBRIDE, TODD—PHOTOGRAPHS
PH10220 710 (June 15, 1995) p52. "At The Uptown: McBride, Veal, John Crist, Michael Gibson (from left)" (Clinch, Danny)
MCCABE, NICK—PHOTOGRAPHS
PH10221 660-661 (July 8, 1993) p96. "Verve (clockwise from top left): Ashcroft, Peter Salisbury, Simon Jones And McCabe" (Sharp, Ken)
MCCABE, ZIA—PHOTOGRAPHS
PH10222 721 (November 16, 1995) p78. "Peter Holmstrom, Courtney Taylor, Zia McCabe, Eric Hedford (from left): They're Exploding, Plastic And Inevitable, Andy Would Approve!" (Winters, Dan)
MCCAIN, GILLIAN—BOOKS
PH10223 737 (June 27, 1996) p55. "Please Kill Me"
MCCANN, BRIAN—PHOTOGRAPHS
PH10224 743 (September 19, 1996) p72. "Comedy Is A Great Passive-Aggressive Tool" (Seliger, Mark)
MCCARROLL, TONY—PHOTOGRAPHS
PH10225 691 (September 22, 1994) p37. "Arthurs, McCarroll, Liam Gallagher, McGuigan, Noel Gallagher (from left)"
MCCARROLL, TONY—PHOTOGRAPHS—PORTRAITS
PH10226 708 (May 18, 1995) p52. "From Left: McGuigan, McCarroll And 'Bonehead'" (Bailey, David)
MCCARRON, DOUG—PHOTOGRAPHS
PH10227 669 (November 11, 1993) p36. "Doug McCarron And His Union Came To The Aid Of The Striking Mexican Dry Wallers" (Reed, Dudley)
MCCARTHY, CAROLYN—PHOTOGRAPHS
PH10228 746 (October 31, 1996) p62. "Assault-Weapon Widow Carolyn McCarthy: Running For Congress Against The NRA"
MCCARTHY, JENNY—ILLUSTRATIONS
PH10229 742 (September 5, 1996) p16. "Trash" (Pendergrast, James T.)
MCCARTHY, JENNY—PHOTOGRAPHS
PH10230 738-739 (July 11, 1996) p34. "At Age 16, During Her High-School Hell Years"
PH10231 738-739 (July 11, 1996) pp[cover]. "The Girl With The Most Mustard: MTV's Jenny McCarthy" (Seliger, Mark)
PH10232 738-739 (July 11, 1996) p38. "In L.A. With Agent-Boyfriend Manzella" (Kravitz, Jeff)
PH10233 738-739 (July 11, 1996) p33. "[Jenny McCarthy]" (Seliger, Mark)
PH10234 738-739 (July 11, 1996) p34. "Playmate Of The Year, 1994"
PH10235 738-739 (July 11, 1996) p38. "With A 'Singled Out' Male"
PH10236 750-751 (December 26, 1996) p90. "Russ Meyer Flick? No, McCarthy (left) And Electra" (Rose, Lisa)
MCCARTHY, JENNY—PHOTOGRAPHS—PORTRAITS
PH10237 738-739 (July 11, 1996) p34. "At Age 5"
MCCARTHY, KEVIN—PHOTOGRAPHS
PH10238 669 (November 11, 1993) p80. "Fright Sights (from left): 'Body Snatchers' 1956, 1978, 1993"
MCCARTHY, STEPHEN—PHOTOGRAPHS
PH10239 660-661 (July 8, 1993) p101. "Gutterball: Johnny Hott, Bryan Harvey, Steve Wynn, Bob Rupe, Stephen McCarthy"
PH10240 663 (August 19, 1993) p15. "Rupe, Hott, Harvey, Wynn And McCarthy (from left)" (Callahan, Walter)
MCCARTHY, THOMAS—PHOTOGRAPHS
PH10241 704 (March 23, 1995) pp102-103. "Class of '95" (Tavee, Tom)
PH10242 704 (March 23, 1995) p102. "Onstage" (Tavee, Tom)
MCCARTNEY, FRASER—PHOTOGRAPHS
PH10243 715 (August 24, 1995) pp90-91. "On The Court In Thompkins Park" (Danelian, Stephen)
MCCARTNEY, LINDA—PHOTOGRAPHS
PH10244 672-673 (December 23, 1993) p37. "Above: Linda, Paul And Lang At Earth Day" (Preston, Neal)
PH10245 675 (February 10, 1994) p12. "Paul And Linda Backstage: Five Continents, 78 Shows, 2 Million Satisfied Fans" (Borris, Dan)
MCCARTNEY, PAUL—ALBUMS
PH10246 619-620 (December 12, 1991) p178. "Snovav CCCP"
PH10247 671 (December 9, 1993) p31. "Paul Is Live" (MacMillan, Iain)
PH10248 672-673 (December 23, 1993) pp153,156. "Paul Is Live"
MCCARTNEY, PAUL—ILLUSTRATIONS
PH10249 650 (February 18, 1993) p56. "Is This The Summer Of Love?" (Guy, Edmund)
MCCARTNEY, PAUL—ILLUSTRATIONS—PORTRAITS
PH10250 641 (October 15, 1992) p61. "[Paul McCartney]" (Nelson, Bill)
MCCARTNEY, PAUL—PHOTOGRAPHS
PH10251 619-620 (December 12, 1991) p60. "Paul McCartney At His Classical Digs" (Modell, David)
PH10252 619-620 (December 12, 1991) p71. "Paul McCartney Gets 'Unplugged'"
PH10253 621 (January 9, 1992) p17. "Mercury Joins Paul McCartney And Other Stars In The Live Aid Finale, 1985" (Preston, Neal)
PH10254 633 (June 25, 1992) p12. "Murphy With McCartney And Producer Trenten Gumbs (from left)"
PH10255 640 (October 1, 1992) p9. "McCartney (above)..." (Meyers, Tim)
PH10256 643 (November 12, 1992) p70. "Michael Cooper (left) Photographed The Cover Of 'Sgt. Pepper'" (Cooper, Michael)

PH10257 649 (February 4, 1993) p9. "McCartney Onstage At The MTV Taping" (Mazur, Kevin)
PH10258 653 (April 1, 1993) p13. "Paul McCartney" (Mazur, Kevin)
PH10259 657 (May 27, 1993) p9. "Lang And McCartney Onstage" (Preston, Neal)
PH10260 658 (June 10, 1993) p34. "McCartney Does Vegas" (Winter, Ken)
PH10261 672-673 (December 23, 1993) p37. "Above: Linda, Paul And Lang At Earth Day" (Preston, Neal)
PH10262 675 (February 10, 1994) p12. "Paul And Linda Backstage: Five Continents, 78 Shows, 2 Million Satisfied Fans" (Borris, Dan)
PH10263 675 (February 10, 1994) p11. "[Paul McCartney]" (Borris, Dan)
PH10264 677 (March 10, 1994) p27. "Imagine: Paul McCartney And Yoko Ono" (Mazur, Kevin)
PH10265 722 (November 30, 1995) p26. "Ringo Starr, John Lennon, Paul McCartney And George Harrison During The Filming Of 'Help!' In 1965: 'So Much Younger Than Today'" (Kindahl, Chris)
PH10266 726 (January 25, 1996) p46. "Starr, McCartney, Harrison, Lennon"
PH10267 744 (October 3, 1996) p20. "Young At Heart, McCartney, Right, Accompanies Ginsberg In London" (McCartney, Linda)

MCCARTNEY, PAUL—PHOTOGRAPHS—PORTRAITS
PH10268 643 (November 12, 1992) p196. "Paul McCartney" (Watson, Albert)
PH10269 720 (November 2, 1995) p49. "Stu Sutcliffe & Paul McCartney" (Kirchherr, Astrid)

MCCARTY, JIM—PHOTOGRAPHS
PH10270 623 (February 6, 1992) p51. "The Yardbirds, Circa 1964 (from left): Chris Dreja, Keith Reif, Paul Samwell-Smith, Eric Clapton And Jim McCarty"

MCCARTY, JIM—PHOTOGRAPHS—PORTRAITS
PH10271 655 (April 29, 1993) p34. "Slowhand (at bottom left) With The Yardbirds: Chris Dreja, Jim McCarty, Paul Samwell-Smith And Keith Relf (clockwise from top left)"

MCCARY, MICHAEL—PHOTOGRAPHS
PH10272 625 (March 5, 1992) p21. "Michael McCary, Wanya Morris, Shawn Stockman And Nate Morris (clockwise from top left)" (Graham, Jim)
PH10273 709 (June 1, 1995) p23. "Boyz II Men: Shawn Stockman, Michael McCary, Wanya Morris, Nate Morris" (Granitz, Steve)

MCCAUGHEY, SCOTT—PHOTOGRAPHS
PH10274 677 (March 10, 1994) p55. "Scott McCaughey Lights Up The Stockroom At Popllama" (Smale, Brian)
PH10275 714 (August 10, 1995) p16. "The New Math: McCaughey, Buck, Tweedy And Greenberg (from left)" (Perez, Marty)
PH10276 717 (September 21, 1995) p20. "Three Beatle Maniacs: Lord, Buck And McCaughey (from left)" (Clinch, Danny)

MCCLAFFERTY, SEAN—PHOTOGRAPHS
PH10277 666 (September 30, 1993) p90. "Hunt (third from left, bottom row) With Delta Lambda Phi Brothers (clockwise from top right): Peter Colohan, Sean McClafferty, Rob Corwin, Price, Stephen Smith And Oligmueller"

MCCLAIN, MIGHTY SAM—ALBUMS
PH10278 667 (October 14, 1993) p123. "Give It Up To Love"

MCCLOUD, SCOTT—PHOTOGRAPHS
PH10279 721 (November 16, 1995) p75. "Johnny Temple, Scott McCloud, Alexis Fleisig And Eli Janney (from left) Enjoy An All-American Snack" (Exum)

MCCLURE, ANDY—PHOTOGRAPHS
PH10280 709 (June 1, 1995) p27. "PC Free: Stewart, Wener, McClure, Osman (from left)" (Westenberg, Kevin)

MCCLURE, SUZETTE—PHOTOGRAPHS—PORTRAITS
PH10281 715 (August 24, 1995) p58. "Suzette McClure, December '94"

MCCLUSKY, JEFF—PHOTOGRAPHS
PH10282 741 (August 22, 1996) p34. "Jeff McClusky"

MCCOLLUM, RICK—PHOTOGRAPHS
PH10283 695 (November 17, 1994) p78. "Afghan Whigs" (Lixenberg, Dana)

MCCOLLUM, RICK—PHOTOGRAPHS—PORTRAITS
PH10284 671 (December 9, 1993) p21. "The Whig Club: Rick McCollum, Greg Dulli, Steve Earle And John Curley" (Broad, Julian)

MCCOMBS, DOUG—PHOTOGRAPHS
PH10285 658 (June 10, 1993) p29. "Wink O'Bannon, Janet Beveridge Bean, Rick Rizzo And Doug McCombs (from left)" (Guip, Andy)

MCCONAUGHEY, MATTHEW—ILLUSTRATIONS
PH10286 740 (August 8, 1996) p67. "Summer Gets Serious" (Brodner, Steve)
PH10287 744 (October 3, 1996) p16. "Credibility" (Pendergrast, James T.)

MCCONAUGHEY, MATTHEW—PHOTOGRAPHS
PH10288 738-739 (July 11, 1996) p98. "Sayles (left) Directs McConaughey"
PH10289 741 (August 22, 1996) pp44-45. "[Matthew McConaughey]" (Sirota, Peggy)
PH10290 741 (August 22, 1996) p48. "McConaughey Onscreen"
PH10291 741 (August 22, 1996) p48. "McConaughey With His Mother, Kay, At The Premiere Of 'A Time To Kill'" (Granitz, Steve)
PH10292 741 (August 22, 1996) p46. "The Star Of 'A Time To Kill' Is A Texas Rebel Who Can Handle Being The Next Big Thing" (Sirota, Peggy)
PH10293 743 (September 19, 1996) p90. "[Summer...]"
PH10294 748 (November 28, 1996) p25. "Crow Flirting With Matthew McConaughey" (Kravitz, Jeff)

MCCONNELL, PAGE—PHOTOGRAPHS
PH10295 631 (May 28, 1992) p16. "Phish (from left): Trey Anastasio, Mike Gordon, Page McConnell, Jon Fishman" (Halsband, Michael)

MCCORMACK, LEIGH—PHOTOGRAPHS
PH10296 658 (June 10, 1993) p78. "Fifties Kid McCormack Finds Magic At The Movies"

MCCREADY, MIKE—PHOTOGRAPHS
PH10297 616 (October 31, 1991) p15. "Pearl Jam (from left): Mike McCready, David Abbruzzese, Eddie Vedder, Jeff Ament And Stone Gossard" (Cuffaro, Chris)
PH10298 634-635 (July 9, 1992) p13. "Pearl Jam's Mike McCready, Dave Abbruzzese, Eddie Vedder, Gossard And Jeff Ament (from left)" (Mercer, Lance)
PH10299 639 (September 17, 1992) p60. "Eddie Vedder, Mike McCready, Jeff Ament And Stone Gossard (from left) Of Pearl Jam" (Blakesberg, Jay)
PH10300 650 (February 18, 1993) p11. "Richards Flanked By Young-uns Mike McCready (left) And Vedder" (Natkin, Paul)
PH10301 659 (June 24, 1993) p15. "McCready, Eitzel, Ament, AMC's Vudi And Dan Pearson (from left)" (Blakesberg, Jay)
PH10302 665 (September 16, 1993) p31. "[Elvis Costello, Jeff Ament, Mike McCready]" (Mercer, Lance)
PH10303 668 (October 28, 1993) p60. "Ament, Vedder And McCready Write A Set List" (Seliger, Mark)
PH10304 668 (October 28, 1993) p51. "The Sun Shines On The Five Musketeers: Jeff Ament, Eddie Vedder (We're Not Kidding), Dave Abbruzzese, Stone Gossard And Mike McCready (from left)" (Seliger, Mark)
PH10305 672-673 (December 23, 1993) p69. "Us 'Vs.' The World: Gossard, Mike McCready, Dave Abbruzzese, Vedder, Jeff Ament (from left)" (Seliger, Mark)
PH10306 681 (May 5, 1994) p12. "Mike McCready: Escape From Pensacola" (Mercer, Lance)
PH10307 697 (December 15, 1994) p17. "Clowin' Around: Gacy Fans McCready (left) And Staley" (Mercer, Lance)

PH10308 702 (February 23, 1995) p26. "Pirate Music: McCready, Vedder, Ament, Irons And Stone Gossard (from left)" (Mercer, Lance)
PH10309 711 (June 29, 1995) p12. "Barrett Martin, Peter Buck And Mike McCready (from left)" (Mercer, Lance)
PH10310 714 (August 10, 1995) p20. "Mad Season: Guitarist Mike McCready" (Mazur, Kevin)
PH10311 726 (January 25, 1996) p17. "Mike McCready, Jeff Ament, Harper, Eddie Vedder, Jack Irons And Stone Gossard (from left)"
PH10312 727 (February 8, 1996) p17. "Mike McReady, Jeff Ament And Eddie Vedder (from left) Dropped Plans For A Live Pearl Jam Album But Allowed Radio Stations To Distribute Their '95 Concert Recordings For Free" (Ge
PH10313 732 (April 18, 1996) p20. "'This Is For Rolling Stone!' Alice In Chains' Layne Staley (left) And Pearl Jam's Mike McCready Express Themselves" (Mazur, Kevin)
PH10314 735 (May 30, 1996) p27. "Stupid Pet Tricks"
MCCREADY, MIKE—PHOTOGRAPHS—PORTRAITS
PH10315 704 (March 23, 1995) p33. "Barrett Martin, Layne Staley, Baker Saunder And Mike McCready (from left)" (Mercer, Lance)
MCCULLOCH, BRUCE—PHOTOGRAPHS—PORTRAITS
PH10316 733 (May 2, 1996) p62. "Kids Foley, McKinney, McCulloch, McDonald And Thompson"
MCDONALD, JEFF—PHOTOGRAPHS
PH10317 685 (June 30, 1994) p41. "Gimme A Head With Hair, Long Beautiful Hair: McDonald (left), Simmons"
MCDONALD, KEVIN—PHOTOGRAPHS—PORTRAITS
PH10318 733 (May 2, 1996) p62. "Kids Foley, McKinney, McCulloch, McDonald And Thompson"
MCDONALD, MICHAEL—PHOTOGRAPHS
PH10319 637 (August 20, 1992) p11. "Rock And Soul (from left): Boz Scaggs, Walter Becker, Donald Fagen, Michael McDonald, Phoebe Snow And Chuck Jackson" (Hamilton, James)
MCDONALD, ROY—PHOTOGRAPHS
PH10320 735 (May 30, 1996) p13. "Muffs Roy McDonald And Kim Shattuck, Sean Ono Lennon, Muff Ronnie Barnett, Sideman Bill Bartell, And Eric Erlandson" (Phalen, Tom)
MCDONNELL, MARY—ILLUSTRATIONS
PH10321 648 (January 21, 1993) p54. "A Few Good Women" (Witte, Michael)
MCDONNELL, MARY—PHOTOGRAPHS
PH10322 648 (January 21, 1993) p55. "Woodard And McDonnell Fight Dependency"
MCDORMAND, FRANCES—PHOTOGRAPHS
PH10323 730 (March 21, 1996) p104. "Frances McDormand On Duty"
PH10324 750-751 (December 26, 1996) p206. "Frances McDormand In 'Fargo'"
MCELHONE, NATASCHA—PHOTOGRAPHS
PH10325 744 (October 3, 1996) p78. "Hopkins As Picasso With Mistress McElhone"
MCENTIRE, JOHN—PHOTOGRAPHS
PH10326 721 (November 16, 1995) p67. "The Sea And Cake: Art-Pop Aficionados Sam Prekop, John McEntire, Archer Prewitt And Eric Claridge (middle row, from left)" (Guip, Amy)
MCFERRIN, BOBBY—ALBUMS
PH10327 625 (March 5, 1992) p68. "Play"
MCGARRY, JIM—PHOTOGRAPHS—PORTRAITS
PH10328 680 (April 21, 1994) p38. "John McGarry In '78, When Tip O'Neill Tapped Him For The FEC"
MCGATHY, BILL—PHOTOGRAPHS
PH10329 741 (August 22, 1996) p34. "Bill McGathy With Black Crowes' Chris Robinson"
MCGAW, PATRICK—PHOTOGRAPHS
PH10330 652 (March 18, 1993) p47. "Patrick McGaw, Joseph Lindsey And Steve Parlavecchio (from left) Of 'Amongst Friends'" (Michaelson, Randall)
PH10331 662 (August 5, 1993) p73. "Guy Talk From Parlavecchio, McGaw And Lambson"
PH10332 704 (March 23, 1995) p128. "Dicaprio, With McGaw (left), Takes A Dive"
MCGEE, SCHIAVONE—PHOTOGRAPHS
PH10333 730 (March 21, 1996) p55. "The Boys In The Bus: Schiavone McGee, David Triano, Eric Lawson, Chris Leitch, Karl Vonklein, David Peterson And Mike Boyd (clockwise from left)" (Clinch, Danny)
PH10334 730 (March 21, 1996) p56. "Frontman McGee Fires Up The UVA Crowd" (Clinch, Danny)
PH10335 730 (March 21, 1996) p56. "McGee, Peterson, Triano And Lawson (from left) Rehearse In The Bus" (Clinch, Danny)
MCGHEE, BROWNIE—PHOTOGRAPHS
PH10336 731 (April 4, 1996) p37. "[Brownie McGhee]"
MCGILLIS, TRISHA—PHOTOGRAPHS
PH10337 722 (November 30, 1995) pp[enc.6]. "Jenny Cool (left) And Trisha" (McLeod, William Mercer)
MCGINLEY, RAYMOND—PHOTOGRAPHS
PH10338 630 (May 14, 1992) p50. "Guitarist Norman Blake, Bassist Gerry Love, Drummer Brendan O'Hare And Guitarist Raymond McGinley (from left)" (Broad, Julian)
PH10339 701 (February 9, 1995) p33. "Join The Club: Norman Blake, Raymond McGinley, Paul Quinn And Gerard Love (clockwise from top left)" (Dyer, Alison)
MCGLONE, MICHAEL—PHOTOGRAPHS
PH10340 741 (August 22, 1996) p105. "Burns, Bahns, Diaz, Aniston, McGlone"
MCGLONE, MIKE—PHOTOGRAPHS
PH10341 715 (August 24, 1995) p110. "Mulcahy, Burns, Bahns And McGlone (from left)"
MCGOVERN, GEORGE—ILLUSTRATIONS
PH10342 645-646 (December 10, 1992) p148. "George McGovern, 1972"
MCGOWAN, JOHNNY—PHOTOGRAPHS
PH10343 743 (September 19, 1996) p38. "Vocalist 'Lana' LeFleur And Producer 'Jay Ski' McGowan"
MCGOWAN, ROSE—PHOTOGRAPHS
PH10344 721 (November 16, 1995) p117. "Duval, McGowan, Schaech (from left)"
MCGRAW, TIM—ALBUMS
PH10345 685 (June 30, 1994) p88. "Not A Moment Too Soon"
MCGREGOR, EWAN—ILLUSTRATIONS
PH10346 740 (August 8, 1996) p67. "Summer Gets Serious" (Brodner, Steve)
MCGREGOR, EWAN—PHOTOGRAPHS
PH10347 702 (February 23, 1995) p81. "Fox, McGregor And Eccleston Find The Body"
PH10348 741 (August 22, 1996) p80. "[Ewan McGregor]" (Agius, Lorenzo)
MCGUIGAN, PAUL—PHOTOGRAPHS
PH10349 691 (September 22, 1994) p37. "Arthurs, McCarroll, Liam Gallagher, McGuigan, Noel Gallagher (from left)"
PH10350 718 (October 5, 1995) p34. "White, Arthurs, Liam Gallagher, Noel Gallagher, McGuigan (from left)" (Jones, Michael Spenser)
PH10351 733 (May 2, 1996) p34. "McGuigan, White And Noel (from left)" (Goldberg, Nathaniel)
MCGUIGAN, PAUL—PHOTOGRAPHS—PORTRAITS
PH10352 708 (May 18, 1995) p52. "From Left: McGuigan, McCarroll And 'Bonehead'" (Bailey, David)
MCGUINN, ROGER—ALBUMS
PH10353 619-620 (December 12, 1991) p165. "Back From Rio"
MCGUINN, ROGER—PHOTOGRAPHS
PH10354 643 (November 12, 1992) p179. "Roger McGuinn" (Markus, Kurt)
PH10355 644 (November 26, 1992) p17. "The Great Garden Party: Dylan Center Stage For The Grand Finale" (Mazur, Kevin)
PH10356 644 (November 26, 1992) p15. "Kantner, Darby Gould, Jack Casady, Tim Gorman, Prairie Prince, Papa John Creach,

McGuinn And Slick Aguilar (from left)" (Mazur, Kevin)
PH10357 685 (June 30, 1994) p40. "Velvet's Paul Chastain, Jeffrey Borchardt And Menck With McGuinn (from left)"
MCKAGAN, DUFF—ILLUSTRATIONS
PH10358 672-673 (December 23, 1993) p10. "Duff!" (Pendergrast, James T.)
MCKAGAN, DUFF—PHOTOGRAPHS
PH10359 672-673 (December 23, 1993) p70. "Duff McKagan Bears All On 'Believe In Me'" (Cuffaro, Chris)
PH10360 721 (November 16, 1995) p26. "Momentary Hipster McKagan With Jones And Pop (from left)" (Kravitz, Jeff)
PH10361 731 (April 4, 1996) p18. "Jones (left) And McKagan In Seattle" (Doughty, Curt)
MCKAGAN, DUFF—PHOTOGRAPHS—PORTRAITS
PH10362 669 (November 11, 1993) p16. "'It's My Heart And Soul,' Says McKagan Of His First Solo Album, 'Believe In Me'" (Cuffaro, Chris)
MCKEAN, MICHAEL—PHOTOGRAPHS
PH10363 662 (August 5, 1993) p33. "Chris Guest, Harry Shearer, Michael McKean, With Carpenter" (Cohen, Lester)
MCKEE, MARIA—ALBUMS
PH10364 666 (September 30, 1993) p106. "You Gotta Sin To Get Saved"
MCKEE, MARIA—PHOTOGRAPHS
PH10365 636 (August 6, 1992) p11. "Michael Penn, Maria McKee And Robbie Robertson (from left) At The Whiskey" (Cavolina, Robbie)
PH10366 660-661 (July 8, 1993) p33. "Almost Lone Justice: Marvin Etzioni, McKee And Don Heffington" (Cohen, Lester)
PH10367 666 (September 30, 1993) p27. "Tom Petty, Along With Maria McKee And Others, Raised Some Big Money For A Worthy Cause" (Matheu, Robert)
MCKEEGAN, MICHAEL—PHOTOGRAPHS—PORTRAITS
PH10368 654 (April 15, 1993) p21. "In Need Of Therapy?: Fyfe Ewing, Michael McKeegan And Andy Cairns (from left)" (Gullick, Steve)
MCKEEHAN, TOBY—PHOTOGRAPHS
PH10369 744 (October 3, 1996) p24. "DC Talk Singer Toby McKeehan (left) And The Trio's Backing Guitarist" (Palmer, Robert)
MCKELLAN, IAN—PHOTOGRAPHS
PH10370 726 (January 25, 1996) p64. "Richard III"
MCKENNA, GREG—PHOTOGRAPHS
PH10371 690 (September 8, 1994) p42. "Cleo's Hanley, McKenna And Scott Riebling (from left)" (Capak, R. J.)
PH10372 710 (June 15, 1995) p39. "Eisenstein, Scott Riebling, Hanley, Stacy Jones, Greg McKenna (from left)" (McDonough, Patricia)
MCKERNAN, RON—PHOTOGRAPHS
PH10373 616 (October 31, 1991) p40. "Bill Kreutzmann, Ron "Pigpen" McKernan, Bob Weir, Garcia And Phil Lesh (clockwise from top left) In 1966" (Greene, Herb)
PH10374 664 (September 2, 1993) p46. "The Dead At Rest in 1966: Phil Lesh, Bill Kreutzman, Ron 'Pigpen' McKernan, Bob Weir And Jerry Garcia (clockwise from left)" (Greene, Herb)
PH10375 676 (February 24, 1994) p46. "The Early Grateful Dead (clockwise from left): Jerry Garcia, Bill Kreutzmann, Ron 'Pigpen' McKernan, Bob Weir, Percussionist Mickey Hart And Phil Lesh" (Marshall, Jim)
PH10376 717 (September 21, 1995) p52. "Before The Dead, They Were The Warlocks" (Greene, Herbi)
PH10377 717 (September 21, 1995) p71. "A Couple Of Good-Time Pirates: Garcia (left) With Pigpen In 1967" (Marshall, Jim)
PH10378 717 (September 21, 1995) p54. "The Dead In '66 At The Crossroads, the Corner Of Haight And Ashbury: Garcia, Pigpen, Lesh, Weir, Kreutzmann (from left)" (Greene, Herbi)
PH10379 717 (September 21, 1995) p65. "The Dead In Front Of Their Ashbury St. House, 1967: Jerry Garcia, Ron 'Pigpen' McKernan, Bob Weir, Phil Lesh, Co-Managers Danny Rifkin And Rock Scully, And Bill Kreutzmann..."
PH10380 717 (September 21, 1995) p48. "Janis Joplin And Ron 'Pigpen' McKernan At The Northern California Folk Rock, In San Jose, Calif., 1968" (Marshall, Jim)
PH10381 717 (September 21, 1995) p67. "Jerry Garcia, Phil Lesh, Bill Kreutzmann, Bob Weir And Ron 'Pigpen' McKernan (clockwise from bottom right) Huddled In San Francisco's Golden Gate Park, 1967" (Marshall, Jim)
PH10382 717 (September 21, 1995) p66. "Keyboardist Ron 'Pigpen' McKernan Takes His Hog For A Spin On Ashbury Street, 1967" (Wolman, Baron)
PH10383 717 (September 21, 1995) p73. "marrying Acid-Damaged Art Music And The Funky Snort Of Live Rock & Roll: The Dead As A Lysergic-Dance Band In 1969 With Tom Constanten, Weir, Kreutzmann, Pigpen, Lesh, Hart..."
PH10384 717 (September 21, 1995) p69. "The Original Quintet At Home At 710 Ashbury St., In 1966: Phil Lesh, Bob Weir, Bill Kreutzmann, Ron 'Pigpen' McKernan And Jerry Garcia (from left)" (Anthony, Gene)
MCKINION, MICKEY—PHOTOGRAPHS
PH10385 684 (June 16, 1994) p61. "James Dixon (center) With Teammates Shane Spry And Mickey McKinion" (Borris, Dan)
MCKINNEY, CYNTHIA—PHOTOGRAPHS
PH10386 682 (May 19, 1994) p43. "Reps. Cynthia McKinney, D-Ga., Carrie Meek, D-Fla., And Eva Clayton, D-N.C. (from left), Are Among The New Black Congresswomen..." (Borris, Dan)
MCKINNEY, CYNTHIA—PHOTOGRAPHS—PORTRAITS
PH10387 642 (October 29, 1992) p49. "[Cynthia McKinney]"
MCKINNEY, MARK—PHOTOGRAPHS—PORTRAITS
PH10388 733 (May 2, 1996) p62. "Kids Foley, McKinney, McCulloch, McDonald And Thompson"
MCKNIGHT, BRIAN—ALBUMS
PH10389 717 (September 21, 1995) p83. "I Remember You"
MCLACHLAN, SARAH—ALBUMS
PH10390 684 (June 16, 1994) p109. "Fumbling Towards Ecstasy"
PH10391 708 (May 18, 1995) p92. "The Freedom Sessions"
MCLACHLAN, SARAH—PHOTOGRAPHS
PH10392 707 (May 4, 1995) p20. "[Sarah McLachlan & Paula Cole]" (Olson, Sheryl)
PH10393 746 (October 31, 1996) p18. "Sisters Are Doin' It For Themselves: McLachlan (left) And Harris At Lilith Fair" (Nemchin, Tracy)
MCLACHLAN, SARAH—PHOTOGRAPHS—PORTRAITS
PH10394 623 (February 6, 1992) p32. "[Sarah McLachlan]" (Moss, Wallace)
MCLAGAN, IAN—PHOTOGRAPHS
PH10395 653 (April 1, 1993) p11. "Kenny Jones, Stewart, Wyman, Wood And Ian McLagan" (Hutchson, Mick)
MCLAREN, MALCOLM—ALBUMS
PH10396 708 (May 18, 1995) p92. "Paris"
MCLEAN, JILL—PHOTOGRAPHS
PH10397 677 (March 10, 1994) p57. "Left: Twin Tone's McLean And Jesperson" (Smale, Brian)
MCLENNAN, G. W.—ALBUMS
PH10398 619-620 (December 12, 1991) pp187,189. "Watershed"
MCLENNAN, GRANT—ILLUSTRATIONS
PH10399 702 (February 23, 1995) p76. "Grant McLennan" (Greve, Margie)
MCMAHON, KEVIN—PHOTOGRAPHS
PH10400 714 (August 10, 1995) p15. "Prick Singer Kevin McMahon (left) And Reznor At Tipitina's" (Smith, Sean C.)
MCMURTRY, JAMES—ALBUMS
PH10401 639 (September 17, 1992) p94. "Candyland"
PH10402 716 (September 7, 1995) p73. "Where'd You Hide The Body"
MCNALLY, DENNIS—PHOTOGRAPHS
PH10403 745 (October 17, 1996) p123. "[Dennis McNally]"
MCNAUGHT, MARK—PHOTOGRAPHS
PH10404 706 (April 20, 1995) pp[enc.3]. "Mark McNaught With Daughter Chanel At The Newport Beach, Calif., Pier" (Seliger,

Mark)
MCNAUGHTON, JOHN—PHOTOGRAPHS
PH10405 630 (May 14, 1992) p73. "[John McNaughton]" (Mahurin, Matt)
MCNEIL, LEGS—BOOKS
PH10406 737 (June 27, 1996) p55. "Please Kill Me"
MCNEILLY, MAC—PHOTOGRAPHS
PH10407 653 (April 1, 1993) p20. "The Jesus Lizard (clockwise from top left): McNeilly, Yow, Denison And Sims" (Ewolf)
PH10408 714 (August 10, 1995) p48. "David Sims, Mac McNeilly, David Yow, Duane Denison, From Left" (Seliger, Mark)
PH10409 736 (June 13, 1996) p20. "Jockey Lavern Hostetler Has A Lot To Discuss With Jesus Lizard Members David Sims, David Yow, Mac McNeilly And Duane Denison (from left)" (Gilson, Matthew)
MCVIE, JOHN—PHOTOGRAPHS
PH10410 655 (April 29, 1993) p34. "Clapton With John Mayall's Bluesbreakers At The Height Of God-mania in '66: Mayall, Hughie Flint, God And John McVie (from left)"
PH10411 670 (November 25, 1993) pp78-79. "[Fleetwood Mac]" (Seliger, Mark)
PH10412 720 (November 2, 1995) p49. "Mick Fleetwood & John McVie" (Seliger, Mark)
MCVIE, JOHN—PHOTOGRAPHS—PORTRAITS
PH10413 643 (November 12, 1992) p117. "Mick Fleetwood & John McVie" (Seliger, Mark)
ME PHI ME—ALBUMS
PH10414 645-646 (December 10, 1992) p174. "One"
ME PHI ME—PHOTOGRAPHS—PORTRAITS
PH10415 636 (August 6, 1992) p24. "[Me Phi Me]" (Corio, David)
MEADE, TODD—PHOTOGRAPHS—PORTRAITS
PH10416 630 (May 14, 1992) p32. "Chainsaw Kittens (clockwise from top left): McBay, Meade, Preston, Bell And Metzger" (Mazur, Kevin)
MEANEY, COLM—PHOTOGRAPHS
PH10417 671 (December 9, 1993) p78. "Daddy's Girl: Kellegher With Meaney"
MEAT BEAT MANIFESTO—ALBUMS
PH10418 744 (October 3, 1996) p74. "Subliminal Sandwich"
MEAT LOAF—ALBUMS
PH10419 668 (October 28, 1993) p83. "Bat Out Of Hell II"
MEAT LOAF—PHOTOGRAPHS
PH10420 670 (November 25, 1993) p15. "[Meat Loaf]" (Rosenberg, Merlyn)
PH10421 670 (November 25, 1993) p16. "With Singer Karla De Vito On Tour During 'Bat I'" (Putland, Michael)
PH10422 672-673 (December 23, 1993) p69. "It's Not Over Till The Fat Man Stops Singing" (Mazur, Kevin)
PH10423 674 (January 27, 1994) p44. "The Meat Man Shares His Divine Experiences"
PH10424 678 (March 24, 1994) p22. "Hot And Heavy: Meat Loaf Delivers Live" (Mazur, Kevin)
PH10425 704 (March 23, 1995) p25. "Bowie (left) Greets Art Lover Meat Loaf" (Bentham, John)
PH10426 733 (May 2, 1996) p24. "Artists Challenging The Record Clubs Include Meat Loaf" (Blakesberg, Jay)
MEAT LOAF—PHOTOGRAPHS—PORTRAITS
PH10427 698-699 (December 29, 1994) p36. "Meat Loaf's "Back Into Hell" Tour: No Sweat" (Smith, Brian)
MEAT PUPPETS
PH10428 654 (April 15, 1993) p24. "Meat Me In Court: The Puppets"
MEAT PUPPETS—ALBUMS
PH10429 683 (June 2, 1994) p69. "Too High To Die"
PH10430 720 (November 2, 1995) p68. "No Joke!"
MEAT PUPPETS—PHOTOGRAPHS
PH10431 682 (May 19, 1994) p21. "Puppet Masters: Curt And Cris Kirkwood And Derrick Bostrom (from left)" (Halsband, Michael)
PH10432 695 (November 17, 1994) p145. "Meat Puppets" (Seliger, Mark)
PH10433 710 (June 15, 1995) p48. "Hey, Mow! Cris And Curt Kirkwood And Derrick Bostrom (from left)" (Gipe, Jon)
MECCA NORMAL—ALBUMS
PH10434 706 (April 20, 1995) p73. "Sitting On Snaps"
MECCA NORMAL—PHOTOGRAPHS—PORTRAITS
PH10435 660-661 (July 8, 1993) p95. "Mecca Normal: David Lester, Jean Smith" (Karpa, Robert)
MEDESKI MARTIN AND WOOD—ALBUMS
PH10436 748 (November 28, 1996) p130. "Shack-Man"
MEDIUM COOL—ALBUMS
PH10437 618 (November 28, 1991) p98. "Imagination"
MEEK, CARRIE—PHOTOGRAPHS
PH10438 682 (May 19, 1994) p43. "Reps. Cynthia McKinney, D-Ga., Carrie Meek, D-Fla., And Eva Clayton, D-N.C. (from left), Are Among The New Black Congresswomen..." (Borris, Dan)
MEETING VENUS (FILM)—PHOTOGRAPHS
PH10439 618 (November 28, 1991) p104. "Diva Glenn Close Enjoys A Nonfatal Attraction"
MEGADETH—ALBUMS
PH10440 640 (October 1, 1992) p67. "Countdown To Extinction"
PH10441 697 (December 15, 1994) p120. "Youthanasia"
MEHTA, ZUBIN—PHOTOGRAPHS
PH10442 674 (January 27, 1994) p13. "Conducting The L.A. Philharmonic With Zubin Mehta (above)" (Axelrod, Joel)
MEIER, BARBARA—PHOTOGRAPHS
PH10443 740 (August 8, 1996) p39. "Maui, Hawaii, January 1993: Meier And Garcia"
MEISEL, STEVEN—PHOTOGRAPHS
PH10444 615 (October 17, 1991) p66. "Steven Meisel And Herb Ritts, New York City, 1990" (Pigozzi, Jean)
PH10445 643 (November 12, 1992) p240. "Shooting Stars: Madonna And Steven Meisel At Work On Her New Book, 'Sex'" (Lew, Darren)
PH10446 644 (November 26, 1992) p13. "Madonna Risks Overexposure With Photographer Steven Meisel" (Mazur, Kevin)
PH10447 645-646 (December 10, 1992) p91. "Madonna And Photog Steven Meisel Do 'Sex'" (Mazur, Kevin)
MEKONS—ALBUMS
PH10448 675 (February 10, 1994) p44. "I Love Mekons"
PH10449 729 (March 7, 1996) p50. "Pussy, King Of The Pirates"
MEKONS—PHOTOGRAPHS
PH10450 667 (October 14, 1993) p37. "Mekons Sarah Corina (left) And Jon Langford" (Mazur, Kevin)
PH10451 694 (November 3, 1994) p22. "Mekons Singer Sally Timms, Gibby Haynes And Jon Langford Belt It Out Onstage" (Crawford, Michael)
PH10452 736 (June 13, 1996) p19. "Where's Sammy And Frank?" (Herdon, David)
MELLE MEL—PHOTOGRAPHS
PH10453 672-673 (December 23, 1993) p142. "Pumping Irony: Melle Mel Was 'Thinking Of Getting High' As He Cut 'White Lines'" (Wessel, Cathrine)
MELLENCAMP, JOHN—ALBUMS
PH10454 616 (October 31, 1991) p91. "Whenever We Wanted"
PH10455 666 (September 30, 1993) p101. "Human Wheels"
PH10456 672-673 (December 23, 1993) p151. "Human Wheels"
PH10457 686-687 (July 14, 1994) p102. "Dance Naked"
PH10458 698-699 (December 29, 1994) p180. "Dance Naked"
PH10459 743 (September 19, 1996) p82. "Mr. Happy Go Lucky"
MELLENCAMP, JOHN—ILLUSTRATIONS
PH10460 623 (February 6, 1992) p3. "John Mellencamp" (Burke, Philip)
MELLENCAMP, JOHN—PHOTOGRAPHS
PH10461 616 (October 31, 1991) p11. "John Mellencamp At Carnegie Hall" (Regan, Ken)
PH10462 619-620 (December 12, 1991) p79. "John Mellencamp, Black Tie Optional" (Regan, Ken)

PH10463 621 (January 9, 1992) p11. "Fergie And John Mellencamp" (Bernstein, Bill)
PH10464 623 (February 6, 1992) p15. "[John Mellencamp]" (Markus, Kurt)
PH10465 625 (March 5, 1992) p78. "Hemingway And Mellencamp Make Peace"
PH10466 626 (March 19, 1992) p11. "John Mellencamp Wants Johnson City, Tennessee, To Have Its MTV" (Mazur, Kevin)
PH10467 627 (April 2, 1992) p23. "[John Mellencamp]" (Alford, Bob)
PH10468 629 (April 30, 1992) p11. "John Mellencamp At Farm Aid V" (Mazur, Kevin)
PH10469 640 (October 1, 1992) p9. "[John Mellencamp, Elaine Irwin]" (Ortega, Albert)
PH10470 665 (September 16, 1993) p13. "John Mellencamp (center) Tears It Up At The Indianapolis Show" (Conroy, Michael)
PH10471 672-673 (December 23, 1993) p53. "Mellencamp Does His Share For The Heartland" (Jewell, Fred)
PH10472 675 (February 10, 1994) p23. "Hoosier Fan Mellencamp" (Mazur, Kevin)
PH10473 690 (September 8, 1994) p64. "On The Beach: Mellencamp With His Wife, Elaine Irwin" (Seliger, Mark)
PH10474 696 (December 1, 1994) p33. "[John Mellencamp]" (Seliger, Mark)
PH10475 703 (March 9, 1995) p36. "Mellencamp On The Mend" (Mazur, Kevin)
PH10476 716 (September 7, 1995) p22. "John Mellencamp Lends A Hand" (Seliger, Mark)
PH10477 736 (June 13, 1996) p32. "Mellencamp, Left, And Junior Vasquez At New York's Hit Factory In April" (Knight, Kevin)
PH10478 748 (November 28, 1996) p26. "Neil Young, John Mellencamp And Willie Nelson, Talking, Presumably, About The Plight Of The Family Farmer" (Roberts, Ebet)

MELLENCAMP, JOHN—PHOTOGRAPHS—PORTRAITS
PH10479 690 (September 8, 1994) pp62-63. "[John Mellencamp]" (Seliger, Mark)

MELODY MAKERS—ALBUMS
PH10480 664 (September 2, 1993) p62. "Joy And Blues"

MELROSE PLACE (TELEVISION SHOW)—ILLUSTRATIONS
PH10481 682 (May 19, 1994) p53. "[Chart]" (Klein, Renee)
PH10482 685 (June 30, 1994) p10. "Dressing Room" (Pendergrast, James T.)

MELVINS—ALBUMS
PH10483 700 (January 26, 1995) p62. "Stone Witch"

MELVINS—PHOTOGRAPHS
PH10484 675 (February 10, 1994) p22. "Crover, Simmons, King Buzzo And Mark Deutrom" (Cohen, Lester)

MELVOIN, JONATHAN—PHOTOGRAPHS
PH10485 741 (August 22, 1996) p32. "Melvoin's Body Is Taken From The Hotel"
PH10486 743 (September 19, 1996) p29. "Melvoin (left) With L.A. Punk Band The Dickies In The Early '90s" (Colver, Ed)

MELVOIN, JONATHAN—PHOTOGRAPHS—PORTRAITS
PH10487 741 (August 22, 1996) p32. "Melvoin (left) And Chamberlin" (Colver, Ed)

MEMNOCH THE DEVIL (BOOK)—ILLUSTRATIONS
PH10488 712-713 (July 13, 1995) pp92-93. "[Anne Rice]" (Collier, John)

MEMOIRS OF AN INVISIBLE MAN (FILM)—PHOTOGRAPHS
PH10489 626 (March 19, 1992) p104. "Invisibility Hampers Chevy Chase's Game"

MEN—ILLUSTRATIONS
PH10490 626 (March 19, 1992) p62. "[Men's Movement]" (Tavee, Tom)

MEN BEHAVING BADLY (TELEVISION SHOW)—PHOTOGRAPHS
PH10491 743 (September 19, 1996) pp94,96. "[Television]"

MENACE II SOCIETY (FILM)—PHOTOGRAPHS
PH10492 660-661 (July 8, 1993) p121. "Turner Menaces Martin Davis"
PH10493 665 (September 16, 1993) p77. "Best Picture"
PH10494 672-673 (December 23, 1993) p172. "New Talent"
PH10495 678 (March 24, 1994) p100. "Missing In Oscar Action"

MENCK, RIC—PHOTOGRAPHS
PH10496 627 (April 2, 1992) p19. "Jeffrey Borchardt, Paul Chastain And Ric Menck (from left)" (Lavine, Michael)
PH10497 685 (June 30, 1994) p40. "Velvet's Paul Chastain, Jeffrey Borchardt And Menck With McGuinn (from left)"

MENDEL, NATE—PHOTOGRAPHS
PH10498 726 (January 25, 1996) p37. "Foo Fighters Are, From Left, Nate Mendel, Pat Smear, Dave Grohl And William Goldsmith" (Seliger, Mark)
PH10499 730 (March 21, 1996) p32. "Horsing Around: David Grohl (top and bottom) And Fellow Foo Fighters William Goldsmith, Pat Smear And Nate Mendel (middle, from left)" (Gougenheim, Kim)

MENDOZA, GEORGE—PHOTOGRAPHS—PORTRAITS
PH10500 659 (June 24, 1993) p64. "George Mendoza, The Shelter's Post-Traumatic Stress Specialist, Is A Veteran Of Argentina's 'Dirty War.'" (Agulera-Helwig, Max)

MENENDEZ, ERIK—PHOTOGRAPHS
PH10501 672-673 (December 23, 1993) p90. "Watching Erik Menendez Watch His Trial"

MENGEDE, PETER—PHOTOGRAPHS
PH10502 637 (August 20, 1992) p15. "Helmet (from left): Stanier, Bogdan, Mengede And Hamilton" (Ockenfels, Frank W.)
PH10503 689 (August 25, 1994) p64. "Original Guitarist Mengede, Bogdan, Hamilton, Stanier (from left)" (Brice, Lindsay)

MERCADO, SCOTT—PHOTOGRAPHS
PH10504 674 (January 27, 1994) p24. "Bardi Martin, Klett, Kevin Martin, Mercado (from left)" (Knight, Kevin)
PH10505 702 (February 23, 1995) p23. "Candlebox (from left): Peter Klett, Scott Mercado, Kevin Martin, Bardi Martin" (Ford, Charles)

MERCHANT, JIMMY—PHOTOGRAPHS
PH10506 651 (March 4, 1993) p16. "Dick Clark With Teenagers Herman Santiago (left) And Jimmy Merchant" (Mazur, Kevin)

MERCHANT, NATALIE—ALBUMS
PH10507 711 (June 29, 1995) p43. "Tigerlily"

MERCHANT, NATALIE—ILLUSTRATIONS
PH10508 640 (October 1, 1992) p62. "10,000 Maniacs: This Side Of Paradise" (Sis, Peter)

MERCHANT, NATALIE—PHOTOGRAPHS
PH10509 622 (January 23, 1992) p6. "Natalie Merchant And Michael Stipe In Boston" (Robicheau, Paul)
PH10510 637 (August 20, 1992) p17. "Natalie Merchant With Producer Paul Fox" (Granitz, Steve)
PH10511 647 (January 7, 1993) p9. "Merchant And Stipe Onstage In Atlanta" (Diamond, Rick)
PH10512 657 (May 27, 1993) p11. "Natalie Merchant Croons With The Wallflowers' Jakob Dylan" (Taft, Mike)
PH10513 667 (October 14, 1993) p40. "Below: Merchant, Bragg, Founder Harry Horgan, Tanya Donelly, Janovitz" (Robicheau, Paul)
PH10514 672-673 (December 23, 1993) p57. "Merchant: No Longer In Her Tribe" (Mazur, Kevin)
PH10515 674 (January 27, 1994) p29. "Gabriel, Merchant And Odetta In Boston" (Robicheau, Paul)
PH10516 679 (April 7, 1994) p39. "Maniac Meets Monks" (Bentham, John)
PH10517 684 (June 16, 1994) p36. "Merchant, Greg Richling" (Forsman, Shelly)
PH10518 695 (November 17, 1994) p100. "Natalie Merchant" (Picayo, Jose)
PH10519 721 (November 16, 1995) p32. "Merchant: Chipping Away At The Eternal-Ingenue Image" (Mazur, Kevin)

MERCHANT, NATALIE—PHOTOGRAPHS—PORTRAITS
PH10520 652 (March 18, 1993) p37. "[Natalie Merchant]"

(Ockenfels, Frank W.)
PH10521 652 (March 18, 1993) pp[cover]. "Natalie Merchant: These Are Her Days" (Thurnher, Jeffrey)
PH10522 652 (March 18, 1993) pp34-35. "Rob Buck, Dennis Drew, Natalie Merchant, Jerome Augustyniak, Steven Gustafson (from left)" (Ockenfels, Frank W.)
PH10523 672-673 (December 23, 1993) p188. "[Covers]" (Thurnher, Jeffrey)
PH10524 721 (November 16, 1995) p31. "[Natalie Merchant]" (Koralik, Cheryl)
PH10525 729 (March 7, 1996) p10. "Our Bodies, Ourselves: Merchant (left) And Steinem" (Katz, Bruce)
PH10526 730 (March 21, 1996) p33. "Merchant: Helping To Save The Trees" (Sullivan, Cleo)

MERCURY REV—PHOTOGRAPHS
PH10527 652 (March 18, 1993) p27. "Jonathan Donahue (left) And Grasshopper"
PH10528 664 (September 2, 1993) p24. "They're All Revved Up: Donahue, Thorpe, Baker, Chambers, Fridmann And Grasshopper (from left)" (Gullick, Steve)

MERCURY, FREDDIE—ILLUSTRATIONS
PH10529 621 (January 9, 1992) p3. "Freddie Mercury" (Burke, Philip)

MERCURY, FREDDIE—PHOTOGRAPHS
PH10530 621 (January 9, 1992) p13. "[Freddie Mercury]" (Hogan, Dave)
PH10531 621 (January 9, 1992) p14. "Freddie Struts His Stuff On A '78 U.S. Tour" (Preston, Neal)
PH10532 621 (January 9, 1992) p17. "Mercury Joins Paul McCartney And Other Stars In The Live Aid Finale, 1985" (Preston, Neal)
PH10533 621 (January 9, 1992) p17. "Mercury With Longtime Friend Mary Austin" (Davidson, Alan)
PH10534 621 (January 9, 1992) p17. "Mercury, Ailing, In London Last September"
PH10535 629 (April 30, 1992) p15. "Freddie Mercury" (Hoffman)

MERCURY, FREDDIE—PHOTOGRAPHS—PORTRAITS
PH10536 621 (January 9, 1992) p14. "Queen In The Mid-Seventies (from left): Deacon, Mercury, May And Taylor" (Rock, Mick)

MERCY RULE—PHOTOGRAPHS
PH10537 698-699 (December 29, 1994) p47. "Mercy Rule" (Callahan, Kristin)

MERRITT, STEPHIN—PHOTOGRAPHS
PH10538 712-713 (July 13, 1995) p48. "Stephin Merritt: Low-Fi Svengali" (Lass, Imke)

MERRITT, STEPHIN—PHOTOGRAPHS—PORTRAITS
PH10539 728 (February 22, 1996) p34. "Merritt: A Man Of Many Band Names" (O'Hara, Gail)

METAKSA, TANYA—PHOTOGRAPHS
PH10540 746 (October 31, 1996) p60. "Tanya Metaksa, The NRA's Chief Lobbyist: Concentrating On The House And The Senate" (Peterson, Mark)

METAKSA, TANYA—PHOTOGRAPHS—PORTRAITS
PH10541 710 (June 15, 1995) p58. "Metaksa" (Peterson, Mark)
PH10542 720 (November 2, 1995) p58. "NRA Powerhouse Tanya Metaksa" (Warburg, Jennifer)

METALLICA—ALBUMS
PH10543 615 (October 17, 1991) p112. "Metallica"
PH10544 619-620 (December 12, 1991) p172. "Metallica"
PH10545 674 (January 27, 1994) p52. "Live Shit: Binge And Purge"
PH10546 738-739 (July 11, 1996) p85. "Load"

METALLICA—ILLUSTRATIONS
PH10547 667 (October 14, 1993) p26. "Metallica"
PH10548 711 (June 29, 1995) p10. "Black Album" (Pendergrast, James T.)
PH10549 738-739 (July 11, 1996) p85. "Into The Groove" (Ryden, Mark)
PH10550 741 (August 22, 1996) p20. "[Note]" (Pendergrast, James T.)

METALLICA—PHOTOGRAPHS
PH10551 617 (November 14, 1991) p53. "Metallica In Paris: With Its New LP, The Band Is On The Right Track" (Seliger, Mark)
PH10552 619-620 (December 12, 1991) p67. "...And Metallica (below)" (Halfin, Ross)
PH10553 619-620 (December 12, 1991) p26. "Metallica (left) And The Black Crowes (right)" (Seliger, Mark)
PH10554 625 (March 5, 1992) p55. "Metallica's All Smiles Over Honors" (Seliger, Mark)
PH10555 652 (March 18, 1993) p13. "Metallica Takes Over A Store" (Gershoff, Gary)
PH10556 708 (May 18, 1995) p74. "Metallica In 1991, From Left: Hammett, Ulrich, Newsted, Hetfield" (Seliger, Mark)
PH10557 727 (February 8, 1996) p12. "Fifty And Fabulous! Kilmister (center) Flanked By Metallica's Jason Newsted, James Hetfield, Kirk Hammett And Lars Ulrich (from left)" (Disanto, Annamaria)
PH10558 728 (February 22, 1996) p25. "Metallica's James Hetfield, Kirk Hammett, Lars Ulrich And Jason Newsted (from left)"
PH10559 737 (June 27, 1996) pp[cover]. "Metallica: They're Back With Summer's Biggest Album & Tour" (Corbijn, Anton)
PH10560 737 (June 27, 1996) p36. "Not Just Riding Shotgun: Newsted (left), Hammett" (Corbijn, Anton)
PH10561 737 (June 27, 1996) pp32-33. "Ready To Rumble" (Corbijn, Anton)
PH10562 750-751 (December 26, 1996) p62. "Makeover" (Leialoha, Mark)
PH10563 750-751 (December 26, 1996) p62. "[Metallica]" (Davila, Bill)

METALLICA—PHOTOGRAPHS—PORTRAITS
PH10564 617 (November 14, 1991) p49. "[Metallica]" (Seliger, Mark)
PH10565 617 (November 14, 1991) pp[cover]. "Metallica: From Metal To Main Street" (Seliger, Mark)
PH10566 619-620 (December 12, 1991) pp[cover]. "1991 Yearbook" (Seliger, Mark)

METHAMPHETAMINE—PHOTOGRAPHS
PH10567 681 (May 5, 1994) p39. "[Methamphetamine]" (Frailey, Stephen)

METHENY, PAT—PHOTOGRAPHS—PORTRAITS
PH10568 685 (June 30, 1994) p32. "[Pat Metheny]" (Lenquette, Youri)

METHOD MAN—PHOTOGRAPHS
PH10569 702 (February 23, 1995) p32. "Wu-Tangin': Meth (third from left)" (Berg, Bob)
PH10570 745 (October 17, 1996) p42. "Method Man Inspects The Wares" (Smart, Miguel)

METHOD MAN—PHOTOGRAPHS—PORTRAITS
PH10571 702 (February 23, 1995) p29. "[Method Man]" (Claiborne, Barron)

METZGER, MARK—PHOTOGRAPHS—PORTRAITS
PH10572 630 (May 14, 1992) p32. "Chainsaw Kittens (clockwise from top left): McBay, Meade, Preston, Bell And Metzger" (Mazur, Kevin)

METZGER, TOM—PHOTOGRAPHS—PORTRAITS
PH10573 710 (June 15, 1995) p57. "Metzger" (Smale, Brian)

MEWES, JASON—PHOTOGRAPHS
PH10574 720 (November 2, 1995) p74. "Mallrats Smith And Mewes"

MEXICO—ILLUSTRATIONS
PH10575 694 (November 3, 1994) pp83-84,87-88+. "[Mexico]" (Smith, Owen)

MEXICO—PHOTOGRAPHS
PH10576 668 (October 28, 1993) p40. "Early Victims Of NAFTA? When Mexican Autoworkers Went On Strike, VW Smashed Their Union" (Rojas, Juan Carlos)

PH10577 668 (October 28, 1993) p41. "...Mexican Autoworkers Face The Same Fight Today" (Rojas, Juan Carlos)
PH10578 741 (August 22, 1996) p80. "[Mexico]"
MI VIDA LOCA (FILM)—PHOTOGRAPHS
PH10579 686-687 (July 14, 1994) p99. "Latina Gangs Face Off In The Los Angeles Barrio"
MIAMI BLUES (FILM)—PHOTOGRAPHS
PH10580 722 (November 30, 1995) p61. "Leigh Didn't Have To Walk Out Of 'Miami Blues'—Her Work Opposite Balwin Ranks With Her Best"
MIAMI RHAPSODY (FILM)—ILLUSTRATIONS
PH10581 701 (February 9, 1995) p61. "New Age Funny Girl" (Meinhardt, Brook)
MIAMI RHAPSODY (FILM)—PHOTOGRAPHS
PH10582 701 (February 9, 1995) p62. "Farrow Catches Parker And Banderas"
MICHAEL COLLINS (FILM)—PHOTOGRAPHS
PH10583 746 (October 31, 1996) p76. "Michael Collins"
MICHAEL, GEORGE—PHOTOGRAPHS
PH10584 617 (November 14, 1991) p13. "John (left) And Michael" (Mazur, Kevin)
PH10585 618 (November 28, 1991) p35. "[George Michael]" (Mazur, Kevin)
PH10586 619-620 (December 12, 1991) p18. "Andrew Ridgeley (left) And George Michael" (Mazur, Kevin)
PH10587 623 (February 6, 1992) p13. "The Wacky, Fun-Loving George Michael" (Mazur, Kevin)
PH10588 627 (April 2, 1992) p11. "The Wacky, Fun-Loving George Michael (left) With Jody Watley And Bernie Taupin" (Mazur, Kevin)
PH10589 644 (November 26, 1992) p22. "Goldberg, Richie, Taylor, John, Michael And Hornsby (from left) At The Garden" (Mazur, Kevin)
PH10590 655 (April 29, 1993) p16. "Michael (left) And The Chili Peppers' Kiedis Are Raising Money For AIDS Patients" (Mazur, Kevin)
PH10591 656 (May 13, 1993) p15. "George Michael" (Mazur, Kevin)
PH10592 662 (August 5, 1993) p59. "George Michael" (Micelotta, Frank)
PH10593 671 (December 9, 1993) p16. "Nice Suit: Michael Exits London Court" (Murray, Andrew)
PH10594 672-673 (December 23, 1993) p17. "George Michael Wants His Freedom" (Mazur, Kevin)
PH10595 688 (August 11, 1994) p28. "Wham Bam: Michael After The Decision" (Mark, Stewart)
PH10596 724-725 (December 28, 1995) p49. "George Michael (right): Free To Shake His Moneymaker" (Murray, Andrew)
PH10597 748 (November 28, 1996) p25. "George Michael Looking Like The God Of Hellfire" (MacPherson, Andrew)
MICHAEL, GEORGE—PHOTOGRAPHS—PORTRAITS
PH10598 647 (January 7, 1993) p14. "[George Michael]" (Gallo, Armando)
PH10599 711 (June 29, 1995) p20. "George Michael: Freedom '95?" (Fisher, David)
MICHEL, PRAKAZREL—PHOTOGRAPHS
PH10600 734 (May 16, 1996) p66. "Rappin' At The House Of Blues: Fugees' Hill, Jean And Michel (from left)" (Kravitz, Jeff)
MICHEL, PRAKAZREL—PHOTOGRAPHS—PORTRAITS
PH10601 742 (September 5, 1996) p42. "Prakazrel Michel" (Rolston, Matthew)
MICHELE, DANETTE—PHOTOGRAPHS—PORTRAITS
PH10602 645-646 (December 10, 1992) p140. "[Danette Michele]" (Eccles, Andrew)
MICKEY MOUSE—ILLUSTRATIONS
PH10603 718 (October 5, 1995) p21. "Wally World" (Freda, Anthony)
MIDLER, BETTE—ILLUSTRATIONS
PH10604 744 (October 3, 1996) p77. "Men Behaving Badly" (Brodner, Steve)
MIDLER, BETTE—ILLUSTRATIONS—PORTRAITS
PH10605 645-646 (December 10, 1992) p152. "Bette Midler, 1973"
MIDLER, BETTE—PHOTOGRAPHS
PH10606 744 (October 3, 1996) p78. "First Wives Keaton, Midler And Hawn Out For Revenge"
MIDNIGHT OIL—ALBUMS
PH10607 617 (November 14, 1991) p154. "Diesel And Dust" (Duncan, Ken)
PH10608 617 (November 14, 1991) p154. "Diesel And Dust" (Midnight Oil)
PH10609 617 (November 14, 1991) p154. "Diesel And Dust" (Morriss, Gary)
PH10610 617 (November 14, 1991) p154. "Diesel And Dust" (Wart)
PH10611 634-635 (July 9, 1992) p104. "Scream In Blue"
PH10612 663 (August 19, 1993) p78. "Earth And Sun And Moon"
PH10613 672-673 (December 23, 1993) p152. "Earth And Sun And Moon"
PH10614 748 (November 28, 1996) p130. "Breathe"
MIDNIGHT OIL—PHOTOGRAPHS
PH10615 652 (March 18, 1993) p13. "Midnight Oil" (Vella, John)
PH10616 656 (May 13, 1993) p13. "Midnight Oil Under The Brooklyn Bridge" (Mazur, Kevin)
PH10617 658 (June 10, 1993) p19. "Burnin' Again: Hillman, Garrett, Moginie, Hirst, Rotsey (from left)" (Seliger, Mark)
PH10618 672-673 (December 23, 1993) p30. "Midnight Oil: The Big Green Machine" (Mazur, Kevin)
MIGHTY APHRODITE (FILM)—ILLUSTRATIONS
PH10619 721 (November 16, 1995) p115. "Woody's Hooker Adventure" (Brodner, Steve)
MIGHTY APHRODITE (FILM)—PHOTOGRAPHS
PH10620 721 (November 16, 1995) p116. "Mira Sorvino's Hooker And Woody Allen"
MIHALY—PHOTOGRAPHS
PH10621 696 (December 1, 1994) p66. "[Mihaly]" (Elledge, Paul)
MILITARY (UNITED STATES)—ILLUSTRATIONS
PH10622 618 (November 28, 1991) p39. "[United States Military]" (Cronin, Brian)
PH10623 651 (March 4, 1993) p35. "Option A, Option B, Option C, Option D" (Cronin, Brian)
PH10624 652 (March 18, 1993) p10. "Straight Troops—Gay Troops" (Pendergrast, James T.)
MILITARY (UNITED STATES)—PHOTOGRAPHS
PH10625 653 (April 1, 1993) p46. "Crossing The Green Line: Marines escort A Food Convoy North Out Of Mogadishu" (Morris, Christopher)
PH10626 653 (April 1, 1993) p49. "Marines On The Move In The Countryside Near Baidoa After Securing The Airfield" (Morris, Christopher)
PH10627 653 (April 1, 1993) p43. "Securing The Area: A Marine On Patrol In Mogadishu Near The American Embassy" (Morris, Christopher)
PH10628 653 (April 1, 1993) p41. "[Somalia]" (Morris, Christopher)
MILITIAS—PHOTOGRAPHS
PH10629 710 (June 15, 1995) p58. "War Games: The Self-Styled Michigan Militia Takes Its Weapons And Hits The Field For A Training Session In November 1994 In Brutus, Mich." (Howe, Cynthia)
PH10630 720 (November 2, 1995) p54. "[Gun Control]" (Winters, Dan)
MILK, HARVEY—PHOTOGRAPHS
PH10631 666 (September 30, 1993) p49. "On Election Night With Milk In '78" (Savage, Steve)
MILLA—ALBUMS
PH10632 680 (April 21, 1994) p84. "The Divine Comedy"

MILLENNIUM (TELEVISION SHOW)—PHOTOGRAPHS
PH10633 743 (September 19, 1996) pp94,96. "[Television]"
THE MILLENNIUM WHOLE EARTH CATALOG (BOOK)—ILLUSTRATIONS
PH10634 696 (December 1, 1994) p24. "Tool Tome" (Goldin, David)
MILLER, CHRIS—PHOTOGRAPHS
PH10635 639 (September 17, 1992) p76. "Miller And Amherst Coed In 1962" (Deleon)
MILLER, EDDIE—PHOTOGRAPHS
PH10636 722 (November 30, 1995) p29. "Giordano, Westerberg And Assistant Engineer Eddie Miller (from left)" (Keeley, Dennis)
MILLER, HEIDI—PHOTOGRAPHS
PH10637 664 (September 2, 1993) p53. "Heidi Miller And Linda Fannon At Gary's Benefit In Pittsburgh, 1993" (Borris, Dan)
MILLER, JERRY—PHOTOGRAPHS
PH10638 670 (November 25, 1993) p38. "Jerry Miller, Don Stevenson, Plant, Peter Lewis And Skip Spence" (Blakesberg, Jay)
MILLER, JIMMY—PHOTOGRAPHS
PH10639 697 (December 15, 1994) p34. "Jimmy Miller: Great Grooves And Dirty R&B" (Miller, Steve)
MILLER, KENNY—PHOTOGRAPHS
PH10640 689 (August 25, 1994) p77. "Kenny Miller And Rachel Leventhal At The Viacom Office In Times Square, New York City" (Newton, Philip)
PH10641 689 (August 25, 1994) p78. "Miller And Leventhal At Their Loft in Tribeca, New York City" (Newton, Philip)
MILLER, NICOLE—PHOTOGRAPHS
PH10642 704 (March 23, 1995) p96. "Landau With His Boss Nicole Miller: He Was Told The Company Wasn't Hiring, But He Didn't Buy It" (Pluchino, Joseph)
MILLER, PENELOPE ANN—PHOTOGRAPHS
PH10643 617 (November 14, 1991) p182. "DeVito Turns On The Charm For Legal Cupcake Miller"
PH10644 671 (December 9, 1993) p76. "Deja Vu: Pacino's Carlito With Miller (left)"
PH10645 688 (August 11, 1994) p62. "The Shadow"
MILLER, RICK—PHOTOGRAPHS
PH10646 721 (November 16, 1995) p38. "The Party Has Rolled Back Into Town: Huff, Miller And Hartman (from left)" (Elledge, Paul)
MILLER, ROGER—PHOTOGRAPHS—PORTRAITS
PH10647 645-646 (December 10, 1992) p102. "Roger Miller"
MILLER, SCOTT—PHOTOGRAPHS
PH10648 660-661 (July 8, 1993) p97. "The Loud Family: Paul Wieneke, Zachary Smith, Miller, Jozef Becker And Rob Poor" (Blakesberg, Jay)
MILLER, SHANNON—PHOTOGRAPHS
PH10649 628 (April 16, 1992) pp[enc.22]. "[Shannon Miller]" (Newton, Philip)
MILLER, STEVE—ALBUMS
PH10650 617 (November 14, 1991) p149. "The Joker" (Van Hamerweld, John)
PH10651 617 (November 14, 1991) p149. "The Joker" (Seeff, Norman)
PH10652 667 (October 14, 1993) p114. "Wide River"
MILLER, STEVE—ILLUSTRATIONS
PH10653 736 (June 13, 1996) p61. "Steve Miller" (Cowles, David)
MILLER, STEVE—PHOTOGRAPHS
PH10654 664 (September 2, 1993) pp21-22. "[Steve Miller]" (Rapoport, Aaron)
MILLER, TOBI—PHOTOGRAPHS
PH10655 636 (August 6, 1992) p13. "The Wallflowers (from left): Barrie Maguire, Jakob Dylan, Rami Jaffee, Peter Yanowitz And Tobi Miller" (Mark, Mary Ellen)
MILLI VANILLI—PHOTOGRAPHS
PH10656 645-646 (December 10, 1992) p40. "Milli Vanilli" (Mazur, Kevin)
MILLIONS—PHOTOGRAPHS
PH10657 625 (March 5, 1992) p27. "Lori Allison, Marty Amsler, Harry Dingman II, Greg Hill (from left)" (Natkin, Paul)
MILLS, MIKE—PHOTOGRAPHS
PH10658 628 (April 16, 1992) p11. "R.E.M.'s Mike Mills, Michael Stipe, Peter Buck And Bill Berry (from left)" (Mazur, Kevin)
PH10659 640 (October 1, 1992) p20. "Michael Stipe, Peter Buck, Mike Mills And Bill Berry (clockwise from left)" (Corbijn, Anton)
PH10660 647 (January 7, 1993) p9. "From Left: Mike Mills, Buck, Bill Berry and Stipe" (Colletti, Steve)
PH10661 651 (March 4, 1993) p32. "Ad-hoc Automatic Baby: Mike Mills, Adam Clayton, Michael Stipe, Larry Mullen Jr." (Mazur, Kevin)
PH10662 672-673 (December 23, 1993) p16. "Mills, Clayton, Stipe And Mullen (from left)" (Mazur, Kevin)
PH10663 676 (February 24, 1994) p29. "'Backbeat' Boys: Dulli, Fleming, Mike Mills, Dave Grohl And Thurston Moore"
PH10664 678 (March 24, 1994) p28. "[MTV's Rock n' Jock Softball Challenge]"
PH10665 680 (April 21, 1994) p64. "Twist And Shout: Fleming, Dulli, Grohl And Mills (from left) At A 'Backbeat' Session" (Cuffaro, Chris)
PH10666 688 (August 11, 1994) p17. "At The Movie Awards: Backbeaters Mike Mills, Don Fleming, Dave Pirner, Greg Dulli, Dave Grohl And Thurston Moore (above, from left)" (Kravitz, Jeff)
PH10667 689 (August 25, 1994) p15. "Michael Stipe, Phillips And Mike Mills (from left)" (Allen, Greg)
PH10668 693 (October 20, 1994) p60. "Mike Mills" (Seliger, Mark)
PH10669 693 (October 20, 1994) p27. "R.E.M.'s Bill Berry, Michael Stipe, Peter Buck, Mike Mills" (Mazur, Kevin)
PH10670 698-699 (December 29, 1994) p50. "Dulli, Fleming, Mills, Grohl, Moore, Pirner Went Out For A Smoke" (Cuffaro, Chris)
PH10671 704 (March 23, 1995) p32. "Band On The Run: Berry, Mills, Stipe And Buck (above, from left)" (Sheehan, Tom)
PH10672 704 (March 23, 1995) p30. "The Well-Dressed bassist: Mike Mills" (Liguz, Andrzej)
PH10673 726 (January 25, 1996) p42. "Peter Buck, Michael Stipe, Bill Berry, Mike Mills" (Jensen, David)
PH10674 737 (June 27, 1996) p29. "R.E.M.'s Mike Mills, Bill Berry, Stipe And Buck (from left) Have Split With Their Longtime Manager" (Rider, Paul)
MIN, ALBERT—PHOTOGRAPHS
PH10675 722 (November 30, 1995) p42. "Utter Confusion Caused Exactly That: Albert Min, Len Longo And J. M. Burr" (Dipeso, Debra)
MIND PLAYING TRICKS ON ME (VIDEO)—PHOTOGRAPHS
PH10676 667 (October 14, 1993) p80. "Geto Boys: 'Playing' With Our Minds"
MINIDISC PLAYERS—PHOTOGRAPHS
PH10677 674 (January 27, 1994) p59. "Sony MZ-E2 Portable MiniDisc Player, $550" (Miller, Greg)
MINISTRY—ALBUMS
PH10678 639 (September 17, 1992) p91. "Psalm 69: The Way To Succeed And The Way To Suck Eggs"
PH10679 728 (February 22, 1996) p59. "Filth Pig"
MINISTRY—ILLUSTRATIONS
PH10680 728 (February 22, 1996) p59. "The Enemy Within" (Rosen, Jonathon)
MINKS—PHOTOGRAPHS
PH10681 709 (June 1, 1995) p52. "[Minks]" (Nelson, Andy)
MINOR, AUSTIN—PHOTOGRAPHS—PORTRAITS
PH10682 715 (August 24, 1995) p63. "Charlie With His Wife Danica And Daughter Austin"

MINOR, CHARLIE—PHOTOGRAPHS
PH10683 715 (August 24, 1995) p59. "Charlie At His Beach House In Malibu, Where He Always Kept A Place By The Fire For Visiting Radio Program Directors"
PH10684 715 (August 24, 1995) p60. "Charlie With Girlfriend Dara Sewell During Their Trip To New Orleans For Mardi Gras This Year"
PH10685 715 (August 24, 1995) p62. "Charlie, Sting And Suzanne Vega" (Cohen, Lester)
PH10686 715 (August 24, 1995) p62. "With Janet Jackson And Her Producer Jimmy Jam, '90"
MINOR, CHARLIE—PHOTOGRAPHS—PORTRAITS
PH10687 715 (August 24, 1995) p63. "Charlie With His Wife Danica And Daughter Austin"
PH10688 715 (August 24, 1995) p64. "Portrait Of A Young Promo Man, 1965"
MINOR, DANICA—PHOTOGRAPHS—PORTRAITS
PH10689 715 (August 24, 1995) p63. "Charlie With His Wife Danica And Daughter Austin"
MINUS 5—PHOTOGRAPHS
PH10690 714 (August 10, 1995) p16. "The New Math: McCaughey, Buck, Tweedy And Greenberg (from left)" (Perez, Marty)
MINUTEMEN—PHOTOGRAPHS
PH10691 693 (October 20, 1994) p38. "Minutemen D. Boon, Watt And George Hurley In 1985 (from left)" (Pasley, Richard)
MIRACLE LEGION—ALBUMS
PH10692 622 (January 23, 1992) p47. "Drenched"
THE MIRROR HAS TWO FACES (FILM)—PHOTOGRAPHS
PH10693 743 (September 19, 1996) p88. "Divas"
PH10694 749 (December 12, 1996) p90. "Streisand: Bookworm Before; Bombshell After"
MISERY (FILM)—PHOTOGRAPHS
PH10695 656 (May 13, 1993) p114. "Above, More King Characters Show Their Dark Side: Kathy Bates ('Misery'), Jack Nicholson ('The Shining'), Sissy Spacek ('Carrie')"
MISSION IMPOSSIBLE (FILM)—PHOTOGRAPHS
PH10696 736 (June 13, 1996) p58. "Blockbusters"
PH10697 738-739 (July 11, 1996) p98. "Bang For The Buck Movie Chart"
MISSISSIPPI MASALA (FILM)—PHOTOGRAPHS
PH10698 624 (February 20, 1992) p50. "Washington And Choudhury At Odds"
MISTRESS (FILM)—PHOTOGRAPHS
PH10699 637 (August 20, 1992) p60. "Deal Makings: De Niro (left) And Wuhl"
MITCHELL, JONI—ALBUMS
PH10700 617 (November 14, 1991) p100. "Hejira" (Mitchell, Joni)
PH10701 617 (November 14, 1991) p100. "Hejira" (Seeff, Norman)
PH10702 617 (November 14, 1991) p100. "Hejira" (Bernstein, Joel)
PH10703 697 (December 15, 1994) p98. "Turbulent Indigo"
MITCHELL, JONI—ILLUSTRATIONS
PH10704 619-620 (December 12, 1991) p5. "[Joni Mitchell]" (Burke, Philip)
PH10705 641 (October 15, 1992) p167. "[Joni Mitchell]" (Grace, Alexa)
MITCHELL, JONI—PHOTOGRAPHS
PH10706 663 (August 19, 1993) p28. "Joni Mitchell At Uncle Miltie's Bash" (Gough, Janet)
PH10707 704 (March 23, 1995) p46. "Joni Mitchell: Unplugged" (Gimple, Melodie)
PH10708 720 (November 2, 1995) p50. "Joni Mitchell" (Seeff, Norman)
PH10709 732 (April 18, 1996) p19. "Joni Mitchell And Coolio Reminisce About All The Good Times They've Shared Together" (Mazur, Kevin)
MITCHELL, JONI—PHOTOGRAPHS—PORTRAITS
PH10710 643 (November 12, 1992) p162. "Joni Mitchell" (Ritts, Herb)
PH10711 686-687 (July 14, 1994) p41. "INXS's Michael Hutchence And Joni Mitchell"
PH10712 692 (October 6, 1994) p52. "Joni Mitchell" (Diltz, Henry)
PH10713 697 (December 15, 1994) p32. "[Joni Mitchell]" (Heisler, Gregory)
MITCHELL, LARRY—PHOTOGRAPHS
PH10714 730 (March 21, 1996) pp86-87. "Duard Kleyn (opposite) Is The Drummer For Friday Nights' Squeezebox, And Larry Mitchell Is A Solo Performer" (Witkin, Christian)
MITCHELL, MITCH—PHOTOGRAPHS
PH10715 625 (March 5, 1992) p17. "Mitch Mitchell, Noel Redding, Young And Al Hendrix (from left)" (Elgar, Nick)
PH10716 643 (November 12, 1992) p65. "Clapton, Lennon, Mitchell And Richards (from left) In 1968" (Russell, Ethan)
PH10717 712-713 (July 13, 1995) p45. "The Experience, Circa '67: Drummer Mitch Mitchell (left), Hendrix, bassist Redding"
MITCHELL, MITCH—PHOTOGRAPHS—PORTRAITS
PH10718 623 (February 6, 1992) p45. "Hendrix Found His Perfect Musical Accomplices In Noel Redding (left) And Mitch Mitchell (right)" (Mankowitz, Gered)
MITCHELL, SHARON—PHOTOGRAPHS
PH10719 693 (October 20, 1994) p75. "Actress Miss Sharon Mitchell"
MITCHUM, ROBERT—PHOTOGRAPHS
PH10720 618 (November 28, 1991) p103. "Robert Mitchum Harassed Polly Bergen In 1962"
PH10721 630 (May 14, 1992) p69. "[Robert Mitchum]"
MITNICK, KEVIN—PHOTOGRAPHS
PH10722 707 (May 4, 1995) p43. "Mitnick Going To His Hearing In Raleigh On Feb. 15" (Bounds, Jim)
MIXNER, DAVID—PHOTOGRAPHS
PH10723 656 (May 13, 1993) p39. "Leading The Charge: David Mixner" (Little, Blake)
MIYAMOTO, SIGERU—PHOTOGRAPHS
PH10724 621 (January 9, 1992) p45. "Grown-Up Business: One Of Miyamoto's Video Games Made Nintendo $445 Million" (Parsons, Caroline)
MIZRAHI, ISAAC—PHOTOGRAPHS
PH10725 678 (March 24, 1994) p49. "Isaac Mizrahi" (Eccles, Andrew)
MOBB DEEP—PHOTOGRAPHS
PH10726 749 (December 12, 1996) p32. "Mobb Rules" (Frohman, Lesse)
MOBY—CD-ROMS
PH10727 722 (November 30, 1995) p71. "Disk"
MOBY—ILLUSTRATIONS
PH10728 707 (May 4, 1995) p11. "Moby" (Burke, Philip)
MOBY—PHOTOGRAPHS
PH10729 707 (May 4, 1995) p59. "[Moby]" (Guip, Amy)
PH10730 707 (May 4, 1995) p60. "Moby Spins A Melee Of Sounds And Emotion" (Gershoff, Gary)
PH10731 742 (September 5, 1996) p24. "Moby Inside Manhattan's Lower East Side Needle Exchange" (Tavee, Tom)
PH10732 742 (September 5, 1996) p24. "Volunteers Distribute Free Condoms And Clean Needles To Clients" (Tavee, Tom)
MOBY—PHOTOGRAPHS—PORTRAITS
PH10733 695 (November 17, 1994) p103. "Moby" (Ockenfels, Frank, 3)
PH10734 726 (January 25, 1996) p51. "Everybody's A Critic: Techno Artist Moby Listened To More Than Dance Music In '95" (Eichner, Steve)
MOBY GRAPE—PHOTOGRAPHS
PH10735 670 (November 25, 1993) p38. "Jerry Miller, Don Stevenson, Plant, Peter Lewis And Skip Spence" (Blakesberg, Jay)

PH10736 697 (December 15, 1994) p41. "Death By Hype: The Late, Great Moby Grape In 1967" (Marshall, Jim)
MODINE, MATTHEW—PHOTOGRAPHS
PH10737 667 (October 14, 1993) pp104-105,108+. "[Matthew Modine]" (Stupakoff, Bico)
PH10738 667 (October 14, 1993) pp103-104. "[Matthew Modine & Julianne Moore]" (Stupakoff, Bico)
PH10739 667 (October 14, 1993) p109. "Modine And Moore As Ralph And Marian Wyman in 'Short Cuts'" (Rudolph, Joyce)
MODINE, MATTHEW—PHOTOGRAPHS—PORTRAITS
PH10740 667 (October 14, 1993) p106. "[Matthew Modine & Julianne Moore]" (Stupakoff, Bico)
MOE.—PHOTOGRAPHS
PH10741 747 (November 14, 1996) p53. "[Moe.]" (Alston, Kwaku)
MOE, TOMMY—PHOTOGRAPHS
PH10742 624 (February 20, 1992) p36. "[Tommy Moe]" (Eccles, Andrew)
MOGINIE, JIM—PHOTOGRAPHS
PH10743 658 (June 10, 1993) p19. "Burnin' Again: Hillman, Garrett, Moginie, Hirst, Rotsey (from left)" (Seliger, Mark)
MOHR, TODD—PHOTOGRAPHS
PH10744 690 (September 8, 1994) p21. "[The H.O.R.D.E. Tour]" (Lilly, Michael A.)
MOL, GRETCHEN—PHOTOGRAPHS
PH10745 747 (November 14, 1996) p126. "Gretchen Mol Mourns Vincent Gallo"
MOLEN, MIRANDA—PHOTOGRAPHS
PH10746 736 (June 13, 1996) p20. "Miranda Molen, Ron 'Rondonna' Dinkens, Watt And Daniela Eden (from left)" (Temme, Marty)
MOLINARI, SUSAN—PHOTOGRAPHS
PH10747 697 (December 15, 1994) p18. "Etheridge, Waters, "Politically Incorrect" Host Bill Maher, Molinari And Baio (from left)"
MOLL FLANDERS (FILM)—PHOTOGRAPHS
PH10748 738-739 (July 11, 1996) p98. "Robin Wright Relies On Morgan Freeman"
MOLLOY, MATT—PHOTOGRAPHS
PH10749 621 (January 9, 1992) p10. "Kevin Conneff, Paddy Moloney, Charlie Watts And Matt Molloy (from left)"
MOLONEY, PADDY—PHOTOGRAPHS
PH10749 621 (January 9, 1992) p10. "Kevin Conneff, Paddy Moloney, Charlie Watts And Matt Molloy (from left)"
MO' MONEY (ALBUM)—ILLUSTRATIONS
PH10750 637 (August 20, 1992) p49. "New Sounds In Black And White" (Mahurin, Matt)
MONACO, DEBRA—PHOTOGRAPHS
PH10751 665 (September 16, 1993) pp[enc.45]. "Above From Left: Chris Colbourn, Friend Debra Monaco, Tom Maginnis And Bill Janovitz" (Newton, Philip)
PH10752 665 (September 16, 1993) pp[enc.44]. "[Bill Janovitz & Debra Monaco]" (Newton, Philip)
PH10753 665 (September 16, 1993) pp[enc.5]. "[Buffalo Tom]" (Newton, Philip)
PH10754 665 (September 16, 1993) pp[enc.50]. "[Tom Maginnis & Debra Monaco]" (Newton, Philip)
MONASTERIO, JUAN—PHOTOGRAPHS—PORTRAITS
PH10755 733 (May 2, 1996) p26. "Killing Retro: Tim Taylor, Juan Monasterio, John Schmersal And Tyler Trent (from top)" (McGuire, Leeann)
MONEY MARK—ALBUMS
PH10756 732 (April 18, 1996) p70. "Mark's Keyboard Repair"
MONEY MARK—PHOTOGRAPHS
PH10757 738-739 (July 11, 1996) p26. "Money Mark Sees The Light" (Cardillichio, Nick)
MONEY MIKE—PHOTOGRAPHS
PH10758 676 (February 24, 1994) p24. "Spank Dog, Money Mike, Mr. Watts, Peter Jorge, D-Smooth, G (from left)" (Hastings, Daniel)
MONEY TRAIN (FILM)—PHOTOGRAPHS
PH10759 723 (December 14, 1995) p92. "Race For The Money: Harrelson And Snipes"
MONEY, BOSCO—PHOTOGRAPHS
PH10760 617 (November 14, 1991) p34. "Bosco Money (left) And Sam Sever" (Lavine, Michael)
MONICA—PHOTOGRAPHS
PH10761 729 (March 7, 1996) p10. "Baseball Been Bery, Bery Good To Me: Morris, Monica And B-Real (from left)" (Kravitz, Jeff)
MONKEES—ALBUMS
PH10762 724-725 (December 28, 1995) p122. "Headquarters"
MONKS—PHOTOGRAPHS
PH10763 712-713 (July 13, 1995) p42. "The Monks On The Reeperbahn"
MONROE, BILL—ILLUSTRATIONS
PH10764 746 (October 31, 1996) p11. "Bluegrass Legend Bill Monroe" (Ulriksen, Mark)
MONROE, BILL—PHOTOGRAPHS
PH10765 684 (June 16, 1994) p25. "Bill Monroe, The Focus Of The Film "High Lonesome""
PH10766 746 (October 31, 1996) p20. "Goodbye, Old Pal: Monroe Onstage In 1994" (Stephens, J. Brian)
PH10767 746 (October 31, 1996) p23. "Pride Of The Opry: The Legendary Bluegrass Boys Lineup Of Monroe, Chubby Wise, Flatt, Scruggs And Monroe's Brother Birch, Circa 1947 (from left)"
MONROE, BILL—PHOTOGRAPHS—PORTRAITS
PH10768 746 (October 31, 1996) p20. "[Bill Monroe]"
PH10769 750-751 (December 26, 1996) p94. "[Bill Monroe]"
MONROE, BIRCH—PHOTOGRAPHS
PH10770 746 (October 31, 1996) p23. "Pride Of The Opry: The Legendary Bluegrass Boys Lineup Of Monroe, Chubby Wise, Flatt, Scruggs And Monroe's Brother Birch, Circa 1947 (from left)"
MONSTER MAGNET—PHOTOGRAPHS
PH10771 710 (June 15, 1995) p54. "Boys In The Attic (clockwise from upper left): Ed Mundell, Jon Kleiman, Wyndorf And Joe Calandra" (Toliver, Chris)
MONSTER MAGNET—PHOTOGRAPHS—PORTRAITS
PH10772 716 (September 7, 1995) p34. "Dopes To Infinity: Wyndorf, Mundell, Kleiman And Calandra (from left)" (Lavine, Michael)
MONTANA, COUNTRY DICK—ALBUMS
PH10773 742 (September 5, 1996) p64. "The Devil Lied To Me"
MONTGOMERY, JOHN MICHAEL—ALBUMS
PH10774 678 (March 24, 1994) p112. "Kickin' It Up"
MONTOYA, CRAIG—PHOTOGRAPHS
PH10775 709 (June 1, 1995) p17. "Alexakis, Craig Montoya And Greg Eklund With Banner From Kids" (Grossman, Amanda)
PH10776 718 (October 5, 1995) p28. "Distortion-Fuzzed Alterna-Rockers Montoya, Alexakis And Eklund (from left)" (Westenberg, Kevin)
PH10777 726 (January 25, 1996) p18. "Everclear's Alexakis (left) And Bassist Craig Montoya Treat The Crowd To A Free Gig In Cali."
MONTREAL, CANADA—PHOTOGRAPHS
PH10778 639 (September 17, 1992) p32. "[Riot]"
MONTY PYTHON AND THE HOLY GRAIL (FILM)—PHOTOGRAPHS
PH10779 639 (September 17, 1992) p81. "You Must Remember This Line"
MOON, KEITH—ILLUSTRATIONS
PH10780 641 (October 15, 1992) p53. "[Keith Moon]" (Risko)
MOON, KEITH—PHOTOGRAPHS
PH10781 619-620 (December 12, 1991) p100. "Graham With The Who's Roger Daltrey, Keith Moon And Pete Townshend, In 1976" (Zagaris, Michael)
MOON, KEITH—PHOTOGRAPHS—PORTRAITS
PH10782 674 (January 27, 1994) p24. "Moon: Museum-Quality

Artifacts" (Dagmar)
MOONEY, TIM—PHOTOGRAPHS
PH10783 695 (November 17, 1994) p131. "American Music Club" (Duke, William)
MOONEY, TIM—PHOTOGRAPHS—PORTRAITS
PH10784 656 (May 13, 1993) p77. "American Music Club (from left): Danny Pearson, Tim Mooney, Vudi, Bruce Kaphan And Mark Eitzel" (Ockenfels, Frank, 3)
MOONLIGHT AND VALENTINO (FILM)—PHOTOGRAPHS
PH10785 720 (November 2, 1995) p77. "Female-Bonding Movies"
MOONSTRUCK (FILM)—PHOTOGRAPHS
PH10786 721 (November 16, 1995) p94. "The Baker In 'Moonstruck'"
MOORE, ANGELO—PHOTOGRAPHS
PH10787 633 (June 25, 1992) p11. "...And Fishbone's Angelo Moore (right) On Earth Day" (Robicheau, Paul)
PH10788 662 (August 5, 1993) p13. "Angelo Moore Of Fishbone Checks Out The View From The Pit" (Blakesberg, Jay)
MOORE, ARCHIE—PHOTOGRAPHS—PORTRAITS
PH10789 655 (April 29, 1993) p24. "Revving It Up: Velocity's Shannon, Spellman, Nelson, Riles And Moore (from left)" (Falls, John)
MOORE, CHANTE—ALBUMS
PH10790 655 (April 29, 1993) p63. "Precious"
MOORE, DELANO—PHOTOGRAPHS
PH10791 671 (December 9, 1993) p59. "Delano Moore, 17, Works As A Peer Counselor In Staggers' Clinic At Fremont High School" (Light, Ken)
MOORE, DEMI—ILLUSTRATIONS
PH10792 655 (April 29, 1993) p67. "Fiscal Attraction" (Friedman, Drew)
PH10793 736 (June 13, 1996) p56. "[Demi Moore]" (Brodner, Steve)
MOORE, DEMI—PHOTOGRAPHS
PH10794 617 (November 14, 1991) p182. "Jeff Daniels Seeks The Truth From Clairvoyant Demi Moore"
PH10795 655 (April 29, 1993) p68. "Demi's Choice: Robert Redford (left) Or Woody Harrelson?"
PH10796 698-699 (December 29, 1994) p199. "Moore And Douglas In "Disclosure""
PH10797 701 (February 9, 1995) p40. "Moore Partying With Husband Bruce Willis" (Spellman, John)
PH10798 721 (November 16, 1995) p117. "Demi Moore With Gary Oldman"
PH10799 740 (August 8, 1996) p68. "'Independence Day,' Travolta In 'Phenomenon,' Schwarzenegger In 'Eraser,' Moore In 'Striptease'"
PH10800 743 (September 19, 1996) p90. "[Summer...]"
MOORE, DEMI—PHOTOGRAPHS—PORTRAITS
PH10801 701 (February 9, 1995) pp38-39. "[Demi Moore]" (Rolston, Matthew)
PH10802 701 (February 9, 1995) p41. "Freshman Moore: Redondo Union High, 1977" (Poppel, Seth)
MOORE, GARY—PHOTOGRAPHS
PH10803 630 (May 14, 1992) p13. "Tom Petty, George Harrison, Gary Moore And B. B. King (from left)"
MOORE, JULIANNE—PHOTOGRAPHS
PH10804 667 (October 14, 1993) pp105,108. "[Julianne Moore]" (Stupakoff, Bico)
PH10805 667 (October 14, 1993) pp103-104. "[Matthew Modine & Julianne Moore]" (Stupakoff, Bico)
PH10806 667 (October 14, 1993) p109. "Modine And Moore As Ralph And Marian Wyman in 'Short Cuts'" (Rudolph, Joyce)
PH10807 694 (November 3, 1994) p106. "Shawn Works Magic On Moore And Smith"
PH10808 731 (April 4, 1996) p66. "Moore, 'Safe'"
MOORE, JULIANNE—PHOTOGRAPHS—PORTRAITS
PH10809 667 (October 14, 1993) p106. "[Matthew Modine & Julianne Moore]" (Stupakoff, Bico)
MOORE, SAM—PHOTOGRAPHS
PH10810 625 (March 5, 1992) p13. "Billy Joel (left) With Sam Moore" (Elgar, Nick)
PH10811 628 (April 16, 1992) p13. "Mavis Staples, MC Lyte, Sam Moore And Bobby 'Blue' Bland (from left)" (Mazur, Kevin)
PH10812 645-646 (December 10, 1992) p33. "Moore (center) And Friends" (Mazur, Kevin)
PH10813 744 (October 3, 1996) p26. "Dole Brother No. 1: Presidential Candidate Robert Dole (left) Clinches With Sam Moore Of Sam And Dave At A GOP Rally"
MOORE, SAM—PHOTOGRAPHS—PORTRAITS
PH10814 623 (February 6, 1992) p51. "Stax's Soul Men Sam Moore (top) And Dave Prater"
MOORE, SCOTTY—PHOTOGRAPHS
PH10815 742 (September 5, 1996) p20. "Scotty Moore (left) Attempts Some Sort Of Hand Ritual With The Ageless Richards" (Herrington, Jim)
PH10816 750-751 (December 26, 1996) p68. "Pleased To Meet You, Hope You Guessed My Name: Elvis Presley's Guitar Player Scotty Moore With Keith Richards" (Herrington, Jim)
MOORE, SUSIE—PHOTOGRAPHS
PH10817 691 (September 22, 1994) p58. "Moore, At Age 7, And His Sister Susie"
MOORE, THURSTON—ALBUMS
PH10818 709 (June 1, 1995) p60. "Psychic Hearts"
MOORE, THURSTON—ILLUSTRATIONS
PH10819 709 (June 1, 1995) p60. "Sonic Boom" (Deen, Georganne)
MOORE, THURSTON—PHOTOGRAPHS
PH10820 633 (June 25, 1992) p12. "Dim Stars (from left): Richard Hell, Steve Shelley, Thurston Moore And Don Fleming" (Busacca, Larry)
PH10821 634-635 (July 9, 1992) p33. "Steve Shelley, Kim Gordon, Lee Ranaldo And Thurston Moore (from left)"
PH10822 637 (August 20, 1992) p9. "Steve Shelley, Kim Gordon, Lee Ranaldo, Shake-A-Leg's Harry Horgan, Moore, Hersh And David Narcizo (from left)" (Robicheau, Paul)
PH10823 656 (May 13, 1993) p15. "Moore, Fleming, Firehose's Mike Watt And J Mascis (from left)" (Callahan, Kristin)
PH10824 676 (February 24, 1994) p29. "'Backbeat' Boys: Dulli, Fleming, Mike Mills, Dave Grohl And Thurston Moore"
PH10825 688 (August 11, 1994) p17. "At The Movie Awards: Backbeaters Mike Mills, Don Fleming, Dave Pirner, Greg Dulli, Dave Grohl And Thurston Moore (above, from left)" (Kravitz, Jeff)
PH10826 691 (September 22, 1994) p58. "Ax Maniac: Moore In The Early 1980s"
PH10827 691 (September 22, 1994) p58. "Moore (right) And Ranaldo (center) With Glenn Branca"
PH10828 691 (September 22, 1994) p56. "Moore And Gordon In '87" (Moore-Erdman, Susan)
PH10829 691 (September 22, 1994) p58. "Moore, At Age 7, And His Sister Susie"
PH10830 691 (September 22, 1994) p56. "Ranaldo, Gordon, Moore, Shelley (from left)" (Petersen, Naomi)
PH10831 691 (September 22, 1994) p53. "[Thurston Moore]" (Ockenfels, Frank W.)
PH10832 695 (November 17, 1994) p84. "Sonic Youth" (Mark, Mary Ellen)
PH10833 698-699 (December 29, 1994) p50. "Dulli, Fleming, Mills, Grohl, Moore, Pirner Went Out For A Smoke" (Cuffaro, Chris)
PH10834 702 (February 23, 1995) p20. "Lee Ranaldo, Moore, Coco And Watt (from left)" (Callahan, Kristin)
PH10835 712-713 (July 13, 1995) p32. "All The Way To Memphis: Moore, Shelley, Gordon And Ranaldo (from left)" (Day, Corinne)
PH10836 715 (August 24, 1995) p43. "Thurston Moore Of Sonic Youth In Midfeedback Orgasm" (Blakesberg, Jay)

PH10837 721 (November 16, 1995) p25. "Sonic Youth's Lee Ranaldo, Thurston Moore, Kim Gordon And Steve Shelley (from left) After Their 'State' Taping In New York" (Capak, R. J.)

MOORE, THURSTON—PHOTOGRAPHS—PORTRAITS

PH10838 691 (September 22, 1994) p54. "Sonic Parents: Moore And Kim Gordon" (Vadukal, Nitin)

PH10839 679 (April 7, 1994) p24. "The Sonic Set: Gordon, Moore, Ranaldo, Shelley (clockwise from top left)" (Watson, Norman)

PH10840 691 (September 22, 1994) p52. "[Thurston Moore]" (Ockenfels, Frank W.)

MOR-X, DARREN—PHOTOGRAPHS

PH10841 721 (November 16, 1995) p78. "Mike Morasky, Darren Mor-X And Dale Flattum (from left) Briefly Considered The Name Rusty Nail Shower Stall But Soon Thought Better of It" (Winters, Dan)

MORALES, GONZALO—PHOTOGRAPHS

PH10842 670 (November 25, 1993) p22. "Lewin, Infarinato, Morales (from left)"

MORALES, PABLO—PHOTOGRAPHS

PH10843 634-635 (July 9, 1992) p93. "...And Pablo Morales" (Zander, Peter)

MORASKY, MIKE—PHOTOGRAPHS

PH10844 721 (November 16, 1995) p78. "Mike Morasky, Darren Mor-X And Dale Flattum (from left) Briefly Considered The Name Rusty Nail Shower Stall But Soon Thought Better of It" (Winters, Dan)

MORAVEC, HANS—PHOTOGRAPHS

PH10845 658 (June 10, 1993) pp[enc.14-15]. "Hans Moravec With (from left) The Tessellator, Uranus And Navlab 2" (Llewellyn, Michael)

MORELLO, TOM—PHOTOGRAPHS

PH10846 664 (September 2, 1993) p31. "Rage's Timmy C., Zack De La Rocha, Brad Wilk And Tom Morello (from left)" (Johnson, William)

PH10847 735 (May 30, 1996) p27. "Rage Against The Machine"

PH10848 737 (June 27, 1996) p15. "Dr. Ruth...And Morello" (Allocca, David)

MOREY, DOUGLAS G.—PHOTOGRAPHS

PH10849 642 (October 29, 1992) p59. "At The Races, England, 1987"

PH10850 642 (October 29, 1992) p58. "Stalking Wildlife In Kenya, 1975"

PH10851 642 (October 29, 1992) p58. "With Mom, Syracuse, New York, 1967"

MORIARTY, CATHY—ILLUSTRATIONS

PH10852 626 (March 19, 1992) p101. "Playing Songs Of Love" (Kelley, Gary)

MORIARTY, CATHY—PHOTOGRAPHS

PH10853 651 (March 4, 1993) p74. "John Goodman Directs Cathy Moriarty And Tacky Monster"

PH10854 716 (September 7, 1995) p84. "Bless This House (left) With Cathy Moriarty And Andrew Clay: No Dice"

MORISSETTE, ALANIS—ALBUMS

PH10855 722 (November 30, 1995) p84. "Jagged Little Pill"

PH10856 729 (March 7, 1996) p64. "Jagged Little Pill"

MORISSETTE, ALANIS—ILLUSTRATIONS

PH10857 716 (September 7, 1995) p100. "Alanis Morissette: Know-It-All" (Rosen, Jonathon)

PH10858 723 (December 14, 1995) p20. "Sex Object" (Pendergrast, James T.)

PH10859 750-751 (December 26, 1996) p73. "[Alanis Morissette]" (Marten, Ruth)

MORISSETTE, ALANIS—PHOTOGRAPHS

PH10860 720 (November 2, 1995) p42. "[Alanis Morissette]" (Ockenfels, Frank W.)

PH10861 720 (November 2, 1995) pp[cover]. "Alanis Morissette: Angry White Female" (Ockenfels, Frank W.)

PH10862 720 (November 2, 1995) p44. "Onstage, Morissette Goes To An Emotional Level That's Almost Over The Top" (Mazur, Kevin)

PH10863 723 (December 14, 1995) p31. "Alanis Morissette" (Mazur, Kevin)

PH10864 726 (January 25, 1996) p37. "Alanis Morissette: Singer And Theater Fan" (Sirota, Peggy)

PH10865 727 (February 8, 1996) p24. "Coming Attractions: Alanis Morissette" (Blakesberg, Jay)

PH10866 732 (April 18, 1996) p19. "I Win, But I'm Humble: Morissette" (Mazur, Kevin)

PH10867 741 (August 22, 1996) p25. "Morissette Sez, 'I'm The Baby Of The Group.' Ga Ga." (Mazur, Kevin)

PH10868 743 (September 19, 1996) p34. "Summer's Young And Old" (Van Iperen, Neils)

PH10869 750-751 (December 26, 1996) p54. "Grammys: Isn't It...Alanis!"

MORISSETTE, ALANIS—PHOTOGRAPHS—PORTRAITS

PH10870 719 (October 19, 1995) p16. "Alanis Morissette Beams" (Gerber, M.)

PH10871 720 (November 2, 1995) p41. "[Alanis Morissette]" (Ockenfels, Frank W.)

PH10872 720 (November 2, 1995) p46. "Alanis Morissette The Dance-Pop Diva At 16" (Shark, Marko)

PH10873 724-725 (December 28, 1995) p54. "Alanis Morissette Did Her Thang" (Sands, Steve)

PH10874 724-725 (December 28, 1995) pp[cover]. "Rock & Roll Yearbook" (Foreman, Richard)

PH10875 736 (June 13, 1996) pp[cover]. "Rock & Roll Summer!" (Ockenfels, Frank W.)

MORPHINE—ALBUMS

PH10876 674 (January 27, 1994) p44. "Cure For Pain"

PH10877 678 (March 24, 1994) p94. "Cure For Pain"

PH10878 704 (March 23, 1995) p124. "Yes"

MORPHINE—PHOTOGRAPHS

PH10879 672-673 (December 23, 1993) p46. "[Morphine]" (Eichner, Steve)

PH10880 677 (March 10, 1994) p17. "Morphine Make 'Late Night' Noise For Conan O'Brien" (Mazur, Kevin)

PH10881 686-687 (July 14, 1994) p36. "Morphine's Sandman, Conway And Colley (from left)" (Lyden, Paul)

PH10882 711 (June 29, 1995) p20. "Masters Of 'Implied Grunge': Colley, Sandman, Conway (from left)" (Ockenfels, Frank, 3)

MORPHINE—PHOTOGRAPHS—PORTRAITS

PH10883 667 (October 14, 1993) p30. "Mark Sandman, Dana Colley And Bill Conway" (Eichner, Steve)

MORPURGO, KEVIN—PHOTOGRAPHS

PH10884 718 (October 5, 1995) p20. "B-Real Flanked By Carl Hinds (left) And Morpurgo" (Shapiro, Stephen)

MORRIS, DICK—PHOTOGRAPHS

PH10885 750-751 (December 26, 1996) p81. "The 'Star' Revealed That Dick Morris Paid For A Foot Job" (Vinomen, Ilkka)

MORRIS, DOUG—PHOTOGRAPHS

PH10886 714 (August 10, 1995) p24. "Doug Morris (center) With Alex And Eddie Van Halen" (Kravitz, Jeff)

MORRIS, KEITH—PHOTOGRAPHS

PH10887 712-713 (July 13, 1995) p25. "Zander Schloss (left), Gibson And Morris At CBGB" (Toliver, Chris)

PH10888 719 (October 19, 1995) p24. "Reuniting Hasn't Been Easy For The Circle Jerks: Keith Morris, Zander Schloss And Keith Clark (from left)" (Garcia, Willie)

PH10889 724-725 (December 28, 1995) p42. "Guest Punkette Debbie Gibson Joined Circle Jerks' Keith Morris" (Toliver, Chris)

MORRIS, MARK—PHOTOGRAPHS

PH10890 619-620 (December 12, 1991) p154. "'He's An Old-Fashioned Choreographer,' Says Baryshnikov (left), Rehearsing With Morris At White Oak Plantation" (Leibovitz, Annie)

PH10891 619-620 (December 12, 1991) p158. "Maxine Presents Mark With The 1991 Dance Magazine Award" (Brazil, Tom)

PH10892 619-620 (December 12, 1991) p153. "White Oak Plantation, Yulee, Florida, July 1990: Morris Collaborated With Baryshnikov's White Oak Dance Project, A Troupe That Dances Mostly Morris" (Leibovitz, Annie)
MORRIS, MARK—PHOTOGRAPHS—PORTRAITS
PH10893 619-620 (December 12, 1991) pp150-151. "[Mark Morris]" (Leibovitz, Annie)
MORRIS, MAXINE—PHOTOGRAPHS
PH10894 619-620 (December 12, 1991) p158. "Maxine Presents Mark With The 1991 Dance Magazine Award" (Brazil, Tom)
MORRIS, NATE—PHOTOGRAPHS
PH10895 625 (March 5, 1992) p21. "Michael McCary, Wanya Morris, Shawn Stockman And Nate Morris (clockwise from top left)" (Graham, Jim)
PH10896 709 (June 1, 1995) p23. "Boyz II Men: Shawn Stockman, Michael McCary, Wanya Morris, Nate Morris" (Granitz, Steve)
PH10897 729 (March 7, 1996) p10. "Baseball Been Bery, Bery Good To Me: Morris, Monica And B-Real (from left)" (Kravitz, Jeff)
MORRIS, WANYA—PHOTOGRAPHS
PH10898 625 (March 5, 1992) p21. "Michael McCary, Wanya Morris, Shawn Stockman And Nate Morris (clockwise from top left)" (Graham, Jim)
PH10899 709 (June 1, 1995) p23. "Boyz II Men: Shawn Stockman, Michael McCary, Wanya Morris, Nate Morris" (Granitz, Steve)
MORRISON, DAVE—PHOTOGRAPHS
PH10900 700 (January 26, 1995) p30. "From Left: Morrison, Cheek, Erhardt, Cleaver" (Ockenfels, Frank, 3)
MORRISON, JIM—ILLUSTRATIONS
PH10901 641 (October 15, 1992) p42. "[Jim Morrison]" (Woodruff, Tom)
PH10902 679 (April 7, 1994) p10. "I'm Outta Here" (Pendergrast, James T.)
MORRISON, JIM—PHOTOGRAPHS
PH10903 649 (February 4, 1993) p52. "The Doors (from left): keyboardist Ray Manzarek, Drummer John Densmore, Guitarist Robbie Krieger, Shaman Jim Morrison" (Diltz, Henry)
PH10904 686-687 (July 14, 1994) p23. "Jim Morrison (above left) And Janis Joplin (left) Are Both Represented With Collections" (Teske, Edmund)
PH10905 718 (October 5, 1995) p45. "Jim Morrison" (Bez, Frank)
PH10906 718 (October 5, 1995) p51. "Jim Morrison With The Doors: 'The Shadow Side Of Rock & Roll's Dionysian Impulse'"
MORRISON, JIM—PHOTOGRAPHS—PORTRAITS
PH10907 619-620 (December 12, 1991) pp[cover]. "1991 Yearbook" (Brodsky, Joel)
PH10908 645-646 (December 10, 1992) p149. "Jim Morrison, 1981"
PH10909 645-646 (December 10, 1992) p161. "Jim Morrison, 1971"
MORRISON, MARTHA—PHOTOGRAPHS
PH10910 728 (February 22, 1996) p18. "Martha Morrison, Tucker, Cale And Reed (from left) Celebrate The Velvets' Induction" (Mazur, Kevin)
PH10911 750-751 (December 26, 1996) p45. "Martha Morrison, The Wife Of Sterling, Moe Tucker, John Cale, And Lou Reed (from left) Celebrate The Velvets' Induction" (Mazur, Kevin)
MORRISON, STERLING—PHOTOGRAPHS
PH10912 648 (January 21, 1993) p11. "Lou Reed, John Cale And Sterling Morrison (from left) At NYU" (Andersen, Nancy)
PH10913 718 (October 5, 1995) p46. "The Velvet Underground (clockwise from bottom left): Nico, Reed, Morrison, Cale And Tucker"
PH10914 719 (October 19, 1995) p22. "The Acute Mind At Work: Morrison As A Velvet In '66" (Malanga, Gerard)
PH10915 724-725 (December 28, 1995) p64. "[Sterling Morrison]"
MORRISON, STERLING—PHOTOGRAPHS—PORTRAITS
PH10916 659 (June 24, 1993) p17. "Tucker, Morrison, Cale And Reed Today (from left)" (Wood, Graham)
PH10917 719 (October 19, 1995) p22. "Morrison In 1994: 'I Was Never A Hippie, And I Never Sold Out'" (Palmer, Dave)
MORRISON, TONI—BOOKS
PH10918 639 (September 17, 1992) p80. "Beloved"
MORRISON, VAN—ALBUMS
PH10919 615 (October 17, 1991) p94. "Hymns To The Silence"
PH10920 662 (August 5, 1993) p66. "Too Long In Exile"
PH10921 672-673 (December 23, 1993) p146. "Too Long In Exile"
PH10922 674 (January 27, 1994) p45. "Too Long In Exile"
PH10923 686-687 (July 14, 1994) p102. "A Night In San Francisco"
PH10924 712-713 (July 13, 1995) p110. "Days Like This"
PH10925 727 (February 8, 1996) p49. "How Long Has This Been Going On"
MORRISON, VAN—ILLUSTRATIONS—PORTRAITS
PH10926 641 (October 15, 1992) p149. "[Van Morrison]" (Maffia, Daniel)
MORRISON, VAN—PHOTOGRAPHS
PH10927 617 (November 14, 1991) p75. "The Last Waltz, 1976: Robertson, Danko And Manuel, With Neil Young (left), Bob Dylan (back to camera) And Van Morrison" (Leibovitz, Annie)
PH10928 648 (January 21, 1993) p11. "Van Morrison" (Blakesberg, Jay)
PH10929 649 (February 4, 1993) p52. "[Van Morrison]" (Gahr, David)
PH10930 651 (March 4, 1993) p31. "Van Morrison" (Blakesberg, Jay)
PH10931 658 (June 10, 1993) p16. "Wells (left) and Morrison" (Michelove, Mim)
PH10932 668 (October 28, 1993) p36. "[Van Morrison, Shane MacGowan, Fiachna O'Braonain]"
PH10933 736 (June 13, 1996) p80. "Van Morrison Gets Intimate In New York" (Capak, R. J.)
MORRISON, VAN—PHOTOGRAPHS—PORTRAITS
PH10934 720 (November 2, 1995) p50. "Van Morrison"
PH10935 740 (August 8, 1996) p23. "A Queen Fave: Van Morrison"
MORRISSEY—ALBUMS
PH10936 642 (October 29, 1992) p69. "Your Arsenal"
PH10937 679 (April 7, 1994) p73. "Vauxhall And I"
PH10938 705 (April 6, 1995) p60. "World Of Morrissey"
PH10939 718 (October 5, 1995) p68. "Southpaw Grammar"
MORRISSEY—ILLUSTRATIONS
PH10940 705 (April 6, 1995) p60. "Boys To Men" (Morse, Joe)
PH10941 705 (April 6, 1995) p9. "Morrissey" (Burke, Philip)
MORRISSEY—PHOTOGRAPHS
PH10942 648 (January 21, 1993) p24. "Morrissey Turns On His Narcissism" (Diamond, Rick)
PH10943 684 (June 16, 1994) p36. "The Celibate King Signs For Fans" (Mazur, Kevin)
MORRISSEY—PHOTOGRAPHS—PORTRAITS
PH10944 645-646 (December 10, 1992) p71. "[Morrissey]" (Owen, Mike)
MORRISSEY, BILL—ALBUMS
PH10945 624 (February 20, 1992) p41. "Inside"
PH10946 669 (November 11, 1993) p74. "Friend Of Mine"
PH10947 735 (May 30, 1996) p48. "You'll Never Get To Heaven"
MORROW, ROB—ILLUSTRATIONS
PH10948 735 (May 30, 1996) p55. "Dead Babe Walking" (Brodner, Steve)
MORROW, ROB—PHOTOGRAPHS
PH10949 691 (September 22, 1994) p104. "Robert Redford, Left, Directs Actor Rob Morrow"
MORSE, CHRISTO—PHOTOGRAPHS
PH10950 715 (August 24, 1995) p95. "Hanging Out In New

York's Central Park" (Danelian, Stephen)
PH10951 715 (August 24, 1995) pp90-91. "On The Court In Thompkins Park" (Danelian, Stephen)
MORTAL KOMBAT (FILM)—PHOTOGRAPHS
PH10952 709 (June 1, 1995) p68. "Toys As Movies"
MORTON, PETER—PHOTOGRAPHS
PH10953 617 (November 14, 1991) p18. "Peter Morton At The L.A. Hard Rock (top)" (Rapoport, Aaron)
MORTON, ROBERT—PHOTOGRAPHS
PH10954 735 (May 30, 1996) p30. "In The Pre-Suit, Pre-CBS Days, Producer Robert Morton Backs Up Dave" (Smeal, James)
MOSELEY-BRAUN, CAROL—PHOTOGRAPHS
PH10955 679 (April 7, 1994) p22. "Moseley-Braun With Photographer" (Lambert, Kenneth)
MOSHING—ILLUSTRATIONS
PH10956 718 (October 5, 1995) p16. "Mosh Pit" (Pendergrast, James T.)
PH10957 742 (September 5, 1996) p16. "Mosh Chart" (Pendergrast, James T.)
MOSHING—PHOTOGRAPHS
PH10958 708 (May 18, 1995) p25. "And Calms The Crowd With A Call For Peace" (Mazur, Kevin)
PH10959 708 (May 18, 1995) p23. "High Steppin: The View From The Pit" (Mazur, Kevin)
PH10960 708 (May 18, 1995) p25. "Reaches In To Catch A Surfer" (Mazur, Kevin)
PH10961 708 (May 18, 1995) p25. "Sadofsky (in glasses) Gets Ready For Action" (Mazur, Kevin)
PH10962 708 (May 18, 1995) p23. "Steve Sadofsky (front, right) Prepares To Catch A Mosher" (Mazur, Kevin)
PH10963 738-739 (July 11, 1996) p20. "Serious Concert Injuries Have Risen With The Mosh Pit's Popularity" (Eichner, Steve)
MOTHER NIGHT (FILM)—PHOTOGRAPHS
PH10964 748 (November 28, 1996) p143. "Nick Nolte And Sheryl Lee Get Cozy"
MOTHERHEAD BUG—PHOTOGRAPHS
PH10965 660-661 (July 8, 1993) p101. "Motherhead Bug (from left): Anthony Lee, Steven Ovenden, April Chung, Cyril Mazzard, Jez Aspinal, Tomoyo, And Dave Ouimet" (Leopardi, N.)
MOTHERS OF INVENTION—PHOTOGRAPHS
PH10966 674 (January 27, 1994) p12. "The '60s And '70s Mothers (below)"
MOTHERSBAUGH, BOB—PHOTOGRAPHS
PH10967 730 (March 21, 1996) p17. "Beck, Devo's Mark Mothersbaugh, Bob Casale, Josh Freese, Bob Mothersbaugh, Jerry Casale" (Anderson, Vera)
MOTHERSBAUGH, MARK—PHOTOGRAPHS
PH10967 730 (March 21, 1996) p17. "Beck, Devo's Mark Mothersbaugh, Bob Casale, Josh Freese, Bob Mothersbaugh, Jerry Casale" (Anderson, Vera)
MOTLEY CRUE—ALBUMS
PH10968 680 (April 21, 1994) pp8789. "Motley Crue"
MOTLEY CRUE—PHOTOGRAPHS
PH10969 645-646 (December 10, 1992) p33. "[Motley Crue]" (Gorman, Greg)
MOTLEY CRUE—PHOTOGRAPHS—PORTRAITS
PH10970 627 (April 2, 1992) p13. "Motley Crue's Tommy Lee, Nikki Sixx, Mick Mars And The Defrocked Vince Neil (clockwise from top left)" (Double, Steve)
MOTORIN, SERGEI—PHOTOGRAPHS—PORTRAITS
PH10971 711 (June 29, 1995) p38. "Motorin, KGB: Killed"
MOTTOLA, TOMMY—PHOTOGRAPHS
PH10972 672-673 (December 23, 1993) p41. "Right: Carey And Mottola" (Somoza, Gerardo)
PH10973 726 (January 25, 1996) p26. "Mariah Carey And Sony Music Chief Tommy Mottola With Cyndi Lauper (from left)" (Capak, R. J.)
MOULD, BOB—ALBUMS
PH10974 734 (May 16, 1996) p66. "Bob Mould"
MOULD, BOB—ILLUSTRATIONS
PH10975 692 (October 6, 1994) p87. "Bob Mould" (Manning, Garrian)
PH10976 694 (November 3, 1994) p11. "Sugar's Bob Mould" (Burke, Philip)
MOULD, BOB—PHOTOGRAPHS
PH10977 637 (August 20, 1992) p9. "Sugar (clockwise from left): Bob Mould, Malcolm Travis And David Barbe"
PH10978 647 (January 7, 1993) p24. "Bob Mould" (Robicheau, Paul)
PH10979 670 (November 25, 1993) p33. "Sugarless Bob Mould Struts His Stuff In Chi-Town" (Natkin, Paul)
PH10980 694 (November 3, 1994) p73. "Barbe (left) And Mould, Athens, Ga. July 1992" (Double, Steve)
PH10981 694 (November 3, 1994) p71. "David Barbe, Malcolm Travis Ad Bob Mould (from left)" (Broad, Julian)
PH10982 694 (November 3, 1994) p72. "Poison Years: Husker Du's Grant Hart, Greg Norton And Mould" (Corrigan, Daniel)
PH10983 695 (November 17, 1994) p39. "Bob Mould Of Sugar" (Barker, Kent)
PH10984 701 (February 9, 1995) p17. "[Sugar]" (Hermer, Ken)
PH10985 747 (November 14, 1996) p44. "[Bob Mould]" (Capak, R. J.)
MOUNTAIN GIRL—PHOTOGRAPHS
PH10986 616 (October 31, 1991) p40. "Jerry Garcia And Mountain Girl At Golden Gate Park In 1968" (Greene, Herb)
MOUNTFIELD, JOHN—PHOTOGRAPHS—PORTRAITS
PH10987 706 (April 20, 1995) p30. "The Stone Roses (clockwise from top left): Mountfield, Wren, Squire And Brown" (Ragel, Jon)
MOUQUET, ERIC—PHOTOGRAPHS—PORTRAITS
PH10988 680 (April 21, 1994) p26. "Deep Forest's Sanchez And Mouquet And Director Tarsem (from left)" (Kuczala, John)
MOZAMBIQUE—PHOTOGRAPHS
PH10989 698-699 (December 29, 1994) pp120-129. "[Mozambique Refugees]" (Salgado, Sebastiao)
MR. BUNGLE—ALBUMS
PH10990 619-620 (December 12, 1991) p182. "Mr. Bungle"
MR. FUNKE—PHOTOGRAPHS
PH10991 664 (September 2, 1993) p20. "The Lords Of Newark (from left): DJ Lord Jazz, Mr. Funke And DoItAll" (Apicella-Hitchcock, Stephen)
MR. HOLLAND'S OPUS (FILM)—PHOTOGRAPHS
PH10992 727 (February 8, 1996) p46. "Richard Dreyfuss Teaches Music To Alicia Witt"
MR. RHODES (TELEVISION SHOW)—PHOTOGRAPHS
PH10993 743 (September 19, 1996) pp94,96. "[Television]"
MR. SATURDAY NIGHT (FILM)—PHOTOGRAPHS
PH10994 642 (October 29, 1992) p78. "In Or Out Of Old-Age Makeup, Billy Crystal Gets Laughs"
MR. SCARFACE—ALBUMS
PH10995 671 (December 9, 1993) p70. "The World Is Yours"
MR. T—PHOTOGRAPHS—PORTRAITS
PH10996 662 (August 5, 1993) p60. "Mr. T" (Mazur, Kevin)
MRS. DOUBTFIRE (FILM)—PHOTOGRAPHS
PH10997 678 (March 24, 1994) p100. "Missing In Oscar Action"
PH10998 680 (April 21, 1994) p96. "Mrs. Doubtfire"
MRS. PARKER AND THE VICIOUS CIRCLE (FILM)—PHOTOGRAPHS
PH10999 697 (December 15, 1994) p104. "Leigh, Third From Left, At The Famed Round Table"
PH11000 705 (April 6, 1995) p69. "Oscar Rejects"
MTV—ILLUSTRATIONS
PH11001 619-620 (December 12, 1991) p71. "[Happy Birthday MTV]"
PH11002 658 (June 10, 1993) p12. "MTV" (Pendergrast, James T.)
PH11003 688 (August 11, 1994) p18. "Reality Bites MTV" (Rosenthal, Marc)

PH11004 689 (August 25, 1994) p15. "Flaming Curry" (Rosenthal, Marc)
PH11005 733 (May 2, 1996) pp18-19. "[MTV]" (Friedman, Drew)
PH11006 736 (June 13, 1996) p16. "You Are Getting Sleepy" (Pendergrast, James T.)
PH11007 737 (June 27, 1996) p12. "Snacks" (Pendergrast, James T.)
PH11008 740 (August 8, 1996) p14. "MTV" (Pendergrast, James T.)
PH11009 745 (October 17, 1996) p24. "Reality" (Pendergrast, James T.)
MTV—PHOTOGRAPHS
PH11010 743 (September 19, 1996) p32. "[MTV Awards]"
MUCH ADO ABOUT NOTHING (FILM)—PHOTOGRAPHS
PH11011 657 (May 27, 1993) p56. "Awry: Washington, Branagh, Thompson"
PH11012 665 (September 16, 1993) p77. "Worst Supporting Actor"
PH11013 672-673 (December 23, 1993) p172. "Overrated"
PH11014 678 (March 24, 1994) p100. "Missing In Oscar Action"
MUDHONEY—ALBUMS
PH11015 647 (January 7, 1993) p46. "Piece Of Cake"
PH11016 705 (April 6, 1995) p64. "My Brother The Cow"
MUDHONEY—PHOTOGRAPHS
PH11017 628 (April 16, 1992) p48. "Mudhoney's Lukin, Turner, Peters And Arm (from left)" (Seliger, Mark)
PH11018 695 (November 17, 1994) p90. "Mudhoney" (Ragel, Jon)
PH11019 700 (January 26, 1995) p32. "Lukin, Arm, Turner (from left)" (Blakesberg, Jay)
PH11020 709 (June 1, 1995) p48. "Seattle Mudslingers: Turner, Arm, Lukin And Peters (from left)" (Winters, Dan)
MUDHONEY—PHOTOGRAPHS—PORTRAITS
PH11021 645-646 (December 10, 1992) p92. "Seattle's Mudhoney" (Mottram, Tony)
MUELLER, JEFF—PHOTOGRAPHS
PH11022 686-687 (July 14, 1994) p74. "Getting The Point Across: Rodan's Tara Jane O'Neil, Noble, Mueller And Kevin Coultas (from left)" (Clinch, Danny)
MUELLER, KARL—PHOTOGRAPHS
PH11023 644 (November 26, 1992) p31. "Karl Mueller, Dave Pirner, Dan Murphy, Grant Young (clockwise from top left)" (Breiehagen, Per)
PH11024 672-673 (December 23, 1993) p57. "Mueller, Dave Pirner, Dan Murphy (from left)" (Franklin, Ross D.)
PH11025 695 (November 17, 1994) p55. "Soul Asylum—Photographs" (Smale, Brian)
PH11026 702 (February 23, 1995) p32. "Strummin' In Stereo: Dave Pirner, Butch Vig, Karl Mueller, Dan Murphy (from left)" (Cuffaro, Chris)
PH11027 711 (June 29, 1995) p31. "'I Want To Put Myself On A Pedestal And Hate Myself For Being There': Pirner, Murphy, Mueller, Campbell (from left)" (Mahurin, Matt)
MUFFS—PHOTOGRAPHS
PH11028 718 (October 5, 1995) pp[enc.4]. "The Muffs In Los Angeles" (Exum)
PH11029 718 (October 5, 1995) pp[enc.30-32 +]. "[The Muffs]" (Exum)
PH11030 735 (May 30, 1996) p13. "Muffs Roy McDonald And Kim Shattuck, Sean Ono Lennon, Muff Ronnie Barnett, Sideman Bill Bartell, And Eric Erlandson" (Phalen, Tom)
MUGGS—PHOTOGRAPHS
PH11031 631 (May 28, 1992) p18. "Muggs, Sen Dog And B-Real (from left)" (Moss, Gary)
PH11032 672-673 (December 23, 1993) p53. "Muggs, B-Real And Sen-Dog (from left) Pay Homage To The Wicked Weed On 'Black Sunday'" (Borris, Dan)
PH11033 731 (April 4, 1996) p30. "Sen Dog, Muggs, B-Real (from left)" (McClelland, P.)
MUGGS—PHOTOGRAPHS—PORTRAITS
PH11034 669 (November 11, 1993) p64. "The Dope On The Hill: B-real, Sen Dog And Muggs (bottom row, from left)" (Borris, Dan)
PH11035 671 (December 9, 1993) p31. "House's Danny Boy, DJ Lethal And Everlast With Cypress' B-Real And Muggs (from left)" (Blakesberg, Jay)
MUHAMMAD, ALI SHAHEED—ILLUSTRATIONS
PH11036 695 (November 17, 1994) p129. "A Tribe Called Quest" (Shurley, Hugh)
MUHAMMED, ALI SHAHEED—PHOTOGRAPHS
PH11038 660-661 (July 8, 1993) p26. "Tribe's Malik 'Phife' Taylor, Ali Shaheed Muhammed And Jonathan 'Q-Tip' Davis (from left)" (Mazur, Kevin)
MUHAMMAD, ALI SHAHEED—PHOTOGRAPHS—PORTRAITS
PH11038a 678 (March 24, 1994) p9. "Quest (clockwise from top): Q-Tip, Ali And Phife Dog" (Seliger, Mark)
MULCAHY, JACK—PHOTOGRAPHS
PH11039 715 (August 24, 1995) p110. "Mulcahy, Burns, Bahns And McGlone (from left)"
MULDAUR, MARIA—RECORDS
PH11040 650 (February 18, 1993) p60. "Louisiana Love Call"
MULDER, KAREN—PHOTOGRAPHS
PH11041 742 (September 5, 1996) p20. "[Jarvis Cocker & Karen Mulder]" (Barritt, Craig)
MULLEN, LARRY, JR.—PHOTOGRAPHS
PH11042 618 (November 28, 1991) p48. "Another Shot From Carnival In The Canary Islands: 'Larry In Rick Wakeman's Hotel Room'" (Corbijn, Anton)
PH11043 618 (November 28, 1991) pp44-45. "Larry And Bono In Berlin, Where Much Of The Album Was Recorded" (Corbijn, Anton)
PH11044 636 (August 6, 1992) p11. "Adam Clayton, The Edge, Bono And Larry Mullen Jr. (from left)" (Thomas, Justin)
PH11045 640 (October 1, 1992) p48. "...And Drummer Larry Mullen Jr." (Preston, Neal)
PH11046 651 (March 4, 1993) p32. "Ad-hoc Automatic Baby: Mike Mills, Adam Clayton, Michael Stipe, Larry Mullen Jr." (Mazur, Kevin)
PH11047 651 (March 4, 1993) p50. "Larry Mullen Jr. Wins On The Skins" (Corbijn, Anton)
PH11048 667 (October 14, 1993) p54. "The Zoo Gang On Tour: The Edge, Bono, Larry Mullen Jr. And Adam Clayton (from left)" (Corbijn, Anton)
PH11049 672-673 (December 23, 1993) p16. "Mills, Clayton, Stipe And Mullen (from left)" (Mazur, Kevin)
PH11050 710 (June 15, 1995) p17. "[U2]" (Mazur, Kevin)
PH11051 714 (August 10, 1995) p30. "U2 Can Do Film Scores: Adam Clayton, Bono, The Edge, Larry Mullen (from left)" (Mazur, Kevin)
PH11052 726 (January 25, 1996) p30. "U2's Bono, Adam Clayton, The Edge And Larry Mullen Jr. (from left)" (Pasley, Richard)
MULLEN, LARRY, JR.—PHOTOGRAPHS—PORTRAITS
PH11053 738-739 (July 11, 1996) p16. "Etheridge And Mullen At A Party In A UCLA Parking Lot" (Berliner, Alan)
MULLIGAN, GERRY—PHOTOGRAPHS—PORTRAITS
PH11054 729 (March 7, 1996) p24. "[Gerry Mulligan]" (Friedman, Carol)
MULTIPLICITY (FILM)—PHOTOGRAPHS
PH11055 736 (June 13, 1996) p61. "Funny Guys"
PH11056 740 (August 8, 1996) p70. "Close Shave For Keaton And Keaton"
MUNDELL, ED—PHOTOGRAPHS
PH11057 710 (June 15, 1995) p54. "Boys In The Attic (clockwise from upper left): Ed Mundell, Jon Kleiman, Wyndorf And Joe Calandra" (Toliver, Chris)
MUNDELL, ED—PHOTOGRAPHS—PORTRAITS
PH11058 716 (September 7, 1995) p34. "Dopes To Infinity: Wyndorf, Mundell, Kleiman And Calandra (from left)" (Lavine,

Michael)

MUNDY, MATT—PHOTOGRAPHS

PH11059 631 (May 28, 1992) p16. "The Rescue Unit (from left): Matt Mundy, Oteil Burbridge, Col. Bruce Hampton, Jimmy Herring And Apt. Q258" (Frazier, Jeff)

MUNICH PHILHARMONIC ORCHESTRA—ALBUMS

PH11060 628 (April 16, 1992) p84. "The Munich Philharmonic Orchestra Plays Abba Classic"

MURATORE, JOHN—PHOTOGRAPHS

PH11061 705 (April 6, 1995) p57. "Mutiny On The Bounty: NASA's Pirates Perrine, Anderson And Muratore (from left)" (Turner, Danny)

MURDER IN THE FIRST (FILM)—PHOTOGRAPHS

PH11062 701 (February 9, 1995) p63. "Slater And Bacon Fight Injustice"

PH11063 731 (April 4, 1996) p66. "Bacon, 'Murder'"

MURDER ONE (TELEVISION SHOW)—PHOTOGRAPHS

PH11064 716 (September 7, 1995) p83. "Murder One: Opposite ER And Thus Presumed Dead"

MURDERS—ILLUSTRATIONS

PH11065 632 (June 11, 1992) p129. "[Murders]" (Cronin, Brian)

PH11066 632 (June 11, 1992) p169. "[Violence]" (Cronin, Brian)

PH11067 632 (June 11, 1992) p171. "[Violence]" (Mahurin, Matt)

PH11068 666 (September 30, 1993) p32. "No. 1 With A Bullet" (Klein, Renee)

PH11069 696 (December 1, 1994) p18. "Nursery" (Pendergrast, James T.)

MURDOCK, ROGER—PHOTOGRAPHS—PORTRAITS

PH11070 654 (April 15, 1993) p17. "Murdock, Hall, Xefos, Rick (from left)" (Seliger, Mark)

MURIEL'S WEDDING (FILM)—PHOTOGRAPHS

PH11071 704 (March 23, 1995) p128. "The Big Day Is Here At Last For Toni Collette"

MURPH—PHOTOGRAPHS

PH11072 656 (May 13, 1993) p17. "Don't Call Us Slackers: Mike Johnson, Murph And J Mascis" (Ockenfels, Frank, 3)

MURPHY BROWN (TELEVISION SHOW)—PHOTOGRAPHS

PH11073 619-620 (December 12, 1991) p202. "Anything For A Ratings Point: Candice Bergen's Murphy Brown Got Pregnant In A Season-Ending Cliffhanger"

MURPHY, CHRIS—PHOTOGRAPHS

PH11074 691 (September 22, 1994) pp[enc.17]. "Chris Murphy On The Violin" (Wessel, Cathrine)

PH11075 691 (September 22, 1994) pp[enc.18]. "Murphy And Della Penna At 12th And Porter In Nashville" (Wessel, Cathrine)

PH11076 691 (September 22, 1994) pp[enc.20]. "Murphy Loading In At Lucy's Record Shop, In Nashville" (Wessel, Cathrine)

MURPHY, DAN—ILLUSTRATIONS

PH11077 672-673 (December 23, 1993) p35. "[Dave Pirner & Dan Murphy]" (Corio, Paul)

MURPHY, DAN—PHOTOGRAPHS

PH11078 633 (June 25, 1992) p11. "Golden Smog (from left): Gary Louris, Chris Mars, Dan Murphy, Craig Johnson And Marc Perlman" (Butler, Bonnie Lynn)

PH11079 644 (November 26, 1992) p31. "Karl Mueller, Dave Pirner, Dan Murphy, Grant Young (clockwise from top left)" (Breiehagen, Per)

PH11080 672-673 (December 23, 1993) p70. "Live From New York: Hamilton, Pirner, Williams, Henry And Murphy (clockwise from top left)" (Mazur, Kevin)

PH11081 672-673 (December 23, 1993) p57. "Mueller, Dave Pirner, Dan Murphy (from left)" (Franklin, Ross D.)

PH11082 674 (January 27, 1994) p29. "Backstage At McCabe's" (Kravitz, Jeff)

PH11083 691 (September 22, 1994) p20. "Hawks Gary Louris, Mark Perlman, Dan Murphy, Noah Levy, Tweedy" (Smiley, Jay)

PH11084 695 (November 17, 1994) p55. "Soul Asylum—Photographs" (Smale, Brian)

PH11085 702 (February 23, 1995) p32. "Strummin' In Stereo: Dave Pirner, Butch Vig, Karl Mueller, Dan Murphy (from left)" (Cuffaro, Chris)

PH11086 711 (June 29, 1995) p31. "'I Want To Put Myself On A Pedestal And Hate Myself For Being There': Pirner, Murphy, Mueller, Campbell (from left)" (Mahurin, Matt)

PH11087 715 (August 24, 1995) p23. "[Soul Asylum]" (Naumann, Ellen)

PH11088 729 (March 7, 1996) p9. "Dave Pirner (left) And Danny Murphy Of Soul Asylum Flank Grant Hart" (Garrity, Brian)

PH11089 735 (May 30, 1996) p50. "Golden Smog's Murphy And Kraig Johnson (from left)" (Capak, R. J.)

PH11090 644 (November 26, 1992) p31. "Karl Mueller, Dave Pirner, Dan Murphy, Grant Young (clockwise from top left)" (Breiehagen, Per)

PH11091 672-673 (December 23, 1993) p70. "Live From New York: Hamilton, Pirner, Williams, Henry And Murphy (clockwise from top left)" (Mazur, Kevin)

PH11092 672-673 (December 23, 1993) p57. "Mueller, Dave Pirner, Dan Murphy (from left)" (Franklin, Ross D.)

PH11093 695 (November 17, 1994) p55. "Soul Asylum—Photographs" (Smale, Brian)

PH11094 702 (February 23, 1995) p32. "Strummin' In Stereo: Dave Pirner, Butch Vig, Karl Mueller, Dan Murphy (from left)" (Cuffaro, Chris)

PH11095 711 (June 29, 1995) p31. "'I Want To Put Myself On A Pedestal And Hate Myself For Being There': Pirner, Murphy, Mueller, Campbell (from left)" (Mahurin, Matt)

PH11096 715 (August 24, 1995) p23. "[Soul Asylum]" (Naumann, Ellen)

PH11097 729 (March 7, 1996) p9. "Dave Pirner (left) And Danny Murphy Of Soul Asylum Flank Grant Hart" (Garrity, Brian)

MURPHY, EDDIE—ILLUSTRATIONS

PH11098 636 (August 6, 1992) p63. "Depreciating Eddie Murphy" (Brodner, Steven)

PH11099 738-739 (July 11, 1996) p95. "Freaks Of Comedy" (Brodner, Steve)

MURPHY, EDDIE—PHOTOGRAPHS

PH11100 626 (March 19, 1992) p11. "Michael Jackson With Eddie Murphy And Producer Trenten Gumbs (from left)"

PH11101 633 (June 25, 1992) p12. "Murphy With McCartney And Producer Trenten Gumbs (from left)"

PH11102 636 (August 6, 1992) p64. "Robin Givens Has The Nails, But Eddie Murphy's Got The Claws"

PH11103 639 (September 17, 1992) p102. "Worst Picture, Worst Actor"

PH11104 649 (February 4, 1993) p72. "[Boomerang]"

PH11105 680 (April 21, 1994) p74. "With His Co-Stars In 'Boomerang' David Alan Grier (left) And Eddie Murphy"

PH11106 685 (June 30, 1994) p81. "Eddie Murphy Fires Off A New Volley Of "Cop" Action"

PH11107 691 (September 22, 1994) p106. "Falling Ego"

PH11108 706 (April 20, 1995) p86. "The 'SNL' Legacy Of Screen Shame"

PH11109 738-739 (July 11, 1996) p96. "Murphy's Nutty Professor As A Fat Slob (left) And Sexist Pig"

PH11110 743 (September 19, 1996) p90. "[Summer...]"

MURPHY, EDDIE—PHOTOGRAPHS—PORTRAITS

PH11111 722 (November 30, 1995) p76. "Eddie Murphy Bites It"

PH11112 737 (June 27, 1996) p42. "Bustin' Out With Pal Eddie Murphy At New York's Paladium Nightclub For A 'Saturday Night Live' Party, 1985"

MURPHY, ELLIOT—ALBUMS

PH11113 645-646 (December 10, 1992) p180. "Diamonds By The Yard"

MURPHY, MICHAEL—PHOTOGRAPHS

PH11114 644 (November 26, 1992) p78. "[Tanner '88]"

PH11115 653 (April 1, 1993) p11. "Navarro, Michael Murphy And Avery" (Cohen, Lester)
MURPHY, PATRICK—PHOTOGRAPHS
PH11116 742 (September 5, 1996) p21. "Fruit O'the Loon: Lemonhead Dando Rocks Hard (can't ya tell?) With Patrick Murphy, Dina Waxman And Bill Gibson (from left)"
MURPHY, PETER—ALBUMS
PH11117 633 (June 25, 1992) p42. "Holy Smoke"
MURPHY, THOMAS—PHOTOGRAPHS
PH11118 724-725 (December 28, 1995) p51. "Disney's Michael Eisner (left), ABC's Thomas Murphy" (Tannenbaum)
MURRAY, BILL—PHOTOGRAPHS
PH11119 654 (April 15, 1993) p69. "Mad Dog"
PH11120 706 (April 20, 1995) p86. "The 'SNL' Legacy Of Screen Shame"
PH11121 743 (September 19, 1996) p88. "Dickheads"
PH11122 748 (November 28, 1996) p143. "Dead On Arrival"
MURRAY, DAVID—ALBUMS
PH11123 627 (April 2, 1992) p46. "Shakill's Warrior"
MURRAY, DEE—PHOTOGRAPHS
PH11124 645-646 (December 10, 1992) p102. "Dee Murray"
MUSBURGER, MIKE—PHOTOGRAPHS
PH11125 660-661 (July 8, 1993) p101. "The Posies (from left): Jon Auer, Dave Fox, Ken Stringfellow And Mike Musburger" (Natkin, Paul)
PH11126 730 (March 21, 1996) p17. "Fastbacks' Kurt Bloch, Mike Musburger, Vedder, Fastbacks' Kim Warnick, Lu Lu Gargiulo" (Michelson, Randall)
MUSHROOM—PHOTOGRAPHS
PH11127 616 (October 31, 1991) p25. "Massive Attack (from left): 3-D, Mushroom And Daddy G"
MUSHROOMS—ILLUSTRATIONS
PH11128 719 (October 19, 1995) p94. "Magical Mushrooms, Mischievous Molds"
MUSIC—BOOKS
PH11129 660-661 (July 8, 1993) p23. "[Incredibly Strange Music, Volume 1]"
MUSIC—ILLUSTRATIONS
PH11130 645-646 (December 10, 1992) p23. "The Year In Music" (Blechman, R. O.)
MUSIC INDUSTRY—ILLUSTRATIONS
PH11131 619-620 (December 12, 1991) p64. "[Music Industry]" (Allen, Terry)
PH11132 647 (January 7, 1993) p18. "Baby Troll Wants More" (Seibold, Jotto)
PH11133 649 (February 4, 1993) p7. "Through The Looking Glass" (Pendergrast, James T.)
PH11134 654 (April 15, 1993) p8. "Fame-O-Meter" (Pendergrast, James T.)
PH11135 662 (August 5, 1993) p8. "Welcome To The Record Biz" (Pendergrast, James T.)
PH11136 672-673 (December 23, 1993) p10. "[Times They Are A-Changin']" (Pendergrast, James T.)
PH11137 684 (June 16, 1994) p17. "Admit One" (Corio, Paul)
PH11138 692 (October 6, 1994) p26. "[Compact Disc Prices]" (Kuper, Peter)
PH11139 697 (December 15, 1994) p25. "[Warner Brothers Records]" (Rosen, Jonathon)
PH11140 729 (March 7, 1996) p6. "Critics" (Pendergrast, James T.)
MUSIC INDUSTRY—PHOTOGRAPHS
PH11141 692 (October 6, 1994) p21. "[Concert]" (Blakesberg, Jay)
MUSICALS—ALBUMS
PH11142 691 (September 22, 1994) p33. "Songs From Chippy"
MUSICIANS—ILLUSTRATIONS
PH11143 683 (June 2, 1994) p15. "[Summer Tours '94]" (Cowles, David)
PH11144 715 (August 24, 1995) p25. "Schoolhouse Rock" (Mericle, Cherise)
PH11145 727 (February 8, 1996) p10. "Stage Bathrooms" (Pendergrast, James T.)
MUSICIANS—ILLUSTRATIONS—LETTERING
PH11146 628 (April 16, 1992) p62. "[Hot Picks]" (Allen, Terry)
PH11147 628 (April 16, 1992) p51. "[New Faces]" (Allen, Terry)
MUSSELWHITE, CHARLIE—ALBUMS
PH11148 689 (August 25, 1994) p89. "In My Time"
MUSSER, JEFF—PHOTOGRAPHS
PH11149 702 (February 23, 1995) p20. "Flag's Jason Zasky, Stesney And Jeff Musser (from left)" (Toliver, Chris)
MUSTAINE, DAVE—PHOTOGRAPHS
PH11150 704 (March 23, 1995) p46. "Dave Mustaine With Flying V And Flying Hair" (Mazur, Kevin)
MUTABARUKA—PHOTOGRAPHS
PH11151 662 (August 5, 1993) p14. "Jamaican Dub Poet Mutabaruka Found Some Of The Bands A Little Hard To Get Used To" (Blakesberg, Jay)
MUTE WITNESS (FILM)—PHOTOGRAPHS
PH11152 712-713 (July 13, 1995) p116. "Big Winners On Small Budgets"
MUZE (COMPUTER SYSTEM)—ILLUSTRATIONS
PH11153 653 (April 1, 1993) p22. "[Muze]" (Rosenthal, Marc)
MY BLOODY VALENTINE—PHOTOGRAPHS—PORTRAITS
PH11154 623 (February 6, 1992) p20. "Clockwise From Top Left: Butcher, Shields, Googe, O'Ciosoig" (Double, Steve)
MY COUSIN VINNY (FILM)—PHOTOGRAPHS
PH11155 627 (April 2, 1992) p42. "Fred Gwynne Referees For Joe Pesci And Marisa Tomei"
MY LIFE WITH THE THRILL KILL KULT—PHOTOGRAPHS
PH11156 618 (November 28, 1991) p30. "Groovie Mann, Jacky Blaque And Buzz McCoy (from left)" (Elledge, Paul)
PH11157 723 (December 14, 1995) p32. "Lambert (in back) And My Life With The Thrill Kill Kult"
MY OWN PRIVATE IDAHO (FILM)—PHOTOGRAPHS
PH11158 615 (October 17, 1991) p100. "River Phoenix (left) And Keanu Reeves Are Bad Boys Of The Road"
PH11159 627 (April 2, 1992) p41. "Phoenix In 'My Own Private Idaho'"
MY SO-CALLED LIFE (TELEVISION SHOW)—PHOTOGRAPHS
PH11160 682 (May 19, 1994) p56. "[Claire Danes]"
MYDLAND, BRENT—PHOTOGRAPHS
PH11161 717 (September 21, 1995) p72. "The Music Never Stopped: Garcia, Weir, Lesh, Brent Mydland, Kreutzmann And Hart (from left) In 1979" (Greene, Herbi)
MYERS, MIKE—PHOTOGRAPHS
PH11162 626 (March 19, 1992) p40. "Director Spheeris Advised Her Stars To 'Keep It Subtle'" (Schiffman, Bonnie)
PH11163 626 (March 19, 1992) p39. "Myers Parties On With Babe Tia Carrere And Carvey" (Schiffman, Bonnie)
PH11164 626 (March 19, 1992) pp34-35. "[Wayne's World]" (Schiffman, Bonnie)
PH11165 626 (March 19, 1992) pp[cover]. "Wayne's World: It's Party Time! It's Excellent!" (Schiffman, Bonnie)
PH11166 656 (May 13, 1993) p15. "Mike Myers (left) And Elton John" (Mazur, Kevin)
PH11167 656 (May 13, 1993) p52. "Myers And Carvey: Partners Who Aren't Really Partners"
PH11168 663 (August 19, 1993) p82. "A Lovely Ax Murderer Leaves Mike Myers Hanging"
PH11169 706 (April 20, 1995) p86. "The 'SNL' Legacy Of Screen Shame"
MYERS, MIKE—PHOTOGRAPHS—PORTRAITS
PH11170 645-646 (December 10, 1992) pp[cover]. "1992 Yearbook" (Schiffman, Bonnie)
PH11171 645-646 (December 10, 1992) p190. "Mike Myers And Dana Carvey"
MYST (CD-ROM)—ILLUSTRATIONS
PH11172 692 (October 6, 1994) p15. "I Myst You" (Blackwell, Patrick)

MYST (CD-ROM)—PHOTOGRAPHS
PH11173 679 (April 7, 1994) p45. "A Scene From One Of The Worlds Of 'Myst'"
MYSTERY SCIENCE THEATER 3000: THE MOVIE (FILM)—PHOTOGRAPHS
PH11174 733 (May 2, 1996) p62. "Nelson And The 'Mst3k' Bots View 'This Island Earth'"

N

NADER, RALPH—ILLUSTRATIONS
PH11175 724-725 (December 28, 1995) p20. "Huge Corporate Profits" (Pendergrast, James T.)
NADER, RALPH—PHOTOGRAPHS
PH11176 721 (November 16, 1995) p86. "In The Beginning: Nader Testifies Before Congress In 1966 On Proposed Auto-Safety regulation, The First Crusade That Brought Him Into The Public Spotlight"
PH11177 721 (November 16, 1995) p91. "Nader Speaks To Supporters Outside Seabrook's Nuclear Power Plant, In New Hampshire, In November 1991, During His Short-Lived Presidential Bid" (Wyman, Ira)
PH11178 721 (November 16, 1995) p88. "Nader's Devotion To Real Democracy Led Him To Endorse Mark Green For New York's Public Advocate In 1993" (Albans, Michael)
PH11179 721 (November 16, 1995) p85. "[Ralph Nader]" (Meeks, Raymond)
NADJA (FILM)—PHOTOGRAPHS
PH11180 715 (August 24, 1995) p108. "The Man Eaters"
NAJIMY, KATHY—PHOTOGRAPHS
PH11181 633 (June 25, 1992) p48. "Goldberg (left) And Najimy Are Singing Nuns On The Run"
PH11182 639 (September 17, 1992) p102. "Best Supporting Actress"
NAKATANI, MICHIE—PHOTOGRAPHS
PH11183 654 (April 15, 1993) pp[enc.29]. "Michie Nakatani, Atsuko Yamano And Naoko Yamano (from left)" (Simons, Chip)
NAKED (FILM)—PHOTOGRAPHS
PH11184 672-673 (December 23, 1993) p174. "[Naked]"
PH11185 674 (January 27, 1994) p48. "Acting Vehicles Include 'The Pelican Brief,' 'In The Name Of The Father,' 'What's Eating Gilbert Grape,' 'Shadowlands,' 'Naked,' And 'Grumpy Old Men'"
PH11186 678 (March 24, 1994) p100. "Missing In Oscar Action"
NAKED GUN 33 1/3
PH11187 680 (April 21, 1994) p93. "Smith Gives Cop Nielsen Double Trouble"
NAKED IN NEW YORK (FILM)—PHOTOGRAPHS
PH11188 681 (May 5, 1994) p49. "Soap Star Turner Puts The Moves On Writer Stoltz"
NAKED LUNCH (BOOK)—PHOTOGRAPHS
PH11189 652 (March 18, 1993) pp[enc.6]. "Naked Lunch"
NAKED LUNCH (FILM)—ILLUSTRATIONS
PH11190 623 (February 6, 1992) p87. "Literary Freak Shows" (Rosen, Jonathon)
NAKED LUNCH (FILM)—PHOTOGRAPHS
PH11191 623 (February 6, 1992) p88. "Peter Weller Confronts His Literary Nightmares"
NALL, ANITA—PHOTOGRAPHS
PH11192 634-635 (July 9, 1992) p96. "Anita Nall" (Zander, Peter)
NANCE, TODD—PHOTOGRAPHS
PH11193 631 (May 28, 1992) p17. "Widespread Panic (from left): John Bell, Michael Houser, Todd Nance, David Schools And Domingo Ortiz" (Messer, Alan)
NAPOLITANO, JOHNETTE—PHOTOGRAPHS
PH11194 628 (April 16, 1992) p13. "World Party Guitarist Jeffrey Trott (left) With Napolitano And Prieboy" (Karas, Steve)
PH11195 670 (November 25, 1993) p37. "Johnette Napolitano Toasts Johnny Depp" (Kravitz, Jeff)
PH11196 678 (March 24, 1994) p22. "Concrete Proof: Napolitano" (Natkin, Paul)
PH11197 681 (May 5, 1994) p22. "Napolitano Puts Concrete Blonde To Bed" (Diltz, Henry)
NARCIZO, DAVID—PHOTOGRAPHS
PH11198 637 (August 20, 1992) p9. "Steve Shelley, Kim Gordon, Lee Ranaldo, Shake-A-Leg's Harry Horgan, Moore, Hersh And David Narcizo (from left)" (Robicheau, Paul)
PH11199 703 (March 9, 1995) p54. "Giving In To The Muses: Drummer David Narcizo, Hersh And Bassist Bernard Georges (from left)" (Seliger, Mark)
PH11200 703 (March 9, 1995) p55. "The Throwing Muses Lineup In 1989 (from left): Hersh, Leslie Langston, Tanya Donelly And Narcizo" (Musto, Ilpo)
NAS—ALBUMS
PH11201 684 (June 16, 1994) p124. "Illmatic For The People: NAS" (Allen, Terry)
PH11202 743 (September 19, 1996) p82. "It Was Written"
NAS—PHOTOGRAPHS
PH11203 682 (May 19, 1994) p64. "[Nas]" (Seliger, Mark)
NASA—ILLUSTRATIONS
PH11204 632 (June 11, 1992) p72. "USA" (Cronin, Brian)
PH11205 708 (May 18, 1995) p14. "Mars" (Pendergrast, James T.)
NASA—PHOTOGRAPHS
PH11206 632 (June 11, 1992) p73. "[NASA]" (Leibovitz, Annie)
PH11207 705 (April 6, 1995) p56. "The Apollo Capsule In Which Three Astronauts Died"
PH11208 705 (April 6, 1995) p56. "'Hubble' Telescope Gets Eye Surgery"
PH11209 705 (April 6, 1995) p54. "Off-The-Shelf Desktop Computers In The New Control Room"
PH11210 705 (April 6, 1995) p56. "A Rogues' Gallery: 'Challenger' Explodes"
PH11211 705 (April 6, 1995) p54. "Then And Now: Retro-NASA's Mainframe Terminals (above)"
NASH, GRAHAM—PHOTOGRAPHS
PH11212 625 (March 5, 1992) p18. "Sara Lee, Crimmins, Graham Nash, Amy Ray, Emily Saliers, David Crosby, Etheridge, Carpenter (from left)" (Berg, Lisa)
PH11213 672-673 (December 23, 1993) p74. "Graham Nash, Van Halen And Young" (Blakesberg, Jay)
PH11214 679 (April 7, 1994) p37. "Ain't Gonna Work On Yasgur's Farm No More: Phil Lesh, Crosby, Nash, Jorma Kaukonen" (Blakesberg, Jay)
NASH, JIM—PHOTOGRAPHS
PH11215 722 (November 30, 1995) p31. "Industrial-Music Pioneers Dannie Flesher And Jim Nash At The Wax Trax! Offices In Chicago's Wicker Park, October 1994" (Chung, Andre F.)
NASH RAMBLERS—ALBUMS
PH11216 625 (March 5, 1992) p70. "At The Ryman"
NASTANOVICH, BOB—PHOTOGRAPHS
PH11217 686-687 (July 14, 1994) p20. "Ibold, Nastanovich And Kannberg (from left)" (Blakesberg, Jay)
PH11218 686-687 (July 14, 1994) p19. "Pavement (clockwise from left): Mark Ibold, Steve West, Bob Nastanovich And Stephen Malkmus" (Blakesberg, Jay)
PH11219 695 (November 17, 1994) p78. "Pavement" (Hanauer, Mark)
NASTASE, ILIE—PHOTOGRAPHS
PH11220 750-751 (December 26, 1996) p63. "[Ilie Nastase]"
NATION OF ULYSSES—PHOTOGRAPHS
PH11221 615 (October 17, 1991) p20. "Nation Of Ulysses" (Harrison, Mark)
NATIONAL ENDOWMENT FOR THE ARTS—ILLUSTRATIONS
PH11222 722 (November 30, 1995) p14. "The Humanities" (Pendergrast, James T.)

NATIONAL RIFLE ASSOCIATION—ILLUSTRATIONS
PH11223 709 (June 1, 1995) p32. "All He Says Is He Ain't Bambi, Senator" (Witte, Michael)
PH11224 723 (December 14, 1995) p22. "Welcome To Fear Itself" (Pendergrast, James T.)
PH11225 749 (December 12, 1996) p16. "Choose Your Neighbors" (Pendergrast, James T.)
NATIONAL RIFLE ASSOCIATION—PHOTOGRAPHS
PH11226 720 (November 2, 1995) p57. "At The NRA Convention, A Display Of Rifles Covered By The Semiautomatic-Weapons Ban" (Winters, Dan)
PH11227 720 (November 2, 1995) p56. "NRA Conventioneers Show Off Their Gun Patches" (Winters, Dan)
NATIONAL SERVICE—PHOTOGRAPHS
PH11228 691 (September 22, 1994) p44. "Boston Director Ron Homer Jr. (center left) And Supervisor Wilbur Brown (center, right) Let The Kids Find Their Own Remedies To Urban Blight" (Ng, Karjean)
PH11229 691 (September 22, 1994) p41. "Young Baltimore Participants Perform Calisthenics Weekday Mornings At City Hall" (Wolfe, Tom)
NATIONAL TECHNOLOGICAL UNIVERSITY—ILLUSTRATIONS
PH11230 666 (September 30, 1993) p60. "[Higher Education]"
THE NATIVE AMERICANS (TELEVISION SHOW)—PHOTOGRAPHS
PH11231 692 (October 6, 1994) p27. "[The Native Americans]"
NATURAL BORN KILLERS (FILM)—PHOTOGRAPHS
PH11232 684 (June 16, 1994) p116. "Bloody: Lewis And Harrelson In "Natural Born Killers""
NATURAL BORN KILLERS (FILM)—ILLUSTRATIONS
PH11233 690 (September 8, 1994) p83. "Blood From A Stone" (Gosfield, Josh)
NATURAL BORN KILLERS (FILM)—PHOTOGRAPHS
PH11234 690 (September 8, 1994) p84. "Crimescape: Juliette Lewis With Cop Tom Sizemore"
PH11235 690 (September 8, 1994) p84. "Killer Lover Boy Woody Harrelson"
PH11236 690 (September 8, 1994) p84. "Lewis And Harrelson"
PH11237 698-699 (December 29, 1994) p199. "[Natural Born Killers]"
NAUGHTY BY NATURE—ALBUMS
PH11238 655 (April 29, 1993) p61. "19 Naughty III"
PH11239 672-673 (December 23, 1993) p156. "19 Naughty III"
PH11240 710 (June 15, 1995) p80. "Poverty's Paradise"
NAUGHTY BY NATURE—PHOTOGRAPHS
PH11241 615 (October 17, 1991) p27. "Naughty By Nature: DJ Kay Gee, Treach And Vinnie (from left)" (Larsen, Kristine)
PH11242 619-620 (December 12, 1991) p86. "You Down Wit' Naughty By Nature?"
PH11243 656 (May 13, 1993) p32. "Naughty By Nature With Flavor Flav (center)" (Capak, R. J.)
PH11244 658 (June 10, 1993) p30. "From Illtown To Chilltown: Naughty's Treach, Vinnie And DJ KayGee" (Larsen, Kristine)
PH11245 663 (August 19, 1993) pp66-68,70. "[Naughty By Nature]" (Gregoire, Jean Louis)
PH11246 695 (November 17, 1994) p110. "Naughty By Nature" (Callis, Chris)
NAVARRO, DAVE—ILLUSTRATIONS
PH11247 736 (June 13, 1996) p38. "Dave Navarro" (Cowles, David)
NAVARRO, DAVE—PHOTOGRAPHS
PH11248 653 (April 1, 1993) p11. "Navarro, Michael Murphy And Avery" (Cohen, Lester)
PH11249 668 (October 28, 1993) p17. "Through The Pepper Mill: The Newest Member Is Dave Navarro" (Dokus, Peter)
PH11250 692 (October 6, 1994) p17. "Peppers Roast: Flea, Anthony Kiedis, Dave Navarro, Chad Smith (from left)" (Mazur, Kevin)
PH11251 706 (April 20, 1995) p16. "[Dave Navarro]" (Johanson, Karen)
PH11252 709 (June 1, 1995) p21. "RHCPs (from left): Flea, Chad Smith, Dave Navarro And Anthony Kiedis" (Streiber, Art)
PH11253 715 (August 24, 1995) p54. "Jane's Addiction, 1990: Farrell, Perkins, Dave Navarro And Eric Avery (from left)" (Miller, Peter Darley)
PH11254 719 (October 19, 1995) p55. "Guitarist Navarro (left) Bonds With Drummer Smith" (Corbijn, Anton)
PH11255 719 (October 19, 1995) p58. "Red Hot Chili Peppers, '95: Dave Navarro, Anthony Kiedis, Flea An Chad Smith (from left)" (Corbijn, Anton)
PH11256 722 (November 30, 1995) p19. "[Red Hot Chili Peppers]" (Musto, Ilpo)
PH11257 731 (April 4, 1996) p17. "Bush Covers? Chili Peppers Frontman Anthony Kiedis, Bassist Flea, The Not-Unattractive Navarro And Drummer Chad Smith (from left)" (Baehler, Chapman)
PH11258 749 (December 12, 1996) p19. "Rhapsody In Blues: Navarro And His Lady Friend, Monet Mazur" (Mazur, Kevin)
NAVARRO, DAVE—PHOTOGRAPHS—PORTRAITS
PH11259 672-673 (December 23, 1993) p65. "Below: Dave Navarro, The New Red-Hot Guitarist" (Cuffaro, Chris)
PH11260 703 (March 9, 1995) p21. "Red Hot Chili Peppers Anthony Kiedis (left) And Dave Navarro At The Slayer Blowout In Los Angeles" (Cohen, Lester)
N.D.—PHOTOGRAPHS
PH11261 689 (August 25, 1994) p44. "All Together Now: Trombino, Atom, Kennedy, Reis, N.D., Petey X, Apollo 9, Froberg (from left)" (Cuffaro, Chris)
NDEGEOCELLO, ME' SHELL—ALBUMS
PH11262 669 (November 11, 1993) p76. "Plantation Lullabies"
PH11263 738-739 (July 11, 1996) p86. "Peace Beyond Passion"
NDEGEOCELLO, ME' SHELL—ILLUSTRATIONS
PH11264 698-699 (December 29, 1994) p38. "[Me'shell NdegeOcello]" (Brown, Calef)
PH11265 742 (September 5, 1996) p13. "Me'Shell Ndegeocello" (Dionisi, Sandra)
PH11266 745 (October 17, 1996) p24. "Grits Lake" (Pendergrast, James T.)
NDEGEOCELLO, ME' SHELL—PHOTOGRAPHS
PH11267 693 (October 20, 1994) p52. "Unpredictable Me'shell NdegeOcello" (Mazur, Kevin)
PH11268 736 (June 13, 1996) p51. "NdegeOcello Offers A Molotov Cocktail Of Funk And Politics" (Smith, Gavin)
NDEGEOCELLO, ME' SHELL—PHOTOGRAPHS—PORTRAITS
PH11269 670 (November 25, 1993) p32. "[Me'shell NdegeOcello]" (Lass, Imke)
PH11270 674 (January 27, 1994) p42. "The Bright Stuff: Me'shell" (Daks, Michael)
PH11271 692 (October 6, 1994) p50. "Me'shell NdegeOcello" (Vial, Veronique)
PH11272 695 (November 17, 1994) p33. "Me'Shell NdegeOcello" (Watson, Albert)
PH11273 742 (September 5, 1996) p32. "[Me'shell NdegeOcello]" (Seliger, Mark)
N'DOUR, YOUSSOU—ALBUMS
PH11274 638 (September 3, 1992) p67. "Eyes Open"
N'DOUR, YOUSSOU—PHOTOGRAPHS
PH11275 655 (April 29, 1993) p12. "Cherry (left) And N'Dour" (Gershoff, Gary)
PH11276 686-687 (July 14, 1994) p42. "Seven Seconds With Cherry And N'Dour"
N'DOUR, YOUSSOU—PHOTOGRAPHS—PORTRAITS
PH11277 689 (August 25, 1994) p45. "Breaking The Language Barrier: Youssou N'Dour" (Gougenheim, Kim)
NEDDE, DOUG—PHOTOGRAPHS
PH11278 691 (September 22, 1994) pp[enc.28]. "Heidi Tappan And Friend Doug Nedde At Sweetwaters, In Burlington, Vt." (Borris, Dan)
NED'S ATOMIC DUSTBIN—ALBUMS
PH11279 652 (March 18, 1993) p52. "Are You Normal?"

NED'S ATOMIC DUSTBIN—PHOTOGRAPHS
PH11280 627 (April 2, 1992) p19. "Ned's Atomic Dustbin (from left): Rat, Alex, Jonn, Dan And Mat" (Double, Steve)
PH11281 645-646 (December 10, 1992) p57. "Ned's Atomic Dustbin"
NEESON, LIAM—PHOTOGRAPHS
PH11282 672-673 (December 23, 1993) p174. "[Schindler's List]"
PH11283 698-699 (December 29, 1994) p199. "Foster And Neeson In "Nell""
PH11284 707 (May 4, 1995) p74. "Roth And Neeson In 'Rob Roy'"
PH11285 730 (March 21, 1996) p106. ""Before" (from left): Neeson, Furlong And Streep"
NEFERTITI—PHOTOGRAPHS
PH11286 684 (June 16, 1994) p30. "The "L.I.F.E." And Times Of Nefertiti" (Posey, Carl)
NEGATIVLAND—ALBUMS
PH11287 624 (February 20, 1992) p11. "The Cover Of Negativland's Parody 'U2'"
NEGATIVLAND—PHOTOGRAPHS
PH11288 689 (August 25, 1994) p36. "Gee, We're Sorry: Negativland In 1991"
NEIL, VINCE—ALBUMS
PH11289 664 (September 2, 1993) p62. "Exposed"
NEIL, VINCE—PHOTOGRAPHS
PH11290 744 (October 3, 1996) p21. "Neil Gives His Fans Their Own Theater Of Pain"
NEIL, VINCE—PHOTOGRAPHS—PORTRAITS
PH11291 627 (April 2, 1992) p13. "Motley Crue's Tommy Lee, Nikki Sixx, Mick Mars And The Defrocked Vince Neil (clockwise from top left)" (Double, Steve)
NEILL, SAM—PHOTOGRAPHS
PH11292 659 (June 24, 1993) p36. "Dern (with Joseph Mazzello And Sam Neill) Perks Up A Sick Dino" (Close, Murray)
PH11293 703 (March 9, 1995) p72. "Sam Neill Flares Up"
NELL (FILM)—PHOTOGRAPHS
PH11294 698-699 (December 29, 1994) p199. "Foster And Neeson In "Nell""
NELSON—PHOTOGRAPHS
PH11295 619-620 (December 12, 1991) p19. "Nelson Releases Its Patriotic Urges" (Granitz, Steve)
NELSON, BRIAN—PHOTOGRAPHS—PORTRAITS
PH11296 655 (April 29, 1993) p24. "Revving It Up: Velocity's Shannon, Spellman, Nelson, Riles And Moore (from left)" (Falls, John)
NELSON, GEORGE—PHOTOGRAPHS—PORTRAITS
PH11297 659 (June 24, 1993) p48. "The Orioles: Sonny Til, Johnny Reed, Tommy Gaither, George Nelson And Alexander Sharp"
NELSON, HARRIET—PHOTOGRAPHS—PORTRAITS
PH11298 698-699 (December 29, 1994) p85. "Harriet Nelson, The Ultimate TV Mom"
NELSON, MARC—PHOTOGRAPHS
PH11299 628 (April 16, 1992) p57. "Carleen Anderson, Marc Nelson And Femi Williams (from left)"
NELSON, MIKE—PHOTOGRAPHS
PH11300 733 (May 2, 1996) p62. "Nelson And The 'Mst3k' Bots View 'This Island Earth'"
NELSON, RICKY—PHOTOGRAPHS
PH11301 638 (September 3, 1992) p72. "Brad Pitt Worships At The Altar Of Idol Ricky Nelson"
NELSON, SEAN—PHOTOGRAPHS
PH11302 690 (September 8, 1994) p87. "Drug Runner Nelson Plays Chess With Dad Jackson"
PH11303 693 (October 20, 1994) p30. "Sean Nelson, Star Of "Fresh," With The Wu-Tang Clan In New York City" (Friedman, Steve)
NELSON, SHARA—ALBUMS
PH11304 696 (December 1, 1994) p122. "What Silence Knows"
NELSON, SHARA—PHOTOGRAPHS—PORTRAITS
PH11305 692 (October 6, 1994) p32. "British Soul Singer Shara Nelson Speaks Out" (Cultice, Joseph)
NELSON, WILLIE—ALBUMS
PH11306 656 (May 13, 1993) p110. "Across The Borderline"
PH11307 672-673 (December 23, 1993) p157. "Across The Borderline"
NELSON, WILLIE—PHOTOGRAPHS
PH11308 619-620 (December 12, 1991) p94. "The All-Star Jam Finale At The Bridge Concert" (Blakesberg, Jay)
PH11309 629 (April 30, 1992) p11. "Nelson (left) With Young Backstage" (Mazur, Kevin)
PH11310 645-646 (December 10, 1992) p39. "Farm Aid Hero Willie Nelson" (Mazur, Kevin)
PH11311 658 (June 10, 1993) p17. "Willie Nelson (left) And Neil Young" (Roberts, Ebet)
PH11312 659 (June 24, 1993) p13. "Edie Brickell And Paul Simon Join Nelson (left) For His Televised Birthday Celebration" (Kennedy, Bill)
PH11313 672-673 (December 23, 1993) p30. "Above: Nelson (left) With Well_wisher Dylan" (Kennedy, Bill)
PH11314 685 (June 30, 1994) p40. "[Willie Nelson & Bubba Dodd]" (Sanchez, Bobby)
PH11315 702 (February 23, 1995) p48. "Willie Nelson (left) With Rev. Al Green" (Mazur, Kevin)
PH11316 703 (March 9, 1995) p34. "[Willie Nelson]" (Lange, George)
PH11317 707 (May 4, 1995) p19. "Nelson, Rick Sims, Spaghetti (from left)" (Davis, Lisa)
PH11318 721 (November 16, 1995) p25. "Nelson, Supersuckers Eddie Spaghetti And Dan Bolton (from left) Lend A Hand" (Roberts, Ebet)
PH11319 743 (September 19, 1996) p40. "Country Rastaman: Nelson And His Faithful Guitar Trigger" (Carrico, John)
PH11320 748 (November 28, 1996) p26. "Neil Young, John Mellencamp And Willie Nelson, Talking, Presumably, About The Plight Of The Family Farmer" (Roberts, Ebet)
NELSON, WILLIE—PHOTOGRAPHS—PORTRAITS
PH11321 750-751 (December 26, 1996) p175. "Willie Nelson" (Seliger, Mark)
NEPKIE, JANET—PHOTOGRAPHS—PORTRAITS
PH11322 639 (September 17, 1992) p84. "Janet Nepkie Is All Business" (Borris, Dan)
NESHEIM, JAKE—PHOTOGRAPHS
PH11323 721 (November 16, 1995) p33. "John Kirsch, Braden Blake, Jake Nesheim And Chris Lockwood (from left)" (Moskowitz, Karen)
NESMITH, MIKE—PHOTOGRAPHS
PH11324 626 (March 19, 1992) p25. "[Mike Nesmith]" (Granitz, Steve)
NESS, MIKE—PHOTOGRAPHS
PH11325 634-635 (July 9, 1992) p32. "Chris Reece, Mike Ness, John Maurer And Dennis Danell (from left)" (Cuffaro, Chris)
PH11326 666 (September 30, 1993) p28. "SD's Mike Ness" (Mercer, Lance)
PH11327 693 (October 20, 1994) p30. "Social Distortion's Ness" (Bain, Rick)
PH11328 711 (June 29, 1995) p12. "Orange County's Punk Finery: SD's Mike Ness" (Johnson, Lisa)
NESS, MIKE—PHOTOGRAPHS—PORTRAITS
PH11329 750-751 (December 26, 1996) p58. "Mike Ness Of Social Distortion"
THE NET (FILM)—PHOTOGRAPHS
PH11330 715 (August 24, 1995) p108. "Dangerous Women: Michelle Pfeiffer, Sandra Bullock, Julia Roberts, Cindy Crawford And Natasha Henstridge"
NEUFELD, MACE—PHOTOGRAPHS
PH11331 696 (December 1, 1994) p116. "Tom Clancy And Harrison Ford On The Set Of "Clear And Present Danger""

NEUWIRTH, BOB—ALBUMS
PH11332 700 (January 26, 1995) p61. "Last Day On Earth"
NEUWIRTH, BOB—PHOTOGRAPHS
PH11333 678 (March 24, 1994) p27. "Bob Neuwirth (left) And John Cale" (Mark, Mary Ellen)
NEVELS, COREY—PHOTOGRAPHS
PH11334 678 (March 24, 1994) p89. "Corey Nevels With Young Farmers In Just Hall, At Howard University" (Wolff, Tom)
NEVILLE, AARON—ALBUMS
PH11335 619-620 (December 12, 1991) p182. "Warm Your Heart"
PH11336 662 (August 5, 1993) p68. "The Grand Tour"
PH11337 709 (June 1, 1995) p61. "The Tattooed Heart"
NEVILLE, AARON—PHOTOGRAPHS
PH11338 625 (March 5, 1992) p17. "Neil Young Takes Center Stage During The All-Star-Jam Finale" (Gershoff, Gary)
PH11339 625 (March 5, 1992) p11. "Neville, Longhair's Son Alexander Byrd" (Mazur, Kevin)
PH11340 682 (May 19, 1994) p38. "Marsalis (left) And Neville, Pre-Show" (Mazur, Kevin)
NEVILLE, ART—PHOTOGRAPHS
PH11341 711 (June 29, 1995) p18. "B. B. King, Robert Cray, Buddy Guy, Art Neville, Jimmie Vaughan, Clapton, Raitt And Tommy Shannon" (Long, Andrew)
NEVILLE BROTHERS—ALBUMS
PH11342 634-635 (July 9, 1992) p102. "Family Groove"
NEVOLO, GREG—PHOTOGRAPHS
PH11343 668 (October 28, 1993) p73. "At Cafe O'Lake" (Newton, Philip)
PH11344 668 (October 28, 1993) p73. "At The Bridge Tender" (Newton, Philip)
PH11345 668 (October 28, 1993) p70. "Greg At Granite Chief, In Squaw Valley" (Newton, Philip)
PH11346 668 (October 28, 1993) pp70,72. "[Greg Nevolo]" (Newton, Philip)
PH11347 668 (October 28, 1993) p73. "Greg With His Dog" (Newton, Philip)
NEW EDITION—ALBUMS
PH11348 745 (October 17, 1996) p132. "Home Again"
NEW ENGLAND SHELTER FOR HOMELESS VETERANS—PHOTOGRAPHS
PH11349 659 (June 24, 1993) p66. "The Cafeteria And Rec Room" (Agulera-Helwig, Max)
NEW JACK CITY (FILM)—PHOTOGRAPHS
PH11350 619-620 (December 12, 1991) p31. "Ice-T In 'New Jack City'"
NEW KIDS ON THE BLOCK—PHOTOGRAPHS
PH11351 619-620 (December 12, 1991) p80. "[New Kids On The Block]" (Mazur, Kevin)
PH11352 645-646 (December 10, 1992) p30. "[New Kids On The Block]" (Mazur, Kevin)
NEW KINGDOM—ALBUMS
PH11353 745 (October 17, 1996) p132. "Paradise Don't Come Cheap"
NEW MEDIA—ILLUSTRATIONS
PH11354 666 (September 30, 1993) p10. "Home Alone 3!" (Pendergrast, James T.)
NEW ORDER—ALBUMS
PH11355 617 (November 14, 1991) p102. "Power, Corruption And Lies" (Saville, Peter)
PH11356 659 (June 24, 1993) p77. "Republic"
PH11357 660-661 (July 8, 1993) p136. "Republic"
NEW ORDER—ILLUSTRATIONS
PH11358 659 (June 24, 1993) p77. "The New 'Republic' Of Desire" (Lardy, Philippe)
NEW ORLEANS, LOUISIANA—PHOTOGRAPHS
PH11359 710 (June 15, 1995) p46. "[Mid City Lanes Rock 'N Bowl]" (Knapp, Bevil)
NEW YORK CITY, NEW YORK—PHOTOGRAPHS
PH11360 621 (January 9, 1992) p24. "Ruby Welcomes The Crowd In New York" (Pulin, Chuck)
PH11361 660-661 (July 8, 1993) p38. "In 1990, People Gathered In New York's Central Park To Mark The Tenth Anniversary Of John Lennon's Murder" (Everke, Tobias)
PH11362 672-673 (December 23, 1993) p137. "Above: The Corner Where It Began For Him"
PH11363 701 (February 9, 1995) pp48,51-52. "[Graffiti]"
PH11364 701 (February 9, 1995) pp48-49. "[Graffiti]" (Fink, Larry)
PH11365 717 (September 21, 1995) p24. "Strawberry Fields In New York's Central Park On The Night Of Aug. 9" (Berkwitz, David)
NEW YORK DOLLS—PHOTOGRAPHS
PH11366 718 (October 5, 1995) p50. "New York Dolls, In Full Glam Regalia, Performing On Television In The Mid-'70s" (Gruen, Bob)
NEW YORK POST (PUBLICATION)—PHOTOGRAPHS
PH11367 734 (May 16, 1996) p72. "The 'Post' Headline"
NEW YORK ROCK (STAGE MUSICAL)—PHOTOGRAPHS
PH11368 679 (April 7, 1994) p28. "'New York' Rockers: Yoko Ono (center) And Cast" (Borris, Dan)
NEWARK, NEW JERSEY—PHOTOGRAPHS
PH11369 640 (October 1, 1992) p35. "Even The Kids Wait For The Show To Start" (Mark, Mary Ellen)
NEWELL, MARTIN—ALBUMS
PH11370 689 (August 25, 1994) p90. "The Greatest Living Englishman"
NEWMAN, JIM—PHOTOGRAPHS
PH11371 644 (November 26, 1992) p64. "[Jim Newman]" (Noble, Chris)
NEWMAN, PAUL—PHOTOGRAPHS
PH11372 678 (March 24, 1994) p105. "Robbins (left) And Newman Play Office Politics, While Leigh (far right) Gets The Story"
PH11373 698-699 (December 29, 1994) p199. "Newman In "Fool""
PH11374 733 (May 2, 1996) p14. "[Gwyneth Paltrow, Brad Pitt, & Paul Newman]" (Ferreir, Albert)
NEWMAN, RANDY—ALBUMS
PH11375 723 (December 14, 1995) p84. "Faust"
NEWMAN, RANDY—PHOTOGRAPHS
PH11376 697 (December 15, 1994) p28. "[Randy Newman]" (Feingold, Deborah)
NEWS MEDIA—ILLUSTRATIONS
PH11377 616 (October 31, 1991) p101. "[News Media]" (Kuper, Peter)
PH11378 625 (March 5, 1992) p33. "News At 5" (Cronin, Brian)
PH11379 628 (April 16, 1992) p31. "Policy" (Cronin, Brian)
PH11380 645-646 (December 10, 1992) p115. "[Elections]" (Cronin, Brian)
PH11381 660-661 (July 8, 1993) p10. "Goldilocks, The Journalist" (Pendergrast, James T.)
PH11382 662 (August 5, 1993) p8. "Minimum Security" (Pendergrast, James T.)
PH11383 670 (November 25, 1993) p48. "What's Black And White And Goes Unread?" (Klein, Renee)
NEWSRADIO (TELEVISION SHOW)—ILLUSTRATIONS
PH11384 729 (March 7, 1996) p57. "[Dave Foley]" (Fishman, Miriam)
NEWSTED, JASON—PHOTOGRAPHS
PH11385 681 (May 5, 1994) p21. "Primus's Les Claypool And Metallica's Jason Newsted" (Blakesberg, Jay)
PH11386 708 (May 18, 1995) p74. "Metallica In 1991, From Left: Hammett, Ulrich, Newsted, Hetfield" (Seliger, Mark)
PH11387 727 (February 8, 1996) p12. "Fifty And Fabulous! Kilmister (center) Flanked By Metallica's Jason Newsted, James Hetfield, Kirk Hammett And Lars Ulrich (from left)" (Disanto, Annamaria)
PH11388 728 (February 22, 1996) p25. "Metallica's James Hetfield, Kirk Hammett, Lars Ulrich And Jason Newsted (from

left)"
PH11389 737 (June 27, 1996) p36. "Not Just Riding Shotgun: Newsted (left), Hammett" (Corbijn, Anton)
NEWSWEEK (PUBLICATION)—PHOTOGRAPHS
PH11390 670 (November 25, 1993) p48. "[Newsweek, Time]"
NEWTON, THANDIE—PHOTOGRAPHS
PH11391 706 (April 20, 1995) p89. "Nolte's Jefferson Toys With Slave Thandie Newton"
NGUYEN, MARY—PHOTOGRAPHS
PH11392 617 (November 14, 1991) pp56-58,61,65. "They Call Her Mom" (Winters, Dan)
NICE, PETE—ALBUMS
PH11393 669 (November 11, 1993) p76. "Dust To Dust"
NICHOLS, BOB—PHOTOGRAPHS
PH11394 740 (August 8, 1996) p35. "Egypt, September 1978" (Boot, Adrian)
NICHOLS, TAYLOR—PHOTOGRAPHS
PH11395 688 (August 11, 1994) p63. "It's Ole To Nichols, Bergen, Eigeman And Sorvino"
NICHOLSEN, JACK—PHOTOGRAPHS
PH11396 616 (October 31, 1991) p25. "The Leslie Spit Treeo (from left): Jack Nicholsen, Laura Hubert, Pat Langner And Tag" (Counts, Wyatt)
NICHOLSON, JACK—ILLUSTRATIONS—PORTRAITS
PH11397 647 (January 7, 1993) p49. "The Two Jacks" (Payne, C. F.)
NICHOLSON, JACK—PHOTOGRAPHS
PH11398 615 (October 17, 1991) p65. "Jack Nicholson And Family, 1990" (Pigozzi, Jean)
PH11399 619-620 (December 12, 1991) p22. "Lifer Bob Dylan With Jack Nicholson" (Mazur, Kevin)
PH11400 645-646 (December 10, 1992) p190. "Jack Nicholson"
PH11401 645-646 (December 10, 1992) p153. "Jack Nicholson, 1981"
PH11402 647 (January 7, 1993) p50. "...And Danny DeVito"
PH11403 647 (January 7, 1993) p50. "Jack Nicholson: On The Spot With To Cruise (left)..."
PH11404 649 (February 4, 1993) p72. "[Man Trouble]"
PH11405 656 (May 13, 1993) p114. "Above, More King Characters Show Their Dark Side: Kathy Bates ('Misery'), Jack Nicholson ('The Shining'), Sissy Spacek ('Carrie')"
PH11406 684 (June 16, 1994) p116. "Creepy: Nicholson Puts The Bite On Pfeiffer In "Wolf""
PH11407 686-687 (July 14, 1994) p98. "Nicholson And Pfeiffer ("Wolf")"
PH11408 722 (November 30, 1995) p75. "Regrets For Nicholson And Huston"
PH11409 727 (February 8, 1996) p13. "[Jack Nicholson & Elle Macpherson]"
NICK OF TIME (FILM)—PHOTOGRAPHS
PH11410 718 (October 5, 1995) p76. "Pulp To Come"
PH11411 723 (December 14, 1995) p92. "Race Against Time: Chase And Depp"
NICKLES, DON—PHOTOGRAPHS—PORTRAITS
PH11412 719 (October 19, 1995) p49. "Nickles" (Downing, Larry)
NICKS, STEVIE—ALBUMS
PH11413 690 (September 8, 1994) p78. "Street Angel"
NICKS, STEVIE—PHOTOGRAPHS
PH11414 651 (March 4, 1993) p21. "Gala Groove: Hillary, Chelsea, Bill, Michael Jackson And Stevie Nicks" (Mazur, Kevin)
PH11415 731 (April 4, 1996) p30. "Stevie Nicks In Full Gypsy Regalia" (Bodnar, George)
NICKS, STEVIE—PHOTOGRAPHS—PORTRAITS
PH11416 643 (November 12, 1992) p101. "Stevie Nicks" (Rolston, Matthew)
PH11417 691 (September 22, 1994) p34. "[Stevie Nicks]" (Lachappell, David)
NICO—PHOTOGRAPHS
PH11418 718 (October 5, 1995) p46. "The Velvet Underground (clockwise from bottom left): Nico, Reed, Morrison, Cale And Tucker"
NICOL, SIMON—PHOTOGRAPHS
PH11419 691 (September 22, 1994) p21. "Ric Sanders, Simon Nicol And Richard Thompson (from left)" (Robicheau, Paul)
NICOLETTE—PHOTOGRAPHS
PH11420 718 (October 5, 1995) p32. "Nicolette, Stephen Lewinson, Daddy G (from left)" (Mazur, Kevin)
NICOLO, JOE—PHOTOGRAPHS
PH11421 741 (August 22, 1996) p72. "[Ruffhouse]" (Whitt, Christina)
NIELSEN, LESLIE—PHOTOGRAPHS
PH11422 680 (April 21, 1994) p93. "Smith Gives Cop Nielsen Double Trouble"
NIELSEN, RICK—PHOTOGRAPHS
PH11423 723 (December 14, 1995) p27. "The Chicago Eight: D'Arcy, Petersson, Carlos, Corgan, Nielsen, Iha, Chamberlin And Zander (from left)" (Elledge, Paul)
NIES, ERIC—ILLUSTRATIONS
PH11424 684 (June 16, 1994) p11. "Rope" (Pendergrast, James T.)
NIES, ERIC—PHOTOGRAPHS
PH11425 680 (April 21, 1994) pp[enc.20]. "At Football Practice In 1988"
PH11426 680 (April 21, 1994) pp[enc.18]. "Below, Amid His Sneaker Collection On The Floor Of His Closet" (Rossi, Aldo)
PH11427 680 (April 21, 1994) pp[enc.5]. "[Eric Nies]" (Rossi, Aldo)
PH11428 680 (April 21, 1994) pp[enc.40]. "Eric Nies At The Little Ones Nursey School, In Deal, N.J., Where His Mother Teaches" (Rossi, Aldo)
PH11429 680 (April 21, 1994) pp[enc.17]. "Eric Nies In-line Skating In Asbury Park, N.J." (Rossi, Aldo)
PH11430 680 (April 21, 1994) pp[enc.21]. "A Guy And His Car At The Old Amusement Park In Asbury Park, N.J." (Rossi, Aldo)
PH11431 680 (April 21, 1994) pp[enc.20]. "In Little League, At Age 12"
PH11432 680 (April 21, 1994) pp[enc.19]. "Opposite, At The Jersey Shore Fitness Shop, In Bradley Beach, Where He Works Out" (Rossi, Aldo)
PH11433 680 (April 21, 1994) pp[enc.20]. "Top Right, At The Windmill Restaurant, Long Branch, N.J." (Rossi, Aldo)
PH11434 680 (April 21, 1994) pp[enc.20]. "With Brother John And Mother"
PH11435 680 (April 21, 1994) pp[enc.18]. "The Young Man And The Sea: Nies At Asbury, N.J." (Rossi, Aldo)
NIES, ERIC—PHOTOGRAPHS—PORTRAITS
PH11436 680 (April 21, 1994) pp[enc.20]. "[Eric Nies]" (Rossi, Aldo)
NIES, JOHN—PHOTOGRAPHS
PH11437 680 (April 21, 1994) pp[enc.20]. "With Brother John And Mother"
NIGHT AND THE CITY (FILM)—PHOTOGRAPHS
PH11438 642 (October 29, 1992) p77. "Night And The City"
NIGHT OF THE LIVING BASEHEADS (VIDEO)—PHOTOGRAPHS
PH11439 667 (October 14, 1993) p85. "'Baseheads': PE's Flav Brings The News"
NIGHT OF THE LIVING DEAD (FILM)—ILLUSTRATIONS
PH11440 669 (November 11, 1993) p80. "The 10 Scariest Movies On Video"
NIGHT ON EARTH (FILM)—ILLUSTRATIONS
PH11441 630 (May 14, 1992) p111. "When Worlds Collide In A Taxicab" (Woolley, Janet)
NIGHT ON EARTH (FILM)—PHOTOGRAPHS
PH11442 630 (May 14, 1992) p112. "Jim Jarmusch Dispatches Driver Winona Ryder"
NIGHTCLUBS—PHOTOGRAPHS
PH11443 630 (May 14, 1992) p89. "[Showers]" (Seliger, Mark)

NIGHTMARE BEFORE CHRISTMAS (FILM)—PHOTOGRAPHS
PH11444 669 (November 11, 1993) p80. "'Nightmare' Lovers Jack And Sally"
NILSEN, JAN—PHOTOGRAPHS
PH11445 644 (November 26, 1992) pp62-63. "[Jan Nilsen]" (Noble, Chris)
NILSSON, HARRY—PHOTOGRAPHS
PH11446 698-699 (December 29, 1994) p83. "Singer-Songwriter Harry Nilsson In 1970"
NILSSON, HARRY—PHOTOGRAPHS—PORTRAITS
PH11447 677 (March 10, 1994) p25. "[Harry Nilsson]"
NINE INCH NAILS—ALBUMS
PH11448 645-646 (December 10, 1992) p184. "Broken"
PH11449 678 (March 24, 1994) p92. "The Downward Spiral"
PH11450 698-699 (December 29, 1994) p173. "The Downward Spiral"
NINE INCH NAILS—ILLUSTRATIONS
PH11451 678 (March 24, 1994) p92. "Hammering" (Drescher, Henrik)
NINE INCH NAILS—PHOTOGRAPHS
PH11452 690 (September 8, 1994) p54. "Vrenna, Woolley, Reznor, Finck, Lohner (from left)" (Cultice, Joseph)
PH11453 692 (October 6, 1994) p17. "[Nine Inch Nails & Larry "Bud" Melman]" (Cultice, Joseph)
PH11454 698-699 (December 29, 1994) p61. "[Nine Inch Nails]" (Mazur, Kevin)
PH11455 700 (January 26, 1995) p51. "Runner-Up Ain't Enough: Trent Reznor Of Nine Inch Nails Drives Home His Point" (Mazur, Kevin)
NINE MONTHS (FILM)—PHOTOGRAPHS
PH11456 709 (June 1, 1995) p68. "Too Much Hugh Grant"
PH11457 714 (August 10, 1995) p62. "Nine Months"
1950S—ILLUSTRATIONS
PH11458 698-699 (December 29, 1994) p153. "Gingrich's Ideal '50s America: When People Thought McCarthy And Father Knew Best" (Plunkert, David)
1994—ILLUSTRATIONS
PH11459 698-699 (December 29, 1994) p169. "The Year In Recordings" (Corio, Paul)
PH11460 702 (February 23, 1995) p16. "[1994]" (Pendergrast, James T.)
1991—ILLUSTRATIONS
PH11461 619-620 (December 12, 1991) p14. "The Sands Of Time" (Pendergrast, James T.)
1991—ILLUSTRATIONS—LETTERING
PH11462 619-620 (December 12, 1991) pp[cover]. "1991 Yearbook" (Ortiz-Lopez, Dennis)
1993 WORLD PEACE AND HEALING GATHERING OF THE RAINBOW FAMILY OF LIVING LIGHT—PHOTOGRAPHS
PH11463 672-673 (December 23, 1993) p120. "Bam-Bam In The Drummers' Circle, 'Blasting Out Babylon'" (Borris, Dan)
PH11464 672-673 (December 23, 1993) p. "Felipe And Lynn Chavez And Children (opposite) Were The Seed People For Kid Village" (Borris, Dan)
PH11465 672-673 (December 23, 1993) p124. "The Herbal Armamentarium At The Center For Alternative-Living Medicine" (Borris, Dan)
PH11466 672-673 (December 23, 1993) p122. "High Camp? The Scene At Faerie Land, The Gathering's Gay Enclave" (Borris, Dan)
PH11467 672-673 (December 23, 1993) p118. "A Rainbow Named Bam-Bam (above) Howls At The Sky" (Borris, Dan)
PH11468 672-673 (December 23, 1993) p126. "Stoking The Breakfast Fire At Kid Village Kitchen: Only Communal Cooking Fires Are Allowed At The Gathering" (Borris, Dan)
PH11469 672-673 (December 23, 1993) p120. "An Unidentified Hare Krishna Rainbow With Homemade Sun Protection" (Borris, Dan)
1992—ILLUSTRATIONS
PH11470 645-646 (December 10, 1992) p7. "[1992]" (Blechman, R. O.)
PH11471 645-646 (December 10, 1992) p208. "Endpaper" (Blechman, R. O.)
PH11472 645-646 (December 10, 1992) p20. "Playing With Fire" (Pendergrast, James T.)
NIRVANA—ALBUMS
PH11473 618 (November 28, 1991) p120. "Nevermind"
PH11474 625 (March 5, 1992) p54. "Nevermind"
PH11475 648 (January 21, 1993) p48. "Incesticide"
PH11476 665 (September 16, 1993) p63. "In Utero"
PH11477 669 (November 11, 1993) p88. "In Utero"
PH11478 676 (February 24, 1994) p16. "In Utero"
PH11479 696 (December 1, 1994) p120. "MTV Unplugged In New York"
PH11480 698-699 (December 29, 1994) p170. "MTV Unplugged in New York"
PH11481 745 (October 17, 1996) p129. "From The Muddy Banks Of The Wishkah"
NIRVANA—ILLUSTRATIONS
PH11482 665 (September 16, 1993) p63. "Sleepless In Seattle" (Brown, Calef)
PH11483 695 (November 17, 1994) p58. "Nirvana" (Ryden, Mark)
PH11484 745 (October 17, 1996) p129. "One Last Blast: The Way We Were—Nirvana Plugged In And Onstage" (Rosen, Jonathon)
NIRVANA—ILLUSTRATIONS—LETTERING
PH11485 628 (April 16, 1992) p37. "[Nirvana]" (Allen, Terry)
NIRVANA—ILLUSTRATIONS—PORTRAITS
PH11486 696 (December 1, 1994) p120. "Might Have Been" (Woolley, Janet)
NIRVANA—PHOTOGRAPHS
PH11487 619-620 (December 12, 1991) p45. "Seattle's Nirvana (above)..." (Cuffaro, Chris)
PH11488 625 (March 5, 1992) p53. "Sending Readers To A Higher Plane" (Cuffaro, Chris)
PH11489 628 (April 16, 1992) pp[cover]. "Nirvana: Inside The Heart And Mind Of Kurt Cobain" (Seliger, Mark)
PH11490 645-646 (December 10, 1992) p79. "Nirvana Backstage At The MTV Awards" (Mazur, Kevin)
PH11491 653 (April 1, 1993) p20. "Nirvana's Chris Novoselic, Kurt Cobain And Dave Grohl (clockwise from top)" (Watermann, Greg)
PH11492 659 (June 24, 1993) p21. "Nirvs: Grohl, Novoselic, Cobain (from left)" (Sirrs, Ed)
PH11493 666 (September 30, 1993) p28. "Kurt Cobain (left) And Chris Novoselic" (Andeel, Michael)
PH11494 667 (October 14, 1993) p67. "'Spirit' In The Sky: Nirvana's First Single Hits No. 2"
PH11495 670 (November 25, 1993) p77. "[Nirvana]" (Seliger, Mark)
PH11496 674 (January 27, 1994) p36. "Team Spirit: Novoselic, Smear, Grohl, Cobain And Touring Cellist Lori Goldston (from left)" (Seliger, Mark)
PH11497 674 (January 27, 1994) p38. "Young Nirvana: Ex-Drummer Chad Channing, Novoselic, Cobain In '88 (from left)" (Peterson, Charles)
PH11498 682 (May 19, 1994) p18. "The Band And The Family: Grohl, Novoselic And Cobain (above)" (Huntington, Jane)
PH11499 683 (June 2, 1994) p52. "Channing, Short-term Guitarist Jason Everman, Novoselic, Cobain 1989" (Wheeler, Alice)
PH11500 683 (June 2, 1994) p66. "Nirvana In L.A. On The Set Of Their Final Video, "Heart-Shaped Box"" (Corbijn, Anton)
PH11501 683 (June 2, 1994) p38. "Nirvana Photographed By Anton Corbijn During A Brief Seattle Session In June 1993" (Corbijn, Anton)
PH11502 691 (September 22, 1994) p19. "Nirvana's Grohl (drums), Simon Fair (at mike), Novoselic (bass)" (Doughty, Curt)

PH11503 698-699 (December 29, 1994) p86. "Kurt Cobain" (Seliger, Mark)
PH11504 720 (November 2, 1995) p51. "Nirvana" (Seliger, Mark)
PH11505 727 (February 8, 1996) p22. "Nirvana Was Always Political: Novoselic, Cobain And Grohl (from left) In London, 1993"
PH11506 742 (September 5, 1996) p25. "Live Nirvana" (Mazur, Kevin)
PH11507 750-751 (December 26, 1996) p82. "Nirvana" (Anker, Matt)
NIRVANA—PHOTOGRAPHS—PORTRAITS
PH11508 645-646 (December 10, 1992) pp[cover]. "1992 Yearbook" (Seliger, Mark)
PH11509 674 (January 27, 1994) p42. "Band And Album Winners: Achieving Nirvana" (Frohman, Jesse)
PH11510 674 (January 27, 1994) pp[cover]. "Nirvana: Success Doesn't Suck" (Seliger, Mark)
PH11511 718 (October 5, 1995) p43. "Nirvana In 1993 During The 'In Utero' Tour: Pat Smear, Kurt Cobain, Dave Grohl, Krist Novoselic (clockwise from right)" (Lenquette, Youri)
NIRVANA—SINGLES
PH11512 653 (April 1, 1993) p20. "Oh, The Guilt (song)"
NISSAN (COMPANY)—PHOTOGRAPHS
PH11513 750-751 (December 26, 1996) p81. "GI Joe Shilling, For Nissan"
NIXON (FILM)—ILLUSTRATIONS
PH11514 726 (January 25, 1996) p63. "Natural Born Tricksters" (Coe, Sue)
NIXON (FILM)—PHOTOGRAPHS
PH11515 726 (January 25, 1996) p64. "Nixon Confers With Haldeman (James Woods)"
PH11516 726 (January 25, 1996) p64. "Nixon Say's He's 'Not A Crook'"
PH11517 726 (January 25, 1996) p64. "Oliver Stone Directs Joan Allen And Anthony Hopkins"
NIXON, RICHARD—ILLUSTRATIONS
PH11518 684 (June 16, 1994) p44. "RS 140, Aug. 2, 1973: Illustration By Ralph Steadman" (Steadman, Ralph)
PH11519 684 (June 16, 1994) p39. "RS 144, Sept. 27, 1973: Cover Illustration By Ralph Steadman" (Steadman, Ralph)
PH11520 684 (June 16, 1994) p45. "The White House Gang: Illustration by Edward Sorel For "Ramparts," 1972" (Sorel, Edward)
PH11521 688 (August 11, 1994) p10. "Still A Crook" (Pendergrast, James T.)
PH11522 726 (January 25, 1996) p63. "Natural Born Tricksters" (Coe, Sue)
NIXON, RICHARD—PHOTOGRAPHS
PH11523 633 (June 25, 1992) p6. "[Richard Nixon]"
PH11524 636 (August 6, 1992) p8. "[Richard Nixon]"
PH11525 645-646 (December 10, 1992) p148. "Richard Nixon, 1974"
PH11526 690 (September 8, 1994) p48. "Above, In A Photo From The CD-ROM: Nixon, Ehrlichman, Kissinger, Haldeman"
PH11527 690 (September 8, 1994) p47. "The Author's Bosses: Future Chief Of Staff H. R. Haldeman (left) And Richard Nixon During The 1968 Campaign"
PH11528 715 (August 24, 1995) p89. "Hot Politician" (Halstead, Dirk)
NIXON, RICHARD—PHOTOGRAPHS—PORTRAITS
PH11529 684 (June 16, 1994) p42. "The Quitter"
NIXONS—PHOTOGRAPHS
PH11530 733 (May 2, 1996) p14. "Nixons' Bassist Ricky Brooks (left) And Maloy" (Burton, Eric)
NO ALTERNATIVE (ALBUM)—PHOTOGRAPHS
PH11531 742 (September 5, 1996) p23. "Red Hot's Rainbow Coalition"
NO DOUBT—PHOTOGRAPHS
PH11532 741 (August 22, 1996) p40. "[No Doubt]" (Cultice, Joseph)
PH11533 750-751 (December 26, 1996) p50. "Breakthrough" (Cultice, Joseph)
NOBODY'S FOOL (FILM)—PHOTOGRAPHS
PH11534 698-699 (December 29, 1994) p199. "Newman In "Fool""
NOEL, KATHY—PHOTOGRAPHS
PH11535 690 (September 8, 1994) p60. "Jeff Phillips And Family In December 1992 (above): Kathy And Keith Noel With Daughter Leighann, Hilda Phillips, Michael Noel, Jeff And Charles Phillips (from left)"
NOEL, KEITH—PHOTOGRAPHS
PH11535 690 (September 8, 1994) p60. "Jeff Phillips And Family In December 1992 (above): Kathy And Keith Noel With Daughter Leighann, Hilda Phillips, Michael Noel, Jeff And Charles Phillips (from left)"
NOEL, LEIGHANN—PHOTOGRAPHS
PH11535 690 (September 8, 1994) p60. "Jeff Phillips And Family In December 1992 (above): Kathy And Keith Noel With Daughter Leighann, Hilda Phillips, Michael Noel, Jeff And Charles Phillips (from left)"
NOEL, MICHAEL—PHOTOGRAPHS
PH11535 690 (September 8, 1994) p60. "Jeff Phillips And Family In December 1992 (above): Kathy And Keith Noel With Daughter Leighann, Hilda Phillips, Michael Noel, Jeff And Charles Phillips (from left)"
NOLAN, JERRY—PHOTOGRAPHS—PORTRAITS
PH11536 645-646 (December 10, 1992) p102. "[Jerry Nolan]" (Gruen, Bob)
NOLTE, BRAWLEY—PHOTOGRAPHS
PH11537 748 (November 28, 1996) p142. "Gibson With Son Nolte"
NOLTE, NICK—PHOTOGRAPHS
PH11538 619-620 (December 12, 1991) p194. "Male Wimps And Female Warriors"
PH11539 621 (January 9, 1992) p55. "Streisand And Nick Nolte In Therapy"
PH11540 684 (June 16, 1994) p116. "Flirty: Roberts And Nolte In "Trouble""
PH11541 688 (August 11, 1994) p62. "I Love Trouble"
PH11542 691 (September 22, 1994) p106. "Acting Valleys"
PH11543 706 (April 20, 1995) p89. "Nolte's Jefferson Toys With Slave Thandie Newton"
PH11544 742 (September 5, 1996) p68. "With Nolte In 'Cape Fear'"
PH11545 748 (November 28, 1996) p143. "Nick Nolte And Sheryl Lee Get Cozy"
NOODLES—PHOTOGRAPHS
PH11546 695 (November 17, 1994) p78. "Offspring" (Danelian, Stephen)
NORDAL, JENS—PHOTOGRAPHS—PORTRAITS
PH11547 652 (March 18, 1993) pp[enc.37]. "Jens Nordal" (Seliger, Mark)
NORMA JEAN AND MARILYN (FILM)—PHOTOGRAPHS
PH11548 735 (May 30, 1996) p56. "Now Playing"
NORMAL LIFE (FILM)—PHOTOGRAPHS
PH11549 747 (November 14, 1996) p124. "Mad Housewife Judd"
NORTE, MARISELA—PHOTOGRAPHS
PH11550 656 (May 13, 1993) p27. "[Marisela Norte]" (McDaniel, Melodie)
NORTH AMERICAN FREE TRADE AGREEMENT—ILLUSTRATIONS
PH11551 656 (May 13, 1993) p35. "[NAFTA]" (Cronin, Brian)
PH11552 671 (December 9, 1993) p7. "Clean Air" (Pendergrast, James T.)
NORTH, OLIVER—PHOTOGRAPHS
PH11553 698-699 (December 29, 1994) p74. "Two Close For Comfort: The Voters Went South On Ollie North's Senate Campaign" (Mathieson, Greg E.)

PH11554 741 (August 22, 1996) p104. "Ollie North Gives Voters The High Sign"

NORTHERN IRELAND—PHOTOGRAPHS

PH11555 656 (May 13, 1993) p18. "Voices Carry: A Recent Demonstration After An IRA Bomb Killed Two Children" (Farrell, Eamonn)

NORTON, EDWARD—PHOTOGRAPHS

PH11556 732 (April 18, 1996) p80. "From Left: Linney And Gere Huddle; Norton Broods"

NORTON, GREG—PHOTOGRAPHS

PH11557 694 (November 3, 1994) p72. "Poison Years: Husker Du's Grant Hart, Greg Norton And Mould" (Corrigan, Daniel)

NOT BAD FOR A GIRL (FILM)—PHOTOGRAPHS

PH11558 748 (November 28, 1996) p36. "Babes In Toyland's Kat Bjelland In 'Not Bad'"

NOTHING BUT THE BLUES (BOOK)—PHOTOGRAPHS

PH11559 683 (June 2, 1994) p17. "Nothing But The Blues"

NOTHING COMPARES 2 U (VIDEO)—PHOTOGRAPHS

PH11560 667 (October 14, 1993) p68. "O'Connor: The Bald And The Beautiful"

NOTORIOUS B.I.G.—ALBUMS

PH11561 694 (November 3, 1994) p96. "Ready To Die"

NOTORIOUS B.I.G.—ILLUSTRATIONS

PH11562 705 (April 6, 1995) p80. "The Notorious B.I.G.: Real Big Poppa" (Marten, Ruth)

NOTORIOUS B.I.G.—PHOTOGRAPHS

PH11563 709 (June 1, 1995) p24. "[Notorious B.I.G.]" (Cardillicchio, Nick)

PH11564 721 (November 16, 1995) p25. "It Takes A B.I.G. Man To Say 'No Glove, No Love'" (Mazur, Kevin)

PH11565 729 (March 7, 1996) p10. "Large And In Charge: B.I.G. (left) And Pal Partner" (Hopkins, T.)

NOVA, HEATHER—PHOTOGRAPHS

PH11566 723 (December 14, 1995) p41. "[Heather Nova]" (Nissen, Melanie)

NOVOSELIC, KRIST—ILLUSTRATIONS

PH11567 695 (November 17, 1994) p58. "Nirvana" (Ryden, Mark)

PH11568 727 (February 8, 1996) p7. "Krist Novoselic" (Burke, Philip)

PH11569 730 (March 21, 1996) p14. "Welcome To Politics" (Pendergrast, James T.)

NOVOSELIC, KRIST—PHOTOGRAPHS

PH11570 622 (January 23, 1992) p40. "Krist Novoselic" (Broad, Julian)

PH11571 628 (April 16, 1992) p38. "Bassist Krist Novoselic" (Seliger, Mark)

PH11572 653 (April 1, 1993) p20. "Nirvana's Krist Novoselic, Kurt Cobain And Dave Grohl (clockwise from top)" (Watermann, Greg)

PH11573 659 (June 24, 1993) p21. "Nirvs: Grohl, Novoselic, Cobain (from left)" (Sirrs, Ed)

PH11574 666 (September 30, 1993) p28. "Kurt Cobain (left) And Krist Novoselic" (Andeel, Michael)

PH11575 674 (January 27, 1994) p28. "Nirvana's Dave Grohl And Krist Novoselic With Madcap MTV Hosts Anthony Kiedis And Flea" (Mazur, Kevin)

PH11576 674 (January 27, 1994) p36. "Team Spirit: Novoselic, Smear, Grohl, Cobain And Touring Cellist Lori Goldston (from left)" (Seliger, Mark)

PH11577 674 (January 27, 1994) p38. "Young Nirvana: Ex-Drummer Chad Channing, Novoselic, Cobain In '88 (from left)" (Peterson, Charles)

PH11578 682 (May 19, 1994) p18. "The Band And The Family: Grohl, Novoselic And Cobain (above)" (Huntington, Jane)

PH11579 683 (June 2, 1994) p52. "Channing, Short-term Guitarist Jason Everman, Novoselic, Cobain 1989" (Wheeler, Alice)

PH11580 683 (June 2, 1994) p38. "Dave Grohl And Fiancee Jennifer Youngblood, Krist Novoselic And Wife Shelli Enter The Memorial Service On April 10" (Banner, Ellen M.)

PH11581 691 (September 22, 1994) p19. "Nirvana's Grohl (drums), Simon Fair (at mike), Novoselic (bass)" (Doughty, Curt)

PH11582 692 (October 6, 1994) p15. "Novoselic, Vedder And Earnie Bailey (from left) Get Loose" (Van Wey, Charles)

PH11583 698-699 (December 29, 1994) p60. "Yoyo A Gaga: Stinky Puffs With Special Guests Dave Grohl And Krist Novoselic" (Doughty, Curt)

PH11584 704 (March 23, 1995) p33. "Rock & Roll Lobbyist Novoselic" (Sorbo, Robert)

PH11585 706 (April 20, 1995) p16. "Krist Novoselic Lays Down The Law" (Kravitz, Jeff)

PH11586 711 (June 29, 1995) p12. "[Artists For A Hate Free America]" (Doughty, Curt)

PH11587 716 (September 7, 1995) p28. "Sweet 75's Krist Novoselic" (Peterson, Charles)

PH11588 727 (February 8, 1996) p22. "Nirvana Was Always Political: Novoselic, Cobain And Grohl (from left) In London, 1993"

PH11589 727 (February 8, 1996) p24. "Sweet 75's Novoselic Plays For JAMPAC, 1995" (Peterson, Charles)

NOVOSELIC, KRIST—PHOTOGRAPHS—PORTRAITS

PH11590 693 (October 20, 1994) p28. "Krist Novoselic And Chris Cornell" (Mazur, Kevin)

PH11591 718 (October 5, 1995) p43. "Nirvana In 1993 During The 'In Utero' Tour: Pat Smear, Kurt Cobain, Dave Grohl, Krist Novoselic (clockwise from right)" (Lenquette, Youri)

PH11592 727 (February 8, 1996) p19. "Novoselic Takes The Clout And Capital He Earned In Concert Halls Into The Corridors Of Political Power" (Ockenfels, Frank W.)

NOVOSELIC, SHELLI—PHOTOGRAPHS

PH11593 683 (June 2, 1994) p38. "Dave Grohl And Fiancee Jennifer Youngblood, Krist Novoselic And Wife Shelli Enter The Memorial Service On April 10" (Banner, Ellen M.)

NOW AND THEN (FILM)—PHOTOGRAPHS

PH11594 720 (November 2, 1995) p77. "Female-Bonding Movies"

NOWELL, BRAD—PHOTOGRAPHS

PH11595 750-751 (December 26, 1996) p58. "Sublime's Brad Nowell"

NRBQ—ALBUMS

PH11596 690 (September 8, 1994) p81. "Message For The Mess Age"

NUCLEAR POWER—ILLUSTRATIONS

PH11597 632 (June 11, 1992) p92. "[Nuclear Power]" (Cronin, Brian)

NUCLEAR POWER—PHOTOGRAPHS

PH11598 658 (June 10, 1993) p53. "The Command Hall Of A Kozlodui Reactor In 1985"

PH11599 658 (June 10, 1993) p53. "Kozlodui In 1976: Two Reactor Units And Adding On"

PH11600 658 (June 10, 1993) p51. "[Nuclear Power]" (Mahurin, Matt)

NUCLEAR WEAPONS—ILLUSTRATIONS

PH11601 622 (January 23, 1992) p19. "[Nuclear Weapons]" (Cronin, Brian)

PH11602 676 (February 24, 1994) p36. "The Politics Of Testing" (Klein, Renee)

NUCLEAR WEAPONS—PHOTOGRAPHS

PH11603 657 (May 27, 1993) p43. "[Soviet Bomb]" (Mahurin, Matt)

PH11604 657 (May 27, 1993) p45. "The Soviets Copied Fat Man, The Nagasaki Bomb..."

PH11605 657 (May 27, 1993) p45. "...To Build Joe 1, Their First Bomb, Ensuring Success"

PH11606 676 (February 24, 1994) p31. "[Nuclear Weapons]" (Tavee, Tom)

PH11607 676 (February 24, 1994) p33. "Scene From An Arms Race: Researchers Working On A Fusion Experiment At Los Alamos In 1958" (Eyeman, JR)

NUDESTOCK (FESTIVAL)—PHOTOGRAPHS
PH11608 740 (August 8, 1996) p18. "'I Love The Freedom!' Said A 40ish Newcomer At Nudestock (doing a festive shimmy to emphasize her point)" (Whitall, Robert, Jr.)
PH11609 750-751 (December 26, 1996) p67. "Cheeks Ahoy! A Sea Of Heinies At Nudestock '96" (Whitall, Robert, Jr.)
NUGENT, TED—PHOTOGRAPHS
PH11610 697 (December 15, 1994) p20. "[Ted Nugent]" (Saleito, Max)
PH11611 730 (March 21, 1996) p18. "A Buffalo Tries Desperately To Shake Off The Nuge" (Settle, Ken)
THE NUTTY PROFESSOR (FILM)—PHOTOGRAPHS
PH11612 736 (June 13, 1996) p61. "Funny Guys"
PH11613 738-739 (July 11, 1996) p96. "Jerry Lewis: The Original Mr. Two-Face"
PH11614 738-739 (July 11, 1996) p96. "Murphy's Nutty Professor As A Fat Slob (left) And Sexist Pig"
N.W.A.—ALBUMS
PH11615 619-620 (December 12, 1991) p178. "Efil4zaggin"
N.W.A.—PHOTOGRAPHS
PH11616 619-620 (December 12, 1991) p86. "This Year's Success Story: N.W.A." (Preston, Neal)
PH11617 619-620 (December 12, 1991) p39. "Wanted: N.W.A." (Preston, Neal)
PH11618 634-635 (July 9, 1992) p17. "N.W.A. (clockwise from top left): MC Ren, Yella, Eazy-E And Dr. Dre" (Preston, Neal)
PH11619 639 (September 17, 1992) p19. "N.W.A. (from left): D.J. Yella, Dr. Dre, Eazy-E And M.C. Ren"
PH11620 666 (September 30, 1993) p42. "Serious Attitude: Ex-N.W.A. Members Ice Cube, Yella, Eazy-E, Dre And MC Ren" (Rosenberg, Howard)
PH11621 707 (May 4, 1995) p25. "Eazy-E (taking aim) With N.W.A. In 1991"
NYPD BLUE (TELEVISION SHOW)—PHOTOGRAPHS
PH11622 666 (September 30, 1993) p115. "How Blue Can You Get? '68's 'N.Y.P.D.' (left)"
PH11623 666 (September 30, 1993) p115. "'93's 'NYPD Blue'"
NYRO, LAURA—PHOTOGRAPHS
PH11624 655 (April 29, 1993) p55. "Manager Geffen With An Early Client, Singer-Songwriter Laura Nyro, 1968" (Paley, Stephen)

O

OASIS—ALBUMS
PH11625 701 (February 9, 1995) p72. "Definitely Maybe"
PH11626 719 (October 19, 1995) p147. "(What's The Story) Morning Glory?"
PH11627 730 (March 21, 1996) p116. "(What's The Story) Morning Glory?"
PH11628 733 (May 2, 1996) p72. "(What's The Story) Morning Glory"
PH11629 734 (May 16, 1996) p80. "(What's The Story) Morning Glory?"
OASIS—ILLUSTRATIONS
PH11630 711 (June 29, 1995) p10. "Oasis Fan After Show" (Pendergrast, James T.)
PH11631 719 (October 19, 1995) p147. "Remaking History" (Russo, Anthony)
PH11632 729 (March 7, 1996) p64. "Oasis: He Ain't Heavy, He's My Brother" (MacDonald, Ross)
OASIS—PHOTOGRAPHS
PH11633 691 (September 22, 1994) p37. "Arthurs, McCarroll, Liam Gallagher, McGuigan, Noel Gallagher (from left)"
PH11634 698-699 (December 29, 1994) p48. "Oasis"
PH11635 703 (March 9, 1995) p24. "Definitely Maybe: Oasis Lead The New British Invasion" (Slattery, Paul)
PH11636 718 (October 5, 1995) p34. "White, Arthurs, Liam Gallagher, Noel Gallagher, McGuigan (from left)" (Jones, Michael Spenser)
PH11637 727 (February 8, 1996) p13. "The Brothers Grim: Liam (left) And Noel Gallagher Of Oasis" (Hole, Danny)
PH11638 733 (May 2, 1996) p34. "Liam And Arthurs (right) Onstage In ;95" (Rasic, Brian)
PH11639 733 (May 2, 1996) p34. "McGuigan, White And Noel (from left)" (Goldberg, Nathaniel)
PH11640 733 (May 2, 1996) p35. "Noel, Liam And Hutchence (from left) At Awards" (Fisher, David)
PH11641 733 (May 2, 1996) p34. "Oasis '94—McGuigan, McCarroll, Liam, Arthurs And Noel (from left)" (Sirrs, Ed)
OASIS—PHOTOGRAPHS—PORTRAITS
PH11642 733 (May 2, 1996) pp[cover]. "Oasis" (Goldberg, Nathaniel)
O'BANNON, WINK—PHOTOGRAPHS
PH11643 658 (June 10, 1993) p29. "Wink O'Bannon, Janet Beveridge Bean, Rick Rizzo And Doug McCombs (from left)" (Guip, Andy)
OBERLIN COLLEGE—PHOTOGRAPHS
PH11644 693 (October 20, 1994) p89. "Oberlin R.A. Andrea Emmons (top left) Leads A Stress-Reliever Session"
PH11645 719 (October 19, 1995) p92. "Queen For A Day At Oberlin's Drag Ball" (Lefkowitz, Lisa)
O'BRAONAIN, FIACHNA—PHOTOGRAPHS
PH11646 668 (October 28, 1993) p36. "[Van Morrison, Shane MacGowan, Fiachna O'Braonain]"
O'BRIAN, HUGH—PHOTOGRAPHS
PH11647 684 (June 16, 1994) p114. "TV Echoes"
O'BRIAN, PATRICK—PHOTOGRAPHS—PORTRAITS
PH11648 630 (May 14, 1992) p83. "[Patrick O'Brian]"
O'BRIEN, CONAN—ILLUSTRATIONS
PH11649 746 (October 31, 1996) p14. "Sacrifice Chart" (Pendergrast, James T.)
O'BRIEN, CONAN—PHOTOGRAPHS
PH11650 715 (August 24, 1995) p113. "[Conan O'Brien]" (Fishman, Miriam)
PH11651 743 (September 19, 1996) p72. "Comedy Is A Great Passive-Aggressive Tool" (Seliger, Mark)
PH11652 743 (September 19, 1996) p69. "The Crest Of The Wave: His Sidekick, Andy Richter; And The 'Late Night' Bandleader, Max Weinberg" (Seliger, Mark)
PH11653 743 (September 19, 1996) p68. "In The Year 1968: Conan O'Brien, Age 5, With The Family Cat In Rhode Island"
PH11654 743 (September 19, 1996) p74. "Infinite Jester: At Harvard In 1984, O'Brien (left, with a friend) Became Known For Pulling Wacky Ivy League Pranks"
O'BRIEN, CONAN—PHOTOGRAPHS—PORTRAITS
PH11655 743 (September 19, 1996) pp[cover]. "The Big Red One: Conan O'Brien's Three-Year Overnight Success" (Seliger, Mark)
PH11656 743 (September 19, 1996) p67. "[Conan O'Brien]" (Seliger, Mark)
O'BRIEN, DAN—PHOTOGRAPHS
PH11657 626 (March 19, 1992) p81. "[Dan O'Brien]" (Hanauer, Mark)
O'BRIEN, ED—PHOTOGRAPHS
PH11658 660-661 (July 8, 1993) p95. "Radiohead: Ed O'Brien, Colin Greenwood, Phil Selway, Yorke, Jonny Greenwood" (Sharp, Ken)
PH11659 716 (September 7, 1995) p19. "Colin Greenwood, Ed O'Brien, Thom Yorke, Jonny Greenwood And Phil Selway (from left)" (Blakesberg, Jay)
PH11660 738-739 (July 11, 1996) p15. "Thom Yorke, Colin Greenwood, Roseanne, Ed O'Brien, Phil Selway And Jonny Greenwood" (Diltz, Henry)
O'BRIEN, SEAN—PHOTOGRAPHS
PH11661 654 (April 15, 1993) p22. "They've Arrived: Arthur Johnson, Sean O'Brien, Thalia Zedek And Chris Brokaw" (Westenberg, Kevin)

PH11662 660-661 (July 8, 1993) p100. "Come (from left): Arthur Johnson, Sean O'Brien, Chris Brokaw And Thalia Zedek" (Apicella-Hitchcock, Stephen)

OCASEK, RIC—PHOTOGRAPHS

PH11663 706 (April 20, 1995) p16. "'God' Producer Ocasek (left) And Bad Brains" (Johnson, Lisa)

PH11664 722 (November 30, 1995) p19. "Graffin, Ocasek, Jay Bentley, Brian Baker, Greg Hetson And Bobby Schayer (from left)" (Mazur, Kevin)

O'CIOSOIG, COLM—PHOTOGRAPHS—PORTRAITS

PH11665 623 (February 6, 1992) p20. "Clockwise From Top Left: Butcher, Shields, Googe, O'Ciosoig" (Double, Steve)

O'CONNELL, BILLY—PHOTOGRAPHS

PH11666 748 (November 28, 1996) p30. "Hersh, On Tour With Her Husband, Billy O'Connell, And Son Ryder" (Chiarella, Frank)

O'CONNELL, JERRY—PHOTOGRAPHS

PH11667 741 (August 22, 1996) p105. "Now Playing"

O'CONNELL, MAURA—PHOTOGRAPHS—PORTRAITS

PH11668 616 (October 31, 1991) p24. "[Maura O'Connell]" (Feingold, Deborah)

O'CONNOR, SINEAD—ALBUMS

PH11669 644 (November 26, 1992) p72. "Am I Not Your Girl?"

PH11670 692 (October 6, 1994) p84. "Universal Mother"

O'CONNOR, SINEAD—ILLUSTRATIONS

PH11671 647 (January 7, 1993) p7. "Tonight! Sinead Performs!" (Pendergrast, James T.)

O'CONNOR, SINEAD—PHOTOGRAPHS

PH11672 619-620 (December 12, 1991) p39. "Sting, Sinead O'Connor, Peter Gabriel (from left)" (Linsen, M.)

PH11673 622 (January 23, 1992) p6. "[Sinead O'Connor]" (Shaw, Eugene)

PH11674 636 (August 6, 1992) p11. "Sinead O'Connor Hits The Clubs" (Coughlin, Kevin P.)

PH11675 644 (November 26, 1992) p19. "Am I Not Your Girl?: Sinead Reacts Angrily To The Mixed Reception From The Crowd" (Mazur, Kevin)

PH11676 645-646 (December 10, 1992) p65. "[Sinead O'Connor]" (Coughlin, Kevin P.)

PH11677 656 (May 13, 1993) p15. "[Sinead O'Connor]" (Farrell, Leon)

PH11678 663 (August 19, 1993) p28. "Sinead O'Connor Sings For Peace"

PH11679 675 (February 10, 1994) p22. "[Bono & Sinead O'Connor]"

PH11680 703 (March 9, 1995) p20. "[Sinead O'Connor]"

PH11681 714 (August 10, 1995) p30. "Sinead O'Connor, Sick Of It All In Jerusalem"

PH11682 715 (August 24, 1995) p43. "A Warm, Elegant And Sanctified Sinead O'Connor" (Blakesberg, Jay)

PH11683 724-725 (December 28, 1995) p48. "Universal Bad Mutha: Sinead O'Connor Struck Back In Jerusalem" (Lemmer, Yoav)

O'CONNOR, SINEAD—PHOTOGRAPHS—PORTRAITS

PH11684 619-620 (December 12, 1991) pp[cover]. "1991 Yearbook" (Ritts, Herb)

PH11685 619-620 (December 12, 1991) p60. "Sinead O'Connor" (Preston, Neal)

PH11686 642 (October 29, 1992) pp50-51,53. "[Sinead O'Connor]" (Watson, Albert)

PH11687 642 (October 29, 1992) pp[cover]. "Sinead: On Axl Rose, Feminism, Mike Tyson And God" (Watson, Albert)

PH11688 643 (November 12, 1992) p88. "Sinead O'Connor" (Weber, Bruce)

PH11689 645-646 (December 10, 1992) pp[cover]. "1992 Yearbook" (Watson, Albert)

PH11690 667 (October 14, 1993) p68. "O'Connor: The Bald And The Beautiful"

PH11691 692 (October 6, 1994) p53. "Sinead O'Connor"

O'CONNOR, TIM—PHOTOGRAPHS—PORTRAITS

PH11692 684 (June 16, 1994) p30. "Simon Austin, Angie Hart, Alistair Barden And Tim O'Connor (from left)" (Westenberg, Kevin)

OCTET, DAVID MURRAY—ALBUMS

PH11693 742 (September 5, 1996) p65. "Dark Star"

O'DELL, KELLY—PHOTOGRAPHS

PH11694 693 (October 20, 1994) p75. "Actress Kelly O'Dell"

ODENKIRK, BOB—ILLUSTRATIONS

PH11695 747 (November 14, 1996) p121. "[Mr. Show With Bob And David]" (Ciardiello, Joe)

ODETTA—PHOTOGRAPHS

PH11696 674 (January 27, 1994) p29. "Gabriel, Merchant And Odetta In Boston" (Robicheau, Paul)

O'DONNELL, CHRIS—ILLUSTRATIONS

PH11697 670 (November 25, 1993) p124. "Disney's Toy Boys" (Kunz, Anita)

O'DONNELL, CHRIS—PHOTOGRAPHS

PH11698 670 (November 25, 1993) p125. "De Mornay Seduces Guppy O'Donnell (below)"

PH11699 670 (November 25, 1993) p125. "Four Stooges: Sutherland, Sheen, O'Donnell, Platt (above)"

PH11700 704 (March 23, 1995) p129. "Driver's Irish Eyes Smile At O'Donnell"

PH11701 709 (June 1, 1995) p17. "Maxine Jones, Robinson, O'Donnell, Cindy Herron, Terry Ellis" (Nelson, Ralph)

PH11702 710 (June 15, 1995) p88. "Barrymore And O'Donnell Before The Fall"

PH11703 712-713 (July 13, 1995) p114. "Good Guys: Kilmer's Batman, Kidman's Dr. Chase Meridian, O'Donnell's Robin"

O'DONNELL, CHRIS—PHOTOGRAPHS—PORTRAITS

PH11704 747 (November 14, 1996) p124. "The Chamber: John Grisham's First Screen Strikeout"

O'DONNELL, NOREEN—PHOTOGRAPHS

PH11705 644 (November 26, 1992) p24. "Hansard, Noreen O'Donnell, Colm Mac Con Iomaire, Brennan, David Odlum And John Carney (from left)" (Marsden, Barry)

O'DONNELL, ROGER—PHOTOGRAPHS

PH11706 733 (May 2, 1996) p22. "Partial To Shades: The Cure's New Lineup Is Simon Gallup, Roger O'Donnell, Robert Smith, Perry Bamonte And Jason Cooper (from left)" (Cox, Paul)

O'DONNELL, ROSIE—ILLUSTRATIONS

PH11707 741 (August 22, 1996) p107. "[Rosie O'Donnell]" (Witte, Michael)

O'DONNELL, ROSIE—PHOTOGRAPHS

PH11708 634-635 (July 9, 1992) p111. "Davis, O'Donnell, Madonna And Petty In A Man's Game"

PH11709 684 (June 16, 1994) p116. "Kinky: O'Donnell And Aykroyd In "Eden""

O'DONNELL, ROSIE—PHOTOGRAPHS—PORTRAITS

PH11710 736 (June 13, 1996) p54. "Rosie O'Donnell: Miss Mike Douglas?"

O'DONOGHUE, MICHAEL—PHOTOGRAPHS—PORTRAITS

PH11711 698-699 (December 29, 1994) p84. "[Michael O'Donoghue]" (Baskin, Edie)

OFELT, JEFFREY—PHOTOGRAPHS

PH11712 652 (March 18, 1993) pp[enc.35]. "Jeffrey Ofelt" (Seliger, Mark)

OFFSPRING—ILLUSTRATIONS

PH11713 690 (September 8, 1994) p96. "Children of The Damned: Offspring" (Todd, Mark)

OFFSPRING—PHOTOGRAPHS

PH11714 686-687 (July 14, 1994) p45. "[Offspring]" (Johnson, Lisa)

PH11715 688 (August 11, 1994) p33. "Straight Out Of Orange County: Offspring" (Hole, Jimmy)

PH11716 691 (September 22, 1994) p25. "Shakin' Thing Up: Ron Welty, Greg K, Noodles, Dexter Holland (from left)" (Seliger, Mark)

PH11717 695 (November 17, 1994) p78. "Offspring" (Danelian, Stephen)
PH11718 698-699 (December 29, 1994) p45. "Offspring" (Seliger, Mark)
PH11719 700 (January 26, 1995) p56. "Offspring's Noodles (left) Prefers...Weezer?" (Seliger, Mark)
PH11720 701 (February 9, 1995) pp42-43. "Greg Kriesel, Bryan Holland, Kevin Wasserman And Ron Welty (from left)" (Seliger, Mark)
PH11721 711 (June 29, 1995) p12. "The Offspring's Dexter Holland Takes On The Spitting Crowd At The Skatefest" (Johnson, Lisa)
PH11722 723 (December 14, 1995) p31. "Offspring" (Malluk, Eddie)
PH11723 736 (June 13, 1996) p33. "Columbia-Bound: The Offspring's Members Are Noodles, Dexter Holland, Greg K., Ron Welty (from left)" (Johnson, Lisa)
PH11724 737 (June 27, 1996) p19. "Offspring's Dexter Holland, Noodles, Ron Welty And Greg K. (from left)" (Mott, Tony)
OFFSPRING—PHOTOGRAPHS—PORTRAITS
PH11725 750-751 (December 26, 1996) p54. "The Offspring: Greener Pastures" (Thurnher, Jeffrey)
O'HALLORAN, BRIAN—PHOTOGRAPHS
PH11726 694 (November 3, 1994) p104. "Clerks Anderson And O'Halloran Discuss The Forbidden"
O'HARE, BRENDAN—PHOTOGRAPHS
PH11727 630 (May 14, 1992) p50. "Guitarist Norman Blake, Bassist Gerry Love, Drummer Brendan O'Hare And Guitarist Raymond McGinley (from left)" (Broad, Julian)
O'HEIR, TIM—PHOTOGRAPHS
PH11728 708 (May 18, 1995) p28. "Producers O'Heir, Smith And Slade (from left)" (Pasley, Richard)
OHIO PLAYERS—ALBUMS
PH11729 617 (November 14, 1991) p149. "Honey" (Kotleba, John)
PH11730 617 (November 14, 1991) p149. "Honey" (Fegley, Richard)
OISIN—PHOTOGRAPHS
PH11731 690 (September 8, 1994) p44. "K1, Oisin, Phrase And Hollis (from left)" (Cross, Brian)
OJE, BABA—PHOTOGRAPHS
PH11732 648 (January 21, 1993) p9. "Arrested Development (from left): Speech, Aerle Taree, Headliner, Rasa Don, Baba Oje And Montsho Eshe" (Mazur, Kevin)
O'KEEFE, MICHAEL—PHOTOGRAPHS
PH11733 619-620 (December 12, 1991) p37. "[Bonnie Raitt, Michael O'Keefe]"
PH11734 645-646 (December 10, 1992) p98. "Clinton With Bonnie Raitt And Her Husband, Michael O'Keefe" (Jacobs, Michael)
OKLAHOMA CITY, OKLAHOMA—PHOTOGRAPHS
PH11735 724-725 (December 28, 1995) p45. "Aftermath: Oklahoma City Fell Prey To Hatred"
OL' DIRTY BASTARD—ILLUSTRATIONS
PH11736 706 (April 20, 1995) p78. "Langston Hughes (left) And Ol' Dirty Bastard" (Pauley, Lynn)
OL' DIRTY BASTARD—PHOTOGRAPHS
PH11737 721 (November 16, 1995) p33. "O.D.B. And Carey On The Set At Rye beach, N.Y." (Toy, Joann)
OLATUNJI, BABATUNDE—PHOTOGRAPHS
PH11738 717 (September 21, 1995) p28. "Olatunji With Kantner, Two Drummers, John Perry Barlow, Weir And Koons Garcia (from left) At The Aug. 13 Memorial At The Polo Field" (Blakesberg, Jay)
OLDHAM, TODD—PHOTOGRAPHS
PH11739 630 (May 14, 1992) p83. "[Todd Oldham, Queen Latifah]" (Baratta, Nicholas)
OLDHAM, TODD—PHOTOGRAPHS—PORTRAITS
PH11740 678 (March 24, 1994) p50. "Todd Oldham" (Ockenfels, Frank W.)
OLDHAM, WILL—PHOTOGRAPHS—PORTRAITS
PH11741 735 (May 30, 1996) p26. "[Will Oldham]" (Gullick, Steve)
OLDMAN, GARY—ILLUSTRATIONS
PH11742 675 (February 10, 1994) p51. "Playing Rough" (Panter, Gary)
OLDMAN, GARY—PHOTOGRAPHS
PH11743 675 (February 10, 1994) p52. "Cop Gary Oldman Beds Down With Devil Lena Olin"
PH11744 700 (January 26, 1995) p66. "Oldman, Rossellini"
PH11745 721 (November 16, 1995) p117. "Demi Moore With Gary Oldman"
PH11746 741 (August 22, 1996) p105. "Wright, Bowie, Oldman, Hopper"
OLDS, MIKE—PHOTOGRAPHS
PH11747 669 (November 11, 1993) p35. "Rebuilding The Carpenters Union: Ubaldo Vasquez, Mike Olds And Jesus Gomez (foreground, from left)" (Reed, Dudley)
O'LEARY, HAZEL—PHOTOGRAPHS
PH11748 678 (March 24, 1994) p33. "[Hazel O'Leary]" (Wolff, Tom)
OLIGMUELLER, STEIVAN—PHOTOGRAPHS
PH11749 666 (September 30, 1993) p90. "Hunt (third from left, bottom row) With Delta Lambda Phi Brothers (clockwise from top right): Peter Colohan, Sean McClafferty, Rob Corwin, Price, Stephen Smith And Oligmueller"
PH11750 666 (September 30, 1993) p88. "Wade Price, Steivan Oligmueller And Bert Childs (from left)" (Himmel, Lizzie)
OLIN, LENA—PHOTOGRAPHS
PH11751 675 (February 10, 1994) p52. "Cop Gary Oldman Beds Down With Devil Lena Olin"
OLIVER OLIVER (FILM)—PHOTOGRAPHS
PH11752 650 (February 18, 1993) p66. "Gregoire Colin Is More Than A Brother To Marina Golovine"
OLNEY, DAVID—ALBUMS
PH11753 623 (February 6, 1992) p79. "Roses"
OLSEN, KEITH—PHOTOGRAPHS
PH11754 735 (May 30, 1996) pp[enc.12]. "Producer Keith Olsen Is Bringing Surround To Music Discs"
OLSON, MARK—PHOTOGRAPHS
PH11755 644 (November 26, 1992) p27. "Louris, Callahan, Olson And Perlman (from left)" (Capak, R. J.)
PH11756 697 (December 15, 1994) p31. ""We Had A Retro Tag, But This Isn't Like Our Last Album," Says Olson (center), With Perlman And Louris" (Dyer, Alison)
OLSON, MARK—PHOTOGRAPHS—PORTRAITS
PH11757 628 (April 16, 1992) p57. "Perlman, Olson, Louris And Callahan (from left)" (Crouser, Michael)
OMAR—ALBUMS
PH11758 710 (June 15, 1995) p81. "For Pleasure"
ON DEADLY GROUND (FILM)—PHOTOGRAPHS
PH11759 679 (April 7, 1994) p83. "Bombs Away"
ON OUR OWN (TELEVISION SHOW)—PHOTOGRAPHS
PH11760 692 (October 6, 1994) p93. "Family In Crisis: Ralph Harris Of "On Our Own" Wears His Mom's Clothes"
ONASSIS, BLACKIE—PHOTOGRAPHS
PH11761 664 (September 2, 1993) p12. "Urge A Go-Go (clockwise from left): Onassis, Kato, Roeser" (Robert, Francis)
PH11762 685 (June 30, 1994) p40. "Etheridge With Kato, Tony Stull, Blackie Onassis And "Eddie" King Roeser (from left)" (Mazur, Kevin)
ONASSIS, BLACKIE—PHOTOGRAPHS—PORTRAITS
PH11763 664 (September 2, 1993) p11. "[Urge Overkill]" (Robert, Francis)
ONASSIS, JACKIE—PHOTOGRAPHS
PH11764 698-699 (December 29, 1994) p80. "[Jacqueline Onassis]"
ONCE IN A LIFETIME (VIDEO)—PHOTOGRAPHS
PH11765 667 (October 14, 1993) p73. "'Lifetime' Achievement: David Byrne"

ONE DOVE—PHOTOGRAPHS
PH11766 671 (December 9, 1993) p25. "One Dove: Suede Of The Moment" (Clunn, Chris)
ONE FALSE MOVE (FILM)—PHOTOGRAPHS
PH11767 644 (November 26, 1992) p78. "[One False Move]"
PH11768 653 (April 1, 1993) p57. "One False Move"
101 DALMATIANS (FILM)—PHOTOGRAPHS
PH11769 743 (September 19, 1996) p88. "Going For The Gold"
O'NEAL, LAWRENCE—PHOTOGRAPHS
PH11770 708 (May 18, 1995) p61. "Lawrence O'Neal (with granddaughter) Began Questioning Principal Humphries' Behavior In The '80s" (Mark, Mary Ellen)
O'NEAL, RYAN—PHOTOGRAPHS
PH11771 733 (May 2, 1996) p62. "'Faithfull': Cher, Palminteri, O'Neal"
O'NEAL, SHAQUILLE—ILLUSTRATIONS
PH11772 656 (May 13, 1993) p7. "Shaquille O'Neal On The Hot List, Of Course" (Burke, Philip)
O'NEAL, SHAQUILLE—PHOTOGRAPHS
PH11773 667 (October 14, 1993) p39. "Snoop, Shaquille O'Neal, George Clinton" (Mazur, Kevin)
PH11774 669 (November 11, 1993) p28. "The Shaq" (Mazur, Kevin)
PH11775 670 (November 25, 1993) p57. "Gotta Sell It: Shaq Pitches For Pepsi (above), Reebok And Spalding"
PH11776 670 (November 25, 1993) p58. "Home Boy: With Father Philip, Mother Lucille, Brother Jamal And Sister Lateefah (from left) In His Parents' Orlando Home Last Year" (Chiasson, John)
PH11777 670 (November 25, 1993) p58. "Jammin': Bringing Down The House On The New Jersey Nets" (Trotman, Noren)
PH11778 670 (November 25, 1993) p57. "Shaq As Rapper: At A Paris Concert Earlier This Year" (Robert, Eric)
PH11779 670 (November 25, 1993) pp52-53. "[Shaquille O'Neal]" (Seliger, Mark)
PH11780 670 (November 25, 1993) pp[cover]. "Shaquille O'Neal: He Jams He Raps He Acts He Sells" (Seliger, Mark)
PH11781 672-673 (December 23, 1993) p188. "[Covers]" (Seliger, Mark)
O'NEAL, SHAQUILLE—PHOTOGRAPHS—PORTRAITS
PH11782 656 (May 13, 1993) p87. "[Shaquille O'Neal]" (O'Neill, Michael)
PH11783 670 (November 25, 1993) p55. "Two Portraits Of The Young Shaq: At 2 And 16"
O'NEIL, TARA JANE—PHOTOGRAPHS
PH11784 686-687 (July 14, 1994) p74. "Getting The Point Across: Rodan's Tara Jane O'Neil, Noble, Mueller And Kevin Coultas (from left)" (Clinch, Danny)
ONLY YOU (FILM)—PHOTOGRAPHS
PH11785 693 (October 20, 1994) p157. "Tomei, Downey And Scene-Stealing Italy"
ONO, YOKO—ALBUMS
PH11786 722 (November 30, 1995) p67. "Rising"
ONO, YOKO—ILLUSTRATIONS—PORTRAITS
PH11787 630 (May 14, 1992) p104. "Yoko Ono: 'Fly' Girl Soars" (Kralyevich, Vincent)
ONO, YOKO—PHOTOGRAPHS
PH11788 626 (March 19, 1992) p29. "Performing With Elephant's Memory On The 'Dick Cavett Show' 1972" (Gruen, Bob)
PH11789 645-646 (December 10, 1992) p148. "John Lennon And Yoko Ono, 1968"
PH11790 655 (April 29, 1993) p56. "Geffen With John Lennon And Yoko Ono, New York, 1980" (Senecal, Michel)
PH11791 674 (January 27, 1994) p13. "Jamming With John And Yoko In 1971 (below)" (Sia, Joseph)
PH11792 677 (March 10, 1994) p27. "Imagine: Paul McCartney And Yoko Ono" (Mazur, Kevin)
PH11793 679 (April 7, 1994) p28. "'New York' Rockers: Yoko Ono (center) And Cast" (Borris, Dan)
PH11794 696 (December 1, 1994) p38. "Ono With :Sgt. Pepper" Uniform" (Capak, R. J.)
PH11795 698-699 (December 29, 1994) p68. "Ono With Lennon's Guitar" (Capak, R. J.)
PH11796 710 (June 15, 1995) p18. "AmFar Head Mathilde Krim With Ono" (Mazur, Kevin)
PH11797 724-725 (December 28, 1995) p56. "Jann Wenner, Yoko Ono, Little Richard, Paul Shaffer Cut Loose" (Mazur, Kevin)
PH11798 729 (March 7, 1996) p18. "[Yoko Ono]" (Camp, E. J.)
PH11799 733 (May 2, 1996) p13. "Nothing's Shocking: Perry Farrell Gazes Fondly At His Unlikely New Pal Yoko Ono"
PH11800 738-739 (July 11, 1996) p68. "Tommy Smothers, John Lennon, Yoko Ono, Rosemary And Timothy Leary (from left) During The Bed-In For Peace In Montreal, 1969"
PH11801 740 (August 8, 1996) p22. "Yoko Ono Does Scream Therapy" (Blakesberg, Jay)
PH11802 742 (September 5, 1996) p21. "[Yoko Ono, Sean Lennon, Adam Yauch]" (Atlas, David)
PH11803 746 (October 31, 1996) p27. "Ono, Richards, Watts, Jagger And Jones (from left) With Circus Friends"
ONO, YOKO—PHOTOGRAPHS—PORTRAITS
PH11804 626 (March 19, 1992) p17. "[Kate Pierson, Yoko Ono]" (Seliger, Mark)
PH11805 643 (November 12, 1992) p110. "Yoko Ono" (Rolston, Matthew)
PH11806 643 (November 12, 1992) p256. "Yoko Ono & John Lennon" (Leibovitz, Annie)
PH11807 645-646 (December 10, 1992) p149. "John Lennon And Yoko Ono, 1982"
PH11808 645-646 (December 10, 1992) p161. "John Lennon And Yoko Ono, 1981"
PH11809 692 (October 6, 1994) p52. "Yoko Ono"
ONYX—ALBUMS
PH11810 672-673 (December 23, 1993) p165. "Bacdafucup"
PH11811 674 (January 27, 1994) p45. "Bacdafucup"
ONYX—PHOTOGRAPHS—PORTRAITS
PH11812 659 (June 24, 1993) p21. "Fredro Starr, Suave Sonny Caesar, Sticky Fingaz And Big D.S. (from left)" (Spector, Gary)
PH11813 672-673 (December 23, 1993) p46. "[Onyx]"
OPTIMISM—ILLUSTRATIONS
PH11814 715 (August 24, 1995) p82. "Hot Annoyance" (Faiola, Susan)
ORANGE 9MM—ALBUMS
PH11815 707 (May 4, 1995) p84. "Driver Not Included"
ORB—ALBUMS
PH11816 693 (October 20, 1994) p146. "Pomme Fritz"
PH11817 706 (April 20, 1995) p69. "Orbus Terrarum"
ORB—ILLUSTRATIONS
PH11818 706 (April 20, 1995) p69. "Thrill Out" (Tarlofsky, Malcolm)
ORBISON, BARBARA—PHOTOGRAPHS
PH11819 644 (November 26, 1992) p13. "Barbara Orbison And Robbie Robertson" (Sallow, Jacki)
PH11820 651 (March 4, 1993) p17. "Bonnie Raitt, K. D. Lang And Barbara Orbison (from left)" (Mazur, Kevin)
ORBISON, ROY—ALBUMS
PH11821 645-646 (December 10, 1992) p178. "King Of Hearts"
ORBISON, ROY—ILLUSTRATIONS
PH11822 641 (October 15, 1992) p135. "[Roy Orbison]" (Gosfield, Josh)
ORBISON, ROY—PHOTOGRAPHS
PH11823 619-620 (December 12, 1991) p32. "[Good Rockin' Tonight]"
PH11824 669 (November 11, 1993) p13. "Orbison: Fair Use Vs. Artistic Vision" (Wyner, Isaiah)
ORBISON, ROY—PHOTOGRAPHS—PORTRAITS
PH11825 645-646 (December 10, 1992) p161. "Roy Orbison, 1989"

ORBITAL—PHOTOGRAPHS
PH11826 679 (April 7, 1994) p19. "Orbital: The Brothers Hartnoll's Future Vision" (Capak, R. J.)
ORBITZ (FOOD)—PHOTOGRAPHS
PH11827 741 (August 22, 1996) p82. "[Orbitz]"
OREGON STATE UNIVERSITY—PHOTOGRAPHS
PH11828 709 (June 1, 1995) p57. "The ALF Owns Up To Deeds At Oregon State University" (Nelson, Andy)
ORIOLES—PHOTOGRAPHS
PH11829 659 (June 24, 1993) p43. "Chessler, Til (on her right) And The Orioles After A Show In 1952, No Longer Penniless"
PH11830 659 (June 24, 1993) p48. "The Orioles And Chessler Honored At The Apollo (1950)"
ORIOLES—PHOTOGRAPHS—PORTRAITS
PH11831 659 (June 24, 1993) p48. "The Orioles: Sonny Til, Johnny Reed, Tommy Gaither, George Nelson And Alexander Sharp"
PH11832 Number not assigned.
O'RIORDAN, DOLORES—PHOTOGRAPHS
PH11833 664 (September 2, 1993) p28. "Lawler, Mike Hogan, O'Riordan, Noel Hogan"
PH11834 680 (April 21, 1994) pp[enc.cover]. "Dolores O'Riordan Of The Cranberries" (Broad, Julian)
PH11835 680 (April 21, 1994) pp[enc.5]. "[Dolores O'Riordan]" (Broad, Julian)
PH11835a 690 (September 8, 1994) p24. "The Newlyweds Greet Fans Outside The Abbey" (Boland, Laurence)
PH11836 695 (November 17, 1994) p37. "The Cranberries" (Meeks, Raymond)
PH11837 696 (December 1, 1994) p44. "Lead Singer Dolores O'Riordan Lets It Linger" (Sirrs, Ed)
PH11838 704 (March 23, 1995) pp[cover]. "The Improbable Rise of Dolores O'Riordan" (Day, Corinne)
PH11839 704 (March 23, 1995) p60. "O'Riordan And Don Burton On Their Wedding Day, July 1994"
PH11840 704 (March 23, 1995) p60. "O'Riordan At London's Royal Albert Hall In January" (Parker, Steven)
PH11841 704 (March 23, 1995) pp56-57. "[Strange Fruit]" (Day, Corinne)
PH11842 711 (June 29, 1995) p13. "The Cranberries' Dolores O'Riordan Before The Melee" (Liu, Brian)
PH11843 736 (June 13, 1996) p52. "Summer Of '96 Road Warriors"
PH11844 743 (September 19, 1996) p44. "'Klonk' O'Riordan Slips Her Message To The Masses" (Rystedt, Rex)
O'RIORDAN, DOLORES—PHOTOGRAPHS—PORTRAITS
PH11845 704 (March 23, 1995) p59. "Dolores O'Riordan" (Day, Corinne)
PH11846 729 (March 7, 1996) p29. "Donating Her Talents: Dolores O'Riordan" (Bodnar, George)
ORLANDO (FILM)—PHOTOGRAPHS
PH11847 659 (June 24, 1993) p89. "Orlando As He (above right), With Charlotte Valandrey"
PH11848 659 (June 24, 1993) p89. "Orlando As She (below) With Billy Zane"
ORMOND, JULIA—ILLUSTRATIONS
PH11849 700 (January 26, 1995) p65. "Legends For The Mall" (Osborn, Kathy)
ORMOND, JULIA—PHOTOGRAPHS
PH11850 700 (January 26, 1995) p66. "Film Legends In The Making: Julia Ormond And Brad Pitt"
PH11851 726 (January 25, 1996) p66. "Unlucky In Love: Ormond Flanked By Kinnear And Ford"
O'ROURKE, P. J.—ILLUSTRATIONS
PH11852 670 (November 25, 1993) p61. "[P. J. O'Rourke]" (Peck, Everett)
PH11853 712-713 (July 13, 1995) p53. "[P. J. O'Rourke]" (Witte, Michael)
PH11854 712-713 (July 13, 1995) p67. "[William Greider & P. J. O'Rourke]" (Witte, Michael)
PH11855 734 (May 16, 1996) pp47,49-50. "[P. J. O'Rourke]" (Blitt, Barry)
PH11856 738-739 (July 11, 1996) pp57,64. "[P. J. O'Rourke]" (Blitt, Barry)
PH11857 743 (September 19, 1996) pp58,61. "[P. J. O'Rourke]" (Blitt, Barry)
PH11858 750-751 (December 26, 1996) p26. "P.J. Lite" (Pendergrast, James T.)
O'ROURKE, P. J.—PHOTOGRAPHS
PH11859 632 (June 11, 1992) p157. "P. J. O'Rourke Kicks Back After Another Day Of Reporting In Manila"
PH11860 639 (September 17, 1992) p42. "At The Table (from left): Greider, O'Rourke, Wenner, Thompson And Clinton" (Seliger, Mark)
ORRIS, JASON—PHOTOGRAPHS
PH11861 711 (June 29, 1995) p23. "Blending '60s Who With Atmospheric Noise: Jurgens, Orris, Ackerson And Wilson (from left)" (Elledge, Paul)
ORTIZ, DOMINGO—PHOTOGRAPHS
PH11862 631 (May 28, 1992) p17. "Widespread Panic (from left): John Bell, Michael Houser, Todd Nance, David Schools And Domingo Ortiz" (Messer, Alan)
ORTMANN, MARK—PHOTOGRAPHS
PH11863 730 (March 21, 1996) p21. "Bottle Rockets Tom Parr, Tom Ray, Brian Henneman, Mark Ortmann (from left)"
OSBORNE, JOAN—ALBUMS
PH11864 716 (September 7, 1995) p100. "Relish"
OSBORNE, JOAN—ILLUSTRATIONS
PH11865 707 (May 4, 1995) p69. "Joan Osborne" (Deen, Georganne)
PH11866 728 (February 22, 1996) p76. "One Of Us! One Of Us!—Joan Osborne" (Angel, Vinnie)
OSBORNE, JOAN—PHOTOGRAPHS
PH11867 730 (March 21, 1996) p47. "[Joan Osborne]" (Seliger, Mark)
PH11868 730 (March 21, 1996) p48. "Osborne Singing "I Heard It Through The Grapevine" At The 1996 Hall Of Fame Ceremony" (Mazur, Kevin)
PH11869 730 (March 21, 1996) p46. "Osborne With Bobby Sheehan Of Blues Traveler (left) And Craig Dreyer, 1991"
PH11870 732 (April 18, 1996) p20. "Joan Osborne, Left, Escorted By Sis Sara" (Mazur, Kevin)
PH11871 736 (June 13, 1996) p19. "The Iggy-esque Guy With Joan Osborne At The VH1 Honors' Benefit? Bryan Adams" (Mazur, Kevin)
OSBORNE, JOAN—PHOTOGRAPHS—PORTRAITS
PH11872 628 (April 16, 1992) p57. "[Joan Osborne]" (Vaccaro, Nick)
PH11873 730 (March 21, 1996) pp45,47. "[Joan Osborne]" (Seliger, Mark)
PH11874 730 (March 21, 1996) pp[cover]. "Joan Osborne: Saved By God, Sex And The Blues" (Seliger, Mark)
OSBORNE, SARA—PHOTOGRAPHS
PH11875 732 (April 18, 1996) p20. "Joan Osborne, Left, Escorted By Sis Sara" (Mazur, Kevin)
OSBOURNE, OZZY—ILLUSTRATIONS
PH11876 741 (August 22, 1996) p20. "Rolling Stone" (Pendergrast, James T.)
OSBOURNE, OZZY—PHOTOGRAPHS
PH11877 640 (October 1, 1992) p10. "Osbourne On The Road" (Leialoha, Mark)
PH11878 645-646 (December 10, 1992) p91. "Ozzy Osbourne Says Goodbye To Life On The Road" (Kirkland, Gene)
PH11879 647 (January 7, 1993) p9. "Ozzy (center) With Members Of Black Sabbath" (Granitz, Steve)
PH11880 666 (September 30, 1993) p18. "[Ozzy Osbourne]" (Seliger, Mark)
PH11881 696 (December 1, 1994) p25. "Ozzy And Main Squeeze Miss Piggy"

PH11882 738-739 (July 11, 1996) p92. "Osbourne '96: Retirement Sucks, But So Does His Return"
OSBOURNE, OZZY—PHOTOGRAPHS—PORTRAITS
PH11883 643 (November 12, 1992) p138. "Ozzy Osbourne" (Seliger, Mark)
PH11884 662 (August 5, 1993) p60. "Ozzy Osbourne" (Kirkland, Gene)
OSEARY, GUY—PHOTOGRAPHS
PH11885 732 (April 18, 1996) pp[enc.7]. "[Guy Oseary]" (Witkin, Christian)
OSMAN, DIID—PHOTOGRAPHS
PH11886 709 (June 1, 1995) p27. "PC Free: Stewart, Wener, McClure, Osman (from left)" (Westenberg, Kevin)
OSMAN, MAT—PHOTOGRAPHS
PH11887 657 (May 27, 1993) p15. "Ultra Suede: Gilbert, Anderson, Osman, Butler (from left)" (Broad, Julian)
OSMOND, DONNY—PHOTOGRAPHS
PH11888 678 (March 24, 1994) p28. "Bonaduce And Osmond"
OSWALD, JOHN—ALBUMS
PH11889 693 (October 20, 1994) p43. "Gray Folded"
OTHELLO (FILM)—PHOTOGRAPHS
PH11890 626 (March 19, 1992) p104. "Jealousy Destroys Welles And Cloutier"
PH11891 726 (January 25, 1996) p64. "Othello"
OTHER PEOPLE'S MONEY (FILM)—ILLUSTRATIONS
PH11892 617 (November 14, 1991) p179. "Selling Short" (Cowles, David)
OTHER PEOPLE'S MONEY (FILM)—PHOTOGRAPHS
PH11893 617 (November 14, 1991) p182. "DeVito Turns On The Charm For Legal Cupcake Miller"
OTIS, JOHNNY—PHOTOGRAPHS—PORTRAITS
PH11894 676 (February 24, 1994) p49. "Johnny Otis, Who Helped The Birth Of Rhythm & Blues"
OUIMET, DAVE—PHOTOGRAPHS
PH11895 660-661 (July 8, 1993) p101. "Motherhead Bug (from left): Anthony Lee, Steven Ovenden, April Chung, Cyril Mazzard, Jez Aspinal, Tomoyo, And Dave Ouimet" (Leopardi, N.)
OUT (PUBLICATION)—ALBUMS
PH11896 631 (May 28, 1992) p11. "Get Out"
OUT (PUBLICATION)—PHOTOGRAPHS
PH11897 630 (May 14, 1992) p90. "[Out]" (Rossi, Aldo)
PH11898 630 (May 14, 1992) p90. "[Out]" (Shirek, Jane)
OUTBREAK (FILM)—PHOTOGRAPHS
PH11899 706 (April 20, 1995) p89. "Now Playing"
OUTKAST—ALBUMS
PH11900 746 (October 31, 1996) p66. "Atliens"
OUTKAST—PHOTOGRAPHS
PH11901 747 (November 14, 1996) p136. "[OutKast]" (Alston, Kwaku)
OUTKAST—PHOTOGRAPHS—PORTRAITS
PH11902 686-687 (July 14, 1994) p79. "[The OutKast]"
OUTSIDE IS AMERICA (BOOK)—PHOTOGRAPHS
PH11903 645-646 (December 10, 1992) p87. "[Outside Is America]"
OVENDEN, STEVEN—PHOTOGRAPHS
PH11904 660-661 (July 8, 1993) p101. "Motherhead Bug (from left): Anthony Lee, Steven Ovenden, April Chung, Cyril Mazzard, Jez Aspinal, Tomoyo, And Dave Ouimet" (Leopardi, N.)
OVERNIGHT SENSATION (BOOK)—PHOTOGRAPHS
PH11905 685 (June 30, 1994) p32. "[Raspberries]"
OWENS, BUCK—PHOTOGRAPHS
PH11906 750-751 (December 26, 1996) pp170-171. "Buck Owens" (Seliger, Mark)
OWENS, ROBERT—PHOTOGRAPHS
PH11907 704 (March 23, 1995) p38. "DJ Robert Owens Spins At A Jungle Night Party" (Titlow, David)

P

P—ALBUMS
PH11908 721 (November 16, 1995) p112. "P"
P-NUT—PHOTOGRAPHS
PH11909 747 (November 14, 1996) p25. "311 Bassist P-Nut Shows Off His Tattoos" (Diamond, Rick)
PACINO, AL—ILLUSTRATIONS
PH11910 616 (October 31, 1991) p95. "Love In A Greasy Spoon" (Risko, Robert)
PH11911 671 (December 9, 1993) p75. "Son Of Scarface" (Cober, Alan E.)
PH11912 745 (October 17, 1996) p17. "'I'm Still Here, What The Hell? Why Not Direct?'—Al Pacino" (Ventura, Andrea)
PACINO, AL—PHOTOGRAPHS
PH11913 615 (October 17, 1991) p102. "Superegos On The Loose"
PH11914 616 (October 31, 1991) p97. "Pacino And Pfeiffer Hit A Brick Wall In Love"
PH11915 647 (January 7, 1993) p50. "Blind Al Pacino Savors A Last Tango With Gabrielle Anwar"
PH11916 653 (April 1, 1993) p57. "Scent Of A Woman"
PH11917 671 (December 9, 1993) p76. "Deja Vu: Pacino's Carlito With Miller (left)"
PH11918 671 (December 9, 1993) p76. "Pacino's Scarface With Pfeiffer"
PH11919 678 (March 24, 1994) p100. "Missing In Oscar Action"
PH11920 723 (December 14, 1995) p92. "Al Pacino"
PH11921 724-725 (December 28, 1995) p138. "De Niro, Pacino And Kilmer In 'Heat'"
PH11922 729 (March 7, 1996) p53. "Pacino Says His Piece As A Mayor Under Suspicion"
PH11923 734 (May 16, 1996) p17. "[Johnny Depp & Al Pacino]" (Davila, Bill)
PH11924 745 (October 17, 1996) p68. "The Master Onstage Recently In 'Hughie'"
PH11925 745 (October 17, 1996) p64. "Pacino Directs: Co-Star Kevin Spacey Pays Heed To His Liege On The Set Of 'Looking For Richard'"
PH11926 745 (October 17, 1996) p65. "'The Godfather' (1972): Brando And Pacino Flank Director Coppola"
PH11927 745 (October 17, 1996) p65. "'The Godfather III' (1990): Coppola Directs Pacino As The Aging Don"
PACINO, AL—PHOTOGRAPHS—PORTRAITS
PH11928 745 (October 17, 1996) p63. "[Al Pacino]" (Watson, Albert)
PH11929 745 (October 17, 1996) p68. "The Novice Takes Hollywood In 1974" (Galella, Ron)
PH11930 746 (October 31, 1996) p78. "Big, Bad Hunchbacked King Al Pacino"
PAGE, JIMMY—ALBUMS
PH11931 654 (April 15, 1993) p62. "Coverdale-Page"
PAGE, JIMMY—ILLUSTRATIONS
PH11932 641 (October 15, 1992) p69. "[Led Zeppelin]" (Burke, Philip)
PH11933 697 (December 15, 1994) p92. "Robert Plant And Jimmy Page" (Cowles, David)
PAGE, JIMMY—PHOTOGRAPHS
PH11934 625 (March 5, 1992) p11. "Jeff Beck (left) And Jimmy Page" (Mazur, Kevin)
PH11935 645-646 (December 10, 1992) p30. "The Famous Party-Ending Jam (above)" (Mazur, Kevin)
PH11936 670 (November 25, 1993) p19. "Page On A Zeppelin Reunion Tour: 'Don't Hold Your Breath'" (Seliger, Mark)
PH11937 675 (February 10, 1994) p23. "Page Moving Van Halen" (Granitz, Steve)
PH11938 696 (December 1, 1994) p29. "[Jimmy Page & Robert Plant]" (Mahurin, Matt)
PH11939 696 (December 1, 1994) p31. "Plant (left) And Page On

Led Zep's 1975 U.S. Tour" (Preston, Neal)
PH11940 698-699 (December 29, 1994) p75. "[Jimmy Page & Robert Plant]"
PH11941 702 (February 23, 1995) p48. "Aerosmith's Joe Perry And Steven Tyler Get Chummy With Led Zep's Robert Plant And Jimmy Page" (Mazur, Kevin)
PH11942 702 (February 23, 1995) p46. "...Getting Chummy With Plant In Rehearsal In 1975" (Preston, Neal)
PH11943 702 (February 23, 1995) p47. "Getting Ledded At Live Aid In '85: 'It Made Us Look Like Loonies,' Says Plant"
PH11944 702 (February 23, 1995) p46. "The Golden Boys: Page, Jones, Bonham And Plant (from left)"
PH11945 702 (February 23, 1995) p47. "Jones, Plant And Page Trample England Underfoot On Tour In 1970"
PH11946 702 (February 23, 1995) pp44-45. "[Robert Plant & Jimmy Page]" (Corbijn, Anton)
PH11947 702 (February 23, 1995) p48. "The Song Remains The Same: Robert Plant, Jimmy Page And Neil Young (from left)" (Mazur, Kevin)
PH11948 706 (April 20, 1995) p38. "Robert Plant (center) And Jimmy Page (right)" (Mazur, Kevin)
PH11949 715 (August 24, 1995) p30. "Jimmy Page: Smokin'!" (Seliger, Mark)
PH11950 720 (November 2, 1995) p49. "Robert Plant & Jimmy Page" (Greene, Herb)
PH11951 724-725 (December 28, 1995) p45. "Page Brought Out The Best In People" (Mazur, Kevin)
PH11952 724-725 (December 28, 1995) p39. "Robert Plant, Jimmy Page, Young (from left)" (Mazur, Kevin)
PH11953 726 (January 25, 1996) p28. "Page, Grant And Plant (from left) In 1975" (Preston, Neal)
PH11954 747 (November 14, 1996) p36. "Page (left) And Plant Have Begun Writing Material For A New Record" (Guzman)

PAGE, JIMMY—PHOTOGRAPHS—PORTRAITS
PH11955 625 (March 5, 1992) pp14-15. "On The Evening Of The Seventh Annual Hall Of Fame Induction Ceremony, 'Rolling Stone' Gathered These Nine Legendary Guitarists At The Waldorf-Astoria For A Once-In-A-Lifetime..."
PH11956 643 (November 12, 1992) p120. "Jimmy Page" (Seliger, Mark)
PH11957 702 (February 23, 1995) p46. "Page As King Yardbird In 1967 (above left)..." (Goodwin, Harry)
PH11958 702 (February 23, 1995) pp[cover]. "The Second Coming: Led Zeppelin's Robert Plant & Jimmy Page" (Corbijn, Anton)

PAGLIA, CAMILLE—PHOTOGRAPHS—PORTRAITS
PH11959 693 (October 20, 1994) pp87,92. "[Camille Paglia]" (Gougenheim, Kim)

PALAC, LISA—PHOTOGRAPHS
PH11960 682 (May 19, 1994) p72. "[Lisa Palac]" (Morey, Craig)

PALACE MUSIC—ALBUMS
PH11961 720 (November 2, 1995) p70. "Viva Last Blues"

PALACE SONGS—ALBUMS
PH11962 701 (February 9, 1995) p58. "Hope"

PALEFACE—PHOTOGRAPHS—PORTRAITS
PH11963 626 (March 19, 1992) p20. "[Paleface]" (Gahr, David)

THE PALLBEARER (FILM)—PHOTOGRAPHS
PH11964 733 (May 2, 1996) p62. "Schwimmer With Paltrow"

PALMER, ROBERT—PHOTOGRAPHS
PH11965 632 (June 11, 1992) p40. "In 1988, Robert Palmer Gets Back Into The Mystic With Master Musician Bachir Attar" (Katzenstein, David)

PALMINTERI, CHAZZ—PHOTOGRAPHS
PH11966 694 (November 3, 1994) p104. "Palminteri Runs With No-Talent Boss Tilly"
PH11967 733 (May 2, 1996) p62. "'Faithfull': Cher, Palminteri, O'Neal"

PALTROW, GWYNETH—ILLUSTRATIONS
PH11968 741 (August 22, 1996) p103. "Hot And Bothered" (Brodner, Steve)

PALTROW, GWYNETH—PHOTOGRAPHS
PH11969 670 (November 25, 1993) p126. "Gwyneth Paltrow (right) Steals The Film"
PH11970 678 (March 24, 1994) p100. "Missing In Oscar Action"
PH11971 682 (May 19, 1994) p57. "[Gwyneth Paltrow]" (Seliger, Mark)
PH11972 733 (May 2, 1996) p14. "[Gwyneth Paltrow, Brad Pitt, & Paul Newman]" (Ferreir, Albert)
PH11973 733 (May 2, 1996) p62. "Schwimmer With Paltrow"
PH11974 741 (August 22, 1996) p104. "Paltrow As Matchmaking Emma"
PH11975 744 (October 3, 1996) p20. "Ethan 'Pip' Hawke And Gwyneth 'Stella' Paltrow" (Schwartzwald, Lawrence)

PALTROW, GWYNETH—PHOTOGRAPHS—PORTRAITS
PH11976 718 (October 5, 1995) p76. "Cop Brad Pitt Battles A Serial Killer To Protect Gwyneth Paltrow"
PH11977 743 (September 19, 1996) p90. "[Summer...]"

PAMER, JOHN—PHOTOGRAPHS
PH11978 696 (December 1, 1994) p32. "Thomson, John Pamer, Toomey And Andrew Webster" (Owen, Tim)

PANACCIONE, CHIN-A—PHOTOGRAPHS
PH11979 708 (May 18, 1995) p38. "Queenie's Panaccione, Schlecter" (Shirk, Alison)

PANIC—PHOTOGRAPHS
PH11980 615 (October 17, 1991) p28. "Jack Coy, George Hernandez, Jeff Braimes, Martin Chandler (from left)" (Mason, Karen)

PANOZZO, JOHN—PHOTOGRAPHS
PH11981 742 (September 5, 1996) p26. "[John Panozzo]" (Walter, Chris)

PANSY DIVISION—PHOTOGRAPHS
PH11982 708 (May 18, 1995) p42. "Beyond The Pop Pales: Pansy Division" (Geller, Marc)

PANTERA—PHOTOGRAPHS
PH11983 685 (June 30, 1994) p24. "Rex, Dimebag Darrell, Vinnie Paul And Phil Anselmo (clockwise from left)" (Winters, Dan)

PANTHER (FILM)—ILLUSTRATIONS
PH11984 708 (May 18, 1995) p95. "Fight The Power" (Kunz, Anita)

PANTHER (FILM)—PHOTOGRAPHS
PH11985 708 (May 18, 1995) p96. "Vance And Chong Front The Panthers"

PANTHER DREAM (BOOK)—ILLUSTRATIONS
PH11986 619-620 (December 12, 1991) p75. "[Panther Dream]" (Weir, Wendy)

PAPA'S CULTURE—PHOTOGRAPHS—PORTRAITS
PH11987 660-661 (July 8, 1993) p96. "Papa's Culture: White (left) And Davis" (Alicino, Christine)

THE PAPER (FILM)—ILLUSTRATIONS
PH11988 679 (April 7, 1994) p81. "The Sleaze Factor" (Guy, Edmund)

THE PAPER (FILM)—PHOTOGRAPHS
PH11989 679 (April 7, 1994) p82. "Metro Editor Michael Keaton (standing) Rouses The Staff For A Hot Story"

PAQUIN, ANNA—PHOTOGRAPHS
PH11990 671 (December 9, 1993) p76. "Grace Notes: Holly Hunter (left) And Anna Paquin"

PARADIS, VANESSA—PHOTOGRAPHS
PH11991 735 (May 30, 1996) p12. "[Lenny Kravitz & Vanessa Paradis]"
PH11992 750-751 (December 26, 1996) p56. "Paradis (left) And Kravitz In Midscuffle"

PARASKEVIN-YOUNG, CONNIE—PHOTOGRAPHS
PH11993 626 (March 19, 1992) p79. "[Connie Paraskevin-Young]" (Hanauer, Mark)

PARENTS MUSIC RESOURCE CENTER—ILLUSTRATIONS
PH11994 723 (December 14, 1995) p20. "Free Speech" (Pendergrast, James T.)

PARILLAUD, ANNE—PHOTOGRAPHS
PH11995 619-620 (December 12, 1991) p194. "Male Wimps And Female Warriors"
PH11996 642 (October 29, 1992) p77. "Innocent Blood"
PH11997 654 (April 15, 1993) p72. "Bridget Fonda (left) Can't Match The Sizzle of Anne Parillaud in 'Le Femme Nikita'"
PARISH, JOHN—ALBUMS
PH11998 745 (October 17, 1996) p130. "Dance Hall At Louse Point"
PARISH, JOHN—PHOTOGRAPHS
PH11999 738-739 (July 11, 1996) p28. "John Parish And Polly Jean Harvey Team Up"
PARISH, STEVE—PHOTOGRAPHS
PH12000 740 (August 8, 1996) p36. "1990: Diving Off The Coast Of Kona, Hawaii, With Steve Parish" (Jensen, Victoria)
PARK CITY, UTAH—PHOTOGRAPHS
PH12001 652 (March 18, 1993) p47. "Park City, Utah" (Michaelson, Randall)
PARKER, CHARLIE—PHOTOGRAPHS—PORTRAITS
PH12002 735 (May 30, 1996) p3. "[The Faces Of Heroin]"
PARKER, COLONEL TOM—PHOTOGRAPHS
PH12003 643 (November 12, 1992) p56. "While Wertheimer Followed Elvis, Catching Colonel Parker Stoking The Starmaking Machine..." (Wertheimer, Alfred)
PARKER, GRAHAM—ALBUMS
PH12004 617 (November 14, 1991) p140. "The Parkerilla" (Bubbles, Barney)
PH12005 617 (November 14, 1991) p140. "The Parkerilla" (Griffin, Brian)
PH12006 639 (September 17, 1992) p94. "Burning Questions"
PARKER, GRAHAM—PHOTOGRAPHS—PORTRAITS
PH12007 645-646 (December 10, 1992) p71. "Graham Parker" (Parker, Jolie)
PARKER, GREG—PHOTOGRAPHS
PH12008 678 (March 24, 1994) p69. "Brothers Under The Skin: Martin Phillips, Greg Parker, Mike Williams, Dexter Wilson, Rick Brown, Greg Jackson, Everett Whiteside, Roderick Bradford, Lacell Sherman..." (Smith, Bria
PARKER, KARREN—PHOTOGRAPHS
PH12009 708 (May 18, 1995) p58. "Karren Parker, Right, With Boyfriend Lovell Knight, Claims Humphries Asked Her 'Why Can't You Black Girls Not Have So Many Babies?'" (Mark, Mary Ellen)
PARKER, MARY-LOUISE—PHOTOGRAPHS
PH12010 702 (February 23, 1995) p81. "Actresses Goldberg, Parker And Barrymore Blow It"
PARKER, NATHANIEL—PHOTOGRAPHS
PH12011 656 (May 13, 1993) p116. "Sex Is Hot For Lombard (top) And Parker"
PARKER, SARAH JESSICA—ILLUSTRATIONS
PH12012 701 (February 9, 1995) p61. "New Age Funny Girl" (Meinhardt, Brook)
PARKER, SARAH JESSICA—PHOTOGRAPHS
PH12013 639 (September 17, 1992) p103. "Cage (left) And Caan Vie For Parker"
PH12014 701 (February 9, 1995) p62. "Farrow Catches Parker And Banderas"
PH12015 730 (March 21, 1996) p106. "Now Playing"
PH12016 745 (October 17, 1996) p144. "Grant And Parker Do The ER Thing"
PARLAVECCHIO, STEVE—PHOTOGRAPHS
PH12017 652 (March 18, 1993) p47. "Patrick McGaw, Joseph Lindsey And Steve Parlavecchio (from left) Of 'Amongst Friends'" (Michaelson, Randall)
PH12018 662 (August 5, 1993) p73. "Guy Talk From Parlavecchio, McGaw And Lambson"
PH12019 665 (September 16, 1993) pp[enc.34]. "[Rob Weiss, Steve Parlavecchio, Michael Arturro]" (Nystrom, Dick)
PARNASS, ALEXANDRA—PHOTOGRAPHS
PH12020 719 (October 19, 1995) p129. "Alexandra Parnass Moved Up By Asking For Jobs No One Else Wanted" (Toy, Joann)
PARR, TOM—PHOTOGRAPHS
PH12021 730 (March 21, 1996) p21. "Bottle Rockets Tom Parr, Tom Ray, Brian Henneman, Mark Ortmann (from left)"
PARSONS, DAVE—PHOTOGRAPHS
PH12022 710 (June 15, 1995) p49. "Dave Parsons, Rossdale, Robin Goodridge, Pulsford (from left)" (Westenberg, Kevin)
PH12023 712-713 (July 13, 1995) p29. "Zen Careerists: Pulsford, Parsons, Rossdale, And Goodridge (from left)" (Mahurin, Matt)
PARSONS, DAVE—PHOTOGRAPHS—PORTRAITS
PH12024 732 (April 18, 1996) p41. "Robin Goodridge, Gavin Rossdale, Dave Parsons And Nigel Pulsford" (Seliger, Mark)
PARSONS, GRAM—PHOTOGRAPHS—PORTRAITS
PH12025 619-620 (December 12, 1991) p32. "[Hickory Wind]"
PH12026 735 (May 30, 1996) p3. "[The Faces Of Heroin]"
PARSONS, KARYN—PHOTOGRAPHS
PH12027 633 (June 25, 1992) p48. "Kid (left) 'N Play Rap With Rogers (left) And Parsons"
PARTON, DOLLY—ALBUMS
PH12028 660-661 (July 8, 1993) p111. "Slow Dancing With The Moon"
PARTON, DOLLY—ILLUSTRATIONS
PH12029 632 (June 11, 1992) p114. "[Dolly Parton]" (Cronin, Brian)
PARTON, DOLLY—PHOTOGRAPHS
PH12030 632 (June 11, 1992) p117. "Parton And Flippo In 1977 At The Waldorf-Astoria Hotel In New York City" (Gahr, David)
PARTON, DOLLY—PHOTOGRAPHS—PORTRAITS
PH12031 632 (June 11, 1992) p115. "[Dolly Parton, Arnold Schwarzenegger]" (Leibovitz, Annie)
PARTRIDGE FAMILY—ILLUSTRATIONS
PH12032 632 (June 11, 1992) p51. "[Partridge Family]" (Cronin, Brian)
PARTRIDGE, ANDY—ALBUMS
PH12033 689 (August 25, 1994) p90. "The Greatest Living Englishman"
PARTRIDGE, ANDY—PHOTOGRAPHS
PH12034 674 (January 27, 1994) p29. "Mann Is Joined by Troubadour Partridge" (Busacca, Larry)
PARTY GIRL (FILM)—PHOTOGRAPHS
PH12035 704 (March 23, 1995) p128. "Parker Posey Makes The N.Y. Party Scene"
PASCAL, ADAM—PHOTOGRAPHS
PH12036 734 (May 16, 1996) p54. "[Adam Pascal]" (Hom, Marc)
PASCUA YAQUI RESERVATION—PHOTOGRAPHS
PH12037 709 (June 1, 1995) p56. "Coronado Lived In This Room For Six Months In 1994 On The Pascua Yaqui Reservation, About 10 Miles Southwest Of Tucson, Ariz." (Aguilera-Hellweg, Max)
PASQUINI, DOMINIC—PHOTOGRAPHS
PH12038 647 (January 7, 1993) p30. "Dunlavy, Dominic Pasquini, Matt Hensler" (Mark, Mary Ellen)
PASSENGERS—ALBUMS
PH12039 723 (December 14, 1995) p82. "Original Soundtracks I"
PASSION (STAGE MUSICAL)—PHOTOGRAPHS
PH12040 683 (June 2, 1994) p76. "Passion"
PASSION FISH (FILM)—ILLUSTRATIONS
PH12041 648 (January 21, 1993) p54. "A Few Good Women" (Witte, Michael)
PASSION FISH (FILM)—PHOTOGRAPHS
PH12042 648 (January 21, 1993) p55. "Woodard And McDonnell Fight Dependency"
PH12043 653 (April 1, 1993) p57. "Passion Fish"
PATCH, BRIAN—PHOTOGRAPHS
PH12044 706 (April 20, 1995) pp[enc.18]. "Skating At Chicken's Pool" (Seliger, Mark)

PATCH, STEVE—PHOTOGRAPHS
PH12045 719 (October 19, 1995) p131. "A&R Man Steve Patch's Jumping-Off Point Was 'Tape Coordinator'" (Toy, Joann)
PATRA—PHOTOGRAPHS
PH12046 715 (August 24, 1995) p23. "Guru, Patra And Byrd At The 'Jazzmatazz II' Release Party" (Capak, R. J.)
PATRA—PHOTOGRAPHS—PORTRAITS
PH12047 695 (November 17, 1994) p132. "Patra" (White, Steven)
PATRIC, JASON—PHOTOGRAPHS
PH12048 621 (January 9, 1992) p55. "Jason Patric And Jennifer Jason Leigh In Danger"
PH12049 746 (October 31, 1996) p76. "Pitt And Patric Bend The Truth"
PATRICK, RICHARD—PHOTOGRAPHS
PH12050 712-713 (July 13, 1995) p37. "The Touring Filter, With Patrick (left) And Liesegang (foreground)" (Norcross, Deborah)
PH12051 715 (August 24, 1995) pp68-69. "Brian Liesegang, Richard Patrick, Geno Lenardo, Matt Walker, Frank Cavanagh (from left)" (Ockenfels, Frank W.)
PH12052 715 (August 24, 1995) p70. "Liesegang (left) And Patrick Crank It Out In Houston" (Haveman, Kathy)
PH12053 720 (November 2, 1995) p16. "Robert And Richard Patrick With Brian Liesegang In L.A. (from left)" (Phillips, Ken)
PATRICK, RICHARD—PHOTOGRAPHS—PORTRAITS
PH12054 715 (August 24, 1995) p70. "For All Filter's Noisy, Bile-Soaked Music, Liesegang (left) And Patrick Are Shy, Thoughtful Guys—Eggheads, Really" (Ockenfels, Frank W.)
PATRICK, ROBERT—PHOTOGRAPHS
PH12055 720 (November 2, 1995) p16. "Robert And Richard Patrick With Brian Liesegang In L.A. (from left)" (Phillips, Ken)
PATRIOT GAMES (FILM)—PHOTOGRAPHS
PH12056 634-635 (July 9, 1992) p114. "A Flag-Waving Thriller Pits Ford Against Terrorists"
PATTON, CHARLIE—ALBUMS
PH12057 625 (March 5, 1992) p63. "King Of The Delta Blues: The Music Of Charlie Patton"
PATTON, CHARLIE—ILLUSTRATIONS—PORTRAITS
PH12058 625 (March 5, 1992) p63. "Deeper Into The Delta" (Allen, Thomas B.)
PATTON, MIKE—PHOTOGRAPHS
PH12059 618 (November 28, 1991) p11. "Patton" (Blakesberg, Jay)
PH12060 645-646 (December 10, 1992) p66. "Faith No More's Mike Patton" (Hutson, Mick)
PAUL, LES—ALBUMS
PH12061 618 (November 28, 1991) p94. "The Legend And The Legacy"
PAUL, LES—PHOTOGRAPHS
PH12062 702 (February 23, 1995) p35. "Albert Lee, Arlen Roth And Les Paul (from left)" (Capak, R. J.)
PAUL, VINNIE—PHOTOGRAPHS
PH12063 685 (June 30, 1994) p24. "Rex, Dimebag Darrell, Vinnie Paul And Phil Anselmo (clockwise from left)" (Winters, Dan)
PH12064 707 (May 4, 1995) p20. "Icky Wail's Mike Teis, Pantera's Dimebag Darrell And Vinnie Paul (from left)" (Stone, John)
PAULIDES, BROOKE—PHOTOGRAPHS
PH12065 644 (November 26, 1992) pp60-61,63. "[Brooke Paulides]" (Noble, Chris)
PAULSON, CHARLIE—PHOTOGRAPHS
PH12066 738-739 (July 11, 1996) p116. "Pfeiffer, Feldmann, Williams And Paulson (from left)"
PAVAROTTI, LUCIANO—PHOTOGRAPHS
PH12067 694 (November 3, 1994) p22. "Pavarotti (left) And Adams"
PAVAROTTI, LUCIANO—PHOTOGRAPHS—PORTRAITS
PH12068 682 (May 19, 1994) p38. "Rain-Forest Crunch: Sting And His Pal Pav" (Mazur, Kevin)
PAVEMENT—ALBUMS
PH12069 664 (September 2, 1993) p64. "Westing"
PH12070 676 (February 24, 1994) p55. "Crooked Rain, Crooked Rain"
PH12071 680 (April 21, 1994) p104. "Crooked Rain, Crooked Rain"
PH12072 706 (April 20, 1995) p70. "Wowee Zowee"
PH12073 731 (April 4, 1996) p76. "Give It A Day"
PAVEMENT—ILLUSTRATIONS
PH12074 676 (February 24, 1994) p55. "Paving The Way" (Deen, Georganne)
PAVEMENT—PHOTOGRAPHS
PH12075 686-687 (July 14, 1994) p20. "Crooked Reign: Pavement Take Over "The Tonight Show""
PH12076 686-687 (July 14, 1994) p20. "Ibold, Nastanovich And Kannberg (from left)" (Blakesberg, Jay)
PH12077 686-687 (July 14, 1994) p19. "Pavement (clockwise from left): Mark Ibold, Steve West, Bob Nastanovich And Stephen Malkmus" (Blakesberg, Jay)
PH12078 695 (November 17, 1994) p78. "Pavement" (Hanauer, Mark)
PH12079 698-699 (December 29, 1994) p37. "Slop Rockers Pavement Hit The Ground Stumbling" (Hanauer, Mark)
PH12080 709 (June 1, 1995) p23. "Lollapalooza Puts Pavement's Mark Ibold (left) And Stephen Malkmus On The Road" (Corio, David)
PH12081 715 (August 24, 1995) p44. "Limbo Rock: Malkmus Of Pavement" (Blakesberg, Jay)
PH12082 742 (September 5, 1996) p23. "[Pavement]"
PH12083 748 (November 28, 1996) p34. "Elastica Meet Go-Go: Kannberg And Ibold With Malkmus (from left)" (Tavee, Tom)
PAVITT, BRUCE—PHOTOGRAPHS
PH12084 628 (April 16, 1992) p44. "Sub Pop's Jonathan Poneman (left) And Bruce Pavitt" (Seliger, Mark)
PAYMAR, JIM—PHOTOGRAPHS
PH12085 650 (February 18, 1993) p43. "'The Reporters': Jim Paymar, Dunlop, Bradford, Abramovitz, And Dunleavy (from left)"
PAYNE, LYNN—PHOTOGRAPHS
PH12086 721 (November 16, 1995) p81. "The Tribe That Sticks Together: Slade Bellum, Lynn Breedlove, Leslie Mah, Lynn Payne, Lynn Flipper (from left)" (Yemchuk, Yelena)
PEARCE, GUY—PHOTOGRAPHS
PH12087 689 (August 25, 1994) p97. "Drag Queens On A Bus: Pearce, Stamp And Weaving"
PEARL JAM—ALBUMS
PH12088 669 (November 11, 1993) p72. "Vs." (Considine, J. D.)
PH12089 672-673 (December 23, 1993) p146. "Vs."
PH12090 674 (January 27, 1994) p45. "Vs."
PH12091 697 (December 15, 1994) p91. "Vitalogy"
PH12092 698-699 (December 29, 1994) p170. "Vitalogy"
PH12093 700 (January 26, 1995) p76. "Vitalogy"
PH12094 701 (February 9, 1995) p72. "Vitalogy"
PH12095 702 (February 23, 1995) p84. "Vitalogy"
PH12096 703 (March 9, 1995) p80. "Vitalogy"
PH12097 704 (March 23, 1995) p144. "Vitalogy"
PH12098 705 (April 6, 1995) p80. "Vitalogy"
PH12099 707 (May 4, 1995) p84. "Vitalogy"
PH12100 708 (May 18, 1995) p108. "Vitalogy"
PH12101 728 (February 22, 1996) p76. "Merkinball"
PH12102 742 (September 5, 1996) p59. "No Code"
PEARL JAM—ILLUSTRATIONS
PH12103 671 (December 9, 1993) p7. "Pearl Jam" (Pendergrast, James T.)
PH12104 700 (January 26, 1995) p76. "Pearl Jam: Seattle Supersonics" (Clayton, Christian)
PH12105 701 (February 9, 1995) p14. "Pearl Jam" (Pendergrast, James T.)
PH12106 715 (August 24, 1995) p18. "Pearl Jam: Contains Filler" (Pendergrast, James T.)

PH12107 728 (February 22, 1996) p16. "Ticketmaster-Pearl Jam" (Pendergrast, James T.)
PH12108 742 (September 5, 1996) p59. "No Limits, No Fear" (Pollock, Ian)
PEARL JAM—PHOTOGRAPHS
PH12109 616 (October 31, 1991) p15. "Pearl Jam (from left): Mike McCready, David Abbruzzese, Eddie Vedder, Jeff Ament And Stone Gossard" (Cuffaro, Chris)
PH12110 619-620 (December 12, 1991) p68. "Pearl Jam, Seattle's Newest Stars" (Cuffaro, Chris)
PH12111 634-635 (July 9, 1992) p13. "Pearl Jam's Mike McCready, Dave Abbruzzese, Eddie Vedder, Gossard And Jeff Ament (from left)" (Mercer, Lance)
PH12112 639 (September 17, 1992) p60. "Eddie Vedder, Mike McCready, Jeff Ament And Stone Gossard (from left) Of Pearl Jam" (Blakesberg, Jay)
PH12113 651 (March 4, 1993) p48. "Pearl Jam: Best New American Band" (Gullick, Steve)
PH12114 662 (August 5, 1993) p34. "Vedder (left) With Jeff Ament" (Rachlin, Amy)
PH12115 667 (October 14, 1993) p100. "It's 'Alive'! 'Give The People A Chance To Visualize Their Own Ideas,' Says Ament"
PH12116 668 (October 28, 1993) p61. "Pearl Jam In Their Nightly Pre-Gig Huddle" (Seliger, Mark)
PH12117 668 (October 28, 1993) p51. "The Sun Shines On The Five Musketeers: Jeff Ament, Eddie Vedder (We're Not Kidding), Dave Abbruzzese, Stone Gossard And Mike McCready (from left)" (Seliger, Mark)
PH12118 668 (October 28, 1993) p56. "Vedder (on his back) And Bassist Jeff Ament Get Crazy Onstage" (Preston, Neal)
PH12119 668 (October 28, 1993) p57. "Vedder And Ament (flying): Thriving On The Weirdness" (Preston, Neal)
PH12120 668 (October 28, 1993) pp[cover]. "A Year In The Life" (Seliger, Mark)
PH12121 672-673 (December 23, 1993) p188. "[Covers]" (Seliger, Mark)
PH12122 672-673 (December 23, 1993) p69. "Us 'Vs.' The World: Gossard, Mike McCready, Dave Abbruzzese, Vedder, Jeff Ament (from left)" (Seliger, Mark)
PH12123 674 (January 27, 1994) p40. "Pearl Jam On A Roll: A Near Sweep" (Preston, Neal)
PH12124 683 (June 2, 1994) p28. "[Pearl Jam]" (Mercer, Lance)
PH12125 688 (August 11, 1994) p30. "Ament (left) And Gossard To Testify Before A House Subcommittee" (Brennan, Shayna)
PH12126 692 (October 6, 1994) p22. "Pearl Jam Ament (left) And Gossard Testify"
PH12127 692 (October 6, 1994) p24. "Pearl Jam, With Abbruzzese (left)" (Rikken, Clemens)
PH12128 696 (December 1, 1994) p23. "The Annual Bridge School Benefit: Pearl Jam's Jeff Ament And Eddie Vedder (above)" (Blakesberg, Jay)
PH12129 698-699 (December 29, 1994) p60. "Pearl Jam's Jeff Ament And Stone Gossard"
PH12130 698-699 (December 29, 1994) p68. "Young, Vedder And Stone Gossard (from left) Do The Right Thing For The Kids" (Hashimoto, Mike)
PH12131 702 (February 23, 1995) p26. "Pirate Music: McCready, Vedder, Ament, Irons And Stone Gossard (from left)" (Mercer, Lance)
PH12132 703 (March 9, 1995) p36. "Rockin' In The Free World: Pearl Jam With Neil Young" (Mazur, Kevin)
PH12133 714 (August 10, 1995) p19. "[Pearl Jam]" (Mazur, Kevin)
PH12134 726 (January 25, 1996) p17. "Mike McCready, Jeff Ament, Harper, Eddie Vedder, Jack Irons And Stone Gossard (from left)"
PH12135 727 (February 8, 1996) p17. "Mike McReady, Jeff Ament And Eddie Vedder (from left) Dropped Plans For A Live Pearl Jam Album But Allowed Radio Stations To Distribute Their '95 Concert Recordings For Free" (Gehring, Karl A.)
PH12136 733 (May 2, 1996) p24. "Pearl Jam's Jeff Ament And Eddie Vedder" (Popplewell, John)
PH12137 748 (November 28, 1996) p57. "Pearl Jam Mug For A Backstage Shot A Finsbury Park, In London, 1992" (Halfin, Ross)
PEARL JAM—PHOTOGRAPHS—PORTRAITS
PH12138 619-620 (December 12, 1991) p45. "...And Pearl Jam (below) Proved Themselves The Pride Of The Evergreen State" (Giron, Joe)
PEARSON, DAN—PHOTOGRAPHS
PH12139 659 (June 24, 1993) p15. "McCready, Eitzel, Ament, AMC's Vudi And Dan Pearson (from left)" (Blakesberg, Jay)
PEARSON, DANNY—PHOTOGRAPHS
PH12140 695 (November 17, 1994) p131. "American Music Club" (Duke, William)
PEARSON, DANNY—PHOTOGRAPHS—PORTRAITS
PH12141 656 (May 13, 1993) p77. "American Music Club (from left): Danny Pearson, Tim Mooney, Vudi, Bruce Kaphan And Mark Eitzel" (Ockenfels, Frank, 3)
PEARSON, J. J.—PHOTOGRAPHS
PH12142 741 (August 22, 1996) p61. "J. J. Pearson Prepares For Action" (Maxwell, Robert)
PEARSON, RIDLEY—PHOTOGRAPHS
PH12143 634-635 (July 9, 1992) p13. "Authorial Intrusion: Stephen King, Dave Barry And Ridley Pearson (from left)" (Foothorap, Robert)
PECK, M. SCOTT—ILLUSTRATIONS
PH12144 719 (October 19, 1995) p81. "[M. Scott Peck]" (Cronin, Brian)
PECK, M. SCOTT—PHOTOGRAPHS
PH12145 719 (October 19, 1995) p86. "One Of The Highest-Priced Inspirational Speakers, Peck Lectured Across The Country" (Vazquez, William)
PH12146 719 (October 19, 1995) p82. "The Self-Help Guru Near The Woods God Was Walking In 'When He Decided He Wanted A Book Written'" (Tavee, Tom)
PEEBLES, ANN—ALBUMS
PH12147 633 (June 25, 1992) p42. "Full Time Love"
PEEL, JOHN—PHOTOGRAPHS
PH12148 663 (August 19, 1993) p19. "[John Peel]" (Indge, Alaister)
PEEPSHOW (PUBLICATION)—PHOTOGRAPHS
PH12149 682 (May 19, 1994) p69. "[Peepshow]"
PEI, I. M.—PHOTOGRAPHS
PH12150 662 (August 5, 1993) p18. "Architect I. M. Pei Greets Chuck Berry" (Mazur, Kevin)
PH12151 662 (August 5, 1993) p18. "Diggin' In The Dirt: The Celebrity Crew Does The Honors" (Mazur, Kevin)
THE PELICAN BRIEF (FILM)—PHOTOGRAPHS
PH12152 674 (January 27, 1994) p48. "Acting Vehicles Include 'The Pelican Brief,' 'In The Name Of The Father,' 'What's Eating Gilbert Grape,' 'Shadowlands,' 'Naked,' And 'Grumpy Old Men'"
PELL, CLAIBORNE—PHOTOGRAPHS—PORTRAITS
PH12153 719 (October 19, 1995) p120. "Sen. Claiborne Pell, A GI Bill Success Story, Is Defending Equal Access To College"
PELL MELL—ALBUMS
PH12154 711 (June 29, 1995) p42. "Interstate"
PELL MELL—PHOTOGRAPHS
PH12155 723 (December 14, 1995) p44. "Pell Mell: Soundtracks For The Road" (Galinsky, Michael)
PELT, LANCE—PHOTOGRAPHS
PH12156 715 (August 24, 1995) p94. "Keane With Empire State Building Guards Darren Hicks, Lance Pelt And Peter Vargas" (Danelian, Stephen)
PENGILLY, KIRK—PHOTOGRAPHS
PH12157 671 (December 9, 1993) p18. "INXS Marks Their Spot: Pengilly; Beers, Tim, Andrew And Jon Farriss; Hutchence (from left)" (Borris, Dan)

PENN, DAN—ALBUMS
PH12158 684 (June 16, 1994) p110. "Do Right Man"
PENN, LEO—PHOTOGRAPHS
PH12159 731 (April 4, 1996) p48. "Parents Leo Penn And Eileen Ryan" (Dominguez, Ralph)
PENN, MICHAEL—ALBUMS
PH12160 644 (November 26, 1992) p72. "Free-For-All"
PENN, MICHAEL—PHOTOGRAPHS
PH12161 636 (August 6, 1992) p11. "Michael Penn, Maria McKee And Robbie Robertson (from left) At The Whiskey" (Cavolina, Robbie)
PH12162 636 (August 6, 1992) p22. "Penn (left) In The Studio With Berg" (Cohen, Lester)
PH12163 675 (February 10, 1994) p22. "Penn, Williams And Himmelman At The Gimme Shelter Benefit For The Homeless" (Mayer, Jeffrey)
PH12164 700 (January 26, 1995) p17. "Michael Penn Does His Share For The Homeless" (Kravitz, Jeff)
PENN, SEAN—ILLUSTRATIONS
PH12165 734 (May 16, 1996) p14. "The Sean Penn Library" (Pendergrast, James T.)
PENN, SEAN—PHOTOGRAPHS
PH12166 654 (April 15, 1993) p69. "We're No Angels"
PH12166a 678 (March 24, 1994) p100. "Missing In Oscar Action"
PH12167 716 (September 7, 1995) p14. "Jewel Of The Aisle: Kilcher And Penn Get Acquainted Backstage" (Young, P.)
PH12168 724-725 (December 28, 1995) p139. "An Image To Remember: Penn And Sarandon"
PH12169 726 (January 25, 1996) p18. "Light Up Or Leave Me Alone: Penn At 'Heat'" (Davis, Ron)
PH12170 731 (April 4, 1996) p48. "Out On The Town With Supermodel Elle MacPherson In 1996"
PH12171 731 (April 4, 1996) p48. "Penn Protecting Then Wife Madonna From The Paparazzi In 1986" (Savignano, Anthony)
PH12172 731 (April 4, 1996) p49. "Penn Wrangles With Photographers In 1986" (Zuffante, Vinnie)
PH12173 731 (April 4, 1996) p47. "[Sean Penn]" (Seliger, Mark)
PH12174 731 (April 4, 1996) p48. "With Robin Wright, The Mother Of His Two Children, In 1991" (Ortega, Albert)
PH12175 736 (June 13, 1996) p19. "Doing The Right Thing At The VH1 Honors Benefit: Eddie Vedder, Who Looks Eerily Like Harrison Ford, Michael Stipe And Recent Newlywed Sean Penn" (Mazur, Kevin)
PENN, SEAN—PHOTOGRAPHS—PORTRAITS
PH12176 731 (April 4, 1996) pp[cover]. "Cool Jerk: Is Sean Penn The Greatest Actor Of His Generation Or A Menace To Society?" (Seliger, Mark)
PH12177 731 (April 4, 1996) p48. "Penn In High School In 1977"
PH12178 731 (April 4, 1996) pp44-45. "[Sean Penn]" (Seliger, Mark)
PENNSYLVANIA STATE UNIVERSITY—PHOTOGRAPHS
PH12179 659 (June 24, 1993) p60. "Blues Traveler Has An Embryonic And Mobile Following Much Like The Grateful Dead's" (Fink, Larry)
PH12180 659 (June 24, 1993) p58. "Save His Soul: A Fan Takes A Break From The Festivities" (Fink, Larry)
THE PEOPLE VS. LARRY FLYNT (FILM)—PHOTOGRAPHS
PH12181 743 (September 19, 1996) p88. "Divas"
PEOPLES, DAVID WEBB—PHOTOGRAPHS
PH12182 656 (May 13, 1993) p73. "[David Webb Peoples]" (Adams, Eddie)
PEPA—PHOTOGRAPHS
PH12183 671 (December 9, 1993) p31. "Spinderella, Blaze Berdahl Of 'Ghostwriter,' Pepa And Salt (from left)" (Leibowitz, Eric)
PH12184 723 (December 14, 1995) p28. "[Salt-N-Pepa & Patti Smith]" (Mazur, Kevin)
PEPA—PHOTOGRAPHS—PORTRAITS
PH12185 695 (November 17, 1994) p140. "Salt-N-Pepa" (Demarchelier, Patrick)
PH12186 696 (December 1, 1994) p24. "Reach, Pepa And LL Cool J" (Sands, Steve)
PERE UBU—ALBUMS
PH12187 663 (August 19, 1993) p78. "Story Of My Life"
PH12188 718 (October 5, 1995) p69. "Ray Gun Suitcase"
PH12189 746 (October 31, 1996) p68. "Datapanik In The Year Zero"
PERE UBU—PHOTOGRAPHS
PH12190 619-620 (December 12, 1991) p67. "Down And Out, High And Mighty: Pere Ubu (left)..." (Vaccaro, Nick)
PERELLA, MARCO—PHOTOGRAPHS
PH12191 642 (October 29, 1992) p59. "1967: Eighteen And Ready"
PH12192 642 (October 29, 1992) p59. "Today: Eight By Ten"
PERETZ, JESSE—PHOTOGRAPHS
PH12193 742 (September 5, 1996) p26. "Ex-Rocker Finds Sweetness In Videos" (Dyer, Alison)
THE PEREZ FAMILY (FILM)—PHOTOGRAPHS
PH12194 709 (June 1, 1995) p70. "Early Starters"
PEREZ, LOUIS—PHOTOGRAPHS
PH12195 616 (October 31, 1991) p13. "Cesar Rosas, Louis Perez, Conrad Lozano, David Hidalgo And Steve Berlin (from left)" (Granitz, Steve)
PEREZ, ROSIE—PHOTOGRAPHS
PH12196 653 (April 1, 1993) p57. "White Men"
PH12197 674 (January 27, 1994) p48. "Best Supporting Actress"
PH12198 688 (August 11, 1994) p62. "It's A Jackpot-Lottery Win For Fonda, Cage And Perez"
PEREZ, ROSIE—PHOTOGRAPHS—PORTRAITS
PH12199 697 (December 15, 1994) p18. "Shakoor, Stipe And Perez (from left) Give Their Achin' Dogs A Rest After AIDS Walk Atlanta"
PEREZ, VINCENT—PHOTOGRAPHS
PH12200 743 (September 19, 1996) p90. "Now Playing"
PERFECT—ALBUMS
PH12201 741 (August 22, 1996) p96. "When Squirrels Play Chicken"
A PERFECT CANDIDATE (FILM)—PHOTOGRAPHS
PH12202 741 (August 22, 1996) p104. "Chuck Robb Hits The Stump"
PH12203 741 (August 22, 1996) p104. "Ollie North Gives Voters The High Sign"
A PERFECT WORLD (FILM)—PHOTOGRAPHS
PH12204 671 (December 9, 1993) p76. "Star Team: Ranger Eastwood (left) And Convict Costner"
PERFUMES—PHOTOGRAPHS
PH12205 618 (November 28, 1991) p84. "[Perfumes]" (Robert, Francois)
PH12206 638 (September 3, 1992) pp[enc.59]. "[Perfumes]" (Steele, Bill)
PH12207 645-646 (December 10, 1992) pp143,145. "[Perfumes]" (Steele, Bill)
PERKINS, CARL—PHOTOGRAPHS—PORTRAITS
PH12208 638 (September 3, 1992) p16. "Carl Perkins" (Figen, Peter)
PERKINS, STEPHEN—PHOTOGRAPHS
PH12209 715 (August 24, 1995) p54. "Jane's Addiction, 1990: Farrell, Perkins, Dave Navarro And Eric Avery (from left)" (Miller, Peter Darley)
PERKINS, STEPHEN—PHOTOGRAPHS—PORTRAITS
PH12210 656 (May 13, 1993) p54. "Stephen Perkins" (Seliger, Mark)
PERKINS, TEX—PHOTOGRAPHS
PH12211 712-713 (July 13, 1995) p46. "High Sea: Gormly, Elliot, And Perkins (from left)" (Capak, R. J.)
PERLICH, MAX—PHOTOGRAPHS
PH12212 630 (May 14, 1992) p69. "[Max Perlich]" (Little,

Blake)
PH12213 732 (April 18, 1996) pp[enc.10,12]. "[Max Perlich]" (Witkin, Christian)
PERLMAN, MARC—PHOTOGRAPHS
PH12214 633 (June 25, 1992) p11. "Golden Smog (from left): Gary Louris, Chris Mars, Dan Murphy, Craig Johnson And Marc Perlman" (Butler, Bonnie Lynn)
PH12215 644 (November 26, 1992) p27. "Louris, Callahan, Olson And Perlman (from left)" (Capak, R. J.)
PH12216 691 (September 22, 1994) p20. "Hawks Gary Louris, Marc Perlman, Dan Murphy, Noah Levy, Tweedy" (Smiley, Jay)
PH12217 697 (December 15, 1994) p31. ""We Had A Retro Tag, But This Isn't Like Our Last Album," Says Olson (center), With Perlman And Louris" (Dyer, Alison)
PH12218 709 (June 1, 1995) p16. "Jayhawk Gary Louris, Crowes Marc Ford And Robinson, Perlman (from left)" (Diamond, Rick)
PERLMAN, MARC—PHOTOGRAPHS—PORTRAITS
PH12219 628 (April 16, 1992) p57. "Perlman, Olson, Louris And Callahan (from left)" (Crouser, Michael)
PERON, JEAN-HERVE—PHOTOGRAPHS
PH12220 685 (June 30, 1994) p38. "The Devil's Work: Peron Of Faust" (Capak, R. J.)
PEROT, ROSS—ILLUSTRATIONS
PH12221 640 (October 1, 1992) pp50-52,54. "[Ross Perot]" (Burke, Philip)
PEROT, ROSS—ILLUSTRATIONS—PORTRAITS
PH12222 636 (August 6, 1992) p31. "[Ross Perot]" (Payne, C. F.)
PEROT, ROSS—PHOTOGRAPHS
PH12223 747 (November 14, 1996) p76. "With Presidential Candidate Ross Perot In October 1992"
PERRINE, LINDA—PHOTOGRAPHS
PH12224 705 (April 6, 1995) p57. "Mutiny On The Bounty: NASA's Pirates Perrine, Anderson And Muratore (from left)" (Turner, Danny)
PERRUGORIA, JORGE—PHOTOGRAPHS
PH12225 701 (February 9, 1995) p63. "Perrugoria And Cruz Do The Forbidden"
PERRY, BRENDAN—PHOTOGRAPHS
PH12226 686-687 (July 14, 1994) p35. ""We Aim To Wake up That Other Self We Have": Lisa Gerrard And Brendan Perry" (Grecco, Michael)
PERRY, CHARLES—PHOTOGRAPHS
PH12227 632 (June 11, 1992) p86. "Our Copy Chief And Resident Arabist, Charles Perry, In 1975" (Hellweg, Max)
PH12228 632 (June 11, 1992) p62. "Staff Members And Contributing Writers At The 1971 Editorial Conference, At Esalen, In Big Sur" (Leibovitz, Annie)
PERRY, JOE—PHOTOGRAPHS
PH12229 634-635 (July 9, 1992) p11. "Tom Hamilton, Joe Perry And Tyler (from left) With Museum Curator Helaine Posner" (Putnam, Sarah)
PH12230 668 (October 28, 1993) p36. "Steven Tyler (left) And Joe Perry At The Walden Woods Benefit" (Robicheau, Paul)
PH12231 679 (April 7, 1994) p38. "Joe Perry, Wolf, Tyler" (Lyden, Paul)
PH12232 694 (November 3, 1994) p58. "Aerodynamics: Tyler (left) And Joe Perry Live" (Mazur, Kevin)
PH12233 694 (November 3, 1994) p60. "Early Daze: Whitford, Tyler, Hamilton, Perry And Kramer At Boston College, 1973" (Pownall, Ron)
PH12234 702 (February 23, 1995) p48. "Aerosmith's Joe Perry And Steven Tyler Get Chummy With Led Zep's Robert Plant And Jimmy Page" (Mazur, Kevin)
PH12235 722 (November 30, 1995) p20. "[Master Musicians Of Jajouka]" (Robicheau, Paul)
PERRY, JOE—PHOTOGRAPHS—PORTRAITS
PH12236 619-620 (December 12, 1991) p67. "Joe Perry (left) And Steve Tyler" (Double, Steve)
PH12237 643 (November 12, 1992) p193. "Joe Perry" (Watson, Albert)
PERRY, LINDA—PHOTOGRAPHS
PH12238 662 (August 5, 1993) p21. "Brunets Have Fun, Too: Hillhouse, Rocha, Perry And Richardson (from left)" (MacNaughtan, Andrew)
PH12239 674 (January 27, 1994) p40. "Nonblond Ambition: Linda Perry" (Mazur, Kevin)
PERRY, LUKE—PHOTOGRAPHS
PH12240 638 (September 3, 1992) p75. "Luke Perry And Kristy Swanson Fight The Bloodsuckers"
PERRY, LUKE—PHOTOGRAPHS—PORTRAITS
PH12241 624 (February 20, 1992) pp[cover]. "Beverly Hills, 90210: Smells Like Teen Spirit" (Eccles, Andrew)
PH12242 624 (February 20, 1992) p23. "Luke Perry" (Eccles, Andrew)
PH12243 624 (February 20, 1992) p26. "Perry Has Been Hampered By The Show's Success" (Eccles, Andrew)
PH12244 645-646 (December 10, 1992) pp[cover]. "1992 Yearbook" (Eccles, Andrew)
PERRY, MATTHEW—PHOTOGRAPHS
PH12245 708 (May 18, 1995) pp[cover]. "Fast Friends: No Sex Bad Jobs Hit Show Go Figure" (Seliger, Mark)
PH12246 708 (May 18, 1995) p. "Matt LeBlanc, Jennifer Aniston, David Schwimmer, Courteney Cox, Lisa Kudrow, Matthew Perry" (Seliger, Mark)
PERRY, STEVE—PHOTOGRAPHS
PH12247 694 (November 3, 1994) p18. "Dynamic Duo: Greenway (left), Perry" (Mayer, Jeffrey)
PERSONALITIES—ILLUSTRATIONS
PH12248 656 (May 13, 1993) p10. "How Stardom Works" (Pendergrast, James T.)
PH12249 675 (February 10, 1994) p6. "SSSSSS..." (Pendergrast, James T.)
PERSUASION (FILM)—PHOTOGRAPHS
PH12250 719 (October 19, 1995) p159. "Austen's Vision Realized"
PH12251 724-725 (December 28, 1995) p136. "Unusual Pleasure"
PERU—ILLUSTRATIONS
PH12252 670 (November 25, 1993) p62. "Personally, I Believe A Hammock, A Cigar And A Gin And Tonic Is The Best Way To Save The Planet" (Peck, Everett)
PH12253 670 (November 25, 1993) p68. "Thoreau Took Bad Ideas About Nature And Made Them Worse" (Peck, Everett)
PERU—PHOTOGRAPHS
PH12254 616 (October 31, 1991) p48. "A Peruvian Mother Has Her Baby Immunized For Polio" (Gaggero, Carlos)
PESCI, JOE—ILLUSTRATIONS
PH12255 723 (December 14, 1995) p89. "Goodfellas Go Vegas" (Brodner, Steve)
PESCI, JOE—PHOTOGRAPHS
PH12256 627 (April 2, 1992) p42. "Fred Gwynne Referees For Joe Pesci And Marisa Tomei"
PH12257 642 (October 29, 1992) p77. "The Public Eye"
PH12258 680 (April 21, 1994) p95. "Christian Slater And Joe Pesci Go Hollywood"
PH12259 682 (May 19, 1994) p106. "Higher Education For Pesci (right) And Fraser"
PH12260 723 (December 14, 1995) p90. "The Lady Gambles: Stone With The Dice; With Jealous Husband Robert De Niro; Gangster Lover Joe Pesci; And Director Martin Scorsese (from top)"
PESO, FRED—PHOTOGRAPHS—PORTRAITS
PH12261 736 (June 13, 1996) p74. "Fred Peso, Former Vice President Of The Mescalero Council" (Barker, Kent)
PET SHOP BOYS—ALBUMS
PH12262 670 (November 25, 1993) p112. "Very"
PH12263 746 (October 31, 1996) p70. "Bilingual"

PETERS, DAN—PHOTOGRAPHS
PH12264 628 (April 16, 1992) p48. "Mudhoney's Lukin, Turner, Peters And Arm (from left)" (Seliger, Mark)
PH12265 695 (November 17, 1994) p90. "Mudhoney" (Ragel, Jon)
PH12266 709 (June 1, 1995) p48. "Seattle Mudslingers: Turner, Arm, Lukin And Peters (from left)" (Winters, Dan)
PETERS, JOEY—PHOTOGRAPHS
PH12267 663 (August 19, 1993) p24. "[Grant Lee Buffalo]" (Azimi, Mojgan B.)
PH12268 695 (November 17, 1994) p94. "Grant Lee Buffalo" (Samuel, Deborah)
PH12269 696 (December 1, 1994) pp98-99. "American Icons: Joey Peters, Grant Lee Phillips And Paul Kimble (from left)" (Ockenfels, Frank, 3)
PETERSON, DAVID—PHOTOGRAPHS
PH12270 730 (March 21, 1996) p55. "The Boys In The Bus: Schiavone McGee, David Triano, Eric Lawson, Chris Leitch, Karl Vonklein, David Peterson And Mike Boyd (clockwise from left)" (Clinch, Danny)
PH12271 730 (March 21, 1996) p56. "McGee, Peterson, Triano And Lawson (from left) Rehearse In The Bus" (Clinch, Danny)
PH12272 730 (March 21, 1996) p62. "Peterson (left) Snags Sushi At Princeton, Where, Triano Say, "You're Definitely The Hired Help."" (Clinch, Danny)
PH12273 730 (March 21, 1996) p62. "Peterson (left) And Leitch Rest For The Next Show" (Clinch, Danny)
PH12274 730 (March 21, 1996) p60. "Peterson Takes His Turn Driving The Bus Between Gigs" (Clinch, Danny)
PETERSSON, TOM—PHOTOGRAPHS
PH12275 723 (December 14, 1995) p27. "The Chicago Eight: D'Arcy, Petersson, Carlos, Corgan, Nielsen, Iha, Chamberlin And Zander (from left)" (Elledge, Paul)
PETEY X—PHOTOGRAPHS
PH12276 689 (August 25, 1994) p44. "All Together Now: Trombino, Atom, Kennedy, Reis, N.D., Petey X, Apollo 9, Froberg (from left)" (Cuffaro, Chris)
PETIT BASSET GRIFFON VENDEEN (PBGV)—PHOTOGRAPHS
PH12277 630 (May 14, 1992) p89. "[PBGV]" (Braun, Paulette)
PETTY, LORI—PHOTOGRAPHS
PH12278 634-635 (July 9, 1992) p111. "Davis, O'Donnell, Madonna And Petty In A Man's Game"
PH12279 707 (May 4, 1995) p74. "Petty ('Tank')"
PETTY, TOM—ALBUMS
PH12280 694 (November 3, 1994) p95. "Wildflowers"
PH12281 742 (September 5, 1996) p60. "She's The One"
PETTY, TOM—ILLUSTRATIONS
PH12282 680 (April 21, 1994) p104. "Still A Chart Breaker: Tom Petty" (Brown, Calef)
PH12283 694 (November 3, 1994) p95. "American Boys" (Ulriksen, Mark)
PETTY, TOM—PHOTOGRAPHS
PH12284 616 (October 31, 1991) p21. "Tom Petty" (Caudle, Todd)
PH12285 630 (May 14, 1992) p13. "Tom Petty, George Harrison, Gary Moore And B. B. King (from left)"
PH12286 633 (June 25, 1992) p12. "Tom Petty" (Caudle, Todd)
PH12287 644 (November 26, 1992) p17. "The Great Garden Party: Dylan Center Stage For The Grand Finale" (Mazur, Kevin)
PH12288 645-646 (December 10, 1992) p53. "Petty Sings For Peace" (Mazur, Kevin)
PH12289 648 (January 21, 1993) p9. "Tom Petty And Harrison" (Mazur, Kevin)
PH12290 666 (September 30, 1993) p27. "Tom Petty, Along With Maria McKee And Others, Raised Some Big Money For A Worthy Cause" (Matheu, Robert)
PH12291 670 (November 25, 1993) p78. "[Tom Petty]" (Seliger, Mark)
PH12292 674 (January 27, 1994) p28. "Jeff Lynne, Tom Petty, Johnny Cash And Rick Rubin (from left) At The Viper Room" (Kirkland, Gene)
PH12293 697 (December 15, 1994) p20. "Petty, Droge And Dylan At The Viper Room (from left)"
PH12294 707 (May 4, 1995) p52. "Backstage With The Boss And The Band (below, from left): Steve Ferrone, Mike Campbell, Petty, Benmont Tench, Howie Epstein And Scott Thurston" (Seliger, Mark)
PH12295 707 (May 4, 1995) p53. "Petty Rolling Down The Highway (above): 'I'm 44 Now, And I Don't Really Feel Like I'm Too Old To Do It...'" (Seliger, Mark)
PH12296 707 (May 4, 1995) p50. "Road Warrior: Petty Waits For Show Time Outside The Peoria Civic Center In Illinois" (Seliger, Mark)
PH12297 707 (May 4, 1995) p53. "Still Life On Tour Bus (below)" (Seliger, Mark)
PH12298 707 (May 4, 1995) pp[cover]. "Tom Petty: King Of The Road" (Seliger, Mark)
PH12299 707 (May 4, 1995) p52. "Writing The Tunes, Calling The Shots (above): Petty At Sound Check In Peoria" (Seliger, Mark)
PH12300 738-739 (July 11, 1996) p16. "Sharon Stone And Petty Look Related" (Charbonneau, Eric)
PH12301 750-751 (December 26, 1996) p88. "Producer Rick Rubin, Benmont Tench, Petty And Cash (from left) Work Their Magic"
PETTY, TOM—PHOTOGRAPHS—PORTRAITS
PH12302 619-620 (December 12, 1991) pp[cover]. "1991 Yearbook" (Seliger, Mark)
PH12303 643 (November 12, 1992) p122. "Tom Petty" (Seliger, Mark)
PH12304 645-646 (December 10, 1992) p153. "Tom Petty And Bob Dylan, 1986"
PH12305 670 (November 25, 1993) p78. "[Tom Petty]" (Seliger, Mark)
PH12306 707 (May 4, 1995) p48. "[Tom Petty]" (Seliger, Mark)
PH12307 707 (May 4, 1995) p54. "Young Blood: Tom Petty In His 1966 High-School Yearbook Photo" (Poppell, Seth)
PFAFF, KRISTEN—PHOTOGRAPHS
PH12308 683 (June 2, 1994) p42. "Hole: Patty Schemel, Love, Kristen Pfaff, Eric Erlandson" (Seliger, Mark)
PFAFF, KRISTEN—PHOTOGRAPHS—PORTRAITS
PH12309 688 (August 11, 1994) p30. "[Kristen Pfaff]" (Pobuda, Brian)
PFAHLER, ADAM—PHOTOGRAPHS
PH12310 660-661 (July 8, 1993) p100. "Jawbreaker (from left): Adam Pfahler, Chris Blake And Blake Schwarzenbach" (Lewis, Don)
PFEIFFER, DARRIN—PHOTOGRAPHS
PH12311 738-739 (July 11, 1996) p116. "Pfeiffer, Feldmann, Williams And Paulson (from left)"
PFEIFFER, MICHELLE—ILLUSTRATIONS
PH12312 616 (October 31, 1991) p95. "Love In A Greasy Spoon" (Risko, Robert)
PH12313 634-635 (July 9, 1992) p109. "Bat Girls On The Line" (Risko, Robert)
PH12314 648 (January 21, 1993) p54. "A Few Good Women" (Witte, Michael)
PH12315 666 (September 30, 1993) p111. "Mean Street Circa 1870" (De Seve, Peter)
PH12316 715 (August 24, 1995) p107. "Woman As Male Fear & Fantasy" (Ryden, Mark)
PFEIFFER, MICHELLE—ILLUSTRATIONS—LETTERING
PH12317 638 (September 3, 1992) pp37-38. "The Bat's Meow" (Karl, Anita)
PFEIFFER, MICHELLE—PHOTOGRAPHS
PH12318 616 (October 31, 1991) p97. "Pacino And Pfeiffer Hit A Brick Wall In Love"
PH12319 634-635 (July 9, 1992) p41. "Michelle Pfeiffer's Sexy, Leather-Bound Catwoman Reveals A Soul In Torment" (Rosenthal, Zade)

PH12320 634-635 (July 9, 1992) p111. "Pfeiffer Puts Keaton In His Place"
PH12321 638 (September 3, 1992) p41. "[Michelle Pfeiffer]" (Ritts, Herb)
PH12322 639 (September 17, 1992) p102. "Best Actress"
PH12323 644 (November 26, 1992) p78. "[Batman Returns]"
PH12324 645-646 (December 10, 1992) p190. "Michelle Pfeiffer"
PH12325 648 (January 21, 1993) p55. "Pfeiffer (left) Battles Racism"
PH12326 666 (September 30, 1993) p112. "Daniel Day-Lewis Nuzzles Michelle Pfeiffer"
PH12327 671 (December 9, 1993) p76. "Pacino's Scarface With Pfeiffer"
PH12328 672-673 (December 23, 1993) p172. "Hot Romance"
PH12329 678 (March 24, 1994) p100. "Missing In Oscar Action"
PH12330 684 (June 16, 1994) p116. "Creepy: Nicholson Puts The Bite On Pfeiffer In "Wolf""
PH12331 686-687 (July 14, 1994) p98. "Nicholson And Pfeiffer ("Wolf")"
PH12332 709 (June 1, 1995) p68. "back-To-School Bashes"
PH12333 715 (August 24, 1995) p108. "Dangerous Women: Michelle Pfeiffer, Sandra Bullock, Julia Roberts, Cindy Crawford And Natasha Henstridge"
PH12334 730 (March 21, 1996) p104. "Pfeiffer And Redford Face Off (left)"

PFEIFFER, MICHELLE—PHOTOGRAPHS—PORTRAITS
PH12335 638 (September 3, 1992) pp36,38. "[Michelle Pfeiffer]" (Ritts, Herb)
PH12336 638 (September 3, 1992) pp[cover]. "Michelle Pfeiffer: The Problems Of Being Perfect" (Ritts, Herb)
PH12337 645-646 (December 10, 1992) pp[cover]. "1992 Yearbook" (Ritts, Herb)

PFLEGER, GISELA—PHOTOGRAPHS—PORTRAITS
PH12338 703 (March 9, 1995) p61. "Victims: Gisela Pfleger (above) Lost Her Life"

PHAIR, LIZ—ALBUMS
PH12339 691 (September 22, 1994) p91. "Whip-Smart"
PH12340 698-699 (December 29, 1994) p173. "Whip-Smart"

PHAIR, LIZ—ILLUSTRATIONS
PH12341 691 (September 22, 1994) p91. "Out Of Exile" (Becker, Polly)
PH12342 696 (December 1, 1994) p18. "[Women]" (Pendergrast, James T.)

PHAIR, LIZ—PHOTOGRAPHS
PH12343 660-661 (July 8, 1993) p95. "Liz Phair: Sexual Subversion" (Maday, Tom)
PH12344 667 (October 14, 1993) p24. "[Liz Phair]" (Southam, Andrew)
PH12345 674 (January 27, 1994) p29. "Backstage At McCabe's" (Kravitz, Jeff)
PH12346 691 (September 22, 1994) p23. "Liz Phair Rocks The Casbah, A Den of Slack" (Hoffman, Randy)
PH12347 692 (October 6, 1994) pp42-43. "[Liz Phair]" (Vadukel, Max)
PH12348 692 (October 6, 1994) pp[cover]. "Liz Phair: A Rock & Roll Star Is Born" (Ockenfels, Frank, 3)
PH12349 692 (October 6, 1994) p45. "Winona Ryder, Phair And Rosanna Arquette In Santa Monica, 1994" (Kravitz, Jeff)
PH12350 698-699 (December 29, 1994) p66. "[Liz Phair]" (Ockenfels, Frank, 3)
PH12351 698-699 (December 29, 1994) p1. "Liz Phair: A Rock & Roll Star Is Born" (Ockenfels, Frank, 3)
PH12352 700 (January 26, 1995) p16. "[Liz Phair]" (Mazur, Kevin)
PH12353 709 (June 1, 1995) p30. "Liz Phair's Stage Fright Is History" (Capak, R. J.)
PH12354 712-713 (July 13, 1995) p25. "[Liz Phair & Material Issue]" (Natkin, Paul)
PH12355 737 (June 27, 1996) p20. "Liz Phair Has Been Matador's Biggest Seller" (Hitchcock, S. Apicella)

PHAIR, LIZ—PHOTOGRAPHS—PORTRAITS
PH12356 672-673 (December 23, 1993) p37. "Below: Liz Phair, A Stunningly Candid Debut" (Southam, Andrew)
PH12357 674 (January 27, 1994) p20. "[Liz Phair]" (Danelian, Stephen)
PH12358 695 (November 17, 1994) p104. "Liz Phair" (Ockenfels, Frank, 3)
PH12359 700 (January 26, 1995) p56. "Liz Phair Opts For The British Pop Soul Of Des'ree" (Danelian, Stephen)
PH12360 721 (November 16, 1995) p40. "Liz Phair Lends A Sympathetic Ear" (Ockenfels, Frank W.)
PH12361 726 (January 25, 1996) p30. "Liz Phair: Jamming With R.E.M." (Jennings, Steve)

THE PHANTOM (FILM)—PHOTOGRAPHS
PH12362 737 (June 27, 1996) p62. "Zane Unmasked And In Phantom Drag"

PHANTON, SLIM JIM—PHOTOGRAPHS
PH12363 652 (March 18, 1993) p15. "Cheap Dates (from left): Phantom, Baxter, Sales, Stanton And James" (Matheu, Robert)

PHARCYDE—PHOTOGRAPHS
PH12364 660-661 (July 8, 1993) p97. "The Pharcyde: Romye Robinson, Imani Wilcox, Derrick Stewart And Tre Hardson" (Azimi, Mojgan B.)
PH12365 672-673 (December 23, 1993) p49. "[The Pharcyde]" (Jonze, Spike)
PH12366 722 (November 30, 1995) p38. "Hip-Hop's Cosmic Voyagers: Wilcox, Robinson, Hardson And Stewart (from left)" (McClelland, Philippe)

PHELAN, JACQUIE—PHOTOGRAPHS
PH12367 634-635 (July 9, 1992) p84. "Bike Builder Charlie Cunningham With His Legendary Racer Wife, Jacquie Phelan" (Stone, Pete)

PHENOMENON (FILM)—PHOTOGRAPHS
PH12368 736 (June 13, 1996) p58. "Oscar Seekers"
PH12369 740 (August 8, 1996) p68. "'Independence Day,' Travolta In 'Phenomenon,' Schwarzenegger In 'Eraser,' Moore In 'Striptease'"

PHIFE DAWG—ILLUSTRATIONS
PH12370 695 (November 17, 1994) p129. "A Tribe Called Quest" (Shurley, Hugh)

PHIFE DOG—PHOTOGRAPHS
PH12371 678 (March 24, 1994) p10. "Mifnight Marauding: Phife (left) and Tip" (Gehring, Karl A.)

PHIFE DOG—PHOTOGRAPHS—PORTRAITS
PH12372 678 (March 24, 1994) p9. "Quest (clockwise from top): Q-Tip, Ali And Phife Dog" (Seliger, Mark)

PHIFER, MEKHI—PHOTOGRAPHS
PH12373 717 (September 21, 1995) p89. "Keitel And Lee On The Case"
PH12374 717 (September 21, 1995) p89. "Phifer On The Spot"
PH12375 732 (April 18, 1996) pp[enc.19-20]. "[Mekhi Phifer]" (Witkin, Christian)

PHILADELPHIA (FILM)—PHOTOGRAPHS
PH12376 672-673 (December 23, 1993) p174. "[Philadelphia]"
PH12377 678 (March 24, 1994) p100. "Missing In Oscar Action"

PHILIPPINES—ILLUSTRATIONS
PH12378 632 (June 11, 1992) p155. "[Philippines]" (Cronin, Brian)

PHILLIPS, CHARLES—PHOTOGRAPHS
PH12379 690 (September 8, 1994) p60. "Jeff Phillips And Family In December 1992 (above): Kathy And Keith Noel With Daughter Leighann, Hilda Phillips, Michael Noel, Jeff And Charles Phillips (from left)"

PHILLIPS, GLENN—ALBUMS
PH12380 648 (January 21, 1993) p50. "Echoes 1975-1985"

PHILLIPS, GRANT LEE—ILLUSTRATIONS
PH12381 736 (June 13, 1996) p51. "Grant Lee Phillips" (Cowles, David)

PHILLIPS, GRANT LEE—PHOTOGRAPHS
PH12382 663 (August 19, 1993) p24. "[Grant Lee Buffalo]" (Azimi, Mojgan B.)
PH12383 695 (November 17, 1994) p94. "Grant Lee Buffalo" (Samuel, Deborah)
PH12384 696 (December 1, 1994) pp98-99. "American Icons: Joey Peters, Grant Lee Phillips And Paul Kimble (from left)" (Ockenfels, Frank, 3)
PH12385 696 (December 1, 1994) p100. "Grant Lee Phillips Onstage In Detroit, August 1993" (Malerba, Gary)
PH12386 700 (January 26, 1995) p52. "Grant Lee Phillips" (Malerba, Gary)
PHILLIPS, HILDA—PHOTOGRAPHS
PH12387 690 (September 8, 1994) p60. "Jeff Phillips And Family In December 1992 (above): Kathy And Keith Noel With Daughter Leighann, Hilda Phillips, Michael Noel, Jeff And Charles Phillips (from left)"
PHILLIPS, JEFF—ILLUSTRATIONS
PH12388 690 (September 8, 1994) pp56-57. "[Jeff Phillips]" (Exum)
PHILLIPS, JEFF—PHOTOGRAPHS
PH12389 690 (September 8, 1994) p61. "Dallas, 1992: Jeff Shows His Mastery Of Street Style At The Skate Park That Bore His Name And Crashed His Dream" (Walgren, Judy)
PH12390 690 (September 8, 1994) p58. "Dallas, March 20, 1990: The King Of Texas Skateboarding In Repose" (Walgren, Judy)
PH12391 690 (September 8, 1994) p60. "Jeff And His Girlfriend, Alison Young, At His Skate Park In 1992" (Walgren, Judy)
PH12392 690 (September 8, 1994) p60. "Jeff Phillips And Family In December 1992 (above): Kathy And Keith Noel With Daughter Leighann, Hilda Phillips, Michael Noel, Jeff And Charles Phillips (from left)"
PHILLIPS, MARTIN—PHOTOGRAPHS
PH12393 678 (March 24, 1994) p69. "Brothers Under The Skin: Martin Phillips, Greg Parker, Mike Williams, Dexter Wilson, Rick Brown, Greg Jackson, Everett Whiteside, Roderick Bradford, Lacell Sherman..." (Smith, Bria
PHILLIPS, SAM (SINGER)—ALBUMS
PH12394 678 (March 24, 1994) p93. "Martinis And Bikinis"
PHILLIPS, SAM (SINGER)—PHOTOGRAPHS
PH12395 623 (February 6, 1992) p11. "Sam Phillips Joins Bruce Cockburn Onstage" (Ienner, Jimmy, Jr.)
PH12396 670 (November 25, 1993) p37. "Naomi Judd, Phillips, Ashley And Wynonna (from left)" (Kravitz, Jeff)
PH12397 689 (August 25, 1994) p15. "Michael Stipe, Phillips And Mike Mills (from left)" (Allen, Greg)
PH12398 700 (January 26, 1995) p52. "Sam Phillips At The Head Of The Class" (McDaniel, Melodie)
PH12399 703 (March 9, 1995) p20. "Terrorist Sam Phillips Shares A Love Scene With Jeremy Irons"
PHILLIPS, SAM (SINGER)—PHOTOGRAPHS—PORTRAITS
PH12400 615 (October 17, 1991) p24. "[Sam Phillips (singer)]" (Roth, David)
PH12401 619-620 (December 12, 1991) p49. "Sam Phillips" (Dill, Nicola)
PH12402 625 (March 5, 1992) p58. "Best New Female Singer" (Roth, David)
PH12403 666 (September 30, 1993) p17. "Sam Phillips: New LP" (Nissen, Melanie)
PHILOSOPHY—PHOTOGRAPHS
PH12404 682 (May 19, 1994) p58. "[Philosophy]"
PHISH—ALBUMS
PH12405 715 (August 24, 1995) p99. "A Live One"
PH12406 746 (October 31, 1996) p65. "Billy Breathes"
PHISH—ILLUSTRATIONS
PH12407 715 (August 24, 1995) p99. "Wet Noodle" (Choy, Dee Dee)
PH12408 746 (October 31, 1996) p65. "A Breath Of Fresh Air: The New Phish Album—More 'Abbey Road' Than 'Live-Dead'" (Allen, Terry)
PH12409 749 (December 12, 1996) p16. "Obnoxo-Meter" (Pendergrast, James T.)
PHISH—PHOTOGRAPHS
PH12410 631 (May 28, 1992) p16. "Phish (from left): Trey Anastasio, Mike Gordon, Page McConnell, Jon Fishman" (Halsband, Michael)
PH12411 744 (October 3, 1996) p35. "Phish"
PHOENIX, ARIZONA—PHOTOGRAPHS
PH12412 710 (June 15, 1995) p48. "[307 Lounge]" (Archibald, Timothy)
PHOENIX, JOAQUIN—PHOTOGRAPHS
PH12413 719 (October 19, 1995) p156. "She Glides Her TV-Form Divine Past Gawkers Phoenix, Affleck And Folland"
PHOENIX, RAIN—PHOTOGRAPHS
PH12414 615 (October 17, 1991) pp84,86. "[River Phoenix And Rain Phoenix]" (Uchitel, Diego)
PH12415 669 (November 11, 1993) p62. "'Cowgirls' Lineup: Rain Phoenix, Victoria Williams And Heather Graham" (Markus, Kurt)
PHOENIX, RIVER—ILLUSTRATIONS—PORTRAITS
PH12416 676 (February 24, 1994) p61. "River's End" (Woolley, Janet)
PHOENIX, RIVER—PHOTOGRAPHS
PH12417 615 (October 17, 1991) pp83,85,87. "[River Phoenix]" (Uchitel, Diego)
PH12418 615 (October 17, 1991) p100. "River Phoenix (left) And Keanu Reeves Are Bad Boys Of The Road"
PH12419 615 (October 17, 1991) pp84,86. "[River Phoenix And Rain Phoenix]" (Uchitel, Diego)
PH12420 616 (October 31, 1991) p62. "Van Sant And Phoenix, Who Signed On Before 'Idaho' Was Financed" (Edwards, Eric)
PH12421 627 (April 2, 1992) p41. "Phoenix In 'My Own Private Idaho'"
PH12422 672-673 (December 23, 1993) p79. "Below: River Phoenix" (Uchitel, Diego)
PH12423 676 (February 24, 1994) p62. "A Grieving Phoenix Stands Guard in 'Silent Tongue'"
PH12424 676 (February 24, 1994) p62. "Phoenix Comforts A Pal In 'Stand By Me'"
PHOENIX, RIVER—PHOTOGRAPHS—PORTRAITS
PH12425 672-673 (December 23, 1993) p172. "Farewell"
PHOTOGRAPHY—ILLUSTRATIONS—LETTERING
PH12426 643 (November 12, 1992) p53. "Being There" (Karl, Anita)
PH12427 643 (November 12, 1992) pp[cover]. "Portraits" (Bloch, Anthony)
PHOTOGRAPHY EQUIPMENT—PHOTOGRAPHS
PH12428 702 (February 23, 1995) p83. "[Cameras]" (Grant, Bob)
PHRASE—PHOTOGRAPHS
PH12429 690 (September 8, 1994) p44. "K1, Oisin, Phrase And Hollis (from left)" (Cross, Brian)
THE PIANO (FILM)—PHOTOGRAPHS
PH12430 671 (December 9, 1993) p76. "Grace Notes: Holly Hunter (left) And Anna Paquin"
PH12431 672-673 (December 23, 1993) p173. "Power Women Of The Year"
PH12432 674 (January 27, 1994) p48. "Best Actress"
PH12433 678 (March 24, 1994) p100. "Oscar's Choices: 'Schindler's List,' 'The Piano,' 'The Remains Of the Day,' 'In The Name Of The Father,' 'The Fugitive' (from left)"
PICCOLI, MICHEL—PHOTOGRAPHS
PH12434 616 (October 31, 1991) p99. "Artist And Model: Michel Piccoli And Emmanuelle Beart"
PICIOTTO, GUY—PHOTOGRAPHS
PH12435 633 (June 25, 1992) p18. "Guy Piciotto" (Callahan, Kristin)
PH12436 670 (November 25, 1993) p33. "Ian MacKaye Flanked By Guy Piciotto (left) And Joe Lally" (Mazur, Kevin)

PICKETT, WILSON—PHOTOGRAPHS
PH12437 650 (February 18, 1993) p52. "Wicked Wilson Pickett Had A Flash-And-Fury Singing Style" (Paley, Stephen)
PH12438 654 (April 15, 1993) p13. "Hammer, Pickett And Brown (from left)" (Mazur, Kevin)
PICNIC (DRAMA)—PHOTOGRAPHS
PH12439 683 (June 2, 1994) p76. "Picnic"
PIDGEON, REBECCA—ILLUSTRATIONS
PH12440 688 (August 11, 1994) p70. "Rebecca Pidgeon" (Deacon, Jim)
PIERCE, BETTY—PHOTOGRAPHS
PH12441 741 (August 22, 1996) p62. "Betty Pierce, A Recent Grad Of The National Institute Of Bail Enforcement" (Maxwell, Robert)
PIERCE, JEFFREY LEE—PHOTOGRAPHS
PH12442 734 (May 16, 1996) p22. "[Jeffrey Lee Pierce]" (Miller, Brad)
PIERCE, JENNIFER—PHOTOGRAPHS
PH12443 689 (August 25, 1994) p41. "Pierce, MacLeod, Hartling, Stein (from top)" (Crump, James)
PIERSON, KATE—PHOTOGRAPHS
PH12444 619-620 (December 12, 1991) p59. "Women In Rock Band Together For Prochoice" (Berkwitz, David Neil)
PH12445 630 (May 14, 1992) p13. "Kate Pierson, Fred Schneider And Kim Bassinger (from left) At The Brown Fund-Raiser" (Mazur, Kevin)
PH12446 637 (August 20, 1992) p11. "The B-52's (from left): Fred Schneider, Kate Pierson, Julee Cruise, Keith Strickland, Sue Hadjopoulos And Pat Irwin" (Michelson, Eric T.)
PH12447 652 (March 18, 1993) p27. "Kate Pierson And Fred Schneider"
PH12448 669 (November 11, 1993) p27. "Jailhouse Rocker Pierson" (Roberts, Ebet)
PH12449 702 (February 23, 1995) p49. "Schneider And Pierson Sandwich The Vandellas" (Mazur, Kevin)
PIERSON, KATE—PHOTOGRAPHS—PORTRAITS
PH12450 626 (March 19, 1992) p17. "[Kate Pierson, Yoko Ono]" (Seliger, Mark)
PIGG, MIKE—PHOTOGRAPHS
PH12451 665 (September 16, 1993) pp[enc.25]. "From Left: Greg Welsh, Ray Browning, Mike Pigg, Wes Hobson, Chuckie V, Scott Tinley, Nate Llerandi And Bill Braun" (Hanauer, Mark)
PIGOZZI, JEAN—PHOTOGRAPHS
PH12452 615 (October 17, 1991) p65. "Andy Warhol And Jean Pigozzi, New York City, 1986" (Pigozzi, Jean)
PH12453 615 (October 17, 1991) p63. "Jasmine, Jean Pigozzi And Jerry Hall, 1987" (Pigozzi, Jean)
PIGS—PHOTOGRAPHS
PH12454 656 (May 13, 1993) p88. "[Vietnamese Pigs]"
PINK FLOYD—ALBUMS
PH12455 617 (November 14, 1991) p149. "Atom Heart Mother" (Thorgerson, Strom)
PH12456 617 (November 14, 1991) p149. "Atom Heart Mother" (Powell, Aubrey)
PH12457 617 (November 14, 1991) p149. "Atom Heart Mother" (Blake, John)
PH12458 617 (November 14, 1991) p122. "Dark Side Of The Moon" (Thorgerson, Strom)
PH12459 617 (November 14, 1991) p122. "Dark Side Of The Moon" (Powell, Aubrey)
PH12460 617 (November 14, 1991) p128. "Wish You Were Here" (Thorgerson, Strom)
PH12461 617 (November 14, 1991) p128. "Wish You Were Here" (Powell, Aubrey)
PH12462 634-635 (July 9, 1992) p4. "The Wall"
PH12463 637 (August 20, 1992) p4. "Dark Side Of The Moon"
PH12464 683 (June 2, 1994) p82. "The Division Bell"
PH12465 684 (June 16, 1994) p105. "The Division Bell"
PH12466 715 (August 24, 1995) p102. "Pulse"
PINK FLOYD—ILLUSTRATIONS
PH12467 619-620 (December 12, 1991) p32. "[Saucerful Of Secrets]"
PH12468 684 (June 16, 1994) p105. "The Floyd" (Marten, Ruth)
PH12469 688 (August 11, 1994) p10. "[Pink Floyd]" (Pendergrast, James T.)
PINK FLOYD—PHOTOGRAPHS
PH12470 684 (June 16, 1994) p16. "The '70s Floyd With Roger Waters (right)"
PH12471 684 (June 16, 1994) p15. "[Pink Floyd]" (Mazur, Kevin)
PH12472 691 (September 22, 1994) p33. "A $103.5-Million Generator: "Division Bell" Set" (Mazur, Kevin)
PH12473 698-699 (December 29, 1994) p55. "Pink Floyd On The Road, 1994: Pure And Simple" (Blakesberg, Jay)
PH12474 728 (February 22, 1996) p19. "Pink Floyd's Richard Wright (left) And Gilmour Flank Special Guest Corgan" (Mazur, Kevin)
PINKUS, JEFF—PHOTOGRAPHS
PH12475 659 (June 24, 1993) p25. "Gibby Haynes, Jeff Pinkus, Paul Leary And King Coffey (clockwise from top)" (Watermann, Greg)
PIRNER, DAVE—ILLUSTRATIONS
PH12476 665 (September 16, 1993) p6. "Items From Fame's Toy Box" (Pendergrast, James T.)
PH12477 672-673 (December 23, 1993) p35. "[Dave Pirner & Dan Murphy]" (Corio, Paul)
PIRNER, DAVE—PHOTOGRAPHS
PH12478 634-635 (July 9, 1992) p11. "Booker T. In The Studio With Producer Michael Beinhorn And Dave Pirner (from left)" (Soica, Alex)
PH12479 644 (November 26, 1992) p31. "Karl Mueller, Dave Pirner, Dan Murphy, Grant Young (clockwise from top left)" (Breiehagen, Per)
PH12480 658 (June 10, 1993) p16. "Lulu And Pirner" (Mazur, Kevin)
PH12481 662 (August 5, 1993) p42. "Dave Pirner" (Seliger, Mark)
PH12482 662 (August 5, 1993) p18. "Diggin' In The Dirt: The Celebrity Crew Does The Honors" (Mazur, Kevin)
PH12483 662 (August 5, 1993) p18. "One Big Happy Family: Pirner, Berry, Townshend, Joel (from left)" (Mazur, Kevin)
PH12484 667 (October 14, 1993) p39. "Below: Dave Pirner (left) With Peter Buck" (Mazur, Kevin)
PH12485 669 (November 11, 1993) p27. "Winona Boy Toy With Victoria Williams" (Mazur, Kevin)
PH12486 672-673 (December 23, 1993) p39. "Diggin' In The Dirt: Soul Asylum's Dave Pirner, Chuck Berry, Townshend, Billy Joel" (Mazur, Kevin)
PH12487 672-673 (December 23, 1993) p70. "Live From New York: Hamilton, Pirner, Williams, Henry And Murphy (clockwise from top left)" (Mazur, Kevin)
PH12488 672-673 (December 23, 1993) p57. "Mueller, Dave Pirner, Dan Murphy (from left)" (Franklin, Ross D.)
PH12489 674 (January 27, 1994) p29. "Backstage At McCabe's" (Kravitz, Jeff)
PH12490 677 (March 10, 1994) p28. "Pirner With Animals Valentine, Chas Chandler And John Steel" (Mazur, Kevin)
PH12491 677 (March 10, 1994) p46. "Ryder At The 'Age Of Innocence' Premiere With Dave Pirner Of Soul Asylum" (Elgar, Nick)
PH12492 688 (August 11, 1994) p17. "At The Movie Awards: Backbeaters Mike Mills, Don Fleming, Dave Pirner, Greg Dulli, Dave Grohl And Thurston Moore (above, from left)" (Kravitz, Jeff)
PH12493 692 (October 6, 1994) p15. "Pirner (left) And Williams" (Phipps, Sandra-Lee)
PH12494 695 (November 17, 1994) p55. "Soul Asylum—Photographs" (Smale, Brian)

PH12495 702 (February 23, 1995) p32. "Strummin' In Stereo: Dave Pirner, Butch Vig, Karl Mueller, Dan Murphy (from left)" (Cuffaro, Chris)
PH12496 709 (June 1, 1995) p23. "Dave Pirner Hosts A Roving Minifest" (Hutson, Mick)
PH12497 711 (June 29, 1995) p30. "Frustrated Incorporated: Pirner Onstage In August 1993" (Malerba, Gary)
PH12498 711 (June 29, 1995) p31. "'I Want To Put Myself On A Pedestal And Hate Myself For Being There': Pirner, Murphy, Mueller, Campbell (from left)" (Mahurin, Matt)
PH12499 711 (June 29, 1995) p32. "In The Limelight: Pirner With Girlfriend Winona Ryder At This Year's Oscar Ceremony, In Los Angeles" (Trapper, Frank)
PH12500 711 (June 29, 1995) p33. "Ryder, Pirner, Band Manager Heaps, Murphy (background) And Ex-Drummer Young Greet Clinton (foreground) At The White House (from left)" (Markowitz, Jeffrey)
PH12501 715 (August 24, 1995) p23. "[Soul Asylum]" (Naumann, Ellen)
PH12502 729 (March 7, 1996) p9. "Dave Pirner (left) And Danny Murphy Of Soul Asylum Flank Grant Hart" (Garrity, Brian)
PH12503 747 (November 14, 1996) p25. "This Hall Was Made For You And Me: Arlo Guthrie, Bruce Springsteen, Tim Robbins, Dave Pirner And Billy Bragg (from left) At The Rock & Roll Hall Of Fame's Woody Guthrie..." (Pre

PIRNER, DAVE—PHOTOGRAPHS—PORTRAITS
PH12504 706 (April 20, 1995) p16. "Springsteen (left) And Dave Pirner Played Tramps For An Evening" (Galindo, Andrew)
PH12505 711 (June 29, 1995) p29. "[Dave Pirner]" (Mahurin, Matt)

PIROG, ERNEST—PHOTOGRAPHS
PH12506 748 (November 28, 1996) p86. "In A Bold Move, Ernest Pirog Took A Saw To His $20,000 Speakers" (Pluchino, Joseph)

PITT, BRAD—ILLUSTRATIONS
PH12507 700 (January 26, 1995) p65. "Legends For The Mall" (Osborn, Kathy)
PH12508 700 (January 26, 1995) p14. "Quiet! Sensitive Vampire Sleeping" (Pendergrast, James T.)
PH12509 746 (October 31, 1996) p75. "Getting Away With Murder: Prosecutor Brad Pitt Lies To Save His Boyhood Pals From Being Sent Away As Killers In A Film That Weaves A Tangled Web Of Fact And Fiction" (Brodner, St

PITT, BRAD—PHOTOGRAPHS
PH12510 630 (May 14, 1992) p59. "[Brad Pitt]" (Thurnher, Jeffrey)
PH12511 638 (September 3, 1992) p72. "Brad Pitt Worships At The Altar Of Idol Ricky Nelson"
PH12512 642 (October 29, 1992) p78. "Redford (left) Directs Look-Alike Brad Pitt"
PH12513 665 (September 16, 1993) p78. "Lewis (left) And Pitt Share A Kiss"
PH12514 684 (June 16, 1994) p35. "Brad Pitt" (Kravitz, Jeff)
PH12515 692 (October 6, 1994) p76. "Brad Pitt And Craig Sheffer Take Direction On "A River Runs Through It""
PH12516 696 (December 1, 1994) pp92,95,97. "[Brad Pitt]" (Seliger, Mark)
PH12517 696 (December 1, 1994) pp[cover]. "Brad Pitt Bites: Rolling Stone's Interview With The Vampire" (Seliger, Mark)
PH12518 696 (December 1, 1994) p94. "In "Vampire," Pitt And Tom Cruise Are Star Bloodsuckers"
PH12519 696 (December 1, 1994) p96. "Pitt Has Dated "Thelma And Louise" Co-Star Davis (top) And "Kalifornia" Girl Lewis (below)"
PH12520 697 (December 15, 1994) p102. "Prowling Vampires Kirsten Dunst, Brad Pitt And Tom Cruise"
PH12521 698-699 (December 29, 1994) p194. "Cruise Bites Pitt In "Vampire""
PH12522 700 (January 26, 1995) p66. "Film Legends In The Making: Julia Ormond And Brad Pitt"
PH12523 705 (April 6, 1995) p69. "Oscar Rejects"
PH12524 726 (January 25, 1996) p66. "Into The Cuckoo's Nest With Willis And Pitt"
PH12525 733 (May 2, 1996) p14. "[Gwyneth Paltrow, Brad Pitt, & Paul Newman]" (Ferreira, Albert)
PH12526 746 (October 31, 1996) p76. "Pitt And Patric Bend The Truth"

PITT, BRAD—PHOTOGRAPHS—PORTRAITS
PH12527 630 (May 14, 1992) pp54-55. "[Brad Pitt]" (Thurnher, Jeffrey)
PH12528 718 (October 5, 1995) p76. "Cop Brad Pitt Battles A Serial Killer To Protect Gwyneth Paltrow"

PITTS, CURTIS—PHOTOGRAPHS
PH12529 677 (March 10, 1994) p54. "Curtis Pitts Gives Two-Fisted Phone At The Sub Pop Office, In Seattle" (Smale, Brian)

PIXIES—ALBUMS
PH12530 621 (January 9, 1992) p60. "Trompe Le Monde"

PIXIES—PHOTOGRAPHS
PH12531 682 (May 19, 1994) p90. "Old Deal: Kim With Pixies David Lovering, Black Francis, Joey Santiago (from left)" (Blakesberg, Jay)

PIXIES—PHOTOGRAPHS—PORTRAITS
PH12532 652 (March 18, 1993) p15. "Ex-Pixies David Lovering, Deal, Joey Santiago, Black Francis (clockwise from left)" (Catlin, A.)

PIZZICATO FIVE—ALBUMS
PH12533 694 (November 3, 1994) p120. "Five By Five"
PH12534 722 (November 30, 1995) p68. "The Sound Of Music"

PJ HARVEY—ALBUMS
PH12535 645-646 (December 10, 1992) p182. "Dry"
PH12536 658 (June 10, 1993) p68. "Rid Of Me"
PH12537 670 (November 25, 1993) p112. "4-Track Demos"
PH12538 672-673 (December 23, 1993) p159. "Rid Of Me"
PH12539 703 (March 9, 1995) p63. "To Bring You My Love"
PH12540 706 (April 20, 1995) p104. "To Bring You My Love"

PLAKAS, DEE—PHOTOGRAPHS
PH12541 628 (April 16, 1992) p56. "Finch, Sparks, Gardner And Plakas (from left)" (Cuffaro, Chris)
PH12542 644 (November 26, 1992) p15. "Dee Plakas, Jennifer Finch, Jett, Donita Sparks And Suzi Gardner (clockwise from left)" (Lewis, Don)
PH12543 652 (March 18, 1993) p22. "Feminist Majority Rules: L7's Finch, Gardner, Sparks, Dee Plakas (from left)" (Johnson, Lisa)
PH12544 688 (August 11, 1994) p25. "Dee Plakas, Donita Sparks, Jennifer Finch, Suzi Gardner (from left)" (Broad, Julian)
PH12545 692 (October 6, 1994) p16. "At Philly's Lollapalooza: L7's Donita Sparks (left), Dee Plakas, Suzi Gardner And Jennifer Finch With Bad Seeds Mick Harvey, James Johnston And Nick Cave" (Weiner, Scott)
PH12546 695 (November 17, 1994) p52. "L7" (Broad, Julian)
PH12547 696 (December 1, 1994) p23. "Elvismania: L7's Suzi Gardner, Dee Plakas, Sparks And Jennifer Finch (from left)" (Mazur, Kevin)
PH12548 698-699 (December 29, 1994) p42. "L7's Donita Sparks, Vedder, L7's Dee Plakas And Her Husband, Kurk Canning (from left)" (Mercer, Lance)

PLANET OF THE APES (FILM)—PHOTOGRAPHS
PH12549 736 (June 13, 1996) p54. "You Damn Dirty Apes! It's 'Planet Of The Apes' Week On The Sci-Fi Channel"

PLANT, ROBERT—ALBUMS
PH12550 660-661 (July 8, 1993) p114. "Fate Of Nations"

PLANT, ROBERT—ILLUSTRATIONS
PH12551 641 (October 15, 1992) p69. "[Led Zeppelin]" (Burke, Philip)
PH12552 696 (December 1, 1994) p13. "Robert Plant" (Burke, Philip)
PH12553 697 (December 15, 1994) p92. "Robert Plant And Jimmy Page" (Cowles, David)

PLANT, ROBERT—PHOTOGRAPHS
PH12554 645-646 (December 10, 1992) p88. "[Stairway To Heaven]"
PH12555 670 (November 25, 1993) p38. "Jerry Miller, Don Stevenson, Plant, Peter Lewis And Skip Spence" (Blakesberg, Jay)
PH12556 696 (December 1, 1994) p29. "[Jimmy Page & Robert Plant]" (Mahurin, Matt)
PH12557 696 (December 1, 1994) p31. "Plant (left) And Page On Led Zep's 1975 U.S. Tour" (Preston, Neal)
PH12558 698-699 (December 29, 1994) p75. "[Jimmy Page & Robert Plant]"
PH12559 702 (February 23, 1995) p48. "Aerosmith's Joe Perry And Steven Tyler Get Chummy With Led Zep's Robert Plant And Jimmy Page" (Mazur, Kevin)
PH12560 702 (February 23, 1995) p46. "...Getting Chummy With Plant In Rehearsal In 1975" (Preston, Neal)
PH12561 702 (February 23, 1995) p47. "Getting Ledded At Live Aid In '85: 'It Made Us Look Like Loonies,' Says Plant"
PH12562 702 (February 23, 1995) p47. "Jones, Plant And Page Trample England Underfoot On Tour In 1970"
PH12563 702 (February 23, 1995) pp44-45. "[Robert Plant & Jimmy Page]" (Corbijn, Anton)
PH12564 702 (February 23, 1995) p48. "The Song Remains The Same: Robert Plant, Jimmy Page And Neil Young (from left)" (Mazur, Kevin)
PH12565 706 (April 20, 1995) p38. "Robert Plant (center) And Jimmy Page (right)" (Mazur, Kevin)
PH12566 720 (November 2, 1995) p49. "Robert Plant & Jimmy Page" (Greene, Herb)
PH12567 723 (December 14, 1995) p28. "Robert Plant And Tracy Bonham" (Robicheau, Paul)
PH12568 724-725 (December 28, 1995) p39. "Robert Plant, Jimmy Page, Young (from left)" (Mazur, Kevin)
PH12569 726 (January 25, 1996) p28. "Page, Grant And Plant (from left) In 1975" (Preston, Neal)
PH12570 730 (March 21, 1996) p33. "Ratner Captures Robert Plant In 1975" (Ratner, Laurence)
PH12571 747 (November 14, 1996) p36. "Page (left) And Plant Have Begun Writing Material For A New Record" (Guzman)
PLANT, ROBERT—PHOTOGRAPHS—PORTRAITS
PH12572 660-661 (July 8, 1993) p25. "[Robert Plant]" (Seliger, Mark)
PH12573 702 (February 23, 1995) pp[cover]. "The Second Coming: Led Zeppelin's Robert Plant & Jimmy Page" (Corbijn, Anton)
PLATOON (FILM)—PHOTOGRAPHS
PH12574 711 (June 29, 1995) p48. "Best On Laser Disc: 'Platoon'"
PLATT, OLIVER—PHOTOGRAPHS
PH12575 670 (November 25, 1993) p125. "Four Stooges: Sutherland, Sheen, O'Donnell, Platt (above)"
PH12576 706 (April 20, 1995) p88. "Jerry Lewis And Oliver Platt Do Battle"
THE PLAYBOYS (FILM)—PHOTOGRAPHS
PH12577 653 (April 1, 1993) p57. "Playboys"
THE PLAYER (FILM)—ILLUSTRATIONS
PH12578 629 (April 30, 1992) p63. "Setting Up Hollywood For The Kill" (Drawson, Blair)
THE PLAYER (FILM)—PHOTOGRAPHS
PH12579 629 (April 30, 1992) p64. "Mill Watches Rival Larry Levy (Peter Gallagher)"
PH12580 629 (April 30, 1992) p64. "Studio Player Griffin Mill (Tim Robbins) At Work"
PH12581 648 (January 21, 1993) p56. "The Player"
PH12582 653 (April 1, 1993) p57. "The Player"
PH12583 656 (May 13, 1993) p114. "'The Player' On Laser"
PM DAWN—ALBUMS
PH12584 654 (April 15, 1993) p60. "The Bliss Album?"
PH12585 720 (November 2, 1995) p66. "Jesus Wept"
PM DAWN—ILLUSTRATIONS
PH12586 654 (April 15, 1993) p60. "'The Bliss Album': A New Dawn" (Ryden, Mark)
PH12587 720 (November 2, 1995) p66. "Two Princes" (Faiola, Susan)
PM DAWN—PHOTOGRAPHS
PH12588 645-646 (December 10, 1992) p31. "PM Dawn" (Capak, R. J.)
PH12589 660-661 (July 8, 1993) p32. "Above: Phat Cats P.M. Dawn" (Granitz, Steve)
PH12590 719 (October 19, 1995) p20. "Influenced By The Beatles And Kraftwerk, PM Dawn Played Their Version Of World Music On 1995's WOMAD Tour" (Blakesberg, Jay)
PM DAWN—PHOTOGRAPHS—PORTRAITS
PH12591 616 (October 31, 1991) p25. "DJ Minutemix (left) And Prince Be" (Brusso, Andrew)
PH12592 630 (May 14, 1992) p79. "Prince Be (left) And His Brother DJ Minutemix" (Watson, Albert)
PNEUMOCYSTIS—PHOTOGRAPHS
PH12593 679 (April 7, 1994) p59. "A Cluster From The Lung Of An AIDS Patient" (Cushion, Melanie)
PH12594 679 (April 7, 1994) p59. "A Cluster Of Pneumocystis From A Rat Lung Shows Many Of Its Forms, Including Spherical Cysts With Daughter Forms Inside" (Ruffolo, John)
POCAHONTAS (FILM)—ILLUSTRATIONS
PH12595 709 (June 1, 1995) p68. "Men In Wigs"
PH12596 709 (June 1, 1995) p68. "Potential Goldmines"
PH12597 712-713 (July 13, 1995) p113. "Fire Rockets 1, 2, 3" (Allen, Terry)
PH12598 712-713 (July 13, 1995) p116. "Pocahontas Flirts With John Smith"
PH12599 716 (September 7, 1995) p78. "Summer Wrap-Up]"
PODGE—PHOTOGRAPHS—PORTRAITS
PH12600 652 (March 18, 1993) pp[enc.37]. "Podge And Sean Bates" (Seliger, Mark)
POE—PHOTOGRAPHS
PH12601 747 (November 14, 1996) p44. "]Poe]" (Capak, R. J.)
PH12602 748 (November 28, 1996) p97. "Poe Uses Her PCs For Writing And Sampling" (Elledge, Paul)
POERSCH, SUSAN—PHOTOGRAPHS
PH12603 691 (September 22, 1994) pp[enc.27]. "In The Burton Office With Co-Worker Susan Poersch" (Borris, Dan)
POETIC JUSTICE (FILM)—ILLUSTRATIONS
PH12604 663 (August 19, 1993) p81. "Girlz N The Hood" (Kelley, Gary)
POETIC JUSTICE (FILM)—PHOTOGRAPHS
PH12605 663 (August 19, 1993) p82. "Janet Jackson With Her Boyz: Director John Singleton (left) And Co-Star Tupac Shakur"
POINT OF NO RETURN (FILM)—PHOTOGRAPHS
PH12606 654 (April 15, 1993) p72. "Bridget Fonda (left) Can't Match The Sizzle of Anne Parillaud in 'Le Femme Nikita'"
POISON—ALBUMS
PH12607 652 (March 18, 1993) p40. "Native Tongue"
POISON IVY (FILM)—ILLUSTRATIONS
PH12608 631 (May 28, 1992) p59. "A Nineties Lolita From Hell" (Drawson, Blair)
POISON IVY (FILM)—PHOTOGRAPHS
PH12609 631 (May 28, 1992) p60. "Barrymore Flashes Tattoo And Toes To Lure Skerritt"
PH12610 631 (May 28, 1992) p60. "Barrymore Plays Moody Babe With Costar Gilbert"
PH12611 644 (November 26, 1992) p78. "[Poison Ivy]"
POLARA—PHOTOGRAPHS
PH12612 711 (June 29, 1995) p23. "Blending '60s Who With Atmospheric Noise: Jurgens, Orris, Ackerson And Wilson (from left)" (Elledge, Paul)
POLICE—ALBUMS
PH12613 715 (August 24, 1995) p101. "Live!"
POLICE OFFICERS—ILLUSTRATIONS
PH12614 648 (January 21, 1993) p30. "[Cop Killers]"

(Kroninger, Stephen)
PH12615 672-673 (December 23, 1993) p10. "Karma Tornado" (Pendergrast, James T.)
POLITICALLY INCORRECT (TELEVISION SHOW)—ILLUSTRATIONS
PH12616 697 (December 15, 1994) p18. "Etheridge, Waters, "Politically Incorrect" Host Bill Maher, Molinari And Baio (from left)"
PH12617 730 (March 21, 1996) p109. "[Politically Incorrect]" (Fishman, Miriam)
POLITICS—ILLUSTRATIONS
PH12618 632 (June 11, 1992) p196. "[Politics]" (Cronin, Brian)
PH12619 705 (April 6, 1995) p14. "Enthusiasm, Cynicism, Hope" (Pendergrast, James T.)
PH12620 706 (April 20, 1995) p12. "Ballot Box" (Pendergrast, James T.)
PH12621 716 (September 7, 1995) p10. "Wisdom" (Pendergrast, James T.)
PH12622 717 (September 21, 1995) p16. "Choose Your Weapon" (Pendergrast, James T.)
PH12623 746 (October 31, 1996) p56. "[Democratics-Republicans]"
POLLAK, KEVIN—ILLUSTRATIONS
PH12624 716 (September 7, 1995) p75. "A Summer Sleeper" (Ulriksen, Mark)
POLLARD, ALISON—PHOTOGRAPHS
PH12625 730 (March 21, 1996) p80. "Jean Pollard (right) With Allison, Her Eldest Daughter And The Last To Develop CFS" (Tavee, Tom)
POLLARD, ALISON—PHOTOGRAPHS—PORTRAITS
PH12626 730 (March 21, 1996) p78. "Alison, Megan, Libby And Hannah Pollard (from left) In 1979"
POLLARD, HANNAH—PHOTOGRAPHS—PORTRAITS
PH12626 730 (March 21, 1996) p78. "Alison, Megan, Libby And Hannah Pollard (from left) In 1979"
POLLARD, JEAN—PHOTOGRAPHS
PH12627 730 (March 21, 1996) p80. "Jean Pollard (right) With Allison, Her Eldest Daughter And The Last To Develop CFS" (Tavee, Tom)
POLLARD, JIM—PHOTOGRAPHS—PORTRAITS
PH12628 686-687 (July 14, 1994) p74. "Kevin Fennell, Toby Sprout, Pollard, Jim Pollard, Greg Demos (from left)" (Rice, Ted)
POLLARD, LIBBY—PHOTOGRAPHS
PH12629 730 (March 21, 1996) p82. "The Pollard Twins, Libby (left) And Megan, Grew Up Under The Cloud Of CFS" (Tavee, Tom)
POLLARD, LIBBY—PHOTOGRAPHS—PORTRAITS
PH12630 730 (March 21, 1996) p78. "Alison, Megan, Libby And Hannah Pollard (from left) In 1979"
POLLARD, MEGAN—PHOTOGRAPHS
PH12631 730 (March 21, 1996) p82. "The Pollard Twins, Libby (left) And Megan, Grew Up Under The Cloud Of CFS" (Tavee, Tom)
POLLARD, MEGAN—PHOTOGRAPHS—PORTRAITS
PH12632 730 (March 21, 1996) p78. "Alison, Megan, Libby And Hannah Pollard (from left) In 1979"
POLLARD, ROBERT—ALBUMS
PH12633 748 (November 28, 1996) p130. "Not In My Airforce"
POLLARD, ROBERT—PHOTOGRAPHS—PORTRAITS
PH12634 686-687 (July 14, 1994) p74. "Kevin Fennell, Toby Sprout, Pollard, Jim Pollard, Greg Demos (from left)" (Rice, Ted)
POLLOCK, COURTENAY—PHOTOGRAPHS
PH12635 740 (August 8, 1996) p35. "Egypt, September 1978" (Boot, Adrian)
POLLOCK, JASON—PHOTOGRAPHS
PH12636 731 (April 4, 1996) p36. "The Two Jasons (Pollock and Ross), Khalsa And Daniel" (Clinch, Danny)
POLO—ILLUSTRATIONS
PH12637 697 (December 15, 1994) pp44-48,50,52+. "[Polo]" (Steadman, Ralph)
POLONSKY, JONNY—PHOTOGRAPHS
PH12638 728 (February 22, 1996) p34. "Do-It-Yourselfer Polonsky Got Help From Frank Black"
POMERANC, MAX—PHOTOGRAPHS
PH12639 664 (September 2, 1993) p70. "Fishburne Challenges Chess Prodigy Pomeranc"
POMUS, DOC—PHOTOGRAPHS—PORTRAITS
PH12640 619-620 (December 12, 1991) p112. "Doc Pomus" (Gahr, David)
PH12641 623 (February 6, 1992) p54. "[Doc Pomus]"
POND—ALBUMS
PH12642 655 (April 29, 1993) p65. "Pond"
PONEMAN, JONATHAN—PHOTOGRAPHS
PH12643 628 (April 16, 1992) p44. "Sub Pop's Jonathan Poneman (left) And Bruce Pavitt" (Seliger, Mark)
PH12644 678 (March 24, 1994) p56. "Ex-KCMU Volunteer Poneman, Co-Owner Of Sub-Pop: 'It was A Fertile Breeding Ground.'" (Lavine, Michael)
PONTIAC BROTHERS—RECORDS
PH12645 650 (February 18, 1993) p59. "Fuzzy Little Piece Of The World"
POOR RIGHTEOUS TEACHERS—ALBUMS
PH12646 617 (November 14, 1991) p173. "Pure Poverty"
POOR, ROB—PHOTOGRAPHS
PH12647 660-661 (July 8, 1993) p97. "The Loud Family: Paul Wieneke, Zachary Smith, Miller, Jozef Becker And Rob Poor" (Blakesberg, Jay)
POP, IGGY—ALBUMS
PH12648 617 (November 14, 1991) p144. "The Idiot" (Kent, Andrew)
PH12649 667 (October 14, 1993) p117. "American Caesar"
PH12650 728 (February 22, 1996) p62. "Naughty Little Doggie"
POP, IGGY—ILLUSTRATIONS
PH12651 666 (September 30, 1993) p7. "Iggy Pop" (Burke, Philip)
PH12652 721 (November 16, 1995) p18. "Iggy" (Pendergrast, James T.)
PH12653 736 (June 13, 1996) p38. "Iggy Pop" (Cowles, David)
POP, IGGY—PHOTOGRAPHS
PH12654 617 (November 14, 1991) p11. "Cinque And Joie Lee With Pop" (Busacca, Larry)
PH12655 652 (March 18, 1993) p13. "Iggy Pop" (Elgar, Nick)
PH12656 658 (June 10, 1993) p60. "As Ziggy, With Iggy Pop And Lou Reed Circa 1972: 'We Knew We Were On The Wave Of Something'"
PH12657 663 (August 19, 1993) p27. "INXS's Garry Gary Beers, Iggy Pop, Andrew Fariss And Jon Fariss (from left)" (Mazur, Kevin)
PH12658 666 (September 30, 1993) p14. "The Bad Boy Of Rock In His Hellion Days" (Rock, Mick)
PH12659 666 (September 30, 1993) p13. "[Iggy Pop]" (Hom, Marc)
PH12660 680 (April 21, 1994) p34. "[Iggy Pop, Evan Dando, Chainsaw Kittens]" (Peterson, Charles)
PH12661 683 (June 2, 1994) p28. "Depp (left) And Pop At The "Serial Mom" Premiere" (Banks, Kathy)
PH12662 689 (August 25, 1994) p15. "[Lemonheads-Buffalo Tom-Gigolo Aunts]" (Busacca, Larry)
PH12663 692 (October 6, 1994) p17. "Strange Bedfellows: Iggy Pop (left) And Killing Joke's Jaz Coleman" (Knaeps, Gie)
PH12664 718 (October 5, 1995) p45. "Iggy Pop" (Rock, Mick)
PH12665 718 (October 5, 1995) p54. "Iggy Pop In '73: 'The Attitude Of Juvenile Delinquency And General Mental Grievance'" (Rock, Mick)
PH12666 720 (November 2, 1995) p16. "Funtime: Iggy Caught Bowie's Set During A Public Theater Benefit, In New York" (Mazur, Kevin)
PH12667 720 (November 2, 1995) p50. "Iggy Pop" (Gassian, Claude)

PH12668 721 (November 16, 1995) p26. "Momentary Hipster McKagan With Jones And Pop (from left)" (Kravitz, Jeff)
PH12669 727 (February 8, 1996) p12. "Woodpussy's Michel Cicero, Rancid's Tim Armstrong, Iggy, The Offspring's Dexter Holland (from left)" (Buzzerio, Johnny)
PH12670 747 (November 14, 1996) p36. "Iggy Pop Shot By Lavine" (Lavine, Michael)
POP, IGGY—PHOTOGRAPHS—PORTRAITS
PH12671 666 (September 30, 1993) p14. "I'd Like To Be A Sort Of Respectable Citizen" (Hom, Marc)
PH12672 697 (December 15, 1994) p20. "Little Pete (Danny Tamberelli) And Pop"
PH12673 719 (October 19, 1995) p38. "Iggy Pop" (Corbijn, Anton)
POP WILL EAT ITSELF—ALBUMS
PH12674 704 (March 23, 1995) p144. "Dos Dedos Mis Amigos"
POPEIL, RON—PHOTOGRAPHS
PH12675 656 (May 13, 1993) p63. "[Ron Popeil]"
POPES—ALBUMS
PH12676 715 (August 24, 1995) p100. "The Snake"
POPINJAYS—PHOTOGRAPHS
PH12677 650 (February 18, 1993) p13. "Peter Tork (left) With The 'Jays' Hancock, Robinson And Ben Kesteven" (Mayer, Jeffrey)
POPPER, JOHN—ILLUSTRATIONS
PH12678 736 (June 13, 1996) p11. "Enit's Perry Farrell And H.O.R.D.E.'s John Popper" (Grossman, Robert)
POPPER, JOHN—PHOTOGRAPHS
PH12679 622 (January 23, 1992) p10. "Clockwise From Top Left: Bobby Sheehan, Brendan Hill, John Popper, Chan Kinchla" (Carroll, Chris)
PH12680 631 (May 28, 1992) p17. "Blues Traveler (from left): Chan Kinchla, John Popper, Brendan Hill And Bobby Sheehan" (Aresu, Paul)
PH12681 659 (June 24, 1993) p57. "Band Of Gypsies: Brendan Hill, Chan Kinchla, John Popper And Bobby Sheehan (from left)" (Fink, Larry)
PH12682 659 (June 24, 1993) p58. "Popper, Temporarily Confined To A Wheelchair, Is Escorted Onstage At Penn State" (Fink, Larry)
PH12683 659 (June 24, 1993) p60. "Volunteers Hold Popper's Chair So He Doesn't Topple" (Fink, Larry)
PH12684 663 (August 19, 1993) p12. "Blues Traveler's John Popper (upper left)" (Caudle, Todd)
PH12685 714 (August 10, 1995) p16. "Blues Traveler's Chan Kinchla, Bobby Sheehan, Brendan Hill And Popper (from left) With Ice-T (second from left)" (Kravitz, Jeff)
PH12686 729 (March 7, 1996) p9. "Hemlock Anyone? Today's Socrates Stern (left) And His Disciple Popper"
PH12687 732 (April 18, 1996) p20. "Great Bar Mitzvah, Huh? Crow Perches On John Popper Of Blues Travelers" (Mazur, Kevin)
POPPER, JOHN—PHOTOGRAPHS—PORTRAITS
PH12688 736 (June 13, 1996) p38. "H.O.R.D.E. Honcho John Popper" (Clinch, Danny)
PH12689 736 (June 13, 1996) pp[cover]. "Rock & Roll Summer!" (Wolff, Tom)
PORCARO, JEFF—PHOTOGRAPHS
PH12690 639 (September 17, 1992) p28. "[Jeff Porcaro]" (Van Houten, Laurens)
PH12691 645-646 (December 10, 1992) p101. "[Jeff Porcaro]" (Van Houten, Laurens)
PORNO FOR PYROS—ALBUMS
PH12692 660-661 (July 8, 1993) p114. "Porno For Pyros"
PH12693 662 (August 5, 1993) p77. "Porno For Pyros"
PH12694 736 (June 13, 1996) p80. "Good God's Urge"
PORNO FOR PYROS—PHOTOGRAPHS
PH12695 672-673 (December 23, 1993) p30. "Porno For Pyros: A Friend In Need" (Seliger, Mark)
PORNOGRAPHY—ILLUSTRATIONS
PH12696 696 (December 1, 1994) p18. "Porn Zone" (Pendergrast, James T.)
PH12697 697 (December 15, 1994) p14. "Porn Store" (Pendergrast, James T.)
PORTASTATIC—ALBUMS
PH12698 714 (August 10, 1995) p72. "Slow Note From A Sinking Ship"
PORTER, JAMES, FATHER—PHOTOGRAPHS
PH12699 669 (November 11, 1993) p54. "The Sins Of The Father: Porter Being Led To His Arraignment At Superior Court In New Bedford, Mass., On Sept. 23, 1992..." (Stockwell, Mark)
PORTER, JAMES, FATHER—PHOTOGRAPHS—PORTRAITS
PH12700 669 (November 11, 1993) p48. "Father James Porter, Photographed For Church Files In The 1960s..."
PORTISHEAD—ALBUMS
PH12701 703 (March 9, 1995) p80. "Dummy"
PORTISHEAD—ILLUSTRATIONS
PH12702 703 (March 9, 1995) p66. "Portishead" (Miller, David)
PORTISHEAD—PHOTOGRAPHS
PH12703 702 (February 23, 1995) p38. "Noir-Agers Beth Gibbons (left) And Geoff Barrow" (Cultice, Joseph)
PORTMAN, NATALIE—PHOTOGRAPHS
PH12704 694 (November 3, 1994) p106. "Hitman Reno Teaches Orphan Portman A Trade"
PH12705 729 (March 7, 1996) p53. "Crazy Love Timothy Hutton And Natalie Portman"
THE PORTRAIT OF A LADY (FILM)—PHOTOGRAPHS
PH12706 743 (September 19, 1996) p90. "Quality Control"
POSEY, PARKER—PHOTOGRAPHS
PH12707 704 (March 23, 1995) p128. "Parker Posey Makes The N.Y. Party Scene"
PH12708 717 (September 21, 1995) p90. "Parker Posey As A Coed From Hell"
PH12709 718 (October 5, 1995) pp[enc.13]. "[Parker Posey]" (Seliger, Mark)
PH12710 718 (October 5, 1995) pp[enc.8-9]. "Parker Posey And Benicio Del Toro At La Meia Ristorante, In Little Italy, In New York" (Seliger, Mark)
PH12711 718 (October 5, 1995) pp[enc.16]. "Posey Posing" (Seliger, Mark)
PH12712 718 (October 5, 1995) pp[enc.13]. "Posey With Friends In Den Of Thieves, In New York" (Seliger, Mark)
POSIES—ALBUMS
PH12713 737 (June 27, 1996) p59. "Amazing Disgrace"
POSIES—PHOTOGRAPHS
PH12714 660-661 (July 8, 1993) p101. "The Posies (from left): Jon Auer, Dave Fox, Ken Stringfellow And Mike Musburger" (Natkin, Paul)
PH12715 706 (April 20, 1995) p17. "[Seattle]" (Doughty, Curt)
PH12716 710 (June 15, 1995) p40. "Posies Brian Young, Auer, Stringfellow, Joe Bass (from left)" (Moskowitz, Karen)
THE POSITIVELY TRUE ADVENTURES OF THE ALLEGED TEXAS CHEERLEADER-MURDERING MOM (TELEVISION FILM)—PHOTOGRAPHS
PH12717 655 (April 29, 1993) p68. "Cheerleader-Murdering Mom"
POSNER, HELAINE—PHOTOGRAPHS
PH12718 634-635 (July 9, 1992) p11. "Tom Hamilton, Joe Perry And Tyler (from left) With Museum Curator Helaine Posner" (Putnam, Sarah)
POSSE (FILM)—PHOTOGRAPHS
PH12719 658 (June 10, 1993) p74. "The Magnificent Six (from left): Stephen Baldwin, Big Daddy Kane, Mario Van Peebles, Tiny Lister Jr., Charles Lane, Tone Loc"
PH12720 709 (June 1, 1995) p68. "back-To-School Bashes"
POST, KRISTIN—PHOTOGRAPHS
PH12721 678 (March 24, 1994) p86. "Play Ball: Big-Buddy Post With Maurio At Jordan Lake, In Chapel Hill" (Surowiecki, David)

POST, LOUISE—PHOTOGRAPHS
PH12722 686-687 (July 14, 1994) p73. "Salt Of The Earth: Lack, Gordon, Post And Shapiro (from left)" (Elledge, Paul)
PH12723 700 (January 26, 1995) p20. "Angry Post-Feminists Don't Wear Fur: Post And Gordon" (Seliger, Mark)
PH12724 700 (January 26, 1995) p19. "Gordon, Lack, Post And Shapiro (from left)" (Seliger, Mark)
PH12725 701 (February 9, 1995) p16. "Louise Post, Johnston, Nina Gordon And Pete Droge do D.C." (Harrington, John)
PH12726 709 (June 1, 1995) p17. "Veruca Salt's Louise Post, Jim Shapiro And Gordon (from left)" (Peters, Karen A.)
POST, MARKIE—PHOTOGRAPHS
PH12727 645-646 (December 10, 1992) p196. "His Half-Brother, Roger, Serenaded John Ritter And Markie Post On 'Hearts Afire'"
POSTER ART—ILLUSTRATIONS
PH12728 672-673 (December 23, 1993) pp131-133. "[Poster Art]" (Kozik, Frank)
POSTER CHILDREN—PHOTOGRAPHS—PORTRAITS
PH12729 628 (April 16, 1992) p63. "Poster Children" (Carroll, Chris)
THE POSTMAN (FILM)—PHOTOGRAPHS
PH12730 731 (April 4, 1996) p66. "'The Postman,' With Troisi"
POTTER, SALLY—PHOTOGRAPHS—PORTRAITS
PH12731 659 (June 24, 1993) p90. "[Sally Potter]" (Huba, John)
POTTER, TREVOR—PHOTOGRAPHS
PH12732 680 (April 21, 1994) p40. "Friends Warned Trevor Potter That Going To The FEC Would Hurt His Career" (Patterson, Laura)
POUNDCAKE (VIDEO)—PHOTOGRAPHS
PH12733 619-620 (December 12, 1991) p33. "'Poundcake' By Van Halen"
POVERTY—ILLUSTRATIONS
PH12734 630 (May 14, 1992) p37. "Vote" (Cronin, Brian)
POWDER (FILM)—PHOTOGRAPHS
PH12735 724-725 (December 28, 1995) p134. "The 10 Worst Movies Of 1995 (degrees of sleaze)"
POWELL, COLIN—ILLUSTRATIONS
PH12736 721 (November 16, 1995) p45. "Please, Baby, Please, Baby, Please, Baby, Please" (Witte, Michael)
POWELL, COLIN—PHOTOGRAPHS
PH12737 724-725 (December 28, 1995) p54. "Cuddly Conservative Colin Powell Threw In The Towel"
POWELL, COLIN—PHOTOGRAPHS—PORTRAITS
PH12738 721 (November 16, 1995) p46. "Top Secret: Powell's Presidential Strategy" (Stone, Les)
POWER RANGERS (FILM)—PHOTOGRAPHS
PH12739 709 (June 1, 1995) p68. "Toys As Movies"
POZ (PUBLICATION)—PHOTOGRAPHS
PH12740 715 (August 24, 1995) p75. "Hot Magazine"
PRAGUE, CZECHOSLOVAKIA—PHOTOGRAPHS
PH12741 746 (October 31, 1996) p26. "A Statue Jackson Erected Of Himself (top) On The Spot Where A Stalin Monument Once Stood"
PRAIRIE PRINCE—PHOTOGRAPHS
PH12742 644 (November 26, 1992) p15. "Kantner, Darby Gould, Jack Casady, Tim Gorman, Prairie Prince, Papa John Creach, McGuinn And Slick Aguilar (from left)" (Mazur, Kevin)
PRATER, DAVE—PHOTOGRAPHS—PORTRAITS
PH12743 623 (February 6, 1992) p51. "Stax's Soul Men Sam Moore (top) And Dave Prater"
PRATT, LARRY—PHOTOGRAPHS—PORTRAITS
PH12744 720 (November 2, 1995) p56. "Waiting For Armageddon: Pratt At The Preparedness Expo '95, Getting Ready For Disasters, Natural And Man-Made" (Winters, Dan)
THE PREACHER'S WIFE (FILM)—PHOTOGRAPHS
PH12745 743 (September 19, 1996) p88. "Divas"
PREFONTAINE, STEVE—PHOTOGRAPHS
PH12746 741 (August 22, 1996) p76. "[Steve Prefontaine]" (Drake, James)
PREKOP, SAM—PHOTOGRAPHS
PH12747 721 (November 16, 1995) p67. "The Sea And Cake: Art-Pop Aficionados Sam Prekop, John McEntire, Archer Prewitt And Eric Claridge (middle row, from left)" (Guip, Amy)
PRELUDE TO A KISS (FILM)—PHOTOGRAPHS
PH12748 637 (August 20, 1992) p57. "Soul-Searching: Ryan (left) And Baldwin"
PRENDERGAST, SHARON MARLEY—PHOTOGRAPHS
PH12749 626 (March 19, 1992) p13. "Sharon Marley Prendergrast, Cedella Marley, Ziggy, Stephen Marley (from left)"
PRESIDENTS OF THE UNITED STATES OF AMERICA—ALBUMS
PH12750 748 (November 28, 1996) p132. "II"
PRESIDENTS OF THE UNITED STATES OF AMERICA—ILLUSTRATIONS
PH12751 723 (December 14, 1995) p104. "Presidents Of The USA: Just Say Lump!" (Gabor, Tim)
PRESIDENTS OF THE UNITED STATES OF AMERICA—PHOTOGRAPHS
PH12752 707 (May 4, 1995) p29. "A Couple Of Crazy Presidents" (Clay, Jennifer)
PH12753 718 (October 5, 1995) p35. "The Right Stuff: Jason Finn, Chris Ballew And Dave Dederer (from left)" (Mason, Karen)
PH12754 723 (December 14, 1995) p31. "The Presidents Of The United States Of America" (Temme, Marty)
PH12755 724-725 (December 28, 1995) p42. "P.U.S.A.: Dave Dederer, Chris Ballew And Jason Finn (from left)"
PH12755a 729 (March 7, 1996) p32. "The Presidents Pay Tribute To The Seattle Sonics" (Westenberg, Kevin)
PRESIDENTS OF THE UNITED STATES OF AMERICA—PHOTOGRAPHS—PORTRAITS
PH12756 729 (March 7, 1996) p30. "One Band Indivisible With Power, Pop And Jokes For All" (Westenberg, Kevin)
PH12757 Number not assigned.
PRESLEY, ELVIS—ALBUMS
PH12758 617 (November 14, 1991) p137. "50,000,000 Elvis Fans Can't Be Wrong" (Parker, Tom, Colonel)
PH12759 617 (November 14, 1991) p137. "50,000,000 Elvis Fans Can't Be Wrong" (Robertson And Fresh)
PH12760 617 (November 14, 1991) p124. "Elvis Presley" (Parker, Tom, Colonel)
PH12761 617 (November 14, 1991) p124. "Elvis Presley" (Popsie)
PH12762 636 (August 6, 1992) p55. "The King Of Rock 'N' Roll: The Complete '50's Masters"
PH12763 651 (March 4, 1993) p55. "The King Of Rock 'N' Roll"
PRESLEY, ELVIS—ILLUSTRATIONS
PH12764 629 (April 30, 1992) p12. "[Elvis Stamps]"
PH12765 632 (June 11, 1992) p119. "[Elvis Presley]" (Cronin, Brian)
PH12766 636 (August 6, 1992) p55. "Elvis Lives—In This Music" (Burns, Charles)
PH12767 645-646 (December 10, 1992) p66. "[Elvis Presley]"
PH12768 669 (November 11, 1993) p76. "[Elvis Presley]"
PH12769 721 (November 16, 1995) p26. "VIP DNA" (Bartholomew, Beth)
PRESLEY, ELVIS—ILLUSTRATIONS—PORTRAITS
PH12770 672-673 (December 23, 1993) p16. "Above: The Official Elvis"
PRESLEY, ELVIS—PHOTOGRAPHS
PH12771 619-620 (December 12, 1991) p32. "[Good Rockin' Tonight]"
PH12772 619-620 (December 12, 1991) p68. "Never Say Die: Elvis Presley"
PH12773 632 (June 11, 1992) p121. "At The Warwick Hotel, In New York, On March 17th, 1956, Elvis Fine-Tunes Before A Television Appearance" (Wertheimer, Alfred)
PH12774 634-635 (July 9, 1992) p25. "Good Rockin' Tonight: Elvis In The Fifties"

PH12775 643 (November 12, 1992) p21. "Baby Let's Play House: It Is June 30th, 1956, And Alfred Wertheimer Is Backstage To Photograph The Young King" (Wertheimer, Alfred)
PH12776 643 (November 12, 1992) p54. "One Boy's Journey Into American Myth: Elvis On The Train To Memphis, 1956" (Wertheimer, Alfred)
PH12777 710 (June 15, 1995) p25. "Live On TV, '68: The King Is Back"
PH12778 720 (November 2, 1995) p49. "Elvis Presley"
PRESLEY, ELVIS—PHOTOGRAPHS—PORTRAITS
PH12779 645-646 (December 10, 1992) p161. "Elvis Presley, 1977"
PRESLEY, LISA MARIE—ILLUSTRATIONS
PH12780 750-751 (December 26, 1996) p45. "[Michael Jackson & Lisa Marie Presley]" (Ryden, Mark)
PRESLEY, LISA MARIE—PHOTOGRAPHS
PH12781 691 (September 22, 1994) p19. "[Michael Jackson & Lisa Marie Presley]" (Zimmerman, Dick)
PH12782 693 (October 20, 1994) p28. "Mr. (left) And Mrs. Michael Jackson" (Kravitz, Jeff)
PH12783 719 (October 19, 1995) p16. "Michael Jackson And The Missis" (Kravitz, Jeff)
PH12784 724-725 (December 28, 1995) p48. "No Glove, And Definitely No Love: Sawyer, Jacksons"
PRESLEY, LISA MARIE—PHOTOGRAPHS—PORTRAITS
PH12785 698-699 (December 29, 1994) p55. "[Michael Jackson & Lisa Marie Presley]" (Zimmerman, Dick)
PRESTON, AARON—PHOTOGRAPHS—PORTRAITS
PH12786 630 (May 14, 1992) p32. "Chainsaw Kittens (clockwise from top left): McBay, Meade, Preston, Bell And Metzger" (Mazur, Kevin)
PRESTON, JOHN—PHOTOGRAPHS
PH12787 698-699 (December 29, 1994) p66. "John Travolta And His Wife, Kelly Preston" (Spellman, John)
PRET-A-PORTER (FILM)—PHOTOGRAPHS
PH12788 698-699 (December 29, 1994) p199. "Roberts And Robbins in "Pret""
THE PRETENDER (TELEVISION SHOW)—PHOTOGRAPHS
PH12789 743 (September 19, 1996) pp94,96. "[Television]"
PRETENDERS—ALBUMS
PH12790 683 (June 2, 1994) p69. "Last Of The Independents"
PH12791 723 (December 14, 1995) p84. "The Isle Of View"
PRETENDERS—PHOTOGRAPHS
PH12792 712-713 (July 13, 1995) p33. "The Pretenders With Chrissie Hynde" (Fowler, Simon)
PREWITT, ARCHER—PHOTOGRAPHS
PH12793 721 (November 16, 1995) p67. "The Sea And Cake: Art-Pop Aficionados Sam Prekop, John McEntire, Archer Prewitt And Eric Claridge (middle row, from left)" (Guip, Amy)
PRICE, ALAN—PHOTOGRAPHS
PH12794 676 (February 24, 1994) p48. "The Angry Young Animals (from left): Drummer John Steel, Organist Alan Price, bass Player Chas Chandler, Lead Singer Eric Burdon And Guitarist Hilton Valentine"
PRICE, CHAD—PHOTOGRAPHS
PH12795 719 (October 19, 1995) p24. "No Mall Punks For All: Chad Price, Stephen Egerton, Karl Alvarez, Bill Stevenson (from left)" (Corrigan, Daniel)
PRICE, WADE—PHOTOGRAPHS
PH12796 666 (September 30, 1993) p90. "Hunt (third from left, bottom row) With Delta Lambda Phi Brothers (clockwise from top right): Peter Colohan, Sean McClafferty, Rob Corwin, Price, Stephen Smith And Oligmueller"
PH12797 666 (September 30, 1993) p88. "Wade Price, Steivan Oligmueller And Bert Childs (from left)" (Himmel, Lizzie)
PRIDE AND GLORY—PHOTOGRAPHS
PH12798 686-687 (July 14, 1994) p72. "LoMenzo, Wylde And Tischy (from left)" (Ragel, Jon)
PRIEBOY, ANDY—PHOTOGRAPHS
PH12799 628 (April 16, 1992) p13. "World Party Guitarist Jeffrey Trott (left) With Napolitano And Prieboy" (Karas, Steve)
PRIEST (FILM)—PHOTOGRAPHS
PH12800 705 (April 6, 1995) p70. "Priest"
PH12801 724-725 (December 28, 1995) p136. "Unusual Pleasure"
PRIESTLEY, JASON—PHOTOGRAPHS
PH12802 647 (January 7, 1993) p11. "Dr. Hunter S. Thompson (left) And Jason Priestley" (Elgar, Nick)
PRIESTLEY, JASON—PHOTOGRAPHS—PORTRAITS
PH12803 624 (February 20, 1992) pp[cover]. "Beverly Hills, 90210: Smells Like Teen Spirit" (Eccles, Andrew)
PH12804 624 (February 20, 1992) p24. "Is Jason Priestley's Brandon 2 Good 2 B 4 Real?" (Eccles, Andrew)
PH12805 624 (February 20, 1992) pp22-23. "Jason Priestley" (Eccles, Andrew)
PH12806 645-646 (December 10, 1992) pp[cover]. "1992 Yearbook" (Eccles, Andrew)
PRIMAL FEAR (FILM)—PHOTOGRAPHS
PH12807 732 (April 18, 1996) p80. "From Left: Linney And Gere Huddle; Norton Broods"
PRIMAL SCREAM—PHOTOGRAPHS
PH12808 684 (June 16, 1994) p26. "A Slice Of Scream: Keyboardist Martin Duffy, Gillespie And Innes (from left)" (Sheehan, Tom)
PRIME TIME—ALBUMS
PH12809 723 (December 14, 1995) p84. "Tone Dialing"
PRIMITIVE RADIO GODS—PHOTOGRAPHS
PH12810 742 (September 5, 1996) p29. "Radio Gods" (Johnson, Lisa)
PRIMUS—ALBUMS
PH12811 658 (June 10, 1993) p71. "Pork Soda"
PRIMUS—PHOTOGRAPHS
PH12812 662 (August 5, 1993) p14. "Les Claypool, Tim Alexander And Larry LaLonde (from left) Of Primus" (Blakesberg, Jay)
PRIMUS—PHOTOGRAPHS—PORTRAITS
PH12813 616 (October 31, 1991) p81. "Smooth Sailing: Guitarist Larry Lalonde, Drummer Tim Alexander And Bassist Les Claypool (clockwise from left)" (Seliger, Mark)
PRINCE—ALBUMS
PH12814 615 (October 17, 1991) p92. "Diamonds And Pearls"
PH12815 617 (November 14, 1991) p147. "Sign O' The Times" (LiPuma, Laura)
PH12816 617 (November 14, 1991) p147. "Sign O' The Times" (Katz, Jeff)
PH12817 619-620 (December 12, 1991) p168. "Diamonds And Pearls"
PH12818 644 (November 26, 1992) p70. "[Symbol]"
PH12819 667 (October 14, 1993) p113. "The Hits: Volume 1 & II"
PH12820 690 (September 8, 1994) p75. "Come"
PH12821 720 (November 2, 1995) p66. "The Gold Experience"
PH12822 741 (August 22, 1996) p98. "Chaos And Disorder"
PRINCE—ILLUSTRATIONS
PH12823 655 (April 29, 1993) p5. "Prince" (Burke, Philip)
PH12824 667 (October 14, 1993) p113. "Secrets Of Seduction" (Ryden, Mark)
PH12825 690 (September 8, 1994) p75. "Oh, Whoever" (Brown, Calef)
PH12826 693 (October 20, 1994) p22. "Critic" (Pendergrast, James T.)
PH12827 720 (November 2, 1995) p66. "Two Princes" (Faiola, Susan)
PH12828 748 (November 28, 1996) p62. "[Prince]" (Kelley, Gary)
PRINCE—PHOTOGRAPHS
PH12829 619-620 (December 12, 1991) p80. "Prince"
PH12830 654 (April 15, 1993) p13. "A Thinly Veiled Prince" (Mazur, Kevin)

PH12831 655 (April 29, 1993) p15. "[Prince]" (Busacca, Larry)
PH12832 655 (April 29, 1993) p16. "Signing Of The Times: Prince Autographs His New Record At A Store In Atlanta" (Busacca, Larry)
PH12833 662 (August 5, 1993) p17. "[Prince]" (Camp, E. J.)
PH12834 672-673 (December 23, 1993) p40. "Below: Prince, Or Late To Dinner To You" (Blakesberg, Jay)
PH12835 672-673 (December 23, 1993) p27. "Who Is This Masked Symbol Man?" (Mazur, Kevin)
PH12836 679 (April 7, 1994) p37. "Symbol Man Prince Parties"
PH12837 681 (May 5, 1994) p22. "[Prince]" (Barrett, Fitzroy)
PH12838 688 (August 11, 1994) p18. "You Recognize The Guy, Don't You? Don't Make Us Say It" (Kravitz, Jeff)
PH12839 714 (August 10, 1995) p17. "Santana (left) And His Glyphness In Florida" (Craig, Tom)
PH12840 733 (May 2, 1996) p13. "[Prince & Mayte Garcia]" (Amati, Ray)
PH12841 741 (August 22, 1996) p26. "[Prince]" (Mazur, Kevin)
PH12842 745 (October 17, 1996) p36. "Talk Like An Egyptian"
PH12843 750-751 (December 26, 1996) p48. "Happy Couple Garcia And Prince" (Rasic, Brian)

PRINCE—PHOTOGRAPHS—PORTRAITS
PH12844 645-646 (December 10, 1992) p85. "[Prince]"
PH12845 658 (June 10, 1993) p22. "He's Got 500 Unreleased Tracks Ready To Go" (Katz, Jeff)
PH12846 678 (March 24, 1994) p18. "[Prince]" (Poole, Edward)
PH12847 Number not assigned.

PRINCE ALWALEED BIN TALAL BIN ABDULAZIZ AL-SAUD—PHOTOGRAPHS
PH12848 750-751 (December 26, 1996) p54. "[Michael Jackson & Prince Alwaleed Bin Talal Bin Abdulaziz Al-Saud]" (Rabbo, Ammar Abd)

PRINCE BE—ILLUSTRATIONS
PH12849 719 (October 19, 1995) p7. "prince Be Of P.M. Dawn" (Burke, Philip)
PH12850 734 (May 16, 1996) p21. "The Truth, And The Tunes, Are Out There..." (Friedman, Drew)

PRINCE BE—PHOTOGRAPHS
PH12851 629 (April 30, 1992) p12. "P.M. Dawn's Prince Be Gets People Dancing" (Pitney, Layne)
PH12852 657 (May 27, 1993) p9. "P.M. Dawn's Prince Be" (Preston, Neal)
PH12853 662 (August 5, 1993) p59. "Prince Be" (Barrett, Fitzroy)
PH12854 672-673 (December 23, 1993) p27. "Hippie, Dippy DJ Minutemix (left) And Prince Be" (Natkin, Paul)
PH12855 719 (October 19, 1995) p19. "P.M. Dawn's Prince Be (left) And J.C. The Eternal Are Redefining What It Means To Be A Black Artists" (Thomas, Katrin)

PRINCE BE—PHOTOGRAPHS—PORTRAITS
PH12856 616 (October 31, 1991) p25. "DJ Minutemix (left) And Prince Be" (Brusso, Andrew)
PH12857 630 (May 14, 1992) p79. "Prince Be (left) And His Brother DJ Minutemix" (Watson, Albert)

THE PRINCE OF TIDES (FILM)—PHOTOGRAPHS
PH12858 619-620 (December 12, 1991) p194. "Male Wimps And Female Warriors"
PH12859 621 (January 9, 1992) p55. "Streisand And Nick Nolte In Therapy"

PRINCE PAUL—PHOTOGRAPHS
PH12860 733 (May 2, 1996) p22. "From Left: Prince Paul, Reid And Teo Macero At The Manhattan Center" (Gershoff, Gary)

PRINCE WILLIAM SOUND, ALASKA—PHOTOGRAPHS
PH12861 632 (June 11, 1992) p176. "The Massive Disaster (opposite page)..."
PH12862 632 (June 11, 1992) p177. "...Produced An Often-Misguided Response (above)" (Schultz, J.)

PRINCESS CAROLINE—PHOTOGRAPHS
PH12863 615 (October 17, 1991) p65. "Stefano Casiraghi And Princess Caroline, 1990" (Pigozzi, Jean)

PRINE, JOHN—ALBUMS
PH12864 622 (January 23, 1992) p46. "The Missing Years"

PRINE, JOHN—PHOTOGRAPHS
PH12865 621 (January 9, 1992) p10. "Margo Timmins And John Prine"
PH12866 624 (February 20, 1992) p15. "[John Prine]" (Smith, Brian)
PH12867 631 (May 28, 1992) p24. "John Prine (below)" (Willett, Robert)

PRINE, JOHN—PHOTOGRAPHS—PORTRAITS
PH12868 717 (September 21, 1995) p36. "[John prine]" (Smith, Brian)

PRINGLE, CHRIS—PHOTOGRAPHS
PH12869 716 (September 7, 1995) p30. "Tough Love: The Chocolate Swiping Homey Chris Pringle (left) And Skee-Lo" (Gougenheim, Kim)

PRISONERS—ILLUSTRATIONS
PH12870 711 (June 29, 1995) p13. "Book 'Em" (Faiola, Susan)

PROCLAIMERS—ALBUMS
PH12871 685 (June 30, 1994) p74. "Hit The Highway"

PRODIGY—PHOTOGRAPHS
PH12872 715 (August 24, 1995) p34. "Reality Raps While Flint Gets Down (from left)" (Capak, R. J.)

THE PROFESSIONAL (FILM)—PHOTOGRAPHS
PH12873 694 (November 3, 1994) p106. "Hitman Reno Teaches Orphan Portman A Trade"

PROFESSOR LONGHAIR—PHOTOGRAPHS—PORTRAITS
PH12874 623 (February 6, 1992) p52. "[Professor Longhair]"

PROFILER (TELEVISION SHOW)—PHOTOGRAPHS
PH12875 743 (September 19, 1996) pp94,96. "[Television]"

THE PROGRAM (FILM)—PHOTOGRAPHS
PH12876 672-673 (December 23, 1993) p172. "Old Controversy"

PROSPERO'S BOOKS (FILM)—PHOTOGRAPHS
PH12877 617 (November 14, 1991) p184. "Gielgud (with two lovers) Can't Tell Truth From Illusion"

PROSTITUTION—PHOTOGRAPHS
PH12878 618 (November 28, 1991) p65. "At 5:00 a.m., Near The End Of Another Long Night In Patpong, Some Locals Wait For Their Girlfriends, Who Work As Bar Girls" (Zachmann, Patrick)
PH12879 618 (November 28, 1991) p70. "Bangkok Prostitutes Await The Results Of HIV Tests For Their Health Identity Cards, Which Are Demanded By Some Bars" (Zachmann, Patrick)
PH12880 618 (November 28, 1991) p66. "A Bankok Streetwalker Reads A Pamphlet On AIDS Distributed By A Support Organization For Prostitutes, Empower" (Zachmann, Patrick)
PH12881 618 (November 28, 1991) p66. "A Health Worker Gives A Lesson In AIDS Prevention In A Red-Light District" (Zachmann, Patrick)
PH12882 618 (November 28, 1991) pp62-66,69-70. "In A Bangkok Hospital, An Eight-Month-Old Child Suffers From AIDS" (Zachmann, Patrick)
PH12883 618 (November 28, 1991) p65. "In A Bar In Pattaya, A Beach Resort, A Customer Tries To Examine A Possible Purchase" (Zachmann, Patrick)
PH12884 618 (November 28, 1991) p69. "Male Dancers Perform At A Bar In Patpong" (Zachmann, Patrick)
PH12885 618 (November 28, 1991) p69. "A Male Sex Worker Displays His Government Health Identity Card, Which Certifies He's Been Tested This Month For HIV" (Zachmann, Patrick)
PH12886 618 (November 28, 1991) p62. "The Red-Light District Of Patpong" (Zachmann, Patrick)
PH12887 618 (November 28, 1991) p64. "Some Children Are Sold Into Prostitution By Their Parents" (Zachmann, Patrick)
PH12888 618 (November 28, 1991) p63. "Streetwalkers In Another Of The City's Night-Life Sections" (Zachmann, Patrick)
PH12889 618 (November 28, 1991) pp62-66,69-70. "Two Addicts With AIDS Who Have Found Refuge In A Shelter In Bangkok" (Zachmann, Patrick)

PH12890 618 (November 28, 1991) p64. "Where East Meets West: A Bar Girl Encourages A Client" (Zachmann, Patrick)
PROTEST—PHOTOGRAPHS
PH12891 715 (August 24, 1995) p84. "Hot Mind Set"
PROTESTS—PHOTOGRAPHS
PH12892 638 (September 3, 1992) p16. "A Group Of Protesters Outside The Meeting" (Crane, David)
PH12893 667 (October 14, 1993) pp58-59. "Anti-Abortionists Protesting At Windle's Clinic In Port St. Lucie" (Smale, Brian)
PH12894 667 (October 14, 1993) p62. "Below: In April, A Policeman Leads Away A Father And Son For Violating The Buffer Zone At Windle's Clinic" (Brown, Michael)
PH12895 715 (August 24, 1995) p77. "Hot Diversion"
PH12896 724-725 (December 28, 1995) p48. "Protests: Because Of A Few, All Suffered" (Capak, R. J.)
PROVINCETOWN, MASSACHUSETTS—PHOTOGRAPHS
PH12897 686-687 (July 14, 1994) p46. "[Provincetown]" (Palmieri, Lou)
PRYCE, JONATHAN—PHOTOGRAPHS
PH12898 731 (April 4, 1996) p66. "Pryce, 'Carrington'"
PRYCE, JONATHAN—PHOTOGRAPHS—PORTRAITS
PH12899 722 (November 30, 1995) p74. "Is Jonathan Pryce's Lytton Strachey Wittier Than Jim Carrey's Ace? You Betcha"
PSYCHOLOGY—PHOTOGRAPHS
PH12900 652 (March 18, 1993) pp[enc.19]. "Double Fantasy" (Kern, Geof)
PH12901 652 (March 18, 1993) pp[enc.6]. "[Where The Jobs Are]"
PH12902 719 (October 19, 1995) p94. "The Mind And Sleep"
PUBLIC ENEMY—ALBUMS
PH12903 619-620 (December 12, 1991) p162. "Apocalypse 91...The Enemy Strikes Black"
PH12904 645-646 (December 10, 1992) p174. "Greatest Misses"
PH12905 666 (September 30, 1993) p59. "It Takes A Nation Of Millions To Hold Us Back"
PH12906 686-687 (July 14, 1994) p101. "Muse Sick N Hour Mess Age"
PUBLIC ENEMY—ILLUSTRATIONS
PH12907 686-687 (July 14, 1994) p101. "Bust This" (Rosenthal, Marc)
PUBLIC ENEMY—ILLUSTRATIONS—LETTERING
PH12908 622 (January 23, 1992) pp34-37. "[Public Enemy]" (Ortiz-Lopez, Dennis)
PUBLIC ENEMY—PHOTOGRAPHS
PH12909 619-620 (December 12, 1991) p88. "PE And Anthrax" (Natkin, Paul)
PH12910 619-620 (December 12, 1991) p19. "Public Enemy" (Natkin, Paul)
PH12911 619-620 (December 12, 1991) p90. "[Public Enemy]" (Ng, N.)
PH12912 619-620 (December 12, 1991) p84. "The Tune In Package Tour Didn't Turn Many Fans On" (Natkin, Paul)
PH12913 622 (January 23, 1992) pp34-35. "From Left: Chuck D, Flavor Flav And Terminator X" (Ockenfels, Frank W.)
PH12914 625 (March 5, 1992) p54. "Public Enemy Sweeps Rap Honors" (Seliger, Mark)
PH12915 645-646 (December 10, 1992) p31. "[Public Enemy]" (Seliger, Mark)
PH12916 667 (October 14, 1993) p85. "'Baseheads': PE's Flav Brings The News"
PH12917 685 (June 30, 1994) p30. "New "Mess Age": Flavor Flav, Chuck D And Terminator X (from front)" (Seliger, Mark)
PH12918 702 (February 23, 1995) p20. "[Public Enemy]"
THE PUBLIC EYE (FILM)—PHOTOGRAPHS
PH12919 642 (October 29, 1992) p77. "The Public Eye"
PUBLIC IMAGE, LTD.—ALBUMS
PH12920 617 (November 14, 1991) p132. "Metal Box" (Lydon, John)
PH12921 617 (November 14, 1991) p132. "Metal Box" (Dimont, Charles)
PH12922 624 (February 20, 1992) p41. "That What Is Not"
PUBLIC TELEVISION—ILLUSTRATIONS
PH12923 697 (December 15, 1994) p17. "Kin Flicks" (Friske, Maria)
PUCKETT, CHRIS—PHOTOGRAPHS—PORTRAITS
PH12924 645-646 (December 10, 1992) pp139,141. "[Chris Puckett]" (Eccles, Andrew)
PULLMAN, BILL—PHOTOGRAPHS
PH12925 708 (May 18, 1995) p97. "Sandra Bullock Wears Down Bill Pullman's Resistance"
PULNOC—ALBUMS
PH12926 618 (November 28, 1991) p94. "City Of Hysteria"
PULP—ALBUMS
PH12927 731 (April 4, 1996) p61. "Different Class"
PULP—PHOTOGRAPHS
PH12928 732 (April 18, 1996) p22. "[Pulp]" (Hogan, Dave)
PH12929 732 (April 18, 1996) p24. "A Wildly Unorthodox Mixture Of Influence Gathered Around The Table: Pulp's Candida Doyle, Mark Webber, Cocker, Steve Mackey, Russell Senior And Nick Banks (from left)" (Rankin)
PULP FICTION (FILM)—ILLUSTRATIONS
PH12930 692 (October 6, 1994) p79. "Tarantino's Twist" (Todd, Mark)
PH12931 700 (January 26, 1995) p16. "Fasten Your Seat Belts" (Fisher, Carolyn)
PULP FICTION (FILM)—PHOTOGRAPHS
PH12932 692 (October 6, 1994) p80. "Arquette Gets Pierced"
PH12933 692 (October 6, 1994) p80. "Keitel Deals"
PH12934 692 (October 6, 1994) p80. "Tarantino Directs"
PH12935 692 (October 6, 1994) p80. "Thurman And Travolta Twist"
PH12936 692 (October 6, 1994) p80. "Travolta And Jackson Shoot"
PH12937 692 (October 6, 1994) p80. "Willis And De Medeiros Screw"
PH12938 698-699 (December 29, 1994) p196. "[Pulp Fiction]"
PH12939 698-699 (December 29, 1994) p194. "Thurman And Travolta Twist In "Pulp""
PH12940 700 (January 26, 1995) p68. "Best Actor (tie)"
PH12941 705 (April 6, 1995) p69. "The Envelope, Please: Nominated For best Picture: Forrest Gump, Pulp Fiction, Quiz Show, Four Weddings And A Funeral, And The Shawshank Redemption"
PH12942 727 (February 8, 1996) p46. "Home Video"
PH12943 728 (February 22, 1996) p43. "Travolta Puts On The Moves In 'Pulp Fiction,' 'Saturday Night Fever' And 'Broken Arrow'"
PULSFORD, NIGEL—PHOTOGRAPHS
PH12944 710 (June 15, 1995) p49. "Dave Parsons, Rossdale, Robin Goodridge, Pulsford (from left)" (Westenberg, Kevin)
PH12945 712-713 (July 13, 1995) p30. "Pulsford (left) And Rossdale In New York In March" (Olson, Sheryl)
PH12946 712-713 (July 13, 1995) p29. "Zen Careerists: Pulsford, Parsons, Rossdale, And Goodridge (from left)" (Mahurin, Matt)
PULSFORD, NIGEL—PHOTOGRAPHS—PORTRAITS
PH12947 732 (April 18, 1996) p41. "Robin Goodridge, Gavin Rossdale, Dave Parsons And Nigel Pulsford" (Seliger, Mark)
PUNK ROCK—ILLUSTRATIONS
PH12948 649 (February 4, 1993) p61. "Do It Yourself: Punk Will Never Die" (Turk, Steve)
PH12949 649 (February 4, 1993) p64. "Punk Will Never Die, Part 2" (Downs, Richard)
PURSUIT OF HAPPINESS—ALBUMS
PH12950 658 (June 10, 1993) p70. "The Downward Road"
PUTTERS—ALBUMS
PH12951 700 (January 26, 1995) p63. "Fear Of Women"
PYLE, ARTIMUS—PHOTOGRAPHS
PH12952 727 (February 8, 1996) p12. "Skynyrd's Bob Burns, Leon Wilkeson, Artimus Pyle (from left)" (Diamond, Rick)

PYLE, CHRIS—PHOTOGRAPHS
PH12953 710 (June 15, 1995) p36. "Brown, Herrema, Hagerty And Pyle (from left): 'We're A Marketing Nightmare'" (Westenberg, Kevin)
PYRAMIDS—ILLUSTRATIONS
PH12954 632 (June 11, 1992) p11. "[Pyramids]" (Cronin, Brian)
PYRAMIDS—PHOTOGRAPHS
PH12955 632 (June 11, 1992) p88. "Prophetic Postcards From The Original Pyramid Expedition"
PYRO, HOWIE—PHOTOGRAPHS
PH12956 701 (February 9, 1995) p19. "D Gen (from left): Danny Sage, Richard Bacchus, Howie Pyro, Jesse Malin, Michael Wildwood" (Seliger, Mark)
PH12957 710 (June 15, 1995) p41. "D Gen (from left): Pyro, Michael Wildwood, Malin, Sage, Richard Bacchus And Gomez" (Ragel, Jon)
PH12958 735 (May 30, 1996) p13. "Do You Feel Lucky Today?"
PYST (CD-ROM)—ILLUSTRATIONS
PH12959 746 (October 31, 1996) p78. "Multimedia"

Q

Q-TIP—ILLUSTRATIONS
PH12960 695 (November 17, 1994) p129. "A Tribe Called Quest" (Shurley, Hugh)
Q-TIP—PHOTOGRAPHS
PH12961 678 (March 24, 1994) p10. "Mifnight Marauding: Phife (left) and Tip" (Gehring, Karl A.)
PH12962 678 (March 24, 1994) p10. "Reaching Creative Extremes: Q-Tip"
PH12963 742 (September 5, 1996) p28. "Q-Tip Of A Tribe Called Quest" (Kravitz, Jeff)
Q-TIP—PHOTOGRAPHS—PORTRAITS
PH12964 678 (March 24, 1994) p9. "Quest (clockwise from top): Q-Tip, Ali And Phife Dog" (Seliger, Mark)
QUAID, DENNIS—PHOTOGRAPHS
PH12965 670 (November 25, 1993) p126. "Dennis Quaid And Meg Ryan Steal A Kiss"
PH12966 737 (June 27, 1996) p62. "Dennis Quaid's Knight Feels Sean Connery's Dragon Breath"
QUALYE, DAN—ILLUSTRATIONS
PH12967 634-635 (July 9, 1992) p8. "Laid Fresh Every Day!" (Pendergrast, James T.)
QUARRY MEN—PHOTOGRAPHS
PH12968 690 (September 8, 1994) p36. "Lennon (center) With The Quarry Men, In Liverpool, England, July 1957" (Rhind, Geoff)
QUEEN—PHOTOGRAPHS—PORTRAITS
PH12969 621 (January 9, 1992) p14. "Queen In The Mid-Seventies (from left): Deacon, Mercury, May And Taylor" (Rock, Mick)
QUEEN LATIFAH—ALBUMS
PH12970 616 (October 31, 1991) p92. "Nature Of A Sista'"
PH12971 619-620 (December 12, 1991) p174. "Nature Of A Sista'"
PH12972 666 (September 30, 1993) p59. "All Hail The Queen"
QUEEN LATIFAH—PHOTOGRAPHS
PH12973 619-620 (December 12, 1991) p37. "Queen Latifah (left)" (Robicheau, Paul)
PH12974 630 (May 14, 1992) p83. "[Todd Oldham, Queen Latifah]" (Baratta, Nicholas)
PH12975 720 (November 2, 1995) p17. "Hoop Dreams: Latifah And Teammate Coolio" (Kravitz, Jeff)
PH12976 724-725 (December 28, 1995) p49. "Quick-Acting Queen Latifah Refused To Be A Victim"
PH12977 748 (November 28, 1996) p143. "Latifah"
QUEEN LATIFAH—PHOTOGRAPHS—PORTRAITS
PH12978 615 (October 17, 1991) p19. "[Queen Latifah]" (Ockenfels, Frank W.)
PH12979 625 (March 5, 1992) p54. "Latifah Raps Up A Win" (Ockenfels, Frank W.)
PH12980 715 (August 24, 1995) p30. "Latifah Gets Car-Jacked" (Hartman, Rose)
QUEEN MARGOT (FILM)—PHOTOGRAPHS
PH12981 700 (January 26, 1995) p66. "Smart Women, Foolish Choices"
QUEENSRYCHE—PHOTOGRAPHS
PH12982 696 (December 1, 1994) p24. "Queensryche Take A Break At Their Listening Party" (Mercer, Lance)
QUEERS—PHOTOGRAPHS
PH12983 747 (November 14, 1996) p42. "Takes One To Know One: O'Neill, King And B-Face (from left)" (Horton, Nancy G.)
THE QUEST (FILM)—PHOTOGRAPHS
PH12984 734 (May 16, 1996) p72. "Jean-Claude Van Damme"
THE QUICK AND THE DEAD (FILM)—ILLUSTRATIONS
PH12985 703 (March 9, 1995) p69. "Sharon And The Wild Bunch" (Payne, C. F.)
THE QUICK AND THE DEAD (FILM)—PHOTOGRAPHS
PH12986 703 (March 9, 1995) p70. "Leonardo Dicaprio And Gene Hackman Face Off In Familial Fury"
PH12987 703 (March 9, 1995) p70. "Sharon Stone Takes Aim"
QUINN, AIDAN—PHOTOGRAPHS
PH12988 675 (February 10, 1994) p52. "Cop Aidan Quinn Beds Angel Madeleine Stowe"

R

RA, SUN—ILLUSTRATIONS
PH12989 651 (March 4, 1993) p63. "Images Of Tomorrow Disguised As Jazz" (Clayton, Christian)
RA, SUN—PHOTOGRAPHS—PORTRAITS
PH12990 660-661 (July 8, 1993) p24. "Sun Ra: 1914-1993" (Watermann, Greg)
PH12991 672-673 (December 23, 1993) p80. "Sun Ra" (Watermann, Greg)
RABIN, YITZBAK—PHOTOGRAPHS
PH12992 724-725 (December 28, 1995) p63. "The Funeral Of Peacemaker Yitzbak Rabin"
RACISM—ILLUSTRATIONS
PH12993 617 (November 14, 1991) p8. "Millie Sees Something Scary" (Pendergrast, James T.)
PH12994 631 (May 28, 1992) p30. "Talk" (Cronin, Brian)
PH12995 633 (June 25, 1992) p22. "[Racism]" (Cronin, Brian)
PH12996 665 (September 16, 1993) p6. "Chemistry 101" (Pendergrast, James T.)
PH12997 666 (September 30, 1993) p10. "Quiet!" (Pendergrast, James T.)
PH12998 690 (September 8, 1994) p16. "Racial ID Card" (Pendergrast, James T.)
PH12999 696 (December 1, 1994) p18. "Educated Chicken—Intelligent Chicken" (Pendergrast, James T.)
PH13000 711 (June 29, 1995) p10. "Racism" (Pendergrast, James T.)
RADIO STATIONS—ILLUSTRATIONS
PH13001 701 (February 9, 1995) p24. "[Radio Formats]" (McCauley, Adam)
RADIOHEAD—ALBUMS
PH13002 672-673 (December 23, 1993) p151. "Pablo Honey"
PH13003 708 (May 18, 1995) p88. "The Bends"
RADIOHEAD—PHOTOGRAPHS
PH13004 660-661 (July 8, 1993) p95. "Radiohead: Ed O'Brien, Colin Greenwood, Phil Selway, Yorke, Jonny Greenwood" (Sharp, Ken)
PH13005 665 (September 16, 1993) p22. "Radiohead With Yorke (center): Appealing To The Creep In Everyone" (Sharp, Ken)
PH13006 672-673 (December 23, 1993) p45. "[Radiohead]"

(Anker, Matt)
PH13007 716 (September 7, 1995) p19. "Colin Greenwood, Ed O'Brien, Thom Yorke, Jonny Greenwood And Phil Selway (from left)" (Blakesberg, Jay)
PH13008 716 (September 7, 1995) p21. "Radiohead At This Year's Live 105 Festival, In San Francisco" (Blakesberg, Jay)
RADIOLAND MURDERS (FILM)—PHOTOGRAPHS
PH13009 696 (December 1, 1994) p134. "Misfires"
RADIOS—ILLUSTRATIONS
PH13010 727 (February 8, 1996) p10. "Etc." (Pendergrast, James T.)
RADIOS—PHOTOGRAPHS
PH13011 686-687 (July 14, 1994) pp46-47. "[Toys]" (Grant, Bob)
RADLE, CARL—PHOTOGRAPHS
PH13012 655 (April 29, 1993) p35. "Derek And The Dominos: Jim Gordon, Carl Radle, Bobby Whitlock And Clapton (from left)..."
RAE, STEPHEN—PHOTOGRAPHS
PH13013 644 (November 26, 1992) p80. "An Identity Crisis For Jaye Davidson (left) And Stephen Rea"
RAEKWON—ALBUMS
PH13014 718 (October 5, 1995) p68. "Only Built Fir Cuban Linx"
RAGE AGAINST THE MACHINE—ALBUMS
PH13015 732 (April 18, 1996) p67. "Evil Empire"
PH13016 737 (June 27, 1996) p72. "Evil Empire"
RAGE AGAINST THE MACHINE—ILLUSTRATIONS
PH13017 732 (April 18, 1996) p67. "Blows Against The Empire" (Bartholomew, Beth)
PH13018 736 (June 13, 1996) p92. "Evil Empire: All The Rage" (Ciardiello, Joe)
PH13019 750-751 (December 26, 1996) p56. "[Rage Against The Machine]" (Coe, Sue)
RAGE AGAINST THE MACHINE—PHOTOGRAPHS
PH13020 664 (September 2, 1993) p31. "Rage's Timmy C., Zack De La Rocha, Brad Wilk And Tom Morello (from left)" (Johnson, William)
PH13021 735 (May 30, 1996) p27. "Rage Against The Machine"
PH13022 744 (October 3, 1996) p34. "Singer De La Rocha (right) And Bassist Tim Bob Fight The Power" (Mazur, Kevin)
RAGING BULL (FILM)—PHOTOGRAPHS
PH13023 654 (April 15, 1993) p69. "Raging Bull"
RAGING SLAB—ALBUMS
PH13024 663 (August 19, 1993) p77. "Dynamite Monster Boogie Concert"
RAIN FOREST—PHOTOGRAPHS
PH13025 727 (February 8, 1996) p40. "The Headwaters Forest, 1989, Following Charles Hurwitz's Raid On Pacific Lumber" (King, Greg)
PH13026 727 (February 8, 1996) pp38-39. "[Rain Forest]" (King, Greg)
RAINBOW FAMILY OF LIVING LIGHT—ILLUSTRATIONS
PH13027 675 (February 10, 1994) p6. "Entrance To Babylon" (Pendergrast, James T.)
RAINCOATS—ALBUMS
PH13028 736 (June 13, 1996) p78. "Looking In The Shadows"
RAISING CAIN (FILM)—PHOTOGRAPHS
PH13029 636 (August 6, 1992) p65. "Psychotic John Lithgow Lends A Hand"
PH13030 649 (February 4, 1993) p72. "[Raising Cain]"
RAITT, BONNIE—ALBUMS
PH13031 619-620 (December 12, 1991) p178. "Luck Of The Draw"
PH13032 679 (April 7, 1994) p71. "Longing In Theirs Hearts"
PH13033 682 (May 19, 1994) p120. "Longing In Theirs Hearts"
RAITT, BONNIE—ILLUSTRATIONS—PORTRAITS
PH13034 641 (October 15, 1992) p171. "[Bonnie Raitt]" (Carver, Steve)
PH13035 679 (April 7, 1994) p71. "The Raitt Stuff" (Smith, Owen)
RAITT, BONNIE—PHOTOGRAPHS
PH13036 619-620 (December 12, 1991) p37. "[Bonnie Raitt, Michael O'Keefe]"
PH13037 619-620 (December 12, 1991) p90. "Henley, Sting, Joel, Raitt" (Kaplan, Todd)
PH13038 619-620 (December 12, 1991) p18. "The Rock And Roll Hall Of Fame Jam" (Bellissimo, J.)
PH13039 627 (April 2, 1992) p11. "The Going Raitts: Bonnie And John"
PH13040 637 (August 20, 1992) p11. "Raitt And Clapton At Wembley" (Ollerenshow, Philip)
PH13041 645-646 (December 10, 1992) p98. "Clinton With Bonnie Raitt And Her Husband, Michael O'Keefe" (Jacobs, Michael)
PH13042 645-646 (December 10, 1992) p66. "Raitt Joins Slowhand Onstage At Wembley" (Ollerenshaw, Philip)
PH13043 651 (March 4, 1993) p17. "Bonnie Raitt, K. D. Lang And Barbara Orbison (from left)" (Mazur, Kevin)
PH13044 651 (March 4, 1993) p15. "Ruth Brown With Bonnie Raitt (left)" (Mazur, Kevin)
PH13045 671 (December 9, 1993) p32. "Raitt, Wallace And Browne (from left)" (Gardner, Christopher M.)
PH13046 678 (March 24, 1994) p27. "Bonnie Raitt Rocks For Choice" (Katz, Bruce)
PH13047 680 (April 21, 1994) p21. "[Bonnie Raitt]" (Naras)
PH13048 681 (May 5, 1994) p15. "Martha Reeves, Brown, Fred Schneider, Richard And Raitt At The Recent Awards (from left)" (Micelotta, Frank)
PH13049 691 (September 22, 1994) p38. "Bonnie Raitt Gives It Up In Philly" (Weiner, Scott)
PH13050 703 (March 9, 1995) p21. "Bonnie Raitt, Tom Hanks, Melissa Etheridge (from left)" (Berliner, A.)
PH13051 706 (April 20, 1995) p15. "Bonnie Raitt, Mistress Of Sensitivity Lennox, Carly Simon And Crow (from left)" (Busacca, Larry)
PH13052 711 (June 29, 1995) p18. "B. B. King, Robert Cray, Buddy Guy, Art Neville, Jimmie Vaughan, Clapton, Raitt And Tommy Shannon" (Long, Andrew)
PH13053 718 (October 5, 1995) p21. "[Bonnie Raitt & Jackson Browne]" (Paul, Jonathan)
PH13054 741 (August 22, 1996) p36. "Environmentally Sound Performer Bonnie Raitt" (Greyshock, Caroline)
PH13055 745 (October 17, 1996) p28. "Bonnie Raitt (left) Joins Bella Abzug In Mocking Bob Dole In Chicago" (Natkin, Paul)
RAITT, BONNIE—PHOTOGRAPHS—PORTRAITS
PH13056 619-620 (December 12, 1991) p53. "...And Bonnie Raitt (below) Release Their Creations" (Oida, Hideo)
PH13057 643 (November 12, 1992) p92. "Bonnie Raitt" (Weber, Bruce)
PH13058 750-751 (December 26, 1996) p78. "Bonnie Raitt"
RAITT, JOHN—PHOTOGRAPHS
PH13059 627 (April 2, 1992) p11. "The Going Raitts: Bonnie And John"
RAJASTHAN CANAL WORKS, INDIA—PHOTOGRAPHS
PH13060 665 (September 16, 1993) pp54-58. "Workers of The World" (Salgado, Sebastiao)
RAKIM—PHOTOGRAPHS—PORTRAITS
PH13061 707 (May 4, 1995) p32. "He's Baack!: Rap Master Rakim" (Abbott, W.)
RAMONE, DEE DEE—PHOTOGRAPHS
PH13062 628 (April 16, 1992) p13. "Dee Dee Ramone Onstage In Detroit" (Schwab, Bill)
RAMONE, JOEY—PHOTOGRAPHS
PH13063 652 (March 18, 1993) p23. "Jett Joins Two Ramones At New York Gig" (Mazur, Kevin)
PH13064 677 (March 10, 1994) p15. "Joey Ramone In A Pinhead Power Salute" (Mott, Tony)

PH13065 678 (March 24, 1994) p16. "[Joey Ramone]" (Danelian, Stephen)
PH13066 688 (August 11, 1994) p18. "Debbie Harry Greets Joey, The Big Birthday Boy" (Banks, Paul)
PH13067 735 (May 30, 1996) p13. "Do You Feel Lucky Today?"
PH13068 741 (August 22, 1996) p31. "Soundgarden's Cornell,. Psychotica's Briggs And Joey Ramone" (Blakesberg, Jay)
PH13069 743 (September 19, 1996) p19. "Soundgarden's Chris Cornell (left) With Joey Ramone And His Little Pals, The New York Dolls" (Di Santo, Anna)
RAMONES—ALBUMS
PH13070 617 (November 14, 1991) p137. "The Ramones" (Bayley, Roberta)
PH13071 642 (October 29, 1992) p74. "Mondo Bizarro"
PH13072 712-713 (July 13, 1995) p111. "Adios Amigos"
RAMONES—PHOTOGRAPHS
PH13073 670 (November 25, 1993) p38. "The Ramones get Psychedelic With Their New Album Of Cover Tunes" (DuBose, George)
PH13074 711 (June 29, 1995) p23. "Adios: End Of The Road For The Ramones?" (Roberts, Ebet)
PH13075 724-725 (December 28, 1995) p48. "Johnny, Joey, Marky And Dee Dee (from left) Called It Quits" (Roberts, Ebet)
RANALDO, LEE—PHOTOGRAPHS
PH13076 634-635 (July 9, 1992) p33. "Steve Shelley, Kim Gordon, Lee Ranaldo And Thurston Moore (from left)"
PH13077 637 (August 20, 1992) p9. "Steve Shelley, Kim Gordon, Lee Ranaldo, Shake-A-Leg's Harry Horgan, Moore, Hersh And David Narcizo (from left)" (Robicheau, Paul)
PH13078 691 (September 22, 1994) p58. "Moore (right) And Ranaldo (center) With Glenn Branca"
PH13079 691 (September 22, 1994) p56. "Ranaldo, Gordon, Moore, Shelley (from left)" (Petersen, Naomi)
PH13080 695 (November 17, 1994) p84. "Sonic Youth" (Mark, Mary Ellen)
PH13081 702 (February 23, 1995) p20. "Lee Ranaldo, Moore, Coco And Watt (from left)" (Callahan, Kristin)
PH13082 712-713 (July 13, 1995) p32. "All The Way To Memphis: Moore, Shelley, Gordon And Ranaldo (from left)" (Day, Corinne)
PH13083 721 (November 16, 1995) p25. "Sonic Youth's Lee Ranaldo, Thurston Moore, Kim Gordon And Steve Shelley (from left) After Their 'State' Taping In New York" (Capak, R. J.)
RANALDO, LEE—PHOTOGRAPHS—PORTRAITS
PH13084 679 (April 7, 1994) p24. "The SOnic Set: Gordon, Moore, Ranaldo, Shelley (clockwise from top left)" (Watson, Norman)
RANCID—ALBUMS
PH13085 720 (November 2, 1995) p92. "And Out Come The Wolves"
RANCID—ILLUSTRATIONS
PH13086 719 (October 19, 1995) p10. "Punk Scale" (Pendergrast, James T.)
RANCID—PHOTOGRAPHS
PH13087 716 (September 7, 1995) p56. "Frederiksen And Armstrong Perfect The Art Of Speed Skanking At A Milwaukee Gig" (Garrity, Brian)
PH13088 716 (September 7, 1995) pp54-55. "Rancid: Lars Frederiksen, Tim Armstrong, Brett Reed, Matt Freeman (clockwise from top left)" (Vadukul, Nitin)
PH13089 724-725 (December 28, 1995) p48. "[Rancid]" (Johnson, Lisa)
PH13090 726 (January 25, 1996) p38. "Rancid's Tim Armstrong (left) And Lara Frederiksen" (Garrity, Brian)
RANCID—PHOTOGRAPHS—PORTRAITS
PH13091 701 (February 9, 1995) p29. "Mohawk Nation: Reed, Freeman, Armstrong And Frederiksen (from left)" (Muller, Michael)
RANDLE, THERESA—ILLUSTRATIONS
PH13092 732 (April 18, 1996) p77. "Phone Sex, Spike Style" (Brodner, Steve)
RANDLE, THERESA—PHOTOGRAPHS
PH13093 732 (April 18, 1996) p78. "Girl 6 Theresa Randle Heats Up The Line"
PH13094 732 (April 18, 1996) p78. "Leonard Thomas And Randle Fulfill A Blaxploitation Fantasy"
PH13095 732 (April 18, 1996) p78. "Madonna And Randle Flank Director Spike Lee"
RANKINE, LESLEY—PHOTOGRAPHS
PH13096 733 (May 2, 1996) p13. "David Byrne Visits Rankine's After-Show Party"
PH13097 741 (August 22, 1996) p36. "Jones And Rankine Try 'Kung Fu'" (Temme, Marty)
RANKINE, LESLEY—PHOTOGRAPHS—PORTRAITS
PH13098 729 (March 7, 1996) p24. "Lesley Rankine Of Ruby Co-Creates A Trip-Hop Dirge You Can Dance To" (Cultice, Joseph)
RANKS, SHABBA—ALBUMS
PH13099 645-646 (December 10, 1992) p169. ""X"-Tra Naked"
RANKS, SHABBA—PHOTOGRAPHS
PH13100 656 (May 13, 1993) p21. "...And Ranks" (Haddi, Michael)
PH13101 672-673 (December 23, 1993) p28. "Below: Shabba Ranks" (Ford, Larry)
PH13102 676 (February 24, 1994) p44. "Shabba Ranks, The King Of Hard-Core Slackness" (Ford, Larry)
RANSOM (FILM)—ILLUSTRATIONS
PH13103 748 (November 28, 1996) p141. "Daddy Braveheart: Mel Gibson Shows The Rebel Chops Of A Scottish Warrior As A New York Tycoon Out To Save His Kidnapped Son By Whatever Means Necessary" (Brodner, Steve)
RANSOM (FILM)—PHOTOGRAPHS
PH13104 743 (September 19, 1996) p88. "Going For The Gold"
PH13105 748 (November 28, 1996) p142. "Gibson With Son Nolte"
RAP MUSIC—ILLUSTRATIONS
PH13106 645-646 (December 10, 1992) p79. "[Rap Music]" (Aitken, Doug)
PH13107 666 (September 30, 1993) p56. "[Hip Hop]"
PH13108 679 (April 7, 1994) p73. "Rap Up" (Beck, Melinda)
RAPAPORT, MICHAEL—PHOTOGRAPHS
PH13109 642 (October 29, 1992) p77. "Zebrahead"
RAPP, ANTHONY—PHOTOGRAPHS
PH13110 734 (May 16, 1996) p58. "[Anthony Rapp]" (Hom, Marc)
THE RAPTURE (FILM)—PHOTOGRAPHS
PH13111 615 (October 17, 1991) p101. "A Presaved Mimi Rogers Tries A Three-Way"
RAPTURE (VIDEO)—PHOTOGRAPHS
PH13112 667 (October 14, 1993) p98. "'Rapture': Debbie Harry's Rap Video"
RASPBERRIES—PHOTOGRAPHS—PORTRAITS
PH13113 685 (June 30, 1994) p32. "[Raspberries]"
RATDOG—PHOTOGRAPHS
PH13114 726 (January 25, 1996) p24. "Wasserman (left) And Weir Perform As Ratdog" (Franckling, Ken)
PH13115 750-751 (December 26, 1996) p68. "Dead Again: Ratdog At This Summer's Further Festival" (Millman, Susana)
RATHER, DAN—PHOTOGRAPHS
PH13116 667 (October 14, 1993) p45. "Bussing Connie Chung At A Press Conference Earlier This Year"
PH13117 667 (October 14, 1993) p45. "In A Shoving Match With Security Guards At The '68 Democratic Convention"
PH13118 667 (October 14, 1993) p45. "In Tiananmen Square In '89"
PH13119 667 (October 14, 1993) p44. "Rather At Rest: After Saying Goodbye To Richard Milhous Nixon On Aug. 9, 1974"
PH13120 667 (October 14, 1993) p45. "With An Afgan Rebel In '80"

RAVENSWOOD, WEST VIRGINIA—PHOTOGRAPHS
PH13121 629 (April 30, 1992) p46. "At Local 5668: The Waiting Has Been Going On For A Year And A Half" (De Keyzer, Carl)
PH13122 629 (April 30, 1992) p46. "At The Union Checkpoint" (De Keyzer, Carl)
PH13123 629 (April 30, 1992) pp44-45. "[Union Members]" (De Keyzer, Carl)
RAVES—PHOTOGRAPHS
PH13124 679 (April 7, 1994) p19. "The Center Of A West Coast Rave" (Blakesberg, Jay)
PH13125 679 (April 7, 1994) p15. "A San Francisco Rave" (Blakesberg, Jay)
RAWHIDE (TELEVISION SHOW)—PHOTOGRAPHS
PH13126 637 (August 20, 1992) p57. "Eastwood's Grizzled Face Reflects The Long Road He's Traveled Since 'Rawhide' (right)"
RAY, AMY—PHOTOGRAPHS
PH13127 684 (June 16, 1994) p36. "Indigo Girl Emily Saliers, Nanci Griffith, Browne, Carpenter, Indigo Girl Amy Ray" (Diamond, Rick)
PH13128 695 (November 17, 1994) p95. "Indigo Girls" (Ford, Charles)
PH13129 712-713 (July 13, 1995) p45. "Indigo Girls Emily Saliers (left), Amy Ray (center) On The White Earth Reservation, In Minnesota" (Pickett, Keri)
PH13130 733 (May 2, 1996) p22. "Indigo Girls Emily Saliers (left) And Amy Ray"
RAY AND GLOVER—ALBUMS
PH13131 682 (May 19, 1994) p103. "Picture Has Faded"
RAY, TOM—PHOTOGRAPHS
PH13132 730 (March 21, 1996) p21. "Bottle Rockets Tom Parr, Tom Ray, Brian Henneman, Mark Ortmann (from left)"
RAYNE, APRIL—PHOTOGRAPHS—PORTRAITS
PH13133 693 (October 20, 1994) p75. "Actress April Rayne, Who Crossed Over With A Role In A Mainstream Movie"
REA, STEPHEN—PHOTOGRAPHS
PH13135 653 (April 1, 1993) p57. "The Crying Game"
READMAN, ALICE—PHOTOGRAPHS
PH13136 657 (May 27, 1993) p16. "Auteur, Auteur: Banbury, Haines, Collins And Readman (clockwise from left)" (Lass, Imke)
REAGAN, RONALD—PHOTOGRAPHS
PH13137 664 (September 2, 1993) p39. "What Difference Does A Decade Make? Gergen With Ronald Reagan And Larry Speakes, May 1982" (Kennerly, David Hume)
THE REAL WORLD (TELEVISION SHOW)—ILLUSTRATIONS
PH13138 742 (September 5, 1996) p71. "[The Real World]" (Matcho, Mark)
THE REAL WORLD (TELEVISION SHOW)—PHOTOGRAPHS
PH13139 670 (November 25, 1993) p100. "Even Better Than The Real Thing: Dominic And Tami Pucker Up For The Camera" (Ragel, Jon)
PH13140 670 (November 25, 1993) p104. "Now I Wanna Be Your Dog: Last Year's 'World' Crew Gets Down In Soho Loft"
PH13141 670 (November 25, 1993) p99. "The 'Real' Deal: Jon, Beth A., Irene, Beth, Dominic, Tami And Glen (from left) On A Venice, Calif., Beach" (Ragel, Jon)
REALITY BITES (FILM)—ILLUSTRATIONS
PH13142 677 (March 10, 1994) p59. "Twenty Something" (Ryden, Mark)
REALITY BITES (FILM)—PHOTOGRAPHS
PH13143 677 (March 10, 1994) p47. "Future Hazy, Try Again: Ryder And Her 'Reality Bites' Boyfriend, Ethan Hawke"
PH13144 677 (March 10, 1994) p60. "Stiller (right) Directs"
PH13145 677 (March 10, 1994) p60. "Zahn, Ryder, Garofalo And Hawke Face A Shaky Future (from left)"
PH13146 703 (March 9, 1995) p49. "Reality Bites Back: Hawke On The Set With Ryder" (Redin, Van)
REALITY, MAXIM—PHOTOGRAPHS
PH13147 715 (August 24, 1995) p34. "Reality Raps While Flint Gets Down (from left)" (Capak, R. J.)
A REASON TO BELIEVE (FILM)—PHOTOGRAPHS
PH13148 717 (September 21, 1995) p90. "Frat Brothers At A Toga Party That Ends In Rape"
REATEGUI, EDDIE—PHOTOGRAPHS
PH13149 706 (April 20, 1995) pp[enc.18]. "Skating At Chicken's Pool" (Seliger, Mark)
RECORD COMPANIES—ILLUSTRATIONS
PH13150 666 (September 30, 1993) p15. "[Baby Boomers]" (Plunkert, David)
RECORD STORES—PHOTOGRAPHS
PH13151 638 (September 3, 1992) p14. "Most Chain Stores Are A Huge Bore" (Mazur, Kevin)
PH13152 638 (September 3, 1992) p13. "The Virgin Megastore In Paris" (Mounir)
RECORDS—ILLUSTRATIONS
PH13153 624 (February 20, 1992) p42. "Replays"
PH13154 629 (April 30, 1992) p57. "Replays"
PH13155 634-635 (July 9, 1992) p102. "On The Edge"
PH13156 636 (August 6, 1992) p66. "Replays"
PH13157 639 (September 17, 1992) p96. "On The Edge"
PH13158 642 (October 29, 1992) p28. "[CD]" (Corio, Paul)
PH13159 645-646 (December 10, 1992) p177. "On The Edge"
PH13160 645-646 (December 10, 1992) p163. "The Year In Records" (Blechman, R. O.)
PH13161 648 (January 21, 1993) p50. "[Replays]"
PH13162 649 (February 4, 1993) p18. "[Singles]" (McCauley, Adam)
PH13163 660-661 (July 8, 1993) p113. "On The Edge"
PH13164 664 (September 2, 1993) p64. "Replays"
PH13165 667 (October 14, 1993) p121. "On The Edge"
PH13166 669 (November 11, 1993) p77. "Replays"
PH13167 672-673 (December 23, 1993) p154. "On The Edge"
PH13168 682 (May 19, 1994) p100. "Replays"
PH13169 685 (June 30, 1994) p77. "Replays"
PH13170 684 (June 16, 1994) p110. "On The Edge"
PH13171 700 (January 26, 1995) p22. "[Records]" (Steinberg, James)
PH13172 705 (April 6, 1995) p62. "Replays"
PH13173 710 (June 15, 1995) p82. "Spoken Word" (Caldicott, Karen)
PH13174 714 (August 10, 1995) p59. "Replays"
PH13175 720 (November 2, 1995) p69. "On The Edge"
PH13176 723 (December 14, 1995) p86. "How Ya Doin' Poughkeepsie" (Corio, Paul)
PH13177 736 (June 13, 1996) p85. "On The Edge"
PH13178 740 (August 8, 1996) p62. "On The Edge"
RECORDS—LETTERING
PH13179 750-751 (December 26, 1996) p183. "The Year In Recordings" (MacDonald, Ross)
RED (FILM)—PHOTOGRAPHS
PH13180 702 (February 23, 1995) p80. "Red"
PH13181 705 (April 6, 1995) p69. "Oscar Rejects"
RED AUNTS—PHOTOGRAPHS
PH13182 710 (June 15, 1995) p42. "[Red Aunts]" (Hole, Jimmy)
RED FIVE—PHOTOGRAPHS
PH13183 743 (September 19, 1996) p20. "Red Five"
RED HOT + RIO (ALBUM)—PHOTOGRAPHS
PH13184 742 (September 5, 1996) p23. "Red Hot's Rainbow Coalition"
RED HOT CHILI PEPPERS—ALBUMS
PH13185 619-620 (December 12, 1991) p174. "BloodSugarSexMagik"
PH13186 625 (March 5, 1992) p61. "BloodSugarSexMagik"
PH13187 718 (October 5, 1995) p67. "One Hot Minute"
PH13188 720 (November 2, 1995) p92. "One Hot Minute"
PH13189 721 (November 16, 1995) p128. "One Hot Minute"
RED HOT CHILI PEPPERS—ILLUSTRATIONS
PH13190 670 (November 25, 1993) p8. "Campbell Soup" (Pendergrast, James T.)

PH13191 718 (October 5, 1995) p67. "Heartbreak Kids" (Rosen, Jonathon)
PH13192 722 (November 30, 1995) p14. "[Red Hot Chili Peppers]" (Pendergrast, James T.)

RED HOT CHILI PEPPERS—PHOTOGRAPHS
PH13193 629 (April 30, 1992) p23. "John Frusciante, Anthony Kiedis, Chad Smith And Flea (from left)" (Cuffaro, Chris)
PH13194 639 (September 17, 1992) p60. "Chili Peppers Flea (left) And Kiedis" (Blakesberg, Jay)
PH13195 639 (September 17, 1992) p64. "Ice-T And The Boo-Yaa Tribe Join The Chili Peppers" (Blakesberg, Jay)
PH13196 645-646 (December 10, 1992) p69. "The Chili Peppers (below)..." (Blakesberg, Jay)
PH13197 660-661 (July 8, 1993) p17. "Man Overboard: Smith, Kiedis, Marshall And Flea" (Leialoha, Mark)
PH13198 667 (October 14, 1993) p77. "Peppers: The Video That Keeps On Giving"
PH13199 670 (November 25, 1993) p88. "[Red Hot Chili Peppers]" (Seliger, Mark)
PH13200 679 (April 7, 1994) p49. "We Three: Hillel Slovak, Kiedis And Flea In '82 (from left)" (Shear, Jack)
PH13201 691 (September 22, 1994) p62. "The Chili Peppers Salute Jimi Hendrix" (Mazur, Kevin)
PH13202 692 (October 6, 1994) p17. "Peppers Roast: Flea, Anthony Kiedis, Dave Navarro, Chad Smith (from left)" (Mazur, Kevin)
PH13203 709 (June 1, 1995) p21. "RHCPs (from left): Flea, Chad Smith, Dave Navarro And Anthony Kiedis" (Streiber, Art)
PH13204 719 (October 19, 1995) p56. "'86: Irons, Slovak, Flea, Kiedis (from left) Backstage At The Ritz, In New York" (Gershoff, Gary)
PH13205 719 (October 19, 1995) pp52-53. "Anthony Kiedis And Flea" (Corbijn, Anton)
PH13206 719 (October 19, 1995) pp54-55. "Flea, Kiedis" (Corbijn, Anton)
PH13207 719 (October 19, 1995) p55. "Guitarist Navarro (left) Bonds With Drummer Smith" (Corbijn, Anton)
PH13208 719 (October 19, 1995) p58. "Red Hot Chili Peppers, '95: Dave Navarro, Anthony Kiedis, Flea An Chad Smith (from left)" (Corbijn, Anton)
PH13209 719 (October 19, 1995) pp[cover[. "Red Hot Chili Peppers: Sound Bodies, Warped Minds" (Corbijn, Anton)
PH13210 719 (October 19, 1995) p60. "Woodstock 1994: Flea And Kiedis" (Weiner, Scott)
PH13211 720 (November 2, 1995) p51. "Red Hot Chili Peppers" (Seliger, Mark)
PH13212 722 (November 30, 1995) p19. "[Red Hot Chili Peppers]" (Musto, Ilpo)
PH13213 731 (April 4, 1996) p17. "Bush Covers? Chili Peppers Frontman Anthony Kiedis, Bassist Flea, The Not-Unattractive Navarro And Drummer Chad Smith (from left)" (Baehler, Chapman)

RED HOT CHILI PEPPERS—PHOTOGRAPHS—PORTRAITS
PH13214 633 (June 25, 1992) pp26-28. "[Red Hot Chili Peppers]" (Seliger, Mark)
PH13215 633 (June 25, 1992) pp[cover]. "Red Hot Chili Peppers" (Seliger, Mark)
PH13216 645-646 (December 10, 1992) pp[cover]. "1992 Yearbook" (Seliger, Mark)
PH13217 645-646 (December 10, 1992) p153. "The Red Hot Chili Peppers, 1992"

RED HOUSE PAINTERS—ALBUMS
PH13218 670 (November 25, 1993) p120. "Red House Painters"
PH13219 741 (August 22, 1996) p100. "Songs For A Blue Guitar"

RED HOUSE PAINTERS—PHOTOGRAPHS
PH13220 665 (September 16, 1993) p25. "In The Red: Mack, Vessel, Kozelek, Koutsos (from left)" (Blakesberg, Jay)
PH13221 693 (October 20, 1994) p48. "Red House Painters Make 4AD Party" (Blakesberg, Jay)

RED LANTERN (FILM)—PHOTOGRAPHS
PH13222 653 (April 1, 1993) p57. "Red Lantern"

RED RED MEAT—ALBUMS
PH13223 680 (April 21, 1994) pp8587. "Jimmywine Majestic"

RED ROAD—ALBUMS
PH13224 698-699 (December 29, 1994) p170. "Music For The Native Americans"

RED ROCK WEST (FILM)—PHOTOGRAPHS
PH13225 681 (May 5, 1994) p48. "Now Playing"
PH13226 705 (April 6, 1995) p69. "Oscar Rejects"

REDDING, NOEL—PHOTOGRAPHS
PH13227 625 (March 5, 1992) p17. "Mitch Mitchell, Noel Redding, Young And Al Hendrix (from left)" (Elgar, Nick)
PH13228 625 (March 5, 1992) p17. "Neil Young Takes Center Stage During The All-Star-Jam Finale" (Gershoff, Gary)
PH13229 712-713 (July 13, 1995) p45. "The Experience, Circa '67: Drummer Mitch Mitchell (left), Hendrix, bassist Redding"

REDDING, NOEL—PHOTOGRAPHS—PORTRAITS
PH13230 623 (February 6, 1992) p45. "Hendrix Found His Perfect Musical Accomplices In Noel Redding (left) And Mitch Mitchell (right)" (Mankowitz, Gered)

REDDING, OTIS—ILLUSTRATIONS
PH13231 669 (November 11, 1993) p76. "[Otis Redding]"

REDDING, OTIS—PHOTOGRAPHS
PH13232 720 (November 2, 1995) p51. "Otis Redding"

REDFORD, ROBERT—ILLUSTRATIONS
PH13233 655 (April 29, 1993) p67. "Fiscal Attraction" (Friedman, Drew)
PH13234 730 (March 21, 1996) p103. "The Sundance Kid Takes On TV" (Brodner, Steve)

REDFORD, ROBERT—PHOTOGRAPHS
PH13235 640 (October 1, 1992) p72. "Kingsley (left) Puts Redford On The Spot"
PH13236 642 (October 29, 1992) p78. "Redford (left) Directs Look-Alike Brad Pitt"
PH13237 652 (March 18, 1993) p47. "Sundance Founder Redford" (Michaelson, Randall)
PH13238 655 (April 29, 1993) p68. "Demi's Choice: Robert Redford (left) Or Woody Harrelson?"
PH13239 691 (September 22, 1994) p104. "Robert Redford, Left, Directs Actor Rob Morrow"
PH13240 692 (October 6, 1994) p76. "Brad Pitt And Craig Sheffer Take Direction On "A River Runs Through It""
PH13241 692 (October 6, 1994) p74. "In "Quiz Show," Director Redford (with actor Ralph Fiennes) Exposes An Infamous 1950s Television Scandal"
PH13242 692 (October 6, 1994) p76. "Redford And Actor Timothy Hutton Both Earned Oscars For "Ordinary People""
PH13243 692 (October 6, 1994) p76. "Redford Shares A Laugh With Freddy Fender And Ruben Blades On "The Milagro Beanfield War" Set"
PH13244 692 (October 6, 1994) p77. "With Ex-Wife Wagenen, 1975" (Claxton, William)
PH13245 730 (March 21, 1996) p104. "Pfeiffer And Redford Face Off (left)"
PH13246 730 (March 21, 1996) p104. "The SUndance Kid Gives A Press Conference"

REDFORD, ROBERT—PHOTOGRAPHS—PORTRAITS
PH13247 692 (October 6, 1994) p77. "The High-School Grad, 1954"
PH13248 692 (October 6, 1994) p72. "[Robert Redford]" (Watson, Albert)
PH13249 703 (March 9, 1995) p70. "Redford faces Tough Questions At Sundance" (Michelson, Randall)

REDGRAVE, VANESSA—PHOTOGRAPHS
PH13250 653 (April 1, 1993) p57. "Howards End"

REDI, JIM—PHOTOGRAPHS
PH13251 692 (October 6, 1994) p29. "The Jesus And Mary Chain's Jim Reid Croons To Mazzy Star Hope Sandoval" (Mayer, Jeffrey)

PH13252 Number not assigned.
REDMAN, JOSHUA—PHOTOGRAPHS
PH13253 700 (January 26, 1995) p53. "Young Jazz Turk Joshua Redman" (Ettlinger, Marion)
PH13254 708 (May 18, 1995) p18. "Velvet At The Vanguard: Lou Reed (left) with Joshua Redman" (Jackson, Gregory)
REDMAN, JOSHUA—PHOTOGRAPHS—PORTRAITS
PH13254a 656 (May 13, 1993) p72. "[Josh Redman]"
REECE, CHRIS—PHOTOGRAPHS
PH13255 634-635 (July 9, 1992) p32. "Chris Reece, Mike Ness, John Maurer And Dennis Danell (from left)" (Cuffaro, Chris)
REED, BRETT—PHOTOGRAPHS
PH13256 716 (September 7, 1995) pp54-55. "Rancid: Lars Frederiksen, Tim Armstrong, Brett Reed, Matt Freeman (clockwise from top left)" (Vadukul, Nitin)
REED, BRETT—PHOTOGRAPHS—PORTRAITS
PH13257 701 (February 9, 1995) p29. "Mohawk Nation: Reed, Freeman, Armstrong And Frederiksen (from left)" (Muller, Michael)
REED, ERIC—PHOTOGRAPHS
PH13258 686-687 (July 14, 1994) p78. "[Eric Reed]"
REED, JOHNNY—PHOTOGRAPHS—PORTRAITS
PH13259 659 (June 24, 1993) p48. "The Orioles: Sonny Til, Johnny Reed, Tommy Gaither, George Nelson And Alexander Sharp"
REED, LOU—ALBUMS
PH13260 622 (January 23, 1992) p43. "Magic And Loss"
PH13261 626 (March 19, 1992) p112. "Magic And Loss"
PH13262 645-646 (December 10, 1992) p164. "Magic And Loss"
PH13263 729 (March 7, 1996) p48. "Set The Twilight Reeling"
REED, LOU—ILLUSTRATIONS
PH13264 622 (January 23, 1992) p43. "Lou Reed's Death Letter" (Woodruff, Thomas)
REED, LOU—PHOTOGRAPHS
PH13265 621 (January 9, 1992) p11. "The Literary Lou Reed" (Uchitel, Diego)
PH13266 638 (September 3, 1992) p11. "Stewart And Reed At Leysin With Chrissie Hynde (from left)" (Allen, David)
PH13267 645-646 (December 10, 1992) p31. "Lou Reed" (Uchitel, Diego)
PH13268 645-646 (December 10, 1992) p85. "Lou Reed" (Mazur, Kevin)
PH13269 647 (January 7, 1993) p11. "Lou Reed Chats Up A Guest" (Elgar, Nick)
PH13270 648 (January 21, 1993) p11. "Lou Reed, John Cale And Sterling Morrison (from left) At NYU" (Andersen, Nancy)
PH13271 649 (February 4, 1993) p8. "Cash, Cockburn And Reed (from left)" (Ienner, Jimmy, Jr.)
PH13272 653 (April 1, 1993) p24. "Cash, Reed And Bloom Onstage In New York" (Capak, R. J.)
PH13273 658 (June 10, 1993) p60. "As Ziggy, With Iggy Pop And Lou Reed Circa 1972: 'We Knew We Were On The Wave Of Something'"
PH13274 662 (August 5, 1993) p28. "John Cale (left) And Lou Reed Doing The Velvet Underground" (Paton, Tim)
PH13275 665 (September 16, 1993) p32. "Gano, Lou Reed And Penn Jillette" (Capak, R. J.)
PH13276 669 (November 11, 1993) p27. "Lou Reed (left) Dropped In On Depeche Mode During Their Plugged Press Conference" (Mazur, Kevin)
PH13277 678 (March 24, 1994) p28. "Kristofferson, Williams, Vega, DJ Vin Scelsa And Lou Reed (from left)" (Roberts, Ebet)
PH13278 683 (June 2, 1994) p28. "Weir, Bruce Hornsby, Reed And Wasserman (from left) At The Trios Show" (Mazur, Kevin)
PH13279 702 (February 23, 1995) p50. "Moon Zappa Accepts Her Father's Award From Lou Reed" (Mazur, Kevin)
PH13280 708 (May 18, 1995) p18. "Velvet At The Vanguard: Lou Reed (left) with Joshua Redman" (Jackson, Gregory)
PH13281 718 (October 5, 1995) p46. "The Velvet Underground (clockwise from bottom left): Nico, Reed, Morrison, Cale And Tucker"
PH13282 719 (October 19, 1995) p42. "This Magic Moment: Lou Reed Gives His Best To Laurie Anderson Backstage" (Corbijn, Anton)
PH13283 720 (November 2, 1995) p49. "Lou Reed" (Kent, Andrew)
PH13284 723 (December 14, 1995) p53. "Jagger (middle) Celebrating Androgyny In The Glam-Rock '70s With Lou Reed (left) And David Bowie, Two Of The Many Who Followed In Jagger's Gender-Bending Footsteps"
PH13285 728 (February 22, 1996) p18. "Martha Morrison, Tucker, Cale And Reed (from left) Celebrate The Velvets' Induction" (Mazur, Kevin)
PH13286 729 (March 7, 1996) p9. "Don't You Know Who I Am, Damn It? Lou Reed Is Felt Up" (Ferreira, Albert)
PH13287 735 (May 30, 1996) p13. "Laurie Anderson, Reed And Wareham (from left) Post-Gig At Josie's, In New York" (Roberts, Ebet)
REED, LOU—PHOTOGRAPHS—PORTRAITS
PH13288 643 (November 12, 1992) p207. "Lou Reed" (Watson, Albert)
PH13289 659 (June 24, 1993) p17. "Tucker, Morrison, Cale And Reed Today (from left)" (Wood, Graham)
REED, NATHANIEL—PHOTOGRAPHS
PH13290 733 (May 2, 1996) p46. "Barley And Reed, The Greens' Secret Weapons" (Tavee, Tom)
REED, RALPH—PHOTOGRAPHS
PH13291 698-699 (December 29, 1994) p162. "Reed Assures The Faithful That Conservatism Will Be Rewarded In This Life" (Warburg, Jennifer)
PH13292 698-699 (December 29, 1994) p159. "Reed With Robertson At The Annual Convention Of The Christian Coalition" (Reinhard, Rick)
PH13293 729 (March 7, 1996) p42. "Reed Hands Out The Gospel At A Christian Coalition Convention In Washington, D.C." (Fink, Larry)
REEDER, SCOTT—PHOTOGRAPHS
PH13294 692 (October 6, 1994) p24. "Desert Storm: Kyuss' Homme, Reeder, Garcia And Hernandez (from left)" (Miller, Michael)
REESE, DELLA—PHOTOGRAPHS
PH13295 619-620 (December 12, 1991) p202. "Redd Foxx (with his 'Royal Family' costar, Della Reese) Died In 'Real Life'"
REEVES, KEANU—ILLUSTRATIONS
PH13296 685 (June 30, 1994) p79. "Die Hard On A Bus" (Pastrana, Robert M.)
REEVES, KEANU—PHOTOGRAPHS
PH13297 615 (October 17, 1991) p100. "River Phoenix (left) And Keanu Reeves Are Bad Boys Of The Road"
PH13298 665 (September 16, 1993) p77. "Worst Supporting Actor"
PH13299 685 (June 30, 1994) p80. "Swat Dude Keanu Reeves Puts Sandra Bullock In The Driver's Seat"
PH13300 698-699 (December 29, 1994) p194. "Reeves And Bullock Ride In "Speed""
PH13301 711 (June 29, 1995) p49. "Reeves in Something Fishy"
PH13302 715 (August 24, 1995) p110. "Lovers At Last: Sanchez-Gijon And Reeves"
PH13303 717 (September 21, 1995) p19. "Don't Quit Your Day Job: Reeves" (Mazur, Kevin)
PH13304 742 (September 5, 1996) p68. "Now Playing"
PH13305 742 (September 5, 1996) p21. "Yo! Lighten Up! It's Rock & Roll! Reeves Goes Sad-Core In Paris" (Roussier)
PH13306 744 (October 3, 1996) p78. "Cameron Diaz, Keanu Reeves" With 'Feeling'"
REEVES, MARTHA—PHOTOGRAPHS
PH13307 674 (January 27, 1994) p29. "Heat Wave: Dulli Onstage With Reeves" (Schwab, Bill)
PH13308 681 (May 5, 1994) p15. "Martha Reeves, Brown, Fred Schneider, Richard And Raitt At The Recent Awards (from left)"

(Micelotta, Frank)
PH13309 724-725 (December 28, 1995) p56. "The Time Was Right: Crow, Hynde, Browne And Reeves (from left)" (Mazur, Kevin)
REEVES, PERREY—PHOTOGRAPHS
PH13310 734 (May 16, 1996) p41. "With His Fictional Vampire Lover And Real-Life Ex-Girlfriend, Perrey Reeves"
THE REF (FILM)—PHOTOGRAPHS
PH13311 679 (April 7, 1994) p83. "Denis Leary Refs Judy Davis And Kevin Spacey"
REFRESHMENTS—PHOTOGRAPHS
PH13312 740 (August 8, 1996) p76. "P. H. Naffah, Roger Clyne, Brian Blush And Arthur 'Buddy' Edwards (from left)" (Ragel, Jon)
REGARDING HENRY (FILM)—PHOTOGRAPHS
PH13313 619-620 (December 12, 1991) p194. "Male Wimps And Female Warriors"
REID, ELLEN—PHOTOGRAPHS
PH13314 681 (May 5, 1994) p16. "Big Dummies: Dan And Brad Roberts, Darvill, Dorge And Reid (from left)" (Blakesberg, Jay)
REID, JIM—PHOTOGRAPHS
PH13315 698-699 (December 29, 1994) p60. "Jim Reid Pairs Up With Hope Sandoval" (Roberts, Ebet)
PH13316 720 (November 2, 1995) p25. "JAMC's Jim (left) And William Reid Vent"
REID, L. A.—PHOTOGRAPHS
PH13317 696 (December 1, 1994) p105. "The Dream Team: Daryl Simmons, Babyface And L.A. Reid At The 1993 Grammys" (Deguire, Greg)
REID, L. A.—PHOTOGRAPHS—PORTRAITS
PH13318 724-725 (December 28, 1995) p45. "Babyface (top) And L.A. Reid"
REID, VERNON—PHOTOGRAPHS
PH13319 622 (January 23, 1992) p11. "Vernon Reid (left) And Melvin Gibbs" (Mazur, Kevin)
PH13320 623 (February 6, 1992) p13. "Vernon Reid, Will Calhoun And Melvin Gibbs (from left)" (Mazur, Kevin)
PH13321 629 (April 30, 1992) p11. "Chapman Onstage With Accordionist Roy Bittan And Vernon Reid" (Mazur, Kevin)
PH13322 637 (August 20, 1992) p9. "Living Colour's Vernon Reid, Corey Glover And Doug Wimbish (from left)" (Mazur, Kevin)
PH13323 648 (January 21, 1993) p18. "Corey Glover, Will Calhoun, Vernon Reid And Doug Wimbish (from left)" (Leialoha, Mark)
PH13324 660-661 (July 8, 1993) p92. "Reid: 'The Ghost Of Hendrix Moves Over This Music In So Many Ways.'" (Delany, Ron)
PH13325 686-687 (July 14, 1994) p42. "Media Ho Henry Rollins, Vernon Reid And Rollins Guitarist Chris Haskett" (Malluk, Eddie)
PH13326 692 (October 6, 1994) p15. "Vernon Reid Salutes The Late Sonny Sharrock" (Atlan, David)
PH13327 733 (May 2, 1996) p22. "From Left: Prince Paul, Reid And Teo Macero At The Manhattan Center" (Gershoff, Gary)
REID, VERNON—PHOTOGRAPHS—PORTRAITS
PH13328 660-661 (July 8, 1993) p88. "The Band (from left): Will Calhoun, Vernon Reid, Doug Wimbish And Corey Glover" (Malfer)
PH13329 660-661 (July 8, 1993) p87. "[Vernon Reid]" (Watson, Albert)
PH13330 695 (November 17, 1994) p42. "Vernon Reid Of Living Colour" (Ravid, Joyce)
REID, WILLIAM—PHOTOGRAPHS
PH13331 720 (November 2, 1995) p25. "JAMC's Jim (left) And William Reid Vent"
REILLY, JOHN C.—PHOTOGRAPHS
PH13332 693 (October 20, 1994) p156. "Woman Warrior Streep (above, with Reilly and Bacon) Braves The Rapids To Save Son Mazzello And Husband Strathairn (left)"
REINER, ROB—PHOTOGRAPHS
PH13333 722 (November 30, 1995) p76. "Rob Reiner Directs Michael Douglas As The Prez"
REIS, JOHN—PHOTOGRAPHS
PH13334 689 (August 25, 1994) p44. "All Together Now: Trombino, Atom, Kennedy, Reis, N.D., Petey X, Apollo 9, Froberg (from left)" (Cuffaro, Chris)
PH13335 745 (October 17, 1996) p28. "A Silver-Lame Clad John Reis At The Reading Festival, In Britain" (Gordon, Jonathan)
REISER, PAUL—PHOTOGRAPHS
PH13336 706 (April 20, 1995) pp[enc.6-9,12]. "[Paul Reiser]" (Avenaim, Jerry)
PH13337 706 (April 20, 1995) pp[enc.cover]. "Spring 95" (Avenaim, Jerry)
REISER, PAUL—PHOTOGRAPHS—PORTRAITS
PH13338 706 (April 20, 1995) pp[enc.10]. "[Paul Reiser]" (Avenaim, Jerry)
REISS, VALERIE—PHOTOGRAPHS
PH13339 704 (March 23, 1995) p84. "Answer Lady: Reiss, A K A Madame Exotica Of Beloit College" (Kuehn, Karen)
RELATIVITY (TELEVISION SHOW)—PHOTOGRAPHS
PH13340 743 (September 19, 1996) pp94,96. "[Television]"
RELF, KEITH—PHOTOGRAPHS
PH13341 623 (February 6, 1992) p51. "The Yardbirds, Circa 1964 (from left): Chris Dreja, Keith Reif, Paul Samwell-Smith, Eric Clapton And Jim McCarty"
RELF, KEITH—PHOTOGRAPHS—PORTRAITS
PH13342 655 (April 29, 1993) p34. "Slowhand (at bottom left) With The Yardbirds: Chris Dreja, Jim McCarty, Paul Samwell-Smith And Keith Relf (clockwise from top left)"
RELIGION—ILLUSTRATIONS
PH13343 729 (March 7, 1996) p41. "[Christian Right]" (Holland, Brad)
PH13344 732 (April 18, 1996) p16. "The Path Of Righteousness—The Path Of Self-Righteousness" (Pendergrast, James T.)
R.E.M.—ALBUMS
PH13345 617 (November 14, 1991) p149. "Document" (Meister, Michael)
PH13346 617 (November 14, 1991) p149. "Document" (McKay, Jim)
PH13347 619-620 (December 12, 1991) p165. "Out Of Time"
PH13348 642 (October 29, 1992) p68. "Automatic For The People"
PH13349 645-646 (December 10, 1992) p164. "Automatic For The People"
PH13350 650 (February 18, 1993) p72. "Automatic For The People"
PH13351 651 (March 4, 1993) p80. "Automatic For The People"
PH13352 692 (October 6, 1994) p83. "Monster"
PH13353 696 (December 1, 1994) p144. "Monster"
PH13354 698-699 (December 29, 1994) p170. "Monster"
PH13355 743 (September 19, 1996) p79. "New Adventures In Hi-Fi"
R.E.M.—ILLUSTRATIONS
PH13356 642 (October 29, 1992) p68. "A Kinder, Gentler R.E.M." (Coe, Sue)
PH13357 692 (October 6, 1994) p83. "Evolve Or Die" (Hungry Dog Studio)
PH13358 697 (December 15, 1994) p120. "R.E.M.: Monster Mash" (Clayton, Christian)
PH13359 743 (September 19, 1996) p79. "New Day Rising" (Fotheringham, Edwin)
PH13360 748 (November 28, 1996) p22. "Employees-Geeks" (Pendergrast, James T.)
R.E.M.—ILLUSTRATIONS—LETTERING
PH13361 625 (March 5, 1992) p45. "R.E.M.: Artist Of The Year" (Karl, Anita)
R.E.M.—PHOTOGRAPHS
PH13362 619-620 (December 12, 1991) pp[cover]. "1991 Yearbook" (Ockenfels, Frank W.)

PH13363 619-620 (December 12, 1991) p37. "Billy Bragg (second from right) Joins R.E.M. On 'Mountain Stage'" (Cohrssen, James)
PH13364 619-620 (December 12, 1991) p79. "Life's Rich Pageant: R.E.M., Short A Buck" (Mazur, Kevin)
PH13365 619-620 (December 12, 1991) p29. "R.E.M. Graduated From College-Rock Darling To Big-Time Hero With 'Out Of Time'" (Ockenfels, Frank W.)
PH13366 619-620 (December 12, 1991) p33. "R.E.M.'s 'Losing My Religion'"
PH13367 625 (March 5, 1992) p48. "At The Home In Athens: Bill Berry, Peter Buck, Michael Stipe And Mike Mills" (Watson, Albert)
PH13368 625 (March 5, 1992) p53. "R.E.M. Conquers World, Readers, Critics" (Ockenfels, Frank W.)
PH13369 628 (April 16, 1992) p11. "R.E.M.'s Mike Mills, Michael Stipe, Peter Buck And Bill Berry (from left)" (Mazur, Kevin)
PH13370 640 (October 1, 1992) p20. "Michael Stipe, Peter Buck, Mike Mills And Bill Berry (clockwise from left)" (Corbijn, Anton)
PH13371 645-646 (December 10, 1992) p32. "R.E.M." (Mazur, Kevin)
PH13372 647 (January 7, 1993) p9. "From Left: Mike Mills, Buck, Bill Berry and Stipe" (Colletti, Steve)
PH13373 667 (October 14, 1993) p68. "'Losing' Is Winning: Stipe And Company Make R.E.M.'s Video A Religious Experience"
PH13374 680 (April 21, 1994) p34. "Stephanopoulos (right) Meets R.E.M." (Mazur, Kevin)
PH13375 693 (October 20, 1994) p27. "R.E.M.'s Bill Berry, Michael Stipe, Peter Buck, Mike Mills" (Mazur, Kevin)
PH13376 698-699 (December 29, 1994) p37. "Buck Stops Here: R.E.M. And Stephanopoulos (with grin)" (Mazur, Kevin)
PH13377 698-699 (December 29, 1994) p66. "We Are The World: R.E.M. Score With A Monster Of A Hit" (Carter, Keith)
PH13378 704 (March 23, 1995) p32. "Band On The Run: Berry, Mills, Stipe And Buck (above, from left)" (Sheehan, Tom)
PH13379 704 (March 23, 1995) p32. "Boy In The Hood: Stipe Onstage In Sydney (top)" (Liguz, Andrzej)
PH13380 704 (March 23, 1995) p24. "[R.E.M.]"
PH13381 726 (January 25, 1996) p42. "Peter Buck, Michael Stipe, Bill Berry, Mike Mills" (Jensen, David)
PH13382 737 (June 27, 1996) p29. "R.E.M.'s Mike Mills, Bill Berry, Stipe And Buck (from left) Have Split With Their Longtime Manager" (Rider, Paul)
PH13383 745 (October 17, 1996) pp[cover]. "R.E.M." (Corbijn, Anton)

R.E.M.—PHOTOGRAPHS—PORTRAITS

PH13384 625 (March 5, 1992) pp[cover]. "R.E.M.: Artist Of The Year" (Watson, Albert)
PH13385 643 (November 12, 1992) p181. "R.E.M." (Markus, Kurt)
PH13386 645-646 (December 10, 1992) pp[cover]. "1992 Yearbook" (Watson, Albert)
PH13387 645-646 (December 10, 1992) p91. "The Dark Side Of R.E.M." (Corbijn, Anton)
PH13388 693 (October 20, 1994) pp[cover]. "R.E.M.: Sex & Noise" (Seliger, Mark)
PH13389 700 (January 26, 1995) p52. "Crush With Eyeglasses: R.E.M. Wow Critics Again" (Seliger, Mark)

THE REMAINS OF THE DAY (FILM)—PHOTOGRAPHS

PH13390 670 (November 25, 1993) p125. "Love Unspoken: Anthony Hopkins And Emma Thompson"
PH13391 672-673 (December 23, 1993) p173. "Repressed Man Of The Year"
PH13392 678 (March 24, 1994) p100. "Oscar's Choices: 'Schindler's List,' 'The Piano,' 'The Remains Of the Day,' 'In The Name Of The Father,' 'The Fugitive' (from left)"

REN & STEMPY—ILLUSTRATIONS

PH13393 630 (May 14, 1992) p52. "[Ren & Stempy]"

RENAISSANCE MAN (FILM)—PHOTOGRAPHS

PH13394 684 (June 16, 1994) p116. "Funny: DeVito Instructs Mark In "Renaissance man""

RENFRO, BRAD—PHOTOGRAPHS

PH13395 688 (August 11, 1994) p62. "It's A Day In Court For Lawyer Sarandon And Renfro"

RENI—PHOTOGRAPHS

PH13396 724-725 (December 28, 1995) p39. "Stoned, Dethroned: Mani, Squire, Brown, Reni (from left)" (Otte, Sylvia)

RENO, JEAN—PHOTOGRAPHS

PH13397 694 (November 3, 1994) p106. "Hitman Reno Teaches Orphan Portman A Trade"

RENT (OPERA)—PHOTOGRAPHS

PH13398 737 (June 27, 1996) p59. "The 'Rent' Cast Look Like The Hippies In 'Hair,' With Thrift-Store Garb And East Village 'Tudes"

REPLACEMENTS—PHOTOGRAPHS

PH13399 619-620 (December 12, 1991) p19. "The Replacements" (Corrigan, Daniel)
PH13400 659 (June 24, 1993) p54. "Early Mats: Westerberg, Bob Stinson, Mars And Tommy Stinson (from left)" (Pasley, Richard)
PH13401 659 (June 24, 1993) p52. "The Later Mats Incarnation: Tommy Stinson, Westerberg, Slim Dunlap And Chris Mars (from left)" (Matheu, Robert)

REPUBLICA—PHOTOGRAPHS

PH13402 744 (October 3, 1996) p84. "Andy Todd, Saffron And Tim Dorney (from left)" (Garner, Kate)

REPUBLICAN PARTY—ILLUSTRATIONS

PH13403 622 (January 23, 1992) p4. "GOP Hats In The Ring" (Pendergrast, James T.)
PH13404 627 (April 2, 1992) p25. "[Democratic Party, Republican Party]" (Cronin, Brian)
PH13405 700 (January 26, 1995) pp35-36. "[Contract With America]" (Kuper, Peter)
PH13406 702 (February 23, 1995) p16. "Follow Me" (Pendergrast, James T.)
PH13407 703 (March 9, 1995) p16. "GOP Fat Cat Lounge" (Pendergrast, James T.)
PH13408 705 (April 6, 1995) p40. "The GOP Is Dining At The Libertarian Cafe, But Not Everyone Likes What's Cooking" (Witte, Michael)
PH13409 706 (April 20, 1995) p41. "The GOP's Trojan Horse Is Trampling Environmental Safeguards" (Witte, Michael)
PH13410 709 (June 1, 1995) p14. "Business—Regulations" (Pendergrast, James T.)
PH13411 710 (June 15, 1995) p14. "GOP Caucus" (Pendergrast, James T.)
PH13412 716 (September 7, 1995) p39. "Take A Right..." (Witte, Michael)
PH13413 719 (October 19, 1995) p45. "Yikes! It's The Attack Of The Dead White Males" (Witte, Michael)
PH13414 722 (November 30, 1995) p14. "The Humanities" (Pendergrast, James T.)
PH13415 727 (February 8, 1996) p30. "I Said, I Can't Hear You"
PH13416 746 (October 31, 1996) p56. "[Democratics-Republicans]"
PH13417 750-751 (December 26, 1996) p48. "[Republicans]" (Brodner, Steve)

REPUBLICAN PARTY—PHOTOGRAPHS

PH13418 724-725 (December 28, 1995) p112. "Pre-Game Warm-Up: GOP Candidates In Manchester For A Debate" (Kraft, Brooks)

RESCUE UNIT—PHOTOGRAPHS

PH13419 631 (May 28, 1992) p16. "The Rescue Unit (from left): Matt Mundy, Oteil Burbridge, Col. Bruce Hampton, Jimmy Herring And Apt. Q258" (Frazier, Jeff)

RESERVOIR DOGS (FILM)—PHOTOGRAPHS

PH13420 642 (October 29, 1992) p77. "Reservoir Dogs"

PH13421 648 (January 21, 1993) p56. "Reservoir Dogs"
PH13422 653 (April 1, 1993) p57. "Reservoir Dogs"
THE RESIDENTS FREAK SHOW (CD-ROM)—ILLUSTRATIONS
PH13423 679 (April 7, 1994) p43. "Tex The Barker, One Of Wanda's Co-Stars, Was Previously A lion Tamer"
PH13424 679 (April 7, 1994) p43. "Wanda The Worm Woman, A Featured Freak In 'The Residents Freak SHow'"
RESTORATION (FILM)—PHOTOGRAPHS
PH13425 726 (January 25, 1996) p67. "Dressed To Kill: Robert Downey Jr."
RETTIG, TOMMY—PHOTOGRAPHS—PORTRAITS
PH13426 684 (June 16, 1994) p114. "TV Echoes"
THE RETURN OF MARTIN GUERRE (FILM)—PHOTOGRAPHS
PH13427 650 (February 18, 1993) p66. "A Decade After 'The Return Of Martin Guerre' With Depardieu And Baye (top)..."
REVEREND HORTON HEAT—ILLUSTRATIONS
PH13428 736 (June 13, 1996) p41. "Reverend Horton Heat" (Cowles, David)
REVEREND HORTON HEAT—PHOTOGRAPHS
PH13429 660-661 (July 8, 1993) p96. "The Reverend Horton Heat: Jimbo Wallace, Jim Heath And Patrick 'Taz' Bentley" (Watermann, Greg)
REVEREND HORTON HEAT—PHOTOGRAPHS—PORTRAITS
PH13430 692 (October 6, 1994) p28. "Country-Fried Rock: Taz, Jimbo And The Sultan Of Psychobilly, The Rev. Horton Heat" (Seliger, Mark)
REX—PHOTOGRAPHS
PH13431 685 (June 30, 1994) p24. "Rex, Dimebag Darrell, Vinnie Paul And Phil Anselmo (clockwise from left)" (Winters, Dan)
REYNOLDS, ROBERT—PHOTOGRAPHS
PH13432 682 (May 19, 1994) p74. "[Mavericks]" (Tucker, Mark)
PH13433 691 (September 22, 1994) p22. "[The Mavericks]" (Harris, Brad)
PH13434 707 (May 4, 1995) p19. "Maverick's Raul Malo (left) And Reynolds In L.A." (Soqui, Ted)
REZNOR, TRENT—ILLUSTRATIONS
PH13435 648 (January 21, 1993) p5. "Trent Reznor Of Nine Inch Nails" (Burke, Philip)
PH13436 693 (October 20, 1994) p22. "[Trent Reznor]" (Pendergrast, James T.)
PH13437 693 (October 20, 1994) p22. "You're A Star" (Pendergrast, James T.)
REZNOR, TRENT—PHOTOGRAPHS
PH13438 645-646 (December 10, 1992) p85. "The Nails' Trent Reznor" (Preston, Neal)
PH13439 648 (January 21, 1993) p25. "Reznor At Lollapalooza '91" (Blakesberg, Jay)
PH13440 648 (January 21, 1993) p13. "[Trent Reznor]" (Westenberg, Kevin)
PH13441 681 (May 5, 1994) p21. "Reznor Rants" (Blakesberg, Jay)
PH13442 690 (September 8, 1994) p53. "Onstage During Lollapalooza I, 1991" (Blakesberg, Jay)
PH13443 690 (September 8, 1994) p52. "Reznor (center) In The Mercer, PA., High-School Band, 1983"
PH13444 690 (September 8, 1994) p53. "Sign Of Things To Come: Reznor In High School"
PH13445 690 (September 8, 1994) p54. "Vrenna, Woolley, Reznor, Finck, Lohner (from left)" (Cultice, Joseph)
PH13446 691 (September 22, 1994) p62. "Nine Inch Nails' Trent Reznor (center)" (Mazur, Kevin)
PH13447 692 (October 6, 1994) p17. "[Nine Inch Nails & Larry "Bud" Melman]" (Cultice, Joseph)
PH13448 700 (January 26, 1995) p51. "Runner-Up Ain't Enough: Trent Reznor Of Nine Inch Nails Drives Home His Point" (Mazur, Kevin)
PH13449 702 (February 23, 1995) p19. "[Trent Reznor & Adam Ant]" (Cultice, Joseph)
PH13450 714 (August 10, 1995) p15. "Prick Singer Kevin McMahon (left) And Reznor At Tipitina's" (Smith, Sean C.)
PH13451 720 (November 2, 1995) p28. "David Bowie (left) Tangos With Trent Reznor" (Capak, R. J.)
PH13452 724-725 (December 28, 1995) p39. "Goody-Two-Shoes Trent Reznor Helped Resurrect Adam Ant (left)" (Cultice, Joseph)
PH13453 745 (October 17, 1996) p47. "Malignant Delight: Reznor" (Callahan, Kristin)
REZNOR, TRENT—PHOTOGRAPHS—PORTRAITS
PH13454 690 (September 8, 1994) pp[cover]. "Nine Inch nails' Killer Instinct: Inside Trent Reznor's Dark World Of Sex, Pain And Rock & Roll" (Mahurin, Matt)
PH13455 690 (September 8, 1994) p51. "[Trent Reznor]" (Corbijn, Anton)
PH13456 695 (November 17, 1994) p26. "Trent Reznor Of Nine Inch Nails" (Mahurin, Matt)
RHODES, LYDIA—PHOTOGRAPHS
PH13457 706 (April 20, 1995) pp[enc.22]. "At Big Coffee Shop, In New York" (Tavee, Tom)
RHODES, NICK—PHOTOGRAPHS
PH13458 653 (April 1, 1993) p20. "Nick Rhodes, Simon LeBon, John Taylor And Warren Cuccurullo (from left)" (Heungman)
RHODES, PHILLIP—PHOTOGRAPHS
PH13459 726 (January 25, 1996) p30. "Gin Blossoms: Robin Wilson, Phillip Rhodes, Bill Lien, Jesse Valenzuela, Scott Johnson (from left)" (Jennings, Steve)
RHUDY, JONATHAN—PHOTOGRAPHS
PH13460 730 (March 21, 1996) p51. "Dogger Rhudy"
RHYTHM THIEF (FILM)—PHOTOGRAPHS
PH13461 722 (November 30, 1995) p74. "Quick Sex: Flynn, Andrews"
RIA DE VIGO, SPAIN—PHOTOGRAPHS
PH13462 665 (September 16, 1993) pp54-58. "Workers of The World" (Salgado, Sebastiao)
RICCI, CHRISTINA—PHOTOGRAPHS
PH13463 618 (November 28, 1991) p53. "They're Altogether Ooky" (Seliger, Mark)
RICE UNIVERSITY—PHOTOGRAPHS
PH13464 730 (March 21, 1996) p65. "Rice University: The Lone Star's Loan Star"
RICE, ANNE—ILLUSTRATIONS
PH13465 716 (September 7, 1995) p10. "Literary Immortality" (Pendergrast, James T.)
RICE, ANNE—PHOTOGRAPHS
PH13466 712-713 (July 13, 1995) p94. "Anne Rice In Her Garden District Home, March 1995" (Ravid, Joyce)
RICH, CHARLIE—ALBUMS
PH13467 636 (August 6, 1992) p60. "Pictures And Paintings"
RICH, CHARLIE—PHOTOGRAPHS
PH13468 724-725 (December 28, 1995) p66. "[Charlie Rich]"
RICH, CHARLIE—PHOTOGRAPHS—PORTRAITS
PH13469 716 (September 7, 1995) p35. "[Charlie Rich]" (Gahr, David)
RICH, MARC—PHOTOGRAPHS
PH13470 629 (April 30, 1992) p45. "Marc Rich, Who The Union Says Controls The Ravenswood Plant"
RICH, TONY—ALBUMS
PH13471 727 (February 8, 1996) p50. "Words"
RICH, TONY—ILLUSTRATIONS
PH13472 730 (March 21, 1996) p116. "Words Up! The Tony Rich Project" (MacDonald, Ross)
RICH, TONY—PHOTOGRAPHS
PH13473 732 (April 18, 1996) pp[enc.8-9]. "[Tony Rich]" (Witkin, Christian)
RICHARD III (FILM)—PHOTOGRAPHS
PH13474 726 (January 25, 1996) p64. "Richard III"
PH13475 729 (March 7, 1996) p53. "'Richard' Pacino's Sundance Debut As A Director"

RICHARDS, ELLA ROSE—PHOTOGRAPHS

PH13476 748 (November 28, 1996) p25. "Richards And Hansen With De La Falaise Holding Little Ella Rose At The New York Film Festival" (Brady, Jay)

RICHARDS, KEITH—ALBUMS

PH13477 621 (January 9, 1992) p51. "Live At The Hollywood Palladium, December 15, 1988"

PH13478 644 (November 26, 1992) p20. "Main Offender"

PH13479 645-646 (December 10, 1992) p179. "Main Offender"

RICHARDS, KEITH—ILLUSTRATIONS—PORTRAITS

PH13480 641 (October 15, 1992) p87. "[Keith Richards]" (Helnwein, Gottfried)

RICHARDS, KEITH—PHOTOGRAPHS

PH13481 618 (November 28, 1991) p11. "Keith Richards" (Natkin, Paul)

PH13482 619-620 (December 12, 1991) p90. "...And Jagger (left)" (Mazur, Kevin)

PH13483 619-620 (December 12, 1991) p104. "Graham And Keith Richards In 1972" (Regan, Ken)

PH13484 619-620 (December 12, 1991) p90. "Like A Rolling Stone: Richards With Dylan (above)..." (Putland, Michael)

PH13485 621 (January 9, 1992) p10. "Tyler (left) And Richards At The Bill Graham Tribute" (Blankenhorn, C.)

PH13486 625 (March 5, 1992) p11. "Johnny Cash" (Mazur, Kevin)

PH13487 625 (March 5, 1992) p17. "Neil Young Takes Center Stage During The All-Star-Jam Finale" (Gershoff, Gary)

PH13488 625 (March 5, 1992) p17. "Young With Keith Richards" (Elgar, Nick)

PH13489 639 (September 17, 1992) p19. "Wood (left) And Richards" (Elgar, Nick)

PH13490 643 (November 12, 1992) p65. "Clapton, Lennon, Mitchell And Richards (from left) In 1968" (Russell, Ethan)

PH13491 643 (November 12, 1992) p74. "On The Rolling Stones' 1975 Tour, Annie Leibovitz's Lens Captured Keith, Mick And Real-Life Rock & Roll" (Leibovitz, Annie)

PH13492 645-646 (December 10, 1992) p30. "The Famous Party-Ending Jam (above)" (Mazur, Kevin)

PH13493 645-646 (December 10, 1992) p87. "[Keith Richards]"

PH13494 647 (January 7, 1993) p11. "Keith Richards And Patti Hansen" (Elgar, Nick)

PH13495 649 (February 4, 1993) p22. "Keith Richards" (Taylor, Chris)

PH13496 650 (February 18, 1993) p11. "Richards Flanked By Young-uns Mike McCready (left) And Vedder" (Natkin, Paul)

PH13497 660-661 (July 8, 1993) p104. "[Keith Richards & Marlon Richards]" (Regan, Ken)

PH13498 662 (August 5, 1993) p33. "Watts, Jagger And Richards In Barbados"

PH13499 665 (September 16, 1993) p32. "[Keith Richards]"

PH13500 668 (October 28, 1993) p35. "[Rolling Stones]"

PH13501 675 (February 10, 1994) p22. "[Keith Richards & Phil Spector]" (Blankenhorn, C.)

PH13502 681 (May 5, 1994) p18. "Nashville Cats: Jones And Richards"

PH13503 683 (June 2, 1994) p16. "Jagger And Richards Roll It Out One More Time" (Mazur, Kevin)

PH13504 686-687 (July 14, 1994) pp68-69. "And Then There Were Four: Charlie Watts, Ron Wood, Mick Jagger And Keith Richards" (Seliger, Mark)

PH13505 686-687 (July 14, 1994) p71. "Lounge Lizards: Don Was Confers With Keith Richards And Mick Jagger In The Studio" (Adebari, Eugene)

PH13506 689 (August 25, 1994) pp56-57. "Four Play In Toronto..." (Corbijn, Anton)

PH13507 689 (August 25, 1994) p61. "The Glimmer Twins, Still In The Swing Of Things: "It's Just You And Your mates," Says Richards" (Corbijn, Anton)

PH13508 689 (August 25, 1994) pp58-59. "[Mick Jagger & Keith Richards]" (Corbijn, Anton)

PH13509 689 (August 25, 1994) p60. ""We Risk reputation, And That's Everything," Says Watts, With A Masked Richards And Wood" (Corbijn, Anton)

PH13510 690 (September 8, 1994) p21. "Mick Jagger, Charlie Watts And Keith Richards (from left) Get Warmed Up In Toronto" (Halsband, Michael)

PH13511 694 (November 3, 1994) p28. "En Route To Philadelphia, Richards Plays Dominoes On The Plane" (Seliger, Mark)

PH13512 694 (November 3, 1994) p28. "Richards And Wood "Warming Up The Hands" In Their Dressing Room" (Seliger, Mark)

PH13513 694 (November 3, 1994) p26. "Wood And Richards" (Seliger, Mark)

PH13514 697 (December 15, 1994) p17. "[Keith Richards, Tom Cruise, & Bruce Springsteen]" (Ferreira, Albert)

PH13515 697 (December 15, 1994) p17. "[Rolling Stones]" (Jones, Steve)

PH13516 712-713 (July 13, 1995) p34. "Stoned In Amsterdam: Wood, Jagger, Richards And Watts (from left) Get Their Ya-Yas Out At The Paradiso" (Corbijn, Anton)

PH13517 715 (August 24, 1995) p37. "Jones, Richards, Watts, Jagger, Wyman (from left) [Watts, Richards, Jones, Jagger, Wyman (from left)]" (Mankowitz, Gered)

PH13518 723 (December 14, 1995) p62. "Wasted Elegance: Jagger And Richards Together In The 1970s"

PH13519 723 (December 14, 1995) p50. "Jagger And Richards Performing With The Stones At The Tower Ballroom, Near Liverpool, 1964"

PH13520 730 (March 21, 1996) p17. "You Can't Always Get What You Want: Richards And Mick Jagger's Ex Faithfull" (Goldsmith, Lynn)

PH13521 734 (May 16, 1996) p18. "Wood, Richards And Fowler (from left) Kicking It"

PH13522 742 (September 5, 1996) p20. "Scotty Moore (left) Attempts Some Sort Of Hand Ritual With The Ageless Richards" (Herrington, Jim)

PH13523 746 (October 31, 1996) p27. "Ono, Richards, Watts, Jagger And Jones (from left) With Circus Friends"

PH13524 748 (November 28, 1996) p25. "Richards And Hansen With De La Falaise Holding Little Ella Rose At The New York Film Festival" (Brady, Jay)

PH13525 750-751 (December 26, 1996) p68. "Pleased To Meet You, Hope You Guessed My Name: Elvis Presley's Guitar Player Scotty Moore With Keith Richards" (Herrington, Jim)

RICHARDS, KEITH—PHOTOGRAPHS—PORTRAITS

PH13526 625 (March 5, 1992) pp14-15. "On The Evening Of The Seventh Annual Hall Of Fame Induction Ceremony, 'Rolling Stone' Gathered These Nine Legendary Guitarists At The Waldorf-Astoria For A Once-In-A-Lifetime..."

PH13527 629 (April 30, 1992) p16. "Keith Richards: 'I Guess Rock & Roll Demands A Pure, Monastic Life'" (Goldsmith, Lynn)

PH13528 643 (November 12, 1992) p199. "Keith Richards" (Watson, Albert)

PH13529 645-646 (December 10, 1992) p157. "Mick Jagger And Keith Richards, 1989"

PH13530 645-646 (December 10, 1992) p157. "Mick Jagger And Keith Richards, 1975"

PH13531 662 (August 5, 1993) p59. "Keith Richards" (Mazur, Kevin)

PH13532 728 (February 22, 1996) p26. "Keith Richards: Playing Solo Again" (Brown, Jane)

PH13533 735 (May 30, 1996) p18. "Richards' Legendary Addiction Virtually Defined Rock Authenticity..." (Gahr, David)

PH13534 735 (May 30, 1996) p3. "[The Faces Of Heroin]"

RICHARDS, MARLON—PHOTOGRAPHS

PH13535 660-661 (July 8, 1993) p104. "[Keith Richards & Marlon Richards]" (Regan, Ken)

PH13536 660-661 (July 8, 1993) pp103,106. "[Marlon Richards]" (Pfriender, Stephanie)

PH13537 660-661 (July 8, 1993) pp104-106. "[Marlon Richards & Lucie De La Falaise]" (Pfriender, Stephanie)
RICHARDS, MARLON—PHOTOGRAPHS—PORTRAITS
PH13538 660-661 (July 8, 1993) p102. "[Marlon Richards]" (Pfriender, Stephanie)
RICHARDS, MICHAEL—PHOTOGRAPHS
PH13539 660-661 (July 8, 1993) p42. "Kramer Vs. Richards" (Seliger, Mark)
PH13540 660-661 (July 8, 1993) p41. "Nothing On: Jason Alexander, Julia Louis-Dreyfus, Jerry Seinfeld And Michael Richards" (Seliger, Mark)
PH13541 660-661 (July 8, 1993) pp[cover]. "Seinfeld Rules!" (Seliger, Mark)
PH13542 672-673 (December 23, 1993) p188. "[Covers]" (Seliger, Mark)
PH13543 698-699 (December 29, 1994) p58. "Jackson With "Seinfeld" Ham Michael Richards" (Kravitz, Jeff)
PH13544 717 (September 21, 1995) p90. "Watt Is Flanked By Uncles Chaykin And Richards"
RICHARDS, MICHAEL—PHOTOGRAPHS—PORTRAITS
PH13545 656 (May 13, 1993) p72. "[Michael Richards]" (Schiffman, Bonnie)
RICHARDS, RICK—PHOTOGRAPHS
PH13546 650 (February 18, 1993) p13. "Baird, Kevin Kinney And Richards (from left)" (Diamond, Rick)
RICHARDSON, DAWN—PHOTOGRAPHS
PH13547 662 (August 5, 1993) p21. "Brunets Have Fun, Too: Hillhouse, Rocha, Perry And Richardson (from left)" (MacNaughtan, Andrew)
RICHARDSON, JASON—PHOTOGRAPHS
PH13548 647 (January 7, 1993) p39. "Road Manager Jason Richardson Counts The Cash" (Seliger, Mark)
RICHARDSON, MIRANDA—PHOTOGRAPHS
PH13549 700 (January 26, 1995) p66. "Dafoe, Richardson"
PH13550 741 (August 22, 1996) p104. "Richardson (left) And Leigh In Peril In Kansas City"
RICHIE, LIONEL—PHOTOGRAPHS
PH13551 644 (November 26, 1992) p22. "Goldberg, Richie, Taylor, John, Michael And Hornsby (from left) At The Garden" (Mazur, Kevin)
RICHLING, GREG—PHOTOGRAPHS
PH13552 684 (June 16, 1994) p36. "Merchant, Greg Richling" (Forsman, Shelly)
RICHMOND, CALIFORNIA—PHOTOGRAPHS
PH13553 696 (December 1, 1994) pp106-108,110+. "[Richmond, California]" (Shames, Stephen)
RICHTER, ANDY—PHOTOGRAPHS
PH13554 743 (September 19, 1996) p69. "The Crest Of The Wave: His Sidekick, Andy Richter; And The 'Late Night' Bandleader, Max Weinberg" (Seliger, Mark)
RICK, DAVE—PHOTOGRAPHS—PORTRAITS
PH13555 654 (April 15, 1993) p17. "Murdock, Hall, Xefos, Rick (from left)" (Seliger, Mark)
RICKLES, DON—PHOTOGRAPHS
PH13556 726 (January 25, 1996) p17. "You Hockey Puck! Dylan, Rickles And Bruce Springsteen" (Mazur, Kevin)
RICKMAN, ALAN—PHOTOGRAPHS
PH13557 639 (September 17, 1992) p102. "Robbins (right) And Rickman Hit The Campaign Trail"
RIDE—ALBUMS
PH13558 732 (April 18, 1996) p69. "Tarantula"
RIDE—PHOTOGRAPHS
PH13559 619-620 (December 12, 1991) p46. "Ride (above) And The La's (below) Brought The Guitar Back To Pop"
PH13560 630 (May 14, 1992) p92. "[Creation]" (Sheehan, T.)
RIDGELEY, ANDREW—PHOTOGRAPHS
PH13561 619-620 (December 12, 1991) p18. "Andrew Ridgeley (left) And George Michael" (Mazur, Kevin)
RIEBLING, SCOTT—PHOTOGRAPHS
PH13562 690 (September 8, 1994) p42. "Cleo's Hanley, McKenna And Scott Riebling (from left)" (Capak, R. J.)
PH13563 710 (June 15, 1995) p39. "Eisenstein, Scott Riebling, Hanley, Stacy Jones, Greg McKenna (from left)" (McDonough, Patricia)
RIFKIN, DANNY—PHOTOGRAPHS
PH13564 717 (September 21, 1995) p65. "The Dead In Front Of Their Ashbury St. House, 1967: Jerry Garcia, Ron 'Pigpen' McKernan, Bob Weir, Phil Lesh, Co-Managers Danny Rifkin And Rock Scully, And Bill Kreutzmann..."
PH13565 717 (September 21, 1995) p66. "Lesh, Early Dead Co-Managers Scully And Rifkin, Weir And Garcia At A Press Conference Following The Oct. 2, 1967, drug Bust At The Dead's House" (Wolman, Baron)
RIGBY, AMY—ALBUMS
PH13566 747 (November 14, 1996) p114. "Diary Of A Mod Housewife"
RIGHT SAID FRED—ALBUMS
PH13567 627 (April 2, 1992) p45. "Up"
RILES, KELLY—PHOTOGRAPHS—PORTRAITS
PH13568 655 (April 29, 1993) p24. "Revving It Up: Velocity's Shannon, Spellman, Nelson, Riles And Moore (from left)" (Falls, John)
RILEY, MARKELL—PHOTOGRAPHS
PH13569 654 (April 15, 1993) pp[enc.3]. "[Spring Collection]" (Seliger, Mark)
RILEY, MARKELL—PHOTOGRAPHS—PORTRAITS
PH13570 654 (April 15, 1993) pp[enc.4,7,10]. "[Markell Riley]" (Seliger, Mark)
PH13571 654 (April 15, 1993) pp[enc.4]. "Wreckx-n-Effect's Markell Riley And Aqil Davidson" (Seliger, Mark)
RILEY, STEVE—PHOTOGRAPHS
PH13572 656 (May 13, 1993) p88. "[Big Black]"
RILEY, TIMOTHY CHRISTIAN—PHOTOGRAPHS
PH13573 666 (September 30, 1993) p16. "Tony3: Dwayne And Raphael Wiggins, Riley (from left)" (Cuffaro, Chris)
PH13574 695 (November 17, 1994) p81. "Tony! Toni! Tone!" (Rolston, Matthew)
RIMES, LEANN—PHOTOGRAPHS
PH13575 744 (October 3, 1996) p32. "[Leann Rimes]"
RIMES, LEANN—PHOTOGRAPHS—PORTRAITS
PH13576 750-751 (December 26, 1996) p54. "Leann Rimes: Teen Country Sensation"
RINGLING SCHOOL OF ART AND DESIGN—ILLUSTRATIONS
PH13577 666 (September 30, 1993) p60. "[Higher Education]"
RIO DE JANEIRO, BRAZIL—ILLUSTRATIONS
PH13578 637 (August 20, 1992) pp36-37,41. "[Earth Summit]" (Peck, Everett)
RIOT GRRRLS—ILLUSTRATIONS
PH13579 664 (September 2, 1993) p8. "Stage Doors" (Pendergrast, James T.)
RISING SONS—ALBUMS
PH13580 652 (March 18, 1993) p42. "Rising Sons"
RISING SUN (FILM)—PHOTOGRAPHS
PH13581 664 (September 2, 1993) p69. "Thriller Tempura: Connery And Snipes Dine Japanese"
RITCHER, SCOTT—PHOTOGRAPHS
PH13582 693 (October 20, 1994) p92. "Guy Who Does It: Scott Ritcher, 21" (Pipes, Breck)
RITCHEY, TOM—PHOTOGRAPHS
PH13583 634-635 (July 9, 1992) p82. "'The Initiative To Build The Bikes Was Mine,' Says Tom Ritchey" (Stone, Pete)
RITTER, JOHN—PHOTOGRAPHS
PH13584 645-646 (December 10, 1992) p196. "His Half-Brother, Roger, Serenaded John Ritter And Markie Post On 'Hearts Afire'"
RITTS, HERB—ILLUSTRATIONS
PH13585 643 (November 12, 1992) p151. "[Herb Ritts]" (Russo, Anthony)
RITTS, HERB—ILLUSTRATIONS—LETTERING
PH13586 643 (November 12, 1992) p151. "[Herb Ritts]" (Karl, Anita)

RITTS, HERB—PHOTOGRAPHS
PH13587 615 (October 17, 1991) p66. "Steven Meisel And Herb Ritts, New York City, 1990" (Pigozzi, Jean)
PH13588 643 (November 12, 1992) p230. "Ritts Got Ahead By Teaming Up With Madonna" (Day, Lorraine)
A RIVER RUNS THROUGH IT (FILM)—PHOTOGRAPHS
PH13589 642 (October 29, 1992) p78. "Redford (left) Directs Look-Alike Brad Pitt"
THE RIVER WILD (FILM)—PHOTOGRAPHS
PH13590 693 (October 20, 1994) p156. "Woman Warrior Streep (above, with Reilly and Bacon) Braves The Rapids To Save Son Mazzello And Husband Strathairn (left)"
RIVERA, TAMIKA—PHOTOGRAPHS
PH13591 718 (October 5, 1995) pp[enc.13]. "Posey With Friends In Den Of Thieves, In New York" (Seliger, Mark)
RIZZO, RICK—PHOTOGRAPHS
PH13592 658 (June 10, 1993) p29. "Wink O'Bannon, Janet Beveridge Bean, Rick Rizzo And Doug McCombs (from left)" (Guip, Andy)
ROACH, ARCHIE—ALBUMS
PH13593 645-646 (December 10, 1992) p184. "Charcoal Lane"
PH13594 664 (September 2, 1993) p65. "Jamu Dreaming"
THE ROAD TO WELLVILLE (BOOK)—ILLUSTRATIONS
PH13595 654 (April 15, 1993) pp48-49. "[The Road To Wellville]" (Tarlofsky, Malcolm)
THE ROAD TO WELLVILLE (FILM)—PHOTOGRAPHS
PH13596 696 (December 1, 1994) p134. "Misfires"
ROB AND FAB—ALBUMS
PH13597 658 (June 10, 1993) p70. "Rob And Fab"
ROB ROY (FILM)—PHOTOGRAPHS
PH13598 707 (May 4, 1995) p74. "Roth And Neeson In 'Rob Roy'"
ROBACK, DAVID—PHOTOGRAPHS—PORTRAITS
PH13599 695 (November 17, 1994) p49. "Mazzy Star" (Sebring, Steven)
ROBB, CHUCK—PHOTOGRAPHS
PH13600 741 (August 22, 1996) p104. "Chuck Robb Hits The Stump"
ROBBINS, J.—PHOTOGRAPHS
PH13601 678 (March 24, 1994) p20. "Barocas, Robbins, Coletta, Barbot (from left)" (Falls, John)
ROBBINS, TIM—ILLUSTRATIONS
PH13602 629 (April 30, 1992) p63. "Setting Up Hollywood For The Kill" (Drawson, Blair)
PH13603 639 (September 17, 1992) p101. "The Player As Candidate" (Kunz, Anita)
ROBBINS, TIM—PHOTOGRAPHS
PH13604 629 (April 30, 1992) p64. "Mill Watches Rival Larry Levy (Peter Gallagher)"
PH13605 629 (April 30, 1992) p64. "Studio Player Griffin Mill (Tim Robbins) At Work"
PH13606 639 (September 17, 1992) p102. "Robbins (right) And Rickman Hit The Campaign Trail"
PH13607 645-646 (December 10, 1992) p190. "Artists Or Hitmakers? You Decide: Director Robert Altman And Tim Robbins"
PH13608 648 (January 21, 1993) p56. "The Player"
PH13609 653 (April 1, 1993) p57. "The Player"
PH13610 667 (October 14, 1993) p126. "Above: A Cop (Tim Robbins) And A Clown (Anne Archer) Enjoy A Chance Encounter"
PH13611 678 (March 24, 1994) p105. "Robbins (left) And Newman Play Office Politics, While Leigh (far right) Gets The Story"
PH13612 692 (October 6, 1994) p81. "Morgan Freeman And Tim Robbins Plot An Escape"
PH13613 698-699 (December 29, 1994) p199. "Roberts And Robbins in "Pret""
PH13614 747 (November 14, 1996) p25. "This Hall Was Made For You And Me: Arlo Guthrie, Bruce Springsteen, Tim Robbins, Dave Pirner And Billy Bragg (from left) At The Rock & Roll Hall Of Fame's Woody Guthrie..." (Pre
ROBBINS, TIM—PHOTOGRAPHS—PORTRAITS
PH13615 642 (October 29, 1992) p54. "[Tim Robbins]" (Watson, Albert)
ROBBINS, TOM—PHOTOGRAPHS—PORTRAITS
PH13616 669 (November 11, 1993) p62. "Author Tom Robbins Visits The Set In Oregon" (Markus, Kurt)
ROBERTS, BRAD—PHOTOGRAPHS
PH13617 617 (November 14, 1991) p13. "Crash Test Dummies' Brad Roberts With Simon" (Roberts, Ebet)
PH13618 681 (May 5, 1994) p16. "Big Dummies: Dan And Brad Roberts, Darvill, Dorge And Reid (from left)" (Blakesberg, Jay)
ROBERTS, DAN—PHOTOGRAPHS
PH13618 681 (May 5, 1994) p16. "Big Dummies: Dan And Brad Roberts, Darvill, Dorge And Reid (from left)" (Blakesberg, Jay)
ROBERTS, ERIC—PHOTOGRAPHS
PH13619 686-687 (July 14, 1994) p60. "Roberts Siblings, 1984: Julia, Eric, Lisa" (Walz, Barbara)
ROBERTS, JULIA—ILLUSTRATIONS
PH13620 621 (January 9, 1992) p54. "Nothing To Crow About" (Payne, C. F.)
PH13621 674 (January 27, 1994) p47. "[Julia Roberts]" (Brodner, Steven)
PH13622 689 (August 25, 1994) p12. "Exposuremeter" (Pendergrast, James T.)
PH13623 715 (August 24, 1995) p107. "Woman As Male Fear & Fantasy" (Ryden, Mark)
ROBERTS, JULIA—PHOTOGRAPHS
PH13624 663 (August 19, 1993) p28. "Lyle Lovett And Julia Roberts"
PH13625 672-673 (December 23, 1993) p41. "Above: Roberts Poses With Her Best man, Lovett"
PH13626 674 (January 27, 1994) p48. "Acting Vehicles Include 'The Pelican Brief,' 'In The Name Of The Father,' 'What's Eating Gilbert Grape,' 'Shadowlands,' 'Naked,' And 'Grumpy Old Men'"
PH13627 684 (June 16, 1994) p116. "Flirty: Roberts And Nolte In "Trouble""
PH13628 686-687 (July 14, 1994) pp56-57,59. "[Julia Roberts]" (Ritts, Herb)
PH13629 686-687 (July 14, 1994) p60. "The Roberts' Acting School, 1969: Julia (in diapers), Family And Students" (Werner, Paul)
PH13630 686-687 (July 14, 1994) p60. "Roberts Siblings, 1984: Julia, Eric, Lisa" (Walz, Barbara)
PH13631 686-687 (July 14, 1994) pp[cover]. "The Rolling Stone Interview: Julia Roberts" (Ritts, Herb)
PH13632 686-687 (July 14, 1994) p65. "The Sneak Wedding Day: June 27, 1993"
PH13633 686-687 (July 14, 1994) p65. "While Divorce Rumors Swirl, Mr. And Mrs. Lovett Stroll In Paris" (Ginies, Michael)
PH13634 688 (August 11, 1994) p62. "I Love Trouble"
PH13635 691 (September 22, 1994) p106. "Acting Valleys"
PH13636 698-699 (December 29, 1994) p199. "Roberts And Robbins in "Pret""
ROBERTS, JULIA—PHOTOGRAPHS—PORTRAITS
PH13637 685 (June 30, 1994) p41. "[Julia Roberts]" (Davila, Bill)
PH13638 686-687 (July 14, 1994) p58. "High-School Grad Roberts (1985)"
PH13639 715 (August 24, 1995) p108. "Dangerous Women: Michelle Pfeiffer, Sandra Bullock, Julia Roberts, Cindy Crawford And Natasha Henstridge"
ROBERTS, LISA—PHOTOGRAPHS
PH13640 686-687 (July 14, 1994) p60. "Roberts Siblings, 1984: Julia, Eric, Lisa" (Walz, Barbara)
ROBERTSON, PAT—PHOTOGRAPHS
PH13641 698-699 (December 29, 1994) p159. "Reed With Robertson At The Annual Convention Of The Christian Coalition" (Reinhard, Rick)

ROBERTSON, ROBBIE—ALBUMS
PH13642 616 (October 31, 1991) p87. "Storyville"
PH13643 619-620 (December 12, 1991) p184. "Storyville"
PH13644 698-699 (December 29, 1994) p170. "Music For The Native Americans"
ROBERTSON, ROBBIE—ILLUSTRATIONS—PORTRAITS
PH13645 616 (October 31, 1991) p87. "Robbie Robertson: The Saga Of 'Storyville'" (Payne, C. F.)
ROBERTSON, ROBBIE—PHOTOGRAPHS
PH13646 617 (November 14, 1991) p75. "The Last Waltz, 1976: Robertson, Danko And Manuel, With Neil Young (left), Bob Dylan (back to camera) And Van Morrison" (Leibovitz, Annie)
PH13647 617 (November 14, 1991) p72. "Levon And The Hawks, Circa 1963: Sax Player Jerry Field, Rick Danko, Levon Helm, Richard Manuel, Garth Hudson And Robertson (from left)"
PH13648 617 (November 14, 1991) pp68-69,71. "[Robbie Robertson]" (Uchitel, Diego)
PH13649 625 (March 5, 1992) p11. "Edge, Robertson" (Mazur, Kevin)
PH13650 636 (August 6, 1992) p11. "Michael Penn, Maria McKee And Robbie Robertson (from left) At The Whiskey" (Cavolina, Robbie)
PH13651 644 (November 26, 1992) p13. "Barbara Orbison And Robbie Robertson" (Sallow, Jacki)
PH13652 647 (January 7, 1993) p11. "Robbie Robertson" (Lowitt, Roxanne)
PH13653 651 (March 4, 1993) p17. "Creedence Clearwater Revisited: Springsteen, Was, Fogerty And Robertson" (Mazur, Kevin)
PH13654 651 (March 4, 1993) p16. "Eric Clapton And Robbie Robertson" (Granitz, Steve)
PH13655 669 (November 11, 1993) p66. "The Hawks At Ontario's Brass Rail Circa '63: Danko, Manuel, Hawkins, Helm, Robertson And Hudson (from left)"
PH13656 676 (February 24, 1994) p46. "The Band (clockwise from top left): Guitarist Robbie Robertson, Drummer Levon Helm, Organist Garth Hudson, Bassist Rock Danko And Pianist Richard Manuel" (Gahr, David)
PH13657 677 (March 10, 1994) p29. "With The Band: Clapton And Robertson" (Mazur, Kevin)
PH13658 698-699 (December 29, 1994) p36. "Famers Eric Clapton And Robbie Robertson (below)" (Mazur, Kevin)
PH13659 719 (October 19, 1995) p38. "'Cleveland Was Just On Fire,' Robbie Robertson Said" (Corbijn, Anton)
ROBERTSON, ROBBIE—PHOTOGRAPHS—PORTRAITS
PH13660 625 (March 5, 1992) pp14-15. "On The Evening Of The Seventh Annual Hall Of Fame Induction Ceremony, 'Rolling Stone' Gathered These Nine Legendary Guitarists At The Waldorf-Astoria For A Once-In-A-Lifetime..."
PH13661 643 (November 12, 1992) pp86-87. "Robbie Robertson" (Weber, Bruce)
PH13662 692 (October 6, 1994) p27. "[Robbie Robertson]" (Williams, David)
PH13663 722 (November 30, 1995) p19. "'Casino' Director Martin Scorsese (left) And Robbie Robertson" (Corbijn, Anton)
ROBIN HOOD: MEN IN TIGHTS (FILM)—PHOTOGRAPHS
PH13664 665 (September 16, 1993) p77. "Worst Supporting Actress"
ROBIN HOOD: PRINCE OF THIEVES (FILM)—PHOTOGRAPHS
PH13665 617 (November 14, 1991) p184. "Is Mastrantonio Wondering If Costner's Aim Is True?"
ROBINSON, BILL—PHOTOGRAPHS—PORTRAITS
PH13666 643 (November 12, 1992) p60. "Kriegsmann Dignified Black Stars Like Bill Robinson" (Kriegsmann, James)
ROBINSON, CHRIS—ILLUSTRATIONS
PH13667 694 (November 3, 1994) p95. "American Boys" (Ulriksen, Mark)
ROBINSON, CHRIS—PHOTOGRAPHS
PH13668 619-620 (December 12, 1991) p76. "Hellion Chris Robinson" (Mazur, Kevin)
PH13669 621 (January 9, 1992) p11. "Marc Ford (left) And Chris Robinson" (Matheu, Robert)
PH13670 631 (May 28, 1992) p9. "Chris (left) And Rich Robinson" (Diamond, Rick)
PH13671 637 (August 20, 1992) p22. "Chris Robinson" (Green, Bil)
PH13672 639 (September 17, 1992) p19. "Chris Robinson Onstage In Detroit" (Schwab, Bill)
PH13673 642 (October 29, 1992) p19. "Black Crowes Marc Ford, Johnny Colt And Chris Robinson (from left) With Guest Rehearser And Show Host Dana Carvey" (Mazur, Kevin)
PH13674 645-646 (December 10, 1992) p36. "Chris Robinson Of The Black Crowes" (Mazur, Kevin)
PH13675 652 (March 18, 1993) p15. "Robinson And His Big Toe" (Schwartz, Michelle)
PH13676 670 (November 25, 1993) p74. "[Black Crowes]" (Seliger, Mark)
PH13677 689 (August 25, 1994) p25. "Silent Partners: Chris (left) And Rich Robinson Share A Happy Moment" (Dyer, Alison)
PH13678 692 (October 6, 1994) p16. "Chris Robinson Lets His Freak Flag Fly" (Diamond, Rick)
PH13679 695 (November 17, 1994) p75. "The Black Crowes" (Luchford, Glen)
PH13680 708 (May 18, 1995) p42. "Chris Robinson: A 'Remedy' That Cures All Ills" (Capak, R. J.)
PH13681 709 (June 1, 1995) p16. "Jayhawk Gary Louris, Crowes Marc Ford And Robinson, Perlman (from left)" (Diamond, Rick)
PH13682 712-713 (July 13, 1995) p25. "Don't Fear The Reefer" (Blakesberg, Jay)
PH13683 736 (June 13, 1996) p41. "The Black Crowes In '94: Chris Robinson, Chris Trujilo, Rich Robinson (from left)" (Blakesberg, Jay)
PH13684 741 (August 22, 1996) p34. "Bill McGathy With Black Crowes' Chris Robinson"
PH13685 746 (October 31, 1996) p35. "[Chris Robinson]" (Halfin, Ross)
ROBINSON, CYNTHIA—PHOTOGRAPHS
PH13686 649 (February 4, 1993) p51. "Rose Stone, Sly, Freddie Stone, Graham, Robinson, Errico And Martini Of Sly And The Family Stone"
ROBINSON, DAWN—PHOTOGRAPHS
PH13687 709 (June 1, 1995) p17. "Maxine Jones, Robinson, O'Donnell, Cindy Herron, Terry Ellis" (Nelson, Ralph)
ROBINSON, DAWN—PHOTOGRAPHS—PORTRAITS
PH13688 660-661 (July 8, 1993) p66. "Dawn Robinson" (Rolston, Matthew)
PH13689 660-661 (July 8, 1993) pp64-65. "En Vogue's Sheer Beauties: Terry Ellis, Maxine Jones, Dawn Robinson And Cindy Herron (from left)" (Rolston, Matthew)
ROBINSON, RICH—ILLUSTRATIONS
PH13690 637 (August 20, 1992) p3. "Rich Robinson Of The Black Crowes" (Burke, Philip)
ROBINSON, RICH—PHOTOGRAPHS
PH13691 631 (May 28, 1992) p9. "Chris (left) And Rich Robinson" (Diamond, Rick)
PH13692 670 (November 25, 1993) p74. "[Black Crowes]" (Seliger, Mark)
PH13693 689 (August 25, 1994) p25. "Silent Partners: Chris (left) And Rich Robinson Share A Happy Moment" (Dyer, Alison)
PH13694 695 (November 17, 1994) p75. "The Black Crowes" (Luchford, Glen)
PH13695 712-713 (July 13, 1995) p25. "Don't Fear The Reefer" (Blakesberg, Jay)
PH13696 736 (June 13, 1996) p41. "The Black Crowes In '94: Chris Robinson, Chris Trujilo, Rich Robinson (from left)" (Blakesberg, Jay)

ROBINSON, ROMYE—PHOTOGRAPHS
PH13697 660-661 (July 8, 1993) p97. "The Pharcyde: Romye Robinson, Imani Wilcox, Derrick Stewart And Tre Hardson" (Azimi, Mojgan B.)
PH13698 722 (November 30, 1995) p38. "Hip-Hop's Cosmic Voyagers: Wilcox, Robinson, Hardson And Stewart (from left)" (McClelland, Philippe)
ROBINSON, SMOKEY—PHOTOGRAPHS
PH13699 631 (May 28, 1992) p11. "Alice Cooper, Smokey Robinson And Bob Seger (from left)" (Plummer, Sue)
PH13700 658 (June 10, 1993) p16. "Gloria Estefan, Smokey Robinson, Franklin, John (from left)" (Mazur, Kevin)
ROBINSON, SMOKEY—PHOTOGRAPHS—PORTRAITS
PH13701 643 (November 12, 1992) p108. "Smokey Robinson" (Rolston, Matthew)
ROBINSON, SYLVIA—PHOTOGRAPHS
PH13702 672-673 (December 23, 1993) p142. "The House That Rap Built: Sugarhill's Sylvia Robinson At Home In '83" (Saunders, Red)
ROBINSON, WENDY—PHOTOGRAPHS
PH13703 650 (February 18, 1993) p13. "Peter Tork (left) With The 'Jays' Hancock, Robinson And Ben Kesteven" (Mayer, Jeffrey)
ROCHA, ROGER—PHOTOGRAPHS
PH13704 662 (August 5, 1993) p21. "Brunets Have Fun, Too: Hillhouse, Rocha, Perry And Richardson (from left)" (MacNaughtan, Andrew)
ROCHELEAU, RON—PHOTOGRAPHS—PORTRAITS
PH13705 741 (August 22, 1996) p77. "[Concrete T.V.]" (Pluchino, Joseph)
ROCHES—ALBUMS
PH13706 638 (September 3, 1992) p67. "A Dove"
ROCHON, LELA—PHOTOGRAPHS
PH13707 724-725 (December 28, 1995) p138. "Houston, Devine, Rochon And Bassett In 'Exhale' (from left)"
THE ROCK (FILM)—ILLUSTRATIONS
PH13708 737 (June 27, 1996) p61. "Bad Boy Son Alcatraz" (Brodner, Steve)
THE ROCK (FILM)—PHOTOGRAPHS
PH13709 737 (June 27, 1996) p62. "Sean Connery Watches Nicholas Cage Defuse A Poison-Gas Bomb On Alcatraz"
ROCK AND ROLL CIRCUS (FILM)—PHOTOGRAPHS
PH13710 746 (October 31, 1996) p27. "Ono, Richards, Watts, Jagger And Jones (from left) With Circus Friends"
ROCK AND ROLL HALL OF FAME—PHOTOGRAPHS
PH13711 662 (August 5, 1993) p18. "Diggin' In The Dirt: The Celebrity Crew Does The Honors" (Mazur, Kevin)
PH13712 670 (November 25, 1993) p86. "[Rock & Roll Hall Of Fame]" (Seliger, Mark)
PH13713 686-687 (July 14, 1994) p23. "Yes, Virginia, There Is A Hall"
PH13714 698-699 (December 29, 1994) p76. "[Hall Of Fame]" (Tucker, Mort)
PH13715 706 (April 20, 1995) p29. "Exhibits: Run-D.M.C.'s Hat And Adidas, Grace Slick's fringed Vest, Roger Daltrey's T-Shirt And Curtis Mayfield's Suit"
PH13716 706 (April 20, 1995) p29. "House Of Pei: The Museum Takes Shape On The Waterfront" (Tucker, Mort)
PH13717 711 (June 29, 1995) p18. "Hall Of Fame: Rock Mannequins"
ROCK CONCERTS (SOVIET UNION)—PHOTOGRAPHS
PH13718 617 (November 14, 1991) p25. "The Scene At Tushino Airfield, Where 500,000 Fans Converged For The Show" (Giron, Joe)
PH13719 617 (November 14, 1991) p25. "Skirmishes At The Concert Sent Fifty-Three People To Local Hospitals"
ROCK FOR CHOICE—ILLUSTRATIONS
PH13720 692 (October 6, 1994) p55. "Rock For Choice"
ROCK MUSIC—ILLUSTRATIONS
PH13721 644 (November 26, 1992) pp49-50,52,55 +. "Our Lives, Our Music" (Lardy, Philippe)
PH13722 704 (March 23, 1995) p119. "Voices Carry" (Northeast, Christian)
PH13723 748 (November 28, 1996) p91. "[Recording Technology]" (King, J. D.)
ROCK MUSIC—ILLUSTRATIONS—LETTERING
PH13724 628 (April 16, 1992) p35. "[Alternative Music]" (Allen, Terry)
ROCK SHE WROTE (BOOK)—PHOTOGRAPHS
PH13725 723 (December 14, 1995) p96. "Rock She Wrote"
ROCK THE VOTE—ILLUSTRATIONS
PH13726 637 (August 20, 1992) p17. "[Rock The Vote]"
ROCK, CHRIS—PHOTOGRAPHS
PH13727 706 (April 20, 1995) p86. "The 'SNL' Legacy Of Screen Shame"
ROCK, CRISSY—PHOTOGRAPHS
PH13728 697 (December 15, 1994) p104. "Crissy Rock"
ROCK, PETE—ALBUMS
PH13729 645-646 (December 10, 1992) p174. "Mecca And The Soul Brother"
ROCKET FROM THE CRYPT—ALBUMS
PH13730 721 (November 16, 1995) p111. "Scream, Dracula, Scream!"
ROCKET FROM THE CRYPT—PHOTOGRAPHS
PH13731 689 (August 25, 1994) p44. "All Together Now: Trombino, Atom, Kennedy, Reis, N.D., Petey X, Apollo 9, Froberg (from left)" (Cuffaro, Chris)
PH13732 728 (February 22, 1996) p29. "Rocket From The Crypt: Atom, J.C. 2000, Petey X, N.D., Speedo And Apollo 9" (Dyer, Alison)
PH13733 738-739 (July 11, 1996) p25. "Rocket From The Crypt" (Cuffan, Chris)
ROCKIN' DOPSIE—PHOTOGRAPHS
PH13734 667 (October 14, 1993) p36. "[Rockin' Dopsie]" (Byrd, Sydney)
ROCKING KINGS—PHOTOGRAPHS
PH13735 623 (February 6, 1992) p44. "Hendrix (second from left) With His First Band, The Rocking Kings"
ROCKIT (VIDEO)—PHOTOGRAPHS
PH13736 667 (October 14, 1993) p93. "'Rockit': Hancock's Video Used Crude Techniques To Create Cool 'Video Scratching'"
RODAN—PHOTOGRAPHS
PH13737 686-687 (July 14, 1994) p74. "Getting The Point Across: Rodan's Tara Jane O'Neil, Noble, Mueller And Kevin Coultas (from left)" (Clinch, Danny)
RODGERS, NILE—PHOTOGRAPHS
PH13738 658 (June 10, 1993) p64. "In The Studio Recording 'Let's Dance' With Nile Rodgers, 1983" (Rosenthal, Cindy)
RODGERS, PAUL—ALBUMS
PH13739 660-661 (July 8, 1993) p114. "Muddy Water Blues"
RODMAN, DENNIS—PHOTOGRAPHS
PH13740 745 (October 17, 1996) p27. "Gavin Rossdale, Gwen Stefani And Dennis Rodman, At A Pre-Show Bash" (Mazur, Kevin)
PH13741 749 (December 12, 1996) pp41-42. "[Dennis Rodman]" (Watson, Albert)
PH13742 750-751 (December 26, 1996) p54. "[Dennis Rodman]"
RODMAN, DENNIS—PHOTOGRAPHS—PORTRAITS
PH13743 749 (December 12, 1996) pp40,45. "[Dennis Rodman]" (Watson, Albert)
PH13744 749 (December 12, 1996) pp[cover]. "Dennis Rodman's Fun House" (Watson, Albert)
RODRIGUEZ, RAY—PHOTOGRAPHS
PH13745 706 (April 20, 1995) pp[enc.18]. "Skating At Chicken's Pool" (Seliger, Mark)
RODRIGUEZ, ROBERT—PHOTOGRAPHS—PORTRAITS
PH13746 652 (March 18, 1993) p47. "[Robert Rodriguez]"

ROE, JEFF—PHOTOGRAPHS
PH13747 678 (March 24, 1994) p80. "Students Jeff Roe (left center) And Mike Weber (right center) Look Out On The World From The Calarts Campus" (Little, Blake)
ROEMER, ROY—PHOTOGRAPHS—PORTRAITS
PH13748 671 (December 9, 1993) p36. "Profiles In Courage"
ROESER, EDDIE KING—PHOTOGRAPHS
PH13749 664 (September 2, 1993) p12. "Urge A Go-Go (clockwise from left): Onassis, Kato, Roeser" (Robert, Francis)
PH13749a 685 (June 30, 1994) p40. "Etheridge With Kato, Tony Stull, Blackie Onassis And "Eddie" King Roeser (from left)" (Mazur, Kevin)
PH13749b 695 (September 2, 1993) p12. "Urge Overkill" (Clinch, Danny)
ROESER, EDDIE KING—PHOTOGRAPHS—PORTRAITS
PH13750 664 (September 2, 1993) p11. "[Urge Overkill]" (Robert, Francis)
ROESSLER, KIRA—PHOTOGRAPHS—PORTRAITS
PH13751 672-673 (December 23, 1993) p112. "Hardcore Heroes Black Flag In March 1984: Bill Stevenson, Kira Roessler, Greg Ginn And Rollins (from left)" (Rosenberg, Howard)
ROGERS, ALYSIA—PHOTOGRAPHS
PH13752 633 (June 25, 1992) p48. "Kid (left) 'N Play Rap With Rogers (left) And Parsons"
ROGERS, ELYSE—PHOTOGRAPHS
PH13753 721 (November 16, 1995) p25. "DHC's Rogers (left) And Karina Denike" (Chambers, Brian)
ROGERS, JIMMY—PHOTOGRAPHS
PH13754 637 (August 20, 1992) p9. "Jagger (left) With Bluesman Jimmy Rogers" (Dent, Phil)
PH13755 645-646 (December 10, 1992) p69. "Jagger And Jimmy Rogers Share The Stage"
ROGERS, MIMI—PHOTOGRAPHS
PH13756 615 (October 17, 1991) p101. "A Presaved Mimi Rogers Tries A Three-Way"
ROGERS, TIM—PHOTOGRAPHS
PH13757 705 (April 6, 1995) p23. "The Joys Of Noise: Adalita Of Magic Dirt (left) And You Am I's Tim Rogers" (Mott, Tony)
ROKER, ROXIE—PHOTOGRAPHS
PH13758 722 (November 30, 1995) p52. "Fun In The Sun: Kravitz And Mom Roxie Roker On The Beach In California, 1967"
ROLAND, DEAN—PHOTOGRAPHS
PH13759 686-687 (July 14, 1994) p30. "Soul Men: Childress, Evans, Dean Roland, Turpin And Ed Roland (clockwise from top left)" (Callahan, Kristin)
ROLAND, ED—PHOTOGRAPHS
PH13759 686-687 (July 14, 1994) p30. "Soul Men: Childress, Evans, Dean Roland, Turpin And Ed Roland (clockwise from top left)" (Callahan, Kristin)
ROLLER-SKATES—PHOTOGRAPHS
PH13760 686-687 (July 14, 1994) pp46-47. "[Toys]" (Grant, Bob)
ROLLERBLADES—PHOTOGRAPHS
PH13761 660-661 (July 8, 1993) p123. "Rollerblade Metroblade And Removable Shoe, $299 A Pair" (Miller, Greg)
ROLLING STONE (PUBLICATION)—ILLUSTRATIONS
PH13762 641 (October 15, 1992) p95. "[Rolling Stone]" (Bishofs, Maris)
PH13763 665 (September 16, 1993) p6. "Rolling Stone" (Pendergrast, James T.)
PH13764 668 (October 28, 1993) p8. "Rolling Stone" (Pendergrast, James T.)
PH13765 670 (November 25, 1993) p8. "Rolling Stone" (Pendergrast, James T.)
PH13766 674 (January 27, 1994) p8. "Rolling Stone: The Whole Truth" (Pendergrast, James T.)
PH13767 675 (February 10, 1994) p6. "Rolling Stone" (Pendergrast, James T.)
PH13768 676 (February 24, 1994) p10. "Rolling Stone" (Pendergrast, James T.)
PH13769 677 (March 10, 1994) p12. "Piss 'n' Vinegar" (Pendergrast, James T.)
PH13770 680 (April 21, 1994) p8. "Candy" (Pendergrast, James T.)
PH13771 681 (May 5, 1994) p8. "RS" (Pendergrast, James T.)
PH13772 682 (May 19, 1994) p14. "In Case Of Fire" (Pendergrast, James T.)
PH13773 693 (October 20, 1994) p22. "[Rolling Stone]" (Pendergrast, James T.)
PH13774 703 (March 9, 1995) p16. "Bandwagon" (Pendergrast, James T.)
PH13775 704 (March 23, 1995) p18. "Editors" (Pendergrast, James T.)
PH13776 710 (June 15, 1995) p14. "D. Parker" (Pendergrast, James T.)
PH13777 710 (June 15, 1995) p14. "Rolling Stone" (Pendergrast, James T.)
PH13778 724-725 (December 28, 1995) p24. "Napkin" (Pendergrast, James T.)
PH13779 729 (March 7, 1996) p6. "Rolling Stone" (Pendergrast, James T.)
PH13780 738-739 (July 11, 1996) p12. "Rolling Stone" (Pendergrast, James T.)
ROLLING STONE (PUBLICATION)—ILLUSTRATIONS—LETTERING
PH13781 632 (June 11, 1992) pp[cover]. "25" (Ortiz-Lopez, Dennis)
THE ROLLING STONE ILLUSTRATED HISTORY OF ROCK & ROLL (BOOK)—PHOTOGRAPHS
PH13782 645-646 (December 10, 1992) p87. "[History Of Rock & Roll]"
ROLLING STONES—ALBUMS
PH13783 617 (November 14, 1991) p93. "Exile On Main Street" (Van Hamersveld, John)
PH13784 617 (November 14, 1991) p93. "Exile On Main Street" (Frank, Robert)
PH13785 617 (November 14, 1991) p154. "Some Girls" (Corristan, Peter)
PH13786 617 (November 14, 1991) p93. "Sticky Fingers" (Braun, Craig)
PH13787 617 (November 14, 1991) p93. "Sticky Fingers" (Warhol, Andy)
PH13788 634-635 (July 9, 1992) p4. "Exile On Main Street"
PH13789 637 (August 20, 1992) p4. "Exile On Main Street"
PH13790 688 (August 11, 1994) p65. "Voodoo Lounge"
PH13791 698-699 (December 29, 1994) p170. "Voodoo Lounge"
ROLLING STONES—ILLUSTRATIONS
PH13792 632 (June 11, 1992) p57. "[Rolling Stones]" (Cronin, Brian)
PH13793 688 (August 11, 1994) p65. "Raw Stones" (Kelley, Gary)
PH13794 691 (September 22, 1994) p14. "Still Rolling" (Pendergrast, James T.)
PH13795 692 (October 6, 1994) p12. "[Rolling Stones]" (Pendergrast, James T.)
ROLLING STONES—PHOTOGRAPHS
PH13796 619-620 (December 12, 1991) p90. "...And Jagger (left)" (Mazur, Kevin)
PH13797 643 (November 12, 1992) p73. "Beth Sunflower Captured The Hell Of Altamont" (Sunflower, Beth)
PH13798 662 (August 5, 1993) p33. "Watts, Jagger And Richards In Barbados"
PH13799 668 (October 28, 1993) p35. "[Rolling Stones]"
PH13800 683 (June 2, 1994) p16. "Jagger And Richards Roll It Out One More Time" (Mazur, Kevin)
PH13801 684 (June 16, 1994) p35. "[Rolling Stones]" (Mazur, Kevin)

PH13802 686-687 (July 14, 1994) pp68-69. "And Then There Were Four: Charlie Watts, Ron Wood, Mick Jagger And Keith Richards" (Seliger, Mark)
PH13803 686-687 (July 14, 1994) p71. "Lounge Lizards: Don Was Confers With Keith Richards And Mick Jagger In The Studio" (Adebari, Eugene)
PH13804 689 (August 25, 1994) pp56-57. "Four Play In Toronto..." (Corbijn, Anton)
PH13805 689 (August 25, 1994) p61. "The Glimmer Twins, Still In The Swing Of Things: "It's Just You And Your mates," Says Richards" (Corbijn, Anton)
PH13806 689 (August 25, 1994) pp58-59. "[Mick Jagger & Keith Richards]" (Corbijn, Anton)
PH13807 689 (August 25, 1994) pp[cover]. "The Rolling Stones: Out For Blood" (Corbijn, Anton)
PH13808 689 (August 25, 1994) p60. ""We Risk reputation, And That's Everything," Says Watts, With A Masked Richards And Wood" (Corbijn, Anton)
PH13809 690 (September 8, 1994) p21. "Mick Jagger, Charlie Watts And Keith Richards (from left) Get Warmed Up In Toronto" (Halsband, Michael)
PH13810 693 (October 20, 1994) p27. "The Lifetime Achievers The Rolling Stones" (Mazur, Kevin)
PH13811 694 (November 3, 1994) p28. "Band On The Runway: The Stones Arrive At The Columbia Airport (left)" (Seliger, Mark)
PH13812 694 (November 3, 1994) p26. "The Final Bow" (Seliger, Mark)
PH13813 694 (November 3, 1994) p26. "Putting The Squeeze Play On Watts" (Seliger, Mark)
PH13814 694 (November 3, 1994) p28. "Richards And Wood "Warming Up The Hands" In Their Dressing Room" (Seliger, Mark)
PH13815 694 (November 3, 1994) p25. "[Rolling Stones]" (Seliger, Mark)
PH13816 694 (November 3, 1994) p26. "Wood And Richards" (Seliger, Mark)
PH13817 698-699 (December 29, 1994) p61. "[Rolling Stones]" (Mazur, Kevin)
PH13818 698-699 (December 29, 1994) p1. "The Rolling Stones: Out For Blood" (Corbijn, Anton)
PH13819 712-713 (July 13, 1995) p34. "Stoned In Amsterdam: Wood, Jagger, Richards And Watts (from left) Get Their Ya-Yas Out At The Paradiso" (Corbijn, Anton)
PH13820 715 (August 24, 1995) p37. "Jones, Richards, Watts, Jagger, Wyman (from left) [Watts, Richards, Jones, Jagger, Wyman (from left)]" (Mankowitz, Gered)
PH13821 720 (November 2, 1995) p49. "The Rolling Stones" (Kane, Art)
PH13822 723 (December 14, 1995) p52. "During Downtime On Tour, Jagger Lounging On A Hotel Bed With Watts On The Isle Of Man, 1964"
PH13823 723 (December 14, 1995) p56. "Jagger (with Charlie Watts, right) Performing 'Brown Sugar' From A Flatbed Truck In New York to Publicize The Stones' 1975 Tour Of The Americas" (Laffont, Jean Pierre)
PH13824 723 (December 14, 1995) p50. "Jagger And Richards Performing With The Stones At The Tower Ballroom, Near Liverpool, 1964"
PH13825 723 (December 14, 1995) p58. "Jagger Gets His Ya-Yas Out During A Spring And Summer 1976 Tour Of Europe"
PH13826 723 (December 14, 1995) p52. "The Rolling Stones Onstage At London's Marquee Club, 1963 (roadie, pal and sometimes pianist Ian Stewart is on maracas)"
PH13827 723 (December 14, 1995) pp54-55. "[The Rolling Stones]" (Marshall, Jim)
PH13828 723 (December 14, 1995) p62. "Wasted Elegance: Jagger And Richards Together In The 1970s"
PH13829 746 (October 31, 1996) p27. "Ono, Richards, Watts, Jagger And Jones (from left) With Circus Friends"

ROLLING STONES—PHOTOGRAPHS—PORTRAITS
PH13830 643 (November 12, 1992) p222. "Photographers Like Hiro, Who Shot The Stones' Album 'Black And Blue,' Helped Raise Cover Art To A New High" (Hiro)

ROLLING STONES—TAPES
PH13831 710 (June 15, 1995) p32. "Prehistoric Stones Fetch A Bundle"

ROLLINS BAND—ALBUMS
PH13832 626 (March 19, 1992) p92. "The End Of Silence"

ROLLINS BAND—PHOTOGRAPHS
PH13833 664 (September 2, 1993) p31. "Part Animal, Rollins" (Capak, R. J.)

ROLLINS, HENRY—ALBUMS
PH13834 680 (April 21, 1994) p83. "Weight"

ROLLINS, HENRY—BOOKS
PH13835 698-699 (December 29, 1994) p65. "Get In The Van"

ROLLINS, HENRY—ILLUSTRATIONS
PH13836 628 (April 16, 1992) p3. "Henry Rollins" (Burke, Philip)
PH13837 676 (February 24, 1994) p10. "What I Say—What I Do" (Pendergrast, James T.)
PH13838 680 (April 21, 1994) p83. "Pretty Hate Machines" (Habermacher, Rene)

ROLLINS, HENRY—ILLUSTRATIONS—LETTERING
PH13839 628 (April 16, 1992) p59. "[Henry Rollins]" (Allen, Terry)

ROLLINS, HENRY—PHOTOGRAPHS
PH13840 619-620 (December 12, 1991) p59. "Henry Rollins Stalks Lollapalooza" (Blakesberg, Jay)
PH13841 631 (May 28, 1992) p9. "Skate-Master Tate, MCA, Ad-Rock, Anthony Kiedis, Henry Rollins (from left)" (Cohen, Lester)
PH13842 650 (February 18, 1993) p18. "[Henry Rollins]" (Corbijn, Anton)
PH13843 664 (September 2, 1993) p31. "Part Animal, Rollins" (Capak, R. J.)
PH13844 676 (February 24, 1994) p28. "Henry Rollins Playing FAIR" (Jones, Sam)
PH13845 686-687 (July 14, 1994) p42. "Media Ho Henry Rollins, Vernon Reid And Rollins Guitarist Chris Haskett" (Malluk, Eddie)
PH13846 686-687 (July 14, 1994) p45. "[Rollins Band]" (Halfin, Ross)
PH13847 688 (August 11, 1994) p36. "More Days Of Peace And Music: Aerosmith (above) And Rollins (right)" (Davis, Katharine)
PH13848 688 (August 11, 1994) p36. "More Days Of Peace And Music: Aerosmith (above) And Rollins (right)" (Hutson, Mick)
PH13849 702 (February 23, 1995) p19. "Henry Rollins And Joe Strummer With Cash In L.A. (from left)" (Granitz, Steve)

ROLLINS, HENRY—PHOTOGRAPHS—PORTRAITS
PH13850 628 (April 16, 1992) p58. "[Henry Rollins]" (Klein, Steven)
PH13851 672-673 (December 23, 1993) p112. "Hardcore Heroes Black Flag In March 1984: Bill Stevenson, Kira Roessler, Greg Ginn And Rollins (from left)" (Rosenberg, Howard)
PH13852 672-673 (December 23, 1993) p111. "[Henry Rollins]" (Watson, Albert)
PH13853 672-673 (December 23, 1993) p16. "Henry Rollins: The Mouth That Roared" (Ockenfels, Frank W.)
PH13854 695 (November 17, 1994) p105. "Henry Rollins" (Mahurin, Matt)
PH13855 708 (May 18, 1995) p17. "Erickson (left) And Rollins In Austin" (Chernikowski, Stephanie)

ROLLINS, RIZ—PHOTOGRAPHS
PH13856 678 (March 24, 1994) p55. "Rollins On His Old Home, KCMU: 'You Used To Turn It On To Be Enlightened, Now You Turn It On As Background.'" (Lavine, Michael)

ROLSTON, MATTHEW—ILLUSTRATIONS
PH13857 643 (November 12, 1992) p97. "[Matthew Rolston]" (Russo, Anthony)
ROLSTON, MATTHEW—ILLUSTRATIONS—LETTERING
PH13858 643 (November 12, 1992) p97. "[Matthew Rolston]" (Karl, Anita)
ROLSTON, MATTHEW—PHOTOGRAPHS
PH13859 643 (November 12, 1992) p246. "Moving On: Photographer Matthew Rolston (seated right) Directs The En Vogue Video 'My Lovin'" (House, Troy)
ROMANCE—PHOTOGRAPHS
PH13860 719 (October 19, 1995) pp137-138,140+. "[Dating]"
ROMANO, RAY—ILLUSTRATIONS
PH13861 745 (October 17, 1996) p139. "[Ray Romano]" (Witte, Michael)
ROMEO IS BLEEDING (FILM)—ILLUSTRATIONS
PH13862 675 (February 10, 1994) p51. "Playing Rough" (Panter, Gary)
PH13863 679 (April 7, 1994) p10. "Violence" (Pendergrast, James T.)
ROMEO IS BLEEDING (FILM)—PHOTOGRAPHS
PH13864 675 (February 10, 1994) p52. "Cop Gary Oldman Beds Down With Devil Lena Olin"
ROMPER STOMPER (FILM)—PHOTOGRAPHS
PH13865 658 (June 10, 1993) p78. "Aussie Skinheads Find A Way Of Life In Race Hatred"
RONSON, MICK—ALBUMS
PH13866 681 (May 5, 1994) p13. "Heaven 'N Hull"
RONSON, MICK—ILLUSTRATIONS
PH13867 682 (May 19, 1994) p103. "Mick Ronson" (Bartholomew, Caty)
RONSON, MICK—PHOTOGRAPHS
PH13868 658 (June 10, 1993) p64. "Onstage With His Longtime Collaborator Mick Ronson During The Spiders' 1973 Japanese Tour"
PH13869 659 (June 24, 1993) p28. "Bowie (with sax) And Ronson (with axe) Were Reunited On Record This Year"
PH13870 659 (June 24, 1993) p28. "Ronson At Work In The Studio In 1981" (Goldsmith, Lynn)
PH13871 672-673 (December 23, 1993) p80. "Below: Ziggy Sidekick Mick Ronson" (Goldsmith, Lynn)
PH13872 681 (May 5, 1994) p13. "Ronson On Stage With His Old Pal Ian Hunter (left) Back In 1975" (Putland, Michael)
RONSTADT, LINDA—ALBUMS
PH13873 623 (February 6, 1992) p77. "Mas Canciones"
PH13874 671 (December 9, 1993) p66. "Winter Light"
RONSTADT, LINDA—PHOTOGRAPHS
PH13875 630 (May 14, 1992) p22. "Jerry Brown In The Late Seventies With Linda Ronstadt, Jackson Browne (right), The Eagles And Other West Coast Musicians" (Pulin, Chuck)
RONSTADT, LINDA—PHOTOGRAPHS—PORTRAITS
PH13876 645-646 (December 10, 1992) p147. "Linda Ronstadt, 1976"
PH13877 712-713 (July 13, 1995) p40. "[Linda Ronstadt]" (Crum, Lee)
ROOMMATES—PHOTOGRAPHS
PH13878 682 (May 19, 1994) p57. "[Electronic Bulletin Boards]"
ROONEY, ANDY—ILLUSTRATIONS
PH13879 740 (August 8, 1996) p65. "[Andy Rooney]" (Allen, Terry)
ROOTS—ALBUMS
PH13880 747 (November 14, 1996) p114. "Illadelph Halflife"
ROOTS—PHOTOGRAPHS
PH13881 715 (August 24, 1995) p87. "Hot Rappers" (Johnson, Eric)
PH13882 748 (November 28, 1996) p44. "In The Groove" (Lavine, Michael)
ROSAS, CESAR—PHOTOGRAPHS
PH13883 616 (October 31, 1991) p13. "Cesar Rosas, Louis Perez, Conrad Lozano, David Hidalgo And Steve Berlin (from left)" (Granitz, Steve)
PH13884 640 (October 1, 1992) p34. "Los Lobos Guitarist Cesar Rosas" (Granitz, Steve)
ROSE, AXL—ILLUSTRATIONS
PH13885 619-620 (December 12, 1991) p5. "[Axl Rose]" (Burke, Philip)
PH13886 641 (October 15, 1992) p191. "[Axl Rose]" (Collier, John)
ROSE, AXL—PHOTOGRAPHS
PH13887 619-620 (December 12, 1991) p55. "Axl Rose" (Mazur, Kevin)
PH13888 619-620 (December 12, 1991) p59. "Axl Rose In St. Louis" (Mazur, Kevin)
PH13889 619-620 (December 12, 1991) p55. "The Dynamic Duo? Axl And Slash (above)" (Mazur, Kevin)
PH13890 622 (January 23, 1992) p11. "Axl Rose" (Kirkland, Gene)
PH13891 625 (March 5, 1992) p19. "Axl Rose (left) And Slash" (Mazur, Kevin)
PH13892 625 (March 5, 1992) p55. "'Comeback' From The 'Worst' Band" (Kirkland, Gene)
PH13893 627 (April 2, 1992) pp32,35,37. "[Axl Rose]" (Ritts, Herb)
PH13894 633 (June 25, 1992) p17. "An Emotional High Point: Elton And Axl At The End Of 'Bohemian Rhapsody'" (Mazur, Kevin)
PH13895 637 (August 20, 1992) p19. "Axl Rose" (Redferns)
PH13896 637 (August 20, 1992) p17. "Axl To Police: 'You Guys Are A Riot'"
PH13897 639 (September 17, 1992) p19. "Axl Rose Skips The Vegetarian Platter"
PH13898 642 (October 29, 1992) p19. "Elton John (left) And Axl Rose" (Mazur, Kevin)
PH13899 642 (October 29, 1992) p26. "Happier Days: Izzy With Axl" (Funk, Harrison)
PH13900 645-646 (December 10, 1992) p49. "Axl Rose Hangs With The Men In Blue"
PH13901 645-646 (December 10, 1992) p45. "John And Rose (below)" (Mazur, Kevin)
PH13902 649 (February 4, 1993) p9. "Let's See, A Is For Apple, Asshole, Assault..."
PH13903 662 (August 5, 1993) p59. "Axl Rose" (Mazur, Kevin)
PH13904 671 (December 9, 1993) p14. "Citizen Rose Leaving Court" (Butkus, Mary)
PH13905 672-673 (December 23, 1993) p17. "Axl Rose Vacationing In Brazil"
PH13906 672-673 (December 23, 1993) p74. "Slash And Axl: Punks For A Day" (Mazur, Kevin)
PH13907 676 (February 24, 1994) p28. "Producer Waddy Wachtel And Gunmen Gilby And Axl" (John, Robert)
PH13908 677 (March 10, 1994) p28. "Springsteen And Rose Come Together" (Mazur, Kevin)
PH13909 680 (April 21, 1994) p20. "[Axl Rose]" (Mazur, Kevin)
PH13910 693 (October 20, 1994) p79. "A Friend In Deed: Jeremy (left) And Axl Rose At Ciro's" (Jeremy, Ron)
ROSE, AXL—PHOTOGRAPHS—PORTRAITS
PH13911 627 (April 2, 1992) pp[cover]. "Axl Rose: The Rolling Stone Interview" (Ritts, Herb)
PH13912 643 (November 12, 1992) p158. "Axl Rose" (Ritts, Herb)
PH13913 645-646 (December 10, 1992) pp[cover]. "1992 Yearbook" (Ritts, Herb)
PH13914 645-646 (December 10, 1992) p147. "Axl Rose, 1992"
ROSE, JIM—PHOTOGRAPHS
PH13915 639 (September 17, 1992) p62. "Jim Rose And The Amazing Mr. Lifto" (Blakesberg, Jay)
ROSE, TRICIA—BOOKS
PH13916 698-699 (December 29, 1994) p64. "Black Noise"

ROSEANNE—ILLUSTRATIONS
PH13917 682 (May 19, 1994) p68. "[White Trash]" (Friedman, Drew)
ROSEANNE—PHOTOGRAPHS
PH13918 698-699 (December 29, 1994) p66. "MTV Host Roseanne With Salt-N-Pepa" (Kravitz, Jeff)
PH13919 738-739 (July 11, 1996) p15. "Thom Yorke, Colin Greenwood, Roseanne, Ed O'Brien, Phil Selway And Jonny Greenwood" (Diltz, Henry)
ROSEN, FRED—PHOTOGRAPHS—PORTRAITS
PH13920 692 (October 6, 1994) p22. "Ticketmaster CEO Fred Rosen"
ROSENBERG, MICA—PHOTOGRAPHS
PH13921 745 (October 17, 1996) p103. "Headed For Brown? Mica Rosenberg, A High-School Senior In Albuquerque, With Consultant Rusty Haynes" (Ford, Charles)
ROSS, DIANA—PHOTOGRAPHS
PH13922 735 (May 30, 1996) p50. "Ross, Sting, Taylor And Williams (from left)" (Mazur, Kevin)
PH13923 735 (May 30, 1996) p12. "Swing Out, Sister" (Mazur, Kevin)
PH13924 750-751 (December 26, 1996) p57. "The Rainforest All-Star Supremes Tribute" (Mazur, Kevin)
ROSS, DIANA—PHOTOGRAPHS—PORTRAITS
PH13925 643 (November 12, 1992) p191. "Diana Ross" (Watson, Albert)
PH13926 643 (November 12, 1992) p78. "Diana Ross Turned To Scavullo For Her Post-Supremes Look" (Scavullo, Francesco)
ROSS, JASON—PHOTOGRAPHS
PH13927 731 (April 4, 1996) p36. "The Two Jasons (Pollock and Ross), Khalsa And Daniel" (Clinch, Danny)
ROSS, RHONDA—PHOTOGRAPHS
PH13928 694 (November 3, 1994) p22. "Ross With Saxaphonist Reggie Woods" (Mazur, Kevin)
ROSSDALE, GAVIN—PHOTOGRAPHS
PH13929 710 (June 15, 1995) p49. "Dave Parsons, Rossdale, Robin Goodridge, Pulsford (from left)" (Westenberg, Kevin)
PH13930 712-713 (July 13, 1995) p30. "Pulsford (left) And Rossdale In New York In March" (Olson, Sheryl)
PH13931 712-713 (July 13, 1995) p29. "Zen Careerists: Pulsford, Parsons, Rossdale, And Goodridge (from left)" (Mahurin, Matt)
PH13932 732 (April 18, 1996) p44. "Rossdale Onstage At RFK Stadium, In Washington, D.C., June '95" (Mendelsohn, Matt)
PH13933 732 (April 18, 1996) pp[cover]. "Three Million Albums, Five Hit Singles...Bush: Why Won't Anyone Take Gavin Rossdale Seriously?" (Seliger, Mark)
PH13934 743 (September 19, 1996) p20. "[Gavin Rossdale & Robert Smith]" (Davies, Meredith)
PH13935 745 (October 17, 1996) p27. "Gavin Rossdale, Gwen Stefani And Dennis Rodman, At A Pre-Show Bash" (Mazur, Kevin)
ROSSDALE, GAVIN—PHOTOGRAPHS—PORTRAITS
PH13936 718 (October 5, 1995) p20. "Oh, The Indignity: Rossdale" (Pope, Pat)
PH13937 732 (April 18, 1996) p42. "[Gavin Rossdale]" (Seliger, Mark)
PH13938 732 (April 18, 1996) p41. "Robin Goodridge, Gavin Rossdale, Dave Parsons And Nigel Pulsford" (Seliger, Mark)
ROSSELLINI, ISABELLA—PHOTOGRAPHS
PH13939 615 (October 17, 1991) p64. "Anjelica Huston And Isabella Rossellini, 1990" (Pigozzi, Jean)
PH13940 700 (January 26, 1995) p66. "Oldman, Rossellini"
ROSSITER, MARTIN—PHOTOGRAPHS
PH13941 719 (October 19, 1995) p33. "At The Forefront: Martin Rossiter Of Gene" (Moore, Suzan)
ROSTENKOWSKI, DAN—PHOTOGRAPHS—PORTRAITS
PH13942 698-699 (December 29, 1994) p152. "[Dan Rostenkowski]"
ROTH, ARLEN—PHOTOGRAPHS
PH13943 702 (February 23, 1995) p35. "Albert Lee, Arlen Roth And Les Paul (from left)" (Capak, R. J.)
ROTH, DAVID LEE—ALBUMS
PH13944 685 (June 30, 1994) p74. "Your Filthy Little Mouth"
ROTH, DAVID LEE—ILLUSTRATIONS
PH13945 708 (May 18, 1995) p14. "[Roth, David Lee]" (Pendergrast, James T.)
ROTH, DAVID LEE—PHOTOGRAPHS
PH13946 657 (May 27, 1993) p9. "[David Lee Roth]" (Arrigo, Charles A.)
PH13947 745 (October 17, 1996) p27. "David Lee Roth With Pumpkin Billy Corgan And Eddie Van Halen" (Kravitz, Jeff)
PH13948 750-751 (December 26, 1996) p78. "Van Halen's Michael Anthony, And Alex And Eddie Van Halen With Roth (from left)" (Christensen, Jeff)
ROTH, TIM—PHOTOGRAPHS
PH13949 707 (May 4, 1995) p74. "Roth And Neeson In 'Rob Roy'"
PH13950 741 (August 22, 1996) p26. "Roth (right) With Shakur, Who Says, 'We're The Most Unlikely Action Stars.'" (Goode, Nicola)
ROTHBERG, PATTI—PHOTOGRAPHS
PH13951 744 (October 3, 1996) p30. "Rothberg Between Her Guitar And A Chair" (Clinch, Danny)
ROTHCHILD, PAUL—PHOTOGRAPHS
PH13952 708 (May 18, 1995) p33. "Producer Rothchild: He Was The Fifth Door"
ROTSEY, MARTIN—PHOTOGRAPHS
PH13953 658 (June 10, 1993) p19. "Burnin' Again: Hillman, Garrett, Moginie, Hirst, Rotsey (from left)" (Seliger, Mark)
PH13954 669 (November 11, 1993) p28. "The Oils' Peter Garrett With Guitarist Martin Rotsey" (Blakesberg, Jay)
ROTTEN, JOHNNY—PHOTOGRAPHS
PH13955 734 (May 16, 1996) p17. "Matlock, Rotten, Jones And Cook Now" (Gruen, Bob)
PH13956 734 (May 16, 1996) p17. "The Pistols' Rotten, Glen Matlock, Steve Jones And Paul Cook In '76" (Gruen, Bob)
PH13957 736 (June 13, 1996) p52. "Pistols '96: Glen Matlock, Steve Jones, Paul Cook And Johnny Rotten (from left)" (Thomas, Justin)
PH13958 740 (August 8, 1996) p30. "A Public Image: Rotten Sells Out At Finsbury Park" (Plummer, Barry)
PH13959 744 (October 3, 1996) p19. "Humperdinck, Who Looks Like A Senator From Nevada, And His Pal Rotten"
PH13960 750-751 (December 26, 1996) p64. "Rotten Getting Filthy In The U.S.A."
ROUNTREE, DAVE—PHOTOGRAPHS—PORTRAITS
PH13961 720 (November 2, 1995) p19. "'Great Escape' Artists Coxon, Albarn, James And Rountree (from left)" (Westenberg, Kevin)
ROURKE, MICKEY—PHOTOGRAPHS
PH13962 630 (May 14, 1992) p114. "Dafoe (left) Suspects Rourke And Mastrantonio"
ROWAN, VICTORIA—PHOTOGRAPHS
PH13963 666 (September 30, 1993) p82. "Rowan: 'If You Show Up In Jeans And A Sweat Shirt, They'll Treat You Like A Kid'" (Irish, Len)
ROWLANDS, GENA—ILLUSTRATIONS
PH13964 630 (May 14, 1992) p111. "When Worlds Collide In A Taxicab" (Woolley, Janet)
ROWNTREE, DAVE—PHOTOGRAPHS
PH13965 694 (November 3, 1994) p34. "Social Distortion: Blur's Coxon, Albarn, Rowntree And James (from left)" (Westenberg, Kevin)
ROWNTREE, DAVE—PHOTOGRAPHS—PORTRAITS
PH13966 623 (February 6, 1992) p32. "Alex James, Damon Albarn, Graham Coxon, Dave Rowntree (clockwise from top)" (Lavine, Michael)
ROXY MUSIC—ALBUMS
PH13967 617 (November 14, 1991) p132. "Country Life" (Ferry, Bryan)

PH13968 617 (November 14, 1991) p132. "Country Life" (Boman, Eric)
ROYAL FAMILY (TELEVISION SHOW)—PHOTOGRAPHS
PH13969 619-620 (December 12, 1991) p202. "Redd Foxx (with his 'Royal Family' costar, Della Reese) Died In 'Real Life'"
ROYAL THEATER (BALTIMORE, MARYLAND)—PHOTOGRAPHS
PH13970 659 (June 24, 1993) p46. "The Royal Theater in 1949, The Heart Of Black Night Life In Baltimore"
ROYAL TRUX—ALBUMS
PH13971 664 (September 2, 1993) p66. "Cats And Dogs"
PH13972 711 (June 29, 1995) p42. "Thank You"
ROYAL TRUX—PHOTOGRAPHS
PH13973 710 (June 15, 1995) p36. "Brown, Herrema, Hagerty And Pyle (from left): 'We're A Marketing Nightmare'" (Westenberg, Kevin)
ROZALLA—ALBUMS
PH13974 645-646 (December 10, 1992) p184. "Everybody's Free"
PH13975 717 (September 21, 1995) p84. "Look No Further"
RUBIN, JERRY—PHOTOGRAPHS
PH13976 738-739 (July 11, 1996) p70. "Leary Plotting With Abbie Hoffman (left) And Jerry Rubin, 1968"
RUBIN, MARK—PHOTOGRAPHS—PORTRAITS
PH13977 697 (December 15, 1994) p40. "Bad Boys: Barnes, Rubin And White (from left)" (Cardillicchio, Nick)
RUBIN, RICK—PHOTOGRAPHS
PH13978 644 (November 26, 1992) p15. "Rubin (left) And Jagger" (Mazur, Kevin)
PH13979 667 (October 14, 1993) p40. "Al Sharpton Escorts Rick Rubin To The Funeral" (Granitz, Steve)
PH13980 674 (January 27, 1994) p28. "Jeff Lynne, Tom Petty, Johnny Cash And Rick Rubin (from left) At The Viper Room" (Kirkland, Gene)
PH13981 719 (October 19, 1995) p64. "Johnny Cash Was The First Music Veteran Whose Career Rubin Revitalized" (McDaniel, Melodie)
PH13982 719 (October 19, 1995) pp62-63. "[Rick Rubin]" (McDaniel, Melodie)
PH13983 719 (October 19, 1995) p67. "Rubin In A Los Angeles Studio Working With Donovan On The Singer's Comeback" (McDaniel, Melodie)
PH13984 719 (October 19, 1995) p64. "Rubin, In White T-Shirt And Beard, With Members Of The Beasties, Slayer And Run-D.M.C. In 1985"
PH13985 750-751 (December 26, 1996) p88. "Producer Rick Rubin, Benmont Tench, Petty And Cash (from left) Work Their Magic"
PH13986 750-751 (December 26, 1996) p74. "Stipe, Rick Rubin, Nusrat Ali Khan, Stephen Dorff And Flea (from left)" (Cohen, Lester)
RUBY (FILM)—PHOTOGRAPHS
PH13987 628 (April 16, 1992) p93. "Danny Aiello As Jack Ruby Chats Up Sherilyn Fenn"
RUBY IN PARADISE (FILM)—PHOTOGRAPHS
PH13988 672-673 (December 23, 1993) p172. "Debut"
PH13989 678 (March 24, 1994) p100. "Missing In Oscar Action"
RUCKER, DARIUS—ILLUSTRATIONS
PH13990 710 (June 15, 1995) p9. "Hootie's Darius Rucker" (Burke, Philip)
RUCKER, DARIUS—PHOTOGRAPHS
PH13991 691 (September 22, 1994) p19. "Hootie Goes to Washington: Soni, Dean Felber, The Prez, Darius Rucker, Bryan (from left)"
PH13992 705 (April 6, 1995) p36. "Rucker Boots And Hollers" (Smith, Sean C.)
PH13993 714 (August 10, 1995) p44. "Darius Rucker: It Would Be Nice To Get Respect As A Band" (Seliger, Mark)
PH13994 714 (August 10, 1995) pp42-43. "Darius Rucker, Dean Felber, Mark Bryan And Jim Sonefeld" (Seliger, Mark)
PH13995 724-725 (December 28, 1995) p58. "Hootie's Darius Rucker At The Bridge School Benefit" (Blakesberg, Jay)
PH13996 726 (January 25, 1996) p37. "Hootie And The Blowfish: Jim Sonefeld, Darius Rucker, Dean Felber And Mark Bryan (from left)" (Seliger, Mark)
PH13997 733 (May 2, 1996) p24. "Hootie's Darius Rucker" (Steinwehe, M.)
RUDGE, DAVID—PHOTOGRAPHS
PH13998 648 (January 21, 1993) p41. "Dead Or Alive? Diane And Peter (left) With His Brother David" (Klicker, John)
RUDGE, FRANCIE—PHOTOGRAPHS
PH13999 648 (January 21, 1993) p42. "Home Alone: Francie Rudge Kept A Vigil For Her Missing Son" (Klicker, John)
RUDGE, PETER JAY—PHOTOGRAPHS
PH14000 648 (January 21, 1993) p41. "Dead Or Alive? Diane And Peter (left) With His Brother David" (Klicker, John)
RUDIN, SCOTT—PHOTOGRAPHS
PH14001 618 (November 28, 1991) p58. "Mysterious And Spooky (from left): Rudin, Sonnenfeld And Tattersall" (Gordon, Melinda Sue)
RUDZITIS—PHOTOGRAPHS—PORTRAITS
PH14002 634-635 (July 9, 1992) p20. "Love Battery (from left): Kevin Whitworth, Rod Rudzitis And Jason Finn" (Lavine, Michael)
RUE, CAROLINE—PHOTOGRAPHS—PORTRAITS
PH14003 637 (August 20, 1992) p15. "Hole's Jill Emery, Eric Erlandson, Love And Caroline Rue (from left)" (Lavine, Michael)
RUEHL, MERCEDES—PHOTOGRAPHS
PH14004 657 (May 27, 1993) p58. "Lost: Coolidge And Ruehl Flank Simon"
RUFFIN, DAVID—PHOTOGRAPHS—PORTRAITS
PH14005 619-620 (December 12, 1991) p109. "David Ruffin"
RUMBLE MILITIA—PHOTOGRAPHS
PH14006 669 (November 11, 1993) p18. "...But Threatens Leftist Rumble Militia (below)"
RUN—ILLUSTRATIONS
PH14007 660-661 (July 8, 1993) p7. "Run Of Run-D.M.C." (Burke, Philip)
RUN—PHOTOGRAPHS
PH14008 667 (October 14, 1993) p73. "'Walk This Way': Run, Stephen Tyler"
PH14009 718 (October 5, 1995) p26. "Rev. Run Revs It Up" (Camp, E. J.)
RUN—PHOTOGRAPHS—PORTRAITS
PH14010 724-725 (December 28, 1995) p54. "The Reverend Run Put A Spin On Gospel Rap" (Friedman, Glen E.)
RUN-D.M.C.—ALBUMS
PH14011 659 (June 24, 1993) p83. "Down With The King"
RUN-D.M.C.—PHOTOGRAPHS
PH14012 660-661 (July 8, 1993) p16. "Days Of Gold: Run-D.M.C. At The Ritz In New York City, 1988" (Elgar, Nick)
PH14013 719 (October 19, 1995) p64. "Rubin, In White T-Shirt And Beard, With Members Of The Beasties, Slayer And Run-D.M.C. In 1985"
RUN-D.M.C.—PHOTOGRAPHS—PORTRAITS
PH14014 660-661 (July 8, 1993) p15. "[Run-D.M.C.]" (Frohman, Jesse)
PH14015 672-673 (December 23, 1993) p30. "Right: The Kings, Run-D.M.C." (Vaccaro, Nick)
THE RUN OF THE COUNTRY (FILM)—PHOTOGRAPHS
PH14016 718 (October 5, 1995) p79. "Matt Keesler And Victoria Smurfit Skinny-Dip"
RUNDGREN, TODD—PHOTOGRAPHS
PH14017 616 (October 31, 1991) p13. "Rundgren, Eric Gardner, Janis Gardner, Little Richard, Spector (from left)" (Granitz, Steve)
PH14018 623 (February 6, 1992) p11. "Isaak With Todd Rundgren" (Blakesberg, Jay)
RUNDGREN, TODD—PHOTOGRAPHS—PORTRAITS
PH14019 677 (March 10, 1994) p24. "Rundgren: L.A. Concert

Shake-Up" (Blakesberg, Jay)
RUPAUL—PHOTOGRAPHS
PH14020 667 (October 14, 1993) p39. "Above: Nirvana's Dave Grohl And Kurt Cobain Flanking RuPaul And Frances Cobain" (Kravitz, Jeff)
PH14021 667 (October 14, 1993) p90. "Work It, Girl: RuPaul Shows His Roots"
PH14022 672-673 (December 23, 1993) p41. "Supermodel Of The World: RuPaul" (Eichner, Steve)
PH14023 710 (June 15, 1995) p41. "[RuPaul]" (Marzullo, Joseph)
PH14024 718 (October 5, 1995) p77. "Rupal, Keitel And Gorham Boogie"
RUPAUL—PHOTOGRAPHS—PORTRAITS
PH14025 662 (August 5, 1993) p24. "[RuPaul]" (Contrato, Mark)
RUPE, BOB—PHOTOGRAPHS
PH14026 660-661 (July 8, 1993) p101. "Gutterball: Johnny Hott, Bryan Harvey, Steve Wynn, Bob Rupe, Stephen McCarthy"
PH14027 663 (August 19, 1993) p15. "Rupe, Hott, Harvey, Wynn And McCarthy (from left)" (Callahan, Walter)
PH14028 732 (April 18, 1996) p47. "Playing Cowboys In The Desert: Bob Rupe, Charlie Quintana, David Lowery And Johnny Hickman (from left)" (Maxwell, Robert)
PH14029 737 (June 27, 1996) p15. "Tjinder Singh With Cracker's Johnny Hickman And Bob Rupe (from left)" (Roberts, Ebet)
RUSH (FILM)—PHOTOGRAPHS
PH14030 617 (November 14, 1991) p13. "Allman (right) In 'Rush'" (Birmelin, Bruce)
PH14031 621 (January 9, 1992) p55. "Jason Patric And Jennifer Jason Leigh In Danger"
RUSH RUSH (VIDEO)—PHOTOGRAPHS
PH14032 619-620 (December 12, 1991) p33. "Paula Abdul's 'Rush Rush'"
RUSH, BOBBY—PHOTOGRAPHS—PORTRAITS
PH14033 642 (October 29, 1992) p49. "[Bobby Rush]"
RUSH, OTIS—ALBUMS
PH14034 689 (August 25, 1994) p89. "Ain't Enough Comin' In"
RUSH, OTIS—PHOTOGRAPHS
PH14035 717 (September 21, 1995) p19. "The Blues Had A Baby, And It Named It Punk Rock: Vedder (left) And Rush"
RUSHDIE, SALMAN—PHOTOGRAPHS
PH14036 666 (September 30, 1993) p27. "Salman Rushdie (left) Give Bono Macphisto An Earful Of Fashion Advice" (Rasic, Brian)
PH14037 667 (October 14, 1993) p54. "Their Satanic Majesties: Bono As The Fly And Salman Rushdie" (Corbijn, Anton)
PH14038 672-673 (December 23, 1993) p57. "Satan, In Disguise (left) Meets The 'Outed' Author Of 'The Santanic Verse' In London" (Corbijn, Anton)
RUSHTON, PHILIPPE—PHOTOGRAPHS—PORTRAITS
PH14039 693 (October 20, 1994) p107. "Philippe Rushton Of The University Of Western Ontario" (Gajdel, Edward)
RUSSELL, KURT—PHOTOGRAPHS
PH14040 742 (September 5, 1996) p68. "Kurt Russell Returns AS Snake Plissken"
RUSSELL, LEON—ALBUMS
PH14041 631 (May 28, 1992) p54. "Anything Can Happen"
RUSSELL, LUTHER—PHOTOGRAPHS
PH14042 622 (January 23, 1992) p14. "Clockwise From Top Left: Davel Sobel, Luther Russell, Chris Joyner, John Hofer, Jason Hiller" (Annalisa)
RUSSELL, TOM—ALBUMS
PH14043 670 (November 25, 1993) p117. "Hillbilly Voodoo"
RUSSIA—PHOTOGRAPHS
PH14044 750-751 (December 26, 1996) p73. "Comrades! Just One More Jell-O Shot For Inspiration!"
RUSSO, DAVID—PHOTOGRAPHS—PORTRAITS
PH14045 631 (May 28, 1992) p22. "David Russo And Joan Jones" (Lewis, Robert)
RUSSO, RENE—PHOTOGRAPHS
PH14046 678 (March 24, 1994) p100. "Missing In Oscar Action"
PH14047 720 (November 2, 1995) p74. "Travolta And Russo Take A Meeting"
RUSTED ROOT—ALBUMS
PH14048 749 (December 12, 1996) p82. "Remember"
RUTGERS UNIVERSITY—PHOTOGRAPHS
PH14049 730 (March 21, 1996) p65. "New Jersey's Rutgers University"
RUTHERFORD, MIKE—PHOTOGRAPHS
PH14050 624 (February 20, 1992) p17. "Genesis, From Left: Tony Banks, Mike Rutherford And Phil Collins" (Ockenfels, Frank W.)
RWANDA—ILLUSTRATIONS
PH14051 694 (November 3, 1994) p14. "Apathy" (Pendergrast, James T.)
RWANDA—PHOTOGRAPHS
PH14052 712-713 (July 13, 1995) pp86-91. "[Rwanda]" (Salgado, Sebastiao)
RWANDANS—PHOTOGRAPHS
PH14053 691 (September 22, 1994) pp67,69-74,76+. "[Rwandan Refugees In Zaire]" (Salgado, Sebastiao)
RYAN, DAVE—PHOTOGRAPHS
PH14054 675 (February 10, 1994) p39. "The Squeaky Clean, Endlessly Cute Power-Pop Trio: Drummer Ryan, Dando And Bassist Dalton" (Rheims, Bettina)
RYAN, EILEEN—PHOTOGRAPHS
PH14055 731 (April 4, 1996) p48. "Parents Leo Penn And Eileen Ryan" (Dominguez, Ralph)
RYAN, MEG—ILLUSTRATIONS
PH14056 660-661 (July 8, 1993) p119. "Date-Night Film Frenzy" (Blitt, Barry)
PH14057 740 (August 8, 1996) p67. "Summer Gets Serious" (Brodner, Steve)
RYAN, MEG—PHOTOGRAPHS
PH14058 637 (August 20, 1992) p57. "Soul-Searching: Ryan (left) And Baldwin"
PH14059 660-661 (July 8, 1993) p120. "'Someday My Prince Will Come' Is A Theme For Ryan (with Hanks, above)"
PH14060 670 (November 25, 1993) p126. "Dennis Quaid And Meg Ryan Steal A Kiss"
PH14061 682 (May 19, 1994) p107. "Stormy Triangle Garcia, Ryan And Booze"
PH14062 705 (April 6, 1995) p69. "Oscar Rejects"
PH14063 708 (May 18, 1995) p96. "Meg Ryan Mixes It Up With French Kisser Kevin Kline"
PH14064 740 (August 8, 1996) p68. "Moriarty (left), Washington"
PH14065 740 (August 8, 1996) p68. "Ryan Under Fire"
RYAN, MEG—PHOTOGRAPHS—PORTRAITS
PH14066 686-687 (July 14, 1994) p42. "[Meg Ryan]" (Robert, Eric)
PH14067 700 (January 26, 1995) p66. "Smart Women, Foolish Choices"
RYAN-HARRIS, DAVID—PHOTOGRAPHS
PH14068 618 (November 28, 1991) p11. "Clockwise From Left: Buck, Enrique, Ryan-Harris, Chris Tinsley, Kinney, Billy Fields And Jamie Turner (wearing glasses)" (Diamond, Rick)
PH14069 625 (March 5, 1992) p27. "Jamie Turner, David Ryan-Harris, Billy Fields, Chris Tinsley, Enrique (from left)" (Leitman, Ruth)
RYDER, MITCH—PHOTOGRAPHS
PH14070 681 (May 5, 1994) p21. "Ryder And Dr. Death: Devil With A Blue Sweater On?"
RYDER, PAUL—PHOTOGRAPHS
PH14071 638 (September 3, 1992) p11. "Weymouth, Shaun Ryder, Frantz And Paul Ryder (clockwise from lower left)" (Gershoff, Gary)

RYDER, SHAUN—PHOTOGRAPHS
PH14071 638 (September 3, 1992) p11. "Weymouth, Shaun Ryder, Frantz And Paul Ryder (clockwise from lower left)" (Gershoff, Gary)
PH14072 727 (February 8, 1996) p13. "Run For The Border: Ryder (left) And Bez In Cuba" (Ayanian, Ryan)
RYDER, SHAUN—PHOTOGRAPHS—PORTRAITS
PH14073 723 (December 14, 1995) p40. "Kermit, Bez And Ryder (from left) Mix An Intoxicating Musical Cocktail" (Westenberg, Kevin)
RYDER, WINONA—ILLUSTRATIONS
PH14074 630 (May 14, 1992) p111. "When Worlds Collide In A Taxicab" (Woolley, Janet)
PH14075 677 (March 10, 1994) p59. "Twenty Something" (Ryden, Mark)
RYDER, WINONA—PHOTOGRAPHS
PH14076 619-620 (December 12, 1991) pp[cover]. "1991 Yearbook" (Ritts, Herb)
PH14077 630 (May 14, 1992) p112. "Jim Jarmusch Dispatches Driver Winona Ryder"
PH14078 677 (March 10, 1994) p47. "Future Hazy, Try Again: Ryder And Her 'Reality Bites' Boyfriend, Ethan Hawke"
PH14079 677 (March 10, 1994) p46. "Ryder At The 'Age Of Innocence' Premiere With Dave Pirner Of Soul Asylum" (Elgar, Nick)
PH14080 677 (March 10, 1994) p48. "Ryder, With Klaas' Grandfather Joe Klaas And A Neighbor, Learns Of Polly's Death" (Manchester, Scott)
PH14081 677 (March 10, 1994) p60. "Streep And Close Play Ball (left), While Ryder And Her Lover, Banderas, Play Around"
PH14082 677 (March 10, 1994) pp44-45. "[Winona Ryder]" (Ritts, Herb)
PH14083 677 (March 10, 1994) p47. "With Daniel Day-Lewis In 'The Age Of Innocence'"
PH14084 677 (March 10, 1994) p60. "Zahn, Ryder, Garofalo And Hawke Face A Shaky Future (from left)"
PH14085 692 (October 6, 1994) p45. "Winona Ryder, Phair And Rosanna Arquette In Santa Monica, 1994" (Kravitz, Jeff)
PH14086 703 (March 9, 1995) p49. "Reality Bites Back: Hawke On The Set With Ryder" (Redin, Van)
PH14087 711 (June 29, 1995) p32. "In The Limelight: Pirner With Girlfriend Winona Ryder At This Year's Oscar Ceremony, In Los Angeles" (Trapper, Frank)
PH14088 711 (June 29, 1995) p33. "Ryder, Pirner, Band Manager Heaps, Murphy (background) And Ex-Drummer Young Greet Clinton (foreground) At The White House (from left)" (Markowitz, Jeffrey)
PH14089 735 (May 30, 1996) p56. "Preppy Haas His Way With Ryder"
PH14090 737 (June 27, 1996) p15. "[Winona Ryder]" (Somoza, Gerardo)
PH14091 749 (December 12, 1996) p90. "Ryder And Woodard Cast A Spell"
PH14092 750-751 (December 26, 1996) p81. "Winona Ryder, Giorgio Armani, And Jakob Dylan (from left)" (Mazur, Kevin)
RYDER, WINONA—PHOTOGRAPHS—PORTRAITS
PH14093 677 (March 10, 1994) pp[cover]. "Winona Ryder: Venus In Bluejeans" (Ritts, Herb)
PH14094 700 (January 26, 1995) p66. "Smart Women, Foolish Choices"
RZEZNIK, JOHNNY—PHOTOGRAPHS
PH14095 710 (June 15, 1995) p31. "A Boy Named Johnny Rzeznik: Loud, Fast, Funny" (Capak, R. J.)
PH14096 723 (December 14, 1995) p36. "Hungry For Success And Searching For Dinner: Johnny Rzeznik, Robby Takac And Mike Malinin" (Ockenfels, Frank W.)

S

SABATO, ANTONIO, JR.—PHOTOGRAPHS
PH14097 741 (August 22, 1996) pp90,92. "[Antonio Sabato Jr.]" (Churilla, Lynda)
SABBAG, ROBERT—PHOTOGRAPHS
PH14098 663 (August 19, 1993) p58. "Our Spy At The Party: The Author At The White House"
SABBAG, ROBERT—PHOTOGRAPHS—PORTRAITS
PH14099 663 (August 19, 1993) p58. "The Author In 1968: Tet Began The Year, Nixon Ended It"
SABIN, ALBERT—PHOTOGRAPHS
PH14100 626 (March 19, 1992) p57. "Dr. Albert Sabin, Whose Vaccine Helped Eradicate Polio, Pictured In 1962" (Eppridge, Bill)
SABRINA—PHOTOGRAPHS—PORTRAITS
PH14101 686-687 (July 14, 1994) p72. "Girl World: Sensi, Linda, Charmaine, Sabrina (from left)" (Borris, Dan)
SABRINA (FILM)—PHOTOGRAPHS
PH14102 726 (January 25, 1996) p66. "Unlucky In Love: Ormond Flanked By Kinnear And Ford"
SADE—ALBUMS
PH14103 645-646 (December 10, 1992) p166. "Love Deluxe"
SADIER, LAETITIA—PHOTOGRAPHS
PH14104 691 (September 22, 1994) p38. "Stereolab's Hansen (left) And Sadier Wax Etheral" (Clinch, Danny)
PH14105 731 (April 4, 1996) p40. "Always The Same, Always Different: Stereolab's Mary Hansen, Tim Gane, Laetitia Sadier And Morgane Lhote (from left)" (Perou, Ralph)
SADOFSKY, STEVE—PHOTOGRAPHS
PH14106 708 (May 18, 1995) p25. "And Calms The Crowd With A Call For Peace" (Mazur, Kevin)
PH14107 708 (May 18, 1995) p25. "Reaches In To Catch A Surfer" (Mazur, Kevin)
PH14108 708 (May 18, 1995) p25. "Sadofsky (in glasses) Gets Ready For Action" (Mazur, Kevin)
PH14109 708 (May 18, 1995) p23. "Steve Sadofsky (front, right) Prepares To Catch A Mosher" (Mazur, Kevin)
SAFE (FILM)—PHOTOGRAPHS
PH14110 714 (August 10, 1995) p64. "Allergic To Life? Try 'Safe'"
PH14111 731 (April 4, 1996) p66. "Moore, 'Safe'"
SAFE PASSAGE (FILM)—PHOTOGRAPHS
PH14112 700 (January 26, 1995) p66. "Smart Women, Foolish Choices"
SAFETY—ILLUSTRATIONS
PH14113 709 (June 1, 1995) p16. "Scaredy-Catalogs" (Rosen, Jonathon)
SAFFERY, ANTHONY—PHOTOGRAPHS
PH14114 728 (February 22, 1996) p32. "Cornershop's Simms, Saffery, Tjinder Singh, Ayres And Hall (from left)" (Wonderland, Alison)
SAFFRON—PHOTOGRAPHS
PH14115 747 (November 14, 1996) p26. "Republica's Saffron, Kidlike In New Orleans" (Olivier, Rick)
SAGE, DANNY—PHOTOGRAPHS
PH14116 701 (February 9, 1995) p19. "D Gen (from left): Danny Sage, Richard Bacchus, Howie Pyro, Jesse Malin, Michael Wildwood" (Seliger, Mark)
PH14117 701 (February 9, 1995) p20. "Glam Rabble-Rousers Wildwood, Malin And Sage (from left) In New York City" (Mazur, Kevin)
PH14118 705 (April 6, 1995) p16. "Label Flava Of The Month: D Gen's Jesse malin (left) And Danny Sage" (Brown, Christy)
PH14119 710 (June 15, 1995) p41. "D Gen (from left): Pyro, Michael Wildwood, Malin, Sage, Richard Bacchus And Gomez" (Ragel, Jon)
SAGER, MIKE—PHOTOGRAPHS
PH14120 632 (June 11, 1992) p174. "Sager: Everybody Has An

Agent Now" (Dressler, Michael)
SAHARA (FILM)—PHOTOGRAPHS
PH14121 744 (October 3, 1996) p52. "Quel Drag: In Her 1984 Flop, 'Sahara'"
SAHM, DOUG—PHOTOGRAPHS
PH14122 681 (May 5, 1994) p14. "Doug Sahm And His Crew" (Virobik-Adams, Kevin)
SAIGON, VIETNAM—PHOTOGRAPHS
PH14123 634-635 (July 9, 1992) p66. "In Saigon The Japanese Are Back And Selling Hard, But Not The Americans" (Giannini, John)
SAINT ETIENNE—ALBUMS
PH14124 662 (August 5, 1993) p65. "So Tough"
SAINTE-MARIE, BUFFY—ALBUMS
PH14125 644 (November 26, 1992) p74. "Coincidence And Likely Stories"
SAJAK, PAT—PHOTOGRAPHS
PH14126 684 (June 16, 1994) p36. "[Wheel Of Fortune]" (Slenzak, Ron)
SALEM, KEVIN—ALBUMS
PH14127 700 (January 26, 1995) p62. "Soma City"
SALEM, KEVIN—PHOTOGRAPHS
PH14128 701 (February 9, 1995) p32. "[Kevin Salem]" (Irish, Len)
SALES, HUNT—PHOTOGRAPHS
PH14129 622 (January 23, 1992) p7. "Brad Whitford, David Bowie, Steven Tyler, Hunt Sales, Tony Sales, Reeves Gabrels, Joey Kramer" (McAlpine, Paul)
SALES, HUNT—PHOTOGRAPHS—PORTRAITS
PH14130 616 (October 31, 1991) p76. "David Bowie, Hunt Sales, Tony Sales And Reeves Gabrels (from left)" (Uchitel, Diego)
PH14130a 616 (October 31, 1991) pp74-75. "[Tim Machine]" (Uchitel, Diego)
SALES, TONY—PHOTOGRAPHS
PH14131 622 (January 23, 1992) p7. "Brad Whitford, David Bowie, Steven Tyler, Hunt Sales, Tony Sales, Reeves Gabrels, Joey Kramer" (McAlpine, Paul)
PH14132 652 (March 18, 1993) p15. "Cheap Dates (from left): Phantom, Baxter, Sales, Stanton And James" (Matheu, Robert)
SALES, TONY—PHOTOGRAPHS—PORTRAITS
PH14133 616 (October 31, 1991) p76. "David Bowie, Hunt Sales, Tony Sales And Reeves Gabrels (from left)" (Uchitel, Diego)
PH14134 616 (October 31, 1991) pp74-75. "[Tim Machine]" (Uchitel, Diego)
SALGADO, SEBASTIAO—PHOTOGRAPHS
PH14135 619-620 (December 12, 1991) p138. "Salgado And His Son Rodrigo In The House The Family Rented In Maine In The Summer Of 1991" (Nofziger, Christopher)
PH14136 619-620 (December 12, 1991) p135. "Salgado; His Wife, Lelia Deliuz Wanick; And Their Sons, Rodrigo (seated) And Juliano" (Nofziger, Christopher)
SALGADO, SEBASTIAO—PHOTOGRAPHS—PORTRAITS
PH14137 619-620 (December 12, 1991) p133. "[Sebastiao Salgado]" (Nofziger, Christopher)
PH14138 702 (February 23, 1995) p66. "Sebastiao Salgado" (Nofziger, Chris)
SALIERS, EMILY—PHOTOGRAPHS
PH14139 625 (March 5, 1992) p18. "Sara Lee, Crimmins, Graham Nash, Amy Ray, Emily Saliers, David Crosby, Etheridge, Carpenter (from left)" (Berg, Lisa)
PH14140 684 (June 16, 1994) p36. "Indigo Girl Emily Saliers, Nanci Griffith, Browne, Carpenter, Indigo Girl Amy Ray" (Diamond, Rick)
PH14141 695 (November 17, 1994) p95. "Indigo Girls" (Ford, Charles)
PH14142 712-713 (July 13, 1995) p45. "Indigo Girls Emily Saliers (left), Amy Ray (center) On The White Earth Reservation, In Minnesota" (Pickett, Keri)
PH14143 733 (May 2, 1996) p22. "Indigo Girls Emily Saliers (left) And Amy Ray"
SALISBURY, MIKE—PHOTOGRAPHS
PH14144 643 (November 12, 1992) p49. "'Rolling Stone' Art Directors (from left): Bob Kingsbury (1968-73), Tony Lane (1974-76), Annie Leibovitz, Mike Salisbury (1973-74), Roger Black (1976-78), Jann S. Wenner, Derek..
SALISBURY, PETER—PHOTOGRAPHS
PH14145 660-661 (July 8, 1993) p96. "Verve (clockwise from top left): Ashcroft, Peter Salisbury, Simon Jones And McCabe" (Sharp, Ken)
SALK, JONAS—PHOTOGRAPHS
PH14146 616 (October 31, 1991) p47. "The Inventor Of Polio Vaccine, Jonas Salk (left), And Dr. Ciro de Quadros" (Gaggero, Carlos)
PH14147 626 (March 19, 1992) p56. "Dr. Jonas Salk, Pioneer Of The Polio Vaccine, In His Laboratory In 1954" (Eisenstaedt, Alfred)
SALT—PHOTOGRAPHS
PH14148 671 (December 9, 1993) p31. "Spinderella, Blaze Berdahl Of 'Ghostwriter,' Pepa And Salt (from left)" (Leibowitz, Eric)
PH14149 723 (December 14, 1995) p28. "[Salt-N-Pepa & Patti Smith]" (Mazur, Kevin)
SALT—PHOTOGRAPHS—PORTRAITS
PH14150 695 (November 17, 1994) p140. "Salt-N-Pepa" (Demarchelier, Patrick)
SALT-N-PEPA—ILLUSTRATIONS
PH14151 678 (March 24, 1994) p112. "Salt-N-Pepa: Whatta Trio, Whatta Hit" (Cowles, David)
SALT-N-PEPA—PHOTOGRAPHS
PH14152 625 (March 5, 1992) p18. "Pepa, Salt, Monie Love And Spinderella (from left)" (Shaw, Gene)
PH14153 671 (December 9, 1993) p31. "Spinderella, Blaze Berdahl Of 'Ghostwriter,' Pepa And Salt (from left)" (Leibowitz, Eric)
PH14154 674 (January 27, 1994) p45. "Salt-N-Pepa On What Women Wanted To Hear Last Year"
PH14155 693 (October 20, 1994) p27. "Salt-N-Pepa" (Mazur, Kevin)
PH14156 698-699 (December 29, 1994) p66. "MTV Host Roseanne With Salt-N-Pepa" (Kravitz, Jeff)
PH14157 700 (January 26, 1995) p53. "Salt-N-Pepa Win For Best Rap Group" (Micelotta, Frank)
PH14158 701 (February 9, 1995) p16. "Salt-N-Pepa At The AIDS Dance-A-Thon" (Colliton, Paul)
PH14159 706 (April 20, 1995) p15. "Toujours Glamour: Salt-N-Pepa Score" (Mazur, Kevin)
PH14160 717 (September 21, 1995) p32. "A She Thing: Salt-N-Pepa"
PH14161 723 (December 14, 1995) p28. "[Salt-N-Pepa & Patti Smith]" (Mazur, Kevin)
PH14162 726 (January 25, 1996) p27. "Home Alone: Pepa (Sandi Denton, left) And Salt (Cheryl James)" (Arnold, Alice)
SALT-N-PEPA—PHOTOGRAPHS—PORTRAITS
PH14163 685 (June 30, 1994) p21. "Recipe For Success: Pepa (left) And Salt" (Rolston, Matthew)
PH14164 695 (November 17, 1994) p140. "Salt-N-Pepa" (Demarchelier, Patrick)
SALVATION ARMY (ORGANIZATION)—PHOTOGRAPHS
PH14165 680 (April 21, 1994) pp[enc.37]. "Aisles Of Smiles: Looking Around, One Shopper Says 'I See A Million Questions But Only One Answer: Dry-Clean It'" (Ragel, Jon)
SALVI, AL—PHOTOGRAPHS
PH14166 746 (October 31, 1996) p60. "The NRA's Man In Illinois: Al Salvi (right), GOP Senate Candidate"
SAM AND DAVE—PHOTOGRAPHS
PH14167 720 (November 2, 1995) p50. "Sam And Dave"

SAM AND DAVE—PHOTOGRAPHS—PORTRAITS
PH14168 623 (February 6, 1992) p51. "Stax's Soul Men Sam Moore (top) And Dave Prater"
SAM GOODY (STORE)—PHOTOGRAPHS
PH14169 734 (May 16, 1996) p24. "Out Of Business: Another Sam Goody Record Store Closes Its Doors For Good" (Capak, R. J.)
SAMBORA, RICHIE—PHOTOGRAPHS
PH14170 615 (October 17, 1991) p14. "Sambora (left), Bon Jovi" (Mazur, Kevin)
PH14171 747 (November 14, 1996) p25. "[Bon Jovi & Friends]" (Souliers, Philippe)
SAMBORA, RICHIE—PHOTOGRAPHS—PORTRAITS
PH14172 692 (October 6, 1994) p17. "Bon Jovi, Foster, Sambora (from left)" (Mazur, Kevin)
SAMMY—PHOTOGRAPHS
PH14173 721 (November 16, 1995) p98. "Sammy, Arthur, Charlie And Civ (from left)" (GS, Jamil)
SAMPRAS, PETE—PHOTOGRAPHS
PH14174 730 (March 21, 1996) p17. "[Elton John & Pete Sampras]" (Diamond, Rick)
SAMTON, DAN—PHOTOGRAPHS
PH14175 715 (August 24, 1995) p96. "[Dan Samton]" (Danelian, Stephen)
PH14176 715 (August 24, 1995) pp90-91. "On The Court In Thompkins Park" (Danelian, Stephen)
SAMWELL-SMITH, PAUL—PHOTOGRAPHS
PH14177 623 (February 6, 1992) p51. "The Yardbirds, Circa 1964 (from left): Chris Dreja, Keith Reif, Paul Samwell-Smith, Eric Clapton And Jim McCarty"
SAMWELL-SMITH, PAUL—PHOTOGRAPHS—PORTRAITS
PH14178 655 (April 29, 1993) p34. "Slowhand (at bottom left) With The Yardbirds: Chris Dreja, Jim McCarty, Paul Samwell-Smith And Keith Relf (clockwise from top left)"
SAN DIEGO, CALIFORNIA—PHOTOGRAPHS
PH14179 691 (September 22, 1994) p23. "Pec City, U.S.A.: South Mission Beach" (Chang, Aaron)
SAN FRANCISCO, CALIFORNIA—ILLUSTRATIONS
PH14180 740 (August 8, 1996) p47. "San Francisco's Faults Run Parallel To Its Highways"
SAN FRANCISCO, CALIFORNIA—PHOTOGRAPHS
PH14181 679 (April 7, 1994) p15. "A San Francisco Rave" (Blakesberg, Jay)
PH14182 717 (September 21, 1995) p23. "A Crowd Of Nearly 2,000 Mourners Assembled Around A Makeshift Shrine At The Polo Field, In San Francisco's Golden Gate Park, On The Night Of Garcia's Death" (Blakesberg, Jay)
PH14183 740 (August 8, 1996) p44. "San Francisco, October 1989" (Scott, Paul X.)
SANCHEZ, MICHEL—PHOTOGRAPHS—PORTRAITS
PH14184 680 (April 21, 1994) p26. "Deep Forest's Sanchez And Mouquet And Director Tarsem (from left)" (Kuczala, John)
SANCHEZ-GIJON, AITANA—PHOTOGRAPHS
PH14185 715 (August 24, 1995) p110. "Lovers At Last: Sanchez-Gijon And Reeves"
SANDERS, RIC—PHOTOGRAPHS
PH14186 691 (September 22, 1994) p21. "Ric Sanders, Simon Nicol And Richard Thompson (from left)" (Robicheau, Paul)
SANDLER, ADAM—PHOTOGRAPHS
PH14187 680 (April 21, 1994) p34. "Airheads Buscemi, Sandler And Fraser" (Wallace, Merie W.)
PH14188 689 (August 25, 1994) p97. "Rock Wanna-Be's: Sandler, Fraser, Buscemi"
PH14189 706 (April 20, 1995) p86. "'SNL' Movie Hell: Chris Farley With David Spade In 'Tommy Boy,' Al Franken With Bear In 'Stuart' And Adam Sandler With Dunces In 'Billy Madison' (from left)"
PH14190 743 (September 19, 1996) p88. "Dickheads"
PH14191 744 (October 3, 1996) p78. "Now Playing"
SANDMAN, MARK—PHOTOGRAPHS
PH14192 686-687 (July 14, 1994) p36. "Morphine's Sandman, Conway And Colley (from left)" (Lyden, Paul)
PH14193 704 (March 23, 1995) p25. "Buffalo Tom's Bill Janovitz, Kristin Hersh, Morphine's Mark Sandman, Gigolo Aunts' Steve Hurley (from left)" (Robicheau, Paul)
PH14194 711 (June 29, 1995) p20. "Masters Of 'Implied Grunge': Colley, Sandman, Conway (from left)" (Ockenfels, Frank, 3)
SANDMAN, MARK—PHOTOGRAPHS—PORTRAITS
PH14195 667 (October 14, 1993) p30. "Mark Sandman, Dana Colley And Bill Conway" (Eichner, Steve)
SANDOVAL, HOPE—ILLUSTRATIONS
PH14196 693 (October 20, 1994) p11. "Mazzy Star's Hope Sandoval" (Burke, Philip)
SANDOVAL, HOPE—PHOTOGRAPHS
PH14197 664 (September 2, 1993) p28. "Mazzy Star's Hope Sandoval" (Levine, Laura)
PH14198 692 (October 6, 1994) p29. "The Jesus And Mary Chain's Jim Reid Croons To Mazzy Star Hope Sandoval" (Mayer, Jeffrey)
PH14199 693 (October 20, 1994) p34. "Wan Countenance, Entrancing Wail: Sandoval In N.Y.C., '90" (Roberts, Ebet)
PH14200 698-699 (December 29, 1994) p60. "Jim Reid Pairs Up With Hope Sandoval" (Roberts, Ebet)
SANDOVAL, HOPE—PHOTOGRAPHS—PORTRAITS
PH14201 695 (November 17, 1994) p49. "Mazzy Star" (Sebring, Steven)
SANDS, JULIAN—PHOTOGRAPHS
PH14202 652 (March 18, 1993) p47. "Sands And Lynch Of 'Boxing Helena'" (Michaelson, Randall)
SANTANA—ALBUMS
PH14203 617 (November 14, 1991) p100. "Abraxas" (Klarwein, Mati)
PH14204 638 (September 3, 1992) p68. "Milagro"
SANTANA—PHOTOGRAPHS
PH14205 722 (November 30, 1995) p70. "Santana: Sensuous Mexicali-Blues Maneuvers" (Pulin, Chuck)
SANTANA, CARLOS—PHOTOGRAPHS
PH14206 618 (November 28, 1991) p35. "[Carlos Santana]" (Micelotta, Frank)
PH14207 619-620 (December 12, 1991) p104. "Graham And Close Friend Carlos Santana" (Roberts, Ebet)
PH14208 625 (March 5, 1992) p17. "Neil Young Takes Center Stage During The All-Star-Jam Finale" (Gershoff, Gary)
PH14209 630 (May 14, 1992) p13. "Carlos Santana" (Cohen, Lester)
PH14210 640 (October 1, 1992) p10. "Santana (left) And Guy" (Granitz, Steve)
PH14211 665 (September 16, 1993) p31. "Carlos Santana And Bob Dylan" (Granitz, Steven)
PH14212 688 (August 11, 1994) p37. "return To Woodstock: Santana" (Mazur, Kevin)
PH14213 707 (May 4, 1995) p20. "Dirnt (left) And Perennial Bammie Fave Carlos Santana" (Blakesberg, Jay)
PH14214 714 (August 10, 1995) p17. "Santana (left) And His Glyphness In Florida" (Craig, Tom)
SANTANA, CARLOS—PHOTOGRAPHS—PORTRAITS
PH14215 625 (March 5, 1992) pp14-15. "On The Evening Of The Seventh Annual Hall Of Fame Induction Ceremony, 'Rolling Stone' Gathered These Nine Legendary Guitarists At The Waldorf-Astoria For A Once-In-A-Lifetime Pho
PH14216 643 (November 12, 1992) p116. "Carlos Santana" (Seliger, Mark)
PH14217 671 (December 9, 1993) p24. "Santana: Bringing Historic Last Shows To Light" (Seliger, Mark)
SANTANA, CARLOS—PHOTOGRAPHS—PORTRAITS
PH14218 717 (September 21, 1995) p74. "Garcia With Carlos Santana In Oakland, 1988" (Blakesberg, Jay)

SANTIAGO, HERMAN—PHOTOGRAPHS
PH14219 651 (March 4, 1993) p16. "Dick Clark With Teenagers Herman Santiago (left) And Jimmy Merchant" (Mazur, Kevin)
SANTIAGO, JOEY—PHOTOGRAPHS
PH14220 682 (May 19, 1994) p90. "Old Deal: Kim With Pixies David Lovering, Black Francis, Joey Santiago (from left)" (Blakesberg, Jay)
SANTIAGO, JOEY—PHOTOGRAPHS—PORTRAITS
PH14221 652 (March 18, 1993) p15. "Ex-Pixies David Lovering, Deal, Joey Santiago, Black Francis (clockwise from left)" (Catlin, A.)
SANZ, JORGE—PHOTOGRAPHS
PH14222 681 (May 5, 1994) p49. "Sanz Nuzzles Verdu For A Beautiful Time"
SAO PAULO, BRAZIL—PHOTOGRAPHS
PH14223 750-751 (December 26, 1996) pp125-133. "[Sao Paulo, Brazil]" (Salgado, Sebastiao)
SARAFINA! (FILM)—PHOTOGRAPHS
PH14224 642 (October 29, 1992) p77. "Sarafina!"
SARANDON, SUSAN—ILLUSTRATIONS
PH14225 648 (January 21, 1993) p54. "A Few Good Women" (Witte, Michael)
SARANDON, SUSAN—PHOTOGRAPHS
PH14226 619-620 (December 12, 1991) p194. "Male Wimps And Female Warriors"
PH14227 623 (February 6, 1992) p90. "Susan Sarandon (left) And Geena Davis Get Even"
PH14228 626 (March 19, 1992) p104. "Sarandon And Dafoe Try To Find A New Life After Drug Dealing"
PH14229 648 (January 21, 1993) p55. "Sarandon Tackles Medicine"
PH14230 688 (August 11, 1994) p62. "It's A Day In Court For Lawyer Sarandon And Renfro"
PH14231 691 (September 22, 1994) p106. "Woman Redeemed"
PH14232 744 (October 3, 1996) p50. "'Healthy' Is Not A Word I'd Use To Describe My Childhood: With Susan Sarandon In 1978's 'Pretty Baby'"
PH14233 744 (October 3, 1996) p50. "Pretty Baby (film)—Photographs"
SARANDON, SUSAN—PHOTOGRAPHS—PORTRAITS
PH14234 700 (January 26, 1995) p66. "Smart Women, Foolish Choices"
SARGENT, STEFANIE ANN—PHOTOGRAPHS
PH14235 645-646 (December 10, 1992) p102. "Stefanie Ann Sargent" (Hawkes, David)
SASSER, JIM—PHOTOGRAPHS—PORTRAITS
PH14236 698-699 (December 29, 1994) p152. "[Jim Sasser]" (Ashe, Terry)
SATURDAY NIGHT FEVER (FILM)—PHOTOGRAPHS
PH14237 728 (February 22, 1996) p43. "Travolta Puts On The Moves In 'Pulp Fiction,' 'Saturday Night Fever' And 'Broken Arrow'"
SATURDAY NIGHT LIVE (TELEVISION SHOW)—ILLUSTRATIONS
PH14238 693 (October 20, 1994) p28. ""Live" Text" (Watson, Esther)
PH14239 706 (April 20, 1995) p85. "Saturday Night Jive" (Peck, Everett)
PH14240 709 (June 1, 1995) p14. "Hollywood" (Pendergrast, James T.)
PH14241 721 (November 16, 1995) p119. "[Saturday Night Live]" (Fishman, Miriam)
SATYRICON (NIGHTCLUB)—PHOTOGRAPHS
PH14242 630 (May 14, 1992) p92. "[Portland, Oregon]" (Dipaola, Steve)
SAUCERFUL OF SECRETS (BOOK)—PHOTOGRAPHS
PH14243 619-620 (December 12, 1991) p32. "[Saucerful Of Secrets]"
SAUNDER, BAKER—PHOTOGRAPHS—PORTRAITS
PH14244 704 (March 23, 1995) p33. "Barrett Martin, Layne Staley, Baker Saunder And Mike McCready (from left)" (Mercer, Lance)
SAVAGE NIGHTS (FILM)—PHOTOGRAPHS
PH14245 675 (February 10, 1994) p53. "Unsafe Sex: Collard (left) And Bohringer"
SAVAGE, JON—PHOTOGRAPHS
PH14246 655 (April 29, 1993) p12. "Authors Lydon (right) And Jon Savage Fly The British Bird"
SAVAGE, RICK—PHOTOGRAPHS
PH14247 629 (April 30, 1992) p39. "Def Leppard Guitarist Phil Collen And Bass Player Rick Savage" (Seliger, Mark)
PH14248 667 (October 14, 1993) p26. "Rick Savage, Phil Collen, Vivian Campbell, Rick Allen And Joe Elliott" (Halfin, Ross)
SAVALAS, TELLY—PHOTOGRAPHS—PORTRAITS
PH14249 698-699 (December 29, 1994) p83. "Who Loves Ya, Baby? Sex Symbol Savalas In 1962"
SAVIO, MARIO—PHOTOGRAPHS
PH14250 750-751 (December 26, 1996) p98. "Mario Savio At Berkeley's Greek Theater, December, 1964"
SAWYER, DIANE—PHOTOGRAPHS
PH14251 724-725 (December 28, 1995) p48. "No Glove, And Definitely No Love: Sawyer, Jacksons"
SAYLES, JOHN—ILLUSTRATIONS
PH14252 671 (December 9, 1993) p3. "John Sayles" (Burke, Philip)
SAYLES, JOHN—PHOTOGRAPHS
PH14253 738-739 (July 11, 1996) p98. "Sayles (left) Directs McConaughey"
SCAGGS, BOZ—ALBUMS
PH14254 617 (November 14, 1991) p149. "Middle Man" (Donald, Nancy)
PH14255 617 (November 14, 1991) p149. "Middle Man" (Bourdain, Guy)
PH14256 681 (May 5, 1994) p51. "Some Change"
SCAGGS, BOZ—ILLUSTRATIONS
PH14257 681 (May 5, 1994) p51. "The Cool Flame" (Kunz, Anita)
SCAGGS, BOZ—PHOTOGRAPHS
PH14258 637 (August 20, 1992) p11. "Rock And Soul (from left): Boz Scaggs, Walter Becker, Donald Fagen, Michael McDonald, Phoebe Snow And Chuck Jackson" (Hamilton, James)
PH14259 682 (May 19, 1994) p26. "[Boz Scaggs]"
SCANLON, PAUL—PHOTOGRAPHS
PH14260 632 (June 11, 1992) p62. "Staff Members And Contributing Writers At The 1971 Editorial Conference, At Esalen, In Big Sur" (Leibovitz, Annie)
PH14261 647 (January 7, 1993) p11. "RS Alumni Photog Annie Leibovitz, Thompson, David Felton, Cameron Crowe, Chris Hodenfield, Ben Fong-Torres, Paul Scanlon (from left)" (Elgar, Nick)
SCARCE—ALBUMS
PH14262 743 (September 19, 1996) p82. "Deadsexy"
SCARCE—PHOTOGRAPHS
PH14263 745 (October 17, 1996) p42. "Alive And Sexy: Graning, Raskin And Propatier (from left)" (Chavez, Marina)
SCARFACE (FILM)—PHOTOGRAPHS
PH14264 671 (December 9, 1993) p76. "Pacino's Scarface With Pfeiffer"
SCARFACE—ALBUMS
PH14265 698-699 (December 29, 1994) p178. "The Diary"
THE SCARLET LETTER (FILM)—PHOTOGRAPHS
PH14266 721 (November 16, 1995) p117. "Demi Moore With Gary Oldman"
PH14267 721 (November 16, 1995) p117. "Lillian Gish (1926)"
SCAVULLO, FRANCESCO—PHOTOGRAPHS
PH14268 615 (October 17, 1991) p66. "Truman Capote And Francesco Scavullo, Studio 54, 1979" (Pigozzi, Jean)
SCELSA, VIN—PHOTOGRAPHS
PH14269 678 (March 24, 1994) p28. "Kristofferson, Williams,

Vega, DJ Vin Scelsa And Lou Reed (from left)" (Roberts, Ebet)
SCENT OF A WOMAN (FILM)—PHOTOGRAPHS
PH14270 647 (January 7, 1993) p50. "Blind Al Pacino Savors A Last Tango With Gabrielle Anwar"
PH14271 653 (April 1, 1993) p57. "Scent Of A Woman"
SCHADER, SETH CASH—PHOTOGRAPHS
PH14272 642 (October 29, 1992) p62. "The Author On An Off Day"
SCHAECH, JOHNATHAN—PHOTOGRAPHS
PH14273 721 (November 16, 1995) p117. "Duval, McGowan, Schaech (from left)"
SCHAYER, BOBBY—PHOTOGRAPHS
PH14274 700 (January 26, 1995) p17. "Bad Religion's Brian Baker, Greg Graffin, Bobby Schayer, Jay Bentley and Greg Hetson" (Kravitz, Jeff)
PH14275 722 (November 30, 1995) p19. "Graffin, Ocasek, Jay Bentley, Brian Baker, Greg Hetson And Bobby Schayer (from left)" (Mazur, Kevin)
SCHAYER, BOBBY—PHOTOGRAPHS—PORTRAITS
PH14276 695 (November 17, 1994) p40. "Bad Religion" (Guip, Amy)
SCHEIDER, ROY—PHOTOGRAPHS
PH14277 666 (September 30, 1993) p115. "Scheider (right) in 'Seaquest'"
SCHELLENBACH, KATE—PHOTOGRAPHS
PH14278 710 (June 15, 1995) p17. "LJ's Schellenbach, Gabby Glaser, Vivian trimble And Jill Cunniff At The Rally For Women's Lives, in D.C. (from left)" (Harrington, John)
PH14279 735 (May 30, 1996) p27. "Glaser, Schellenbach, Producer Lanois And Trimble (from left)" (Olivier, Rick)
SCHELLENBACH, KATE—PHOTOGRAPHS—PORTRAITS
PH14280 660-661 (July 8, 1993) p97. "Luscious Jackson (clockwise from top left): Glaser, Schellenbach, Cunniff, Trimble" (Minchin, James R., III)
SCHEMEL, PATTY—PHOTOGRAPHS
PH14281 683 (June 2, 1994) p42. "Hole: Patty Schemel, Love, Kristen Pfaff, Eric Erlandson" (Seliger, Mark)
PH14282 697 (December 15, 1994) p67. "Hole As One: Bassist Melissa Auf Der Maur (who replaced Kristen Pfaff), Guitarist Eric Erlandson, Drummer Patty Schemel And Love (from left)" (Seliger, Mark)
PH14283 698-699 (December 29, 1994) p50. "Doll Parts: Hole's Eric Erlandson, Melissa Auf der Maur, Patty Schemel And Love" (Seliger, Mark)
PH14284 715 (August 24, 1995) p46. "Courtney Love, Eric Erlandson, Patty Schemel, Melissa Auf Der Maur" (Seliger, Mark)
SCHENKENBERG, MARCUS—PHOTOGRAPHS
PH14285 630 (May 14, 1992) p84. "[Marcus]" (Weber, Bruce)
SCHENKMAN, ERIC—PHOTOGRAPHS
PH14286 631 (May 28, 1992) p15. "The Spin Doctors' Chris Barron, Eric Schenkman And Aaron Comess (from left)" (Mazur, Kevin)
PH14287 647 (January 7, 1993) p36. "Guitarist Eric Schenkman Ties One On Before The Show" (Seliger, Mark)
PH14288 647 (January 7, 1993) p36. "Schenkman, In The Top Bunk, And Comess, Down Below, Enjoy A Rare Moment Of Midtour Shut-Eye" (Seliger, Mark)
PH14289 647 (January 7, 1993) p34. "[Spin Doctors]" (Seliger, Mark)
PH14290 674 (January 27, 1994) p45. "Pet Picks: Eric Schenkman (above, right) Of Spin Doctors Reveals His Favorites"
PH14291 684 (June 16, 1994) p18. "A Force Of Hobbit: Schenkman, White, Barron And Comess Back In The Studio"
PH14292 695 (November 17, 1994) p135. "Spin Doctors" (Seeff, Norman)
SCHIFFER, CLAUDIA—PHOTOGRAPHS
PH14293 715 (August 24, 1995) p87. "Hot Career Move" (Sands, Steve)
SCHINDLER'S LIST (FILM)—PHOTOGRAPHS
PH14294 672-673 (December 23, 1993) p174. "[Schindler's List]"
PH14295 674 (January 27, 1994) p48. "Best Supporting Actor"
PH14296 678 (March 24, 1994) p100. "Missing In Oscar Action"
SCHLABOWSKE, DEAN—PHOTOGRAPHS
PH14297 733 (May 2, 1996) p57. "Durante, Schlabowske, Langford, Dear (from left)" (Swider, Frank)
SCHLECTER, SIVAN—PHOTOGRAPHS
PH14298 708 (May 18, 1995) p38. "Queenie's Panaccione, Schlecter" (Shirk, Alison)
SCHLOSS, ZANDER—PHOTOGRAPHS
PH14299 712-713 (July 13, 1995) p25. "Zander Schloss (left), Gibson And Morris At CBGB" (Toliver, Chris)
PH14300 719 (October 19, 1995) p24. "Reuniting Hasn't Been Easy For The Circle Jerks: Keith Morris, Zander Schloss And Keith Clark (from left)" (Garcia, Willie)
SCHMERSAL, JOHN—PHOTOGRAPHS—PORTRAITS
PH14301 733 (May 2, 1996) p26. "Killing Retro: Tim Taylor, Juan Monasterio, John Schmersal And Tyler Trent (from top)" (McGuire, Leeann)
SCHMIT, TIMOTHY B.—PHOTOGRAPHS
PH14302 685 (June 30, 1994) p23. "Birds Of A Feather: Joe Walsh, Timothy B. Schmit, Don Henley, Don Felder And Glenn Frey (from left)"
SCHMOKE, KURT—PHOTOGRAPHS
PH14303 663 (August 19, 1993) p32. "Mayor Kurt Schmoke Addressing Baltimoreans Angered By The Failure Of City Development To Yield Good Jobs" (Daniels, Craig)
PH14304 663 (August 19, 1993) p33. "Schmoke With Reporters After Pledging A New Social Contract For Local Workers" (Daniels, Kurt)
SCHNEIDER, FRED—ALBUMS
PH14305 733 (May 2, 1996) p54. "Just Fred"
SCHNEIDER, FRED—PHOTOGRAPHS
PH14306 630 (May 14, 1992) p13. "Kate Pierson, Fred Schneider And Kim Bassinger (from left) At The Brown Fund-Raiser" (Mazur, Kevin)
PH14307 637 (August 20, 1992) p11. "The B-52's (from left): Fred Schneider, Kate Pierson, Julee Cruise, Keith Strickland, Sue Hadjopoulos And Pat Irwin" (Michelson, Eric T.)
PH14308 637 (August 20, 1992) p9. "Fred Schneider, Kwame, Weymouth And Frantz (from left) At The 'Paper' Bash"
PH14309 652 (March 18, 1993) p27. "Kate Pierson And Fred Schneider"
PH14310 681 (May 5, 1994) p15. "Martha Reeves, Brown, Fred Schneider, Richard And Raitt At The Recent Awards (from left)" (Micelotta, Frank)
PH14311 683 (June 2, 1994) p27. "Below: Schneider, Kate Pierson, Keith Strickland" (Batzdorff, Rob)
PH14312 702 (February 23, 1995) p49. "Schneider And Pierson Sandwich The Vandellas" (Mazur, Kevin)
SCHNEIDER, RICK—PHOTOGRAPHS
PH14313 722 (November 30, 1995) pp[enc.4]. "Mister 3-D Making Macaroni" (McLeod, William Mercer)
SCHNEIDER, ROB—ILLUSTRATIONS
PH14314 748 (November 28, 1996) p139. "[Men Behaving Badly]" (Ciardiello, Joe)
SCHOCK, GINA—PHOTOGRAPHS
PH14315 616 (October 31, 1991) p11. "Cervenka, Gina Schock, Jane Wiedlin, Kathy Valentine, Charlotte Caffey (clockwise from top left)" (Granitz, Steve)
SCHOLTEN, DAVID—PHOTOGRAPHS
PH14316 719 (October 19, 1995) p70. "Adolphson (left) And Scholten Collecting Petition Signatures At Utah's Arches National Park" (McDonough, Patricia)
SCHOOL OF FISH—PHOTOGRAPHS
PH14317 618 (November 28, 1991) p30. "Josh Clayton-Felt,

Dominic Nardini, M.P. And Michael Ward (from left)" (Cuffaro, Chris)
SCHOOLS, DAVID—PHOTOGRAPHS
PH14318 631 (May 28, 1992) p17. "Widespread Panic (from left): John Bell, Michael Houser, Todd Nance, David Schools And Domingo Ortiz" (Messer, Alan)
SCHWARTZ, CHRIS—PHOTOGRAPHS
PH14319 741 (August 22, 1996) p72. "[Ruffhouse]" (Whitt, Christina)
SCHWARZENBACH, BLAKE—PHOTOGRAPHS
PH14320 660-661 (July 8, 1993) p100. "Jawbreaker (from left): Adam Pfahler, Chris Blake And Blake Schwarzenbach" (Lewis, Don)
SCHWARZENEGGER, ARNOLD—ILLUSTRATIONS
PH14321 659 (June 24, 1993) p87. "Dinosaur Summer" (Witte, Michael)
SCHWARZENEGGER, ARNOLD—PHOTOGRAPHS
PH14322 615 (October 17, 1991) p64. "Mick Jagger And Arnold Schwarzenegger, 1990" (Pigozzi, Jean)
PH14323 619-620 (December 12, 1991) pp[cover]. "1991 Yearbook" (Ritts, Herb)
PH14324 632 (June 11, 1992) p115. "[Dolly Parton, Arnold Schwarzenegger]" (Leibovitz, Annie)
PH14325 645-646 (December 10, 1992) p157. "Arnold Schwarzenegger, 1991"
PH14326 662 (August 5, 1993) p72. "In 'Hero,' Schwarzenegger Carries A Stiff, And We Do Mean The Film"
PH14327 665 (September 16, 1993) p77. "Worst Picture"
PH14328 689 (August 25, 1994) p96. "Schwarzenegger And Curtis Work Out The Kinks"
PH14329 697 (December 15, 1994) p104. "Dr. De Vito Examines A Very Pregnant Ah-nuld"
PH14330 740 (August 8, 1996) p68. "'Independence Day,' Travolta In 'Phenomenon,' Schwarzenegger In 'Eraser,' Moore In 'Striptease'"
SCHWARZENEGGER, ARNOLD—PHOTOGRAPHS—PORTRAITS
PH14331 656 (May 13, 1993) p13. "[Arnold Schwarzenegger]"
SCHWARZKOPF, NORMAN—PHOTOGRAPHS
PH14332 619-620 (December 12, 1991) p201. "Stormin' Norman Schwarzkopf Tells Barbara Walters About The Video Victory In The Gulf"
SCHWIMMER, DAVID—PHOTOGRAPHS
PH14333 708 (May 18, 1995) pp[cover]. "Fast Friends: No Sex Bad Jobs Hit Show Go Figure" (Seliger, Mark)
PH14334 708 (May 18, 1995) p64. "Hey, Hey, Where's The Monkey? (Marcel Is Leaving)"
PH14335 708 (May 18, 1995) p. "Matt LeBlanc, Jennifer Aniston, David Schwimmer, Courteney Cox, Lisa Kudrow, Matthew Perry" (Seliger, Mark)
PH14336 715 (August 24, 1995) p75. "Hot Actor" (Vadukul, Nitin)
PH14337 733 (May 2, 1996) p62. "Schwimmer With Paltrow"
SCIALFA, PATTI—ALBUMS
PH14338 665 (September 16, 1993) p70. "Rumble Doll"
SCIALFA, PATTI—PHOTOGRAPHS
PH14339 636 (August 6, 1992) p42. "Springsteen Onstage With Wife Patti Scialfa At Stockholm's Globe Arena, June 15th" (Preston, Neal)
PH14340 664 (September 2, 1993) p31. "[Rumble Doll]" (Busacca, Larry)
PH14341 702 (February 23, 1995) p50. "Johnson, Tyler, Springsteen And Patti Scialfa Schmooze" (Mazur, Kevin)
SCIALFA, PATTI—PHOTOGRAPHS—PORTRAITS
PH14342 667 (October 14, 1993) p34. "[Patti Scialfa]" (Borris, Dan)
SCIENCE—ILLUSTRATIONS
PH14343 656 (May 13, 1993) p90. "[Nitric Oxide]" (Sevalrud, Thom)
SCOFIELD, PAUL—PHOTOGRAPHS
PH14344 749 (December 12, 1996) p90. "Scofield Drives A Girl To Hysteria"
SCORPIONS—PHOTOGRAPHS
PH14345 623 (February 6, 1992) p11. "Mikhail Gorbachev Greets Members Of Scorpions In Moscow" (Regan, Ken)
SCORSESE, MARTIN—PHOTOGRAPHS
PH14346 627 (April 2, 1992) p41. "'Cape Fear' Director Scorsese"
PH14347 666 (September 30, 1993) p112. "Director Martin Scorsese Sets Up A Lavish Dinner Party"
PH14348 678 (March 24, 1994) p100. "Missing In Oscar Action"
PH14349 723 (December 14, 1995) p90. "The Lady Gambles: Stone With The Dice; With Jealous Husband Robert De Niro; Gangster Lover Joe Pesci; And Director Martin Scorsese (from top)"
SCORSESE, MARTIN—PHOTOGRAPHS—PORTRAITS
PH14350 722 (November 30, 1995) p19. "'Casino' Director Martin Scorsese (left) And Robbie Robertson" (Corbijn, Anton)
PH14351 731 (April 4, 1996) p66. "Scorsese, 'Casino'"
SCOTIA, CALIFORNIA—PHOTOGRAPHS
PH14352 727 (February 8, 1996) p43. "Protesters At An Earth First! Demonstration In 1989 Paraded Through Scotia, Calif., Carrying Paper-Faced Effigies Of Corporate Raider Charles Hurwitz" (King, Greg)
SCOTT THOMAS, KRISTIN—PHOTOGRAPHS
PH14353 743 (September 19, 1996) p90. "Quality Control"
SCOTT THOMAS, KRISTIN—PHOTOGRAPHS—PORTRAITS
PH14354 748 (November 28, 1996) p142. "Scott Thomas, Left, Binoche"
SCOTT, CASEY—PHOTOGRAPHS
PH14355 656 (May 13, 1993) p27. "[Casey Scott]"
SCOTT, JIMMY—ALBUMS
PH14356 640 (October 1, 1992) p69. "All The Way"
SCOTT, MIKE—PHOTOGRAPHS
PH14357 664 (September 2, 1993) p32. "Scott (right) Greets His Former Mate" (Gershoff, Gary)
SCOTT, MIKE—PHOTOGRAPHS—PORTRAITS
PH14358 658 (June 10, 1993) p26. "[Mike Scott]"
SCOTT-HERON, GIL—PHOTOGRAPHS
PH14359 689 (August 25, 1994) p46. "Gil Scott-Heron (above)" (Capak, R. J.)
SCOTT-THOMAS, KRISTIN—PHOTOGRAPHS
PH14360 676 (February 24, 1994) p62. "Shipboard Romance Seigner (left) And Scott-Thomas"
SCRAWL—ALBUMS
PH14361 744 (October 3, 1996) p72. "Travel On, Rider"
SCREAMING TREES—ALBUMS
PH14362 738-739 (July 11, 1996) p86. "Dust"
SCREAMING TREES—PHOTOGRAPHS
PH14363 645-646 (December 10, 1992) p85. "Screaming Trees" (Cuffaro, Chris)
PH14364 650 (February 18, 1993) p15. "Gary Lee Conner, Barrett Martin, Mark Lanegan And Van Conner (from left)" (Winters, Dan)
PH14365 695 (November 17, 1994) p110. "Screaming Trees" (Ragel, Jon)
PH14366 741 (August 22, 1996) p56. "Lanegan (left) And Lee Conner Perform At LollaPalooza On June 27, 1996" (Blakesberg, Jay)
PH14367 741 (August 22, 1996) p55. "Out Of The Woods" (Sednaoui, Stephane)
PH14368 750-751 (December 26, 1996) p68. "Seattle Survivors: Screaming Trees Are Blooming In The Post-Grunge Era" (Ragel, Jon)
SCRUGGS, EARL—PHOTOGRAPHS
PH14369 746 (October 31, 1996) p23. "Pride Of The Opry: The Legendary Bluegrass Boys Lineup Of Monroe, Chubby Wise, Flatt, Scruggs And Monroe's Brother Birch, Circa 1947 (from left)"

SCRUGGS, EARL—PHOTOGRAPHS—PORTRAITS
PH14370 750-751 (December 26, 1996) p172. "Earl Scruggs" (Seliger, Mark)
SCUD MOUNTAIN BOYS—PHOTOGRAPHS
PH14371 750-751 (December 26, 1996) p57. "Breakthrough"
SCULL, JONATHAN—PHOTOGRAPHS
PH14372 748 (November 28, 1996) p81. "Professional Geek Jonathan Scull Pens Voluble Reviews For The High-End Bible 'Stereophile'" (Pluchino, Joseph)
SCULLEY, JOHN—PHOTOGRAPHS
PH14373 731 (April 4, 1996) p55. "Apple's 'Chief Listener,' John Sculley, In '92"
PH14374 731 (April 4, 1996) pp54-55. "Jobs And Sculley In '84" (Kashi, Ed)
PH14375 731 (April 4, 1996) p54. "Jobs, Sculley And Wozniak (from left) Unveil The Apple IIC In '84"
PH14376 732 (April 18, 1996) p61. "John Sculley (left) With Hillary Clinton"
SCULLEY, JOHN—PHOTOGRAPHS—PORTRAITS
PH14377 732 (April 18, 1996) p60. "Sculley With The Newton Prototype, 1992"
SCULLY, ROCK—PHOTOGRAPHS
PH14378 717 (September 21, 1995) p65. "The Dead In Front Of Their Ashbury St. House, 1967: Jerry Garcia, Ron 'Pigpen' McKernan, Bob Weir, Phil Lesh, Co-Managers Danny Rifkin And Rock Scully, And Bill Kreutzmann..."
PH14379 717 (September 21, 1995) p66. "Lesh, Early Dead Co-Managers Scully And Rifkin, Weir And Garcia At A Press Conference Following The Oct. 2, 1967, drug Bust At The Dead's House" (Wolman, Baron)
SEA AND CAKE—PHOTOGRAPHS
PH14380 721 (November 16, 1995) p67. "The Sea And Cake: Art-Pop Aficionados Sam Prekop, John McEntire, Archer Prewitt And Eric Claridge (middle row, from left)" (Guip, Amy)
SEAGAL, STEVEN—PHOTOGRAPHS
PH14381 679 (April 7, 1994) p83. "Bombs Away"
SEAL—ALBUMS
PH14382 625 (March 5, 1992) p60. "Seal"
PH14383 692 (October 6, 1994) p90. "Seal"
SEAL—PHOTOGRAPHS
PH14384 618 (November 28, 1991) pp15,18. "[Seal]" (MacPherson, Andrew)
PH14385 732 (April 18, 1996) p19. "Open Up And Say Ah: D'Angelo (left) And Three-Time Winner Seal Get A Little Crazy" (Mazur, Kevin)
SEAL—PHOTOGRAPHS—PORTRAITS
PH14386 619-620 (December 12, 1991) p44. "Seal" (McClelland, Philippe)
PH14387 689 (August 25, 1994) p36. "[Seal]"
PH14388 695 (November 17, 1994) p32. "Seal" (Koralik, Cheryl)
SEALS, SON—ALBUMS
PH14389 615 (October 17, 1991) p93. "Living In The Danger Zone"
SEAQUEST (TELEVISION SHOW)—PHOTOGRAPHS
PH14390 666 (September 30, 1993) p115. "Scheider (right) in 'Seaquest'"
SEARCH AND DESTROY (FILM)—PHOTOGRAPHS
PH14391 708 (May 18, 1995) p97. "A Deadly Drive For Dunne, Douglas And Walken"
THE SEARCHERS (FILM)—PHOTOGRAPHS
PH14392 658 (June 10, 1993) p74. "Ethan (Wayne) To Niece (Wood): 'Let's Go Home, Debbie'"
SEARCHING FOR BOBBY FISCHER (FILM)—PHOTOGRAPHS
PH14393 664 (September 2, 1993) p70. "Fishburne Challenges Chess Prodigy Pomeranc"
SEATTLE—ILLUSTRATIONS
PH14394 724-725 (December 28, 1995) p20. "Welcome To Seattle" (Pendergrast, James T.)
SEATTLE, WASHINGTON—ILLUSTRATIONS—LETTERING
PH14395 628 (April 16, 1992) p43. "[Seattle, Washington]" (Allen, Terry)
SEATTLE, WASHINGTON—PHOTOGRAPHS
PH14396 628 (April 16, 1992) p43. "Two Of Seattle's Restless Natives" (Seliger, Mark)
PH14397 683 (June 2, 1994) p59. "More Than 5,000 Fans Paid Tribute To Cobain In Seattle On April 10" (Winters, Dan)
PH14398 683 (June 2, 1994) p60. "Police Couldn't Keep Seattle Mourners Out Of The Fountains" (Winters, Dan)
PH14399 735 (May 30, 1996) pp35-40. "[Seattle & Heroin]" (Exum)
SEBADOH—ALBUMS
PH14400 664 (September 2, 1993) p61. "Bubble And Scrape"
PH14401 692 (October 6, 1994) p104. "Bake Sale"
PH14402 696 (December 1, 1994) p126. "Bakesale"
PH14403 742 (September 5, 1996) p60. "Harmacy"
SEBADOH—PHOTOGRAPHS
PH14404 704 (March 23, 1995) p43. "The Sensitive Souls Of Sebadoh: Fay, Barlow And Loewenstein (from left)" (Ockenfels, Frank, 3)
PH14405 736 (June 13, 1996) p53. "Sebadoh's Natural Ones: Bob Fay, Jason Lowenstein And Lou Barlow" (Van Iperen, Neils)
PH14406 744 (October 3, 1996) p56. "The Current Sebadoh Lineup Of Jason Lowenstein, Bob Fay And Barlow (from left)" (Peterson, Charles)
SEBASTIAN—PHOTOGRAPHS
PH14407 670 (November 25, 1993) p79. "[Sebastian]" (Seliger, Mark)
SEBERG, JEAN—PHOTOGRAPHS
PH14408 730 (March 21, 1996) p104. "Hurt (left) Reflects On Seberg As Saint Joan"
SECRET FRIENDS (FILM)—PHOTOGRAPHS
PH14409 624 (February 20, 1992) p50. "Alan Bates (left) And Friends At Dinner"
THE SECRET HISTORY (BOOK)—PHOTOGRAPHS
PH14410 652 (March 18, 1993) pp[enc.6]. "The Secret History"
SECRET OF ROAN INISH (FILM)—PHOTOGRAPHS
PH14411 731 (April 4, 1996) p66. "Inish"
SECRETS AND LIES (FILM)—PHOTOGRAPHS
PH14412 743 (September 19, 1996) p90. "Quality Control"
PH14413 745 (October 17, 1996) p142. "Jean-Bapiste (left) And Blethyn Flank Mike Leigh"
SEDGWICK, KYRA—PHOTOGRAPHS
PH14414 664 (September 2, 1993) p69. "Charles Grodin, Robert Downey Jr., Kyra Sedgwick, Alfre Woodard And Tom Sizemore"
SEEFF, NORMAN—BOOKS
PH14415 698-699 (December 29, 1994) p63. "Sessions" (Seeff, Norman)
SEEGER, PETE—PHOTOGRAPHS
PH14416 637 (August 20, 1992) p23. "The All-Star Lineup Onstage In Central Park" (Mazur, Kevin)
PH14417 728 (February 22, 1996) pp18-19. "Belafonte, Seeger And Guthrie (from left)" (Mazur, Kevin)
SEGAL, ED—PHOTOGRAPHS—PORTRAITS
PH14418 691 (September 22, 1994) p45. "AmeriCorps Head Eli Segal: "Getting Things Done"" (Wolfe, Tom)
SEGAL, ELI—PHOTOGRAPHS
PH14419 659 (June 24, 1993) p33. "Eli Segal (center), White House Director Of National Service, And His Staff" (Grace, Arthur)
SEGER, BOB—ALBUMS
PH14420 615 (October 17, 1991) p93. "The Fire Inside"
SEGER, BOB—PHOTOGRAPHS
PH14421 631 (May 28, 1992) p11. "Alice Cooper, Smokey Robinson And Bob Seger (from left)" (Plummer, Sue)
SEIFERT, JODY—PHOTOGRAPHS
PH14422 703 (March 9, 1995) p29. "Easy As Pie: Jody Seifert, Nina Hellman And Kerri Kenney (from left)" (Falls, John)

SEIGNER, EMMANUELLE—PHOTOGRAPHS
PH14423 676 (February 24, 1994) p62. "Shipboard Romance Seigner (left) And Scott-Thomas"
SEINFELD (TELEVISION SHOW)—ILLUSTRATIONS
PH14424 664 (September 2, 1993) p8. "Thanks For Nothing" (Pendergrast, James T.)
SEINFELD (TELEVISION SHOW)—PHOTOGRAPHS
PH14425 691 (September 22, 1994) p49. "Jerry And Elaine (Julia Louis-Dreyfus) Won't Get Back In The Sack" (Sonnemair, Jan)
SEINFELD, JERRY—ILLUSTRATIONS
PH14426 694 (November 3, 1994) p14. "Drugs 'N' Gravy" (Pendergrast, James T.)
SEINFELD, JERRY—PHOTOGRAPHS
PH14427 660-661 (July 8, 1993) p41. "Nothing On: Jason Alexander, Julia Louis-Dreyfus, Jerry Seinfeld And Michael Richards" (Seliger, Mark)
PH14428 660-661 (July 8, 1993) pp[cover]. "Seinfeld Rules!" (Seliger, Mark)
PH14429 672-673 (December 23, 1993) p188. "[Covers]" (Seliger, Mark)
PH14430 690 (September 8, 1994) p73. "Master Of His Domain: Jerry Seinfeld Has A Typical Warm "Larry Sanders" Moment" (Fallon, Bernard)
PH14431 691 (September 22, 1994) p50. "A 21-Year Age Gap Doesn't Faze Seinfeld Or Shoshanna Lonstein" (Gerber, M.)
PH14432 691 (September 22, 1994) p49. "Jerry And Elaine (Julia Louis-Dreyfus) Won't Get Back In The Sack" (Sonnemair, Jan)
PH14433 691 (September 22, 1994) p46. "[Jerry Seinfeld]" (Seliger, Mark)
PH14434 691 (September 22, 1994) pp[cover]. "Jerry Seinfeld: The King Of Prime-Time Comedy" (Seliger, Mark)
SEINFELD, JERRY—PHOTOGRAPHS—PORTRAITS
PH14435 630 (May 14, 1992) p52. "[Jerry Seinfeld]" (Schiffman, Bonnie)
PH14436 660-661 (July 8, 1993) p45. "Jerry Seinfeld And His Cereal: 'I'm Constantly Working On Better Breakfast Systems.'" (Seliger, Mark)
PH14437 691 (September 22, 1994) p47. "[Jerry Seinfeld]" (Seliger, Mark)
PH14438 691 (September 22, 1994) p48. "Massapequa High-School Grad Seinfeld: 1972"
PH14439 691 (September 22, 1994) p49. "Stand-Up Is Seinfeld's Passion; TV Is "No Big Deal"" (Drinkwater, Paul)
SELENA—ALBUMS
PH14440 716 (September 7, 1995) p72. "Dreaming Of You"
SELENA—PHOTOGRAPHS—PORTRAITS
PH14441 724-725 (December 28, 1995) p64. "[Selena]" (Rinaldi, Maurice)
SELF-ESTEEM—ILLUSTRATIONS
PH14442 678 (March 24, 1994) p6. "Self Esteem" (Pendergrast, James T.)
SELIGER, MARK—ILLUSTRATIONS
PH14443 643 (November 12, 1992) p115. "[Mark Seliger]" (Russo, Anthony)
SELIGER, MARK—ILLUSTRATIONS—LETTERING
PH14444 643 (November 12, 1992) p115. "[Mark Seliger]" (Karl, Anita)
SELIGER, MARK—PHOTOGRAPHS
PH14445 643 (November 12, 1992) p248. "Mark Seliger (right) On Location: Inventiveness, Vitality And A Healthy Dose Of Humor" (Sherman, Steve)
SELWAY, PHIL—PHOTOGRAPHS
PH14446 738-739 (July 11, 1996) p15. "Thom Yorke, Colin Greenwood, Roseanne, Ed O'Brien, Phil Selway And Jonny Greenwood" (Diltz, Henry)
PH14447 660-661 (July 8, 1993) p95. "Radiohead: Ed O'Brien, Colin Greenwood, Phil Selway, Yorke, Jonny Greenwood" (Sharp, Ken)
PH14448 716 (September 7, 1995) p19. "Colin Greenwood, Ed O'Brien, Thom Yorke, Jonny Greenwood And Phil Selway (from left)" (Blakesberg, Jay)
SEMEL, TERRY—PHOTOGRAPHS
PH14449 726 (January 25, 1996) p26. "Warner's Bob Daly (left), Terry Semel" (Smeal, Jim)
SEMEN AND BLOOD III—PHOTOGRAPHS
PH14450 737 (June 27, 1996) p37. "Loaded Image: Serrano's 'Semen And Blood III'" (Serrano, Andres)
SEN DOG—PHOTOGRAPHS
PH14451 631 (May 28, 1992) p18. "Muggs, Sen Dog And B-Real (from left)" (Moss, Gary)
PH14452 662 (August 5, 1993) p16. "Just Another Band From L.A.? Sen Dog, B-Real And DJ Muggs (from left)"
PH14452a 672-673 (December 23, 1993) p53. "Muggs, B-Real And Sen-Dog (from left) Pay Homage To The Wicked Weed On 'Black Sunday'" (Borris, Dan)
PH14453 715 (August 24, 1995) p44. "Sen Dog, B-Real, Bobo (from left)" (Blakesberg, Jay)
PH14454 731 (April 4, 1996) p30. "Sen Dog, Muggs, B-Real (from left)" (McClelland, P.)
SEN DOG—PHOTOGRAPHS—PORTRAITS
PH14455 669 (November 11, 1993) p64. "The Dope On The Hill: B-real, Sen Dog And Muggs (bottom row, from left)" (Borris, Dan)
PH14456 Number not assigned.
SENIOR, RUSSELL—PHOTOGRAPHS
PH14457 732 (April 18, 1996) p24. "A Wildly Unorthodox Mixture Of Influence Gathered Around The Table: Pulp's Candida Doyle, Mark Webber, Cocker, Steve Mackey, Russell Senior And Nick Banks (from left)" (Rankin)
SENSE AND SENSIBILITY (FILM)—PHOTOGRAPHS
PH14458 731 (April 4, 1996) p66. "'Sense And Sensibility,' With Thompson And Kate Winslet"
SENSI—PHOTOGRAPHS—PORTRAITS
PH14459 686-687 (July 14, 1994) p72. "Girl World: Sensi, Linda, Charmaine, Sabrina (from left)" (Borris, Dan)
SEPULTURA—ALBUMS
PH14460 730 (March 21, 1996) p98. "Roots"
SERBEDZIJA, RADE—PHOTOGRAPHS
PH14461 704 (March 23, 1995) p128. "Manchevski Directs Lovers Cartlidge And Serbedzija"
SERBIA—ILLUSTRATIONS
PH14462 657 (May 27, 1993) p6. "Yugoslavian Transportation" (Pendergrast, James T.)
PH14463 728 (February 22, 1996) p16. "The Heart..." (Pendergrast, James T.)
SERCH, MC—ALBUMS
PH14464 640 (October 1, 1992) p68. "Return Of The Product"
SERIAL MOM (FILM)—ILLUSTRATIONS
PH14465 681 (May 5, 1994) p47. "Divine Madness" (Risko, Robert)
SERIAL MOM (FILM)—PHOTOGRAPHS
PH14466 681 (May 5, 1994) p48. "Momhood, John Waters Style: Divine (left) And Turner"
PH14467 705 (April 6, 1995) p69. "Oscar Rejects"
SERPA, PERRY—PHOTOGRAPHS
PH14468 677 (March 10, 1994) p57. "Nasty Men: Martin And Perry Serpa" (Smale, Brian)
SERVING IN SILENCE (FILM)—PHOTOGRAPHS
PH14469 702 (February 23, 1995) p81. "Atten-tion! Close"
SET IT OFF (FILM)—PHOTOGRAPHS
PH14470 748 (November 28, 1996) p143. "Latifah"
SETZER, BRIAN—ALBUMS
PH14471 680 (April 21, 1994) p87. "The Brian Setzer Orchestra"
SETZER, BRIAN—PHOTOGRAPHS
PH14472 737 (June 27, 1996) p16. "Strummer (left) And Setzer"
SEVEN (FILM)—PHOTOGRAPHS
PH14473 718 (October 5, 1995) p76. "Cop Brad Pitt Battles A Serial Killer To Protect Gwyneth Paltrow"
PH14474 731 (April 4, 1996) p66. "Freeman, 'Seven'"

SEVEN MARY THREE—PHOTOGRAPHS
PH14475 731 (April 4, 1996) p36. "The Two Jasons (Pollock and Ross), Khalsa And Daniel" (Clinch, Danny)
7 SECONDS (VIDEO)—PHOTOGRAPHS
PH14476 689 (August 25, 1994) p45. "Breaking The Language Barrier: Youssou N'Dour" (Gougenheim, Kim)
PH14477 689 (August 25, 1994) p45. "Timekeeper Cherry" (Gougenheim, Kim)
7 YEAR BITCH—ALBUMS
PH14478 649 (February 4, 1993) p66. "Sick 'Em"
PH14479 691 (September 22, 1994) p99. "Viva Zapata"
7 YEAR BITCH—PHOTOGRAPHS
PH14480 690 (September 8, 1994) p21. "Mad Lovers Drew Barrymore (top right) And 7 Year Bitch" (Marshak, Bob)
PH14481 692 (October 6, 1994) p55. "7 Year Bitch's Vigil At A 1993 L.A. Benefit" (Cohen, Lester)
PH14482 722 (November 30, 1995) p19. "Who Are You Callin' A Bitch?: To Wit, Elizabeth Davis, Selene Vigil, Agnew And Roisin Dunne Of 7 Year Bitch (from left)" (Blakesberg, Jay)
PH14483 731 (April 4, 1996) p17. "7 Year Bitch's Davis, Selene Vigil (from left)" (Eichner, Steve)
SEVER, SAM—PHOTOGRAPHS
PH14484 617 (November 14, 1991) p34. "Bosco Money (left) And Sam Sever" (Lavine, Michael)
SEVINK, JON—PHOTOGRAPHS
PH14485 630 (May 14, 1992) p32. "The Levellers (from left): Friend, Sevink, Chadwick, Heather And Cunningham" (Doove, Hester)
SEWELL, DARA—PHOTOGRAPHS
PH14486 715 (August 24, 1995) p60. "Charlie With Girlfriend Dara Sewell During Their Trip To New Orleans For Mardi Gras This Year"
SEWELL, RUFUS—PHOTOGRAPHS
PH14487 735 (May 30, 1996) p57. "Life On The Farm"
SEX—ILLUSTRATIONS
PH14488 691 (September 22, 1994) p19. "Holy Hymen!" (Friske, Maria)
SEX PISTOLS—ALBUMS
PH14489 617 (November 14, 1991) p92. "Never Mind The Bollocks Here's The Sex Pistols" (Reid, Jamie)
PH14490 743 (September 19, 1996) p80. "Filthy Lucre Live"
SEX PISTOLS—PHOTOGRAPHS
PH14491 633 (June 25, 1992) p6. "[Sex Pistols]" (Gruen, Bob)
PH14492 636 (August 6, 1992) p8. "[Sex Pistols]" (Gruen, Bob)
PH14493 734 (May 16, 1996) p17. "Matlock, Rotten, Jones And Cook Now" (Gruen, Bob)
PH14494 734 (May 16, 1996) p17. "The Pistols' Rotten, Glen Matlock, Steve Jones And Paul Cook In '76" (Gruen, Bob)
PH14495 736 (June 13, 1996) p52. "Pistols '96: Glen Matlock, Steve Jones, Paul Cook And Johnny Rotten (from left)" (Thomas, Justin)
SEXISM—ILLUSTRATIONS
PH14496 667 (October 14, 1993) p67. "[Women]" (Isip, Jordan)
SEXSMITH, RON—ALBUMS
PH14497 716 (September 7, 1995) p72. "Ron Sexsmith"
SEXTON, CHARLIE—PHOTOGRAPHS
PH14498 630 (May 14, 1992) p25. "Chris Layton, Tommy Shannon, Doyle Bramhall II, Charlie Sexton (from left)" (Pumphrey, Steve)
PH14499 654 (April 15, 1993) pp[enc.16,24]. "[Charlie Sexton]" (Woodward, Fred)
PH14500 654 (April 15, 1993) pp[enc.3]. "[Spring Collection]" (Woodard, Fred)
PH14501 654 (April 15, 1993) pp[enc.cover]. "Spring Fashion 1993" (Woodward, Fred)
SEXTON, CHARLIE—PHOTOGRAPHS—PORTRAITS
PH14502 654 (April 15, 1993) pp[enc.17]. "[Charlie Sexton]" (Woodward, Fred)
SEYMOUR, NICK—PHOTOGRAPHS
PH14503 676 (February 24, 1994) p17. "Four's A Crowd: Neil Finn, Mark Hart, Paul Hester And Nick Seymour (from left)" (Broad, Julian)
THE SHADOW (FILM)—PHOTOGRAPHS
PH14504 684 (June 16, 1994) p114. "Potential Headaches"
PH14505 688 (August 11, 1994) p62. "The Shadow"
SHADOWLANDS (FILM)—PHOTOGRAPHS
PH14506 674 (January 27, 1994) p48. "Acting Vehicles Include 'The Pelican Brief,' 'In The Name Of The Father,' 'What's Eating Gilbert Grape,' 'Shadowlands,' 'Naked,' And 'Grumpy Old Men'"
SHADOWS AND FOG (FILM)—PHOTOGRAPHS
PH14507 645-646 (December 10, 1992) p190. "Woody Allen And Mia Farrow"
PH14508 649 (February 4, 1993) p72. "[Shadows And Fog]"
SHADY—ALBUMS
PH14509 700 (January 26, 1995) p76. "World"
SHAFFER, PAUL—PHOTOGRAPHS
PH14510 724-725 (December 28, 1995) p56. "Jann Wenner, Yoko Ono, Little Richard, Paul Shaffer Cut Loose" (Mazur, Kevin)
SHAFFER, SCOTT—PHOTOGRAPHS
PH14511 652 (March 18, 1993) pp[enc.36]. "Hilary Wall And Scott Shaffer" (Seliger, Mark)
PH14512 652 (March 18, 1993) pp[enc.38]. "Scott Shaffer" (Seliger, Mark)
SHAGGY—ALBUMS
PH14513 716 (September 7, 1995) p70. "Boombastic"
SHAGGY—ILLUSTRATIONS
PH14514 720 (November 2, 1995) p92. "Shaggy: Captain Boombastic" (Menchin, Scott)
SHAGGY—PHOTOGRAPHS
PH14515 672-673 (December 23, 1993) p48. "[Shaggy]" (Hilton, Roger)
SHAI—ALBUMS
PH14516 653 (April 1, 1993) p52. "If I Ever Fall In Love"
SHAKESPEAR'S SISTER—PHOTOGRAPHS
PH14517 653 (April 1, 1993) p13. "Tom Jones And Shakespear's Sister"
SHAKOOR, NADIRAH—PHOTOGRAPHS—PORTRAITS
PH14518 697 (December 15, 1994) p18. "Shakoor, Stipe And Perez (from left) Give Their Achin' Dogs A Rest After AIDS Walk Atlanta"
SHAKUR, AFENI—PHOTOGRAPHS
PH14519 746 (October 31, 1996) p46. "Afeni Shakur, 23 (second from left), And Lumumba Abdul Shakur (right) Were Charged In A Black Panther Bombing Plot, In 1969"
SHAKUR, LUMUMBA ABDUL—PHOTOGRAPHS
PH14519 746 (October 31, 1996) p46. "Afeni Shakur, 23 (second from left), And Lumumba Abdul Shakur (right) Were Charged In A Black Panther Bombing Plot, In 1969"
SHAKUR, TUPAC—ALBUMS
PH14520 707 (May 4, 1995) p68. "Me Against The World"
PH14521 731 (April 4, 1996) p60. "All Eyez On Me"
PH14522 746 (October 31, 1996) p51. "All Eyez On Me"
PH14523 746 (October 31, 1996) p51. "Me Against The World"
SHAKUR, TUPAC—ILLUSTRATIONS
PH14524 708 (May 18, 1995) p108. "2Pac: Caged Heat" (Bartholomew, Beth)
PH14525 731 (April 4, 1996) p76. "All Eyez On Me: Pac In Heat" (MacDonald, Ross)
PH14526 749 (December 12, 1996) p16. "Entering The Freeze Zone" (Pendergrast, James T.)
PH14527 750-751 (December 26, 1996) p78. "[Tupac Shakur]" (Barbour, Karen)
SHAKUR, TUPAC—PHOTOGRAPHS
PH14528 663 (August 19, 1993) p82. "Janet Jackson With Her Boyz: Director John Singleton (left) And Co-Star Tupac Shakur"

PH14529 668 (October 28, 1993) p22. "[Tupac Shakur]" (Clinch, Danny)
PH14530 722 (November 30, 1995) p42. "Shakur Was Upbeat During His Trial Last Fall" (Reuters)
PH14531 724-725 (December 28, 1995) p60. "Shakur" (Benabib, Michael)
PH14532 724-725 (December 28, 1995) p60. "Shakur" (Orris, Darby)
PH14533 728 (February 22, 1996) p64. "2Pac Returns To The Stage In New Orleans" (Smith, Sean)
PH14534 730 (March 21, 1996) p18. "[2Pac Shakur & Snoop Doggy Dogg]" (Mazur, Kevin)
PH14535 732 (April 18, 1996) p19. "Ace Frehley, Paul Stanley, 2Pac, Peter Criss And Gene Simmons (from left)" (Mazur, Kevin)
PH14536 741 (August 22, 1996) p26. "Roth (right) With Shakur, Who Says, 'We're The Most Unlikely Action Stars.'" (Goode, Nicola)
PH14537 745 (October 17, 1996) p40. "Tupac Shakur (left) With Death Row's 'Suge' Knight This Summer"
PH14538 746 (October 31, 1996) p41. "Shakur (left) And Knight Sitting In Knight's Black BMW Sedan In Las Vegas On Sept. 7, Only Moments Before The Shooting" (Corjuni)
PH14539 746 (October 31, 1996) p46. "Shakur (left) And Suge Knight In 1995 At Club 662 On Flamingo Road In Downtown Las Vegas"
PH14540 746 (October 31, 1996) p42. "Shakur Arrives At A Manhattan Courtroom On Dec. 1, 1994, For His Sexual-Abuse Verdict"
PH14541 746 (October 31, 1996) p42. "Shakur With Digital Underground's Money B. (from left) And The D.U. Posse On A Video Shoot In 1991" (Posey, Carl)
PH14542 746 (October 31, 1996) p42. "Shakur With Janet Jackson On The Set Of The Film 'Poetic Justice' In 1993"
PH14543 746 (October 31, 1996) pp38-39. "[Tupac Shakur]" (Winters, Dan)
PH14544 746 (October 31, 1996) p49. "[Tupac Shakur]" (Clinch, Danny)
PH14545 746 (October 31, 1996) pp[cover]. "Tupac Shakur: The Strange & Terrible Saga" (Clinch, Danny)
SHAKUR, TUPAC—PHOTOGRAPHS—PORTRAITS
PH14546 672-673 (December 23, 1993) p74. "Poetic Justice? Shakur In A Peaceful Moment" (Clinch, Danny)
PH14547 714 (August 10, 1995) p30. "Shakur: Up In Smoke?"
SHALHOUB, TONY—PHOTOGRAPHS
PH14548 744 (October 3, 1996) p78. "Cooking With Shalhoub (left) And Tucci"
SHALLOW GRAVE (FILM)—PHOTOGRAPHS
PH14549 702 (February 23, 1995) p81. "Fox, McGregor And Eccleston Find The Body"
SHAMANS—PHOTOGRAPHS
PH14550 630 (May 14, 1992) p91. "[Shamanism]"
SHAME—PHOTOGRAPHS
PH14551 649 (February 4, 1993) p23. "Jeremy Toback, Shawn Smith, Regan Hagar And Stone Gossard (from left)"
SHANA—PHOTOGRAPHS
PH14552 638 (September 3, 1992) pp[enc.2,12]. "[Marky Mark, Shana]" (Klein, Steven)
PH14553 638 (September 3, 1992) pp[enc.11,16]. "[Shana]" (Klein, Steven)
SHANAHAN, JAY—PHOTOGRAPHS
PH14554 693 (October 20, 1994) p75. "Director Jay Shanahan On A Set in The Valley"
SHANAHAN, MARY—PHOTOGRAPHS
PH14555 643 (November 12, 1992) p49. "'Rolling Stone' Art Directors (from left): Bob Kingsbury (1968-73), Tony Lane (1974-76), Annie Leibovitz, Mike Salisbury (1973-74), Roger Black (1976-78), Jann S. Wenner, Derek..
SHANDLING, GARRY—ILLUSTRATIONS
PH14556 690 (September 8, 1994) p67. "[Garry Shandling]" (Risko, Robert)
SHANDLING, GARRY—PHOTOGRAPHS
PH14557 645-646 (December 10, 1992) p198. "Possible Talk-Show Host Dana Carvey With Fake Talk-Show Host Garry Shandling"
PH14558 672-673 (December 23, 1993) p88. "Larry (right) With Helen Hunt" (Fallon, Brenda)
PH14559 690 (September 8, 1994) p71. "Doing "Tonight" In 1984: "One Of The Troubles With A Nightly Talk Show Is That It's Nightly"
PH14560 690 (September 8, 1994) p72. "Many Celebrities Who Appear On "The Larry Sanders Show" Are Fans, Like Alec Baldwin" (Tepper, Randy)
PH14561 690 (September 8, 1994) p73. "Master Of His Domain: Jerry Seinfeld Has A Typical Warm "Larry Sanders" Moment" (Fallon, Bernard)
PH14562 690 (September 8, 1994) p70. "Shandling With Real-Life Fiancee And Fictional Co-Worker Linda Doucett" (Kravitz, Jeff)
PH14563 690 (September 8, 1994) p68. "Sidekick Hank Kingsley (Jeffrey Tambor), Producer Arthur (Rip Torn) And Host Larry Sanders (Shandling)"
PH14564 690 (September 8, 1994) p70. "With Real-Life Co-Worker And Fictional Girlfriend Jessica harper, From "It's Garry Shandling's Show""
PH14565 714 (August 10, 1995) p15. "Shandling, Left, And Beck On The Set Of 'Larry Sanders'" (Hole, Danny)
SHANGHAI TRIAD (FILM)—PHOTOGRAPHS
PH14566 726 (January 25, 1996) p67. "Shanghai Triad"
SHANGRI-LAS—PHOTOGRAPHS
PH14567 692 (October 6, 1994) p50. "The Shangri-Las"
SHANICE—ALBUMS
PH14568 626 (March 19, 1992) p95. "Inner Child"
SHANNON, SARAH—PHOTOGRAPHS—PORTRAITS
PH14569 655 (April 29, 1993) p24. "Revving It Up: Velocity's Shannon, Spellman, Nelson, Riles And Moore (from left)" (Falls, John)
SHANNON, TOMMY—PHOTOGRAPHS
PH14570 630 (May 14, 1992) p25. "Chris Layton, Tommy Shannon, Doyle Bramhall II, Charlie Sexton (from left)" (Pumphrey, Steve)
PH14571 654 (April 15, 1993) pp[enc.20]. "[Tommy Shannon]" (Woodward, Fred)
PH14572 711 (June 29, 1995) p18. "B. B. King, Robert Cray, Buddy Guy, Art Neville, Jimmie Vaughan, Clapton, Raitt And Tommy Shannon" (Long, Andrew)
SHANNON, TOMMY—PHOTOGRAPHS—PORTRAITS
PH14573 654 (April 15, 1993) pp[enc.17]. "[Tommy Shannon]" (Woodward, Fred)
SHAPIRO, JIM—PHOTOGRAPHS
PH14574 686-687 (July 14, 1994) p73. "Salt Of The Earth: Lack, Gordon, Post And Shapiro (from left)" (Elledge, Paul)
PH14575 700 (January 26, 1995) p19. "Gordon, Lack, Post And Shapiro (from left)" (Seliger, Mark)
PH14576 709 (June 1, 1995) p17. "Veruca Salt's Louise Post, Jim Shapiro And Gordon (from left)" (Peters, Karen A.)
SHARP, ALEXANDER—PHOTOGRAPHS—PORTRAITS
PH14577 659 (June 24, 1993) p48. "The Orioles: Sonny Til, Johnny Reed, Tommy Gaither, George Nelson And Alexander Sharp"
SHARP, MATT—PHOTOGRAPHS
PH14578 694 (November 3, 1994) p40. "Matt Sharp, Patrick Wilson, Brian Bell And Rivers Cuomo (from left)" (Elledge, Paul)
PH14579 704 (March 23, 1995) pp62-63. "Matt Sharp, Rivers Cuomo, Brian Bell, Pat Wilson (from left)" (Corbijn, Anton)
SHARPTON, AL—PHOTOGRAPHS
PH14580 667 (October 14, 1993) p40. "Al Sharpton Escorts Rick Rubin To The Funeral" (Granitz, Steve)
SHARROCK, SONNY—PHOTOGRAPHS—PORTRAITS
PH14581 686-687 (July 14, 1994) p26. "[Sonny Sharrock]"

SHIELDS, BROOKE—PHOTOGRAPHS

PH14629 744 (October 3, 1996) p46. "[Brooke Shields]" (Seliger, Mark)

PH14630 744 (October 3, 1996) p48. "Brooke Shields And Her Fiances, Andre Agassi: 'She Gave Great Fax'"

PH14631 744 (October 3, 1996) p50. "Island Girl: With Christopher Atkins In 'The Blue Lagoon'"

PH14632 744 (October 3, 1996) p52. "Must-See Worthy? The Cast Of Shields' New Sitcom, 'Suddenly Susan'"

PH14633 744 (October 3, 1996) p52. "The Plane Truth: Shields Spoofs Herself In 1989's 'Speed Zone!'"

PH14634 744 (October 3, 1996) p52. "Quel Drag: In Her 1984 Flop, 'Sahara'"

PH14635 744 (October 3, 1996) p48. "Shields With Her Mother And Former Omnipresence, Teri" (Barr, Nancy)

PH14636 744 (October 3, 1996) pp[cover]. "Suddenly Sinful: The Continuing Education Of Brooke Shields" (Seliger, Mark)

SHIELDS, BROOKE—PHOTOGRAPHS—PORTRAITS

PH14637 744 (October 3, 1996) p50. "'Healthy' Is Not A Word I'd Use To Describe My Childhood: With Susan Sarandon In 1978's 'Pretty Baby'"

PH14638 Number not assigned.

PH14639 744 (October 3, 1996) p50. "Teen Idyll: Steaming It Up With Martin Hewitt In 1981's 'Endless Love'"

SHIELDS, KEVIN—PHOTOGRAPHS—PORTRAITS

PH14640 623 (February 6, 1992) p20. "Clockwise From Top Left: Butcher, Shields, Googe, O'Ciosoig" (Double, Steve)

SHIELDS, TERI—PHOTOGRAPHS

PH14641 744 (October 3, 1996) p48. "Shields With Her Mother And Former Omnipresence, Teri" (Barr, Nancy)

SHILTS, RANDY—PHOTOGRAPHS

PH14642 657 (May 27, 1993) p31. "Reporter With A Point Of View: Randy Shilts" (Wilson, James D.)

PH14643 666 (September 30, 1993) p49. "On Election Night With Milk In '78" (Savage, Steve)

PH14644 666 (September 30, 1993) p46. "[Randy Shilts]" (Winters, Dan)

PH14645 666 (September 30, 1993) p49. "Shilts At His Desk In The 'San Francisco Chronicle' Newsroom, '78" (Klimak, Martin)

PH14646 666 (September 30, 1993) p48. "Shilts Outside His Home On The Russian River: 'Every Debate Weakens A Taboo'" (Winters, Dan)

PH14647 698-699 (December 29, 1994) p85. "Reporter Randy Shilts" (Winters, Dan)

SHIMOMURA, TSUTOMU—PHOTOGRAPHS

PH14648 707 (May 4, 1995) p42. "At The San Diego Supercomputer Center" (Decker, Alan)

PH14649 707 (May 4, 1995) p42. "Shimomura Stays Wired While Skiing" (Gropp, Gerry)

SHINAS, SOFIA—PHOTOGRAPHS

PH14650 638 (September 3, 1992) pp[enc.26]. "[Sofia Shinas, John Wesley Harding]" (Veyssey, Frederique)

SHINAS, SOFIA—PHOTOGRAPHS—PORTRAITS

PH14651 638 (September 3, 1992) pp[enc.21,23]. "[Sofia Shinas]" (Veyssey, Frederique)

THE SHINING (FILM)—PHOTOGRAPHS

PH14652 656 (May 13, 1993) p114. "Above, More King Characters Show Their Dark Side: Kathy Bates ('Misery'), Jack Nicholson ('The Shining'), Sissy Spacek ('Carrie')"

SHINING THROUGH (FILM)—ILLUSTRATIONS

PH14653 624 (February 20, 1992) p47. "Achtung Baby" (Kunz, Anita)

SHINING THROUGH (FILM)—PHOTOGRAPHS

PH14654 624 (February 20, 1992) p49. "Michael Douglas And Secretary Melanie Griffith At War"

SHINN, RYAN—PHOTOGRAPHS

PH14655 652 (March 18, 1993) pp[enc.37]. "Ryan Shinn" (Seliger, Mark)

SHIRELLES—PHOTOGRAPHS

PH14656 728 (February 22, 1996) p18. "Shirelles Shirley Alston, Lee, Doris Kenner (from left): Dedicating It To The Ones They Love" (Mazur, Kevin)

SHIVERS—ALBUMS

PH14657 728 (February 22, 1996) p62. "The Buried Life"

SHOCKED, MICHELLE—ALBUMS

PH14658 630 (May 14, 1992) p105. "Arkansas Traveler"

PH14659 749 (December 12, 1996) p84. "Kind Hearted Woman"

SHOCKED, MICHELLE—PHOTOGRAPHS

PH14660 638 (September 3, 1992) p11. "Rob Wasserman, Bob Weir, Michelle Shocked And Bruce Cockburn (from left)" (Kravitz, Jeff)

PH14661 653 (April 1, 1993) p24. "Backstage At The Troubadour In L.A." (Granitz, Steve)

SHOES—PHOTOGRAPHS

PH14662 638 (September 3, 1992) pp[enc.53-54]. "[Shoes]" (Robert, Francois)

PH14663 691 (September 22, 1994) pp[enc.36]. "[Shoes]" (Meehan, Arthur)

PH14664 706 (April 20, 1995) pp[enc.32]. "The Patent-Leather Look" (Meehan, Arthur)

PH14665 718 (October 5, 1995) pp[enc.45-46]. "[Shoes]" (Tavee, Tom)

SHONEN KNIFE—PHOTOGRAPHS

PH14666 654 (April 15, 1993) pp[enc.29]. "Michie Nakatani, Atsuko Yamano And Naoko Yamano (from left)" (Simons, Chip)

PH14667 654 (April 15, 1993) pp[enc.29-30 +]. "[Shonen Knife]" (Simons, Chip)

PH14668 668 (October 28, 1993) p36. "Shonen Knife (front) Hang With Gumball" (Boland, Laurence)

SHORE, PAULY—PHOTOGRAPHS

PH14669 633 (June 25, 1992) p48. "Shore (left) And Astin Flank Cave Man Fraser"

SHORE, PAULY—PHOTOGRAPHS—PORTRAITS

PH14670 634-635 (July 9, 1992) p55. "[Pauly Shore]" (Seliger, Mark)

SHORT CUTS (FILM)—ILLUSTRATIONS

PH14671 667 (October 14, 1993) p125. "A Robert Altman Smash" (Dana, Steven)

SHORT CUTS (FILM)—PHOTOGRAPHS

PH14672 648 (January 21, 1993) p9. "Lyle Lovett And Cake"

PH14673 667 (October 14, 1993) p126. "Above: A Cop (Tim Robbins) And A Clown (Anne Archer) Enjoy A Chance Encounter"

PH14674 667 (October 14, 1993) p109. "Director Robert Altman On The Set of 'Short Cuts'" (Rudolph, Joyce)

PH14675 667 (October 14, 1993) p109. "Modine And Moore As Ralph And Marian Wyman in 'Short Cuts'" (Rudolph, Joyce)

PH14676 672-673 (December 23, 1993) p174. "[Short Cuts]"

PH14677 678 (March 24, 1994) p100. "Missing In Oscar Action"

SHORT, MARTIN—PHOTOGRAPHS

PH14678 750-751 (December 26, 1996) p207. "'Mars': Short And Lisa Marie"

SHOWGIRLS (FILM)—PHOTOGRAPHS

PH14679 719 (October 19, 1995) p156. "Elizabeth Berkley Showing Off"

PH14680 724-725 (December 28, 1995) p134. "The 10 Worst Movies Of 1995 (degrees of sleaze)"

SHUDDER TO THINK—PHOTOGRAPHS

PH14681 686-687 (July 14, 1994) p73. "Cute-Band Alert: Shudder To Think's Werdren, Wade, Larson And Hill (from left)" (Clinch, Danny)

SHUDDER TO THINK—PHOTOGRAPHS—PORTRAITS

PH14682 719 (October 19, 1995) p26. "Truly Baroque—Like A Strange Union Of R.E.M. And Queen: Larson, Hill, Wedren And Wade (from left)" (Clinch, Danny)

SHUE, ELIZABETH—PHOTOGRAPHS

PH14683 720 (November 2, 1995) p76. "She (Elizabeth Shue) Is A Hooker"

PH14684 720 (November 2, 1995) p76. "Together: cage And Shue Are Lovers Battling The Odds"

PH14685 721 (November 16, 1995) p94. "And The Drunk (with Elizabeth Shue) In 'Leaving Las Vegas'" (Hanover, Suzanne)
SHUMAN, MORT—PHOTOGRAPHS—PORTRAITS
PH14686 619-620 (December 12, 1991) p95. "Mort Shuman"
SIB, JOE—PHOTOGRAPHS
PH14687 709 (June 1, 1995) p16. "Flava In Ya Ear: Wax's Loomis, Joe Sib, Dave Georgeff And Soda Drop In On Fogelnes In His 'Squirt TV' Bedroom Studio (from left)" (Brown, Christy)
SIBERIA—ILLUSTRATIONS
PH14688 747 (November 14, 1996) pp86,89-90,92+. "[Siberia]" (Banyai, Istvan)
SIBERRY, JANE—ALBUMS
PH14689 717 (September 21, 1995) p84. "Maria"
SIBERRY, JANE—PHOTOGRAPHS—PORTRAITS
PH14690 680 (April 21, 1994) p18. "[Jane Siberry]" (Irish, Len)
SICE—PHOTOGRAPHS
PH14691 719 (October 19, 1995) p33. "Sice Of The Boo Radleys" (Moore, Suzan)
SICKLERVILLE, NEW JERSEY—PHOTOGRAPHS
PH14692 692 (October 6, 1994) p70. "Overbrook Senior High Wasn't A Crumbling Inner-City School With Metal Detectors" (Lixenberg, Dana)
SIEGEL, DAN—PHOTOGRAPHS
PH14693 731 (April 4, 1996) p18. "Jennings (center) With Suckers, Dan Siegel, Dan Bolton, Ron Heathman And Singer Eddie Spaghetti (from left)" (Diamond, Rick)
SILBERMAN, STEVE—BOOKS
PH14694 693 (October 20, 1994) p43. "Skeleton Key"
THE SILENCE OF THE LAMBS (FILM)—PHOTOGRAPHS
PH14695 617 (November 14, 1991) p184. "Art Versus Commerce"
PH14696 619-620 (December 12, 1991) p192. "In 'The Silence Of The Lambs,' Jodie Foster Finds An Affinity With The Male Monster (Anthony Hopkins)"
PH14697 678 (March 24, 1994) p63. "Demme, Flanked By Hanks And Banderas, Denies That The Positive Gay Images In 'Philadelphia' Are A Reaction Against The Gay Killer in 'Lambs' (left)"
SILENT FALL (FILM)—PHOTOGRAPHS
PH14698 694 (November 3, 1994) p106. "Now Playing"
SILENT TONGUE (FILM)—ILLUSTRATIONS
PH14699 676 (February 24, 1994) p61. "River's End" (Woolley, Janet)
SILENT TONGUE (FILM)—PHOTOGRAPHS
PH14700 676 (February 24, 1994) p62. "A Grieving Phoenix Stands Guard in 'Silent Tongue'"
SILK—ALBUMS
PH14701 657 (May 27, 1993) p49. "Lose Control"
SILKWOOD, KAREN—PHOTOGRAPHS
PH14702 632 (June 11, 1992) p95. "Karen Silkwood: Her Death Rallied A Movement Of Doubting Thomases"
SILOS—ALBUMS
PH14703 694 (November 3, 1994) p101. "Susan Across The Ocean"
SILVER, SUSAN—PHOTOGRAPHS
PH14704 684 (June 16, 1994) p52. "Cameron, Thayil, Yamamoto, Cornell, Silver, Tour Manager Eric Johnson (from left) In 1988" (Peterson, Charles)
SILVERCHAIR—ILLUSTRATIONS
PH14705 719 (October 19, 1995) p172. "Silverchair: Tomorrow Never Knows" (Menchin, Scott)
PH14706 731 (April 4, 1996) p14. "Fame" (Pendergrast, James T.)
SILVERCHAIR—PHOTOGRAPHS
PH14707 705 (April 6, 1995) p23. "The Hardcore Roar Of Silverchair (Daniel Johns, left) And Spiderbait" (Mott, Tony)
PH14708 715 (August 24, 1995) p31. "Chris Joannou, Ben Gillies And Daniel Johns (from left): Could You Just Say We're 18?" (Clinch, Danny)
PH14709 723 (December 14, 1995) p31. "Silverchair" (Callahan, Kristin)
PH14710 728 (February 22, 1996) p46. "Gut Feeling: Johns, Joannou And Gillies, From Left, In A Sophisticated Pose (left)" (Seliger, Mark)
PH14711 728 (February 22, 1996) p47. "Johns, Joannou And Gillies (from left) Goof Around—As Usual" (Seliger, Mark)
SILVERCHAIR—PHOTOGRAPHS—PORTRAITS
PH14712 726 (January 25, 1996) p38. "Silverchair: Young, Hard-Rocking Aussies Chris Joannou, Daniel Johns And Ben Gillies (from left)" (Anderson, David)
PH14713 728 (February 22, 1996) p45. "Silverchair's Daniel Johns, Ben Gillies And Chris Joannou (from left) Turn On The Charm" (Seliger, Mark)
SILVERSTONE, ALICIA—ILLUSTRATIONS
PH14714 719 (October 19, 1995) p10. "Rolling Stone" (Pendergrast, James T.)
SILVERSTONE, ALICIA—PHOTOGRAPHS
PH14715 709 (June 1, 1995) p68. "back-To-School Bashes"
PH14716 714 (August 10, 1995) p62. "Dash And Silverstone Phone It In At High School"
PH14717 716 (September 7, 1995) p46. "[Alicia Silverstone]" (Sirota, Peggy)
PH14718 716 (September 7, 1995) pp[cover]. "Alicia Silverstone: Ballad Of A Teenage Queen" (Sirota, Peggy)
PH14719 716 (September 7, 1995) p13. "Clued In: America's 'As If' Girl Alicia Silverstone (center) With Luscious Jackson" (Cohen, Lester)
PH14720 716 (September 7, 1995) p47. "The Doll-Baby Star Of 'Clueless' Says, 'I Really Look Like Crap'" (Sirota, Peggy)
PH14721 716 (September 7, 1995) p50. "Lethal Lolita: Silverstone Does Her Thing In 'The Crush'" (McEwan, Rob)
PH14722 716 (September 7, 1995) p48. "Video Vixens Silverstone And Liv Tyler In Aerosmith's 'Crazy'" (Gougenheim, Kim)
PH14723 741 (August 22, 1996) p104. "Silverstone As Her Clueless Update"
SILVERSTONE, ALICIA—PHOTOGRAPHS—PORTRAITS
PH14724 716 (September 7, 1995) pp44-45. "[Alicia Silverstone]" (Sirota, Peggy)
PH14725 716 (September 7, 1995) p78. "Summer Wrap-Up]"
SIMENON, TIM—PHOTOGRAPHS—PORTRAITS
PH14726 741 (August 22, 1996) p78. "[Tim Simenon]" (Vadukul, Nitin)
SIMIEN, TERRANCE—ILLUSTRATIONS
PH14727 680 (April 21, 1994) p88. "Terrance Simien" (Synarski, Susan)
SIMINS, RUSSELL—PHOTOGRAPHS
PH14728 700 (January 26, 1995) p25. "Blues Demolition Squad: Judah Bauer, Spencer, Russell Simins (from left)" (Ockenfels, Frank, 3)
PH14729 745 (October 17, 1996) p31. "Primitive Cool: Russell Simins, Jon Spencer And Judah Bauer (from left)" (Ockenfels, Frank W.)
SIMMONS, DARYL—PHOTOGRAPHS
PH14730 696 (December 1, 1994) p105. "The Dream Team: Daryl Simmons, Babyface And L.A. Reid At The 1993 Grammys" (Deguire, Greg)
SIMMONS, GENE—PHOTOGRAPHS
PH14731 675 (February 10, 1994) p22. "Crover, Simmons, King Buzzo And Mark Deutrom" (Cohen, Lester)
PH14732 685 (June 30, 1994) p41. "Gimme A Head With Hair, Long Beautiful Hair: McDonald (left), Simmons"
PH14733 715 (August 24, 1995) p25. "Paul Stanley, Gene Simmons, Eric Singer, Bruce Kulick (from left)" (Blakesberg, Jay)
PH14734 724-725 (December 28, 1995) p51. "Kiss' Simmons, Eric Singer, Stanley And Bruce Kulick (from left)" (Blakesberg, Jay)

PH14735 727 (February 8, 1996) p18. "Gene Simmons, Peter Criss And Ace Frehley (from left) Rode 'Kiss Alive!' To Stardom In 1975 And Scored A Second Hit Concert Album With 'Kiss Alive II' In 1977" (Putland, Michael)
PH14736 732 (April 18, 1996) p19. "Ace Frehley, Paul Stanley, 2Pac, Peter Criss And Gene Simmons (from left)" (Mazur, Kevin)
PH14737 736 (June 13, 1996) p52. "Kiss Come Back With Their Makeup Intact: Ace Frehley, Gene Simmons, Peter Criss And Paul Stanley" (Malluk, Eddie)
PH14738 740 (August 8, 1996) p31. "Bloody Mess: Simmons In Detroit Rock City" (Settle, Ken)
PH14739 743 (September 19, 1996) p34. "Summer's Young And Old" (Kohos)

SIMMONS, RICHARD—PHOTOGRAPHS
PH14740 693 (October 20, 1994) p90. "[Nutrition]" (Klein, Renee)

SIMMS, NICK—PHOTOGRAPHS
PH14741 728 (February 22, 1996) p32. "Cornershop's Simms, Saffery, Tjinder Singh, Ayres And Hall (from left)" (Wonderland, Alison)

SIMON AND GARFUNKEL—PHOTOGRAPHS
PH14742 654 (April 15, 1993) p13. "Simon (right) And Garfunkel" (Granitz, Steve)
PH14743 672-673 (December 23, 1993) p70. "Garfunkel And His Soul Mate Simon" (Mazur, Kevin)

SIMON AND THE BAR SINISTER—PHOTOGRAPHS
PH14744 686-687 (July 14, 1994) p78. "[Simon And The Bar Sinister]" (Matson, Gary)

SIMON, CARLY—ALBUMS
PH14745 617 (November 14, 1991) p108. "Playing Possum" (Seeff, Norman)

SIMON, CARLY—PHOTOGRAPHS
PH14746 617 (November 14, 1991) p13. "Crash Test Dummies' Brad Roberts With Simon" (Roberts, Ebet)
PH14747 643 (November 12, 1992) p77. "Carly Simon Got Nasty For Norman Seeff" (Seeff, Norman)
PH14748 698-699 (December 29, 1994) p63. "Sessions" (Seeff, Norman)
PH14749 706 (April 20, 1995) p15. "Bonnie Raitt, Mistress Of Sensitivity Lennox, Carly Simon And Crow (from left)" (Busacca, Larry)

SIMON, NEIL—PHOTOGRAPHS
PH14750 657 (May 27, 1993) p58. "Lost: Coolidge And Ruehl Flank Simon"

SIMON, PAUL (CONGRESSMAN)—PHOTOGRAPHS
PH14751 660-661 (July 8, 1993) p52. "Babbitt On The Campaign Trail: Presidential Candidates Michael Dukakis, Babbitt, Paul Simon, Richard Gephardt, Jesse Jackson And Al Gore (from left) At A New York Forum..." (Peterson

SIMON, PAUL (CONGRESSMAN)—PHOTOGRAPHS—PORTRAITS
PH14752 722 (November 30, 1995) p47. "[Paul Simon]" (Atlan, J. L.)

SIMON, PAUL—ILLUSTRATIONS
PH14753 619-620 (December 12, 1991) p5. "[Paul Simon]" (Burke, Philip)

SIMON, PAUL—PHOTOGRAPHS
PH14754 619-620 (December 12, 1991) p67. "Block Party: Paul Simon In The Park" (Mazur, Kevin)
PH14755 634-635 (July 9, 1992) p11. "Paul Simon (left) And Billy Joel" (Busacca, Larry)
PH14756 640 (October 1, 1992) p9. "Paul Simon Onstage In Montauk" (Mazur, Kevin)
PH14757 645-646 (December 10, 1992) p54. "Billy Joel (left) And Paul Simon" (Busacca, Larry)
PH14758 659 (June 24, 1993) p13. "Edie Brickell And Paul Simon Join Nelson (left) For His Televised Birthday Celebration" (Kennedy, Bill)
PH14759 672-673 (December 23, 1993) p70. "Garfunkel And His Soul Mate Simon" (Mazur, Kevin)

SIMON, PAUL—PHOTOGRAPHS—PORTRAITS
PH14760 643 (November 12, 1992) p175. "Paul Simon" (Markus, Kurt)

SIMON, RAY—PHOTOGRAPHS
PH14761 702 (February 23, 1995) p55. "Ray Simon Beefed Up His Skills, But He Still Works On The Assembly Line, Like His Father And Grandfather Did Before Him" (Kuehn, Karen)

SIMON, SIMONE—PHOTOGRAPHS—PORTRAITS
PH14762 643 (November 12, 1992) p60. "Hurrell Gilded Screen Lilies Like Simone Simon" (Hurrell, George)

SIMONE, DOMINIQUE—PHOTOGRAPHS
PH14763 693 (October 20, 1994) p75. "And Actress Dominique Simone"

SIMONE, NINA—ALBUMS
PH14764 669 (November 11, 1993) p73. "A Single Woman"

SIMPLE MINDS—ALBUMS
PH14765 703 (March 9, 1995) p64. "Good News From The Next World"

SIMPLY RED—ALBUMS
PH14766 721 (November 16, 1995) p110. "Life"

SIMPSON, BART—ILLUSTRATIONS
PH14767 645-646 (December 10, 1992) p156. "Matt Groening's Bart Simpson, 1990"

SIMPSON, HOMER—ILLUSTRATIONS
PH14768 731 (April 4, 1996) p18. "[The Simpsons]" (Groening, Matt)
PH14769 734 (May 16, 1996) p29. "Keep Your Day Job: Sonic Youth Look On In Horror As Homer Simpson Gets Down"

SIMPSON, O. J.—ILLUSTRATIONS
PH14770 690 (September 8, 1994) p24. "Wired For More Juice" (Mayo, Martin)
PH14771 698-699 (December 29, 1994) p26. "The Illustrated History Of The Universe" (Pendergrast, James T.)
PH14772 701 (February 9, 1995) p14. "Juice-Justice" (Pendergrast, James T.)

SIMPSON, O. J.—PHOTOGRAPHS
PH14773 724-725 (December 28, 1995) p58. "The American Way: F. Lee Bailey, Simpson, Johnnie Cochran" (Chun, Myung J.)

SIMPSON, O. J.—PHOTOGRAPHS—PORTRAITS
PH14774 698-699 (December 29, 1994) p58. "[O. J. Simpson]"

THE SIMPSONS (TELEVISION SHOW)—ILLUSTRATIONS
PH14775 682 (May 19, 1994) p57. "[Apu]"

SIMS, DAVID—PHOTOGRAPHS
PH14776 653 (April 1, 1993) p20. "The Jesus Lizard (clockwise from top left): McNeilly, Yow, Denison And Sims" (Ewolf)
PH14777 714 (August 10, 1995) p48. "David Sims, Mac McNeilly, David Yow, Duane Denison, From Left" (Seliger, Mark)
PH14778 736 (June 13, 1996) p20. "Jockey Lavern Hostetler Has A Lot To Discuss With Jesus Lizard Members David Sims, David Yow, Mac McNeilly And Duane Denison (from left)" (Gilson, Matthew)

SIMS, RICK—PHOTOGRAPHS
PH14779 707 (May 4, 1995) p19. "Nelson, Rick Sims, Spaghetti (from left)" (Davis, Lisa)

SINATRA, FRANK—ALBUMS
PH14780 672-673 (December 23, 1993) p148. "The Columbia Years 1943-1952"
PH14781 672-673 (December 23, 1993) p151. "Duets"

SINATRA, FRANK—ILLUSTRATIONS
PH14782 682 (May 19, 1994) p97. "Their Way" (Day, Robert)

SINATRA, FRANK—PHOTOGRAPHS
PH14783 676 (February 24, 1994) p28. "[Bono & Frank Sinatra]" (Corbijn, Anton)
PH14784 680 (April 21, 1994) p33. "Bono, Still Getting Under Sinatra's Skin" (Mazur, Kevin)
PH14785 698-699 (December 29, 1994) p42. "Post-Grammy Bono And Frank Sinatra" (Mazur, Kevin)
PH14786 724-725 (December 28, 1995) p63. "[Frank Sinatra]"

SINATRA, FRANK—PHOTOGRAPHS—PORTRAITS
PH14787 678 (March 24, 1994) p14. "Juggy Gayles, The Moses

Of Promo..."
PH14788 698-699 (December 29, 1994) p75. "Chairman Of The Bored: Sinatra Coasts With "Duets II""
SINGER, BRYAN—PHOTOGRAPHS
PH14789 716 (September 7, 1995) p76. "Director Bryan Singer"
SINGER, ERIC—PHOTOGRAPHS
PH14790 715 (August 24, 1995) p25. "Paul Stanley, Gene Simmons, Eric Singer, Bruce Kulick (from left)" (Blakesberg, Jay)
PH14791 724-725 (December 28, 1995) p51. "Kiss' Simmons, Eric Singer, Stanley And Bruce Kulick (from left)" (Blakesberg, Jay)
SINGH, TJINDER—PHOTOGRAPHS
PH14792 728 (February 22, 1996) p32. "Cornershop's Simms, Saffery, Tjinder Singh, Ayres And Hall (from left)" (Wonderland, Alison)
PH14793 737 (June 27, 1996) p15. "Tjinder Singh With Cracker's Johnny Hickman And Bob Rupe (from left)" (Roberts, Ebet)
A SINGLE GIRL (FILM)—PHOTOGRAPHS
PH14794 749 (December 12, 1996) p90. "Now Playing"
SINGLE WHITE FEMALE (FILM)—ILLUSTRATIONS
PH14795 638 (September 3, 1992) p71. "Achy Breaky And Deadly" (Sadowski, Wiktor)
SINGLE WHITE FEMALE (FILM)—PHOTOGRAPHS
PH14796 638 (September 3, 1992) p72. "Bonding With Leigh (left) Is A Living Hell For Fonda"
PH14797 649 (February 4, 1993) p72. "[Single White Female]"
SINGLES (ALBUM)—ILLUSTRATIONS
PH14798 637 (August 20, 1992) p49. "New Sounds In Black And White" (Mahurin, Matt)
SINGLES (FILM)—PHOTOGRAPHS
PH14799 640 (October 1, 1992) p57. "[Singles]" (Watson, Albert)
SINGLETON, JOHN—PHOTOGRAPHS
PH14800 663 (August 19, 1993) p82. "Janet Jackson With Her Boyz: Director John Singleton (left) And Co-Star Tupac Shakur"
SINISE, GARY—PHOTOGRAPHS
PH14801 688 (August 11, 1994) p56. "[Forrest Gump]"
SINNERS—ALBUMS
PH14802 737 (June 27, 1996) p55. "Find A Door"
SIOUX, SIOUXSIE—PHOTOGRAPHS
PH14803 692 (October 6, 1994) p16. "[Siouxsie Sioux And John Cale]" (Berg, Bob)
PH14804 710 (June 15, 1995) p31. "Siouxsie Sioux, High Priestess Of Goth" (Garrity, Brian)
SIOUX, SIOUXSIE—PHOTOGRAPHS—PORTRAITS
PH14805 692 (October 6, 1994) p52. "Siouxsie Sioux" (Stevenson)
SIOUXSIE AND THE BANSHEES—ALBUMS
PH14806 705 (April 6, 1995) p80. "The Rapture"
SIR DOUGLAS QUINTET—ALBUMS
PH14807 690 (September 8, 1994) p80. "Day Dreaming At Midnight"
SIR MIX-A-LOT—ALBUMS
PH14808 628 (April 16, 1992) p86. "Mack Daddy"
PH14809 645-646 (December 10, 1992) p176. "Mack Daddy"
PH14810 666 (September 30, 1993) p59. "Mack Daddy"
PH14811 691 (September 22, 1994) p94. "Chief Boot Knocka"
SIR MIX-A-LOT—PHOTOGRAPHS
PH14812 645-646 (December 10, 1992) p32. "Sir Mix-A-Lot Got Back" (Moskowitz, Karen)
PH14813 665 (September 16, 1993) p22. "Sir Mix-A-Lot" (Blakesberg, Jay)
PH14814 667 (October 14, 1993) p82. "Butt Seriously, Folks: MTV Kicked Sir Mix-A-Lot's Ass Off The Air"
PH14815 701 (February 9, 1995) p17. "I, Spy: Sir Mix-A-Lot As "The Watcher""
SIR MIX-A-LOT—PHOTOGRAPHS—PORTRAITS
PH14816 693 (October 20, 1994) p44. "[Sir Mix-A-Lot]" (Garner, Kate)
SIRENS (FILM)—PHOTOGRAPHS
PH14817 679 (April 7, 1994) p82. "Flanked By Sirens, Fitzgerald Is Erotically Awakened"
SISTER ACT (FILM)—PHOTOGRAPHS
PH14818 633 (June 25, 1992) p48. "Goldberg (left) And Najimy Are Singing Nuns On The Run"
PH14819 639 (September 17, 1992) p102. "Best Supporting Actress"
PH14820 644 (November 26, 1992) p78. "[Sister Act]"
SISTER SOULJAH—ILLUSTRATIONS
PH14821 636 (August 6, 1992) p3. "Sister Souljah" (Burke, Philip)
SISTER SOULJAH—PHOTOGRAPHS
PH14822 636 (August 6, 1992) p15. "Sister Souljah Signs Autographs Outside The Apollo Theater, In Harlem" (Mazur, Kevin)
PH14823 636 (August 6, 1992) p17. "Souljah Was Well Known In The Black Community Before The Clinton Incident" (Mazur, Kevin)
PH14824 645-646 (December 10, 1992) p65. "Souljah Went Mouth To Mouth With Clinton" (Mazur, Kevin)
SISTERS OF MERCY—PHOTOGRAPHS
PH14825 619-620 (December 12, 1991) p84. "The Tune In Package Tour Didn't Turn Many Fans On" (Natkin, Paul)
SIX DEGREES OF SEPARATION (FILM)—PHOTOGRAPHS
PH14826 672-673 (December 23, 1993) p174. "[Six Degrees Of Separation]"
SIXTEEN HORSEPOWER—PHOTOGRAPHS
PH14827 731 (April 4, 1996) p36. "Roots-Gloom Trio: Sixteen Horsepower's Soll, Tola And Edwards (from left)" (Keeley, Dennis)
6TH AVENUE HEARTACHE (VIDEO)—PHOTOGRAPHS
PH14828 745 (October 17, 1996) p44. "Two Stills From The Wallflowers' Fincher-Directed Video, '6th Avenue Heartache'"
6THS—ALBUMS
PH14829 710 (June 15, 1995) p81. "Wasps' Nests"
60 FT DOLLS—PHOTOGRAPHS
PH14830 747 (November 14, 1996) p52. "[60 Ft Dolls]" (Broad, Julian)
SIXX, NIKKI—PHOTOGRAPHS—PORTRAITS
PH14831 627 (April 2, 1992) p13. "Motley Crue's Tommy Lee, Nikki Sixx, Mick Mars And The Defrocked Vince Neil (clockwise from top left)" (Double, Steve)
SIZEMORE, TOM—PHOTOGRAPHS
PH14832 664 (September 2, 1993) p69. "Charles Grodin, Robert Downey Jr., Kyra Sedgwick, Alfre Woodard And Tom Sizemore"
PH14833 690 (September 8, 1994) p84. "Crimescape: Juliette Lewis With Cop Tom Sizemore"
SKATALITES—PHOTOGRAPHS
PH14834 676 (February 24, 1994) p41. "'60s Ska Pioneers The Skatalites"
SKATE-MASTER TATE—PHOTOGRAPHS
PH14835 631 (May 28, 1992) p9. "Skate-Master Tate, MCA, Ad-Rock, Anthony Kiedis, Henry Rollins (from left)" (Cohen, Lester)
SKEE-LO—PHOTOGRAPHS
PH14836 716 (September 7, 1995) p30. "Tough Love: The Chocolate Swiping Homey Chris Pringle (left) And Skee-Lo" (Gougenheim, Kim)
SKELETON KEY—PHOTOGRAPHS
PH14837 747 (November 14, 1996) p56. "[Skeleton Key]" (Ragel, Jon)
SKELETONS—PHOTOGRAPHS
PH14838 629 (April 30, 1992) p28. "Dave Alvin (right) With Skeletons Lou Whitney (left) And Bobby Lloyd Hicks" (Carrico, John)
SKERRITT, TOM—PHOTOGRAPHS
PH14839 631 (May 28, 1992) p60. "Barrymore Flashes Tattoo And Toes To Lure Skerritt"

SKID ROW—ALBUMS
PH14840 706 (April 20, 1995) p78. "Subhuman Race"
SKIING—PHOTOGRAPHS
PH14841 617 (November 14, 1991) pp161,164. "[Kathy Jarvis]" (Noble, Chris)
PH14842 617 (November 14, 1991) pp159-163. "[Scott Jacobson]" (Noble, Chris)
PH14843 644 (November 26, 1992) pp60-61,63. "[Brooke Paulides]" (Noble, Chris)
PH14844 644 (November 26, 1992) pp62-63. "[Jan Nilsen]" (Noble, Chris)
PH14845 644 (November 26, 1992) p64. "[Jim Newman]" (Noble, Chris)
SKILLINGS, MUZZ—PHOTOGRAPHS—PORTRAITS
PH14846 660-661 (July 8, 1993) p90. "The 'Vivid' Incarnations Of Living Colour, With Muzz Skillings (far right)" (Lavine, Michael)
SKIN CARE PRODUCTS—PHOTOGRAPHS
PH14847 633 (June 25, 1992) p38. "[Skin Care]" (Robledo, Maria)
SKINHEADS—ALBUMS
PH14848 669 (November 11, 1993) p18. "...And Skinhead Albums (above, left)..."
SKINHEADS—PHOTOGRAPHS
PH14849 669 (November 11, 1993) p18. "...Their Fans (above)..."
PH14850 685 (June 30, 1994) p54. "[Skinheads]" (Winters, Dan)
SKINNER, JULIE—PHOTOGRAPHS
PH14851 742 (September 5, 1996) p20. "Kirk Hammett With Model Julie Skinner" (Jordan, Kelly)
SKOLNIK, HEIDI—PHOTOGRAPHS
PH14852 693 (October 20, 1994) p90. "[Nutrition]" (Klein, Renee)
SLADE, SEAN—PHOTOGRAPHS
PH14853 702 (February 23, 1995) p19. "Front: Hatfield, Donelly, Bragg. Rear: Dean Fraser, Gary Smith, Sean Slade" (Robicheau, Paul)
PH14854 708 (May 18, 1995) p28. "Producers O'Heir, Smith And Slade (from left)" (Pasley, Richard)
SLANT 6—ALBUMS
PH14855 712-713 (July 13, 1995) p132. "Inzombia"
SLASH—ALBUMS
PH14856 702 (February 23, 1995) p71. "It's Five O'Clock Somewhere"
SLASH—ILLUSTRATIONS
PH14857 702 (February 23, 1995) p71. "Slash & Burn" (Piven, Hanoch)
PH14858 706 (April 20, 1995) p9. "Slash" (Burke, Philip)
SLASH—PHOTOGRAPHS
PH14859 618 (November 28, 1991) p11. "Kirk Kammett, Slash, Lars Ulrich, Geoff Tate And Armored Saint Drummer Gonzo (from left)" (Blakesberg, Jay)
PH14860 619-620 (December 12, 1991) p55. "The Dynamic Duo? Axl And Slash (above)" (Mazur, Kevin)
PH14861 619-620 (December 12, 1991) p55. "Slash" (Mazur, Kevin)
PH14862 622 (January 23, 1992) p6. "From Left: Hoon, Slash And Duff" (White, Frank)
PH14863 625 (March 5, 1992) p19. "Axl Rose (left) And Slash" (Mazur, Kevin)
PH14864 625 (March 5, 1992) p55. "'Comeback' From The 'Worst' Band" (Kirkland, Gene)
PH14865 633 (June 25, 1992) p12. "Slash: Carole King And I" (Whitall, Bob)
PH14866 638 (September 3, 1992) p18. "Slash" (Kirkland, Gene)
PH14867 645-646 (December 10, 1992) p77. "Slash During The Soon-To-Be-Aborted Set" (Mazur, Kevin)
PH14868 650 (February 18, 1993) p11. "Slash (left) And May Play Dueling Guitars" (Mazur, Kevin)
PH14869 655 (April 29, 1993) p25. "The Plugged Slash" (Hutson, Mick)
PH14870 663 (August 19, 1993) p27. "Izzy (left) Cuddles Up To Buddy Slash" (Kirkland, Greg)
PH14871 670 (November 25, 1993) p76. "[Slash]" (Seliger, Mark)
PH14872 671 (December 9, 1993) p32. "[Slash & Lenny Kravitz]" (Mayer, Jeffrey)
PH14873 672-673 (December 23, 1993) p74. "Slash And Axl: Punks For A Day" (Mazur, Kevin)
PH14874 676 (February 24, 1994) p29. "Slash And Buddy Guy" (Lines, Edward G., Jr.)
PH14875 696 (December 1, 1994) p23. "Snakepit Slash And His Newest Toy" (John, Robert)
PH14875a 706 (April 20, 1995) p53, 55. "[Slash]" (Mahurin, Matt)
PH14876 746 (October 31, 1996) p17. "Bland (left) Duets With A Disturbingly Fit Slash" (De Leon, John)
PH14877 749 (December 12, 1996) p24. "[Slash]" (Seliger, Mark)
SLASH—PHOTOGRAPHS—PORTRAITS
PH14878 619-620 (December 12, 1991) pp[cover]. "1991 Yearbook" (Seliger, Mark)
PH14879 643 (November 12, 1992) p105. "Slash" (Rolston, Matthew)
PH14880 706 (April 20, 1995) pp53,55. "[Slash]" (Mahurin, Matt)
PH14881 711 (June 29, 1995) p13. "[Trouble With Tribbles]" (Mazur, Kevin)
SLATER, CHRISTIAN—PHOTOGRAPHS
PH14882 666 (September 30, 1993) p112. "Slater (right) Comforts A Bloody Arquette"
PH14883 680 (April 21, 1994) p95. "Christian Slater And Joe Pesci Go Hollywood"
PH14884 701 (February 9, 1995) p63. "Slater And Bacon Fight Injustice"
PH14885 729 (March 7, 1996) p54. "Slater And Travolta Confer With Director Woo"
SLAUGHTER—ALBUMS
PH14886 633 (June 25, 1992) p44. "The Wild Life"
SLAYER—ALBUMS
PH14887 701 (February 9, 1995) p58. "Divine Intervention"
PH14888 735 (May 30, 1996) p49. "Undisputed Attitude"
SLAYER—PHOTOGRAPHS
PH14889 705 (April 6, 1995) p36. "Live Evil: Araya (left) And King" (Mazur, Kevin)
PH14890 719 (October 19, 1995) p64. "Rubin, In White T-Shirt And Beard, With Members Of The Beasties, Slayer And Run-D.M.C. In 1985"
SLEATER-KINNEY—ALBUMS
PH14891 736 (June 13, 1996) p82. "Call The Doctor"
SLEATER-KINNEY—PHOTOGRAPHS
PH14892 747 (November 14, 1996) p49. "[Sleater-Kinney]" (Maxwell, Paul)
SLEDGE, ROBERT—PHOTOGRAPHS
PH14893 721 (November 16, 1995) p73. "Power Trio With A Twist: Darren Jessee, Ben Folds And Robert Sledge (from left) Make Absurdity Swing Like Mad" (Guip, Amy)
PH14894 749 (December 12, 1996) p20. "BFF's Robert Sledge, Darren Jessee; Klezmatics Frank London, Alicia Svigals; And Folds" (Mazur, Kevin)
SLEDGEHAMMER (VIDEO)—PHOTOGRAPHS
PH14895 667 (October 14, 1993) p66. "Gabriel: 'Sledgehammer' Pounded The Competition With Its Outrageous And Zany Animation"
PH14896 667 (October 14, 1993) p67. "Personal Trainer: Johnson Outfits Gabriel"
SLEEPER—PHOTOGRAPHS
PH14896a 709 (June 1, 1995) p27. "PC Free: Stewart, Wener, McClure, Osman (from left)" (Westenberg, Kevin)

SLEEPER (FILM)—PHOTOGRAPHS
PH14897 665 (September 16, 1993) p49. "Filming 'Sleeper' (1973) With Diane Keaton"
PH14898 Number not assigned.
SLEEPERS (FILM)—ILLUSTRATIONS
PH14899 746 (October 31, 1996) p75. "Getting Away With Murder: Prosecutor Brad Pitt Lies To Save His Boyhood Pals From Being Sent Away As Killers In A Film That Weaves A Tangled Web Of Fact And Fiction" (Brodner, St
SLEEPERS (FILM)—PHOTOGRAPHS
PH14900 743 (September 19, 1996) p88. "The Young And The Restless"
PH14901 746 (October 31, 1996) p76. "De Niro's Priest Lies On The Stand"
PH14902 746 (October 31, 1996) p76. "Pitt And Patric Bend The Truth"
SLEEPLESS IN SEATTLE (FILM)—ILLUSTRATIONS
PH14903 660-661 (July 8, 1993) p119. "Date-Night Film Frenzy" (Blitt, Barry)
SLEEPLESS IN SEATTLE (FILM)—PHOTOGRAPHS
PH14904 660-661 (July 8, 1993) p75. "Ephron On The 'Sleepless In Seattle' Set With Tom Hanks: 'You Hope To Get The Guys To Cry, Too.'" (McBroom, Bruce)
PH14905 660-661 (July 8, 1993) p120. "'Someday My Prince Will Come' Is A Theme For Ryan (with Hanks, above)"
SLEEPYHEAD—ALBUMS
PH14906 688 (August 11, 1994) p80. "Starduster"
SLICK, GRACE—PHOTOGRAPHS—PORTRAITS
PH14907 643 (November 12, 1992) p73. "The San Francisco Queen Bees Of Rock, Slick And Joplin, Sat For Marshall" (Marshall, Jim)
PH14908 692 (October 6, 1994) p50. "Grace Slick"
SLICK RICK—ALBUMS
PH14909 703 (March 9, 1995) p67. "Behind Bars"
SLING BLADE (FILM)—PHOTOGRAPHS
PH14910 749 (December 12, 1996) p90. "Now Playing"
SLIVER (FILM)—PHOTOGRAPHS
PH14911 659 (June 24, 1993) p88. "Lust: 'Sliver,' With William Baldwin And Sharon Stone"
PH14912 660-661 (July 8, 1993) p120. "Snow White And Stone (with Baldwin)"
PH14913 665 (September 16, 1993) p77. "Worst Actress"
SLOAN—ALBUMS
PH14914 654 (April 15, 1993) p64. "Smeared"
SLOAN, ROSS—PHOTOGRAPHS
PH14915 651 (March 4, 1993) p24. "Sloan, Edwards, Fletcher, Stephens" (Roca, John)
SLOVAK, HILLEL—PHOTOGRAPHS
PH14916 679 (April 7, 1994) p49. "We Three: Hillel Slovak, Kiedis And Flea In '82 (from left)" (Shear, Jack)
PH14917 719 (October 19, 1995) p56. "'86: Irons, Slovak, Flea, Kiedis (from left) Backstage At The Ritz, In New York" (Gershoff, Gary)
SLOVENIA—ILLUSTRATIONS
PH14918 728 (February 22, 1996) p16. "The Heart..." (Pendergrast, James T.)
SLY AND THE FAMILY STONE—ALBUMS
PH14919 617 (November 14, 1991) p144. "There's A Riot Goin' On" (Berg, John)
SLY AND THE FAMILY STONE—PHOTOGRAPHS
PH14920 649 (February 4, 1993) p51. "Rose Stone, Sly, Freddie Stone, Graham, Robinson, Errico And Martini Of Sly And The Family Stone"
PH14921 651 (March 4, 1993) p16. "Sly (center) And The Family Stone" (Granitz, Steve)
SMALL FACES—ALBUMS
PH14922 617 (November 14, 1991) p108. "Ogdens' Nut Gone Flakes" (Small Faces)
PH14923 617 (November 14, 1991) p108. "Ogdens' Nut Gone Flakes" (Brown, P.)
SMARTT, NIGEL—PHOTOGRAPHS
PH14924 708 (May 18, 1995) p82. "On Muscle Beach, In Venice, Calif." (Seliger, Mark)
SMASHING PUMPKINS—ALBUMS
PH14925 665 (September 16, 1993) p65. "Siamese Dream"
PH14926 666 (September 30, 1993) p128. "Siamese Dream"
PH14927 667 (October 14, 1993) p136. "Siamese Dream"
PH14928 672-673 (December 23, 1993) p159. "Siamese Dream"
PH14929 696 (December 1, 1994) p124. "Pisces Iscariot"
PH14930 722 (November 30, 1995) p64. "Mellon Collie And The Infinite Sadness"
PH14931 723 (December 14, 1995) p104. "Mellon Collie And The Infinite Sadness"
PH14932 726 (January 25, 1996) p43. "Mellon Collie And The Infinite Sadness"
PH14933 727 (February 8, 1996) p60. "Mellon Collie And The Infinite Sadness"
PH14934 728 (February 22, 1996) p76. "Mellon Collie And The Infinite Sadness"
PH14935 731 (April 4, 1996) p76. "Mellon Collie And The Infinite Sadness"
PH14936 749 (December 12, 1996) p81. "The Aeroplane Flies High"
SMASHING PUMPKINS—ILLUSTRATIONS
PH14937 684 (June 16, 1994) p11. "Alternative" (Pendergrast, James T.)
PH14938 722 (November 30, 1995) p64. "Up Against The Wall" (Angel, Vinnie)
PH14939 724-725 (December 28, 1995) p116. "Corgan Finds Succor In A Good Tune, A Monster Riff And The Kind Of Languid, Rapturous Guitarscape That Gives Self-Pity A Good Name" (Rosen, Jonathon)
PH14940 724-725 (December 28, 1995) p20. "Pumpkin Patch" (Pendergrast, James T.)
PH14941 746 (October 31, 1996) p14. "Truth" (Pendergrast, James T.)
PH14942 749 (December 12, 1996) p81. "Swinging Singles: The Smashing Pumpkins Put Their B Sides In A Snazzy Box" (Miller, David)
SMASHING PUMPKINS—PHOTOGRAPHS
PH14943 655 (April 29, 1993) p12. "Pumpkins D'Arcy (left) And Corgan" (Diamond, Rick)
PH14944 660-661 (July 8, 1993) p100. "Smashing Pumpkins (from left): Billy Corgan, D'Arcy, Jimmy Chamberlin And James Iha" (Johnson, Lisa)
PH14945 680 (April 21, 1994) pp42-43. "All Pumped Up: Jimmy Chamberlin, James Iha, Billy Corgan And D'Arcy (from left)" (Luchford, Glen)
PH14946 680 (April 21, 1994) p43. "[Smashing Pumpkins]" (Luchford, Glen)
PH14947 680 (April 21, 1994) pp[cover]. "Smashing Pumpkins: Double-Platinum Soap Opera" (Luchford, Glen)
PH14948 684 (June 16, 1994) p35. "The Pumpkins" (Blakesberg, Jay)
PH14949 695 (November 17, 1994) p47. "Smashing Pumpkins" (Ockenfels, Frank, 3)
PH14950 698-699 (December 29, 1994) p50. "Smashing Pumpkins At The Fillmore" (Blakesberg, Jay)
PH14951 705 (April 6, 1995) p16. "Billy Corgan, Drummer Jimmy Chamberlin And James Iha (from left)" (Natkin, Paul)
PH14952 711 (June 29, 1995) p19. "Billy Corgan, D'Arcy, Jimmy Chamberlin, James Iha (from left)" (Elledge, Paul)
PH14953 721 (November 16, 1995) pp50-51. "Billy Corgan Levitates D'Arcy" (Seliger, Mark)
PH14954 721 (November 16, 1995) p52. "Cutting Up: James Iha (left) And Jimmy Chamberlin" (Seliger, Mark)
PH14955 721 (November 16, 1995) pp[cover]. "Disillusionment! Obsession! Confusion! Satisfaction!: Smashing Pumpkins" (Seliger, Mark)

PH14956 721 (November 16, 1995) p56. "Ready To Rock You: D'Arcy, Iha, Corgan, Chamberlin (from left) In 1992" (Lenquette)
PH14957 723 (December 14, 1995) p27. "The Chicago Eight: D'Arcy, Petersson, Carlos, Corgan, Nielsen, Iha, Chamberlin And Zander (from left)" (Elledge, Paul)
PH14958 724-725 (December 28, 1995) p40. "Corgan, Jimmy Chamberlin, James Iha (from left)" (Natkin, Paul)
PH14959 726 (January 25, 1996) p43. "Smashing Pumpkins' Billy Corgan, D'Arcy, James Iha, Jimmy Chamberlin (from left)" (Seliger, Mark)
PH14960 743 (September 19, 1996) p28. "D'Arcy, Corgan And Iha (above, from left) At The Tibet Festival On June 15" (Blakesberg, Jay)
PH14961 747 (November 14, 1996) p42. "Cracking The Whip On Moshers: Smashing Pumpkins Early This Year" (Mazur, Kevin)

SMASHING PUMPKINS—PHOTOGRAPHS—PORTRAITS
PH14962 619-620 (December 12, 1991) p48. "Smashing Pumpkins" (Natkin, Paul)
PH14963 667 (October 14, 1993) p19. "D'Arcy, Jimmy Chamberlim, Billy Corgan, James Iha (clockwise from top left)" (Hom, Marc)
PH14964 672-673 (December 23, 1993) p53. "Chicago's Smashing Pumpkins" (Johnson, Lisa)
PH14965 680 (April 21, 1994) p46. "Just Off The Vine: Smashing Pumpkins In may 1991" (Natkin, Paul)

SMEAL, ELEANOR—PHOTOGRAPHS
PH14966 667 (October 14, 1993) p62. "Left: Windle And Randall Terry Face Off In March, As Eleanor Smeal Looks On" (McGlothlin, Doug)

SMEAR, PAT—PHOTOGRAPHS
PH14967 674 (January 27, 1994) p36. "Team Spirit: Novoselic, Smear, Grohl, Cobain And Touring Cellist Lori Goldston (from left)" (Seliger, Mark)
PH14968 726 (January 25, 1996) p37. "Foo Fighters Are, From Left, Nate Mendel, Pat Smear, Dave Grohl And William Goldsmith" (Seliger, Mark)
PH14969 730 (March 21, 1996) p32. "Horsing Around: David Grohl (top and bottom) And Fellow Foo Fighters William Goldsmith, Pat Smear And Nate Mendel (middle, from left)" (Gougenheim, Kim)
PH14970 732 (April 18, 1996) p20. "Pat Smear ('This is my first suit') And Dave Grohl" (Mazur, Kevin)
PH14971 736 (June 13, 1996) p20. "[Foo Fighters]" (Mazur, Kevin)
PH14972 740 (August 8, 1996) p17. "Smear With, Yes, Joan Jett" (Liu, Brian)
PH14973 745 (October 17, 1996) p27. "Pumpkin James Iha (left) With Foo Fighter Smear" (Mazur, Kevin)

SMEAR, PAT—PHOTOGRAPHS—PORTRAITS
PH14974 718 (October 5, 1995) p43. "Nirvana In 1993 During The 'In Utero' Tour: Pat Smear, Kurt Cobain, Dave Grohl, Krist Novoselic (clockwise from right)" (Lenquette, Youri)

SMELLS LIKE NIRVANA (VIDEO)—PHOTOGRAPHS
PH14975 667 (October 14, 1993) p94. "Smells Like Weird Al: Spoofing Nirvana"

SMELLS LIKE TEEN SPIRIT (VIDEO)—PHOTOGRAPHS
PH14976 667 (October 14, 1993) p67. "'Spirit' In The Sky: Nirvana's First Single Hits No. 2"

SMIF N WESSUN—PHOTOGRAPHS—PORTRAITS
PH14977 686-687 (July 14, 1994) p73. "Straight Outta Brooklyn: Tek And Steele" (Borris, Dan)

SMITH, ANDY—PHOTOGRAPHS
PH14978 686-687 (July 14, 1994) p38. "Brickell, Assistant Engineer Andy Smith And Halee (from left)" (Mazur, Kevin)

SMITH, ANNA NICOLE—PHOTOGRAPHS
PH14979 680 (April 21, 1994) p93. "Smith Gives Cop Nielsen Double Trouble"

SMITH, BRAD—PHOTOGRAPHS
PH14980 639 (September 17, 1992) p20. "Shannon Hoon, Christopher Thorn, Glen Graham, Brad Smith And Rogers Stevens (clockwise from top left)" (Clinch, Danny)
PH14981 640 (October 1, 1992) p27. "Blind Melon (from left): Smith, Stevens, Thorn, Hoon And Graham" (Clinch, Danny)
PH14982 669 (November 11, 1993) pp38-39. "Brad Smith, Glen Graham, Shannon Hood, Rogers Stevens & Christopher Thorn (from left)" (Seliger, Mark)

SMITH, BROOKE—PHOTOGRAPHS
PH14983 694 (November 3, 1994) p106. "Shawn Works Magic On Moore And Smith"

SMITH, CHAD—PHOTOGRAPHS
PH14984 629 (April 30, 1992) p23. "John Frusciante, Anthony Kiedis, Chad Smith And Flea (from left)" (Cuffaro, Chris)
PH14985 660-661 (July 8, 1993) p17. "Man Overboard: Smith, Kiedis, Marshall And Flea" (Leialoha, Mark)
PH14986 692 (October 6, 1994) p17. "Peppers Roast: Flea, Anthony Kiedis, Dave Navarro, Chad Smith (from left)" (Mazur, Kevin)
PH14987 709 (June 1, 1995) p21. "RHCPs (from left): Flea, Chad Smith, Dave Navarro And Anthony Kiedis" (Streiber, Art)
PH14988 719 (October 19, 1995) p55. "Guitarist Navarro (left) Bonds With Drummer Smith" (Corbijn, Anton)
PH14989 719 (October 19, 1995) p58. "Red Hot Chili Peppers, '95: Dave Navarro, Anthony Kiedis, Flea An Chad Smith (from left)" (Corbijn, Anton)
PH14990 724-725 (December 28, 1995) p63. "Chad Smith Took One For The Team" (Beauchemin, Paul)
PH14991 731 (April 4, 1996) p17. "Bush Covers? Chili Peppers Frontman Anthony Kiedis, Bassist Flea, The Not-Unattractive Navarro And Drummer Chad Smith (from left)" (Baehler, Chapman)

SMITH, CHRISTINA—PHOTOGRAPHS—PORTRAITS
PH14992 652 (March 18, 1993) pp[enc.37]. "Christina Smith" (Seliger, Mark)

SMITH, DEBBIE—PHOTOGRAPHS
PH14993 720 (November 2, 1995) p22. "On: Echobelly's Harris, Smith, Johansson, Madan And Henderson (from left)" (Claiborne, Barron)

SMITH, DON—PHOTOGRAPHS
PH14994 689 (August 25, 1994) p75. "Editors Don And Erin Smith Of "Teenage Gang Debs"" (Hill, Britain)

SMITH, ELLIOTT—PHOTOGRAPHS
PH14995 742 (September 5, 1996) p21. "Are We Having Fun Yet?" (Kessler, Joshua)

SMITH, ERIN—PHOTOGRAPHS
PH14996 689 (August 25, 1994) p75. "Editors Don And Erin Smith Of "Teenage Gang Debs"" (Hill, Britain)

SMITH, FRED—PHOTOGRAPHS
PH14997 632 (June 11, 1992) p36. "MC5 (clockwise from top left): Thompson, Tyner, Kramer, Smith"
PH14998 647 (January 7, 1993) p22. "Tom Verlaine, Richard Lloyd, Billy Ficca And Fred Smith (from left)" (Buck, Chris)
PH14999 708 (May 18, 1995) p30. "MC5: Michael Davis, Dennis Thompson, Kramer, Smith, Tyner (from left)"
PH15000 738-739 (July 11, 1996) p48. "Fred And Patti Smith In 1990" (Corkery, Richard)

SMITH, FRED—PHOTOGRAPHS—PORTRAITS
PH15001 698-699 (December 29, 1994) p80. "Fred "Sonic" Smith In 1992 (above)" (Schwab, Bill)

SMITH, G. E.—PHOTOGRAPHS
PH15002 640 (October 1, 1992) p9. "McCartney (above)..." (Meyers, Tim)
PH15003 668 (October 28, 1993) p30. "G. E. Smith (left) And Bruce Henderson" (Mazur, Kevin)

SMITH, GARY—PHOTOGRAPHS
PH15004 702 (February 23, 1995) p19. "Front: Hatfield, Donelly, Bragg. Rear: Dean Fraser, Gary Smith, Sean Slade" (Robicheau, Paul)

PH15005 708 (May 18, 1995) p28. "Producers O'Heir, Smith And Slade (from left)" (Pasley, Richard)
SMITH, GREG—PHOTOGRAPHS
PH15006 616 (October 31, 1991) p11. "Greg Smith, Pete Freezin', Alice Cooper And Stef Burns (from left)" (Mazur, Kevin)
SMITH, JEAN—PHOTOGRAPHS—PORTRAITS
PH15007 660-661 (July 8, 1993) p95. "Mecca Normal: David Lester, Jean Smith" (Karpa, Robert)
SMITH, KEN—PHOTOGRAPHS
PH15008 659 (June 24, 1993) p65. "Ken Smith, A Medic In Vietam, Found Ways To Deal With His Own Post-Traumatic Stress, Then Founded A Shelter After Seeing Vets Living Behind The Vietnam Memorial..." (Agulera-Helwig,
SMITH, KENDRA—ALBUMS
PH15009 716 (September 7, 1995) p73. "Five Ways Of Disappearing"
SMITH, KEVIN—PHOTOGRAPHS
PH15010 720 (November 2, 1995) p74. "Mallrats Smith And Mewes"
SMITH, MARK E.—PHOTOGRAPHS
PH15011 665 (September 16, 1993) p20. "Smith: 'The Difference Between Us And You Is That We Have Brains'" (Irish, Len)
SMITH, MICHAEL—PHOTOGRAPHS
PH15012 750-751 (December 26, 1996) p46. "Harding And Michael Smith, Her Future Ex-Hubby" (McKiernan, Scott)
SMITH, PATTI—ALBUMS
PH15013 617 (November 14, 1991) p113. "Horses" (Heimall, Bob)
PH15014 617 (November 14, 1991) p113. "Horses" (Mapplethorpe, Robert)
PH15015 634-635 (July 9, 1992) p4. "Horses"
PH15016 637 (August 20, 1992) p4. "Horses"
PH15017 737 (June 27, 1996) p53. "Gone Again"
SMITH, PATTI—BOOKS
PH15018 682 (May 19, 1994) p29. "Early Work"
SMITH, PATTI—ILLUSTRATIONS
PH15019 641 (October 15, 1992) p64. "[Patti Smith]" (Brodner, Steve)
PH15020 726 (January 25, 1996) p7. "Patti Smith" (Burke, Philip)
SMITH, PATTI—ILLUSTRATIONS—PORTRAITS
PH15021 737 (June 27, 1996) p53. "About A Grrrl" (Woolley, Janet)
SMITH, PATTI—PHOTOGRAPHS
PH15022 619-620 (December 12, 1991) p42. "Patti Smith Preaches Her Gospel" (Schwab, Bill)
PH15023 643 (November 12, 1992) p77. "The Sexy Seventies: Patti Smith Undressed For Robert Mapplethorpe" (Mapplethorpe, Robert)
PH15024 663 (August 19, 1993) p25. "The Recluse Returns: Patti Smith" (Mazur, Kevin)
PH15025 672-673 (December 23, 1993) p53. "Patti Smith Treats The New York Crowd" (Mazur, Kevin)
PH15026 692 (October 6, 1994) p52. "Patti Smith"
PH15027 705 (April 6, 1995) p16. "Punk Poetess Patti Smith" (Kowalsky, Jeff)
PH15028 717 (September 21, 1995) p19. "Chanting Barefoot: Patti Smith In Central Park" (Atlas, David)
PH15029 723 (December 14, 1995) p28. "[Salt-N-Pepa & Patti Smith]" (Mazur, Kevin)
PH15030 724-725 (December 28, 1995) p45. "[Patti Smith]" (Kowalsky, Jeffrey Alan)
PH15031 726 (January 25, 1996) p74. "Divine Intervention: Dylan And Smith Duet On 'Dark Eyes' At The Beacon" (Beccaris, Rob)
PH15032 726 (January 25, 1996) p18. "[Michael Stipe And Patti Smith]"
PH15033 726 (January 25, 1996) p46. "Patti Smith, Happy To Be Back" (Goldsmith, Lynn)
PH15034 728 (February 22, 1996) p18. "Smith And Her Guitarist Lenny Kaye" (Mazur, Kevin)
PH15035 735 (May 30, 1996) p27. "Artistic Pals Michael Stipe And Patti Smith" (Mazur, Kevin)
PH15036 738-739 (July 11, 1996) p48. "And Patti Singing With Her Hero Bob Dylan In New York During Their 1995 Tour" (Mazur, Kevin)
PH15037 738-739 (July 11, 1996) p55. "Calling Radio Ethiopia: Smith With Lenny Kaye In 1976" (Goldsmith, Lynn)
PH15038 738-739 (July 11, 1996) p48. "Fred And Patti Smith In 1990" (Corkery, Richard)
PH15039 738-739 (July 11, 1996) p42. "[Patti Smith]" (Winters, Dan)
PH15040 738-739 (July 11, 1996) p46. "[Patti Smith]" (Seeff, Norman)
PH15041 738-739 (July 11, 1996) p44. "Smith As A Dead Ringer For Keith Richards In Her New York Loft In The Early 1970s" (Linn, Judy)
PH15042 738-739 (July 11, 1996) p44. "Smith's Great '70s Band"
PH15043 738-739 (July 11, 1996) p44. "Star Time: Patti Smith In Full Cry At A Concert In New York's Central Park, 1976" (Gruen, Bob)
PH15044 749 (December 12, 1996) p19. "Smith, Helped Out By Young, At The Bridge Benefit" (Blakesberg, Jay)
SMITH, PATTI—PHOTOGRAPHS—PORTRAITS
PH15045 736 (June 13, 1996) p53. "Smith (above left) Returns" (Matheu, Robert)
PH15046 742 (September 5, 1996) p23. "[Patti Smith]" (Every, Bart)
SMITH, ROBERT—ILLUSTRATIONS
PH15047 667 (October 14, 1993) p113. "Secrets Of Seduction" (Ryden, Mark)
SMITH, ROBERT—PHOTOGRAPHS
PH15048 631 (May 28, 1992) p11. "Simon Gallup, Porl Thompson, Perry Bamonte, Robert Smith, Boris Williams (from left)" (Cox, Paul)
PH15049 633 (June 25, 1992) p12. "The Cure's Simon Gallup, Perry Bamonte And Smith (from left)" (Elgar, Nick)
PH15050 636 (August 6, 1992) p27. "Musical Mope: Robert Smith" (Turner, Chip)
PH15051 733 (May 2, 1996) p22. "Partial To Shades: The Cure's New Lineup Is Simon Gallup, Roger O'Donnell, Robert Smith, Perry Bamonte And Jason Cooper (from left)" (Cox, Paul)
PH15052 737 (June 27, 1996) p16. "Smith Says He Would Rather Be Asked, 'Why Are You So Scarily Good?'" (Mazur, Kevin)
PH15053 743 (September 19, 1996) p20. "[Gavin Rossdale & Robert Smith]" (Davies, Meredith)
SMITH, ROBERT—PHOTOGRAPHS—PORTRAITS
PH15054 645-646 (December 10, 1992) p47. "The Cure's Gloom King, Robert Smith" (Weiner, Scott)
SMITH, SHAWN—PHOTOGRAPHS
PH15055 649 (February 4, 1993) p23. "Jeremy Toback, Shawn Smith, Regan Hagar And Stone Gossard (from left)"
SMITH, STEPHEN—PHOTOGRAPHS
PH15056 666 (September 30, 1993) p90. "Hunt (third from left, bottom row) With Delta Lambda Phi Brothers (clockwise from top right): Peter Colohan, Sean McClafferty, Rob Corwin, Price, Stephen Smith And Oligmueller"
SMITH, STEVEN W.—PHOTOGRAPHS
PH15057 714 (August 10, 1995) p37. "Lawyer Steven W. Smith Takes A Stand Against Affirmative Action" (Turner, Danny)
SMITH, THOMAS EUGENE—PHOTOGRAPHS
PH15058 696 (December 1, 1994) p44. "Layne, Mr. Brown, Smith, Mrs. Brown" (Capak, R. J.)
SMITH, WILL—ILLUSTRATIONS
PH15059 707 (May 4, 1995) p73. "Bad Boys On The Prowl" (Kelley, Gary)

SMITH, WILL—PHOTOGRAPHS
PH15060 707 (May 4, 1995) p74. "Lawrence And Smith In 'Bad Boys'"
SMITH, ZACHARY—PHOTOGRAPHS
PH15061 660-661 (July 8, 1993) p97. "The Loud Family: Paul Wieneke, Zachary Smith, Miller, Jozef Becker And Rob Poor" (Blakesberg, Jay)
SMITHEREENS—ALBUMS
PH15062 616 (October 31, 1991) p91. "Blow Up"
PH15063 682 (May 19, 1994) p102. "A Date With The Smithereens"
SMITHS—ALBUMS
PH15064 617 (November 14, 1991) p140. "The Smiths" (Warhol, Andy)
SMOKE (FILM)—PHOTOGRAPHS
PH15065 711 (June 29, 1995) p49. "Stockard Channing Blows Smoke At A Wary Harvey Keitel"
PH15066 731 (April 4, 1996) p66. "Smoke"
SMOKIN SUCKAZ WIT LOGIC—PHOTOGRAPHS
PH15067 676 (February 24, 1994) p24. "Spank Dog, Money Mike, Mr. Watts, Peter Jorge, D-Smooth, G (from left)" (Hastings, Daniel)
SMOKING POPES—ALBUMS
PH15068 715 (August 24, 1995) p101. "Born To Quit"
SMOKING POPES—PHOTOGRAPHS
PH15069 746 (October 31, 1996) p18. "Smoking Popes: Bassist Matt Caterer, Drummer Mike Felumlee, Singer Josh Caterer And Guitarist Eli Caterer (from left)" (Robicheau, Paul)
SMOOTH—PHOTOGRAPHS
PH15070 670 (November 25, 1993) p32. "Smooth Heats Up The Box"
SMOOTH, C. L.—ALBUMS
PH15071 645-646 (December 10, 1992) p174. "Mecca And The Soul Brother"
SMOTHERS, TOMMY—PHOTOGRAPHS
PH15072 738-739 (July 11, 1996) p68. "Tommy Smothers, John Lennon, Yoko Ono, Rosemary And Timothy Leary (from left) During The Bed-In For Peace In Montreal, 1969"
SMULDERS, SHERRY—PHOTOGRAPHS
PH15073 668 (October 28, 1993) p73. "At The Bridge Tender" (Newton, Philip)
PH15074 668 (October 28, 1993) p72. "[Eden Carter & Sherry Smulders]" (Newton, Philip)
PH15075 668 (October 28, 1993) p72. "[Sherry Smulders]" (Newton, Philip)
SMURFIT, VICTORIA—PHOTOGRAPHS
PH15076 718 (October 5, 1995) p79. "Matt Keesler And Victoria Smurfit Skinny-Dip"
SNAKEPIT—ALBUMS
PH15077 702 (February 23, 1995) p71. "It's Five O'Clock Somewhere"
THE SNAPPER (FILM)—PHOTOGRAPHS
PH15078 671 (December 9, 1993) p78. "Daddy's Girl: Kellegher With Meaney"
SNAVELY, TODD—PHOTOGRAPHS
PH15079 624 (February 20, 1992) p32. "May The G-Force Be With You: Don't Ask About The Mush Run" (Smale, Brian)
PH15080 624 (February 20, 1992) p29. "Today Calgary, Tomorrow Albertville? From Left: Woodard, Leturgez, Snavely And Leonowicz" (Smale, Brian)
SNEAKERS (FILM)—PHOTOGRAPHS
PH15081 640 (October 1, 1992) p72. "Kingsley (left) Puts Redford On The Spot"
SNEAKERS—PHOTOGRAPHS—PORTRAITS
PH15082 655 (April 29, 1993) p19. "Mitch Easter (left) And Chris Stamey" (Register, Charles)
SNIPES, WESLEY—ILLUSTRATIONS
PH15083 742 (September 5, 1996) p67. "The Psycho Guy" (Brodner, Steve)
SNIPES, WESLEY—PHOTOGRAPHS
PH15084 631 (May 28, 1992) p60. "Forsythe, Stoltz And Snipes (from left) Battle Paralysis"
PH15085 664 (September 2, 1993) p69. "Thriller Tempura: Connery And Snipes Dine Japanese"
PH15086 669 (November 11, 1993) p80. "'Demolition' Men Wesley Snipes And Sylvester Stallone"
PH15087 702 (February 23, 1995) p19. "Wesley Snipes (left) Hands It To Ice Cube" (Mazur, Kevin)
PH15088 717 (September 21, 1995) p89. "Patrick Swayze, Wesley Snipes And John Leguizamo (from left) Hit The Road"
PH15089 723 (December 14, 1995) p92. "Race For The Money: Harrelson And Snipes"
PH15090 742 (September 5, 1996) p68. "Fan De Niro Stalks Snipes At A Ballgame"
PH15091 Number not assigned.
SNOOP DOGGY DOGG—ALBUMS
PH15092 674 (January 27, 1994) p51. "Doggystyle"
PH15093 676 (February 24, 1994) p16. "Doggystyle"
SNOOP DOGGY DOGG—ILLUSTRATIONS
PH15094 674 (January 27, 1994) p51. "Snoop & Cube" (Linn, Warren)
PH15095 731 (April 4, 1996) p11. "Snoop Doggy Dogg" (Guy, Edmund)
SNOOP DOGGY DOGG—PHOTOGRAPHS
PH15096 666 (September 30, 1993) pp38-39. "[Dr. Dre & Snoop Doggy Dogg]" (Seliger, Mark)
PH15097 667 (October 14, 1993) p39. "Snoop, Shaquille O'Neal, George Clinton" (Mazur, Kevin)
PH15098 670 (November 25, 1993) p83. "[Snoop Doggy Dogg & Dr. Dre]" (Seliger, Mark)
PH15099 672-673 (December 23, 1993) p63. "Snoop Dogg" (Seliger, Mark)
PH15100 672-673 (December 23, 1993) p45. "[Snoop Doggy Dogg]" (Seliger, Mark)
PH15101 678 (March 24, 1994) p27. "Wahlberg, Not On Snoop's Dick" (Mazur, Kevin)
PH15102 679 (April 7, 1994) p22. "Snoop Doggy Dogg" (Seliger, Mark)
PH15103 693 (October 20, 1994) p28. "Snoop Doggy Dogg" (Mazur, Kevin)
PH15104 712-713 (July 13, 1995) p33. "Dr. Dre (left), Snoop Doggy Dogg" (Seliger, Mark)
PH15104a 730 (March 21, 1996) p18. "[2Pac Shakur & Snoop Doggy Dogg]" (Mazur, Kevin)
PH15105 731 (April 4, 1996) p26. "Lee And Snoop Give Each Other Support"
PH15106 731 (April 4, 1996) p24. "Snoop (right) And Former Bodyguard McKinley Lee Listen To Trial Testimony"
PH15107 731 (April 4, 1996) pp22-23. "Snoop Leaves The Los Angeles Criminal Courts Building On Feb. 20 With His Son, Corde, After Being Acquitted Of Murder Charges In The 1993 Shooting Of Philip Woldemariam"
PH15108 750-751 (December 26, 1996) p50. "Snoop Leaving A Los Angeles Courthouse With His Mother, Beverly Brodus, And His On, Corde" (Ruymen, Jim)
SNOOP DOGGY DOGG—PHOTOGRAPHS—PORTRAITS
PH15109 666 (September 30, 1993) pp[cover]. "Dr Dre And Snoop Doggy Dogg: One Nation Under A G Thang" (Seliger, Mark)
PH15110 667 (October 14, 1993) p21. "Snoop Dogg (left) And Malik" (Seliger, Mark)
PH15111 672-673 (December 23, 1993) p188. "[Covers]" (Seliger, Mark)
PH15112 695 (November 17, 1994) p64. "Snoop Doggy Dogg" (Mondino, Jean Baptiste)
PH15113 698-699 (December 29, 1994) p68. "[Snoop Doggy Dogg]" (Shafer, F. Scott)
PH15114 720 (November 2, 1995) p50. "Snoop Doggy Dogg" (Mondino, Jean Baptiste)

SNOW—ALBUMS
PH15115 656 (May 13, 1993) p108. "12 Inches Of Snow"
SNOW—ILLUSTRATIONS
PH15116 668 (October 28, 1993) p8. "Snow Job" (Pendergrast, James T.)
SNOW—PHOTOGRAPHS
PH15117 665 (September 16, 1993) p12. "Street-Fightin' Man: Snow Hails From Toronto But Made It In New York" (Nissen, Melanie)
SNOW—PHOTOGRAPHS—PORTRAITS
PH15118 665 (September 16, 1993) p11. "[Snow]" (Ockenfels, Frank W.)
SNOW, PHOEBE—PHOTOGRAPHS
PH15119 622 (January 23, 1992) p6. "Phoebe Snow (left) And Lady Miss Kier At The Reebok Awards" (Robicheau, Paul)
PH15120 637 (August 20, 1992) p11. "Rock And Soul (from left): Boz Scaggs, Walter Becker, Donald Fagen, Michael McDonald, Phoebe Snow And Chuck Jackson" (Hamilton, James)
SO I MARRIED AN AXE MURDERER (FILM)—PHOTOGRAPHS
PH15121 663 (August 19, 1993) p82. "A Lovely Ax Murderer Leaves Mike Myers Hanging"
SOBEL, DAVE—PHOTOGRAPHS
PH15122 622 (January 23, 1992) p14. "Clockwise From Top Left: Davel Sobel, Luther Russell, Chris Joyner, John Hofer, Jason Hiller" (Annalisa)
SOBULE, JILL—PHOTOGRAPHS
PH15123 716 (September 7, 1995) p14. "[Jill Sobule & Freedy Johnston]" (Spellan, Jim)
SOCIAL DISTORTION—ALBUMS
PH15124 744 (October 3, 1996) p71. "White Light White Heat White Trash"
SOCIAL DISTORTION—PHOTOGRAPHS
PH15125 628 (April 16, 1992) p13. "Social Distortion Lights Up Times Square" (Gershoff, Gary)
PH15126 634-635 (July 9, 1992) p32. "Chris Reece, Mike Ness, John Maurer And Dennis Danell (from left)" (Cuffaro, Chris)
PH15127 741 (August 22, 1996) p26. "Bassist John Maurer, Guitarist Dennis Danell And Mike Ness Play Their Hearst Out" (Baehler, Chapman)
PH15128 748 (November 28, 1996) p47. "[Social Distortion]" (Ockenfels, Frank W.)
PH15129 749 (December 12, 1996) p28. "Dennis Danell, Ness, Chuck Biscuits, John Maurer (from left)" (Okeda, Mitch)
SODA—PHOTOGRAPHS
PH15130 709 (June 1, 1995) p16. "Flava In Ya Ear: Wax's Loomis, Joe Sib, Dave Georgeff And Soda Drop In On Fogelnes In His 'Squirt TV' Bedroom Studio (from left)" (Brown, Christy)
SOFT BOYS—ALBUMS
PH15131 676 (February 24, 1994) p59. "1976-81"
SOFTWARE—PHOTOGRAPHS
PH15132 722 (November 30, 1995) p81. "[Instruments]" (Grant, Bob)
PH15133 722 (November 30, 1995) pp[enc.48]. "[Software]" (Grant, Bob)
SOHL, RICHARD—PHOTOGRAPHS
PH15134 738-739 (July 11, 1996) p44. "Smith's Great '70s Band"
SOLANAS, VALERIE—PHOTOGRAPHS—PORTRAITS
PH15135 734 (May 16, 1996) p72. "The Real Solanas"
SOLL, KEVEN—PHOTOGRAPHS
PH15136 731 (April 4, 1996) p36. "Roots-Gloom Trio: Sixteen Horsepower's Soll, Tola And Edwards (from left)" (Keeley, Dennis)
SOMALIA—PHOTOGRAPHS
PH15137 653 (April 1, 1993) p46. "Crossing The Green Line: Marines escort A Food Convoy North Out Of Mogadishu" (Morris, Christopher)
PH15138 653 (April 1, 1993) p49. "Marines On The Move In The Countryside Near Baidoa After Securing The Airfield" (Morris, Christopher)
PH15139 653 (April 1, 1993) p43. "Securing The Area: A Marine On Patrol In Mogadishu Near The American Embassy" (Morris, Christopher)
PH15140 653 (April 1, 1993) p41. "[Somalia]" (Morris, Christopher)
PH15141 672-673 (December 23, 1993) p84. "Celebrating U.S. Failure In Somalia In October" (Watson, Paul)
SOMEDAY (VIDEO)—PHOTOGRAPHS
PH15142 619-620 (December 12, 1991) p33. "Mariah Carey's 'Someday'"
SOMETHING TO TALK ABOUT (FILM)—PHOTOGRAPHS
PH15143 715 (August 24, 1995) p108. "Dangerous Women: Michelle Pfeiffer, Sandra Bullock, Julia Roberts, Cindy Crawford And Natasha Henstridge"
SOMMERSBY (FILM)—ILLUSTRATIONS
PH15144 650 (February 18, 1993) p65. "Con With The Wind" (Cowles, David)
SOMMERSBY (FILM)—PHOTOGRAPHS
PH15145 650 (February 18, 1993) p66. "...Richard Gere Plays Tricks On Jodie Foster"
SON VOLT—PHOTOGRAPHS
PH15146 716 (September 7, 1995) p14. "Son Burning: David Boquist, Farrar, Heidorn And Jim Boquist (from left) Crank Up The Voltage" (Lucas, J.)
SONEFELD, JIM—PHOTOGRAPHS
PH15147 714 (August 10, 1995) pp42-43. "Darius Rucker, Dean Felber, Mark Bryan And Jim Sonefeld" (Seliger, Mark)
PH15148 726 (January 25, 1996) p37. "Hootie And The Blowfish: Jim Sonefeld, Darius Rucker, Dean Felber And Mark Bryan (from left)" (Seliger, Mark)
SONGWRITERS—ILLUSTRATIONS
PH15149 623 (February 6, 1992) p73. "For The Sake Of The Song" (Cronin, Brian)
SONI—PHOTOGRAPHS
PH15150 691 (September 22, 1994) p19. "Hootie Goes to Washington: Soni, Dean Felber, The Prez, Darius Rucker, Bryan (from left)"
SONIC YOUTH—ALBUMS
PH15151 617 (November 14, 1991) p140. "Daydream Nation" (Richter, Gerhard)
PH15152 638 (September 3, 1992) p63. "Dirty"
PH15154 640 (October 1, 1992) p88. "Dirty"
PH15155 651 (March 4, 1993) p57. "Dirty"
PH15156 681 (May 5, 1994) p52. "Experimental Jet Set, Trash And No Star"
PH15157 685 (June 30, 1994) p88. "Experimental Jet Set, Trash And No Star"
PH15158 719 (October 19, 1995) p149. "Washing Machine"
PH15159 721 (November 16, 1995) p128. "Washing Machine"
SONIC YOUTH—ILLUSTRATIONS
PH15160 638 (September 3, 1992) p63. "Noise From Underground" (Burke, Philip)
PH15161 734 (May 16, 1996) p29. "Keep Your Day Job: Sonic Youth Look On In Horror As Homer Simpson Gets Down"
SONIC YOUTH—PHOTOGRAPHS
PH15162 634-635 (July 9, 1992) p33. "Steve Shelley, Kim Gordon, Lee Ranaldo And Thurston Moore (from left)"
PH15163 663 (August 19, 1993) p20. "Future New Wave? Sonic Youth In The Studio With Cypress Hill" (Callahan, Kristin)
PH15164 667 (October 14, 1993) p97. "Sonic Youth: This 'Boots' Is Made For Watching"
PH15165 691 (September 22, 1994) p56. "Ranaldo, Gordon, Moore, Shelley (from left)" (Petersen, Naomi)
PH15166 695 (November 17, 1994) p84. "Sonic Youth" (Mark, Mary Ellen)
PH15167 712-713 (July 13, 1995) p32. "All The Way To Memphis: Moore, Shelley, Gordon And Ranaldo (from left)" (Day, Corinne)

PH15168 721 (November 16, 1995) p25. "Sonic Youth's Lee Ranaldo, Thurston Moore, Kim Gordon And Steve Shelley (from left) After Their 'State' Taping In New York" (Capak, R. J.)
PH15169 740 (August 8, 1996) p22. "Sonic Youth's Kim Gordon And Thurston Moore Do An Afternoon Set" (Blakesberg, Jay)
PH15170 745 (October 17, 1996) p41. "Sonic Youth (above) Do A Film Score For An Eric Bogosian Play" (Lavine, Michael)
SONIC YOUTH—PHOTOGRAPHS—PORTRAITS
PH15171 645-646 (December 10, 1992) p69. "Sonic Youth Gets Down And 'Dirty'" (Badulescu, Enrique)
PH15172 679 (April 7, 1994) p24. "The SOnic Set: Gordon, Moore, Ranaldo, Shelley (clockwise from top left)" (Watson, Norman)
SONNENFELD, BARRY—PHOTOGRAPHS
PH15173 618 (November 28, 1991) p58. "Mysterious And Spooky (from left): Rudin, Sonnenfeld And Tattersall" (Gordon, Melinda Sue)
SONNIER, DANE—PHOTOGRAPHS
PH15174 617 (November 14, 1991) p34. "Ben Huggins, Alan Doss, Monty Colvin And Dane Sonnier (from left)" (Carter, Keith)
SORBO, KEVIN—PHOTOGRAPHS
PH15175 715 (August 24, 1995) p74. "Hot TV Show"
SOREN, TABITHA—PHOTOGRAPHS
PH15176 645-646 (December 10, 1992) p66. "Clinton With MTV's Soren" (Cohen, Lester)
PH15177 745 (October 17, 1996) p33. "Fear And Loathing: Bob Dole With Tabitha Soren (top); A Choose Or Lose Representative Talks With Potential Young Voters"
SORVINO, MIRA—PHOTOGRAPHS
PH15178 688 (August 11, 1994) p63. "It's Ole To Nichols, Bergen, Eigeman And Sorvino"
PH15179 721 (November 16, 1995) p116. "Mira Sorvino's Hooker And Woody Allen"
PH15180 730 (March 21, 1996) p17. "You Are So Beautiful To Me: Dulli, Sorvino" (Mazur, Kevin)
PH15181 735 (May 30, 1996) p56. "Now Playing"
SOUL ASYLUM—ALBUMS
PH15182 647 (January 7, 1993) p60. "Grave Dancers Union"
PH15183 648 (January 21, 1993) p49. "Grave Dancers Union"
PH15184 649 (February 4, 1993) p84. "Grave Dancers Union"
PH15185 672-673 (December 23, 1993) pp159,162. "Grave Dancers Union"
PH15186 710 (June 15, 1995) p79. "Let Your Dim Light Shine"
SOUL ASYLUM—ILLUSTRATIONS
PH15187 710 (June 15, 1995) p79. "No Apologies" (Holley, Jason)
PH15188 715 (August 24, 1995) p18. "Rock History" (Pendergrast, James T.)
SOUL ASYLUM—PHOTOGRAPHS
PH15189 644 (November 26, 1992) p31. "Karl Mueller, Dave Pirner, Dan Murphy, Grant Young (clockwise from top left)" (Breiehagen, Per)
PH15190 660-661 (July 8, 1993) p32. "Soul Asylum: Runaway Hit" (Seliger, Mark)
PH15191 662 (August 5, 1993) p41. "At A Live Radio Gig In New York" (Seliger, Mark)
PH15192 662 (August 5, 1993) p38. "[Soul Asylum]" (Seliger, Mark)
PH15193 662 (August 5, 1993) pp[cover]. "Soul Asylum: Platinum Punks" (Seliger, Mark)
PH15194 662 (August 5, 1993) p43. "Soul Survivors: The Band Tears It Up During A Surprise Performance At Tramps, In New York City" (Seliger, Mark)
PH15195 670 (November 25, 1993) p86. "[Soul Asylum]" (Seliger, Mark)
PH15196 672-673 (December 23, 1993) p188. "[Covers]" (Seliger, Mark)
PH15197 672-673 (December 23, 1993) p57. "Mueller, Dave Pirner, Dan Murphy (from left)" (Franklin, Ross D.)
PH15198 674 (January 27, 1994) p40. "Runaway Single: Soul Asylum" (Seliger, Mark)
PH15199 695 (November 17, 1994) p55. "Soul Asylum—Photographs" (Smale, Brian)
PH15200 702 (February 23, 1995) p32. "Strummin' In Stereo: Dave Pirner, Butch Vig, Karl Mueller, Dan Murphy (from left)" (Cuffaro, Chris)
PH15201 711 (June 29, 1995) p31. "'I Want To Put Myself On A Pedestal And Hate Myself For Being There': Pirner, Murphy, Mueller, Campbell (from left)" (Mahurin, Matt)
PH15202 715 (August 24, 1995) p23. "[Soul Asylum]" (Naumann, Ellen)
SOUL ASYLUM—PHOTOGRAPHS—PORTRAITS
PH15203 645-646 (December 10, 1992) p91. "Soul Asylum: Minneapolis's Finest" (Breiehagen, Per)
PH15204 711 (June 29, 1995) pp[cover]. "Soul Asylum: The Good, The Bad And The Lonely" (Mahurin, Matt)
PH15205 712-713 (July 13, 1995) p33. "Soul Asylum Shine Their Dim Light" (Mason, Karen)
SOUL BLUES BOYS—ALBUMS
PH15206 649 (February 4, 1993) p69. "All Night Long"
SOUL COUGHING—ALBUMS
PH15207 697 (December 15, 1994) p96. "Ruby Vroom"
SOUL COUGHING—PHOTOGRAPHS
PH15208 734 (May 16, 1996) p18. "Soul Brothas M. Doughty (left) And Sebastian Steinberg" (Callahan, Kristin)
PH15209 735 (May 30, 1996) p23. "The Rock & Roll Zelig: Doughty Mouthing Off Onstage, 1994" (Banjee)
SOUL COUGHING—PHOTOGRAPHS—PORTRAITS
PH15210 735 (May 30, 1996) p21. "Frontman M. Doughty, Sebastian Steinberg, Mark De Gli Antoni And Yuval Gabay" (Vadukul, Nitin)
SOUL II SOUL—ALBUMS
PH15211 631 (May 28, 1992) p54. "Volume III Just Right"
PH15212 720 (November 2, 1995) p70. "Believe"
SOULE, MICHAEL—PHOTOGRAPHS
PH15213 693 (October 20, 1994) p84. "Michael Soule, Conservation Biologist" (Lee, Monica)
SOUNDGARDEN—ALBUMS
PH15214 619-620 (December 12, 1991) p174. "Badmotorfinger"
PH15215 677 (March 10, 1994) p63. "Superknown"
PH15216 735 (May 30, 1996) p45. "Down On The Upside"
SOUNDGARDEN—CD-ROMS
PH15217 722 (November 30, 1995) p71. "Alive In The Superunknown"
SOUNDGARDEN—ILLUSTRATIONS
PH15218 677 (March 10, 1994) p63. "Super Band" (Downs, Richard)
PH15219 688 (August 11, 1994) p10. "Label" (Pendergrast, James T.)
PH15220 702 (February 23, 1995) p16. "Honesty" (Pendergrast, James T.)
PH15221 735 (May 30, 1996) p45. "Superknown" (Borda, Juliette)
SOUNDGARDEN—PHOTOGRAPHS
PH15222 618 (November 28, 1991) p12. "Members Of Soundgarden Join Spinal Tap Backstage At 'RIP' Party" (Mayer, Jeffrey)
PH15223 639 (September 17, 1992) p64. "Soundgarden" (Blakesberg, Jay)
PH15224 645-646 (December 10, 1992) p69. "...And Soundgarden (right) Rocked The Lolla II Crowd" (Blakesberg, Jay)
PH15225 674 (January 27, 1994) p17. "Cameron, Shepherd, Cornell, Thayil (from left)" (Westenberg, Kevin)
PH15226 684 (June 16, 1994) p52. "Cameron, Thayil, Yamamoto, Cornell, Silver, Tour Manager Eric Johnson (from left) In 1988" (Peterson, Charles)
PH15227 684 (June 16, 1994) p50. "Cornell, Thayil, Sundquist, Yamamoto In Mid-'80s" (Peterson, Charles)

PH15228 684 (June 16, 1994) p50. "Ditto Tavern, '86: Thayil And Cornell" (Peterson, Charles)
PH15229 684 (June 16, 1994) p49. "Sit 'N' Spin: Cameron, Shepherd, Thayil And Cornell (from left) In Seattle" (Seliger, Mark)
PH15230 684 (June 16, 1994) pp[cover]. "Soundgarden" (Seliger, Mark)
PH15231 695 (November 17, 1994) p131. "Soundgarden" (Seliger, Mark)
PH15232 698-699 (December 29, 1994) p106. "From Sub Pop To Superstardom: Kim Thayil, Cornell, Ben Shepherd And Matt Cameron (from left)" (Seliger, Mark)
PH15233 698-699 (December 29, 1994) p42. "Superunknown No More: Soundgarden" (Cuffaro, Chris)
PH15234 700 (January 26, 1995) p16. "[Soundgarden]" (Doughty, Curt)
PH15235 727 (February 8, 1996) p26. "Soundgarden's Chris Cornell, Kim Thayil, Ben Shepherd And Matt Cameron (from left) In Seattle's Studio Litho" (Westenberg, Kevin)
PH15236 737 (June 27, 1996) p56. "Soundgarden's Cornell, Ben Shepherd, Thayil And Matt Cameron (from left)"

SOUNDGARDEN—PHOTOGRAPHS—PORTRAITS
PH15237 619-620 (December 12, 1991) p90. "North By Northwest: Soundgarden" (Lavine, Michael)
PH15238 634-635 (July 9, 1992) p45. "[Soundgarden]" (Seliger, Mark)

SOUNDS OF BLACKNESS—PHOTOGRAPHS—PORTRAITS
PH15239 686-687 (July 14, 1994) p39. "Sounds Of Blackness: 30 Voices, 10 Musicians And A Whole Lotta Heart" (May, Sandy)

SOUNDTRACKS—ALBUMS
PH15240 619-620 (December 12, 1991) p178. "The Commitments"
PH15241 619-620 (December 12, 1991) p165. "New Jack City"
PH15242 623 (February 6, 1992) p77. "Juice"
PH15243 624 (February 20, 1992) p40. "Until The End Of The World"
PH15244 625 (March 5, 1992) p65. "The Mambo Kings"
PH15245 627 (April 2, 1992) p44. "Falling From Grace"
PH15246 630 (May 14, 1992) p124. "Wayne's World"
PH15247 637 (August 20, 1992) p49. "Mo' Money"
PH15248 637 (August 20, 1992) p49. "Singles"
PH15249 645-646 (December 10, 1992) p166. "Deep Blues"
PH15250 645-646 (December 10, 1992) p169. "South Central"
PH15251 648 (January 21, 1993) p60. "The Bodyguard"
PH15252 649 (February 4, 1993) p84. "The Bodyguard"
PH15253 650 (February 18, 1993) p58. "The Bodyguard"
PH15254 651 (March 4, 1993) p80. "The Bodyguard"
PH15255 652 (March 18, 1993) p52. "The Bodyguard"
PH15256 653 (April 1, 1993) p68. "The Bodyguard"
PH15257 657 (May 27, 1993) p49. "CB4"
PH15258 657 (May 27, 1993) p63. "The Bodyguard"
PH15259 659 (June 24, 1993) p96. "The Bodyguard"
PH15260 666 (September 30, 1993) p100. "Judgment Night"
PH15261 676 (February 24, 1994) p42. "The Harder They Come"
PH15262 681 (May 5, 1994) p53. "Backbeat"
PH15263 684 (June 16, 1994) p124. "The Crow"
PH15264 688 (August 11, 1994) p34. "Above The Rim"
PH15265 688 (August 11, 1994) p34. "The Crow"
PH15266 688 (August 11, 1994) p34. "Reality Bites"
PH15267 689 (August 25, 1994) p104. "The Lion King"
PH15268 690 (September 8, 1994) p96. "The Lion King"
PH15269 691 (September 22, 1994) p120. "The Lion King"
PH15270 692 (October 6, 1994) p104. "The Lion King"
PH15271 697 (December 15, 1994) p120. "Murder Was The Case"
PH15272 698-699 (December 29, 1994) p178. "Pulp Fiction"
PH15273 705 (April 6, 1995) p25. "Tank Girl"
PH15274 726 (January 25, 1996) p69. "Dead Man Walking"
PH15275 741 (August 22, 1996) p100. "Phenomenon"
PH15276 749 (December 12, 1996) p82. "Evita"

SOUTHERN CULTURE ON THE SKIDS—ALBUMS
PH15277 684 (June 16, 1994) p109. "Ditch Diggin'"
PH15278 718 (October 5, 1995) p88. "Dirt Track Date"

SOUTHERN CULTURE ON THE SKIDS—PHOTOGRAPHS
PH15279 721 (November 16, 1995) p38. "The Party Has Rolled Back Into Town: Huff, Miller And Hartman (from left)" (Elledge, Paul)

SOUTHERN, TERRY—PHOTOGRAPHS—PORTRAITS
PH15280 724-725 (December 28, 1995) p66. "[Terry Southern]" (McDarrah, Fred W.)

SOUTHSIDE JOHNNY AND THE ASBURY JUKES—ALBUMS
PH15281 617 (November 14, 1991) p169. "Better Days"

SOUTHSIDE JOHNNY AND THE ASBURY JUKES—ILLUSTRATIONS
PH15282 617 (November 14, 1991) p169. "Southside Johnny: The Juke Also Rises" (Peck, Everett)

SOUTHSIDE JOHNNY AND THE ASBURY JUKES—PHOTOGRAPHS
PH15283 617 (November 14, 1991) p11. "Springsteen, Southside Johnny, Little Steven (from left)" (Busacca, Larry)
PH15284 691 (September 22, 1994) p20. "Springsteen (left) And Southside Johnny" (Hunter, Alicia)

SOVIET UNION—ILLUSTRATIONS
PH15285 615 (October 17, 1991) p8. "Millie Comes Upon A Sticky Situation" (Pendergrast, James T.)
PH15286 616 (October 31, 1991) p8. "Millie Checks The Pantry" (Pendergrast, James T.)

SOVIET UNION—PHOTOGRAPHS
PH15287 615 (October 17, 1991) p77. "[Soviet Union Coup]" (Wallis, Robert)
PH15288 617 (November 14, 1991) p25. "The Scene At Tushino Airfield, Where 500,000 Fans Converged For The Show" (Giron, Joe)
PH15289 617 (November 14, 1991) p25. "Skirmishes At The Concert Sent Fifty-Three People To Local Hospitals"

SPACE JAM (FILM)—PHOTOGRAPHS
PH15290 743 (September 19, 1996) p88. "Dickheads"

SPACEHOG—PHOTOGRAPHS
PH15291 734 (May 16, 1996) p32. "Fighting For Time In Front Of The Mirror: Brothers Antony And Royston Langdon, Richard Steel, And Jonny Cragg (from left)" (Clinch, Danny)

SPACEK, SISSY—PHOTOGRAPHS
PH15292 656 (May 13, 1993) p114. "Above, More King Characters Show Their Dark Side: Kathy Bates ('Misery'), Jack Nicholson ('The Shining'), Sissy Spacek ('Carrie')"

SPACEY, KEVIN—ILLUSTRATIONS
PH15293 716 (September 7, 1995) p75. "A Summer Sleeper" (Ulriksen, Mark)

SPACEY, KEVIN—PHOTOGRAPHS
PH15294 745 (October 17, 1996) p64. "Pacino Directs: Co-Star Kevin Spacey Pays Heed To His Liege On The Set Of 'Looking For Richard'"
PH15295 748 (November 28, 1996) p142. "Kevin Spacey, Left, Directs Matt Dillon"

SPACEY, KEVIN—PHOTOGRAPHS—PORTRAITS
PH15296 715 (August 24, 1995) p80. "Hot Character Actor" (Capak, R. J.)
PH15297 716 (September 7, 1995) p76. "Gabriel Byrne (left) And Kevin Spacey Face A Lineup"

SPADE, DAVID—PHOTOGRAPHS
PH15298 706 (April 20, 1995) p86. "'SNL' Movie Hell: Chris Farley With David Spade In 'Tommy Boy,' Al Franken With Bear In 'Stuart' And Adam Sandler With Dunces In 'Billy Madison' (from left)"
PH15299 729 (March 7, 1996) p54. "Now Playing"

SPADER, JAMES—PHOTOGRAPHS
PH15300 683 (June 2, 1994) p78. "Amick Gets Spader In Her Sex Vise"

PH15301 745 (October 17, 1996) p142. "Now Playing"
SPAGHETTI, EDDIE—PHOTOGRAPHS
PH15302 707 (May 4, 1995) p19. "Nelson, Rick Sims, Spaghetti (from left)" (Davis, Lisa)
PH15303 719 (October 19, 1995) p15. "Eddie Spaghetti And Dan Bolton Of The Supersuckers (top) And Cult Folkie Ani DiFranco Get Down At Seattle's Bumbershoot" (Doughty, Curt)
PH15304 721 (November 16, 1995) p25. "Nelson, Supersuckers Eddie Spaghetti And Dan Bolton (from left) Lend A Hand" (Roberts, Ebet)
PH15305 731 (April 4, 1996) p18. "Jennings (center) With Suckers, Dan Siegel, Dan Bolton, Ron Heathman And Singer Eddie Spaghetti (from left)" (Diamond, Rick)
SPAGHETTI, EDDIE—PHOTOGRAPHS—PORTRAITS
PH15306 721 (November 16, 1995) p43. "[Eddie Spaghetti]" (Moskowitz, Karen)
SPAIN—PHOTOGRAPHS
PH15307 665 (September 16, 1993) pp54-58. "Workers of The World" (Salgado, Sebastiao)
SPANK DOG—PHOTOGRAPHS
PH15308 676 (February 24, 1994) p24. "Spank Dog, Money Mike, Mr. Watts, Peter Jorge, D-Smooth, G (from left)" (Hastings, Daniel)
SPANKING THE MONKEY (FILM)—PHOTOGRAPHS
PH15309 682 (May 19, 1994) p63. "[Incest]"
PH15310 686-687 (July 14, 1994) p98. "Mom Watson And Son Davies"
PH15311 691 (September 22, 1994) p106. "Best Little Film"
SPANN, OTIS—ALBUMS
PH15312 640 (October 1, 1992) p67. "The Complete Candid Otis Spann-Lightnin' Hopkins Sessions"
SPARKS, DONITA—PHOTOGRAPHS
PH15313 628 (April 16, 1992) p56. "Finch, Sparks, Gardner And Plakas (from left)" (Cuffaro, Chris)
PH15314 644 (November 26, 1992) p15. "Dee Plakas, Jennifer Finch, Jett, Donita Sparks And Suzi Gardner (clockwise from left)" (Lewis, Don)
PH15315 652 (March 18, 1993) p22. "Feminist Majority Rules: L7's Finch, Gardner, Sparks, Dee Plakas (from left)" (Johnson, Lisa)
PH15316 688 (August 11, 1994) p25. "Dee Plakas, Donita Sparks, Jennifer Finch, Suzi Gardner (from left)" (Broad, Julian)
PH15317 692 (October 6, 1994) p16. "At Philly's Lollapalooza: L7's Donita Sparks (left), Dee Plakas, Suzi Gardner And Jennifer Finch With Bad Seeds Mick Harvey, James Johnston And Nick Cave" (Weiner, Scott)
PH15318 695 (November 17, 1994) p52. "L7" (Broad, Julian)
PH15319 696 (December 1, 1994) p23. "Elvismania: L7's Suzi Gardner, Dee Plakas, Sparks And Jennifer Finch (from left)" (Mazur, Kevin)
PH15320 698-699 (December 29, 1994) p42. "L7's Donita Sparks, Vedder, L7's Dee Plakas And Her Husband, Kurk Canning (from left)" (Mercer, Lance)
PH15321 703 (March 9, 1995) p36. "Choose Or Lose: L7's Donita Sparks" (Sandler, Harry)
SPEAKERS—PHOTOGRAPHS
PH15322 678 (March 24, 1994) p107. "Bose Acoustimass-3 Multimedia Speaker System ($699)" (Miller, Greg)
PH15323 686-687 (July 14, 1994) pp46-47. "[Toys]" (Grant, Bob)
PH15324 741 (August 22, 1996) pp84-85. "[Hot Technology]" (Grant, Bob)
SPEAKES, LARRY—PHOTOGRAPHS
PH15325 664 (September 2, 1993) p39. "What Difference Does A Decade Make? Gergen With Ronald Reagan And Larry Speakes, May 1982" (Kennerly, David Hume)
SPEARHEAD—ALBUMS
PH15326 698-699 (December 29, 1994) p173. "Home"
SPEARHEAD—PHOTOGRAPHS
PH15327 684 (June 16, 1994) p30. "Franti (foreground) With Spearhead" (Miller, Michael)
PH15328 700 (January 26, 1995) p24. "[Spearhead]"
SPECIAL SAUCE—ALBUMS
PH15329 684 (June 16, 1994) p108. "G. Love And Special Sauce"
THE SPECIALIST (FILM)—PHOTOGRAPHS
PH15330 694 (November 3, 1994) p106. "Now Playing"
SPECIES (FILM)—PHOTOGRAPHS
PH15331 715 (August 24, 1995) p108. "Dangerous Women: Michelle Pfeiffer, Sandra Bullock, Julia Roberts, Cindy Crawford And Natasha Henstridge"
PH15332 715 (August 24, 1995) p108. "The Man Eaters"
SPECTOR, PHIL—ALBUMS
PH15333 618 (November 28, 1991) p87. "Back To Mono (1958-1969)"
SPECTOR, PHIL—ILLUSTRATIONS
PH15334 618 (November 28, 1991) p87. "Songs Lasting Three Minutes—And Forever" (Day, Rob)
PH15335 641 (October 15, 1992) p45. "[Phil Spector]" (Blitt, Barry)
SPECTOR, PHIL—PHOTOGRAPHS
PH15336 616 (October 31, 1991) p13. "Rundgren, Eric Gardner, Janis Gardner, Little Richard, Spector (from left)" (Granitz, Steve)
PH15337 651 (March 4, 1993) p17. "Dion, Phil Spector And Springsteen" (Mazur, Kevin)
PH15338 651 (March 4, 1993) p18. "Phil Spector And Friends" (Granitz, Steve)
PH15339 675 (February 10, 1994) p22. "[Keith Richards & Phil Spector]" (Blankenhorn, C.)
SPECTOR, RONNIE—PHOTOGRAPHS
PH15340 639 (September 17, 1992) p20. "Love (left) With Spector" (Granitz, Steve)
SPEECH—ALBUMS
PH15341 727 (February 8, 1996) p50. "Speech"
SPEECH—ILLUSTRATIONS
PH15342 647 (January 7, 1993) p3. "Speech Of Arrested Development" (Burke, Philip)
SPEECH—PHOTOGRAPHS
PH15343 647 (January 7, 1993) p25. "AD's Headliner (left) And Speech" (States, Ann)
PH15344 647 (January 7, 1993) p13. "Arrested Development's Headliner, Taree, Eshe And Speech (from left): Talkin' About A Different Kind Of Nirvana" (States, Ann)
PH15345 648 (January 21, 1993) p9. "Arrested Development (from left): Speech, Aerle Taree, Headliner, Rasa Don, Baba Oje And Montsho Eshe" (Mazur, Kevin)
PH15346 657 (May 27, 1993) p17. "Arrested Development's Aerle taree, Headliner And Speech (from left)" (Arnold, Alice)
PH15347 685 (June 30, 1994) p29. "Speech Of Arrested Development" (Blakesberg, Jay)
PH15348 688 (August 11, 1994) p17. "Nelson Mandela (left) And AD's Speech"
SPEECH—PHOTOGRAPHS—PORTRAITS
PH15349 634-635 (July 9, 1992) p20. "Arrested Development (from left): Headliner, Montsho Eshe, Aerle Taree, Rasa Don And Speech" (Lavine, Michael)
PH15350 634-635 (July 9, 1992) p20. "Love Battery (from left): Kevin Whitworth, Rod Rudzitis And Jason Finn" (Lavine, Michael)
PH15351 667 (October 14, 1993) p94. "Arrested Development: Speech Pursues A Dialogue With God In 'Tennessee'"
SPEECHLESS (FILM)—PHOTOGRAPHS
PH15352 700 (January 26, 1995) p66. "Smart Women, Foolish Choices"
SPEED (FILM)—ILLUSTRATIONS
PH15353 685 (June 30, 1994) p79. "Die Hard On A Bus" (Pastrana, Robert M.)
SPEED (FILM)—PHOTOGRAPHS
PH15354 685 (June 30, 1994) p80. "Swat Dude Keanu Reeves

Puts Sandra Bullock In The Driver's Seat"
PH15355 684 (June 16, 1994) p114. "Potential Blockbusters"
PH15356 698-699 (December 29, 1994) p194. "Reeves And Bullock Ride In "Speed""
PH15357 705 (April 6, 1995) p69. "Oscar Rejects"
SPEED ZONE! (FILM)—PHOTOGRAPHS
PH15358 744 (October 3, 1996) p52. "The Plane Truth: Shields Spoofs Herself In 1989's 'Speed Zone!'"
SPELLMAN, JIM—PHOTOGRAPHS—PORTRAITS
PH15359 655 (April 29, 1993) p24. "Revving It Up: Velocity's Shannon, Spellman, Nelson, Riles And Moore (from left)" (Falls, John)
SPENCE, SKIP—PHOTOGRAPHS
PH15360 670 (November 25, 1993) p38. "Jerry Miller, Don Stevenson, Plant, Peter Lewis And Skip Spence" (Blakesberg, Jay)
SPENCER, JAMES—PHOTOGRAPHS
PH15361 693 (October 20, 1994) p89. "Evergreen Senior Spencer, Enforcer"
SPENCER, JON—ALBUMS
PH15362 644 (November 26, 1992) p74. "The Jon Spencer Blues Explosion"
PH15363 744 (October 3, 1996) p72. "Now I Got Worry"
SPENCER, JON—PHOTOGRAPHS
PH15364 700 (January 26, 1995) p25. "Blues Demolition Squad: Judah Bauer, Spencer, Russell Simins (from left)" (Ockenfels, Frank, 3)
PH15365 701 (February 9, 1995) p17. "Jon Spencer Bowling Explosion" (Laureen, Dawn)
PH15366 745 (October 17, 1996) p31. "Primitive Cool: Russell Simins, Jon Spencer And Judah Bauer (from left)" (Ockenfels, Frank W.)
PH15367 745 (October 17, 1996) p36. "Spencer Channels The King" (Olson, Sheryl)
SPHEERIS, PENELOPE—PHOTOGRAPHS
PH15368 626 (March 19, 1992) p40. "Director Spheeris Advised Her Stars To 'Keep It Subtle'" (Schiffman, Bonnie)
SPICE 1—PHOTOGRAPHS—PORTRAITS
PH15369 670 (November 25, 1993) p32. "Spice 1: This Year's Model"
SPIDERBAIT—PHOTOGRAPHS
PH15370 705 (April 6, 1995) p23. "The Hardcore Roar Of Silverchair (Daniel Johns, left) And Spiderbait" (Mott, Tony)
SPIEGEL, JAY—PHOTOGRAPHS
PH15371 691 (September 22, 1994) p38. "Revoke-Your-License Velocity: Gumball Drummer Jay Spiegel, Fleming And Bassist Eric Vermillion (from left)" (Capak, R. J.)
SPIEGEL, JEFF—PHOTOGRAPHS
PH15372 677 (March 10, 1994) p57. "Above: Skene! Man Spiegel" (Smale, Brian)
SPIELBERG, STEVEN—PHOTOGRAPHS
PH15373 659 (June 24, 1993) p36. "Dern And Jeff Goldblum, Flanking Steven Spielberg, Fell In Love On The Set" (Close, Murray)
PH15374 678 (March 24, 1994) p100. "Oscar's Choices: 'Schindler's List,' 'The Piano,' 'The Remains Of the Day,' 'In The Name Of The Father,' 'The Fugitive' (from left)"
PH15375 698-699 (December 29, 1994) p42. "Bridesmaid Revisited, Not: Spielberg Scores"
SPIELBERG, STEVEN—PHOTOGRAPHS—PORTRAITS
PH15376 698-699 (December 29, 1994) p68. "Geffen, Katzenberg, Spielberg (from left)" (Berliner)
SPIN CITY (TELEVISION SHOW)—PHOTOGRAPHS
PH15377 743 (September 19, 1996) pp94,96. "[Television]"
SPIN DOCTORS—ALBUMS
PH15378 686-687 (July 14, 1994) p110. "Turn It Upside Down"
SPIN DOCTORS—PHOTOGRAPHS
PH15379 631 (May 28, 1992) p15. "The Spin Doctors' Chris Barron, Eric Schenkman And Aaron Comess (from left)" (Mazur, Kevin)
PH15380 647 (January 7, 1993) p36. "The Boys On The Bus" (Seliger, Mark)
PH15381 647 (January 7, 1993) p39. "The Fans Go Bonkers Later That Night" (Seliger, Mark)
PH15382 647 (January 7, 1993) pp[cover]. "On Tour With Spin Doctors Rock's Road Warriors" (Seliger, Mark)
PH15383 647 (January 7, 1993) pp35-39. "[Spin Doctors]" (Seliger, Mark)
PH15384 647 (January 7, 1993) p39. "The Spin Doctors Pose With Their Crew In Poughkeepsie" (Seliger, Mark)
PH15385 660-661 (July 8, 1993) p33. "The Doctors Are In" (Mazur, Kevin)
PH15386 672-673 (December 23, 1993) p188. "[Covers]" (Seliger, Mark)
PH15387 674 (January 27, 1994) p45. "Pet Picks: Eric Schenkman (above, right) Of Spin Doctors Reveals His Favorites"
PH15388 684 (June 16, 1994) p18. "A Force Of Hobbit: Schenkman, White, Barron And Comess Back In The Studio"
PH15389 695 (November 17, 1994) p135. "Spin Doctors" (Seeff, Norman)
SPIN DOCTORS—PHOTOGRAPHS—PORTRAITS
PH15390 647 (January 7, 1993) p34. "[Spin Doctors]" (Seliger, Mark)
SPINAL TAP—ALBUMS
PH15391 627 (April 2, 1992) p45. "Break Like The Wind"
SPINAL TAP—PHOTOGRAPHS
PH15392 615 (October 17, 1991) p13. "Spinal Tap's Nigel Tufnel, David St. Hubbins And Derek Smalls (from left)" (Mazur, Kevin)
PH15393 618 (November 28, 1991) p12. "Members Of Soundgarden Join Spinal Tap Backstage At 'RIP' Party" (Mayer, Jeffrey)
SPINANES—PHOTOGRAPHS—PORTRAITS
PH15394 677 (March 10, 1994) p22. "[The Spinanes]"
SPINDERELLA—PHOTOGRAPHS
PH15395 625 (March 5, 1992) p18. "Pepa, Salt, Monie Love And Spinderella (from left)" (Shaw, Gene)
PH15396 671 (December 9, 1993) p31. "Spinderella, Blaze Berdahl Of 'Ghostwriter,' Pepa And Salt (from left)" (Leibowitz, Eric)
PH15397 723 (December 14, 1995) p28. "[Salt-N-Pepa & Patti Smith]" (Mazur, Kevin)
SPINDERELLA—PHOTOGRAPHS—PORTRAITS
PH15398 685 (June 30, 1994) p22. "Spinderella Control: Whatta DJ" (Rolston, Matthew)
PH15399 695 (November 17, 1994) p140. "Salt-N-Pepa" (Demarchelier, Patrick)
SPINDLER, MICHAEL—PHOTOGRAPHS
PH15400 732 (April 18, 1996) p63. "Spindler (left) And Markkula Were Barraged By Questions At Apple's 1996 Shareholders' Meeting"
SPIRITUALIZED—ALBUMS
PH15401 708 (May 18, 1995) p93. "Pure Phase"
THE SPITFIRE GRILL (FILM)—PHOTOGRAPHS
PH15402 742 (September 5, 1996) p68. "Elliott, Burstyn And Harden"
SPITZ, DAN—PHOTOGRAPHS
PH15403 656 (May 13, 1993) p31. "Noisemakers Ian, Dan Spitz, Bush, Frankie Bello And Benante (from left)" (Mazur, Kevin)
SPITZ, MARK—ILLUSTRATIONS—PORTRAITS
PH15404 645-646 (December 10, 1992) p157. "Mark Spitz, 1973"
SPONGE—ALBUMS
PH15405 738-739 (July 11, 1996) p90. "Wax Ecstatic"
SPONGE—PHOTOGRAPHS
PH15406 706 (April 20, 1995) p36. "Motor City Five: Mazzola, Grover, Dombrowski, Tim And Mike Cross (from left)" (Halsband, Michael)
PH15407 708 (May 18, 1995) p17. "Mike Cross (left), Dombrowski Rock Detroit" (Schwab, Bill)

PH15408 710 (June 15, 1995) p49. "Mike Cross, Dombrowski, Charlie Grover, Joey Mazzola, Tim Cross (from left)" (Tavee, Tom)
PH15409 718 (October 5, 1995) p26. "'Saturday Morning' Special: Sponge" (Cultice, Joseph)
PH15410 736 (June 13, 1996) p53. "Sponge (below) Try To Beat The Sophomore Slump" (Berg, Bob)
PH15411 742 (September 5, 1996) p37. "[Sponge]" (Ockenfels, Frank W.)
SPORE—ALBUMS
PH15412 686-687 (July 14, 1994) p124. "Giant"
SPORTS—PHOTOGRAPHS
PH15413 630 (May 14, 1992) p90. "[Ibuprofen]" (Beck, Robert)
SPRINGSTEEN, BRUCE—ALBUMS
PH15414 617 (November 14, 1991) p110. "Born To Run" (Berg, John)
PH15415 617 (November 14, 1991) p110. "Born To Run" (Engel, Andy)
PH15416 617 (November 14, 1991) p110. "Born To Run" (Meola, Eric)
PH15417 617 (November 14, 1991) p147. "Greetings From Asbury Park, N.J." (Berg, John)
PH15418 629 (April 30, 1992) p53. "Human Touch"
PH15419 634-635 (July 9, 1992) p4. "Born To Run"
PH15420 637 (August 20, 1992) p4. "Born To Run"
PH15421 645-646 (December 10, 1992) p164. "Human Touch"
PH15422 705 (April 6, 1995) p60. "Greatest Hits"
PH15423 724-725 (December 28, 1995) p127. "The Ghost of Tom Joad"
SPRINGSTEEN, BRUCE—ILLUSTRATIONS
PH15424 629 (April 30, 1992) p3. "Bruce Springsteen" (Burke, Philip)
PH15425 641 (October 15, 1992) pp130-131. "[Bruce Springsteen]" (Payne, C. F.)
PH15426 705 (April 6, 1995) p60. "Boys To Men" (Morse, Joe)
PH15427 707 (May 4, 1995) p84. "Springsteen: Broooce! Brooooce!" (Bartholomew, Beth)
SPRINGSTEEN, BRUCE—ILLUSTRATIONS—PORTRAITS
PH15428 629 (April 30, 1992) p53. "New Bruce: Lose Your Illusions" (Collier, John)
SPRINGSTEEN, BRUCE—PHOTOGRAPHS
PH15429 617 (November 14, 1991) p11. "Springsteen, Southside Johnny, Little Steven (from left)" (Busacca, Larry)
PH15430 619-620 (December 12, 1991) p18. "The Rock And Roll Hall Of Fame Jam" (Bellissimo, J.)
PH15431 625 (March 5, 1992) p24. "Springsteen At The Christie Benefits, Where He Debuted Some Of His New Material" (Preston, Neal)
PH15432 627 (April 2, 1992) p11. "Springsteen Onstage With The Iguanas" (Gerber, Cheryl)
PH15433 633 (June 25, 1992) p11. "Springsteen At The Bottom Line" (Cunningham, Peter)
PH15434 636 (August 6, 1992) p15. "Springsteen Onstage With Band Member Crystal Taliefero" (Preston, Neal)
PH15435 636 (August 6, 1992) p42. "Springsteen Onstage With Wife Patti Scialfa At Stockholm's Globe Arena, June 15th" (Preston, Neal)
PH15436 639 (September 17, 1992) p20. "Springsteen With Taliefero" (Preston, Neal)
PH15437 644 (November 26, 1992) p13. "Springsteen Plugs In For 'Unplugged'" (Preston, Neal)
PH15438 645-646 (December 10, 1992) p53. "Bruce Does 'SNL'" (Ng, Norman)
PH15439 645-646 (December 10, 1992) p35. "Bruce Goes E Street-less" (Mazur, Kevin)
PH15440 645-646 (December 10, 1992) p87. "[Down Thunder Road]"
PH15441 650 (February 18, 1993) p11. "The Boss And Bon Jovi Share A Stage" (Picknally, Pete)
PH15442 651 (March 4, 1993) p17. "Creedence Clearwater Revisited: Springsteen, Was, Fogerty And Robertson" (Mazur, Kevin)
PH15443 651 (March 4, 1993) p17. "Dion, Phil Spector And Springsteen" (Mazur, Kevin)
PH15444 656 (May 13, 1993) p13. "Springsteen Onstage In The Garden State" (Longfield, Scott D.)
PH15445 659 (June 24, 1993) p30. "[Bruce Springsteen]" (Hutson, Mick)
PH15446 662 (August 5, 1993) p34. "[Bruce Springsteen]" (Mazur, Kevin)
PH15447 664 (September 2, 1993) p31. "[Rumble Doll]" (Busacca, Larry)
PH15448 667 (October 14, 1993) p94. "'Brilliant Disguise': Bruce Springsteen Wears It Well"
PH15449 677 (March 10, 1994) p28. "Springsteen And Rose Come Together" (Mazur, Kevin)
PH15450 678 (March 24, 1994) p28. "Bruce At AIDS Project L.A." (Kravitz, Jeff)
PH15451 678 (March 24, 1994) p12. "Springsteen's CD Features Early '70s Demos" (Preston, Neal)
PH15452 684 (June 16, 1994) p35. "Magic Johnson, Springsteen, James Brown" (Kravitz, Jeff)
PH15453 688 (August 11, 1994) p20. "Pull Up A Stool: John Wesley Harding (left) Is Joined By Buddy Bruce Springsteen" (Glade, Gary)
PH15454 691 (September 22, 1994) p20. "Springsteen (left) And Southside Johnny" (Hunter, Alicia)
PH15455 697 (December 15, 1994) p17. "[Keith Richards, Tom Cruise, & Bruce Springsteen]" (Ferreira, Albert)
PH15456 702 (February 23, 1995) p50. "Johnson, Tyler, Springsteen And Patti Scialfa Schmooze" (Mazur, Kevin)
PH15457 705 (April 6, 1995) p17. "Springsteen And Etheridge team Up For 'MTV Unplugged'" (Micelotta, Frank)
PH15458 709 (June 1, 1995) p16. "Elvis Is Everywhere: Bruce Springsteen (left) And Sting Channel The King" (Mazur, Kevin)
PH15459 717 (September 21, 1995) p20. "Bruce! In New Jersey! Onstage! In A Bar! How Novel!" (Liebowitz, Alyse)
PH15460 719 (October 19, 1995) p36. "Bruce Springsteen Before His Performance" (Corbijn, Anton)
PH15461 722 (November 30, 1995) p20. "Rapt Fans Worship At Springsteen's Altar In New York" (Burmiston, Ray)
PH15462 724-725 (December 28, 1995) p56. "Forever Young: Bob Dylan And Bruce Springsteen" (Mazur, Kevin)
PH15463 726 (January 25, 1996) p17. "You Hockey Puck! Dylan, Rickles And Bruce Springsteen" (Mazur, Kevin)
PH15464 729 (March 7, 1996) p12. "A Tale Of Two Tours: The Small-Theater Tour By Springsteen (left) Was A Field Day For Scalpers, But Corgan And The Pumpkins Shut Them Out" (Capak, R. J.)
PH15465 729 (March 7, 1996) p12. "A Tale Of Two Tours: The Small-Theater Tour By Springsteen (left) Was A Field Day For Scalpers, But Corgan And The Pumpkins Shut Them Out" (Liu, Brian)
PH15466 743 (September 19, 1996) p34. "[Bruce Springsteen]" (Preston, Neal)
PH15467 747 (November 14, 1996) p25. "This Hall Was Made For You And Me: Arlo Guthrie, Bruce Springsteen, Tim Robbins, Dave Pirner And Billy Bragg (from left) At The Rock & Roll Hall Of Fame's Woody Guthrie..." (Pre
PH15468 750-751 (December 26, 1996) p90. "Jesse Jackson And Bruce Springsteen Led The Rally"
SPRINGSTEEN, BRUCE—PHOTOGRAPHS—PORTRAITS
PH15469 628 (April 16, 1992) p15. "[Bruce Springsteen]" (Springsteen, Pam)
PH15470 636 (August 6, 1992) pp39-40. "[Bruce Springsteen]" (Ritts, Herb)
PH15471 636 (August 6, 1992) pp[cover]. "Bruce: The Rolling Stone Interview" (Ritts, Herb)

PH15472 643 (November 12, 1992) p161. "Bruce Springsteen" (Ritts, Herb)
PH15473 645-646 (December 10, 1992) pp[cover]. "1992 Yearbook" (Ritts, Herb)
PH15474 645-646 (December 10, 1992) p147. "Bruce Springsteen, 1987"
PH15475 706 (April 20, 1995) p15. "Bennett (left) And Springsteen Bagged A Few" (Mazur, Kevin)
PH15476 706 (April 20, 1995) p16. "Springsteen (left) And Dave Pirner Played Tramps For An Evening" (Galindo, Andrew)
PH15477 712-713 (July 13, 1995) p33. "Bruce: Playing And Paying Tribute" (Preston, Neal)
PH15478 720 (November 2, 1995) p51. "Bruce Springsteen" (Kennedy, David Michael)

SPROUT, TOBY—PHOTOGRAPHS—PORTRAITS
PH15479 686-687 (July 14, 1994) p74. "Kevin Fennell, Toby Sprout, Pollard, Jim Pollard, Greg Demos (from left)" (Rice, ted)

SPRY, SHANE—PHOTOGRAPHS
PH15480 684 (June 16, 1994) p61. "James Dixon (center) With Teammates Shane Spry And Mickey McKinion" (Borris, Dan)

SPUNGEN, NANCY—PHOTOGRAPHS
PH15481 720 (November 2, 1995) p49. "Nancy Spungen & Sid Vicious"

SPY HARD (FILM)—PHOTOGRAPHS
PH15482 738-739 (July 11, 1996) p98. "Bang For The Buck Movie Chart"

SQUIRE, JOHN—PHOTOGRAPHS
PH15483 724-725 (December 28, 1995) p39. "Stoned, Dethroned: Mani, Squire, Brown, Reni (from left)" (Otte, Sylvia)

SQUIRE, JOHN—PHOTOGRAPHS—PORTRAITS
PH15484 706 (April 20, 1995) p30. "The Stone Roses (clockwise from top left): Mountfield, Wren, Squire And Brown" (Ragel, Jon)

ST. JOHN, BOB—PHOTOGRAPHS
PH15485 636 (August 6, 1992) p21. "Extreme's Nuno Bettencourt (seated, right) At The Boards With Bob St. John"

ST. JOHN, DICK—BOOKS
PH15486 670 (November 25, 1993) p19. "Rock & Roll Cookbook"

ST. JOHN, SANDY—BOOKS
PH15486 670 (November 25, 1993) p19. "Rock & Roll Cookbook"

ST. JOHNNY—ALBUMS
PH15487 670 (November 25, 1993) p114. "High As A Kite"

ST. LAWRENCE, JES—PHOTOGRAPHS
PH15488 666 (September 30, 1993) p55. "St. Lawrence Of Quackenbush's In His Cups" (McSpadden, Wyatt)

ST. LOUIS, MISSOURI—PHOTOGRAPHS
PH15489 616 (October 31, 1991) p11. "Anti-Axl Protesters At St. Louis Rally" (Newcomb, Peter)
PH15490 619-620 (December 12, 1991) p55. "[Axl Rose Protest]" (Newcomb, Peter)

STAGGERS, BARBARA—PHOTOGRAPHS
PH15491 671 (December 9, 1993) p55. "Dr. Barbara Staggers" (Light, Ken)
PH15492 671 (December 9, 1993) p57. "Staggers Hugging A Patient At Her Clinic" (Light, Ken)

STAIRWAY TO HEAVEN: LED ZEPPELIN UNCENSORED (BOOK)—PHOTOGRAPHS
PH15493 645-646 (December 10, 1992) p88. "[Stairway To Heaven]"

STALEY, LAYNE—ILLUSTRATIONS
PH15494 644 (November 26, 1992) p1. "Layne Staley Of Alice In Chains" (Burke, Philip)
PH15495 695 (November 17, 1994) p129. "Alice In Chains" (Holley, Jason)
PH15496 730 (March 21, 1996) p14. "[Alice In Chains]" (Pendergrast, James T.)

STALEY, LAYNE—PHOTOGRAPHS
PH15497 624 (February 20, 1992) p12. "From Left: Layne Staley, Ann Wilson, Stone Gossard, Jerry Cantrell" (Mason, Karen)
PH15498 644 (November 26, 1992) p45. "[Alice In Chains]" (Winters, Dan)
PH15499 657 (May 27, 1993) p17. "Alice In Chains' Layne Staley" (Granitz, Steve)
PH15500 662 (August 5, 1993) p60. "Layne Staley" (Blakesberg, Jay)
PH15501 662 (August 5, 1993) p13. "Mike Inez, Layne Staley, Jerry Cantrell And Sean Kinney (clockwise from top left) Of Alice In Chains" (Blakesberg, Jay)
PH15502 672-673 (December 23, 1993) p39. "Too Much Fun For Alice's Layne Staley?" (Blakesberg, Jay)
PH15503 676 (February 24, 1994) p18. "Chain Reaction: Sean Kinney, Jerry Cantrell, Layne Staley And Mike Inez (from left)" (Moskowitz, Karen)
PH15504 697 (December 15, 1994) p17. "Clowin' Around: Gacy Fans McCready (left) And Staley" (Mercer, Lance)
PH15505 711 (June 29, 1995) p12. "It's A Mad, Mad World: Alice In Chains' Staley (top)" (Mercer, Lance)
PH15506 723 (December 14, 1995) p28. "Mike Inez, A Fan, Layne Staley, Cantrell (from left) And Ghoulish Pals" (Doughty, Curt)
PH15507 727 (February 8, 1996) p33. "Kinney, Cantrell, Staley And Inez (from left)" (Seliger, Mark)
PH15508 727 (February 8, 1996) p35. "Kinney, Cantrell, Staley And Mike Starr In 1990 (from left)"
PH15509 727 (February 8, 1996) p36. "Staley (left) And Cantrell Performing During LollaPalooza '93" (Eichner, Steve)
PH15510 732 (April 18, 1996) p20. "'This Is For Rolling Stone!' Alice In Chains' Layne Staley (left) And Pearl Jam's Mike McCready Express Themselves" (Mazur, Kevin)

STALEY, LAYNE—PHOTOGRAPHS—PORTRAITS
PH15511 676 (February 24, 1994) p20. "Singer Layne Staley: 'I Never Planned Out My Life. Shit Just Happens.'" (Moskowitz, Karen)
PH15512 704 (March 23, 1995) p33. "Barrett Martin, Layne Staley, Baker Saunder And Mike McCready (from left)" (Mercer, Lance)
PH15513 727 (February 8, 1996) pp[cover]. "The Needle And The Damage Done: Alice In Chains' Layne Staley" (Seliger, Mark)
PH15514 727 (February 8, 1996) p34. "Staley: If I Live On Just A Strictly Sugar Diet, Hey, I Like It" (Seliger, Mark)
PH15515 735 (May 30, 1996) p3. "[The Faces Of Heroin]"

STALIN, JOSEPH—PHOTOGRAPHS
PH15516 741 (August 22, 1996) p74. "[The Cold War]"

STALKERS—ILLUSTRATIONS
PH15517 750-751 (December 26, 1996) p26. "[Target]" (Pendergrast, James T.)

STALLONE, SYLVESTER—ILLUSTRATIONS
PH15518 659 (June 24, 1993) p87. "Dinosaur Summer" (Witte, Michael)

STALLONE, SYLVESTER—PHOTOGRAPHS
PH15519 615 (October 17, 1991) p67. "Sylvester Stallone Signing An Autograph, 1990" (Pigozzi, Jean)
PH15520 659 (June 24, 1993) p88. "Thrills: 'Cliffhanger,' With Stallone"
PH15521 669 (November 11, 1993) p80. "'Demolition' Men Wesley Snipes And Sylvester Stallone"
PH15522 716 (September 7, 1995) p78. "Summer Wrap-Up]"

STAMEY, CHRIS—ALBUMS
PH15523 619-620 (December 12, 1991) p184. "Mavericks"

STAMEY, CHRIS—PHOTOGRAPHS—PORTRAITS
PH15524 655 (April 29, 1993) p19. "Mitch Easter (left) And Chris Stamey" (Register, Charles)

STAMP, TERENCE—PHOTOGRAPHS
PH15525 689 (August 25, 1994) p97. "Drag Queens On A Bus: Pearce, Stamp And Weaving"

STAMP, TERENCE—PHOTOGRAPHS—PORTRAITS
PH15526 705 (April 6, 1995) p69. "Oscar Rejects"
STAMPS—ILLUSTRATIONS
PH15527 644 (November 26, 1992) p24. "[Next Year]"
STAND BY ME (FILM)—PHOTOGRAPHS
PH15528 676 (February 24, 1994) p62. "Phoenix Comforts A Pal In 'Stand By Me'"
STANFIELD, LISA—ALBUMS
PH15529 621 (January 9, 1992) p51. "Real Love"
STANFORD UNIVERSITY—PHOTOGRAPHS
PH15530 719 (October 19, 1995) p91. "Underdressed At The Exotic Erotic Party (above)" (Christian, Michael)
STANIER, JOHN—PHOTOGRAPHS
PH15531 637 (August 20, 1992) p15. "Helmet (from left): Stanier, Bogdan, Mengede And Hamilton" (Ockenfels, Frank W.)
PH15532 689 (August 25, 1994) p63. "John Stanier, Henry Bogdan, Page Hamilton And Rob Echeverria (clockwise from top left)" (Wessel, Cathrine)
PH15533 689 (August 25, 1994) p64. "Original Guitarist Mengede, Bogdan, Hamilton, Stanier (from left)" (Brice, Lindsay)
PH15534 695 (November 17, 1994) p92. "Helmet" (Huba, John)
STANLEY, PAUL—PHOTOGRAPHS
PH15535 664 (September 2, 1993) p32. "Paul Stanley (left) With David Cassidy" (Plummer, Sue)
PH15536 690 (September 8, 1994) p24. "Stanley And Baby"
PH15537 715 (August 24, 1995) p25. "Paul Stanley, Gene Simmons, Eric Singer, Bruce Kulick (from left)" (Blakesberg, Jay)
PH15538 724-725 (December 28, 1995) p51. "Kiss' Simmons, Eric Singer, Stanley And Bruce Kulick (from left)" (Blakesberg, Jay)
PH15539 732 (April 18, 1996) p19. "Ace Frehley, Paul Stanley, 2Pac, Peter Criss And Gene Simmons (from left)" (Mazur, Kevin)
PH15540 736 (June 13, 1996) p52. "Kiss Come Back With Their Makeup Intact: Ace Frehley, Gene Simmons, Peter Criss And Paul Stanley" (Malluk, Eddie)
STANLEY, PAUL—PHOTOGRAPHS—PORTRAITS
PH15541 750-751 (December 26, 1996) p45. "Paul Stanley Of Kiss" (Mazur, Kevin)
STANSHALL, VIVIAN—PHOTOGRAPHS
PH15542 706 (April 20, 1995) p32. "Doo-Dah Man: Stanshall In His Bonzo Days"
STANT, SHANE—PHOTOGRAPHS
PH15543 686-687 (July 14, 1994) p86. "Stant In Phoenix (below)" (Gero, Paul)
STANTON, HARRY DEAN—PHOTOGRAPHS
PH15544 652 (March 18, 1993) p15. "Cheap Dates (from left): Phantom, Baxter, Sales, Stanton And James" (Matheu, Robert)
STAPLES, MAVIS—PHOTOGRAPHS
PH15545 628 (April 16, 1992) p13. "Mavis Staples, MC Lyte, Sam Moore And Bobby 'Blue' Bland (from left)" (Mazur, Kevin)
STAPLES, POP—ALBUMS
PH15546 637 (August 20, 1992) p53. "Peace To The Neighbor-hood"
STAPLES, STUART—PHOTOGRAPHS
PH15547 682 (May 19, 1994) p32. "Gloom Patrol: Brit-Crit Faves Tindersticks With Stuart Staples (center)" (Westenberg, Kevin)
STAPLETON, WENDY—PHOTOGRAPHS
PH15548 680 (April 21, 1994) pp[enc.38]. "It's Not Just Shopping, It's An Adventure" (Ragel, Jon)
STAR TREK (TELEVISION SHOW)—PHOTOGRAPHS
PH15549 682 (May 19, 1994) p72. "[Nonlethal Weapons]"
STAR TREK: FIRST CONTACT (FILM)—PHOTOGRAPHS
PH15550 743 (September 19, 1996) p88. "Going For The Gold"
STAR TREK: VOYAGER (TELEVISION SHOW)—PHOTOGRAPHS
PH15551 704 (March 23, 1995) p131. "UPN's New 'Star Trek: Voyager': The Captain And The Neelix"
STAR WARS TRILOGY (VIDEO DISCS)—PHOTOGRAPHS
PH15552 669 (November 11, 1993) p81. "[Star Wars Trilogy]"
STARGATE (FILM)—PHOTOGRAPHS
PH15553 696 (December 1, 1994) p134. "Misfires"
STARK, KOO—PHOTOGRAPHS
PH15554 615 (October 17, 1991) p66. "Graham Greene And Koo Stark, 1986" (Pigozzi, Jean)
STARKEY, LEE—PHOTOGRAPHS
PH15555 719 (October 19, 1995) p25. "Starr And Daughter Starkey" (Busacca, Larry)
STARR, FREDRO—PHOTOGRAPHS
PH15556 659 (June 24, 1993) p21. "Fredro Starr, Suave Sonny Caesar, Sticky Fingaz And Big D.S. (from left)" (Spector, Gary)
STARR, MIKE—PHOTOGRAPHS
PH15557 644 (November 26, 1992) p45. "[Alice In Chains]" (Winters, Dan)
PH15558 727 (February 8, 1996) p35. "Kinney, Cantrell, Staley And Mike Starr In 1990 (from left)"
STARR, RINGO—PHOTOGRAPHS
PH15559 631 (May 28, 1992) p9. "Ringo Starr, Julian Lennon And George Harrison (from left)" (Young, Richard)
PH15560 680 (April 21, 1994) p64. "Ticket To Ride: Starr And Lennon With Photographer Astrid Kirchherr" (Scheler, Max)
PH15561 719 (October 19, 1995) p25. "Starr And Daughter Starkey" (Busacca, Larry)
PH15562 722 (November 30, 1995) p26. "Ringo Starr, John Lennon, Paul McCartney And George Harrison During The Filming Of 'Help!' In 1965: 'So Much Younger Than Today'" (Kindahl, Chris)
PH15563 726 (January 25, 1996) p46. "Starr, McCartney, Harrison, Lennon"
STARR, RINGO—PHOTOGRAPHS—PORTRAITS
PH15564 634-635 (July 9, 1992) pp87-89. "[Ringo Starr]" (Seliger, Mark)
PH15565 643 (November 12, 1992) p121. "Ringo Starr" (Seliger, Mark)
PH15566 701 (February 9, 1995) p24. "On Their Wedding Day: Starr, Cox" (Freeman, Robert)
STARSKI, LOVEBUG—PHOTOGRAPHS
PH15567 672-673 (December 23, 1993) p137. "Left: Lovebug Starski Today" (Wessel, Cathrine)
PH15568 672-673 (December 23, 1993) p139. "Lovebug (left) With Early Rapper Eddie Cheba In 1978"
PH15569 672-673 (December 23, 1993) p139. "Lovebug Starski Working The Mike And Spinning His Wheels At Disco Fever, In The South Bronx, In 1983" (Mark, Mary Ellen)
STATMORE, MELISSA—PHOTOGRAPHS
PH15570 704 (March 23, 1995) p99. "Statmore Of J. Walter Thompson: 'Use Connections. We Love Referrals.'" (Pluchino, Joseph)
STAY (VIDEO)—PHOTOGRAPHS
PH15571 675 (February 10, 1994) p13. "[Bono]"
STEADMAN, ALISON—PHOTOGRAPHS
PH15572 627 (April 2, 1992) p41. "'Life Is Sweet' And Stars Horrocks And Alison Steadman"
STEADMAN, CARL—PHOTOGRAPHS
PH15573 745 (October 17, 1996) p119. "Suck Co-Creator Carl Steadman At HotWired's Office (above) And In The Bedroom He Keeps At Work (right)" (Duke, William)
STEALING BEAUTY (FILM)—PHOTOGRAPHS
PH15574 737 (June 27, 1996) p63. "Irons (left) And Tyler Talk Sex And Art"
STEARNS, CLIFF—PHOTOGRAPHS—PORTRAITS
PH15575 719 (October 19, 1995) p49. "Stearns"
STECKLER, JEREMY—PHOTOGRAPHS
PH15576 693 (October 20, 1994) p137. "Steckler" (White, Steven)
STEEL, JOHN—PHOTOGRAPHS
PH15577 676 (February 24, 1994) p48. "The Angry Young Animals (from left): Drummer John Steel, Organist Alan Price,

bass Player Chas Chandler, Lead Singer Eric Burdon And Guitarist Hilton Valentine"
PH15578 677 (March 10, 1994) p28. "Pirner With Animals Valentine, Chas Chandler And John Steel" (Mazur, Kevin)
STEEL POOL BATH TUB—PHOTOGRAPHS
PH15579 721 (November 16, 1995) p78. "Mike Morasky, Darren Mor-X And Dale Flattum (from left) Briefly Considered The Name Rusty Nail Shower Stall But Soon Thought Better of It" (Winters, Dan)
STEEL PULSE—PHOTOGRAPHS
PH15580 706 (April 20, 1995) p17. "Steel Pulse Play Marley Tribute" (Kravitz, Jeff)
STEEL, RICHARD—PHOTOGRAPHS
PH15581 734 (May 16, 1996) p32. "Fighting For Time In Front Of The Mirror: Brothers Antony And Royston Langdon, Richard Steel, And Jonny Cragg (from left)" (Clinch, Danny)
STEELE—PHOTOGRAPHS—PORTRAITS
PH15582 686-687 (July 14, 1994) p73. "Straight Outta Brooklyn: Tek And Steele" (Borris, Dan)
STEELE, ALISON—PHOTOGRAPHS
PH15583 721 (November 16, 1995) p38. "[Alison Steele]"
STEELE, ROBERT D.—PHOTOGRAPHS—PORTRAITS
PH15584 682 (May 19, 1994) p46. "[Robert D. Steele]"
STEELY DAN—PHOTOGRAPHS
PH15585 664 (September 2, 1993) p32. "Walter Becker And Donald Fagen" (Mazur, Kevin)
PH15586 667 (October 14, 1993) p37. "Walter Becker (left), Donald Fagen Get Back, Jack" (Mazur, Kevin)
PH15587 672-673 (December 23, 1993) p58. "Below: Walter Becker And Donald Fagen" (Mazur, Kevin)
STEFANI, GWEN—PHOTOGRAPHS
PH15588 740 (August 8, 1996) p17. "Stefani, Left, And Manson, Who Obviously Eats Her Spinach" (Cohen, Lester)
PH15589 742 (September 5, 1996) p28. "Slinky Temptress Stefani" (Popplewell, John)
PH15590 745 (October 17, 1996) p27. "Gavin Rossdale, Gwen Stefani And Dennis Rodman, At A Pre-Show Bash" (Mazur, Kevin)
STEFANI, GWEN—PHOTOGRAPHS—PORTRAITS
PH15591 750-751 (December 26, 1996) p73. "Gwen Stefani Of No Doubt" (Cultice, Joseph)
STEIN, LAURA—PHOTOGRAPHS
PH15592 689 (August 25, 1994) p41. "Pierce, MacLeod, Hartling, Stein (from top)" (Crump, James)
STEINBERG, LEWIS—PHOTOGRAPHS
PH15593 625 (March 5, 1992) p13. "Lewis Steinberg, Steve Cropper, Booker T. Jones, Marion Jackson, Randall Jackson, Duck Dunn, Jim Stewart (from left)" (Elgar, Nick)
STEINBERG, SEBASTIAN—PHOTOGRAPHS
PH15594 734 (May 16, 1996) p18. "Soul Brothas M. Doughty (left) And Sebastian Steinberg" (Callahan, Kristin)
STEINBERG, SEBASTIAN—PHOTOGRAPHS—PORTRAITS
PH15595 735 (May 30, 1996) p21. "Frontman M. Doughty, Sebastian Steinberg, Mark De Gli Antoni And Yuval Gabay" (Vadukul, Nitin)
STEINEM, GLORIA—PHOTOGRAPHS—PORTRAITS
PH15596 729 (March 7, 1996) p10. "Our Bodies, Ourselves: Merchant (left) And Steinem" (Katz, Bruce)
PH15597 749 (December 12, 1996) p20. "Proud Mom At Son's College Graduation? No, It's Steinem With Vedder, Post-Rally" (Warburg, Jenny)
STEINER, JOSH—ILLUSTRATIONS
PH15598 691 (September 22, 1994) p20. "Wonkful Conduct" (Friske, Maria)
STEINMILLER, ROBERT J., JR.—PHOTOGRAPHS
PH15599 655 (April 29, 1993) p69. "DeVito Is Dad To Steinmiller And Hughes"
STEMPLE, HERBERT—PHOTOGRAPHS
PH15600 691 (September 22, 1994) p104. "Van Doren, Left, And Stemple Flank Host Jack Barry On "Twenty-One," Circa 1956"
STENMOE, KARI—PHOTOGRAPHS
PH15601 652 (March 18, 1993) pp[enc.37]. "Sandra Symington And Kari Stenmoe" (Seliger, Mark)
STEPHANOPOULOS, GEORGE—PHOTOGRAPHS
PH15602 664 (September 2, 1993) p39. "With Bill Clinton And George Stephanopoulos, may 1993"
PH15603 670 (November 25, 1993) p126. "Stephanopoulos (left) And Carville Cheer For Clinton"
PH15604 671 (December 9, 1993) p42. "[The Rolling Stone Interview of Bill Clinton]" (Seliger, Mark)
PH15605 680 (April 21, 1994) p34. "Stephanopoulos (right) Meets R.E.M." (Mazur, Kevin)
PH15606 698-699 (December 29, 1994) p37. "Buck Stops Here: R.E.M. And Stephanopoulos (with grin)" (Mazur, Kevin)
STEPHENS, JODY—PHOTOGRAPHS
PH15607 658 (June 10, 1993) p17. "Auer, Chilton, Stephens And Stringfellow" (Perez, Marty)
PH15608 668 (October 28, 1993) p15. "Big Star On The Steps Of Alex Chilton's Memphis, Tenn., Home In 1972: Andy Hummel, Jody Stephens, Chris Bell And Chilton (above, from left)" (Manning, Carole)
PH15609 668 (October 28, 1993) p15. "Chilton And Stephens On Reunion Day 1993 (left)" (Rosenberg, Merlyn)
STEPHENS, TOBY—PHOTOGRAPHS
PH15610 747 (November 14, 1996) p124. "Stubbs, In Drag, Deceives Stephens"
STEPHENS, VICTOR—PHOTOGRAPHS
PH15611 651 (March 4, 1993) p24. "Sloan, Edwards, Fletcher, Stephens" (Roca, John)
STEREO EQUIPMENT—AMPLIFIERS—PHOTOGRAPHS
PH15612 658 (June 10, 1993) pp[enc.25]. "Good Breeding: The Naim 72 Pre-Amp, $1455, And Naim 140 Amp, Have An English Accent" (Rosa And Rosa)
PH15613 658 (June 10, 1993) pp[enc.28]. "The NAD 2400 Amp, $600, Provides Sonic Oomph Galore" (Rosa And Rosa)
STEREO EQUIPMENT—PHOTOGRAPHS
PH15614 621 (January 9, 1992) p39. "Close And Play: Krell's Top-Loading CD-DSP Compact-Disc Player Has Long-Playing Appeal" (Gaz, Stab)
PH15615 621 (January 9, 1992) p40. "Hard To Find: The Onix OA21S Integrated Amplifier Is Well Worth Pursuing, However" (Gaz, Stab)
PH15616 621 (January 9, 1992) p40. "Speakers Of The House: The Atlantic Technology Pattern Home Theater System" (Gaz, Stab)
PH15617 621 (January 9, 1992) p38. "An Industrial Work Of Art: The JBL Pro III Speakers Will Not Shred Eardrums Or Foster A Subconscious Longing To Stop And Read A Book" (Gaz, Stab)
PH15618 627 (April 2, 1992) p48. "Theta's DS Pre Converter (top) And Data Transport" (Joel, Seth)
PH15619 630 (May 14, 1992) p117. "Alpine 7980 3D In-Dash Tuner-CD Changer; Quart QM335CX Speaker System" (Grant, Bob)
PH15620 633 (June 25, 1992) p52. "Panasonic SL-NP1A Portable CD Player, Sherwood RX-4100R Receiver And M Technology Persona One Speakers" (Coleman, Gene)
PH15621 634-635 (July 9, 1992) pp122-123. "[Toys]" (Goldin, David)
PH15622 653 (April 1, 1993) p61. "Party Central: The Bose Lifestyle Music Center With Satellites" (Cubillo, Enrique)
PH15623 656 (May 13, 1993) p121. "Faces To Like: The Alpine 7513 (top) And The Clarion 5740" (Rosa, Doug)
PH15623a 658 (June 10, 1993) pp[enc.30]. "Cable Ready: Straight Wire Pleases The Most Ardent Audiophiles"
PH15624 660-661 (July 8, 1993) p124. "Cicena HipHugger Personal Tape Player And Radio, $39" (Miller, Greg)
PH15625 660-661 (July 8, 1993) p123. "Sony CFD-970 Sports Series Portable Stereo, 4345" (Miller, Greg)
PH15626 664 (September 2, 1993) p73. "Kawasaki Ks-301, $300" (Miller, Greg)

PH15627 664 (September 2, 1993) p73. "Sharp WQ-CH600, $249" (Miller, Greg)
PH15628 674 (January 27, 1994) p59. "Bang And Olufsen Beosound 2000 Music System, $1,995" (Miller, Greg)
PH15629 680 (April 21, 1994) p99. "Alpine 5960 CD Shuttle ($420)" (Miller, Greg)
PH15630 680 (April 21, 1994) p99. "Arkon Sound Feeder SF100 ($49.95)" (Miller, Greg)
PH15631 680 (April 21, 1994) p99. "Denon DCT-950R RDS Receiver CD Player-Controller ($750)" (Miller, Greg)
PH15632 680 (April 21, 1994) p99. "MB Quart QM 218.02 CX Two-Way Speakers ($389 The Set)" (Miller, Greg)
PH15633 680 (April 21, 1994) p99. "Sony MDX-400 Mini Disc Changer ($1,299.95)" (Miller, Greg)
PH15634 684 (June 16, 1994) p92. "Advent Laureates Make The Best Of Any Components" (Miller, Greg)
PH15635 684 (June 16, 1994) p99. "Almost Perfect: The Cello Pallette Equalizer" (Miller, Greg)
PH15636 684 (June 16, 1994) p94. "Altec Speakers, Onkyo Works, Technics' Classic Turntable" (Miller, Greg)
PH15637 684 (June 16, 1994) p92. "Bookshelf Amp: The Creek 4240 Gives You Accurate Sound With No Frills" (Miller, Greg)
PH15638 684 (June 16, 1994) p100. "Keypads By Ada, Audioease And Audioaccess (from left) Control Sound Throughout The Home" (Miller, Greg)
PH15639 684 (June 16, 1994) p101. "Pioneer's CDL-97 Makes CD's And Laserdiscs Shine" (Miller, Greg)
PH15640 684 (June 16, 1994) p91. "Plug In A Portable CD Or Tape Player And Bose's Wave Radio Becomes A Minisystem" (Miller, Greg)
PH15641 684 (June 16, 1994) p101. "Programming The Panasonic PV-4464 Stereo VCR Is Practically Possible" (Miller, Greg)
PH15642 684 (June 16, 1994) p91. "PSB Alpha Speakers Fit Anywhere: JVC's Compu Link Components Simplify Your Life" (Miller, Greg)
PH15643 684 (June 16, 1994) p101. "The Rear Loudspeakers For The JBL Home Theater" (Miller, Greg)
PH15644 684 (June 16, 1994) p94. "The Sony CDP-X707ES CD Player Is 36 Pounds Of High-Tech Performance" (Miller, Greg)
PH15645 684 (June 16, 1994) p99. "Suited For Sensitive Speakers, Luxman's C-383 Preamp Has Multiroom Capability" (Miller, Greg)
PH15646 691 (September 22, 1994) p109. "[Hot Stuff]" (Buck, Monica)
PH15647 697 (December 15, 1994) p107. "[Technology]" (Grant, Bob)
PH15648 708 (May 18, 1995) p101. "[Automobiles]" (Grant, Bob)
PH15649 708 (May 18, 1995) pp[enc.8-12 +]. "[Stereo Equipment]" (Weiss, Mark)
PH15650 712-713 (July 13, 1995) p121. "[Technology]" (Grant, Bob)
PH15651 719 (October 19, 1995) p163. "[Speakers]" (Grant, Bob)
PH15652 730 (March 21, 1996) p111. "[Technology]" (Grant, Bob)
PH15653 731 (April 4, 1996) p70. "Technology" (Grant, Bob)
PH15654 735 (May 30, 1996) pp[enc.10-12 +]. "[Stereo Equipment]" (Akashi, Shu)

STEREO EQUIPMENT—PRE-AMPS—PHOTOGRAPHS
PH15655 658 (June 10, 1993) pp[enc.25]. "Good Breeding: The Naim 72 Pre-Amp, $1455, And Naim 140 Amp, Have An English Accent" (Rosa And Rosa)

STEREO EQUIPMENT—RECEIVERS—PHOTOGRAPHS
PH15656 658 (June 10, 1993) pp[enc.24]. "Overpowering Sound: the Sony STR-311 Receiver, $220, Delivers Seventy Watts Per Channel" (Rosa And Rosa)

STEREO EQUIPMENT—SPEAKERS—PHOTOGRAPHS
PH15657 657 (May 27, 1993) p61. "Burning Up The Highway: The Infinity Kappa 130KD" (Porto, James)
PH15658 658 (June 10, 1993) pp[enc.28]. "Subtle Strength: The Monitor Audio Studio 20 SE Speakers, $4500, Convey An Aura Of Power" (Rosa And Rosa)

STEREO EQUIPMENT—TURNTABLES—PHOTOGRAPHS
PH15659 658 (June 10, 1993) pp[enc.29]. "The Cardas-Benz Ruby Phono Cartridge, $2375, Stands Alone" (Rosa And Rosa)
PH15660 658 (June 10, 1993) pp[enc.26]. "Rock Solid: The Platter Of The Rotel RP 855 Weighs 3.3 Pounds" (Rosa And Rosa)

STEREO MC'S—PHOTOGRAPHS
PH15661 668 (October 28, 1993) p24. "Stereo MC's: Rocked The Main Stage" (Capak, R. J.)

STEREOLAB—ALBUMS
PH15662 698-699 (December 29, 1994) p173. "Mars Audiac Quintet"

STEREOLAB—PHOTOGRAPHS
PH15663 691 (September 22, 1994) p38. "Stereolab's Hansen (left) And Sadier Wax Etheral" (Clinch, Danny)
PH15664 731 (April 4, 1996) p40. "Always The Same, Always Different: Stereolab's Mary Hansen, Tim Gane, Laetitia Sadier And Morgane Lhote (from left)" (Perou, Ralph)

STERN, ALISON—PHOTOGRAPHS
PH15665 675 (February 10, 1994) p32. "Scenes From A Marriage: Stern And Dad Ben Dance At Stern's Wedding In 1978 (above)"
PH15666 675 (February 10, 1994) p32. "Stern And Alison Today" (Mintz, Ari)

STERN, BEN—PHOTOGRAPHS
PH15667 675 (February 10, 1994) p32. "Scenes From A Marriage: Stern And Dad Ben Dance At Stern's Wedding In 1978 (above)"

STERN, DANIEL—PHOTOGRAPHS
PH15668 685 (June 30, 1994) p80. "Crystal, Lovitz And Stern Go West For Box-Office Gold"

STERN, ELLEN—PHOTOGRAPHS
PH15669 675 (February 10, 1994) p30. "At 13, With His Mother And Sister Ellen"

STERN, HOWARD—ILLUSTRATIONS
PH15670 678 (March 24, 1994) p6. "Sexiness Scales" (Pendergrast, James T.)

STERN, HOWARD—PHOTOGRAPHS
PH15671 675 (February 10, 1994) p30. "At 13, With His Mother And Sister Ellen"
PH15672 675 (February 10, 1994) p30. "At 6 Months"
PH15673 675 (February 10, 1994) p30. "At 7"
PH15674 675 (February 10, 1994) p31. "Howard And Ray: He Claims Mom Once Told Him To Wear Her Panties When He Was Out Of Undies" (Mintz, Ari)
PH15675 675 (February 10, 1994) p32. "Scenes From A Marriage: Stern And Dad Ben Dance At Stern's Wedding In 1978 (above)"
PH15676 675 (February 10, 1994) p32. "Stern And Alison Today" (Mintz, Ari)
PH15677 682 (May 19, 1994) p37. "The Stings And The Honorable Howard Stern" (Mazur, Kevin)
PH15678 694 (November 3, 1994) p22. "Stern And Puppet Curt Kirkwood" (Mazur, Kevin)
PH15679 698-699 (December 29, 1994) p42. "The Agony Of Defeat: Ex-candidate Stern"
PH15680 729 (March 7, 1996) p9. "Hemlock Anyone? Today's Socrates Stern (left) And His Disciple Popper"
PH15681 743 (September 19, 1996) p20. "Johnson, With Stern And Angus Young (from left), Calls Stern 'A Good Kid. And His Fans Are A Rowdy Bunch Of Buggers'"

STERN, HOWARD—PHOTOGRAPHS—PORTRAITS
PH15682 675 (February 10, 1994) p30. "At 3"
PH15683 675 (February 10, 1994) pp28-29. "[Howard Stern]" (Seliger, Mark)

PH15684 675 (February 10, 1994) pp[cover]. "Revenge Of The Nerd: Howard Stern" (Seliger, Mark)
PH15685 675 (February 10, 1994) p30. "Stern As A Senior, From His High School Yearbook In 1972"

STERN, RAY—PHOTOGRAPHS
PH15686 675 (February 10, 1994) p30. "At 13, With His Mother And Sister Ellen"
PH15687 675 (February 10, 1994) p31. "Howard And Ray: He Claims Mom Once Told Him To Wear Her Panties When He Was Out Of Undies" (Mintz, Ari)

STESNEY, FRED—PHOTOGRAPHS
PH15688 702 (February 23, 1995) p20. "Flag's Jason Zasky, Stesney And Jeff Musser (from left)" (Toliver, Chris)

STEUER, JONATHAN—PHOTOGRAPHS
PH15689 722 (November 30, 1995) pp[enc.6]. "Jonathan 'Dr. Cheese' Steuer" (McLeod, William Mercer)

STEVENS, CAT—PHOTOGRAPHS—PORTRAITS
PH15690 724-725 (December 28, 1995) p54. "[Cat Stevens]" (Musto, Ilpo)

STEVENS, ROGERS—PHOTOGRAPHS
PH15691 630 (May 14, 1992) p28. "Blind Melon's Hoon (left) And Rogers Stevens" (Kraft, Chris)
PH15692 639 (September 17, 1992) p20. "Shannon Hoon, Christopher Thorn, Glen Graham, Brad Smith And Rogers Stevens (clockwise from top left)" (Clinch, Danny)
PH15693 640 (October 1, 1992) p27. "Blind Melon (from left): Smith, Stevens, Thorn, Hoon And Graham" (Clinch, Danny)
PH15694 669 (November 11, 1993) pp38-39. "Brad Smith, Glen Graham, Shannon Hood, Rogers Stevens & Christopher Thorn (from left)" (Seliger, Mark)

STEVENSON, BILL—PHOTOGRAPHS
PH15695 719 (October 19, 1995) p24. "No Mall Punks For All: Chad Price, Stephen Egerton, Karl Alvarez, Bill Stevenson (from left)" (Corrigan, Daniel)

STEVENSON, BILL—PHOTOGRAPHS—PORTRAITS
PH15696 672-673 (December 23, 1993) p112. "Hardcore Heroes Black Flag In March 1984: Bill Stevenson, Kira Roessler, Greg Ginn And Rollins (from left)" (Rosenberg, Howard)

STEVENSON, DON—PHOTOGRAPHS
PH15697 670 (November 25, 1993) p38. "Jerry Miller, Don Stevenson, Plant, Peter Lewis And Skip Spence" (Blakesberg, Jay)

STEWART, DAVE—ALBUMS
PH15698 704 (March 23, 1995) p122. "Greetings From The Gutter"

STEWART, DAVE—PHOTOGRAPHS
PH15699 626 (March 19, 1992) p13. "Dave Stewart, Robin Zander And Dr. John (from left)" (Tallman, Susie)
PH15700 638 (September 3, 1992) p11. "Stewart And Reed At Leysin With Chrissie Hynde (from left)" (Allen, David)

STEWART, DERRICK—PHOTOGRAPHS
PH15701 660-661 (July 8, 1993) p97. "The Pharcyde: Romye Robinson, Imani Wilcox, Derrick Stewart And Tre Hardson" (Azimi, Mojgan B.)
PH15702 722 (November 30, 1995) p38. "Hip-Hop's Cosmic Voyagers: Wilcox, Robinson, Hardson And Stewart (from left)" (McClelland, Philippe)

STEWART, IAN—PHOTOGRAPHS
PH15703 723 (December 14, 1995) p52. "The Rolling Stones Onstage At London's Marquee Club, 1963 (roadie, pal and sometimes pianist Ian Stewart is on maracas)"

STEWART, JIM—PHOTOGRAPHS
PH15704 625 (March 5, 1992) p13. "Lewis Steinberg, Steve Cropper, Booker T. Jones, Marion Jackson, Randall Jackson, Duck Dunn, Jim Stewart (from left)" (Elgar, Nick)

STEWART, JON—PHOTOGRAPHS
PH15705 682 (May 19, 1994) p63. "[Jon Stewart]" (Seliger, Mark)
PH15706 700 (January 26, 1995) p26. "[Jon Stewart]" (Carroll, Chris)
PH15707 705 (April 6, 1995) p17. "Lara Flynn Boyle And Jon Stewart Groping At The ESPY Awards" (Mazur, Kevin)
PH15708 709 (June 1, 1995) p27. "PC Free: Stewart, Wener, McClure, Osman (from left)" (Westenberg, Kevin)
PH15709 714 (August 10, 1995) p17. "Absolut-ly Fabulous: Bennett And Stewart In New York" (Mazur, Kevin)

STEWART, MELVIN—PHOTOGRAPHS
PH15710 634-635 (July 9, 1992) p97. "Melvin Stewart" (Zander, Peter)

STEWART, PATRICK—PHOTOGRAPHS
PH15711 715 (August 24, 1995) p110. "Friends United: Batt, Stewart, Weber And Weiss"

STEWART, ROD—ALBUMS
PH15712 617 (November 14, 1991) p149. "Never A Dull Moment" (Craig, John)
PH15713 617 (November 14, 1991) p149. "Never A Dull Moment" (Caraeff, Ed)
PH15714 659 (June 24, 1993) p80. "Unplugged...And Unseated"

STEWART, ROD—PHOTOGRAPHS
PH15715 619-620 (December 12, 1991) pp[cover]. "1991 Yearbook" (Eccles, Andrew)
PH15716 619-620 (December 12, 1991) p37. "Rod Stewart (right) And His John" (Adebari, Eugene)
PH15717 619-620 (December 12, 1991) p19. "[Rod Stewart, Rachel Hunter]" (Smeal, James)
PH15718 653 (April 1, 1993) p16. "The Jeff Beck group Circa 1968: Mickey Waller, Beck, Stewart And Wood (from left)"
PH15719 653 (April 1, 1993) p11. "Kenny Jones, Stewart, Wyman, Wood And Ian McLagan" (Hutchson, Mick)
PH15720 653 (April 1, 1993) p11. "Ron Wood (left) And Rod Stewart" (Preston, Neal)
PH15721 672-673 (December 23, 1993) p74. "Below: Sting, Adams And Stewart Pay Homage To Men In Tights" (Wessel, Cathrine)
PH15722 676 (February 24, 1994) p48. "Rod The Mod: Have We Told You Lately That We Love You?" (Putland, Michael)
PH15723 682 (May 19, 1994) p34. "Was Tonight Really The Night? Rod Stewart" (Granitz, Steve)
PH15724 720 (November 2, 1995) p50. "Rod Stewart" (Dickson, Ian)

STEWART, ROD—PHOTOGRAPHS—PORTRAITS
PH15725 643 (November 12, 1992) p118. "Rod Stewart" (Seliger, Mark)

STICKY FINGAZ—PHOTOGRAPHS—PORTRAITS
PH15726 659 (June 24, 1993) p21. "Fredro Starr, Suave Sonny Caesar, Sticky Fingaz And Big D.S. (from left)" (Spector, Gary)

STILES, BOB—PHOTOGRAPHS
PH15727 742 (September 5, 1996) pp52-53. "World-Class Road-Luge Pilots Lee Dansie, Bob Stiles And Shawn Goulet (from left) Take A Break Near The Top Of The X Games' 'Crash Alley'" (Seliger, Mark)

STILLER, BEN—PHOTOGRAPHS
PH15728 677 (March 10, 1994) p60. "Stiller (right) Directs"
PH15729 732 (April 18, 1996) p78. "Kelly And Stiller"

STILLER, BEN—PHOTOGRAPHS—PORTRAITS
PH15730 689 (August 25, 1994) p15. "You've Got A Friend Like Ben—Stiller" (Davis, Lisa O'Conner)

STILLS, STEVE—PHOTOGRAPHS
PH15731 645-646 (December 10, 1992) p98. "Stills Greets Clinton At The Convention" (Jacobs, Michael)

STING—ALBUMS
PH15732 619-620 (December 12, 1991) p182. "The Soul Cages"
PH15733 652 (March 18, 1993) p38. "Ten Summoner's Tales"
PH15734 672-673 (December 23, 1993) p168. "Ten Summoner's Tales"
PH15735 730 (March 21, 1996) p96. "Mercury Falling"

STING—ILLUSTRATIONS
PH15736 652 (March 18, 1993) p38. "Sting Tells His Tales" (Cowles, David)

STING—ILLUSTRATIONS—PORTRAITS
PH15737 641 (October 15, 1992) p115. "[Sting]" (Sadowski, Wiktor)
STING—PHOTOGRAPHS
PH15738 617 (November 14, 1991) p11. "Nell Campbell And Sting" (Granitz, Steve)
PH15739 619-620 (December 12, 1991) pp[cover]. "1991 Yearbook" (Ritts, Herb)
PH15740 619-620 (December 12, 1991) p90. "Henley, Sting, Joel, Raitt" (Kaplan, Todd)
PH15741 619-620 (December 12, 1991) p18. "[Sting]" (Preston, Neal)
PH15742 619-620 (December 12, 1991) p39. "Sting, Sinead O'Connor, Peter Gabriel (from left)" (Linsen, M.)
PH15743 629 (April 30, 1992) p11. "Dress Rehearsal For The Rain-Forest Benefit: Sting, John, Goldberg, Cole, Henley And Taylor (from left)" (Regan, Ken)
PH15744 629 (April 30, 1992) p11. "Natalie Cole Waltzes Sting" (Regan, Ken)
PH15745 640 (October 1, 1992) p9. "Styler, Steed And Sting (from left)" (Aris, Brian)
PH15746 645-646 (December 10, 1992) p39. "[Rain Forest Redux]" (Regan, Ken)
PH15747 645-646 (December 10, 1992) p77. "[Sting & Trudy Styler]" (Phillips, George)
PH15748 648 (January 21, 1993) p9. "Sting And The Studio" (Mazur, Kevin)
PH15749 657 (May 27, 1993) pp36-39. "[Sting]" (MacPherson, Andrew)
PH15750 660-661 (July 8, 1993) p29. "Sting At The Silver Bowl" (Blakesberg, Jay)
PH15751 672-673 (December 23, 1993) p74. "Below: Sting, Adams And Stewart Pay Homage To Men In Tights" (Wessel, Cathrine)
PH15752 672-673 (December 23, 1993) p28. "Left: Sting, Gentleman Farmer" (MacPherson, Andrew)
PH15753 680 (April 21, 1994) p33. "The Stings Cut A Rug" (Elgar, Nick)
PH15754 682 (May 19, 1994) p37. "No Rap, No Hard Stuff: Taylor, Houston, Wynette, John, Sting (from left) At Rehearsal" (Mazur, Kevin)
PH15755 682 (May 19, 1994) p38. "Rain-Forest Crunch: Sting And His Pal Pav" (Mazur, Kevin)
PH15756 682 (May 19, 1994) p37. "Sting And Taylor" (Mazur, Kevin)
PH15757 682 (May 19, 1994) p37. "The Stings And The Honorable Howard Stern" (Mazur, Kevin)
PH15758 693 (October 20, 1994) p37. "Sting Leads The Pack On "Earthrise"" (Somoza, Gerardo)
PH15759 703 (March 9, 1995) p20. "Sting And Man Of The Hour Elton John" (Mazur, Kevin)
PH15760 709 (June 1, 1995) p16. "Elvis Is Everywhere: Bruce Springsteen (left) And Sting Channel The King" (Mazur, Kevin)
PH15761 715 (August 24, 1995) p62. "Charlie, Sting And Suzanne Vega" (Cohen, Lester)
PH15762 724-725 (December 28, 1995) p39. "Behind Closed Doors: Sting And John" (Mazur, Kevin)
PH15763 733 (May 2, 1996) p14. "New York's Where I'd Rather Stay! Sting Scorns Finland"
PH15764 735 (May 30, 1996) p12. "If You're Gonna Love, Wear The Glove" (Mazur, Kevin)
PH15765 735 (May 30, 1996) p50. "Ross, Sting, Taylor And Williams (from left)" (Mazur, Kevin)
PH15766 750-751 (December 26, 1996) p57. "The Rainforest All-Star Supremes Tribute" (Mazur, Kevin)
STING—PHOTOGRAPHS—PORTRAITS
PH15767 643 (November 12, 1992) p210. "Sting" (Watson, Albert)
PH15768 657 (May 27, 1993) pp[cover]. "Sting: The King Of Pain Or Just A Regular Guy?" (MacPherson, Andrew)
PH15769 672-673 (December 23, 1993) p188. "[Covers]" (MacPherson, Andrew)
PH15770 697 (December 15, 1994) p18. "[Elton John & Sting]" (Fisher, David)
PH15771 740 (August 8, 1996) p24. "[Sting]" (Claxton, William)
STINKY PUFFS—PHOTOGRAPHS
PH15772 691 (September 22, 1994) p19. "Nirvana's Grohl (drums), Simon Fair (at mike), Novoselic (bass)" (Doughty, Curt)
PH15773 698-699 (December 29, 1994) p60. "Yoyo A Gaga: Stinky Puffs With Special Guests Dave Grohl And Krist Novoselic" (Doughty, Curt)
STINSON, BOB—PHOTOGRAPHS
PH15774 659 (June 24, 1993) p54. "Early Mats: Westerberg, Bob Stinson, Mars And Tommy Stinson (from left)" (Pasley, Richard)
PH15775 705 (April 6, 1995) p28. "Stinson Performing In 1984" (Pantsios, Anastasia)
PH15776 724-725 (December 28, 1995) p64. "[Bob Stinson]" (Corrigan, Daniel)
STINSON, TOMMY—PHOTOGRAPHS
PH15777 649 (February 4, 1993) p9. "Westerberg (left) And Stinson Shoot The Breeze In Minneapolis" (Beaulieu, Allen)
PH15778 659 (June 24, 1993) p54. "Early Mats: Westerberg, Bob Stinson, Mars And Tommy Stinson (from left)" (Pasley, Richard)
PH15779 659 (June 24, 1993) p52. "The Later Mats Incarnation: Tommy Stinson, Westerberg, Slim Dunlap And Chris Mars (from left)" (Matheu, Robert)
PH15780 666 (September 30, 1993) p20. "Bash And Pop's Tommy Stinson" (Kraft, Chris)
STIPE, MICHAEL—ILLUSTRATIONS—PORTRAITS
PH15781 641 (October 15, 1992) p187. "[Michael Stipe]" (Goldstrom, Robert)
STIPE, MICHAEL—PHOTOGRAPHS
PH15782 615 (October 17, 1991) p13. "Michael Stipe, Arsenio Hall" (Mazur, Kevin)
PH15783 622 (January 23, 1992) p6. "Natalie Merchant And Michael Stipe In Boston" (Robicheau, Paul)
PH15784 628 (April 16, 1992) p11. "R.E.M.'s Mike Mills, Michael Stipe, Peter Buck And Bill Berry (from left)" (Mazur, Kevin)
PH15785 640 (October 1, 1992) p20. "Michael Stipe, Peter Buck, Mike Mills And Bill Berry (clockwise from left)" (Corbijn, Anton)
PH15786 642 (October 29, 1992) p21. "Cherry And Stipe" (Keeley, Dennis)
PH15787 647 (January 7, 1993) p9. "From Left: Mike Mills, Buck, Bill Berry and Stipe" (Colletti, Steve)
PH15788 647 (January 7, 1993) p9. "Merchant And Stipe Onstage In Atlanta" (Diamond, Rick)
PH15789 648 (January 21, 1993) p11. "Baez, Gabriel, Richie Havens And Stipe (from left) At The Reebok Awards" (Robicheau, Paul)
PH15790 651 (March 4, 1993) p32. "Ad-hoc Automatic Baby: Mike Mills, Adam Clayton, Michael Stipe, Larry Mullen Jr." (Mazur, Kevin)
PH15791 652 (March 18, 1993) p22. "Michael Stipe And Pals At L.A. Benefit" (Cohen, Lester)
PH15792 672-673 (December 23, 1993) p16. "Mills, Clayton, Stipe And Mullen (from left)" (Mazur, Kevin)
PH15793 674 (January 27, 1994) p28. "Guided By Voices: Hersh And Stipe"
PH15794 680 (April 21, 1994) p33. "R.E.M.'s Michael Stipe" (Mazur, Kevin)
PH15795 688 (August 11, 1994) p17. "Courtney Love And Michael Stipe (right)" (Kravitz, Jeff)
PH15796 689 (August 25, 1994) p15. "Michael Stipe, Phillips And Mike Mills (from left)" (Allen, Greg)
PH15797 691 (September 22, 1994) p20. "[Michael Stipe & Tori Amos]" (Diamond, Rick)

PH15798 693 (October 20, 1994) p27. "R.E.M.'s Bill Berry, Michael Stipe, Peter Buck, Mike Mills" (Mazur, Kevin)
PH15799 696 (December 1, 1994) p40. "[Michael Stipe]" (Wolff, Jeremy)
PH15800 701 (February 9, 1995) p17. "Spicy (left) And Yogurt, But Shaved, Take A Break" (Kravitz, Jeff)
PH15801 704 (March 23, 1995) p32. "Band On The Run: Berry, Mills, Stipe And Buck (above, from left)" (Sheehan, Tom)
PH15802 704 (March 23, 1995) p32. "Boy In The Hood: Stipe Onstage In Sydney (top)" (Liguz, Andrzej)
PH15803 704 (March 23, 1995) p29. "Not Too Goofy, Not Too Arch—Just Loose And Natural: Stipe Onstage in Oz" (Mott, Tony)
PH15804 704 (March 23, 1995) p27. "[R.E.M.]" (Sheehan, Tom)
PH15805 709 (June 1, 1995) p23. "Michael Stipe Fronts A Monster Tour"
PH15806 711 (June 29, 1995) p26. "A Rejuvenated Stipe: 'Welcome To Aneurysm '95!'" (Blakesberg, Jay)
PH15807 719 (October 19, 1995) p16. "Michael 'Buddha' Stipe" (Mazur, Kevin)
PH15808 722 (November 30, 1995) p19. "Stipe (left) And Yorke In Tel Aviv"
PH15809 724-725 (December 28, 1995) p54. "MTV Video Music Award Performers: Live's Ed Kowalczyk, Michael Stipe And White Zombie's Sean Yseult (from left)" (Mazur, Kevin)
PH15810 726 (January 25, 1996) p18. "[Michael Stipe And Patti Smith]"
PH15811 726 (January 25, 1996) p37. "Michael Stipe Delivers During R.E.M.'s 'Monster' Tour" (Mazur, Kevin)
PH15812 726 (January 25, 1996) p42. "Peter Buck, Michael Stipe, Bill Berry, Mike Mills" (Jensen, David)
PH15813 735 (May 30, 1996) p27. "Artistic Pals Michael Stipe And Patti Smith" (Mazur, Kevin)
PH15814 736 (June 13, 1996) p19. "Doing The Right Thing At The VH1 Honors Benefit: Eddie Vedder, Who Looks Eerily Like Harrison Ford, Michael Stipe And Recent Newlywed Sean Penn" (Mazur, Kevin)
PH15815 737 (June 27, 1996) p29. "R.E.M.'s Mike Mills, Bill Berry, Stipe And Buck (from left) Have Split With Their Longtime Manager" (Rider, Paul)
PH15816 745 (October 17, 1996) pp53,55,58. "[R.E.M.]" (Corbijn, Anton)
PH15817 750-751 (December 26, 1996) p74. "Stipe, Rick Rubin, Nusrat Ali Khan, Stephen Dorff And Flea (from left)" (Cohen, Lester)

STIPE, MICHAEL—PHOTOGRAPHS—PORTRAITS
PH15818 625 (March 5, 1992) p46. "[Michael Stipe]" (Watson, Albert)
PH15819 667 (October 14, 1993) p85. "Stipe: R.E.M.'s Man On The Street"
PH15820 693 (October 20, 1994) p58. "Michael Stipe" (Seliger, Mark)
PH15821 695 (November 17, 1994) p34. "Michael Stipe Of R.E.M." (Seliger, Mark)
PH15822 697 (December 15, 1994) p28. "[Michael Stipe]" (Quigley, Brian)
PH15823 697 (December 15, 1994) p18. "Shakoor, Stipe And Perez (from left) Give Their Achin' Dogs A Rest After AIDS Walk Atlanta"
PH15824 715 (August 24, 1995) p89. "Hot Male Look" (Seliger, Mark)

STIRRATT, JOHN—PHOTOGRAPHS
PH15825 707 (May 4, 1995) p32. "The Buddy System: Johnston, Coomer, Stirratt, Tweedy And Bennett (from left)" (Miller, Brad)

STOCKMAN, SHAWN—PHOTOGRAPHS
PH15826 625 (March 5, 1992) p21. "Michael McCary, Wanya Morris, Shawn Stockman And Nate Morris (clockwise from top left)" (Graham, Jim)
PH15827 709 (June 1, 1995) p23. "Boyz II Men: Shawn Stockman, Michael McCary, Wanya Morris, Nate Morris" (Granitz, Steve)

STOCKMAN, STEVE—PHOTOGRAPHS—PORTRAITS
PH15828 710 (June 15, 1995) p62. "Stockman" (Coomer, Brett)

STOLTZ, ERIC—PHOTOGRAPHS
PH15829 631 (May 28, 1992) p60. "Forsythe, Stoltz And Snipes (from left) Battle Paralysis"
PH15830 681 (May 5, 1994) p49. "Soap Star Turner Puts The Moves On Writer Stoltz"
PH15831 690 (September 8, 1994) p87. "[Killing Zoe]"
PH15832 694 (November 3, 1994) p18. "[Eric Stoltz, Sandra Bullock, Samantha Mathis]"

STONE ROSES—ALBUMS
PH15833 701 (February 9, 1995) p57. "Second Coming"

STONE ROSES—PHOTOGRAPHS
PH15834 724-725 (December 28, 1995) p39. "Stoned, Dethroned: Mani, Squire, Brown, Reni (from left)" (Otte, Sylvia)
PH15835 749 (December 12, 1996) p32. "Wilted And Dead: England's Stone Roses Say Thanks And Call It Quits" (Smith, Pennie)

STONE ROSES—PHOTOGRAPHS—PORTRAITS
PH15836 706 (April 20, 1995) p30. "The Stone Roses (clockwise from top left): Mountfield, Wren, Squire And Brown" (Ragel, Jon)

STONE TEMPLE PILOTS—ALBUMS
PH15837 672-673 (December 23, 1993) p152. "Core"
PH15838 686-687 (July 14, 1994) p106. "Purple"
PH15839 688 (August 11, 1994) p80. "Purple"
PH15840 698-699 (December 29, 1994) p176. "Purple"
PH15841 733 (May 2, 1996) p51. "Tiny Music"
PH15842 735 (May 30, 1996) p68. "Tiny Music"
PH15843 736 (June 13, 1996) p92. "Tiny Music"

STONE TEMPLE PILOTS—ILLUSTRATIONS
PH15844 675 (February 10, 1994) p6. "Identities: One Per Customer" (Pendergrast, James T.)
PH15845 733 (May 2, 1996) p51. "STP's Sugar Fix" (Burns, Charles)
PH15846 750-751 (December 26, 1996) p58. "[Stone Temple Pilots]" (Clayton, Christian)

STONE TEMPLE PILOTS—PHOTOGRAPHS
PH15847 662 (August 5, 1993) p52. "Missing Links: The Pilots Let Off Steam On The Green During A Break From Their Hectic Schedules" (Ragel, Jon)
PH15848 662 (August 5, 1993) p50. "Stone Temple Pilots Eric Kretz, Dean DeLeo, Robert DeLeo And Weiland (from left)" (Ragel, Jon)
PH15849 665 (September 16, 1993) p31. "STP Put Their Best Kissy-Face Forward" (Linn, Jason)
PH15850 672-673 (December 23, 1993) p46. "[Stone Temple Pilots]" (Blakesberg, Jay)
PH15851 698-699 (December 29, 1994) p58. "Laughing All The Way: Stone Temple Pilots Deflect The Critical Slings And Arrows"
PH15852 710 (June 15, 1995) p22. "STP, From Left: Robert And Dean DeLeo, Weiland, Kretz" (Haynes, Loren)
PH15853 747 (November 14, 1996) p45. "[Stone Temple Pilots]" (Eder, John)

STONE, FREDDIE—PHOTOGRAPHS
PH15854 649 (February 4, 1993) p51. "Rose Stone, Sly, Freddie Stone, Graham, Robinson, Errico And Martini Of Sly And The Family Stone"

STONE, OLIVER—PHOTOGRAPHS
PH15855 622 (January 23, 1992) p49. "Kevin Costner Conspires With Director Oliver Stone"
PH15856 655 (April 29, 1993) p68. "Wild Palms"

STONE, ROLAND—ALBUMS
PH15857 668 (October 28, 1993) p80. "Remember Me"

STONE, ROSE—PHOTOGRAPHS
PH15858 649 (February 4, 1993) p51. "Rose Stone, Sly, Freddie Stone, Graham, Robinson, Errico And Martini Of Sly And The Family Stone"

STONE, SHARON—ILLUSTRATIONS
PH15859 703 (March 9, 1995) p69. "Sharon And The Wild Bunch" (Payne, C. F.)
PH15860 723 (December 14, 1995) p89. "Goodfellas Go Vegas" (Brodner, Steve)
PH15861 735 (May 30, 1996) p55. "Dead Babe Walking" (Brodner, Steve)
STONE, SHARON—PHOTOGRAPHS
PH15862 628 (April 16, 1992) p90. "Clothes Off, Heat On, Douglas Romances The Stone"
PH15863 644 (November 26, 1992) p78. "[Basic Instinct]"
PH15864 645-646 (December 10, 1992) p190. "Sharon Stone"
PH15865 649 (February 4, 1993) p72. "Homage Of Ripoff? In 'Body of Evidence,' Madonna And Dafoe (left) Share Stone And Douglas's Basic Instincts"
PH15866 659 (June 24, 1993) p88. "Lust: 'Sliver,' With William Baldwin And Sharon Stone"
PH15867 660-661 (July 8, 1993) p120. "Snow White And Stone (with Baldwin)"
PH15868 665 (September 16, 1993) p77. "Worst Actress"
PH15869 703 (March 9, 1995) p70. "Sharon Stone Takes Aim"
PH15870 723 (December 14, 1995) p90. "The Lady Gambles: Stone With The Dice; With Jealous Husband Robert De Niro; Gangster Lover Joe Pesci; And Director Martin Scorsese (from top)"
PH15871 732 (April 18, 1996) p78. "Stone And Adjani"
PH15872 735 (May 30, 1996) p56. "Jailbird"
PH15873 738-739 (July 11, 1996) p16. "Sharon Stone And Petty Look Related" (Charbonneau, Eric)
STONE, SHARON—PHOTOGRAPHS—PORTRAITS
PH15874 630 (May 14, 1992) pp42-43,46. "[Sharon Stone]" (Watson, Albert)
PH15875 630 (May 14, 1992) pp[cover]. "Starring Sharon Stone" (Watson, Albert)
PH15876 645-646 (December 10, 1992) pp[cover]. "1992 Yearbook" (Watson, Albert)
PH15877 676 (February 24, 1994) p62. "[Intersection]"
STONE, SLY—PHOTOGRAPHS
PH15878 649 (February 4, 1993) p51. "Rose Stone, Sly, Freddie Stone, Graham, Robinson, Errico And Martini Of Sly And The Family Stone"
PH15879 651 (March 4, 1993) p16. "Sly (center) And The Family Stone" (Granitz, Steve)
STORKRAFT—PHOTOGRAPHS
PH15880 669 (November 11, 1993) p18. "Germany Targets Storkraft (left),..."
THE STORY OF QIU JU (FILM)—PHOTOGRAPHS
PH15881 654 (April 15, 1993) p72. "Gong Li May Be The Biggest Star You've Never Heard Of"
STORY—PHOTOGRAPHS—PORTRAITS
PH15882 636 (August 6, 1992) p24. "Jennifer Kimball (left) And Jonatha Brooke" (Horner, Carl J.)
STOWE, MADELEINE—PHOTOGRAPHS
PH15883 675 (February 10, 1994) p52. "Cop Aidan Quinn Beds Angel Madeleine Stowe"
PH15884 678 (March 24, 1994) p104. "Two Babes And A Hunk: Davis (Angie); Stowe (China Moon); Grant (Four Weddings)"
STRADLIN, IZZY—ALBUMS
PH15885 645-646 (December 10, 1992) p179. "Izzy Stradlin And The Ju Ju Hounds"
STRADLIN, IZZY—PHOTOGRAPHS
PH15886 619-620 (December 12, 1991) p55. "Izzy Stradlin (left)" (Mazur, Kevin)
PH15887 634-635 (July 9, 1992) p11. "Yes, He Is: Izzy Stradlin In A Chicago Studio With Jah-T" (Natkin, Paul)
PH15888 642 (October 29, 1992) p26. "Happier Days: Izzy With Axl" (Funk, Harrison)
PH15889 644 (November 26, 1992) p13. "Izzy Stradlin Onstage In Chicago" (Natkin, Paul)
PH15890 663 (August 19, 1993) p27. "Izzy (left) Cuddles Up To Buddy Slash" (Kirkland, Greg)
STRADLIN, IZZY—PHOTOGRAPHS—PORTRAITS
PH15891 642 (October 29, 1992) p23. "[Izzy Stradlin]" (Ockenfels, Frank W.)
PH15892 645-646 (December 10, 1992) p93. "Stradlin And The Ju Ju Hounds Come Out From Under The Gunners' Shadow"
STRAIGHT UP (VIDEO)—PHOTOGRAPHS
PH15893 667 (October 14, 1993) p98. "Forever Your Girl: Paula Abdul's 'Straight Up' Video Tap-Dances Onto The List"
STRAITJACKET FITS—PHOTOGRAPHS
PH15894 615 (October 17, 1991) p28. "John Collie, Shayne Carter, Andrew Brough, David Wood (from left)" (Blakesberg, Jay)
STRANGE DAYS (FILM)—PHOTOGRAPHS
PH15895 719 (October 19, 1995) p158. "Kathryn Bigelow (left) Directs Bassett And Fiennes In A Brutal Parable"
A STRANGER AMONG US (FILM)—PHOTOGRAPHS
PH15896 636 (August 6, 1992) p65. "New York Cop Melanie Griffith Goes Undercover As A Hasidic Jew"
PH15897 639 (September 17, 1992) p102. "Worst Actress"
STRATHAIRN, DAVID—PHOTOGRAPHS
PH15898 693 (October 20, 1994) p156. "Woman Warrior Streep (above, with Reilly and Bacon) Braves The Rapids To Save Son Mazzello And Husband Strathairn (left)"
STRAW, SYD—PHOTOGRAPHS
PH15899 664 (September 2, 1993) p32. "Nick Cave With Syd Straw" (Mazur, Kevin)
STRAW, SYD—PHOTOGRAPHS—PORTRAITS
PH15900 734 (May 16, 1996) p25. "[Syd Straw]" (Elledge, Paul)
STRAWBERRY AND CHOCOLATE (FILM)—PHOTOGRAPHS
PH15901 701 (February 9, 1995) p63. "Perrugoria And Cruz Do The Forbidden"
STREEP, MERYL—ILLUSTRATIONS
PH15902 711 (June 29, 1995) p47. "Bridge Of Tides" (MacDonald, Ross)
STREEP, MERYL—PHOTOGRAPHS
PH15903 637 (August 20, 1992) p57. "Youth Seeking: Hawn (left) And Streep"
PH15904 677 (March 10, 1994) p60. "Streep And Close Play Ball (left), While Ryder And Her Lover, Banderas, Play Around"
PH15905 693 (October 20, 1994) p156. "Woman Warrior Streep (above, with Reilly and Bacon) Braves The Rapids To Save Son Mazzello And Husband Strathairn (left)"
PH15906 711 (June 29, 1995) p48. "New Romantic Triangle: Woman (Meryl Streep), man (Clint Eastwood) And Bridge"
PH15907 730 (March 21, 1996) p106. ""Before" (from left): Neeson, Furlong And Streep"
STREET FIGHTERS (FILM)—PHOTOGRAPHS
PH15908 701 (February 9, 1995) p63. "The Late Raul Julia"
STREISAND, BARBRA—ALBUMS
PH15909 663 (August 19, 1993) p92. "Back To Broadway"
STREISAND, BARBRA—PHOTOGRAPHS
PH15910 619-620 (December 12, 1991) p194. "Male Wimps And Female Warriors"
PH15911 621 (January 9, 1992) p55. "Streisand And Nick Nolte In Therapy"
PH15912 688 (August 11, 1994) p38. "People, People Who Need $16.6 Million: Barbra" (Mazur, Kevin)
PH15913 749 (December 12, 1996) p90. "Streisand: Bookworm Before; Bombshell After"
STREISAND, BARBRA—PHOTOGRAPHS—PORTRAITS
PH15914 743 (September 19, 1996) p88. "Divas"
STRENKERT, CHRIS—PHOTOGRAPHS
PH15915 750-751 (December 26, 1996) p80. "Father Chris Strenkert With His Extra-Large Baby, Zachary" (Davis, Clarence)
STRENKERT, ZACHARY—PHOTOGRAPHS
PH15915 750-751 (December 26, 1996) p80. "Father Chris Strenkert With His Extra-Large Baby, Zachary" (Davis, Clarence)

STRESS—ILLUSTRATIONS
PH15916 650 (February 18, 1993) p6. "Stress Relief" (Pendergrast, James T.)
STRICKLAND, KEITH—PHOTOGRAPHS
PH15917 637 (August 20, 1992) p11. "The B-52's (from left): Fred Schneider, Kate Pierson, Julee Cruise, Keith Strickland, Sue Hadjopoulos And Pat Irwin" (Michelson, Eric T.)
PH15918 683 (June 2, 1994) p27. "Below: Schneider, Kate Pierson, Keith Strickland" (Batzdorff, Rob)
STRICKLAND, MICHAEL—PHOTOGRAPHS
PH15919 704 (March 23, 1995) pp102-103. "Class of '95" (Tavee, Tom)
PH15920 704 (March 23, 1995) p102. "Onstage" (Tavee, Tom)
STRIGENS, DAMIEN—PHOTOGRAPHS
PH15921 689 (August 25, 1994) p24. "Pumpkins' Corgan Joins The Frogs' Damien Strigens And Jimmy Fleming" (Blakesberg, Jay)
STRIKES—PHOTOGRAPHS
PH15922 668 (October 28, 1993) p40. "Early Victims Of NAFTA? When Mexican Autoworkers Went On Strike, VW Smashed Their Union" (Rojas, Juan Carlos)
PH15923 668 (October 28, 1993) p41. "...Mexican Autoworkers Face The Same Fight Today" (Rojas, Juan Carlos)
PH15924 669 (November 11, 1993) p37. "Dry Wallers Picketing At A Construction Site During Their Strike Last Year" (Dimitrov, Slobodan)
STRINGER, HOWARD—PHOTOGRAPHS—PORTRAITS
PH15925 689 (August 25, 1994) p69. "Those Were The Days: CBS President Howard Stringer, QVC Chairman Barry Diller And CBS Chairman Larry Tisch, from left"
STRINGFELLOW, KEN—PHOTOGRAPHS
PH15926 658 (June 10, 1993) p17. "Auer, Chilton, Stephens And Stringfellow" (Perez, Marty)
PH15927 660-661 (July 8, 1993) p101. "The Posies (from left): Jon Auer, Dave Fox, Ken Stringfellow And Mike Musburger" (Natkin, Paul)
PH15928 710 (June 15, 1995) p40. "Posies Brian Young, Auer, Stringfellow, Joe Bass (from left)" (Moskowitz, Karen)
STRIPPERS—ILLUSTRATIONS
PH15929 740 (August 8, 1996) p14. "Exploitation" (Pendergrast, James T.)
STRIPTEASE (FILM)—PHOTOGRAPHS
PH15930 736 (June 13, 1996) p58. "Headaches"
PH15931 738-739 (July 11, 1996) p96. "A Cartoon Moore (left) In 'Hunchback'; In 'Striptease'"
PH15932 740 (August 8, 1996) p68. "'Independence Day,' Travolta In 'Phenomenon,' Schwarzenegger In 'Eraser,' Moore In 'Striptease'"
STRONG, SAMANTHA—PHOTOGRAPHS
PH15933 693 (October 20, 1994) p74. "Actress Samantha Strong Signing Autographs In Las Vegas"
STROWEIS, JACQUES—PHOTOGRAPHS
PH15934 688 (August 11, 1994) p58. "Digital Domain's Jacques Stroweis Checks Work In Progress" (Bruno, John)
PH15935 688 (August 11, 1994) p58. "Digital Domain's Jacques Stroweis Checks Work In Progress" (Legato, Rob)
STRUMMER, JOE—PHOTOGRAPHS
PH15936 618 (November 28, 1991) p12. "Mick Jones (left) And Joe Strummer" (Gruen, Bob)
PH15937 702 (February 23, 1995) p19. "Henry Rollins And Joe Strummer With Cash In L.A. (from left)" (Granitz, Steve)
PH15938 737 (June 27, 1996) p16. "Strummer (left) And Setzer"
STRUNG OUT—ALBUMS
PH15939 737 (June 27, 1996) p72. "Suburban Teenage Wasteland Blues"
STRUNK, RYAN—PHOTOGRAPHS—PORTRAITS
PH15940 652 (March 18, 1993) pp[enc.37]. "Ryan Strunk" (Seliger, Mark)
STRUYCKEN, CAREL—PHOTOGRAPHS
PH15941 618 (November 28, 1991) p53. "They're Altogether Ooky" (Seliger, Mark)
STUART, MARTY—ALBUMS
PH15942 640 (October 1, 1992) p69. "This One's Gonna Hurt You"
STUBBS, IMOGEN—PHOTOGRAPHS
PH15943 724-725 (December 28, 1995) p138. "Lee Directs Winslet, Thompson And Imogen Stubbs In 'Sense' (from left)"
PH15944 747 (November 14, 1996) p124. "Stubbs, In Drag, Deceives Stephens"
STUD, RON—PHOTOGRAPHS
PH15945 628 (April 16, 1992) p55. "DJ Alamo, Grand Puba Maxwell And Ron Stud (from left)" (Seliger, Mark)
STUDI, WES—PHOTOGRAPHS
PH15946 653 (April 1, 1993) p57. "Mohicans"
PH15947 672-673 (December 23, 1993) p174. "[Geronimo]"
STUDS (TELEVISION SHOW)—PHOTOGRAPHS
PH15948 618 (November 28, 1991) p106. "'Studs' Host Mark DeCarlo And Contestants: Men Who Date Women And The Women Who Trash Them"
PH15949 630 (May 14, 1992) p89. "[Studs]"
STULL, TONY—PHOTOGRAPHS
PH15950 685 (June 30, 1994) p40. "Etheridge With Kato, Tony Stull, Blackie Onassis And "Eddie" King Roeser (from left)" (Mazur, Kevin)
STYLER, TRUDY—PHOTOGRAPHS
PH15951 640 (October 1, 1992) p9. "Styler, Steed And Sting (from left)" (Aris, Brian)
PH15952 645-646 (December 10, 1992) p77. "[Sting & Trudy Styler]" (Phillips, George)
SUBDUDES—ALBUMS
PH15953 685 (June 30, 1994) p75. "Annunciation"
SUBLIME—PHOTOGRAPHS
PH15954 708 (May 18, 1995) p32. "Haunted By Their Past: Sublime" (Dunne, John)
SUBTERRANEAN HOMESICK BLUES (VIDEO)—PHOTOGRAPHS
PH15955 667 (October 14, 1993) p69. "Bob Dylan (With Allen Ginsberg At Left): You Don't Need A Weatherman"
SUDDENLY SUSAN (TELEVISION SHOW)—PHOTOGRAPHS
PH15956 743 (September 19, 1996) pp94,96. "[Television]"
PH15957 744 (October 3, 1996) p52. "Must-See Worthy? The Cast Of Shields' New Sitcom, 'Suddenly Susan'"
SUDDENLY, TAMMY!—ALBUMS
PH15958 712-713 (July 13, 1995) p108. "We Get There When We Do"
SUEDE—ALBUMS
PH15959 658 (June 10, 1993) p68. "Suede"
SUEDE—PHOTOGRAPHS
PH15960 657 (May 27, 1993) p15. "Ultra Suede: Gilbert, Anderson, Osman, Butler (from left)" (Broad, Julian)
PH15961 660-661 (July 8, 1993) p26. "Suede: Fall From Grace?" (Sheehan, Tom)
SUEDE—PHOTOGRAPHS—PORTRAITS
PH15962 672-673 (December 23, 1993) p27. "Below: Suede, Trans-Atlantic Hype Of The Year" (Rider, Paul)
SUGAR—ALBUMS
PH15963 642 (October 29, 1992) p71. "Copper Blue"
PH15964 644 (November 26, 1992) p84. "Copper Blue"
PH15965 700 (January 26, 1995) p56. "File Under Easy Listening"
SUGAR—PHOTOGRAPHS
PH15966 637 (August 20, 1992) p9. "Sugar (clockwise from left): Bob Mould, Malcolm Travis And David Barbe"
PH15967 672-673 (December 23, 1993) p30. "Sugar, Dressed Down" (Howell, Dan)
PH15968 694 (November 3, 1994) p73. "Barbe (left) And Mould, Athens, Ga. July 1992" (Double, Steve)
PH15969 694 (November 3, 1994) p71. "David Barbe, Malcolm Travis Ad Bob Mould (from left)" (Broad, Julian)
SUGAR BABYLON—PHOTOGRAPHS
PH15970 697 (December 15, 1994) p61. "[Sugar Babylon]"

SUGARCUBES—ALBUMS
PH15971 625 (March 5, 1992) p65. "Stick Around For Joy"
SUGARCUBES—PHOTOGRAPHS
PH15972 645-646 (December 10, 1992) p33. "The Joyous Sugarcubes" (Blakesberg, Jay)
SUGARPLASTIC—PHOTOGRAPHS
PH15973 732 (April 18, 1996) pp[enc.14-15]. "[The SUgarplastic]" (Witkin, Christian)
SUGGS, DONALD—PHOTOGRAPHS
PH15974 656 (May 13, 1993) p21. "American GLAAD-iator: Donald Suggs" (Del Sol, Michel)
SUI, ANNA—PHOTOGRAPHS—PORTRAITS
PH15975 656 (May 13, 1993) p73. "[Anna Sui]" (Afanador, Ruven)
PH15976 678 (March 24, 1994) p49. "Anna Sui" (Jensen, David)
SUICIDE—ILLUSTRATIONS
PH15977 748 (November 28, 1996) p22. "[Volcano]" (Pendergrast, James T.)
SUKIA—PHOTOGRAPHS
PH15978 747 (November 14, 1996) p52. "[Sukia]" (Ragel, Jon)
SULLIVAN, JOHN PATRICK—PHOTOGRAPHS
PH15979 662 (August 5, 1993) p14. "Cattle Call: 'It's Not The First Time My Art Has been Censored,' Said Scarification Buff John Patrick Sullivan (bottom), Whose Body-Branding Booth Was Quickly Shut Down..." (Blakes
SULT, MARCIA—PHOTOGRAPHS
PH15980 619-620 (December 12, 1991) p100. "Graham With Former Girlfriend Marcia Sult, Son David And Stepson Thomas Sult" (Regan, Ken)
SULT, THOMAS—PHOTOGRAPHS
PH15980 619-620 (December 12, 1991) p100. "Graham With Former Girlfriend Marcia Sult, Son David And Stepson Thomas Sult" (Regan, Ken)
SUMMER, DONNA—PHOTOGRAPHS—PORTRAITS
PH15981 692 (October 6, 1994) p52. "Donna Summer"
SUMMERALL, SHARON—PHOTOGRAPHS
PH15982 712-713 (July 13, 1995) p49. "Henley And Bride Summerall" (Dominguez, Miguel)
SUN-60—PHOTOGRAPHS—PORTRAITS
PH15983 631 (May 28, 1992) p22. "David Russo And Joan Jones" (Lewis, Robert)
SUNDQUIST, SCOTT—PHOTOGRAPHS
PH15984 684 (June 16, 1994) p50. "Cornell, Thayil, Sundquist, Yamamoto In Mid-'80s" (Peterson, Charles)
SUNG, KIM IL—PHOTOGRAPHS
PH15985 698-699 (December 29, 1994) p58. "Jimmy Carter Bonds With The Late Kim Il Sung"
SUNGLASSES—PHOTOGRAPHS
PH15986 660-661 (July 8, 1993) p30. "[John Lennon Ties And Sunglasses]" (Steele, Bill)
PH15987 686-687 (July 14, 1994) pp46-47. "[Toys]" (Grant, Bob)
SUPER DELUXE—PHOTOGRAPHS
PH15988 721 (November 16, 1995) p33. "John Kirsch, Braden Blake, Jake Nesheim And Chris Lockwood (from left)" (Moskowitz, Karen)
SUPER FURRY ANIMALS—ALBUMS
PH15989 745 (October 17, 1996) p132. "Fuzzy Logic"
SUPERCHUNK—ALBUMS
PH15990 628 (April 16, 1992) p84. "Tossing Seeds"
PH15991 654 (April 15, 1993) p61. "On The Mouth"
PH15992 684 (June 16, 1994) p109. "Foolish"
SUPERDRAG—PHOTOGRAPHS
PH15993 741 (August 22, 1996) p39. "From Knoxville To Buzz Bin" (Wong, Michael)
SUPERGRASS—ALBUMS
PH15994 714 (August 10, 1995) p58. "I Should Coco"
SUPERGRASS—PHOTOGRAPHS
PH15995 718 (October 5, 1995) pp[enc.26]. "At The Cricket House, University Park, Oxford" (GS, Jamil)
PH15996 718 (October 5, 1995) pp[enc.22]. "In The Living Room At Their House, In Oxford" (GS, Jamil)
PH15997 718 (October 5, 1995) pp[enc.20-21]. "In The Randolph Hotel Bar, Oxford" (GS, Jamil)
PH15998 718 (October 5, 1995) pp[enc.cover]. "Supergrass On A Guide Friday Tour Bus, Oxford, England" (GS, Jamil)
SUPERSONIC GUIDE (WORLD WIDE WEB)—ILLUSTRATIONS
PH15999 746 (October 31, 1996) p78. "Web Watch"
SUPERSUCKERS—PHOTOGRAPHS
PH16000 628 (April 16, 1992) p43. "The Supersuckers Onstage At RKCNDY" (Seliger, Mark)
PH16001 719 (October 19, 1995) p15. "Eddie Spaghetti And Dan Bolton Of The Supersuckers (top) And Cult Folkie Ani DiFranco Get Down At Seattle's Bumbershoot" (Doughty, Curt)
PH16002 721 (November 16, 1995) p25. "Nelson, Supersuckers Eddie Spaghetti And Dan Bolton (from left) Lend A Hand" (Roberts, Ebet)
PH16003 731 (April 4, 1996) p18. "Jennings (center) With Suckers, Dan Siegel, Dan Bolton, Ron Heathman And Singer Eddie Spaghetti (from left)" (Diamond, Rick)
SUPERTRAMP—ALBUMS
PH16004 617 (November 14, 1991) p119. "Breakfast In America" (Doud, Mike)
PH16005 617 (November 14, 1991) p119. "Breakfast In America" (Rapoport, Aaron)
SUPREME COURT—ALBUMS
PH16006 675 (February 10, 1994) p47. "Supreme Court Goes Electric"
SUPREME COURT OF THE UNITED STATES—ILLUSTRATIONS
PH16007 637 (August 20, 1992) p6. "Supreme Court Coatroom, Summer 1992" (Pendergrast, James T.)
PH16008 639 (September 17, 1992) p3. "The Bush Years: Supreme Cruelty" (Coe, Sue)
SUPREMES—PHOTOGRAPHS—PORTRAITS
PH16009 692 (October 6, 1994) p50. "Supremes"
SURFRIDER FOUNDATION (ORGANIZATION)—PHOTOGRAPHS
PH16010 659 (June 24, 1993) pp70-72,74. "[Surfrider Foundation]" (Hranek, Matthew)
PH16011 659 (June 24, 1993) pp70-72,74. "[Surfrider Foundation]" (Ockenfels, Frank W.)
SURVIVING PICASSO (FILM)—PHOTOGRAPHS
PH16012 744 (October 3, 1996) p78. "Hopkins As Picasso With Mistress McElhone"
SUTCLIFFE, STU—PHOTOGRAPHS
PH16013 720 (November 2, 1995) p49. "Stu Sutcliffe & Paul McCartney" (Kirchherr, Astrid)
PH16014 680 (April 21, 1994) p63. "Hamburg Days: George Harrison, Stuart Sutcliffe And John Lennon" (Kirchherr, Astrid)
SUTHERLAND, DONALD—PHOTOGRAPHS
PH16015 669 (November 11, 1993) p80. "Fright Sights (from left): 'Body Snatchers' 1956, 1978, 1993"
PH16016 672-673 (December 23, 1993) p174. "[Six Degrees Of Separation]"
SUTHERLAND, KIEFER—ILLUSTRATIONS
PH16017 670 (November 25, 1993) p124. "Disney's Toy Boys" (Kunz, Anita)
SUTHERLAND, KIEFER—PHOTOGRAPHS
PH16018 670 (November 25, 1993) p125. "Four Stooges: Sutherland, Sheen, O'Donnell, Platt (above)"
PH16019 685 (June 30, 1994) p81. "Urban Riders: Sutherland And Harrelson"
SVIGALS, ALICIA—PHOTOGRAPHS
PH16020 749 (December 12, 1996) p20. "BFF's Robert Sledge, Darren Jessee; Klezmatics Frank London, Alicia Svigals; And Folds" (Mazur, Kevin)
SWAGGART, JIMMY—ILLUSTRATIONS
PH16021 632 (June 11, 1992) pp164-165. "[Jimmy Swaggart]" (Drescher, Henrik)
SWANS—ALBUMS
PH16022 718 (October 5, 1995) p69. "The Great Annihilation"

SWANSON, GLORIA—PHOTOGRAPHS
PH16023 697 (December 15, 1994) p102. "Glenn Close Onstage Recalls Swanson In "Sunset Blvd.""
SWANSON, KRISTY—PHOTOGRAPHS
PH16024 637 (August 20, 1992) pp44-46. "[Kristy Swanson]" (Veysset, Frederique)
PH16025 638 (September 3, 1992) p75. "Luke Perry And Kristy Swanson Fight The Bloodsuckers"
PH16026 700 (January 26, 1995) p68. "Swanson, Connelly, Epps And Cube Tackle "Learning""
SWARNS, CHRISTINA—PHOTOGRAPHS
PH16027 719 (October 19, 1995) p133. "Attorney Christina Swarns Found The Right Mentor" (Toy, Joann)
SWAYZE, PATRICK—PHOTOGRAPHS
PH16028 629 (April 30, 1992) p65. "Patrick Swayze Does His Bit For The Poor"
PH16029 717 (September 21, 1995) p89. "Patrick Swayze, Wesley Snipes And John Leguizamo (from left) Hit The Road"
SWEAT, KEITH—ALBUMS
PH16030 621 (January 9, 1992) p51. "Keep It Comin'"
SWEDEN—ILLUSTRATIONS
PH16031 734 (May 16, 1996) p52. "[Sweden]" (Blitt, Barry)
PH16032 737 (June 27, 1996) p12. "Welcome To Sweden" (Pendergrast, James T.)
SWEENEY, JULIA—PHOTOGRAPHS
PH16033 691 (September 22, 1994) pp[enc.9-14]. "[Julia Sweeney]" (Scavullo, Francesco)
PH16034 691 (September 22, 1994) pp[enc.cover]. "Julie Sweeney As Pat" (Scavullo, Francesco)
PH16035 691 (September 22, 1994) pp[enc.5]. "Style 94" (Scavullo, Francesco)
PH16036 706 (April 20, 1995) p86. "The 'SNL' Legacy Of Screen Shame"
SWEENEY, JULIA—PHOTOGRAPHS—PORTRAITS
PH16037 691 (September 22, 1994) pp[enc.cover]. "Sweeney" (Scavullo, Francesco)
SWEET DREAMS (VIDEO)—PHOTOGRAPHS
PH16038 667 (October 14, 1993) p100. "Taking Care Of Business In 'Sweet Dreams'"
SWEET LULLABY (VIDEO)—PHOTOGRAPHS
PH16039 680 (April 21, 1994) p26. "Art View: A Recurring Video Image" (Gougenheim, Kim)
SWEET, KATRINA—PHOTOGRAPHS
PH16040 668 (October 28, 1993) p73. "At Cafe O'Lake" (Newton, Philip)
SWEET, MATTHEW—ALBUMS
PH16041 622 (January 23, 1992) p47. "Girlfriend"
PH16042 665 (September 16, 1993) p70. "Altered Beast"
PH16043 705 (April 6, 1995) p61. "100% Fun"
SWEET, MATTHEW—PHOTOGRAPHS
PH16044 626 (March 19, 1992) p11. "Robyn Hitchcock (left), Matthew Sweet" (Capak, R. J.)
PH16045 637 (August 20, 1992) pp44-45,47. "[Matthew Sweet]" (Veysset, Frederique)
PH16046 655 (April 29, 1993) p11. "From Left: A Bongo, Fleetwood, Keyboardist Nicky Hopkins And Sweet" (Di Santo, Annamaria)
PH16047 658 (June 10, 1993) p17. "Sweet And Williams" (Allen, Greg)
PH16048 663 (August 19, 1993) p25. "Sugar Fix: Matthew Sweet" (Settle, Ken)
PH16049 708 (May 18, 1995) p18. "Light And Sweet: Tad, Matthew" (Olson, Sheryl)
SWEET, MATTHEW—PHOTOGRAPHS—PORTRAITS
PH16050 618 (November 28, 1991) p33. "[Matthew Sweet]" (Ockenfels, Frank W.)
PH16051 672-673 (December 23, 1993) p54. "Sweet: Altered Beast" (Lenquette, Youri)
PH16052 695 (November 17, 1994) p49. "Matthew Sweet" (Snyder, Isabel)
SWERVEDRIVER—PHOTOGRAPHS
PH16053 625 (March 5, 1992) p27. "Jimmy Hartridge, Graham Bonnar, Adam Franklin, Adi Vynes (from left)" (Anker, Matt)
SWIFT, KEN—PHOTOGRAPHS
PH16054 638 (September 3, 1992) pp[enc.42]. "[Jossie Harris, Ken Swift, Richard Colon]" (Eccles, Andrew)
PH16055 638 (September 3, 1992) pp[enc.40]. "[Ken Swift]" (Eccles, Andrew)
SWINGERS (FILM)—PHOTOGRAPHS
PH16056 746 (October 31, 1996) p78. "Now Playing"
SWINTON, TILDA—PHOTOGRAPHS
PH16057 627 (April 2, 1992) p42. "Gay King Waddongton Nuzzles A Frustrated Swinton"
PH16058 659 (June 24, 1993) p89. "Orlando As He (above right), With Charlotte Valandrey"
PH16059 659 (June 24, 1993) p89. "Orlando As She (below) With Billy Zane"
SWISS, JO—PHOTOGRAPHS
PH16060 626 (March 19, 1992) p20. "God's Little Monkeys (from left): Dave Allen, Jo Swiss, Dave Wall, Jon Townend" (Byrne, Peter)
SWV
PH16061 672-673 (December 23, 1993) p151. "It's About Time"
SYLVIAN, DAVID—ALBUMS
PH16062 670 (November 25, 1993) p114. "The First Day"
SYMINGTON, SANDRA—PHOTOGRAPHS
PH16063 652 (March 18, 1993) pp[enc.37]. "Sandra Symington And Kari Stenmoe" (Seliger, Mark)

T

T REX—ALBUMS
PH16064 617 (November 14, 1991) p123. "The Slider" (Starr, Ringo)
TAFT, JOSH—PHOTOGRAPHS
PH16065 638 (September 3, 1992) p11. "Josh Taft, Paul Westerberg And Cameron Crowe (from left)" (Mercer, Lance)
TAG—PHOTOGRAPHS
PH16066 616 (October 31, 1991) p25. "The Leslie Spit Treeo (from left): Jack Nicholsen, Laura Hubert, Pat Langner And Tag" (Counts, Wyatt)
TAG TEAM—ALBUMS
PH16067 671 (December 9, 1993) p72. "Whoomp!" (.)
TAKAC, ROBBY—PHOTOGRAPHS
PH16068 723 (December 14, 1995) p36. "Hungry For Success And Searching For Dinner: Johnny Rzeznik, Robby Takac And Mike Malinin" (Ockenfels, Frank W.)
TAKE ANOTHER LITTLE PIECE OF MY HEART (BOOK)—PHOTOGRAPHS
PH16069 652 (March 18, 1993) p30. "[Twisted Sisters]"
TAKE ON ME (VIDEO)—PHOTOGRAPHS
PH16070 667 (October 14, 1993) p70. "A-Ha: Through The Looking Glass, To The Top"
TAKE THAT—PHOTOGRAPHS—PORTRAITS
PH16071 656 (May 13, 1993) p87. "[Take That]"
TAKE THAT—SINGLES
PH16072 720 (November 2, 1995) p70. "Back For Good (song)"
TALES FROM THE HOOD (FILM)—PHOTOGRAPHS
PH16073 710 (June 15, 1995) p86. "Tales from The Hood"
TALIEFERO, CRYSTAL—PHOTOGRAPHS
PH16074 636 (August 6, 1992) p15. "Springsteen Onstage With Band Member Crystal Taliefero" (Preston, Neal)
PH16075 639 (September 17, 1992) p20. "Springsteen With Taliefero" (Preston, Neal)
TALKING HEADS—ALBUMS
PH16076 617 (November 14, 1991) p128. "Fear Of Music" (Harrison, Jerry)

TALKING HEADS—PHOTOGRAPHS
PH16077 675 (February 10, 1994) p14. "Talking Heads Play Their First Show As A Foursome In 1977" (Godlis)
PH16078 720 (November 2, 1995) p50. "Talking Heads" (Goldis)
TALLENT, GARRY—PHOTOGRAPHS
PH16079 644 (November 26, 1992) p15. "Max Weinberg, Clarence Clemons, Darlene Love, Little Steven, Garry Tallent And Danny Federici (from left)" (Mazur, Kevin)
TAMBERELLI, DANNY—PHOTOGRAPHS—PORTRAITS
PH16080 697 (December 15, 1994) p20. "Little Pete (Danny Tamberelli) And Pop"
TAMBOR, JEFFREY—PHOTOGRAPHS
PH16081 690 (September 8, 1994) p68. "Sidekick Hank Kingsley (Jeffrey Tambor), Producer Arthur (Rip Torn) And Host Larry Sanders (Shandling)"
TANK GIRL (FILM)—PHOTOGRAPHS
PH16082 707 (May 4, 1995) p74. "Petty ('Tank')"
TANNER '88 (FILM)—PHOTOGRAPHS
PH16083 644 (November 26, 1992) p78. "[Tanner '88]"
TAPPAN, HEIDI—PHOTOGRAPHS
PH16084 691 (September 22, 1994) pp[enc.28]. "Heidi Tappan And Friend Doug Nedde At Sweetwaters, In Burlington, Vt." (Borris, Dan)
PH16085 691 (September 22, 1994) pp[enc.27]. "Heidi Tappan At Home In Vermont" (Borris, Dan)
PH16086 691 (September 22, 1994) pp[enc.cover]. "Heidi Tappan From Burton Snowboards" (Borris, Dan)
PH16087 691 (September 22, 1994) pp[enc.27]. "In The Burton Office With Co-Worker Susan Poersch" (Borris, Dan)
PH16088 691 (September 22, 1994) pp[enc.28]. "On Lake Champlain" (Borris, Dan)
TARANTINO, QUENTIN—ILLUSTRATIONS
PH16089 697 (December 15, 1994) p14. "Movie Blood" (Pendergrast, James T.)
PH16090 718 (October 5, 1995) p16. "Big Door-Petty Door" (Pendergrast, James T.)
PH16091 721 (November 16, 1995) p18. "Non-Pulp Fiction" (Pendergrast, James T.)
TARANTINO, QUENTIN—PHOTOGRAPHS
PH16092 692 (October 6, 1994) p80. "Tarantino Directs"
PH16093 694 (November 3, 1994) pp76-77. "[Quentin Tarantino]" (Winters, Dan)
PH16094 694 (November 3, 1994) p78. "Tarantino Kisses Travolta To Celebrate The "Pulp Fiction" Victory At Cannes" (Robert, Eric)
PH16095 708 (May 18, 1995) p98. "Tarantino As Destiny"
PH16096 728 (February 22, 1996) p70. "Now Playing"
TARANTINO, QUENTIN—PHOTOGRAPHS—PORTRAITS
PH16097 730 (March 21, 1996) p18. "Keep It In Your Pants: Tarantino (left) And Linklater" (Crawford, Michael)
TARANTULA (BOOK)—PHOTOGRAPHS
PH16098 679 (April 7, 1994) p29. "The Way We Were"
TAREE, AERLE—PHOTOGRAPHS
PH16099 647 (January 7, 1993) p13. "Arrested Development's Headliner, Taree, Eshe And Speech (from left): Talkin' About A Different Kind Of Nirvana" (States, Ann)
PH16100 648 (January 21, 1993) p9. "Arrested Development (from left): Speech, Aerle Taree, Headliner, Rasa Don, Baba Oje And Montsho Eshe" (Mazur, Kevin)
PH16101 657 (May 27, 1993) p17. "Arrested Development's Aerle taree, Headliner And Speech (from left)" (Arnold, Alice)
TAREE, AERLE—PHOTOGRAPHS—PORTRAITS
PH16102 634-635 (July 9, 1992) p20. "Arrested Development (from left): Headliner, Montsho Eshe, Aerle Taree, Rasa Don And Speech" (Lavine, Michael)
PH16103 634-635 (July 9, 1992) p20. "Love Battery (from left): Kevin Whitworth, Rod Rudzitis And Jason Finn" (Lavine, Michael)
TARSEM—PHOTOGRAPHS
PH16104 667 (October 14, 1993) p68. "Tarsem: From R.E.M. To TV Commercials?" (Andrade, Fatima)
TARSEM—PHOTOGRAPHS—PORTRAITS
PH16105 680 (April 21, 1994) p26. "Deep Forest's Sanchez And Mouquet And Director Tarsem (from left)" (Kuczala, John)
TATE, GEOFF—PHOTOGRAPHS
PH16106 615 (October 17, 1991) p14. "Queensryche's Geoff Tate, Billy Idol" (Mazur, Kevin)
PH16107 618 (November 28, 1991) p11. "Kirk Kammett, Slash, Lars Ulrich, Geoff Tate And Armored Saint Drummer Gonzo (from left)" (Blakesberg, Jay)
TATTERSALL, GALE—PHOTOGRAPHS
PH16108 618 (November 28, 1991) p58. "Mysterious And Spooky (from left): Rudin, Sonnenfeld And Tattersall" (Gordon, Melinda Sue)
TAUPIN, BERNIE—PHOTOGRAPHS
PH16109 618 (November 28, 1991) p12. "Bernie Taupin (left) And Elton John" (Mazur, Kevin)
PH16110 627 (April 2, 1992) p11. "The Wacky, Fun-Loving George Michael (left) With Jody Watley And Bernie Taupin" (Mazur, Kevin)
PH16111 677 (March 10, 1994) pp28-29. "John Salutes Longtime Colaborator Bernie Taupin" (Mazur, Kevin)
TAXES—ILLUSTRATIONS
PH16112 626 (March 19, 1992) p31. "In God We Trust, Liberty, 1992" (Cronin, Brian)
TAXI DRIVER (FILM)—PHOTOGRAPHS
PH16113 654 (April 15, 1993) p69. "Taxi Driver"
PH16114 742 (September 5, 1996) p68. "In 'Taxi Driver'"
TAYLOR, CHAD—PHOTOGRAPHS
PH16115 716 (September 7, 1995) p13. "Chad Taylor, Kowalezyk, Pat Dahlheimer (from left)" (Callahan, Kristin)
PH16116 726 (January 25, 1996) p35. "Dahlheimer, Taylor, Kowalczyk And Gracey (from left) At Their York, Pa., High School In 1989" (Broad, Julian)
TAYLOR, CHAD—PHOTOGRAPHS—PORTRAITS
PH16117 696 (December 1, 1994) p51. "Chad Taylor" (Fleischauer, Robert)
PH16118 726 (January 25, 1996) p34. "Taylor, Kowalczyk, Gracey And Dahlheimer (from left) In New York In Late 1995" (Broad, Julian)
TAYLOR, CHRIS—PHOTOGRAPHS
PH16119 718 (October 5, 1995) p61. "Chris Taylor The Month Before The Shooting" (Reynolds, George)
TAYLOR, COURTNEY—PHOTOGRAPHS
PH16120 721 (November 16, 1995) p78. "Peter Holmstrom, Courtney Taylor, Zia McCabe, Eric Hedford (from left): They're Exploding, Plastic And Inevitable, Andy Would Approve!" (Winters, Dan)
TAYLOR, DALLAS—PHOTOGRAPHS
PH16121 617 (November 14, 1991) p13. "Burton Averre, Dallas Taylor, Wilson And Was (from left)" (Preston, Neal)
TAYLOR, DEWEY—PHOTOGRAPHS
PH16122 629 (April 30, 1992) p50. "Joe Uehlein And Dewey Taylor Testifying In The Swiss Parliament, In Bern" (De Keyzer, Carl)
TAYLOR, ELIZABETH—PHOTOGRAPHS
PH16123 644 (November 26, 1992) p22. "Goldberg, Richie, Taylor, John, Michael And Hornsby (from left) At The Garden" (Mazur, Kevin)
PH16124 667 (October 14, 1993) p69. "Jackson: A video Taylor-ed To His Dreams"
TAYLOR, JAMES—ALBUMS
PH16125 666 (September 30, 1993) p101. "Live"
TAYLOR, JAMES—ILLUSTRATIONS—PORTRAITS
PH16126 641 (October 15, 1992) p91. "[James Taylor]" (Schwartz, Daniel)
TAYLOR, JAMES—PHOTOGRAPHS
PH16127 629 (April 30, 1992) p11. "Dress Rehearsal For The

Rain-Forest Benefit: Sting, John, Goldberg, Cole, Henley And Taylor (from left)" (Regan, Ken)
PH16128 645-646 (December 10, 1992) p96. "Taylor, Young And Elton John" (Blakesberg, Jay)
PH16129 682 (May 19, 1994) p37. "No Rap, No Hard Stuff: Taylor, Houston, Wynette, John, Sting (from left) At Rehearsal" (Mazur, Kevin)
PH16130 682 (May 19, 1994) p37. "Sting And Taylor" (Mazur, Kevin)
PH16131 688 (August 11, 1994) p18. "Garth And The Closest Thing To God, James Taylor" (Kravitz, Jeff)
PH16132 735 (May 30, 1996) p50. "Ross, Sting, Taylor And Williams (from left)" (Mazur, Kevin)
PH16133 750-751 (December 26, 1996) p57. "The Rainforest All-Star Supremes Tribute" (Mazur, Kevin)

TAYLOR, JAMES—PHOTOGRAPHS—PORTRAITS
PH16134 643 (November 12, 1992) p169. "James Taylor" (Ritts, Herb)
PH16135 736 (June 13, 1996) pp[cover]. "Rock & Roll Summer!" (Brucker, Andrew)

TAYLOR, JOHN—PHOTOGRAPHS
PH16136 653 (April 1, 1993) p20. "Nick Rhodes, Simon LeBon, John Taylor And Warren Cuccurullo (from left)" (Heungman)

TAYLOR, KOKO—ALBUMS
PH16137 676 (February 24, 1994) p56. "Force Of nature"

TAYLOR, LILI—ILLUSTRATIONS
PH16138 734 (May 16, 1996) p71. "Scum Manifesto" (Brodner, Steve)
PH16139 736 (June 13, 1996) p62. "Lili Taylor" (Cowles, David)

TAYLOR, LILI—PHOTOGRAPHS
PH16140 719 (October 19, 1995) p159. "Vampire Lili Taylor Stalks The Streets"
PH16141 734 (May 16, 1996) p72. "Lili Taylor"
PH16142 742 (September 5, 1996) p68. "Girls Taylor, Grace And Harris"
PH16143 743 (September 19, 1996) p90. "[Summer...]"

TAYLOR, LILI—PHOTOGRAPHS—PORTRAITS
PH16144 736 (June 13, 1996) p20. "Shy Lili Taylor"

TAYLOR, MALIK—PHOTOGRAPHS
PH16145 660-661 (July 8, 1993) p26. "Tribe's Malik 'Phife' Taylor, Ali Shaheed Muhammed And Jonathan 'Q-Tip' Davis (from left)" (Mazur, Kevin)

TAYLOR, MEL—PHOTOGRAPHS—PORTRAITS
PH16146 744 (October 3, 1996) p32. "[Mel Taylor]" (Knott, Phil)

TAYLOR, ROGER—PHOTOGRAPHS—PORTRAITS
PH16147 621 (January 9, 1992) p14. "Queen In The Mid-Seventies (from left): Deacon, Mercury, May And Taylor" (Rock, Mick)

TAYLOR, TIM—PHOTOGRAPHS—PORTRAITS
PH16148 733 (May 2, 1996) p26. "Killing Retro: Tim Taylor, Juan Monasterio, John Schmersal And Tyler Trent (from top)" (McGuire, Leeann)

TAYLOR, TRACY—PHOTOGRAPHS
PH16149 718 (October 5, 1995) p62. "A Bereaved Tracy Taylor Is Consoled As She Walks From Graveside Services For Her Husband Chris" (Gilstrap, Nancy)

TAZ—PHOTOGRAPHS
PH16150 685 (June 30, 1994) p41. "Heat's band Mates Taz And Jimbo; Jourgensen And Heat" (Bland, James)

TAZ—PHOTOGRAPHS—PORTRAITS
PH16151 692 (October 6, 1994) p28. "Country-Fried Rock: Taz, Jimbo And The Sultan Of Psychobilly, The Rev. Horton Heat" (Seliger, Mark)

TEAM DRESCH—PHOTOGRAPHS
PH16152 686-687 (July 14, 1994) p78. "[Team Dresch]" (Abeel, Neilson)

TEARS FOR FEARS—ALBUMS
PH16153 664 (September 2, 1993) p66. "Elemental"

TECHNOLOGY—ILLUSTRATIONS
PH16154 708 (May 18, 1995) p32. "Beep Pop" (Bishofs, Maris)
PH16155 727 (February 8, 1996) p55. "[CD-ROM Games]"

TECHNOLOGY—PHOTOGRAPHS
PH16156 619-620 (December 12, 1991) p197. "[Technology]" (Rosen, Jonathon)
PH16157 634-635 (July 9, 1992) pp122-123. "[Toys]" (Goldin, David)
PH16158 660-661 (July 8, 1993) p124. "Day Runner Personal Organizer And Texas Instruments Timerunner Electronic Organizer, $245" (Miller, Greg)
PH16159 660-661 (July 8, 1993) p124. "Franklin Electronics Digital Book Palm-Size Keyboard, $199, And Book Cards, $29 To 4129 Each" (Miller, Greg)
PH16160 660-661 (July 8, 1993) p123. "Motorola Bravo Express Pocket Pagers, $250 Each" (Miller, Greg)
PH16161 660-661 (July 8, 1993) p124. "Telecraft Pocket Faxxer Portable Fax Machine, $400" (Miller, Greg)
PH16162 664 (September 2, 1993) p73. "Leapfrog, $69.95" (Miller, Greg)
PH16163 668 (October 28, 1993) p91. "VCR Plus + With CallSet, $59.99" (Miller, Greg)
PH16164 697 (December 15, 1994) p107. "[Technology]" (Grant, Bob)
PH16165 700 (January 26, 1995) p70. "[Technology]"
PH16166 705 (April 6, 1995) p73. "[Technology]" (Grant, Bob)
PH16167 716 (September 7, 1995) p92. "[Communications Technology]" (Grant, Bob)
PH16168 720 (November 2, 1995) p81. "[Television Technology]" (Grant, Bob)
PH16169 736 (June 13, 1996) p64. "[Technology]" (Grant, Bob)
PH16170 741 (August 22, 1996) pp84-85. "[Hot Technology]" (Grant, Bob)
PH16171 743 (September 19, 1996) p99. "[Home, Movies]"
PH16172 745 (October 17, 1996) p147. "[Technology]" (Grant, Bob)
PH16173 748 (November 28, 1996) p112. "[Technology]"

TEEN MILK—ILLUSTRATIONS
PH16174 724-725 (December 28, 1995) p20. "The Milk Of Life" (Pendergrast, James T.)

TEENAGE FANCLUB—ALBUMS
PH16175 623 (February 6, 1992) p100. "Bandwagonesque"
PH16176 624 (February 20, 1992) p53. "Bandwagonesque"
PH16177 625 (March 5, 1992) p84. "Bandwagonesque"
PH16178 669 (November 11, 1993) p73. "Thirteen"

TEENAGE FANCLUB—PHOTOGRAPHS
PH16179 628 (April 16, 1992) p62. "Teenage Fanclub" (Lavine, Michael)
PH16180 630 (May 14, 1992) p50. "Guitarist Norman Blake, Bassist Gerry Love, Drummer Brendan O'Hare And Guitarist Raymond McGinley (from left)" (Broad, Julian)
PH16181 675 (February 10, 1994) p23. "Tony Bennett Meets His Teenage Fanclub"
PH16182 701 (February 9, 1995) p33. "Join The Club: Norman Blake, Raymond McGinley, Paul Quinn And Gerard Love (clockwise from top left)" (Dyer, Alison)

TEENAGE GANG DEBS (PUBLICATION)—PHOTOGRAPHS
PH16183 689 (August 25, 1994) p73. "[Teenage Gang Debs]"

TEENGENERATE—ALBUMS
PH16184 689 (August 25, 1994) p28. "Savage"

TEI, TOWA—PHOTOGRAPHS—PORTRAITS
PH16185 639 (September 17, 1992) p37. "Super DJ Dmitry Brill, Lady Kier Kirby And Towa 'Towa' Tei (clockwise from top left)" (Anderson, Patrick)

TEIS, MIKE—PHOTOGRAPHS
PH16186 707 (May 4, 1995) p20. "Icky Wail's Mike Teis, Pantera's Dimebag Darrell And Vinnie Paul (from left)" (Stone, John)

TEK—PHOTOGRAPHS—PORTRAITS
PH16187 686-687 (July 14, 1994) p73. "Straight Outta Brooklyn:

Tek And Steele" (Borris, Dan)
TELEGRAMS—PHOTOGRAPHS
PH16188 659 (June 24, 1993) p43. "The Vibranaires Lost A Competition On 'Arthur Godfrey's Talent Scouts,' And 5000 People Protested"
TELEPHONE—PHOTOGRAPHS
PH16189 682 (May 19, 1994) p58. "[Telephone]"
TELEPHONES—ILLUSTRATIONS
PH16190 741 (August 22, 1996) p72. "[A Tiny Cell Phone]" (Clarke, Greg)
TELEPHONES—PHOTOGRAPHS
PH16191 631 (May 28, 1992) p67. "Tickets To Ride: Autotalk TX, Pioneer PCC-700, Clarion CAL-1000" (Coleman, Gene)
PH16192 664 (September 2, 1993) p73. "Escourt 9000, $399" (Miller, Greg)
TELESCOPES—PHOTOGRAPHS
PH16193 634-635 (July 9, 1992) pp122-123. "[Toys]" (Goldin, David)
TELEVISION—ALBUMS
PH16194 642 (October 29, 1992) p70. "Television"
TELEVISION—ILLUSTRATIONS
PH16195 616 (October 31, 1991) p105. "[Television]" (Allen, Terry)
PH16196 619-620 (December 12, 1991) p197. "[Technology]" (Rosen, Jonathon)
PH16197 645-646 (December 10, 1992) p195. "The Year In Television" (Blechman, R. O.)
PH16198 658 (June 10, 1993) pp[enc.33]. "[Television]" (Allen, Terry)
PH16199 671 (December 9, 1993) p38. "America Confronts Its Problems"
PH16200 680 (April 21, 1994) p22. "[Music Television]" (Corio, Paul)
PH16201 708 (May 18, 1995) p17. "Public Access" (Friske, Maria)
PH16202 716 (September 7, 1995) p81. "[Television Shows]" (Fishman, Miriam)
PH16203 717 (September 21, 1995) p93. "[Television Shows]" (Fishman, Miriam)
PH16204 720 (November 2, 1995) p79. "[Talk Shows]" (Fishman, Miriam)
PH16205 727 (February 8, 1996) p53. "The New Shows: Fewer 'Friends' But Lots Of Old Familiar Faces" (Fishman, Miriam)
PH16206 732 (April 18, 1996) p81. "[Saturday Morning Television]" (Fishman, Miriam)
TELEVISION—PHOTOGRAPHS
PH16207 621 (January 9, 1992) p41. "NAD MR13A Television; Panasonic PV-S4167 Super VHS VCR; Kenwood LVD-700 Combi Player" (Gaz, Stab)
PH16208 636 (August 6, 1992) p68. "Set Design: The Twenty-Inch RCA F20706FT, $519" (Cubillo, Enrique)
PH16209 647 (January 7, 1993) p22. "Tom Verlaine, Richard Lloyd, Billy Ficca And Fred Smith (from left)" (Buck, Chris)
PH16210 664 (September 2, 1993) p73. "Pioneer SD-P5575, $3,999" (Miller, Greg)
PH16211 670 (November 25, 1993) p129. "Magnavox CCR095 9-Inch TVCR, $450" (Miller, Greg)
PH16212 680 (April 21, 1994) p96. "Pioneer 55-Inch Cinema-Wide"
PH16213 680 (April 21, 1994) p96. "Proscan 34-Inch Cinemascreen"
PH16214 686-687 (July 14, 1994) pp46-47. "[Toys]" (Grant, Bob)
PH16215 726 (January 25, 1996) p79. "[Technology]"
PH16216 730 (March 21, 1996) p111. "[Technology]" (Grant, Bob)
PH16217 743 (September 19, 1996) p99. "[Technology]" (Rosa And Rosa)
TELEVISION (1996)—ILLUSTRATIONS
PH16218 743 (September 19, 1996) p93. "[Television]" (Klingensmith, Milt)
TELEVISION PERSONALITIES—ALBUMS
PH16219 659 (June 24, 1993) p84. "Closer To God"
TEMPESTA, JOHN—PHOTOGRAPHS
PH16220 726 (January 25, 1996) p50. "White Zombie: J., Rob Zombie, John Tempesta And Sean Yseult (from left)" (Cuffaro, Chris)
TEMPLE, JOHNNY—PHOTOGRAPHS
PH16221 721 (November 16, 1995) p75. "Johnny Temple, Scott McCloud, Alexis Fleisig And Eli Janney (from left) Enjoy An All-American Snack" (Exum)
10,000 MANIACS—ALBUMS
PH16222 640 (October 1, 1992) p62. "Our Time In Eden"
PH16223 672-673 (December 23, 1993) p157. "MTV Unplugged"
10,000 MANIACS—PHOTOGRAPHS—PORTRAITS
PH16224 645-646 (December 10, 1992) p79. "10,000 Maniacs" (Halsband, Michael)
PH16225 652 (March 18, 1993) pp34-35. "Rob Buck, Dennis Drew, Natalie Merchant, Jerome Augustyniak, Steven Gustafson (from left)" (Ockenfels, Frank W.)
TENCH, BENMONT—PHOTOGRAPHS
PH16226 707 (May 4, 1995) p52. "Backstage With The Boss And The Band (below, from left): Steve Ferrone, Mike Campbell, Petty, Benmont Tench, Howie Epstein And Scott Thurston" (Seliger, Mark)
PH16227 750-751 (December 26, 1996) p88. "Producer Rick Rubin, Benmont Tench, Petty And Cash (from left) Work Their Magic"
TENNANT, NEIL—PHOTOGRAPHS—PORTRAITS
PH16228 651 (March 4, 1993) p28. "...Tennant And Lowe"
PH16229 671 (December 9, 1993) p22. "[Neil Tennant]" (Earl, Andy)
TENNESSEE (VIDEO)—PHOTOGRAPHS
PH16230 667 (October 14, 1993) p94. "Arrested Development: Speech Pursues A Dialogue With God In 'Tennessee'"
TENNILLE, TONI—PHOTOGRAPHS
PH16231 653 (April 1, 1993) p13. "Toni Tennille And Captain (background)" (Erbland, Peter)
TENUTA, JUDY—PHOTOGRAPHS
PH16232 616 (October 31, 1991) p54. "A Petite Howitzer, She Demurely Suggests To Potential Followers, "Worship Me, Pigs!" And They Do, For They Must" (Schiffman, Bonnie)
TERKUHLE, ABBY—PHOTOGRAPHS
PH16233 663 (August 19, 1993) p48. "Writer Tracy Grandstaff, Judge And MTV Exec Abby Terkuhle" (Ockenfels, Frank W.)
TERMINATOR 2 (FILM)—PHOTOGRAPHS
PH16234 619-620 (December 12, 1991) p194. "Male Wimps And Female Warriors"
TERMINATOR X—ILLUSTRATIONS
PH16235 690 (September 8, 1994) p78. "Terminator X" (Dunn, Carl)
TERMINATOR X—PHOTOGRAPHS
PH16236 676 (February 24, 1994) p25. "Whodini With Terminator X (seated)"
PH16237 685 (June 30, 1994) p30. "New "Mess Age": Flavor Flav, Chuck D And Terminator X (from front)" (Seliger, Mark)
TERRY, RANDALL—PHOTOGRAPHS
PH16238 667 (October 14, 1993) p62. "Left: Windle And Randall Terry Face Off In March, As Eleanor Smeal Looks On" (McGlothlin, Doug)
PH16239 710 (June 15, 1995) p64. "Terry" (Tuttle, Jeff)
TESH, JOHN—ILLUSTRATIONS
PH16240 738-739 (July 11, 1996) p101. "[John Tesh]" (Palma, Eric)
THA DOGG POUND—PHOTOGRAPHS
PH16241 720 (November 2, 1995) p32. "Demons Of The Week: Kurupt And Daz (from left)"
PH16242 728 (February 22, 1996) p64. "Daz (left) And Kurupt Of Tha Dogg Pound Pay Tribute" (Smith, Sean)

THAILAND—PHOTOGRAPHS
PH16243 618 (November 28, 1991) p65. "At 5:00 a.m., Near The End Of Another Long Night In Patpong, Some Locals Wait For Their Girlfriends, Who Work As Bar Girls" (Zachmann, Patrick)
PH16244 618 (November 28, 1991) p70. "Bangkok Prostitutes Await The Results Of HIV Tests For Their Health Identity Cards, Which Are Demanded By Some Bars" (Zachmann, Patrick)
PH16245 618 (November 28, 1991) p66. "A Bankok Streetwalker Reads A Pamphlet On AIDS Distributed By A Support Organization For Prostitutes, Empower" (Zachmann, Patrick)
PH16246 618 (November 28, 1991) p66. "A Health Worker Gives A Lesson In AIDS Prevention In A Red-Light District" (Zachmann, Patrick)
PH16247 618 (November 28, 1991) pp62-66,69-70. "In A Bangkok Hospital, An Eight-Month-Old Child Suffers From AIDS" (Zachmann, Patrick)
PH16248 618 (November 28, 1991) p65. "In A Bar In Pattaya, A Beach Resort, A Customer Tries To Examine A Possible Purchase" (Zachmann, Patrick)
PH16249 618 (November 28, 1991) p69. "Male Dancers Perform At A Bar In Patpong" (Zachmann, Patrick)
PH16250 618 (November 28, 1991) p69. "A Male Sex Worker Displays His Government Health Identity Card, Which Certifies He's Been Tested This Month For HIV" (Zachmann, Patrick)
PH16251 618 (November 28, 1991) p62. "The Red-Light District Of Patpong" (Zachmann, Patrick)
PH16252 618 (November 28, 1991) p64. "Some Children Are Sold Into Prostitution By Their Parents" (Zachmann, Patrick)
PH16253 618 (November 28, 1991) p63. "Streetwalkers In Another Of The City's Night-Life Sections" (Zachmann, Patrick)
PH16254 618 (November 28, 1991) pp62-66,69-70. "Two Addicts With AIDS Who Have Found Refuge In A Shelter In Bangkok" (Zachmann, Patrick)
PH16255 618 (November 28, 1991) p64. "Where East Meets West: A Bar Girl Encourages A Client" (Zachmann, Patrick)
THAT NIGHT (FILM)—PHOTOGRAPHS
PH16256 663 (August 19, 1993) p83. "Juliette Lewis Prepares For The Big Night"
THAT THING YOU DO (FILM)—PHOTOGRAPHS
PH16257 743 (September 19, 1996) p88. "The Young And The Restless"
PH16258 745 (October 17, 1996) p142. "Live Tyler Looks On"
THATCHER, MARGARET—PHOTOGRAPHS
PH16259 689 (August 25, 1994) p52. "The Man Who Helped Topple The Iron Curtain Visits The Iron Lady: Gorbachev With Lady Thatcher Late Last Year"
THAT'S ENTERTAINMENT! III (FILM)—PHOTOGRAPHS
PH16260 682 (May 19, 1994) p108. "MTV-Ready Lucille Ball Cracks The Whip"
THAYIL, KIM—ILLUSTRATIONS
PH16261 681 (May 5, 1994) p60. "Soundgardener: Kim Thayil" (Brown, Calef)
PH16262 736 (June 13, 1996) p47. "Kim Thayil" (Cowles, David)
THAYIL, KIM—PHOTOGRAPHS
PH16263 621 (January 9, 1992) p11. "Ben Shepherd, Kim Thayil, Chris Cornell And Matt Cameron (from left)"
PH16264 674 (January 27, 1994) p17. "Cameron, Shepherd, Cornell, Thayil (from left)" (Westenberg, Kevin)
PH16265 684 (June 16, 1994) p52. "Cameron, Thayil, Yamamoto, Cornell, Silver, Tour Manager Eric Johnson (from left) In 1988" (Peterson, Charles)
PH16266 684 (June 16, 1994) p50. "Cornell, Thayil, Sundquist, Yamamoto In Mid-'80s" (Peterson, Charles)
PH16267 684 (June 16, 1994) p50. "Ditto Tavern, '86: Thayil And Cornell" (Peterson, Charles)
PH16268 684 (June 16, 1994) p49. "Sit 'N' Spin: Cameron, Shepherd, Thayil And Cornell (from left) In Seattle" (Seliger, Mark)
PH16269 695 (November 17, 1994) p131. "Soundgarden" (Seliger, Mark)
PH16270 698-699 (December 29, 1994) p106. "From Sub Pop To Superstardom: Kim Thayil, Cornell, Ben Shepherd And Matt Cameron (from left)" (Seliger, Mark)
PH16271 717 (September 21, 1995) p34. "Kim Thayil At The July Session" (Peterson, Charles)
PH16272 727 (February 8, 1996) p26. "Soundgarden's Chris Cornell, Kim Thayil, Ben Shepherd And Matt Cameron (from left) In Seattle's Studio Litho" (Westenberg, Kevin)
PH16273 737 (June 27, 1996) p56. "Soundgarden's Cornell, Ben Shepherd, Thayil And Matt Cameron (from left)"
THAYIL, KIM—PHOTOGRAPHS—PORTRAITS
PH16274 634-635 (July 9, 1992) p45. "[Soundgarden]" (Seliger, Mark)
PH16275 677 (March 10, 1994) p16. "Kim Thayil And Breeder Kelley Deal" (Mott, Tony)
THE THE—ALBUMS
PH16276 649 (February 4, 1993) p66. "Dusk"
THELMA & LOUISE (FILM)—PHOTOGRAPHS
PH16277 619-620 (December 12, 1991) p194. "Male Wimps And Female Warriors"
PH16278 623 (February 6, 1992) p90. "Susan Sarandon (left) And Geena Davis Get Even"
PH16279 696 (December 1, 1994) p96. "Pitt Has Dated "Thelma And Louise" Co-Star Davis (top) And "Kalifornia" Girl Lewis (below)"
THEO—PHOTOGRAPHS
PH16280 728 (February 22, 1996) p20. "Once I Had A Love, And It Was A Gas: Theo At Don Hill's" (Papas, B. J.)
THERAPY?—ALBUMS
PH16281 727 (February 8, 1996) p50. "Infernal Love"
THERAPY?—PHOTOGRAPHS—PORTRAITS
PH16282 654 (April 15, 1993) p21. "In Need Of Therapy?: Fyfe Ewing, Michael McKeegan And Andy Cairns (from left)" (Gullick, Steve)
THERMADORE—PHOTOGRAPHS
PH16283 737 (June 27, 1996) p28. "Smokin' In The Living Room" (Dyer, Alison)
THERON, CHARLIZE—PHOTOGRAPHS
PH16284 745 (October 17, 1996) p142. "Now Playing"
THESE IMMORTAL SOULS—ALBUMS
PH16285 657 (May 27, 1993) p52. "I'm Never Gonna Die Again"
THEWLIS, DAVID—PHOTOGRAPHS
PH16286 674 (January 27, 1994) p48. "Acting Vehicles Include 'The Pelican Brief,' 'In The Name Of The Father,' 'What's Eating Gilbert Grape,' 'Shadowlands,' 'Naked,' And 'Grumpy Old Men'"
PH16287 678 (March 24, 1994) p100. "Missing In Oscar Action"
THEY MIGHT BE CALLED GIANTS—ALBUMS
PH16288 629 (April 30, 1992) p57. "Apollo 18"
THIELE, BOB—PHOTOGRAPHS
PH16289 730 (March 21, 1996) p26. "[Bob Thiele]"
THINGS TO DO IN DENVER WHEN YOU'RE DEAD (FILM)—PHOTOGRAPHS
PH16290 719 (October 19, 1995) p158. "Andy Garcia Sweet-Talks Gabrielle Anwar Into Danger"
THINNER (FILM)—PHOTOGRAPHS
PH16291 748 (November 28, 1996) p143. "Dead On Arrival"
13 ENGINES—PHOTOGRAPHS
PH16292 676 (February 24, 1994) p28. "John Critchley (left) And 13 Engines" (Sigusmondi, Floris)
13TH FLOOR ELEVATORS—PHOTOGRAPHS
PH16293 706 (April 20, 1995) p23. "Spaced Rangers: Erickson (center) With The Elevators Onstage In 1966" (Simmons, Bob)
THIS BOY'S LIFE (FILM)—PHOTOGRAPHS
PH16294 654 (April 15, 1993) p69. "Pick The Psycho: De Niro, Dushku, Barkin Or DiCaprio?"

PH16295 742 (September 5, 1996) p68. "With Dicaprio In 'This Boy's Life'"
THIS IS MY LIFE (FILM)—ILLUSTRATIONS
PH16296 625 (March 5, 1992) p75. "A Sundance Spotlight On Women" (Risko, Robert)
THIS IS MY LIFE (FILM)—PHOTOGRAPHS
PH16297 625 (March 5, 1992) p76. "Hoffman, Kavner And Mathis Turn Trauma Into Laughter"
THIS NOTE'S FOR YOU (VIDEO)—PHOTOGRAPHS
PH16298 667 (October 14, 1993) p68. "This Caption's For Neil: Young's Video Got MTV Mad"
THOMAS, CLARENCE—ILLUSTRATIONS
PH16299 630 (May 14, 1992) p89. "[Yale]" (Cowles, David)
THOMAS, CLARENCE—PHOTOGRAPHS
PH16300 619-620 (December 12, 1991) p201. "American Gladiators: Judge Clarence Thomas Steps Into The Arena And Wins By Hair"
THOMAS, IRMA—PHOTOGRAPHS
PH16301 681 (May 5, 1994) p15. "Ben E. King And Irma Thomas Are Besides Themselves" (Micelotta, Frank)
PH16302 681 (May 5, 1994) p15. "Ben E. King And Irma Thomas Are Besides Themselves"
THOMAS, JAQUELINE—PHOTOGRAPHS
PH16303 651 (March 4, 1993) p23. "Michael Thomas, Jaqueline Thomas, Paul Cassidy, Elvis Costello, Don Belton" (Westenberg, Kevin)
THOMAS, LEONARD—PHOTOGRAPHS
PH16304 732 (April 18, 1996) p78. "Leonard Thomas And Randle Fulfill A Blaxploitation Fantasy"
THOMAS, MICHAEL—PHOTOGRAPHS
PH16305 651 (March 4, 1993) p23. "Michael Thomas, Jaqueline Thomas, Paul Cassidy, Elvis Costello, Don Belton" (Westenberg, Kevin)
THOMAS, ROZONDA—PHOTOGRAPHS
PH16306 631 (May 28, 1992) p22. "TLC (clockwise from top): T-Boz, Chilli, Left Eye" (Cuffaro, Chris)
THOMAS, ROZONDA—PHOTOGRAPHS—PORTRAITS
PH16307 715 (August 24, 1995) p27. "'Left Eye' Lopes, 'T-Boz' Watkins And 'Chilli' Thomas (from left)" (White, Steve)
PH16308 715 (August 24, 1995) p28. "The Younger, Wilder TLC: Watkins, Lopes And Thomas In 1992 (from left)" (Green, Adrian)
THOMAS, SCOTT—PHOTOGRAPHS
PH16309 680 (April 21, 1994) p38. "In '86, Democrat Scott Thomas Inherited The Commission's AFL-CIO Seat"
THOMPSON, DENNIS—PHOTOGRAPHS
PH16310 632 (June 11, 1992) p36. "MC5 (clockwise from top left): Thompson, Tyner, Kramer, Smith"
PH16311 708 (May 18, 1995) p30. "MC5: Michael Davis, Dennis Thompson, Kramer, Smith, Tyner (from left)"
THOMPSON, EMMA—PHOTOGRAPHS
PH16312 627 (April 2, 1992) p41. "Hopkins And Thompson Battle For Home And England"
PH16313 657 (May 27, 1993) p56. "Awry: Washington, Branagh, Thompson"
PH16314 670 (November 25, 1993) p125. "Love Unspoken: Anthony Hopkins And Emma Thompson"
PH16315 724-725 (December 28, 1995) p138. "Lee Directs Winslet, Thompson And Imogen Stubbs In 'Sense' (from left)"
PH16316 731 (April 4, 1996) p66. "'Sense And Sensibility,' With Thompson And Kate Winslet"
THOMPSON, HUNTER S.—ILLUSTRATIONS
PH16317 622 (January 23, 1992) pp22-25,27-28. "[Hunter S. Thompson]" (Steadman, Ralph)
PH16318 622 (January 23, 1992) pp[cover]. "Hunter Thompson: Fear And Loathing In Elko" (Steadman, Ralph)
PH16319 632 (June 11, 1992) p45. "[Hunter S. Thompson]" (Steadman, Ralph)
PH16320 645-646 (December 10, 1992) pp[cover]. "1992 Yearbook" (Steadman, Ralph)
PH16321 701 (February 9, 1995) p14. "Rolling Stone" (Pendergrast, James T.)
PH16322 748 (November 28, 1996) pp65,67,70-71+. "[Hunter S. Thompson]" (Steadman, Ralph)
THOMPSON, HUNTER S.—ILLUSTRATIONS—LETTERING
PH16323 622 (January 23, 1992) pp22-24,26,29. "[Hunter S. Thompson]" (Ortiz-Lopez, Dennis)
THOMPSON, HUNTER S.—PHOTOGRAPHS
PH16324 632 (June 11, 1992) p48. "Dr. Thompson Passes His Sobriety Test At The Big Sur Editorial Conference, In 1971"
PH16325 632 (June 11, 1992) p62. "Staff Members And Contributing Writers At The 1971 Editorial Conference, At Esalen, In Big Sur" (Leibovitz, Annie)
PH16326 639 (September 17, 1992) p42. "At The Table (from left): Greider, O'Rourke, Wenner, Thompson And Clinton" (Seliger, Mark)
PH16327 639 (September 17, 1992) p55. "Dr. Thompson Ponders Clinton's Call For More Cops In The Street" (Seliger, Mark)
PH16328 647 (January 7, 1993) p11. "Dr. Hunter S. Thompson (left) And Jason Priestley" (Elgar, Nick)
PH16329 647 (January 7, 1993) p11. "RS Alumni Photog Annie Leibovitz, Thompson, David Felton, Cameron Crowe, Chris Hodenfield, Ben Fong-Torres, Paul Scanlon (from left)" (Elgar, Nick)
PH16330 747 (November 14, 1996) p25. "Hunter Thompson (right) Flogs A Blow-Up Doll As Johnny Depp Takes In The Good Doctor's, Er, Lecture" (Kravitz, Jeff)
THOMPSON, LINDA—ALBUMS
PH16331 740 (August 8, 1996) p58. "Dreams Fly Away"
THOMPSON, LISA—PHOTOGRAPHS—PORTRAITS
PH16332 656 (May 13, 1993) p94. "Deidre Lang, Jennifer Lopez, Twist, Jossie Harris, Lisa Thompson (from left)"
PH16333 656 (May 13, 1993) p98. "Left Thompson, Right Lang"
THOMPSON, PORL—PHOTOGRAPHS
PH16334 631 (May 28, 1992) p11. "Simon Gallup, Porl Thompson, Perry Bamonte, Robert Smith, Boris Williams (from left)" (Cox, Paul)
THOMPSON, RICHARD—ALBUMS
PH16335 657 (May 27, 1993) p48. "Watching The Dark"
PH16336 678 (March 24, 1994) p96. "Mirror Blue"
PH16337 679 (April 7, 1994) p88. "Mirror Blue"
PH16338 732 (April 18, 1996) p73. "You? Me? Us?"
THOMPSON, RICHARD—ILLUSTRATIONS—PORTRAITS
PH16339 657 (May 27, 1993) p48. "Watch The Dark, See The Light" (Smith, Owen)
THOMPSON, RICHARD—PHOTOGRAPHS
PH16340 630 (May 14, 1992) p13. "David Byrne, Richard Thompson And John Cale (from left) After The Saint Ann Show" (Vartoogian, Jack)
PH16341 662 (August 5, 1993) p34. "Finn (left) With Thompson" (Roth, Greg)
PH16342 691 (September 22, 1994) p21. "Ric Sanders, Simon Nicol And Richard Thompson (from left)" (Robicheau, Paul)
PH16343 745 (October 17, 1996) p46. "[Richard Thompson]" (Wilson, Michael)
THOMPSON, RICHARD—PHOTOGRAPHS—PORTRAITS
PH16344 682 (May 19, 1994) p28. "[Richard Thompson]" (Sanders, Peter)
THOMPSON, SCOTT—PHOTOGRAPHS—PORTRAITS
PH16345 733 (May 2, 1996) p62. "Kids Foley, McKinney, McCulloch, McDonald And Thompson"
THOMSON, JASON—PHOTOGRAPHS
PH16346 652 (March 18, 1993) pp[enc.37]. "Jason Thomson" (Seliger, Mark)
THOMSON, KRISTIN—PHOTOGRAPHS
PH16347 696 (December 1, 1994) p32. "Thomson, John Pamer, Toomey And Andrew Webster" (Owen, Tim)
THORN, CHRISTOPHER—PHOTOGRAPHS
PH16348 639 (September 17, 1992) p20. "Shannon Hoon, Christopher Thorn, Glen Graham, Brad Smith And Rogers

Stevens (clockwise from top left)" (Clinch, Danny)
PH16349 640 (October 1, 1992) p27. "Blind Melon (from left): Smith, Stevens, Thorn, Hoon And Graham" (Clinch, Danny)
PH16350 669 (November 11, 1993) pp38-39. "Brad Smith, Glen Graham, Shannon Hood, Rogers Stevens & Christopher Thorn (from left)" (Seliger, Mark)
THORN, EMILY—PHOTOGRAPHS
PH16351 666 (September 30, 1993) p55. "Thorn At Work: Don't Ask For A Mange Latte" (Krenz, Scott)
THORN, TRACEY—ILLUSTRATIONS
PH16352 738-739 (July 11, 1996) p7. "Everything But The Girl's Ben Watt And Tracey Thorn" (Risko, Robert)
THORN, TRACEY—PHOTOGRAPHS
PH16353 738-739 (July 11, 1996) p22. "Watt And Thorn: Their Relationship Survived His Illness, And Their Music Thrived" (Alston, Kwaku)
THORNE-SMITH, COURTNEY—PHOTOGRAPHS
PH16354 682 (May 19, 1994) p52. "Good Girl Thorne-Smith Deals With Fame, But Billy Misses Alison" (Seliger, Mark)
PH16355 682 (May 19, 1994) pp48-49. "[Melrose Place]" (Seliger, Mark)
PH16356 682 (May 19, 1994) pp[cover]. "Melrose Place's Bod Squad" (Seliger, Mark)
THORPE, SUZANNE—PHOTOGRAPHS
PH16357 664 (September 2, 1993) p24. "They're All Revved Up: Donahue, Thorpe, Baker, Chambers, Fridmann And Grasshopper (from left)" (Gullick, Steve)
THORTON, BILLY BOB—PHOTOGRAPHS
PH16358 749 (December 12, 1996) p90. "Now Playing"
THORTON, BONNIE—PHOTOGRAPHS
PH16359 718 (October 5, 1995) pp[enc.13]. "Posey With Friends In Den Of Thieves, In New York" (Seliger, Mark)
THREADGILL, HENRY—ALBUMS
PH16360 706 (April 20, 1995) p74. "Carry The Day"
3 (FILM)—PHOTOGRAPHS
PH16361 680 (April 21, 1994) p93. "Smith Gives Cop Nielsen Double Trouble"
311—PHOTOGRAPHS
PH16362 720 (November 2, 1995) p16. "Feel The Heat: 311 Raise Cash In Kansas For Needy Kids" (Stump, Jeff)
PH16363 743 (September 19, 1996) p37. "311's Mahoney, Martinez, Hexum, P-Nut And Sexton" (Dyer, Alison)
THE THREE MUSKETEERS (FILM)—ILLUSTRATIONS
PH16364 670 (November 25, 1993) p124. "Disney's Toy Boys" (Kunz, Anita)
THE THREE MUSKETEERS (FILM)—PHOTOGRAPHS
PH16365 670 (November 25, 1993) p125. "De Mornay Seduces Guppy O'Donnell (below)"
PH16366 670 (November 25, 1993) p125. "Four Stooges: Sutherland, Sheen, O'Donnell, Platt (above)"
THREE OF HEARTS (FILM)—PHOTOGRAPHS
PH16367 657 (May 27, 1993) p58. "Gay: Lovers Kelly Lynch And Sherilyn Fenn Before The Fall"
3-D—PHOTOGRAPHS
PH16368 616 (October 31, 1991) p25. "Massive Attack (from left): 3-D, Mushroom And Daddy G"
THREESOME (FILM)—PHOTOGRAPHS
PH16369 680 (April 21, 1994) p93. "Student Union For Charles, Boyle And Baldwin"
THROWING MUSES—ALBUMS
PH16370 702 (February 23, 1995) p72. "University"
PH16371 741 (August 22, 1996) p96. "Limbo"
THROWING MUSES—PHOTOGRAPHS
PH16372 703 (March 9, 1995) p54. "Giving In To The Muses: Drummer David Narcizo, Hersh And Bassist Bernard Georges (from left)" (Seliger, Mark)
PH16373 703 (March 9, 1995) p55. "The Throwing Muses Lineup In 1989 (from left): Hersh, Leslie Langston, Tanya Donelly And Narcizo" (Musto, Ilpo)
PH16374 706 (April 20, 1995) p50. "Throwing Muses Circa 1988" (Pyke, Steve)
PH16375 707 (May 4, 1995) p36. "Georges (left) And Hersh Throw Down" (Blakesberg, Jay)
THUNDER, SHELLY—PHOTOGRAPHS
PH16376 676 (February 24, 1994) p44. "Dance Hall's Shelly Thunder"
THUNDERS, JOHNNY—PHOTOGRAPHS
PH16377 619-620 (December 12, 1991) p109. "Johnny Thunders" (Gruen, Bob)
THUNDERS, JOHNNY—PHOTOGRAPHS—PORTRAITS
PH16378 735 (May 30, 1996) p3. "[The Faces Of Heroin]"
THURMAN, UMA—ILLUSTRATIONS
PH16379 692 (October 6, 1994) p79. "Tarantino's Twist" (Todd, Mark)
THURMAN, UMA—PHOTOGRAPHS
PH16380 652 (March 18, 1993) pp[enc.4]. "[Jennifer 8]"
PH16381 669 (November 11, 1993) pp58-59. "[Uma Thurman]" (Markus, Kurt)
PH16382 669 (November 11, 1993) p60. "'Uma Was Always Sissy Hankshaw To Me,' Says 'Cowgirls' Director Gus Van Sant" (Markus, Kurt)
PH16383 682 (May 19, 1994) p107. "Now Playing"
PH16384 692 (October 6, 1994) p80. "Thurman And Travolta Twist"
PH16385 696 (December 1, 1994) p25. "Ms. Aykroyd (Donna Dixon), Eric Clapton, Uma Thurman And Dan Aykroyd (from left)" (Allen, David)
PH16386 698-699 (December 29, 1994) p194. "Thurman And Travolta Twist In "Pulp""
PH16387 734 (May 16, 1996) p74. "Chaplin, Thurman And Garofalo In Love"
THURMAN, UMA—PHOTOGRAPHS—PORTRAITS
PH16388 669 (November 11, 1993) p58. "[Uma Thurman]" (Markus, Kurt)
THURSTON, SCOTT—PHOTOGRAPHS
PH16389 707 (May 4, 1995) p52. "Backstage With The Boss And The Band (below, from left): Steve Ferrone, Mike Campbell, Petty, Benmont Tench, Howie Epstein And Scott Thurston" (Seliger, Mark)
TIBBETTS, STEVE—ALBUMS
PH16390 692 (October 6, 1994) p87. "The Fall Of Us All"
TIBET—ILLUSTRATIONS
PH16391 743 (September 19, 1996) p12. "Entering Tibet" (Pendergrast, James T.)
TIBETAN FREEDOM CONCERT—PHOTOGRAPHS
PH16392 740 (August 8, 1996) p20. "Praying Buddhist Monks...Crowd Surfers" (Blakesberg, Jay)
TICKETMASTER (COMPANY)—ILLUSTRATIONS
PH16393 691 (September 22, 1994) p14. "Welcome!" (Pendergrast, James T.)
PH16394 692 (October 6, 1994) p12. "Eye Drops" (Pendergrast, James T.)
PH16395 728 (February 22, 1996) p16. "Ticketmaster-Pearl Jam" (Pendergrast, James T.)
TIE-DYED (FILM)—PHOTOGRAPHS
PH16396 718 (October 5, 1995) p79. "Now Playing"
TIES—PHOTOGRAPHS
PH16397 637 (August 20, 1992) p11. "Jerry's Kids"
PH16398 660-661 (July 8, 1993) p30. "[John Lennon Ties And Sunglasses]" (Steele, Bill)
TIGER—ALBUMS
PH16399 666 (September 30, 1993) p104. "Claws Of The Cat"
TIGRETT, ISAAC—PHOTOGRAPHS
PH16400 617 (November 14, 1991) p18. "Isaac Tigrett At Home (below)" (Little, Blake)
TIGRETT, MAUREEN COX STARKEY—PHOTOGRAPHS—PORTRAITS
PH16401 701 (February 9, 1995) p24. "On Their Wedding Day: Starr, Cox" (Freeman, Robert)

TIL, SONNY—PHOTOGRAPHS
PH16402 659 (June 24, 1993) p43. "Chessler, Til (on her right) And The Orioles After A Show In 1952, No Longer Penniless"
TIL, SONNY—PHOTOGRAPHS—PORTRAITS
PH16403 659 (June 24, 1993) p48. "The Orioles: Sonny Til, Johnny Reed, Tommy Gaither, George Nelson And Alexander Sharp"
TILLOTSON, TIM—PHOTOGRAPHS
PH16404 704 (March 23, 1995) p81. "Tim 'The Condom Man' Tillotson Of The University Of Wisconsin-Madison: 'Learning How To Have Good Sex With A Condom Is A Skill Like Riding A Bike'" (Kuehn, Karen)
TILLY, JENNIFER—PHOTOGRAPHS
PH16405 694 (November 3, 1994) p104. "Palminteri Runs With No-Talent Boss Tilly"
PH16406 745 (October 17, 1996) p142. "Now Playing"
TIMBUK 3—ALBUMS
PH16407 617 (November 14, 1991) p177. "Big Shot In The Dark"
TIME (PUBLICATION)—PHOTOGRAPHS
PH16408 670 (November 25, 1993) p48. "[Newsweek, Time]"
TIME COP (FILM)—PHOTOGRAPHS
PH16409 692 (October 6, 1994) p81. "Van Damme Aims A Lethal Kick At Assassin James Lew"
A TIME TO KILL (FILM)—PHOTOGRAPHS
PH16410 736 (June 13, 1996) p58. "Oscar Seekers"
PH16411 740 (August 8, 1996) p68. "McConaughey, Bullock, Schumacher (from left) Kill Time"
PH16412 741 (August 22, 1996) p48. "McConaughey Onscreen"
PH16413 743 (September 19, 1996) p90. "[Summer...]"
TIMMINS, BOB—PHOTOGRAPHS
PH16414 735 (May 30, 1996) p58. "Drug Counselor Bob Timmins" (Soqui, Ted)
TIMMINS, MARGO—PHOTOGRAPHS
PH16415 621 (January 9, 1992) p10. "Margo Timmins And John Prine"
PH16416 628 (April 16, 1992) pp[enc.9]. "[Lyle Lovett, Margo Timmins]" (Laxton, William)
PH16417 628 (April 16, 1992) pp[enc.13]. "[Margo Timmins]" (Laxton, William)
PH16418 631 (May 28, 1992) p24. "Margo Timmins (above)" (Willett, Robert)
TIMMINS, MARGO—PHOTOGRAPHS—PORTRAITS
PH16419 628 (April 16, 1992) pp[enc.17]. "[Margo Timmins]" (Laxton, William)
TIMMS, SALLY—PHOTOGRAPHS
PH16420 694 (November 3, 1994) p22. "Mekons Singer Sally Timms, Gibby Haynes And Jon Langford Belt It Out Onstage" (Crawford, Michael)
TIMONY, SIMON FAIR—PHOTOGRAPHS
PH16421 715 (August 24, 1995) p81. "Hot Preteen Idol" (Kuehn, Karen)
TIN MACHINE—PHOTOGRAPHS
PH16422 622 (January 23, 1992) p7. "Brad Whitford, David Bowie, Steven Tyler, Hunt Sales, Tony Sales, Reeves Gabrels, Joey Kramer" (McAlpine, Paul)
TIN MACHINE—PHOTOGRAPHS—PORTRAITS
PH16423 616 (October 31, 1991) p76. "David Bowie, Hunt Sales, Tony Sales And Reeves Gabrels (from left)" (Uchitel, Diego)
PH16424 616 (October 31, 1991) pp74-75. "[Tim Machine]" (Uchitel, Diego)
TINDERSTICKS—ALBUMS
PH16425 698-699 (December 29, 1994) p181. "Tindersticks"
PH16426 719 (October 19, 1995) p150. "Tindersticks"
TINDERSTICKS—PHOTOGRAPHS
PH16427 682 (May 19, 1994) p32. "Gloom Patrol: Brit-Crit Faves Tindersticks With Stuart Staples (center)" (Westenberg, Kevin)
TINLEY, SCOTT—PHOTOGRAPHS
PH16428 665 (September 16, 1993) pp[enc.25]. "From Left: Greg Welsh, Ray Browning, Mike Pigg, Wes Hobson, Chuckie V, Scott Tinley, Nate Llerandi And Bill Braun" (Hanauer, Mark)
TINSLEY, CHRIS—PHOTOGRAPHS
PH16429 618 (November 28, 1991) p11. "Clockwise From Left: Buck, Enrique, Ryan-Harris, Chris Tinsley, Kinney, Billy Fields And Jamie Turner (wearing glasses)" (Diamond, Rick)
PH16430 625 (March 5, 1992) p27. "Jamie Turner, David Ryan-Harris, Billy Fields, Chris Tinsley, Enrique (from left)" (Leitman, Ruth)
TINY LIGHTS—PHOTOGRAPHS—PORTRAITS
PH16431 637 (August 20, 1992) p20. "John Hamilton, Donna Croughn, Andy Demos, Dave Dreiwitz And Stuart Hake (from left)" (Borris, Dan)
TISCH, LARRY—PHOTOGRAPHS—PORTRAITS
PH16432 689 (August 25, 1994) p69. "Those Were The Days: CBS President Howard Stringer, QVC Chairman Barry Diller And CBS Chairman Larry Tisch, from left"
TISCHY, BRIAN—PHOTOGRAPHS
PH16433 686-687 (July 14, 1994) p72. "LoMenzo, Wylde And Tischy (from left)" (Ragel, Jon)
TITANIC LOVE AFFAIR—PHOTOGRAPHS
PH16434 658 (June 10, 1993) p32. "Clockwise From Left: Lars Gustafsson, Jay Bennett, Ken Hartz And Mike Hazelrigg" (Elledge, Paul)
TLC—ILLUSTRATIONS
PH16435 703 (March 9, 1995) p80. "TLC: Burning Up For Your Love" (Bartholomew, Caty)
TLC—PHOTOGRAPHS
PH16436 631 (May 28, 1992) p22. "TLC (clockwise from top): T-Boz, Chilli, Left Eye" (Cuffaro, Chris)
PH16437 719 (October 19, 1995) p16. "T-Boz, Chilli And Left Eye (from left) Of TLC Cop The Award For Best Video" (Kravitz, Jeff)
PH16438 726 (January 25, 1996) p43. "TLC's 'Boz' Watkins, 'Left Eye' Lopes And 'Chilli' Thomas (from left)" (Jensen, David)
TLC—PHOTOGRAPHS—PORTRAITS
PH16439 715 (August 24, 1995) p27. "'Left Eye' Lopes, 'T-Boz' Watkins And 'Chilli' Thomas (from left)" (White, Steve)
PH16440 715 (August 24, 1995) p28. "The Younger, Wilder TLC: Watkins, Lopes And Thomas In 1992 (from left)" (Green, Adrian)
TO DIE FOR (FILM)—ILLUSTRATIONS
PH16441 719 (October 19, 1995) p155. "Lethal Seduction" (Hungry Dog Studio)
TO DIE FOR (FILM)—PHOTOGRAPHS
PH16442 718 (October 5, 1995) p76. "Pulp To Come"
PH16443 719 (October 19, 1995) p156. "Kidman Gets Dillon In A Sexual Vise"
PH16444 719 (October 19, 1995) p156. "She Glides Her TV-Form Divine Past Gawkers Phoenix, Affleck And Folland"
PH16445 724-725 (December 28, 1995) p136. "Unusual Pleasure"
PH16446 731 (April 4, 1996) p66. "Kidman, 'To Die For'"
TO WONG FOO, THANKS FOR EVERYTHING! JULIE NEWMAR (FILM)—ILLUSTRATIONS
PH16447 717 (September 21, 1995) p87. "Queens Of The Desert" (Stauffer, Brian)
TO WONG FOO, THANKS FOR EVERYTHING, JULIE NEWMAR (FILM)—PHOTOGRAPHS
PH16448 717 (September 21, 1995) p89. "Patrick Swayze, Wesley Snipes And John Leguizamo (from left) Hit The Road"
PH16449 731 (April 4, 1996) p66. "Leguizamo, 'Wong Foo'"
TOBACK, JEREMY—PHOTOGRAPHS
PH16450 649 (February 4, 1993) p23. "Jeremy Toback, Shawn Smith, Regan Hagar And Stone Gossard (from left)"
TOBIAS, JESSE—PHOTOGRAPHS
PH16451 665 (September 16, 1993) p16. "New Pepper Jesse

Tobias (above)" (Cuffaro, Chris)
TOLA, JEAN-YVES—PHOTOGRAPHS
PH16452 731 (April 4, 1996) p36. "Roots-Gloom Trio: Sixteen Horsepower's Soll, Tola And Edwards (from left)" (Keeley, Dennis)
TOM AND VIV (FILM)—PHOTOGRAPHS
PH16453 700 (January 26, 1995) p66. "Dafoe, Richardson"
TOM TOM CLUB—PHOTOGRAPHS
PH16454 637 (August 20, 1992) p9. "Fred Schneider, Kwame, Weymouth And Frantz (from left) At The 'Paper' Bash"
TOMAS—PHOTOGRAPHS
PH16455 716 (September 7, 1995) p32. "Ambient Ace Tomas Gets Busy" (Villand, Kiino)
TOMEI, MARISA—PHOTOGRAPHS
PH16456 627 (April 2, 1992) p42. "Fred Gwynne Referees For Joe Pesci And Marisa Tomei"
PH16457 693 (October 20, 1994) p157. "Tomei, Downey And Scene-Stealing Italy"
TOMEI, MARISA—PHOTOGRAPHS—PORTRAITS
PH16458 656 (May 13, 1993) p62. "[Marisa Tomei]" (Thurnher, Jeffrey)
TOMLIN, LILY—PHOTOGRAPHS
PH16459 669 (November 11, 1993) p81. "Tomlin's Miss Hathaway Welcomes The Clampetts To 90210"
TOMMY (OPERA)—ILLUSTRATIONS
PH16460 652 (March 18, 1993) p21. "[Tommy]"
TOMMY (OPERA)—PHOTOGRAPHS
PH16461 658 (June 10, 1993) p22. "Pinball Wizard On Broadway" (Marcus)
TOMOYO—PHOTOGRAPHS
PH16462 660-661 (July 8, 1993) p101. "Motherhead Bug (from left): Anthony Lee, Steven Ovenden, April Chung, Cyril Mazzard, Jez Aspinal, Tomoyo, And Dave Ouimet" (Leopardi, N.)
TONE LOC—PHOTOGRAPHS
PH16463 658 (June 10, 1993) p74. "The Magnificent Six (from left): Stephen Baldwin, Big Daddy Kane, Mario Van Peebles, Tiny Lister Jr., Charles Lane, Tone Loc"
PH16464 659 (June 24, 1993) p15. "Ride 'Em, Cowboy: Big Daddy Kane (left) And Tone Loc Take New York" (Shaw, Gene)
PH16465 667 (October 14, 1993) p90. "Tone Loc: He Appropriated Palmer For 'Wild Thing'"
TONE LOC—PHOTOGRAPHS—PORTRAITS
PH16466 708 (May 18, 1995) p32. "Loc Answers To The Long Arm" (Micelotta, Frank)
TONIGHT SHOW (TELEVISION SHOW)—PHOTOGRAPHS
PH16467 677 (March 10, 1994) p17. "Polly Jean Harvey Makes Small Talk With Jay Leno" (Norton, Margaret)
PH16468 686-687 (July 14, 1994) p20. "Crooked Reign: Pavement Take Over "The Tonight Show""
PH16469 690 (September 8, 1994) p71. "Doing "Tonight" In 1984: "One Of The Troubles With A Nightly Talk Show Is That It's Nightly"
TONY! TONI! TONE!—PHOTOGRAPHS
PH16470 666 (September 30, 1993) p16. "Tony3: Dwayne And Raphael Wiggins, Riley (from left)" (Cuffaro, Chris)
PH16471 695 (November 17, 1994) p81. "Tony! Toni! Tone!" (Rolston, Matthew)
TOO $HORT—ALBUMS
PH16472 639 (September 17, 1992) p96. "Shorty The Pimp"
TOO MUCH JOY—ALBUMS
PH16473 647 (January 7, 1993) p47. "Mutiny"
TOOHEY, SHERRI—PHOTOGRAPHS
PH16474 652 (March 18, 1993) pp[enc.3]. "[Sherri Toohey]" (Dry, Dan)
TOOL—PHOTOGRAPHS
PH16475 748 (November 28, 1996) p41. "Justin Chancellor, Maynard Keenan, Danny Carey And Adam Jones (from left)" (Hashimoto, Mike)
TOOMEY, JENNY—PHOTOGRAPHS
PH16476 696 (December 1, 1994) p32. "Thomson, John Pamer, Toomey And Andrew Webster" (Owen, Tim)
TOOTS AND THE MAYTALS—PHOTOGRAPHS
PH16477 676 (February 24, 1994) p41. "Jamaican Soulmen Toots And The Maytals"
TORK, PETER—PHOTOGRAPHS
PH16478 650 (February 18, 1993) p13. "Peter Tork (left) With The 'Jays' Hancock, Robinson And Ben Kesteven" (Mayer, Jeffrey)
PH16479 684 (June 16, 1994) p35. "Peter Tork And Wavy Gravy" (Blakesberg, Jay)
TORN, RIP—PHOTOGRAPHS
PH16480 690 (September 8, 1994) p68. "Sidekick Hank Kingsley (Jeffrey Tambor), Producer Arthur (Rip Torn) And Host Larry Sanders (Shandling)"
TORRES, DARA—PHOTOGRAPHS
PH16481 634-635 (July 9, 1992) p92. "Dara Torres (left)..." (Zander, Peter)
PH16482 634-635 (July 9, 1992) p94. "Matt Biondi, Dara Torres And Tom Jager (from left)" (Zander, Peter)
TORRES, EDWIN—PHOTOGRAPHS—PORTRAITS
PH16483 662 (August 5, 1993) p20. "[Edwin Torres]" (Borris, Dan)
TORRES, TICO—PHOTOGRAPHS
PH16484 747 (November 14, 1996) p25. "[Bon Jovi & Friends]" (Souliers, Philippe)
TORTOISE—PHOTOGRAPHS
PH16485 723 (December 14, 1995) p44. "Tortoise: Unorthodox Improvisation" (Taylor, Michele)
TOTO—ALBUMS
PH16486 617 (November 14, 1991) p137. "Turn Back" (Lane, Tony)
PH16487 617 (November 14, 1991) p137. "Turn Back" (Emerson, Sam)
PH16488 617 (November 14, 1991) p137. "Turn Back" (Cosgrove, John)
TOUSSAINT, ALLEN—PHOTOGRAPHS
PH16489 653 (April 1, 1993) p24. "Backstage At The Troubadour In L.A." (Granitz, Steve)
TOWNEND, JON—PHOTOGRAPHS
PH16490 626 (March 19, 1992) p20. "God's Little Monkeys (from left): Dave Allen, Jo Swiss, Dave Wall, Jon Townend" (Byrne, Peter)
TOWNSHEND, PETER—ALBUMS
PH16491 663 (August 19, 1993) p76. "Psychoderelict"
TOWNSHEND, PETER—ILLUSTRATIONS
PH16492 641 (October 15, 1992) p39. "[Pete Townshend]" (English, Mark)
PH16493 690 (September 8, 1994) p76. "Who Story" (Gorgun, Ahmet)
TOWNSHEND, PETER—PHOTOGRAPHS
PH16494 619-620 (December 12, 1991) p100. "Graham With The Who's Roger Daltrey, Keith Moon And Pete Townshend, In 1976" (Zagaris, Michael)
PH16495 656 (May 13, 1993) p15. "Townshend Being Honored By Very Special Arts At Sardi's" (Elgar, Nick)
PH16496 662 (August 5, 1993) p18. "One Big Happy Family: Pirner, Berry, Townshend, Joel (from left)" (Mazur, Kevin)
PH16497 664 (September 2, 1993) p29. "Psychoderelict: Pete Townshend" (Mazur, Kevin)
PH16498 672-673 (December 23, 1993) p106. "A Chorus Line: 'Tommy' Director Des McAnuff, Townshend And Michael Cerveris, Who Plays Tommy (from left)" (Cunningham, Peter)
PH16499 672-673 (December 23, 1993) p39. "Diggin' In The Dirt: Soul Asylum's Dave Pirner, Chuck Berry, Townshend, Billy Joel" (Mazur, Kevin)
PH16500 672-673 (December 23, 1993) p109. "Frills And Thrills: Pete Townshend Onstage In 1968" (Wolman, Baron)
PH16501 679 (April 7, 1994) p20. "Join Together: Daltrey Onstage With Townshend" (Mazur, Kevin)

PH16502 720 (November 2, 1995) p50. "Pete Townsend" (Smith, Pennie)
PH16503 736 (June 13, 1996) p30. "[Peter Townshend]" (O'Neil, Terry)
PH16504 741 (August 22, 1996) p25. "Pete Townshend And Bob Dylan Bond Backstage At The Prince's Trust Concert" (Mazur, Kevin)
TOWNSHEND, PETER—PHOTOGRAPHS—PORTRAITS
PH16505 634-635 (July 9, 1992) p13. "Pete Townshend"
PH16506 652 (March 18, 1993) p21. "[Peter Townshend]"
PH16507 672-673 (December 23, 1993) p105. "[Peter Townshend]" (Eccles, Andrew)
PH16508 745 (October 17, 1996) p41. "Pete Townshend Gets Theatrical, Once Again" (O'Neil, Terry)
TOY STORY (FILM)—ILLUSTRATIONS
PH16509 723 (December 14, 1995) p90. "Megastar Voices: Tim Allen And Tom Hanks"
PH16510 731 (April 4, 1996) p66. "Toy Story"
TOYS—ILLUSTRATIONS
PH16511 697 (December 15, 1994) p18. "Toy Vey!" (Friske, Maria)
TOYS—PHOTOGRAPHS
PH16511a 656 (May 13, 1993) p65. "[Global Positioning System]"
TOYS (FILM)—PHOTOGRAPHS
PH16512 645-646 (December 10, 1992) p97. "[Toys]" (Baldwin, Sidney)
PH16513 648 (January 21, 1993) p55. "Robin Williams (left) And A Huggy L. L. Cool J Play Cousins"
PH16514 649 (February 4, 1993) p72. "[Toys]"
PH16515 Number not assigned.
TRAFFIC—ALBUMS
PH16516 617 (November 14, 1991) p147. "The Low Spark Of High Heeled Boys" (Wright, Tony)
PH16517 617 (November 14, 1991) p147. "The Low Spark Of High Heeled Boys" (Polak, Richard)
PH16518 684 (June 16, 1994) p108. "Far From Home"
TRAINS—ILLUSTRATIONS
PH16519 658 (June 10, 1993) p37. "[Trains]" (Cronin, Brian)
TRAINSPOTTING (FILM)—PHOTOGRAPHS
PH16520 736 (June 13, 1996) p60. "Smart Alternatives"
PH16521 740 (August 8, 1996) p68. "Train Spotters Miller, McGregor, McKidd, Bremner (from left)"
PH16522 743 (September 19, 1996) p90. "[Summer...]"
TRAMPOLINES—PHOTOGRAPHS
PH16523 738-739 (July 11, 1996) p16. "Moms! Dads! This Is What Your Kids Are Really Doing When They Say They're Sleeping Over At Their Fried Jimmy's House!" (Perez, Marty)
TRANSGLOBAL UNDERGROUND—ALBUMS
PH16524 714 (August 10, 1995) p58. "International Times"
TRAPANI, SICILY, ITALY—PHOTOGRAPHS
PH16525 665 (September 16, 1993) pp54-58. "Workers of The World" (Salgado, Sebastiao)
TRASTER, DEE—PHOTOGRAPHS—PORTRAITS
PH16526 685 (June 30, 1994) p59. "Fourth Reicher Tim Traster With His Parents, Roy And Dee" (Winters, Dan)
TRASTER, ROY—PHOTOGRAPHS
PH16526 685 (June 30, 1994) p59. "Fourth Reicher Tim Traster With His Parents, Roy And Dee" (Winters, Dan)
TRASTER, TIM—PHOTOGRAPHS—PORTRAITS
PH16526 685 (June 30, 1994) p59. "Fourth Reicher Tim Traster With His Parents, Roy And Dee" (Winters, Dan)
TRAVEL—ILLUSTRATIONS
PH16527 704 (March 23, 1995) p72. "[Harvard Travel Series]" (Guarnaccia, Steven)
TRAVIS, MALCOLM—PHOTOGRAPHS
PH16528 637 (August 20, 1992) p9. "Sugar (clockwise from left): Bob Mould, Malcolm Travis And David Barbe"
PH16529 694 (November 3, 1994) p71. "David Barbe, Malcolm Travis Ad Bob Mould (from left)" (Broad, Julian)
PH16530 701 (February 9, 1995) p17. "[Sugar]" (Hermer, Ken)
TRAVIS, RANDY—ALBUMS
PH16531 696 (December 1, 1994) p124. "This Is Me"
TRAVOLTA, JOHN—ILLUSTRATIONS
PH16532 692 (October 6, 1994) p79. "Tarantino's Twist" (Todd, Mark)
PH16533 720 (November 2, 1995) p73. "The Mob Goes Hollywood" (Linn, Warren)
PH16534 731 (April 4, 1996) p14. "Card-Carrying Member" (Pendergrast, James T.)
TRAVOLTA, JOHN—ILLUSTRATIONS—PORTRAITS
PH16535 724-725 (December 28, 1995) p73. "[John Travolta]" (Kelley, Gary)
TRAVOLTA, JOHN—PHOTOGRAPHS
PH16536 692 (October 6, 1994) p80. "Thurman And Travolta Twist"
PH16537 692 (October 6, 1994) p80. "Travolta And Jackson Shoot"
PH16538 698-699 (December 29, 1994) p66. "John Travolta And His Wife, Kelly Preston" (Spellman, John)
PH16539 698-699 (December 29, 1994) p194. "Thurman And Travolta Twist In "Pulp""
PH16540 700 (January 26, 1995) p68. "Best Actor (tie)"
PH16541 720 (November 2, 1995) p74. "Hackman (in brace) And DeVito Watch Travolta Operate, Hollywood Style"
PH16542 720 (November 2, 1995) p74. "Travolta And Russo Take A Meeting"
PH16543 723 (December 14, 1995) p92. "Race As An Issue: Belafonte And Travolta"
PH16544 728 (February 22, 1996) pp40-41. "[John Travolta]" (Seliger, Mark)
PH16545 728 (February 22, 1996) p42. "Last Year, Travolta Struck A Family-man Pose With His Wife, Kelly, And His Son, Jett" (Talesnick, Barry)
PH16546 728 (February 22, 1996) p43. "Travolta Puts On The Moves In 'Pulp Fiction,' 'Saturday Night Fever' And 'Broken Arrow'"
PH16547 729 (March 7, 1996) p54. "Slater And Travolta Confer With Director Woo"
PH16548 731 (April 4, 1996) p66. "Travolta, 'Shorty'"
PH16549 740 (August 8, 1996) p68. "'Independence Day,' Travolta In 'Phenomenon,' Schwarzenegger In 'Eraser,' Moore In 'Striptease'"
TRAVOLTA, JOHN—PHOTOGRAPHS—PORTRAITS
PH16550 694 (November 3, 1994) p78. "Tarantino Kisses Travolta To Celebrate The "Pulp Fiction" Victory At Cannes" (Robert, Eric)
PH16551 724-725 (December 28, 1995) pp[cover]. "Rock & Roll Yearbook" (Foreman, Richard)
PH16552 728 (February 22, 1996) p40. "[John Travolta]" (Seliger, Mark)
PH16553 728 (February 22, 1996) pp[cover]. "Mr. Cool: The Rolling Stone Interview With John Travolta" (Seliger, Mark)
TRE COOL—PHOTOGRAPHS
PH16554 691 (September 22, 1994) p25. "Punk's New Breed: Mike Dirnt, Billie Joe And Tre Cool (from left)" (Seliger, Mark)
PH16555 700 (January 26, 1995) pp40-41. "Billie Joe (Opposite), Mike Dirnt And Tre Cool" (Winters, Dan)
PH16556 724-725 (December 28, 1995) p29. "Tre Cool, Billy Joe Armstrong, Mike Dirnt" (Seliger, Mark)
TREACH—PHOTOGRAPHS
PH16557 658 (June 10, 1993) p30. "From Illtown To Chilltown: Naughty's Treach, Vinnie And DJ KayGee" (Larsen, Kristine)
PH16558 663 (August 19, 1993) pp66-68,70. "[Naughty By Nature]" (Gregoire, Jean Louis)
PH16559 695 (November 17, 1994) p110. "Naughty By Nature" (Callis, Chris)
PH16560 715 (August 24, 1995) p34. "Treach: Newark To Motown" (Settle, Ken)

TREACH—PHOTOGRAPHS—PORTRAITS
PH16561 696 (December 1, 1994) p24. "Reach, Pepa And LL Cool J" (Sands, Steve)
PH16562 717 (September 21, 1995) p32. "Sue Tha Police: Treach Of Naughty By Nature" (Clinch, Danny)
TREADWALL—PHOTOGRAPHS
PH16563 630 (May 14, 1992) p89. "[The Treadwall]"
TRENT, TYLER—PHOTOGRAPHS—PORTRAITS
PH16564 733 (May 2, 1996) p26. "Killing Retro: Tim Taylor, Juan Monasterio, John Schmersal And Tyler Trent (from top)" (McGuire, Leeann)
TRESPASS (FILM)—PHOTOGRAPHS
PH16565 649 (February 4, 1993) p75. "Ice Cube (left) And Ice-T Get Fired Up"
TRIAL BY JURY (FILM)—PHOTOGRAPHS
PH16566 691 (September 22, 1994) p106. "Cop Hurt Moves In On Juror Whalley-Kilmer"
TRIALS—ILLUSTRATIONS
PH16567 642 (October 29, 1992) p8. "Parkay On Trial" (Pendergrast, James T.)
TRIANO, ERIC—PHOTOGRAPHS
PH16568 730 (March 21, 1996) p55. "The Boys In The Bus: Schiavone McGee, David Triano, Eric Lawson, Chris Leitch, Karl Vonklein, David Peterson And Mike Boyd (clockwise from left)" (Clinch, Danny)
PH16569 730 (March 21, 1996) p56. "McGee, Peterson, Triano And Lawson (from left) Rehearse In The Bus" (Clinch, Danny)
PH16570 730 (March 21, 1996) p60. "Triano Solos At The Washington College Student Center" (Clinch, Danny)
TRIBE 8—PHOTOGRAPHS
PH16571 708 (May 18, 1995) p38. "San Francisco's Lesbian Warriors Tribe 8 Tailor Political Hardcore For The Slam Pit" (Sherman, Chloe)
PH16572 721 (November 16, 1995) p81. "The Tribe That Sticks Together: Slade Bellum, Lynn Breedlove, Leslie Mah, Lynn Payne, Lynn Flipper (from left)" (Yemchuk, Yelena)
A TRIBE CALLED QUEST—ALBUMS
PH16573 670 (November 25, 1993) p116. "Midnight Marauders"
PH16574 740 (August 8, 1996) p57. "Beats, Rhymes And Life"
A TRIBE CALLED QUEST—ILLUSTRATIONS
PH16575 695 (November 17, 1994) p129. "A Tribe Called Quest" (Shurley, Hugh)
PH16576 740 (August 8, 1996) p57. "Speaking In Tongues" (Clayton, Christian)
A TRIBE CALLED QUEST—PHOTOGRAPHS
PH16577 660-661 (July 8, 1993) p26. "Tribe's Malik 'Phife' Taylor, Ali Shaheed Muhammed And Jonathan 'Q-Tip' Davis (from left)" (Mazur, Kevin)
PH16578 678 (March 24, 1994) p10. "Mifnight Marauding: Phife (left) and Tip" (Gehring, Karl A.)
PH16579 698-699 (December 29, 1994) p60. "A Tribe Called Quest Heat Up The Main Stage" (Blakesberg, Jay)
PH16580 732 (April 18, 1996) p32. "Phife, Q-Tip And Ali Shaheed Muhammad (from left) In Battery Studio" (Posey, Carl)
A TRIBE CALLED QUEST—PHOTOGRAPHS—PORTRAITS
PH16581 678 (March 24, 1994) p9. "Quest (clockwise from top): Q-Tip, Ali And Phife Dog" (Seliger, Mark)
TRICKY—ALBUMS
PH16582 710 (June 15, 1995) p83. "Maxinquaye"
PH16583 741 (August 22, 1996) p98. "Nearly God"
PH16584 741 (August 22, 1996) p98. "Tricky Presents Grassroots"
PH16585 749 (December 12, 1996) p86. "Pre-Millennium Tension"
TRICKY—ILLUSTRATIONS
PH16586 747 (November 14, 1996) p13. "'I'm Proof You Can Get A Life Without Becoming A Gangster'—Tricky" (Marten, Ruth)
TRICKY—PHOTOGRAPHS
PH16587 706 (April 20, 1995) p36. "Trip-Hop Hooray: Martina And Tricky" (Rider, Paul)
PH16588 714 (August 10, 1995) p33. "[Tricky]" (Rider, Paul)
PH16589 726 (January 25, 1996) p50. "Trip-Hopper Tricky (right) With Singer Martine" (Double, Steve)
TRICKY—PHOTOGRAPHS—PORTRAITS
PH16590 747 (November 14, 1996) p46. "[Tricky]" (Afanador, Ruven)
TRIMBLE, VIVIAN
PH16591 710 (June 15, 1995) p17. "LJ's Schellenbach, Gabby Glaser, Vivian trimble And Jill Cunniff At The Rally For Women's Lives, in D.C. (from left)" (Harrington, John)
TRIMBLE, VIVIAN—PHOTOGRAPHS
PH16592 735 (May 30, 1996) p27. "Glaser, Schellenbach, Producer Lanois And Trimble (from left)" (Olivier, Rick)
TRIMBLE, VIVIAN—PHOTOGRAPHS—PORTRAITS
PH16593 660-661 (July 8, 1993) p97. "Luscious Jackson (clockwise from top left): Glaser, Schellenbach, Cunniff, Trimble" (Minchin, James R., III)
TRIPPING DAISY—PHOTOGRAPHS
PH16594 716 (September 7, 1995) p13. "Dye Hard: Daisy's DeLaughter (left) And Wes Berggren" (George, Tryan)
TRIPPLEHORN, JEANNE—PHOTOGRAPHS
PH16595 659 (June 24, 1993) p88. "Suspense: 'The Firm' With Jeanne Tripplehorn And Cruise"
TRISTAN—PHOTOGRAPHS
PH16596 617 (November 14, 1991) p80. "Matthew With His "Spiritual Director," Tristan, A Fifteen-Year-Old Spitz" (Winters, Dan)
TRITT, TRAVIS—PHOTOGRAPHS
PH16597 628 (April 16, 1992) p17. "Allman Brothers Fan Travis Tritt" (Devault, Jim)
TROCHE, ROSE—PHOTOGRAPHS
PH16598 685 (June 30, 1994) p82. "Director Troche (left) With Stars Brodie And Turner"
TROCHE, ROSE—PHOTOGRAPHS—PORTRAITS
PH16599 682 (May 19, 1994) p58. "[Rose Troche]"
TROIANO, JIMMY—PHOTOGRAPHS
PH16600 632 (June 11, 1992) p132. "Accused Killer Jimmy Troiano At The Scene Of The Crime" (Mintz, Ari)
TROISI—PHOTOGRAPHS—PORTRAITS
PH16601 731 (April 4, 1996) p66. "'The Postman,' With Troisi"
TROMBINO, MARK—PHOTOGRAPHS
PH16602 689 (August 25, 1994) p44. "All Together Now: Trombino, Atom, Kennedy, Reis, N.D., Petey X, Apollo 9, Froberg (from left)" (Cuffaro, Chris)
TROSCH, DAVID—PHOTOGRAPHS—PORTRAITS
PH16603 710 (June 15, 1995) p64. "Trosch"
TROTT, JEFFREY—PHOTOGRAPHS
PH16604 628 (April 16, 1992) p13. "World Party Guitarist Jeffrey Trott (left) With Napolitano And Prieboy" (Karas, Steve)
TRUCKS, DEREK—PHOTOGRAPHS—PORTRAITS
PH16605 630 (May 14, 1992) p92. "[Derek Trucks]" (Smith, Brian)
TRUDELL, JOHN—ALBUMS
PH16606 631 (May 28, 1992) p53. "AKA Grafitti Man"
TRUE BELIEVERS—PHOTOGRAPHS
PH16607 681 (May 5, 1994) p14. "The True Believers" (Virobik-Adams, Kevin)
TRUE LIES (FILM)—PHOTOGRAPHS
PH16608 684 (June 16, 1994) p114. "Potential Headaches"
PH16609 688 (August 11, 1994) pp54-55,57. "[True Lies]"
PH16610 689 (August 25, 1994) p96. "Schwarzenegger And Curtis Work Out The Kinks"
PH16611 691 (September 22, 1994) p106. "Woman Demeaned"
TRUE ROMANCE (FILM)—PHOTOGRAPHS
PH16612 666 (September 30, 1993) p112. "Slater (right) Comforts A Bloody Arquette"
PH16613 672-673 (December 23, 1993) p172. "Underrated"
TRUJILO, CHRIS—PHOTOGRAPHS
PH16614 736 (June 13, 1996) p41. "The Black Crowes In '94:

Chris Robinson, Chris Trujilo, Rich Robinson (from left)" (Blakesberg, Jay)
THE TRUTH ABOUT CATS AND DOGS (FILM)—PHOTOGRAPHS
PH16615 734 (May 16, 1996) p74. "Chaplin, Thurman And Garofalo In Love"
TRYNIN, JENNIFER—PHOTOGRAPHS
PH16616 715 (August 24, 1995) p74. "Hot Debut Album" (Ockenfels, Frank W.)
TSONGAS, PAUL—ILLUSTRATIONS
PH16617 627 (April 2, 1992) p5. "Paul Tsongas" (Burke, Philip)
TUATARA—PHOTOGRAPHS
PH16618 748 (November 28, 1996) p26. "Tuatara's Martin, Harwood And Buck (from left)" (Doughty, Curt)
TUCCI, STANLEY—PHOTOGRAPHS
PH16619 744 (October 3, 1996) p78. "Cooking With Shalhoub (left) And Tucci"
TUCKER, C. DELORES—PHOTOGRAPHS
PH16620 679 (April 7, 1994) p22. "Tucker" (Lambert, Kenneth)
TUCKER, MAUREEN—ALBUMS
PH16621 619-620 (December 12, 1991) p189. "I Spent A Week There The Other Night"
TUCKER, MAUREEN—PHOTOGRAPHS
PH16622 692 (October 6, 1994) p53. "Moe Tucker" (Leitman, Ruth)
PH16623 696 (December 1, 1994) p36. "The Mother Of All Drummers: Moe Tucker At Lunch In Douglas, Ga." (Leitman, Ruth)
PH16624 718 (October 5, 1995) p46. "The Velvet Underground (clockwise from bottom left): Nico, Reed, Morrison, Cale And Tucker"
PH16625 728 (February 22, 1996) p18. "Martha Morrison, Tucker, Cale And Reed (from left) Celebrate The Velvets' Induction" (Mazur, Kevin)
TUCKER, MAUREEN—PHOTOGRAPHS—PORTRAITS
PH16626 659 (June 24, 1993) p17. "Tucker, Morrison, Cale And Reed Today (from left)" (Wood, Graham)
TUNE IN, TURN ON, BURN OUT TOUR—PHOTOGRAPHS
PH16627 619-620 (December 12, 1991) p84. "The Tune In Package Tour Didn't Turn Many Fans On" (Natkin, Paul)
TURNER, GUINEVERE—PHOTOGRAPHS
PH16628 685 (June 30, 1994) p82. "Director Troche (left) With Stars Brodie And Turner"
TURNER, IKE—PHOTOGRAPHS
PH16629 663 (August 19, 1993) p28. "Mr. Slap-happy Himself, Ike Turner" (Cohen, Diane)
TURNER, IKE—PHOTOGRAPHS—PORTRAITS
PH16630 659 (June 24, 1993) p89. "Biography: "What's Love Got To Do With It,' With Lawrence Fishburne And Angela Bassett As Ike And Tina Turner (left)"
TURNER, JAMIE—PHOTOGRAPHS
PH16631 618 (November 28, 1991) p11. "Clockwise From Left: Buck, Enrique, Ryan-Harris, Chris Tinsley, Kinney, Billy Fields And Jamie Turner (wearing glasses)" (Diamond, Rick)
PH16632 625 (March 5, 1992) p27. "Jamie Turner, David Ryan-Harris, Billy Fields, Chris Tinsley, Enrique (from left)" (Leitman, Ruth)
TURNER, JANINE—PHOTOGRAPHS—PORTRAITS
PH16633 666 (September 30, 1993) p51. "[Janine Turner]"
TURNER, KATHLEEN—ILLUSTRATIONS
PH16634 681 (May 5, 1994) p47. "Divine Madness" (Risko, Robert)
TURNER, KATHLEEN—PHOTOGRAPHS
PH16635 659 (June 24, 1993) p13. "Waters And Turner (second from right) With Members Of L7" (Caruso, Phillip)
PH16636 681 (May 5, 1994) p48. "Momhood, John Waters Style: Divine (left) And Turner"
PH16637 681 (May 5, 1994) p49. "Soap Star Turner Puts The Moves On Writer Stoltz"
TURNER, KATHLEEN—PHOTOGRAPHS—PORTRAITS
PH16638 705 (April 6, 1995) p69. "Oscar Rejects"
TURNER, STEVE—PHOTOGRAPHS
PH16639 628 (April 16, 1992) p48. "Mudhoney's Lukin, Turner, Peters And Arm (from left)" (Seliger, Mark)
PH16640 670 (November 25, 1993) p38. "Mudhoney Guitarist Steve Turner, Gilmore And Guitarist Mark Arm" (Peterson, Charles)
PH16641 695 (November 17, 1994) p90. "Mudhoney" (Ragel, Jon)
PH16642 700 (January 26, 1995) p32. "Lukin, Arm, Turner (from left)" (Blakesberg, Jay)
PH16643 709 (June 1, 1995) p48. "Seattle Mudslingers: Turner, Arm, Lukin And Peters (from left)" (Winters, Dan)
TURNER, TINA—ALBUMS
PH16644 747 (November 14, 1996) p116. "Wildest Dreams"
TURNER, TINA—ILLUSTRATIONS
PH16645 641 (October 15, 1992) p121. "[Tina Turner]" (Drawson, Blair)
TURNER, TINA—PHOTOGRAPHS
PH16646 638 (September 3, 1992) p59. "Onstage With Tina Turner, 1969"
PH16647 654 (April 15, 1993) p13. "Tina Turner And Bryan Adams" (Mazur, Kevin)
PH16648 698-699 (December 29, 1994) p63. "Sessions" (Seeff, Norman)
TURNER, TINA—PHOTOGRAPHS—PORTRAITS
PH16649 643 (November 12, 1992) p208. "Tina Turner" (Watson, Albert)
PH16650 659 (June 24, 1993) p89. "Biography: "What's Love Got To Do With It,' With Lawrence Fishburne And Angela Bassett As Ike And Tina Turner (left)"
PH16651 726 (January 25, 1996) p17. "La Liaison Dangereuse: Bono And Tina Turner, Livin' On The Edge"
TURNER, TYRIN—PHOTOGRAPHS
PH16652 660-661 (July 8, 1993) p121. "Turner Menaces Martin Davis"
TURNOUT BROTHERS—PHOTOGRAPHS
PH16653 628 (April 16, 1992) p63. "The Turnout Brothers"
TURNTABLES—PHOTOGRAPHS
PH16654 707 (May 4, 1995) p79. "[Technology]" (Grant, Bob)
TUROW, SCOTT—PHOTOGRAPHS—PORTRAITS
PH16655 666 (September 30, 1993) p56. "[Scot Turow]"
TURPIN, WILL—PHOTOGRAPHS
PH16656 686-687 (July 14, 1994) p30. "Soul Men: Childress, Evans, Dean Roland, Turpin And Ed Roland (clockwise from top left)" (Callahan, Kristin)
TURTLE LAKE RESORT, MICHIGAN—PHOTOGRAPHS
PH16657 724-725 (December 28, 1995) p51. "[Nudefest]" (Slocum, Werner)
TURTURRO, JOHN—PHOTOGRAPHS
PH16658 627 (April 2, 1992) p41. "'Barton Fink,' With John Turturro And John Goodman"
PH16659 691 (September 22, 1994) p104. "Onscreen It's Ralph Fiennes, Left, As Van Doren, And John Turturro As Stemple"
TUTTON, BILL—PHOTOGRAPHS
PH16660 720 (November 2, 1995) p24. "Bozulich, Keenan, Tutton, Fitzgerald, Greene (from left)" (Toy, Joann)
TWAIN, SHANIA—ALBUMS
PH16661 670 (November 25, 1993) p112. "Shania Twain"
TWEEDY, JEFF—PHOTOGRAPHS
PH16662 684 (June 16, 1994) p35. "Tupelo's Last Stand: Farrar (left), Tweedy" (Defilippo, Michael)
PH16663 691 (September 22, 1994) p20. "Hawks Gary Louris, Mark Perlman, Dan Murphy, Noah Levy, Tweedy" (Smiley, Jay)
PH16664 707 (May 4, 1995) p32. "The Buddy System: Johnston, Coomer, Stirratt, Tweedy And Bennett (from left)" (Miller, Brad)
PH16665 714 (August 10, 1995) p16. "The New Math: McCaughey, Buck, Tweedy And Greenberg (from left)" (Perez, Marty)
PH16666 721 (November 16, 1995) p26. "Bottle Rocket Henneman (left) And Jeff Tweedy Of Wilco" (Ellenby, Peter)

TWELFTH NIGHT (FILM)—PHOTOGRAPHS
PH16667 747 (November 14, 1996) p124. "Stubbs, In Drag, Deceives Stephens"
TWELVE MONKEYS (FILM)—PHOTOGRAPHS
PH16668 718 (October 5, 1995) p76. "Pulp To Come"
PH16669 726 (January 25, 1996) p66. "Into The Cuckoo's Nest With Willis And Pitt"
24-7 SPYZ—ALBUMS
PH16670 644 (November 26, 1992) p72. "Strength In Numbers"
TWENTY-ONE (FILM)—PHOTOGRAPHS
PH16671 615 (October 17, 1991) p102. "Patsy Kensit Ponders Sex In The Nineties"
TWENTY-ONE (TELEVISION SHOW)—PHOTOGRAPHS
PH16672 691 (September 22, 1994) p104. "Van Doren, Left, And Stemple Flank Host Jack Barry On "Twenty-One," Circa 1956"
TWIN PEAKS: FIRE WALK WITH ME (FILM)—PHOTOGRAPHS
PH16673 639 (September 17, 1992) p103. "Anderson (left) And MacLachlan Lost In Lynchland"
TWIST—PHOTOGRAPHS—PORTRAITS
PH16674 656 (May 13, 1993) p94. "Deidre Lang, Jennifer Lopez, Twist, Jossie Harris, Lisa Thompson (from left)"
PH16675 656 (May 13, 1993) p97. "Twist"
TWISTER (FILM)—PHOTOGRAPHS
PH16676 736 (June 13, 1996) p58. "Blockbusters"
TWITTY, CONWAY—PHOTOGRAPHS
PH16677 672-673 (December 23, 1993) p79. "Conway Twitty" (Tackett, Michael)
TWITTY, CONWAY—PHOTOGRAPHS—PORTRAITS
PH16678 662 (August 5, 1993) p27. "[Conway Twitty]"
TWO BITS (FILM)—PHOTOGRAPHS
PH16679 723 (December 14, 1995) p92. "Al Pacino"
2 DAYS IN THE VALLEY (FILM)—PHOTOGRAPHS
PH16680 745 (October 17, 1996) p142. "Now Playing"
TWO GIRLS IN LOVE (FILM)—PHOTOGRAPHS
PH16681 709 (June 1, 1995) p70. "Rebel Voices"
TWO IF BY SEA (FILM)—ILLUSTRATIONS
PH16682 727 (February 8, 1996) p45. "When The Stars Dumb Out" (Hartland, Jessie)
TWO IF BY SEA (FILM)—PHOTOGRAPHS
PH16683 727 (February 8, 1996) p46. "Denis Leary And Sandra Bullock Mug And Kiss As Lovers On The Run In The First And Maybe Worst Comedy Of 1996"
2 LIVE CREW—PHOTOGRAPHS
PH16684 636 (August 6, 1992) p22. "[2 Live Crew]" (Callahan, Kristin)
PH16684a 720 (November 2, 1995) p16. "Feel The Heat: 311 Raise Cash In Kansas For Needy Kids" (Stump. Jeff)
TYLER, LIV—PHOTOGRAPHS
PH16685 694 (November 3, 1994) pp[cover]. "Family Values" (Watson, Albert)
PH16686 694 (November 3, 1994) pp62-66. "[Liv Tyler]" (Watson, Albert)
PH16687 694 (November 3, 1994) p67. "Rad Dad: Bebe Buell, Tyler And Liv (age 11) In 1988" (Hall, Charles)
PH16688 716 (September 7, 1995) p48. "Video Vixens Silverstone And Liv Tyler In Aerosmith's 'Crazy'" (Gougenheim, Kim)
PH16689 737 (June 27, 1996) p63. "Irons (left) And Tyler Talk Sex And Art"
PH16690 737 (June 27, 1996) p62. "Now Playing"
PH16691 740 (August 8, 1996) p17. "[Liv Tyler & Steven Tyler]" (Kravitz, Jeff)
PH16692 745 (October 17, 1996) p142. "Live Tyler Looks On"
TYLER, LIV—PHOTOGRAPHS—PORTRAITS
PH16693 682 (May 19, 1994) p63. "[Models]" (Hollywood, Barry)
TYLER, RICHARD—PHOTOGRAPHS
PH16694 682 (May 19, 1994) p64. "[Richard Tyler]" (Hanauer, Mark)
TYLER, STEVEN—ILLUSTRATIONS
PH16695 656 (May 13, 1993) p103. "Aerosmith Holds On Loosely" (Sheldon, David K.)
PH16696 677 (March 10, 1994) p72. "Tight Grip: Steven Tyler Of Aerosmith" (Cowles, David)
TYLER, STEVEN—PHOTOGRAPHS
PH16697 615 (October 17, 1991) p13. "Steven Tyler, Don Henley" (Mazur, Kevin)
PH16698 621 (January 9, 1992) p10. "Tyler (left) And Richards At The Bill Graham Tribute" (Blankenhorn, C.)
PH16699 622 (January 23, 1992) p7. "Brad Whitford, David Bowie, Steven Tyler, Hunt Sales, Tony Sales, Reeves Gabrels, Joey Kramer" (McAlpine, Paul)
PH16700 623 (February 6, 1992) p11. "Steven Tyler" (Bernstein, Christopher D.)
PH16701 634-635 (July 9, 1992) p11. "Tom Hamilton, Joe Perry And Tyler (from left) With Museum Curator Helaine Posner" (Putnam, Sarah)
PH16702 659 (June 24, 1993) p13. "Kuriansky, Tyler And Hamilton" (Paul, Tina)
PH16703 667 (October 14, 1993) p101. "Aerosmith: Steve Tyler Acts Out For 'Janie's'"
PH16704 667 (October 14, 1993) p73. "'Walk This Way': Run, Stephen Tyler"
PH16705 668 (October 28, 1993) p36. "Steven Tyler (left) And Joe Perry At The Walden Woods Benefit" (Robicheau, Paul)
PH16706 669 (November 11, 1993) p25. "Dressin' On The Edge: Aerosmith's Steven Tyler" (Capak, R. J.)
PH16707 679 (April 7, 1994) p38. "Joe Perry, Wolf, Tyler" (Lyden, Paul)
PH16708 694 (November 3, 1994) p58. "Aerodynamics: Tyler (left) And Joe Perry Live" (Mazur, Kevin)
PH16709 694 (November 3, 1994) p60. "Early Daze: Whitford, Tyler, Hamilton, Perry And Kramer At Boston College, 1973" (Pownall, Ron)
PH16710 694 (November 3, 1994) pp[cover]. "Family Values" (Watson, Albert)
PH16711 694 (November 3, 1994) p67. "Rad Dad: Bebe Buell, Tyler And Liv (age 11) In 1988" (Hall, Charles)
PH16712 694 (November 3, 1994) pp56-57. "[Steven Tyler]" (Watson, Albert)
PH16713 702 (February 23, 1995) p48. "Aerosmith's Joe Perry And Steven Tyler Get Chummy With Led Zep's Robert Plant And Jimmy Page" (Mazur, Kevin)
PH16714 708 (May 18, 1995) p17. "[Steven Tyler]" (Conde, Dominick)
PH16715 723 (December 14, 1995) p27. "Young, Surprise Guest Steven Tyler And Hynde (from left)" (Blakesberg, Jay)
PH16716 724-725 (December 28, 1995) p40. "Aerosmith's Tom Hamilton, Joey Kramer, Brad Whitford And Steven Tyler (from left)" (Robicheau, Paul)
PH16717 735 (May 30, 1996) p20. "It Took Tyler Four Attempts At Rehab Before He Got Clean" (Bozi, Tibor)
PH16718 740 (August 8, 1996) p17. "[Liv Tyler & Steven Tyler]" (Kravitz, Jeff)

U

U ROY—PHOTOGRAPHS—PORTRAITS
PH16719 676 (February 24, 1994) p42. "Dub Master U Roy (right)" (Corio, David)
U2—ALBUMS
PH16720 617 (November 14, 1991) p154. "The Joshua Tree" (Averill, Steve)
PH16721 617 (November 14, 1991) p154. "The Joshua Tree" (Corbijn, Anton)
PH16722 617 (November 14, 1991) p128. "War" (Averill, Steve)
PH16723 617 (November 14, 1991) p128. "War" (Finlay, Ian)

PH16724 621 (January 9, 1992) p60. "Achtung Baby"
PH16725 634-635 (July 9, 1992) p4. "War"
PH16726 637 (August 20, 1992) p4. "War"
PH16727 651 (March 4, 1993) p50. "Achtung Baby"
PH16728 662 (August 5, 1993) p63. "Zooropa"
PH16729 664 (September 2, 1993) p80. "Zooropa"
PH16730 672-673 (December 23, 1993) p151. "Zooropa"
U2—ILLUSTRATIONS
PH16731 621 (January 9, 1992) p50. "U2's 'Achtung Baby': Bring The Noise" (Linn, Warren)
PH16732 670 (November 25, 1993) p8. "Rolling Stone" (Pendergrast, James T.)
U2—ILLUSTRATIONS—LETTERING
PH16733 640 (October 1, 1992) pp40-42,47-48. "U2" (Karl, Anita)
U2—PHOTOGRAPHS
PH16734 618 (November 28, 1991) p47. "The Big Room At Hansa Studios" (Corbijn, Anton)
PH16735 618 (November 28, 1991) pp42-48,50. "Dublin: Making Cutouts For The Album Cover Under The Guidance Of Steve Averill (second from left)" (Corbijn, Anton)
PH16736 618 (November 28, 1991) p48. "Morocco: 'Sometimes We'd Escape From The Studio...'" (Corbijn, Anton)
PH16737 618 (November 28, 1991) p44. "'This Must Have Been Taken After One Of Anton's Jokes...'" (Corbijn, Anton)
PH16738 618 (November 28, 1991) p42. "[U2]" (Corbijn, Anton)
PH16739 618 (November 28, 1991) pp[cover]. "U2 Exclusive: The Making Of 'Achtung Baby'" (Corbijn, Anton)
PH16740 619-620 (December 12, 1991) pp[cover]. "1991 Yearbook" (Corbijn, Anton)
PH16741 624 (February 20, 1992) p11. "U2"
PH16742 627 (April 2, 1992) p11. "U2 Performs At A London Clothing Store: Bono (left) And Adam Clayton"
PH16743 636 (August 6, 1992) p11. "Adam Clayton, The Edge, Bono And Larry Mullen Jr. (from left)" (Thomas, Justin)
PH16744 645-646 (December 10, 1992) p87. "[Outside Is America]"
PH16745 645-646 (December 10, 1992) p39. "U2 On Zoo TV" (Mazur, Kevin)
PH16746 651 (March 4, 1993) p48. "...U2 Swept This Year's Poll" (Corbijn, Anton)
PH16747 667 (October 14, 1993) p54. "The Zoo Gang On Tour: The Edge, Bono, Larry Mullen Jr. And Adam Clayton (from left)" (Corbijn, Anton)
PH16748 672-673 (December 23, 1993) p37. "Above: His Bononess, In All His Splendor" (Preston, Neal)
PH16749 686-687 (July 14, 1994) p41. "[U2]" (Fisher, David)
PH16750 714 (August 10, 1995) p30. "U2 Can Do Film Scores: Adam Clayton, Bono, The Edge, Larry Mullen (from left)" (Mazur, Kevin)
PH16751 726 (January 25, 1996) p30. "U2's Bono, Adam Clayton, The Edge And Larry Mullen Jr. (from left)" (Pasley, Richard)
PH16752 745 (October 17, 1996) p41. "Too Much Guinness? U2 Delay Release Of Their New Record Till Early Next Year" (Corbijn, Anton)
U2—PHOTOGRAPHS—PORTRAITS
PH16753 643 (November 12, 1992) p153. "U2" (Ritts, Herb)
U2—SINGLES
PH16754 712-713 (July 13, 1995) p111. "Hold Me, Thrill Me, Kiss Me, Kill Me (song)"
UDRIS, DAVID—PHOTOGRAPHS
PH16755 732 (April 18, 1996) pp[enc.23]. "[David And Michael Udris]" (Witkin, Christian)
UDRIS, MICHAEL—PHOTOGRAPHS
PH16755 732 (April 18, 1996) pp[enc.23]. "[David And Michael Udris]" (Witkin, Christian)
UEHLEIN, JOE—PHOTOGRAPHS
PH16756 629 (April 30, 1992) p50. "Joe Uehlein And Dewey Taylor Testifying In The Swiss Parliament, In Bern" (De Keyzer, Carl)
UFO—ALBUMS
PH16757 648 (January 21, 1993) p23. "UFO: BBC Radio Live In Concert"
UGLY KID JOE—PHOTOGRAPHS
PH16758 629 (April 30, 1992) p31. "Ugly Kid Joe (from left): Roger Lahr, Klaus Eichstadt, Whitfield Crane, Cordell Crockett And Mark Davis" (O'Beirne, Andy)
PH16759 Number not assigned.
ULLMAN, TRACEY—PHOTOGRAPHS
PH16760 665 (September 16, 1993) p77. "Worst Supporting Actress"
ULMER, JAMES BLOOD—ALBUMS
PH16761 750-751 (December 26, 1996) p189. "Odyssey"
ULRICH, LARS—PHOTOGRAPHS
PH16762 615 (October 17, 1991) p13. "Metallica's Ulrich (left), James Hetfield" (Mazur, Kevin)
PH16763 618 (November 28, 1991) p11. "Kirk Kammett, Slash, Lars Ulrich, Geoff Tate And Armored Saint Drummer Gonzo (from left)" (Blakesberg, Jay)
PH16764 626 (March 19, 1992) p25. "Lars Ulrich (right)" (Pool, Smiley)
PH16765 655 (April 29, 1993) p11. "Ulrich, Young And Hetfield (from left)" (Blakesberg, Jay)
PH16766 708 (May 18, 1995) p74. "Metallica In 1991, From Left: Hammett, Ulrich, Newsted, Hetfield" (Seliger, Mark)
PH16767 708 (May 18, 1995) p76. "Ulrich Onstage In Miami, 1988" (Desota, George)
PH16768 727 (February 8, 1996) p12. "Fifty And Fabulous! Kilmister (center) Flanked By Metallica's Jason Newsted, James Hetfield, Kirk Hammett And Lars Ulrich (from left)" (Disanto, Annamaria)
PH16769 728 (February 22, 1996) p25. "Metallica's James Hetfield, Kirk Hammett, Lars Ulrich And Jason Newsted (from left)"
ULRICH, LARS—PHOTOGRAPHS—PORTRAITS
PH16770 708 (May 18, 1995) p72. "[Lars Ulrich]" (Ockenfels, Frank W.)
UNCLE TUPELO—ALBUMS
PH16771 626 (March 19, 1992) p97. "Still Feel Gone"
PH16772 671 (December 9, 1993) p73. "Anodyne"
UNCLE TUPELO—PHOTOGRAPHS
PH16773 672-673 (December 23, 1993) p69. "Below: Uncle Tupelo, This Year's Best" (Corrigan, Daniel)
PH16774 684 (June 16, 1994) p35. "Tupelo's Last Stand: Farrar (left), Tweedy" (Defilippo, Michael)
UNDER SIEGE (FILM)—PHOTOGRAPHS
PH16775 709 (June 1, 1995) p68. "Potential Goldmines"
UNDERCOVER OF THE NIGHT (VIDEO)—PHOTOGRAPHS
PH16776 667 (October 14, 1993) p87. "'Undercover': Latin Jagger"
THE UNDERNEATH (FILM)—PHOTOGRAPHS
PH16777 708 (May 18, 1995) p98. "Alison Elliott And Peter Gallagher Conspire"
UNDERWORLD—PHOTOGRAPHS
PH16778 744 (October 3, 1996) p32. "Up From The Techno Depths: Hyde, Smith And Emerson (from left)" (Nash, Peter)
UNFORGIVEN (FILM)—ILLUSTRATIONS
PH16779 637 (August 20, 1992) p55. "An Outlaw At Twilight" (Unruh, Jack)
UNFORGIVEN (FILM)—PHOTOGRAPHS
PH16780 637 (August 20, 1992) p57. "Eastwood's Grizzled Face Reflects The Long Road He's Traveled Since 'Rawhide' (right)"
PH16781 639 (September 17, 1992) p102. "Best Picture, Best Actor"
PH16782 645-646 (December 10, 1992) p190. "Clint Eastwood"
PH16783 648 (January 21, 1993) p56. "Unforgiven"
PH16784 653 (April 1, 1993) p57. "Unforgiven"

UNGLESS, DEREK—PHOTOGRAPHS
PH16785 643 (November 12, 1992) p49. "'Rolling Stone' Art Directors (from left): Bob Kingsbury (1968-73), Tony Lane (1974-76), Annie Leibovitz, Mike Salisbury (1973-74), Roger Black (1976-78), Jann S. Wenner, Derek..
UNHAPPILY EVER AFTER (TELEVISION SHOW)—PHOTOGRAPHS
PH16786 704 (March 23, 1995) p131. "WB's 'Unhappily': Divorced...With Children And A Talking Bunny"
UNIONS—ILLUSTRATIONS
PH16787 615 (October 17, 1991) p39. "Union" (Cronin, Brian)
UNITED AUTO WORKERS—PHOTOGRAPHS
PH16788 668 (October 28, 1993) p41. "Ford Goons Attack A UAW Organizer In 1937..."
UNITED FUTURE ORGANIZATION—PHOTOGRAPHS
PH16789 684 (June 16, 1994) p21. "United Future Organization, From France And Japan" (Schoerner, N.)
UNITED STATES OF AMERICA—ILLUSTRATIONS
PH16790 691 (September 22, 1994) p36. "[Haiti]" (Martin, Matthew)
PH16791 740 (August 8, 1996) p44. "U.S. Fault Lines"
UNIVERSAL SOLDIER (FILM)—PHOTOGRAPHS
PH16792 636 (August 6, 1992) p66. "Van Damme (right) And Lundgren (center) Play Robots"
UNIVERSITY OF ARIZONA—PHOTOGRAPHS
PH16793 719 (October 19, 1995) p92. "Arizona's Camel Jerk: A Whole New World"
UNIVERSITY OF CALIFORNIA-BERKELEY—ILLUSTRATIONS
PH16794 730 (March 21, 1996) p65. "UCAL At Berkeley: California's Crown Jewel"
UNIVERSITY OF COLORADO AT BOULDER—PHOTOGRAPHS
PH16795 719 (October 19, 1995) p91. "Overfed At Alferd Packer Day" (Cooper, Dawn)
UNIVERSITY OF DELAWARE—PHOTOGRAPHS
PH16796 704 (March 23, 1995) p69. "University Of Delaware" (Bennett, Kelly)
UNIVERSITY OF ILLINOIS—PHOTOGRAPHS
PH16797 704 (March 23, 1995) p69. "University Of Illinois" (Widmer, Rick)
UNIVERSITY OF MICHIGAN—PHOTOGRAPHS
PH16798 693 (October 20, 1994) p89. "At The U. Of Michigan Naked Mile: Some Come To Stare" (Rusnak, Benjamin)
PH16799 693 (October 20, 1994) p87. "The Last Night Of Classes, The Jocks Of Michigan Run The Naked Mile" (Thompson, Kyndell)
PH16800 693 (October 20, 1994) p89. "Some Come To Bare" (Thompson, Kyndell)
PH16801 704 (March 23, 1995) p69. "University Of Michigan" (Lurie, Jonathan)
PH16802 719 (October 19, 1995) p101. "During Michigan's Hash Bash, The Police Arrest Participants At Random" (Ravid, Joyce)
PH16803 719 (October 19, 1995) p104. "Michigan Could Lose $10 Million A Year If It Fails To Enforce Drug Laws" (Ravid, Joyce)
PH16804 719 (October 19, 1995) p103. "Sophisticated Student-Run Networks Have Made Drugs Easier To Obtain" (Ravid, Joyce)
PH16805 719 (October 19, 1995) p100. "The University Of Michigan's Hash Bash Draws About 5,000 People A Year" (Ravid, Joyce)
UNIVERSITY OF NORTH CAROLINA—PHOTOGRAPHS
PH16806 704 (March 23, 1995) p69. "University Of North Carolina" (Jones, Craig)
PH16807 730 (March 21, 1996) p65. "Chapel Hill"
UNIVERSITY OF TEXAS-AUSTIN—PHOTOGRAPHS
PH16808 730 (March 21, 1996) p65. "University Of Texas In Rockin' Austin"
UNIVERSITY OF WASHINGTON—PHOTOGRAPHS
PH16809 626 (March 19, 1992) p70. "A Crooked Deck: The University Of Washington Flips The Cards For Caltech At The 1961 Rose Bowl"
UNIVERSITY OF WISCONSIN—PHOTOGRAPHS
PH16810 626 (March 19, 1992) p68. "The Lady In The Lake: The Pail And Shovel Party Buries The Statue Of Liberty In Icy Waters" (Kienitz, Michael)
UNPLUGGED (TELEVISION SHOW)—PHOTOGRAPHS
PH16811 619-620 (December 12, 1991) p71. "Paul McCartney Gets 'Unplugged'"
UNSTRUNG HEROES (FILM)—PHOTOGRAPHS
PH16812 717 (September 21, 1995) p90. "Watt Is Flanked By Uncles Chaykin And Richards"
UNTIL THE END OF THE WORLD (FILM)—PHOTOGRAPHS
PH16813 622 (January 23, 1992) p50. "William Hurt And Solveig Dommartin Face The End"
UNTIL THE END OF THE WORLD (FILM)—ILLUSTRATIONS
PH16814 624 (February 20, 1992) p40. "The End Of The World Feels Fine" (Holland, Brad)
UNWOUND—ALBUMS
PH16815 736 (June 13, 1996) p92. "Repetition"
UNZIPPED (FILM)—PHOTOGRAPHS
PH16816 715 (August 24, 1995) p110. "Models Celebrate Isaac Mizrahi"
PH16817 724-725 (December 28, 1995) p136. "Unusual Pleasure"
PH16818 731 (April 4, 1996) p66. "Unzipped"
UP CLOSE AND PERSONAL (FILM)—PHOTOGRAPHS
PH16819 730 (March 21, 1996) p104. "Pfeiffer And Redford Face Off (left)"
PH16820 730 (March 21, 1996) p104. "The SUndance Kid Gives A Press Conference"
UPDEGRAFF, RUSTY—PHOTOGRAPHS
PH16821 680 (April 21, 1994) pp[enc.38]. "It's Not Just Shopping, It's An Adventure" (Ragel, Jon)
UPSHAW, DAWN—ALBUMS
PH16822 655 (April 29, 1993) p65. "Symphony No. 3"
URBINA, WILBER—PHOTOGRAPHS
PH16823 680 (April 21, 1994) pp[enc.38]. "It's Not Just Shopping, It's An Adventure" (Ragel, Jon)
URBUS ORBIS (COFFEEHOUSE)—PHOTOGRAPHS
PH16824 688 (August 11, 1994) p22. "[Urbus Orbis]" (Natkin, Paul)
URGE OVERKILL—ALBUMS
PH16825 663 (August 19, 1993) p76. "Saturation"
PH16826 674 (January 27, 1994) p44. "Saturation"
PH16827 716 (September 7, 1995) p69. "Exit The Dragon"
URGE OVERKILL—ILLUSTRATIONS
PH16828 716 (September 7, 1995) p69. "Suave Rock Gods" (Dougan, Michael)
URGE OVERKILL—PHOTOGRAPHS
PH16829 663 (August 19, 1993) p28. "Urge Overkill In The Studio" (Tolbert, Mpozi)
PH16830 664 (September 2, 1993) p12. "Urge A Go-Go (clockwise from left): Onassis, Kato, Roeser" (Robert, Francis)
PH16831 664 (September 2, 1993) p11. "[Urge Overkill]" (Robert, Francis)
PH16832 672-673 (December 23, 1993) p40. "Urge Overkill: Serious Fun" (Clinch, Danny)
PH16833 685 (June 30, 1994) p40. "Etheridge With Kato, Tony Stull, Blackie Onassis And "Eddie" King Roeser (from left)" (Mazur, Kevin)
PH16834 688 (August 11, 1994) p22. "[Urge Overkill]" (Elledge, Paul)
PH16835 695 (November 17, 1994) p84. "Urge Overkill" (Clinch, Danny)
URGE OVERKILL—PHOTOGRAPHS—PORTRAITS
PH16836 664 (September 2, 1993) p11. "[Urge Overkill]" (Robert, Francis)
US3—ALBUMS
PH16837 677 (March 10, 1994) p68. "Hand On The Torch"

US3—PHOTOGRAPHS
PH16838 684 (June 16, 1994) p21. "London's Us3" (Natkin, Paul)
USED PEOPLE (FILM)—PHOTOGRAPHS
PH16839 649 (February 4, 1993) p72. "[Used People]"
USELESS PLAYBOYS—ALBUMS
PH16840 709 (June 1, 1995) p27. "The Useless Playboys" (Kozik, Frank)
THE USUAL SUSPECTS (FILM)—ILLUSTRATIONS
PH16841 716 (September 7, 1995) p75. "A Summer Sleeper" (Ulriksen, Mark)
THE USUAL SUSPECTS (FILM)—PHOTOGRAPHS
PH16842 709 (June 1, 1995) p70. "Rebel Voices"
PH16843 716 (September 7, 1995) p76. "Gabriel Byrne (left) And Kevin Spacey Face A Lineup"
PH16844 724-725 (December 28, 1995) p136. "Unusual Pleasure"
UTAH—PHOTOGRAPHS
PH16845 719 (October 19, 1995) p76. "Oil Storage Tanks Tower Above Southern Utah's Wilderness On Land That's Been Leased To An Oil Company" (McDonough, Patricia)
PH16846 719 (October 19, 1995) p75. "Oil Well Located On Federal Land For Which SUWA Seeks Wilderness Designation" (McDonough, Patricia)
PH16847 719 (October 19, 1995) p69. "A Slice Of Southern Utah's Red-Rock Wilderness That Environmentalists Are Fighting To Preserve" (McDonough, Patricia)
PH16848 719 (October 19, 1995) p72. "The Stark And Still Unspoiled Beauty Of Southern Utah's Sprawling Red-Rock Wilderness" (McDonough, Patricia)
UTTER CONFUSION—PHOTOGRAPHS
PH16849 722 (November 30, 1995) p42. "Utter Confusion Caused Exactly That: Albert Min, Len Longo And J. M. Burr" (Dipeso, Debra)

V

V, CHUCKIE—PHOTOGRAPHS
PH16850 665 (September 16, 1993) pp[enc.28]. "At Laura Lee's Salon In Boulder" (Hanauer, Mark)
PH16851 665 (September 16, 1993) pp[enc.27]. "Chuckie Racing In San Diego" (Cruse, Rich)
PH16852 665 (September 16, 1993) pp[enc.24]. "[Chuckie V]" (Hanauer, Mark)
PH16853 665 (September 16, 1993) pp[enc.29]. "[Chuckie V & Bill Braun]" (Hanauer, Mark)
PH16854 665 (September 16, 1993) pp[enc.cover]. "Fall Fashion" (Hanauer, Mark)
PH16855 665 (September 16, 1993) pp[enc.25]. "From Left: Greg Welsh, Ray Browning, Mike Pigg, Wes Hobson, Chuckie V, Scott Tinley, Nate Llerandi And Bill Braun" (Hanauer, Mark)
PH16856 665 (September 16, 1993) pp[enc.28]. "Racing In The Wildflower Triathlon In California" (Oliver, Robert)
PH16857 665 (September 16, 1993) pp[enc.27]. "Shopping At Alphalfa's Markets In Boulder, Colo." (Hanauer, Mark)
VALANDREY, CHARLOTTE—PHOTOGRAPHS
PH16858 659 (June 24, 1993) p89. "Orlando As He (above right), With Charlotte Valandrey"
VALENTI, JON—PHOTOGRAPHS
PH16859 680 (April 21, 1994) pp[enc.38]. "It's Not Just Shopping, It's An Adventure" (Ragel, Jon)
VALENTINE, HILTON—PHOTOGRAPHS
PH16860 676 (February 24, 1994) p48. "The Angry Young Animals (from left): Drummer John Steel, Organist Alan Price, bass Player Chas Chandler, Lead Singer Eric Burdon And Guitarist Hilton Valentine"
PH16861 677 (March 10, 1994) p28. "Pirner With Animals Valentine, Chas Chandler And John Steel" (Mazur, Kevin)
VALENTINE, KATHY—PHOTOGRAPHS
PH16862 616 (October 31, 1991) p11. "Cervenka, Gina Schock, Jane Wiedlin, Kathy Valentine, Charlotte Caffey (clockwise from top left)" (Granitz, Steve)
VALENZUELA, JESSE—PHOTOGRAPHS
PH16863 722 (November 30, 1995) p20. "Gin Blossom's Scott Johnson, Dead Hot's Brian Griffith, Blossom Valenzuela And Dead Hot Curtis Grippe (from left)"
PH16864 726 (January 25, 1996) p30. "Gin Blossoms: Robin Wilson, Phillip Rhodes, Bill Lien, Jesse Valenzuela, Scott Johnson (from left)" (Jennings, Steve)
VALLETTA, AMBER—PHOTOGRAPHS
PH16865 737 (June 27, 1996) p15. "Valletta (left) Hugs Amos, Who Introduced Her Onstage Piano As "My New Little Friend"" (Busacca, Larry)
VAMPIRE IN BROOKLYN (FILM)—PHOTOGRAPHS
PH16866 722 (November 30, 1995) p76. "Eddie Murphy Bites It"
VAN DAMME, JEAN-CLAUDE—PHOTOGRAPHS
PH16867 636 (August 6, 1992) p66. "Van Damme (right) And Lundgren (center) Play Robots"
PH16868 665 (September 16, 1993) p76. "Woo (left) Directs Van Damme For Action"
PH16869 692 (October 6, 1994) p81. "Van Damme Aims A Lethal Kick At Assassin James Lew"
VAN DAMME, JEAN-CLAUDE—PHOTOGRAPHS—PORTRAITS
PH16870 734 (May 16, 1996) p72. "Jean-Claude Van Damme"
VAN DIJK, CAROL—PHOTOGRAPHS
PH16871 653 (April 1, 1993) p22. "Peter Visser, Herman Bunskoeke, Carol Van Dijk And Berend Dubbe (from left)" (Doove, Hester)
VAN DOREN, CHARLES—PHOTOGRAPHS
PH16872 691 (September 22, 1994) p104. "Van Doren, Left, And Stemple Flank Host Jack Barry On "Twenty-One," Circa 1956"
VAN HALEN—ALBUMS
PH16873 617 (November 14, 1991) p144. "1984" (Angelus, Pete)
PH16874 617 (November 14, 1991) p144. "1984" (Seireeni, Richard)
PH16875 617 (November 14, 1991) p144. "1984" (Jellison, David)
PH16876 617 (November 14, 1991) p144. "1984" (Nahas, Margo Zafer)
PH16877 619-620 (December 12, 1991) p187. "For Unlawful Carnal Knowledge"
PH16878 704 (March 23, 1995) p122. "Balance"
VAN HALEN—ILLUSTRATIONS
PH16879 704 (March 23, 1995) p144. "Van Halen: A Delicate Balance" (Martin, Ruth)
VAN HALEN—PHOTOGRAPHS
PH16880 615 (October 17, 1991) p34. "Eddie Van Halen (left) And Sammy Hagar" (Mazur, Kevin)
PH16881 619-620 (December 12, 1991) p33. "'Poundcake' By Van Halen"
PH16882 622 (January 23, 1992) p7. "Eddie Van HAlen And Hagar" (Clark, Shaun)
PH16883 645-646 (December 10, 1992) p79. "Van Halen Took Honors" (Mazur, Kevin)
PH16884 650 (February 18, 1993) p16. "Alex, Eddie, Anthony, Hagar (from left)"
PH16885 654 (April 15, 1993) p13. "Van Halen Onstage At The Whiskey" (Granitz, Steve)
PH16886 663 (August 19, 1993) p25. "Sammy Hagar And Eddie Van Halen" (Settle, Ken)
PH16887 667 (October 14, 1993) p69. "Van Halen And Fenske At '92 MTV Awards" (Micelotta, Frank)
PH16888 667 (October 14, 1993) p78. "Van Halen's 'Teacher'"
PH16889 740 (August 8, 1996) p23. "The Cradlerocksagain: Roth Rejoins Alex And Eddie Van Halen, Michael Anthony (from left)" (Seeff, Norman)

PH16890 750-751 (December 26, 1996) p78. "Van Halen's Michael Anthony, And Alex And Eddie Van Halen With Roth (from left)" (Christensen, Jeff)

VAN HALEN—PHOTOGRAPHS—PORTRAITS

PH16891 619-620 (December 12, 1991) p53. "Van Halen (left)..." (Temme, Marty)

PH16892 643 (November 12, 1992) p129. "Van Halen" (Seliger, Mark)

VAN HALEN, ALEX—PHOTOGRAPHS

PH16893 650 (February 18, 1993) p16. "Alex, Eddie, Anthony, Hagar (from left)"

PH16894 714 (August 10, 1995) p24. "Doug Morris (center) With Alex And Eddie Van Halen" (Kravitz, Jeff)

VAN HALEN, EDDIE—ILLUSTRATIONS

PH16895 615 (October 17, 1991) p5. "Eddie Van Halen In Performance" (Burke, Philip)

VAN HALEN, EDDIE—PHOTOGRAPHS

PH16896 615 (October 17, 1991) p34. "Eddie Van Halen (left) And Sammy Hagar" (Mazur, Kevin)

PH16897 615 (October 17, 1991) p14. "Hagar, Goldberg, Van Halen And Goldberg's Daughter, Alex" (Mazur, Kevin)

PH16898 619-620 (December 12, 1991) p31. "Van Halen And Bertinelli Wait For Wolfgang" (Granitz, Steve)

PH16899 622 (January 23, 1992) p7. "Eddie Van HAlen And Hagar" (Clark, Shaun)

PH16900 645-646 (December 10, 1992) p98. "Valerie Bertinelli, Van Halen And James Wood At A Clinton Rally" (Jacobs, Michael)

PH16901 649 (February 4, 1993) p8. "Van Halen (left) And George Harrison At The Jeff Porcaro Tribute" (Granitz, Steve)

PH16902 650 (February 18, 1993) p16. "Alex, Eddie, Anthony, Hagar (from left)"

PH16903 663 (August 19, 1993) p25. "Sammy Hagar And Eddie Van Halen" (Settle, Ken)

PH16904 672-673 (December 23, 1993) p74. "Graham Nash, Van Halen And Young" (Blakesberg, Jay)

PH16905 675 (February 10, 1994) p23. "Page Moving Van Halen" (Granitz, Steve)

PH16906 683 (June 2, 1994) p27. "Duffers Eddie van Halen (left) And Neil Young" (Granitz, Steve)

PH16907 705 (April 6, 1995) p49. "At Age 11, Behind His First Drum Kit"

PH16908 705 (April 6, 1995) p46. "At Age 12 With Mom Eugenia And His First Guitar"

PH16909 705 (April 6, 1995) p45. "[Eddie Van Halen]" (Seliger, Mark)

PH16910 705 (April 6, 1995) p44. "Right Here, Right Now: Eddie Van Halen With His Wife, Actress Valerie Bertinelli, And Son, Wolfgang" (Seliger, Mark)

PH16911 705 (April 6, 1995) pp[cover]. "The Rolling Stone Interview: Eddie Van Halen" (Seliger, Mark)

PH16912 714 (August 10, 1995) p24. "Doug Morris (center) With Alex And Eddie Van Halen" (Kravitz, Jeff)

PH16913 745 (October 17, 1996) p27. "David Lee Roth With Pumpkin Billy Corgan And Eddie Van Halen" (Kravitz, Jeff)

VAN HALEN, EDDIE—PHOTOGRAPHS—PORTRAITS

PH16914 705 (April 6, 1995) p43. "[Eddie Van Halen]" (Seliger, Mark)

PH16915 705 (April 6, 1995) p48. "Pasadena High Graduation Picture, '73"

VAN HALEN, EUGENIA—PHOTOGRAPHS

PH16916 705 (April 6, 1995) p46. "At Age 12 With Mom Eugenia And His First Guitar"

VAN HALEN, WOLFGANG—PHOTOGRAPHS

PH16917 705 (April 6, 1995) p44. "Right Here, Right Now: Eddie Van Halen With His Wife, Actress Valerie Bertinelli, And Son, Wolfgang" (Seliger, Mark)

VAN PEEBLES, MARIO—ILLUSTRATIONS

PH16918 658 (June 10, 1993) p73. "New Jack Cowboys" (Blitt, Barry)

PH16919 708 (May 18, 1995) p95. "Fight The Power" (Kunz, Anita)

VAN PEEBLES, MARIO—PHOTOGRAPHS

PH16920 658 (June 10, 1993) p74. "The Magnificent Six (from left): Stephen Baldwin, Big Daddy Kane, Mario Van Peebles, Tiny Lister Jr., Charles Lane, Tone Loc"

PH16921 658 (June 10, 1993) p76. "Son Of A Big Gun: Mario Still Leans On The Sweet Back Of His Old Man, Melvin" (Guzman)

PH16922 708 (May 18, 1995) p96. "Mario And Melvin Van Peebles Set Up A Shot"

VAN PEEBLES, MELVIN—PHOTOGRAPHS

PH16923 658 (June 10, 1993) p76. "Son Of A Big Gun: Mario Still Leans On The Sweet Back Of His Old Man, Melvin" (Guzman)

PH16924 708 (May 18, 1995) p96. "Mario And Melvin Van Peebles Set Up A Shot"

PH16925 724-725 (December 28, 1995) p60. "Van peebles" (Elgar, Nick)

VAN ROCK, THEO—PHOTOGRAPHS

PH16926 686-687 (July 14, 1994) p45. "[Rollins Band]" (Halfin, Ross)

VAN SANT, GUS—PHOTOGRAPHS

PH16927 616 (October 31, 1991) p61. "[Gus Van Sant]" (Watson, Norman)

PH16928 616 (October 31, 1991) p62. "Van Sant And Phoenix, Who Signed On Before 'Idaho' Was Financed" (Edwards, Eric)

PH16929 669 (November 11, 1993) p60. "'Uma Was Always Sissy Hankshaw To Me,' Says 'Cowgirls' Director Gus Van Sant" (Markus, Kurt)

VAN SEENUS, GUINEVERE—PHOTOGRAPHS

PH16930 741 (August 22, 1996) p86. "[Guinevere Van Seenus]" (Churilla, Lynda)

VAN ZANDT, STEVE—PHOTOGRAPHS

PH16931 617 (November 14, 1991) p11. "Springsteen, Southside Johnny, Little Steven (from left)" (Busacca, Larry)

PH16932 644 (November 26, 1992) p15. "Max Weinberg, Clarence Clemons, Darlene Love, Little Steven, Garry Tallent And Danny Federici (from left)" (Mazur, Kevin)

PH16933 664 (September 2, 1993) p31. "[Rumble Doll]" (Busacca, Larry)

VAN ZANDT, TOWNES—ALBUMS

PH16934 685 (June 30, 1994) p75. "Roadsongs"

PH16935 704 (March 23, 1995) p124. "No Deeper Blue"

VANCE, COURTNEY B.—PHOTOGRAPHS

PH16936 708 (May 18, 1995) p96. "Vance And Chong Front The Panthers"

VANCOUVER, WASHINGTON—PHOTOGRAPHS

PH16937 744 (October 3, 1996) p23. "The Alternative-Clad Audiences At Jesus Northwest, In Vancouver, Wash., Praises Its Lucky Stars" (Blakesberg, Jay)

VANDROSS, LUTHER—ALBUMS

PH16938 663 (August 19, 1993) p77. "Never Let Me Go"

PH16939 702 (February 23, 1995) p74. "Songs"

VANESSA-MAE—ILLUSTRATIONS

PH16940 731 (April 4, 1996) p17. "G-Strings" (O'Connell, Mitch)

VANILLA ICE—ALBUMS

PH16941 681 (May 5, 1994) p55. "Mind Blowin"

VANILLA ICE—PHOTOGRAPHS

PH16942 619-620 (December 12, 1991) p76. "The Pistol-Packing Ice Man" (Ortega, Albert)

PH16943 619-620 (December 12, 1991) p53. "Stop This Train: Vanilla Ice (below)" (Mazur, Kevin)

VARGAS, PETER—PHOTOGRAPHS

PH16944 715 (August 24, 1995) p94. "Keane With Empire State Building Guards Darren Hicks, Lance Pelt And Peter Vargas" (Danelian, Stephen)

VARIOUS ARTISTS—ALBUMS

PH16945 621 (January 9, 1992) p52. "JazzSpeak"

PH16946 623 (February 6, 1992) p80. "I'm Your Fan"
PH16947 624 (February 20, 1992) p45. "Pimps, Players And Private Eyes"
PH16948 626 (March 19, 1992) p93. "Street Jams"
PH16949 629 (April 30, 1992) p58. "Guitarrorists"
PH16950 639 (September 17, 1992) p91. "Virus 100"
PH16951 640 (October 1, 1992) p68. "The Specter Records Story"
PH16952 645-646 (December 10, 1992) p187. "A Very Special Christmas 2"
PH16953 648 (January 21, 1993) p52. "Freedom Of Choice"
PH16954 648 (January 21, 1993) p52. "Roots N' Blues"
PH16955 648 (January 21, 1993) p50. "Techno Mancer"
PH16956 649 (February 4, 1993) p69. "Across The Great Divide"
PH16957 649 (February 4, 1993) p62. "Anarchy In The UK"
PH16958 649 (February 4, 1993) p63. "The Beat Generation"
PH16959 649 (February 4, 1993) p62. "The Blank Generation"
PH16960 649 (February 4, 1993) p62. "The Modern World"
PH16961 658 (June 10, 1993) p69. "The Cobra Records Story: Chicago Rock And Blues 1956-1958"
PH16962 660-661 (July 8, 1993) p116. "B. Brown Posse"
PH16963 660-661 (July 8, 1993) p109. "Sweet Relief"
PH16964 662 (August 5, 1993) p65. "Rites Of Rhythm & Blues"
PH16965 664 (September 2, 1993) p59. "Menace II Society"
PH16966 665 (September 16, 1993) p72. "Bob Dylan: The 30th Anniversary Concert Celebration"
PH16967 665 (September 16, 1993) p66. "Uptown MTV Unplugged"
PH16968 667 (October 14, 1993) p121. "Go-Man-Go"
PH16969 668 (October 28, 1993) p75. "The Great 1955 Shrine Concert"
PH16970 669 (November 11, 1993) p74. "Common Threads"
PH16971 669 (November 11, 1993) p75. "No Alternative"
PH16972 670 (November 25, 1993) p17. "Born To Choose"
PH16973 670 (November 25, 1993) p17. "In Defense Of Animals"
PH16974 670 (November 25, 1993) p17. "No Alternative"
PH16975 671 (December 9, 1993) p70. "Born To Choose"
PH16976 671 (December 9, 1993) p72. "Sounds Of The South"
PH16977 672-673 (December 23, 1993) p74. "No Alternative"
PH16978 674 (January 27, 1994) p52. "Conmemorative"
PH16979 674 (January 27, 1994) p64. "No Alternative"
PH16980 675 (February 10, 1994) p60. "No Alternative"
PH16981 676 (February 24, 1994) p56. "Stone Free"
PH16982 678 (March 24, 1994) p96. "Back To The Streets"
PH16983 678 (March 24, 1994) p94. "Howls, Raps And Roars"
PH16984 679 (April 7, 1994) p72. "Live At CBGB's"
PH16985 680 (April 21, 1994) p85. "Rhythm Country And Blues"
PH16986 680 (April 21, 1994) p85. "A Tribute To Curtis Mayfield"
PH16987 682 (May 19, 1994) p100. "Alternative NRG"
PH16988 682 (May 19, 1994) p102. "Deep Six"
PH16989 686-687 (July 14, 1994) p109. "Rare On Air Vol. 1"
PH16990 688 (August 11, 1994) p69. "Seattle Women In Rock"
PH16991 693 (October 20, 1994) p37. "Earthrise"
PH16992 694 (November 3, 1994) p100. "Kiss My Ass"
PH16993 698-699 (December 29, 1994) p174. "Rock Stars Kill"
PH16994 698-699 (December 29, 1994) p188. "Woodstock"
PH16995 700 (January 26, 1995) p60. "British Beat Before The Beatles"
PH16996 700 (January 26, 1995) p61. "The Glory Of Gershwin"
PH16997 703 (March 9, 1995) p64. "Beat The Retreat"
PH16998 703 (March 9, 1995) p67. "Just Can't Get Enough"
PH16999 705 (April 6, 1995) p64. "Law Of The Jungle"
PH17000 706 (April 20, 1995) p70. "Till The Night is Gone"
PH17001 716 (September 7, 1995) p70. "Valis 1 Destruction Of Syntax"
PH17002 718 (October 5, 1995) p73. "Spirit Of '73"
PH17003 719 (October 19, 1995) p149. "Country Kickers"
PH17004 721 (November 16, 1995) p110. "It's Hard To Believe It"
PH17005 723 (December 14, 1995) p81. "Def Jam 10th Year Anniversary" (Coleman, Mark)
PH17006 723 (December 14, 1995) p86. "Totally Wired"
PH17007 724-725 (December 28, 1995) p58. "Help"
PH17008 726 (January 25, 1996) p38. "Encomium"
PH17009 728 (February 22, 1996) p60. "American Folk Blues Festival '62-'65"
PH17010 729 (March 7, 1996) p28. "Home Alive"
PH17011 737 (June 27, 1996) p54. "The United States Of Poetry"
PH17012 740 (August 8, 1996) p60. "The Moog Cookbook" (X)
PH17013 741 (August 22, 1996) p95. "Sweet Relief II"
PH17014 742 (September 5, 1996) p62. "The Concert For The Rock & Roll Hall Of Fame"
PH17015 743 (September 19, 1996) p80. "Growin' Up Too Fast"
PH17016 745 (October 17, 1996) p134. "Germs (Tribute)"
PH17017 748 (November 28, 1996) p134. "Supernatural Fairy Tales"
PH17018 750-751 (December 26, 1996) p192. "Cosmic Kurushi Monsters"

VARNEY, JIM—PHOTOGRAPHS
PH17019 669 (November 11, 1993) p81. "Tomlin's Miss Hathaway Welcomes The Clampetts To 90210"

VASQUEZ, JUNIOR—PHOTOGRAPHS
PH17020 706 (April 20, 1995) pp[enc.29]. "At A Club In New York" (Tavee, Tom)
PH17021 706 (April 20, 1995) pp[enc.22]. "At Big Coffee Shop, In New York" (Tavee, Tom)
PH17022 706 (April 20, 1995) pp[enc.23]. "At Home" (Tavee, Tom)
PH17023 706 (April 20, 1995) pp[enc.24]. "On The Road At Soundworks, In New York" (Tavee, Tom)
PH17024 736 (June 13, 1996) p32. "Mellencamp, Left, And Junior Vasquez At New York's Hit Factory In April" (Knight, Kevin)

VASQUEZ, JUNIOR—PHOTOGRAPHS—PORTRAITS
PH17025 706 (April 20, 1995) pp[enc.26]. "At Eight Ball Records, In New York" (Tavee, Tom)

VASQUEZ, UBALDO—PHOTOGRAPHS
PH17026 669 (November 11, 1993) p35. "Rebuilding The Carpenters Union: Ubaldo Vasquez, Mike Olds And Jesus Gomez (foreground, from left)" (Reed, Dudley)

VAUGHAN, JIMMIE—PHOTOGRAPHS
PH17027 711 (June 29, 1995) p18. "B. B. King, Robert Cray, Buddy Guy, Art Neville, Jimmie Vaughan, Clapton, Raitt And Tommy Shannon" (Long, Andrew)

VAUGHAN, STEVIE RAY—ALBUMS
PH17028 618 (November 28, 1991) p94. "The Sky Is Crying"

VAUGHAN, STEVIE RAY—PHOTOGRAPHS
PH17029 615 (October 17, 1991) p47. "Cray, Clapton And Vaughan (from left) On The Night Of The Crash" (Knight, Robert)

VAUGHN, VINCE—PHOTOGRAPHS
PH17030 746 (October 31, 1996) p78. "Now Playing"

VEAL, ROB—PHOTOGRAPHS
PH17031 710 (June 15, 1995) p52. "At The Uptown: McBride, Veal, John Crist, Michael Gibson (from left)" (Clinch, Danny)

VEDDER, EDDIE—ILLUSTRATIONS
PH17032 672-673 (December 23, 1993) p7. "Pearl Jam's Eddie vedder" (Burke, Philip)
PH17033 681 (May 5, 1994) p5. "Eddie Vedder" (Burke, Philip)
PH17034 695 (November 17, 1994) p152. "Eddie Vedder Of Pearl Jam" (Corio, Paul)
PH17035 697 (December 15, 1994) p91. "Life Study" (Cowles, David)
PH17036 701 (February 9, 1995) p14. "Pearl Jam" (Pendergrast, James T.)

PH17037 712-713 (July 13, 1995) p107. "Forever Young" (Kunz, Anita)
PH17038 712-713 (July 13, 1995) p20. "Van" (Pendergrast, James T.)

VEDDER, EDDIE—ILLUSTRATIONS—PORTRAITS
PH17039 669 (November 11, 1993) p72. "Nothin' But A G Thing" (Payne, C. F.)

VEDDER, EDDIE—PHOTOGRAPHS
PH17040 616 (October 31, 1991) p15. "Pearl Jam (from left): Mike McCready, David Abbruzzese, Eddie Vedder, Jeff Ament And Stone Gossard" (Cuffaro, Chris)
PH17041 616 (October 31, 1991) p16. "Vedder Losing Himself Onstage" (Johnson, Lisa)
PH17042 624 (February 20, 1992) p19. "Eddie Vedder" (Constanini, Mark)
PH17043 634-635 (July 9, 1992) p13. "Pearl Jam's Mike McCready, Dave Abbruzzese, Eddie Vedder, Gossard And Jeff Ament (from left)" (Mercer, Lance)
PH17044 639 (September 17, 1992) p60. "Eddie Vedder, Mike McCready, Jeff Ament And Stone Gossard (from left) Of Pearl Jam" (Blakesberg, Jay)
PH17045 642 (October 29, 1992) p19. "Kiedis (left) And Vedder Get Tender" (Mazur, Kevin)
PH17046 645-646 (December 10, 1992) p98. "Eddie Vedder At A Rock The Vote Concert" (Rachlin, Amy)
PH17047 645-646 (December 10, 1992) p79. "Pearl Jam's Eddie Vedder" (Granitz, Steve)
PH17048 645-646 (December 10, 1992) p96. "Vedder (left) With Sammy Hagar" (Blakesberg, Jay)
PH17049 650 (February 18, 1993) p11. "Richards Flanked By Young-uns Mike McCready (left) And Vedder" (Natkin, Paul)
PH17050 651 (March 4, 1993) p16. "Eddie Vedder And The Surviving Doors Light A Fire Together" (Granitz, Steve)
PH17051 651 (March 4, 1993) p49. "Eddie Vedder Moshes To A Different Drum" (Skid)
PH17052 651 (March 4, 1993) p15. "Eddie Vedder Strikes A Lizard King Pose" (Granitz, Steve)
PH17053 660-661 (July 8, 1993) p16. "Jammin' With Eddie: Vedder And Band To Tour Europe" (Allen, Greg)
PH17054 662 (August 5, 1993) p34. "Vedder (left) With Jeff Ament" (Rachlin, Amy)
PH17055 664 (September 2, 1993) p29. "Hair Apparent: Pearl Jam's Vedder" (Mikrut, Jack)
PH17056 667 (October 14, 1993) p39. "Below: Eddie Vedder (left) With Neil Young" (Kravitz, Jeff)
PH17057 668 (October 28, 1993) p60. "Ament, Vedder And McCready Write A Set List" (Seliger, Mark)
PH17058 668 (October 28, 1993) p52. "Before The Frenzy: Vedder At A Sound Check In Spokane, Wash., This Summer" (Seliger, Mark)
PH17059 668 (October 28, 1993) p56. "Subtle He's Not: Vedder Heading To Work Incognito" (Seliger, Mark)
PH17060 668 (October 28, 1993) p51. "The Sun Shines On The Five Musketeers: Jeff Ament, Eddie Vedder (We're Not Kidding), Dave Abbruzzese, Stone Gossard And Mike McCready (from left)" (Seliger, Mark)
PH17061 668 (October 28, 1993) p56. "Vedder (on his back) And Bassist Jeff Ament Get Crazy Onstage" (Preston, Neal)
PH17062 668 (October 28, 1993) p57. "Vedder And Ament (flying): Thriving On The Weirdness" (Preston, Neal)
PH17063 668 (October 28, 1993) p52. "Vedder Crowd-Surfing In 1991: 'A Lot Of That Came Out Of Me Saying Look, This Is How Intense I'm Taking This Moment'" (Cuffaro, Chris)
PH17064 668 (October 28, 1993) p55. "Vedder In A Private Moment Backstage: 'I Can't Seem To Enjoy Success'" (Seliger, Mark)
PH17065 668 (October 28, 1993) p58. "...While Dave Abbruzzese Takes Five And Vedder Mops Up" (Seliger, Mark)
PH17066 671 (December 9, 1993) p26. "Eddie Vedder Onstage In San Francisco" (Blakesberg, Jay)
PH17067 672-673 (December 23, 1993) p63. "Above: Neil Young And Eddie Vedder Share A Moment" (Kravitz, Jeff)
PH17068 672-673 (December 23, 1993) p17. "Above: The Dorrs With Vedder" (Mazur, Kevin)
PH17069 672-673 (December 23, 1993) p58. "Eddie Vedder (left, no mask) With Young" (Preston, Neal)
PH17070 672-673 (December 23, 1993) p69. "Us 'Vs.' The World: Gossard, Mike McCready, Dave Abbruzzese, Vedder, Jeff Ament (from left)" (Seliger, Mark)
PH17071 674 (January 27, 1994) p41. "Song 'N' Sex God Vedder" (Preston, Neal)
PH17072 674 (January 27, 1994) p28. "Vedder And haynes Do The Bus Jam" (Spinelli, Edward)
PH17073 675 (February 10, 1994) p13. "Pearl Jam Broke Sales Records" (Mazur, Kevin)
PH17074 679 (April 7, 1994) p38. "Arm In Arms: Arm, Vedder And Gilmore"
PH17075 679 (April 7, 1994) p20. "Making 'My Generation' His Own: Vedder" (Mazur, Kevin)
PH17076 681 (May 5, 1994) p11. "[Pearl Jam]" (Mahurin, Matt)
PH17077 688 (August 11, 1994) p17. "[Eddie Vedder & Beth Liebling]"
PH17078 692 (October 6, 1994) p15. "Novoselic, Vedder And Earnie Bailey (from left) Get Loose" (Van Wey, Charles)
PH17079 696 (December 1, 1994) p23. "The Annual Bridge School Benefit: Pearl Jam's Jeff Ament And Eddie Vedder (above)" (Blakesberg, Jay)
PH17080 698-699 (December 29, 1994) p42. "L7's Donita Sparks, Vedder, L7's Dee Plakas And Her Husband, Kurk Canning (from left)" (Mercer, Lance)
PH17081 698-699 (December 29, 1994) p107. "Sorry, Wrong Bus: Reluctant Heroes Eddie Vedder (center) And Cornell (right) During The 1992 Lollapalooza Tour" (Mercer, Lance)
PH17082 698-699 (December 29, 1994) p68. "Young, Vedder And Stone Gossard (from left) Do The Right Thing For The Kids" (Hashimoto, Mike)
PH17083 700 (January 26, 1995) p50. "Eddie Vedder At The Helm Of '94's Best band" (Busacca, Larry)
PH17084 702 (February 23, 1995) p26. "Eddie vedder: I Am What I Play" (Mercer, Lance)
PH17085 702 (February 23, 1995) p26. "Pirate Music: McCready, Vedder, Ament, Irons And Stone Gossard (from left)" (Mercer, Lance)
PH17086 708 (May 18, 1995) p28. "Eddie Vedder Gets It Together On The Road" (Mercer, Lance)
PH17087 709 (June 1, 1995) p20. "From Left: Eddie Vedder; Dave Grohl; And Their Guiding Light, Mike Watt" (Mazur, Kevin)
PH17088 709 (June 1, 1995) p20. "Vedder (left) And Watt Preaching The Punk-Rock Gospel" (Mazur, Kevin)
PH17089 710 (June 15, 1995) p17. "Watt (left) And Vedder After A New York Show" (Mazur, Kevin)
PH17090 714 (August 10, 1995) p20. "Vedder: Now He's A Romantic Balladeer" (Mazur, Kevin)
PH17091 716 (September 7, 1995) p25. "Back On The Road—Sort Of: Pearl Jam's Vedder" (Stone, T.)
PH17092 717 (September 21, 1995) p19. "The Blues Had A Baby, And It Named It Punk Rock: Vedder (left) And Rush"
PH17093 724-725 (December 28, 1995) p40. "Eddie Vedder (left) And Neil Young" (Busacca, Larry)
PH17094 724-725 (December 28, 1995) p48. "Vedder Dropped Out" (Mazur, Kevin)
PH17095 726 (January 25, 1996) p37. "Best Make Singer: Eddie Vedder Of Pearl Jam" (Mazur, Kevin)
PH17096 726 (January 25, 1996) p17. "Mike McCready, Jeff Ament, Harper, Eddie Vedder, Jack Irons And Stone Gossard (from left)"
PH17097 730 (March 21, 1996) p17. "Fastbacks' Kurt Bloch, Mike Musburger, Vedder, Fastbacks' Kim Warnick, Lu Lu Gargiulo" (Michelson, Randall)

PH17098 732 (April 18, 1996) p19. "Smokin'! Vedder And Wife Beth Liebling" (Mazur, Kevin)
PH17099 733 (May 2, 1996) p24. "Pearl Jam's Jeff Ament And Eddie Vedder" (Popplewell, John)
PH17100 736 (June 13, 1996) p19. "Doing The Right Thing At The VH1 Honors Benefit: Eddie Vedder, Who Looks Eerily Like Harrison Ford, Michael Stipe And Recent Newlywed Sean Penn" (Mazur, Kevin)
PH17101 743 (September 19, 1996) p32. "Eddie Vedder, Still Battling The Ticket Industry" (Stone, T.)
PH17102 746 (October 31, 1996) p34. "Candidate Vedder? Eddie Addresses The Post-Grunge Nation" (Mazur, Kevin)
PH17103 748 (November 28, 1996) p54. "Beth Liebling And Vedder At The VH1 Honors At The Universal Amphitheater, In L.A., April 1996" (Mazur, Kevin)
PH17104 748 (November 28, 1996) p51. "[Eddie Vedder]" (Halfin, Ross)
PH17105 748 (November 28, 1996) pp[cover]. "Inventing Eddie Vedder: Pearl Jam's Mystery Man" (Halfin, Ross)
PH17106 748 (November 28, 1996) p52. "Mueller, Voted Most Talented At San Dieguito High In 1982, And Jamie Burris"
PH17107 750-751 (December 26, 1996) p78. "Found: Eddie Vedder And Pearl Jam Surface In Seattle" (Mazur, Kevin)

VEDDER, EDDIE—PHOTOGRAPHS—PORTRAITS
PH17108 668 (October 28, 1993) p55. "Young Eddie As A High-School Senior"
PH17109 702 (February 23, 1995) p48. "Come On, Get Happy: Eddie Vedder With Idol Neil Young" (Mazur, Kevin)
PH17110 749 (December 12, 1996) p20. "Proud Mom At Son's College Graduation? No, It's Steinem With Vedder, Post-Rally" (Warburg, Jenny)

VEES, JACK—PHOTOGRAPHS
PH17111 708 (May 18, 1995) p27. "The Dashboard Drummer Changes Your Relationship To Music Says Vees" (Kuehn, Karen)

VEGA, DAPHNE RUBIN—PHOTOGRAPHS
PH17112 734 (May 16, 1996) p55. "[Daphne Rubin Vega]" (Hom, Marc)

VEGA, SUZANNE—ALBUMS
PH17113 640 (October 1, 1992) p63. "99.9 F"
PH17114 748 (November 28, 1996) p136. "Nine Objects Of Desire"

VEGA, SUZANNE—PHOTOGRAPHS
PH17115 634-635 (July 9, 1992) p13. "Vega" (Ettlinger, Marion)
PH17116 645-646 (December 10, 1992) p85. "Suzanne Vega"
PH17117 656 (May 13, 1993) p32. "Vega At The Academy" (Capak, R. J.)
PH17118 678 (March 24, 1994) p28. "Kristofferson, Williams, Vega, DJ Vin Scelsa And Lou Reed (from left)" (Roberts, Ebet)
PH17119 715 (August 24, 1995) p62. "Charlie, Sting And Suzanne Vega" (Cohen, Lester)
PH17120 732 (April 18, 1996) p32. "Sporting A New 'Do: Suzanne Vega"
PH17121 734 (May 16, 1996) p17. "Garofalo (left) And Vega Waxin' And Relaxin'" (Murray, Rebecca)
PH17122 750-751 (December 26, 1996) p70. "[Suzanne Vega]" (Sanchez, Albert)

VEGA, SUZANNE—PHOTOGRAPHS—PORTRAITS
PH17123 692 (October 6, 1994) p53. "Suzanne Vega" (Southam, Andrew)
PH17124 750-751 (December 26, 1996) p70. "Make-Over" (Goldsmith, Lynn)

VELDT—PHOTOGRAPHS
PH17125 683 (June 2, 1994) p24. "Twin Tones: Daniel Chavis, Burris, Danny Chavis And Levi (from left)" (Cardillicchio, Nick)

VELO-DELUXE—ALBUMS
PH17126 697 (December 15, 1994) p96. "Superelastic"

VELOCITY GIRL—ALBUMS
PH17127 658 (June 10, 1993) p71. "Copacetic"
PH17128 686-687 (July 14, 1994) p106. "Simpatico!"

VELOCITY GIRL—PHOTOGRAPHS—PORTRAITS
PH17129 655 (April 29, 1993) p24. "Revving It Up: Velocity's Shannon, Spellman, Nelson, Riles And Moore (from left)" (Falls, John)

VELOSO, CAETANO—ALBUMS
PH17130 633 (June 25, 1992) p45. "Circulado"
PH17131 645-646 (December 10, 1992) p182. "Circulado"

VELOSO, CAETANO—ILLUSTRATIONS
PH17132 688 (August 11, 1994) p69. "[Caetano Veloso & Gil Gilberto]" (Menchin, Scott)

VELVET CRUSH—ALBUMS
PH17133 696 (December 1, 1994) p128. "Teenage Symphonies To God"

VELVET CRUSH—PHOTOGRAPHS
PH17134 627 (April 2, 1992) p19. "Jeffrey Borchardt, Paul Chastain And Ric Menck (from left)" (Lavine, Michael)
PH17135 685 (June 30, 1994) p40. "Velvet's Paul Chastain, Jeffrey Borchardt And Menck With McGuinn (from left)"

VELVET CRUSH—PHOTOGRAPHS—PORTRAITS
PH17136 645-646 (December 10, 1992) p61. "Velvet Crush"

VELVET UNDERGROUND—ALBUMS
PH17137 617 (November 14, 1991) p97. "Velvet Underground And Nico" (Warhol, Andy)
PH17138 670 (November 25, 1993) p107. "Live MCMXCIII"
PH17139 722 (November 30, 1995) p69. "Peel Slowly And See"

VELVET UNDERGROUND—ILLUSTRATIONS
PH17140 663 (August 19, 1993) p4. "Velvet Underground" (Pendergrast, James T.)
PH17141 670 (November 25, 1993) p107. "The Velvet Mainstream" (Woodruff, Thomas)

VELVET UNDERGROUND—PHOTOGRAPHS
PH17142 659 (June 24, 1993) p17. "The Velvets In 1968"
PH17143 659 (June 24, 1993) p18. "The Velvets In Action In 1966"
PH17144 662 (August 5, 1993) p28. "John Cale (left) And Lou Reed Doing The Velvet Underground" (Paton, Tim)
PH17145 718 (October 5, 1995) p46. "The Velvet Underground (clockwise from bottom left): Nico, Reed, Morrison, Cale And Tucker"
PH17146 719 (October 19, 1995) p22. "The Acute Mind At Work: Morrison As A Velvet In '66" (Malanga, Gerard)
PH17147 728 (February 22, 1996) p18. "Martha Morrison, Tucker, Cale And Reed (from left) Celebrate The Velvets' Induction" (Mazur, Kevin)
PH17148 750-751 (December 26, 1996) p45. "Martha Morrison, The Wife Of Sterling, Moe Tucker, John Cale, And Lou Reed (from left) Celebrate The Velvets' Induction" (Mazur, Kevin)

VELVET UNDERGROUND—PHOTOGRAPHS—PORTRAITS
PH17149 659 (June 24, 1993) p17. "Tucker, Morrison, Cale And Reed Today (from left)" (Wood, Graham)

VENICE-VENICE (FILM)—PHOTOGRAPHS
PH17150 642 (October 29, 1992) p77. "Venice-Venice"

VERDU, MARIBEL—PHOTOGRAPHS
PH17151 681 (May 5, 1994) p49. "Sanz Nuzzles Verdu For A Beautiful Time"

VERLAINE, TOM—PHOTOGRAPHS
PH17152 647 (January 7, 1993) p22. "Tom Verlaine, Richard Lloyd, Billy Ficca And Fred Smith (from left)" (Buck, Chris)

VERMILLION, ERIC—PHOTOGRAPHS
PH17153 691 (September 22, 1994) p38. "Revoke-Your-License Velocity: Gumball Drummer Jay Spiegel, Fleming And Bassist Eric Vermillion (from left)" (Capak, R. J.)

VERTIGO (FILM)—PHOTOGRAPHS
PH17154 745 (October 17, 1996) p144. "Vertigo: Alfred Hitchcock's Obsession Is Restored To Its Erotic-Neurotic Glory"

VERUCA SALT—ALBUMS
PH17155 694 (November 3, 1994) p100. "American Thighs"

VERUCA SALT—ILLUSTRATIONS
PH17156 700 (January 26, 1995) p9. "Veruca Salt" (Burke,

Philip)
VERUCA SALT—PHOTOGRAPHS
PH17157 686-687 (July 14, 1994) p73. "Salt Of The Earth: Lack, Gordon, Post And Shapiro (from left)" (Elledge, Paul)
PH17158 698-699 (December 29, 1994) p45. "Veruca Salt" (Elledge, Paul)
PH17159 700 (January 26, 1995) p19. "Gordon, Lack, Post And Shapiro (from left)" (Seliger, Mark)
PH17160 705 (April 6, 1995) p25. "Veruca Salt Lend A Distinctive 'Aurora' To The Project" (Elledge, Paul)
PH17161 709 (June 1, 1995) p17. "Veruca Salt's Louise Post, Jim Shapiro And Gordon (from left)" (Peters, Karen A.)
VERVE—PHOTOGRAPHS
PH17162 660-661 (July 8, 1993) p96. "Verve (clockwise from top left): Ashcroft, Peter Salisbury, Simon Jones And McCabe" (Sharp, Ken)
PH17163 672-673 (December 23, 1993) p45. "[Verve]" (Double, Stephen)
VERVE PIPE—PHOTOGRAPHS
PH17164 741 (August 22, 1996) p116. "[The Verve Pipe]" (Maxwell, Robert)
VESSEL, JERRY—PHOTOGRAPHS
PH17165 665 (September 16, 1993) p25. "In The Red: Mack, Vessel, Kozelek, Koutsos (from left)" (Blakesberg, Jay)
VH1 (TELEVISION NETWORK)—ILLUSTRATIONS
PH17166 712-713 (July 13, 1995) p119. "The New VH1: Too Old For Beavis, Too Young To Die" (Conrad, Jon)
VIBE (PUBLICATION)—PHOTOGRAPHS
PH17167 642 (October 29, 1992) p33. "[Vibe]"
VICIOUS, SID—PHOTOGRAPHS
PH17168 720 (November 2, 1995) p49. "Nancy Spungen & Sid Vicious"
VICIOUS, SID—PHOTOGRAPHS—PORTRAITS
PH17169 735 (May 30, 1996) p3. "[The Faces Of Heroin]"
VICKREY, DAN—PHOTOGRAPHS
PH17170 669 (November 11, 1993) p24. "A '90s Sensibility: Vickrey, Gillingham, Duritz, Bowman, Malley, Bryson (from left)" (Blakesberg, Jay)
PH17171 674 (January 27, 1994) p25. "Crows (from left): Vickrey, Malley, Duritz" (Blakesberg, Jay)
PH17172 685 (June 30, 1994) pp[cover]. "Counting Crows: The Biggest New Band In America" (Seliger, Mark)
PH17173 685 (June 30, 1994) p46. "Free Men In Paris: Dave Bryson, Steve Bowman, Dan Vickrey, Matt Malley And Charlie Gillingham (from left)" (Seliger, Mark)
VIDALE, THEA—PHOTOGRAPHS—PORTRAITS
PH17174 666 (September 30, 1993) p116. "Thea Vidale"
VIDEO—ILLUSTRATIONS
PH17175 631 (May 28, 1992) p60. "Video Hot Sheet"
PH17176 638 (September 3, 1992) p72. "Video & Laser Picks"
VIDEO CAMERAS—ILLUSTRATIONS
PH17177 709 (June 1, 1995) p17. "Tattle Tape" (Rosen, Jonathon)
VIDEO CAMERAS—PHOTOGRAPHS
PH17178 634-635 (July 9, 1992) pp122-123. "[Toys]" (Goldin, David)
PH17179 649 (February 4, 1993) p80. "Parental Guidance: Prepare Yourself With The Canon USC3" (Coleman, Glen)
PH17180 660-661 (July 8, 1993) p124. "Sharp VL-H100U Hi-8 Viewcam Camcorder, $2199" (Miller, Greg)
PH17181 668 (October 28, 1993) p91. "Canon UCS5, $1,900" (Miller, Greg)
PH17182 668 (October 28, 1993) p91. "Sony TR500; $1,800" (Miller, Greg)
PH17183 693 (October 20, 1994) p139. "[Camcorders]" (Miller, Greg)
PH17184 700 (January 26, 1995) p70. "[Technology]"
PH17185 715 (August 24, 1995) p115. "[Video]" (Grant, Bob)
PH17186 721 (November 16, 1995) p122. "[Video Cameras]" (Grant, Bob)
VIDEO DISC PLAYERS—PHOTOGRAPHS
PH17187 647 (January 7, 1993) p53. "For Purists And Couch Potatoes: Panasonic LX-900 (top) And Marantz LV500" (Davies And Starr)
VIDEO DISCS—ILLUSTRATIONS
PH17188 634-635 (July 9, 1992) p111. "Video & Laser Picks"
PH17189 651 (March 4, 1993) p72. "Video & Laser Hot Sheet"
PH17190 665 (September 16, 1993) p78. "[Video Laser]"
VIDEO GAMES—ILLUSTRATIONS
PH17191 656 (May 13, 1993) p67. "[Sonic The Hedgehog 2]"
PH17192 745 (October 17, 1996) p147. "[Technology]" (Grant, Bob)
VIDEO MIXERS—PHOTOGRAPHS
PH17193 674 (January 27, 1994) p59. "Videonics Digital Video Mixer, $1,199" (Miller, Greg)
VIDEO MONITORS—PHOTOGRAPHS
PH17194 656 (May 13, 1993) p64. "[Employment]"
VIDEO PROJECTORS—PHOTOGRAPHS
PH17195 634-635 (July 9, 1992) pp122-123. "[Toys]" (Goldin, David)
VIDEO RECORDERS—PHOTOGRAPHS
PH17196 668 (October 28, 1993) p91. "JVC HR-S6900, $999.95; RCA VR664HF, $519" (Miller, Greg)
PH17197 715 (August 24, 1995) p115. "[Video]" (Grant, Bob)
VIDEOTAPES—ILLUSTRATIONS
PH17198 629 (April 30, 1992) p65. "Video Hot Sheet"
VIDEOTAPES—PHOTOGRAPHS
PH17199 668 (October 28, 1993) p91. "Tale Of The Tape 1993" (Miller, Greg)
VIEIRA, MARY ANN—PHOTOGRAPHS
PH17200 652 (March 18, 1993) p23. "Doodlebug, Ladybug, Butterfly (from left)" (Guzman)
VIETNAM—PHOTOGRAPHS
PH17201 634-635 (July 9, 1992) p73. "Highway 1 Revisited: South Of Nha Trang, A Farmer Herds His Flock Of Ducks" (Giannini, John)
PH17202 634-635 (July 9, 1992) p61. "Honda 50S And Flag Shirts: Pop Culture On The Road From Da Nang To Hoi An" (Giannini, John)
PH17203 634-635 (July 9, 1992) p66. "An Uncle Ho For The Home: Picking Out A Souvenir At The Ho Mausoleum" (Giannini, John)
PH17204 634-635 (July 9, 1992) p70. "The War Museum: Photos Of President 'Gion Xon' And Antiwar Protesters" (Giannini, John)
VIETNAM WAR—ILLUSTRATIONS
PH17205 684 (June 16, 1994) p40. "RS 130, March 15, 1973: Illustration By Ralph Steadman" (Steadman, Ralph)
VIETNAM WAR VETERANS—PHOTOGRAPHS—PORTRAITS
PH17206 659 (June 24, 1993) p62. "A Vietnam Vet, Homeless For More Than A Decade, Is Now Living On His Own After A Stint At The New England Shelter For Homeless Veterans" (Agulera-Helwig, Max)
VIG, BUTCH—PHOTOGRAPHS
PH17207 630 (May 14, 1992) p83. "[Butch Vig]" (Seliger, Mark)
PH17208 702 (February 23, 1995) p32. "Strummin' In Stereo: Dave Pirner, Butch Vig, Karl Mueller, Dan Murphy (from left)" (Cuffaro, Chris)
PH17209 718 (October 5, 1995) p24. "Erikson, Vig And Phil Davis (from left) As Firetown, 1989" (Pantsios, A. J.)
PH17210 718 (October 5, 1995) p23. "Trash Is Where It's At: Erikson, Marker, Vig, Manson (clockwise from left)" (Ockenfels, Frank W.)
VIGIL, SELENE—PHOTOGRAPHS
PH17211 722 (November 30, 1995) p19. "Who Are You Callin' A Bitch?: To Wit, Elizabeth Davis, Selene Vigil, Agnew And Roisin Dunne Of 7 Year Bitch (from left)" (Blakesberg, Jay)
PH17212 731 (April 4, 1996) p17. "7 Year Bitch's Davis, Selene Vigil (from left)" (Eichner, Steve)

PH17213 742 (September 5, 1996) p20. "Selene Vigil Of 7 Year Bitch, Langdon, Alexakis And Bonham" (Morganstein, Barry)
VIGIL, SELENE—PHOTOGRAPHS—PORTRAITS
PH17214 732 (April 18, 1996) p38. "[Selene Vigil]" (Cuffaro, Chris)
VINGE, VERNOR—PHOTOGRAPHS
PH17215 748 (November 28, 1996) p121. "Despite His Day Job As A Math Professor, Vinge Is Best Known For His Visionary Sc-Fi" (Vadukul, Nitin)
VINGE, VERNOR—PHOTOGRAPHS—PORTRAITS
PH17216 748 (November 28, 1996) p119. "[Vernor Vinge]" (Vadukul, Nitin)
VINNIE—PHOTOGRAPHS
PH17217 658 (June 10, 1993) p30. "From Illtown To Chilltown: Naughty's Treach, Vinnie And DJ KayGee" (Larsen, Kristine)
PH17218 695 (November 17, 1994) p110. "Naughty By Nature" (Callis, Chris)
VIOLENCE—ILLUSTRATIONS
PH17219 632 (June 11, 1992) p169. "[Violence]" (Cronin, Brian)
PH17220 632 (June 11, 1992) p171. "[Violence]" (Mahurin, Matt)
PH17221 651 (March 4, 1993) p10. "The Importance Of Defining Your Terms" (Pendergrast, James T.)
PH17222 653 (April 1, 1993) p8. "Things To Do" (Pendergrast, James T.)
PH17223 677 (March 10, 1994) p36. "Homocides And Firearms Homicides Per 100,000" (Klein, Renee)
PH17224 677 (March 10, 1994) p32. "Motor-Vehicles Deaths Compared With Firearms Deaths" (Klein, Renee)
PH17225 677 (March 10, 1994) p34. "Suicides, Homocides And Fatal Accidents Involving Firearms" (Klein, Renee)
PH17226 700 (January 26, 1995) p14. "Victim-Criminal" (Pendergrast, James T.)
PH17227 728 (February 22, 1996) p38. "It All Started After He Watched A Congressional Debate On C-SPAN" (Witte, Michael)
PH17228 732 (April 18, 1996) p16. "Big City" (Pendergrast, James T.)
VIRGINITY—ILLUSTRATIONS
PH17229 691 (September 22, 1994) p19. "Holy Hymen!" (Friske, Maria)
VIRTUAL REALITY—PHOTOGRAPHS
PH17230 735 (May 30, 1996) pp[enc.2-3]. "[Technology]" (Winters, Dan)
VIRTUOSITY (FILM)—PHOTOGRAPHS
PH17231 716 (September 7, 1995) p77. "Denzel Washington Vs. Killer Computer"
VISSER, PETER—PHOTOGRAPHS
PH17232 653 (April 1, 1993) p22. "Peter Visser, Herman Bunskoeke, Carol Van Dijk And Berend Dubbe (from left)" (Doove, Hester)
VISTA (ORGANIZATION)—PHOTOGRAPHS
PH17233 659 (June 24, 1993) p32. "VISTA Revisited? A Volunteer Talks To A Family In Fount, Kentucky, In 1965" (Strode, William)
VITAMINS—ILLUSTRATIONS
PH17234 677 (March 10, 1994) p12. "Runaway Vitamin Hides In Aspirin Bottle" (Pendergrast, James T.)
VOELZ, SUSAN—ALBUMS
PH17235 667 (October 14, 1993) p123. "13 Ribs"
VOGUE (VIDEO)—PHOTOGRAPHS
PH17236 667 (October 14, 1993) p78. "'Vogue': Madonna's Video Is Burning"
VOLKMER, HAROLD—PHOTOGRAPHS—PORTRAITS
PH17237 710 (June 15, 1995) p62. "Volkmer" (McNamee, Wally)
VOLLMER, SREDNI—PHOTOGRAPHS
PH17238 669 (November 11, 1993) p67. "Sredni Vollmer, Helm, Dylan And Danko In NYC in '83 (above)" (Landy, Elliott)
VOLUPTUOUS HORROR OF KAREN BLACK—ALBUMS
PH17239 668 (October 28, 1993) p80. "A National Health Care"
VON FURSTENBERG, DIANE—PHOTOGRAPHS—PORTRAITS
PH17240 689 (August 25, 1994) p70. "Diller, With Close Friend Diane Von Furstenberg, At CBS' 25th-Anniversary Party For "60 Minutes" In 1993" (Lennihn, Mark)
VON FURTH, DAISY—PHOTOGRAPHS
PH17241 692 (October 6, 1994) p60. "Daisy Von Furth In Her New York Apartment" (Hom, Marc)
VON, EERIE—PHOTOGRAPHS
PH17242 678 (March 24, 1994) p42. "Those Evil Mothers In Danzig: Chuck Biscuits, Glenn Danzig, John Christ, Eerie Von (from left)" (Seliger, Mark)
VONKLEIN, KARL—PHOTOGRAPHS
PH17243 730 (March 21, 1996) p55. "The Boys In The Bus: Schiavone McGee, David Triano, Eric Lawson, Chris Leitch, Karl Vonklein, David Peterson And Mike Boyd (clockwise from left)" (Clinch, Danny)
VOODOO GLOW SKULLS—PHOTOGRAPHS
PH17244 704 (March 23, 1995) p44. "Riverside's Finest: The Voodoo Glow Skulls" (Ballard, Mike)
PH17245 706 (April 20, 1995) pp[enc.16]. "The Voodoo Glow Skulls" (Seliger, Mark)
VOYAGE TO THE BOTTOM OF THE SEA (TELEVISION SHOW)—PHOTOGRAPHS
PH17246 666 (September 30, 1993) p115. "All Wet: Basehart (far left) In 'Bottom Of The Sea'"
VOYAGER (FILM)—PHOTOGRAPHS
PH17247 617 (November 14, 1991) p184. "Delpy Hides The Truth From Shepard"
VREELAND, DIANA—PHOTOGRAPHS
PH17248 615 (October 17, 1991) p67. "Diana Vreeland And Alexander Godunov, New York City, 1981" (Pigozzi, Jean)
VRENNA, CHRIS—PHOTOGRAPHS
PH17249 690 (September 8, 1994) p54. "Vrenna, Woolley, Reznor, Finck, Lohner (from left)" (Cultice, Joseph)
VUDI—PHOTOGRAPHS
PH17250 659 (June 24, 1993) p15. "McCready, Eitzel, Ament, AMC's Vudi And Dan Pearson (from left)" (Blakesberg, Jay)
PH17251 690 (September 8, 1994) p25. "[American Music Club]" (Blakesberg, Jay)
PH17252 695 (November 17, 1994) p131. "American Music Club" (Duke, William)
VUDI—PHOTOGRAPHS—PORTRAITS
PH17253 656 (May 13, 1993) p77. "American Music Club (from left): Danny Pearson, Tim Mooney, Vudi, Bruce Kaphan And Mark Eitzel" (Ockenfels, Frank, 3)
VULGAR BOATMEN—ALBUMS
PH17254 631 (May 28, 1992) p54. "Please Panic"
VYNES, ADI—PHOTOGRAPHS
PH17255 625 (March 5, 1992) p27. "Jimmy Hartridge, Graham Bonnar, Adam Franklin, Adi Vynes (from left)" (Anker, Matt)

W

WACHTEL, WADDY—PHOTOGRAPHS
PH17256 676 (February 24, 1994) p28. "Producer Waddy Wachtel And Gunmen Gilby And Axl" (John, Robert)
WACO BROTHERS—PHOTOGRAPHS
PH17257 733 (May 2, 1996) p57. "Durante, Schlabowske, Langford, Dear (from left)" (Swider, Frank)
WADDINGTON, STEVE—PHOTOGRAPHS
PH17258 627 (April 2, 1992) p42. "Gay King Waddongton Nuzzles A Frustrated Swinton"
WADE, ADAM—PHOTOGRAPHS
PH17259 686-687 (July 14, 1994) p73. "Cute-Band Alert: Shudder To Think's Werdren, Wade, Larson And Hill (from left)" (Clinch, Danny)

WADE, ADAM—PHOTOGRAPHS—PORTRAITS
PH17260 719 (October 19, 1995) p26. "Truly Baroque—Like A Strange Union Of R.E.M. And Queen: Larson, Hill, Wedren And Wade (from left)" (Clinch, Danny)
WAHL, JON—PHOTOGRAPHS
PH17261 715 (August 24, 1995) p36. "Bagarozzi, Walther, Lee And Wahl" (Peterson, Charles)
WAHLBERG, DONNIE—PHOTOGRAPHS
PH17262 619-620 (December 12, 1991) p76. "Donnie Wahlberg In A Blaze Of Glory"
PH17263 678 (March 24, 1994) p27. "Wahlberg, Not On Snoop's Dick" (Mazur, Kevin)
WAHLBERG, MARK—PHOTOGRAPHS
PH17264 710 (June 15, 1995) p18. "[Leonardo DiCaprio & Marky Mark]" (Mazur, Kevin)
WAILER, BUNNY—PHOTOGRAPHS—PORTRAITS
PH17265 676 (February 24, 1994) p42. "Blackheart Man: Rasta Moralist Bunny Wailer" (Corio, David)
WAILERS—ALBUMS
PH17266 617 (November 14, 1991) p132. "Catch A Fire" (Dyer, Rod)
PH17267 617 (November 14, 1991) p132. "Catch A Fire" (Weiner, Bob)
WAINWRIGHT, LOUDON, III—ALBUMS
PH17268 651 (March 4, 1993) p64. "History"
PH17269 726 (January 25, 1996) p73. "Grown Man"
WAINWRIGHT, LOUDON, III—PHOTOGRAPHS
PH17270 672-673 (December 23, 1993) p162. "History"
WAITING TO EXHALE (FILM)—PHOTOGRAPHS
PH17271 724-725 (December 28, 1995) p138. "Houston, Devine, Rochon And Bassett In 'Exhale' (from left)"
PH17272 731 (April 4, 1996) p66. "Bassett And Devine, 'Exhale'"
WAITS, TOM—ALBUMS
PH17273 617 (November 14, 1991) p144. "Franks Wild Years" (Price, Jeff)
PH17274 617 (November 14, 1991) p144. "Franks Wild Years" (Mondino, J. B.)
PH17275 623 (February 6, 1992) p79. "Mississippi Lad"
PH17276 642 (October 29, 1992) p69. "Bone Machine"
PH17277 651 (March 4, 1993) p57. "Bone Machine"
PH17278 677 (March 10, 1994) p64. "The Black Rider"
WAITS, TOM—PHOTOGRAPHS
PH17279 649 (February 4, 1993) p8. "Waits Onstage In The Wonderland of Hamburg" (Wollenberger, Thomas)
PH17280 675 (February 10, 1994) p23. "'Black Rider' Creators Wilson, Burroughs And Waits (from left)" (Brinkhoff, Ralf)
PH17281 730 (March 21, 1996) p100. "A Walking Antique: Waits' First U.S. Show In More Than Three Years" (Stolder, Steven)
WAL-MART (COMPANY)—ILLUSTRATIONS
PH17282 682 (May 19, 1994) p14. "Wal-Mart" (Pendergrast, James T.)
WALDEN, DIANE—PHOTOGRAPHS
PH17283 648 (January 21, 1993) p41. "Dead Or Alive? Diane And Peter (left) With His Brother David" (Klicker, John)
PH17284 649 (February 4, 1993) p43. "Diane And Lawyer Marc Blackman, Before She Was Charged With Sexual Abuse" (Jewett, Tim)
PH17285 649 (February 4, 1993) p44. "Diane Walden And Lawyer Blackman Await The Jury's Verdict On April 28th, 1992" (Ellis, Bob)
WALDEN POND—PHOTOGRAPHS
PH17286 615 (October 17, 1991) p53. "[Walden Pond]" (Gall, Sally)
A WALK IN THE CLOUDS (FILM)—PHOTOGRAPHS
PH17287 709 (June 1, 1995) p68. "Sappy Love Stories"
PH17288 715 (August 24, 1995) p110. "Lovers At Last: Sanchez-Gijon And Reeves"
WALK THIS WAY (VIDEO)—PHOTOGRAPHS
PH17289 667 (October 14, 1993) p73. "'Walk This Way': Run, Stephen Tyler"
WALKEN, CHRISTOPHER—PHOTOGRAPHS
PH17290 702 (February 23, 1995) p19. "Walken (right) In A Public Display" (Daniel, Michael)
PH17291 708 (May 18, 1995) p97. "A Deadly Drive For Dunne, Douglas And Walken"
WALKER, JUNIOR—PHOTOGRAPHS
PH17292 726 (January 25, 1996) p28. "DeWalt, a k a Junior Walker, In 1966"
WALKER, MATT—PHOTOGRAPHS
PH17293 715 (August 24, 1995) pp68-69. "Brian Liesegang, Richard Patrick, Geno Lenardo, Matt Walker, Frank Cavanagh (from left)" (Ockenfels, Frank W.)
WALKER, T-BONE—ALBUMS
PH17294 617 (November 14, 1991) p172. "The Complete Imperial Recordings, 1950-1954"
WALL, DAVE—PHOTOGRAPHS
PH17295 626 (March 19, 1992) p20. "God's Little Monkeys (from left): Dave Allen, Jo Swiss, Dave Wall, Jon Townend" (Byrne, Peter)
WALL, HILARY—PHOTOGRAPHS
PH17296 652 (March 18, 1993) pp[enc.36]. "Hilary Wall And Scott Shaffer" (Seliger, Mark)
PH17297 652 (March 18, 1993) pp[enc.35]. "Hilary Wall, Julie French And Heather Freeman" (Seliger, Mark)
WALLACE, BILL—PHOTOGRAPHS
PH17298 671 (December 9, 1993) p32. "Raitt, Wallace And Browne (from left)" (Gardner, Christopher M.)
WALLACE, JOMBO—PHOTOGRAPHS
PH17299 660-661 (July 8, 1993) p96. "The Reverend Horton Heat: Jimbo Wallace, Jim Heath And Patrick 'Taz' Bentley" (Watermann, Greg)
WALLER, MICKEY—PHOTOGRAPHS
PH17300 653 (April 1, 1993) p16. "The Jeff Beck group Circa 1968: Mickey Waller, Beck, Stewart And Wood (from left)"
WALLFLOWERS—ALBUMS
PH17301 644 (November 26, 1992) p74. "The Wallflowers"
PH17302 737 (June 27, 1996) p56. "Bringing Down The Horse"
WALLFLOWERS—PHOTOGRAPHS
PH17303 636 (August 6, 1992) p13. "The Wallflowers (from left): Barrie Maguire, Jakob Dylan, Rami Jaffee, Peter Yanowitz And Tobi Miller" (Mark, Mary Ellen)
PH17304 745 (October 17, 1996) p44. "Two Stills From The Wallflowers' Fincher-Directed Video, '6th Avenue Heartache'"
WALLFLOWERS—PHOTOGRAPHS—PORTRAITS
PH17305 645-646 (December 10, 1992) p62. "The Wallflowers" (Seliger, Mark)
WALLICE, MARC—PHOTOGRAPHS
PH17306 693 (October 20, 1994) p74. "Actors Tom Chapman And Marc Wallice"
WALLINGER, KARL—PHOTOGRAPHS
PH17307 664 (September 2, 1993) p32. "Scott (right) Greets His Former Mate" (Gershoff, Gary)
WALSER, DON—PHOTOGRAPHS
PH17308 733 (May 2, 1996) p57. "Walser" (Virobik-Adams, Kevin)
WALSER, ROBERT—BOOKS
PH17309 669 (November 11, 1993) p24. "Running With The Devil"
WALSH, JOE—PHOTOGRAPHS
PH17310 685 (June 30, 1994) p23. "Birds Of A Feather: Joe Walsh, Timothy B. Schmit, Don Henley, Don Felder And Glenn Frey (from left)"
WALT MINK—PHOTOGRAPHS—PORTRAITS
PH17311 637 (August 20, 1992) p20. "Candice Belanoff, John Kimbrough And Joey Waronker (from left)" (Cuffaro, Chris)
WALTERS, BARBARA—PHOTOGRAPHS
PH17312 619-620 (December 12, 1991) p201. "Stormin' Norman

Schwarzkopf Tells Barbara Walters About The Video Victory In The Gulf"
WALTHER, ROB—PHOTOGRAPHS
PH17313 715 (August 24, 1995) p36. "Bagarozzi, Walther, Lee And Wahl" (Peterson, Charles)
WANICK, LELIA DELUIZ—PHOTOGRAPHS
PH17314 619-620 (December 12, 1991) p135. "Salgado; His Wife, Lelia Deliuz Wanick; And Their Sons, Rodrigo (seated) And Juliano" (Nofziger, Christopher)
THE WAR (FILM)—PHOTOGRAPHS
PH17315 696 (December 1, 1994) p134. "Father, Son: Kevin Costner, Elijah Wood"
THE WAR ROOM (FILM)—PHOTOGRAPHS
PH17316 670 (November 25, 1993) p126. "Stephanopoulos (left) And Carville Cheer For Clinton"
WARD, BRANDON—PHOTOGRAPHS
PH17317 706 (April 20, 1995) pp[enc.14]. "Huntington Beach High Surf Team" (Seliger, Mark)
WAREHAM, DEAN—PHOTOGRAPHS
PH17318 728 (February 22, 1996) p64. "Luna's Wareham, Demeski And Eden (from left)" (Capak, R. J.)
PH17319 735 (May 30, 1996) p13. "Laurie Anderson, Reed And Wareham (from left) Post-Gig At Josie's, In New York" (Roberts, Ebet)
WARHOL, ANDY—PHOTOGRAPHS
PH17320 615 (October 17, 1991) p65. "Andy Warhol And Jean Pigozzi, New York City, 1986" (Pigozzi, Jean)
PH17321 734 (May 16, 1996) p72. "Warhol With Candy Darling"
WARLOCKS—PHOTOGRAPHS
PH17322 717 (September 21, 1995) p52. "Before The Dead, They Were The Warlocks" (Greene, Herbi)
WARNICK, KIM—PHOTOGRAPHS
PH17323 730 (March 21, 1996) p17. "Fastbacks' Kurt Bloch, Mike Musburger, Vedder, Fastbacks' Kim Warnick, Lu Lu Gargiulo" (Michelson, Randall)
WARONKER, JOEY—PHOTOGRAPHS—PORTRAITS
PH17324 637 (August 20, 1992) p20. "Candice Belanoff, John Kimbrough And Joey Waronker (from left)" (Cuffaro, Chris)
WARREN G—ALBUMS
PH17325 688 (August 11, 1994) p69. "Regulate...G Funk Era"
PH17326 700 (January 26, 1995) p55. "Regulate...G Funk Era"
WARREN G—ILLUSTRATIONS
PH17327 683 (June 2, 1994) p72. "Warren G." (Durand, Tylor)
PH17328 691 (September 22, 1994) p120. "Warren G: Regulating A Groove" (Todd, Mark)
WARREN G—PHOTOGRAPHS
PH17329 690 (September 8, 1994) p37. "One Out Of 213: Long Beach's Warren G" (Miller, Michael)
PH17330 700 (January 26, 1995) p16. "Big Brother Is Watching: Dr. Dre (left) With The Birthday Boy" (Cross, Brian)
WARREN G—PHOTOGRAPHS—PORTRAITS
PH17331 War (December 29, 1994) p47. "" (Llewell, Michael)
WARREN, MIKE—PHOTOGRAPHS
PH17332 730 (March 21, 1996) p52. "Warren Of UMass Tapped Out His Hall Mates" (Comjean)
WAS, DAVID—ILLUSTRATIONS
PH17333 734 (May 16, 1996) p21. "The Truth, And The Tunes, Are Out There..." (Friedman, Drew)
WAS, DON—PHOTOGRAPHS
PH17334 617 (November 14, 1991) p13. "Burton Averre, Dallas Taylor, Wilson And Was (from left)" (Preston, Neal)
PH17335 651 (March 4, 1993) p17. "Creedence Clearwater Revisited: Springsteen, Was, Fogerty And Robertson" (Mazur, Kevin)
PH17336 651 (March 4, 1993) p17. "The New P-Folk? George Clinton, Jackson Browne And Don Was (from left)" (Mazur, Kevin)
PH17337 686-687 (July 14, 1994) p71. "Lounge Lizards: Don Was Confers With Keith Richards And Mick Jagger In The Studio" (Adebari, Eugene)
PH17338 704 (March 23, 1995) p24. "Brian Wilson (at piano) And Don Was (right) Play At Sundance" (Michelson, Randall)
WASH, MARTHA—ALBUMS
PH17339 654 (April 15, 1993) p64. "Martha Wash"
WASHING, WHIT—PHOTOGRAPHS
PH17340 715 (August 24, 1995) p95. "Hanging Out In New York's Central Park" (Danelian, Stephen)
PH17341 715 (August 24, 1995) pp90-91. "On The Court In Thompkins Park" (Danelian, Stephen)
WASHINGTON, DENZEL—ILLUSTRATIONS
PH17342 718 (October 5, 1995) p75. "Crime Fiction" (Kelley, Gary)
WASHINGTON, DENZEL—PHOTOGRAPHS
PH17343 624 (February 20, 1992) p50. "Washington And Choudhury At Odds"
PH17344 644 (November 26, 1992) p39. "Denzel And Spike On Location In Egypt" (Lee, David)
PH17345 644 (November 26, 1992) p40. "Denzel And Spike (seated) Prepare For The Film's Barbershop Sequence" (Lee, David)
PH17346 644 (November 26, 1992) p36. "The Two Faces Of Malcolm X: Denzel Before A Mural In New York City" (Watson, Albert)
PH17347 645-646 (December 10, 1992) p192. "Denzel Washington: Trying To Do The Right Thing By Malcolm"
PH17348 648 (January 21, 1993) p56. "Malcolm X"
PH17349 657 (May 27, 1993) p56. "Awry: Washington, Branagh, Thompson"
PH17350 731 (April 4, 1996) p66. "Cheadle And Washington, 'Devil'"
PH17351 743 (September 19, 1996) p90. "[Summer...]"
WASHINGTON, DENZEL—PHOTOGRAPHS—PORTRAITS
PH17352 644 (November 26, 1992) p34. "[Denzel Washington]" (Watson, Albert)
PH17353 644 (November 26, 1992) pp[cover]. "Denzel Washington: Making Malcolm X" (Watson, Albert)
PH17354 645-646 (December 10, 1992) pp[cover]. "1992 Yearbook" (Watson, Albert)
PH17355 678 (March 24, 1994) p100. "Missing In Oscar Action"
PH17356 716 (September 7, 1995) p77. "Denzel Washington Vs. Killer Computer"
PH17357 718 (October 5, 1995) p76. "Detective Denzel Washington Falls Under The Spell Of Devil Jennifer Beals"
WASHINGTON, DINAH—PHOTOGRAPHS—PORTRAITS
PH17358 649 (February 4, 1993) p54. "[Dinah Washington]"
PH17359 692 (October 6, 1994) p50. "Dinah Washington"
WASSER, JOAN—PHOTOGRAPHS
PH17360 693 (October 20, 1994) p30. "Cleo's Hanley, Stacy Jones, Manning; Builders Joan Wasser, Eric Masunaga" (Robicheau, Paul)
PH17361 693 (October 20, 1994) p49. "Kevin March, Dave Derby, Joan Wasser, Eric Masunaga (from left)" (Lass, Imke)
WASSERMAN, KEVIN—PHOTOGRAPHS
PH17362 686-687 (July 14, 1994) p45. "[Offspring]" (Johnson, Lisa)
PH17363 691 (September 22, 1994) p28. "Controlled Chaos: Noodles And Dreads In Action"
PH17364 691 (September 22, 1994) p25. "Shakin' Thing Up: Ron Welty, Greg K, Noodles, Dexter Holland (from left)" (Seliger, Mark)
PH17365 701 (February 9, 1995) pp42-43. "Greg Kriesel, Bryan Holland, Kevin Wasserman And Ron Welty (from left)" (Seliger, Mark)
WASSERMAN, ROB—ALBUMS
PH17366 683 (June 2, 1994) p70. "Trios"
WASSERMAN, ROB—PHOTOGRAPHS
PH17367 638 (September 3, 1992) p11. "Rob Wasserman, Bob Weir, Michelle Shocked And Bruce Cockburn (from left)" (Kravitz, Jeff)

PH17368 683 (June 2, 1994) p28. "Weir, Bruce Hornsby, Reed And Wasserman (from left) At The Trios Show" (Mazur, Kevin)
PH17369 726 (January 25, 1996) p24. "Wasserman (left) And Weir Perform As Ratdog" (Franckling, Ken)
WATANABE, TRESSA—PHOTOGRAPHS
PH17370 652 (March 18, 1993) pp[enc.37]. "Tressa Watanabe" (Seliger, Mark)
THE WATCHER (TELEVISION SHOW)—PHOTOGRAPHS
PH17371 701 (February 9, 1995) p17. "I, Spy: Sir Mix-A-Lot As "The Watcher""
WATCHES—PHOTOGRAPHS
PH17372 628 (April 16, 1992) pp[enc.37]. "[Watches]" (Robert, Francois)
PH17373 638 (September 3, 1992) pp[enc.57]. "[Watches]" (Steele, Bill)
PH17374 660-661 (July 8, 1993) p123. "Avocet Climber's Watch, $120" (Miller, Greg)
PH17375 712-713 (July 13, 1995) p121. "[Technology]" (Grant, Bob)
WATCHMAN—PHOTOGRAPHS—PORTRAITS
PH17376 615 (October 17, 1991) p28. "[The Watchman]" (Carroll, Chris)
WATERBOYS—ALBUMS
PH17377 660-661 (July 8, 1993) p112. "Dream Harder"
THE WATERDANCE (FILM)—PHOTOGRAPHS
PH17378 631 (May 28, 1992) p60. "Forsythe, Stoltz And Snipes (from left) Battle Paralysis"
WATERMAN, JOHN—PHOTOGRAPHS
PH17379 667 (October 14, 1993) p40. "John Waterman, Brian Wood, John McBain, Ben Shepherd And Matt Cameron" (Hapke, Fran)
WATERS, CRYSTAL—ALBUMS
PH17380 619-620 (December 12, 1991) p165. "Surprise"
PH17381 689 (August 25, 1994) p92. "Storyteller"
WATERS, CRYSTAL—PHOTOGRAPHS
PH17382 619-620 (December 12, 1991) p59. "Women In Rock Band Together For Prochoice" (Berkwitz, David Neil)
WATERS, JOHN—PHOTOGRAPHS
PH17383 615 (October 17, 1991) p64. "Patty Hearst And John Waters, 1988" (Pigozzi, Jean)
PH17384 659 (June 24, 1993) p13. "Waters And Turner (second from right) With Members Of L7" (Caruso, Phillip)
PH17385 697 (December 15, 1994) p18. "Etheridge, Waters, "Politically Incorrect" Host Bill Maher, Molinari And Baio (from left)"
PH17386 700 (January 26, 1995) p17. "[John Giorno's AIDS Treatment Project]" (Gruen, Bob)
WATERS, MAXINE—PHOTOGRAPHS—PORTRAITS
PH17387 682 (May 19, 1994) p44. "Maxine Waters, Elected In '90, Sets A Fiery Example For Black Congresswomen" (Borris, Dan)
WATERS, MUDDY—PHOTOGRAPHS
PH17388 655 (April 29, 1993) p35. "Muddy Waters, One Of Clapton's Earliest Blues Idols, Joins The Guitarist Onstage In Chicago In 1979..." (Natkin, Paul)
PH17389 678 (March 24, 1994) p13. "Heaven Sent: Muddy Waters Cutting Tracks At Chess Back In The '60s"
WATERS, ROGER—ALBUMS
PH17390 639 (September 17, 1992) p28. "Amused To Death"
PH17391 645-646 (December 10, 1992) p182. "Amused To Death"
WATERS, ROGER—PHOTOGRAPHS
PH17392 636 (August 6, 1992) p13. "Beck (left) With Waters" (Adebari, Eugene)
PH17393 684 (June 16, 1994) p16. "The '70s Floyd With Roger Waters (right)"
WATERSON, SAM—ILLUSTRATIONS
PH17394 681 (May 5, 1994) p47. "Divine Madness" (Risko, Robert)
WATERWORLD (FILM)—PHOTOGRAPHS
PH17395 709 (June 1, 1995) p68. "Potential Trouble Spots"
PH17396 716 (September 7, 1995) p78. "Summer Wrap-Up]"
WATFORD, MICHAEL—ALBUMS
PH17397 680 (April 21, 1994) p89. "Michael Watford"
WATKINS, TIONNE—PHOTOGRAPHS
PH17398 631 (May 28, 1992) p22. "TLC (clockwise from top): T-Boz, Chilli, Left Eye" (Cuffaro, Chris)
WATKINS, TIONNE—PHOTOGRAPHS—PORTRAITS
PH17399 715 (August 24, 1995) p27. "'Left Eye' Lopes, 'T-Boz' Watkins And 'Chilli' Thomas (from left)" (White, Steve)
PH17400 715 (August 24, 1995) p28. "The Younger, Wilder TLC: Watkins, Lopes And Thomas In 1992 (from left)" (Green, Adrian)
WATLEY, JODY—ALBUMS
PH17401 622 (January 23, 1992) p45. "Affairs Of The Heart"
WATLEY, JODY—PHOTOGRAPHS
PH17402 627 (April 2, 1992) p11. "The Wacky, Fun-Loving George Michael (left) With Jody Watley And Bernie Taupin" (Mazur, Kevin)
WATSON, ALBERT—ILLUSTRATIONS
PH17403 643 (November 12, 1992) p189. "[Albert Watson]" (Russo, Anthony)
WATSON, ALBERT—ILLUSTRATIONS—LETTERING
PH17404 643 (November 12, 1992) p189. "[Albert Watson]" (Karl, Anita)
WATSON, ALBERTA—PHOTOGRAPHS
PH17405 682 (May 19, 1994) p63. "[Incest]"
PH17406 686-687 (July 14, 1994) p98. "Mom Watson And Son Davies"
WATSON, EMILY—PHOTOGRAPHS—PORTRAITS
PH17407 748 (November 28, 1996) p143. "Wave Maker Emily Watson"
WATSON, JOHNNY—PHOTOGRAPHS
PH17408 738-739 (July 11, 1996) p22. "[Johnny 'Guitar' Watson" (Corio, David)
WATT, BEN—ILLUSTRATIONS
PH17409 738-739 (July 11, 1996) p7. "Everything But The Girl's Ben Watt And Tracey Thorn" (Risko, Robert)
WATT, BEN—PHOTOGRAPHS
PH17410 738-739 (July 11, 1996) p22. "Watt And Thorn: Their Relationship Survived His Illness, And Their Music Thrived" (Alston, Kwaku)
WATT, MIKE—ALBUMS
PH17411 704 (March 23, 1995) p119. "Ball-Hog Or Tugboat?"
WATT, MIKE—ILLUSTRATIONS
PH17412 734 (May 16, 1996) p21. "The Truth, And The Tunes, Are Out There..." (Friedman, Drew)
WATT, MIKE—PHOTOGRAPHS
PH17413 633 (June 25, 1992) p11. "Greg Humphreys, Mike Watt, Doug Macmillan, Bill Janovitz, Tom Maginnis And Mike Connell (from left) In Raleigh"
PH17414 656 (May 13, 1993) p15. "Moore, Fleming, Firehose's Mike Watt And J Mascis (from left)" (Callahan, Kristin)
PH17415 658 (June 10, 1993) p34. "Firehose's Watt And Hurley" (Mazur, Kevin)
PH17416 693 (October 20, 1994) p38. "Mike Watt Enjoys His Leisure Time"
PH17417 693 (October 20, 1994) p38. "Minutemen D. Boon, Watt And George Hurley In 1985 (from left)" (Pasley, Richard)
PH17418 702 (February 23, 1995) p20. "Lee Ranaldo, Moore, Coco And Watt (from left)" (Callahan, Kristin)
PH17419 709 (June 1, 1995) p20. "From Left: Eddie Vedder; Dave Grohl; And Their Guiding Light, Mike Watt" (Mazur, Kevin)
PH17420 709 (June 1, 1995) p19. "[Mike Watt]" (Mazur, Kevin)
PH17421 709 (June 1, 1995) p20. "Vedder (left) And Watt Preaching The Punk-Rock Gospel" (Mazur, Kevin)
PH17422 736 (June 13, 1996) p20. "Miranda Molen, Ron 'Rondonna' Dinkens, Watt And Daniela Eden (from left)"

(Temme, Marty)
PH17423 748 (November 28, 1996) p100. "A Veteran Internet User, Mike Watt Has A List Of 150 E-Mail Friends To Whom He Sends Bits Of News" (Maday, Tom)
PH17424 710 (June 15, 1995) p17. "Watt (left) And Vedder After A New York Show" (Mazur, Kevin)
WATT, NATHAN—PHOTOGRAPHS
PH17425 717 (September 21, 1995) p90. "Watt Is Flanked By Uncles Chaykin And Richards"
WATTS, CHARLIE—PHOTOGRAPHS
PH17426 619-620 (December 12, 1991) p53. "Charlie Watts (left)" (Stoddart, John)
PH17427 621 (January 9, 1992) p10. "Kevin Conneff, Paddy Moloney, Charlie Watts And Matt Molloy (from left)"
PH17428 638 (September 3, 1992) p18. "[Charlie Watts]" (Mazur, Kevin)
PH17429 662 (August 5, 1993) p33. "Watts, Jagger And Richards In Barbados"
PH17430 668 (October 28, 1993) p35. "[Rolling Stones]"
PH17431 670 (November 25, 1993) p38. "Charlie Watts" (Morganstein, Barry)
PH17432 686-687 (July 14, 1994) pp68-69. "And Then There Were Four: Charlie Watts, Ron Wood, Mick Jagger And Keith Richards" (Seliger, Mark)
PH17433 689 (August 25, 1994) pp56-57. "Four Play In Toronto..." (Corbijn, Anton)
PH17434 689 (August 25, 1994) p60. ""We Risk reputation, And That's Everything," Says Watts, With A Masked Richards And Wood" (Corbijn, Anton)
PH17435 690 (September 8, 1994) p21. "Mick Jagger, Charlie Watts And Keith Richards (from left) Get Warmed Up In Toronto" (Halsband, Michael)
PH17436 694 (November 3, 1994) p26. "Putting The Squeeze Play On Watts" (Seliger, Mark)
PH17437 712-713 (July 13, 1995) p34. "Stoned In Amsterdam: Wood, Jagger, Richards And Watts (from left) Get Their Ya-Yas Out At The Paradiso" (Corbijn, Anton)
PH17438 715 (August 24, 1995) p37. "Jones, Richards, Watts, Jagger, Wyman (from left) [Watts, Richards, Jones, Jagger, Wyman (from left)]" (Mankowitz, Gered)
PH17439 723 (December 14, 1995) p52. "During Downtime On Tour, Jagger Lounging On A Hotel Bed With Watts On The Isle Of Man, 1964"
PH17440 723 (December 14, 1995) p56. "Jagger (with Charlie Watts, right) Performing 'Brown Sugar' From A Flatbed Truck In New York to Publicize The Stones' 1975 Tour Of The Americas" (Laffont, Jean Pierre)
PH17441 735 (May 30, 1996) p24. "[Charlie Watts]"
PH17442 746 (October 31, 1996) p27. "Ono, Richards, Watts, Jagger And Jones (from left) With Circus Friends"
WAVY GRAVY—PHOTOGRAPHS
PH17443 684 (June 16, 1994) p35. "Peter Tork And Wavy Gravy" (Blakesberg, Jay)
WAVY GRAVY—PHOTOGRAPHS—PORTRAITS
PH17444 705 (April 6, 1995) p17. "Sauce Du Jour, Brown Gravy: Said Sauce Jackson Browne (left), Gravy" (Blakesberg, Jay)
PH17445 747 (November 14, 1996) p26. "Deadhead Tom Konicke (left) With Wavy Gravy" (Mazur, Kevin)
WAX—PHOTOGRAPHS
PH17446 709 (June 1, 1995) p16. "Flava In Ya Ear: Wax's Loomis, Joe Sib, Dave Georgeff And Soda Drop In On Fogelnes In His 'Squirt TV' Bedroom Studio (from left)" (Brown, Christy)
WAXMAN, DINA—PHOTOGRAPHS
PH17447 742 (September 5, 1996) p21. "Fruit O' the Loon: Lemonhead Dando Rocks Hard (can't ya tell?) With Patrick Murphy, Dina Waxman And Bill Gibson (from left)"
WAYANS, DAMON—PHOTOGRAPHS
PH17448 690 (September 8, 1994) p87. "Damon Wayans Is A Tacky Caped Crusader"
PH17449 744 (October 3, 1996) p78. "Now Playing"
WAYLON: AN AUTOBIOGRAPHY (BOOK)—PHOTOGRAPHS
PH17450 750-751 (December 26, 1996) p196. "Books"
WAYNE, JOHN—ILLUSTRATIONS
PH17451 658 (June 10, 1993) p73. "New Jack Cowboys" (Blitt, Barry)
WAYNE, JOHN—PHOTOGRAPHS
PH17452 658 (June 10, 1993) p74. "Ethan (Wayne) To Niece (Wood): 'Let's Go Home, Debbie'"
WAYNE'S WORLD (FILM)—PHOTOGRAPHS
PH17453 626 (March 19, 1992) p40. "Director Spheeris Advised Her Stars To 'Keep It Subtle'" (Schiffman, Bonnie)
PH17454 626 (March 19, 1992) p39. "Myers Parties On With Babe Tia Carrere And Carvey" (Schiffman, Bonnie)
PH17455 626 (March 19, 1992) pp34-35. "[Wayne's World]" (Schiffman, Bonnie)
WEAVER, SIGOURNEY—ILLUSTRATIONS
PH17456 657 (May 27, 1993) p55. "Mr. Myth Goes To Washington" (Risko, Robert)
WEAVER, SIGOURNEY—PHOTOGRAPHS
PH17457 633 (June 25, 1992) p48. "Weaver Is More Sinead Than Sigourney"
PH17458 657 (May 27, 1993) p56. "Dave The Fake Prez (Kevin Kline) Waves With The Real First Lady (Sigourney Weaver)"
PH17459 700 (January 26, 1995) p68. "Weaver And Kingsley Talk "Death""
PH17460 721 (November 16, 1995) p117. "Sigourney Weaver (left) Plays Victim While Cop Holly Hunter Packs Heat"
WEAVING, HUGO—PHOTOGRAPHS
PH17461 689 (August 25, 1994) p97. "Drag Queens On A Bus: Pearce, Stamp And Weaving"
WEBB, CHRISTIAN—PHOTOGRAPHS—PORTRAITS
PH17462 680 (April 21, 1994) p26. "Israel Webb, Lords (from left)" (Marsel, Steve)
WEBB, JIMMY—ALBUMS
PH17463 667 (October 14, 1993) p117. "Suspending Disbelief"
WEBB, JIMMY—PHOTOGRAPHS
PH17464 670 (November 25, 1993) p22. "Webb Went Through 'A Pretty Emotional Time Personally' While Recording His Album" (Borris, Dan)
WEBBER, MARK—PHOTOGRAPHS
PH17465 732 (April 18, 1996) p24. "A Wildly Unorthodox Mixture Of Influence Gathered Around The Table: Pulp's Candida Doyle, Mark Webber, Cocker, Steve Mackey, Russell Senior And Nick Banks (from left)" (Rankin)
WEBER, BRUCE—ILLUSTRATIONS
PH17466 643 (November 12, 1992) p83. "[Bruce Weber]" (Russo, Anthony)
WEBER, BRUCE—ILLUSTRATIONS—LETTERING
PH17467 643 (November 12, 1992) p83. "[Bruce Weber]" (Karl, Anita)
WEBER, JOHN—PHOTOGRAPHS—PORTRAITS
PH17468 660-661 (July 8, 1993) pp54-55. "Pumping Up: Posse Member John Weber And His Rottweiler Puppy" (Smale, Brian)
WEBER, MIKE—PHOTOGRAPHS
PH17469 678 (March 24, 1994) p80. "Students Jeff Roe (left center) And Mike Weber (right center) Look Out On The World From The Calarts Campus" (Little, Blake)
WEBER, STEVEN—PHOTOGRAPHS
PH17470 715 (August 24, 1995) p110. "Friends United: Batt, Stewart, Weber And Weiss"
WEBSTER, ANDREW—PHOTOGRAPHS
PH17471 696 (December 1, 1994) p32. "Thomson, John Pamer, Toomey And Andrew Webster" (Owen, Tim)
WEBSTER, DANIEL—PHOTOGRAPHS
PH17472 678 (March 24, 1994) p69. "Brothers Under The Skin: Martin Phillips, Greg Parker, Mike Williams, Dexter Wilson, Rick Brown, Greg Jackson, Everett Whiteside, Roderick Bradford, Lacell Sherman..." (Smith, Brian)

WEDDING PRESENT—PHOTOGRAPHS
PH17473 749 (December 12, 1996) p36. "The Wedding Present"
WEDOWEE, ALABAMA—PHOTOGRAPHS
PH17474 708 (May 18, 1995) p55. "Aug. 6, 1994: A School Falls To Ashes" (Weiner, Alan S.)
PH17475 708 (May 18, 1995) p55. "Before: Randolph County High School" (Shamsi-Basha, Karim)
PH17476 708 (May 18, 1995) p60. "Black Citizens In A Show Of Unity, April 30, 1994" (Edmondson, Vanessa)
PH17477 708 (May 18, 1995) p61. "Klansmen From Franklin, Ga., Hold A Membership Drive Just Outside Wedowee" (Edmondson, Vanessa)
PH17478 708 (May 18, 1995) p61. "A Lone Skinhead From The Mississippi-Based Nationalist Movement Displays His Wares Inn Wedowee" (Stevenson, John W.)
PH17479 708 (May 18, 1995) p60. "A Mississippi Group Of White Supremacists And Others march On Wedowee, Sept. 17, 1994" (Stevenson, John W.)
WEDREN, CRAIG—PHOTOGRAPHS
PH17480 716 (September 7, 1995) p28. "Sing-Along: Shudder To Think's Wedren" (Doughty, Chris)
WEDREN, CRAIG—PHOTOGRAPHS—PORTRAITS
PH17481 719 (October 19, 1995) p26. "Truly Baroque—Like A Strange Union Of R.E.M. And Queen: Larson, Hill, Wedren And Wade (from left)" (Clinch, Danny)
WEEN—ALBUMS
PH17482 698-699 (December 29, 1994) p176. "Chocolate And Cheese"
PH17483 740 (August 8, 1996) p62. "12 Golden Country Greats"
WEEN, DEAN—PHOTOGRAPHS
PH17484 705 (April 6, 1995) p30. "Dean Ween: Guitar" (Clinch, Danny)
WEEN, GENE—PHOTOGRAPHS
PH17485 705 (April 6, 1995) p30. "Gene Ween: Vocals" (Clinch, Danny)
WEEZER—ALBUMS
PH17486 698-699 (December 29, 1994) p190. "Weezer"
PH17487 746 (October 31, 1996) p66. "Pinkerton"
WEEZER—ILLUSTRATIONS
PH17488 707 (May 4, 1995) p16. "Candy" (Pendergrast, James T.)
WEEZER—PHOTOGRAPHS
PH17489 694 (November 3, 1994) p40. "Matt Sharp, Patrick Wilson, Brian Bell And Rivers Cuomo (from left)" (Elledge, Paul)
PH17490 704 (March 23, 1995) pp62-63. "Matt Sharp, Rivers Cuomo, Brian Bell, Pat Wilson (from left)" (Corbijn, Anton)
PH17491 704 (March 23, 1995) p64. "'Reverb Is Not Good For The Kids': Rehearsing For 'The Word'" (Corbijn, Anton)
WEICKER, LOWELL—PHOTOGRAPHS—PORTRAITS
PH17492 671 (December 9, 1993) p36. "Profiles In Courage"
WEILAND—ILLUSTRATIONS
PH17493 665 (September 16, 1993) p3. "Stone Temple Pilots' Weiland" (Burke, Philip)
PH17494 688 (August 11, 1994) p80. "Weiland: Soaring Fighter Pilot" (Levine, Laura)
PH17495 695 (November 17, 1994) p133. "Weiland of Stone Temple Pilots" (Ulriksen, Mark)
PH17496 733 (May 2, 1996) p9. "Cowles, David" (Scott Weiland)
WEILAND—PHOTOGRAPHS
PH17497 659 (June 24, 1993) p15. "Weiland (left) With King Missile's John S. Hall" (Kravitz, Jeff)
PH17498 662 (August 5, 1993) p50. "Stone Temple Pilots Eric Kretz, Dean DeLeo, Robert DeLeo And Weiland (from left)" (Ragel, Jon)
PH17499 665 (September 16, 1993) p26. "Slacker Pilot Weiland" (Mazur, Kevin)
PH17500 672-673 (December 23, 1993) p39. "Weiland Belts One Out For Choice" (Kravitz, Jeff)
PH17501 692 (October 6, 1994) p35. "Take Me To The Pilot: Weiland Lands In Philly" (Swanson, David)
PH17502 710 (June 15, 1995) p22. "STP, From Left: Robert And Dean DeLeo, Weiland, Kretz" (Haynes, Loren)
PH17503 749 (December 12, 1996) p36. "The Pilots' Scott Weiland Returns" (Mazur, Kevin)
WEILAND—PHOTOGRAPHS—PORTRAITS
PH17504 662 (August 5, 1993) p50. "Weiland Exploring The Possibility That There's A Little Gene Simmons In All Of Us" (Ragel, Jon)
PH17505 675 (February 10, 1994) p18. "[Weiland]" (McDaniel, Melodie)
PH17506 693 (October 20, 1994) p27. "STP's Weiland With Steven Tyler" (Mazur, Kevin)
PH17507 710 (June 15, 1995) p21. "[Scott Weiland]" (Vadukul, Nitin)
PH17508 711 (June 29, 1995) p16. "Busted: STP's Weiland" (Vadukul, Nitin)
PH17509 712-713 (July 13, 1995) p45. "Weiland At His June 5 Court Date"
PH17510 735 (May 30, 1996) p3. "[The Faces Of Heroin]"
WEINBERG, MAX—PHOTOGRAPHS
PH17511 644 (November 26, 1992) p15. "Max Weinberg, Clarence Clemons, Darlene Love, Little Steven, Garry Tallent And Danny Federici (from left)" (Mazur, Kevin)
PH17512 743 (September 19, 1996) p69. "The Crest Of The Wave: His Sidekick, Andy Richter; And The 'Late Night' Bandleader, Max Weinberg" (Seliger, Mark)
WEINBRECHT, DONNA—PHOTOGRAPHS
PH17513 624 (February 20, 1992) p37. "[Donna Weinbrecht]" (Eccles, Andrew)
WEIR, ALISON—PHOTOGRAPHS
PH17514 632 (June 11, 1992) p103. "Kohn, Alison And David Weir And Wenner (from left) In 1975" (Kohn, Diana)
WEIR, BOB—ILLUSTRATIONS
PH17515 736 (June 13, 1996) p38. "Bob Weir" (Cowles, David)
WEIR, BOB—PHOTOGRAPHS
PH17516 616 (October 31, 1991) p40. "Bill Kreutzmann, Ron "Pigpen" McKernan, Bob Weir, Garcia And Phil Lesh (clockwise from top left) In 1966" (Greene, Herb)
PH17517 619-620 (December 12, 1991) p37. "Bob Weir (left) Digs Los Lobos And, In Turn, Is Dug, At The "Deadicated' Party"
PH17518 619-620 (December 12, 1991) p103. "Phil Lesh, Bob Weir, Neil Young And Jerry Garcia (from left) Pay Tribute To Bill Graham" (Blakesberg, Jay)
PH17519 623 (February 6, 1992) p11. "Toys For Tots: Bob Weir With Gregg Allman" (Blakesberg, Jay)
PH17520 638 (September 3, 1992) p11. "Rob Wasserman, Bob Weir, Michelle Shocked And Bruce Cockburn (from left)" (Kravitz, Jeff)
PH17521 657 (May 27, 1993) p9. "Oh Say Can You See?: The Dead's Vince Welnick, Bob Weir And Jerry Garcia" (Blakesberg, Jay)
PH17522 660-661 (July 8, 1993) p29. "The Dead's Phil Lesh, Bob Weir And Jerry Garcia (from left)" (Blakesberg, Jay)
PH17523 664 (September 2, 1993) p46. "The Dead At Rest in 1966: Phil Lesh, Bill Kreutzman, Ron 'Pigpen' McKernan, Bob Weir And Jerry Garcia (clockwise from left)" (Greene, Herb)
PH17524 676 (February 24, 1994) p46. "The Early Grateful Dead (clockwise from left): Jerry Garcia, Bill Kreutzmann, Ron 'Pigpen' McKernan, Bob Weir, Percussionist Mickey Hart And Phil Lesh" (Marshall, Jim)
PH17525 677 (March 10, 1994) p28. "Berry, Weir And Shirli Dixon (from left)" (Mazur, Kevin)
PH17526 677 (March 10, 1994) p27. "The Dead's Lesh, Weir, Vince Welnick, Hornsby, Bill Kreutzmann, Mickey Hart" (Mazur, Kevin)
PH17527 683 (June 2, 1994) p28. "Weir, Bruce Hornsby, Reed And Wasserman (from left) At The Trios Show" (Mazur, Kevin)

PH17528 696 (December 1, 1994) p24. "Bob Weir, Lesh And Garcia (from left)" (Blakesberg, Jay)
PH17529 717 (September 21, 1995) p52. "Before The Dead, They Were The Warlocks" (Greene, Herbi)
PH17530 717 (September 21, 1995) p54. "The Dead In '66 At The Crossroads, the Corner Of Haight And Ashbury: Garcia, Pigpen, Lesh, Weir, Kreutzmann (from left)" (Greene, Herbi)
PH17531 717 (September 21, 1995) p65. "The Dead In Front Of Their Ashbury St. House, 1967: Jerry Garcia, Ron 'Pigpen' McKernan, Bob Weir, Phil Lesh, Co-Managers Danny Rifkin And Rock Scully, And Bill Kreutzmann..."
PH17532 717 (September 21, 1995) p26. "Garcia 'Proved That Great Music Can Make Sad Times Better,' Said Weir" (Seliger, Mark)
PH17533 717 (September 21, 1995) p67. "Jerry Garcia, Phil Lesh, Bill Kreutzmann, Bob Weir And Ron 'Pigpen' McKernan (clockwise from bottom right) Huddled In San Francisco's Golden Gate Park, 1967" (Marshall, Jim)
PH17534 717 (September 21, 1995) p66. "Lesh, Early Dead Co-Managers Scully And Rifkin, Weir And Garcia At A Press Conference Following The Oct. 2, 1967, drug Bust At The Dead's House" (Wolman, Baron)
PH17535 717 (September 21, 1995) p73. "marrying Acid-Damaged Art Music And The Funky Snort Of Live Rock & Roll: The Dead As A Lysergic-Dance Band In 1969 With Tom Constanten, Weir, Kreutzmann, Pigpen, Lesh, Hart..."
PH17536 717 (September 21, 1995) p72. "The Music Never Stopped: Garcia, Weir, Lesh, Brent Mydland, Kreutzmann And Hart (from left) In 1979" (Greene, Herbi)
PH17537 717 (September 21, 1995) p28. "Not Fade Away: Barlow, Hart, Kantner And Weir (from left) Celebrate Garcia In Golden Gate Park" (Blakesberg, Jay)
PH17538 717 (September 21, 1995) p28. "Olatunji With Kantner, Two Drummers, John Perry Barlow, Weir And Koons Garcia (from left) At The Aug. 13 Memorial At The Polo Field" (Blakesberg, Jay)
PH17539 717 (September 21, 1995) p69. "The Original Quintet At Home At 710 Ashbury St., In 1966: Phil Lesh, Bob Weir, Bill Kreutzmann, Ron 'Pigpen' McKernan And Jerry Garcia (from left)" (Anthony, Gene)
PH17540 726 (January 25, 1996) p23. "The Last Incarnation Of The Dead Perform In February 1995: Phil Lesh, Mickey Hart, Bob Weir, Jerry Garcia And Vince Welnick (from left)" (Blakesberg, Jay)
PH17541 726 (January 25, 1996) p24. "Wasserman (left) And Weir Perform As Ratdog" (Franckling, Ken)
WEIR, BOB—PHOTOGRAPHS—PORTRAITS
PH17542 717 (September 21, 1995) p72. "Nonstop Truckin' And Retooled Roots: The Dead's 1970s Lineup, With Keith Godchaux, Garcia, Lesh, kreutzmann, Donna Godchaux And Weir (clockwise from top left)"
WEIR, DAVID—PHOTOGRAPHS
PH17543 632 (June 11, 1992) p103. "Kohn, Alison And David Weir And Wenner (from left) In 1975" (Kohn, Diana)
WEISS, ANDREW—PHOTOGRAPHS
PH17544 705 (April 6, 1995) p30. "Andrew Weiss: bass" (Clinch, Danny)
WEISS, LYDIA—PHOTOGRAPHS
PH17545 665 (September 16, 1993) pp[enc.36]. "[Rob Weiss & Lydia Weiss]" (Nystrom, Dick)
WEISS, MICHAEL T.—PHOTOGRAPHS
PH17546 715 (August 24, 1995) p110. "Friends United: Batt, Stewart, Weber And Weiss"
WEISS, ROB—PHOTOGRAPHS
PH17547 665 (September 16, 1993) pp[enc.33-34 +]. "[Rob Weiss]" (Nystrom, Dick)
PH17548 665 (September 16, 1993) pp[enc.36]. "[Rob Weiss & Lydia Weiss]" (Nystrom, Dick)
PH17549 665 (September 16, 1993) pp[enc.36]. "[Rob Weiss & Michael Arturro]" (Nystrom, Dick)
PH17550 665 (September 16, 1993) pp[enc.34]. "[Rob Weiss, Steve Parlavecchio, Michael Arturro]" (Nystrom, Dick)
WEIST, DIANNE—PHOTOGRAPHS
PH17551 694 (November 3, 1994) p104. "Wiest Puts The Make On Cusack In Central Park"
WELCH, GILLIAN—ALBUMS
PH17552 735 (May 30, 1996) p46. "Revival"
WELCH, GILLIAN—PHOTOGRAPHS
PH17553 745 (October 17, 1996) p47. "Hollywood Goes Nashville: Welch" (Lyden, Paul)
WELCH, JUSTIN—PHOTOGRAPHS
PH17554 707 (May 4, 1995) p23. "Donna Matthews, Justine Frischmann, Annie Holland And Justin Welch (from left)" (Camp, E. J.)
PH17555 723 (December 14, 1995) p28. "Justin Welch, Justine Frischmann And MTV's Daisy Fuentes (from left)" (Mazur, Kevin)
WELCH, KEVIN—PHOTOGRAPHS
PH17556 664 (September 2, 1993) p57. "Kelly Willis With Kevin Welch Onstage In Nashville, Tenn." (Gwinn, Beth)
WELCOME TO THE DOLLHOUSE (FILM)—PHOTOGRAPHS
PH17557 736 (June 13, 1996) p60. "Smart Alternatives"
PH17558 741 (August 22, 1996) p72. "[Critic Proofing]"
WELD (VIDEO)—PHOTOGRAPHS
PH17559 621 (January 9, 1992) p56. "New Ragged Glories"
WELD, WILLIAM—PHOTOGRAPHS
PH17560 750-751 (December 26, 1996) p70. "Everyone Does The Macarena: Gov. William Weld Of Massachusetts Puts His Arms Up"
WELD, WILLIAM—PHOTOGRAPHS—PORTRAITS
PH17561 671 (December 9, 1993) p36. "Profiles In Courage"
WELK, LAWRENCE—PHOTOGRAPHS—PORTRAITS
PH17562 645-646 (December 10, 1992) p102. "Lawrence Welk"
WELLER, MITCH—PHOTOGRAPHS
PH17563 728 (February 22, 1996) p48. "March 1995: D-Mac Crew Parties With Jazz At Mitch Weller's" (Smale, Brian)
WELLER, PAUL—ALBUMS
PH17564 644 (November 26, 1992) p72. "Paul Weller"
PH17565 712-713 (July 13, 1995) p109. "Stanley Road"
WELLER, PETER—PHOTOGRAPHS
PH17566 623 (February 6, 1992) p88. "Peter Weller Confronts His Literary Nightmares"
WELLES, ORSON—PHOTOGRAPHS
PH17567 626 (March 19, 1992) p104. "Jealousy Destroys Welles And Cloutier"
WELLS, JUNIOR—PHOTOGRAPHS
PH17568 618 (November 28, 1991) p74. "Guy, B. B. King And Junior Wells At The 1968 Newport Folk Festival" (Gahr, David)
PH17569 658 (June 10, 1993) p16. "Wells (left) and Morrison" (Michelove, Mim)
WELLS, KITTY—PHOTOGRAPHS
PH17570 750-751 (December 26, 1996) p179. "Kitty Wells & Johnny Wright" (Seliger, Mark)
WELLS, MARY—PHOTOGRAPHS—PORTRAITS
PH17571 638 (September 3, 1992) p17. "[Mary Wells]"
PH17572 645-646 (December 10, 1992) p101. "Mary Wells"
WELNICK, VINCE—PHOTOGRAPHS
PH17573 657 (May 27, 1993) p9. "Oh Say Can You See?: The Dead's Vince Welnick, Bob Weir And Jerry Garcia" (Blakesberg, Jay)
PH17574 677 (March 10, 1994) p27. "The Dead's Lesh, Weir, Vince Welnick, Hornsby, Bill Kreutzmann, Mickey Hart" (Mazur, Kevin)
PH17575 726 (January 25, 1996) p23. "The Last Incarnation Of The Dead Perform In February 1995: Phil Lesh, Mickey Hart, Bob Weir, Jerry Garcia And Vince Welnick (from left)" (Blakesberg, Jay)
WELSH, GREG—PHOTOGRAPHS
PH17576 665 (September 16, 1993) pp[enc.25]. "From Left: Greg Welsh, Ray Browning, Mike Pigg, Wes Hobson, Chuckie V,

Scott Tinley, Nate Llerandi And Bill Braun" (Hanauer, Mark)
WELTY, RON—PHOTOGRAPHS
PH17577 686-687 (July 14, 1994) p45. "[Offspring]" (Johnson, Lisa)
PH17578 691 (September 22, 1994) p25. "Shakin' Thing Up: Ron Welty, Greg K, Noodles, Dexter Holland (from left)" (Seliger, Mark)
PH17579 695 (November 17, 1994) p78. "Offspring" (Danelian, Stephen)
PH17580 701 (February 9, 1995) pp42-43. "Greg Kriesel, Bryan Holland, Kevin Wasserman And Ron Welty (from left)" (Seliger, Mark)
WENDERS, WIM—PHOTOGRAPHS
PH17581 623 (February 6, 1992) p34. "[Wim Wenders]"
WENDT, GEORGE—PHOTOGRAPHS
PH17582 701 (February 9, 1995) p17. "[Sugar]" (Hermer, Ken)
WENER, LOUISE—PHOTOGRAPHS
PH17583 709 (June 1, 1995) p27. "PC Free: Stewart, Wener, McClure, Osman (from left)" (Westenberg, Kevin)
WENNER, JANN—PHOTOGRAPHS
PH17584 632 (June 11, 1992) p103. "Kohn, Alison And David Weir And Wenner (from left) In 1975" (Kohn, Diana)
PH17585 632 (June 11, 1992) p62. "Staff Members And Contributing Writers At The 1971 Editorial Conference, At Esalen, In Big Sur" (Leibovitz, Annie)
PH17586 639 (September 17, 1992) p42. "At The Table (from left): Greider, O' Rourke, Wenner, Thompson And Clinton" (Seliger, Mark)
PH17587 643 (November 12, 1992) p49. "'Rolling Stone' Art Directors (from left): Bob Kingsbury (1968-73), Tony Lane (1974-76), Annie Leibovitz, Mike Salisbury (1973-74), Roger Black (1976-78), Jann S. Wenner, Derek..
PH17588 671 (December 9, 1993) p42. "[The Rolling Stone Interview of Bill Clinton]" (Seliger, Mark)
PH17589 702 (February 23, 1995) p49. "Wenner (left) And Ertegun" (Mazur, Kevin)
PH17590 724-725 (December 28, 1995) p56. "Jann Wenner, Yoko Ono, Little Richard, Paul Shaffer Cut Loose" (Mazur, Kevin)
WERDREN, CRAIG—PHOTOGRAPHS
PH17591 686-687 (July 14, 1994) p73. "Cute-Band Alert: Shudder To Think's Werdren, Wade, Larson And Hill (from left)" (Clinch, Danny)
WE' RE NO ANGELS (FILM)—PHOTOGRAPHS
PH17592 654 (April 15, 1993) p69. "We're No Angels"
WEST, STEVE—PHOTOGRAPHS
PH17593 686-687 (July 14, 1994) p19. "Pavement (clockwise from left): Mark Ibold, Steve West, Bob Nastanovich And Stephen Malkmus" (Blakesberg, Jay)
PH17594 695 (November 17, 1994) p78. "Pavement" (Hanauer, Mark)
WESTERBERG, PAUL—ALBUMS
PH17595 660-661 (July 8, 1993) p116. "14 Songs"
PH17596 663 (August 19, 1993) p92. "14 Songs"
PH17597 664 (September 2, 1993) p80. "14 Songs"
PH17598 672-673 (December 23, 1993) p164. "14 Songs"
PH17599 733 (May 2, 1996) p52. "Eventually"
WESTERBERG, PAUL—ILLUSTRATIONS
PH17600 659 (June 24, 1993) p7. "Paul Westerberg" (Burke, Philip)
PH17601 663 (August 19, 1993) p4. "Instant Music" (Pendergrast, James T.)
WESTERBERG, PAUL—PHOTOGRAPHS
PH17602 616 (October 31, 1991) p11. "Westerberg And Jett" (Busacca, Larry)
PH17603 638 (September 3, 1992) p11. "Josh Taft, Paul Westerberg And Cameron Crowe (from left)" (Mercer, Lance)
PH17604 649 (February 4, 1993) p9. "Westerberg (left) And Stinson Shoot The Breeze In Minneapolis" (Beaulieu, Allen)
PH17605 659 (June 24, 1993) p52. "The Later Mats Incarnation: Tommy Stinson, Westerberg, Slim Dunlap And Chris Mars (from left)" (Matheu, Robert)
PH17606 659 (June 24, 1993) p54. "Early Mats: Westerberg, Bob Stinson, Mars And Tommy Stinson (from left)" (Pasley, Richard)
PH17607 659 (June 24, 1993) p53. "The Last Tour: Westerberg Onstage In New York City" (Rothenberg, Debra L.)
PH17608 663 (August 19, 1993) p27. "Westerberg And Friends In Beantown" (Robicheau, Paul)
PH17609 666 (September 30, 1993) p20. "Westerberg: A Roller-Coaster Ride For Austin" (Kraft, Chris)
PH17610 672-673 (December 23, 1993) p54. "Westerberg: Why Is This Man Smiling?" (Robicheau, Paul)
PH17611 695 (November 17, 1994) p107. "Paul Westerberg" (Borris, Dan)
PH17612 722 (November 30, 1995) p29. "Giordano, Westerberg And Assistant Engineer Eddie Miller (from left)" (Keeley, Dennis)
PH17613 743 (September 19, 1996) p19. "Westerberg Plays On Mats Song, 'Nobody'" (Fineman, Aaron)
WESTERBERG, PAUL—PHOTOGRAPHS—PORTRAITS
PH17614 659 (June 24, 1993) p51. "[Paul Westerberg]" (Mahurin, Matt)
WESTON, RANDY—ALBUMS
PH17615 630 (May 14, 1992) p108. "The Spirits Of Our Ancestors"
WESTSIDE CONNECTION—ALBUMS
PH17616 749 (December 12, 1996) p86. "Bow Down"
WETTON, JOHN—PHOTOGRAPHS
PH17617 655 (April 29, 1993) p20. "The Great Deceivers: John Wetton, David Cross, Fripp And Bill Bruford (from left)"
WEXLER, JERRY—PHOTOGRAPHS
PH17618 650 (February 18, 1993) p51. "Aretha Franklin 'Making Miracles' In The Studio With Wexler In 1969"
PH17619 650 (February 18, 1993) p51. "Bob Dylan and Wexler In 1972 During A Doug Sahm Session" (Gahr, David)
PH17620 650 (February 18, 1993) p52. "White, Franklin, Wexler And Nesuhi And Ahmet Ertegun (from left)" (Gahr, David)
PH17621 650 (February 18, 1993) p52. "Wicked Wilson Pickett Had A Flash-And-Fury Singing Style" (Paley, Stephen)
PH17622 650 (February 18, 1993) p50. "Wexler And Ray Charles Share A Laugh Backstage"
WEXLER, JERRY—PHOTOGRAPHS—PORTRAITS
PH17623 650 (February 18, 1993) p50. "Jerry Wexler (top)" (Gahr, David)
WEYMOUTH, TINA—PHOTOGRAPHS
PH17624 619-620 (December 12, 1991) p59. "Women In Rock Band Together For Prochoice" (Berkwitz, David Neil)
PH17625 637 (August 20, 1992) p9. "Fred Schneider, Kwame, Weymouth And Frantz (from left) At The 'Paper' Bash"
PH17626 638 (September 3, 1992) p11. "Weymouth, Shaun Ryder, Frantz And Paul Ryder (clockwise from lower left)" (Gershoff, Gary)
PH17627 744 (October 3, 1996) p30. "Will The Heads (above) Roll? The Band Was Sued By Byrne" (Ockenfels, Frank W.)
WEYRICH, PAUL—PHOTOGRAPHS
PH17628 729 (March 7, 1996) p45. "Weyrich, The Architect Of The Christian-Right Network" (Peterson, Mark)
WHALE—ALBUMS
PH17629 719 (October 19, 1995) p152. "We Care"
WHALE—PHOTOGRAPHS
PH17630 685 (June 30, 1994) p32. "[Whale]" (Gougenheim, Kim)
WHALLEY-KILMER, JOANNE—PHOTOGRAPHS
PH17631 691 (September 22, 1994) p106. "Cop Hurt Moves In On Juror Whalley-Kilmer"
WHAT'S EATING GILBERT GRAPE (FILM)—PHOTOGRAPHS
PH17632 674 (January 27, 1994) p48. "Acting Vehicles Include 'The Pelican Brief,' 'In The Name Of The Father,' 'What's Eating Gilbert Grape,' 'Shadowlands,' 'Naked,' And 'Grumpy Old

Men'"

WHAT'S LOVE GOT TO DO WITH IT (FILM)—PHOTOGRAPHS
- **PH17633** 659 (June 24, 1993) p89. "Biography: "What's Love Got To Do With It,' With Lawrence Fishburne And Angela Bassett As Ike And Tina Turner (left)"
- **PH17634** 660-661 (July 8, 1993) p33. "What's Love Got To Do With It?" (Stevens, D.)
- **PH17635** 665 (September 16, 1993) p77. "Best Actress"

WHEATON, WIL—PHOTOGRAPHS
- **PH17636** 676 (February 24, 1994) p62. "Phoenix Comforts A Pal In 'Stand By Me'"

WHEEL OF FORTUNE (TELEVISION SHOW)—PHOTOGRAPHS
- **PH17637** 684 (June 16, 1994) p36. "[Wheel Of Fortune]" (Slenzak, Ron)

WHEELER, CARON—ALBUMS
- **PH17638** 655 (April 29, 1993) p63. "Beach Of The War Goddess"

WHEELER, TIM—PHOTOGRAPHS
- **PH17639** 719 (October 19, 1995) p33. "Tim Wheeler (left), Mark Hamilton Of Ash" (Page, Scarlet)

WHEELER, VICKY—PHOTOGRAPHS
- **PH17640** 677 (March 10, 1994) p56. "Vicky Wheeler And Dan Mackta at Autotonic Headquarters, Which Doubles As her apartment, In Manhattan" (Smale, Brian)

WHEN A MAN LOVES A WOMAN (FILM)—PHOTOGRAPHS
- **PH17641** 682 (May 19, 1994) p107. "Stormy Triangle Garcia, Ryan And Booze"
- **PH17642** 705 (April 6, 1995) p69. "Oscar Rejects"

WHEN WE WERE KINGS (FILM)—PHOTOGRAPHS
- **PH17643** 747 (November 14, 1996) p124. "Now Playing"

WHERE IS JOE MERCHANT? (BOOK)—ILLUSTRATIONS
- **PH17644** 636 (August 6, 1992) pp48-49. "[Where Is Joe Merchant?]" (Collier, John)

WHILE YOU WERE SLEEPING (FILM)—PHOTOGRAPHS
- **PH17645** 708 (May 18, 1995) p97. "Sandra Bullock Wears Down Bill Pullman's Resistance"

WHISPERS IN THE DARK (FILM)—PHOTOGRAPHS
- **PH17646** 639 (September 17, 1992) p102. "Worst Supporting Actor"

WHITAKER, FOREST—PHOTOGRAPHS
- **PH17647** 686-687 (July 14, 1994) p99. "Jeff Bridges And Forest Whitaker Go Boom"

WHITE (FILM)—PHOTOGRAPHS
- **PH17648** 702 (February 23, 1995) p80. "White"

WHITE, ALAN—PHOTOGRAPHS
- **PH17649** 718 (October 5, 1995) p34. "White, Arthurs, Liam Gallagher, Noel Gallagher, McGuigan (from left)" (Jones, Michael Spenser)
- **PH17650** 733 (May 2, 1996) p34. "McGuigan, White And Noel (from left)" (Goldberg, Nathaniel)

WHITE, BARRY—PHOTOGRAPHS
- **PH17651** 662 (August 5, 1993) p34. "D'Arby, Cherry And White (from left)" (Robicheau, Paul)

WHITE, BARRY—PHOTOGRAPHS—PORTRAITS
- **PH17652** 696 (December 1, 1994) p23. "Dr. Feelgood, Barry White" (Wolfe, Eddie)
- **PH17653** 701 (February 9, 1995) p30. "[Barry White]" (Casado, John)

WHITE, HARLEY—PHOTOGRAPHS—PORTRAITS
- **PH17654** 660-661 (July 8, 1993) p96. "Papa's Culture: White (left) And Davis" (Alicino, Christine)

WHITE MAN'S BURDEN (FILM)—PHOTOGRAPHS
- **PH17655** 723 (December 14, 1995) p92. "Race As An Issue: Belafonte And Travolta"

WHITE, MARK—PHOTOGRAPHS
- **PH17656** 647 (January 7, 1993) p34. "[Spin Doctors]" (Seliger, Mark)
- **PH17657** 647 (January 7, 1993) p37. "Mark White Takes Time To Flex His Big-Bass Muscles In A Hotel Mirror..." (Seliger, Mark)
- **PH17658** 684 (June 16, 1994) p18. "A Force Of Hobbit: Schenkman, White, Barron And Comess Back In The Studio"
- **PH17659** 695 (November 17, 1994) p135. "Spin Doctors" (Seeff, Norman)

WHITE MEN CAN'T JUMP (FILM)—PHOTOGRAPHS
- **PH17660** 653 (April 1, 1993) p57. "White Men"

WHITE, RALPH—PHOTOGRAPHS—PORTRAITS
- **PH17661** 697 (December 15, 1994) p40. "Bad Boys: Barnes, Rubin And White (from left)" (Cardillicchio, Nick)

WHITE, ROBERT—PHOTOGRAPHS
- **PH17662** 697 (December 15, 1994) p34. "White (center) With Ruth Brown (left) In The Mid-'60s"

WHITE, RYAN—PHOTOGRAPHS
- **PH17663** 629 (April 30, 1992) p18. "AIDS Victim Ryan White With Elton John" (Slocomb, Jeff)

WHITE SANDS (FILM)—PHOTOGRAPHS
- **PH17664** 630 (May 14, 1992) p114. "Dafoe (left) Suspects Rourke And Mastrantonio"

WHITE SQUALL (FILM)—ILLUSTRATIONS
- **PH17665** 728 (February 22, 1996) p69. "The Unsinkable Jeff Bridges" (Allen, Julian)

WHITE SQUALL (FILM)—PHOTOGRAPHS
- **PH17666** 728 (February 22, 1996) p70. "Bridges At The Helm: Strong Actor, Shaky Career"
- **PH17667** 728 (February 22, 1996) p70. "Bridges Finds Home Sweet Hell On Water"

WHITE, TED—PHOTOGRAPHS
- **PH17668** 650 (February 18, 1993) p52. "White, Franklin, Wexler And Nesuhi And Ahmet Ertegun (from left)" (Gahr, David)

WHITE, VANNA—PHOTOGRAPHS
- **PH17669** 684 (June 16, 1994) p36. "[Wheel Of Fortune]" (Slenzak, Ron)

WHITE WEDDING (VIDEO)—PHOTOGRAPHS
- **PH17670** 667 (October 14, 1993) p97. "Idol Pleasures: 'White Wedding'"

WHITE ZOMBIE—ILLUSTRATIONS
- **PH17671** 710 (June 15, 1995) p96. "White Zombie: Songs Of The Living Dead" (Martin, Matthew)

WHITE ZOMBIE—PHOTOGRAPHS
- **PH17672** 671 (December 9, 1993) p13. "Beavis And Butt-head Faves J., Philo, Rob And Sean (from left)" (Ragel, Jon)
- **PH17673** 695 (November 17, 1994) p50. "White Zombie" (Winter, Dan)
- **PH17674** 726 (January 25, 1996) p50. "White Zombie: J., Rob Zombie, John Tempesta And Sean Yseult (from left)" (Cuffaro, Chris)

WHITESIDE, EVERETT—PHOTOGRAPHS
- **PH17675** 678 (March 24, 1994) p69. "Brothers Under The Skin: Martin Phillips, Greg Parker, Mike Williams, Dexter Wilson, Rick Brown, Greg Jackson, Everett Whiteside, Roderick Bradford, Lacell Sherman..." (Smith, Brian)
- **PH17676** 678 (March 24, 1994) p70. "Everett Spinning At 118 Beats Per Minute" (Smith, Brian)
- **PH17677** 678 (March 24, 1994) p72. "Williams, Whiteside, Jackson, Sherman (from left) On The Library Steps" (Smith, Brian)

WHITFIELD, BARRENCE—ALBUMS
- **PH17678** 670 (November 25, 1993) p117. "Hillbilly Voodoo"

WHITFORD, BRAD—PHOTOGRAPHS
- **PH17679** 622 (January 23, 1992) p7. "Brad Whitford, David Bowie, Steven Tyler, Hunt Sales, Tony Sales, Reeves Gabrels, Joey Kramer" (McAlpine, Paul)
- **PH17680** 694 (November 3, 1994) p60. "Early Daze: Whitford, Tyler, Hamilton, Perry And Kramer At Boston College, 1973" (Pownall, Ron)
- **PH17681** 724-725 (December 28, 1995) p40. "Aerosmith's Tom Hamilton, Joey Kramer, Brad Whitford And Steven Tyler (from left)" (Robicheau, Paul)

WHITLEY, CHRIS—ALBUMS
- **PH17682** 619-620 (December 12, 1991) p187. "Living With The

Law"
PH17683 706 (April 20, 1995) p73. "Din Of Ecstasy"
WHITLEY, CHRIS—PHOTOGRAPHS
PH17684 616 (October 31, 1991) p21. "Chris Whitley" (Caudle, Todd)
PH17685 703 (March 9, 1995) p20. "Whitley (left) With Fan Jeff Buckley" (Busacca, Larry)
WHITLOCK, BOBBY—PHOTOGRAPHS
PH17686 655 (April 29, 1993) p35. "Derek And The Dominos: Jim Gordon, Carl Radle, Bobby Whitlock And Clapton (from left)..."
WHITNEY, LOU—PHOTOGRAPHS
PH17687 629 (April 30, 1992) p28. "Dave Alvin (right) With Skeletons Lou Whitney (left) And Bobby Lloyd Hicks" (Carrico, John)
WHITWORTH, KEVIN—PHOTOGRAPHS—PORTRAITS
PH17688 634-635 (July 9, 1992) p20. "Love Battery (from left): Kevin Whitworth, Rod Rudzitis And Jason Finn" (Lavine, Michael)
WHO—ALBUMS
PH17689 617 (November 14, 1991) p154. "Who's Next" (Kosh, John)
PH17690 617 (November 14, 1991) p119. "Tommy" (McInnerney, Mike)
PH17691 617 (November 14, 1991) p119. "Tommy" (Meller, Barrie)
PH17692 617 (November 14, 1991) p154. "Who's Next" (Russell, Ethan A.)
PH17693 718 (October 5, 1995) p71. "The Who Sell Out" (Appleford, Steve)
PH17694 718 (October 5, 1995) p71. "A Quick One" (Appleford, Steve)
WHO—PHOTOGRAPHS
PH17695 619-620 (December 12, 1991) p100. "Graham With The Who's Roger Daltrey, Keith Moon And Pete Townshend, In 1976" (Zagaris, Michael)
PH17696 678 (March 24, 1994) p18. "Who Wants A Box Set? Daltrey (left) With Band"
PH17697 748 (November 28, 1996) p40. "The Who Rock The Isle Of Wight"
WHODINI—PHOTOGRAPHS
PH17698 676 (February 24, 1994) p25. "Whodini With Terminator X (seated)"
WICKED GAME (VIDEO)—PHOTOGRAPHS
PH17699 667 (October 14, 1993) p96. "From Her To Eternity: In 'Wicked Game,' Isaak Nuzzles Christiansen Beachside"
WIDE SARGASSO SEA (FILM)—PHOTOGRAPHS
PH17700 656 (May 13, 1993) p116. "Sex Is Hot For Lombard (top) And Parker"
WIDESPREAD PANIC—PHOTOGRAPHS
PH17701 618 (November 28, 1991) p30. "Widespread Panic (clockwise from top left): Todd Nance, Domingo Ortiz, Dave Schools, T Lavitz, John Bell And Michael Houser" (Blakesberg, Jay)
PH17702 631 (May 28, 1992) p17. "Widespread Panic (from left): John Bell, Michael Houser, Todd Nance, David Schools And Domingo Ortiz" (Messer, Alan)
PH17703 663 (August 19, 1993) p12. "Widespread Panic (above)" (Caudle, Todd)
WIDOWS PEAK (FILM)—PHOTOGRAPHS
PH17704 683 (June 2, 1994) p76. "Mia Farrow ("Widows' Peak")"
WIEDLIN, JANE—PHOTOGRAPHS
PH17705 616 (October 31, 1991) p11. "Cervenka, Gina Schock, Jane Wiedlin, Kathy Valentine, Charlotte Caffey (clockwise from top left)" (Granitz, Steve)
WIENEKE, PAUL—PHOTOGRAPHS
PH17706 660-661 (July 8, 1993) p97. "The Loud Family: Paul Wieneke, Zachary Smith, Miller, Jozef Becker And Rob Poor" (Blakesberg, Jay)
WIEST, DIANE—PHOTOGRAPHS
PH17707 700 (January 26, 1995) p68. "Best Supporting Actress"
WIGGINS, DWAYNE—PHOTOGRAPHS
PH17708 666 (September 30, 1993) p16. "Tony3: Dwayne And Raphael Wiggins, Riley (from left)" (Cuffaro, Chris)
PH17709 695 (November 17, 1994) p81. "Tony! Toni! Tone!" (Rolston, Matthew)
WIGGINS, RAPHAEL—PHOTOGRAPHS
PH17710 666 (September 30, 1993) p16. "Tony3: Dwayne And Raphael Wiggins, Riley (from left)" (Cuffaro, Chris)
PH17711 695 (November 17, 1994) p81. "Tony! Toni! Tone!" (Rolston, Matthew)
WIGGS, JOSEPHINE—PHOTOGRAPHS
PH17712 668 (October 28, 1993) p18. "Not Just Another Girl Group: Wiggs, Kim Deal, Macpherson And Kelley Deal (from left)" (Lass, Imke)
PH17713 682 (May 19, 1994) p89. "[The Breeders]" (Seliger, Mark)
PH17714 695 (November 17, 1994) p131. "The Breeders" (Seliger, Mark)
WIGGS, JOSEPHINE—PHOTOGRAPHS—PORTRAITS
PH17715 660-661 (July 8, 1993) p101. "Breeders: Jim MacPherson, Kelley Deal, Kim Deal And Josephine Wiggs" (Mart, K.)
WILCO—ALBUMS
PH17716 705 (April 6, 1995) p62. "A.M."
PH17717 708 (May 18, 1995) p108. "A.M."
PH17718 747 (November 14, 1996) p111. "Being There"
WILCO—ILLUSTRATIONS
PH17719 747 (November 14, 1996) p111. "Wheatfield Soul: Wilco Outgrow The Roots-Rock Legacy Of Uncle Tupelo" (Butler, David)
WILCO—PHOTOGRAPHS
PH17720 707 (May 4, 1995) p32. "The Buddy System: Johnston, Coomer, Stirratt, Tweedy And Bennett (from left)" (Miller, Brad)
PH17721 748 (November 28, 1996) p36. "Pulling Up Their Roots?" (Chavez, Marina)
WILCOX, DAVID—ALBUMS
PH17722 690 (September 8, 1994) p80. "Big Horizon"
WILCOX, IMANI—PHOTOGRAPHS
PH17723 660-661 (July 8, 1993) p97. "The Pharcyde: Romye Robinson, Imani Wilcox, Derrick Stewart And Tre Hardson" (Azimi, Mojgan B.)
PH17724 722 (November 30, 1995) p38. "Hip-Hop's Cosmic Voyagers: Wilcox, Robinson, Hardson And Stewart (from left)" (McClelland, Philippe)
WILD AT HEART (FILM)—PHOTOGRAPHS
PH17725 721 (November 16, 1995) p94. "The Elvis Wanna-Be (with William Dafoe) In 'Wild At Heart'"
WILD BILL (FILM)—PHOTOGRAPHS
PH17726 709 (June 1, 1995) p68. "Potential Trouble Spots"
PH17727 723 (December 14, 1995) p92. "Jeff Bridges"
THE WILD BUNCH (FILM)—PHOTOGRAPHS
PH17728 703 (March 9, 1995) p72. "Aging Cowboy William Holden Goes For The Big Gun In The Final Shootout"
PH17729 727 (February 8, 1996) p46. "Home Video"
WILD THING (VIDEO)—PHOTOGRAPHS
PH17730 667 (October 14, 1993) p90. "Tone Loc: He Appropriated Palmer For 'Wild Thing'"
WILD THINGS—ILLUSTRATIONS
PH17731 645-646 (December 10, 1992) p152. "Maurice Sendak's Wild Things, 1976"
WILD, WILD WEST (TELEVISION SHOW)—PHOTOGRAPHS
PH17732 666 (September 30, 1993) p116. "Gee-Whiz Men: 'Wild, Wild West' (left)"
WILDER, ALAN—PHOTOGRAPHS
PH17733 670 (November 25, 1993) p94. "1982: Fletcher, Gahan, Gore And Wilder (from left)"
PH17734 670 (November 25, 1993) p92. "In Madrid, Making Their Last Record: Gahan, Gore, Wilder, Fletcher (from left)"

(Corbijn, Anton)
PH17735 670 (November 25, 1993) p94. "1985: Gore, Wilder, Gahan And Fletcher (clockwise from left)" (Nosotti, Fabio)
WILDWOOD, MICHAEL—PHOTOGRAPHS
PH17736 701 (February 9, 1995) p20. "Glam Rabble-Rousers Wildwood, Malin And Sage (from left) In New York City" (Mazur, Kevin)
PH17737 701 (February 9, 1995) p19. "D Gen (from left): Danny Sage, Richard Bacchus, Howie Pyro, Jesse Malin, Michael Wildwood" (Seliger, Mark)
PH17738 710 (June 15, 1995) p41. "D Gen (from left): Pyro, Michael Wildwood, Malin, Sage, Richard Bacchus And Gomez" (Ragel, Jon)
WILDWOOD, NEW JERSEY—PHOTOGRAPHS
PH17739 638 (September 3, 1992) pp46-47,50-51+. "[Wildwood, New Jersey]" (Mark, Mary Ellen)
WILES, ELIZABETH ANN—PHOTOGRAPHS—PORTRAITS
PH17740 666 (September 30, 1993) p28. "[Elizabeth Ann Wiles & Aten Julius Bushaw Calhoun]"
WILK, BRAD—PHOTOGRAPHS
PH17741 664 (September 2, 1993) p31. "Rage's Timmy C., Zack De La Rocha, Brad Wilk And Tom Morello (from left)" (Johnson, William)
PH17742 735 (May 30, 1996) p27. "Rage Against The Machine"
WILKESON, LEON—PHOTOGRAPHS
PH17743 727 (February 8, 1996) p12. "Skynyrd's Bob Burns, Leon Wilkeson, Artimus Pyle (from left)" (Diamond, Rick)
WILL, GEORGE—PHOTOGRAPHS
PH17744 747 (November 14, 1996) p81. "Washington, D.C., 1988: Writer George Will With Larry And Herb Cohen (from left)" (Naltchayan, Neshan)
WILLIAM SHAKESPEARE'S ROMEO AND JULIET (FILM)—PHOTOGRAPHS
PH17744a 743 (September 19, 1996) p88. "The Young And The Restless"
PH17745 747 (November 14, 1996) p124. "The Bright Angel Meets Her Knight At A Costume Ball"
PH17746 747 (November 14, 1996) p124. "Danes Juliet Pines For Her Love"
PH17747 747 (November 14, 1996) p124. "Dicaprio's Desperate Romeo Takes A Hostage"
WILLIAMS, BORIS—PHOTOGRAPHS
PH17748 631 (May 28, 1992) p11. "Simon Gallup, Porl Thompson, Perry Bamonte, Robert Smith, Boris Williams (from left)" (Cox, Paul)
WILLIAMS, CHRISTOPHER—ALBUMS
PH17749 651 (March 4, 1993) p65. "Changes"
WILLIAMS, FEMI—PHOTOGRAPHS
PH17750 628 (April 16, 1992) p57. "Carleen Anderson, Marc Nelson And Femi Williams (from left)"
WILLIAMS, FREEDOM—PHOTOGRAPHS
PH17751 626 (March 19, 1992) p11. "Freedom Williams, David Cole, Robert Clivilles, Zelma Davis (from left)" (Mazur, Kevin)
WILLIAMS, HANK, JR.—ILLUSTRATIONS
PH17752 682 (May 19, 1994) p68. "[White Trash]" (Friedman, Drew)
WILLIAMS, HAROLD—PHOTOGRAPHS
PH17753 684 (June 16, 1994) p61. "Harold Williams Signs Autographs" (Borris, Dan)
WILLIAMS, LUCINDA—ALBUMS
PH17754 638 (September 3, 1992) p68. "Sweet Old World"
WILLIAMS, LUCINDA—PHOTOGRAPHS
PH17755 637 (August 20, 1992) p11. "Williams (left) And Cash" (Gershoff, Gary)
PH17756 645-646 (December 10, 1992) p77. "Lucinda Williams" (Gershoff, Gary)
PH17757 650 (February 18, 1993) p29. "Lucinda Williams" (Kraft, Chris)
WILLIAMS, MARION—ALBUMS
PH17758 677 (March 10, 1994) p66. "Can't Keep It To Myself"
WILLIAMS, MARION—PHOTOGRAPHS—PORTRAITS
PH17759 689 (August 25, 1994) p32. "[Marion Williams]" (Gahr, David)
PH17760 698-699 (December 29, 1994) p80. "[Marion Williams]"
WILLIAMS, MIKE—PHOTOGRAPHS
PH17761 678 (March 24, 1994) p69. "Brothers Under The Skin: Martin Phillips, Greg Parker, Mike Williams, Dexter Wilson, Rick Brown, Greg Jackson, Everett Whiteside, Roderick Bradford, Lacell Sherman..." (Smith, Brian)
PH17762 678 (March 24, 1994) p72. "Williams, Whiteside, Jackson, Sherman (from left) On The Library Steps" (Smith, Brian)
WILLIAMS, ROBBIE—PHOTOGRAPHS
PH17763 716 (September 7, 1995) p35. "Williams Splits, Teens In Tailspin"
WILLIAMS, ROBIN—ILLUSTRATIONS
PH17764 615 (October 17, 1991) p99. "That Old Black Magic" (Payne, C. F.)
PH17765 670 (November 25, 1993) p81. "[Robin Williams]" (Seliger, Mark)
WILLIAMS, ROBIN—PHOTOGRAPHS
PH17766 615 (October 17, 1991) p100. "Street Sorcery From Robin Williams And His Homeless Knights"
PH17767 621 (January 9, 1992) p55. "Robin Williams (left) And Dustin Hoffman In Conflict"
PH17768 645-646 (December 10, 1992) p97. "[Toys]" (Baldwin, Sidney)
PH17769 648 (January 21, 1993) p55. "Robin Williams (left) And A Huggy L. L. Cool J Play Cousins"
PH17770 649 (February 4, 1993) p72. "[Toys]"
PH17771 670 (November 25, 1993) p81. "[Robin Williams]" (Seliger, Mark)
PH17772 678 (March 24, 1994) p100. "Missing In Oscar Action"
PH17773 683 (June 2, 1994) p76. "Robin Williams Plays The Ages Of Man"
PH17774 735 (May 30, 1996) p12. "If You're Gonna Love, Wear The Glove" (Mazur, Kevin)
PH17775 735 (May 30, 1996) p12. "Williams Gives A Big 'Nanu, Nanu' To Pal Elton John" (Mazur, Kevin)
PH17776 735 (May 30, 1996) p50. "Ross, Sting, Taylor And Williams (from left)" (Mazur, Kevin)
PH17777 742 (September 5, 1996) p68. "Francis Ford Coppola Directs Robin Williams To Act Like A 10-Year-Old In 'Jack'"
PH17778 750-751 (December 26, 1996) p57. "The Rainforest All-Star Supremes Tribute" (Mazur, Kevin)
WILLIAMS, ROBIN—PHOTOGRAPHS—PORTRAITS
PH17779 616 (October 31, 1991) p55. "His Maelstrom Brain Marauds Over Everything In Its Path, Trailing A High-Octane Wake Of Spent Adrenaline" (Schiffman, Bonnie)
PH17780 619-620 (December 12, 1991) pp[cover]. "1991 Yearbook" (Seliger, Mark)
PH17781 670 (November 25, 1993) p81. "[Robin Williams]" (Seliger, Mark)
WILLIAMS, SIMON—PHOTOGRAPHS
PH17782 738-739 (July 11, 1996) p116. "Pfeiffer, Feldmann, Williams And Paulson (from left)"
WILLIAMS, VANESSA—ALBUMS
PH17783 703 (March 9, 1995) p64. "The Sweetest Days"
WILLIAMS, VICTORIA—ALBUMS
PH17784 696 (December 1, 1994) p128. "Loose"
WILLIAMS, VICTORIA—ILLUSTRATIONS
PH17785 660-661 (July 8, 1993) p109. "'Sweet Relief': Sweet Emotions" (Frinta, Dagmar)
WILLIAMS, VICTORIA—PHOTOGRAPHS
PH17786 658 (June 10, 1993) p17. "Sweet And Williams" (Allen, Greg)
PH17787 664 (September 2, 1993) p13. "When She Got Sick, Williams Had To Depend On Her Pals" (Allen, Greg)

PH17788 669 (November 11, 1993) p62. "'Cowgirls' Lineup: Rain Phoenix, Victoria Williams And Heather Graham" (Markus, Kurt)
PH17789 669 (November 11, 1993) p27. "Winona Boy Toy With Victoria Williams" (Mazur, Kevin)
PH17790 672-673 (December 23, 1993) p58. "Above: Victoria Williams Gets Some Relief" (Allen, Greg)
PH17791 672-673 (December 23, 1993) p70. "Live From New York: Hamilton, Pirner, Williams, Henry And Murphy (clockwise from top left)" (Mazur, Kevin)
PH17792 675 (February 10, 1994) p22. "Penn, Williams And Himmelman At The Gimme Shelter Benefit For The Homeless" (Mayer, Jeffrey)
PH17793 678 (March 24, 1994) p28. "Kristofferson, Williams, Vega, DJ Vin Scelsa And Lou Reed (from left)" (Roberts, Ebet)
PH17794 692 (October 6, 1994) p15. "Pirner (left) And Williams" (Phipps, Sandra-Lee)
PH17795 700 (January 26, 1995) p32. "Victoria Williams Unleashes Her Heavy Mettle" (Capak, R. J.)
PH17796 734 (May 16, 1996) p18. "Vic Chesnutt And Victoria Williams Feel The Love" (Diltz, Henry)
WILLIAMS, VICTORIA—PHOTOGRAPHS—PORTRAITS
PH17797 690 (September 8, 1994) p45. "Williams: "I Feel Positive About My Health."" (Cuffaro, Chris)
PH17798 695 (November 17, 1994) p140. "Victoria Williams" (Ockenfels, Frank, 3)
WILLIAMS, WENDY—PHOTOGRAPHS
PH17799 628 (April 16, 1992) pp[enc.27]. "[Norman Bellingham, Wendy Williams, Kent Ferguson]" (Nicks, Dewey)
PH17800 628 (April 16, 1992) pp[enc.28]. "[Wendy Williams]" (Nicks, Dewey)
PH17801 628 (April 16, 1992) pp[enc.29]. "[Wendy Williams, Kent Ferguson]" (Nicks, Dewey)
PH17802 628 (April 16, 1992) pp[enc.34]. "[Wendy Williams, Norman Bellingham]" (Nicks, Dewey)
WILLIAMS-CHAPPEL, FIONA—PHOTOGRAPHS—PORTRAITS
PH17803 745 (October 17, 1996) p44. "[Fiona Williams-Chappel]"
WILLIS, BRUCE—ILLUSTRATIONS
PH17804 710 (June 15, 1995) p85. "Die Hard In A Kilt" (Payne, C. F.)
WILLIS, BRUCE—PHOTOGRAPHS
PH17805 691 (September 22, 1994) p106. "Bombs Away"
PH17806 692 (October 6, 1994) p80. "Willis And De Medeiros Screw"
PH17807 701 (February 9, 1995) p40. "Moore Partying With Husband Bruce Willis" (Spellman, John)
PH17808 710 (June 15, 1995) p86. "Jackson And Willis Try To Undo A Bad Situation In 'Die Hard With A Vengeance'"
PH17809 726 (January 25, 1996) p66. "Into The Cuckoo's Nest With Willis And Pitt"
PH17810 745 (October 17, 1996) p144. "Bruce Willis Plays Samurai In A Suit"
WILLIS, KELLY—PHOTOGRAPHS
PH17811 664 (September 2, 1993) p57. "Kelly Willis With Kevin Welch Onstage In Nashville, Tenn." (Gwinn, Beth)
WILLIS, KELLY—PHOTOGRAPHS—PORTRAITS
PH17812 664 (September 2, 1993) p56. "[Kelly Willis]" (Hom, Marc)
WILLIS, WESLEY—PHOTOGRAPHS—PORTRAITS
PH17813 747 (November 14, 1996) p36. "[Wesley Willis]" (Gougenheim, Kim)
WILMINGTON, NORTH CAROLINA—PHOTOGRAPHS
PH17814 688 (August 11, 1994) p20. "[Wilmington, North Carolina]" (Craft, Terry)
WILSEY, SHANNON—PHOTOGRAPHS
PH17815 693 (October 20, 1994) p80. "Allman And Shannon, Circa 1986"
PH17816 693 (October 20, 1994) p76. "At The Zoo In 1973: Shannon Always Loved To Dance"
PH17817 693 (October 20, 1994) pp72-73. "[Savannah]" (Gittler, Ian)
PH17818 693 (October 20, 1994) p77. "Los Angeles 1992: If You Don't Love Me, I'm Sorry" (Gittler, Ian)
PH17819 693 (October 20, 1994) p79. "A Teen In Texas, 1985: A Rare Turn At The Sink"
WILSON, ANN—PHOTOGRAPHS
PH17820 624 (February 20, 1992) p12. "From Left: Layne Staley, Ann Wilson, Stone Gossard, Jerry Cantrell" (Mason, Karen)
PH17821 649 (February 4, 1993) p9. "Ann Wilson At The Seattle Benefit" (Mercer, Lance)
PH17822 696 (December 1, 1994) p25. "Howard Leese, John Paul Jones, Ann Wilson, Denny Fongheiser And Nancy Wilson"
WILSON, BRIAN—ILLUSTRATIONS
PH17823 663 (August 19, 1993) p73. "The Boys Of Summer" (Cowles, David)
PH17824 724-725 (December 28, 1995) p118. "The Beached Boy Finds New Inspiration In Ancient History—His Heart Survived The Bad Trip, Even If Parts Of His Head Didn't" (Kunz, Anita)
WILSON, BRIAN—ILLUSTRATIONS—PORTRAITS
PH17825 641 (October 15, 1992) p79. "[Brian Wilson]" (Day, Rob)
WILSON, BRIAN—PHOTOGRAPHS
PH17826 617 (November 14, 1991) p13. "Burton Averre, Dallas Taylor, Wilson And Was (from left)" (Preston, Neal)
PH17827 704 (March 23, 1995) p24. "Brian Wilson (at piano) And Don Was (right) Play At Sundance" (Michelson, Randall)
PH17828 707 (May 4, 1995) p33. "Wilson (standing) In The Studio"
PH17829 717 (September 21, 1995) p89. "Brian And Melinda Wilson"
PH17830 733 (May 2, 1996) p22. "Wilson (right) With Collaborator Tony Asher" (Schwartz, Michael)
WILSON, BRIAN—PHOTOGRAPHS—PORTRAITS
PH17831 643 (November 12, 1992) p100. "Brian Wilson" (Rolston, Matthew)
PH17832 707 (May 4, 1995) p33. "Sail On, Sailor: Brian Wilson Today" (Little, Blake)
WILSON, CASSANDRA—ALBUMS
PH17833 678 (March 24, 1994) p93. "Blue Light 'Til Dawn"
PH17834 730 (March 21, 1996) p100. "New Moon Daughter"
WILSON, CASSANDRA—PHOTOGRAPHS
PH17835 682 (May 19, 1994) pp76-77. "[Cassandra Wilson]" (Seliger, Mark)
WILSON, CINDY—PHOTOGRAPHS
PH17836 678 (March 24, 1994) p27. "Cindy Wilson Flies With The B-52's" (Rives, Bob)
WILSON, DEXTER—PHOTOGRAPHS
PH17837 678 (March 24, 1994) p69. "Brothers Under The Skin: Martin Phillips, Greg Parker, Mike Williams, Dexter Wilson, Rick Brown, Greg Jackson, Everett Whiteside, Roderick Bradford, Lacell Sherman..." (Smith, Brian)
WILSON, JACKIE—ALBUMS
PH17838 649 (February 4, 1993) p64. "Mr. Excitement!"
WILSON, JACKIE—PHOTOGRAPHS
PH17839 720 (November 2, 1995) p50. "Jackie Wilson"
WILSON, MATT—PHOTOGRAPHS
PH17840 711 (June 29, 1995) p23. "Blending '60s Who With Atmospheric Noise: Jurgens, Orris, Ackerson And Wilson (from left)" (Elledge, Paul)
WILSON, MELINDA—PHOTOGRAPHS
PH17841 717 (September 21, 1995) p89. "Brian And Melinda Wilson"
WILSON, NANCY—PHOTOGRAPHS
PH17842 696 (December 1, 1994) p25. "Howard Leese, John Paul Jones, Ann Wilson, Denny Fongheiser And Nancy Wilson"
WILSON, PATRICK—PHOTOGRAPHS
PH17843 694 (November 3, 1994) p40. "Matt Sharp, Patrick

Wilson, Brian Bell And Rivers Cuomo (from left)" (Elledge, Paul)
PH17844 704 (March 23, 1995) pp62-63. "Matt Sharp, Rivers Cuomo, Brian Bell, Pat Wilson (from left)" (Corbijn, Anton)
WILSON, PETE—PHOTOGRAPHS
PH17845 750-751 (December 26, 1996) p80. "The Cruel And Unusual California Gov. Pete Wilson" (Groshong, Dan)
WILSON PHILLIPS—ALBUMS
PH17846 634-635 (July 9, 1992) p100. "Shadows And Light"
WILSON PHILLIPS—PHOTOGRAPHS—PORTRAITS
PH17847 619-620 (December 12, 1991) pp[cover]. "1991 Yearbook" (Eccles, Andrew)
WILSON, RICKY—PHOTOGRAPHS—PORTRAITS
PH17848 629 (April 30, 1992) p16. "Ricky Wilson: The B-52's Waited A Year Before Admitting He Died Of AIDS" (Goldsmith, Lynn)
WILSON, RITA—PHOTOGRAPHS
PH17849 652 (March 18, 1993) pp[enc.37]. "Rita Wilson" (Seliger, Mark)
WILSON, ROBERT—PHOTOGRAPHS
PH17850 675 (February 10, 1994) p23. "'Black Rider' Creators Wilson, Burroughs And Waits (from left)" (Brinkhoff, Ralf)
WILSON, ROBIN—PHOTOGRAPHS
PH17851 726 (January 25, 1996) p30. "Gin Blossoms: Robin Wilson, Phillip Rhodes, Bill Lien, Jesse Valenzuela, Scott Johnson (from left)" (Jennings, Steve)
WILSON, RODNEY—PHOTOGRAPHS
PH17852 692 (October 6, 1994) p68. "Rodney Wilson In Front Of His House, Where Ernie Bought His .38" (Lixenberg, Dana)
WIMBISH, DOUG—PHOTOGRAPHS
PH17853 637 (August 20, 1992) p9. "Living Colour's Vernon Reid, Corey Glover And Doug Wimbish (from left)" (Mazur, Kevin)
PH17854 648 (January 21, 1993) p18. "Corey Glover, Will Calhoun, Vernon Reid And Doug Wimbish (from left)" (Leialoha, Mark)
WIMBISH, DOUG—PHOTOGRAPHS—PORTRAITS
PH17855 660-661 (July 8, 1993) p88. "The Band (from left): Will Calhoun, Vernon Reid, Doug Wimbish And Corey Glover" (Malfer)
WINCHELL, WALTER—PHOTOGRAPHS
PH17856 697 (December 15, 1994) p102. ""Winchell" The Book Recalls "Sweet Smell Of Success""
WINDLE, PATRICIA—PHOTOGRAPHS
PH17857 667 (October 14, 1993) p62. "Left: Windle And Randall Terry Face Off In March, As Eleanor Smeal Looks On" (McGlothlin, Doug)
WINDLE, PATRICIA—PHOTOGRAPHS—PORTRAITS
PH17858 667 (October 14, 1993) p57. "[Patricia Windle]" (Smale, Brian)
WINDLE, TED—PHOTOGRAPHS
PH17859 667 (October 14, 1993) p61. "Ted Windle, A Retired Air Force major, Helps His Wife Manage Her Three Clinics" (Smale, Brian)
WINDLE, TOD—PHOTOGRAPHS
PH17860 667 (October 14, 1993) p60. "Family Affair: Windle's Son Tod In The Port St. Lucie Clinic, Which He Runs" (Smale, Brian)
WINFREY, OPRAH—PHOTOGRAPHS
PH17861 672-673 (December 23, 1993) p20. "Winfrey And Jackson Yukking It Up On The Air" (Emerson, Sam)
WINGER, DEBRA—PHOTOGRAPHS
PH17862 674 (January 27, 1994) p48. "Acting Vehicles Include 'The Pelican Brief,' 'In The Name Of The Father,' 'What's Eating Gilbert Grape,' 'Shadowlands,' 'Naked,' And 'Grumpy Old Men'"
WINK, JOSH—PHOTOGRAPHS
PH17863 746 (October 31, 1996) p32. "[Josh Wink]" (Royce, Mark)
WINNINGHAM, MARE—PHOTOGRAPHS—PORTRAITS
PH17864 722 (November 30, 1995) p58. "Leigh (with 'Georgia' sister Winningham) Would Like An Oscar But Says, 'It Doesn't Change Your Life'" (Demarchelier, Patrick)
WINSLET, KATE—PHOTOGRAPHS
PH17865 724-725 (December 28, 1995) p138. "Lee Directs Winslet, Thompson And Imogen Stubbs In 'Sense' (from left)"
PH17866 731 (April 4, 1996) p66. "'Sense And Sensibility,' With Thompson And Kate Winslet"
WINTER, JOHNNY—PHOTOGRAPHS—PORTRAITS
PH17867 720 (November 2, 1995) p49. "Johnny Winter" (Seeff, Norman)
WINTERS, JONATHAN—PHOTOGRAPHS—PORTRAITS
PH17868 616 (October 31, 1991) p55. "Forever Left To His Own Devices, He Is The Eternal Only Child, Whose Favorite Toy Is Life" (Schiffman, Bonnie)
WINTERSON, JEANNETTE—PHOTOGRAPHS—PORTRAITS
PH17869 656 (May 13, 1993) p82. "[Jeannette Winterson]" (Edelstein, Jillian)
WINWOOD, STEVE—ALBUMS
PH17870 617 (November 14, 1991) p154. "Arc Of A Diver" (Wright, Tony)
WINWOOD, STEVE—PHOTOGRAPHS
PH17871 630 (May 14, 1992) p15. "Steve Winwood And Etta James" (Cooper, Dick)
PH17872 655 (April 29, 1993) p35. "The Aptly Named Blind Faith: Steve Winwood, Rick Grech, Ginger Baker And Clapton (from left)"
PH17873 680 (April 21, 1994) p34. "Capaldi Backs Winwood" (Corbijn, Anton)
PH17874 689 (August 25, 1994) p46. "Traffic's Steve Winwood (right)" (Tackett, Michael)
WINWOOD, STEVE—PHOTOGRAPHS—PORTRAITS
PH17875 643 (November 12, 1992) p205. "Steve Winwood" (Watson, Albert)
WISE, CHUBBY—PHOTOGRAPHS
PH17876 746 (October 31, 1996) p23. "Pride Of The Opry: The Legendary Bluegrass Boys Lineup Of Monroe, Chubby Wise, Flatt, Scruggs And Monroe's Brother Birch, Circa 1947 (from left)"
WITH HONORS (FILM)—PHOTOGRAPHS
PH17877 682 (May 19, 1994) p106. "Higher Education For Pesci (right) And Fraser"
WITT, ALICIA—PHOTOGRAPHS
PH17878 707 (May 4, 1995) p74. "Humphrey, Witt ('Fun')"
PH17879 727 (February 8, 1996) p46. "Richard Dreyfuss Teaches Music To Alicia Witt"
WOLDEMARIAM, KIDUSAN—PHOTOGRAPHS
PH17880 731 (April 4, 1996) p26. "Philip Woldemariam's Mother, Kidusan (left), And Sister Zee React To Testimony During The Trial"
WOLDEMARIAM, ZEE—PHOTOGRAPHS
PH17880 731 (April 4, 1996) p26. "Philip Woldemariam's Mother, Kidusan (left), And Sister Zee React To Testimony During The Trial"
WOLF (FILM)—ILLUSTRATIONS
PH17881 686-687 (July 14, 1994) p97. "The Wolf, The Lion And The Lamb" (Fisher, Jeffrey)
WOLF (FILM)—PHOTOGRAPHS
PH17882 684 (June 16, 1994) p116. "Creepy: Nicholson Puts The Bite On Pfeiffer In "Wolf""
PH17883 686-687 (July 14, 1994) p98. "Nicholson And Pfeiffer ("Wolf")"
WOLF, PETER—PHOTOGRAPHS
PH17884 671 (December 9, 1993) p31. "J. Geils-less Peter Wolf In Detroit" (Settle, Ken)
PH17885 679 (April 7, 1994) p38. "Joe Perry, Wolf, Tyler" (Lyden, Paul)
PH17886 696 (December 1, 1994) p44. "Give It To Him: A Howlin' Wolf" (Mazur, Kevin)

WOLF, PETER—PHOTOGRAPHS—PORTRAITS
PH17887 736 (June 13, 1996) p20. "Willie, We're Pulling For Ya! Willie Alexander (left) And Peter Wolf, Together Again" (Robicheau, Paul)
WOLFE, TOM—ILLUSTRATIONS
PH17888 749 (December 12, 1996) p11. "New Fiction By Tom Wolfe" (Risko, Robert)
WOLFE, TOM—PHOTOGRAPHS
PH17889 632 (June 11, 1992) p75. "Tom Wolfe At Cape Kennedy, Florida, 1972" (Leibovitz, Annie)
PH17890 647 (January 7, 1993) p11. "Tom Wolfe" (Elgar, Nick)
WOLFMAN JACK—PHOTOGRAPHS—PORTRAITS
PH17891 714 (August 10, 1995) p30. "The Wolfman Signs Off"
WOLINSKY, STEVE—PHOTOGRAPHS
PH17892 679 (April 7, 1994) p57. "At Northwestern University, Steve Wolinsky Is Leading A Team Of Researchers Who Are Studying The Transmission Of HIV As Well As Its Methods Within The Body" (Winters, Dan)
WOLVES—PHOTOGRAPHS
PH17893 693 (October 20, 1994) pp82-83. "[Wolf]" (Balog, James)
WOMEN—ILLUSTRATIONS
PH17894 632 (June 11, 1992) p169. "[Violence]" (Cronin, Brian)
PH17895 632 (June 11, 1992) p171. "[Violence]" (Mahurin, Matt)
PH17896 666 (September 30, 1993) p10. "Boss" (Pendergrast, James T.)
PH17897 667 (October 14, 1993) p67. "[Women]" (Isip, Jordan)
PH17898 669 (November 11, 1993) p8. "Girls Guitar" (Pendergrast, James T.)
PH17899 692 (October 6, 1994) pp57-58. "[Women In The Music Industry]" (Allen, Terry)
WON LUMP SOME—ALBUMS
PH17900 735 (May 30, 1996) p68. "Clean Hits"
WONDER, STEVIE—ALBUMS
PH17901 617 (November 14, 1991) p137. "Journey Through The Secret Life Of Plants" (Cavaika, John)
PH17902 617 (November 14, 1991) p137. "Journey Through The Secret Life Of Plants" (Nahas, Margo)
PH17903 704 (March 23, 1995) p121. "Conversation Peace"
PH17904 726 (January 25, 1996) p72. "Natural Wonder"
WONDER, STEVIE—ILLUSTRATIONS
PH17905 645-646 (December 10, 1992) p152. "Stevie Wonder, 1975"
WONDER, STEVIE—PHOTOGRAPHS
PH17906 712-713 (July 13, 1995) pp80-81. "Still Believes In The Healing Power Of Music In A Gangsta-Rap World" (Mahurin, Matt)
PH17907 712-713 (July 13, 1995) p82. "The Golden Age Of High Funk: Stevie Wonder In London, 1974" (Putland, Michael)
PH17908 712-713 (July 13, 1995) p84. "Wonder Boy: Little Stevie In The Early 1960s"
PH17909 728 (February 22, 1996) p19. "Stevie Wonder With Darlynn And Keith John, The Son Of The Late Soul Singer Little Willie John" (Mazur, Kevin)
WONG, RUSSELL—PHOTOGRAPHS
PH17910 666 (September 30, 1993) p113. "Yu Fei Hong Finds No Joy Dancing With Russell Wong"
WOO, JOHN—PHOTOGRAPHS
PH17911 656 (May 13, 1993) p87. "[John Woo]" (Moseley, Melissa)
PH17912 665 (September 16, 1993) p76. "Woo (left) Directs Van Damme For Action"
PH17913 729 (March 7, 1996) p54. "Slater And Travolta Confer With Director Woo"
WOOD, BRIAN—PHOTOGRAPHS
PH17914 667 (October 14, 1993) p40. "John Waterman, Brian Wood, John McBain, Ben Shepherd And Matt Cameron" (Hapke, Fran)
WOOD, DAVID—PHOTOGRAPHS
PH17915 615 (October 17, 1991) p28. "John Collie, Shayne Carter, Andrew Brough, David Wood (from left)" (Blakesberg, Jay)
WOOD, ED—ILLUSTRATIONS
PH17916 693 (October 20, 1994) p155. "The Remarkable Personal And Tacky Touch Of Ed Wood Can Be Seen In The Advertising For His 1953 Debut Film"
WOOD, ELIJAH—PHOTOGRAPHS
PH17917 696 (December 1, 1994) p134. "Father, Son: Kevin Costner, Elijah Wood"
WOOD, NATALIE—PHOTOGRAPHS
PH17918 658 (June 10, 1993) p74. "Ethan (Wayne) To Niece (Wood): 'Let's Go Home, Debbie'"
WOOD, RON—ILLUSTRATIONS—PORTRAITS
PH17919 698-699 (December 29, 1994) p70. "[Ron Wood]" (Payne, C. F.)
WOOD, RON—PHOTOGRAPHS
PH17920 637 (August 20, 1992) p16. "Ron Wood" (Weiner, S.)
PH17921 639 (September 17, 1992) p19. "Wood (left) And Richards" (Elgar, Nick)
PH17922 647 (January 7, 1993) p24. "Bernard Fowler (left) And Wood" (Diamond, Richard)
PH17923 653 (April 1, 1993) p11. "Kenny Jones, Stewart, Wyman, Wood And Ian McLagan" (Hutchson, Mick)
PH17924 653 (April 1, 1993) p16. "The Jeff Beck group Circa 1968: Mickey Waller, Beck, Stewart And Wood (from left)"
PH17925 653 (April 1, 1993) p11. "Ron Wood (left) And Rod Stewart" (Preston, Neal)
PH17926 668 (October 28, 1993) p35. "[Rolling Stones]"
PH17927 686-687 (July 14, 1994) pp68-69. "And Then There Were Four: Charlie Watts, Ron Wood, Mick Jagger And Keith Richards" (Seliger, Mark)
PH17928 689 (August 25, 1994) pp56-57. "Four Play In Toronto..." (Corbijn, Anton)
PH17929 689 (August 25, 1994) p60. ""We Risk reputation, And That's Everything," Says Watts, With A Masked Richards And Wood" (Corbijn, Anton)
PH17930 694 (November 3, 1994) p26. "Wood And Richards" (Seliger, Mark)
PH17931 694 (November 3, 1994) p28. "Richards And Wood "Warming Up The Hands" In Their Dressing Room" (Seliger, Mark)
PH17932 694 (November 3, 1994) p28. "Wood Gets The Final Touch before The Columbia Show (left)" (Seliger, Mark)
PH17933 697 (December 15, 1994) p17. "[Rolling Stones]" (Jones, Steve)
PH17934 712-713 (July 13, 1995) p34. "Stoned In Amsterdam: Wood, Jagger, Richards And Watts (from left) Get Their Ya-Yas Out At The Paradiso" (Corbijn, Anton)
PH17935 734 (May 16, 1996) p18. "Wood, Richards And Fowler (from left) Kicking It"
WOODARD, ALFRE—ILLUSTRATIONS
PH17936 648 (January 21, 1993) p54. "A Few Good Women" (Witte, Michael)
WOODARD, ALFRE—PHOTOGRAPHS
PH17937 648 (January 21, 1993) p55. "Woodard And McDonnell Fight Dependency"
PH17938 653 (April 1, 1993) p57. "Passion Fish"
PH17939 664 (September 2, 1993) p69. "Charles Grodin, Robert Downey Jr., Kyra Sedgwick, Alfre Woodard And Tom Sizemore"
WOODARD, CHARLAYNE—PHOTOGRAPHS
PH17940 749 (December 12, 1996) p90. "Ryder And Woodard Cast A Spell"
WOODARD, JEFF—PHOTOGRAPHS
PH17941 624 (February 20, 1992) p29. "Today Calgary, Tomorrow Albertville? From Left: Woodard, Leturgez, Snavely And Leonowicz" (Smale, Brian)
PH17942 624 (February 20, 1992) p32. "May The G-Force Be With You: Don't Ask About The Mush Run" (Smale, Brian)

PH17943 624 (February 20, 1992) p31. "Jeff Woodard, Brakeman And Pusher: He's No Crybaby" (Smale, Brian)
WOODS, JAMES—PHOTOGRAPHS
PH17944 645-646 (December 10, 1992) p98. "Valerie Bertinelli, Van Halen And James Wood At A Clinton Rally" (Jacobs, Michael)
PH17945 726 (January 25, 1996) p64. "Nixon Confers With Haldeman (James Woods)"
PH17946 743 (September 19, 1996) p90. "Quality Control"
WOODS, REGGIE—PHOTOGRAPHS
PH17947 694 (November 3, 1994) p22. "Ross With Saxaphonist Reggie Woods" (Mazur, Kevin)
WOODSTOCK '94—ILLUSTRATIONS
PH17948 691 (September 22, 1994) p14. "Woodstock II" (Pendergrast, James T.)
PH17949 694 (November 3, 1994) p14. "[Woodstock '94]" (Pendergrast, James T.)
WOODSTOCK '94—PHOTOGRAPHS
PH17950 691 (September 22, 1994) p64. "Peaceful, Easy Feeling: Fans Take A Break From The Action" (Goldsmith, Lynn)
PH17951 691 (September 22, 1994) p62. "Dusk At Winston Farm: The Population Would Swell To A High Of 350,000" (Grossmann, Andre)
PH17952 691 (September 22, 1994) p61. "[Woodstock '94]" (Kraft, Brooks)
PH17953 691 (September 22, 1994) p62. "Tents Pitched On Concert Fields, In Paths And On Creek Beds"
PH17954 694 (November 3, 1994) p37. "Some Of The Souvenirs Found At Woodstock '94" (Goldsmith, Lynn)
PH17955 700 (January 26, 1995) p53. "In The Mud At Woodstock 1994" (Laforet, Vincent)
PH17956 700 (January 26, 1995) p45. "The Now-Famous Mud Fight At Woodstock" (Olson, Jonathan)
PH17957 738-739 (July 11, 1996) p19. "The Muddy Mosh Pit At Woodstock '94, Where Hundreds Of Festival Injuries Were Reported" (Fields, Alexander C.)
WOODSTOCK—PHOTOGRAPHS
PH17958 645-646 (December 10, 1992) p149. "Woodstock, 1969"
PH17959 667 (October 14, 1993) p36. "Naked Greed: Rival Promoters Go To War Over Next Summer's Woodstock II"
PH17960 684 (June 16, 1994) p18. "Woodstock: Soon On A TV Near You"
WOODSTOCK, NEW YORK—ILLUSTRATIONS
PH17961 691 (September 22, 1994) p100. "Real Woodstock" (Hussey, Tim)
WOODWARD, FRED—PHOTOGRAPHS
PH17962 643 (November 12, 1992) p49. "'Rolling Stone' Art Directors (from left): Bob Kingsbury (1968-73), Tony Lane (1974-76), Annie Leibovitz, Mike Salisbury (1973-74), Roger Black (1976-78), Jann S. Wenner, Derek..
WOOLLEY, JAMES—PHOTOGRAPHS
PH17963 690 (September 8, 1994) p54. "Vrenna, Woolley, Reznor, Finck, Lohner (from left)" (Cultice, Joseph)
WORKERS: AN ARCHAEOLOGY OF THE INDUSTRIAL AGE (BOOK)—PHOTOGRAPHS
PH17964 665 (September 16, 1993) pp54-58. "Workers of The World" (Salgado, Sebastiao)
WORKMAN, JIMMY—PHOTOGRAPHS
PH17965 618 (November 28, 1991) p53. "They're Altogether Ooky" (Seliger, Mark)
WORL-A-GIRL—PHOTOGRAPHS—PORTRAITS
PH17966 686-687 (July 14, 1994) p72. "Girl World: Sensi, Linda, Charmaine, Sabrina (from left)" (Borris, Dan)
WORLD MUSIC—ILLUSTRATIONS
PH17967 615 (October 17, 1991) p94. "The Global Beat"
PH17968 626 (March 19, 1992) p95. "The Global Beat"
PH17969 633 (June 25, 1992) p43. "The Global Beat"
PH17970 640 (October 1, 1992) p75. "The Global Beat"
PH17971 645-646 (December 10, 1992) p187. "The Global Beat"
PH17971 650 (February 18, 1993) p59. "The Global Beat"
PH17972 658 (June 10, 1993) p78. "[The Global Beat]"
PH17973 670 (November 25, 1993) p108. "Global Beat"
PH17974 672-673 (December 23, 1993) p163. "Global Beat"
PH17975 680 (April 21, 1994) p90. "Global Beat"
PH17976 689 (August 25, 1994) p92. "Global Beat"
PH17977 698-699 (December 29, 1994) p182. "Global Beat"
PH17978 709 (June 1, 1995) p62. "Global Beat"
WORLD PARTY—ALBUMS
PH17979 660-661 (July 8, 1993) p112. "Bang!"
WORLD WIDE WEB—ILLUSTRATIONS
PH17980 726 (January 25, 1996) p18. "666.com" (Meshon, Aaron)
WORLD WIDE WEB—PHOTOGRAPHS
PH17981 710 (June 15, 1995) p91. "[World Wide Web Pages]"
PH17982 722 (November 30, 1995) pp[enc.16]. "Digital Piecework: Each Surfer Is Expected To Post About 150 New Sites A Day" (Blakesberg, Jay)
PH17983 734 (May 16, 1996) p68. "[Rocktropolis]"
WORTHINGTON, TRACE—PHOTOGRAPHS
PH17984 676 (February 24, 1994) p51. "Trace Worthington On The Trampoline Behind His House" (Hanauer, Mark)
PH17985 676 (February 24, 1994) p51. "Worthington Eating Breakfast At Morning Ray Cafe, In Park City, Utah" (Hanauer, Mark)
PH17986 676 (February 24, 1994) p53. "Signing Autographs At A Gart Bros. In Park City..." (Hanauer, Mark)
PH17987 676 (February 24, 1994) p51. "[Coach Chris "Hatchet' Haslock]" (Hanauer, Mark)
PH17988 676 (February 24, 1994) p51. "Hitting The Slopes At 2 Years Old"
WORTHINGTON, TRACE—PHOTOGRAPHS—PORTRAITS
PH17989 676 (February 24, 1994) p53. "At The Wasatch Brew Pub With Heidi Boissonneau..." (Hanauer, Mark)
WOZNIAK, STEVE—PHOTOGRAPHS
PH17990 731 (April 4, 1996) p54. "Jobs, Sculley And Wozniak (from left) Unveil The Apple IIC In '84"
PH17991 731 (April 4, 1996) p55. "Woz (left), Jobs And Some Serious Circuitry In '76"
WRECKX-N-EFFECT—PHOTOGRAPHS—PORTRAITS
PH17992 654 (April 15, 1993) pp[enc.4]. "Wreckx-n-Effect's Markell Riley And Aqil Davidson" (Seliger, Mark)
WREN, ALAN—PHOTOGRAPHS—PORTRAITS
PH17993 706 (April 20, 1995) p30. "The Stone Roses (clockwise from top left): Mountfield, Wren, Squire And Brown" (Ragel, Jon)
WRIGHT, JEFFREY—PHOTOGRAPHS
PH17994 741 (August 22, 1996) p105. "Wright, Bowie, Oldman, Hopper"
WRIGHT, JOHNNY—PHOTOGRAPHS
PH17995 750-751 (December 26, 1996) p179. "Kitty Wells & Johnny Wright" (Seliger, Mark)
WRIGHT, LAWRENCE—PHOTOGRAPHS
PH17996 632 (June 11, 1992) p166. "Author Lawrence Wright On A Trail In Texas In 1988"
WRIGHT, RICHARD—PHOTOGRAPHS
PH17997 728 (February 22, 1996) p19. "Pink Floyd's Richard Wright (left) And Gilmour Flank Special Guest Corgan" (Mazur, Kevin)
WRIGHT, ROBIN—PHOTOGRAPHS
PH17998 686-687 (July 14, 1994) p98. "Robin Wright And Hanks ("Forrest Gump")"
PH17999 731 (April 4, 1996) p48. "With Robin Wright, The Mother Of His Two Children, In 1991" (Ortega, Albert)
PH18000 738-739 (July 11, 1996) p98. "Robin Wright Relies On Morgan Freeman"
WU, JENNIFER S.—PHOTOGRAPHS
PH18001 642 (October 29, 1992) p63. "At College, Post-

Recovery"
PH18002 642 (October 29, 1992) p63. "The End Of The World, And I Feel Fine"
WU-TANG CLAN—PHOTOGRAPHS
PH18003 675 (February 10, 1994) p23. "[Wu-Tang Clan]"
PH18004 693 (October 20, 1994) p30. "Sean Nelson, Star Of "Fresh," With The Wu-Tang Clan In New York City" (Friedman, Steve)
WUERTHNER, GEORGE—PHOTOGRAPHS
PH18005 693 (October 20, 1994) p84. "Matteson And Wuerthner In Absaroka-Bear Tooth Wilderness" (Wuerthner, George)
WUHL, ROBERT—PHOTOGRAPHS
PH18006 637 (August 20, 1992) p60. "Deal Makings: De Niro (left) And Wuhl"
WUORNOS, AILEEN—PHOTOGRAPHS
PH18007 677 (March 10, 1994) p60. "[Aileen Wuornos]"
WYATT EARP (FILM)—PHOTOGRAPHS
PH18008 688 (August 11, 1994) p62. "Wyatt Earp"
PH18009 691 (September 22, 1994) p106. "Worst Big Film"
PH18010 698-699 (December 29, 1994) p199. "[Wyatt Earp]"
WYATT, ROBERT—ALBUMS
PH18011 623 (February 6, 1992) p82. "Dondestan"
WYLDE, ZAKK—PHOTOGRAPHS
PH18012 686-687 (July 14, 1994) p72. "LoMenzo, Wylde And Tischy (from left)" (Ragel, Jon)
WYMAN, BILL—PHOTOGRAPHS
PH18013 648 (January 21, 1993) p25. "The Latest Stone To Leave The Fold" (Williams, Jo)
PH18014 653 (April 1, 1993) p11. "Kenny Jones, Stewart, Wyman, Wood And Ian McLagan" (Hutchson, Mick)
PH18015 655 (April 29, 1993) p37. "Clapton, Bill Wyman And Jeff Beck Onstage At London's Royal Albert Hall In September 1983, Performing At The ARMS Benefit Concerts" (Zuffante, Vinnie)
PH18016 672-673 (December 23, 1993) p17. "Wyman: No Longer Rolling" (Mazur, Kevin)
PH18017 715 (August 24, 1995) p37. "Jones, Richards, Watts, Jagger, Wyman (from left) [Watts, Richards, Jones, Jagger, Wyman (from left)]" (Mankowitz, Gered)
WYNDORF, DAVE—PHOTOGRAPHS
PH18018 710 (June 15, 1995) p54. "Boys In The Attic (clockwise from upper left): Ed Mundell, Jon Kleiman, Wyndorf And Joe Calandra" (Toliver, Chris)
WYNDORF, DAVE—PHOTOGRAPHS—PORTRAITS
PH18019 716 (September 7, 1995) p34. "Dopes To Infinity: Wyndorf, Mundell, Kleiman And Calandra (from left)" (Lavine, Michael)
WYNETTE, TAMMY—PHOTOGRAPHS
PH18020 625 (March 5, 1992) p19. "Tammy Wynette With Musical Friends"
PH18021 682 (May 19, 1994) p37. "No Rap, No Hard Stuff: Taylor, Houston, Wynette, John, Sting (from left) At Rehearsal" (Mazur, Kevin)
PH18022 682 (May 19, 1994) p37. "Show Stopper Tammy Wynette" (Mazur, Kevin)
PH18023 750-751 (December 26, 1996) p173. "Tammy Wynette" (Seliger, Mark)
WYNETTE, TAMMY—PHOTOGRAPHS—PORTRAITS
PH18024 692 (October 6, 1994) p50. "Tammy Wynette"
WYNN, STEVE—ALBUMS
PH18025 634-635 (July 9, 1992) p105. "Dazzling Display"
WYNN, STEVE—PHOTOGRAPHS
PH18026 660-661 (July 8, 1993) p101. "Gutterball: Johnny Hott, Bryan Harvey, Steve Wynn, Bob Rupe, Stephen McCarthy"
PH18027 663 (August 19, 1993) p15. "Rupe, Hott, Harvey, Wynn And McCarthy (from left)" (Callahan, Walter)

X

X—ALBUMS
PH18028 617 (November 14, 1991) p140. "Los Angeles" (Gargani, Frank)
PH18029 664 (September 2, 1993) p64. "Hey Zeus!"
X—PHOTOGRAPHS
PH18030 659 (June 24, 1993) p23. "'Xdream: Gilkyson, Doe, Cervenka, Bonebrake (from left)"
X-FILES (TELEVISION SHOW)—ILLUSTRATIONS
PH18031 722 (November 30, 1995) p79. "[X-Files]" (Fishman, Miriam)
PH18032 737 (June 27, 1996) p12. "Rolling Stone" (Pendergrast, James T.)
X-FILES (TELEVISION SHOW)—PHOTOGRAPHS
PH18033 734 (May 16, 1996) p40. "When They're Not Chasing UFOs, Mulder And Scully Battle The Occasional Flukeman (above)"
X GAMES—PHOTOGRAPHS
PH18034 742 (September 5, 1996) p53. "Preparing For Takeoff" (Seliger, Mark)
PH18035 742 (September 5, 1996) p54. "Terminal Velocity: Pilots Often Reach Freeway Speeds" (Seliger, Mark)
PH18036 742 (September 5, 1996) p56. "A BMX Competitor Dazzles The Onlooking Crowd With A Serious Show Of Extreme Air" (Seliger, Mark)
PH18037 742 (September 5, 1996) p57. "In-Line And Ready To Rip: Racers Prepare To Descend The College Hill Course" (Seliger, Mark)
X, MALCOLM—ILLUSTRATIONS
PH18038 648 (January 21, 1993) p7. "1960's - 1990's" (Pendergrast, James T.)
X, MALCOLM—PHOTOGRAPHS
PH18039 644 (November 26, 1992) p36. "The Two Faces Of Malcolm X: Denzel Before A Mural In New York City" (Watson, Albert)
X-PENSIVE WINOS—ALBUMS
PH18040 621 (January 9, 1992) p51. "Live At The Hollywood Palladium, December 15, 1988"
XEFOS, CHRIS—PHOTOGRAPHS—PORTRAITS
PH18041 654 (April 15, 1993) p17. "Murdock, Hall, Xefos, Rick (from left)" (Seliger, Mark)
XTC—ALBUMS
PH18042 631 (May 28, 1992) p55. "Nonsuch"
PH18043 634-635 (July 9, 1992) p128. "Nonsuch"
PH18044 636 (August 6, 1992) p80. "Nonsuch"
PH18045 648 (January 21, 1993) p23. "'XTC' Live In Concert 1980"
XU, LI—PHOTOGRAPHS
PH18046 642 (October 29, 1992) p62. "From Red Songs To Rock 'N' Roll"

Y

YALE UNIVERSITY—PHOTOGRAPHS
PH18047 626 (March 19, 1992) p67. "Nation's Disgrace: Jolly Yalies Down Temperance Crusader"
YAMAMOTO, HIRO—PHOTOGRAPHS
PH18048 684 (June 16, 1994) p50. "Cornell, Thayil, Sundquist, Yamamoto In Mid-'80s" (Peterson, Charles)
PH18049 684 (June 16, 1994) p52. "Cameron, Thayil, Yamamoto, Cornell, Silver, Tour Manager Eric Johnson (from left) In 1988" (Peterson, Charles)
YAMANO, ATSUKO—PHOTOGRAPHS
PH18050 654 (April 15, 1993) pp[enc.29]. "Michie Nakatani, Atsuko Yamano And Naoko Yamano (from left)" (Simons, Chip)

YAMANO, NAOKO—PHOTOGRAPHS
PH18050 654 (April 15, 1993) pp[enc.29]. "Michie Nakatani, Atsuko Yamano And Naoko Yamano (from left)" (Simons, Chip)
YAMATSUKA, EYE—PHOTOGRAPHS
PH18051 712-713 (July 13, 1995) p45. "Boredoms Singer Eye Yamatsuka" (Toliver, Chris)
YANG, JERRY—PHOTOGRAPHS
PH18052 722 (November 30, 1995) pp[enc.19]. "Young, In Charge And Tired: Yang (left) And Filo" (Blakesberg, Jay)
PH18053 722 (November 30, 1995) pp[enc.15]. "Yang (left) And Filo, Creators Of The Yahoo! Directory: They Found A Way To 'Deliver Eyeballs'" (Winters, Dan)
YANG, NU YENG—PHOTOGRAPHS—PORTRAITS
PH18054 703 (March 9, 1995) p61. "Nu Yeng Yang (below) Lost His Son" (Bartholomew, Bart)
YANG, XOU—PHOTOGRAPHS—PORTRAITS
PH18055 703 (March 9, 1995) p56. "[Xou Yang]"
YANKOVIC, AL—ILLUSTRATIONS
PH18056 735 (May 30, 1996) p68. "Yankin' Yer Chain: 'Weird Al' Yankovic" (Hungry Dog Studio)
YANKOVIC, AL—PHOTOGRAPHS
PH18057 667 (October 14, 1993) p94. "Smells Like Weird Al: Spoofing Nirvana"
YANOWITZ, PETER—PHOTOGRAPHS
PH18058 636 (August 6, 1992) p13. "The Wallflowers (from left): Barrie Maguire, Jakob Dylan, Rami Jaffee, Peter Yanowitz And Tobi Miller" (Mark, Mary Ellen)
YARDBIRDS—PHOTOGRAPHS
PH18059 623 (February 6, 1992) p51. "The Yardbirds, Circa 1964 (from left): Chris Dreja, Keith Reif, Paul Samwell-Smith, Eric Clapton And Jim McCarty"
YARDBIRDS—PHOTOGRAPHS—PORTRAITS
PH18060 655 (April 29, 1993) p34. "Slowhand (at bottom left) With The Yardbirds: Chris Dreja, Jim McCarty, Paul Samwell-Smith And Keith Relf (clockwise from top left)"
YATES, DON—PHOTOGRAPHS
PH18061 678 (March 24, 1994) p57. "Cursed? KCMU-FM Management: Knab, Now Resigned, Yates And Mara (from left)" (Lavine, Michael)
YATSURA—PHOTOGRAPHS
PH18062 747 (November 14, 1996) p60. "[Yatsura]" (Christie, Donald)
YAUCH, ADAM—ILLUSTRATIONS
PH18063 740 (August 8, 1996) p7. "The Beastie Boys' Adam Yauch Interviews The Dalai Lama" (Kunz, Anita)
YAUCH, ADAM—PHOTOGRAPHS
PH18064 678 (March 24, 1994) p43. "Beasties In The Jungle: Mike Diamond, Adam Horovitz And Adam Yauch (clockwise from top left)" (Simons, Chip)
PH18065 681 (May 5, 1994) p21. "Beasties Adam Yauch (left) And Mike D With Joey DiPaolo"
PH18066 684 (June 16, 1994) p36. "United Beastie Service: Adam Horowitz, Mike Diamond, Adam Yauch" (Kravitz, Jeff)
PH18067 688 (August 11, 1994) p49. "Yauch, Diamond, Horovitz (clockwise from top) In 1986"
PH18068 692 (October 6, 1994) p16. "Mellow Monks Chill With Beastie Boy Adam Yauch" (Weiner, Scott)
PH18069 693 (October 20, 1994) p28. "Beasties Adam Yauch, Mike D, Adam Horowitz Warming Up At Radio City Music Hall During Rehearsal (from left)" (Mazur, Kevin)
PH18070 720 (November 2, 1995) p17. "Adam Yauch Gets Political In New York" (Johnson, Nancy Jo)
PH18071 740 (August 8, 1996) p21. "The Dalai Lama And Yauch Meet In Rome" (Suekwon)
PH18072 742 (September 5, 1996) p21. "[Yoko Ono, Sean Lennon, Adam Yauch]" (Atlas, David)
PH18073 750-751 (December 26, 1996) p64. "Beastie Boys Adam Yauch Takes The Stage With A Plethora Of Tibetan Monks" (Blakesberg, Jay)
YAUCH, ADAM—PHOTOGRAPHS—PORTRAITS
PH18074 688 (August 11, 1994) p48. "Adam Yauch" (Rolston, Matthew)
YEARWOOD, TRISHA—ALBUMS
PH18075 640 (October 1, 1992) p63. "Hearts In Armor"
PH18076 674 (January 27, 1994) p54. "The Song Remembers When"
PH18077 705 (April 6, 1995) p65. "Thinkin' About You"
YELLA—PHOTOGRAPHS
PH18078 634-635 (July 9, 1992) p17. "N.W.A. (clockwise from top left): MC Ren, Yella, Eazy-E And Dr. Dre" (Preston, Neal)
PH18079 666 (September 30, 1993) p42. "Serious Attitude: Ex-N.W.A. Members Ice Cube, Yella, Eazy-E, Dre And MC Ren" (Rosenberg, Howard)
YELTSIN, BORIS—ILLUSTRATIONS
PH18080 743 (September 19, 1996) p54. "[Boris Yeltsin]" (Blitt, Barry)
PH18081 743 (September 19, 1996) p9. "Russian President Boris Yeltsin" (Panter, Gary)
YELTSIN, BORIS—PHOTOGRAPHS
PH18082 750-751 (December 26, 1996) p70. "Yeltsin: Fear And Dancing On The Campaign Trail"
YES—ALBUMS
PH18083 617 (November 14, 1991) p102. "Relayer" (Dean, Roger)
PH18084 691 (September 22, 1994) p94. "Talk"
YO LA TENGO—ALBUMS
PH18085 711 (June 29, 1995) p60. "Electr-O-Pura"
YO-YO—ALBUMS
PH18086 636 (August 6, 1992) p59. "Black Pearl"
YO-YO—PHOTOGRAPHS
PH18087 653 (April 1, 1993) p13. "Ed Lover And Yo-Yo"
YO-YO—PHOTOGRAPHS—PORTRAITS
PH18088 619-620 (December 12, 1991) p88. "Yo-Yo" (Little, Blake)
PH18089 645-646 (December 10, 1992) p66. "The Black Pearl, Yo-Yo" (Blakesberg, Jay)
YOAKUM, DWIGHT—ALBUMS
PH18090 658 (June 10, 1993) p67. "This Time"
PH18091 672-673 (December 23, 1993) p165. "This Time"
PH18092 716 (September 7, 1995) p72. "Dwight Live"
PH18093 723 (December 14, 1995) p84. "Gone"
YOAKUM, DWIGHT—ILLUSTRATIONS
PH18094 658 (June 10, 1993) p67. "The Time Has Come For Dwight" (Davis, Paul)
PH18095 669 (November 11, 1993) p8. "Sexy Chart" (Pendergrast, James T.)
YOAKUM, DWIGHT—PHOTOGRAPHS
PH18096 657 (May 27, 1993) p11. "Yoakum (left, no tongue) And Fonda" (Kravitz, Jeff)
PH18097 666 (September 30, 1993) p64. "[Dwight Yoakum]"
PH18098 666 (September 30, 1993) p63. "In Columbus, Ohio, 1959, Left"
PH18099 666 (September 30, 1993) p64. "[Dwight Yoakum]" (Mosenfelder, Tim)
PH18100 666 (September 30, 1993) p63. "And Today On Hollywood Boulevard" (Seliger, Mark)
PH18101 666 (September 30, 1993) p66. "When He Wears The Hat, He Is A Star, Bigger Than Life" (Seliger, Mark)
PH18102 666 (September 30, 1993) p65. "Yoakum (right) Performing At A High School Variety Show In 1973"
YOGA—ILLUSTRATIONS
PH18103 660-661 (July 8, 1993) p10. "Pie Charts" (Pendergrast, James T.)
YORKE, THOM—PHOTOGRAPHS
PH18104 665 (September 16, 1993) p22. "Radiohead With Yorke (center): Appealing To The Creep In Everyone" (Sharp, Ken)
PH18105 671 (December 9, 1993) p31. "Yorke And Donnelly Share A Moment"

PH18106 716 (September 7, 1995) p19. "Colin Greenwood, Ed O'Brien, Thom Yorke, Jonny Greenwood And Phil Selway (from left)" (Blakesberg, Jay)
PH18107 716 (September 7, 1995) p21. "Yorke At Glastonbury, 1994" (Putland, Michael)
PH18108 722 (November 30, 1995) p19. "Stipe (left) And Yorke In Tel Aviv"
PH18109 733 (May 2, 1996) p20. "Buzz Clips: Spearhead's Michael Franti (below); Radioheads' Thom Yorke (above, left)"
PH18110 738-739 (July 11, 1996) p15. "Thom Yorke, Colin Greenwood, Roseanne, Ed O'Brien, Phil Selway And Jonny Greenwood" (Diltz, Henry)

YOTHU YINDI—PHOTOGRAPHS—PORTRAITS
PH18111 640 (October 1, 1992) p29. "Yothu Yindi: Crossover Stars" (Low, Dorothy)

YOU MIGHT THINK (VIDEO)—PHOTOGRAPHS
PH18112 667 (October 14, 1993) p78. "The Cars' 'You Might Think': When Ric Ocasek Sang It, He Sang A Mouthful"

YOU SEND ME (BOOK)—PHOTOGRAPHS
PH18113 701 (February 9, 1995) p28. "You Send Me"

YOU SO CRAZY (FILM)—PHOTOGRAPHS
PH18114 677 (March 10, 1994) p60. "Martin Lawrence From Sitcom To Stand-Up"

YOUNG, ALISON—PHOTOGRAPHS
PH18115 690 (September 8, 1994) p60. "Jeff And His Girlfriend, Alison Young, At His Skate Park In 1992" (Walgren, Judy)

YOUNG, ANGUS—PHOTOGRAPHS
PH18116 640 (October 1, 1992) p10. "AC-DC's Angus Young"
PH18117 743 (September 19, 1996) p20. "Johnson, With Stern And Angus Young (from left), Calls Stern 'A Good Kid. And His Fans Are A Rowdy Bunch Of Buggers'"

YOUNG BLACK TEENAGERS—ALBUMS
PH18118 651 (March 4, 1993) p66. "Dead End Kidz Doin' Lifetime Bidz"

YOUNG, BRIAN—PHOTOGRAPHS
PH18119 710 (June 15, 1995) p40. "Posies Brian Young, Auer, Stringfellow, Joe Bass (from left)" (Moskowitz, Karen)

YOUNG, CARL—PHOTOGRAPHS—PORTRAITS
PH18120 700 (January 26, 1995) p24. "[Spearhead]"

YOUNG, CHARLES M.—PHOTOGRAPHS
PH18121 632 (June 11, 1992) p126. "Young And Belushi Meet The Dead Boys, December 1977" (Kearney, Mitch)

YOUNG, DAMIAN—PHOTOGRAPHS
PH18122 706 (April 20, 1995) p88. "Young, Huppert, Donovan And Lowensohn Run"

YOUNG DISCIPLES—PHOTOGRAPHS
PH18123 628 (April 16, 1992) p57. "Carleen Anderson, Marc Nelson And Femi Williams (from left)"

YOUNG, GRANT—PHOTOGRAPHS
PH18124 644 (November 26, 1992) p31. "Karl Mueller, Dave Pirner, Dan Murphy, Grant Young (clockwise from top left)" (Breiehagen, Per)
PH18125 695 (November 17, 1994) p55. "Soul Asylum—Photographs" (Smale, Brian)
PH18126 711 (June 29, 1995) p33. "Ryder, Pirner, Band Manager Heaps, Murphy (background) And Ex-Drummer Young Greet Clinton (foreground) At The White House (from left)" (Markowitz, Jeffrey)

YOUNG, LA MONTE—ALBUMS
PH18127 669 (November 11, 1993) p77. "Just Stompin'"

YOUNG MC—PHOTOGRAPHS—PORTRAITS
PH18128 666 (September 30, 1993) p55. "[Young MC]"

YOUNG, NEIL—ALBUMS
PH18129 617 (November 14, 1991) p171. "Weld"
PH18130 619-620 (December 12, 1991) p165. "Weld"
PH18131 625 (March 5, 1992) p61. "Weld"
PH18132 644 (November 26, 1992) p71. "Harvest Moon"
PH18133 655 (April 29, 1993) p62. "Lucky Thirteen"
PH18134 663 (August 19, 1993) p76. "Unplugged"
PH18135 689 (August 25, 1994) p87. "Sleeps With Angels"
PH18136 712-713 (July 13, 1995) p107. "Mirror Ball"
PH18137 740 (August 8, 1996) p58. "Broken Arrow"

YOUNG, NEIL—ILLUSTRATIONS
PH18138 641 (October 15, 1992) p145. "[Neil Young]" (Mahurin, Matt)
PH18139 645-646 (December 10, 1992) p152. "Neil Young, 1979"
PH18140 689 (August 25, 1994) p87. "Forever Young" (Ulriksen, Mark)
PH18141 693 (October 20, 1994) p168. "Neil Young: A Fine Vintage Whine" (Gorgun, Ahmet)
PH18142 712-713 (July 13, 1995) p107. "Forever Young" (Kunz, Anita)

YOUNG, NEIL—ILLUSTRATIONS—LETTERING
PH18143 648 (January 21, 1993) pp35-37. "Forever Young" (Karl, Anita)

YOUNG, NEIL—PHOTOGRAPHS
PH18144 617 (November 14, 1991) p75. "The Last Waltz, 1976: Robertson, Danko And Manuel, With Neil Young (left), Bob Dylan (back to camera) And Van Morrison" (Leibovitz, Annie)
PH18145 618 (November 28, 1991) p20. "[Neil Young]" (Roberts, Ebet)
PH18146 619-620 (December 12, 1991) p94. "The All-Star Jam Finale At The Bridge Concert" (Blakesberg, Jay)
PH18147 619-620 (December 12, 1991) p103. "Phil Lesh, Bob Weir, Neil Young And Jerry Garcia (from left) Pay Tribute To Bill Graham" (Blakesberg, Jay)
PH18148 619-620 (December 12, 1991) p26. "Neil Young" (Mazur, Kevin)
PH18149 625 (March 5, 1992) p17. "Young With Keith Richards" (Elgar, Nick)
PH18150 625 (March 5, 1992) p17. "Mitch Mitchell, Noel Redding, Young And Al Hendrix (from left)" (Elgar, Nick)
PH18151 625 (March 5, 1992) p17. "Neil Young Takes Center Stage During The All-Star-Jam Finale" (Gershoff, Gary)
PH18152 625 (March 5, 1992) p25. "Booker T. And The MG's, With Neil Young" (Mazur, Kevin)
PH18153 629 (April 30, 1992) p11. "Nelson (left) With Young Backstage" (Mazur, Kevin)
PH18154 638 (September 3, 1992) p11. "Warren Zevon (left) And Neil Young" (Goldman, Paul)
PH18155 644 (November 26, 1992) p17. "The Great Garden Party: Dylan Center Stage For The Grand Finale" (Mazur, Kevin)
PH18156 644 (November 26, 1992) p19. "Neil Young's Performance Was One Of The Many Highlights Of The Evening" (Mazur, Kevin)
PH18157 645-646 (December 10, 1992) p96. "Taylor, Young And Elton John" (Blakesberg, Jay)
PH18158 645-646 (December 10, 1992) p30. "The Famous Party-Ending Jam (above)" (Mazur, Kevin)
PH18159 645-646 (December 10, 1992) p93. "[Neil Young]" (Mazur, Kevin)
PH18160 648 (January 21, 1993) p36. "[Neil Young]" (Seliger, Mark)
PH18161 655 (April 29, 1993) p11. "Ulrich, Young And Hetfield (from left)" (Blakesberg, Jay)
PH18162 658 (June 10, 1993) p17. "Willie Nelson (left) And Neil Young" (Roberts, Ebet)
PH18163 664 (September 2, 1993) p29. "Grunge Guru Young (left) And Steve Cropper" (Mikrut, Jack)
PH18164 667 (October 14, 1993) p39. "Below: Eddie Vedder (left) With Neil Young" (Kravitz, Jeff)
PH18165 667 (October 14, 1993) p68. "This Caption's For Neil: Young's Video Got MTV Mad"
PH18166 672-673 (December 23, 1993) p28. "Above: Gregg Allman, John Fogerty And Neil Young" (Blakesberg, Jay)
PH18167 672-673 (December 23, 1993) p74. "Graham Nash, Van Halen And Young" (Blakesberg, Jay)

PH18168 672-673 (December 23, 1993) p63. "Above: Neil Young And Eddie Vedder Share A Moment" (Kravitz, Jeff)
PH18169 672-673 (December 23, 1993) p58. "Eddie Vedder (left, no mask) With Young" (Preston, Neal)
PH18170 674 (January 27, 1994) p42. "Forever Young: With Booker T.,MG's" (Blakesberg, Jay)
PH18171 683 (June 2, 1994) p27. "Duffers Eddie van Halen (left) And Neil Young" (Granitz, Steve)
PH18172 694 (November 3, 1994) p17. "Young" (Smith, Sean)
PH18173 696 (December 1, 1994) p23. "The Mighty Neil Young (right)" (Blakesberg, Jay)
PH18174 698-699 (December 29, 1994) p68. "Young, Vedder And Stone Gossard (from left) Do The Right Thing For The Kids" (Hashimoto, Mike)
PH18175 702 (February 23, 1995) p48. "The Song Remains The Same: Robert Plant, Jimmy Page And Neil Young (from left)" (Mazur, Kevin)
PH18176 703 (March 9, 1995) p36. "Rockin' In The Free World: Pearl Jam With Neil Young" (Mazur, Kevin)
PH18177 723 (December 14, 1995) p27. "Young, Surprise Guest Steven Tyler And Hynde (from left)" (Blakesberg, Jay)
PH18178 724-725 (December 28, 1995) p40. "Eddie Vedder (left) And Neil Young" (Busacca, Larry)
PH18179 724-725 (December 28, 1995) p39. "Robert Plant, Jimmy Page, Young (from left)" (Mazur, Kevin)
PH18180 728 (February 22, 1996) p24. "Young And Briggs At 1995's Rock & Roll Hall Of Fame Inductions" (Briggs, Bettina)
PH18181 737 (June 27, 1996) p29. "Young Has Reunited With Crazy Horse For A New Album And Tour" (Hashimoto, Mike)
PH18182 744 (October 3, 1996) p35. "Young Rockin' In The Free South" (Capak, R. J.)
PH18183 748 (November 28, 1996) p26. "Neil Young, John Mellencamp And Willie Nelson, Talking, Presumably, About The Plight Of The Family Farmer" (Roberts, Ebet)
PH18184 749 (December 12, 1996) p19. "Smith, Helped Out By Young, At The Bridge Benefit" (Blakesberg, Jay)

YOUNG, NEIL—PHOTOGRAPHS—PORTRAITS
PH18185 643 (November 12, 1992) p201. "Neil Young" (Watson, Albert)
PH18186 648 (January 21, 1993) pp[cover]. "How Neil Stays Forever Young" (Seliger, Mark)
PH18187 648 (January 21, 1993) pp34-35. "[Forever Young]" (Seliger, Mark)
PH18188 672-673 (December 23, 1993) p188. "[Covers]" (Seliger, Mark)
PH18189 681 (May 5, 1994) p22. "Neil Young (left) And Elton John Go Hollywood At Elton's Oscar Party" (Mazur, Kevin)
PH18190 702 (February 23, 1995) p48. "Come On, Get Happy: Eddie Vedder With Idol Neil Young" (Mazur, Kevin)
PH18191 731 (April 4, 1996) p17. "[Neil Young & Jim Jarmusch]" (Hashimoto, Mike)

YOUNG, NEIL—VIDEOS
PH18192 621 (January 9, 1992) p56. "New Ragged Glories"

YOUNG, RICHARD—PHOTOGRAPHS
PH18193 668 (October 28, 1993) p30. "Greg Martin, Johnnie Johnson And Richard Young (from left)" (Natkin, Paul)

YOUNG, SEAN—PHOTOGRAPHS
PH18194 669 (November 11, 1993) p81. "Assante And Young Get Smoke In Their Eyes"

YOUNGBERG, ROB—PHOTOGRAPHS—PORTRAITS
PH18195 685 (June 30, 1994) p28. "Tragi-Pop Wuss Rockers: Lotion's Youngberg, Zajkowski, Bill And Jim Ferguson (from left)" (Cardillicchio, Nick)

YOUNGBLOOD, JENNIFER—PHOTOGRAPHS
PH18196 683 (June 2, 1994) p38. "Dave Grohl And Fiancee Jennifer Youngblood, Krist Novoselic And Wife Shelli Enter The Memorial Service On April 10" (Banner, Ellen M.)

YOW, DAVID—ILLUSTRATIONS
PH18197 714 (August 10, 1995) p7. "The Jesus Lizard's David Yow" (Burke, Philip)

YOW, DAVID—PHOTOGRAPHS
PH18198 653 (April 1, 1993) p20. "The Jesus Lizard (clockwise from top left): McNeilly, Yow, Denison And Sims" (Ewolf)
PH18199 714 (August 10, 1995) p48. "David Sims, Mac McNeilly, David Yow, Duane Denison, From Left" (Seliger, Mark)
PH18200 714 (August 10, 1995) p51. "The Ones To Watch At LollaPalooza: Denison, Yow And Sims (from left)" (Perez, Marty)
PH18201 715 (August 24, 1995) p43. "David Yow Of The Jesus Lizard In All His Brutal Beauty—But With His Clothes on" (Blakesberg, Jay)
PH18202 716 (September 7, 1995) p13. "[David Yow]" (Oh, Viviane)
PH18203 724-725 (December 28, 1995) p60. "Yow" (Oh, Viviane)
PH18204 736 (June 13, 1996) p20. "Jockey Lavern Hostetler Has A Lot To Discuss With Jesus Lizard Members David Sims, David Yow, Mac McNeilly And Duane Denison (from left)" (Gilson, Matthew)

YOW, DAVID—PHOTOGRAPHS—PORTRAITS
PH18205 714 (August 10, 1995) p49. "[David Yow]" (Seliger, Mark)

YSEULT, SEAN—PHOTOGRAPHS
PH18206 671 (December 9, 1993) p13. "Beavis And Butt-head Faves J., Philo, Rob And Sean (from left)" (Ragel, Jon)
PH18207 695 (November 17, 1994) p50. "White Zombie" (Winter, Dan)
PH18208 715 (August 24, 1995) p23. "Sean Yseult Of White Zombie Burns It Up At KROQ's Weenie Roast" (Johnson, Lisa)
PH18209 724-725 (December 28, 1995) p54. "MTV Video Music Award Performers: Live's Ed Kowalczyk, Michael Stipe And White Zombie's Sean Yseult (from left)" (Mazur, Kevin)
PH18210 726 (January 25, 1996) p50. "White Zombie: J., Rob Zombie, John Tempesta And Sean Yseult (from left)" (Cuffaro, Chris)

YUAN, LIU—PHOTOGRAPHS
PH18211 720 (November 2, 1995) p28. "Up Against The Great Wall: Liu (left) And Cui" (Pulin, Chuck)

YUGOSLAVIA—ILLUSTRATIONS
PH18212 647 (January 7, 1993) pp40-41. "Yugoslavia" (Peck, Everett)
PH18213 657 (May 27, 1993) p6. "Yugoslavian Transportation" (Pendergrast, James T.)
PH18214 728 (February 22, 1996) p16. "The Heart..." (Pendergrast, James T.)

Z

Z—PHOTOGRAPHS
PH18215 680 (April 21, 1994) p30. "Making Dad Proud: Z's Ahmet And Dweezil Zappa" (Capak, R. J.)

Z Z TOP—ALBUMS
PH18216 675 (February 10, 1994) p41. "Antenna"
PH18217 744 (October 3, 1996) p72. "Rhythmeen"

Z Z TOP—ILLUSTRATIONS
PH18218 675 (February 10, 1994) p41. "Hip As The Blues" (Corio, Paul)

Z Z TOP—PHOTOGRAPHS
PH18219 631 (May 28, 1992) p11. "ZZ Top's Dusty Hill, Frank Beard And Billy Gibbons (from left)" (Reitzel, Bill)
PH18220 645-646 (December 10, 1992) p65. "ZZ Top" (Mazur, Kevin)
PH18221 647 (January 7, 1993) p9. "The Brothers ZZ" (Elgar, Nick)
PH18222 670 (November 25, 1993) p37. "[Eric Clapton, Z Z Top]" (Mason, Colin)

ZAHN, STEVE—ILLUSTRATIONS
PH18223 677 (March 10, 1994) p59. "Twenty Something" (Ryden, Mark)
ZAHN, STEVE—PHOTOGRAPHS
PH18224 677 (March 10, 1994) p60. "Zahn, Ryder, Garofalo And Hawke Face A Shaky Future (from left)"
ZAIRE—PHOTOGRAPHS
PH18225 691 (September 22, 1994) pp67,69-74,76+. "[Rwandan Refugees In Zaire]" (Salgado, Sebastiao)
ZAJKOWSKI, TONY—PHOTOGRAPHS
PH18226 685 (June 30, 1994) p28. "Tragi-Pop Wuss Rockers: Lotion's Youngberg, Zajkowski, Bill And Jim Ferguson (from left)" (Cardillicchio, Nick)
ZANDER, ROBIN—PHOTOGRAPHS
PH18227 626 (March 19, 1992) p13. "Dave Stewart, Robin Zander And Dr. John (from left)" (Tallman, Susie)
PH18228 723 (December 14, 1995) p27. "The Chicago Eight: D'Arcy, Petersson, Carlos, Corgan, Nielsen, Iha, Chamberlin And Zander (from left)" (Elledge, Paul)
ZANE, BILLY—PHOTOGRAPHS
PH18229 659 (June 24, 1993) p89. "Orlando As She (below) With Billy Zane"
PH18230 737 (June 27, 1996) p62. "Zane Unmasked And In Phantom Drag"
ZAP MAMA—PHOTOGRAPHS
PH18231 708 (May 18, 1995) p18. "Members Of Zap mama With Spearhead's Michael Franti (rear)" (Roberts, Ebet)
ZAPATA, MIA—PHOTOGRAPHS
PH18232 664 (September 2, 1993) p13. "[Miz Zapata]" (Djie, Richard)
ZAPPA, AHMET—PHOTOGRAPHS
PH18233 680 (April 21, 1994) p30. "Making Dad Proud: Z's Ahmet And Dweezil Zappa" (Capak, R. J.)
ZAPPA, AHMET—PHOTOGRAPHS—PORTRAITS
PH18234 674 (January 27, 1994) p15. "The Zappas: Dweezil, Diva, Gail, Frank, Moon And Ahmet (from left)" (Goldsmith, Lynn)
ZAPPA, DIVA—PHOTOGRAPHS—PORTRAITS
PH18234 674 (January 27, 1994) p15. "The Zappas: Dweezil, Diva, Gail, Frank, Moon And Ahmet (from left)" (Goldsmith, Lynn)
ZAPPA, DWEEZIL—PHOTOGRAPHS
PH18235 680 (April 21, 1994) p30. "Making Dad Proud: Z's Ahmet And Dweezil Zappa" (Capak, R. J.)
ZAPPA, DWEEZIL—PHOTOGRAPHS—PORTRAITS
PH18236 674 (January 27, 1994) p15. "The Zappas: Dweezil, Diva, Gail, Frank, Moon And Ahmet (from left)" (Goldsmith, Lynn)
ZAPPA, FRANK—ALBUMS
PH18237 617 (November 14, 1991) p116. "Weasels Ripped My Flesh" (Park, Neon)
PH18238 617 (November 14, 1991) p153. "We're Only In It For The Money" (Schatzberg, Jerrold)
PH18239 617 (November 14, 1991) p153. "We're Only In It For The Money" (Schenkel, Cal)
PH18240 674 (January 27, 1994) p15. "Absolutely Free"
PH18241 674 (January 27, 1994) p15. "Broadway The Hard Way"
PH18242 674 (January 27, 1994) p15. "Hot Rats"
PH18243 715 (August 24, 1995) p104. "Civilization Phaze III"
PH18244 724-725 (December 28, 1995) p122. "Strictly Commercial"
PH18245 744 (October 3, 1996) p71. "Lather"
ZAPPA, FRANK—ILLUSTRATIONS
PH18246 674 (January 27, 1994) p3. "Frank Zappa" (Burke, Philip)
PH18247 677 (March 10, 1994) p12. "Frank" (Pendergrast, James T.)
ZAPPA, FRANK—PHOTOGRAPHS
PH18248 674 (January 27, 1994) p13. "Conducting The L.A. Philharmonic With Zubin Mehta (above)" (Axelrod, Joel)
PH18249 674 (January 27, 1994) p12. "Greasy Kids Stuff: Zappa Behind The Drums With The Black-Outs (above)"
PH18250 674 (January 27, 1994) p13. "Zappa With Captain Beefheart (left)" (Pulin, Chuck)
PH18251 674 (January 27, 1994) p13. "Jamming With John And Yoko In 1971 (below)" (Sia, Joseph)
PH18252 727 (February 8, 1996) p12. "[Frank Zappa Bust]"
ZAPPA, FRANK—PHOTOGRAPHS—PORTRAITS
PH18253 621 (January 9, 1992) p22. "[Frank Zappa]" (Etra, Amy)
PH18254 640 (October 1, 1992) p20. "[Frank Zappa]" (Grecco, Michael)
PH18255 674 (January 27, 1994) p15. "The Zappas: Dweezil, Diva, Gail, Frank, Moon And Ahmet (from left)" (Goldsmith, Lynn)
PH18256 674 (January 27, 1994) p11. "[Frank Zappa]" (Seeff, Norman)
PH18257 674 (January 27, 1994) p16. "Zappa Gives Capitol Hill An Earful In '85"
PH18258 674 (January 27, 1994) p16. "Zappa In '93: He Never Stopped Working"
PH18259 696 (December 1, 1994) p38. "Zappa" (Etra, Amy)
ZAPPA, GAIL—PHOTOGRAPHS—PORTRAITS
PH18260 674 (January 27, 1994) p15. "The Zappas: Dweezil, Diva, Gail, Frank, Moon And Ahmet (from left)" (Goldsmith, Lynn)
ZAPPA, MOON UNIT—PHOTOGRAPHS
PH18261 702 (February 23, 1995) p50. "Moon Zappa Accepts Her Father's Award From Lou Reed" (Mazur, Kevin)
ZAPPA, MOON UNIT—PHOTOGRAPHS—PORTRAITS
PH18262 674 (January 27, 1994) p15. "The Zappas: Dweezil, Diva, Gail, Frank, Moon And Ahmet (from left)" (Goldsmith, Lynn)
ZASKY, JASON—PHOTOGRAPHS
PH18263 702 (February 23, 1995) p20. "Flag's Jason Zasky, Stesney And Jeff Musser (from left)" (Toliver, Chris)
ZEBRAHEAD (FILM)—PHOTOGRAPHS
PH18264 642 (October 29, 1992) p77. "Zebrahead"
ZEDEK, THALIA—PHOTOGRAPHS
PH18265 654 (April 15, 1993) p22. "They've Arrived: Arthur Johnson, Sean O'Brien, Thalia Zedek And Chris Brokaw" (Westenberg, Kevin)
PH18266 660-661 (July 8, 1993) p100. "Come (from left): Arthur Johnson, Sean O'Brien, Chris Brokaw And Thalia Zedek" (Apicella-Hitchcock, Stephen)
ZEHR, MINDY—PHOTOGRAPHS
PH18267 706 (April 20, 1995) pp[enc.17]. "At Garf's" (Seliger, Mark)
ZELENKE, MIKE—PHOTOGRAPHS
PH18268 712-713 (July 13, 1995) p25. "[Liz Phair & Material Issue]" (Natkin, Paul)
ZELLWEGER, RENEE—PHOTOGRAPHS
PH18269 750-751 (December 26, 1996) p138. "Crowe—Script In Hand—Directs Cruise And Zellweger"
PH18270 750-751 (December 26, 1996) p207. "Tom Cruise And Renee Zellweger"
ZELLWEGER, RENEE—PHOTOGRAPHS—PORTRAITS
PH18271 750-751 (December 26, 1996) p141. "Zellweger Won The Hardest Part To Cast"
ZEVON, WARREN—ALBUMS
PH18272 618 (November 28, 1991) p98. "Mr. Bad Example"
PH18273 663 (August 19, 1993) p76. "Learning To Flinch"
ZEVON, WARREN—PHOTOGRAPHS
PH18274 638 (September 3, 1992) p11. "Warren Zevon (left) And Neil Young" (Goldman, Paul)
ZILLATRON—ALBUMS
PH18275 693 (October 20, 1994) p147. "Lord Of The Harvest"
ZIMMERMAN, KEITH—BOOKS
PH18276 680 (April 21, 1994) p28. "Rotten: No Irish, No Blacks,

No Dogs"
ZIMMERMAN, KEN—BOOKS
PH18276 680 (April 21, 1994) p28. "Rotten: No Irish, No Blacks, No Dogs"
ZINAM, DAVID—ALBUMS
PH18277 655 (April 29, 1993) p65. "Symphony No. 3"
ZINN, HOWARD—ILLUSTRATIONS
PH18278 748 (November 28, 1996) p22. "Coffee" (Pendergrast, James T.)
ZINN, HOWARD—PHOTOGRAPHS—PORTRAITS
PH18279 745 (October 17, 1996) pp93,98. "[Howard Zinn]" (Vadukul, Nitin)
ZOCKS, ADAM—PHOTOGRAPHS
PH18280 666 (September 30, 1993) p80. "Zocks The Jock: His Internship Helped Him Find A Way To Sidestep The Freeze" (Irish, Len)
ZOMBIE, ROB—PHOTOGRAPHS
PH18281 671 (December 9, 1993) p13. "Beavis And Butt-head Faves J., Philo, Rob And Sean (from left)" (Ragel, Jon)
PH18282 671 (December 9, 1993) p14. "Rob: 'My Motivation Is That I Hate Everything'" (Ragel, Jon)
PH18283 695 (November 17, 1994) p50. "White Zombie" (Winter, Dan)
PH18284 715 (August 24, 1995) p34. "Rob Zombie Works A 12-Year-Old's Dream Job" (Capak, R. J.)
PH18285 719 (October 19, 1995) p15. "[Rob Zombie]" (Callahan, Kristin)
PH18286 726 (January 25, 1996) p50. "White Zombie: J., Rob Zombie, John Tempesta And Sean Yseult (from left)" (Cuffaro, Chris)
PH18287 744 (October 3, 1996) p36. "[Rob Zombie]" (Cuffaro, Chris)
ZUCKERMAN, DEAN—PHOTOGRAPHS
PH18288 651 (March 4, 1993) p28. "Dean Zuckerman, Kevin Costigan, Jennifer Barry, Eddie Fagin (from left)" (Lavine, Michael)
ZUG, SWITZERLAND—PHOTOGRAPHS
PH18289 629 (April 30, 1992) p48. "Zug, Switzerland: More Than A Tax Paradise, It's Home To Marc Rich's Firm" (De Keyzer, Carl)
ZULU, DUDU—PHOTOGRAPHS
PH18290 632 (June 11, 1992) p183. "'There's Always Been A Hidden, Invisible Middle Ground In South Africa Of Connections Between People And Cultures,' Said Clegg, Shown Here With Savuka Percussionist Dudu Zulu" (Kat
PH18291 632 (June 11, 1992) p184. "The Nexus Between Music And Social Change: Clegg And Dudu Zulu (left) In Johannesburg" (Katzenstein, David)
ZULU, RAS I—PHOTOGRAPHS
PH18292 700 (January 26, 1995) p24. "[Spearhead]"
ZUNIGA, DAPHNE—PHOTOGRAPHS
PH18293 682 (May 19, 1994) pp[cover]. "Melrose Place's Bod Squad" (Seliger, Mark)
PH18294 682 (May 19, 1994) pp48-49. "[Melrose Place]" (Seliger, Mark)

Photographer/Illustrator Index to
Photographs & Illustrations

A

Aaron, Peter PH02805
Abbott, Waring PH02139, PH08565, PH08596, PH13061
Abeel, Neilson PH16152
Abrahams, Mark PH05099
Adams, Eddie PH06192, PH06197, PH12182
Adaskaveg, Michael PH05733
Adebari, Eugene PH01036, PH07890, PH07942, PH08224, PH13505, PH13803, PH15716, PH17337, PH17392
Adel, Daniel PH07341
Adolphe, Joseph PH03252
Afanador, Ruven PH02391, PH02393, PH08848, PH15975, PH16590
Agius, Lorenzo PH10348
Aguiar, Mariah PH00499, PH05561
Aguilera-Hellweg, Max PH00582, PH03365, PH03366, PH03367, PH03368, PH12037
Agulera-Helwig, Max PH06909, PH10500, PH11349, PH15008, PH17206
Aitken, Doug PH00265, PH03408, PH13106
Akashi, Shu PH15654
Albans, Michael PH06362, PH11178
Alexander, David PH04646
Alford, Bob PH10467
Alfred PH01157
Alicino, Christine PH02019, PH03909, PH09975, PH11987, PH17654
Allen, David PH00597, PH00840, PH02738, PH04313, PH04900, PH05839, PH06616, PH07973, PH09676, PH09877, PH13266, PH15700, PH16385
Allen, Ethan PH10104
Allen, Greg PH01094, PH02360, PH10667, PH12397, PH15796, PH16047, PH17053, PH17786, PH17787, PH17790
Allen, Julian PH01739, PH09523, PH09582, PH17665
Allen, Terry PH00035, PH00226, PH00448, PH00862, PH00888, PH01012, PH01804, PH02282, PH03172, PH04786, PH06671, PH07167, PH07169, PH08660, PH08891, PH11131, PH11146, PH11147, PH11201, PH11485, PH12408, PH12597, PH13724, PH13839, PH13879, PH14395, PH16195, PH16198, PH17899
Allen, Thomas B. PH12058
Allocca, David PH07912, PH07970, PH10848
Alston, Kwaku PH04981, PH07527, PH09527, PH10741, PH11901, PH16353, PH17410
Altman, Robert PH09122, PH09129
Altshuler, Lev PH00272
Amati, Ray PH05797, PH06883, PH09875, PH12840
Anchor, Mat PH01100
Andeel, Michael PH02957, PH11493, PH11574
Andersen, Nancy PH02142, PH10912, PH13270
Anderson, David PH05976, PH08166, PH08268, PH14712
Anderson, Patrick PH01754, PH04067, PH08954, PH16185
Anderson, Vera PH01024, PH02358, PH04213, PH05527, PH10967
Andrade, Fatima PH16104
Angel, Vinnie PH02546, PH05380, PH05418, PH07166, PH07168, PH08559, PH08918, PH11866, PH14938
Angelus, Pete PH16873
Anker, Matt PH00042, PH00390, PH00630, PH01143, PH01464, PH02436, PH05480, PH06815, PH08723, PH09759, PH11507, PH13006, PH16053, PH17255
Annalisa PH01022, PH05443, PH05528, PH07202, PH07237, PH08404, PH14042, PH15122
Anthony, Gene PH00062, PH05762, PH05764, PH06318, PH08872, PH09331, PH10384, PH17539
Apicella-Hitchcock, Stephen PH01766, PH03119, PH04324, PH04350, PH08276, PH08297, PH09576, PH10991, PH11662, PH12355, PH18266
Appleby, David PH03128
Appleford, Steve PH17693, PH17694
Archibald, Timothy PH07364, PH12412
Aresu, Paul PH01394, PH07188, PH08673, PH12680, PH14591
Aris, Brian PH06788, PH15745, PH15951
Arnold, Alice PH00529, PH03233, PH06932, PH07517, PH14162, PH15346, PH16101
Arrigo, Charles A. PH13946
Ascencios, N. PH02268, PH04751, PH05711
Ashe, Terry PH01550, PH07132, PH14236
Aslan PH07971
Asnin, Marc PH00158, PH06819, PH06820, PH06821, PH06822, PH08548
Astor, Josef PH03972
Atashian, John PH00320a, PH01400
Atkins, Martin PH04146
Atlan, David PH13326
Atlan, J. L. PH14752
Atlas, David PH09294, PH11802, PH15028, PH18072
Avenaim, Jerry PH13336, PH13337, PH13338
Averill, Steve PH16720, PH16722
Axelrod, Joel PH10442, PH18248
Ayanian, Ryan PH01210, PH14072
Ayeroff, Jeffrey Kent PH09839
Azimi, Mojgan B. PH02336, PH06284, PH06544, PH06725, PH08666, PH12267, PH12364, PH12382, PH13697, PH15701, PH17723

B

Badulescu, Enrique PH15171
Baehler, Chapman PH00952, PH05294, PH05500, PH08650, PH11257, PH13213, PH14991, PH15127
Bailey, David PH00544, PH01622, PH05682, PH05691, PH07975, PH10226, PH10352
Bain, Rick PH00072, PH11327
Baker, Bernie PH05389, PH05393
Baker, Lenny PH03723
Baldwin, Sidney PH08923, PH16512, PH17768
Ballard, Mike PH17244
Balog, James PH17893
Banjee PH04429, PH15209
Banks, Kathy PH04160, PH12661
Banks, Paul PH06792, PH13066
Banner, Ellen M. PH06435, PH11580, PH11593, PH18196
Banyai, Istvan PH09627, PH09850, PH14688
Baratta, Nicholas PH11739, PH12974
Barbour, Bob PH05390
Barbour, Karen PH06210, PH07212, PH14527
Barker, Kent PH00325, PH02603, PH03006, PH05907, PH09094, PH10983, PH12261
Barocas, Melanie PH08385
Barr, John PH07183, PH08010
Barr, Nancy PH14635, PH14641
Barrett, Fitzroy PH02816, PH12853, PH12837
Barritt, Craig PH03016, PH11041
Barry, David PH01993, PH09214, PH09314, PH09372
Bartholomew, Bart PH18054
Bartholomew, Beth PH00785, PH08221, PH08434, PH12769, PH13017, PH14524, PH15427
Bartholomew, Caty PH00969, PH03454, PH13867, PH16435
Baseman, Gary PH03559, PH05387
Basil PH01032, PH07453
Baskin, Edie PH09789, PH11711
Batzdorff, Rob PH00608, PH05325, PH14311, PH15918
Bauer, Randy PH05572
Bauknight, Catherine PH02888
Bayer, Sam PH01616
Bayley, Roberta PH13070
Bean, Janet PH00923, PH00924
Beauchemin, Paul PH14990
Beaulieu, Allen PH15777, PH17604
Beauvais, Yves PH08294
Beccaris, Rob PH02737, PH04624, PH15031
Bechtel, Doug PH05983
Beck, Lawrence PH05388
Beck, Melinda PH13108
Beck, Robert PH01216, PH15413
Becker, Polly PH12341
Beckman, Janette PH07072
Beckner, Greg PH02545, PH05701, PH07442
Bell, Bruse PH05602
Bell, Colin PH04792, PH05563, PH07276
Bell, Pedro PH05601, PH05604
Bellissimo, John PH01877, PH02088, PH05157, PH09078, PH13038, PH15430
Benabib, Michael PH01817, PH04476, PH04477, PH08474, PH14531
Bennett, Kelly PH16796
Bentham, John PH01605, PH10425, PH10516
Berg, Bob PH02145, PH03393, PH03773, PH05930, PH08598, PH09581, PH09829, PH10569, PH14803, PH15410
Berg, John PH03929, PH04580, PH14919, PH15414, PH15417
Berg, Lisa PH02272, PH03507, PH03539, PH04935, PH09197, PH11212, PH14139
Berkwitz, David Neil PH03331, PH06160, PH08952, PH11365, PH12444, PH17382, PH17624
Berliner PH05856, PH08501, PH15376
Berliner, A. PH04943, PH06683, PH13050
Berliner, Alan PH04957, PH11053
Berliner, Alex PH07879, PH09857
Berman, Nina PH04719, PH08796
Berman, Steve PH05271
Berndt, Jerry PH08582
Bernstein, Andrea PH07235
Bernstein, Bill PH05147, PH10463
Bernstein, Christopher D. PH16700
Bernstein, Joel PH10702
Berry, Jim PH00018, PH00020, PH05346, PH07493
Beukers, Alan PH05647
Bez, Frank PH10905
Biafra, Jello PH04009
Bilderback PH05394
Bilham, Maryanne PH06088

Binder, Donna PH00621, PH04060
Birmelin, Bruce PH00250, PH14030
Bishofs, Maris PH02454, PH02827, PH03216, PH04805, PH13762, PH16154
Blackwell, Patrick PH03127, PH05095, PH11172
Blake, John PH12457
Blake, Peter PH00959
Blakesberg, Jay PH00126, PH00188, PH00202, PH00220, PH00251, PH00253, PH00257, PH00279, PH00284, PH00285, PH00296, PH00330, PH00331, PH00334, PH00368, PH00485, PH00531, PH00551, PH00578, PH00613, PH00618, PH00631, PH00689, PH00782, PH00795, PH00796, PH00953, PH01021, PH01023, PH01045, PH01053, PH01142, PH01242, PH01267, PH01268, PH01290, PH01417, PH01519, PH01523, PH01628, PH01725, PH01753, PH01790, PH01811, PH01892, PH01908, PH01930, PH02062, PH02217, PH02333, PH02334, PH02503, PH02782, PH02783, PH02784, PH02785, PH02786, PH02787, PH02893, PH02954, PH02964, PH03015, PH03086, PH03232, PH03245, PH03307, PH03336, PH03337, PH03353, PH03399, PH03400, PH03401, PH03442, PH03465, PH03480, PH03540, PH03659, PH03709, PH03712, PH03841, PH03876, PH03912, PH03970, PH04016, PH04017, PH04018, PH04019, PH04036, PH04262, PH04298, PH04308, PH04323, PH04421, PH04505, PH04558, PH04570, PH04571, PH04618, PH04776, PH04778, PH04975, PH05057, PH05058, PH05068, PH05075, PH05079, PH05080, PH05185, PH05256, PH05277, PH05314, PH05339, PH05350, PH05447, PH05474, PH05498, PH05566, PH05587, PH05643, PH05734, PH05735, PH05739, PH05740, PH05747, PH05753, PH05755, PH05768, PH05785, PH05791, PH05828, PH05874, PH05980, PH06060, PH06133, PH06172, PH06214, PH06297, PH06298, PH06300, PH06301, PH06302, PH06304, PH06308, PH06320, PH06377, PH06382, PH06585, PH06650, PH06712, PH06809, PH06811, PH06847, PH07068, PH07099, PH07115, PH07125, PH07312, PH07313, PH07507, PH07567, PH07568, PH07579, PH07580, PH07589, PH07603, PH07604, PH07614, PH07635, PH07692, PH07751, PH07752, PH07772, PH08046, PH08233, PH08393, PH08477, PH08483, PH08484, PH08503, PH08628, PH08629, PH08630, PH08683, PH08739, PH08756, PH08757, PH08807a, PH08813, PH08827, PH08847, PH08902, PH08903, PH08963, PH09317, PH09318, PH09322, PH09323, PH09332, PH09333, PH09412, PH09533, PH09534, PH09535, PH09536, PH09538, PH09540, PH09597, PH09654, PH09656, PH09691, PH09737, PH09748, PH09796, PH09930, PH09934, PH09935, PH10299, PH10301, PH10426, PH10638, PH10648, PH10735, PH10788, PH10836, PH10865, PH10928, PH10930, PH11019, PH11035, PH11141, PH11151, PH11213, PH11214, PH11217, PH11218, PH11308, PH11385, PH11659, PH11682, PH11738, PH11801, PH12059, PH12076, PH12077, PH12081, PH12112, PH12128, PH12139, PH12473, PH12531, PH12555, PH12590, PH12647, PH12812, PH12834, PH13007, PH13008, PH13068, PH13124, PH13125, PH13194, PH13195, PH13196, PH13220, PH13221, PH13314, PH13439, PH13441, PH13442, PH13618, PH13682, PH13683, PH13695, PH13696, PH13840, PH13915, PH13954, PH13995, PH14018, PH14019, PH14181, PH14182, PH14213, PH14218, PH14220, PH14366, PH14448, PH14453, PH14482, PH14733, PH14734, PH14790, PH14791, PH14813, PH14859, PH14948, PH14950, PH14960, PH15044, PH15061, PH15169, PH15223, PH15224, PH15347, PH15360, PH15500, PH15501, PH15502, PH15537, PH15538, PH15697, PH15750, PH15806, PH15850, PH15894, PH15921, PH15972, PH15979, PH16107, PH16128, PH16375, PH16392, PH16479, PH16579, PH16614, PH16642, PH16715, PH16763, PH16765, PH16904, PH16937, PH17044, PH17048, PH17066, PH17079, PH17165, PH17170, PH17171, PH17211, PH17250, PH17251, PH17443, PH17444, PH17518, PH17519, PH17521, PH17522, PH17528, PH17537, PH17538, PH17540, PH17573, PH17575, PH17593, PH17701, PH17706, PH17915, PH17982, PH18052, PH18073, PH18089, PH18106, PH18146, PH18147, PH18157, PH18161, PH18166, PH18167, PH18170, PH18173, PH18177, PH18184, PH18201
Bland, James PH06960, PH08159, PH08396, PH16150
Blankenhorn, C. PH13485, PH13501, PH15339, PH16698
Blankenhorn, Craig PH05476, PH07454
Blanshard, Richard PH02722
Blechman, R. O. PH02652, PH11130, PH11470, PH11471, PH13160, PH16197
Blitt, Barry PH00224, PH02315, PH02628, PH03649, PH03949, PH04142, PH05454, PH06669, PH07077, PH07241, PH08516, PH09054, PH09342, PH09964, PH11855, PH11856, PH11857, PH14056, PH14903, PH15335, PH16031, PH16918, PH17451, PH18080
Bloch, Anthony PH12427
Bodnar, George PH11415, PH11846
Bodtke, Peter PH03302
Bogren, Martin PH02238
Boland, Laurence PH02015, PH06506, PH11835a, PH14668
Boman, Eric PH13968
Boot, Adrian PH04785, PH05719, PH05765, PH05770, PH07033, PH09578, PH10034, PH11394, PH12635
Borda, Juliette PH15221
Borris, Dan PH00612, PH00617, PH00634, PH00744, PH00745, PH00784, PH00857, PH00858, PH00916, PH00987, PH01056, PH01270, PH01271, PH01527, PH01538, PH01573, PH01802, PH01803, PH01902, PH02266, PH02356, PH02525, PH02532, PH02798, PH03550, PH03708, PH03711, PH03908, PH04130, PH04314, PH04315, PH04490, PH05025, PH05032, PH05083, PH06068, PH06224, PH06599, PH06627, PH07070, PH07228, PH07230, PH07504, PH07539, PH07733, PH07996, PH08097, PH08098, PH08099, PH08100, PH08101, PH08102, PH08103, PH08104, PH08105, PH08106, PH08107, PH08108, PH08109, PH08110, PH08111, PH08300, PH08468, PH08469, PH08470, PH08471, PH08488, PH09105, PH09106, PH09107, PH09445, PH10245, PH10262, PH10263, PH10385, PH10386, PH10438, PH10637, PH11032, PH11034, PH11278, PH11322, PH11368, PH11463, PH11464, PH11465, PH11466, PH11467, PH11468, PH11469, PH11793, PH12157, PH12603, PH14101, PH14342, PH14452a, PH14455, PH14459, PH14977, PH15480, PH15582, PH16084, PH16085, PH16086, PH16087, PH16088, PH16187, PH16431, PH16483, PH17387, PH17464, PH17611, PH17753, PH17966
Bounds, Jim PH10722
Bourdain, Guy PH14255
Bowles, Murray PH00501
Bozi, Tibor PH02584, PH16717
Brack, Dennis PH00718, PH00907, PH06198, PH08795
Brady, Jay PH03964, PH06700, PH13476, PH13524
Brainard, George PH10150
Bralds, Braldt PH09264
Braley, Colin PH01969
Brandenstein, Gabriela PH01062, PH04109, PH06889
Braun, Cory Wells PH08909
Braun, Craig PH13786
Braun, Paulette PH12277
Brazil, Tom PH10891, PH10894
Breiehagen, Per PH11023, PH11079, PH11090, PH12479, PH15189, PH15203, PH18124
Brennan, Shayna PH00295, PH06218, PH12125
Brice, Lindsay PH01429, PH02467, PH06635, PH06996, PH10503, PH15533
Briggs, Bettina PH01751, PH18180
Bright, Matt PH05599
Brinkhoff, Ralf PH02011, PH17280, PH17850
Brinkley, Christie PH08195
Broad, Julian PH00112, PH00383, PH00779, PH01258, PH01326, PH01327, PH02068, PH02937, PH02946, PH03458, PH03590, PH03679, PH03761, PH03762, PH04116, PH04426, PH04546, PH04660, PH05194, PH05197, PH05206, PH05613, PH05807, PH05809, PH05969, PH06233, PH06234, PH06408, PH06425, PH06803, PH07107, PH08821, PH08823, PH08824, PH08900, PH08936, PH08939, PH09300, PH09304, PH09490, PH09492, PH09493, PH09682, PH10284, PH10338, PH10981, PH11570, PH11727, PH11834, PH11835, PH11887, PH12544, PH12546, PH14503, PH14830, PH15316, PH15318, PH15960, PH15969, PH16116, PH16118, PH16180, PH16529
Brodner, Steve PH00031, PH00227, PH01186, PH01528, PH02112, PH02283, PH02404, PH02629, PH02630, PH02669, PH02670, PH02675, PH03226, PH03598, PH03814, PH03978, PH03979, PH04125, PH04236, PH04840, PH05018, PH05949, PH06045, PH06057, PH06673, PH06760, PH06901, PH07353, PH07487, PH07559, PH08320, PH08517, PH08767, PH09049, PH09200, PH10286, PH10346, PH10604, PH10619, PH10793, PH10948, PH11098, PH11099, PH11968, PH12255, PH12509, PH13092, PH13103, PH13234, PH13417, PH13621, PH13708, PH14057, PH14899, PH15019, PH15083, PH15860, PH15861, PH16138
Brodsky, Joel PH04407, PH10907
Brown, Calef PH00936, PH01013, PH04569, PH07211, PH08843, PH11264, PH11482, PH12282, PH12825, PH13532, PH16261
Brown, Calet PH01013
Brown, Christy PH03727, PH05345, PH05872, PH09561, PH09924, PH14118, PH14687, PH15130, PH17446
Brown, Jane PH13532
Brown, Michael PH12894
Brown, P. PH14923
Brucker, Andrew PH16135
Bruno, John PH15934
Brusso, Andrew PH03713, PH04326, PH12591, PH12856
Bryan-Brown, Marc PH10043

Bubbles, Barney PH12004
Buchsbaum, Jay David PH09071
Buck, Chris PH01946, PH05165, PH09511, PH09733, PH14998, PH16209, PH17152
Buck, Monica PH15646
Burbridge, Richard PH02439
Burke, Philip PH00048, PH00163, PH00358, PH00382, PH00478, PH00498, PH00609, PH00811, PH01011, PH01034, PH01241, PH01344, PH01584, PH01585, PH01814, PH01912, PH01919, PH01939, PH02052, PH02113, PH02781, PH02824, PH02938, PH02941, PH03258, PH03297, PH03334, PH03558, PH03737, PH03780, PH03848, PH03935, PH03936, PH04032, PH04259, PH04586, PH05186, PH05347, PH05629, PH05649, PH05669, PH05723, PH05803, PH05823, PH05972, PH06025, PH06471, PH06630, PH06829, PH07093, PH07277, PH07530, PH07531, PH07597, PH07639, PH07919, PH08220, PH08296, PH08622, PH08988, PH09263, PH09298, PH09717, PH09847, PH09977, PH10083, PH10179, PH10460, PH10529, PH10704, PH10728, PH10941, PH10976, PH11568, PH11772, PH11932, PH12221, PH12551, PH12552, PH12651, PH12823, PH12849, PH13435, PH13690, PH13836, PH13885, PH13990, PH14007, PH14196, PH14252, PH14753, PH14821, PH14858, PH15020, PH15160, PH15342, PH15424, PH15494, PH16617, PH16895, PH17032, PH17033, PH17156, PH17493, PH17600, PH18197, PH18246
Burniston, Ray PH04489, PH15461
Burns, Charles PH00667, PH01468, PH08539, PH09472, PH09481, PH10007, PH12766, PH15845
Burrington, Robert PH09703
Burton, Eric PH01800, PH09946, PH11530
Busacca, Larry PH00032, PH00365, PH01446, PH01952, PH03038, PH03568, PH04280, PH04614, PH04748, PH05055, PH05071, PH05307, PH06980, PH08142, PH08194, PH08197, PH08204, PH08205, PH09187, PH09190, PH09302, PH09637, PH09971, PH10820, PH12034, PH12654, PH12662, PH12831, PH12832, PH13051, PH14340, PH14601, PH14749, PH14755, PH14757, PH15283, PH15429, PH15447, PH15555, PH15561, PH16865, PH16931, PH16933, PH17083, PH17093, PH17602, PH17685, PH18178
Buscarro, Larry PH09532
Bustamante, Gerald PH02154, PH07152
Butkus, Mary PH13904
Butler, Bonnie Lynn PH06110, PH08280, PH09604, PH10051, PH11078, PH12214
Butler, David PH17719
Butler, Geoff PH01615, PH08016
Butler, Henrietta PH01794
Butler, Kimberly PH09443
Butler, Robert PH03176
Buzzerio, Johnny PH00505, PH02626, PH07286, PH12669
Byram, Stephen PH00929
Byrd, Sydney PH13734
Byrne, Peter PH00214, PH06084, PH16060

C

Cadiente, Tim PH00503, PH05056
Cahn, Lee PH04659
Calahan, Walter PH02509
Caldicott, Karen PH13173
Callahan, Kristin PH02592, PH03078, PH03350, PH03707, PH03760, PH04428, PH04965, PH05264, PH05308, PH05576, PH06634, PH07389, PH07759, PH07781, PH08826, PH09006, PH09489, PH09798, PH10009, PH10537, PH10823, PH10834, PH12435, PH13081, PH13453, PH13759, PH14709, PH15163, PH15208, PH15594, PH16115, PH16656, PH16684, PH17414, PH17418, PH18285
Callahan, Walter PH06562, PH06825, PH07400, PH10240, PH14027, PH18027
Callis, Chris PH05846, PH11246, PH16559, PH17218
Calson, Judith PH04011
Calver, Dave PH01586
Camp, E. J. PH00638, PH00702, PH00937, PH01274, PH01941, PH03112, PH03738, PH04789, PH04873, PH04874, PH05559, PH07275, PH07382, PH10155, PH10209, PH11798, PH12833, PH14009, PH17554
Campbell, William PH02273
Cancalosi, John PH02424
Cantor, David PH05661
Capa, Cornell PH08570
Capak, R. J. PH00386, PH00552, PH00602, PH01069, PH01376, PH01611, PH01764, PH01853, PH01866, PH01947, PH01950, PH02086, PH02093, PH02095, PH02096, PH02158, PH02255, PH02399, PH03020, PH03319, PH03604, PH03783, PH03901, PH04117, PH04269, PH04285, PH04403, PH04427, PH04522, PH04609, PH04733, PH04762, PH04823, PH04855, PH05114, PH05261, PH05267, PH05312, PH05323, PH05640, PH05671, PH05708, PH05738, PH06005, PH06111, PH06117, PH06173, PH06209, PH06485, PH06507, PH06551, PH06631, PH06687, PH06691, PH06729, PH06962, PH07111, PH07196, PH07226, PH07284, PH07656, PH08057, PH08148, PH08158, PH08208, PH08244, PH08284, PH08533, PH08560, PH08926, PH08956, PH09075, PH09097, PH09175, PH09359, PH09605, PH09741, PH09940, PH10371, PH10837, PH10933, PH10973, PH10985, PH11089, PH11243, PH11755, PH11794, PH11795, PH11826, PH12046, PH12062, PH12211, PH12215, PH12220, PH12353, PH12588, PH12601, PH12872, PH12896, PH13083, PH13147, PH13272, PH13275, PH13451, PH13562, PH13680, PH13833, PH13843, PH13943, PH14095, PH14169, PH14359, PH14607, PH15058, PH15168, PH15296, PH15371, PH15464, PH15661, PH16044, PH16706, PH17117, PH17153, PH17318, PH17795, PH18182, PH18215, PH18233, PH18235, PH18284
Capozzola, Lou PH09469
Caraeff, Ed PH15713
Cardenas, Jeffrey PH01968
Cardillicchio, Nick PH00670, PH00804, PH01619, PH02008, PH02533, PH04333, PH05148, PH06087, PH06921, PH09079, PH09371, PH09594, PH09680, PH09909, PH10757, PH11563, PH13977, PH17125, PH17661, PH18195, PH18226
Carrico, John PH00276, PH07145, PH11319, PH14838, PH17687
Carroll, Chris PH01393, PH03040, PH05845, PH07187, PH07229, PH08672, PH10218, PH12679, PH12729, PH14590, PH15706, PH17376
Carroll, Tim PH00427
Carter, Keith PH03109, PH04423, PH05664, PH06008, PH07456, PH13377, PH15174
Caruso, Phillip PH08934, PH16635, PH17384
Carver, Steve PH13034
Casado, John PH17653
Cassidy, Chris PH00738, PH06343
Catlin, A. PH04040, PH04396, PH05475, PH09692, PH12532, PH14221
Caudle, Todd PH01226, PH05736, PH06660, PH07373, PH12284, PH12286, PH12684, PH17684, PH17703
Cavaika, John PH17901
Cavolina, Robbie PH10365, PH12161, PH13650
Chambers, Brian PH03776, PH04132, PH13753
Chambers, Bruce PH04662
Champagne, Kim PH08022
Chang, Aaron PH14179
Charbonneau, Eric PH02883, PH02884, PH02896, PH02897, PH12300, PH15873
Chavez, Marina PH02133, PH03647, PH07659, PH09513, PH14263, PH14621, PH17721
Chernikowski, Stephanie PH04895, PH04896, PH13855
Cheuse, Josh PH04927
Chiarella, Frank PH07101, PH11666
Chiasson, John PH01194, PH01465, PH04524, PH06396, PH06784, PH11776
Choy, Dee Dee PH12407
Christensen, Jeff PH13948, PH16890
Christian, Michael PH15530
Christie, Donald PH18062
Chun, Myung J. PH00698, PH03007, PH14773
Chung, Andre F. PH05317, PH11215
Churilla, Lynda PH03798, PH09745, PH14097, PH16930
Ciardiello, Joe PH02502, PH03069, PH03542, PH11695, PH13018, PH14314
Claiborne, Barron PH04703, PH06759, PH07003, PH08214, PH09827, PH10571, PH14993
Clark, Bill PH05881, PH06037
Clark, John PH07350
Clark, Shaun PH06584, PH16882, PH16899
Clarke, Greg PH00318, PH01014, PH16190
Claxton, William PH13244, PH15771
Clay, Jennifer PH12752
Clayton, Christian PH00317, PH02695, PH07705, PH12104, PH12989, PH13358, PH15846, PH16576
Cleere, Carol PH01847
Cleland, Jane PH01671
Clements, Geoffrey PH00537
Clinch, Danny PH01316, PH01356, PH01357, PH01364, PH01416, PH01460, PH01635, PH01932, PH02023, PH03067, PH03375, PH03394, PH03451, PH03515, PH03827, PH03881, PH04305, PH05180, PH05181, PH05182, PH05209, PH05960, PH05975, PH06022, PH06079, PH06255, PH06256, PH06697, PH06907, PH07200, PH07201, PH07318, PH07319, PH07325, PH08165, PH08266, PH08499, PH08593, PH09007, PH09011, PH09040, PH09041, PH09095, PH09096, PH09247, PH09248, PH09542, PH09554, PH09574, PH09754, PH10220, PH10276, PH10333, PH10334, PH10335, PH11022, PH11784, PH12270, PH12271, PH12272, PH12273, PH12274, PH12636, PH12688, PH13737, PH13749b, PH13927, PH13951, PH14104, PH14475, PH14529, PH14544, PH14545, PH14546, PH14681, PH14682, PH14708, PH14980, PH14981, PH15291, PH15581, PH15663, PH15692, PH15693, PH16348, PH16349, PH16562, PH16568, PH16569, PH16570, PH16832, PH16835, PH17031, PH17243, PH17259, PH17260, PH17481, PH17484, PH17485, PH17544, PH17591
Clinton, George PH05603
Close, Murray PH04179, PH04180, PH06107, PH08448, PH08449, PH10191, PH11292, PH15373
Clunn, Chris PH11766
Cobb, Rachel PH02547, PH02548, PH02549,

PH06605, PH06606, PH06607, PH06608, PH06609
Cober, Alan E. PH02259, PH07542, PH07595, PH11911
Coe, Sue PH02041, PH02044, PH03703, PH04866, PH07352, PH11514, PH11522, PH13019, PH13356, PH16008
Cohen, Diane PH16629
Cohen, Lester PH00568, PH00590, PH01146, PH01525, PH02274, PH02854, PH03537, PH03552, PH03561, PH04062, PH04194, PH04418, PH04556, PH04752, PH04960, PH05115, PH05296, PH05362, PH06490, PH06494, PH06975, PH07045, PH07383, PH07535, PH08311, PH08359, PH08627, PH08654, PH08696, PH09751, PH09980, PH10210, PH10363, PH10366, PH10484, PH10685, PH11115, PH11248, PH11260, PH12162, PH13841, PH13986, PH14209, PH14481, PH14589, PH14719, PH14731, PH14835, PH15176, PH15588, PH15761, PH15791, PH15817, PH17119
Cohrssen, James PH01669, PH13363
Coleman, Gene PH02409, PH15620, PH16191
Coleman, Glen PH17179
Coleman, Mark PH17005
Coles, Rogan PH07550
Colletti, Steve PH01166, PH01923, PH10660, PH13372, PH15787
Collier, John PH02694, PH02839, PH03980, PH04012, PH10488, PH13886, PH15428, PH17644
Collins, John PH06715
Colliton, Paul PH09866, PH14158
Colver, Ed PH02485, PH04249, PH10486, PH10487
Comjean PH17332
Conde, Dominick PH01607, PH16714
Conrad, Jon PH17166
Conroy, Michael PH10470
Considine, J. D. PH12088
Constanini, Mark PH02947, PH08625, PH17042
Constantine, Elaine PH05338
Contrato, Mark PH14025
Contratto, Mark PH10018
Cook, Nick PH00351
Coomer, Brett PH15828
Cooper, Dawn PH16795
Cooper, Dick PH08003, PH17871
Cooper, Michael PH00961, PH03284, PH10256
Corbijn, Anton PH00256, PH00399, PH00588, PH01075, PH01165, PH01182, PH01183, PH01450, PH01470, PH01471, PH01472, PH01473, PH01474, PH01475, PH01493, PH01494, PH01496, PH01499, PH01844, PH01845, PH01888, PH01922, PH01992, PH02226, PH02332, PH02378, PH02793, PH03570, PH03667, PH03668, PH04155, PH04345, PH04619, PH04620, PH04684, PH04734, PH04735, PH04742, PH04861, PH04862, PH04863, PH04951, PH05290, PH05291, PH05292, PH05320, PH05333, PH05334, PH05485, PH05652, PH05654, PH06196, PH06654, PH06836, PH07122, PH07552, PH07943, PH07944, PH07945, PH07946, PH07951, PH08390, PH08645, PH08646, PH08647, PH09024, PH09025, PH09400, PH10559, PH10560, PH10561, PH10659, PH11042, PH11043, PH11047, PH11048, PH11254, PH11255, PH11389, PH11500, PH11501, PH11946, PH11958, PH12563, PH12573, PH12673, PH13205, PH13206, PH13207, PH13208, PH13209, PH13282, PH13370, PH13383, PH13387, PH13455, PH13506, PH13507, PH13508, PH13509, PH13516, PH13659, PH13663, PH13804, PH13805, PH13806, PH13807, PH13808, PH13818, PH13819, PH13842, PH14037, PH14038, PH14350, PH14579, PH14783, PH14988, PH14989, PH15460, PH15785, PH15816, PH16721, PH16734, PH16735, PH16736, PH16737, PH16738, PH16739, PH16740, PH16746, PH16747, PH16752, PH17433, PH17434, PH17437, PH17490, PH17491, PH17734, PH17844, PH17873, PH17928, PH17929, PH17934
Corio, David PH01571, PH01827, PH06023, PH07570, PH08478, PH09765, PH09932, PH10033, PH10415, PH12080, PH16719, PH17265, PH17408
Corio, Paul PH02664, PH03142, PH05395, PH06531, PH06970, PH07157, PH07172, PH07213, PH09213, PH09424, PH11077, PH11137, PH11459, PH12477, PH13158, PH13176, PH16200, PH17034, PH18218
Corjuni PH08789, PH14538
Corkery, Richard PH08190, PH09683, PH15000, PH15038
Coro, Ron PH02310, PH04582
Corrigan, Daniel PH00213, PH00273, PH04766, PH06799, PH07529, PH10982, PH11557, PH12795, PH13399, PH15695, PH15776, PH16773
Corristan, Peter PH13785
Corriston, Peter PH09159
Cosgrove, John PH16488
Costello PH08761
Costello, Paul PH02818
Costello, Thomas P. PH01104
Coughlin, Kevin P. PH11674, PH11676
Counts, Wyatt PH00366, PH00367, PH00370, PH07438, PH09019, PH09335, PH10161, PH11396, PH16066
Courtney, Mark PH00463
Cowles, David PH00249, PH00275, PH01852, PH02061, PH02314, PH02641, PH02825, PH03012, PH03035, PH03171, PH03648, PH04025, PH04031, PH04200, PH04587, PH04817, PH05433, PH05541, PH05817, PH05886, PH06798, PH07036, PH07186, PH07304, PH07467, PH07573, PH07799, PH08187, PH09341, PH10653, PH11143, PH11247, PH11892, PH11933, PH12381, PH12553, PH12653, PH13428, PH14151, PH15144, PH15736, PH16139, PH16262, PH16299, PH16696, PH17035, PH17515, PH17823
Cox, Paul PH00747, PH00749, PH03283, PH03674, PH03676, PH05698, PH05700, PH11706, PH15048, PH15051, PH16334, PH17748
Craft, Terry PH17814
Craig, John PH15712
Craig, Tom PH12839, PH14214
Crane, David PH12892
Crawford, Michael PH05199, PH06918, PH09016, PH09452, PH10451, PH16097, PH16420
Criss, Lydia PH03510
Croft, Richard PH02305
Cronin, Brian PH00316, PH00444, PH00767, PH00988, PH01109, PH01691, PH01911, PH02045, PH02823, PH02826, PH02828, PH02829, PH04122, PH04123, PH04124, PH04655, PH04705, PH04708, PH04709, PH04755, PH04799, PH05991, PH06938, PH07295, PH07690, PH07707, PH07840, PH07989, PH07993, PH08783, PH08814, PH09414, PH10004, PH10205, PH10622, PH10623, PH11065, PH11066, PH11204, PH11378, PH11379, PH11380, PH11551, PH11597, PH11601, PH12029, PH12032, PH12144, PH12378, PH12618, PH12734, PH12765, PH12954, PH12994, PH12995, PH13404, PH13792, PH15149, PH16112, PH16519, PH16787, PH17219, PH17894
Cross, Brian PH04468, PH07290, PH08461, PH10099, PH11731, PH12429, PH17330
Crouser, Michael PH02159, PH08061, PH09610, PH10052, PH11757, PH12219
Crum, Lee PH01174, PH13877
Crumb, R. PH01221, PH03631, PH08367
Crump, James PH06813, PH07990, PH09806, PH12443, PH15592
Cruse, Rich PH16851
Cubillo, Enrique PH15622, PH16208
Cuffan, Chris PH13733
Cuffaro, Chris PH00002, PH00282, PH00447a, PH00569, PH00664, PH01068, PH01534, PH02000, PH03591, PH03785, PH03802, PH03813, PH04419, PH04482, PH04497, PH04537, PH04542, PH04642, PH04954, PH05054, PH05191, PH05276, PH05310, PH05313, PH05565, PH05570, PH05804, PH06211, PH06433, PH06438, PH07433, PH07444, PH07778, PH08091, PH08569, PH08626, PH08669, PH08931, PH09092, PH09562, PH09760, PH10162, PH10297, PH10359, PH10362, PH10665, PH10670, PH10833, PH11026, PH11085, PH11094, PH11259, PH11261, PH11325, PH11487, PH11488, PH12109, PH12110, PH12276, PH12495, PH12541, PH13193, PH13255, PH13334, PH13573, PH13731, PH14317, PH14363, PH14984, PH15126, PH15200, PH15233, PH15313, PH16220, PH16306, PH16436, PH16451, PH16470, PH16602, PH17040, PH17063, PH17208, PH17214, PH17311, PH17324, PH17398, PH17674, PH17708, PH17710, PH17797, PH18210, PH18286, PH18287
Cultice, Joseph PH00428, PH00429, PH00438, PH00825, PH01086, PH01116, PH02050, PH04082, PH04192, PH05201, PH05935, PH06492, PH07566, PH08603, PH09531, PH10010, PH11305, PH11452, PH11453, PH11532, PH11533, PH12703, PH13098, PH13445, PH13447, PH13449, PH13452, PH15409, PH15591, PH17249, PH17963
Cummins, Jim PH02715, PH04089
Cummins, Kevin PH01488, PH01489, PH01490, PH02425, PH04523, PH08458
Cunningham, Peter PH02468, PH10215, PH15433, PH16498
Cushion, Melanie PH00148, PH12593
Cuta, Anthony PH06361

D

Dagmar PH10782
Dah-Len PH01698
Daks, Michael PH11270
Dana, Steven PH14671
Danelian, Stephen PH00036, PH00473, PH01150, PH01881, PH01883, PH03261, PH04782, PH04938, PH05458, PH05459, PH06864, PH06870, PH07144, PH07280, PH08459, PH08513, PH08514, PH08515, PH08828, PH08957, PH09001, PH09002, PH10243, PH10950, PH10951, PH11546, PH11717, PH12156, PH12357, PH12359, PH13065, PH14175, PH14176, PH16944, PH17340, PH17341, PH17579
Daniel, Michael PH17290
Daniels, Craig PH14303
Daniels, Kurt PH14304
Darrios, H. PH09976
Datz, Margot PH05241
Davey, Randy PH01971
Davidson, Alan PH00583, PH10533

Davies And Starr PH03377, PH17187
Davies, Meredith PH13934, PH15053
Davila, Bill PH04168, PH09660, PH10563, PH11923, PH13637
Davis, Chris PH07720
Davis, Clarence PH15915
Davis, Katharine PH00093, PH01248, PH13847
Davis, Lisa PH04917, PH11317, PH14779, PH15302
Davis, Lisa O'Conner PH15730
Davis, Paul PH05729, PH09845, PH18094
Davis, Ron PH09881, PH12169
Day, Corinne PH03460, PH06171, PH07253, PH07256, PH09082, PH10835, PH11838, PH11841, PH11845, PH13082, PH14606, PH15167
Day, Jeff PH02953
Day, Lorraine PH09859, PH13588
Day, Rob PH15334, PH17825
Day, Robert PH02366, PH14782
De Guire, Gregg PH01837, PH03746
De Keyzer, Carl PH13121, PH13122, PH13123, PH16122, PH16756, PH18289
De Leon, John PH01331, PH14876
De Roos, Govert PH04212
De Seve, Peter PH00119, PH03950, PH12315
Deacon, Jim PH00686a, PH06796, PH12440
Dean, Roger PH18083
Debourbon, Yvonne PH04924
Decker, Alan PH14648
Deen, Georganne PH07706, PH10819, PH11865, PH12074
Defilippo, Michael PH05049, PH16662, PH16774
Deguire, Greg PH00639, PH00640, PH01710, PH13317, PH14730
DeJoseph, Dominic PH03763
Del Grecco, Maria PH00103
Del Sol, Michel PH15974
Delany, Ron PH13324
Deleon PH10635
Delessert, Etienne PH01279
Demarchelier, Patrick PH07806, PH07813, PH07826, PH09235, PH09241, PH12185, PH14150, PH14164, PH15399, PH17864
Dent, Phil PH07927, PH13754
Dervaux, Isabelle PH06470
Desota, George PH16767
Devault, Jim PH16597
Dexters, Bernaded PH03306
Di Biase, Vince PH05773, PH05796
Di Santo, Anna PH03354, PH13069
Di Santo, Annamaria PH05302, PH07367, PH16046
Diamond, Rick PH00363, PH00703, PH01283, PH01285, PH01289, PH01437, PH01568, PH01831, PH01885, PH01920, PH01953, PH01999, PH02275, PH02307, PH03299, PH03562, PH03882, PH03887, PH04864, PH05170, PH05207, PH05411, PH05456, PH05511, PH06407, PH06736, PH06965, PH07685, PH08060, PH08095, PH08252, PH08254, PH08736, PH08825, PH09398, PH09415, PH09608, PH09779, PH10511, PH10942, PH11909, PH12218, PH12952, PH13127, PH13546, PH13670, PH13678, PH13681, PH13691, PH14068, PH14140, PH14174, PH14693, PH14943, PH15305, PH15788, PH15797, PH16003, PH16429, PH16631, PH17743, PH17922
Dickson, Ian PH15724
Dickson, Nigel PH09401
Dill, Nicola PH01955, PH12401
Diltz, Henry PH01788, PH03113, PH04138, PH04408, PH04818, PH06378, PH06383, PH07753, PH07880, PH07886, PH08874, PH09993, PH10712, PH10903, PH11197, PH11660, PH13919, PH14446, PH17796, PH18110
Dilyard, Matt PH01606, PH08314
Dimitrov, Slobodan PH15924
Dimont, Charles PH12921
Dionisi, Sandra PH07272, PH09962, PH11265
Dipaola, Steve PH14242
Dipaolo, Debra PH01015, PH06899, PH09555
Dipeso, Debra PH02007, PH09558, PH10675, PH16849
Disanto, Annamaria PH06652, PH07120, PH08664, PH10557, PH11387, PH16768
Dixon, Dean PH01858
Djie, Richard PH18232
Dodge, Tom PH00098
Dodson, Jeff PH00108
Dokus, Peter PH04697, PH05444, PH11249
Dominguez, Miguel PH07050, PH15982
Dominguez, Ralph PH12159, PH14055
Donald, Nancy PH14254
Donaldson, Matthew PH03054
Doove, Hester PH01197, PH01989, PH02469, PH03662, PH04525, PH05547, PH06964, PH09365, PH14485, PH16871, PH17232
Dorst, Chris PH05937
Double, Steve PH00064, PH00778, PH01101, PH01481, PH02066, PH02551, PH03013, PH03498, PH03764, PH04838, PH05693, PH05830, PH05864, PH06118, PH06153, PH06324, PH06846, PH06913, PH08292, PH08901, PH09212, PH09366, PH10058, PH10092, PH10199, PH10970, PH10980, PH11154, PH11280, PH11291, PH11665, PH12236, PH14640, PH14831, PH15968, PH16589, PH17163
Doud, Mike PH09158, PH16004
Dougan, Michael PH16828
Doughty, Chris PH17480
Doughty, Curt PH00205, PH00546, PH01435, PH01935, PH02219, PH02540, PH04260, PH04999, PH05069, PH06437, PH06439, PH06440, PH06734, PH06850, PH07694, PH08352, PH10078, PH10361, PH11502, PH11581, PH11583, PH11586, PH12715, PH15234, PH15303, PH15506, PH15772, PH15773, PH16001, PH16618
Douglas Brothers PH03098
Douthart, Bill PH03108
Downie, Scott PH01124, PH05279, PH08632
Downing, Larry PH02925, PH04362, PH05361, PH11412
Downs, Richard PH12949, PH15218
Drake, James PH12746
Drawson, Blair PH00651, PH00831, PH03298, PH07843, PH12578, PH12608, PH13602, PH16645
Drescher, Henrik PH05865, PH06529, PH11451, PH16021
Dressler, Michael PH14120
Drinkwater, Paul PH14439
Dry, Dan PH16474
DuBose, George PH13073
Dugdale, Bruce PH00481, PH02518
Duke, William PH00332, PH01729, PH04511, PH04779, PH05179, PH07079, PH08181, PH10783, PH12140, PH15573, PH17252
Duncan, Ken PH10607
Dunn, Carl PH16235
Dunne, John PH08267, PH15954
Dunnick, Regan PH05924
Durand, Tylor PH17327
Duttmann, Uwe PH03817
Dye, Bruce PH02374
Dyer, Alison PH01287, PH01328, PH04970, PH05811, PH05858, PH06453, PH06810, PH08059, PH08836, PH09607, PH09681, PH10339, PH11756, PH12193, PH12217, PH13677, PH13693, PH13732, PH16182, PH16283, PH16363
Dyer, Rod PH10026, PH17266
Dykinga, Jack W. PH05417
Dylan, Bob PH04583

E

Earl, Andy PH01576, PH16229
Eccles, Andrew PH01322, PH01338, PH01894, PH02263, PH03102, PH03103, PH03688, PH04346, PH04347, PH04348, PH05252, PH06763, PH06764, PH07505, PH08040, PH08571, PH08766, PH10602, PH10725, PH10742, PH12241, PH12242, PH12243, PH12244, PH12803, PH12804, PH12805, PH12806, PH12924, PH15715, PH16054, PH16055, PH16507, PH17513, PH17847
Eckstein, Ed PH00150, PH08965
Edelstein, Jillian PH17869
Eder, John PH08702, PH15853
Edmondson, Vanessa PH08897, PH17476, PH17477
Edwards, Eric PH12420, PH16928
Egan, Nick PH01575
Eichner, Steve PH00208, PH01849, PH02222, PH03085, PH03223, PH03240, PH03913, PH04702, PH04941, PH06505, PH07434, PH08093, PH09000, PH09722, PH09978, PH10734, PH10879, PH10883, PH10963, PH14022, PH14195, PH14483, PH15509, PH17212
Eidrigevicius, Stasys PH01587
Eisenstaedt, Alfred PH14147
Elgar, Nick PH00748, PH01329, PH01522, PH03531, PH03594, PH03675, PH04553, PH05138, PH05375, PH05699, PH06319, PH06359, PH06699, PH07007, PH07008, PH07043, PH07236, PH07833, PH07845, PH07893, PH08193, PH08198, PH08307, PH08685, PH09225, PH09852, PH10715, PH10810, PH12491, PH12655, PH12802, PH13227, PH13269, PH13488, PH13489, PH13494, PH14012, PH14079, PH14261, PH15049, PH15593, PH15704, PH15753, PH16328, PH16329, PH16495, PH16925, PH17890, PH17921, PH18149, PH18150, PH18221
Elledge, Paul PH00041, PH00923, PH00926, PH01074, PH01122, PH02262, PH02477, PH02480, PH02541, PH03273, PH03311, PH03666, PH03860, PH03863, PH04420, PH04765, PH04803, PH04912, PH05512, PH05841, PH06178, PH06554, PH06814, PH06817, PH06928, PH07452, PH07644, PH07647, PH08453, PH08780, PH08949, PH10621, PH10646, PH11156, PH11423, PH11861, PH12275, PH12602, PH12612, PH12722, PH14574, PH14578, PH14952, PH14957, PH15279, PH15900, PH16434, PH16834, PH17157, PH17158, PH17160, PH17489, PH17840, PH17843, PH18228
Ellenby, Peter PH07057, PH16666
Ellis, Bob PH01318, PH17285
Emerson, Sam PH07578, PH07601, PH07825, PH07863, PH07889, PH16487, PH17861
Engel, Andy PH15415
England, Thomas S. PH02890
English, Mark PH16492
Eppridge, Bill PH14100
Erbland, Peter PH02234, PH16231
Erickson, Sam PH04629, PH10151
Erikson, Wendy PH02317, PH04576
Erwitt, Elliot PH09160
Estrada, Kevin PH02507
Estrine, Darryl PH03073, PH04431,

PH07006, PH07010
Etra, Amy PH18253, PH18259
Ettlinger, Marion PH13253, PH17115
Evans, Marty PH03242
Evans, Paul PH08020a
Everke, Tobias PH09273, PH11361
Every, Bart PH15046
Ewolf PH04133, PH08135, PH10407, PH14776, PH18198
Exum PH00078, PH02622, PH04261, PH04332, PH05306, PH06050, PH06872, PH07083, PH07305, PH07411, PH08029, PH10279, PH11028, PH11029, PH12388, PH14399, PH16221
Eyerman, JR PH11607

F

Factor, Davis PH03800
Faiola, Susan PH03369, PH05096, PH06727, PH11814, PH12587, PH12827, PH12870
Fallon, Bernard PH14430, PH14561
Fallon, Brenda PH07490, PH09036, PH14558
Falls, John PH00786, PH00808, PH02132, PH03074, PH06982, PH08052, PH08573, PH10149, PH10789, PH11296, PH13568, PH13601, PH14422, PH14569, PH15359, PH17129
Farrell, Eamonn PH11555
Farrell, Leon PH11677
Farrell, Perry PH08023
Farrington, Tom PH07633
Feanny, Najlah PH08592
Fegley, Richard PH11730
Feingold, Deborah PH01099, PH04312, PH04394, PH04592, PH04630, PH04633, PH05659, PH05813, PH06205, PH06208, PH06252, PH06730, PH06731, PH09973, PH11376, PH11668
Fenton, Steve PH05681
Ferreira, Albert PH03616, PH04169, PH05746, PH08807, PH11374, PH11972, PH12525, PH13286, PH13514, PH15455
Ferry, Bryan PH13967
Fields, Alexander C. PH17957
Figen, Peter PH12208
Fine, Sean PH05578
Fineman, Aaron PH17613
Fink, Larry PH01395, PH01396, PH01397, PH01398, PH01914, PH01915, PH01916, PH02613, PH04764, PH04802, PH05399, PH07189, PH07784, PH08674, PH08675, PH11364, PH12179, PH12180, PH12681, PH12682, PH12683, PH13293, PH14592
Finlay, Ian PH16723
Fish, James PH01940
Fish, Jim PH02768, PH08278
Fisher, Carolyn PH00073, PH02441, PH07161, PH12931
Fisher, David PH01502, PH04744, PH05678, PH05690, PH07540, PH08259, PH10599, PH11640, PH15770, PH16749
Fisher, Jeffrey PH05422, PH09458, PH17881
Fishman, Miriam PH00917, PH04643, PH05359, PH08808, PH11384, PH11650, PH12617, PH14241, PH16202, PH16203, PH16204, PH16205, PH16206, PH18031
Fitzgerald, Ralph PH04825
Fleischauer, Robert PH03759, PH06232, PH08817, PH16117
Flesher, Vivienne PH00686
Florence, John PH03784, PH07537
Foo, Sharlyn PH05392
Foothorap, Robert PH00826, PH08724, PH12143
Ford, Charles PH02206, PH04919, PH06638, PH06926, PH07686, PH08286, PH08773, PH10074, PH10086, PH10505, PH13128, PH13921, PH14141
Ford, Larry PH07588, PH08277, PH13101, PH13102
Foreman, Richard PH10874, PH16551
Forsman, Shelly PH10517, PH13552
Fotheringham, Edwin PH13359
Fowler, Simon PH00044, PH07551, PH12792
Fox, John Gilbert PH03872, PH03874
Fox, Robert PH00146, PH00147
Frailey, Stephen PH04513, PH07179, PH07180, PH10567
Frampton, Jerald PH04512, PH10005
France, Neil A. PH08535
Franckling, Ken PH04263, PH13114, PH17369, PH17541
Frank, Robert PH13784
Franken, O. PH09267, PH09268
Franklin, Ross D. PH11024, PH11081, PH11092, PH12488, PH15197
Frazier, Jeff PH00466, PH01990, PH06659, PH07086, PH11059, PH13419
Freda, Anthony PH02591, PH06971, PH10603
Freeman, Robert PH00963, PH15566, PH16401
Fricke, David PH03724
Friedman, Carol PH11054
Friedman, Drew PH00510, PH01298, PH01414, PH02046, PH02321, PH02837, PH05052, PH05549, PH06714, PH06740, PH07674, PH09357, PH10792, PH11005, PH12850, PH13233, PH13917, PH17333, PH17412, PH17752
Friedman, Glen E. PH14010
Friedman, Steve PH11303, PH18004
Frinta, Dagmar PH17785
Friske, Maria PH04961, PH12923, PH14488, PH15598, PH16201, PH16511, PH17229
Frohman, Jesse PH07590, PH07624, PH07626, PH11509, PH14014
Frohman, Lesse PH10726
Frost, Frankie PH05745, PH08806
Funk, Harrison PH06538, PH13899, PH15888
Furmanovsky, Jill PH02730

G

Gabor, Tim PH00030, PH01588, PH12751
Gaggero, Carlos PH04004, PH06466, PH06939, PH06940, PH12254, PH14146
Gagnon, Mark PH02873
Gahr, David PH00758, PH01948, PH02716, PH02755, PH03837, PH03942, PH04320, PH04597, PH04603, PH04908, PH04911, PH05331, PH05483, PH06566, PH06990, PH07432, PH07448, PH08684, PH09991, PH10929, PH11963, PH12030, PH12640, PH13469, PH13533, PH13656, PH17568, PH17619, PH17620, PH17623, PH17668, PH17759
Gajdel, Edward PH14039
Galbraith, Robert PH05771
Gale, Tony PH00716, PH01900, PH02754, PH03497
Galella, Ron PH00837, PH11929
Galindo, Andrew PH12504, PH15476
Galinsky, Michael PH12155
Gall, Sally PH17286
Gallagher, James PH03288
Gallo, Armando PH09677, PH10598
Garcia, Fernie PH09728, PH09730
Garcia, Frederic PH07862
Garcia, Willie PH02672, PH02765, PH10888, PH14300
Gardner, Christopher M. PH01882, PH13045, PH17298
Gardner, Elysa PH01761, PH03378
Gargani, Frank PH18028
Garner, Kate PH01988, PH04578, PH05063, PH06728, PH06841, PH09972, PH13402, PH14816
Garrity, Brian PH00500, PH00504, PH01018, PH04767, PH04953, PH05513, PH05515, PH06800, PH11088, PH11097, PH12502, PH13087, PH13090, PH14804
Gassian, Claude PH04616, PH04622, PH07953, PH07969, PH12667
Gates, Stephen PH07484
Gaynor, Adrian PH00671
Gaz, Stab PH15614, PH15615, PH15616, PH15617, PH16207
Gehring, Karl A. PH00301, PH05655, PH05656, PH10312, PH12135, PH12371, PH12961, PH16578
Geller, Marc PH11982
General Cartography PH09043
George, Tryan PH01151, PH04090, PH16594
Gerber, Cheryl PH07638, PH15432
Gerber, M. PH00404, PH07650, PH09210, PH09559, PH09879, PH10870, PH14431
Gerber, Mitchell PH00405, PH01362, PH07320, PH09211
Gero, Paul PH15543
Gershoff, Gary PH01243, PH01670, PH02003, PH02369, PH02397, PH02566, PH04554, PH05289, PH05502, PH05859, PH05933, PH07740, PH08643, PH09790, PH10555, PH10730, PH11275, PH11338, PH12860, PH13204, PH13228, PH13327, PH13487, PH14071, PH14208, PH14357, PH14917, PH15125, PH17307, PH17626, PH17755, PH17756, PH18151
Giannini, John PH06694, PH14123, PH17201, PH17202, PH17203, PH17204
Gifford PH04365
Giger, H. R. PH04836, PH06786
Gilson, Matthew PH04136, PH07395, PH08139, PH10409, PH14778, PH18204
Gilstrap, Nancy PH16149
Gimple, Melodie PH10707
Gindreau, J. C. PH00555, PH04893
Ginies, Michael PH09702, PH13633
Giordano, Ann PH06908
Gipe, Jon PH01259, PH01566, PH08536, PH08537, PH08747, PH08751, PH09569, PH10433
Giron, Joe PH05445, PH12138, PH13718, PH15288
Gittler, Ian PH17817, PH17818
Glackmeyer, Kevin PH01577, PH01825
Glade, Gary PH06713, PH15453
Glaser, Milton PH07917
Godber, Barry PH08703
Godlis PH16077
Goldberg, Nathaniel PH05689, PH10351, PH11639, PH11642, PH17650
Goldin, David PH00655a, PH01212, PH01409, PH02163, PH02419, PH03177, PH07158, PH07164, PH10634, PH15621, PH16157, PH16193, PH17178, PH17195
Goldis PH16078
Goldman, Paul PH18154, PH18274
Goldsmith, Lynn PH01312, PH01375, PH03514, PH04471, PH05008, PH05269, PH08511, PH13520, PH13527, PH13870, PH13871, PH15033, PH15037, PH17124, PH17848, PH17950, PH17954, PH18234, PH18236, PH18255, PH18260, PH18262
Goldstrom, Robert PH15781
Gonson, J. J. PH07231
Goode, Nicola PH13950, PH14536
Goodwin, Harry PH07982, PH11957
Gordon, Jonathan PH13335
Gordon, Melinda Sue PH14001, PH15173, PH16108
Gorgun, Ahmet PH01647, PH03257, PH16493, PH18141
Gorman, Greg PH10969

Gorson, Arthur H. PH10029
Gosfield, Josh PH06741, PH07838, PH09402, PH11233, PH11822
Goude, Jean-Paul PH08319
Gougenheim, Kim PH00278, PH02573, PH03967, PH05384, PH05519, PH05953, PH06122, PH06446, PH07232, PH07326, PH09732, PH10008, PH10499, PH11277, PH11959, PH12869, PH14476, PH14477, PH14722, PH14836, PH14969, PH16039, PH16688, PH17630, PH17813
Gough, Janet PH10706
Govoni, Tricia PH00467
Grace, Alexa PH10705
Grace, Arthur PH14419
Graham, Jim PH01648, PH01654, PH10272, PH10895, PH10898, PH15826
Grahn, Geoffrey PH08979
Granitz, Steve PH00087, PH00847, PH01158, PH01189, PH01310, PH01653, PH01942, PH02109, PH02198, PH02377, PH02464, PH02519, PH02711, PH02764, PH04340, PH04409, PH04606, PH04649, PH04687, PH04834, PH04950, PH05348, PH05467, PH05543, PH05799, PH05802, PH06075, PH06567, PH06778, PH07041, PH07048, PH07146, PH07538, PH07822, PH08238, PH08557, PH09473, PH09588, PH09629, PH09661, PH09678, PH09726, PH10273, PH10291, PH10510, PH10896, PH10899, PH11295, PH11324, PH11879, PH11937, PH12195, PH12589, PH13654, PH13849, PH13883, PH13884, PH13979, PH14017, PH14210, PH14211, PH14315, PH14580, PH14661, PH14742, PH14921, PH15336, PH15338, PH15340, PH15499, PH15723, PH15738, PH15827, PH15879, PH15937, PH16489, PH16862, PH16885, PH16898, PH16901, PH16905, PH16906, PH17047, PH17050, PH17052, PH17705, PH18171
Grant, Bob PH01215, PH02162, PH02171, PH02172, PH02173, PH02174, PH02175, PH02176, PH02440, PH02446, PH02447, PH02448, PH03167, PH03193, PH03194, PH03196, PH03198, PH03199, PH03204, PH03205, PH03206, PH03207, PH03208, PH03695, PH06504, PH06936, PH06998, PH08591, PH12428, PH13011, PH13760, PH15132, PH15133, PH15323, PH15324, PH15619, PH15647, PH15648, PH15650, PH15651, PH15652, PH15653, PH15987, PH16164, PH16166, PH16167, PH16168, PH16169, PH16170, PH16172, PH16214, PH16216, PH16654, PH17185, PH17186, PH17192, PH17197, PH17375
Gray, Todd PH07581, PH07605
Grecco, Michael PH01217, PH03063, PH04007, PH05908, PH12226, PH18254
Green And Read PH09010
Green, Adrian PH09565, PH16308, PH16440, PH17400
Green, Bil PH13671
Green, Martha PH04757
Greenberg, Jill PH06621
Greene, Herb PH05730, PH05731, PH05741, PH05767, PH05780, PH06253, PH06296, PH06303, PH06321, PH06397, PH08084, PH08862, PH08863, PH09171, PH09316, PH09319, PH10373, PH10374, PH10986, PH11950, PH12566, PH17516, PH17523
Greene, Herbi PH03234, PH05748, PH05751, PH05757, PH05761, PH05763, PH05784, PH05786, PH05789, PH06309, PH06311, PH06316, PH06317, PH06807, PH06808, PH08866, PH08867, PH08870, PH08871, PH09324, PH09325, PH09329, PH09330, PH10376, PH10378, PH10383, PH11161, PH17322, PH17529, PH17530, PH17535, PH17536
Gregoire, Jean Louis PH01869, PH08508, PH11245, PH16558
Grenon, Martha PH04892
Greve, Margie PH08392, PH10399
Greyshock, Caroline PH08700, PH13054
Griffin, Brian PH04147, PH07831, PH12005
Griffin, Rick PH06291, PH06293
Groening, Matt PH03704, PH14768
Gropp, Gerry PH00281, PH14649
Groshong, Dan PH17845
Grossman, Amanda PH00175, PH04783, PH10775
Grossman, Robert PH05053, PH12678
Grossmann, Andre PH17951
Gruen, Bob PH03248, PH03249, PH03794, PH04811, PH06170, PH06793, PH07808, PH08331, PH08353, PH08354, PH09266, PH09287, PH10140, PH10141, PH11366, PH11536, PH11788, PH13955, PH13956, PH14491, PH14492, PH14493, PH14494, PH15043, PH15936, PH16377, PH17386
GS, Jamil PH00540, PH00980, PH02523, PH02524, PH02680, PH02681, PH03274, PH04452, PH05608, PH05609, PH06089, PH08975, PH08976, PH09598, PH14173, PH15995, PH15996, PH15997, PH15998
Guarnaccia, Steven PH01232, PH16527
Guastella, Mike PH01879, PH06693
Guip, Amy PH00280, PH00707, PH01137, PH02759, PH05357, PH06239, PH07129, PH08121, PH10326, PH10729, PH12747, PH12793, PH14276, PH14380, PH14893
Guip, Andy PH00924, PH04813, PH10285, PH11643, PH13592
Gullick, Steve PH00709, PH02130, PH02486, PH04385, PH04984, PH05545, PH06289, PH10368, PH10528, PH11741, PH12113, PH16282, PH16357
Gunther, Steve A. PH02111
Gustafsson, Per PH08845, PH08857
Guy, Edmund PH02561, PH02660, PH03170, PH04509, PH04668, PH05947, PH07596, PH07664, PH07918, PH10100, PH10249, PH11988, PH15095
Guzman PH00442, PH01943, PH02069, PH02930, PH02932, PH02972, PH02977, PH02979, PH02982, PH03447, PH04266, PH04267, PH07139, PH07746, PH09635, PH09646, PH09658, PH09721, PH11954, PH12571, PH16921, PH16923, PH17200
Gwinn, Beth PH01787, PH02383, PH17556, PH17811

H

Habermacher, Rene PH09624, PH13838
Haddi, Michael PH05275, PH13100
Hales-Tooke, Hugh PH01017, PH01030, PH03522
Haley, Thomas PH01510, PH01690
Halfin, Ross PH00219, PH02129, PH02201, PH02766, PH03080, PH04077, PH04826, PH05940, PH06852, PH10552, PH12137, PH13685, PH13846, PH14248, PH16926, PH17104, PH17105
Hall, Charles PH01959, PH16687, PH16711
Halles-Tooke, Hugh PH03517, PH03518, PH03519, PH03520, PH03521, PH03523, PH03524, PH03525
Hallisey, John PH00341
Halsband, Michael PH00377, PH01564, PH03544, PH03547, PH04370, PH05242, PH05473, PH06177, PH06457, PH07947, PH08745, PH08748, PH10193, PH10295, PH10431, PH12410, PH13510, PH13809, PH15406, PH16224, PH17435
Halstead, Dirk PH04363, PH11528
Hambly, Bob PH05094
Hames, William PH08943
Hamill, Brian PH00237, PH00238
Hamilton, James PH01046, PH04991, PH07789, PH10061, PH10319, PH14258, PH15120
Hamilton, Richard PH00962
Hanauer, Mark PH00497, PH01300, PH01433, PH01700, PH01701, PH01896, PH02270, PH03246, PH04770, PH06853, PH07135, PH07233, PH07569, PH08563, PH08941, PH09483, PH09509, PH09712, PH09931, PH11219, PH11657, PH11993, PH12078, PH12079, PH12451, PH16428, PH16694, PH16850, PH16852, PH16853, PH16854, PH16855, PH16857, PH17576, PH17594, PH17984, PH17985, PH17986, PH17987, PH17989
Hanover, Suzanne PH02119, PH09145, PH14685
Hapke, Fran PH02179, PH10216, PH14613, PH17379, PH17914
Harders, Marian PH01563
Hardie, George PH09157
Harrington, John PH03660, PH04502, PH06061, PH06181, PH08298, PH09750, PH12725, PH14278, PH16591
Harrington, Russ PH08839
Harris, Brad PH04021, PH08475, PH09939, PH10165, PH13433
Harrison, Jerry PH16076
Harrison, Mark PH00957, PH11221
Hartland, Jessie PH16682
Hartman, Rose PH12980
Harvey, William S. PH04406
Hashimoto, Mike PH06220, PH08043, PH12130, PH16475, PH17082, PH18174, PH18181, PH18191
Hastings, Daniel PH03743, PH05614, PH08391, PH10758, PH15067, PH15308
Haveman, Kathy PH05189, PH09434, PH12052
Hawkes, David PH14235
Haworth, Jann PH00960
Haynes, Loren PH04092, PH04094, PH08861, PH15852, PH17502
Haynsworth, John PH01967
Heimall, Bob PH15013
Heisler, George PH07005
Heisler, Gregory PH06368, PH10713
Heller, Steven A. PH09585
Hellweg, Max PH12227
Helnwein, Gottfried PH13480
Hendrickson, Matt PH09609
Hening, Lu PH04790, PH05560, PH10156
Henley, Don PH04645
Herdon, David PH01079, PH06370, PH09018, PH09762, PH10452
Hermer, Ken PH00780, PH10984, PH16530, PH17582
Herrington, Jim PH01659, PH10815, PH10816, PH13522, PH13525
Hershiko, Eli PH09008
Herzhaft, Beth PH05904
Hess, Fred PH07548
Heungman PH03652, PH04565, PH09151, PH13458, PH16136
Hildenhagen, Michael PH05630, PH09023
Hill, Britain PH01153, PH01572, PH06724, PH07288, PH09029, PH10000, PH10106, PH14994, PH14996
Hilton, Roger PH14515
Himmel, Lizzie PH02593, PH03101, PH03373, PH04110, PH04111, PH04112, PH07488, PH07489, PH10277, PH11749, PH11750, PH12796, PH12797, PH15056
Hiro PH01111, PH03944, PH13830
Hirschfeld, Al PH08709, PH09340
Hirst, Edward PH07549

Hoeffler, Jonathan PH02695a
Hoefler, Jonathan PH07173
Hoffman PH10535
Hoffman, Dezo PH00972
Hoffman, Randy PH12346
Hogan, Dave PH04695, PH05677, PH09768, PH10530, PH12928
Hole, Danny PH00799, PH01020, PH05673, PH05688, PH09180, PH11637, PH14565
Hole, Jimmy PH11715, PH13182
Holland, Brad PH02514, PH13343, PH16814
Holley, Jason PH00199, PH02214, PH07691, PH08737, PH15187, PH15495
Hollywood, Barry PH09249, PH16693
Holmes, J. F. PH00244
Hom, Marc PH00903, PH02138, PH02484, PH03326, PH03865, PH05620, PH06166, PH06168, PH06707, PH07067, PH07652, PH10082, PH12036, PH12659, PH12671, PH13110, PH14963, PH17112, PH17241, PH17812
Hooks Brothers PH08689
Hopkins, T. PH11565
Horner, Carl J. PH01770, PH08665, PH15882
Horton, Nancy G. PH12983
Horwood, Annie PH04010
Hoselton, Charles B. PH02992
House, Troy PH13859
Howe, Cynthia PH10629
Howell, Dan PH15967
Hranek, Matthew PH01543, PH16010
Huba, John PH01430, PH04700, PH06636, PH06997, PH12731, PH15534
Huber, William PH07455
Hungry Dog Studio PH00264, PH02060, PH03175, PH04342, PH05580, PH07547, PH07575, PH08264, PH08348, PH08604, PH09849, PH13357, PH16441, PH18056
Hunter, Alicia PH15284, PH15454
Hunter, George PH07770
Huntington, Jane PH02966, PH06434, PH11498, PH11578
Hurrell, George PH02101, PH14762
Hurschmann, Paul PH01820, PH03911, PH07417
Hussey, Tim PH17961
Hutchson, Mick PH04989, PH05633, PH08327, PH10395, PH15719, PH17923, PH18014
Hutson, Mick PH00094, PH02951, PH03566, PH07110, PH09697, PH12060, PH12496, PH13848, PH14869, PH15445

I

Ienner, Jimmy, Jr. PH02398, PH03009, PH03011, PH06896, PH12395, PH13271
Indge, Alaister PH12148
Irish, Len PH01129, PH02149, PH02418, PH04330, PH04731, PH05706, PH06550, PH07904, PH08460, PH08810, PH09444, PH10160, PH13963, PH14128, PH14690, PH15011, PH18280
Ishioka, Eiko PH03931
Isip, Jordan PH14496, PH17897
Isip, Jordin PH01303, PH06596
Israelson, Nels PH01893
Ivansco, Joey PH05882
Iwasa PH08799

J

Jackson, Gregory PH01709, PH10183, PH13254, PH13280
Jacobs, Michael PH00117, PH01190, PH02853, PH02855, PH08250, PH11734, PH13041, PH15731, PH16900, PH17944
Jana PH00394, PH03305
Jellison, David PH16875
Jennings, Steve PH00493, PH02600, PH03587, PH06021, PH06478, PH07123, PH08290, PH09431, PH09651, PH09724, PH12361, PH13459, PH16864, PH17851
Jensen, David PH01170, PH01171, PH01933, PH10673, PH13381, PH15812, PH15976, PH16438
Jensen, Victoria PH05769, PH12000
Jeremy, Ron PH08115, PH13910
Jerome, Tony PH08495
Jetter, Frances PH06828
Jewell, Fred PH10471
Jewett, Tim PH01317, PH17284
Joel, Seth PH15618
Joel, Yale PH08809
Johanson, Karen PH11251
John, Robert PH02769, PH13907, PH14875, PH17256
Johnson, C. PH06579
Johnson, Eric PH04334, PH05597, PH10170, PH13881
Johnson, Lisa PH00663, PH02474, PH02770, PH03300, PH03857, PH05193, PH05806, PH06115, PH06522, PH06523, PH07278, PH07285, PH07640, PH08876, PH08933, PH08935, PH08938, PH11328, PH11663, PH11714, PH11721, PH11723, PH12543, PH12810, PH13089, PH14944, PH14964, PH15315, PH17041, PH17362, PH17577, PH18208
Johnson, Nancy Jo PH18070
Johnson, William PH02104, PH03966, PH10846, PH13020, PH17741
Johnston, Daniel PH00413
Jones, Craig PH16806
Jones, Michael Spenser PH00542, PH05672, PH05686, PH10350, PH11636, PH17649
Jones, Sam PH09385, PH13844
Jones, Steve PH08719, PH13515, PH17933
Jonze, Spike PH06223, PH12365
Jordan, Kelly PH06655, PH14851
Judge, Mike PH00999, PH01000, PH01001, PH01002, PH01004, PH01005

K

Kahn, Lee PH04658
Kaltman, Naomi PH03563, PH03565
Kane, Art PH13821
Kaplan, Todd PH07039, PH08191, PH13037, PH15740
Kaplin, Todd PH04139, PH04413, PH08875, PH09994
Karas, Steve PH11194, PH12799, PH16604
Karl, Anita PH01469, PH03608, PH04669a, PH04730, PH05463, PH10025, PH12317, PH12426, PH13361, PH13586, PH13858, PH14444, PH16733, PH17404, PH17467, PH18143
Karpa, Robert PH09336, PH10435, PH15007
Kashi, Ed PH05831, PH08175, PH14374
Katz, Bruce PH10525, PH13046, PH15596
Katz, Jeff PH05230, PH05240, PH08326, PH12816, PH12845
Katz, Shelly PH08423
Katzenstein, David PH00571, PH02803, PH02804, PH05518, PH11965, PH18290, PH18291
Kearney, Mitch PH01110, PH04006, PH18121
Keeley, Dennis PH00333, PH01019, PH02359, PH02562, PH04760, PH06044, PH10636, PH14827, PH15136, PH15786, PH16452, PH17612
Keeling, Jason PH05582
Keiser, Beth PH02194
Kelley, Gary PH00558, PH00920, PH01692, PH02693, PH03607, PH04157, PH04195, PH05112, PH07800, PH09085, PH09948, PH10852, PH12604, PH12828, PH13793, PH15059, PH16535, PH17342
Kelly, James M. PH02362
Kelly, John PH05007, PH07963
Kelly, Roz PH07023
Kelly-Mouse Studios PH05720, PH06290
Kennedy, Bill PH01733, PH04611, PH11312, PH11313, PH14758
Kennedy, David Michael PH15478
Kennerly, David Hume PH05896, PH13137, PH15325
Kent, Andrew PH12648, PH13283
Kern, Geof PH02434, PH07470, PH07471, PH07472, PH07473, PH07474, PH12900
Kessler, Joshua PH03742, PH03906, PH04548, PH07430, PH09575, PH14995
Keyser, James PH09074
Kidd, Tom PH06158
Kienitz, Michael PH16810
Kilby, Jak PH04988
Kindahl, Chris PH00983, PH06780, PH09278, PH10265, PH15562
King, David PH07013
King, Don PH05391
King, Greg PH13025, PH13026, PH14352
King, J. D. PH08075, PH13723
Kino PH00940
Kirchherr, Astrid PH00976, PH00981, PH06779, PH09275, PH09288, PH10269, PH16013, PH16014
Kirkland, Douglas PH08177
Kirkland, Gene PH00092, PH00648, PH02373, PH06535, PH06536, PH06537, PH07321, PH09778, PH11878, PH11884, PH12292, PH13890, PH13892, PH13980, PH14864, PH14866
Kirkland, Greg PH06539, PH14870, PH15890
Kirschbaum, Jed PH07392
Kittner, Sam PH09557
Klarwein, Mati PH03930, PH14203
Kleiman, Dennis PH02623, PH02624, PH06871, PH06873, PH07195, PH09292, PH09295
Klein, Renee PH04711, PH04715, PH04795, PH06227, PH07156, PH07163, PH08947, PH10481, PH11068, PH11383, PH11602, PH14740, PH14852, PH17223, PH17224, PH17225
Klein, Steven PH03793, PH10013, PH10014, PH10017, PH13850, PH14552, PH14553
Klicker, John PH13998, PH13999, PH14000, PH17283
Klimak, Martin PH14645
Klingensmith, Milt PH16218
Knaeps, Gie PH03070, PH05295, PH06840, PH12663
Knapp, Bevil PH11359
Kneten, Rocky PH07410
Knight, Kevin PH02204, PH08590, PH08772, PH08885, PH10072, PH10084, PH10477, PH10504, PH17024
Knight, Robert PH02701, PH03479, PH17029
Knott, Phil PH16146
Kohn, Diana PH08802, PH17514, PH17543, PH17584
Kohos PH14739
Konte, Keba PH07612
Koralik, Cheryl PH10524, PH14388
Korody, T. PH08176
Kosh PH04644
Kosh, John PH17689
Kotleba, John PH11729
Kowalsky, Jeffrey Alan PH15030, PH15027
Kozik, Frank PH12728, PH16840
Kraft, Brooks PH04422, PH05038, PH13418, PH17952
Kraft, Chris PH01218, PH01355, PH01818,

PH06894, PH07317, PH08333, PH08816, PH08990, PH09764, PH15691, PH15780, PH17609, PH17757
Kralyevich, Vincent PH11787
Kramer, Daniel PH04581
Kravitz, Jeff PH00364, PH00403, PH00517, PH00615, PH00675, PH00705, PH00943, PH01016, PH01126, PH01135, PH01399, PH01793, PH01841, PH02306, PH02928, PH02936, PH02958, PH02965, PH02967, PH02986, PH02990, PH03010, PH03211, PH03260, PH03262, PH03324, PH03569, PH04170, PH03581, PH03818, PH03822, PH04219a, PH04246, PH04425, PH04539, PH05065, PH05278, PH05283, PH05311, PH05373, PH05583, PH06093, PH06237, PH06429, PH06436, PH06618, PH06832, PH07127, PH07147, PH07190, PH07194, PH07281, PH07282, PH07385, PH07610, PH07757, PH07817, PH07866, PH07869, PH07888, PH08078, PH08285, PH08351, PH08409, PH08417, PH08425, PH08637, PH08676, PH08794, PH09209, PH09631, PH09636, PH09653, PH09995, PH10138, PH10232, PH10294, PH10360, PH10600, PH10666, PH10761, PH10825, PH10886, PH10897, PH11082, PH11195, PH11585, PH12164, PH12345, PH12349, PH12396, PH12489, PH12492, PH12514, PH12668, PH12685, PH12782, PH12783, PH12838, PH12963, PH12975, PH13543, PH13918, PH13947, PH14020, PH14085, PH14156, PH14274, PH14562, PH14593, PH14660, PH15450, PH15452, PH15580, PH15795, PH15800, PH16131, PH16330, PH16437, PH16691, PH16718, PH16894, PH16912, PH16913, PH17056, PH17067, PH17367, PH17497, PH17500, PH17520, PH18066, PH18096, PH18164, PH18168
Krementz, Jill PH02382
Krenz, Scott PH16351
Kriegsmann, James PH13666
Kron, Daniel PH05836
Kroninger, Stephen PH02636, PH12614
Krueger, Brian PH06463
Krueger, Gary PH08784, PH08785
Kuczala, John PH04068, PH10988, PH14184, PH16105
Kuehn, Karen PH04653, PH06666, PH07177, PH07178, PH09446, PH13339, PH14761, PH16404, PH16421, PH17111
Kuhmsted, B. PH08928
Kuhn, Shane PH09136
Kunz, Anita PH01411, PH02579, PH02589, PH02838, PH06400, PH06670, PH08188, PH11697, PH11984, PH13603, PH14257, PH14595, PH14653, PH16017, PH16364, PH16919, PH17037, PH17824, PH18063, PH18142
Kuper, Peter PH04713, PH04714, PH04800, PH06026, PH06595, PH08906, PH11138, PH11377, PH13405

L

Lachappell, David PH11417
Lacombe, Brigitte PH02402
Ladwig, Jim PH04986
Laffont, Jean Pierre PH07958, PH13823, PH17440
Laforet, Vincent PH17955
Lambert, Kenneth PH10955, PH16620
Lance, James L. PH06758, PH09753
Landy, Elliott PH00757, PH00759, PH03836, PH04610, PH04621, PH04641, PH06984, PH06986, PH06988, PH17238
Lane, Tony PH16486
Lange, George PH11316
Lantry, Christian PH03364
Lardy, Philippe PH11358, PH13721
Larsen, Kristine PH01868, PH03509, PH04322, PH06054, PH11241, PH11244, PH16557, PH17217
Lass, Imke PH00585, PH00751, PH01720, PH02157, PH03092, PH03748, PH03775, PH04026, PH04033, PH04174, PH06134, PH06546, PH06593, PH09148, PH09811, PH09999, PH10132, PH10538, PH11269, PH13136, PH17361, PH17712
Laureen, Dawn PH15365
Lavine, Michael PH00169, PH00532, PH00533, PH00828, PH01406, PH01545, PH01639, PH01956, PH02102, PH02135, PH02437, PH02530, PH03114, PH03386, PH03439, PH03443, PH04382, PH04383, PH04450, PH04506, PH04837, PH04906, PH04922, PH04923, PH04962, PH04963, PH04996, PH05204, PH05257, PH06604, PH06933, PH06934, PH07271, PH07773, PH07998, PH08146, PH08150, PH08345, PH08530, PH08552, PH08770, PH08781, PH08883, PH09093, PH09307, PH09441, PH09506, PH09616, PH09667, PH09742, PH09749, PH09899, PH09997, PH10496, PH10760, PH10772, PH11058, PH12644, PH12670, PH13856, PH13882, PH13966, PH14002, PH14003, PH14484, PH14846, PH15170, PH15237, PH15349, PH15350, PH16102, PH16103, PH16179, PH17134, PH17688, PH18019, PH18061, PH18288
Laxton, William PH09695, PH09696, PH09704, PH16416, PH16417, PH16419
Le, Thi-Linh PH06854
Lee, David PH09202, PH09203, PH17344, PH17345
Lee, John PH09539
Lee, Johnny PH02311
Lee, Lilly PH08369
Lee, Monica PH15213
Lefkowitz, Lisa PH11645
Legato, Rob PH15935
Lego PH02410, PH08306
Leialoha, Mark PH02152, PH05280, PH06071, PH08634, PH09503, PH10066, PH10562, PH11877, PH13197, PH13323, PH14985, PH17854
Leibovitz, Annie PH00398, PH00696, PH00755, PH00853, PH01309, PH02125, PH02415, PH02609, PH03551, PH03833, PH04591, PH04909, PH04928, PH05137, PH05153, PH05335, PH05374, PH05732, PH05758, PH05850, PH05853, PH06246, PH06369, PH07365, PH07910, PH07925, PH07926, PH07928, PH08257, PH08727, PH08728, PH08815, PH08837, PH08969, PH08977, PH09062, PH09224, PH09281, PH09286, PH09390, PH09988, PH10031, PH10032, PH10890, PH10892, PH10893, PH10927, PH11206, PH11806, PH12031, PH12228, PH13491, PH13646, PH14144, PH14260, PH14324, PH14555, PH16325, PH16785, PH17585, PH17587, PH17889, PH17962, PH18144
Leibowitz, Eric PH01141, PH12183, PH14148, PH14153, PH15396
Leitman, Ruth PH03736, PH04865, PH05081, PH05171, PH05365, PH05366, PH09524, PH09529, PH14069, PH16430, PH16622, PH16623, PH16632
Lemmer, Yoav PH11683
Lennihn, Mark PH04275, PH17240
Lennon, John PH09260
Lenquette, Youri PH00165, PH00387, PH01404, PH02479, PH02999, PH03315, PH03862, PH06450, PH06488, PH07646, PH10568, PH11511, PH11591, PH14956, PH14974, PH16051
Leonard, Herman PH03940, PH03941
Leopardi, N. PH00556, PH02616, PH09177, PH10190, PH10965, PH11895, PH11904, PH16462
Levenson, Alan PH09668, PH09669
Levine, Laura PH01118, PH03796, PH06176, PH06481, PH07683, PH07684, PH09026, PH09970, PH14197, PH17494
Levine, Linda PH06167
Lew, Darren PH09860, PH10445
Lewis, Don PH01325, PH05192, PH05805, PH08053, PH08143, PH08932, PH12310, PH12542, PH14320, PH15314
Lewis, Gary PH02625, PH09889, PH09890
Lewis, Robert PH08322, PH14045, PH15983
Lichfield, P. PH07911, PH07966
Liebowitz, Alyse PH15459
Liepke, Skip PH02696, PH02697, PH04589, PH09201
Light, Ken PH06905, PH10791, PH15491, PH15492
Liguz, Andrzej PH01169, PH01928, PH10672, PH13379, PH15802
Lilly, Michael A. PH10744
Lindberg, Peter PH07984, PH07985
Lindbergh, Peter PH09883
Linden, John Edward PH00475
Lines, Edward G., Jr. PH06569, PH14874
Linn, Jason PH15849
Linn, Judy PH15041
Linn, Warren PH05911, PH06597, PH07574, PH15094, PH16533, PH16731
Lins, Rico PH04806
Linsen, M. PH05631, PH11672, PH15742
Liotta Patrick PH09885
LiPuma, Laura PH12815
Little, Blake PH04349, PH05857, PH06038, PH07477, PH07478, PH08800, PH10723, PH12212, PH13747, PH16400, PH17469, PH17832, PH18088
Liu, Brian PH03320, PH03329, PH03461, PH03968, PH04545, PH06838, PH08149, PH09929, PH11842, PH14972, PH15465
Lixenberg, Dana PH00110, PH03677, PH04541, PH04656, PH06391, PH06392, PH10283, PH14692, PH17852
Llewell, Michael PH17331
Llewellyn, Michael PH00771, PH00772, PH00773, PH01801, PH02164, PH09686, PH10845
Loftus, Phil PH07883
Long, Andrew PH02740, PH03482, PH06570, PH08688, PH11341, PH13052, PH14572, PH17027
Longfield, Scott D. PH15444
Lopex, Bret PH03279
Low, Dorothy PH00116, PH09387, PH18111
Lowitt, Roxanne PH01596, PH02708, PH13652
Lowry, Ray PH02773
Lucas, J. PH01544, PH05050, PH06976, PH15146
Luchford, Glen PH01288, PH02160, PH03304, PH03858, PH07641, PH13679, PH13694, PH14945, PH14946, PH14947
Lujan, Marcos PH06667
Lurie, Jonathan PH16801
Lyden, Paul PH03083, PH03238, PH10881, PH12231, PH14192, PH16707, PH17553, PH17885
Lydon, John PH12920

M

MacDonald, Ross PH01736, PH04669, PH05015, PH11632, PH13179, PH13472, PH14525, PH15902
Mack, Andrew PH00912
MacLennan, Philippe PH06119
MacMillan, Iain PH10247

MacNaughtan, Andrew PH05446, PH07203, PH12238, PH13547, PH13704
MacPherson, Andrew PH01492, PH01515, PH01516, PH04741, PH04749, PH04750, PH04964, PH09770, PH09802, PH09804, PH10597, PH14384, PH15749, PH15752, PH15768, PH15769
Maday, Tom PH12343, PH17423
Madden, Hayley PH06845
Maffia, Daniel PH00865, PH10926
Mafford, Spike PH06241
Mahurin, Matt PH00128, PH00360, PH00371, PH02031, PH02199, PH04510, PH05166, PH05636, PH06151, PH07303, PH10405, PH10750, PH11027, PH11067, PH11086, PH11095, PH11600, PH11603, PH11938, PH12023, PH12498, PH12505, PH12556, PH12946, PH13454, PH13456, PH13854, PH13931, PH14875a, PH14798, PH14880, PH15201, PH15204, PH17076, PH17220, PH17614, PH17895, PH17906, PH18138
Malanga, Gerard PH10914, PH17146
Malerba, Gary PH12385, PH12386, PH12497
Malfer PH02153, PH06072, PH09505, PH13328, PH17855
Malige, Didier PH00887, PH05509
Malluk, Eddie PH03513, PH05532, PH06851, PH08760, PH11722, PH13325, PH13845, PH14737, PH15540
Maloney, Wren PH01699
Manchester, Scott PH08768, PH14080
Mankowitz, Gered PH07025, PH07026, PH07027, PH07029, PH07952, PH07962, PH07967, PH07986, PH08162, PH08312, PH10718, PH13230, PH13517, PH13820, PH17438, PH18017
Manning, Carole PH01076, PH01233, PH01234, PH02596, PH02597, PH07466, PH15608
Manning, Garrian PH10975
Mantel, John M. PH09963
Mapplethorpe, Robert PH15014, PH15023
Marander, Tracy PH02976
Marcus PH16461
Marcus, Joan PH04666, PH09952
Marek, Mark PH04074
Margolis, Lisa B. PH02599
Mark, Mary Ellen PH01578, PH01693, PH02144, PH02583, PH02767, PH04551, PH04634, PH05028, PH05023, PH05024, PH05029, PH05033, PH05287, PH05966, PH06169, PH06951, PH07064, PH07440, PH07441, PH07443, PH07908, PH08787, PH09910, PH10655, PH10832, PH11333, PH11369, PH11770, PH12009, PH12038, PH13080, PH14605, PH15166, PH15569, PH17303, PH17739, PH18058
Mark, Stewart PH10595
Markel, B. PH01664, PH02881, PH04287
Markowitz, Jeffrey PH00490, PH02870, PH06950, PH08494, PH12500, PH14088, PH18126
Marks, Elliot PH06972
Markus, Kurt PH00690, PH01791, PH01796, PH01797, PH01798, PH01891, PH04181, PH04182, PH04184, PH04966, PH06258, PH07314, PH08693, PH08701, PH10354, PH10464, PH12415, PH13385, PH13616, PH14760, PH16381, PH16382, PH16388, PH16929, PH17788
Marquette, Joe PH00810
Marsden, Barry PH01730, PH02264, PH05471, PH06696, PH07735, PH11705
Marsel, Steve PH00720, PH07767, PH09464, PH09577, PH17462
Marshak, Bob PH00839, PH14480
Marshall, Jim PH02380, PH02521, PH04020, PH04596, PH05183, PH05744, PH05750, PH05759, PH06042, PH06245, PH06305, PH06310, PH06313, PH06314, PH06752, PH06805, PH07019, PH07955, PH07965, PH08370, PH08372, PH08373, PH08375, PH08377, PH08380, PH08864, PH08869, PH09132, PH09320, PH09327, PH10068, PH10375, PH10377, PH10380, PH10381, PH10736, PH13827, PH14907, PH17524, PH17533
Mart, K. PH01724, PH04029, PH04041, PH09814, PH17715
Marten, Ruth PH07337, PH10859, PH11562, PH12468, PH16586
Martin, Christopher T. PH04828
Martin, J. Michelle PH03444, PH04507, PH05258, PH07774, PH08346
Martin, Matthew PH02615, PH06598, PH08838, PH10148, PH16790, PH17671
Martin, Ruth PH16879
Marzullo, Joseph PH14023
Maser, Wayne PH04686, PH09411
Masi, Agenzia PH01508
Mason, Colin PH02733, PH18222
Mason, Karen PH00737, PH01358, PH01678, PH02205, PH02215, PH02491, PH03093, PH03441, PH04063, PH04791, PH05202, PH06212, PH07075, PH10073, PH10085, PH11980, PH12753, PH15205, PH15497, PH17820
Massar, Eli PH07905, PH08811
Mastroianni, Roger PH03100
Matcho, Mark PH13138
Matheu, Robert PH00913, PH02536, PH04550, PH05409, PH08007, PH10054, PH10367, PH12290, PH12363, PH13401, PH13669, PH14132, PH15045, PH15544, PH15779, PH17605
Mathieson, Greg E. PH11553
Mats PH01372, PH06672, PH07162
Matson, Gary PH14744
Mauro, Aldo PH02156, PH03747, PH06545, PH09147
Maxwell, Paul PH14892
Maxwell, Robert PH02014, PH03448, PH03506, PH07140, PH08679, PH09723, PH12142, PH12441, PH14028, PH17164
Maxwell, Robert Paul PH05102, PH05103, PH05104, PH10153, PH10154
May, Sandy PH15239
Mayer, Jeffrey PH02712, PH03634, PH04367, PH05062, PH06375, PH06664, PH07206, PH08587, PH08846, PH12163, PH12247, PH12677, PH13251, PH13703, PH14198, PH14872, PH15222, PH15393, PH16478, PH17792
Mayforth, Hal PH07150, PH07151, PH09844
Mayo, Martin PH05867, PH14770
Mazur, Kevin PH00049, PH00050, PH00051, PH00058, PH00095, PH00101, PH00115, PH00127, PH00192, PH00248, PH00255, PH00262, PH00299, PH00385, PH00407, PH00415, PH00437, PH00468, PH00488, PH00525, PH00527, PH00528, PH00604, PH00676, PH00706, PH00715, PH00812, PH00821, PH00872, PH00938, PH00942, PH00947, PH00992, PH01026, PH01029, PH01035, PH01041, PH01047, PH01048, PH01049, PH01055, PH01067, PH01073, PH01080, PH01085, PH01095, PH01115, PH01125, PH01128, PH01130, PH01131, PH01136, PH01164, PH01167, PH01175, PH01176, PH01177, PH01179, PH01180, PH01181, PH01184, PH01200, PH01245, PH01265, PH01275, PH01284, PH01313, PH01330, PH01345, PH01431, PH01438, PH01444, PH01445, PH01448, PH01451, PH01478, PH01485, PH01486, PH01487, PH01500, PH01501, PH01503, PH01504, PH01507, PH01521, PH01589, PH01593, PH01594, PH01595, PH01612, PH01613, PH01618, PH01638, PH01650, PH01667, PH01668, PH01697, PH01734, PH01822, PH01835, PH01836, PH01838, PH01840, PH01846, PH01862, PH01876, PH01880, PH01884, PH01889, PH01898, PH01899, PH01921, PH01924, PH01926, PH01957, PH02004, PH02049, PH02076, PH02084, PH02087, PH02091, PH02097, PH02103, PH02127, PH02147, PH02151, PH02246, PH02247, PH02250, PH02251, PH02256, PH02343, PH02357, PH02368, PH02370, PH02372, PH02375, PH02381, PH02394, PH02400, PH02432, PH02472, PH02488, PH02504, PH02505, PH02506, PH02517, PH02699, PH02710, PH02720, PH02731, PH02735, PH02736, PH02739, PH02744, PH02745, PH02761, PH02772, PH02792, PH02794, PH02795, PH02796, PH02806, PH02856, PH02867, PH02882, PH02887, PH02889, PH02892, PH02901, PH02903, PH02907, PH02927, PH02929, PH02949, PH02956, PH02959, PH02960, PH02961, PH02970, PH03048, PH03049, PH03053, PH03057, PH03058, PH03062, PH03105, PH03115, PH03120, PH03265, PH03268, PH03281, PH03318, PH03321, PH03322, PH03325, PH03332, PH03358, PH03360, PH03384, PH03403, PH03481, PH03488, PH03493, PH03494, PH03496, PH03512, PH03564, PH03571, PH03572, PH03573, PH03585, PH03643, PH03726, PH03732, PH03734, PH03740, PH03750, PH03770, PH03786, PH03795, PH03824, PH03838, PH03850, PH03910, PH03923, PH03948, PH04076, PH04152, PH04191, PH04224, PH04226, PH04241, PH04292, PH04316, PH04317, PH04318, PH04351, PH04381, PH04388, PH04410, PH04424, PH04459, PH04466, PH04538, PH04544, PH04594, PH04598, PH04599, PH04604, PH04613, PH04623, PH04625, PH04626, PH04627, PH04628, PH04638, PH04639, PH04650, PH04729, PH04737, PH04740, PH04743, PH04745, PH04824, PH04886, PH04910, PH04921, PH04925, PH04936, PH04955, PH04956, PH04992, PH04993, PH04994, PH05045, PH05072, PH05073, PH05074, PH05128, PH05142, PH05198, PH05218, PH05272, PH05282, PH05284, PH05286, PH05324, PH05349, PH05358, PH05385, PH05410, PH05440, PH05472, PH05484, PH05487, PH05489, PH05529, PH05531, PH05544, PH05562, PH05573, PH05577, PH05585, PH05618, PH05634, PH05635, PH05637, PH05737, PH05810, PH05812, PH05938, PH05939, PH05944, PH06001, PH06002, PH06003, PH06011, PH06012, PH06013, PH06014, PH06018, PH06055, PH06064, PH06070, PH06092, PH06094, PH06098, PH06123, PH06206, PH06225, PH06238, PH06267, PH06306, PH06357, PH06358, PH06379, PH06430, PH06441, PH06442, PH06443, PH06447, PH06448, PH06449, PH06533, PH06534, PH06540, PH06541, PH06556, PH06557, PH06565, PH06568, PH06582, PH06583, PH06603, PH06610, PH06611, PH06633, PH06645, PH06648, PH06649, PH06776, PH06777, PH06804, PH06806, PH06830, PH06912, PH06916, PH06931, PH07004, PH07038, PH07040, PH07047, PH07049, PH07052, PH07053, PH07061, PH07071, PH07076, PH07108, PH07112, PH07113, PH07128, PH07224, PH07225, PH07227, PH07323, PH07379, PH07380, PH07381, PH07387, PH07414, PH07415, PH07421, PH07422,

Mazur, Kevin (continued)
PH07439, PH07449, PH07512, PH07536, PH07564, PH07587, PH07607, PH07608, PH07613, PH07632, PH07651, PH07655, PH07732, PH07758, PH07761, PH07763, PH07765, PH07801, PH07811, PH07818, PH07827, PH07846, PH07850, PH07852, PH07853, PH07854, PH07855, PH07861, PH07867, PH07868, PH07923, PH07929, PH07935, PH07939, PH07940, PH07948, PH07981, PH08004, PH08051, PH08083, PH08122, PH08144, PH08147, PH08192, PH08196, PH08199, PH08201, PH08202, PH08203, PH08206, PH08207, PH08209, PH08210, PH08211, PH08216, PH08222, PH08223, PH08228, PH08229, PH08230, PH08231, PH08232, PH08234, PH08235, PH08236, PH08237, PH08239, PH08240, PH08241, PH08242, PH08245, PH08246, PH08247, PH08248, PH08251, PH08253, PH08255, PH08258, PH08260, PH08281, PH08304, PH08315, PH08332, PH08336, PH08339, PH08394, PH08424, PH08482, PH08485, PH08498, PH08504, PH08510, PH08572, PH08595, PH08631, PH08633, PH08636, PH08638, PH08641, PH08644, PH08677, PH08708, PH08749, PH08753, PH08759, PH08764, PH08774, PH08786, PH08792, PH08803, PH08804, PH08820, PH08859, PH08865, PH08879, PH08919, PH08925, PH08940, PH08991, PH08992, PH08993, PH08997, PH08998, PH08999, PH09004, PH09015, PH09064, PH09119, PH09152, PH09165, PH09178, PH09182, PH09299, PH09301, PH09303, PH09315, PH09321, PH09346, PH09380, PH09429, PH09430, PH09463, PH09474, PH09475, PH09478, PH09501, PH09502, PH09526, PH09546, PH09628, PH09630, PH09640, PH09650, PH09664, PH09679, PH09689, PH09740, PH09747, PH09767, PH09799, PH09854, PH09861, PH09862, PH09863, PH09876, PH09880, PH09882, PH09884, PH09923, PH09987, PH10001, PH10039, PH10045, PH10059, PH10069, PH10070, PH10087, PH10118, PH10168, PH10174, PH10189, PH10211, PH10217, PH10257, PH10258, PH10264, PH10310, PH10313, PH10355, PH10356, PH10416, PH10422, PH10424, PH10446, PH10447, PH10450, PH10466, PH10468, PH10472, PH10475, PH10506, PH10514, PH10519, PH10572, PH10584, PH10585, PH10586, PH10587, PH10588, PH10589, PH10590, PH10591, PH10594, PH10616, PH10618, PH10656, PH10658, PH10661, PH10662, PH10669, PH10709, PH10811, PH10812, PH10862, PH10863, PH10866, PH10867, PH10880, PH10910, PH10911, PH10943, PH10958, PH10959, PH10960, PH10961, PH10962, PH10996, PH11038, PH11046, PH11049, PH11050, PH11051, PH11080, PH11091, PH11150, PH11166, PH11250, PH11258, PH11267, PH11309, PH11310, PH11315, PH11339, PH11340, PH11351, PH11352, PH11399, PH11414, PH11420, PH11454, PH11455, PH11490, PH11506, PH11564, PH11575, PH11590, PH11664, PH11675, PH11732, PH11762, PH11773, PH11774, PH11792, PH11796, PH11797, PH11820, PH11868, PH11870, PH11871, PH11875, PH11934, PH11935, PH11941, PH11947, PH11948, PH11951, PH11952, PH12068, PH12132, PH12133, PH12150, PH12151, PH12175, PH12184, PH12232, PH12234, PH12239, PH12287, PH12288, PH12289, PH12352, PH12436, PH12438, PH12445, PH12449, PH12471, PH12472, PH12474, PH12480, PH12482, PH12483, PH12484, PH12485, PH12486, PH12487, PH12490, PH12547, PH12559, PH12564, PH12565, PH12568, PH12657, PH12666, PH12687, PH12742, PH12786, PH12830, PH12835, PH12841, PH13022, PH13043, PH13044, PH13063, PH13151, PH13201, PH13202, PH13268, PH13276, PH13278, PH13279, PH13285, PH13303, PH13309, PH13319, PH13320, PH13321, PH13322, PH13364, PH13369, PH13371, PH13374, PH13375, PH13376, PH13446, PH13448, PH13482, PH13486, PH13492, PH13503, PH13531, PH13551, PH13556, PH13561, PH13649, PH13653, PH13657, PH13658, PH13668, PH13673, PH13674, PH13700, PH13711, PH13740, PH13749a, PH13796, PH13800, PH13801, PH13810, PH13817, PH13887, PH13888, PH13889, PH13891, PH13894, PH13898, PH13901, PH13903, PH13906, PH13908, PH13909, PH13922, PH13923, PH13924, PH13928, PH13935, PH13978, PH14092, PH14106, PH14107, PH14108, PH14109, PH14117, PH14149, PH14155, PH14159, PH14161, PH14170, PH14172, PH14212, PH14219, PH14275, PH14286, PH14306, PH14312, PH14341, PH14385, PH14416, PH14417, PH14510, PH14534, PH14535, PH14656, PH14736, PH14743, PH14754, PH14756, PH14759, PH14784, PH14785, PH14822, PH14823, PH14824, PH14860, PH14861, PH14863, PH14867, PH14868, PH14873, PH14881, PH14889, PH14894, PH14961, PH14970, PH14971, PH14973, PH14978, PH14986, PH15003, PH15006, PH15024, PH15025, PH15029, PH15034, PH15035, PH15036, PH15052, PH15087, PH15097, PH15101, PH15103, PH15104a, PH15180, PH15319, PH15337, PH15345, PH15379, PH15385, PH15392, PH15397, PH15403, PH15439, PH15442, PH15443, PH15446, PH15449, PH15456, PH15458, PH15462, PH15463, PH15475, PH15510, PH15539, PH15541, PH15545, PH15578, PH15585, PH15586, PH15587, PH15590, PH15605, PH15606, PH15677, PH15678, PH15707, PH15709, PH15748, PH15754, PH15755, PH15756, PH15757, PH15759, PH15760, PH15762, PH15764, PH15765, PH15766, PH15782, PH15784, PH15790, PH15792, PH15794, PH15798, PH15807, PH15809, PH15811, PH15813, PH15814, PH15886, PH15899, PH15912, PH15950, PH16020, PH16079, PH16100, PH16106, PH16109, PH16110, PH16111, PH16123, PH16129, PH16130, PH16132, PH16133, PH16145, PH16496, PH16497, PH16499, PH16501, PH16504, PH16577, PH16625, PH16647, PH16697, PH16708, PH16713, PH16745, PH16750, PH16762, PH16833, PH16861, PH16880, PH16883, PH16896, PH16897, PH16932, PH16943, PH17045, PH17068, PH17073, PH17075, PH17087, PH17088, PH17089, PH17090, PH17094, PH17095, PH17098, PH17100, PH17102, PH17103, PH17107, PH17109, PH17147, PH17148, PH17263, PH17264, PH17335, PH17336, PH17368, PH17402, PH17415, PH17419, PH17420, PH17421, PH17424, PH17428, PH17445, PH17499, PH17503, PH17506, PH17511, PH17525, PH17526, PH17527, PH17555, PH17574, PH17589, PH17590, PH17736, PH17751, PH17774, PH17775, PH17776, PH17778, PH17789, PH17791, PH17853, PH17886, PH17909, PH17947, PH17997, PH18016, PH18021, PH18022, PH18069, PH18148, PH18152, PH18153, PH18155, PH18156, PH18158, PH18159, PH18175, PH18176, PH18179, PH18189, PH18190, PH18209, PH18220, PH18261
McAlpine, Paul PH01591, PH05622, PH08830, PH14129, PH16422, PH16699, PH17679
McBroom, Bruce PH04872, PH06674, PH14904
McCartney, Linda PH06043, PH10267
McCauley, Adam PH13001, PH13162
McClelland, P. PH00616, PH03710, PH06726, PH11033, PH12366, PH13698, PH14386, PH14454, PH15702, PH17724
McDaniel, Melodie PH02379, PH04399, PH05903, PH11550, PH12398, PH13981, PH13982, PH13983, PH17505
McDarrah, Fred W. PH15280
McDean, Craig PH06491, PH06842
McDermand, Jo PH02719, PH07431
McDonough, Patricia PH00079, PH01156, PH02807, PH04773, PH06421, PH06689, PH08350, PH10372, PH13563, PH14316, PH16845, PH16846, PH16847, PH16848
McEwan, Rob PH03633, PH14721
McGee, Henry PH07185
McGlothlin, Doug PH14966, PH16238, PH17857
McGuire, Leeann PH01680, PH10755, PH14301, PH16148, PH16564
McInnerney, Mike PH17690
McIntyre, Will PH02552
McKay, Jim PH13346
McKiernan, Scott PH06723, PH15012
McLeah, Jill PH06083
McLeod, William Mercer PH00408, PH00692, PH03200, PH03202, PH03203, PH03255, PH03696, PH03697, PH03698, PH04386, PH07106, PH09530, PH10337, PH14313, PH15689
McManus, Jeri PH09838
McMullan, James PH01874
McMullan, Patrick PH01161, PH09652
McNamara-Zamur PH01557
McNamee, Wally PH17237
McSpadden, Wyatt PH15488
McVey, Cameron PH09836
Medina, Lope PH09223
Meehan, Arthur PH14663, PH14664
Meeks, Raymond PH03459, PH07252, PH07255, PH09081, PH11179, PH11836
Meier, Raymond PH00369
Meinhardt, Brook PH10581, PH12012
Meisel, Steven PH09851, PH09891, PH09892
Meister, Michael PH13345
Mella, Michael PH07522
Meller, Barrie PH17691
Menchin, Scott PH01454, PH05965, PH07159, PH09396, PH14514, PH14705, PH17132
Mendelsohn, Matt PH13932
Meola, Eric PH15416
Mercer, Lance PH00003, PH00008, PH00283, PH00287, PH00294, PH00298, PH00303, PH01929, PH02213, PH02466, PH03349, PH03382, PH03592, PH05648, PH06213, PH06221, PH07257, PH07739, PH08580, PH08942, PH09824, PH10044, PH10077, PH10079, PH10169, PH10298, PH10302, PH10306, PH10307, PH10308, PH10309, PH10315, PH11326, PH12111, PH12124, PH12131, PH12548, PH12982, PH14244, PH15320, PH15504, PH15505, PH15512, PH16065, PH17043, PH17080, PH17081, PH17084, PH17085, PH17086, PH17603, PH17821
Mericle, Charise PH00629, PH07710
Mericle, Cherise PH02590, PH11144
Merillon, Georges PH00375

Meshon, Aaron PH02457, PH10116, PH17980
Messer, Alan PH01078, PH07407, PH11193, PH11862, PH14318, PH17702
Meyer, Jeffrey PH02734
Meyers, Tim PH10255, PH15002
Micelotta, Frank PH01863, PH02983, PH02993, PH04944, PH05146, PH06451, PH06647, PH07388, PH07872, PH08694, PH08822, PH08921, PH09476, PH10592, PH13048, PH13308, PH14157, PH14206, PH14310, PH15457, PH16301, PH16466, PH16887
Michaelson, Randall PH06767, PH08408, PH09447, PH09773, PH10330, PH12001, PH12017, PH13237, PH14202
Michaut, Valerie PH00565
Michelove, Mim PH10931, PH17569
Michelson, Eric T. PH00605, PH03605, PH06580, PH07576, PH07749, PH12446, PH14307, PH15917
Michelson, Randall PH01371, PH05108, PH05814, PH11126, PH13249, PH17097, PH17323, PH17338, PH17827
Midnight Oil PH10608
Mikrut, Jack PH03532, PH17055, PH18163
Miles, Steve PH06041, PH08586
Miller, Brad PH01123, PH03276, PH07294, PH08303, PH12442, PH15825, PH16664, PH17720
Miller, David PH12702, PH14942
Miller, Ethan PH03323
Miller, Greg PH00432, PH00854, PH00855, PH00856, PH00905, PH01213, PH01214, PH02165, PH02166, PH02167, PH02168, PH02169, PH02170, PH03130, PH03169, PH03178, PH03179, PH03180, PH03181, PH03182, PH03183, PH03184, PH03185, PH03186, PH03187, PH03188, PH03189, PH03190, PH03191, PH03192, PH06935, PH07704, PH10677, PH13761, PH15322, PH15624, PH15625, PH15626, PH15627, PH15628, PH15629, PH15630, PH15631, PH15632, PH15633, PH15634, PH15635, PH15636, PH15637, PH15638, PH15639, PH15640, PH15641, PH15642, PH15643, PH15644, PH15645, PH16158, PH16159, PH16160, PH16161, PH16162, PH16163, PH16192, PH16210, PH16211, PH17180, PH17181, PH17182, PH17183, PH17193, PH17196, PH17199, PH17374
Miller, Karen PH05158
Miller, Michael PH03259, PH04374, PH05495, PH05795, PH07074, PH07302, PH08913, PH13294, PH15327, PH17329
Miller, Peter Darley PH00591, PH05066, PH08027, PH11253, PH12209
Miller, Steve PH10639
Millman, Susana PH03466, PH05756, PH06418, PH08585, PH13115
Mills, Doug PH02265, PH02869
Millson, P. J. PH09442
Milne, Donald PH04793
Minchin, James R., III PH03658, PH06063, PH09755, PH14280, PH16593
Mintz, Ari PH15666, PH15674, PH15676, PH15687, PH16600
Missbrenner, Kevin PH10046
Mitchell, Joni PH10700
Modell, David PH10251
Mondino, Jean Baptiste PH06472, PH15112, PH15114, PH17274
Montalbetti-Campbell PH00391, PH00393, PH02322, PH04527, PH04529
Montgomery, David PH07014
Moore, Michael PH00109, PH04540, PH07100
Moore, Suzan PH13941, PH14691
Moore, T. PH02980, PH06163
Moore-Erdman, Susan PH06164, PH10828
Morey, Craig PH11960
Morganstein, Barry PH00179, PH01461, PH09012, PH17213, PH17431
Moriarity, Pat PH03126
Morin, Jim PH02836
Morris, Christopher PH10625, PH10626, PH10627, PH10628, PH15137, PH15138, PH15139, PH15140
Morris, Dennis PH10036, PH10037
Morriss, Gary PH10609
Morse, Joe PH10940, PH15426
Morse, Paul PH07860
Morse, Ralph PH08174
Moseley, Melissa PH17911
Mosenfeld, Tim PH03263, PH07450
Mosenfelder, Tim PH01537, PH03316, PH03533, PH05594, PH06067, PH08687, PH18099
Moskowitz, Karen PH00203, PH00575, PH00876, PH01324, PH02218, PH04503, PH07265, PH07693, PH08740, PH08752, PH09518, PH09639, PH11323, PH12716, PH14812, PH15306, PH15503, PH15511, PH15928, PH15988, PH18119
Moss, Gary PH00610, PH02208, PH03705, PH11031, PH14451
Moss, Wallace PH10394
Mott, Tony PH00046, PH01223, PH01224, PH01315, PH01723, PH03303, PH03339, PH03859, PH04030, PH04034, PH05386, PH05607, PH06477, PH08265, PH10012, PH11724, PH13064, PH13757, PH14707, PH15370, PH15803, PH16275
Mottram, Tony PH01281, PH11021
Mounir PH13152
Muhammad, Ozier PH05815
Muller, Michael PH00507, PH05516, PH05523, PH06352, PH13091, PH13257
Mundahl, Kurt PH05494
Murray, Andrew PH05674, PH08576, PH10593, PH10596
Murray, Rebecca PH05821, PH17121
Murrey, Ron PH07565, PH08395
Musto, Ilpo PH04392, PH07097, PH08649, PH09021, PH11200, PH11256, PH13212, PH15690, PH16373

N

Nachtwey, James PH06467
Nahas, Margo PH17902
Nahas, Margo Zafer PH16876
Nahoum, Ken PH04470
Nakamura, Joel PH08421
Naltchayan, Neshan PH03032, PH08716, PH17744
Nannarello, Spike PH00642, PH09896
Naras PH13047
Nash, Peter PH03722, PH16778
Nation, Bill PH06231
Natkin, Paul PH00028, PH00243, PH00374, PH00425, PH00436, PH00534, PH00574, PH01792, PH01843, PH02012, PH02476, PH02481, PH02729, PH03301, PH03310, PH03383, PH04284, PH04325, PH04832, PH05460, PH05641, PH06831, PH07193, PH07322, PH07643, PH07648, PH07988, PH08058, PH08094, PH08282, PH08487, PH08578, PH09174, PH10081, PH10134, PH10300, PH10657, PH10979, PH11125, PH11196, PH12354, PH12714, PH12854, PH12909, PH12910, PH12912, PH13055, PH13481, PH13496, PH14825, PH14951, PH14958, PH14962, PH14965, PH15887, PH15889, PH15927, PH16627, PH16824, PH16838, PH17049, PH17388, PH18193, PH18268
Naumann, Ellen PH11087, PH11096, PH12501, PH15202
Navizet, Albane PH03247
Neema, Frederic PH06190, PH06200
Nelson, Andy PH10681, PH11828
Nelson, Bill PH10250
Nelson, Mike PH01758, PH04693
Nelson, Ralph PH04829, PH04848, PH07088, PH08328, PH11701, PH13687
Nelson, Tony PH10055
Nemchin, Tracy PH06757, PH10393
Newcomb, Peter PH15489, PH15490
Newton, Philip PH01961, PH01962, PH01963, PH01964, PH02323, PH02324, PH02325, PH02326, PH03041, PH03042, PH03043, PH03094, PH05962, PH05963, PH06668, PH07376, PH07377, PH08031, PH08032, PH08033, PH08034, PH08035, PH09368, PH09369, PH09903, PH09904, PH09905, PH09906, PH10640, PH10641, PH10649, PH10751, PH10752, PH10753, PH10754, PH11343, PH11344, PH11345, PH11346, PH11347, PH15073, PH15074, PH15075, PH16040
Ng, Karjean PH01870, PH03583, PH07301, PH11228
Ng, Norman PH03272, PH09761, PH12911, PH15438
Nicks, Dewey PH01082, PH01083, PH01084, PH01706, PH05149, PH05150, PH05151, PH17799, PH17800, PH17801, PH17802
Nicoli, Fabio PH04835
Niemann, Christoph PH00200, PH00736
Nissen, Melanie PH09794, PH11566, PH12403, PH15117
Niviere, D. PH07875
Noble, Chris PH07906, PH08047, PH11371, PH11445, PH12065, PH14841, PH14842, PH14843, PH14844, PH14845
Nofziger, Christopher PH00143, PH00144, PH00145, PH01675, PH14135, PH14136, PH14137, PH14138, PH17314
Norcross, Deborah PH05187, PH09432, PH12050
Northeast, Christian PH13722
Norton, Margaret PH06834, PH09308, PH16467
Nosotti, Fabio PH04154, PH05319, PH05651, PH06194, PH17735
Nubile, James PH05875, PH05876, PH05877, PH05878
Nystrom, Dick PH00547, PH00548, PH00620, PH03371, PH03965, PH12019, PH17545, PH17547, PH17548, PH17549, PH17550

O

O'Beirne, Andy PH03463, PH03527, PH03925, PH04769, PH08958, PH16758
Ockenfels, Frank W. PH00182, PH00335, PH00557, PH00581, PH00623, PH00624, PH00770, PH00798, PH00863, PH00910, PH00911, PH01031, PH01134, PH01377, PH01389, PH01427, PH01462, PH01624, PH01661, PH01677, PH01936, PH02191, PH02193, PH02426, PH02475, PH02508, PH02544, PH02801, PH02899, PH02985, PH03084, PH03097, PH03237, PH03239, PH03309, PH03330, PH03346, PH03359, PH03361, PH03859a, PH04290, PH04493, PH04780, PH04781, PH04889, PH04898, PH04995, PH05119, PH05188, PH05503, PH05713, PH05870, PH06135, PH06187, PH06271, PH06286, PH06553, PH06632, PH06783, PH06848, PH06995, PH07012, PH07618, PH07642, PH07771, PH07780, PH08287, PH08431, PH08432, PH08433, PH08486, PH08668, PH09259, PH09355,

PH09433, PH09436, PH09519, PH09520, PH09670, PH09927, PH09979, PH10019, PH10502, PH10520, PH10522, PH10733, PH10784, PH10831, PH10840, PH10860, PH10861, PH10871, PH10875, PH10882, PH10900, PH11072, PH11592, PH11740, PH12051, PH12054, PH12141, PH12269, PH12348, PH12350, PH12351, PH12358, PH12360, PH12384, PH12913, PH12978, PH12979, PH13362, PH13365, PH13368, PH13853, PH14050, PH14096, PH14194, PH14404, PH14728, PH14729, PH14949, PH15118, PH15128, PH15364, PH15366, PH15411, PH15531, PH15891, PH16011, PH16050, PH16068, PH16225, PH16233, PH16616, PH16770, PH17210, PH17253, PH17293, PH17627, PH17798
O'Connell, Mitch PH00536, PH04516, PH16940
Oh, Viviane PH08138, PH18202, PH18203
O'Hara, Gail PH10539
Oida, Hideo PH13056
Okeda, Mitch PH15129
O'Keefe, Cora PH07457
O'Leary, Bill PH08126
Oleski, Dan PH06839, PH08819
Oliphant PH02830, PH02900
Oliveira, Alex PH06748, PH09665
Oliver, Benjamin PH01823
Oliver, Robert PH16856
Olivier, Rick PH06062, PH09027, PH09752, PH14115, PH14279, PH16592
Ollerenshaw, Philip PH02707, PH13042
Ollerenshow, Philip PH02684, PH13040
Olsen, K. Thor PH10047
Olson, Jonathan PH06340, PH06346, PH17956
Olson, Sheryl PH00495, PH02030, PH03065, PH03653, PH04300, PH04453, PH06269, PH06351, PH06483, PH06892, PH09154, PH09725, PH10392, PH12945, PH13930, PH15367, PH16049
Omes, World B. PH00930
O'Neal, Jane PH03593
O'Neil, Terry PH16503, PH16508
O'Neill, Michael PH11782
O'Neill, Terry PH07954
Ono, Yoko PH09261
Orris, Darby PH14532
Ortega, Albert PH07747, PH07924, PH10469, PH12174, PH16942, PH17999
Ortiz-Lopez, Dennis PH00319, PH02367, PH03529, PH05728, PH07016, PH11462, PH12908, PH13781, PH16323
Osborn, Kathy PH09218, PH11849, PH12507
Otte, Sylvia PH01463, PH01832, PH03744, PH04566, PH05037, PH09967, PH13396, PH15483, PH15834
Owen, Mike PH10944
Owen, Tim PH11978, PH16347, PH16476, PH17471

P

P.A.G. PH00516, PH02121
Page, Scarlet PH00549, PH02483, PH06629, PH17639
Paley, Stephen PH05851, PH11624, PH12437, PH17621
Palma, Eric PH16240
Palmer, Brian PH00829
Palmer, Dave PH10917
Palmer, Robert PH10369
Palmieri, Lou PH12897
Paniccioli, Ernie PH02063
Panter, Gary PH06337, PH07598, PH11742, PH13862, PH18081
Pantsios, A. J. PH03946, PH04897, PH05220, PH17209
Pantsios, Anastasia PH15775
Papas, B. J. PH00045, PH00950, PH06746, PH10213, PH16280
Paraskevas, Michael PH09500
Park, Neon PH09470, PH18237
Parker, Jolie PH12007
Parker, Steven PH11840
Parker, Tom, Colonel PH12758, PH12760
Parsons, Caroline PH10724
Pasley, Richard PH01509, PH01533, PH02797, PH03782, PH04746, PH06862, PH07513, PH07783, PH09256, PH10053, PH10691, PH11052, PH11728, PH13400, PH14854, PH15005, PH15774, PH15778, PH16751, PH17417, PH17606
Pastrana, Robert M. PH07369, PH13296, PH15353
Paton, Tim PH02143, PH04788, PH05558, PH13274, PH17144
Patterson, Laura PH12732
Paul, Jonathan PH01887, PH13053
Paul, Tina PH06640, PH08908, PH16702
Pauley, Lynn PH07460, PH11736
Payne, C. F. PH01848, PH02354, PH02844, PH04356, PH05235, PH05948, PH06031, PH06594, PH07037, PH07240, PH07308, PH08008, PH11397, PH12222, PH12985, PH13620, PH13645, PH15425, PH15859, PH17039, PH17764, PH17804, PH17919
Payne, Gary PH05833
Payne, Malcolm PH09045
Peck, Everett PH04369, PH04434, PH05013, PH11852, PH12252, PH12253, PH13578, PH14239, PH15282, PH18212
Pedota, Jack PH00896, PH04202
Peellart, Guy PH01581
Pendergrast, James T. PH00021, PH00023, PH00024, PH00074, PH00075, PH00086, PH00225, PH00311, PH00326, PH00359, PH00379, PH00412, PH00416, PH00455, PH00662, PH00731, PH00766, PH00797, PH00832, PH01006, PH01093, PH01552, PH01554, PH01719, PH01913, PH01966, PH02027, PH02028, PH02033, PH02034, PH02035, PH02036, PH02037, PH02038, PH02039, PH02040, PH02042, PH02043, PH02053, PH02281, PH02423, PH02451, PH02452, PH02455, PH02458, PH02459, PH02462, PH02612, PH02663, PH02822, PH02831, PH02832, PH02833, PH02835, PH02939, PH02942, PH02943, PH02944, PH03047, PH03096, PH03152, PH03173, PH03174, PH03215, PH03235, PH03398, PH03455, PH03504, PH03505, PH03526, PH03560, PH03650, PH03849, PH03879, PH04054, PH04118, PH04228, PH04508, PH04515, PH04517, PH04518, PH04519, PH04526, PH04663, PH04706, PH04707, PH04710, PH04716, PH04718, PH04756, PH04796, PH04797, PH04798, PH04801, PH04844, PH04867, PH04869, PH04870, PH04934, PH04972, PH05020, PH05021, PH05022, PH05051, PH05097, PH05098, PH05243, PH05255, PH05423, PH05548, PH05581, PH05712, PH05726, PH05727, PH05868, PH06032, PH06120, PH06155, PH06185, PH06240, PH06294, PH06336, PH06338, PH06424, PH06464, PH06511, PH06512, PH06513, PH06514, PH06515, PH06516, PH06517, PH06716, PH06879, PH07080, PH07081, PH07154, PH07155, PH07165, PH07171, PH07263, PH07315, PH07338, PH07339, PH07340, PH07708, PH07709, PH07920, PH08009, PH08134, PH08401, PH08623, PH08624, PH08710, PH08844, PH08892, PH08896, PH08960, PH08989, PH09125, PH09141, PH09163, PH09255, PH09339, PH09344, PH09345, PH09422, PH09423, PH09537, PH09625, PH09626, PH10229, PH10287, PH10358, PH10482, PH10548, PH10550, PH10624, PH10858, PH10902, PH10956, PH10957, PH11002, PH11006, PH11007, PH11008, PH11009, PH11069, PH11133, PH11134, PH11135, PH11136, PH11140, PH11145, PH11175, PH11205, PH11222, PH11224, PH11225, PH11266, PH11354, PH11381, PH11382, PH11424, PH11460, PH11461, PH11472, PH11521, PH11552, PH11569, PH11630, PH11649, PH11671, PH11858, PH11876, PH11994, PH12103, PH12105, PH12106, PH12107, PH12165, PH12248, PH12249, PH12342, PH12409, PH12469, PH12476, PH12508, PH12615, PH12619, PH12620, PH12621, PH12622, PH12652, PH12696, PH12697, PH12826, PH12967, PH12993, PH12996, PH12997, PH12998, PH12999, PH13000, PH13010, PH13027, PH13086, PH13190, PH13192, PH13344, PH13360, PH13403, PH13406, PH13407, PH13410, PH13411, PH13414, PH13436, PH13437, PH13465, PH13579, PH13622, PH13763, PH13764, PH13765, PH13766, PH13767, PH13768, PH13769, PH13770, PH13771, PH13772, PH13773, PH13774, PH13775, PH13776, PH13777, PH13778, PH13779, PH13780, PH13794, PH13795, PH13837, PH13863, PH13945, PH14051, PH14240, PH14394, PH14424, PH14426, PH14442, PH14462, PH14463, PH14526, PH14706, PH14714, PH14771, PH14772, PH14918, PH14937, PH14940, PH14941, PH15116, PH15188, PH15219, PH15220, PH15285, PH15286, PH15496, PH15517 PH15670, PH15844, PH15916, PH15929, PH15977, PH16007, PH16032, PH16089, PH16090, PH16091, PH16174, PH16321, PH16391, PH16393, PH16394, PH16395, PH16534, PH16567, PH16732, PH17036, PH17038, PH17140, PH17221, PH17222, PH17226, PH17228, PH17234, PH17282, PH17488, PH17601, PH17896, PH17898, PH17948, PH17949, PH18032, PH18038, PH18095, PH18103, PH18213, PH18214, PH18247, PH18278
Penn, Irving PH03933
Pereira, Al PH04777, PH10135
Peretz, Jesse PH03799
Perez, Marty PH00573, PH01931, PH02595, PH04135, PH06363, PH08137, PH10275, PH10690, PH15607, PH15926, PH16523, PH16665, PH18200
Perou, Ralph PH05702, PH06698, PH09418, PH14105, PH15664
Perry, David PH07063
Pessin, Annalisa PH05093
Peters, Doug PH03437a
Peters, Karen A. PH06182, PH12726, PH14576, PH17161
Petersen, Naomi PH06165, PH10830 , PH13079, PH14604, PH15165
Peterson, Charles PH00111, PH00178, PH00482, PH00545, PH00691, PH02181, PH02392, PH02471, PH02492, PH02779, PH02963, PH02968, PH02973, PH02975, PH02987, PH02989, PH03340, PH03341, PH03342, PH03348, PH03356, PH03678, PH03792, PH03907, PH04543, PH06006, PH06480, PH06482, PH07828, PH08281a, PH09183, PH09573, PH10159, PH11497, PH11577, PH11587, PH11589, PH12660, PH14406, PH14704, PH15226, PH15227, PH15228, PH15984, PH16265, PH16266, PH16267, PH16271, PH16640, PH17261, PH17313, PH18048, PH18049
Peterson, Mark PH00622, PH04534,

PH05883, PH06186, PH07828, PH10540, PH10541, PH14751, PH17628
Pfriender, Stephanie PH03963, PH04084, PH13536, PH13537, PH13538
Phalen, Tom PH00805, PH00851, PH01027, PH04905, PH09293, PH10320, PH11030, PH14583
Phillips, George PH15747, PH15952
Phillips, Ken PH09435, PH12053, PH12055
Phillips, Robert PH00114, PH06941
Philo, Celia PH01580
Philo, Duffy PH01579
Phipps, Sandra-Lee PH12493, PH17794
Picayo, Jose PH10518
Pickett, Keri PH07687, PH13129, PH14142
Picknally, Pete PH01447, PH15441
Pigozzi, Jean PH01756, PH02212, PH02232, PH02407, PH06085, PH06364, PH06613, PH06614, PH06954, PH07370, PH07532, PH07914, PH07921, PH07922, PH08048, PH08189, PH08948, PH10114, PH10444, PH11398, PH12452, PH12453, PH12863, PH13587, PH13939, PH14268, PH14322, PH15519, PH15554PH17248, PH17320, PH17383
Pilon, Alain PH06914
Pipes, Breck PH13582
Pitney, Layne PH12851
Piven, Hanoch PH04588, PH08755, PH14857
Piven, Hanoch Ernesto PH01422, PH09846
Pizzarello, Charlie PH04976, PH07404 . PH09595
Pluchino, Joseph PH01728, PH06272, PH08509, PH08973, PH09788, PH10642, PH12506, PH13705, PH14372, PH15570
Plummer, Barry PH03072, PH07870, PH13958
Plummer, Sue PH02412, PH03282, PH07756, PH08283, PH13699, PH14421, PH15535
Plunkert, David PH04402, PH11458, PH13150
Pobuda, Brian PH12309
Polak, Richard PH16517
Pollock, Arthur PH01246
Pollock, Ian PH12108
Pool, Smiley PH02065, PH07109, PH16764
Poole, Edward PH12846
Pope, Pat PH05684, PH13936
Poppel, Seth PH10802
Poppell, Seth PH12307
Popplewell, John PH00302, PH00492, PH12136, PH15589, PH17099
Popsie PH12761
Porto, James PH15657
Porto, Jim PH05100
Posey, Carl PH04273, PH11286, PH14541, PH16580
Powell, Aubrey PH05626, PH09156, PH12456, PH12459, PH12461
Powell, D. PH00245
Powell, Ricky PH00939, PH00945
Powers, Dan PH00807, PH08735
Pownall, Ron PH00096, PH00097, PH06641, PH08831, PH12233, PH16709, PH17680
Prato, Rodica PH00113
Preston, Neal PH00291, PH00292, PH00589, PH01484, PH01495, PH01514, PH01590, PH01674, PH02752, PH03584, PH04225, PH04227, PH04457, PH04688, PH05861, PH06076, PH06287, PH06558, PH07044, PH07600, PH07874, PH08994, PH08996, PH09164, PH09166, PH09172, PH09494, PH09870, PH09874, PH10105, PH10200, PH10244, PH10253, PH10259, PH10261, PH10531, PH10532, PH11045, PH11616, PH11617, PH11618, PH11685, PH11939, PH11942, PH11953, PH12118, PH12119, PH12123, PH12503, PH12557, PH12560, PH12569, PH12852, PH13438, PH13614, PH14339, PH15431, PH15434, PH15435, PH15436, PH15437, PH15451, PH15466, PH15467, PH15477, PH15720, PH15741, PH16074, PH16075, PH16121, PH16748, PH17061, PH17062, PH17069, PH17071, PH17334, PH17826, PH17925, PH18078, PH18169
Preuitt, Clayton PH01945, PH04096, PH07160
Price, Jeff PH17273
Pugliano, Bill PH08904
Pulin, Chuck PH01042, PH01850, PH01878, PH02236, PH04647, PH06307, PH07602, PH08157, PH11360, PH13875, PH14205, PH18211, PH18250
Pumphrey, Steve PH00470, PH01681, PH09098, PH14498, PH14570
Putland, Michael PH01608, PH01610, PH02558, PH02741, PH03511, PH04210, PH04595, PH05010, PH05530, PH06646, PH07503, PH08758, PH10421, PH13484, PH13872, PH14735, PH15722, PH17907, PH18107
Putnam, Jamie PH06952
Putnam, Sarah PH00088, PH06639, PH12229, PH12718, PH16701
Pyke, Steve PH16374

Q

Quigley, Brian PH10015, PH15822

R

Raban, Duncan PH07913, PH07960
Rabbo, Ammar Abd PH07877, PH07878, PH12848
Rachlin, Amy PH00286, PH12114, PH17046, PH17054
Ragel, Jon PH00484, PH00646, PH00803, PH01833, PH01960, PH02605, PH02891, PH02898, PH03221, PH03225, PH03728, PH04003, PH04091, PH04093, PH05441, PH05819, PH06019, PH06128, PH07435, PH07776, PH08366, PH08860, PH08982, PH09543, PH09736, PH09925, PH10076, PH10987, PH11018, PH12265, PH12798, PH12957, PH13139, PH13141, PH13312, PH14119, PH14165, PH14365, PH14368, PH14837, PH15484, PH15548, PH15836, PH15847, PH15848, PH15978, PH16433, PH16641, PH16821, PH16823, PH16859, PH17498, PH17504, PH17672, PH17738, PH17993, PH18012, PH18206, PH18281, PH18282
Rall, Ted PH02231, PH02834, PH04121, PH04712, PH06228, PH07469
Rama, Raj PH00060
Randolph, Popsie PH00447b
Rankin PH00769, PH03014, PH04451, PH06484, PH09800, PH12929, PH14457, PH17465
Rapoport, Aaron PH03895, PH03896, PH03899, PH03904, PH10654, PH10953, PH16005
Rapp, Frank PH09375
Rapport, Steve PH07623
Rasic, Brian PH00543, PH01299, PH01491, PH02713, PH02721, PH05675, PH05798, PH11638, PH12843, PH14036
Ratner, Laurence PH12570
Ravid, Joyce PH04514, PH08302, PH13330, PH13466, PH16802, PH16803, PH16804, PH16805
Ray, Bill PH02543
Redfern, David PH07983
Redferns PH13895
Redin, Van PH06890, PH13146, PH14086
Reed, Dudley PH06130, PH10227, PH11747, PH17026
Reese, Tom PH02974
Regan, Ken PH00053, PH00054, PH00055, PH00057, PH03059, PH03060, PH04593, PH06095, PH06100, PH06156, PH06243, PH06247, PH06249, PH06250, PH06254, PH07042, PH08227, PH09495, PH09496, PH10461, PH10462, PH13483, PH13497, PH13535, PH14345, PH15743, PH15744, PH15746, PH15980, PH16127
Register, Charles PH04664, PH15082, PH15524
Reid, Jamie PH14489
Reilly, John PH06347
Reinhard, Rick PH13292, PH13641
Reitzel, Bill PH00040, PH00927, PH05936, PH07192, PH18219
Reuters PH03285, PH14530
Rex PH02054
Rexroad, James PH02931, PH09634
Reynolds, George PH16119
Reynolds, Tamara PH04657
Rheims, Bettina PH03767, PH03789, PH03791, PH09258, PH14054
Rhind, Geoff PH09277, PH12968
Rice, Ted PH03090, PH04131, PH05145, PH06499, PH12628, PH12634, PH15479
Rich, Nina PH01239
Richardson, Alan PH03201
Richter, Gerhard PH15151
Rider, Paul PH01172, PH01676, PH01934, PH02702, PH05696, PH06771, PH08858, PH10091, PH10674, PH13382, PH15815, PH15962, PH16587, PH16588
Ridgers, Derek PH00372
Rieker, Edward PH05754
Rikken, Clemens PH00009, PH08818, PH12127
Rinaldi, Maurice PH14441
Risko PH10780
Risko, Robert PH00895, PH00968, PH03884, PH03914, PH04156, PH04723, PH04980, PH05478, PH08505, PH08776, PH09109, PH09843, PH11910, PH12312, PH12313, PH14465, PH14556, PH16296, PH16352, PH16634, PH17394, PH17409, PH17456, PH17888
Ritts, Herb PH00887a, PH00887b, PH00991, PH01482, PH01483, PH01513, PH01592, PH01598, PH01625, PH02291, PH02292, PH03469, PH03470, PH03472, PH03475, PH04171, PH04739, PH05488, PH05854, PH05973, PH05974, PH06532, PH07802, PH07823, PH07847, PH07881, PH07884, PH07885, PH08225, PH08256, PH09479, PH09840, PH10710, PH11684, PH12321, PH12335, PH12336, PH12337, PH13628, PH13631, PH13893, PH13911, PH13912, PH13913, PH14076, PH14082, PH14093, PH14323, PH15470, PH15471, PH15472, PH15473, PH15739, PH16134, PH16753
Rives, Bob PH17836
Robathon, Peter PH05683, PH05692
Robert, Eric PH11778, PH14066, PH16094, PH16550
Robert, Francis PH08496, PH08500, PH11761, PH11763, PH13749, PH13750, PH16830, PH16831, PH16836
Robert, Francois PH01542, PH12205, PH14662, PH17372
Roberts, Ebet PH00400, PH01096, PH01198, PH01436, PH02390, PH03449, PH05003, PH05496, PH06244, PH06866, PH07141, PH07782, PH08145, PH08653, PH08886, PH09070, PH10478, PH11311, PH11318, PH11320, PH12448, PH13074, PH13075, PH13277, PH13287, PH13315, PH13617,

PH14029, PH14199, PH14200, PH14207, PH14269, PH14746, PH14793, PH15304, PH16002, PH17118, PH17319, PH17793, PH18145, PH18162, PH18183, PH18231
Robertson And Fresh PH12759
Robicheau, Paul PH00090, PH00091, PH00100, PH00102, PH00190, PH00378, PH00580, PH00688, PH01459, PH01672, PH01673, PH01965, PH02557, PH02567, PH03044, PH03045, PH03774, PH03856, PH04188, PH04389, PH04391, PH05000, PH05415, PH05510, PH05632, PH05642, PH05645, PH05824, PH05825, PH05829, PH06162, PH06261, PH06642, PH06688, PH06869, PH06876, PH07094, PH07098, PH07374, PH07375, PH07514, PH08036, PH08037, PH08038, PH08039, PH08128, PH08334, PH08349, PH08832, PH08953, PH09360, PH09907, PH09974, PH10120, PH10131, PH10509, PH10513, PH10515, PH10787, PH10822, PH10978, PH11198, PH11419, PH11696, PH12230, PH12235, PH12567, PH12973, PH13077, PH14186, PH14193, PH14603, PH14853, PH15004, PH15069, PH15119, PH15783, PH15789, PH16342, PH16705, PH16716, PH17360, PH17608, PH17610, PH17651, PH17681, PH17887
Robledo, Maria PH14847
Roca, John PH04761, PH05321, PH14915, PH15611
Rock, Mick PH01600, PH04005, PH05006, PH10175, PH10536, PH12658, PH12664, PH12665, PH12969, PH16147
Roemer, Mike PH08583
Rojas, Juan Carlos PH10576, PH10577, PH15922, PH15923
Rolston, Matthew PH00059, PH00461, PH00944, PH00948, PH00955, PH02100, PH03741, PH04185, PH04221, PH04830, PH04831, PH04850, PH05436, PH05584, PH05586, PH07055, PH07089, PH07090, PH07197, PH07390, PH08079, PH08329, PH08330, PH08639, PH08651, PH08652, PH08678, PH08851, PH08853, PH09076, PH09077, PH09982, PH10212, PH10601, PH10801, PH11416, PH11805, PH13574, PH13688, PH13689, PH13701, PH14163, PH14879, PH15398, PH16471, PH17709, PH17711, PH17831, PH18074
Rosa, Alison PH09181
Rosa And Rosa PH03131, PH03132, PH03133, PH03134, PH03135, PH03195, PH03197, PH15612, PH15613, PH15655, PH15656, PH15658, PH15659, PH15660, PH16217
Rosa, Doug PH00320, PH15623
Rose, Lisa PH04807, PH10236
Rosen, Jonathon PH01392, PH02227, PH02683, PH03553, PH03673, PH03977, PH06530, PH07464, PH08463, PH09184, PH09487, PH10680, PH10857, PH11139, PH11190, PH11484, PH13191, PH14113, PH14939, PH16156, PH16196, PH17177
Rosenberg, Howard PH01292, PH04464, PH04691, PH06039, PH07584, PH10202, PH11620, PH13751, PH13851, PH15696, PH18079
Rosenberg, Merlyn PH02598, PH10420, PH15609
Rosenthal, Cindy PH01599, PH13738
Rosenthal, Marc PH02456, PH03004, PH11003, PH11004, PH11153, PH12907
Rosenthal, Zade PH00897, PH02017, PH02177, PH08523, PH12319
Ross, Michael PH07830
Rossi, Aldo PH11426, PH11427, PH11428, PH11429, PH11430, PH11432, PH11433, PH11435, PH11436, PH11897
Roth, David PH04849, PH05082, PH12400, PH12402
Roth, Greg PH05208, PH16341
Rothenberg, Debra L. PH17607
Roussier PH13305
Royce, Mark PH17863
Rubinstein, Bill PH00089
Rudolph, Joyce PH00269, PH10739, PH10806, PH14674, PH14675
Ruffolo, John PH00149, PH12594
Rusnak, Benjamin PH16798
Russell, Ethan PH02706, PH09269, PH10716, PH13490, PH17692
Russo, Anthony PH05540, PH07035, PH10024, PH11631, PH13585, PH13857, PH14443, PH17403, PH17466
Ruthless PH04472
Ruymen, Jim PH01763, PH15108
Ryden, Mark PH01467, PH02280, PH02926, PH02945, PH03468, PH05816, PH06423, PH06877, PH07844, PH09343, PH09623, PH09848, PH10107, PH10549, PH11483, PH11567, PH12316, PH12586, PH12780, PH12824, PH13142, PH13623, PH14075, PH15047, PH18223
Rystedt, Rex PH06454, PH08797, PH09780, PH11844

S

Sadowski, Wiktor PH05367, PH14795, PH15737
Saleito, Max PH11610
Salgado, Sebastiao PH00732, PH01237, PH01441, PH01555, PH02161, PH03651, PH04216, PH04720, PH04721, PH04722, PH06465, PH07436, PH07653, PH07681, PH07689, PH07769, PH08407, PH08507, PH08911, PH09919, PH10989, PH13060, PH13462, PH14052, PH14053, PH14223, PH15307, PH16525, PH17964, PH18225
Salicki PH07807, PH07832
Salisbury, Mike PH03241
Sallow, Jacki PH11819, PH13651
Salvadori, Honey PH05195
Salvatori, Lou PH03680, PH06849, PH07287
Samuel, Deborah PH06285, PH08667, PH12268, PH12383
Sanchez, Albert PH17122
Sanchez, Bobby PH04338, PH11314
Sanders, David PH01917
Sanders, Peter PH16344
Sanders, Timothy Greenfield PH02110, PH08489
Sandler, Harry PH15321
Sands, Steve PH02197, PH07851, PH09808, PH09898, PH10873, PH12186, PH14293, PH16561
Saunders, Red PH06268, PH13702
Savage, Steve PH10631, PH14643
Savignano, Anthony PH09887, PH12171
Saville, Peter PH11355
Scavullo, Francesco PH13926, PH16033, PH16034, PH16035, PH16037
Schacher, Stephen PH01466
Schafer, F. Scott PH02207, PH02329, PH04251
Schatzberg, Jerrold PH18238
Scheid, Jeff PH00741
Scheinmann, David PH02556
Scheler, Max PH00977, PH08744, PH09276, PH15560
Scheltema, Sandy PH09673
Schenkel, Cal PH18239
Schienmann, David PH05646
Schiffman, Bonnie PH02278, PH02339, PH02340, PH02341, PH02342, PH02350, PH03641, PH06626, PH07882, PH09413, PH09709, PH11162, PH11163, PH11164, PH11165, PH11170, PH13545, PH14435, PH15368, PH16232, PH17453, PH17454, PH17455, PH17779, PH17868
Schoerner, N. PH16789
Schultz, J. PH12862
Schultz, Nina PH04039, PH09388
Schumaker, Ward PH01058, PH04103, PH06878
Schwab, Bill PH01789, PH03545, PH04371, PH04535, PH08397, PH13062, PH13307, PH13672, PH15001, PH15022, PH15407
Schwartz, Daniel PH16126
Schwartz, Michael PH00553, PH17830
Schwartz, Michelle PH13675
Schwartz, Murray PH00750
Schwartz, Sara PH06643
Schwartzwald, Lawrence PH06891, PH07873, PH11975
Scott, Paul X. PH14183
Sebring, Steven PH10196, PH10197, PH13599, PH14201
Sednaoui, Stephane PH06489, PH14367
Seeff, Norman PH00099, PH00460, PH00823, PH02233, PH02520, PH03124, PH08180, PH08490, PH10651, PH10701, PH10708, PH14292, PH14415, PH14745, PH14747, PH14748, PH15040, PH15389, PH16648, PH16889, PH17659, PH17867, PH18256
Seibold, Jotto PH11132
Seidemann, Bob PH01350
Seidman, Amy PH09306
Seidmann, Bob PH08379
Seireeni, Richard PH16874
Seliger, Mark PH00004, PH00005, PH00006, PH00007, PH00067, PH00068, PH00104, PH00183, PH00184, PH00185, PH00186, PH00189, PH00206, PH00218, PH00221, PH00222, PH00258, PH00288, PH00289, PH00290, PH00293, PH00376, PH00405b, PH00417, PH00418, PH00420, PH00421, PH00479, PH00491, PH00494, PH00564, PH00576, PH00577, PH00579, PH00645, PH00647, PH00774, PH00813, PH00814, PH00815, PH00816, PH00817, PH00818, PH00819, PH00820, PH00824, PH00830, PH00844, PH00885, PH00886, PH01037, PH01040, PH01043, PH01044, PH01050, PH01054, PH01097, PH01098, PH01173, PH01192, PH01201, PH01244, PH01260, PH01261, PH01262, PH01263, PH01264, PH01280, PH01282, PH01286, PH01291, PH01347, PH01348, PH01360, PH01361, PH01365, PH01367, PH01565, PH01629, PH01630, PH01721, PH01722, PH01890, PH01906, PH01907, PH01909, PH01910, PH01925, PH02032, PH02094, PH02182, PH02183, PH02184, PH02187, PH02195, PH02220, PH02224, PH02308, PH02309, PH02318, PH02347, PH02352, PH02353, PH02376, PH02384, PH02387, PH02388, PH02389, PH02478, PH02482, PH02511, PH02576, PH02611, PH02671, PH02788, PH02848, PH02849, PH02850, PH02863, PH02864, PH02865, PH02866, PH02872, PH02874, PH02875, PH02878, PH02935, PH02948, PH02962, PH02984, PH02991, PH02995, PH02998, PH03027, PH03079, PH03121, PH03122, PH03125, PH03312, PH03313, PH03314, PH03317, PH03328, PH03343, PH03345, PH03347, PH03355, PH03357, PH03362, PH03402, PH03404, PH03429, PH03434, PH03435, PH03535, PH03536, PH03579, PH03580, PH03586, PH03663, PH03664, PH03725, PH03733, PH03777, PH03778, PH03842, PH03847, PH03851, PH03852, PH03853, PH03861, PH03864, PH03890, PH03891, PH03903,

Seliger, Mark (continued)
PH04027, PH04028, PH04037, PH04038, PH04045, PH04046, PH04047, PH04048, PH04049, PH04050, PH04075, PH04079, PH04080, PH04086, PH04087, PH04088, PH04134, PH04230, PH04233, PH04247, PH04296, PH04299, PH04310, PH04321, PH04329, PH04376, PH04377, PH04387, PH04395, PH04460, PH04461, PH04462, PH04463, PH04465, PH04467, PH04469, PH04473, PH04475, PH04572, PH04574, PH04575, PH04747, PH04827, PH04878, PH04899, PH04901, PH04902, PH04904, PH04931, PH04983, PH05061, PH05067, PH05076, PH05077, PH05078, PH05132, PH05133, PH05154, PH05270, PH05281, PH05300, PH05301, PH05303, PH05304, PH05305, PH05351, PH05352, PH05354, PH05383, PH05412, PH05520, PH05521, PH05534, PH05668, PH05707, PH05714, PH05742, PH05743, PH05749, PH05774, PH05775, PH05776, PH05777, PH05778, PH05779, PH05781, PH05782, PH05788, PH05792, PH05793, PH05826, PH05827, PH05873, PH05898, PH05977, PH05978, PH05979, PH05981, PH05982, PH06121, PH06124, PH06129, PH06152, PH06179, PH06180, PH06204, PH06207, PH06216, PH06217, PH06226, PH06257, PH06264, PH06266, PH06339, PH06341, PH06348, PH06349, PH06350, PH06380, PH06387, PH06388, PH06426, PH06431, PH06444, PH06503, PH06552, PH06591, PH06619, PH06651, PH06657, PH06782, PH06887, PH06893, PH06963, PH07096, PH07103, PH07114, PH07116, PH07117, PH07119, PH07124, PH07133, PH07136, PH07204, PH07216, PH07264, PH07266, PH07267, PH07268, PH07269, PH07270, PH07279, PH07283, PH07324, PH07345, PH07346, PH07347, PH07348, PH07349, PH07351, PH07437, PH07479, PH07533, PH07616, PH07617, PH07619, PH07620, PH07621, PH07625, PH07627, PH07628, PH07630, PH07645, PH07649, PH07695, PH07748, PH07941, PH07949, PH07950, PH08136, PH08160, PH08167, PH08168, PH08169, PH08212, PH08269, PH08270, PH08271, PH08272, PH08310, PH08317, PH08318, PH08357, PH08414, PH08436, PH08438, PH08439, PH08635, PH08692, PH08720, PH08731, PH08732, PH08741, PH08746, PH08750, PH08877, PH08878, PH08884, PH08898, PH08899, PH08950, PH08964, PH09005, PH09089, PH09104, PH09130, PH09149, PH09150, PH09195, PH09196, PH09217, PH09243, PH09244, PH09245, PH09246, PH09310, PH09352, PH09353, PH09354, PH09448, PH09510, PH09514, PH09515, PH09516, PH09599, PH09600, PH09601, PH09602, PH09612, PH09633, PH09642, PH09643, PH09644, PH09649, PH09655, PH09671, PH09674, PH09775, PH09787, PH09812, PH09813, PH09921, PH09922, PH09926, PH09936, PH09937, PH09981, PH10023, PH10094, PH10180, PH10184, PH10214, PH10224, PH10231, PH10233, PH10303, PH10304, PH10305, PH10404, PH10408, PH10411, PH10412, PH10413, PH10432, PH10473, PH10474, PH10476, PH10479, PH10498, PH10551, PH10553, PH10554, PH10556, PH10564, PH10565, PH10566, PH10617, PH10668, PH10743, PH11017, PH11038a, PH11070, PH11199, PH11203, PH11273, PH11321, PH11386, PH11443, PH11489, PH11495, PH11496, PH11503, PH11504, PH11508, PH11510, PH11547, PH11571, PH11576, PH11651, PH11652, PH11655, PH11656, PH11712, PH11716, PH11718, PH11719, PH11720, PH11779, PH11780, PH11781, PH11804, PH11860, PH11867, PH11873, PH11874, PH11880, PH11883, PH11906, PH11936, PH11949, PH11955, PH11956, PH11971, PH12024, PH12044, PH12084, PH12116, PH12117, PH12120, PH12121, PH12122, PH12173, PH12176, PH12178, PH12210, PH12245, PH12246, PH12264, PH12291, PH12294, PH12295, PH12296, PH12297, PH12298, PH12299, PH12302, PH12303, PH12305, PH12306, PH12308, PH12372, PH12450, PH12481, PH12516, PH12517, PH12572, PH12600, PH12643, PH12695, PH12709, PH12710, PH12711, PH12712, PH12723, PH12724, PH12813, PH12914, PH12915, PH12917, PH12947, PH12956, PH12964, PH13149, PH13199, PH13211, PH13214, PH13215, PH13216, PH13388, PH13389, PH13430, PH13463, PH13504, PH13511, PH13512, PH13513, PH13526, PH13539, PH13540, PH13541, PH13542, PH13548, PH13554, PH13555, PH13569, PH13570, PH13571, PH13591, PH13660, PH13676, PH13692, PH13712, PH13745, PH13802, PH13811, PH13812, PH13813, PH13814, PH13815, PH13816, PH13933, PH13937, PH13938, PH13953, PH13993, PH13994, PH13996, PH14116, PH14215, PH14216, PH14217, PH14247, PH14281, PH14282, PH14283, PH14284, PH14287, PH14288, PH14289, PH14333, PH14335, PH14370, PH14396, PH14407, PH14427, PH14428, PH14429, PH14433, PH14434, PH14436, PH14437, PH14511, PH14512, PH14575, PH14615, PH14616, PH14617, PH14620, PH14629, PH14636, PH14655, PH14670, PH14710, PH14711, PH14713, PH14777, PH14871, PH14877, PH14878, PH14924, PH14953, PH14954, PH14955, PH14959, PH14967, PH14968, PH14982, PH14992, PH15096, PH15098, PH15099, PH15100, PH15102, PH15104, PH15109, PH15110, PH15111, PH15147, PH15148, PH15190, PH15191, PH15192, PH15193, PH15194, PH15195, PH15196, PH15198, PH15229, PH15230, PH15231, PH15232, PH15238, PH15380, PH15381, PH15382, PH15383, PH15384, PH15386, PH15390, PH15507, PH15513, PH15514, PH15564, PH15565, PH15601, PH15604, PH15683, PH15684, PH15694, PH15705, PH15725, PH15727, PH15820, PH15821, PH15824, PH15940, PH15941, PH15945, PH16000, PH16063, PH16151, PH16226, PH16237, PH16268, PH16269, PH16270, PH16274, PH16326, PH16327, PH16346, PH16350, PH16354, PH16355, PH16356, PH16359, PH16372, PH16389, PH16544, PH16552, PH16553, PH16554, PH16556, PH16581, PH16639, PH16766, PH16892, PH16909, PH16910, PH16911, PH16914, PH16917, PH17057, PH17058, PH17059, PH17060, PH17064, PH17065, PH17070, PH17159, PH17172, PH17173, PH17207, PH17242, PH17245, PH17296, PH17297, PH17305, PH17317, PH17364, PH17365, PH17370, PH17432, PH17436, PH17512, PH17532, PH17570, PH17578, PH17580, PH17586, PH17588, PH17656, PH17657, PH17713, PH17714, PH17737, PH17765, PH17771, PH17780, PH17781, PH17835, PH17849, PH17927, PH17930, PH17931, PH17932, PH17965, PH17992, PH17995, PH18023, PH18034, PH18035, PH18036, PH18037, PH18041, PH18100, PH18101, PH18160, PH18186, PH18187, PH18188, PH18199, PH18205, PH18267, PH18293, PH18294
Senecal, Michel PH05848, PH09272, PH11790
Serrano, Andres PH14450
Sestini, Massimo PH02978, PH09632
Settle, Ken PH00665, PH04282, PH06587, PH07118, PH08763, PH11611, PH14738, PH16048, PH16560, PH16886, PH16903, PH17884
Sevalrud, Thom PH14343
Sferra, Rik PH00633, PH00783, PH01269, PH07069
Shacter, Susan PH00704
Shafer, F. Scott PH15113
Shames, Stephen PH13553
Shamsi-Basha, Karim PH17475
Shapiro, Stephen PH00614, PH07207, PH10884
Shark, Marko PH10872
Sharp, Ken PH00550, PH06376, PH06381, PH08347, PH10221, PH11658, PH13004, PH13005, PH14145, PH14447, PH17162, PH18104
Sharp, Martin PH03489
Sharp, Tim PH06263
Sharratt, Marc PH03495
Shaw, Eugene PH01815, PH07412, PH11673
Shaw, Gene PH01222, PH09685, PH14152, PH15395, PH16464
Shear, Jack PH05285, PH08640, PH13200, PH14916
Sheehan, Tom PH01168, PH01518, PH01927, PH03099, PH04533, PH05676, PH05971, PH07700, PH09367, PH10671, PH12808, PH13378, PH13560, PH15801, PH15804, PH15961
Sheldon, David K. PH16695
Sherman, Chloe PH16571
Sherman, Steve PH14445
Shirek, Jane PH11898
Shirk, Alison PH11979, PH14298
Shulman, Scott C. PH03781, PH06861
Shurley, Hugh PH00522, PH11036, PH12370, PH12960, PH16575
Sia, Joseph PH02742, PH09274, PH11791, PH18251
Sibert, Jody PH01252, PH02128
Sievert, Jon PH03087
Sigmon, Jim PH04605
Sigusmondi, Floris PH03516, PH16292
Silfen, Alan PH00015
Silva, Joao PH05048, PH09961
Simmons, Bob PH04894, PH16293
Simon, Martin PH00908, PH04364, PH06855
Simon, Peter PH08013
Simon, Tom PH14623
Simons, Chip PH00941, PH04219, PH07384, PH11183, PH14666, PH14667, PH18050, PH18064
Sinclair, Jodie PH01548, PH07051
Sirota, Peggy PH03700, PH04945, PH04947, PH04948, PH04949, PH07734, PH10289, PH10292, PH10864, PH14717, PH14718, PH14720, PH14724
Sirrs, Ed PH02955, PH06428, PH07491, PH09826, PH09928, PH11492, PH11573, PH11641, PH11837
Siry, Eric PH07174
Sis, Peter PH10508
Skid PH17051
Skwish, Andrew PH06592, PH09466
Slattery, Paul PH05657, PH11635
Slenzak, Ron PH01842, PH09477, PH14126, PH17637, PH17669
Slobin, Barry PH03293
Slocomb, Jeff PH08226, PH17663
Slocum, Werner PH16657

Smale, Brian PH00321, PH00322, PH00462, PH00464, PH00465, PH01102, PH01103, PH01418, PH02188, PH03875, PH06326, PH06327, PH06385, PH08120, PH08961, PH08962, PH09311, PH09312, PH09361, PH09362, PH10088, PH10274, PH10397, PH10573, PH11025, PH11084, PH11093, PH12494, PH12529, PH12893, PH14468, PH15079, PH15080, PH15199, PH15372, PH17468, PH17563, PH17640, PH17858, PH17859, PH17860, PH17941, PH17942, PH17943, PH18125
Smart, Miguel PH10570
Smeal, James PH03771, PH07506, PH09350, PH10954, PH14449, PH15717
Smiley, Jay PH09376, PH09606, PH11083, PH12216, PH16663
Smith, Bob PH06911
Smith, Brian PH01663, PH01861, PH02682, PH04652, PH06355, PH06356, PH06701, PH06702, PH07615, PH07792, PH07793, PH08426, PH08427, PH10427, PH12008, PH12393, PH12866, PH12868, PH14624, PH14625, PH16605, PH17472, PH17675, PH17676, PH17677, PH17761, PH17762, PH17837
Smith, Elwood PH02644, PH02667
Smith, F. Carter PH09727, PH09729
Smith, Gavin PH11268
Smith, Jack PH05265
Smith, Kelly PH02319, PH04166, PH06919, PH08090
Smith, Lane PH07839, PH08399
Smith, Matthew Jordan PH01696
Smith, Owen PH10575, PH13035, PH16339
Smith, Pennie PH02774, PH15835, PH16502
Smith, Robert PH05644, PH08602, PH10060
Smith, Sean PH01366, PH14533, PH16242, PH18172
Smith, Sean C. PH10400, PH13450, PH13992
Snowden, Lord PH02055
Snyder, Isabel PH16052
Soares, John PH00801
Soest, Steve PH03828
Soica, Alex PH01065, PH08308, PH12478
Solomon, Mark PH02791
Somoza, Gerardo PH02252, PH03267, PH08850, PH10972, PH14090, PH15758
Sonnemair, Jan PH09603, PH14425, PH14432
Soqui, Ted PH09941, PH10166, PH13434, PH16414
Sorbo, Robert PH11584
Sorel, Edward PH00223, PH05084, PH07523, PH11520
Souliers, Philippe PH07104, PH09517, PH14171, PH16484
Southam, Andrew PH05838, PH08155, PH12344, PH12356, PH17123
Spector, Gary PH01225, PH02108, PH11812, PH15556, PH15726
Spellan, Jim PH08299, PH15123
Spellman, John PH06366, PH10797, PH12787, PH16538, PH17807
Spencer, Robert PH04215
Spinelli, Edward PH06917, PH17072
Springsteen, Pam PH00954, PH02401, PH06007, PH07583, PH15469
St. Nicholas, Randee PH01785, PH05885, PH07788, PH08130
Stabile, K. Wiles PH05266
Staedler, Lance PH00850, PH08995, PH09003
Stahnke, Paul PH06588
Starr, Ringo PH16064
Starr, Steve PH06720
Stasys PH04754
States, Ann PH00524, PH04920, PH06929, PH06930, PH15343, PH15344, PH16099
Stauffer, Brian PH07711, PH16447
Stavato, Michael PH09795
Steadman, Ralph PH05121, PH07468, PH11518, PH11519, PH12637, PH16317, PH16318, PH16319, PH16320, PH16322, PH17205
Steele, Bill PH12206, PH12207, PH15986, PH16398, PH17373
Steinberg, James PH02453, PH05660, PH13171
Steinwehe, M. PH13997
Stephens, J. Brian PH10766
Sterkel, Mark P. PH05662
Stevens, D. PH00878, PH05231, PH07629, PH17634
Stevens, John PH07223
Stevens, Joseph PH02751
Stevenson PH14805
Stevenson, John W. PH17478, PH17479
Stewart, Chris PH04617
Stockwell, Mark PH06706, PH12699
Stoddart PH01512
Stoddart, John PH17426
Stolder, Steven PH17281
Stone, Dennis PH01476, PH04736
Stone, John PH04283, PH12064, PH16186
Stone, Les PH00476, PH12738
Stone, Pete PH01727, PH03661, PH05239, PH08550, PH12367, PH13583
Stone, T. PH17091, PH17101
Stratton, Jim PH01537a
Strauss, Jay PH03222
Streiber, Art PH05288, PH08642, PH11252, PH13203, PH14987
Strick, David PH05140
Strobel, Desmond PH05298
Strode, William PH17233
Struzan, Drew PH03278
Stubbs, Charles PH03162
Studna, Carl PH02704, PH06772, PH06773
Stump, Jeff PH16362, PH16684a
Stupakoff, Bico PH10737, PH10738, PH10740, PH10804, PH10805, PH10809
Suekwon PH03765, PH18071
Sullivan, Cleo PH10526
Sullivan, Lorinda PH06262, PH08335
Summers, Mark PH01163
Sundland, Steen PH02550, PH03574, PH03575, PH03582
Sunflower, Beth PH13797
Surowiecki, David PH12721
Sutton, Ward PH03022, PH07703
Swanson, David PH17501
Sweeny, Glynis PH07842
Swider, Frank PH04051, PH04568, PH09017, PH14297, PH17257
Synarski, Susan PH14727

T

Tackett, Michael PH16677, PH17874
Taft, Mike PH04636, PH10512
Talesnick, Barry PH01819, PH16545
Tallman, Susie PH04481, PH15699, PH18227
Tanabe, Hiroshi PH07425
Tanhauser, Gary PH00768
Tannenbaum PH04774, PH11118
Tapogna, Mary PH06721
Tarlofsky, Malcolm PH08156, PH11818, PH13595
Tavee, Tom PH00152, PH00153, PH00434, PH00710, PH00711, PH00794, PH01077, PH01333, PH01334, PH01711, PH02444, PH02811, PH03500, PH03546, PH03548, PH03636, PH04186, PH04187, PH04372, PH04973, PH04974, PH06131, PH06143, PH06412, PH06458, PH06622, PH06623, PH07085, PH07209, PH07210, PH07343, PH07344, PH08344, PH08574, PH09066, PH09067, PH10194, PH10241, PH10242, PH10490, PH10731, PH10732, PH11606, PH12083, PH12146, PH12625, PH12627, PH12629, PH12631, PH13290, PH13457, PH14665, PH15408, PH15919, PH15920, PH17020, PH17021, PH17022, PH17023, PH17025
Taylor, Chris PH00480, PH02431, PH02950, PH13495
Taylor, Michele PH16485
Taylor, Randy PH00157
Telemans, Al PH06656
Teller, Juergen PH02559
Temme, Marty PH04286, PH04732, PH08358, PH10746, PH12754, PH13097, PH16891, PH17422
Tepper, Randy PH00725, PH09037, PH14560
Teske, Edmund PH04411, PH10904
Thomas, Huw PH03295
Thomas, Justin PH01479, PH02790, PH03250, PH04738, PH08355, PH10142, PH11044, PH13957, PH14495, PH16743
Thomas, Katrin PH08077, PH12855
Thompson, D. Kent PH00261, PH02257, PH04277, PH06138, PH07483
Thompson, Jay PH09170
Thompson, Kyndell PH16799, PH16800
Thorgerson, Strom PH05625, PH09155, PH12455, PH12458, PH12460
Thurnher, Jeffrey PH01949, PH01951, PH06977, PH09638, PH10521, PH10523, PH11725, PH12510, PH12527, PH16458
Tighe, Michael PH07754
Tillery, Bob PH02918, PH08614
Tillery, Val PH02919, PH08615
Tisman, Jeff PH01359, PH09900
Titlow, David PH11907
Tobiishi, Tsukasa PH05598
Todd, Mark PH01305, PH06235, PH07002, PH07403, PH08502, PH11713, PH12930, PH16379, PH16532, PH17328
Tolbert, Mpozi PH07611, PH16829
Toliver, Chris PH02134, PH05946, PH05945, PH08769, PH10771, PH10887, PH10889, PH11057, PH11149, PH14299, PH15688, PH18018, PH18051, PH18263
Tonge, David PH03735, PH05274
Torno, Pattiy PH02580, PH03880, PH08567, PH09525, PH09528
Toy, Joann PH01657, PH02254, PH05246, PH05884, PH06365, PH08532, PH11737, PH12020, PH12045, PH16027, PH16660
Trachtenberg, Robert PH01652
Trappe, David PH01337
Trapper, Frank PH03618, PH08608, PH12499, PH14087
Treick, Tom PH06718
Treml, Alex PH06865, PH07060
Trippett, Robert PH02462a, PH02845, PH06142, PH06999, PH07698, PH09426, PH09916
Trotman, Noren PH11777
Trott, Greg PH01072
Tucker, Mark PH01795, PH04022, PH04115, PH08476, PH09942, PH10167, PH13432
Tucker, Mort PH13714, PH13716
Turk, Steve PH07153, PH12948
Turnball, Ann PH08894
Turner, Arnold PH01346
Turner, Chip PH15050
Turner, Danny PH00388, PH03947, PH07372, PH12224, PH15057
Tuttle, Jeff PH16239
Tytler, Scott PH02064

U

Uchitel, Diego PH01620, PH01621, PH05623, PH05624, PH12414, PH12417, PH12419, PH12422, PH13265, PH13267, PH13648, PH14130, PH14130a, PH14133, PH14134, PH16423, PH16424
Ulriksen, Mark PH00726, PH04085, PH04235, PH06555, PH06559, PH10764, PH12283, PH12624, PH13667, PH15293, PH16841, PH17495, PH18140
Umland, Steve PH10056, PH10057
Unruh, Jack PH04667, PH16779
Usa, Rex PH02554, PH02685, PH02700

V

Vaccaro, Nick PH02249, PH11872, PH12190, PH14015
Vadukel, Max PH12347
Vadukul, Nitin PH00204, PH00502, PH02079, PH02080, PH02081, PH03026, PH03962, PH04430, PH04833, PH05514, PH05522, PH05616, PH06175, PH06924, PH06925, PH10838, PH13088, PH13256, PH14336, PH14726, PH15210, PH15595, PH17215, PH17216, PH17507, PH17508, PH18279
Vallbona, Nuri PH02058
Van Ess, Mark PH03372
Van Hamersveld, John PH13783
Van Hamerweld, John PH10650
Van Houten, Laurens PH12690, PH12691
Van Iperen, Neils PH00800, PH05120, PH09716, PH10152, PH10868, PH14405
Van Overbeek, Will PH02077, PH02078, PH03024, PH03025, PH06920, PH06922, PH09120, PH09121
Van Vliet, Don PH02235
Van Wey, Charles PH00697, PH11582, PH17078
Vargas, Alberto PH02312
Vartoogian, Jack PH01954, PH02092, PH02141, PH05113, PH16340
Vazquez, William PH12145
Vella, John PH10615
Vellekoop, Maurice PH02662
Ventura, Andrea PH00970, PH11912
Verene, Chris PH07249
Veronsky, Frank PH05117
Veysset, Frederique PH16024, PH16045
Veyssey, Frederique PH06710, PH06711, PH14650, PH14651
Vial, Veronique PH11271
Victor, Pascal PH00397
Villand, Kiino PH01133, PH16455
Vinomen, Ilkka PH10885
Virobik-Adams, Kevin PH00181, PH03344, PH14122, PH16607, PH17308
Vogt, Andy PH04379
Von Buhler, Cynthia PH05902
Von Jansky, Ladi PH05421, PH09662
Von Unwerth, Ellen PH01162, PH02564, PH02565, PH02571, PH02572, PH07105, PH07805, PH07824, PH09153

W

Wagg, Peter PH06787
Wakefield, Michael PH07234
Walgren, Judy PH12389, PH12390, PH12391, PH18115
Walker, Diana PH00906, PH08171, PH08172, PH08173
Wallace, Merie W. PH02020, PH05506, PH14187
Wallis, Robert PH15287
Walsh, Nick PH04035
Walter, Chris PH10048, PH11981
Walz, Barbara PH13619, PH13630, PH13640
Warburg, Jennifer PH04753, PH09781, PH09797, PH10542, PH13291
Warburg, Jenny PH15597, PH17110
Warhol, Andy PH13787, PH15064, PH17137
Wart PH10610
Watermann, Greg PH01138, PH02075, PH02952, PH03023, PH06427, PH06833, PH06915, PH06961, PH08927, PH09118, PH11491, PH11572, PH12475, PH12990, PH12991, PH13429, PH17299
Watson, Albert PH00271, PH01185, PH01247, PH01623, PH01634, PH01821, PH02018, PH02746, PH02747, PH02748, PH02749, PH02753, PH02757, PH03264, PH03266, PH03476, PH03530, PH03623, PH03624, PH03625, PH03893, PH04120, PH04250, PH04327, PH05653, PH06090, PH06091, PH06195, PH06342, PH06360, PH06571, PH07418, PH07419, PH07420, PH07976, PH08681, PH08793, PH09348, PH09356, PH09381, PH09384, PH09769, PH10268, PH11272, PH11686, PH11687, PH11689, PH11928, PH12237, PH12592, PH12857, PH13248, PH13288, PH13329, PH13367, PH13384, PH13386, PH13528, PH13615, PH13741, PH13743, PH13744, PH13852, PH13925, PH14799, PH15767, PH15818, PH15874, PH15875, PH15876, PH16649, PH16685, PH16686, PH16710, PH16712, PH17346, PH17352, PH17353, PH17354, PH17875, PH18039, PH18185
Watson, Esther PH02940, PH08554, PH14238
Watson, Norman PH06174, PH10839, PH13084, PH14608, PH15172, PH16927
Watson, Paul PH15141
Watts, Mychal PH02895, PH03089
Wayland, Pat PH07176
Weber, Bruce PH00708, PH02516, PH02522, PH03037, PH05009, PH06794, PH08343, PH11688, PH13057, PH13661, PH14285
Weber, Uli PH01633
Weiner, Alan S. PH17474
Weiner, Bob PH10027, PH17267
Weiner, S. PH17920
Weiner, Scott PH00681, PH02433, PH05196, PH05273, PH05293, PH05808, PH06826, PH08301, PH08648, PH08937, PH12545, PH13049, PH13210, PH15054, PH15317, PH18068
Weir, Wendy PH11986
Weiss, Mark PH15649
Welch, Matthew PH07062
Weller, Bonnie PH04083
Wells, Tony PH06486
Welt, Susan PH03932
Wentzell, Barrie PH02717
Wentzell, Barry PH08249
Werner, John PH06812
Werner, Paul PH13629
Wertheimer, Alfred PH12003, PH12773, PH12775, PH12776
Wescott, Stacey PH01159, PH06733, PH09083
Wessel, Cathrine PH00052, PH01363, PH01428, PH03973, PH04097, PH04098, PH04099, PH04100, PH04101, PH04102, PH04140, PH04270, PH04699, PH06270, PH06637, PH06946, PH06947, PH06948, PH06949, PH10125, PH10126, PH10127, PH10128, PH10129, PH10130, PH10453, PH11074, PH11075, PH11076, PH15532, PH15567, PH15721, PH15751
West, Kirk PH00247, PH00252, PH01199
Westenberg, Kevin PH00164, PH00166, PH00170, PH00176, PH00584, PH00739, PH00740, PH00788, PH01106, PH01188, PH01302, PH01403, PH01405, PH01407, PH01762, PH01765, PH01826, PH02029, PH02180, PH02185, PH02416, PH03118, PH03289, PH03338, PH03351, PH03381, PH03437, PH03438, PH03440, PH04064, PH04065, PH04784, PH04968, PH05203, PH05205, PH05536, PH05555, PH06116, PH06150, PH06589, PH06797, PH06837, PH07084, PH07997, PH07999, PH08275, PH09370, PH10280, PH10776, PH11661, PH11692, PH11886, PH12022, PH12755a, PH12756, PH12944, PH12953, PH13440, PH13929, PH13961, PH13965, PH13973, PH14073, PH14614, PH14618, PH14896a, PH15225, PH15235, PH15547, PH15708, PH16264, PH16272, PH16303, PH16305, PH16427, PH17583, PH18265
Westenberger PH06036
Westheimer, Bill PH02449
Wexler, Lane PH02099
Wheat, Jody PH06692
Wheeler, Alice PH02493, PH02969, PH04978, PH05835, PH09571, PH09572, PH11499, PH11579
Whitaker, Bob PH03490
Whitall, Bob PH08698, PH14865
Whitall, Robert PH05416
Whitall, Robert, Jr. PH11608, PH11609
White, Brian Ashley PH02192
White, E. Lee PH03385, PH03905
White, Frank PH04532, PH07316, PH14862
White, James PH05159
White, Steven PH05126, PH06154, PH06867, PH09564, PH12047, PH15576, PH16307, PH16439, PH17399
White, Timothy PH03503, PH08200
Whiteside, George PH09188
Whitt, Christina PH11421, PH14319
Whorf, Christopher PH06910
Widmer, Rick PH16797
Willett, Robert PH12867, PH16418
Williams, David PH13662
Williams, Jo PH18013
Williamson, Tucker PH05658, PH08152
Wilson, James D. PH14642
Wilson, Michael PH16343
Wiltshire, Graham PH01636, PH02718
Winter, Dan PH04173, PH07777, PH17673, PH18207, PH18283
Winter, Ken PH10260
Winter, Kevin PH01160, PH04443, PH05064
Winters Dan
Winters, Dan PH00019, PH00076, PH00077, PH00151, PH00201, PH00304, PH00305, PH00306, PH00307, PH00308, PH00309, PH00426, PH00486, PH00487, PH01025, PH01249, PH02123, PH02216, PH02607, PH02996, PH03220, PH03224, PH03689, PH03812, PH04281, PH04297, PH05184, PH05228, PH05263, PH05381, PH05382, PH05464, PH05465, PH06344, PH06345, PH06353, PH06519, PH06737, PH06973, PH07082, PH07184, PH07297, PH08014, PH08015, PH08738, PH08980, PH08981, PH09427, PH09738, PH10075, PH10158, PH10222, PH10630, PH10841, PH10844, PH11020, PH11226, PH11227, PH11392, PH11983, PH12063, PH12266, PH12744, PH13431, PH14364, PH14397, PH14398, PH14543, PH14644, PH14646, PH14647, PH14850, PH15039, PH15498, PH15557, PH15579, PH16093, PH16120, PH16526, PH16555, PH16596, PH16643, PH17230, PH17892, PH18053
Wise, Alexandra PH03731
Witkin, Christian PH00512, PH05101, PH06761, PH07191, PH08775, PH08798, PH09391, PH10172, PH10714, PH11885, PH12213, PH12375, PH13473, PH15973,

PH16755
Witte, Michael PH00022, PH00234, PH02460, PH02627, PH02840, PH02841, PH02842, PH02843, PH03606, PH04126, PH04127, PH04354, PH04355, PH04677, PH04717, PH04868, PH05468, PH06027, PH06028, PH06029, PH06030, PH06371, PH06372, PH06373, PH06386, PH06386a, PH07170, PH08447, PH09579, PH09617, PH10321, PH11223, PH11707, PH11853, PH11854, PH12041, PH12314, PH12736, PH13408, PH13409, PH13412, PH13413, PH13861, PH14225, PH14321, PH15518, PH17227, PH17936
Wojahn, Brent PH04704, PH06722
Wolfe, Eddie PH07815, PH17652
Wolfe, Jerry PH03816, PH06868
Wolfe, Tom PH00743, PH11229, PH14418
Wolff, Jeremy PH15799
Wolff, Richard PH09289
Wolff, Tom PH00746, PH03446, PH07138, PH07459, PH09690, PH09719, PH09720, PH11334, PH11748, PH12689
Wolfson, Ron PH01786, PH08011
Wolfson, Todd V. PH01974, PH04918
Wollenberger, Thomas PH17279
Wolman, Baron PH02820, PH03251, PH03499, PH05353, PH05355, PH05752, PH05760, PH05787, PH06299, PH06312, PH06315, PH07934, PH08382, PH08868, PH09138, PH09139, PH09326, PH09328, PH10379, PH10382, PH13564, PH13565, PH14378, PH14379, PH16500, PH17531, PH17534
Wonderland, Alison PH00599, PH03363, PH06620, PH14114, PH14741, PH14792
Wong, Michael PH15993
Woo, David PH06518
Wood, Graham PH02148, PH10916, PH13289, PH16626, PH17149
Woodard, Fred PH06473, PH06474, PH06475, PH06487, PH06874, PH14500
Woode, Theodore PH04162, PH09793
Woodruff, Thomas PH02812, PH05122, PH10901, PH13264, PH17141
Woodward, Fred PH01682, PH04343, PH06409, PH09099, PH09100, PH09101, PH09102, PH14499, PH14501, PH14502, PH14571, PH14573
Woolley, Janet PH05722, PH11441, PH11486, PH12416, PH13964, PH14074, PH14699, PH15021
Worthington, Herbert PH05299
Wright, Tom PH04987
Wright, Tony PH16516, PH17870
Wuerthner, George PH01656, PH10143, PH18005
Wyman, Ira PH01335, PH04353, PH04357, PH08568, PH11177
Wyman, Jay PH06790
Wyner, Isaiah PH11824

Y

Yaccarino, Dan PH02666, PH03150
Yemchuk, Yelena PH01087, PH01726, PH05330, PH09911, PH12086, PH16572
Yoder, Dave PH05237
Young, Dale PH02276
Young, P. PH08657, PH12167
Young, Richard PH02435, PH02723, PH03017, PH06479, PH06617, PH06775, PH06835, PH06843, PH07974, PH09291, PH15559
Young, Russell PH03445, PH03450, PH05040, PH07137, PH09718
Yurkovic, Gerhard PH00526

Z

Zachmann, Patrick PH00130, PH00131, PH00132, PH00133, PH00134, PH00135, PH00136, PH00137, PH00138, PH00139, PH00140, PH00141, PH00142, PH12878, PH12879, PH12880, PH12881, PH12882, PH12883, PH12884, PH12885, PH12886, PH12887, PH12888, PH12889, PH12890, PH16243, PH16244, PH16245, PH16246, PH16247, PH16248, PH16249, PH16250, PH16251, PH16252, PH16253, PH16254, PH16255
Zagaris, Michael PH03768, PH06251, PH10781, PH16494, PH17695
Zander, Peter PH01256, PH07909, PH10843, PH11192, PH15710, PH16481, PH16482
Zielenbach, Tim PH01028
Zimmerman, Dick PH07865, PH07891, PH12781, PH12785
Zlozower, Neil PH00674, PH01139, PH06236, PH06543, PH07126
Zuffante, Vinnie PH00012, PH01039, PH01456, PH02725, PH02728, PH04056, PH04816, PH07810, PH08852, PH12172, PH18015

Poetry

B

BEATTY, PAUL

PR00867 "No Tag Backs [excerpt]." 662 (August 5, 1993) p20.

Only one poem was published in *Rolling Stone* during the time period covered by this volume. For an alphabetical listing of poets and their works published in *RS* prior to this volume, see the Poetry sections in ***The Rolling Stone Index: Twenty-Five Years of Popular Culture, 1967-1991***.

RANDOM NOTES

A

ABBOTT AND COSTELLO
RN36916 659 (June 24, 1993) pp13,15.
RN36917 704 (March 23, 1995) pp24-25.
ABBRUZZESE, DAVE
RN36918 634-635 (July 9, 1992) pp11,13.
RN36919 703 (March 9, 1995) pp20-21.
ABDUL, PAULA
RN36920 622 (January 23, 1992) pp6-7.
RN36921 627 (April 2, 1992) pp11,13.
RN36922 703 (March 9, 1995) pp20-21.
RN36923 730 (March 21, 1996) pp17-18.
ABU-JAMAL, MUMIA
RN36924 718 (October 5, 1995) pp20-21.
ABZUG, BELLA
RN36925 745 (October 17, 1996) pp27-28.
AC-DC
RN36926 640 (October 1, 1992) pp9-10.
RN36927 649 (February 4, 1993) pp8-9.
RN36928 659 (June 24, 1993) pp13,15.
RN36929 743 (September 19, 1996) pp19-20.
ACE OF BASE
RN36930 700 (January 26, 1995) pp16-17.
ACKERMAN, MICHAEL
RN36931 712-713 (July 13, 1995) pp25-26.
AD-ROCK
RN36932 726 (January 25, 1996) pp17-18.
ADAMS, BRYAN
RN36933 616 (October 31, 1991) pp11,13.
RN36934 640 (October 1, 1992) pp9-10.
RN36935 642 (October 29, 1992) pp19,21.
RN36936 654 (April 15, 1993) pp11,13.
RN36937 693 (October 20, 1994) pp27-28,30.
RN36938 694 (November 3, 1994) pp17-18,22.
RN36939 696 (December 1, 1994) pp23-25.
RN36940 736 (June 13, 1996) pp19-20.
ADKINS, MARK
RN36941 711 (June 29, 1995) pp12-13.
RN36942 715 (August 24, 1995) pp23,25.
ADLER, LARRY
RN36943 682 (May 19, 1994) pp37-38.
AEROSMITH
RN36944 615 (October 17, 1991) pp13-14.
RN36945 622 (January 23, 1992) pp6-7.
RN36946 623 (February 6, 1992) pp11,13.
RN36947 626 (March 19, 1992) pp11,13.
RN36948 627 (April 2, 1992) pp11,13.
RN36949 634-635 (July 9, 1992) pp11,13.
RN36950 657 (May 27, 1993) pp9,11.
RN36951 659 (June 24, 1993) pp13,15.
RN36952 664 (September 2, 1993) pp31-32.
RN36953 667 (October 14, 1993) pp39-40.
RN36954 668 (October 28, 1993) pp35-36.
RN36955 679 (April 7, 1994) pp37-39.
RN36956 680 (April 21, 1994) pp33-34.
RN36957 683 (June 2, 1994) pp27-28.
RN36958 684 (June 16, 1994) pp35-36.
RN36959 688 (August 11, 1994) pp17-18,20.
RN36960 693 (October 20, 1994) pp27-28,30.
RN36961 701 (February 9, 1995) pp16-17.
RN36962 708 (May 18, 1995) pp17-18.
RN36963 722 (November 30, 1995) pp19-20.
RN36964 745 (October 17, 1996) pp27-28.
AFGHAN WHIGS
RN36965 674 (January 27, 1994) pp28-29.
RN36966 676 (February 24, 1994) pp28-29.
RN36967 685 (June 30, 1994) pp40-41.
RN36968 691 (September 22, 1994) pp19-21.
RN36969 708 (May 18, 1995) pp17-18.
RN36970 730 (March 21, 1996) pp17-18.
RN36971 740 (August 8, 1996) pp17-18.
AFRIKA BAMBAATAA
RN36972 670 (November 25, 1993) pp37-38.
AGASSI, ANDRE
RN36973 721 (November 16, 1995) pp25-26.
RN36974 730 (March 21, 1996) pp17-18.
AGNEW, VALERIE
RN36975 722 (November 30, 1995) pp19-20.
AGUILAR, SLICK
RN36976 644 (November 26, 1992) pp13,15.
AKRE, CARRIE
RN36977 666 (September 30, 1993) pp27-28.
ALABAMA
RN36978 727 (February 8, 1996) pp12-13.
ALBARN, DAMON
RN36979 737 (June 27, 1996) pp15-16.
ALBINI, STEVE
RN36980 743 (September 19, 1996) pp19-20.
ALEXAKIS, ANNABELLA
RN36981 740 (August 8, 1996) pp17-18.
ALEXAKIS, ART
RN36982 709 (June 1, 1995) pp16-17.
RN36983 726 (January 25, 1996) pp17-18.
RN36984 740 (August 8, 1996) pp17-18.
RN36985 742 (September 5, 1996) pp20-21.
ALEXANDER, ARTHUR
RN36986 689 (August 25, 1994) pp15-16.
ALEXANDER, WILLIE
RN36987 736 (June 13, 1996) pp19-20.
ALI
RN36988 669 (November 11, 1993) pp27-28.
ALI, MUHAMMAD
RN36989 712-713 (July 13, 1995) pp25-26.
ALICE IN CHAINS
RN36990 618 (November 28, 1991) pp11-12.
RN36991 624 (February 20, 1992) pp11-12.
RN36992 660-661 (July 8, 1993) pp32-33.
RN36993 676 (February 24, 1994) pp28-29.
RN36994 697 (December 15, 1994) pp17-18,20.
RN36995 711 (June 29, 1995) pp12-13.
RN36996 723 (December 14, 1995) pp27-28.
RN36997 729 (March 7, 1996) pp9-10.
RN36998 732 (April 18, 1996) pp19-20.
ALL-STAR GARAGE BAND
RN36999 748 (November 28, 1996) pp25-26.
ALLEN, PAUL
RN37000 738-739 (July 11, 1996) pp15-16.
ALLEY, KIRSTIE
RN37001 688 (August 11, 1994) pp17-18,20.
ALLMAN BROTHERS
RN37002 617 (November 14, 1991) pp11,13.
RN37003 621 (January 9, 1992) pp10-11.
RN37004 624 (February 20, 1992) pp11-12.
RN37005 658 (June 10, 1993) pp16-17.
RN37006 681 (May 5, 1994) pp21-22.
RN37007 686-687 (July 14, 1994) pp41-42.
RN37008 690 (September 8, 1994) pp21,24.
RN37009 729 (March 7, 1996) pp9-10.
RN37010 731 (April 4, 1996) pp17-18.
RN37011 746 (October 31, 1996) pp17-18.
ALLMAN, GREGG
RN37012 617 (November 14, 1991) pp11,13.
RN37013 623 (February 6, 1992) pp11,13.
RN37014 624 (February 20, 1992) pp11-12.
RN37015 746 (October 31, 1996) pp17-18.
ALTMAN, ROBERT
RN37016 648 (January 21, 1993) pp9,11.
AMBER
RN37017 736 (June 13, 1996) pp19-20.
AMENT, JEFF
RN37018 634-635 (July 9, 1992) pp11,13.
RN37019 659 (June 24, 1993) pp13,15.
RN37020 665 (September 16, 1993) pp31-32.
RN37021 681 (May 5, 1994) pp21-22.
RN37022 696 (December 1, 1994) pp23-25.
RN37023 726 (January 25, 1996) pp17-18.
AMERICAN MUSIC CLUB
RN37024 659 (June 24, 1993) pp13,15.
RN37025 670 (November 25, 1993) pp37-38.
RN37026 684 (June 16, 1994) pp35-36.
AMOS, TORI
RN37027 691 (September 22, 1994) pp19-21.
RN37028 701 (February 9, 1995) pp16-

17.
RN37029 737 (June 27, 1996) pp15-16.
ANDERSON, AL
RN37030 680 (April 21, 1994) pp33-34.
ANDERSON, JON
RN37031 685 (June 30, 1994) pp40-41.
ANDERSON, LAURIE
RN37032 719 (October 19, 1995) pp15-16.
RN37033 729 (March 7, 1996) pp9-10.
RN37034 735 (May 30, 1996) pp12-13.
ANDERSON, PAMELA
RN37035 703 (March 9, 1995) pp20-21.
RN37036 705 (April 6, 1995) pp16-17.
RN37037 706 (April 20, 1995) pp15-17.
RN37038 708 (May 18, 1995) pp17-18.
ANGELOU, MAYA
RN37039 717 (September 21, 1995) pp19-20.
ANIMALS
RN37040 691 (September 22, 1994) pp19-21.
ANKA, PAUL
RN37041 621 (January 9, 1992) pp10-11.
ANN-MARGRET
RN37042 631 (May 28, 1992) pp9,11.
ANSANI, TED
RN37043 712-713 (July 13, 1995) pp25-26.
ANT, ADAM
RN37044 702 (February 23, 1995) pp19-20.
ANTHRAX
RN37045 628 (April 16, 1992) pp11,13.
RN37046 637 (August 20, 1992) pp9,11.
RN37047 665 (September 16, 1993) pp31-32.
RN37048 681 (May 5, 1994) pp21-22.
RN37049 692 (October 6, 1994) pp15-17.
APHEX TWIN
RN37050 701 (February 9, 1995) pp16-17.
AQUANETTAS
RN37051 668 (October 28, 1993) pp35-36.
AQUIAR, MARIA
RN37052 640 (October 1, 1992) pp9-10.
ARAFAT, YASSER
RN37053 703 (March 9, 1995) pp20-21.
ARAYA, TOM
RN37053 703 (March 9, 1995) pp20-21.
ARCHERS OF LOAF
RN37054 700 (January 26, 1995) pp16-17.
ARM, MARK
RN37055 655 (April 29, 1993) pp11-12.
RN37056 668 (October 28, 1993) pp35-36.
RN37057 670 (November 25, 1993) pp37-38.
RN37058 679 (April 7, 1994) pp37-39.
RN37059 683 (June 2, 1994) pp27-28.
ARMANI
RN37060 746 (October 31, 1996) pp17-18.
ARMORED SAINT
RN37061 618 (November 28, 1991) pp11-12.
RN37062 637 (August 20, 1992) pp9,11.
ARMSTRONG, TIM
RN37063 712-713 (July 13, 1995) pp25-26.
RN37064 718 (October 5, 1995) pp20-21.
RN37065 727 (February 8, 1996) pp12-13.
RN37066 735 (May 30, 1996) pp12-13.
ARNOLD, TOM
RN37067 678 (March 24, 1994) pp27-28.
RN37068 693 (October 20, 1994) pp27-28,30.
ARQUETTE, PATRICIA
RN37069 708 (May 18, 1995) pp17-18.
ARQUETTE, ROSANNA
RN37070 733 (May 2, 1996) pp13-14.
ARRESTED DEVELOPMENT
RN37071 648 (January 21, 1993) pp9,11.
RN37072 654 (April 15, 1993) pp11,13.
RN37073 660-661 (July 8, 1993) pp32-33.
RN37074 688 (August 11, 1994) pp17-18,20.
RN37075 690 (September 8, 1994) pp21,24.
RN37076 697 (December 15, 1994) pp17-18,20.
ARTIS THE SPOONMAN
RN37077 681 (May 5, 1994) pp21-22.
RN37078 700 (January 26, 1995) pp16-17.
ASH
RN37079 742 (September 5, 1996) pp20-21.
ASTBURY, IAN
RN37080 628 (April 16, 1992) pp11,13.
ATCHA
RN37081 731 (April 4, 1996) pp17-18.
ATKINS, CHET
RN37082 631 (May 28, 1992) pp9,11.
ATKINS, JAMES
RN37083 636 (August 6, 1992) pp11,13.
ATTRACTIONS
RN37084 675 (February 10, 1994) pp22-23.
AUER, JON
RN37085 658 (June 10, 1993) pp16-17.
AUGUSTE, ROSE-ANNE
RN37086 701 (February 9, 1995) pp16-17.
AUSTIN, DALLAS
RN37087 735 (May 30, 1996) pp12-13.
AVERRE, BURTON
RN37088 617 (November 14, 1991) pp11,13.
AVERY, ERIC
RN37089 653 (April 1, 1993) pp11,13.
AVERY, TEX
RN37090 719 (October 19, 1995) pp15-16.
AYKROYD, DAN
RN37091 696 (December 1, 1994) pp23-25.

B

B-52S
RN37092 630 (May 14, 1992) pp13,15.
RN37093 637 (August 20, 1992) pp9,11.
RN37094 669 (November 11, 1993) pp27-28.
RN37095 678 (March 24, 1994) pp27-28.
RN37096 683 (June 2, 1994) pp27-28.
B-REAL
RN37097 671 (December 9, 1993) pp31-32.
RN37098 718 (October 5, 1995) pp20-21.
RN37099 729 (March 7, 1996) pp9-10.
BABYFACE
RN37100 704 (March 23, 1995) pp24-25.
RN37101 738-739 (July 11, 1996) pp15-16.
BACH, JOHANN SEBASTIAN
RN37102 722 (November 30, 1995) pp19-20.
BACH, SEBASTIAN
RN37103 640 (October 1, 1992) pp9-10.
BACHARACH, BURT
RN37104 716 (September 7, 1995) pp13-14.
BAD BRAINS
RN37105 704 (March 23, 1995) pp24-25.
RN37106 706 (April 20, 1995) pp15-17.
BAD RELIGION
RN37107 700 (January 26, 1995) pp16-17.
RN37108 711 (June 29, 1995) pp12-13.
RN37109 722 (November 30, 1995) pp19-20.
RN37110 731 (April 4, 1996) pp17-18.
BAD SEEDS
RN37111 692 (October 6, 1994) pp15-17.
BAEZ, JOAN
RN37112 648 (January 21, 1993) pp9,11.
RN37113 649 (February 4, 1993) pp8-9.
RN37114 737 (June 27, 1996) pp15-16.
RN37115 742 (September 5, 1996) pp20-21.
BAILEY, EARNIE
RN37116 692 (October 6, 1994) pp15-17.
BAIO, SCOTT
RN37117 697 (December 15, 1994) pp17-18,20.
BAIRD, DAN
RN37118 650 (February 18, 1993) pp11,13.
BAKER
RN37119 711 (June 29, 1995) pp12-13.
BAKER, BRIAN
RN37120 700 (January 26, 1995) pp16-17.
RN37121 722 (November 30, 1995) pp19-20.
BALDWIN, STEPHEN
RN37122 730 (March 21, 1996) pp17-18.
BALIN, MARTY
RN37123 644 (November 26, 1992) pp13,15.
BAMONTE, PERRY
RN37124 631 (May 28, 1992) pp9,11.
RN37125 633 (June 25, 1992) pp11-12.
BAND
RN37126 669 (November 11, 1993) pp27-28.
RN37127 697 (December 15, 1994) pp17-18,20.
RN37128 710 (June 15, 1995) pp17-18.
RN37129 742 (September 5, 1996) pp20-21.
BANGLES
RN37130 668 (October 28, 1993) pp35-36.
BARASCH, MATT
RN37131 727 (February 8, 1996) pp12-13.
BARBE, DAVID
RN37132 637 (August 20, 1992) pp9,11.
RN37133 701 (February 9, 1995) pp16-17.
BARENAKED LADIES
RN37134 662 (August 5, 1993) pp33-34.
RN37135 668 (October 28, 1993) pp35-36.
BARLOW, LOU
RN37136 700 (January 26, 1995) pp16-17.
RN37137 706 (April 20, 1995) pp15-17.
BARNETT, RONNIE
RN37138 735 (May 30, 1996) pp12-13.
BARNEY
RN37139 676 (February 24, 1994) pp28-29.
BARRETT, SYD
RN37140 689 (August 25, 1994) pp15-16.

BARRY, DAVE
RN37141 634-635 (July 9, 1992) pp11,13.
BARRYMORE, DREW
RN37142 616 (October 31, 1991) pp11,13.
RN37143 681 (May 5, 1994) pp21-22.
RN37144 690 (September 8, 1994) pp21,24.
RN37145 694 (November 3, 1994) pp17-18,22.
RN37146 709 (June 1, 1995) pp16-17.
RN37147 734 (May 16, 1996) pp17-18.
BARTELL, BILL
RN37148 735 (May 30, 1996) pp12-13.
BASH AND POP
RN37149 649 (February 4, 1993) pp8-9.
BASINGER, KIM
RN37150 630 (May 14, 1992) pp13,15.
BASQUIAT, JEAN-MICHEL
RN37151 714 (August 10, 1995) pp15-17.
BASSETT, ANGELA
RN37152 660-661 (July 8, 1993) pp32-33.
BAXTER, JEFF
RN37153 652 (March 18, 1993) pp13,15.
RN37154 733 (May 2, 1996) pp13-14.
BEACH BOYS
RN37155 617 (November 14, 1991) pp11,13.
RN37156 652 (March 18, 1993) pp13,15.
RN37157 704 (March 23, 1995) pp24-25.
BEAR, BOOGA
RN37158 642 (October 29, 1992) pp19,21.
BEARD, FRANK
RN37159 631 (May 28, 1992) pp9,11.
BEASTIE BOYS
RN37159 631 (May 28, 1992) pp9,11.
RN37160 660-661 (July 8, 1993) pp32-33.
RN37161 676 (February 24, 1994) pp28-29.
RN37162 681 (May 5, 1994) pp21-22.
RN37163 684 (June 16, 1994) pp35-36.
RN37164 692 (October 6, 1994) pp15-17.
RN37165 693 (October 20, 1994) pp27-28,30.
RN37166 700 (January 26, 1995) pp16-17.
RN37167 710 (June 15, 1995) pp17-18.
RN37168 711 (June 29, 1995) pp12-13.
RN37169 720 (November 2, 1995) pp16-17.
RN37170 726 (January 25, 1996) pp17-18.
RN37171 736 (June 13, 1996) pp19-20.
RN37172 742 (September 5, 1996) pp20-21.
BEATLES
RN37173 630 (May 14, 1992) pp13,15.
RN37174 631 (May 28, 1992) pp9,11.
RN37175 633 (June 25, 1992) pp11-12.
RN37176 648 (January 21, 1993) pp9,11.
RN37177 649 (February 4, 1993) pp8-9.
RN37178 653 (April 1, 1993) pp11,13.
RN37179 668 (October 28, 1993) pp35-36.
RN37180 676 (February 24, 1994) pp28-29.
RN37181 717 (September 21, 1995) pp19-20.
RN37182 721 (November 16, 1995) pp25-26.
RN37183 749 (December 12, 1996) pp19-20.
BEAUSOLEIL
RN37184 658 (June 10, 1993) pp16-17.
BECK
RN37185 674 (January 27, 1994) pp28-29.
RN37186 702 (February 23, 1995) pp19-20.
RN37187 714 (August 10, 1995) pp15-17.
RN37188 723 (December 14, 1995) pp27-28.
RN37189 730 (March 21, 1996) pp17-18.
RN37190 738-739 (July 11, 1996) pp15-16.
RN37191 743 (September 19, 1996) pp19-20.
RN37192 745 (October 17, 1996) pp27-28.
BECK, JEFF
RN37193 625 (March 5, 1992) pp11,13-15,17+.
RN37194 636 (August 6, 1992) pp11,13.
BECKER, WALTER
RN37195 637 (August 20, 1992) pp9,11.
RN37196 664 (September 2, 1993) pp31-32.
BEE GEES
RN37197 662 (August 5, 1993) pp33-34.
BEERS, GARRY GARY
RN37198 663 (August 19, 1993) pp27-28.
BEINHORN, MICHAEL
RN37199 634-635 (July 9, 1992) pp11,13.
BEL BIV DEVOE
RN37200 650 (February 18, 1993) pp11,13.
BELL, ANDY
RN37201 722 (November 30, 1995) pp19-20.
BELL, CHRIS
RN37202 658 (June 10, 1993) pp16-17.
BELL, RICO
RN37203 736 (June 13, 1996) pp19-20.
BELLADONNA, JOEY
RN37204 628 (April 16, 1992) pp11,13.
BELLY
RN37205 659 (June 24, 1993) pp13,15.
RN37206 663 (August 19, 1993) pp27-28.
RN37207 666 (September 30, 1993) pp27-28.
RN37208 667 (October 14, 1993) pp39-40.
RN37209 671 (December 9, 1993) pp31-32.
RN37210 691 (September 22, 1994) pp19-21.
RN37211 702 (February 23, 1995) pp19-20.
BELUSHI, JIM
RN37212 720 (November 2, 1995) pp16-17.
BELUSHI, JOHN
RN37213 693 (October 20, 1994) pp27-28,30.
BENNETT, TONY
RN37214 654 (April 15, 1993) pp11,13.
RN37215 657 (May 27, 1993) pp9,11.
RN37216 667 (October 14, 1993) pp39-40.
RN37217 674 (January 27, 1994) pp28-29.
RN37218 675 (February 10, 1994) pp22-23.
RN37219 680 (April 21, 1994) pp33-34.
RN37220 683 (June 2, 1994) pp27-28.
RN37221 702 (February 23, 1995) pp19-20.
RN37222 706 (April 20, 1995) pp15-17.
RN37223 714 (August 10, 1995) pp15-17.
BENNETT, WILLIAM
RN37224 723 (December 14, 1995) pp27-28.
BENTLEY, JAY
RN37225 700 (January 26, 1995) pp16-17.
RN37226 722 (November 30, 1995) pp19-20.
BENZEDRINE MONKS
RN37227 692 (October 6, 1994) pp15-17.
BERDAHL, BLAZE
RN37228 671 (December 9, 1993) pp31-32.
BERGGREN, WES
RN37229 716 (September 7, 1995) pp13-14.
BERLE, MILTON
RN37230 663 (August 19, 1993) pp27-28.
RN37231 667 (October 14, 1993) pp39-40.
BERLIN, STEVE
RN37232 616 (October 31, 1991) pp11,13.
BERNHARD, SANDRA
RN37233 700 (January 26, 1995) pp16-17.
RN37234 705 (April 6, 1995) pp16-17.
BERRY, BILL
RN37235 628 (April 16, 1992) pp11,13.
RN37236 647 (January 7, 1993) pp9,11.
RN37237 693 (October 20, 1994) pp27-28,30.
BERRY, CHUCK
RN37238 697 (December 15, 1994) pp17-18,20.
BETTENCOURT, NUNO
RN37239 692 (October 6, 1994) pp15-17.
BETTER THAN EZRA
RN37240 714 (August 10, 1995) pp15-17.
BETTIE SERVEERT
RN37241 691 (September 22, 1994) pp19-21.
BETTS, DICKEY
RN37242 624 (February 20, 1992) pp11-12.
RN37243 658 (June 10, 1993) pp16-17.
RN37244 746 (October 31, 1996) pp17-18.
BETTS, DUANE
RN37244 746 (October 31, 1996) pp17-18.
BEVERLY, FRANKIE
RN37245 717 (September 21, 1995) pp19-20.
BEZ
RN37246 727 (February 8, 1996) pp12-13.
BIALIK, MAYIM
RN37247 630 (May 14, 1992) pp13,15.
BIG DADDY KANE
RN37248 659 (June 24, 1993) pp13,15.
BIG DIPPER
RN37249 683 (June 2, 1994) pp27-28.
BIG HEAD TODD
RN37250 690 (September 8, 1994) pp21,24.
BIG HEAD TODD AND THE MONSTERS
RN37251 718 (October 5, 1995) pp20-21.
BIG STAR
RN37252 658 (June 10, 1993) pp16-17.
RN37253 678 (March 24, 1994) pp27-28.
RN37254 688 (August 11, 1994) pp17-18,20.

BIG TOE
RN37255 652 (March 18, 1993) pp13,15.
BIGELOW, JIM
RN37256 716 (September 7, 1995) pp13-14.
BIKINI KILL
RN37257 659 (June 24, 1993) pp13,15.
RN37258 690 (September 8, 1994) pp21,24.
RN37259 715 (August 24, 1995) pp23,25.
RN37260 720 (November 2, 1995) pp16-17.
RN37261 738-739 (July 11, 1996) pp15-16.
BILLIE JOE
RN37262 689 (August 25, 1994) pp15-16.
RN37263 693 (October 20, 1994) pp27-28,30.
RN37264 694 (November 3, 1994) pp17-18,22.
RN37265 707 (May 4, 1995) pp19-20.
BINGENHEIMER, RODNEY
RN37266 734 (May 16, 1996) pp17-18.
BIOHAZARD
RN37267 690 (September 8, 1994) pp21,24.
RN37268 707 (May 4, 1995) pp19-20.
BIRTHDAY PARTY
RN37269 642 (October 29, 1992) pp19,21.
BISCUITS, CHUCK
RN37270 741 (August 22, 1996) pp25-26.
BLACK, BILL
RN37271 742 (September 5, 1996) pp20-21.
BLACK, CLINT
RN37272 629 (April 30, 1992) pp11-12.
RN37273 630 (May 14, 1992) pp13,15.
RN37274 660-661 (July 8, 1993) pp32-33.
BLACK CROWES
RN37275 621 (January 9, 1992) pp10-11.
RN37276 631 (May 28, 1992) pp9,11.
RN37277 639 (September 17, 1992) pp19-20.
RN37278 642 (October 29, 1992) pp19,21.
RN37279 644 (November 26, 1992) pp13,15.
RN37280 652 (March 18, 1993) pp13,15.
RN37281 692 (October 6, 1994) pp15-17.
RN37282 693 (October 20, 1994) pp27-28,30.
RN37283 709 (June 1, 1995) pp16-17.
RN37284 712-713 (July 13, 1995) pp25-26.
RN37285 714 (August 10, 1995) pp15-17.
BLACK FLAG
RN37286 741 (August 22, 1996) pp25-26.
BLACK, FRANK
RN37287 674 (January 27, 1994) pp28-29.
RN37288 693 (October 20, 1994) pp27-28,30.
RN37289 702 (February 23, 1995) pp19-20.
BLACK GRAPE
RN37290 727 (February 8, 1996) pp12-13.
RN37291 745 (October 17, 1996) pp27-28.
BLACK, KAREN
RN37292 676 (February 24, 1994) pp28-29.
BLACK ROCK COALITION ORCHESTRA
RN37293 692 (October 6, 1994) pp15-17.
BLACK SABBATH
RN37294 647 (January 7, 1993) pp9,11.
RN37295 690 (September 8, 1994) pp21,24.
BLACK VELVET FLAG
RN37295 690 (September 8, 1994) pp21,24.
RN37296 702 (February 23, 1995) pp19-20.
BLACKFOOT
RN37297 727 (February 8, 1996) pp12-13.
BLACKHEARTS
RN37298 706 (April 20, 1995) pp15-17.
BLACKSTREET
RN37299 748 (November 28, 1996) pp25-26.
BLACKWELL, OTIS
RN37300 674 (January 27, 1994) pp28-29.
BLADES, RUBEN
RN37301 623 (February 6, 1992) pp11,13.
BLAKE BABIES
RN37302 627 (April 2, 1992) pp11,13.
BLAND, BOBBY
RN37303 625 (March 5, 1992) pp11,13-15,17+.
RN37304 628 (April 16, 1992) pp11,13.
RN37305 746 (October 31, 1996) pp17-18.
BLEYLE, JODY
RN37306 709 (June 1, 1995) pp16-17.
BLIGE, MARY J.
RN37307 704 (March 23, 1995) pp24-25.
RN37308 707 (May 4, 1995) pp19-20.
RN37309 717 (September 21, 1995) pp19-20.
BLIND MELON
RN37310 622 (January 23, 1992) pp6-7.
RN37311 639 (September 17, 1992) pp19-20.
RN37312 666 (September 30, 1993) pp27-28.
RN37313 667 (October 14, 1993) pp39-40.
RN37314 674 (January 27, 1994) pp28-29.
RN37315 685 (June 30, 1994) pp40-41.
RN37316 692 (October 6, 1994) pp15-17.
RN37317 723 (December 14, 1995) pp27-28.
BLOCK, KURT
RN37318 730 (March 21, 1996) pp17-18.
BLONDIE
RN37319 700 (January 26, 1995) pp16-17.
BLOOM, LUKA
RN37320 693 (October 20, 1994) pp27-28,30.
BLUE OYSTER CULT
RN37321 718 (October 5, 1995) pp20-21.
BLUERUNNERS
RN37322 618 (November 28, 1991) pp11-12.
BLUES BROTHERS
RN37323 720 (November 2, 1995) pp16-17.
BLUES EXPLOSION
RN37324 742 (September 5, 1996) pp20-21.
BLUES TRAVELER
RN37325 663 (August 19, 1993) pp27-28.
RN37326 690 (September 8, 1994) pp21,24.
RN37327 714 (August 10, 1995) pp15-17.
RN37328 729 (March 7, 1996) pp9-10.
RN37329 732 (April 18, 1996) pp19-20.
BLUR
RN37330 709 (June 1, 1995) pp16-17.
RN37331 718 (October 5, 1995) pp20-21.
RN37332 737 (June 27, 1996) pp15-16.
BOGOSIAN, ERIC
RN37333 621 (January 9, 1992) pp10-11.
BOLTON, DAN
RN37334 719 (October 19, 1995) pp15-16.
RN37335 721 (November 16, 1995) pp25-26.
RN37336 731 (April 4, 1996) pp17-18.
BOLTON, MICHAEL
RN37337 628 (April 16, 1992) pp11,13.
RN37338 702 (February 23, 1995) pp19-20.
BON JOVI
RN37339 686-687 (July 14, 1994) pp41-42.
RN37340 705 (April 6, 1995) pp16-17.
RN37341 715 (August 24, 1995) pp23,25.
RN37342 747 (November 14, 1996) pp25-26.
BON JOVI, JON
RN37343 615 (October 17, 1991) pp13-14.
RN37344 617 (November 14, 1991) pp11,13.
RN37345 623 (February 6, 1992) pp11,13.
RN37346 650 (February 18, 1993) pp11,13.
RN37347 691 (September 22, 1994) pp19-21.
RN37348 692 (October 6, 1994) pp15-17.
RN37349 709 (June 1, 1995) pp16-17.
RN37350 715 (August 24, 1995) pp23,25.
RN37351 749 (December 12, 1996) pp19-20.
BONADUCE, DANNY
RN37352 678 (March 24, 1994) pp27-28.
BONHAM, TRACY
RN37353 723 (December 14, 1995) pp27-28.
RN37354 742 (September 5, 1996) pp20-21.
BONO
RN37355 624 (February 20, 1992) pp11-12.
RN37356 627 (April 2, 1992) pp11,13.
RN37357 636 (August 6, 1992) pp11,13.
RN37358 639 (September 17, 1992) pp19-20.
RN37359 655 (April 29, 1993) pp11-12.
RN37360 663 (August 19, 1993) pp27-28.
RN37361 666 (September 30, 1993) pp27-28.
RN37362 675 (February 10, 1994) pp22-23.
RN37363 676 (February 24, 1994) pp28-29.
RN37364 680 (April 21, 1994) pp33-34.
RN37365 686-687 (July 14, 1994) pp41-42.
RN37366 704 (March 23, 1995) pp24-25.
RN37367 707 (May 4, 1995) pp19-20.
RN37368 721 (November 16, 1995) pp25-26.
RN37369 726 (January 25, 1996) pp17-18.
RN37370 728 (February 22, 1996) p20.

RN37371 731 (April 4, 1996) pp17-18.
RN37372 735 (May 30, 1996) pp12-13.
BOOKER, CEDELLA MARLEY
RN37373 734 (May 16, 1996) pp17-18.
BOOKER T & THE M.G.'S
RN37374 625 (March 5, 1992) pp11,13-15,17+.
RN37375 685 (June 30, 1994) pp40-41.
BOOTH, TIM
RN37376 686-687 (July 14, 1994) pp41-42.
BOQUIST, DAVE
RN37377 716 (September 7, 1995) pp13-14.
BOQUIST, JIM
RN37377 716 (September 7, 1995) pp13-14.
BORCHARDT, JEFFREY
RN37378 685 (June 30, 1994) pp40-41.
BORMAN, GARY
RN37379 658 (June 10, 1993) pp16-17.
BOSS
RN37380 668 (October 28, 1993) pp35-36.
BOSS HOG
RN37381 729 (March 7, 1996) pp9-10.
BOTTLE ROCKETS
RN37382 721 (November 16, 1995) pp25-26.
BOURKE, STEPHANIE
RN37383 715 (August 24, 1995) pp23,25.
BOWIE, DAVID
RN37384 622 (January 23, 1992) pp6-7.
RN37385 647 (January 7, 1993) pp9,11.
RN37386 670 (November 25, 1993) pp37-38.
RN37387 674 (January 27, 1994) pp28-29.
RN37388 675 (February 10, 1994) pp22-23.
RN37389 704 (March 23, 1995) pp24-25.
RN37390 712-713 (July 13, 1995) pp25-26.
RN37391 714 (August 10, 1995) pp15-17.
RN37392 720 (November 2, 1995) pp16-17.
RN37393 722 (November 30, 1995) pp19-20.
RN37394 723 (December 14, 1995) pp27-28.
RN37395 747 (November 14, 1996) pp25-26.
RN37396 749 (December 12, 1996) pp19-20.
BOY GEORGE
RN37397 678 (March 24, 1994) pp27-28.
BOYLE, LARA FLYNN
RN37398 705 (April 6, 1995) pp16-17.
BOYZ II MEN
RN37399 644 (November 26, 1992) pp13,15.
RN37400 706 (April 20, 1995) pp15-17.
RN37401 711 (June 29, 1995) pp12-13.
RN37402 729 (March 7, 1996) pp9-10.
BRADLEE, BEN
RN37403 647 (January 7, 1993) pp9,11.
BRADLEY, ED
RN37403 647 (January 7, 1993) pp9,11.
BRAGG, BILLY
RN37404 616 (October 31, 1991) pp11,13.
RN37405 623 (February 6, 1992) pp11,13.
RN37406 667 (October 14, 1993) pp39-40.
RN37407 702 (February 23, 1995) pp19-20.
RN37408 747 (November 14, 1996) pp25-26.
BRAMLETT, BEKKA
RN37409 663 (August 19, 1993) pp27-28.
BRANDY
RN37410 711 (June 29, 1995) pp12-13.
RN37411 723 (December 14, 1995) pp27-28.
RN37412 748 (November 28, 1996) pp25-26.
BRAXTON, TONI
RN37413 680 (April 21, 1994) pp33-34.
RN37414 711 (June 29, 1995) pp12-13.
RN37415 745 (October 17, 1996) pp27-28.
BREEDERS
RN37416 652 (March 18, 1993) pp13,15.
RN37417 663 (August 19, 1993) pp27-28.
RN37418 674 (January 27, 1994) pp28-29.
RN37419 676 (February 24, 1994) pp28-29.
RN37420 736 (June 13, 1996) pp19-20.
BRICKELL, EDIE
RN37421 634-635 (July 9, 1992) pp11,13.
RN37422 659 (June 24, 1993) pp13,15.
RN37423 679 (April 7, 1994) pp37-39.
BROOKLYN FUNK ESSENTIALS
RN37424 717 (September 21, 1995) pp19-20.
BROOKS, GARTH
RN37425 625 (March 5, 1992) pp11,13-15,17+.
RN37426 627 (April 2, 1992) pp11,13.
RN37427 628 (April 16, 1992) pp11,13.
RN37428 630 (May 14, 1992) pp13,15.
RN37429 648 (January 21, 1993) pp9,11.
RN37430 649 (February 4, 1993) pp8-9.
RN37431 688 (August 11, 1994) pp17-18,20.
BROOKS, RICKY
RN37432 733 (May 2, 1996) pp13-14.
BROWN, BOBBY
RN37433 622 (January 23, 1992) pp6-7.
RN37434 638 (September 3, 1992) pp9,11.
RN37435 642 (October 29, 1992) pp19,21.
RN37436 680 (April 21, 1994) pp33-34.
RN37437 684 (June 16, 1994) pp35-36.
BROWN, HELEN GURLEY
RN37438 617 (November 14, 1991) pp11,13.
BROWN, IAN
RN37439 712-713 (July 13, 1995) pp25-26.
BROWN, JAMES
RN37440 615 (October 17, 1991) pp13-14.
RN37441 626 (March 19, 1992) pp11,13.
RN37442 653 (April 1, 1993) pp11,13.
RN37443 654 (April 15, 1993) pp11,13.
RN37444 662 (August 5, 1993) pp33-34.
RN37445 666 (September 30, 1993) pp27-28.
RN37446 680 (April 21, 1994) pp33-34.
RN37447 684 (June 16, 1994) pp35-36.
RN37448 686-687 (July 14, 1994) pp41-42.
RN37449 694 (November 3, 1994) pp17-18,22.
RN37450 737 (June 27, 1996) pp15-16.
BROWN, JERRY
RN37451 630 (May 14, 1992) pp13,15.
BROWN, JULIE (DOWNTOWN)
RN37452 649 (February 4, 1993) pp8-9.
BROWN, JUNIOR
RN37453 668 (October 28, 1993) pp35-36.
RN37454 691 (September 22, 1994) pp19-21.
BROWN, RON
RN37455 647 (January 7, 1993) pp9,11.
BROWN, RUTH
RN37456 680 (April 21, 1994) pp33-34.
BROWN, SCOTT
RN37457 684 (June 16, 1994) pp35-36.
BROWNE, JACKSON
RN37458 617 (November 14, 1991) pp11,13.
RN37459 618 (November 28, 1991) pp11-12.
RN37460 621 (January 9, 1992) pp10-11.
RN37461 622 (January 23, 1992) pp6-7.
RN37462 671 (December 9, 1993) pp31-32.
RN37463 684 (June 16, 1994) pp35-36.
RN37464 686-687 (July 14, 1994) pp41-42.
RN37465 697 (December 15, 1994) pp17-18,20.
RN37466 705 (April 6, 1995) pp16-17.
RN37467 718 (October 5, 1995) pp20-21.
RN37468 745 (October 17, 1996) pp27-28.
BROWNSTONE
RN37469 702 (February 23, 1995) pp19-20.
BRYAN, MARK
RN37470 691 (September 22, 1994) pp19-21.
BUBBLES
RN37471 630 (May 14, 1992) pp13,15.
BUCHANAN, PATRICK
RN37472 629 (April 30, 1992) pp11-12.
BUCK, PETER
RN37473 618 (November 28, 1991) pp11-12.
RN37474 628 (April 16, 1992) pp11,13.
RN37475 647 (January 7, 1993) pp9,11.
RN37476 667 (October 14, 1993) pp39-40.
RN37477 693 (October 20, 1994) pp27-28,30.
RN37478 704 (March 23, 1995) pp24-25.
RN37479 711 (June 29, 1995) pp12-13.
RN37480 714 (August 10, 1995) pp15-17.
RN37481 717 (September 21, 1995) pp19-20.
RN37482 719 (October 19, 1995) pp15-16.
RN37483 748 (November 28, 1996) pp25-26.
BUCKELEW, DYAN
RN37484 630 (May 14, 1992) pp13,15.
BUCKINGHAM, LINDSEY
RN37484 630 (May 14, 1992) pp13,15.
BUCKLEY, JEFF
RN37485 703 (March 9, 1995) pp20-21.
RN37486 709 (June 1, 1995) pp16-17.
RN37487 710 (June 15, 1995) pp17-18.
RN37488 727 (February 8, 1996) pp12-13.
BUCKSHOT LEFONQUE
RN37489 685 (June 30, 1994) pp40-41.
BUDDHA
RN37490 727 (February 8, 1996) pp12-13.
BUFFALO SPRINGFIELD
RN37491 657 (May 27, 1993) pp9,11.
BUFFALO TOM
RN37492 633 (June 25, 1992) pp11-12.

RN37493 667 (October 14, 1993) pp39-40.
RN37494 683 (June 2, 1994) pp27-28.
RN37495 684 (June 16, 1994) pp35-36.
RN37496 689 (August 25, 1994) pp15-16.

BUFFETT, JIMMY
RN37497 642 (October 29, 1992) pp19,21.
RN37498 668 (October 28, 1993) pp35-36.
RN37499 696 (December 1, 1994) pp23-25.

BUGGIN, CRITTERS
RN37500 748 (November 28, 1996) pp25-26.

BUKOWSKI, CHARLES
RN37501 734 (May 16, 1996) pp17-18.

BULLOCK, SANDRA
RN37502 694 (November 3, 1994) pp17-18,22.

BURNETT, T-BONE
RN37503 636 (August 6, 1992) pp11,13.
RN37504 639 (September 17, 1992) pp19-20.
RN37505 675 (February 10, 1994) pp22-23.
RN37506 689 (August 25, 1994) pp15-16.

BURNING SPEAR
RN37507 694 (November 3, 1994) pp17-18,22.

BURNING TREE
RN37508 621 (January 9, 1992) pp10-11.

BURNS, BOB
RN37509 727 (February 8, 1996) pp12-13.

BURNS, STEF
RN37510 616 (October 31, 1991) pp11,13.

BURROUGHS, WILLIAM
RN37511 675 (February 10, 1994) pp22-23.
RN37512 722 (November 30, 1995) pp19-20.
RN37513 747 (November 14, 1996) pp25-26.

BURTON, DON
RN37514 690 (September 8, 1994) pp21,24.

BUSCEMI, STEVE
RN37515 680 (April 21, 1994) pp33-34.
RN37516 747 (November 14, 1996) pp25-26.

BUSH
RN37517 718 (October 5, 1995) pp20-21.
RN37518 731 (April 4, 1996) pp17-18.
RN37519 745 (October 17, 1996) pp27-28.

BUSH, DAVE
RN37520 746 (October 31, 1996) pp17-18.

BUSH, GEORGE
RN37521 640 (October 1, 1992) pp9-10.
RN37522 658 (June 10, 1993) pp16-17.

BUSH, JOHN
RN37523 637 (August 20, 1992) pp9,11.

BUSH, KATE
RN37524 686-687 (July 14, 1994) pp41-42.

BUSTA RHYMES
RN37525 742 (September 5, 1996) pp20-21.
RN37526 748 (November 28, 1996) pp25-26.

BUTLER, RICHARD
RN37527 701 (February 9, 1995) pp16-17.

BUTTHOLE SURFERS
RN37528 674 (January 27, 1994) pp28-29.
RN37529 694 (November 3, 1994) pp17-18,22.
RN37530 703 (March 9, 1995) pp20-21.
RN37531 709 (June 1, 1995) pp16-17.
RN37532 747 (November 14, 1996) pp25-26.

BUZZIN' COUSINS
RN37533 623 (February 6, 1992) pp11,13.

BYRD, ALEXANDER
RN37534 625 (March 5, 1992) pp11,13-15,17+.

BYRD, DONALD
RN37535 715 (August 24, 1995) pp23,25.

BYRDS
RN37536 726 (January 25, 1996) pp17-18.

BYRNE, DAVID
RN37537 618 (November 28, 1991) pp11-12.
RN37538 630 (May 14, 1992) pp13,15.
RN37539 631 (May 28, 1992) pp9,11.
RN37540 634-635 (July 9, 1992) pp11,13.
RN37541 683 (June 2, 1994) pp27-28.
RN37542 706 (April 20, 1995) pp15-17.
RN37543 719 (October 19, 1995) pp15-16.
RN37544 733 (May 2, 1996) pp13-14.

BYTCHES WITH PROBLEMS
RN37545 659 (June 24, 1993) pp13,15.

C

C + C MUSIC FACTORY
RN37546 615 (October 17, 1991) pp13-14.
RN37547 626 (March 19, 1992) pp11,13.

C., TIMMY
RN37548 664 (September 2, 1993) pp31-32.

CADWELLADER, SCOTT
RN37549 654 (April 15, 1993) pp11,13.

CAESAR, SID
RN37550 663 (August 19, 1993) pp27-28.

CAFFEY, CHARLOTTE
RN37551 616 (October 31, 1991) pp11,13.

CAGE, NICHOLAS
RN37552 628 (April 16, 1992) pp11,13.
RN37553 708 (May 18, 1995) pp17-18.

CALE, J. J.
RN37554 711 (June 29, 1995) pp12-13.

CALE, JOHN
RN37555 630 (May 14, 1992) pp13,15.
RN37556 648 (January 21, 1993) pp9,11.
RN37557 678 (March 24, 1994) pp27-28.
RN37558 692 (October 6, 1994) pp15-17.
RN37559 708 (May 18, 1995) pp17-18.

CALHOUN, ATEN JULIUS BUSHAW
RN37560 666 (September 30, 1993) pp27-28.

CALHOUN, WILL
RN37561 623 (February 6, 1992) pp11,13.

CAMERON, MATT
RN37562 621 (January 9, 1992) pp10-11.
RN37563 667 (October 14, 1993) pp39-40.
RN37564 743 (September 19, 1996) pp19-20.

CAMPBELL, GLEN
RN37565 660-661 (July 8, 1993) pp32-33.

CAMPBELL, JOHN
RN37566 665 (September 16, 1993) pp31-32.

CAMPBELL, LUTHER
RN37567 676 (February 24, 1994) pp28-29.
RN37568 685 (June 30, 1994) pp40-41.

CAMPBELL, NAOMI
RN37569 630 (May 14, 1992) pp13,15.
RN37570 654 (April 15, 1993) pp11,13.
RN37571 658 (June 10, 1993) pp16-17.
RN37572 723 (December 14, 1995) pp27-28.

CAMPBELL, NELL
RN37573 617 (November 14, 1991) pp11,13.

CAMPER VAN BEETHOVEN
RN37574 626 (March 19, 1992) pp11,13.

CANDLEBOX
RN37575 686-687 (July 14, 1994) pp41-42.

CANTRELL, JERRY
RN37576 624 (February 20, 1992) pp11-12.
RN37577 723 (December 14, 1995) pp27-28.
RN37578 729 (March 7, 1996) pp9-10.

CAPALDI, JIM
RN37579 680 (April 21, 1994) pp33-34.

CAPOTE, TRUMAN
RN37580 637 (August 20, 1992) pp9,11.

CAPRA, FRANK
RN37581 697 (December 15, 1994) pp17-18,20.

CAPTAIN AND TENNILLE
RN37582 653 (April 1, 1993) pp11,13.

CAREY, MARIAH
RN37583 615 (October 17, 1991) pp13-14.
RN37584 616 (October 31, 1991) pp11,13.
RN37585 626 (March 19, 1992) pp11,13.
RN37585 626 (March 19, 1992) pp11,13.
RN37586 657 (May 27, 1993) pp9,11.
RN37587 691 (September 22, 1994) pp19-21.
RN37588 702 (February 23, 1995) pp19-20.
RN37589 732 (April 18, 1996) pp19-20.

CARLOS, BUN E.
RN37590 723 (December 14, 1995) pp27-28.

CARLOS THE JACKAL
RN37591 701 (February 9, 1995) pp16-17.

CARMELLINI, BETTY
RN37592 743 (September 19, 1996) pp19-20.

CARPENTER, MARY-CHAPIN
RN37593 625 (March 5, 1992) pp11,13-15,17+.
RN37594 638 (September 3, 1992) pp9,11.
RN37595 662 (August 5, 1993) pp33-34.
RN37596 684 (June 16, 1994) pp35-36.
RN37597 697 (December 15, 1994) pp17-18,20.
RN37598 706 (April 20, 1995) pp15-17.
RN37599 718 (October 5, 1995) pp20-21.

CARR, KRISTEN ANN
RN37600 660-661 (July 8, 1993) pp32-33.

CARREY, JIM
RN37601 705 (April 6, 1995) pp16-17.

CARROLL, LEWIS

RN37602 649 (February 4, 1993) pp8-9.
CARS
RN37603 722 (November 30, 1995) pp19-20.
CARSON, JOHNNY
RN37604 624 (February 20, 1992) pp11-12.
CARSON, LORI
RN37605 712-713 (July 13, 1995) pp25-26.
CARTER, BILL
RN37606 709 (June 1, 1995) pp16-17.
CARTER, BILLY
RN37607 650 (February 18, 1993) pp11,13.
CARTER, JIMMY
RN37608 622 (January 23, 1992) pp6-7.
CARVER, RAYMOND
RN37609 648 (January 21, 1993) pp9,11.
CARVEY, DANA
RN37610 642 (October 29, 1992) pp19,21.
CASADY, JACK
RN37611 644 (November 26, 1992) pp13,15.
CASALE, BOB
RN37612 730 (March 21, 1996) pp17-18.
CASALE, JERRY
RN37612 730 (March 21, 1996) pp17-18.
CASE, PETER
RN37613 623 (February 6, 1992) pp11,13.
CASH, JOHNNY
RN37614 625 (March 5, 1992) pp11,13-15,17+.
RN37615 640 (October 1, 1992) pp9-10.
RN37616 660-661 (July 8, 1993) pp32-33.
RN37617 674 (January 27, 1994) pp28-29.
RN37618 692 (October 6, 1994) pp15-17.
RN37619 693 (October 20, 1994) pp27-28,30.
RN37620 694 (November 3, 1994) pp17-18,22.
RN37621 702 (February 23, 1995) pp19-20.
RN37622 741 (August 22, 1996) pp25-26.
CASH, ROSANNE
RN37623 625 (March 5, 1992) pp11,13-15,17+.
RN37624 637 (August 20, 1992) pp9,11.
RN37625 649 (February 4, 1993) pp8-9.
CASSIDY, DAVID
RN37626 664 (September 2, 1993) pp31-32.
RN37627 678 (March 24, 1994) pp27-28.
RN37628 689 (August 25, 1994) pp15-16.
CATERER, EL
RN37629 746 (October 31, 1996) pp17-18.
CATERER, JOSH
RN37629 746 (October 31, 1996) pp17-18.
CATERER, MATT
RN37629 746 (October 31, 1996) pp17-18.
CATES, JOE
RN37630 689 (August 25, 1994) pp15-16.
CAVE, NICK
RN37631 637 (August 20, 1992) pp9,11.
RN37632 642 (October 29, 1992) pp19,21.
RN37633 664 (September 2, 1993) pp31-32.
RN37634 692 (October 6, 1994) pp15-17.
RN37635 704 (March 23, 1995) pp24-25.
RN37636 716 (September 7, 1995) pp13-14.
RN37637 733 (May 2, 1996) pp13-14.
CEASE, JEFF
RN37638 621 (January 9, 1992) pp10-11.
CERVENKA, EXENE
RN37639 616 (October 31, 1991) pp11,13.
RN37640 640 (October 1, 1992) pp9-10.
RN37641 666 (September 30, 1993) pp27-28.
RN37642 668 (October 28, 1993) pp35-36.
RN37643 675 (February 10, 1994) pp22-23.
CHAINSAW KITTENS
RN37644 680 (April 21, 1994) pp33-34.
CHALFONT, KEVIN
RN37645 670 (November 25, 1993) pp37-38.
CHAMBERLAIN, WILT
RN37646 697 (December 15, 1994) pp17-18,20.
CHAMBERLIN, JIMMY
RN37647 705 (April 6, 1995) pp16-17.
RN37648 723 (December 14, 1995) pp27-28.
CHAPMAN, TRACY
RN37649 629 (April 30, 1992) pp11-12.
CHARLES, RAY
RN37650 654 (April 15, 1993) pp11,13.
RN37651 659 (June 24, 1993) pp13,15.
RN37652 662 (August 5, 1993) pp33-34.
RN37653 668 (October 28, 1993) pp35-36.
RN37654 669 (November 11, 1993) pp27-28.
RN37655 697 (December 15, 1994) pp17-18,20.
CHARO
RN37656 655 (April 29, 1993) pp11-12.
CHASE, CHEVY
RN37657 640 (October 1, 1992) pp9-10.
CHASTAIN, PAUL
RN37658 685 (June 30, 1994) pp40-41.
CHEAP DATES
RN37659 652 (March 18, 1993) pp13,15.
CHEAP TRICK
RN37660 626 (March 19, 1992) pp11,13.
RN37661 706 (April 20, 1995) pp15-17.
RN37662 723 (December 14, 1995) pp27-28.
CHECKER, CHUBBY
RN37663 622 (January 23, 1992) pp6-7.
CHENZIRA, AYOKA
RN37664 697 (December 15, 1994) pp17-18,20.
CHER
RN37665 696 (December 1, 1994) pp23-25.
RN37666 715 (August 24, 1995) pp23,25.
RN37667 726 (January 25, 1996) pp17-18.
RN37668 740 (August 8, 1996) pp17-18.
CHERONE, GARY
RN37669 683 (June 2, 1994) pp27-28.
CHERRY, DON
RN37670 708 (May 18, 1995) pp17-18.
CHERRY, NENEH
RN37671 617 (November 14, 1991) pp11,13.
RN37672 642 (October 29, 1992) pp19,21.
RN37673 655 (April 29, 1993) pp11-12.
RN37674 662 (August 5, 1993) pp33-34.
RN37675 686-687 (July 14, 1994) pp41-42.
RN37676 707 (May 4, 1995) pp19-20.
RN37677 708 (May 18, 1995) pp17-18.
CHESNUTT, VIC
RN37678 636 (August 6, 1992) pp11,13.
RN37679 676 (February 24, 1994) pp28-29.
RN37680 689 (August 25, 1994) pp15-16.
RN37681 734 (May 16, 1996) pp17-18.
RN37682 742 (September 5, 1996) pp20-21.
CHICKENWOLF
RN37683 720 (November 2, 1995) pp16-17.
CHIEFTAINS
RN37684 621 (January 9, 1992) pp10-11.
CHILLI
RN37685 719 (October 19, 1995) pp15-16.
RN37686 732 (April 18, 1996) pp19-20.
CHILTON, ALEX
RN37687 658 (June 10, 1993) pp16-17.
RN37688 678 (March 24, 1994) pp27-28.
RN37689 688 (August 11, 1994) pp17-18,20.
CHIPPERFIELD, SHEILA
RN37690 746 (October 31, 1996) pp17-18.
CHRIST, JESUS
RN37691 683 (June 2, 1994) pp27-28.
RN37692 706 (April 20, 1995) pp15-17.
RN37693 726 (January 25, 1996) pp17-18.
RN37694 740 (August 8, 1996) pp17-18.
CHRISTOPHER, JOE
RN37695 729 (March 7, 1996) pp9-10.
CHURCHILL, WINSTON
RN37696 658 (June 10, 1993) pp16-17.
CIBO MATTO
RN37697 729 (March 7, 1996) pp9-10.
CICERO, MICHEL
RN37698 727 (February 8, 1996) pp12-13.
CIRCLE JERKS
RN37699 706 (April 20, 1995) pp15-17.
RN37700 707 (May 4, 1995) pp19-20.
RN37701 712-713 (July 13, 1995) pp25-26.
RN37702 726 (January 25, 1996) pp17-18.
CLAPTON, ERIC
RN37703 615 (October 17, 1991) pp13-14.
RN37704 618 (November 28, 1991) pp11-12.
RN37705 625 (March 5, 1992) pp11,13-15,17+.
RN37706 637 (August 20, 1992) pp9,11.
RN37707 642 (October 29, 1992) pp19,21.
RN37708 647 (January 7, 1993) pp9,11.
RN37709 654 (April 15, 1993) pp11,13.
RN37710 670 (November 25, 1993) pp37-38.
RN37711 675 (February 10, 1994) pp22-23.
RN37712 691 (September 22, 1994) pp19-21.
RN37713 696 (December 1, 1994) pp23-25.
RN37714 701 (February 9, 1995) pp16-17.
RN37715 702 (February 23, 1995) pp19-20.
RN37716 726 (January 25, 1996) pp17-18.

CLAPTON, ERIC (continued)
RN37717 738-739 (July 11, 1996) pp15-16.
RN37718 741 (August 22, 1996) pp25-26.
RN37719 746 (October 31, 1996) pp17-18.
CLARK, DICK
RN37720 674 (January 27, 1994) pp28-29.
CLARKE, GILBY
RN37721 663 (August 19, 1993) pp27-28.
RN37722 676 (February 24, 1994) pp28-29.
RN37723 690 (September 8, 1994) pp21,24.
CLARKE, VINCE
RN37724 722 (November 30, 1995) pp19-20.
CLASH
RN37725 618 (November 28, 1991) pp11-12.
RN37726 706 (April 20, 1995) pp15-17.
RN37727 737 (June 27, 1996) pp15-16.
CLAYPOOL, LES
RN37728 681 (May 5, 1994) pp21-22.
RN37729 686-687 (July 14, 1994) pp41-42.
CLAYTON, ADAM
RN37730 627 (April 2, 1992) pp11,13.
RN37731 636 (August 6, 1992) pp11,13.
RN37732 658 (June 10, 1993) pp16-17.
RN37733 675 (February 10, 1994) pp22-23.
RN37734 710 (June 15, 1995) pp17-18.
RN37735 738-739 (July 11, 1996) pp15-16.
CLAYTON, MERRY
RN37736 730 (March 21, 1996) pp17-18.
CLAYTON, ROBERT F., JR.
RN37737 631 (May 28, 1992) pp9,11.
CLEMONS, CLARENCE
RN37738 644 (November 26, 1992) pp13,15.
CLEOPATRA
RN37738 644 (November 26, 1992) pp13,15.
CLIFF, JIMMY
RN37739 692 (October 6, 1994) pp15-17.
CLINTON, BILL
RN37740 647 (January 7, 1993) pp9,11.
RN37741 684 (June 16, 1994) pp35-36.
RN37742 691 (September 22, 1994) pp19-21.
RN37743 720 (November 2, 1995) pp16-17.
CLINTON, CHELSEA
RN37744 743 (September 19, 1996) pp19-20.
CLINTON, GEORGE
RN37745 667 (October 14, 1993) pp39-40.
RN37746 675 (February 10, 1994) pp22-23.
RN37747 680 (April 21, 1994) pp33-34.
RN37748 712-713 (July 13, 1995) pp25-26.
RN37749 730 (March 21, 1996) pp17-18.
RN37750 741 (August 22, 1996) pp25-26.
RN37751 743 (September 19, 1996) pp19-20.
CLINTON, HILLARY
RN37752 678 (March 24, 1994) pp27-28.
RN37753 691 (September 22, 1994) pp19-21.
CLINTON, ROGER
RN37754 650 (February 18, 1993) pp11,13.
RN37755 658 (June 10, 1993) pp16-17.
CLIVILLES, ROBERT
RN37756 626 (March 19, 1992) pp11,13.
CLOWES, DANIEL
RN37757 688 (August 11, 1994) pp17-18,20.
COBAIN, FRANCES BEAN
RN37758 667 (October 14, 1993) pp39-40.
RN37759 720 (November 2, 1995) pp16-17.
COBAIN, KURT
RN37760 642 (October 29, 1992) pp19,21.
RN37761 655 (April 29, 1993) pp11-12.
RN37762 664 (September 2, 1993) pp31-32.
RN37763 666 (September 30, 1993) pp27-28.
RN37764 667 (October 14, 1993) pp39-40.
RN37765 668 (October 28, 1993) pp35-36.
RN37766 676 (February 24, 1994) pp28-29.
RN37767 686-687 (July 14, 1994) pp41-42.
RN37768 690 (September 8, 1994) pp21,24.
RN37769 692 (October 6, 1994) pp15-17.
COBB, TY
RN37770 719 (October 19, 1995) pp15-16.
COBURN, JAMES
RN37771 747 (November 14, 1996) pp25-26.
COCKBURN, BRUCE
RN37772 623 (February 6, 1992) pp11,13.
RN37773 638 (September 3, 1992) pp9,11.
RN37774 649 (February 4, 1993) pp8-9.
RN37775 657 (May 27, 1993) pp9,11.
COCKER, JARVIS
RN37776 737 (June 27, 1996) pp15-16.
RN37777 742 (September 5, 1996) pp20-21.
COCO
RN37778 702 (February 23, 1995) pp19-20.
COCTAILS
RN37779 714 (August 10, 1995) pp15-17.
COFFEY, KING
RN37780 703 (March 9, 1995) pp20-21.
COHEN, HERB
RN37781 657 (May 27, 1993) pp9,11.
COHEN, JASON
RN37782 690 (September 8, 1994) pp21,24.
RN37783 694 (November 3, 1994) pp17-18,22.
COHEN, LEONARD
RN37784 618 (November 28, 1991) pp11-12.
RN37785 648 (January 21, 1993) pp9,11.
COLBOURN, CHRIS
RN37786 683 (June 2, 1994) pp27-28.
COLE, DAVID
RN37787 615 (October 17, 1991) pp13-14.
RN37788 626 (March 19, 1992) pp11,13.
COLE, LLOYD
RN37789 618 (November 28, 1991) pp11-12.
COLE, NATALIE
RN37790 628 (April 16, 1992) pp11,13.
RN37791 629 (April 30, 1992) pp11-12.
RN37792 665 (September 16, 1993) pp31-32.
COLE, PAULA
RN37793 693 (October 20, 1994) pp27-28,30.
RN37794 707 (May 4, 1995) pp19-20.
RN37795 719 (October 19, 1995) pp15-16.
RN37796 746 (October 31, 1996) pp17-18.
COLEMAN, JAZ
RN37797 692 (October 6, 1994) pp15-17.
COLEMAN, ORNETTE
RN37798 688 (August 11, 1994) pp17-18,20.
COLLEN, PHIL
RN37799 640 (October 1, 1992) pp9-10.
COLLINS, ALBERT
RN37800 630 (May 14, 1992) pp13,15.
COLLINS, BOOTSY
RN37801 723 (December 14, 1995) pp27-28.
RN37802 737 (June 27, 1996) pp15-16.
COLLINS, PHIL
RN37803 719 (October 19, 1995) pp15-16.
COLOR ME BADD
RN37804 628 (April 16, 1992) pp11,13.
COLT, JOHNNY
RN37805 642 (October 29, 1992) pp19,21.
COLUMBUS, CHRIS
RN37806 644 (November 26, 1992) pp13,15.
COLVIN, SHAWN
RN37807 667 (October 14, 1993) pp39-40.
COMBUSTIBLE EDISON
RN37808 690 (September 8, 1994) pp21,24.
CONCRETE BLONDE
RN37809 628 (April 16, 1992) pp11,13.
RN37810 668 (October 28, 1993) pp35-36.
RN37811 670 (November 25, 1993) pp37-38.
RN37812 681 (May 5, 1994) pp21-22.
CONNEFF, KEVIN
RN37813 621 (January 9, 1992) pp10-11.
CONNELL, MIKE
RN37814 633 (June 25, 1992) pp11-12.
CONNELLS
RN37814 633 (June 25, 1992) pp11-12.
CONNICK, HARRY, JR.
RN37815 650 (February 18, 1993) pp11,13.
RN37816 654 (April 15, 1993) pp11,13.
CONSOLIDATED
RN37817 671 (December 9, 1993) pp31-32.
COODER, RY
RN37818 624 (February 20, 1992) pp11-12.
RN37819 671 (December 9, 1993) pp31-32.
RN37820 686-687 (July 14, 1994) pp41-42.
RN37821 707 (May 4, 1995) pp19-20.
COOK, PAUL
RN37822 734 (May 16, 1996) pp17-18.
COOK, RONALD
RN37823 721 (November 16, 1995) pp25-26.
COOKE, SAM
RN37824 650 (February 18, 1993) pp11,13.
COOLIO

RN37825 693 (October 20, 1994) pp27-28,30.
RN37826 703 (March 9, 1995) pp20-21.
RN37827 706 (April 20, 1995) pp15-17.
RN37828 710 (June 15, 1995) pp17-18.
RN37829 720 (November 2, 1995) pp16-17.
RN37830 723 (December 14, 1995) pp27-28.
RN37831 727 (February 8, 1996) pp12-13.
RN37832 731 (April 4, 1996) pp17-18.
RN37833 732 (April 18, 1996) pp19-20.
COOMBES, GAZ
RN37834 726 (January 25, 1996) pp17-18.
COOPER, ALICE
RN37835 616 (October 31, 1991) pp11,13.
RN37836 631 (May 28, 1992) pp9,11.
COOPER, DOUGLAS
RN37837 701 (February 9, 1995) pp16-17.
COPPOLA, SOFIA
RN37838 710 (June 15, 1995) pp17-18.
CORDES, JARETT
RN37839 720 (November 2, 1995) pp16-17.
CORGAN, BILLY
RN37840 655 (April 29, 1993) pp11-12.
RN37841 684 (June 16, 1994) pp35-36.
RN37842 693 (October 20, 1994) pp27-28,30.
RN37843 694 (November 3, 1994) pp17-18,22.
RN37844 705 (April 6, 1995) pp16-17.
RN37845 723 (December 14, 1995) pp27-28.
RN37846 728 (February 22, 1996) p20.
RN37847 731 (April 4, 1996) pp17-18.
RN37848 737 (June 27, 1996) pp15-16.
CORNELL, CHRIS
RN37849 621 (January 9, 1992) pp10-11.
RN37850 638 (September 3, 1992) pp9,11.
RN37851 681 (May 5, 1994) pp21-22.
RN37852 693 (October 20, 1994) pp27-28,30.
RN37853 706 (April 20, 1995) pp15-17.
RN37854 719 (October 19, 1995) pp15-16.
RN37855 743 (September 19, 1996) pp19-20.
CORNERSHOP
RN37856 736 (June 13, 1996) pp19-20.
RN37857 737 (June 27, 1996) pp15-16.
COSTELLO, ELVIS
RN37858 621 (January 9, 1992) pp10-11.
RN37859 626 (March 19, 1992) pp11,13.
RN37860 655 (April 29, 1993) pp11-12.
RN37861 665 (September 16, 1993) pp31-32.
RN37862 675 (February 10, 1994) pp22-23.
RN37863 679 (April 7, 1994) pp37-39.
RN37864 683 (June 2, 1994) pp27-28.
RN37865 686-687 (July 14, 1994) pp41-42.
RN37866 689 (August 25, 1994) pp15-16.
RN37867 692 (October 6, 1994) pp15-17.
RN37868 734 (May 16, 1996) pp17-18.
COSTNER, KEVIN
RN37869 627 (April 2, 1992) pp11,13.
RN37870 637 (August 20, 1992) pp9,11.
RN37871 648 (January 21, 1993) pp9,11.
COUNTING CROWS
RN37872 688 (August 11, 1994) pp17-18,20.
RN37873 689 (August 25, 1994) pp15-16.
RN37874 707 (May 4, 1995) pp19-20.
RN37875 742 (September 5, 1996) pp20-21.
COWBOY JUNKIES
RN37876 621 (January 9, 1992) pp10-11.
RN37877 749 (December 12, 1996) pp19-20.
COX, LARRY
RN37878 682 (May 19, 1994) pp37-38.
COXEN, GRAHAM
RN37879 709 (June 1, 1995) pp16-17.
CRACKER
RN37880 626 (March 19, 1992) pp11,13.
RN37881 665 (September 16, 1993) pp31-32.
RN37882 674 (January 27, 1994) pp28-29.
RN37883 685 (June 30, 1994) pp40-41.
RN37884 686-687 (July 14, 1994) pp41-42.
RN37885 712-713 (July 13, 1995) pp25-26.
RN37886 737 (June 27, 1996) pp15-16.
CRAFT, PHILIP
RN37887 708 (May 18, 1995) pp17-18.
CRAMPS
RN37888 676 (February 24, 1994) pp28-29.
CRANBERRIES
RN37889 684 (June 16, 1994) pp35-36.
RN37890 690 (September 8, 1994) pp21,24.
RN37891 711 (June 29, 1995) pp12-13.
RN37892 731 (April 4, 1996) pp17-18.
CRANE, WHITFIELD
RN37893 667 (October 14, 1993) pp39-40.
CRASH TEST DUMMIES
RN37894 617 (November 14, 1991) pp11,13.
CRAY, ROBERT
RN37895 616 (October 31, 1991) pp11,13.
RN37896 624 (February 20, 1992) pp11-12.
RN37897 658 (June 10, 1993) pp16-17.
CREACH, PAPA JOHN
RN37898 644 (November 26, 1992) pp13,15.
CREEDENCE CLEARWATER REVIVAL
RN37899 630 (May 14, 1992) pp13,15.
RN37900 681 (May 5, 1994) pp21-22.
RN37901 711 (June 29, 1995) pp12-13.
CRENSHAW, MARSHALL
RN37902 689 (August 25, 1994) pp15-16.
CRIMMINS, BARRY
RN37903 625 (March 5, 1992) pp11,13-15,17+.
CRISS, PETER
RN37904 638 (September 3, 1992) pp9,11.
RN37905 732 (April 18, 1996) pp19-20.
CRITCHLEY, JOHN
RN37906 676 (February 24, 1994) pp28-29.
CROCE, A. J.
RN37907 707 (May 4, 1995) pp19-20.
CROCE, JIM
RN37907 707 (May 4, 1995) pp19-20.
CRONKITE, BETSY
RN37908 696 (December 1, 1994) pp23-25.
CRONKITE, WALTER
RN37909 647 (January 7, 1993) pp9,11.
RN37910 696 (December 1, 1994) pp23-25.
RN37911 716 (September 7, 1995) pp13-14.
CROPPER, STEVE
RN37912 625 (March 5, 1992) pp11,13-15,17+.
RN37913 685 (June 30, 1994) pp40-41.
RN37914 697 (December 15, 1994) pp17-18,20.
CROSBY & NASH
RN37915 625 (March 5, 1992) pp11,13-15,17+.
CROSBY, BING
RN37916 623 (February 6, 1992) pp11,13.
CROSBY, DAVID
RN37917 625 (March 5, 1992) pp11,13-15,17+.
RN37918 679 (April 7, 1994) pp37-39.
RN37919 700 (January 26, 1995) pp16-17.
RN37920 718 (October 5, 1995) pp20-21.
CROSBY, STILLS AND NASH
RN37921 678 (March 24, 1994) pp27-28.
CROSS, MIKE
RN37922 708 (May 18, 1995) pp17-18.
CROVER, DALE
RN37923 675 (February 10, 1994) pp22-23.
RN37924 733 (May 2, 1996) pp13-14.
CROW, SHERYL
RN37925 681 (May 5, 1994) pp21-22.
RN37926 701 (February 9, 1995) pp16-17.
RN37927 702 (February 23, 1995) pp19-20.
RN37928 703 (March 9, 1995) pp20-21.
RN37929 706 (April 20, 1995) pp15-17.
RN37930 707 (May 4, 1995) pp19-20.
RN37931 732 (April 18, 1996) pp19-20.
RN37932 746 (October 31, 1996) pp17-18.
RN37933 748 (November 28, 1996) pp25-26.
CROWDED HOUSE
RN37934 662 (August 5, 1993) pp33-34.
RN37935 681 (May 5, 1994) pp21-22.
RN37936 707 (May 4, 1995) pp19-20.
CROWE, CAMERON
RN37937 638 (September 3, 1992) pp9,11.
RN37938 647 (January 7, 1993) pp9,11.
CRUISE, JULEE
RN37939 637 (August 20, 1992) pp9,11.
CRUISE, TOM
RN37940 697 (December 15, 1994) pp17-18,20.
RN37941 738-739 (July 11, 1996) pp15-16.
CRUMB, R.
RN37942 719 (October 19, 1995) pp15-16.
CRUZ, BRANDON
RN37943 702 (February 23, 1995) pp19-20.
CUCCURULLO, WARREN
RN37944 708 (May 18, 1995) pp17-18.
CULKIN, MACAULAY
RN37945 644 (November 26, 1992) pp13,15.
CULT
RN37946 628 (April 16, 1992) pp11,13.
CUNNIFF, JILL
RN37947 710 (June 15, 1995) pp17-18.
CURE
RN37948 631 (May 28, 1992) pp9,11.
RN37949 633 (June 25, 1992) pp11-12.

RN37950 728 (February 22, 1996) p20.
RN37951 737 (June 27, 1996) pp15-16.
RN37952 743 (September 19, 1996) pp19-20.
CURRY, ADAM
RN37953 689 (August 25, 1994) pp15-16.
CYPRESS HILL
RN37954 644 (November 26, 1992) pp13,15.
RN37955 648 (January 21, 1993) pp9,11.
RN37956 671 (December 9, 1993) pp31-32.
RN37957 674 (January 27, 1994) pp28-29.
RN37958 710 (June 15, 1995) pp17-18.
RN37959 714 (August 10, 1995) pp15-17.
RN37960 718 (October 5, 1995) pp20-21.
RN37961 729 (March 7, 1996) pp9-10.
RN37962 731 (April 4, 1996) pp17-18.
RN37963 742 (September 5, 1996) pp20-21.
CYRUS, BILLY RAY
RN37964 652 (March 18, 1993) pp13,15.
RN37965 654 (April 15, 1993) pp11,13.
RN37966 655 (April 29, 1993) pp11-12.

D

D, CHUCK
RN37967 624 (February 20, 1992) pp11-12.
RN37968 664 (September 2, 1993) pp31-32.
RN37969 670 (November 25, 1993) pp37-38.
RN37970 693 (October 20, 1994) pp27-28,30.
RN37971 733 (May 2, 1996) pp13-14.
RN37972 735 (May 30, 1996) pp12-13.
D GENERATION
RN37973 705 (April 6, 1995) pp16-17.
RN37974 735 (May 30, 1996) pp12-13.
D. J. JAZZY JEFF AND THE FRESH PRINCE
RN37975 628 (April 16, 1992) pp11,13.
D, MIKE
RN37976 660-661 (July 8, 1993) pp32-33.
RN37977 681 (May 5, 1994) pp21-22.
RN37978 693 (October 20, 1994) pp27-28,30.
RN37979 710 (June 15, 1995) pp17-18.
RN37980 736 (June 13, 1996) pp19-20.
DA BRAT
RN37981 707 (May 4, 1995) pp19-20.
DA BUSH BABES
RN37982 719 (October 19, 1995) pp15-16.
DA LENCH MOB
RN37983 644 (November 26, 1992) pp13,15.
DAHLHEIMER, PAT
RN37984 716 (September 7, 1995) pp13-14.
DALE, DICK
RN37985 659 (June 24, 1993) pp13,15.
DALEY, RICHARD
RN37986 745 (October 17, 1996) pp27-28.
DALLAS COWBOY CHEERLEADERS
RN37987 629 (April 30, 1992) pp11-12.
DALTREY, ROGER
RN37988 653 (April 1, 1993) pp11,13.
RN37989 700 (January 26, 1995) pp16-17.
RN37990 741 (August 22, 1996) pp25-26.
DAMBUILDERS
RN37991 693 (October 20, 1994) pp27-28,30.
DAMN YANKEES
RN37992 631 (May 28, 1992) pp9,11.
DANCE HALL CRASHERS
RN37993 721 (November 16, 1995) pp25-26.
DANDELION
RN37994 718 (October 5, 1995) pp20-21.
DANDO, EVAN
RN37995 627 (April 2, 1992) pp11,13.
RN37996 662 (August 5, 1993) pp33-34.
RN37997 666 (September 30, 1993) pp27-28.
RN37998 679 (April 7, 1994) pp37-39.
RN37999 680 (April 21, 1994) pp33-34.
RN38000 683 (June 2, 1994) pp27-28.
RN38001 700 (January 26, 1995) pp16-17.
RN38002 708 (May 18, 1995) pp17-18.
RN38003 710 (June 15, 1995) pp17-18.
RN38004 742 (September 5, 1996) pp20-21.
DANELL, DENNIS
RN38005 741 (August 22, 1996) pp25-26.
DANES, CLAIRE
RN38006 700 (January 26, 1995) pp16-17.
RN38007 740 (August 8, 1996) pp17-18.
RN38008 749 (December 12, 1996) pp19-20.
D'ANGELO
RN38009 732 (April 18, 1996) pp19-20.
DANIELS, CHARLIE
RN38010 727 (February 8, 1996) pp12-13.
DANILO
RN38011 669 (November 11, 1993) pp27-28.
DANKO, RICK
RN38012 742 (September 5, 1996) pp20-21.
DANNEMANN, MONIKA
RN38013 734 (May 16, 1996) pp17-18.
DANNY BOY
RN38014 671 (December 9, 1993) pp31-32.
DANZA, TONY
RN38015 716 (September 7, 1995) pp13-14.
D'ARBY, TERENCE TRENT
RN38016 662 (August 5, 1993) pp33-34.
D'ARCY
RN38017 723 (December 14, 1995) pp27-28.
DAS EFX
RN38018 642 (October 29, 1992) pp19,21.
RN38019 675 (February 10, 1994) pp22-23.
DASHBOARD SAVIORS
RN38020 689 (August 25, 1994) pp15-16.
DAULNE, MARIE
RN38021 708 (May 18, 1995) pp17-18.
DAVES, JENNIFER
RN38022 730 (March 21, 1996) pp17-18.
DAVIES, RAY
RN38023 633 (June 25, 1992) pp11-12.
RN38024 734 (May 16, 1996) pp17-18.
DAVIES, RICHARD
RN38025 742 (September 5, 1996) pp20-21.
DAVIS, ELIZABETH
RN38026 722 (November 30, 1995) pp19-20.
RN38027 731 (April 4, 1996) pp17-18.
DAVIS, JULIE
RN38028 717 (September 21, 1995) pp19-20.
DAVIS, KERRY
RN38029 736 (June 13, 1996) pp19-20.
DAVIS, RENNIE
RN38030 745 (October 17, 1996) pp27-28.
DAVIS, SAMMY, JR.
RN38031 736 (June 13, 1996) pp19-20.
DAVIS, ZELMA
RN38032 626 (March 19, 1992) pp11,13.
DAY, DORIS
RN38033 652 (March 18, 1993) pp13,15.
DAY-LEWIS, DANIEL
RN38034 675 (February 10, 1994) pp22-23.
D.C. TALK
RN38035 691 (September 22, 1994) pp19-21.
DE FUEGOS
RN38036 683 (June 2, 1994) pp27-28.
DE LA FALAISE, LUCIE
RN38037 748 (November 28, 1996) pp25-26.
DE LA ROCHA, ZACK
RN38038 664 (September 2, 1993) pp31-32.
RN38039 674 (January 27, 1994) pp28-29.
RN38040 706 (April 20, 1995) pp15-17.
RN38041 715 (August 24, 1995) pp23,25.
RN38042 718 (October 5, 1995) pp20-21.
DE NIRO, ROBERT
RN38043 701 (February 9, 1995) pp16-17.
RN38044 726 (January 25, 1996) pp17-18.
DEAD BOYS
RN38045 642 (October 29, 1992) pp19,21.
RN38046 662 (August 5, 1993) pp33-34.
DEAD HOT WORKSHOP
RN38047 722 (November 30, 1995) pp19-20.
DEAD KENNEDYS
RN38048 631 (May 28, 1992) pp9,11.
DEAL, KELLEY
RN38049 736 (June 13, 1996) pp19-20.
DEAL, KIM
RN38050 652 (March 18, 1993) pp13,15.
RN38051 674 (January 27, 1994) pp28-29.
RN38052 746 (October 31, 1996) pp17-18.
DECONSTRUCTION
RN38053 653 (April 1, 1993) pp11,13.
DEE, KIKI
RN38054 666 (September 30, 1993) pp27-28.
DEF JEF
RN38055 669 (November 11, 1993) pp27-28.
DEF LEPPARD
RN38056 640 (October 1, 1992) pp9-10.
RN38057 642 (October 29, 1992) pp19,21.
DEFILLO, MARLON
RN38058 704 (March 23, 1995) pp24-25.
DEFORREST, CALVERT
RN38059 692 (October 6, 1994) pp15-17.
DEFRANCO, TONY
RN38060 653 (April 1, 1993) pp11,13.
DEFUNKT

RN38061 623 (February 6, 1992) pp11,13.
DEGARMO, CHRIS
RN38062 615 (October 17, 1991) pp13-14.
RN38063 696 (December 1, 1994) pp23-25.
DEL THA FUNKEE HOMOSAPIEN
RN38064 659 (June 24, 1993) pp13,15.
DELANEY AND BONNIE
RN38065 663 (August 19, 1993) pp27-28.
DELAUGHTER, TIM
RN38066 716 (September 7, 1995) pp13-14.
DELAY, RANDY
RN38067 650 (February 18, 1993) pp11,13.
DELFIN, BEN
RN38068 710 (June 15, 1995) pp17-18.
DELORENZO, VICTOR
RN38069 658 (June 10, 1993) pp16-17.
DELUCA, MIKE
RN38070 707 (May 4, 1995) pp19-20.
DEMME, TED
RN38071 730 (March 21, 1996) pp17-18.
DENIKE, KARINA
RN38072 721 (November 16, 1995) pp25-26.
DENISON, DUANE
RN38073 736 (June 13, 1996) pp19-20.
DENVER, JOHN
RN38074 669 (November 11, 1993) pp27-28.
DEPECHE MODE
RN38075 650 (February 18, 1993) pp11,13.
RN38076 667 (October 14, 1993) pp39-40.
RN38077 669 (November 11, 1993) pp27-28.
RN38078 696 (December 1, 1994) pp23-25.
DEPP, JOHNNY
RN38079 666 (September 30, 1993) pp27-28.
RN38080 670 (November 25, 1993) pp37-38.
RN38081 674 (January 27, 1994) pp28-29.
RN38082 679 (April 7, 1994) pp37-39.
RN38083 683 (June 2, 1994) pp27-28.
RN38084 696 (December 1, 1994) pp23-25.
RN38085 709 (June 1, 1995) pp16-17.
RN38086 714 (August 10, 1995) pp15-17.
RN38087 734 (May 16, 1996) pp17-18.
RN38088 738-739 (July 11, 1996) pp15-16.
RN38089 744 (October 3, 1996) pp19-21.
RN38090 747 (November 14, 1996) pp25-26.
DERRINGER, RICK
RN38091 630 (May 14, 1992) pp13,15.
DERSHOWITZ, ALAN
RN38092 657 (May 27, 1993) pp9,11.
DEUTROM, MARK
RN38093 675 (February 10, 1994) pp22-23.
DEVILHEAD
RN38094 748 (November 28, 1996) pp25-26.
DEVILLE, C. C.
RN38095 626 (March 19, 1992) pp11,13.
RN38096 633 (June 25, 1992) pp11-12.
DEVITO, DANNY
RN38097 734 (May 16, 1996) pp17-18.
DEVITO, LIBERTY
RN38098 689 (August 25, 1994) pp15-16.
DEVO
RN38099 633 (June 25, 1992) pp11-12.
RN38100 717 (September 21, 1995) pp19-20.
RN38101 730 (March 21, 1996) pp17-18.
DFL
RN38102 736 (June 13, 1996) pp19-20.
DI
RN38103 721 (November 16, 1995) pp25-26.
DIAMOND DARRELL
RN38104 689 (August 25, 1994) pp15-16.
DIAMOND, JULIE LEWITT
RN38105 720 (November 2, 1995) pp16-17.
DIAMOND, MIKE
RN38106 684 (June 16, 1994) pp35-36.
DIAMOND, NEIL
RN38107 659 (June 24, 1993) pp13,15.
RN38108 665 (September 16, 1993) pp31-32.
RN38109 711 (June 29, 1995) pp12-13.
DIAZ, CAMERON
RN38110 749 (December 12, 1996) pp19-20.
DICAPRIO, LEONARDO
RN38111 710 (June 15, 1995) pp17-18.
RN38112 749 (December 12, 1996) pp19-20.
DICKSON, THOMAS GRAY, JR.
RN38113 703 (March 9, 1995) pp20-21.
DIDDLEY, BO
RN38114 733 (May 2, 1996) pp13-14.
DIE KRUPPS
RN38115 668 (October 28, 1993) pp35-36.
DIFRANCO, ANI
RN38116 719 (October 19, 1995) pp15-16.
RN38117 738-739 (July 11, 1996) pp15-16.
RN38118 747 (November 14, 1996) pp25-26.
DIG
RN38119 691 (September 22, 1994) pp19-21.
DILLON FENCE
RN38120 633 (June 25, 1992) pp11-12.
DILLON, MATT
RN38121 681 (May 5, 1994) pp21-22.
DIM STARS
RN38122 633 (June 25, 1992) pp11-12.
DIMEBAG DARRELL
RN38123 689 (August 25, 1994) pp15-16.
RN38124 707 (May 4, 1995) pp19-20.
DINIZIO, PAT
RN38125 648 (January 21, 1993) pp9,11.
DINKENS, RON
RN38126 736 (June 13, 1996) pp19-20.
DINOSAUR JR.
RN38127 656 (May 13, 1993) pp13,15.
RN38128 659 (June 24, 1993) pp13,15.
RN38129 660-661 (July 8, 1993) pp32-33.
RN38130 665 (September 16, 1993) pp31-32.
RN38131 715 (August 24, 1995) pp23,25.
DIPAOLO, JOEY
RN38132 681 (May 5, 1994) pp21-22.
DIRNT, MIKE
RN38133 707 (May 4, 1995) pp19-20.
DISNEY, WALT
RN38134 621 (January 9, 1992) pp10-11.
DIXON, DONNA
RN38135 696 (December 1, 1994) pp23-25.
DIXON, WILLIE
RN38136 691 (September 22, 1994) pp19-21.
RN38137 697 (December 15, 1994) pp17-18,20.
DJ LETHAL
RN38138 671 (December 9, 1993) pp31-32.
DJ MINUTE-MIX
RN38139 657 (May 27, 1993) pp9,11.
DJ POOH
RN38140 706 (April 20, 1995) pp15-17.
DJ PREMIER
RN38141 685 (June 30, 1994) pp40-41.
RN38142 715 (August 24, 1995) pp23,25.
D.J. YELLA
RN38143 639 (September 17, 1992) pp19-20.
DODD, BUBBA
RN38144 685 (June 30, 1994) pp40-41.
DOE, JOHN
RN38145 618 (November 28, 1991) pp11-12.
RN38146 650 (February 18, 1993) pp11,13.
RN38147 663 (August 19, 1993) pp27-28.
RN38148 666 (September 30, 1993) pp27-28.
RN38149 676 (February 24, 1994) pp28-29.
RN38150 700 (January 26, 1995) pp16-17.
DOGSTAR
RN38151 717 (September 21, 1995) pp19-20.
RN38152 742 (September 5, 1996) pp20-21.
DOHERTY, SHANNEN
RN38153 648 (January 21, 1993) pp9,11.
RN38154 688 (August 11, 1994) pp17-18,20.
DOLE, ELIZABETH
RN38155 744 (October 3, 1996) pp19-21.
DOLE, ROBERT
RN38156 723 (December 14, 1995) pp27-28.
RN38157 745 (October 17, 1996) pp27-28.
RN38158 747 (November 14, 1996) pp25-26.
DOLENZ, MICKEY
RN38159 702 (February 23, 1995) pp19-20.
DOLLAR, JOHNNY
RN38160 655 (April 29, 1993) pp11-12.
DOMBROWSKI, VINNIE
RN38161 708 (May 18, 1995) pp17-18.
DOMINO
RN38162 690 (September 8, 1994) pp21,24.
DON, RASA
RN38163 648 (January 21, 1993) pp9,11.
DONAHUE, TOM
RN38164 722 (November 30, 1995) pp19-20.
DONELLY, TANYA
RN38165 659 (June 24, 1993) pp13,15.
RN38166 663 (August 19, 1993) pp27-28.
RN38167 666 (September 30, 1993) pp27-28.
RN38168 667 (October 14, 1993) pp39-

40.
RN38169 671 (December 9, 1993) pp31-32.
RN38170 702 (February 23, 1995) pp19-20.
DOOBIE BROTHERS
RN38171 733 (May 2, 1996) pp13-14.
DOORS
RN38172 648 (January 21, 1993) pp9,11.
RN38173 666 (September 30, 1993) pp27-28.
DORGAN, STEPHANIE
RN38174 704 (March 23, 1995) pp24-25.
DORKIN, EVAN
RN38175 690 (September 8, 1994) pp21,24.
DORNEY, TIM
RN38176 747 (November 14, 1996) pp25-26.
DORSEY, ELIAS
RN38177 707 (May 4, 1995) pp19-20.
DOUCET, MICHAEL
RN38178 658 (June 10, 1993) pp16-17.
DOUGHTY
RN38179 719 (October 19, 1995) pp15-16.
DOUGHTY, M.
RN38180 734 (May 16, 1996) pp17-18.
DOYLE, TAD
RN38181 666 (September 30, 1993) pp27-28.
RN38182 708 (May 18, 1995) pp17-18.
DR. DRE
RN38183 634-635 (July 9, 1992) pp11,13.
RN38184 639 (September 17, 1992) pp19-20.
RN38185 653 (April 1, 1993) pp11,13.
RN38186 659 (June 24, 1993) pp13,15.
RN38187 668 (October 28, 1993) pp35-36.
RN38188 670 (November 25, 1993) pp37-38.
RN38189 678 (March 24, 1994) pp27-28.
RN38190 692 (October 6, 1994) pp15-17.
RN38191 700 (January 26, 1995) pp16-17.
RN38192 702 (February 23, 1995) pp19-20.
DR. HOOK AND THE MEDICINE SHOW
RN38193 680 (April 21, 1994) pp33-34.
DR. JOHN
RN38194 626 (March 19, 1992) pp11,13.
RN38195 640 (October 1, 1992) pp9-10.
DREAM SYNDICATE
RN38196 616 (October 31, 1991) pp11,13.
DREW, DENNIS
RN38197 633 (June 25, 1992) pp11-12.
DREW, EMILY ANN
RN38197 633 (June 25, 1992) pp11-12.
DREW, KERRY
RN38197 633 (June 25, 1992) pp11-12.
D.R.I.
RN38198 721 (November 16, 1995) pp25-26.
DRIVIN' AND CRYIN'
RN38199 618 (November 28, 1991) pp11-12.
RN38200 650 (February 18, 1993) pp11,13.
DROGE, PETE
RN38201 697 (December 15, 1994) pp17-18,20.
RN38202 701 (February 9, 1995) pp16-17.
RN38203 711 (June 29, 1995) pp12-13.
DUDAS, CHRIS
RN38204 700 (January 26, 1995) pp16-17.
DUFF
RN38205 622 (January 23, 1992) pp6-7.
DUKE, DAVID
RN38206 618 (November 28, 1991) pp11-12.
DULLI, GREG
RN38207 674 (January 27, 1994) pp28-29.
RN38208 676 (February 24, 1994) pp28-29.
RN38209 685 (June 30, 1994) pp40-41.
RN38210 688 (August 11, 1994) pp17-18,20.
RN38211 691 (September 22, 1994) pp19-21.
RN38212 708 (May 18, 1995) pp17-18.
RN38213 730 (March 21, 1996) pp17-18.
RN38214 740 (August 8, 1996) pp17-18.
DUNAWAY, FAYE
RN38214 740 (August 8, 1996) pp17-18.
DUNN, DUCK
RN38215 625 (March 5, 1992) pp11,13-15,17+.
RN38216 685 (June 30, 1994) pp40-41.
DUNNE, ROISIN
RN38217 722 (November 30, 1995) pp19-20.
DUNST, KIRSTEN
RN38218 714 (August 10, 1995) pp15-17.
DURAN DURAN
RN38219 675 (February 10, 1994) pp22-23.
RN38220 686-687 (July 14, 1994) pp41-42.
RN38221 690 (September 8, 1994) pp21,24.
RN38222 708 (May 18, 1995) pp17-18.
DURANTE, JIMMY
RN38223 667 (October 14, 1993) pp39-40.
DURITZ, ADAM
RN38224 712-713 (July 13, 1995) pp25-26.
RN38225 742 (September 5, 1996) pp20-21.
DYLAN, BOB
RN38226 617 (November 14, 1991) pp11,13.
RN38227 634-635 (July 9, 1992) pp11,13.
RN38228 636 (August 6, 1992) pp11,13.
RN38229 648 (January 21, 1993) pp9,11.
RN38230 652 (March 18, 1993) pp13,15.
RN38231 655 (April 29, 1993) pp11-12.
RN38232 658 (June 10, 1993) pp16-17.
RN38233 659 (June 24, 1993) pp13,15.
RN38234 665 (September 16, 1993) pp31-32.
RN38235 670 (November 25, 1993) pp37-38.
RN38236 686-687 (July 14, 1994) pp41-42.
RN38237 704 (March 23, 1995) pp24-25.
RN38238 710 (June 15, 1995) pp17-18.
RN38239 712-713 (July 13, 1995) pp25-26.
RN38240 717 (September 21, 1995) pp19-20.
RN38241 721 (November 16, 1995) pp25-26.
RN38242 726 (January 25, 1996) pp17-18.
RN38243 741 (August 22, 1996) pp25-26.
RN38244 742 (September 5, 1996) pp20-21.
RN38245 743 (September 19, 1996) pp19-20.
DYLAN, JAKOB
RN38246 636 (August 6, 1992) pp11,13.
RN38247 657 (May 27, 1993) pp9,11.
RN38248 697 (December 15, 1994) pp17-18,20.
RN38249 746 (October 31, 1996) pp17-18.

E

E STREET BAND
RN38250 644 (November 26, 1992) pp13,15.
RN38251 662 (August 5, 1993) pp33-34.
EAGLES
RN38252 681 (May 5, 1994) pp21-22.
RN38253 697 (December 15, 1994) pp17-18,20.
RN38254 707 (May 4, 1995) pp19-20.
RN38255 734 (May 16, 1996) pp17-18.
EARLE, STEVE
RN38256 629 (April 30, 1992) pp11-12.
RN38257 741 (August 22, 1996) pp25-26.
EARTH, WIND AND FIRE
RN38258 717 (September 21, 1995) pp19-20.
EASTON, SHEENA
RN38259 624 (February 20, 1992) pp11-12.
EAZY-E
RN38260 639 (September 17, 1992) pp19-20.
RN38261 670 (November 25, 1993) pp37-38.
RN38262 674 (January 27, 1994) pp28-29.
RN38263 690 (September 8, 1994) pp21,24.
RN38264 712-713 (July 13, 1995) pp25-26.
EDEN, DANIELA
RN38265 736 (June 13, 1996) pp19-20.
EDGE
RN38266 625 (March 5, 1992) pp11,13-15,17+.
RN38267 636 (August 6, 1992) pp11,13.
RN38268 686-687 (July 14, 1994) pp41-42.
EDMUNDS, DAVE
RN38269 685 (June 30, 1994) pp40-41.
EDWARDS, EDWIN
RN38270 637 (August 20, 1992) pp9,11.
EITZEL, MARK
RN38271 659 (June 24, 1993) pp13,15.
RN38272 670 (November 25, 1993) pp37-38.
EKLUND, GREG
RN38273 709 (June 1, 1995) pp16-17.
ELASTICA
RN38274 712-713 (July 13, 1995) pp25-26.
RN38275 715 (August 24, 1995) pp23,25.
RN38276 723 (December 14, 1995) pp27-28.
RN38277 746 (October 31, 1996) pp17-18.
ELDERS, JOYCELYN
RN38278 708 (May 18, 1995) pp17-18.
ELECTRA, CARMEN
RN38279 748 (November 28, 1996) pp25-26.

ELLIOT, SAM
RN38280 617 (November 14, 1991) pp11,13.
ELLIOTT, JOE
RN38281 640 (October 1, 1992) pp9-10.
ELLIS, TERRY
RN38282 709 (June 1, 1995) pp16-17.
ELLISON, JIM
RN38283 712-713 (July 13, 1995) pp25-26.
ELY, JOE
RN38284 623 (February 6, 1992) pp11,13.
RN38285 660-661 (July 8, 1993) pp32-33.
RN38286 747 (November 14, 1996) pp25-26.
EMF
RN38287 636 (August 6, 1992) pp11,13.
RN38288 653 (April 1, 1993) pp11,13.
EN VOGUE
RN38289 642 (October 29, 1992) pp19,21.
RN38290 650 (February 18, 1993) pp11,13.
RN38291 665 (September 16, 1993) pp31-32.
RN38292 693 (October 20, 1994) pp27-28,30.
RN38293 709 (June 1, 1995) pp16-17.
ENO, BRIAN
RN38294 647 (January 7, 1993) pp9,11.
RN38295 731 (April 4, 1996) pp17-18.
ENRIQUE
RN38296 618 (November 28, 1991) pp11-12.
ERASURE
RN38297 722 (November 30, 1995) pp19-20.
ERICKSON, ROKY
RN38298 708 (May 18, 1995) pp17-18.
ERLANDSON, ERIC
RN38299 644 (November 26, 1992) pp13,15.
RN38300 694 (November 3, 1994) pp17-18,22.
RN38301 734 (May 16, 1996) pp17-18.
RN38302 735 (May 30, 1996) pp12-13.
ESHE, MONTSHO
RN38303 648 (January 21, 1993) pp9,11.
ESPY, MIKE
RN38304 694 (November 3, 1994) pp17-18,22.
ESQUIVEL, JUAN
RN38305 690 (September 8, 1994) pp21,24.
ESTEFAN, GLORIA
RN38306 642 (October 29, 1992) pp19,21.
RN38307 658 (June 10, 1993) pp16-17.
ESTEVEZ, EMILIO
RN38308 627 (April 2, 1992) pp11,13.
ETHERIDGE, MELISSA
RN38309 625 (March 5, 1992) pp11,13-15,17+.
RN38310 685 (June 30, 1994) pp40-41.
RN38311 697 (December 15, 1994) pp17-18,20.
RN38312 703 (March 9, 1995) pp20-21.
RN38313 705 (April 6, 1995) pp16-17.
RN38314 706 (April 20, 1995) pp15-17.
RN38315 728 (February 22, 1996) p20.
RN38316 738-739 (July 11, 1996) pp15-16.
RN38317 748 (November 28, 1996) pp25-26.
EVERCLEAR
RN38318 718 (October 5, 1995) pp20-21.
RN38319 726 (January 25, 1996) pp17-18.
RN38320 740 (August 8, 1996) pp17-18.
RN38321 742 (September 5, 1996) pp20-21.
EVERLAST
RN38322 671 (December 9, 1993) pp31-32.
RN38323 681 (May 5, 1994) pp21-22.
EXTRA FANCY
RN38324 723 (December 14, 1995) pp27-28.
RN38325 746 (October 31, 1996) pp17-18.
EXTREME
RN38326 659 (June 24, 1993) pp13,15.
RN38327 683 (June 2, 1994) pp27-28.
RN38328 692 (October 6, 1994) pp15-17.

F

FABULOUS THUNDERBIRDS
RN38329 634-635 (July 9, 1992) pp11,13.
RN38330 640 (October 1, 1992) pp9-10.
FACES
RN38331 653 (April 1, 1993) pp11,13.
FAGEN, DONALD
RN38332 637 (August 20, 1992) pp9,11.
RN38333 649 (February 4, 1993) pp8-9.
RN38334 664 (September 2, 1993) pp31-32.
FAIR, JAD
RN38335 691 (September 22, 1994) pp19-21.
FAIR, SHEENAH
RN38335 691 (September 22, 1994) pp19-21.
FAIR, SIMON
RN38335 691 (September 22, 1994) pp19-21.
FAIRPORT CONVENTION
RN38335 691 (September 22, 1994) pp19-21.
FAITH NO MORE
RN38336 618 (November 28, 1991) pp11-12.
RN38337 639 (September 17, 1992) pp19-20.
RN38338 652 (March 18, 1993) pp13,15.
FAITHFULL, MARIANNE
RN38339 636 (August 6, 1992) pp11,13.
RN38340 683 (June 2, 1994) pp27-28.
RN38341 716 (September 7, 1995) pp13-14.
RN38342 730 (March 21, 1996) pp17-18.
FALL
RN38343 746 (October 31, 1996) pp17-18.
FARAGHER, DAVEY
RN38344 626 (March 19, 1992) pp11,13.
FARISS, ANDREW
RN38345 663 (August 19, 1993) pp27-28.
FARISS, JON
RN38345 663 (August 19, 1993) pp27-28.
FARLEY, CHRIS
RN38346 740 (August 8, 1996) pp17-18.
FARRAR, JAY
RN38347 684 (June 16, 1994) pp35-36.
RN38348 716 (September 7, 1995) pp13-14.
FARRELL, PERRY
RN38349 617 (November 14, 1991) pp11,13.
RN38350 631 (May 28, 1992) pp9,11.
RN38351 638 (September 3, 1992) pp9,11.
RN38352 648 (January 21, 1993) pp9,11.
RN38353 676 (February 24, 1994) pp28-29.
RN38354 700 (January 26, 1995) pp16-17.
RN38355 707 (May 4, 1995) pp19-20.
RN38356 715 (August 24, 1995) pp23,25.
RN38357 723 (December 14, 1995) pp27-28.
RN38358 727 (February 8, 1996) pp12-13.
RN38359 733 (May 2, 1996) pp13-14.
RN38360 746 (October 31, 1996) pp17-18.
FASTBACKS
RN38361 730 (March 21, 1996) pp17-18.
FAT BOYS
RN38362 726 (January 25, 1996) pp17-18.
FATEH ALI KHAN, NUSRAT
RN38363 727 (February 8, 1996) pp12-13.
FEDERICI, DANNY
RN38364 644 (November 26, 1992) pp13,15.
FEELIES
RN38365 636 (August 6, 1992) pp11,13.
FELBER, DEAN
RN38366 691 (September 22, 1994) pp19-21.
FELDMAN, JOHN
RN38367 745 (October 17, 1996) pp27-28.
FELL, NORMAN
RN38368 678 (March 24, 1994) pp27-28.
FELLINI, FEDERICO
RN38369 625 (March 5, 1992) pp11,13-15,17+.
FELTON, DAVID
RN38370 647 (January 7, 1993) pp9,11.
FELUMLEE, MIKE
RN38371 746 (October 31, 1996) pp17-18.
FENDER, LEO
RN38372 625 (March 5, 1992) pp11,13-15,17+.
FENDER, PHYLLIS
RN38372 625 (March 5, 1992) pp11,13-15,17+.
FERGIE
RN38373 621 (January 9, 1992) pp10-11.
FERRY, BRYAN
RN38374 657 (May 27, 1993) pp9,11.
FIELDS, BILLY
RN38375 618 (November 28, 1991) pp11-12.
FIGGS
RN38376 746 (October 31, 1996) pp17-18.
FILTER
RN38377 720 (November 2, 1995) pp16-17.
RN38378 723 (December 14, 1995) pp27-28.
RN38379 743 (September 19, 1996) pp19-20.
FINCH, JENNIFER
RN38380 644 (November 26, 1992) pp13,15.
RN38381 692 (October 6, 1994) pp15-17.
RN38382 696 (December 1, 1994) pp23-25.
RN38383 718 (October 5, 1995) pp20-21.
FINN, TIM

RN38384 662 (August 5, 1993) pp33-34.
RN38385 707 (May 4, 1995) pp19-20.
FIREHOSE
RN38386 616 (October 31, 1991) pp11,13.
RN38387 627 (April 2, 1992) pp11,13.
RN38388 633 (June 25, 1992) pp11-12.
RN38389 656 (May 13, 1993) pp13,15.
FIRM
RN38390 675 (February 10, 1994) pp22-23.
FISHBONE
RN38391 631 (May 28, 1992) pp9,11.
RN38392 633 (June 25, 1992) pp11-12.
RN38393 634-635 (July 9, 1992) pp11,13.
RN38394 660-661 (July 8, 1993) pp32-33.
RN38395 676 (February 24, 1994) pp28-29.
FISHBURNE, LAURENCE
RN38396 660-661 (July 8, 1993) pp32-33.
RN38397 689 (August 25, 1994) pp15-16.
RN38398 735 (May 30, 1996) pp12-13.
FISHER, NORWOOD
RN38399 676 (February 24, 1994) pp28-29.
FLAT DUO JETS
RN38400 633 (June 25, 1992) pp11-12.
FLAVOR FLAV
RN38401 624 (February 20, 1992) pp11-12.
RN38402 664 (September 2, 1993) pp31-32.
RN38403 671 (December 9, 1993) pp31-32.
RN38404 689 (August 25, 1994) pp15-16.
RN38405 693 (October 20, 1994) pp27-28,30.
RN38406 704 (March 23, 1995) pp24-25.
RN38407 723 (December 14, 1995) pp27-28.
FLEA
RN38408 631 (May 28, 1992) pp9,11.
RN38409 642 (October 29, 1992) pp19,21.
RN38410 648 (January 21, 1993) pp9,11.
RN38411 654 (April 15, 1993) pp11,13.
RN38412 667 (October 14, 1993) pp39-40.
RN38413 674 (January 27, 1994) pp28-29.
RN38414 692 (October 6, 1994) pp15-17.
RN38415 731 (April 4, 1996) pp17-18.
RN38416 744 (October 3, 1996) pp19-21.
FLEETWOOD MAC
RN38417 624 (February 20, 1992) pp11-12.
RN38418 630 (May 14, 1992) pp13,15.
RN38419 655 (April 29, 1993) pp11-12.
RN38420 663 (August 19, 1993) pp27-28.
RN38421 722 (November 30, 1995) pp19-20.
FLEETWOOD, MICK
RN38422 655 (April 29, 1993) pp11-12.
RN38423 659 (June 24, 1993) pp13,15.
FLEMING, DON
RN38424 633 (June 25, 1992) pp11-12.
RN38425 656 (May 13, 1993) pp13,15.
RN38426 668 (October 28, 1993) pp35-36.
RN38427 676 (February 24, 1994) pp28-29.
RN38428 688 (August 11, 1994) pp17-18,20.
FLETCHER, ANDY
RN38429 669 (November 11, 1993) pp27-28.
FLETCHER, JOHN
RN38430 650 (February 18, 1993) pp11,13.
FLINT, KEITH
RN38431 749 (December 12, 1996) pp19-20.
FLOKSMEN
RN38432 662 (August 5, 1993) pp33-34.
FLUKER, DAVID
RN38433 728 (February 22, 1996) p20.
FLYNT, LARRY
RN38434 741 (August 22, 1996) pp25-26.
RN38435 748 (November 28, 1996) pp25-26.
FOGELNES, JAKE
RN38436 709 (June 1, 1995) pp16-17.
FOGERTY, JOHN
RN38437 625 (March 5, 1992) pp11,13-15,17+.
RN38438 630 (May 14, 1992) pp13,15.
FOGHAT
RN38439 660-661 (July 8, 1993) pp32-33.
RN38440 705 (April 6, 1995) pp16-17.
FOLDS, BEN
RN38441 749 (December 12, 1996) pp19-20.
FOLLOW FOR NOW
RN38442 618 (November 28, 1991) pp11-12.
FONDA, PETER
RN38443 653 (April 1, 1993) pp11,13.
RN38444 657 (May 27, 1993) pp9,11.
FONG-TORRES, BEN
RN38445 647 (January 7, 1993) pp9,11.
FONGHEISER, DENNY
RN38446 696 (December 1, 1994) pp23-25.
FONTANA, D. J.
RN38447 742 (September 5, 1996) pp20-21.
FOO FIGHTERS
RN38448 706 (April 20, 1995) pp15-17.
RN38449 732 (April 18, 1996) pp19-20.
RN38450 736 (June 13, 1996) pp19-20.
RN38451 740 (August 8, 1996) pp17-18.
RN38452 745 (October 17, 1996) pp27-28.
FORD, HARRISON
RN38453 735 (May 30, 1996) pp12-13.
RN38454 736 (June 13, 1996) pp19-20.
FORD, MARC
RN38455 621 (January 9, 1992) pp10-11.
RN38456 642 (October 29, 1992) pp19,21.
RN38457 709 (June 1, 1995) pp16-17.
FOREIGNER
RN38458 642 (October 29, 1992) pp19,21.
RN38459 718 (October 5, 1995) pp20-21.
FORMAN, MILOS
RN38460 741 (August 22, 1996) pp25-26.
FOSTER
RN38461 746 (October 31, 1996) pp17-18.
FOSTER, JODIE
RN38462 692 (October 6, 1994) pp15-17.
4 NON BLONDES
RN38463 671 (December 9, 1993) pp31-32.
RN38464 681 (May 5, 1994) pp21-22.
FOWLER, BERNARD
RN38465 670 (November 25, 1993) pp37-38.
RN38466 734 (May 16, 1996) pp17-18.
FRAMPTON, PETER
RN38467 731 (April 4, 1996) pp17-18.
FRANCIS, BLACK
RN38468 616 (October 31, 1991) pp11,13.
RN38469 652 (March 18, 1993) pp13,15.
FRANK, ANTHONY
RN38470 624 (February 20, 1992) pp11-12.
FRANKLIN, ARETHA
RN38471 658 (June 10, 1993) pp16-17.
RN38472 665 (September 16, 1993) pp31-32.
RN38473 680 (April 21, 1994) pp33-34.
RN38474 717 (September 21, 1995) pp19-20.
FRANTI, MICHAEL
RN38475 708 (May 18, 1995) pp17-18.
RN38476 719 (October 19, 1995) pp15-16.
RN38477 738-739 (July 11, 1996) pp15-16.
FRANTZ, CHRIS
RN38478 637 (August 20, 1992) pp9,11.
RN38479 638 (September 3, 1992) pp9,11.
FRASER, BRENDAN
RN38480 680 (April 21, 1994) pp33-34.
FRASER, DEAN
RN38481 702 (February 23, 1995) pp19-20.
FREAKWATER
RN38482 709 (June 1, 1995) pp16-17.
FREAKY CHAKRA
RN38483 715 (August 24, 1995) pp23,25.
FREDRO
RN38484 729 (March 7, 1996) pp9-10.
FREEMAN, MATT
RN38485 727 (February 8, 1996) pp12-13.
FREESE, JOSH
RN38486 730 (March 21, 1996) pp17-18.
FREEZIN', PETE
RN38487 616 (October 31, 1991) pp11,13.
FREHLEY, ACE
RN38488 732 (April 18, 1996) pp19-20.
FRISCHMANN, JUSTINE
RN38489 712-713 (July 13, 1995) pp25-26.
RN38490 715 (August 24, 1995) pp23,25.
RN38491 723 (December 14, 1995) pp27-28.
RN38492 746 (October 31, 1996) pp17-18.
FROOM, MITCHELL
RN38493 634-635 (July 9, 1992) pp11,13.
FRUSCIANTE, JOHN
RN38494 667 (October 14, 1993) pp39-40.
FSK
RN38495 712-713 (July 13, 1995) pp25-26.
FUENTES, DAISY
RN38496 723 (December 14, 1995) pp27-28.
FUGAZI
RN38497 744 (October 3, 1996) pp19-21.
FUGEES
RN38498 741 (August 22, 1996) pp25-26.
RN38499 746 (October 31, 1996) pp17-18.

FULSON, LOWELL
RN38500 697 (December 15, 1994) pp17-18,20.
FUN LOVIN' CRIMINALS
RN38501 747 (November 14, 1996) pp25-26.
FUNKADELIC
RN38502 654 (April 15, 1993) pp11,13.
RN38503 692 (October 6, 1994) pp15-17.
FUNKDOOBIEST
RN38504 671 (December 9, 1993) pp31-32.
RN38505 710 (June 15, 1995) pp17-18.

G

GABRELS, REEVES
RN38506 622 (January 23, 1992) pp6-7.
GABRIEL, PETER
RN38507 615 (October 17, 1991) pp13-14.
RN38508 617 (November 14, 1991) pp11,13.
RN38509 629 (April 30, 1992) pp11-12.
RN38510 648 (January 21, 1993) pp9,11.
RN38511 653 (April 1, 1993) pp11,13.
RN38512 654 (April 15, 1993) pp11,13.
RN38513 663 (August 19, 1993) pp27-28.
RN38514 674 (January 27, 1994) pp28-29.
RN38515 679 (April 7, 1994) pp37-39.
RN38516 691 (September 22, 1994) pp19-21.
RN38517 693 (October 20, 1994) pp27-28,30.
RN38518 701 (February 9, 1995) pp16-17.
RN38519 736 (June 13, 1996) pp19-20.
GACY BUNCH
RN38520 697 (December 15, 1994) pp17-18,20.
GACY, JOHN WAYNE
RN38520 697 (December 15, 1994) pp17-18,20.
GAHAN, DAVE
RN38521 696 (December 1, 1994) pp23-25.
GALLAGHER, LIAM
RN38522 727 (February 8, 1996) pp12-13.
RN38523 731 (April 4, 1996) pp17-18.
RN38524 735 (May 30, 1996) pp12-13.
RN38525 737 (June 27, 1996) pp15-16.
RN38526 745 (October 17, 1996) pp27-28.
RN38527 749 (December 12, 1996) pp19-20.
GALLAGHER, NOEL
RN38528 718 (October 5, 1995) pp20-21.
RN38529 727 (February 8, 1996) pp12-13.
RN38530 742 (September 5, 1996) pp20-21.
RN38531 749 (December 12, 1996) pp19-20.
GALLO, JOEY
RN38532 634-635 (July 9, 1992) pp11,13.
GALLUP, SIMON
RN38533 631 (May 28, 1992) pp9,11.
RN38534 633 (June 25, 1992) pp11-12.
GANDHI
RN38535 664 (September 2, 1993) pp31-32.
GANG STARR
RN38536 685 (June 30, 1994) pp40-41.
RN38537 690 (September 8, 1994) pp21,24.
RN38538 708 (May 18, 1995) pp17-18.
RN38539 715 (August 24, 1995) pp23,25.
GANO, GORDON
RN38540 665 (September 16, 1993) pp31-32.
GARBAGE
RN38541 740 (August 8, 1996) pp17-18.
GARCIA, DEBRA KOONS
RN38542 734 (May 16, 1996) pp17-18.
GARCIA, JERRY
RN38543 637 (August 20, 1992) pp9,11.
RN38544 639 (September 17, 1992) pp19-20.
RN38545 656 (May 13, 1993) pp13,15.
RN38546 657 (May 27, 1993) pp9,11.
RN38547 678 (March 24, 1994) pp27-28.
RN38548 679 (April 7, 1994) pp37-39.
RN38549 691 (September 22, 1994) pp19-21.
RN38550 696 (December 1, 1994) pp23-25.
RN38551 703 (March 9, 1995) pp20-21.
RN38552 704 (March 23, 1995) pp24-25.
RN38553 705 (April 6, 1995) pp16-17.
RN38554 730 (March 21, 1996) pp17-18.
RN38555 738-739 (July 11, 1996) pp15-16.
GARCIA, MAYTE
RN38556 733 (May 2, 1996) pp13-14.
GARDNER, ERIC
RN38557 616 (October 31, 1991) pp11,13.
GARDNER, JANIS
RN38557 616 (October 31, 1991) pp11,13.
GARDNER, SUZI
RN38558 627 (April 2, 1992) pp11,13.
RN38559 644 (November 26, 1992) pp13,15.
RN38560 692 (October 6, 1994) pp15-17.
RN38561 696 (December 1, 1994) pp23-25.
GARDNER, TED
RN38562 723 (December 14, 1995) pp27-28.
GARFUNKEL, ART
RN38563 654 (April 15, 1993) pp11,13.
GARGIULO, LU LU
RN38564 730 (March 21, 1996) pp17-18.
GAROFALO, JANEANE
RN38565 734 (May 16, 1996) pp17-18.
RN38566 740 (August 8, 1996) pp17-18.
GARRETT, PETER
RN38567 633 (June 25, 1992) pp11-12.
RN38568 652 (March 18, 1993) pp13,15.
RN38569 669 (November 11, 1993) pp27-28.
RN38570 690 (September 8, 1994) pp21,24.
GAULTIER, JEAN PAUL
RN38571 694 (November 3, 1994) pp17-18,22.
GAUTREAU, AIMEE
RN38572 731 (April 4, 1996) pp17-18.
GAYE, MARVIN
RN38573 683 (June 2, 1994) pp27-28.
RN38574 707 (May 4, 1995) pp19-20.
RN38575 717 (September 21, 1995) pp19-20.
GAYE, NONA
RN38576 683 (June 2, 1994) pp27-28.
GEGGY TAH
RN38577 719 (October 19, 1995) pp15-16.
GELDOF, BOB
RN38578 715 (August 24, 1995) pp23,25.
GELLER, SARAH
RN38579 685 (June 30, 1994) pp40-41.
GENERAL PUBLIC
RN38580 674 (January 27, 1994) pp28-29.
GEORGEFF, DAVE
RN38581 709 (June 1, 1995) pp16-17.
GEORGIA SATELLITES
RN38582 650 (February 18, 1993) pp11,13.
GERMS
RN38583 700 (January 26, 1995) pp16-17.
GERSHWIN, GEORGE
RN38584 629 (April 30, 1992) pp11-12.
RN38585 686-687 (July 14, 1994) pp41-42.
GHOST FACE KILLER
RN38586 730 (March 21, 1996) pp17-18.
GIBBONS, BILLY
RN38587 631 (May 28, 1992) pp9,11.
GIBBS, DAVE
RN38588 689 (August 25, 1994) pp15-16.
GIBBS, MELVIN
RN38589 623 (February 6, 1992) pp11,13.
GIBSON, BILL
RN38590 742 (September 5, 1996) pp20-21.
GIBSON, BRIAN
RN38591 660-661 (July 8, 1993) pp32-33.
GIBSON, DEBBIE
RN38592 624 (February 20, 1992) pp11-12.
RN38593 707 (May 4, 1995) pp19-20.
RN38594 712-713 (July 13, 1995) pp25-26.
GIBSON, MEL
RN38595 740 (August 8, 1996) pp17-18.
GIGOLO AUNTS
RN38596 689 (August 25, 1994) pp15-16.
GILLEY, MICKEY
RN38597 694 (November 3, 1994) pp17-18,22.
GILMAN, LENNY
RN38598 706 (April 20, 1995) pp15-17.
GILMORE, JIMMIE DALE
RN38599 665 (September 16, 1993) pp31-32.
RN38600 670 (November 25, 1993) pp37-38.
RN38600a 678 (March24, 1994) pp27-28.
RN38601 679 (April 7, 1994) pp37-39.
RN38602 697 (December 15, 1994) pp17-18,20.
RN38603 706 (April 20, 1995) pp15-17.
RN38604 729 (March 7, 1996) pp9-10.
GILMOUR, DAVID
RN38605 689 (August 25, 1994) pp15-16.
GILMOUR, JIMMIE DALE
RN38606 678 (March 24, 1994) pp27-28.
GILREATH, CHARLIE
RN38607 723 (December 14, 1995) pp27-28.
GIN BLOSSOMS
RN38608 665 (September 16, 1993) pp31-32.
RN38609 681 (May 5, 1994) pp21-22.
RN38610 722 (November 30, 1995) pp19-20.
GINGRICH, NEWT

RN38611 708 (May 18, 1995) pp17-18.
RN38612 726 (January 25, 1996) pp17-18.
RN38613 729 (March 7, 1996) pp9-10.
GINSBERG, ALLEN
RN38614 679 (April 7, 1994) pp37-39.
RN38615 690 (September 8, 1994) pp21,24.
RN38616 705 (April 6, 1995) pp16-17.
RN38617 706 (April 20, 1995) pp15-17.
RN38618 744 (October 3, 1996) pp19-21.
GIORNO, JOHN
RN38619 700 (January 26, 1995) pp16-17.
GIRLS AGAINST BOYS
RN38620 736 (June 13, 1996) pp19-20.
GITS
RN38621 666 (September 30, 1993) pp27-28.
RN38622 689 (August 25, 1994) pp15-16.
RN38623 706 (April 20, 1995) pp15-17.
GIULIANI, RUDY
RN38624 716 (September 7, 1995) pp13-14.
GLASER, GABBY
RN38625 710 (June 15, 1995) pp17-18.
GLASS, PHILIP
RN38626 647 (January 7, 1993) pp9,11.
RN38627 701 (February 9, 1995) pp16-17.
RN38628 706 (April 20, 1995) pp15-17.
RN38629 733 (May 2, 1996) pp13-14.
RN38630 744 (October 3, 1996) pp19-21.
GLITTER, GARY
RN38631 741 (August 22, 1996) pp25-26.
GLOVER, COREY
RN38632 637 (August 20, 1992) pp9,11.
GLUE
RN38633 723 (December 14, 1995) pp27-28.
GO-GO'S
RN38634 616 (October 31, 1991) pp11,13.
GOATS
RN38635 707 (May 4, 1995) pp19-20.
GOD
RN38636 626 (March 19, 1992) pp11,13.
GOD STREET WINE
RN38637 702 (February 23, 1995) pp19-20.
GOFFEY, DANNY
RN38638 726 (January 25, 1996) pp17-18.
GOFFRIER, BILL
RN38639 683 (June 2, 1994) pp27-28.
GOLD, TODD
RN38640 617 (November 14, 1991) pp11,13.
GOLDBERG, ALEX
RN38641 615 (October 17, 1991) pp13-14.
GOLDBERG, WHOOPI
RN38641 615 (October 17, 1991) pp13-14.
RN38642 629 (April 30, 1992) pp11-12.
GOLDEN PALOMINOS
RN38643 686-687 (July 14, 1994) pp41-42.
RN38644 712-713 (July 13, 1995) pp25-26.
GOLDEN SMOG
RN38645 633 (June 25, 1992) pp11-12.
RN38646 729 (March 7, 1996) pp9-10.
GOLDFINGER
RN38647 740 (August 8, 1996) pp17-18.
RN38648 745 (October 17, 1996) pp27-28.
GOLDIE
RN38648 745 (October 17, 1996) pp27-28.
GOLDMAN, EMMA
RN38649 691 (September 22, 1994) pp19-21.
GOLDSMITH, WILLIAM
RN38650 736 (June 13, 1996) pp19-20.
GOLUB, ALEX
RN38651 694 (November 3, 1994) pp17-18,22.
GONZO
RN38652 618 (November 28, 1991) pp11-12.
GOO GOO DOLLS
RN38653 721 (November 16, 1995) pp25-26.
GORBACHEV, MIKHAIL
RN38654 623 (February 6, 1992) pp11,13.
RN38655 657 (May 27, 1993) pp9,11.
GORDON, IRVING
RN38656 628 (April 16, 1992) pp11,13.
RN38657 634-635 (July 9, 1992) pp11,13.
GORDON, KIM
RN38658 637 (August 20, 1992) pp9,11.
RN38659 683 (June 2, 1994) pp27-28.
RN38660 693 (October 20, 1994) pp27-28,30.
RN38661 700 (January 26, 1995) pp16-17.
RN38662 702 (February 23, 1995) pp19-20.
RN38663 721 (November 16, 1995) pp25-26.
GORDON, NINA
RN38664 701 (February 9, 1995) pp16-17.
RN38665 709 (June 1, 1995) pp16-17.
GORDY, BERRY
RN38666 679 (April 7, 1994) pp37-39.
GORE, ALBERT
RN38667 720 (November 2, 1995) pp16-17.
GORMAN, TIM
RN38668 644 (November 26, 1992) pp13,15.
GORMAN, TOM
RN38669 663 (August 19, 1993) pp27-28.
GORTON, SLADE
RN38670 708 (May 18, 1995) pp17-18.
GOSSARD, STONE
RN38671 624 (February 20, 1992) pp11-12.
RN38672 634-635 (July 9, 1992) pp11,13.
RN38673 662 (August 5, 1993) pp33-34.
RN38674 726 (January 25, 1996) pp17-18.
GOTTI, JOHN
RN38675 734 (May 16, 1996) pp17-18.
GOULD, BILLY
RN38676 652 (March 18, 1993) pp13,15.
GOULD, DARBY
RN38677 644 (November 26, 1992) pp13,15.
GRAFFIN, GREG
RN38678 700 (January 26, 1995) pp16-17.
RN38679 722 (November 30, 1995) pp19-20.
GRAHAM, BILL
RN38680 621 (January 9, 1992) pp10-11.
RN38681 625 (March 5, 1992) pp11,13-15,17+.
RN38682 681 (May 5, 1994) pp21-22.
GRAHAM, GLEN
RN38683 639 (September 17, 1992) pp19-20.
GRAMM, LOU
RN38684 642 (October 29, 1992) pp19,21.
GRANDMASTER FLASH
RN38685 670 (November 25, 1993) pp37-38.
RN38686 708 (May 18, 1995) pp17-18.
GRANING, CHICK
RN38687 704 (March 23, 1995) pp24-25.
GRANT, EDDIE
RN38688 662 (August 5, 1993) pp33-34.
GRANT LEE BUFFALO
RN38689 676 (February 24, 1994) pp28-29.
RN38690 704 (March 23, 1995) pp24-25.
GRATEFUL DEAD
RN38691 639 (September 17, 1992) pp19-20.
RN38692 640 (October 1, 1992) pp9-10.
RN38693 657 (May 27, 1993) pp9,11.
RN38694 666 (September 30, 1993) pp27-28.
RN38695 670 (November 25, 1993) pp37-38.
RN38696 679 (April 7, 1994) pp37-39.
RN38697 681 (May 5, 1994) pp21-22.
RN38698 691 (September 22, 1994) pp19-21.
RN38699 696 (December 1, 1994) pp23-25.
RN38700 715 (August 24, 1995) pp23,25.
RN38701 738-739 (July 11, 1996) pp15-16.
RN38702 746 (October 31, 1996) pp17-18.
RN38703 747 (November 14, 1996) pp25-26.
GRAVITY KILLS
RN38703 747 (November 14, 1996) pp25-26.
GRAY, DOUG
RN38704 740 (August 8, 1996) pp17-18.
GREEN, AL
RN38705 686-687 (July 14, 1994) pp41-42.
RN38706 706 (April 20, 1995) pp15-17.
GREEN DAY
RN38707 689 (August 25, 1994) pp15-16.
RN38708 693 (October 20, 1994) pp27-28,30.
RN38709 694 (November 3, 1994) pp17-18,22.
RN38710 701 (February 9, 1995) pp16-17.
RN38711 707 (May 4, 1995) pp19-20.
RN38712 734 (May 16, 1996) pp17-18.
GREENBERG, MARK
RN38713 714 (August 10, 1995) pp15-17.
GREENE, RICHARD
RN38714 718 (October 5, 1995) pp20-21.
GREENHALGH, TOM
RN38715 736 (June 13, 1996) pp19-20.
GREENWAY, BARNEY
RN38716 694 (November 3, 1994) pp17-18,22.
GREENWOOD, COLIN
RN38717 738-739 (July 11, 1996) pp15-16.
GREENWOOD, GAIL
RN38718 663 (August 19, 1993) pp27-28.
GREENWOOD, JONNY

RN38719 738-739 (July 11, 1996) pp15-16.
GREENWOOD, LEE
RN38720 684 (June 16, 1994) pp35-36.
GRIFFIN, RICK
RN38721 666 (September 30, 1993) pp27-28.
GRIFFITH, BRIAN
RN38722 722 (November 30, 1995) pp19-20.
GRIFFITH, MELANIE
RN38723 647 (January 7, 1993) pp9,11.
GRIFFITH, NANCI
RN38724 637 (August 20, 1992) pp9,11.
RN38725 663 (August 19, 1993) pp27-28.
RN38726 684 (June 16, 1994) pp35-36.
RN38727 729 (March 7, 1996) pp9-10.
GRILLO, BRIAN
RN38728 746 (October 31, 1996) pp17-18.
GRIPPE, CURTIS
RN38729 722 (November 30, 1995) pp19-20.
GROHL, DAVE
RN38730 667 (October 14, 1993) pp39-40.
RN38731 674 (January 27, 1994) pp28-29.
RN38732 676 (February 24, 1994) pp28-29.
RN38733 688 (August 11, 1994) pp17-18,20.
RN38734 691 (September 22, 1994) pp19-21.
RN38735 693 (October 20, 1994) pp27-28,30.
RN38736 702 (February 23, 1995) pp19-20.
RN38737 706 (April 20, 1995) pp15-17.
RN38738 710 (June 15, 1995) pp17-18.
RN38739 732 (April 18, 1996) pp19-20.
RN38740 736 (June 13, 1996) pp19-20.
RN38741 745 (October 17, 1996) pp27-28.
GRUND, ANDY
RN38742 708 (May 18, 1995) pp17-18.
GRUSHECKY, JOE
RN38743 717 (September 21, 1995) pp19-20.
RN38744 722 (November 30, 1995) pp19-20.
GRYPHON
RN38745 679 (April 7, 1994) pp37-39.
GUDMUNDSDOTTIR, BJORK
RN38746 658 (June 10, 1993) pp16-17.
RN38747 679 (April 7, 1994) pp37-39.
RN38748 697 (December 15, 1994) pp17-18,20.
RN38749 704 (March 23, 1995) pp24-25.
RN38750 745 (October 17, 1996) pp27-28.
GUESS WHO
RN38751 740 (August 8, 1996) pp17-18.
GUEST, CHRISTOPHER
RN38752 662 (August 5, 1993) pp33-34.
GUISSMANN, WOODY
RN38753 683 (June 2, 1994) pp27-28.
GUMBALL
RN38754 633 (June 25, 1992) pp11-12.
RN38755 656 (May 13, 1993) pp13,15.
RN38756 668 (October 28, 1993) pp35-36.
RN38757 676 (February 24, 1994) pp28-29.
GUMBS, TRENTEN
RN38758 626 (March 19, 1992) pp11,13.
RN38759 633 (June 25, 1992) pp11-12.
GUNN, DAVID
RN38760 671 (December 9, 1993) pp31-32.
GUNN, DAVID, JR.
RN38760 671 (December 9, 1993) pp31-32.
GUNS N' ROSES
RN38761 616 (October 31, 1991) pp11,13.
RN38762 622 (January 23, 1992) pp6-7.
RN38763 625 (March 5, 1992) pp11,13-15,17+.
RN38764 634-635 (July 9, 1992) pp11,13.
RN38765 639 (September 17, 1992) pp19-20.
RN38766 642 (October 29, 1992) pp19,21.
RN38767 644 (November 26, 1992) pp13,15.
RN38768 648 (January 21, 1993) pp9,11.
RN38769 650 (February 18, 1993) pp11,13.
RN38770 652 (March 18, 1993) pp13,15.
RN38771 663 (August 19, 1993) pp27-28.
RN38772 671 (December 9, 1993) pp31-32.
RN38773 676 (February 24, 1994) pp28-29.
RN38774 690 (September 8, 1994) pp21,24.
RN38775 696 (December 1, 1994) pp23-25.
RN38776 721 (November 16, 1995) pp25-26.
RN38777 746 (October 31, 1996) pp17-18.
GURU
RN38778 690 (September 8, 1994) pp21,24.
RN38779 708 (May 18, 1995) pp17-18.
RN38780 711 (June 29, 1995) pp12-13.
RN38781 715 (August 24, 1995) pp23,25.
GUTHRIE, ARLO
RN38782 679 (April 7, 1994) pp37-39.
RN38783 747 (November 14, 1996) pp25-26.
GUTHRIE, WOODY
RN38783 747 (November 14, 1996) pp25-26.
GUTTERMOUTH
RN38784 711 (June 29, 1995) pp12-13.
RN38785 715 (August 24, 1995) pp23,25.
RN38786 718 (October 5, 1995) pp20-21.
GUY, BUDDY
RN38787 615 (October 17, 1991) pp13-14.
RN38788 640 (October 1, 1992) pp9-10.
RN38789 676 (February 24, 1994) pp28-29.

H

HADJOPOULOS, SUE
RN38790 637 (August 20, 1992) pp9,11.
HAGAR, SAMMY
RN38791 615 (October 17, 1991) pp13-14.
RN38792 622 (January 23, 1992) pp6-7.
RN38793 648 (January 21, 1993) pp9,11.
RN38794 654 (April 15, 1993) pp11,13.
RN38795 681 (May 5, 1994) pp21-22.
RN38796 729 (March 7, 1996) pp9-10.
RN38797 731 (April 4, 1996) pp17-18.
HALF JAPANESE
RN38798 691 (September 22, 1994) pp19-21.
HALFORD, ROB
RN38799 642 (October 29, 1992) pp19,21.
HALL AND OATES
RN38800 704 (March 23, 1995) pp24-25.
HALL, ARSENIO
RN38801 615 (October 17, 1991) pp13-14.
HALL, JERRY
RN38802 624 (February 20, 1992) pp11-12.
RN38803 653 (April 1, 1993) pp11,13.
RN38804 731 (April 4, 1996) pp17-18.
RN38805 748 (November 28, 1996) pp25-26.
HALL, JOHN S.
RN38806 659 (June 24, 1993) pp13,15.
HALL, ROSIE
RN38807 731 (April 4, 1996) pp17-18.
HALL, VONDIE CURTIS
RN38808 741 (August 22, 1996) pp25-26.
HALLUCINATIONS
RN38809 736 (June 13, 1996) pp19-20.
HAMILTON, JULIAN FORREST
RN38810 627 (April 2, 1992) pp11,13.
HAMILTON, PAGE
RN38811 669 (November 11, 1993) pp27-28.
HAMILTON, TERRY
RN38812 627 (April 2, 1992) pp11,13.
HAMILTON, TOM
RN38812 627 (April 2, 1992) pp11,13.
RN38813 634-635 (July 9, 1992) pp11,13.
RN38814 659 (June 24, 1993) pp13,15.
HAMLISCH, MARVIN
RN38815 665 (September 16, 1993) pp31-32.
HAMMER
RN38816 630 (May 14, 1992) pp13,15.
RN38817 631 (May 28, 1992) pp9,11.
RN38818 640 (October 1, 1992) pp9-10.
RN38819 654 (April 15, 1993) pp11,13.
HAMMER, M. C.
RN38820 615 (October 17, 1991) pp13-14.
HAMMERBOX
RN38821 666 (September 30, 1993) pp27-28.
HAMMETT, KIRK
RN38822 618 (November 28, 1991) pp11-12.
RN38823 628 (April 16, 1992) pp11,13.
RN38824 655 (April 29, 1993) pp11-12.
RN38825 665 (September 16, 1993) pp31-32.
RN38826 681 (May 5, 1994) pp21-22.
RN38827 727 (February 8, 1996) pp12-13.
RN38828 742 (September 5, 1996) pp20-21.
HANCOCK, JOHN
RN38829 729 (March 7, 1996) pp9-10.
HANCOCK, POLLY
RN38830 650 (February 18, 1993) pp11,13.
HANKS, TOM
RN38831 703 (March 9, 1995) pp20-21.
HANLEY, KAY
RN38832 693 (October 20, 1994) pp27-28,30.
HANNA, KATHLEEN
RN38833 690 (September 8, 1994)

pp21,24.
RN38834 720 (November 2, 1995) pp16-17.
RN38835 738-739 (July 11, 1996) pp15-16.
HANSEN, PATTI
RN38836 647 (January 7, 1993) pp9,11.
RN38837 748 (November 28, 1996) pp25-26.
HAPPY MONDAYS
RN38838 638 (September 3, 1992) pp9,11.
HARDING, JOHN WESLEY
RN38839 627 (April 2, 1992) pp11,13.
RN38840 649 (February 4, 1993) pp8-9.
RN38841 688 (August 11, 1994) pp17-18,20.
HARDWICK, CHRIS
RN38842 748 (November 28, 1996) pp25-26.
HARLOW, LISA
RN38843 700 (January 26, 1995) pp16-17.
HARMFUL IF SWALLOWED
RN38844 702 (February 23, 1995) pp19-20.
HARNOY, OFRA
RN38845 731 (April 4, 1996) pp17-18.
HARPER, BEN
RN38846 717 (September 21, 1995) pp19-20.
RN38847 726 (January 25, 1996) pp17-18.
HARRELL, ANDRE
RN38848 712-713 (July 13, 1995) pp25-26.
HARRELSON, WOODY
RN38849 691 (September 22, 1994) pp19-21.
RN38850 741 (August 22, 1996) pp25-26.
RN38851 748 (November 28, 1996) pp25-26.
HARRIS, EMMYLOU
RN38852 746 (October 31, 1996) pp17-18.
HARRIS, LISA
RN38853 749 (December 12, 1996) pp19-20.
HARRISON, GEORGE
RN38854 630 (May 14, 1992) pp13,15.
RN38855 631 (May 28, 1992) pp9,11.
RN38856 648 (January 21, 1993) pp9,11.
RN38857 649 (February 4, 1993) pp8-9.
RN38858 653 (April 1, 1993) pp11,13.
RN38859 683 (June 2, 1994) pp27-28.
HARRY, DEBBIE
RN38860 621 (January 9, 1992) pp10-11.
RN38861 688 (August 11, 1994) pp17-18,20.
RN38862 700 (January 26, 1995) pp16-17.
RN38863 723 (December 14, 1995) pp27-28.
RN38864 728 (February 22, 1996) p20.
HART, BETSY
RN38865 747 (November 14, 1996) pp25-26.
HART, GRANT
RN38866 729 (March 7, 1996) pp9-10.
HART, JOHN
RN38867 692 (October 6, 1994) pp15-17.
HART, MARK
RN38868 662 (August 5, 1993) pp33-34.
HART, MICKEY
RN38869 648 (January 21, 1993) pp9,11.
RN38870 733 (May 2, 1996) pp13-14.
RN38871 738-739 (July 11, 1996) pp15-16.
HART, TERRY
RN38872 744 (October 3, 1996) pp19-21.
HARTMAN, PHIL
RN38873 693 (October 20, 1994) pp27-28,30.
HARTNOLL, PHIL
RN38874 745 (October 17, 1996) pp27-28.
HARVEY, MICK
RN38875 692 (October 6, 1994) pp15-17.
HARVEY, POLLY JEAN
RN38876 669 (November 11, 1993) pp27-28.
RN38877 679 (April 7, 1994) pp37-39.
RN38878 733 (May 2, 1996) pp13-14.
HARVEY, RICHARD
RN38879 679 (April 7, 1994) pp37-39.
HARWOOD, JUSTIN
RN38880 748 (November 28, 1996) pp25-26.
HASKETT, CHRIS
RN38881 686-687 (July 14, 1994) pp41-42.
HATER
RN38882 667 (October 14, 1993) pp39-40.
HATFIELD, JULIANA
RN38883 627 (April 2, 1992) pp11,13.
RN38884 662 (August 5, 1993) pp33-34.
RN38885 671 (December 9, 1993) pp31-32.
RN38886 691 (September 22, 1994) pp19-21.
RN38887 700 (January 26, 1995) pp16-17.
RN38888 702 (February 23, 1995) pp19-20.
RN38889 703 (March 9, 1995) pp20-21.
HATORI, HONDA
RN38890 729 (March 7, 1996) pp9-10.
HATORI, MIHO
RN38890 729 (March 7, 1996) pp9-10.
HATZIYANNIS, ROBIN
RN38891 730 (March 21, 1996) pp17-18.
HAVEL, VACLAV
RN38892 717 (September 21, 1995) pp19-20.
RN38893 729 (March 7, 1996) pp9-10.
HAVENS, RICHIE
RN38894 648 (January 21, 1993) pp9,11.
RN38895 679 (April 7, 1994) pp37-39.
HAWKE, ETHAN
RN38896 688 (August 11, 1994) pp17-18,20.
RN38897 744 (October 3, 1996) pp19-21.
RN38898 749 (December 12, 1996) pp19-20.
HAWKINS, ERSKINE
RN38899 654 (April 15, 1993) pp11,13.
HAWKINS, SOPHIE B.
RN38900 631 (May 28, 1992) pp9,11.
RN38901 714 (August 10, 1995) pp15-17.
HAWKINS, TED
RN38902 700 (January 26, 1995) pp16-17.
HAYDEN
RN38903 747 (November 14, 1996) pp25-26.
RN38904 749 (December 12, 1996) pp19-20.
HAYDEN, ROBERT
RN38905 732 (April 18, 1996) pp19-20.
HAYDEN, TOM
RN38906 745 (October 17, 1996) pp27-28.
HAYES, ISAAC
RN38907 716 (September 7, 1995) pp13-14.
RN38908 733 (May 2, 1996) pp13-14.
RN38909 737 (June 27, 1996) pp15-16.
HAYES, ROBERT PAUL
RN38910 631 (May 28, 1992) pp9,11.
HAYES, RUTHERFORD B.
RN38911 710 (June 15, 1995) pp17-18.
HAYNES, GIBBY
RN38912 674 (January 27, 1994) pp28-29.
RN38913 694 (November 3, 1994) pp17-18,22.
RN38914 709 (June 1, 1995) pp16-17.
RN38915 747 (November 14, 1996) pp25-26.
HAYNES, WARREN
RN38916 746 (October 31, 1996) pp17-18.
HAYWARD, RICHIE
RN38917 615 (October 17, 1991) pp13-14.
HAZEL
RN38918 709 (June 1, 1995) pp16-17.
HEADLINER
RN38919 648 (January 21, 1993) pp9,11.
HEADON, TOPPER
RN38920 706 (April 20, 1995) pp15-17.
HEALEY, JACK
RN38921 654 (April 15, 1993) pp11,13.
HEART
RN38922 624 (February 20, 1992) pp11-12.
RN38923 649 (February 4, 1993) pp8-9.
RN38924 696 (December 1, 1994) pp23-25.
HEARTBREAKERS
RN38925 633 (June 25, 1992) pp11-12.
RN38926 738-739 (July 11, 1996) pp15-16.
HEATHMAN, RON
RN38927 731 (April 4, 1996) pp17-18.
HEAVY D
RN38928 720 (November 2, 1995) pp16-17.
HEFNER, CHRISTIE
RN38929 737 (June 27, 1996) pp15-16.
HEIDORN, MIKE
RN38930 716 (September 7, 1995) pp13-14.
HELL, RICHARD
RN38931 633 (June 25, 1992) pp11-12.
HELM, LEVON
RN38932 742 (September 5, 1996) pp20-21.
HELMET
RN38933 666 (September 30, 1993) pp27-28.
RN38934 669 (November 11, 1993) pp27-28.
RN38935 693 (October 20, 1994) pp27-28,30.
HELMS, CHET
RN38936 681 (May 5, 1994) pp21-22.
HELMS, JESSE
RN38937 749 (December 12, 1996) pp19-20.
HENDRIX, AL
RN38938 625 (March 5, 1992) pp11,13-15,17+.
RN38939 719 (October 19, 1995) pp15-16.
HENDRIX, JIMI
RN38940 625 (March 5, 1992) pp11,13-15,17+.
RN38941 633 (June 25, 1992) pp11-12.
RN38942 640 (October 1, 1992) pp9-10.
RN38943 657 (May 27, 1993) pp9,11.
RN38944 676 (February 24, 1994) pp28-29.

RN38945 680 (April 21, 1994) pp33-34.
RN38946 689 (August 25, 1994) pp15-16.
RN38947 697 (December 15, 1994) pp17-18,20.
RN38948 719 (October 19, 1995) pp15-16.
RN38949 734 (May 16, 1996) pp17-18.
HENLEY, DON
RN38950 615 (October 17, 1991) pp13-14.
RN38951 617 (November 14, 1991) pp11,13.
RN38952 626 (March 19, 1992) pp11,13.
RN38953 629 (April 30, 1992) pp11-12.
RN38954 630 (May 14, 1992) pp13,15.
RN38955 639 (September 17, 1992) pp19-20.
RN38956 647 (January 7, 1993) pp9,11.
RN38957 649 (February 4, 1993) pp8-9.
RN38958 654 (April 15, 1993) pp11,13.
RN38959 657 (May 27, 1993) pp9,11.
RN38960 668 (October 28, 1993) pp35-36.
RN38961 681 (May 5, 1994) pp21-22.
RN38962 696 (December 1, 1994) pp23-25.
RN38963 735 (May 30, 1996) pp12-13.
RN38964 748 (November 28, 1996) pp25-26.
HENNEMAN, BRIAN
RN38965 721 (November 16, 1995) pp25-26.
HENRY, JOE
RN38966 669 (November 11, 1993) pp27-28.
RN38967 671 (December 9, 1993) pp31-32.
HERBERT, HERBIE
RN38968 670 (November 25, 1993) pp37-38.
HERMAN, BOB
RN38969 719 (October 19, 1995) pp15-16.
HERMAN, PEE-WEE
RN38970 615 (October 17, 1991) pp13-14.
HERMAN'S HERMITS
RN38971 693 (October 20, 1994) pp27-28,30.
HERRON, CINDY
RN38972 709 (June 1, 1995) pp16-17.
HERSH, KRISTIN
RN38973 637 (August 20, 1992) pp9,11.
RN38974 674 (January 27, 1994) pp28-29.
RN38975 688 (August 11, 1994) pp17-18,20.
RN38976 704 (March 23, 1995) pp24-25.
RN38977 718 (October 5, 1995) pp20-21.
HERVEY, JASON
RN38978 616 (October 31, 1991) pp11,13.
HERZIGOVA, EVA
RN38979 747 (November 14, 1996) pp25-26.
HETFIELD, JAMES
RN38980 615 (October 17, 1991) pp13-14.
RN38981 628 (April 16, 1992) pp11,13.
RN38982 655 (April 29, 1993) pp11-12.
RN38983 727 (February 8, 1996) pp12-13.
RN38984 742 (September 5, 1996) pp20-21.
HETSON, GREG
RN38985 700 (January 26, 1995) pp16-17.
RN38986 722 (November 30, 1995) pp19-20.
HEXUM, NICK
RN38987 720 (November 2, 1995) pp16-17.
HIATT, JOHN
RN38988 665 (September 16, 1993) pp31-32.
HICKMAN, JOHNNY
RN38989 626 (March 19, 1992) pp11,13.
RN38990 737 (June 27, 1996) pp15-16.
HIDALGO, DAVID
RN38991 616 (October 31, 1991) pp11,13.
RN38992 668 (October 28, 1993) pp35-36.
RN38993 679 (April 7, 1994) pp37-39.
RN38994 707 (May 4, 1995) pp19-20.
HIGHWAYMEN
RN38995 640 (October 1, 1992) pp9-10.
RN38996 712-713 (July 13, 1995) pp25-26.
HIJAZI, TANYA
RN38997 648 (January 21, 1993) pp9,11.
HIJUELOS, OSCAR
RN38998 616 (October 31, 1991) pp11,13.
HILFIGER, TOMMY
RN38999 731 (April 4, 1996) pp17-18.
HILL, BRENDAN
RN39000 714 (August 10, 1995) pp15-17.
HILL, DUSTY
RN39001 631 (May 28, 1992) pp9,11.
RN39002 647 (January 7, 1993) pp9,11.
HILL, LAURYN
RN39003 741 (August 22, 1996) pp25-26.
RN39004 746 (October 31, 1996) pp17-18.
HILL, WALTER
RN39005 621 (January 9, 1992) pp10-11.
HIMMELMAN, PETER
RN39006 675 (February 10, 1994) pp22-23.
HINDS, CARL
RN39007 718 (October 5, 1995) pp20-21.
HINDS, DAVID
RN39008 706 (April 20, 1995) pp15-17.
HIRST, ROB
RN39009 656 (May 13, 1993) pp13,15.
RN39010 658 (June 10, 1993) pp16-17.
RN39011 669 (November 11, 1993) pp27-28.
HITCHCOCK, ROBYN
RN39012 616 (October 31, 1991) pp11,13.
RN39013 626 (March 19, 1992) pp11,13.
RN39014 663 (August 19, 1993) pp27-28.
HITLER, ADOLPH
RN39015 648 (January 21, 1993) pp9,11.
HOCHBERG, BURT
RN39016 697 (December 15, 1994) pp17-18,20.
HODENFIELD, CHRIS
RN39017 647 (January 7, 1993) pp9,11.
HOFFMAN, ABBIE
RN39018 745 (October 17, 1996) pp27-28.
HOLE
RN39019 644 (November 26, 1992) pp13,15.
RN39020 690 (September 8, 1994) pp21,24.
RN39021 693 (October 20, 1994) pp27-28,30.
RN39022 694 (November 3, 1994) pp17-18,22.
RN39023 700 (January 26, 1995) pp16-17.
RN39024 704 (March 23, 1995) pp24-25.
RN39025 705 (April 6, 1995) pp16-17.
RN39026 715 (August 24, 1995) pp23,25.
RN39027 735 (May 30, 1996) pp12-13.
RN39028 741 (August 22, 1996) pp25-26.
HOLIDAY, BILLIE
RN39029 684 (June 16, 1994) pp35-36.
HOLLAND, DEXTER
RN39030 700 (January 26, 1995) pp16-17.
RN39031 711 (June 29, 1995) pp12-13.
RN39032 727 (February 8, 1996) pp12-13.
HOOKER, JOHN LEE
RN39033 624 (February 20, 1992) pp11-12.
RN39034 629 (April 30, 1992) pp11-12.
RN39035 649 (February 4, 1993) pp8-9.
RN39036 659 (June 24, 1993) pp13,15.
RN39037 697 (December 15, 1994) pp17-18,20.
RN39038 705 (April 6, 1995) pp16-17.
HOON, NICO BLUE
RN39039 726 (January 25, 1996) pp17-18.
HOON, SHANNON
RN39040 622 (January 23, 1992) pp6-7.
RN39041 639 (September 17, 1992) pp19-20.
RN39042 666 (September 30, 1993) pp27-28.
RN39043 674 (January 27, 1994) pp28-29.
RN39044 692 (October 6, 1994) pp15-17.
RN39045 723 (December 14, 1995) pp27-28.
RN39046 726 (January 25, 1996) pp17-18.
HOOTIE AND THE BLOWFISH
RN39047 691 (September 22, 1994) pp19-21.
RN39048 727 (February 8, 1996) pp12-13.
RN39049 748 (November 28, 1996) pp25-26.
HOPKINS, NICKY
RN39050 655 (April 29, 1993) pp11-12.
HOPPER, DENNIS
RN39051 628 (April 16, 1992) pp11,13.
RN39052 717 (September 21, 1995) pp19-20.
HORGAN, HARRY
RN39053 637 (August 20, 1992) pp9,11.
RN39054 667 (October 14, 1993) pp39-40.
HORNSBY, BRUCE
RN39055 626 (March 19, 1992) pp11,13.
RN39056 683 (June 2, 1994) pp27-28.
RN39057 729 (March 7, 1996) pp9-10.
HORNSBY, KATHY
RN39058 626 (March 19, 1992) pp11,13.
HORNSBY, KEITH RANDALL
RN39058 626 (March 19, 1992) pp11,13.
HORNSBY, RUSSELL IVES
RN39058 626 (March 19, 1992) pp11,13.
HOROVITZ, ADAM
RN39059 631 (May 28, 1992) pp9,11.
RN39060 684 (June 16, 1994) pp35-36.
RN39061 693 (October 20, 1994) pp27-28,30.
RN39062 736 (June 13, 1996) pp19-20.
HOSKINS, ROBERT DEWEY
RN39063 728 (February 22, 1996) p20.
HOSLER, MARK

RN39064 624 (February 20, 1992) pp11-12.
HOSTETLER, LAVERN
RN39065 736 (June 13, 1996) pp19-20.
HOTEI, TOMOYASU
RN39066 686-687 (July 14, 1994) pp41-42.
HOTHOUSE FLOWERS
RN39067 636 (August 6, 1992) pp11,13.
RN39068 668 (October 28, 1993) pp35-36.
RN39069 691 (September 22, 1994) pp19-21.
HOUSE OF PAIN
RN39070 654 (April 15, 1993) pp11,13.
RN39071 671 (December 9, 1993) pp31-32.
RN39072 681 (May 5, 1994) pp21-22.
HOUSTON, WHITNEY
RN39073 622 (January 23, 1992) pp6-7.
RN39074 627 (April 2, 1992) pp11,13.
RN39075 638 (September 3, 1992) pp9,11.
RN39076 650 (February 18, 1993) pp11,13.
RN39077 662 (August 5, 1993) pp33-34.
RN39078 678 (March 24, 1994) pp27-28.
RN39079 680 (April 21, 1994) pp33-34.
RN39080 682 (May 19, 1994) pp37-38.
RN39081 738-739 (July 11, 1996) pp15-16.
HOWLE, DANIELLE
RN39082 742 (September 5, 1996) pp20-21.
HOWLETT, LIAM
RN39083 749 (December 12, 1996) pp19-20.
HOWLIN' WOLF
RN39084 693 (October 20, 1994) pp27-28,30.
HR
RN39085 706 (April 20, 1995) pp15-17.
HUDSON, GARTH
RN39086 742 (September 5, 1996) pp20-21.
HUES CORPORATION
RN39087 712-713 (July 13, 1995) pp25-26.
HUEY
RN39088 747 (November 14, 1996) pp25-26.
HUFF, MARY
RN39089 746 (October 31, 1996) pp17-18.
HUMAN LEAGUE
RN39090 694 (November 3, 1994) pp17-18,22.
HUMMEL, ANDY
RN39091 658 (June 10, 1993) pp16-17.
HUMPERDINCK, ENGELBERT
RN39092 744 (October 3, 1996) pp19-21.
HUMPHREYS, GREG
RN39093 633 (June 25, 1992) pp11-12.
HUNTER, RACHEL
RN39094 621 (January 9, 1992) pp10-11.
HUNTER, ROBERT
RN39095 670 (November 25, 1993) pp37-38.
HUSK, BRYAN
RN39096 718 (October 5, 1995) pp20-21.
HUSKER DU
RN39097 637 (August 20, 1992) pp9,11.
RN39098 729 (March 7, 1996) pp9-10.
HUTCHENCE, MICHAEL
RN39099 631 (May 28, 1992) pp9,11.
RN39100 659 (June 24, 1993) pp13,15.
RN39101 662 (August 5, 1993) pp33-34.
RN39102 669 (November 11, 1993) pp27-28.
RN39103 683 (June 2, 1994) pp27-28.
RN39104 686-687 (July 14, 1994) pp41-42.
RN39105 696 (December 1, 1994) pp23-25.
HUTSELL, MELANIE
RN39106 693 (October 20, 1994) pp27-28,30.
HUTTON, LAUREN
RN39107 682 (May 19, 1994) pp37-38.
HYENAS IN THE DESERT
RN39108 735 (May 30, 1996) pp12-13.
HYNDE, CHRISSIE
RN39109 638 (September 3, 1992) pp9,11.
RN39110 650 (February 18, 1993) pp11,13.
RN39111 655 (April 29, 1993) pp11-12.
RN39112 668 (October 28, 1993) pp35-36.
RN39113 689 (August 25, 1994) pp15-16.
RN39114 696 (December 1, 1994) pp23-25.
RN39115 720 (November 2, 1995) pp16-17.
RN39116 723 (December 14, 1995) pp27-28.
RN39117 733 (May 2, 1996) pp13-14.

I

IAN, SCOTT
RN39118 665 (September 16, 1993) pp31-32.
RN39119 692 (October 6, 1994) pp15-17.
ICE CUBE
RN39120 618 (November 28, 1991) pp11-12.
RN39121 621 (January 9, 1992) pp10-11.
RN39122 638 (September 3, 1992) pp9,11.
RN39123 644 (November 26, 1992) pp13,15.
RN39124 664 (September 2, 1993) pp31-32.
RN39125 675 (February 10, 1994) pp22-23.
RN39126 683 (June 2, 1994) pp27-28.
RN39127 693 (October 20, 1994) pp27-28,30.
RN39128 702 (February 23, 1995) pp19-20.
RN39129 706 (April 20, 1995) pp15-17.
RN39130 710 (June 15, 1995) pp17-18.
ICE-T
RN39131 621 (January 9, 1992) pp10-11.
RN39132 622 (January 23, 1992) pp6-7.
RN39133 636 (August 6, 1992) pp11,13.
RN39134 653 (April 1, 1993) pp11,13.
RN39135 659 (June 24, 1993) pp13,15.
RN39136 664 (September 2, 1993) pp31-32.
RN39137 678 (March 24, 1994) pp27-28.
RN39138 683 (June 2, 1994) pp27-28.
RN39139 702 (February 23, 1995) pp19-20.
RN39140 708 (May 18, 1995) pp17-18.
RN39141 714 (August 10, 1995) pp15-17.
RN39142 733 (May 2, 1996) pp13-14.
RN39143 749 (December 12, 1996) pp19-20.
ICKY WAIL
RN39144 707 (May 4, 1995) pp19-20.
IDOL, BILLY
RN39145 615 (October 17, 1991) pp13-14.
RN39146 621 (January 9, 1992) pp10-11.
RN39147 622 (January 23, 1992) pp6-7.
RN39148 636 (August 6, 1992) pp11,13.
RN39149 638 (September 3, 1992) pp9,11.
RN39150 644 (November 26, 1992) pp13,15.
RN39151 707 (May 4, 1995) pp19-20.
RN39152 749 (December 12, 1996) pp19-20.
IGUANAS
RN39153 627 (April 2, 1992) pp11,13.
IHA, JAMES
RN39154 705 (April 6, 1995) pp16-17.
RN39155 723 (December 14, 1995) pp27-28.
RN39156 735 (May 30, 1996) pp12-13.
RN39157 745 (October 17, 1996) pp27-28.
IMA
RN39158 733 (May 2, 1996) pp13-14.
INDIGO GIRLS
RN39159 625 (March 5, 1992) pp11,13-15,17+.
RN39160 684 (June 16, 1994) pp35-36.
RN39161 710 (June 15, 1995) pp17-18.
RN39162 712-713 (July 13, 1995) pp25-26.
RN39163 745 (October 17, 1996) pp27-28.
INEZ, MIKE
RN39164 723 (December 14, 1995) pp27-28.
INNER CIRCLE
RN39165 706 (April 20, 1995) pp15-17.
INSPECTOR DECK
RN39166 730 (March 21, 1996) pp17-18.
INTERIOR, LUX
RN39167 676 (February 24, 1994) pp28-29.
INXS
RN39168 630 (May 14, 1992) pp13,15.
RN39169 631 (May 28, 1992) pp9,11.
RN39170 659 (June 24, 1993) pp13,15.
RN39171 663 (August 19, 1993) pp27-28.
RN39172 669 (November 11, 1993) pp27-28.
RN39173 686-687 (July 14, 1994) pp41-42.
IRON BUTTERFLY
RN39174 718 (October 5, 1995) pp20-21.
IRONS, JACK
RN39175 726 (January 25, 1996) pp17-18.
IRONS, JEREMY
RN39176 702 (February 23, 1995) pp19-20.
RN39177 703 (March 9, 1995) pp20-21.
IRWIN, ELAINE
RN39178 640 (October 1, 1992) pp9-10.
RN39179 711 (June 29, 1995) pp12-13.
IRWIN, PAT
RN39180 637 (August 20, 1992) pp9,11.
ISAAK, CHRIS
RN39181 615 (October 17, 1991) pp13-14.
RN39182 623 (February 6, 1992) pp11,13.
RN39183 629 (April 30, 1992) pp11-12.
RN39184 644 (November 26, 1992) pp13,15.
RN39185 648 (January 21, 1993) pp9,11.
RN39186 662 (August 5, 1993) pp33-34.
RN39187 668 (October 28, 1993) pp35-36.

RN39188 679 (April 7, 1994) pp37-39.
RN39189 696 (December 1, 1994) pp23-25.
RN39190 716 (September 7, 1995) pp13-14.
RN39191 733 (May 2, 1996) pp13-14.
ISLEY BROTHERS
RN39192 625 (March 5, 1992) pp11,13-15,17+.
RN39193 733 (May 2, 1996) pp13-14.
ISLEY, ERNIE
RN39194 625 (March 5, 1992) pp11,13-15,17+.
ISLEY, MARVIN
RN39194 625 (March 5, 1992) pp11,13-15,17+.
ISLEY, RONALD
RN39194 625 (March 5, 1992) pp11,13-15,17+.

J

J.
RN39195 648 (January 21, 1993) pp9,11.
J. GEILS BAND
RN39196 671 (December 9, 1993) pp31-32.
RN39197 679 (April 7, 1994) pp37-39.
J MASCIS
RN39198 656 (May 13, 1993) pp13,15.
RN39199 659 (June 24, 1993) pp13,15.
RN39200 683 (June 2, 1994) pp27-28.
RN39201 706 (April 20, 1995) pp15-17.
JACKSON, CHUCK
RN39202 637 (August 20, 1992) pp9,11.
JACKSON, JANET
RN39203 615 (October 17, 1991) pp13-14.
RN39204 623 (February 6, 1992) pp11,13.
RN39205 629 (April 30, 1992) pp11-12.
RN39206 654 (April 15, 1993) pp11,13.
RN39207 667 (October 14, 1993) pp39-40.
RN39208 683 (June 2, 1994) pp27-28.
RN39208 685 (June 30, 1994) pp40-41.
RN39209 697 (December 15, 1994) pp17-18,20.
RN39210 711 (June 29, 1995) pp12-13.
RN39211 717 (September 21, 1995) pp19-20.
RN39212 749 (December 12, 1996) pp19-20.
JACKSON, JESSE
RN39213 629 (April 30, 1992) pp11-12.
JACKSON, KATHERINE
RN39214 679 (April 7, 1994) pp37-39.
JACKSON, MARION
RN39215 625 (March 5, 1992) pp11,13-15,17+.
JACKSON, MICHAEL
RN39216 617 (November 14, 1991) pp11,13.
RN39217 626 (March 19, 1992) pp11,13.
RN39218 630 (May 14, 1992) pp13,15.
RN39219 633 (June 25, 1992) pp11-12.
RN39220 636 (August 6, 1992) pp11,13.
RN39221 638 (September 3, 1992) pp9,11.
RN39222 642 (October 29, 1992) pp19,21.
RN39223 650 (February 18, 1993) pp11,13.
RN39224 654 (April 15, 1993) pp11,13.
RN39225 656 (May 13, 1993) pp13,15.
RN39226 660-661 (July 8, 1993) pp32-33.
RN39227 662 (August 5, 1993) pp33-34.
RN39228 666 (September 30, 1993) pp27-28.
RN39229 671 (December 9, 1993) pp31-32.
RN39230 679 (April 7, 1994) pp37-39.
RN39231 690 (September 8, 1994) pp21,24.
RN39232 691 (September 22, 1994) pp19-21.
RN39233 693 (October 20, 1994) pp27-28,30.
RN39234 697 (December 15, 1994) pp17-18,20.
RN39235 716 (September 7, 1995) pp13-14.
RN39236 719 (October 19, 1995) pp15-16.
RN39237 720 (November 2, 1995) pp16-17.
RN39238 726 (January 25, 1996) pp17-18.
RN39239 735 (May 30, 1996) pp12-13.
RN39240 737 (June 27, 1996) pp15-16.
JACKSON, RANDALL
RN39241 625 (March 5, 1992) pp11,13-15,17+.
JACKSON, RANDY
RN39242 679 (April 7, 1994) pp37-39.
JACKSON, RANDY, JR.
RN39242 679 (April 7, 1994) pp37-39.
JACKSON, REBBIE
RN39242 679 (April 7, 1994) pp37-39.
JACKSON, TITO
RN39242 679 (April 7, 1994) pp37-39.
JACKSONS
RN39242 679 (April 7, 1994) pp37-39.
JACKYL
RN39243 664 (September 2, 1993) pp31-32.
JACOBSON, JAY
RN39244 704 (March 23, 1995) pp24-25.
JAFFEE, RAMI
RN39245 636 (August 6, 1992) pp11,13.
JAGGER, CHRIS
RN39246 731 (April 4, 1996) pp17-18.
JAGGER, GEORGIA MAY AYEESHA
RN39247 624 (February 20, 1992) pp11-12.
JAGGER, MICK
RN39247 624 (February 20, 1992) pp11-12.
RN39248 625 (March 5, 1992) pp11,13-15,17+.
RN39249 637 (August 20, 1992) pp9,11.
RN39250 639 (September 17, 1992) pp19-20.
RN39251 644 (November 26, 1992) pp13,15.
RN39252 652 (March 18, 1993) pp13,15.
RN39253 653 (April 1, 1993) pp11,13.
RN39254 659 (June 24, 1993) pp13,15.
RN39255 662 (August 5, 1993) pp33-34.
RN39256 665 (September 16, 1993) pp31-32.
RN39257 668 (October 28, 1993) pp35-36.
RN39258 683 (June 2, 1994) pp27-28.
RN39259 690 (September 8, 1994) pp21,24.
RN39260 692 (October 6, 1994) pp15-17.
RN39261 693 (October 20, 1994) pp27-28,30.
RN39262 701 (February 9, 1995) pp16-17.
RN39263 717 (September 21, 1995) pp19-20.
RN39264 730 (March 21, 1996) pp17-18.
RN39265 731 (April 4, 1996) pp17-18.
RN39266 735 (May 30, 1996) pp12-13.
RN39267 738-739 (July 11, 1996) pp15-16.
RN39268 741 (August 22, 1996) pp25-26.
RN39269 748 (November 28, 1996) pp25-26.
JAH KINGS
RN39270 718 (October 5, 1995) pp20-21.
JAH-T
RN39271 634-635 (July 9, 1992) pp11,13.
JAINOE
RN39272 746 (October 31, 1996) pp17-18.
JAM, JIMMY
RN39273 749 (December 12, 1996) pp19-20.
JAMES
RN39274 686-687 (July 14, 1994) pp41-42.
RN39275 691 (September 22, 1994) pp19-21.
JAMES, ELMORE
RN39276 625 (March 5, 1992) pp11,13-15,17+.
RN39277 691 (September 22, 1994) pp19-21.
JAMES, ETTA
RN39278 630 (May 14, 1992) pp13,15.
JAMES, JAMIE
RN39279 652 (March 18, 1993) pp13,15.
JAMES, RICK
RN39280 648 (January 21, 1993) pp9,11.
RN39281 678 (March 24, 1994) pp27-28.
RN39282 680 (April 21, 1994) pp33-34.
RN39283 691 (September 22, 1994) pp19-21.
RN39284 744 (October 3, 1996) pp19-21.
JAMIROQUAI
RN39285 711 (June 29, 1995) pp12-13.
JAMPA, TENZIN
RN39286 692 (October 6, 1994) pp15-17.
JANE'S ADDICTION
RN39287 615 (October 17, 1991) pp13-14.
RN39288 616 (October 31, 1991) pp11,13.
RN39289 617 (November 14, 1991) pp11,13.
RN39290 628 (April 16, 1992) pp11,13.
RN39291 653 (April 1, 1993) pp11,13.
RN39292 667 (October 14, 1993) pp39-40.
RN39293 731 (April 4, 1996) pp17-18.
JANOVITZ, BILL
RN39294 633 (June 25, 1992) pp11-12.
RN39295 667 (October 14, 1993) pp39-40.
RN39296 683 (June 2, 1994) pp27-28.
RN39297 684 (June 16, 1994) pp35-36.
JARECKE, KEN
RN39298 640 (October 1, 1992) pp9-10.
JARMUSCH, JIM
RN39299 659 (June 24, 1993) pp13,15.
RN39300 714 (August 10, 1995) pp15-17.
RN39301 726 (January 25, 1996) pp17-18.
RN39302 731 (April 4, 1996) pp17-18.
RN39303 738-739 (July 11, 1996) pp15-16.
JASPER, CHRIS
RN39304 625 (March 5, 1992) pp11,13-15,17+.
JAYHAWKS
RN39305 633 (June 25, 1992) pp11-12.

RN39306 658 (June 10, 1993) pp16-17.
RN39307 691 (September 22, 1994) pp19-21.
RN39308 692 (October 6, 1994) pp15-17.
RN39309 709 (June 1, 1995) pp16-17.
RN39310 718 (October 5, 1995) pp20-21.
J.C. THE ETERNAL
RN39311 720 (November 2, 1995) pp16-17.
JEFFERSON AIRPLANE
RN39312 679 (April 7, 1994) pp37-39.
RN39313 722 (November 30, 1995) pp19-20.
JEFFERSON STARSHIP
RN39314 644 (November 26, 1992) pp13,15.
JENCO, SAL
RN39315 709 (June 1, 1995) pp16-17.
JENKINS, TAMARA
RN39316 697 (December 15, 1994) pp17-18,20.
JENNINGS, CHRISTOPHER
RN39317 715 (August 24, 1995) pp23,25.
JENNINGS, PETER
RN39318 625 (March 5, 1992) pp11,13-15,17+.
RN39319 715 (August 24, 1995) pp23,25.
JENNINGS, WAYLON
RN39320 640 (October 1, 1992) pp9-10.
RN39321 658 (June 10, 1993) pp16-17.
RN39322 693 (October 20, 1994) pp27-28,30.
RN39323 719 (October 19, 1995) pp15-16.
RN39324 731 (April 4, 1996) pp17-18.
JEREMY, RON
RN39325 740 (August 8, 1996) pp17-18.
JERNIGAN, JOSEPH
RN39326 712-713 (July 13, 1995) pp25-26.
JESS
RN39327 664 (September 2, 1993) pp31-32.
JESSEE, DARREN
RN39328 749 (December 12, 1996) pp19-20.
JESUS AND MARY CHAIN
RN39329 627 (April 2, 1992) pp11,13.
RN39330 638 (September 3, 1992) pp9,11.
RN39331 700 (January 26, 1995) pp16-17.
RN39332 714 (August 10, 1995) pp15-17.
JESUS JONES
RN39333 615 (October 17, 1991) pp13-14.
JESUS LIZARD
RN39334 716 (September 7, 1995) pp13-14.
RN39335 718 (October 5, 1995) pp20-21.
RN39336 736 (June 13, 1996) pp19-20.
JETHRO TULL
RN39337 628 (April 16, 1992) pp11,13.
JETT, JOAN
RN39338 616 (October 31, 1991) pp11,13.
RN39339 617 (November 14, 1991) pp11,13.
RN39340 644 (November 26, 1992) pp13,15.
RN39341 668 (October 28, 1993) pp35-36.
RN39342 689 (August 25, 1994) pp15-16.
RN39343 690 (September 8, 1994) pp21,24.
RN39344 696 (December 1, 1994) pp23-25.
RN39345 706 (April 20, 1995) pp15-17.
RN39346 710 (June 15, 1995) pp17-18.
RN39347 728 (February 22, 1996) p20.
RN39348 740 (August 8, 1996) pp17-18.
JEWEL
RN39349 716 (September 7, 1995) pp13-14.
RN39350 740 (August 8, 1996) pp17-18.
RN39351 745 (October 17, 1996) pp27-28.
RN39352 748 (November 28, 1996) pp25-26.
JILLETTE, PENN
RN39353 665 (September 16, 1993) pp31-32.
JIMBO
RN39354 685 (June 30, 1994) pp40-41.
JIMMY EAT WORLD
RN39355 746 (October 31, 1996) pp17-18.
JODECI
RN39356 712-713 (July 13, 1995) pp25-26.
RN39357 721 (November 16, 1995) pp25-26.
JODY GRIND
RN39358 631 (May 28, 1992) pp9,11.
JOEL, BILLY
RN39359 625 (March 5, 1992) pp11,13-15,17+.
RN39360 631 (May 28, 1992) pp9,11.
RN39361 634-635 (July 9, 1992) pp11,13.
RN39362 642 (October 29, 1992) pp19,21.
RN39363 647 (January 7, 1993) pp9,11.
RN39364 657 (May 27, 1993) pp9,11.
RN39365 662 (August 5, 1993) pp33-34.
RN39366 689 (August 25, 1994) pp15-16.
RN39367 709 (June 1, 1995) pp16-17.
JOHANSEN, DAVID
RN39368 700 (January 26, 1995) pp16-17.
JOHN, ELTON
RN39369 617 (November 14, 1991) pp11,13.
RN39370 618 (November 28, 1991) pp11-12.
RN39371 629 (April 30, 1992) pp11-12.
RN39372 634-635 (July 9, 1992) pp11,13.
RN39373 637 (August 20, 1992) pp9,11.
RN39374 642 (October 29, 1992) pp19,21.
RN39375 655 (April 29, 1993) pp11-12.
RN39376 656 (May 13, 1993) pp13,15.
RN39377 658 (June 10, 1993) pp16-17.
RN39378 666 (September 30, 1993) pp27-28.
RN39379 668 (October 28, 1993) pp35-36.
RN39380 669 (November 11, 1993) pp27-28.
RN39381 674 (January 27, 1994) pp28-29.
RN39382 681 (May 5, 1994) pp21-22.
RN39383 682 (May 19, 1994) pp37-38.
RN39384 689 (August 25, 1994) pp15-16.
RN39385 697 (December 15, 1994) pp17-18,20.
RN39386 703 (March 9, 1995) pp20-21.
RN39387 709 (June 1, 1995) pp16-17.
RN39388 721 (November 16, 1995) pp25-26.
RN39389 730 (March 21, 1996) pp17-18.
RN39390 733 (May 2, 1996) pp13-14.
RN39391 735 (May 30, 1996) pp12-13.
RN39392 740 (August 8, 1996) pp17-18.
RN39393 749 (December 12, 1996) pp19-20.
JOHNS, DANIEL
RN39394 720 (November 2, 1995) pp16-17.
JOHNSON, BETSY
RN39395 708 (May 18, 1995) pp17-18.
JOHNSON, BRIAN
RN39396 743 (September 19, 1996) pp19-20.
JOHNSON, CRAIG
RN39397 633 (June 25, 1992) pp11-12.
JOHNSON, DON
RN39398 647 (January 7, 1993) pp9,11.
JOHNSON, KENNEY DALE
RN39399 668 (October 28, 1993) pp35-36.
JOHNSON, MAGIC
RN39400 684 (June 16, 1994) pp35-36.
JOHNSON, MIKE
RN39401 659 (June 24, 1993) pp13,15.
JOHNSON, SCOTT
RN39402 722 (November 30, 1995) pp19-20.
JOHNSTON, DANIEL
RN39403 700 (January 26, 1995) pp16-17.
JOHNSTON, FREDDY
RN39403 700 (January 26, 1995) pp16-17.
RN39404 701 (February 9, 1995) pp16-17.
RN39405 716 (September 7, 1995) pp13-14.
JOHNSTON, JAMES
RN39406 692 (October 6, 1994) pp15-17.
JOHNSTON, NICK
RN39407 722 (November 30, 1995) pp19-20.
JONES, BOOKER T.
RN39408 625 (March 5, 1992) pp11,13-15,17+.
RN39409 634-635 (July 9, 1992) pp11,13.
RN39410 685 (June 30, 1994) pp40-41.
JONES, DUNCAN
RN39411 712-713 (July 13, 1995) pp25-26.
JONES, GEORGE
RN39412 693 (October 20, 1994) pp27-28,30.
JONES, JOHN PAUL
RN39413 696 (December 1, 1994) pp23-25.
JONES, KENDALL REY
RN39414 676 (February 24, 1994) pp28-29.
JONES, KENNY
RN39415 653 (April 1, 1993) pp11,13.
JONES, MAXINE
RN39416 709 (June 1, 1995) pp16-17.
JONES, MICK
RN39417 618 (November 28, 1991) pp11-12.
RN39418 642 (October 29, 1992) pp19,21.
RN39419 718 (October 5, 1995) pp20-21.
JONES, RICKIE LEE
RN39420 663 (August 19, 1993) pp27-28.
RN39421 669 (November 11, 1993) pp27-28.
JONES, STACY
RN39422 693 (October 20, 1994) pp27-28,30.

JONES, STEVE
RN39423 721 (November 16, 1995) pp25-26.
RN39424 731 (April 4, 1996) pp17-18.
RN39425 734 (May 16, 1996) pp17-18.
JONES, TOM
RN39426 630 (May 14, 1992) pp13,15.
RN39427 653 (April 1, 1993) pp11,13.
RN39428 654 (April 15, 1993) pp11,13.
RN39429 693 (October 20, 1994) pp27-28,30.
RN39430 697 (December 15, 1994) pp17-18,20.
JONG, ERICA
RN39431 617 (November 14, 1991) pp11,13.
JONZE, SPIKE
RN39432 705 (April 6, 1995) pp16-17.
RN39433 710 (June 15, 1995) pp17-18.
JORDAN, MICHAEL
RN39434 671 (December 9, 1993) pp31-32.
JORDAN, MONTELL
RN39435 748 (November 28, 1996) pp25-26.
JOURGENSEN, AL
RN39436 665 (September 16, 1993) pp31-32.
RN39437 685 (June 30, 1994) pp40-41.
JOURNEY
RN39438 670 (November 25, 1993) pp37-38.
RN39439 694 (November 3, 1994) pp17-18,22.
JOVOVICH, MILLA
RN39440 688 (August 11, 1994) pp17-18,20.
JU JU HOUNDS
RN39441 634-635 (July 9, 1992) pp11,13.
RN39442 644 (November 26, 1992) pp13,15.
RN39443 650 (February 18, 1993) pp11,13.
RN39444 652 (March 18, 1993) pp13,15.
JUDAS PRIEST
RN39445 640 (October 1, 1992) pp9-10.
RN39446 642 (October 29, 1992) pp19,21.
JUDD, ASHLEY
RN39447 670 (November 25, 1993) pp37-38.
RN39448 726 (January 25, 1996) pp17-18.
JUDD, NAOMI
RN39449 670 (November 25, 1993) pp37-38.
JUDD, WYNONNA
RN39450 630 (May 14, 1992) pp13,15.
RN39451 660-661 (July 8, 1993) pp32-33.
RN39452 670 (November 25, 1993) pp37-38.
RN39453 685 (June 30, 1994) pp40-41.
JULIUS, ANTHONY
RN39454 748 (November 28, 1996) pp25-26.
JUNIOR REID
RN39455 706 (April 20, 1995) pp15-17.

K

KAHN, CHAKA
RN39456 680 (April 21, 1994) pp33-34.
KAMOZE, INI
RN39457 711 (June 29, 1995) pp12-13.
KANE, MARI
RN39458 705 (April 6, 1995) pp16-17.
KANSAS
RN39459 718 (October 5, 1995) pp20-21.
KANTNER, PAUL
RN39460 644 (November 26, 1992) pp13,15.
RN39461 679 (April 7, 1994) pp37-39.
KAPLAN, IRA
RN39462 736 (June 13, 1996) pp19-20.
KASPAROV, GARY
RN39463 663 (August 19, 1993) pp27-28.
KATO, NASH
RN39463 663 (August 19, 1993) pp27-28.
RN39464 668 (October 28, 1993) pp35-36.
RN39465 685 (June 30, 1994) pp40-41.
KAUFMAN, ANDY
RN39466 705 (April 6, 1995) pp16-17.
KAUKONEN, JORMA
RN39467 679 (April 7, 1994) pp37-39.
KAY, TONY
RN39468 660-661 (July 8, 1993) pp32-33.
KAYE, LENNY
RN39469 717 (September 21, 1995) pp19-20.
RN39470 744 (October 3, 1996) pp19-21.
KAYE, TONY
RN39471 666 (September 30, 1993) pp27-28.
KC AND THE SUNSHINE BAND
RN39472 686-687 (July 14, 1994) pp41-42.
KEITEL, HARVEY
RN39473 708 (May 18, 1995) pp17-18.
RN39474 719 (October 19, 1995) pp15-16.
KELLEY, ARCH, III
RN39475 685 (June 30, 1994) pp40-41.
KELLY, JOHN
RN39476 693 (October 20, 1994) pp27-28,30.
KELLY, R.
RN39477 736 (June 13, 1996) pp19-20.
KELLY, TIM
RN39478 654 (April 15, 1993) pp11,13.
KEMP, GARY
RN39479 627 (April 2, 1992) pp11,13.
KEMP, SHAWN
RN39480 720 (November 2, 1995) pp16-17.
KENNEDY
RN39481 667 (October 14, 1993) pp39-40.
RN39482 693 (October 20, 1994) pp27-28,30.
KENSIT, PATSY
RN39483 731 (April 4, 1996) pp17-18.
KERRIGAN, NANCY
RN39484 696 (December 1, 1994) pp23-25.
KESEY, KEN
RN39485 690 (September 8, 1994) pp21,24.
KESTER, JIMMY
RN39486 691 (September 22, 1994) pp19-21.
KESTEVEN, BEN
RN39487 650 (February 18, 1993) pp11,13.
KEVORKIAN, JACK
RN39488 681 (May 5, 1994) pp21-22.
KHAN, CHAKA
RN39489 691 (September 22, 1994) pp19-21.
RN39490 708 (May 18, 1995) pp17-18.
RN39491 711 (June 29, 1995) pp12-13.
RN39492 716 (September 7, 1995) pp13-14.
KID CREOLE
RN39493 741 (August 22, 1996) pp25-26.
KIDJO, ANGELIQUE
RN39494 691 (September 22, 1994) pp19-21.
KIEDIS, ANTHONY
RN39495 631 (May 28, 1992) pp9,11.
RN39496 638 (September 3, 1992) pp9,11.
RN39497 642 (October 29, 1992) pp19,21.
RN39498 649 (February 4, 1993) pp8-9.
RN39499 654 (April 15, 1993) pp11,13.
RN39500 667 (October 14, 1993) pp39-40.
RN39501 674 (January 27, 1994) pp28-29.
RN39502 692 (October 6, 1994) pp15-17.
RN39503 694 (November 3, 1994) pp17-18,22.
RN39504 703 (March 9, 1995) pp20-21.
RN39505 719 (October 19, 1995) pp15-16.
RN39506 722 (November 30, 1995) pp19-20.
RN39507 731 (April 4, 1996) pp17-18.
KILL SYBIL
RN39508 666 (September 30, 1993) pp27-28.
KILLING JOKE
RN39509 692 (October 6, 1994) pp15-17.
KILMISTER, LEMMY
RN39510 727 (February 8, 1996) pp12-13.
RN39511 743 (September 19, 1996) pp19-20.
KINCHLA, CHAN
RN39512 714 (August 10, 1995) pp15-17.
KING, B. B.
RN39513 616 (October 31, 1991) pp11,13.
RN39514 625 (March 5, 1992) pp11,13-15,17+.
RN39515 630 (May 14, 1992) pp13,15.
RN39516 640 (October 1, 1992) pp9-10.
RN39517 697 (December 15, 1994) pp17-18,20.
RN39518 722 (November 30, 1995) pp19-20.
RN39519 735 (May 30, 1996) pp12-13.
RN39520 748 (November 28, 1996) pp25-26.
KING, BILLIE JEAN
RN39521 656 (May 13, 1993) pp13,15.
KING BUZZO
RN39522 675 (February 10, 1994) pp22-23.
KING, CAROLE
RN39523 633 (June 25, 1992) pp11-12.
RN39524 636 (August 6, 1992) pp11,13.
RN39525 639 (September 17, 1992) pp19-20.
KING CRIMSON
RN39526 676 (February 24, 1994) pp28-29.
KING, LITTLE JIMMY
RN39527 697 (December 15, 1994) pp17-18,20.
KING, MARTIN LUTHER
RN39528 624 (February 20, 1992) pp11-12.
RN39529 664 (September 2, 1993) pp31-32.

RN39530 733 (May 2, 1996) pp13-14.
KING MISSILE
RN39531 636 (August 6, 1992) pp11,13.
RN39532 659 (June 24, 1993) pp13,15.
KING, STEPHEN
RN39533 634-635 (July 9, 1992) pp11,13.
KINGSTON TRIO
RN39534 662 (August 5, 1993) pp33-34.
KINISON, SAM
RN39535 622 (January 23, 1992) pp6-7.
KINKS
RN39536 633 (June 25, 1992) pp11-12.
KINNEY, KEVIN
RN39537 618 (November 28, 1991) pp11-12.
RN39538 650 (February 18, 1993) pp11,13.
KIRKWOOD, CHRIS
RN39539 694 (November 3, 1994) pp17-18,22.
KIRKWOOD, CURT
RN39540 700 (January 26, 1995) pp16-17.
KIRSHNER, MIA
RN39541 708 (May 18, 1995) pp17-18.
KISS
RN39542 638 (September 3, 1992) pp9,11.
RN39543 640 (October 1, 1992) pp9-10.
RN39544 664 (September 2, 1993) pp31-32.
RN39545 665 (September 16, 1993) pp31-32.
RN39546 675 (February 10, 1994) pp22-23.
RN39547 685 (June 30, 1994) pp40-41.
RN39548 690 (September 8, 1994) pp21,24.
RN39549 691 (September 22, 1994) pp19-21.
RN39550 715 (August 24, 1995) pp23,25.
RN39551 732 (April 18, 1996) pp19-20.
KISSER, ANDREAS
RN39552 689 (August 25, 1994) pp15-16.
KISSINGER, HENRY
RN39553 659 (June 24, 1993) pp13,15.
KLEZMATICS
RN39554 749 (December 12, 1996) pp19-20.
KLF
RN39555 625 (March 5, 1992) pp11,13-15,17+.
KLINE, KEVIN
RN39556 686-687 (July 14, 1994) pp41-42.
KNIGHT, GLADYS
RN39557 722 (November 30, 1995) pp19-20.
KOLM, RON
RN39558 708 (May 18, 1995) pp17-18.
KONICKE, TOM
RN39559 747 (November 14, 1996) pp25-26.
KOOL DJ HERC
RN39560 670 (November 25, 1993) pp37-38.
KOONS, DEBORAH
RN39561 678 (March 24, 1994) pp27-28.
RN39562 679 (April 7, 1994) pp37-39.
RN39563 691 (September 22, 1994) pp19-21.
KORESH, DAVID
RN39564 655 (April 29, 1993) pp11-12.
KOTTKE, LEO
RN39565 669 (November 11, 1993) pp27-28.
KOTZEN, RICHIE
RN39566 633 (June 25, 1992) pp11-12.
KOWALCZYK, ED
RN39567 701 (February 9, 1995) pp16-17.
RN39568 714 (August 10, 1995) pp15-17.
RN39569 716 (September 7, 1995) pp13-14.
RN39570 721 (November 16, 1995) pp25-26.
KRAMER, JOEY
RN39571 622 (January 23, 1992) pp6-7.
KRAVITZ, LENNY
RN39572 644 (November 26, 1992) pp13,15.
RN39573 656 (May 13, 1993) pp13,15.
RN39574 666 (September 30, 1993) pp27-28.
RN39575 667 (October 14, 1993) pp39-40.
RN39576 671 (December 9, 1993) pp31-32.
RN39577 683 (June 2, 1994) pp27-28.
RN39578 711 (June 29, 1995) pp12-13.
RN39579 723 (December 14, 1995) pp27-28.
RN39580 735 (May 30, 1996) pp12-13.
RN39581 740 (August 8, 1996) pp17-18.
KRICFALUSI, JOHN
RN39582 719 (October 19, 1995) pp15-16.
KRIM, MATHILDE
RN39583 710 (June 15, 1995) pp17-18.
KRISTOFFERSON, KRIS
RN39584 640 (October 1, 1992) pp9-10.
RN39585 659 (June 24, 1993) pp13,15.
RN39586 678 (March 24, 1994) pp27-28.
RN39587 694 (November 3, 1994) pp17-18,22.
RN39588 712-713 (July 13, 1995) pp25-26.
KRS-ONE
RN39589 642 (October 29, 1992) pp19,21.
RN39590 741 (August 22, 1996) pp25-26.
KRUGMAN, MICHAEL
RN39591 690 (September 8, 1994) pp21,24.
RN39592 694 (November 3, 1994) pp17-18,22.
KULICK, BRUCE
RN39593 715 (August 24, 1995) pp23,25.
KUNSTLER, WILLIAM
RN39594 745 (October 17, 1996) pp27-28.
KURIANSKY, JUDY
RN39595 659 (June 24, 1993) pp13,15.
KWAME
RN39596 637 (August 20, 1992) pp9,11.

L

L. L. COOL J
RN39597 615 (October 17, 1991) pp13-14.
RN39598 628 (April 16, 1992) pp11,13.
RN39599 659 (June 24, 1993) pp13,15.
RN39600 664 (September 2, 1993) pp31-32.
RN39601 680 (April 21, 1994) pp33-34.
RN39602 696 (December 1, 1994) pp23-25.
RN39603 736 (June 13, 1996) pp19-20.
L7
RN39604 627 (April 2, 1992) pp11,13.
RN39605 644 (November 26, 1992) pp13,15.
RN39606 659 (June 24, 1993) pp13,15.
RN39607 660-661 (July 8, 1993) pp32-33.
RN39608 667 (October 14, 1993) pp39-40.
RN39609 671 (December 9, 1993) pp31-32.
RN39610 683 (June 2, 1994) pp27-28.
RN39611 688 (August 11, 1994) pp17-18,20.
RN39612 692 (October 6, 1994) pp15-17.
RN39613 696 (December 1, 1994) pp23-25.
RN39614 711 (June 29, 1995) pp12-13.
RN39615 718 (October 5, 1995) pp20-21.
RN39616 719 (October 19, 1995) pp15-16.
RN39617 731 (April 4, 1996) pp17-18.
LABELLE, PATTI
RN39618 638 (September 3, 1992) pp9,11.
LADY MISS KIER
RN39619 622 (January 23, 1992) pp6-7.
LADYSMITH BLACK MAMBAZO
RN39619 622 (January 23, 1992) pp6-7.
LAGUARDIA HIGH SCHOOL CHOIR
RN39620 682 (May 19, 1994) pp37-38.
LALAS, ALEXI
RN39621 689 (August 25, 1994) pp15-16.
LAMAS, LORENZO
RN39622 746 (October 31, 1996) pp17-18.
LANAHAN, BRIAN
RN39623 688 (August 11, 1994) pp17-18,20.
LANDY, EUGENE
RN39624 617 (November 14, 1991) pp11,13.
LANE, JANI
RN39625 655 (April 29, 1993) pp11-12.
LANEGAN, MARK
RN39626 711 (June 29, 1995) pp12-13.
LANG, K. D.
RN39627 631 (May 28, 1992) pp9,11.
RN39628 640 (October 1, 1992) pp9-10.
RN39629 652 (March 18, 1993) pp13,15.
RN39630 654 (April 15, 1993) pp11,13.
RN39631 657 (May 27, 1993) pp9,11.
RN39632 658 (June 10, 1993) pp16-17.
RN39633 674 (January 27, 1994) pp28-29.
RN39634 683 (June 2, 1994) pp27-28.
LANGDON, ROYSTON
RN39635 742 (September 5, 1996) pp20-21.
LANGFORD, JON
RN39636 694 (November 3, 1994) pp17-18,22.
RN39637 736 (June 13, 1996) pp19-20.
LANOIS, DANIEL
RN39638 617 (November 14, 1991) pp11,13.
LAS VEGAS, YVA
RN39639 711 (June 29, 1995) pp12-13.
LATVALA, DICK
RN39640 670 (November 25, 1993) pp37-38.
LAUDERDALE, JIM
RN39641 691 (September 22, 1994) pp19-21.
LAUPER, CYNDI
RN39642 621 (January 9, 1992) pp10-11.
RN39643 717 (September 21, 1995) pp19-20.

LAWRENCE, JOEY
RN39644 678 (March 24, 1994) pp27-28.
RN39645 704 (March 23, 1995) pp24-25.
LEACH, ROBIN
RN39646 644 (November 26, 1992) pp13,15.
LEARY, DENIS
RN39647 659 (June 24, 1993) pp13,15.
RN39648 693 (October 20, 1994) pp27-28,30.
LEAVELL, CHUCK
RN39649 710 (June 15, 1995) pp17-18.
LEBON, SIMON
RN39650 708 (May 18, 1995) pp17-18.
LED ZEPPELIN
RN39651 631 (May 28, 1992) pp9,11.
RN39652 652 (March 18, 1993) pp13,15.
RN39653 655 (April 29, 1993) pp11-12.
RN39654 675 (February 10, 1994) pp22-23.
LEE, BEN
RN39655 710 (June 15, 1995) pp17-18.
LEE, CINQUE
RN39656 617 (November 14, 1991) pp11,13.
LEE, CRAIG
RN39657 616 (October 31, 1991) pp11,13.
LEE, JOIE
RN39658 617 (November 14, 1991) pp11,13.
LEE, SARA
RN39659 625 (March 5, 1992) pp11,13-15,17+.
LEE, SPIKE
RN39660 617 (November 14, 1991) pp11,13.
RN39661 680 (April 21, 1994) pp33-34.
RN39662 685 (June 30, 1994) pp40-41.
RN39663 733 (May 2, 1996) pp13-14.
LEE, TOMMY
RN39664 627 (April 2, 1992) pp11,13.
RN39665 705 (April 6, 1995) pp16-17.
RN39666 706 (April 20, 1995) pp15-17.
RN39667 708 (May 18, 1995) pp17-18.
LEECH, MARK
RN39668 711 (June 29, 1995) pp12-13.
LEEN, BILL
RN39669 665 (September 16, 1993) pp31-32.
LEESE, HOWARD
RN39670 696 (December 1, 1994) pp23-25.
LEFT EYE
RN39671 719 (October 19, 1995) pp15-16.
LEIBOVITZ, ANNIE
RN39672 647 (January 7, 1993) pp9,11.
LEIGH, JENNIFER JASON
RN39673 617 (November 14, 1991) pp11,13.
LEMMY
RN39674 676 (February 24, 1994) pp28-29.
LEMONHEADS
RN39675 627 (April 2, 1992) pp11,13.
RN39676 662 (August 5, 1993) pp33-34.
RN39695 679 (April 7, 1994) pp37-39.
RN39695a 689 (August 25, 1994) pp15-16.
RN39678 742 (September 5, 1996) pp20-21.
LENNON, JOHN
RN39679 647 (January 7, 1993) pp9,11.
RN39680 653 (April 1, 1993) pp11,13.
RN39681 710 (June 15, 1995) pp17-18.
RN39682 717 (September 21, 1995) pp19-20.
RN39683 727 (February 8, 1996) pp12-13.
LENNON, JULIAN
RN39684 631 (May 28, 1992) pp9,11.
LENNON, SEAN
RN39685 662 (August 5, 1993) pp33-34.
RN39686 729 (March 7, 1996) pp9-10.
RN39687 733 (May 2, 1996) pp13-14.
RN39688 735 (May 30, 1996) pp12-13.
RN39689 742 (September 5, 1996) pp20-21.
LENNOX, ANNIE
RN39690 653 (April 1, 1993) pp11,13.
RN39691 706 (April 20, 1995) pp15-17.
RN39692 732 (April 18, 1996) pp19-20.
LENO, JAY
RN39693 624 (February 20, 1992) pp11-12.
RN39694 705 (April 6, 1995) pp16-17.
RN39695 Number not assigned.
LESH, PHIL
RN39695 679 (April 7, 1994) pp37-39.
RN39696 696 (December 1, 1994) pp23-25.
LETTERMAN, DAVID
RN39697 693 (October 20, 1994) pp27-28,30.
LETTERS TO CLEO
RN39697 693 (October 20, 1994) pp27-28,30.
LEVY, NOAH
RN39698 691 (September 22, 1994) pp19-21.
LEWIS, HUEY
RN39699 629 (April 30, 1992) pp11-12.
LEWIS, JERRY
RN39700 669 (November 11, 1993) pp27-28.
LEWIS, JERRY LEE
RN39701 668 (October 28, 1993) pp35-36.
RN39702 690 (September 8, 1994) pp21,24.
RN39703 693 (October 20, 1994) pp27-28,30.
RN39704 694 (November 3, 1994) pp17-18,22.
RN39705 741 (August 22, 1996) pp25-26.
LEWIS, KERRIE
RN39706 694 (November 3, 1994) pp17-18,22.
LEWIS, PETER
RN39707 670 (November 25, 1993) pp37-38.
LEWIS, SHAWN
RN39708 694 (November 3, 1994) pp17-18,22.
LEWIS, TERRY
RN39709 749 (December 12, 1996) pp19-20.
LIEBLING, BETH
RN39710 686-687 (July 14, 1994) pp41-42.
RN39711 688 (August 11, 1994) pp17-18,20.
RN39712 732 (April 18, 1996) pp19-20.
LIESEGANG, BRIAN
RN39713 720 (November 2, 1995) pp16-17.
LIMBAUGH, RUSH
RN39714 686-687 (July 14, 1994) pp41-42.
RN39715 706 (April 20, 1995) pp15-17.
LINCOLN, ABRAHAM
RN39716 721 (November 16, 1995) pp25-26.
LINK, JOHNSON
RN39717 703 (March 9, 1995) pp20-21.
LINKLATER, RICHARD
RN39718 730 (March 21, 1996) pp17-18.
LIPPERT, PATRICK
RN39719 680 (April 21, 1994) pp33-34.
RN39720 733 (May 2, 1996) pp13-14.
LIPPS, INC.
RN39721 719 (October 19, 1995) pp15-16.
LITTLE RICHARD
RN39722 616 (October 31, 1991) pp11,13.
RN39723 625 (March 5, 1992) pp11,13-15,17+.
RN39724 654 (April 15, 1993) pp11,13.
RN39725 676 (February 24, 1994) pp28-29.
RN39726 680 (April 21, 1994) pp33-34.
RN39727 684 (June 16, 1994) pp35-36.
LITTLE WILLIE JOHN
RN39728 722 (November 30, 1995) pp19-20.
LIVE
RN39729 701 (February 9, 1995) pp16-17.
RN39730 714 (August 10, 1995) pp15-17.
RN39731 716 (September 7, 1995) pp13-14.
RN39732 721 (November 16, 1995) pp25-26.
RN39733 737 (June 27, 1996) pp15-16.
LIVING COLOUR
RN39734 621 (January 9, 1992) pp10-11.
RN39735 629 (April 30, 1992) pp11-12.
RN39736 636 (August 6, 1992) pp11,13.
RN39737 637 (August 20, 1992) pp9,11.
RN39738 692 (October 6, 1994) pp15-17.
LOCKLEAR, HEATHER
RN39739 747 (November 14, 1996) pp25-26.
LOGAN, JACK
RN39740 689 (August 25, 1994) pp15-16.
LOGGINS, KENNY
RN39741 657 (May 27, 1993) pp9,11.
LONDON, FRANK
RN39742 749 (December 12, 1996) pp19-20.
LONDON SYMPHONY ORCHESTRA
RN39743 683 (June 2, 1994) pp27-28.
LONE JUSTICE
RN39744 660-661 (July 8, 1993) pp32-33.
LOOMIS
RN39745 709 (June 1, 1995) pp16-17.
LOPES, LISA
RN39746 688 (August 11, 1994) pp17-18,20.
LORD, MARY LOU
RN39747 717 (September 21, 1995) pp19-20.
RN39748 742 (September 5, 1996) pp20-21.
LOS LOBOS
RN39749 616 (October 31, 1991) pp11,13.
RN39750 634-635 (July 9, 1992) pp11,13.
RN39751 668 (October 28, 1993) pp35-36.
RN39752 679 (April 7, 1994) pp37-39.
RN39753 707 (May 4, 1995) pp19-20.
LOST
RN39754 736 (June 13, 1996) pp19-20.
LOUNGE LIZARDS
RN39755 692 (October 6, 1994) pp15-17.
LOURIS, GARY

RN39756 633 (June 25, 1992) pp11-12.
RN39757 691 (September 22, 1994) pp19-21.
RN39758 709 (June 1, 1995) pp16-17.
RN39759 718 (October 5, 1995) pp20-21.
LOVE, COURTNEY
RN39760 642 (October 29, 1992) pp19,21.
RN39761 644 (November 26, 1992) pp13,15.
RN39762 650 (February 18, 1993) pp11,13.
RN39763 660-661 (July 8, 1993) pp32-33.
RN39764 667 (October 14, 1993) pp39-40.
RN39765 668 (October 28, 1993) pp35-36.
RN39766 688 (August 11, 1994) pp17-18,20.
RN39767 689 (August 25, 1994) pp15-16.
RN39768 690 (September 8, 1994) pp21,24.
RN39769 694 (November 3, 1994) pp17-18,22.
RN39770 703 (March 9, 1995) pp20-21.
RN39771 704 (March 23, 1995) pp24-25.
RN39772 705 (April 6, 1995) pp16-17.
RN39773 714 (August 10, 1995) pp15-17.
RN39774 720 (November 2, 1995) pp16-17.
RN39775 734 (May 16, 1996) pp17-18.
RN39776 741 (August 22, 1996) pp25-26.
RN39777 745 (October 17, 1996) pp27-28.
RN39778 748 (November 28, 1996) pp25-26.
LOVE, DARLENE
RN39779 639 (September 17, 1992) pp19-20.
RN39780 644 (November 26, 1992) pp13,15.
RN39781 730 (March 21, 1996) pp17-18.
LOVE, MONIE
RN39782 625 (March 5, 1992) pp11,13-15,17+.
LOVEMONGERS
RN39783 649 (February 4, 1993) pp8-9.
LOVER, ED
RN39784 653 (April 1, 1993) pp11,13.
RN39785 659 (June 24, 1993) pp13,15.
LOVERBOY
RN39786 740 (August 8, 1996) pp17-18.
LOVERING, DAVID
RN39787 652 (March 18, 1993) pp13,15.
LOVETT, LYLE
RN39788 625 (March 5, 1992) pp11,13-15,17+.
RN39789 648 (January 21, 1993) pp9,11.
RN39790 653 (April 1, 1993) pp11,13.
RN39791 658 (June 10, 1993) pp16-17.
RN39792 662 (August 5, 1993) pp33-34.
RN39793 663 (August 19, 1993) pp27-28.
RN39794 693 (October 20, 1994) pp27-28,30.
RN39795 705 (April 6, 1995) pp16-17.
RN39796 733 (May 2, 1996) pp13-14.
LOWE, NICK
RN39797 675 (February 10, 1994) pp22-23.
RN39798 691 (September 22, 1994) pp19-21.
LOWE, ROB
RN39799 709 (June 1, 1995) pp16-17.
RN39800 736 (June 13, 1996) pp19-20.
LOWE, STACY
RN39801 648 (January 21, 1993) pp9,11.
LOWERY, DAVID
RN39802 626 (March 19, 1992) pp11,13.
RN39803 712-713 (July 13, 1995) pp25-26.
LOZANO, CONRAD
RN39804 616 (October 31, 1991) pp11,13.
LULU
RN39805 658 (June 10, 1993) pp16-17.
LUNA
RN39806 735 (May 30, 1996) pp12-13.
RN39807 748 (November 28, 1996) pp25-26.
LUNACHICKS
RN39808 728 (February 22, 1996) p20.
LURIE, JOHN
RN39809 692 (October 6, 1994) pp15-17.
LUSCIOUS JACKSON
RN39810 685 (June 30, 1994) pp40-41.
RN39811 704 (March 23, 1995) pp24-25.
RN39812 710 (June 15, 1995) pp17-18.
RN39813 716 (September 7, 1995) pp13-14.
LUSH
RN39814 638 (September 3, 1992) pp9,11.
RN39815 693 (October 20, 1994) pp27-28,30.
LUTZ, BARBARA
RN39816 729 (March 7, 1996) pp9-10.
LYCETT, KEVIN
RN39817 736 (June 13, 1996) pp19-20.
LYDON, JOHNNY
RN39818 655 (April 29, 1993) pp11-12.
RN39819 707 (May 4, 1995) pp19-20.
RN39820 723 (December 14, 1995) pp27-28.
LYNCH, STAN
RN39821 666 (September 30, 1993) pp27-28.
LYNNE, JEFF
RN39822 674 (January 27, 1994) pp28-29.
LYNYRD SKYNYRD
RN39823 727 (February 8, 1996) pp12-13.
RN39824 736 (June 13, 1996) pp19-20.
LYTE, MC
RN39825 618 (November 28, 1991) pp11-12.
RN39826 625 (March 5, 1992) pp11,13-15,17+.
RN39827 628 (April 16, 1992) pp11,13.
RN39828 696 (December 1, 1994) pp23-25.
RN39829 748 (November 28, 1996) pp25-26.

M

MACGOWAN, SHANE
RN39830 616 (October 31, 1991) pp11,13.
RN39831 668 (October 28, 1993) pp35-36.
RN39832 696 (December 1, 1994) pp23-25.
MACK, RUSSELL
RN39833 689 (August 25, 1994) pp15-16.
MACKAYE, IAN
RN39834 744 (October 3, 1996) pp19-21.
MACLEOD, SCOTT
RN39835 720 (November 2, 1995) pp16-17.
MACMILLAN, DOUG
RN39836 633 (June 25, 1992) pp11-12.
MACPHERSON, ELLE
RN39837 727 (February 8, 1996) pp12-13.
MAD SEASON
RN39838 711 (June 29, 1995) pp12-13.
MADDER ROSE
RN39839 700 (January 26, 1995) pp16-17.
MADONNA
RN39840 616 (October 31, 1991) pp11,13.
RN39841 636 (August 6, 1992) pp11,13.
RN39842 644 (November 26, 1992) pp13,15.
RN39843 649 (February 4, 1993) pp8-9.
RN39844 657 (May 27, 1993) pp9,11.
RN39845 664 (September 2, 1993) pp31-32.
RN39846 665 (September 16, 1993) pp31-32.
RN39847 667 (October 14, 1993) pp39-40.
RN39848 668 (October 28, 1993) pp35-36.
RN39849 669 (November 11, 1993) pp27-28.
RN39850 688 (August 11, 1994) pp17-18,20.
RN39851 693 (October 20, 1994) pp27-28,30.
RN39852 694 (November 3, 1994) pp17-18,22.
RN39853 703 (March 9, 1995) pp20-21.
RN39854 704 (March 23, 1995) pp24-25.
RN39855 707 (May 4, 1995) pp19-20.
RN39856 712-713 (July 13, 1995) pp25-26.
RN39857 715 (August 24, 1995) pp23,25.
RN39858 717 (September 21, 1995) pp19-20.
RN39859 719 (October 19, 1995) pp15-16.
RN39860 728 (February 22, 1996) p20.
RN39861 729 (March 7, 1996) pp9-10.
RN39862 731 (April 4, 1996) pp17-18.
RN39863 732 (April 18, 1996) pp19-20.
RN39864 734 (May 16, 1996) pp17-18.
RN39865 735 (May 30, 1996) pp12-13.
RN39866 736 (June 13, 1996) pp19-20.
MADONNABES
RN39866 736 (June 13, 1996) pp19-20.
MAGINNIS, TOM
RN39867 633 (June 25, 1992) pp11-12.
MAGNUSON, ANN
RN39868 621 (January 9, 1992) pp10-11.
MAGUIRE, BARRY
RN39869 636 (August 6, 1992) pp11,13.
MAHARISHI MAHESH YOGI
RN39870 631 (May 28, 1992) pp9,11.
MAHER, BILL
RN39871 697 (December 15, 1994) pp17-18,20.
RN39872 733 (May 2, 1996) pp13-14.
RN39873 747 (November 14, 1996) pp25-26.
MAJIDI, ARMAND
RN39874 726 (January 25, 1996) pp17-18.
MALIN, JESSE
RN39875 705 (April 6, 1995) pp16-17.
MALKMUS, STEPHEN
RN39876 685 (June 30, 1994) pp40-41.
MALLEY, MIKE

RN39877 707 (May 4, 1995) pp19-20.
MALLORY, BILL
RN39878 675 (February 10, 1994) pp22-23.
MALO, RAUL
RN39879 707 (May 4, 1995) pp19-20.
MALOY, ZAC
RN39880 733 (May 2, 1996) pp13-14.
MANCINI, HENRY
RN39881 688 (August 11, 1994) pp17-18,20.
MANDELA, NELSON
RN39882 685 (June 30, 1994) pp40-41.
RN39883 688 (August 11, 1994) pp17-18,20.
MANILOW, BARRY
RN39884 660-661 (July 8, 1993) pp32-33.
MANKEY, JAMES
RN39885 681 (May 5, 1994) pp21-22.
MANN, AIMEE
RN39886 674 (January 27, 1994) pp28-29.
MANNING, BARBARA
RN39887 693 (October 20, 1994) pp27-28,30.
MANSON, SHIRLEY
RN39888 740 (August 8, 1996) pp17-18.
MANZAREK, RAY
RN39889 648 (January 21, 1993) pp9,11.
MARILYN MANSON
RN39890 714 (August 10, 1995) pp15-17.
RN39891 745 (October 17, 1996) pp27-28.
MARK, MARKY
RN39892 650 (February 18, 1993) pp11,13.
RN39893 654 (April 15, 1993) pp11,13.
MARKIEWICZ, CLARISSA
RN39894 686-687 (July 14, 1994) pp41-42.
MARLEY, BOB
RN39895 639 (September 17, 1992) pp19-20.
RN39896 675 (February 10, 1994) pp22-23.
RN39897 694 (November 3, 1994) pp17-18,22.
RN39898 706 (April 20, 1995) pp15-17.
RN39899 734 (May 16, 1996) pp17-18.
RN39900 736 (June 13, 1996) pp19-20.
MARLEY, CEDELLA
RN39901 626 (March 19, 1992) pp11,13.
MARLEY, RITA
RN39901 626 (March 19, 1992) pp11,13.
RN39902 639 (September 17, 1992) pp19-20.
MARLEY, STEPHEN
RN39903 626 (March 19, 1992) pp11,13.
MARLEY, ZIGGY
RN39903 626 (March 19, 1992) pp11,13.
RN39904 634-635 (July 9, 1992) pp11,13.
RN39905 653 (April 1, 1993) pp11,13.
RN39906 694 (November 3, 1994) pp17-18,22.
RN39907 714 (August 10, 1995) pp15-17.
RN39908 734 (May 16, 1996) pp17-18.
MARS, CHRIS
RN39909 627 (April 2, 1992) pp11,13.
RN39910 633 (June 25, 1992) pp11-12.
RN39911 712-713 (July 13, 1995) pp25-26.
MARS, MICK
RN39912 627 (April 2, 1992) pp11,13.
MARSALIS, BRANFORD
RN39913 624 (February 20, 1992) pp11-12.
RN39914 682 (May 19, 1994) pp37-38.
RN39915 685 (June 30, 1994) pp40-41.
RN39916 691 (September 22, 1994) pp19-21.
RN39917 697 (December 15, 1994) pp17-18,20.
RN39918 708 (May 18, 1995) pp17-18.
MARSHALL, ARIK
RN39919 667 (October 14, 1993) pp39-40.
MARSHALL TUCKER BAND
RN39920 681 (May 5, 1994) pp21-22.
RN39921 740 (August 8, 1996) pp17-18.
MARTELL, T. J.
RN39922 729 (March 7, 1996) pp9-10.
MARTIN, BARDIE
RN39923 686-687 (July 14, 1994) pp41-42.
MARTIN, BARRETT
RN39924 711 (June 29, 1995) pp12-13.
RN39925 748 (November 28, 1996) pp25-26.
MARTIN, DEAN
RN39926 669 (November 11, 1993) pp27-28.
MARTIN, KEVIN
RN39927 686-687 (July 14, 1994) pp41-42.
MARTIN, STEVE
RN39928 654 (April 15, 1993) pp11,13.
RN39929 693 (October 20, 1994) pp27-28,30.
MARTINEZ, CHRISTINA
RN39930 729 (March 7, 1996) pp9-10.
MARX, GROUCHO
RN39931 710 (June 15, 1995) pp17-18.
MARX, RICHARD
RN39932 640 (October 1, 1992) pp9-10.
MARY'S DANISH
RN39933 665 (September 16, 1993) pp31-32.
MASON, DAVE
RN39934 680 (April 21, 1994) pp33-34.
MASSIVE ATTACK
RN39935 655 (April 29, 1993) pp11-12.
RN39936 707 (May 4, 1995) pp19-20.
MASTER MUSICIANS OF JAJOUKA
RN39937 722 (November 30, 1995) pp19-20.
MASUNAGA, ERIC
RN39938 693 (October 20, 1994) pp27-28,30.
MATERIAL ISSUE
RN39939 712-713 (July 13, 1995) pp25-26.
MATHIS, JOHNNY
RN39940 670 (November 25, 1993) pp37-38.
MATHIS, SAMANTHA
RN39941 694 (November 3, 1994) pp17-18,22.
RN39942 740 (August 8, 1996) pp17-18.
MATLOCK, GLEN
RN39943 734 (May 16, 1996) pp17-18.
MATTHEWS, DAVE
RN39944 716 (September 7, 1995) pp13-14.
RN39945 721 (November 16, 1995) pp25-26.
RN39946 743 (September 19, 1996) pp19-20.
MATTHEWS, DONNA
RN39947 746 (October 31, 1996) pp17-18.
MAURER, JOHN
RN39948 741 (August 22, 1996) pp25-26.
MAVERICKS
RN39949 707 (May 4, 1995) pp19-20.
MAX, PETER
RN39950 657 (May 27, 1993) pp9,11.
MAXI PRIEST
RN39951 685 (June 30, 1994) pp40-41.
MAY, BRIAN
RN39952 650 (February 18, 1993) pp11,13.
MAYALL, JOHN
RN39953 697 (December 15, 1994) pp17-18,20.
MAYFIELD, CURTIS
RN39954 676 (February 24, 1994) pp28-29.
RN39955 680 (April 21, 1994) pp33-34.
MAZUR, KEVIN
RN39956 674 (January 27, 1994) pp28-29.
MAZUR, MONET
RN39957 749 (December 12, 1996) pp19-20.
M.C. REN
RN39958 639 (September 17, 1992) pp19-20.
MC5
RN39959 628 (April 16, 1992) pp11,13.
MCA
RN39960 631 (May 28, 1992) pp9,11.
RN39961 726 (January 25, 1996) pp17-18.
MCBAIN, JOHN
RN39962 667 (October 14, 1993) pp39-40.
MCCABE, NICK
RN39963 710 (June 15, 1995) pp17-18.
MCCARTHY, JENNY
RN39964 748 (November 28, 1996) pp25-26.
MCCARTNEY, LINDA
RN39965 694 (November 3, 1994) pp17-18,22.
MCCARTNEY, PAUL
RN39966 633 (June 25, 1992) pp11-12.
RN39967 640 (October 1, 1992) pp9-10.
RN39968 649 (February 4, 1993) pp8-9.
RN39969 653 (April 1, 1993) pp11,13.
RN39970 657 (May 27, 1993) pp9,11.
RN39971 671 (December 9, 1993) pp31-32.
RN39972 683 (June 2, 1994) pp27-28.
RN39973 704 (March 23, 1995) pp24-25.
RN39974 744 (October 3, 1996) pp19-21.
MCCAUGHEY, SCOTT
RN39975 714 (August 10, 1995) pp15-17.
RN39976 717 (September 21, 1995) pp19-20.
MCCLINTON, DELBERT
RN39977 628 (April 16, 1992) pp11,13.
MCCONAUGHEY, MATTHEW
RN39978 748 (November 28, 1996) pp25-26.
MCCONNELL, PAGE
RN39979 744 (October 3, 1996) pp19-21.
MCCORD, KEVIN
RN39980 691 (September 22, 1994) pp19-21.
MCCREADY, MIKE
RN39981 634-635 (July 9, 1992) pp11,13.
RN39982 650 (February 18, 1993) pp11,13.
RN39983 659 (June 24, 1993) pp13,15.
RN39984 665 (September 16, 1993) pp31-32.
RN39985 697 (December 15, 1994) pp17-18,20.

RN39986 711 (June 29, 1995) pp12-13.
RN39987 726 (January 25, 1996) pp17-18.
RN39988 732 (April 18, 1996) pp19-20.
RN39989 748 (November 28, 1996) pp25-26.
MCDONALD, COUNTRY JOE
RN39990 679 (April 7, 1994) pp37-39.
MCDONALD, JEFF
RN39991 685 (June 30, 1994) pp40-41.
MCDONALD, MICHAEL
RN39992 637 (August 20, 1992) pp9,11.
MCDONALD, ROY
RN39993 735 (May 30, 1996) pp12-13.
MCELRATH, JENNI
RN39994 743 (September 19, 1996) pp19-20.
MCFERRIN, BOBBY
RN39995 616 (October 31, 1991) pp11,13.
MCGOWAN, SHANE
RN39996 666 (September 30, 1993) pp27-28.
MCGUIGAN, PAUL
RN39997 720 (November 2, 1995) pp16-17.
MCGUINN, ROGER
RN39998 644 (November 26, 1992) pp13,15.
RN39999 662 (August 5, 1993) pp33-34.
RN40000 685 (June 30, 1994) pp40-41.
RN40001 719 (October 19, 1995) pp15-16.
MCGUINNESS, PAUL
RN40002 624 (February 20, 1992) pp11-12.
RN40003 663 (August 19, 1993) pp27-28.
MCINTOSH, DAVID
RN40004 706 (April 20, 1995) pp15-17.
MCKAGAN, DUFF
RN40005 721 (November 16, 1995) pp25-26.
RN40006 731 (April 4, 1996) pp17-18.
MCKAY, JIM
RN40007 648 (January 21, 1993) pp9,11.
MCKEAN, MICHAEL
RN40008 662 (August 5, 1993) pp33-34.
MCKEE, MARIA
RN40009 636 (August 6, 1992) pp11,13.
RN40010 660-661 (July 8, 1993) pp32-33.
RN40011 666 (September 30, 1993) pp27-28.
MCLACHLAN, SARAH
RN40012 707 (May 4, 1995) pp19-20.
RN40013 746 (October 31, 1996) pp17-18.
MCLAGAN, IAN
RN40014 653 (April 1, 1993) pp11,13.
MCLAREN, MALCOLM
RN40015 710 (June 15, 1995) pp17-18.
RN40016 734 (May 16, 1996) pp17-18.
MCMAHON, KEVIN
RN40017 714 (August 10, 1995) pp15-17.
MCMURTRY, JAMES
RN40018 623 (February 6, 1992) pp11,13.
MCNEILLY, MAC
RN40019 736 (June 13, 1996) pp19-20.
MCVEY, CAMERON
RN40020 655 (April 29, 1993) pp11-12.
MEADE, TYSON
RN40021 680 (April 21, 1994) pp33-34.
MEAT LOAF
RN40022 686-687 (July 14, 1994) pp41-42.
RN40023 704 (March 23, 1995) pp24-25.
RN40024 705 (April 6, 1995) pp16-17.
RN40025 731 (April 4, 1996) pp17-18.
MEAT PUPPETS
RN40026 685 (June 30, 1994) pp40-41.
RN40027 694 (November 3, 1994) pp17-18,22.
RN40028 700 (January 26, 1995) pp16-17.
MEGADETH
RN40029 628 (April 16, 1992) pp11,13.
RN40030 652 (March 18, 1993) pp13,15.
RN40031 664 (September 2, 1993) pp31-32.
MEINE, KLAUS
RN40032 623 (February 6, 1992) pp11,13.
MEISEL, STEVEN
RN40033 644 (November 26, 1992) pp13,15.
MEKONS
RN40034 694 (November 3, 1994) pp17-18,22.
RN40035 709 (June 1, 1995) pp16-17.
RN40036 736 (June 13, 1996) pp19-20.
MELLE MEL
RN40037 670 (November 25, 1993) pp37-38.
MELLENCAMP, JOHN
RN40038 616 (October 31, 1991) pp11,13.
RN40039 618 (November 28, 1991) pp11-12.
RN40040 621 (January 9, 1992) pp10-11.
RN40041 622 (January 23, 1992) pp6-7.
RN40042 623 (February 6, 1992) pp11,13.
RN40043 626 (March 19, 1992) pp11,13.
RN40044 629 (April 30, 1992) pp11-12.
RN40045 640 (October 1, 1992) pp9-10.
RN40046 658 (June 10, 1993) pp16-17.
RN40047 675 (February 10, 1994) pp22-23.
RN40048 676 (February 24, 1994) pp28-29.
RN40049 694 (November 3, 1994) pp17-18,22.
RN40050 711 (June 29, 1995) pp12-13.
RN40051 721 (November 16, 1995) pp25-26.
RN40052 748 (November 28, 1996) pp25-26.
MELLENCAMP, SPECK
RN40053 711 (June 29, 1995) pp12-13.
MELODY MAKERS
RN40054 653 (April 1, 1993) pp11,13.
MELVINS
RN40055 675 (February 10, 1994) pp22-23.
RN40056 688 (August 11, 1994) pp17-18,20.
RN40057 733 (May 2, 1996) pp13-14.
RN40058 736 (June 13, 1996) pp19-20.
MENCK, RIC
RN40059 685 (June 30, 1994) pp40-41.
MERCHANT, NATALIE
RN40060 622 (January 23, 1992) pp6-7.
RN40061 647 (January 7, 1993) pp9,11.
RN40062 656 (May 13, 1993) pp13,15.
RN40063 657 (May 27, 1993) pp9,11.
RN40064 665 (September 16, 1993) pp31-32.
RN40065 667 (October 14, 1993) pp39-40.
RN40066 674 (January 27, 1994) pp28-29.
RN40067 679 (April 7, 1994) pp37-39.
RN40068 684 (June 16, 1994) pp35-36.
RN40069 697 (December 15, 1994) pp17-18,20.
RN40070 706 (April 20, 1995) pp15-17.
RN40071 729 (March 7, 1996) pp9-10.
MERCURY, FREDDIE
RN40072 650 (February 18, 1993) pp11,13.
RN40073 656 (May 13, 1993) pp13,15.
RN40074 720 (November 2, 1995) pp16-17.
ME'SHELL NDEGEOCELLO
RN40075 708 (May 18, 1995) pp17-18.
MESSINA, JIM
RN40076 657 (May 27, 1993) pp9,11.
METALLICA
RN40077 615 (October 17, 1991) pp13-14.
RN40078 618 (November 28, 1991) pp11-12.
RN40079 628 (April 16, 1992) pp11,13.
RN40080 629 (April 30, 1992) pp11-12.
RN40081 634-635 (July 9, 1992) pp11,13.
RN40082 639 (September 17, 1992) pp19-20.
RN40083 652 (March 18, 1993) pp13,15.
RN40084 655 (April 29, 1993) pp11-12.
RN40085 665 (September 16, 1993) pp31-32.
RN40086 668 (October 28, 1993) pp35-36.
RN40087 681 (May 5, 1994) pp21-22.
RN40088 719 (October 19, 1995) pp15-16.
RN40089 727 (February 8, 1996) pp12-13.
RN40090 742 (September 5, 1996) pp20-21.
RN40091 745 (October 17, 1996) pp27-28.
MICHAEL, GEORGE
RN40092 617 (November 14, 1991) pp11,13.
RN40093 623 (February 6, 1992) pp11,13.
RN40094 627 (April 2, 1992) pp11,13.
RN40095 654 (April 15, 1993) pp11,13.
RN40096 656 (May 13, 1993) pp13,15.
RN40097 669 (November 11, 1993) pp27-28.
RN40098 674 (January 27, 1994) pp28-29.
RN40099 703 (March 9, 1995) pp20-21.
RN40100 748 (November 28, 1996) pp25-26.
MICHAELS, BRET
RN40101 626 (March 19, 1992) pp11,13.
RN40102 633 (June 25, 1992) pp11-12.
RN40103 703 (March 9, 1995) pp20-21.
MICHAELS, CAROLYN
RN40104 718 (October 5, 1995) pp20-21.
MIDGET STOOGES
RN40105 715 (August 24, 1995) pp23,25.
MIDNIGHT OIL
RN40106 633 (June 25, 1992) pp11-12.
RN40107 652 (March 18, 1993) pp13,15.
RN40108 656 (May 13, 1993) pp13,15.
RN40109 658 (June 10, 1993) pp16-17.
RN40110 669 (November 11, 1993) pp27-28.
RN40111 690 (September 8, 1994) pp21,24.
MILLER, DENNIS
RN40112 636 (August 6, 1992) pp11,13.
MILLER, GLEN
RN40113 681 (May 5, 1994) pp21-22.
MILLER, JERRY

RN40114 670 (November 25, 1993) pp37-38.
MILLER, RAND
RN40115 692 (October 6, 1994) pp15-17.
MILLER, RICK
RN40116 746 (October 31, 1996) pp17-18.
MILLER, ROBYN
RN40117 692 (October 6, 1994) pp15-17.
MILLER, STEVE
RN40118 633 (June 25, 1992) pp11-12.
RN40119 657 (May 27, 1993) pp9,11.
RN40120 681 (May 5, 1994) pp21-22.
RN40121 684 (June 16, 1994) pp35-36.
MILLER, TOBI
RN40122 636 (August 6, 1992) pp11,13.
MILLI VANILLI
RN40123 621 (January 9, 1992) pp10-11.
MILLS, MIKE
RN40124 628 (April 16, 1992) pp11,13.
RN40125 647 (January 7, 1993) pp9,11.
RN40126 676 (February 24, 1994) pp28-29.
RN40127 678 (March 24, 1994) pp27-28.
RN40128 688 (August 11, 1994) pp17-18,20.
RN40129 689 (August 25, 1994) pp15-16.
RN40130 693 (October 20, 1994) pp27-28,30.
MILOS, MARILYN
RN40131 716 (September 7, 1995) pp13-14.
MINISTRY
RN40132 638 (September 3, 1992) pp9,11.
RN40133 665 (September 16, 1993) pp31-32.
RN40134 685 (June 30, 1994) pp40-41.
RN40135 696 (December 1, 1994) pp23-25.
MINNELLI, LIZA
RN40136 669 (November 11, 1993) pp27-28.
RN40137 678 (March 24, 1994) pp27-28.
RN40138 680 (April 21, 1994) pp33-34.
MINOR THREAT
RN40139 721 (November 16, 1995) pp25-26.
MINUS 5
RN40140 714 (August 10, 1995) pp15-17.
RN40141 717 (September 21, 1995) pp19-20.
MITCHELL, JONI
RN40142 636 (August 6, 1992) pp11,13.
RN40143 662 (August 5, 1993) pp33-34.
RN40144 663 (August 19, 1993) pp27-28.
RN40145 686-687 (July 14, 1994) pp41-42.
RN40146 732 (April 18, 1996) pp19-20.
RN40147 733 (May 2, 1996) pp13-14.
MITCHELL, MITCH
RN40148 625 (March 5, 1992) pp11,13-15,17+.
MIXMASTER MORRIS
RN40149 738-739 (July 11, 1996) pp15-16.
MOBY
RN40150 715 (August 24, 1995) pp23,25.
RN40151 716 (September 7, 1995) pp13-14.
MOBY GRAPE
RN40152 670 (November 25, 1993) pp37-38.
MOHR, TODD
RN40153 690 (September 8, 1994) pp21,24.
RN40154 718 (October 5, 1995) pp20-21.
MOLEN, MIRANDA
RN40155 736 (June 13, 1996) pp19-20.
MOLINARI, SUSAN
RN40156 697 (December 15, 1994) pp17-18,20.
MOLLOY, MATT
RN40157 621 (January 9, 1992) pp10-11.
MOLONEY, PADDY
RN40157 621 (January 9, 1992) pp10-11.
MONICA
RN40158 729 (March 7, 1996) pp9-10.
MONIE LOVE
RN40159 621 (January 9, 1992) pp10-11.
MONK, THELONIOUS
RN40160 703 (March 9, 1995) pp20-21.
MONKEES
RN40161 629 (April 30, 1992) pp11-12.
RN40162 657 (May 27, 1993) pp9,11.
RN40163 663 (August 19, 1993) pp27-28.
RN40164 702 (February 23, 1995) pp19-20.
MONROE, MARILYN
RN40165 688 (August 11, 1994) pp17-18,20.
RN40166 721 (November 16, 1995) pp25-26.
MONTOYA, CRAIG
RN40167 709 (June 1, 1995) pp16-17.
RN40168 726 (January 25, 1996) pp17-18.
MOONEY, TIM
RN40169 684 (June 16, 1994) pp35-36.
MOORE, ANGELO
RN40170 633 (June 25, 1992) pp11-12.
MOORE, GARY
RN40171 630 (May 14, 1992) pp13,15.
MOORE, SAM
RN40172 625 (March 5, 1992) pp11,13-15,17+.
RN40173 628 (April 16, 1992) pp11,13.
MOORE, SCOTTY
RN40174 742 (September 5, 1996) pp20-21.
MOORE, THURSTON
RN40175 633 (June 25, 1992) pp11-12.
RN40176 637 (August 20, 1992) pp9,11.
RN40177 656 (May 13, 1993) pp13,15.
RN40178 676 (February 24, 1994) pp28-29.
RN40179 683 (June 2, 1994) pp27-28.
RN40180 688 (August 11, 1994) pp17-18,20.
RN40181 702 (February 23, 1995) pp19-20.
RN40182 715 (August 24, 1995) pp23,25.
RN40183 721 (November 16, 1995) pp25-26.
RN40184 734 (May 16, 1996) pp17-18.
MORELLO, TOM
RN40185 664 (September 2, 1993) pp31-32.
RN40186 718 (October 5, 1995) pp20-21.
RN40187 737 (June 27, 1996) pp15-16.
MORISSETTE, ALANIS
RN40188 719 (October 19, 1995) pp15-16.
RN40189 721 (November 16, 1995) pp25-26.
RN40190 732 (April 18, 1996) pp19-20.
RN40191 741 (August 22, 1996) pp25-26.
MORITSUGU, JOHN
RN40192 697 (December 15, 1994) pp17-18,20.
MORPHINE
RN40193 691 (September 22, 1994) pp19-21.
RN40194 704 (March 23, 1995) pp24-25.
MORPURGO, KEVIN
RN40195 718 (October 5, 1995) pp20-21.
MORRIS, KEITH
RN40196 712-713 (July 13, 1995) pp25-26.
MORRIS, NATE
RN40197 729 (March 7, 1996) pp9-10.
MORRISON, STERLING
RN40198 648 (January 21, 1993) pp9,11.
MORRISON, VAN
RN40198 648 (January 21, 1993) pp9,11.
RN40199 655 (April 29, 1993) pp11-12.
RN40200 658 (June 10, 1993) pp16-17.
RN40201 668 (October 28, 1993) pp35-36.
MORRISSEY
RN40202 631 (May 28, 1992) pp9,11.
RN40203 684 (June 16, 1994) pp35-36.
RN40204 688 (August 11, 1994) pp17-18,20.
RN40205 726 (January 25, 1996) pp17-18.
RN40206 748 (November 28, 1996) pp25-26.
MOSS, KATE
RN40207 727 (February 8, 1996) pp12-13.
RN40208 747 (November 14, 1996) pp25-26.
MOTHER LOVE BONE
RN40209 741 (August 22, 1996) pp25-26.
MOTHER TERESA
RN40210 701 (February 9, 1995) pp16-17.
RN40211 728 (February 22, 1996) p20.
MOTHER TONGUE
RN40212 664 (September 2, 1993) pp31-32.
MOTHERSBAUGH, BOB
RN40213 730 (March 21, 1996) pp17-18.
MOTHERSBAUGH, MARK
RN40213 730 (March 21, 1996) pp17-18.
MOTLEY CRUE
RN40214 622 (January 23, 1992) pp6-7.
RN40215 627 (April 2, 1992) pp11,13.
RN40216 628 (April 16, 1992) pp11,13.
RN40217 705 (April 6, 1995) pp16-17.
RN40218 744 (October 3, 1996) pp19-21.
MOTORHEAD
RN40219 676 (February 24, 1994) pp28-29.
RN40220 727 (February 8, 1996) pp12-13.
RN40221 743 (September 19, 1996) pp19-20.
MOTTOLA, TOMMY
RN40222 657 (May 27, 1993) pp9,11.
MOULD, BOB
RN40223 637 (August 20, 1992) pp9,11.
RN40224 686-687 (July 14, 1994) pp41-42.
RN40225 701 (February 9, 1995) pp16-17.
RN40226 742 (September 5, 1996) pp20-21.
MOUSE, MICKEY
RN40227 726 (January 25, 1996) pp17-18.
MOYET, ALISON
RN40228 697 (December 15, 1994) pp17-18,20.
MR. T
RN40229 716 (September 7, 1995) pp13-14.

MR. T EXPERIENCE
RN40230 636 (August 6, 1992) pp11,13.
MUDHONEY
RN40231 624 (February 20, 1992) pp11-12.
RN40232 644 (November 26, 1992) pp13,15.
RN40233 655 (April 29, 1993) pp11-12.
RN40234 666 (September 30, 1993) pp27-28.
RN40235 668 (October 28, 1993) pp35-36.
RN40236 670 (November 25, 1993) pp37-38.
RN40237 679 (April 7, 1994) pp37-39.
RN40238 683 (June 2, 1994) pp27-28.
RN40239 719 (October 19, 1995) pp15-16.
MUFFS
RN40240 711 (June 29, 1995) pp12-13.
RN40241 735 (May 30, 1996) pp12-13.
MUGGS
RN40242 671 (December 9, 1993) pp31-32.
MULDER, KAREN
RN40243 742 (September 5, 1996) pp20-21.
MULLEN, LARRY, JR.
RN40244 636 (August 6, 1992) pp11,13.
RN40245 710 (June 15, 1995) pp17-18.
RN40246 738-739 (July 11, 1996) pp15-16.
MULLIS, KARY
RN40247 721 (November 16, 1995) pp25-26.
MURMURS
RN40248 712-713 (July 13, 1995) pp25-26.
MURPHY, DAN
RN40249 633 (June 25, 1992) pp11-12.
RN40250 674 (January 27, 1994) pp28-29.
RN40251 691 (September 22, 1994) pp19-21.
RN40252 715 (August 24, 1995) pp23,25.
RN40253 729 (March 7, 1996) pp9-10.
MURPHY, EDDIE
RN40254 626 (March 19, 1992) pp11,13.
RN40255 630 (May 14, 1992) pp13,15.
RN40256 633 (June 25, 1992) pp11-12.
MURPHY, MICHAEL
RN40257 653 (April 1, 1993) pp11,13.
MURPHY, PATRICK
RN40258 742 (September 5, 1996) pp20-21.
MURPHY, PETER
RN40259 716 (September 7, 1995) pp13-14.
MURRAY, BILL
RN40260 747 (November 14, 1996) pp25-26.
MURRAY, DEE
RN40261 629 (April 30, 1992) pp11-12.
MUSBURGER, MIKE
RN40262 730 (March 21, 1996) pp17-18.
MUSSER, JEFF
RN40263 702 (February 23, 1995) pp19-20.
MUSTAINE, DAVE
RN40264 628 (April 16, 1992) pp11,13.
RN40265 664 (September 2, 1993) pp31-32.
MUSTAINE, JUSTIS DAVID
RN40266 628 (April 16, 1992) pp11,13.
MUSTAINE, PAM
RN40266 628 (April 16, 1992) pp11,13.
MUTTER, ANNE-SOPHIE
RN40267 731 (April 4, 1996) pp17-18.
MY LIFE WITH THE THRILL KILL KULT
RN40268 666 (September 30, 1993) pp27-28.
MYERS, MIKE
RN40269 656 (May 13, 1993) pp13,15.
RN40270 693 (October 20, 1994) pp27-28,30.

N

NAPALM DEATH
RN40271 694 (November 3, 1994) pp17-18,22.
NAPOLITANO, JOHNETTE
RN40272 628 (April 16, 1992) pp11,13.
RN40273 668 (October 28, 1993) pp35-36.
RN40274 670 (November 25, 1993) pp37-38.
RN40275 681 (May 5, 1994) pp21-22.
NARCIZO, DAVID
RN40276 637 (August 20, 1992) pp9,11.
NAS
RN40277 690 (September 8, 1994) pp21,24.
NASH, GRAHAM
RN40278 625 (March 5, 1992) pp11,13-15,17+.
RN40279 679 (April 7, 1994) pp37-39.
RN40280 718 (October 5, 1995) pp20-21.
RN40281 745 (October 17, 1996) pp27-28.
NAUGHTY BY NATURE
RN40282 622 (January 23, 1992) pp6-7.
RN40283 659 (June 24, 1993) pp13,15.
RN40284 664 (September 2, 1993) pp31-32.
RN40285 667 (October 14, 1993) pp39-40.
RN40286 679 (April 7, 1994) pp37-39.
RN40287 696 (December 1, 1994) pp23-25.
RN40288 720 (November 2, 1995) pp16-17.
RN40289 729 (March 7, 1996) pp9-10.
NAVARRO, DAVE
RN40290 616 (October 31, 1991) pp11,13.
RN40291 653 (April 1, 1993) pp11,13.
RN40292 667 (October 14, 1993) pp39-40.
RN40293 692 (October 6, 1994) pp15-17.
RN40294 703 (March 9, 1995) pp20-21.
RN40295 706 (April 20, 1995) pp15-17.
RN40296 722 (November 30, 1995) pp19-20.
RN40297 731 (April 4, 1996) pp17-18.
RN40298 749 (December 12, 1996) pp19-20.
NDEGEOCELLO, ME'SHELL
RN40299 711 (June 29, 1995) pp12-13.
RN40300 712-713 (July 13, 1995) pp25-26.
RN40301 746 (October 31, 1996) pp17-18.
N'DOUR, YOUSSOU
RN40302 655 (April 29, 1993) pp11-12.
RN40303 686-687 (July 14, 1994) pp41-42.
NEALSON, KEVIN
RN40304 693 (October 20, 1994) pp27-28,30.
NEFERTITI
RN40305 707 (May 4, 1995) pp19-20.
NEGATIVLAND
RN40306 624 (February 20, 1992) pp11-12.
NEIL, VINCE
RN40307 627 (April 2, 1992) pp11,13.
RN40308 644 (November 26, 1992) pp13,15.
RN40309 683 (June 2, 1994) pp27-28.
RN40310 696 (December 1, 1994) pp23-25.
RN40311 744 (October 3, 1996) pp19-21.
NELSON, JUDD
RN40312 616 (October 31, 1991) pp11,13.
NELSON, SEAN
RN40313 693 (October 20, 1994) pp27-28,30.
NELSON, WILLIE
RN40314 629 (April 30, 1992) pp11-12.
RN40315 631 (May 28, 1992) pp9,11.
RN40316 640 (October 1, 1992) pp9-10.
RN40317 652 (March 18, 1993) pp13,15.
RN40318 658 (June 10, 1993) pp16-17.
RN40319 659 (June 24, 1993) pp13,15.
RN40320 660-661 (July 8, 1993) pp32-33.
RN40321 685 (June 30, 1994) pp40-41.
RN40322 694 (November 3, 1994) pp17-18,22.
RN40323 705 (April 6, 1995) pp16-17.
RN40324 707 (May 4, 1995) pp19-20.
RN40325 712-713 (July 13, 1995) pp25-26.
RN40326 721 (November 16, 1995) pp25-26.
RN40327 731 (April 4, 1996) pp17-18.
RN40328 748 (November 28, 1996) pp25-26.
NESS, MIKE
RN40329 666 (September 30, 1993) pp27-28.
RN40330 693 (October 20, 1994) pp27-28,30.
RN40331 711 (June 29, 1995) pp12-13.
RN40332 741 (August 22, 1996) pp25-26.
NEUROTIC BOY OUTSIDER
RN40333 721 (November 16, 1995) pp25-26.
NEUWIRTH, BOBBY
RN40334 678 (March 24, 1994) pp27-28.
NEVILLE, AARON
RN40335 625 (March 5, 1992) pp11,13-15,17+.
RN40336 633 (June 25, 1992) pp11-12.
RN40337 682 (May 19, 1994) pp37-38.
RN40338 696 (December 1, 1994) pp23-25.
NEVILLE BROTHERS
RN40339 633 (June 25, 1992) pp11-12.
RN40340 684 (June 16, 1994) pp35-36.
RN40341 738-739 (July 11, 1996) pp15-16.
NEW KIDS ON THE BLOCK
RN40342 678 (March 24, 1994) pp27-28.
NEW ORDER
RN40343 662 (August 5, 1993) pp33-34.
NEW POWER GENERATION
RN40344 637 (August 20, 1992) pp9,11.
NEW YORK DOLLS
RN40345 700 (January 26, 1995) pp16-17.
RN40346 743 (September 19, 1996) pp19-20.
NEWMAN, PAUL
RN40347 733 (May 2, 1996) pp13-14.
NEWS
RN40348 629 (April 30, 1992) pp11-12.
NEWSTED, JASON

RN40349 628 (April 16, 1992) pp11,13.
RN40350 665 (September 16, 1993) pp31-32.
RN40351 681 (May 5, 1994) pp21-22.
RN40352 727 (February 8, 1996) pp12-13.
NEWTON, JOE
RN40353 703 (March 9, 1995) pp20-21.
NEWTON, THANDIE
RN40354 741 (August 22, 1996) pp25-26.
NEWTON, WAYNE
RN40355 634-635 (July 9, 1992) pp11,13.
NICE, PETE
RN40356 631 (May 28, 1992) pp9,11.
NICHOLSON, JACK
RN40357 707 (May 4, 1995) pp19-20.
RN40358 727 (February 8, 1996) pp12-13.
NICKLEBAG
RN40359 734 (May 16, 1996) pp17-18.
NICKS, STEVIE
RN40360 624 (February 20, 1992) pp11-12.
RN40361 663 (August 19, 1993) pp27-28.
NICOL, SIMON
RN40362 691 (September 22, 1994) pp19-21.
NIELSON, RICK
RN40363 723 (December 14, 1995) pp27-28.
NIGHT RANGER
RN40364 685 (June 30, 1994) pp40-41.
NILSSON, HARRY
RN40365 702 (February 23, 1995) pp19-20.
NINE INCH NAILS
RN40366 634-635 (July 9, 1992) pp11,13.
RN40367 654 (April 15, 1993) pp11,13.
RN40368 679 (April 7, 1994) pp37-39.
RN40369 681 (May 5, 1994) pp21-22.
RN40370 692 (October 6, 1994) pp15-17.
RN40371 702 (February 23, 1995) pp19-20.
RN40372 714 (August 10, 1995) pp15-17.
RN40373 723 (December 14, 1995) pp27-28.
NIRVANA
RN40374 642 (October 29, 1992) pp19,21.
RN40375 655 (April 29, 1993) pp11-12.
RN40376 664 (September 2, 1993) pp31-32.
RN40377 666 (September 30, 1993) pp27-28.
RN40378 667 (October 14, 1993) pp39-40.
RN40379 674 (January 27, 1994) pp28-29.
RN40380 676 (February 24, 1994) pp28-29.
RN40381 689 (August 25, 1994) pp15-16.
RN40382 691 (September 22, 1994) pp19-21.
RN40383 692 (October 6, 1994) pp15-17.
RN40384 693 (October 20, 1994) pp27-28,30.
RN40385 702 (February 23, 1995) pp19-20.
RN40386 711 (June 29, 1995) pp12-13.
NIXON, MOJO
RN40387 639 (September 17, 1992) pp19-20.
NIXON, RICHARD
RN40388 685 (June 30, 1994) pp40-41.
NIXONS
RN40389 733 (May 2, 1996) pp13-14.
NO DOUBT
RN40390 740 (August 8, 1996) pp17-18.
RN40391 743 (September 19, 1996) pp19-20.
NORMAN, JESSY
RN40392 709 (June 1, 1995) pp16-17.
NOTORIOUS B.I.G.
RN40393 714 (August 10, 1995) pp15-17.
RN40394 721 (November 16, 1995) pp25-26.
RN40395 729 (March 7, 1996) pp9-10.
NOVELLO, IVER
RN40396 686-687 (July 14, 1994) pp41-42.
NOVOSELIC, KRIST
RN40397 666 (September 30, 1993) pp27-28.
RN40398 674 (January 27, 1994) pp28-29.
RN40399 676 (February 24, 1994) pp28-29.
RN40400 691 (September 22, 1994) pp19-21.
RN40401 692 (October 6, 1994) pp15-17.
RN40402 693 (October 20, 1994) pp27-28,30.
RN40403 706 (April 20, 1995) pp15-17.
RN40404 711 (June 29, 1995) pp12-13.
RN40405 732 (April 18, 1996) pp19-20.
NRBQ
RN40406 680 (April 21, 1994) pp33-34.
NUEROTIC OUTSIDERS
RN40407 731 (April 4, 1996) pp17-18.
NUGENT, TED
RN40408 623 (February 6, 1992) pp11,13.
RN40409 631 (May 28, 1992) pp9,11.
RN40410 652 (March 18, 1993) pp13,15.
RN40411 696 (December 1, 1994) pp23-25.
RN40412 697 (December 15, 1994) pp17-18,20.
RN40413 730 (March 21, 1996) pp17-18.
N.W.A.
RN40414 634-635 (July 9, 1992) pp11,13.
RN40415 639 (September 17, 1992) pp19-20.
RN40416 690 (September 8, 1994) pp21,24.
RN40417 718 (October 5, 1995) pp20-21.

O

OASIS
RN40418 710 (June 15, 1995) pp17-18.
RN40419 718 (October 5, 1995) pp20-21.
RN40420 720 (November 2, 1995) pp16-17.
RN40421 727 (February 8, 1996) pp12-13.
RN40422 731 (April 4, 1996) pp17-18.
RN40423 735 (May 30, 1996) pp12-13.
RN40424 737 (June 27, 1996) pp15-16.
RN40425 742 (September 5, 1996) pp20-21.
RN40426 745 (October 17, 1996) pp27-28.
RN40427 746 (October 31, 1996) pp17-18.
RN40428 749 (December 12, 1996) pp19-20.
O'BRAONAIN, FIACHNA
RN40429 668 (October 28, 1993) pp35-36.
O'BRIAN, BERNADETTE
RN40430 737 (June 27, 1996) pp15-16.
O'BRIEN, ED
RN40431 738-739 (July 11, 1996) pp15-16.
OCASEK, RIC
RN40432 706 (April 20, 1995) pp15-17.
RN40433 722 (November 30, 1995) pp19-20.
O'CONNOR, SINEAD
RN40434 622 (January 23, 1992) pp6-7.
RN40435 636 (August 6, 1992) pp11,13.
RN40436 652 (March 18, 1993) pp13,15.
RN40437 656 (May 13, 1993) pp13,15.
RN40438 663 (August 19, 1993) pp27-28.
RN40439 667 (October 14, 1993) pp39-40.
RN40440 675 (February 10, 1994) pp22-23.
RN40441 703 (March 9, 1995) pp20-21.
ODETTA
RN40442 674 (January 27, 1994) pp28-29.
O'DONNELL, CHRIS
RN40443 709 (June 1, 1995) pp16-17.
OFFSPRING
RN40444 700 (January 26, 1995) pp16-17.
RN40445 711 (June 29, 1995) pp12-13.
RN40446 727 (February 8, 1996) pp12-13.
OJE, BABA
RN40447 648 (January 21, 1993) pp9,11.
RN40448 660-661 (July 8, 1993) pp32-33.
OLDMAN, GARY
RN40449 663 (August 19, 1993) pp27-28.
OLSON, MARK
RN40450 718 (October 5, 1995) pp20-21.
OMAR
RN40451 717 (September 21, 1995) pp19-20.
ONASSIS, BLACKIE
RN40452 685 (June 30, 1994) pp40-41.
112
RN40453 748 (November 28, 1996) pp25-26.
ONE INCH PUNCH
RN40454 749 (December 12, 1996) pp19-20.
O'NEAL, SHAQUILLE
RN40455 652 (March 18, 1993) pp13,15.
RN40456 667 (October 14, 1993) pp39-40.
RN40457 669 (November 11, 1993) pp27-28.
ONO, YOKO
RN40458 621 (January 9, 1992) pp10-11.
RN40459 647 (January 7, 1993) pp9,11.
RN40460 662 (August 5, 1993) pp33-34.
RN40461 710 (June 15, 1995) pp17-18.
RN40462 727 (February 8, 1996) pp12-13.
RN40463 729 (March 7, 1996) pp9-10.
RN40464 733 (May 2, 1996) pp13-14.
RN40465 742 (September 5, 1996) pp20-21.
ONYX
RN40466 668 (October 28, 1993) pp35-36.
RN40467 675 (February 10, 1994) pp22-23.
RN40468 729 (March 7, 1996) pp9-10.

ORBISON, BARBARA
RN40469 644 (November 26, 1992) pp13,15.
ORBITAL
RN40470 745 (October 17, 1996) pp27-28.
ORCHESTRA OF ST. LUKE'S
RN40471 682 (May 19, 1994) pp37-38.
O' RIORDAN, DOLORES
RN40472 684 (June 16, 1994) pp35-36.
RN40473 690 (September 8, 1994) pp21,24.
RN40474 711 (June 29, 1995) pp12-13.
OSBORNE, JOAN
RN40475 727 (February 8, 1996) pp12-13.
RN40476 732 (April 18, 1996) pp19-20.
RN40477 736 (June 13, 1996) pp19-20.
OSBORNE, SARA
RN40478 732 (April 18, 1996) pp19-20.
OSBOURNE, BUZZ
RN40479 733 (May 2, 1996) pp13-14.
OSBOURNE, OZZY
RN40480 621 (January 9, 1992) pp10-11.
RN40481 640 (October 1, 1992) pp9-10.
RN40482 647 (January 7, 1993) pp9,11.
RN40483 690 (September 8, 1994) pp21,24.
RN40484 696 (December 1, 1994) pp23-25.
RN40485 728 (February 22, 1996) p20.
OSMOND BROTHERS
RN40486 678 (March 24, 1994) pp27-28.
OSMOND, DONNY
RN40487 625 (March 5, 1992) pp11,13-15,17+.
RN40488 678 (March 24, 1994) pp27-28.
OSMONDS
RN40489 696 (December 1, 1994) pp23-25.
OUTLAWS
RN40490 681 (May 5, 1994) pp21-22.

P

P
RN40491 709 (June 1, 1995) pp16-17.
P-FUNK ALL-STARS
RN40492 654 (April 15, 1993) pp11,13.
P-NUT
RN40493 747 (November 14, 1996) pp25-26.
PACINO, AL
RN40494 726 (January 25, 1996) pp17-18.
RN40495 734 (May 16, 1996) pp17-18.
PAGE, JIMMY
RN40496 625 (March 5, 1992) pp11,13-15,17+.
RN40497 655 (April 29, 1993) pp11-12.
RN40498 675 (February 10, 1994) pp22-23.
RN40499 708 (May 18, 1995) pp17-18.
RN40500 723 (December 14, 1995) pp27-28.
RN40501 741 (August 22, 1996) pp25-26.
PAGE, STEVEN
RN40502 662 (August 5, 1993) pp33-34.
RN40503 668 (October 28, 1993) pp35-36.
PALTROW, GWYNETH
RN40504 728 (February 22, 1996) p20.
RN40505 733 (May 2, 1996) pp13-14.
RN40506 742 (September 5, 1996) pp20-21.
RN40507 744 (October 3, 1996) pp19-21.
RN40508 745 (October 17, 1996) pp27-28.
RN40509 749 (December 12, 1996) pp19-20.
PANTERA
RN40510 689 (August 25, 1994) pp15-16.
RN40511 707 (May 4, 1995) pp19-20.
PAPP, JOSEPH
RN40512 720 (November 2, 1995) pp16-17.
PARACHUTE EXPRESS
RN40512 720 (November 2, 1995) pp16-17.
PARADIS, VANESSA
RN40513 735 (May 30, 1996) pp12-13.
PARLIAMENT
RN40514 654 (April 15, 1993) pp11,13.
RN40515 692 (October 6, 1994) pp15-17.
PARSONS, ALAN
RN40516 718 (October 5, 1995) pp20-21.
PARTON, DOLLY
RN40517 696 (December 1, 1994) pp23-25.
PARTRIDGE, ANDY
RN40518 674 (January 27, 1994) pp28-29.
PARTRIDGE FAMILY
RN40519 664 (September 2, 1993) pp31-32.
RN40520 678 (March 24, 1994) pp27-28.
PATRA
RN40521 715 (August 24, 1995) pp23,25.
PATRIC, JASON
RN40522 617 (November 14, 1991) pp11,13.
PATRICK, RICHARD
RN40523 720 (November 2, 1995) pp16-17.
RN40524 723 (December 14, 1995) pp27-28.
PATRICK, ROBERT
RN40525 720 (November 2, 1995) pp16-17.
PATTON, MIKE
RN40526 618 (November 28, 1991) pp11-12.
PAUL, VINNIE
RN40527 707 (May 4, 1995) pp19-20.
PAULSON, CHARLIE
RN40528 745 (October 17, 1996) pp27-28.
PAVAROTTI, LUCIANO
RN40529 682 (May 19, 1994) pp37-38.
RN40530 694 (November 3, 1994) pp17-18,22.
RN40531 721 (November 16, 1995) pp25-26.
RN40532 731 (April 4, 1996) pp17-18.
PAVEMENT
RN40533 663 (August 19, 1993) pp27-28.
RN40534 685 (June 30, 1994) pp40-41.
RN40535 693 (October 20, 1994) pp27-28,30.
PAW
RN40536 686-687 (July 14, 1994) pp41-42.
PEARCY, STEPHEN
RN40537 630 (May 14, 1992) pp13,15.
PEARL JAM
RN40538 618 (November 28, 1991) pp11-12.
RN40539 634-635 (July 9, 1992) pp11,13.
RN40540 638 (September 3, 1992) pp9,11.
RN40541 642 (October 29, 1992) pp19,21.
RN40542 650 (February 18, 1993) pp11,13.
RN40543 658 (June 10, 1993) pp16-17.
RN40544 659 (June 24, 1993) pp13,15.
RN40545 662 (August 5, 1993) pp33-34.
RN40546 663 (August 19, 1993) pp27-28.
RN40547 665 (September 16, 1993) pp31-32.
RN40548 667 (October 14, 1993) pp39-40.
RN40549 674 (January 27, 1994) pp28-29.
RN40550 676 (February 24, 1994) pp28-29.
RN40551 681 (May 5, 1994) pp21-22.
RN40552 683 (June 2, 1994) pp27-28.
RN40553 688 (August 11, 1994) pp17-18,20.
RN40554 696 (December 1, 1994) pp23-25.
RN40555 697 (December 15, 1994) pp17-18,20.
RN40556 703 (March 9, 1995) pp20-21.
RN40557 706 (April 20, 1995) pp15-17.
RN40558 717 (September 21, 1995) pp19-20.
RN40559 726 (January 25, 1996) pp17-18.
RN40560 732 (April 18, 1996) pp19-20.
RN40561 747 (November 14, 1996) pp25-26.
RN40562 748 (November 28, 1996) pp25-26.
RN40563 749 (December 12, 1996) pp19-20.
PEARSON, DAN
RN40564 659 (June 24, 1993) pp13,15.
PEARSON, RIDLEY
RN40565 634-635 (July 9, 1992) pp11,13.
PEI, I. M.
RN40566 690 (September 8, 1994) pp21,24.
PELTIER, LEONARD
RN40567 684 (June 16, 1994) pp35-36.
PELZL, HANS-MICHAEL
RN40568 718 (October 5, 1995) pp20-21.
PENN, MICHAEL
RN40569 636 (August 6, 1992) pp11,13.
RN40570 649 (February 4, 1993) pp8-9.
RN40571 675 (February 10, 1994) pp22-23.
RN40572 700 (January 26, 1995) pp16-17.
PENN, SEAN
RN40573 663 (August 19, 1993) pp27-28.
RN40574 689 (August 25, 1994) pp15-16.
RN40575 716 (September 7, 1995) pp13-14.
RN40576 726 (January 25, 1996) pp17-18.
RN40577 736 (June 13, 1996) pp19-20.
PENNYWISE
RN40578 718 (October 5, 1995) pp20-21.
PEPA
RN40579 671 (December 9, 1993) pp31-32.
RN40580 696 (December 1, 1994) pp23-25.
RN40581 723 (December 14, 1995) pp27-28.
PERDIE, BERNARD
RN40582 715 (August 24, 1995) pp23,25.

PERE UBU
RN40583 742 (September 5, 1996) pp20-21.
PEREZ, LOUIS
RN40584 616 (October 31, 1991) pp11,13.
PEREZ, ROSIE
RN40585 697 (December 15, 1994) pp17-18,20.
PERKINS, CARL
RN40586 640 (October 1, 1992) pp9-10.
RN40587 693 (October 20, 1994) pp27-28,30.
PERKINS, ELIZABETH
RN40588 715 (August 24, 1995) pp23,25.
PERLMAN, MARC
RN40589 633 (June 25, 1992) pp11-12.
RN40590 691 (September 22, 1994) pp19-21.
RN40591 709 (June 1, 1995) pp16-17.
PERON, EVA
RN40592 729 (March 7, 1996) pp9-10.
PERRY, JOE
RN40593 634-635 (July 9, 1992) pp11,13.
RN40594 657 (May 27, 1993) pp9,11.
RN40595 664 (September 2, 1993) pp31-32.
RN40596 668 (October 28, 1993) pp35-36.
RN40597 679 (April 7, 1994) pp37-39.
RN40598 722 (November 30, 1995) pp19-20.
PERRY, LINDA
RN40599 671 (December 9, 1993) pp31-32.
PERRY, STEVE
RN40600 670 (November 25, 1993) pp37-38.
RN40601 694 (November 3, 1994) pp17-18,22.
PET SHOP BOYS
RN40602 697 (December 15, 1994) pp17-18,20.
PETA
RN40603 730 (March 21, 1996) pp17-18.
PETERSSON, TOM
RN40604 723 (December 14, 1995) pp27-28.
PETTY, JANE
RN40605 637 (August 20, 1992) pp9,11.
PETTY, TOM
RN40606 629 (April 30, 1992) pp11-12.
RN40607 630 (May 14, 1992) pp13,15.
RN40608 633 (June 25, 1992) pp11-12.
RN40609 637 (August 20, 1992) pp9,11.
RN40610 648 (January 21, 1993) pp9,11.
RN40611 666 (September 30, 1993) pp27-28.
RN40612 667 (October 14, 1993) pp39-40.
RN40613 674 (January 27, 1994) pp28-29.
RN40614 693 (October 20, 1994) pp27-28,30.
RN40615 697 (December 15, 1994) pp17-18,20.
RN40616 702 (February 23, 1995) pp19-20.
RN40617 716 (September 7, 1995) pp13-14.
RN40618 719 (October 19, 1995) pp15-16.
RN40619 738-739 (July 11, 1996) pp15-16.
RN40620 740 (August 8, 1996) pp17-18.
PFEIFFER, DARRIN
RN40621 745 (October 17, 1996) pp27-28.
PHAIR, LIZ
RN40622 674 (January 27, 1994) pp28-29.
RN40623 700 (January 26, 1995) pp16-17.
RN40624 712-713 (July 13, 1995) pp25-26.
PHANTOM, SLIM JIM
RN40625 652 (March 18, 1993) pp13,15.
PHARCYDE
RN40626 717 (September 21, 1995) pp19-20.
PHILLIPS, GRANT LEE
RN40627 676 (February 24, 1994) pp28-29.
RN40628 710 (June 15, 1995) pp17-18.
PHILLIPS, PAUL
RN40629 714 (August 10, 1995) pp15-17.
PHILLIPS, SAM
RN40630 675 (February 10, 1994) pp22-23.
PHILLIPS, SAM (SINGER)
RN40631 623 (February 6, 1992) pp11,13.
RN40632 670 (November 25, 1993) pp37-38.
RN40633 686-687 (July 14, 1994) pp41-42.
RN40634 689 (August 25, 1994) pp15-16.
RN40635 702 (February 23, 1995) pp19-20.
RN40636 703 (March 9, 1995) pp20-21.
PHISH
RN40637 686-687 (July 14, 1994) pp41-42.
RN40638 744 (October 3, 1996) pp19-21.
PICCIOTTO, GUY
RN40638 744 (October 3, 1996) pp19-21.
PICKETT, WILSON
RN40639 633 (June 25, 1992) pp11-12.
RN40640 654 (April 15, 1993) pp11,13.
PIERSON, KATE
RN40641 630 (May 14, 1992) pp13,15.
RN40642 637 (August 20, 1992) pp9,11.
RN40643 669 (November 11, 1993) pp27-28.
RN40644 683 (June 2, 1994) pp27-28.
PILATE, PONTIUS
RN40644 683 (June 2, 1994) pp27-28.
RN40645 689 (August 25, 1994) pp15-16.
PILATUS, ROB
RN40646 621 (January 9, 1992) pp10-11.
PINERA, MIKE
RN40647 718 (October 5, 1995) pp20-21.
PINK FLOYD
RN40648 636 (August 6, 1992) pp11,13.
RN40649 722 (November 30, 1995) pp19-20.
PIRNER, DAVE
RN40650 634-635 (July 9, 1992) pp11,13.
RN40651 658 (June 10, 1993) pp16-17.
RN40652 660-661 (July 8, 1993) pp32-33.
RN40653 666 (September 30, 1993) pp27-28.
RN40654 667 (October 14, 1993) pp39-40.
RN40655 669 (November 11, 1993) pp27-28.
RN40656 674 (January 27, 1994) pp28-29.
RN40657 676 (February 24, 1994) pp28-29.
RN40658 688 (August 11, 1994) pp17-18,20.
RN40659 692 (October 6, 1994) pp15-17.
RN40660 706 (April 20, 1995) pp15-17.
RN40661 715 (August 24, 1995) pp23,25.
RN40662 729 (March 7, 1996) pp9-10.
RN40663 747 (November 14, 1996) pp25-26.
PISTONE, JOE
RN40664 734 (May 16, 1996) pp17-18.
PITT, BRAD
RN40665 637 (August 20, 1992) pp9,11.
RN40666 684 (June 16, 1994) pp35-36.
RN40667 714 (August 10, 1995) pp15-17.
RN40668 723 (December 14, 1995) pp27-28.
RN40669 733 (May 2, 1996) pp13-14.
RN40670 744 (October 3, 1996) pp19-21.
PIXIES
RN40671 616 (October 31, 1991) pp11,13.
RN40672 652 (March 18, 1993) pp13,15.
PJ HARVEY
RN40673 714 (August 10, 1995) pp15-17.
RN40674 721 (November 16, 1995) pp25-26.
RN40675 741 (August 22, 1996) pp25-26.
PLAKAS, DEE
RN40676 644 (November 26, 1992) pp13,15.
RN40677 692 (October 6, 1994) pp15-17.
RN40678 696 (December 1, 1994) pp23-25.
PLANT, ROBERT
RN40679 670 (November 25, 1993) pp37-38.
RN40680 689 (August 25, 1994) pp15-16.
RN40681 708 (May 18, 1995) pp17-18.
RN40682 723 (December 14, 1995) pp27-28.
RN40683 741 (August 22, 1996) pp25-26.
PLASTERCASTER, CYNTHIA
RN40684 657 (May 27, 1993) pp9,11.
PLIMSOULS
RN40685 623 (February 6, 1992) pp11,13.
PM DAWN
RN40686 627 (April 2, 1992) pp11,13.
RN40687 629 (April 30, 1992) pp11-12.
RN40688 649 (February 4, 1993) pp8-9.
RN40689 657 (May 27, 1993) pp9,11.
RN40690 660-661 (July 8, 1993) pp32-33.
RN40691 669 (November 11, 1993) pp27-28.
RN40692 710 (June 15, 1995) pp17-18.
RN40693 720 (November 2, 1995) pp16-17.
POGUES
RN40694 616 (October 31, 1991) pp11,13.
POISON
RN40695 615 (October 17, 1991) pp13-14.
RN40696 626 (March 19, 1992) pp11,13.
RN40697 633 (June 25, 1992) pp11-12.
RN40698 703 (March 9, 1995) pp20-21.
POLLACK, JEFF
RN40699 626 (March 19, 1992) pp11,13.
POLLOCK, JACKSON
RN40700 736 (June 13, 1996) pp19-20.
POLO, MARCO

RN40701 711 (June 29, 1995) pp12-13.
POMUS, DOC
RN40702 625 (March 5, 1992) pp11,13-15,17+.
RN40703 634-635 (July 9, 1992) pp11,13.
POP, IGGY
RN40704 617 (November 14, 1991) pp11,13.
RN40705 652 (March 18, 1993) pp13,15.
RN40706 659 (June 24, 1993) pp13,15.
RN40707 663 (August 19, 1993) pp27-28.
RN40708 675 (February 10, 1994) pp22-23.
RN40709 679 (April 7, 1994) pp37-39.
RN40710 680 (April 21, 1994) pp33-34.
RN40711 683 (June 2, 1994) pp27-28.
RN40712 689 (August 25, 1994) pp15-16.
RN40713 692 (October 6, 1994) pp15-17.
RN40714 697 (December 15, 1994) pp17-18,20.
RN40715 714 (August 10, 1995) pp15-17.
RN40716 720 (November 2, 1995) pp16-17.
RN40717 721 (November 16, 1995) pp25-26.
RN40718 723 (December 14, 1995) pp27-28.
RN40719 727 (February 8, 1996) pp12-13.
RN40720 736 (June 13, 1996) pp19-20.
POPES
RN40721 696 (December 1, 1994) pp23-25.
POPINJAYS
RN40722 650 (February 18, 1993) pp11,13.
POPPER, JOHN
RN40723 690 (September 8, 1994) pp21,24.
RN40724 714 (August 10, 1995) pp15-17.
RN40725 729 (March 7, 1996) pp9-10.
RN40726 732 (April 18, 1996) pp19-20.
PORCARO, JEFF
RN40727 649 (February 4, 1993) pp8-9.
PORNO FOR PYROS
RN40728 631 (May 28, 1992) pp9,11.
RN40729 638 (September 3, 1992) pp9,11.
RN40730 653 (April 1, 1993) pp11,13.
RN40731 676 (February 24, 1994) pp28-29.
RN40732 706 (April 20, 1995) pp15-17.
RN40733 707 (May 4, 1995) pp19-20.
RN40734 723 (December 14, 1995) pp27-28.
RN40735 727 (February 8, 1996) pp12-13.
PORTER, COLE
RN40736 629 (April 30, 1992) pp11-12.
PORTISHEAD
RN40737 718 (October 5, 1995) pp20-21.
POSIES
RN40738 658 (June 10, 1993) pp16-17.
RN40739 706 (April 20, 1995) pp15-17.
POSNER, HELAINE
RN40740 634-635 (July 9, 1992) pp11,13.
POST, LOUISE
RN40741 701 (February 9, 1995) pp16-17.
RN40742 709 (June 1, 1995) pp16-17.
POUNDSTONE, PAULA
RN40743 691 (September 22, 1994) pp19-21.
POWELL, COLIN
RN40744 640 (October 1, 1992) pp9-10.
PRAIRIE PRINCE
RN40745 644 (November 26, 1992) pp13,15.
PRATER, DAVE
RN40746 625 (March 5, 1992) pp11,13-15,17+.
PRATER, ROSEMARY
RN40746 625 (March 5, 1992) pp11,13-15,17+.
PRAY, DOUG
RN40747 730 (March 21, 1996) pp17-18.
PRENDERGAST, SHARON MARLEY
RN40748 626 (March 19, 1992) pp11,13.
PRESIDENTS OF THE UNITED STATES OF AMERICA
RN40749 719 (October 19, 1995) pp15-16.
RN40750 740 (August 8, 1996) pp17-18.
PRESLEY, ELVIS
RN40751 624 (February 20, 1992) pp11-12.
RN40752 629 (April 30, 1992) pp11-12.
RN40753 630 (May 14, 1992) pp13,15.
RN40754 631 (May 28, 1992) pp9,11.
RN40755 633 (June 25, 1992) pp11-12.
RN40756 644 (November 26, 1992) pp13,15.
RN40757 650 (February 18, 1993) pp11,13.
RN40758 693 (October 20, 1994) pp27-28,30.
RN40759 696 (December 1, 1994) pp23-25.
RN40760 702 (February 23, 1995) pp19-20.
RN40761 709 (June 1, 1995) pp16-17.
RN40762 716 (September 7, 1995) pp13-14.
RN40763 721 (November 16, 1995) pp25-26.
RN40764 736 (June 13, 1996) pp19-20.
RN40765 742 (September 5, 1996) pp20-21.
PRESLEY, LISA MARIE
RN40766 690 (September 8, 1994) pp21,24.
RN40767 691 (September 22, 1994) pp19-21.
RN40768 693 (October 20, 1994) pp27-28,30.
PRESLEY, PRISCILLA
RN40769 629 (April 30, 1992) pp11-12.
PRESTON, BILLY
RN40770 644 (November 26, 1992) pp13,15.
PRETENDERS
RN40771 655 (April 29, 1993) pp11-12.
RN40772 720 (November 2, 1995) pp16-17.
RN40773 723 (December 14, 1995) pp27-28.
PRICK
RN40774 714 (August 10, 1995) pp15-17.
PRIEBOY, ANDY
RN40775 628 (April 16, 1992) pp11,13.
PRIESTLEY, JASON
RN40776 630 (May 14, 1992) pp13,15.
RN40777 647 (January 7, 1993) pp9,11.
PRIMUS
RN40778 631 (May 28, 1992) pp9,11.
RN40779 676 (February 24, 1994) pp28-29.
RN40780 681 (May 5, 1994) pp21-22.
RN40781 721 (November 16, 1995) pp25-26.
PRINCE
RN40782 615 (October 17, 1991) pp13-14.
RN40783 637 (August 20, 1992) pp9,11.
RN40784 654 (April 15, 1993) pp11,13.
RN40785 656 (May 13, 1993) pp13,15.
RN40786 664 (September 2, 1993) pp31-32.
RN40787 679 (April 7, 1994) pp37-39.
RN40788 681 (May 5, 1994) pp21-22.
RN40789 683 (June 2, 1994) pp27-28.
RN40790 688 (August 11, 1994) pp17-18,20.
RN40791 692 (October 6, 1994) pp15-17.
RN40792 696 (December 1, 1994) pp23-25.
RN40793 701 (February 9, 1995) pp16-17.
RN40794 714 (August 10, 1995) pp15-17.
RN40795 727 (February 8, 1996) pp12-13.
RN40796 733 (May 2, 1996) pp13-14.
RN40797 741 (August 22, 1996) pp25-26.
PRINCE BE
RN40798 629 (April 30, 1992) pp11-12.
RN40799 649 (February 4, 1993) pp8-9.
RN40800 657 (May 27, 1993) pp9,11.
PRINCE CHARLES
RN40801 741 (August 22, 1996) pp25-26.
PRINCESS DIANA
RN40802 748 (November 28, 1996) pp25-26.
PRINCESS STEPHANIE
RN40803 737 (June 27, 1996) pp15-16.
PRINE, JOHN
RN40804 621 (January 9, 1992) pp10-11.
RN40805 623 (February 6, 1992) pp11,13.
RN40806 647 (January 7, 1993) pp9,11.
RN40807 671 (December 9, 1993) pp31-32.
PROCHAZKA, AURE
RN40808 689 (August 25, 1994) pp15-16.
PRODIGY
RN40809 743 (September 19, 1996) pp19-20.
RN40810 745 (October 17, 1996) pp27-28.
RN40811 749 (December 12, 1996) pp19-20.
PROFESSOR LONGHAIR
RN40812 625 (March 5, 1992) pp11,13-15,17+.
RN40813 714 (August 10, 1995) pp15-17.
PROPER GROUNDS
RN40814 636 (August 6, 1992) pp11,13.
PRYOR, RICHARD
RN40815 633 (June 25, 1992) pp11-12.
PSYCHOTICA
RN40816 728 (February 22, 1996) pp20.
PUBLIC ENEMY
RN40817 622 (January 23, 1992) pp6-7.
RN40818 624 (February 20, 1992) pp11-12.
RN40819 628 (April 16, 1992) pp11,13.
RN40820 664 (September 2, 1993) pp31-32.
RN40821 670 (November 25, 1993) pp37-38.
RN40822 675 (February 10, 1994) pp22-23.
RN40823 676 (February 24, 1994) pp28-29.

RN40824 693 (October 20, 1994) pp27-28,30.
RN40825 702 (February 23, 1995) pp19-20.
RN40826 723 (December 14, 1995) pp27-28.
RN40827 742 (September 5, 1996) pp20-21.
PULP
RN40827 742 (September 5, 1996) pp20-21.
PYLE, ARTIMUS
RN40828 727 (February 8, 1996) pp12-13.
PYLON
RN40829 621 (January 9, 1992) pp10-11.
PYRO, HOWIE
RN40830 735 (May 30, 1996) pp12-13.

Q

Q-TIP
RN40831 742 (September 5, 1996) pp20-21.
QUAID, DENNIS
RN40832 656 (May 13, 1993) pp13,15.
QUASAR
RN40833 736 (June 13, 1996) pp19-20.
QUEEN
RN40834 650 (February 18, 1993) pp11,13.
RN40835 656 (May 13, 1993) pp13,15.
RN40836 720 (November 2, 1995) pp16-17.
QUEEN ELIZABETH II
RN40837 701 (February 9, 1995) pp16-17.
QUEEN LATIFAH
RN40838 622 (January 23, 1992) pp6-7.
RN40839 628 (April 16, 1992) pp11,13.
RN40840 629 (April 30, 1992) pp11-12.
RN40841 649 (February 4, 1993) pp8-9.
RN40842 701 (February 9, 1995) pp16-17.
RN40843 706 (April 20, 1995) pp15-17.
RN40844 720 (November 2, 1995) pp16-17.
QUEENSRYCHE
RN40845 615 (October 17, 1991) pp13-14.
RN40846 618 (November 28, 1991) pp11-12.
RN40847 696 (December 1, 1994) pp23-25.
QUINN, ALICE
RN40848 708 (May 18, 1995) pp17-18.

R

RABIN, YITZHAK
RN40849 703 (March 9, 1995) pp20-21.
RADIOHEAD
RN40850 671 (December 9, 1993) pp31-32.
RN40851 718 (October 5, 1995) pp20-21.
RN40852 722 (November 30, 1995) pp19-20.
RN40853 738-739 (July 11, 1996) pp15-16.
RADLOFF, RITA
RN40854 692 (October 6, 1994) pp15-17.
RAGE AGAINST THE MACHINE
RN40855 664 (September 2, 1993) pp31-32.
RN40856 671 (December 9, 1993) pp31-32.
RN40857 674 (January 27, 1994) pp28-29.
RN40858 684 (June 16, 1994) pp35-36.
RN40859 706 (April 20, 1995) pp15-17.
RN40860 715 (August 24, 1995) pp23,25.
RN40861 718 (October 5, 1995) pp20-21.
RN40862 737 (June 27, 1996) pp15-16.
RAITT, BONNIE
RN40863 624 (February 20, 1992) pp11-12.
RN40864 627 (April 2, 1992) pp11,13.
RN40865 628 (April 16, 1992) pp11,13.
RN40866 637 (August 20, 1992) pp9,11.
RN40867 648 (January 21, 1993) pp9,11.
RN40868 652 (March 18, 1993) pp13,15.
RN40869 658 (June 10, 1993) pp16-17.
RN40870 671 (December 9, 1993) pp31-32.
RN40871 678 (March 24, 1994) pp27-28.
RN40872 680 (April 21, 1994) pp33-34.
RN40873 703 (March 9, 1995) pp20-21.
RN40874 705 (April 6, 1995) pp16-17.
RN40875 706 (April 20, 1995) pp15-17.
RN40876 718 (October 5, 1995) pp20-21.
RN40877 729 (March 7, 1996) pp9-10.
RN40878 731 (April 4, 1996) pp17-18.
RN40879 732 (April 18, 1996) pp19-20.
RN40880 733 (May 2, 1996) pp13-14.
RN40881 745 (October 17, 1996) pp27-28.
RN40882 748 (November 28, 1996) pp25-26.
RAITT, JOHN
RN40883 627 (April 2, 1992) pp11,13.
RAJLICH, JANA
RN40884 748 (November 28, 1996) pp25-26.
RAMONE, DEE DEE
RN40885 628 (April 16, 1992) pp11,13.
RAMONE, JOEY
RN40886 670 (November 25, 1993) pp37-38.
RN40887 680 (April 21, 1994) pp33-34.
RN40888 688 (August 11, 1994) pp17-18,20.
RN40889 693 (October 20, 1994) pp27-28,30.
RN40890 735 (May 30, 1996) pp12-13.
RN40891 738-739 (July 11, 1996) pp15-16.
RN40892 743 (September 19, 1996) pp19-20.
RAMONE, JOHNNY
RN40892 743 (September 19, 1996) pp19-20.
RAMONES
RN40893 624 (February 20, 1992) pp11-12.
RN40894 636 (August 6, 1992) pp11,13.
RN40895 640 (October 1, 1992) pp9-10.
RN40896 670 (November 25, 1993) pp37-38.
RN40897 676 (February 24, 1994) pp28-29.
RN40898 719 (October 19, 1995) pp15-16.
RN40899 743 (September 19, 1996) pp19-20.
RANALDO, LEE
RN40900 637 (August 20, 1992) pp9,11.
RN40901 702 (February 23, 1995) pp19-20.
RN40902 717 (September 21, 1995) pp19-20.
RN40903 721 (November 16, 1995) pp25-26.
RANCID
RN40904 712-713 (July 13, 1995) pp25-26.
RN40905 715 (August 24, 1995) pp23,25.
RN40906 718 (October 5, 1995) pp20-21.
RN40907 727 (February 8, 1996) pp12-13.
RN40908 734 (May 16, 1996) pp17-18.
RN40909 735 (May 30, 1996) pp12-13.
RN40910 743 (September 19, 1996) pp19-20.
RANKINE, LESLEY
RN40911 733 (May 2, 1996) pp13-14.
RAT SCABIES
RN40912 702 (February 23, 1995) pp19-20.
RATT
RN40913 630 (May 14, 1992) pp13,15.
RAY, AMY
RN40914 625 (March 5, 1992) pp11,13-15,17+.
RN40915 684 (June 16, 1994) pp35-36.
REAGAN, RONALD
RN40916 658 (June 10, 1993) pp16-17.
REAGAN YOUTH
RN40917 726 (January 25, 1996) pp17-18.
RED AUNTS
RN40918 736 (June 13, 1996) pp19-20.
RED FIVE
RN40919 743 (September 19, 1996) pp19-20.
RED HOT CHILI PEPPERS
RN40920 631 (May 28, 1992) pp9,11.
RN40921 638 (September 3, 1992) pp9,11.
RN40922 642 (October 29, 1992) pp19,21.
RN40923 644 (November 26, 1992) pp13,15.
RN40924 648 (January 21, 1993) pp9,11.
RN40925 649 (February 4, 1993) pp8-9.
RN40926 654 (April 15, 1993) pp11,13.
RN40927 664 (September 2, 1993) pp31-32.
RN40928 667 (October 14, 1993) pp39-40.
RN40929 692 (October 6, 1994) pp15-17.
RN40930 694 (November 3, 1994) pp17-18,22.
RN40931 703 (March 9, 1995) pp20-21.
RN40932 706 (April 20, 1995) pp15-17.
RN40933 720 (November 2, 1995) pp16-17.
RN40934 722 (November 30, 1995) pp19-20.
RN40935 731 (April 4, 1996) pp17-18.
RN40936 744 (October 3, 1996) pp19-21.
RN40937 749 (December 12, 1996) pp19-20.
RED ROAD ENSEMBLE
RN40938 710 (June 15, 1995) pp17-18.
REDD KROSS
RN40939 685 (June 30, 1994) pp40-41.
RN40940 688 (August 11, 1994) pp17-18,20.
REDDING, NOEL
RN40941 625 (March 5, 1992) pp11,13-15,17+.
REDFORD, ROBERT
RN40942 696 (December 1, 1994) pp23-25.
REDMAN, JOSHUA
RN40943 708 (May 18, 1995) pp17-18.
REED, LOU
RN40944 617 (November 14, 1991) pp11,13.

RN40945 621 (January 9, 1992) pp10-11.
RN40946 622 (January 23, 1992) pp6-7.
RN40947 638 (September 3, 1992) pp9,11.
RN40948 647 (January 7, 1993) pp9,11.
RN40949 648 (January 21, 1993) pp9,11.
RN40950 649 (February 4, 1993) pp8-9.
RN40951 665 (September 16, 1993) pp31-32.
RN40952 669 (November 11, 1993) pp27-28.
RN40953 678 (March 24, 1994) pp27-28.
RN40954 679 (April 7, 1994) pp37-39.
RN40955 683 (June 2, 1994) pp27-28.
RN40956 708 (May 18, 1995) pp17-18.
RN40957 716 (September 7, 1995) pp13-14.
RN40958 719 (October 19, 1995) pp15-16.
RN40959 729 (March 7, 1996) pp9-10.
RN40960 735 (May 30, 1996) pp12-13.
RN40961 736 (June 13, 1996) pp19-20.

REEVES, JIM
RN40962 629 (April 30, 1992) pp11-12.

REEVES, KEANU
RN40963 717 (September 21, 1995) pp19-20.
RN40964 742 (September 5, 1996) pp20-21.

REEVES, MARTHA
RN40965 654 (April 15, 1993) pp11,13.
RN40966 674 (January 27, 1994) pp28-29.

REID, VERNON
RN40967 623 (February 6, 1992) pp11,13.
RN40968 629 (April 30, 1992) pp11-12.
RN40969 636 (August 6, 1992) pp11,13.
RN40970 637 (August 20, 1992) pp9,11.
RN40971 686-687 (July 14, 1994) pp41-42.
RN40972 692 (October 6, 1994) pp15-17.

REID, WILLIAM
RN40973 700 (January 26, 1995) pp16-17.

REIS, JOHN
RN40974 745 (October 17, 1996) pp27-28.

REISER, PAUL
RN40975 706 (April 20, 1995) pp15-17.

R.E.M.
RN40976 615 (October 17, 1991) pp13-14.
RN40977 617 (November 14, 1991) pp11,13.
RN40978 618 (November 28, 1991) pp11-12.
RN40979 628 (April 16, 1992) pp11,13.
RN40980 636 (August 6, 1992) pp11,13.
RN40981 642 (October 29, 1992) pp19,21.
RN40982 647 (January 7, 1993) pp9,11.
RN40983 678 (March 24, 1994) pp27-28.
RN40984 680 (April 21, 1994) pp33-34.
RN40985 689 (August 25, 1994) pp15-16.
RN40986 693 (October 20, 1994) pp27-28,30.
RN40987 697 (December 15, 1994) pp17-18,20.
RN40988 704 (March 23, 1995) pp24-25.
RN40989 705 (April 6, 1995) pp16-17.
RN40990 714 (August 10, 1995) pp15-17.
RN40991 716 (September 7, 1995) pp13-14.
RN40992 717 (September 21, 1995) pp19-20.
RN40993 719 (October 19, 1995) pp15-16.
RN40994 722 (November 30, 1995) pp19-20.
RN40995 734 (May 16, 1996) pp17-18.
RN40996 748 (November 28, 1996) pp25-26.

REMBRANDTS
RN40997 720 (November 2, 1995) pp16-17.

RENO, MIKE
RN40998 740 (August 8, 1996) pp17-18.

REPLACEMENTS
RN40999 616 (October 31, 1991) pp11,13.
RN41000 627 (April 2, 1992) pp11,13.
RN41001 633 (June 25, 1992) pp11-12.
RN41002 638 (September 3, 1992) pp9,11.
RN41003 649 (February 4, 1993) pp8-9.
RN41004 663 (August 19, 1993) pp27-28.
RN41005 712-713 (July 13, 1995) pp25-26.
RN41006 743 (September 19, 1996) pp19-20.

REPUBLICA
RN41007 747 (November 14, 1996) pp25-26.
RN41008 749 (December 12, 1996) pp19-20.

REVEREND HORTON HEAT
RN41009 685 (June 30, 1994) pp40-41.
RN41010 720 (November 2, 1995) pp16-17.

REYNOLDS, ROBERT
RN41011 707 (May 4, 1995) pp19-20.

REZNOR, TRENT
RN41012 681 (May 5, 1994) pp21-22.
RN41013 692 (October 6, 1994) pp15-17.
RN41014 702 (February 23, 1995) pp19-20.
RN41015 714 (August 10, 1995) pp15-17.

RHODES, NICK
RN41016 686-687 (July 14, 1994) pp41-42.

RICH, RICHIE
RN41017 631 (May 28, 1992) pp9,11.

RICHARDS, ELLA ROSE
RN41018 748 (November 28, 1996) pp25-26.

RICHARDS, KEITH
RN41019 618 (November 28, 1991) pp11-12.
RN41020 621 (January 9, 1992) pp10-11.
RN41021 625 (March 5, 1992) pp11,13-15,17+.
RN41022 639 (September 17, 1992) pp19-20.
RN41023 647 (January 7, 1993) pp9,11.
RN41024 650 (February 18, 1993) pp11,13.
RN41025 662 (August 5, 1993) pp33-34.
RN41026 665 (September 16, 1993) pp31-32.
RN41027 668 (October 28, 1993) pp35-36.
RN41028 675 (February 10, 1994) pp22-23.
RN41029 684 (June 16, 1994) pp35-36.
RN41030 697 (December 15, 1994) pp17-18,20.
RN41031 730 (March 21, 1996) pp17-18.
RN41032 734 (May 16, 1996) pp17-18.
RN41033 742 (September 5, 1996) pp20-21.
RN41034 748 (November 28, 1996) pp25-26.

RICHARDS, RICK
RN41035 650 (February 18, 1993) pp11,13.

RICHIE, LIONEL
RN41036 652 (March 18, 1993) pp13,15.
RN41037 748 (November 28, 1996) pp25-26.

RICHLING, GREG
RN41038 684 (June 16, 1994) pp35-36.

RICKLES, DON
RN41039 726 (January 25, 1996) pp17-18.

RILEY, PAT
RN41040 688 (August 11, 1994) pp17-18,20.

RISON, ANDRE
RN41040 688 (August 11, 1994) pp17-18,20.

RITCHIE, SIMON
RN41041 655 (April 29, 1993) pp11-12.

RITTER, JOHN
RN41042 639 (September 17, 1992) pp19-20.

RITTER, THOMAS J.
RN41043 716 (September 7, 1995) pp13-14.

ROBBINS, TIM
RN41044 747 (November 14, 1996) pp25-26.

ROBERTS, BRAD
RN41045 617 (November 14, 1991) pp11,13.

ROBERTS, ELLIOT
RN41046 726 (January 25, 1996) pp17-18.

ROBERTS, JULIA
RN41047 662 (August 5, 1993) pp33-34.
RN41048 663 (August 19, 1993) pp27-28.
RN41049 685 (June 30, 1994) pp40-41.

ROBERTSON, ROBBIE
RN41050 625 (March 5, 1992) pp11,13-15,17+.
RN41051 628 (April 16, 1992) pp11,13.
RN41052 636 (August 6, 1992) pp11,13.
RN41053 644 (November 26, 1992) pp13,15.
RN41054 647 (January 7, 1993) pp9,11.
RN41055 710 (June 15, 1995) pp17-18.
RN41056 722 (November 30, 1995) pp19-20.
RN41057 746 (October 31, 1996) pp17-18.

ROBINSON, BOBBY
RN41058 625 (March 5, 1992) pp11,13-15,17+.

ROBINSON, CHRIS
RN41059 621 (January 9, 1992) pp10-11.
RN41060 631 (May 28, 1992) pp9,11.
RN41061 639 (September 17, 1992) pp19-20.
RN41062 642 (October 29, 1992) pp19,21.
RN41063 652 (March 18, 1993) pp13,15.
RN41064 692 (October 6, 1994) pp15-17.
RN41065 709 (June 1, 1995) pp16-17.
RN41066 712-713 (July 13, 1995) pp25-26.

ROBINSON, DARREN
RN41067 726 (January 25, 1996) pp17-18.

ROBINSON, DAVID
RN41068 679 (April 7, 1994) pp37-39.

ROBINSON, DAWN
RN41069 709 (June 1, 1995) pp16-17.

ROBINSON, RICH
RN41070 631 (May 28, 1992) pp9,11.
RN41071 712-713 (July 13, 1995) pp25-26.

ROBINSON, SMOKEY
RN41072 631 (May 28, 1992) pp9,11.
RN41073 658 (June 10, 1993) pp16-17.
ROBINSON, WENDY
RN41074 650 (February 18, 1993) pp11,13.
ROCK BOTTOM REMAINDERS
RN41075 634-635 (July 9, 1992) pp11,13.
ROCKET FROM THE CRYPT
RN41076 745 (October 17, 1996) pp27-28.
RODGERS, JIMMIE
RN41077 679 (April 7, 1994) pp37-39.
RODGERS, NILE
RN41078 630 (May 14, 1992) pp13,15.
RODMAN, DENNIS
RN41079 719 (October 19, 1995) pp15-16.
RN41080 745 (October 17, 1996) pp27-28.
ROESER, KING
RN41081 668 (October 28, 1993) pp35-36.
RN41082 685 (June 30, 1994) pp40-41.
ROESSLER, PAUL
RN41083 714 (August 10, 1995) pp15-17.
ROGERS, ELYSE
RN41084 721 (November 16, 1995) pp25-26.
ROGERS, JIMMY
RN41085 637 (August 20, 1992) pp9,11.
ROLLING STONES
RN41086 618 (November 28, 1991) pp11-12.
RN41087 656 (May 13, 1993) pp13,15.
RN41088 668 (October 28, 1993) pp35-36.
RN41089 670 (November 25, 1993) pp37-38.
RN41090 674 (January 27, 1994) pp28-29.
RN41091 684 (June 16, 1994) pp35-36.
RN41092 690 (September 8, 1994) pp21,24.
RN41093 692 (October 6, 1994) pp15-17.
RN41094 693 (October 20, 1994) pp27-28,30.
RN41095 697 (December 15, 1994) pp17-18,20.
RN41096 702 (February 23, 1995) pp19-20.
RN41097 710 (June 15, 1995) pp17-18.
RN41098 717 (September 21, 1995) pp19-20.
RN41099 734 (May 16, 1996) pp17-18.
RN41100 742 (September 5, 1996) pp20-21.
RN41101 748 (November 28, 1996) pp25-26.
ROLLINS BAND
RN41102 631 (May 28, 1992) pp9,11.
RN41103 664 (September 2, 1993) pp31-32.
RN41104 686-687 (July 14, 1994) pp41-42.
ROLLINS, HENRY
RN41105 631 (May 28, 1992) pp9,11.
RN41106 640 (October 1, 1992) pp9-10.
RN41107 662 (August 5, 1993) pp33-34.
RN41108 664 (September 2, 1993) pp31-32.
RN41109 674 (January 27, 1994) pp28-29.
RN41110 676 (February 24, 1994) pp28-29.
RN41111 683 (June 2, 1994) pp27-28.
RN41112 686-687 (July 14, 1994) pp41-42.
RN41113 702 (February 23, 1995) pp19-20.
RN41114 704 (March 23, 1995) pp24-25.
RN41115 708 (May 18, 1995) pp17-18.
RN41116 742 (September 5, 1996) pp20-21.
ROOTS
RN41117 717 (September 21, 1995) pp19-20.
ROSAS, CESAR
RN41118 616 (October 31, 1991) pp11,13.
ROSE, AXL
RN41118 616 (October 31, 1991) pp11,13.
RN41119 622 (January 23, 1992) pp6-7.
RN41120 625 (March 5, 1992) pp11,13-15,17+.
RN41121 639 (September 17, 1992) pp19-20.
RN41122 642 (October 29, 1992) pp19,21.
RN41123 644 (November 26, 1992) pp13,15.
RN41124 649 (February 4, 1993) pp8-9.
RN41125 650 (February 18, 1993) pp11,13.
RN41126 667 (October 14, 1993) pp39-40.
RN41127 670 (November 25, 1993) pp37-38.
RN41128 676 (February 24, 1994) pp28-29.
RN41129 706 (April 20, 1995) pp15-17.
ROSE, JIM
RN41130 638 (September 3, 1992) pp9,11.
ROSE, RICHARD
RN41131 705 (April 6, 1995) pp16-17.
ROSEANNE
RN41132 693 (October 20, 1994) pp27-28,30.
RN41133 708 (May 18, 1995) pp17-18.
RN41134 738-739 (July 11, 1996) pp15-16.
ROSENBLATT, ROGER
RN41135 691 (September 22, 1994) pp19-21.
ROSS, DIANA
RN41136 694 (November 3, 1994) pp17-18,22.
RN41137 707 (May 4, 1995) pp19-20.
RN41138 715 (August 24, 1995) pp23,25.
RN41139 735 (May 30, 1996) pp12-13.
ROSS, KEN
RN41140 650 (February 18, 1993) pp11,13.
ROSS, RHONDA
RN41141 694 (November 3, 1994) pp17-18,22.
ROSSDALE, GAVIN
RN41142 718 (October 5, 1995) pp20-21.
RN41143 743 (September 19, 1996) pp19-20.
RN41144 745 (October 17, 1996) pp27-28.
ROSSINGTON, GARY
RN41145 727 (February 8, 1996) pp12-13.
ROSSNEY, ROBERT
RN41146 701 (February 9, 1995) pp16-17.
ROSTROPOVICH, MSTISLAV
RN41147 735 (May 30, 1996) pp12-13.
ROTH, DAVID LEE
RN41148 657 (May 27, 1993) pp9,11.
RN41149 745 (October 17, 1996) pp27-28.
ROTH, TIM
RN41150 689 (August 25, 1994) pp15-16.
RN41151 741 (August 22, 1996) pp25-26.
ROTSEY, MARTIN
RN41152 669 (November 11, 1993) pp27-28.
ROTTEN, JOHNNY
RN41153 734 (May 16, 1996) pp17-18.
RN41154 744 (October 3, 1996) pp19-21.
ROURKE, MICKEY
RN41155 678 (March 24, 1994) pp27-28.
RUBIN, RICK
RN41156 644 (November 26, 1992) pp13,15.
RN41157 660-661 (July 8, 1993) pp32-33.
RN41158 667 (October 14, 1993) pp39-40.
RN41159 674 (January 27, 1994) pp28-29.
RUBY
RN41160 733 (May 2, 1996) pp13-14.
RN41161 736 (June 13, 1996) pp19-20.
RUCKER, DARIUS
RN41162 691 (September 22, 1994) pp19-21.
RUFFNER, MASON
RN41163 655 (April 29, 1993) pp11-12.
RUN WESTY RUN
RN41164 633 (June 25, 1992) pp11-12.
RN41165 729 (March 7, 1996) pp9-10.
RUN-D.M.C.
RN41166 628 (April 16, 1992) pp11,13.
RN41167 668 (October 28, 1993) pp35-36.
RN41168 696 (December 1, 1994) pp23-25.
RUNAWAYS
RN41169 644 (November 26, 1992) pp13,15.
RN41170 668 (October 28, 1993) pp35-36.
RUNDGREN, TODD
RN41171 616 (October 31, 1991) pp11,13.
RN41172 623 (February 6, 1992) pp11,13.
RN41173 648 (January 21, 1993) pp9,11.
RN41174 678 (March 24, 1994) pp27-28.
RUPAUL
RN41175 666 (September 30, 1993) pp27-28.
RN41176 667 (October 14, 1993) pp39-40.
RN41177 710 (June 15, 1995) pp17-18.
RN41178 723 (December 14, 1995) pp27-28.
RUPE, BOB
RN41179 737 (June 27, 1996) pp15-16.
RUSH
RN41180 640 (October 1, 1992) pp9-10.
RN41181 658 (June 10, 1993) pp16-17.
RN41182 705 (April 6, 1995) pp16-17.
RUSH, OTIS
RN41183 717 (September 21, 1995) pp19-20.
RUSHDIE, SALMAN
RN41184 666 (September 30, 1993) pp27-28.
RN41185 729 (March 7, 1996) pp9-10.
RUTTENBER, TIMOTHY TYSON
RN41186 631 (May 28, 1992) pp9,11.
RYAN, MEG

RN41187 686-687 (July 14, 1994) pp41-42.
RYAN-HARRIS, DAVID
RN41188 618 (November 28, 1991) pp11-12.
RYDER, MITCH
RN41189 681 (May 5, 1994) pp21-22.
RYDER, PAUL
RN41190 638 (September 3, 1992) pp9,11.
RYDER, SHAUN
RN41190 638 (September 3, 1992) pp9,11.
RN41191 727 (February 8, 1996) pp12-13.
RYDER, WINONA
RN41192 674 (January 27, 1994) pp28-29.
RN41193 737 (June 27, 1996) pp15-16.
RN41194 749 (December 12, 1996) pp19-20.
RZA
RN41195 730 (March 21, 1996) pp17-18.

S

SAFFRON
RN41196 747 (November 14, 1996) pp25-26.
SAGAL, KATEY
RN41197 746 (October 31, 1996) pp17-18.
SAGE, DANNY
RN41198 705 (April 6, 1995) pp16-17.
SAGET, BOB
RN41199 709 (June 1, 1995) pp16-17.
SALEM, KEVIN
RN41200 704 (March 23, 1995) pp24-25.
SALES, HUNTER
RN41201 622 (January 23, 1992) pp6-7.
SALES, TONY
RN41201 622 (January 23, 1992) pp6-7.
RN41202 652 (March 18, 1993) pp13,15.
SALIERS, EMILY
RN41203 625 (March 5, 1992) pp11,13-15,17+.
RN41204 684 (June 16, 1994) pp35-36.
SALT
RN41205 671 (December 9, 1993) pp31-32.
RN41206 723 (December 14, 1995) pp27-28.
SALT-N-PEPA
RN41207 621 (January 9, 1992) pp10-11.
RN41208 625 (March 5, 1992) pp11,13-15,17+.
RN41209 639 (September 17, 1992) pp19-20.
RN41210 671 (December 9, 1993) pp31-32.
RN41211 679 (April 7, 1994) pp37-39.
RN41212 693 (October 20, 1994) pp27-28,30.
RN41213 696 (December 1, 1994) pp23-25.
RN41214 701 (February 9, 1995) pp16-17.
RN41215 703 (March 9, 1995) pp20-21.
RN41216 706 (April 20, 1995) pp15-17.
RN41217 707 (May 4, 1995) pp19-20.
RN41218 710 (June 15, 1995) pp17-18.
RN41219 717 (September 21, 1995) pp19-20.
RN41220 720 (November 2, 1995) pp16-17.
RN41221 721 (November 16, 1995) pp25-26.
RN41222 723 (December 14, 1995) pp27-28.
SAM AND DAVE
RN41223 625 (March 5, 1992) pp11,13-15,17+.
SAMBORA, RICHIE
RN41224 615 (October 17, 1991) pp13-14.
RN41225 692 (October 6, 1994) pp15-17.
RN41226 747 (November 14, 1996) pp25-26.
SAMPRAS, PETE
RN41227 730 (March 21, 1996) pp17-18.
SANDERS, RIC
RN41228 691 (September 22, 1994) pp19-21.
SANDLER, ADAM
RN41229 680 (April 21, 1994) pp33-34.
SANTANA
RN41230 714 (August 10, 1995) pp15-17.
SANTANA, CARLOS
RN41231 625 (March 5, 1992) pp11,13-15,17+.
RN41232 630 (May 14, 1992) pp13,15.
RN41233 640 (October 1, 1992) pp9-10.
RN41234 655 (April 29, 1993) pp11-12.
RN41235 665 (September 16, 1993) pp31-32.
RN41236 707 (May 4, 1995) pp19-20.
RN41237 714 (August 10, 1995) pp15-17.
SANTANA, JORGE
RN41238 630 (May 14, 1992) pp13,15.
SANTANA, JOSE
RN41238 630 (May 14, 1992) pp13,15.
SANTIAGO, JOEY
RN41239 652 (March 18, 1993) pp13,15.
SATAN
RN41240 726 (January 25, 1996) pp17-18.
SATCHEL
RN41241 691 (September 22, 1994) pp19-21.
SATRIANI, JOE
RN41242 684 (June 16, 1994) pp35-36.
SAUSAGE
RN41243 686-687 (July 14, 1994) pp41-42.
SAVAGE, JON
RN41244 655 (April 29, 1993) pp11-12.
SCAGGS, BOZ
RN41245 616 (October 31, 1991) pp11,13.
RN41246 633 (June 25, 1992) pp11-12.
RN41247 637 (August 20, 1992) pp9,11.
SCANLON, PAUL
RN41248 647 (January 7, 1993) pp9,11.
SCARCE
RN41249 704 (March 23, 1995) pp24-25.
SCHAYER, BOBBY
RN41250 700 (January 26, 1995) pp16-17.
RN41251 722 (November 30, 1995) pp19-20.
SCHELLENBACH, KATE
RN41252 710 (June 15, 1995) pp17-18.
RN41253 716 (September 7, 1995) pp13-14.
SCHNEIDER, FRED
RN41254 630 (May 14, 1992) pp13,15.
RN41255 637 (August 20, 1992) pp9,11.
RN41256 683 (June 2, 1994) pp27-28.
RN41257 706 (April 20, 1995) pp15-17.
SCHNEIDER, ROB
RN41258 693 (October 20, 1994) pp27-28,30.
SCHOCK, GINA
RN41259 616 (October 31, 1991) pp11,13.
SCHOOL OF FISH
RN41260 665 (September 16, 1993) pp31-32.
SCHRODI, ERIK
RN41261 654 (April 15, 1993) pp11,13.
SCHWARTZ, DEBORAH
RN41262 668 (October 28, 1993) pp35-36.
SCHWARZENEGGER, ARNOLD
RN41263 656 (May 13, 1993) pp13,15.
SCHWIMMER, DAVID
RN41264 749 (December 12, 1996) pp19-20.
SCIALFA, PATTI
RN41265 624 (February 20, 1992) pp11-12.
RN41266 664 (September 2, 1993) pp31-32.
RN41267 691 (September 22, 1994) pp19-21.
SCORPIONS
RN41268 623 (February 6, 1992) pp11,13.
SCORSESE, MARTIN
RN41269 647 (January 7, 1993) pp9,11.
RN41270 722 (November 30, 1995) pp19-20.
SCOTT, JIMMY
RN41271 654 (April 15, 1993) pp11,13.
SCOTT, MIKE
RN41272 618 (November 28, 1991) pp11-12.
RN41273 664 (September 2, 1993) pp31-32.
SCREAMING TREES
RN41274 660-661 (July 8, 1993) pp32-33.
RN41275 667 (October 14, 1993) pp39-40.
RN41276 711 (June 29, 1995) pp12-13.
RN41277 748 (November 28, 1996) pp25-26.
SEAL
RN41278 732 (April 18, 1996) pp19-20.
RN41279 740 (August 8, 1996) pp17-18.
SEAM
RN41280 709 (June 1, 1995) pp16-17.
SEBADOH
RN41281 697 (December 15, 1994) pp17-18,20.
RN41282 706 (April 20, 1995) pp15-17.
SEEFF, NORMAN
RN41283 697 (December 15, 1994) pp17-18,20.
SEEGER, PETE
RN41284 722 (November 30, 1995) pp19-20.
RN41285 747 (November 14, 1996) pp25-26.
SEGER, BOB
RN41286 631 (May 28, 1992) pp9,11.
SELVIN, JOEL
RN41287 648 (January 21, 1993) pp9,11.
SELWAY, PHIL
RN41288 738-739 (July 11, 1996) pp15-16.
SEPULTURA
RN41289 689 (August 25, 1994) pp15-16.
SERCH, MC
RN41290 631 (May 28, 1992) pp9,11.
SERMON, ERIC
RN41291 669 (November 11, 1993) pp27-28.
SETZER, BRIAN
RN41292 737 (June 27, 1996) pp15-16.

7 YEAR BITCH
RN41293 690 (September 8, 1994) pp21,24.
RN41294 722 (November 30, 1995) pp19-20.
RN41295 731 (April 4, 1996) pp17-18.
RN41296 742 (September 5, 1996) pp20-21.
SEX PISTOLS
RN41297 655 (April 29, 1993) pp11-12.
RN41298 718 (October 5, 1995) pp20-21.
RN41299 731 (April 4, 1996) pp17-18.
RN41300 734 (May 16, 1996) pp17-18.
SEYMOUR, JANE
RN41301 712-713 (July 13, 1995) pp25-26.
SEYMOUR, STEPHANIE
RN41302 667 (October 14, 1993) pp39-40.
RN41303 706 (April 20, 1995) pp15-17.
SHADES
RN41304 656 (May 13, 1993) pp13,15.
SHAI
RN41305 664 (September 2, 1993) pp31-32.
SHAKESPEARE, WILLIAM
RN41306 704 (March 23, 1995) pp24-25.
SHAKESPEAR'S SISTER
RN41307 653 (April 1, 1993) pp11,13.
SHAKOOR, NADIRAH
RN41308 697 (December 15, 1994) pp17-18,20.
SHAKUR, TUPAC
RN41309 671 (December 9, 1993) pp31-32.
RN41310 700 (January 26, 1995) pp16-17.
RN41311 715 (August 24, 1995) pp23,25.
RN41312 730 (March 21, 1996) pp17-18.
RN41313 732 (April 18, 1996) pp19-20.
RN41314 741 (August 22, 1996) pp25-26.
RN41315 745 (October 17, 1996) pp27-28.
RN41316 747 (November 14, 1996) pp25-26.
SHANDLING, GARY
RN41317 714 (August 10, 1995) pp15-17.
SHANNON, KYLE
RN41318 722 (November 30, 1995) pp19-20.
SHAPIRO, JIM
RN41319 709 (June 1, 1995) pp16-17.
SHARPTON, AL
RN41320 667 (October 14, 1993) pp39-40.
RN41321 715 (August 24, 1995) pp23,25.
SHARROCK, SONNY
RN41322 692 (October 6, 1994) pp15-17.
SHATTUCK, KIM
RN41323 735 (May 30, 1996) pp12-13.
SHAW, ARTIE
RN41324 681 (May 5, 1994) pp21-22.
SHAW, TOMMY
RN41325 631 (May 28, 1992) pp9,11.
SHEARER, HARRY
RN41326 662 (August 5, 1993) pp33-34.
SHEEHAN, BOBBY
RN41327 714 (August 10, 1995) pp15-17.
SHELLEY, STEVE
RN41328 633 (June 25, 1992) pp11-12.
RN41329 637 (August 20, 1992) pp9,11.
RN41330 721 (November 16, 1995) pp25-26.
SHEPHERD, BEN
RN41331 621 (January 9, 1992) pp10-11.
RN41332 667 (October 14, 1993) pp39-40.
SHEPHERD, KENNY WAYNE
RN41333 748 (November 28, 1996) pp25-26.
SHIELDS, BROOKE
RN41334 654 (April 15, 1993) pp11,13.
SHIRELLES
RN41335 665 (September 16, 1993) pp31-32.
RN41336 680 (April 21, 1994) pp33-34.
RN41337 722 (November 30, 1995) pp19-20.
SHOCKED, MICHELLE
RN41338 638 (September 3, 1992) pp9,11.
RN41339 658 (June 10, 1993) pp16-17.
RN41340 678 (March 24, 1994) pp27-28.
RN41341 691 (September 22, 1994) pp19-21.
RN41342 700 (January 26, 1995) pp16-17.
RN41343 705 (April 6, 1995) pp16-17.
SHONEN KNIFE
RN41344 668 (October 28, 1993) pp35-36.
SHORT, MARTIN
RN41345 722 (November 30, 1995) pp19-20.
SHUDDER TO THINK
RN41346 690 (September 8, 1994) pp21,24.
RN41347 714 (August 10, 1995) pp15-17.
RN41348 719 (October 19, 1995) pp15-16.
SHUE, ANDREW
RN41349 681 (May 5, 1994) pp21-22.
SHUMAN, MORT
RN41350 634-635 (July 9, 1992) pp11,13.
SIB, JOE
RN41351 709 (June 1, 1995) pp16-17.
SIBELIUS
RN41352 731 (April 4, 1996) pp17-18.
SICK OF IT ALL
RN41353 726 (January 25, 1996) pp17-18.
SIEGEL, DAN
RN41354 731 (April 4, 1996) pp17-18.
SIEGFRIED AND ROY
RN41355 745 (October 17, 1996) pp27-28.
SILK
RN41356 664 (September 2, 1993) pp31-32.
SILLEN, PETE
RN41357 676 (February 24, 1994) pp28-29.
SILVER BULLET BAND
RN41358 631 (May 28, 1992) pp9,11.
SILVER, SUSAN
RN41359 730 (March 21, 1996) pp17-18.
SILVERCHAIR
RN41360 720 (November 2, 1995) pp16-17.
RN41361 726 (January 25, 1996) pp17-18.
RN41362 729 (March 7, 1996) pp9-10.
SILVERSTONE, ALICIA
RN41363 688 (August 11, 1994) pp17-18,20.
RN41364 716 (September 7, 1995) pp13-14.
SIMMONS, GENE
RN41365 675 (February 10, 1994) pp22-23.
RN41366 680 (April 21, 1994) pp33-34.
RN41367 685 (June 30, 1994) pp40-41.
RN41368 691 (September 22, 1994) pp19-21.
RN41369 715 (August 24, 1995) pp23,25.
RN41370 732 (April 18, 1996) pp19-20.
SIMMONS, JOSEPH
RN41371 628 (April 16, 1992) pp11,13.
SIMMONS, RUSSELL
RN41372 748 (November 28, 1996) pp25-26.
SIMON AND GARFUNKEL
RN41373 654 (April 15, 1993) pp11,13.
RN41374 722 (November 30, 1995) pp19-20.
SIMON, CARLY
RN41375 617 (November 14, 1991) pp11,13.
RN41376 653 (April 1, 1993) pp11,13.
RN41377 706 (April 20, 1995) pp15-17.
SIMON, PAUL
RN41378 622 (January 23, 1992) pp6-7.
RN41379 634-635 (July 9, 1992) pp11,13.
RN41380 640 (October 1, 1992) pp9-10.
RN41381 652 (March 18, 1993) pp13,15.
RN41382 654 (April 15, 1993) pp11,13.
RN41383 659 (June 24, 1993) pp13,15.
RN41384 679 (April 7, 1994) pp37-39.
SIMONE, SONIA
RN41385 701 (February 9, 1995) pp16-17.
SIMPLE TRUTH
RN41386 637 (August 20, 1992) pp9,11.
SIMPSON, ARNELLE
RN41387 723 (December 14, 1995) pp27-28.
SIMPSON, O. J.
RN41388 689 (August 25, 1994) pp15-16.
RN41389 690 (September 8, 1994) pp21,24.
RN41390 706 (April 20, 1995) pp15-17.
RN41391 723 (December 14, 1995) pp27-28.
SIMS, DAVID
RN41392 736 (June 13, 1996) pp19-20.
SIMS, RICK
RN41393 707 (May 4, 1995) pp19-20.
SINATRA, FRANK
RN41394 665 (September 16, 1993) pp31-32.
RN41395 669 (November 11, 1993) pp27-28.
RN41396 676 (February 24, 1994) pp28-29.
RN41397 680 (April 21, 1994) pp33-34.
RN41398 696 (December 1, 1994) pp23-25.
RN41399 726 (January 25, 1996) pp17-18.
RN41400 736 (June 13, 1996) pp19-20.
SINGER, ERIC
RN41401 715 (August 24, 1995) pp23,25.
SINGH, TJINDER
RN41402 737 (June 27, 1996) pp15-16.
SINGLETON, JOHN
RN41403 629 (April 30, 1992) pp11-12.
SINISE, GARY
RN41404 737 (June 27, 1996) pp15-16.
SIOUX, SIOUXSIE
RN41405 692 (October 6, 1994) pp15-17.
SIR MIX-A-LOT
RN41406 654 (April 15, 1993) pp11,13.
RN41407 701 (February 9, 1995) pp16-17.

SIXX, NIKKI
RN41408 627 (April 2, 1992) pp11,13.
SKATE-MASTER TATE
RN41409 631 (May 28, 1992) pp9,11.
SKERIK
RN41410 748 (November 28, 1996) pp25-26.
SKID ROW
RN41411 640 (October 1, 1992) pp9-10.
SKILLINGS, MUZZ
RN41412 621 (January 9, 1992) pp10-11.
SKINNER, JULIE
RN41413 742 (September 5, 1996) pp20-21.
SLADE, SEAN
RN41414 702 (February 23, 1995) pp19-20.
SLASH
RN41415 618 (November 28, 1991) pp11-12.
RN41416 622 (January 23, 1992) pp6-7.
RN41417 625 (March 5, 1992) pp11,13-15,17+.
RN41418 626 (March 19, 1992) pp11,13.
RN41419 633 (June 25, 1992) pp11-12.
RN41420 644 (November 26, 1992) pp13,15.
RN41421 650 (February 18, 1993) pp11,13.
RN41422 663 (August 19, 1993) pp27-28.
RN41423 671 (December 9, 1993) pp31-32.
RN41424 674 (January 27, 1994) pp28-29.
RN41425 676 (February 24, 1994) pp28-29.
RN41426 696 (December 1, 1994) pp23-25.
RN41427 711 (June 29, 1995) pp12-13.
RN41428 727 (February 8, 1996) pp12-13.
RN41429 737 (June 27, 1996) pp15-16.
RN41430 746 (October 31, 1996) pp17-18.
SLATER, CHRISTIAN
RN41431 667 (October 14, 1993) pp39-40.
SLAUGHTER
RN41432 639 (September 17, 1992) pp19-20.
RN41433 654 (April 15, 1993) pp11,13.
SLAUGHTER, MARK
RN41434 639 (September 17, 1992) pp19-20.
SLAYER
RN41435 703 (March 9, 1995) pp20-21.
RN41436 721 (November 16, 1995) pp25-26.
SLEDGE, PERCY
RN41437 628 (April 16, 1992) pp11,13.
SLEDGE, ROBERT
RN41438 749 (December 12, 1996) pp19-20.
SLICK, GRACE
RN41439 686-687 (July 14, 1994) pp41-42.
RN41440 712-713 (July 13, 1995) pp25-26.
SLICK RICK
RN41441 715 (August 24, 1995) pp23,25.
SMASHING PUMPKINS
RN41442 655 (April 29, 1993) pp11-12.
RN41443 674 (January 27, 1994) pp28-29.
RN41444 684 (June 16, 1994) pp35-36.
RN41445 685 (June 30, 1994) pp40-41.
RN41446 691 (September 22, 1994) pp19-21.
RN41447 693 (October 20, 1994) pp27-28,30.
RN41448 694 (November 3, 1994) pp17-18,22.
RN41449 705 (April 6, 1995) pp16-17.
RN41450 723 (December 14, 1995) pp27-28.
RN41451 728 (February 22, 1996) p20.
RN41452 731 (April 4, 1996) pp17-18.
RN41453 735 (May 30, 1996) pp12-13.
RN41454 737 (June 27, 1996) pp15-16.
RN41455 745 (October 17, 1996) pp27-28.
SMEAR, PAT
RN41456 732 (April 18, 1996) pp19-20.
RN41457 736 (June 13, 1996) pp19-20.
RN41458 740 (August 8, 1996) pp17-18.
RN41459 745 (October 17, 1996) pp27-28.
SMITH, BRAD
RN41460 639 (September 17, 1992) pp19-20.
SMITH, CHAD
RN41461 692 (October 6, 1994) pp15-17.
RN41462 731 (April 4, 1996) pp17-18.
SMITH, ELLIOTT
RN41463 742 (September 5, 1996) pp20-21.
SMITH, FRED
RN41464 617 (November 14, 1991) pp11,13.
RN41465 705 (April 6, 1995) pp16-17.
SMITH, G. E.
RN41466 640 (October 1, 1992) pp9-10.
SMITH, GARY
RN41467 702 (February 23, 1995) pp19-20.
SMITH, GREG
RN41468 616 (October 31, 1991) pp11,13.
SMITH, MANDY
RN41469 656 (May 13, 1993) pp13,15.
SMITH, PATSY
RN41469 656 (May 13, 1993) pp13,15.
SMITH, PATTI
RN41470 617 (November 14, 1991) pp11,13.
RN41471 705 (April 6, 1995) pp16-17.
RN41472 717 (September 21, 1995) pp19-20.
RN41473 723 (December 14, 1995) pp27-28.
RN41474 726 (January 25, 1996) pp17-18.
RN41475 749 (December 12, 1996) pp19-20.
SMITH, ROBERT
RN41476 631 (May 28, 1992) pp9,11.
RN41477 633 (June 25, 1992) pp11-12.
RN41478 737 (June 27, 1996) pp15-16.
RN41479 743 (September 19, 1996) pp19-20.
SMITH, TODD
RN41480 705 (April 6, 1995) pp16-17.
SMITHEREENS
RN41481 648 (January 21, 1993) pp9,11.
SMITHS
RN41482 684 (June 16, 1994) pp35-36.
SMOKING POPES
RN41483 746 (October 31, 1996) pp17-18.
SNIPES, WESLEY
RN41484 702 (February 23, 1995) pp19-20.
RN41485 748 (November 28, 1996) pp25-26.
SNOOP DOGGY DOGG
RN41486 665 (September 16, 1993) pp31-32.
RN41487 667 (October 14, 1993) pp39-40.
RN41488 668 (October 28, 1993) pp35-36.
RN41489 670 (November 25, 1993) pp37-38.
RN41490 678 (March 24, 1994) pp27-28.
RN41491 693 (October 20, 1994) pp27-28,30.
RN41492 700 (January 26, 1995) pp16-17.
RN41493 702 (February 23, 1995) pp19-20.
RN41494 704 (March 23, 1995) pp24-25.
RN41495 707 (May 4, 1995) pp19-20.
RN41496 723 (December 14, 1995) pp27-28.
RN41497 730 (March 21, 1996) pp17-18.
SNOW, PHOEBE
RN41498 621 (January 9, 1992) pp10-11.
RN41499 622 (January 23, 1992) pp6-7.
RN41500 637 (August 20, 1992) pp9,11.
SOBULE, JILL
RN41501 716 (September 7, 1995) pp13-14.
SOCIAL DISTORTION
RN41502 628 (April 16, 1992) pp11,13.
RN41503 666 (September 30, 1993) pp27-28.
RN41504 693 (October 20, 1994) pp27-28,30.
RN41505 711 (June 29, 1995) pp12-13.
RN41506 741 (August 22, 1996) pp25-26.
SOCRATES
RN41507 729 (March 7, 1996) pp9-10.
SODA
RN41508 709 (June 1, 1995) pp16-17.
SOLANIS, VALERIE
RN41509 716 (September 7, 1995) pp13-14.
SOLOMON, TIM
RN41510 694 (November 3, 1994) pp17-18,22.
SOMERS, SUZANNE
RN41511 639 (September 17, 1992) pp19-20.
SON VOLT
RN41512 716 (September 7, 1995) pp13-14.
SONI
RN41513 691 (September 22, 1994) pp19-21.
SONIC YOUTH
RN41514 633 (June 25, 1992) pp11-12.
RN41515 637 (August 20, 1992) pp9,11.
RN41516 656 (May 13, 1993) pp13,15.
RN41517 660-661 (July 8, 1993) pp32-33.
RN41518 665 (September 16, 1993) pp31-32.
RN41519 670 (November 25, 1993) pp37-38.
RN41520 700 (January 26, 1995) pp16-17.
RN41521 702 (February 23, 1995) pp19-20.
RN41522 704 (March 23, 1995) pp24-25.
RN41523 715 (August 24, 1995) pp23,25.
RN41524 717 (September 21, 1995) pp19-20.
RN41525 721 (November 16, 1995) pp25-26.
RN41526 731 (April 4, 1996) pp17-18.

SORUM, MATT
RN41527 721 (November 16, 1995) pp25-26.
RN41528 731 (April 4, 1996) pp17-18.
SORVINO, MIRA
RN41529 730 (March 21, 1996) pp17-18.
SOUL ASYLUM
RN41530 633 (June 25, 1992) pp11-12.
RN41531 634-635 (July 9, 1992) pp11,13.
RN41532 658 (June 10, 1993) pp16-17.
RN41533 660-661 (July 8, 1993) pp32-33.
RN41534 666 (September 30, 1993) pp27-28.
RN41535 669 (November 11, 1993) pp27-28.
RN41536 674 (January 27, 1994) pp28-29.
RN41537 691 (September 22, 1994) pp19-21.
RN41538 692 (October 6, 1994) pp15-17.
RN41539 706 (April 20, 1995) pp15-17.
RN41540 715 (August 24, 1995) pp23,25.
RN41541 729 (March 7, 1996) pp9-10.
RN41542 747 (November 14, 1996) pp25-26.
SOUL COUGHING
RN41543 719 (October 19, 1995) pp15-16.
RN41544 734 (May 16, 1996) pp17-18.
RN41545 736 (June 13, 1996) pp19-20.
SOUNDGARDEN
RN41546 618 (November 28, 1991) pp11-12.
RN41547 621 (January 9, 1992) pp10-11.
RN41548 624 (February 20, 1992) pp11-12.
RN41549 633 (June 25, 1992) pp11-12.
RN41550 638 (September 3, 1992) pp9,11.
RN41551 663 (August 19, 1993) pp27-28.
RN41552 666 (September 30, 1993) pp27-28.
RN41553 667 (October 14, 1993) pp39-40.
RN41554 681 (May 5, 1994) pp21-22.
RN41555 700 (January 26, 1995) pp16-17.
RN41556 719 (October 19, 1995) pp15-16.
RN41557 730 (March 21, 1996) pp17-18.
RN41558 743 (September 19, 1996) pp19-20.
SOUP DRAGONS
RN41559 653 (April 1, 1993) pp11,13.
SOUTHERN CULTURE ON THE SKIDS
RN41560 746 (October 31, 1996) pp17-18.
SOUTHSIDE JOHNNY AND THE ASBURY JUKES
RN41561 617 (November 14, 1991) pp11,13.
RN41562 650 (February 18, 1993) pp11,13.
RN41563 691 (September 22, 1994) pp19-21.
SPACEHOG
RN41564 742 (September 5, 1996) pp20-21.
SPAGHETTI, EDDIE
RN41565 707 (May 4, 1995) pp19-20.
RN41566 719 (October 19, 1995) pp15-16.
RN41567 721 (November 16, 1995) pp25-26.
RN41568 731 (April 4, 1996) pp17-18.
SPANDAU BALLET
RN41569 627 (April 2, 1992) pp11,13.
SPARKLEHORSE
RN41570 742 (September 5, 1996) pp20-21.
SPARKS, DONITA
RN41571 644 (November 26, 1992) pp13,15.
RN41572 671 (December 9, 1993) pp31-32.
RN41573 688 (August 11, 1994) pp17-18,20.
RN41574 692 (October 6, 1994) pp15-17.
RN41575 696 (December 1, 1994) pp23-25.
RN41576 718 (October 5, 1995) pp20-21.
SPARROW
RN41577 708 (May 18, 1995) pp17-18.
SPEARHEAD
RN41577 708 (May 18, 1995) pp17-18.
RN41578 717 (September 21, 1995) pp19-20.
RN41579 719 (October 19, 1995) pp15-16.
RN41580 738-739 (July 11, 1996) pp15-16.
RN41581 742 (September 5, 1996) pp20-21.
SPECTOR, PHIL
RN41582 616 (October 31, 1991) pp11,13.
RN41583 625 (March 5, 1992) pp11,13-15,17+.
RN41584 639 (September 17, 1992) pp19-20.
RN41585 647 (January 7, 1993) pp9,11.
RN41586 675 (February 10, 1994) pp22-23.
SPECTOR, PHILLIP, JR.
RN41587 625 (March 5, 1992) pp11,13-15,17+.
SPECTOR, RONNIE
RN41588 639 (September 17, 1992) pp19-20.
SPEECH
RN41589 648 (January 21, 1993) pp9,11.
RN41590 654 (April 15, 1993) pp11,13.
RN41591 688 (August 11, 1994) pp17-18,20.
SPENCE, SKIP
RN41592 670 (November 25, 1993) pp37-38.
SPENCER, JON
RN41593 701 (February 9, 1995) pp16-17.
RN41594 729 (March 7, 1996) pp9-10.
RN41595 742 (September 5, 1996) pp20-21.
SPIN DOCTORS
RN41596 659 (June 24, 1993) pp13,15.
RN41597 660-661 (July 8, 1993) pp32-33.
RN41598 694 (November 3, 1994) pp17-18,22.
RN41599 729 (March 7, 1996) pp9-10.
SPINAL TAP
RN41600 615 (October 17, 1991) pp13-14.
RN41601 618 (November 28, 1991) pp11-12.
RN41602 622 (January 23, 1992) pp6-7.
RN41603 626 (March 19, 1992) pp11,13.
RN41604 662 (August 5, 1993) pp33-34.
RN41605 667 (October 14, 1993) pp39-40.
SPINDERELLA
RN41606 625 (March 5, 1992) pp11,13-15,17+.
RN41607 671 (December 9, 1993) pp31-32.
RN41608 723 (December 14, 1995) pp27-28.
SPONGE
RN41609 708 (May 18, 1995) pp17-18.
RN41610 717 (September 21, 1995) pp19-20.
RN41611 719 (October 19, 1995) pp15-16.
SPRING, MIKE
RN41612 711 (June 29, 1995) pp12-13.
SPRINGSTEEN, BRUCE
RN41613 617 (November 14, 1991) pp11,13.
RN41614 624 (February 20, 1992) pp11-12.
RN41615 627 (April 2, 1992) pp11,13.
RN41616 631 (May 28, 1992) pp9,11.
RN41617 633 (June 25, 1992) pp11-12.
RN41618 639 (September 17, 1992) pp19-20.
RN41619 644 (November 26, 1992) pp13,15.
RN41620 650 (February 18, 1993) pp11,13.
RN41621 656 (May 13, 1993) pp13,15.
RN41622 660-661 (July 8, 1993) pp32-33.
RN41623 662 (August 5, 1993) pp33-34.
RN41624 664 (September 2, 1993) pp31-32.
RN41625 669 (November 11, 1993) pp27-28.
RN41626 676 (February 24, 1994) pp28-29.
RN41627 678 (March 24, 1994) pp27-28.
RN41628 681 (May 5, 1994) pp21-22.
RN41629 684 (June 16, 1994) pp35-36.
RN41630 688 (August 11, 1994) pp17-18,20.
RN41631 691 (September 22, 1994) pp19-21.
RN41632 693 (October 20, 1994) pp27-28,30.
RN41633 697 (December 15, 1994) pp17-18,20.
RN41634 702 (February 23, 1995) pp19-20.
RN41635 705 (April 6, 1995) pp16-17.
RN41636 706 (April 20, 1995) pp15-17.
RN41637 709 (June 1, 1995) pp16-17.
RN41638 717 (September 21, 1995) pp19-20.
RN41639 722 (November 30, 1995) pp19-20.
RN41640 723 (December 14, 1995) pp27-28.
RN41641 726 (January 25, 1996) pp17-18.
RN41642 747 (November 14, 1996) pp25-26.
SQUEEZE
RN41643 675 (February 10, 1994) pp22-23.
STALEY, LAYNE
RN41644 624 (February 20, 1992) pp11-12.
RN41645 697 (December 15, 1994) pp17-18,20.
RN41646 711 (June 29, 1995) pp12-13.
RN41647 723 (December 14, 1995) pp27-28.
RN41648 732 (April 18, 1996) pp19-20.
STALLONE, SYLVESTER
RN41649 712-713 (July 13, 1995) pp25-26.
STANLEY, EVAN SHANE

RN41650 690 (September 8, 1994) pp21,24.
STANLEY, PAUL
RN41651 664 (September 2, 1993) pp31-32.
RN41652 690 (September 8, 1994) pp21,24.
RN41653 715 (August 24, 1995) pp23,25.
RN41654 732 (April 18, 1996) pp19-20.
STANSFIELD, LISA
RN41655 656 (May 13, 1993) pp13,15.
STANTON, HARRY DEAN
RN41656 652 (March 18, 1993) pp13,15.
STAPLES, MAVIS
RN41657 628 (April 16, 1992) pp11,13.
STARR, RINGO
RN41658 631 (May 28, 1992) pp9,11.
RN41659 649 (February 4, 1993) pp8-9.
RN41660 653 (April 1, 1993) pp11,13.
RN41661 657 (May 27, 1993) pp9,11.
RN41662 683 (June 2, 1994) pp27-28.
STEEL PULSE
RN41662 685 (June 30, 1994) pp40-41.
RN41663 706 (April 20, 1995) pp15-17.
STEELY DAN
RN41664 664 (September 2, 1993) pp31-32.
RN41665 733 (May 2, 1996) pp13-14.
STEFANI, GWEN
RN41666 740 (August 8, 1996) pp17-18.
RN41667 745 (October 17, 1996) pp27-28.
STEIN, CHRIS
RN41668 700 (January 26, 1995) pp16-17.
STEINBERG, LEWIS
RN41669 625 (March 5, 1992) pp11,13-15,17+.
STEINBERG, SEBASTIAN
RN41670 734 (May 16, 1996) pp17-18.
STEINEM, GLORIA
RN41671 729 (March 7, 1996) pp9-10.
RN41672 749 (December 12, 1996) pp19-20.
STEINER, JOSH
RN41673 691 (September 22, 1994) pp19-21.
STEPHANOPOULOS, GEORGE
RN41674 680 (April 21, 1994) pp33-34.
RN41675 691 (September 22, 1994) pp19-21.
STEPHENS, JAY
RN41675 691 (September 22, 1994) pp19-21.
STEPHENS, JODY
RN41676 658 (June 10, 1993) pp16-17.
STERN, HOWARD
RN41677 680 (April 21, 1994) pp33-34.
RN41678 682 (May 19, 1994) pp37-38.
RN41679 694 (November 3, 1994) pp17-18,22.
RN41680 729 (March 7, 1996) pp9-10.
RN41681 743 (September 19, 1996) pp19-20.
STESNEY, FRED
RN41682 702 (February 23, 1995) pp19-20.
STEVENS, CAT
RN41683 666 (September 30, 1993) pp27-28.
RN41684 719 (October 19, 1995) pp15-16.
STEVENS, ROGERS
RN41685 639 (September 17, 1992) pp19-20.
STEVENS, STEVE
RN41686 636 (August 6, 1992) pp11,13.
RN41687 644 (November 26, 1992) pp13,15.
STEVENSON, DON
RN41688 670 (November 25, 1993) pp37-38.
STEWART, DAVE
RN41689 626 (March 19, 1992) pp11,13.
RN41690 638 (September 3, 1992) pp9,11.
STEWART, DAVID W.
RN41691 709 (June 1, 1995) pp16-17.
STEWART, JIM
RN41692 625 (March 5, 1992) pp11,13-15,17+.
STEWART, JON
RN41693 680 (April 21, 1994) pp33-34.
RN41694 693 (October 20, 1994) pp27-28,30.
RN41695 701 (February 9, 1995) pp16-17.
RN41696 705 (April 6, 1995) pp16-17.
RN41697 714 (August 10, 1995) pp15-17.
STEWART, KEN
RN41698 722 (November 30, 1995) pp19-20.
STEWART, ROD
RN41699 621 (January 9, 1992) pp10-11.
RN41700 653 (April 1, 1993) pp11,13.
RN41701 658 (June 10, 1993) pp16-17.
RN41702 702 (February 23, 1995) pp19-20.
STICKY FINGAZ
RN41703 729 (March 7, 1996) pp9-10.
STILLER, BEN
RN41704 689 (August 25, 1994) pp15-16.
STILLS, STEVE
RN41705 745 (October 17, 1996) pp27-28.
STING
RN41706 617 (November 14, 1991) pp11,13.
RN41707 629 (April 30, 1992) pp11-12.
RN41708 640 (October 1, 1992) pp9-10.
RN41709 648 (January 21, 1993) pp9,11.
RN41710 654 (April 15, 1993) pp11,13.
RN41711 659 (June 24, 1993) pp13,15.
RN41712 668 (October 28, 1993) pp35-36.
RN41713 680 (April 21, 1994) pp33-34.
RN41714 682 (May 19, 1994) pp37-38.
RN41715 694 (November 3, 1994) pp17-18,22.
RN41716 697 (December 15, 1994) pp17-18,20.
RN41717 703 (March 9, 1995) pp20-21.
RN41718 709 (June 1, 1995) pp16-17.
RN41719 733 (May 2, 1996) pp13-14.
RN41720 735 (May 30, 1996) pp12-13.
STINKY PUFFS
RN41721 691 (September 22, 1994) pp19-21.
STINSON, BOB
RN41722 743 (September 19, 1996) pp19-20.
STINSON, TOMMY
RN41723 649 (February 4, 1993) pp8-9.
STIPE, MICHAEL
RN41724 615 (October 17, 1991) pp13-14.
RN41725 622 (January 23, 1992) pp6-7.
RN41726 628 (April 16, 1992) pp11,13.
RN41727 642 (October 29, 1992) pp19,21.
RN41728 644 (November 26, 1992) pp13,15.
RN41729 647 (January 7, 1993) pp9,11.
RN41730 648 (January 21, 1993) pp9,11.
RN41731 674 (January 27, 1994) pp28-29.
RN41732 678 (March 24, 1994) pp27-28.
RN41733 680 (April 21, 1994) pp33-34.
RN41734 681 (May 5, 1994) pp21-22.
RN41735 688 (August 11, 1994) pp17-18,20.
RN41736 689 (August 25, 1994) pp15-16.
RN41737 691 (September 22, 1994) pp19-21.
RN41738 693 (October 20, 1994) pp27-28,30.
RN41739 697 (December 15, 1994) pp17-18,20.
RN41740 701 (February 9, 1995) pp16-17.
RN41741 719 (October 19, 1995) pp15-16.
RN41742 722 (November 30, 1995) pp19-20.
RN41743 726 (January 25, 1996) pp17-18.
RN41744 736 (June 13, 1996) pp19-20.
STOCKWELL, DEAN
RN41745 717 (September 21, 1995) pp19-20.
STOLTZ, ERIC
RN41746 694 (November 3, 1994) pp17-18,22.
STONE, MIKE
RN41747 748 (November 28, 1996) pp25-26.
STONE, OLIVER
RN41748 648 (January 21, 1993) pp9,11.
RN41749 727 (February 8, 1996) pp12-13.
RN41750 736 (June 13, 1996) pp19-20.
RN41751 748 (November 28, 1996) pp25-26.
STONE ROSES
RN41752 712-713 (July 13, 1995) pp25-26.
RN41753 745 (October 17, 1996) pp27-28.
STONE, SHARON
RN41754 656 (May 13, 1993) pp13,15.
RN41755 738-739 (July 11, 1996) pp15-16.
STONE, SLY
RN41756 712-713 (July 13, 1995) pp25-26.
STONE TEMPLE PILOTS
RN41757 659 (June 24, 1993) pp13,15.
RN41758 665 (September 16, 1993) pp31-32.
RN41759 684 (June 16, 1994) pp35-36.
RN41760 685 (June 30, 1994) pp40-41.
RN41761 693 (October 20, 1994) pp27-28,30.
RN41762 694 (November 3, 1994) pp17-18,22.
RN41763 700 (January 26, 1995) pp16-17.
RN41764 721 (November 16, 1995) pp25-26.
STOOGES
RN41765 652 (March 18, 1993) pp13,15.
STRADLIN, IZZY
RN41766 616 (October 31, 1991) pp11,13.
RN41767 634-635 (July 9, 1992) pp11,13.
RN41768 644 (November 26, 1992) pp13,15.
RN41769 663 (August 19, 1993) pp27-28.

STRANDBERG, TODD
RN41770 726 (January 25, 1996) pp17-18.
STRAUSS, PAUL
RN41771 744 (October 3, 1996) pp19-21.
STRAW, SYD
RN41772 664 (September 2, 1993) pp31-32.
RN41773 686-687 (July 14, 1994) pp41-42.
RN41774 688 (August 11, 1994) pp17-18,20.
STRAY CATS
RN41775 652 (March 18, 1993) pp13,15.
RN41776 737 (June 27, 1996) pp15-16.
STREISAND, BARBRA
RN41777 678 (March 24, 1994) pp27-28.
STRICKLAND, KEITH
RN41778 637 (August 20, 1992) pp9,11.
RN41779 683 (June 2, 1994) pp27-28.
STRINGFELLOW, KEN
RN41780 658 (June 10, 1993) pp16-17.
STRUMMER, JOE
RN41781 616 (October 31, 1991) pp11,13.
RN41782 618 (November 28, 1991) pp11-12.
RN41783 702 (February 23, 1995) pp19-20.
RN41784 737 (June 27, 1996) pp15-16.
STULL, TONY
RN41785 685 (June 30, 1994) pp40-41.
STYLER, TRUDIE
RN41786 629 (April 30, 1992) pp11-12.
RN41787 640 (October 1, 1992) pp9-10.
RN41788 735 (May 30, 1996) pp12-13.
SUBLIME
RN41789 711 (June 29, 1995) pp12-13.
SUGAR
RN41790 637 (August 20, 1992) pp9,11.
RN41791 667 (October 14, 1993) pp39-40.
RN41792 701 (February 9, 1995) pp16-17.
SUGAR HILL GANG
RN41793 746 (October 31, 1996) pp17-18.
SUGARCUBES
RN41794 658 (June 10, 1993) pp16-17.
SUI, ANNA
RN41795 749 (December 12, 1996) pp19-20.
SUMMERS, ANDY
RN41796 617 (November 14, 1991) pp11,13.
SUPER DELUXE
RN41797 743 (September 19, 1996) pp19-20.
SUPERCHUNK
RN41798 693 (October 20, 1994) pp27-28,30.
SUPERGRASS
RN41799 726 (January 25, 1996) pp17-18.
SUPERSUCKERS
RN41800 707 (May 4, 1995) pp19-20.
RN41801 719 (October 19, 1995) pp15-16.
RN41802 721 (November 16, 1995) pp25-26.
RN41803 731 (April 4, 1996) pp17-18.
RN41804 741 (August 22, 1996) pp25-26.
RN41805 745 (October 17, 1996) pp27-28.
SUPREMES
RN41806 717 (September 21, 1995) pp19-20.
RN41807 730 (March 21, 1996) pp17-18.
SURRAN, RENE
RN41808 644 (November 26, 1992) pp13,15.
SVEN VATH
RN41809 715 (August 24, 1995) pp23,25.
SVIGALS, ALICIA
RN41810 749 (December 12, 1996) pp19-20.
SWAGGART, JIMMY
RN41811 694 (November 3, 1994) pp17-18,22.
SWEENEY, JULIA
RN41812 693 (October 20, 1994) pp27-28,30.
SWEET, MATTHEW
RN41813 626 (March 19, 1992) pp11,13.
RN41814 655 (April 29, 1993) pp11-12.
RN41815 658 (June 10, 1993) pp16-17.
RN41816 663 (August 19, 1993) pp27-28.
RN41817 667 (October 14, 1993) pp39-40.
RN41818 700 (January 26, 1995) pp16-17.
RN41819 708 (May 18, 1995) pp17-18.
RN41820 712-713 (July 13, 1995) pp25-26.
SWV
RN41821 664 (September 2, 1993) pp31-32.
RN41822 675 (February 10, 1994) pp22-23.
RN41823 690 (September 8, 1994) pp21,24.
SYKES, JOHN
RN41824 748 (November 28, 1996) pp25-26.

T

T-BOZ
RN41825 719 (October 19, 1995) pp15-16.
TACKHEAD
RN41826 637 (August 20, 1992) pp9,11.
TAD
RN41827 666 (September 30, 1993) pp27-28.
RN41828 708 (May 18, 1995) pp17-18.
TAFT, JOSH
RN41829 638 (September 3, 1992) pp9,11.
TALIEFERO, CRYSTAL
RN41830 639 (September 17, 1992) pp19-20.
TALKING HEADS
RN41831 638 (September 3, 1992) pp9,11.
TALLENT, GARY
RN41832 644 (November 26, 1992) pp13,15.
TAMAKI, KOJI
RN41833 686-687 (July 14, 1994) pp41-42.
TAMBERELLI, DANNY
RN41834 697 (December 15, 1994) pp17-18,20.
TARANTINO, QUENTIN
RN41835 700 (January 26, 1995) pp16-17.
RN41836 714 (August 10, 1995) pp15-17.
RN41837 730 (March 21, 1996) pp17-18.
TAREE, AERLE
RN41838 648 (January 21, 1993) pp9,11.
TARSEM
RN41839 615 (October 17, 1991) pp13-14.
TATE, GEOFF
RN41839 615 (October 17, 1991) pp13-14.
RN41840 618 (November 28, 1991) pp11-12.
RN41841 696 (December 1, 1994) pp23-25.
TAUPIN, BERNIE
RN41842 618 (November 28, 1991) pp11-12.
RN41843 627 (April 2, 1992) pp11,13.
RN41844 634-635 (July 9, 1992) pp11,13.
TAYLOR, CHAD
RN41845 716 (September 7, 1995) pp13-14.
RN41846 721 (November 16, 1995) pp25-26.
TAYLOR, DALLAS
RN41847 617 (November 14, 1991) pp11,13.
TAYLOR, ELIZABETH
RN41848 679 (April 7, 1994) pp37-39.
TAYLOR, JAMES
RN41849 629 (April 30, 1992) pp11-12.
RN41850 654 (April 15, 1993) pp11,13.
RN41851 682 (May 19, 1994) pp37-38.
RN41852 688 (August 11, 1994) pp17-18,20.
RN41853 709 (June 1, 1995) pp16-17.
RN41854 735 (May 30, 1996) pp12-13.
TAYLOR, JOHN
RN41855 721 (November 16, 1995) pp25-26.
RN41856 731 (April 4, 1996) pp17-18.
TAYLOR, KOKO
RN41857 697 (December 15, 1994) pp17-18,20.
TAYLOR, LILI
RN41858 736 (June 13, 1996) pp19-20.
TAZ
RN41859 685 (June 30, 1994) pp40-41.
TCHAIKOVSKY, BRAM
RN41860 731 (April 4, 1996) pp17-18.
TEENAGE FANCLUB
RN41861 675 (February 10, 1994) pp22-23.
TEIS, MIKE
RN41862 707 (May 4, 1995) pp19-20.
TELEVISION
RN41863 617 (November 14, 1991) pp11,13.
TEMPLE, SHIRLEY
RN41864 726 (January 25, 1996) pp17-18.
10,000 MANIACS
RN41865 633 (June 25, 1992) pp11-12.
RN41866 647 (January 7, 1993) pp9,11.
RN41867 656 (May 13, 1993) pp13,15.
RN41868 657 (May 27, 1993) pp9,11.
RN41869 664 (September 2, 1993) pp31-32.
RN41870 665 (September 16, 1993) pp31-32.
RN41871 679 (April 7, 1994) pp37-39.
RN41872 697 (December 15, 1994) pp17-18,20.
TENNILLE, TONI
RN41873 653 (April 1, 1993) pp11,13.
TERMINATOR X
RN41874 664 (September 2, 1993) pp31-32.
TERRIO, DENNY
RN41875 685 (June 30, 1994) pp40-41.
THAYIL, KIM

RN41876 621 (January 9, 1992) pp10-11.
THELONIOUS MONSTER
RN41877 648 (January 21, 1993) pp9,11.
THEO
RN41878 728 (February 22, 1996) p20.
THERAPY?
RN41879 690 (September 8, 1994) pp21,24.
THIN LIZZY
RN41880 630 (May 14, 1992) pp13,15.
3RD BASS
RN41881 631 (May 28, 1992) pp9,11.
13 ENGINES
RN41882 676 (February 24, 1994) pp28-29.
13TH FLOOR ELEVATORS
RN41883 708 (May 18, 1995) pp17-18.
38 SPECIAL
RN41884 681 (May 5, 1994) pp21-22.
RN41885 727 (February 8, 1996) pp12-13.
THOMAS, CARLA
RN41886 654 (April 15, 1993) pp11,13.
THOMAS, IRMA
RN41887 680 (April 21, 1994) pp33-34.
RN41888 683 (June 2, 1994) pp27-28.
THOMAS, JEREMY
RN41889 681 (May 5, 1994) pp21-22.
RN41890 Number not assigned.
THOMPSON, CHERYLANNE
RN41891 636 (August 6, 1992) pp11,13.
THOMPSON, HUNTER S.
RN41892 647 (January 7, 1993) pp9,11.
RN41893 747 (November 14, 1996) pp25-26.
THOMPSON, PORL
RN41894 631 (May 28, 1992) pp9,11.
THOMPSON, RICHARD
RN41895 630 (May 14, 1992) pp13,15.
RN41896 662 (August 5, 1993) pp33-34.
RN41897 686-687 (July 14, 1994) pp41-42.
RN41898 691 (September 22, 1994) pp19-21.
RN41899 719 (October 19, 1995) pp15-16.
THORN, CHRISTOPHER
RN41900 639 (September 17, 1992) pp19-20.
311
RN41901 720 (November 2, 1995) pp16-17.
RN41902 747 (November 14, 1996) pp25-26.
THROWING MUSES
RN41903 637 (August 20, 1992) pp9,11.
RN41904 674 (January 27, 1994) pp28-29.
RN41905 704 (March 23, 1995) pp24-25.
RN41906 715 (August 24, 1995) pp23,25.
RN41907 718 (October 5, 1995) pp20-21.
THURMAN, UMA
RN41908 696 (December 1, 1994) pp23-25.
RN41909 748 (November 28, 1996) pp25-26.
RN41910 749 (December 12, 1996) pp19-20.
TILTON, CHARLENE
RN41911 681 (May 5, 1994) pp21-22.
TIME
RN41912 749 (December 12, 1996) pp19-20.
TIMMINS, MARGO
RN41913 621 (January 9, 1992) pp10-11.
TIMMS, SALLY
RN41914 694 (November 3, 1994) pp17-18,22.
TIN MACHINE
RN41915 622 (January 23, 1992) pp6-7.
RN41916 637 (August 20, 1992) pp9,11.
RN41917 652 (March 18, 1993) pp13,15.
TINSLEY, CHRIS
RN41918 618 (November 28, 1991) pp11-12.
TITANIC LOVE AFFAIR
RN41919 709 (June 1, 1995) pp16-17.
TLC
RN41920 660-661 (July 8, 1993) pp32-33.
RN41921 707 (May 4, 1995) pp19-20.
RN41922 719 (October 19, 1995) pp15-16.
RN41923 732 (April 18, 1996) pp19-20.
RN41924 735 (May 30, 1996) pp12-13.
TOAD THE WET SPROCKET
RN41925 684 (June 16, 1994) pp35-36.
TOBIAS, JESSE
RN41926 667 (October 14, 1993) pp39-40.
TOKYO NEW PHILHARMONIC ORCHESTRA
RN41927 686-687 (July 14, 1994) pp41-42.
TOM TOM CLUB
RN41928 637 (August 20, 1992) pp9,11.
RN41929 638 (September 3, 1992) pp9,11.
TONE LOC
RN41930 659 (June 24, 1993) pp13,15.
TOOL
RN41931 686-687 (July 14, 1994) pp41-42.
RN41932 718 (October 5, 1995) pp20-21.
TORK, PETER
RN41933 629 (April 30, 1992) pp11-12.
RN41934 650 (February 18, 1993) pp11,13.
RN41935 684 (June 16, 1994) pp35-36.
TORME, MEL
RN41936 702 (February 23, 1995) pp19-20.
RN41937 719 (October 19, 1995) pp15-16.
TORRES, TICO
RN41938 747 (November 14, 1996) pp25-26.
TOSH, ANDREW
RN41939 694 (November 3, 1994) pp17-18,22.
TOSH, PETER
RN41939 694 (November 3, 1994) pp17-18,22.
TOTO
RN41940 649 (February 4, 1993) pp8-9.
RN41941 704 (March 23, 1995) pp24-25.
TOURE, ALI FARKA
RN41942 668 (October 28, 1993) pp35-36.
TOWNSEND, MITCH
RN41943 743 (September 19, 1996) pp19-20.
TOWNSEND, ROBERT
RN41944 710 (June 15, 1995) pp17-18.
TOWNSHEND, PETER
RN41945 634-635 (July 9, 1992) pp11,13.
RN41946 656 (May 13, 1993) pp13,15.
RN41947 670 (November 25, 1993) pp37-38.
RN41948 736 (June 13, 1996) pp19-20.
RN41949 741 (August 22, 1996) pp25-26.
RN41950 749 (December 12, 1996) pp19-20.
TRAFFIC
RN41951 680 (April 21, 1994) pp33-34.
TRAMMPS
RN41952 686-687 (July 14, 1994) pp41-42.
TRAVELING WILBURYS
RN41953 629 (April 30, 1992) pp11-12.
TRAVIS, MALCOLM
RN41954 637 (August 20, 1992) pp9,11.
RN41955 701 (February 9, 1995) pp16-17.
TRAVOLTA, JOHN
RN41956 729 (March 7, 1996) pp9-10.
RN41957 738-739 (July 11, 1996) pp15-16.
TRE COOL
RN41958 707 (May 4, 1995) pp19-20.
TREACH
RN41959 696 (December 1, 1994) pp23-25.
RN41960 729 (March 7, 1996) pp9-10.
A TRIBE CALLED QUEST
RN41961 659 (June 24, 1993) pp13,15.
RN41962 669 (November 11, 1993) pp27-28.
RN41963 742 (September 5, 1996) pp20-21.
RN41964 748 (November 28, 1996) pp25-26.
TRICKY
RN41965 745 (October 17, 1996) pp27-28.
RN41966 749 (December 12, 1996) pp19-20.
TRIMBLE, VIVIAN
RN41967 685 (June 30, 1994) pp40-41.
RN41968 710 (June 15, 1995) pp17-18.
TRIPPING DAISY
RN41969 716 (September 7, 1995) pp13-14.
TRITT, TRAVIS
RN41970 648 (January 21, 1993) pp9,11.
RN41971 652 (March 18, 1993) pp13,15.
TROTT, JEFFREY
RN41972 628 (April 16, 1992) pp11,13.
TRUCKS, BUTCH
RN41973 624 (February 20, 1992) pp11-12.
RN41974 746 (October 31, 1996) pp17-18.
TRUDELL, JOHN
RN41975 705 (April 6, 1995) pp16-17.
TRUJILLO, KIMBERLEE
RN41976 702 (February 23, 1995) pp19-20.
TSHABALALA, HEADMAN
RN41977 622 (January 23, 1992) pp6-7.
TUATARA
RN41978 748 (November 28, 1996) pp25-26.
TUCKER, MAUREEN
RN41979 648 (January 21, 1993) pp9,11.
TURLINGTON, CHRISTY
RN41980 702 (February 23, 1995) pp19-20.
TURNER, IKE
RN41981 660-661 (July 8, 1993) pp32-33.
RN41982 663 (August 19, 1993) pp27-28.
TURNER, JAMIE
RN41983 618 (November 28, 1991) pp11-12.
TURNER, KATHLEEN
RN41984 659 (June 24, 1993) pp13,15.
RN41985 683 (June 2, 1994) pp27-28.
TURNER, STEVE
RN41986 670 (November 25, 1993) pp37-38.

TURNER, TED
RN41987 655 (April 29, 1993) pp11-12.
TURNER, TINA
RN41988 654 (April 15, 1993) pp11,13.
RN41989 660-661 (July 8, 1993) pp32-33.
RN41990 663 (August 19, 1993) pp27-28.
RN41991 726 (January 25, 1996) pp17-18.
RN41992 728 (February 22, 1996) p20.
RN41993 736 (June 13, 1996) pp19-20.
TURTLES
RN41994 740 (August 8, 1996) pp17-18.
TWEEDY, JEFF
RN41995 684 (June 16, 1994) pp35-36.
RN41996 691 (September 22, 1994) pp19-21.
RN41997 714 (August 10, 1995) pp15-17.
RN41998 716 (September 7, 1995) pp13-14.
RN41999 721 (November 16, 1995) pp25-26.
TWITTY, CONWAY
RN42000 692 (October 6, 1994) pp15-17.
2 LIVE CREW
RN42001 676 (February 24, 1994) pp28-29.
TYLER, LIV
RN42002 740 (August 8, 1996) pp17-18.
TYLER, STEVEN
RN42003 615 (October 17, 1991) pp13-14.
RN42004 621 (January 9, 1992) pp10-11.
RN42005 622 (January 23, 1992) pp6-7.
RN42006 623 (February 6, 1992) pp11,13.
RN42007 626 (March 19, 1992) pp11,13.
RN42008 627 (April 2, 1992) pp11,13.
RN42009 634-635 (July 9, 1992) pp11,13.
RN42010 659 (June 24, 1993) pp13,15.
RN42011 668 (October 28, 1993) pp35-36.
RN42012 679 (April 7, 1994) pp37-39.
RN42013 680 (April 21, 1994) pp33-34.
RN42014 684 (June 16, 1994) pp35-36.
RN42015 693 (October 20, 1994) pp27-28,30.
RN42016 701 (February 9, 1995) pp16-17.
RN42017 708 (May 18, 1995) pp17-18.
RN42018 723 (December 14, 1995) pp27-28.
RN42019 740 (August 8, 1996) pp17-18.
RN42020 745 (October 17, 1996) pp27-28.
RN42021 749 (December 12, 1996) pp19-20.
TYLER, TAJ MONROE
RN42022 627 (April 2, 1992) pp11,13.
TYLER, TERESA
RN42022 627 (April 2, 1992) pp11,13.
TYNER, ROB
RN42023 628 (April 16, 1992) pp11,13.

U

U2
RN42024 617 (November 14, 1991) pp11,13.
RN42025 624 (February 20, 1992) pp11-12.
RN42026 627 (April 2, 1992) pp11,13.
RN42027 636 (August 6, 1992) pp11,13.
RN42028 639 (September 17, 1992) pp19-20.
RN42029 642 (October 29, 1992) pp19,21.
RN42030 654 (April 15, 1993) pp11,13.
RN42031 658 (June 10, 1993) pp16-17.
RN42032 663 (August 19, 1993) pp27-28.
RN42033 666 (September 30, 1993) pp27-28.
RN42034 675 (February 10, 1994) pp22-23.
RN42035 686-687 (July 14, 1994) pp41-42.
RN42036 704 (March 23, 1995) pp24-25.
RN42037 710 (June 15, 1995) pp17-18.
RN42038 738-739 (July 11, 1996) pp15-16.
UGLY KID JOE
RN42039 667 (October 14, 1993) pp39-40.
ULF
RN42040 700 (January 26, 1995) pp16-17.
ULRICH, LARS
RN42041 615 (October 17, 1991) pp13-14.
RN42042 618 (November 28, 1991) pp11-12.
RN42043 628 (April 16, 1992) pp11,13.
RN42044 652 (March 18, 1993) pp13,15.
RN42045 655 (April 29, 1993) pp11-12.
RN42046 727 (February 8, 1996) pp12-13.
UNBEARABLES
RN42047 708 (May 18, 1995) pp17-18.
UNCLE TUPELO
RN42048 684 (June 16, 1994) pp35-36.
RN42049 716 (September 7, 1995) pp13-14.
UNSANE
RN42050 697 (December 15, 1994) pp17-18,20.
URBAN MASAYA
RN42051 691 (September 22, 1994) pp19-21.
URGE OVERKILL
RN42052 663 (August 19, 1993) pp27-28.
RN42053 668 (October 28, 1993) pp35-36.
RN42054 685 (June 30, 1994) pp40-41.
RN42055 689 (August 25, 1994) pp15-16.

V

VAI, STEVE
RN42056 622 (January 23, 1992) pp6-7.
VALENTINE, KATHY
RN42057 616 (October 31, 1991) pp11,13.
VALENZUELA, JESSE
RN42058 722 (November 30, 1995) pp19-20.
VALLETTA, AMBER
RN42059 737 (June 27, 1996) pp15-16.
VAN HALEN
RN42060 615 (October 17, 1991) pp13-14.
RN42061 622 (January 23, 1992) pp6-7.
RN42062 654 (April 15, 1993) pp11,13.
RN42063 683 (June 2, 1994) pp27-28.
RN42064 745 (October 17, 1996) pp27-28.
VAN HALEN, ALEX
RN42065 733 (May 2, 1996) pp13-14.
VAN HALEN, EDDIE
RN42066 615 (October 17, 1991) pp13-14.
RN42067 622 (January 23, 1992) pp6-7.
RN42068 649 (February 4, 1993) pp8-9.
RN42069 654 (April 15, 1993) pp11,13.
RN42070 663 (August 19, 1993) pp27-28.
RN42071 675 (February 10, 1994) pp22-23.
RN42072 683 (June 2, 1994) pp27-28.
RN42073 733 (May 2, 1996) pp13-14.
RN42074 745 (October 17, 1996) pp27-28.
RN42075 748 (November 28, 1996) pp25-26.
VAN PEEBLES, MARIO
RN42076 707 (May 4, 1995) pp19-20.
VAN PEEBLES, MELVIN
RN42076 707 (May 4, 1995) pp19-20.
VAN ZANDT, STEVE
RN42077 617 (November 14, 1991) pp11,13.
RN42078 644 (November 26, 1992) pp13,15.
RN42079 664 (September 2, 1993) pp31-32.
RN42080 717 (September 21, 1995) pp19-20.
VAN ZANDT, TOWNES
RN42081 659 (June 24, 1993) pp13,15.
VANDALS
RN42082 711 (June 29, 1995) pp12-13.
VANDROSS, LUTHER
RN42083 665 (September 16, 1993) pp31-32.
VANESSA-MAE
RN42084 731 (April 4, 1996) pp17-18.
VANILLA ICE
RN42085 676 (February 24, 1994) pp28-29.
RN42086 681 (May 5, 1994) pp21-22.
VAPORS
RN42087 712-713 (July 13, 1995) pp25-26.
VAUGHAN, STEVIE RAY
RN42088 640 (October 1, 1992) pp9-10.
VEDDER, EDDIE
RN42089 634-635 (July 9, 1992) pp11,13.
RN42090 638 (September 3, 1992) pp9,11.
RN42091 642 (October 29, 1992) pp19,21.
RN42092 650 (February 18, 1993) pp11,13.
RN42093 658 (June 10, 1993) pp16-17.
RN42094 662 (August 5, 1993) pp33-34.
RN42095 667 (October 14, 1993) pp39-40.
RN42096 674 (January 27, 1994) pp28-29.
RN42097 679 (April 7, 1994) pp37-39.
RN42098 683 (June 2, 1994) pp27-28.
RN42099 686-687 (July 14, 1994) pp41-42.
RN42100 688 (August 11, 1994) pp17-18,20.
RN42101 692 (October 6, 1994) pp15-17.
RN42102 696 (December 1, 1994) pp23-25.
RN42103 707 (May 4, 1995) pp19-20.
RN42104 710 (June 15, 1995) pp17-18.
RN42105 717 (September 21, 1995) pp19-20.
RN42106 726 (January 25, 1996) pp17-18.

RN42107 727 (February 8, 1996) pp12-13.
RN42108 730 (March 21, 1996) pp17-18.
RN42109 732 (April 18, 1996) pp19-20.
RN42110 736 (June 13, 1996) pp19-20.
RN42111 738-739 (July 11, 1996) pp15-16.
RN42112 743 (September 19, 1996) pp19-20.
RN42113 749 (December 12, 1996) pp19-20.
VEGA, SUZANNE
RN42114 634-635 (July 9, 1992) pp11,13.
RN42115 653 (April 1, 1993) pp11,13.
RN42116 678 (March 24, 1994) pp27-28.
RN42117 708 (May 18, 1995) pp17-18.
RN42118 734 (May 16, 1996) pp17-18.
VELECESCU, ADRIAN
RN42119 697 (December 15, 1994) pp17-18,20.
VELVET CRUSH
RN42120 685 (June 30, 1994) pp40-41.
VELVET UNDERGROUND
RN42121 648 (January 21, 1993) pp9,11.
RN42122 692 (October 6, 1994) pp15-17.
RN42123 714 (August 10, 1995) pp15-17.
RN42124 716 (September 7, 1995) pp13-14.
RN42125 722 (November 30, 1995) pp19-20.
RN42126 735 (May 30, 1996) pp12-13.
RN42127 736 (June 13, 1996) pp19-20.
VERLAINE, TOM
RN42128 674 (January 27, 1994) pp28-29.
VERSACE, GIANNI
RN42129 749 (December 12, 1996) pp19-20.
VERSCHOOR, GEORGE
RN42130 688 (August 11, 1994) pp17-18,20.
VERUCA SALT
RN42131 690 (September 8, 1994) pp21,24.
RN42132 701 (February 9, 1995) pp16-17.
RN42133 709 (June 1, 1995) pp16-17.
RN42134 721 (November 16, 1995) pp25-26.
VERVE
RN42135 710 (June 15, 1995) pp17-18.
VIAN, JOSEPH
RN42136 626 (March 19, 1992) pp11,13.
VICIOUS, SID
RN42137 655 (April 29, 1993) pp11-12.
VIGDOR, LUIS
RN42138 702 (February 23, 1995) pp19-20.
VIGIL, SELENE
RN42139 722 (November 30, 1995) pp19-20.
RN42140 731 (April 4, 1996) pp17-18.
RN42141 742 (September 5, 1996) pp20-21.
VINSON-KAFURA, JANE
RN42142 717 (September 21, 1995) pp19-20.
VINYL, KOSMO
RN42143 618 (November 28, 1991) pp11-12.
VIOLENT FEMMES
RN42144 630 (May 14, 1992) pp13,15.
RN42145 633 (June 25, 1992) pp11-12.
RN42146 658 (June 10, 1993) pp16-17.
RN42147 665 (September 16, 1993) pp31-32.
RN42148 668 (October 28, 1993) pp35-36.
RN42149 691 (September 22, 1994) pp19-21.
VOLMAN, MARK
RN42150 740 (August 8, 1996) pp17-18.
VOODOO CHILDREN
RN42151 665 (September 16, 1993) pp31-32.
VUDI
RN42152 659 (June 24, 1993) pp13,15.
VULLO, MARIA
RN42153 722 (November 30, 1995) pp19-20.

W

WACHTEL, WADDY
RN42154 676 (February 24, 1994) pp28-29.
WAHLBERG, DONNIE
RN42155 678 (March 24, 1994) pp27-28.
WAHLBERG, MARK
RN42156 710 (June 15, 1995) pp17-18.
WAILER, BUNNY
RN42157 694 (November 3, 1994) pp17-18,22.
WAITS, TOM
RN42158 634-635 (July 9, 1992) pp11,13.
RN42159 649 (February 4, 1993) pp8-9.
RN42160 659 (June 24, 1993) pp13,15.
RN42161 675 (February 10, 1994) pp22-23.
WALKEN, CHRISTOPHER
RN42162 702 (February 23, 1995) pp19-20.
WALKER, ALBERTINA
RN42163 706 (April 20, 1995) pp15-17.
WALL OF VOODOO
RN42164 628 (April 16, 1992) pp11,13.
WALLACE, BILL
RN42165 671 (December 9, 1993) pp31-32.
WALLFLOWERS
RN42166 636 (August 6, 1992) pp11,13.
RN42167 652 (March 18, 1993) pp13,15.
RN42168 657 (May 27, 1993) pp9,11.
RN42169 697 (December 15, 1994) pp17-18,20.
RN42170 746 (October 31, 1996) pp17-18.
WALLINGER, KARL
RN42171 664 (September 2, 1993) pp31-32.
WALLMEN
RN42172 712-713 (July 13, 1995) pp25-26.
WAREHAM, DEAN
RN42173 735 (May 30, 1996) pp12-13.
WARHOL, ANDY
RN42174 714 (August 10, 1995) pp15-17.
RN42175 716 (September 7, 1995) pp13-14.
RN42176 736 (June 13, 1996) pp19-20.
WARNICK, KIM
RN42177 730 (March 21, 1996) pp17-18.
WARRANT
RN42178 655 (April 29, 1993) pp11-12.
WARREN G
RN42179 700 (January 26, 1995) pp16-17.
WAS, DON
RN42180 617 (November 14, 1991) pp11,13.
RN42181 630 (May 14, 1992) pp13,15.
RN42182 640 (October 1, 1992) pp9-10.
RN42183 652 (March 18, 1993) pp13,15.
RN42184 704 (March 23, 1995) pp24-25.
RN42185 716 (September 7, 1995) pp13-14.
WASHINGTON, GEORGE
RN42186 721 (November 16, 1995) pp25-26.
WASSER, JOAN
RN42187 693 (October 20, 1994) pp27-28,30.
WASSERMAN, ROB
RN42188 638 (September 3, 1992) pp9,11.
RN42189 683 (June 2, 1994) pp27-28.
RN42190 718 (October 5, 1995) pp20-21.
WATERBOYS
RN42191 664 (September 2, 1993) pp31-32.
WATERMAN, JOHN
RN42192 667 (October 14, 1993) pp39-40.
WATERS, CRYSTAL
RN42193 704 (March 23, 1995) pp24-25.
WATERS, JOHN
RN42194 659 (June 24, 1993) pp13,15.
RN42195 683 (June 2, 1994) pp27-28.
RN42196 697 (December 15, 1994) pp17-18,20.
RN42197 700 (January 26, 1995) pp16-17.
RN42198 707 (May 4, 1995) pp19-20.
WATERS, MUDDY
RN42199 640 (October 1, 1992) pp9-10.
WATERS, ROGER
RN42200 630 (May 14, 1992) pp13,15.
RN42201 636 (August 6, 1992) pp11,13.
WATLEY, JODY
RN42202 627 (April 2, 1992) pp11,13.
WATT, MIKE
RN42202 627 (April 2, 1992) pp11,13.
RN42203 633 (June 25, 1992) pp11-12.
RN42204 656 (May 13, 1993) pp13,15.
RN42205 702 (February 23, 1995) pp19-20.
RN42206 710 (June 15, 1995) pp17-18.
RN42207 714 (August 10, 1995) pp15-17.
RN42208 719 (October 19, 1995) pp15-16.
RN42209 736 (June 13, 1996) pp19-20.
WATTS, CHARLIE
RN42210 621 (January 9, 1992) pp10-11.
RN42211 637 (August 20, 1992) pp9,11.
RN42212 662 (August 5, 1993) pp33-34.
RN42213 668 (October 28, 1993) pp35-36.
RN42214 670 (November 25, 1993) pp37-38.
RN42215 690 (September 8, 1994) pp21,24.
RN42216 734 (May 16, 1996) pp17-18.
WAVY GRAVY
RN42217 679 (April 7, 1994) pp37-39.
RN42218 684 (June 16, 1994) pp35-36.
RN42219 705 (April 6, 1995) pp16-17.
RN42220 747 (November 14, 1996) pp25-26.
WAX
RN42221 709 (June 1, 1995) pp16-17.
WAXMAN, DINA
RN42222 742 (September 5, 1996) pp20-21.
WEDREN, CRAIG
RN42223 714 (August 10, 1995) pp15-17.
WEEN

RN42224 705 (April 6, 1995) pp16-17.
WEEZER
RN42225 723 (December 14, 1995) pp27-28.
WEILAND
RN42226 659 (June 24, 1993) pp13,15.
RN42227 665 (September 16, 1993) pp31-32.
RN42228 684 (June 16, 1994) pp35-36.
RN42229 693 (October 20, 1994) pp27-28,30.
RN42230 700 (January 26, 1995) pp16-17.
RN42231 721 (November 16, 1995) pp25-26.
WEINBERG, MAX
RN42232 644 (November 26, 1992) pp13,15.
RN42233 717 (September 21, 1995) pp19-20.
WEINSTEIN, JOSH
RN42234 731 (April 4, 1996) pp17-18.
WEIR, BOB
RN42235 623 (February 6, 1992) pp11,13.
RN42236 638 (September 3, 1992) pp9,11.
RN42237 657 (May 27, 1993) pp9,11.
RN42238 683 (June 2, 1994) pp27-28.
RN42239 696 (December 1, 1994) pp23-25.
RN42240 706 (April 20, 1995) pp15-17.
RN42241 718 (October 5, 1995) pp20-21.
RN42242 734 (May 16, 1996) pp17-18.
RN42243 738-739 (July 11, 1996) pp15-16.
WEIR, WENDY
RN42244 706 (April 20, 1995) pp15-17.
WEISS, PETE
RN42245 648 (January 21, 1993) pp9,11.
WELCH, JUSTIN
RN42246 723 (December 14, 1995) pp27-28.
RN42247 746 (October 31, 1996) pp17-18.
WELK, LAWRENCE
RN42248 640 (October 1, 1992) pp9-10.
WELLS, JUNIOR
RN42249 658 (June 10, 1993) pp16-17.
WELNICK, VINCE
RN42250 657 (May 27, 1993) pp9,11.
WENDERS, WIM
RN42251 617 (November 14, 1991) pp11,13.
RN42252 704 (March 23, 1995) pp24-25.
WENDT, GEORGE
RN42253 701 (February 9, 1995) pp16-17.
WENNER, JANN
RN42254 693 (October 20, 1994) pp27-28,30.
WEST, KEVIN E.
RN42255 727 (February 8, 1996) pp12-13.
WESTERBERG, PAUL
RN42256 616 (October 31, 1991) pp11,13.
RN42257 638 (September 3, 1992) pp9,11.
RN42258 649 (February 4, 1993) pp8-9.
RN42259 663 (August 19, 1993) pp27-28.
RN42260 743 (September 19, 1996) pp19-20.
WEXLER, JERRY
RN42261 630 (May 14, 1992) pp13,15.
WEYMOUTH, TINA
RN42262 637 (August 20, 1992) pp9,11.
RN42263 638 (September 3, 1992) pp9,11.
WHAM!
RN42264 748 (November 28, 1996) pp25-26.
WHITAKER, FOREST
RN42265 642 (October 29, 1992) pp19,21.
WHITE, BARRY
RN42266 662 (August 5, 1993) pp33-34.
RN42267 696 (December 1, 1994) pp23-25.
RN42268 707 (May 4, 1995) pp19-20.
WHITE, MARK
RN42269 660-661 (July 8, 1993) pp32-33.
WHITE ZOMBIE
RN42270 680 (April 21, 1994) pp33-34.
RN42271 715 (August 24, 1995) pp23,25.
RN42272 719 (October 19, 1995) pp15-16.
WHITFORD, BRAD
RN42273 622 (January 23, 1992) pp6-7.
WHITLEY, CHRIS
RN42274 703 (March 9, 1995) pp20-21.
WHO
RN42275 657 (May 27, 1993) pp9,11.
RN42276 662 (August 5, 1993) pp33-34.
RN42277 666 (September 30, 1993) pp27-28.
RN42278 670 (November 25, 1993) pp37-38.
RN42279 700 (January 26, 1995) pp16-17.
RN42280 741 (August 22, 1996) pp25-26.
WHODINI
RN42281 650 (February 18, 1993) pp11,13.
RN42282 664 (September 2, 1993) pp31-32.
WIEDLIN, JANE
RN42283 616 (October 31, 1991) pp11,13.
WILCO
RN42284 684 (June 16, 1994) pp35-36.
RN42285 691 (September 22, 1994) pp19-21.
RN42286 714 (August 10, 1995) pp15-17.
RN42287 716 (September 7, 1995) pp13-14.
RN42288 721 (November 16, 1995) pp25-26.
WILDER, ALAN
RN42289 650 (February 18, 1993) pp11,13.
WILES, ELIZABETH ANN
RN42290 666 (September 30, 1993) pp27-28.
WILK, BRAD
RN42291 664 (September 2, 1993) pp31-32.
WILKESON, LEON
RN42292 727 (February 8, 1996) pp12-13.
WILKINS, DOMINIQUE
RN42293 679 (April 7, 1994) pp37-39.
WILLIAMS, ANDY
RN42294 706 (April 20, 1995) pp15-17.
WILLIAMS, BORIS
RN42295 631 (May 28, 1992) pp9,11.
WILLIAMS BROTHERS
RN42296 692 (October 6, 1994) pp15-17.
WILLIAMS, FREEDOM
RN42297 626 (March 19, 1992) pp11,13.
WILLIAMS, HANK
RN42298 657 (May 27, 1993) pp9,11.
WILLIAMS, LUCINDA
RN42299 637 (August 20, 1992) pp9,11.
RN42300 667 (October 14, 1993) pp39-40.
WILLIAMS, MONTEL
RN42301 654 (April 15, 1993) pp11,13.
WILLIAMS, ROBIN
RN42302 617 (November 14, 1991) pp11,13.
RN42303 705 (April 6, 1995) pp16-17.
RN42304 735 (May 30, 1996) pp12-13.
WILLIAMS, SIMON
RN42305 745 (October 17, 1996) pp27-28.
WILLIAMS, VANESSA
RN42306 680 (April 21, 1994) pp33-34.
RN42307 707 (May 4, 1995) pp19-20.
WILLIAMS, VICTORIA
RN42308 636 (August 6, 1992) pp11,13.
RN42309 658 (June 10, 1993) pp16-17.
RN42310 669 (November 11, 1993) pp27-28.
RN42311 671 (December 9, 1993) pp31-32.
RN42312 675 (February 10, 1994) pp22-23.
RN42313 678 (March 24, 1994) pp27-28.
RN42314 683 (June 2, 1994) pp27-28.
RN42315 692 (October 6, 1994) pp15-17.
RN42316 700 (January 26, 1995) pp16-17.
RN42317 706 (April 20, 1995) pp15-17.
RN42318 718 (October 5, 1995) pp20-21.
RN42319 721 (November 16, 1995) pp25-26.
RN42320 734 (May 16, 1996) pp17-18.
WILSON, ANN
RN42321 624 (February 20, 1992) pp11-12.
RN42322 649 (February 4, 1993) pp8-9.
RN42323 667 (October 14, 1993) pp39-40.
RN42324 696 (December 1, 1994) pp23-25.
WILSON, BRIAN
RN42325 617 (November 14, 1991) pp11,13.
RN42326 704 (March 23, 1995) pp24-25.
WILSON, CINDY
RN42327 630 (May 14, 1992) pp13,15.
RN42328 637 (August 20, 1992) pp9,11.
RN42329 678 (March 24, 1994) pp27-28.
WILSON, NANCY
RN42330 649 (February 4, 1993) pp8-9.
RN42331 667 (October 14, 1993) pp39-40.
RN42332 696 (December 1, 1994) pp23-25.
WILSON PHILLIPS
RN42333 676 (February 24, 1994) pp28-29.
WILSON, ROBERT
RN42334 675 (February 10, 1994) pp22-23.
WILSON, ROBIN
RN42335 665 (September 16, 1993) pp31-32.
WIMBISH, DOUG
RN42336 637 (August 20, 1992) pp9,11.
WINGS
RN42337 657 (May 27, 1993) pp9,11.
WINKLER, ERIC
RN42338 692 (October 6, 1994) pp15-17.
WINWOOD, STEVE
RN42339 630 (May 14, 1992) pp13,15.
RN42340 680 (April 21, 1994) pp33-34.
RN42341 748 (November 28, 1996) pp25-26.

WIRE
RN42342 746 (October 31, 1996) pp17-18.
WITHERS, BILL
RN42343 644 (November 26, 1992) pp13,15.
WOBBLE, JAH
RN42344 636 (August 6, 1992) pp11,13.
WOLF, PETER
RN42345 658 (June 10, 1993) pp16-17.
RN42346 671 (December 9, 1993) pp31-32.
RN42347 679 (April 7, 1994) pp37-39.
RN42348 736 (June 13, 1996) pp19-20.
WOLFE, TOM
RN42349 647 (January 7, 1993) pp9,11.
WOLMAN, BARON
RN42350 652 (March 18, 1993) pp13,15.
WONDER, STEVIE
RN42351 717 (September 21, 1995) pp19-20.
RN42352 732 (April 18, 1996) pp19-20.
WOOD, ANDREW
RN42353 741 (August 22, 1996) pp25-26.
WOOD, BRIAN
RN42354 667 (October 14, 1993) pp39-40.
WOOD, CHRIS
RN42355 680 (April 21, 1994) pp33-34.
WOOD, RON
RN42356 637 (August 20, 1992) pp9,11.
RN42357 639 (September 17, 1992) pp19-20.
RN42358 653 (April 1, 1993) pp11,13.
RN42359 662 (August 5, 1993) pp33-34.
RN42360 668 (October 28, 1993) pp35-36.
RN42361 697 (December 15, 1994) pp17-18,20.
RN42362 734 (May 16, 1996) pp17-18.
RN42363 741 (August 22, 1996) pp25-26.
WOODPUSSY
RN42364 727 (February 8, 1996) pp12-13.
WOODS, REGGIE
RN42365 694 (November 3, 1994) pp17-18,22.
WORLD PARTY
RN42366 628 (April 16, 1992) pp11,13.
RN42367 664 (September 2, 1993) pp31-32.
WRECKX-N-EFFECT
RN42368 659 (June 24, 1993) pp13,15.
WRIGHT, STEVEN
RN42369 634-635 (July 9, 1992) pp11,13.
WU-TANG CLAN
RN42370 675 (February 10, 1994) pp22-23.
RN42371 690 (September 8, 1994) pp21,24.
RN42372 693 (October 20, 1994) pp27-28,30.
RN42373 730 (March 21, 1996) pp17-18.
RN42374 741 (August 22, 1996) pp25-26.
WYMAN, BILL
RN42375 653 (April 1, 1993) pp11,13.
RN42376 656 (May 13, 1993) pp13,15.
RN42377 670 (November 25, 1993) pp37-38.
WYMAN, STEPHEN
RN42378 656 (May 13, 1993) pp13,15.
WYNETTE, TAMMY
RN42379 625 (March 5, 1992) pp11,13-15,17+.
RN42380 682 (May 19, 1994) pp37-38.

X

X
RN42381 616 (October 31, 1991) pp11,13.
RN42382 618 (November 28, 1991) pp11-12.
RN42383 663 (August 19, 1993) pp27-28.
RN42384 666 (September 30, 1993) pp27-28.
RN42385 668 (October 28, 1993) pp35-36.
RN42386 671 (December 9, 1993) pp31-32.
RN42387 676 (February 24, 1994) pp28-29.
RN42388 716 (September 7, 1995) pp13-14.
X-PENSIVE WINOS
RN42389 618 (November 28, 1991) pp11-12.
XSCAPE
RN42390 748 (November 28, 1996) pp25-26.
XTC
RN42391 674 (January 27, 1994) pp28-29.

Y

YA YA'S
RN42392 720 (November 2, 1995) pp16-17.
YANOWITZ, PETER
RN42393 636 (August 6, 1992) pp11,13.
YARDBIRDS
RN42394 625 (March 5, 1992) pp11,13-15,17+.
RN42395 675 (February 10, 1994) pp22-23.
YASGUR, MAX
RN42396 679 (April 7, 1994) pp37-39.
YAUCH, ADAM
RN42397 681 (May 5, 1994) pp21-22.
RN42398 684 (June 16, 1994) pp35-36.
RN42399 692 (October 6, 1994) pp15-17.
RN42400 693 (October 20, 1994) pp27-28,30.
RN42401 720 (November 2, 1995) pp16-17.
RN42402 736 (June 13, 1996) pp19-20.
RN42403 742 (September 5, 1996) pp20-21.
YES
RN42404 685 (June 30, 1994) pp40-41.
YO LA TENGO
RN42405 736 (June 13, 1996) pp19-20.
YO-YO
RN42406 642 (October 29, 1992) pp19,21.
RN42407 644 (November 26, 1992) pp13,15.
RN42408 653 (April 1, 1993) pp11,13.
YOAKUM, DWIGHT
RN42409 622 (January 23, 1992) pp6-7.
RN42410 623 (February 6, 1992) pp11,13.
RN42411 628 (April 16, 1992) pp11,13.
RN42412 653 (April 1, 1993) pp11,13.
RN42413 657 (May 27, 1993) pp9,11.
RN42414 668 (October 28, 1993) pp35-36.
RN42415 694 (November 3, 1994) pp17-18,22.
YORKE, THOM
RN42416 671 (December 9, 1993) pp31-32.
RN42417 722 (November 30, 1995) pp19-20.
RN42418 738-739 (July 11, 1996) pp15-16.
YOUNG, ANGUS
RN42419 640 (October 1, 1992) pp9-10.
RN42420 743 (September 19, 1996) pp19-20.
YOUNG, NEIL
RN42421 625 (March 5, 1992) pp11,13-15,17+.
RN42422 629 (April 30, 1992) pp11-12.
RN42423 630 (May 14, 1992) pp13,15.
RN42424 638 (September 3, 1992) pp9,11.
RN42425 654 (April 15, 1993) pp11,13.
RN42426 655 (April 29, 1993) pp11-12.
RN42427 658 (June 10, 1993) pp16-17.
RN42428 663 (August 19, 1993) pp27-28.
RN42429 665 (September 16, 1993) pp31-32.
RN42430 666 (September 30, 1993) pp27-28.
RN42431 667 (October 14, 1993) pp39-40.
RN42432 681 (May 5, 1994) pp21-22.
RN42433 683 (June 2, 1994) pp27-28.
RN42434 694 (November 3, 1994) pp17-18,22.
RN42435 696 (December 1, 1994) pp23-25.
RN42436 697 (December 15, 1994) pp17-18,20.
RN42437 714 (August 10, 1995) pp15-17.
RN42438 717 (September 21, 1995) pp19-20.
RN42439 721 (November 16, 1995) pp25-26.
RN42440 723 (December 14, 1995) pp27-28.
RN42441 726 (January 25, 1996) pp17-18.
RN42442 731 (April 4, 1996) pp17-18.
RN42443 743 (September 19, 1996) pp19-20.
RN42444 744 (October 3, 1996) pp19-21.
RN42445 745 (October 17, 1996) pp27-28.
RN42446 748 (November 28, 1996) pp25-26.
RN42447 749 (December 12, 1996) pp19-20.
YOW, DAVID
RN42448 716 (September 7, 1995) pp13-14.
RN42449 736 (June 13, 1996) pp19-20.
YSEULT, SEAN
RN42450 715 (August 24, 1995) pp23,25.

Z

Z Z TOP
RN42451 631 (May 28, 1992) pp9,11.
RN42452 647 (January 7, 1993) pp9,11.
RN42453 670 (November 25, 1993) pp37-38.
ZANDER, ROBIN
RN42454 626 (March 19, 1992) pp11,13.
RN42455 723 (December 14, 1995) pp27-28.

ZAP MAMA
RN42456 708 (May 18, 1995) pp17-18.
ZAPATA, MIA
RN42457 666 (September 30, 1993) pp27-28.
RN42458 689 (August 25, 1994) pp15-16.
RN42459 706 (April 20, 1995) pp15-17.
ZAPPA, FRANK
RN42460 727 (February 8, 1996) pp12-13.
ZASKY, JASON
RN42461 702 (February 23, 1995) pp19-20.
ZELENKO, MIKE
RN42462 712-713 (July 13, 1995) pp25-26.
ZEVON, WARREN
RN42463 638 (September 3, 1992) pp9,11.
ZOMBIE, ROB
RN42464 714 (August 10, 1995) pp15-17.
RN42465 719 (October 19, 1995) pp15-16.
ZORN, JOHN
RN42466 742 (September 5, 1996) pp20-21.
ZUCKERT, ADAM
RN42467 743 (September 19, 1996) pp19-20.

Record Reviews

A

ABANA BA NASERY
Nursery Boys Go Ahead
RR10382 645-646 (December 10, 1992) p187. (McLane, Daisann)
ABBA
Gold
RR10383 672-673 (December 23, 1993) p156. (Evans, Paul)
Thank You For The Music
RR10384 714 (August 10, 1995) p59. (Considine, J. D.)
ABDUL, PAULA
Head Over Heals
RR10385 715 (August 24, 1995) p102. (Gardner, Elysa)
ABERCROMBIE, JOHN
Witchcraft
RR10386 711 (June 29, 1995) p44. (Futterman, Steve)
ABYSSINIANS
Satta Massagana
RR10387 676 (February 24, 1994) p42. (McLane, Daisann)
AC-DC
Ballbreaker
RR10388 721 (November 16, 1995) p112. (Dunn, Jancee)
RR10389 724-725 (December 28, 1995) p125. (Fricke, David)
ACKER, KATHY
Pussy, King Of The Pirates
RR10390 729 (March 7, 1996) p50. (Kot, Greg)
ADAMS, BRYAN
Waking Up The Neighbours
RR10391 615 (October 17, 1991) pp92-93. (Hunter, James)
ADAMS, OLETA
Evolution
RR10392 671 (December 9, 1993) pp72-73. (Dyson, Michael Eric)
ADAMSON, BARRY
The Negro Inside Me
RR10393 665 (September 16, 1993) p72. (Helmore, Edward)
Oedipus Schmoedipus
RR10394 746 (October 31, 1996) p70. (Vincentelli, Elisabeth)
AEROSMITH
Get A Grip
RR10395 656 (May 13, 1993) pp103-104. (Coleman, Mark)
Pandora's Box
RR10396 619-620 (December 12, 1991) p177. (McLeese, Don)
AFGHAN WHIGS
Black Love
RR10397 730 (March 21, 1996) pp95-96. (Strauss, Neil)
Gentlemen
RR10398 674 (January 27, 1994) pp52,54. (Diehl, Matt)
AINTS
Ascension
RR10399 619-620 (December 12, 1991) p168. (Fricke, David)
S.L.S.Q.
RR10400 619-620 (December 12, 1991) p168. (Fricke, David)
AITKEN, LAUREL
The Long Hot Summer—Jamaican Ska 1963
RR10401 619-620 (December 12, 1991) p168. (Fricke, David)
The Original Skatalites And Laurel Aitken
RR10402 664 (September 2, 1993) p16. (Fricke, David)
ALDEN, HOWARD
Your Song
RR10403 711 (June 29, 1995) p44. (Futterman, Steve)
ALDEN, HOWARD (TRIO)
A Good Likeness
RR10404 659 (June 24, 1993) p84. (Futterman, Steve)
ALEXANDER, ARTHUR
Lonely Just Like Me
RR10404a 662 (August 5, 1993) p64. (Altman, Billy)
ALEXANDER, WILLIE
Willie Loco Boom Boom Ga Ga: 1975-1991
RR10405 625 (March 5, 1992) p70. (Fricke, David)
ALI, NAZAKAT
Salamat And Nazakat Ali
RR10406 628 (April 16, 1992) p85. (Fricke, David)
ALI, SALAMAT
Salamat And Nazakat Ali
RR10407 628 (April 16, 1992) p85. (Fricke, David)
ALICE IN CHAINS
Alice In Chains
RR10408 722 (November 30, 1995) pp63-64,66. (Wiederhorn, Jon)
Dirt
RR10409 645-646 (December 10, 1992) p179. (Coleman, Mark)
Jar Of Flies
RR10410 678 (March 24, 1994) p95. (Evans, Paul)
Unplugged
RR10411 744 (October 3, 1996) pp71-72. (Masuo, Sandy)
ALLAN, DAVE
Loud Lose And Savage
RR10412 716 (September 7, 1995) p73. (Fricke, David)
ALLEN, DEBORAH
Delta Dreamland
RR10413 656 (May 13, 1993) p110. (McLeese, Don)
ALLEN, TERRY
The Silent Majority
RR10414 662 (August 5, 1993) p67. (McLeese, Don)
ALLMAN BROTHERS
2nd Street
RR10415 711 (June 29, 1995) p45. (Swenson, John)
Where It All Begins
RR10416 686-687 (July 14, 1994) p104. (Evans, Paul)
A.L.T.
Stone Cold World
RR10417 676 (February 24, 1994) p59. (Santiago, Roberto)
ALTAMIRA BANDA SHOW
Altamira Banda Show
RR10418 626 (March 19, 1992) p95. (McLane, Daisann)
ALVIN, DAVE
Blue Blvd
RR10419 619-620 (December 12, 1991) p168. (Fricke, David)
King Of California
RR10420 686-687 (July 14, 1994) p104. (Evans, Paul)
AMERICAN MUSIC CLUB
Everclear
RR10421 619-620 (December 12, 1991) p187. (Fricke, David)
Mercury
RR10422 654 (April 15, 1993) p61. (O'Connor, Rob)
San Francisco
RR10423 696 (December 1, 1994) p122. (Ali, Lorraine)
AMOS, TORI
Boys For Pele
RR10424 727 (February 8, 1996) pp48-49. (McDonnell, Evelyn)
Little Earthquakes
RR10425 627 (April 2, 1992) p46. (Woodard, Josef)

Under The Pink
RR10426 676 (February 24, 1994) p59. (St. Leger, Marie Elsie)
RR10427 698-699 (December 29, 1994) p185. (Evans, Paul)
AMPS
Pacer
RR10428 723 (December 14, 1995) p82. (Appleford, Steve)
RR10429 724-725 (December 28, 1995) pp124-125. (Fricke, David)
ANDERSEN, ERIC
Danko-Fjeld-Andersen
RR10430 674 (January 27, 1994) p54. (Evans, Paul)
ANDERSON, JOHN
Solid Ground
RR10431 663 (August 19, 1993) p77. (McLeese, Don)
ANDERSON, LAURIE
Bright Red
RR10432 697 (December 15, 1994) p95. (Isler, Scott)
ANDERSON, PETE
Working Class
RR10433 693 (October 20, 1994) p150. (McLeese, Don)
ANDERSON, THOMAS
Blues For The Flying Dutchman
RR10434 653 (April 1, 1993) p54. (Jurek, Thom)
CX-9 (song)
RR10435 662 (August 5, 1993) p24. (DeCurtis, Anthony)
Uranium Road (song)
RR10436 662 (August 5, 1993) p24. (DeCurtis, Anthony)
ANDERSON, TOM
Alright It Was Frank
RR10437 677 (March 10, 1994) p65. (Evans, Paul)
ANGULO, MOISES
Fusion
RR10438 709 (June 1, 1995) p62. (McLane, Daisann)
ANONYMOUS 4
An English Ladymass
RR10439 662 (August 5, 1993) p24. (DeCurtis, Anthony)
ANT, ADAM
Wonderful
RR10440 706 (April 20, 1995) p80. (Evans, Paul)
ANTENNA
Hideout
RR10441 655 (April 29, 1993) p65. (George-Warren, Holly)
Sway
RR10442 618 (November 28, 1991) p96. (Evans, Paul)
ANTHRAX
Sound Of White Noise
RR10443 659 (June 24, 1993) p83. (Sinclair, Tom)
APACHE INDIAN
No Reservations
RR10444 672-673 (December 23, 1993) p163. (McLane, Daisann)
APARTMENTS
A Life Full Of Farewells
RR10445 711 (June 29, 1995) pp43,45. (O'Connor, Rob)
APHEX TWIN
I Care Because You Do
RR10446 707 (May 4, 1995) pp65,68. (Prince, David J.)
Selected Ambient Works Vol. II
RR10447 685 (June 30, 1994) p72. (Wiederhorn, Jon)
APPLES IN STEREO
Fun Trick Noisemaker
RR10448 750-751 (December 26, 1996) p192. (Fricke, David)
Science Faire
RR10449 750-751 (December 26, 1996) p192. (Fricke, David)
APRIL MARCH
Voo Doo Doll (song)
RR10450 667 (October 14, 1993) p121. (Fricke, David)
ARANBEE POP SYMPHONY ORCHESTRA
The Aranbee Pop Symphony Orchestra
RR10451 624 (February 20, 1992) p42. (McLeese, Don)
ARC ANGELS
Arc Angels
RR10452 634-635 (July 9, 1992) p107. (Evans, Paul)
ARCHER, TASMIN
Great Expectations
RR10453 659 (June 24, 1993) p83. (Smith, Danyel)
ARCHERS OF LOAF
Vee Vee
RR10454 704 (March 23, 1995) p125. (Evans, Paul)
ARENA, TINA
Chains (song)
RR10455 736 (June 13, 1996) p78. (Kenny, Glenn)
ARMSTRONG, FRANKIE
Let No One Deceive You: Songs Of Bertolt Brecht
RR10456 634-635 (July 9, 1992) p102. (Fricke, David)
ARMSTRONG, LOUIS
Portrait Of The Artist As A Young Man 1923-1934
RR10457 698-699 (December 29, 1994) p180. (Futterman, Steve)
ARNOLD, BILLY BOY
Back Where I Belong
RR10458 672-673 (December 23, 1993) p154. (Fricke, David)
ARRESTED DEVELOPMENT
3 Years, 5 Months And 2 Days In The Life Of...
RR10459 645-646 (December 10, 1992) p164. (Coleman, Mark)
Zingalamaduni
RR10460 685 (June 30, 1994) pp71-72. (White, Armond)
ARROWS
Loud Lose And Savage
RR10461 716 (September 7, 1995) p73. (Fricke, David)
ASA NISI MASA
Asa Nisi Masa
RR10463 716 (September 7, 1995) p73. (Fricke, David)
ASLEEP AT THE WHEEL
Tribute To The Music Of Bob Wills And The Texas Playboys
RR10464 672-673 (December 23, 1993) p158. (McLeese, Don)
ASTAIRE, FRED
Stepping Out
RR10465 692 (October 6, 1994) p89. (Futterman, Steve)
ATKINS, CHET
Chet Atkins: The RCA Years
RR10466 645-646 (December 10, 1992) p174. (McLeese, Don)
ATTAR, BACHIR
Apocalypse Across The Sky
RR10467 637 (August 20, 1992) p52. (Fricke, David)
The Next Dream
RR10468 660-661 (July 8, 1993) p113. (Fricke, David)
ATTAWAY, MURRAY
In Thrall
RR10469 662 (August 5, 1993) p64. (Okamoto, David)
AUTEURS
After Murder Park
RR10470 734 (May 16, 1996) p68. (Berger, Arion)
Now I'm A Cowboy
RR10471 684 (June 16, 1994) p106. (Evans, Paul)
AXIOM FUNK
Funkcronomicon
RR10472 712-713 (July 13, 1995) p108. (Fernando, S. H., Jr.)
AZTEC CAMERA
Dreamland
RR10473 666 (September 30, 1993) pp104,106. (Sarig, Roni)

B

B-52S
Good Stuff
RR10474 634-635 (July 9, 1992) p101. (Gardner, Elysa)
B-TRIBE
Fiesta Total
RR10475 689 (August 25, 1994) p92. (McLane, Daisann)
BABES IN TOYLAND
Nemesisters
RR10476 709 (June 1, 1995) p64. (Evans, Paul)
BABYFACE
For The Cool In You
RR10477 668 (October 28, 1993) p76. (Toure)
BAD BRAINS
God Of Love
RR10478 710 (June 15, 1995) p81. (Kot, Greg)
Rise
RR10479 660-661 (July 8, 1993) p20. (Fricke, David)
BAD COMPANY
Company Of Strangers
RR10480 715 (August 24, 1995) p104. (Darzin, Daina)
BAD LIVERS
Horses In The Mine
RR10481 683 (June 2, 1994) p70. (McLeese, Don)
BAD RELIGION
The Gray Race
RR10482 729 (March 7, 1996) p48. (Appleford, Steve)
Stranger Than Fiction
RR10483 694 (November 3, 1994) pp98,100. (Kot, Greg)
BAD SEEDS
Henry's Dream
RR10484 636 (August 6, 1992) p57. (George-Warren, Holly)
Let Love In
RR10485 684 (June 16, 1994) p110. (O'Connor, Rob)
Murder Ballads
RR10486 730 (March 21, 1996) p96. (Van Parys, Bill)
BADALAMENTI, ANGELO
Booth And The Bad Angel
RR10487 745 (October 17, 1996) pp134,136. (Coleman, Mark)
BAERWALD, DAVID
Triage
RR10488 653 (April 1, 1993) p54. (Wright, Christian)
BAEZ, JOAN
Play Me Backwards
RR10489 648 (January 21, 1993) p49. (Holden, Stephen)
Rare, Live And Classic
RR10490 675 (February 10, 1994) p43. (Isler, Scott)
BAHIA BLACK
Ritual Beating System
RR10491 629 (April 30, 1992) p59. (McLane, Daisann)
BAILEY, PHILIP
Philip Bailey
RR10492 691 (September 22, 1994) p97. (Dyson, Michael Eric)
BAIRD, DAN
Love Songs For The Hearing Impaired
RR10493 648 (January 21, 1993) p49. (Coleman, Mark)
BAKER, ANITA
Rhythm Of Love
RR10494 702 (February 23, 1995) p74. (Dyson, Michael Eric)
BAKER, CHET
The Pacific Jazz Years
RR10495 698-699 (December 29, 1994) p180. (Futterman, Steve)
BAKER, GINGER
Going Back Home
RR10496 693 (October 20, 1994) pp148,150. (Futterman, Steve)
BALL, DAVID
Thinkin' Problem
RR10497 683 (June 2, 1994) p70. (McLeese, Don)
BALL, MARCIA
Blue House
RR10498 701 (February 9, 1995) p57. (McLeese, Don)
BAND
Across The Great Divide
RR10499 698-699 (December 29, 1994) p188. (Considine, J. D.)
Basement Tapes
RR10500 689 (August 25, 1994) p34. (Barron, Chris)
Jericho
RR10501 670 (November 25, 1993) p28. (Dylan, Jakob)
RR10502 676 (February 24, 1994) pp57,59. (Walls, Richard C.)
BAND OF SUSANS
Here Comes Success
RR10503 708 (May 18, 1995) p90. (Evans, Paul)
Veil
RR10504 664 (September 2, 1993) p62. (Palmer, Robert)
BAR-KAYS
The Best Of The Bar-Kays
RR10505 667 (October 14, 1993) p118. (Toure)
BARDO POND
Amanita
RR10506 750-751 (December 26, 1996) p198.
BARLOW, LOUIS
Winning Losers
RR10507 696 (December 1, 1994) pp126-127. (Kemp, Mark)
BARNEY
Barney's Favorites Vol. 1
RR10508 669 (November 11, 1993) p74. (Eddy, Chuck)
BARONE, RICHARD
Clouds Over Eden
RR10509 675 (February 10, 1994) p45. (O'Connor, Rob)
BARRETT, SYD
Crazy Diamond
RR10510 406 (June 16, 1994) pp105-106. (Graves, Tom)
Opel
RR10511 679 (April 7, 1994) p30. (Hoon, Shannon)
BARRON, KENNY
Lemuria-Seascape
RR10512 623 (February 6, 1992) p80. (Futterman, Steve)
BASEHEAD
Not In Kansas Anymore
RR10513 656 (May 13, 1993) p108. (Smith, Danyel)
Play With Toys
RR10514 634-635 (July 9, 1992) pp102,104. (Powell, Kevin)
BASH AND POP
Friday Night Is Killing Me
RR10515 649 (February 4, 1993) p64. (Mirkin, Steven)
BEACH BOYS
Good Vibrations
RR10516 663 (August 19, 1993) pp73-74. (Milward, John)
BEACON HILL BILLIES
More Songs Of Love And Murder
RR10517 691 (September 22, 1994) p97. (McLeese, Don)
BEASTIE BOYS
Check Your Head
RR10518 633 (June 25, 1992) p41. (Powell, Kevin)
Ill Communication
RR10519 683 (June 2, 1994) pp68-69. (Diehl, Matt)
Some Old Bullshit
RR10520 683 (June 2, 1994) pp68-69. (Diehl, Matt)
BEAT
The Beat
RR10521 690 (September 8, 1994) p78. (Evans, Paul)
BEAT HAPPENING
You Turn Me On

RR10522 649 (February 4, 1993) pp68-69. (Azerrad, Michael)
BEATLES
Anthology 2
RR10523 731 (April 4, 1996) pp59-60. (McCulley, Jerry)
Anthology 3
RR10524 749 (December 12, 1996) p84. (Puterbaugh, Parke)
The Beatles Compact Discs Singles Collection
RR10525 645-646 (December 10, 1992) p170. (Considine, J. D.)
Compact Disc EP Collection
RR10526 636 (August 6, 1992) p59. (Puterbaugh, Parke)
I Want To Hold Your Hand (song)
RR10527 675 (February 10, 1994) p18. (D'Arby, Terence Trent)
Live At The BBC
RR10528 700 (January 26, 1995) pp59-60. (DeCurtis, Anthony)
She Loves You (song)
RR10529 675 (February 10, 1994) p18. (D'Arby, Terence Trent)
BEAU BRUMMELS
San Fran Sessions
RR10530 750-751 (December 26, 1996) pp190,192.
BEAVIS & BUTT-HEAD
The Beavis And Butt-Head Experience
RR10531 671 (December 9, 1993) p66. (Sinclair, Tom)
BECK
Mellow Gold
RR10532 679 (April 7, 1994) p72. (Azerrad, Michael)
RR10533 698-699 (December 29, 1994) pp190-191. (Evans, Paul)
Odelay
RR10534 736 (June 13, 1996) pp77-78. (Kemp, Mark)
RR10535 750-751 (December 26, 1996) p184.
One Foot In The Grave
RR10536 698-699 (December 29, 1994) p174. (Fricke, David)
BECK, JEFF
Beckology
RR10537 619-620 (December 12, 1991) p177. (McLeese, Don)
Crazy Legs
RR10538 665 (September 16, 1993) pp70,72. (Milward, John)
BEIRACH, RICHIE
Convergence
RR10539 618 (November 28, 1991) p96. (Futterman, Steve)
BELL BIV DEVOE
Hootie Mack
RR10540 663 (August 19, 1993) pp74,76. (Toure)
BELL, CHRIS
I Am The Cosmos
RR10541 626 (March 19, 1992) pp87-88. (Puterbaugh, Parke)
BELL, VINCE
Phoenix
RR10542 686-687 (July 14, 1994) p107. (McLeese, Don)
BELLY
Star
RR10543 654 (April 15, 1993) p64. (Ransom, Kevin)
BENATAR, PAT
Gravity's Rainbow
RR10544 666 (September 30, 1993) p108. (Odintz, Andrea)
BENEDICTINE MONKS OF SANTO DOMINGO DE SILOS
Chant
RR10545 684 (June 16, 1994) p106. (Evans, Paul)
BENNETT, TONY
MTV Unplugged
RR10546 689 (August 25, 1994) p90. (Evans, Paul)
Steppin' Out
RR10547 672-673 (December 23, 1993) p151. (Evans, Paul)
BERG, MATRACA
The Speed Of Grace
RR10548 682 (May 19, 1994) pp100,102. (McLeese, Don)
BERRYHILL, CINDY LEE
Garage Orchestra
RR10549 689 (August 25, 1994) p90. (Evans, Paul)
BETTER THAN EZRA
Friction, Baby
RR10550 743 (September 19, 1996) p82. (Gardner, Elysa)
BETTIE SERVEERT
Lamprey
RR10551 702 (February 23, 1995) p77. (Flaum, Eric)
Palomine
RR10552 655 (April 29, 1993) p61. (Ali, Lorraine)
BHATT, V. M.
A Meeting By The River
RR10553 656 (May 13, 1993) pp108,110. (Woodard, Josef)
BICKERT, ED
Sketches
RR10554 678 (March 24, 1994) p97. (Futterman, Steve)
BIG BLACK
The Rich Man's Eight Track Tape
RR10555 649 (February 4, 1993) pp66,68. (Kot, Greg)
BIG STAR
Big Star Live
RR10556 626 (March 19, 1992) pp87-88. (Puterbaugh, Parke)
Columbia
RR10557 670 (November 25, 1993) p117. (George-Warren, Holly)
No. 1 Record
RR10558 645-646 (December 10, 1992) p180. (Coleman, Mark)
Radio City
RR10559 645-646 (December 10, 1992) p180. (Coleman, Mark)
Third-Sister Lovers
RR10560 626 (March 19, 1992) pp87-88. (Puterbaugh, Parke)
BIG TOWN PLAYBOYS
Crazy Legs
RR10561 665 (September 16, 1993) pp70,72. (Milward, John)
BIG YOUTH
Dreadlocks Dread
RR10562 676 (February 24, 1994) p42. (McLane, Daisann)
BIKINI KILL
Bikini Kill
RR10563 649 (February 4, 1993) p68. (Eddy, Chuck)
Reject All American
RR10564 734 (May 16, 1996) p68. (Kemp, Mark)
Yeah Yeah Yeah Yeah
RR10565 666 (September 30, 1993) p104. (McDonnell, Evelyn)
BILLY PILGRIM
Billy Pilgrim
RR10566 683 (June 2, 1994) p72. (Dean, Chuck)
BLACK CATS
Fever
RR10567 689 (August 25, 1994) p92. (McLane, Daisann)
BLACK, CLINT
No Time To Kill
RR10567a 666 (September 30, 1993) p105. (McLeese, Don)
BLACK CROWES
Amorica
RR10568 694 (November 3, 1994) pp95-96. (Evans, Paul)
The Southern Harmony And Musical Companion
RR10569 633 (June 25, 1992) pp40-41. (Curtis, Gregory)
Three Snakes And One Charm
RR10570 736 (June 13, 1996) p53. (Wiederhorn, Jon)
RR10571 740 (August 8, 1996) p60. (Huffman, Eddie)
BLACK, FRANK
Frank Black
RR10571a 653 (April 1, 1993) p54. (Wright, Christian)

Teenager Of The Year
RR10571b 689 (August 25, 1994) p89. (Weisel, Al)
BLACK GRAPE
It's Great When You're Straight...Yeah
RR10572 721 (November 16, 1995) pp111-112. (Cohen, Jason)
BLACK MOON
Enta Da Stage
RR10573 679 (April 7, 1994) p73. (Toure)
BLACK ROCK COALITION
The History Of Our Future
RR10574 617 (November 14, 1991) pp173,177. (Fricke, David)
BLACK SABBATH
Forbidden
RR10575 715 (August 24, 1995) p104. (Darzin, Daina)
BLACK SHEEP
Non-Fiction
RR10576 701 (February 9, 1995) pp55-56. (Toure)
BLACK STALIN
Rebellion
RR10577 680 (April 21, 1994) p90. (McLane, Daisann)
Roots Rock Soca
RR10578 626 (March 19, 1992) p95. (McLane, Daisann)
BLACK UHURU
Anthem
RR10579 676 (February 24, 1994) p42. (McLane, Daisann)
Liberations
RR10580 672-673 (December 23, 1993) p163. (McLane, Daisann)
RR10581-83 Numbers not assigned.
BLACKSTREET
Another Level
RR10584 750-751 (December 26, 1996) p186.
BLACKWELL, ED
What It Is?
RR10585 679 (April 7, 1994) p74. (McLeod, Rodd)
BLADES, RUBEN
Tras La Tormenta
RR10586 709 (June 1, 1995) p62. (McLane, Daisann)
BLAKELY, ART
The Complete Blue Note Recordings Of Art Blakely's 1960 Jazz Messengers
RR10587 645-646 (December 10, 1992) p180. (Futterman, Steve)
The History Of Art Blakely And The Jazz Messengers
RR10588 645-646 (December 10, 1992) p180. (Futterman, Steve)
BLANCHARD, TERENCE
Terence Blanchard
RR10589 618 (November 28, 1991) p96. (Futterman, Steve)
BLEGVAD, PETER
Just Woke Up
RR10590 728 (February 22, 1996) p62. (DeRogatis, Jim)
BLESSID UNION OF SOULS
Home
RR10591 709 (June 1, 1995) p64. (Evans, Paul)
BLEY, CARLA
Go Together
RR10592 665 (September 16, 1993) p67. (Futterman, Steve)
BLEY, PAUL
Fusion
RR10593 631 (May 28, 1992) p61. (Futterman, Steve)
Memoirs
RR10594 642 (October 29, 1992) p75. (Futterman, Steve)
Thesis
RR10595 631 (May 28, 1992) p61. (Futterman, Steve)
BLIGE, MARY J.
What's The 411?
RR10596 645-646 (December 10, 1992) p166. (Coleman, Mark)
BLIND FAITH
Blind Faith
RR10597 655 (April 29, 1993) p42. (Futterman, Steve)
BLIND MELON
Blind Melon
RR10598 672-673 (December 23, 1993) pp159,162. (Evans, Paul)
Soup
RR10599 716 (September 7, 1995) p72. (Drozdowski, Ted)
BLK
Black 47
RR10600 626 (March 19, 1992) p93. (Manning, Kara)
BLONDIE
The Platinum Collection
RR10601 698-699 (December 29, 1994) p188. (Considine, J. D.)
BLONDY, ALPHA
Live Au Zenith
RR10602 680 (April 21, 1994) p90. (McLane, Daisann)
BLOOD CIRCUS
Primal Rock Therapy
RR10603 648 (January 21, 1993) pp48-49. (Alden, Grant)
BLOOD OF ABRAHAM
Future Profits
RR10604 675 (February 10, 1994) pp43-44. (Diehl, Matt)
BLOOD ORANGES
The Crying Tree
RR10605 685 (June 30, 1994) p74. (Mirkin, Steven)
BLOOM, LUKA
The Acoustic Motorbike
RR10606 623 (February 6, 1992) pp73,77. (Gardner, Elysa)
BLUE AEROPLANES
Beatsongs
RR10607 619-620 (December 12, 1991) p187. (Fricke, David)
BLUE NILE
Peace At Last
RR10608 737 (June 27, 1996) p56. (Diehl, Matt)
BLUE OYSTER CULT
Cult Classic
RR10609 701 (February 9, 1995) p59. (Diehl, Matt)
Workshop Of The Telescopes
RR10610 724-725 (December 28, 1995) p122. (Coleman, Mark)
BLUES EXPLOSION
Now I Got Worry
RR10611 744 (October 3, 1996) p72. (Diehl, Matt)
BLUES MOB
Bloodlines
RR10612 698-699 (December 29, 1994) p174. (Fricke, David)
BLUES RODEO
Lost Together
RR10613 648 (January 21, 1993) p52. (Milward, John)
BLUES TRAVELER
Four
RR10614 724-725 (December 28, 1995) p129. (Fricke, David)
Live From The Fall
RR10615 741 (August 22, 1996) p96. (Puterbaugh, Parke)
BLUETONES
Expecting To Fly
RR10616 742 (September 5, 1996) p62. (Sinclair, David)
BLUR
The Great Escape
RR10617 724-725 (December 28, 1995) pp120,124. (Fricke, David)
Parklife
RR10618 685 (June 30, 1994) p73. (Evans, Paul)
RR10619 698-699 (December 29, 1994) pp185,190. (Evans, Paul)

BODEANS
Go Slow Down
RR10620 677 (March 10, 1994) p64. (Jurek, Thom)
BODY COUNT
Born Dead
RR10621 694 (November 3, 1994) p98. (Evans, Paul)
BOLLIN, ZUZU
Texas Bluesman
RR10622 624 (February 20, 1992) pp42,45. (Santelli, Robert)
BOMB THE BASS
Clear
RR10623 732 (April 18, 1996) p69. (Palmer, Tamara)
BON JOVI
Keep The Faith
RR10624 645-646 (December 10, 1992) pp168-169. (Coleman, Mark)
These Days
RR10625 711 (June 29, 1995) p42. (Darzin, Daina)
BONE THUGS-N-HARMONY
E. 1999 Eternal
RR10626 720 (November 2, 1995) pp69-70. (Fernando, S. H., Jr.)
BONNER, JOSEPH
Impressions Of Copenhagen
RR10627 645-646 (December 10, 1992) p177. (Fricke, David)
RR10628 Number not assigned.
BOOKER, CEDELLA MARLEY
Smilin' Island Of Song
RR10629 650 (February 18, 1993) p59. (McLane, Daisann)
BOOKER, JAMES
Minute Waltz (song)
RR10630 666 (September 30, 1993) p18. (Wild, David)
BOOKER T & THE M.G.'S
That's The Way It Should Be
RR10630a 693 (October 20, 1994) p148. (Milward, John)
BOOTH, TIM
Booth And The Bad Angel
RR10631 745 (October 17, 1996) pp134,136. (Coleman, Mark)
BOOTSY'S NEW RUBBER BAND
Blasters Of The Universe
RR10632 693 (October 20, 1994) pp147-148. (Fernando, S. H., Jr.)
BOREDOMS
Chocolate Synthesizer
RR10633 712-713 (July 13, 1995) p111. (Wiederhorn, Jon)
BOSS HOG
Boss Hog
RR10634 721 (November 16, 1995) p113. (O'Connor, Rob)
BOSTON
Walk On
RR10635 689 (August 25, 1994) p90. (Evans, Paul)
BOTTLE ROCKETS
The Brooklyn Side
RR10636 719 (October 19, 1995) p150. (Kemp, Mark)
BOUKMAN EKSPERYANS
Kalfou Danjere
RR10637 645-646 (December 10, 1992) p187. (McLane, Daisann)
Libete
RR10638 707 (May 4, 1995) p68. (St. Leger, Marie Elsie)
Vodou Adjae
RR10639 626 (March 19, 1992) p95. (McLane, Daisann)
BOWIE, DAVID
Black Tie White Noise
RR10640 655 (April 29, 1993) pp59,61. (Evans, Paul)
Bowie: The Singles 1969 To 1993
RR10641 672-673 (December 23, 1993) p148. (Considine, J. D.)
Hunky Dory
RR10642 680 (April 21, 1994) p21. (Hutchence, Michael)
Outside
RR10643 719 (October 19, 1995) p148. (Fricke, David)
RR10644 724-725 (December 28, 1995) p126. (Fricke, David)
Santa Monica '72
RR10645 706 (April 20, 1995) p72. (Fricke, David)
BOX TOPS
Soul Deep
RR10646 750-751 (December 26, 1996) p189. (Coleman, Mark)
BOYS II MEN
II
RR10647 698-699 (December 29, 1994) p176. (Evans, Paul)
BR5-49
BR5-49
RR10648 748 (November 28, 1996) p132. (Coleman, Mark)
BRAGG, BILLY
Don't Try This At Home
RR10649 616 (October 31, 1991) p92. (Tannenbaum, Rob)
William Bloke
RR10650 743 (September 19, 1996) p84. (Moon, Tom)
BRAIN SURGEONS
Eponymous
RR10651 701 (February 9, 1995) p59. (Diehl, Matt)
BRAND NEW HEAVIES
Brother Sister
RR10652 679 (April 7, 1994) pp74,76. (St. Leger, Marie Elsie)
Heavy Rhyme Experience: Vol. 1
RR10653 639 (September 17, 1992) p94. (Ehrlich, Dimitri)
BRAXTON, TONI
Secrets
RR10654 750-751 (December 26, 1996) p190.
Toni Braxton
RR10655 670 (November 25, 1993) p114. (McAlley, John)
BREAD
Retrospective
RR10656 750-751 (December 26, 1996) p189. (Coleman, Mark)
BREEDERS
The Breeders' Last Splash
RR10657 665 (September 16, 1993) p17. (Mundy, Chris)
Last Splash
RR10658 667 (October 14, 1993) p116. (Rust, Ned)
RR10659 672-673 (December 23, 1993) p162. (Evans, Paul)
BRICKELL, EDIE
Picture Perfect Morning
RR10660 697 (December 15, 1994) pp97-98. (McAlley, John)
BRIGMAN, GEORGE
I Can Hear The Ants Dancin'
RR10661 706 (April 20, 1995) p72. (Fricke, David)
BRODSKY QUARTET
The Juliet Letters
RR10662 652 (March 18, 1993) pp39-40. (Gardner, Elysa)
BRONX STYLE BOB
Grandma's Ghost
RR10663 645-646 (December 10, 1992) pp182,184. (Coleman, Mark)
BROOKS AND DUNN
Hard Workin' Man
RR10664 656 (May 13, 1993) p107. (Drozdowski, Ted)
BROOKS, GARTH
The Chase
RR10665 645-646 (December 10, 1992) p184. (Coleman, Mark)
In Pieces
RR10666 667 (October 14, 1993) p114. (Evans, Paul)
Ropin' The Wind
RR10667 619-620 (December 12, 1991) p162. (Fricke, David)

BROOKS, HADDA
Time Was When
RR10668 729 (March 7, 1996) p50. (Himes, Geoffrey)
BROTHER PHELPS
Let Go
RR10669 666 (September 30, 1993) p105. (McLeese, Don)
BROWN, BOBBY
Bobby
RR10670 639 (September 17, 1992) pp90-91. (Considine, J. D.)
RR10671 645-646 (December 10, 1992) p168. (Coleman, Mark)
BROWN, CHARLES
Driftin' Blues
RR10672 636 (August 6, 1992) p66. (Considine, J. D.)
These Blues
RR10673 702 (February 23, 1995) p76. (St. Leger, Marie Elsie)
BROWN, GREG
Friend Of Mine
RR10674 669 (November 11, 1993) pp74,76. (Ransom, Kevin)
BROWN, JAMES
Love Power Peace: Live At The Olympia, Paris, 1971
RR10675 636 (August 6, 1992) p66. (Considine, J. D.)
The Payback
RR10676 648 (January 21, 1993) p50. (Considine, J. D.)
Star Time
RR10677 619-620 (December 12, 1991) p162. (Fricke, David)
RR10678 Number not assigned.
BROWN, JUNIOR
Guit With It
RR10679 666 (September 30, 1993) p105. (McLeese, Don)
Semi-crazy
RR10680 736 (June 13, 1996) p86. (Corcoran, Michael)
12 Shades Of Brown
RR10680a 666 (September 30, 1993) p105. (McLeese, Don)
BROWN, MARTY
Cryin', Lovin', Leavin'
RR10681 686-687 (July 14, 1994) p107. (McLeese, Don)
Wild Kentucky Skies
RR10682 660-661 (July 8, 1993) p116. (McLeese, Don)
BROWNE, JACKSON
I'm Alive
RR10683 669 (November 11, 1993) p74. (Manning, Kara)
RR10684 672-673 (December 23, 1993) p162. (Evans, Paul)
Looking East
RR10685 729 (March 7, 1996) pp48,50. (Gardner, Elysa)
BRUBECK, DAVE
Time Signatures
RR10686 672-673 (December 23, 1993) p164. (Futterman, Steve)
BRUCE, JACK
Cities Of The Heart
RR10687 682 (May 19, 1994) p103. (Evans, Paul)
Monkjack
RR10688 720 (November 2, 1995) p69. (Fricke, David)
BRUCE, LENNY
Lenny Bruce Originals: Volume 1
RR10689 627 (April 2, 1992) p46. (Evans, Paul)
Lenny Bruce Originals: Volume 2
RR10690 627 (April 2, 1992) p46. (Evans, Paul)
BRUTON, STEPHEN
What It Is
RR10691 663 (August 19, 1993) p77. (McLeese, Don)
BUCKINGHAM, LINDSEY
Out Of The Cradle
RR10692 634-635 (July 9, 1992) pp99-100. (Considine, J. D.)
RR10693 645-646 (December 10, 1992) p169. (Coleman, Mark)
BUCKLEY, JEFF
Grace
RR10694 694 (November 3, 1994) p101. (Zacharek, Stephanie)
Live At Sin-e
RR10695 677 (March 10, 1994) p65. (Evans, Paul)
BUKEM, L. T. J.
Logical Progression
RR10696 744 (October 3, 1996) p74. (Micallef, Ken)
BULL, SANDY
Vehicles
RR10697 619-620 (December 12, 1991) p168. (Fricke, David)
BURNETT, T-BONE
The Criminal Under My Own Hat
RR10698 638 (September 3, 1992) pp67-68. (Milward, John)
BURNING SPEAR
Garvey's Ghost
RR10699 676 (February 24, 1994) p42. (McLane, Daisann)
Marcus Garvey
RR10700 676 (February 24, 1994) p42. (McLane, Daisann)
BURNSIDE, R. L.
A Ass Pocket Of Whiskey
RR10701 741 (August 22, 1996) p100. (Kemp, Mark)
Too Bad Jim
RR10702 690 (September 8, 1994) p80. (Santelli, Robert)
BURROUGHS, WILLIAM
The Priest, They Called Him
RR10703 670 (November 25, 1993) p116. (Weisel, Al)
Spare Ass Annie And Other Tales
RR10704 670 (November 25, 1993) p116. (Weisel, Al)
BUSH
Razorblade Suitcase
RR10705 749 (December 12, 1996) p84. (Diehl, Matt)
BUSH, KATE
The Red Shoes
RR10706 670 (November 25, 1993) p120. (Walls, Richard C.)
BUSTA RHYMES
The Coming
RR10707 733 (May 2, 1996) p54. (Berman, Eric)
BUTTER 08
Butter
RR10708 747 (November 14, 1996) p116. (Brackett, Nathan)
BUTTERFIELD, PAUL
East-West Live
RR10709 748 (November 28, 1996) p136. (Futterman, Steve)
Strawberry Jam
RR10710 710 (June 15, 1995) pp81,83. (Evans, Paul)
BUTTHOLE SURFERS
Electriclarryland
RR10711 750-751 (December 26, 1996) p190.
Independent Worm Saloon
RR10712 658 (June 10, 1993) p70. (Robbins, Ira)
BUZZCOCKS
Trade Test Transmission
RR10713 667 (October 14, 1993) p121. (Fricke, David)
BYRD, BOBBY
Bobby Byrd Got Soul
RR10714 718 (October 5, 1995) pp70,73. (Torres, Richard)
BYRNE, DAVID
David Byrne
RR10715 686-687 (July 14, 1994) p110. (Wright, Christian)
Uh-Oh
RR10716 626 (March 19, 1992) p89. (Woodard, Josef)
BYRON, DON
Tuskegee Experiments
RR10717 631 (May 28, 1992) p61. (Futterman, Steve)

C

CAIFANES
El Nervio Del Volcan
RR10718 696 (December 1, 1994) p122. (Morales, Ed)
CAKE LIKE
Delicious
RR10719 702 (February 23, 1995) pp76-77. (Azerrad, Michael)
CALE, J. J.
Number 10
RR10720 647 (January 7, 1993) p54. (McLeese, Don)
CALE, JOHN
Last Day On Earth
RR10721 700 (January 26, 1995) p61. (McLeese, Don)
Seducing Down The Door
RR10722 700 (January 26, 1995) p61. (McLeese, Don)
CAMEO
The Best Of Cameo
RR10723 667 (October 14, 1993) p118. (Toure)
CAMPBELL, JOHN
Howlin Mercy
RR10724 653 (April 1, 1993) pp53-54. (Milward, John)
CAMPBELL, SARAH ELIZABETH
Running With You
RR10725 679 (April 7, 1994) p77. (McLeese, Don)
CAN
Cannibalism 1
RR10726 724-725 (December 28, 1995) p122. (Coleman, Mark)
The Peel Sessions
RR10727 736 (June 13, 1996) p85. (Fricke, David)
Soundtracks
RR10728 724-725 (December 28, 1995) p122. (Coleman, Mark)
CANDLEBOX
Lucy
RR10729 720 (November 2, 1995) p70. (Eddy, Chuck)
CAPTAIN BEEFHEART
I May Be Hungry But I Sure Ain't Weird
RR10730 639 (September 17, 1992) p96. (Fricke, David)
CARCASS
Heartwork
RR10731 681 (May 5, 1994) p52. (Darzin,Daina)
CARDIGANS
First Band On The Moon
RR10732 747 (November 14, 1996) pp112,114. (Cohen, Jason)
RR10732 747 (November 14, 1996) pp112,114. (Cohen, Jason)
CAREY, MARIAH
Emotions
RR10733 617 (November 14, 1991) pp170-171. (Tannenbaum, Rob)
Music Box
RR10734 668 (October 28, 1993) pp76,78. (Holden, Stephen)
CARLISLE, BELINDA
Live Your Life Be Free
RR10735 622 (January 23, 1992) pp44-45. (Kirk, Deborah)
CARPENTER, KAREN
Karen Carpenter
RR10736 746 (October 31, 1996) pp68,70. (Hardy, Ernest)
CARPENTER, MARY-CHAPIN
Come On Come On
RR10737 638 (September 3, 1992) p68. (Berger, Arion)
CARPENTERS
From The Top
RR10738 619-620 (December 12, 1991) p177. (McLeese, Don)
The Originals
RR10739 693 (October 20, 1994) p142. (Weisel, Al)
CARROLL, BARBARA
This Heart Of Mine
RR10740 692 (October 6, 1994) p89. (Futterman, Steve)
CARS
Just What I Needed
RR10741 724-725 (December 28, 1995) p122. (Coleman, Mark)
CARSON, LORI
Where It Goes
RR10742 708 (May 18, 1995) pp90,92. (Mirkin, Steve)
CARTER FAMILY
Anchored In Love
RR10743 675 (February 10, 1994) p46. (McLeese, Don)
My Clinch Mountain Home
RR10744 675 (February 10, 1994) p46. (McLeese, Don)
CARTER, BENNY
Harlem Renaissance
RR10745 642 (October 29, 1992) p75. (Futterman, Steve)
CARTER, CARLENE
Little Love Letters
RR10746 664 (September 2, 1993) p66. (O'Connor, Rob)
Unbreakable Heart (song)
RR10747 666 (September 30, 1993) p18. (Wild, David)
CARTER, JAMES
Conversin' With The Elders
RR10748 738-739 (July 11, 1996) p90. (Fine, Jason)
JC On The Set
RR10749 696 (December 1, 1994) p129. (Stern, Chip)
CASH, JOHNNY
American Recordings
RR10750 682 (May 19, 1994) pp97-98,100. (DeCurtis, Anthony)
RR10751 698-699 (December 29, 1994) p176. (Evans, Paul)
The Essential Johnny Cash
RR10752 629 (April 30, 1992) p57. (Considine, J. D.)
Unchained
RR10753 750-751 (December 26, 1996) p198.
CASH, ROSANNE
10 Song Demo
RR10754 733 (May 2, 1996) pp52,54. (Himes, Geoffrey)
The Wheel
RR10755 652 (March 18, 1993) p40. (Moon, Tom)
CATHERINE WHEEL
Happy Days
RR10756 710 (June 15, 1995) p80. (Drozdowski, Ted)
CAVE, NICK
Henry's Dream
RR10757 636 (August 6, 1992) p57. (George-Warren, Holly)
Let Love In
RR10758 684 (June 16, 1994) p110. (O'Connor, Rob)
Murder Ballads
RR10759 730 (March 21, 1996) p96. (Van Parys, Bill)
CELL
Slo-Blo
RR10760 650 (February 18, 1993) pp59-60. (Sinclair, Tom)
CHADBOURNE, EUGENE
Terror Has Some Strange Kinfolk
RR10761 667 (October 14, 1993) p121. (Fricke, David)
CHALOFF, SERGE
The Complete Serge Chaloff Sessions
RR10762 665 (September 16, 1993) p67. (Futterman, Steve)
CHAPMAN, TRACY
Matters Of The Heart
RR10763 630 (May 14, 1992) p103. (Holden, Stephen)
New Beginning
RR10764 721 (November 16, 1995) p111. (Torres, Richard)
CHARALAMBIDES

Union
RR10765 684 (June 16, 1994) p24. (Moore, Thurston)
CHARLATANS UK
Between 10th And 11th
RR10766 634-635 (July 9, 1992) p105. (O'Connor, Rob)
CHARLES, RAY
Berlin, 1962
RR10767 740 (August 8, 1996) p62. (Fricke, David)
The Birth Of Soul
RR10768 619-620 (December 12, 1991) p177. (McLeese, Don)
My World
RR10769 656 (May 13, 1993) p110. (Holden, Stephen)
CHEAP TRICK
Sex, America, Cheap Trick
RR10770 746 (October 31, 1996) p68. (Fricke, David)
Woke Up With A Monster
RR10771 683 (June 2, 1994) p69. (Sinclair, Tom)
CHEATHAM, DOC
The Eighty Seven Years Of Doc Cheatham
RR10772 671 (December 9, 1993) p70. (Futterman, Steve)
CHERRY, DON
Complete Communion
RR10773 665 (September 16, 1993) p67. (Futterman, Steve)
Symphony For Improvisors
RR10774 665 (September 16, 1993) p67. (Futterman, Steve)
Where Is Brooklyn?
RR10775 665 (September 16, 1993) p67. (Futterman, Steve)
CHERRY, NENEH
Homebrew
RR10776 644 (November 26, 1992) pp69-70. (Coleman, Mark)
CHESTERFIELD KINGS
Let's Go Get Stoned
RR10777 684 (June 16, 1994) p110. (Fricke, David)
CHESTNUTT, MARK
What A Way To Live
RR10778 691 (September 22, 1994) p97. (McLeese, Don)
CHESTNUTT, VIC
About To Choke
RR10779 749 (December 12, 1996) p86. (Robbins, Ira)
CHIC
Chic-ism
RR10780 626 (March 19, 1992) pp89,92. (Powell, Kevin)
Dance, Dance, Dance
RR10781 624 (February 20, 1992) p42. (McLeese, Don)
Greatest Hits
RR10782 682 (May 19, 1994) p21. (Queen Latifah)
CHICAGO
Group Portrait
RR10783 619-620 (December 12, 1991) p177. (McLeese, Don)
CHICO SCIENCE AND NACAO ZUMBI
Da Lama Ao Caos
RR10784 698-699 (December 29, 1994) p182. (McLane, Daisann)
CHIEFTAINS
The Bells Of Dublin
RR10785 619-620 (December 12, 1991) p189. (Fricke, David)
An Irish Evening
RR10786 625 (March 5, 1992) p72. (Swenson, John)
The Long Black Veil
RR10787 701 (February 9, 1995) pp56-57. (Swenson, John)
CHILDS, TONI
The Woman's Boat
RR10788 686-687 (July 14, 1994) p104. (Evans, Paul)
CHILLS
Soft Bomb
RR10789 638 (September 3, 1992) p68. (McDonnell, Evelyn)
CHINO XL
Here To Save You All
RR10790 735 (May 30, 1996) p50. (Hardy, Ernest)
CHOICE
Stick-N-Moove
RR10791 631 (May 28, 1992) p55. (Marlowe, Ann)
CHURCH
Priest = Aura
RR10792 628 (April 16, 1992) p84. (Robbins, Ira)
Sometime Anywhere
RR10793 693 (October 20, 1994) p151. (Ahearn, Kim)
CIBO MATTO
Viva! La Woman
RR10794 727 (February 8, 1996) pp50-51. (Weisel, Al)
RR10795-7 Numbers not assigned.
CLAPTON, ERIC
Bluesbreakers With Eric Clapton
RR10798 655 (April 29, 1993) p42. (Futterman, Steve)
Crossroads 2
RR10799 731 (April 4, 1996) p61. (Fricke, David)
Eric Clapton
RR10800 655 (April 29, 1993) p42. (Futterman, Steve)
461 Ocean Boulevard
RR10800a 655 (April 29, 1993) p42. (Futterman, Steve)
From The Cradle
RR10801 693 (October 20, 1994) pp141-142. (Fricke, David)
RR10802 698-699 (December 29, 1994) pp180-181. (Evans, Paul)
Journeyman
RR10803 655 (April 29, 1993) p42. (Futterman, Steve)
Just One Night
RR10804 655 (April 29, 1993) p42. (Futterman, Steve)
Money And Cigarettes
RR10805 655 (April 29, 1993) p42. (Futterman, Steve)
Rush
RR10806 655 (April 29, 1993) p42. (Futterman, Steve)
Slowhand
RR10807 655 (April 29, 1993) p42. (Futterman, Steve)
24 Nights
RR10807a 616 (October 31, 1991) p91. (Woodard, Josef)
RR10807b 619-620 (December 12, 1991) p174. (Fricke, David)
Unplugged
RR10808 645-646 (December 10, 1992) pp180,182. (Coleman, Mark)
RR10809 655 (April 29, 1993) p42. (Futterman, Steve)
CLARK, GLEN
Looking For A Connection
RR10810 686-687 (July 14, 1994) p107. (McLeese, Don)
CLARK, GUY
Boats To Build
RR10811 647 (January 7, 1993) p54. (McLeese, Don)
CLARKE, GILBEY
Pawn Shop Guitars
RR10812 689 (August 25, 1994) p90. (Evans, Paul)
CLASH
Clash On Broadway
RR10813 619-620 (December 12, 1991) p177. (McLeese, Don)
CLAY, JAMES
Cookin' At The Continental
RR10814 623 (February 6, 1992) p80. (Futterman, Steve)
CLAY, OTIS
I'll Treat You Right
RR10815 633 (June 25, 1992) p42. (Palmer, Robert)
Soul Man: Live In Japan
RR10816 624 (February 20, 1992) p42. (McLeese, Don)
CLEMENTS, VASSAR
Once In A While

RR10817 656 (May 13, 1993) p110. (McLeese, Don)
CLINE, PATSY
The Patsy Cline Collection
RR10818 619-620 (December 12, 1991) p177. (McLeese, Don)
CLINTON, GEORGE
Go Fer Yer Funk
RR10819 664 (September 2, 1993) p64. (Considine, J. D.)
Hey Man...Smell My Finger
RR10820 674 (January 27, 1994) p54. (Smith, Danyel)
Live—The Funkadelic Collection
RR10821 676 (February 24, 1994) p57. (Fricke, David)
'P' Is The Funk
RR10822 664 (September 2, 1993) p64. (Considine, J. D.)
T.A.P.O.A.F.O.M.
RR10823 736 (June 13, 1996) p51. (Wiederhorn, Jon)
RR10824 738-739 (July 11, 1996) p87. (Kemp, Mark)
RR10825 750-751 (December 26, 1996) p194.
CLINTON, ROGER
Nothing Good Comes Easy
RR10826 696 (December 1, 1994) p124. (Swenson, John)
COAL PORTERS
Rebels Without Applause (EP)
RR10827 628 (April 16, 1992) p85. (Fricke, David)
COASTERS
50 Coastin' Hits
RR10828 648 (January 21, 1993) p50. (Considine, J. D.)
COBAIN, KURT
The Priest, They Called Him
RR10829 670 (November 25, 1993) p116. (Weisel, Al)
COBRA VERDE
Viva La Muerte
RR10830 698-699 (December 29, 1994) p174. (Fricke, David)
COCKBURN, BRUCE
Christmas
RR10831 672-673 (December 23, 1993) p169. (Howard, Pete)
COCTEAU TWINS
Four-Calendar Cafe
RR10832 677 (March 10, 1994) pp64,66. (Drozdowski, Ted)
COHEN, LEONARD
The Future
RR10833 647 (January 7, 1993) p45. (Wright, Christian)
COLE, LLOYD
Bad Vibes
RR10834 693 (October 20, 1994) pp150-151. (McDonnell, Evelyn)
Don't Get Weird On Me, Babe
RR10835 623 (February 6, 1992) p83. (Drozdowski, Ted)
COLE, NAT KING
The Capitol Years
RR10836 645-646 (December 10, 1992) p180. (Futterman, Steve)
COLE, NATALIE
Take A Look
RR10837 664 (September 2, 1993) p61. (Gardner, Elysa)
COLEMAN, GEORGE
Convergence
RR10838 618 (November 28, 1991) p96. (Futterman, Steve)
James Williams Meets The Saxophone Masters
RR10839 653 (April 1, 1993) p53. (Futterman, Steve)
COLEMAN, ORNETTE
Beauty Is A Rare Thing
RR10840 672-673 (December 23, 1993) p164. (Futterman, Steve)
Tone Dialing
RR10841 723 (December 14, 1995) pp84,86. (Fricke, David)
COLEMAN, STEVE
Rhythm In Mind
RR10842 649 (February 4, 1993) p75. (Futterman, Steve)
COLLECTIVE SOUL
Collective Soul
RR10843 710 (June 15, 1995) p83. (Evans, Paul)
COLLINS, ALBERT
The Complete Imperial Recordings
RR10844 617 (November 14, 1991) pp172-173. (Palmer, Robert)
COLLINS, BOOTSY
Blasters Of The Universe
RR10845 693 (October 20, 1994) pp147-148. (Fernando, S. H., Jr.)
COLLINS, EDWYN
Gorgeous George
RR10846 719 (October 19, 1995) p153. (Micallef, Ken)
COLLINS, PHIL
Both Sides
RR10847 675 (February 10, 1994) p43. (McAlley, John)
COLON, WILLIE
Hecho En Puerto Rico
RR10848 670 (November 25, 1993) p108. (McLane, Daisann)
Tras La Tormenta
RR10849 709 (June 1, 1995) p62. (McLane, Daisann)
COLTRANE, JOHN
A John Coltrane Retrospective: The Impulse Years
RR10850 645-646 (December 10, 1992) p180. (Futterman, Steve)
Live In Seattle
RR10851 708 (May 18, 1995) pp87-88. (Fricke, David)
The Thelonious Monk Quartet Live At The Five Spot Featuring John Coltrane
RR10852 653 (April 1, 1993) p53. (Futterman, Steve)
COLVIN, SHAWN
Cover Girl
RR10853 697 (December 15, 1994) p98. (Manning, Kara)
Fat City
RR10854 647 (January 7, 1993) p47. (D'Erasmo, Stacey)
COME
Eleven: Eleven
RR10855 655 (April 29, 1993) p63. (Palmer, Robert)
Near Life Experience
RR10856 740 (August 8, 1996) p58. (Wiederhorn, Jon)
COMMON SENSE
Resurrection
RR10857 701 (February 9, 1995) pp55-56. (Toure)
CON FUNK SHUN
The Best Of Con Funk Shun
RR10858 667 (October 14, 1993) p118. (Toure)
CONCRETE BLONDE
Walking In London
RR10859 627 (April 2, 1992) pp45-46. (Jurek, Thom)
CONGOS
Heart Of The Congos
RR10860 730 (March 21, 1996) p98. (Fricke, David)
CONNELLY, CHRIS
Shipwreck
RR10861 703 (March 9, 1995) p66. (Evans, Paul)
CONRAD, TONY
Slapping Pythagoras
RR10862 716 (September 7, 1995) p73. (Fricke, David)
CONTINENTAL DRIFTERS
Continental Drifters
RR10863 698-699 (December 29, 1994) p182. (Evans, Paul)
COODER, RY
A Meeting By The River
RR10864 656 (May 13, 1993) pp108,110. (Woodard, Josef)
Rising Sons
RR10865 652 (March 18, 1993) p42. (Fricke, David)
COOKE, SAM
Sam Cooke's SAR Records Story 1959-1965
RR10866 696 (December 1, 1994) p121. (Palmer, Robert)

COOLIO
Gangsta's Paradise
RR10867 724-725 (December 28, 1995) p118. (Fricke, David)
It Takes A Thief
RR10868 689 (August 25, 1994) p88. (Toure)
COOPER, ALICE
The Last Temptation
RR10869 686-687 (July 14, 1994) p110. (Eddy, Chuck)
COPE, JULIAN
Autogeddon
RR10870 693 (October 20, 1994) p148. (Evans, Paul)
Floored Genius 2
RR10871 684 (June 16, 1994) p110. (Fricke, David)
Jehovahkill
RR10872 647 (January 7, 1993) p47. (O'Connor, Rob)
Peggy Suicide
RR10873 619-620 (December 12, 1991) p178. (Fricke, David)
COREA, CHICK
Play
RR10874 625 (March 5, 1992) p68. (Chambers, Gordon)
CORNERSHOP
Lock Stock & Double-Barrel (EP)
RR10875 664 (September 2, 1993) p16. (Fricke, David)
Woman's Gotta Have It
RR10876 724-725 (December 28, 1995) p125. (Fricke, David)
RR10877-8 Numbers not assigned.
COSTELLO, ELVIS
All This Useless Beauty
RR10879 735 (May 30, 1996) p49. (Farber, Jim)
Brutal Youth
RR10880 678 (March 24, 1994) p96. (O'Connor, Rob)
Get Happy!!
RR10881 682 (May 19, 1994) p100. (Considine, J. D.)
The Juliet Letters
RR10882 652 (March 18, 1993) pp39-40. (Gardner, Elysa)
Kojak Variety
RR10883 711 (June 29, 1995) p43. (Walls, Richard C.)
2 1
RR108883a 669 (November 11, 1993) p77. (Considine, J. D.)
Years
RR108883b 669 (November 11, 1993) p77. (Considine, J. D.)
COUNTING CROWS
August And Everything After
RR10884 668 (October 28, 1993) p76. (Jurek, Thom)
RR10885 672-673 (December 23, 1993) p153. (Evans, Paul)
Recovering The Satellites
RR10886 748 (November 28, 1996) p134. (DeCurtis, Anthony)
COUNTRY JOE AND THE FISH
Section 43 (song)
RR10887 720 (November 2, 1995) p69. (Fricke, David)
COVERDALE, DAVID
Coverdale-Page
RR10888 654 (April 15, 1993) p62. (Considine, J. D.)
COWBOY JUNKIES
Black Eyed Man
RR10889 623 (February 6, 1992) pp73,77. (Gardner, Elysa)
Pale Sun Crescent Moon
RR10890 677 (March 10, 1994) p66. (Zacharek, Stephanie)
COX FAMILY
I Know Who Holds Tomorrow
RR10891 675 (February 10, 1994) p46. (McLeese, Don)
COX, ANTHONY
Falling Man
RR10892 618 (November 28, 1991) p96. (Futterman, Steve)
CRAMPS
Flamejob
RR10893 703 (March 9, 1995) p66. (Evans, Paul)
CRANBERRIES
Everybody Else Is Doing It, So Why Can't We?
RR10894 672-673 (December 23, 1993) pp146,151. (Evans, Paul)
No Need To Argue
RR10895 697 (December 15, 1994) p94. (Stenger, Wif)
To The Faithful Departed
RR10896 735 (May 30, 1996) pp46,48. (Ali, Lorraine)
CRANES
Wings Of Joy
RR10897 627 (April 2, 1992) p46. (Berger, Arion)
CRAY, ROBERT
I Was Warned
RR10898 642 (October 29, 1992) pp70-71. (McGee, David)
Shame + A Sin
RR10899 669 (November 11, 1993) p73. (Milward, John)
RR10899 669 (November 11, 1993) p73. (Milward, John)
CRAZY HORSE
Broken Arrow
RR10900 740 (August 8, 1996) p58. (O'Connor, Rob)
Sleeps With Angels
RR10901 689 (August 25, 1994) pp87-88. (Fricke, David)
RR10902 698-699 (December 29, 1994) p191. (Evans, Paul)
Weld
RR10903 617 (November 14, 1991) pp171-172. (McLeese, Don)
RR10904 619-620 (December 12, 1991) p165. (Fricke, David)
CREAM
Disraeli Gears
RR10905 648 (January 21, 1993) p50. (Considine, J. D.)
RR10906 655 (April 29, 1993) p42. (Futterman, Steve)
Fresh Cream
RR10907 648 (January 21, 1993) p50. (Considine, J. D.)
RR10908 655 (April 29, 1993) p42. (Futterman, Steve)
Wheels Of Fire
RR10909 648 (January 21, 1993) p50. (Considine, J. D.)
RR10910 655 (April 29, 1993) p42. (Futterman, Steve)
CREATION REBEL
Historic Moments Vol. 1
RR10911 703 (March 9, 1995) p65. (Fernando, S. H., Jr.)
CRENSHAW, MARSHALL
Life's Too Short
RR10912 619-620 (December 12, 1991) p184. (Fricke, David)
Miracle Of Science
RR10913 743 (September 19, 1996) p84. (Hoskyns, Barney)
CROKER, BRENDAN
The Great Indoors
RR10914 637 (August 20, 1992) p53. (McLeese, Don)
CROSBY, DAVID
Thousand Roads
RR10915 665 (September 16, 1993) p72. (Gardner, Elysa)
CROSBY, STILLS & NASH
Crosby, Stills & Nash
RR10916 686-687 (July 14, 1994) p32. (Nicks, Stevie)
CROW, SHERYL
Sheryl Crow
RR10917 744 (October 3, 1996) pp69,71. (Gardner, Elysa)
RR10918 750-751 (December 26, 1996) p186.
CROWDED HOUSE
Together Alone
RR10919 679 (April 7, 1994) p76. (Wright, Christian)
CROWELL, RODNEY
Let The Picture Paint Itself
RR10920 691 (September 22, 1994) p99. (Ransom, Kevin)
Life Is Messy
RR10921 636 (August 6, 1992) p60. (McGee, David)
CRUEL SEA
The Honeymoon Is Over
RR10922 704 (March 23, 1995) p124. (Gardner, Elysa)
CRYNER, BOBBIE

Bobbie Cryner
RR10923 663 (August 19, 1993) p77. (McLeese, Don)
Girl Of Your Dreams
RR10924 726 (January 25, 1996) p73. (Himes, Geoffrey)
CUL DE SAC
China Gate
RR10925 737 (June 27, 1996) p59. (Sprague, David)
CULT
The Cult
RR10926 698-699 (December 29, 1994) p173. (Evans, Paul)
CULTURE
Two Sevens Clash
RR10927 676 (February 24, 1994) p42. (McLane, Daisann)
Wings Of A Dove
RR10928 650 (February 18, 1993) p59. (McLane, Daisann)
CURE
Paris
RR10929 672-673 (December 23, 1993) p168. (Evans, Paul)
Show
RR10930 667 (October 14, 1993) pp113-114. (Wright, Christian)
RR10931 672-673 (December 23, 1993) p168. (Evans, Paul)
Wild Mood Swings
RR10932 736 (June 13, 1996) p83. (DeCurtis, Anthony)
Wish
RR10933 630 (May 14, 1992) pp101,103. (Hunter, James)
RR10934 645-646 (December 10, 1992) pp179-180. (Coleman, Mark)
CURRY, MARK
It's Only Time
RR10935 676 (February 24, 1994) p17. (Browne, Jackson)
CURVE
Doppelganger
RR10936 630 (May 14, 1992) p107. (Berger, Arion)
CYPRESS HILL
Black Sunday
RR10937 665 (September 16, 1993) p64. (Diehl, Matt)
RR10938 672-673 (December 23, 1993) p146. (Evans, Paul)
Temples Of Boom
RR10939 721 (November 16, 1995) pp109-110. (Fernando, S. H., Jr.)
RR10940 724-725 (December 28, 1995) p124. (Fricke, David)
CYRUS, BILLY RAY
It Won't Be The Last
RR10941 665 (September 16, 1993) p66. (Swenson, John)
Some Gave All
RR10942 636 (August 6, 1992) p60. (Berger, Arion)
RR10943 645-646 (December 10, 1992) p166. (Coleman, Mark)

D

D GENERATION
D Generation
RR10944 704 (March 23, 1995) p125. (Evans, Paul)
No Lunch
RR10945 743 (September 19, 1996) p84. (Fricke, David)
No Way Out (song)
RR10946 667 (October 14, 1993) p121. (Fricke, David)
D, CHUCK
Autobiography Of Mistachuck
RR10947 744 (October 3, 1996) pp72,74. (DeCurtis, Anthony)
DA BRAT
Funkdafied
RR10948 698-699 (December 29, 1994) pp182,185. (Evans, Paul)
DADDY RICH
Dust To Dust
RR10949 669 (November 11, 1993) pp76-77. (Diehl, Matt)
DAISY
The Hum Of D.A.I.S.Y.
RR10950 652 (March 18, 1993) p42. (Fricke, David)
DALE, DICK
Tribal Thunder
RR10951 668 (October 28, 1993) p81. (Palmer, Robert)
D'ANGELO
Brown Sugar
RR10952 716 (September 7, 1995) pp71-72. (Coker, Cheo H.)
DANKO, RICK
Danko-Fjeld-Andersen
RR10953 674 (January 27, 1994) p54. (Evans, Paul)
DANZIG
Danzig
RR10954 698-699 (December 29, 1994) p173. (Evans, Paul)
Danzig III: How The Gods Kill
RR10955 634-635 (July 9, 1992) p105. (Palmer, Robert)
D'ARBY, TERENCE TRENT
Symphony Or Damn
RR10956 660-661 (July 8, 1993) pp110-111. (Volk, Steven)
RR10957 672-673 (December 23, 1993) p153. (Evans, Paul)
Vibrator
RR10958 709 (June 1, 1995) pp61-62. (McElfresh, Suzanna)
DARLING, HELEN
Jenny Come Back (song)
RR10959 716 (September 7, 1995) p70. (Eddy, Chuck)
DAS EFX
Dead Serious
RR10960 631 (May 28, 1992) p55. (Light, Alan)
DAVIS, MILES
The Complete Columbia Studio Recordings
RR10961 750-751 (December 26, 1996) pp195-196.
Doo-Bop
RR10962 636 (August 6, 1992) p60. (Moon, Tom)
Miles Smiles
RR10963 631 (May 28, 1992) p61. (Futterman, Steve)
Sketches Of Spain
RR10964 680 (April 21, 1994) p21. (Hutchence, Michael)
RR10965 Number not assigned.
DE LA SOUL
Buhloone Mind State
RR10966 672-673 (December 23, 1993) p156. (Evans, Paul)
Stakes Is High
RR10967 740 (August 8, 1996) p60. (Sprague, David)
3 Feet High And Rising
RR10967a 666 (September 30, 1993) p59. (Kelley, Robin D.G.)
DEAD CAN DANCE
Toward The Within
RR10968 702 (February 23, 1995) p76. (Evans, Paul)
DEADEYE DICK
A Different Story
RR10969 691 (September 22, 1994) p98. (Evans, Paul)
DEAL, KELLEY
Go To The Sugar Alter
RR10970 744 (October 3, 1996) p74. (O'Connor, Rob)
DEBARGE, EL
In The Storm
RR10971 631 (May 28, 1992) p55. (Eddy, Chuck)
DECONSTRUCTION
Deconstruction
RR10972 693 (October 20, 1994) p151. (Sinclair, Tom)
DEEE-LITE
Infinity Within
RR10973 634-635 (July 9, 1992) pp101-102. (Wright, Christian)
DEF LEPPARD
Adrenalize

RR10974 628 (April 16, 1992) pp79-80. (Considine, J. D.)
Retro Active
RR10975 670 (November 25, 1993) pp114,116. (Evans, Paul)
Slang
RR10976 736 (June 13, 1996) p85. (Wiederhorn, Jon)
DEFINITION OF SOUND
Experience
RR10977 736 (June 13, 1996) p85. (Sprague, David)
DEFLOWERS
Just What It's Like (song)
RR10978 667 (October 14, 1993) p121. (Fricke, David)
Uhhh (song)
RR10979 667 (October 14, 1993) p121. (Fricke, David)
DELEVANTES
Long About That Time
RR10980 709 (June 1, 1995) pp64-65. (Santelli, Robert)
DELTA 72
The R&B Of Membership
RR10981 740 (August 8, 1996) p62. (Fricke, David)
DEMENT, IRIS
Infamous Angel
RR10982 672-673 (December 23, 1993) p168. (Evans, Paul)
My Life
RR10983 688 (August 11, 1994) pp66,69. (Okamoto, David)
DEPECHE MODE
Songs Of Faith And Devotion
RR10984 654 (April 15, 1993) p65. (Berger, Arion)
RR10985 672-673 (December 23, 1993) p151. (Evans, Paul)
DEREK AND THE DOMINOS
Layla
RR10986 655 (April 29, 1993) p42. (Futterman, Steve)
Live At The Fillmore
RR10987 677 (March 10, 1994) p67. (Considine, J. D.)
DEREK AND THE RUINS
Saisoro
RR10988 730 (March 21, 1996) p98. (Fricke, David)
DESTROY ALL MONSTERS
Destroy All Monsters 1974-1976
RR10989 706 (April 20, 1995) p72. (Fricke, David)
DEVLINS
Drift
RR10990 658 (June 10, 1993) p70. (Gardner, Elysa)
DEVO
Devo Live: The Mongoloid Years
RR10991 645-646 (December 10, 1992) p177. (Fricke, David)
DEYOUNG, DENNIS
10 On Broadway
RR10992 696 (December 1, 1994) p129. (Diehl, Matt)
DIAMOND, NEIL
Glory Road: 1968 To 1972
RR10993 636 (August 6, 1992) pp56-57. (Wild, David)
The Greatest Hits 1966-1992
RR10994 636 (August 6, 1992) pp56-57. (Wild, David)
In My Lifetime
RR10995 750-751 (December 26, 1996) p189. (Coleman, Mark)
DIBANGO, MANU
Wakafrika
RR10996 688 (August 11, 1994) p70. (Evans, Paul)
DICTATORS
I Am Right (single)
RR10997 745 (October 17, 1996) p135. (Fricke, David)
Loyola (song)
RR10998 745 (October 17, 1996) p135. (Fricke, David)
DIED PRETTY
Doughboy Hollow
RR10999 625 (March 5, 1992) p70. (Jurek, Thom)
Trace
RR11000 678 (March 24, 1994) p95. (Evans, Paul)
DIFRANCO, ANI
Dilate
RR11001 736 (June 13, 1996) p85. (O'Connor, Rob)
Not A Pretty Girl
RR11002 715 (August 24, 1995) pp102,104. (Goodman, Fred)
DIG
Believe (song)
RR11003 680 (April 21, 1994) p21. (Hutchence, Michael)
DIGABLE PLANETS
Blowout Comb
RR11004 696 (December 1, 1994) p127. (Berman, Eric)
Reachin'
RR11005 650 (February 18, 1993) p60. (Powell, Kevin)
RR11006 672-673 (December 23, 1993) p157. (Evans, Paul)
DIGITAL UNDERGROUND
The Body-Hat Syndrome
RR11007 670 (November 25, 1993) p121. (Toure)
DIM STARS
Dim Stars
RR11008 638 (September 3, 1992) pp63-65. (Palmer, Robert)
DINOSAUR JR.
Green Mind
RR11009 619-620 (December 12, 1991) p182. (Fricke, David)
Where You Been
RR11010 650 (February 18, 1993) p58. (Azerrad, Michael)
Without A Sound
RR11011 692 (October 6, 1994) pp90-91. (Diehl, Matt)
DIORIO, JOE
Rare Birds
RR11012 711 (June 29, 1995) p44. (Futterman, Steve)
DIRE STRAITS
On Every Street
RR11013 615 (October 17, 1991) pp91-92. (McLeese, Don)
DIRTY THREE
Dirty Three
RR11014 724-725 (December 28, 1995) p125. (Fricke, David)
Horse Stories
RR11015 746 (October 31, 1996) p70. (Fine, Jason)
Sad And Defeated
RR11016 724-725 (December 28, 1995) p125. (Fricke, David)
DISPOSABLE HEROES OF HIPHOPRISY
Hypocrisy Is The Greatest Luxury
RR11017 630 (May 14, 1992) p108. (Dyson, Michael Eric)
DJURA, DJUR
The Voice Of Silence
RR11018 670 (November 25, 1993) p108. (McLane, Daisann)
DOE, JOHN
Kissingsohard
RR11019 717 (September 21, 1995) p84. (Flaum, Eric)
DOGG POUND
Dogg Food
RR11020 724-725 (December 28, 1995) p124. (Fricke, David)
DOKKEN
Dysfunctional
RR11021 715 (August 24, 1995) p104. (Darzin, Daina)
DOMINO
Sweet Potatoe Pie
RR11022 682 (May 19, 1994) p21. (Queen Latifah)
DOMINO, FATS
They Call Me The Fat Man
RR11023 619-620 (December 12, 1991) p177. (McLeese, Don)
DONOVAN
Sutras
RR11024 748 (November 28, 1996) pp134,136. (Himmelsbach, Erik)
Troubadour: The Definitive Collection 1964-1976
RR11025 645-646 (December 10, 1992) pp166,168. (Coleman, Mark)

Funky Divas
RR11076 629 (April 30, 1992) p56. (Smith, Danyel)
RR11077 645-646 (December 10, 1992) p166. (Coleman, Mark)
Whatta Man (song)
RR11078 678 (March 24, 1994) p16. (Donelly, Tanya)
ENIGMA
The Cross Of Changes
RR11079 680 (April 21, 1994) p88. (Evans, Paul)
ENO, BRIAN
The Essential Fripp And Eno
RR11080 682 (May 19, 1994) p100. (Considine, J. D.)
II
RR11081 672-673 (December 23, 1993) p148. (Considine, J. D.)
Nerve Net
RR11082 645-646 (December 10, 1992) p182. (Coleman, Mark)
Spinner
RR11083 723 (December 14, 1995) pp82,84. (DeRogatis, Jim)
ENTOMBED
Wolverine Blues
RR11084 681 (May 5, 1994) p52. (Darzin,Daina)
ENYA
The Memory Of Trees
RR11085 726 (January 25, 1996) p73. (Gardner, Elysa)
EPMD
Business Never Personal
RR11086 639 (September 17, 1992) pp95-96. (Nelson, Havelock)
ERASURE
Abba-Esque
RR11087 645-646 (December 10, 1992) p182. (Coleman, Mark)
I Say, I Say, I Say
RR11088 697 (December 15, 1994) p96. (White, Armond)
ERIC B. AND RAKIM
Don't Sweat The Technique
RR11089 634-635 (July 9, 1992) p106. (Nelson, Havelock)
Paid In Full
RR11090 666 (September 30, 1993) p56. (Kelley, Robin D.G.)
ERICKSON, ROKY
All That May Do My Rhyme
RR11091 708 (May 18, 1995) p90. (Hill, Trent)
We Are Never Talking (song)
RR11092 698-699 (December 29, 1994) p174. (Fricke, David)
ESCOVEDO, ALEJANDRO
Gravity
RR11093 640 (October 1, 1992) pp67-68. (McLeese, Don)
Thirteen Years
RR11094 682 (May 19, 1994) p102. (George-Warren, Holly)
With These Hands
RR11095 732 (April 18, 1996) pp71,73. (Kemp, Mark)
ESTEFAN, GLORIA
Mi Tierra
RR11096 682 (May 19, 1994) p21. (Queen Latifah)
ESTEP, MAGGIE
No More Mister Nice Girl
RR11097 684 (June 16, 1994) pp106,108. (O'Dair, Barbara)
ETERNAL
Always And Forever
RR11098 692 (October 6, 1994) pp87-88. (Smith, Danyel)
ETHERIDGE, MELISSA
Never Enough
RR11099 630 (May 14, 1992) p103. (Cullen, Jim)
Your Little Secret
RR11100 722 (November 30, 1995) p68. (Gardner, Elysa)
ETHYL MEATPLOW
Happy Days, Sweetheart
RR11101 664 (September 2, 1993) pp61-62. (Ali, Lorraine)
ETZIONI, MARVIN
The Mandolin Man
RR11102 626 (March 19, 1992) p97. (Gardner, Elysa)
EUGENIUS
Mary Queen Of Scots
RR11103 678 (March 24, 1994) p95. (Evans, Paul)
EVANS, BILL
Jazz At The Maintenance Shop
RR11104 665 (September 16, 1993) p67. (Futterman, Steve)
EVANS, GIL
The Complete Columbia Studio Recordings
RR11105 750-751 (December 26, 1996) pp195-196.
EVANS, JOHN
Terror Has Some Strange Kinfolk
RR11106 667 (October 14, 1993) p121. (Fricke, David)
EVERLY BROTHERS
Heartaches And Harmonies
RR11107 698-699 (December 29, 1994) p188. (Considine, J. D.)
Walk Right Back
RR11108 672-673 (December 23, 1993) p148. (Considine, J. D.)
EVERYTHING BUT THE GIRL
Walking Wounded
RR11109 736 (June 13, 1996) p85. (Hardy, Ernest)

F

FAGEN, DONALD
Kamakiriad
RR11110 662 (August 5, 1993) p65. (Holden, Stephen)
FAITH NO MORE
Angel Dust
RR11111 638 (September 3, 1992) p65. (Sinclair, Tom)
King For A Day, Fool For A Lifetime
RR11112 709 (June 1, 1995) p61. (Weisel, Al)
FAITHFULL, MARIANNE
A Collection Of Her Best Recordings
RR11113 693 (October 20, 1994) p150. (Mirkin, Steven)
FALL
Kimble (E.P.)
RR11114 660-661 (July 8, 1993) p113. (Fricke, David)
FALL-OUTS
Here I Come And Other Hits
RR11115 672-673 (December 23, 1993) p154. (Fricke, David)
FAMBRO, MICHE
The Chapel Session
RR11116 740 (August 8, 1996) p62. (Fricke, David)
FARMER, ART
The Company I Keep
RR11117 692 (October 6, 1994) p89. (Futterman, Steve)
FARRIS, DIONNE
Wild Seed—Wild Flower
RR11118 700 (January 26, 1995) p62. (Coker, Cheo H.)
FASTBACKS
Every Day Is Saturday (EP)
RR11119 628 (April 16, 1992) p85. (Fricke, David)
Fastbacks...And His Orchestra
RR11120 628 (April 16, 1992) p85. (Fricke, David)
Play Five Of Their Favorites (EP)
RR11121 628 (April 16, 1992) p85. (Fricke, David)
Zucker
RR11122 655 (April 29, 1993) p63. (McDonnell, Evelyn)
FAT JOE
Jealous One's Envy
RR11123 721 (November 16, 1995) p113. (Coker, Cheo H.)

FAT JOE DA GANGSTA
Represent
RR11124 668 (October 28, 1993) p83. (Ehrlich, Dimitri)
FATEH ALI KHAN, NUSRAT
Night Song
RR11125 728 (February 22, 1996) pp60,62. (Richardson, Susan)
FATIMA MANSIONS
Viva Dead Ponies
RR11126 619-620 (December 12, 1991) p187. (Fricke, David)
FAUST
Rien
RR11127 736 (June 13, 1996) p85. (Fricke, David)
FEAR
Fear: The Record
RR11128 624 (February 20, 1992) p42. (McLeese, Don)
FERRY, BRYAN
Mamouna
RR11129 696 (December 1, 1994) pp124,126. (Volk, Steven)
Taxi
RR11130 659 (June 24, 1993) pp78,80. (Wright, Christian)
FILTER
Short Bus
RR11131 724-725 (December 28, 1995) p124. (Fricke, David)
FIRE IN THE KITCHEN
Cold Rain And Snow (single)
RR11132 645-646 (December 10, 1992) p177. (Fricke, David)
Simple English (song)
RR11133 645-646 (December 10, 1992) p177. (Fricke, David)
Theory Of Everything
RR11134 645-646 (December 10, 1992) p177. (Fricke, David)
FIREHOSE
The Live Totem Pole EP
RR11135 623 (February 6, 1992) pp82-83. (Stenger, Wif)
Mr. Machinery Operator
RR11136 657 (May 27, 1993) p52. (Dougan, John)
FIREHOUSE
3
RR11137 715 (August 24, 1995) p104. (Darzin, Daina)
FIREMAN
Strawberries Oceans Ships Forest
RR11138 685 (June 30, 1994) p76. (Gaar, Gillian G.)
FISHBONE
The Reality Of My Surroundings
RR11139 619-620 (December 12, 1991) p178. (Fricke, David)
FIVE BLIND BOYS OF ALABAMA
Deep River
RR11140 649 (February 4, 1993) p68. (Hunter, James)
5 ROYALS
Monkey Hips And Rice
RR11141 688 (August 11, 1994) p71. (Palmer, Robert)
FJELD, JONAS
Danko-Fjeld-Andersen
RR11142 674 (January 27, 1994) p54. (Evans, Paul)
FLAMIN' GROOVIES
Rock Juice
RR11143 645-646 (December 10, 1992) p177. (Fricke, David)
FLAMING LIPS
Clouds Taste Metallic
RR11144 720 (November 2, 1995) p68. (Weisel, Al)
Transmissions From The Satellite Heart
RR11145 668 (October 28, 1993) pp81,83. (Kot, Greg)
FLANAGAN, TOMMY
Let's
RR11146 678 (March 24, 1994) p97. (Futterman, Steve)
RR11147 Number not assigned.
FLEETWOOD MAC
Live At The BBC
RR11148 750-751 (December 26, 1996) p189. (Coleman, Mark)
25 Years: The Chain
RR11148a 645-646 (December 10, 1992) p170. (Considine, J. D.)
FLESHTONES
Beautiful Light
RR11149 679 (April 7, 1994) p74. (Evans, Paul)
FLIPPEN, BENTON
Old Times, New Times
RR11150 698-699 (December 29, 1994) p174. (Fricke, David)
FLORES, ROSIE
Once More With Feeling
RR11151 666 (September 30, 1993) p105. (McLeese, Don)
FLOWERED UP
A Life With Brian
RR11152 625 (March 5, 1992) pp68,70. (Berger, Arion)
FLYING SAUCER ATTACK
Chorus
RR11153 731 (April 4, 1996) p61. (Wiederhorn, Jon)
Further
RR11154 715 (August 24, 1995) p102. (O'Connor, Rob)
FOETUS
Gash
RR11155 709 (June 1, 1995) pp62,64. (Diehl, Matt)
FOLDS, BEN
Ben Folds Five
RR11156 718 (October 5, 1995) p70. (Cohen, Jason)
FOLEY
7 Years Ago...Directions In Smart-Alec Music
RR11157 660-661 (July 8, 1993) p20. (Fricke, David)
FOLLOW FOR NOW
Follow For Now
RR11158 618 (November 28, 1991) p98. (Sinclair, Tom)
FOO FIGHTERS
Foo Fighters
RR11159 714 (August 10, 1995) pp56-57. (Foege, Alec)
RR11160 724-725 (December 28, 1995) p120. (Fricke, David)
FOR REAL
It's A Natural Thing
RR11161 692 (October 6, 1994) pp87-88. (Smith, Danyel)
FOR SQUIRRELS
Example
RR11162 726 (January 25, 1996) pp72-73. (O'Connor, Rob)
FORBERT, STEVE
The American In Me
RR11163 623 (February 6, 1992) pp73,77. (Gardner, Elysa)
FORD, RICKY
Hard Groovin'
RR11164 618 (November 28, 1991) p96. (Futterman, Steve)
FORDHAM, JULIA
Falling Forward
RR11165 691 (September 22, 1994) pp97,99. (Gardner, Elysa)
FOREIGNER
Mr. Moonlight
RR11166 707 (May 4, 1995) p68. (Evans, Paul)
FOREVER BAD BLUES BAND
Just Stompin'
RR11167 669 (November 11, 1993) p77. (Fricke, David)
FORMANEK, MICHAEL
Low Profile
RR11168 692 (October 6, 1994) p89. (Futterman, Steve)
FORSTER, ROBERT
Danger In The Past
RR11169 619-620 (December 12, 1991) pp187,189. (Fricke, David)
FOULA
Foula
RR11170 645-646 (December 10, 1992) p187. (McLane, Daisann)
FOUNTAIN, CLARENCE

Deep River
RR11171 649 (February 4, 1993) p68. (Hunter, James)
FRACASSO, MICHAEL
When I Lived In The Wild
RR11172 707 (May 4, 1995) p70. (McLeese, Don)
FRAMPTON, PETER
Frampton Comes Alive II
RR11173 723 (December 14, 1995) p86. (Kot, Greg)
Peter Frampton
RR11174 678 (March 24, 1994) p95. (Evans, Paul)
FRANKLIN, ARETHA
Queen Of Soul: The Atlantic Recordings
RR11175 645-646 (December 10, 1992) p170. (Considine, J. D.)
FREE
Molten Gold
RR11176 672-673 (December 23, 1993) p148. (Considine, J. D.)
FRENTE!
Marvin The Album
RR11177 685 (June 30, 1994) p73. (Evans, Paul)
Shape
RR11178 740 (August 8, 1996) pp60,62. (Ali, Lorraine)
FRIEDMAN, KINKY
Old Testaments And New Revelations
RR11179 656 (May 13, 1993) p107. (Wild, David)
FRIGGS
Juiced Up (song)
RR11180 720 (November 2, 1995) p69. (Fricke, David)
Mama Blew A Hoody (song)
RR11181 720 (November 2, 1995) p69. (Fricke, David)
FRIPP, ROBERT
The Essential Fripp And Eno
RR11182 682 (May 19, 1994) p100. (Considine, J. D.)
The First Day
RR11183 670 (November 25, 1993) p114. (Lyman, Andy)
FRISELL, BILL
Have A Little Faith
RR11184 656 (May 13, 1993) pp107-108. (Moon, Tom)
This Land
RR11185 691 (September 22, 1994) p94. (Woodard, Josef)
FROM GOOD HOMES
Open Up The Sky
RR11186 709 (June 1, 1995) p64. (Evans, Paul)
FUGAZI
In On The Kill Taker
RR11187 664 (September 2, 1993) p16. (Fricke, David)
RR11188 666 (September 30, 1993) p106. (Diehl, Matt)
Red Medicine
RR11189 712-713 (July 13, 1995) p109. (Kemp, Mark)
Steady Diet Of Nothing
RR11190 619-620 (December 12, 1991) p168. (Fricke, David)
FUGEES
The Score
RR11191 730 (March 21, 1996) pp96,98. (Powers, Ann)
RR11192 750-751 (December 26, 1996) pp186,190.
FUGS
The Fugs First Album
RR11193 670 (November 25, 1993) pp112,114. (Isler, Scott)
FUN LOVIN' CRIMINALS
Come Find Yourself
RR11194 731 (April 4, 1996) p60. (Sarig, Roni)
FUNKADELIC
The Electric Spanking Of War Babies
RR11195 664 (September 2, 1993) p64. (Considine, J. D.)
Live—The Funkadelic Collection
RR11196 676 (February 24, 1994) p57. (Fricke, David)
Music For Your Mother
RR11197 664 (September 2, 1993) p64. (Considine, J. D.)
One Nation Under A Groove
RR11198 664 (September 2, 1993) p64. (Considine, J. D.)
Uncle Jam Wants You
RR11199 664 (September 2, 1993) p64. (Considine, J. D.)
FUNKI PORCINI
Love, Pussycats And Carwrecks
RR11200 748 (November 28, 1996) pp136-137. (Micallef, Ken)
FURY IN THE SLAUGHTERHOUSE
Mono
RR11201 685 (June 30, 1994) p73. (Evans, Paul)
FUTURE SOUND OF LONDON
Dead Cities
RR11202 750-751 (December 26, 1996) p195.

G

G. LOVE
G. Love And Special Sauce
RR11203 684 (June 16, 1994) p108. (Moon, Tom)
GABRIEL, ANA
Mi Mexico
RR11204 623 (February 6, 1992) pp77,79. (McLane, Daisann)
GABRIEL, PETER
Secret World Live
RR11205 693 (October 20, 1994) pp142,146. (Richardson, Susan)
Us
RR11206 640 (October 1, 1992) p63. (Kot, Greg)
GAINES, REG E.
Please Don't Take My Air Jordans
RR11207 684 (June 16, 1994) p108. (Toure)
GALAS, DIAMANDA
The Singer
RR11208 633 (June 25, 1992) p44. (Cullman, Brian)
The Sporting Life
RR11209 692 (October 6, 1994) p87. (Evans, Paul)
GALAXIE 500
Galaxie 500
RR11210 747 (November 14, 1996) p116. (Wiederhorn, Jon)
GANG STARR
Daily Operation
RR11211 634-635 (July 9, 1992) p105. (Smith, Danyel)
Hard To Earn
RR11212 683 (June 2, 1994) p70. (Nelson, Havelock)
RR11213 698-699 (December 29, 1994) p173. (Evans, Paul)
GARBAGE
Garbage
RR11214 717 (September 21, 1995) p82. (Hunter, James)
GARCIA, JERRY
Not For Kids Only
RR11215 672-673 (December 23, 1993) p151. (Evans, Paul)
Shady Grove
RR11216 750-751 (December 26, 1996) p199.
GATTON, DANNY
The Humbler
RR11217 750-751 (December 26, 1996) p192. (Fricke, David)
GAYE, MARVIN
Marvin Gaye The Master 1961-84
RR11218 724-725 (December 28, 1995) p122. (Coleman, Mark)
The Norman Whitfield Sessions
RR11219 694 (November 3, 1994) p100. (Considine, J. D.)
GAYLE, CHARLES
Kingdom Come
RR11220 708 (May 18, 1995) pp87-88. (Fricke, David)
More Live At The Knitting Factory
RR11221 672-673 (December 23, 1993) p154. (Fricke, David)

GEGGY TAH
Grand Opening
RR11222 686-687 (July 14, 1994) p104. (Evans, Paul)
GELB, HOWE
Dreaded Brown Recluse
RR11223 619-620 (December 12, 1991) p168. (Fricke, David)
GELDOF, BOB
The Happy Club
RR11224 663 (August 19, 1993) p78. (Jurek, Thom)
GENE
Olympian
RR11225 711 (June 29, 1995) p45. (Cohen, Jason)
GENERAL PUBIC
Rub It Better
RR11226 708 (May 18, 1995) p92. (Manning, Kara)
GENESIS
We Can't Dance
RR11227 621 (January 9, 1992) p51. (Manning, Kara)
GENIUS
Liquid Swords
RR11228 722 (November 30, 1995) pp66-67. (Fernando, S. H., Jr.)
GERMANO, LISA
Excerpts From A Love Circus
RR11229 742 (September 5, 1996) p64. (Ali, Lorraine)
Geek The Girl
RR11230 694 (November 3, 1994) p98. (Evans, Paul)
Happiness
RR11231 666 (September 30, 1993) p106. (Kemp, Mark)
On The Way Down From The Moon Palace
RR11232 617 (November 14, 1991) p177. (Bessman, Jim)
GERMS
MIA
RR11233 676 (February 24, 1994) p57. (Hill, Trent)
GETO BOYS
The Resurrection
RR11234 734 (May 16, 1996) p68. (Huffman, Eddie)
Till Death Do Us Part
RR11235 658 (June 10, 1993) p69. (Nelson, Havelock)
We Can't Be Stopped
RR11236 619-620 (December 12, 1991) p184. (Fricke, David)
GHORWANE
Majurugenta
RR11237 672-673 (December 23, 1993) p163. (McLane, Daisann)
GHOSTFACE KILLAH
Ironman
RR11238 749 (December 12, 1996) p82. (Fernando, S. H., Jr.)
GIANT SAND
Glum
RR11239 690 (September 8, 1994) p78. (Drozdowski, Ted)
Purge And Slouch
RR11240 689 (August 25, 1994) p92. (Drozdowski, Ted)
GIBSON, DEBBIE
Body Mind Soul
RR11241 651 (March 4, 1993) p65. (Eddy, Chuck)
GIL, GILBERTO
Parabolic
RR11242 645-646 (December 10, 1992) p187. (McLane, Daisann)
Tropicalia 2
RR11243 688 (August 11, 1994) p69. (McLane, Daisann)
GILL, VINCE
When Love Finds You
RR11244 686-687 (July 14, 1994) p107. (McLeese, Don)
GILLESPIE, DIZZY
Dizzy's Diamonds: Best Of The Verve Years
RR11245 645-646 (December 10, 1992) p180. (Futterman, Steve)
Shaw 'Nuff
RR11246 665 (September 16, 1993) p67. (Futterman, Steve)
GILMORE, JIMMIE DALE
After Awhile
RR11247 619-620 (December 12, 1991) p184. (Fricke, David)
Braver Newer World
RR11248 738-739 (July 11, 1996) pp87,90. (Fricke, David)
Spinning Around The Sun
RR11249 665 (September 16, 1993) p17. (Mundy, Chris)
RR11250 667 (October 14, 1993) pp114,116. (Milward, John)
GIN BLOSSOMS
Congratulations I'm Sorry
RR11251 730 (March 21, 1996) p98. (Manning, Kara)
New Miserable Experience
RR11252 672-673 (December 23, 1993) pp146,151. (Evans, Paul)
GINN, GREG
Dick
RR11253 667 (October 14, 1993) p34. (Neely, Kim)
GIRA, M.
Drainland
RR11254 718 (October 5, 1995) p69. (Walls, Richard C.)
GIRLS AGAINST BOYS
House Of GVSB
RR11255 733 (May 2, 1996) p54. (Azerrad, Michael)
GIUFFRE, JIMMY
Fusion
RR11256 631 (May 28, 1992) p61. (Futterman, Steve)
Thesis
RR11257 631 (May 28, 1992) p61. (Futterman, Steve)
GLASS, PHILIP
Contrary Motion
RR11258 682 (May 19, 1994) p98. (Schwarz, K. Robert)
Einstein On The Beach
RR11259 682 (May 19, 1994) p98. (Schwarz, K. Robert)
Hydrogen Jukebox
RR11260 682 (May 19, 1994) p98. (Schwarz, K. Robert)
Music In Fifths
RR11261 682 (May 19, 1994) p98. (Schwarz, K. Robert)
Music In Similar Motion
RR11262 682 (May 19, 1994) p98. (Schwarz, K. Robert)
Music With Changing Parts
RR11263 682 (May 19, 1994) p98. (Schwarz, K. Robert)
Two Pages
RR11264 682 (May 19, 1994) p98. (Schwarz, K. Robert)
GO-GO'S
Return To The Valley Of The Go-Go's
RR11265 698-699 (December 29, 1994) p173. (Evans, Paul)
GOATS
No Goats, No Glory
RR11266 696 (December 1, 1994) pp127-128. (Diehl, Matt)
Tricks Of The Shade
RR11267 650 (February 18, 1993) p60. (Levy, Joe)
GOD STREET WINE
Red
RR11268 737 (June 27, 1996) p56. (Gardner, Elysa)
GODFATHERS OF THREATT
Super Bad
RR11269 690 (September 8, 1994) p78. (Evans, Paul)
GOD'S FAVORITE BAND
Shacknasty
RR11270 637 (August 20, 1992) p50. (Robbins, Ira)
GOLDEN PALOMINOS
Drunk With Passion
RR11271 618 (November 28, 1991) p98. (McKenna, Kristine)
GOLDEN SMOG
Down By The Old Mainstream
RR11272 729 (March 7, 1996) p50. (Drozdowski, Ted)
GOODMAN, BENNY

A Study Of Frustration
RR11273 692 (October 6, 1994) p89. (Futterman, Steve)
GOODMAN, STEVE
The Easter Tapes
RR11274 750-751 (December 26, 1996) p192. (Fricke, David)
No Big Surprise
RR11275 698-699 (December 29, 1994) p188. (Considine, J. D.)
GOODRICK, MICK
Rare Birds
RR11276 711 (June 29, 1995) p44. (Futterman, Steve)
GORDON, ROBERT
The Humbler
RR11277 750-751 (December 26, 1996) p192. (Fricke, David)
GORECKI, HENRYK
Symphony No. 3
RR11278 655 (April 29, 1993) p65. (Schwarz, K. Robert)
RR11279 657 (April 29, 1993) p6. (Schwarz, K. Robert)
GORKY'S ZYGOTIC MYNCI
Introducing Gorky's Zygotic Mynci
RR11280 745 (October 17, 1996) p132. (Wiederhorn, Jon)
GORODETSKY, EDDIE
Christmas Party With Eddie G.
RR11281 672-673 (December 23, 1993) p169. (Howard, Pete)
GOV'T MULE
Gov't Mule
RR11282 711 (June 29, 1995) p45. (Swenson, John)
GP'S
Saturday Rolling Around
RR11283 639 (September 17, 1992) p96. (Fricke, David)
GRAND PUBA
Reel To Reel
RR11284 647 (January 7, 1993) p46. (Ehrlich, Dimitri)
GRANT LEE BUFFALO
Copperopolis
RR11285 736 (June 13, 1996) p78. (DeRogatis, Jim)
Fuzzy
RR11286 652 (March 18, 1993) p42. (Fricke, David)
Mighty Joe Moon
RR11287 692 (October 6, 1994) p84. (Weisel, Al)
RR11288 698-699 (December 29, 1994) p190. (Evans, Paul)
GRATEFUL DEAD
Grayfolded
RR11289 724-725 (December 28, 1995) p120. (Fricke, David)
Hundred Year Hall
RR11290 724-725 (December 28, 1995) p120. (Fricke, David)
Infrared Roses
RR11291 625 (March 5, 1992) p70. (Fricke, David)
GRAVEDIGGAZ
Six Feet Deep
RR11292 692 (October 6, 1994) p90. (Fernando, S. H., Jr.)
GREAT SOCIETY
Born To Be Burned
RR11293 741 (August 22, 1996) p100. (Futterman, Steve)
GREEN DAY
Dookie
RR11294 698-699 (December 29, 1994) p191. (Evans, Paul)
Insomniac
RR11295 720 (November 2, 1995) pp65,68. (Coleman, Mark)
RR11296 724-725 (December 28, 1995) p129. (Fricke, David)
GREGG, JONATHAN
Blue On Blonde
RR11297 625 (March 5, 1992) p72. (Puterbaugh, Parke)
GREY GHOST
Grey Ghost
RR11298 652 (March 18, 1993) p42. (Fricke, David)
GRIFFIN, JOHNNY
Chicago, New York, Paris
RR11299 711 (June 29, 1995) p44. (Futterman, Steve)
GRIFFITH, NANCI
Flyer
RR11300 696 (December 1, 1994) pp122,124. (Galvin, Peter)
Other Voices, Other Rooms
RR11301 654 (April 15, 1993) pp62,64. (Manning, Kara)
GRIFTERS
Ain't My Lookout
RR11302 728 (February 22, 1996) p62. (O'Connor, Rob)
Crappin' You Negative
RR11303 701 (February 9, 1995) pp57-58. (Kot, Greg)
GRISMAN, DAVID
Not For Kids Only
RR11304 672-673 (December 23, 1993) p151. (Evans, Paul)
Shady Grove
RR11305 750-751 (December 26, 1996) p199.
GROSSMAN, STEFAN
Black Melodies On A Clear Afternoon
RR11306 630 (May 14, 1992) p109. (Milward, John)
How To Play Blues Guitar
RR11307 630 (May 14, 1992) p109. (Milward, John)
GROSSMAN, STEVE
Do It
RR11308 678 (March 24, 1994) p97. (Futterman, Steve)
GROUP HOME
Livin' Proof
RR11309 729 (March 7, 1996) p50. (Fernando, S. H., Jr.)
GRUSHECKY, JOE
American Babylon
RR11310 724-725 (December 28, 1995) p126. (Fricke, David)
End Of The Century
RR11311 645-646 (December 10, 1992) p177. (Fricke, David)
GUDMUNDSDOTTIR, BJORK
Debut
RR11312 664 (September 2, 1993) p66. (Graves, Tom)
Human Behaviour (song)
RR11313 666 (September 30, 1993) p18. (Wild, David)
Post
RR11314 711 (June 29, 1995) pp41-42. (Ali, Lorraine)
GUERRA, JUAN LUIS
Areito
RR11315 654 (April 15, 1993) p65. (McLane, Daisann)
GUIDED BY VOICES
Alien Lanes
RR11316 704 (March 23, 1995) pp119-121. (Diehl, Matt)
Bee Thousand
RR11317 688 (August 11, 1994) p66. (Azerrad, Michael)
Box
RR11318 704 (March 23, 1995) pp119-121. (Diehl, Matt)
Under The Bushes Under The Stars
RR11319 731 (April 4, 1996) pp60-61. (Corcoran, Michael)
GUMBALL
Super Tasty
RR11320 650 (February 18, 1993) pp59-60. (Sinclair, Tom)
GUMBO
Droppin' Soulful H2O On The Fiber
RR11321 667 (October 14, 1993) p123. (Ferguson, Kate)
GUNS N' ROSES
The Spaghetti Incident?
RR11322 671 (December 9, 1993) pp65-66. (Gold, Jonathan)
Use Your Illusion I
RR11323 615 (October 17, 1991) pp89,91. (Fricke, David)
RR11324 619-620 (December 12, 1991) p162. (Fricke, David)
Use Your Illusion II
RR11325 615 (October 17, 1991) pp89,91. (Wright, Christian)
RR11326 619-620 (December 12, 1991) p162. (Fricke, David)
GURU
Jazzmatazz
RR11327 659 (June 24, 1993) pp83-84. (Ferguson, Kate)
RR11328 672-673 (December 23, 1993) p157. (Evans, Paul)

RR11329 715 (August 24, 1995) p102. (Walls, Richard C.)
GUTTERBALL
Gutterball
RR11330 666 (September 30, 1993) p108. (George-Warren, Holly)
GUY, BUDDY
Alone And Acoustic
RR11331 623 (February 6, 1992) p79. (Santelli, Robert)
Buddy Guy & Junior Wells Play The Blues
RR11332 636 (August 6, 1992) p66. (Considine, J. D.)
Damn Right, I've Got The Blues
RR11333 619-620 (December 12, 1991) pp174,178. (Fricke, David)
RR11334 623 (February 6, 1992) p79. (Santelli, Robert)
Feels Like Rain
RR11335 653 (April 1, 1993) p53. (Palmer, Robert)
Slippin' In
RR11336 698-699 (December 29, 1994) p181. (Evans, Paul)
The Very Best Of Buddy Guy
RR11337 636 (August 6, 1992) p66. (Considine, J. D.)
GZA
Liquid Swords
RR11338 722 (November 30, 1995) pp66-67. (Fernando, S. H., Jr.)

H

H. P. LOVECRAFT
Live—May 11, 1968
RR11339 619-620 (December 12, 1991) p168. (Fricke, David)
H-TOWN
Fever For Da Flavor
RR11340 662 (August 5, 1993) p65. (Rabhan, Jeffrey)
HACKBERRY RAMBLERS
Cajun Boogie
RR11341 672-673 (December 23, 1993) p154. (Fricke, David)
HADEN, CHARLIE
As Long As There's Music
RR11342 671 (December 9, 1993) p70. (Futterman, Steve)
Memoirs
RR11343 642 (October 29, 1992) p75. (Futterman, Steve)
Now Is The Hour
RR11344 734 (May 16, 1996) p66. (Fine, Jason)
HAGAR, SAMMY
Unboxed
RR11345 685 (June 30, 1994) p74. (Drozdowski, Ted)
HAGGARD, MERLE
Down Every Road
RR11346 733 (May 2, 1996) p54. (Kemp, Mark)
Same Train, A Different Time
RR11347 707 (May 4, 1995) p70. (McLeese, Don)
HAKMOUN, HASSAN
Trance
RR11348 680 (April 21, 1994) p90. (McLane, Daisann)
HAMMER
The Funky Headhunter
RR11349 680 (April 21, 1994) p88. (Evans, Paul)
Too Legit To Quit
RR11350 618 (November 28, 1991) p90. (Light, Alan)
HAMMOND, JOHN
Trouble No More
RR11351 677 (March 10, 1994) p65. (Evans, Paul)
HAMPTON, BRUCE
Col. Bruce Hampton And The Aquarium Rescue Unit
RR11351a 626 (March 19, 1992) p95. (Palmer, Robert)
HAMPTON GREASE BAND
Music To Eat
RR11352 730 (March 21, 1996) p98. (Fricke, David)
RR11353 750-751 (December 26, 1996) p189. (Coleman, Mark)
RR11354 Number not assigned.
HANCOCK, BUTCH
Eats Away The Night
RR11355 706 (April 20, 1995) pp78,81. (McLeese, Don)
Own The Way Over Here
RR11356 662 (August 5, 1993) p67. (McLeese, Don)
HANCOCK, HERBIE
Dis Is Da Drum
RR11357 710 (June 15, 1995) p83. (Moon, Tom)
HANDY, W. C.
W. C. Handy's Memphis Blues Band
RR11358 704 (March 23, 1995) p123. (Santelli, Robert)
HARDIN, TIM
Hang On To A Dream
RR11359 692 (October 6, 1994) p90. (Isler, Scott)
HARMONY ROCKETS
Paralyzed Mind Of The Archangel Void
RR11360 724-725 (December 28, 1995) p125. (Fricke, David)
HARRIS, EMMYLOU
At The Ryman
RR11361 625 (March 5, 1992) p70. (Hunter, James)
Cowgirl's Prayer
RR11362 669 (November 11, 1993) p73. (Bessman, Jim)
Portraits
RR11363 750-751 (December 26, 1996) p189. (Coleman, Mark)
Wrecking Ball
RR11364 721 (November 16, 1995) p110. (Richardson, Susan)
HARRISON, GEORGE
Live In Japan With Eric Clapton And Band
RR11365 636 (August 6, 1992) p59. (Puterbaugh, Parke)
HARRY, DEBBIE
Debravation
RR11366 667 (October 14, 1993) pp118,121. (McDonnell, Evelyn)
HARVEY, POLLY JEAN
Dance Hall At Louse Point
RR11367 745 (October 17, 1996) p130. (McDonnell, Evelyn)
HATER
Hater
RR11368 667 (October 14, 1993) p34. (Neely, Kim)
HATFIELD, JULIANA
Become What You Are
RR11369 668 (October 28, 1993) p81. (Mirkin, Steve)
RR11370 672-673 (December 23, 1993) p162. (Evans, Paul)
Hey Babe
RR11371 634-635 (July 9, 1992) pp106-107. (Tannenbaum, Rob)
RR11372 645-646 (December 10, 1992) p182. (Coleman, Mark)
Only Everything
RR11373 704 (March 23, 1995) p124. (Zacharek, Stephanie)
HAWES, HAMPTON
As Long As There's Music
RR11374 671 (December 9, 1993) p70. (Futterman, Steve)
HAWKINS, SOPHIE B.
Tongues And Tails
RR11375 631 (May 28, 1992) p53. (Wright, Christian)
Whaler
RR11376 688 (August 11, 1994) p70. (Evans, Paul)
HAWKINS, TED
The Next Hundred Years
RR11377 689 (August 25, 1994) p90. (Jurek, Thom)
HAYDEN
Everything I Long For
RR11378 734 (May 16, 1996) p68. (Wyman, Bill)
HAYNES, WARREN

Tales Of Ordinary Madness
RR11379 657 (May 27, 1993) p53. (Swenson, John)
HEADS
No Talking Just Head
RR11380 745 (October 17, 1996) pp130,132. (Moon, Tom)
HEALTH AND HAPPINESS SHOW
Tonic
RR11381 675 (February 10, 1994) p45. (O'Connor, Rob)
RR11382 Number not assigned.
HEAVY D AND THE BOYS
Blue Funk
RR11383 654 (April 15, 1993) p62. (Ehrlich, Dimitri)
HEFFINGTON, DON
In The Red
RR11384 707 (May 4, 1995) p70. (McLeese, Don)
HELMET
Betty
RR11385 692 (October 6, 1994) p91. (Wiederhorn, Jon)
Meantime
RR11386 639 (September 17, 1992) pp91,94. (Azerrad, Michael)
HELTAH SKELTAH
Nocturnal
RR11387 741 (August 22, 1996) pp98,100. (Fernando, S. H., Jr.)
HENDERSON, JOE
The Blue Note Years
RR11388 672-673 (December 23, 1993) p164. (Futterman, Steve)
James Williams Meets The Saxophone Masters
RR11389 653 (April 1, 1993) p53. (Futterman, Steve)
Lush Life
RR11390 623 (February 6, 1992) p80. (Futterman, Steve)
The Milestone Years
RR11391 698-699 (December 29, 1994) p180. (Futterman, Steve)
So Near, So Far
RR11392 653 (April 1, 1993) p53. (Futterman, Steve)
HENDERSON, MIKE
Country Music Made Me Do It
RR11393 679 (April 7, 1994) p77. (McLeese, Don)
HENDRIX, JIMI
Blues
RR11394 682 (May 19, 1994) p100. (Considine, J. D.)
The Jimi Hendrix Experience Box Set
RR11395 669 (November 11, 1993) p77. (Considine, J. D.)
Stages
RR11396 619-620 (December 12, 1991) p177. (McLeese, Don)
HENRY, JOE
Kindness Of The World
RR11397 672-673 (December 23, 1993) p158. (McLeese, Don)
Trampoline
RR11398 732 (April 18, 1996) p69. (Sarig, Roni)
HERSCH, KRISTIN
Hips And Makers
RR11399 679 (April 7, 1994) pp72-73. (Zacharek, Stephanie)
HIATT, JOHN
Perfectly Good Guitar
RR11400 668 (October 28, 1993) p78. (Cohen, Jason)
HIGHWAYMEN
The Road Goes On Forever
RR11401 712-713 (July 13, 1995) p110. (McGee, David)
HILL, ANDREW
Judgment!
RR11402 692 (October 6, 1994) p89. (Futterman, Steve)
HILL, FAITH
Take Me As I Am
RR11403 675 (February 10, 1994) p46. (McLeese, Don)
HINOJOSA, TISH
Destiny's Gate
RR11404 686-687 (July 14, 1994) p107. (McLeese, Don)
HITCHCOCK, ROBYN
A Day In The Life (song)
RR11405 634-635 (July 9, 1992) p102. (Fricke, David)
Moss Elixir
RR11406 745 (October 17, 1996) p137. (Robbins, Ira)
Mossy Liquor
RR11407 745 (October 17, 1996) p137. (Robbins, Ira)
HITCHCOCK, ROBYN (& THE EGYPTIANS)
Black Snake Diamond Role
RR11408 705 (April 6, 1995) p62. (Considine, J. D.)
Element Of Light
RR11409 705 (April 6, 1995) p62. (Considine, J. D.)
Fegmania!
RR11410 705 (April 6, 1995) p62. (Considine, J. D.)
Gotta Let This Hen Out!
RR11411 705 (April 6, 1995) p62. (Considine, J. D.)
Gravy Deco
RR11412 705 (April 6, 1995) p62. (Considine, J. D.)
Groovy Decay
RR11413 705 (April 6, 1995) p62. (Considine, J. D.)
Groovy Decoy
RR11414 705 (April 6, 1995) p62. (Considine, J. D.)
I Often Dream Of Trains
RR11415 705 (April 6, 1995) p62. (Considine, J. D.)
Perspex Island
RR11416 619-620 (December 12, 1991) pp182,184. (Fricke, David)
Respect
RR11417 654 (April 15, 1993) p62. (McDonnell, Evelyn)
HOGAN, KELLY
The Whistle Only Dogs Can Hear
RR11418 742 (September 5, 1996) p65. (Hunter, James)
HOLCOMB, ROBIN
Rockabye
RR11419 642 (October 29, 1992) pp69-70. (Stenger, Wif)
HOLE
Ask For It
RR11420 724-725 (December 28, 1995) pp124-125. (Fricke, David)
Live Through This
RR11421 680 (April 21, 1994) pp83-84. (Fricke, David)
RR11422 698-699 (December 29, 1994) p191. (Evans, Paul)
HOLIDAY, BILLIE
Billie Holiday: The Legacy 1933-1958
RR11423 616 (October 31, 1991) p89. (Harrington, Spencer)
The Complete Billie Holiday On Verve 1945-1959
RR11424 645-646 (December 10, 1992) p180. (Futterman, Steve)
HOLLY, BUDDY
The Buddy Holly Collection
RR11425 672-673 (December 23, 1993) p148. (Considine, J. D.)
HOLMES BROTHERS
Jubilation
RR11426 636 (August 6, 1992) pp59-60. (Jurek, Thom)
Where It's At
RR11427 624 (February 20, 1992) p45. (Swenson, John)
HOLSAPPLE, PETER
Mavericks
RR11428 619-620 (December 12, 1991) p184. (Fricke, David)
HOOKER, JOHN LEE
Boom Boom
RR11429 655 (April 29, 1993) p65. (Swenson, John)
Mr. Lucky
RR11430 619-620 (December 12, 1991) pp174,178. (Fricke, David)

HOOKER, WILLIAM
Shamballa
RR11431 672-673 (December 23, 1993) p154. (Fricke, David)
HOOTIE AND THE BLOWFISH
Cracked Rear View
RR11432 693 (October 20, 1994) p148. (Evans, Paul)
RR11433 724-725 (December 28, 1995) p116. (Fricke, David)
Fairweather Johnson
RR11434 734 (May 16, 1996) pp63-64. (Gardner, Elysa)
RR11435 750-751 (December 26, 1996) p186.
HOPKINS, LIGHTNIN'
The Complete Candid Otis Spann-Lightnin' Hopkins Sessions
RR11436 640 (October 1, 1992) p67. (Fricke, David)
The Complete Prestige-Bluesville Recordings
RR11437 619-620 (December 12, 1991) p177. (McLeese, Don)
HORMONES
Sell Out Young (song)
RR11438 716 (September 7, 1995) p73. (Fricke, David)
You Can't Win (song)
RR11439 716 (September 7, 1995) p73. (Fricke, David)
HORNSBY, BRUCE
Harbor Lights
RR11440 658 (June 10, 1993) pp69-70. (Evans, Paul)
HORTA, TONINHO
Once I Loved
RR11441 649 (February 4, 1993) p68. (Palmer, Robert)
HOTHOUSE FLOWERS
Songs From The Rain
RR11442 657 (May 27, 1993) p52. (Manning, Kara)
HOUSE OF PAIN
Fine Malt Lyrics
RR11443 642 (October 29, 1992) p70. (Nelson, Havelock)
HOUSTON, PENELOPE
Cut You
RR11444 731 (April 4, 1996) p62. (Farber, Jim)
HOVERCRAFT
Hovercraft (EP)
RR11445 745 (October 17, 1996) p135. (Fricke, David)
HOWARD, ADINA
Do You Wanna Ride
RR11446 708 (May 18, 1995) p90. (Evans, Paul)
HOWLIN WOLF
Ain't Gonna Be Your Dog
RR11447 682 (May 19, 1994) p100. (Considine, J. D.)
Howlin' Wolf
RR11448 619-620 (December 12, 1991) p177. (McLeese, Don)
HUBBARD, RAY WYLIE
Loco Gringo's Lament
RR11449 707 (May 4, 1995) p70. (McLeese, Don)
HUGGY BEAR
Our Troubled Youth
RR11450 666 (September 30, 1993) p104. (McDonnell, Evelyn)
HUGHES, LANGSTON
The Voice Of Langston Hughes
RR11451 706 (April 20, 1995) p78. (Toure)
HUMAN LEAGUE
Octopus
RR11452 707 (May 4, 1995) p69. (Evans, Paul)
HUMBLE PIE
In Concert
RR11453 740 (August 8, 1996) p62. (Fricke, David)
HUNTER, LONG JOHN
Ride With Me
RR11454 672-673 (December 23, 1993) p154. (Fricke, David)
HURRICANE
The Hurra
RR11455 709 (June 1, 1995) p65. (McElfresh, Suzanna)
HURT, MISSISSIPPI JOHN
Avalon Blues 1963
RR11456 624 (February 20, 1992) p42. (McLeese, Don)
Worried Blues 1963
RR11457 624 (February 20, 1992) p42. (McLeese, Don)
HUSKER DU
The Living End
RR11458 681 (May 5, 1994) pp53,55. (Zacharek, Stephanie)
HYENAS IN THE DESERT
Die Laughing
RR11459 742 (September 5, 1996) pp62,64. (Coleman, Mark)

I

I MOTHER EARTH
Dig
RR11460 667 (October 14, 1993) p34. (Neely, Kim)
IAN, JANIS
Breaking Silence
RR11461 665 (September 16, 1993) pp65-66. (D'Erasmo, Stacey)
IBRAHIM, ABDULLAH
Mantra Mode
RR11462 623 (February 6, 1992) p80. (Futterman, Steve)
ICE CUBE
Death Certificate
RR11463 619-620 (December 12, 1991) p165. (Fricke, David)
Lethal Injection
RR11464 674 (January 27, 1994) pp51-52. (Toure)
The Predator
RR11465 647 (January 7, 1993) p46. (Smith, Danyel)
ICE-T
Body Count
RR11466 630 (May 14, 1992) pp105,107. (Considine, J. D.)
Home Invasion
RR11467 653 (April 1, 1993) pp51-52. (DeCurtis, Anthony)
RR11468 672-673 (December 23, 1993) p165. (Evans, Paul)
VI: Return Of The Real
RR11469 737 (June 27, 1996) pp56,59. (Harris, Carter)
IDOL, BILLY
Cyberpunk
RR11470 662 (August 5, 1993) pp64-65. (Coleman, Mark)
IMPERIAL DRAG
Imperial Drag
RR11471 740 (August 8, 1996) p60. (Van Parys, Bill)
IMPERIAL TEEN
Seasick
RR11472 734 (May 16, 1996) p68. (McDonnell, Evelyn)
IMPRESSIONS
The Anthology 1961-1977
RR11473 649 (February 4, 1993) p69. (McEwen, Joe)
INCOGNITO
100 Degrees And Rising
RR11474 719 (October 19, 1995) pp150,152. (Torres, Rick)
INCREDIBLE CASUALS
Your Sounds
RR11475 625 (March 5, 1992) p70. (Fricke, David)
INDIA
Llego La India
RR11476 645-646 (December 10, 1992) p187. (McLane, Daisann)
INDIGO GIRLS
Swamp Ophelia
RR11477 689 (August 25, 1994) pp89-90. (Matteo, Steve)
INFIDELS
Infidels
RR11478 621 (January 9, 1992) p53. (Sauter, Michael)

INNER CIRCLE
Bad Boys
RR11479 660-661 (July 8, 1993) p20. (Fricke, David)
INSPIRAL CARPETS
Devil Hopping
RR11480 682 (May 19, 1994) p103. (Evans, Paul)
INTRUDERS
Cowboys To Girls
RR11481 724-725 (December 28, 1995) p122. (Coleman, Mark)
INXS
Full Moon, Dirty Hearts
RR11482 676 (February 24, 1994) pp56-57. (Wright, Christian)
Welcome To Wherever You Are
RR11483 638 (September 3, 1992) pp65,67. (Garbarini, Vic)
RR11484 675 (February 10, 1994) p18. (D'Arby, Terence Trent)
IRON CITY HOUSEROCKERS
End Of The Century
RR11485 645-646 (December 10, 1992) p177. (Fricke, David)
IRON PROSTATE
Bring Me The Head Of Jerry Garcia (single)
RR11486 625 (March 5, 1992) p70. (Fricke, David)
ISAACS, GREGORY
Night Nurse
RR11487 676 (February 24, 1994) p42. (McLane, Daisann)
ISAAK, CHRIS
San Francisco Days
RR11488 656 (May 13, 1993) p104. (Wright, Christian)
IVORY LIBERTY
Dissolve
RR11489 628 (April 16, 1992) p85. (Fricke, David)
J MASCIS
Martin And Me
RR11490 733 (May 2, 1996) p56. (DeRogatis, Jim)

J

JACKSON FIVE
Soulsation!
RR11491 714 (August 10, 1995) p59. (Considine, J. D.)
RR11492 724-725 (December 28, 1995) p122. (Coleman, Mark)
JACKSON, JANET
Design Of A Decade
RR11493 724-725 (December 28, 1995) p125. (Fricke, David)
Janet
RR11494 659 (June 24, 1993) p78. (Toure)
RR11495 672-673 (December 23, 1993) p152. (Evans, Paul)
JACKSON, MICHAEL
Dangerous
RR11496 621 (January 9, 1992) pp49-51. (Light, Alan)
History
RR11497 714 (August 10, 1995) pp55,57-58. (Hunter, James)
RR11498 724-725 (December 28, 1995) p125. (Fricke, David)
JAGGER, MICK
Wandering Spirit
RR11499 650 (February 18, 1993) pp56,58. (Puterbaugh, Parke)
RR11500 672-673 (December 23, 1993) p146. (Evans, Paul)
JAM
Live Jam
RR11501 693 (October 20, 1994) p146. (Sinclair, Tom)
JAMAL, AHMAD
Chicago Revisited: Live At Joe Segal's Jazz Showcase
RR11502 659 (June 24, 1993) p84. (Futterman, Steve)
JAMES
Laid
RR11503 698-699 (December 29, 1994) p190. (Evans, Paul)
Wah Wah
RR11504 698-699 (December 29, 1994) p190. (Evans, Paul)
JAMES, COLIN
Colin James And The Little Big Band
RR11505 679 (April 7, 1994) p74. (Evans, Paul)
JAMES, ELMORE
King Of The Slide Guitar
RR11506 645-646 (December 10, 1992) p170. (Considine, J. D.)
JAMES, ETTA
The Right Time
RR11507 644 (November 26, 1992) p75. (Swenson, John)
JAMES, WENDY
Now Ain't The Time For Your Tears
RR11508 665 (September 16, 1993) p70. (Robbins, Ira)
JAMIROQUAI
The Return Of The Space Cowboy
RR11509 704 (March 23, 1995) p125. (Evans, Paul)
JARBOE
Sacrificial Cake
RR11510 718 (October 5, 1995) p69. (Walls, Richard C.)
JARVIS, DUANE
DJ's Front Porch
RR11511 683 (June 2, 1994) p70. (McLeese, Don)
JASON
On Foot In The Honky Tonk
RR11512 637 (August 20, 1992) pp52-53. (Hunter, James)
JASON AND THE SCORCHERS
A Blazing Grace
RR11513 703 (March 9, 1995) p66. (McLeese, Don)
Essential Jason And The Scorchers Volume One: Are You Ready For The Country
RR11514 647 (January 7, 1993) p54. (McLeese, Don)
JAYHAWKS
Hollywood Town Hall
RR11515 642 (October 29, 1992) p70. (Mundy, Chris)
Tomorrow The Green Grass
RR11516 703 (March 9, 1995) pp66-67. (O'Connor, Rob)
JAZZ FUTURES
Live In Concert
RR11517 665 (September 16, 1993) p67. (Futterman, Steve)
J.B.'S
Funky Good Time
RR11518 705 (April 6, 1995) p62. (Considine, J. D.)
JEFFERSON AIRPLANE
Jefferson Airplane Loves You
RR11519 645-646 (December 10, 1992) pp166,168. (Coleman, Mark)
JEFFREYS, GARLAND
Don't Call Me Buckwheat
RR11520 628 (April 16, 1992) pp80,84. (Sinclair, Tom)
RR11521 645-646 (December 10, 1992) p178. (Coleman, Mark)
JENNINGS, WAYLON
Only Daddy That'll Walk The Line
RR11522 672-673 (December 23, 1993) p158. (McLeese, Don)
Waymore's Blues (Part II)
RR11523 691 (September 22, 1994) p97. (McLeese, Don)
JESUS AND MARY CHAIN
Honey's Dead
RR11524 630 (May 14, 1992) p107. (Robbins, Ira)
Stoned And Dethroned
RR11525 697 (December 15, 1994) pp94-95. (Seymour, Corey)
JESUS JONES

Doubt
RR11526 619-620 (December 12, 1991) p182. (Fricke, David)
Perverse
RR11527 650 (February 18, 1993) p60. (Blardinelli, Jill)
JESUS LIZARD
Down
RR11528 697 (December 15, 1994) p97. (Ali, Lorraine)
(Fly) On (The Wall) (song)
RR11529 676 (February 24, 1994) p57. (Fricke, David)
Shot
RR11530 733 (May 2, 1996) p52. (O'Connor, Rob)
Show
RR11531 697 (December 15, 1994) p97. (Ali, Lorraine)
JETT, JOAN
Love Is All Around (song)
RR11532 736 (June 13, 1996) p78. (Kenny, Glenn)
Notorious
RR11533 615 (October 17, 1991) p93. (Sinclair, Tom)
Pure And Simple
RR11534 691 (September 22, 1994) pp94,97. (Zacharek, Stephanie)
JIMENEZ, FLACO
Flaco Jimenez
RR11535 698-699 (December 29, 1994) p178. (McLeese, Don)
Partners
RR11536 637 (August 20, 1992) p53. (McLeese, Don)
JOCQUE, BEAU
Pick Up On This!
RR11537 684 (June 16, 1994) p110. (Fricke, David)
JODECI
The Show, The After-Party, The Hotel
RR11538 719 (October 19, 1995) pp152-153. (Gardner, Elysa)
RR11539 724-725 (December 28, 1995) p126. (Fricke, David)
JOEL, BILLY
River Of Dreams
RR11540 663 (August 19, 1993) p74. (Manning, Kara)
RR11541 672-673 (December 23, 1993) p156. (Evans, Paul)
JOHN AND MARY
The Weedkiller's Daughter
RR11542 656 (May 13, 1993) pp104,107. (Mell, A. J.)
JOHN, ELTON
Duets
RR11543 671 (December 9, 1993) pp66,70. (Gardner, Elysa)
Made In England
RR11544 707 (May 4, 1995) p65. (Galvin, Peter)
The One
RR11545 638 (September 3, 1992) p67. (Farber, Jim)
JOHN, MABLE
Stay Out Of The Kitchen
RR11546 660-661 (July 8, 1993) p20. (Fricke, David)
JOHNSON, BIG JACK
The Oil Man
RR11547 679 (April 7, 1994) p74. (Evans, Paul)
JOHNSON, BLIND WILLIE
The Complete Blind Willie Johnson
RR11548 664 (September 2, 1993) p64. (Considine, J. D.)
JOHNSON, LINTON KWESI
Making History
RR11549 676 (February 24, 1994) p42. (McLane, Daisann)
JOHNSON, MIKE
Year Of Mondays
RR11550 733 (May 2, 1996) p56. (DeRogatis, Jim)
JOHNSON, SLY
Back In The Game
RR11551 706 (April 20, 1995) p72. (Fricke, David)
JOHNSTON, DANIEL
Artistic Vice
RR11552 624 (February 20, 1992) pp41-42. (Robbins, Ira)
Fun
RR11553 698-699 (December 29, 1994) p176. (Evans, Paul)
JOHNSTON, FREDDY
This Perfect World
RR11554 686-687 (July 14, 1994) p102. (O'Dair, Barbara)
JOI
The Pendulum Vibe
RR11555 700 (January 26, 1995) p62. (Coker, Cheo H.)
JOLLY BOYS
Beer Joint And Tailoring
RR11556 628 (April 16, 1992) p85. (Fricke, David)
JONES, ELVIN
Youngblood
RR11557 649 (February 4, 1993) p75. (Futterman, Steve)
JONES, GEORGE
The Bradley Barn Sessions
RR11558 693 (October 20, 1994) p150. (McLeese, Don)
Cup Of Loneliness
RR11559 698-699 (December 29, 1994) p178. (McLeese, Don)
High-Tech Redneck
RR11560 672-673 (December 23, 1993) p158. (McLeese, Don)
The Spirit Of Country
RR11561 698-699 (December 29, 1994) p178. (McLeese, Don)
JONES, HOWARD
In The Running
RR11562 630 (May 14, 1992) p103. (Wright, Christian)
JONES, JOHN PAUL
The Sporting Life
RR11563 692 (October 6, 1994) p87. (Evans, Paul)
JONES, QUINCY
This Is How I Feel About Jazz
RR11564 649 (February 4, 1993) p75. (Futterman, Steve)
JONES, RICKIE LEE
Pop Pop
RR11565 616 (October 31, 1991) p93. (Woodard, Josef)
Traffic From Paradise
RR11566 668 (October 28, 1993) p80. (Manning, Kara)
JONES, SPIKE
Musical Depreciation Revue
RR11567 691 (September 22, 1994) p93. (McGee, David)
Spiked!
RR11568 691 (September 22, 1994) p93. (McGee, David)
JONES, THAD
The Complete Solid State Recordings Of The Thad Jones - Mel Lewis Big Band
RR11569 698-699 (December 29, 1994) p180. (Futterman, Steve)
JOPLIN, JANIS
Janis
RR11570 672-673 (December 23, 1993) p148. (Considine, J. D.)
JORDAN, SASS
Rats
RR11571 681 (May 5, 1994) p54. (Evans, Paul)
JU JU HOUNDS
Izzy Stradlin And The Ju Ju Hounds
RR11572 645-646 (December 10, 1992) p179. (Coleman, Mark)
JUDD, WYNONNA
Tell Me Why
RR11573 660-661 (July 8, 1993) p114. (Dean, Chuck)
Wynonna
RR11574 631 (May 28, 1992) pp51-52. (McGee, David)
RR11575 645-646 (December 10, 1992) pp164,166. (Coleman, Mark)
JUDDS

The Judds Collection 1983-1990
RR11576 645-646 (December 10, 1992) p174. (McLeese, Don)
JUNGLE BROTHERS
J. Beez Wit The Remedy
RR11577 668 (October 28, 1993) p83. (Thigpen, David)

K

K, PAUL
The Blue Sun
RR11578 645-646 (December 10, 1992) p177. (Fricke, David)
KAISER, HENRY
Hope You Like Our New Direction
RR11579 619-620 (December 12, 1991) p168. (Fricke, David)
KALEIDOSCOPE
Egyptian Candy
RR11580 629 (April 30, 1992) p57. (Considine, J. D.)
KALESIJSKI SVUCI
Bosnia Breakdown
RR11581 698-699 (December 29, 1994) p174. (Fricke, David)
KANE, KIERAN
Dead Rekoning
RR11582 707 (May 4, 1995) p70. (McLeese, Don)
Find My Way Home
RR11583 675 (February 10, 1994) p46. (McLeese, Don)
KANSAS
Kansas
RR11584 696 (December 1, 1994) p129. (Diehl, Matt)
KANTNER, PAUL
A Guide Through The Chaos
RR11585 747 (November 14, 1996) p114. (Damsker, Matt)
KASSAV
Tekit Izi
RR11586 670 (November 25, 1993) p108. (McLane, Daisann)
KEB' MO'
Keb' Mo'
RR11587 697 (December 15, 1994) p98. (Lyman, Andy)
KEEN, ROBERT EARL
A Bigger Piece Of Sky
RR11588 662 (August 5, 1993) p67. (McLeese, Don)
Gringo Honeymoon
RR11589 693 (October 20, 1994) p150. (McLeese, Don)
RR11590 698-699 (December 29, 1994) p181. (Evans, Paul)
KEITA, SALIF
Folon...The Past
RR11591 727 (February 8, 1996) p51. (Moon, Tom)
KELLAWAY, ROGER
Life's A Take
RR11592 659 (June 24, 1993) p84. (Futterman, Steve)
KELLY, PAUL
The Best Of Paul Kelly
RR11593 747 (November 14, 1996) p116. (Morris, Chris)
Deeper Water
RR11594 724-725 (December 28, 1995) p118. (Fricke, David)
Wanted Man
RR11595 698-699 (December 29, 1994) pp176,178. (Evans, Paul)
KELLY, R.
R. Kelly
RR11596 726 (January 25, 1996) p72. (DeRogatis, Jim)
KENNEDY, MAURA
River Of Fallen Stars
RR11597 707 (May 4, 1995) p70. (McLeese, Don)
KENNEDY, PETE
River Of Fallen Stars
RR11598 707 (May 4, 1995) p70. (McLeese, Don)
KENTUCKY HEADHUNTERS
Rave On!!
RR11599 657 (May 27, 1993) p53. (Swenson, John)
KERSHAW, SAMMY
Haunted Heart
RR11600 656 (May 13, 1993) p110. (McLeese, Don)
KETCHUM, HAL
Every Little Word
RR11601 683 (June 2, 1994) p70. (McLeese, Don)
Sure Love
RR11602 653 (April 1, 1993) p52. (McGee, David)
KHALED
N'ssi N'ssi
RR11603 680 (April 21, 1994) p90. (McLane, Daisann)
KHAN, CHAKA
The Woman I Am
RR11604 628 (April 16, 1992) p84. (Chambers, Gordon)
KID FROST
East Side Story
RR11605 631 (May 28, 1992) p54. (Santiago, Roberto)
KIERMYER, FRANKLIN
Solomon's Daughter
RR11606 698-699 (December 29, 1994) p174. (Fricke, David)
KIG MISSILE
Happy Hour
RR11607 652 (March 18, 1993) p39. (Harris, Michael C.)
KILLDOZER
When The Levee Breaks (song)
RR11608 720 (November 2, 1995) p69. (Fricke, David)
KILLER JOE
Scene Of The Crime
RR11609 622 (January 23, 1992) pp46-47. (Swenson, John)
KIMBROUGH, JUNIOR
All Night Long
RR11610 649 (February 4, 1993) p69. (Santelli, Robert)
Sad Days, Lonely Nights
RR11611 698-699 (December 29, 1994) p181. (Evans, Paul)
KING, B. B.
King Of The Blues
RR11611a 645-646 (December 10, 1992) p170. (Considine, J. D.)
KING, CAROLE
Colour Of Your Dreams
RR11611b 659 (June 24, 1993) pp80,83. (Manning, Kara)
In Concert
RR11611c 680 (April 21, 1994) p88. (Evans, Paul)
A Natural Woman
RR11611d 694 (November 3, 1994) p100. (Considine, J. D.)
KING CRIMSON
B'Boom
RR11612 730 (March 21, 1996) p98. (Fricke, David)
The Essential King Crimson: Frame By Frame
RR11613 619-620 (December 12, 1991) p177. (McLeese, Don)
The Great Deceiver
RR11614 645-646 (December 10, 1992) p170. (Considine, J. D.)
Thrak
RR11615 711 (June 29, 1995) p43. (Bambarger, Bradley)
Thrakattak
RR11616 750-751 (December 26, 1996) p198.
Vroom
RR11617 698-699 (December 29, 1994) p174. (Fricke, David)
KING JAMMY
Computer Style
RR11618 629 (April 30, 1992) p57. (Considine, J. D.)
Hits Style
RR11619 629 (April 30, 1992) p57. (Considine, J. D.)
A Man And His Music, Vol. II—Computer Style
RR11620 676 (February 24, 1994) p42. (McLane, Daisann)

RR11621-24 Numbers not assigned.
KING'S X
King's X
RR11625 629 (April 30, 1992) pp56-57. (Neely, Kim)
KINKS
Phobia
RR11626 654 (April 15, 1993) p64. (Evans, Paul)
To The Bone
RR11627 706 (April 20, 1995) p72. (Fricke, David)
KINNEY, KEVN
Down Out Law
RR11628 680 (April 21, 1994) pp89-90. (O'Connor, Rob)
KIRCHEN, BILL
Tombstone Every Mile
RR11629 693 (October 20, 1994) p150. (McLeese, Don)
KIRK, ANDY
Mary's Idea
RR11630 659 (June 24, 1993) p84. (Futterman, Steve)
KMFDM
'Xtort'
RR11631 736 (June 13, 1996) p53. (Wiederhorn, Jon)
RR11632 738-739 (July 11, 1996) p90. (Masuo, Sandy)
KOERNER, SPIDER JOHN
Running Jumping Standing Still
RR11633 682 (May 19, 1994) p103. (Swenson, John)
KOOL AND THE GANG
The Best Of Kool And The Gang 1969-1976
RR11634 667 (October 14, 1993) p118. (Toure)
KOSTAS
S In Moderation
RR11635 693 (October 20, 1994) p150. (McLeese, Don)
KOUROS, ANDY
Goodbye
RR11636 689 (August 25, 1994) p92. (McLane, Daisann)
KRAMER, WAYNE
The Hard Stuff
RR11637 704 (March 23, 1995) p122. (Drozdowski, Ted)
KRAUSS, ALISON
I Know Who Holds Tomorrow
RR11638 675 (February 10, 1994) p46. (McLeese, Don)
Now That I've Found You
RR11639 706 (April 20, 1995) p80. (Evans, Paul)
KRAVITZ, LENNY
Are You Gonna Go My Way
RR11640 655 (April 29, 1993) pp61-62. (Poulson-Bryant, Scott)
RR11641 672-673 (December 23, 1993) p153. (Evans, Paul)
Circus
RR11642 717 (September 21, 1995) pp81-83. (Kemp, Mark)
RR11643 724-725 (December 28, 1995) p126. (Fricke, David)
KRIS KROSS
Da Bomb
RR11644 667 (October 14, 1993) p117. (Nelson, Havelock)
Totally Krossed Out
RR11645 645-646 (December 10, 1992) pp176,178. (Coleman, Mark)
KRONOS QUARTET
Pieces Of Africa
RR11646 628 (April 16, 1992) p86. (Richardson, Susan)
Short Stories
RR11647 658 (June 10, 1993) p71. (Schwarz, K. Robert)
KRS-ONE
KRS-One
RR11648 721 (November 16, 1995) p113. (Coker, Cheo H.)
Return Of The Boom Bap
RR11649 670 (November 25, 1993) p120. (Ehrlich, Dimitri)
KULA SHAKER
K
RR11650 750-751 (December 26, 1996) p195.
KURIOUS JORGE
Constipated Monkey
RR11651 679 (April 7, 1994) p73. (Toure)
KUSTOMIZED
The Battle For Space
RR11652 706 (April 20, 1995) p81. (Diehl, Matt)
KWEDER, KENN
Kenn Kweder
RR11653 716 (September 7, 1995) p73. (Fricke, David)

L

L. L. COOL J
14 Shots To The Dome
RR11654 656 (May 13, 1993) p107. (Toure)
Mama Said Knock You Out
RR11655 619-620 (December 12, 1991) p184. (Fricke, David)
Mr. Smith
RR11656 727 (February 8, 1996) pp49-50. (Coker, Cheo H.)
L7
Bricks Are Heavy
RR11657 639 (September 17, 1992) p94. (Berger, Arion)
Hungry For Stink
RR11658 698-699 (December 29, 1994) pp182,185. (Evans, Paul)
LAFAVE, JIMMY
Austin Skyline
RR11659 683 (June 2, 1994) p70. (McLeese, Don)
Highway Trance
RR11660 683 (June 2, 1994) p70. (McLeese, Don)
LANDRETH, SONNY
Outward Bound
RR11661 637 (August 20, 1992) p53. (McLeese, Don)
South Of I-10
RR11662 706 (April 20, 1995) pp73-74. (Milward, John)
LANEGAN, MARK
Whiskey For The Holy Ghost
RR11663 680 (April 21, 1994) pp89-90. (O'Connor, Rob)
LANG, K. D.
All You Can Eat
RR11664 721 (November 16, 1995) p112. (Walters, Barry)
Even Cowgirls Get The Blues
RR11665 677 (March 10, 1994) p65. (Evans, Paul)
Ingenue
RR11666 629 (April 30, 1992) p57. (Milward, John)
LANOIS, DANIEL
For The Beauty Of Wynona
RR11667 657 (May 27, 1993) p49. (Evans, Paul)
LAROSE
Democratie
RR11668 626 (March 19, 1992) p95. (McLane, Daisann)
LATIN PLAYBOYS
Latin Playboys
RR11669 684 (June 16, 1994) pp109-110. (Jurek, Thom)
LAUDERDALE, JIM
Planet Of Love
RR11670 623 (February 6, 1992) p83. (Sauter, Michael)
Pretty Close To The Truth
RR11671 691 (September 22, 1994) p97. (McLeese, Don)
LAUGHNER, PETER
Take The Guitar Player For A Ride
RR11672 698-699 (December 29, 1994) p174. (Fricke, David)
LAUPER, CYNDI
Hat Full Of Stars
RR11673 664 (September 2, 1993) pp60-61. (George-Warren, Holly)
LAWRENCE, TRACY
Alibis

RR11674 656 (May 13, 1993) p110. (McLeese, Don)
LEARY, DENIS
No Cure For Cancer
RR11675 651 (March 4, 1993) p65. (Evans, Paul)
LED ZEPPELIN
The Complete Studio Recordings
RR11676 669 (November 11, 1993) p77. (Considine, J. D.)
LEE, ARTHUR
5 String Serenade (song)
RR11677 664 (September 2, 1993) p16. (Fricke, David)
Girl On Fire (song)
RR11677a 698-699 (December 29, 1994) p174. (Fricke, David)
7 And 7 Is (song)
RR11678 698-699 (December 29, 1994) p174. (Fricke, David)
RR11679 Number not assigned.
LEE, BEN
Grandpaw Would
RR11680 708 (May 18, 1995) pp92-93. (Kelly, Christina)
LEMONHEADS
Car Button Cloth
RR11681 748 (November 28, 1996) pp132,134. (Hoskyns, Barney)
Come On Feel The Lemonheads
RR11682 670 (November 25, 1993) pp108,112. (Ali, Lorraine)
LENNON, JULIAN
Help Yourself
RR11683 616 (October 31, 1991) p93. (Puterbaugh, Parke)
LENNOX, ANNIE
Diva
RR11684 633 (June 25, 1992) p41. (Evans, Paul)
Medusa
RR11685 706 (April 20, 1995) p70. (Gardner, Elysa)
LEVELLERS
Levelling The Land
RR11686 633 (June 25, 1992) p45. (Gardner, Elysa)
LEWD, TREY
Drop The Line
RR11687 645-646 (December 10, 1992) p180. (Coleman, Mark)
LEWIS, EPHRAIM
Skin
RR11688 637 (August 20, 1992) p53. (Powell, Kevin)
LEWIS, HUEY
Four Chords And Several Years Ago
RR11689 684 (June 16, 1994) p106. (Evans, Paul)
LEWIS, JERRY LEE
Jerry Lee Lewis
RR11690 624 (February 20, 1992) p42. (McLeese, Don)
Rockin' My Life Away
RR11691 624 (February 20, 1992) p42. (McLeese, Don)
Young Blood
RR11692 712-713 (July 13, 1995) p111. (Drozdowski, Ted)
LEWIS, MEL
The Complete Solid State Recordings Of The Thad Jones - Mel Lewis Big Band
RR11693 698-699 (December 29, 1994) p180. (Futterman, Steve)
LEWIS, PETER
Peter Lewis
RR11694 720 (November 2, 1995) p69. (Fricke, David)
LIGHTFOOT, GORDON
Waiting For You
RR11695 664 (September 2, 1993) p62. (Altman, Billy)
LINCOLN, ABBEY
You Gotta Pay The Band
RR11696 618 (November 28, 1991) p96. (Futterman, Steve)
LIQUID COURAGE
Liquid Courage
RR11697 686-687 (July 14, 1994) p104. (Evans, Paul)
LIQUOR CABINET
Mood Elevator
RR11698 726 (January 25, 1996) p71. (Moon, Tom)
LIQUOR GIANTS
Here
RR11699 698-699 (December 29, 1994) p174. (Fricke, David)
LISA LISA
LL77
RR11700 681 (May 5, 1994) p54. (Evans, Paul)
LITTLE AXE
The Wolf That House Built
RR11701 703 (March 9, 1995) p65. (Fernando, S. H., Jr.)
LITTLE JACK MELODY WITH HIS YOUNG TURKS
On The Blank Generation
RR11702 634-635 (July 9, 1992) p102. (Fricke, David)
LITTLE VILLAGE
Little Village
RR11703 624 (February 20, 1992) p42. (Okamoto, David)
LITTLE, BOOKER
Fantastic Frank Strozier: Plus
RR11704 678 (March 24, 1994) p97. (Futterman, Steve)
LIVE
Throwing Copper
RR11705 688 (August 11, 1994) p70. (Evans, Paul)
LIVING COLOUR
Stain
RR11706 652 (March 18, 1993) p39. (Considine, J. D.)
RR11707 672-673 (December 23, 1993) p157. (Evans, Paul)
LLOYD, BILL
Set To Pop
RR11708 683 (June 2, 1994) p70. (McLeese, Don)
LO, ISMAEL
Iso
RR11709 698-699 (December 29, 1994) p182. (McLane, Daisann)
LOGAN, JACK
Bulk
RR11710 691 (September 22, 1994) pp100-101. (Fricke, David)
Mood Elevator
RR11711 726 (January 25, 1996) p71. (Moon, Tom)
Out Of Whack (EP)
RR11712 720 (November 2, 1995) p69. (Fricke, David)
LONDON SINFONIETTA
Symphony No. 3
RR11713 655 (April 29, 1993) p65. (Schwarz, K. Robert)
RR11714 657 (April 29, 1993) p6. (Schwarz, K. Robert)
LONDON SUEDE
Dog Man Star
RR11715 698-699 (December 29, 1994) pp185,190. (Evans, Paul)
LONDON SYMPHONY ORCHESTRA
Symphonic Music Of The Rolling Stones
RR11716 686-687 (July 14, 1994) p104. (Evans, Paul)
LONESOME DEBONAIRES
Blue On Blonde
RR11717 625 (March 5, 1992) p72. (Puterbaugh, Parke)
LOOSE DIAMONDS
New Location
RR11718 707 (May 4, 1995) p70. (McLeese, Don)
LOOSE GRAVEL
Thanks For The Memories
RR11719 652 (March 18, 1993) p42. (Fricke, David)
LORD KITCHENER
Klassic Kitchener
RR11720 680 (April 21, 1994) p90. (McLane, Daisann)
LOS HURACANES DEL NORTE
Vientos

RR11721 672-673 (December 23, 1993) p163. (McLane, Daisann)
LOS LOBOS
Colossal Head
RR11722 732 (April 18, 1996) p70. (Himes, Geoffrey)
Just Another Band From East L.A.
RR11723 669 (November 11, 1993) p77. (Considine, J. D.)
Kiko
RR11724 633 (June 25, 1992) pp41-42. (Okamoto, David)
LOUD FAMILY
Plants And Birds And Rocks And Things
RR11725 656 (May 13, 1993) p104. (Considine, J. D.)
The Tape Of Only Linda
RR11726 698-699 (December 29, 1994) p182. (Evans, Paul)
LOUD MACHINE 5000
Go Grace Go (song)
RR11727 676 (February 24, 1994) p57. (Fricke, David)
Lord Of Nothing Pt. 1 (song)
RR11728 676 (February 24, 1994) p57. (Fricke, David)
LOUVIN BROTHERS
Satan Is Real
RR11729 750-751 (December 26, 1996) p189. (Coleman, Mark)
Tragic Songs Of Life
RR11730 750-751 (December 26, 1996) p189. (Coleman, Mark)
LOVANO, JOE
From The Soul
RR11731 642 (October 29, 1992) p75. (Futterman, Steve)
Memoirs
RR11732 642 (October 29, 1992) p75. (Futterman, Steve)
Tenor Legacy
RR11733 678 (March 24, 1994) p97. (Futterman, Steve)
LOVE
5 String Serenade (song)
RR11734 664 (September 2, 1993) p16. (Fricke, David)
RR11735 Number not assigned.
Forever Changes
RR11736 724-725 (December 28, 1995) p122. (Coleman, Mark)
Girl On Fire (song)
RR11737 698-699 (December 29, 1994) p174. (Fricke, David)
Love Story
RR11738 724-725 (December 28, 1995) p122. (Coleman, Mark)
7 And 7 Is (song)
RR11738a 698-699 (December 29, 1994) p174. (Fricke, David)
LOVE AND ROCKETS
Sweet F.A.
RR11739 736 (June 13, 1996) p86. (Hendrickson, Matt)
LOVE SPIT LOVE
Love Spit Love
RR11740 697 (December 15, 1994) pp95-96. (Welchman, Geoffrey)
LOVE, MONIE
In A Word Or 2
RR11741 658 (June 10, 1993) p69. (McDonnell, Evelyn)
LOVETT, LYLE
I Love Everybody
RR11742 692 (October 6, 1994) pp88,90. (Milward, John)
Joshua Judges Ruth
RR11743 629 (April 30, 1992) p56. (McLeese, Don)
The Road To Ensenada
RR11744 738-739 (July 11, 1996) p90. (Gardner, Elysa)
LOW
The Curtain Hits The Cast
RR11745 745 (October 17, 1996) pp136-137. (O'Connor, Rob)
LOWE, NICK
The Impossible Bird
RR11746 698-699 (December 29, 1994) p190. (Evans, Paul)
LUCAS, GARY
Gods And Monsters
RR11747 649 (February 4, 1993) p68. (Palmer, Robert)
LULU
Independence
RR11748 663 (August 19, 1993) p78. (Berger, Arion)
LUNACHICKS
Binge And Purge
RR11749 653 (April 1, 1993) p54. (Szabo, Julia)
LUSCIOUS JACKSON
In Search Of Manny
RR11750 679 (April 7, 1994) p30. (Hoon, Shannon)
Natural Ingredients
RR11751 691 (September 22, 1994) pp92,94. (St. Leger, Marie Elsie)
LUSH
Split
RR11752 690 (September 8, 1994) p78. (Evans, Paul)
Spooky
RR11753 628 (April 16, 1992) p86. (Reynolds, Simon)
LYNN, LORETTA
Honky Tonk Angels
RR11754 672-673 (December 23, 1993) p158. (McLeese, Don)
Honky Tonk Girl
RR11755 698-699 (December 29, 1994) p178. (McLeese, Don)
LYNNE, SHELBY
Temptation
RR11756 666 (September 30, 1993) p105. (McLeese, Don)
LYNYRD SKYNYRD
The Last Rebel
RR11757 657 (May 27, 1993) p53. (Swenson, John)
Lynyrd Skynyrd
RR11758 619-620 (December 12, 1991) p177. (McLeese, Don)
LYRES
Some Lyrics
RR11759 684 (June 16, 1994) p110. (Fricke, David)
LYTE, MC
Ain't No Other
RR11760 668 (October 28, 1993) pp78,80. (Nelson, Havelock)
Lyte As A Rock
RR11761 666 (September 30, 1993) p56. (Walser, Robert)

M

M PEOPLE
Bizarre Fruit
RR11762 714 (August 10, 1995) p58. (Panahpour, Nilou)
M., LISA
Ahora Vengo Alborota
RR11763 658 (June 10, 1993) p78. (McLane, Daisann)
MACCOLL, KIRSTY
Titanic Days
RR11764 675 (February 10, 1994) pp44-45. (White, Armond)
MACGOWAN, SHANE
The Snake
RR11765 715 (August 24, 1995) pp100-101. (Flaum, Eric)
MACHITO
Machito And His Afro-Cubans Cubop City
RR11766 640 (October 1, 1992) p75. (McLane, Daisann)
MAD PROFESSOR
It's A Mad, Mad, Mad, Mad Professor
RR11767 705 (April 6, 1995) p65. (Fernando, S. H., Jr.)

No Protection
RR11768 734 (May 16, 1996) pp64,66. (Hardy, Ernest)
MAD RIVER
A Gazelle (song)
RR11769 720 (November 2, 1995) p69. (Fricke, David)
MAD SEASON
Above
RR11770 706 (April 20, 1995) p74. (Davies, Barbara)
MADDER ROSE
Panic On
RR11771 678 (March 24, 1994) p16. (Donelly, Tanya)
RR11772 685 (June 30, 1994) p76. (Manning, Kara)
MADONNA
Bedtime Stories
RR11773 697 (December 15, 1994) pp93-94. (O'Dair, Barbara)
Erotica
RR11774 644 (November 26, 1992) p70. (Berger, Arion)
MAGIC DIRT
Friends In Danger
RR11775 750-751 (December 26, 1996) p192.
Magic Dirt
RR11776 732 (April 18, 1996) pp68-69. (Fricke, David)
MAGIC SAM
Magic Sam 1957-1966: West Side Guitar
RR11777 625 (March 5, 1992) p70. (Fricke, David)
Magic Touch
RR11778 659 (June 24, 1993) p81. (Sandmel, Ben)
MAGNAPOP
Hot Boxing
RR11779 698-699 (December 29, 1994) p190. (Evans, Paul)
MAGNOLIAS
Off The Hook
RR11780 637 (August 20, 1992) p50. (Robbins, Ira)
MAHAL, TAJ
Rising Sons
RR11781 652 (March 18, 1993) p42. (Fricke, David)
MAKAVELI
The Don Killuminati
RR11782 750-751 (December 26, 1996) p184.
MAKE-UP
Destination: Love
RR11783 740 (August 8, 1996) p62. (Fricke, David)
MAN OR ASTRO-MAN?
Is It...Man Or Astro-Man?
RR11784 667 (October 14, 1993) p121. (Fricke, David)
MANIC STREET PREACHERS
Everything Must Go
RR11785 750-751 (December 26, 1996) p199.
From Despair To Where (song)
RR11786 664 (September 2, 1993) p16. (Fricke, David)
MANN, AIMEE
Whatever
RR11787 662 (August 5, 1993) p68. (Manning, Kara)
MANZAREK, RAY
Myth And Reality
RR11788 747 (November 14, 1996) p114. (Damsker, Matt)
MARILYN MANSON
Antichrist Superstar
RR11789 748 (November 28, 1996) pp129-130. (Ali, Lorraine)
MARKIE, BIZ
All Samples Cleared!
RR11790 666 (September 30, 1993) p101. (Toure)
MARLEY, BOB
One Love
RR11791 628 (April 16, 1992) p81. (Palmer, Robert)
Songs Of Freedom
RR11792 645-646 (December 10, 1992) p170. (Considine, J. D.)
MARLEY, ZIGGY
Joy And Blues
RR11793 664 (September 2, 1993) pp62,64. (Mirkin, Steven)
MARS, CHRIS
75% Less Fat
RR11794 657 (May 27, 1993) pp50,52. (Weisel, Al)
MARSALIS, WYNTON
Blue Interlude
RR11795 637 (August 20, 1992) p52. (Futterman, Steve)
Citi Movement
RR11796 653 (April 1, 1993) p52. (Stern, Chip)
MARTHA AND THE VANDELLAS
Live Wire
RR11797 672-673 (December 23, 1993) p148. (Considine, J. D.)
MARTYN, JOHN
Sweet Little Mysteries
RR11798 685 (June 30, 1994) p77. (Considine, J. D.)
MARY'S DANISH
American Standard
RR11799 647 (January 7, 1993) p47. (Young, Jon)
MASSAKER
Koksofen
RR11800 672-673 (December 23, 1993) p154. (Fricke, David)
MASSENGIL, DAVID
Coming Up For Air
RR11801 645-646 (December 10, 1992) p177. (Fricke, David)
MASSIVE ATTACK
No Protection
RR11802 734 (May 16, 1996) pp64,66. (Hardy, Ernest)
Protection
RR11803 705 (April 6, 1995) p64. (Evans, Paul)
MASTER MUSICIANS OF JAJOUKA
Apocalypse Across The Sky
RR11804 637 (August 20, 1992) p52. (Fricke, David)
MASTERS OF REALITY
Sunrise On The Sufferbus
RR11805 652 (March 18, 1993) p40. (Drozdowski, Ted)
MATERIAL
Hallucination Engine
RR11806 677 (March 10, 1994) p65. (Evans, Paul)
MATERIAL ISSUE
Destination Universe
RR11807 637 (August 20, 1992) p50. (Robbins, Ira)
Freak City Soundtrack
RR11808 683 (June 2, 1994) p69. (Sinclair, Tom)
MATTHEWS, DAVE
Crash
RR11809 734 (May 16, 1996) p64. (DeRogatis, Jim)
Under The Table And Dreaming
RR11810 698-699 (December 29, 1994) pp181-182. (Evans, Paul)
RR11811 724-725 (December 28, 1995) p129. (Fricke, David)
MATTHEWS, ERIC
It's Heavy In Here
RR11812 719 (October 19, 1995) p150. (O'Connor, Rob)
MAVERICKS
From Hell To Paradise
RR11813 637 (August 20, 1992) p53. (McLeese, Don)
What A Crying Shame
RR11814 677 (March 10, 1994) p65. (Evans, Paul)
MAXWELL
Maxwell's Urban Hang Suite
RR11815 750-751 (December 26, 1996) p186.
MAY, BRIAN
Back To The Light
RR11816 657 (May 27, 1993) p50. (Altman, Billy)
MAYALL, JOHN
Bluesbreakers With Eric Clapton

RR11817 655 (April 29, 1993) p42. (Futterman, Steve)
MAYFIELD, CURTIS
The Anthology 1961-1977
RR11818 649 (February 4, 1993) p69. (McEwen, Joe)
New World Order
RR11819 747 (November 14, 1996) p112. (Coleman, Mark)
People Get Ready!
RR11820 750-751 (December 26, 1996) p189. (Coleman, Mark)
MAYFIELD, PERCY
Percy Mayfield Live
RR11821 649 (February 4, 1993) p66. (Swenson, John)
MAZZY STAR
Into Dust (song)
RR11822 666 (September 30, 1993) p18. (Wild, David)
So Tonight That I Might See
RR11823 671 (December 9, 1993) p73. (Ali, Lorraine)
MC 900 FT. JESUS
One Step Ahead Of The Spider
RR11824 690 (September 8, 1994) p78. (Evans, Paul)
MC SOLAAR
Prose Combat
RR11825 697 (December 15, 1994) p97. (Ehrlich, Dimitri)
MC5
Back In The USA
RR11826 645-646 (December 10, 1992) pp174,176. (Coleman, Mark)
High Time
RR11827 645-646 (December 10, 1992) pp174,176. (Coleman, Mark)
Kick Out The Jams
RR11828 624 (February 20, 1992) p42. (McLeese, Don)
Power Trip
RR11829 698-699 (December 29, 1994) p174. (Fricke, David)
MCBRIDE, MARTINA
The Way That I Am
RR11830 675 (February 10, 1994) p46. (McLeese, Don)
MCCARTNEY, PAUL
Off The Ground
RR11831 650 (February 18, 1993) pp56,58. (Puterbaugh, Parke)
Paul Is Live
RR11832 672-673 (December 23, 1993) pp153,156. (Evans, Paul)
The Russian Album
RR11833 619-620 (December 12, 1991) pp178,182. (Fricke, David)
Unplugged: The Official Bootleg
RR11834 619-620 (December 12, 1991) pp178,182. (Fricke, David)
MCCLAIN, MIGHTY SAM
Give It Up To Love
RR11835 667 (October 14, 1993) p123. (Drozdowski, Ted)
MCCLINTON, DELBERT
Never Been Rocked Enough
RR11836 637 (August 20, 1992) p53. (McLeese, Don)
MCCONELL, ROB
Sketches
RR11837 678 (March 24, 1994) p97. (Futterman, Steve)
MCFERRIN, BOBBY
Play
RR11838 625 (March 5, 1992) p68. (Chambers, Gordon)
MCGUINN, ROGER
Back From Rio
RR11839 619-620 (December 12, 1991) p165. (Fricke, David)
MCKEE, MARIA
You Gotta Sin To Get Saved
RR11840 666 (September 30, 1993) pp106,108. (Stenger, Wif)
MCKNIGHT, BRIAN
I Remember You
RR11841 717 (September 21, 1995) pp83-84. (Torres, Richard)
MCLACHLAN, SARAH
The Freedom Sessions
RR11842 708 (May 18, 1995) p92. (Odintz, Andrea)
Fumbling Towards Ecstasy
RR11843 684 (June 16, 1994) p109. (Gardner, Elysa)
MCLAREN, MALCOLM
Paris
RR11844 708 (May 18, 1995) p92. (Panahpour, Nilou)
MCLENNAN, G. W.
Watershed
RR11845 619-620 (December 12, 1991) pp187,189. (Fricke, David)
MCLENNAN, GRANT
Horsebreaker Star
RR11846 702 (February 23, 1995) p76. (Evans, Paul)
MCMURTRY, JAMES
Candyland
RR11847 639 (September 17, 1992) p94. (Drozdowski, Ted)
Where'd You Hide The Body
RR11848 716 (September 7, 1995) p73. (Ahearn, Kim)
MCTELL, BLIND WILLIE
The Definitive Blind Willie McTell
RR11849 685 (June 30, 1994) p77. (Considine, J. D.)
ME PHI ME
One
RR11850 645-646 (December 10, 1992) p174. (Coleman, Mark)
MEAT BEAT MANIFESTO
Subliminal Sandwich
RR11851 744 (October 3, 1996) p74. (Van Parys, Bill)
MEAT LOAF
Bat Out Of Hell II
RR11852 668 (October 28, 1993) p83. (Birkbeck, Matt)
MEAT PUPPETS
No Joke!
RR11853 720 (November 2, 1995) pp68-69. (Flaum, Eric)
Too High To Die
RR11854 683 (June 2, 1994) pp69-70. (Weisel, Al)
MECCA NORMAL
Jarred Up
RR11855 665 (September 16, 1993) p17. (Mundy, Chris)
Sitting On Snaps
RR11856 706 (April 20, 1995) p73. (McDonnell, Evelyn)
MEDESKI MARTIN AND WOOD
Shack-Man
RR11857 748 (November 28, 1996) p130. (Gehr, Richard)
MEDIUM COOL
Imagination
RR11858 618 (November 28, 1991) p98. (Palmer, Robert)
MEDNICK, LISA
Artifacts Of Love
RR11859 679 (April 7, 1994) p77. (McLeese, Don)
MEGADETH
Youthanasia
RR11860 698-699 (December 29, 1994) p173. (Evans, Paul)
MEKONS
The Curse Of The Mekons
RR11861 619-620 (December 12, 1991) p168. (Fricke, David)
I Love Mekons
RR11862 675 (February 10, 1994) p44. (Kot, Greg)
Pussy, King Of The Pirates
RR11863 729 (March 7, 1996) p50. (Kot, Greg)
MELLENCAMP, JOHN
Dance Naked
RR11864 686-687 (July 14, 1994) p102. (Bessman, Jim)
RR11865 698-699 (December 29, 1994) pp180-181. (Evans, Paul)

Human Wheels
RR11866 666 (September 30, 1993) p101. (McLeese, Don)
RR11867 672-673 (December 23, 1993) p151. (Evans, Paul)
Mr. Happy Go Lucky
RR11868 743 (September 19, 1996) p82. (Damsker, Matt)
Whenever We Wanted
RR11869 616 (October 31, 1991) p91. (Evans, Paul)
MELLESSE, NETSANET
Spirit Of Sheba
RR11870 658 (June 10, 1993) p78. (McLane, Daisann)
RR11871 672-673 (December 23, 1993) p163. (McLane, Daisann)
MELLOW MAN ACE
Brother With Two Tongues
RR11872 631 (May 28, 1992) p54. (Santiago, Roberto)
MELODY MAKERS
Joy And Blues
RR11873 664 (September 2, 1993) pp62,64. (Mirkin, Steven)
MELVINS
Stone Witch
RR11874 700 (January 26, 1995) p62. (Alden, Grant)
MENDELSSOHN, JOHN
Masterpieces
RR11875 716 (September 7, 1995) p73. (Fricke, David)
MENSAH, E. T.
All For You
RR11876 650 (February 18, 1993) p59. (McLane, Daisann)
Day By Day
RR11877 650 (February 18, 1993) p59. (McLane, Daisann)
MENSWEAR
Nuisance
RR11878 724-725 (December 28, 1995) pp120,124. (Fricke, David)
MERCHANT, NATALIE
Tigerlily
RR11879 711 (June 29, 1995) p43. (Weisel, Al)
RR11880 724-725 (December 28, 1995) p116. (Fricke, David)
MERCURY REV
Boces
RR11880a 660-661 (July 8, 1993) p20. (Fricke, David)
See You On The Other Side
RR11881 724-725 (December 28, 1995) p125. (Fricke, David)
Yerself Is Steam
RR11882 645-646 (December 10, 1992) p177. (Fricke, David)
RR11883 Number not assigned.
MERCURY, DANIELA
O Canto Da Cidada
RR11884 658 (June 10, 1993) p78. (McLane, Daisann)
MERMAN
A Glorious Lethal Euphoria
RR11885 724-725 (December 28, 1995) p125. (Fricke, David)
MESSIAH
Twenty-First Century Jesus
RR11886 685 (June 30, 1994) p73. (Evans, Paul)
METALLICA
Live Shit: Binge And Purge
RR11887 674 (January 27, 1994) p52. (Considine, J. D.)
Load
RR11888 736 (June 13, 1996) p51. (Wiederhorn, Jon)
RR11889 738-739 (July 11, 1996) pp85-86. (Sprague, David)
RR11890 750-751 (December 26, 1996) p190.
Metallica
RR11891 619-620 (December 12, 1991) pp172,174. (Fricke, David)
METERS
Funkify Your Life
RR11892 705 (April 6, 1995) p62. (Considine, J. D.)
METHOD MAN
Tical
RR11893 698-699 (December 29, 1994) pp178,180. (Evans, Paul)
MICHAEL, GEORGE
Older
RR11894 736 (June 13, 1996) p83. (Weisel, Al)
MIDNIGHT OIL
Breathe
RR11895 748 (November 28, 1996) pp130,132. (Moon, Tom)
Earth And Sun And Moon
RR11896 663 (August 19, 1993) p78. (Puterbaugh, Parke)
RR11897 672-673 (December 23, 1993) p152. (Evans, Paul)
Scream In Blue
RR11898 634-635 (July 9, 1992) pp104-105. (Fricke, David)
MIDWEST CREOLE ENSEMBLE
Jack Salmon And Derby Sauce
RR11899 652 (March 18, 1993) p42. (Fricke, David)
MIGHTY SPARROW
Volume 1
RR11900 658 (June 10, 1993) p78. (McLane, Daisann)
Volume 2
RR11901 658 (June 10, 1993) p78. (McLane, Daisann)
Volume 3
RR11902 658 (June 10, 1993) p78. (McLane, Daisann)
Volumes 1, 2, And 3
RR11903 672-673 (December 23, 1993) p163. (McLane, Daisann)
MILLA
The Divine Comedy
RR11904 680 (April 21, 1994) pp84-85. (McAlley, John)
MILLER, STEVE
Box Set
RR11905 698-699 (December 29, 1994) p188. (Considine, J. D.)
Wide River
RR11906 667 (October 14, 1993) p114. (Evans, Paul)
MINISTRY
Filth Pig
RR11907 728 (February 22, 1996) pp59-60. (Wiederhorn, Jon)
Psalm 69: The Way To Succeed And The Way To Suck Eggs
RR11908 639 (September 17, 1992) p91. (Kot, Greg)
MIRACLE LEGION
Drenched
RR11909 622 (January 23, 1992) p47. (Robbins, Ira)
MIRACLES
The 35th Anniversary Collection
RR11910 682 (May 19, 1994) p100. (Considine, J. D.)
MIRROR-DASH
Electric Pen (single)
RR11911 639 (September 17, 1992) p96. (Fricke, David)
MISSILE 727
Democratie
RR11912 626 (March 19, 1992) p95. (McLane, Daisann)
MISSISSIPPI SHEIKS
Stop And Listen
RR11913 648 (January 21, 1993) p50. (Considine, J. D.)
MITCHELL, JONI
Court And Spark
RR11914 686-687 (July 14, 1994) p32. (Nicks, Stevie)
Turbulent Indigo
RR11915 697 (December 15, 1994) p98. (Milward, John)
MITCHELL, RED
Finally
RR11916 659 (June 24, 1993) p84. (Futterman, Steve)
Jive At Five
RR11917 659 (June 24, 1993) p84. (Futterman, Steve)
Life's A Take
RR11918 659 (June 24, 1993) p84. (Futterman, Steve)
Talking
RR11919 623 (February 6, 1992) p80. (Futterman, Steve)

MOBB DEEP
The Infamous
RR11920 721 (November 16, 1995) p113. (Coker, Cheo H.)
MOBY
Everything Is Wrong
RR11921 704 (March 23, 1995) p125. (Evans, Paul)
RR11922 724-725 (December 28, 1995) p120. (Fricke, David)
MODERN JAZZ QUARTET
MJQ40
RR11923 619-620 (December 12, 1991) p177. (McLeese, Don)
MOLES
What's The New Mary Jane (single)
RR11924 639 (September 17, 1992) p96. (Fricke, David)
MOMPOSINA, TOTO LA
Toto La Momposina Y Sus Tambores—La Candela Viva
RR11925 670 (November 25, 1993) p108. (McLane, Daisann)
MONEY MARK
Mark's Keyboard Repair
RR11926 732 (April 18, 1996) pp70-71. (Hardy, Ernest)
MONK, THELONIOUS
The Complete Blue Note Recordings
RR11927 698-699 (December 29, 1994) p180. (Futterman, Steve)
The Thelonious Monk Quartet Live At The Five Spot Featuring John Coltrane
RR11928 653 (April 1, 1993) p53. (Futterman, Steve)
MONKEES
Headquarters
RR11929 724-725 (December 28, 1995) p122. (Coleman, Mark)
Listen To The Band
RR11930 619-620 (December 12, 1991) p177. (McLeese, Don)
The Monkees
RR11931 724-725 (December 28, 1995) p122. (Coleman, Mark)
More Of
RR11932 724-725 (December 28, 1995) p122. (Coleman, Mark)
Pisces, Aquarius, Capricorn And Jones Ltd.
RR11933 724-725 (December 28, 1995) p122. (Coleman, Mark)
MONROE, BILL
The Music Of Bill Monroe: From 1936 To 1994
RR11934 691 (September 22, 1994) p97. (McLeese, Don)
MONTANA, COUNTRY DICK
The Devil Lied To Me
RR11935 742 (September 5, 1996) pp64-65. (George-Warren, Holly)
MONTE, MARISA
Rose And Charcoal
RR11936 698-699 (December 29, 1994) p182. (McLane, Daisann)
MONTGOMERY, JOHN MICHAEL
Kickin' It Up
RR11937 679 (April 7, 1994) p77. (McLeese, Don)
MONTGOMERY, WES
The Complete Riverside Recordings
RR11938 672-673 (December 23, 1993) p164. (Futterman, Steve)
MOODY BLUES
Time Traveller
RR11939 698-699 (December 29, 1994) p188. (Considine, J. D.)
MOORE, CHANTE
Precious
RR11940 655 (April 29, 1993) p63. (Dyson, Michael Eric)
MOORE, THURSTON
Psychic Hearts
RR11941 709 (June 1, 1995) pp60-61. (Kemp, Mark)
MORE, BENY
Magia Antillana
RR11942 640 (October 1, 1992) p75. (McLane, Daisann)
The Most From Beny More
RR11943 640 (October 1, 1992) p75. (McLane, Daisann)
Y Hoy Como Ayer
RR11944 640 (October 1, 1992) p75. (McLane, Daisann)
MORISSETTE, ALANIS
Ironic (song)
RR11945 736 (June 13, 1996) p78. (Kenny, Glenn)
Jagged Little Pill
RR11946 724-725 (December 28, 1995) p116. (Fricke, David)
MORPHINE
Cure For Pain
RR11947 678 (March 24, 1994) p94. (Berger, Arion)
Yes
RR11948 704 (March 23, 1995) p124. (Garelick, Jon)
MORRISON, VAN
The Best Of Van Morrison Volume Two
RR11949 662 (August 5, 1993) pp66,68. (O'Connor, Rob)
Days Like This
RR11950 712-713 (July 13, 1995) p110. (Moon, Tom)
How Long Has This Been Going On
RR11951 727 (February 8, 1996) p49. (Himes, Geoffrey)
Hymns To The Silence
RR11952 615 (October 17, 1991) p94. (Gardner, Elysa)
A Night In San Francisco
RR11953 686-687 (July 14, 1994) p102. (Puterbaugh, Parke)
Too Long In Exile
RR11954 662 (August 5, 1993) pp66,68. (O'Connor, Rob)
RR11955 672-673 (December 23, 1993) p146. (Evans, Paul)
MORRISSEY
Southpaw Grammar
RR11956 718 (October 5, 1995) pp68-69. (Weisel, Al)
Vauxhall And I
RR11957 679 (April 7, 1994) pp73-74. (Volk, Steven)
World Of Morrissey
RR11958 705 (April 6, 1995) pp60-61. (Evans, Paul)
Your Arsenal
RR11959 642 (October 29, 1992) p69. (Coleman, Mark)
MORRISSEY, BILL
Friend Of Mine
RR11960 669 (November 11, 1993) pp74,76. (Ransom, Kevin)
Inside
RR11961 624 (February 20, 1992) p41. (Evans, Paul)
Night Train
RR11962 669 (November 11, 1993) pp74,76. (Ransom, Kevin)
You'll Never Get To Heaven
RR11963 735 (May 30, 1996) p48. (DeCurtis, Anthony)
MOTHERS OF INVENTION
We're Only In It For The Money
RR11964 724-725 (December 28, 1995) p122. (Coleman, Mark)
MOTIAN, PAUL
Ants To The Moon
RR11965 711 (June 29, 1995) p44. (Futterman, Steve)
Paul Motian In Tokyo
RR11966 642 (October 29, 1992) p75. (Futterman, Steve)
MOTLEY CRUE
Motley Crue
RR11967 680 (April 21, 1994) pp87,89. (Berger, Arion)
MOULD, BOB
Bob Mould
RR11968 734 (May 16, 1996) p66. (O'Connor, Rob)
MOVE
Black Country Rock
RR11969 676 (February 24, 1994) p57. (Fricke, David)

Great Move!
RR11970 694 (November 3, 1994) p100. (Considine, J. D.)
MR. BUNGLE
Mr. Bungle
RR11971 619-620 (December 12, 1991) p182. (Fricke, David)
MR. SCARFACE
The World Is Yours
RR11972 671 (December 9, 1993) p70. (Nelson, Havelock)
MUDHONEY
My Brother The Cow
RR11973 705 (April 6, 1995) pp64-65. (Alden, Grant)
Piece Of Cake
RR11974 647 (January 7, 1993) pp46-47. (Hill, Trent)
MUFFINS
Manna-Mirage
RR11975 634-635 (July 9, 1992) p102. (Fricke, David)
MULDAUR, MARIA
Louisiana Love Call
RR11976 650 (February 18, 1993) pp60-61. (Swenson, John)
MUNICH PHILHARMONIC ORCHESTRA
The Munich Philharmonic Orchestra Plays Abba Classic
RR11977 628 (April 16, 1992) p84. (Eddy, Chuck)
MURPHY, ELLIOTT
Diamonds By The Yard
RR11978 645-646 (December 10, 1992) p180. (Coleman, Mark)
MURPHY, PETER
Holy Smoke
RR11979 633 (June 25, 1992) p42. (Volk, Steve)
MURPHY, WILLIE
Running Jumping Standing Still
RR11980 682 (May 19, 1994) p103. (Swenson, John)
MURRAY, DAVID
Shakill's Warrior
RR11981 627 (April 2, 1992) p46. (Futterman, Steve)
MURRAY, SUNNY
Kingdom Come
RR11982 708 (May 18, 1995) pp87-88. (Fricke, David)
MUSIC MACHINE
Beyond The Garage
RR11983 730 (March 21, 1996) p98. (Fricke, David)
MUSSELWHITE, CHARLIE
In My Time
RR11984 689 (August 25, 1994) p89. (Swenson, John)
MY BLOODY VALENTINE
Loveless
RR11985 625 (March 5, 1992) p68. (Robbins, Ira)
MY DYING BRIDE
Turn Loose The Swans
RR11986 681 (May 5, 1994) p52. (Darzin,Daina)
MYLES, RAYMOND ANTHONY
A Taste Of Heaven
RR11987 720 (November 2, 1995) p69. (Fricke, David)

N

NAKED CITY
Torture Garden
RR11988 619-620 (December 12, 1991) p182. (Fricke, David)
NAS
Illmatic
RR11989 689 (August 25, 1994) p88. (Toure)
It Was Written
RR11990 736 (June 13, 1996) pp51,53. (Wiederhorn, Jon)
RR11991 743 (September 19, 1996) pp82,84. (Coleman, Mark)
RR11992 750-751 (December 26, 1996) pp194-195.
NASH RAMBLERS
At The Ryman
RR11993 625 (March 5, 1992) p70. (Hunter, James)
NAUGHTY BY NATURE
Naughty By Nature
RR11993a 666 (September 30, 1993) p59. (Dyson, Michael Eric)
19 Naughty III
RR11994 655 (April 29, 1993) p61. (Toure)
RR11995 672-673 (December 23, 1993) pp156-157. (Evans, Paul)
RR11996 Number not assigned.
Poverty's Paradise
RR11997 710 (June 15, 1995) p80. (Coker, Cheo H.)
NDEGEOCELLO, ME'SHELL
Peace Beyond Passion
RR11998 736 (June 13, 1996) p53. (Wiederhorn, Jon)
RR11999 738-739 (July 11, 1996) p86. (Hardy, Ernest)
RR12000 750-751 (December 26, 1996) p190.
Plantation Lullabies
RR12001 669 (November 11, 1993) p76. (Gardner, Elysa)
N'DOUR, YOUSSOU
Eyes Open
RR12002 638 (September 3, 1992) p67. (McLane, Daisann)
Youssou N'Dour
RR12003 680 (April 21, 1994) p90. (McLane, Daisann)
NEGATIVLAND
The Willsaphone Stupid Show
RR12004 684 (June 16, 1994) p110. (Fricke, David)
NEIL, VINCE
Exposed
RR12005 664 (September 2, 1993) p62. (Eddy, Chuck)
NELSON, SHARA
What Silence Knows
RR12006 696 (December 1, 1994) p122. (Panahpour, Nilou)
NELSON, WILLIE
Across The Borderline
RR12007 656 (May 13, 1993) p110. (Holden, Stephen)
RR12008 672-673 (December 23, 1993) p157. (Evans, Paul)
The Early Years: The Complete Liberty Recordings Plus More
RR12009 686-687 (July 14, 1994) p107. (McLeese, Don)
Healing Hands Of Time
RR12010 698-699 (December 29, 1994) p176. (Evans, Paul)
Moonlight Becomes You
RR12011 679 (April 7, 1994) p77. (McLeese, Don)
Spirit
RR12012 750-751 (December 26, 1996) p198.
Who'll Buy My Memories?
RR12013 619-620 (December 12, 1991) p162. (Fricke, David)
NEUWIRTH, BOB
Last Day On Earth
RR12014 700 (January 26, 1995) p61. (McLeese, Don)
NEVILLE, AARON
The Grand Tour
RR12014a 662 (August 5, 1993) p68. (Milward, John)
The Tattooed Heart
RR12014b 709 (June 1, 1995) p61. (Galvin, Peter)
Warm Your Heart
RR12014c 619-620 (December 12, 1991) p182. (Fricke, David)
NEVILLE BROTHERS
Family Groove
RR12015 634-635 (July 9, 1992) p102. (Walls, Richard C.)
Mitakuye Oyasin Oyasin
RR12016 735 (May 30, 1996) p49. (Himes, Geoffrey)
RR12017-20 Numbers not assigned.
NEW AGE STEPPERS
Massive Hits Vol. 1
RR12021 703 (March 9, 1995) p65. (Fernando, S. H., Jr.)

NEW DYLANS
Warren Piece
RR12022 681 (May 5, 1994) p54. (Evans, Paul)
NEW EDITION
Home Again
RR12023 745 (October 17, 1996) p132. (Hardy, Ernest)
NEW KINGDOM
Paradise Don't Come Cheap
RR12024 745 (October 17, 1996) pp132,134. (Fernando, S. H., Jr.)
NEW ORDER
Republic
RR12025 659 (June 24, 1993) pp77-78. (White, Armond)
NEW 2 LIVE CREW
Back At Your Ass For The Nine-4
RR12025a 679 (April 7, 1994) p74. (Evans, Paul)
NEW YORK COMPOSERS ORCHESTRA
First Program In Standard Time
RR12026 649 (February 4, 1993) p75. (Futterman, Steve)
NEW YORK DOLLS
Endless Party
RR12027 660-661 (July 8, 1993) p20. (Fricke, David)
NEW YORK STORIES
New York Stories
RR12028 642 (October 29, 1992) p75. (Futterman, Steve)
NEWCOMER, CARRIE
An Angel At My Shoulder
RR12029 683 (June 2, 1994) p70. (McLeese, Don)
NEWELL, MARTIN
The Greatest Living Englishman
RR12030 689 (August 25, 1994) p90. (Lyman, Andy)
NEWMAN, RANDY
Faust
RR12031 723 (December 14, 1995) p84. (Weisel, Al)
Randy Newman
RR12032 714 (August 10, 1995) p59. (Considine, J. D.)
NEWPORT ALL-STARS
Swing That Music
RR12033 671 (December 9, 1993) p70. (Futterman, Steve)
NICE, PETE
Dust To Dust
RR12034 669 (November 11, 1993) pp76-77. (Diehl, Matt)
NICHOLSON, GIMMER
Christopher Idylls
RR12035 724-725 (December 28, 1995) p125. (Fricke, David)
NICKS, STEVIE
Street Angel
RR12036 690 (September 8, 1994) pp78,80. (Manning, Kara)
NILSSON, HARRY
Personal Best
RR12037 714 (August 10, 1995) p59. (Considine, J. D.)
RR12038 724-725 (December 28, 1995) p122. (Coleman, Mark)
NINE INCH NAILS
Broken
RR12039 645-646 (December 10, 1992) pp184,187. (Coleman, Mark)
The Downward Spiral
RR12040 678 (March 24, 1994) pp92-93. (Gold, Jonathan)
RR12041 698-699 (December 29, 1994) p173. (Evans, Paul)
NIRVANA
From The Muddy Banks Of The Wishkah
RR12042 745 (October 17, 1996) pp129-130. (Ali, Lorraine)
RR12043 750-751 (December 26, 1996) p186.
In Utero
RR12044 665 (September 16, 1993) pp63-64. (Fricke, David)
RR12045 672-673 (December 23, 1993) p146. (Evans, Paul)
Incesticide
RR12046 648 (January 21, 1993) pp48-49. (Alden, Grant)
MTV Unplugged In New York
RR12047 696 (December 1, 1994) pp120-122. (O'Dair, Barbara)
RR12048 698-699 (December 29, 1994) p170. (Evans, Paul)
Nevermind
RR12049 618 (November 28, 1991) pp96,98. (Robbins, Ira)
NO DOUBT
Tragic Kingdom
RR12050 750-751 (December 26, 1996) p195.
NO WALLS
No Walls
RR12051 634-635 (July 9, 1992) p102. (Fricke, David)
NOTORIOUS B.I.G.
Ready To Die
RR12052 694 (November 3, 1994) pp96,98. (Coker, Cheo H.)
NOVA MOB
Ballad No. 19 (song)
RR12053 634-635 (July 9, 1992) p102. (Fricke, David)
Nova Mob
RR12054 691 (September 22, 1994) p98. (Evans, Paul)
Shoot Your Way To Freedom (song)
RR12055 634-635 (July 9, 1992) p102. (Fricke, David)
NRBQ
Message For The Mess Age
RR12056 690 (September 8, 1994) p81. (George-Warren, Holly)
Stay With Me
RR12057 660-661 (July 8, 1993) p20. (Fricke, David)
N.W.A.
Efil4zaggin
RR12058 619-620 (December 12, 1991) p178. (Fricke, David)
Straight Outta Compton
RR12059 666 (September 30, 1993) p59. (Dyson, Michael Eric)
NYRO, LAURA
Walk The Dog And Light The Light
RR12060 667 (October 14, 1993) pp117-118. (McAlley, John)

O

OASIS
Definitely Maybe
RR12061 698-699 (December 29, 1994) pp185,190. (Evans, Paul)
(What's The Story) Morning Glory?
RR12062 719 (October 19, 1995) pp147-149. (Wiederhorn, Jon)
RR12063 724-725 (December 28, 1995) pp120,124. (Fricke, David)
O'BRIAN, DILLON
Scenes From My Last Confession
RR12064 694 (November 3, 1994) p98. (Evans, Paul)
OBSESSED
The Church Within
RR12065 681 (May 5, 1994) p54. (Evans, Paul)
O'CONNELL, MAURA
Blue Is The Color Of Hope
RR12066 647 (January 7, 1993) p54. (McLeese, Don)
O'CONNOR, SINEAD
Am I Not Your Girl?
RR12067 644 (November 26, 1992) p72. (Gardner, Elysa)
Universal Mother
RR12068 692 (October 6, 1994) pp84,87. (Zacharek, Stephanie)
OCTET, DAVID MURRAY
Dark Star
RR12069 742 (September 5, 1996) p65. (Fine, Jason)
ODOM, ANDREW 'B.B.'

Goin' To California
RR12070 659 (June 24, 1993) p81. (Sandmel, Ben)
OFFSPRING
Smash
RR12071 694 (November 3, 1994) pp98,100. (Kot, Greg)
O'HARA, JAMIE
Rise Above It
RR12072 683 (June 2, 1994) p70. (McLeese, Don)
OL' DIRTY BASTARD
Return To The 36 Chambers
RR12073 706 (April 20, 1995) p78. (Toure)
OLIVIA TREMOR CONTROL
Dusk At Cubist Castle
RR12074 750-751 (December 26, 1996) p192. (Fricke, David)
OLNEY, DAVID
Roses
RR12075 623 (February 6, 1992) p79. (Bessman, Jim)
OLSON, CARLA
Reap The Whirlwind
RR12076 698-699 (December 29, 1994) p182. (Evans, Paul)
OMAR
For Pleasure
RR12077 710 (June 15, 1995) p81. (Moon, Tom)
ONO, YOKO
Onobox
RR12078 630 (May 14, 1992) p104. (Fricke, David)
Rising
RR12079 722 (November 30, 1995) p67. (Fricke, David)
ONYX
Bacdafucup
RR12080 672-673 (December 23, 1993) p165. (Evans, Paul)
ORB
Orbus Terrarum
RR12081 706 (April 20, 1995) pp69-70. (Wiederhorn, Jon)
Pomme Fritz
RR12082 693 (October 20, 1994) pp146-147. (Wiederhorn, Jon)
ORBISON, ROY
King Of Hearts
RR12083 645-646 (December 10, 1992) pp178-179. (Coleman, Mark)
ORBITAL
In Sides
RR12084 740 (August 8, 1996) p62. (Galtney, Smith)
ORCHESTRA BAOBAB
Bamba
RR12085 672-673 (December 23, 1993) p163. (McLane, Daisann)
ORIGINAL SKATALITES
The Long Hot Summer—Jamaican Ska 1963
RR12086 619-620 (December 12, 1991) p168. (Fricke, David)
OSBORNE, JOAN
Relish
RR12087 707 (May 4, 1995) p69. (Evans, Paul)
OSWALD, JOHN
Gray Folded
RR12088 693 (October 20, 1994) p43. (Strauss, Neil)
RR12089 724-725 (December 28, 1995) p120. (Fricke, David)
OUTKAST
Atliens
RR12090 746 (October 31, 1996) pp66,68. (Powell, Kevin)
OVERTONES
Western Beat
RR12091 637 (August 20, 1992) p53. (McLeese, Don)
OVIEDO, ISAAC
Routes Of Rhythm Vol. 3
RR12092 640 (October 1, 1992) p75. (McLane, Daisann)
OWENS, BUCK
The Buck Owens Collection
RR12093 645-646 (December 10, 1992) p174. (McLeese, Don)

P

P
P
RR12094 721 (November 16, 1995) pp112-113. (Foege, Alec)
PABLO, AUGUSTUS
King Tubby Meets The Rockers Uptown
RR12095 676 (February 24, 1994) p42. (McLane, Daisann)
PAGE, JIMMY
Coverdale-Page
RR12096 654 (April 15, 1993) p62. (Considine, J. D.)
No Quarter
RR12097 697 (December 15, 1994) p92. (DeCurtis, Anthony)
RR12098 698-699 (December 29, 1994) p170. (Evans, Paul)
PALACE BROTHERS
Palace Brothers
RR12099 701 (February 9, 1995) pp58-59. (O'Connor, Rob)
PALACE MUSIC
Viva Last Blues
RR12100 720 (November 2, 1995) p70. (Panahpour, Nilou)
PALACE SONGS
Hope
RR12101 701 (February 9, 1995) pp58-59. (O'Connor, Rob)
PANTERA
Far Beyond Driven
RR12102 682 (May 19, 1994) p103. (Evans, Paul)
The Great Southern Trendkill
RR12103 736 (June 13, 1996) p83. (Masuo, Sandy)
PAPA WEMBA
Emotion
RR12104 709 (June 1, 1995) p62. (McLane, Daisann)
PARISH, JOHN
Dance Hall At Louse Point
RR12105 745 (October 17, 1996) p130. (McDonnell, Evelyn)
RR12106 Number not assigned.
PARKER, GRAHAM
Burning Questions
RR12107 639 (September 17, 1992) p94. (Gardner, Elysa)
Passion Is No Ordinary Word
RR12108 672-673 (December 23, 1993) p148. (Considine, J. D.)
12 Haunted Episodes
RR12108a 707 (May 4, 1995) p69. (Evans, Paul)
PARKER, WILLIAM
Kingdom Come
RR12109 708 (May 18, 1995) pp87-88. (Fricke, David)
PARKS, VAN DYKE
Orange Crate Art
RR12110 724-725 (December 28, 1995) p118. (Fricke, David)
PARLIAMENT
Live—The Funkadelic Collection
RR12111 676 (February 24, 1994) p57. (Fricke, David)
Tear The Roof Off 1974-1980
RR12112 667 (October 14, 1993) p118. (Toure)
PARNELL, LEE ROY
On The Road
RR12113 675 (February 10, 1994) p46. (McLeese, Don)
PARRISH, MICHAEL
Automobility
RR12114 716 (September 7, 1995) p73. (Fricke, David)
PARTON, DOLLY
Heartsongs
RR12115 698-699 (December 29, 1994) p178. (McLeese, Don)

Honky Tonk Angels
RR12116 672-673 (December 23, 1993) p158. (McLeese, Don)
The RCA Years 1967-1986
RR12117 672-673 (December 23, 1993) p158. (McLeese, Don)
Slow Dancing With The Moon
RR12118 660-661 (July 8, 1993) pp111-112. (D'Erasmo, Stacey)
PARTRIDGE, ANDY
The Greatest Living Englishman
RR12119 689 (August 25, 1994) p90. (Lyman, Andy)
PASS, JOE
Finally
RR12120 659 (June 24, 1993) p84. (Futterman, Steve)
PASSENGERS
Original Soundtracks I
RR12121 723 (December 14, 1995) pp82,84. (DeRogatis, Jim)
PATTON, BIG JOHN
Let 'Em Roll
RR12122 671 (December 9, 1993) p70. (Futterman, Steve)
PATTON, CHARLES
Founder Of The Delta Blues: 1929-34
RR12123 625 (March 5, 1992) pp63,65. (Palmer, Robert)
King Of The Delta Blues: The Music Of Charlie Patton
RR12124 625 (March 5, 1992) pp63,65. (Palmer, Robert)
PAUL, LES
The Legend And The Legacy
RR12125 618 (November 28, 1991) p94. (Drozdowski, Ted)
PAVEMENT
Crooked Rain, Crooked Rain
RR12126 676 (February 24, 1994) pp55-56. (Diehl, Matt)
Slanted And Enchanted
RR12127 678 (March 24, 1994) p16. (Donelly, Tanya)
Westing
RR12128 664 (September 2, 1993) p64. (Berger, Arion)
Wowee Zowee
RR12129 706 (April 20, 1995) p70. (Kemp, Mark)
PAVONE, MARIO
Song For
RR12130 692 (October 6, 1994) p89. (Futterman, Steve)
PAYCHECK, JOHNNY
The Real Mr. Heartache
RR12131 750-751 (December 26, 1996) p189. (Coleman, Mark)
PEARL JAM
No Code
RR12132 742 (September 5, 1996) pp59-60. (Fricke, David)
RR12133 750-751 (December 26, 1996) p186.
Ten
RR12134 619-620 (December 12, 1991) p174. (Fricke, David)
Vitalogy
RR12135 697 (December 15, 1994) pp91-93. (Weisel, Al)
RR12136 698-699 (December 29, 1994) p170. (Evans, Paul)
Vs.
RR12137 669 (November 11, 1993) pp72-73. (Considine, J. D.)
RR12138 672-673 (December 23, 1993) p146. (Evans, Paul)
PEEBLES, ANN
Full Time Love
RR12139 633 (June 25, 1992) p42. (Palmer, Robert)
PELL MELL
Flow
RR12140 628 (April 16, 1992) p85. (Fricke, David)
Interstate
RR12141 711 (June 29, 1995) p42. (Davies, Barbara)
PENN, DAN
Do Right Man
RR12142 684 (June 16, 1994) p110. (Nicolucci, Guy)
PENN, MICHAEL
Free-For-All
RR12143 644 (November 26, 1992) p72. (Evans, Paul)
PEPLOWSKI, KEN
Steppin' With Peps
RR12144 671 (December 9, 1993) p70. (Futterman, Steve)
PERE UBU
Datapanik In The Year Zero
RR12145 746 (October 31, 1996) p68. (Fricke, David)
Ray Gun Suitcase
RR12146 718 (October 5, 1995) pp69-70. (Drozdowski, Ted)
Story Of My Life
RR12147 663 (August 19, 1993) p78. (Sprague, David)
PERFECT
When Squirrels Play Chicken
RR12148 741 (August 22, 1996) pp96,98. (Gardner, Elysa)
PERKINS, PINETOP
Portrait Of A Delta Bluesman
RR12149 659 (June 24, 1993) p81. (Sandmel, Ben)
PET SHOP BOYS
Bilingual
RR12150 746 (October 31, 1996) p70. (Hoskyns, Barney)
Very
RR12151 670 (November 25, 1993) p112. (Considine, J. D.)
PETERSON, OSCAR
Saturday Night At The Blue Note
RR12152 618 (November 28, 1991) p96. (Futterman, Steve)
PETERSON, RALPH
Ornettology
RR12153 631 (May 28, 1992) p61. (Futterman, Steve)
PETTY, TOM
She's The One
RR12154 742 (September 5, 1996) pp60,62. (Puterbaugh, Parke)
Wildflowers
RR12155 694 (November 3, 1994) pp95-96. (Gardner, Elysa)
RR12156 698-699 (December 29, 1994) pp180-181. (Evans, Paul)
PHAIR, LIZ
Exile In Guyville
RR12157 658 (June 10, 1993) pp68-69. (Kot, Greg)
RR12158 665 (September 16, 1993) p17. (Mundy, Chris)
Whip-Smart
RR12159 691 (September 22, 1994) pp91-92. (O'Dair, Barbara)
RR12160 698-699 (December 29, 1994) p173. (Evans, Paul)
PHARCYDE
Bizarre Ride II The Pharcyde
RR12161 672-673 (December 23, 1993) p165. (Evans, Paul)
PHILLIPS, GLENN
Echoes 1975-1985
RR12162 648 (January 21, 1993) p50. (Puterbaugh, Parke)
PHILLIPS, SAM
Martinis And Bikinis
RR12163 678 (March 24, 1994) p93. (Manning, Kara)
RR12164 698-699 (December 29, 1994) p185. (Evans, Paul)
PHISH
Billy Breathes
RR12165 746 (October 31, 1996) pp65-66. (Gehr, Richard)
RR12166 750-751 (December 26, 1996) p194.
A Live One
RR12167 715 (August 24, 1995) pp99-100. (Moon, Tom)
RR12168 724-725 (December 28, 1995) p129. (Fricke, David)
PICKETT, WILSON
A Man And A Half
RR12169 636 (August 6, 1992) p66. (Considine, J. D.)
PIDGEON, REBECCA
The Raven
RR12170 688 (August 11, 1994) p70. (Evans, Paul)

PIERCE, BILLY
James Williams Meets The Saxophone Masters
RR12171 653 (April 1, 1993) p53. (Futterman, Steve)
PIERCE, WEBB
King Of The Honky-Tonk
RR12172 691 (September 22, 1994) p97. (McLeese, Don)
PINK FLOYD
Dark Side Of The Moon
RR12173 675 (February 10, 1994) p18. (D'Arby, Terence Trent)
The Division Bell
RR12174 684 (June 16, 1994) pp105-106. (Graves, Tom)
Pulse
RR12175 715 (August 24, 1995) p102. (O'Connor, Rob)
Shine On
RR12176 648 (January 21, 1993) p50. (Considine, J. D.)
PIZZICATO FIVE
The Sound Of Music
RR12177 722 (November 30, 1995) p68. (Wiesel, Al)
RR12178 Number not assigned.
PJ HARVEY
RR12179 672-673 (December 23, 1993) p159. (Evans, Paul)
Dry
RR12180 645-646 (December 10, 1992) p182. (Coleman, Mark)
4-Track Demos
RR12180a 670 (November 25, 1993) p112. (McDonnell, Evelyn)
Rid Of Me
RR12181 658 (June 10, 1993) pp68-69. (Kot, Greg)
RR12182 672-673 (December 23, 1993) p159. (Evans, Paul)
To Bring You My Love
RR12183 703 (March 9, 1995) pp63-64. (O'Dair, Barbara)
RR12184 724-725 (December 28, 1995) pp118,120. (Fricke, David)
PLANT, ROBERT
Fate Of Nations
RR12185 660-661 (July 8, 1993) p114. (Frost, Deborah)
No Quarter
RR12186 697 (December 15, 1994) p92. (DeCurtis, Anthony)
RR12187 698-699 (December 29, 1994) p170. (Evans, Paul)
PLAY THE TRACKS OF
Beautycase
RR12188 750-751 (December 26, 1996) p192. (Fricke, David)
PM DAWN
The Bliss Album?
RR12189 654 (April 15, 1993) pp60-61. (Hunter, James)
Jesus Wept
RR12190 720 (November 2, 1995) p66. (Kemp, Mark)
POISON
Native Tongue
RR12191 652 (March 18, 1993) p40. (Frost, Deborah)
POLARA
Polara
RR12192 702 (February 23, 1995) p76. (Evans, Paul)
POLICE
Live!
RR12193 715 (August 24, 1995) p101. (Hunter, James)
Message In A Box
RR12194 669 (November 11, 1993) p77. (Considine, J. D.)
POLLARD, ROBERT
Not In My Airforce
RR12195 748 (November 28, 1996) p130. (Diehl, Matt)
POND
Pond
RR12196 655 (April 29, 1993) p65. (Alden, Grant)
PONTIAC BROTHERS
Fuzzy Little Piece Of The World
RR12197 650 (February 18, 1993) p59. (McLeese, Don)
POOR RIGHTEOUS TEACHERS
Pure Poverty
RR12198 617 (November 14, 1991) p173. (Powell, Kevin)
POP, IGGY
American Caesar
RR12199 667 (October 14, 1993) p117. (Kemp, Mark)
Naughty Little Doggie
RR12200 728 (February 22, 1996) p62. (Fricke, David)
POPES
The Snake
RR12201 715 (August 24, 1995) pp100-101. (Flaum, Eric)
POPO, SUNDAR
Is The Spanner She Want
RR12202 672-673 (December 23, 1993) p163. (McLane, Daisann)
PORK
Grand Slam Baby (single)
RR12203 672-673 (December 23, 1993) p154. (Fricke, David)
PORNO FOR PYROS
Good God's Urge
RR12204 736 (June 13, 1996) pp80,82. (Berger, Arion)
Porno For Pyros
RR12205 660-661 (July 8, 1993) p114. (Berger, Arion)
PORTISHEAD
Dummy
RR12206 703 (March 9, 1995) p66. (Evans, Paul)
POSIES
Amazing Disgrace
RR12207 737 (June 27, 1996) p59. (Himes, Geoffrey)
POSTER CHILDREN
Daisychain Reaction
RR12208 637 (August 20, 1992) p50. (Robbins, Ira)
POWDER
Biff! Bang! Powder
RR12209 676 (February 24, 1994) p57. (Fricke, David)
POWELL, BUD
Complete Blue Note And Roost Recordings
RR12210 698-699 (December 29, 1994) p180. (Futterman, Steve)
The Complete Bud Powell
RR12211 698-699 (December 29, 1994) p180. (Futterman, Steve)
PRADO, PEREZ
Havana, 3 A.M.
RR12212 640 (October 1, 1992) p75. (McLane, Daisann)
PRESIDENTS OF THE UNITED STATES OF AMERICA
The Presidents Of The United States Of America
RR12213 724-725 (December 28, 1995) pp. (Fricke, David)
II
RR12214 748 (November 28, 1996) p132. (Cohen, Jason)
PRESLEY, ELVIS
Amazing Grace
RR12215 698-699 (December 29, 1994) p188. (Considine, J. D.)
Elvis From Nashville To Memphis
RR12216 669 (November 11, 1993) p76. (Evans, Paul)
The King Of Rock 'N' Roll: The Complete '50's Masters
RR12217 636 (August 6, 1992) pp55-56. (Light, Alan)
PRETENDERS
The Isle Of View
RR12218 723 (December 14, 1995) p84. (Farber, Jim)
RR12219 724-725 (December 28, 1995) p129. (Fricke, David)
Last Of The Independents
RR12220 683 (June 2, 1994) p69. (O'Dair, Barbara)
RR12221 698-699 (December 29, 1994) pp182,185. (Evans, Paul)
PREVITE, BOBBY
Slay The Suitors
RR12222 692 (October 6, 1994) p89. (Futterman, Steve)

PRICE, MARYANN
Etched In Swing
RR12223 666 (September 30, 1993) p105. (McLeese, Don)
PRICE, TONI
Swim Away
RR12224 663 (August 19, 1993) p77. (McLeese, Don)
PRIME TIME
Tone Dialing
RR12225 723 (December 14, 1995) pp84,86. (Fricke, David)
PRIMITIVE RADIO GODS
Rocket
RR12226 750-751 (December 26, 1996) p190.
PRIMUS
Pork Soda
RR12227 658 (June 10, 1993) p71. (Sinclair, Tom)
PRINCE
Chaos And Disorder
RR12228 741 (August 22, 1996) p98. (Hardy, Ernest)
Come
RR12229 690 (September 8, 1994) pp75-76,78. (Moon, Tom)
Diamonds And Pearls
RR12230 615 (October 17, 1991) p92. (Light, Alan)
RR12231 619-620 (December 12, 1991) pp168,172. (Fricke, David)
The Gold Experience
RR12232 720 (November 2, 1995) p66. (Cooper, Carol)
RR12233 724-725 (December 28, 1995) p124. (Fricke, David)
The Hits: Volume 1 & II
RR12234 667 (October 14, 1993) pp113-114. (Wright, Christian)
[Symbol]
RR12235 644 (November 26, 1992) pp70-71. (Considine, J. D.)
PRINE, JOHN
Great Days
RR12236 672-673 (December 23, 1993) p148. (Considine, J. D.)
A John Prine Christmas
RR12237 672-673 (December 23, 1993) p169. (Howard, Pete)
The Missing Years
RR12238 622 (January 23, 1992) p46. (Milward, John)
PROCLAIMERS
Hit The Highway
RR12239 685 (June 30, 1994) pp74-75. (Galvin, Peter)
PRODIGY
Music For The Jilted Generation
RR12240 706 (April 20, 1995) p80. (Evans, Paul)
PUBLIC ENEMY
Apocalypse 91...The Enemy Strikes Black
RR12241 619-620 (December 12, 1991) p162. (Fricke, David)
Fear Of A Black Planet
RR12242 666 (September 30, 1993) p56. (Walser, Robert)
Greatest Misses
RR12243 645-646 (December 10, 1992) p174. (Coleman, Mark)
It Takes A Nation Of Millions To Hold Us Back
RR12244 666 (September 30, 1993) pp56,59. (Kelley, Robin D.G.)
RR12245 666 (September 30, 1993) p59. (Dyson, Michael Eric)
Muse Sick N Hour Mess Age
RR12246 686-687 (July 14, 1994) pp101-102. (Toure)
RR12247 698-699 (December 29, 1994) pp173,176. (Evans, Paul)
PUBLIC IMAGE, LTD.
That What Is Not
RR12248 624 (February 20, 1992) p41. (Eddy, Chuck)
PULNOC
City Of Hysteria
RR12249 618 (November 28, 1991) pp94,96. (Fricke, David)
PULP
Different Class
RR12250 731 (April 4, 1996) pp61-62. (Fricke, David)
PURSUIT OF HAPPINESS
The Downward Road
RR12251 658 (June 10, 1993) p70. (Isler, Scott)
PUTTERS
Fear Of Women
RR12252 700 (January 26, 1995) p63. (Dean, Chuck)

Q

QUEEN
Made In Heaven
RR12253 724-725 (December 28, 1995) p116. (Fricke, David)
QUEEN LATIFAH
All Hail The Queen
RR12254 666 (September 30, 1993) p59. (Dyson, Michael Eric)
Nature Of A Sista'
RR12255 616 (October 31, 1991) pp92-93. (Cardwell, Diane)
RR12256 619-620 (December 12, 1991) p174. (Fricke, David)

R

RA, SUN
Art Forms Of Dimensions Tomorrow
RR12257 651 (March 4, 1993) pp63-64. (Swenson, John)
Bad And Beautiful
RR12258 651 (March 4, 1993) pp63-64. (Swenson, John)
Cosmic Tones For Mental Therapy
RR12259 651 (March 4, 1993) pp63-64. (Swenson, John)
Holiday For Soul Dance
RR12260 623 (February 6, 1992) p80. (Futterman, Steve)
RR12261 651 (March 4, 1993) pp63-64. (Swenson, John)
Interstellar Low Ways
RR12262 651 (March 4, 1993) pp63-64. (Swenson, John)
Jazz In Silhouette
RR12263 623 (February 6, 1992) p80. (Futterman, Steve)
RR12264 651 (March 4, 1993) pp63-64. (Swenson, John)
Monorails And Satellites
RR12265 623 (February 6, 1992) p80. (Futterman, Steve)
RR12266 651 (March 4, 1993) pp63-64. (Swenson, John)
My Brother The Wind Volume II
RR12267 651 (March 4, 1993) pp63-64. (Swenson, John)
Other Planets Of There
RR12268 651 (March 4, 1993) pp63-64. (Swenson, John)
The Singles
RR12269 750-751 (December 26, 1996) pp195-196.
Sound Of Joy
RR12270 711 (June 29, 1995) p44. (Futterman, Steve)
Sound Sun Pleasure
RR12271 623 (February 6, 1992) p80. (Futterman, Steve)
RR12272 651 (March 4, 1993) pp63-64. (Swenson, John)
Sun Ra Visits Planet Earth
RR12273 651 (March 4, 1993) pp63-64. (Swenson, John)
Super-Sonic Jazz
RR12274 623 (February 6, 1992) p80. (Futterman, Steve)
RR12275 651 (March 4, 1993) pp63-64. (Swenson, John)
We Travel The Spaceways
RR12276 651 (March 4, 1993) pp63-64. (Swenson, John)
RACHEL
Music For Egon Schiele
RR12277 730 (March 21, 1996) p98. (Fricke, David)
RADIOHEAD

The Bends
RR12278 708 (May 18, 1995) p88. (Drozdowski, Ted)
Pablo Honey
RR12279 672-673 (December 23, 1993) p151. (Evans, Paul)
RAEKWON
Only Built Fir Cuban Linx
RR12280 718 (October 5, 1995) p68. (Fernando, S. H., Jr.)
RAGE AGAINST THE MACHINE
Evil Empire
RR12281 732 (April 18, 1996) pp67-68. (Wiederhorn, Jon)
RR12282 750-751 (December 26, 1996) p184.
RAGING SLAB
Dynamite Monster Boogie Concert
RR12283 663 (August 19, 1993) p77. (Frost, Deborah)
RAINCOATS
Looking In The Shadows
RR12284 736 (June 13, 1996) p78. (McDonnell, Evelyn)
RAITT, BONNIE
Longing In Theirs Hearts
RR12285 679 (April 7, 1994) pp71-72. (Kot, Greg)
Luck Of The Draw
RR12286 619-620 (December 12, 1991) p178. (Fricke, David)
Road Tested
RR12287 723 (December 14, 1995) p86. (Kot, Greg)
RAMONES
Acid Eaters
RR12288 677 (March 10, 1994) p65. (Evans, Paul)
Adios Amigos
RR12289 712-713 (July 13, 1995) p111. (Diehl, Matt)
Mondo Bizarro
RR12290 642 (October 29, 1992) p74. (Thompson, Dave)
RAMZY, HOSSAM
Egyptian Rai
RR12291 709 (June 1, 1995) p62. (McLane, Daisann)
RANKS, SHABBA
X-Tra Naked
RR12292 645-646 (December 10, 1992) p169. (Coleman, Mark)
RARA MACHINE
Break The Chain
RR12293 626 (March 19, 1992) p95. (McLane, Daisann)
Voudou Nou
RR12294 689 (August 25, 1994) p92. (McLane, Daisann)
RAY AND GLOVER
Picture Has Faded
RR12295 682 (May 19, 1994) p103. (Swenson, John)
REAL KIDS
Grown Up Wrong
RR12296 667 (October 14, 1993) p121. (Fricke, David)
The Real Kids
RR12297 625 (March 5, 1992) p70. (Fricke, David)
RED DRESS
The Collection
RR12298 706 (April 20, 1995) p72. (Fricke, David)
RED FOOTED GENIUS
Hydraulic
RR12299 667 (October 14, 1993) p34. (Neely, Kim)
RED HOT CHILI PEPPERS
BloodSugarSexMagik
RR12300 619-620 (December 12, 1991) p174. (Fricke, David)
One Hot Minute
RR12301 718 (October 5, 1995) pp67-68. (Darzin, Daina)
RED HOUSE PAINTERS
Ocean Beach
RR12302 708 (May 18, 1995) p90. (Evans, Paul)
Red House Painters I
RR12303 670 (November 25, 1993) p120. (O'Connor, Rob)
Red House Painters II
RR12304 670 (November 25, 1993) p120. (O'Connor, Rob)
Songs For A Blue Guitar
RR12305 741 (August 22, 1996) p100. (DeCurtis, Anthony)
RED RED MEAT
Jimmywine Majestic
RR12306 680 (April 21, 1994) pp85,87. (Kot, Greg)
RED ROAD
Music For The Native Americans
RR12307 694 (November 3, 1994) p98. (Evans, Paul)
RR12308 698-699 (December 29, 1994) pp170,173. (Evans, Paul)
RED, TAMPA
The Guitar Wizard
RR12309 685 (June 30, 1994) p77. (Considine, J. D.)
REDDING, OTIS
Otis!
RR12310 669 (November 11, 1993) p76. (Evans, Paul)
Remember Me
RR12311 636 (August 6, 1992) p66. (Considine, J. D.)
REDMAN
Dare Iz A Darkside
RR12312 701 (February 9, 1995) pp55-56. (Toure)
REDMAN, JOSHUA
Wish
RR12313 671 (December 9, 1993) p70. (Futterman, Steve)
REDS
Cry Tomorrow
RR12314 634-635 (July 9, 1992) p102. (Fricke, David)
REED, LOU
Magic And Loss
RR12315 622 (January 23, 1992) pp43-44. (Fricke, David)
RR12316 645-646 (December 10, 1992) p164. (Coleman, Mark)
Set The Twilight Reeling
RR12317 729 (March 7, 1996) p48. (Fricke, David)
REEVES, MARTHA
Live Wire
RR12318 672-673 (December 23, 1993) p148. (Considine, J. D.)
REID, VERNON
Mistaken Identity
RR12319 750-751 (December 26, 1996) p194.
REINHARDT, DJANGO
Djangology
RR12320 672-673 (December 23, 1993) p164. (Futterman, Steve)
R.E.M.
Automatic For The People
RR12321 642 (October 29, 1992) pp68-69. (Evans, Paul)
RR12322 645-646 (December 10, 1992) p164. (Coleman, Mark)
Monster
RR12323 692 (October 6, 1994) pp83-84. (Palmer, Robert)
RR12324 698-699 (December 29, 1994) p170. (Evans, Paul)
New Adventures In Hi-Fi
RR12325 743 (September 19, 1996) pp79-80. (Kemp, Mark)
RR12326 750-751 (December 26, 1996) p190.
Out Of Time
RR12327 619-620 (December 12, 1991) p165. (Fricke, David)
REPLACEMENTS
Alex Chilton (song)
RR12328 659 (June 24, 1993) p53. (Mundy, Chris)
Can't Hardly Wait (song)
RR12329 659 (June 24, 1993) p53. (Mundy, Chris)
Color Me Impressed (song)
RR12330 659 (June 24, 1993) p53. (Mundy, Chris)
I Will Dare (song)
RR12331 659 (June 24, 1993) p53. (Mundy, Chris)
I'll Be You (song)
RR12332 659 (June 24, 1993) p53. (Mundy, Chris)

Left Of The Dial (song)
RR12333 659 (June 24, 1993) p53. (Mundy, Chris)
Little Mascara (song)
RR12334 659 (June 24, 1993) p53. (Mundy, Chris)
Sadly Beautiful (song)
RR12335 659 (June 24, 1993) p53. (Mundy, Chris)
Unsatisfied (song)
RR12336 659 (June 24, 1993) p53. (Mundy, Chris)
Within Your Reach (song)
RR12337 659 (June 24, 1993) p53. (Mundy, Chris)
REVEREND HORTON HEAT
Smoke 'Em If You Got 'Em
RR12337a 625 (March 5, 1992) p70. (Fricke, David)
REVOLUTIONARY DUB WARRIORS
Reaction Dub part 1: Deliverance
RR12338 703 (March 9, 1995) p65. (Fernando, S. H., Jr.)
REX DAISY
Brand New Friend (song)
RR12339 720 (November 2, 1995) p69. (Fricke, David)
Walls Scream (song)
RR12340 720 (November 2, 1995) p69. (Fricke, David)
RICH, CHARLIE
Boss Man
RR12341 707 (May 4, 1995) p70. (McLeese, Don)
The Fabulous Charlie Rich
RR12342 707 (May 4, 1995) p70. (McLeese, Don)
Pictures And Paintings
RR12343 636 (August 6, 1992) p60. (Coleman, Mark)
Set Me Free
RR12344 707 (May 4, 1995) p70. (McLeese, Don)
RICH, TONY
Words
RR12345 727 (February 8, 1996) p50. (Cooper, Carol)
RICHARDS, KEITH
Live At The Hollywood Palladium, December 15, 1988
RR12346 621 (January 9, 1992) p51. (Palmer, Robert)
Main Offender
RR12347 645-646 (December 10, 1992) p179. (Coleman, Mark)
RICHARDSON, SCOTT
Tornado Souvenirs
RR12348 652 (March 18, 1993) p42. (Fricke, David)
RIDE
Going Blank Again
RR12349 645-646 (December 10, 1992) pp179-180. (Coleman, Mark)
Live Light
RR12350 732 (April 18, 1996) pp69-70. (DeRogatis, Jim)
Tarantula
RR12351 732 (April 18, 1996) pp69-70. (DeRogatis, Jim)
RIGBY, AMY
Diary Of A Mod Housewife
RR12352 747 (November 14, 1996) p114. (McCormick, Moira)
RIGHT SAID FRED
Up
RR12353 627 (April 2, 1992) p45. (Hunter, Jim)
RILEY, BILLY LEE
Blue Collar Blues
RR12354 647 (January 7, 1993) p54. (McLeese, Don)
RISING SONS
Rising Sons
RR12355 652 (March 18, 1993) p42. (Fricke, David)
ROACH, ARCHIE
Charcoal Lane
RR12356 633 (June 25, 1992) p43. (McLane, Daisann)
RR12357 645-646 (December 10, 1992) p184. (Coleman, Mark)
Jamu Dreaming
RR12358 664 (September 2, 1993) pp65-66. (Lyman, Andy)
ROACH, MAX
Percussion Bitter Sweet
RR12359 653 (April 1, 1993) p53. (Futterman, Steve)
ROARING LION
Roaring Loud, Standing Proud
RR12360 658 (June 10, 1993) p78. (McLane, Daisann)
ROB AND FAB
Rob And Fab
RR12361 658 (June 10, 1993) pp70-71. (Eddy, Chuck)
ROBERTSON, ROBBIE
Music For The Native Americans
RR12362 694 (November 3, 1994) p98. (Evans, Paul)
RR12363 698-699 (December 29, 1994) pp170,173. (Evans, Paul)
Storyville
RR12364 616 (October 31, 1991) pp87,89,91. (DeCurtis, Anthony)
RR12365 619-620 (December 12, 1991) pp184,187. (Fricke, David)
ROBINSON, SMOKEY
The 35th Anniversary Collection
RR12366 682 (May 19, 1994) p100. (Considine, J. D.)
ROCHES
A Dove
RR12367 638 (September 3, 1992) p67. (Manning, Kara)
ROCK, PETE
Mecca And The Soul Brother
RR12368 645-646 (December 10, 1992) p174. (Coleman, Mark)
ROCKET FROM THE CRYPT
Scream, Dracula, Scream!
RR12369 721 (November 16, 1995) p111. (Ali, Lorraine)
RODGERS, JIMMIE
Last Sessions
RR12370 629 (April 30, 1992) p57. (Considine, J. D.)
No Hard Times
RR12371 629 (April 30, 1992) p57. (Considine, J. D.)
RODGERS, PAUL
Muddy Water Blues
RR12372 660-661 (July 8, 1993) pp114,116. (Evans, Paul)
RODRIGUEZ, ARSENIO
Afro-Cuban Classic: Los 24 Exitos Originales de Arsenio Rodriguez
RR12373 640 (October 1, 1992) p75. (McLane, Daisann)
A Todos Los Barrios
RR12374 640 (October 1, 1992) p75. (McLane, Daisann)
ROGERS, TAMMY
In The Red
RR12375 707 (May 4, 1995) p70. (McLeese, Don)
ROGIE, S. E.
Dead Men Don't Smoke Marijuana
RR12376 698-699 (December 29, 1994) p182. (McLane, Daisann)
ROLLING STONES
Stripped
RR12377 724-725 (December 28, 1995) p118. (Fricke, David)
Voodoo Lounge
RR12378 688 (August 11, 1994) pp65-66. (O'Dair, Barbara)
RR12379 698-699 (December 29, 1994) p170. (Evans, Paul)
ROLLINS BAND
The End Of Silence
RR12380 626 (March 19, 1992) p92. (Sinclair, Tom)
ROLLINS, HENRY
Rollins: The Boxed Life
RR12381 649 (February 4, 1993) pp63-64. (Powell, Kevin)
Weight
RR12382 680 (April 21, 1994) pp83-84. (Welchman, Geoffrey)
ROLLINS, SONNY
The Complete Prestige Recordings

RR12383 645-646 (December 10, 1992) p180. (Futterman, Steve)
RONETTES
The Best Of The Ronettes
RR12384 648 (January 21, 1993) p50. (Considine, J. D.)
The Early Years
RR12385 648 (January 21, 1993) p50. (Considine, J. D.)
RONSON, MICK
Heaven And Hull
RR12386 682 (May 19, 1994) p103. (Evans, Paul)
RONSTADT, LINDA
Feels Like Home
RR12387 705 (April 6, 1995) p65. (Galvin, Peter)
Mas Canciones
RR12388 623 (February 6, 1992) pp77,79. (McLane, Daisann)
Winter Light
RR12389 671 (December 9, 1993) p66. (Galvin, Peter)
ROOTS
Illadelph Halflife
RR12390 747 (November 14, 1996) p114. (Powell, Kevin)
ROSS, ANNIE
Conversation On A Barstool (song)
RR12391 666 (September 30, 1993) p18. (Wild, David)
ROSS, DIANA
Forever Diana
RR12392 672-673 (December 23, 1993) p148. (Considine, J. D.)
ROSS, TAL
AKA Detrimental Vasoline
RR12393 724-725 (December 28, 1995) p125. (Fricke, David)
ROSSY
One Eye On The Future, One Eye On The Past
RR12394 658 (June 10, 1993) p78. (McLane, Daisann)
ROTH, DAVID LEE
A Little Ain't Enough
RR12395 619-620 (December 12, 1991) p187. (Fricke, David)
Your Filthy Little Mouth
RR12396 685 (June 30, 1994) p74. (Drozdowski, Ted)
ROTHBERG, PATTI
Between The 1 And The 9
RR12397 735 (May 30, 1996) p46. (Powers, Ann)
ROWLES, JIMMY
If I'm Lucky
RR12398 649 (February 4, 1993) p75. (Futterman, Steve)
The Peacocks
RR12399 678 (March 24, 1994) p97. (Futterman, Steve)
ROYAL TRUX
Cats And Dogs
RR12400 664 (September 2, 1993) p66. (Reynolds, Simon)
Thank You
RR12401 711 (June 29, 1995) pp42-43. (Palmer, Robert)
RR12402 724-725 (December 28, 1995) p126. (Fricke, David)
ROZALLA
Everybody's Free
RR12403 645-646 (December 10, 1992) p184. (Coleman, Mark)
Look No Further
RR12404 717 (September 21, 1995) pp84-85. (Weisel, Al)
RR
Dangerhouse, Volume One
RR12405 619-620 (December 12, 1991) p168. (Fricke, David)
RUN C&W
Into The Twangy-First Century
RR12406 656 (May 13, 1993) p110. (McLeese, Don)
RUN ON
Start Packing
RR12407 730 (March 21, 1996) p98. (Fricke, David)
RUN-D.M.C.
Down With The King
RR12408 659 (June 24, 1993) p83. (Coleman, Mark)
RR12409 672-673 (December 23, 1993) pp156-157. (Evans, Paul)
Raising Hell
RR12410 666 (September 30, 1993) p59. (Dyson, Michael Eric)
Together Forever
RR12411 619-620 (December 12, 1991) p184. (Fricke, David)
RUSH, OTIS
Ain't Enough Comin' In
RR12412 689 (August 25, 1994) p89. (Milward, John)
Otis Rush, 1956-1958
RR12413 625 (March 5, 1992) p70. (Fricke, David)
RUSSELL, ARTHUR
Another Night
RR12414 706 (April 20, 1995) p72. (Fricke, David)
RUSSELL, LEON
Anything Can Happen
RR12415 631 (May 28, 1992) p54. (Graves, Tom)
RUSSELL, TOM
Box Of Visions
RR12416 670 (November 25, 1993) pp117,120. (Jurek, Thom)
Hillbilly Voodoo
RR12417 670 (November 25, 1993) pp117,120. (Jurek, Thom)
Hurricane Season
RR12418 624 (February 20, 1992) p45. (Swenson, John)
RUSTED ROOT
Remember
RR12419 749 (December 12, 1996) pp82,84. (Damsker, Matt)

S

SADE
Love Deluxe
RR12420 645-646 (December 10, 1992) p166. (Coleman, Mark)
RR12421 669 (November 11, 1993) p20. (Kravitz, Lenny)
SAINT ETIENNE
So Tough
RR12422 662 (August 5, 1993) p65. (White, Armond)
SAINTE-MARIE, BUFFY
Coincidence And Likely Stories
RR12423 644 (November 26, 1992) p74. (Graves, Tom)
SAKAMOTO, RYUICHI
Heartbeat
RR12424 645-646 (December 10, 1992) p182. (Coleman, Mark)
SALEM, KEVIN
Soma City
RR12425 700 (January 26, 1995) pp62-63. (George-Warren, Holly)
SALT-N-PEPA
Hot, Cool & Vicious
RR12426 666 (September 30, 1993) p56. (Kelley, Robin D.G.)
Whatta Man (song)
RR12427 678 (March 24, 1994) p16. (Donelly, Tanya)
SAM AND DAVE
Sweat 'N' Soul
RR12428 664 (September 2, 1993) p64. (Considine, J. D.)
SANTANA
Milagro
RR12429 638 (September 3, 1992) p68. (Swenson, John)
SATAN AND ADAM
Harlem Blues
RR12430 619-620 (December 12, 1991) p168. (Fricke, David)
SCAGGS, BOZ
Some Change
RR12431 681 (May 5, 1994) p51. (Evans, Paul)

SCARCE
Deadsexy
RR12432 743 (September 19, 1996) p82. (Wiederhorn, Jon)
SCARFACE
The Diary
RR12433 698-699 (December 29, 1994) pp178,180. (Evans, Paul)
SCENIC
Acquatica
RR12434 746 (October 31, 1996) p70. (Fine, Jason)
Incident At Cima
RR12435 724-725 (December 28, 1995) p125. (Fricke, David)
SCHNEIDER, FRED
Just Fred
RR12436 733 (May 2, 1996) pp54,56. (Appleford, Steve)
SCIALFA, PATTI
Rumble Doll
RR12437 665 (September 16, 1993) p70. (Gardner, Elysa)
SCOTS PIRATES
Revolutionary Means
RR12438 724-725 (December 28, 1995) p124. (Fricke, David)
Scots Pirates
RR12439 672-673 (December 23, 1993) p154. (Fricke, David)
SCOTT, CASEY
Creep City
RR12440 663 (August 19, 1993) p19. (Neely, Kim)
SCOTT, JIMMY
All The Way
RR12441 640 (October 1, 1992) p69. (Wright, Christian)
SCOTT, RAYMOND
The Music Of Raymond Scott: Reckless Nights And Turkish Twilights
RR12442 663 (August 19, 1993) p19. (Neely, Kim)
SCOTT, STEPHEN
Aminah's Dream
RR12443 653 (April 1, 1993) p53. (Futterman, Steve)
SCRATCH
Scratch
RR12444 667 (October 14, 1993) p34. (Neely, Kim)
SCRAWL
Travel On, Rider
RR12445 744 (October 3, 1996) p72. (McDonnell, Evelyn)
SCREAMING TREES
Dust
RR12446 736 (June 13, 1996) p51. (Wiederhorn, Jon)
RR12447 738-739 (July 11, 1996) pp86-87. (O'Connor, Rob)
RR12448 750-751 (December 26, 1996) pp184,186.
SCREECHING WEASEL
Kill The Musicians
RR12449 716 (September 7, 1995) p73. (Fricke, David)
SEAL
Seal
RR12450 692 (October 6, 1994) p90. (Wright, Christian)
SEALS, SON
Living In The Danger Zone
RR12451 615 (October 17, 1991) p93. (Brauer, Laurence)
SEBADOH
Bakesale
RR12452 696 (December 1, 1994) pp126-127. (Kemp, Mark)
Bubble And Scrape
RR12453 664 (September 2, 1993) p61. (Hill, Trent)
Harmacy
RR12454 742 (September 5, 1996) p60. (Kemp, Mark)
SEGER, BOB
The Fire Inside
RR12455 615 (October 17, 1991) pp93-94. (Milward, John)
SELENA
Dreaming Of You
RR12456 716 (September 7, 1995) pp72-73. (Eddy, Chuck)
SEMISONIC
Great Divide
RR12457 750-751 (December 26, 1996) pp196,198.
SENTRIDOH
Winning Losers
RR12458 684 (June 16, 1994) p110. (Fricke, David)
SEPULTURA
Chaos A.D.
RR12459 681 (May 5, 1994) p52. (Darzin,Daina)
Roots
RR12460 730 (March 21, 1996) pp98,100. (Wiederhorn, Jon)
SERCH, MC
Return Of The Product
RR12461 640 (October 1, 1992) p68. (Tannenbaum, Rob)
SETTERS
The Setters
RR12462 694 (November 3, 1994) p101. (Mirkin, Steven)
SETZER, BRIAN
The Brian Setzer Orchestra
RR12463 680 (April 21, 1994) p87. (Lyman, Andy)
7 YEAR BITCH
Sick 'Em
RR12464 649 (February 4, 1993) p66. (Dougan, John)
Viva Zapata
RR12465 691 (September 22, 1994) pp99-100. (Berger, Arion)
SEX PISTOLS
Filthy Lucre Live
RR12466 743 (September 19, 1996) pp80,82. (Robbins, Ira)
SEXSMITH, RON
Ron Sexsmith
RR12467 716 (September 7, 1995) p72. (Scoppa, Bud)
SEXTON, CHARLIE
Under The Wishing Tree
RR12468 706 (April 20, 1995) p80. (Evans, Paul)
SHADOW
Columbus Lied
RR12469 626 (March 19, 1992) p95. (McLane, Daisann)
SHADOWS OF KNIGHT
Raw 'N Alive At The Cellar, 1966
RR12470 645-646 (December 10, 1992) p177. (Fricke, David)
SHAGGY
Boombastic
RR12471 716 (September 7, 1995) p70. (Weisel, Al)
SHAI
If I Ever Fall In Love
RR12472 653 (April 1, 1993) pp52-53. (Dyson, Michael)
SHAKUR, TUPAC
All Eyez On Me
RR12473 731 (April 4, 1996) p60. (Jamison, Laura)
RR12474 750-751 (December 26, 1996) p184.
Me Against The World
RR12475 707 (May 4, 1995) pp68,70. (Coker, Cheo H.)
SHAMS
Quilt
RR12476 645-646 (December 10, 1992) p177. (Fricke, David)
SHANICE
Inner Child
RR12477 626 (March 19, 1992) pp95,97. (Dyson, Michael Eric)
SHANNON'S DRESS
Shannon's Dress (EP)
RR12478 672-673 (December 23, 1993) p154. (Fricke, David)
SHAVER
Unshaven
RR12479 716 (September 7, 1995) p72. (McLeese, Don)
SHAVER, BILLY JOE
Tramp On Your Street
RR12480 663 (August 19, 1993) p77. (McLeese, Don)
SHEAR, JULES
The Great Puzzle

RR12481 623 (February 6, 1992) pp73,77. (Gardner, Elysa)
Healing Bones
RR12482 692 (October 6, 1994) p87. (Evans, Paul)
SHEIK, DUNCAN
Duncan Sheik
RR12483 745 (October 17, 1996) p136. (Hunter, James)
SHELLAC
At Action Park
RR12484 698-699 (December 29, 1994) p174. (Fricke, David)
The Rude Gesture
RR12485 684 (June 16, 1994) p110. (Fricke, David)
Uranus
RR12486 684 (June 16, 1994) p110. (Fricke, David)
SHELLEYAN ORPHAN
Humroot
RR12487 642 (October 29, 1992) p74. (Odintz, Andrea)
SHERMAN, BIM
Miracle
RR12488 750-751 (December 26, 1996) p192. (Fricke, David)
SHINES
The Shines
RR12489 625 (March 5, 1992) p70. (Fricke, David)
SHIPP, MATTHEW
Circular Temple
RR12490 708 (May 18, 1995) pp87-88. (Fricke, David)
SHIVERS
The Buried Life
RR12491 728 (February 22, 1996) p62. (Himes, Geoffrey)
SHOCKED, MICHELLE
Arkansas Traveler
RR12492 630 (May 14, 1992) p105. (Kemp, Mark)
Kind Hearted Woman
RR12493 749 (December 12, 1996) pp84,86. (Appleford, Steve)
SHOES
Silhouette
RR12494 624 (February 20, 1992) p42. (McLeese, Don)
SHONEN KNIFE
Rock Animals
RR12495 677 (March 10, 1994) p65. (Evans, Paul)
SHOUKICHI KINA
Peppermint Tea House
RR12496 680 (April 21, 1994) p90. (McLane, Daisann)
SHULL, TAD
In The Land Of The Tenor
RR12497 665 (September 16, 1993) p67. (Futterman, Steve)
SHYHEIM
AKA The Rugged Child
RR12498 689 (August 25, 1994) p88. (Toure)
SIBERRY, JANE
Maria
RR12499 717 (September 21, 1995) p84. (Dean, Chuck)
When I Was A Boy
RR12500 670 (November 25, 1993) p120. (Walls, Richard C.)
SIDIBE, SALI
Wassoulou Foli
RR12501 680 (April 21, 1994) p90. (McLane, Daisann)
SILK
Lose Control
RR12502 657 (May 27, 1993) pp49-50. (Considine, J. D.)
SILOS
Susan Across The Ocean
RR12503 694 (November 3, 1994) p101. (Mirkin, Steven)
SILVERCHAIR
Frogstomp
RR12504 724-725 (December 28, 1995) p120. (Fricke, David)
SIMIEN, TERRANCE
There's Room For Us All
RR12505 680 (April 21, 1994) p88. (Evans, Paul)
SIMON, PAUL
Paul Simon 1964-1993
RR12506 669 (November 11, 1993) p77. (Considine, J. D.)
SIMONE, NINA
A Single Woman
RR12507 669 (November 11, 1993) p73. (Berger, Arion)
SIMPLE MINDS
Good News From The Next World
RR12508 703 (March 9, 1995) p64. (Manning, Kara)
SIMPLY RED
Life
RR12509 721 (November 16, 1995) p110. (Hunter, James)
SIMPLY SAUCER
Cyborgs Revisted
RR12510 645-646 (December 10, 1992) p177. (Fricke, David)
SIMS, ZOOT
If I'm Lucky
RR12511 649 (February 4, 1993) p75. (Futterman, Steve)
SINATRA, FRANK
The Columbia Years 1943-1952
RR12512 672-673 (December 23, 1993) p148. (Considine, J. D.)
Duets
RR12513 672-673 (December 23, 1993) p151. (Evans, Paul)
Sinatra And Sextet: Live In Paris
RR12514 682 (May 19, 1994) pp97-98,100. (DeCurtis, Anthony)
The Song Is You
RR12515 698-699 (December 29, 1994) p188. (Considine, J. D.)
SINNERS
Find A Door
RR12516 737 (June 27, 1996) pp55-56. (DeCurtis, Anthony)
SIR DOUGLAS QUINTET
Day Dreaming At Midnight
RR12517 690 (September 8, 1994) p80. (Mirkin, Steven)
SIR MIX-A-LOT
Chief Boot Knocka
RR12518 691 (September 22, 1994) p94. (Berman, Eric)
Mack Daddy
RR12519 628 (April 16, 1992) p86. (Coleman, Mark)
RR12520 645-646 (December 10, 1992) pp176,178. (Coleman, Mark)
RR12521 666 (September 30, 1993) p56. (Walser, Robert)
SIX FINGER SATELLITE
The Pigeon Is The Most Popular Bird
RR12522 667 (October 14, 1993) p121. (Fricke, David)
6THS
Wasps' Nests
RR12523 710 (June 15, 1995) p81. (Manning, Kara)
SKATALITES
The Original Skatalites And Laurel Aitken
RR12524 664 (September 2, 1993) p16. (Fricke, David)
SKELETONS
In The Flesh!
RR12525 619-620 (December 12, 1991) p168. (Fricke, David)
SKID ROW
Subhuman Race
RR12526 706 (April 20, 1995) p78. (Gold, Jonathan)
SLASH
It's Five O'Clock Somewhere
RR12527 702 (February 23, 1995) pp71-72. (Considine, J. D.)
RR12528 724-725 (December 28, 1995) p126. (Fricke, David)
SLAUGHTER
The Wild Life
RR12529 633 (June 25, 1992) p44. (Eddy, Chuck)
SLAYER
Divine Intervention
RR12530 701 (February 9, 1995) p58. (Palmer, Robert)

Undisputed Attitude
RR12531 735 (May 30, 1996) p49. (Masuo, Sandy)
SLEATER-KINNEY
Call The Doctor
RR12532 736 (June 13, 1996) p82. (Ali, Lorraine)
SLEEPY LABEEF
Strange Things Happening
RR12533 683 (June 2, 1994) p70. (McLeese, Don)
SLICK RICK
Behind Bars
RR12534 703 (March 9, 1995) p67. (Coker, Cheo H.)
SLINT
Spiderland
RR12535 619-620 (December 12, 1991) p168. (Fricke, David)
SLOAN
Smeared
RR12536 654 (April 15, 1993) p64. (Robbins, Ira)
SLOWDRIVE
Just For A Day
RR12537 625 (March 5, 1992) p68. (Robbins, Ira)
SLY AND THE FAMILY STONE
Dance To The Music
RR12538 717 (September 21, 1995) p85. (Coleman, Mark)
Life
RR12539 717 (September 21, 1995) p85. (Coleman, Mark)
A Whole New Thing
RR12540 717 (September 21, 1995) p85. (Coleman, Mark)
SMALL FACES
The Anthology 1965-1967
RR12541 750-751 (December 26, 1996) p189. (Coleman, Mark)
There Are But Four Small Faces
RR12542 624 (February 20, 1992) p42. (McLeese, Don)
SMASHING PUMPKINS
The Aeroplane Flies High
RR12543 749 (December 12, 1996) pp81-82. (Moon, Tom)
Mellon Collie And The Infinite Sadness
RR12544 722 (November 30, 1995) pp64,66. (DeRogatis, Jim)
RR12545 724-725 (December 28, 1995) p116. (Fricke, David)
Pisces Iscariot
RR12546 696 (December 1, 1994) p124. (Weisel, Al)
Siamese Dream
RR12547 665 (September 16, 1993) p17. (Mundy, Chris)
RR12548 665 (September 16, 1993) p65. (Ali, Lorraine)
RR12549 672-673 (December 23, 1993) p159. (Evans, Paul)
SMITH, KENDRA
Five Ways Of Disappearing
RR12550 716 (September 7, 1995) p73. (Davies, Barbara)
SMITH, PATTI
Gone Again
RR12551 736 (June 13, 1996) p51. (Wiederhorn, Jon)
RR12552 737 (June 27, 1996) pp53-54. (Carson, Tom)
RR12553 750-751 (December 26, 1996) p184.
Piss Factory
RR12554 668 (October 28, 1993) p26. (DeCurtis, Anthony)
SMITHEREENS
Blow Up
RR12555 616 (October 31, 1991) pp91-92. (King, Wayne)
A Date With The Smithereens
RR12556 682 (May 19, 1994) pp102-103. (Odintz, Andrea)
SMOKING POPES
Born To Quit
RR12557 715 (August 24, 1995) pp101-102. (Kot, Greg)
SMOOTH, C. L.
Mecca And The Soul Brother
RR12558 645-646 (December 10, 1992) p174. (Coleman, Mark)
SMUGGLERS
Atlanta Whiskey Flats
RR12559 652 (March 18, 1993) p42. (Fricke, David)
SNAKEPIT
It's Five O'Clock Somewhere
RR12560 702 (February 23, 1995) pp71-72. (Considine, J. D.)
RR12561 724-725 (December 28, 1995) p126. (Fricke, David)
SNIDER, TODD
Songs For The Daily Planet
RR12562 707 (May 4, 1995) p70. (McLeese, Don)
SNOOP DOGGY DOGG
Doggystyle
RR12563 674 (January 27, 1994) pp51-52. (Toure)
SNOW
12 Inches Of Snow
RR12564 656 (May 13, 1993) p108. (Eddy, Chuck)
SOCIAL DISTORTION
White Light White Heat White Trash
RR12565 744 (October 3, 1996) p71. (Robbins, Ira)
SOFT BOYS
1976-81
RR12566 676 (February 24, 1994) p59. (Mirkin, Steve)
SON VOLT
Trace
RR12567 724-725 (December 28, 1995) p120. (Fricke, David)
SONIC YOUTH
Dirty
RR12568 638 (September 3, 1992) pp63-65. (Palmer, Robert)
Experimental Jet Set, Trash And No Star
RR12569 681 (May 5, 1994) pp52-53. (O'Dair, Barbara)
Live At The Continental Club
RR12570 634-635 (July 9, 1992) p102. (Fricke, David)
Washing Machine
RR12571 719 (October 19, 1995) p149. (Moon, Tom)
RR12572 724-725 (December 28, 1995) p125. (Fricke, David)
SONNIER, JO-EL
Cajun Roots
RR12573 686-687 (July 14, 1994) p107. (McLeese, Don)
SOUL ASYLUM
Grave Dancers Union
RR12574 648 (January 21, 1993) pp49-50. (Diehl, Matt)
RR12575 672-673 (December 23, 1993) pp159,162. (Evans, Paul)
Let Your Dim Light Shine
RR12576 710 (June 15, 1995) pp79-80. (Gardner, Elysa)
RR12577 724-725 (December 28, 1995) p116. (Fricke, David)
SOUL BLUES BOYS
All Night Long
RR12578 649 (February 4, 1993) p69. (Santelli, Robert)
SOUL COUGHING
Ruby Vroom
RR12579 697 (December 15, 1994) pp96-97. (Azerrad, Michael)
SOUL II SOUL
Believe
RR12580 720 (November 2, 1995) p70. (St. Leger, Marie Elsie)
Volume III Just Right
RR12581 631 (May 28, 1992) p54. (Coleman, Mark)
SOUNDGARDEN
Badmotorfinger
RR12582 619-620 (December 12, 1991) p174. (Fricke, David)
Down On The Upside
RR12583 735 (May 30, 1996) pp45-46. (O'Connor, Rob)
RR12584 750-751 (December 26, 1996) p184.
Superunknown
RR12585 677 (March 10, 1994) pp63-64. (Considine, J. D.)
RR12586 698-699 (December 29, 1994) p176. (Evans, Paul)
SOUTHERN CULTURE ON THE SKIDS
Ditch Diggin'
RR12587 684 (June 16, 1994) p109. (Welchman, Geoffrey)
SOUTHSIDE JOHNNY AND THE ASBURY JUKES
Better Days

RR12588 617 (November 14, 1991) pp169-170. (Santelli, Robert)
SPACIOUS MIND
Sleepy Eyes And Butterflies
RR12589 720 (November 2, 1995) p69. (Fricke, David)
SPANIC BOYS
Dream Your Life Away
RR12590 666 (September 30, 1993) p18. (Wild, David)
SPANN, OTIS
The Complete Candid Otis Spann-Lightnin' Hopkins Sessions
RR12591 640 (October 1, 1992) p67. (Fricke, David)
SPEARHEAD
Home
RR12592 698-699 (December 29, 1994) pp173,176. (Evans, Paul)
SPECIAL SAUCE
G. Love And Special Sauce
RR12593 684 (June 16, 1994) p108. (Moon, Tom)
SPECTOR, PHIL
Back To Mono (1958-1969)
RR12594 618 (November 28, 1991) pp87,90,94. (Loder, Kurt)
SPEECH
Speech
RR12595 727 (February 8, 1996) p50. (Fernando, S. H., Jr.)
SPENCER, JON
The Jon Spencer Blues Explosion
RR12596 644 (November 26, 1992) p74. (Levy, Joe)
Now I Got Worry
RR12597 744 (October 3, 1996) p72. (Diehl, Matt)
Orange
RR12598 698-699 (December 29, 1994) p181. (Evans, Paul)
SPICE 1
187 He Wrote
RR12599 670 (November 25, 1993) p121. (Toure)
SPIN DOCTORS
Turn It Upside Down
RR12600 686-687 (July 14, 1994) p110. (Swenson, John)
You've Got To Believe In Something
RR12601 734 (May 16, 1996) p64. (DeRogatis, Jim)
SPINAL TAP
Break Like The Wind
RR12602 627 (April 2, 1992) p45. (Wright, Christian)
SPINNERS
A One Of A Kind Love Affair—The Anthology
RR12603 624 (February 20, 1992) p42. (McLeese, Don)
SPIRIT
Chronicles
RR12604 628 (April 16, 1992) p85. (Fricke, David)
SPIRITUALIZED
Pure Phase
RR12605 708 (May 18, 1995) p93. (Kot, Greg)
SPLIT
I Can Hear The Ants Dancin'
RR12606 706 (April 20, 1995) p72. (Fricke, David)
SPONGE
Wax Ecstatic
RR12607 736 (June 13, 1996) p51. (Wiederhorn, Jon)
RR12608 738-739 (July 11, 1996) p90. (Diehl, Matt)
SPOON
Telephono
RR12609 734 (May 16, 1996) p66. (Wiederhorn, Jon)
SPRINGSTEEN, BRUCE
The Ghost Of Tom Joad
RR12610 724-725 (December 28, 1995) p127. (Gilmore, Mikal)
Greatest Hits
RR12611 705 (April 6, 1995) pp60-61. (Evans, Paul)
Human Touch
RR12612 629 (April 30, 1992) pp53,56,67. (DeCurtis, Anthony)
RR12613 645-646 (December 10, 1992) p164. (Coleman, Mark)
Lucky Town
RR12614 629 (April 30, 1992) pp53,56,67. (DeCurtis, Anthony)
RR12615 645-646 (December 10, 1992) p164. (Coleman, Mark)
SPROUT, TOBIN
Carnival Boy
RR12616 748 (November 28, 1996) p130. (Diehl, Matt)
SRC
Lost Masters
RR12617 672-673 (December 23, 1993) p154. (Fricke, David)
ST. JOHNNY
High As A Kite
RR12618 670 (November 25, 1993) p114. (Ro, Ronin)
STAMEY, CHRIS
Christmas Time
RR12619 672-673 (December 23, 1993) p169. (Howard, Pete)
Mavericks
RR12620 619-620 (December 12, 1991) p184. (Fricke, David)
STANDELLS
Dirty Water
RR12621 684 (June 16, 1994) p110. (Fricke, David)
The Hot Ones!
RR12622 684 (June 16, 1994) p110. (Fricke, David)
Try It
RR12623 684 (June 16, 1994) p110. (Fricke, David)
Why Pick On Me
RR12624 684 (June 16, 1994) p110. (Fricke, David)
STANLEY, RALPH
Saturday Night And Sunday Morning
RR12625 677 (March 10, 1994) p18. (Duritz, Adam)
STANSFIELD, LISA
Real Love
RR12626 621 (January 9, 1992) p51. (Holden, Stephen)
STAPLES, POP
Peace To The Neighborhood
RR12627 637 (August 20, 1992) p53. (Altman, Billy)
STARR, RINGO
Time Takes Time
RR12628 636 (August 6, 1992) p59. (Puterbaugh, Parke)
STEEL POLE BATH TUB
Auf Wiedersehen (song)
RR12629 720 (November 2, 1995) p69. (Fricke, David)
Surrender (song)
RR12630 720 (November 2, 1995) p69. (Fricke, David)
STEEL PULSE
True Democracy
RR12631 676 (February 24, 1994) p42. (McLane, Daisann)
STEELY DAN
Alive In America
RR12632 723 (December 14, 1995) p86. (Kot, Greg)
Citizen
RR12633 677 (March 10, 1994) p67. (Considine, J. D.)
STEREOLAB
Mars Audiac Quintet
RR12634 698-699 (December 29, 1994) p173. (Evans, Paul)
Transient Random-Noise Bursts With Announcements
RR12635 672-673 (December 23, 1993) p154. (Fricke, David)
STEWART, DAVE
Greetings From The Gutter
RR12636 704 (March 23, 1995) p122. (Gardner, Elysa)
STEWART, GARY
Gary's Greatest
RR12637 624 (February 20, 1992) p42. (McLeese, Don)
I'm A Texan
RR12638 675 (February 10, 1994) p46. (McLeese, Don)
STEWART, ROD
Unplugged...And Unseated

RR12639 659 (June 24, 1993) p80. (Considine, J. D.)
STING
Mercury Falling
RR12640 730 (March 21, 1996) p96. (Gardner, Elysa)
The Soul Cages
RR12641 619-620 (December 12, 1991) p182. (Fricke, David)
Ten Summoner's Tales
RR12642 652 (March 18, 1993) pp38-39. (DeCurtis, Anthony)
RR12643 672-673 (December 23, 1993) p168. (Evans, Paul)
STONE ROSES
Second Coming
RR12644 701 (February 9, 1995) p57. (Volk, Steven)
STONE TEMPLE PILOTS
Core
RR12645 672-673 (December 23, 1993) pp152-153. (Evans, Paul)
Purple
RR12646 686-687 (July 14, 1994) p106. (Ali, Lorraine)
RR12647 698-699 (December 29, 1994) p176. (Evans, Paul)
Tiny Music
RR12648 733 (May 2, 1996) pp51-52. (Ali, Lorraine)
RR12649 750-751 (December 26, 1996) p186.
STONE, ROLAND
Remember Me
RR12650 668 (October 28, 1993) pp80-81. (Palmer, Robert)
STONE, SLY
Precious Stone
RR12651 706 (April 20, 1995) p72. (Fricke, David)
STRADLIN, IZZY
Izzy Stradlin And The Ju Ju Hounds
RR12652 645-646 (December 10, 1992) p179. (Coleman, Mark)
STREISAND, BARBRA
Just For The Record
RR12653 619-620 (December 12, 1991) p177. (McLeese, Don)
STROZIER, FRANK
Fantastic Frank Strozier: Plus
RR12654 678 (March 24, 1994) p97. (Futterman, Steve)
STUART, MARTY
Love And Luck
RR12655 679 (April 7, 1994) p77. (McLeese, Don)
This One's Gonna Hurt You
RR12656 640 (October 1, 1992) p69. (George-Warren, Holly)
STUTTERING JOHN
Stuttering John
RR12657 684 (June 16, 1994) p106. (Evans, Paul)
STYRENES
It's Artastic
RR12658 628 (April 16, 1992) p85. (Fricke, David)
SUBDUDES
Annunciation
RR12659 685 (June 30, 1994) pp75-76. (Sulcas, Adele)
SUBLIME
Sublime
RR12660 750-751 (December 26, 1996) p186.
SUDDENLY, TAMMY!
We Get There When We Do
RR12661 712-713 (July 13, 1995) pp108-109. (Hunter, James)
SUEDE
The Drowners (single)
RR12662 639 (September 17, 1992) p96. (Fricke, David)
My Insatiable (single)
RR12663 639 (September 17, 1992) p96. (Fricke, David)
Suede
RR12664 658 (June 10, 1993) p68. (Fricke, David)
To The Birds (single)
RR12665 639 (September 17, 1992) p96. (Fricke, David)
SUGAR
Copper Blue
RR12666 642 (October 29, 1992) pp71,74. (Ransom, Kevin)
File Under Easy Listening
RR12667 692 (October 6, 1994) p87. (Evans, Paul)
RR12668 698-699 (December 29, 1994) p190. (Evans, Paul)
SUGARCUBES
Stick Around For Joy
RR12669 625 (March 5, 1992) p65. (Azerrad, Michael)
SUMMER, DONNA
The Donna Summer Anthology
RR12670 672-673 (December 23, 1993) p148. (Considine, J. D.)
SUN DIAL
Reflecter
RR12671 652 (March 18, 1993) p42. (Fricke, David)
SUNRAYS
Vintage Rays
RR12672 750-751 (December 26, 1996) pp190,192.
SUPER BLUE
Bacchanal Time
RR12673 658 (June 10, 1993) p78. (McLane, Daisann)
SUPER FURRY ANIMALS
Fuzzy Logic
RR12674 745 (October 17, 1996) p132. (Wiederhorn, Jon)
SUPERCHUNK
Foolish
RR12675 684 (June 16, 1994) p109. (Diehl, Matt)
On The Mouth
RR12676 654 (April 15, 1993) pp61-62. (Diehl, Matt)
Tossing Seeds
RR12677 628 (April 16, 1992) pp84,86. (Eddy, Chuck)
SUPERGRASS
I Should Coco
RR12678 714 (August 10, 1995) p58. (Wiederhorn, Jon)
RR12679 724-725 (December 28, 1995) pp126,129. (Fricke, David)
SUPREME COURT
Supreme Court Goes Electric
RR12680 675 (February 10, 1994) p47. (Puterbaugh, Parke)
SWAINSON, NEIL
Sketches
RR12681 678 (March 24, 1994) p97. (Futterman, Steve)
SWALLOW, STEVE
Fusion
RR12682 631 (May 28, 1992) p61. (Futterman, Steve)
Go Together
RR12683 665 (September 16, 1993) p67. (Futterman, Steve)
Thesis
RR12684 631 (May 28, 1992) p61. (Futterman, Steve)
SWANS
The Great Annihilation
RR12685 718 (October 5, 1995) p69. (Walls, Richard C.)
SWEAT, KEITH
Keep It Comin'
RR12686 621 (January 9, 1992) pp51-52. (Chambers, Gordon)
RR12687 Number not assigned.
SWEET, MATTHEW
Altered Beast
RR12688 665 (September 16, 1993) p70. (O'Connor, Rob)
Girlfriend
RR12689 622 (January 23, 1992) p47. (Evans, Paul)
100% Fun
RR12689a 705 (April 6, 1995) pp61-62. (Jurek, Thom)
SWELL
41
RR12690 686-687 (July 14, 1994) p104. (Evans, Paul)
SWV
It's About Time
RR12691 672-673 (December 23, 1993) p151. (Evans, Paul)
SYKES, KEITH
RR12692 637 (August 20, 1992) p53. (McLeese, Don)

SYLVIAN, DAVID
The First Day
RR12693 670 (November 25, 1993) p114. (Lyman, Andy)
RR12694 Number not assigned.

T

T REX
The Essential Collection
RR12695 619-620 (December 12, 1991) p177. (McLeese, Don)
TADPOLES
Far Out
RR12696 735 (May 30, 1996) p50. (DeRogatis, Jim)
TAG TEAM
Whoomp!
RR12697 671 (December 9, 1993) p72. (Hopkins, Tracy E.)
TAHITIAN CHOIR
Rapa Iti
RR12698 650 (February 18, 1993) p59. (McLane, Daisann)
RR12699 672-673 (December 23, 1993) p163. (McLane, Daisann)
TAKE THAT
Back For Good (song)
RR12700 720 (November 2, 1995) p70. (Hunter, James)
TARRAS, DAVE
Yiddish-American Klezmer Music: 1925-1956
RR12701 629 (April 30, 1992) p57. (Considine, J. D.)
TASHIAN, BARRY
Ready For Love
RR12702 656 (May 13, 1993) p110. (McLeese, Don)
TASHIAN, HOLLY
RR12702 656 (May 13, 1993) p110. (McLeese, Don)
TATE, HOWARD
Get It While You Can
RR12703 724-725 (December 28, 1995) p126. (Fricke, David)
TAYLOR, ART
Mr. A. T.
RR12704 631 (May 28, 1992) p61. (Futterman, Steve)
TAYLOR, JAMES
Live
RR12705 666 (September 30, 1993) pp101-104. (McAlley, John)
TAYLOR, KOKO
Force Of Nature
RR12706 676 (February 24, 1994) p56. (McLeese, Don)
TEAM DRESCH
Captain My Captain
RR12707 736 (June 13, 1996) p82. (Ali, Lorraine)
TEARS FOR FEARS
Elemental
RR12708 664 (September 2, 1993) p66. (Manning, Kara)
TEENAGE FANCLUB
Bandwagonesque
RR12709 623 (February 6, 1992) pp80,82. (Berger, Arion)
Thirteen
RR12710 669 (November 11, 1993) pp73-74. (Azerrad, Michael)
TELEVISION
Television
RR12711 642 (October 29, 1992) p70. (Fricke, David)
TELEVISION PERSONALITIES
Closer To God
RR12712 659 (June 24, 1993) p84. (Robbins, Ira)
TEMPTATIONS
Emperors Of Soul
RR12713 698-699 (December 29, 1994) p188. (Considine, J. D.)
10,000 MANIACS
Few And Far Between
RR12714 668 (October 28, 1993) p26. (DeCurtis, Anthony)
MTV Unplugged
RR12715 672-673 (December 23, 1993) p157. (Evans, Paul)
Our Time In Eden
RR12716 640 (October 1, 1992) pp62-63. (DeCurtis, Anthony)
TERMINATOR X
Super Bad
RR12717 690 (September 8, 1994) p78. (Evans, Paul)
TERRY, CLARK
Jive At Five
RR12718 659 (June 24, 1993) p84. (Futterman, Steve)
TEXAS TORNADOS
4 Aces
RR12719 740 (August 8, 1996) p62. (Himes, Geoffrey)
Hangin' On By A Thread
RR12720 647 (January 7, 1993) p54. (McLeese, Don)
THE THE
Dusk
RR12721 649 (February 4, 1993) p66. (Jurek, Thom)
THEE SPEAKING CANARIES
Songs For The Terrestrially Challenged
RR12722 716 (September 7, 1995) p73. (Fricke, David)
THERAPY?
Infernal Love
RR12723 727 (February 8, 1996) p50. (Gardner, Elysa)
THESE IMMORTAL SOULS
I'm Never Gonna Die Again
RR12724 657 (May 27, 1993) p52. (Palmer, Robert)
THEY MIGHT BE GIANTS
Apollo 18
RR12725 629 (April 30, 1992) pp57-58. (Robbins, Ira)
THIN WHITE ROPE
The One That Got Away
RR12726 660-661 (July 8, 1993) p113. (Fricke, David)
THIS MORTAL COIL
This Mortal Coil
RR12727 655 (April 29, 1993) p62. (Considine, J. D.)
THOMAS, IRMA
Walk Around Heaven
RR12728 684 (June 16, 1994) p110. (Fricke, David)
THOMPSON, LINDA
Dreams Fly Away
RR12729 740 (August 8, 1996) pp58,60. (Berman, Leslie)
THOMPSON, LUCKY
Tricotism
RR12730 678 (March 24, 1994) p97. (Futterman, Steve)
THOMPSON, RICHARD
Mirror Blue
RR12731 678 (March 24, 1994) p96. (Gardner, Elysa)
Watching The Dark
RR12732 657 (May 27, 1993) pp48-49. (Walls, Richard C.)
You? Me? Us?
RR12733 732 (April 18, 1996) p73. (Fricke, David)
THOMPSON, RON
Just Like A Devil
RR12734 649 (February 4, 1993) p66. (Swenson, John)
THREADGILL, HENRY
Carry The Day
RR12735 706 (April 20, 1995) pp74,78. (Woodard, Josef)
THREE FISH
Three Fish
RR12736 737 (June 27, 1996) p56. (Fricke, David)
THROWING MUSES
Limbo
RR12737 741 (August 22, 1996) p96. (Ali, Lorraine)
University
RR12738 702 (February 23, 1995) pp72,74. (O'Dair, Barbara)

TIBBETTS, STEVE
The Fall Of Us All
RR12739 692 (October 6, 1994) p87. (Fricke, David)
TIGER
Claws Of The Cat
RR12740 666 (September 30, 1993) p104. (Weisel, Al)
TILLIS, PAM
Sweetheart's Dance
RR12741 683 (June 2, 1994) p70. (McLeese, Don)
TIMBUK 3
Big Shot In The Dark
RR12742 617 (November 14, 1991) p177. (Webster, Andy)
A Hundred Lovers
RR12743 705 (April 6, 1995) p64. (Evans, Paul)
TINDERSTICKS
Tindersticks
RR12744 698-699 (December 29, 1994) p181. (Evans, Paul)
RR12745 719 (October 19, 1995) p150. (Kot, Greg)
TONE-LOC
Cool Hand Loc
RR12746 618 (November 28, 1991) p90. (Light, Alan)
RR12747 Number not assigned.
TOO MUCH JOY
Mutiny
RR12748 647 (January 7, 1993) p47. (Milward, John)
TOO SHORT
Get In Where Fit In
RR12749 670 (November 25, 1993) p121. (Toure)
Shorty The Pimp
RR12749a 639 (September 17, 1992) p96. (Smith, Danyel)
TOOL
Aenima
RR12750 750-751 (December 26, 1996) p190.
TOOTS AND THE MAYTALS
Funky Kingston
RR12751 689 (August 25, 1994) p34. (Barron, Chris)
TOPHAM, TOP
Lookin' Down The Backtracks, 1963-1969
RR12752 639 (September 17, 1992) p96. (Fricke, David)
TORTOISE
Millions Now Living Will Never Die
RR12753 750-751 (December 26, 1996) p198.
TOSH, PETER
Equal Rights
RR12754 676 (February 24, 1994) p42. (McLane, Daisann)
TOWERING INFERNO
Kaddish
RR12755 737 (June 27, 1996) p59. (Stenger, Wif)
TOWNSHEND, PETER
Psychoderelict
RR12756 663 (August 19, 1993) p76. (Evans, Paul)
TRACTORS
The Tractors
RR12757 691 (September 22, 1994) p97. (McLeese, Don)
RR12758 698-699 (December 29, 1994) pp181-182. (Evans, Paul)
TRAFFIC
Far From Home
RR12759 684 (June 16, 1994) pp108-109. (Considine, J. D.)
TRANSGLOBAL UNDERGROUND
International Times
RR12760 714 (August 10, 1995) p58. (Ali, Lorraine)
TRAVIS, MERLE
Folk Songs Of The Hills
RR12761 750-751 (December 26, 1996) p189. (Coleman, Mark)
TRAVIS, RANDY
This Is Me
RR12762 696 (December 1, 1994) p124. (Bessman, Jim)
A TRIBE CALLED QUEST
Award Tour (song)
RR12763 682 (May 19, 1994) p21. (Queen Latifah)
Beats, Rhymes And Life
RR12764 740 (August 8, 1996) pp57-58. (Hardy, Ernest)
Midnight Marauders
RR12765 670 (November 25, 1993) pp116-117. (Kenny, Glenn)
TRICKY
Maxinquaye
RR12766 710 (June 15, 1995) p83. (Hunter, James)
RR12767 724-725 (December 28, 1995) p120. (Fricke, David)
Nearly God
RR12768 741 (August 22, 1996) p98. (Hunter, James)
Pre-Millennium Tension
RR12769 749 (December 12, 1996) p86. (Fine, Jason)
Tricky Presents Grassroots
RR12770 741 (August 22, 1996) p98. (Hunter, James)
TRISCHKA, TONY
World Turning
RR12771 672-673 (December 23, 1993) p158. (McLeese, Don)
TRITT, TRAVIS
Ten Feet Tall And Bulletproof
RR12772 696 (December 1, 1994) p124. (Bessman, Jim)
TRUDELL, JOHN
AKA Grafitti Man
RR12773 631 (May 28, 1992) pp53-54. (Jurek, Thom)
Johnny Damas And Me
RR12774 677 (March 10, 1994) p65. (Evans, Paul)
TRUE BELIEVERS
Hard Road
RR12775 682 (May 19, 1994) p102. (George-Warren, Holly)
TRY N' BE
Try N' Be
RR12776 658 (June 10, 1993) pp70-71. (Eddy, Chuck)
TSUNAMI
Be Like That (song)
RR12777 684 (June 16, 1994) p110. (Fricke, David)
Newspaper (song)
RR12778 684 (June 16, 1994) p110. (Fricke, David)
TUCKER, MOE
I Spent A Week There The Other Night
RR12779 619-620 (December 12, 1991) p189. (Fricke, David)
TURNER, JOE
Big, Bad And Blue
RR12780 677 (March 10, 1994) p67. (Considine, J. D.)
TURNER, TINA
The Collected Recordings, '60s to '90s
RR12781 698-699 (December 29, 1994) p188. (Considine, J. D.)
Wildest Dreams
RR12782 747 (November 14, 1996) p116. (Gardner, Elysa)
TWAIN, SHANIA
Shania Twain
RR12783 670 (November 25, 1993) p112. (McGee, David)
24-7 SPYZ
Strength In Numbers
RR12784 644 (November 26, 1992) p72. (Powell, Kevin)
TWITTY, CONWAY
The Conway Twitty Collection
RR12785 698-699 (December 29, 1994) p178. (McLeese, Don)
TYNER, MCCOY
44th Street
RR12786 618 (November 28, 1991) p96. (Futterman, Steve)
TYPE O NEGATIVE
Bloody Kisses
RR12787 702 (February 23, 1995) p74. (Szabo, Julia)

TYSON, IAN
Eighteen Inches Of Rain
RR12788 679 (April 7, 1994) p77. (McLeese, Don)

U

U ROY
Dread In A Babylon
RR12789 676 (February 24, 1994) p42. (McLane, Daisann)
U2
Achtung Baby
RR12790 621 (January 9, 1992) p50. (Gardner, Elysa)
Hold Me, Thrill Me, Kiss Me, Kill Me (song)
RR12791 712-713 (July 13, 1995) p111. (Gardner, Elysa)
Where The Streets Have No Name (song)
RR12792 686-687 (July 14, 1994) p32. (Nicks, Stevie)
Zooropa
RR12793 662 (August 5, 1993) pp63-64. (DeCurtis, Anthony)
RR12794 672-673 (December 23, 1993) pp151-152. (Evans, Paul)
ULMER, JAMES BLOOD
Odyssey
RR12795 750-751 (December 26, 1996) p189. (Coleman, Mark)
UNCLE TUPELO
Anodyne
RR12796 671 (December 9, 1993) p73. (Kemp, Mark)
Still Feel Gone
RR12797 626 (March 19, 1992) p97. (Mundy, Chris)
UNREST
Isabel Bishop E.P.
RR12798 660-661 (July 8, 1993) p113. (Fricke, David)
UP
Killer Up!
RR12799 716 (September 7, 1995) p73. (Fricke, David)
UPSHAW, DAWN
Symphony No. 3
RR12800 655 (April 29, 1993) p65. (Schwarz, K. Robert)
RR12801 657 (April 29, 1993) p6. (Schwarz, K. Robert)
URGE OVERKILL
Exit The Dragon
RR12802 716 (September 7, 1995) pp69-70. (Mundy, Chris)
RR12803 724-725 (December 28, 1995) p116. (Fricke, David)
Saturation
RR12804 663 (August 19, 1993) p76. (Kot, Greg)
RR12805 665 (September 16, 1993) p17. (Mundy, Chris)
US3
Hand On The Torch
RR12806 677 (March 10, 1994) p68. (Ehrlich, Dimitri)
UTAH SAINTS
Utah Saints
RR12807 648 (January 21, 1993) pp50,52. (Hunter, James)

V

VALDEZ, MERCEDITAS
Cuba
RR12808 658 (June 10, 1993) p78. (McLane, Daisann)
RR12809 672-673 (December 23, 1993) p163. (McLane, Daisann)
VAMPIRES SOUND INCORPORATION
Vampyros Lesbos Sexadelic Dance Party
RR12810 734 (May 16, 1996) p68. (Vam Pyros, Bill)
VAN BERGEYK, TOM
Black Melodies On A Clear Afternoon
RR12811 630 (May 14, 1992) p109. (Milward, John)
VAN HALEN
Balance
RR12812 704 (March 23, 1995) p122. (Evans, Paul)
For Unlawful Carnal Knowledge
RR12813 619-620 (December 12, 1991) p187. (Fricke, David)
VAN PEEBLES, MELVIN
Ghetto Gothic
RR12814 705 (April 6, 1995) p64. (Evans, Paul)
VAN RONK, DAVE
Let No One Deceive You: Songs Of Bertolt Brecht
RR12815 634-635 (July 9, 1992) p102. (Fricke, David)
VAN ZANDT, TOWNES
No Deeper Blue
RR12816 704 (March 23, 1995) p124. (Swenson, John)
Roadsongs
RR12817 660-661 (July 8, 1993) p113. (Fricke, David)
RR12818 685 (June 30, 1994) p75. (Palmer, Robert)
VANDROSS, LUTHER
Never Let Me Go
RR12819 663 (August 19, 1993) pp77-78. (Considine, J. D.)
Songs
RR12820 702 (February 23, 1995) p74. (Dyson, Michael Eric)
VANILLA ICE
Mind Blowin
RR12821 681 (May 5, 1994) p55. (Smith, Danyel)
VARTTINA
Aitara
RR12822 709 (June 1, 1995) p62. (McLane, Daisann)
VAUGHAN, STEVIE RAY
In The Beginning
RR12823 645-646 (December 10, 1992) p166. (Coleman, Mark)
The Sky Is Crying
RR12824 618 (November 28, 1991) p94. (McLeese, Don)
VEGA, SUZANNE
Nine Objects Of Desire
RR12825 748 (November 28, 1996) p136. (Altman, Billy)
99.9 F
RR12826 640 (October 1, 1992) pp63,67. (Woodard, Josef)
VELO-DELUXE
Superelastic
RR12827 697 (December 15, 1994) p96. (Puterbaugh, Parke)
VELOCITY GIRL
Copacetic
RR12828 658 (June 10, 1993) p71. (Diehl, Matt)
Simpatico!
RR12829 686-687 (July 14, 1994) pp106,109. (Ahearn, Kim)
VELOSO, CAETANO
Circulado
RR12830 633 (June 25, 1992) p45. (Holden, Stephen)
RR12831 645-646 (December 10, 1992) p182. (Coleman, Mark)
Fina Estampa
RR12832 698-699 (December 29, 1994) p182. (McLane, Daisann)
Tropicalia 2
RR12833 688 (August 11, 1994) p69. (McLane, Daisann)
VELVET CRUSH
In The Presence Of Greatness
RR12834 625 (March 5, 1992) p68. (Robbins, Ira)
Teenage Symphonies To God
RR12835 696 (December 1, 1994) pp128-129. (Zinman, Greg)
VELVET UNDERGROUND
Live MCMXCIII
RR12836 670 (November 25, 1993) pp107-108. (McLeese, Don)
Peel Slowly And See
RR12837 722 (November 30, 1995) p69. (Palmer, Robert)
VENTURES
The Ventures' Christmas Album

RR12838 672-673 (December 23, 1993) p169. (Howard, Pete)
VERMONSTER
The Holy Sound Of American Pipe
RR12839 667 (October 14, 1993) p121. (Fricke, David)
VERUCA SALT
American Thighs
RR12840 694 (November 3, 1994) p100. (Ahearn, Kim)
VIDALIAS
Melodyland
RR12841 703 (March 9, 1995) p66. (Evans, Paul)
VIVES, CARLOS
Clasicos De La Provincia
RR12842 689 (August 25, 1994) p92. (McLane, Daisann)
VIX, JENN
Jenn Vix
RR12843 683 (June 2, 1994) p72. (Evans, Paul)
VOELZ, SUSAN
13 Ribs
RR12844 667 (October 14, 1993) p123. (Bessman, Jim)
VOLUPTUOUS HORROR OF KAREN BLACK
A National Health Care
RR12845 668 (October 28, 1993) p80. (Szabo, Julia)
VULGAR BOATMEN
Please Panic
RR12846 631 (May 28, 1992) pp54-55. (Robbins, Ira)

W

WAILER, BUNNY
Rock 'N' Groove
RR12847 676 (February 24, 1994) p42. (McLane, Daisann)
WAILERS
One Love
RR12848 628 (April 16, 1992) p81. (Palmer, Robert)
WAINWRIGHT, LOUDON, III
Career Moves
RR12849 672-673 (December 23, 1993) pp162,164. (Evans, Paul)
Grown Man
RR12850 726 (January 25, 1996) p73. (McLeese, Don)
History
RR12851 651 (March 4, 1993) pp64-65. (Wild, David)
RR12852 672-673 (December 23, 1993) pp162,164. (Evans, Paul)
I Wish I Was A Lesbian (song)
RR12853 668 (October 28, 1993) p26. (DeCurtis, Anthony)
WAITS, TOM
The Black Rider
RR12854 677 (March 10, 1994) p64. (Ali, Lorraine)
Bone Machine
RR12855 642 (October 29, 1992) p69. (O'Connor, Rob)
Mississippi Lad
RR12856 623 (February 6, 1992) p79. (Palmer, Robert)
Rain Dogs
RR12857 679 (April 7, 1994) p30. (Hoon, Shannon)
WALKABOUTS
Scavenger
RR12858 625 (March 5, 1992) p70. (Fricke, David)
WALKER, JERRY JEFF
Hill Country Rain
RR12859 637 (August 20, 1992) p53. (McLeese, Don)
Viva Luckenbach!
RR12860 683 (June 2, 1994) p70. (McLeese, Don)
WALKER, T-BONE
The Complete Imperial Recordings, 1950-1954
RR12861 617 (November 14, 1991) pp172-173. (Palmer, Robert)
WALL, CHRIS
Cowboy Nation
RR12862 686-687 (July 14, 1994) p107. (McLeese, Don)
WALLFLOWERS
Bringing Down The Horse
RR12863 737 (June 27, 1996) p56. (Altman, Billy)
The Wallflowers
RR12864 644 (November 26, 1992) pp74-75. (Evans, Paul)
WARDEN, MONTE
Monte Warden
RR12865 663 (August 19, 1993) p77. (McLeese, Don)
WARE, DAVID S.
Cryptology
RR12866 708 (May 18, 1995) pp87-88. (Fricke, David)
WAREHAM, DEAN
Anesthesia (song)
RR12867 634-635 (July 9, 1992) p102. (Fricke, David)
I Don't Care (song)
RR12868 634-635 (July 9, 1992) p102. (Fricke, David)
WARREN G
Regulate...G Funk Era
RR12869 688 (August 11, 1994) pp69,71. (Fernando, S. H., Jr.)
WASH, MARTHA
Martha Wash
RR12870 654 (April 15, 1993) pp64-65. (Chambers, Gordon)
WASHBOARD SAM
Rockin' My Blues Away
RR12871 629 (April 30, 1992) p57. (Considine, J. D.)
WASSERMAN, ROB
Trios
RR12872 683 (June 2, 1994) pp70,72. (Bessman, Jim)
WATERBOYS
Dream Harder
RR12873 660-661 (July 8, 1993) pp112,114. (Swenson, John)
WATERS, CRYSTAL
Storyteller
RR12874 689 (August 25, 1994) p92. (Wilson, Michael)
Surprise
RR12875 619-620 (December 12, 1991) p165. (Fricke, David)
WATERS, MUDDY
The Complete Plantation Recordings
RR12876 664 (September 2, 1993) p64. (Considine, J. D.)
Folk Singer
RR12877 677 (March 10, 1994) p67. (Considine, J. D.)
One More Mile
RR12878 682 (May 19, 1994) p100. (Considine, J. D.)
WATERS, ROGER
Amused To Death
RR12879 645-646 (December 10, 1992) p182. (Coleman, Mark)
WATFORD, MICHAEL
Michael Watford
RR12880 680 (April 21, 1994) p89. (Ressler, Darren)
WATLEY, JODIE
Affairs Of The Heart
RR12881 622 (January 23, 1992) p45. (Cardwell, Diane)
WATT, MIKE
Ball-Hog Or Tugboat?
RR12882 704 (March 23, 1995) pp119,121. (Azerrad, Michael)
WEATHERMEN
The Blue Sun
RR12883 645-646 (December 10, 1992) p177. (Fricke, David)
WEAVERS
Wasn't That A Time
RR12884 675 (February 10, 1994) p43. (Isler, Scott)
WEBB, JIMMY
Suspending Disbelief
RR12885 667 (October 14, 1993) pp117-118. (McAlley, John)

WEEN
Chocolate And Cheese
RR12886 698-699 (December 29, 1994) p176. (Evans, Paul)
12 Golden Country Greats
RR12887 740 (August 8, 1996) p62. (Flaum, Eric)
WEEZER
Pinkerton
RR12888 746 (October 31, 1996) p66. (O'Connor, Rob)
Weezer
RR12889 698-699 (December 29, 1994) p190. (Evans, Paul)
WEIN, GEORGE
Swing That Music
RR12890 671 (December 9, 1993) p70. (Futterman, Steve)
WELCH, GILLIAN
Revival
RR12891 735 (May 30, 1996) p46. (Powers, Ann)
WELCH, KEVIN
Western Beat
RR12892 637 (August 20, 1992) p53. (McLeese, Don)
WELLER, PAUL
Paul Weller
RR12893 644 (November 26, 1992) pp72,74. (Manning, Kara)
Stanley Road
RR12894 712-713 (July 13, 1995) pp109-110. (McDonnell, Evelyn)
Wild Wood
RR12895 693 (October 20, 1994) p146. (Sinclair, Tom)
WELLS, JUNIOR
Alone And Acoustic
RR12896 623 (February 6, 1992) p79. (Santelli, Robert)
Buddy Guy & Junior Wells Play The Blues
RR12897 636 (August 6, 1992) p66. (Considine, J. D.)
WESLEY, FRED
A Blow For Me, A Toot For You
RR12898 682 (May 19, 1994) p100. (Considine, J. D.)
Say Blow By Blow Backwards
RR12899 682 (May 19, 1994) p100. (Considine, J. D.)
WESTERBERG, PAUL
Eventually
RR12899a 733 (May 2, 1996) p52. (Fricke, David)
14 Songs
RR12900 660-661 (July 8, 1993) p116. (George-Warren, Holly)
RR12901 672-673 (December 23, 1993) pp164-165. (Evans, Paul)
RR12902 Number not assigned.
WESTON, RANDY
The Spirits Of Our Ancestors
RR12903 630 (May 14, 1992) p108. (Palmer, Robert)
WESTSIDE CONNECTION
Bow Down
RR12904 749 (December 12, 1996) p86. (Powell, Kevin)
WET WET WET
Part One
RR12905 693 (October 20, 1994) p148. (Evans, Paul)
WHALE
We Care
RR12906 719 (October 19, 1995) p152. (Hunter, James)
WHEELER, CARON
Beach Of The War Goddess
RR12907 655 (April 29, 1993) pp63,65. (Coleman, Mark)
WHITE, BARRY
Just For You
RR12908 645-646 (December 10, 1992) p170. (Considine, J. D.)
WHITE, BUKKA
The Complete Bukka White
RR12909 685 (June 30, 1994) p77. (Considine, J. D.)
WHITE, JOY
Between Midnight And Hindsight
RR12910 647 (January 7, 1993) p54. (McLeese, Don)
WHITE, JOY LYNN
Wild Love
RR12911 691 (September 22, 1994) p97. (McLeese, Don)
WHITE, LARI
Lead Me Not
RR12912 656 (May 13, 1993) p110. (McLeese, Don)
WHITFIELD, BARRENCE
Hillbilly Voodoo
RR12913 670 (November 25, 1993) pp117,120. (Jurek, Thom)
WHITFIELD, MARK
Patrice
RR12914 618 (November 28, 1991) p96. (Futterman, Steve)
WHITLEY, CHRIS
Din Of Ecstasy
RR12915 706 (April 20, 1995) pp73-74. (Milward, John)
Living With The Law
RR12916 619-620 (December 12, 1991) p187. (Fricke, David)
WHO
Live At Leeds
RR12917 705 (April 6, 1995) p62. (Considine, J. D.)
RR12918 718 (October 5, 1995) p71. (Appleford, Steve)
Live At The Isle Of Wight Festival 1970
RR12919 750-751 (December 26, 1996) p199.
A Quick One
RR12920 718 (October 5, 1995) p71. (Appleford, Steve)
Thirty Years Of Maximum R & B
RR12921 690 (September 8, 1994) p76. (Swenson, John)
The Who Sell Out
RR12922 718 (October 5, 1995) p71. (Appleford, Steve)
WIDESPREAD PANIC
Ain't Life Grand
RR12923 698-699 (December 29, 1994) pp181-182. (Evans, Paul)
WILCO
A.M.
RR12924 705 (April 6, 1995) pp62,64. (George-Warren, Holly)
Being There
RR12925 747 (November 14, 1996) pp111-112. (Kot, Greg)
WILCOX, DAVID
Big Horizon
RR12926 690 (September 8, 1994) pp80-81. (McAlley, John)
WILDER, WEBB
Town And County
RR12927 705 (April 6, 1995) p64. (Evans, Paul)
WILLIAMS, CHRISTOPHER
Changes
RR12928 651 (March 4, 1993) p65. (Dyson, Michael Eric)
WILLIAMS, HANK, JR.
The Bocephus Box: The Hand Williams Jr. Collection 1979-1992
RR12929 645-646 (December 10, 1992) p174. (McLeese, Don)
Living Proof: The MGM Recordings 1963-1975
RR12930 645-646 (December 10, 1992) p174. (McLeese, Don)
Out Of Left Field
RR12931 656 (May 13, 1993) p110. (McLeese, Don)
WILLIAMS, JAMES
James Williams Meets The Saxophone Masters
RR12932 653 (April 1, 1993) p53. (Futterman, Steve)
WILLIAMS, LUCINDA
Sweet Old World
RR12933 638 (September 3, 1992) p68. (Jurek, Thom)
WILLIAMS, MARION
Can't Keep It To Myself
RR12934 677 (March 10, 1994) pp66,68. (Evans, Paul)
WILLIAMS, MARY LOU
Mary's Idea

RR12935 659 (June 24, 1993) p84. (Futterman, Steve)
WILLIAMS, VANESSA
The Sweetest Days
RR12936 703 (March 9, 1995) pp64,66. (Dyson, Michael Eric)
WILLIAMS, VICTORIA
Loose
RR12937 696 (December 1, 1994) p128. (Jurek, Thom)
This Moment In Toronto
RR12938 724-725 (December 28, 1995) p129. (Fricke, David)
WILLIS, KELLY
Kelly Willis
RR12939 663 (August 19, 1993) p77. (McLeese, Don)
WILLS, BOB
Bob Wills: The Country Music Hall Of Fame
RR12940 636 (August 6, 1992) p66. (Considine, J. D.)
RR12941 Number not assigned.
WILSON, BRIAN
I Just Wasn't Made For These Times
RR12942 724-725 (December 28, 1995) p118. (Fricke, David)
Orange Crate Art
RR12943 724-725 (December 28, 1995) p118. (Fricke, David)
WILSON, CASSANDRA
Blue Light 'Til Dawn
RR12944 678 (March 24, 1994) pp93-94. (Milward, John)
New Moon Daughter
RR12945 730 (March 21, 1996) p100. (Himes, Geoffrey)
WILSON, JACKIE
Mr. Excitement!
RR12946 649 (February 4, 1993) pp64,66. (Palmer, Robert)
WILSON, KIM
Tigerman
RR12947 689 (August 25, 1994) p89. (Swenson, John)
WILSON PHILLIPS
Shadows And Light
RR12947a 634-635 (July 9, 1992) pp100-101. (Berger, Arion)
WINTER, JOHNNY
A Rock & Roll Collection
RR12948 677 (March 10, 1994) p67. (Considine, J. D.)
WINWOOD, STEVE
The Finer Things
RR12949 705 (April 6, 1995) p62. (Considine, J. D.)
WIPERS
Silver Sail
RR12950 676 (February 24, 1994) p57. (Fricke, David)
WOBBLE, JAH
Spinner
RR12951 723 (December 14, 1995) pp82,84. (DeRogatis, Jim)
WOLF, PETER
Long Line
RR12952 736 (June 13, 1996) pp82-83. (Gardner, Elysa)
WOMACK, BOBBY
Communication
RR12953 694 (November 3, 1994) p100. (Considine, J. D.)
Facts Of Life
RR12954 694 (November 3, 1994) p100. (Considine, J. D.)
Lookin' For A Love Again
RR12955 694 (November 3, 1994) p100. (Considine, J. D.)
Midnight Mover
RR12956 677 (March 10, 1994) p67. (Considine, J. D.)
Understanding
RR12957 694 (November 3, 1994) p100. (Considine, J. D.)
WONDER, STEVIE
Conversation Peace
RR12958 704 (March 23, 1995) pp121-122. (Milward, John)
Natural Wonder
RR12959 726 (January 25, 1996) p72. (Altman, Billy)
WOOD, RON
Slide On This
RR12960 645-646 (December 10, 1992) p179. (Coleman, Mark)
WOODRUFF, BOB
Dreams And Saturday Nights
RR12961 679 (April 7, 1994) p77. (McLeese, Don)
WORKMAN, REGGIE
Summit Conference
RR12962 692 (October 6, 1994) p89. (Futterman, Steve)
WORLD PARTY
Bang!
RR12963 660-661 (July 8, 1993) p112. (Sprague, David)
WU-TNAG CLAN
Enter The Wu-Tang
RR12964 679 (April 7, 1994) p73. (Toure)
WYATT, ROBERT
Dondestan
RR12965 623 (February 6, 1992) p82. (Robbins, Ira)
WYNETTE, TAMMY
Honky Tonk Angels
RR12966 672-673 (December 23, 1993) p158. (McLeese, Don)
Tears Of Fire: The 25th Anniversary Collection
RR12967 645-646 (December 10, 1992) p174. (McLeese, Don)
Without Walls
RR12968 698-699 (December 29, 1994) p176. (Evans, Paul)
WYNN, STEVE
Dazzling Display
RR12969 634-635 (July 9, 1992) pp105-106. (Sinclair, Tom)
Fluorescent
RR12970 683 (June 2, 1994) p72. (Evans, Paul)
Melting In The Dark
RR12971 740 (August 8, 1996) p58. (Wiederhorn, Jon)

X

X
Hey Zeus!
RR12972 664 (September 2, 1993) pp64-65. (Kemp, Mark)
Unclogged
RR12973 717 (September 21, 1995) p84. (Flaum, Eric)
X-PENSIVE WINOS
Live At The Hollywood Palladium, December 15, 1988
RR12974 621 (January 9, 1992) p51. (Palmer, Robert)
XTC
Nonsuch
RR12975 631 (May 28, 1992) p55. (Azerrad, Michael)

Y

YARDBIRDS
Five Live Yardbirds
RR12976 655 (April 29, 1993) p42. (Futterman, Steve)
YEARWOOD, TRISHA
Hearts In Armor
RR12977 640 (October 1, 1992) p63. (McGee, David)
RR12978 645-646 (December 10, 1992) pp164,166. (Coleman, Mark)
The Song Remembers When
RR12979 674 (January 27, 1994) p54. (McAlley, John)
Thinkin' About You
RR12980 705 (April 6, 1995) p65. (Galvin, Peter)
YES
Talk
RR12981 691 (September 22, 1994) p94. (Birkbeck, Matt)
YO LA TENGO
May I Sing With Me
RR12982 634-635 (July 9, 1992) p102. (Fricke, David)

YO-YO
Black Pearl
RR12983 636 (August 6, 1992) p59. (Cardwell, Diane)
Make Way For The Motherlode
RR12984 619-620 (December 12, 1991) p174. (Fricke, David)
YOAKUM, DWIGHT
Dwight Live
RR12985 716 (September 7, 1995) p72. (McLeese, Don)
Gone
RR12986 723 (December 14, 1995) p84. (Himes, Geoffrey)
This Time
RR12987 658 (June 10, 1993) pp67-68. (McLeese, Don)
RR12988 672-673 (December 23, 1993) p165. (Evans, Paul)
YOTHU YINDI
Tribal Voice
RR12989 633 (June 25, 1992) p43. (McLane, Daisann)
YOUNG BLACK TEENAGERS
Dead End Kidz Doin' Lifetime Bidz
RR12990 651 (March 4, 1993) p66. (Smith, Danyel)
YOUNG, LA MONTE
Just Stompin'
RR12991 669 (November 11, 1993) p77. (Fricke, David)
YOUNG, NEIL
Broken Arrow
RR12992 740 (August 8, 1996) p58. (O'Connor, Rob)
Harvest Moon
RR12993 644 (November 26, 1992) pp71-72. (Kot, Greg)
Lucky Thirteen
RR12994 655 (April 29, 1993) pp62-63. (Hunter, James)
Mirror Ball
RR12995 712-713 (July 13, 1995) pp107-108. (Considine, J. D.)
RR12996 724-725 (December 28, 1995) p126. (Fricke, David)
Sleeps With Angels
RR12997 689 (August 25, 1994) pp87-88. (Fricke, David)
RR12998 698-699 (December 29, 1994) p191. (Evans, Paul)
Unplugged
RR12999 663 (August 19, 1993) pp76-77. (Gilyard, Burl)
RR13000 672-673 (December 23, 1993) p157. (Evans, Paul)
Weld
RR13001 617 (November 14, 1991) pp171-172. (McLeese, Don)
RR13002 619-620 (December 12, 1991) p165. (Fricke, David)
YOUNG, STEVE
Switchblades Of Love
RR13003 675 (February 10, 1994) p46. (McLeese, Don)

Z

Z Z TOP
Antenna
RR13004 675 (February 10, 1994) pp41,43. (Milward, John)
Rhythmeen
RR13005 744 (October 3, 1996) p72. (Diehl, Matt)
ZAHAR
Trance
RR13006 680 (April 21, 1994) p90. (McLane, Daisann)
ZAP MAMA
Africa Invades Europe
RR13007 650 (February 18, 1993) p59. (McLane, Daisann)
RR13008 672-673 (December 23, 1993) p163. (McLane, Daisann)
Sabsylma
RR13009 689 (August 25, 1994) p92. (McLane, Daisann)
ZAPPA, FRANK
Absolutely Free
RR13010 674 (January 27, 1994) p15. (Swenson, John)
Ahead Of Their Time
RR13011 660-661 (July 8, 1993) p113. (Fricke, David)
Apostrophe
RR13012 674 (January 27, 1994) p15. (Swenson, John)
Broadway The Hard Way
RR13013 674 (January 27, 1994) p15. (Swenson, John)
Civilization Phaze III
RR13014 715 (August 24, 1995) p104. (Fricke, David)
Fillmore East
RR13015 674 (January 27, 1994) p15. (Swenson, John)
Frank Zappa Meets The Mothers Of Prevention
RR13016 674 (January 27, 1994) p15. (Swenson, John)
Freak Out!
RR13017 674 (January 27, 1994) p15. (Swenson, John)
Hot Rats
RR13018 674 (January 27, 1994) p15. (Swenson, John)
RR13019 724-725 (December 28, 1995) p122. (Coleman, Mark)
Joe's Garage
RR13020 674 (January 27, 1994) p15. (Swenson, John)
Lather
RR13021 744 (October 3, 1996) p71. (Gehr, Richard)
Over-Nite Sensation
RR13022 674 (January 27, 1994) p15. (Swenson, John)
Playground Psychotics
RR13023 660-661 (July 8, 1993) p113. (Fricke, David)
Sheik Yerbouti
RR13024 674 (January 27, 1994) p15. (Swenson, John)
Shut Up 'N Play Yer Guitar
RR13025 674 (January 27, 1994) p15. (Swenson, John)
Strictly Commercial
RR13026 724-725 (December 28, 1995) p122. (Coleman, Mark)
Uncle Meat
RR13027 674 (January 27, 1994) p15. (Swenson, John)
We're Only In It For The Money
RR13028 674 (January 27, 1994) p15. (Swenson, John)
The Yellow Shark
RR13029 674 (January 27, 1994) p15. (Swenson, John)
You Can't Do That On Stage Anymore
RR13030 674 (January 27, 1994) p15. (Swenson, John)
ZE, TOM
The Hips Of Tradition
RR13031 645-646 (December 10, 1992) p187. (McLane, Daisann)
ZENI GEVA
Desire For Agony
RR13032 676 (February 24, 1994) p57. (Fricke, David)
ZEVON, WARREN
Learning To Flinch
RR13033 663 (August 19, 1993) pp76-77. (Gilyard, Burl)
Mr. Bad Example
RR13034 618 (November 28, 1991) p98. (Gardner, Elysa)
ZILLATRON
Lord Of The Harvest
RR13035 693 (October 20, 1994) pp147-148. (Fernando, S. H., Jr.)
ZINAM, DAVID
Symphony No. 3
RR13036 655 (April 29, 1993) p65. (Schwarz, K. Robert)
RR13037 657 (April 29, 1993) p6. (Schwarz, K. Robert)
ZORN, JOHN
Masada
RR13038 711 (June 29, 1995) p44. (Futterman, Steve)
ZUZU'S PETALS
When No One's Looking
RR13039 660-661 (July 8, 1993) p20. (Fricke, David)
ZYDECO, BUCKWHEAT
On Track
RR13040 626 (March 19, 1992) pp92-93. (Swenson, John)
ZYDECO HI-ROLLERS
Pick Up On This!
RR13041 684 (June 16, 1994) p110. (Fricke, David)

Soundtracks, Anthologies & Various Artists Collections

A

ABORIGINAL CHOIRS OF CENTRAL AUSTRALIA
RR13042 633 (June 25, 1992) p43. (McLane, Daisann)
ABOVE THE RIM
RR13043 683 (June 2, 1994) p72. (Evans, Paul)
ACROSS THE GREAT DIVIDE
RR13044 649 (February 4, 1993) p69. (McLeese, Don)
AFRICANDO VOLUME 1
RR13045 658 (June 10, 1993) p78. (McLane, Daisann)
RR13046 672 (December 23, 1993) p163. (McLane, Daisann)
AFRO BRASIL
RR13047 650 (February 18, 1993) p59. (McLane, Daisann)
RR13048 672 (December 23, 1993) p163. (McLane, Daisann)
ALTERNATIVE NRG
RR13049 682 (May 19, 1994) p100. (McAlley, John)
ALTERNATIVE WOODSTOCK
RR13050 691 (September 22, 1994) p100. (Milward, John)
AMERICA IS DYING
RR13051 736 (June 13, 1996) p53. (Wiederhorn, Jon)
AMERICAN FOLK BLUES FESTIVAL '62-'65
RR13052 728 (February 22, 1996) p60. (Fricke, David)
ANARCHY IN THE UK
RR13053 649 (February 4, 1993) pp61-63. (Robbins, Ira)
THE ART OF FINGERSTYLE GUITAR
RR13054 630 (May 14, 1992) p109. (Milward, John)
ARTIFICIAL INTELLIGENCE II
RR13055 702 (February 23, 1995) p73. (Prince, David J.)

B

B. BROWN POSSE
RR13056 660 (July 8, 1993) p116. (Toure)
BACK TO THE STREETS
RR13057 678 (March 24, 1994) pp96-97. (Swenson, John)
BACKBEAT
RR13058 681 (May 5, 1994) p53. (Azerrad, Michael)
BATAK OF NORTH SUMATRA
RR13059 645 (December 10, 1992) p177. (Fricke, David)
THE BEAT GENERATION
RR13060 649 (February 4, 1993) pp63-64. (Powell, Kevin)
BEAT THE RETREAT
RR13061 703 (March 9, 1995) p64. (Hunter, B. R.)
BERSERKLEY'S BEST
RR13062 677 (March 10, 1994) p67. (Considine, J. D.)
THE BEST OF COOL YULE
RR13063 672 (December 23, 1993) p169. (Howard, Pete)
BEST OF STUDIO ONE, VOLS, I, II AND III
RR13064 676 (February 24, 1994) p42. (McLane, Daisann)
BLACK AND TAN CLUB
RR13065 621 (January 9, 1992) pp52-53. (McDonnell, Evelyn)
BLACK BOX
RR13066 700 (January 26, 1995) p63. (Kot, Greg)
THE BLANK GENERATION
RR13067 649 (February 4, 1993) pp61-63. (Robbins, Ira)
BLOWUP
RR13068 636 (August 6, 1992) p66. (Considine, J. D.)
BLUES CLASSICS
RR13069 750 (December 26, 1996) p189. (Coleman, Mark)
BLUES ORIGINALS
RR13070 655 (April 29, 1993) p62. (Considine, J. D.)
BLUES REVIVAL
RR13071 655 (April 29, 1993) p62. (Considine, J. D.)
BLUES ROOTS
RR13072 655 (April 29, 1993) p62. (Considine, J. D.)
BLUES WITH A FEELING
RR13073 664 (September 2, 1993) p64. (Considine, J. D.)
BOB DYLAN: THE 30TH ANNIVERSARY CONCERT CELEBRATION
RR13074 665 (September 16, 1993) p72. (Richardson, Susan)
THE BODYGUARD
RR13075 650 (February 18, 1993) pp58-59. (Berger, Arion)
BOGLE
RR13076 650 (February 18, 1993) p59. (McLane, Daisann)
BOILING POINT
RR13077 615 (October 17, 1991) p94. (McLane, Daisann)
BORDERLANDS
RR13078 686 (July 14, 1994) p107. (McLeese, Don)
RR13079 689 (August 25, 1994) p92. (McLane, Daisann)
BORN TO CHOOSE
RR13080 671 (December 9, 1993) pp70,72. (Berger, Arion)
BOSSA NOVA BRASIL
RR13081 650 (February 18, 1993) p59. (McLane, Daisann)
RR13082 672 (December 23, 1993) p163. (McLane, Daisann)
BOYZ IN THE HOOD
RR13083 619 (December 12, 1991) pp165,168. (Fricke, David)
THE BRILL BUILDING SOUND
RR13084 672 (December 23, 1993) p148. (Considine, J. D.)
BRING IT ON HOME
RR13085 691 (September 22, 1994) p100. (Milward, John)
BRITISH BEAT BEFORE THE BEATLES
RR13086 700 (January 26, 1995) pp60-61. (Isler, Scott)
THE BUDDAH BOX
RR13087 683 (June 30, 1994) p77. (Considine, J. D.)

C

CAGED-UNCAGED
RR13088 672 (December 23, 1993) p154. (Fricke, David)
THE CASABLANCA RECORDS STORY
RR13089 694 (November 3, 1994) p100. (Considine, J. D.)
RR13090 657 (May 27, 1993) p49. (Rabhan, Jeffrey)
A CHANCE OPERATION
RR13091 676 (February 24, 1994) p57. (Fricke, David)
CHESS BLUES
RR13092 655 (April 29, 1993) p62. (Considine, J. D.)
THE CHISWICK STORY
RR13093 649 (February 4, 1993) p64. (Isler, Scott)
A CHRISTMAS GIFT FOR YOU
RR13094 672 (December 23, 1993) p169. (Howard, Pete)
CHRISTMAS IN THE CITY
RR13095 672 (December 23, 1993) p169. (Howard, Pete)
THE COBRA RECORDS STORY: CHICAGO ROCK AND BLUES 1956-1958
RR13096 658 (June 10, 1993) p69. (Palmer, Robert)
COLOR AND LIGHT
RR13097 711 (June 29, 1995) p44. (Futterman, Steve)
COME OUT AND PLAY
RR13098 649 (February 4, 1993) pp61-63. (Robbins, Ira)
COME TOGETHER
RR13099 709 (June 1, 1995) p64. (Evans, Paul)
COME TOGETHER: MOTOWN SINGS THE BEATLES
RR13100 683 (June 30, 1994) p76. (Gaar, Gillian G.)
THE COMMITMENTS
RR13101 619 (December 12, 1991) p178. (Fricke, David)
COMMON THREADS
RR13102 669 (November 11, 1993) p74. (Manning, Kara)
THE COMPLETE STAX-VOLT SINGLES VOL 2: 1968-1971
RR13103 669 (November 11, 1993) p77. (Considine, J. D.)
THE COMPLETE STAX-VOLT SOUL SINGLES, VOL. III 1972-1975

RR13104 698 (December 29, 1994) p188. (Considine, J. D.)
THE CONCERT FOR THE ROCK & ROLL HALL OF FAME
RR13105 742 (September 5, 1996) p62. (DeCurtis, Anthony)
CONMEMORATIVO
RR13106 674 (January 27, 1994) p52. (Seymour, Corey)
COSMIC KURUSHI MONSTERS
RR13107 750 (December 26, 1996) p192. (Fricke, David)
COUNTRY KICKERS
RR13108 719 (October 19, 1995) pp149-150. (Eddy, Chuck)
COWABUNGA!
RR13109 750 (December 26, 1996) p189. (Coleman, Mark)
THE CROW
RR13110 686 (July 14, 1994) p104. (Evans, Paul)
CUBA: FULLY CHARGED
RR13111 658 (June 10, 1993) p78. (McLane, Daisann)
RR13112 672 (December 23, 1993) p163. (McLane, Daisann)
CUBAN CLASSICS VOL. 3: DIABLO AL INFIERNO
RR13113 640 (October 1, 1992) p75. (McLane, Daisann)
CUBAN COUNTERPOINT: A HISTORY OF THE SON MONTUNO
RR13114 640 (October 1, 1992) p75. (McLane, Daisann)
CUBAN GOLD
RR13115 672 (December 23, 1993) p163. (McLane, Daisann)

D

DANCE CLUB COUNTRY
RR13116 719 (October 19, 1995) pp149-150. (Eddy, Chuck)
DANCEHALL REGGAESPANOL
RR13117 626 (March 19, 1992) p95. (McLane, Daisann)
DANGEROUS MINDS
RR13118 724 (December 28, 1995) p118. (Fricke, David)
DEAD MEN WALKING
RR13119 726 (January 25, 1996) pp69,71. (Ali, Lorraine)
DEEP BLUES
RR13120 645 (December 10, 1992) p166. (Coleman, Mark)
DEEP SIX
RR13121 682 (May 19, 1994) p102. (Gaar, Gillian)
DEF JAM 10TH YEAR ANNIVERSARY
RR13122 723 (December 14, 1995) pp81-82. (Coleman, Mark)
DIGGIN' IN THE CRATES
RR13123 683 (June 30, 1994) p77. (Considine, J. D.)
DIY
RR13124 649 (February 4, 1993) pp61-63. (Robbins, Ira)
THE DOO WOP BOX
RR13125 686 (July 14, 1994) p108. (McGee, David)
DUENDE: THE PASSION AND DAZZLING VIRTUOSITY OF FLAMENCO
RR13126 698 (December 29, 1994) p182. (McLane, Daisann)

E

THE EAST SIDE SOUND
RR13127 740 (August 8, 1996) p62. (Fricke, David)
ENCOMIUM
RR13128 708 (May 18, 1995) p90. (Evans, Paul)
ETERNAL CHANT
RR13129 698 (December 29, 1994) p188. (Considine, J. D.)
EVITA
RR13130 749 (December 12, 1996) p82. (Gardner, Elysa)

F

FALLING FROM GRACE
RR13131 627 (April 2, 1992) pp44-45. (Cullen, Jim)
FIFTY YEARS OF SUNSHINE
RR13132 672 (December 23, 1993) p154. (Fricke, David)
FIRE OF THE AMAZONES
RR13133 645 (December 10, 1992) p177. (Fricke, David)
THE FIRE-FURY RECORDS STORY
RR13134 655 (April 29, 1993) p62. (Considine, J. D.)
FLATPICKING GUITAR FESTIVAL
RR13135 630 (May 14, 1992) p109. (Milward, John)
FORREST GUMP
RR13136 691 (September 22, 1994) p98. (Evans, Paul)
FORRO, ETC.
RR13137 615 (October 17, 1991) p94. (McLane, Daisann)
FREEDOM OF CHOICE
RR13138 648 (January 21, 1993) p52. (McDonnell, Evelyn)
FRIDAY
RR13139 707 (May 4, 1995) p69. (Evans, Paul)
FROM PHILLY WITH LOVE
RR13140 724 (December 28, 1995) p122. (Coleman, Mark)
FROM THE BUSH
RR13141 633 (June 25, 1992) p43. (McLane, Daisann)
FUNK ESSENTIALS
RR13142 667 (October 14, 1993) p118. (Toure)
FUNKY STUFF
RR13143 667 (October 14, 1993) p118. (Toure)

G

GERMS (TRIBUTE)
RR13144 745 (October 17, 1996) p134. (Robbins, Ira)
GLOBAL CELEBRATION
RR13145 672 (December 23, 1993) p163. (McLane, Daisann)
THE GLORY OF GERSHWIN
RR13146 700 (January 26, 1995) pp61-62. (Gardner, Elysa)
GO IN THE DARK
RR13147 684 (June 16, 1994) p24. (Moore, Thurston)
GO-MAN-GO
RR13148 667 (October 14, 1993) p121. (McLane, Daisann)
RR13149 672 (December 23, 1993) p163. (McLane, Daisann)
THE GOSPEL SOUND
RR13150 686 (July 14, 1994) p104. (Evans, Paul)
GRAND SLAM!
RR13151 710 (June 15, 1995) p82. (McDonnell, Evelyn)
THE GREAT 1955 SHRINE CONCERT
RR13152 668 (October 28, 1993) pp75-76. (Dyson, Michael Eric)
GREAT AMERICAN SONGWRITERS
RR13153 680 (April 21, 1994) p87. (Milward, John)
THE GREAT GOSPEL MEN
RR13154 668 (October 28, 1993) pp75-76. (Dyson, Michael Eric)
THE GREAT GOSPEL WOMEN
RR13155 668 (October 28, 1993) pp75-76. (Dyson, Michael Eric)
GROWIN' UP TOO FAST
RR13156 743 (September 19, 1996) p80. (McDonnell, Evelyn)
GS I LOVE YOU
RR13157 750 (December 26, 1996) p192. (Fricke, David)
GUITAR PARADISE OF EAST AFRICA
RR13158 615 (October 17, 1991) p94. (McLane, Daisann)
GUITARRORISTS
RR13159 629 (April 30, 1992) p58. (Drozdowski, Ted.)

H

HANDLE LIKE EGGS
RR13160 660 (July 8, 1993) p113. (Fricke, David)
THE HARDER THEY COME
RR13161 676 (February 24, 1994) p42. (McLane, Daisann)
HARMONICA CLASSICS
RR13162 648 (January 21, 1993) p50. (Considine, J. D.)

HI TIMES: THE HI RECORDS R&B YEARS
RR13163 705 (April 6, 1995) p62. (Considine, J. D.)
HIP HOP GREATS: CLASSIC RAPS
RR13164 666 (September 30, 1993) p56. (Walser, Robert)
RR13165 666 (September 30, 1993) p56. (Kelley, Robin D.G.)
THE HISTORY OF SPACE AGE POP
RR13166 724 (December 28, 1995) p116. (Fricke, David)
HITSVILLE USA: THE MOTOWN SINGLES COLLECTION 1959-1971
RR13167 645 (December 10, 1992) p170. (Considine, J. D.)
HITSVILLE U.S.A., VOLUME II
RR13168 672 (December 23, 1993) p148. (Considine, J. D.)
HOWLS, RAPS AND ROARS
RR13169 678 (March 24, 1994) pp94,96. (Evans, Paul)

I

IF I WERE A CARPENTER
RR13170 693 (October 20, 1994) p142. (Weisel, Al)
ILLUMINATIONS
RR13171 615 (October 17, 1991) p94. (McLane, Daisann)
I'M YOUR FAN
RR13172 623 (February 6, 1992) p80. (Wright, Christian)
IN THEIR OWN WORDS: VOLUME ONE
RR13173 693 (October 20, 1994) p148. (Evans, Paul)
INTERNAL JOURNAL, VOL II
RR13174 710 (June 15, 1995) p82. (McDonnell, Evelyn)
ISTANBUL 1925
RR13175 709 (June 1, 1995) p62. (McLane, Daisann)
IT CAME FROM MEMPHIS
RR13176 730 (March 21, 1996) p98. (Fricke, David)
IT'S HARD TO BELIEVE IT
RR13177 721 (November 16, 1995) pp110-111. (Walls, Richard C.)

J

JAZZSPEAK
RR13178 621 (January 9, 1992) pp52-53. (McDonnell, Evelyn)
JESUS CHRIST SUPERSTAR: A RESURRECTION
RR13179 702 (February 23, 1995) p76. (Evans, Paul)
THE JEWEL-PAULA RECORDS STORY: THE BLUES, RHYTHM AND BLUES AND SOUL RECORDINGS
RR13180 658 (June 10, 1993) p69. (Palmer, Robert)
JIVE SOWETO: THE INDESTRUCTIBLE BEAT OF SOWETO VOL. 4
RR13181 645 (December 10, 1992) p187. (McLane, Daisann)
JOYAS DE LA MUSICA CUBANA, VOL. 1
RR13182 640 (October 1, 1992) p75. (McLane, Daisann)
JUDGMENT NIGHT
RR13183 666 (September 30, 1993) pp100-101. (Azerrad, Michael)
JUICE
RR13184 623 (February 6, 1992) p77. (Powell, Kevin)
JUMP BLUES CLASSICS
RR13185 648 (January 21, 1993) p50. (Considine, J. D.)
JUST CAN'T GET ENOUGH
RR13186 703 (March 9, 1995) p67. (Manning, Kara)

K

KISS MY ASS
RR13187 694 (November 3, 1994) pp100-101. (Odintz, Andrea)

L

LAW OF THE JUNGLE
RR13188 705 (April 6, 1995) p64. (Fernando, S. H., Jr.)
THE LION KING
RR13189 698 (December 29, 1994) p178. (Evans, Paul)
LIVE AT CBGB'S
RR13190 679 (April 7, 1994) p72. (O'Dair, Barbara)

M

MAMA'S HUNGRY EYES
RR13191 698 (December 29, 1994) p178. (McLeese, Don)
THE MAMBO KINGS
RR13192 625 (March 5, 1992) pp65,68. (McLane, Daisann)
THE MANSON FAMILY: AN OPERA
RR13193 639 (September 17, 1992) p96. (Fricke, David)
MAS! A CARIBBEAN CHRISTMAS PARTY
RR13194 645 (December 10, 1992) p187. (McLane, Daisann)
MASS. AVE.
RR13195 649 (February 4, 1993) pp61-63. (Robbins, Ira)
MASTER OF THE DELTA BLUES: THE FRIENDS OF CHARLIE PATTON
RR13196 625 (March 5, 1992) pp63,65. (Palmer, Robert)
MEAN OLD WORLD
RR13197 750 (December 26, 1996) p189. (Coleman, Mark)
MEDIUM RARE
RR13198 667 (October 14, 1993) p121. (Fricke, David)
MEMPHIS BLUES CARAVAN, VOL. I
RR13199 704 (March 23, 1995) p123. (Santelli, Robert)
MEMPHIS BLUES CARAVAN, VOL. II
RR13200 704 (March 23, 1995) p123. (Santelli, Robert)
MEMPHIS COUNTRY BLUES, VOL. I
RR13201 704 (March 23, 1995) p123. (Santelli, Robert)
MEMPHIS TOWN
RR13202 704 (March 23, 1995) p123. (Santelli, Robert)
MENACE II SOCIETY
RR13203 664 (September 2, 1993) pp59-60. (Toure)
MEXICAN R 'N' B
RR13204 639 (September 17, 1992) p96. (Fricke, David)
MISSISSIPPI DELTA BLUES
RR13205 655 (April 29, 1993) p62. (Considine, J. D.)
MO' MONEY
RR13206 637 (August 20, 1992) pp49-50. (Dyson, Michael)
THE MODERN WORLD
RR13207 649 (February 4, 1993) pp61-63. (Robbins, Ira)
THE MONTEREY INTERNATIONAL POP FESTIVAL
RR13208 645 (December 10, 1992) pp166,168. (Coleman, Mark)
THE MOOG COOKBOOK
RR13209 740 (August 8, 1996) p60. (Van Parys, Bill)
RR13210 744 (October 3, 1996) p16.
THE MOTHER OF ALL FLAGPOLE CHRISTMAS ALBUMS
RR13211 672 (December 23, 1993) p154. (Fricke, David)
MTV UNPLUGGED (EP)
RR13212 645 (December 10, 1992) pp180,182. (Coleman, Mark)
MURDER WAS THE CASE
RR13213 698 (December 29, 1994) p178. (Evans, Paul)
THE MUSIC NEVER STOPPED
RR13214 724 (December 28, 1995) p120. (Fricke, David)
THE MUSIC OF DISNEY: A LEGACY IN SONG
RR13215 645 (December 10, 1992) p170. (Considine, J. D.)

N

NATURAL BORN KILLERS
RR13216 698 (December 29, 1994) p178. (Evans, Paul)

NEW JACK CITY
RR13217 619 (December 12, 1991) pp165,168. (Fricke, David)
NEW JERSEY DRIVE, VOL I
RR13218 710 (June 15, 1995) p80. (Coker, Cheo H.)
NEW JERSEY DRIVE, VOL. II
RR13219 710 (June 15, 1995) p80. (Coker, Cheo H.)
NEW YORK EYE AND EAR CONTROL
RR13220 619 (December 12, 1991) p168. (Fricke, David)
NO ALTERNATIVE
RR13221 669 (November 11, 1993) p75. (Sinclair, Tom)
NO PRIMA DONNA
RR13222 703 (March 9, 1995) p64. (Hunter, B. R.)
NORDESTE BRASIL
RR13223 650 (February 18, 1993) p59. (McLane, Daisann)
RR13224 672 (December 23, 1993) p163. (McLane, Daisann)

O

1-800 NEW FUNK
RR13225 690 (September 8, 1994) pp75-76,78. (Moon, Tom)
THE ORIGINAL MAMBO KINGS: AN INTRODUCTION TO AFRO-CUBOP 1948-1954
RR13226 659 (June 24, 1993) p84. (Futterman, Steve)
ORLANDO
RR13227 667 (October 14, 1993) p121. (Fricke, David)
OUT ON THE ROLLING SEA
RR13228 698 (December 29, 1994) p182. (McLane, Daisann)

P

PEENI WAALI
RR13229 634 (July 9, 1992) p102. (Fricke, David)
PHAT TRAX
RR13230 694 (November 3, 1994) p100. (Considine, J. D.)
PHENOMENON
RR13231 741 (August 22, 1996) p100. (Himes, Geoffrey)
PIANO NIGHT AT TIPITINA'S
RR13232 736 (June 13, 1996) p85. (Fricke, David)
PIMPS, PLAYERS AND PRIVATE EYES
RR13233 624 (February 20, 1992) p45. (Light, Alan)
POETIC JUSTICE
RR13234 664 (September 2, 1993) pp59-60. (Toure)
POSTMODERN BLUES
RR13235 655 (April 29, 1993) p62. (Considine, J. D.)
POSTWAR CHICAGO
RR13236 648 (January 21, 1993) p50. (Considine, J. D.)
PULP FICTION
RR13237 698 (December 29, 1994) p178. (Evans, Paul)
PUTUMAYO PRESENTS THE BEST OF WORLD MUSIC
RR13238 667 (October 14, 1993) p121. (McLane, Daisann)

R

THE R&B BOX: 30 YEARS OF RHYTHM & BLUES
RR13239 698 (December 29, 1994) p188. (Considine, J. D.)
RARE ON AIR VOL. 1
RR13240 686 (July 14, 1994) pp109-110. (McAlley, John)
RARE SURF
RR13241 724 (December 28, 1995) p125. (Fricke, David)
RED HOT AND COUNTRY
RR13242 693 (October 20, 1994) p150. (McLeese, Don)
REGGAE CHRISTMAS
RR13243 672 (December 23, 1993) p169. (Howard, Pete)
RELATIONSHIPS FROM HELL
RR13244 710 (June 15, 1995) p82. (McDonnell, Evelyn)
RENT
RR13245 750 (December 26, 1996) pp192,194.
RHYTHM COUNTRY AND BLUES
RR13246 680 (April 21, 1994) p85. (McGee, David)
RIG ROCK TRUCKSTOP
RR13247 675 (February 10, 1994) p46. (McLeese, Don)
RITES OF RHYTHM & BLUES
RR13248 662 (August 5, 1993) pp65-66. (Swenson, John)
ROCK STARS KILL
RR13249 698 (December 29, 1994) p174. (Fricke, David)
THE ROLLING STONES ROCK & ROLL CIRCUS
RR13250 750 (December 26, 1996) p199.
ROOTS N' BLUES
RR13251 648 (January 21, 1993) p52. (Palmer, Robert)

S

SAMBA BRASIL
RR13252 650 (February 18, 1993) p59. (McLane, Daisann)
RR13253 672 (December 23, 1993) p163. (McLane, Daisann)
THE SCEPTER RECORDS STORY
RR13254 640 (October 1, 1992) pp68-69. (Santelli, Robert)
SEATTLE WOMEN IN ROCK
RR13255 688 (August 11, 1994) p69. (McDonnell, Evelyn)
SHAKE IT UP!
RR13256 649 (February 4, 1993) pp61-63. (Robbins, Ira)
SIDES 1-4 (SINGLE)
RR13257 745 (October 17, 1996) p135. (Fricke, David)
SIF SAFAA
RR13258 724 (December 28, 1995) p125. (Fricke, David)
SINGLES
RR13259 637 (August 20, 1992) pp49-50,52. (Sinclair, Tom)
THE SINGLES (1993-1994) LOVERLY MUSIC
RR13260 745 (October 17, 1996) p135. (Fricke, David)
SKA BONANZA: THE STUDIO ONE SKA YEARS
RR13261 628 (April 16, 1992) p81. (Palmer, Robert)
SKYNYRD FRYNDS
RR13262 693 (October 20, 1994) p150. (McLeese, Don)
SLY AND ROBBIE PRESENT TAXI
RR13263 676 (February 24, 1994) p42. (McLane, Daisann)
A SNAKE IN THE HEART
RR13264 710 (June 15, 1995) p82. (McDonnell, Evelyn)
SOCA CARNIVAL 93
RR13265 672 (December 23, 1993) p163. (McLane, Daisann)
SONGS FROM CHIPPY
RR13266 691 (September 22, 1994) p97. (McLeese, Don)
SONGS OF THE WEST
RR13267 672 (December 23, 1993) p148. (Considine, J. D.)
THE SOUL OF BLACK PERU
RR13268 709 (June 1, 1995) p62. (McLane, Daisann)
SOUL OF VIETNAM
RR13269 677 (March 10, 1994) p67. (Considine, J. D.)
SOUL TRAIN 25TH ANNIVERSARY
RR13270 723 (December 14, 1995) pp81-82. (Coleman, Mark)
SOUNDS OF THE SOUTH
RR13271 671 (December 9, 1993) p72. (Fricke, David)
SOUTH CENTRAL
RR13272 645 (December 10, 1992) p169. (Coleman, Mark)
THE SPECIALTY STORY
RR13273 683 (June 30, 1994) p77. (Considine, J. D.)
SPIRIT OF '73
RR13274 718 (October 5, 1995) p73. (Dunn, Jancee)
STARRY EYES
RR13275 649 (February 4, 1993) pp61-63. (Robbins, Ira)
THE STIFF RECORDS BOX SET
RR13276 649 (February 4, 1993) p64. (Isler, Scott)
STONE FREE
RR13277 676 (February 24, 1994) p56. (O'Connor, Rob)

STONE ROCK BLUES
RR13278 683 (June 30, 1994) p77. (Considine, J. D.)
STREET JAMS
RR13279 626 (March 19, 1992) pp93,95. (Light, Alan)
THE SUN RECORDS COLLECTION
RR13280 698 (December 29, 1994) p188. (Considine, J. D.)
SUNSET PARK
RR13281 735 (May 30, 1996) pp48-49. (Hardy, Ernest)
SUPERNATURAL FAIRY TALES
RR13282 748 (November 28, 1996) p134. (Eddy, Chuck)
SWEET RELIEF
RR13283 660 (July 8, 1993) pp109-110. (Jurek, Thom)
RR13284 665 (September 16, 1993) p17. (Mundy, Chris)
SWEET RELIEF II
RR13285 736 (June 13, 1996) p53. (Wiederhorn, Jon)
RR13286 741 (August 22, 1996) pp95-96. (Moon, Tom)
SWING THAT MUSIC!
RR13287 672 (December 23, 1993) p164. (Futterman, Steve)
SWING TIME!
RR13288 672 (December 23, 1993) p164. (Futterman, Steve)

T

TABALA WOLOF SUFI DRUMMING OF SENEGAL
RR13289 670 (November 25, 1993) p108. (McLane, Daisann)
TECHNO MANCER
RR13290 648 (January 21, 1993) pp50,52. (Hunter, James)
TEENAGE KICKS
RR13291 649 (February 4, 1993) pp61-63. (Robbins, Ira)
A TEJANO COUNTRY CHRISTMAS
RR13292 698 (December 29, 1994) p178. (McLeese, Don)
TEMPLE OF THE DOG
RR13293 619 (December 12, 1991) p168. (Fricke, David)
TEXAS BLUES
RR13294 648 (January 21, 1993) p50. (Considine, J. D.)
THEY CAME, THEY PLAYED, THEY BLOCKED THE DRIVEWAY
RR13295 676 (February 24, 1994) p57. (Fricke, David)
TILL THE NIGHT IS GONE
RR13296 706 (April 20, 1995) pp70,73. (McGee, David)
TONITE LET'S ALL MAKE LOVE IN LONDON
RR13297 624 (February 20, 1992) p42. (McLeese, Don)
TOTALLY WIRED
RR13298 723 (December 14, 1995) p86. (Dunn, Jancee)
TOUGHER THAN MUSIC
RR13299 676 (February 24, 1994) p42. (McLane, Daisann)
TOUGHER THAN TOUGH
RR13300 670 (November 25, 1993) p108. (McLane, Daisann)
RR13301 672 (December 23, 1993) p148. (Considine, J. D.)
TRANCE PLANET
RR13302 689 (August 25, 1994) p92. (McLane, Daisann)
A TRIBUTE TO BLACK ENTERTAINERS
RR13303 655 (April 29, 1993) p62. (Considine, J. D.)
A TRIBUTE TO CURTIS MAYFIELD
RR13304 680 (April 21, 1994) p85. (Considine, J. D.)
TULARE DUST
RR13305 698 (December 29, 1994) p178. (McLeese, Don)

U

THE UNITED STATES OF POETRY
RR13306 737 (June 27, 1996) pp54-55. (McDonnell, Evelyn)
UNSETTLED SCORES
RR13307 736 (June 13, 1996) p85. (Fricke, David)
UNTIL THE END OF THE WORLD
RR13308 624 (February 20, 1992) pp40-41. (Mundy, Chris)
UPTOWN MTV UNPLUGGED
RR13309 665 (September 16, 1993) pp66,70. (Dyson, Michael Eric)
URBAN BLUES
RR13310 648 (January 21, 1993) p50. (Considine, J. D.)

V

THE V-DISCS
RR13311 694 (November 3, 1994) p100. (Considine, J. D.)
VALIS 1 DESTRUCTION OF SYNTAX
RR13312 716 (September 7, 1995) pp70-71. (Fernando, S. H., Jr.)
A VERY SPECIAL CHRISTMAS 2
RR13313 645 (December 10, 1992) p187. (Coleman, Mark)
VIRUS 100
RR13314 639 (September 17, 1992) p91. (McDonnell, Evelyn)
VOIX DU SOLEIL
RR13315 698 (December 29, 1994) p182. (McLane, Daisann)

W

WAVELENGTH INFINITY
RR13316 736 (June 13, 1996) p85. (Fricke, David)
WEIRD NIGHTMARE
RR13317 642 (October 29, 1992) p75. (Futterman, Steve)
WE'RE DESPERATE
RR13318 649 (February 4, 1993) pp61-63. (Robbins, Ira)
WHAT IS BHANGRA?
RR13319 689 (August 25, 1994) p92. (McLane, Daisann)
WHERE WOODSTOCK LIVES
RR13320 691 (September 22, 1994) p100. (Milward, John)
WHITE COUNTRY BLUES (1926-1938)
RR13321 664 (September 2, 1993) p64. (Considine, J. D.)
WHITE MEN CAN'T RAP
RR13322 645 (December 10, 1992) p169. (Coleman, Mark)
WILD THINGS: WYLD KIWI GARAGE 1966-69
RR13323 660 (July 8, 1993) p113. (Fricke, David)
WIND YOUR WAIST
RR13324 626 (March 19, 1992) p95. (McLane, Daisann)
WOODSTOCK
RR13325 698 (December 29, 1994) p188. (Considine, J. D.)
WOODSTOCK '94
RR13326 698 (December 29, 1994) p188. (Considine, J. D.)
WORD UP
RR13327 710 (June 15, 1995) p82. (McDonnell, Evelyn)

Y

YULETUNES
RR13328 619 (December 12, 1991) p. (Fricke, David)

Reviewer Index to Record Reviews

A

Ahearn, Kim RR10793, RR11848, RR12829, RR12840
Alden, Grant RR10603, RR11874, RR11973, RR12046, RR12196
Ali, Lorraine RR10423, RR10552, RR10896, RR11034, RR11101, RR11178, RR11229, RR11314, RR11528, RR11531, RR11682, RR11789, RR11823, RR12042, RR12369, RR12532, RR12548, RR12646, RR12648, RR12707, RR12737, RR12760, RR12854, RR13119
Altman, Billy RR10404a, RR11695, RR11816, RR12627, RR12825, RR12863, RR12959
Appleford, Steve RR10428, RR10482, RR12436, RR12493, RR12918, RR12920, RR12922
Azerrad, Michael RR10522, RR10532, RR10719, RR11010, RR11255, RR11317, RR11386, RR12579, RR12669, RR12710, RR12882, RR12975, RR13058, RR13183

B

Bambarger, Bradley RR11615
Barron, Chris RR10500, RR11044, RR12751,
Berger, Arion RR10470, RR10737, RR10897, RR10936, RR10942, RR10984, RR11152, RR11657, RR11748, RR11774, RR11947, RR11967, RR12128, RR12204, RR12205, RR12465, RR12507, RR12709, RR12947a, RR13075, RR13080
Berman, Eric RR10707, RR11004, RR12518
Berman, Leslie RR12729
Bessman, Jim RR11232, RR11362, RR11864, RR12075, RR12762, RR12772, RR12844, RR12872
Birkbeck, Matt RR11852, RR12981
Blardinelli, Jill RR11035, RR11527
Brackett, Nathan RR10708
Brauer, Laurence RR12451
Browne, Jackson RR10935

C

Cardwell, Diane RR12255, RR12881, RR12983
Carson, Tom RR12552
Chambers, Gordon RR10874, RR11604, RR11838, RR12686, RR12870
Cohen, Jason RR10572, RR10732, RR11156, RR11225, RR11400, RR12214
Coker, Cheo H. RR10952, RR11118, RR11123, RR11555, RR11648, RR11656, RR11920, RR11997, RR12052, RR12475, RR12534, RR13218, RR13219
Coleman, Mark RR10395, RR10409, RR10459, RR10487, RR10493, RR10558, RR10559, RR10596, RR10610, RR10624, RR10631, RR10646, RR10648, RR10656, RR10663, RR10665, RR10671, RR10693, RR10726, RR10728, RR10741, RR10776, RR10808, RR10934, RR10943, RR10995, RR11025, RR11027, RR11077, RR11082, RR11087, RR11148, RR11218, RR11295, RR11353, RR11363, RR11372, RR11459, RR11470, RR11481, RR11492, RR11519, RR11521, RR11572, RR11575, RR11645, RR11687, RR11729, RR11730, RR11736, RR11738, RR11819, RR11820, RR11826, RR11827, RR11850, RR11929, RR11931, RR11932, RR11933, RR11959, RR11964, RR11978, RR11991, RR12038, RR12039, RR12083, RR12131, RR12180, RR12243, RR12292, RR12316, RR12322, RR12343, RR12347, RR12349, RR12357, RR12368, RR12403, RR12408, RR12420, RR12424, RR12519, RR12520, RR12538, RR12539, RR12540, RR12541, RR12558, RR12581, RR12613, RR12615, RR12652, RR12761, RR12795, RR12823, RR12831, RR12879, RR12907, RR12960, RR12978, RR13019, RR13026, RR13069, RR13109, RR13120, RR13122, RR13140, RR13197, RR13208, RR13212, RR13270, RR13272, RR13313, RR13322
Considine, J. D. RR10384, RR10499, RR10525, RR10601, RR10641, RR10670, RR10672, RR10675, RR10676, RR10692, RR10752, RR10819, RR10822, RR10828, RR10881, RR10883a, RR10883b, RR10888, RR10905, RR10907, RR10909, RR10974, RR10987, RR11026, RR11043, RR11056, RR11066, RR11080, RR11081, RR11107, RR11108, RR11148a, RR11175, RR11176, RR11182, RR11195, RR11197, RR11198, RR11199, RR11219, RR11275, RR11332, RR11337, RR11394, RR11395, RR11408, RR11409, RR11410, RR11411, RR11412, RR11413, RR11414, RR11415, RR11425, RR11447, RR11466, RR11491, RR11506, RR11518, RR11548, RR11570, RR11580, RR11611a, RR11611d, RR11614, RR11618, RR11619, RR11676, RR11706, RR11723, RR11725, RR11792, RR11797, RR11798, RR11849, RR11887, RR11892, RR11905, RR11910, RR11913, RR11939, RR11970, RR12032, RR12037, RR12096, RR12108, RR12137, RR12151, RR12169, RR12176, RR12194, RR12215, RR12235, RR12236, RR12309, RR12311, RR12318, RR12366, RR12370, RR12371, RR12384, RR12385, RR12392, RR12428, RR12502, RR12506, RR12512, RR12515, RR12527, RR12560, RR12585, RR12633, RR12639, RR12670, RR12701, RR12713, RR12727, RR12759, RR12780, RR12781, RR12819, RR12871, RR12876, RR12877, RR12878, RR12897, RR12898, RR12899, RR12908, RR12909, RR12917, RR12940, RR12948, RR12949, RR12953, RR12954, RR12955, RR12956, RR12957, RR12995, RR13062, RR13068, RR13070, RR13071, RR13072, RR13073, RR13084, RR13087, RR13089, RR13092, RR13103, RR13104, RR13123, RR13129, RR13134, RR13162, RR13163, RR13167, RR13168, RR13185, RR13205, RR13215, RR13230, RR13235, RR13236, RR13239, RR13267, RR13269, RR13273, RR13278, RR13280, RR13294, RR13303, RR13310, RR13321, RR13301, RR13304, RR13311, RR13325, RR13326
Cooper, Carol RR12232, RR12345
Corcoran, Michael RR10680, RR11319
Cullen, Jim RR11099, RR13131
Cullman, Brian RR11208
Curtis, Gregory RR10569

D

Damsker, Matt RR11585, RR11788, RR11868, RR12419
D'Arby, Terence Trent RR10527, RR10529, RR11484, RR12173
Darzin, Daina RR10480, RR10575, RR10625, RR10731, RR11021, RR11084, RR11137, RR11986, RR12301, RR12459
Davies, Barbara RR11770, RR12141, RR12550
Dean, Chuck RR10566, RR11573, RR12252, RR12499
DeCurtis, Anthony RR10435, RR10436, RR10439, RR10528, RR10750, RR10886, RR10932, RR10947, RR11029, RR11036, RR11051, RR11467, RR11963, RR12097, RR12186, RR12305, RR12364, RR12514, RR12516, RR12554, RR12612, RR12614, RR12642, RR12714, RR12716, RR12793, RR12853, RR13105
D'Erasmo, Stacey RR10854, RR11461, RR12118
DeRogatis, Jim RR10590, RR11083, RR11285, RR11490, RR11550, RR11596, RR11809, RR12121, RR12350, RR12351, RR12544, RR12601, RR12696, RR12951
Diehl, Matt RR10398, RR10519, RR10520, RR10604, RR10608, RR10609, RR10611, RR10651, RR10705, RR10937, RR10949, RR10992, RR11011, RR11155, RR11188, RR11266, RR11316, RR11318, RR11584, RR11652, RR12034, RR12126, RR12195, RR12289, RR12574, RR12597, RR12608, RR12616, RR12675, RR12676, RR12828, RR13005
Donelly, Tanya RR11078, RR11771, RR12127, RR12427
Dougan, John RR11136, RR12464
Drozdowski, Ted RR10599, RR10664, RR10756, RR10832, RR10835, RR11239, RR11240, RR11272, RR11345, RR11637, RR11692, RR11805, RR11835, RR11847, RR12125, RR12146, RR12278, RR12396, RR13159
Dunn, Jancee RR10388, RR13274, RR13298
Duritz, Adam RR12625
Dylan, Jakob RR10501
Dyson, Michael Eric RR10392, RR10492, RR10494, RR11017, RR11940, RR11993a, RR12059, RR12245, RR12254, RR12410, RR12472, RR12477, RR12820, RR12928, RR12936, RR13152, RR13154, RR13155, RR13206, RR13309

E

Eddy, Chris RR10959
Eddy, Chuck RR10508, RR10563, RR10729, RR10869, RR10971, RR11241, RR11977, RR12005, RR12248, RR12361, RR12456, RR12529, RR12564, RR12677, RR12776, RR13108, RR13116, RR13282
Ehrlich, Dimitri RR10653, RR11124, RR11284, RR11383, RR11649, RR11825, RR12806
Evans, Paul RR10383, RR10410, RR10416, RR10420, RR10427, RR10430, RR10437, RR10440,

Evans, Paul (continued)
RR10442, RR10452, RR10454, RR10471, RR10476, RR10503, RR10521, RR10533, RR10545, RR10546, RR10547, RR10549, RR10568, RR10591, RR10598, RR10618, RR10619, RR10621, RR10635, RR10640, RR10647, RR10659, RR10666, RR10684, RR10687, RR10689, RR10690, RR10695, RR10710, RR10751, RR10788, RR10802, RR10812, RR10843, RR10861, RR10863, RR10870, RR10885, RR10893, RR10894, RR10902, RR10926, RR10929, RR10931, RR10938, RR10944, RR10948, RR10953, RR10954, RR10957, RR10966, RR10968, RR10969, RR10975, RR10982, RR10985, RR10996, RR11000, RR11006, RR11030, RR11032, RR11033, RR11042, RR11050, RR11052, RR11058, RR11069, RR11079, RR11103, RR11142, RR11149, RR11166, RR11174, RR11177, RR11186, RR11201, RR11209, RR11213, RR11215, RR11222, RR11230, RR11252, RR11265, RR11269, RR11288, RR11294, RR11304, RR11328, RR11336, RR11349, RR11351, RR11370, RR11376, RR11422, RR11432, RR11440, RR11446, RR11452, RR11468, RR11480, RR11495, RR11500, RR11503, RR11504, RR11505, RR11509, RR11541, RR11547, RR11553, RR11563, RR11571, RR11590, RR11595, RR11611, RR11611c, RR11626, RR11639, RR11641, RR11658, RR11665, RR11667, RR11675, RR11684, RR11689, RR11697, RR11700, RR11705, RR11707, RR11715, RR11716, RR11726, RR11746, RR11752, RR11779, RR11803, RR11806, RR11810, RR11814, RR11824, RR11832, RR11846, RR11860, RR11865, RR11867, RR11869, RR11886, RR11893, RR11897, RR11906, RR11921, RR11955, RR11958, RR11961, RR11995, RR12008, RR12010, RR12022, RR12025a, RR12041, RR12045, RR12048, RR12054, RR12061, RR12064, RR12065, RR12076, RR12080, RR12087, RR12098, RR12102, RR12108a, RR12136, RR12138, RR12143, RR12156, RR12160, RR12161, RR12164, RR12170, RR12179, RR12182, RR12187, RR12192, RR12206, RR12216, RR12221, RR12240, RR12247, RR12279, RR12288, RR12302, RR12307, RR12308, RR12310, RR12321, RR12324, RR12362, RR12363, RR12372, RR12379, RR12386, RR12409, RR12431, RR12433, RR12468, RR12482, RR12495, RR12505, RR12513, RR12549, RR12575, RR12586, RR12592, RR12598, RR12611, RR12634, RR12643, RR12645, RR12647, RR12657, RR12667, RR12668, RR12689, RR12690, RR12691, RR12715, RR12717, RR12743, RR12744, RR12756, RR12758, RR12774, RR12794, RR12812, RR12814, RR12841, RR12843, RR12849, RR12852, RR12864, RR12886, RR12889, RR12901, RR12905, RR12923, RR12927, RR12934, RR12968, RR12970, RR12988, RR12998, RR13000, RR13043, RR13099, RR13110, RR13128, RR13136, RR13139, RR13150, RR13169, RR13173, RR13179, RR13189, RR13213, RR13216, RR13237

F

Farber, Jim RR10879, RR11444, RR11545, RR12218

Ferguson, Kate RR11321, RR11327

Fernando, S. H., Jr. RR10472, RR10626, RR10632, RR10845, RR10911, RR10939, RR11228, RR11238, RR11292, RR11309, RR11338, RR11387, RR11701, RR11767, RR12021, RR12024, RR12280, RR12338, RR12595, RR12869, RR13035, RR13188, RR13312

Fine, Jason RR10748, RR11015, RR11344, RR12069, RR12434, RR12769

Flaum, Eric RR10551, RR11019, RR11765, RR11853, RR12201, RR12887, RR12973

Foege, Alec RR11159, RR12094

Fricke, David RR10389, RR10399, RR10400, RR10401, RR10402, RR10405, RR10406, RR10407, RR10412, RR10419, RR10421, RR10429, RR10448, RR10449, RR10450, RR10456, RR10458, RR10461, RR10463, RR10467, RR10468, RR10479, RR10536, RR10574, RR10607, RR10612, RR10614, RR10617, RR10627, RR10643, RR10644, RR10645, RR10661, RR10667, RR10677, RR10688, RR10697, RR10713, RR10727, RR10730, RR10761, RR10767, RR10770, RR10777, RR10785, RR10799, RR10801, RR10807b, RR10821, RR10827, RR10830, RR10841, RR10851, RR10860, RR10862, RR10865, RR10867, RR10871, RR10873, RR10875, RR10876, RR10887, RR10901, RR10904, RR10912, RR10940, RR10945, RR10946, RR10950, RR10978, RR10979, RR10981, RR10988, RR10989, RR10991, RR10997, RR10998, RR11009, RR11014, RR11016, RR11020, RR11037, RR11045, RR11049, RR11070, RR11073, RR11074, RR11075, RR11092, RR11106, RR11114, RR11115, RR11116, RR11119, RR11120, RR11121, RR11126, RR11127, RR11131, RR11132, RR11133, RR11134, RR11139, RR11143, RR11150, RR11157, RR11160, RR11167, RR11169, RR11180, RR11181, RR11187, RR11190, RR11196, RR11217, RR11220, RR11221, RR11223, RR11236, RR11247, RR11248, RR11274, RR11277, RR11283, RR11286, RR11289, RR11290, RR11291, RR11296, RR11298, RR11310, RR11311, RR11323, RR11324, RR11326, RR11333, RR11339, RR11341, RR11352, RR11360, RR12337a, RR11405, RR11416, RR11420, RR11421, RR11428, RR11430, RR11431, RR11433, RR11436, RR11438, RR11439, RR11445, RR11453, RR11454, RR11463, RR11475, RR11479, RR11485, RR11486, RR11489, RR11493, RR11498, RR11526, RR11529, RR11537, RR11539, RR11546, RR11551, RR11556, RR11578, RR11579, RR11581, RR11594, RR11606, RR11608, RR11612, RR11617, RR11627, RR11643, RR11653, RR11655, RR11672, RR11677, RR11677a, RR11678, RR11694, RR11699, RR11702, RR11710, RR11712, RR11719, RR11727, RR11728, RR11734, RR11737, RR11738a, RR11759, RR11769, RR11776, RR11777, RR11781, RR11783, RR11784, RR11786, RR11800, RR11801, RR11804, RR11811, RR11829, RR11833, RR11834, RR11839, RR11845, RR11861, RR11875, RR11878, RR11880, RR11880a, RR11881, RR11882, RR11885, RR11891, RR11898, RR11899, RR11911, RR11922, RR11924, RR11946, RR11969, RR11971, RR11975, RR11982, RR11983, RR11987, RR11988, RR12004, RR12013, RR12014c, RR12027, RR12035, RR12044, RR12051, RR12053, RR12055, RR12057, RR12058, RR12063, RR12074, RR12078, RR12079, RR12086, RR12089, RR12109, RR12110, RR12111, RR12114, RR12132, RR12134, RR12140, RR12145, RR12168, RR12184, RR12188, RR12200, RR12203, RR12209, RR12213, RR12219, RR12225, RR12231, RR12233, RR12241, RR12249, RR12250, RR12253, RR12256, RR12277, RR12286, RR12296, RR12297, RR12298, RR12300, RR12314, RR12315, RR12317, RR12327, RR12339, RR12340, RR12348, RR12355, RR12365, RR12377, RR12393, RR12395, RR12402, RR12405, RR12407, RR12411, RR12413, RR12414, RR12430, RR12435, RR12438, RR12439, RR12449, RR12458, RR12470, RR12476, RR12478, RR12484, RR12485, RR12486, RR12488, RR12489, RR12490, RR12504, RR12510, RR12522, RR12524, RR12525, RR12528, RR12535, RR12545, RR12559, RR12561, RR12567, RR12570, RR12572, RR12577, RR12582, RR12589, RR12591, RR12604, RR12606, RR12617, RR12620, RR12621, RR12622, RR12623, RR12624, RR12629, RR12630, RR12635, RR12641, RR12651, RR12658, RR12662, RR12663, RR12664, RR12665, RR12671, RR12679, RR12703, RR12711, RR12722, RR12726, RR12728, RR12733, RR12736, RR12739, RR12752, RR12767, RR12777, RR12778, RR12779, RR12798, RR12799, RR12803, RR12813, RR12815, RR12817, RR12839, RR12858, RR12866, RR12867, RR12868, RR12875, RR12883, RR12899a, RR12916, RR12938, RR12942, RR12943, RR12950, RR12982, RR12984, RR12991, RR12996, RR12997, RR13002, RR13011, RR13014, RR13023, RR13032, RR13039, RR13041, RR13052, RR13059, RR13083, RR13088, RR13091, RR13101, RR13107, RR13118, RR13127, RR13132, RR13133, RR13157, RR13160, RR13166, RR13176, RR13193, RR13198, RR13204, RR13211, RR13214, RR13217, RR13220, RR13227, RR13229, RR13232, RR13241, RR13249, RR13257, RR13258, RR13260, RR13271, RR13293, RR13295, RR13307, RR13316, RR13323, RR13328

Frost, Deborah RR12185, RR12191, RR12283

Futterman, Steve RR10386, RR10403, RR10404, RR10457, RR10465, RR10495, RR10496, RR10512, RR10539, RR10554, RR10587, RR10588, RR10589, RR10592, RR10593, RR10594, RR10595, RR10597, RR10686, RR10709, RR10717, RR10740, RR10745, RR10762, RR10772, RR10773, RR10774, RR10775, RR10798, RR10800, RR10800a, RR10803, RR10804, RR10805, RR10806, RR10807, RR10809, RR10814, RR10836, RR10838, RR10839, RR10840, RR10842, RR10850, RR10852, RR10892, RR10906, RR10908, RR10910,

Futterman, Steve (continued)
RR10963, RR10986, RR11012, RR11061, RR11062, RR11068, RR11104, RR11117, RR11146, RR11164, RR11168, RR11245, RR11246, RR11256, RR11257, RR11273, RR11276, RR11293, RR11299, RR11308, RR11342, RR11343, RR11374, RR11388, RR11389, RR11390, RR11391, RR11392, RR11402, RR11424, RR11462, RR11502, RR11517, RR11557, RR11564, RR11569, RR11592, RR11630, RR11693, RR11696, RR11704, RR11731, RR11732, RR11733, RR11795, RR11817, RR11837, RR11916, RR11917, RR11918, RR11919, RR11927, RR11928, RR11938, RR11965, RR11966, RR11981, RR12026, RR12028, RR12033, RR12120, RR12122, RR12130, RR12144, RR12152, RR12153, RR12171, RR12210, RR12211, RR12222, RR12260, RR12263, RR12265, RR12270, RR12271, RR12274, RR12313, RR12320, RR12359, RR12383, RR12398, RR12399, RR12443, RR12497, RR12511, RR12654, RR12681, RR12682, RR12683, RR12684, RR12704, RR12718, RR12730, RR12786, RR12890, RR12914, RR12932, RR12935, RR12962, RR12976, RR13038, RR13097, RR13226, RR13287, RR13288, RR13317

G

Gaar, Gillian G. RR11138, RR13100, RR13121
Galtney, Smith RR12084
Galvin, Peter RR11300, RR11544, RR12014b, RR12239, RR12387, RR12389, RR12980
Garbarini, Vic RR11483
Gardner, Elysa RR10385, RR10474, RR10550, RR10606, RR10662, RR10685, RR10837, RR10882, RR10889, RR10915, RR10917, RR10922, RR10990, RR11085, RR11100, RR11102, RR11163, RR11165, RR11268, RR11434, RR11538, RR11543, RR11685, RR11686, RR11744, RR11843, RR11952, RR12001, RR12067, RR12107, RR12148, RR12155, RR12437, RR12481, RR12576, RR12636, RR12640, RR12723, RR12731, RR12782, RR12790, RR12791, RR12952, RR13034, RR13130, RR13146
Garelick, Jon RR11948
Gehr, Richard RR11857, RR12165, RR13021
George-Warren, Holly RR10441, RR10484, RR10557, RR10757, RR11094, RR11330, RR11673, RR11935, RR12056, RR12425, RR12656, RR12775, RR12900, RR12924
Gilmore, Mikal RR12610
Gilyard, Burl RR12999, RR13033
Gold, Jonathan RR11322, RR12040, RR12526
Goodman, Fred RR11002
Graves, Tom RR10510, RR11312, RR12174, RR12415, RR12423

H

Hardy, Ernest RR10736, RR10790, RR11109, RR11768, RR11802, RR11926, RR11999, RR12023, RR12228, RR12764, RR13281
Harrington, Spencer RR11423
Harris, Carter RR11469
Harris, Michael C. RR11607
Helmore, Edward RR10393
Hendrickson, Matt RR11739
Hill, Trent RR11091, RR11233, RR11974, RR12453
Himes, Geoffrey RR10668, RR10754, RR10924, RR11722, RR11951, RR12016, RR12207, RR12491, RR12719, RR12945, RR12986, RR13231
Himmelsbach, Erik RR11024
Holden, Stephen RR10489, RR10734, RR10763, RR10769, RR11110, RR12007, RR12626, RR12830
Hoon, Shannon RR10511, RR11750, RR12857
Hopkins, Tracy E. RR12697
Hoskyns, Barney RR10913, RR11681, RR12150
Howard, Pete RR10831, RR11281, RR12237, RR12619, RR12838, RR13063, RR13094, RR13095, RR13243
Huffman, Eddie RR10571, RR11234
Hunter, B.R. RR13061, RR13222
Hunter, James RR10391, RR10933, RR11055, RR11140, RR11171, RR11214, RR11361, RR11418, RR11497, RR11512, RR11993, RR12189, RR12193, RR12353, RR12483, RR12509, RR12661, RR12700, RR12766, RR12768, RR12770, RR12807, RR12906, RR12994, RR13290
Hutchence, Michael RR10642, RR10964, RR11003

I

Isler, Scott RR10432, RR10490, RR11193, RR11359, RR12251, RR12884, RR13086, RR13093, RR13276

J

Jamison, Laura RR12473
Jurek, Thom RR10434, RR10620, RR10859, RR10884, RR10999, RR11224, RR11377, RR11426, RR11669, RR12416, RR12417, RR12689a, RR12721, RR12773, RR12913, RR12933, RR12937, RR13283

K

Kelley, Robin D.G. RR10967a, RR11090, RR12244, RR12426, RR13165
Kelly, Christina RR11680
Kemp, Mark RR10507, RR10534, RR10564, RR10636, RR10701, RR10824, RR11095, RR11189, RR11231, RR11346, RR11642, RR11941, RR12129, RR12190, RR12199, RR12325, RR12452, RR12454, RR12492, RR12796, RR12972
Kenny, Glenn RR10455, RR11532, RR11945, RR12765
King, Wayne RR12555
Kirk, Deborah RR10735
Kot, Greg RR10390, RR10478, RR10483, RR10555, RR11145, RR11173, RR11206, RR11303, RR11862, RR11863, RR11908, RR12071, RR12157, RR12181, RR12285, RR12287, RR12306, RR12557, RR12605, RR12632, RR12745, RR12804, RR12925, RR12993, RR13066
Kravitz, Lenny RR12421

L

Levy, Joe RR11267, RR12596
Light, Alan RR10960, RR11350, RR11496, RR12217, RR12230, RR12746, RR13233, RR13279
Loder, Kurt RR12594
Lyman, Andy RR11183, RR11587, RR12030, RR12119, RR12358, RR12463, RR12693

M

Manning, Kara RR10600, RR10683, RR10853, RR11226, RR11227, RR11251, RR11301, RR11442, RR11540, RR11566, RR11611b, RR11772, RR11787, RR12036, RR12163, RR12367, RR12508, RR12523, RR12708, RR12893, RR13102, RR13186
Marlowe, Ann RR10791
Masuo, Sandy RR10411, RR11632, RR12103, RR12531
Matteo, Steve RR11477
McAlley, John RR10655, RR10660, RR10847, RR11904, RR12060, RR12705, RR12885, RR12926, RR12979, RR13049, RR13240
McCormick, Moira RR12352
McCulley, Jerry RR10523
McDonnell, Evelyn RR10424, RR10565, RR10789, RR10834, RR11122, RR11366, RR11367, RR11417, RR11450, RR11472, RR11741, RR11856, RR12105, RR12180a, RR12284, RR12445, RR12894, RR13065, RR13138, RR13151, RR13156, RR13174, RR13178, RR13244, RR13255, RR13264, RR13306, RR13314, RR13327
McElfresh, Suzanna RR10958, RR11455
McEwen, Joe RR11473, RR11818
McGee, David RR10898, RR10921, RR11401, RR11567, RR11568, RR11574, RR11602, RR12783, RR12977, RR13125, RR13246, RR13296
McKenna, Kristine RR11271
McLane, Daisann RR10382, RR10387, RR10418, RR10438, RR10444, RR10475, RR10491, RR10562, RR10567, RR10577, RR10578, RR10579, RR10580, RR10586, RR10602, RR10629, RR10637, RR10639, RR10699, RR10700, RR10784, RR10848, RR10849, RR10927, RR10928, RR11018, RR11064, RR11170, RR11204, RR11237, RR11242, RR11243, RR11348, RR11476, RR11487, RR11549, RR11586, RR11603, RR11620, RR11636, RR11668, RR11709, RR11720, RR11721, RR11763, RR11766, RR11870, RR11871, RR11884, RR11900, RR11901, RR11902, RR11903, RR11912, RR11925, RR11936, RR11942, RR11943, RR11944, RR12002, RR12003, RR12085, RR12092, RR12095, RR12104, RR12202, RR12212, RR12291, RR12293, RR12294, RR12356, RR12360, RR12373, RR12374, RR12376, RR12388, RR12394, RR12469, RR12496, RR12501, RR12631, RR12673, RR12699, RR12754, RR12789, RR12808, RR12809, RR12822, RR12832, RR12833, RR12842, RR12847, RR12989, RR13006, RR13008, RR13009, RR13031, RR13042, RR13045, RR13046, RR13047, RR13048, RR13064, RR13076, RR13077, RR13079, RR13081, RR13082, RR13111, RR13112, RR13113, RR13114, RR13115, RR13117, RR13126, RR13137, RR13141, RR13145, RR13148, RR13149, RR13158, RR13161, RR13171, RR13175, RR13181, RR13182, RR13192, RR13194, RR13223, RR13224, RR13228, RR13238, RR13252, RR13253, RR13263, RR13265, RR13268, RR13289, RR13299, RR13300, RR13302, RR13319, RR13315
McLeese, Don RR10396, RR10413, RR10414, RR10431, RR10433, RR10451, RR10464, RR10466, RR10481, RR10497, RR10498, RR10517, RR10537, RR10542, RR10548, RR10567a, RR10669, RR10679, RR10680a, RR10681, RR10682, RR10691,

McLeese, Don (continued)
RR10720, RR10721, RR10722, RR10725, RR10738, RR10743, RR10744, RR10768, RR10778, RR10781, RR10783, RR10810, RR10811, RR10813, RR10816, RR10817, RR10818, RR10891, RR10903, RR10914, RR10923, RR11013, RR11023, RR11031, RR11053, RR11054, RR11071, RR11072, RR11093, RR11128, RR11151, RR11172, RR11244, RR11347, RR11355, RR11356, RR11384, RR11393, RR11396, RR11397, RR11403, RR11404, RR11437, RR11448, RR11449, RR11456, RR11457, RR11511, RR11513, RR11514, RR11522, RR11523, RR11535, RR11536, RR11558, RR11559, RR11560, RR11561, RR11576, RR11582, RR11583, RR11588, RR11589, RR11597, RR11598, RR11600, RR11601, RR11613, RR11629, RR11635, RR11638, RR11659, RR11660, RR11661, RR11671, RR11674, RR11690, RR11691, RR11708, RR11718, RR11743, RR11754, RR11755, RR11756, RR11758, RR11813, RR11828, RR11830, RR11836, RR11859, RR11866, RR11923, RR11930, RR11934, RR11937, RR12009, RR12011, RR12014, RR12029, RR12066, RR12072, RR12091, RR12093, RR12113, RR12115, RR12116, RR12117, RR12172, RR12197, RR12223, RR12224, RR12341, RR12342, RR12344, RR12354, RR12375, RR12406, RR12479, RR12480, RR12494, RR12533, RR12542, RR12562, RR12573, RR12603, RR12637, RR12638, RR12653, RR12655, RR12692, RR12695, RR12702, RR12706, RR12720, RR12741, RR12757, RR12771, RR12785, RR12788, RR12824, RR12836, RR12850, RR12859, RR12860, RR12862, RR12865, RR12892, RR12910, RR12911, RR12912, RR12929, RR12930, RR12931, RR12939, RR12961, RR12966, RR12967, RR12985, RR12987, RR13001, RR13003, RR13044, RR13078, RR13191, RR13242, RR13247, RR13262, RR13266, RR13292, RR13297, RR13305

McLeod, Rodd RR10585

Mell, A. J. RR11542

Micallef, Ken RR10696, RR10846, RR11200

Milward, John RR10516, RR10538, RR10561, RR10613, RR10630a, RR10698, RR10724, RR10899, RR11250, RR11306, RR11307, RR11662, RR11666, RR11742, RR11915, RR12014a, RR12238, RR12412, RR12455, RR12748, RR12811, RR12915, RR12944, RR12958, RR13004, RR13050, RR13054, RR13085, RR13135, RR13153, RR13320

Mirkin, Steven RR10515, RR10605, RR10742, RR11113, RR11369, RR11793, RR11873, RR12462, RR12503, RR12517, RR12566

Moon, Tom RR10650, RR10755, RR10962, RR11184, RR11203, RR11357, RR11380, RR11591, RR11698, RR11711, RR11895, RR11950, RR12077, RR12167, RR12229, RR12543, RR12571, RR12593, RR13225, RR13286

Moore, Thurston RR10765, RR13147, RR13284, RR13308

Morales, Ed RR10718

Morris, Chris RR11593

Mundy, Chris RR10657, RR11249, RR11515, RR11855, RR12158, RR12328, RR12329, RR12330, RR12331, RR12332, RR12333, RR12334, RR12335, RR12336, RR12337, RR12547, RR12797, RR12802, RR12805

N

Neely, Kim RR11253, RR11368, RR11460, RR11625, RR12299, RR12440, RR12442, RR12444

Nelson, Havelock RR11028, RR11086, RR11089, RR11212, RR11235, RR11443, RR11644, RR11760, RR11972

Nicks, Stevie RR10916, RR11040, RR11914, RR12792

Nicolucci, Guy RR12142

O

O'Connor, Rob RR10422, RR10445, RR10485, RR10509, RR10634, RR10746, RR10758, RR10766, RR10872, RR10880, RR10900, RR10970, RR11001, RR11057, RR11063, RR11154, RR11162, RR11302, RR11381, RR11516, RR11530, RR11628, RR11663, RR11745, RR11812, RR11949, RR11954, RR11968, RR12099, RR12101, RR12175, RR12303, RR12304, RR12447, RR12583, RR12688, RR12855, RR12888, RR12992, RR13277

O'Dair, Barbara RR11097, RR11554, RR11773, RR12047, RR12159, RR12183, RR12220, RR12378, RR12569, RR12738, RR13190

Odintz, Andrea RR10544, RR11041, RR11842, RR12487, RR12556, RR13187

Okamoto, David RR10469, RR10983, RR11703, RR11724

P

Palmer, Robert RR10504, RR10815, RR10844, RR10855, RR10866, RR10951, RR10955, RR11008, RR11059, RR11141, RR11335, RR11351a, RR11441, RR11747, RR11791, RR11858, RR12123, RR12124, RR12139, RR12323, RR12346, RR12401, RR12530, RR12568, RR12650, RR12724, RR12818, RR12837, RR12848, RR12856, RR12861, RR12903, RR12946, RR12974, RR13096, RR13180, RR13196, RR13251, RR13261

Palmer, Tamara RR10623, RR13096, RR13180, RR13196, RR13251, RR13261

Panahpour, Nilou RR11065, RR11762, RR11844, RR12006, RR12100

Poulson-Bryant, Scott RR11640

Powell, Kevin RR10514, RR10518, RR10780, RR11005, RR11688, RR12090, RR12198, RR12381, RR12390, RR12784, RR12904, RR13184, RR13060

Powers, Ann RR11191, RR12397, RR12891

Prince, David J. RR10446, RR11038, RR11039, RR13055

Puterbaugh, Parke RR10524, RR10526, RR10541, RR10556, RR10560, RR10615, RR11297, RR11365, RR11499, RR11683, RR11717, RR11831, RR11896, RR11953, RR12154, RR12162, RR12628, RR12680, RR12827

Q

Queen Latifah RR10782, RR11022, RR11096, RR12763

R

Rabhan, Jeffrey RR11340, RR13090

Ransom, Kevin RR10543, RR10674, RR10920, RR11960, RR11962, RR12666

Ressler, Darren RR12880

Reynolds, Simon RR11753, RR12400

Richardson, Susan RR11047, RR11048, RR11125, RR11205, RR11364, RR11646, RR13074

Ro, Ronin RR12618

Robbins, Ira RR10712, RR10779, RR10792, RR11270, RR11406, RR11407, RR11508, RR11524, RR11552, RR11780, RR11807, RR11909, RR11985, RR12049, RR12208, RR12466, RR12536, RR12537, RR12565, RR12712, RR12725, RR12834, RR12846, RR12965, RR13053, RR13067, RR13098, RR13124, RR13195, RR13207, RR13256, RR13275, RR13291, RR13318, RR13144

Rust, Ned RR10658

S

Sandmel, Ben RR11778, RR12070, RR12149

Santelli, Robert RR10622, RR10702, RR10980, RR11331, RR11334, RR11358, RR11610, RR12578, RR12588, RR12896, RR13199, RR13200, RR13201, RR13202, RR13254

Santiago, Roberto RR10417, RR11605, RR11872

Sarig, Roni RR10473, RR11194, RR11398

Sauter, Michael RR11478, RR11670

Schwarz, K. Robert RR11258, RR11259, RR11260, RR11261, RR11262, RR11263, RR11264, RR11278, RR11279, RR11647, RR11713, RR11714, RR12800, RR12801, RR13036, RR13037

Scoppa, Bud RR12467

Seymour, Corey RR11525, RR13106

Sinclair, David RR10616

Sinclair, Tom RR10443, RR10531, RR10760, RR10771, RR10972, RR11111, RR11158, RR11320, RR11501, RR11520, RR11533, RR11808, RR12227, RR12380, RR12895, RR12969, RR13221, RR13259

Smith, Danyel RR10453, RR10513, RR10820, RR11076, RR11098, RR11161, RR11211, RR11465, RR12749a, RR12821, RR12990

Sprague, David RR10925, RR10967, RR10977, RR11889, RR12147, RR12963

St. Leger, Marie Elsie RR10426, RR10638, RR10652, RR10673, RR11751, RR12580

Stenger, Wif RR10895, RR11135, RR11419, RR11840, RR12755

Stern, Chip RR10749, RR11796

Strauss, Neil RR10397, RR12088

Sulcas, Adele RR12659

Swenson, John RR10415, RR10786, RR10787, RR10826, RR10941, RR11282, RR11379, RR11427, RR11429, RR11507, RR11599, RR11609, RR11633, RR11757, RR11821, RR11976, RR11980, RR11984, RR12257, RR12258, RR12259, RR12261, RR12262, RR12264, RR12266, RR12267, RR12268, RR12272, RR12273, RR12275, RR12276, RR12295, RR12418, RR12429, RR12600, RR12734, RR12816, RR12873, RR12921, RR12947, RR13010, RR13012, RR13013, RR13015, RR13016, RR13017, RR13018, RR13020, RR13022, RR13024, RR13025, RR13027, RR13028, RR13029, RR13030, RR13040, RR13248, RR13057

Szabo, Julia RR11749, RR12787, RR12845

T

Tannenbaum, Rob RR10649,

RR10733, RR11371, RR12461
Thigpen, David RR11577
Thompson, Dave RR12290
Torres, Richard RR10714, RR10764, RR11841
Torres, Rick RR11474
Toure RR10477, RR10505, RR10540, RR10573, RR10576, RR10723, RR10857, RR10858, RR10868, RR11007, RR11207, RR11451, RR11464, RR11494, RR11634, RR11651, RR11654, RR11790, RR11989, RR11994, RR12073, RR12112, RR12246, RR12312, RR12498, RR12563, RR12599, RR12749, RR12964, RR13056, RR13142, RR13143, RR13203, RR13234

V

"Vam Pyros, Bill" RR12810
Van Parys, Bill RR10486, RR10759, RR11471, RR11851, RR12810, RR13209
Vincentelli, Elisabeth RR10394
Volk, Steven RR10956, RR11129, RR11957, RR11979, RR12644

W

Walls, Richard C. RR10502, RR10706, RR10883, RR11254, RR11329, RR11510, RR12015, RR12500, RR12685, RR12732, RR13177
Walser, Robert RR11761, RR12242, RR12521, 13164
Walters, Barry RR11664
Webster, Andy RR12742
Weisel, Al RR10571b, RR10703, RR10704, RR10739, RR10794, RR10829, RR11112, RR11144, RR11287, RR11794, RR11854, RR11879, RR11894, RR11956, RR12031, RR12135, RR12404, RR12471, RR12546, RR12740, RR13170
Welchman, Geoffrey RR11740, RR12382, RR12587
White, Armond RR10460, RR11088, RR11764, RR12025, RR12422
Wiederhorn, Jon RR10408, RR10447, RR10570, RR10633, RR10823, RR10856, RR10976, RR11153, RR11210, RR11280, RR11385, RR11631, RR11888, RR11907, RR11990, RR11998, RR12062, RR12081, RR12082, RR12281, RR12432, RR12446, RR12460, RR12551, RR12607, RR12609, RR12674, RR12678, RR12971, RR13051, RR13285
Wiesel, Al RR12177
Wild, David RR10630, RR10747, RR10993, RR10994, RR11046, RR11179, RR11313, RR11822, RR12391, RR12590, RR12851
Wilson, Michael RR12874
Woodard, Josef RR10425, RR10553, RR10716, RR10807a, RR10864, RR11185, RR11565, RR12735, RR12826
Wright, Christian RR10488, RR10571a, RR10715, RR10833, RR10919, RR10930, RR10973, RR11130, RR11325, RR11375, RR11482, RR11488, RR11562, RR12234, RR12441, RR12450, RR12602, RR13172
Wyman, Bill RR11378

Y

Young, Jon RR11067, RR11799

Z

Zacharek, Stephanie RR10694, RR10890, RR11373, RR11399, RR11458, RR11534, RR12068
Zinman, Greg RR12835

Title Index to Record Reviews

A

A.M. RR12924
Abba-Esque RR11087
Aboriginal Choirs Of Central Australia RR13042
About To Choke RR10779
Above RR11770
Above The Rim RR13043
Absolutely Free RR13010
Achtung Baby RR12790
Acid Eaters RR12288
The Acoustic Motorbike RR10606
Acquatica RR12434
Across The Borderline RR12007, RR12008
Across The Great Divide RR10499, RR13044
Adios Amigos RR12289
Adrenalize RR10974
The Aeroplane Flies High RR12543
Affairs Of The Heart RR12881
Africa Invades Europe RR13007, RR13008
Africando Volume 1 RR13045, RR13046
Afro Brasil RR13047, RR13048
Afro-Cuban Classic: Los 24 Exitos Originales de Arsenio Rodriguez RR12373
After Awhile RR11247
After Murder Park RR10470
Ahead Of Their Time RR13011
Ahora Vengo Alborota RR11763
Ain't Enough Comin' In RR12412
Ain't Gonna Be Your Dog RR11447
Ain't Life Grand RR12923
Ain't My Lookout RR11302
Ain't No Other RR11760
Aitara RR12822
AKA Detrimental Vasoline RR12393
AKA Grafitti Man RR12773
AKA The Rugged Child RR12498
Alex Chilton (song) RR12328
Alibis RR11674
Alice In Chains RR10408
Alien Lanes RR11316
Alive In America RR12632
All Eyez On Me RR12473, RR12474
All For You RR11876
All Hail The Queen RR12254
All Night Long RR11610, RR12578
All Samples Cleared! RR11790
All That May Do My Rhyme RR11091
All The Way RR12441
All This Useless Beauty RR10879
All You Can Eat RR11664
Alone And Acoustic RR11331, RR12896
Alright It Was Frank RR10437
Altamira Banda Show RR10418
Altered Beast RR12688
Alternative NRG RR13049
Alternative Woodstock RR13050
Always And Forever RR11098
Am I Not Your Girl? RR12067
Amanita RR10506
Amazing Disgrace RR12207
Amazing Grace RR12215
America Is Dying RR13051
American Babylon RR11310
American Caesar RR12199
American Folk Blues Festival '62-'65 RR13052
The American In Me RR11163
American Recordings RR10750, RR10751
American Standard RR11799
American Thighs RR12840
Aminah's Dream RR12443
Amorica RR10568
Amused To Death RR12879
Anarchy In The UK RR13053
Anchored In Love RR10743
Anesthesia (song) RR12867
An Angel At My Shoulder RR12029
Angel Dust RR11111
Annunciation RR12659
Anodyne RR12796
Another Level RR10584
Another Night RR12414
Antenna RR13004
Anthem RR10579
The Anthology 1961-1977 RR11473, RR11818
The Anthology 1965-1967 RR12541
Anthology 2 RR10523
Anthology 3 RR10524
Antichrist Superstar RR11789
Ants To The Moon RR11965
Anything Can Happen RR12415
Apocalypse Across The Sky RR10467, RR11804
Apocalypse 91...The Enemy Strikes Black RR12241
Apollo 18 RR12725
Apostrophe RR13012
The Aranbee Pop Symphony Orchestra RR10451
Arc Angels RR10452
Are You Gonna Go My Way RR11640, RR11641
Areito RR11315
Arkansas Traveler RR12492
Art Forms Of Dimensions Tomorrow RR12257
The Art Of Fingerstyle Guitar RR13054
Artifacts Of Love RR11859
Artificial Intelligence II RR13055
Artistic Vice RR11552
As Long As There's Music RR11342, RR11374
Asa Nisi Masa RR10463
Ascension RR10399
Ask For It RR11420
A Ass Pocket Of Whiskey RR10701
At Action Park RR12484
At The Ryman RR11361, RR11993
Atlanta Whiskey Flats RR12559
Atliens RR12090
Auf Wiedersehen (song) RR12629
August And Everything After RR10884, RR10885
Austin Skyline RR11659
Autobiography Of Mistachuck RR10947
Autogeddon RR10870
Automatic For The People RR12321, RR12322
Automobility RR12114
Avalon Blues 1963 RR11456
Award Tour (song) RR12763

B

B. Brown Posse RR13056
Bacchanal Time RR12673
Bacdafucup RR12080
Back At Your Ass For The Nine-4 RR12025a
Back For Good (song) RR12700
Back From Rio RR11839
Back In The Game RR11551
Back In The USA RR11826
Back To Mono (1958-1969) RR12594
Back To The Light RR11816
Back To The Streets RR13057
Back Where I Belong RR10458
Backbeat RR13058
Bad And Beautiful RR12258
Bad Boys RR11479
Bad Vibes RR10834
Badmotorfinger RR12582
Bakesale RR12452
Balance RR12812
Ball-Hog Or Tugboat? RR12882
Ballad No. 19 (song) RR12053
Ballbreaker RR10388, RR10389
Bamba RR12085
Bandwagonesque RR12709
Bang! RR12963
Barney's Favorites Vol. 1 RR10508
Basement Tapes RR10500, RR11044
Bat Out Of Hell II RR11852
Batak Of North Sumatra RR13059
The Battle For Space RR11652
B'Boom RR11612
Be Like That (song) RR12777
Beach Of The War Goddess RR12907
The Beat RR10521
The Beat Generation RR13060
Beat The Retreat RR13061
The Beatles Compact Discs Singles Collection RR10525
Beats, Rhymes And Life RR12764
Beatsongs RR10607
Beautiful Freak RR11060
Beautiful Light RR11149
Beauty Is A Rare Thing RR10840
Beautycase RR12188
The Beavis And Butt-Head Experience RR10531
Beckology RR10537
Become What You Are RR11369, RR11370
Bedtime Stories RR11773
Bee Thousand RR11317
Beer Joint And Tailoring RR11556
Behind Bars RR12534
Being There RR12925
Believe RR12580
Believe (song) RR11003
The Bells Of Dublin RR10785
Ben Folds Five RR11156
The Bends RR12278
Berlin, 1962 RR10767
Berserkley's Best RR13062
The Best Of Cameo RR10723
The Best Of Con Funk Shun RR10858
The Best Of Cool Yule RR13063
The Best Of Kool And The Gang 1969-1976 RR11634
The Best Of Paul Kelly RR11593
Best Of Studio One, Vols, I, II And III RR13064
The Best Of The Bar-Kays RR10505
The Best Of The Ronettes RR12384
The Best Of Van Morrison Volume Two RR11949
Better Days RR12588
Betty RR11385
Between Midnight And Hindsight RR12910
Between 10th And 11th RR10766
Between The 1 And The 9 RR12397

Beyond The Garage RR11983
Biff! Bang! Powder RR12209
Big, Bad And Blue RR12780
Big Horizon RR12926
Big Shot In The Dark RR12742
Big Star Live RR10556
A Bigger Piece Of Sky RR11588
Bikini Kill RR10563
Bilingual RR12150
Billie Holiday: The Legacy 1933-1958 RR11423
Billy Breathes RR12165, RR12166
Billy Pilgrim RR10566
Binge And Purge RR11749
The Birth Of Soul RR10768
Bizarre Fruit RR11762
Bizarre Ride II The Pharcyde RR12161
Black And Tan Club RR13065
Black Box RR13066
Black Country Rock RR11969
Black Eyed Man RR10889
Black 47 RR10600
Black Love RR10397
Black Melodies On A Clear Afternoon RR11306, RR12811
Black Pearl RR12983
The Black Rider RR12854
Black Snake Diamond Role RR11408
Black Sunday RR10937, RR10938
Black Tie White Noise RR10640
The Blank Generation RR13067
Blasters Of The Universe RR10632, RR10845
A Blazing Grace RR11513
Blind Faith RR10597
Blind Melon RR10598
The Bliss Album? RR12189
Bloodlines RR10612
BloodSugarSexMagik RR12300
Bloody Kisses RR12787
A Blow For Me, A Toot For You RR12898
Blow Up RR12555, RR13068
Blowout Comb RR11004
Blue Blvd RR10419
Blue Collar Blues RR12354
Blue Funk RR11383
Blue House RR10498
Blue Interlude RR11795
Blue Is The Color Of Hope RR12066
Blue Light 'Til Dawn RR12944
The Blue Note Years RR11388
Blue On Blonde RR11297, RR11717
The Blue Sun RR11578, RR12883
Blues RR11394
Blues Classics RR13069
Blues For The Flying Dutchman RR10434
Blues Originals RR13070
Blues Revival RR13071
Blues Roots RR13072
Blues With A Feeling RR13073
Bluesbreakers With Eric Clapton RR10798, RR11817
Boats To Build RR10811
Bob Dylan: The 30th Anniversary Concert Celebration RR13074
Bob Mould RR11968
Bob Wills: The Country Music Hall Of Fame RR12940
Bobbie Cryner RR10923
Bobby RR10670, RR10671
Bobby Byrd Got Soul RR10714
The Bocephus Box: The Hand Williams Jr. Collection 1979-1992 RR12929
Boces RR11880a
Body Count RR11466
Body Mind Soul RR11241
The Bodyguard RR13075
The Body-Hat Syndrome RR11007
Bogle RR13076
Boiling Point RR13077
Bone Machine RR12855
Boom Boom RR11429
Boombastic RR12471
Booth And The Bad Angel RR10487, RR10631
The Bootleg Series: Volumes 1-3 RR11045
Borderlands RR13078, RR13079
Born Dead RR10621
Born To Be Burned RR11293
Born To Choose RR13080
Born To Quit RR12557
Bossa Nova Brasil RR13081, RR13082
Bosnia Breakdown RR11581
Boss Hog RR10634
Boss Man RR12341
Both Sides RR10847
Bow Down RR12904
Bowie: The Singles 1969 To 1993 RR10641
Box RR11318
Box Of Visions RR12416
Box Set RR11905
Boys For Pele RR10424
Boyz In The Hood RR13083
BR5-49 RR10648
The Bradley Barn Sessions RR11558
Brand New Friend (song) RR12339
Braver Newer World RR11248
Break Like The Wind RR12602
Break The Chain RR12293
Breaking Silence RR11461
Breathe RR11895
The Breeders' Last Splash RR10657
The Brian Setzer Orchestra RR12463
Bricks Are Heavy RR11657
Bright Red RR10432
The Brill Building Sound RR13084
Bring It On Home RR13085
Bring Me The Head Of Jerry Garcia (single) RR11486
Bringing Down The Horse RR12863
British Beat Before The Beatles RR13086
Broadway The Hard Way RR13013
Broken RR12039
Broken Arrow RR10900, RR12992
The Brooklyn Side RR10636
Brother Sister RR10652
Brother With Two Tongues RR11872
Brown Sugar RR10952
Brutal Youth RR10880
Bubble And Scrape RR12453
The Buck Owens Collection RR12093
The Buddah Box RR13087
Buddy Guy & Junior Wells Play The Blues RR11332, RR12897
The Buddy Holly Collection RR11425
Buhloone Mind State RR10966
Bulk RR11710
The Buried Life RR12491
Burning Questions RR12107
Business Never Personal RR11086
Butter RR10708

C

Caged-Uncaged RR13088
Cajun Boogie RR11341
Cajun Roots RR12573
Call The Doctor RR12532
Can You Hear A Motion? RR11061
Candyland RR11847
Cannibalism 1 RR10726
Can't Hardly Wait (song) RR12329
Can't Keep It To Myself RR12934
The Capitol Years RR10836
Captain My Captain RR12707
Car Button Cloth RR11681
Career Moves RR12849
Carnival Boy RR12616
Carry The Day RR12735
The Casablanca Records Story RR13089
Cats And Dogs RR12400
CB4 RR13090
Chains (song) RR10455
A Chance Operation RR13091
Changes RR12928
Chant RR10545
Chaos A.D. RR12459
Chaos And Disorder RR12228
The Chapel Session RR11116
Charcoal Lane RR12356, RR12357
The Chase RR10665
Check Your Head RR10518
Chess Blues RR13092
Chet Atkins: The RCA Years RR10466
Chicago Revisited: Live At Joe Segal's Jazz Showcase RR11502
Chicago, New York, Paris RR11299
Chic-ism RR10780
Chief Boot Knocka RR12518
China Gate RR10925
The Chiswick Story RR13093
Chocolate And Cheese RR12886
Chocolate Synthesizer RR10633
Chorus RR11153
Christmas RR10831
A Christmas Gift For You RR13094
Christmas In The City RR13095
Christmas Party With Eddie G. RR11281
Christmas Time RR12619
Christopher Idylls RR12035
The Chronic RR11028, RR11029, RR11030
Chronicles RR12604
The Church Within RR12065
Circulado RR12830, RR12831
Circular Temple RR12490
Circus RR11642, RR11643
Citi Movement RR11796
Cities Of The Heart RR10687
Citizen RR12633
City Of Hysteria RR12249
Civilization Phaze III RR13014
Clash On Broadway RR10813
Clasicos De La Provincia RR12842
Claws Of The Cat RR12740
Clear RR10623
Closer To God RR12712
Clouds Over Eden RR10509
Clouds Taste Metallic RR11144
The Cobra Records Story: Chicago Rock And Blues 1956-1958 RR13096
Coincidence And Likely Stories RR12423
Col. Bruce Hampton And The Aquarium Rescue Unit RR11351a
Cold Rain And Snow (single) RR11132
Colin James And The Little Big Band RR11505
The Collected Recordings, '60s to '90s RR12781
The Collection RR12298
A Collection Of Her Best Recordings RR11113
Collective Soul RR10843
Color And Light RR13097
Color Me Impressed (song) RR12330
Colossal Head RR11722
Colour Of Your Dreams RR11611b
Columbia RR10557
The Columbia Years 1943-1952 RR12512
Columbus Lied RR12469
Come RR12229
Come Find Yourself RR11194
Come On Come On RR10737
Come On Feel The Lemonheads RR11682

Come Out And Play RR13098
Come Together RR13099
Come Together: Motown Sings The Beatles RR13100
The Coming RR10707
Coming Up For Air RR11801
The Commitments RR13101
Common Threads RR13102
Communication RR12953
Compact Disc EP Collection RR10526
The Company I Keep RR11117
Company Of Strangers RR10480
The Complete Billie Holiday On Verve 1945-1959 RR11424
The Complete Blind Willie Johnson RR11548
Complete Blue Note And Roost Recordings RR12210
The Complete Blue Note Recordings Of Art Blakely's 1960 Jazz Messengers RR10587
The Complete Blue Note Recordings RR11927
The Complete Bud Powell RR12211
The Complete Bukka White RR12909
The Complete Candid Otis Spann-Lightnin' Hopkins Sessions RR11436, RR12591
The Complete Columbia Studio Recordings RR10961, RR11105
Complete Communion RR10773
The Complete Imperial Recordings RR10844
The Complete Imperial Recordings, 1950-1954 RR12861
The Complete Plantation Recordings RR12876
The Complete Prestige-Bluesville Recordings RR11437
The Complete Prestige Recordings RR12383
The Complete Riverside Recordings RR11938
The Complete Serge Chaloff Sessions RR10762
The Complete Solid State Recordings Of The Thad Jones - Mel Lewis Big Band RR11569, RR11693
The Complete Stax-Volt Singles Vol 2: 1968-1971 RR13103
The Complete Stax-Volt Soul Singles, Vol. III 1972-1975 RR13104
The Complete Studio Recordings RR11676
Computer Style RR11618
The Concert For The Rock & Roll Hall Of Fame RR13105
Congratulations I'm Sorry RR11251
Conmemorativo RR13106
Constipated Monkey RR11651
Continental Drifters RR10863
Contrary Motion RR11258
Convergence RR10539, RR10838
Conversation On A Barstool (song) RR12391
Conversation Peace RR12958
Conversin' With The Elders RR10748
The Conway Twitty Collection RR12785
Cookin' At The Continental RR10814
Cool Hand Loc RR12746
Copacetic RR12828
Copper Blue RR12666
Copperopolis RR11285
Core RR12645
Cosmic Kurushi Monsters RR13107
Cosmic Tones For Mental Therapy RR12259
Country Kickers RR13108
Country Music Made Me Do It RR11393
Court And Spark RR11914
Cover Girl RR10853
Coverdale-Page RR10888, RR12096
Cowabunga! RR13109
Cowboy Nation RR12862
Cowboys To Girls RR11481
Cowgirl's Prayer RR11362
Cracked Rear View RR11432, RR11433
Crappin' You Negative RR11303
Crash RR11809
Crazy Diamond RR10510
Crazy Legs RR10538, RR10561
Creep City RR12440
The Criminal Under My Own Hat RR10698
Crooked Rain, Crooked Rain RR12126
Crosby, Stills & Nash RR10916
The Cross Of Changes RR11079
Crossroads 2 RR10799
The Crow RR13110
Cry Tomorrow RR12314
Cryin', Lovin', Leavin' RR10681
The Crying Tree RR10605
Cryptology RR12866
Cuba RR12808, RR12809
Cuba: Fully Charged RR13111, RR13112
Cuban Classics Vol. 3: Diablo al Infierno RR13113
Cuban Counterpoint: A History Of The Son Montuno RR13114
Cuban Gold RR13115
The Cult RR10926
Cult Classic RR10609
Cup Of Loneliness RR11559
Cure For Pain RR11947
The Curse Of The Mekons RR11861
The Curtain Hits The Cast RR11745
Cut You RR11444
CX-9 (song) RR10435
Cyberpunk RR11470
Cyborgs Revisted RR12510

D

D Generation RR10944
Da Bomb RR11644
Da Lama Ao Caos RR10784
Daily Operation RR11211
Daisychain Reaction RR12208
Damn Right, I've Got The Blues RR11333, RR11334
Dance Club Country RR13116
Dance, Dance, Dance RR10781
Dance Hall At Louse Point RR11367, RR12105
Dance Naked RR11864, RR11865
Dance To The Music RR12538
Dancehall Reggaespanol RR13117
Danger In The Past RR11169
Dangerhouse, Volume One RR12405
Dangerous RR11496
Dangerous Minds RR13118
Danko-Fjeld-Andersen RR10430, RR10953, RR11142
Danzig RR10954
Danzig III: How The Gods Kill RR10955
Dare Iz A Darkside RR12312
Dark Side Of The Moon RR12173
Dark Star RR12069
Datapanik In The Year Zero RR12145
A Date With The Smithereens RR12556
David Byrne RR10715
Day By Day RR11877
Day Dreaming At Midnight RR12517
A Day In The Life (song) RR11405
Days Like This RR11950
Dazzling Display RR12969
Dead Cities RR11202
Dead End Kidz Doin' Lifetime Bidz RR12990
Dead Men Don't Smoke Marijuana RR12376
Dead Men Walking RR13119
Dead Rekoning RR11582
Dead Serious RR10960
Deadsexy RR12432
Death Certificate RR11463
Death Travels West (EP) RR11073
Debravation RR11366
Debut RR11312
Deconstruction RR10972
Deep Blues RR13120
Deep River RR11140, RR11171
Deep Six RR13121
Deeper Water RR11594
Def Jam 10th Year Anniversary RR13122
Definitely Maybe RR12061
The Definitive Blind Willie McTell RR11849
Delicious RR10719
Delta Dreamland RR10413
Democratie RR11668, RR11912
Design Of A Decade RR11493
Desire For Agony RR13032
Destination: Love RR11783
Destination Universe RR11807
Destiny's Gate RR11404
Destroy All Monsters 1974-1976 RR10989
Devil Hopping RR11480
The Devil Lied To Me RR11935
Devo Live: The Mongoloid Years RR10991
Diamonds And Pearls RR12230, RR12231
Diamonds By The Yard RR11978
The Diary RR12433
Diary Of A Mod Housewife RR12352
Dick RR11253
Die Laughing RR11459
Different Class RR12250
A Different Story RR10969
Dig RR11460
Diggin' In The Crates RR13123
Dilate RR11001
Dim Stars RR11008
Din Of Ecstasy RR12915
Dirt RR10409
Dirty RR12568
Dirty Three RR11014
Dirty Water RR12621
Dis Is Da Drum RR11357
Disraeli Gears RR10905, RR10906
Dissolve RR11489
Ditch Diggin' RR12587
Diva RR11684
The Divine Comedy RR11904
Divine Intervention RR12530
The Division Bell RR12174
DiY RR13124
Dizzy's Diamonds: Best Of The Verve Years RR11245
Djangology RR12320
DJ's Front Porch RR11511
Do It RR11308
Do Right Man RR12142
Do You Wanna Ride RR11446
Dog Man Star RR11715
Dogg Food RR11020
Doggystyle RR12563
The Don Killuminati RR11782
Dondestan RR12965
The Donna Summer Anthology RR12670
Don't Call Me Buckwheat RR11520, RR11521
Don't Get Weird On Me, Babe RR10835
Don't Sweat The Technique RR11089
Don't Try This At Home RR10649
The Doo Wop Box RR13125
Doo-Bop RR10962
Dookie RR11294
Doppelganger RR10936
Doubt RR11526
Doughboy Hollow RR10999
A Dove RR12367
Down RR11528
Down By The Old Mainstream RR11272

Down Every Road RR11346
Down On The Upside RR12583, RR12584
Down Out Law RR11628
Down With The King RR12408, RR12409
The Downward Road RR12251
The Downward Spiral RR12040, RR12041
Drainland RR11254
Dread In A Babylon RR12789
Dreaded Brown Recluse RR11223
Dreadlocks Dread RR10562
Dream Harder RR12873
Dream Your Life Away RR12590
Dreaming Of You RR12456
Dreamland RR10473
Dreams And Saturday Nights RR12961
Dreams Fly Away RR12729
Drenched RR11909
Drift RR10990
Driftin' Blues RR10672
Drop The Line RR11687
The Dropouts RR11037
Droppin' Soulful H2O On The Fiber RR11321
The Drowners (single) RR12662
Drums Are Dangerous RR11038
Drunk With Passion RR11271
Dry RR12180
Duende: The Passion And Dazzling Virtuosity Of Flamenco RR13126
Duets RR11543, RR12513
Dummy RR12206
Duncan Sheik RR12483
Duran Duran RR11041, RR11042
Dusk RR12721
Dusk At Cubist Castle RR12074
Dust RR12446, RR12447, RR12448
Dust To Dust RR10949, RR12034
Dwight Live RR12985
Dynamite Monster Boogie Concert RR12283
Dysfunctional RR11021

E

E. 1999 Eternal RR10626
The Early Years RR12385
The Early Years: The Complete Liberty Recordings Plus More RR12009
Earth And Sun And Moon RR11896, RR11897
The East Side Sound RR13127
East Side Story RR11605
East-West Live RR10709
The Easter Tapes RR11274
Eats Away The Night RR11355
Echoes 1975-1985 RR12162
Efil4zaggin RR12058
Egyptian Candy RR11580
Egyptian Rai RR12291
Eighteen Inches Of Rain RR12788
The Eighty Seven Years Of Doc Cheatham RR10772
Einstein On The Beach RR11259
El Moodio RR11067
El Nervio Del Volcan RR10718
Elastica RR11065
Electric Pen (single) RR11911
The Electric Spanking Of War Babies RR11195
Electriclarryland RR10711
Element Of Light RR11409
Elemental RR12708
Eleven: Eleven RR10855
Elvis From Nashville To Memphis RR12216
Emotion RR12104
Emotions RR10733
Emperors Of Soul RR12713
Encomium RR13128
The End Of Silence RR12380
End Of The Century RR11311, RR11485
Endless Party RR12027
An English Ladymass RR10439
Enta Da Stage RR10573
Enter The Wu-Tang RR12964
Eponymous RR10651
Equal Rights RR12754
Eric Clapton RR10800
Erotica RR11774
The Essential Collection RR12695
The Essential Fripp And Eno RR11080, RR11182
Essential Jason And The Scorchers Volume One: Are You Ready For The Country RR11514
The Essential Johnny Cash RR10752
The Essential King Crimson: Frame By Frame RR11613
Essential Steve Earle RR11053
Etched In Swing RR12223
Eternal Chant RR13129
The Eternal Dance RR11056
Even Cowgirls Get The Blues RR11665
Eventually RR12899a
Everclear RR10421
Every Day Is Saturday (EP) RR11119
Every Little Word RR11601
Everybody Else Is Doing It, So Why Can't We? RR10894
Everybody's Free RR12403
Everything I Long For RR11378
Everything Is Wrong RR11921, RR11922
Everything Must Go RR11785
Evil Empire RR12281, RR12282
Evita RR13130
Evolution RR10392
Example RR11162
Excerpts From A Love Circus RR11229
Exile In Guyville RR12157, RR12158
Exit The Dragon RR12802, RR12803
Expecting To Fly RR10616
Experience RR10977
Experimental Jet Set, Trash And No Star RR12569
Exposed RR12005
Eyes Open RR12002

F

The Fabulous Charlie Rich RR12342
Facts Of Life RR12954
Fairweather Johnson RR11434, RR11435
The Fall Of Us All RR12739
Falling Forward RR11165
Falling From Grace RR13131
Falling Man RR10892, RR11062
Family Groove RR12015
Fantastic Frank Strozier: Plus RR11704, RR12654
Far Beyond Driven RR12102
Far East Suite RR11068
Far From Home RR12759
Far Out RR12696
Fastbacks...And His Orchestra RR11120
Fat City RR10854
Fate Of Nations RR12185
Faust RR12031
Fear Of A Black Planet RR12242
Fear Of Women RR12252
Fear: The Record RR11128
Feels Like Home RR12387
Feels Like Rain RR11335
Fegmania! RR11410
Fever RR10567
Fever For Da Flavor RR11340
Few And Far Between RR12714
Fiesta Total RR10475
50 Coastin' Hits RR10828
Fifty Years Of Sunshine RR13132
File Under Easy Listening RR12667, RR12668
Fillmore East RR13015
Filth Pig RR11907
Filthy Lucre Live RR12466
Fina Estampa RR12832
Finally RR11916, RR12120
Find A Door RR11036, RR12516
Find My Way Home RR11583
Fine Malt Lyrics RR11443
The Finer Things RR12949
The Fire Inside RR12455
Fire Of The Amazones RR13133
The Fire-Fury Records Story RR13134
First Band On The Moon RR10732
The First Day RR11183, RR12693
First Program In Standard Time RR12026
Five Live Yardbirds RR12976
5 String Serenade (song) RR11677, RR11734
Five Ways Of Disappearing RR12550
Flaco Jimenez RR11535
Flamejob RR10893
Flatpicking Guitar Festival RR13135
Floored Genius 2 RR10871
Flow RR12140
Fluorescent RR12970
(Fly) On (The Wall) (song) RR11529
Flyer RR11300
Folk Singer RR12877
Folk Songs Of The Hills RR12761
Follow For Now RR11158
Folon...The Past RR11591
Foo Fighters RR11159, RR11160
Foolish RR12675
For Pleasure RR12077
For The Beauty Of Wynona RR11667
For The Cool In You RR10477
For Unlawful Carnal Knowledge RR12813
Forbidden RR10575
Force Of nature RR12706
Forever Changes RR11736
Forever Diana RR12392
Forrest Gump RR13136
Forro, Etc. RR13137
44th Street RR12786
41 RR12690
Foula RR11170
Founder Of The Delta Blues: 1929-34 RR12123
Four RR10614
4 Aces RR12719
Four Chords And Several Years Ago RR11689
461 Ocean Boulevard RR10800a
Four-Calendar Cafe RR10832
14 Shots To The Dome RR11654
14 Songs RR12900, RR12901
4-Track Demos RR12179, RR12180a
Frampton Comes Alive II RR11173
Frank Black RR10571a
Frank Zappa Meets The Mothers Of Prevention RR13016
Freak City Soundtrack RR11808
Freak Out! RR13017
Freedom Of Choice RR13138
Free-For-All RR12143
The Freedom Sessions RR11842
Fresh Cream RR10907, RR10908
Friction, Baby RR10550
Friday RR13139
Friday Night Is Killing Me RR10515
Friend Of Mine RR10674, RR11960
Friends In Danger RR11775
Frogstomp RR12504
From Despair To Where (song) RR11786
From Hell To Paradise RR11813
From Philly With Love RR13140

From The Bush RR13141
From The Cradle RR10801, RR10802
From The Muddy Banks Of The Wishkah RR12042, RR12043
From The Soul RR11731
From The Top RR10738
The Fugs First Album RR11193
Full Moon, Dirty Hearts RR11482
Full Time Love RR12139
Fumbling Towards Ecstasy RR11843
Fun RR11553
Fun Trick Noisemaker RR10448
Funk Essentials RR13142
Funkcronomicon RR10472
Funkdafied RR10948
Funkify Your Life RR11892
Funky Divas RR11076, RR11077
Funky Good Time RR11518
The Funky Headhunter RR11349
Funky Kingston RR12751
Funky Stuff RR13143
Further RR11154
Fusion RR10438, RR10593, RR11256, RR12682
The Future RR10833
Future Profits RR10604
Fuzzy RR11286
Fuzzy Little Piece Of The World RR12197
Fuzzy Logic RR12674

G

G. Love And Special Sauce RR11203, RR12593
Galaxie 500 RR11210
Gangsta's Paradise RR10867
Garage Orchestra RR10549
Garbage RR11214
Garvey's Ghost RR10699
Gary's Greatest RR12637
Gash RR11155
A Gazelle (song) RR11769
Geek The Girl RR11230
Gentlemen RR10398
Germs (Tribute) RR13144
Get A Grip RR10395
Get Happy!! RR10881
Get In Where Fit In RR12749
Get It While You Can RR12703
Ghetto Gothic RR12814
The Ghost Of Tom Joad RR12610
Girl Of Your Dreams RR10924
Girl On Fire (song) RR11677a, RR11737
Girlfriend RR12689
Give It Up To Love RR11835
Global Celebration RR13145
A Glorious Lethal Euphoria RR11885
The Glory Of Gershwin RR13146
Glory Road: 1968 To 1972 RR10993
Glum RR11239
Go Fer Yer Funk RR10819
Go Grace Go (song) RR11727
Go In The Dark RR13147
Go Slow Down RR10620
Go To The Sugar Alter RR10970
Go Together RR10592, RR12683
God Of Love RR10478
Gods And Monsters RR11747
Goin' Back To New Orleans RR11031
Goin' To California RR12070
Going Back Home RR10496
Going Blank Again RR12349
Gold RR10383
The Gold Experience RR12232, RR12233
Go-Man-Go RR13148, RR13149
Gone RR12986
Gone Again RR12551, RR12552, RR12553
Good As I Been To You RR11046
Good God's Urge RR12204
A Good Likeness RR10404
Good News From The Next World RR12508
Good Stuff RR10474
Good Vibrations RR10516
Goodbye RR11636
Gorgeous George RR10846
The Gospel Sound RR13150
Gotta Let This Hen Out! RR11411
Gov't Mule RR11282
Grace RR10694
Grand Opening RR11222
Grand Slam! RR13151
Grand Slam Baby (single) RR12203
The Grand Tour RR12014a
Grandma's Ghost RR10663
Grandpaw Would RR11680
Grave Dancers Union RR12574, RR12575
Gravity RR11093
Gravity's Rainbow RR10544
Gravy Deco RR11412
Gray Folded RR12088, RR12089
The Gray Race RR10482
Grayfolded RR11289
Great American Songwriters RR13153
The Great Annihilation RR12685
Great Days RR12236
The Great Deceiver RR11614
Great Divide RR12457
The Great Escape RR10617
Great Expectations RR10453
The Great Gospel Men RR13154
The Great Gospel Women RR13155
The Great Indoors RR10914
Great Move! RR11970
The Great 1955 Shrine Concert RR13152
The Great Puzzle RR12481
The Great Southern Trendkill RR12103
Greatest Hits RR10782, RR12611
The Greatest Hits 1966-1992 RR10994
Greatest Hits, Vol. III RR11047
The Greatest Living Englishman RR12030, RR12119
Greatest Misses RR12243
Green Mind RR11009
Greetings From The Gutter RR12636
Grey Ghost RR11298
Gringo Honeymoon RR11589, RR11590
Groovy Decay RR11413
Groovy Decoy RR11414
Group Portrait RR10783
Growin' Up Too Fast RR13156
Grown Man RR12850
Grown Up Wrong RR12296
GS I Love You RR13157
A Guide Through The Chaos RR11585
Guit With It RR10679
Guitar Paradise Of East Africa RR13158
The Guitar Wizard RR12309
Guitarrorists RR13159
Gutterball RR11330

H

Hallucination Engine RR11806
Hand On The Torch RR12806
Handle Like Eggs RR13160
Hang On To A Dream RR11359
Hangin' On By A Thread RR12720
Happiness RR11231
The Happy Club RR11224
Happy Days RR10756
Happy Days, Sweetheart RR11101
Happy Hour RR11607
Harbor Lights RR11440
Hard Groovin' RR11164
Hard Road RR12775
The Hard Stuff RR11637
Hard To Earn RR11212, RR11213
Hard Workin' Man RR10664
The Harder They Come RR13161
Harlem Blues RR12430
Harlem Renaissance RR10745
Harmacy RR12454
Harmonica Classics RR13162
Harvest Moon RR12993
Hat Full Of Stars RR11673
Hater RR11368
Haunted Heart RR11600
Havana, 3 A.M. RR12212
Have A Little Faith RR11184
Head Over Heals RR10385
Headquarters RR11929
Healing Bones RR12482
Healing Hands Of Time RR12010
Heart Of The Congos RR10860
Heartaches And Harmonies RR11107
Heartbeat RR12424
Hearts In Armor RR12977, RR12978
Heartsongs RR12115
Heartwork RR10731
Heaven And Hull RR12386
Heavy Rhyme Experience: Vol. 1 RR10653
Hecho En Puerto Rico RR10848
Hell Freezes Over RR11051, RR11052
Help Yourself RR11683
Henry's Dream RR10484, RR10757
Here RR11699
Here Comes Success RR10503
Here I Come And Other Hits RR11115
Here To Save You All RR10790
Hey Babe RR11371, RR11372
Hey Man...Smell My Finger RR10820
Hey Zeus! RR12972
Heyday 1979-83 RR11074
Hi Times: The Hi Records R&B Years RR13163
Hideout RR10441
High As A Kite RR12618
High Time RR11827
High-Tech Redneck RR11560
Highway Trance RR11660
Hill Country Rain RR12859
Hillbilly Voodoo RR12417, RR12913
Hip Hop Greats: Classic Raps RR13164, RR13165
Hips And Makers RR11399
The Hips Of Tradition RR13031
Historic Moments Vol. 1 RR10911
History RR11497, RR11498, RR12851, RR12852
The History Of Art Blakely And The Jazz Messengers RR10588
The History Of Our Future RR10574
The History Of Space Age Pop RR13166
Hit The Highway RR12239
Hits Style RR11619
The Hits: Volume 1 & II RR12234
Hitsville USA: The Motown Singles Collection 1959-1971 RR13167
Hitsville U.S.A., Volume II RR13168
Hold Me, Thrill Me, Kiss Me, Kill Me (song) RR12791
Holiday For Soul Dance RR12260, RR12261
Hollywood Town Hall RR11515
Holy Smoke RR11979
The Holy Sound Of American Pipe RR12839
Home RR10591, RR12592
Home Again RR12023
Home Invasion RR11467, RR11468
Homebrew RR10776
The Honeymoon Is Over RR10922
Honey's Dead RR11524
Honky Tonk Angels RR11754, RR12116, RR12966

Honky Tonk Girl RR11755
Hootie Mack RR10540
Hope RR12101
Hope You Like Our New Direction RR11579
Horse Stories RR11015
Horsebreaker Star RR11846
Horses In The Mine RR10481
Hot Boxing RR11779
Hot, Cool & Vicious RR12426
The Hot Ones! RR12622
Hot Rats RR13018, RR13019
House Of GVSB RR11255
Hovercraft (EP) RR11445
How Long Has This Been Going On RR11951
How To Play Blues Guitar RR11307
Howlin Mercy RR10724
Howlin' Wolf RR11448
Howls, Raps And Roars RR13169
The Hum Of D.A.I.S.Y. RR10950
Human Behaviour (song) RR11313
Human Touch RR12612, RR12613
Human Wheels RR11866, RR11867
The Humbler RR11217, RR11277
Humroot RR12487
A Hundred Lovers RR12743
Hundred Year Hall RR11290
Hungry For Stink RR11658
Hunky Dory RR10642
The Hurra RR11455
Hurricane Season RR12418
Hydraulic RR12299
Hydrogen Jukebox RR11260
Hymns To The Silence RR11952
Hypocrisy Is The Greatest Luxury RR11017

I

I Am Right (single) RR10997
I Am The Cosmos RR10541
I Can Hear The Ants Dancin' RR10661, RR12606
I Can't Make you Love Me (song) RR11040
I Care Because You Do RR10446
I Don't Care (song) RR12868
I Feel Alright RR11054
I Just Wasn't Made For These Times RR12942
I Know Who Holds Tomorrow RR10891, RR11638
I Love Everybody RR11742
I Love Mekons RR11862
I May Be Hungry But I Sure Ain't Weird RR10730
I Often Dream Of Trains RR11415
I Remember You RR11841
I Say, I Say, I Say RR11088
I Should Coco RR12678, RR12679
I Spent A Week There The Other Night RR12779
I Want To Hold Your Hand (song) RR10527
I Was Warned RR10898
I Will Dare (song) RR12331
I Wish I Was A Lesbian (song) RR12853
If I Ever Fall In Love RR12472
If I Were A Carpenter RR13170
If I'm Lucky RR12398, RR12511
II RR10647, RR11081, RR12214
I'll Be You (song) RR12332
Ill Communication RR10519
I'll Treat You Right RR10815
Illadelph Halflife RR12390
Illmatic RR11989
Illuminations RR13171
I'm A Texan RR12638
I'm Alive RR10683, RR10684
I'm Never Gonna Die Again RR12724
I'm Your Fan RR13172
Imagination RR11858
Imperial Drag RR11471
The Impossible Bird RR11746
Impressions Of Copenhagen RR10627
In A Word Or 2 RR11741
In Concert RR11453, RR11611c
In My Lifetime RR10995
In My Time RR11984
In On The Kill Taker RR11187, RR11188
In Pieces RR10666
In Search Of Manny RR11750
In Sides RR12084
In The Beginning RR11027, RR12823
In The Flesh! RR12525
In The Land Of The Tenor RR12497
In The Presence Of Greatness RR12834
In The Red RR11384, RR12375
In The Running RR11562
In The Storm RR10971
In Their Own Words: Volume One RR13173
In Thrall RR10469
In Utero RR12044, RR12045
Incesticide RR12046
Incident At Cima RR12435
Independence RR11748
Independent Worm Saloon RR10712
The Infamous RR11920
Infamous Angel RR10982
Infernal Love RR12723
Infidels RR11478
Infinity Within RR10973
Infrared Roses RR11291
Ingenue RR11666
Inner Child RR12477
Inside RR11961
Insomniac RR11295, RR11296
Internal Journal, Vol II RR13174
International Times RR12760
Interstate RR12141
Interstellar Low Ways RR12262
Into Dust (song) RR11822
Into The Twangy-First Century RR12406
Introducing Gorky's Zygotic Mynci RR11280
An Irish Evening RR10786
Ironic (song) RR11945
Ironman RR11238
Is It...Man Or Astro-Man? RR11784
Is The Spanner She Want RR12202
Isabel Bishop E.P. RR12798
The Isle Of View RR12218, RR12219
Iso RR11709
Istanbul 1925 RR13175
It Came From Memphis RR13176
It Takes A Nation Of Millions To Hold Us Back RR12244, RR12245
It Takes A Thief RR10868
It Was Written RR11990, RR11991, RR11992
It Won't Be The Last RR10941
It's A Mad, Mad, Mad, Mad Professor RR11767
It's A Natural Thing RR11161
It's About Time RR12691, RR12692
It's Artastic RR12658
It's Five O'Clock Somewhere RR12527, RR12528, RR12560, RR12561
It's Great When You're Straight...Yeah RR10572
It's Hard To Believe It RR13177
It's Heavy In Here RR11812
It's Only Time RR10935
Izzy Stradlin And The Ju Ju Hounds RR11572, RR12652

J

J. Beez Wit The Remedy RR11577
Jack Salmon And Derby Sauce RR11899
Jagged Little Pill RR11946
James Williams Meets The Saxophone Masters RR10839, RR11389, RR12171, RR12932
Jamu Dreaming RR12358
Janet RR11494, RR11495
Janis RR11570
Jar Of Flies RR10410
Jarred Up RR11855
Jazz At The Maintenance Shop RR11104
Jazz In Silhouette RR12263, RR12264
Jazzmatazz RR11327, RR11328, RR11329
JazzSpeak RR13178
JC On The Set RR10749
Jealous One's Envy RR11123
Jefferson Airplane Loves You RR11519
Jehovahkill RR10872
Jenn Vix RR12843
Jenny Come Back (song) RR10959
Jericho RR10501, RR10502
Jerry Lee Lewis RR11690
Jesus Christ Superstar: A Resurrection RR13179
Jesus Wept RR12190
The Jewel-Paula Records Story: The Blues, Rhythm And Blues And Soul Recordings RR13180
The Jimi Hendrix Experience Box Set RR11395
Jimmywine Majestic RR12306
Jive At Five RR11917, RR12718
Jive Soweto: The Indestructible Beat Of Soweto Vol. 4 RR13181
Joe's Garage RR13020
A John Coltrane Retrospective: The Impulse Years RR10850
A John Prine Christmas RR12237
Johnny Damas And Me RR12774
The Jon Spencer Blues Explosion RR12596
Joshua Judges Ruth RR11743
Journeyman RR10803
Joy And Blues RR11793, RR11873
Joyas de la Musica Cubana, Vol. 1 RR13182
Jubilation RR11426
The Judds Collection 1983-1990 RR11576
Judgment! RR11402
Judgment Night RR13183
Juice RR13184
Juiced Up (song) RR11180
The Juliet Letters RR10662, RR10882
Jump Blues Classics RR13185
Just Another Band From East L.A. RR11723
Just Can't Get Enough RR13186
Just For A Day RR12537
Just For The Record RR12653
Just For You RR12908
Just Fred RR12436
Just Like A Devil RR12734
Just One Night RR10804
Just Stompin' RR11167, RR12991
Just What I Needed RR10741
Just What It's Like (song) RR10978
Just Woke Up RR10590

K

K RR11650
Kaddish RR12755
Kalfou Danjere RR10637
Kamakiriad RR11110
Kansas RR11584
Karen Carpenter RR10736
Keb' Mo' RR11587
Keep It Comin' RR12686
Keep The Faith RR10624
Kelly Willis RR12939
Kenn Kweder RR11653
Kick Out The Jams RR11828
Kickin' It Up RR11937
Kiko RR11724

Kill The Musicians RR12449
Killer Up! RR12799
Kimble (E.P.) RR11114
Kind Hearted Woman RR12493
Kindness Of The World RR11397
King For A Day, Fool For A Lifetime RR11112
King Of California RR10420
King Of Hearts RR12083
The King Of Rock 'N' Roll: The Complete '50's Masters RR12217
King Of The Blues RR11611a
King Of The Delta Blues: The Music Of Charlie Patton RR12124
King Of The Honky-Tonk RR12172
King Of The Slide Guitar RR11506
King Tubby Meets The Rockers Uptown RR12095
Kingdom Come RR11220, RR11982, RR12109
King's X RR11625
Kiss My Ass RR13187
Kissingsohard RR11019
Klassic Kitchener RR11720
Kojak Variety RR10883
Koksofen RR11800
KRS-One RR11648

L

Laid RR11503
Lamprey RR10551
Last Day On Earth RR10721, RR12014
Last Of The Independents RR12220, RR12221
The Last Rebel RR11757
Last Sessions RR12370
Last Splash RR10658, RR10659
The Last Temptation RR10869
Lather RR13021
Latin Playboys RR11669
Law Of The Jungle RR13188
Layla RR10986
Lead Me Not RR12912
Learning To Flinch RR13033
Left Of The Dial (song) RR12333
The Legend And The Legacy RR12125
Lemuria-Seascape RR10512
Lenny Bruce Originals: Volume 1 RR10689
Lenny Bruce Originals: Volume 2 RR10690
Let 'Em Roll RR12122
Let Go RR10669
Let Love In RR10485, RR10758
Let No One Deceive You: Songs Of Bertolt Brecht RR10456, RR12815
Let The Picture Paint Itself RR10920
Let Your Dim Light Shine RR12576, RR12577
Lethal Injection RR11464
Let's RR11146
Let's Go Get Stoned RR10777
Letter To Laredo RR11070
Levelling The Land RR11686
Liberations RR10580
Libete RR10638
Life RR12509, RR12539
A Life Full Of Farewells RR10445
Life Is Messy RR10921
A Life With Brian RR11152
Life's A Take RR11592, RR11918
Life's Too Short RR10912
Limbo RR12737
The Lion King RR13189
Liquid Courage RR11697
Liquid Swords RR11228, RR11338
Listen To The Band RR11930
A Little Ain't Enough RR12395
Little Earthquakes RR10425
Little Love Letters RR10746
Little Mascara (song) RR12334
Little Village RR11703
Live RR12705
Live! RR12193
Live At CBGB's RR13190
Live At Leeds RR12917, RR12918
Live At Sin-e RR10695
Live At The BBC RR10528, RR11148
Live At The Continental Club RR12570
Live At The Fillmore RR10987
Live At The Hollywood Palladium, December 15, 1988 RR12346, RR12974
Live At The Isle Of Wight Festival 1970 RR12919
Live Au Zenith RR10602
Live From The Fall RR10615
Live In Concert RR11517
Live In Japan With Eric Clapton And Band RR11365
Live In Seattle RR10851
Live Jam RR11501
Live Light RR12350
Live—May 11, 1968 RR11339
Live MCMXCIII RR12836
A Live One RR12167, RR12168
Live Shit: Binge And Purge RR11887
Live Shots RR11071
Live—The Funkadelic Collection RR10821, RR11196, RR12111
Live Through This RR11421, RR11422
The Live Totem Pole EP RR11135
Live Wire RR11797, RR12318
Live Your Life Be Free RR10735
Livin' Proof RR11309
The Living End RR11458
Living In The Danger Zone RR12451
Living Proof: The MGM Recordings 1963-1975 RR12930
Living With The Law RR12916
LL77 RR11700
Llego La India RR11476
Load RR11888, RR11889, RR11890
Lock Stock & Double-Barrel (EP) RR10875
Loco Gringo's Lament RR11449
Logical Progression RR10696
Lonely Just Like Me RR10404a
Long About That Time RR10980
The Long Black Veil RR10787
The Long Hot Summer—Jamaican Ska 1963 RR10401, RR12086
Long Line RR12952
Longing In Theirs Hearts RR12285
Look No Further RR12404
Lookin' Down The Backtracks, 1963-1969 RR12752
Lookin' For A Love Again RR12955
Looking East RR10685
Looking For A Connection RR10810
Looking In The Shadows RR12284
Loose RR12937
Lord Of Nothing Pt. 1 (song) RR11728
Lord Of The Harvest RR13035
Lose Control RR12502
Lost Masters RR12617
Lost Together RR10613
Loud Lose And Savage RR10412, RR10461
Louisiana Love Call RR11976
Love And Danger RR11072
Love And Luck RR12655
Love Deluxe RR12420, RR12421
Love Is All Around (song) RR11532
Love Power Peace: Live At The Olympia, Paris, 1971 RR10675
Love Songs For The Hearing Impaired RR10493
Love Spit Love RR11740
Love Story RR11738
Love, Pussycats And Carwrecks RR11200
Loveless RR11985
Low Profile RR11168
Loyola (song) RR10998
Luck Of The Draw RR12286
Lucky Thirteen RR12994
Lucky Town RR12614, RR12615
Lucy RR10729
Lush Life RR11390
Lynyrd Skynyrd RR11758
Lyte As A Rock RR11761

M

Machito And His Afro-Cubans Cubop City RR11766
Mack Daddy RR12519, RR12520, RR12521
Made In England RR11544
Made In Heaven RR12253
Magia Antillana RR11942
Magic And Loss RR12315, RR12316
Magic Dirt RR11776
Magic Sam 1957-1966: West Side Guitar RR11777
Magic Touch RR11778
Main Offender RR12347
Majurugenta RR11237
Make Way For The Motherlode RR12984
Making History RR11549
Mama Blew A Hoody (song) RR11181
Mama Said Knock You Out RR11655
Mama's Hungry Eyes RR13191
The Mambo Kings RR13192
Mamouna RR11129
A Man And A Half RR12169
A Man And His Music, Vol. II—Computer Style RR11620
The Mandolin Man RR11102
Manna-Mirage RR11975
The Manson Family: An Opera RR13193
Mantra Mode RR11462
Marcus Garvey RR10700
Maria RR12499
Mark's Keyboard Repair RR11926
Mars Audiac Quintet RR12634
Martha Wash RR12870
Martin And Me RR11490
Martinis And Bikinis RR12163, RR12164
Marvin Gaye The Master 1961-84 RR11218
Marvin The Album RR11177
Mary Queen Of Scots RR11103
Mary's Idea RR11630, RR12935
Mas! A Caribbean Christmas Party RR13194
Mas Canciones RR12388
Masada RR13038
Mass. Ave. RR13195
Massive Hits Vol. 1 RR12021
Master Of The Delta Blues: The Friends Of Charlie Patton RR13196
Masterpieces RR11875
Matters Of The Heart RR10763
Mavericks RR11428, RR12620
Maxinquaye RR12766, RR12767
Maxwell's Urban Hang Suite RR11815
May I Sing With Me RR12982
Me Against The World RR12475
Mean Old World RR13197
Meantime RR11386
Mecca And The Soul Brother RR12368, RR12558
Medium Rare RR13198
Medusa RR11685
A Meeting By The River RR10553, RR10864
Mel RR11057
Mellon Collie And The Infinite Sadness RR12544, RR12545
Mellow Gold RR10532, RR10533
Melodyland RR12841

Melting In The Dark RR12971
Memoirs RR10594, RR11343, RR11732
The Memory Of Trees RR11085
Memphis Blues Caravan, Vol. I RR13199
Memphis Blues Caravan, Vol. II RR13200
Memphis Country Blues, Vol. I RR13201
Memphis Town RR13202
Menace II Society RR13203
Mercury RR10422
Mercury Falling RR12640
Message For The Mess Age RR12056
Message In A Box RR12194
Metallica RR11891
Mexican R'N' B RR13204
Mi Mexico RR11204
Mi Tierra RR11096
MIA RR11233
Michael Watford RR12880
Midnight Marauders RR12765
Midnight Mover RR12956
Mighty Joe Moon RR11287, RR11288
Milagro RR12429
Miles Smiles RR10963
The Milestone Years RR11391
Millions Now Living Will Never Die RR12753
Mind Blowin RR12821
Minute Waltz (song) RR10630
Miracle RR12488
Miracle Of Science RR10913
Mirror Ball RR12995, RR12996
Mirror Blue RR12731
The Missing Years RR12238
Mississippi Delta Blues RR13205
Mississippi Lad RR11059, RR12856
Mistaken Identity RR12319
Mitakuye Oyasin Oyasin RR12016
MJQ40 RR11923
Mo' Money RR13206
The Modern World RR13207
Molten Gold RR11176
Mondo Bizarro RR12290
Money And Cigarettes RR10805
The Monkees RR11931
Monkey Hips And Rice RR11141
Monkjack RR10688
Mono RR11201
Monorails And Satellites RR12265, RR12266
Monster RR12323, RR12324
Monte Warden RR12865
The Monterey International Pop Festival RR13208
Mood Elevator RR11698, RR11711
The Moog Cookbook RR13209, RR13210
Moonlight Becomes You RR12011
More Live At The Knitting Factory RR11221
More Of RR11932
More Songs Of Love And Murder RR10517
Moss Elixir RR11406
Mossy Liquor RR11407
The Most From Beny More RR11943
The Mother Of All Flagpole Christmas Albums RR13211
Motley Crue RR11967
Mr. A. T. RR12704
Mr. Bad Example RR13034
Mr. Bungle RR11971
Mr. Excitement! RR12946
Mr. Happy Go Lucky RR11868
Mr. Lucky RR11430
Mr. Machinery Operator RR11136
Mr. Moonlight RR11166
Mr. Smith RR11656
MTV Unplugged RR10546, RR11048, RR11049, RR12715
MTV Unplugged (EP) RR13212
MTV Unplugged In New York RR12047, RR12048
Muddy Water Blues RR12372
Muevelo Con El General RR11064
The Munich Philharmonic Orchestra Plays Abba Classic RR11977
Murder Ballads RR10486, RR10759
Murder Was The Case RR13213
Muse Sick N Hour Mess Age RR12246, RR12247
Music Box RR10734
Music For Egon Schiele RR12277
Music For The Jilted Generation RR12240
Music For The Native Americans RR12307, RR12308, RR12362, RR12363
Music For Your Mother RR11197
Music In Fifths RR11261
Music In Similar Motion RR11262
The Music Never Stopped RR13214
The Music Of Bill Monroe: From 1936 To 1994 RR11934
The Music Of Disney: A Legacy In Song RR13215
The Music Of Raymond Scott: Reckless Nights And Turkish Twilights RR12442
Music To Eat RR11352, RR11353
Music With Changing Parts RR11263
Musical Depreciation Revue RR11567
Mutiny RR12748
My Brother The Cow RR11973
My Brother The Wind Volume II RR12267
My Clinch Mountain Home RR10744
My Insatiable (single) RR12663
My Life RR10983
My World RR10769
Myth And Reality RR11788

N

A National Health Care RR12845
Native Tongue RR12191
Natural Born Killers RR13216
Natural Ingredients RR11751
A Natural Woman RR11611d
Natural Wonder RR12959
Nature Of A Sista' RR12255, RR12256
Naughty By Nature RR11993a
Naughty Little Doggie RR12200
Near Life Experience RR10856
Nearly God RR12768
The Negro Inside Me RR10393
Nemesisters RR10476
Nerve Net RR11082
Never Been Rocked Enough RR11836
Never Enough RR11099
Never Let Me Go RR12819
Nevermind RR12049
New Adventures In Hi-Fi RR12325, RR12326
New Beginning RR10764
New Jack City RR13217
New Jersey Drive, Vol I RR13218
New Jersey Drive, Vol. II RR13219
New Location RR11718
New Miserable Experience RR11252
New Moon Daughter RR12945
New World Order RR11819
New York Eye And Ear Control RR13220
New York Stories RR12028
Newspaper (song) RR12778
The Next Dream RR10468
The Next Hundred Years RR11377
A Night In San Francisco RR11953
Night Nurse RR11487
Night Song RR11125
Night Train RR11962
Nine Objects Of Desire RR12825
19 Naughty III RR11994, RR11995
1976-81 RR12566
99.9 F RR12826
No Alternative RR13221
No Big Surprise RR11275
No Code RR12132, RR12133
No Cure For Cancer RR11675
No Deeper Blue RR12816
No Goats, No Glory RR11266
No Hard Times RR12371
No Joke! RR11853
No Lunch RR10945
No More Mister Nice Girl RR11097
No Need To Argue RR10895
No. 1 Record RR10558
No Prima Donna RR13222
No Protection RR11768, RR11802
No Quarter RR12097, RR12098, RR12186, RR12187
No Reservations RR10444
No Talking Just Head RR11380
No Time To Kill RR10567a
No Walls RR12051
No Way Out (song) RR10946
Nocturnal RR11387
Non-Fiction RR10576
Nonsuch RR12975
Nordeste Brasil RR13223, RR13224
The Norman Whitfield Sessions RR11219
Not A Pretty Girl RR11002
Not For Kids Only RR11215, RR11304
Not In Kansas Anymore RR10513
Not In My Airforce RR12195
Nothing Good Comes Easy RR10826
Notorious RR11533
Nova Mob RR12054
Now Ain't The Time For Your Tears RR11508
Now I Got Worry RR10611, RR12597
Now I'm A Cowboy RR10471
Now Is The Hour RR11344
Now That I've Found You RR11639
N'ssi N'ssi RR11603
Nuisance RR11878
Number 10 RR10720
Nursery Boys Go Ahead RR10382

O

O Canto Da Cidada RR11884
Ocean Beach RR12302
Octopus RR11452
Odelay RR10534, RR10535
Odyssey RR12795
Oedipus Schmoedipus RR10394
Off The Ground RR11831
Off The Hook RR11780
The Oil Man RR11547
Old Testaments And New Revelations RR11179
Old Times, New Times RR11150
Older RR11894
Olympian RR11225
Omettology RR12153
On Every Street RR11013
On Foot In The Honky Tonk RR11512
On The Blank Generation RR11702
On The Mouth RR12676
On The Road RR12113
On The Way Down From The Moon Palace RR11232
On Track RR13040
Once I Loved RR11441
Once In A While RR10817
Once More With Feeling RR11151
The One RR11545
One RR11850
1-800 New Funk RR13225
One Eye On The Future, One Eye On The Past RR12394

One Foot In The Grave RR10536
One Hot Minute RR12301
100 Degrees And Rising RR11474
187 He Wrote RR12599
100% Fun RR12689a
One Love RR11791, RR12848
One More Mile RR12878
One Nation Under A Groove RR11198
A One Of A Kind Love Affair—The Anthology RR12603
One Step Ahead Of The Spider RR11824
The One That Got Away RR12726
Only Built Fir Cuban Linx RR12280
Only Daddy That'll Walk The Line RR11522
Only Everything RR11373
Onobox RR12078
Opel RR10511
Open Up The Sky RR11186
Orange RR12598
Orange Crate Art RR12110, RR12943
Orbus Terrarum RR12081
The Original Mambo Kings: An Introduction To Afro-Cubop 1948-1954 RR13226
The Original Skatalites And Laurel Aitken RR10402, RR12524
Original Soundtracks I RR12121
The Originals RR10739
Orlando RR13227
Other Planets Of There RR12268
Other Voices, Other Rooms RR11301
Otis! RR12310
Otis Rush, 1956-1958 RR12413
Our Time In Eden RR12716
Our Troubled Youth RR11450
Out Of Left Field RR12931
Out Of The Cradle RR10692, RR10693
Out Of Time RR12327
Out Of Whack (EP) RR11712
Out On The Rolling Sea RR13228
Outside RR10643, RR10644
Outward Bound RR11661
Over-Nite Sensation RR13022
Own The Way Over Here RR11356

P

P RR12094
'P' Is The Funk RR10822
Pablo Honey RR12279
Pacer RR10428, RR10429
The Pacific Jazz Years RR10495
Paid In Full RR11090
Palace Brothers RR12099
Pale Sun Crescent Moon RR10890
Palomine RR10552
Pandora's Box RR10396
Panic On RR11771, RR11772
Parabolic RR11242
Paradise Don't Come Cheap RR12024
Paralyzed Mind Of The Archangel Void RR11360
Paris RR10929, RR11844
Parklife RR10618, RR10619
Part One RR12905
Partners RR11536
Passion Is No Ordinary Word RR12108
Patrice RR12914
The Patsy Cline Collection RR10818
Paul Is Live RR11832
Paul Motian In Tokyo RR11966
Paul Simon 1964-1993 RR12506
Paul Weller RR12893
Pawn Shop Guitars RR10812
The Payback RR10676
Peace At Last RR10608
Peace Beyond Passion RR11998, RR11999, RR12000
Peace To The Neighborhood RR12627
The Peacocks RR12399
The Peel Sessions RR10727
Peel Slowly And See RR12837
Peeni Waali RR13229
Peggy Suicide RR10873
The Pendulum Vibe RR11555
Pentastar RR11055
People Get Ready! RR11820
Peppermint Tea House RR12496
Percussion Bitter Sweet RR12359
Percy Mayfield Live RR11821
Perfectly Good Guitar RR11400
Personal Best RR12037, RR12038
Perspex Island RR11416
Perverse RR11527
Peter Frampton RR11174
Peter Lewis RR11694
Phat Trax RR13230
Phenomenon RR13231
Philip Bailey RR10492
Phobia RR11626
Phoenix RR10542
Piano Night At Tipitina's RR13232
Pick Up On This! RR11537, RR13041
Picture Has Faded RR12295
Picture Perfect Morning RR10660
Pictures And Paintings RR12343
Piece Of Cake RR11974
Pieces Of Africa RR11646
The Pigeon Is The Most Popular Bird RR12522
Pimps, Players And Private Eyes RR13233
Pinkerton RR12888
Pisces Iscariot RR12546
Pisces, Aquarius, Capricorn And Jones Ltd. RR11933
Piss Factory RR12554
Planet Of Love RR11670
Plantation Lullabies RR12001
Plants And Birds And Rocks And Things RR11725
The Platinum Collection RR10601
Play RR10874, RR11838
Play Five Of Their Favorites (EP) RR11121
Play Me Backwards RR10489
Play With Toys RR10514
Playground Psychotics RR13023
Please Don't Take My Air Jordans RR11207
Please Panic RR12846
Plugged In RR11058
Poetic Justice RR13234
Polara RR12192
Pomme Fritz RR12082
Pond RR12196
Pop Pop RR11565
Pork Soda RR12227
Porno For Pyros RR12205
Portrait Of A Delta Bluesman RR12149
Portrait Of The Artist As A Young Man 1923-1934 RR10457
Portraits RR11363
Post RR11314
Postmodern Blues RR13235
Postwar Chicago RR13236
Poverty's Paradise RR11997
Power Trip RR11829
Precious RR11940
Precious Stone RR12651
The Predator RR11465
Pre-Millennium Tension RR12769
The Presidents Of The United States Of America RR12213
Pretty Close To The Truth RR11671
Priest = Aura RR10792
The Priest, They Called Him RR10703, RR10829
Primal Rock Therapy RR10603
Prose Combat RR11825
Protection RR11803
Psalm 69: The Way To Succeed And The Way To Suck Eggs RR11908
Psychic Hearts RR11941
Psychoderelict RR12756
Pulp Fiction RR13237
Pulse RR12175
Pure And Simple RR11534
Pure Phase RR12605
Pure Poverty RR12198
Purge And Slouch RR11240
Purple RR12646, RR12647
Pussy, King Of The Pirates RR10390, RR11863
Putumayo Presents The Best Of World Music RR13238

Q

Queen Of Soul: The Atlantic Recordings RR11175
A Quick One RR12920
Quilt RR12476

R

The R&B Box: 30 Years Of Rhythm & Blues RR13239
The R&B Of Membership RR10981
R. Kelly RR11596
Radio City RR10559
Rain Dogs RR12857
Raising Hell RR12410
Randy Newman RR12032
Rapa Iti RR12698, RR12699
Rare Birds RR11012, RR11276
Rare, Live And Classic RR10490
Rare On Air Vol. 1 RR13240
Rare Surf RR13241
Rats RR11571
Rave On!! RR11599
The Raven RR12170
Raw 'N Alive At The Cellar, 1966 RR12470
Ray Gun Suitcase RR12146
Razorblade Suitcase RR10705
The RCA Years 1967-1986 RR12117
Reachin' RR11005, RR11006
Reaction Dub part 1: Deliverance RR12338
Ready For Love RR12702
Ready To Die RR12052
The Real Kids RR12297
Real Love RR12626
The Real Mr. Heartache RR12131
The Reality Of My Surroundings RR11139
Reap The Whirlwind RR12076
Rebellion RR10577
Rebels Without Applause (EP) RR10827
Recovering The Satellites RR10886
Red RR11268
Red Hot And Country RR13242
Red House Painters I RR12303
Red House Painters II RR12304
Red Medicine RR11189
The Red Shoes RR10706
Reel To Reel RR11284
Reflecter RR12671
Reggae Christmas RR13243
Regulate...G Funk Era RR12869
Reject All American RR10564
Relationships From Hell RR13244
Relish RR12087
Remember RR12419
Remember Me RR12311, RR12650
Rent RR13245
Represent RR11124
Republic RR12025
Respect RR11417

Resurrection RR10857
The Resurrection RR11234
Retro Active RR10975
Retrospective RR10656
Return Of The Boom Bap RR11649
Return Of The Product RR12461
The Return Of The Space Cowboy RR11509
Return To The 36 Chambers RR12073
Return To The Valley Of The Go-Go's RR11265
Revival RR12891
Revolutionary Means RR12438
Rhythm Country And Blues RR13246
Rhythm In Mind RR10842
Rhythm Of Love RR10494
Rhythmeen RR13005
The Rich Man's Eight Track Tape RR10555
Rid Of Me RR12181, RR12182
Ride With Me RR11454
Rien RR11127
Rig Rock Truckstop RR13247
The Right Time RR11507
Rise RR10479
Rise Above It RR12072
Rising RR12079
Rising Sons RR10865, RR11781, RR12355
Rites Of Rhythm & Blues RR13248
Ritual Beating System RR10491
River Of Dreams RR11540, RR11541
River Of Fallen Stars RR11597, RR11598
The Road Goes On Forever RR11401
Road Tested RR12287
The Road To Ensenada RR11744
Roadsongs RR12817, RR12818
Roaring Loud, Standing Proud RR12360
Rob And Fab RR12361
A Rock & Roll Collection RR12948
Rock Animals RR12495
Rock Juice RR11143
Rock 'N' Groove RR12847
Rock Stars Kill RR13249
Rockabye RR11419
Rocket RR12226
Rockin' My Blues Away RR12871
Rockin' My Life Away RR11691
The Rolling Stones Rock & Roll Circus RR13250
Rollins: The Boxed Life RR12381
Ron Sexsmith RR12467
Roots RR12460
Roots N' Blues RR13251
Roots Rock Soca RR10578
Ropin' The Wind RR10667
Rose And Charcoal RR11936
Roses RR12075
Routes Of Rhythm Vol. 3 RR12092
Rub It Better RR11226
Ruby Vroom RR12579
The Rude Gesture RR12485
Rumble Doll RR12437
Running Jumping Standing Still RR11633, RR11980
Running With You RR10725
Rush RR10806
The Russian Album RR11833

S

S In Moderation RR11635
Sabsylma RR13009
Sacrificial Cake RR11510
Sad And Defeated RR11016
Sad Days, Lonely Nights RR11611
Sadly Beautiful (song) RR12335
Saisoro RR10988
Salamat And Nazakat Ali RR10406, RR10407
Sam Cooke's SAR Records Story 1959-1965 RR10866
Samba Brasil RR13252, RR13253
Same Train, A Different Time RR11347
San Fran Sessions RR10530
San Francisco RR10423
San Francisco Days RR11488
Santa Monica '72 RR10645
Satan Is Real RR11729
Satta Massagana RR10387
Saturation RR12804, RR12805
Saturday Night And Sunday Morning RR12625
Saturday Night At The Blue Note RR12152
Saturday Rolling Around RR11283
Say Blow By Blow Backwards RR12899
Scavenger RR12858
Scene Of The Crime RR11609
Scenes From My Last Confession RR12064
The Scepter Records Story RR13254
Schubert Dip RR11075
Science Faire RR10449
The Score RR11191, RR11192
Scots Pirates RR12439
Scratch RR12444
Scream In Blue RR11898
Scream, Dracula, Scream! RR12369
Seal RR12450
Seasick RR11472
Seattle Women In Rock RR13255
Second Coming RR12644
2nd Street RR10415
Secret World Live RR11205
Secrets RR10654
Section 43 (song) RR10887
Seducing Down The Door RR10722
See You On The Other Side RR11881
Selected Ambient Works Vol. II RR10447
Sell Out Young (song) RR11438
Semi-crazy RR10680
Set Me Free RR12344
Set The Twilight Reeling RR12317
Set To Pop RR11708
The Setters RR12462
7 And 7 Is (song) RR11678, RR11738a
7 Years Ago...Directions In Smart-Alec Music RR11157
75% Less Fat RR11794
Sex, America, Cheap Trick RR10770
Shack-Man RR11857
Shacknasty RR11270
Shadows And Light RR12947a
Shady Grove RR11216, RR11305
Shake It Up! RR13256
Shakill's Warrior RR11981
Shamballa RR11431
Shame + A Sin RR10899
Shania Twain RR12783
Shannon's Dress (EP) RR12478
Shape RR11178
Shaw 'Nuff RR11246
She Loves You (song) RR10529
Sheik Yerbouti RR13024
Sheryl Crow RR10917, RR10918
She's The One RR12154
Shine On RR12176
The Shines RR12489
Shipwreck RR10861
Shoot Your Way To Freedom (song) RR12055
Short Bus RR11131
Short Stories RR11647
Shorty The Pimp RR12749a
Shot RR11530
Show RR10930, RR10931, RR11531
The Show, The After-Party, The Hotel RR11538, RR11539
Shut Up 'N Play Yer Guitar RR13025
Siamese Dream RR12547, RR12548, RR12549
Sick 'Em RR12464
Sides 1-4 (single) RR13257
Sif Safaa RR13258
The Silent Majority RR10414
Silhouette RR12494
Silver Sail RR12950
Simpatico! RR12829
Simple English (song) RR11133
Sinatra And Sextet: Live In Paris RR12514
The Singer RR11208
A Single Woman RR12507
The Singles RR12269, RR13259
The Singles (1993-1994) Loverly Music RR13260
Sitting On Snaps RR11856
Six Feet Deep RR11292
VI: Return Of The Real RR11469
60 Watt Silver Lining RR11063
Ska Bonanza: The Studio One Ska Years RR13261
Sketches RR10554, RR11837, RR12681
Sketches Of Spain RR10964
Skin RR11688
The Sky Is Crying RR12824
Skynyrd Frynds RR13262
Slang RR10976
Slanted And Enchanted RR12127
Slapping Pythagoras RR10862
Slay The Suitors RR12222
Sleeps With Angels RR10901, RR10902, RR12997, RR12998
Sleepy Eyes And Butterflies RR12589
Slide On This RR12960
Slippin' In RR11336
Slo-Blo RR10760
Slow Dancing With The Moon RR12118
Slowhand RR10807
S.L.S.Q. RR10400
Sly And Robbie Present Taxi RR13263
Smash RR12071
Smeared RR12536
Smilin' Island Of Song RR10629
Smoke RR11035
Smoke 'Em If You Got 'Em RR11337a
The Snake RR11765, RR12201
A Snake In The Heart RR13264
So Near, So Far RR11392
So Tonight That I Might See RR11823
So Tough RR12422
Soca Carnival 93 RR13265
Soft Bomb RR10789
Solid Ground RR10431
Solomon's Daughter RR11606
Soma City RR12425
Some Change RR12431
Some Gave All RR10942, RR10943
Some Lyrics RR11759
Some Old Bullshit RR10520
Sometime Anywhere RR10793
Song For RR12130
The Song Is You RR11026, RR12515
The Song Remembers When RR12979
Songs RR12820
Songs For A Blue Guitar RR12305
Songs For The Daily Planet RR12562
Songs For The Terrestrially Challenged RR12722
Songs From Chippy RR13266
Songs From The Rain RR11442
Songs Of Faith And Devotion RR10984, RR10985
Songs Of Freedom RR11792
Songs Of The West RR13267
The Soul Cages RR12641
Soul Deep RR10646
Soul Man: Live In Japan RR10816
The Soul Of Black Peru RR13268

Soul Of Vietnam RR13269
Soul Train 25th Anniversary RR13270
Soulsation! RR11491, RR11492
Sound Of Joy RR12270
The Sound Of Music RR12177
Sound Of White Noise RR10443
Sound Sun Pleasure RR12271, RR12272
Sound System RR11039
Sounds Of The South RR13271
Soundtracks RR10728
Soup RR10599
South Central RR13272
South Of I-10 RR11662
The Southern Harmony And Musical Companion RR10569
Southpaw Grammar RR11956
The Spaghetti Incident? RR11322
Spare Ass Annie And Other Tales RR10704
The Specialty Story RR13273
Speech RR12595
The Speed Of Grace RR10548
Spiderland RR12535
Spiked! RR11568
Spinner RR11083, RR12951
Spinning Around The Sun RR11249, RR11250
Spirit RR12012
The Spirit Of Country RR11561
Spirit Of '73 RR13274
Spirit Of Sheba RR11870, RR11871
The Spirits Of Our Ancestors RR12903
Split RR11752
Spooky RR11753
The Sporting Life RR11209, RR11563
Stages RR11396
Stain RR11706, RR11707
Stakes Is High RR10967
Stanley Road RR12894
Star RR10543
Star Time RR10677
Starry Eyes RR13275
Start Packing RR12407
Stay Out Of The Kitchen RR11546
Stay With Me RR12057
Steady Diet Of Nothing RR11190
Steppin' Out RR10547
Steppin' With Peps RR12144
Stepping Out RR10465
Stick Around For Joy RR12669
Stick-N-Moove RR10791
The Stiff Records Box Set RR13276
Still Feel Gone RR12797
Stone Cold World RR10417
Stone Free RR13277
Stone Rock Blues RR13278
Stone Witch RR11874
Stoned And Dethroned RR11525
Stop And Listen RR11913
Storm Warning RR11069
Story Of My Life RR12147
Storyteller RR12874
Storyville RR12364, RR12365
Straight Outta Compton RR12059
Strange Magic RR11066
Strange Things Happening RR12533
Stranger Than Fiction RR10483
Strawberries Oceans Ships Forest RR11138
Strawberry Jam RR10710
Street Angel RR12036
Street Jams RR13279
Strength In Numbers RR12784
Strictly Commercial RR13026
Stripped RR12377
A Study Of Frustration RR11273
Stuttering John RR12657
Subhuman Race RR12526
Sublime RR12660
Subliminal Sandwich RR11851
Suede RR12664
Summit Conference RR12962
Sun Ra Visits Planet Earth RR12273
The Sun Records Collection RR13280
Sunrise On The Sufferbus RR11805
Sunset Park RR13281
Super Bad RR11269, RR12717
Super Tasty RR11320
Superelastic RR12827
Supernatural Fairy Tales RR13282
Super-Sonic Jazz RR12274, RR12275
Superunknown RR12585, RR12586
Supreme Court Goes Electric RR12680
Sure Love RR11602
Surprise RR12875
Surrender (song) RR12630
Susan Across The Ocean RR12503
Suspending Disbelief RR12885
Sutras RR11024
Swamp Ophelia RR11477
Sway RR10442
Sweat 'N' Soul RR12428
Sweet F.A. RR11739
Sweet Little Mysteries RR11798
Sweet Old World RR12933
Sweet Potatoe Pie RR11022
Sweet Relief RR13283, RR13284
Sweet Relief II RR13285, RR13286
The Sweetest Days RR12936
Sweetheart's Dance RR12741
Swim Away RR12224
Swing That Music RR12033, RR12890, RR13287
Swing Time! RR13288
Switchblades Of Love RR13003
[Symbol] RR12235
Symphonic Music Of The Rolling Stones RR11716
Symphony For Improvisors RR10774
Symphony No. 3 RR11278, RR11279, RR11713, RR11714, RR12800, RR12801, RR13036, RR13037
Symphony Or Damn RR10956, RR10957

T

Tabala Wolof Sufi Drumming Of Senegal RR13289
Take A Look RR10837
Take Me As I Am RR11403
Take The Guitar Player For A Ride RR11672
Tales Of Ordinary Madness RR11379
Talk RR12981
Talking RR11919
The Tape Of Only Linda RR11726
T.A.P.O.A.F.O.M. RR10823, RR10824, RR10825
Tarantula RR12351
A Taste Of Heaven RR11987
The Tattooed Heart RR12014b
Taxi RR11130
Tear The Roof Off 1974-1980 RR12112
Tears Of Fire: The 25th Anniversary Collection RR12967
Techno Mancer RR13290
Teenage Kicks RR13291
Teenage Symphonies To God RR12835
Teenager Of The Year RR10571b
A Tejano Country Christmas RR13292
Tekit Izi RR11586
Telephono RR12609
Television RR11032, RR12711
Tell Me Why RR11573
Temple Of The Dog RR13293
Temples Of Boom RR10939, RR10940
Temptation RR11756
Ten RR12134
Ten Feet Tall And Bulletproof RR12772
10 On Broadway RR10992
10 Song Demo RR10754
Ten Summoner's Tales RR12642, RR12643
Tenor Legacy RR11733
Terence Blanchard RR10589
Terror Has Some Strange Kinfolk RR10761, RR11106
Texas Blues RR13294
Texas Bluesman RR10622
Thank You RR11043, RR12401, RR12402
Thank You For The Music RR10384
Thanks For The Memories RR11719
That What Is Not RR12248
That's The Way It Should Be RR10630a
The Thelonious Monk Quartet Live At The Five Spot Featuring John Coltrane RR10852, RR11928
Theory Of Everything RR11134
There Are But Four Small Faces RR12542
There's Room For Us All RR12505
These Blues RR10673
These Days RR10625
Thesis RR10595, RR11257, RR12684
They Call Me The Fat Man RR11023
They Came, They Played, They Blocked The Driveway RR13295
Thinkin' About You RR12980
Thinkin' Problem RR10497
Third-Sister Lovers RR10560
Thirteen RR12710
13 Ribs RR12844
Thirteen Years RR11094
The 35th Anniversary Collection RR11910, RR12366
Thirty Years Of Maximum R & B RR12921
This Heart Of Mine RR10740
This Is How I Feel About Jazz RR11564
This Is Me RR12762
This Land RR11185
This Moment In Toronto RR12938
This Mortal Coil RR12727
This One's Gonna Hurt You RR12656
This Perfect World RR11554
This Time RR12987, RR12988
Thousand Roads RR10915
Thrak RR11615
Thrakattak RR11616
3 RR11137
3 Feet High And Rising RR10967a
Three Fish RR12736
Three Snakes And One Charm RR10570, RR10571
3 Years, 5 Months And 2 Days In The Life Of... RR10459
Throwing Copper RR11705
Tical RR11893
Tigerlily RR11879, RR11880
Tigerman RR12947
Till Death Do Us Part RR11235
Till The Night is Gone RR13296
Time Signatures RR10686
Time Takes Time RR12628
Time Traveller RR11939
Time Was When RR10668
Tindersticks RR12744, RR12745
Tiny Music RR12648, RR12649
Titanic Days RR11764
To Bring You My Love RR12183, RR12184
To The Birds (single) RR12665
To The Bone RR11627
To The Faithful Departed RR10896
A Todos Los Barrios RR12374
Together Alone RR10919
Together Forever RR12411
Tombstone Every Mile RR11629

Tomorrow The Green Grass RR11516
Tone Dialing RR10841, RR12225
Tongues And Tails RR11375
Toni Braxton RR10655
Tonic RR11381
Tonite Let's All Make Love In London RR13297
Too Bad Jim RR10702
Too High To Die RR11854
Too Legit To Quit RR11350
Too Long In Exile RR11954, RR11955
Tornado Souvenirs RR12348
Torture Garden RR11988
Tossing Seeds RR12677
Totally Krossed Out RR11645
Totally Wired RR13298
Toto La Momposina Y Sus Tambores—La Candela Viva RR11925
Tougher Than Music RR13299
Tougher Than Tough RR13300, RR13301
Toward The Within RR10968
Town And County RR12927
Trace RR11000, RR12567
The Tractors RR12757, RR12758
Trade Test Transmission RR10713
Traffic From Paradise RR11566
Tragic Kingdom RR12050
Tragic Songs Of Life RR11730
Tramp On Your Street RR12480
Trampoline RR11398
Trance RR11348, RR13006
Trance Planet RR13302
Transient Random-Noise Bursts With Announcements RR12635
Transmissions From The Satellite Heart RR11145
Tras La Tormenta RR10586, RR10849
Travel On, Rider RR12445
Triage RR10488
Tribal Thunder RR10951
Tribal Voice RR12989
A Tribute To Black Entertainers RR13303
A Tribute To Curtis Mayfield RR13304
Tribute To The Music Of Bob Wills And The Texas Playboys RR10464
Tricks Of The Shade RR11267
Tricky Presents Grassroots RR12770
Tricotism RR12730
Trios RR12872
Tropicalia 2 RR11243, RR12833
Troubadour: The Definitive Collection 1964-1976 RR11025
Trouble No More RR11351
True Democracy RR12631
Try It RR12623
Try N' Be RR12776
Tulare Dust RR13305
Turbulent Indigo RR11915
Turn It Upside Down RR12600
Turn Loose The Swans RR11986
Tuskegee Experiments RR10717
12 Golden Country Greats RR12887
12 Haunted Episodes RR12108a
12 Inches Of Snow RR12564
12 Shades Of Brown RR10680a
Twenty-First Century Jesus RR11886
25 Years: The Chain RR11148a
24 Nights RR10807a, RR10807b
2 1 RR10883a
II [Two] RR10647, RR11081, RR12214
Two Pages RR11264
Two Sevens Clash RR10927

U

Uh-Oh RR10716
Uhhh (song) RR10979
Unboxed RR11345
Unbreakable Heart (song) RR10747
Unchained RR10753
Uncle Jam Wants You RR11199
Uncle Meat RR13027
Unclogged RR12973
Under The Bushes Under The Stars RR11319
Under The Pink RR10426, RR10427
Under The Table And Dreaming RR11810, RR11811
Under The Wishing Tree RR12468
Understanding RR12957
Undisputed Attitude RR12531
Union RR10765
The United States Of Poetry RR13306
Universal Mother RR12068
University RR12738
Unplugged RR10411, RR10808, RR10809, RR12999, RR13000
Unplugged...And Unseated RR12639
Unplugged: The Official Bootleg RR11834
Unsatisfied (song) RR12336
Unsettled Scores RR13307
Unshaven RR12479
Until The End Of The World RR13308
Up RR12353
Uptown MTV Unplugged RR13309
Uranium Road (song) RR10436
Uranus RR12486
Urban Blues RR13310
Us RR11206
Use Your Illusion I RR11323, RR11324
Use Your Illusion II RR11325, RR11326
Utah Saints RR12807

V

Valis 1 Destruction Of Syntax RR13312
Vampyros Lesbos Sexadelic Dance Party RR12810
Vauxhall And I RR11957
The V-Discs RR13311
Vee Vee RR10454
Vehicles RR10697
Veil RR10504
The Ventures' Christmas Album RR12838
Very RR12151
The Very Best Of Buddy Guy RR11337
A Very Special Christmas 2 RR13313
VI: Return Of The Real RR11469
Vibrator RR10958
Vientos RR11721
Vintage Rays RR12672
Virus 100 RR13314
Vitalogy RR12135, RR12136
Viva Dead Ponies RR11126
Viva La Muerte RR10830
Viva! La Woman RR10794
Viva Last Blues RR12100
Viva Luckenbach! RR12860
Viva Zapata RR12465
Vodou Adjae RR10639
The Voice Of Langston Hughes RR11451
The Voice Of Silence RR11018
Voix Du Soleil RR13315
Volume 1 RR11900
Volume 2 RR11901
Volume 3 RR11902
Volume III Just Right RR12581
Volumes 1, 2, And 3 RR11903
Voo Doo Doll (song) RR10450
Voodoo Lounge RR12378, RR12379
Voudou Nou RR12294
Vroom RR11617
Vs. RR12137, RR12138

W

W. C. Handy's Memphis Blues Band RR11358
Wah Wah RR11504
Waiting For You RR11695
Wakafrika RR10996
Waking Up The Neighbours RR10391
Walk Around Heaven RR12728
Walk On RR10635
Walk Right Back RR11108
Walk The Dog And Light The Light RR12060
Walking In London RR10859
Walking Wounded RR11109
The Wallflowers RR12864
Walls Scream (song) RR12340
Wandering Spirit RR11499, RR11500
Wanted Man RR11595
Warm Your Heart RR12014c
Warren Piece RR12022
Washing Machine RR12571, RR12572
Wasn't That A Time RR12884
Wasps' Nests RR12523
Wassoulou Foli RR12501
Watching The Dark RR12732
Watershed RR11845
Wavelength Infinity RR13316
Wax Ecstatic RR12607, RR12608
The Way That I Am RR11830
Way To Blue RR11033
Waymore's Blues (Part II) RR11523
We Are Never Talking (song) RR11092
We Can't Be Stopped RR11236
We Can't Dance RR11227
We Care RR12906
We Get There When We Do RR12661
We Travel The Spaceways RR12276
The Weedkiller's Daughter RR11542
Weezer RR12889
Weight RR12382
Weird Nightmare RR13317
Welcome To Wherever You Are RR11483, RR11484
Weld RR10903, RR10904, RR13001, RR13002
We're Desperate RR13318
We're Only In It For The Money RR11964, RR13028
Western Beat RR12091, RR12892
Westing RR12128
Whaler RR11376
What A Crying Shame RR11814
What A Way To Live RR10778
What Is Bhangra? RR13319
What It Is RR10585, RR10691
What Silence Knows RR12006
Whatever RR11787
What's The 411? RR10596
What's The New Mary Jane (single) RR11924
(What's The Story) Morning Glory? RR12062, RR12063
Whatta Man (song) RR11078, RR12427
The Wheel RR10755
Wheels Of Fire RR10909, RR10910
When I Lived In The Wild RR11172
When I Was A Boy RR12500
When Love Finds You RR11244
When No One's Looking RR13039
When Squirrels Play Chicken RR12148
When The Levee Breaks (song) RR11608
Whenever We Wanted RR11869
Where Is Brooklyn? RR10775
Where It All Begins RR10416
Where It Goes RR10742
Where It's At RR11427
Where The Streets Have No Name (song) RR12792
Where Woodstock Lives RR13320
Where You Been RR11010
Where'd You Hide The Body RR11848
Whip-Smart RR12159, RR12160
Whiskey For The Holy Ghost RR11663

The Whistle Only Dogs Can Hear RR11418
White Country Blues (1926-1938) RR13321
White Light White Heat White Trash RR12565
White Men Can't Rap RR13322
The Who Sell Out RR12922
A Whole New Thing RR12540
Who'll Buy My Memories? RR12013
Whoomp! RR12697
Why Pick On Me RR12624
Wide River RR11906
Wild Kentucky Skies RR10682
The Wild Life RR12529
Wild Love RR12911
Wild Mood Swings RR10932
Wild Seed—Wild Flower RR11118
Wild Things: Wyld Kiwi Garage 1966-69 RR13323
Wild Wood RR12895
Wildest Dreams RR12782
Wildflowers RR12155, RR12156
William Bloke RR10650
Willie Loco Boom Boom Ga Ga: 1975-1991 RR10405
The Willsaphone Stupid Show RR12004
Wind Your Waist RR13324
Wings Of A Dove RR10928
Wings Of Joy RR10897
Winning Losers RR10507, RR12458
Winter Light RR12389
Wish RR10933, RR10934, RR12313
Witchcraft RR10386
With These Hands RR11095
Within Your Reach (song) RR12337
Without A Sound RR11011
Without Walls RR12968
Woke Up With A Monster RR10771
The Wolf That House Built RR11701
Wolverine Blues RR11084
The Woman I Am RR11604
The Woman's Boat RR10788
Woman's Gotta Have It RR10876
Wonderful RR10440
Woodstock RR13325
Woodstock '94 RR13326
Word Up RR13327
Words RR12345
Working Class RR10433
Workshop Of The Telescopes RR10610
World Gone Wrong RR11050
The World Is Yours RR11972
World Of Morrissey RR11958
World Turning RR12771
Worried Blues 1963 RR11457
Wowee Zowee RR12129
Wrecking Ball RR11364
Wynonna RR11574, RR11575

X

Xtort RR11631, RR11632
X-Tra Naked RR12292

Y

Y Hoy Como Ayer RR11944
Yank Crime RR11034
Yeah Yeah Yeah Yeah RR10565
Year Of Mondays RR11550
Years RR10883b
The Yellow Shark RR13029
Yerself Is Steam RR11882
Yes RR11948
Yiddish-American Klezmer Music: 1925-1956 RR12701
You Can't Do That On Stage Anymore RR13030
You Can't Win (song) RR11439
You Gotta Pay The Band RR11696
You Gotta Sin To Get Saved RR11840
You? Me? Us? RR12733
You Turn Me On RR10522
You'll Never Get To Heaven RR11963
Young Blood RR11692
Youngblood RR11557
Your Arsenal RR11959
Your Filthy Little Mouth RR12396
Your Little Secret RR11100
Your Song RR10403
Your Sounds RR11475
Youssou N'Dour RR12003
Youthanasia RR11860
You've Got To Believe In Something RR12601
Yuletunes RR13328

Z

Zingalamaduni RR10460
Zooropa RR12793, RR12794
Zucker RR11122

The Rolling Stone Index

Master Indexes

Master Index to
Author & Reviewer Names

A

Aaron, Charles AR12916
Aasen, Arin LE08034
Abbey, Marc LE08035
Abbring, Lance LE08036
Abel, Brad LE08037
Abernathy, Brian LE08038
Abowitz, Richard CR00699, CR00714
Abraham, Jacob (Resident Psychiatrist, Columbia-Presbyterian Medical Center) LE08039
Abramowitz, Andy LE08040
Abramson, Greg LE08041
Acosta, Joshua LE08042
Adamidis, Harry LE08043
Adams, Jeff LE08044
Adams, Scott LE08045
Adams, Todd LE08046
Adkins, G. P., Captain (Fort Leonard Wood) LE08047
Adkins, Suzi L. LE08048
Adler, William M. AR12917
Aggers, William LE08049
Ahearn, Kim AR12918, AR12919, AR12920, AR12921, AR12922, CR00760, RR10793, RR11848, RR12829, RR12840
Aiges, Scott AR12923, AR12924, CR00748
Alatorre, Laura LE08050
Albano, Dawn LE08051
Alden, Grant AR12925, RR10603, RR11874, RR11973, RR12046, RR12196
Alejandro, Hannah LE08052
Alexakis, Art AR12926
Ali, Lorraine AR12927, AR12928, AR12929, AR12930, AR12931, AR12932, AR12933, AR12934, AR12935, AR12936, AR12937, AR12938, AR12939, AR12940, AR12941, AR12942, AR12943, AR12944, RR10423, RR10552, RR10896, RR11034, RR11101, RR11178, RR11229, RR11314, RR11528, RR11531, RR11682, RR11789, RR11823, RR12042, RR12369, RR12532, RR12548, RR12646, RR12648, RR12707, RR12737, RR12760, RR12854, RR13119
Alicandro, Bill AR12945
Allen, Jennifer AR12946, AR12947
Allen, Laura LE08053
Allgood, Desiree LE08054
Alterman, Eric AR12948, AR12949, AR12950, AR12951, AR12952, AR12953, AR12954, AR12955, AR12956
Altman, Ann LE08055
Altman, Billy RR10404a, RR11695, RR11816, RR12627, RR12825, RR12863, RR12959
Ambs, Daryl LE08056
Ament, Jeff LE08057
Amerman, Dale LE08058
Amos, Tori AR12957, AR12958, BR01100, MR01892
Amsden, Stephen E. LE08059
Anderson, David J. LE08060
Anderson, Mark Kendall CR00701
Anderson, Phyllis (U.S. Department of Energy) LE08061
Andler, Matthew LE08062
Andrews, Paul D. LE08063
Angeline, Mary LE08064
Anstadt, Douglas LE08065
Apodaca, Tim LE08066
Appleford, Steve AR12960, AR12961, AR12962, AR12963, AR12964, AR12965, AR12966, AR12967, AR12968, AR12969, RR10428, RR10482, RR12436, RR12493, RR12918, RR12920, RR12922
Apter, Lauren E. LE08067
Archer, Brian LE08068
Archer-Weinstein, Linda (T.J. Martell Foundation) LE08069
Arendt, A. J. LE08070
Armor, Perry LE08071
Armstrong, Adam LE08072
Armstrong, Lynn LE08073
Armstrong, Sherri LE08074
Arnold, Gina BR01111, CR00828, CR00839, CR00862
Arnold, Kerry LE08075
Arrington, Carl AR12970, AR12971, AR12972, AR12973, CR00798
Artley, Melanie LE08076
Asel, Eric LE08077
Ash, Debbie LE08078
Ashby, Kelso, III LE08079
Ashdown, David LE08080
Askew, Roger LE08081
Atkins, Norman AR12981, AR12982
Atkins, Vance LE08082
Atkinson, Bishop LE08083
Aubrey, Joy LE08084
AuBuchon, Mark LE08085
Audevart, Pete LE08086
Auer, Nicole J. LE08087
Aufdenkampe, Nick LE08088
Austin, Michael D. LE08089 AR12983, AR12984
Aykroyd, Dan AR12985
Azerrad, Michael AR12986, AR12987, AR12988, AR12989, AR12990, AR12991, AR12992, AR12993, AR12994, AR12995, AR12996, AR12997, AR12998, AR12999, AR13000, AR13001, AR13002, AR13003, AR13004, AR13005, AR13006, AR13007, AR13008, AR13009, AR13010, AR13011, AR13012, AR13013, AR13014, AR13015, AR13016, AR13017, AR13018, AR13019, BR01056, CR00641, CR00683, CR00722, CR00831, CR00848, CR00868, RR10522, RR10532, RR10719, RR11010, RR11255, RR11317, RR11386, RR12579, RR12669, RR12710, RR12882, RR12975, RR13058, RR13183
Azevedo, Rob. LE08090

B

B., Anna LE08091
Baber, Michael LE08092
Bach, Sebastian LE08093, LE08094
Backous, Mike LE08095
Bae, Nelson LE08096
Baerwald, David LE08097
Baich, Karielle LE08098
Baikal, Alison LE08099
Bailey, Andrew AR13020
Bailey, B. J. LE08100
Baird, Robert AR13021
Baker, Alex LE08101
Baker, Carl F. LE08102
Baker, Eric LE08103
Baker, Josh LE08104
Baker, Roger LE08105
Ballard, Chris LE08106
Ballou, Melissa LE08107
Bambarger, Bradley RR11615
Barber, Scott LE08108
Barendse, Nathan LE08109
Barich, Bill AR13022
Barlow, J. A. LE08110
Barrett, Johanna LE08111
Barris, Lyn LE08112
Barritt, T. R. LE08113
Barron, Chris AR13023, BR01080, MR01973, RR10500, RR11044, RR12751
Barrymore, Drew LE08114
Barth, Jack AR13024, AR13025
Bartholomew, Danielle LE08115
Basson, Duncan LE08116
Bataille, Georges BR01120
Battis, Amy LE08117
Bauer, Nanci LE08118
Baugh, Danny Scott LE08119
Bayles, Martha BR01078
Beam, M. J. LE08120
Beard, Michael A. LE08121
Bearden, Donna LE08122
Beare, Stephen LE08123
Beatty, Dan LE08124, LE08125
Beatty, Paul PR00867
Beck, Henry Cabot AR13026
Becker, Matt LE08126
Bedwell, Audrey LE08127
Beiser, Vince AR13027
Bejarano, Richard Xavier, Sr. LE08128
Belch, John LE08129
Belden, Heath LE08130
Belinski, Jules LE08131
Bellace, Matt LE08132
Bellen, Brian AR13028
Bellino, Teresa LE08133
Benn, Evan LE08134
Bennett, Bill LE08135
Bennett, Courtney LE08136
Benoit, Raymond S. LE08137
BenSreti, E. LE08138
Bentley, Cory Ann LE08139
Benzakein, Ariel LE08140
Benzie, Robert LE08141
Beran, Geoff LE08142
Berce, Steven LE08143
Berger, Arion AR13029, RR10470, RR10737, RR10897, RR10936, RR10942, RR10984, RR11152, RR11657, RR11748, RR11774, RR11947, RR11967, RR12128, RR12204, RR12205, RR12465, RR12507, RR12709, RR12947a, RR13075, RR13080
Berger, Diane Harris AR13030
Bergman, Barry LE08144
Berk, Lori AR13031, AR13032
Berka, Anthony S. LE08145
Berkowitz, Roger LE08146
Berman, Eric AR13033, RR10707, RR11004, RR12518
Berman, Joseph LE08147
Berman, Leslie RR12729
Bermant, Charles AR13034
Bernhard, Lisa AR13035
Bertram, Michelle LE08148
Berube, Michael LE08149
Bessman, Jim RR11232, RR11362, RR11864, RR12075, RR12762, RR12772, RR12844, RR12872
Best, Daisy LE08150
Betts, Michael C. LE08151
Bezzag, Loesa LE08152
Bibler, Jon LE08153
Bilafer, Steve AR13036
Bilenkin, Sharone LE08154
Billera, Joe LE08155
Bilyeau, Nancy AR13037
Binelli, Mark AR13038, AR13039, AR13040, AR13041, AR13042, CR00782
Birkbeck, Matt RR11852, RR12981
Birt, Raymond LE08156
Bishop, Elaine LE08157
Bishop, Jake LE08158
Bitopoulos, Bill LE08159
Bittner, Marlena LE08160
Black, Clint LE08161
Black, David AR13044
Black, Jason LE08162
Black, Kent AR13045, AR13046

Blackburn, Jay LE08163
Blackstock, Peter AR13047, AR13048
Blackstone, Eve LE08164
Blair, Tiffany LE08165
Blake, D. M. LE08166
Blakesberg, Jay AR13049, AR13050
Blanchard, Jake LE08167
Blankholm, Becky LE08168
Blardinelli, Jill RR11035, RR11527
Blechman, R. O. AR13051, AR13052, AR13053, AR13054, AR13055
Blecksmith, Emily LE08169
Blum, Matthew Gregg LE08170
Bly, Robert AR13057
Boehlert, Eric AR13058, AR13059, AR13060, AR13061, AR13062, AR13063, AR13064, AR13065, AR13066, AR13067, AR13068, AR13069, AR13070, AR13071, AR13072, AR13073, AR13074, AR13075, AR13076, AR13077, AR13078, AR13079, AR13080, AR13081, AR13082, AR13083, AR13084, AR13085, AR13086, AR13087, AR13088, AR13089, AR13090, AR13091, AR13092, AR13093, AR13094, AR13095
Boggeri, Lisa LE08171
Bohannon, Allen LE08172
Bon Jovi, Jon LE08173
Bono AR13097
Bonsol, Allan LE08174
Book, Kevin LE08175 AR13098, AR13099
Boopkins, Billy LE08176
Booth, Stephen A. AR13100, AR13101, AR13102, AR13103, AR13104, AR13105, AR13106, AR13107, AR13108, AR13109, AR13110, AR13111, AR13112, AR13113, AR13114, AR13115, AR13116, AR13117, AR13118, AR13119, AR13120, AR13121, AR13122, AR13123, AR13124, AR13125, AR13126, AR13127, AR13128
Borris, Dan AR13129, AR13130
Bosch, Nika LE08177
Bosley, Rachael K. LE08178
Boss, Kit AR13131
Boswinkle, Bill LE08179
Bove, Richie X. LE08180
Bowers, Carol LE08181
Bowie, David LE08182
Boydston, Barbara LE08183
Boykin, Ben LE08184
Boyle, T. Coraghessan AR13132
Bozowski, Nicole LE08185
Bozza, Anthony AR13133, AR13134, AR13135, AR13136, AR13137, AR13138
Braam, Thomas LE08186
Brackett, Nathan AR13139, BR01107, BR01109, RR10708
Bradford, Krista AR13140
Bradford, Meredith LE08187
Bradshaw, Mike LE08188
Brady, Sarah (Chair, Handgun Control, Inc.) LE08189
Brand, Joel AR13141
Brannon, Patrick T. LE08190, LE08191
Brant, James LE08192
Bratto, David LE08193
Brauer, Laurence RR12451
Bream, Jon AR13142
Breckenridge, Darcy LE08194
Breskin, David AR13143, AR13144, AR13145, AR13146, AR13147, AR13148
Bret, Kathryn A. LE08195
Brewer, Lynn A. LE08196
Brewster, Josh LE08197
Brillman, Dan LE08198
Brodsky, Andrew LE08199
Brooks, David LE08200
Brooks, Robert A. LE08201
Broscheid, Deborah LE08202
Brothers, Joyce AR13150
Broughton, Frank AR13151
Brown, Dee BR01055
Brown, Elissa LE08203
Brown, Jeffrey C. LE08204
Brown, Jennie LE08205
Brown, Joseph LE08206
Brown, Kevin LE08207
Brown, Lee P. (Director, Office Of National Drug Control Policy) LE08208
Brown, Martha LE08209
Brown, Patsy LE08210
Browne, Jackson AR13152, BR01113, CR00684, MR01809, RR10935
Brunetti, Maureen LE08211
Bryan, Matthew W. LE08212
Bryant, Kevin LE08213
Bryant, Merriken LE08214
Buchanan, Rob AR13153
Buckingham, Brian LE08215
Buckley, Christopher LE08216
Buckley, Jeff AR13154
Budoff, Irene LE08217
Buell, Bebe LE08218
Buffett, Jimmy AR13155, AR13156
Buffkin, Meg LE08219
Bukovica, Emir LE08220
Bunch, Aimee J. LE08221
Bunn, Torie LE08222
Bures, Juliana LE08223
Burford, Katie LE08224
Burger, Bob LE08225
Burk, Ronnie LE08226
Burke, J. Michael LE08227
Burkert, Tim LE08228
Burkett, Elinor AR13158, BR01074
Burkhardt, Louis LE08229
Burns, Joe AR13160
Burns, Rick, Jr. LE08230
Busby, Robert LE08231
Bussell, Adam LE08232
Buth, Marianne LE08233
Butler, Dave LE08234
Butler, Keith D. (Military Journalist - Staff Sergeant, U.S. Army) LE08235
Byrd, Esther Brock LE08236

C

C. D. LE08284
Cain, David LE08237
Calcagno, Jo Ann (Assistant Program Director, WQBK-FM) LE08238
Caldwell, Mikie LE08239
Cale, John LE08240
Calhoun, Aaron LE08241
Calhoun, Mike LE08242
Callahan, Jim LE08243
Cameron, Sean LE08244
Camino, Anna LE08245
Campbell, Archibald W. LE08246
Campbell, Jack LE08247
Campbell, Leann LE08248
Campbell, Luther BR01043
Canady, Charles T. LE08249
Candler, Jonas LE08250
Canedo, Ken, Father LE08251
Cao, Andy LE08252
Cappello, Robin LE08253
Cappello, Victoria LE08254
Cardwell, Diane AR13162, RR12255, RR12881, RR12983
Carlin, T. M. LE08255
Carman, Colin LE08256
Carmichael, Marni LE08257
Carmona, Oliver LE08258
Carothers, Frank LE08259
Carr, Timothy M. LE08260
Carrico, Monica A. LE08261
Carroll, Bill AR13163
Carroll, Gregg LE08262
Carroll, Lisa LE08263
Carson, Tom AR13164, RR12552
Carter, Stacie LE08264
Carter, Thomas LE08265
Carulli, Frank LE08266
Carvaines, Michael LE08267
Casanta, Sharon LE08268
Case, J. Marshall LE08269
Case, Rachel LE08270
Caselnova, Andrew LE08271
Caserta, Peggy BR01073
Casertano, Matt LE08272
Casey, Mike LE08273
Cash, Rosanne LE08274
Casida, Chris LE08275
Castleberry, Janet LE08276
Cataldi, Anna AR13165
Cate, Thom LE08277
Catfish LE08278
Cathy AR13166
Caudell, Kim Feathers LE08279
Caulder, Lisa LE08280
Cauthen, Karin LE08281
Cave, Nick LE08282
Cavendish, Dave LE08283
Cejas, F. LE08285
Cekinovich, Nicholas LE08286 AR13169
Cenote, Monarcha LE08287
Chafee, John H. (U.S. Senate) LE08288
Chambers, Gordon AR13170, RR10874, RR11604, RR11838, RR12686, RR12870
Chatfield, Lucas LE08289
Cheek, William LE08290
Cheney, Alan LE08291, LE08292
Cheney, Deidre LE08293
Cherico, Mark A. LE08294
Cherniavsky, Neva LE08295
Chetwin, Susan (General Manager, Muzak) LE08296
Child, Desmond LE08297
Childs, Clancy LE08298
Choate, Rob LE08299
Chonin, Neva AR13184, CR00883
Choy, Cindy Cup LE08300
Christianson, Dan LE08301
Christmas, Andrew LE08302
Chung, Bernard LE08303
Chung, Jae LE08304
Cignoli, Christine LE08305
Ciluffo, Jason LE08306
Cioffi, Tara M. LE08307
Ciolek, Danna G. LE08308
Cipollo, Lisa LE08309
Clark, Aaron LE08310
Clark, Beki LE08311
Clark, Charity LE08312
Clark, Tim LE08313
Clark, William Scott LE08314
Clarke, Zane LE08315
Claypool, Les AR13187, LE08316, LE08317
Clear, Randy LE08318
Clemens, Jim LE08319
Clements, Marcelle AR13188
Clohessy, David (Survivors Network Of Those Abused By Priests) LE08320
Coccoli, Christine LE08321
Cocker, Jarvis AR13190
Coe, Sue AR13191, AR13192, AR13193
Coffey, Michael J. AR13194
Cohen, Elizabeth AR13195
Cohen, Jason AR13196, AR13197, AR13198, AR13199, AR13200, AR13201, AR13202, AR13203, AR13204, AR13205, AR13206, AR13207, AR13208, AR13209, AR13210, AR13211, CR00777, CR00800, CR00832, CR00907, RR10572, RR10732, RR11156, RR11225, RR11400, RR12214
Cohen, Patricia AR13212
Cohen, Randee Dawn LE08322
Cohen, Rich AR13213, AR13214, AR13215, AR13216, AR13217, AR13218, AR13219, AR13220, AR13221, AR13222, AR13223, AR13224, AR13225, AR13226, AR13227, AR13228, AR13229, AR13230, AR13231, AR13232, AR13233, AR13234, AR13235, AR13236, AR13237, AR13238, AR13239, AR13240, AR13241, AR13242, AR13243, AR13244,

Cohen, Rich (continued)
AR13245, AR13246, AR13247, AR13248, AR13249, AR13250, AR13251, AR13252, AR13253, AR13254, AR13255, AR13256, AR13257, AR13258, AR13259, AR13260, AR13261, AR13262, AR13263, AR13264, AR13265, AR13266, AR13267, AR13268
Cohn, Jonathan AR13269
Cohn, Nik BR01044
Coke, Gordon P. AR13270
Coker, Cheo H. AR13271, RR10952, RR11118, RR11123, RR11555, RR11648, RR11656, RR11920, RR11997, RR12052, RR12475, RR12534, RR13218, RR13219
Colalillo, Christina LE08323
Colapinto, John AR13272, AR13273, AR13274, AR13275, AR13276, AR13277, AR13278, AR13279, AR13280, AR13281, AR13282, AR13283, AR13284, AR13285
Colatrella, Elizabeth LE08324
Colby, Shannon LE08325
Cole, Lewis AR13286
Cole, Natalie LE08326
Coleman, Mark AR13287, AR13288, AR13289, AR13290, AR13291, AR13292, AR13293, AR13294, AR13295, AR13296, AR13297, AR13298, AR13299, AR13300, AR13301, BR01040, BR01044, BR01046, BR01051, BR01052, BR01053, BR01054, BR01057, BR01058, BR01059, BR01060, BR01064, BR01067, BR01072, BR01077, BR01078, BR01084, BR01087, BR01096, BR01098, BR01108, BR01114, BR01115, BR01118, BR01124, BR01125, BR01126, BR01130, BR01131, CR00673, CR00803, RR10395, RR10409, RR10459, RR10487, RR10493, RR10558, RR10559, RR10596, RR10610, RR10624, RR10631, RR10646, RR10648, RR10656, RR10663, RR10665, RR10671, RR10693, RR10726, RR10728, RR10741, RR10776, RR10808, RR10934, RR10943, RR10995, RR11025, RR11027, RR11077, RR11082, RR11087, RR11148, RR11218, RR11295, RR11353, RR11363, RR11372, RR11459, RR11470, RR11481, RR11492, RR11519, RR11521, RR11572, RR11575, RR11645, RR11687, RR11729, RR11730, RR11736, RR11738, RR11819, RR11820, RR11826, RR11827, RR11850, RR11929, RR11931, RR11932, RR11933, RR11959, RR11964, RR11978, RR11991, RR12038, RR12039, RR12083, RR12131, RR12180, RR12243, RR12292, RR12316, RR12322, RR12343, RR12347, RR12349, RR12357, RR12368, RR12403, RR12408, RR12420, RR12424, RR12519, RR12520, RR12538, RR12539, RR12540, RR12541, RR12558, RR12581, RR12613, RR12615, RR12652, RR12761, RR12795, RR12823, RR12831, RR12879, RR12907, RR12960, RR12978, RR13019, RR13026, RR13069, RR13109, RR13120, RR13122, RR13140, RR13197, RR13208, RR13212, RR13270, RR13272, RR13313, RR13322
Coleman, Rick AR13302
Collins, Barbara (Librarian, Central High School, Knoxville, Tennessee) LE08327
Collins, Edwyn AR13303
Collins, Phil LE08328
Colman, Chris LE08329
Comes, John F. LE08330
Compton, Jeffrey R. LE08331
Comstock, Christina LE08332
Concerned Reader LE08333
Conlon, Cinder LE08334
Connell, David LE08335
Conner, Kathy LE08336
Conners, Janet LE08337
Conrod, Jonan LE08338
Considine, J. D. AR13312, AR13313, AR13314, AR13315, CR00727, CR00774, CR00840, CR00841, CR00945, CR00946, RR10384, RR10499, RR10525, RR10601, RR10641, RR10670, RR10672, RR10675, RR10676, RR10692, RR10752, RR10819, RR10822, RR10828, RR10881, RR10883a, RR10883b, RR10888, RR10905, RR10907, RR10909, RR10974, RR10987, RR11026, RR11043, RR11056, RR11066, RR11080, RR11081, RR11107, RR11108, RR11148a, RR11175, RR11176, RR11182, RR11195, RR11197, RR11198, RR11199, RR11219, RR11275, RR11332, RR11337, RR11394, RR11395, RR11408, RR11409, RR11410, RR11411, RR11412, RR11413, RR11414, RR11415, RR11425, RR11447, RR11466, RR11491, RR11506, RR11518, RR11548, RR11570, RR11580, RR11611a, RR11611d, RR11614, RR11618, RR11619, RR11676, RR11706, RR11723, RR11725, RR11792, RR11797, RR11798, RR11849, RR11887, RR11892, RR11905, RR11910, RR11913, RR11939, RR11970, RR12032, RR12037, RR12096, RR12108, RR12137, RR12151, RR12169, RR12176, RR12194, RR12215, RR12235, RR12236, RR12309, RR12311, RR12318, RR12366, RR12370, RR12371, RR12384, RR12385, RR12392, RR12428, RR12502, RR12506, RR12512, RR12515, RR12527, RR12560, RR12585, RR12633, RR12639, RR12670, RR12701, RR12713, RR12727, RR12759, RR12780, RR12781, RR12819, RR12871, RR12876, RR12877, RR12878, RR12897, RR12898, RR12899, RR12908, RR12909, RR12917, RR12940, RR12948, RR12949, RR12953, RR12954, RR12955, RR12956, RR12957, RR12995, RR13062, RR13068, RR13070, RR13071, RR13072, RR13073, RR13084, RR13087, RR13089, RR13092, RR13103, RR13104, RR13123, RR13129, RR13134, RR13162, RR13163, RR13167, RR13168, RR13185, RR13205, RR13215, RR13230, RR13235, RR13236, RR13239, RR13267, RR13269, RR13273, RR13278, RR13280, RR13294, RR13301, RR13303, RR13304, RR13310, RR13311, RR13321, RR13325, RR13326
Constantino, Mario T. LE08339
Contreras, Frankie LE08340
Contreras, Joseph AR13316 AR13317, AR13318
Conty, Tony LE08341
Conyers, John (United States House of Representatives-Democrat, Michigan) LE08342
Cook, Christine A. LE08343
Cook, Jim LE08344
Cook, Stu LE08345
Coolio AR13319
Coon, Kiersten LE08346
Cooper, Carol AR13320, AR13321, AR13322, RR12232, RR12345
Cooper, Rich AR13323, AR13324
Coover, Kris W. LE08348
Coppola, Angela LE08349
Corbin, Rosemary M. (Mayor, Richmond, California) LE08350
Corcoran, Joel LE08351
Corcoran, Michael RR10680, RR11319
Corrigan, Jeff LE08352
Corsetti, Lorrie LE08353
Costello, Elvis LE08354
Costic, Jeff LE08355
Cott, Jonathan AR13339, AR13340, AR13341, AR13342
Cotton, Mark LE08356
Cotts, Cynthia AR13343
Counts, Kyle LE08357
County, Jayne BR01088
Coupland, Douglas BR01099
Coyle, John LE08358
Crain, William LE08359
Cramer, Erin LE08360
Cramer, Richard Ben AR13345
Cran, Kathy LE08361
Crane, Jessica LE08362, LE08363
Cranston, Alan AR13346, AR13347
Cranston, Michael S. LE08364
Crawford, Miles LE08365, LE08366
Crawford, Paul, J. LE08367
Creasy LE08368
Crenshaw, Marshall BR01079
Cresse, Mark E. AR13349
Creswell, Toby CR00648
Criblez, David J. LE08369, LE08370
Crim, Rick LE08371
Crisafulli, Chuck AR13350, AR13351
Croghan, Peggy LE08372
Cross, Charles R. AR13355, AR13356, AR13357, BR01093, CR00689, CR00842
Crowe, Cameron AR13358, AR13359, AR13360, AR13361
Crowe, Joshua LE08373
Crowley, Aleister BR01062
Crutcher, Michael J. LE08374
Crutcher, Will LE08375
Cruz, Brian LE08376
Cullen, Jim RR11099, RR13131
Culley, Erin AR13362, AR13363, AR13364, AR13365
Cullman, Brian RR11208
Cummings, Sue AR13366, AR13367
Cunningham, Carl LE08377
Curran, Betsy LE08378
Curtis, Gregory RR10569
Curtis, Jeff LE08379
Curtis, Tom AR13368, AR13369
Cuthbertson, Timothy LE08380

D

D.A. LE08381
D. J. LE08424
Da Silva, Ana AR13370
Dagelen, Mark LE08382
Dahl, Shawn AR13371
Dalbesio, Jamie LE08383
Daly, James AR13372, AR13373, AR13374, AR13375
Daly, Steven AR13376, AR13377, AR13378, AR13379, AR13380, AR13381, AR13382, AR13383, AR13384
Damron, Vicki L. LE08384
Damsker, Matt AR13385, BR01045, BR01071, BR01090, BR01103, BR01110, BR01111, BR01121, BR01123, CR00649, RR11585, RR11788, RR11868, RR12419
Dana, Will AR13386
D'Antico, Paul AR13387
D'Arby, Terence Trent AR13388, AR13389, CR00896, LE08385, MR01299, RR10527, RR10529, RR11484, RR12173
D'Arcy AR13390
Darling, Nicolett LE08386
Darzin, Daina AR13391, AR13392, AR13393, AR13394, AR13395, AR13396, AR13397, AR13398, AR13399, AR13400, CR00642, CR00668, CR00670, CR00706, CR00720, CR00723, CR00733, CR00781, CR00795,

CR00799, CR00833, CR00870, CR00881, CR00902, RR10480, RR10575, RR10625, RR10731, RR11021, RR11084, RR11137, RR11986, RR12301, RR12459
Davidson, John AR13401
Davies, Barbara RR11770, RR12141, RR12550
Davies, Jim LE08387
Davies, Pete LE08388
Davies, Ray BR01134
Davis, Christine LE08389
Davis, Elite (Elite Professional Services) LE08390
Davis, Francis LE08391
Davis, Greg LE08392
Davis, Rachel LE08393
Davis, Stephen AR13402
Davis, Steven LE08394
Davis, Virginia B. LE08395
Dawson, Amy E. LE08396
Day, Pamela LE08397
Dayton, Elizabeth LE08398
Dayton, Mark LE08399
De Jong, Jonathan LE08400
De Rosier, Sarah LE08401
De Vaul, Philip Hart, Esq. LE08402
Dean, Chuck AR13403, AR13404, AR13405, AR13406, AR13407, AR13408, AR13409, AR13410, CR00921, RR10566, RR11573, RR12252, RR12499
Dean, John AR13411, AR13412
Dean, Roger LE08403
Dean, Wayne LE08404
DeCurtis, Anthony AR13413, AR13414, AR13415, AR13416, AR13417, AR13418, AR13419, AR13420, AR13421, AR13422, AR13423, AR13424, AR13425, AR13426, AR13427, AR13428, AR13429, AR13430, AR13431, AR13432, AR13433, AR13434, AR13435, AR13436, AR13437, AR13438, AR13439, AR13440, AR13441, AR13442, AR13443, AR13444, AR13445, AR13446, AR13447, BR01043, BR01049, BR01073, BR01081, CR00675, CR00707, CR00801, CR00875, CR00932, MR01356, MR01398, RR10435, RR10436, RR10439, RR10528, RR10750, RR10886, RR10932, RR10947, RR11029, RR11036, RR11051, RR11467, RR11963, RR12097, RR12186, RR12305, RR12364, RR12514, RR12516, RR12554, RR12612, RR12614, RR12642, RR12714, RR12716, RR12793, RR12853, RR13105
DeFalco, Ritch LE08405
DeFoer, Damon LE08406
DeGrazia-Sanders, John LE08407
Deitz, Alex LE08408
DeLuca, Dan CR00860
DeLuca, Shannon LE08409
Denny, Jyrone, Jr. LE08410
Dentico, Todd LE08411
DePaola, John AR13449
DeParrie, Paul (Editor, Life Advocate) LE08412
Depoto, Marc D. LE08413
D'Erasmo, Stacey AR13450, RR10854, RR11461, RR12118
DeRogatis, Jim AR13451, AR13452, AR13453, AR13454, AR13455, AR13456, AR13457, AR13458, AR13459, BR01099, CR00697, CR00708, CR00886, RR10590, RR11083, RR11285, RR11490, RR11550, RR11596, RR11809, RR12121, RR12350, RR12351, RR12544, RR12601, RR12696, RR12951
Dery, Johanna LE08414
Dery, Mark AR13460, AR13461
Des Barres, Pamela BR01106, BR01122
DeWitt, Carey A. LE08415
Diane LE08416
Dickson, Harvey LE08417
Diehl, Matt AR13462, AR13463, AR13464, AR13465, AR13466, AR13467, AR13468, AR13469, AR13470, AR13471, AR13472, CR00752, CR00815, RR10398, RR10519, RR10520, RR10604, RR10608, RR10609, RR10611, RR10651, RR10705, RR10937, RR10949, RR10992, RR11011, RR11155, RR11188, RR11266, RR11316, RR11318, RR11584, RR11652, RR12034, RR12126, RR12195, RR12289, RR12574, RR12597, RR12608, RR12616, RR12675, RR12676, RR12828, RR13005
Diehl, Mindy LE08418
Digby, Alan LE08419
Dillard, L. R. LE08420
Dillon, Alex LE08421
DiMartino, Dave CR00903
Dinsmore, Jeff LE08422
Dionne, Paul A. LE08423
Dizney, Joe AR13473
Dmytryk, Vicky LE08425
Dockery, Sue Ellen LE08426
Doctorow, E. L. AR13474
Dodd, David BR01096
Dodge, Brian LE08427
Dominicis, Jorge (Flo-Sun Inc.) LE08428
Donahoe, Tom LE08429
Donald, Kyra LE08430
Donald, Tom CR00694
Donelly, Tanya AR13475, BR01095, MR01693, MR01759, RR11078, RR11771, RR12127, RR12427
Donnelly, Jason LE08431
Donnerstag, Roslyn LE08432
Donohue, John LE08433
Donovan, Scott LE08434
Dougan, John RR11136, RR12464
Douglass, Amy LE08435
Dowdy, Julie LE08436
Dowell, Susannah LE08437
Doyle, Larry AR13478
Doyle, Macreena LE08438
Dr. John BR01126
Drago, Karen LE08439
Drake, G. L. LE08440
Drake, Joanne LE08441
Drake, Pamela AR13479
Drakeford, Dale B. LE08442
Drew, Dan LE08443
Drew, Marilyn LE08444
Dreyfuss, Robert AR13480, AR13481
Drinnon, Richard BR01066
Driscoll, Kevin LE08445
Drozdowski, Ted AR13482, AR13483, CR00741, CR00778, CR00811, CR00918, CR00937, RR10599, RR10664, RR10756, RR10832, RR10835, RR11239, RR11240, RR11272, RR11345, RR11637, RR11692, RR11805, RR11835, RR11847, RR12125, RR12146, RR12278, RR12396, RR13159
Drozdyk, Charlie AR13484
Du Plessis, Adrian LE08446
Dubin, K. L. LE08447
Dudman, Joe LE08448
Duex, Steven LE08449
Duffy, Thom AR13486, CR00690, CR00790
Dugan, Renee LE08450
Dugan, Sarah LE08451
Dunlap, Barbara J. LE08452
Dunn, Jancee AR13487, AR13488, AR13489, AR13490, AR13491, AR13492, AR13493, AR13494, AR13495, AR13496, AR13497, AR13498, AR13499, AR13500, AR13501, AR13502, AR13503, AR13504, AR13505, AR13506, AR13507, AR13508, AR13509, AR13510, AR13511, AR13512, AR13513, AR13514, AR13515, AR13516, AR13517, AR13518, AR13519, AR13520, AR13521, AR13522, AR13523, AR13524, AR13525, AR13526, AR13527, AR13528, AR13529, AR13530, AR13531, AR13532, AR13533, AR13534, AR13535, AR13536, AR13537, AR13538, AR13539, AR13540, AR13541, AR13542, AR13543, AR13544, AR13545, AR13546, AR13547, AR13548, AR13549, AR13550, AR13551, AR13552, AR13553, AR13554, AR13555, AR13556, AR13557, AR13558, AR13559, AR13560, AR13561, AR13562, AR13563, AR13564, AR13565, AR13566, AR13567, AR13568, AR13569, AR13570, AR13571, AR13572, AR13573, BR01106, RR10388, RR13274, RR13298
Dunning, Thomas N. LE08453
Durant, Wendy LE08454
Durham, Curtis W., Jr. LE08455
Duritz, Adam AR13574, MR01228, RR12625
Dylan, Bob BR01123
Dylan, Jakob AR13575, CR00664, CR00717, RR10501
Dyrek, Mark LE08456
Dyson, Michael Eric RR10392, RR10492, RR10494, RR11017, RR11940, RR11993a, RR12059, RR12245, RR12254, RR12410, RR12472, RR12477, RR12820, RR12928, RR12936, RR13152, RR13154, RR13155, RR13206, RR13309

E

E., Rebecca LE08457
AR13576
Earle, Simon LE08458
Easterling, Shan LE08459, LE08460
E.B. LE08461
Ebert, Crissy LE08462
Eberth, Garrett LE08463
Eccles, Andrew AR13577
Eccles, Bert LE08464
Echlin, Hobey CR00821
Ecke, Ray LE08465
Eddy, Chuck RR10508, RR10563, RR10729, RR10869, RR10959, RR10971, RR11241, RR11977, RR12005, RR12248, RR12361, RR12456, RR12529, RR12564, RR12677, RR12776, RR13108, RR13116, RR13282
Edmonson, G. Huey, Jr. LE08466
Edwards, Lew LE08467
Efstathiou, Jim AR13579
Eggers, Paul W. LE08468
Ehrlich, Dimitri AR13580, AR13581, AR13582, AR13583, AR13584, AR13585, AR13586, AR13587, AR13588, AR13589, AR13590, AR13591, AR13592, AR13593, AR13594, AR13595, CR00725, CE00750, CR00766, CR00873, RR10653, RR11124, RR11284, RR11383, RR11649, RR11825, RR12806
Ehrmann, Eric AR13596, LE08469
Eichhorn, Dennis LE08470
Eidson, Matt LE08471
Eilberg, Jonathan S. LE08472
Eisenhour, Andrew LE08473
Eitzel, Mark AR13597
Eldridge, Corinne LE08474
Eldridge, Matt LE08475
Elias LE08476
Ellingsworth, Linda LE08477
Elliot, Joe LE08478
Ellsworth, Matt LE08479
Emanuel, Matt LE08480
Engeler, Amy AR13599
Englender, Jonathan LE08481
Englert, Francis LE08482
Eno, Brian AR13600, LE08483
Enriquez, Eric LE08484
Erdman, Ed LE08485
Erickson, Steve AR13601,

AR13602, AR13603
Erstad, Sped LE08486
Escott, Colin BR01077
Eshleman, Kristen LE08487
Esquerra, Teresa C. LE08488
Eszterhas, Joe AR13604
Ethan S. LE08489
Etheridge, Eric AR13605, AR13606, AR13607
Etheridge, Melissa AR13608, LE08490
Evangelisto, Christie LE08491
Evans, Bob LE08492
Evans, Daniel R. LE08493
Evans, John G. LE08494
Evans, Krista LE08495
Evans, Paul CR00814, CR00942, RR10383, RR10410, RR10416, RR10420, RR10427, RR10430, RR10437, RR10440, RR10442, RR10452, RR10454, RR10471, RR10476, RR10503, RR10521, RR10533, RR10545, RR10546, RR10547, RR10549, RR10568, RR10591, RR10598, RR10618, RR10619, RR10621, RR10635, RR10640, RR10647, RR10659, RR10666, RR10684, RR10687, RR10689, RR10690, RR10695, RR10710, RR10751, RR10788, RR10802, RR10812, RR10843, RR10861, RR10863, RR10870, RR10885, RR10893, RR10894, RR10902, RR10926, RR10929, RR10931, RR10938, RR10944, RR10948, RR10953, RR10954, RR10957, RR10966, RR10968, RR10969, RR10975, RR10982, RR10985, RR10996, RR11000, RR11006, RR11030, RR11032, RR11033, RR11042, RR11050, RR11052, RR11058, RR11069, RR11079, RR11103, RR11142, RR11149, RR11166, RR11174, RR11177, RR11186, RR11201, RR11209, RR11213, RR11215, RR11222, RR11230, RR11252, RR11265, RR11269, RR11288, RR11294, RR11304, RR11328, RR11336, RR11349, RR11351, RR11370, RR11376, RR11422, RR11432, RR11440, RR11446, RR11452, RR11468, RR11480, RR11495, RR11500, RR11503, RR11504, RR11505, RR11509, RR11541, RR11547, RR11553, RR11563, RR11571, RR11590, RR11595, RR11611, RR11611c, RR11626, RR11639, RR11641, RR11658, RR11665, RR11667, RR11675, RR11684, RR11689, RR11697, RR11700, RR11705, RR11707, RR11715, RR11716, RR11726, RR11746, RR11752, RR11779, RR11803, RR11806, RR11810, RR11814, RR11824, RR11832, RR11846, RR11860, RR11865, RR11867, RR11869, RR11886, RR11893, RR11897, RR11906, RR11921, RR11955, RR11958, RR11961, RR11995, RR12008, RR12010, RR12022, RR12025a, RR12041, RR12045, RR12048, RR12054, RR12061, RR12064, RR12065, RR12076, RR12080, RR12087, RR12098, RR12102, RR12108a, RR12136, RR12138, RR12143, RR12156, RR12160, RR12161, RR12164, RR12170, RR12179, RR12182, RR12187, RR12192, RR12206, RR12216, RR12221, RR12240, RR12247, RR12279, RR12288, RR12302, RR12307, RR12308, RR12310, RR12321, RR12324, RR12362, RR12363, RR12372, RR12379, RR12386, RR12409, RR12431, RR12433, RR12468, RR12482, RR12495, RR12505, RR12513, RR12549, RR12575, RR12586, RR12592, RR12598, RR12611, RR12634, RR12643, RR12645, RR12647, RR12657, RR12667, RR12668, RR12689, RR12690, RR12691, RR12715, RR12717, RR12743, RR12744, RR12756, RR12758, RR12774, RR12794, RR12812, RR12814, RR12841, RR12843, RR12849, RR12852, RR12864, RR12886, RR12889, RR12901, RR12905, RR12923, RR12927, RR12934, RR12968, RR12970, RR12988, RR12998, RR13000, RR13043, RR13099, RR13110, RR13128, RR13136, RR13139, RR13150, RR13169, RR13173, RR13179, RR13189, RR13213, RR13216, RR13237
Eviston, Todd LE08496
Ewald, Russ AR13610
Ewert, Marc E. LE08497, LE08498
Ewing, Rose LE08499

F

Fabb, Charlie LE08500 AR13611
Failor, Thomas LE08501
Faithfull, Marianne BR01067
Falk, Bradley LE08502
Falk, Stephen LE08503
Fallon, Melanie LE08504
Fallow, John LE08505
Fannon, Gary AR13612, LE08506
Fannon, Linda LE08507
Farber, Jim AR13613, AR13614, AR13615, AR13616, AR13617, AR13618, AR13619, AR13620, RR10879, RR11444, RR11545, RR12218
Fargo, Hank LE08508
Farkas, Rachel LE08509
Farland, Adam LE08510
Farmer, Greg LE08511
Farrell, Kevin LE08512
Farsi, Linda LE08513
Fayer, Steve BR01129
Fayner, Scott LE08514
Featherstone, Peter J. LE08515
Fein, Art BR01083
Feldman, Mark LE08516
Feldman, Richard J. (Executive Director, American Shooting Sports Council) LE08517
Feldt, Gloria (President, Planned Parenthood Of America) LE08518
Felton, David AR13625
Fentoff, Herb LE08519
Ferdon, Ricky LE08520
Ferguson, Jeanne LE08521
Ferguson, Kate RR11321, RR11327
Fernando, S. H., Jr. AR13626, AR13627, AR13628, CR00793, RR10472, RR10626, RR10632, RR10845, RR10911, RR10939, RR11228, RR11238, RR11292, RR11309, RR11338, RR11387, RR11701, RR11767, RR12021, RR12024, RR12280, RR12338, RR12595, RR12869, RR13035, RR13188, RR13312
Ferraro, Tony LE08522
Ferren, Scott LE08523
Fidler, Danielle LE08524
Fierst, David LE08525
Finch, Jannette LE08526
Fine, Jason AR13629, AR13630, AR13631, AR13632, AR13633, AR13634, CR00669, CR00692, CR00724, CR00767, CR00792, CR00818, CR00820, CR00922, RR10748, RR11015, RR11344, RR12069, RR12434, RR12769
Finney, Stephen C., Jr. LE08527
Fischer, Ron LE08528
Fischia LE08529
Fisher, Carrie AR13635
Fisher, Chase LE08530
Fisher, Liz LE08531
Fitzgerald, Mike LE08532
Fitzhugh, Chrissie LE08533
Fitzpatrick, Sean LE08534
Flanagan, J. Brian AR13637
Flaum, Eric CR00899, RR10551, RR11019, RR11765, RR11853, RR12201, RR12887, RR12973
Fleck, Joe LE08535
Fleischmann, Mark AR13638, AR13639, AR13640, AR13641, AR13642, AR13643, AR13644, AR13645, AR13646, AR13647, AR13648, AR13649, AR13650
Fleming, Ross LE08536
Fletcher, Andrew LE08537
Fletcher, Doug (Publisher, Journal Of Nursing Jocularity) LE08538
Fletcher, Matthew J. LE08539
Flippo, Chet AR13651
Flowers, Stephen W. LE08540
Foege, Alec AR13652, AR13653, AR13654, AR13655, AR13656, AR13657, AR13658, AR13659, AR13660, AR13661, AR13662, AR13663, AR13664, AR13665, AR13666, AR13667, AR13668, AR13669, AR13670, AR13671, AR13672, BR01057, CR00705, CR00865, CR00866, CR00908, CR00941, RR11159, RR12094
Fogarty, Kelly P. LE08541
Fogg, Eric LE08542
Fogle, Thomas LE08543
Fong-Torres, Ben AR13673, AR13674
Fontaine, Heather LE08544
Fontenote, Troy LE08545
Fortini, Ellen J. LE08546
Fortner, Lynn LE08547
Foss, Nicholas LE08548
Foster, Douglas AR13684
Foster, Nick LE08549
France, Kim AR13685, AR13686, AR13687, AR13688
Francine, Lisa LE08550
Frank, Philly LE08551
Frankel, Alex LE08552
Frascella, Lawrence AR13689, BR01048
Fraser, Donovan LE08553
Fream, Rob LE08554
Fredrickson, Dan LE08555
Freedman, Samuel G. AR13690
Freeman, Priscilla (Humans Against Nuclear-Waste Dumps) LE08556
French, David T. LE08557
French, Valerie LE08558
Fricke, David AR13691, AR13692, AR13693, AR13694, AR13695, AR13696, AR13697, AR13698, AR13699, AR13700, AR13701, AR13702, AR13703, AR13704, AR13705, AR13706, AR13707, AR13708, AR13709, AR13710, AR13711, AR13712, AR13713, AR13714, AR13715, AR13716, AR13717, AR13718, AR13719, AR13720, AR13721, AR13722, AR13723, AR13724, AR13725, AR13726, AR13727, AR13728, AR13729, AR13730, AR13731, AR13732, AR13733, AR13734, AR13735, AR13736, AR13737, AR13738, AR13739, AR13740, AR13741, AR13742, AR13743, AR13744, AR13745, AR13746, AR13747, AR13748, AR13749, AR13750, AR13751, AR13752, AR13753, AR13754, AR13755, AR13756, AR13757, AR13758, AR13759, BR01065, BR01082, BR01083, BR01133, CR00646, CR00676, CR00679, CR00716, CR00734, CR00745, CR00746, CR00761, CR00776, CR00786, CR00871, CR00927, CR00928, RR10389, RR10399, RR10400, RR10401, RR10402, RR10405, RR10406, RR10407, RR10412, RR10419, RR10421, RR10429, RR10448, RR10449, RR10450, RR10456, RR10458, RR10461, RR10463, RR10467, RR10468, RR10479, RR10536,

Fricke, David (continued) RR10574, RR10607, RR10612, RR10614, RR10617, RR10627, RR10643, RR10644, RR10645, RR10661, RR10667, RR10677, RR10688, RR10697, RR10713, RR10727, RR10730, RR10761, RR10767, RR10770, RR10777, RR10785, RR10799, RR10801, RR10807b, RR10821, RR10827, RR10830, RR10841, RR10851, RR10860, RR10862, RR10865, RR10867, RR10871, RR10873, RR10875, RR10876, RR10887, RR10901, RR10904, RR10912, RR10940, RR10945, RR10946, RR10950, RR10978, RR10979, RR10981, RR10988, RR10989, RR10991, RR10997, RR10998, RR11009, RR11014, RR11016, RR11020, RR11037, RR11045, RR11049, RR11070, RR11073, RR11074, RR11075, RR11092, RR11106, RR11114, RR11115, RR11116, RR11119, RR11120, RR11121, RR11126, RR11127, RR11131, RR11132, RR11133, RR11134, RR11139, RR11143, RR11150, RR11157, RR11160, RR11167, RR11169, RR11180, RR11181, RR11187, RR11190, RR11196, RR11217, RR11220, RR11221, RR11223, RR11236, RR11247, RR11248, RR11274, RR11277, RR11283, RR11286, RR11289, RR11290, RR11291, RR11296, RR11298, RR11310, RR11311, RR11323, RR11324, RR11326, RR11333, RR11339, RR11341, RR11352, RR11360, RR11405, RR11416, RR11420, RR11421, RR11428, RR11430, RR11431, RR11433, RR11436, RR11438, RR11439, RR11445, RR11453, RR11454, RR11463, RR11475, RR11479, RR11485, RR11486, RR11489, RR11493, RR11498, RR11526, RR11529, RR11537, RR11539, RR11546, RR11551, RR11556, RR11578, RR11579, RR11581, RR11594, RR11606, RR11608, RR11612, RR11617, RR11627, RR11643, RR11653, RR11655, RR11672, RR11677, RR11677a, RR11678, RR11694, RR11699, RR11702, RR11710, RR11712, RR11719, RR11727, RR11728, RR11734, RR11737, RR11738a, RR11759, RR11769, RR11776, RR11777, RR11781, RR11783, RR11784, RR11786, RR11800, RR11801, RR11804, RR11811, RR11829, RR11833, RR11834, RR11839, RR11845, RR11861, RR11875, RR11878, RR11880, RR11880a, RR11881, RR11882, RR11885, RR11891, RR11898, RR11899, RR11911, RR11922, RR11924, RR11946, RR11969, RR11971, RR11975, RR11982, RR11983, RR11987, RR11988, RR12004, RR12013, RR12014c, RR12027, RR12035, RR12044, RR12051, RR12053, RR12055, RR12057, RR12058, RR12063, RR12074, RR12078, RR12079, RR12086, RR12089, RR12109, RR12110, RR12111, RR12114, RR12132, RR12134, RR12140, RR12145, RR12168, RR12184, RR12188, RR12200, RR12203, RR12209, RR12213, RR12219, RR12225, RR12231, RR12233, RR12241, RR12249, RR12250, RR12253, RR12256, RR12277, RR12286, RR12296, RR12297, RR12298, RR12300, RR12314, RR12315, RR12317, RR12327, RR12337a, RR12339, RR12340, RR12348, RR12355, RR12365, RR12377, RR12393, RR12395, RR12402, RR12405, RR12407, RR12411, RR12413, RR12414, RR12430, RR12435, RR12438, RR12439, RR12449, RR12458, RR12470, RR12476, RR12478, RR12484, RR12485, RR12486, RR12488, RR12489, RR12490, RR12504, RR12510, RR12522, RR12524, RR12525, RR12528, RR12535, RR12545, RR12559, RR12561, RR12567, RR12570, RR12572, RR12577, RR12582, RR12589, RR12591, RR12604, RR12606, RR12617, RR12620, RR12621, RR12622, RR12623, RR12624, RR12629, RR12630, RR12635, RR12641, RR12651, RR12658, RR12662, RR12663, RR12664, RR12665, RR12671, RR12679, RR12694, RR12703, RR12711, RR12722, RR12726, RR12728, RR12733, RR12736, RR12739, RR12752, RR12767, RR12777, RR12778, RR12779, RR12798, RR12799, RR12803, RR12813, RR12815, RR12817, RR12839, RR12858, RR12866, RR12867, RR12868, RR12875, RR12883, RR12899a, RR12916, RR12938, RR12942, RR12943, RR12950, RR12982, RR12984, RR12991, RR12996, RR12997, RR13002, RR13011, RR13014, RR13023, RR13032, RR13039, RR13041, RR13052, RR13059, RR13083, RR13088, RR13091, RR13101, RR13107, RR13118, RR13127, RR13132, RR13133, RR13157, RR13160, RR13166, RR13176, RR13193, RR13198, RR13204, RR13211, RR13214, RR13217, RR13220, RR13227, RR13229, RR13232, RR13241, RR13249, RR13257, RR13258, RR13260, RR13271, RR13293, RR13295, RR13307, RR13316, RR13323, RR13328

Friedline, Rick LE08559

Friedman, Caroline LE08560

Friedman, David Benioff LE08561

Friel, Gillian LE08562

Friesen, Dale LE08563

Friesen, Jeffrey LE08564

Frisbie, Fritz LE08565

Frischmann, Justine AR13760

Fritz, Matthew LE08566

Fritz, Matthew R. LE08567

Frost, Deborah AR13762, CR00887, RR12185, RR12191, RR12283

Frost, Nicholas LE08568

Fryman, Avi LE08569

Fuller, Graham AR13763

Fuller, John LE08570

Fuller, Kimberly A. LE08571

Futey, Jason LE08572

Futterman, Ellen AR13764

Futterman, Steve AR13765, AR13766, AR13767, AR13768, AR13769, AR13770, AR13771, AR13772, AR13773, AR13774, AR13775, AR13776, AR13777, AR13778, AR13779, AR13780, AR13781, AR13782, AR13783, AR13784, AR13785, AR13786, BR01117, CR00657, CR00672, CR00729, CR00771, CR00812, CR00864, CR00872, CR00934, RR10386, RR10403, RR10404, RR10457, RR10465, RR10495, RR10496, RR10512, RR10539, RR10554, RR10587, RR10588, RR10589, RR10592, RR10593, RR10594, RR10595, RR10597, RR10686, RR10709, RR10717, RR10740, RR10745, RR10762, RR10772, RR10773, RR10774, RR10775, RR10798, RR10800, RR10800a, RR10803, RR10804, RR10805, RR10806, RR10807, RR10809, RR10814, RR10836, RR10838, RR10839, RR10840, RR10842, RR10850, RR10852, RR10892, RR10906, RR10908, RR10910, RR10963, RR10986, RR11012, RR11061, RR11062, RR11068, RR11104, RR11117, RR11146, RR11164, RR11168, RR11245, RR11246, RR11256, RR11257, RR11273, RR11276, RR11293, RR11299, RR11308, RR11342, RR11343, RR11374, RR11388, RR11389, RR11390, RR11391, RR11392, RR11402, RR11424, RR11462, RR11502, RR11517, RR11557, RR11564, RR11569, RR11592, RR11630, RR11693, RR11696, RR11704, RR11731, RR11732, RR11733, RR11795, RR11817, RR11837, RR11916, RR11917, RR11918, RR11919, RR11927, RR11928, RR11938, RR11965, RR11966, RR11981, RR12026, RR12028, RR12033, RR12120, RR12122, RR12130, RR12144, RR12152, RR12153, RR12171, RR12210, RR12211, RR12222, RR12260, RR12263, RR12265, RR12270, RR12271, RR12274, RR12313, RR12320, RR12359, RR12383, RR12398, RR12399, RR12443, RR12497, RR12511, RR12654, RR12681, RR12682, RR12683, RR12684, RR12704, RR12718, RR12730, RR12786, RR12890, RR12914, RR12932, RR12935, RR12962, RR12976, RR13038, RR13097, RR13226, RR13287, RR13288, RR13317

G

G., Jenny LE08573

Gaal, Gary LE08574

Gaar, Gillian G. AR13787, AR13788, BR01116, CR00855, CR00878, RR11138, RR13100, RR13121

Gaboury, Dennis AR13789

Gaenir, Palyne LE08575

Gaines, Donna AR13790

Gaines, Gregory LE08576

Galeano, Eduardo BR01094

Gallagher, Hugh AR13791

Gallagher, Noel AR13792

Galtney, Smith RR12084

Galvin, Peter RR11300, RR11544, RR12014b, RR12239, RR12387, RR12389, RR12980

Gambaccini, Paul AR13793

Gans, David AR13794

Garbarini, Vic RR11483

Gardner, Elysa AR13795, AR13796, AR13797, AR13798, AR13799, AR13800, AR13801, AR13802, AR13803, AR13804, AR13805, AR13806, AR13807, AR13808, AR13809, AR13810, AR13811, AR13812, AR13813, AR13814, AR13815, AR13816, AR13817, AR13818, AR13819, AR13820, AR13821, AR13822, AR13823, AR13824, AR13825, AR13826, AR13827, AR13828, AR13829, AR13830, AR13831, BR01116, BR01122, CR00638, CR00682, CR00742, CR00751, CR00756, CR00759, CR00763, CR00879, CR00898, CR00920, RR10385, RR10474, RR10550, RR10606, RR10662, RR10685, RR10837, RR10882, RR10889, RR10915, RR10917, RR10922, RR10990, RR11085, RR11100, RR11102, RR11163, RR11165, RR11268, RR11434, RR11538, RR11543, RR11685, RR11686, RR11744, RR11843, RR11952, RR12001, RR12067, RR12107, RR12148, RR12155, RR12437, RR12481, RR12576, RR12636, RR12640, RR12723, RR12731, RR12782, RR12790, RR12791, RR12952, RR13034, RR13130, RR13146

Gardner, M. Victoria LE08577
Garelick, Jon AR13832, RR11948
Garfield, Simon AR13833
Garland, Eric LE08578
Garlick, Erin LE08579
Garneau, Bill LE08580
Garofalo, Janeane AR13834
Garrard, Dale LE08581
Garrett, Larry Alton LE08582
Gauthier, Martina LE08583
Gehr, Richard AR13835, AR13836, AR13837, AR13838, RR11857, RR12165, RR13021
Geitner, Paul AR13839, AR13840, AR13841
Gelber, Eric LE08584
Geller, Keith LE08585
George, Jenny LE08586
George-Warren, Holly AR13843, AR13844, AR13845, AR13846, AR13847, AR13848, AR13849, AR13850, BR01050, RR10441, RR10484, RR10557, RR10757, RR11094, RR11330, RR11673, RR11935, RR12056, RR12425, RR12656, RR12775, RR12900, RR12924
Gerardo LE08587
Gerstein, Lawrence (Director, International Tibet Movement) LE08588
Getman, Josh LE08589
GhosstMyst@aol.com LE08590
Gibbons, Billy AR13851
Gibson, William AR13852
Gideon, Tim LE08591
Gilbert, Debbie LE08592
Giles, Jeff AR13853, AR13854, AR13855, AR13856, AR13857, AR13858, AR13859, AR13860, AR13861, AR13862, AR13863, AR13864, AR13865, AR13866, AR13867, AR13868, AR13869, AR13870, AR13871, AR13872, AR13873, AR13874, AR13875, AR13876, AR13877, AR13878, AR13879, AR13880, AR13881, AR13882, AR13883, AR13884, AR13885, AR13886, AR13887, AR13888, AR13889, AR13890, AR13891, AR13892, AR13893, AR13894, AR13895, AR13896, AR13897, AR13898, AR13899, AR13900, AR13901, AR13902, AR13903, AR13904, AR13905, AR13906
Gill, Mark Stuart AR13907
Gillen, James LE08593
Gilmartin, Eric LE08594
Gilmore, Mikal AR13908, AR13909, AR13910, AR13911, AR13912, AR13913, AR13914, AR13915, AR13916, RR12610
Gilstrap, Peter AR13917, AR13918
Gilyard, Burl RR12999, RR13033
Gimarc, George BR01101
Gionfriddo, Gina LE08595
Giordano, A. J. LE08596
Giraudo, Angie LE08597
Gitter, Mike AR13919, CR00696, CR00719, CR00735, CR00796
Gladstone, Eric CR00758
Glaser, Milton AR13921
Glass, Daniel LE08598
Glebbeek, Caesar BR01082
Glenn, Amanda LE08599
Glick, Daniel AR13922, AR13923
Glinert, Ed BR01107
Gnoshita, Mikk LE08600
Gold, Jonathan AR13924, AR13925, AR13926, AR13927, RR11322, RR12040, RR12526
Goldammer, Rosmarie LE08601
Goldberg, Michael AR13928, AR13929, AR13930, AR13931, AR13932, AR13933, AR13934, AR13935, AR13936, AR13937, AR13938, AR13939, AR13940, AR13941, AR13942, AR13943, AR13944, AR13945, AR13946, AR13947, AR13948, AR13949, AR13950, AR13951, AR13952, AR13953, AR13954, AR13955, AR13956, AR13957, AR13958, AR13959, AR13960, AR13961, AR13962, AR13963, AR13964, AR13965, AR13966, AR13967, AR13968, AR13969, AR13970, AR13971, AR13972, AR13973, AR13974, AR13975, AR13976, AR13977, AR13978, AR13979, AR13980, AR13981, AR13982, AR13983, AR13984, AR13985, AR13986, AR13987, AR13988, AR13989, AR13990, AR13991, AR13992, AR13993, AR13994, AR13995, AR13996, CR00640, CR00757, CR00843, CR00905
Goldschmid, Eyal LE08602
Goldstein, Patrick AR13998, AR13999, AR14000
Goldstein, Paul LE08603
Goldstein, Steve LE08604
Gollin, Randi AR14002, AR14003
Golpinar, Derya LE08605
Gonos, Michael LE08606
Gonzales, Laurence AR14004
Gonzales, Mindy LE08607
Gonzalez, J. LE08608
Gonzalez, Jim LE08609
Goodell, Jeff AR14005, AR14006, AR14007, AR14008, AR14009, AR14010, AR14011, AR14012, AR14013, AR14014, AR14015, AR14016
Goodman, Fred AR14017, AR14018, AR14019, AR14020, AR14021, AR14022, AR14023, AR14024, AR14025, AR14026, AR14027, AR14028, AR14029, AR14030, AR14031, AR14032, AR14033, AR14034, AR14035, AR14036, AR14037, RR11002
Goodman, Ryan J. LE08610
Goodwin, Andrew CR00858
Goodyear, Sarah AR14038
Goosens, Miles LE08611
Goraieb, Rob LE08612
Gordon, Robert AR14039, AR14040
Gordy, Berry BR01125
Gorenfeld, John LE08613
Goslow, Paul LE08614
Gould, Sean LE08615
Gowdy, Stephanie LE08616
Gowen, Anne AR14041, AR14042
Graczyk, T. J. LE08617
Graff, Gary AR14043
Graham, Bill BR01049
Graham, Gary LE08618
Graham, Holly A. LE08619
Graham, Ken LE08620
Graham, Lamar AR14044, AR14045, AR14046
Grant, Duncan LE08621
Graves, D'Ann LE08622
Graves, Tom RR11312, RR12174, RR12415, RR12423
Graves, Troy C. LE08623
Grayson, George T. LE08624
Greber, Jonathan LE08625
Greeder, Chris LE08626
Green, John LE08627
Green, Robin AR14055
Greenberg, Corey AR14056
Greenfield, Robert AR14057, AR14058, BR01049, BR01060
Greenfield, Steve LE08628
Greenlaw, Rob LE08629
Greenlees, Teresa LE08630
Greenwood, Jane A. LE08631
Gregersen, Andrea M. LE08632
Gregg, Allison LE08633
Gregory, V. LE08634
Greider, William AR14059, AR14060, AR14061, AR14062, AR14063, AR14064, AR14065, AR14066, AR14067, AR14068, AR14069, AR14070, AR14071, AR14072, AR14073, AR14074, AR14075, AR14076, AR14077, AR14078, AR14079, AR14080, AR14081, AR14082, AR14083, AR14084, AR14085, AR14086, AR14087, AR14088, AR14089, AR14090, AR14091, AR14092, AR14093, AR14094, AR14095, AR14096, AR14097, AR14098, AR14099, AR14100, AR14101, AR14102, AR14103, AR14104, AR14105, AR14106, AR14107, AR14108, AR14109, AR14110, AR14111, AR14112, AR14113, AR14114, AR14115, AR14116, AR14117, AR14118, AR14119, AR14120, AR14121, AR14122, LE08635
Grey, Ellen LE08636
Griffin, Rob LE08637
Grigsby, Camilla LE08638
Grogan, Emmett BR01105
Groshner, Gary LE08639
Gross, Allison LE08640
Gross, Allison Levie LE08641
Gross, Wendy LE08642
Grossman, Dan AR14123
Grubb, Karen LE08643
Grunke, Chris LE08644
Gudmundsdottir, Bjork AR14124, BR01120, MR02057
Guender, Suki LE08645
Guida-Colonno, Laurie LE08646
Guill, Mark LE08647
Gunderloy, Mike BR01133
Gunning, Jonathan LE08648
Guralnick, Peter BR01084
Gustafson, Carey LE08649
Gutman, David BR01054
Guy, Ed LE08650
Gyde, Amelia LE08651

H

Haber, Matt LE08652
Haberman, Mary LE08653
Hadley, Jess LE08654
Haefeker, Amy LE08655
Hagadorn, N. LE08656
Hagan, Brian LE08657
Haik, Mac LE08658, LE08659
Haik, Mack LE08660
Haislip, Theresa LE08661
Hajdu, David BR01087 AR14126, AR14127, AR14128
Hall, Jane LE08662
Hall, Justin AR14129
Hall, Kaylan LE08663
Hall, Roger AR14130
Hamerlinck, John LE08664
Hamilton, Diane LE08665
Hamilton, John LE08666
Hamilton, Tish AR14131, AR14132, AR14133
Hamilton, Woody LE08667
Hammer, Joshua AR14134
Hampton, Henry BR01129
Hanauer, Amy LE08668
Handelman, David AR14135, AR14136, AR14137
Hanfman, Edward LE08669
Hannigan, Jim LE08670
Hansen, Peter LE08671
Hansen, Robyn LE08672
Hanson, Mary Kay LE08673
Hardy, Ernest AR14138, RR10736, RR10790, RR11109, RR11768, RR11802, RR11926, RR11999, RR12023, RR12228, RR12764, RR13281
Hardy, Jon A. LE08674
Hargett, Gayle LE08675
Haring, Bruce AR14139, BR01093
Harland, Dave LE08676
Harp, Nicholas Allen LE08677
Harrelson, Woody LE08678
Harrington, Spencer RR11423
Harris, Anthony LE08679
Harris, Carter RR11469
Harris, David AR14140, AR14141, AR14142
Harris, Emmylou AR14143
Harris, Jason C. AR14144
Harris, Michael C. CR00686, CR00764, CR00770, CR00884, RR11607
Harris, Patricia LE08680

Harrison, Andrew CR00740, CR00837
Harrison, Jody-Kate Fisher LE08681
Harrison, Lisa A. LE08682
Harrold, Jamie LE08683
Harstad, Dave LE08684
Hart, Daniel War LE08685, LE08686, LE08687
Hartley, Bruce (Mercury Records) LE08688
Hartley, K. LE08689
Hartner, George LE08690
Hartsig, Beth LE08691
Hartwiger, Alexander G. LE08692
Harvey, Kevin LE08693
Haselmann, Ralph, Jr. LE08694
Hatch, Michael LE08695
Hatfield, Juliana AR14145
Hatto, Melissa LE08696
Haun, Tom LE08697
Hauser, Robert LE08698
Haveman, Kathy LE08699
Hawk, R. D. LE08700
Hawthorne, Kate LE08701
Haydock, Patricia LE08702
Hayes, Jen LE08703
Hayes, Misty LE08704
Heath, Chris AR14147, AR14148
Heatom, Cambriah LE08705
Hechinger, Brian LE08706
Heffner, Josh LE08707
Heidgerken, Tanya LE08708
Heldman, Kevin AR14149, AR14150
Helin, Jeanine LE08709
Heller, Chris BR01070
Helm, Levon AR14151, BR01124
Helmeczi, Monica L. LE08710
Helmore, Edward RR10393
Helmuth, Tina LE08711
Helton, Shannon LE08712
Hendrickson, F. LE08713
Hendrickson, Matt AR14152, AR14153, AR14154, AR14155, AR14156, AR14157, AR14158, AR14159, AR14160, AR14161, AR14162, AR14163, AR14164, AR14165, AR14166, AR14167, AR14168, AR14169, AR14170, AR14171, AR14172, AR14173, AR14174, AR14175, AR14176, AR14177, AR14178, AR14179, AR14180, AR14181, AR14182, AR14183, AR14184, AR14185, AR14186, AR14187, AR14188, AR14189, AR14190, AR14191, AR14192, AR14193, AR14194, AR14195, RR11739
Hendrikson, Andrew LE08714
Henera, Richard LE08715
Henke, James AR14196, AR14197, AR14198, AR14199, AR14200, AR14201, AR14202
Henley, Don AR14203
Henniger, Michael LE08716
Henry, George LE08717
Henry, Megan Anne LE08718
Herbst, Peter AR14204
Herczog, Mary AR14205, AR14206
Herlands, Jason LE08719
Herndon, David AR14207, AR14208
Herrera, Timothy LE08720
Hersh, Kristin AR14209
Herz, Dayna LE08721
Herz, J. C. AR14210, AR14211, AR14212
Hesse, Angus LE08722
Hetzel, Karen LE08723
Heylin, Clinton BR01053
Hiatt, John LE08724
Higginbotham, Adam AR14213
Hildebrand, Larry LE08725
Hill, Meg LE08726
Hill, Trent RR11091, RR11233, RR11974, RR12453
Hiller, Eddie LE08727
Himes, Geoffrey AR14214, AR14215, AR14216, AR14217, AR14218, RR10668, RR10754, RR10924, RR11722, RR11951, RR12016, RR12207, RR12491, RR12719, RR12945, RR12986, RR13231
Himmelsbach, Erik RR11024
Hinerfeld, Daniel S. AR14219
Hinkle, Katie J. LE08728
Hirshey, Gerri AR14220, AR14221, AR14222, AR14223
Hochman, Steve AR14224, AR14225, AR14226, AR14227, AR14228, AR14229, AR14230, AR14231, AR14232, AR14233, AR14234, AR14235, AR14236, AR14237, AR14238, AR14239, CR00732, CR00785, CR00852, CR00900, CR00901
Hodenfield, Chris AR14240
Hoffer, Julie LE08729
Hoffman, A. M. LE08730
Hoffman, Alan LE08731
Hoffman, John LE08732
Hoffman, Len LE08733
Hoffner, Aidan LE08734
Holden, Chris LE08735
Holden, Joy LE08736
Holden, Ryan LE08737, LE08738
Holden, Stephen RR10489, RR10734, RR10763, RR10769, RR11110, RR12007, RR12626, RR12830
Holland, Pam LE08739
Holliday, Art AR14241
Hollinger, Andrew LE08740
Holoran, Michael (Program Director, KUPR) LE08741
Holthouse, David CR00830
Homer BR01080
Honda, Yuka AR14243
Honeck, John LE08742
Hood, S. LE08743
Hoon, Shannon AR14244, BR01042, MR01236, RR10511, RR11750, RR12857
Hooper, Laurence AR14245
Hooten, Joe LE08744
Hooton, Rachel LE08745
Hopkins, Ellen AR14246
Hopkins, Jerry AR14247, AR14248
Hopkins, Tracy AR14249, AR14250, AR14251, CR00700
Hopkins, Tracy E. RR12697
Hopper, Justin LE08746
Horn, Linda J. LE08747
Horne, Paula Major LE08748
Hornsby, Mark LE08749
Horovitz, Pamela (National Association Of Recording Merchandisers) LE08750
Horrigan, Timothy LE08751
Horton, Lori LE08752
Horton, Rich LE08753
Horton, Tom AR14252
Hoskyns, Barney AR14253, BR01130, RR10913, RR11681, RR12150
Hosselton, Garold LE08754 AR14254, AR14255, AR14256
Houchins, Elizabeth LE08755, LE08756
Houghton, Leah LE08757
Houser, Melissa LE08758
Hovav, Adi LE08759 MR01583, AR14257
Howard, Pete AR14258, AR14259, AR14260, AR14261, AR14262, AR14263, AR14264, AR14265, AR14266, AR14267, AR14268, AR14269, AR14270, AR14271, AR14272, AR14273, AR14274, AR14275, RR10831, RR11281, RR12237, RR12619, RR12838, RR13063, RR13094, RR13095, RR13243
Howell, Jackie LE08760
Howell, Scott LE08761
Hubbard, Mark A. LE08762
Huber, Kevin R., Rev. LE08763
Hudgins, Conny LE08764
Hudson, Angela LE08765
Huegelmann, Mark LE08766
Huffman, Eddie RR10571, RR11234
Hughes, Chris LE08767
Hughes, Kathie LE08768
Huhn, Mary AR14276, AR14277, AR14278, AR14279
Hulka, Evan LE08769
Huml, A. LE08770
Hunt, J. LE08771, LE08772
Hunter, B. R. RR13061, RR13222
Hunter, James AR14280, AR14281, AR14282, AR14283, BR01061, CR00681, CR00693, CR00810, RR10391, RR10933, RR11055, RR11140, RR11171, RR11214, RR11361, RR11418, RR11497, RR11512, RR11993, RR12189, RR12193, RR12353, RR12483, RR12509, RR12661, RR12700, RR12766, RR12768, RR12770, RR12807, RR12906, RR12994, RR13290
Hunter, Robert AR14284
Hutchence, Michael AR14285, BR01132, MR02016, RR10642, RR10964, RR11003
Hutchinson, James LE08773
Hynde, Chrissie AR14286 AR14287

I

Ian, Janis LE08774
Ian, Scott LE08775
Ice Cube LE08776
Idzkowski, Mai LE08777
Infusino, Divina AR14289
Ingram, Susan LE08778
Irving, David LE08779
Isaacs, Steve (MTV) LE08780
Isler, Scott RR10432, RR10490, RR11193, RR11359, RR12251, RR12884, RR13086, RR13093, RR13276
Israel, Dulcy AR14291, AR14292, AR14293, AR14294, AR14295, AR14296
Iveson, Suzanne LE08781 AR14301

J

J.A.M. LE08788
J.D. LE08793
J.E.B. LE08794
J.J. LE08800
J.T. LE08823
Jackson, Biff LE08782
Jackson, Devon AR14302, AR14303
Jackson, Lara LE08783
Jacobowitz, Eden LE08784
Jacobs, Karrie AR14304
Jacobs, Sally AR14305
Jaffe, Eriq LE08785
Jaffe, Jonathan LE08786
Jafloat, Craig LE08787
James, Etta BR01102
Jamison, Laura AR14306, CR00769, RR12473
Janczyn, Melinda LE08789
Janecek, Rebecca LE08790
Janice, Cari Goldberg BR01133
Jasniewicz, Lisabeth LE08791
Jaynes, Simon LE08792
Jeff LE08795, LE08796
Jeffries, Sara LE08797
Jenkins, Sacha AR14309
Jennings, Matt LE08798
Jennings, Waylon BR01131
Jensen, Sheila LE08799
Joel, Billy LE08801
Johanssen, Pascal LE08802
John, Robert BR01076
Johnson, Amber LE08803
Johnson, Aran AR14312
Johnson, Charles LE08804
Johnson, Cory AR14313, AR14314, AR14315
Johnson, Dean AR14316
Johnson, Debra A. LE08805
Johnson, Denis BR01081
Johnson, Hillary AR14317

Johnson, Jerry C. LE08806
Johnson, Martin AR14318, AR14319, AR14320
Johnson, Ray LE08807
Johnson, Sarah LE08808
Johnson, Shaun LE08809
Johnson, Tanya LE08810
Johnson, Tiffany D. LE08811
Johnston, David AR14321
Jones, Adam LE08812
Jones, J. Marcus LE08813
Jones, Kelly LE08814
Jones, Kristine LE08815
Jones, Mick AR14322
Jones, Natalie LE08816
Jones, Patric LE08817
Jones, Rickie Lee AR14323, CR00653
Jones, Tim A. LE08818
Joplin, Janis AR14324
Joplin, Laura AR14325
Jorgensen, Lori LE08819
Jorgensen, Vidar J. (Thoreau Country Conservation Alliance) LE08820
Joyce, Matt LE08821
Joyner, Dan LE08822
Judd, Brian LE08824
Julig, Louise LE08825
Juon, Steve "Flash" LE08826
Jurek, Thom CR00687, CR00802, CR00804, CR00912, CR00924, RR10434, RR10620, RR10859, RR10884, RR10999, RR11224, RR11377, RR11426, RR11669, RR12416, RR12417, RR12689a, RR12721, RR12773, RR12913, RR12933, RR12937, RR13283

K

K.B. LE08842
K.M. LE08881
Kahlmorgan, Andree LE08827
Kahn, Carole E. LE08828
Kalinoski, Pamela LE08829
Kalitowski, Susanna LE08830
Kaprelian, Peter LE08831
Karlen, Neal BR01045, BR01046
Karnes, Randall T. LE08832
Karr, Kathy Jo LE08833
Karr, Sunny LE08834
Kasendorf, Jesse LE08835
Kasprzak, Michelle LE08836
Kathol, Jon LE08837
Katson, Trisha LE08838
Katz, Adam LE08839
Katz, Jon AR14326, AR14327, AR14328, AR14329, AR14330, AR14331, AR14332, AR14333, AR14334, AR14335, AR14336, AR14337, AR14338, AR14339, AR14340, AR14341, AR14342, AR14343
Kay, Jill LE08840
Kaye, Lenny BR01131
Kazdoy, Amanda LE08841
Keadle, Dianne L. LE08843
Kearse, Ashley LE08844
Keebler, Ed LE08845
Keefe, Tom LE08846
Kehoe, John AR14344
Keigwin, Mark LE08847
Keller, Eugene LE08848
Keller, Martin AR14345
Kelley, Collin LE08849
Kelley, Robin D.G. RR10967a, RR11090, RR12244, RR12426, RR13165
Kelly, Chaz LE08850
Kelly, Chris AR14346
Kelly, Christina AR14347, AR14348, AR14349, AR14350, CR00791, RR11680
Kelly, Kate LE08851
Kelly, Rob LE08852
Kemp, Mark AR14351, AR14352, AR14353, AR14354, AR14355, AR14356, AR14357, AR14358, AR14359, CR00730, RR10507, RR10534, RR10564, RR10636, RR10701, RR10824, RR11095, RR11189, RR11231, RR11346, RR11642, RR11941, RR12129, RR12190, RR12199, RR12325, RR12452, RR12454, RR12492, RR12796, RR12972
Kendall, Steven L. LE08853
Kening, Dan AR14360
Kennedy, Daniel LE08854
Kennedy, Mike LE08855
Kennedy, William BR01104
Kenney, Glenn
Kenny, Glenn AR14361, AR14362, AR14363, AR14364, AR14365, AR14366, AR14367, AR14368, AR14369, AR14370, AR14371, AR14372, AR14373, AR14374, AR14375, AR14376, AR14377, AR14378, AR14379, AR14380, AR14381, AR14382, AR14383, AR14384, AR14385, AR14386, AR14387, AR14388, AR14389, AR14390, AR14391, AR14392, AR14393, AR14394, AR14395, AR14396, AR14397, AR14398, AR14399, AR14400, AR14401, AR14402, AR14403, AR14404, AR14405, AR14406, AR14407, AR14408, AR14409, AR14410, AR14411, AR14412, AR14413, AR14414, AR14415, BR01086, CR00743, RR10455, RR11532, RR11945, RR12765
Kent, Nick BR01061
Kern, Geof AR14416
Kerr, Jim AR14417
Kesey, Ken AR14418
Kester, T. S. LE08856
Kevorkian, Maureen LE08857
Kibler, Martha LE08858
Kight, Matt LE08859
Kilpatrick, Eva LE08860
Kim, Ben LE08861
Kim, Jae-Ha AR14419, AR14420, CR00755
Kim, Linda AR14421
Kim, Wook AR14422, AR14423
Kimball, Jaclyn LE08862
Kimbrough, Walter LE08863
Kinel, Traci LE08864
King, B. B. BR01052
King, Bill LE08865
King, Kelli LE08866
King, Wayne RR12555
Kingsley, Kim LE08867
Kinkada, Chris LE08869
Kipp, Brian K. LE08870
Kirie, V. LE08871
Kirk, Deborah AR14424, RR10735
Kirk, Ken LE08872
Kirka, Mike LE08873
Kiss LE08874
Kjeldergaard, Dennis LE08875
Klavans, Anne LE08876
Klein, Morgan LE08877
Klein, Steven AR14425
Klemke, Anita BR01050
Klien, Joe AR14426
Klockner, Cathy Lute LE08878
Klofkorn, Warren LE08879
Klop, J. Michael LE08880
Knapp, John R., Jr. LE08882
Knight, Kristy LE08883
Knoedelseder, William BR01119
Knopper, Steve AR14427
Knudson, Heather LE08884
Koback, Todd J. LE08885
Koenigsmann, Heidi LE08886
Kohn, Howard AR14428, AR14429
Kollock, Paul LE08887
Konigsberg, Eric AR14430, AR14431, AR14432
Konlack, Shanna LE08888
Koppel, Jeffrey LE08889
Koppel, Jeffrey D. LE08890
Korthals, Jim LE08891
Kosslow, Kenny LE08892
Kot, Greg AR14433, AR14434, AR14435, AR14436, AR14437, AR14438, AR14439, CR00644, CR00753, CR00834, CR00913, CR00944, RR10390, RR10478, RR10483, RR10555, RR11145, RR11173, RR11206, RR11303, RR11862, RR11863, RR11908, RR12071, RR12157, RR12181, RR12285, RR12287, RR12306, RR12557, RR12605, RR12632, RR12745, RR12804, RR12925, RR12993, RR13066
Kouri, James J. (Vice-President And Associate Editor, 'Chief of Police') LE08893
Kowaleski, Michael LE08894
Kraemer, George P. LE08895
Krakora, Christopher LE08896
Krakuer, Jon AR14440
Kramer, B. LE08897
Kramer, Dan LE08898
Kramer, Kathleen J. LE08899
Krantz, Michael AR14441
Kravitz, Lenny AR14442, BR01047, CR00877, RR12421
Krell, Eric AR14443
Krieger, Chris LE08900
KRS-One Metaphysician LE08901
Krubeck, Jim LE08902
Krugman, Michael AR14444, AR14445
Kuhn, Kelly LE08903
Kuipers, Dean AR14446, AR14447
Kulick, Bruce LE08904
Kutch, Stephani LE08905
Kyriazi, Linda LE08906

L

L., John LE08907
L.M.W. LE08968
Ladd, Carol LE08908
Ladybug AR14448
LaGuerre, Harvey LE08909
Laing, D. Brent LE08910
Lambert, Kelsey LE08911
Lamssies, Dominique LE08912
Landsea, Chris LE08913
Lane, Karen LE08914
Langbehn, Josh LE08915
Langenburg, Lea LE08916
Langie, Matthew LE08917
Langro, Robert LE08918
Lanier, Emmett Mike LE08919
LaPierre, Wayne R., Jr. (National Rifle Association Of America) LE08920
Large, Kim LE08921
Lari, Erika LE08922, LE08923
Larkin, Carol BR01075
Lasher, Grant B. LE08924
Laudati, Niel LE08925
Lauzon, Timothy LE08926
Lawrence, Dana J. LE08927
Lawrence, Sharron Lesley LE08928
Lawrence, Tina LE08929
Laxton, William AR14449
Lay, Carrie LE08930
Lazar, Shelley LE08931
Leach, Steve LE08932
Leahy, Deborah LE08933
Leahy, Josie LE08934
Leber, Rebecca (Rhode Island School Of Design) LE08935
LeBlanc, Angie LE08936
LeConte, Robert (President, National Association Of Veteran Police Officers) LE08937
Lee, Janet LE08939
Lee, Mee Sun LE08940
Lee, Ricky AR14451, AR14452
Lee, Roberta LE08941, LE08942
Lee, Roy LE08943
Leech, John LE08944
Lefsetz, Robert Scott LE08945
Lehrer, Eli LE08946
Leibovitz, Annie AR14453, AR14454
Leiby, Richard AR14455
Leigh, Vivian LE08947
Lenquette, Youri LE08948
Leonard, Mike AR14456, AR14457
Leonetti, Chuck LE08949
Lepsche, Michele LE08950

Lerner, Gerda BR01068
Lesco, Barbara LE08951
Leurquin, Chris LE08952
Levesque, Richard L. LE08953
Levin, Michael LE08954
Levine, Robert AR14458, AR14459
Levy, Douglas LE08955
Levy, Joe RR11267, RR12596
Lewis, Jennifer LE08956
Lewis, Jeremy LE08957
Lewis, Monnica LE08958
Lewis, Neil A. AR14460
Lewis, Richard LE08959
Lewman, Mark AR14461
L'Heureux, Susan A. LE08960
Lidman, Eric LE08961
Lieb, Kristin AR14462, AR14463
Light, Alan AR14464, AR14465, AR14466, AR14467, AR14468, AR14469, AR14470, AR14471, AR14472, AR14473, AR14474, AR14475, AR14476, AR14477, AR14478, AR14479, AR14480, AR14481, AR14482, AR14483, AR14484, AR14485, AR14486, AR14487, AR14488, AR14489, AR14490, AR14491, AR14492, AR14493, AR14494, AR14495, AR14496, AR14497, AR14498, AR14499, AR14500, AR14501, CR00660, CR00739, CR00754, CR00762, CR00947, RR10960, RR11350, RR11496, RR12217, RR12230, RR12746, RR13233, RR13279
Lilly, Jean LE08962
Lilly, Ned LE08963
Limes, Patrick LE08964
Lin, Edward AR14502
Linden, Amy AR14503
Linderman, Allison LE08965
Lindsay, K. LE08966
Lipsky, David AR14504, AR14505, AR14506, AR14507, AR14508
Little, Craig (Librarian, Rich Central High School) LE08967
Lochridge, Eric LE08969
Lockhart, Judy AR14510
Lockman, Darcy AR14511, AR14512
Loder, Kurt AR14513, AR14514, AR14515, AR14516, AR14517, AR14518, RR12594
Loeb, Lisa AR14519
Loewen, James W. BR01085
Logan, Penelope LE08970
Lomax, Louisa LE08971
Lombardo, Dave LE08972
Long, Daniel M. LE08973
Lorch, Donatella AR14521
Lose, E. Heather LE08974
Louderback, Daylin C. LE08975
Louie, Lisa LE08976
Louis, Paul C. LE08977
Louis, Scott M. LE08978
Love, Courtney AR14522
Love, Mary Jane LE08979
Love, Robert AR14523, AR14524, BR01074
Lovett, Anthony R. AR14525
Lowenstein, Tim LE08980
Lowry, Pam LE08981
Lozaw, Tristram CR00935
Luciano, Manfredi LE08982
Ludwig, Erin Z. LE08983
Ludwig, Louie LE08984
Lueders, Jane LE08985
Lugar, Richard (Chairman, U.S. Senate Agriculture Committee) LE08986
Lukin, Chloe LE08987
Lundgren, Eric LE08988
Lundgren, Julie LE08989
Luoma, Marc AR14526
Lurie, Elizabeth B. (President and COO, Net, Inc.) LE08990
Lyden, John BR01110
Lyman, Andy RR11183, RR11587, RR12030, RR12119, RR12358, RR12463, RR12693
Lynch, Amanda LE08991
Lynd, Alice BR01091
Lynn, Adam LE08992, LE08993
Lyon, Dennis LE08994, LE08995, LE08996, LE08997

M

Maasz LE08998
MacAdams, Lewis AR14527, AR14528, AR14529
MacAllister, Jules LE08999
Macanke, Mike LE09000
MacAyeal, James LE09001
MacAyeal, Jim LE09002
Mace, Luther, III LE09003
Machcinski, Dawn LE09004
Macht, Dave LE09005
Mackey, Kristopher LE09006
MacNeil, Timothy L. LE09007
Macnie, Jim AR14530, AR14531
MacPherson, Andrew AR14532
Madorsky, Jordan LE09008
Madrid, Ben, III LE09009
Maggin, Donald L. BR01118
Mahaffy, Scott William LE09010, LE09011
Majerus, Elizabeth LE09012
Malige, Didier AR14534
Malley, Stephen AR14535
Malone, Ryan LE09013
Malonee, James LE09014
Maloof, Aaron LE09015
Mancini, Dante LE09016
Mandel, Gerry LE09017
Mandelbaum, Syd LE09018
Manegold, Catherine S. AR14536
Mankad, Nimitt LE09019
Mannes, George AR14537
Manning, Kara AR14538, AR14539, AR14540, AR14541, AR14542, AR14543, AR14544, AR14545, AR14546, AR14547, AR14548, AR14549, AR14550, AR14551, AR14552, AR14553, AR14554, AR14555, AR14556, AR14557, AR14558, CR00718, CR00788, CR00911, RR10600, RR10683, RR10853, RR11226, RR11227, RR11251, RR11301, RR11442, RR11540, RR11566, RR11611b, RR11772, RR11787, RR12036, RR12163, RR12367, RR12508, RR12523, RR12708, RR12893, RR13102, RR13186
Manning, Todd M. LE09020
Manos, Jessica LE09021
Manson, Mike LE09022
Manson, Shirley AR14559
Manticos, Stephanie LE09023
Marcus, Greil AR14560, AR14561, AR14562, BR01103
Margasak, Peter AR14563
Margeas, Sam LE09024
Marin, Rick AR14564, AR14565, AR14566, AR14567, AR14568, AR14569, AR14570, AR14571, AR14572, AR14573, AR14574
Markotay, John LE09025
Markunas, Christina LE09026
Markus, Kurt AR14575
Marlowe, Ann RR10791
Marsh, Dave AR14576, BR01086, LE09027
Martel, Jay AR14577, AR14578, AR14579, AR14580, AR14581, AR14582, AR14583, AR14584, AR14585, AR14586, AR14587, AR14588, AR14589, AR14590, AR14591, AR14592, AR14593, AR14594
Martens, Patrick LE09028
Martin, Cherie A. LE09029
Martin, George BR01040
Martin, Kevin AR14595
Martin, Mary LE09030
Martin, Sarah LE09031
Martin, V. N. LE09032
Martinez, Elizabeth BR01069
Martinez, Janie LE09033
Masline, Gary W. LE09034
Mason, Stewart Allensworth LE09035
Masserat, Sassan LE09036
Massing, Michael AR14596
Masterson, Holly LE09037
Masuo, Sandy AR14597, AR14598, AR14599, AR14600, RR10411, RR11632, RR12103, RR12531
Mathews, Randy LE09038
Matteo, Steve RR11477
Matthei, Julie LE09039
Matthews, Brenda AR14601
Matthews, Dave AR14602, AR14603
Matthews, Merill LE09040
Matthews, Nick LE09041
Matthews, Tom LE09042
Mattson, Rosemary LE09043
Matusak, Ron LE09044
May, Alex LE09045
Maynor, L. Bryce LE09046
Maynther, Andrea LE09047
McAllen, Jim LE09048
McAlley, John CR00666, RR10655, RR10660, RR10847, RR11904, RR12060, RR12705, RR12885, RR12926, RR12979, RR13049, RR13240
McCain, Gillian BR01097, BR01098
McCarty, Kelly S. LE09049
McClafferty, Jennifer LE09050
McClellan, Mike LE09051
McCormick, Moira AR14605, CR00651, CR00685, CR00816, RR12352
McCulley, Jerry AR14606, RR10523
McDonald, Mike LE09052
McDonnell, Evelyn AR14607, AR14608, AR14609, AR14610, AR14611, AR14612, AR14613, CR00713, CR00726, CR00738, CR00773, CR00859, RR10424, RR10565, RR10789, RR10834, RR11122, RR11366, RR11367, RR11417, RR11450, RR11472, RR11741, RR11856, RR12105, RR12180a, RR12284, RR12445, RR12894, RR13065, RR13138, RR13151, RR13156, RR13174, RR13178, RR13244, RR13255, RR13264, RR13306, RR13314, RR13327
McDougal, Roger LE09053
McDowell, Evelyn BR01108
McElfresh, Suzanne RR10958, RR11455
McEwen, Joe RR11473, RR11818
McEwen, Matt LE09054
McGann, Rachel LE09055
McGarr, Michael LE09056
McGarrah, C. LE09057
McGasko, J. LE09058
McGee, David AR14614, BR01072, RR10898, RR10921, RR11401, RR11567, RR11568, RR11574, RR11602, RR12783, RR12977, RR13125, RR13246, RR13296
McGee, Matt J. LE09059
McGlinn, Evan AR14615, AR14616, AR14617
McGovern, George AR14618
McGrath, Judith (President, MTV) LE09060
McGuigan, Christine LE09061
McGuire, Roxanne LE09062
McIntyre, Roger LE09063
McKagan, Duff LE09064
McKenna, Kristine AR14619, RR11271
McLachlan, Sarah AR14620
McLane, Daisann AR14621, AR14622, AR14623, BR01092, RR10382, RR10387, RR10418, RR10438, RR10444, RR10475, RR10491, RR10562, RR10567, RR10577, RR10578, RR10579, RR10580, RR10586, RR10602, RR10629, RR10637, RR10639, RR10699, RR10700, RR10784, RR10848, RR10849, RR10927,

McLane, Daisann (continued)
RR10928, RR11018, RR11064, RR11170, RR11204, RR11237, RR11242, RR11243, RR11315, RR11348, RR11476, RR11487, RR11549, RR11586, RR11603, RR11620, RR11636, RR11668, RR11709, RR11720, RR11721, RR11763, RR11766, RR11870, RR11871, RR11876, RR11877, RR11884, RR11900, RR11901, RR11902, RR11903, RR11912, RR11925, RR11936, RR11942, RR11943, RR11944, RR12002, RR12003, RR12085, RR12092, RR12095, RR12104, RR12202, RR12212, RR12291, RR12293, RR12294, RR12356, RR12360, RR12373, RR12374, RR12376, RR12388, RR12394, RR12469, RR12496, RR12501, RR12631, RR12673, RR12698, RR12699, RR12754, RR12789, RR12808, RR12809, RR12822, RR12832, RR12833, RR12842, RR12847, RR12989, RR13006, RR13007, RR13008, RR13009, RR13031, RR13042, RR13045, RR13046, RR13047, RR13048, RR13064, RR13076, RR13077, RR13079, RR13081, RR13082, RR13111, RR13112, RR13113, RR13114, RR13115, RR13117, RR13126, RR13137, RR13141, RR13145, RR13148, RR13149, RR13158, RR13161, RR13171, RR13175, RR13181, RR13182, RR13192, RR13194, RR13223, RR13224, RR13228, RR13238, RR13252, RR13253, RR13263, RR13265, RR13268, RR13289, RR13299, RR13300, RR13302, RR13315, RR13319, RR13324
McLaughlin, Kelly LE09065
McLeese, Don AR14624, AR14625, AR14626, AR14627, AR14628, AR14629, AR14630, AR14631, CR00639, CR00647, CR00650, CR00652, CR00663, CR00691, CR00695, CR00702, CR00783, CR00805, CR00819, CR00857, CR00861, CR00893, CR00917, CR00936, CR00939, RR10396, RR10413, RR10414, RR10431, RR10433, RR10451, RR10464, RR10466, RR10481, RR10497, RR10498, RR10517, RR10537, RR10542, RR10548, RR10576a, RR10669, RR10679, RR10680a, RR10681, RR10682, RR10691, RR10720, RR10721, RR10722, RR10725, RR10738, RR10743, RR10744, RR10768, RR10778, RR10781, RR10783, RR10810, RR10811, RR10813, RR10816, RR10817, RR10818, RR10891, RR10903, RR10914, RR10923, RR11013, RR11023, RR11031, RR11053, RR11054, RR11071, RR11072, RR11093, RR11128, RR11151, RR11172, RR11244, RR11347, RR11355, RR11356, RR11384, RR11393, RR11396, RR11397, RR11403, RR11404, RR11437, RR11448, RR11449, RR11456, RR11457, RR11511, RR11513, RR11514, RR11522, RR11523, RR11535, RR11536, RR11558, RR11559, RR11560, RR11561, RR11576, RR11582, RR11583, RR11588, RR11589, RR11597, RR11598, RR11600, RR11601, RR11613, RR11629, RR11635, RR11638, RR11659, RR11660, RR11661, RR11671, RR11674, RR11690, RR11691, RR11708, RR11718, RR11743, RR11754, RR11755, RR11756, RR11758, RR11813, RR11828, RR11830, RR11836, RR11859, RR11866, RR11923, RR11930, RR11934, RR11937, RR12009, RR12011, RR12014, RR12029, RR12066, RR12072, RR12091, RR12093, RR12113, RR12115, RR12116, RR12117, RR12172, RR12197, RR12223, RR12224, RR12341, RR12342, RR12344, RR12354, RR12375, RR12406, RR12479, RR12480, RR12494, RR12533, RR12542, RR12562, RR12573, RR12603, RR12637, RR12638, RR12653, RR12655, RR12692, RR12695, RR12702, RR12706, RR12720, RR12741, RR12757, RR12771, RR12785, RR12788, RR12824, RR12836, RR12850, RR12859, RR12860, RR12862, RR12865, RR12892, RR12910, RR12911, RR12912, RR12929, RR12930, RR12931, RR12939, RR12961, RR12966, RR12967, RR12985, RR12987, RR13001, RR13003 , RR13044, RR13078, RR13191, RR13242, RR13247, RR13262, RR13266, RR13292, RR13297, RR13305
McLeese, Maria AR14632
McLemore, Tod LE09066
McLeod, Ernest LE09067
McLeod, Rodd RR10585
McManus, Sam LE09068
McNaughton, Craig LE09069
McNeil, Legs BR01097, BR01098
McNeill, Rebecca LE09070
McNulty, Bill (General Manager, KCXX) LE09071
McNutly, Lori LE09072
McPherson, Rich LE09073
McQueen, Gregg LE09074
McRae, Victoria LE09075
McTig, Alex LE09076
McTigue, Leo LE09077
Meathrell, Carrie LE09078
Meda, Tony LE09079
Meehan, Arthur AR14633
Megan, Sheila LE09080
Meis, Marcia LE09081
Melara, John LE09082
Mell, A. J. RR11542
Mer LE09083
Mercer, Michael LE09084
Mercer, Mike LE09085
Merchant, Ismail AR14634
Merovich, Heather LE09086
Messick, Jaymelin LE09087
Metallica LE09088
Metzler, Jeff LE09089
Meyer, Sharon LE09090
Micallef, Ken RR10696, RR10846, RR11200
Mike L. LE09091
Mikesell, Brian G. LE09092
Miklas, Jolene LE09093
Milam, Doug LE09094
Milchen, Jeff LE09095
Miles, Frank LE09096
Militano, M. LE09097
Miller, Adam AR14635, AR14636
Miller, Bruce A. AR14637
Miller, Chris AR14638
Miller, Dan (U.S. House Of Representatives) LE09098
Miller, Ellen LE09099
Miller, Greg LE09100
Miller, Hillary LE09101
Miller, Jennifer LE09102
Miller, Joanna LE09103
Miller, John R. BR01043
Miller, Justin LE09104
Miller, Rhonda LE09105
Miller, Russell AR14639
Miller, Steve AR14640
Miller, Susan S. LE09106
Miller, Tim AR14641
Milliken, Skye LE09107
Mills, Sophie LE09108
Milner, Andrew LE09109
Milward, John AR14642, AR14643, AR14644, AR14645, CR00635, CR00737, RR10516, RR10538, RR10561, RR10613, RR10630a, RR10698, RR10724, RR10899, RR11250, RR11306, RR11307, RR11662, RR11666, RR11742, RR11915, RR12014a, RR12238, RR12412, RR12455, RR12748, RR12811, RR12915, RR12944, RR12958, RR13004, RR13050, RR13054, RR13085, RR13135, RR13153, RR13320
Minard, Ron LE09110
Minor, Margo LE09111
Minton, Jonathan LE09112
Mirkin, Steven AR14646, RR10515, RR10605, RR10742, RR11113, RR11369, RR11793, RR11873, RR12462, RR12503, RR12517, RR12566
Mislow, Bradley S. LE09113
Mitani, Karen LE09114
Mitchell, Deborah AR14647
Mitchell, Lee LE09115
Mitro, Tina LE09116
Mobley, Diane LE09117
Moe, Jackie LE09118
Moeller, Karin LE09119
Moerer, Keith CR00894, CR00930, CR00933
Moffitt, Gary S. LE09120
Molanphy, Chris LE09121
Molidor, Rod, Jr. LE09122
Molyneux, Guy AR14648, AR14649, AR14650
Monica And Gabriella LE09123
Monk LE09124
Montalbano, Liz LE09125
Montgomery, Liz LE09126
Montgomery, Matt LE09127
Montgomery, Sarah LE09128
Montgomery, Stephanie LE09129
Moody, Eugenie LE09130
Moomaw, Bruce LE09131
Moon, Robyn LE09132, LE09133
Moon, Tom AR14651, CR00784, CR00904, CR00940, RR10650, RR10755, RR10962, RR11184, RR11203, RR11357, RR11380, RR11591, RR11698, RR11711, RR11895, RR11950, RR12077, RR12167, RR12229, RR12543, RR12571, RR12593, RR13225, RR13286
Moore, David LE09134
Moore, Douglas LE09135
Moore, Kimberly LE09136
Moore, Thomas LE09137
Moore, Thurston AR14652, BR01105, CR00775, LE09138, MR01979, RR10765, RR13147
Morales, Ed AR14653, AR14654, RR10718
Morgenstern, Hans LE09139
Morgenstern, Steve AR14655, AR14656, AR14657, AR14658, AR14659, AR14660, AR14661, AR14662, AR14663, AR14664, AR14665, AR14666, AR14667
Morris, Bob AR14668
Morris, Chris RR11593
Morris, Jason LE09140
Morris, Karlene LE09141
Morrison, Melissa AR14669
Morrissey, Sandy LE09142
Moser, Jeffrey AR14670
Moss, Shayna LE09143
Moszynski, Meegan LE09144
Mott, David LE09145
Mount, Jimmy LE09146
Mr. Riot LE09147
Mueller, Frederick LE09148
Muetz, Roman LE09149
Mulrooney, C. LE09150
Mundy, Chris AR14672, AR14673, AR14674, AR14675, AR14676, AR14677, AR14678, AR14679, AR14680, AR14681, AR14682, AR14683, AR14684, AR14685, AR14686, AR14687, AR14688, AR14689, AR14690, AR14691, AR14692, AR14693, AR14694, AR14695, AR14696, AR14697, AR14698, AR14699, AR14700, AR14701, AR14702, AR14703, AR14704, AR14705, AR14706, AR14707, AR14708,

Mundy, Chris (continued) AR14709, AR14710, AR14711, AR14712, AR14713, AR14714, AR14715, AR14716, AR14717, AR14718, AR14719, AR14720, AR14721, AR14722, AR14723, AR14724, AR14725, AR14726, AR14727, AR14728, AR14729, AR14730, AR14731, AR14732, AR14733, BR01056, CR00838, MR01387, RR10657, RR11249, RR11515, RR11855, RR12158, RR12328, RR12329, RR12330, RR12331, RR12332, RR12333, RR12334, RR12335, RR12336, RR12337, RR12547, RR12797, RR12802, RR12805, RR13284, RR13308
Murphy, Darren LE09151
Murphy, Elliott LE09152
Murphy, Joseph LE09153
Musil, Robert K. (Physicians For Social Responsibility) LE09154
Mustafaa, I'dris Abdul LE09155
Myers, Mike LE09156
Mynatt, Julie LE09157

N

Nadelmann, Ethan AR14736, AR14737
Nadler, Eric AR14738
Nakamura, Lauren LE09158
Name Withheld LE09159, LE09160, LE09161, LE09162, LE09163, LE09164, LE09165, LE09166, LE09167, LE09168, LE09169, LE09170, LE09171, LE09172, LE09173
Neal, Mim (Rotary International) LE09174
Neely, Kim AR14739, AR14740, AR14741, AR14742, AR14743, AR14744, AR14745, AR14746, AR14747, AR14748, AR14749, AR14750, AR14751, AR14752, AR14753, AR14754, AR14755, AR14756, AR14757, AR14758, AR14759, AR14760, AR14761, AR14762, AR14763, AR14764, AR14765, AR14766, AR14767, AR14768, AR14769, AR14770, AR14771, AR14772, AR14773, AR14774, AR14775, AR14776, AR14777, AR14778, AR14779, AR14780, AR14781, AR14782, AR14783, AR14784, AR14785, AR14786, AR14787, AR14788, BR01076, CR00910, MR01531, RR11253, RR11368, RR11460, RR11625, RR12299, RR12440, RR12442, RR12444
Nefsky, Brian LE09175
Neill, Danielle LE09176
Neiswender, Kate M. LE09177
Nelson, Havelock RR11028, RR11086, RR11089, RR11212, RR11235, RR11443, RR11644, RR11760, RR11972
Nemec, Michael Paul LE09178
Neumann, Rita E. LE09179
Newbauer, James L. LE09180
Newbold, Renee LE09181
Newcomb, Doug AR14795
Newman, Elizabeth LE09182
Newman, Herbert E. LE09183
Newman, Judith AR14796, AR14797
Newton, Philip AR14799
Nicholson, Anthony LE09184
Nickels, Mark LE09185
Nicks, Dewey AR14801
Nicks, Stevie AR14802, BR01062, BR01128, RR10916, RR11040, RR11914, RR12792
Nicolucci, Guy RR12142
Nielson, Rick AR14803
Nigara, Mark LE09186
Nilan LE09187
Nilson, Kai LE09188
Nobis, J. G. LE09189
Noble, Danielle LE09190
Nolan, A. M. AR14806
Noon, Rebecca LE09191
Norland, John LE09192
Norlander, Linda LE09193
Norman, Philip AR14807
Notorious B.A.E. LE09194
Novoselic, Krist LE09195, LE09196
Nudo, Sal LE09197

O

O'Brien, Conan AR14811
O'Brien, Jill LE09198
O'Brien, Patti AR14812, AR14813, AR14814, AR14815, AR14816, AR14817, AR14818, AR14819, AR14820, AR14821, AR14822, AR14823, AR14824, AR14825, AR14826, AR14827, AR14828, AR14829, AR14830, AR14831, AR14832, AR14833, AR14834, AR14835, AR14836, AR14837, AR14838, AR14839, AR14840, AR14841, AR14842, AR14843, AR14844, AR14845, AR14846, AR14847, AR14848, AR14849, AR14850, AR14851, AR14852, AR14853, AR14854, AR14855, AR14856, AR14857, AR14858, AR14859, AR14860, AR14861, AR14862, AR14863, AR14864, AR14865
Ocel, Natalie LE09200
O'Connell, Tom LE09201
O'Connor, Rob AR14866, AR14867, AR14868, RR10422, RR10445, RR10485, RR10509, RR10634, RR10746, RR10758, RR10766, RR10872, RR10880, RR10900, RR10970, RR11001, RR11057, RR11063, RR11154, RR11162, RR11302, RR11381, RR11516, RR11530, RR11628, RR11663, RR11745, RR11812, RR11949, RR11954, RR11968, RR12099, RR12101, RR12175, RR12303, RR12304, RR12447, RR12583, RR12688, RR12855, RR12888, RR12992, RR13277
O'Dair, Barbara AR14869, CR00747, RR11097, RR11554, RR11773, RR12047, RR12159, RR12183, RR12220, RR12378, RR12569, RR12738, RR13190
Odintz, Andrea RR10544, RR11041, RR11842, RR12487, RR12556, RR13187
Odom, Gary LE09202
Oehling, Rick LE09203
Oeser, Kristen LE09204
Okamoto, Chris CR00844, CR00938
Okamoto, David RR10469, RR10983, RR11703, RR11724
Olszewski, Shellie LE09205
Oltarzewski, John LE09206, LE09207
132 University Of Wisconsin Students LE09208
O'Neill, Dan LE09209
Ono, Yoko LE09210
Oransky, Michael LE09211
Orloff, Peter LE09212
Orloffsky, George LE09213
Orosco, Janice L. LE09214
O'Rourke, P. J. AR14993, AR14994, AR14995, AR14996, AR14997, AR14998, AR14999, AR15000, AR15001, AR15002, AR15003, AR15004, AR15005, AR15006, AR15007, AR15008, AR15009, AR15010, AR15011, AR15012, AR15013
Orsborn, Mikel LE09215
Orwell, Bruce AR15014
Osbourne, Ozzy AR15015
Osbourne, Sharon LE09216
Osojnak, Jake S. LE09217
Ossian, Richard E. LE09218
Oswald, Eric LE09219
Owen, Frank CR00856
Ozegovix, Georgiana LE09220

P

Pabst, Bobbi LE09221
Pagaza, Joy LE09222
Page, Carolyn D. LE09223
Pagnac, Dawn LE09224
Paguaga, A. LE09225
Palac, Lisa AR15019
Palmer, Bryant (News Editor, Vanderbilt Hustler, Vanderbilt University) LE09226
Palmer, Robert AR15020, AR15021, AR15022, AR15023, AR15024, AR15025, AR15026, AR15027, RR10504, RR10815, RR10844, RR10855, RR10866, RR10951, RR10955, RR11008, RR11059, RR11141, RR11335, RR11351a, RR11441, RR11747, RR11791, RR11858, RR12123, RR12124, RR12139, RR12323, RR12346, RR12401, RR12530, RR12568, RR12650, RR12724, RR12818, RR12837, RR12848, RR12856, RR12861, RR12903, RR12946, RR12974, RR13096, RR13180, RR13196, RR13251, RR13261
Palmer, Tamara RR10623
Pan, Wilber LE09227
Panahpour, Nilou AR15028, AR15029, AR15030, AR15031, AR15032, AR15033, AR15034, AR15035, AR15036, AR15037, CR00636, CR00780, CR00823, CR00914, CR00929, RR11065, RR11762, RR11844, RR12006, RR12100
Park, Brad LE09228
Park, Emmet LE09229
Parker, Chris LE09230
Parker, Chriss LE09231
Parker, John LE09232
Parker, Renee LE09233
Parkinson, Mandy LE09234
Parks, Cheri LE09235
Parrott, David LE09236
Partridge, Margaret LE09237
Pasha, J. LE09238
Passalaqua, William LE09239
Patellis, Tony LE09240
Patrias, R. J. LE09241
Patrick, Brian LE09242
Patrick, Deval L. (Assistant Attorney General) LE09243
Peaches LE09244
Pearce, Greg LE09245
Pearce, Matt LE09246
Peavy, Allison LE09247
Peckham, David LE09248
Peers, James H., III LE09249
Pelekakis, Steve LE09250
Pell, Saint James LE09251
Pellegrini, Christina LE09252
Pellone, Michelle LE09253
Pendergrast, James T. AR15039, AR15040, AR15041, AR15042, AR15043, AR15044, AR15045, AR15046, AR15047, AR15048, AR15049, AR15050, AR15051, AR15052, AR15053, AR15054, AR15055, AR15056, AR15057, AR15058, AR15059, AR15060, AR15061, AR15062, AR15063, AR15064, AR15065, AR15066, AR15067, AR15068, AR15069, AR15070, AR15071, AR15072, AR15073, AR15074, AR15075, AR15076, AR15077
Pendon, Mike LE09254
Pensiero, Nicole LE09255
Pereira, Chris LE09256
Perez, Jennifer LE09257
Perez, Somer LE09258
Perkins, Carl BR01072
Perolli, Agim LE09259
Perrin, Debbie LE09260
Perry, Charles AR15078
Perry, Jim BR01107
Perry, Joe LE09261
Perry, Luke LE09262
Perry, Tom LE09263
Perse, Tobias AR15079, AR15080, AR15081, AR15082, AR15083,

CR00849
Persinger, Michael LE09264
Peters, Anthony LE09265
Peters, Matt LE09266
Peterson, Charles BR01114
Peterson, Dele LE09267
Peterson, Gary LE09268
Petri, Tom (House Of Representatives) LE09269
Petrone, Joe LE09270
Pette, Finn J. LE09271
Petty, Alan LE09272
Pfeiffer, Kappy LE09273
Pflieger, Aimee LE09274
Phalen, Tom AR15084, AR15085, AR15086, AR15087, AR15088, AR15089
Philips, Chuck AR15090, AR15091
Phillips, David AR15092
Phillips, Glen AR15093
Phillips, Grant Lee AR15094
Phythian, Michael LE09275
Picard, Billy LE09276
Picha, Bill LE09277
Pickering, Jake LE09278
Pierson, Erica LE09279
Pierson, Kate AR15095
Pietradura, Edie LE09280
Pigozzi, Jean AR15096
Pigza, Jeff LE09281
Pike, Melissa LE09282
Pilar Soaring Hawk LE09283
Pinhead The Cenobite LE09284
Pirozzi, Anthony A. LE09285
Pitts, Cindy LE09286
Place, Michelle LE09287
Plake, Jonathan LE09288
Platt, Aren LE09289
Ploszay, Aimee LE09290
Polasek, Aron LE09291
Pollard, Rock & Roll Peg LE09292
Pond, Steve AR15099, AR15100, AR15101, AR15102, AR15103, AR15104, CR00678, CR00712, CR00768, CR00825, CR00876, CR00919
Pope, Christy Lynn LE09293
Porter, Bruce AR15105
Posies LE09294
Potter, Christopher Beach LE09295
Potter, Elaine LE09296
Poulin, David J. LE09297
Poulson-Bryant, Scott RR11640
Powell, Bryan C. LE09298
Powell, Kevin AR15107, AR15108, RR10514, RR10518, RR10780, RR11005, RR11688, RR12090, RR12198, RR12381, RR12390, RR12784, RR12904, RR13060, RR13184
Powell, Michael AR15109
Powers, Ann AR15110, AR15111, AR15112, AR15113, BR01108, BR01112, CR00654, CR00671, CR00674, CR00829, CR00863, RR11191, RR12397, RR12891
Prater, Francine LE09299
Pratt, Jennifer LE09300
Pratt, Monica (Project Director, Families Against Mandatory Minimums) LE09301
Prepsky, Todd Alan LE09302
Prescott, Norma LE09303
Price, Anna LE09304
Price, Mark LE09305
Price, Michael L. LE09306
Pricone, Steven LE09307
Prince, David AR15115, AR15116, AR15117
Prince, David J. AR15118, RR10446, RR11038, RR11039, RR13055
Prince, Malcolm D. LE09308
Proctor, Maggie LE09309
Pugh, Monica LE09310
Punky II LE09311
Puterbaugh, Parke AR15120, AR15121, AR15122, AR15123, AR15124, AR15125, AR15126, AR15127, AR15128, AR15129, AR15130, AR15131, AR15132, AR15133, AR15134, CR00637, CR00662, CR00680, CR00688, CR00698, CR00794, CR00817, CR00835, CR00836, CR00850, CR00854, CR00909, CR00923, CR00925, CR00948, CR00950, RR10524, RR10526, RR10541, RR10556, RR10560, RR10615, RR11297, RR11365, RR11499, RR11683, RR11717, RR11831, RR11896, RR11953, RR12154, RR12162, RR12628, RR12680, RR12827

Q

Q-Tip AR15135
Quattlebaum, Jon LE09312
Queen Latifah AR15136, BR01089, CR00824, MR01453, RR10782, RR11022, RR11096, RR12763
Quirk, Michael "Fucking" LE09313

R

Rabbat, Paul LE09314
Rabhan, Jeffrey RR11340, RR13090
Rachel LE09315
Rafter, Jim LE09316
Raftery, Brian M. LE09317
Raines, Greg LE09318
Rainnie, Michael LE09319
Rais, Michael LE09320
Rak, John L. LE09321
Ralph, Anne Elizabeth LE09322
Ramirez, Alfonso LE09323
Ramirez, Joan LE09324
Ramirez, Robert LE09325
Raml, John LE09326
Ramon, Vida LE09327
Ramone, Joey LE09328
Ramsey, Leah LE09329
Rand, Kristen AR15138
Randall, Leo LE09330
Randall, Robert LE09331, LE09332
Ransom, Kevin RR10543, RR10674, RR10920, RR11960, RR11962, RR12666
Rapattoni, R. LE09333
Rascher, J. LE09334
Rather, Dan AR15140
Rawley, Kim LE09335
Ray, Christopher A. AR15141
Ray, Eric LE09336
Ray, Michael LE09337
Ray, Michael K. LE09338
Redmond, Todd LE09339
Reed, Andrew D. LE09340
Reed, Thomas Grady, III LE09341
Reeher, Jason Chaffey LE09342
Rees, Robert LE09343
Reeves, John LE09344
Reger, Nathan LE09345
Reich, Robert (Secretary Of Labor) LE09346
Reich, Robert B. AR15148
Reichart, Joel LE09347
Reichl, Peter AR15149
Reimelt, Christine LE09348
Reinardt, Tony LE09349
Reindollar, Brett LE09350
Reinhardt, Mel LE09351
Reiniche, Josh LE09352
Relic, Peter J. AR15150, AR15151, AR15152
Renfro, Rodney LE09353, LE09354
Reno, James AR15155
Rensin, David AR15156, AR15157
Resnicoff, Matt AR15159
Ressler, Darren RR12880
Ressler, Robin E. LE09355
Ressler-Bunk, Amanda LE09356
Ressner, Jeffrey AR15160, AR15161, AR15162, AR15163, AR15164, AR15165, AR15166, AR15167, AR15168, AR15169, AR15170, AR15171, AR15172, AR15173, AR15174, CR00915
Reynolds, Simon AR15176, AR15177, AR15178, RR11753, RR12400
Reznikoff, Charlie LE09357
Rhodes, David C. LE09358
Rhodes, Richard AR15179, AR15180, AR15181, AR15182, AR15183
Rice, Anne AR15184
Rice, Noah LE09359
Richards, B. J. LE09360
Richards, Brigid (Project Assistant, Richmond High School) LE09361
Richardson, J. LE09362
Richardson, Susan AR15185, AR15186, AR15187, AR15188, BR01070, BR01102, BR01135, CR00709, CR00715, RR11047, RR11048, RR11125, RR11205, RR11364, RR11646, RR13074
Richart, M. LE09363
Richmond, Rebecca LE09364
Rickenbach, John AR15189
Ridenour, Heather Amanda LE09365
Riedmuller, Kevin G. LE09366
Riegler, Jennifer LE09367
Riffle, Dale (Director, P.I.G.S.) LE09368
Rifkin, Glenn AR15190
Rifkind, Nina F. LE09369
Ring, James LE09370
Ripley, J. F. LE09371
Ritts, Herb AR15191, AR15192
Ritz, David AR15193, AR15194, AR15195, AR15196, AR15197, AR15198, BR01052, BR01102
Rizer, Jasmine LE09372
Rizzi, Danny LE09373
Ro, Ronin RR12618
Robb, Phillip Michael LE09374
Robbins, Ira AR15199, AR15200, AR15201, AR15202, AR15203, AR15204, AR15205, AR15206, AR15207, AR15208, AR15209, BR01075, CR00634, CR00779, CR00787, CR00882, RR10712, RR10779, RR10792, RR11270, RR11406, RR11407, RR11508, RR11524, RR11552, RR11780, RR11807, RR11909, RR11985, RR12049, RR12208, RR12466, RR12536, RR12537, RR12565, RR12712, RR12725, RR12834, RR12846, RR12965, RR13053, RR13067, RR13098, RR13124, RR13144, RR13195, RR13207, RR13256, RR13275, RR13291, RR13318
Robbins, Michael AR15210
Robert, Francois AR15211, AR15212
Roberts, Christa A. LE09375
Roberts, Eliza LE09376
Roberts, Sara LE09377
Roberts, Todd AR15213
Robicheau, Paul AR15214, AR15215, CR00704, CR00721, CR00847
Robinson, Brent LE09378
Robinson, Chris AR15216, LE09379
Robinson, Katherine LE09380
Robinson, Scott AR15217
Robinson, Todd LE09381
Roche, Laura Anne LE09382
Rochester, Aaron LE09383
A Rock & Roll Fan LE09384
Rodin, Jenny LE09385
Rodrick, Tamara LE09386
Rodrigues, Marcus LE09387
Rogers, Ray AR15219, AR15220
Rogers, Sara LE09388
Rollins, Henry LE09389
Rolston, Matthew AR15223, BR01048
Roof, Dennis LE09390
Rosado, Jen LE09391
Rose, Catherine LE09392
Rose, Starlette LE09393

Rose, Tricia BR01051
Roseen, Eryk LE09394
Rosenbaum, David LE09395
Rosenberg, Tina AR15224, AR15225
Rosewall, Laura LE09396
Ross, Kristin LE09397
Ross, Linda LE09398
Ross, Michael (President, Delicious Vinyl) LE09399
Roth, Melissa AR15226, AR15227, AR15228, AR15229, AR15230, AR15231
Rothwell, Adam LE09400
Rowe, Jonathan AR15232
Rowell, Bob LE09401
Royte, Elizabeth AR15233, AR15234
Rozell, Teresa LE09402
Rubiner, Michael AR15235, AR15236, AR15237, AR15238, AR15239, AR15240, AR15241, AR15242, AR15243, AR15244, AR15245, AR15246, AR15247, AR15248, AR15249, AR15250, AR15251, AR15252, AR15253, AR15254, AR15255, AR15256, AR15257, AR15258, AR15259, AR15260, AR15261, AR15262, AR15263, AR15264, AR15265, AR15266, AR15267, AR15268, AR15269, AR15270, AR15271, AR15272, AR15273, AR15274, AR15275, AR15276, AR15277, AR15278, AR15279, AR15280, AR15281, AR15282, AR15283, AR15284, AR15285, AR15286, AR15287, AR15288, AR15289, AR15290, AR15291, AR15292, AR15293, AR15294, AR15295, AR15296, AR15297, AR15298, AR15299, AR15300, AR15301, AR15302, AR15303, AR15304, AR15305, AR15306, AR15307, AR15308, AR15309, AR15310, AR15311, AR15312, AR15313, AR15314, AR15315, AR15316, AR15317, AR15318, AR15319, AR15320, AR15321, AR15322, AR15323, AR15324, AR15325
Rubinstein, Julian AR15326
Rubright, Jeannie LE09403
Rubsam, David LE09404
Rucker, Darius AR15327
Rudd, Larry LE09405
Rude Grrl LE09406
Ruef, Bill A. LE09407
Ruggiero, Bob LE09408
Rule, Kristin LE09409
Ruscitto, Chris LE09410
Rush, Todd LE09411
Rushton, J. Philippe LE09412
Rushton, Jerry L. LE09413
Rust, Ned RR10658
Ruzicka, Alexander LE09414
Ryall, Rich LE09415
Ryan, Jenn LE09416
Ryder, Shaun AR15328
Rye, Ramsey LE09417

S

S.E.A. LE09460
S., Kyle LE09418
S., Lily LE09419
S.R.M. LE09547
Saalberg, Amy LE09420
Sabbag, Robert AR15329, AR15330, AR15331
Sager, Mike AR15332, AR15333, AR15334, AR15335, AR15336, AR15337, AR15338
Sahm, Doug LE09421
Saia, Geoffrey LE09422
Salcedo, Helen LE09423
Salgado, Sebastiao AR15339, AR15340, AR15341, AR15342, AR15343, AR15344, AR15345 AR15346
Saltzman, Tanya LE09424
Samson, Kate LE09425
Samuels, David AR15347, AR15348, AR15349
Samuels, Wendell, Jr. LE09426 RR10530
Sanaulla, Jabeen LE09427
Sanders, Jack P. LE09428
Sandmel, Ben RR11778, RR12070, RR12149
Sane, Hoon LE09429
Sanger, Brian LE09430
Santelli, Robert AR15350, AR15351, CR00656, CR00926, RR10622, RR10702, RR10980, RR11331, RR11334, RR11358, RR11610, RR12578, RR12588, RR12896, RR13199, RR13200, RR13201, RR13202, RR13254
Santiago, Javier BR01092
Santiago, Roberto AR15352, RR10417, RR11605, RR11872
Santos, Tony LE09431
Sarig, Roni RR10473, RR11194, RR11398
Sattler, Tina LE09432
Sauder, R. L. LE09433
Sauer, Lucas K. LE09434
Saul, Thomas LE09435
Saunders, Dudley AR15353, AR15354, CR00851
Saunders, Marguerite T. LE09436
Sauter, Michael RR11478, RR11670
Sautner, Grant LE09437
Savage, Chad L. LE09438
Savage, John C. LE09439
Savage, Jon BR01065
Savaglia, Kenny LE09440
Savan, Leslie AR15355
Sayles, John AR15356
Scalzo, Greg J. LE09441
Scatena, Dino AR15357
Scavullo, Francesco AR15358
Schansberg, D. Eric (Indiana University-Southeast) LE09442
Scheel, Michelle LE09443
Schemer, Karen AR15359
Schiffman, Bonnie AR15360
Schildbach, J. C. LE09444
Schipper, Henry AR15361
Schirmer, David W. LE09445
Schleich, Kathryn LE09446
Schlosberg, Jeremy LE09447
Schlosser, Kurt LE09448
Schmidt, Bill LE09449
Schmidt, George LE09450
Schmidt, Patty LE09451
Schmoke, Kurt AR15362
Schmoll, David LE09452
Schnabel, Jason LE09453
Schneck, Diane LE09454
Schneider, Fred AR15363
Schoemer, Karen AR15364, AR15365, AR15366, AR15367
Schoonbeck, Lucinda LE09455
Schott, John LE09456
Schruers, Fred AR15368, AR15369, AR15370, AR15371, AR15372, AR15373, AR15374, AR15375, AR15376, AR15377, AR15378, BR01097, CR00845
Schwartz, Stephen (Staff Writer, San Francisco Chronicle) LE09457
Schwarz, K. Robert RR11258, RR11259, RR11260, RR11261, RR11262, RR11263, RR11264, RR11278, RR11279, RR11647, RR11713, RR11714, RR12800, RR12801, RR13036, RR13037
Schwinghammer, Michelle LE09458
Scoppa, Bud RR12467
Scott, Taylor LE09459
Scribner, Sara AR15379, AR15380, AR15381
Sedgwick, Kyra LE09461
Seeboth, Martin LE09462
Seeff, Norman BR01115
Segal, Eli J. LE09463
Segal, Robert LE09464
Segal, Stephanie LE09465
Segale, Lisa LE09466
Seibel, Bob LE09467
Sekulic, Mike LE09468
Seliger, Mark AR15382, AR15383, AR15384
Selvin, Joel BR01121
Sendecke, Anne C. LE09469
Sexton, Scott LE09470
Seymour, Corey AR15385, AR15386, AR15387, AR15388, AR15389, RR11525, RR13106
Shabino, Bruce LE09471
Shakur, Sanyika BR01089
Shannon, David LE09472
Shapiro, Harry BR01082
Sharp, Matt AR15390
Sharp, Rae LE09473
Shaturd, Paulie LE09474
Shaw, Dana LE09475
Shaw, Jocelyn LE09476
Shaw, Steve LE09477
Shaw, Thomas Edward BR01050
Shawna J LE09478
Shea, Brian LE09479
Shea, Mack D. LE09480
Sheff, David AR15391
Sheff-Cahan, Vicki AR15392
Shelley, N. LE09481
Shenk, David BR01117
Shepherd John LE09482
Sheppard, Scott Robert LE09483
Sherer, Alan AR15393
Sherrill, Stephen AR15394, AR15395, AR15396, AR15397, AR15398, AR15399, AR15400, AR15401, AR15402, AR15403
Sherwood, Frances BR01128
Shetler, Darren LE09484
Shields, Ben LE09485
Shiner, Lewis BR01071
Shipley, James LE09486
Shirley, David CR00897
Shoemaker, Bill LE09487
Shore, Tony LE09488
Shriver, Sargent LE09489
Shulman, Seth AR15404
Siddoway, Mark LE09490
Sieler, Mark J. LE09491
Siff, Andrew E. AR15405
Silberger, Kathy AR15406
Silberman, Steve BR01117
Silman, S. Jack LE09492
Silversher, Michael LE09493
Silvidi, Alan LE09494
Simmons, D. Michael LE09495
Simmons, Gene LE09496
Simmons, Michael AR15407
Simon, Paul (Senator) LE09497
Simon, Susan LE09498
Simonson, Kevin P. AR15408
Simpson, John AR15409
Simpson, Peter G. LE09499
Sinclair, David AR15414, AR15415, AR15416, AR15417, AR15418, AR15419, AR15420, AR15421, AR15422, AR15423, AR15424, AR15425, AR15426, AR15427, AR15428, AR15429, AR15430, AR15431, AR15432, AR15433, AR15434, AR15435, AR15436, AR15437, AR15438, AR15439, AR15440, CR00677, CR00711, CR00853, CR00867, CR00874, CR00895, CR00943, RR10616
Sinclair, Tom AR15441, AR15442, CR00655, CR00736, CR00749, CR00806, CR00808, RR10443, RR10531, RR10760, RR10771, RR10972, RR11111, RR11158, RR11320, RR11501, RR11520, RR11533, RR11808, RR12227, RR12380, RR12895, RR12969, RR13221, RR13259
Singh, Matt LE09500
Singletary, M. J. LE09501
Singleton, John LE09502
Sintes, Mac LE09503
Sirloin LE09504
Skaalrud, Lee LE09505
Skala, Gene LE09506
Skalski, Paul LE09507
Skoric, Ivo LE09508
Skrok, Rachel LE09509
Slater, Christian LE09510
Slick, Laurie L. LE09511

Small, John LE09512
Smear, Pat AR15444
Smicklas, Lisa LE09513
Smith, Adam LE09514
Smith, Christine LE09515
Smith, Danyel AR15445, AR15446, AR15447, AR15448, AR15449, AR15450, AR15451, AR15452, RR10453, RR10513, RR10820, RR11076, RR11098, RR11161, RR11211, RR11465, RR12749a, RR12821, RR12990
Smith, Dwight A. AR15453
Smith, Erin LE09516
Smith, G. E. (Music Director, Saturday Night Live) LE09517
Smith, Jen LE09518
Smith, Jennifer LE09519
Smith, Jonathan LE09520
Smith, Ken (Executive Director, New England Shelter For Homeless Veterans) LE09521
Smith, Kevin J. AR15454
Smith, Marty LE09522
Smith, Mat AR15455, AR15456
Smith, Matt LE09523
Smith, Patti BR01058, BR01064, LE09524
Smith, R. LE09525
Smith, Stephanie Lynn LE09526
Smith, Virginia A. LE09527
Smith-Pearson, Stephany LE09528
Snyder, Ed B. LE09529
Snyder, Julene LE09530
Snyder, Kenneth LE09531
So, Conway LE09532
Sodano, Todd M. LE09533
Solotaroff, Paul AR15457, AR15458
Somach, Denny (President, Cinema Records) LE09534
Soocher, Stan AR15459, BR01119
Sorensen, Charlie LE09536
Soto, Alfred LE09537
Souther, Matt LE09538
Souza, Kenneth J. LE09539
Sparacio, Bob LE09540
Sparling, Steven W. LE09541
Spector, Phil LE09542
Speece, Andy LE09543
Speer, Keith L. AR15460
Spella, Arnold R., Jr. AR15461
Spencer, Peter AR15462
Spencer, Scott AR15463, AR15464, AR15465
Spera, Keith AR15466, AR15467
Spinelli, Nicole K. LE09544
Spinney, Constance LE09545
Sprague, David AR15468, AR15469, AR15470, AR15471, AR15472, AR15473, AR15474, CR00789, RR10925, RR10967, RR10977, RR11889, RR12147, RR12963
Spriggs, James D. LE09546
Squires, Jim AR15475
St. John, Dick BR01106
St. Leger, Marie Elsie RR10426, RR10673, AR15476, CR00661, RR10638, RR10652, RR11751, RR12580
Stacey C. LE09548
Stachler, Joseph LE09549
Staggs, Jeffrey LE09550
Stains, Laurence AR15477, AR15478
Stambaugh, Scott LE09551
Stamberg, Eric LE09552
Stankovich, Hajira D. LE09553
Stankowitz, Anne M. LE09554
Stanley, Ginger LE09555
Stanley, Paul LE09556
Starnes, G. Brian LE09557
Stasko, Michael A. LE09558
Steele, Bill AR15482, AR15483
Stefani, Gwen AR15485
Steinberg, Neil AR15486, AR15487, AR15488
Steinhauer, Josie LE09559
Stenger, Wif RR10895, RR11135, RR11419, RR11840, RR12755
Stenmo, Art LE09560
Stephens, Marc LE09561
Stephens, Ron LE09562
Stephenson, Lisa LE09563
Stern, Chip RR10749, RR11796
Sterne, Hilary AR15490
Stevens, Phil LE09564
Stewart, Jenn LE09565
Stewart, Jon AR15491
Stipe, Michael LE09566
Stolder, Steven AR15492, AR15493, AR15494, AR15495, AR15496, CR00916, CR00931
Stone, Kassy LE09567
Stone, Kelly LE09568, LE09569
Stone, Oliver LE09570
Stone, Peter H. AR15497
Stone, Robert AR15498
Stott, Daemon LE09571
Strauss, Neil AR15499, AR15500, AR15501, AR15502, AR15503, AR15504, AR15505, AR15506, AR15507, AR15508, AR15509, AR15510, AR15511, AR15512, AR15513, AR15514, AR15515, AR15516, AR15517, AR15518, AR15519, AR15520, AR15521, AR15522, AR15523, AR15524, AR15525, AR15526, AR15527, AR15528, AR15529, AR15530, AR15531, AR15532, AR15533, AR15534, AR15535, AR15536, AR15537, AR15538, RR10397, RR12088
Strittmatter, Greta LE09572
Stromme, Renee D. LE09573
Studley, Kevin A. LE09574
Sturdivant, Wade LE09575
Sudetic, Chuck AR15539
Suematsu, Daisuke LE09576
Sugarmann, Josh AR15540
Sulcas, Adele RR12659
Sulikowski, Stefan LE09577
Sullivan, Andy LE09578
Sullivan, Randall AR15541, AR15542, AR15543, AR15544, AR15545, AR15546
Sullivan, Robert AR15547, AR15548, AR15549, AR15550, AR15551
Summers, Audrey LE09579
Summers, Corey LE09580
Sundberg, Greg LE09581
Super DJ Dmitry AR15554
Suskind, Chad LE09582
Sutter, J. Paul LE09583
Svabodan, Chelsea LE09584
Swallow, Erik LE09585
Swanson, Pete LE09586
Sweeney, Jan LE09587
Sweet, Matthew AR15555
Swenson, John AR15556, AR15557, AR15558, AR15559, AR15560, AR15561, CR00643, CR00665, CR00744, CR00885, CR00949, RR10415, RR10786, RR10787, RR10826, RR10941, RR11282, RR11379, RR11427, RR11429, RR11507, RR11599, RR11609, RR11633, RR11757, RR11821, RR11976, RR11980, RR11984, RR12257, RR12258, RR12259, RR12261, RR12262, RR12264, RR12266, RR12267, RR12268, RR12272, RR12273, RR12275, RR12276, RR12295, RR12418, RR12429, RR12600, RR12734, RR12816, RR12873, RR12921, RR12947, RR13010, RR13012, RR13013, RR13015, RR13016, RR13017, RR13018, RR13020, RR13022, RR13024, RR13025, RR13027, RR13028, RR13029, RR13030, RR13040, RR13057, RR13248
Swierczynski, Duane (Research Editor, Philadelphia Magazine) LE09588
Swisher, Shawn LE09589
Syman, Stefanie AR15562, AR15563, AR15564, AR15565
Szabo, Julia RR11749, RR12787, RR12845
Szada, Shelly LE09590

T

T. LE09591
Taddeo, Annie LE09592
Tague, Susan Mathis LE09593
Takacs, Robert P. AR15566
Takaki, Ron BR01063
Talley, John LE09594
Tankersley, Joel LE09595
Tannenbaum, Rob AR15567, AR15568, AR15569, AR15570, AR15571, AR15572, CR00703, CR00728, CR00765, CR00822, CR00869, RR10649, RR10733, RR11371, RR12461
Tant, Ed LE09596
Taranto, Michael LE09597
Taree, Aerle LE09598
Taroli, Garry S. LE09599
Taylor, Corey LE09600
Taylor, Dane LE09601
Taylor, Jeremy LE09602
Taylor, Jodi LE09603
Taylor, Kristen LE09604
Taylor, Lili AR15573
Taylor, Linda LE09606
Teitsworth, Charles LE09607
Temoney, Kate E. LE09608
Terence, Danielle LE09609
Terry, Sara AR15577
Testa, Jim AR15578, AR15579, AR15580, AR15581
Tews, Eddie LE09610
Thayil, Kim AR15582, LE09611
Thelander, Mari LE09612
Thigpen, David AR15583, AR15584, AR15585, AR15586, AR15587, AR15588, AR15589, AR15590, RR11577
Thomas, D. M. BR01132
Thomas, Michael AR15592
Thomas, Stewart LE09613
Thompson, Bruce LE09614
Thompson, Christopher L. LE09615
Thompson, Dave AR15593, RR12290
Thompson, Gavin LE09616
Thompson, Hunter S. AR15594, AR15595, AR15596, AR15597, AR15598, AR15599, AR15600, AR15601, AR15602, LE09617, LE09618
Thompson, Page LE09619
Thompson, Stephen LE09620
Thomson, Elizabeth BR01054
Thomson, Stephanie LE09621
Thorne-Smith, Courtney LE09622
Thornton, Jerry LE09623
Thornton, Kyan LE09624
Thorpe, Helen AR15603
Thurman, Poppy LE09625
Tien, Ellen AR15604, AR15605
Tierney, Michael AR15606
Tim LE09626
Timmins, Margo LE09627
Tims, Stan LE09628
Tippens, Elizabeth AR15608
Tirella, Joseph V. AR15609
Tisch, Jerry LE09629
Todd, E. LE09630
Tolley, Bridget LE09631
Tomaselli, Mindy Ruben LE09632
Torres, Richard RR10714, RR10764, RR11474, RR11841
Tosches, Nick BR01059
Toure AR15612, AR15613, AR15614, AR15615, AR15616, AR15617, AR15618, AR15619, AR15620, AR15621, AR15622, AR15623, AR15624, AR15625, AR15626, AR15627, AR15628, AR15629, AR15630, AR15631, AR15632, AR15633, AR15634, AR15635, AR15636, RR10477, RR10505, RR10540, RR10573, RR10576, RR10723, RR10857, RR10858, RR10868, RR11007, RR11207, RR11451, RR11464, RR11494, RR11634, RR11651, RR11654, RR11790, RR11989,

RR11994, RR12073, RR12112, RR12246, RR12312, RR12498, RR12563, RR12599, RR12749, RR12964, RR13056, RR13142, RR13143, RR13203, RR13234
Tout, Deborah LE09633
Towey, Shaun LE09634
Travers, Peter AR15637, AR15638, AR15639, AR15640, AR15641, AR15642, AR15643, AR15644, AR15645, AR15646, AR15647, AR15648, AR15649, AR15650, AR15651, AR15652, AR15653, AR15654, AR15655, AR15656, AR15657, AR15658, AR15659, AR15660, AR15661, AR15662, AR15663, AR15664, AR15665, AR15666, AR15667, AR15668, AR15669, AR15670, AR15671, AR15672, AR15673, AR15674, AR15675, AR15676, AR15677, AR15678, AR15679, AR15680, AR15681, AR15682, AR15683, AR15684, AR15685, AR15686, CR00906, LE09635, MR01189, MR01190, MR01191, MR01192, MR01194, MR01195, MR01196, MR01197, MR01198, MR01199, MR01200, MR01201, MR01202, MR01203, MR01204, MR01205, MR01206, MR01207, MR01208, MR01209, MR01210, MR01211, MR01212, MR01213, MR01214, MR01215, MR01216, MR01217, MR01218, MR01219, MR01220, MR01221, MR01222, MR01223, MR01224, MR01226, MR01227, MR01229, MR01230, MR01231, MR01232, MR01233, MR01234, MR01235, MR01237, MR01238, MR01239, MR01240, MR01241, MR01243, MR01244, MR01245, MR01246, MR01247, MR01248, MR01249, MR01250, MR01251, MR01252, MR01253, MR01254, MR01255, MR01256, MR01257, MR01258, MR01259, MR01260, MR01261, MR01262, MR01264, MR01265, MR01266, MR01267, MR01268, MR01269, MR01270, MR01271, MR01272, MR01273, MR01274, MR01275, MR01276, MR01277, MR01278, MR01279, MR01280, MR01281, MR01282, MR01283, MR01284, MR01285, MR01286, MR01287, MR01288, MR01289, MR01290, MR01291, MR01292, MR01293, MR01294, MR01295, MR01297, MR01298, MR01300, MR01301, MR01302, MR01303, MR01304, MR01305, MR01306, MR01307, MR01308, MR01309, MR01310, MR01311, MR01312, MR01313, MR01315, MR01316, MR01317, MR01318, MR01319, MR01320, MR01321, MR01322, MR01323, MR01324, MR01325, MR01328, MR01329, MR01330, MR01331, MR01332, MR01333, MR01334, MR01335, MR01336, MR01337, MR01338, MR01339, MR01340, MR01341, MR01342, MR01343, MR01344, MR01345, MR01346, MR01347, MR01348, MR01349, MR01350, MR01351, MR01352, MR01353, MR01354, MR01355, MR01357, MR01358, MR01360, MR01361, MR01362, MR01364, MR01365, MR01366, MR01367, MR01368, MR01369, MR01370, MR01371, MR01372, MR01374, MR01375, MR01376, MR01378, MR01379, MR01380, MR01381, MR01382, MR01383, MR01384, MR01385, MR01386, MR01388, MR01391, MR01392,MR01393, MR01394, MR01395, MR01396, MR01397, MR01399, MR01400, MR01401, MR01402, MR01403, MR01404, MR01405, MR01406, MR01407, MR01408, MR01409, MR01412, MR01413, MR01414, MR01415, MR01416, MR01417, MR01418, MR01420, MR01421, MR01422, MR01423, MR01425, MR01426, MR01427, MR01428, MR01429, MR01430, MR01431, MR01432, MR01433, MR01434, MR01435, MR01436, MR01437, MR01439, MR01440, MR01441, MR01442, MR01443, MR01444, MR01445, MR01447, MR01448, MR01449, MR01450, MR01451, MR01452, MR01454, MR01455, MR01456, MR01458, MR01459, MR01461, MR01462, MR01464, MR01465, MR01466, MR01467, MR01469, MR01470, MR01471, MR01472, MR01473, MR01477, MR01478, MR01479, MR01480, MR01481, MR01482, MR01483, MR01484, MR01485, MR01486, MR01487, MR01489, MR01490, MR01491, MR01492, MR01493, MR01494, MR01496, MR01498, MR01499, MR01500, MR01501, MR01502, MR01504, MR01505, MR01506, MR01507, MR01508, MR01509, MR01510, MR01511, MR01512, MR01513, MR01514, MR01515, MR01516, MR01517, MR01518, MR01519, MR01520, MR01521, MR01522, MR01523, MR01524, MR01525, MR01526, MR01527, MR01528, MR01529, MR01530, MR01532, MR01533, MR01534, MR01535, MR01536, MR01537, MR01538, MR01539, MR01540, MR01541, MR01542, MR01543, MR01544, MR01545, MR01546, MR01547, MR01548, MR01551, MR01552, MR01553, MR01554, MR01555, MR01556, MR01557, MR01559, MR01560, MR01561, MR01562, MR01563, MR01564, MR01565, MR01566, MR01567, MR01568, MR01569, MR01570, MR01571, MR01572, MR01574, MR01575, MR01576, MR01577, MR01578, MR01579, MR01580, MR01581, MR01582, MR01584, MR01585, MR01586, MR01587, MR01588, MR01589, MR01590, MR01591, MR01592, MR01593, MR01594, MR01595, MR01596, MR01597, MR01598, MR01599, MR01600, MR01601, MR01602, MR01603, MR01604, MR01605, MR01606, MR01607, MR01608, MR01609, MR01610, MR01611, MR01612, MR01613, MR01614, MR01615, MR01616, MR01617, MR01618, MR01619, MR01620, MR01621, MR01622, MR01623, MR01624, MR01625, MR01626, MR01627, MR01628, MR01629, MR01630, MR01631, MR01632, MR01633, MR01634, MR01635, MR01636, MR01637, MR01638, MR01639, MR01640, MR01641, MR01642, MR01643, MR01644, MR01645, MR01646, MR01647, MR01648, MR01649, MR01650, MR01651, MR01652, MR01653, MR01654, MR01655, MR01656, MR01657, MR01658, MR01659, MR01660, MR01661, MR01662, MR01663, MR01664, MR01665, MR01666, MR01667, MR01668, MR01670, MR01671, MR01672, MR01673, MR01674, MR01675, MR01676, MR01677, MR01678, MR01679, MR01680, MR01681, MR01682, MR01683, MR01684, MR01685, MR01686, MR01687, MR01688, MR01689, MR01690, MR01691, MR01692, MR01694, MR01695, MR01696, MR01697, MR01698, MR01699, MR01700, MR01701, MR01702, MR01703, MR01704, MR01705, MR01706, MR01707, MR01708, MR01709, MR01710, MR01711, MR01712, MR01713, MR01714, MR01715, MR01716, MR01717, MR01718, MR01719, MR01721, MR01722, MR01723, MR01724, MR01725, MR01726, MR01727, MR01728, MR01729, MR01730, MR01731, MR01732, MR01733, MR01734, MR01735, MR01736, MR01737, MR01738, MR01739, MR01740, MR01741, MR01742, MR01743, MR01744, MR01745, MR01746, MR01747, MR01748, MR01749, MR01750, MR01751, MR01752, MR01753, MR01754, MR01755, MR01756, MR01757, MR01758, MR01761, MR01762, MR01763, MR01764, MR01765, MR01766, MR01767, MR01768, MR01769, MR01770, MR01771, MR01772, MR01773, MR01774, MR01775, MR01776, MR01777, MR01778, MR01779, MR01780, MR01781, MR01782, MR01783, MR01784, MR01785, MR01786, MR01787, MR01789, MR01790, MR01791, MR01792, MR01793, MR01794, MR01795, MR01797, MR01798, MR01799, MR01800, MR01801, MR01802, MR01803, MR01804, MR01805, MR01806, MR01807, MR01808, MR01810, MR01811, MR01812, MR01813, MR01814, MR01815, MR01816, MR01817, MR01818, MR01819, MR01820, MR01821, MR01822, MR01823, MR01824, MR01825, MR01826, MR01827, MR01828, MR01829, MR01830, MR01831, MR01832, MR01833, MR01834, MR01835, MR01836, MR01837, MR01838, MR01839, MR01840, MR01841, MR01842, MR01843, MR01844, MR01845, MR01846, MR01847, MR01848, MR01849, MR01850, MR01851, MR01852, MR01853, MR01854, MR01855, MR01856, MR01857, MR01858, MR01859, MR01860, MR01861, MR01862, MR01863, MR01864, MR01865, MR01866, MR01867, MR01868, MR01869, MR01870, MR01871, MR01873, MR01874, MR01875, MR01876, MR01877, MR01878, MR01879, MR01880, MR01881, MR01882, MR01883, MR01884, MR01885, MR01886, MR01887, MR01888, MR01889, MR01890, MR01891, MR01893, MR01894, MR01895, MR01896, MR01897, MR01898, MR01899, MR01900, MR01901, MR01902, MR01903, MR01904, MR01905, MR01906, MR01907, MR01908, MR01909, MR01910, MR01911, MR01912, MR01913, MR01914, MR01915, MR01916, MR01917, MR01918, MR01919, MR01920, MR01921, MR01922, MR01923, MR01924, MR01925, MR01926, MR01927, MR01928, MR01929, MR01930, MR01931, MR01932, MR01933, MR01934, MR01935, MR01936, MR01937, MR01938, MR01939, MR01940, MR01941, MR01942, MR01943, MR01944, MR01945, MR01946, MR01947, MR01948, MR01949, MR01950, MR01951, MR01952, MR01953, MR01954, MR01955, MR01956, MR01957, MR01958, MR01959, MR01960, MR01961, MR01962, MR01963, MR01964, MR01966, MR01967, MR01968, MR01969, MR01970, MR01971, MR01972, MR01975, MR01976, MR01977, MR01978, MR01980, MR01981, MR01982, MR01983, MR01984, MR01985, MR01986, MR01987, MR01988, MR01989, MR01990, MR01991, MR01992, MR01993, MR01994, MR01995, MR01996, MR01997, MR01998, MR01999,

Travers, Peter (continued) MR02000, MR02001, MR02003, MR02004, MR02005, MR02006, MR02007, MR02008, MR02009, MR02010, MR02011, MR02012, MR02013, MR02014, MR02015, MR02017, MR02018, MR02019, MR02020, MR02021, MR02022, MR02023, MR02024, MR02025, MR02026, MR02027, MR02028, MR02029, MR02030, MR02031, MR02032, MR02033, MR02034, MR02035, MR02036, MR02037, MR02038, MR02039, MR02040, MR02041, MR02042, MR02043, MR02044, MR02045, MR02046, MR02047, MR02048, MR02049, MR02050, MR02051, MR02052, MR02053, MR02054, MR02055, MR02056, MR02058, MR02059, MR02060, MR02061, MR02062, MR02064, MR02065, MR02066, MR02067, MR02068, MR02069, MR02070, MR02071, MR02072, MR02073, MR02074, MR02075, MR02076, MR02077, MR02078, MR02079, MR02080, MR02081, MR02082, MR02084, MR02085, MR02086, MR02087, MR02088, MR02089, MR02090, MR02091, MR02092, MR02093, MR02094, MR02095, MR02096, MR02097, MR02098, MR02099, MR02100, MR02101, MR02102, MR02103, MR02104, MR02105, MR02106, MR02108, MR02109, MR02110, MR02111, MR02112, MR02113, MR02114, MR02115, MR02116, MR02117, MR02118, MR02119, MR02120, MR02121, MR02122, MR02123, MR02124, MR02125, MR02126, MR02127, MR02128, MR02129, MR02130, MR02131, MR02132, MR02133, MR02134, MR02135, MR02136, MR02137, MR02138, MR02139, MR02140, MR02141, MR02142, MR02143, MR02144, MR02145, MR02146, MR02147, MR02148, MR02149, MR02150, MR02151, MR02152, MR02153, MR02154, MR02155, MR02156, MR02157, MR02158, MR02159, MR02160, MR02161, MR02162
Tre LE09636
Treadaway, Trey LE09637
Treguboff, Jeff LE09638
Tremain, Kerry LE09639
Tremblay, Mike LE09640
Treubig, Dennis LE09641
Trinchera, Tom LE09642
Trisha LE09643
Tritt, Travis LE09644
Troiano, Larry LE09645
Troitsky, Artemy AR15690, AR15691
Trumbo, Keith LE09646
Tuck, Stephanie AR15692, AR15693, AR15694, AR15695, AR15696
Tudir, Susan LE09647
Tullos, Julie LE09648
Turkman, S. U. LE09649
Turner, Kirk LE09650
Turner, Mark LE09651
Tyler, Sarah LE09652
Tyler, Steven LE09653, LE09654, LE09655, LE09656
Tzu, Sun BR01042

U

Udovitch, Mim AR15697, AR15698, AR15699, AR15700, AR15701, AR15702, AR15703, AR15704
Ullenberg, Susan LE09657
Unger, Russ LE09658
Unholz, John LE09659
Untermyer, Alexander LE09660

V

Vagelatos, Alex LE09661
Valence, Rick LE09662
Valium, Judea LE09663
"Vam Pyros, Bill" RR12810
Van Bakel, Rogier AR15716
Van Buskirk, Elizabeth M. LE09664
Van Do, Dave LE09665
Van Dusen, Christie LE09666
Van Parys, Bill AR15717, AR15718, AR15719, AR15720, BR01088, BR01101, CR00880, RR10486, RR10759, RR11471, RR11851, RR12810, RR13209
Van Wagner, Chad LE09667
Van Zeipel, Jayson LE09668
VanAlstyne, Kirstie LE09669
Vanto-Fhym, Aser LE09670
Varela, Roger LE09671
Vaughn, Wendi LE09672
Vedder, Eddie LE09673
Velazquez, Brian LE09674
Veysset, Frederique AR15722 AR15724, AR15725
Vig, Butch AR15726
Villasana, Tina LE09675
Vincentelli, Elisabeth AR15726a, AR15727, AR15728, RR10394
Virshup, Amy AR15729
Vishnesky, Phillip C. LE09676 AR15730
Vitas, Jason A. LE09677
Vitek, Robin L. LE09678
Vizard, Frank AR15731, AR15732
Vller, Josh LE09679
Voida, Steven M. LE09680
Volk, Steven RR10956, RR11129, RR11957, RR11979, RR12644
Vykruta, Ron LE09681

W

Wacheldorf, Shelley LE09682
Wade, Jesse LE09683
Walk, Hunter LE09684
Walker, Alice BR01100
Walker, John AR15733
Walker, Murray LE09685
Walker, Scott LE09686
Wallace, Kristin LE09687
Wallior, Susan M. LE09688
Walls, Richard C. RR10502, RR10706, RR10883, RR11254, RR11329, RR11510, RR12015, RR12500, RR12685, RR12732, RR13177
Walser, Robert BR01112, RR11761, RR12242, RR12521, RR13164
Walsh, Jim AR15734, AR15735, CR00645, CR00731
Walsh, John LE09689
Walsh, Kirk AR15736
Walters, Barry RR11664
Walters, James LE09690
Ward, Matthew B. LE09691
Ward, Sandy LE09692
Wareham, Dean AR15737
Warner, Justin LE09693
Warnock, Mickey AR15738
Warren, Brad LE09694
Wasylkiw, Blaine LE09695
Waters, Martha LE09696
Watkins, Glenn A. LE09697
Watkins, Neil LE09698
Watley, Jody LE09699
Watson, Albert AR15739
Watson, Dave LE09700
Watson, Jason R. LE09701
Watson, Kevin LE09702
Watson, Melissa Audra LE09703
Watson, Terri M. LE09704
Webb, Pete AR15741
Weber, Bruce AR15742
Weber, Kurt T. (Program Director, Cascade Policy Institute) LE09705
Webster, Andy RR12742
Webster, Christopher A. LE09706
Weedman, Jeff LE09707
Weicker, Lowell P., Jr. LE09708
Weidler, Bob LE09709
Weil, Elizabeth AR15743, AR15744, AR15745, AR15746
Weil, Holly J. LE09710
Weill, Sue LE09711
Weiner, Kirsten LE09712
Weiner, Tim AR15747
Weingarten, Marc AR15748, AR15749, AR15750
Weinger, Harry AR15751
Weir, David AR15752
Weis, Shyama LE09713
Weisel, Al AR15753, AR15754, AR15755, AR15756, AR15757, AR15758, AR15759, AR15760, AR15761, AR15762, AR15763, AR15764, AR15765, AR15766, AR15767, AR15768, AR15769, AR15770, AR15771, AR15772, AR15773, AR15774, AR15775, BR01079, CR00658, CR00826, RR10571b, RR10703, RR10704, RR10739, RR10794, RR10829, RR11112, RR11144, RR11287, RR11794, RR11854, RR11879, RR11894, RR11956, RR12031, RR12135, RR12404, RR12471, RR12546, RR12740, RR13170
Weisner, Aron LE09714
Weiss, Michael F. LE09715
Welchman, Geoffrey RR11740, RR12382, RR12587
Wells, Jo Ann LE09716
Wenner, Jann AR15776, AR15777, AR15778, AR15779, AR15780, AR15781, AR15782, AR15783, AR15784, AR15785, AR15786, AR15787, AR15788, AR15789, AR15790, AR15791, AR15792, AR15793, AR15794, AR15795, AR15796, AR15797, AR15798, AR15799, AR15800, AR15801
Wentworth, Liz LE09717
Wessel, Cathrine AR15802
West, Faith LE09718
West, Jill LE09719
Westfield, Alisha LE09720
Wexler, Jerry AR15804
Weymouth, Tina AR15805
Wheatley, Jack LE09721
Whinery, Megan LE09722
Whisler, Casey LE09723
White, Aaron LE09724
White, Armond AR15808, RR10460, RR11088, RR11764, RR12025, RR12422
White, Chris LE09725
White, Richard LE09726
White, Richard J. LE09727
White, S. Tracy LE09728
White, Timothy AR15809, BR01090
Whitehead, John C. (Asst. Prof., Dept. of Economics, East Carolina Univ.) LE09729
Whiteley, Stephen LE09730
Whitmer, Mike LE09731
Whitney, Stu LE09732
Wiatt, Jody LE09733
Wiederhorn, Jon AR15812, AR15813, AR15814, AR15815, AR15816, AR15817, AR15818, AR15819, AR15820, AR15821, AR15822, AR15823, AR15824, AR15825, AR15826, AR15827, AR15828, AR15829, AR15830, AR15831, AR15832, AR15833, AR15834, AR15835, AR15836, AR15837, AR15838, AR15839, AR15840, AR15841, AR15842, AR15843, AR15844, AR15845, AR15846, AR15847, AR15848, AR15849, AR15850, AR15851, AR15852, AR15853, AR15854, AR15855, AR15856, AR15857, AR15858, AR15859, AR15860, AR15861, AR15862, AR15863, AR15864, AR15865, CR00659, CR00827, RR10408, RR10447, RR10570, RR10633, RR10823, RR10856, RR10976, RR11153, RR11210, RR11280, RR11385, RR11631, RR11888, RR11907, RR11990, RR11998, RR12062, RR12081, RR12082, RR12281,

Wiederhorn, Jon (continued) RR12432, RR12446, RR12460, RR12551, RR12607, RR12609, RR12674, RR12678, RR12971, RR13051, RR13285
Wielenga, Dave AR15866, AR15867, AR15868, AR15869
Wiesel, Al RR12177
Wieser, Adam J. LE09734
Wiest, Randy LE09735
Wilber, Catie LE09736
Wild, David AR15870, AR15871, AR15872, AR15873, AR15874, AR15875, AR15876, AR15877, AR15878, AR15879, AR15880, AR15881, AR15882, AR15883, AR15884, AR15885, AR15886, AR15887, AR15888, AR15889, AR15890, AR15891, AR15892, AR15893, AR15894, AR15895, AR15896, AR15897, AR15898, AR15899, AR15900, AR15901, AR15902, AR15903, AR15904, AR15905, AR15906, AR15907, AR15908, AR15909, AR15910, AR15911, AR15912, AR15913, AR15914, AR15915, AR15916, AR15917, AR15918, AR15919, AR15920, AR15921, AR15922, AR15923, AR15924, AR15925, AR15926, AR15927, AR15928, AR15929, AR15930, AR15931, AR15932, AR15933, AR15934, AR15935, AR15936, AR15937, AR15938, AR15939, AR15940, AR15941, AR15942, AR15943, AR15944, AR15945, AR15946, AR15947, AR15948, AR15949, AR15950, AR15951, AR15952, AR15953, AR15954, AR15955, AR15956, AR15957, AR15958, AR15959, AR15960, AR15961, AR15962, AR15963, AR15964, AR15965, AR15966, AR15967, AR15968, AR15969, AR15970, AR15971, AR15972, AR15973, AR15974, AR15975, AR15976, AR15977, AR15978, AR15979, AR15980, AR15981, AR15982, AR15983, AR15984, AR15985, AR15986, AR15987, AR15988, AR15989, AR15990, AR15991, AR15992, AR15993, AR15994, AR15995, AR15996, AR15997, AR15998, AR15999, AR16000, AR16001, AR16002, AR16003, AR16004, AR16005, AR16006, AR16007, AR16008, AR16009, AR16010, AR16011, AR16012, AR16013, AR16014, AR16015, AR16016, AR16017, AR16018, AR16019, BR01104, BR01134, CR00667, CR00710, CR00772, CR00797, CR00807, CR00809, CR00813, RR10630, RR10747, RR10993, RR10994, RR11046, RR11179, RR11313, RR11822, RR12391, RR12590, RR12851
Wiley, Audrey LE09737
Wilkinson, Francis AR16020, AR16021, AR16022, AR16023, AR16024, AR16025, AR16026, AR16027, AR16028, AR16029, AR16030, AR16031, AR16032, AR16033, AR16034, AR16035, AR16036, AR16037, AR16038, AR16039, AR16040, AR16041, AR16042, AR16043, AR16044, AR16045
Wilkinson, George Mark LE09738
Wilkinson, Peter AR16046, AR16047, AR16048, AR16049, AR16050, AR16051
Wilkison, Chad LE09739
Wilkofsky, Marc LE09740
Willey, Lisa LE09741
Williams, A. LE09742
Williams, Allen LE09743
Williams, Fern Baum LE09744
Williams, Isaac LE09745
Williams, Jenny LE09746
Williams, Linda LE09747
Williams, S. LE09748
Williamson, Roger LE09749
Willis, Aaron LE09750
Willis, Jessica AR16052
Wills, Garry AR16053
Wilson, Bob LE09751
Wilson, Ian LE09752
Wilson, Larry LE09753
Wilson, LeAnne LE09754
Wilson, Linda M. LE09755
Wilson, Michael RR12874
Wilson, Peter LE09756
Wilson, Rona H. LE09757
Wilson, Susan LE09758
Wing, Eliza AR16054, AR16055, AR16056
Winterson, Jeanette BR01095
Winthrop, D. L. LE09759
Wischer, David LE09760
Withycombe, Mary LE09761
Witkin, Christian AR16057
Wofford, Emmett LE09762
Wolf, John A. LE09763
Wolfe, Bill AR16058
Wolfe, Tom AR16059, AR16060, AR16061
Wolff, Daniel BR01135
Wolman, Kris LE09764
Wolpin, Stewart AR16062, AR16063, AR16064, AR16065, AR16066, AR16067, AR16068, AR16069, AR16070, AR16071, AR16072, AR16073, AR16074, AR16075, AR16076, AR16077, AR16078, AR16079, AR16080, AR16081, AR16082, AR16083, AR16084, AR16085
Wood, Joe AR16086, AR16087
Wood, T. (Andy Wood's Mother) LE09765
Woodard, Josef AR16088, RR10425, RR10553, RR10716, RR10807a, RR10864, RR11185, RR11565, RR12735, RR12826
Woodie, John D. F. LE09766
Woodward, Fred AR16089
Woodward, Mike LE09767
Wool, Rachel LE09768
Wooster, Chris LE09769
Worthington, Beth LE09770
Wright, Christian AR16090, RR10488, RR10571a, RR10715, RR10833, RR10919, RR10930, RR10973, RR11130, RR11325, RR11375, RR11482, RR11488, RR11562, RR12234, RR12441, RR12450, RR12602, RR13172
Wright, Kelly LE09771
Wright, Lawrence AR16091, AR16092
Wyar, Sue LE09772
Wyman, Ben LE09773
Wyman, Bill AR16093, AR16094, AR16095, AR16096, RR11378
Wyndham, Charles LE09774

Y

Yackley, Ayla Jean LE09775
Yaegel, Mark S. LE09776, LE09777
Yankovic, Al AR16097
Yarlas, Aaron LE09778
Yauch, Adam AR16098
Yearwood, Trisha LE09779
Yednock, Kimberly LE09780
Yellen, Samuel BR01041
Yo-Yo LE09781
Yockey, W. H. LE09782
Yocom, Travis C. LE09783
Yoffe, Emily AR16101
York, Kristi LE09784
Youchison, Steven LE09785
Youells, M. LE09786
Young, Amy LE09787
Young, Bob AR16102
Young, Charles M. AR16103, AR16104, AR16105, AR16106, AR16107, AR16108, AR16109
Young, Hilarie LE09788
Young, J. A. LE09789
Young, John LE09790
Young, Jon RR11067, RR11799
Young, Marilyn BR01127
Youngs, Ben AR16110
Yousuf, Sara LE09791
Yow, David AR16111

Z

Zaccherio, Michael LE09792, LE09793, LE09794
Zacharek, Stephanie RR10694, RR10890, RR11373, RR11399, RR11458, RR11534, RR12068
Zani, Cheri LE09795, LE09796
Zanti, Hope LE09797
Zartman, David C. LE09798
Zarzecki, Tom LE09799
Zawadzki, Trinette LE09800
Zay, Laura LE09801
Zehme, Bill AR16112, AR16113, AR16114, AR16115, AR16116, AR16117, AR16118, AR16119, AR16120
Zerbe, Allison LE09802
Zeskind, Leonard AR16121, AR16122
Zevin, Dan AR16123, AR16124, AR16125, AR16126, AR16127, AR16128, AR16129, AR16130, AR16131, AR16132
Zicklin, Eric AR16133
Zima, Dan LE09803
Zimmerman, Keith BR01110
Zinman, Greg RR12835
Zinn, Howard BR01041, BR01055, BR01063, BR01066, BR01068, BR01069, BR01085, BR01091, BR01094, BR01127, BR01129
Zulaica, Don LE09804
Zweiback, Richard LE09805

Master Index to Titles

A

The A List: Celebrity Guidance Counselors Recommend One Book, One Movie, One Recording That Will Change Your Life AR15394
A.M. RR12924
Abba-Esque RR11087
ABC Television Boots Concert-Tape Traders Off Its America Online Site AR14458
Aboriginal Choirs Of Central Australia RR13042
About Facing Chairman Nunn: Inside The Gay Lobby AR16020
About To Choke RR10779
Above RR11770
Above The Rim RR13043
Absolutely Free RR13010
An Abuse Of Trust? Michael Jackson Defends His Honor AR13928
Achin' To Be Understood: The Rolling Stone Interview With Paul Westerberg AR14672
Achtung, Babies! A New U2 Album! AR13691
Achtung Baby RR12790
Acid Damage: The Strange, Tragic Tale Of Psychedelic Icon Roky Erickson's Descent Into Madness AR14624
Acid Eaters RR12288
The Acid Test: Deadheads Face Hard Time In LSD Crackdown AR15499
The Acoustic Motorbike RR10606
Acquatica RR12434
Acquired Taste: G. Love Serves A New Platter With Special Sauce AR13795
Across The Borderline RR12007, RR12008
Across The Great Divide RR10499, RR13044
Acting!!! Genius!!! Brilliant!!! AR13213, AR14812
Adios Amigos RR12289
Adrenalize RR10974
The Adventures Of Miss Thing: In 4 Months Alanis Morissette Has Gone From Washed-Up Child Star To Queen Of This Year's Pop Culture Prom AR15870
The Aeroplane Flies High RR12543
Aerosmith: Albany, N.Y. CR00635
Aerosmith Box: A Hard-Rock Primer AR14739
Aerosmith In A Hard Place: New Album Is Delayed Amid Rumors Of Drugs, Bickering And Behind-The-Scenes Firings AR13272, AR14152
Aerosmith's Hot Grip: Steven Tyler Promises New Album To Be The Band's Biggest, Scariest Yet AR15871
Affairs Of The Heart RR12881
Afghan Whigs Get Soulful On Their New LP 'Black Love' AR15593
Afghan Whigs: Washington CR00636
Africa Invades Europe RR13007, RR13008
Africando Volume 1 RR13045, RR13046
Afro-Cuban Classic: Los 24 Exitos Originales de Arsenio Rodriguez RR12373
After Awhile RR11247
After Murder Park RR10470
After South Central: The White Conscience AR14059
After The Storm: Billy Joel Turns To Beethoven For 'Dreams' AR13796
Aftermath: In Rwanda A Year After The Massacre, There Is Still No Justice, No Peace AR14521, AR15339
Afro Brasil RR13047, RR13048
The Agony And The Ecstasy: Evan Dando On The Highs And Lows Of Being The King Of College Charts AR13853
Agony And The Ecstasy: Kevin Salem Turns Bitter Times Into Blissful Blasts AR14039
Ah, The Smell Of It: L7 Bask In The Sweet Stink Of Success AR13391
Ahead Of Their Time RR13011
Ahora Vengo Alborota RR11763
AIDS And Rock: Sound Of Silence AR14205, AR14224
AIDS And The Media: Shifting Out Of Neutral AR14326
Aimee Mann AR13487
Ain't Enough Comin' In RR12412
Ain't Gonna Be Your Dog RR11447
Ain't Life Grand RR12923
Ain't My Lookout RR11302
Ain't No Other RR11760
Aitara RR12822
AKA Detrimental Vasoline RR12393
AKA Grafitti Man RR12773
AKA The Rugged Child RR12498
Al Pacino: The Rolling Stone Interview AR13413
Albert Collins 1932-1993 AR13765
Albert Goldman 1927-1994 AR14361
Albert King: 1923-1992 AR15556
Albert Watson AR15739
Alejandro Escovedo AR13692
Alex Chilton (song) RR12328
Alibis RR11674
Alice In Chains RR10408
Alice Through The Looking Glass: The Dark Brooding Side Of The Seattle Scene AR15160
Alien Lanes RR11316
Alison Steele: 1937-1995 AR14539
Alive In America RR12632
All Eyez On Me RR12473, RR12474
All For You RR11876
All Guns, No Butter: Inside Somalia, A Starving Nation Armed To The Teeth AR14993
All Hail The Queen RR12254
All I Want For Christmas AR16062
All Night Long RR11610, RR12578
All Samples Cleared! RR11790
All She Wants AR13797
An All-Star Experience: Jimi Hendrix Is Feted On Tribute Album AR13929
All Systems Go: Whether It's Budget Audio For A Dorm Room Or Home Theater For A Mansion, One Of These New Setups Is Right For You AR13638
All That May Do My Rhyme RR11091
All The President's Men AR16021
All The Way RR12441
All They Need To Know They Learned In Hollywood AR13478
All This Useless Beauty RR10879
All You Can Eat RR11664
All You Need Is Ears BR01040
Alone And Acoustic RR11331, RR12896
Alright It Was Frank RR10437
Altamira Banda Show RR10418
Altered Beast RR12688
Altered Stakes: Don Law Cuts Out The Middleman AR13058
Alternative Music AR14740
Alternative NRG RR13049
The Alternative Underground: Bands On The Real Cutting Edge Turn Out For Six-day Washington Festival AR15199
Alternative Woodstock RR13050
Alt.Rock AR14276
Always And Forever RR11098
Am I Not Your Girl? RR12067
Amanita RR10506
Amateur Home-Theater Setups Created A Look Of High-Tech Chaos That Might Come To Typify Video In The Nineties: The TV Room As Booby Trap AR15637
Amazing Disgrace RR12207
Amazing Grace RR12215
Ambersunshower AR13184
Ambush At Fort Bragg: Conclusion AR16059
A.M.C.'s S.F. AR15235
America Is Dying RR13051
American Babylon RR11310
American Caesar RR12199
American Folk Blues Festival '62-'65 RR13052
The American In Me RR11163
American Labor Struggles BR01041
American Recordings RR10750, RR10751
American Standard RR11799
American Stars N' Bars: Living History Steals The Show At SXSW AR13693
American Thighs RR12840
Aminah's Dream RR12443
Amorica RR10568
Amused To Death RR12879
A-Muze Yourself: From Abba To Zappa: A New Computer Gives Fans Fingertip Access To Disc Data AR14362
Anarchy In The UK RR13053
Anatomy Of A Murder: How Corporate Lobbyists Plotted To Kill Of Direct Student Lending AR13269
Anchored In Love RR10743
And A Happy New Gear AR13100
And Don't Forget... AR16063
And If You Still Don't Get It... AR14994
And We Bid You Good Night: Artists And Colleagues Pay Tribute To Garcia AR12959
The Andy-Hero: In A Few Minutes, We Learn How Andy Rooney Has Survived 'Dateline,' Molly Ivins And Kurt Cobain AR15872
Anesthesia (song) RR12867
An Angel At My Shoulder RR12029
Angel Dust RR11111
Angelique Kidjo: Politics With A Beat AR12986
Ani DiFranco AR14607
Animated Arguments: Why The Show's Critics Just Don't Get It AR14327
Annie Lennox: New York CR00780
Annunciation RR12659
Anodyne RR12796
Another Level RR10584
Another Night RR12414
Antenna RR13004
Anthem RR10579
The Anthology 1961-1977 RR11473, RR11818
The Anthology 1965-1967 RR12541
Anthology 2 RR10523
Anthology 3 RR10524

Anthrax Brings The 'Noise': The Thrash-Metal Kings Find A New Voice AR15873
Antichrist Superstar RR11789
Antonio Carlos Jobim: 1927-1994 AR13766
Ants To The Moon RR11965
Anything Can Happen RR12415
Apocalypse Across The Sky RR10467, RR11804
Apocalypse 91...The Enemy Strikes Black RR12241
Apollo 18 RR12725
Apostrophe RR13012
The Aranbee Pop Symphony Orchestra RR10451
Arc Angels RR10452
Are The Kids All Right? As More Moms Enter The Pop-Music Work Force, Rock & Roll Nannies Have Their Hands Full AR13488
Are You Gonna Go My Way RR11640, RR11641
Are You Xperienced?: On The Fashion Tip With Kim Gordon Of Sonic Youth AR14813, AR15385
Areito RR11315
Aren't Stickers Enough? A Revived PMRC Pushes For A Stringent New Record-Ratings System AR15492
Arkansas Traveler RR12492
Armed And Dangerous: The NRA, Militias And White Supremacists Are Fostering A Network Of Right Wing Warriors AR16121
Arrested Development: Relaying Positive Messages AR15107
[Art Department] AR12974
Art Forms Of Dimensions Tomorrow RR12257
Art Garfunkel AR13489
The Art Of Fingerstyle Guitar RR13054
The Art Of Noise: The New Rock-Poster Genius Of Frank Kozik AR14344
The Art Of The Deal: The Real Arithmetic Behind The New Superstar Contracts AR13930
The Art Of War BR01042
Art Students In America AR13214
Art Versus Commerce AR13613
Arthur Alexander: 1940-1993 AR13287
Artifacts Of Love RR11859
Artificial Intelligence II RR13055
Artist Biographies AR12918
Artist Biographies [cont.] AR12919
Artistic Vice RR11552
Artists Join Forces For AIDS Album AR15874
Artists' Picks AR12975
Artists' Picks: 1992 Music Awards AR12976
Artists' Picks: 1993 Music Awards AR12977
As Long As There's Music RR11342, RR11374
As Nasty As They Wanna Be BR01043
As The World 'Terns: More Weird Tales Of Internships AR15226
Asa Nisi Masa RR10463
[ASCAP-Deems Taylor Award] AR12978
[ASCAP-Deems Taylor Awards] AR12979, AR12980
Ascension RR10399
Ask A Marine AR14140
Ask For It RR11420
A Ass Pocket Of Whiskey RR10701
Ass Ponys AR15028
The Astral Jane: Jane Siberry Makes Metaphysical Pop With Heart AR12970
Astro Freaks: 2000 AR13392
At Action Park RR12484
At The Ryman RR11361, RR11993
Atco Folds; More Cuts Expected AR13931
Atlanta AR13038
Atlanta Whiskey Flats RR12559
Atliens RR12090
Atomic Logic: The Bomb In The Post-Cold War World AR15179
Attack Of The Cyber-Rockers: New Computer Rocker Jocks Get Their Modems Working AR13932
Attack Of The Fall Flicks AR15638
Audio Power To The People: Now Is The Time To Exercise—And Enjoy—Your Right To Low-Cost Hi-Fi AR13639
Auf Wiedersehen (song) RR12629
August And Everything After RR10884, RR10885
Aunts' Indie Plans AR15150
Austin Skyline RR11659
Australia's Other Stars: Aboriginal Bands Are Making Their Mark On Music From Down Under AR13694
Autobiography Of Mistachuck RR10947
Autogeddon RR10870
Automatic For The People RR12321, RR12322
Automobility RR12114
Avalon Blues 1963 RR11456
Award Tour (song) RR12763
[Awards] AR12983, AR12984
Awopbopaloobop: The Golden Age Of Rock BR01044
Axl On Trial AR13764
Axl Rose AR14741
Axl's St. Louis Blues: Singer Arrested In New York For Riot Charges AR14673

B

B. Brown Posse RR13056
The B-52s, Juliana Hatfield: Radio City Music Hall CR00638, CR00742
Babes In Toyland: The Making And Selling Of A Rock And Roll Band BR01045, BR01046
Bacchanal Time RR12673
Bacdafucup RR12080
Back At Your Ass For The Nine-4 RR12025a
Back For Good (song) RR12700
Back From Rio RR11839
Back In The Game RR11551
Back In The Saddle: C&W Outlaw Steve Earle Returns From His Lost Years AR14214
Back In The USA RR11826
Back To Mono (1958-1969) RR12594
Back To The Back Of The Bus?: Clinton's Mixed Signals On Civil Rights AR14060
Back To The Garden AR14017
Back To The Light RR11816
Back To The Streets RR13057
Back Where I Belong RR10458
Backbeat RR13058
Backbeat: For The Soundtrack Of The Beatles Biopic, An Alternative Supergroup Came Together AR13196
Bad And Beautiful RR12258
Bad Boys RR11479
Bad Livers AR13393
Bad To The Bone: John Mellencamp Strips Down To Fighting Trim On "Dance Naked" AR13414
Bad Vibes RR10834
Badmotorfinger RR12582
Bakesale RR12452
Balance RR12812
Balancing Act: Eddie Van Halen AR15875
Ball-Hog Or Tugboat? RR12882
Ballad No. 19 (song) RR12053
Ballad Of A Teenage Queen AR13215
The Ballad Of Yoko: The B-52's Kate Pierson Talks With Yoko Ono AR15095
Ballbreaker RR10388, RR10389
Ballroom Blitz AR13933
Bamba RR12085
Band On The Run: Life On The Road With The Health And Happiness Show AR15236, AR15802
Banding Together: Underground Rockers Fight For Abortion Rights AR12927
Bandwagonesque RR12709
Bang! RR12963
Barbra Streisand: New York City CR00906
Barney's Favorites Vol. 1 RR10508
Barry Diller: The Rolling Stone Interview AR14005
Barry White AR13490
Basehead: Charting A New Course For The Hip-Hop Generation AR14464
Basement Tapes RR10500, RR11044
Bassman's Holiday: Mike Watt Casts An All-Star Solo Album AR13462
Bat Out Of Hell II RR11852
Batak Of North Sumatra RR13059
The Bat's Meow: Catwoman Michelle Pfeiffer AR14220
The Battle For Space RR11652
The Battle For Walden Woods: Don Henley Helped Save The Trees, But Some Preservationists Say He Doesn't Know When To Quit AR14427
BBC Bonanza: Vintage U.K. Radio Concerts Now On CD AR13767
B'Boom RR11612
Be Like That (song) RR12777
Beach Of The War Goddess RR12907
Beached Monster AR15237
Beastie Boys: New York CR00642
Beastie Boys, Rollins Band: Roseland Ballroom CR00641, CR00868
The Beat RR10521
The Beat Generation RR13060
Beat The Retreat RR13061
Beatle On The Block: Rare Tape Of An Early John Lennon Performance To Be Auctioned In London AR14363
The Beatles Compact Discs Singles Collection RR10525
Beats, Rhymes And Life RR12764
Beatsongs RR10607
Beausoleil CR00643
Beautiful Freak RR11060
Beautiful Light RR11149
Beautiful Loser: Video Director Steve Hanft's Scruffy Style Has Taken Him From Beck To Hootie AR13629
Beauty Is A Rare Thing RR10840
Beautycase RR12188
The Beavis And Butt-Head Experience RR10531
Beck Is Back: The Reclusive Guitarist Returns With Two Albums AR15414
Beck: Minneapolis CR00645
Beck: Resident Alien AR13491
Beck: Thanks To 'Loser,' This Hip-Hop Folk Rocker Is The Most Unlikely Success Story Of The Year AR15876
Beck: The Metro CR00644
Beckology RR10537
Become What You Are RR11369, RR11370
Becoming Juliana Hatfield AR13685
Bedtime Stories RR11773
Bee Thousand RR11317
Beer Joint And Tailoring RR11556
Before You Sign On The Dotted Line...: What The Republicans' Contract With America Means To You AR16022
Behind Bars RR12534
Behind Beavis And Butt-Head: The Stercoraceous Vision Of Mike Judge AR16103

Behind The Fly: Bono AR14465
Behind The Sheen: Butch Vig AR15726
Behind The Zines: The Chronic Urges And Ultraobsessions Of Do-It-Yourself Publishing AR15395
Being There RR12925
Being There: Wherever The Celebrated And Notorious Set Down In The Eighties, Jean Pigozzi Was There AR15096
Being There; The History Of Rock & Roll Photography AR14221
Believe RR12580
Believe (song) RR11003
The Bells Of Dublin RR10785
Belly: Tanya Donelly Finds Her Lucky 'Star' AR14674
Ben Folds Five RR11156
Ben Lee AR12920
The Bends RR12278
Benedictine Brawl AR14742
The Benefit Blitz: Rockers Put Out For Various Pet Projects AR14743
Berlin, 1962 RR10767
Bernard Edwards 1952-1996 AR14215
Berserkley's Best RR13062
The Best In Video Laser AR15639
The Best Little Sinecure In Washington: No One Does Less With More Than The Federal Election Commission AR16023
Best New Band: Elastica AR13451
The Best Of Cameo RR10723
The Best Of Con Funk Shun RR10858
The Best Of Cool Yule RR13063
The Best Of Kool And The Gang 1969-1976 RR11634
The Best Of Paul Kelly RR11593
Best Of Studio One, Vols, I, II And III RR13064
The Best Of The Bar-Kays RR10505
The Best Of The Ronettes RR12384
The Best Of Van Morrison Volume Two RR11949
Better Days RR12588
Better Red Than Dead: Learning To Live With Conan O'Brien AR15877
Better Workers Or Better Jobs? AR14061
Bettie Serveert: A Dutch Band Plays A Sweeter Kind Of Grunge AR15200
Betty RR11385
Between Midnight And Hindsight RR12910
Between 10th And 11th RR10766
Between The 1 And The 9 RR12397
Beyond Cool AR15878
Beyond The Garage RR11983
Beyond The Low Water Mark: A Treasure Diver Learns That Some Customers Can Drive A Hard Bargain, In This Excerpt From The New Novel 'Where Is Joe Merchant?' AR13155
Beyond The Reruns AR15879
The Bible BR01047
Biff! Bang! Powder RR12209
Big Audio Dynamite II; Public Image Ltd.; Live; Blind Melon CR00647, CR00652, CR00783, CR00857
Big, Bad And Blue RR12780
The Big Black Boot: What Do Loggers, Hipsters, Bikers And Hikers Have In Common? AR13216
Big Boom In Industrial Metal: Helmet Signs Million-Dollar Deal With Interscope AR12987
Big Daze Out: Goin' Off The Deep End At The Big Day Out AR13695
Big Hits, Bigger Misses AR15640
Big Horizon RR12926
The Big Lie: A Republican Majority Doesn't Mean A Reactionary Mandate AR14648
Big Names, Big Bucks AR13059
The Big Noise In The Hood AR16064
The Big Pay Back: The R&B Foundation Honors Its Stars AR14018
The Big Payback: Coolio Gets A Phat Return On His Dues With "Fantastic Voyage" AR13320
The B.I.G. Payback: Notorious B.I.G. Is Living Large—The Legal Way AR13626
Big Pictures BR01048
The Big Scare: Heart Attack Trips Up Mellencamp AR14456
Big Shot In The Dark RR12742
The Big Show: Hall Of Fame's Labor Day Lineup AR13288
The Big Sleaze AR13140
Big Sound Tiny Package AR16065
The Big Squeeze: Tuition Is Up, Salaries Are Down, And The Government Couldn't Care Less AR15347
Big Star Live RR10556
Big Star: The Strange Life And Resurrection Of An American Power-Pop Legend AR15120
Big Sugar Vs. The Everglades AR13922
Big Talk In Little Rock AR14062
The Big Three's Best Bets AR14655
Big Time: Being Hip Is Something That Dwight Yoakum Does Best AR15364
Big Tours Buoy Promoters' Spirits [and other news] AR13934
A Bigger Piece Of Sky RR11588
Bikini Kill RR10563
Bilingual RR12150
Bill And Hillary Will See You Now AR14063
Bill Clinton For President: A Rolling Stone Editorial AR15776
Bill Clinton: The Rolling Stone Interview AR14064, AR14995, AR15594, AR15777
Bill Graham Presents BR01049
Bill Graham's Last Waltz AR13935
Bill Monroe: Father Of Bluegrass Is Dead At 84 AR13415
Bill 2982: No Sale AR13197
Billie Holiday: The Legacy 1933-1958 RR11423
[Billie Joe] AR13652
Bill's Mix: Right Ends, Left Means AR14065
Billy Breathes RR12165, RR12166
Billy Corgan Talks: The Smashing Pumpkins Leader On Death, Drugs And The Future Of His Band AR13696
Billy Joel AR13492, AR15809
Billy Joel & Elton John: East Rutherford, N.J. CR00763
Billy Joel's New Legal Firestorm AR13936
Billy Pilgrim RR10566
Binge And Purge RR11749
Birds On A Wire: Counting Crows Fight The Hype And Battle The Backlash As They Revitalize The Sound And Tradition of Classic Rock AR15880
Birmingham, Alabama AR13043
The Birth Of Soul RR10768
Birth Of The Gearhead Nation: Out For A Clunk With The Pioneers Of Mountain Biking As They Come To Grips With Their Funky Past And Muddy Future AR13153
Bis AR14213
A Bit Of Guitar Heaven: Austin's Arc Angels Prove They're More Than Just Another Blues-Rock Band AR14625
Bittersweet Relief: Rockers Face The Health-Care Blues AR14019
Bizarre Fruit RR11762
Bizarre Ride II The Pharcyde RR12161
[Bjork] AR15697
Black & Blue: Me'shell NdegeOcello Fights For Your Rights On 'Peace Beyond Passion' AR15110
Black And Tan Club RR13065
Black Box RR13066
Black Country Rock RR11969
The Black Crowes AR14225, CR00648
The Black Crowes: Upper Darby, PA CR00649
Black Eyed Man RR10889
Black 47 RR10600
Black Francis's Name Game: The Pixies Frontman Nutures Another Persona With 'Frank Black' AR13798
Black Like Me AR15477
Black Love RR10397
Black Melodies On A Clear Afternoon RR11306, RR12811
Black Monk Time BR01050
Black Noise BR01051
Black Pearl RR12983
The Black Rider RR12854
Black Snake Diamond Role RR11408
Black Sunday RR10937, RR10938
Black Tie White Noise RR10640
The Blank Generation RR13067
Blasters Of The Universe RR10632, RR10845
A Blazing Grace RR11513
Blind Faith RR10597
Blind Melon RR10598
Blind Melon: Chicago CR00651
The Bliss Album? RR12189
Blood And Vengeance: One Family's Story Of The Massacre At Srebrenica And The Unending War In Bosnia AR15539
Blood On The Tracks: Warner Bros. Gets Hit In A Boardroom Shootout AR14642
Bloodlines RR10612
BloodSugarSexMagik RR12300
Bloody Kisses RR12787
A Blow For Me, A Toot For You RR12898
Blow: How A Small-Town Boy Made $100 Million With The Medellin Cocaine Cartel And Lost It All AR15105
Blow Up RR12555, RR13068
Blowout Comb RR11004
Blue Blvd RR10419
Blue Collar Blues RR12354
Blue Funk RR11383
Blue Hawaii AR14560
Blue House RR10498
Blue Interlude RR11795
Blue Is The Color Of Hope RR12066
Blue Light 'Til Dawn RR12944
The Blue Note Years RR11388
Blue On Blonde RR11297, RR11717
The Blue Sun RR11578, RR12883
Bluegrass: Then And Now AR13768
Blues RR11394
Blues All Around Me BR01052
Blues Classics RR13069
Blues For The Flying Dutchman RR10434
Blues From On High: The Arc Angels Bring A Li'l Bit Of Heaven To Austin AR14626, AR16089
Blues Originals RR13070
Blues Power: Stevie Ray Vaughan Honored At Fete AR14627
Blues Revival RR13071
Blues Roots RR13072
The Blues Traveler Rock & Roll Medicine Show AR15121
Blues With A Feeling RR13073
Blues With A Fuse: Jon Spencer Sparks An Explosive Trio AR15812
Bluesbreakers With Eric Clapton RR10798, RR11817
Bluesman Willie Dixon: 1915-1992 AR13056
Blur: The New 'Leisure' Class AR14866

Bo Diddley AR13133
Boardroom Shuffle: Baby Boomers Take Over At Major Labels AR15881
Boats To Build RR10811
Bob Dylan AR14513
Bob Dylan: Jones Beach, N.Y. CR00707
Bob Dylan: New York CR00709
Bob Dylan—Santana: Wantagh, N.Y. CR00706, CR00870
Bob Dylan: The Beacon Theater CR00708
Bob Dylan: The Recording Sessions (1960-1994) BR01053
Bob Dylan: The 30th Anniversary Concert Celebration RR13074
Bob Dylan Tribute: All-Star Show Tentatively Set For October AR15882
Bob Mould RR11968
Bob Mould: Chicago CR00816
Bob Mould: Irving Plaza CR00815
Bob Stinson: 1959-1995 AR14675
Bob Thiele 1922-1996 AR13769
Bob Wills: The Country Music Hall Of Fame RR12940
Bobbie Cryner RR10923
Bobby RR10670, RR10671
Bobby Brown, Shabba Ranks, TLC, Mary J. Blige: Reunion Arena CR00650, CR00663, CR00861, CR00917
Bobby Byrd Got Soul RR10714
Bobby Short: Live At New York City's Cafe Carlyle CR00877
The Bocephus Box: The Hand Williams Jr. Collection 1979-1992 RR12929
Boces RR11880a
Body Count RR11466
Body Count Shows Canceled, 'Cop Killer' Protest Continues As Police Refuse To Provide Security AR14466
Body Count: The Academy CR00655, CR00749
Body Mind Soul RR11241
The Bodyguard RR13075
The Body-Hat Syndrome RR11007
Bogle RR13076
Boiling Point RR13077
Bombay: Despite Crushing Poverty And Overpopulation, A Mighty Middle-Class Economy Has Turned Bombay Into A City Of Hope AR14634, AR15340
Bon Jovi CR00656
Bone Machine RR12855
Bone Of Contention: Fishbone Bassist Accused Of Attempted Kidnapping AR14020
Boning Up: Neither Drum-Beating Nor Breast Beating, Men's Studies Comes Into Its Own AR13907
Bonnie Raitt AR13493, AR14196
Bonnie Raitt: Philadelphia CR00860
Bono On Bob AR13097
The Book On Genesis: Collins, Rutherford And Banks Write Another Chapter With Their New Album, 'We Can't Dance' AR15883
Booker T. And The MG's CR00657
Books AR13098, AR13099
Boom Boom RR11429
The Boom Goes Bust AR13452
Boombastic RR12471
Booth And The Bad Angel RR10487, RR10631
The Bootleg Series: Volumes 1-3 RR11045
Borderlands RR13078, RR13079
Born Dead RR10621
Born To Be Burned RR11293
Born To Be The Boss: All The Hail New Queen Of Hardcore Rap AR15612
Born To Choose RR13080
Born To Quit RR12557
Bosnia Breakdown RR11581
Boss Hog RR10634
Boss Man RR12341
Bossa Nova Brasil RR13081, RR13082
Both Sides RR10847
Bounty Hunter AR13045
Bow Down RR12904
The Bowie Companion BR01054
Bowie: The Singles 1969 To 1993 RR10641
Bowie's Wedding Album: The Thin White Duke Returns With His First Solo Album In Six Years AR15884
Box RR11318
Box Of Visions RR12416
Box Set RR11905
A Boy And His Gun: An American Tragedy AR13273
Boy George AR13494
Boy George Plays 'The Crying Game' AR14364
Boys For Pele RR10424
Boys: Hanging With The Spur Posse AR12946
Boys' Life: Silverchair, Food Fights Are More Fun Than Selling Millions Of Records AR13697
Boys To Men AR14467
Boys To Men: The Pharcyde Break Boundaries On 'LabCabin' AR12928
Boyz In The Hood RR13083
BR5-49 RR10648
Brace Yourself! Whale Sink Their Teeth Into Your TV AR14365
The Bradley Barn Sessions RR11558
The Braids Update Queen For The Hip-Hop Crowd AR15753
Brand New Friend (song) RR12339
The Brand New Heavies: New York City CR00661
Brave New Home: Couch Potatoes Of The Future, Fear Not AR14441
Braver Newer World RR11248
Break Like The Wind RR12602
Break The Chain RR12293
Breaking Silence RR11461
Breaking Silence: Scott Weiland Of Stone Temple Pilots Opens Up And Gets Busy AR13362
Breathe RR11895
A Breed Apart: Powered by The Musical Vision Of Kim Deal And The Free Spirit Of Her Sister, Kelley, The Breeders Bring Soul And Sass To Punk Rock AR15365
The Breeders' Last Splash RR10657
The Brian Setzer Orchestra RR12463
Brian Wilson AR13625
Bricks Are Heavy RR11657
Briggs, David 1944-1995 AR13149
Bright Red RR10432
The Brill Building Sound RR13084
Bring It On Home RR13085
Bring Me The Head Of Jerry Garcia (single) RR11486
Bringing Down The Horse RR12863
Bringing Up Baby: A Behind-The-Scenes Look At The Making Of U2's New Album AR13600
Britain's Class Act: Blur Stand Up For Their Mod-Rock Roots On "Parklife" AR13376
The British Aren't Coming: Is The Newest Wave From The U.K. A Washout? AR15415
British Beat Before The Beatles RR13086
Broadway The Hard Way RR13013
Broken RR12039
Broken Arrow RR10900, RR12992
The Brooklyn Side RR10636
Brother Ray Is At It Again: Ray Charles Moves Into The Nineties With His New Release, 'My World' AR15885
Brother Sister RR10652
Brother With Two Tongues RR11872
The Brothers Grim: Ray And Dave Davies Ponder Their Ongoing Sibling Rivalry On 'Phobia' AR15886
Brown Sugar RR10952
Brownie McGhee 1915-1996 AR14216
Bruce Babbitt: Is He Tough Enough To Save The Environment? AR16024
Bruce Kaplan: 1945-1992 AR15161
Bruce Plans Late-Summer Tour [and other news] AR13937
Bruce Springsteen: Sheffield Arena CR00895
Bruce: Still The Boss In Europe AR13312
Bruce Weber AR15742
Bruce's Lucky Touch: Two New Albums Put Springsteen Back In The Rock & Roll Spotlight AR14197
Brutal Youth RR10880
Bryan Adams CR00634
Bryan Ferry AR13416
Bryan Ferry: New York CR00718
Bubble And Scrape RR12453
Buchanan Rethinks The American Empire AR14066
The Buck Owens Collection RR12093
The Buddah Box RR13087
Buddy Guy & Junior Wells Play The Blues RR11332, RR12897
Buddy Guy: His Time Is Now AR15463
Buddy Guy: The Chance CR00737
The Buddy Holly Collection RR11425
The Buddy System: The Networks' New fall Shows Ask, 'Can't We All Be Friends?' AR15887
Buffalo Stance: Boston's Buffalo Tom Steer Clear Of The Musical Wildlife AR14676
Buhloone Mind State RR10966
Building On Rock: A Summer '95 Opening Is Expected On The Long-Awaited Rock Hall Of Fame AR13653
Bulk RR11710
Bulletin Boards: News From Cyberspace AR14328
Bullets & Bombs AR13157
Bummer Summer: The First Harvest Of A Gutless Film Season Offers Slim Pickings AR15641
The Buried Life RR12491
Burlington, Vermont AR13159
Burn, Baby, Burn: The Women Of TLC Stay Cool Under Fire AR13321
Burnin' And Lootin': Tony Toni Tone Fire Up The Funk AR14226
Burning Questions RR12107
Burning Rubber: Elastica Hit The U.S. At Full Throttle AR14540
Bury My Heart At Wounded Knee BR01055
Bush: Nirvana Wanna Bes AR13377
Bush Whacked! An Unknown English Band Takes America By Surprise AR14346
The Bush Years: Staying The Course AR13191
The Bush Years: Supreme Cruelty AR13192
The Bush Years: The Environmental President AR13193
Bush's Hits AR15238
Bush's Tax-Cut Follies: Rich Entertainment AR14067
Business Never Personal RR11086
Bustin' Loose AR14814, AR15604
But Can He Win? AR14649
Butter RR10708
The Butthole Surfers AR16104
Butthole Surfers—Stone Temple Pilots—Flaming Lips: New York Coty CR00670,

CR00720, CR00902
Buy One, Get One Free: Rocket From The Crypt And Drive Like Jehu Put San Diego On The Rock Map AR14289
The Buzz At Sundance AR13161
Buzz Been: Did Radio Kill MTV's Video Star? AR13060

C

Caged-Uncaged RR13088
Cajun Boogie RR11341
Cajun Roots RR12573
Cake AR15813
Cake Like AR12988
The Call Of The Wild: To The People On The Edge Of The Environmental Movement, The Program To Bring Back The Wolf Has A Big Problem—It Isn't Natural AR14527
Call The Doctor RR12532
Cameron Diaz AR13495
Camille Paglia: Lit Crit's Snit Fits AR14421
The Campaign AR15039
The Campaign: Clinton Takes A Side Trip AR15040
The Campaign: G.H.W. Bush Sees His 1st Bar Code AR15047
The Campaign: George B. In Free Fall AR15041
The Campaign: George B. Packs For Japan AR15042
The Campaign: George B's Economic Plan AR15043
The Campaign: George Bush Makes A Decision AR15044
The Campaign: George Bush, The Candidate Of Change AR15045
The Campaign: George's Solution For Domestic Problems AR15046
The Campaign: G.H.W. Bush Thinks About The Common Man AR15048
The Campaign: GOP Hats In The Ring AR15049
The Campaign: Laid Fresh Every Day! AR15050
The Campaign: Movin' On AR15051
The Campaign: Old Math AR15052
The Campaign: President Bush Tours U.S. Cities AR15053
The Campaign-Reform Game AR16025
The Campaign: Supreme Court Coatroom, Summer 1992 AR15054
The Campaign: Trust-O-Meter AR15055
Can Clinton Put Life In The Party? AR14068
Can Doug Wilder's G.O.P. Tricks Save The Democrats? AR14639
Can Janet Reno Bust The War On Drugs?: The New Attorney General Tries To Change The Debate On Drugs And Crime AR16026
Can Seal Handle Fame?: Or Will Success Drive The British Singer 'Crazy'? AR15567
Can The Media Do The Right Thing? AR14329
Can The Presidents Of The United States Of America Live Up To The Majesty & Stupidity Of Their Name? AR13355
Can You Hear A Motion? RR11061
Candlebox AR13654
Candyland RR11847
Cannibalism 1 RR10726
Can't Hardly Wait (song) RR12329
Can't Keep It To Myself RR12934
Canter's Rock On Rye: The Kibitz Room Serves Up An Electric Menu Of Matzo And Music AR15888
The Capital Gang Bang: The Failure Of The Washington Press Corps AR14330
A Capital Idea: Rockers Run Labels For Fun 'N' Profit AR15219
The Capitol Years RR10836
Captain My Captain RR12707
Car Button Cloth RR11681
Car Stereos For Spring '96: Roadworthy Companions With Distinct Personalities AR13101
The Cardigans Wear Their Loopy '60s Influences On Their Sleeves AR15029
Career Moves RR12849
Carnival Boy RR12616
Carpenters Collection AR13496
Carry The Day RR12735
The Cartels Would Like A Second Chance AR15329
The Casablanca Records Story RR13089
Casey Scott: 'City' Slacker AR15162
Casualties Of War AR15341
Cat Power AR15353
Cathy Dennis: One From The Heart AR13799
Cats And Dogs RR12400
Caught in The Net: The Cautionary Tale Of A Cornell Student Who Posted A Suicide Note In Cyberspace AR14744
CB4 RR13090
CD News AR13167, AR13168, AR14258, AR14259, AR14260, AR14261, AR14262, AR14263, AR14264, AR14265, AR14266, AR14267, AR14268, AR14269, AR14270, AR14271, AR14272, AR14273
CD-Package Standard Set AR13938
CDs Put A New Spin On Your PC: Multimedia Software Brings Video And Sound Together With Your Computer AR13034
Cease Fire AR15138, AR15540
Celebrity Guidance Counselors AR13169
Certified Punk: Claw Hammer Nail It With 'Thank' AR13403
Chains (song) RR10455
Chainsaw Kittens: Grungy Glam, Oklahoma Style AR15441
The Chairman Of The Board: My Life In The Studio With Brother Ray, Lady Soul, Bob Dylan And The Wicked Pickett AR15193, AR15804
A Chance Operation RR13091
Changes RR12928
Channel Surfing AR13171, AR13172, AR13173, AR13174, AR13175, AR13176, AR13177, AR13178, AR15889, AR15890, AR15891, AR15892, AR15893, AR15894, AR15895, AR15896, AR15897, AR15898, AR15899, AR15900
Channel Surfing: Cable TV Spawns Four New Outlets With Their Eyes On MTV AR14139
Chant RR10545
Chaos A.D. RR12459
Chaos And Disorder RR12228
The Chapel Session RR11116
Charcoal Lane RR12356, RR12357
[Charles Bukowski] AR13179
Charlie Rich: 1932-1995 AR13289
Charlie Watts AR13453, CR00934
Chas Chandler: 1938-1996 AR14153
The Chase RR10665
Cheap Seats At The Video Revolution: HDTV's On Its Way, But In The Meantime You Still Need Something To Watch AR13640
Cheap Trick: Labels Buy Hits By Giving Away Bargain-Price Cassette Singles AR13061
Cheating Time: How Some High-School Students From California Improved Their SAT Scores AR14219
Check It Out AR13180, AR13181, AR13182, AR13183
Check Your Head RR10518
Cheeky Monkeys AR15239
Chemical Brothers Explode Underground With Their New EP, 'Loops Of Fury' AR12929
The Chemical Brothers Mix It Up With Noel Gallagher AR15754
Cher AR13497
Chess Blues RR13092
Chet Atkins: The RCA Years RR10466
Chicago AR14419
Chicago, New York, Paris RR11299
Chicago Revisited: Live At Joe Segal's Jazz Showcase RR11502
Chic-ism RR10780
Chief Boot Knocka RR12518
Children Of The Damned Never Mind The Sex Pistols: Here's Their Offspring AR13655
Chill Factor: DJs Cool Down L.A.'s Post-Rave Club Scene AR14351
China Gate RR10925
China Syndrome: CD Piracy Results In A Trade War AR14302
Chip Trick: Big Brother Is Trying To Get On Line AR14006
The Chiswick Story RR13093
Chocolate And Cheese RR12886
Chocolate Synthesizer RR10633
Choose Your Poison: Newt & Co. Roll Back A Generation Of Environmental Protections AR12948
Chorus RR11153
Chow Manhattan: Parker Posey And Benicio Del Toro Treat Themselves To A Bottle Of Wine, A Little Red Sauce And Some Italian Dressing AR13498, AR14815
Chris Cornell Of Soundgarden: The End Of The Innocence AR13656
Chris Harford: A Rocker With A Sense Of Direction AR12989
Chris Isaak: Beacon Theater CR00751
Chris Isaak's Twin Peaks: The Pop Heartthrob Takes Two Steps Forward With A New Album And Movie AR15901
Chris Knox: New York CR00773
Chris Robinson Of The Black Crowes AR13499
Chrissie Hynde Of The Pretenders AR15902
Christmas RR10831
A Christmas Gift For You RR13094
Christmas In The City RR13095
Christmas Party With Eddie G. RR11281
Christmas Time RR12619
Christopher Idylls RR12035
The Chronic RR11028, RR11029, RR11030
Chronicle AR13185
Chronicles RR12604
[Chronology of Female Rock Musicians] AR13186
Chuck D Is Back With More Agendas Than Ever AR13463
Chuckie's In Love: Triathlete Chuckie V Swims, Cycles And Runs With The Best—And He Doesn't Do it For The Money AR13217
The Church Within RR12065
Cindy: A Portfolio AR15191
The Cindy Chronicles: The Body, The Marriage, The Mole AR16112
Circulado RR12830, RR12831
Circular Temple RR12490
Circus RR11642, RR11643
Citi Movement RR11796
Cities Of The Heart RR10687
Citizen RR12633
Citizen GE: How Multinationals Like General Electric Have Seized Power In The United

States AR14069
City Of Hysteria RR12249
Civilization Phaze III RR13014
Civilizing Cyberspace: The Rolling Stone Interview With Mitch Kapor AR14007
Clarification AR13411
Clash On Broadway RR10813
Clasico Rock AR14653
Clasicos De La Provincia RR12842
Class Conflict: Zappa Vid Gets Teacher Suspended AR14366
The Class Of '92 AR13770
Class Of '93: The Rock And Roll Hall Of Fame AR13771
Claws Of The Cat RR12740
Clean Sweep: Garbage's Masterminds Craft Murky Pop Into An Album That's Impossible To Refuse AR13198
Clear RR10623
Cleo's Mass. Appeal AR15240
"Clerks"—Dangerous Talk AR15642
Clint Eastwood AR15903
Clint Eastwood: The Rolling Stone Interview AR13143
Clinton And Brown Sound Off: The Candidates Talk About Music, From Miles Davis To The Mothers Of Invention AR15361
Clinton And Campaign Reform: The Sounds Of Silence AR16027
Clinton At Midterm? What Went Wrong AR14070
Clinton For President AR15778
Clinton Goes Right Toward Consensus AR14071
Clinton: I Want The MTV Vote AR14745
Clinton Rocked The Vote, Now It's Rocking Him: Young Democrats Are Turning Their Back On The President And Politics AR12949
Clinton's Choice: Jobs Or Mexico AR14072
Clinton's Credit: The 72-Hour Student Loan AR16028
Clinton's Health Plan: More Funk 4U AR15613
Close Encounters: Youssou N'Dour And Neneh Cherry Make Record Time In "7 Seconds" AR14541
Close To You AR13189
Closer To God RR12712
Clouds Over Eden RR10509
Clouds Taste Metallic RR11144
Clown 'N' Dirty: Mariah Carey's Twisted 'Fantasy' AR13500
The Cobra Records Story: Chicago Rock And Blues 1956-1958 RR13096
Cocteau Twins—Moose: Atlanta CR00681, CR00810
Coincidence And Likely Stories RR12423
Col. Bruce Hampton And The Aquarium Rescue Unit RR1151a
Cold Rain And Snow (single) RR11132
Colin James And The Little Big Band RR11505
Colin-Izing America: The Best Thing Colin Powell Could Do For The Nation Is Run For President AR14073
The Collected Recordings, '60s to '90s RR12781
The Collection RR12298
A Collection Of Her Best Recordings RR11113
Collective Soul RR10843
College 94 Notebook AR15396
College Notebook AR13854, AR15227
Color And Light RR13097
Color Me Impressed (song) RR12330
Colossal Head RR11722
Colour Of Your Dreams RR11611b
Columbia RR10557
The Columbia Years 1943-1952 RR12512
Columbus Lied RR12469
Come RR12229
Come As You Are AR14561
Come As You Are: The Story Of Nirvana BR01056
Come Find Yourself RR11194
Come Gather Round, People AR15904
Come On Come On RR10737
Come On Feel The Lemonheads RR11682
Come Out And Play RR13098
Come Together RR13099
Come Together: Motown Sings The Beatles RR13100
Comedy AR13304
The Coming RR10707
Coming To A Screen Near You AR16066
Coming Up For Air RR11801
The Commitments RR13101
Common Threads RR13102
Communication RR12953
Compact Disc EP Collection RR10526
The Company I Keep RR11117
Company Of Strangers RR10480
The Complete Billie Holiday On Verve 1945-1959 RR11424
The Complete Blind Willie Johnson RR11548
Complete Blue Note And Roost Recordings RR12210
The Complete Blue Note Recordings RR11927
The Complete Blue Note Recordings Of Art Blakely's 1960 Jazz Messengers RR10587
The Complete Bud Powell RR12211
The Complete Bukka White RR12909
The Complete Candid Otis Spann-Lightnin' Hopkins Sessions RR11436, RR12591
The Complete Clapton: In His Own Words AR13305
The Complete Clapton: Living On Blues Power AR15020
The Complete Clapton: Plugged In AR13772
The Complete Columbia Studio Recordings RR10961, RR11105
Complete Communion RR10773
The Complete Imperial Recordings RR10844
The Complete Imperial Recordings, 1950-1954 RR12861
The Complete Plantation Recordings RR12876
The Complete Prestige-Bluesville Recordings RR11437
The Complete Prestige Recordings RR12383
The Complete Riverside Recordings RR11938
The Complete Serge Chaloff Sessions RR10762
The Complete Solid State Recordings Of The Thad Jones - Mel Lewis Big Band RR11569, RR11693
The Complete Stax-Volt Singles Vol 2: 1968-1971 RR13103
The Complete Stax-Volt Soul Singles, Vol. III 1972-1975 RR13104
The Complete Studio Recordings RR11676
Computer Style RR11618
The Concert For The Rock & Roll Hall Of Fame RR13105
Concrete Blonde: Chicago CR00685
Confessions Of Sir Psycho Sexy: The Rolling Stone Interview With Anthony Kiedis Of The Red Hot Chili Peppers AR14746
Confusion Is Next BR01057
Congrats AR13306, AR13307
Congratulations AR13308, AR13309, AR13310, AR13311
Congratulations I'm Sorry RR11251
Congress: Kill NAFTA AR14074
Conmemorativo RR13106
Constipated Monkey RR11651
Continental Drifters RR10863
Contrary Motion RR11258
The Contributors AR13317, AR13318
Conventional Wisdom: Why The Bottle Rockets And Other Bands Pay To Play At Industry Schmoozefests AR13062
Convergence RR10539, RR10838
Conversation On A Barstool (song) RR12391
Conversation Peace RR12958
Conversin' With The Elders RR10748
Conway Twitty: 1933-1993 AR14628
The Conway Twitty Collection RR12785
Cookin' At The Continental RR10814
Cool Hand Loc RR12746
Cool Jerk: How Sean Penn Reconciles Being The Best Actor Of His Generation With Being A Menace To Society AR14677
'Cop Killer' Aftershocks: Labels Asking Rap Artists To Remove Controversial Tracks From Albums AR14747
'Cop Killer' Is Iced: Ice-T Pulls Song From His Album In Response To Death Threats AR15163
Cop Killer: The Sequel AR15814
'Cop Killer': Yielding To Censors Never Works In The Long Run AR13417
Cop Killers? The Media Target The Police AR14331
Copacetic RR12828
Copper Blue RR12666
Copperopolis RR11285
The Coral Sea BR01058
Core RR12645
[Correction] AR13325, AR13326, AR13327, AR13328, AR13329, AR13330, AR13331, AR13332, AR13333, AR13334, AR13335, CR00846
[Corrections] AR13336, AR13337, AR13338
Cosmic Comeback: Julian Cope's Music Of The Spheres AR13199
Cosmic Kurushi Monsters RR13107
Cosmic Tones For Mental Therapy RR12259
The Cost Of Living Clean AR12981
Counting Crows AR13939
Counting Crows: Detroit CR00687
Country AR14629
Country Artist Of The Year AR14530
Country Kickers RR13108
Country Music Has Become The Refuge Of Older Rock Fans AR13418
Country Music Made Me Do It RR11393
Country Punk'ins: Nelson Covers Bridge Rebel Cultures AR12925
Country Roundup AR15568
The Country That Stayed Out In The Cold AR14075
Country: The Twisted Roots Of Rock & Roll BR01059
Country's New Gold Rush: With Garth Brooks Leading The Way, Nashville Is Booming AR15569
Court And Spark RR11914
Courtney Love AR14748
Cover Girl RR10853
Coverdale-Page RR10888, RR12096
The Covers 1993 AR13344
Cowabunga! RR13109
Cowboy Junkies; John Prine CR00688, CR00854
Cowboy Nation RR12862
Cowboys To Girls RR11481
Cowgirl's Prayer RR11362
The Crack-Up AR15475
Cracked Rear View RR11432, RR11433

Crackers With Attitude: When The Alternative Press Gets Predictable, Cracker Get Weird AR15122
The Cradle Will Rock: Silverchair Make Music Beyond Their Years AR14433
The Cranberries AR14542, CR00689
The Cranberries: London CR00690
The Crap Is Out There: The Search For Signs Of Intelligent Life On Fall TV AR15905
Crappin' You Negative RR11303
Crash RR11809
Crazy Diamond RR10510
Crazy Legs RR10538, RR10561
[Credit] AR13348
Credit Where Credit's Due AR14076
Creep City RR12440
Crime Pays: Beleaguered Interscope Passes From Hot Potato To Hot Property AR13063
The Criminal Under My Own Hat RR10698
Critics Comments AR12930, AR13039, AR13271, AR13350, AR13385, AR13404, AR13832, AR13835, AR13843, AR14227, AR14249, AR14352, AR14434, AR14444, AR14614, AR15201, AR15726a
Critics' Picks: 1992 Music Awards AR13352
Critics' Picks: 1993 Music Awards AR13353
Critics Poll: 1996 AR13354
Crooked Rain, Crooked Rain RR12126
Crosby, Stills & Nash RR10916
The Cross Of Changes RR11079
Crossover Acts: Bridging The Gap Between Simplicity And Sophistication, These Cameras Are Shooting For A Wider Audience AR13102
Crossroads 2 RR10799
The Crow RR13110
Crowded House, Sheryl Crow: Atlanta CR00693
Crowes Take Flight AR15906
Crowning Moment: Tanya Donelly & Belly Hit The Big Time With King AR13501
Cruel Sea: New York CR00694
A Cry In The Dark: Love Reads Cobain's Note To Vigil AR14522
Cry Tomorrow RR12314
Cryin', Lovin', Leavin' RR10681
'The Crying Game' Star Jaye Davidson Breaks The Silence: Oscar's Big Surprise AR13855
The Crying Tree RR10605
Cryptology RR12866
Cub AR13134
Cuba RR12808, RR12809
Cuba: Fully Charged RR13111, RR13112
Cuban Classics Vol. 3: Diablo al Infierno RR13113
Cuban Counterpoint: A History Of The Son Montuno RR13114
Cuban Gold RR13115
Cubanomics: In Fidel Castro's Crumbling Socialist Paradise, The Rum Is Older Than The Whores, The Currency Is Worthless, And Everybody's Working For The Yankee Dollar AR14996
Cui Jian: New York CR00761
The Cult RR10926
Cult Classic RR10609
The Cult Of Ray: 'Seinfeld' Meets The Suburbs On CBS' 'Everybody Loves Raymond' AR15907
Cultural Healing: Choir Marries Gospel And Hip-Hop AR14318
Culture Wars: The GOP's Version Of American History Is 'Don't Worry, Be Happy' AR12950
Cumbersome Combo: Seven Mary Three Churn It Out AR15468
Cup Of Loneliness RR11559
The Cure CR00691, CR00695
Cure For Pain RR11947
The Curse Of The Mekons RR11861
The Curtain Hits The Cast RR11745
Cut To The Chase AR14313, AR14816
Cut You RR11444
Cuts Like A Knife AR15908
Cutting Edge Colleges: Four Schools That Are Preparing Their Students For The 21st Century AR15486
CX-9 (song) RR10435
Cyber Funk U: Berklee College Of Music Has Seen The Future And Wants You To Write The Score AR15190
Cyberpunk RR11470
Cyberstuff AR14656
Cyborgs Revisted RR12510

D

D Generatings AR15030
D Generation RR10944
Da Bomb RR11644
Da Lama Ao Caos RR10784
Dad, I'm A Degenerate: New York's D Generation Spark A New Glam-Rock Scene Behind The Green Door AR14347
Dada: Strange Characters Take Center Stage In 'Puzzle' AR12990
Daily Operation RR11211
Daisychain Reaction RR12208
Dambuilders AR15214
Damn Right, I've Got The Blues RR11333, RR11334
Dan Baird's Dixie-Fried Love: The Former Georgia Satellite Ruffles Some Feathers With His Solo Effort AR15123
Danamania! AR16113
Dance Club Country RR13116
Dance, Dance, Dance RR10781
Dance Hall At Louse Point RR11367, RR12105
Dance Naked RR11864, RR11865
Dance Of Death AR15233
Dance To The Music RR12538
Dancehall Reggaespanol RR13117
Dancin' With The Devil: White Zombie Mint Gold From Goth AR13394
Dancing In The Seats: Roll Over Beethoven, The Professors Of Pop Have Arrived AR16123
Danger In The Past RR11169
Dangerhouse, Volume One RR12405
Dangerous RR11496
Dangerous, Dedicated And Wild At heart, Nicolas Cage Is A Hollywood Samurai AR15368
Dangerous Minds RR13118
Daniel Lanois Finds His Own Voice: Known For The LPs He's Made For U2 And Bob Dylan, The Producer Turns One Out For Himself AR15099
Danko-Fjeld-Andersen RR10430, RR10953, RR11142
Danny Gatton: 1945-1994 AR13698
Danny Gatton Tribute AR15557
Danzig RR10954
Danzig: Roseland CR00696
Danzig III: How The Gods Kill RR10955
Dare Iz A Darkside RR12312
The Dark Side Of 'Amused': Roger Waters Tackles War And Andrew Lloyd Webber On His New Album AR13699
Dark Side Of The Moon RR12173
Dark Star BR01060, RR12069
The Dark Stuff BR01061
Darkness On The Edge of Bedrock: Kyle MacLachlan Brings His All-American Weirdness To "The Flintstones" AR13218, AR14532, AR14817
Datapanik In The Year Zero RR12145
A Date With The Smithereens RR12556
The Dating Dame AR13502
Dave Matthews Band: Raleigh, N.C. CR00794
Dave Vs. Dave: Forget Leno & Koppel—Letterman May Be His Own Worst Enemy AR15369
David Bowie AR14514
David Bowie: Roseland Ballroom CR00659
David Bowie Rumbles In The Jungle On 'Earthling' AR13464
David Byrne AR13503, RR10715
David Cronenberg: The Rolling Stone Interview AR13144
David Geffen: The Rolling Stone Interview AR13998
David Letterman: The Rolling Stone Interview AR16114
Dawn Of The Dead: The Duo Dead Can Dance Get Back To Nature With Their Album "Into The Labyrinth" AR12971
Day By Day RR11877
Day Dreaming At Midnight RR12517
A Day In The Life AR13020
A Day In The Life (song) RR11405
Day Of The Dre: Dr. Dre And His Protege, Snoop Doggy Dogg, Take Hardcore Rap From South Central L.A. To Your House AR13924
Days Like This RR11950
Dazzling Display RR12969
Dead Aim: Filter Hit The Bull's Eye With The Controversial Track 'Hey Man, Nice Shot' AR13504
Dead Cities RR11202
Dead End Kidz Doin' Lifetime Bidz RR12990
Dead End: The Grateful Dead Call It Quits AR13794
Dead Flowers?: Gilbey Clarke Ponders The Troubled State Of Guns N' Roses AR12931
Dead Flowers?: Stone Roses Rise For A 'Second Coming' AR15909
Dead Man Talking: How Newt Gingrich Went From Being The Life Of The Party To The GOP's Pariah In Two Revolutionary Years AR14077
Dead Men Don't Smoke Marijuana RR12376
Dead Men Walking RR13119
Dead Rekoning RR11582
Dead Reckoning: Garcia's Passing Brings To An End A Heroic Journey Of Self-Discovery AR13022
Dead Serious RR10960
Deadsexy RR12432
Dear Diary: The Secret World Of Kate Bush AR15416
Death Becomes Him: Nick Cave Acquires A Taste For Murder AR13700
Death Certificate RR11463
Death In The Candy Store: The Prostitution Capital Of The World, Thailand Is Committing Sexual Suicide By HIV Infection AR15180
A Death In The Family AR13908
Death Of A Cheerleader AR15541
Death Of A Salesman AR16046
Death Travels West (EP) RR11073
Debravation RR11366
Debut RR11312
Deception & Reality: If You're Wondering Why Bill Clinton And Bob Dole Haven't Addressed The Economic Woes Of The '90s, Don't Ask The Media AR14078
Decking The Hall: As The Hall Of Fame Goes

Up, The Collection Comes To Life AR13290
Deconstruction RR10972
Dee Murray: 1946-1992 AR13448
Deee-Lusions Of Grandeur: Deee-Lite Searches For A New Groove On 'Infinity Within' AR13856
Deep Blues RR13120
Deep Cover AR13610, AR14818
Deep Forest's Lush 'Lullaby' AR15755
Deep In The Heart Of Siberia AR14997
Deep River RR11140, RR11171
Deep Six RR13121
Deeper Water RR11594
Deep-River Blues: John Mellencamp And Blind Melon Rock For Flood Victims AR14457
Def Jam 10th Year Anniversary RR13122
Def Leppard CR00698
Def Leppard: Ready To Roar? AR13701
Definitely Maybe RR12061
The Definitive Blind Willie McTell RR11849
Delicious RR10719
Delta Dreamland RR10413
Demi Moore =Sex AR15698
Democratie RR11668, RR11912
Dennis Rodman's Floating World AR14147
Denny Cordell: 1943-1995 AR14021
Denzel On Malcolm AR16086
Depeche Mode: The Rock & Roll Rebirth Of Everybody's Favorite Euroweenies AR13378
Descendents: The Warehouse CR00699
Desert Bloom: With Spacey Rock And Country Ballads, Cracker Reinvent Themselves In The California Sun AR12960
Desert-Island Videos: What's Your No. 1? AR14543
Design Of A Decade RR11493
Desire For Agony RR13032
Des'ree Moves On AR15476
Destination: Love RR11783
Destination Universe RR11807
Destiny's Gate RR11404
Destroy All Monsters 1974-1976 RR10989
The Devil And Anne Rice AR13909
The Devil And John Holmes AR15332
Devil Hopping RR11480
The Devil Inside: For Danzig — The Man And The Band — That Old Black Magic Isn't Just A Sales Gimmick AR15910
The Devil Lied To Me RR11935
Devil Or Angel? Either Way, South Africa's Winnie Mandela Has Grass-Roots Support AR15140
Devo Live: The Mongoloid Years RR10991
Devolution Rock: Brainiac Are Taking Retro To The Future AR15469
Diamonds And Pearls RR12230, RR12231
Diamonds By The Yard RR11978
The Diary RR12433
Diary Of A Drug Fiend BR01062
Diary Of A Mod Housewife RR12352
Dick RR11253
Die Laughing RR11459
Different Class RR12250
A Different Mirror BR01063
A Different Story RR10969
Dig RR11460
Digable Planets: New York CR00700
Digable Planets: The Trio Pays Homage To Early Jazz Greats AR14319
Digital Hollywood: How Computers Are Remaking Movie Making AR14245
Digital-Tape War Heats Up AR13940
Digital Underground: Bootlegging Makes Inroads On The Info Superhighway AR13372
Diggin' In The Crates RR13123
Dilate RR11001
Dillon Fence: Pop With A Melody AR15124
Dim Stars RR11008
Din Of Ecstasy RR12915
Dinosaur Jr.: Northhampton, Mass. CR00701
Dinosaur Summer: A T. Rex And A Terminator Aim To Stomp All Rivals, From Clint To The Coneheads AR15643
Dionne Farris AR13580, AR15241
Dire Straits CR00703
Dirt RR10409
Dirty RR12568
Dirty Three RR11014
Dirty Water RR12621
Dis Is Da Drum RR11357
Disc Contentment: Digital Components Challenge CD-Hating Audiophiles' Claims Of Vinyl Supremacy AR13641
Disc-O-Mania!!! AR16067
The Disciples Of Pot: Cypress Hill Says Marijuana's Getting A Bad Rap AR15570
The Dish AR14657
Dishwalla And Styx Fuse Their Illusions AR14348
Disraeli Gears RR10905, RR10906
Dissolve RR11489
Ditch Diggin' RR12587
Diva RR11684
The Divine Comedy RR11904
Divine Inspiration: Sixteen Horsepower Conjure Up That Old-Time Religion AR13844
Divine Intervention RR12530
The Division Bell RR12174
DiY RR13124
Dizzy Gillespie: 1917-1993 AR13773
Dizzy's Diamonds: Best Of The Verve Years RR11245
Djangology RR12320
DJ's Front Porch RR11511
Do It RR11308
Do Right Man RR12142
Do You Wanna Ride RR11446
Dr. Dre Stares Down DWI Rap AR15614
Dr. Hunter S. Thompson: On The Occasion Of The 25th Anniversary Of The Publication Of Fear And Loathing In Las Vegas, An Unfettered Discussion On The Values Of The '60s, The Addictive Properties Of Professional Journalism And The Definition Of Gonzo AR14998
Does Primus Really Suck?: The San Francisco Trio, Whose Music Mixes Thrash, Funk And Progressive Rock, Has Built A Devoted Following Of Fans On The Alternative Scene AR12991
The Dog Is Us AR13188
Dog Man Star RR11715
Dogg Food RR11020
The Dogg Walks AR15866
Doggystyle RR12563
Dollars And Dancing Bears AR14277
Dolly Parton AR13651
Domino AR15090
Don Cherry: 1936-1995 AR14217
Don Henley & Glenn Frey AR13419
The Don Killuminati RR11782
Donald Cammell 1934-1996 AR13064
Donald Fagen: Doing It Again AR15911
Dondestan RR12965
The Donna Summer Anthology RR12670
Don't Call Me Buckwheat RR11520, RR11521
Don't Call Me Slacker: Student Volunteers Speak For Themselves About Changing The World Little By Little AR13476
Don't Ever Change: Buzzcocks Make Pure Punk-Pop For Now People AR13200
Don't Get Weird On Me, Babe RR10835
Don't Leave Home Without It AR16068
Don't Look Back: Two New Films Expand On The Story Of Grunge AR13356
Don't Sweat The Technique RR11089
Don't Tread On Me: Metallica's James Hetfield AR13702
Don't Try This At Home RR10649
Don't Try This At Home: At The End Of Its Second Season, 'The Real World' Gets A Reality Check AR13164
The Doo Wop Box RR13125
Doo-Bop RR10962
Dookie RR11294
Doomed To Succeed: The Princes Of Twitch Take Cybergore To A New Level AR14044
The Dope On Health Care AR13477
Doppelganger RR10936
A Dose Of Reality: Kurt Cobain Recovers From A Drug-And-Alcohol Induced Coma AR15500
Double Dose Of Springsteen AR13941
Double Fantasy AR13274, AR14154
Double Trouble: Luke And Murphy Jensen Are The new Rude Dudes Of Tennis AR14615
Doubt RR11526
Doughboy Hollow RR10999
A Dove RR12367
Down RR11528
Down But Not Out: Chicago's Eleventh Dream Day Picks Up The Pieces With 'El Moodio' AR16090
Down But Not Out: Labor Struggles To Find Its Voice AR14079
Down By The Old Mainstream RR11272
Down Every Road RR11346
Down On The Upside RR12583, RR12584
Down Out Law RR11628
Down With The King RR12408, RR12409
Down-Home Souls: Jayhawks Fly High On Their "Green Grass" AR12932
Downtown Science: A Broad Spectrum Of Sounds AR14468
The Downward Road RR12251
The Downward Spiral RR12040, RR12041
The Downward Spiral: The Last Days Of Nirvana's Leader AR13657, AR15501
Drainland RR11254
Dread In A Babylon RR12789
The Dread Zone: Bad Brains Are One Of Rock's Most Volatile Bands—In Music And Temper AR12961
Dreaded Brown Recluse RR11223
Dreadlocks Dread RR10562
Dream Girl AR16047
Dream Harder RR12873
Dream Your Life Away RR12590
Dreaming Of You RR12456
Dreamland RR10473
Dreams And Saturday Nights RR12961
Dreams Fly Away RR12729
Drenched RR11909
Drift RR10990
Driftin' Blues RR10672
Drinkin' And Draggin' AR13917
Drop In, Turn On, Tune Out: Replacing Factory-Installed Car Speakers Will Change Your Life AR14795
Drop The Line RR11687
The Dropout 'Zine AR15397
The Dropouts RR11037
Droppin' Soulful H2O On The Fiber RR11321
The Drowners (single) RR12662
Drug News AR13485

The Drug War: Prohibition Fails Again AR13605
Drugs Claim Sublime's Singer; Depeche Mode's Gahan OD's AR14155
Drugstore Cowgirl: It's Sex, Peyote And Poetry As Uma Thurman Thumbs A Ride Aboard A Counterculture Classic AR13339
Drums Are Dangerous RR11038
Drunk With Passion RR11271
Dry RR12180
Dubious Summer Trends AR15644
Duck And Cover: The Three Most Important Issues Of The Campaign And Why The Candidates Won't Talk About Them AR14080
Duende: The Passion And Dazzling Virtuosity Of Flamenco RR13126
Duets RR11543, RR12513
Duff's Single-Gun Theory: Duff McKagan Strikes Out On His Own AR14678
Dumb About Disc Players: A Guide To Choosing The Best Laser Players Without Straining Brain Or Budget AR15645
Dummy RR12206
Duncan Sheik RR12483
Duran Duran RR11041, RR11042
Duran Duran: New York City CR00705
Dusk RR12721
Dusk At Cubist Castle RR12074
Dust RR12446, RR12447, RR12448
The Dust Brothers Take The Past Into The Future AR13630
The Dust Of Life AR15333
Dust To Dust RR10949, RR12034
Dutch Treat: The Stones Go Back To Clubland For A New Live LP AR13703
Dwayne Goettel: 1964-1995 AR15815
Dwight Live RR12985
Dynamite Monster Boogie Concert RR12283
Dysfunction Junction: The New Oprahs And Little Rickies Prove Talk Is Cheap AR15912
Dysfunctional RR11021

E

E: A Tender Pop Sensibility AR13800
E. 1999 Eternal RR10626
E!'s So Fine: A Network Boldly Says There's No Business But Show Business AR15913
The Eagles: Irvine, Calif. CR00710
Early Delivery: Brandy Breaks Out at 16 with 'Baby' AR13322
Early Starters AR15646
Early Work BR01064
The Early Years RR12385
The Early Years: The Complete Liberty Recordings Plus More RR12009
Earth And Sun And Moon RR11896, RR11897
Earth Summit: Going For The Green In Rio AR14999
The East Side Sound RR13127
East Side Story RR11605
East-West Live RR10709
The Easter Tapes RR11274
Easy Target: Why Tupac Should Be Heard Before He's Buried AR13910
Eating For A's: Nutrition Experts Chew The No-Fat AR15242
Eats Away The Night RR11355
Eazy-E: Down By Law AR15583
Eazy-E: 1963-1995 AR15816, AR15914
Echobelly: London CR00711
Echoes 1975-1985 RR12162
Eco-Tech: Green Components For These PC Times AR13103
Eddie Hazel: 1950-1992 AR14469
Eddie Hinton: 1944-1995 AR13704
Eddie Kendricks: 1939-1992 AR14470
Eddie Spaghetti of Supersuckers AR13505
Eden's Children: 10,000 Maniacs Grapple With The Pleasures & Perils Of Success in The Real World AR13686
Edie's New "Morning": Solo Brickell Takes It Simple And Soulful AR13420
[Editorial] AR13275, AR13578, AR15779, AR15780, AR15781, AR15782, AR15783, AR15784, AR15785, AR15915
Editor's Notebook AR15786, AR15787, AR15788, AR15789
Eels AR15817
Efil4zaggin RR12058
Egyptian Candy RR11580
Egyptian Rai RR12291
8: Leave Me Alone AR14367
Eighteen Inches Of Rain RR12788
18: Kiss AR14368
88: She Blinded Me With Science AR14679
85: Little Red Corvette AR14369
84: Alive AR14749
89: Thunderstruck AR13031
81: Free Your Mind AR13506
87: The Thunder Rolls AR13801
The Eighty Seven Years Of Doc Cheatham RR10772
86: Sweet Dreams AR13802
80: Straight Up AR13507
83: It Was A Good Day AR15615
82: Rapture AR13508
Einstein On The Beach RR11259
El Mariachi And The Sundance Kid AR15647
El Moodio RR11067
El Nervio Del Volcan RR10718
Elastica RR11065
Election '92 AR13598
Election Post-Mortem: The Price Of Failure AR14081
Election Watch AR14544, AR14545, AR14546, AR14547
The Electric Dorm—Tune In, Turn On, Veg Out With Cool Compact Components AR14658
Electric Pen (single) RR11911
The Electric Spanking Of War Babies RR11195
Electriclarryland RR10711
An Elegy For Jerry AR14284
Element Of Light RR11409
Elemental RR12708
Eleven: Eleven RR10855
11: Walk This Way AR15616
Ella Fitzgerald: 1917-1996 AR13911
Elton John Leads Fight Against AIDS AR13803
Elvis Costello And The Attractions: Tinley Park, Ill. CR00686
Elvis Costello's Classical Gas: The Pop Poet Teams Up With A String Quartet On 'The Juliet Letters' AR13291
Elvis From Nashville To Memphis RR12216
Elvis's Stamp Of Approval: Postal Service To Pay Tribute To Presley And Other Rock Stars In New Series AR13942
[E-Mail] AR13576
The Emergency Plan To Bail Out The Banks AR14082
EMI Gives Old Artists New Deal [and other news] AR13943
Emotion RR12104
Emotions RR10733
Emperors Of Soul RR12713
Emperors Of The Air AR14616, AR14819
Empty Gesture Department AR15056
Encomium RR13128
The End Of Silence RR12380
End Of The Beginning: Jerry Garcia And The Grateful Dead's Music Was The Last Remnant Of A Magic Vision AR15498
End Of The Century RR11311, RR11485
Endless Party RR12027
Endpaper AR13051, AR14416
Enemies Of The Arts: The Republicans' Hit Men AR15079
The Enemy Within: An Exclusive Excerpt From The Upcoming Book 'Betrayal' Tells The Inside Story of The Hunt For Aldrich Ames, The Deadliest Traitor In The History Of The CIA AR14321, AR14460, AR15747
Engine Of Aggression: Anthrax Accelerate To The Forefront On 'Stomp 442' AR15818
England's Dreaming: Anarchy, Sex Pistols, Punk Rock And Beyond BR01065
An English Ladymass RR10439
ENIT Festival AR13139
Enta Da Stage RR10573
Enter The Wu-Tang RR12964
Ephraim Lewis: Sensual Soul AR13162
Eponymous RR10651
Equal Rights RR12754
Eric Clapton AR15021, RR10800
Eric Clapton: New York City CR00676
Eric Clapton: Royal Albert Hall CR00677
Erotica RR11774
Esquivel AR13509
The Essential Collection RR12695
The Essential Fripp And Eno RR11080, RR11182
Essential Jason And The Scorchers Volume One: Are You Ready For The Country RR11514
The Essential Johnny Cash RR10752
The Essential King Crimson: Frame By Frame RR11613
Essential Steve Earle RR11053
The Essential Zappa AR15558
Etched In Swing RR12223
Eternal Chant RR13129
The Eternal Dance RR11056
Ethan Hawke: Renaissance Boy AR14680
Eugene, Oregon AR13609
Eugenius: The Former Captain America Invades The U.S. AR14681
Europe's Drug Prescription: Innovative Approaches To The Drug Problem From Over There AR14736
[Evan Dando] AR13395
Evan Dando Of The Lemonheads AR13405
Even Cowgirls Get The Blues RR11665
The Evening Mirror: Can The 'NBC Nightly News' Succeed By Doing Fewer Stories About Washington And More About Peoria? AR14332
Evening The Score: Affirmative Action Cracks Open The Great Divide AR12917
Eventually RR12899a
Everclear RR10421
Every Day Is Saturday (EP) RR11119
Every Little Word RR11601
Everybody Else Is Doing It, So Why Can't We? RR10894
Everybody's Free RR12403
Everything But The Girl's Ben Watt Makes Pleasant Pop From Personal Misery AR15819
Everything I Long For RR11378
Everything Is Wrong RR11921, RR11922
Everything Must Go RR11785
Everything Old Is New Again AR13104
Evil Empire RR12281, RR12282
Evita RR13130
Evolution RR10392

Ex-Blossom Dies: Songwriter Hopkins, 32, Commits Suicide After Battle With Alcohol AR13021
The Ex-Im Files: How The Taxpayer-Funded Export-Import Bank Helps Ship Jobs Overseas AR14083
Example RR11162
Excerpts From A Love Circus RR11229
Executive Sweet: Music Execs Name Their Price As Salaries Soar AR13065
Exile In Guyville RR12157, RR12158
Exile In Guyville: A Report On How Women Are Faring In The Music Industry AR12933
Exile On Main Street: Small-Town Life Suits Jack Logan Just Fine AR13705
Exiles On Main Street AR15457
Exit The Dragon RR12802, RR12803
Expecting To Fly RR10616
Experience RR10977
An Experiment In Terror: 7 Days And Seven Nights Alone With MTV AR13791
Experimental Jet Set, Trash And No Star RR12569
Exploding Tickets: Pearl Jam Wage An Anti-Trust War Against Ticketmaster On Capitol Hill AR15502
Exposed RR12005
Extreme's Triple Play AR14750
Eye Candy AR13105
Eyes Open RR12002
Eyes Wide Open, Hearts Full Of Hope AR14084
Ezra's Better, Bigger Easy AR15243

F

F Troop: The GOP Raids Public Schools AR14085
The Fabulous Charlie Rich RR12342
Faces Of Violence AR13611
Facing West BR01066
Facts Of Life RR12954
Fairweather Johnson RR11434, RR11435
Faith No More AR15916
Faithfull BR01067
The Fall Group Grope: The New Season Offers Yuks For Blacks, Fake Feminism For Women, Familiar Faces For The Old, Pecs And Posing For The Young AR14577
The Fall Of Animal House: For Dartmouth's Alpha Delta Fraternity, The Choice Is Change Or Die AR14430
The Fall Of Us All RR12739
Falling Forward RR11165
Falling From Grace RR13131
Falling Man RR10892, RR11062
False Messiah AR16091
Fame-O-Meter AR15057
Family Groove RR12015
Famous By Association: Vic Chestnutt Joins His Rock & Roll Heroes In The Spotlight AR14353
Fantastic Frank Strozier: Plus RR11704, RR12654
FAQ: Frequently Asked Questions About The World Wide Web AR16069
Far Beyond Driven RR12102
Far East Suite RR11068
Far From Home RR12759
Far Out RR12696
Farewell AR13621, AR13622, AR13623, AR13624
Fast Start For 'Dangerous' AR13944
Fastbacks...And His Orchestra RR11120
Fat City RR10854
Fate Of Nations RR12185
Fats Is Back! AR13302
Faust RR12031
Faust: Hartford, Conn. CR00716
Fear And Loathing In Elko AR15595
Fear And Loathing In Las Vegas AR15596
Fear Of A Black Planet RR12242
Fear Of A Hip Hop Syllabus: Three Professors Reveal What The Required Listening Will Be When Rap Goes To College AR15398
Fear Of Women RR12252
Fear: The Record RR11128
Federal Payola Probe Continues [and other news] AR13945
Feeling The Space: Yoko Ono Enters A New World—The Theater AR14370
Feels Like Home RR12387
Feels Like Rain RR11335
Fegmania! RR11410
The Female Experience BR01068
Female Rappers Laud Reno AR13581
Fever RR10567
Fever For Da Flavor RR11340
The Fevered Rise Of America Online AR14008
Few And Far Between RR12714
Fiesta Total RR10475
Fifteen Essential Albums AR13774
15: Once In A Lifetime AR13510
50 Coastin' Hits RR10828
Fifty Years Of Sunshine RR13132
58: Manchild AR14751
The Fifty-First State: P. J. O'Rourke Road-Trips Vietnam AR15000
55: Wild Thing AR14371
54: And She Was AR14372
59: Justified And Ancient AR14373
51: Back To My Roots AR13511
57: Fish Heads AR14374
56: Faith AR13512
53: Shock The Monkey AR14375
52: Black Or White AR15617
50: When I Think Of You AR13513
The Fight For The Right To Choose: L7 And Friends Rock For Reproductive Freedom AR14752
Fighting Hype And The Weight of His Father's Legend, Jeff Buckley Finds His Own Voice On "Grace" AR13465
File Under Easy Listening RR12667, RR12668
Filed Of Dreams: The Big Business Behind Woodstock '94 AR14643
Fillmore East RR13015
Filth Pig RR11907
Filthy Lucre Live RR12466
Fina Estampa RR12832
Finally RR11916, RR12120
Find A Door RR11036, RR12516
Find My Way Home RR11583
Fine Malt Lyrics RR11443
The Finer Things RR12949
Fiona Apple AR15820
The Fire Inside RR12455
Fire Of The Amazones RR13133
The Fire This Time: Midnight Oil Reignites With A New Album AR13706
The Fire-Fury Records Story RR13134
Firehose: The Grand CR00719
First Band On The Moon RR10732
The First Day RR11183, RR12693
First Place Watches AR15482
First Program In Standard Time RR12026
The First Reform: Campaign Finance AR14086
Fish Out Of Water AR15125
Fishin' For Tuition: Students Talk About Their Jobs AR13857
5 Against The World: Pearl Jam Emerge From The Strange Daze Of Superstardom With A New Album Full Of Rage And Warrior Soul AR13358
Five Hundred Years Of Chicano History In Pictures BR01069
Five Live Yardbirds RR12976
5: Nothing Compares 2 U AR13804
5 String Serenade (song) RR11677, RR11734
Five Ways Of Disappearing RR12550
Fix The Grammys AR13636
Fixing The Vote: The Grammys Set Up A Secret Panel To Make Nominations Hipper AR16093
Flaco Jimenez RR11535
Flamejob RR10893
Flatpicking Guitar Festival RR13135
[Flea] AR14753
Flood Of Box Sets Due AR14274
Floored Genius 2 RR10871
Flow RR12140
Flower Grrrl: After 12 Years With 10,000 Maniacs, Natalie Merchant makes The Most Of Liberation On 'Tigerlily' AR13707
Fluffy May Be Pretty, But They're Hardly Vacant AR13466
Fluorescent RR12970
(Fly) On (The Wall) (song) RR11529
Flyer RR11300
Flying Boats: Why 'Netizen' Works And 'Salon' Doesn't AR14009
Folk Singer RR12877
Folk Songs Of The Hills RR12761
Follow For Now RR11158
Follow For Now: A Hard-Rockin' Guitar Band AR12992
Folon...The Past RR11591
Foo Fighters AR14682, RR11159, RR11160
Foolish RR12675
For Pleasure RR12077
For The Beauty Of Wynona RR11667
For The Cool In You RR10477
For The Record AR13675, AR13676, AR13677, AR13678, AR13679, AR13680, AR13681, AR13682, AR13683
For Unlawful Carnal Knowledge RR12813
Forbidden RR10575
Force Of Nature RR12706
Foreigner—The Doobie Brothers: Mansfield, Mass. CR00704, CR00721
Forever Changes RR11736
Forever Diana RR12392
Forever Young: Neil Young Proves Life In Rock & Roll Can Begin Again At Fortysomething AR14471
The Forgotten Epidemic AR14317
Former Lemonhead Jesse Peretz Gets Behind The Lens AR13467
Forrest Gump RR13136
Forro, Etc. RR13137
Fortunate Son: John Fogerty Looks Back On The Glory Days Of Creedence Clearwater Revival AR13946
40: Baby Got Back AR14564
48: China Girl AR14376
45 Special: A New Label Flourishes In A Funky Format AR13631
45: Whip It AR14377
44: Night Of The Living Baseheads AR15618
44th Street RR12786
49: By The Time I Get To Arizona AR15619
41 RR12690
41: Man On The Moon AR14565
47: Undercover Of The Night AR14378
46: Goin' Back To Cali AR15620
43: Justify My Love AR15621
42: Series Of Dreams AR14538
Forward Into The Past: Paul McCartney Wraps Up A World Tour And Gets Ready For A Beatles Reunion AR15917

Foula RR11170
Founder Of The Delta Blues: 1929-34 RR12123
Fountains Of Wayne Bubble With Power Pop AR15202
Four RR10614
4 Aces RR12719
Four Chords And Several Years Ago RR11689
461 Ocean Boulevard RR10800a
400 Years In A Convent, 50 Years In A Whorehouse AR15001
4 Non Blondes AR13839
4: This Note's For You AR14566
Four-Calendar Cafe RR10832
14 Shots To The Dome RR11654
14 Songs RR12900, RR12901
4-Track Demos RR12179, RR12180a
The Frames: Bringing A Different Mix To Their Irish Stew AR15399
Frampton Comes Alive II RR11173
Frank Black RR10571a
Frank Zappa Meets The Mothers Of Prevention RR13016
Frank Zappa: 1940-1993 AR13708
Frank Zappa Stricken With Cancer: But Family Says He's Fighting It Successfully AR14754
The Frat Trap: After A Decade As A Big College Band, Fighting Gravity Are Ready To Move Off Campus AR15918
Freak City Soundtrack RR11808
Freak Out! RR13017
Freddie Mercury: 1946-1991 AR15164
Freddy Krueger Does D.C.: Meet Bob Dole, Nightmare On Capitol Hill AR13346
A Free Man On Death Row: White Knight Bails Out Shakur AR15867
The Free Your Mind Spoken-Word Tour CR00713, CR00726, CR00738
Freedie's Royal Send-Off: Show Also Marks Rock's First Major Rallying Cry In The Fight Against AIDS AR14755
Freedom '93: That's What George Michael Gets If He Wins A Groundbreaking Suit Against Sony AR13833
Freedom Of Choice RR13138
Freedom Rock: Rock Out Censorship Leads The Fight AR15756
The Freedom Sessions RR11842
Free-For-All RR12143
The Freewheelers: After-Hours Rock AR15400
Frente AR12921
Fresh Cream RR10907, RR10908
The Fresh Ones: Foo Fighters Weird Candy Fantasies AR13514
Friction, Baby RR10550
Friday RR13139
Friday Night Is Killing Me RR10515
Friend Of Mine RR10674, RR11960
Friends In Danger RR11775
Friends: Six Lives On Videotape AR15919
Frogstomp RR12504
From A (Allman) To Z (Zappa) AR13761
From Despair To Where (song) RR11786
From Folk City To Fat City: Shawn Colvin Finds Her Place In The Sun AR15100
From Graceland To Cleveland AR13292
From Hell To Paradise RR11813
From Metal To Mozart BR01070
From Philly With Love RR13140
From The Bush RR13141
From The Cradle RR10801, RR10802
From The Muddy Banks Of The Wishkah RR12042, RR12043
From The Soul RR11731
From The Top RR10738
Fugazi CR00722
Fugazi: New York City CR00723
Fugees: Leaders Of The New Cool AR13658
The Fugs First Album RR11193
Full Moon, Dirty Hearts RR11482
Full Time Love RR12139
Fumbling Towards Ecstasy RR11843
Fun RR11553
Fun Lovin' Criminals Take Their Horseplay Seriously AR13515
Fun Trick Noisemaker RR10448
Funeral For A Friend: Deadheads Flock To San Francisco To Honor Jerry Garcia AR13659
Funk Essentials RR13142
Funkcronomicon RR10472
Funkdafied RR10948
Funkify Your Life RR11892
Funky Divas RR11076, RR11077
Funky, Futuristic Beck Channels Cosmic Debris AR12934
Funky Good Time RR11518
The Funky Headhunter RR11349
Funky Kingston RR12751
Funky Stuff RR13143
Further RR11154
Fusion RR10438, RR10593, RR11256, RR12682
The Future RR10833
Future Profits RR10604
Fuzzy RR11286
Fuzzy Little Piece Of The World RR12197
Fuzzy Logic RR12674

G

G. E. Smith & The High Plains Drifters: Amagansett, N. Y. CR00744, CR00885
G. Love And Special Sauce RR11203, RR12593
Gag U.: From Caltech's Card Trick To Amherst's Run-Around Sabrina, These Pranks Are Total Classics AR15487
The Galactic Boys: Art-Metal Buckaroos AR13709
Galaxie 500 RR11210
Gang Bang Bang: Welcome To Ex-Yugoslavia, Land Of A Thousand Grievances, Where The Christians Hate The Muslims, The Serbs Hate The Croats, The Bosnians Hate The Montenegrins, And Everyone Has A Gun AR15002
Gang Murder In The Heartland AR14635
Gang Of Seven: All Talk, No Music AR13947
Gang Starr AR13293
Gangsta's Paradise RR10867
Garage Orchestra RR10549
Garbage RR11214
Garcia: Truckin' Again AR13948
Garth Brooks: Charlotte, N.C. CR00662
Garvey's Ghost RR10699
Gary's Greatest RR12637
Gash RR11155
A Gathering Of The Tribes: A Report From The 1993 World Peace And Healing Gathering Of The Rainbow Family Of Living Light AR14528
A Gazelle (song) RR11769
Geddy Lee Of Rush AR13516
Geek Love: Stepping Out From John Mellencamp's Shadow, Singer And Violinist Lisa Germano Hits A Nerve On "Geek The Girl" AR14354
Geek Love: Strange But True Tales Of Stereo Obsession AR15716
Geek The Girl RR11230
Generation Latex: Sex On Campus!! AR14504
Generation Next AR13842
Generation Next: The Smokin' Sounds Of Summer '94 AR13396, AR13517, AR13582, AR14548, AR14683
Gentlemen RR10398
George Bush's Heroin Connection AR14738
George Clinton And The P-Funk All-Stars CR00679, CR00680
George Harrison: Live And Low-Key AR14536
George Herbert Hoover Walker Bush AR14087
George Jones AR13406
George Jones: Tramps CR00765
George Michael CR00807
Germ Warfare AR15181
Germany Stomps Skinhead Music: Authorities Bust Third Reich & Roll AR14304
Germs (Tribute) RR13144
Geronimo Vs. Cochise: As Apaches Fight To Build A Nuclear Waste Dump On Their New Mexico Reservation, The Descendants Of Two Legendary Warriors Are Locked In A Battle For The Soul Of The Tribe AR14529
Gerry Mulligan 1927-1996 AR13775
Get A Grip RR10395
Get Happy!! RR10881
Get Happy: Perry Farrell Finds Nirvana On The Way To LollaPalooza '95 And A New LP AR12962
Get In Where Fit In RR12749
Get It While You Can RR12703
Gettin' Mighty Crowded: Summer Tours '94 AR14022
Getting Ahead: Upgrade Now! AR14578
Getting Better: Work In Progress AR13518
Getting In: Everybody Goes To Rusty AR14431
Getting It All On Tape AR16070
Getting Lost: Chronicle Of A Death Foretold AR13276
Getting Real: Silicon Flame Out AR14010
Getting The Led Out: Jimmy Page And Robert Plant Are Back In Business AR13519
Getting Wise: Howard Zinn's Rage Against The Machine AR16105
Ghetto Gothic RR12814
The Ghost Of Tom Joad RR12610
Ghosts In The Machine: The CD-ROM Of "The Haldeman Diaries" And A New Documentary Finally Tell The Full Watergate Story AR13412
Giant Sand: Hoboken, N.J. CR00728
Gibby Haynes Of The Butthole Surfers AR13520
Gil Scott-Heron: New York City CR00873
Gillian Welch: Cajun And Bluegrass Festival CR00935
The Girl Friend AR13219
The Girl In The Tweed Jacket AR14621
Girl Of Your Dreams RR10924
Girl On Fire (song) RR11677a, RR11737
Girlfriend RR12689
The Girlie Show AR15699
Girls Against Boys AR15470
Give It Up To Love RR11835
Give Pot A Chance: Voters In California And Arizona Strike A Blow Against The War On Drugs AR15407
Giving Working People A Break AR13920
The GLAAD Hit List AR13614
Glam Slam 2: The Auteurs AR14280
Glimpses BR01071
Global Celebration RR13145
The Global Sweatshop: Indonesian Workers Struggle For Rights And Help From Clinton AR14088
Global Village: WOMAD Returns For A Tour

Of The U.S. AR13583
A Glorious Lethal Euphoria RR11885
The Glory Of Gershwin RR13146
Glory Road: 1968 To 1972 RR10993
Glum RR11239
Go, Cat Go! BR01072
Go Fer Yer Funk RR10819
Go Grace Go (song) RR11727
Go In The Dark RR13147
Go Slow Down RR10620
Go To The Sugar Alter RR10970
Go Together RR10592, RR12683
God Of Love RR10478
The Godfathers Of Rap: The Rise And Fall Of The First Heroes Of Hip-Hop AR13033
Gods And Monsters RR11747
God's Little Monkeys: A Sardonic Political Edge AR13858
Goin' Back To New Orleans RR11031
Goin' To California RR12070
Going Back Home RR10496
Going Blank Again RR12349
Going Down With Janis BR01073
Going For The Gold: Monet Talks As Golden-Circle Seating Divides Concert Audiences AR14023
Gold RR10383
The Gold Experience RR12232, RR12233, RR12694
Gold Medals And Platinum Blondes: The Dream Team At Atlanta's Largest Strip Club Gets Pumped For The Summer Olympics AR13277
Golden Smog CR00730
Goldfinger AR13997
Go-Man-Go RR13148, RR13149
Gone RR12986
Gone Again RR12551, RR12552, RR12553
Gone But Not Forgotten: Though Virtually Extinct, Vinyl Record Albums Still Have Their Defenders AR15126
Goo Goo Dolls: Minneapolis CR00731
Good As I Been To You RR11046
Good God's Urge RR12204
A Good Likeness RR10404
Good News From The Next World RR12508
Good Stuff RR10474
Good Times: Morning Has Broken The Newest Looks Pop And Shine To Keep You Suited Up Long Past The Twilight's Last Gleaming AR14820, AR15605
Good Vibrations RR10516
Good Vibrations: The Fugees Score One For Positivity AR15471
Goodbye RR11636
The GOP's Strike Force: The Right-Wing Propaganda Machine Churns Out Money, Activists And Lies AR12951
Gorgeous George RR10846
The Gospel Sound RR13150
Got The Foreclosed, Bankrupt GOP Blues AR14089
Gotta Let This Hen Out! RR11411
Gov't Mule RR11282
Grace RR10694
Grace Under Fire: The NRA Takes Potshots At Assault-Weapons Opponents AR12952
Grand Jury Attacks Arena Security [and other news] AR13949
The Grand, New York CR00824
Grand Opening RR11222
Grand Slam! RR13151
Grand Slam Baby (single) RR12203
The Grand Tour RR12014a
Grandma's Ghost RR10663
Grandpaw Would RR11680
Grant Lee Buffalo AR15111
Grapevine AR14047, AR14048, AR14049, AR14050, AR14051, AR14052, AR14156, AR14157, AR14158, AR14159, AR14160, AR14161, AR14162, AR14163, AR14164, AR14165, AR14166, AR14167, AR14168, AR14169, AR14170, AR14171, AR14172
Grateful Dead Cut Staff AR15493
The Grateful Dead, Sting: Las Vegas, Nevada CR00732, CR00901
Grave Dancers Union RR12574, RR12575
The Gravest Show On Earth BR01074
Gravity RR11093
Gravity's Rainbow RR10544
Gravy Deco RR11412
Gray Folded RR12088, RR12089
The Gray Race RR10482
Grayfolded RR11289
Great American Songwriters RR13153
The Great Annihilation RR12685
Great Days RR12236
The Great Deceiver RR11614
Great Divide RR12457
The Great Escape RR10617
Great Expectations RR10453
The Great Gospel Men RR13154
The Great Gospel Women RR13155
The Great Indoors RR10914
Great Moments In College Journalism: 1 AR14053
Great Moments In College Journalism: 2 AR14054
Great Move! RR11970
The Great 1955 Shrine Concert RR13152
Great Performances: The Year's Best AR15648, AR15649
The Great Price War: Used CDs Become The Center Of A Retail Battle AR13950
The Great Puzzle RR12481
Great Reduced Expectations AR15550
The Great Southern Trendkill RR12103
The Great Western Cave-In: For Now, Political Forces Beat Market Forces AR16029
Greatest Hits RR10782, RR12611
The Greatest Hits 1966-1992 RR10994
Greatest Hits, Vol. III RR11047
The Greatest Living Englishman RR12030, RR12119
Greatest Misses RR12243
Greed Or Need?: CDs Hit $17.98 In Record Biz's Banner Year AR15757
The Greek Theater, Los Angeles CR00896
Green Day AR13660
Green Daze AR14684
Green Jelly's Bubblegum Punk AR13294
Green Mind RR11009
Greetings From The Gutter RR12636
Greg Dulli Of Afghan Whigs AR13521
Greg Graffin Of Bad Religion AR13661
Grey Ghost RR11298
Gringo Honeymoon RR11589, RR11590
Grok The Vote AR14090
Groovy Decay RR11413
Groovy Decoy RR11414
Group Gets Youth Vote On Bandwagon AR14756
Group Portrait RR10783
Growin' Up Too Fast RR13156
Grown Man RR12850
Grown Up Wrong RR12296
Grrrls At War AR13687
Grunge City: For Real Rockers Seattle Is The Ultimate Wet Dream AR12993
GS I Love You RR13157
Guess Who's Coming To Legislate AR16030
Guess Who's Coming To Washington AR13036
A Guide Through The Chaos RR11585
The Guinness Encyclopedia Of Popular Music BR01075
Guit With It RR10679
Guitar Note: The DTS-I Changes Tunings In Seconds AR14443
Guitar Paradise Of East Africa RR13158
The Guitar Wizard RR12309
Guitarrorists RR13159
Gumball: New York CR00733
Gunning For Guns: Clinton Calls For Ideas On Confronting Violence AR16031
Guns N' Roses AR14125, CR00734
Guns N' Roses; Metallica CR00736, CR00806
Guns N' Roses: New Haven Coliseum CR00735, CR00796
Guns N' Roses: The Photographic History BR01076
Guns N' Roses To Play AIDS Benefit [and other news] AR13951
Guns Or Budget? Clinton's Options AR14091
Gus Van Sant's Northwest Passage: The Director Of 'Drugstore Cowboy' Continues To Explore Uncharted Territory With 'My Own Private Idaho' AR14135
Gut Check In The Heartland AR15334
Gutterball RR11330
Gutterball Take A Working Vacation AR15203
Guy Clark, Joe Ely, Paul Kelly, Michelle Shocked, Allen Toussaint: The Troubadour CR00678, CR00712, CR00768, CR00876, CR00919
Guyville Java Jive AR14420

H

Hail Hail Rock & Roll: Behind The Scenes And Onstage At The Concert For The Hall Of Fame AR13522
Haiti AR15003
Haitian Flight Song: World Music Artists At The Mercy Of Global Politics AR15462
Half Way Home: Soliciting The Hospitality Of Their Extended Family AR14228
Hall Gets Joplin Haul AR14126
Hall Of Fame AR13295, AR14127
Hall Of Fame '95: Led Zeppelin And Neil Young Highlight The 10th Anniversary Celebration AR13523
Hall Of Fame '96 AR13524, AR15031
Hall Of Fame Groundbreaking: At Long Last, The Site Is Ready For The Country's First Rock Shrine AR15352
Hall Of Fame Inductees AR14128
Hall Of Fame Inductees Announced AR13776
Hall Of Fame Nominees AR14173
Hall Of Fame: See You In September AR13296
Hall Of Fame To Break Ground AR13952
Hallucination Engine RR11806
Hammer; Boyz II Men; Jodeci CR00660, CR00739, CR00762
Hammer Hurting; Shops For New Label AR15584
Hand On The Torch RR12806
Handle Like Eggs RR13160
Hang On To A Dream RR11359
Hangin' On By A Thread RR12720
Hank Williams: The Biography BR01077
Happiness RR11231
The Happy Club RR11224
Happy Days RR10756
Happy Days, Sweetheart RR11101
Happy Hour RR11607
Harbor Lights RR11440
The Hard-Core Curriculum: Despite A Decade Of 'Just Say No' And Get-Tough Laws, Drugs Are Back On Campus With A Vengeance AR14505

A Hard Dazed Night: Soul Asylum's Dave Pirner Burns The Midnight Oil, Defending His Band, His Music And His Punk Credibility AR15503
Hard Groovin' RR11164
Hard Road RR12775
The Hard Stuff RR11637
Hard To Earn RR11212, RR11213
Hard To Handle: The Black Crowes Throw A Snit And Toughen Their Sound On The New LP AR14229
Hard To The Core AR14757
Hard Workin' Man RR10664
The Harder They Come RR13161
Harlem Blues RR12430
Harlem Renaissance RR10745
Harmacy RR12454
Harmonica Classics RR13162
Harry Nilsson 1941-1994 AR14379
Harvest Moon RR12993
Hat Full Of Stars RR11673
The Hate Squad: The Religious Right Is Making A Killing From Bashing Clinton AR16032
Hater RR11368
Haunted Heart RR11600
Havana, 3 A.M. RR12212
Have A Little Faith RR11184
He Had Faced His Demon: Deborah Koons Garcia Speaks Out AR13710
He Was A Crook AR15597
'He Was A Geek And A God:' The Story Behind The Tragic Death Of Kurt Cobain AR15504
Head Case AR13468
Head Count, $ Amount AR14146
Head Over Heals RR10385
Headquarters RR11929
Healing Bones RR12482
Healing Hands Of Time RR12010
The Healing Of Daniel Johnston: A Punk-Rock Cult Hero's Roller-Coaster Ride Toward Wider Recognition AR14630
Heard The About The Welfare Queen? AR14092
The Heart And Sole Of The City: The Right Sneaker Keeps You In The Action AR15211
The Heart Of Darkness: The Boston Band Come Makes Soul Music For The Slacker Generation AR13482
Heart Of The Congos RR10860
Heartaches And Harmonies RR11107
Heartbeat RR12424
Hearts In Armor RR12977, RR12978
Heart-Shaped Noise: The Music And The Legacy AR13711
Heartsongs RR12115
Heartwork RR10731
The Heat Puppets AR15244
Heather Nova Weathers The Quiet Storm AR12963
Heaven And Hull RR12386
Heaven Is Under Our Feet: Voices For Walden Woods AR13057, AR13474, AR14203
A 'Heavier, Funkier' Living Colour: Vernon Reid And Company Set To Release 'Stain' AR14472
Heavy Rhyme Experience: Vol. 1 RR10653
Hecho En Puerto Rico RR10848
Hell Freezes Over RR11051, RR11052
Help Wanted: Red Hot Guitarist AR14758
Help Yourself RR11683
Hendrix To Tour U.S.: Traveling Exhibit Hits The States In April AR15165
Henley To Buy Walden Site AR15920
Henry Kaiser: San Francisco CR00767
Henry Rollins' L.A. AR15245
Henry Rollins: Rocks Angriest Voice Rises From The Ashes Of Black Flag AR14685
Henry's Dream RR10484, RR10757
Her Back Pages AR14608
Herb Ritts AR15192
Here RR11699
Here Comes Success RR10503
Here I Come And Other Hits RR11115
Here, There And Everywhere AR14606
Here To Save You All RR10790
Heroin AR13278
Heroin: Back On The Charts AR14230
He's A Loser, Baby: Court Rejects George Michael's Plea To Break His Contract With Sony AR15417
Hey Babe RR11371, RR11372
Hey Man...Smell My Finger RR10820
Hey Zeus! RR12972
Heyday 1979-83 RR11074
Hi Times: The Hi Records R&B Years RR13163
Hickory Smoke AR13129, AR13220, AR14821
The Hidden Power Of Dreams: The Cranberries Speak Softly But Carry A Big Hit AR14686, AR14822
Hideout RR10441
High As A Kite RR12618
High Interactivity: CD's Bring Movies, Games And Books To A TV Near You AR13106
High School Confidential: Amy Heckerling, The Writer And Director Of 'Clueless," Celebrates Adolescence As A State Of Mind AR13221
High Time RR11827
High-Plains Surfers AR15246
High-Quality TV's, Big And Small, For Tight Spaces Or Going Places AR13107
High-Quality Video Adds Sizzle To CD-ROMs AR14659
High-Tech Redneck RR11560
High Times: Meat Puppets Make Bong Rock Fro Now People AR12994
Highway Trance RR11660
Hill Country Rain RR12859
The Hill People: They Only Come Out At Night At Don Hill's, New York's Glam Mecca For The Dusk-Till-Dawn Set AR14823
Hillbilly Voodoo RR12417, RR12913
Hip Hop Greats: Classic Raps RR13164, RR13165
Hip-Hop Nation Is Shaken By Tupac Shakur Ambush Off Las Vegas Strip AR15868
Hips And Makers RR11399
The Hips Of Tradition RR13031
Hire Education: The Secretary Of Labor Tells You Where The Jobs Will Be In The New Economy AR15148
His Name Was Prince... AR13142
Historic Moments Vol. 1 RR10911
History RR11497, RR11498, RR12851, RR12852
The History Of Art Blakely And The Jazz Messengers RR10588
The History Of Our Future RR10574
The History Of Space Age Pop RR13166
Hit Patrol AR13805
Hit The Highway RR12239
Hit, With A Bullet: Filter On Target With "Nice Shot" AR15758
Hits Style RR11619
The Hits: Volume 1 & II RR12234
Hitsville USA: The Motown Singles Collection 1959-1971 RR13167
Hitsville U.S.A., Volume II RR13168
Hold Me, Thrill Me, Kiss Me, Kill Me (song) RR12791
Hole In Our Sole BR01078
Hole Is A Band: While The Courtney Saga Continues, Hole Prove That A Rock & Roll Band Is The Sum Of Its Parts AR13201
Hole: New York CR00747
Holiday For Soul Dance RR12260, RR12261
Holiday Hits And Misses AR15650
Hollywood AR14242
Hollywood Director David Fincher Returns To Video AR15921
Hollywood Rock BR01079
Hollywood Swingin': Film Soundtracks Go Out On The Cutting Edge AR13662
Hollywood Town Hall RR11515
Holy Rap Session AR16098
Holy Rock & Rollers AR13066
Holy Smoke RR11979
The Holy Sound Of American Pipe RR12839
Home RR10591, RR12592
Home Again RR12023
The Home Front: In The War Against AIDS, Some Of The Bravest Battles Are Fought Far From Laboratories And Demonstrations AR13279
Home Invasion RR11467, RR11468
Home On The Strange AR13712
Home Video: Broadway Goes Hollywood AR15651
Homebrew RR10776
Homestyle: Neneh Cherry on Love, Music And The Pursuit Of Happiness AR14759
Homeward Bound: Spearhead Redefine The Meaning Of Roots Rock AR15922
Honey, I Shrunk The Cineplex: Home Is Where The Theater Is AR14056
The Honeymoon Is Over RR10922
Honey's Dead RR11524
Honky Tonk Angels RR11754, RR12116, RR12966
Honky Tonk Girl RR11755
Honky-Tonk Men: George Jones And Keith Richards Pair Up For Jones' Upcoming Album AR14281
Honky-Tonk Woman AR13845
The Hood The Bad & The Ugly: For Naughty By Nature, The Question Is Not Can You Take East Orange Out Of The Boyz, But Can You Take The Boyz Out Of East Orange? AR13222, AR14824
Hootie And The Blowfish: New Orleans CR00748
Hootie Mack RR10540
Hope RR12101
Hope & Hard Times: For The Workers At Ravenswood Aluminum, The Struggle To Regain Their Union Jobs Took Them From Small-Town Appalachia To The Glass Canyons Of International Finance AR15464
Hope You Like Our New Direction RR11579
H.O.R.D.E. Of Hearing: The New Jamming Generation Hits The Road To Swap Solos And Party Down AR15559
Horse Stories RR11015
Horsebreaker Star RR11846
Horses In The Mine RR10481
Hot AR14254
Hot Accessory AR13859, AR15247
Hot Actor AR13223, AR13860, AR15248, AR15249
Hot Actor: Dogging It With Brad Pitt, The Good Ol' Bad Boy From 'Thelma And Louise' AR14579
Hot Actress AR13224, AR13280, AR13861, AR15250, AR15251
Hot Alternative Subgenre: One-Hype Wonders AR15759
Hot Appliance AR13225, AR15252

Hot Architect AR13862, AR15253
Hot Arms AR13226, AR15254
Hot Art Form AR13863, AR15255
Hot Art Show: The Gramercy Art Fair AR14580
Hot Athlete AR13227, AR13864, AR15256, AR15257
Hot Athlete: Steve Prefontaine AR15326
Hot Author: Stephen Hunter AR15743
Hot Band AR13228, AR15258, AR15366
Hot Band: A College-Rock Favorite, Teenage Fanclub Is Now Earning Mainstream Pop Acceptance AR14687
Hot Boxing RR11779
Hot Brit: Ewan McGregor AR15370
Hot Bulletin Board AR13229, AR15259
Hot Bullshit Compliment AR13865, AR15260
Hot Car AR13866, AR15261
Hot Career Move: Quitting AR14581
Hot Cartoonist: Pat Moriarity AR13135
Hot Comic Book AR13230, AR15262
Hot, Cool & Vicious RR12426
Hot Country Act AR13231, AR15263
Hot Country Act: BR5-49 AR13067
Hot Country Singer AR13867, AR15264
Hot Cover: Ask Killer Babe Sharon Stone About Sex And You'll Find She Has A Basic Instinct For It AR16115
Hot Dates AR13868, AR15265
Hot Debut AR13869, AR15266
Hot Designer AR13232, AR13870, AR15267, AR15268
Hot Director AR13233, AR13871, AR15269, AR15270, AR16048
Hot Director: James Mangold AR15744
Hot Disease: Ulcers AR16124
Hot Drink: Orbitz AR16125
Hot Drug AR13872, AR15271
Hot Drug: Claritin AR13024
Hot Exercise AR13234, AR15272
Hot Fashion AR14825, AR15692
Hot Founding Father: Ben Franklin AR15228
Hot Gadget AR13873, AR15273
Hot Hollywood Hangout: Hamilton's AR13136
Hot Infomercial AR13874, AR15274
Hot Jazz Artist AR13235, AR14826, AR15275
Hot Jazz Artist: Kenny Garrett AR13777
Hot Jazz Artists AR13778
Hot Jazzman AR13779
Hot Judd AR13875, AR15276
Hot Label: Ruffhouse AR15760
The Hot List AR13236, AR13237, AR13876, AR14506, AR15277, AR15278, AR15279, AR16126
Hot Look AR14511, AR14827, AR15484, AR15490
Hot Loser AR13238, AR15280
Hot Magazine: Loaded AR16127
Hot Marketing Ploy: Critic Proofing AR14582
Hot Medical Equipment AR13877, AR15281
Hot Models AR13239, AR15282
Hot Molecule AR13878, AR15283
Hot Mood: Confusion AR13386
Hot Movie Critic AR13240, AR15284
Hot Movie Theme AR13241, AR15285
The Hot Ones! RR12622
Hot Performance Artist AR13242, AR15286
Hot Picks: An Insider's Guide To the Season's New Faces AR14549
Hot Picks: Rock & Roll Is Their Business Here's Who They're Listening To AR14255
Hot Picks: When Music Insiders Kick Back, These Are The Bands They Listen To AR14256
Hot Playwright AR13879, AR15287
Hot Producer AR13880, AR15288
Hot Producer: Tim Simenon AR15761
Hot Rap Trend AR13881, AR15289
Hot Rapper AR13243, AR15290
Hot Rappers AR13806
Hot Rats RR13018, RR13019
Hot Record Label AR13882, AR15291
Hot Resurrection AR13883, AR15292
Hot Retro Ethos AR13884, AR15293
Hot Revival AR13885, AR15294
Hot Revival: The Cold War AR15229
Hot Scam AR13886, AR15295
Hot Screenwriter AR13887, AR15296
Hot Sex Symbol AR13888, AR15297
Hot Sitcom Twist: Depressing Season Finales AR14583
Hot Stand-Up AR13244, AR15298
Hot Standup AR13889, AR15299
Hot Status Symbol: A Tiny Cell Phone AR13025
Hot Stuff: New Electronics So Cool They Sizzle AR16071
Hot Stuff: Plugging In The New AR13108
Hot Style AR13245, AR14828
Hot Subculture AR13246, AR13890, AR15300, AR15301
Hot Technology AR14660
Hot Teen Idols AR13891, AR15302
Hot Threat AR13892, AR15303
Hot Threat: Cyberterrorism AR15230
Hot Turn-On: Seventies Porn AR13525
Hot TV Show AR13247, AR15304
Hot TV Show: Concrete T.V. AR14584
Hot TV Star: Brandy AR16128
Hot Unprotected Minority AR13248, AR15305
Hot Vacation Spot AR13249, AR15306
Hot Vacation Spot: Anywhere That's Like Somewhere Else 20 Years Ago AR14585
Hot Vice AR13250, AR15307
Hot Video Game AR13893, AR15308
House Of Cards: Crowded House Mix Whimsy And Melancholy On 'Together Alone' AR15923
House Of GVSB RR11255
House Of Pain: The Fight Against Gansta Rap Hits Captiol Hill AR15445
A House With No Closets AR13195
Hovercraft (EP) RR11445
How Bad Can It Be? NBC's Hit Sitcom 'Men Behaving Badly' Is Pretty Good, But It Should Be Worse AR15924
How Long Has This Been Going On RR11951
How Many Times Will Bill Blink?: Courage And The President AR14093
How Stardom Works AR15058
How Swede It Is: Ace Of Base Invade U.S. Airwaves AR14380
How To Be A Road Scholar AR13109
How To Fake A Resume: Entry-Level Lessons For The Real World AR16129
How To Play Blues Guitar RR11307
How To Vote In Fifty States AR14257
How We Export Jobs And Disease AR14094
Howlin Mercy RR10724
Howlin' Wolf RR11448
Howls, Raps And Roars RR13169
Huh-huh, Huh-huh: MTV's Beavis And Butt-Head On What's Cool And What Sucks AR16106
The Hum Of D.A.I.S.Y. RR10950
Human Behaviour (song) RR11313
Human Touch RR12612, RR12613
Human Wheels RR11866, RR11867
The Humbler RR11217, RR11277
Humroot RR12487
A Hundred Lovers RR12743
Hundred Year Hall RR11290
Hungry For Stink RR11658
Hunky Dory RR10642
The Hurra RR11455
Hurricane AR13469
Hurricane Season RR12418
Hush AR13170
Hydraulic RR12299
Hydrogen Jukebox RR11260
Hymns To The Silence RR11952
HyperViolence: A Generation Of Kids In Richmond, Calif., Is Growing Up In The Shadow Of Guns, Drugs And Death AR13286
Hypocrisy Is The Greatest Luxury RR11017

I

I Am Free And I Want To Thank Rolling Stone And Its Readers For Returning My Life To Me AR13612
I Am Right (single) RR10997
I Am Somebody: After A Wildly Successful Duet With Coolio, L.V. Surfaces With His Own Gangsta's Paradise AR15406
I Am The Cosmos RR10541
I Can Hear The Ants Dancin' RR10661, RR12606
I Can't Make you Love Me (song) RR11040
I Care Because You Do RR10446
I Don't Care (song) RR12868
I Feel Alright RR11054
I Fought The Law AR14287
I Just Wasn't Made For These Times RR12942
I Know Who Holds Tomorrow RR10891, RR11638
I Love Everybody RR11742
I Love Mekons RR11862
I May Be Hungry But I Sure Ain't Weird RR10730
I Often Dream Of Trains RR11415
I Remember You RR11841
I Say, I Say, I Say RR11088
I Should Coco RR12678, RR12679
I Spent A Week There The Other Night RR12779
I Want My DVD AR13110
I Want To Hold Your Hand (song) RR10527
I Was A Campus Lab Rat AR15309
I Was Warned RR10898
I Will Dare (song) RR12331
I Wish I Was A Lesbian (song) RR12853
Ian Anderson AR13763
Ice-T AR14473
Ice-T: The Rolling Stone Interview AR14474
Ice-T's Declaration Of Independence: The Truth Behind His Split With Time Warner AR14475
Iceland's Sugarcubes AR13713
If I Ever Fall In Love RR12472
If I Only Had A Brain AR14638
If I Were A Carpenter RR13170
If I'm Lucky RR12398, RR12511
If The Symptoms Are Rapid Increases In Teen Deaths From Murder, Suicide And Car Crashes, Alcohol And Drugs...The Disease Is Adolescence AR13684
If You Think You Made A Mistake In 1992, Think Again AR16033
If You Want Your Summer To Be A Movable Feast, You'll Need Tech With Some Get-Up-And-Go AR13111
Iggy Still Pops: The Original Punk Is In Royal Form On American Caesar AR14760
II RR10647, RR11081, RR12214
The Iliad BR01080
I'll Be You (song) RR12332

Ill Communication RR10519
I'll Treat You Right RR10815
Illadelph Halflife RR12390
Illmatic RR11989
Illuminations RR13171
I'm A Texan RR12638
I'm Alive RR10683, RR10684
I'm Never Gonna Die Again RR12724
I'm Your Fan RR13172
Imagination RR11858
Imperial Drag RR11471
Imperial Teen Chart Their Own Course On 'Seasick' AR13632
The Importance Of Defining Your Terms AR15059, AR15060
The Impossible Bird RR11746
Impressions Of Copenhagen RR10627
Improve Your Images AR13112
In A Bjork State Of Mind: The Former Sugarcube Finds Life Is Sweet As A Soloist AR13807
In A Word Or 2 RR11741
In Concert RR11453, RR11611c
In Living Color AR15808
In Living Color: Vernon Reid Goes Solo With A Stellar Cast AR13714
In My Lifetime RR10995
In My Room AR13642
In My Time RR11984
[In November...] AR14288
In On The Kill Taker RR11187, RR11188
In Pieces RR10666
In Search Of Manny RR11750
In Search Of The Cure For AIDS: A Special Report From The Frontiers Of Science AR15547
In Sides RR12084
In The Beginning RR11027, RR12823
In The Dogg House: Tha Dogg Pound Get Caught In The Middle AR15869
In The Flesh! RR12525
In The Land Of The Tenor RR12497
In The News AR13194, AR13953, AR13954, AR13955, AR13956, AR13957, AR13958, AR13959, AR13960, AR13961, AR13962, AR13963, AR13964, AR13965, AR13966, AR13967, AR13968, AR13969, AR14024, AR14025, AR14026, AR14027, AR14028, AR14029, AR14030, AR14031, AR14381, AR14382, AR14476, AR14477, AR14478, AR14479, AR14550, AR15455, AR15505, AR15506, AR15507, AR15508, AR15509, AR15510, AR15511, AR15512, AR15513, AR15514, AR15515, AR15516, AR15517, AR15518, AR15519, AR15520, AR15521, AR15821, AR15822, AR15823, AR15824, AR15825, AR15826, AR15827, AR15828, AR15829, AR15830, AR15831, AR15832, AR15833, AR15834, AR15835, AR15836, AR15837, AR15925
In The Presence Of Greatness RR12834
In The Red RR11384, RR12375
In The Running RR11562
In The Storm RR10971
In The Zone Of Perceived Faith: Report From New Hampshire AR13601
In Their Own Words: Club Series Spawns A Tour By Some Of Music's Most Distinguished Songwriters AR14136
In Their Own Words: Volume One RR13173
In Thrall RR10469
In Through The Back Door: The Butthole Surfers Are The Certified Shock Jocks Of The Next Wave AR13202
In Utero RR12044, RR12045
In With The Outtakes: Def Leppard Issues New Odds & Sods LP AR13715
Incense And Insolence: Mazzy Star Carry The Torch For '60s Psychedelia And The Importance Of Being Difficult AR13663
Incesticide RR12046
Incident At Cima RR12435
Independence RR11748
Independent Worm Saloon RR10712
Indie Speedway: Sonicnet Launches An On-Line Service For Music AR14383
Industrial Era: Jim Nash, Co-Founder Of Wax Trax!, Is Claimed By AIDS AR15118
The Infamous RR11920
Infamous Angel RR10982
Infernal Love RR12723
Infidels RR11478
Infinity Within RR10973
Infrared Roses RR11291
Ingenue RR11666
Inner Child RR12477
Insane In The Brain (song) AR12957
Insane In The Brain: For Biker Wayne Croasdale Life Is Going Downhill AR13251, AR14829
Inside RR11961
Insomniac RR11295, RR11296
Internal Journal, Vol II RR13174
International Times RR12760
Interstate RR12141
Interstellar Low Ways RR12262
Into Dust (song) RR11822
Into The Loop: How To Get The Job You Want After Graduation AR13484
Into The Twangy-First Century RR12406
Into The Unknown: Soundgarden Explore Rock & Roll's Heart Of Darkness AR14761
Introducing Gorky's Zygotic Mynci RR11280
Introduction AR14290
INXS Get Real: More Than Hooks And Looks AR13808
INXS: New York City CR00750
An Irish Evening RR10786
Ironic (song) RR11945
Ironman RR11238
Is It...Man Or Astro-Man? RR11784
Is Moshing Murder? AR13068
Is P.M. Dawn's Prince Be the Brian Wilson Of Hip-Hop? God Only Knows AR14503
Is The Spanner She Want RR12202
Is This Any Way To Renew An Economy? AR14095
Is This Any Way To Run A White House?: Clinton Finally Brings Change To Washington—A New Chief Of Staff AR16034
Is This The Woman Who Invented Rock & Roll?: The Deborah Chessler Story AR14562
Isabel Bishop E.P. RR12798
The Isle Of View RR12218, RR12219
Isn't It Alanis? 'Ironic' Parodies Flood The Airwaves AR14349
Isn't That Conveeenient! AR13113
Iso RR11709
Istanbul 1925 RR13175
It Came From Memphis RR13176
It Came From The Course Catalog AR14297
It Came From The Course Catalog No. 2 AR14298
It Came From The Course Catalog No. 3 AR14299
It Came From The Course Catalog No. 4 AR14300
It Takes A Nation Of Millions To Hold Us Back RR12244, RR12245
It Takes A Thief RR10868
It Was Written RR11990, RR11991, RR11992
It Won't Be The Last RR10941
It's A Mad, Mad, Mad About You World AR14830, AR15926
It's A Mad, Mad, Mad, Mad Professor RR11767
It's A Natural Thing RR11161
It's About Time RR12691, RR12692
It's All Coming Into Focus AR13114
It's Artastic RR12658
It's Five O'Clock Somewhere RR12527, RR12528, RR12560, RR12561
It's Great When You're Straight...Yeah RR10572
It's Hard To Believe It RR13177
It's Heavy In Here RR11812
It's Only Time RR10935
It's Party Time—It's Excellent: 'Wayne's World' Will Change The History Of Cinema—And Monkeys Might Fly Out Of Our Butt! AR16101
It's Pat: Julia Sweeney's Gender-Bending Character Goes To Hollywood AR15358, AR15603
It's Show Time! AR13252
It's The Jesus And Nirvana Chain! AR14435
Izzy Or Isn't He?: Stradlin May Be Splitting With Guns N' Roses AR14762
Izzy Quits Guns N' Roses AR14301
Izzy Stradlin And The Ju Ju Hounds RR11572, RR12652

J

J. Beez Wit The Remedy RR11577
J Mascis: New York City CR00752
Jack Logan: New York CR00784
Jack Salmon And Derby Sauce RR11899
Jackson: $20 Million From HBO AR15927
Jackson Browne AR13421
Jackson Browne: New York City CR00666
Jackson Charity Off To A Slow Start [and other news] AR13970
Jackson's Dangerous Game: The Self-Crowned King Of Pop Ruled On Prime Time, But Did We Get The Truth? AR14480
Jackson's Double Play: The Singer Steps Up To The Plate With A New Album And Movie AR15928
Jagged Little Pill RR11946
Jagger Remembers: The Rolling Stone Interview AR15790
Jailhouse Ragga: Snow Busts Out Of The Big House And Up The Pop Charts AR14622
Jale AR14806
James CR00755
James Carville's Hot List AR13894, AR15310
The James Gang: With 'Laid,' These British Lads Finally Get Over AR13809
James Taylor AR14204
James Williams Meets The Saxophone Masters RR10839, RR11389, RR12171, RR12932
Jampac Benefit AR15084
Jamu Dreaming RR12358
Janeane Garofalo's Hot List AR13834
Janet RR11494, RR11495
Janet Jackson: Rosemont, Ill. CR00753
Janis RR11570
[Japan] AR14307
Japanese Corporations; U.S. Corporations AR15061
Jar Of Flies RR10410
Jarred Up RR11855
Jason Bentley AR13633
Jawbox AR14384
Jay Leno AR15929
The Jayhawks CR00756
Jazz At The Maintenance Shop RR11104
Jazz In Silhouette RR12263, RR12264
Jazzmatazz RR11327, RR11328, RR11329

JazzSpeak RR13178
JC On The Set RR10749
Jealous One's Envy RR11123
Jeff Ament Of Pearl Jam AR15762
Jeff Buckley: New York City CR00668
Jeff Porcaro: 1954-1992 AR14308
Jefferson Airplane Loves You RR11519
Jeffrey Gaines: Real-Life Sketches AR14605
Jeffrey Lee Pierce 1958-1996 AR14355
Jehovahkill RR10872
Jello Biafra Attacked AR13971
Jenn Vix RR12843
Jennifer Jason Leigh: She's The Queen of The Ravaged, Boozed Up And Strung Out AR13526
Jenny Come Back (song) RR10959
Jericho RR10501, RR10502
Jerry & George & Kramer & Elaine: Exposing The Secrets Of SEINFELD's Success AR16116
Jerry Brown For President: A Rolling Stone Editorial AR15791
Jerry Brown's Grass-Roots Call To Arms: An Interview With The Editors Of Rolling Stone AR14310
Jerry Garcia AR14198, AR14453
Jerry Garcia: 1942-1995 AR13912, AR13921
Jerry Garcia Ill; Dead Cancel Tour AR13972
Jerry Lee Lewis RR11690
The 'Jerry Maguire' Journal AR13359
Jerry Nolan: 1946-1992 AR14311
The Jesus And Mary Chain Rage Against The Machine On 'I Hate Rock & Roll' AR15838
The Jesus And Mary Chain: Washington, D.C. CR00758
The Jesus & Mazzy Chain AR14174
Jesus Christ Superstar: A Resurrection RR13179
Jesus Jones, Stereo MC's: Roseland CR00759, CR00898
Jesus' Son BR01081
Jesus Wept RR12190
The Jewel-Paula Records Story: The Blues, Rhythm And Blues And Soul Recordings RR13180
Jim Carrey: Bare Facts And Shocking Revelations AR15371
Jim Lauderdale: An Eclectic 'Debut' AR15166
Jim Morrison AR14247
Jimi Hendrix: Electric Gypsy BR01082
The Jimi Hendrix Experience Box Set RR11395
Jimi: The Man And The Music AR13716
Jimmy Buffett AR14356
Jimmy Miller 1942-1994 AR13780
Jimmy Page And Robert Plant: Miami CR00836, CR00850
Jimmywine Majestic RR12306
Jive At Five RR11917, RR12718
Jive Soweto: The Indestructible Beat Of Soweto Vol. 4 RR13181
Joan Baez AR14515
Joan Jett And The Blackhearts: New York City CR00760
Joan Osborne: Holy Roller Finds Salvation In God And Good Sex AR15112
Joe Henry Bounces From Rural Rock To An Urban Groove AR14175
Joe Henry: On His Own AR15401
Joel Sues Lawyers: Singer Claims Fraud In $90 Million Lawsuit AR14763
Joe's Garage RR13020
Joey Ramone AR14385
John Cage: 1912-1992 AR15185
John Cale AR15763
John Campbell: A Modern Bluesman AR13473
John Campbell: 1952-1993 AR15560
A John Coltrane Retrospective: The Impulse Years RR10850
John Hiatt: New York City CR00743
John Lennon AR15792
John Lydon AR13527
John Mellencamp CR00802
John Mellencamp: Gets Serious And Funky AR15186
John Mellencamp: Grand Rapids, Mich. CR00801
John Panozzo: 1948-1996 AR14176
John Parish & Polly Jean Harvey: Fleece And Firkin CR00740, CR00837
John Peel AR12995
John Prine AR14551
A John Prine Christmas RR12237
John Travolta AR15930
Johnnie Johnson & The Kentucky Headhunters: Chicago CR00764, CR00770
Johnny B. Gone AR15931
Johnny Cash AR13528
Johnny Cash: New York CR00673
Johnny Cash: The Hard Reign Of A Country-Music King AR15101
Johnny Clegg's War On Apartheid AR13690
Johnny Damas And Me RR12774
Johnny 'Guitar' Watson 1935-1996 AR15194
The Jon Spencer Blues Explosion RR12596
The Jon Spencer Blues Explosion Throw A Punky, Bluesy Party On 'Now I Got Worry' AR14350
Jon Stewart AR15311
Jon Stewart's Hot List AR15491
Jonathan Demme: The Rolling STone Interview AR13422
Joni Mitchell AR13529, AR15932
Joni Mitchell: Los Angeles CR00809
Josh Wink Lands Techno At A Major Label AR13151
Joshua Judges Ruth RR11743
Journeyman RR10803
Joy And Blues RR11793, RR11873
Joy In Mudville: Against All Odds, Woodstock '94 Gave Another Generation Three Days Of Peace, Muck And Understanding AR14644
Joyas de la Musica Cubana, Vol. 1 RR13182
The Joys Of Noise: Soundgarden Throw A High-Frequency Sludgefest AR13357
Jubilation RR11426
The Judds Collection 1983-1990 RR11576
Judgment! RR11402
Judgment Night RR13183
Juice RR13184
Juiced Up (song) RR11180
Julia Makes Trouble: The Rolling Stone Interviews AR15156
The Juliet Letters RR10662, RR10882
Jump Blues Classics RR13185
Jungle Boogie AR15176
Junior Brown: New York CR00665
Junior Brown: Warfield Theater CR00664
Junkie Town AR14507
Jurassic Spark: Laura Dern AR15933
Just Another Band From East L.A. RR11723
Just Can't Get Enough RR13186
Just Desserts AR15934
Just Desserts: Can Ben And Jerry Make A Company As Good As Their Ice Cream? AR15551
Just For A Day RR12537
Just For The Record RR12653
Just For You RR12908
Just Fred RR12436
Just Like A Devil RR12734
Just One Night RR10804
Just Say Moe: The Heartbeat Of The VU Makes A Solo Noise AR13040
Just Say 'Yes': Morphine Shoot To Low-Fi Stardom AR13281
Just Stompin' RR11167, RR12991
Just What I Needed RR10741
Just What It's Like (song) RR10978
Just Woke Up RR10590
Justice Denied AR14432

K

K RR11650
K. D. Lang AR12935
K. D. Lang: How Did A Lesbian, Feminist, Vegetarian Canadian Win A Grammy And The Hearts Of America? AR15700
Kaddish RR12755
Kalfou Danjere RR10637
Kamakiriad RR11110
Kansas RR11584
Karen Carpenter RR10736
Kat Bjelland Of Babes In Toyland AR14688
Katell Keineg AR14646
Keb' Mo' RR11587
Keep It Comin' RR12686
Keep On Pushing!: The Strange And Twisted Tale Of The United States Olympic Bobsled Team AR16130
Keep That Wallet Out AR13643
Keep The Faith RR10624
Keepers Of The Flame: Defying The Alternative-Rock Trend, Candlebox Break Out Of Seattle With Traditional Pop Metal AR13203
Keeping Time AR15356
Keeping Up With The Jones: A Colorful Romp From Zeppelin To The Buttholes AR13204
Keith Moon AR14248
Keith Richards AR14516
Keith Richards And The X-Pensive Winos: Town And Country CR00867, CR00943
Keith: Rock's Main Offender AR14764
Kelly Hogan AR13041
Kelly Willis RR12939
Kenn Kweder RR11653
Kenny Wayne Shepherd AR13810
Kick Out The Jams RR11828
Kickin' It Up RR11937
A Kid Makes 'News': Dave Foley Grows Up To Be A 'Newsradio' Star AR15935
The Kids Are Alright: Green Day AR13664
The Kids Are Alright: Offspring AR12936
Kids In The Dark AR13145
Kiko RR11724
Kill The Musicians RR12449
Killer Up! RR12799
Kimble (E.P.) RR11114
Kind Hearted Woman RR12493
Kind Of Blue: Does Songwriter Lou Barlow—The Heart And Soul Of Sebadoh, Sentridoh And The Folk Implosion—Care Too Much? AR12937
Kindness Of The World RR11397
The King & I AR13253
The King And I AR13254
King Crimson: New York CR00771
King For A Day: First Graceland Concert Planned For October AR15522
King For A Day, Fool For A Lifetime RR11112
King Of California RR10420
King Of Hearts RR12083
The King Of Prime-Time Comedy AR15372
The King Of Rain AR14869
The King Of Rock 'N' Roll: The Complete '50's Masters RR12217

King Of The Blues RR11611a
King Of The Delta Blues: The Music Of Charlie Patton RR12124
King Of The Goons AR13604
King Of The Honky-Tonk RR12172
King Of The Slide Guitar RR11506
King Tubby Meets The Rockers Uptown RR12095
Kingdom Come RR11220, RR11982, RR12109
Kings Of Comedy AR15360, AR16117
King's X RR11625
Kiss My Ass RR13187
Kiss: Tiger Stadium CR00772
Kissingsohard RR11019
Kitsch Me, Stupid: Seattle's Super Deluxe Pucker Up AR15839
Klassic Kitchener RR11720
KMFDM Make Industrial Music The Old-Fashion Way—They Thrash Their Hardware AR15840
Knee-Deep In The Hoopla, From Cub Scouts To Bee Girls, With Some Raw Deals & Rough Living In Between, Blind Melon Has Taken The Long, Hard Road To The Top AR14765
Kojak Variety RR10883
Koksofen RR11800
Kristen Pfaff : 1967-1994 AR15523
KRS-One AR15622, RR11648
Kula Shaker AR14253
Kurt Cobain 1967-1994 AR13423
Kurt Markus AR14575
Kyuss The Sky: Retrodelic Generator Parties Breed An Electric Genre AR15841

L

L.A. Confidential AR12964, AR12965, AR12966, AR15936, AR15937, AR15938, AR15939, AR15940, AR15941, AR15942, AR15943, AR15944, AR15945, AR15946
The L. A. Musical History Tour BR01083
L. A. Rappers Speak Out AR14481
Laid RR11503
Lamprey RR10551
Land O' Babes AR15312
Land Of The Dead: San Francisco Was Where It All Began AR13673
Last But Not Lost: Santana's New Label AR13781
Last Day On Earth RR10721, RR12014
The Last Nixon AR14618
Last Of The Independents RR12220, RR12221
The Last Rebel RR11757
Last Sessions RR12370
Last Splash RR10658, RR10659
The Last Stand AR14141
The Last Temptation RR10869
Last Train To Memphis BR01084
The Last Wave AR16049
A Lasting Impression: The Rolling Stone Interview With Curtis Mayfield AR14482
Lather RR13021
Latin Playboys RR11669
Laura Dern AR15157
Laurie Anderson AR15717
Law Of The Jungle RR13188
The Law Of Unintended Consequences: Mandatory Minimum Sentencing Puts First-Time Offenders In Jail For Life And Lets Drug Kingpins Bargain For Their Freedom AR15488
Lawsuit Over Lymon Song Settled AR13973
Lawyers, Punks And Money: SST Records Battle Of Writs And Wills Against Former Acts AR13974
Layla RR10986
Lead Me Not RR12912
Leader Of The Old School: Juggy Gayles Hyped Records The Old-Fashion Way—With Style AR13846
Leann Rimes Sees 'Blue' Skies AR14531
Leapin' Lizard: LollaPaloozers Aren't Likely To Forget The Jesus Lizard If Lead Singer David Yow Has Anything To Say About It AR13470
Learning To Flinch RR13033
Leather & Lace AR14450
Led Zep: The Boxed Life AR15947
Led Zeppelin AR13360
Left Of The Dial (song) RR12333
The Left Stuff: Consolidated Mix Politics With Humor AR15113
The Legacy AR15167
The Legend And The Legacy RR12125
Legends Of Country Music AR13847, AR15382
Lemon Fresh Joy AR15948
Lemonheads CR00741, CR00778
Lemonheads: New York City CR00777
Lemonheads: The Academy CR00779, CR00787, CR00882
Lemuria-Seascape RR10512
Lennon's Family Ties: Beatle's Accessories Hot Summer Sellers AR15386
Lenny Bruce Originals: Volume 1 RR10689
Lenny Bruce Originals: Volume 2 RR10690
[Lenny Kravitz] AR15949
Lenny Kravitz: Mystic, Mimic, Father, Lover, Which Is The Real Lenny The Kid? AR15524
Leonard Bernstein AR13340
Leonard Cohen: New York City CR00682
Les Claypool Of Primus AR14436
Leslie Spit Treeo: Canadian Psycho Folk AR14552
Let 'Em Roll RR12122
Let Go RR10669
Let It Flow: River Phoenix Plays It Cool On And Off The Screen AR13035, AR14831
Let Love In RR10485, RR10758
Let No One Deceive You: Songs Of Bertolt Brecht RR10456, RR12815
Let The Good Times Bowl AR12923
Let The Picture Paint Itself RR10920
Let Your Dim Light Shine RR12576, RR12577
Lethal Injection RR11464
Let's RR11146
Let's Book AR14832, AR15127
Let's Go Get Stoned RR10777
Let's Go Or Let's Not And Say We Did: Why You Can't trust The Best-Selling Harvard Travel Series AR16131
Let's Interactive AR13115
Let's Interactive: Breakthroughs In Digital Technology Promise To Bring A New Look To Your Television Set AR15731
A Letter From The Editor AR15793, AR15794, AR15795
Letter To Laredo RR11070
Letters To Cleo: New York City CR00781
The Levellers: A Foot-Stompin' News Service AR12996
Levelling The Land RR11686
Liberations RR10580
Libete RR10638
Lies My Teacher Told Me BR01085
Life RR12509, RR12539
Life After Death: The Rolling Stone Interview With Courtney Love AR13717
Life After Def: The Post-Rap, Post-Metal World Of Rick Rubin AR15950
Life After Garcia AR13913
Life After Guns N' Roses: With The Release Of His Album, Izzy Stradlin Finally Breaks His Silence AR13718
A Life Full Of Farewells RR10445
A Life In The Balance: Jackson Browne Gets Serious About Love AR15951
Life In The Indie Cities: From Bad Weather And Obstacles Comes Great Music—If You Know Where To Look AR13255, AR14833
Life Is Messy RR10921
Life Of Brian: Don Was Frames A Beach Boys Saga AR13205
Life On The Duplex Planet AR13836
A Life With Brian RR11152
Life's A Take RR11592, RR11918
Life's Too Short RR10912
The Lilys Blossom With Seductive '60s Sounds AR15032
Limbo RR12737
Limited Access: Behind-The-Scenes Ticket Maneuvering Leaves Concert Fans With Second-rate Seats AR13069
Linda Ronstadt AR14689
Lindsey Buckingham: The Wiltern Theater CR00667
The Lion King RR13189
Liquid Courage RR11697
Liquid Swords RR11228, RR11338
Lisa Palac's Hot List AR15019
Listen To The Band RR11930
A Little Ain't Enough RR12395
Little Earthquakes RR10425
A Little Holiday Gear AR13116
Little Love Letters RR10746
Little Mascara (song) RR12334
Little Richard AR15128
Little Rock, Arkansas AR14509
A Little Strange Music AR14386
Little Village RR11703
Liv In The Fast Lane: Actress Liv Tyler Wraps Her Inner Charm In Men's Outerwear AR13256, AR14834
Live RR12705
Live! RR12193
Live: Artist Of The Year AR13206
Live At CBGB's RR13190
Live At Leeds RR12917, RR12918
Live At Sin-e RR10695
Live At The BBC RR10528, RR11148
Live At The Continental Club RR12570
Live At The Fillmore RR10987
Live At The Hollywood Palladium, December 15, 1988 RR12346, RR12974
Live At The Isle Of Wight Festival 1970 RR12919
Live: Athens, Ga. CR00782
Live Au Zenith RR10602
Live From The Fall RR10615
Live, From Vietnam!: Bryan Adams Experiences Life After Wartime When He Plays Ho Chi Minh City AR14690
Live In Concert RR11517
Live In Japan With Eric Clapton And Band RR11365
Live In Seattle RR10851
Live Jam RR11501
Live Light RR12350
Live—May 11, 1968 RR11339
Live MCMXCIII RR12836
A Live One RR12167, RR12168
Live Shit: Binge And Purge RR11887
Live Shots RR11071
Live Stiffs: Full-Blown Concert Albums Play To Less Applause AR13070
Live—The Funkadelic Collection RR10821, RR11196, RR12111
Live Through This RR11421, RR11422
Live Through This: A Year On The Road With Nirvana AR12997

The Live Totem Pole EP RR11135
Live Wire RR11797, RR12318
Live Your Life Be Free RR10735
Livin' Proof RR11309
The Living End RR11458
Living In The Danger Zone RR12451
Living In The USA: Revenge Of The Doughnut Boys AR15335
Living In The USA: The Case Of Gary Fannon AR15336
Living Proof: The MGM Recordings 1963-1975 RR12930
Living With The Law RR12916
Liz Phair AR13530
Liz Phair: Last Train To Guyville AR14691
Liz Phair: Los Angeles CR00845
LL Cool J AR15764
LL77 RR11700
Llego La India RR11476
Lloyd Cole CR00683
Lo Rez Skyline AR13852
Load RR11888, RR11889, RR11890
Lock Stock & Double-Barrel (EP) RR10875
Loco Gringo's Lament RR11449
Logical Progression RR10696
Lois AR14553
LollaPalooza: Family Affair AR15842
Lollapalooza Jr.: Tomorrow's Stars Are On The Second Stage Today AR15525
Lollapalooza '92 AR14766
Lollapalooza '93 AR14767
London Bridge: Cornershop Curry Western Flavor AR15843
London Calling AR15418, AR15419, AR15420, AR15421, AR15422, AR15423, AR15424, AR15425, AR15426, AR15427, AR15428
London Confidential AR15429
The London Suede: New York CR00907
Lonely Just Like Me RR10404a
Long About That Time RR10980
The Long Black Veil RR10787
Long Fin Killie AR14597
The Long Hot Summer—Jamaican Ska 1963 RR10401, RR12086
Long Line RR12952
The Long Road Home AR13316, AR15342
The Long Road To Little Village: Four Distinguished Musicians Find A New Home AR15952
The Longest War AR14596
Longing In Theirs Hearts RR12285
The Look: In A New Book, Rolling Stone Celebrates 40 Years Of Rock Photography AR14520
Look No Further RR12404
Lookin' Down The Backtracks, 1963-1969 RR12752
Lookin' For A Love Again RR12955
Looking East RR10685
Looking For A Connection RR10810
Looking For The Next Revolution: The Rolling Stone Interview With Steve Jobs AR14011
Looking In The Shadows RR12284
Looks Like Team Spirit: On Their Way To Barcelona, Four Athletes Take A Break From Their Olympic Training To Try On American Clothes AR14801, AR15693
Loose RR12937
Loosening The Beltway: Everybody's A Pundit On 'Politically Incorrect' AR15953
Lord Of Nothing Pt. 1 (song) RR11728
Lord Of The Harvest RR13035
Los Angeles AR13363
Los Lobos CR00785
Lose Control RR12502
Losing The Right To Choose: Republicans In Congress Wage War On Abortion AR12953
Losing Their Religion: Rev. Horton Heat Lets The Spirits Move Him AR13531
The Lost Boy: The Life Of Kurt Cobain AR14692
The Lost Boys: With 'Sweet Oblivion,' Screaming Trees Finally Come Out Of The Woods AR12998
Lost In America: A Father, A Family And An Entire Community Struggle To Understand How One Of Their Sons Could Go So Wrong AR15330
Lost In America—Not!: Navigation Systems And Cellular Phones Will Help You Get There From Here AR15732
Lost In Space: Outlaw Engineers Are Struggling To Save NASA With A New Generation Of Secret Technology AR14004
Lost Masters RR12617
Lost Together RR10613
Lotion AR12999
Lou Reed: Beyond The Underground AR13719
Loud Lose And Savage RR10412, RR10461
Louie Louie BR01086
Louisiana Love Call RR11976
Lounge's Last Call AR13071
Love And Danger RR11072
Love And Luck RR12655
Love Battery: Modifying The Northwest Sound AR13000
The Love Boat AR14586
Love Deluxe RR12420, RR12421
Love Featuring Arthur Lee: New York CR00776, CR00786
Love Is All Around (song) RR11532
Love It To Death: Trent Reznor Of Nine Inch Nails Preaches the Dark Gospel Of Sex, Pain And Rock & Roll AR13925
Love Janis: Janis Joplin's Rise To Stardom Is Chronicled In These Letters Written To Her Family In Texas AR14324, AR14325
Love Power Peace: Live At The Olympia, Paris, 1971 RR10675
Love, Pussycats And Carwrecks RR11200
Love Songs For The Hearing Impaired RR10493
Love Spit Love RR11740
Love Story RR11738
Loveless RR11985
Low Profile RR11168
Low-Fi Romantics: Sebadoh Flirt With The Mainstream AR13483
Loyola (song) RR10998
Lucinda Williams: La Zona Rosa CR00939
Luck Of The Draw RR12286
Lucky Thirteen RR12994
Lucky Town RR12614, RR12615
Lucy RR10729
Luka Bloom, David Byrne, Rosanne Cash, Lou Reed: The Bottom Line CR00654, CR00671, CR00674, CR00863
Luka Bloom Doesn't Want To Be Just Another Boring Folkie: Songs From The Heart AR13001
Luka Bloom: The Troubadour CR00653
Luna CR00789
Lunatic Behavior: Soul Asylum Fight The Follow-Up-Album Blues AR15954
Luscious Jackson: Record In New Orleans AR15466
Luscious Jackson Stray From Home On 'Fever In Fever Out' AR13471
Luscious Life AR15718
Lush Life BR01087, RR11390
Lynyrd Skynyrd RR11758
Lyte As A Rock RR11761

M

M. Scott Peck At The End Of The Road AR13282
M Speak For Newbies AR13117
Machine Dreams: Rage Take On The Rights Of Native Americans AR13397
Machito And His Afro-Cubans Cubop City RR11766
Mack Daddy RR12519, RR12520, RR12521
Made In England RR11544
Made In Heaven RR12253
Madonna AR13635
Madonna: London CR00790
Madonna To Sign $60 Million Deal [and other news] AR13975
Magia Antillana RR11942
Magic And Loss RR12315, RR12316
Magic And Loss: Lida Husik Meshes Indie With Ambient AR13532
Magic Dirt RR11776
Magic Sam 1957-1966: West Side Guitar RR11777
Magic Touch RR11778
Magnapop: Georgia's Finest? AR14177
Magnetic Field AR16072
Main Offender RR12347
Majek Faskek: A Messenger Of World Music AR15955
Majurugenta RR11237
Make Way For The Motherlode RR12984
Making Art From Chaos: Jimmy Webb Is Writing His New Songs In The Key Of Life AR12972
Making Education Work AR14533
Making History RR11549
Making History? A Marketing Blitz of Epic Proportions AR15844
Making Money The Old-Fashion Way: Despite Promises Of A High-Tech Revolution, College-Educated Americans Earn It Working On The Line AR15548
The Making Of The Soviet Bomb AR15182
Making The Scene: A Filmmaker's Diary AR13361
Malignant Giant AR14428
Mall Rap: The Million Man March Draws A Crew Of Hip-Hop Artists To Washington, D.C. AR15494
Mall Rats: Beleaguered Chain Record Stores Are Sinking Fast AR13072
Mama Blew A Hoody (song) RR11181
Mama Said Knock You Out RR11655
Mama's Hungry Eyes RR13191
The Mambo Kings RR13192
Mamouna RR11129
A Man And A Half RR12169
A Man And His Music, Vol. II—Computer Style RR11620
Man Enough To Be A Woman BR01088
Man, Monkeys And Disease AR13368
Man Of The Year: David Letterman AR15373
Man Or Mouth?: The Rolling Stone Interview With Howard Stern AR14567
The Man Who Would Be King Of Country: Billy Ray Cyrus Scores With 'Some Gave All' AR15571
Man With A Plan AR13002
Mandatory Minimums: Eight More Victims AR15080
The Mandolin Man RR11102
Manna-Mirage RR11975
Mannequins With A Twist AR13297
The Manson Family: An Opera RR13193
Mantra Mode RR11462
Marcus Garvey RR10700
Maria RR12499
Marian Wright Edelman: On The Front Lines Of The Battle To Save America's Children

AR12982
Marilyn Manson: Convention Hall CR00791
Marion Williams: 1927-1994 AR15187
Mario's Big Brother: From 'Donkey Kong' To New Super Nintendo, Sigeru Miyamoto Has Shaped A Generation AR15391
Marisela Norte AR13848
Mark E. Smith's Wrath & Roll: With Their 17th LP, The Fall Are Back In Your Face AR13207
Mark Morris Says He's Not Just A Hard-Drinking, Chain-Smoking, Long-Haired Beats From Modern-Dance Hell AR14222
Mark Seliger AR15383
Mark's Keyboard Repair RR11926
Married To Metal: The Rolling Stone Interview With Metallica's Lars Ulrich AR13720
Mars Audiac Quintet RR12634
Martha Wash RR12870
Martin And Me RR11490
Martin Lawrence AR14587, AR15446
Martinis And Bikinis RR12163, RR12164
Marty Brown: More Than A Country Throwback AR14360
Marvin Gaye The Master 1961-84 RR11218
Marvin The Album RR11177
Marxman AR13811
Mary Queen Of Scots RR11103
Mary Wells: 1943-1992 AR14483
Mary's Idea RR11630, RR12935
Mas! A Caribbean Christmas Party RR13194
Mas Canciones RR12388
Masada RR13038
Mass. Ave. RR13195
Massive Attack: Infectious Dance Pop AR15956
Massive Attack: New York CR00793
Massive Hits Vol. 1 RR12021
Master Class AR13460
Master Of The Delta Blues: The Friends Of Charlie Patton RR13196
Master Of War: Novelist Tom Clancy Keeps Making New Enemies AR13257
Mastering Madonna AR15608
Masterpieces RR11875
Masters Of The Game: Over The Mountain And Through The Woods With Three Young Designers Who Show The Brand Names How To Play AR13130, AR14617
Matters Of The Heart RR10763
Matthew McConaughey AR15374
Matthew Rolston AR15223
Matthew Sweet: Detroit CR00912
Maureen Cox Starkey Tigrett: 1946-1994 AR15957
Mavericks RR11428, RR12620
The Mavericks Beach Country AR15313
The Mavericks: New York City CR00795
Maxinquaye RR12766, RR12767
Maxwell AR15765
Maxwell's Urban Hang Suite RR11815
May I Sing With Me RR12982
MC Lyte AR15447
MC5's Rob Tyner Dies AR14604
Me Against The World RR12475
Me Phi Me: Up From The Ashes Of Flint AR13895
Mean & Sober: Ego And Innuendo Run Amok As The Music Industry Feuds Over Drug Treatment AR13283
Mean Old World RR13197
Mean Streaks: Amped, Angry And In Your Face, Graffiti Refuses To Die AR14149
Meantime RR11386
Meat Loaf: New York City CR00798
Meat Loaf: The Man Who Saw Paradise By The Dashboard Lights Is Back With 'Bat Out Of Hell II' AR14693
Meat Puppets AR15526
Mecca And The Soul Brother RR12368, RR12558
The Media's Myth Of The Bloody Campaign AR14333
The Media's War On Kids: From The Beatles To Beavis And Butt-head AR14334
Medium Rare RR13198
Medusa RR11685
Meet The Beavis!: The Last Word From America's Phenomenal Pop Combo AR16107
A Meeting By The River RR10553, RR10864
Megadeth: New York CR00799
Mekons: New York City CR00800
Mel RR11057
Melissa Etheridge AR13450
Melissa Etheridge: In Through The Out Door AR13258
Melissa Etheridge On Janis Joplin AR13608
Melissa Etheridge: Target Center CR00714
Mellon Collie And The Infinite Sadness RR12544, RR12545
Mellow Gold RR10532, RR10533
Melodyland RR12841
'Melrose Place' Is A Really Good Show AR15958
Melting In The Dark RR12971
Melvin Franklin: 1942-1995 AR15845
Members Only: Record Clubs Feel Retailers' And Artists' Heat AR13073
Memnoch The Devil AR15184
Memo From The National Affairs Desk AR15598
Memo To The Academy On Its 64th Birthday: Retire Or Reform AR15652
Memoirs RR10594, RR11343, RR11732
Memorial Tribute To Eazy-E AR15467
Memory Of A Gonzo Christmas Past AR14523
The Memory Of Trees RR11085
Memphis Blues Caravan, Vol. I RR13199
Memphis Blues Caravan, Vol. II RR13200
Memphis Country Blues, Vol. I RR13201
Memphis Town RR13202
Menace To Society AR13401
Menace II Society RR13203
Mercury RR10422
Mercury Falling RR12640
Mercury Rev: Irving Plaza CR00803
Mercury Rev Rising: They Were Too Weird Even For Lollapalooza AR14387
Me'shell NdegeOcello AR14609, AR15623
Me'shell NdegeOcello: New York City CR00823
Message For The Mess Age RR12056
Message In A Bottle: Shane MacGowan Serves It Straight Up AR12938
Message In A Box RR12194
Metal Machine Music AR14537
Metal Metheny Music AR14388
Metallica CR00805, RR11891
Metallica: Clarkston, Mich. CR00804
Metallica: Once The Scourge Of The Mainstream, The Titans Of Thrash Are On Top Of The Charts AR13721
The Method Of His Madness AR14240
Mexican R'N' B RR13204
Mi Mexico RR11204
Mi Tierra RR11096
MIA RR11233
Miami AR14451
Michael Jackson AR14223, CR00754
Michael Jackson Plans Summer Tour [and other news] AR13976
Michael Jackson: The Making Of 'The King Of Pop' AR13977
Michael Nesmith CR00825
Michael O'Donoghue AR12985
Michael Richards's Hot List AR13896, AR15314
[Michael Stipe] AR13424
Michael Stipe AR13722
Michael Stipe: The Rolling Stone Interview AR13723
Michael Sues Sony: Fights To Break Contract With Record Company AR13978
Michael Watford RR12880
Mick Jagger AR13341
Mick Ronson: 1946-1993 AR14694
Mick: Third Time A Charm? AR15959
Mickey Hart & Robert Hunter AR13837
Middle-Class Funk AR14096
Midnight Marauders RR12765
Midnight Mover RR12956
Midseason Pre-Mortem AR15960
Mighty Joe Moon RR11287, RR11288
Mike Clarke 1944-1993 AR14389
Mike Love Sues Brian Wilson: Claims He Co-Wrote Several Beach Boys Classics AR15961
Mike Scott's Spiritual Renewal: The Leader Of The Waterboys Gets Back To Basics On 'Dream Harder' AR13849
Milagro RR12429
Miles Smiles RR10963
The Milestone Years RR11391
Millie Checks The Pantry AR15062
Millie Comes Upon A Sticky Situation AR15063
Millie Sees Something Scary AR15064
Millie Visits The Senate AR15065
The Millions: A Gimmick-Free Sound AR15408
Millions Now Living Will Never Die RR12753
Mind Blowin RR12821
Mining For Gold: Jewel Takes The Long, Slow Road To Success AR13074
Ministry: The Paramount CR00808
Minor Threat AR13047
Minute Waltz (song) RR10630
Miracle RR12488
Miracle Cure: In The Age Of Grunge, The Spin Doctors Score With A Joyful Noise AR13897
Miracle Of Science RR10913
Mirror Ball RR12995, RR12996
Mirror Blue RR12731
The Missing Years RR12238
Mississippi Delta Blues RR13205
Mississippi Lad RR11059, RR12856
Mistaken Identity RR12319
Misty Mountain Hop: Amateurs And Pros Jump Around In Aspen Highlands AR14535, AR14835
Misty Mountain Memories: Robert Plant Embraces His Past On 'Fate Of Nations' AR14768
Mitakuye Oyasin Oyasin RR12016
The Mitch Is Back: Toweling Off For 'Baywatch Nights' AR15962
MJQ40 RR11923
Mo' Better Multimedia AR13118
Mo' Money RR13206
Mo' Wax Captures The Trip-Hop Vibe AR14563
Mobb Deep Deliver 'Hell On Earth' To The Faithful AR13627
[Moby] AR15527
Moby: The Great White Wail AR12939
Mod Jobs: Strange And Twisted Paths To Contentment And Prosperity AR16133
Mod Squad: With 'I Should Coco' The U.K. Trio Supergrass Bring Their Freshly

Manicured Pop To America AR14836, AR15430
The Modern World RR13207
Moe. AR13838
Molten Gold RR11176
Mondo Bizarro RR12290
Money And Cigarettes RR10805
The Money Hunt: A Shrinking Pie Changes D.C. Budget Games AR14097
Money, It's A Gas: Pink Floyd Eclipse Stones' Ticket-Sales Record AR15528
The Monkees RR11931
Monkees Redux?: Fox's New Show 'The Heights' Zeroes In On A Made-For-Television Blue-Collar Rock Band AR15963
Monkey Hips And Rice RR11141
Monkjack RR10688
Mono RR11201
Monorails And Satellites RR12265, RR12266
Monster BR01089, RR12323, RR12324
Monster Madness AR13425
Monster Magnetism AR13298
Monster On The Loose: R.E.M. Open Their First Tour In Five Years, In Australia AR13724
Monte Warden RR12865
The Monterey International Pop Festival RR13208
Monterey Pop, Airplane Sets Due AR14275
Mood Elevator RR11698, RR11711
The Moog Cookbook RR13209, RR13210
Moon Struck: Grant Lee Buffalo Roam The Margins Of American Gothic On Might Joe Moon AR15529
Moonlight Becomes You RR12011
More Blues For Music Biz: Layoffs And Cutbacks Continue Into The New Year AR14032
More Live At The Knitting Factory RR11221
More Of RR11932
More Songs Of Love And Murder RR10517
More Stunts, More Overpaid Stars, More Demi Moore Naked And More To The Point: Is Anything Any Good? AR15653
More Washington Show Talk: In Today's Episode, TV Ruins Everything AR16035
Morphine: Boston CR00811
Morphine: The Band's Low-Rock Music Is Nearly As Addictive As Its Pharmaceutical Namesake AR14769
Morrissey: Atlantic Civic Center CR00814
Moscow's Metal Melee: An Eyewitness Report From The Monsters Of Rock Tour AR15690
Mosh Unit: The Muffs' Two-Minute Bursts Of melodic Noise Are Clamorous Punk Postcards From The Edge AR12967, AR14837
Moss Elixir RR11406
Mossy Liquor RR11407
The Most Dangerous Man In America AR15232
The Most From Beny More RR11943
The Mother Of All Flagpole Christmas Albums RR13211
Mothers Of Invention: Women In Rock Talk About Scents, Sensibility And Sexism AR15701
Motley Crue RR11967
Motor Voter: Goin' Mobile AR14041
Motown's Baby Boyz: Philadelphia's Boyz II Men Become The Label's Hottest Act In Years AR14484
Movie Directors Who Toy With Tape AR14291
Movie Extras AR15654
Mr. A. T. RR12704
Mr. Bad Example RR13034
Mr. Bill's Neighborhood AR15599
Mr. Bungle RR11971
Mr. Excitement! RR12946
Mr. Happy Go Lucky RR11868
Mr. Lucky RR11430
Mr. Machinery Operator RR11136
Mr. Microsoftee: Paul Allen, Shy Billionaire, Tries To Rock The I-Way AR13131
Mr. Moonlight RR11166
Mr. Natural AR14695
Mr. Smith RR11656
MTV AR15066
MTV Awards Lure The Stars AR13075
MTV Turns Ten AR14671
MTV Unplugged RR10546, RR11048, RR11049, RR12715
MTV Unplugged (EP) RR13212
MTV Unplugged In New York RR12047, RR12048
Muddy Water Blues RR12372
Mudhoney: San Francisco CR00818
Mudhoney: The First Great Seattle Band Of The '80s Has The Last Laugh In The '90s AR13398
Muevelo Con El General RR11064
Multimedia AR14210, AR14390
Multimedia: The Season's Must-Have CD-ROMs AR14661
The Munich Philharmonic Orchestra Plays Abba Classic RR11977
Murder Ballads RR10486, RR10759
Murder Mystery AR15085
Murder Was The Case RR13213
Muscle & Melody AR14696
Muscle Machines AR16073
Muse Sick N Hour Mess Age RR12246, RR12247
Music Awards: 1995 AR14734
Music Biz Blues AR14735
Music Biz Rebounds In '93: Sales Increases Give Industry Hope AR15530
Music Box RR10734
Music By Modem: On-Line Services Provide A High-Tech Option To Music Distribution AR13373
Music For Egon Schiele RR12277
Music For The Jilted Generation RR12240
Music For The Native Americans RR12307, RR12308, RR12362, RR12363
Music For Your Mother RR11197
Music For Your Mother: Lords Of The Underground Bring Family Values To Hardcore Rap AR13584
Music In Fifths RR11261
Music In Similar Motion RR11262
The Music Never Stopped RR13214
The Music Never Stops: The Rolling Stone Interview With Jerry Garcia AR13426
The Music Of Bill Monroe: From 1936 To 1994 RR11934
The Music Of Disney: A Legacy In Song RR13215
The Music Of Raymond Scott: Reckless Nights And Turkish Twilights RR12442
Music To Eat RR11352, RR11353
Music Versus Muscle AR14770
Music Videos AR13615
Music With Changing Parts RR11263
Musical Chairs? Executive-Shuffle Rumors Rage On AR15964
Musical Depreciation Revue RR11567
Mutiny RR12748
Muzak Attack AR13840
My Bloody Valentine; Dinosaur Jr. CR00702, CR00819
My Brother The Cow RR11973
My Brother The Wind Volume II RR12267
My Clinch Mountain Home RR10744
My Insatiable (single) RR12663
My Life RR10983
My Life With The Thrill Kill Kult: Straight Out Of The Seventies AR13371
My So-Called Double Life: Kristin Hersh Of Throwing Muses Finds The Common Ground Between Motherhood And Rock & Roll AR15531
My Way Or The Highway: Despite Accusations That He's Stuck In The Past, Lenny Kravitz Is Now In Vogue AR14771
My World RR10769
Myth And Reality RR11788

N

Naked Lunch Box AR14055
The Naked Transcript AR13427
Nanci Griffith Comes Home: The Singer-Songwriter Settles Down After Years Of Late Nights And Hotels AR16054
The Nasty Truth: Field-Tested techniques To Get The Love You Deserve AR15745
Nathan Daniel: 1912-1994 AR15159
A Nation Of Nomads: As The Presidential Campaign Begins, The Republican Wanna-Be's Encounter An American Electorate Wandering Between Hope And Rage AR13602
A National Health Care RR12845
Native American Son: Robbie Robertson Finds A Common Bond Between His Heritage And His Music AR14231
Native Tongue RR12191
Native Tongues: New Poets With A Rock & Roll Attitude AR14610
Natural Born Killers RR13216
Natural Ingredients RR11751
A Natural Woman RR11611d
Natural Wonder RR12959
Nature Of A Sista' RR12255, RR12256
Naughty As They Wanna Be: The Hood Comes First When Naughty By Nature Hits The Mike AR14485
Naughty By Nature RR11993a
Naughty By Nature: Detroit CR00821
Naughty By Nature's Surprise Success AR13428
Naughty Little Doggie RR12200
Near Life Experience RR10856
The Nearest Faraway Place BR01090
Nearly God RR12768
Ned's Atomic Dustbin: A Band With A Nonattitude AR14867
Negativland And SST Settle AR13979
The Negro Inside Me RR10393
Neil Diamond AR13533
Neil Jordan AR15375
Neil Tennant Of The Pet Shop Boys AR15572
Neil Young AR14199, CR00947
Neil Young: Going To Extremes AR13725
Neil Young—Pearl Jam: Stockholm, Sweden CR00840, CR00945
Neil Young: Virginia Beach Amphitheater CR00948
Nemesisters RR10476
Nerve Net RR11082
The Nerve Of Her AR13787
Net Worst" The 'New' Networks Go Where The Boys Already Are AR14588
Never Been Rocked Enough RR11836
Never Enough RR11099
Never Let Me Go RR12819
Nevermind RR12049
New Adventures In Hi-Fi RR12325, RR12326
New Bands Strike Gold With Majors AR13003
New Beginning RR10764

[New Book] AR14789
New Deal Redux Or Great Society II? AR14098
New Faces AR14790, AR14791, AR14792, AR14793, AR14794
New Faces: A Guide To This Summer's Coolest Music—And The Artists Making It AR15204
New Facts On Porcaro Death AR15965
New Film Or No Film? Cameras In The Digital Age Require Your To Choose A Format AR13119
A New 'Girlfriend' For Matthew Sweet: Hard-Edged Album Documents Romantic Turmoil AR13004
New Jack And Jill AR14232, AR15384
New Jack City RR13217
New Jersey Drive, Vol I RR13218
New Jersey Drive, Vol. II RR13219
New Kids Top Money List AR15168
New Labels Face Tough Times AR13980
New Location RR11718
New Miserable Experience RR11252
New Moon Daughter RR12945
New Music From Mexico AR14654
New Ragged Glories AR13616
The New Road Warriors: For The Members Of Blues Traveler, Life Is One Big, Happy Tour AR13812
The New Skitcoms: Sketches Of Pain AR14508
A New Wave: Rasin Music Catches Fire At Haitian Fest AR14623
New World Order RR11819
A New World Party: Peter Gabriel brings WOMAD To U.S. AR14207
New York City AR15719
New York Eye And Ear Control RR13220
New York Stories RR12028
Newport, Rhode Island AR14798
Newspaper (song) RR12778
Newt Vs. The '60s: The Values Of The Counterculture Top Gingrich's Hit List AR12954
The Next Big Thing AR13726
The Next Dream RR10468
The Next Hundred Years RR11377
The Next Wave: The Fusion Of Jazz And Hip-Hop Is Bringing A New Groove To The Dance Floor AR13585
Next Wave: The Last Word On All Things Computer AR15562
Next Wave: The Last Word On All Things Digital AR15563
Nice Guys Finish First: Live Make The Leap From Small Town To Big Time AR14178
Nicholas Schaffner AR14800
Nick Cave AR13534
Nicky Hopkins: 1944-1994 AR14697
A Night In San Francisco RR11953
Night Nurse RR11487
Night Song RR11125
Night Train RR11962
Nine Inch Nails—David Bowie: Camden, N.J. CR00658, CR00826
Nine Inch Nails: Irving Plaza CR00827
Nine Objects Of Desire RR12825
9: Take On Me AR13535
19: Bastards Of Young AR14698
19 Naughty III RR11994, RR11995
1994 Music Awards AR13727
1991 CMJ Music Marathon AR13005
The 1996 Presidential Yearbook: What Were They Then? AR14804
1993: The Year In Movies AR15655
1976-81 RR12566
1960's - 1990's AR15067
1926 Miles 1991: The Man Who Changed Music AR15022
98: Silent All These Years AR14391
95: Janie's Got A Gun AR14699
94: Beethoven AR14772
'94 Gleason Awards AR14805
99: One AR14292
99.9 F RR12826
91: Freedom 90 AR14392
97: Groove Is In The Heart AR14250
96: Human Behaviour AR14422
90: The Perfect Kiss AR14393
93: Orange Crush AR14394
92: Back On The Chain Gang AR13813
Nipped In The Bid: High Hopes Dampen Rock Auction AR14179
Nirvana: After Giving Birth To The Surprise Hit Of The Year, The Guys From Seattle Fight The Demons Of Fame AR14700
Nirvana: Cow Palace CR00829
Nirvana: Inside The Heart And Mind Of Kurt Cobain AR13006
Nirvana: Noise For '93 AR13007
Nirvana Projects On Hold AR15532
Nirvana To 'Newsweek': Drop Dead AR14033
Nirvana Tops Album Charts: 'Nevermind' Bumps 'Dangerous' Out Of Number One Position AR14773
Nixon's Record AR14099
No Alternative RR13221
No Big Surprise RR11275
No Code RR12132, RR12133
No Cure For Cancer RR11675
No Deeper Blue RR12816
No Doubt CR00830
No Fear Of Frying: The Hard Rock Cafe Celebrates Twenty Years Of Rock And Rolls AR13898
No Goats, No Glory RR11266
No Hard Times RR12371
No Heat Wave For Summer Tours AR13981
No Joke! RR11853
No Lunch RR10945
No Mercy: Leonard Cohen's Tales from The Dark Side AR13429
No More Mister Nice Girl RR11097
No More Years: Why George Must Go AR14100
No Need To Argue RR10895
No. 1 Record RR10558
No Pain, No Gain: The Rolling Stone Interview With Henry Rollins AR13728
No Peace In The Valley AR14208
No Prima Donna RR13222
No Protection RR11768, RR11802
No Quarter RR12097, RR12098, RR12186, RR12187
No Reservations RR10444
No Tag Backs [excerpt] PR00867
No Talking Just Head RR11380
No Time To Kill RR10567a
No Vision Whatsoever: Why We Are All Strangers In The Everglades AR13156
No Walls RR12051
No Way Out (song) RR10946
Noam Chomsky: Anarchy In The U.S.A. AR16108
Nocturnal RR11387
The Noise On The Bus: MTV News & Rock The Vote Put Youth Issues On The '96 Campaign Agenda AR14459
None-A-Day: Is The FDA Out To Take Your Vitamins? AR16036
Non-Fiction RR10576
Nonsuch RR12975
Nonviolence In America BR01091
Nora Ephron: On The Front Lines Of The Sexual Battlefield With The Writer And Director Of 'Sleepless In Seattle' AR13689
Nordeste Brasil RR13223, RR13224
Normal Weirdness In Seattle AR14838, AR15367
The Norman Whitfield Sessions RR11219
Not A Pretty Girl RR11002
Not Fade Away: Everclear Triumph Over Demons Of The Past AR15846
Not For Kids Only RR11215, RR11304
Not Guided By Voices: The return of Instrumental Rock AR15748
Not In Kansas Anymore RR10513
Not In My Airforce RR12195
Not Just Blowing Smoke: Cypress Hill Light Up On 'Black Sunday' AR13586
Not Out Of The Woods Yet: Don Henley Responds To Developer's Accusations AR15966
Nothing But A G Thang: Warren G Hits With "Regulate" AR13926
Nothing Good Comes Easy RR10826
Notorious RR11533
Nova Mob RR12054
Now Ain't The Time For Your Tears RR11508
Now Ear This: Noses Are Fine, And Navels Are Cool, But This Is Still The Classic Rock & Roll Pierce AR15387
Now I Got Worry RR10611, RR12597
Now I'm A Cowboy RR10471
Now Is The Hour RR11344
Now That I've Found You RR11639
Nowhere To Run AR14246
The NRA Sees Red AR16122
NRA's Last Hurrah? AR13480
NRBQ: New York City CR00831
N'ssi N'ssi RR11603
Nueva Ola Portoricensis BR01092
Nuisance RR11878
Number 10 RR10720
Nursery Boys Go Ahead RR10382
Nusrat Fateh Ali Khan: Radio City Music Hall CR00715

O

O Canto Da Cidada RR11884
Oasis AR14180
Oasis Cancel Last Third Of U.S. Tour After Rocky Start AR15456
Oasis: Hoboken, N.J. CR00832
Oasis: The Trouble Boys AR13208
Obituaries AR14808, AR14809, AR14810
Obscenity Bill Passed In Washington [and other news] AR13982
Ocean Beach RR12302
Octopus RR11452
Odelay RR10534, RR10535
Odyssey RR12795
Oedipus Schmoedipus RR10394
Of Lunch And War: There Was Suppose To Be A Revolution In Mexico, But The Mexicans Got In The Way AR15004
Off The Bandwagon: Teenage Fanclub Battle The Ghost Of Albums Past AR14233
Off The Charts BR01093
Off The Ground RR11831
Off The Hook RR11780
Off The Street And Onto Center Stage: Rock Steady Crew And Jossie Harris Turn Break Dancing Into An Art AR13577, AR13814
The Offspring: New York CR00833
Oh, What A Night AR13076
Oi! Did They Have Troubles AR13579
The Oil Man RR11547
Old Punks In Peril: No Green Day For '70s And '80s Pioneers AR15578
Old Testaments And New Revelations

RR11179
Old Times, New Times RR11150
Older RR11894
Old-School Cool AR15315
The Olympia Spirit: The Ticket Is Love Rock And Minimalism At Yoyo A Go Go AR14611
Olympian RR11225
Omettology RR12153
On A High Horse: Shudder To Think Shatter Convention With 'Pony Express' AR13008
On A Role: What The Jobs Of The 21st Century Will Be—And How To Prepare For Them Now AR14045
On Every Street RR11013
On Foot In The Honky Tonk RR11512
On The Blank Generation RR11702
On The Couch With Smashing Pumpkins: The Final Analysis AR13150
On The Cover Of Rolling Stone AR15388
On The Edge AR13729, AR13730, AR13731
On The Mouth RR12676
On The Range, Political Forces Still Beat Market Forces AR16037
On The Road AR14870, AR14871, AR14872, RR12113
On The Road...Again: A Troupe Of New Bands Is Taking Its Old-Time Rock & Roll Across America AR13899
On The Row AR15224
On The Way Down From The Moon Palace RR11232
On Track RR13040
Once Death-Defying Clowns, The Red Hot Chili Peppers Grow Up To Be Sensitive White Males AR13665
Once I Loved RR11441
Once In A While RR10817
Once More With Feeling RR11151
The One RR11545
One RR11850
1-800 New Funk RR13225
One Eye On The Future, One Eye On The Past RR12394
One Foot In The Grave RR10536
One Hot Minute AR13137, AR13536, AR14512, AR14839, AR15746, AR15967, AR16057, RR12301
One Hot Mother Of A Pepper: The Red Hot Chili Peppers Finally Get A New Guitarist And Gear Up To Make Their Next LP AR15968
100 Classic Album Covers AR14873
100 Classic Album Covers: A Broken Frame AR14874
100 Classic Album Covers: Abraxas AR14875
100 Classic Album Covers: Aladdin Sane AR14876
100 Classic Album Covers: America Beauty AR14877
100 Classic Album Covers: Aoxomoxoa AR14878
100 Classic Album Covers: Arc Of A Diver AR14879
100 Classic Album Covers: Atom Heart Mother AR14880
100 Classic Album Covers: Bitches Brew AR14881
100 Classic Album Covers: Blind Faith AR14882
100 Classic Album Covers: Born To Run AR14883
100 Classic Album Covers: Brain Salad Surgery AR14884
100 Classic Album Covers: Breakfast In America AR14885
100 Classic Album Covers: Bringing It All Back Home AR14886
100 Classic Album Covers: Candy-O AR14887
100 Classic Album Covers: Catch A Fire AR14888
100 Classic Album Covers: Cats Under The Stars AR14889
100 Classic Album Covers: Cheap Thrills AR14890
100 Classic Album Covers: Cosmic Slop AR14891
100 Classic Album Covers: Country Life AR14892
100 Classic Album Covers: Dark Side Of The Moon AR14893
100 Classic Album Covers: Daydream Nation AR14894
100 Classic Album Covers: Diamond Dogs AR14895
100 Classic Album Covers: Diesel And Dust AR14896
100 Classic Album Covers: Disraeli Gears AR14897
100 Classic Album Covers: Doc At The Radar Station AR14898
100 Classic Album Covers: Document AR14899
100 Classic Album Covers: Eat A Peach AR14900
100 Classic Album Covers: Electric Ladyland AR14901
100 Classic Album Covers: Elvis Presley AR14902
100 Classic Album Covers: Exile On Main Street AR14903
100 Classic Album Covers: Fear Of Music AR14904
100 Classic Album Covers: 50,000,000 Elvis Fans Can't Be Wrong AR14905
100 Classic Album Covers: Franks Wild Years AR14906
100 Classic Album Covers: Fresh Fruit For Rotting Vegetables AR14907
100 Classic Album Covers: Greetings From Asbury Park, N.J. AR14908
100 Classic Album Covers: Hardcore Jollies AR14909
100 Classic Album Covers: Hejira AR14910
100 Classic Album Covers: Honey AR14911
100 Classic Album Covers: Horses AR14912
100 Classic Album Covers: Hot Buttered Soul AR14913
100 Classic Album Covers: Hotel California AR14914
100 Classic Album Covers: House Of The Holy AR14915
100 Classic Album Covers: In The Court Of The Crimson King AR14916
100 Classic Album Covers: Into The Purple Valley AR14917
100 Classic Album Covers: It's A Beautiful Day AR14918
100 Classic Album Covers: Journey Through The Secret Life Of Plants AR14919
100 Classic Album Covers: Koo Koo AR14920
100 Classic Album Covers: Led Zeppelin AR14921
100 Classic Album Covers: Licensed To Ill AR14922
100 Classic Album Covers: Live Peace In Toronto AR14923
100 Classic Album Covers: London Calling AR14924
100 Classic Album Covers: Look Sharp AR14925
100 Classic Album Covers: Los Angeles AR14926
100 Classic Album Covers: Metal Box AR14927
100 Classic Album Covers: Middle Man AR14928
100 Classic Album Covers: Never A Dull Moment AR14929
100 Classic Album Covers: Never Mind The Bollocks Here's The Sex Pistols AR14930
100 Classic Album Covers: 1984 AR14931
100 Classic Album Covers: Nothing's Shocking AR14932
100 Classic Album Covers: Ogdens' Nut Gone Flakes AR14933
100 Classic Album Covers: One Step Beyond AR14934
100 Classic Album Covers: Ooh La La AR14935
100 Classic Album Covers: Peter Gabriel AR14936
100 Classic Album Covers: Physical Graffiti AR14937
100 Classic Album Covers: Playing Possum AR14938
100 Classic Album Covers: Power, Corruption And Lies AR14939
100 Classic Album Covers: Relayer AR14940
100 Classic Album Covers: Rumours AR14941
100 Classic Album Covers: Sailin' Shoes AR14942
100 Classic Album Covers: See Jungle! See Jungle! Go Join Your Gang Yeah!... AR14943
100 Classic Album Covers: Self Portrait AR14944
100 Classic Album Covers: Sgt. Pepper's Lonely Hearts Club Band AR14945
100 Classic Album Covers: Sign O' The Times AR14946
100 Classic Album Covers: Slave To The Rhythm AR14947
100 Classic Album Covers: Some Girls AR14948
100 Classic Album Covers: Sticky Fingers AR14949
100 Classic Album Covers: Strange Days AR14950
100 Classic Album Covers: The Beatles AR14951
100 Classic Album Covers: The Idiot AR14952
100 Classic Album Covers: The Joker AR14953
100 Classic Album Covers: The Joshua Tree AR14954
100 Classic Album Covers: The Low Spark Of High Heeled Boys AR14955
100 Classic Album Covers: The Parkerilla AR14956
100 Classic Album Covers: The Ramones AR14957
100 Classic Album Covers: The Slider AR14958
100 Classic Album Covers: The Smiths AR14959
100 Classic Album Covers: There's A Riot Goin' On AR14960
100 Classic Album Covers: Tommy AR14962
100 Classic Album Covers: True Blue AR14963
100 Classic Album Covers: Trust AR14964
100 Classic Album Covers: Turn Back AR14965
100 Classic Album Covers: Tutu AR14966
100 Classic Album Covers: Velvet Underground And Nico AR14967
100 Classic Album Covers: War AR14968

100 Classic Album Covers: Weasels Ripped My Flesh AR14969
100 Classic Album Covers: Welcome To My Nightmare AR14970
100 Classic Album Covers: We're Only In It For The Money AR14971
100 Classic Album Covers: Who's Next AR14972
100 Classic Album Covers: Wish You Were Here AR14973
100 Classic Album Covers: With The Beatles AR14974
100 Degrees And Rising RR11474
187 He Wrote RR12599
101 Reasons To Watch TV AR15969
100% Fun RR12689a
100: Satisfaction AR14395
The 100 Top Music Videos AR13617
One Love AR15023, RR11791, RR12848
One More For The Road AR16074
One More Mile RR12878
One More 'Saturday Night': Will This Season Be A Fresh Start Or The Long Buh-Bye? AR15970
One More Time With Feeling: Defying Time And Trends, The Rolling Stones Return With More Of That Voodoo They Do So Well AR13732
One Nation Under A Groove RR11198
A One Of A Kind Love Affair—The Anthology RR12603
One Of Us! One Of Us! One Of... AR13537, AR14641
1: Sledgehammer AR14396
One Step Ahead Of The Spider RR11824
The One That Got Away RR12726
Online AR14975, AR14976, AR14977, AR14978, AR14979, AR14980, AR14981, AR14982, AR14983, AR14984, AR14985, AR14986, AR14987, AR14988, AR14989, AR14990
Only Built Fir Cuban Linx RR12280
Only Daddy That'll Walk The Line RR11522
Only Everything RR11373
Onobox RR12078
Ono's Season Of Grief AR13430
Onward Christian Soldiers: Bob Dole, Phil Gramm And The Other Republican Candidates Are Kowtowing To The Religious Right, But Conservative Christians Are Searching For A True Believer AR13603
Onyx: Bringing Old-School Hip-Hop To The Mosh Pit AR14320
Opel RR10511
Open Up The Sky RR11186
Open Views Of Latin America BR01094
Opera Man: The Rolling Stone Interview With Pete Townshend AR13431
Opinion AR14774
Opinion: Blaming Hardcore For Murder Is Taking The Lazy Way Out AR14486
Opinion: Chapman Killed Lennon To Achieve This Kind Of Notoriety AR13432
Opinion: Tribute LPs Filled With Quirky Covers Are Just No Fun Anymore AR13733
Orange RR12598
Orange County Crush AR13364
Orange Crate Art RR12110, RR12943
Orange Day: In This Southern California County, The Punk Spirit Never Died AR13365, AR14840
Oranges Are Not The Only Fruit BR01095
The Orb: Chicago CR00834
Orbus Terrarum RR12081
Organically Grown: Blind Melon Parlays Its Small-Town Roots Into A Big-City Sound AR14775
The Origin Of AIDS: A Startling New Theory Attempts To Answer The Question 'Was It An Act Of God Or An Act Of Man?' AR13369
'Origin Of AIDS' Update: Clarification AR14991
The Original Mambo Kings: An Introduction To Afro-Cubop 1948-1954 RR13226
The Original Riot Grrrl: Joan Jett Lives Up To Her Bad Reputation AR13379
The Original Skatalites And Laurel Aitken RR10402, RR12524
Original Soundtracks I RR12121
The Originals RR10739
The Orioles Discography AR14992
Orlando RR13227
Oscar '95: The Fix Is In AR15656
Oscar '96: Soo-Ey! AR15657
Oscar Blindness AR15658
Oscar Rejects: A Racist, Sexist And Gutless Academy Screws Up Big Time AR15659
Other Planets Of There RR12268
The Other Summer Tour AR13983
Other Voices, Other Rooms RR11301
Otis! RR12310
Otis Rush, 1956-1958 RR12413
Our Lives, Our Music: Abbey Road AR13270
Our Lives, Our Music: Angel Dust AR15409
Our Lives, Our Music: Appetite For Destruction AR13166, AR14312
Our Lives, Our Music: Are You Experienced? AR13387
Our Lives, Our Music: Armed Forces AR13449
Our Lives, Our Music: Bat Out Of Hell AR16110
Our Lives, Our Music: Born To Run AR15149
Our Lives, Our Music: Bringing It All Back Home AR13637
Our Lives, Our Music: By The Readers Of 'Rolling Stone' AR15016
Our Lives, Our Music: Catch Bull At Four AR13349
Our Lives, Our Music: Daydream Nation AR15210
Our Lives, Our Music: Exile On Main Street AR12945
Our Lives, Our Music: Freak Out! AR15393
Our Lives, Our Music: Get Your Wings AR14601
Our Lives, Our Music: Goodbye Yellow Brick Road AR15189
Our Lives, Our Music: Horses AR13479
Our Lives, Our Music: Hotcakes AR15461
Our Lives, Our Music: Led Zeppelin IV AR15738
Our Lives, Our Music: Live At The Apollo AR15141
Our Lives, Our Music: Mud Slide Slim And The Blue Horizon AR15454
Our Lives, Our Music: Murmur AR13163
Our Lives, Our Music: Nevermind AR15741
Our Lives, Our Music: Out Of Time AR14637
Our Lives, Our Music: Psychocandy AR14502
Our Lives, Our Music: Ritual De Lo Habitual AR16052
Our Lives, Our Music: Scarecrow AR15460
Our Lives, Our Music: Sgt. Pepper's Lonely Hearts Club Band AR14670
Our Lives, Our Music: Shake Your Money Maker AR15566
Our Lives, Our Music: Songs Of Leonard Cohen AR13030
Our Lives, Our Music: Stand! AR15733
Our Lives, Our Music: The Joshua Tree AR15453
Our Lives, Our Music: The Stranger AR15405
Our Lives, Our Music: The Unforgettable Fire AR14526
Our Lives, Our Music: The Wall AR15092
Our Lives, Our Music: The White Album AR14144, AR14510
Our Lives, Our Music: Use Your Illusion I AR14130
Our Lives, Our Music: Velvet Underground And Nico AR15606
Our Lives, Our Music: What's Going On AR14241
Our Lives, Our Music: Workingman's Dead AR13028
Our Lives, Our Times: By The Readers Of 'Rolling Stone' AR15017
Our Man In Nirvana Rages On (And On) About Stardom, Fatherhood, His Feud With Pearl Jam, The Death Of Grunge And Why He's Never Been Happier In His Life: The Rolling Stone Interview AR13734
Our Time In Eden RR12716
Our Troubled Youth RR11450
Out Of Left Field RR12931
Out Of The Closet: Yoko Ono Lends Rare Lennon Gear To The Hall Of Fame AR15766
Out Of The Copy Room: How To Make Your First Job Work For You AR14796
Out Of The Cradle RR10692, RR10693
Out Of The Ordinary AR15971
Out Of The Shadows...Into The Night AR14841, AR15316
Out Of Time RR12327
Out Of Whack (EP) RR11712
Out On The Rolling Sea RR13228
Out There AR15018
OutKast AR14309
Outside RR10643, RR10644
Outtakes: On The Road And Behind The Scenes With Rolling Stone's Chief Photographer AR15972
Outward Bound RR11661
Over There: The U.S. Military's Toxic Reach AR14123, AR15404
Over To You, Dan: How Cronkite's Heir Became Chung's Sidekick AR14335
Over-Nite Sensation RR13022
Own The Way Over Here RR11356
Ozzy Osbourne AR14776, CR00835

P

P RR12094
'P' Is The Funk RR10822
Pablo Honey RR12279
Pacer RR10428, RR10429
The Pacific Jazz Years RR10495
Package Goods AR15847
Paid In Full RR11090
Paisley Is Out AR13984
Palace Brothers RR12099
Pale Sun Crescent Moon RR10890
Paleface: Tempering Venom With Glee AR14002
Palmer On Rock AR15749
Palomine RR10552
Pandora's Box RR10396
Panic: Metal Shot Through With Rock AR13900
Panic On RR11771, RR11772
Papa John Creach: 1917-1994 AR13735
Papa Was A Rolling Stone: But Marlon Richards Is Not Just A Chip Off The Old Rock AR13259, AR14842
Parabolic RR11242
Paradise Don't Come Cheap RR12024
Paradise Found: Coolio Completes His Fantastic Voyage From The Mean Streets

Of Los Angeles To The Top Of The Pop Charts AR14357
Paradise Lost AR14252
Paralyzed Mind Of The Archangel Void RR11360
Paris RR10929, RR11844
Parkay On Trial AR15068
Parklife RR10618, RR10619
Part One RR12905
Partners RR11536
Party Culture: Strange Customs, Quaint Traditions And Stupid Parlor Tricks AR14554
Party Out Of Bounds: On The Bus And Out Of Control With The Cypress Hill—House Of Pain Tour AR15448
Passion Is No Ordinary Word RR12108
Pat Boone AR13538
Patent Pending AR15081
Patrice RR12914
Patrick Lippert: 1958-1993 AR15014
Pat's Kids AR13260
The Patsy Cline Collection RR10818
Patti Rothberg Brings Her Subterranean Lovesick Blues To The Surface AR13138
Patti Scialfa AR15102
Patti Smith CR00886
Patti Smith: New York City CR00887
Patti Smith: The Rolling Stone Interview AR13736
Paul Is Live RR11832
Paul K AR15205
Paul McCartney AR13793
Paul McCartney: Sam Boyd Silver Bowl CR00797
Paul Motian In Tokyo RR11966
Paul Rothchild: 1935-1995 AR14034
Paul Simon 1964-1993 RR12506
Paul Weller RR12893
[Paul Westerberg] AR15973
Paul Westerberg—Bash And Pop: Austin, Texas CR00639, CR00936
Paul Westerberg Looks Back, Moves Forward On New LP AR15734
Pavement: London CR00838
Pavement Smooth Out The Edges On 'Corners' AR13472
Pawn Shop Guitars RR10812
Pay To Play: Independent Promoters Cash In On The Hits As Alternative Radio Becomes Big Business AR13077
The Payback RR10676
Peace At Last RR10608
Peace Beyond Passion RR11998, RR11999, RR12000
Peace To The Neighborhood RR12627
The Peacocks RR12399
Pearl Jam Drummer Beats It AR14777
Pearl Jam: Key Arena CR00842
Pearl Jam On The Road AR15038
Pearl Jam: San Francisco CR00843
Pearl Jam: Taking On Ticketmaster AR13078
Pearl Jammin' AR15585
Pedal To The Medal: These Olympic Contenders Shift Into Casual Gear AR14314, AR14843
The Peel Sessions RR10727
Peel Slowly And See RR12837
Peeni Waali RR13229
Peggy Suicide RR10873
The Pendulum Vibe RR11555
Penn's 'Free-For-All': Singer Releases Stunning Second Effort AR15974
The Pentagon Vs. The Budget: Still Hot For The Cold War AR14101
Pentastar RR11055
People Get Ready! RR11820
People Hold On AR13388
The Pepper Chase AR13539
Peppermint Tea House RR12496
Percussion Bitter Sweet RR12359
Percy Mayfield Live RR11821
Perfectly Good Guitar RR11400
Performance AR14358, CR00724, CR00894, CR00930, CR00933
The Perils Of Pauly AR14589
Peripheral Vision AR15564
Perry Farrell AR12940
Perry Farrell Busted For Drugs [and other news] AR13985
Personal Best RR12037, RR12038
Personal Best: Whether You're Hitting The Slopes Or An Indoor Pool, You Need Lotions And Shampoos To Counteract The Drying Effects Of The Winter Workout AR14131, AR14844
Perspex Island RR11416
Perverse RR11527
Pervert Designer AR14452
Pete Townshend AR15975
Pete Townshend: New York City CR00920
Peter Frampton RR11174
Peter Gabriel: The Academy CR00725
Peter Gabriel's Secret World AR15431
Peter Gabriel's 'Us': Singer Releases First Album Since 1986's 'So' AR13815
Peter Lewis RR11694
Peter Townshend AR15796
Peter Wolf: New York CR00941
Phat Cats And Punks: Rappers Meet Metalheads On 'Judgment Night' AR13587
Phat Trax RR13230
Phenomenon RR13231
Phil Spector AR15797
Philip Bailey RR10492
Phish: Boston CR00847
Phobia RR11626
Phoenix RR10542
Phony Campaign Reform: Update AR16038
Photographers Who See Some Screen Action AR14293
Piano Night At Tipitina's RR13232
Pick Up On This! RR11537, RR13041
Picture Has Faded RR12295
Picture Perfect Morning RR10660
Picture This: The Best Of Rock-Photography Book AR15389
Pictures And Paintings RR12343
Piece Of Cake RR11974
Pieces Of Africa RR11646
The Pigeon Is The Most Popular Bird RR12522
Pimps, Players And Private Eyes RR13233
Pinkerton RR12888
Pisces, Aquarius, Capricorn And Jones Ltd. RR11933
Pisces Iscariot RR12546
Piss Factory RR12554
A Pistol-Whipped Nation: Pass The Brady Bill—Then Ban Handguns AR14102
Pit Master Wanted: Large, Mellow Men To Keep Peace At Live Shows AR15234
P.J. Gets The Last Word: Why I Still Think I'm Right, No Matter What Greider Says AR15005
PJ Harvey AR15533, CR00848
PJ Harvey: London CR00849
The Plague Years AR13044
Planet Of Love RR11670
Planets' World AR15317
Plans For Dylan Tribute: Clapton, Harrison And Others To Perform AR15976
Plantation Lullabies RR12001
Plants And Birds And Rocks And Things RR11725
Plastic Fantastic Punk Rock: Urge Overkill Bring The '70s Back To Life AR14701
The Plastic Ono McCartney Band AR13737
The Platinum Collection RR10601
Play RR10874, RR11838
Play Five Of Their Favorites (EP) RR11121
Play It By Ear: CD Game A Hit AR15169
Play Me Backwards RR10489
Play With Toys RR10514
The Player: Shaquille O'Neal, A Celebrity For The New World AR13999
The Players 1992 AR15660
Players Stumped By Myst Can Now Get Pyst AR14662
Playground Psychotics RR13023
Playing 'God": The Brains Behind Crash Test Dummies AR13841
Playing In The Band: The Music Of The Grateful Dead AR13738
Playing It Straight BR01096
Playing With Fire AR15069
Please Don't Take My Air Jordans RR11207
Please Kill Me BR01097, BR01098
Please Panic RR12846
The Pleasure Of Pain: Nine Inch Nails' Trent Reznor Dances On The Edge Of Madness AR14234
The Plight Of The Crowes: The Band Cancels Show After Trouble With Police AR15217
The Pluck Of The Irish: Musicians Unite To Protest Sectarian Violence AR13816
Plugged In RR11058
The Plugged-In Voter: The New News Has Reconnected People And Politics AR14336
PM Dawn: Metaphysical Graffiti AR13009
Poe: Toad's Place CR00851
Poetic Justice RR13234
Point And Click Picks AR13120
Polara AR14181, RR12192
Polaroids From The Dead BR01099
Police Blotter AR15097, AR15098
Police Sweep L.A. In The Wake Of Shakur Murder: Death Row Reportedly Under FBI Investigation AR15609
Polo Is My Life: Fear And Loathing In Horse Country AR15600
Pomme Fritz RR12082
Pond RR12196
Pop Journal AR13079, AR13080, AR13081, AR13082, AR13083, AR13084
Pop Pop RR11565
Pop Singer Riles Israeli Right AR13027
Pop Tarts: Orchestrated Rock Maneuvers Its Way Through The Grungy Darkness AR13454
The Pop Wizardry Of Sam Phillips AR16088
Pork Soda RR12227
Pork To The People AR16039
Porno For Pyros CR00852, RR12205
Portishead AR15767
Portland, Maine AR15106
Portrait Of A Delta Bluesman RR12149
Portrait Of Defeat: Is The End Near For The NRA? AR13481
Portrait Of The Artist A A Journalist AR15798
Portrait Of The Artist As A Young Man 1923-1934 RR10457
Portraits RR11363
Posies: Inside Out AR15231
Positive PE: After A Hiatus, Public Enemy Return With A Fierce But Soulful Album AR15449
'Posse' Leader Mario Van Peebles Shoots From The Lip AR15661
Possessing The Secret Of Joy BR01100
Post RR11314

Post Mac Attack AR15977
Postmodern Blues RR13235
Post-Orbal Remorse AR16060
Postwar Chicago RR13236
Poverty's Paradise RR11997
Powder To The People: Connoisseurs Of The Cold Rip Through Their Favorite Brand Of Snow AR14440, AR14845
Power Play: Meet The Men Who Rule Modern-Rock Radio AR16094
Power Surge: Multimedia Systems AR13121
Power To The People: Bulgaria Struggles With The Peaceful Atom & Post-Cold War Politics AR15183
Power To The People: Hazel O'Leary Rewires The Department Of Energy AR16040
Power Trip RR11829
Prai$e The Lord AR14182
Precious RR11940
Precious Stone RR12651
The Predator RR11465
Pre-Millennium Tension RR12769
Prescentable: This Holiday Season, Make More Than Just A Suitable Impression By Giving—Or Wearing—One Of These Fragrances Or Aftershaves AR14846
Prescription Refilled: Spin Doctors' "Turn It Upside Down" Is More That Meets The Ear AR14702
[Present Tense] AR15114
President Clinton: The Rolling Stone Interview AR14103, AR15799
Presidential Candidates Discover America AR14104
Presidents Of The United States Of America AR15379
The Presidents Of The United States Of America RR12213
Pre-Teenage Wasteland: Catching Saturday-Morning Fever AR15978
The Pretenders: London CR00853
Pretty Close To The Truth RR11671
Pretty Hate Machine: On Their New Album, 'Load,' Metallica Explore The Devil Inside AR13739
Pretty On The Inside: Blur Get Introspective On Their New Album AR15472
Pretty On The Outside: Echobelly Coat Perversity With Sugar Pop AR15848
Price Busters: Green Day Lower Ticket Prices And One-Up Pearl Jam AR14183
The Price Is Not Right: Is Ticketmaster Taking These People For A Ride? AR14035
The Price Of Politics—Student Loans AR15348
Priest = Aura RR10792
The Priest, They Called Him RR10703, RR10829
Primal Rock Therapy RR10603
Primed And Ticking: PJ Harvey Beat The Sophomore Jinx And Get Their Mojo Workin' With An American Tour And Their Powerful New Album, 'Rid Of Me' AR13762
Primitive Radio Gods Get The Blues AR15768
Primus Choices AR13049
Prince: Free At Last AR13433
The Prince Of Wildwood: Jack Brian Searches The Jersey Shore For Love, Girls And A Future AR14337
Prince Records Three Hours Of 'Emancipation' AR13434
Prince Retires—Maybe: He Says He's Quitting Studio Work, But Don't Hold Your Breath AR13986
Prodigal Son: The Battle Over New Bruce, Dead CDs AR14036
Prodigy CR00855
The Prodigy: New York CR00856
Professors Of Hate: Academia's Dirty Secret AR14636
Profiles In College: Books, CD-ROMs And Web Sites That Tell You Where To Go AR15119
Promoters Hurt By Summer Flops AR13987
Prose Combat RR11825
Protection RR11803
Provincetown AR13160
Psalm 69: The Way To Succeed And The Way To Suck Eggs RR11908
Psychic Hearts RR11941
Psychoderelict RR12756
Public Enemy #1: Rap's Top Group Focuses On Gold Brains, Not Gold Chains AR14487
Pulling The Donkey Lever AR15006
Pulp CR00858
Pulp Fiction RR13237
Pulp Friction: Frontman Jarvis Cocker Wreaks Revenge For The 'Common People' AR15432
Pulse RR12175
Pumpkins Plan Double Disc: Billy Corgan And The Band Have A Smashing Good Time In The Studio AR14437
Punk Diary 1970-1979 BR01101
The Punk-Rock Talking Blues: Henry Rollins Bares All With The Spoken Word AR14778
Punk's Holy Rollers: Bad Religion Have Come A Long Way From Their Garage-Rock Roots AR14397
Pure And Simple RR11534
Pure & Simple: Kelly Willis, County Waif AR14847, AR15359
Pure Phase RR12605
Pure Poverty RR12198
Purge And Slouch RR11240
Purple RR12646, RR12647
Push It Good: Salt-N-Pepa Are Going To The Edge AR15188
Pussy, King Of The Pirates RR10390, RR11863
Putumayo Presents The Best Of World Music RR13238

Q

Quad City DJ's Are On The Right Track AR14138
Queen Latifah's New Gambit: Her New Album Reaches Out To A Larger Audience AR14488
Queen Of Soul: The Atlantic Recordings RR11175
Queen's Reich: Queer Punk Comes Out of The Closet—Loudly AR15220
A Quick One RR12920
Quilt RR12476

R

The R&B Box: 30 Years Of Rhythm & Blues RR13239
The R&B Of Membership RR10981
R. Kelly CR00769, RR11596
Race, Money And The Meaningless Search For The Center: Who Really Won The Election Of 1996 And Why AR14105
Racers, Rockers And Roaches Star In The Best New CD-ROM Games AR14663
Radio City RR10559
Radio Daze AR13740
Radio Free Vedder: Pearl Jam Hijack The Airwaves For A Free-Form Throw-Down AR13788
Radio Land Rush: The Industry's Biggest Station Owners Get Bigger While The Small Ones Sign Off AR13085
Radiohead: 'Creep' Is The Most Audacious Pop Move Since The Police's 'Every Breath You Take' AR14398
Rage Against The Machine: Roseland Ballroom CR00859
Rage To Survive BR01102
The Raging Optimism And Multiple Personalities Of Dave Matthews AR13284
Rain Dogs RR12857
Rainforest Foundation Benefit AR13618
Raising Hell RR12410
Ralph J. Gleason Awards AR14184, AR15137
Rancid AR14185
Random Access: Dispatches From Cyberspace AR14664
Randy Newman RR12032
Randy Shilts: The Rolling Stone Interview AR16053
Range Wars: Should COllege Radio Be Making Waves Or Making Money? AR14668
Ranters And Crowd Pleasers: Punk In Pop Music 1977-92 BR01103
Rap AR14489
Rap Wrap AR15139
Rapa Iti RR12698, RR12699
Rapid Transit AR14665
Rappers Get Roughed Up: John 'Ecstacy' Fletcher And Friends File Complaint Against New York Police AR12916
Rappers Sound Warning: The Violence In Los Angeles Didn't Surprise Those Who Were Paying Attention AR14490
Rare Birds RR11012, RR11276
Rare, Live And Classic RR10490
Rare On Air Vol. 1 RR13240
Rare Surf RR13241
Rats RR11571
Rave AR15485
Rave On!! RR11599
The Raven RR12170
Raves AR12926, AR12958, AR13023, AR13152, AR13154, AR13187, AR13190, AR13303, AR13319, AR13370, AR13389, AR13390, AR13435, AR13475, AR13574, AR13575, AR13597, AR13741, AR13760, AR13792, AR13851, AR14124, AR14143, AR14145, AR14209, AR14243, AR14244, AR14285, AR14286, AR14322, AR14323, AR14417, AR14442, AR14448, AR14519, AR14559, AR14595, AR14602, AR14603, AR14620, AR14640, AR14652, AR14703, AR14779, AR14780, AR14802, AR14803, AR15015, AR15093, AR15094, AR15135, AR15136, AR15216, AR15327, AR15328, AR15363, AR15390, AR15444, AR15554, AR15555, AR15573, AR15582, AR15737, AR15805, AR15980, AR16097, AR16111, CR00745, CR00775
Ravestock AR15769
Ravi Shankar At Carnegie Hall CR00875
Raw And Chunky: A Tribe Called Quest Go Minimalist AR14306
Raw 'N Alive At The Cellar, 1966 RR12470
Ray Charles AR13674
Ray Davies CR00697
Ray Gun Suitcase RR12146
Razorblade Suitcase RR10705
The RCA Years 1967-1986 RR12117
Reachin' RR11005, RR11006
Reaction Dub part 1: Deliverance RR12338
Readers' Picks: 1992 Music Awards AR15142
Readers' Picks: 1993 Music Awards AR15143

Readers Poll: 1996 AR15144
The Reading Festival AR13010, AR14445
The Reading List AR15145
Ready For Love RR12702
Ready To Die RR12052
The Real Dirt: Alice In Chains Take A Hard Look At The Dark Side Of Seattle On The New EP 'Jar Of Flies' AR13399
The Real Kids RR12297
Real Love RR12626
The Real Mr. Heartache RR12131
The Real New Deal: The Breeders Get Wet And Wild As They Dive Back Into Action On 'Last Splash' AR13011
The Real World AR14797
Reality Bites Back: In It's Fifth Season, 'The Real World' Spins Off Into Orbit AR15981
The Reality Of My Surroundings RR11139
Reap The Whirlwind RR12076
Rebecca Coupe Franks: Young Woman With A Horn AR14038
Rebel Yellers: Pantera Take Metal To No. 1 With Their New "Far Beyond Driven" AR13400
Rebellion RR10577
Rebels Without Applause (EP) RR10827
The Rebirth Of Elton John AR14807
Record-Chain Blacklist: Super Club Establishes Policy On Rating Lyrics AR14781
Record High AR13988
Recovering The Satellites RR10886
Red RR11268
Red Alert AR13261
Red Hot And Country RR13242
Red Hot + Positive AR14186
Red Hot Chili Peppers' Naked Truth AR13742
Red Hot Chili Peppers Nirvana Pearl Jam CR00828, CR00839, CR00862
Red-Hot Lollapalooza: Chili Peppers Will Headline This Summer's Alternative-Music Meld AR13990
Red House Painters AR13989
Red House Painters I RR12303
Red House Painters II RR12304
Red Medicine RR11189
The Red Shoes RR10706
Redbaiter Liar Warmonger Crook: Richard Milhous Nixon 1913-1994 AR15146
Reel To Reel RR11284
Reflecter RR12671
The Refreshments AR15147
Refueled & Reborn: While Led Zeppelin Take Their Rightful Place In The Rock & Roll Hall Of Fame, Jimmy Page And Robert Plant Draw Up New Flight Plans AR13436
Reggae Christmas RR13243
Regulate...G Funk Era RR12869
Reject All American RR10564
Relationships From Hell RR13244
Relish RR12087
R.E.M. AR14148
R.E.M.: Mountain View, Calif. CR00865
R.E.M.: Tour On? AR15849
The Remaking Of The President AR14106
Remember RR12419
Remember Me RR12311, RR12650
Remembering Bill AR15153
Remembering Miles AR15154
Rent RR13245
Rent Strikes AR14848, AR15850
Replays AR13313
Report From Sundance AR15662
Represent RR11124
Republic RR12025
Republica AR15770
Requiem For A Heavyweight AR15349
Requiescat In Pace AR15158
Respect RR11417
Restricted Access: A Major Record Chain Hits Rap And Rock With 18-To-Buy Labels AR15586
Resurrection RR10857
The Resurrection RR11234
Retread Sneakers: The Duo Releases A Collection Of New Old Songs AR15206
Retro Active RR10975
Retrospective RR10656
Return Mail AR15175
The Return Of Dr. Feelgood AR15982
Return Of The All-Day Sucker AR13991
Return Of The Boom Bap RR11649
Return Of The Crimson King: Robert Fripp And Company Rejoin Forces For The First Time In Ten Years AR13743
Return Of The King: Robert Fripp Keeps His Word AR13744
Return Of The Product RR12461
The Return Of The Space Cowboy RR11509
Return To The 36 Chambers RR12073
Return To The Valley Of The Go-Go's RR11265
Revenge Of The Weezer Nerds: They're Not Punk, They're Not Pop, They're Not Pretty, But They're Huge AR15702
Reverend Horton Heat: New York City CR00866
Revival RR12891
Revolutionary Means RR12438
Rhythm Country And Blues RR13246
Rhythm In Mind RR10842
Rhythm Nation AR15115, AR15116, AR15117
Rhythm Of Love RR10494
Rhythmeen RR13005
The Rich Man's Eight Track Tape RR10555
Richard Linklater's Hot List AR13901, AR15318
Richard Thompson AR13540
Rickie Lee Jones: New York CR00766
Rid Of Me RR12181, RR12182
Ride With Me RR11454
Riding The Yellow Trolley Car BR01104
Rien RR11127
Rig Rock Truckstop RR13247
The Right Computer For You: It's The Soul Of The System That Counts AR13122
Right Hair, Right Now: An Unkempt Mop Top Complements Today's Radical Biker Chic AR14849, AR15694
Right Here, Right Now: The Seattle Rock Band Pearl Jam Learns How To Celebrate Life AR14782
The Right Time RR11507
Ringo: Confident And Sober, The Former Beatle Releases His Best Album In Nearly Two Decades AR15983
Ringolevio BR01105
Riots Mar G N' R Tour AR14491
Rise RR10479
Rise Above It RR12072
The Rise And Fall Of A Super Freak AR15337
The Rise And Fall Of Apple Inc AR14012
The Rise And Fall Of Apple Inc. [Part Two] AR14013
Rising RR12079
Rising Sons RR10865, RR11781, RR12355
Rites Of Rhythm & Blues RR13248
Ritual Beating System RR10491
River Of Dreams RR11540, RR11541
River Of Fallen Stars RR11597, RR11598
The Road From Nowhere: Walking The Streets Of Aberdeen, Wash. AR13914
The Road Goes On Forever RR11401
The Road Less Traveled AR15851
The Road Less Traveled: Pavement's Crooked Path To Stardom AR13209
Road Tested RR12287
The Road To Ensenada RR11744
The Road To Wellville AR13132
Road Trips AR15402
Road Woes: What It Costs AR13086
Roadsongs RR12817, RR12818
Roaring Loud, Standing Proud RR12360
Rob And Fab RR12361
Rob Collins: 1963-1996 AR14187
Rob Zombie AR15151
Robbie Robertson: The Rolling Stone Interview AR15024
Robert Altman: The Rolling Stone Interview AR13146
Robert F. Kennedy Jr.: Getting Down To Earth With A Leading Eco-Activist AR15392
Robert Redford: The Rolling Stone Interview AR13437
Robert Rodriguez AR15663
Robert White 1936-1994 AR15751
Robyn Hitchcock AR13407
Robyn Hitchcock And The Egyptians CR00746
Robyn Hitchcock's Wild Kingdom: In The Land Of Odds, The Leader Of The Egyptians Rules AR15129
Rock Against AIDS, 1993 AR14206, AR14235
Rock And Rap Comics AR14399
A Rock & Roll Collection RR12948
Rock & Roll Cookbook BR01106
Rock & Roll Hall Of Fame AR13541, AR13782, AR14705, AR15170, AR15984
The Rock & Roll Hall Of Fame '94 AR13783, AR15130
Rock & Roll Music AR15218
Rock & Roll Must Not Let Broadway Blunt Its Visceral Power AR13438
Rock & Roll Summer: Artist's Picks AR15086
Rock & Roll Summer: Athens AR13042
Rock & Roll Summer: Austin AR14631, AR14632
Rock & Roll Summer: Boston AR14316
Rock & Roll Summer: Detroit AR14043
Rock & Roll Summer: Jersey Shore AR15350
Rock & Roll Summer: London AR13486
Rock & Roll Summer: Los Angeles AR15152
Rock & Roll Summer: Minneapolis AR15735
Rock & Roll Summer: New Orleans AR12924
Rock & Roll Summer: New York AR15033
Rock & Roll Summer: Phoenix AR13918
Rock & Roll Summer: Seattle AR15087
Rock & Roll Traveler USA BR01107
Rock & Roll Yearbook AR13542, AR13543, AR13544, AR13902, AR14704, AR14706, AR14707, AR15034, AR15319, AR15852
Rock Animals RR12495
Rock Hall Announces Inductees AR13784
Rock Juice RR11143
Rock 'N' Groove RR12847
Rock Radio Make-Over: Two New Formats Echo Listeners' Changing Tastes AR13087
Rock, Rap And Movies Bring You The News AR14338
Rock She Wrote BR01108
Rock Stars Kill RR13249
Rock: The Rough Guide BR01109
Rock The Vote's New Campaign: Organization Gets Out The Vote In New Hampshire Primary AR14492
Rockabye RR11419
Rocket RR12226
Rocket Takes Off: San Diego's Favorite Sons Get Fans Fired Up AR15750

Rockin' And 'Rolling' Into Cyberspace AR15853
Rockin' Dopsie: 1932-1993 AR15561
Rockin' In The Heart Of Texas: Unsigned Bands Reign Supreme At Austin's Annual Music Blowout AR13745
Rockin' My Blues Away RR12871
Rockin' My Life Away RR11691
Rock's Dream Team: Legends Meet At Hall Of Fame's Opening-Day Show AR13817
Rock's Greatest Showman AR13992
Rock's Royal Jesters: King Missile Makes Merry On College Radio With 'Detachable Penis' AR12973
Rod Stewart: Anaheim, Calif. CR00900
[Rolling Stone...] AR15221
The Rolling Stone Interview AR14783
The Rolling Stone Interview: Eric Clapton AR14200
The Rolling Stone Interview: Jerry Garcia AR14201
The Rolling Stone Interview With Sonic Youth's Thurston Moore: Better Living Through Feedback AR13746
Rolling Stone Online AR15222
The Rolling Stones On Tour AR14057
The Rolling Stones Rock & Roll Circus RR13250
The Rolling Stones' 'Rock & Roll Circus' Is Back In Town AR14359
Rollins: The Boxed Life RR12381
Rom & Roll: Hanging With Wanda The Worm Women And Friends AR14339
Ron Sexsmith RR12467
Ron Wood Of The Rolling Stones AR13545
Ronnie Wood: The Roxy Theater CR00942
Roommatism: How To Live With Others Without Killing Yourself AR16132
Roots RR12460
Roots N' Blues RR13251
Roots Rock Soca RR10578
The Roots Roll Away From The Jazz-Hip-Hop Tree AR14651
Ropin' The Whirl Wind: Garth Brooks The Rolling Stone Interview AR13439
Ropin' The Wind RR10667
Rory Gallagher: 1948-1995 AR15433
Rose And Charcoal RR11936
A Rose In Gloom: Madder Rose Balance Prettiness With Dissonance On "Panic On" AR13380
Roses RR12075
Ross Perot Talks, Washington Squawks AR14107
Rotten: No Irish—No Blacks—No Dogs BR01110
'Round Midnight: A Tribe Called Quest Shift Into High Gear With Their New Album AR15624
Route 666: On The Road To Nirvana BR01111
Routes Of Rhythm Vol. 3 RR12092
Roy Acuff: 1903-1992 AR14493
Roy Orbison AR15103
Royal Spoils: Royal Trux Keep Everyone Guessing With 'Thank You' AR15380
The Royal Treatment: The Beastie Boys Fight For Their Right To Prosper AR12941
The Royalty Scam: R&B Foundation Rewards Underpaid Musical Pioneers AR15854
Rub It Better RR11226
Rubber Souls AR14132, AR14633
Ruby Doomsday: Ruby Sparkle With Their Bleak Bravado AR13546
Ruby Vroom RR12579
The Rude Gesture RR12485
Ruling Asses: Oasis Have Conquered America, And They Won't Shut Up About It AR14708
Rumble Doll RR12437
Run-D.M.C.: Back On The Throne AR15625
Run-D.M.C., Naughty By Nature: Radio City Music Hall CR00822, CR00869
Run, Newt, Run: Would A Presidential Bid Finally Expose The Real Newt Gingrich? AR12955
Running Jumping Standing Still RR11633, RR11980
Running With The Devil BR01112
Running With You RR10725
RuPaul AR15703
Rush RR10806
The Rushdie Letters BR01113
The Russian Album RR11833
Russian Roulette AR15007
Rwanda: The Death Of A Nation AR14134, AR15343
Rx Now, Pay Later: Will Health Reform Be Clinton's Reaganomics? AR14108

S

S In Moderation RR11635
Sabsylma RR13009
A Sacrifice To The Lords Of Yesterday AR13606
Sacrificial Cake RR11510
Sad And Defeated RR11016
A Sad Day For Comedy AR16118
Sad Days, Lonely Nights RR11611
Sadly Beautiful (song) RR12335
Safe & Sound: Home Alive Unites The Seattle Music Community While Teaching Self-Defense AR15088
Saisoro RR10988
Salamat And Nazakat Ali RR10406, RR10407
Saline Solution: Veruca Salt Wrap Their Hardcore Inside A Candy-Pop Coating AR15771
Sally Potter: Introducing 'Orlando' Director AR15664
Salt Lake City, Utah AR15346
Sam Cooke's SAR Records Story 1959-1965 RR10866
Sam Kinison: 1953-1992 AR15985
Samba Brasil RR13252, RR13253
Same Train, A Different Time RR11347
Samshing Pumpkins: Chicago CR00884
The Samurai And The Cyberthief: How The World's Most-Wanted Computer Criminal Was Hunted Down By One Of His Targets—The Master Of Cybersecurity AR14014
San Diego AR15155
San Fran Sessions RR10530
San Francisco AR13050, RR10423
San Francisco Days RR11488
Sandra Bernhard AR15626
The Sands Of Time AR15070
Santa Monica '72 RR10645
Santana CR00872
Santana-Jeff Beck CR00646, CR00871
Sao Paulo Megacity AR14142
Sarah McLachlan: Happy To Be Unhappy AR13818
Satan Is Real RR11729
Satta Massagana RR10387
Saturation RR12804, RR12805
Saturday Night And Sunday Morning RR12625
Saturday Night At The Blue Note RR12152
Saturday Night Jive AR15665
Saturday Rolling Around RR11283
Saviors' Haven AR15320
Say Blow By Blow Backwards RR12899
Say Of The Lucas AR15772
Scarce Survive Tragedy And Release Belated Debut AR15855
Scavenger RR12858
Scene Of The Crime RR11609
Scenes From My Last Confession RR12064
Scenes From The Cast Struggle In Beverly Hills:Mauled In Malls By Rabid Fans, The Stars Of 'Beverly Hills, 90210' Deal With Their Teen Minutes Of Fames AR14590
Scents Of Style: Fragrances For The Holiday Season AR14850
Scentsual Pleasures AR15483, AR15489
The Scepter Records Story RR13254
School Of Fish: Confounding Critics AR14868
School Ties Stars Unbutton Their Shirts AR14315, AR14534
Schubert Dip RR11075
Science Faire RR10449
The Score RR11191, RR11192
Scots Pirates RR12439
Scrambling For Dollars: Will Cable Companies Break The Promise Of New Video Technologies? AR13644
Scratch RR12444
Scream, Dracula, Scream! RR12369
Scream In Blue RR11898
Screaming Life BR01114
Screaming Trees AR13634
Screaming Trees: Woodshed For Success AR14188
Screen Saviors AR16075
The Sea And Cake AR15177
Seal RR12450
Seal, Delivered: "Seal" Chronicles Two Years Of Inner And Outer Turmoil AR15587
The Search For The Secret Pyramid AR14418, AR15078
Seasick RR11472
Seattle Women In Rock RR13255
Sebastiao Salgado: The Rolling Stone Interview AR13342
Second Coming RR12644
The Second Coming! AR15986
Second Helping AR13088
2nd Street RR10415
The Secret Life Of Jerry Garcia AR14058
The Secret Of St. Mary's AR13158, AR13789
Secret World Live RR11205
Secrets RR10654
Section 43 (song) RR10887
Seducing Down The Door RR10722
The Seduction Of Peter Jay Rudge: Part One AR15542
The Seduction Of Peter Jay Rudge: Part Two AR15543
See You On The Other Side RR11881
Seeking Soul Asylum: At Home With The Loud Fast Rulers Of The Minneapolis Music Scene AR14709
Seizing The Light AR13165
Selected Ambient Works Vol. II RR10447
Selene Vigil Of 7 Year Bitch AR13547
Sell Out Young (song) RR11438
Selling Out AR16095
Selling Sex In 'Showgirls' AR15666
Semi-crazy RR10680
Senator Krist: Krist Novoselic Talks About Politics, Censorship And Life After Nirvana AR13455
The Sensual Christian: Father Matthew Fox Extols The Joys Of Passion And Lust Over The Shame Of Original Sin True Believers AR16092
A Separate Peace: The Clinton Administration Has Abandoned The Rhetoric Of The War On Drugs, But It Hasn't Stopped Fighting The War AR16041
Sessions! BR01115

Set Me Free RR12344
Set The Twilight Reeling RR12317
Set To Pop RR11708
The Setters RR12462
7 And 7 Is (song) RR11678, RR11735
Seven Inches Of Pleasure: For Bands And Fans, The Single Is The New Format Of Choice AR13012
7: Subterranean Homesick Blues AR14400
7 Years Ago...Directions In Smart-Alec Music RR11157
17: Been Caught Stealing AR13548
78: Dirty Boots AR14401
75: One AR14402
75% Less Fat RR11794
'75% Less Fat,' 100% Rock: Former Mat Chris Mars Sheds Some Excess Weight On His Second Solo LP AR14236
74: Psycho Therapy AR14403
70: I Want Your AR13819
79: Voices Carry AR13549
71: Rosalita AR13820
77: White Wedding AR14568
76: Mysterious Ways AR13821
73: Wicked Game AR13822
72: Shadrach AR14404
Sex, America, Cheap Trick RR10770
Sex At Sundance AR15667
The Sex Pistols: Finsbury Park CR00874
Sexual Healing: Janet Jackson Finds Peace, Inspiration And Chart Success Through Carnal Knowledge AR15195
Shack-Man RR11857
Shacknasty RR11270
Shadows And Light RR12947a
Shady Grove RR11216, RR11305
Shake It Up! RR13256
Shakill's Warrior RR11981
Shamballa RR11431
Shame + A Sin RR10899
Shania Twain RR12783
Shannon Hood: 1967-1995 AR13456
Shannon's Dress (EP) RR12478
Shape RR11178
The Shape Of Things To Come AR16076
Shara Nelson AR14282
Shaw 'Nuff RR11246
She Loves You (song) RR10529
Sheik Yerbouti RR13024
Sheryl Crow AR14283, RR10917, RR10918
Sheryl Crow: She Only Wants To Be With You AR15376
She's A Rebel BR01116
She's The One RR12154
Shine On RR12176
The Shines RR12489
Shipwreck RR10861
Shoot Your Way To Freedom (song) RR12055
Shop Therapy: Kerri Kenney Of 'The State' Prowls Manhattan's Lower East Side AR14851, AR15035
Shopping At Sal's: Searching For The Look Of The Future At The Salvation Army AR13262, AR14852
Short Bus RR11131
The Short Life And Death Of Tupac Shakur: Bury Me Like A G AR15108
Short Stories RR11647
Shorty The Pimp RR12749a
Shot RR11530
Shot In The Heart AR13915
Should We Throw The Bums Out? AR14109
Show RR10930, RR10931, RR11531
The Show, The After-Party, The Hotel RR11538, RR11539
Shut Up 'N Play Yer Guitar RR13025
Siamese Dream RR12547, RR12548, RR12549
Sick 'Em RR12464
Sick Of It All: Searching For Breakthroughs In Musicians' Health Care AR14189
Side Effects: A Concerned Public Official Says We Need To Shift The Way We Think About Drugs Before We Lose Even More Young Lives To AIDS An Violence AR15362
Sides 1-4 (single) RR13257
Sidewalks For Sale: Libertarians Are Flourishing On Capitol Hill, On Campus And On Line AR16042
Sif Safaa RR13258
The Silent Majority RR10414
Silhouette RR12494
Silver Sail RR12950
Simmering Chili: Peppers Stir Up A Red-Hot New Album AR13351
Simon Bonney: The Singer Changes Directions On 'Forever' AR13850
Simon LeBon Of Duran Duran AR14710
Simpatico! RR12829
Simple English (song) RR11133
Simple Minds: Seattle CR00878
Simple Minds: Stereolab Make Suprisingly Seductive Minimalist Pop AR15178
A Simple Twist Of Fate AR14426
Simply Red CR00879
Simply The Best: Tracy Bonham Enjoys Her Winning Streak AR14462
Sinatra And Sextet: Live In Paris RR12514
Since Then AR15410, AR15411, AR15412, AR15413
Sinead Speaks AR14494
Sinful Wages: Clinton Wavers On Raising Workers' Pay AR14110
The Singer RR11208
Singer, Actor, Director: With A Movie And A New Album, John Mellencamp Branches Out AR13823
A Singer Finds Her Voice: Maura O'Connell Redefines The Songstress As A Force To Be Reckoned With AR16055
Singin' In The Rain: Artists Unite To Benefit Rain-Forest Charity AR13824
Singing From The Heart: Tracy Chapman Explores Some New Territory On Her Third Album AR14495
A Single Woman RR12507
The Singles RR12269, RR13259
The Singles (1993-1994) Loverly Music RR13260
The Sinkable Carol Browner: New EPA Chief Finds Herself In Over Her Head AR16043
Sins Of The Innocent: Children Are Falling Victim To A New Kind Of Sexual Offender—Other Children AR15577
Sioux Indians File Suit Against The Cult [and other news] AR13993
Siouxsie And The Banshees: New York CR00880
Sir Mix-A-Lot AR13550
Site Seeing On The Web AR16077
Sitting On Snaps RR11856
Six Feet Deep RR11292
VI: Return Of The Real RR11469
6: Right Now AR14569
16: Thriller AR15627
68: Smells Like Nirvana AR14570
60: Epic AR14405
65: Jazzin' For Blue Jean AR14406
60 Ft Dolls AR14598
64: Brilliant Disguise AR14571
69: Tennessee AR14294
61: Every Breath You Take AR14555
67: Money For Nothing AR13825
66: Oh Father AR14556
63: Rockit AR14407
62: It's My Life AR13551
60 Watt Silver Lining RR11063
Size Counts: With The Right Audio System, You'll Have A Good Relationship With Music AR13645
Ska Bonanza: The Studio One Ska Years RR13261
Skate Dreams: Roller Basketball Is A Game Of Fast Breaks And Fast Breaking AR13263, AR14853
Skate Till You Die: The Fast Times And Tragic Death of Jeff Phillips, The King Of Texas Skateboarding AR16050
Skee-Lo Is As Skee-Lo Does In 'I Wish' AR13552
Skeleton Key AR15354, BR01117
Sketches RR10554, RR11837, RR12681
Sketches Of Spain RR10964
Skids' Mark: Southern Culture Hit It Big With 'Date' AR13408
Skin RR11688
Skin Deep: Republican Front-Runner Bob Dole Will Do Anything For A Buck AR15497
Skit Happens: On HBO's New Sketch-Comedy Series, There's No Business Like 'Mr. Show' Business AR15987
The Sky Is Crying RR12824
Skynyrd Frynds RR13262
Slang RR10976
Slanted And Enchanted RR12127
Slapping Pythagoras RR10862
Slash Leaves Guns N' Roses: Cites Differences With Axl Rose AR14190
Slave To The Grind: Can Eric Nies Escape MTV's Star-Breaker Machinery? AR13264, AR14854
Slaves To The Grind: The Most Important Job In A College Town Is Supplying The Jolt AR15403
Slay The Suitors RR12222
Slayer: New York CR00881
Sleater-Kinney AR15727
Sleeper AR15434
Sleeping With The Enemy?: Indie Meets Major As Matador And Atlantic Records Join Forces AR15207
Sleeps With Angels RR10901, RR10902, RR12997, RR12998
Sleepy Eyes And Butterflies RR12589
Slide On This RR12960
Slippin' Around On The Road With Brad Pitt AR14711
Slippin' In RR11336
Slo-Blo RR10760
Slow Dancing With The Moon RR12118
Slowhand RR10807
S.L.S.Q. RR10400
Sly And Robbie Present Taxi RR13263
Small Audio Dynamite: When It Comes To Stereo Systems, Bigger Is Not Always Better AR13646
The Small One: After Decades Of Preparing For A Big Earthquake Along The San Andreas Fault, California Scientists Now Believe It's The Increasingly Frequent Quakes That May Lay Waste To San Francisco Or Los Angeles AR15549
Smart Alternative AR15443
Smart Money AR13343
Smash RR12071
Smashing Pumpkins AR14712, AR14713
Smashing Pumpkins' Keyboardist Dies Of Drug Overdose; Drummer Charged With Possession AR14191
Smashing Pumpkins' Sudden Impact: The Band's 'Siamese Dream' Comes True

AR13013
Smashing Pumpkins: The Rolling Stone Interview With Billy Corgan AR13747
The Smashing Pumpkins: Thomas And Mack Center CR00883
A Smashing Time: At South By Southwest, If You Schmooze, You Lose AR13748
Smeared RR12536
Smells Like Team Spirit: Clinton Seeks A Few Good Students To Fix Up America AR14111
Smilin' Island Of Song RR10629
Smoke RR11035
Smoke 'Em If You Got 'Em RR12337a
Smokin' Groovies CR00669, CR00692, CR00792, CR00820, CR00922
Smokin Suckaz Wit Logic AR13588
The Snake RR11765, RR12201
A Snake In The Heart RR13264
Snakin Around AR14425, AR15988
Snoop In The Doghouse: Dr. Dre Protege And Bodyguard Face Murder Charge AR13927
So Near, So Far RR11392
So Tonight That I Might See RR11823
So Tough RR12422
So Where's The Fire?: Perry Farrell Talks About Sex, Drugs, Karma, Everything But His New Band, Porno For Pyros AR14784
So You Finally Put Together The Ideal Audio System AR13647
Soaking Up Inspiration From The Local Bowling Alley, Sponge Move From Grim-Faced Grunge To Blue-Collar Glam AR15856
Social Distortion Find Their New Highs On The Road With 'White Trash' AR12942
Soca Carnival 93 RR13265
Soft Bomb RR10789
Sole Singers AR15495
Solid Ground RR10431
Solid-State Family Values: When It Comes Time To Do Something For Posterity, Buy A Camcorder AR16078
Solomon's Daughter RR11606
Soma City RR12425
Some Change RR12431
Some Gave All RR10942, RR10943
Some Kind Of Wonderful: Boz Scaggs Rediscovers The Joys Of Rock & Soul AR14237
Some Lyrics RR11759
Some Old Bullshit RR10520
Sometime Anywhere RR10793
Son Of Samurai AR16109
Song For RR12130
The Song Is You RR11026, RR12515
The Song Remains The Same: L.A.'s Social Distortion Brings Its Punk Roots To The MTV Generation AR14714
The Song Remembers When RR12979
Songs RR12820
Songs For A Blue Guitar RR12305
Songs For The Daily Planet RR12562
Songs For The Terrestrially Challenged RR12722
Songs From Chippy RR13266
Songs From The Rain RR11442
Songs Of Faith And Devotion RR10984, RR10985
Songs Of Freedom RR11792
Songs Of The West RR13267
Sonic Bloom: Oasis Return With 'Morning Glory' LP AR13826
Sonic Solutions AR13123
Sonic Youth: Go Guitar Crazy On Lucky 13th Release AR14040
Sonic Youth's 'Dirty' Set For July Release AR13014
Sonny Sharrock 1940-1994 AR14408
Sophie's Choice: Sophie B. Hawkins Realizes Her Vision And Creates A Smash Single AR15989
Sophmore Humps: The Modern-Rock Trail Is Littered With One-Hit Wonders AR13089
Soul Asylum AR13553, AR14855
Soul Asylum: After 11 Long Years Of Virtual Obscurity, The Little Punk Band That Couldn't Finally Does With The Success Of 'Grave Dancers Union' AR14715
Soul Asylum: Dave Pirner & Dan Murphy AR13554
The Soul Behind The Face: Babyface Steps Out from Behind The Boards To The Top Of The Charts AR15196
The Soul Cages RR12641
Soul Coughing: Hack Out A Hearty Blend Of Beat Poetry, Hip-Hop And Art Rock AR15473
Soul Deep RR10646
Soul Man: Live In Japan RR10816
The Soul Of Black Peru RR13268
The Soul Of The New Machine: Tin Machine Is More Than David Bowie's Latest Invention AR15990
Soul Of Vietnam RR13269
Soul Train 25th Anniversary RR13270
Souled Out: Has The New Technology Finally Sucked The Revolution Out Of Rock & Roll—Or Given It A New Lease On Life? AR13749
Souljah's Bad Rap: Candidate Clinton Thrusts The Rapper-Activist Into The Spotlight AR14785
Soulsation! RR11491, RR11492
Sound Factory: In Computer Labs, Dedicated Wireheads Give Pop Music A Digital Make-Over AR15565
Sound Of Joy RR12270
The Sound Of Music RR12177
The Sound Of The Future: With Its First Two Albums, My Bloody Valentine Has Redefined Rock AR13015
Sound Of White Noise RR10443
Sound Sun Pleasure RR12271, RR12272
Sound System RR11039
Soundgarden: Houston CR00893
Soundgarden: The Veteran Band From Seattle Proves There's Life After Nirvana AR14786
The Sounds Of Cyberspace AR15579, AR15580
Sounds Of The South RR13271
Soundtracks RR10728
Soup RR10599
South Central RR13272
South Of I-10 RR11662
Southern Comfort: Hootie And The Blowfish Take Their Deep-Fried Jams And Sweet Love Songs To The Top Of The Charts AR13265
Southern Comfort: How Come There Are Billions To Bail Out Mexico But Nada For U.S. Cities? AR14112
The Southern Harmony And Musical Companion RR10569
Southpaw Grammar RR11956
Space Is The Place: Rockers Look To The Skies In Search Of UFOs AR14345
Space Oddity: Bootsy Collins Orbits Higher With "Zillatron" And "Blasters Of The Universe" AR14424
Spacehog: Revive Glam, Gender Bending And Mascara AR15857
The Spaghetti Incident? RR11322
Spaghetti Western: The Singing Cowboy Junkie Margo Timmins And The Lone Star State's Own Lyle Lovett Get Duded Up Italian-Like AR14449, AR15991
Spare Ass Annie And Other Tales RR10704
The Specialty Story RR13273
Speech RR12595
Speech Therapy: Arrested Development Calls For A Revolution Of The Mind AR14716
Speed Mettle: The Fastest Americans In Their Sports, These Skaters And Skiers Hope To Bring Home The Olympic Gold AR13323, AR14856
The Speed Of Grace RR10548
The Spice Of Life: Salt-N-Pepa Prove That Hip-Hop Is Not Just A Man's Game AR13555
Spiderland RR12535
Spiked! RR11568
Spin Doctor: Club DJ Junior Vasquez Remixes The Soundtrack Of New York At Night AR13266, AR14857
Spin Doctors AR13666
Spinal Tap AR15992
The Spinanes AR13688
Spinner RR11083, RR12951
Spinning Around The Sun RR11249, RR11250
Spirit RR12012
The Spirit Of Country RR11561
Spirit Of '73 RR13274
Spirit Of Sheba RR11870, RR11871
The Spirits Of Our Ancestors RR12903
Splash, Point And Shoot: When Your Destination Is All Wet, These Are The Right Cameras to Take Along AR13124
Split RR11752
Sponge AR12968
Sponge City AR15321
Spooky RR11753
The Sporting Life RR11209, RR11563
Springsteen AR14517
Springsteen Settles Suits With Roadies [and other news] AR13994
Springsteen: The Rolling Stone Interview AR14202
Squeeze Box: The Who Get The Deluxe Treatment AR15534
Squeezed Pay AR13212
Stages RR11396
Stain RR11706, RR11707
Stakes Is High RR10967
Stalkers: Is The Threat To Rock Stars Growing? AR12943
Stamping Out Hate AR13048
[Stamps] AR15480
Stan Getz: A Life In Jazz BR01118
Stanley Road RR12894
Star RR10543
Star Scribes AR15481
Star-Studded Soundtrack: U2, Talking Heads, R.E.M. And Others Provide Music For Wenders Film AR14496
Star Systems 1992 AR13648
Star Systems '93: Audio For Every Room And Budget AR13649
Star Time RR10677
Star Trek: Melissa Etheridge Takes The Long Hard Road From The Heartland To Hollywood AR13556
The 'Star Wars' Trilogy On Laser AR15668
Starr Time For Ringo AR15993
Starry Eyes RR13275
Stars Sing For Williams AR15171
Start Packing RR12407
Starting Over: Wilco See A New Dawn With 'A.M.' AR14192
State Of The Reunion AR15331
Static Electricity: Radiohead Transform Emotional Turmoil Into Kinetic Pop

AR15858
Station To Station: On A Personal Tour Of Ziggy's London, David Bowie Looks Back At His Days As The Glam King Of England AR15435
Stay Out Of The Kitchen RR11546
Stay With Me RR12057
Steady Diet Of Nothing RR11190
Steal This Diploma: Higher Education At Lower Prices AR15322
The Stealth War Against Abortion: In Rural States Like Mississippi, Abortion May Still Be Legal, But Lawmakers Have Made It Nearly Impossible For Women To Make The Choice For Themselves AR15225
Steely Dan: New York City CR00897
Stephen Dorff: Playing The Forgotten Beatle AR13210
Steppin' Out RR10547
Steppin' With Peps RR12144
Stepping Out RR10465
Stereolab: Hoboken, N.J. CR00899
Sterling Morrison: 1942-1995 AR13750
Steve Miller: The Space Cowboy And Gangster Of Love Proves There's Life After His Greatest Hits AR14238
Stevie Nicks AR13557
Stevie Wonder: Never-Ending Song Of Peace AR15197
Stick Around For Joy RR12669
Stick-N-Moove RR10791
Sticks & Stones: Whether You're Heading For The Great Outdoors Or The Urban Jungle, Durable Watches And Rugged Boots Ease Your Trek Off The Beaten Path AR15212
Sticky Situation: A New Warning Label On MC Eiht's Hit CD Raises Some Epic Questions AR15773
The Stiff Records Box Set RR13276
Stiffed: A True Story Of MCA, The Music Business, And The Mafia BR01119
Still Feel Gone RR12797
Still First In Space: Pink Floyd Rocket Back To The Top With The Division Bell AR15535
Still Rocking: PCs, The Web, Multimedia...Despite The Hype Computer Technology Can't Compare With The Elegance Reliability And Value Of Today's Audio Systems AR13650
Sting AR14619
'Stock Footage AR13026
Stockholm Syndrome AR15008
Stone Alone: Pearl Jam's Stone Gossard Goes Solo With Shame AR13299
Stone Cold World RR10417
Stone Free RR13277
Stone Rock Blues RR13278
Stone Temple Pilots: Philadelphia CR00904
Stone Temple Pilots: Universal Amphitheater CR00903
Stone Witch RR11874
Stoned And Dethroned RR11525
Stones Sign Deal With Virgin AR15172
Stones Take It To The Max: 'At The Max' Shows The Rolling Stones As They've Never Been Seen Before AR15994
Stones Uncovered AR13300
Stop And Listen RR11913
Storm Warning RR11069
The Story: A Signature Sound AR16056
Story Of My Life RR12147
Story Of My Life: Personal Publishing On The Web AR14129
Story Of The Eye BR01120
Storyteller RR12874
Storyville RR12364, RR12365
Straight Outta Compton RR12059
Straight Shooters: Seattle Rockers Take A Sober Side Trip With Mad Season AR15089
Straight Troops—Gay Troops AR15071
Straitjacket Fits: New Zealand's Pop Export AR14717
Straitjacket Fits—The Bats—The Jean-Paul Sarte Experience: San Francisco CR00640, CR00757, CR00905
The Strand, Los Angeles CR00684
The Strange And Mysterious Death Of Mrs. Jerry Lee Lewis AR13345
Strange Fruit: Black Grape Uncork A Distinctive Vintage AR15436
Strange Fruit: The Improbable Rise Of Dolores O'Riordan And The Cranberries AR13667
The Strange Loves Of Lyle Lovett AR15995
Strange Magic RR11066
Strange Things Happening RR12533
Stranger Than Fiction RR10483
Strawberries Oceans Ships Forest RR11138
Strawberry Jam RR10710
Street Angel RR12036
Street Jams RR13279
Street News AR13589, AR13590, AR13591, AR13592, AR13593, AR13594, AR13595, AR15450, AR15451, AR15452, AR15628
Strength In Numbers RR12784
Stress Relief AR15072
Strictly Commercial RR13026
Stripped RR12377
Studio Of The Moment: At Fort Apache, The Motto Is 'Great Big Guitars And No Rules' AR14463
A Study Of Frustration RR11273
Stupid And Contagious AR15009
Stupid Is As Stupid Does AR15669
Stuttering John RR12657
Styling A Greater Green Empire: Sebastian Inc. Gives Something Back To The Earth AR15695
Subhuman Race RR12526
Sublime RR12660
Subliminal Sandwich RR11851
Suede RR12664
Suede: All That Glitters AR13381
Suede: New York City CR00908
Sugar: Cat's Cradle CR00817, CR00909
Sugar: Turning Bitter Into Sweet AR14718
Suicidal Tendencies: Kurt Did Not Die For You AR13790
Suicide Watch AR12922
Sukia AR15728
Summer Concert Season Comes Up Short AR13090
Summer Movie Report Card AR15552, AR15670
Summer Of Love BR01121
Summer With A Vengence: Why Hollywood Will Die Hard Trying To Bust Last Summer's Record AR15671
Summer Wrap-Up AR15672
Summit Conference RR12962
Sun Ra Arkestra At The Bottom Line CR00910
Sun Ra: 1914-1993 AR13785
Sun Ra Visits Planet Earth RR12273
The Sun Records Collection RR13280
Sun Strategies: The Best Defense Is A Good Dose Of SPF AR15553
The Sundays: The Academy CR00788, CR00911
Sunrise On The Sufferbus RR11805
Sunset Park RR13281
Sun-60: A Dynamic Duo AR15173
Super Bad RR11269, RR12717
Super Highway Sounds AR16079
Super Tasty RR11320
Superbad!: The Elusive Prince Returns Triumphant AR14497
Superdrag Take Off For The Big Time At Top Speed AR15859
Superegos On The Loose AR13619
Superelastic RR12827
Supermodel City AR15036
Supernatural Fairy Tales RR13282
Super-Sonic Jazz RR12274, RR12275
Superunknown RR12585, RR12586
Supreme Court Goes Electric RR12680
Supreme Justice: Rap's Day In Court AR15459
Sure Love RR11602
Surfing's Eco-Warriors: The Members Of The Surfrider Foundation Are Making Waves For Cleaner Coastal Waters AR15996
Surprise RR12875
Surrender (song) RR12630
Surviving The Crusades AR15458
Susan Across The Ocean RR12503
Suspending Disbelief RR12885
Sutras RR11024
Suzanne Vega: The Academy CR00926
Swamp Ophelia RR11477
Sway RR10442
Sweat 'N' Soul RR12428
Sweet F.A. RR11739
Sweet Little Mysteries RR11798
Sweet Old World RR12933
Sweet Potatoe Pie RR11022
Sweet Relief RR13283, RR13284
Sweet Relief II RR13285, RR13286
The Sweet Smell Of Success: The Punks Of Rancid Match Wits With The Corporate Rock Machine AR13668
Sweet Soul Music: Retro Rockers Collective Soul Take A Shine To The Airwaves AR14409
Sweet Surrender: Donning Dress-To-Kill Leather Jackets, The Midwestern Singer And The Vampire Slayer Give Themselves Up To A Day At The Beach AR14858, AR15696
The Sweetest Days RR12936
Sweetheart's Dance RR12741
Swervedriver: Chaos, Distortion And Feedback AR14719
Swim Away RR12224
A Swing And A Miss: The Senate Crime Bill AR13607
Swing That Music RR12033, RR12890, RR13287
Swing Time! RR13288
Switchblades Of Love RR13003
Syd Straw Plays With The Skeletons In Her Closet AR13457
[Symbol] RR12235
Sympathy For The Flip Side: Collector Turns Penchant For The Obscure Into A&R Dream AR13366
Symphonic Music Of The Rolling Stones RR11716
Symphony For Improvisors RR10774
Symphony No. 3 RR11278, RR11279, RR11713, RR11714, RR12800, RR12801, RR13036, RR13037
Symphony Or Damn RR10956, RR10957
Systems Theory: Carefully Chosen Components + The Right Software = A Computer That Works The Way You Do AR13125

T

Tabala Wolof Sufi Drumming Of Senegal RR13289
Take A Look RR10837

Take Another Little Piece Of My Heart BR01122
Take Me As I Am RR11403
Take The Guitar Player For A Ride RR11672
A Tale Of 2 Indies: Epitaph Records... AR14193
A Tale Of 2 Indies: Matador... AR13091
Tales From The Crib: Dormitory Resident Advisers Explain How They Deal With Bongs, Beer, Stress And...Uh...Noisy Couples AR15323
Tales From The Downside: Freedy Johnston Writes Perfect pop Songs About Hard Times And Heartbreak AR13669
Tales Of Ordinary Madness RR11379
Talk RR12981
Talk This Way: The Rolling Stone Interview With Aerosmith's Steven Tyler AR13751
Talking RR11919
Tania's World AR14429, AR15752
Tanks For The Memories: Michael Jackson Imposes 'HIStory' On The Czech Republic AR14669
The Tape Of Only Linda RR11726
T.A.P.O.A.F.O.M. RR10823, RR10824, RR10825
Tara Key AR14612
Tarantula BR01123, RR12351
A Taste Of Heaven RR11987
Tattoo You: Lou Deangelis Gets Crazy On His Mountain Bike AR14461, AR14859
The Tattooed Heart RR12014b
Taxi RR11130
Tear The Roof Off 1974-1980 RR12112
Tears Of Fire: The 25th Anniversary Collection RR12967
Techno Mancer RR13290
Technology: A Three-Way Video-Game Battle Begins AR14666
Technology: Getting Up To Speed On The Web With ISDN AR14667
Technology: New Home-Theater Products Adapt Themselves To Smaller Spaces AR13126
Technopop AR15574
Ted Hawkins: 1936-1995 AR15381
The Ted Offensive: How Ted Koppel's 'Nightline' Rules The World AR15997
Teenage Kicks RR13291
Teenage Symphonies To God RR12835
Teenager Of The Year RR10571b
Tejano Country Christmas RR13292
Tekit Izi RR11586
Telephono RR12609
Television AR13752, RR11032, RR12711
Television's Refined Tuning: The New York Punk-Guitar Godfathers Pick Up Where They Left Off AR13440
Tell Me Why RR11573
Tell Us About Your Life AR15575
Tell Us About Your Music AR15576
Temple Of The Dog RR13293
Temples Of Boom RR10939, RR10940
The Temporary Miracle: How One Good Job Becomes Three Lousy Ones AR14113
Temptation RR11756
Ten RR12134
Ten Best Movies Of 1992 AR15673
The 10 Best Movies Of 1994 AR15674
10: Express Yourself AR13558
Ten Feet Tall And Bulletproof RR12772
10 On Broadway RR10992
10 Song Demo RR10754
Ten Summoner's Tales RR12642, RR12643
Ten Things In 1993 That Didn't Suck AR14340
10,000 Maniacs On The Loose Again AR15998
The 10 Worst Movies Of 1994 AR15675
Tenor Legacy RR11733
Terence Blanchard RR10589
Terminators: The Robots That Rodney Brooks And Hans Moravec Imagine Will Succeed Humans, Not Serve Them AR13461
Terror Has Some Strange Kinfolk RR10761, RR11106
Texas Blues RR13294
Texas Bluesman RR10622
Thank You RR11043, RR12401, RR12402
Thank You For The Music RR10384
Thanks For The Memories RR11719
That Girl AR13559
That What Is Not RR12248
That's Entertainment AR13127
That's The Way It Should Be RR10630a
The Thelonious Monk Quartet Live At The Five Spot Featuring John Coltrane RR10852, RR11928
Theory Of Everything RR11134
Therapy?: From The Land Of Bombings And Bono AR13919
There Are But Four Small Faces RR12542
There's Room For Us All RR12505
Thermadore Try Not To Get Worried AR14599
These Blues RR10673
These Days RR10625
These Heads Are Meant To Roll: Manufacturers Put A New—Not To Mention Detachable—Face On Car Audio AR16058
Thesis RR10595, RR11257, RR12684
They Call Me The Fat Man RR11023
They Came, They Played, They Blocked The Driveway RR13295
They Might Be Giants CR00915
They Might Be Giants: New York CR00914
They Say They Want A Revolution: In The Ukraine And Georgia, Nothing Secedes Like Secession AR15010
They're Here, They're The Queers And They're Not What You Think AR15208
Things To Do AR15073
Thinkin' About You RR12980
Thinkin' Problem RR10497
Third-Sister Lovers RR10560
Thirteen RR12710
13: Love Will Never Do AR15629
13 Ribs RR12844
Thirteen Years RR11094
38: Ashes To Ashes AR14410
The 35th Anniversary Collection RR11910, RR12366
35: Love Shack AR13560
34: Slave To The Rhythm AR15630
39: In Bloom AR13561
31: Kool Thing AR13562
37: Atlantic City AR14573
36: Jeremy AR14572
33: Mind Playing Tricks On Me AR14251
32: Burning Down The House AR13563
Thirty Years Of Maximum R & B RR12921
30: You Might Think AR13032
This Ain't No Mudd Club: CBGB Celebrates Its 20 Years Of Rock & Roll AR13016
This Heart Of Mine RR10740
This Is How I Feel About Jazz RR11564
This Is Me RR12762
This Land RR11185
This Moment In Toronto RR12938
[This Month...] AR15591
This Mortal Coil RR12727
This Old 'Palooza AR14438
This One's Gonna Hurt You RR12656
This Perfect World RR11554
This Show Was About Every Critic's Desire: To Rock It Like You Write It AR13753
This Time RR12987, RR12988
This Wheel's On Fire AR13402, AR14151, BR01124
Thorn EMI Buys Virgin AR13995
Thoroughly Modern Bjork AR15704
Those Were The Days: New Home Video Captures The Beatles During Their First Visit To America AR13827
Thousand Roads RR10915
Thrak RR11615
Thrakattak RR11616
3 RR11137
Three Days At The Barricades: How Rock & Roll, Fax Machines And The Hip Crowd Helped Crack The Coup AR15691
3 Feet High And Rising RR10967a
Three Fish RR12736
311 Kiss Up To Hippies And Skate Punks AR14600
Three In A Van: Mike Watt Hits The Road Econo Style With Dave Grohl And Eddie Vedder AR13670
3: Losing My Religion AR14411
Three Snakes And One Charm RR10570, RR10571
3 Tribes AR13382
3 Years, 5 Months And 2 Days In The Life Of... RR10459
Through The Looking Glass AR15074
Throwing Copper RR11705
Throwing Muses CR00916
Thunder Down Under: Australia Takes An Alterna-Rock Holiday With Big Day Out AR15357
Tical RR11893
Ticket Jam: Pearl Jam's Concert Sales Spur New Controversy AR13092
Ticket Masters: How Smashing Pumpkins, Nine Inch Nails And Others Thwart Concert Scalpers AR13093
Tickets To Ride: Pearl Jam Hit The Road Their Way AR15860
Tigerlily RR11879, RR11880
Tigerman RR12947
Till Death Do Us Part RR11235
Till The Night is Gone RR13296
Tim Burton: The Rolling Stone Interview AR13147
Tim Ferguson: The Mint CR00717
Tim Finn: Apart From The Crowd AR13828
Tim Robbins: The Running Man AR16119
Time Signatures RR10686
Time Takes Time RR12628
Time Traveller RR11939
Time Warner Runs Up The White Flag: The Media Help Drag Down One Of Their Own AR14341
Time Was When RR10668
The Times Have Indeed Changed: The Band Follows Dylan In Selling Their Songs As Ads AR14037
The "Times" They Are A-Changin' AR15607
Timing Is Everything AR14576
Timothy Leary: 1920-1996 AR13916
Tindersticks AR15437, RR12744, RR12745
Tiny Lights: Shining In Hoboken AR13829
Tiny Music RR12648, RR12649
Tipper: Dems Send Wrong Message AR13441
Tipper Gore Quits PMRC: But Has The First Lady of 'Parental Advisory' Really Given Up The Fight? AR14042
Titanic Days RR11764
Titanic Love Affair: Sunk Once, The Band Returns With 'No Charisma' AR14720
TLC: Street-Level Feminism AR14498
To Be Loved BR01125
To Bring You My Love RR12183, RR12184
To Hell & Back: They Say They're Not

Jinxed, But The Members Of Def Leppard Have Had To Endure A String Of Tragedies That Would Have Destroyed Most Other Bands AR13754
To Hell And Back AR15861
To Rolling Stone Readers AR15610, AR15611
To The Birds (single) RR12665
To The Bone RR11627
To The Faithful Departed RR10896
To The Readers Of Rolling Stone AR15800
Toasting Townshend: Roger Daltrey Does Carnegie Hall AR15536
A Todos Los Barrios RR12374
Together Alone RR10919
Together Forever RR12411
Toking Down With The MC5 AR13596
Tom Cruise: Pushing Thirty, The Star Of 'Far And Away' Gets His Life Together With The Help Of Scientology And His Wife Nicole Kidman AR14000
Tom Hanks Rides Again AR15676
Tom Jones AR13564
Tom Petty And The Heartbreakers—Chris Whitley CR00844, CR00938
Tom Petty: This IS How It Feels On The Road AR15377
Tom Waits: Paramount Theater CR00931
Tombstone Every Mile RR11629
'Tommy' Scores Again: An Old Tale Gets A New Twist On The Stage AR15999
'Tommy' Sells Out AR15588
Tomorrow The Green Grass RR11516
Tone Dialing RR10841, RR12225
Tongues And Tails RR11375
Toni Braxton RR10655
Tonic RR11381
Tonight! Sinead Performs! AR15075
Tonite Let's All Make Love In London RR13297
Tony Bennett AR13565
The Tonya Harding Fall: The Transformation of A Young Figure-Skating Champion Into The World's Most Visible Villainess AR15544
Too Bad Jim RR10702
Too High To Die RR11854
Too Legit To Quit RR11350
Too Long In Exile RR11954, RR11955
Tool: Boston CR00918
Tool Get Spiritual And Scatological With 'Aenima' AR15862
Topcat: The Making Of "The Lion King" AR16000
Topical Disease AR15324
[Tori Amos] AR14721
Tori Amos: Ethereal Earthquakes AR13830
Tori Amos: The Power And The Passion AR15631
Tornado Souvenirs RR12348
Torture Garden RR11988
Tossing Seeds RR12677
Totally Krossed Out RR11645
Totally Stoned: Primal Scream Return To Rock Roots With "Give Out But Don't Give Up" AR13383
Totally Wired AR13374, AR13375, RR13298
Toto La Momposina Y Sus Tambores—La Candela Viva RR11925
Tough Times For Rock Auctions AR13903
Tougher Than Music RR13299
Tougher Than Tough RR13300, RR13301
Tour De Force: The Rolling Stones Rake It In And Rock The House AR13267
Tours: From Sex Pistols To Kiss, The Summer Of...'76? AR16001
Toward A Sane National Drug Policy AR14737, AR15801
Toward The Within RR10968
Town And County RR12927
Toy Caldwell: 1948-1993 AR15131
Toys From The Attic AR14722
The Toys Of Summer AR16080, AR16081, AR16102
Toys Of Summer: Look Here For Something New Under The Sun AR16082
Trace RR11000, RR12567
A Trace Of Gold: The Ace Catches Air On The Way To Lillehammer AR13324, AR14860
The Tracks Of The Coyote AR14446
The Tractors RR12757, RR12758
Tracy Chapman CR00675
Trade Test Transmission RR10713
Traffic: Charlotte, N.C. CR00921
Traffic From Paradise RR11566
Tragic Kingdom RR12050
A Tragic Miscarriage Of Justice Continues: The State Of Michigan Vs. Gary Fannon AR15338
Tragic Songs Of Life RR11730
Tramp On Your Street RR12480
Trampoline RR11398
Trance RR11348, RR13006
Trance Planet RR13302
Transient Random-Noise Bursts With Announcements RR12635
Transmissions From The Satellite Heart RR11145
Trapped in Mr. Bill's Neighborhood AR15601
Tras La Tormenta RR10586, RR10849
Trash Collection: Sonic Youth Go Artcore On New LP AR14412
Travel On, Rider RR12445
Travolta: The Rolling Stone Interview AR15378
[Trent Hill's Essay] AR15687
Tri And Mighty: To Brave The Hawaii Ironman, It Takes Big Kahunas AR14133, AR14861
Triage RR10488
Tribal Thunder RR10951
Tribal Voice RR12989
A Tribe Called Quest AR15442
Tribute AR15688
Tribute: David Briggs 1944-1995 AR15132
Tribute: Junior Walker 1931-1995 AR14218
Tribute: Pete Grant 1935-1995 AR13458
A Tribute To Black Entertainers RR13303
A Tribute To Curtis Mayfield RR13304
Tribute To The Music Of Bob Wills And The Texas Playboys RR10464
A Tribute To Woody: Artists Gather To Commemorate Singer's Birthday AR13442
Tributes AR15037, AR15689
Tricks Of The Shade RR11267
Tricky AR13384, AR15438
Tricky Presents Grassroots RR12770
Tricotism RR12730
Trios RR12872
Trippy Lip Shtick: Flaming Lips Rain Cosmic Debris AR13409
Tropicalia 2 RR11243, RR12833
Troubadour: The Definitive Collection 1964-1976 RR11025
Trouble In Paradise: Violence Erupts After MTV Event In New Jersey AR14723
Trouble No More RR11351
True Democracy RR12631
"True Lies" And Sexual Violence AR15677
True Lies: On "The Larry Sanders Show," Garry Shandling Turns The Talk-Show Brouhaha Into The Funniest Thing On TV AR14591
A Truly Democratic Party: The MTV And VH-1 Generations Swing Together At Clinton's Inaugural AR14239, AR14724
Try A Little Tenderness AR15082
Try It RR12623
Try N' Be RR12776
Tulare Dust RR13305
Tumble Weeds: Competing In A Sport That Demands Youth And Artistry, Gymnasts Shannon Miller And Jarrod Hanks Make The Leap From Athlete To Performer AR13599, AR14799
Tuning Into Prine Time: John Prine Scores High In The Ratings With 'The Missing Years' AR16002
Turbulent Indigo RR11915
Turn It Upside Down RR12600
Turn Loose The Swans RR11986
Turning Half Japanese AR14413
The Turning Point: Annie Lennox Finds Life After Eurythmics AR15439
Tuskegee Experiments RR10717
12: Beat It AR15632
12 Golden Country Greats RR12887
12 Haunted Episodes RR12108a
12 Inches Of Snow RR12564
12 Shades Of Brown RR10680a
28: Vogue AR13566
Twenty-First Century Jesus RR11886
25: Give It Away AR13567
25 Years Of Fear And Loathing AR15602
25 Years: The Chain RR11148a
24: Borderline AR14414
24 Nights RR10807a, RR10807b
20: Like A Prayer AR15633
29: Close AR14295
21: Gett Off AR15634
27: Billie Jean AR13568
26: Hot For Teacher AR13569
23: Boys Of Summer AR13831
22: Girls Just Want To Have Fun AR13570
Twilight Of The Greens AR13923
Twisted Twang: Geraldine Fibbers Take It To The Limit AR12944
II [Two] RR10647, RR11081, RR12214
Two For The Road: On The Move With Those Sexual Screwups From 'Short Cuts,' Matthew Modine & Julianne Moore AR14862, AR15720
2 1 RR10883a
2: Smells Like Teen Spirit AR14725
Two Pages RR11264
Two Sevens Clash RR10927
2pac's Gospel Truth: In A Year When His Song Was On Trial For A Murder, The Rapper Seeks Calm In The Storm AR15091

U

U2 CR00923
U2: Finds What It's Looking For AR13755
U2 Get Their Wings AR14415
U2: The Zoo Tour Move Outdoors AR13996
Ugly Kid Joe: Living Out Their Fantasies AR14003
Uh-Oh RR10716
Uhhh (song) RR10979
Unboxed RR11345
Unbreakable Heart (song) RR10747
The Un-Candidate AR14015
Unchained RR10753
Uncharted Territory: 12 Artists On The Edge AR15705
Uncle Jam Wants You RR11199
Uncle Meat RR13027
Unclogged RR12973
Under A Hoodoo Moon BR01126
Under The Bushes Under The Stars RR11319

Under The Pink RR10426, RR10427
Under The Table And Dreaming RR11810, RR11811
Under The Wishing Tree RR12468
Under Your Thumb: New Hand-Held Electronics Put Technology In The Grasp Of Your Hand AR15736
Understanding RR12957
Underworld Find Their Voice Behind Beats And Riffs AR15213
Undisputed Attitude RR12531
Union RR10765
The United States Of Poetry RR13306
Universal Mother RR12068
University RR12738
Unplugged RR10411, RR10808, RR10809, RR12999, RR13000
Unplugged...And Unseated RR12639
Unplugged: The Official Bootleg RR11834
[Unprecedented Sweep] AR15706
Unreasonable Doubt AR15545
Unreasonable Doubt: Part 2 AR15546
Unsatisfied (song) RR12336
Unsettled Scores RR13307
Unshaven RR12479
Until The End Of The World RR13308
Unusual Suspects: Loud Lucy & Civ Defy Alterna-Rock Convention And Live To Talk About It AR14863, AR15581, AR15774
Up RR12353
Up Against The Drywall: Mexican-American Carpenters Remake The U.S. Labor Movement In Orange County, Calif. AR14114
Up Against The Wal: Wal-Mart Keeps Albums—And Customers?—Out AR15589
Up The Amazon: Chasing Sloths, Drinking Bootleg Rum And Getting Tight With Chiggers AR15011
Up The Mountain AR15025
Update AR14447, AR15707, AR15708, AR15709, AR15710, AR15711, AR15712, AR15713, AR15714
Uptown MTV Unplugged RR13309
Uranium Road (song) RR10436
Uranus RR12486
Urban Blues RR13310
Urge Overkill Indoors AR15325
Us RR11206
U.S. Literacy Sinks To New Low AR15076
Use Your Illusion I RR11323, RR11324
Use Your Illusion II RR11325, RR11326
Utah Saints RR12807

V

The 'Vad' Fad: Making Music-Video Commercials AR15355
Valis 1 Destruction Of Syntax RR13312
Valuing The Family AR15715
Vampyros Lesbos Sexadelic Dance Party RR12810
Van Halen CR00637, CR00925
Van Halen: Clarkston, Michigan CR00924
Van Halen: Here, Now AR16003
Van Morrison AR16004, CR00812
Van Morrison: The Nob Hill Masonic Center CR00813
Vauxhall And I RR11957
The V-Discs RR13311
Vee Vee RR10454
Vehicles RR10697
Veil RR10504
The Veldt AR13671
Velocity Girl AR13904
Velvet Crush: A Slovenly Rock & Roll Spirit AR14726
The Velvet Underground: London CR00927
The Ventures' Christmas Album RR12838
Vernon Reid, Will Calhoun And Melvin Gibbs CR00672, CR00729, CR00864
Verve At The Anshe Slonim Synagogue CR00928
The Verve: New York CR00929
The Verve Pipe AR15721
Very RR12151
The Very Best Of Buddy Guy RR11337
A Very Special Christmas 2 RR13313
VI: Return Of The Real RR11469
'Vibe' Baptized By Fire: Debut Issue Of Hip-Hop Magazine Hits The Street To Attacks And Praise AR13443
Vibrator RR10958
Victoria Williams: New York CR00940
Victoria's Secret: Victoria Williams Gets Real "Loose" On Her New LP AR15104
Video & Laser Hot Sheet AR15724
The Video File AR13029, AR15775
Video Files AR15725
Video Laser Hot Picks AR15678
Video-Laser News AR15679
Videomakers Who Vault To The Big Screen AR14296
Videos By Number AR14423
Vientos RR11721
The Vietnam Wars BR01127
A View To Kill AR12956
Vindication BR01128
Vintage Rays RR12672
Virtual Dylan: Bob Dylan Goes Electric Again—On CD-ROM AR15537
Virus 100 RR13314
The Vision Thing AR15730
Vision Thing AR13756
The Visionary Light AR15344
Vitalogy RR12135, RR12136
Viva Dead Ponies RR11126
Viva La Divas AR15198
Viva La Muerte RR10830
Viva! La Woman RR10794
Viva Last Blues RR12100
Viva Luckenbach! RR12860
Viva Zapata RR12465
Vivian Stanshall: 1943-1995 AR15209
Vodou Adjae RR10639
A Voice In The Night AR14518
Voice Of Experience: Iris DeMent Turns Her Life Into Song AR14727
The Voice Of Langston Hughes RR11451
The Voice Of Silence RR11018
Voices Of Freedom BR01129
Voix Du Soleil RR13315
Volley Of The Dolls: The Goo Goo Dolls Turn It Up And Kick Out The Jams, Replacements Style AR14728
Volume 1 RR11900
Volume 2 RR11901
Volume 3 RR11902
Volume III Just Right RR12581
Volumes 1, 2, And 3 RR11903
Voo Doo Doll (song) RR10450
Voodoo Child: Hendrix Jr. Sues Estate AR14455
Voodoo Child: The Rolling Stone Interview With Living Colour's Vernon Reid AR13148
Voodoo Lounge RR12378, RR12379
Voters For A Choice Benefit: Washington CR00727, CR00774, CR00841, CR00946
Voudou Nou RR12294
Voyage To The Bottom Of The Season AR14592
Vroom RR11617
Vs. RR12137, RR12138

W

W. C. Handy's Memphis Blues Band RR11358
Wah Wah RR11504
Wailing Souls: A Reggae Hall Of Fame AR13314
Waist Deep In Whitewater: P. J. O'Rourke Gets His Mind Right With Pols, Pickles And Catfish AR15012
Waiting For The Band AR13757
Waiting For The Sun BR01130
Waiting For You RR11695
Wakafrika RR10996
Waking Up The Neighbours RR10391
Walk Around Heaven RR12728
Walk On RR10635
Walk On The West Side AR13037, AR15722
Walk On The Wild Side: The Secret History Of The Alternative-Rock Revolution AR15026
Walk Right Back RR11108
Walk The Dog And Light The Light RR12060
Walking In London RR10859
Walking Wounded RR11109
The Wallflowers RR12864
The Wallflowers At The Chance, Poughkeepsie, N.Y. CR00932
Wal-Mart: No 'Utero' AR13571
Walls Scream (song) RR12340
Walt Mink: Power-Trio Rock AR13017
Walter Hyatt 1949-1996 AR13094
Wandering Spirit RR11499, RR11500
Wanted Man RR11595
Wanted! 10 Things You Can Do To Make A Difference AR15109
The War At Home: How The Media Miss The Story On 34,000 Gun Deaths Each Year AR14342
War At Warners: Power Struggle Plagues World's Largest Label AR16005
War College AR13141
Warm Your Heart RR12014c
Warner Bros.: A New Regime AR16006
Warren Beatty AR16120
Warren Piece RR12022
Washing Machine RR12571, RR12572
Wasn't That A Time RR12884
Wasps' Nests RR12523
Wassoulou Foli RR12501
Watching The Dark RR12732
The Watchman: Straightforward Ballsy Folk AR13018
Watershed RR11845
Wavelength Infinity RR13316
Wax Ecstatic RR12607, RR12608
The Wax Factor: Major Labels Get Back Into The 12-Inch Groove Thang AR15133
The Way That I Am RR11830
Way To Blue RR11033
Waylon: An Autobiography BR01131
Waymore's Blues (Part II) RR11523
Wayne's World: For The MC5's Kramer, The Future Is Now AR12969
We Are Golden: Woodstock '94 Is Headed Into The Black AR14645
We Are Never Talking (song) RR11092
[We Are Proud...] AR15740
We Are Tibet: The Beastie Boys And Smashing Pumpkins Headline The Largest Benefit Concert Of The 1990s AR15496
We Can't Be Stopped RR11236
We Can't Dance RR11227
We Care RR12906
We Get There When We Do RR12661
We Should Have Seen It Coming: Riots Are The Latest Rock Fad AR14787
We Travel The Spaceways RR12276
We Were Just Happy Freaks, Man: Garcia In

His Own Words AR13301
Web Watch: Because You're Mine, I Walk Online AR14278
Webb Of Sound AR15215
Webheads On Ramona Street: Jonathan 'Dr. Cheeze' Steuer Makes His Million-Dollar Cyborganic Dream Garden Become Reality AR14016
Wedowee: When An Alabama Principal Said No To Interracial Dating, A Small Community Was Forced To Confront Its Racist Heritage AR14305
The Weedkiller's Daughter RR11542
Ween AR13410
Weezer AR14557, RR12889
Weight RR12382
Weiland Arrested For Drugs AR15863
Weiland In Drug Treatment; Pilots Grounded AR14194
Weiland: Of Stone Temple Pilots AR14729
Weird Nightmare RR13317
The 'Weird' Side Of R.E.M.: 'Automatic For The People' Features Slow, Dark, Brooding Songs AR13758
The Weiss Man Cometh: Introducing Rob Weiss—Director, Bigmouth, Suburban Success Story AR16007
Welcome To The Information Superdorm: The Digital Future Is Being Shaped On Campus Right Now AR14211
Welcome To The Jungle AR14150
Welcome To The Machine: The Music Revolution Comes To Your Town AR13367
Welcome To Wherever You Are RR11483, RR11484
Weld RR10903, RR10904, RR13001, RR13002
Well Armed: 'Tank Girl' LP Snags A-List Punks AR14303
We're Desperate RR13318
We're Not Gonna Take It: Gay And Lesbian Activists Battle The Rise Of Homophobia In Pop Music AR13620
We're Only In It For The Money RR11964, RR13028
West Des Moines, Iowa AR15803
Western Beat RR12091, RR12892
Westing RR12128
WH Down & Dirty: The Rolling Stone Interview AR13444
Whaler RR11376
What A Crying Shame RR11814
What A Way To Live RR10778
What A Wonderful Web It Could Be: Netscape's Co-Inventor Charts The Digital Future AR14212
What Clinton Can Do For The Economy AR14115
What Does Conan O'Brien Have That You Don't? AR14730
What Is Bhangra? RR13319
What It Is RR10691
What It Is? RR10585
What Silence Knows RR12006
What To Do The Morning After AR15083
What TV Movies Are Doing Right AR15680
What You Can Do AR15806
Whatever RR11787
What's In A 'Name'? Goo Goo Dolls Score A Hit Nine Years In The Making AR15474
What's New, Democrat? Clinton's Politics Look Awfully Familiar AR14116
What's The 411? RR10596
What's The New Mary Jane (single) RR11924
(What's The Story) Morning Glory? RR12062, RR12063
(What's The Story) With Brit Pop Sites? AR14279
Whatta Man (song) RR11078, RR12427
The Wheel RR10755
Wheels Of Fire RR10909, RR10910
When Elvis Was King: New Box Set Compiles All Of Presley's Recordings From The Fifties AR16008
When I Lived In The Wild RR11172
When I Was A Boy RR12500
When Love Finds You RR11244
When No One's Looking RR13039
When Squirrels Play Chicken RR12148
When Success fails: What Really Bugs The GOP About Student Loans And Americorps is That They Work AR14650
When The Levee Breaks (song) RR11608
When The Mightiest Television Network Meets Up With The Lords Of Testosterone, Someone's Bound To Get Hurt AR16061
When The Senate Comes Around: Cooler Heads Are Prevailing In That Other House On Capitol Hill AR16044
Whenever We Wanted RR11869
Where Angels Fear To Tread: Pearl Jam Open Their Spring Tour On A Wing And A Prayer AR14788
Where Is Brooklyn? RR10775
Where It All Begins RR10416
Where It Goes RR10742
Where It's At RR11427
Where The Jobs Are AR15807
Where The Streets Have No Name (song) RR12792
Where The Wild Things Are: The Beastie Boys Become Kings Of Their Own Urbane Jungle AR14731
Where There's Smoke: Method Man Ignited Hip-Hop With Blunt Rhyme AR15635
Where You Been RR11010
Where Woodstock Lives RR13320
Where'd You Hide The Body RR11848
Whigging Out: Afghan Whigs Join Sub Pop Alumni With A Major-Label Debut, 'Gentlemen' AR13019
Whip Smart: The Tricks Of The Trade For Better Grades AR14046
Whip-Smart RR12159, RR12160
Whiskey For The Holy Ghost RR11663
The Whistle Only Dogs Can Hear RR11418
White Country Blues (1926-1938) RR13321
The White Hotel BR01132
White Light White Heat White Trash RR12565
White Men Can't Rap RR13322
White Men Can't Rule: A Melting Pot Revolt AR14343
White Zombie: Mansfield, Mass. CR00937
Who Are You? Pearl Jam's Eddie Vedder AR13095, AR13285, AR14195
Who Is This Guy? AR14864, AR16009
Who Lost Russia?: The Ex-Reds Need Our Greenbacks AR14117
The Who Sell Out RR12922
Whole Lotta Lolla AR15538
Whole Lotta Rosie: With 'The Rosie O'Donnell Show' Around, Talk Becomes Slightly Less Cheap AR16010
Whole Lotta Shakin' Up Goin' On AR14732
A Whole New Thing RR12540
Who'll Buy My Memories? RR12013
Whoomp! RR12697
Who's On Broadway?: Pete Townshend Discusses Bringing The Rock Opera To The Great White Way AR16011
Who's On First?: Lollapalooza Hunts For A Headliner AR15864
Who's Pulling Bill Clinton's Strings? AR14118
Why Are We In Haiti? AR15810
Why Brooke, Why Now AR16012
Why I Believe What I Believe AR15013
Why I Don't Believe What He Believes AR14119
Why Pick On Me RR12624
Why The Mighty GE Can't Strike Out AR14120
Why The Rich Get Richer: Because The Fed Is Engineering A Recession For The Rest Of Us AR14121
Wichita, Kansas AR15811
Wide River RR11906
Wide-Lapel Hell: VH1 Drags 'Bandstand' Out Of The Fashion Closet AR13572
The Wide-Screen Factor AR15681
Widespread Panic: Not Just Another Southern Band AR15351
Wilbert Harrison 1929-1994 AR13786
Wild Kentucky Skies RR10682
The Wild Life RR12529
Wild Love RR12911
Wild Mood Swings RR10932
Wild Seed—Wild Flower RR11118
The Wild Side Of Paradise AR15592
Wild Thing: Drew Barrymore AR14733
Wild Things: Wyld Kiwi Garage 1966-69 RR13323
Wild Wood RR12895
Wildest Dreams RR12782
Wildflowers RR12155, RR12156
Will Oldham Of Palace: King Of Appalachian Indie Rock AR14439
Will The Fed Stiff Clinton? AR14122
William Bloke RR10650
William Kunstler: 1919-1995 AR15465
William M. Gaines (1922-1992) AR14524
Willie Loco Boom Boom Ga Ga: 1975-1991 RR10405
Willie Nelson AR13573
Willie Nelson Throws A Reggae Party AR13211
Willie's Dream: Blues Heaven Buys Chess Studio AR16096
The Willsaphone Stupid Show RR12004
Wilmington, N.C. AR15134
Wilson Phillips AR16013
Win, Lose Or Drawl: Redneck Comic Jeff Foxworthy Tries To Prove That The South Can Do It Again—Again AR16014
Wind Your Waist RR13324
Wings Of A Dove RR10928
Wings Of Joy RR10897
Wings Over America: The Eagles Reunite For Their First Tour In 14 Years AR16015
Winning Losers RR10507, RR12458
Winona AR13905
Winter Light RR12389
Wired For Love: Three Tales Of Computer Romance AR13268, AR14865
Wired For Sound: With The Advent Of Cyberspace, Music May Never Be The Same AR16083
Wired In California: Meth, The Drug That Snuffed Out The Summer Of Love, Is Back, And California IS Exporting It All Over The Nation AR14525
Wish RR10933, RR10934, RR12313
Witchcraft RR10386
With A Little Help From His Mates: Mick Ronson's Posthumous 'Heaven 'N Hull' To Be Released AR13672
With These Hands RR11095
Within Your Reach (song) RR12337
Without A Sound RR11011
Without Walls RR12968
Woke Up With A Monster RR10771
The Wolf That House Built RR11701

Wolverine Blues RR11084
WOMAD On The Road AR14558
The Woman I Am RR11604
The Woman's Boat RR10788
Woman's Gotta Have It RR10876
Wonderful RR10440
Woodstock RR13325
Woodstock '94 RR13326
Woody Allen: The Rolling Stone Interview AR13445
Word Up RR13327
Words RR12345
Words From The 'Home' Front AR14499
Workers Of The World: A Portfolio AR15345, AR16045
Working Class RR10433
Working For The Dead AR14647
Workshop Of The Telescopes RR10610
The World According To Gorby: Over Lunch In Moscow, The Former Senator From California Talks Politics With The Former Head Of the Soviet Union AR13347
World Gone Wrong RR11050
The World Is Yours RR11972
World Music On The Hill: The Grateful Dead Bring The Rain Forest To Washington AR13315
World Of Morrissey RR11958
The World Of Zines BR01133
World Turning RR12771
The World's Biggest Rerun: Why Is The Addams Family Making Hollywood Ghoul Crazy? AR14137
Worried Blues 1963 RR11457
Worth Bragging About: Billy Bragg Takes A Leap Forward With A Stunning New Album AR13906
Would You Please Welcome...: Dave, Conan, Jay And Arsenio Pump Up The Volume AR14574
Wowee Zowee RR12129
Wrecking Ball RR11364
Wu Tang Clan Deliver The Goods With 'Wu Wear' AR13628
Wyman Quits The Stones AR14500
Wynonna RR11574, RR11575
Wynonna Leaves Home: One-Half Of Country Music's Judds Declares Her Independence AR14501
Wysiwys: With These Camcorders, What You See Is What You Shot AR16084

X

X: Can Denzel Washington Make Malcolm Speak To A New Generation Of Americans? AR16087
X Files: Undercover AR16016
X-Ploitation: Paranoids Terrorized By Copycat Thriller Series! AR16017
X-Ray BR01134
X-Tra Naked RR12292
Xs New World Order: L.A.'s Seminal Punkers Reunite On 'Hey Zeus!' AR14613
Xtort RR11631, RR11632
Xtreme Prejudice: At The X Games, ESPN's Alterna-Lympics, The Road Lugers Tried To Go Straight, The Network Tried To Get Radical, And Street Cred Was Just A Marketing Concept AR13046

Y

Y Hoy Como Ayer RR11944
Yabba-Dabba-Doo-Doo: A Summer Movie Guide To What's Fun Among The Dumb AR15682
Yahoo!: How Two Stanford Students Created The Little Search Engine That Could AR15729
Yank Crime RR11034
Yatsura AR15865
Yeah Yeah Yeah Yeah RR10565
The Year In Movies AR13052, AR15683, AR15684, AR15685, AR15686
The Year In Music AR13053, AR13446, AR16099
The Year In Records AR13054
The Year In Television AR13055, AR14593, AR14594
The Year In TV AR16018
Year Of Mondays RR11550
The Year Of The Near Miss AR14811
The Yearn To Earn: Gang Starr Hit Pay Dirt With Streetwise Sounds AR15590
Years RR10883b
The Year's Best In Laser AR16100
The Yellow Shark RR13029
Yerself Is Steam RR11882
Yes RR11948
Yiddish-American Klezmer Music: 1925-1956 RR12701
Yo La Tengo—Teenage Fanclub CR00913, CR00944
Yoko Ono AR15027
Yoko Ono & John Lennon AR14454
You Can Take it With You AR13128
You Can't Always Get What You Want AR15174
You Can't Do That On Stage Anymore RR13030
You Can't Win (song) RR11439
You Gotta Pay The Band RR11696
You Gotta Sin To Get Saved RR11840
You? Me? Us? RR12733
You Send Me BR01135
You Shoulda Been There AR13759
You Turn Me On RR10522
You'll Never Get To Heaven RR11963
The Young And The Reckless: The Pot Is Stronger, The Acid Milder, And The Kids Who Are Turning On Are Younger Than Ever AR16051
Young Blood RR11692
Young, Gifted And Bad AR15636
Young, White And Surrounded AR12947
Youngblood RR11557
Your Arsenal RR11959
Your Filthy Little Mouth RR12396
Your Little Secret RR11100
Your Own Private Audio AR16085
Your Song RR10403
Your Sounds RR11475
Youssou N'Dour RR12003
Youthanasia RR11860
You've Got To Believe In Something RR12601
Yugoslavian Transportation AR15077
Yuletunes RR13328
Yum-Yum Make Sugary-Sweet Pop (With Strings) AR13459

Z

Z: New York City CR00949
Z Z Top CR00950
Zappa Premiere Set: European Ensemble To Debut 'The Yellow Shark' AR16019
Ziggy's Axeman: Mick Ronson Was A Sideman Extraordinaire AR15440
Zingalamaduni RR10460
Zoo World Order: With A Lot Of Help From The Edge, U2 Are Reborn With A Case of The Giggles—And A New Sense Of Mission AR13447
Zooropa RR12793, RR12794
Zucker RR11122